VOLUME 26 Sumatra to Trampoline

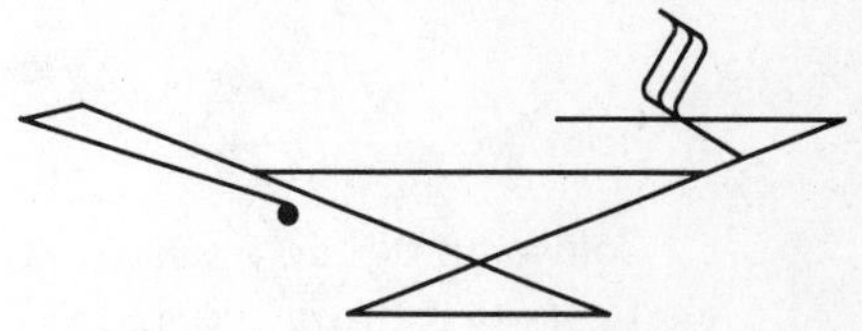

THE ENCYCLOPEDIA AMERICANA

INTERNATIONAL EDITION

COMPLETE IN THIRTY VOLUMES FIRST PUBLISHED IN 1829

AMERICANA CORPORATION International Headquarters: 575 Lexington Avenue, New York, New York 10022

Library of Congress Cataloging in Publication Data
Main entry under title:

The Encyclopedia Americana.

Published 1829–1858 under title: Encyclopaedia
Americana; 1907–1912: The Americana.
Includes bibliographical references.
1. Encyclopedias and dictionaries.
AE5.E333 1975 031 74–11347
ISBN 0–7172–0106–6

Manufactured in the U.S.A.

MIRIAM BUCHER, FROM PHOTO RESEARCHERS, INC.

A small community hugs the Musi River near Palembang, Sumatra.

SUMATRA, soo-mä'trə, is the westernmost of the major islands of Indonesia and, after Borneo, the largest of the Greater Sunda group. It is situated between the Indian Ocean and the Malay Archipelago's interior seas. Sumatra is separated from the Malay Peninsula to the northeast by the Strait of Malacca and from Java to the southeast by the Sunda Strait. Extending about 1,100 miles (1,750 km) from northwest to southeast, the island reaches a width of 250 miles (400 km) at the equator, which bisects it. Its area is about 167,000 square miles (433,000 sq km); exclusive of fringing islands.

The Land. Sumatra is divided lengthwise into two main topographic zones. One, the Barisan mountains, actually consists of two parallel mountain chains that closely flank the entire west coast. These chains contain some 80 volcanic peaks, another dozen active volcanoes, and several enclosed plateaus. They reach their maximum elevation of almost 12,500 feet (3,800 meters) atop Mt. Kerintji. They also contain five major lakes, the largest being Toba, a crater lake, in the north. Extending inland from the east coast is the second major topographic zone, a lowland plain occupying some 60% of the island. A narrow coastal strip in the north, this zone widens to over 150 miles (240 km) in the south.

Most of the rivers draining the west coast are short, with steep gradients, and are little used for transportation. The rivers draining the eastern slopes are longer, tap extensive watersheds, and are generally navigable by large ships. Several of Sumatra's chief ports—Palembang, Djambi, Pakanbaru—are located along these rivers at a considerable distance from the sea.

Sumatra has a tropical climate with little seasonal temperature variation. The mean annual temperature at 4,000 feet (1,200 meters) in the north is 68° F (20° C), as against 80° F (27° C) in lowland south Sumatra. Annual rainfall averages 95 to 140 inches (2,400–3,550 mm) with an October-November maximum north of the equator and a December-January maximum south of it.

Vegetation is luxuriant and highly diversified, especially according to altitude. Along the east coast are huge tidal bush-mangrove marshlands. Extensive stretches of savanna, supporting imperata grasses, palms, and bamboos, range upward from 200 feet (60 meters), and vast stands of equatorial forest stretch from 400 feet (120 meters) to the highest peaks. Besides deciduous trees like chestnuts and oaks, this forest contains valuable tropical hardwoods such as teak, ebony, and ironwood, as well as lianas, resin trees, camphor, and sandalwoods.

Sumatra's wildlife includes two types of apes (the gibbon and orangutan), members of the lemur and tarsier families, Malayan bears, elephants, tigers, tapirs, two almost extinct varieties of rhinoceros, civet cats, and many kinds of reptiles and birds.

The People. Sumatra and its fringing islands supported about 20 million inhabitants in 1970, or 16% of Indonesia's total population. Some 15 languages are spoken, excluding dialects. Yet about 75% of the people belong to one of the four major ethno-linguistic groups—the Malay (7 million), Menangkabau (4.4 million), Batak (2.3 million), and Achinese (over 2 million).

The Malays occupy the coastline and river basins of the eastern lowlands but are widely scattered elsewhere as well. The Menangkabau inhabit the densely settled Padang highlands of west central Sumatra. Farther northwest in the interior uplands surrounding Lake Toba live the Bataks. The Achinese dwell farthest northwest, along the coastal plain encircling Sumatra's northern end. Minor groups include the Alas and the Gajo, who are mountaineers living between the Batak and Achinese; the Rejang-Lampung-Kubu speakers of the south; and the peoples of the eastern and western offshore islands.

Except within the minority European and Chinese communities, Sumatra's peoples are physically of a generalized Malayan phenotype. Their languages, while mutually unintelligible, reveal a definite common ancestry within the west Austronesian language family. Most Sumatrans are Muslim, except for the Batak, almost half of whom are Christian. Local customs continue to modify religious identities. For example, Menangkabau matrilineal clan duties still counteract orthodox Muslim family law, and the Christian Batak still observe pagan rites.

Economy. Agriculture is the primary economic activity, with rice the staple food crop. Corn (maize) and root crops, especially cassava, are important secondary staples in many areas. Cash crops grown by farmers with small holdings are peanuts, rubber, pepper, cotton, tobacco, copra, cloves, nutmeg, kapok, coffee, and betelnuts. Sumatra accounts for over 50% of Indonesia's smallholder rubber export, but rice must be imported to feed the urban population and plantation workers. Large estates produce the bulk of the island's agricultural exports. Plantation crops include rubber, tobacco, palm oil, tea, coffee, and fibers such as sisal and ramie. Tobacco and rubber estates are concentrated in the northeastern coastal region.

Petroleum, tin, and bauxite are the leading mineral products of Sumatra and its offshore islands. Over 70% of Indonesia's crude oil comes from the coastal plains around Palembang, Djambi, and Pakanbaru. The tin mines of Bangka, Billiton, and Singkep islands make Indonesia the world's second-largest tin exporter. Bauxite is mined in the Riouw (Riau) islands, and 75% of Indonesia's coal production comes from the Padang highlands and southern Sumatra.

Primary trading centers, shipping points, and associated land transport systems are found in the Medan-Belawan area of the north, in the Padang highlands, and in the south. Outside of these network areas and the oil company roads of the central plain, transport by river and by mountain trail remains the rule. Sumatra's major cities are also linked by air.

History. During the early centuries of the Christian era, Sumatra was known to the Indians and Chinese because of its position astride the maritime trade routes between India and China. The spread of Indian cultural influence in the island is attested by Sanskritic archaeological remnants in Sumatra. By the 7th century at least two Indianized states were flourishing on the east coast: Melayu (Malayu), with its capital at Djambi, and Srivijaya, with its capital at Palembang. By about 1000, Srivijaya not only controlled the lucrative Malacca Strait trade route but most of Sumatra, western Java, and the Malay Peninsula with its Kra Isthmus overland routes. When Marco Polo visited Sumatra in 1292, Srivijaya was a center of Buddhist learning, but its maritime power had waned and it faced growing religious opposition from newly converted Muslim chieftains in north Sumatra. During the 15th century, Islam became established in Acheh (Atjeh), and the Achinese spread their faith south among the Menangkabau and other groups.

Portuguese traders and missionaries reached Sumatra in the 16th century, and the Dutch began their penetration of the island in the 17th. By the early 18th century the Dutch East India Company had established numerous trading forts along both coasts of Sumatra and had concluded defense and trade monopoly agreements with local chieftains. Competition from the British continued until 1824, when Britain ceded to the Dutch its last Sumatran trading footholds on Billiton island and at Bengkulu in return for Malacca and for Dutch recognition of British Singapore. By 1900 there were Dutch mission stations throughout the Batak highlands, and estate, mining, and transportation activities were well established. The Achinese, however, resisted the Dutch until 1908.

During World War II, Sumatra was occupied by the Japanese. Following Japan's surrender in 1945, Sumatrans took part in the struggle against the returning Dutch. Sumatra joined the newly established Republic of Indonesia in 1950. Since then, the island's exports have provided a disproportionately large share of the national income. The Java-centered economic policies of President Sukarno before 1965 generated local dissatisfactions with the central government and contributed to the outbreak of several rebellions and regional movements. Since 1965 the economic policies of President Suharto's government have attracted new foreign investment to Sumatra.

PETER R. GOETHALS
University of North Carolina

SUMBA, sōōm'bə, is one of the Lesser Sunda Islands in Indonesia. It was formerly known as *Sandalwood Island,* from the once abundant trees that furnished its chief export. The island, south of Flores and west of Timor, is about 145 miles (230 km) long and 50 miles (80 km) wide and has an area of 4,305 square miles (11,150 sq km).

Most of the Sundanese are farmers. Corn (maize) is their chief crop. Horses and water buffalo are bred, many for export. The people live in villages of houses with steeply pitched roofs. Many of them are animists. The chief town is Waingapu on the north coast. Population: (1961) 251,126.

SUMBAWA, sōōm-bä'wə, is one of the larger islands of the Lesser Sunda group in Indonesia. It lies between Flores to the east and Lombok to the west. Irregularly shaped, Sumbawa (Soembawa) has a length of 175 miles (280 km) and a maximum width of 55 miles (85 km). The island is very mountainous, with a few narrow plains along the coast. The highest peak is a volcano, Mt. Tambora, 9,350 feet (2,850 meters) high. Saleh Bay on the north coast almost bisects Sumbawa. On Bima Bay, farther east, lies Raba, the largest town, the administrative center, and a port of call for interisland shipping.

Sumbawans, most of whom are Muslims, are of mixed Malay and Papuan stock. They grow rice, corn (maize), coffee, tobacco, fruits, and vegetables, moving to new fields as the old ones are exhausted. Livestock raising is important to the export economy. Population: (1961) 507,596.

PETER R. INGOLD, *University of Vermont*

SUMER

TEL-VIGNEAU

Stele commemorating Naramsin's victory over a west Iranian chieftain dates from the 3d millennium B. C.

SUMER, sōō'mər, the homeland of the world's earliest known civilization, was roughly the same territory as modern southern Iraq from around Baghdad to the Persian Gulf. It consisted largely of a bleak, windswept, but potentially fertile plain formed over thousands of years by silt deposits from the Tigris and Euphrates rivers. Its climate was hot and dry, but with the help of irrigation the people of Sumer made the land so productive that modern scholars tend to identify it with the Biblical Garden of Eden.

HISTORY

Sumer was first settled about 4500 B. C. by the Ubaidians, a people whose stone farming implements and clay artifacts were first uncovered in the ruins of al-Ubaid and later in the lowest levels of other archaeological sites in southern Iraq. The Ubaidians founded villages that later became important Sumerian urban centers. In the course of the next 1,000 years these settlements were infiltrated by Semitic nomads from the Arabian and Syrian deserts. From this cross-fertilization of peoples evolved a relatively high culture in which the Semitic element was predominant.

The Sumerians, whose original home may have been in the region of the Caspian Sea, probably did not reach Sumer before 3300 B. C. Their arrival and subsequent ethnic and cultural fusion with the existing population led to the creation of man's first high civilization, now commonly known as Sumerian primarily because Sumerian was the prevailing language of the land.

City-States. The first notable ruler of Sumer was Etana, a king of Kish in northern Sumer who lived about 2800 B. C. The Kish dynasty succeeded to some extent in unifying the rival city-states that had developed in Sumer.

Not long after Etana, however, a king named Meskiagsher founded at Erech (Biblical Uruk;

modern Warka) a dynasty whose martial exploits ushered in a "heroic age." From this city in southern Sumer, Meskiagsher is said to have extended his rule to the Zagros Mountains (on the eastern border of modern Iraq) and the Mediterranean Sea. His son Enmerkar and the latter's successor, Lugalbanda, were noted for the conquest of Aratta, a city-state in Iran that was renowned for its wealth of metal and stone, resources lacking in Sumer.

Following Lugalbanda's reign, Erech's power was seriously threatened by the last two rulers of Kish, Enmebaraggesi and Agga, who were not only military figures of note but outstanding religious leaders as well. At Nippur, in central Sumer, they founded the Ekur, or temple of Enlil, Sumer's leading deity. Thus they helped make Nippur the religious and cultural center of the land.

Meanwhile, a third power, Ur (Biblical Ur of the Chaldees) had arisen in the south under its ruler, Mesannepadda. The royal tombs of Ur may date from the time of the dynasty he founded. Shortly after his death Erech again became the leading city-state of Sumer, this time under the rule of Gilgamesh, the supreme hero of Sumerian story and legend. See also GILGAMESH EPIC.

As a result of the destructive struggle of Kish, Erech, and Ur for control of Nippur and hegemony over all Sumer, the land was subjugated by the Elamites to the east. But around 2500, it was restored to its former power by Lugalannemundu of Adab, in central Sumer. He is said to have controlled an empire extending over much of the ancient world. Not long after him came Mesilim of Kish, a ruler noted for his building activities and for settling a bitter territorial dispute between two rival southern city-states, Lagash (Telloh) and Umma. This was history's first recorded case of peaceful political arbitration.

In time, Eannatum of Lagash extended his sway over all of Sumer, but the power he established did not last more than a generation after his death. Urukagina, the last king of the Lagash dynasty, was a notable political reformer, and in one of his inscriptions the word "freedom" appears for the first time in written history. He curtailed the oppressive practices of a greedy bureaucracy, reduced taxes, and put an end to gross injustice and exploitation. But Urukagina was overthrown by Lugalzaggesi, the ambitious ruler of Umma, who burned much of Lagash.

Akkadian Dynasty. About 2350 a Semitic leader named Sargon toppled Lugalzaggesi from power and went on to conquer all of Sumer. He established a powerful Semitic dynasty that lasted over 100 years and made its influence felt as far as India and Ethiopia. Sargon founded in northern Sumer a new capital named Agade (Biblical Akkad), which for a brief period became the wealthiest and most powerful city in the ancient world. After Sargon's death, two of his sons were successful rulers. But during the reign of his grandson Naramsin, the Gutians, a semibarbaric people from the Zagros Mountains, invaded Sumer and left it desolate.

It took the Sumerians generations to recover. From about 2150, Lagash was again prominent, especially under its pious governor Gudea, whose features are well known from numerous statues of him excavated in Lagash. Gudea figures prominently in the history of literature. A long hymn celebrating his restoration of the Eninnu, or main temple of Lagash, is a literary masterpiece.

Neo-Sumerian Period. Sumer was finally delivered from the Gutians by Utuhegal of Erech. About 2100 one of his generals, the ambitious Ur-Nammu, made himself master of Ur. After defeating Lagash, Ur-Nammu made Ur once again the capital of Sumer. Parts of his law code, the first in history, have been identified and translated.

Ur-Nammu's son Shulgi was one of the great monarchs of the ancient world—a rare combination of soldier, statesman, and patron of learning and letters. Throughout his reign Sumer prospered and dominated the neighboring lands. But after his death, hordes of Semitic nomads—the Amorites of the Bible—streamed in from the west. About 2000 B. C. the Elamites, Sumer's perennial enemies on its eastern flank, attacked and destroyed Ur and ravaged much of Sumer.

In the following two centuries there was a constant power struggle involving several Sumerian city-states, which were now largely Semitized. Finally, about 1760, the Amorite king Hammurabi succeeded in unifying the land, with Babylon in the north as its capital. With the reign of Hammurabi the history of Sumer comes under the history of Babylonia.

SUMERIAN CULTURE

In its heyday Sumer consisted of more than a dozen city-states. Each was a walled city surrounded by numerous villages and hamlets.

The City. Sumerian cities had from 10,000 to 50,000 inhabitants. Their streets were narrow and winding, without paving or drainage. Traffic moved either on foot or by donkey.

The outstanding feature of each city was the temple, situated on a high terrace and enclosing a high tower, known as a ziggurat. Its central room, or cella, had a niche for the god's statue as well as an offering table and was surrounded by rooms for the use of the priests. The temple's outer walls were built largely of mud brick. The columns of its courts and porticos were resplendent with colored geometric patterns composed of the painted heads of innumerable clay cones inserted in them. The shrine was at times decorated with wall paintings.

The average house was a small one-story mud brick structure with several rooms around an open court. There were also larger, two-story houses, the ground floor of which contained a reception room, kitchen, lavatory, servant quarters, and, sometimes, a private chapel.

Furniture consisted of low tables, stools and high-backed chairs, and beds with wooden frames. The household pots and pans had various shapes and were made of clay, stone, copper, or bronze. Baskets and chests were made of reed and wood. Floors and walls were adorned with reed mats, skin rugs, and woolen hangings. Below the house might be the family mausoleum, where the dead were buried with some of their belongings for use in the Nether World.

Political Power. In theory the entire city belonged to the god to whom it had been assigned on the day the world was created. In practice, however, most of the land belonged not to the temple but to the citizens—farmers and cattle breeders, boatmen and fishermen, merchants and scribes, artisans and craftsmen. Political power originally lay in their hands, and the city governor was no more than a peer among peers.

As the danger of attack by the surrounding peoples increased, kingship came into being, and the king acquired paramount importance. The

Sumerian ruler was a vicar of the gods. His duties were to defend the land from its enemies and enlarge its territory and influence, to improve the irrigation system so essential to its prosperity, to build and repair roads, and to preserve law and justice.

Society. The basic unit of Sumerian society was the family, and marriages were arranged by parents. The betrothal became legal as soon as the groom presented a bridal gift to the father. A wife could hold property, engage in business, and qualify as a witness. But she might be divorced on light grounds, or, if she should have no children, the husband could take a second wife. Children were under the absolute authority of their parents and could even be sold into slavery.

Slaves, originally prisoners of war or impoverished fellow citizens, could be flogged and branded. But they could engage in business, borrow money, buy their freedom, and marry a free person, thus ensuring the freedom of their children.

Technology. Some of Sumer's most far-reaching achievements involved irrigation and agriculture. Engineers constructed intricate systems of canals, dikes, weirs, and reservoirs, and they used leveling instruments, measuring rods, and maps in preparing plans and surveys. Their arithmetic was based on the number 60 rather than 10 and had a form of place notation. Measures were standardized.

Farming developed into a complex, systematized technique. Farmer almanacs were prepared and used as texts in Sumerian schools. Sumerian craftsmen were skilled in metallurgy, fulling, bleaching, dyeing, and preparing paints, pigments, cosmetics, and perfumes. The Sumerian physician made use of an assortment of botanical, zoological, and mineralogical ingredients as *materia medica* in his prescriptions.

Religion. The Sumerians worshiped a pantheon of gods of diverse rank and character. The four leading deities were An (Heaven), Ki (Earth), Enlil (Lord Air), and Enki (Lord of the Deep). Ranking lower in the hierarchy were the gods in charge of the sun, moon, stars, and planets, and of wind, rain and tempest. In addition, there were many lesser deities in charge of the numerous natural and cultural phenomena that constitute the cosmos. The great gods' chief instrument of creation was the divine word, which once pronounced could not be altered. The *me*, or universal laws that even the gods had to obey, kept the universe in continuous, harmonious operation.

The Sumerian believed that man had been fashioned of clay and created solely to provide the gods with food and shelter. Ignorant of his destiny and haunted by insecurity, he sought salvation by praying to his personal god, a kind of good angel. In death, the ghostlike spirit descended to the Nether World, where existence was a dismal reflection of life on earth.

Prayers, offerings, and sacrifices were rendered to the gods at the temple, which had a large priestly personnel. The most joyous festival was the prolonged New Year celebration, which culminated in a sacred marriage—actually a fertility rite—between the king, in the role of the god Dumuzi, and Inanna, goddess of love and procreation.

Mythology. The gods of Sumer resembled men in appearance and behavior, and a rich mythology concerned their deeds and misdeeds. One of the most striking myths is about the god Enlil

HIRMER FOTOARCHIV

BRONZE HEAD from Nineveh is believed to represent King Sargon, founder of the Akkadian dynasty.

and his beloved, Ninlil. She followed him to the Nether World, to which he had been banished by the other gods. Several myths concern Enki, the divine culture hero, who brought civilization to mankind and saved man from destruction by the Flood, but who almost suffered death after eating the forbidden plants of Dilmun, the paradise of the gods. The deity that most inspired poets was Inanna, the ambitious and cruel but not unattractive goddess who descended to the Nether World in disregard of the divine laws. She reascended to the earth only after her husband, Dumuzi, took her place in the "Land of No Return"—hence the wailing for Dumuzi prevalent throughout the ancient Middle East.

The Arts. Religion inspired much of Sumerian art, such as temple statues, plaques, friezes, decorative inlays, and engraved cylinder seals. The sculptors modeled the temple statues in both abstract and naturalistic styles. Men were bearded or clean-shaven and wore a flounced skirt, sometimes covered by a long cloak, or a long shirt with a fringed shawl wrapped over it. Women had pigtails wound about the head and wore long tufted dresses that left the right arm bare.

Music, too, was largely temple-inspired, but song accompanied by instrumental music also resounded in the palace during feasts and celebrations. Beautifully constructed harps and lyres have been recovered from the royal tombs.

UNIVERSITY MUSEUM, PHILADELPHIA

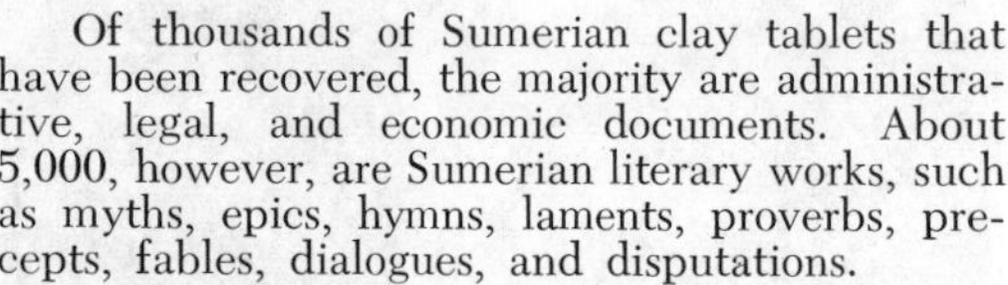

Bull's head (*above*) is a detail of a harp from Ur. Seated statue (*right*) is of Gudea, governor of Lagash.

GIRAUDON

Of thousands of Sumerian clay tablets that have been recovered, the majority are administrative, legal, and economic documents. About 5,000, however, are Sumerian literary works, such as myths, epics, hymns, laments, proverbs, precepts, fables, dialogues, and disputations.

Language, Writing, and Education. Sumerian was an agglutinative language, resembling Turkish and Hungarian in some of its structural and grammatical features. The most important Sumerian contribution to civilization was the development of the cuneiform system of writing this language. Later, other languages also were written in cuneiform.

The writing, which was done on clay tablets, originated about 3000 B. C. with a series of pictographic signs devised by Sumerian temple administrators for the purpose of keeping their accounts. It was used at first only to inscribe the simplest memoranda and notations. Over the centuries, however, it became a phonetic system of writing in which each sign stood for one or more syllables. See also CUNEIFORM.

Learning to read and write the complex cuneiform syllabary required years of attendance at the Sumerian school, called the "tablet-house." The head of the school was the "school father," the professor was known as the "expert," and assistants were "big brothers." The students, or "school sons," came from well-to-do families, but the tuition was probably minimal.

Teaching methods were dull and uninspiring. Discipline was harsh, and "drop-outs" were numerous. The curriculum consisted primarily of copying and memorizing long lists of words and phrases. Other major subjects were mathematics and literature.

Sumerian Character. A psychological drive for power and prestige colored the Sumerian character and was responsible in large part for the civil and foreign wars that finally destroyed Sumerian political power. Polarized into poor and rich and weak and strong, Sumerian society professed such ideals as justice, equity, and compassion, but injustice, inequity, and oppression abounded. The short-sighted Sumerians upset nature's delicate ecological balance by overirrigating their fields and orchards and thus "salted" and "silted" them into sterility. There is evidence also that Sumer suffered from cheating merchants and the "generation gap" between parents and children, teachers and students.

Despite these failings and shortcomings, Sumer dominated the ancient world spiritually and culturally for more than a millennium. Observant, reflective, and pragmatic, the Sumerians evolved a way of life that struck a balance between reason and fancy, freedom and authority. As a consequence, they made outstanding technological and ideological breakthroughs.

The Legacy of Sumer. It is now generally agreed that Sumer was in some respects the cradle of civilization. Among the Sumerian contributions to human development are such technological devices as the potter's wheel, the wheeled vehicle, the sailboat, and the seed plow. Sumerian temples and ziggurats are architectural prototypes of the synagogue, church, and mosque. The Sumerians were the first to develop a system of writing. The first coherent musical system centering on a diatonic scale can also be traced back to Sumerian sources. The city-state originated in Sumer, and Sumerian written law is the forerunner of Biblical, Greek, and Roman law. The division of the circle into 360 degrees and of the hour into 60 minutes of 60 seconds goes back to the Sumerian sexagesimal (base 60) system of numbers.

Judaeo-Christian ideas about the creation of the universe and man, the creative power of the divine Word, the Flood, the confusion of tongues, man's personal god, suffering and submission, death and the Nether World—all have their counterparts in Sumerian religious thought. Such Biblical books as Psalms, Lamentations, Proverbs, and the Song of Songs have their forerunners among the Sumerian literary works.

DISCOVERY OF SUMERIAN CIVILIZATION

The existence of the Sumerians is entirely a discovery of modern archaeology and scholarship. The ancient Hebrews and Greeks knew the land of Sumer as Babylonia, the home of the Semitic-speaking Babylonians. This was also the belief of the explorers and archaeologists who began excavating in the area in the early 1800's.

Most of the cuneiform documents excavated in those early days were written in the Semitic tongue now known as Akkadian, and the Semites were therefore assumed to have been the original inhabitants of the land and to have invented cuneiform. As study of the documents progressed, it became apparent that there were no signs for certain characteristic Semitic sounds, such as guttural and emphatic stops. Moreover, some of the excavated tablets were recognizably bilingual, with Semitic translations of words and phrases of a language that was not Semitic in vocabulary or structure.

In 1869, the French scholar Jules Oppert suggested that the name of the people who spoke this strange tongue was found in the inscriptions of the early rulers, who were designated "kings of Sumer and Akkad." Since Akkad, he argued, certainly referred to a Semitic land, Sumer must be the name of the non-Semitic land whose people, the Sumerians, originated cuneiform.

Not all scholars accepted Oppert's identification, but soon the French excavations at Lagash, which began in 1877, started to unearth what were to be thousands of Sumerian clay tablets and many statues and plaques. Twelve years later the Americans began digging at Nippur, where some 3,000 Sumerian literary tablets and fragments were unearthed. Since then excavations in various sites have uncovered Sumerian temples, palaces, and other buildings, as well as innumerable artifacts and inscriptions. As a result, the Sumerians are becoming one of the best-known peoples of the ancient world.

SAMUEL NOAH KRAMER
Author of "History Begins at Sumer"

Bibliography

Cambridge University Press, *The Cambridge Ancient History,* rev. ed., vol. 1 (New York and London 1970).
Kramer, Samuel Noah, *Cradle of Civilization* (New York 1969).
Kramer, Samuel Noah, *History Begins at Sumer* (New York 1959).
Kramer, Samuel Noah, *Sumerian Mythology* (Philadelphia 1944).
Kramer, Samuel Noah, *The Sumerians* (Chicago 1963).
Saggs, Henry W. F., *The Greatness that Was Babylon* (New York 1962).

SUMMARY COURT-MARTIAL. See COURT-MARTIAL.

SUMMARY JUDGMENT, in law, a means of obtaining a judgment in a civil lawsuit where there appears to be no triable issue. This avoids waiting the usual period of months, or even years, for the case to be reached on the regular trial calendar. The procedure is often used in the United States in both state and federal courts. It was developed to prevent a defendant who had no defense from delaying judgment—often in an effort to put his property out of reach of the plaintiff—by filing a sham answer and demanding a jury trial. The procedure was later expanded to include the much rarer case in which the defendant proved that a plaintiff had stated a sham claim for some ulterior purpose.

Defenses: Sham or in Good Faith? In a typical case, the plaintiff who claims a right to an immediate judgment without waiting for the case to be reached on the regular trial calendar makes a motion for a summary judgment. It is not enough for the plaintiff merely to charge that the other party's defense is without merit; to expose a sham denial he must first produce evidence, usually by means of affidavits, tending to prove that the facts alleged in his own statement are probably true. If the defendant making the denial produces evidence tending to show that the facts adduced by the plaintiff are not true, the motion is denied and the case must await its turn on the trial calendar. If, however, the defendant does not produce evidence to support his denial, the motion for summary judgment is granted.

In order to expose a sham statement of claim or defense, the party making the motion must produce evidence tending to prove that the other side's statement is false. If he fails, the motion is denied, and the case must be tried in regular course. If he succeeds, the party making the statement must then produce evidence to support its truth. If no such proof is forthcoming, judgment will be rendered immediately.

Basis for Summary Judgment. In summary judgment proceedings, supporting and opposing affidavits must be made on personal knowledge by persons competent to testify and must contain facts admissible in evidence. Generally a summary judgment is justified only if no material issue of fact survives the pleadings, affidavits, and depositional proof. If questions of fact appear, a trial is required.

English and American Legislation. Application of an 1855 English statute on summary judgments was limited to action on bills of exchange and promissory notes. Before the adoption in 1938 of the federal rules of civil procedure for the district courts of the United States, summary judgment procedure was not available in all types of cases. The first provision in California, for example, authorized the procedure only "in an action to recover upon a debt or upon a liquidated demand including an action to enforce or foreclose a lien or mortgage." The federal rules were the first to provide that the procedure should be available in every type of action without restriction.

WILLIAM WIRT BLUME
Author of "American Civil Procedure"

SUMMARY JURISDICTION. See SUMMARY JUDGMENT.

SUMMER, one of the four seasons. The seasons result from the tilt of the earth's axis to the plane of its orbit. As the earth moves around the sun, the relative lengths of day and night at a given latitude on earth—and hence the amount of solar heat received there—go through a yearly cycle of changes that man has divided into four periods, or seasons. Summer, on the average, is the warmest of these periods.

In the Northern Hemisphere, summer begins on the summer solstice (about June 22), when the hemisphere faces the sun most fully. Because the earth stores summer heat, the hottest days tend to occur about two months later. The season ends on the autumnal equinox (about September 22), when the hemisphere begins to be tipped away from the sun. In the Southern Hemisphere, summer begins about December 22 and ends about March 21.

SUMMER SOLSTICE. See SOLSTICE; SUMMER.

SUMMER SQUASH. See SQUASH.

SUMMERSIDE is a town on the south shore of Prince Edward Island, Canada, on Bedeque Bay of Northumberland Strait, about 40 miles (64 km) west of Charlottetown. It is the center of an agricultural region in which fox farming is important.

Daniel Green, a Quaker Loyalist from Pennsylvania, was the first settler (1780), and the growing community was called Green's Shores. In 1840 an inn, the Summerside House, was opened, and its name was stamped on mailbags for the town, which became known as Summerside. Population: 9,439.

SUMMIT, a village in northeastern Illinois, in Cook county, is about 10 miles (16 km) southwest of the center of Chicago. The village has a large corn refinery and makes corn products. Summit is situated on the low divide between the Great Lakes and the Mississippi River. It was incorporated in 1890. Government is by mayor and council. Population: 11,569.

SUMMIT, a city in northeastern New Jersey, in Union county, is about 10 miles (16 km) west of Newark. It includes the crest of First Watchung Mountain, a ridge that was an observation point for the Americans during the Revolution. Summit is a residential community and a shopping center for a large area. It also has chemical, pharmaceutical, and synthetic-fabrics laboratories. Publishing and insurance are also important to the economy.

Summit was settled in 1795. It was incorporated as a township in 1869 and as a city in 1899. Government is by mayor and council. Population: 23,620.

SUMMONS, in American law, a formal document that gives notice to a person, in a criminal case, to appear in court to answer a charge against him or informs him, in a civil proceeding, that an action is being started against him.

Although, in form, it often resembles a court order, a summons is rarely issued by a judge. Policemen usually issue criminal summonses, and lawyers usually issue civil summonses.

Although a criminal summons is best known for its use in traffic cases, in which it is called a "ticket," it is also used for alleged violations of municipal ordinances, such as those relating to sanitation and building safety. Experimental projects, such as one conducted in 1964 by the Vera Institute of Justice in association with the New York City Police Department, have established the utility of issuing summonses in other minor criminal matters, for example, in shoplifting. This avoids unnecessary incarceration and allows the policeman to remain on his beat. See ARREST.

A civil summons usually contains notice of what will happen if the person served fails to contest the action. In most cases the consequence is entry of a judgment for the amount of damages claimed. This requires proof that the summons was served as required by law. Sometimes corrupt professional process servers are shown to have engaged in "sewer service," the term given to the practice of filing false affidavits when actually the summons was never served on the designated person.

RICHARD A. GREEN, *Director, American Bar Association Project on Standards for Criminal Justice*

SUMNER, Charles (1811–1874), American political leader. In a long career in the U.S. Senate, he was a powerful, articulate opponent of slavery, and he labored devotedly to secure the equal rights of black men. Always guided by moral conviction, Sumner embodied the Puritan spirit in politics.

Early Career. Sumner was born in Boston on Jan. 6, 1811. He was brought up in an atmosphere of frugality, industry, and piety and was given the best education available—at the Boston Latin School, Harvard College, and Harvard Law School, receiving his law degree in 1833. Admitted to the bar in 1834, he was more interested in legal theory than in his practice, and in 1837 he went to Europe to study judicial institutions.

Returning to America in 1840, Sumner found Boston provincial and his law practice tedious. Friends sought to interest him in civic affairs. Sumner eagerly embraced humanitarian causes and in 1845 proclaimed himself a reformer in an Independence Day address attacking all war. The social ostracism that followed had its compensations. His dedication to principle won the admiration of such reformers as Theodore Parker and William Lloyd Garrison.

Election to the Senate. The issues of slavery and territorial expansionism led Sumner into politics. He became one of the "Conscience Whigs," who tried unsuccessfully to pledge the Massachusetts Whig party to a strong antislavery stand, but bolted the party in 1848 and supported Martin Van Buren, the presidential candidate of the Free Soilers. A coalition of Democrats and Free Soilers gained control of the Massachusetts legislature and in 1851 elected Sumner to the U.S. Senate seat he was to occupy until his death.

In the Senate, Sumner was a member of a tiny antislavery minority. In 1852 he proposed repeal of the Fugitive Slave Act of 1850, arguing that while freedom was national, slavery was sectional and no federal act should give it recognition. Stephen A. Douglas' Kansas-Nebraska bill of 1854 revived the slavery issue in Congress, and Sumner was among those who fought what they considered a new example of proslavery aggression. Though unable to defeat the bill, they aroused the North and organized the antislavery men into the newly formed Republican party.

Assault by Brooks. On May 19 and 20, 1856, Sumner delivered an oration in the Senate called "The Crime Against Kansas." He characterized Sen. Andrew Pickens Butler of South Carolina as a Don Quixote paying his vows to "the harlot, Slavery," and branded Douglas as Sancho Panza, "the squire of Slavery . . . ready to do its humiliating offices." On May 22, after the close of the day's session, Sumner was confronted at his desk by a tall stranger, who said, "I have read your speech twice over carefully; it is a libel on South Carolina, and Mr. Butler, who is a relative of mine." Down on Sumner's head crashed a heavy cane. Sumner tried to rise while blows rained upon him. At length he fell bleeding and unconscious in the aisle. His assailant was Rep. Preston Smith Brooks of South Carolina. See also BROOKS, PRESTON SMITH.

The assault evoked sympathy for Sumner throughout the North, even among those who had hitherto deplored his extremism. Sumner visited doctors in Europe and America and underwent a cauterization of the spinal skin tissue.

Not until 1859 was he able regularly to resume his Senate seat. To many Northerners his vacant chair spoke eloquently of the evils of slavery; to most Southerners, his illness seemed "shamming" for political purposes. There is some medical opinion that his ailments were psychosomatic.

Civil War. On June 4, 1860, Sumner delivered before the Senate a massive indictment of "The Barbarism of Slavery." When Lincoln's election precipitated secession, Sumner at first welcomed this opportunity to rid the nation of slavery. But when secession led to war, he strongly supported the Union effort.

Sumner was made chairman of the Senate Committee on Foreign Relations in 1861. During the war his personal acquaintance with European leaders helped him plead the Northern cause abroad and transmit, unofficially, the views of European statesmen to President Lincoln. His moderating role was seen in the *Trent* affair of November-December 1861, when he persuaded Lincoln to release two Confederate envoys seized from a British vessel. Sumner, however, could not forgive the English for their allegedly pro-Southern conduct, and after the war he pressed for claiming a staggering amount in wartime damages.

A Radical Republican, Sumner sought to repeal all fugitive slave laws, to abolish slavery in the District of Columbia, and to create a Freedmen's Bureau as "a bridge from slavery to freedom." Though he respected Lincoln's good intentions, he thought the President dilatory.

Postwar Career. Toward Lincoln's successor, Andrew Johnson, Sumner felt neither loyalty nor respect. Attacking Johnson's moderate reconstruction plans, he declared that the Southern states in seceding had committed suicide, and called for a thorough reorganization of Southern society. He proposed that the freedmen should be given homesteads carved out of their former masters' estates and that state legislatures should be required to maintain a system of public schools open to all races. Because President Johnson opposed these Radical measures, Sumner considered him "a public enemy," and he supported the impeachment proceedings against Johnson in 1868.

At the same time Sumner came increasingly to differ with members of his own party. His devotion to "absolute human equality" seemed pious eyewash to the new generation of Republicans, who considered him archaic and pedantic.

Almost from the outset Sumner opposed President Grant's administration. When Grant considered annexing Santo Domingo, Sumner said this would lead to a "dance of blood." Secretary of State Hamilton Fish learned that Sumner's extreme position regarding wartime claims against Britain was jeopardizing their settlement, and he concluded with Grant that Sumner was untrustworthy. In 1871 the executive department supported Sumner's senatorial foes, who removed him as chairman of the Foreign Relations Committee.

Sumner was now without a party. He was also alone. His wife had left him within a year of their marriage in 1866. He supported Horace Greeley against Grant in 1872, but his influence was not sufficient to help his candidate. Thereafter a heart condition prevented Sumner from taking an active part in Congressional proceedings. His motion in 1872 to strike the names of Civil War battles from the regimental colors angered Northern veterans. The Massachusetts legislature condemned the resolutions, but loyal followers succeeded in having the vote rescinded.

Sumner made his last Senate appearance on March 10, 1874. He died of a heart attack the next day. His body lay in state in the Capitol rotunda before burial in Cambridge, Mass.

DAVID DONALD, *Johns Hopkins University*

Further Reading: Donald, David, *Charles Sumner and the Coming of the Civil War* (New York 1960); id., *Charles Sumner and the Rights of Man* (New York 1970); Pierce, Edward L., *Memoirs and Letters of Charles Sumner*, 4 vols. (Boston 1877–1893; reprinted, New York 1969); Storey, Moorfield, *Charles Sumner* (Boston 1900; reprinted, New York 1969).

SUMNER, James Batcheller (1887–1955), American biochemist, who was awarded the 1946 Nobel Prize in chemistry for his work on enzymes. He shared the award with two other American biochemists, John Howard Northrup and Wendell Meredith Stanley, who also worked on enzymes.

Sumner thought that enzymes were proteins and set out in 1917 to prepare a pure enzyme. Since jackbean meal (*Canavalia ensiformis*) is rich in the enzyme urease, which is easily detected because of its capacity to liberate ammonia from urea, Sumner set out to identify the various components of the meal. In 1926 he succeeded in isolating tiny crystals that showed very strong urease activity as well as satisfying the various tests for proteins. His discovery that enzymes were proteins was not accepted for several years, but in 1930, Sumner's position was confirmed when Northrup crystallized three other enzymes —pepsin, trypsin, and chymotrypsin—and showed that they were proteins.

Sumner was born in Canton, Mass., on Nov. 19, 1887, and educated at Harvard, where he received his Ph.D. in 1914. He took a biochemistry position in the Cornell Medical School, where he remained until a few weeks before his death in Buffalo, N. Y., on Aug. 12, 1955.

AARON J. IHDE, *University of Wisconsin*

SUMNER, William Graham (1840–1910), American sociologist, who was one of the first and most influential teachers of sociology in the United States. Sumner was born in Paterson, N. J., on Oct. 30, 1840, graduated from Yale University in 1863, and was ordained an Episcopal priest in 1869. His concern with economic, political, and social problems caused him to give up his parish in Morristown, N. J., and return to Yale University as professor of political science in 1872. His principal interest was in teaching. His first and most influential book, *Folkways,* was not published until 1907, three years before his death in Englewood, N. J., on April 12, 1910. His other writings were published as *The Science of Society* (4 vols., 1927–1928).

In *Folkways,* Sumner maintained that people's behavior in society is governed by two types of rules that evolved gradually through trial and error. They are called *folkways* if they tend to be obeyed routinely, as a matter of conditioning and habit. Thus folkways determine how people dress, what foods they eat, or the other things they do to conform to a certain way of life. General conformity is ensured because folkways are the socially accepted forms of behavior.

The second type, *mores,* are rules that are crucial to the very survival of the group or society. Violations of the *mores*—for example, cannibalism or incest—are strongly censured. Mores, if institutionalized, became laws.

In Sumner's view the basic problem for any

society is its continued existence. Folkways and mores protect a group. They give it coherence and security. Members of a group are loyal to it because they consider their own mores and folkways superior to that of any other group. This attitude Sumner calls "ethnocentrism."

As a theory, Sumner's approach is usually referred to as a form of social Darwinism or evolutionism. It assumes constant conflict and competition between groups. Social phenomena—for example, folkways and mores—are explained as functioning primarily for the survival of the group. This view has been criticized on two grounds. First, its assumptions are too one-sided because group relationships include cooperation as well as conflict. Secondly, its conclusions are not confirmed by fact. Instances have been found in which the mores of a group are detrimental to its survival. See also FOLKWAYS AND MORES.

RUTH HEYDEBRAND, *Washington University*

SUMO. See WRESTLING–*Sumo.*

SUMPTUARY LAWS, sum'chə-wer-ē, are laws that attempt to regulate or restrict excessive expenditures by private individuals for food or drink, dress, personal adornment, or other luxuries. The theories behind the laws have been economic, social, moral, or religious, but all have proved difficult or impossible to enforce for long. The chief modern example was the 18th Amendment to the U.S. Constitution, which from 1919 to 1933 banned the sale of alcoholic beverages.

Early Experiments. In the 6th century B.C. the laws of Solon limited lavish Athenian funerals and weddings. Three centuries later, other edicts regulated the amount of jewelry and the quality of gowns worn by Roman matrons. But by the 2d century A.D. the Emperor Tiberius was quoted by Tacitus as confessing that "sumptuary laws are in disgrace . . . and by moderate penalties the evil could not be suppressed."

Varied Motives. The Greek and Roman laws stemmed from the conviction that extravagance was injurious to public policy, undermined the morale of the citizen, and distracted him from his public duties. In medieval Europe excessive displays of riches or exotic food and drink were considered pagan threats to the Christian's soul. Rulers strove to control even such details as lengths of robes, heights of headdresses, and points of shoes. Sumptuary laws also enforced social distinctions within the feudal system. Thus, in England, the quality of textiles permitted for wearing apparel was strictly graded. The greatest lords were entitled to finest quality linens and woolens with bright colors, yeomen could have durable but drab fabrics, and villeins could wear rough worsteds. In the 14th century a law of the English King Edward III decreed that because indulgence in costly meats was impoverishing many subjects and preventing them from meeting their feudal obligations all classes should limit such viands to two per course, with only two such courses per meal.

Moral Function. Although the modern age, under the gradual influence of democratic ideas, made many of these distinctions obsolete, the moral function of sumptuary laws remained strong. In the New World the Puritans, although primarily stressing religious conformity, had shared this view. In 1634 the Massachusetts General Court, because of "the greate, superfluous and unnecessary expenses occasioned by some new and immodest fashions," prohibited a list of luxury imports. Virginia in 1662 banned commodities such as "silk stuffe in garments" and "ribbands wrought with silver or gold." The 18th century French philosopher Montesquieu wrote that laws limiting the right to indulge individual tastes were beneficial because they preserved "the proportion between our wants and the means of satisfying them."

Frontier austerity and democracy rendered sumptuary laws largely irrelevant in 19th century America, and the rise of free enterprise capitalism and mass production of consumer goods throughout the Western world rendered them generally obsolete. See also BLUE LAWS.

WILLIAM F. SWINDLER
School of Law, College of William and Mary

SUMTER, Thomas (1734–1832), American Revolutionary officer. Sumter was born near Charlottesville, Va., on Aug. 14, 1734. He fought in the French and Indian War, and in 1765 he settled near Eutaw Springs, S. C.

When the British conquered South Carolina in 1780, Sumter organized an irregular force and aided considerably in reconquering the colony. After the war he founded Stateburg, S. C., and served in the U. S. House of Representatives and the Senate, retiring in 1810. Sumter died near Stateburg on June 1, 1832.

SUMTER, a city in central South Carolina, the seat of Sumter county, is 44 miles (70 km) southeast of Columbia. It is the commercial center of an agricultural area that raises cotton and soybeans. Sumter's industries include food-processing, chemical, lumber, furniture, and textile plants, foundries, and machine shops.

Morris College and a branch of Clemson University are in Sumter. The Iris Gardens in the city produce magnificent blooms in May and June. Poinsett State Park is nearby.

Incorporated in 1845 as Sumterville and named for Thomas Sumter, a Revolutionary War officer, it was chartered as a city in 1887 and the name changed to Sumter. Government is by council and manager. Population: 23,895.

CHAPMAN J. MILLING, JR.
Sumter County Library

SUMTER, Fort. See FORT SUMTER NATIONAL MONUMENT.

SUMY, sōō'mi, is a city and oblast in the USSR. The city is on the Psel River, 90 miles (145 km) northwest of Kharkov. The capital of the oblast, it is the center of a sugar beet district and has a large sugar-refining industry. The city also produces machinery for chemical and sugar factories and manufactures woolen cloth, tobacco products, and superphosphate fertilizer.

Sumy oblast is in the northern part of the Ukrainian SSR and has an area of 9,200 square miles (23,800 sq km). It is in wooded steppe country, drained by the Sula and Psel rivers. The oblast is primarily agricultural, with wheat and sugar beets the main crops. Industry is largely limited to processing farm products, but there is a small oil field at Kachanovka. The principal cities are Sumy, Konotop, and Shostka. Population: (1969 est.) of the oblast, 1,494,000; of the city, 149,000.

THEODORE SHABAD, *Editor "Soviet Geography"*

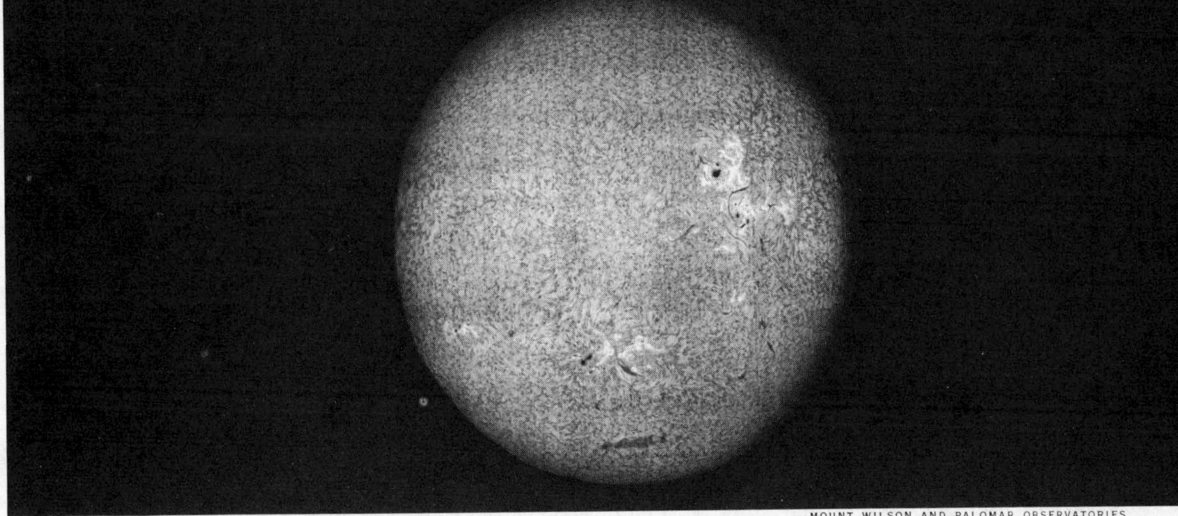

MOUNT WILSON AND PALOMAR OBSERVATORIES

The sun's turbulent disk, viewed in a spectral zone showing hydrogen, is marked by several active regions.

SUN, the central controlling body of the solar system. It is by far the largest member of the system, being 740 times more massive than its nine major planets together and 10 times wider than the largest planet, Jupiter.

The sun's rays supply the earth with heat and light, contribute to the growth of plant life, evaporate water from the ocean and other bodies of water, play a role in the production of winds, and perform many other functions that are vital to the existence of life on earth.

As a star the sun is a typically yellow dwarf, inconspicuously located in a spiral arm near the outer edge of our Milky Way galaxy. In orbiting the center of the galaxy, it whirls toward the constellation Cygnus at a velocity of about 140 miles (220 km) per second. At the same time it speeds toward a point in the constellation Hercules at 12 miles (20 km) per second, in a transverse motion that is perpendicular to its galactic orbit. See STAR.

THE EVOLUTION OF THE SUN

Formation. The sun and its planets were formed several billion years ago from a cloud of interstellar matter. Because the sun contains a larger proportion of heavy elements such as iron than do many other stars, astronomers conclude that it is a second-generation star. This means that the gas cloud out of which the sun formed was itself the ashes of earlier stars that had burned out. See also SOLAR SYSTEM.

Local irregularities in the gas cloud formed the nuclei around which condensations began. After the condensations reached a certain critical density, they developed sufficient gravitational attraction to draw in ever-increasing amounts of matter from the surrounding volumes of the cloud. Eventually the proto-sun gathered in so much matter that its interior pressure and temperature became high enough for nuclear reactions to begin. Thus it became, in effect, a large hydrogen nuclear reactor, releasing energy in such quantities that condensation ceased.

By that time the sun was a stable object that could exist for a long time on its ample fuel supply. The tremendous forces produced by the release of energy within the sun, as hydrogen was transmuted to helium by nuclear reactions, were held in check by the equally strong and oppositely directed gravitational forces.

The Death of the Sun. Life cycles of stars are counted in billions of years. The sun has enough fuel to sustain its present rate of energy production for some 10 billion years. During that time it will change but little.

However, the solar fuel eventually will begin to be exhausted. At that time the sun will expand slowly, becoming cooler at its surface. Its luminosity will be greater because of the increase in size. The expansion process will accelerate until eventually the sun becomes a red giant star and then a red supergiant, perhaps 1,000 times more luminous than it is now. During this expansion phase the sun's core will be almost pure helium, but the burning of hydrogen will continue in a shell of ever-increasing radius around the core.

The core eventually will begin to collapse, igniting the helium. Theories of stellar evolution are uncertain about what will happen after the helium flash. However, it seems very probable that the flash will mark the beginning of an unstable stage during which the sun will eject a substantial portion of its mass back into space—there to begin a new life cycle as part of some future star. The remnants of the sun will ultimately collapse and condense to a relatively inert, low-luminosity state similar to that of white dwarf stars. In this form the sun will slowly burn out.

GENERAL CHARACTERISTICS

The sun is a glowing ball of gases about 865,000 miles (1,393,000 km) in diameter. In terms of relative mass, it consists of 69.5% hydrogen and 28% helium—an element first discovered on the sun. Carbon, nitrogen, and oxygen account for 2% of the mass, and magnesium, sulfur, silicon, and iron account for 0.5%. Other elements are present in the sun in trace amounts only.

Although the sun is gaseous throughout its entire structure, it appears to have a definite surface when viewed through a suitable filter. This is an illusion caused by the sun's great distance from the earth, which averages about 92,960,000 miles (149,660,000 km) from the center of the sun to the center of the earth. The distance actually varies through the year because the earth's orbit is slightly elliptical. Early in January, when the earth is closest to the sun, the distance is about 91,400,000 miles (147,150,000 km). Early in July, when the earth is farthest away, the distance is about 94,500,000 miles (152,140,000 km).

As Galileo Galilei discovered in 1610, the sun rotates about an axis that is approximately aligned with the earth's axis. The rotational movement is from east to west, as viewed from the earth, and the speed decreases from a period of nearly 27 days at the solar equator to a period of more than 30 days near the poles. That is, the gaseous sun rotates more rapidly at the equator than at the poles.

This rotating ball of gases has a mass of 2.19×10^{27} tons (nearly 2×10^{30} kg), which is 330,000 times the mass of the earth. Its average density is 88 pounds per cubic foot (1.41 grams per cu cm), which is 1.41 times the density of water but only a little more than 0.25 times the average density of the earth. However, the sun's density increases greatly toward the interior. The gas pressure at the apparent surface is only 1/10 that of the earth's standard atmospheric pressure at sea level, and its density is only about 1/3,500 that of terrestrial air at sea level, but at the center of the sun the gases are highly compressed by the great mass of material above them. The gas density there is nearly 100 times the density of water, or nearly 9 times the density of lead, and the pressure is 200 billion atmospheres.

Temperature also increases toward the interior, from about 10,000° F (6,000° C) at the apparent surface to more than 18,000,000° F (10,000,000° C) at the center. Above the apparent surface the temperature first decreases to about 7,200° F (4,000° C) and then increases rapidly to more than 1,800,000° F (1,000,000° C) in the outer atmosphere of the sun.

The gravitational pull at the surface of the sun is 28 times as strong as the gravitational pull at the earth's surface. So strong is the sun's gravity that it exceeds the earth's gravitational pull for any object that is more than 160,000 miles (nearly 258,000 km) from the earth. Thus the moon experiences a stronger gravitational pull from the sun than from the earth.

SOLAR ENERGY

To appreciate the vastness of the power that is inherent in sunlight, one need only reflect that all the power represented in the winds and in dams and rivers and all the power contained in natural fuels such as wood, coal, and oil is nothing more than sunlight that has been stored up by a tiny planet 93 million miles away from the sun.

Energy Output. The sunlight received at the top of the earth's atmosphere supplies energy to the earth at the rate of about 2 calories per square centimeter (about 0.15 sq inch) per minute—a figure known as the *solar constant.* This amounts to a steady supply of 2.4×10^{14} horsepower (25.6×10^{14} kg-calories per minute) for the earth as a whole. Yet the earth intercepts only 2.2 billionths of the power generated by the sun. During observations made over a period of 50 years, this output of solar power has varied by no more than a few tenths of 1%.

Source of the Sun's Energy. Scientists have recognized that only one known process, atomic transmutation, is capable of generating sufficient energy to maintain the sun's output of power. In fact, the first practical investigation into atomic energy was made as part of the attempt to explain the source of solar power.

The sequence of nuclear reactions within the sun was worked out independently in 1938 by the German-American physicist Hans Bethe and the German astronomer Carl von Weizsäcker. Two main cycles of reactions may be described, of which the most important is the *proton-proton reaction.* In this sequence, protons collide to form hydrogen nuclei, which in turn collide with further protons to produce unstable helium nuclei. The latter react and form stable helium nuclei, at the same time producing more protons and other subatomic particles. The net result of the cycle of proton-proton reactions is that hydrogen is transmuted into helium.

The *carbon cycle* is more complex but the net result is the same. Nuclei of heavier elements such as carbon, nitrogen, and oxygen are involved, but in the end it is the star's hydrogen

The relatively small height of the chromosphere is exaggerated. The corona extends into the solar wind.

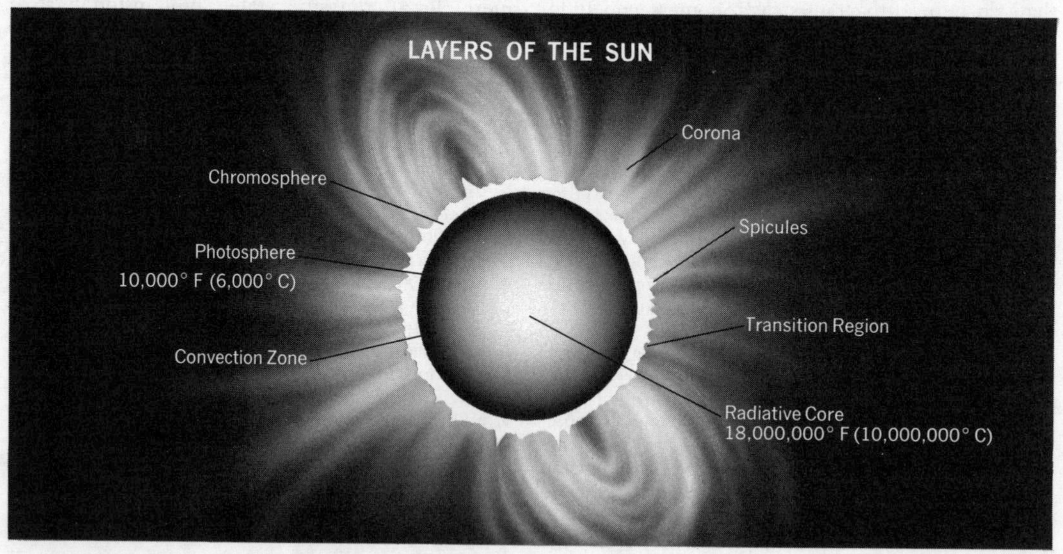

LARGE PROMINENCE loops high into the coronal region. The material of the prominence moves along lines of force of the localized magnetic field, sinking back toward the sun.

YERKES OBSERVATORY PHOTOGRAPH, UNIVERSITY OF CHICAGO

supplies that are converted into helium. The proton-proton sequence apparently predominates in less massive stars such as the sun.

Thus the sun is a giant thermonuclear furnace that transforms hydrogen into helium, and energy released near the center of the sun continually pushes outward in an effort to escape. The force of this outward push is offset by the strong gravitational pull of the sun on the gases composing its outer layers.

Convective Cells. Most of the sun is in a highly stable configuration, and mixing of the solar gases is extremely slow. However, just below the apparent surface or *photosphere* the sun is convectively unstable. That is, it transfers heat in a circulatory process from hotter regions below to cooler regions above. Numerous convective cells in this region keep the gases in the outer layers well mixed.

The convective cells are manifest to telescopes on earth as small, bright *granules* and larger *supergranules* covering the "surface" of the sun. Because of their relatively small size and their importance in understanding the structure and interior processes of the sun, the granules present a challenging observational problem.

THE OUTER LAYERS

The most familiar solar phenomena, such as sunspots and prominences, take place in the outer layers of the sun.

Early eclipse observers were able to see the sun's extensive, pearly-white *corona* surrounding the obscuring disk of the moon. Bright, rose-colored *prominences* were sometimes seen extending above the edge of the moon's disk and into the corona. However, observational progress became more rapid after the introduction of photographic techniques at the eclipse of 1851. Thus in 1860 the Italian astronomer Angelo Secchi was able to prove that prominences in fact were part of the sun rather than of the moon, as early observers had tended to believe.

In 1869 the U. S. astronomers Charles Young and William Harkness discovered an unknown emission line superimposed on the continuous spectrum of the solar corona. Attempts to explain the processes that caused this strange new line and several similar lines discovered in following years were to lead to revolutionary concepts of the sun's atmosphere (see below, under the discussion of *Corona*).

In 1870, Young also observed the spectrum of a shallow layer of gases between the photosphere and the corona—the so-called *reversing layer*—which flashed into view for a few seconds at the beginning and the end of a total eclipse. The region from which this flash spectrum arose was given the name *chromosphere,* because of its rosy-red appearance.

Since that time, eclipse observations have added a wealth of detail to the astronomer's knowledge of the chromosphere, corona, and prominences. In addition, instrument techniques have been developed that permit astronomers to observe the corona and other phenomena of the outer layers without waiting for an eclipse of the sun.

Chromosphere. The chromosphere is an irregular layer of gases, varying in depth from 1,000 to 10,000 miles (1,600 to 16,000 km). It extends upward from the visible edge of the sun—that is, the photosphere—to join with the overlying corona. At heights greater than 3,000 miles (4,800 km) above the photosphere, the extensions of the chromosphere consist almost entirely of small, high-speed jets of gas called *spicules.* These jets are ejected from the low chromosphere into the less dense corona.

A typical spicule "lives" only about 4 to 5 minutes. During this time it rises with a speed of about 17 miles (27 km) per second from its base at a height of about 1,000 miles to a maximum height of about 10,000 miles.

The spectrum of the chromosphere shows numerous bright emission lines that are produced by hydrogen and helium and by many neutral and ionized atoms of metals. Again, the temperature gradient is reversed in the chromosphere, so that temperature increases with distance outward from the sun. The exact manner of this temperature rise is fundamental to an understanding of solar processes. It can only be mentioned here that the temperature in the upper photosphere is at a minimum of about 7,200° F (4,000° C), and that it rises in the low chromosphere to about 10,800° F (6,000° C). In the high chromosphere the temperature is over 36,000° F (20,000° C).

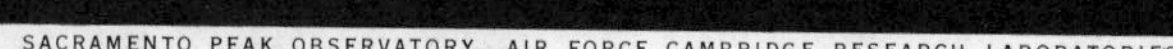

SACRAMENTO PEAK OBSERVATORY, AIR FORCE CAMBRIDGE RESEARCH LABORATORIES

Spicules—rapid jets of gas—shoot up from the chromosphere into the corona, each lasting about 5 minutes.

Prominences. Solar prominences extend into the region of the corona. They appear to be similar in many respects to the chromosphere. That is, their spectra show emission lines of the same neutral and ionized atoms as do chromosphere spectra. However, different kinds of prominences show marked differences in the relative intensities of their spectral lines, a fact that indicates differences in temperature and density.

Knots of material in a prominence move predominantly downward, usually along gently curved trajectories that follow the lines of force in localized magnetic fields. Even though the matter in prominences is seen through telescopes to move downward, however, this does not mean that it is falling freely under the force of gravity. Instead, the magnetic forces that are present tend to balance the force of gravity and keep the downward velocity constant. And some kinds of prominences, such as eruptives, surges, and sprays, show a predominantly outward motion.

Prominences generally move at speeds of about 100 miles (160 km) per second. The fastest such motion ever observed was a surge that moved outward at 830 miles (1,330 km) per second. Since the velocity for escape from the sun is 380 miles (610 km) per second, this means that the material in the surge and similar fast-moving prominences escapes the sun's gravitational pull.

Corona. The corona is the tenuous outermost part of the solar atmosphere. In a total solar eclipse the corona shines with the brightness of the full moon, and may be seen extending out to several times the diameter of the sun. In fact, it extends beyond the orbit of Jupiter, thus encompassing the earth. At these distances it is very tenuous and is known as the *solar wind,* the effects of which are discussed below under *The Sun and the Earth.*

It has been mentioned that an unknown coronal line was discovered at the eclipse of 1869, and that this was followed by the discovery of other emission lines on the coronal spectrum. When astronomers failed to identify these lines with any known set of laboratory spectra, they were prompted to invent a new element, "coronium." It was not until 1940 that the Swedish physicist Bengt Edlen identified several of the lines with familiar terrestrial atoms—atoms subjected, however, to extremely "abnormal" conditions in terms of the earth's environment. Thus the "green" line discovered in 1869 was identified with iron atoms having 13 of their normal 26 electrons removed. Other lines were identified as iron atoms missing 9 to 14 electrons, and still others were identified with similarly stripped atoms of nickel, calcium, and argon. Such high stages of ionization, it was determined, require temperatures of about 1,800,000° F (1,000,000° C), and this was verified by other data.

It is these high temperatures that cause the corona to expand continually outward, forming the solar wind that sweeps past the earth into the far limits of the solar system. The high temperatures also produce intense amounts of X-rays and far ultraviolet photons, and give rise to intense noise-like signals at radio wavelengths. It is believed that the chromosphere and corona are heated by shock waves generated in the sun's subphotospheric convection zone.

THE TRANSITION REGION of the sun's outer layers corresponds to the region in the photograph above in which brighter and darker gases merge. Gas pressure drops slowly from the convection zone to the corona, but temperature and density change sharply.

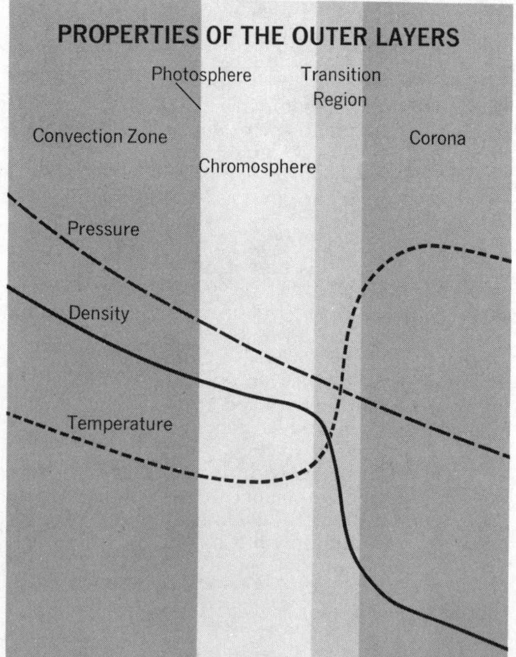

SOLAR ACTIVITY

Sunspots are the most familiar example of solar activity, but the emphasis they are given as a measure of such activity arises primarily from the ease with which they are observed. Frequently a wide variety of complex phenomena, requiring refined observational techniques, are found in association with sunspots. These phenomena are referred to collectively as *solar activity,* and those regions that show a marked degree of activity are called *active regions.*

Sunspots. As early as 28 B.C., Chinese annals carried records of dark areas observed on the sun. However, they were attributed to flying birds. In 1610, while surveying the wonders of the heavens revealed by his newly perfected telescope, Galileo observed the same small, dark spots on the face of the sun. By watching these spots appear on the eastern edge of the sun and then drift across the solar disk to disappear off the western edge, Galileo determined that the spots were in fact on the sun and not shadows cast by some other object or objects.

It has since been learned that the average lifetime for a given sunspot is about one week. However, some spots live for only a few hours, while others may live as long as 18 months. The spots range in size from the smallest observable objects, about 500 miles (800 km) in diameter, to huge areas that are over 50,000 miles (80,000 km) in diameter. The spots are related to magnetic activity in the sun's outer layers, but the processes are not yet fully understood. They appear as dark areas simply because they are somewhat cooler than the surrounding gases.

Spots may occur singly or in groups of two to more than 100. There is also a marked tendency for the spots to occur in pairs, in which case the two spots tend to have opposite magnetic polarities. Furthermore, the more westerly or "leader" spots in the sun's northern hemisphere tend to have an opposite polarity to the leader spots in the southern hemisphere. The strength of the magnetic field associated with any given spot is closely related to the spot's size, and the largest have fields of about 3,500 gauss.

Galileo and later astronomers recognized that the number of sunspots varies from year to year, but it was not until 1843 that a German amateur astronomer, Heinrich Schwabe, observed that the number follows a periodic cycle of maxima and minima.

Records of sunspots show that there is no strict periodicity either in the time when maximum or minimum numbers occur, or in the total number of spots. The average period between minima is 11.08 years, but individual sunspot cycles have varied in length from 8 to 13 years. The number of sunspots at maximum has varied from 46 to 154.

At the beginning of a new sunspot cycle, there are usually remnant spots of the preceding cycle at latitudes 5° to 10° from the solar equator. The spots of the new cycle begin at latitudes 25° to 40° from the equator, in both hemispheres. As the cycle progresses, the newer spots tend to form closer and closer to the equator. There is also a reversal in the magnetic polarities of spot groups in both hemispheres as a new cycle begins. That is, if the "leader" spots were of north polarity in the preceding cycle, they change to south polarity for the new cycle.

Active Regions. In the photosphere surrounding sunspots there are usually bright veinlike features known as *faculae*, a word derived from a Latin word meaning "torch." Faculae are observed in normal white light without the aid of special devices. However, they are seen only near the edge of the sun, where they stand out in greater contrast with the photosphere. They are much longer-lived than sunspots.

The chromosphere over sunspot regions also shows bright areas of longer lifetime and greater extent than the spots themselves. These areas are called *plages*, from a French word meaning "beach," but they may also be known as *bright flocculi*, from a Latin word meaning "flock of wool." Above the plages, the chromosphere is mottled by alternately bright and dark features of fainter contrast than the plages. Not uncommonly, dark ribbonlike features known as *dark filaments* are scattered over the solar surface in association with the plages, although other filaments may be at high solar latitudes outside of the sunspot zone. At the edge of the sun's disk the filaments show up as prominences elevated above the chromosphere.

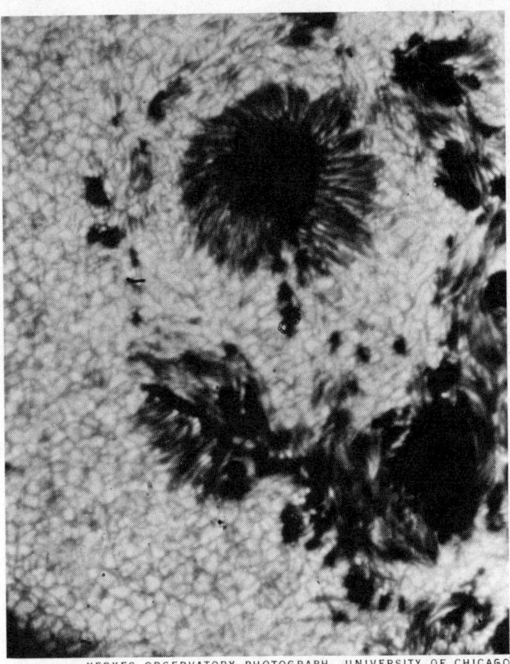

YERKES OBSERVATORY PHOTOGRAPH, UNIVERSITY OF CHICAGO

SUNSPOT GROUP, photographed with a telescope carried high into the atmosphere by a balloon, shows fine structures of the spots. It also reveals the granules marking convective cells below the surface.

The corona itself is both hotter and denser than average above the active regions. Temperatures of several million degrees are not uncommon there, and coronal structures above such regions display the intricate patterns of magnetic fields that are associated with sunspots and their surroundings. Most of the coronal radiations—including X-rays and radio waves—are more intense in the active regions, and the lines in their spectra are stronger.

Prominences that are associated with active regions are characteristically short-lived. They often appear as closed loops or as violent ejections of matter in sprays and surges.

Flares. The most spectacular and in many ways the most interesting phenomena of active regions are flares. Flares are observed in the chromosphere as short-lived explosive brightenings of plages. They begin with a sudden brightening in part of the plage, usually near sunspots, and increase to maximum brightness in 5 to 10 minutes. During this time the flare spreads to surrounding areas of the plage. The most favorable times for flares to occur are when sunspot groups are decaying or growing. Large bright flares usually last an hour or more. Smaller ones may disappear in a few minutes.

Intense bursts of X-rays and radio signals emitted from the corona are associated with many flares. These radiations are observed simultaneously with the flare, but following intense flares there are often greatly enhanced fluxes of energetic protons and alpha particles in a half hour to a few days, as recorded by particle detectors near the earth. The protons and alpha particles are accelerated from the corona above chromospheric flare regions at the time of the visual flare. Their arrival at the earth is delayed because their velocity is lower than the velocity of electromagnetic radiations, and sometimes by their complicated trajectories in the solar magnetic fields.

THE SUN AND THE EARTH

Solar ultraviolet and X-radiation produce the earth's ionosphere. That is, the photons of radiation are absorbed by the gases of the atmosphere high above the earth. The variable intensity of the radiation causes continuous fluctuations in the ionosphere, producing irregularities in radio transmission and reception on the earth's surface. The 11-year cycle of solar activity generates a similar cycle of variations in the ionosphere.

Short-term outbreaks of solar activity, particularly flares, may seriously disturb and even black out high-frequency communications for short periods. Increased ultraviolet and X-radiation from the sun also produce added heat in the earth's atmosphere, causing the atmosphere to swell and to extend farther into space. Orbiting satellites encounter increased drag when this occurs.

One of the spectacular achievements of satellite research has been the direct observation of the solar wind, together with many associated and previously unsuspected phenomena. As the wind blows past the earth, the earth's magnetic field far out in space is caught up and blown with it. This confines the magnetic field upwind and produces a long magnetic "tail" downwind. Some of the particles of the solar wind—mainly protons and electrons—leak inside the magnetic field to produce the vast Van Allen belts that girdle the earth. See VAN ALLEN RADIATION BELTS.

The solar wind becomes gusty as activity occurs on the sun. Buffeting of the earth's magnetic field by these gusts produces geomagnetic storms. Some of the trapped particles are accelerated and penetrate deeper into the earth's atmosphere, where they produce aurorae and possibly other effects.

When certain flares of unusual character occur, the sun ejects particles of cosmic-ray energies—that is, up to a million times the energy of particles in the solar wind. Large numbers of particles of intermediate energies about 10,000 times that of the solar wind particles are also emitted. These particle bursts are known as *proton storms.* Because of their energy range and their density, proton storms present a definite hazard to astronauts who venture beyond the protective shield of the earth's magnetic field. Space travelers have to be aware of solar and space "weather" conditions.

STUDY OF THE SUN

All that is known of the sun's structure and interior processes has been learned or inferred from the light and other radiation that the sun emits. Light carries with it indelible "fingerprints" of its source. The visible light of the sun closely resembles blackbody radiation, or ideal radiation, emitted at a temperature of 30,000° F (6,000° C), but closer spectroscopic inspection reveals thousands of dark, narrow lines crossing the bands of spectral colors. Each of the lines is caused by the absorption of light by atoms or molecules of a particular element in the solar atmosphere, and elements present in the sun are identified in this manner.

Thus spectroscopy is one of the astronomer's most powerful tools in solar research. From the solar spectrum detailed information has been obtained on a great number of solar properties, including composition, variations of temperature and pressure in the solar atmosphere, and the total energy generated by the sun.

Ordinary optical observatories with specially designed solar telescopes continue to provide the major focal point of solar studies. Typically, such observatories are located where they can provide the best conditions for particular kinds of observations. For example, clean and tenuous air is needed for studying the corona, and this is best found on high mountaintops. Studies of the chromosphere and corona also demand steady, quiet atmospheric conditions combined with a low frequency of cloud cover so that the highest possible angular resolution can be achieved.

Certain aspects of the corona and chromosphere can be properly studied only at times of total solar eclipse. Thus, expeditions to eclipse sites, often in remote areas of the earth, are a vital part of solar research. See ECLIPSE.

Orbiting solar observatories as well as high-altitude rockets and balloons permit observations of the sun from outside most of the earth's atmosphere. This permits observations of spectral regions that are inaccessible from the ground, notably extreme ultraviolet and X-ray wavelengths. The principal radiations of the corona and chromosphere occur at these wavelengths. Astronomers have also begun to employ infrared telescopes, both from the ground and from high-flying aircraft, so that regions of the sun which are not readily observable by other techniques may be studied.

Large radio antennas have been placed around the world to keep daily watch on the sun, both to determine the character of solar radiation at radio wavelengths and to detect transient solar events such as flares and energetic particle ejections. Each new extension of observations into different spectral regions reveals important new solar phenomena and increases the supply of data from which astronomers piece together their concepts of the physical properties of the sun and its activities.

R. GRANT ATHAY
High Altitude Observatory
National Center for Atmospheric Research

Bibliography

Billings, Donald E., *A Guide to the Solar Corona* (New York 1966).

Kuiper, Gerard P., ed., *The Sun* (Chicago 1953).

Parker, Eugene N., *Interplanetary Dynamical Processes* (New York 1963).

Smith, Henry J., and Elske, V. P., *Solar Flares* (New York 1963).

Tandberg-Hanssen, Eimer, *Solar Activity* (Waltham, Mass., 1967).

Thomas, Richard N., and Athay, R. Grant, *Physics of the Chromosphere* (New York 1961).

Zirin, Harold, *The Solar Atmosphere* (Waltham, Mass., 1966).

SUN ALSO RISES, The, first novel by Ernest Hemingway, published in 1926. It tells of American and British expatriates in France and Spain in 1925. The narrator is Jake Barnes, a newspaperman and wounded veteran of World War I. His associates include Lady Brett Ashley, an international adventuress; Robert Cohn, minor editor and novelist; and Bill Gorton, a humorist. The action is simple, moving from the café life on the Left Bank in Paris to the fiesta of San Fermín in Pamplona, Spain, where we meet the real hero of the novel, a young bullfighter named Pedro Romero. With Brett as queen bee, a quadrangular affair develops. Barnes' war wound prevents consummation of his love for Brett, but she has brief affairs with Cohn and Romero, finally rejecting both. Cohn, an amateur boxer, interrupts a séance between the bullfighter and the lady, hurting Romero badly. Next day, at the climactic bullfight of the fiesta, Romero proves his manhood in a magnificent triumph. A deflated Cohn departs the scene, and the novel ends with a sardonic interview between Brett and Jake in a Madrid taxicab.

One of Hemingway's epigraphs is a statement ascribed to Gertrude Stein: "You are all a lost generation." The novel rapidly became a handbook for so-called "lost-generationism" among young people who had survived the war, lived a hand–to–mouth existence in foreign capitals, and spent their days in continuous motion from bar to bar. But Hemingway later explained that the novel's real theme is in the quotation from Ecclesiastes that gives him his title. The story's true hero is the abiding earth itself, while such generations as that of Jake, Brett, Romero, and Cohn come and depart between sun and sun.

CARLOS BAKER, *Princeton University*

SUN BEAR. See BEAR.

SUN BITTERN, bit'ûrn, a large, timid wading bird found in tropical rain forests from southern Mexico to Bolivia and southeastern Brazil. It has a stout body 18 inches (46 cm) long, a slender neck, and long, slender, orange legs. The full, soft plumage is of varying shades of mottled black, gray, brown, and white. When the wings are spread in display they show a striking pattern of black, chestnut, pale olive, yellow, and white.

Sun bitterns feed on insects, crustaceans, and small fish. Their nests are bulky structures of sticks and mud constructed by both sexes in trees 12 to 30 feet (4–9 meters) above the ground. The two or three nearly oval eggs are buff-colored with reddish-brown spots.

The sun bittern, *Eurypyga helias,* is the sole member of the family Eurypygidae.

KENNETH E. STAGER
Los Angeles County Museum of Natural History

SUN CH'ING-LING, sōōn ching ling (1892–), Chinese public figure and widow of Sun Yat-sen, founder of the Chinese Republic. Madame Sun was born in Shanghai into the influential Soong family. She is an elder sister of Mme. Chiang Kai-shek.

Graduating from Wesleyan College in Macon, Ga., in 1913, Ch'ing-ling returned to Shanghai and became Sun Yat-sen's secretary. They were married in Tokyo the next year. Ch'ing-ling helped Sun in his work and remained dedicated to his revolutionary ideals after his death in 1925. Following the break between the Nationalists and Communists in 1927 she claimed that Sun's policies had been violated and left for the Soviet Union. Returning in 1929 she associated with dissident political elements and opposed Chiang Kai-shek's leadership, except during World War II.

Under China's Communist regime, Madame Sun was a vice chairman of the People's Republic. She headed welfare and women's organizations, was active in Soviet friendship and world peace associations, and traveled abroad.

HARRY J. LAMLEY, *University of Hawaii*

SUN DANCE, the most spectacular of the religious ceremonies of the Plains Indians of North America. The name derives from the Dakota (Sioux) term for the dance, because the Dakota followed the custom of gazing at the sun as they danced. Other tribes, which usually do not gaze at the sun during the ceremony, call it a fasting or thirst dance or a holy ("medicine") lodge dance. The dance is held annually. The participants pray for the general welfare and for personal wants, and they expect to experience visions during the course of the ceremony.

Probably through the influence of tribes such as the Hidatsa and Mandan, who held elaborate indoor fasting and torture ceremonies, the Cheyenne and Arapaho were inspired to build open-air, circular lodges for their dances. The usual lodge is built around a central pole—a ceremonially cut and decorated cottonwood. This is surrounded by a circular row of posts supporting a wall of boughs, with rafters extending from the pole to the wall. The Dakota and some other tribes do not use rafters. Altars, sometimes very elaborate, and medicine bundles—collections of sacred or magical objects—are associated with some dances.

The form of dance varies. The Cheyenne, Arapaho, and Plains Ojibwa dance in place facing the pole. The Dakota dance in place but

Sun bittern (*Eurypyga helias*)

ARTHUR AMBLER, FROM NATIONAL AUDUBON SOCIETY

COURTESY OF THE AMERICAN MUSEUM OF NATURAL HISTORY

Teton Dakota sun dance, depicted in painting by Short Bull, a member of the tribe.

periodically move to face the four cardinal points of the compass or the sun. The Shoshoni, Ute, and Crow run to the pole and then dance backwards to booths inside the lodge wall. The men shrill eagle bone whistles while dancing, and some groups also permit women to use the whistles. The dance itself, irrespective of preparations and intrusive ceremonies, usually lasts three days and part of the nights, with frequent intermissions.

The dance sometimes involved ordeals until the U. S. government banned such practices late in the 19th century. In the most common form of torture, skewers were run through a dancer's chest muscles and fastened by cords to the central pole. The dancer pulled at the cords until the skewers tore out of his chest.

The Sun Dance is particularly popular with the northern Arapaho, the Shoshoni, and the Crow. The Dakota no longer continuously observe the fast, and dance only part of the day.

STEPHEN E. FERACA
Bureau of Indian Affairs

SUN GREBE. See FINFOOT.

SUN VALLEY, a resort village in south-central Idaho, in Blaine county, is situated in a valley of the Sawtooth Mountains, at an altitude of about 6,000 feet, about 90 miles (144 km) in an air line east of Boise. It was organized in 1936 by W. Averell Harriman, then chairman of the Union Pacific Railroad, as a ski resort to compete with the best in Europe. Sun Valley is now a winter and summer resort, with facilities for all sports. It is a starting point for hiking and fishing excursions into the primitive area of the Sawtooths. The small city of Ketchum, about one mile (0.6 km) to the south, was the last home of Ernest Hemingway, the novelist, who died there and is buried in the Ketchum cemetery.

The incorporated village of Sun Valley is governed by a mayor and council. Population: 317.

SUN WORSHIP. The worship or adoration of the sun is found among many religions in all parts of the world. The sun, usually personified, is considered a major divinity or powerful spirit. In ancient Egypt the cult of the sun god Ra was centered at Heliopolis, "City of the Sun." There, sun worship was one aspect of a complex polytheism. Similarly, the ancient Greeks had their sun god in Phoebus Apollo, who was represented as racing the sun chariot across the sky. Vedic Hinduism had its sun deity in Surya or Mitra. The ancient Persian religion of Mithraism centered on the "Invincible Sun."

Sun deities also have often been identified with the origin of royal lineages. Thus, the royal house of Japan traces its descent from the sun goddess Amaterasu, while the Inca of Peru similarly claimed to be the children of the sun. In the beliefs of the Inca, the sun was the most important of a group of sky gods, who themselves were the servants of the creator god, Viracocha. The Temple of the Sun in Cuzco is a major religious edifice of the Inca period.

Beliefs and rituals centering on a solar deity are not limited to societies with elaborate priestly and political hierarchies. Belief in a sun deity was widespread among both South and North American Indians, who were organized on a tribal rather than on a state level. Among the North American Indians of the Great Plains, the Sun Dance was a central ritual of great importance. During this ceremony, men implored the sun for blessings and visions, often undergoing extreme types of self-torture. See SUN DANCE.

Remnants of sun worship are found in various European folk practices. Rites associated with the winter solstice have been incorporated into Christmas rituals. Another key date was the summer solstice—Midsummer Day, or St. John's Day. A St. John's Eve custom was to build great bonfires, particularly on mountain tops.

ERIKA BOURGUIGNON
The Ohio State University

EASTFOTO

Sun Yat-sen

SUN YAT-SEN, sōōn yät sen (1866–1925), Chinese revolutionary leader and national hero. In Nationalist China he is revered as the "father of the republic." In Communist China he is hailed as the "pioneer of the revolution."

Early Life. Sun was born on Nov. 12, 1866, in Hsiangshan county, Kwangtung province, South China. His parents were of peasant stock. When he was 12 he was able to join his elder brother, who had emigrated to Hawaii. There Sun attended Iolani School, an Anglican academy in Honolulu, and displayed an aptitude for English and for Western studies. After graduating in 1882 he returned to China. A rebellious youth, he was banished from his village for desecrating a temple idol. He then went to Hong Kong, where he was baptized a Christian and in 1892 became a physician.

Soon abandoning medicine, he went to Tientsin and tried to interest the powerful Chinese official Li Hung-chang in a proposal for broad reform. Rebuffed by Li and already strongly opposed to the ruling Ch'ing (Manchu) dynasty, Sun began his career as a revolutionary.

The Revolutionary. In 1894, Sun left China for Hawaii, where he formed the Hsing Chung Hui (Revive China Society) among the local Chinese. He set up a main branch in Hong Kong in January 1895 and, in league with secret societies, staged an abortive revolt at Canton that October.

Sun spent the next 16 years in exile traveling about the world in search of support for his revolutionary movement. He became a familiar figure among overseas Chinese and gained international fame after Ch'ing government agents in 1896 attempted to kidnap him in London. During his exile Sun spent considerable time in Japan. The rising tide of revolutionary sentiment among Chinese students abroad led in 1905 to the founding of the T'ung Meng Hui (Revolutionary Alliance) in Tokyo, with Sun as its elected head. Thereafter he was able to broaden the base of his support by attracting intellectuals from throughout China to his cause.

In 1905, Sun first propounded his Three Principles of the People: nationalism, democracy, and livelihood. His influence spread and revolutionary activity in China increased, yet attempts to foment uprisings continued to fail. Sun helped direct no less than 10 abortive uprisings prior to the successive revolt that broke out unexpectedly in Wuchang on Oct. 10, 1911.

The Statesman. On learning of the Wuchang Revolt, Sun proceeded to London and Paris on a diplomatic mission in behalf of the revolution. He returned to China in late December 1911 amid great fanfare. Elected provisional president of the Republic of China, he assumed office on Jan. 1, 1912, at Nanking. In February, however, he resigned in favor of a rival—the powerful northern military leader Yüan Shih-k'ai—in order to avert civil war.

After the transfer of the republican capital to Peking, the T'ung Meng Hui was formed into a legitimate political party, the Kuomintang, or Nationalist party. Sun was elected party director but proved to be more attentive to schemes for national reconstruction, including railroad development, than to party issues.

Sun became immersed in politics again in 1913 after Yüan Shih-k'ai acted to suppress the Kuomintang and to make himself emperor. Sun supported anti-Yüan forces in a short-lived resistance, then took refuge in Japan. There, in 1914, he sought Japanese aid and reorganized the Kuomintang, placing it under his direct control and renaming it the Chung-hua Komingtang (Chinese Revolutionary Party).

Sun returned to China shortly before Yüan's death in 1916, intent upon implementing his revolutionary program. However, he had to contend with military leaders who succeeded Yüan in power at Peking. Sun set up a rival regime at Canton in 1917, but withdrew his support the following year, when southern warlords on whom he depended for support moved to dominate his regime. After a two-year sojourn in Shanghai, he returned to Canton determined to establish a base from which his party might reunify China.

Sun inaugurated a republican government at Canton and fostered a regional military buildup, despite opposition from southern warlords. He also accepted Soviet and international Communist backing, which in 1923–1924 led him into an alliance with the Chinese Communists. The result was the restructuring of the Kuomintang and the creation of a party-directed army. Sun died in Peking on March 12, 1925.

Throughout his career Sun was a fervent nationalist and visionary who strove to make China strong and modern. Mainly Western-trained, he was more detached from traditional influences than most of his compatriots in China. His revolutionary principles were broad and flexible, encompassing ideas he learned from the world at large. Although impulsive in his actions, Sun was a natural leader whose patriotism, courage, and integrity endeared him to his countrymen.

HARRY J. LAMLEY, *University of Hawaii*

Bibliography

Hsü, Leonard S., ed. and tr., *Sun Yat-sen, His Political and Social Ideals* (Los Angeles 1933).

Jansen, Marius B., *The Japanese and Sun Yat-sen* (Cambridge, Mass., 1954).

Linebarger, Paul N., *Sun Yat-sen and the Chinese Republic* (New York 1925).

Schiffrin, Harold Z., *Sun Yat-sen and the Origins of the Chinese Revolution* (Berkeley 1968).

Sharman, Lyon, *Sun Yat-sen: His Life and Its Meaning* (New York 1934).

A. W. AMBLER, FROM NATIONAL AUDUBON SOCIETY

Kenya amethyst sunbird

SUNBIRD, any of over 100 species of small, brightly colored, nectar- and insect-eating birds. More than half of the species live in Africa; the rest live in India, Ceylon, Burma, Malaya, the East Indies, and Australia. Several atypical species are often called "spider hunters" because of their feeding habits. Sunbirds are the ecological equivalents of New World hummingbirds.

Sunbirds are 3½ to 8½ inches (9–22 cm) long. They have long, slender, down-curved bills; extensible tubular tongues forked at the tip; rounded wings; rounded or square-tipped tails; and short, stout legs. Both male and female spider hunters are drably colored, but the males of other sunbirds are brilliantly colored.

Sunbirds feed on both flower nectar and insects, but unlike hummingbirds they tend to perch on the flower being probed rather than to hover around it. Occasionally they puncture long flowers to get at the nectar. They travel through flowering areas according to the blossoming season. They are nongregarious and nonmigratory.

The female alone builds a purselike nest, with a porticolike roof, suspended from a branch. The nest is made of plant fibers held together with spider webs and raggedly camouflaged with coarse vegetation and lined with hair, down, or feathers. One to three eggs are laid, white or pale blue and streaked or blotched. The female alone usually incubates the eggs for 13 or 14 days, but the male may help feed the young.

Sunbirds make up the family Nectariniidae of the order Passeriformes.

CARL WELTY, *Beloit College*

SUNBURN is a painful redness of the skin caused by exposure to sunlight. It is caused not by heat but by rays of ultraviolet light (UVL). These rays are filtered out of the atmosphere by smoke and smog, and most of them are blocked by ordinary window glass. Clouds, though, do not filter ultraviolet rays, so a person can be sunburned on a cloudy day. Also, the rays can be reflected by snow and sand, so one can be sunburned while sitting under an umbrella at the beach.

Redness of the skin develops from 30 minutes to 24 hours after exposure. If the sunburn is mild, there may be a barely noticeable flaking of the skin accompanied by tanning. More severe sunburns result in blisters that rupture and leave a peeling surface. In very severe cases there may be general discomfort, headache, chills, fever, and even shock. Talcum powder and aspirin may be used to alleviate the discomfort of mild cases of sunburn. More severe cases require stronger pain-killers and the administration of corticosteroids.

The skin is normally protected from the effects of ultraviolet rays by the outermost layer of the epidermis (stratum corneum) and by particles of dark pigment (melanin) in the epidermis. However, this protection is not total and even dark-skinned people, such as Negroes, may become sunburned if exposure to UVL is prolonged. Eventually enough rays penetrate the epidermis and cause chemical changes in the underlying dermis. It is believed that such changes may lead to skin cancer.

STEPHEN E. SILVER, M. D.
Montefiore Hospital, New York

SUNBURY, a city in central Pennsylvania, the seat of Northumberland county, is on the Susquehanna River, 55 miles (88 km) north of Harrisburg. The city ships coal, a natural resource of the region, and makes textiles, clothing, metal products, and machine tools.

A replica of Fort Augusta, which was built in 1756 during the French and Indian War, is in Sunbury, and the state maintains a historical museum at the site. Sunbury was platted in 1772 on the site of the ancient Indian settlement of Shamokin. It was incorporated as a borough in 1797 and as a city in 1921. Government is by commission. Population: 13,025.

SUNDA ISLANDS, sun'də, a part of the Indonesian Archipelago in Southeast Asia. Extending some 2,200 miles (3,500 km) from west to east and 1,100 miles (1,750 km) from north to south, they are divided into two groups. The Greater Sundas comprise Sumatra, Java, Borneo, and Sulawesi (Celebes); the Lesser Sundas, stretching eastward from Java, include Bali, Lombok, Sumbawa, Sumba, Flores, and Timor. Except for portions of Borneo and Timor, the Sunda Islands belong to Indonesia. See also INDONESIA and articles on individual islands.

SUNDAY, Billy (1862–1935), American Presbyterian revivalist. William Ashley Sunday was born in Ames, Iowa, on Nov. 19, 1862. He spent his childhood in an orphanage. He worked at odd jobs until 1883 when he began a baseball career with the Chicago White Sox, playing later with teams in Pittsburgh and Philadelphia. He underwent a conversion experience in 1886, and when he married Helen A. Thompson in 1888 he became a Presbyterian.

Interest in religious affairs led Billy Sunday to work for the Chicago Y.M.C.A. and then to be an assistant to J. Wilbur Chapman, a noted evangelist. By 1896, Sunday had begun his own career as a revivalist. Licensed to preach by the Chicago Presbytery in 1898, he was ordained, with an examination waived, in 1903.

With Homer A. Rodeheaver as song leader, Sunday held mass meetings in towns and cities all over the country, the largest of which was in New York City in 1917. He preached a vivid version of an evangelical-fundamentalist theology, and he was noted for flamboyant acrobatics in the pulpit. His converts were estimated at one million. Funds for his work came through free-will offerings and contributions from wealthy businessmen. His popularity waned after 1920. Sunday died in Chicago, on Nov. 6, 1935.

JAMES H. SMYLIE
Union Theological Seminary, Richmond, Va.

SUNDAY is the first day of the week, traditionally assigned for Christian worship. Literally "Sunday" means "day of the sun." It derives its name from the ancient pagan week, whose days were named after the sun, moon, and five visible planets. Sunday, like the other days of the week in the Western calendar, is reckoned from midnight to midnight. Other calendars measure their days from sunset to sunset—for example, the Hebrew Sabbath is so measured. The liturgical observance of Sunday among Roman Catholics traditionally begins with the first vespers on the preceding Saturday. Though the pagan name, "Sunday," survives in English, the importance of the day is due to its Christian significance.

The observance of a specific day during each week as a time of worship is widespread; for example, Jews observe the Sabbath (Saturday) and Muslims observe Friday. What is unique about the Christian observance of Sunday is not the choice of one day a week for worship, but the specifically Christian meaning given this day.

Origins of Christian Observance. Christ observed the Sabbath but opposed legalistic interpretations of it. Likewise, Christ's Jewish followers, apparently not wishing to abandon a traditional religious practice, observed the Sabbath in addition to their specifically Christian worship. This tradition of Sabbath observance was absent in the non-Jewish areas to which Christianity soon spread. Also, the developing conviction that Christian beliefs superseded the Jewish Covenant implied that Christians were not bound to Sabbath observance. Nonetheless, both the Sabbath and Sunday were observed by Christians for some time. Eventually, Sunday became the distinctive day for Christian worship, since Sunday is the day of Christ's Resurrection, and the day of the coming of the Holy Spirit (Pentecost).

In the early church the term that gradually gained widest acceptance was "the Lord's Day," an expression used in the New Testament (Revelation 1:10). Its Latin form, *dies dominica,* survives in modern French *dimanche,* Spanish *domingo,* and Italian *domenica.* Though the pagan term, *dies solis,* or "day of the sun," continued in use, it was frequently given Christian significance by describing Christ as the "Sun of Justice" bringing light into a world of darkness. Furthermore, as the "first day" of the week, Sunday was reverenced as the day of new creation through Christ, in contrast to the Sabbath, which was sacred to the Jews as the day on which creation was completed. In a variant of this idea, God is portrayed as resting on the Sabbath from His work of creation and then on Sunday, "the eighth day," inaugurating His new creation, the church.

A Day of Worship. From the apostolic era to the present it has been customary for Christians to assemble for communal Sunday services. A wide variety of liturgical practices, such as sermons, Scriptural readings, processions, vigils, and Vespers became associated with Sunday at various times and places. However, the most characteristic act of Christian worship is the celebration of the Eucharist, or the Lord's Supper. In Christian theology, the Eucharist has been viewed as a historical commemoration of Christ's Last Supper, death, and Resurrection; as a present encounter with the risen Christ; and as a sign of expectation of the resurrection of all Christians with Christ. Sunday, as the weekly celebration of the Resurrection, also has been considered an appropriate day for administering Baptism, symbolizing the recipient's death to sin and resurrection to new life in Christ.

A Day of Rest. While Sunday was observed as a day of worship in apostolic times, the observance of Sunday as a day of rest became established later. Though many early Christians undoubtedly were constrained to work on Sunday, as Christianity increased in adherents, it gradually became customary to observe Sunday as a day wholly dedicated to God. Abstaining from unnecessary work on Sunday has an obvious parallel in the Jewish Sabbath observance, which required avoidance of all mundane activities. Both observances have been given theological interpretations. The Sabbath rest has been viewed as imitating God's rest on the seventh day of creation, while the Sunday rest has been seen as symbolizing the freedom acquired through Christian redemption.

Just as pagan festivals were celebrated as holidays, Christians frequently celebrated Sunday with various amusements. At times, ecclesiastical authorities have deemed it necessary to oppose some popular but unseemly amusements, and some have opposed any type of amusement on Sunday. The 4th century councils of Elvira and Laodicea mark the first of many ecclesiastical regulations enjoining church attendance and forbidding unnecessary work, public transactions, and some types of amusement on Sundays.

Civil Legislation. Civil laws requiring the observance of Sunday date back at least to Emperor Constantine the Great, who designated Sunday as a legal day of rest and worship in 321. This law, however, was not specifically Christian, since Sunday was the day of the sun-god for pagans as well as the Lord's day for Christians. While Constantine thus managed to please the two major religious groups in the Roman Empire, numerous later laws regulating behavior on Sunday have been avowedly Christian.

In English law, Sunday legislation, which first appeared in the 13th century, was enlarged in the 16th and 17th centuries by the addition of numerous specific provisions and penalties. Similar Sunday laws were soon introduced into the British colonies in North America. Some colonial blue laws, for example, made failure to attend Sunday church services a criminal offense. Vestiges of colonial legislation on compulsory Sunday worship survived through the early part of the 19th century.

Though laws requiring Sunday worship have disappeared from American codes, prohibitions of Sunday labor and some types of amusement still survive in modified form. In some places laws require stores to be closed on Sunday, and restrict the sale of liquor. Businessmen affected by such restrictions have argued that these laws unreasonably interfere with their freedom of religion and freedom of enterprise. The legality of such laws has generally been sustained in American courts on the basis of implied social value, not religious implications. Such a secular value has been judged legally justifiable, although the designation of Sunday as a day of rest indirectly aids the religious observance of Christians.

Numerous exceptions have been legislated to allow some kinds of work and amusements on Sundays. In many areas the existing laws are rarely enforced. See also BLUE LAWS.

JOHN T. FORD, C. S. C.
Catholic University of America

SUNDAY SCHOOL is an institution for the moral and religious instruction of children and, less often, of adolescents and adults. The church school, or Sabbath school, as it is also called, usually meets in a church building on Sundays for an hour or so. Although now a worldwide, ecumenical phenomenon, the Sunday school still reflects its Protestant, Anglo-American origins. It is most visible in the English-speaking nations, especially in the United States, where it has long been the primary mode of religious instruction for Protestants. The Protestant churches in North America and Britain furnish a vast majority of the world's Sunday school enrollment. In 1970, for example, U. S. and Canadian Protestant churches reported a total enrollment of about 30 million.

The Sunday school is part of the broader topic of religious instruction, which is covered in such articles as CATHOLIC CHURCH, ROMAN—*Activities;* and RELIGIOUS EDUCATION.

Origins of the Movement. No one knows for sure the date of the first Sunday school. In the 18th century there were countless attempts at religious teaching on Sundays. The origins of the Sunday school movement are easier to locate. Robert Raikes, a newspaper publisher in Gloucester, England, had devoted years to the cause of prison reform. Gradually, however, his interest moved from detention to the prevention of crime among the children of the poor. Since most of these children worked grueling hours during the week, they could not attend the only schools available to them—charity schools sponsored by upper-class patrons. Raikes' solution was the Sunday school, a one-day charity school in which lower-class children would learn to read the Scriptures, improve their manners and morals, and stay out of mischief on Sunday. His first Sunday school, which opened in late 1780 in Sooty Alley, Gloucester, was a failure, but an attempt in 1783 was more successful.

Raikes was a far better publicist than a schoolman. Through his writings the Sunday school became the newest cause among benevolent-minded gentlemen. In 1785 a London merchant, William Fox, launched the Sunday School Society, an organization that quickly developed a miniature school system for the poor in London and other cities. By 1787 there were about 250,000 children in the Sunday charity schools.

The American Pattern. Shortly after news about Raikes' innovation reached the New World, a handful of Philadelphia churchmen formed the First Day, or Sabbath, School Society in 1791. Their organization, a replica of Fox's venture, was the first transatlantic imitation. Most of the societies founded in the ensuing years—Pittsburgh (1808), New York (1816), and Boston (1817)—reflected the English model. The American Sunday School Union (1824) openly copied the books produced by its counterpart in Britain, the London Sunday School Union (1803).

By the middle decades of the 19th century, however, the American Sunday school was beginning to show distinctive traits. In 1830 the ASSU vowed to establish a Sunday school "in every destitute place" in the Mississippi Valley. On the western frontier, where there were few congregations, the new Sunday schools often evolved into churches. This pattern of development created a stronger link between school and congregation than was generally true in England.

The American Sunday school could not succeed as long as it remained a school for the poor; neither the rich nor the poor would accept its offerings. Church leaders worked hard to make the Sunday school appeal to all white families. The American Sunday school reflected the country's caste system. Black and white schools existed separately in both the North and South.

The establishment of universal public education came eariler in the United States than in England. The existence of the public school freed the Sunday school from the task of teaching the "Three R's." Its scope was now limited to instruction in the Bible and Christian life. This proved to be a more manageable program and contributed to the growth of the movement between the Civil War and World War I.

Growth and Decline. The success of the movement in its peak period, 1865 to 1920, was largely due to the Sunday school convention. The earlier national conventions (1832, 1833, and 1859) had not made much impact. But after the Civil War the convention system—a series of interconnected annual county and state meetings and a triennial "international" convention—replaced the ASSU as the organizing center for interdenominational cooperation.

The International Sunday School Convention, which included Canadians as well as Americans after 1872, sparked significant developments. In 1872 it organized the International Uniform Lesson Plan, a scheme that promoted the study of the same Biblical passage by persons of all ages in every Sunday school. The "Uniform Lesson" became a fixture in most Sunday schools in the English-speaking nations. With its British counterpart it was a major stimulus to the growth of Sunday schools in Asia, Africa, and South America. Out of this Anglo-American alliance came the World Sunday School Convention (1889) and the World Sunday School Association (1907).

In the 20th century the Sunday school experienced reform and decline. After 1900 the "religious education" movement, the religious wing of progressive education, attempted to reform the Sunday school by introducing "graded" lessons (material adapted to the needs of each group), the critical study of the Bible, and professional leadership. By the 1920's most denominations were using graded lessons, although the Uniform Lesson remained popular in many congregations. Critical Biblical study is not universally practiced in Sunday schools. Professionally trained leadership is a rarity.

Sunday school enrollment declined after 1920 except for the years of the post–World War II "religious revival." Some reasons for this decline are changing leisure patterns, the availability of other "character building" agencies, and the pervasive power of secularization with a consequent loss of direction and purpose among Sunday school workers. Even so, this institution continues to be American Protestantism's major instrument for Christian nurture.

ROBERT W. LYNN
Union Theological Seminary, New York

Further Reading: Kennedy, William Bean, *The Shaping of Protestant Education* (New York 1966); Nelson, C. Ellis, *Where Faith Begins* (Richmond 1967); Rice, Edwin Wilbur, *The Sunday School Movement and the American Sunday School Union* (Philadelphia 1917); Smart, James D., *The Teaching Ministry of the Church* (Philadelphia 1955).

SUNDERLAND, 2d Earl of (1640–1702), English courtier and diplomat. He was born Robert Spencer in Paris on Aug. 4, 1640, the son of Henry Spencer, 1st Earl of Sunderland (1620–1643), and educated at Oxford. He carried out various diplomatic missions for Charles II and in 1679 was appointed secretary of state.

An ambitious and crafty politician, Sunderland reached the height of his power under James II. He carried out the royal policy of giving political equality to Roman Catholics and in 1688 declared that he had been converted to that faith. When the Glorious Revolution occurred he fled to Rotterdam disguised as a woman. But, as an able administrator, he was admitted to England again in 1691 by the new king, William III, and became his political adviser. A cynic and gambler, Sunderland was called by a contemporary "the subtillest, workingest villain that is on the face of the earth." He died in Althorp, England, on Sept. 22, 1702.

MAURICE ASHLEY
University of Loughborough, England

SUNDERLAND, 3d Earl of (1674–1722), English diplomat and bibliophile. Charles Spencer was the son of Robert Spencer, 2d Earl of Sunderland. He returned to England in 1691 from Holland, where he had been in exile with his father, and was elected in 1695 a Whig member of Parliament. His second wife was Anne Churchill, daughter of the 1st Duke of Marlborough. He entered the House of Lords in 1702, and, partly through pressure by his mother-in-law, the Duchess of Marlborough, became envoy extraordinary to Vienna and in 1706 a secretary of state. He was a literary patron of Defoe, Steele, and Addison.

In 1710 he was dismissed by Queen Anne. But when George I came to the throne in 1714, Sunderland's posts were in turn lord lieutenant of Ireland, lord privy seal, secretary of state, and first lord of the treasury. In 1720 he was involved in the scandal growing out of the collapse of the South Sea Company but was acquitted of fraud. He died in London on April 19, 1722.

MAURICE ASHLEY
University of Loughborough, England

SUNDERLAND, a county borough on the northeast coast of England in Durham county, where the West River flows into the North Sea, is 10 miles (16 km) southeast of Newcastle-upon-Tyne. Sunderland is a trading and manufacturing center. Two large curving piers protect the entrance to its harbor.

Sunderland has been building ships at least since the 14th century and in modern times has become well known for its large tankers. Glass was made here in the 8th century, and heatproof glass is still one of the town's specialties. There are large engineering works and several busy industrial estates. Modern buildings include the Civic Centre, the Central Library, the Museum and Art Gallery, the Polytechnic School, and the Civic Theatre. There are fine sandy beaches at the northern end of the borough. Population: (1961) 189,686.

GORDON STOKES, *Author, "English Place-Names"*

SUNDEW, any of a group of small insectivorous plants bearing clusters of white, pink, or red flowers on slender stems above rosettes of leaves. Each leaf is covered with sticky hairs. When an insect becomes entangled in the hairs, the leaf edges gradually bend inward toward the center, trapping the insect. Digestive enzymes secreted by leaf glands then break down the insect's body tissues, and the nutrients are absorbed by the plant. Like other insectivorous plants, sundews live mostly in bogs and swamps, where there is little nitrogen in the soil. It is believed that their digestion of insects makes up for this need.

Sundews make up the genus *Drosera* of the family Droseraceae. Though found on all continents, they are most abundant in Australia and southern Africa. A common species in North America and Eurasia is *D. rotundifolia.* It has round glistening leaves and white to red flowers on stems that reach a height of 10 inches (25 cm). Another common species, *D. filiformis,* has threadlike leaves covered with glistening purple hairs and white to purple flowers borne on stems that grow as tall as 2 feet (60 cm). *D. angelica* is another North American species.

J. A. YOUNG, *U. S. Department of Agriculture*

SUNDEW LEAF, after entangling a fly in its sticky hairs, folds over to trap it and digest its tissues.

ANNAN PHOTO

SUNDIAL, an instrument that tells time by measuring the apparent passage of the sun through its daily course in the sky. The vast majority of sundials consist of a pointer, called a style or gnomon, and a calibrated plate upon which the pointer casts a shadow.

The horizontal sundial illustrated in Figure 6 is designed for use anywhere at 52° north latitude. The plate is fastened to a horizontal surface and turned so that the right angle at the base of the style points due north. The acute angle that the hypotenuse of the style makes with the base is equal to the angle of latitude (in this case 52°), ensuring that the hypotenuse is parallel to the earth's axis (Figure 1). At the instant of midday, when the sun is at its zenith, or directly overhead, the sun, style, and axis of the earth will be in one plane, so that the shadow cast by the style will be on the 12 o'clock line. The calibration of the dial, based on the orientation of the sun to the earth during the course of the day, makes it possible to read the correct solar time as the shadow moves around the dial.

The calibration of the dial can be understood by imagining a sundial placed so that the style lies on the earth's north-south axis and the plate is secured to a horizontal surface on the north pole. Thus the plate would be perpendicular to the style and parallel to the earth's equator. As the earth rotates about its axis, the shadow cast by the style would sweep out equal periods of time, since the earth rotates at an approximately constant velocity. Therefore the plate of the sundial could be calibrated by dividing it into 24 equal arcs. If the dial were moved from the north pole to any other place on earth and the plate kept parallel to the equator, these calibrations would not need to be changed. This type of sundial is called an equatorial or equinoctial sundial.

If the sundial is to have a plate in any position other than one parallel to the equatorial plane, such as horizontal, vertical, or in another plane, equal arcs on the plate will not correspond to equal periods of time. However, the correct calibrations can be determined by means of either geometry or trigonometry.

Time Measurement. Sundial time, or solar time, does not correspond to clock time, or mean solar time. Clock time corresponds to a period measured by the sun's apparent movement from zenith to zenith, assuming fictitiously a sun rotating at constant velocity around the earth in the equatorial plane. Actually, the earth revolves around the sun in an elliptical orbit, and the plane of the orbit is inclined about 23° from the plane of the earth's equator. As a result of these two factors the sun's apparent velocity fluctuates. Solar time, therefore, varies from clock time according to the day of the year, except at the equinoxes and solstices. The difference between solar time and clock time (mean solar time) is called the equation of time. See also TIME.

Types of Sundials. There are three major types of sundials. The dials discussed above depend basically only upon the rotation of the earth about its axis. These dials are often given names corresponding to the placement of the calibrated surface—horizontal, vertical, inclined, or equatorial. All sundials of this class are called directional sundials because their styles must always be aligned with the north-south axis of the earth.

Another type of sundial depends not only upon the rotation of the earth about its axis but also upon the changes in position of the sun above and below the equator in the course of a year. The advantage of this type of dial, called an altitude sundial, is that it does not require a compass for orientation. Typical of altitude sundials is the pillar, or shepherd's sundial (Figure 4). The calibrations of the instrument reflect the change in the altitude of the sun in the sky with the succeeding months. The months are marked off by the vertical lines and the hours by the diagonal lines. When the dial is suspended from its rings, with the pointer, or gnomon, erected over the line of the proper month, the instrument is rotated until the shadow falls directly beneath the gnomon, indicating the time.

A third group of sundials measures the sun's azimuth (horizontal angle between the sun and the south point of the horizon), rather than its altitude. Some dials incorporate the principles of two types. For example, the universal ring dial (Figure 3) is an equatorial dial with a time-indicating device that must be changed from month to month.

History. The most ancient of scientific instruments is probably the sundial. A stick placed in the ground gave early man a simple way to tell time. The most important early develop-

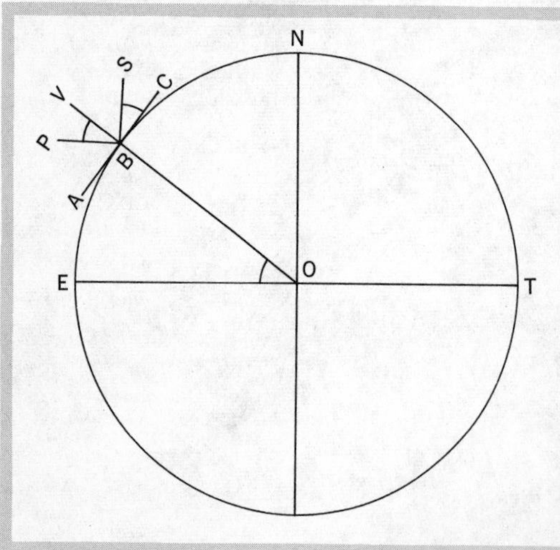

Figure 1. This diagram shows the use of horizontal and equatorial sundials at a point, *B*, on the earth's surface. *N* represents the north pole. Angle *EOB* measures latitude. *BC* is the plate of a horizontal sundial and *BS*, the style. If *CBS*, the angle made by the style and the plate, equals the angle of latitude, *BS* is parallel to *ON*, the earth's axis. The ring on an equatorial dial represented by *BP* is parallel to the equator *ET*, when angle *PBV* equals the angle of latitude. Latitude on an equatorial dial is measured from the vertical to the horizontal, as seen in Figure 5.

Figure 2. Portable diptych sundial made of ivory with brass fitting measures 4½ by 3½ inches. It is German, dating from 1602.

Figure 3. Universal ring dial has a diameter of 8½ inches. It is of English make, dating from about 1707-1730.

Figure 4. Pillar dial made of fruitwood has a height of 3 inches. It is European, of the 18th or 19th century.

Figure 5. Portable equatorial sundial made of brass with silver fittings. The diameter of the compass plate is 5⅛ inches. It is German, dating about 1725.

Figure 6, below, is a garden sundial made of brass, measuring 6¼ inches in height. It is English, from the late 18th century.

Figure 7, above, a portable equatorial sundial with a minute wheel, is English, from the first half of the 18th century.

SUNDIALS

ALL PHOTOS COURTESY OF THE METROPOLITAN MUSEUM OF ART, GIFT OF MRS. STEPHEN D. TUCKER

ments in the construction of sundials occurred in Egypt, Babylonia, and Greece. Most sundials from these civilizations divide daylight into equal hours, called temporary hours, taking no account of the variation in the period of daylight during the year.

By the beginning of the Christian era, the principles of construction of most of the sundials discussed above were known. Before the invention of the compass, portable sundials were mainly of the self-orienting altitude type because of the difficulty in aligning a sundial of the directional class.

The introduction of trigonometry into mathematics by the Greeks by about 150 A. D. supplied the tool for plotting the hour lines with simple arithmetical calculations instead of the more cumbersome geometric constructions. The method was exploited by the Arabs and subsequently by European Renaissance sundial makers.

The great age of the European sundial lasted from the 16th to the 19th century. The development of the mechanical clock spurred the search for more accurate sundials for their regulation. With the increasing accuracy of the watch and the wide adoption of standard time in the 19th century, the sundial lost its practical value. Nevertheless, sundials have not gone completely out of use.

Clare Vincent
Metropolitan Museum of Art
Bruce Chandler
New York University

Bibliography

Cousins, Frank W., *Sundials: The Art and Science of Gnomonics* (New York 1970).

Higgins, Kathleen, "The Classification of Sundials," *Annals of Science*, Vol. IX, no. 4, pp. 243–358, 1953.

Marshall, Roy K., *Sundials* (New York 1963).

Mayall, R. Newton, and Mayall, Margaret, *Sundials: How to Know, Use, and Make Them* (Boston 1938).

Price, Derek J., "Precision Instruments: to 1500," *A History of Technology*, ed. by Charles Singer, Vol. III, Ch. 22 (Oxford 1957).

Zinner, Ernst, *Deutsche und Niederländische Astronomische Instrumente des 11.-18. Jahrhunderts* (Munich 1956).

LYNWOOD M. CHACE, FROM NATIONAL AUDUBON SOCIETY

Male sunfish sweeps a place in the sand for his mate to lay her eggs.

ALVIN STAFFAN, FROM NATIONAL AUDUBON SOCIETY

Long-eared sunfish (*Lepomis megalotis*)

SUNDIATA, so͞on-dē-ä'tä (died about 1255), king of the Mandingo (Mande) people, who is credited with founding the West African empire of Mali. Although Sundiata is the great hero of Mandingo legend, little is reliably known about his career. He was a member of a southern Mandingo clan called the Keita. The Keita were traders who settled in the upper Niger Valley, where they may have been viceroys of the rulers of Ghana.

When the Ghana empire collapsed after its conquest by the Almoravids about 1076, the Keita became independent. By about 1200 paramountcy on the upper Niger had passed to the Susu. But about 1235, Sundiata defeated the Susu king, Sumanguru. He established his capital at Niani and laid the foundations of an empire stretching from the Atlantic to modern Nigeria.

J. D. FAGE
Author of "A History of West Africa"

SUNDROP. See EVENING PRIMROSE.

SUNFISH, any of a family of over 30 species of freshwater fishes native to the lakes and streams of North America. The sunfish family includes many well-known angling favorites, such as the large mouth and smallmouth basses (genus *Micropterus*), the crappies (genus *Pomoxis*), the rock bass (genus *Ambloplites*), and several small and colorful species known as pumpkinseed, longear, bluegill, and green sunfishes (genus *Lepomis*). The small species of sunfish are also popular in home aquariums.

Members of the family are called "sunfishes" probably for any of three reasons—the bright coloring of the males, the circular appearance of some species when they are viewed from the side, and the circular nest that sunfishes usually build.

All sunfishes occur naturally east of the Rocky Mountains, except one species—the Sacramento perch (*Archoplites interruptus*), which is found in the Sacramento and San Joaquin regions of California. Some species, such as the largemouth bass (*M. salmoides*), have also been introduced into Europe and other regions.

Description. Sunfishes of the genus *Lepomis* are generally deep-bodied and laterally compressed. They have small mouths and well-developed opercular flaps that are sometimes erroneously called "ears." Each also has one long dorsal fin, the anterior part of which is composed of strong spines, while the posterior part is made up only of soft rays. The pelvic fin consists of one spine and five soft rays, while the anal fin has three spines and many soft rays. The caudal fin is only slightly forked.

Sunfishes range in size from the 1½-inch (3.7-cm) banded sunfish (*Elassoma zonatum*) and mottled sunfish (*E. evergladei*) to the largemouth bass, which may measure up to 32 inches (81 cm). Two common species are the 3-inch (7.5 cm) black-banded sunfish (*Enneacanthus chaetodon*), found in freshwater from New Jersey to northern Florida, and the slightly larger, pigmy, or blue-spotted, sunfish (*Enneacanthus gloriosus*), found throughout the eastern and southeastern United States. The various species of sunfishes, when overcrowded, may become dwarfed, or they may hybridize and produce offspring that may be difficult to distinguish from one another.

Behavior and Life Cycle. Sunfishes are somewhat aggressive, especially during the spawning period, which begins in the spring when the temperature rises. The males move inshore, select nesting sites, and begin to prepare nests. Each male, with a series of fanlike motions of its tail and body, clears a circular area and forms a shallow depression. He then lures females to the nest where they deposit eggs, each nest normally containing the eggs of more than one female. He then fertilizes the eggs, guards the nest zealously, and aerates them by fanning them with his fins. If he is caught or removed from the nest at this critical time, the young will quickly perish. After the eggs hatch, the fry rise to the surface and are soon abandoned by the male. The life of a typical sunfish is short, seldom more than 10 years.

All sunfishes are carnivorous. They eat a variety of smaller creatures, such as terrestrial and aquatic insects, crustaceans, and mollusks, as well as smaller fishes. Most species travel in schools and prefer the quiet weedy waters of ponds or lakes.

Classification. The freshwater sunfishes are classified in 10 genera, making up the family Centrarchidae, of the order Perciformes. The name "sunfish" is also sometimes applied to the ocean sunfish (*Mola mola*).

See also BASS; CRAPPIE.

WILLIAM B. SCOTT, *University of Toronto*

SUNFLOWER, any of a group of tall, coarse annual or perennial plants with large flower heads that turn to follow the path of the sun. The daisylike flower heads have yellow ray flowers surrounding a center of brown, yellow, purple, or nearly black disk flowers.

Sunflowers make up the genus *Helianthus* of the composite family (Compositae). One of the most familiar species, the common sunflower (*H. annuus*), sometimes reaches a height of 15 feet (4.5 meters) and bears huge flower heads over 1 foot (0.3 meter) in diameter. It is widespread in the western prairies of the United States and is the official state flower of Kansas. Several horticultural varieties of this species have been developed, some with attractive yellow and orange disk flowers. In the Soviet Union, India, Argentina, and Egypt, it is widely cultivated for its oily seeds. The oil obtained from the seeds is used in making salad oil, margarine, and candy. The cake that is left after the oil has been pressed out is used as a feed for livestock.

Another well-known sunflower is the Jerusalem artichoke or girasole (*H. tuberosus*). In Italian the word *girasole* means "turning to the sun." This perennial plant grows 5 to 10 feet (1.5-3 meters) tall and bears all-yellow flower heads about 3 inches (76 mm) in diameter. Sometimes it is cultivated for its underground club-shaped tubers that are about 4 inches (10 cm) long. The tubers are edible and are occasionally eaten as a vegetable or used as food for livestock.

Common sunflower (*Helianthus annuus*)

ROCHE

Other common sunflowers in North America include the thin-leaved sunflower (*H. decapetalus*), the woodland sunflower (*H. divaricatus*), the swamp sunflower (*H. angustifolius*), the silverleaf sunflower (*H. argophyllus*), the giant sunflower (*H. giganteus*), and the showy sunflower (*H. laetiflorus*).

J. A. YOUNG
U. S. Department of Agriculture

SUNG DYNASTY, sŏŏng, a dynasty that ruled in China from 960 to 1279. It was founded by Gen. Chao K'uang-yin (Sung T'ai Tsu), the last successful usurper in Chinese history. He subdued the warlords, who had restricted central authority since the 8th century, and fixed the principle of civilian control over the military in Chinese tradition. The period is divided into two parts: the Northern Sung (960–1126), when the dynasty ruled all China, and the Southern Sung (1127–1279).

During the Sung period, Chinese culture developed unusually rapidly. An agricultural and commercial revolution based on technological developments brought greatly increased productivity. New shipbuilding techniques and the use of the compass stimulated foreign trade. Huge cities and urban problems appeared. Accompanying economic strains brought the invention of paper currency, and modern economic thought was foreshadowed in the reforms of the minister Wang An-shih.

Neo-Confucianism, as synthesized by Chu Hsi, became the dominant philosophy in China to the 20th century. Sung achievements in poetry, landscape painting, and porcelain were high. Movable type appeared, and Sung books are prized for the excellence of their printing. The status of women declined, however, with the expansion of the custom of footbinding.

Although the dynasty was not noted for its military power, Sung resistance to the Mongol invaders led by Genghis Khan is remarkable. After a generation of conflict, the Sung empire fell to Genghis Khan's grandson Kublai Khan. See also CHINA—*History; Philosophy and Religion; Art and Architecture;* and *Literature.*

JAMES R. SHIRLEY, *Northern Illinois University*

SUNGARI RIVER, sŏŏn'gä'rē', in China, the chief tributary of the Amur River (Heilung Kiang). Its course of 1,215 miles (1,956 km) lies entirely within Manchuria. The river drains an area of 201,930 square miles (523,000 sq km), which includes the richest forest resources in China, the largest coal deposits in Manchuria, and extensive land under corn (maize), soybeans, and sugar beets.

The Sungari (meaning "Heavenly River" in Manchu) is called Sunghwa Kiang in Chinese. It originates in the Changpai Mountains near the Korean border and flows northwest until it converges with the Nen near Fuyü. Turning sharply northeast it continues past Harbin and joins the Amur at the Soviet border. The river abounds in fish and is navigable for steamers from Harbin downward. The southern (upper) Sungari has great hydroelectric potential.

SEN-DOU CHANG, *University of Hawaii*

SUNGARIA. See DZUNGARIA.

SUNI, sōōn′ē, a small antelope (*Neotragus moschatus*) found in southeastern Africa from South Africa to Kenya and on Zanzibar, Mafia, and other adjacent small islands off the coast. The suni is often separated from its close relatives the royal and pygmy antelopes and placed in a genus of its own, *Nesotragus*. It inhabits mainly dry coastal thickets but also occurs inland, ranging up into mountain forests. It has a rather spotty, or localized, distribution, and the inland populations of the Kenya mountains and Kilimanjaro are isolated.

The suni is about 13 to 15 inches (33–38 cm) high at the shoulders and from 18 to 20 pounds (8–9 kg) in weight. Males have straight, strongly ridged horns about 2½ to 5 inches (6–13 cm) long. Females are hornless. The general color of the suni is reddish or chestnut, with whitish markings below.

Virtually nothing is known of the suni's habits and breeding. It appears to be mainly a browser and to occur usually singly or in pairs. It probably has no closely defined birth season.

W. F. H. ANSELL, *Department of Wildlife, Fisheries and National Parks, Zambia*

SUNLAMP, a lamp that produces ultraviolet radiation at wavelengths that increase metabolism, stimulate formation of a hormone ("vitamin D_3," deficiency of which causes rickets), and tan human skin. The most widely used sunlamp for tanning is the 275-watt RS sunlamp. It has a mercury-vapor lamp tube enclosed in a special glass bulb with an inner metal reflector surface. The mercury-vapor element produces the proper range of ultraviolet radiation, the special glass bulb transmits the radiation, and the reflector directs the radiation for easy skin exposure. This sunlamp has a screw base that fits ordinary light-bulb sockets, and it operates with electricity obtained from household wall receptacles. After the lamp is turned on, an exposure of 8 to 13 minutes will produce a mild sunburn on an average untanned skin 30 inches (76 cm) from the lamp. The reddening of the skin usually is followed by a tan. Ultraviolet radiation from the lamp has wavelengths in the range from 280 to 320 nanometers, as does sunlight.

From earliest times men believed that sunlight possessed tonic, curative, and disinfectant powers. Scientific research on the actual effects of sunlight on the human body began about 1900. One pioneer in this field was the Danish physician Niels Finsen, who won the Nobel Prize in physiology or medicine in 1903 for his discovery that skin tuberculosis can be treated by exposure to sunlight.

CHARLES L. AMICK, *Emerson Electric Company*

SUNNA. See ISLAM–*The Prophetic Tradition* (Sunna).

SUNNITES, sōōn′īts, the majority body of Muslims. They constitute about 90% of all Muslims and are often, though inaccurately, called "orthodox." The usual Arabic term for them is "ahlu-l-sunna wa-l-jamaa," meaning "people who adhere to (Mohammed's) sunna, or customary practice, and to the community." See also ISLAM.

The other main group, the Shia or Shiites, who claim that Ali, Mohammed's son-in-law, was the rightful successor to the prophet and reject the first three caliphs, regards the welfare of the community as depending on the inspiration of a series of imams descended from Ali. The Sunnites, in contrast, hold that Ali was only the fourth caliph and not inspired, and that the life of the community ought to be based on the Koran and the sunna or practice of Mohammed, which are to be interpreted by *ulama*, or jurists.

The sunna is defined by the six collections of Hadith or "traditions" regarded as authoritative, but there is no universally accepted statement of Sunnite doctrine. Within Sunnite Islam there are four equally recognized legal schools or rites, and there are also divergent theological schools. Sunnites hold that Islam was Sunnite from the first, but Western scholars think Sunnism took definitive form only about the fourth Islamic century.

W. MONTGOMERY WATT
University of Edinburgh

SUNNYSIDE is the estate of the American author Washington Irving, in Tarrytown, N. Y., along the Hudson River. The area is famous as the scene of *Rip Van Winkle* and other stories by Irving. See IRVING, WASHINGTON.

SUNNYVALE, a city in western California, is in Santa Clara county, about 40 miles (64 km) southeast of San Francisco. The manufacture of missiles and research in aeronautics and electronics are major contributors to the economy. Other industries include food processing and the making of electrical equipment and chemicals. Moffett Field, a U. S. naval air station, is nearby.

Sunnyvale was settled in 1849 by the family of Martin Murphy, Jr., whose house was built piecemeal in Boston, shipped around Cape Horn, and assembled in Sunnyvale. The community was incorporated in 1912. It has a council-manager government. Population: 95,408.

SUNRISE AND SUNSET. As the earth turns on its axis, the sun appears to rise and set. The times of day when these events occur vary with latitude. Because of the earth's tilt on its axis they also vary throughout the year, except at the poles (see DAY). At the equator day and night are of equal length. At the poles the sun stays in the sky six months before setting, and then stays six months below the horizon.

Daytime lasts about four minutes longer than it would on an earth without air. Refraction of sunlight by the atmosphere causes sunrise to be hastened and sunset to be delayed by about two minutes beyond the actual event.

More daytime is added when the sun's disk is taken into account. That is, sunrise is defined as the moment when the upper rim of the solar disk appears above the sea-level horizon, and sunset as the moment when the upper rim disappears below the horizon. Near the equator this adds another two minutes to the length of the day, and at higher latitudes the sun's increasingly slanted path causes the sun to take even longer to rise above and sink below the horizon.

The striking colors often observed at sunrise and sunset are caused by dust and water particles in the atmosphere. When the sun is near the horizon, shorter wavelengths of light tend to be absorbed by the particles in the greater thickness of air through which they must travel, thus producing an orange or reddish glow.

SUNSET CRATER NATIONAL MONUMENT, in north central Arizona, is 14 miles (22 km) northeast of Flagstaff. The crater is at the summit of a volcanic cone that rises about 1,000 feet (300 meters) above its surroundings and 8,000 feet (2,400 meters) above sea level. The name was suggested by the colors of the peak, which range from yellow near the top through orange to red near the base, with a rim of black ash at the bottom. The crater is about 1,300 feet (395 meters) in diameter and 400 feet (120 meters) deep.

The national monument, which was established in 1930, covers over 3,000 acres (1,215 hectares) and includes ice caves and lava flows.

SUNSPOT, a more or less circular region of physical and magnetic disturbance in the outer layer, or photosphere, of the sun. Sunspots appear singly and in pairs and groups. They look dark only because they are cooler than surrounding gases. Their numbers increase and decrease in a roughly 11-year cycle. See also SUN.

SUNSTONE, or *aventurine oligoclase,* is a variety of feldspar that exhibits a bright golden sparkle when light shines on it. The sparkle is caused by the reflection of light from the surfaces of minute platelike crystals of hematite or goethite enclosed in the mineral parallel to one another. Sunstone is occasionally used as a gem; the finest specimens come from Tvedestrand, Norway. See also FELDSPAR.

SUNSTROKE is a form of heatstroke that is produced by prolonged exposure to the sun. See HEATSTROKE.

SUPERCHARGER, a device for providing surplus air (oxygen) to the cylinders of internal-combustion engines. Supercharging reached a zenith in the days when commercial and military airplanes were powered by reciprocating engines rather than jet engines. It is now used on small planes with reciprocating engines, on many diesel engines, and on some racing automobiles.

Supercharging derives its importance from the fact that the power output of an engine bears a direct relationship to its air (oxygen)-breathing capacity. If the air entering the cylinders is compressed, the power output increases in a direct ratio to the additional weight of air provided per second to the cylinders.

Most superchargers employ centrifugal compressors. These units, operating at rotative speeds up to 30,000 rpm, compress the air both in the impeller and by diffusion action on exit from the impeller. They are usually driven through gearing from the main shaft of the reciprocating engine. But sometimes they are driven by a small turbine powered by energy remaining in the exhaust gases from the reciprocating engine.

Positive-displacement rotary compressors also are used, particularly when the goal is scavenging the exhaust gases along with some supercharging. One of the most common displacement compressors has two rotors, each with two matching lobes. Air, trapped between the rotating rotor lobes and the casing, is then compressed under the meshing action of the mating rotors. The two rotor shafts are geared together to keep the lobes always in proper relative position. See also PUMPS.

BURGESS H. JENNINGS
Northwestern University

SUPERCONDUCTIVITY, one of the most striking phenomena in physics, was discovered in 1911 by Kamerlingh Onnes at Leiden, the Netherlands, only three years after he had learned how to liquefy helium and thus reach the extremely low temperatures required. He found that when cooled to liquid helium temperatures, mercury becomes superconducting, losing all trace of resistance to flow of electricity. It was soon found that many metals and alloys become superconducting when cooled below a transition temperature characteristic of the material. For the discovery of superconductivity, Onnes was awarded the Nobel Prize in physics in 1913.

For nearly 50 years superconductivity defied explanation and was one of the outstanding puzzles of physics. Our present understanding gradually evolved through a long series of experimental and theoretical researches by many people working in laboratories throughout the world. It was not until 1957 that the phenomena was explained by a theory developed by John Bardeen, Leon N. Cooper, and J. Robert Schrieffer at the University of Illinois. It is known as the BCS theory from the initials of its founders. This theory, with its subsequent developments by many people, accounts in a quantitative way for most observed properties of superconductors and has also been used to predict many new effects not previously observed. The theory gave a stimulus to a rapid expansion of research in superconductivity.

Another major stimulus to research has been in the many applications that began to appear in the early 1960's, including superconducting electromagnets and sensitive detecting instruments based on quantum aspects of superconductors.

This article will first discuss the temperature scale used to describe phenomena at very low temperatures. It will then review the key steps that have led to our present scientific understanding and describe some of the applications.

Kelvin Temperature Scale. In the 1860's, Lord Kelvin of Britain proposed an absolute thermo-

Fig. 1. Kelvin temperature scale and superconducting transition temperatures of several metals.

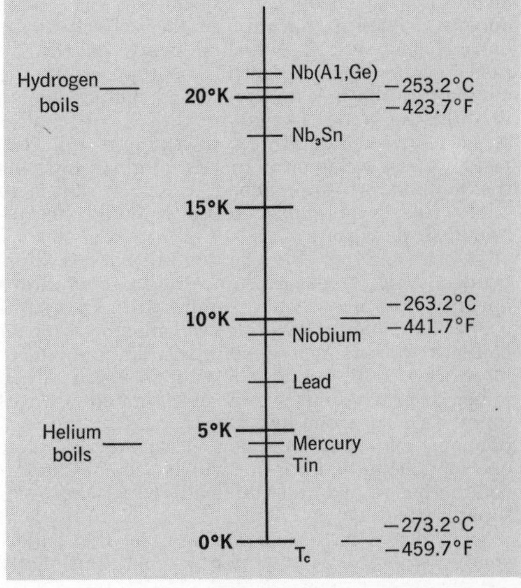

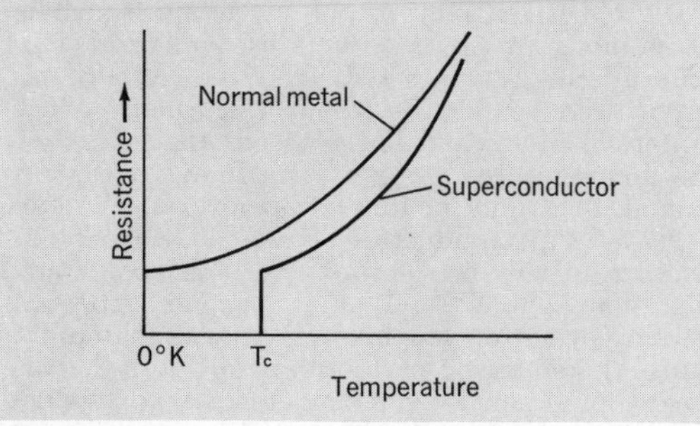

Fig. 2. Temperature dependence of the resistance of normal and superconducting metals (schematic).

dynamic scale of temperatures, defined without reference to the properties of any particular material. On this scale, now called the Kelvin scale, at absolute zero (0° K), matter is in its state of lowest energy. The scale is chosen so that there is a difference of 100° between the freezing and boiling points of water, as in the centigrade scale. Absolute zero, 0° K, is −273.2° C or −459.7° F.

A comparison of the Kelvin, centigrade, and Fahrenheit scales at very low temperatures is given in Fig. 1. Also indicated are the superconducting transition temperatures, T_c, of a few materials and the boiling points of hydrogen (20.4° K) and of helium (4.2° K). The highest known superconducting transition temperature, almost 21° K, is in a ternary alloy of niobium, germanium, and aluminum.

Discovery of Superconductivity. In a crystal of normal metal the atoms are arranged in a regular array known as a lattice. In metals that can conduct electricity the atoms give up their outer, or valence, electrons, which become free to move about within the metal. Atoms that have lost electrons in this fashion are called ions. When a voltage is applied to the metal these free, or conduction, electrons move toward the positive terminal of the voltage source, producing an electric current. If the array of atoms is not absolutely regular—which is true for all metals—the electrons will encounter resistance. The resistance is defined as the ratio of the voltage to the current flow, R-V/I, which depends on the dimensions and on an intrinsic property of the conductor, the resistivity. When Onnes began an investigation of the properties of matter at very low temperatures, he thought that the resistivity of very pure metals might vanish as the temperature approached 0° K. He chose to study frozen mercury because it could be obtained in pure form.

Quite unexpectedly, he found that, as illustrated in Fig. 2, the resistance of mercury drops abruptly to zero when a temperature of 4.2° K is reached. Soon it was observed that high purity is not required, that a considerable number of impurities could be added without much effect. When other metals were investigated it was found that superconductivity is a fairly common phenomenon. Two common elements that have been much studied are tin, which becomes superconducting at 3.2° K, and lead, which becomes superconducting at 7.2° K.

To show that the resistance in the superconducting state is not merely small but really vanishes for all practical purposes, Onnes showed that persistent currents flow indefinitely in a ring or solenoid with no battery or other source of power. As long as the temperature is kept below the transition temperature, there is no appreciable decay in the current.

Early Research. Further work by the successors of Onnes at Leiden showed that superconductivity is associated with an ordering of the structure of the electrons in the metal into some sort of condensed state. A major advance occurred in 1933 when Walther Meissner in Germany discovered a property of superconductors that is perhaps even more basic than the vanishing of the resistance. Superconductors exclude a magnetic field. If a superconductor is cooled below its transition temperature in the absence of a magnetic field, and then a magnetic field is applied, eddy currents will be induced in a thin surface layer that will keep the magnetic field from changing in the interior, so that the field will remain zero. In the absence of scattering, these currents persist indefinitely. What Meissner showed is that even if the specimen is cooled in the presence of a magnetic field, as illustrated in Fig. 3, the field is expelled when the specimen becomes superconducting. This state with the field excluded is the unique stable state.

Not long after, in 1935, two brothers, Heinz and Fritz London, who were refugees in England from Nazi Germany, proposed equations that describe both vanishing resistance and the Meissner effect. The equations have been widely used since that time to describe the electromagnetic properties of superconductors.

Type I and Type II Superconductors and Superconducting Magnets. With increasing magnetic field, magnetic flux can penetrate the interior of superconductors in two different ways, depending on the type of superconductor. In a Type I superconductor, when the field reaches a critical value, H_c, the superconductor goes into an intermediate state that consists of alternate layers of normal and superconducting regions. The field in the normal regions is equal to H_c but vanishes in the superconducting regions. At higher fields than H_c the metal reverts to normal. Normally H_c is only a few hundred gauss. (For reference, the earth's magnetic field is about half a gauss and typical magnetic fields in electrical machinery may be of the order of 10,000 gauss.)

In Type II superconductors, which were discovered in 1937 by the Russian physicist L. V. Shubnikov and explained by another Russian, A. A. Abrikosov, 20 years later, flux penetrates in a surprising way. When the applied field is between a lower critical field, H_{c1}, which is lower than H_c, and an upper critical field, H_{c2}, which can be considerably higher than H_c, flux can penetrate in the form of an array of quantized vortex lines. A vortex line consists of currents circulating about the axis of the vortex and associated magnetic field lines along the axis.

The upper critical field, H_{c2}, can in some cases be as high as several hundred thousand gauss. The discovery of such materials in 1961 made possible the design of superconducting electromagnets with fields of well over 100,000 gauss. Such magnets are now widely used in physics laboratories throughout the world. Since the windings are superconducting, there is no dissipation of electricity. Power is required only to establish the current flow, not to maintain it.

Microscopic Theory. Clues to the nature of the interaction between electrons that is responsible for their condensation into the superconducting state came from two directions in 1950, one experimental and the other theoretical. Both indicated that superconductivity arises from an interaction between the free electrons and the vibrational motions of the ions about their equilibrium positions. These motions increase as the temperature of the metal increases. Since lattice vibrations are one cause of the irregularities in the lattice, they are closely related to the resistance. In a pure metal at 0° K the resistance practically, but not entirely, vanishes. This lowering of resistance, however, does not explain the complete vanishing of resistance in superconductors at temperatures above 0° K. Superconductivity represents a phenomenon that is not explainable in terms of classical physics but must be understood in terms of the quantum theory developed by Werner Heisenberg, Erwin Schrödinger, Paul Dirac, and others in 1925–1927.

The first to propose the idea that superconductivity should depend essentially on quantum theory was Fritz London. As early as 1935 he suggested that a superconductor should behave as a single large, or macroscopic, quantum system. One prediction of this theory was that the total flux threading a superconducting ring will be quantized as an integral multiple of the flux quantum, $hc/2e$, where h is Planck's constant, c is the velocity of light, and e is the charge of an electron. The flux quantum $hc/2e$ is approximately 2×10^{-7} gauss per cm^2. The predicted quantization was first observed experimentally by two groups in 1962.

The next significant step toward a theory of superconductivity was made by the German-born English physicist Herbert Fröhlich, who showed that the interaction between the electrons and the lattice vibrations could result in an effective attractive interaction between electrons. Essentially this interaction depends on the transfer of energy from an electron to the lattice and from the lattice to another electron.

In 1956, Leon Cooper showed that an attractive force, no matter how weak, would cause a pair of conduction electrons to condense into a bound state. The following year Bardeen, Cooper, and Schrieffer showed how the many electrons in a metal can be associated in pairs. When the paired states all have the same total momentum, the superconductor can best take advantage of the electron-lattice interaction to give a low energy state. The common momentum of the pairs results from a cooperative interaction among them and is responsible for the supercurrent flow. It is this cooperative behavior of the pairs that implies the existence of a macroscopic quantum state.

If values of a small number of material properties are determined from experiment, the theory can be used to calculate in a quantitative way most of the many properties of superconductors. The theory also has been used to predict many unusual properties in advance of experiment. Since it can be used both for analysis of experimental data and prediction of new phenomena, it has provided a great stimulus to the field.

Josephson Effect. One of the most striking predictions is the Josephson effect. In 1962, when Brian D. Josephson was a graduate student at Cambridge University, England, he predicted on the basis of the BCS theory that a supercurrent could flow through a thin insulating barrier separating two superconducting metals by the quantum-mechanical process of tunneling. He also predicted that if a direct voltage, V, is applied across the barrier, an alternating current should flow with a frequency given by

$$\nu = 2eV/h,$$

where e is the electronic charge and h is Planck's constant. If V is the order of millivolts, ν is in the microwave range. If a microwave field of frequency ν_a is applied, he suggested that it could beat against the Josephson current, causing characteristic steps in the direct-current voltage when V is such that $n\nu_a = 2eV/h$, and n is an integer. These predictions, later verified experimentally, illustrate the macroscopic quantization suggested by London.

Since all that is required is a measurement of frequency and of voltage, the Josephson effect has been used to make very precise measurements of the ratio of the fundamental constants, $2e/h$, that enter the frequency condition.

Superconducting Materials. One factor limiting the applications of superconductors is the very low temperature required. Considerable effort has gone into attempts to find superconductors with higher transition temperatures. Although a great many superconducting alloys and compounds have been discovered, particularly by the German-born American physicist B. T. Matthias and co-workers, the maximum transition temperature has increased quite slowly over the years, from about 18° K in 1954 to 21° K in 1970.

Suggestions have been given for systems that should be superconducting to much higher temperatures, but it is not at all certain that any of these is feasible. Calculations indicate that a metallic form of hydrogen, which should exist at extremely high pressures, would be superconducting at room temperature. The interior of Jupiter may consist of hydrogen in this form. It has also been suggested that the interior of neutron stars (pulsars) may be superconducting.

Applications. Applications of superconductors so far have been mainly to instruments for use in other fields of science. Superconducting magnets have been used for many purposes, including large bubble chamber magnets to de-

Fig. 3. Two aspects of superconductivity. (a) Persistent current flow in a ring with no battery or other source of power. (b) Meissner effect: If a magnetic field is applied in the normal state, the field goes through the specimen. When cooled into the superconducting state, the field is expelled.

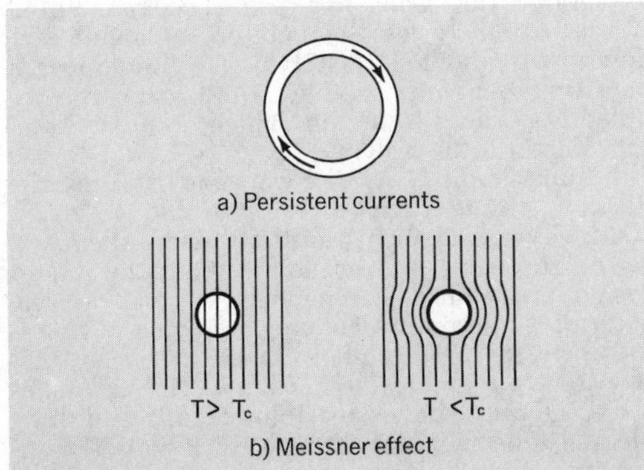

ARGONNE NATIONAL LABORATORY

Fig. 4. One of the two pancake assemblies containing the superconducting coils for a 20,000-gauss bubble-chamber magnet with a bore of 15.7 ft. (4.8 meters), in use at the Argonne National Laboratory.

flect high energy particles, as illustrated in Fig. 4. If fusion energy ever becomes practical, superconducting magnets will be used to contain the hot plasma.

Another application in high-energy physics is the use of superconductors in the cavity walls of linear accelerators used to produce high-energy particles. Because the energy loss in the walls is very small, superconducting accelerators can be used for continuous rather than pulsed operation, thus allowing much more data to be collected in a given time. A 500-foot (152-meter) superconducting accelerator is under construction at Stanford University. The present Stanford 2-mile (3-km) accelerator may be converted for superconducting operation.

The Josephson effect is used in superconducting quantum interference devices (SQUID's) to measure magnetic fields as small as 10^{-9} gauss and to measure voltages as small as 10^{-16} volt. Both values are at least 100 times smaller than those that can be obtained with nonsuperconducting devices. Studies are being made for possible application of the effect of components for electronic computers that require very large memory arrays.

Serious consideration is being given to the use of superconductors in underground power-transmission cables. The problem is simpler for direct current than for alternating current operation. Calculations indicate that it may be feasible if it is necessary to go underground in any case or if transmission of extremely large amounts of power is required.

One of the most spectacular applications of superconductivity being considered is for magnetic levitation of high-speed trains. Superconducting magnets would be used to lift the train off the road bed and thus reduce friction. Speeds of the order of 300 mph are contemplated. A model of such a train was exhibited at the 1970 World's Fair in Osaka, Japan.

JOHN BARDEEN
Nobel Prize Winner in Physics
University of Illinois

Further Reading: Cohen, Morrel H., ed., *Superconductivity in Science and Technology* (Chicago 1968); Fishlock, David, ed., *A Guide to Superconductivity* (London 1969); Lynton, Ernest A., *Superconductivity* (London 1969); Parks, R. D., ed., *Superconductivity*, vols. 1 and 2 (New York 1969); Shoenberg, David, *Superconductivity* (London 1960).

SUPERCOOLING is the cooling of a liquid below its freezing point without solidification or crystallization. For example, supercooling occurs when water is cooled below 0° C (32° F) without the formation of ice. This usually occurs only under carefully controlled conditions. With the addition of a crystal of ice to the liquid, much of the water will freeze. If a saturated solution of water and sugar is slowly cooled, the solution becomes supersaturated. The addition of more sugar, or even of dust, causes the crystallization of sugar from solution. In both cases the supercooled condition is highly unstable.

SUPEREGO is a psychoanalytic concept designating a major element of personality. The concept was developed by Sigmund Freud, who gave the name "superego" to the agency responsible for self-imposed standards of conduct and morality and the source of feelings of self-approval or guilt. He presented the concept fully in *The Ego and the Id* (1923), which postulated three major components within man's personality: *id, ego,* and *superego.*

The *id* contains biological and sexual drives seeking immediate gratification and pleasure. The *ego* develops as the child discovers that immediate gratification is not always possible. It is the system of higher mental processes controlling the acquisition of skills and techniques for achieving goals within the bounds of the real world. The *superego* is the internal representative of the values and ideals of the society. It is the moral part of the personality, representing the ideal rather than the actual and demanding goodness rather than pleasure.

Freud held that the superego developed in response to parental rewards and punishments. Transgressions of this internalized code are felt, consciously or unconsciously, as deserving of punishment, following a pattern of guilt and atonement. The child thus incorporates both the approving and punishing features of the all-important parents as a powerful and enduring agency within his own personality. Freud emphasized the early childhood years and basic identification with parents in superego formation. Many psychologists have also studied the considerable importance of later experience in the acquisition and modification of conscience and morality. See also EGO; ID.

ALDEN E. WESSMAN
The City College, New York

SUPERFLUIDITY is the ability of a liquid to flow without friction through very narrow channels. Helium, He^4, is the only substance known to exhibit this behavior. He^4 becomes liquid at the extremely low temperature of about 4.2° Kelvin. At about 2.2° Kelvin, He^4 undergoes a transformation into another liquid state, the so-called superfluid state, in which it exists from 2.2° Kelvin to 0° Kelvin.

Superfluidity was discovered in 1938 by the Russian physicist Pyotr Kapitsa and independently by the British physicists Jack Allen and A. D. Misener. It was found that the liquid flowed easily through channels as small as one tenth of a micron in diameter, implying a viscosity at least 1,000 million times less than that of water. Superfluid flow of liquid He^4 also takes place, as was shown by John Daunt and Kurt Mendelssohn in 1938, through thick films (of approximately 100 atoms thickness) that are spontaneously formed on any surface dipping into the liquid. It was found that as with superconductivity, there is a limiting critical flow rate for superfluid flow. Forced flow above the critical value destroys the superfluid property.

Further features of the superfluid state are the thermomechanical effects and the phenomenon of "second sound." The former effects, which were found by Allen and Harry Jones (1938) and by Daunt and Mendelssohn (1939), involve the spontaneous flow of superfluid from a region of low temperature to a region of higher temperature and conversely the development of a temperature gradient whenever there is a spontaneous flow of superfluid. These effects were explained by Laslo Tisza (1938) and by Heinz London (1939). Second sound, predicted by Tisza (1938) and discovered by V. P. Peshkov (1944), is the transmission of weakly damped temperature waves in the liquid.

Since this early work, considerable theoretical and experimental research has been done on superfluidity. The phenomenon is considered to be fundamentally due to the type of quantum statistics (Bose-Einstein) that are applicable to the particles of He^4, as was originally suggested by Fritz London (1938). Major contributions to the theory have been made by Lev Landau (1941) and Richard Feynman (1955).

The rare isotope of helium of mass 3, He^3, is also liquid at very low temperatures. It has not been found, however, to show properties of the superfluid state at any temperature down to about 2 millidegrees Kelvin, which is the lowest temperature at which tests for superfluidity have been made.

JOHN G. DAUNT
Stevens Institute of Technology

SUPERHETERODYNE RECEIVER. See RADIO—*History* (Heterodyne Reception); and *Radio Communications Systems* (Superheterodyne Receiver).

SUPERINTENDENT OF SCHOOLS. See SCHOOL SUPERINTENDENT.

SUPERIOR, a city in northwestern Wisconsin, the seat of Douglas county, is at the western end of Lake Superior. It is across the St. Louis River from Duluth, Minn., with which it is connected by a toll-free bridge. The port of Superior-Duluth is one of the largest in the United States in cargo tonnage handled. Superior transships coal, iron ore, and grain from rail to water carriers. It is the terminus of an oil pipeline and has an oil refinery. There also is a shipyard. The city manufactures briquets, hardboard, flour, and dairy products.

A campus of Wisconsin State University and a technical institute are in the city. The Douglas County Historical Museum displays Indian artifacts and portraits; local rocks, plants, and birds; and archives of local history. Billings Park, with a 5-mile (3-km) drive along the St. Louis River, is a scenic attraction.

U. S. Senator Stephen A. Douglas of Illinois was a member of the company that developed the site of Superior. The first log cabin in the area was built in 1853. The village government was formed in 1887, and a city charter was granted in 1889. Government is by mayor and aldermen. Population: 32,237.

GRACE HACKER, *Superior Public Library*

SUPERIOR, Lake, in east central North America, the largest freshwater lake in the world. On the U. S.–Canadian border, it is the farthest north and west of the five Great Lakes. Superior is 350 miles (563 km) long, 160 miles (257 km) across at its widest, covers 31,800 square miles (82,362 sq km), and reaches a depth of 1,333 feet (406 meters). It holds 53.8% of the Great Lakes' total water content. Superior, at 600 feet (183 meters), is the highest above sea level of all the Great Lakes. It discharges into Lake Huron, which is about 20 feet (6 meters) lower, via the St. Mary's River.

The Lake Superior region is one of rugged beauty and outstanding natural resources—97% of the U. S. land area there is classified as rural. Huge expanses of Canadian forest and wilderness are studded with lakes and laced with small streams. The U. S. side was heavily logged from 1870 to 1930, but the area has been reforested. The water in Lake Superior is almost pristinely pure, with only localized areas of pollution. The wide expanse of water, strong winds, and a northerly climate cause Superior to have more fog and rougher water than the other Great Lakes.

Fish and wildlife of the region include pike, perch, trout, bass, and muskellunge; songbirds, upland game birds, and waterfowl; and deer, moose, and bear. In western Lake Superior, Isle Royale, the lake's largest island, is a U. S. national park. Ontario's Lake Superior Provincial Park is at the eastern end of the lake.

The Economy. Fewer than one million people live in the Superior basin. They are concentrated on the U. S. side in the Duluth, Minn.–Superior, Wis., area; in the Michigan cities of Sault Ste. Marie, Marquette, Ontonagon, and Houghton; in Ashland, Wis.; and in the Ontario urban areas of Sault Ste. Marie and Thunder Bay (formerly Fort William and Port Arthur).

Manufacturing employs the largest number of people, followed by mining, forest products, sales, and agriculture. Iron ore, copper, and limestone are the most important minerals. The world's largest grain elevators are at Thunder Bay, Ontario's busiest ocean port. The Duluth-Superior district, 2,342 miles (3,770 km) from the sea, leads Great Lakes ports in international tonnage.

After 1840, the Superior region's "copper country" was the main U. S. source of copper, but production dwindled. Iron ore production flourished with the opening of the first Soo lock on

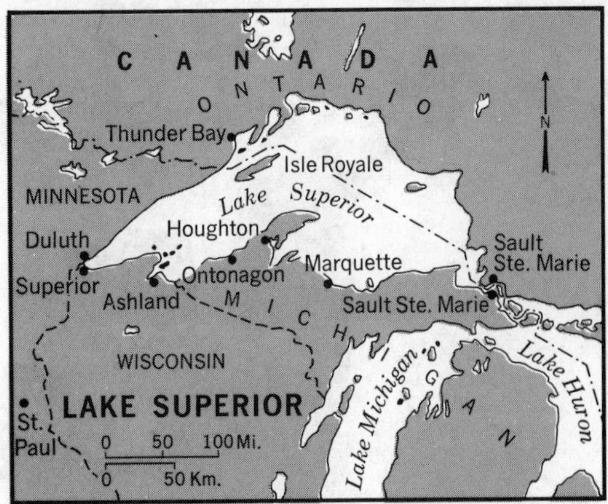

the St. Mary's River in 1855 and supplied America's steel mills until after World War II. The depletion of high-grade ore fostered technological development to exploit the enormous deposits of low-grade iron ores (taconite). Ninety million tons of ore and taconite pellets pass the Soo locks annually—80 per cent of the total United States production.

History. Étienne Brûlé and the Northwest Fur Company traders explored the Lake Superior region in the early 1620's. Indian-white hostilities in the lower lakes forced explorers to follow the Ottawa River northwest to Georgian Bay and Lake Superior. A trading post and Father Jacques Marquette's Jesuit mission were established in 1668 at the Falls of the St. Mary's River, the site of Sault Ste. Marie, Mich. Across the St. Mary's is Sault Ste. Marie, Ont.

LEONARD J. GOODSELL
Great Lakes Commission

SUPERMAN is the usual translation of the German word *Übermensch* (literally "overman"), which was used by Friedrich Nietzsche as a philosophic concept. The superman, according to Nietzsche, is an ideal toward which man should strive. Through his will to power, man should elevate himself to a state of complete self-control. He should possess mental and moral strength but should never use strength to do violence or to force a code on others.

The concept of superman, which had its seeds in the writings of Goethe, was taken up by numerous writers, including George Bernard Shaw. The Nazis distorted the idea in an attempt to fit it into their propaganda attempting to establish the Germans as a master race.

SUPERMARKET, a departmentalized self-service food store. First established in the 1930's, the supermarket achieved rapid growth, and it now accounts for more than three fourths of all grocery store sales in the United States. Its basic appeal has been low prices, but the supermarket also offers the convenience of buying all foods under one roof. Other advantages for customers include ease of parking and, frequently, the convenience of shopping hours that extend far into the evening.

One of the earliest supermarkets was opened in Jamaica, Queens, New York City, in 1930 by independent merchants as a means of combating chain-store competition. By 1932 there were eight supermarkets, including one in a former automobile plant in Elizabeth, N. J The growth of supermarkets has centered in the United States and Canada, but this form of food marketing is gaining acceptance in England, Switzerland, West Germany, Italy, Belgium, and other countries.

Characteristics. Most supermarkets are operated by chains. They sell grocery items by departments, such as meat, produce, or bakery goods. They also sell nonfood items by departments, such as children's clothing, stationery, and hardware.

To achieve high volume, a prerequisite to low prices, supermarket operators advertise extensively and offer national brands. Costs are kept low by self-service operations and a cash-and-carry procedure under which credit and delivery services generally are not offered.

A typical supermarket occupies a large floor space on a single level and is situated on a major street or highway that provides the traf-

The self-service supermarket presents a broad array of goods at low prices, all available under one roof.

GRAND UNION

fic flow needed for a high sales volume. It has a large parking lot. It makes massive outlays for newspaper and in-store advertising, presents elaborate displays of products, and offers broad variety in its goods.

A later development is the small, or "bantam," supermarket, catering to the housewife who needs just a few items, such as bread or milk, and does not want to drive a fairly long distance to a large supermarket and wait in line. Instead, she can go to a bantam market that is situated in her neighborhood and handles only a limited line of brand-name merchandise.

Trends. To overcome store-to-store similarity and to broaden the appeal of supermarkets, operators have added consumer services and wider lines of merchandise. In 1950 the typical supermarket handled about 3,750 items, but by 1970 the number of items handled had increased to about 7,800.

In the late 1950's and early 1960's many supermarkets sought to attract customers through trading stamp plans and contests and games with valuable prizes. Some promotional strategies led to higher profit margins and higher prices, which in turn led to the rediscovery that emphasis on low prices still carried considerable appeal, especially during an inflationary period. Thus, during the mid-1960's, "discount" supermarkets entered the scene with lower margins and lower prices, achieved at least in part by reducing services and promotional expenses. This discount strategy produced sharp increases in store sales and became a very strong force in the supermarket field by the 1970's. See also DISCOUNT RETAILING; TRADING STAMPS.

NEIL M. FORD
University of Wisconsin

SUPERNOVA, sōō-pər-nō'və, a star that explodes and loses a large amount of mass, temporarily increasing in brightness by as much as 100 million times. Supernovae occur in a galaxy once every few hundred years. See STAR.

SUPERPHOSPHATE is the most important phosphorus fertilizer. It is produced by the action of sulfuric acid on phosphate rock. The product is a mixture of calcium sulfate and monocalcium phosphate and contains 16% to 22% water soluble P_2O_5. It is this substance that is used in most phosphate fertilizers. See FERTILIZER.

SUPERSATURATED SOLUTION. See SOLUTIONS—*Concentrations.*

SUPERSONIC FLIGHT is flight at speeds faster than the speed of sound. A sound wave moves through air at about 760 miles (1,220 km) per hour at sea level, but this value decreases in thinner air at higher altitudes.

A plane in flight produces pressure waves, or sound waves. As the plane nears the speed of sound the waves ahead of it are compressed, creating a "sound barrier" that for years was thought to set a limit to flight speeds. This barrier was successfully crossed in 1947 by a rocket plane, and today there are many supersonic aircraft. See also AERODYNAMICS.

SUPERSONIC TRANSPORT. See SST.

SUPERSONICS. See AERODYNAMICS; SOUND.

SUPERSTITION, a term in popular usage for which many anthropologists prefer the more comprehensive term "folk custom and belief." It covers a multitude of notions and is closely related to magic, to the idea that man can use supernatural forces to control the natural world. Imbedded in the culture of the world's peoples, like the belief in spirits, superstition has important functions that continually change with the times.

Function and Scope. Fears of the unknown may lead to "superstitious" acts like knocking on wood or crossing one's fingers. These fears of the unknown are also elements in religion. In primitive society religion, science, and superstitious magic are not easily separated. Observers of human behavior may classify as false the beliefs of subcultures like the folk of the Ozarks, the Chinese Lolos, or the people of southern India. Yet in the stress-filled 1960's and 1970's, many old beliefs, such as those in astrology and witchcraft, have gained new popularity in the sophisticated society of the United States and Europe. Plainly, despite supposed sophistication, human beings are all the folk and thus are still the source for folklore. (See also FOLKLORE.) They are protected only a little by reason.

Retention, Reinterpretation, and Foreignness. The American anthropologist Melville Herskovits remarked that "all human custom is meaningful; nothing without some living value survives in

SUD-AVIATION/BRITISH AIRCRAFT CORPORATIONS

SUPERSONIC AIRCRAFT, the Concorde 001, is a joint French-British project for establishing commercial flights at supersonic speeds. Other nations are also developing supersonic transport systems for passenger flights.

any culture." In all cultures, some old customs are not only retained, but they are reinterpreted and given new meanings. Superstitions, then, are not mere obstinate survivals. Their functions change with changes in the culture's pattern or status among other cultures, but they remain human concerns to human beings. It is said that a girl who takes the last cookie will be an old maid. The American folklorist Wayland Hand surmised that this is basically a taboo enjoined upon girls by older women to teach good manners. Knocking on wood was once, like the pouring of water or oil at a Greek shrine or the throwing of earth over one's shoulder at a Chinese wedding, a gesture to avoid *hubris*—to placate the jealous gods who avenge themselves on a man happy enough to boast about his happiness. It became a cure for pride, a steeling of the boaster against psychological shock if his boast proved false. In the ballad *The Unquiet Grave* excessive weeping for the dead makes the ghost uneasy. Yet it is also true that this superstition —or survival of a custom—may calm the living instead of the dead. No longer do people believe that the rice at a wedding promotes fertility, but the custom of throwing rice contributes to the gaiety of the occasion.

Superstitions are not folly to those who believe and practice them, though a culture different in time or place may reject them as alien. The early Christian propagandist Clement of Alexandria, writing about 200 A. D., accused the heathen of making gods like to themselves, and called this practice the source of all superstition. To the heathen, he said, everything—a mouse boring through an altar, a cock crowing at nightfall—is an omen. They "worship every stick and greasy stone ... dread tufts of tawny wool, and lumps of salt, and torches, and squills, and sulfur, bewitched by sorcerers, in certain impure rites of superstition." In the 20th century, northern Europeans, including the English, despise a diet of horsemeat, once the sacrificial food of the worshipers of the Germanic gods and thus the target of the Christian missionaries from the south. But in the south of Europe horsemeat is a welcome staple. At the beginning of the age of science, the physician Sir Thomas Browne in his *Pseudodoxia epidemica* (1646) laughed at the "vulgar errors" of those less educated than himself. He mentions such beliefs as these: a pot full of ashes contains as much water as an empty one; the mandrake root, shaped like a man, shrieks when pulled up; bitter almonds preserve one against drunkenness; the flesh of peacocks does not decay. Such errors he attributes to Satan, in whom he himself believed, and to the neglect of scientific inquiry. So in his contact with other cultures, Western man rejects active superstitions that better fit these cultures—ritual bathing in the Ganges or ritual cannibalism. Toward his own rituals—such as compulsive handwashing, the heaping up of personal collections of magazines, pins, and old automobile licenses, or the avoidance of the number 13 or cracks in the sidewalks—Western man is more tolerant.

Areas and Subjects of Superstition. All the world, then, has customs and beliefs that may appear irrational to some observers. They can best be studied in the context of culture patterns that include the great rites of passage—birth, marriage, and death—as well as daily routine, animals and plants or "unnatural natural history," ghosts and demons, and formulaic numbers and words. A pioneer of this kind of matrix study, who also insisted on authentic informant sources for the belief, is the American folklorist Wayland Hand.

***Rites of Passage*.** The first great grouping celebrates the life of man: cradle, wedding ring, and grave. Birth and its antecedents begin the chain. If you deny a pregnant woman her yen for strawberry soda her child will have "strawberry marks" on its chest. The day of birth is also important:

Monday's child is fair of face;
Tuesday's child is full of grace;
Wednesday's child is merry and glad;
Thursday's child is sorry and sad;
Friday's child is loving and giving;
Saturday's child works hard for a living;
And the child that is born on the Sabbath day,
Is blithe and bonny, good, and gay.

Childhood is the special epoch of the ills of the body and of folk medicine. Thus, for example, people with large ears live longer than those with small ones. To avoid rabies bite off the dog's tail. Rumanian mothers tie red ribbons around a child's ankles to keep it from being harmed, and Irish mothers bathe their babies in holy wells. Sir Walter Scott was treated for lameness by being wrapped in a sheep's hide. Some believe that kissing a red-haired girl will cure sore eyes, and others believe in putting whiskey on a snake bite, as does Noah in Marc Connelly's *Green Pastures*. Tom Sawyer and Huck Finn went to the graveyard to find a cure for their warts, a childhood affliction for which Wayland Hand recorded some 300 causes and cures. Among the causes are egg white, raindrops from the eaves, jellyfish, and toadstools. Among the cures are being touched by a seventh son, ritual spitting, old bones, horse manure, milkweed juice, and potatoes.

***Daily Life*.** As life proceeds, domestic activities create new beliefs, as the following examples show. Holding a raw potato in the mouth while peeling onions prevents weeping. It is unlucky to spill salt because Judas did it at the Last Supper. Singing in bed means weeping in bed—*hubris* once more. "Friday night's dream on the Saturday told/ Is sure to come true be it never so old." Never lace and tie one shoe before the other is on.

Such daily routines mingle with the larger relationships outside the home—economic and social, travel and communication, as indicated by the following varied beliefs. An itching palm or foam on breakfast coffee may betoken money to come. Male chauvinism has determined that a woman brings bad luck to a ship, a mine, a steel factory, or a lumberyard. The belief has obviously migrated from one occupational sphere to another. No book should be allowed to lie on top of the Bible. When your left ear burns someone is talking about you; cross it with a wet finger and avoid the scandal. A murdered man's wounds bleed in the presence of his murderer. A guilty witch floats, while an innocent witch sinks—modern man has generally called this a rather expensive experiment, yet to the cultures that believe in them, witches are very potent. Clyde Kluckhohn and Dorothy Leighton in *The Navaho* (1962) quote a woman of the pueblos: "Then my baby about two years old got sick. I took her to the hospital at that Mission and they couldn't make her well. She got worse so I brought her home and they had a four-night sing. In two days she was well." An unclinical experiment, but functional for the woman's belief in a cure through witchcraft.

Like birth and death, love and marriage need social reinforcement. In Chinese thought husband and wife are bound by a real though invisible silken cord. In America, if a man balances a broom on his finger, it will fall in the direction his sweetheart lives. "Marry in white, you'll marry all right;/ Marry in blue, your love is true . . ./ Marry in red, you had better be dead."

Death, Ghosts and Demons. According to widespread belief, death warns of its coming by a bird flying in a window, a howling dog, an Irish banshee, or a Cuban owl. Americans embalm corpses as Egyptians did 3,000 years ago. They cremate like the circumpolar tribes from Russia and Scandinavia to North America. But they do not expose their dead as the Parsees of India do. In parts of Illinois, the belief is that you will go to heaven if it rains on your corpse. But in Germany if you have made an enemy of a cat, storms will pound your grave. The ghost is simply one kind of revenant who returns to plague the living or to seek rest and peace. In eastern Europe vampires must be buried at a crossroads with a stake through the heart. In the Scottish ballad *Wife of Usher's Well* and among Central Woodlands Indians the dead come back in earthly flesh and blood to quiet the excessive grief of the living.

Like fears of death and ghosts, superstitions about the devil have a long and varied history. Indeed, it might be said that the devil is a most Christian being, though Clement of Alexandria equated him with pagan gods. In Scandinavian and English ballads he speaks riddles and makes love. In the Kentucky mountains he can be called up by a fiddle. In German folktales and early English plays and in the puppet show *Punch and Judy* he is a buffoon. But in the anxious periods of the late Renaissance, with science questioning all values, both Roman Catholic and Protestant authorities heeded the fancies of feeble minds that accused others of intercourse with the devil. The lore of witches remains in the hex signs on Pennsylvania Dutch barns.

The Seasons, the Fields, and the Stars. Another concern of popular belief is weather prediction. Meteorology is a science, but most of us still repeat the rhyme "Red sky at night, sailor's delight; Red sky at morning, sailors take warning." Does the squirrel cause the hard winter by assembling an unusual supply of nuts, or does he simply predict it? In Spain, timber cut in the light of the moon will warp. To unfasten a pin on New Year's Day will bring bad luck throughout the year.

Animals and Plants. To kill a spider or annoy a cat brings bad luck, whereas to let sparrows or house snakes remain in the home as household gods or mascots brings good luck. In India the cow is revered, in Germany the stork, in ancient Egypt it was the bull, cat, ibis, or scarab beetle. Other popular beliefs about plants and animals are quite varied. Swans change shape—witness Wagner's opera *Lohengrin*—and as they die, they sing their sweetest song. Hoop snakes roll in the American West, blacksnakes milk cows, and rattlesnakes are kept away by a bit of their hide worn on your shoe. Mistletoe encourages Christmas kissing. Cucumbers planted on Saturday are bitter. Burned potato peelings destroy next year's crop.

Words and Numbers. Plotinus interpreted the universe through a theory of numbers, and people still tend to think in terms of formulas. Persons who speak Indo-European languages talk about things in threes, Winnebago Indians in fours, and the Clackamas Indians in fives. Misfortunes, too, come in threes—"What happens twice will happen thrice." Keep what you have for seven years or you'll regret it. Friday the 13th recalls the day of Christ's crucifixion, and office buildings, apartment houses, and hotels avoid the 13th floor. Two is company, three's a crowd. Medieval Jews and Christians believed there were 365 bones in the body, one of which was a key-bone without which there could not be life. The charm of numbers extends to formulaic verse, as in this poetic cure for burns, recorded by Samuel Pepys: "There came Three Angels out of the East;/ The one brought fire, the other brought frost—/Out fire; in frost,/ In the name of the Father, and Son, and Holy Ghost." In North Carolinian belief, warts can be cured by reciting poetry.

Some of these beliefs may seem strange to persons with a conventional Western education in science, technology, or religion. Superstitions can be better understood by studying their ethical, economic, psychological, social, and entertainment value to the people who believe in them.

FRANCIS LEE UTLEY
The Ohio State University

Bibliography

Hand, Wayland, *Popular Beliefs and Superstitions from North Carolina* (Durham, N. C., 1961–1964).
Herskovits, Melville J., "Folklore after a Hundred Years: A Problem in Redefinition," *Journal of American Folklore,* vol. 59, pp. 89–100, 1956.
Hyatt, Harry M., *Folk-Lore from Adams County, Illinois* (New York 1935).
Puckett, Newbell N., *Folk Beliefs of the Southern Negro* (Chapel Hill, N. C., 1926).
Thompson, Stith S., *Motif-Index of Folk-Literature* (Bloomington, Ind., 1955–1960).
Wimberley, Lowry C., *Folklore in the English and Scottish Ballads* (Chicago 1929).

SUPPE, zo͞op'ā, **Franz von** (1819–1895), Austrian composer, who is remembered mainly for his overtures. He was born Francesco Suppé-Demelli, in Spalato, Dalmatia (now Split, Yugoslavia), on April 18, 1819. After studying music in Padua and at the Vienna Conservatory, he became an orchestra conductor in various Viennese theaters—the Theater an der Wien, the Carl Theater, and the Leopoldstadt Theater. Meanwhile he composed voluminously, producing some 30 comic operas and operettas and about 180 other pieces. He died in Vienna on May 21, 1895.

Von Suppe's best-known overtures are *Poet and Peasant, Light Cavalry,* and *Morning, Noon, and Night in Vienna.* Of his operas, those still occasionally performed include *Beautiful Galathea* (1865), *Fatanitza* (1876), *Boccaccio* (1879), and *Donna Juanita* (1880). He also wrote choral works, *Dalmatian Mass,* a symphony, and a number of string quartets.

SUPPLEJACK, sup'əl-jak, a graceful North American twining shrub, sometimes also called *rattan vine.* It is native to the southern and central United States. The supplejack bears oblong-ovate leaves and terminal clusters of small, greenish white flowers. The flowers ripen into attractive bluish black fruits that make the supplejack a desirable ornamental plant for garden trellises. However, it is not always hardy enough to survive the winter in areas north of Virginia and Kentucky.

The supplejack, *Berchemia scandens,* is a member of the buckthorn family (Rhamnaceae). Other plants also known as "supplejack" include a small Australian tree (*Ventilago viminalis*), an Australian clematis (*Clematis aristata*), and tropical woody vines of the genera *Paullinia* and *Serjania.*

J. A. Young
U. S. Department of Agriculture

SUPPLY AND DEMAND. "Supply" and "demand" are headings under which the economist studies the behavior of sellers and buyers and their influence on prices, production, and consumption.

Most commonly, supply and demand are expressed in "schedules"—also called "functions"—relating quantity to price. A supply schedule relates the quantity that sellers will offer for sale to the price they expect to receive. A demand schedule relates the quantity that buyers will purchase to the price they will have to pay. Normally, the higher the prospective selling price, the larger the quantity that sellers will supply; the lower the price, the larger the quantity that buyers will purchase. Strictly speaking, supply and demand schedules apply only to situations where each seller or buyer handles a small volume and adjusts quantity to price as if price were beyond his control.

Effects of Substitution. Supply and demand schedules reflect opportunities for substitution. Consumers may be able to choose among many similar items to meet their needs. Pork can be substituted for beef, and margarine for butter. However, should beef fall in price while the price of pork remains unchanged, buyers will tend to buy more beef. The quantity purchased responds to changes in price according to the *elasticity of demand.* Where substitution is easy, demand tends to be highly elastic. Products with no close substitute, such as salt, tend to have low demand elasticity.

Determinants. The demand schedule for a consumer product depends on the incomes of buyers, their subjective preferences, and the prices of other products. A change in any of these determinants tends to shift the demand schedule.

Demand for productive inputs by business firms is considered to be a *derived demand,* arising from the final demand for the output that these resources can produce. Business firms, when buying input services, may substitute one for another when their prices change. The demand schedule for services of any input reflects the revenue productivity of the input: how much it adds to the output and revenue of a firm. The input's productivity depends on its intrinsic quality, on the technique of production, on the quality and quantity of other inputs, and on the final demand for the product.

In the supply schedule of a product, the quantity supplied tends to be larger at a higher price because of substitutions by producers: a rise in selling price means producers can increase their incomes by producing more of that product and shifting away from other items. The supply schedule depends on the producer's costs, which in turn depend on the technique of production and the prices of needed inputs. With the introduction of mass production methods in the 1950's for poultry production, the supply of chickens and eggs increased substantially.

There are supply schedules for the services of labor, land, and capital. Given the limitations of population size, the supply of labor depends on people's willingness to substitute work for leisure as wage rates change. The supply of land is usually treated as completely inelastic, fixed by nature.

Reaching an Equilibrium. Prices reach an equilibrium at the level where quantity demanded equals quantity supplied. Only at this level are the desires of buyers and sellers mutually consistent. If the price is above the equilibrium level, buyers will not purchase the quantity sellers want to sell, and the price will tend to fall. If the price is below equilibrium, sellers will not furnish the quantity buyers want, and prices will be bid up.

An increase in the demand for a product tends to raise its price. This may result from a change in consumer preference. An increase in supply tends to lower price. Thus chicken and egg prices dropped in the 1950's when supply increased.

Most household incomes are earned from the sale of services of labor, land, and capital. The supply-demand interaction that determines prices for these services also determines the pattern of income distribution among households.

Paul B. Trescott
Southern Methodist University
Author of "The Logic of the Price System"

SUPPURATION is the formation of pus in an inflammation. See Inflammation.

SUPRARENAL GLAND is an alternate name for the adrenal gland. See Adrenal Glands.

SUPREMACY, Acts of, 16th century laws that created a national church in England by transferring control from the pope at Rome to the British sovereign. After the pope refused his consent to Henry VIII's divorce from Catherine of Aragon, papal authority in England was formally abolished by the Act of Supremacy of 1534, in which Parliament declared Henry the only supreme head of the church there and gave him jurisdictional power over ecclesiastical appointments and administration. The Act of Supremacy of 1559 asserted that the sovereign was forever supreme governor of the realm in spiritual as well as temporal matters.

SUPREMACY, Royal, the concept that the British sovereign is the head of the Church of England. The outstanding affirmation of this principle was the Act of Supremacy of 1559. Since 1701, law has required that the sovereign be a member of the Church of England. The sovereign is the supreme governor of the realm in spiritual as well as temporal matters.

In effect, the exercise of royal supremacy in modern times has passed to the ecclesiastical and civil officials, although the sovereign is officially head of the Church. All changes in ecclesiastical laws and the appointment of bishops must be approved by Parliament and the sovereign. See England, Church of.

SUPREMATISM is a form of abstract painting developed by the Russian artist Kasimir Malevich. See Malevich, Kasimir.

D. JORDAN WILSON-PIX

This classic structure in Washington, D. C., designed by Cass Gilbert, has housed the Supreme Court since 1936.

SUPREME COURT OF THE UNITED STATES, the court that heads the judicial branch of the American government. It is undoubtedly the world's most powerful tribunal. The court's unusual authority derives from its dual legal and political roles, for it is the nation's highest appellate law court and at the same time the official interpreter and expounder of the U. S. Constitution. Because many of the most important provisions of the Constitution are extremely broad and offer much room for difference of opinion, the court's influence in the political development of the American republic has been very great, often exceeding that of the president or Congress.

CONTENTS

The Supreme Court was created directly by Article III of the Constitution and entrusted with "the judicial Power of the United States." It is headed by the chief justice of the United States, who in ceremonies of state is the third-ranking official, after the president and vice president. He presides over the court in its public sessions and its private conferences and, acting through the Administrative Office of the U. S. Courts and "the judicial Power of the United States." It is directs the administration of the federal judicial system.

The number of judges on the court is fixed by Congress, not by the Constitution. The Supreme Court was originally composed of six members, but was subsequently both increased and reduced by Congress. Since 1869 the size of the court has remained fixed at nine members. Justices of the Supreme Court and all other federal judges are appointed by the president, by and with the advice and consent of the Senate. They serve "during good Behaviour," which in effect means life tenure.

JURISDICTION

The function of the Supreme Court, according to the U. S. Constitution, is to decide "cases" and "controversies." The cases it hears come to it in three ways. First, the Constitution defines two classes of cases that are in the court's original jurisdiction, that is, that are heard without prior consideration by any other court. Such cases—comparatively few—are (1) those in which a state is a party and (2) those affecting ambassadors and ministers.

Second, the Supreme Court receives appeals from the lower federal courts: 93 district courts, 11 courts of appeals, and a few specialized tribunals such as the U. S. court of claims. Although the Supreme Court has a statutory obligation to hear certain types of appeals, most cases come up for review on the writ of certiorari, a discretionary writ that the court can grant or refuse as it sees fit. The writ is granted on the affirmative vote of four justices. Thus the court is largely free to decide only cases that present issues of public importance.

Third, the court reviews appeals from state supreme courts that present a substantial "federal question," generally where a federal constitutional right has been denied in the state courts. Article VI makes the federal Constitution, laws, and treaties "the supreme Law of the Land" and binding on state judges. Review by the Supreme Court enforces this obligation.

Limitations. Because the Supreme Court has the power to interpret the Constitution and to declare acts of the president and congressional statutes unconstitutional, the American system is often referred to as one of "judicial supremacy." However, the court is limited by the countervailing powers of the other two branches. The president can arouse public opinion against court decisions to which he objects, but his greatest influence on the court is through his appointment of the justices. He must, of course, keep in mind the need to secure Senate confirmation. About one fifth of the nominees to the court have been rejected or not acted on by the Senate; only three nominees have been rejected in the 20th century, however.

Congress exercises pressure on the court principally by initiating legislation or constitutional amendments to reverse judicial interpretations, but it can also threaten impeachment. The Constitution even provides that the appellate jurisdiction of the court is subject to "such Regulations as the Congress shall make." This language suggests the theoretical possibility that an unfriendly Congress could partially or completely deny the Supreme Court its appellate jurisdiction. Although action of this sort has occasionally been threatened, it is highly unlikely to happen.

The Supreme Court is thus a participant in a balance of power, which requires that its great authority be exercised with some regard to the political realities of the time. A perennial division has existed on the court between judicial activists and advocates of self-restraint. The court has often been attacked, but it has survived all crises, for even its opponents agree that it performs an essential function in the American constitutional system.

Conduct of Business. The Supreme Court occupies a stately marble building in Washington, where its annual term runs from October to June. The court sits for four hours daily, Monday through Thursday, to hear cases and to hand down decisions. Oral argument, limited to one hour or less for each side, permits counsel to summarize and clarify positions taken in the written briefs, and allows the justices to put questions. Counsel must be members of the Supreme Court bar; admission is open to any member of a state bar on recommendation by a member of the Supreme Court bar.

On Friday of each week when the court has been sitting, the justices meet in closed conference to decide cases heard that week. The chief justice presents each case that is ready for decisions, with his comments. Discussion is then continued by the associate justices in order of seniority. After all have spoken, the vote is taken, with the most junior justice voting first and the chief justice last. The chief justice decides who shall write the opinion for the court, except that where there is a divided vote and the chief justice is in the minority, the senior associate justice in the majority controls the assignment. Drafts of opinions are circulated among the justices, and the author may revise the final opinion on the basis of his colleagues' comments. Justices who differ from the opinion of the court are free to file concurring or dissenting opinions. Decisions are usually announced on Monday.

POLITICAL HISTORY OF THE COURT

It is possible to distinguish three periods in the history of the Supreme Court's activity as a major participant in the development of national policies. In the first period, extending from the founding of the nation to the Civil War, the court's major emphasis was on strengthening the authority of the national government and establishing its own claim to supremacy in interpreting the Constitution. From the Civil War to the New Deal of the 1930's, the court's mission was principally to protect the growing capitalist industrial development from legislative regulation. In the third period, beginning in 1937, the emphasis shifted from economic freedom to civil liberties, and the court emerged as the national guardian of individual rights.

From the Founding to the Civil War. The first decade of the court's history gave little indication of its subsequent stature. President Washington's appointees were all Federalists sympathetic to the administration, and the entire federal judiciary quickly developed a partisan tone. Two of the first three chief justices, John Jay and Oliver Ellsworth, resigned after a few years, and the other, John Rutledge, was refused confirmation by the Senate after four months in office. Justice Samuel Chase openly pronounced his Federalist political views on the bench, and in 1800 a term of the court could not be held because he was absent campaigning for the reelection of President John Adams. When Jefferson became president, Chase was impeached but escaped conviction.

Though the court heard comparatively few cases during its first decade, it did establish its own authority and that of the new nation. When President Washington submitted some legal questions in the field of foreign relations for judicial advice, the court asserted its independence, declaring that its constitutional role was only to decide actual controversies, not to render advisory opinions.

The court strongly supported federal authority against the states. *Ware* v. *Hylton* (1796) held that the treaty of peace with Britain overrode a Virginia law on the issue of debts owed by Americans to British subjects. In *Chisholm* v. *Georgia* (1793) the court unwisely attacked state sovereignty by interpreting Article III to mean that a state could be sued in federal courts by the citizens of another state. This holding was so bitterly resented by the states that the 11th Amendment was promptly adopted to override it.

One month before Jefferson's inauguration in 1801, John Marshall of Virginia was named chief justice by the outgoing president, John Adams. For 35 years Marshall dominated the court and did more than any other justice to determine its character and that of the federal constitutional system. His courage, his convictions, and the intellectual force of his opinions raised the court to a position of equality with president and Congress.

Marshall's greatest success was *Marbury* v. *Madison* (1803), in which he held that the Supreme Court had the power to declare acts of Congress unconstitutional. This authority was implied by the language of the Constitution, but it was not specifically stated, and the dominant Jeffersonians were hostile to the federal judiciary. In *Marbury*, Marshall fashioned a stunning victory for the court out of a case that had seemed to offer only a choice between two evils.

William Marbury had been appointed a justice of the peace for the District of Columbia by President Adams, but his commission had not been delivered to him by the time Adams left office in March 1801. The new secretary of state, James Madison, found the commission in his office and refused to deliver it to Marbury, who then brought suit in the original jurisdiction of

MEMBERS OF THE SUPREME COURT

Name	Served[1]	Appointed by	From
CHIEF JUSTICES			
John Jay	1790–1795	Washington	N. Y.
John Rutledge	1795[2]	Washington	S. C.
Oliver Ellsworth	1796–1800	Washington	Conn.
John Marshall	1801–1835	J. Adams	Va.
Roger B. Taney	1836–1864	Jackson	Md.
Salmon P. Chase	1864–1873	Lincoln	Ohio
Morrison R. Waite	1874–1888	Grant	Ohio
Melville W. Fuller	1888–1910	Cleveland	Ill.
Edward D. White	1910–1921	Taft	La.
William H. Taft	1921–1930	Harding	Conn.
Charles E. Hughes	1930–1941	Hoover	N. Y.
Harlan F. Stone	1941–1946	F. Roosevelt	N. Y.
Fred M. Vinson	1946–1953	Truman	Ky.
Earl Warren	1953–1969	Eisenhower	Calif.
Warren E. Burger	1969–	Nixon	Minn.
ASSOCIATE JUSTICES			
John Rutledge	1790–1791	Washington	S. C.
William Cushing	1790–1810	Washington	Mass.
James Wilson	1789–1798	Washington	Pa.
John Blair	1790–1796	Washington	Va.
James Iredell	1790–1799	Washington	N. C.
Thomas Johnson	1792–1793	Washington	Md.
William Paterson	1793–1806	Washington	N. J.
Samuel Chase	1796–1811	Washington	Md.
Bushrod Washington	1799–1829	J. Adams	Va.
Alfred Moore	1800–1804	J. Adams	N. C.
William Johnson	1804–1834	Jefferson	S. C.
Henry B. Livingston	1807–1823	Jefferson	N. Y.
Thomas Todd	1807–1826	Jefferson	Ky.
Gabriel Duval	1811–1836	Madison	Md.
Joseph Story	1812–1845	Madison	Mass.
Smith Thompson	1823–1843	Monroe	N. Y.
Robert Trimble	1826–1828	J. Q. Adams	Ky.
John McLean	1830–1861	Jackson	Ohio
Henry Baldwin	1830–1844	Jackson	Pa.
James M. Wayne	1835–1867	Jackson	Ga.
Philip P. Barbour	1836–1841	Jackson	Va.
John Catron	1837–1865	Jackson	Tenn.
John McKinley	1838–1852	Van Buren	Ala.
Peter V. Daniel	1842–1860	Van Buren	Va.
Samuel Nelson	1845–1872	Tyler	N. Y.
Levi Woodbury	1845–1851	Polk	N. H.
Robert C. Grier	1846–1870	Polk	Pa.
Benjamin R. Curtis	1851–1857	Fillmore	Mass.
John A. Campbell	1853–1861	Pierce	Ala.
Nathan Clifford	1858–1881	Buchanan	Me.
Noah H. Swayne	1862–1881	Lincoln	Ohio
Samuel F. Miller	1862–1890	Lincoln	Iowa
David Davis	1862–1877	Lincoln	Ill.
Stephen J. Field	1863–1897	Lincoln	Calif.
William Strong	1870–1880	Grant	Pa.
Joseph P. Bradley	1870–1892	Grant	N. J.
Ward Hunt	1873–1882	Grant	N. Y.
John M. Harlan	1877–1911	Hayes	Ky.
William B. Woods	1881–1887	Hayes	Ga.
Stanley Matthews	1881–1889	Garfield	Ohio
Horace Gray	1882–1902	Arthur	Mass.
Samuel Blatchford	1882–1893	Arthur	N. Y.
Lucius Q. C. Lamar	1888–1893	Cleveland	Miss.
David J. Brewer	1890–1910	B. Harrison	Kans.
Henry B. Brown	1891–1906	B. Harrison	Mich.
George Shiras	1892–1903	B. Harrison	Pa.
Howell E. Jackson	1893–1895	B. Harrison	Tenn.
Edward D. White	1894–1910	Cleveland	La.
Rufus W. Peckham	1896–1909	Cleveland	N. Y.
Joseph McKenna	1898–1925	McKinley	Calif.
Oliver W. Holmes	1902–1932	T. Roosevelt	Mass.
William R. Day	1903–1922	T. Roosevelt	Ohio
William H. Moody	1906–1910	T. Roosevelt	Mass.
Horace H. Lurton	1910–1914	Taft	Tenn.
Charles E. Hughes	1910–1916	Taft	N. Y.
Willis Van Devanter	1911–1937	Taft	Wyo.
Joseph R. Lamar	1911–1916	Taft	Ga.
Mahlon Pitney	1912–1922	Taft	N. J.
James C. McReynolds	1914–1941	Wilson	Tenn.
Louis D. Brandeis	1916–1939	Wilson	Mass.
John H. Clarke	1916–1922	Wilson	Ohio
George Sutherland	1922–1938	Harding	Utah
Pierce Butler	1923–1939	Harding	Minn.
Edward T. Sanford	1923–1930	Harding	Tenn.
Harlan F. Stone	1925–1941	Coolidge	N. Y.
Owen J. Roberts	1930–1945	Hoover	Pa.
Benjamin N. Cardozo	1932–1938	Hoover	N. Y.
Hugo L. Black	1937–1971	F. Roosevelt	Ala.
Stanley Reed	1938–1957	F. Roosevelt	Ky.
Felix Frankfurter	1939–1962	F. Roosevelt	Mass.
William O. Douglas	1939–	F. Roosevelt	Conn.
Frank Murphy	1940–1949	F. Roosevelt	Mich.
James F. Byrnes	1941–1942	F. Roosevelt	S. C.
Robert H. Jackson	1941–1954	F. Roosevelt	N. Y.
Wiley Rutledge	1943–1949	F. Roosevelt	Iowa
Harold H. Burton	1945–1958	Truman	Ohio
Tom C. Clark	1949–1967	Truman	Texas
Sherman Minton	1949–1956	Truman	Ind.
John M. Harlan	1955–1971	Eisenhower	N. Y.
William J. Brennan, Jr.	1956–	Eisenhower	N. J.
Charles E. Whittaker	1957–1962	Eisenhower	Mo.
Potter Stewart	1958–	Eisenhower	Ohio
Byron R. White	1962–	Kennedy	Colo.
Arthur J. Goldberg	1962–1965	Kennedy	Ill.
Abe Fortas	1965–1969	Johnson	D. C.
Thurgood Marshall	1967–	Johnson	Md.
Harry A. Blackmun	1970–	Nixon	Minn.
Lewis F. Powell, Jr.	1972–	Nixon	Va.
William H. Rehnquist	1972–	Nixon	Ariz.

[1] Terms begin with date of actual service, not date of appointment. [2] Appointed by Washington but not confirmed by the Senate.

the Supreme Court for a writ of mandamus to compel Madison to deliver the commission. If Marshall granted the writ, Jefferson would order Madison not to obey it. If Marshall refused to issue the writ, he would admit the impotence of his court.

Marshall avoided both horns of this dilemma and found another issue on which to decide the case. He held that the statute purporting to grant the Supreme Court authority to issue writs of mandamus in its original jurisdiction, under which Marbury had brought the suit, had extended the court's original jurisdiction beyond that provided for in the Constitution. The heart of his opinion, and its enduring contribution, was a logical demonstration that the court was obliged to refuse enforcement of any statute that it found to be contrary to the Constitution.

Having placed the court in a strong position, Marshall's next purpose was to guarantee broad authority for Congress. Here his greatest opinion was *McCulloch* v. *Maryland* (1819), in which he ruled that Congress enjoyed not only the powers specifically granted by the Constitution, but also those implied powers necessary or helpful in carrying out its constitutional purposes. One of the most important of the specifically granted powers—to regulate commerce—was given a broad interpretation in *Gibbons* v. *Ogden* (1824).

Part of Marshall's strategy to promote a strong national government was to win the support of the propertied interests by giving them federal protection. For example, in a series of decisions, such as the Dartmouth College case (*Dartmouth College* v. *Woodward;* 1819), he extended the protection of the contract clause—Article I, Section 10, whereby states were forbidden to pass any "Law impairing the Obligation of Contracts"—to a corporate franchise, which was clearly beyond the intentions of the framers.

Marshall's successor was Roger B. Taney (chief justice, 1836–1864), a Democrat from Maryland appointed by President Jackson. As secretary of the treasury, Taney had carried out Jackson's orders to withdraw federal deposits from the Bank of the United States, and the eastern mercantile and financial interests feared that Taney was a radical democrat who would wreck Marshall's carefully built jurisprudence. But in fact Taney was no less determined than Marshall to preserve the prerogatives of judicial review.

It is true that there was a contrast between Taney's Jacksonian democracy and Marshall's Federalism. States' rights and state police powers were emphasized on the Taney court, rather than central authority. Property rights kept their influence, but it was owners of agrarian property—land and slaves—rather than the commercial creditor class that tended to win judicial favor.

During his first 20 years on the court, Taney's attachment to the economic interests of the South and West made him look like an economic liberal. But this same attachment led to the fateful decision in *Dred Scott* v. *Sandford* (1857), where his court—under the delusion that it could solve the slavery question—denied the power of Congress to control slavery in the territories and the right of Negroes to be citizens. This decision tarnished Taney's reputation and seriously compromised the court, so that it was in no position to challenge the constitutionally questionable actions that President Lincoln took in reacting to the secession crisis. When Taney held Lincoln's suspension of the writ of habeas corpus unconstitutional in *Ex parte Merryman* (1861), Lincoln ignored the ruling. Another confrontation was narrowly averted when the court by a vote of 5 to 4 upheld Lincoln's sea blockade of the Confederacy in the *Prize Cases* (1863).

From the Civil War to the New Deal. The political system that emerged from the Civil War was one of congressional supremacy. Lincoln was dead, and Andrew Johnson, his unfortunate successor, was to be impeached and to escape conviction by a single vote. The Supreme Court, still bearing the burden of the *Dred Scott* decision, was in disrepute. Congress showed its low opinion of the court by changing its size three times in seven years for political reasons. When the court appeared likely to declare some Reconstruction legislation unconstitutional in 1868, Congress simply withdrew the court's jurisdiction to decide the case, and the court acquiesced in *Ex parte McCardle* (1869).

The post-Civil War Congress, lacking members from the secessionist states and dominated by Northern Republican abolitionists, turned to the task of bringing the liberated slaves into the community of free men. With this object Congress secured the ratification of three amendments—the 13th (1865), 14th (1868), and 15th (1870)—and a series of civil rights acts dating from 1866 to 1875. But as part of the settlement in their favor of the disputed Hayes-Tilden election of 1876, the congressional Republicans largely abandoned their concern over the freedmen's fate. What permanent effect the Civil War amendments and the civil rights legislation was to have was left to the Supreme Court.

The post-Civil War court had been chastened by its experiences but by no means reconstructed, and it was still rather traditional in its outlook. Its members at first could not conceive that the 14th Amendment had fundamentally reordered the relations between the nation and the states. That amendment imposed three basic new obligations on the states: they were forbidden to make or enforce any laws abridging the privileges or immunities of citizens of the United States; to deprive any person of life, liberty, or property without due process of law; or to deny any person within their jurisdiction the equal protection of the laws.

When the court was first asked to enforce these new standards, in the *Slaughter-House Cases* (1873), and to declare unconstitutional a state law setting up a slaughtering monopoly in New Orleans, it replied that the 14th Amendment had given no such power. But the pressures for judicial protection of property rights were very great. The postwar period was one of rapid industrial expansion, effected by raw methods. A continent was being crossed by railroads, resources were being exploited, great fortunes were being built. Resentment against the methods of the monopolists and "robber barons," particularly in the agrarian states, had led to the adoption of the regulatory Granger legislation. The Supreme Court was pressed to take sides, and following its ruling in *Munn* v. *Illinois* (1877), it concluded that the due process clause was a directive to the courts to review all legislation regulating the use of property to see whether it accorded with judicial concepts of economic freedom. Thus the doctrine of substantive due process was born, which was to be the major theme of judicial review up to the New Deal.

During this period the chief justices—Salmon P. Chase (served 1864–1873), Morrison R. Waite (served 1874–1888), and Melville W. Fuller (served 1888–1910)—fell far short of the stature of Marshall and Taney, and failed to mold the court in their own image. With no strong leadership, the court for the first time found its intellectual quality among its associate justices, men like Samuel F. Miller, Stephen J. Field, Joseph P. Bradley, and the first John M. Harlan.

By the dawn of the 20th century the conservative, laissez-faire image of the court was firmly established. Its antagonism toward government interference with free enterprise was shown by decisions invalidating a New York 10-hour law for bakers, holding unconstitutional the federal Child Labor Act, and voiding the District of Columbia minimum wage law for women. The court did accept the arguments justifying much legislative intervention, such as regulation of hours for women, and for men in unhealthful occupations; workmen's compensation; zoning; and many other regulatory statutes. But its predominantly conservative character made it a principal target of criticism for the Progressive movement.

Chief Justice Fuller died in 1910, and was succeeded by Edward D. White of Louisiana. He was followed by former President William Howard Taft (1921–1930). The most influential and distinguished member of the court during these years, however, was Associate Justice Oliver Wendell Holmes. Appointed by President Roosevelt in 1902 from the Massachusetts supreme court, he steadily grew in stature and reputation until he resigned in 1932, aged 91.

The public knew Holmes as the great dissenter, and he was generally regarded as a liberal because his dissents were often protests against the denial of civil liberties or against the judicial invalidation of progressive legislation. But some of his protests were less an expression of political liberalism than of a philosophy of limited judicial review, which insisted that judges should not substitute their views for those of legislators so long as the legislative policy remained within the bounds of reason.

Holmes' position was gradually strengthened in the country and on the court by such events as the appointment to the court in 1910 of the reform governor of New York, Charles Evans Hughes, and the election of Woodrow Wilson as president in 1912. Hughes left the court in 1916 to run for president, but that same year Wilson named to the court an ardent Progressive, Louis B. Brandeis, who was confirmed by the Senate in spite of the opposition of the organized bar and big business.

The phrase "Holmes and Brandeis dissenting" quickly became a part of American folklore as these two justices, though proceeding from different premises, joined in case after case to protest the court's policies. In 1925 they were joined by the liberal Harlan F. Stone, who had been U. S. attorney general. In their dissenting opinions over the next few years this trio mapped out an alternative to the doctrinaire conservatism of the court majority.

Hughes returned to the court in 1930 as chief justice. A much more flexible man than Taft, he had the responsibility of guiding the court in its review of the constitutional aspects of the new and experimental legislation enacted by Franklin Roosevelt's New Deal to combat the Great Depression. On the Hughes court, Brandeis and Stone were joined by Benjamin N. Cardozo, who was a sensitive and highly literate chief judge of the New York state court of appeals, when he was appointed by President Hoover in 1932 to fill the Holmes vacancy. These three justices were generally favorable to the New Deal, but they were opposed by four conservatives —Willis Van Devanter, James C. McReynolds, George Sutherland, and Pierce Butler. The balance of power on the court thus rested with Hughes and the ninth member, Owen J. Roberts.

The court at first seemed willing to adapt itself to the new legislative trends of the Depression era. But in 1935 and 1936 the court invalidated a series of important federal and state laws, usually by a vote of 5 to 4 or 6 to 3, depending on whether Roberts alone, or Roberts and Hughes, voted with the conservative bloc.

After his reelection in 1936, President Roosevelt—who had not had a single opportunity to appoint a justice during his first term—sought to eliminate the judicial barrier to reform. He proposed increasing the court to 15 justices. But juggling the size of the court was no longer so acceptable as it had been in the 1860's, and the court-packing plan was defeated in Congress. However, in several key cases in the spring of 1937, Roberts shifted to the liberal side, giving the administration some 5 to 4 victories. Van Devanter then retired, and Roosevelt had his opportunity to begin remaking the court.

From the New Deal to the 1970's. Between 1937 and 1943, Roosevelt appointed eight members to the court, one position being filled twice, and elevated Stone to the chief justiceship as successor to Hughes in 1941. All these appointees were liberals on economic issues, and there ceased to be any danger of the court's invalidating regulatory legislation affecting property. The characteristic problem of the Roosevelt court was civil liberty: the justices quickly found themselves more divided than ever, but now over the nature of their judicial responsibility for the protection of libertarian values. Justices Hugo Black, William O. Douglas, Frank Murphy, and Wiley Rutledge were a cohesive group firmly committed to the use of judicial power to protect civil liberties from legislative or administrative infringement. Justice Felix Frankfurter, the brilliant and influential professor from Harvard Law School, argued contrariwise that the Holmes tradition called for judicial restraint.

The libertarian character of the Roosevelt court was substantially altered by President Truman's four appointments. Chief Justice Fred Vinson succeeded Stone in 1946. Both Rutledge and Murphy died in 1949, leaving only Black and Douglas in the court's activist block. The most difficult problems of the Vinson court were generated by the Cold War. The court upheld the convictions under the Smith Act of the leaders of the American Communist party in *Dennis* v. *United States* (1951), and it refrained from interfering with the hunt for Communists conducted by Sen. Joseph McCarthy and the House Committee on Un-American Activities.

On Vinson's death in 1953, President Eisenhower named Earl Warren, 3-term governor of California, as chief justice. In his first term the court decided *Brown* v. *Board of Education* (1954), unanimously declaring racial segregation in the public schools unconstitutional, and overturning the rule of "separate but equal" facilities which had justified segregation for almost 60 years.

This decision was an appropriate beginning for the Warren court, which during its 16 years was to be the most controversial in American history. Racial segregation was almost the only policy issue on which the court was unanimous. During its early years the Warren court was rather evenly balanced between the activists and the justices who were more cautious in taking new positions. Black and Douglas were joined in the activist camp by Warren and William J. Brennan, Jr., while John M. Harlan, a grandson of the earlier Harlan, was a powerful recruit to the Frankfurter wing. Following Frankfurter's retirement in 1962 and the appointment of four justices by Presidents Kennedy and Johnson, the balance swung substantially toward the activist position. One of Johnson's nominees was Thurgood Marshall, the court's first Negro member.

An initial attack on the Warren court culminated in 1958 when congressional conservatives proposed a series of measures to curb the court or reverse some of its decisions. The proposals were narrowly defeated. In addition to the *Brown* decision, congressional opposition had been aroused by rulings limiting state powers and restricting the operation of both federal and state anti-Communist programs.

During the 1960's the conservative assault on the court became more intense. The first target was a series of "one man, one vote" decisions, in which the court held that the House of Representatives and both houses of state legislatures must be elected from districts roughly equal in population. Conservatives also criticized decisions holding that prayer and Bible-reading in the public schools amounted to an unconstitutional establishment of religion, and they attacked numerous decisions imposing stricter standards for state criminal prosecutions. Again opposition in Congress to the court was largely unsuccessful. Efforts to secure constitutional amendments reversing the prayer and reapportionment decisions failed. In the Omnibus Crime Control and Safe Streets Act of 1968, however, Congress challenged three of the court's decisions in that field.

Richard Nixon made opposition to the court's criminal prosecution decisions a major plank in his 1968 campaign, and promised that as president he would appoint only "strict constructionists" to the court.

In 1968, a few months before the presidential election, Chief Justice Warren notified President Johnson of his desire to retire. To fill this anticipated vacancy, Johnson sent to the Senate the nomination of Abe Fortas, a member of the court since 1965. For a variety of reasons, such as the reluctance of Republicans to see this important post filled by Johnson so near the end of his term, opposition to Fortas' liberal views, and the alleged impropriety of Fortas' close relations with the White House while on the bench, the nomination was subjected to a filibuster in the Senate and had to be withdrawn. Warren then continued to serve as chief justice. Justice Fortas' troubles were not over, however. His acceptance of an annual fee for services to a foundation run by a financier who was under federal indictment forced him to resign in 1969, the first justice in history to leave the court under allegations of unethical conduct.

Warren continued to serve until June 1969, at President Nixon's request. The President then named to be chief justice a judge of the federal court of appeals for the District of Columbia, Warren Earl Burger. Burger, though personally active in criminal law reform, had been outspoken on and off the bench in opposing the criminal prosecution decisions of the Warren court. Having announced that the appointment to the Fortas vacancy would go to a Southern judge, Nixon saw his first two nominees—Clement F. Haynesworth, Jr., of South Carolina and G. Harrold Carswell, of Florida—rejected by the Senate. Angrily charging the Senate with prejudice against the South, Nixon then named a Minnesota federal appeals court judge, Harry A. Blackmun, who was confirmed unanimously.

INTERPRETING THE CONSTITUTION: A CONTINUING PROCESS

The Supreme Court's performance as interpreter of the Constitution can be conveniently considered under five headings: federal-state relations, property rights and economic regulation, civil liberties, criminal justice, and equal protection of the laws.

Federal-State Relations. A basic function of the Supreme Court has been to act as umpire of the federal system. It can perhaps be argued that the court is not an impartial umpire in a federal-state conflict, because it is an agent of one of the parties. Partisans of the states have often contended that this arrangement is unfair, but clearly the basic decisions concerning federal relationships must be made from the vantage point of the whole system.

The Marshall court laid the foundations for federal supremacy. *Fletcher* v. *Peck* (1810) decided that the court could declare state laws unconstitutional. *Martin* v. *Hunter's Lessee* (1816) and *Cohens* v. *Virginia* (1821) established that decisions of state courts denying claims under the federal Constitution were subject to review by the Supreme Court. *McCulloch* v. *Maryland* (1819) held that states could not interfere with a federal activity by use of their taxing power, and *Gibbons* v. *Ogden* (1824) ruled that a federal statute prevails over a conflicting state statute. These basic principles have been restated on countless occasions.

The challenge that the slavery issue presented to the federal system could not be handled by judicial decree, however. Nullification in South Carolina in 1832 and secession in 1861 were crises for the presidency to meet, not the judiciary. The court's principal contribution was the tragic error of the *Dred Scott* decision. After the war was over, the court stated, in *Texas* v. *White* (1869), the fundamental principle of the federal system, which it had cost thousands of lives to reestablish: "The Constitution, in all its provisions, looks to an indestructible Union, composed of indestructible States."

Of the powers delegated to Congress by the Constitution, one of the most important for federal-state relations is the power to regulate commerce. In *Gibbons* v. *Ogden* (1824) Marshall held that this power extended to all forms of commerce among the states. But local activities, such as manufacturing, mining, logging, and agriculture were at first considered intrastate operations, subject to regulation only by the states in which they were located. In *Hammer* v. *Dagenhart* (1918) the court declared the federal Child Labor Act unconstitutional in a 5-to-4 decision that, as Justice Holmes said, mistakenly subordinated the power to regulate commerce to the 10th Amendment. In the *Gibbons* case Marshall had recognized that local commerce could be regulated if it affected other states; and as the nation's economy became increasingly interdependent, the court approved increased federal regulation by using the "effect on commerce" doctrine. For example, in 1922, Chief Justice Taft ruled that the purchase and sale of cattle in the Chicago stockyards were part of an interstate "stream of commerce" and so subject to federal regulation.

This expansive interpretation of the commerce power came to an abrupt but temporary halt in 1935 and 1936 as the court held several major New Deal recovery statutes unconstitutional. But in *NLRB* v. *Jones & Laughlin Steel Corporation* (1937) the court abandoned this policy and upheld the Wagner Act, which required all industries in commerce or affecting commerce to engage in collective bargaining with their employees. *Hammer* v. *Dagenhart* was overruled in 1941 when the federal Wage-Hour law was upheld.

A later federal statute based on the now almost unlimited commerce power was the Civil Rights Act of 1964, which banned racial discrimination in all public accommodations affecting commerce, such as hotels, motels, and restaurants. The court upheld this statute in *Heart of Atlanta Motel* v. *United States* (1964).

Property Rights and Economic Regulation. The Constitution originally protected property chiefly by forbidding the states to impair the obligation of contracts and by barring the federal government from taking private property without due process or compensation. Before the Civil War, the main court activity in this area was Marshall's extension of the contract clause to public contracts, such as corporate charters.

LANDMARK DECISIONS OF THE SUPREME COURT

Marbury v. **Madison** (1803): the Supreme Court can declare acts of Congress unconstitutional.

McCulloch v. **Maryland** (1819): powers granted to Congress by the Constitution are to be broadly construed.

Dartmouth College v. **Woodward** (1819): a corporate franchise is a contract, which the Constitution forbids a state legislature to impair.

Gibbons v. **Ogden** (1824): the power of Congress to regulate commerce extends to all forms of interstate commerce and to local commerce that affects commerce among the states.

Dred Scott v. **Sandford** (1857): Negroes cannot be citizens, and Congress cannot control slavery in the territories; the Missouri Compromise is unconstitutional.

Ex parte Milligan (1866): the president cannot order the trial of civilians by military courts in areas outside the military theater.

Civil Rights Cases (1883): equal protection under the 14th Amendment applies only to state action, not to discrimination by private persons.

Hurtado v. **California** (1884): the 14th Amendment does not incorporate the criminal procedure provisions of the Bill of Rights.

Pollock v. **Farmers' Loan & Trust Co.** (1895): the federal income tax is unconstitutional.

Plessy v. **Ferguson** (1896): under the "separate but equal" doctrine, racial segregation on public carriers does not deny equal protection.

Lochner v. **New York** (1905): a 10-hour-day law for bakers is a denial of freedom of contract.

Hammer v. **Dagenhart** (1918): the federal Child Labor Act is an unconstitutional interference with the right of the states to regulate manufacturing.

Schenck v. **United States** (1919): speech cannot be punished unless there is a "clear and present danger" that it will lead to evils Congress has a right to prevent.

Gitlow v. **New York** (1925): the due process clause of the 14th Amendment makes the 1st Amendment's free speech provisions applicable to the states.

McGrain v. **Daugherty** (1927): Congress has broad but not unlimited power to conduct investigations.

Schechter Poultry Corp. v. **United States** (1935): the National Industrial Recovery Act providing for self-regulation of industry is unconstitutional.

NLRB v. **Jones & Laughlin Steel Corp.** (1937): the court upholds the Wagner Act and returns to a broad interpretation of the commerce power.

West Coast Hotel Co. v. **Parrish** (1937): state minimum wage laws for women are valid; the court abandons substantive due process in the economic field.

Bridges v. **California** (1941): 1st Amendment freedoms have a "preferred position" over other rights.

Dennis v. **United States** (1951): Smith Act conviction of American Communist party leaders is upheld.

Youngstown Sheet & Tube Co. v. **Sawyer** (1952): President Truman's seizure of steel mills to assure munitions for troops in Korea is unconstitutional.

Brown v. **Board of Education** (1954): racial segregation in the public schools denies equal protection.

Roth v. **United States** (1957): obscenity is defined and held not to be protected by the 1st Amendment.

Mapp v. **Ohio** (1961): the court begins to make all criminal procedure provisions of the Bill of Rights effective in state prosecutions.

Engel v. **Vitale** (1962): a state-sponsored program of prayers in the public schools is unconstitutional.

Baker v. **Carr** (1962): courts can hear complaints against unequal apportionment of population among legislative districts.

Gideon v. **Wainwright** (1963): in state criminal prosecutions counsel must be provided if the defendant cannot afford to retain it.

Reynolds v. **Sims** (1964): the rule of "one man, one vote" requires all state legislators to be elected from districts roughly equal in population.

New York Times v. **Sullivan** (1964): public officials can secure libel judgments against newspapers only where falsehoods are known to be such and malicious.

Griswold v. **Connecticut** (1965): state law forbidding birth control information is an unconstitutional invasion of right to privacy.

Miranda v. **Arizona** (1966): suspects under police inquiry must be notified of their rights, including right to counsel, or confessions will be invalid.

Witherspoon v. **Connecticut** (1968): persons with general scruples about death penalty cannot be excluded from juries in capital cases.

Welsh v. **United States** (1970): persons opposed to war on moral or ethical grounds are entitled to draft exemption as conscientious objectors.

The adoption of the 14th Amendment made possible more extensive judicial protection of business and property. Under that amendment the obligation of observing due process, which the 5th Amendment imposed on the federal government, was extended to the states. At first this was not regarded as of great importance, because due process was understood to guarantee only traditional trial procedures such as notice and hearing, and the due process provision in the 5th Amendment had seldom been invoked.

However, after the adoption of the 14th Amendment, efforts were immediately made to use its provisions to block legislative regulation of property. The privileges and immunities clause seemed the most promising for this purpose, but the court gave that language a narrow interpretation in the *Slaughter-House Cases* (1873). Attention then turned to the due process clause, again unsuccessfully at first. In *Munn* v. *Illinois* (1877) the court refused to hold state regulation of grain storage rates a taking of property without due process. But 10 years later the court in *Mugler* v. *Kansas* (1887), while upholding a state law prohibiting the manufacture or sale of liquor, frankly admitted that it would judge the merits of legislation challenged on due process grounds. In another 10 years *Allgeyer* v. *Louisiana* (1897) established the principle that freedom to make contracts was part of the liberty guaranteed by the due process clause, and any interference with that freedom would be held unconstitutional.

Thus due process was expanded from a procedural guarantee to a judicial license to veto legislation. The principal beneficiaries of the new doctrine of substantive due process were business corporations, which in 1886 had been held to be "persons" covered by the 14th Amendment. By the turn of the century every new piece of social legislation was being attacked in court as a taking of property without due process or as a denial of freedom of contract.

An 8-hour day in mines and smelters was approved by the court in *Holden* v. *Hardy* (1898) on grounds of health, as was a law establishing a 10-hour day for women in industry in *Muller* v. *Oregon* (1908). But in *Lochner* v. *New York* (1905) the court held by a vote of 5 to 4 that a 10-hour-day law for bakers was unconstitutional, and in *Adkins* v. *Children's Hospital* (1923) the court struck down a District of Columbia minimum wage law, a ruling repeated in *Morehead* v. *N. Y. ex rel. Tipaldo* (1936).

Justice Holmes charged that in making such decisions the court was acting as a superlegislature. It was in part these substantive due process decisions that caused New Deal opposition to the court. But even before the first Roosevelt appointee took his seat, the court in *West Coast Hotel Co.* v. *Parrish* (1937) had reversed itself and upheld a state minimum wage law for women. The court then abandoned further efforts to apply due process tests to economic legislation.

Civil Liberties. The 1st Amendment forbids Congress to abridge "the freedom of speech, or of the press; or the right of the people peaceably to assemble, and to petition the Government for a redress of grievances." It also directs Congress not to make any law "respecting an establishment of religion, or prohibiting the free exercise thereof."

Surprisingly, the Supreme Court had little occasion to interpret these basic freedoms for more than a century. But during World War I the espionage and sedition acts directed against opponents of the war brought important free speech issues before the court. Justice Holmes was the court's spokesman in the initial cases. In *Schenck* v. *United States* (1919) he developed the "clear and present danger test," which states that the utterance of words cannot be punished unless they are used in such circumstances and are of such a nature as to create a clear and present danger that they will result in violence or some other evil the government has a right to prevent.

In *Gitlow* v. *New York* (1925) the court unexpectedly held that the 1st Amendment's guarantee against congressional abridgement of free speech also applied to the states by reason of the 14th Amendment prohibition against denial of liberty without due process of law. In subsequent decisions all the other guarantees of the 1st Amendment have likewise been given effect against state action, thus making 1st Amendment freedoms uniform throughout the nation.

The clear and present danger test left a great deal to the discretion of judges and juries. The Roosevelt court reenforced it by the concept that the freedoms of the 1st Amendment occupied a "preferred position," freedom of speech and thought being the indispensable conditions for every other form of freedom. Black's statement of this doctrine in *Bridges* v. *California* (1941) was strongly controverted by Frankfurter, who contended that all constitutional freedoms had equal claims to enforcement. In the 1950's and 1960's Frankfurter and Harlan successfully swung the court to the "balancing" test, which weighed conflicting constitutional claims against each other, to determine which should prevail.

Perhaps the most common free speech problem concerned the rights of speakers, picketers, or demonstrators in the streets or other public places. The court held in *Hague* v. *CIO* (1939) that there is a constitutional right to such use of public streets or parks. Because of the problems of traffic control and public safety, permits can be required, but they must be granted on a nondiscriminatory basis, and denial of a permit may be appealed to the courts. *Kovacs* v. *Cooper* (1949) held that sound amplification of speeches in streets or parks can be controlled.

Demonstrators who move through the streets or surround public buildings may raise serious issues of public safety. In *Edwards* v. *South Carolina* (1963) and *Cox* v. *Louisiana* (1965) the court upheld demonstrations by large groups, disagreeing with the police contention that they were a public danger. However, in *Stotland* v. *Pennsylvania* (1970) the court refused to review the validity of an ordinance under which the mayor of Philadelphia had banned all public gatherings for five days after the assassination of Martin Luther King, Jr.

Freedom of the press has not presented so many problems for the court as freedom of speech. A leading free-press decision is *Near* v. *Minnesota* (1931); the court held unconstitutional a state statute allowing malicious and scandalous newspapers to be shut down by injunction. Another important ruling, 6–3, in *New York Times* v. *United States* (1971), refused to prevent publication by the *Times* and the Washington *Post* of the secret Pentagon Papers because the government had not shown a danger to national security justifying prior restraint. See CENSORSHIP.

The American press has always been free to publish any information it can secure about criminal suspects, although such news may prejudice the community against a defendant and make it impossible to secure an impartial jury. The court focused attention on this issue in *Sheppard* v. *Maxwell* (1966), where it held that newspaper publicity tactics had forced an indictment and made the subsequent trial into a carnival. But the court stopped short of suggesting that editors could be forbidden to print news about criminal prosecutions or punished for doing so.

The press has always been subject to libel suits for defamation of character, with truth as a defense. In *New York Times* v. *Sullivan* (1964) the court ruled that even untrue statements about public officials could not be punished unless the falsehood was known to be such, intentional, and malicious.

Obscenity, like libel, has long been punishable under state laws, and there is also a federal statute covering obscenity in the mails. The court upheld these statutes in *Roth* v. *United States* (1957) on the grounds that obscenity is not protected by the 1st Amendment. However, it then had some difficulty in deciding what kinds of material were actually obscene. In *Roth* and subsequent decisions it developed three rules: the material must appeal to the "prurient interest" of the average person, by "contemporary community standards"; it must be "patently offensive"; and it must have no "redeeming social importance." These tests were so lenient that pornographic materials greatly increased in circulation. In 1973 the court held that the three-part test applied only to depictions or descriptions of "sexual conduct"; state instead of federal standards would now prevail; and to be "obscene" a prurient and offensive work need not "utterly" lack value, but merely lack "serious literary, artistic, political, or scientific value."

The right of individuals to organize into groups for various purposes is derived from the right of assembly and the freedoms of speech, press, and religion. The principal challenge to this right has been acts directed against the Communist party. In *Dennis* v. *United States* (1951) the court upheld the conviction of 11 leaders of the American Communist party for violation of the Smith Act (1940), which punished advocating or teaching the violent overthrow of the government. However, the court's subsequent position that Communists can be punished only for their own illegal acts, not for mere membership in the party, largely terminated the use of the Smith Act as well as the Internal Security Act of 1950.

The ban on an establishment of religion has been held by the court to mean no government sponsorship of, government financial support of, or active involvement in religious activity. In *Everson* v. *Board of Education* (1947) the court held that bus fares of children attending parochial schools could be paid from public funds, because it was a benefit to the child rather than to the church school. Providing free textbooks on secular subjects to both public and parochial schoolchildren was upheld on the same basis in *Board of Education* v. *Allen* (1968). But prayers and Bible-reading in the public schools are not permissible. Neither is the use of public school buildings for "released time" programs of religious training (*McCollum* v. *Board of Education*, 1948), but releasing students for religious classes off the school grounds is acceptable (*Zorach* v. *Clauson*, 1952). The contention that tax exemption on church property amounts to a financial subsidy to religion was rejected in *Walz* v. *Tax Commission of the City of New York* (1970).

Charges of interference with the free exercise of religion usually grow out of social welfare laws which unintentionally inflict a hardship on some religious group. Laws requiring businesses to close on Sunday handicap Jewish merchants, whose religion requires that they also close on Saturday. In the Sunday Closing cases (1961) the court upheld such laws on the ground that, while Sunday closing had originally been a religious practice, it had become a secular regulation intended only to provide a uniform day of rest. In *Sherbert* v. *Verner* (1963) the court modified this position and decided that where a secular regulation had a harsh impact on a religious group, it should not be enforced if there was some alternative means whereby the state could accomplish the same end without impairing free exercise of religion. Schoolchildren who object to saluting the flag on religious grounds cannot be compelled to do so (*West Virginia State Board of Education* v. *Barnette*, 1943).

Refusal to serve in the armed forces on the grounds of religiously based conscientious objection to war has always been permitted by the draft laws. In *Welsh* v. *United States* (1970) the court held that moral or ethical objections to war could also justify exemption from the draft.

Criminal Justice. Five of the ten amendments in the Bill of Rights are concerned with the rights of persons who are suspects or defendants in criminal cases. The most important are the protections in the 4th Amendment against unreasonable searches and seizures; the 5th Amendment guarantees of due process, grand jury indictment, and freedom from self-incrimination and double jeopardy; the 6th Amendment guarantee of jury trial and representation by counsel; and the 8th Amendment protection against excessive bail and cruel and unusual punishment.

These provisions, the court held in *Barron* v. *Baltimore* (1833), applied only to federal prosecutions. When the 14th Amendment was adopted, a major new problem of constitutional interpretation was posed for the courts: whether the due process clause incorporated and made applicable to state prosecutions all the guarantees found in the 4th through the 8th Amendments.

For more than half a century the court answered this question in the negative. The court's position was that the due process clause imposed on the states only the general obligation to adopt procedures in criminal cases that were consistent with a system of "ordered liberty" and embodied those principles of justice "so rooted in the traditions and conscience of our people as to be ranked as fundamental." Ordered liberty required adequate notice of the state's charges and fair trial, but it did not include, for example, the right of indictment by grand jury (*Hurtado* v. *California*, 1884), freedom from self-incrimination (*Twining* v. *New Jersey*, 1908), or protection against double jeopardy (*Palko* v. *Connecticut*, 1937). On the other hand, freedom from unreasonable search and seizure was classed by the court as fundamental (*Wolf* v. *Colorado*, 1949).

Throughout the 1950's the court found it increasingly difficult to distinguish between protections that were fundamental and those that were not, or to justify the fact that procedures that could be used in state courts would be unconstitutional if employed in federal courts. Finally, in *Mapp* v. *Ohio* (1961) the court abandoned this effort and began to insist that state standards be the same as federal, which required the overruling of many earlier decisions.

The Warren court was particularly concerned about abuses in the investigative practices used by local police to secure confessions. After holding in *Gideon* v. *Wainwright* (1963) that counsel must be supplied in all criminal cases if defendants were unable to afford it, the court in *Escobedo* v. *Illinois* (1964) extended this requirement of counsel to the pretrial period as well. In later decisions, headed by *Miranda* v. *Arizona* (1966), the court went further and laid down what amounted to a code of conduct for police interrogation of suspects. Substantial congressional and public opposition to these rulings led to the inclusion in the Omnibus Crime Control and Safe Streets Act of 1968 of provisions aimed at reversing several of them.

Equal Protection of the Laws. The equal protection clause of the 14th Amendment was drafted primarily to guarantee equal rights to the newly freed blacks, but for more than three quarters of a century the Supreme Court did very little toward its enforcement. The civil rights statutes adopted between 1866 and 1875 were largely ignored or rendered ineffective by judicial interpretation. The Civil Rights Act of 1875 forbade racial discrimination or separation in public accommodations, but in the Civil Rights Cases (1883) the court ruled that the 14th Amendment forbade only state-imposed discrimination, not discrimination by private individuals or corporations. *Plessy* v. *Ferguson* (1896) held that segregation on public carriers was valid so long as equal facilities were provided.

In 1954 the court reversed the "separate but equal" rule in *Brown* v. *Board of Education*, which declared racial segregation in the public schools unconstitutional. This ruling set in motion the most staggering task any court has ever undertaken—the reversal of several centuries of segregationist practices and thought patterns. The Warren court throughout its 16 years was united in pressing for the elimination of all forms of racial discrimination, though progress was very slow even after Congress undertook to assist it by passing a new series of civil rights acts.

School segregation was in part the result of segregated housing patterns. Some states adopted "open occupancy" laws making it illegal to refuse to sell or rent to persons because of their race or color, but not until 1968 did Congress pass a federal civil rights act making this guarantee nationwide. In the same year the court rather surprisingly decided in *Jones* v. *Alfred H. Mayer Co.* that under the Civil Rights Act of 1866 this had already been the law for 100 years.

Racial discrimination in voting has also concerned the court, though its efforts met with little success until Congress passed the Voting Rights Act of 1965. One of the chief methods of preventing Southern Negroes from voting had been to require them to demonstrate literacy and an understanding of federal and state constitutions—a requirement that could easily be administered by registrars in a manner to disqualify Negroes. The Voting Rights Act forbade any state where 50% of the eligible voters were not registered or did not vote in the 1964 elections to enforce literacy or "understanding" tests, and federal registrars took over registration in counties where the attorney general certified they were needed to enforce the 15th Amendment. The court upheld this statute in *South Carolina* v. *Katzenbach* (1966).

The Warren court also applied the equal protection clause to guarantee fair apportionment of population among election districts. In 1946 the court in *Colegrove* v. *Green* refused to take cognizance of complaints that wide variations in the population of congressional districts denied equal protection of the laws, saying that this was a "political question" in which courts should not get involved. But in 1962, in *Baker* v. *Carr,* it reversed this holding and opened the courts to apportionment problems. In a series of cases, of which *Reynolds* v. *Sims* (1964) was the most important, the court held that the House of Representatives and both houses of state legislatures must follow the rule of "one man, one vote" with election districts roughly equal in population. These decisions had a profound political effect in reducing rural control of state legislatures as urban and suburban residents secured for the first time proportionate representation. The court also extended the one man, one vote rule to local legislative bodies in *Avery* v. *Midland County* (1968) and subsequent rulings.

A UNIQUE INSTITUTION

The example of the United States Supreme Court was influential, after World War II, in causing constitutional courts to be created in several countries, including West Germany, Italy, and India. But the American institution remains unique among the world's high courts in its combination of judicial and political functions. For justices to play this dual role successfully requires special skills and attitudes. Judicial experience in itself has not been regarded as adequate preparation for the post, as is evidenced by the fact that almost half of the justices were appointed to the court without previous judicial service, including such outstanding ones as Marshall, Story, Taney, Miller, Bradley, Hughes, Brandeis, Stone, Black, Frankfurter, and Warren. Interpreting the Constitution is a task that calls, not for narrow technical skills, but for judgment, experience in political affairs, sensitivity to human needs, and understanding of the principles underlying a free society.

Judicial Review. Although the Supreme Court's political function has inevitably made it the periodic target of controversy, even its opponents have generally agreed that its role is essential. It is true that judicial review can create serious problems, for a judiciary serving for life introduces a certain oligarchical element into democratic government. Such a court may get out of touch with the times or become wedded to unworkable constitutional theories, as it did in *Dred Scott* or in its conflict with the New Deal. At the other extreme, it may, according to its constitutional principles, undertake to reform social evils faster than the society finds acceptable, as the experience of the Warren court in certain areas seemed to demonstrate.

Conclusion. All things considered, the advantages of judicial participation in American constitutional policy-making have seemed overwhelming. Judicial review permits a sober second look at actions that the president or Congress may have taken in the heat of controversy or under the pressure of time or electoral threats. Minorities may secure protection from the court when they would not be able to get a hearing in Congress. Supreme Court review of state justice offers some assurance that local practices will not be permitted to fall below acceptable national standards. The Supreme Court can act as a national conscience because of the special obligation imposed on the justices to review governmental action in the light of the enduring standards of the Constitution.

See also CONSTITUTION OF THE UNITED STATES; articles on concepts such as CIVIL RIGHTS AND LIBERTIES and DUE PROCESS OF LAW; and articles on justices and important individual cases.

C. HERMAN PRITCHETT
University of California at Santa Barbara
Author of "The American Constitution"

Bibliography

Beveridge, Albert J., *The Life of John Marshall,* 4 vols. (Boston 1916–1919).
Bickel, Alexander M., *The Supreme Court and the Idea of Progress* (New York 1970).
Bowen, Catherine Drinker, *Yankee from Olympus: Justice Holmes and His Family* (Boston 1944).
Israel, Fred L., and Friedman, Leon, eds., *The Justices of the U. S. Supreme Court 1789–1969,* 4 vols. (New York 1969).
Konvitz, Milton R., *Expanding Liberties* (New York 1966).
Kurland, Philip B., ed., *The Supreme Court Review* (Chicago 1960–1970).
Lewis, Anthony, *Gideon's Trumpet* (New York 1964).
Mason, Alpheus T., *Harlan Fiske Stone: Pillar of the Law* (New York 1956).
Mason, Alpheus T., and Beaney, William M., *The Supreme Court in a Free Society* (New York 1968).
McCloskey, Robert G., *The American Supreme Court* (Chicago 1960).
Murphy, Walter F., *Congress and the Court* (Chicago 1962).
Pfeffer, Leo, *This Honorable Court* (Boston 1965).
Pritchett, C. Herman, *The American Constitution,* 2d ed. (New York 1968).
Pritchett, C. Herman, *The Roosevelt Court* (New York 1948).
Shapiro, Martin, *Law and Politics in the Supreme Court* (New York 1964).
Warren, Charles, *The Supreme Court in United States History,* 3 vols. (Boston 1922).

SUPREME SOVIET, the bicameral legislature of the USSR. See UNION OF SOVIET SOCIALIST REPUBLICS–*Government*.

SUR. See TYRE.

SURABAJA, sŏŏr-ə-bī′ə, is the second-largest city in Indonesia. It is situated on the northeast coast of Java, on Surabaja Strait, opposite Madura island. The city's architecture shows the imprint of Dutch colonial rule, but Surabaja has many newer residential sections and commercial buildings in modern international style. There is also an old, congested downtown district of small shops and markets.

Surabaja (Soerabaja) is the prime trading center for eastern Java. Its coastal location is important for communication with Indonesia's many island components, and the port lies along a major sea-lane from Southeast Asia to Australia. The city has extensive harbor facilities, including the Indonesia's largest naval base.

Among the agricultural goods that move through Surabaja's port are vegetable fibers, sugarcane, tobacco, maize, tapioca, coffee, cocoa, rubber, copra, spices, and rice. The city is one of Indonesia's major manufacturing centers, with food processing, petroleum refining, shipbuilding, textile and chemical production, and auto assembly among its industrial activities.

Airlangga University and also a technical college and a naval college are located in Surabaja. Population: (1961) 1,007,945.

PETER R. INGOLD
University of Vermont

SURAKARTA, sŏŏr-ə-kär′tə, is a city in east-central Java, Indonesia. It is situated on the Solo River on one of the country's most densely populated plains, which is flanked east and west by lofty volcanic peaks. One volcano, Mt. Merapi, is active, and its periodic eruptions shower the plain with fertilizing volcanic ash. Surakarta (Soerakarta) is a commercial center of this region and is linked to all parts of Java by rail and road. Fruits, vegetables, tobacco, sugarcane, cassava, coconuts, and rice enter the city's markets for shipment to other parts of Indonesia. Manufactures include foodstuffs, batik cloth, fine metalcraft products, woodcarvings, and musical instruments.

Formerly called Solo, Surakarta was for centuries the seat of the sultanate of Surakarta. When Indonesia won its independence from the Dutch in 1949, the sultanate was incorporated into Central Java province. Perhaps because of its inland location, the city escaped heavy Europeanization and preserved much of its early Javanese cultural heritage.

Surakarta has several institutions of higher learning, including the Islamic University of Indonesia. The sultan's walled palace, or *kraton,* is an attraction for visitors to the city. Population: (1961) 367,626.

PETER R. INGOLD
University of Vermont

SURAT, sŏŏr′ət, a city in India, is the capital of Surat district in Gujarat state. It is 150 miles (240 km) north of Bombay and 14 miles (23 km) from the mouth of the Tapti River. This ancient city was long the chief port of India, and its population in the 18th century was probably the largest in the country.

Surat was seized by the Mughul emperor Akbar from the kingdom of Ahmadabad in 1573 and soon became the chief point of European trade with the Mughul Empire. It was also the scene of bitter conflict among Portuguese, Dutch, and British traders. In 1612 the British established their first trading station in India at Surat. From 1664 the city's wealth became the object of frequent marauding expeditions by Shivaji, the founder of the Maratha Empire. These raids, the decline of the Mughuls, the transfer of the center of British operations to Bombay, silting of the harbor, a disastrous fire, and floods on the Tapti all combined to bring Surat virtually to ruin.

Surat's recovery began with the cotton and railroad-construction booms in India after 1860. Although insignificant as a port, Surat is a major center for inland trade, cotton and silk milling, high-quality handloom weaving, and other crafts. Population: (1968 est.) 349,384.

JOSEPH E. SCHWARTZBERG
University of Minnesota

SURESNES, sü-rân′, is a town in France in the department of Hauts-de-Seine. A residential suburb of Paris, it lies immediately west of the city, across the Seine River from the Bois de Boulogne. Mont Valérien, on the heights of Suresnes, provides a commanding view of the countryside around Paris.

Suresnes' manufactures include automobiles, metal pipes, printed fabrics, rubber, chemicals, and perfume.

In 1593, Suresnes was the scene of the conferences between Protestant and Roman Catholic leaders that led to the adoption of Catholicism by Henry IV and to his entrance into Paris the following year. At the summit of Mont Valérien is the old fort that was the key to the defense of Paris in the sieges of the city by the Germans in 1870 and by the government of the National Assembly at Versailles in 1871. Population: (1962) 38,980.

SURETYSHIP. See GUARANTY; INDEMNITY.

SURF CASTING. See FISHING–*Surf Fishing*.

SURF PERCH, any of a family of small, mainly marine fishes that resemble perches and bear live young. The fish is also called *sea perch.* Surf perches are most abundant along the California coast. Some also are found northward to Alaska and southward to Baja California. Two species occur off Japan and Korea, and one, the tule perch, lives in fresh water in northern California. Many are found near surf and others in bays and around piers. They are caught by sports fishermen and are of some commercial importance in California.

Surf perches range from 3 to 18 inches (7.5–46 cm) in length. Most are silvery or grayish, but some are vividly colored. Males use modified anal fins to transfer sperm to the females, who store them and delay fertilization. About 10 to 12 months after mating, from 8 to 40 well-developed young are born.

Surf perches make up the family Embiotocidae of the order Perciformes.

MURRAY NEWMAN
Vancouver Public Aquarium

SURF RIDING. See SURFING.

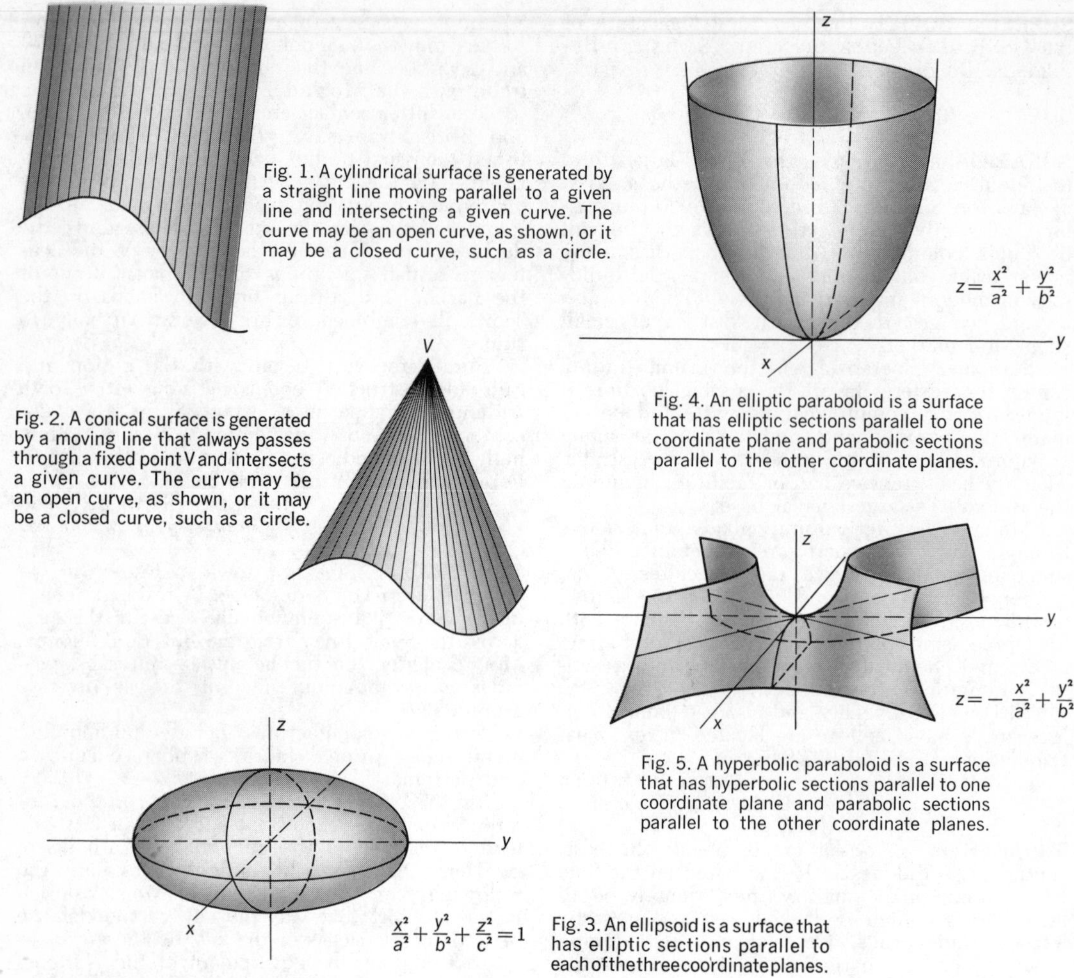

Fig. 1. A cylindrical surface is generated by a straight line moving parallel to a given line and intersecting a given curve. The curve may be an open curve, as shown, or it may be a closed curve, such as a circle.

Fig. 2. A conical surface is generated by a moving line that always passes through a fixed point V and intersects a given curve. The curve may be an open curve, as shown, or it may be a closed curve, such as a circle.

Fig. 4. An elliptic paraboloid is a surface that has elliptic sections parallel to one coordinate plane and parabolic sections parallel to the other coordinate planes.

Fig. 5. A hyperbolic paraboloid is a surface that has hyperbolic sections parallel to one coordinate plane and parabolic sections parallel to the other coordinate planes.

Fig. 3. An ellipsoid is a surface that has elliptic sections parallel to each of the three coordinate planes.

SURFACE. A plane is the simplest surface, but in the axiomatic development of geometry, "plane" is usually an undefined term. In analytic geometry, a surface is often defined as the locus of points whose cartesian coordinates satisfy an equation $f(x,y,z) = 0$. If the function f is a polynomial, the surface S is said to be algebraic. A surface that is not algebraic is said to be transcendental. If f is a polynomial of degree n, S is said to be of order n, and a general line intersects S in n points. If $n = 1$, S is a plane, and if $n = 2$, S is a quadric surface. Surfaces also may be defined by equations of the form $x = f(u,v)$, $y = g(u,v)$, and $z = h(u,v)$, which express the coordinates of a point on the surface as functions of two auxiliary variables, u and v.

For some purposes it is convenient to think of a surface as the locus generated when a straight line or a curve moves through space in a prescribed manner. A surface formed by a moving straight line is called a ruled surface, and the various positions of the moving line are called the generators of the surface. For example, if the generators of a ruled surface S are all parallel, S is a cylinder (see Fig. 1). As another example, if the generators all pass through a fixed point V, the surface is a cone having V as its vertex (see Fig. 2). The surface generated when a curve is rotated about a fixed line l is called a surface of revolution, and l is called its axis. For example, the doughnut-shaped surface formed when a circle rotates about a nonintersecting line in the plane of the circle is called a torus. See also Torus.

After the plane, the simplest surfaces are the quadric surfaces. Besides cones and cylinders, there are five types of quadric surfaces: ellipsoids, elliptic paraboloids, hyperbolic paraboloids, hyperboloids of one sheet, and hyperboloids of two sheets (see Figs. 3–7). The hyperbolic paraboloid and the hyperboloid of one sheet are ruled surfaces. Each is formed by two sets of generators, whereas the cone and the cylinder are formed by a single set of generators.

Types of Points on a Surface. Through an arbitrary point P on a general surface S, there pass infinitely many curves that lie entirely on S. In general, the tangents to these curves at the point P all lie in the same plane. This plane is called the tangent plane to S at the point P, and the line perpendicular to this plane at P is called the normal to S at P.

A point where the tangent plane does not exist is said to be a singular point. A point that is not singular is called a regular point. If the surface S lies entirely on one side of the tangent plane near a regular point P, then P is called an elliptic point. Near an elliptic point, some planes parallel to the tangent plane intersect S in closed

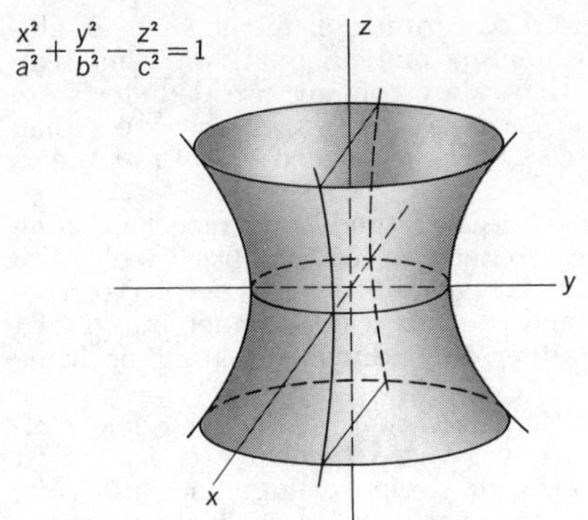

Fig. 6. A hyperboloid of one sheet has elliptic sections in every plane parallel to one of the coordinate planes and hyperbolic sections parallel to the other coordinate planes.

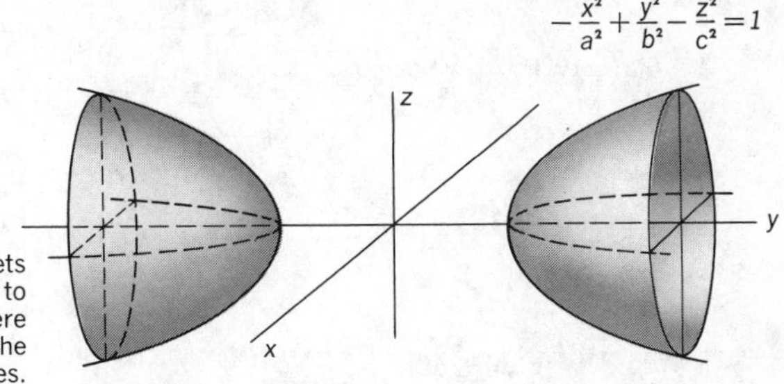

Fig. 7. A hyperboloid of two sheets has hyperbolic sections parallel to two of the coordinate planes. Where they exist, sections parallel to the other coordinate plane are ellipses.

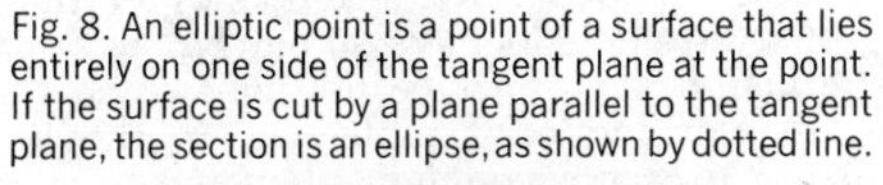

Fig. 8. An elliptic point is a point of a surface that lies entirely on one side of the tangent plane at the point. If the surface is cut by a plane parallel to the tangent plane, the section is an ellipse, as shown by dotted line.

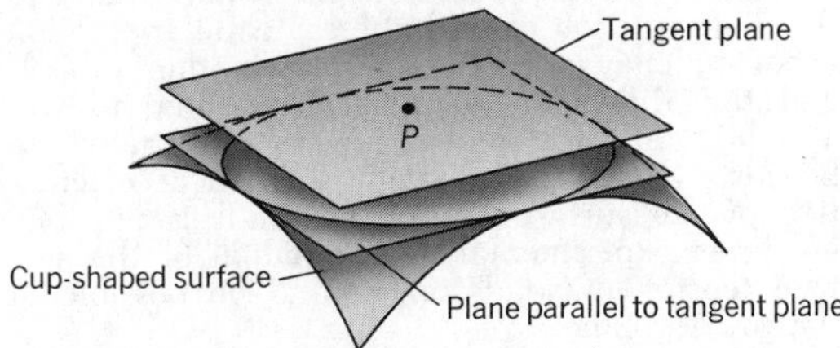

Saddle-shaped surface

Tangent plane

P

Section made by parallel plane above tangent plane

Section made by parallel plane below tangent plane

Fig. 9. A hyperbolic point is a point of a surface that lies on both sides of the tangent plane at the point. If the surface is cut by a plane parallel to the tangent plane, the section resembles a hyperbola.

curves that are approximately ellipses (see Fig. 8). Close to P, the surface resembles a cup. If the surface contains points on each side of the tangent plane near P, then P is called a hyperbolic point. Near such a point, planes parallel to the tangent plane, on each side of it, intersect S in curves that are approximately hyperbolas (see Fig. 9). Close to a hyperbolic point, a surface resembles a saddle. A third type of point is called a parabolic point. Near a parabolic point, a surface has a single curve in common with its tangent plane, instead of two intersecting curves, as at a hyperbolic point, or a single point, as at an elliptic point.

Curvature of a Surface. Consider now the family of planes that passes through the normal to a surface S at a point P. Each such plane intersects S in a curve, and at P each of these curves has associated with it a number called its curvature. Among these curvatures, there is always a maximum curvature K_M and a minimum curvature K_m. These quantities are called the principal curvatures of S at P. The quantity $(K_M + K_m)/2$ is called the mean curvature of S at P, and the quantity $K_M K_m$ is called the total, or gaussian, curvature of S at P. At any elliptic point of a surface S, K_M and K_m always have the same sign, and hence the total curvature is positive. At any hyperbolic point, K_M and K_m always have opposite signs, and hence the total curvature is negative. At any parabolic point, at least one of the principal curvatures is zero, and hence the total curvature is zero.

A sphere is a surface with the same positive curvature at every point. The simplest surface with a constant negative curvature is the pseudosphere, which looks similar to a flared horn. A plane is a surface of zero curvature.

Developable Surfaces. Let S be a surface of constant total curvature K and S' be a surface of constant total curvature K'. A famous theorem given by Gauss guarantees that either surface can be deformed into the other without changing arc lengths or angles if, and only if, $K = K'$.

A developable surface is one that can be rolled out onto a plane without distorting distances or angles. Since the plane has zero curvature, it follows from Gauss' theorem that all developable surfaces have zero curvature. Since a sphere has a positive curvature, it also follows from Gauss' theorem that there are inevitable distortions in any plane map of our world.

The cone and the cylinder are developable surfaces. As for other such surfaces, their generators are all tangent to some twisted curve.

C. Ray Wylie, *Furman University*

Further Reading: Eves, Howard, *A Survey of Geometry* (Boston 1965); Hilbert, David, and Cohn-Vossen, S., *Geometry and the Imagination* (New York 1952).

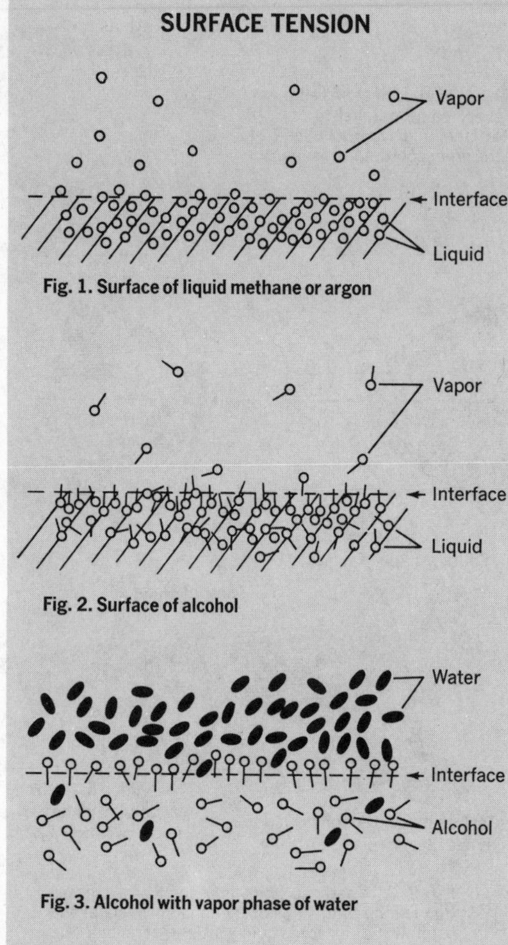

Fig. 1. Surface of liquid methane or argon

Fig. 2. Surface of alcohol

Fig. 3. Alcohol with vapor phase of water

SURFACE-ACTIVE AGENT. See SURFACTANT.

SURFACE-EFFECT SHIP, a vehicle that travels on a cushion of air that is maintained beneath it. See AIR CUSHION VEHICLE.

SURFACE HARDENING is a process for hardening steel parts that require a hard, wear-resistant surface while maintaining a soft, ductile core. Two basic methods are used.

In the first method, a surface alloy layer of carbon or some other hardening agent is built up on a plain or low-carbon steel. This hard-surface layer can be produced by means of carburizing, cyaniding, or nitriding.

Carburizing employs a low-carbon steel that when heated with a solid, liquid, or gaseous material—such as charcoal, carbon, cyanide salt bath, natural gas, or propane—produces an outer layer of high-carbon steel containing 0.8% to 1.4% carbon. Time and temperature determine surface alloy thickness.

Cyaniding is of two kinds. One, used for small parts such as gears, ratchets, pins, and screws, employs a bath of fused sodium salt. The other employs a carbon-rich gas with ammonia, thereby adding nitrogen as well as carbon to the part.

Nitriding uses ammonia gas or molten cyanide salts to add nitrogen to the surface of steel that contains a nitride-forming element, such as aluminum, chromium, molybdenum, or vanadium. Because of their alloy content, nitrided steels are stronger and have greater surface hardness than ordinary steels. Their surfaces also resist corrosion well.

The other basic method of surface hardening adds nothing to the surface, but uses steels with the necessary hardenability. The part or surface to be hardened is exposed to extremely rapid heat treatment, either by induction heating or flame heating.

In induction hardening, a high-frequency alternating current is used to heat the part. Fast operation, freedom from scaling, and little distortion make up for the high cost. Hardening can be localized to such specific areas as gear and ratchet teeth and the wearing surfaces of shafts and cams.

In flame hardening the part is heated with an oxyacetylene flame. Water is sprayed over the surface to cool it as soon as the desired temperature is reached. Large parts can be treated without affecting the entire piece, and the equipment is portable.

ALVIN S. COHAN
Scientific Design Company

SURFACE TENSION is the tendency of the surface of a liquid to behave somewhat like a thin elastic membrane. Surface tension, which results from the attraction of molecules in the liquid, is related to many common phenomena, such as the behavior of soap bubbles, capillary action (the tendency of liquids to rise in thin tubes), and the ability or inability of a liquid to wet a solid. Surface tension is not restricted to liquids. However, although theoretical calculation of the surface tension of solids is possible, no direct experimental determination of the surface tension of solids appears to be possible at the present time.

Causes of Surface Tension. Molecules in the interior of a liquid are subject to a uniform field of force, whereas molecules at the surface of a liquid—that is, at the interface between the liquid and an adjoining liquid or vapor—are subject to a net attraction toward the bulk of the liquid rather than toward the more dispersed molecules in the vapor. Thus all liquid surfaces in the absence of other forces tend to contract to the minimum area. For example, a freely suspended volume of liquid assumes a spherical shape, since the sphere has the minimum surface-to-volume ratio. When the area of an interface is extended, it is necessary for molecules to move from the interior of the liquid into the surface, thereby doing work against the cohesive forces in the liquid. This results in the surface region of the liquid having a higher energy than the bulk of the liquid. Accordingly, surface tension is strictly defined as the work required to create a unit area of surface at constant temperature and volume and with the number of molecules in the system unchanged.

Molecular Arrangement at an Interface. The arrangement of molecules at the liquid-vapor interface of a pure liquid depends on several forces, including van der Waals intermolecular forces and hydrogen bonding forces. For liquid surfaces at temperatures very much lower than the critical temperature (the highest temperature at which a vapor can be liquefied), it is generally thought that the arrangement of liquid molecules at the vapor interface is such that only the order in the first layer of molecules is appreciably different from that in the bulk liquid.

Figure 1 shows the arrangement expected at a surface of liquid methane or liquid argon below the critical temperature. As the critical temperature is approached, the surface region between liquid and vapor becomes thicker, with the third, fourth, and deeper layers of the liquid becoming successively affected as the liquid density decreases and the vapor density increases.

The surface of a pure liquid, such as alcohol, whose molecules have both a polar and a nonpolar end group is shown in Figure 2. The alcohol molecules are asymmetric in both structure and energy. The polar group of each molecule is attracted to the bulk liquid much more strongly than the nonpolar end group, hence the molecules at the surface are strong-oriented at essentially right angles to the surface. The vertically oriented molecules in the surface region render the surface monolayer somewhat thicker than the monolayer at the surface of a liquid made up of spherically symmetric molecules.

If the vapor phase at the liquid surface in Figure 2 is replaced by liquid water, the molecules at the surface reverse their orientation and present their nonpolar portions to the alcohol (Figure 3). This arises because the forces of attraction between the bulk liquid water and the polar groups are much greater than those between the same polar groups and the alcohol.

A wide variety of reliable techniques have been developed for measuring the surface tensions of liquids. Several of the more useful techniques are sessile drop profile, capillary height, Wilhelmy plate, DuNoüy ring, drop weight, and maximum bubble pressure. The accompanying table gives values for the surface tension of several liquids at 20° C (68° F).

SURFACE TENSIONS AT 20° C (68° F)

Liquid	Dynes/cm	Liquid	Dynes/cm
Benzene	28.88	Nitrobenzene	43.35
Carbon tetra-chloride	26.76	n-octane	21.80
Mercury	487.00	Water	72.76

HAROLD SCHONHORN
Bell Telephone Laboratories

Further Reading: Boys, Charles Vernon, *Soap Bubbles and the Forces that Mould Them* (New York 1920); Adamson, Arthur W., *Physical Chemistry of Surfaces* (New York 1967).

SURFACE WATER. See HYDROLOGIC CYCLE; HYDROLOGY; LAKE; RIVERS; WATER SUPPLY; WATERSHED; WATERWAYS OF THE WORLD.

SURFACTANT, sər-fak′tənt, or surface active agent, is a compound that affects the surface tension between two liquid phases. Generally, surfactants lower the surface tension. Materials such as soaps, detergents, and wetting agents are surfactants.

Uses. Because of their detergent behavior, surfactants are important in industrial and household cleaning formulations. Water pollution caused by detergents has led to an increased use of the surfactant LAS because it is more biodegradable than the surfactant ABS. Because nonbiodegradable surfactants are not decomposed by the normal sewage bacteria, they accumulate in rivers and streams and are a major source of pollution. See DETERGENT.

Surfactants are used as antistatic agents in the manufacture of plastic articles and as wetting agents in the formation of plastic coatings. Surfactants solubilize flavor oils in beverages and improve the capacity of paper towels to absorb water. In the tanning of leather they promote wetting and penetration.

Properties. Surfactant compounds contain molecules with substituent groups of differing solubility characteristics. Most frequently, one group is polar and water soluble (hydrophilic), while the other is nonpolar and water insoluble (hydrophobic). As a result, surfactants are soluble in at least one phase of a system containing liquids of differing solubilities. The polar end of the molecule is oriented toward the polar liquid phase and the nonpolar end toward the nonpolar phase. Because of the attraction of opposite ends of surfactant molecules by different liquid phases, the concentration of surfactant molecules is greater in the phase interface than in the bulk of the solution. Consequently the surface tension of the liquid decreases.

Generally, surfactant molecules are large, with molecular weights ranging from about 200 to many thousands. They are classified as anionic, cationic, and non-ionic. In anionic surfactants the hydrophilic group is a polar, negatively charged ion such as carboxylate (COO^-), sulfate (SO_4^{-2}), or phosphate (PO_4^{-3}). Soaps, which are salts of fatty acids, are typical anionic surfactants. In cationic surfactants the hydrophilic group is most often quaternary nitrogen (RNH_3^+). In non-ionic surfactants attraction between one end of the molecule and the polar liquid is caused by hydrogen bonding.

HERBERT LIEBESKIND
The Cooper Union

SURFBIRD, a stocky, short-billed, ploverlike shorebird that breeds in Alaska and migrates down the Pacific coast as far as the Strait of Magellan. It summers in rock-strewn mountain tundra, feeding on insects. The surfbird winters along rocky coasts, searching out small mussels and invertebrates.

The surfbird is 9½ inches (24 cm) long and has a wingspread of 20 inches (50 cm). It has

Surfbird (*Aphriza virgata*)

ALLAN D. CRUICKSHANK, FROM NATIONAL AUDUBON SOCIETY

RON CHURCH, FROM PHOTO RESEARCHERS

Surfing in a heavy swell at Waimea, Oahu, Hawaii, where underlying reefs increase the height of waves.

short yellow legs, distinctive white wing stripes, a white rump, and a white tail with a black triangle at the tip. From August to March it is dark brownish grey on the head, back, and breast and white on the belly. In the spring and early summer it is heavily mottled and streaked with white, rust, and gray-brown.

The surfbird nest is a depression on the ground lined with vegetation. The four eggs are buff-colored, heavily speckled with dark brown. The male incubates the eggs and leads predators away by feigning injury.

The surfbird, *Aphriza virgata*, is an aberrant member of the family Scolopacidae, order Charadriiformes.

GEORGE E. WATSON
Smithsonian Institution

SURFING, also called *surf riding,* is the sport and art of riding an ocean wave. In the most popular form of the sport, the surfer stands on a surfboard. Other forms of surfing make use of bellyboards, kneeboards, inflated rubber mats, canoes, and kayaks. In body surfing, no equipment is used. Whatever the vehicle or the technique, surfing requires great skill and balance.

History of Surfing. Surf riding was a favorite pastime of the ancient Polynesians who inhabited the islands in the Pacific Ocean from New Zealand to Tahiti and who are believed to have brought the sport to Hawaii. The English explorer Capt. James Cook witnessed the sport when he discovered the Sandwich (Hawaiian) Islands in 1778. He wrote in the ship's log that as the surf broke in Kealakekua Bay, native persons on boards "place themselves on the summit of the largest surge by which they are driven along with amazing rapidity toward the shore."

With the arrival in 1820 of New England missionaries, who frowned on the nakedness of surfers and on the gambling that frequently accompanied surfing contests, the sport died out. Its renaissance began in 1908, when Alexander Hume Ford founded the outrigger Canoe Club in Honolulu to foster surfing and canoe riding. Tourist interest, plus the efforts of Duke Kahanamoku, a champion surfer, helped to spread the sport to the West. Surfing developed slowly,

RON CHURCH, FROM RAPHO GUILLUMETTE

THE SURFER has caught the wave and, by shifting his weight, maneuvers the board for the ride to shore.

however, the major drawback being the long (14–18 feet or 4.25–5.5 meters) and heavy (about 150 pounds or 56 kg) redwood boards that few surfers could handle. With the introduction in the 1940's of light balsa boards and, in the mid-1950's, of polyurethane foam boards, which are easily carried and are more maneuverable in the water, interest in the sport grew rapidly throughout the world. Hawaii remains the center of surfing and offers the most challenging waves. A high spot in the career of any surfer is to travel to the North Shore of Oahu during the winter and early spring and contest the heavy swells that roll down on Hawaii from the North Pacific.

The sport of surfing is governed in the United States by the Western, Eastern, and Hawaiian surfing associations. These organizations conduct a series of United States competitions on the East and West coasts and in Hawaii, and winners participate in a biennial world contest. Surfers in competitive runs are judged mostly on form and skill. Officials award points for takeoff, turns, length of ride, and difficulty of wave selected. Judging is done from the beach. Other countries with nationwide programs include Peru, Australia, France, Ireland, Mexico, Britain, and South Africa. The first world competitions were held in Manly, Australia, in 1962.

Boards. The modern surfboard measures 5 to 9 feet (1.5–2.7 meters) long, depending on the surfer's size and style, 18 to 22 inches (45.7–55.8 cm) wide, and 3 to 4 inches (7-10 cm) thick in the center, with the nose and tail sections frequently tapered. Each board has a point of balance, generally a short distance behind its center, in relation to the size and weight of the surfer.

Weighing between 5 and 12 pounds (11–26 kg), the board has one or two foiled fins laminated to the underside at the rear for directional stability. Surfboards are made of polyurethane foam and are covered with fiber-glass reinforced plastic with a coating of wax across the deck for traction.

Fundamentals. A foot-high wave will propel a surfboard, but the average size of a ridden wave is about 3 or 4 feet (0.91–1.2 meters). The fastest surfing is done on waves that reach heights of 15 to 20 feet (4.5 to 6 meters).

To get to the takeoff point offshore where the waves are suitable, the surfer, lying flat or kneeling on the board with his weight slightly aft to keep the nose clear of the water, paddles with his arms. Just before the unbroken wave he has chosen to ride reaches him, he begins paddling shoreward to gain speed. As the wave moves him forward and his paddling speed increases, the board starts sliding down the wave face. At this point the surfer has caught the wave, so he pushes up with his hands and stands, legs apart and flexed, one foot leading the other. Now his objective is to stay involved with the breaking part of the wave. He maneuvers the board close to the breaking section of the wave and travels a path somewhat parallel to the shoreline. The beginning surfer must keep away from the breaking part of the wave, or else he will be knocked from the board or have to ride it straightforward to the shore. He maneuvers the board to the right or left primarily by shifting his weight to the right or left. As the wave diminishes, he leans back and turns the board over the back of the wave. In a spill, the surfer should stay under water a few seconds and then come up with his head protected to avoid being injured by the board.

Surfing experts perform exciting maneuvers, such as riding the nose while going at full speed, turning back and forth, and climbing up and dropping down the face of the wave. One of the most challenging feats is riding completely within the curl of the wave.

Many surfers have come to regard the sport as an aesthetic and spiritual experience, involving the mind as well as the body. The individual operating within a territory of danger feels the power of the wave. The closer he can bring himself to the power, and therefore the danger, the better he is at surfing. It is the same with bullfighting.

In *body surfing*, the swimmer strokes hard down the face of the wave just as the wave begins to break. With one arm and body fully extended or with both arms at his sides, he slides down or across the face of the wave much the same as a board surfer.

JOHN SEVERSON and DREW KAMPION
Editors, "Surfer" magazine

Bibliography

Dixon, Peter, *Complete Book on Surfing* (New York 1965).
Dixon, Peter, *Where the Surfers Are* (New York 1968).
Houston, James D., and Finney, B. R., *Surfing: The Sport of Hawaiian Kings* (Rutland, Vt., 1968).
Olney, R. R., and Graham, R. W., *Kings of the Surf* (New York 1970).
Severson, John Hugh, ed., *Great Surfing* (New York 1967).
Wagenvoord, James, and Bailey, Lynn, *How to Surf* (New York 1968).

SURFPERCH. See SURF PERCH.

SURGEON GENERAL, in the United States government, the chief executive of the Public Health Service in the Department of Health, Education, and Welfare. The service is charged with protecting the health of the American people and collaborating with other nations and international agencies in health activities, and the surgeon general manages its many programs. The title of surgeon general is also held by the chief medical officers of the U. S. Army and the U. S. Air Force.

SURGEONFISH, any of a family of colorful marine fishes found in tropical waters, particularly around rocky and coral reef areas. They are called surgeonfish because they have sharp, scalpel-like spines imbedded on each side of the body just in front of the tail. Although most surgeonfishes have only a single folding spine on each side, some species have as many as six immovable spines.

Surgeonfishes are usually less than 20 inches (50 cm) long. They have deep, laterally compressed bodies and prominent median fins that make them look larger than they are and that may discourage small-mouthed predators. Perhaps the most striking surgeonfishes are those of the genus *Naso*, sometimes called "unicorn fishes" because they have prominent hornlike structures on their foreheads. Surgeonfishes feed mainly by nibbling and scraping encrusted algae. Their silvery, disk-shaped larvae drift around in plankton. Before the larvae transform into adults, they drift over a suitable reef area at night, and then, within four or five days, change into miniature adults.

There are more than 75 species of surgeonfishes, classified in several genera, making up the family Acanthuridae of the order Perciformes.

DANIEL M. COHEN
U. S. Fish and Wildlife Service

Surgeonfish, or doctorfish

RUSS KINNE, FROM PHOTO RESEARCHERS

SURGERY is the branch of medicine that treats diseases, injuries, and deformities primarily through manual operations. Surgery also deals with the diagnosis of disease and the care of the patient before and after the operation. To aid in his treatment of the patient, a variety of pharmaceutical, dietary, and physical forms of therapy are available to the surgeon.

Types of Surgical Procedures. Most surgical procedures fall within one of four broad classifications: the treatment and repair of wounds, extirpative (removal) surgery, reconstructive surgery, and physiological surgery. A fifth type of procedure, replacement surgery, has developed relatively recently and is still the subject of much research and experimentation.

Wound treatment and repair are often commonly thought to be involved in cases in which the patient has a deep cut or other obvious type of wound. However, every surgical operation requires wound treatment and repair since the operation itself creates a potentially dangerous wound.

Extirpative surgery sometimes entails the removal of a part of an organ, as in the removal of a lobe of the lung (lobectomy). In other cases, an entire organ, such as a gallbladder or uterus, may be removed. These operations are known as a cholecystectomy and hysterectomy, respectively. Many operations for cancer involve the extirpation of apparently healthy tissue along with the diseased tissue to help prevent the disease from spreading.

Reconstructive surgery is practiced extensively in plastic surgery and orthopedic surgery. To some extent, however, reconstructive surgery is practiced in all major operations.

Physiological considerations play a key role in all surgical operations. The surgeon must maintain the patient's blood, body fluid, and electrolyte levels by means of transfusions, intravenous feeding, and other measures. In *physiological surgery* the patient's physiological mechanisms are altered when his disease cannot be satisfactorily treated other ways. For example, some vascular conditions, including high blood pressure, can be alleviated through operations on the autonomic nervous system. These operations do not cure the condition because they do not remove the underlying cause.

Replacement surgery entails the replacement of diseased or damaged organs or tissues with artificial devices, such as plastic heart valves, or organs or tissues from living human donors or cadavers. One of the most dramatic achievements in the field of replacement surgery was the successful transplantation of the human heart.

Branches of Surgery. It is sometimes difficult to draw a sharp distinction between general surgery and the various surgical specialties. Many abdominal operations, such as appendectomies, are considered the domain of general surgery, but others are usually performed by specialists in the field of colon and rectal surgery. Conversely, some surgeons specialize in operations on the breast or thyroid—operations that are customarily considered part of general surgery. Chest surgery and orthopedic surgery are performed by general surgeons as well as by specialists.

Most surgical specialties evolved from general surgery during the 19th and 20th centuries. Some specialties, such as obstetrics and gynecology, orthopedics, and plastic surgery, have existed as separate fields for centuries. Before the advent of modern surgery, however, the people who practiced these types of surgery tended to be from outside the regular surgical profession. Other specialties, such as neurosurgery and cardiovascular surgery, are relatively new.

By 1970 there were ten surgical specialty boards, including one for general surgery, in the United States and Canada. In order of their founding, starting with the oldest specialty board, they are: ophthalmology, otolaryngology, obstetrics and gynecology, orthopedics, colon and rectal surgery, urology, plastic surgery, neurosurgery, and thoracic (chest) surgery.

Ophthalmic surgery deals with disorders of the eyes and associated structures. The removal of cataracts and the repair of torn retinas are among the types of operations performed by specialists in this type of surgery. *Otolaryngology* is concerned with disorders of the ears, larynx (voicebox), pharynx, nasal passages, and bronchial passages. One of the most common operations performed by specialists in otolaryngology is the tonsillectomy. Emergency extractions of foreign bodies from the throat are also commonly performed.

Obstetrics and gynecology are combined in the specialty that deals with pregnancy and birth and diseases of the female reproductive system. In addition to delivering babies, these specialists also perform hysterectomies and removals of ovarian cysts. *Orthopedic surgery* is concerned with the bones, joints, tendons, ligaments, and muscles. Among the types of disorders treated by orthopedic surgeons are bone fractures and joint dislocations. *Colon and rectal surgery* is the specialty dealing with disorders of the large intestine. *Urological surgery* deals with disorders of the kidneys, ureters, urinary bladder, prostate, urethra, and the organs and structures of the male reproductive system.

Plastic surgery is performed to improve the appearance and function of external tissues through readjustment and grafting. Congenital deformities, such as cleft palate and harelip, are commonly corrected by plastic surgeons. *Neurosurgery* is concerned with the brain, cranial nerves, spinal cord, and peripheral nerves. Many neurological operations are performed to remove tumors or to repair damage resulting from severe injuries. *Thoracic surgery* treats disorders of the lungs and other structures within the pleural cavity. Cardiovascular surgery, which is concerned with the heart and the major blood vessels leading to and from the heart, has become a subspecialty of thoracic surgery.

Training and Certification. In the United States, medical school graduates who wish to become surgeons must first spend a year as an intern at an accredited hospital. Depending on the field of specialty he wishes to enter, the doctor then spends a period of four or more years of residency at a hospital and sometimes combines residency with graduate school.

Training programs in general surgery require a residency of at least four years. A minimum of three years must be devoted to clinical surgery, and one year may be spent on research. An alternate training program consists of three years of clinical surgical residency followed by two years of practice under a preceptor or two years of graduate courses in surgery and basic sciences. After the candidate has satisfactorily completed a training program, he takes written and oral examinations given by the specialty board. Once he passes these tests, the doctor becomes a fully certified general surgeon.

Training in the other surgical specialties is similar, varying primarily in the amount of time devoted to general surgery. A residency in plastic surgery, for example, consists of three years of general surgery, two years of plastic surgery, and two years of supervised surgical practice. A neurosurgical residency includes one year of general surgery, four years of graduate study of which at least 30 months is devoted to clinical neurosurgery, and two years of supervised practice. As in general surgery, the candidate must pass written and oral examinations before he is certified by the specialty board.

HISTORY OF SURGERY

Although surgery was practiced in ancient times, modern surgery may be said to begin with the rapid progress made in the last quarter of the 19th century, following the introduction of anesthesia and antisepsis. However, important steps in the development of modern surgery occurred prior to the late 19th century. These steps included the raising of the educational standards and social status of the surgeon, the development of a scientific approach to surgery, and the introduction of a number of technical innovations and achievements, such as the effective control of bleeding.

Early Surgery. Paleopathology, the study of disease in fossil plants and animals, indicates that virtually all major categories of disease are as old as man or even older. The surgical treatment of disease almost certainly predates the invention of writing; thus there are no written records of the earliest surgical operations. However, prehistoric skulls reveal that trepanning, or the removal of parts of bone from the skull, was performed in many primitive societies. It is doubtful, though, that the operation was undertaken for therapeutic reasons. It may have been performed as a part of magico-religious ceremonies.

The Edwin Smith Papyrus, a part of an Egyptian manuscript written in the 17th century B. C. and discovered by Edwin Smith in the mid-1800's, is the oldest known Egyptian medical document and the only early document dealing exclusively with surgery. It is actually a copy of a text originally written about 2500 B. C. The surviving fragment of the manuscript contains descriptions of about 50 cases of varying severity, many of which are head injuries. Each description follows the same pattern: the problem is identified, an examination is outlined, and one of three classifications of treatment is recommended. The ailment may be treated, "contended with," or not treated at all. The anatomical descriptions in the papyrus are precise and objective. Especially noteworthy is the absence of magical or religious elements that are prominent in other Egyptian medical writings.

The complete absence of Mesopotamian surgical writings suggests that the practice of surgery there may have been discouraged by the harsh penalties for unsuccessful treatment, as specified, for example, in the Babylonian legal codes. In China, until the 20th century, and in Japan, until the time of the first Western contacts, surgery was generally neglected. Religious and philosophical dogmas were averse to anatomical dissection and operations in which blood

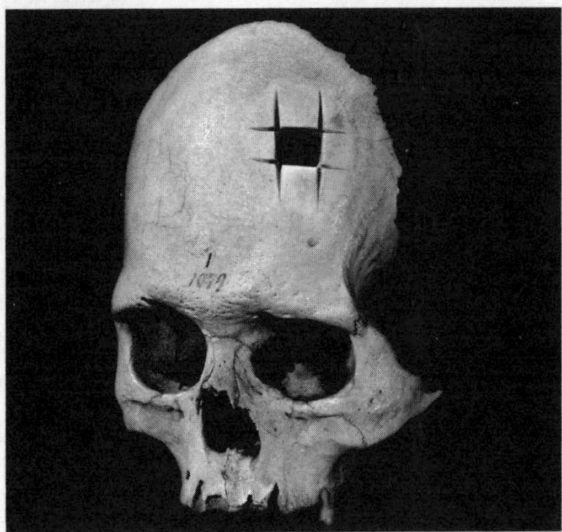

THE AMERICAN MUSEUM OF NATURAL HISTORY

TREPANNING was practiced by many primitive peoples. This ancient skull was found near Cuzco, Peru.

was shed. The scarcity of surgical documents from these ancient civilizations probably means that necessary restorative procedures, such as the care of wounds and the setting of fractures, were avoided by the regular medical practitioners and were relegated to others.

Hindu surgery, on the other hand, was highly developed, as shown by the major surgical text, the *Suśruta Samhita*, which was written sometime between the 6th century B. C. and the 6th century A. D. This work treats surgery as the first and most important branch of medical science. Although the anatomical descriptions are vague, there are precisely detailed accounts of the examination of patients and the prognoses of diseases. More than 100 instruments, the majority of which are blunt rather than cutting, are also mentioned. Some degree of anesthesia was obtained by giving patients alcohol and narcotics. Among the various operations performed were the extraction of urinary bladder stones and plastic surgery. Replacing a destroyed nose was accomplished by transplanting a flap of skin from elsewhere on the patient's body.

Greek and Roman Surgery. In the 5th century B. C., Greek medicine, along with other aspects of Greek civilization, enjoyed a remarkable flowering. Over 70 medical treatises written around that time were gathered together several centuries later by Alexandrian scholars who attributed them to the Greek physician Hippocrates. Today it is generally agreed that these works were composed by many different authors who, like the other physicians at the time, seem to have practiced both medicine and surgery. Although they regard surgery as a last resort, these treatises describe surgical procedures for treating head injuries, fractures, dislocations, hemorrhoids, ulcers, fistulas, and wounds. In contrast to the vague anatomical descriptions found in other medical treatises, the surgical anatomy is accurate and precise. The description and treatment of dislocations of the hip and shoulder and congenital clubfoot are excellent even by modern standards.

During the centuries following the decline of classical Greece, the major scientific as well as political center was Alexandria, Egypt. For the first time in history, large-scale human dissection was legalized, and as a result many anatomical discoveries were made. Only a few fragments of the works of the chief anatomists of this period—Herophilus and Erasistratus—are extant. However, Celsus, a Latin author of the 1st century A. D., summed up the progress of surgery during the 500 years after the writing of the Hippocratic treatises. In general, surgery was less conservative during this time than during the Hippocratic period. Operations not mentioned in the earlier treatises, such as the extraction of urinary bladder stones and operations to treat hernias, are detailed by Celsus. Other notable achievements recorded by Celsus are eye surgery and the use of ligatures to control bleeding. Celsus considered surgery, together with dietary measures and the use of drugs, as one type of therapy available to the doctor. He did not separate surgeons from physicians in either theory or practice.

Galen, the Greek physician who lived during the 2d century A. D., is one of the most famous doctors of antiquity. He is remembered chiefly for his views on physiology and pathology, which dominated medical thought for more than 1,500 years. However, Galen also practiced surgery, and his writings on the ailments that were considered to be surgical diseases—tumors, inflammations, abscesses, and wounds—acquired dogmatic authority during the centuries succeeding Galen's death.

Byzantine and Arabic Surgery. After the death of Galen, medical authorities, especially in the Byzantine Empire, wrote long compilations of earlier medical knowledge. The last of these encyclopedic authors, Paul of Aegina, who lived during the 7th century, summarized the medical works of Hippocrates, Galen, and others. Paul's encyclopedia, in turn, was the source of much Arabic and late Western medieval surgery.

Paul's surgical writings included observations from his own practice, including descriptions of the extraction of arrows lodged near large blood vessels or in the chest. Some procedures, which he apparently derived from surgeons whose works are lost, were definite advances and represent the high point of ancient surgery. Examples of such procedures are tracheotomies and operations to treat aneurysms (abnormal dilations of blood vessels) in the extremities. In other aspects, Byzantine surgery was cruder and crueler than earlier techniques. For example, there was much emphasis on the use of the hot cautery and the encouragement of the formation of pus in wounds.

Surgical knowledge stagnated during the centuries when the culture of antiquity passed over to the Arabic-speaking world. The Islamic religion inhibited anatomical research and any therapy involving bloodshed. Surgery took on the status of a lowly occupation, distinct from medicine and practiced by uneducated craftsmen in cases where it could not be avoided. The only Arabic author to write a separate treatise on surgery was Albucasis, a native of Muslim Spain who lived during the 11th century. Albucasis relied heavily on the surgical writings of Paul of Aegina, and he dealt extensively with eye diseases, frequent ailments in the Muslim lands. His text was exceptional for its many illustrations of surgical instruments, although cauterization was preferred to the knife in the treatment of a variety of diseases. Although his influence on his own culture was slight, Albucasis' text, in a Latin translation, served as a basis for western European surgical authors in the late Middle Ages and later.

Medieval Europe. Little is known about western European surgery during the early medieval period. The church, which controlled most aspects of social and political life, also tried to provide medical and surgical services. Ancient surgical knowledge was first introduced in the 11th century, when Latin translations of Arabic works were written in Italy and Spain.

Constantine the African was the earliest and most renowned of the translators. His work, which was accomplished at the monastery of Monte Cassino near Naples, Italy, stimulated the development of the nearby medical community at Salerno. Several surgical works were produced by the Salernitan school during the 12th century. The manuscript called the *Bamberg Surgery*, written about the middle of the 12th century and later found in a library in Bamberg, Germany, contains a formula for a "soporific sponge," which consisted of opium, mandragora (mandrake root), and other ingredients to reduce the patient's pain during an operation. The surgical text of Roger (Ruggiero Frugardi) mentions suturing the intestine over a hollow tube and treating an exposed intestinal wound by applying the moist intestines of a freshly killed animal. The wet, or open, treatment of wounds, which involved the intentional stimulation of pus formation, is associated with Salernitan surgery. The notion that such pus formation is desirable, which was the origin of the term "laudable pus," remained in favor with a majority of surgeons until the 19th century. Roger's text was copied, commented on, and elaborated by his student Roland of Parma and others.

In the 13th and 14th centuries surgical texts written by educated authors became more plentiful. These men were associated with the early European universities—Bologna, Montpellier, and Paris. As university scholars, they were clergymen and doctors who wrote in Latin. Unlike the majority of their medical colleagues, they did not disdain writing about or even practicing surgery. But these men were few in number, and surgical practice was generally left to barbers and other uneducated workers. The educational and social gap between physicians and most practicing surgeons became wider as the universities developed during the late Middle Ages and the Renaissance. Thus, these surgical authors, including Theodoric, William of Saliceto, Lanfranc, Henri de Mondeville, and Guy de Chauliac, should not be considered representative of the surgical profession. They were acutely aware of the low status of surgery as it then existed, and they urged the recognition of its importance, the need for its improvement, and the need to link it more closely with medicine.

The surgical text of Theodoric, who lived during the 13th century and was associated with the university at Bologna, was based on the teachings of his master Hugh of Lucca. The dry treatment of wounds, which involved bringing the edges of the wound together, and the use of simple dressings were advocated over the Salernitan doctrine. The theory of surgery stressed at Bologna retained many of the features of Arabic medicine, including the preference of cauterization over the knife, bandaging rather than suturing, and the use of drugs in various combinations.

William of Saliceto, who taught at Bologna, wrote a comprehensive surgical text around 1275. He revived the use of the scalpel, stressed the importance of anatomical knowledge for the surgeon, and included case histories of his own patients. His pupil Lanfranc was forced to leave Italy because of his political involvements, and when he arrived in Paris toward the end of the 13th century he taught surgery in the faculty of medicine of the University of Paris. Lanfranc also gave lessons to the guild of Paris surgeons, which had formed during the middle of the 13th century. This surgical group, known as the confraternity of St. Côme, persisted into the 17th century as a small group of learned surgeons. At the time of Lanfranc, and to some extent as a result of his work, surgical leadership in Europe passed from Italy to France.

The two outstanding French surgeons of the 14th century were Henri de Mondeville and Guy de Chauliac. Both of these men studied in Italy as well as at Montpellier and at Paris. Also, they were both doctors of medicine who practiced surgery and deplored the separation of the two professions. Henri de Mondeville was surgeon to several kings of France, and Guy de Chauliac served the popes during their residence at Avignon. The surgical text of Henri de Mondeville, written during the early 14th century, was never completed. In it, he questioned the prevailing devotion to the authority of Galen and the Arabic authors. He also opposed the open treatment of wounds and the use of complicated mixtures of drugs.

Guy de Chauliac's famous work, *Chirurgia Magna* (*The Great Surgery*), was written around 1360 and remained the major surgical text until the 16th century. Abridgments in the form of catechisms for surgical students were published under Chauliac's name as late as the 18th century. Although Chauliac was more conservative in style and content than Mondeville, he was clear and methodical. He also stressed studying cadavers in preference to books.

Renaissance and 17th Century. The fall of Constantinople to the Turks in the middle of the 15th century sent many Greek scholars to the West, particularly to Italy. Classical Greek medical works, which had generally been available in faulty translations from Arabic versions, were now translated directly from Greek into Latin. In addition, outstanding surgical works of antiquity, such as those of Paul of Aegina and Celsus, were rediscovered. About the same time the introduction of printing revolutionized the spread of knowledge. By the beginning of the 16th century, not only had costly editions of the works of Hippocrates and Celsus been printed but there were also inexpensive manuals available to surgical students. Although Latin remained the common language of the European scholarly community, an increasing number of surgical works were published in the vernacular for the benefit of artisans.

The emergence of strong secular states in Italy during the Rennaissance and the emergence of the nation-state in France, Holland, and England in the 16th and 17th centuries were accompanied by a lessening, if not the overthrow, of papal authority in those countries. Religious prohibitions on anatomical dissections and surgical operations were weakened. At the same time, warfare increasingly became the hallmark of European national policy, and the use of firearms permitted more complex fighting and caused more severe and different types of wounds. Skilled surgeons became indispensable to an effective army, and most of the outstanding surgeons of this period, as well as many of the less renowned, gained valuable experience as military surgeons.

The voyages of exploration and the development of overseas commerce required naval medical personnel, and, as in the army, most of these individuals were surgeons. Syphilis was Europe's major new disease, probably introduced by the early explorers returning from the Americas. The treatment of syphilis, which consisted of applications of mercury, was a lucrative part of the practice of many surgeons.

Human anatomical dissection, which had been revived by Mondino of Bologna in the early 14th century, received great impetus during the Renaissance. In Italy, anatomical investigation and naturalism in art were combined by Leonardo da Vinci and others. The publication in 1543 of a magnificently illustrated text, *Fabrica,* by Andreas Vesalius, the professor of anatomy at Padua, led to the overthrow of Galenic doctrine in the field of anatomy. Abridgements of this text were used by surgical students as well as non-university practitioners.

Studies of anatomical changes caused by disease lagged behind the growth of the study of normal anatomy. However, in the late 15th century the Florentine surgeon Antonio Benivieni described pathological changes in more than 100 cases he had studied.

Except in Italy, and later in Holland, surgeons were excluded from the European universities. In 16th century Paris, the surgeons' confraternity of St. Côme received royal support but was unable to achieve its goal of university status. Most of the leading Paris surgeons of the 16th and 17th centuries came from the ranks of the barber surgeons, to whom the small group of educated surgeons left such tasks as bloodletting and the treatment of bruises, abscesses, and minor wounds. In the middle of the 17th century, the barber surgeons of Paris were legally united with the scholarly surgeons, and all university pretensions and forms of equality with the physicians were stripped away from the surgical community. From the modern point of view, the combination of the functions of the barber surgeons and the surgeons seems degrading to the surgeons. But prior to the 18th century, the status of the barber surgeon was not to be scorned. Nor was membership in a guild of artisans considered inferior, at least in economic terms, to association with a university. The barber surgeons performed their tasks adequately at a time when the physicians of the University of Paris were being ridiculed by the French dramatist Molière for their scholarly pretensions and their reactionary medical theories.

In other French cities and in the countryside barber surgeons took charge of most medical as well as surgical ailments. Similar conditions existed in the German state and in England, where the United Company of Barber Surgeons of London was formed in the middle of the 16th century. Major operative procedures, including the extraction of urinary bladder stones, cataract couching (moving the lens of the eye), and amputations, were usually performed by traveling empirics, men who had received no formal training but relied on their experience. Frequently,

JEFFERSON MEDICAL COLLEGE OF PHILADELPHIA: PHOTOGRAPHED BY THE PHILADELPHIA MUSEUM OF ART

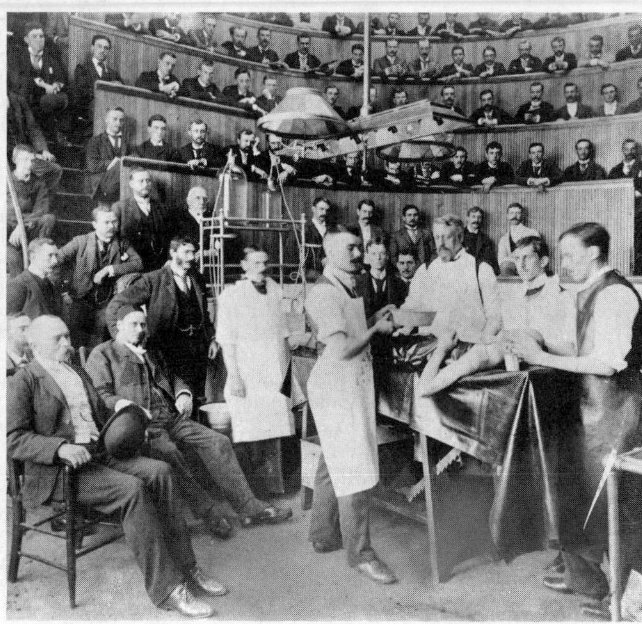

THE BETTMANN ARCHIVE

ANATOMICAL THEATER at Bellevue Hospital (*above*) in New York as it appeared in 1898. Only the surgeons wore gowns, and ether was used as the anesthetic.

THE GROSS CLINIC (*left*), by Thomas Eakins, shows professor and students in ordinary street clothes.

a family would develop a specific operation, technique, or even an instrument and transmit the secret knowledge from one generation to the next. In Italy, the Branca family specialized in plastic surgery of the nose, and the Norsini family specialized in hernia operations. The Colots were a French family specializing in the removal of urinary bladder stones, and the Chamberlens, a French-English dynasty, devised the obstetrical forceps.

France continued its surgical leadership during the 16th and 17th centuries, and the career of Ambroise Paré, the most famous surgeon of the Renaissance, illustrates many aspects of this period. Paré, the son of a poor provincial artisan, served his apprenticeship under a Paris barber surgeon. As a student barber surgeon he worked for three years in a large Paris hospital, the Hôtel Dieu, where he was able to perform autopsies and dissections. Paré then began a long career as a military surgeon, finally attaining the post of first surgeon to successive kings of France. The confraternity of St. Côme acknowledged Paré's stature by seeking his membership and by relaxing the usual scholarly prerequisites for admission. Paré enhanced the prestige of surgery by the example of his career, by his writings, which were in French and stimulated the publication of other treatises in the vernacular, and by his reputation for integrity and humanitarian concern for his patients.

Paré relied heavily on his own experiences and observations and made several fundamental contributions to the development of new techniques. His chance discovery that gunshot wounds heal better when treated without the customary application of boiling oil led him to oppose the prevailing doctrine that such wounds were always poisonous. He was also among the first to control bleeding by ligating (tying off) arteries during an amputation rather than by applying the hot cautery iron. Paré also contributed to the field of obstetrics, although ordinary deliveries for women of all social classes were performed by midwives until well into the 18th century.

Pierre Franco, a contemporary and fellow countryman of Paré, came from even humbler origins. Franco, who worked in various places in France and Switzerland, condemned the ignorance and dishonesty that he observed among the itinerant "cutters." Although he did not achieve a reputation comparable to Paré's, he appears to have been a bolder and more ingenious surgeon. His descriptions of operations for strangulated hernias and the extraction of urinary bladder stones are still considered masterful.

In the German-speaking lands, surgeons of the late 15th and early 16th centuries began writing treatises in German on the treatment of battle wounds and amputation techniques. Wurtz of Switzerland excelled in these procedures, and Fabricius of Hilden, the leading German surgeon of the late 16th and early 17th centuries, was a bold original thinker who discarded the ancient concepts of pathology still followed by his contemporaries, including Paré.

Richard Wiseman, whose career as a military surgeon and eventually as surgeon to King Charles II is reminiscent of Paré's, was the preeminent figure in 17th century British surgery. In Italy, Gasparo Tagliacozzi refined plastic surgery, particularly the restoration of the nose by skin grafting. At Padua, the tradition of Italian university surgeon-anatomists was furthered by the work and teaching of Fabricius ab Aquapendente.

18th Century. During the 18th century the social status of the surgical profession improved

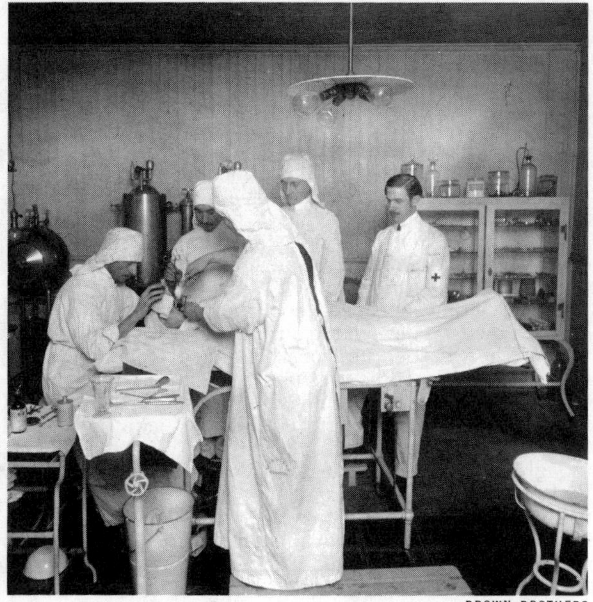

BROWN BROTHERS

BY EARLY 1900's, surgeons (*above*) wore caps and gowns during an operation, but not masks or gloves.

MODERN OPERATING ROOM (*right*) has complex equipment, such as the heart-lung machine shown here. All instruments and clothing have been sterilized.

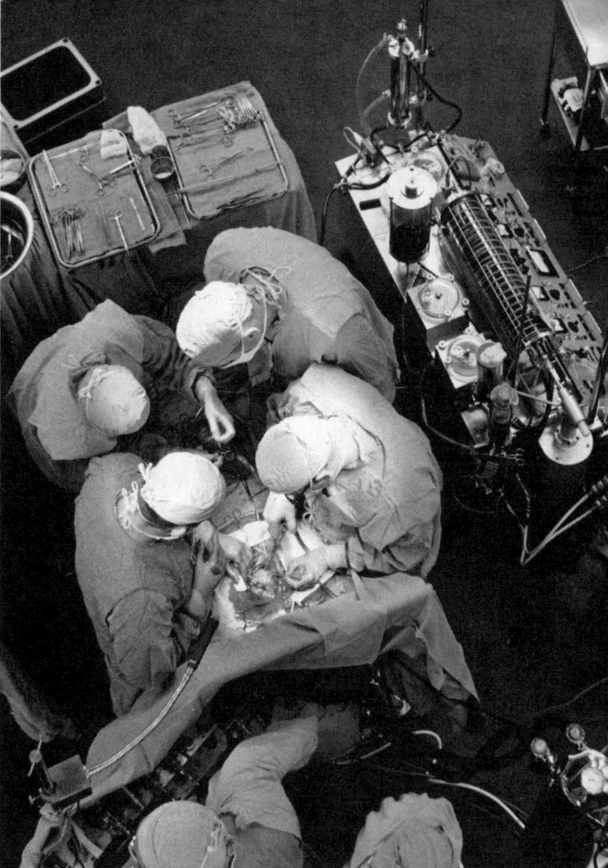

CLINICAL CENTER, NATIONAL INSTITUTES OF HEALTH

markedly. As surgeons ended their association with barbers they approached social equality with physicians. A liberal education, followed by public and private courses in anatomy, surgical operations, physiology, pharmacy, and other subjects, began to supplement the traditional practical surgical training of apprenticeship, hospital work, and military experience. Although there were few completely new operations devised, better methods and instruments for traditional operations were developed and refined. Hernia operations, eye surgery, and bladder stone operations passed from the hands of quacks into those of regular surgeons. Less encumbered than their medical colleagues by obsolete theories, the surgeons related autopsy findings to the clinical course of disease and made some progress in the experimental approach to disease and surgical therapy.

The leading surgical centers during the first half of the 18th century were Amsterdam, Leiden, and Paris. Starting about the middle of the century, London surgery advanced rapidly. Throughout Europe scientific societies flourished in major provincial cities as well as capitals. These societies published memoirs, conducted extensive correspondence, and awarded prizes for essays on scientific problems. In contrast to the universities, which generally continued to exclude surgeons, the societies accepted them and treated them as scientific equals with physicians. The sections devoted to anatomy in society publications included many outstanding surgical articles. The growth of other medical periodicals, their numerous translations, and the mobility of students also facilitated the exchange and spread of surgical knowledge throughout Europe.

The trends in surgery during the 18th century are illustrated in the following story about Frère Jacques (Jacques de Beaulieu), who appeared in Paris in 1697 with a new and initially successful method for operating to remove urinary bladder stones. His ignorance of anatomy was revealed by a surgeon-anatomist of the Academy of Sciences who had been commissioned to dissect the cadavers of many of Frère Jacques' patients. However, even the strongest of his critics thought that his technique had advantages that could be used by a competent surgeon with knowledge of anatomy. In 1704, Frère Jacques went to Holland to teach his technique to the Amsterdam surgeon Johann Jacob Rau, who improved it and refined the instruments. In the 1720's, William Cheselden, a famous London surgeon and member of the Royal Society of London, adopted the method and improved it further. Finally, in 1729, the Paris surgeon François Sauveur Morand was sent to London by the Academy of Sciences to learn Cheselden's technique. Morand reintroduced the method into Paris at the same time that several Paris surgeons were independently demonstrating its value. During the rest of the 18th century, this technique was the preferred method for bladder stone removal, even though a variety of alternate procedures and instruments were devised.

Procedures for amputations also were improved in the 18th century. English, French, and Dutch surgeons in the late 17th and early 18th centuries mastered the techniques of separating a limb at the joint and the application of skin flaps to the stump. Operations on the head, chest, and abdomen were generally avoided, but French surgeons could successfully remove segments of the intestines that had become gangrenous as a result of a hernia. And when a patient's life was endangered, deep-lying abscesses and other collections of fluids were incised and drained. Considerable progress was made in the description and treatment of orthopedic disorders, such as fracture of the clavicle and tearing of the Achilles tendon. New instruments were devised for treating diseases of the urinary system and for removing or cutting off the blood supply to abnormal growths inside body openings. Arterial aneurysms (swellings) in the extremities, which had formerly been untreated or treated by amputation of the limb, were cured by ligating (tying off) the affected artery. The first correct pathological description of eye cataracts was published in the first decade of the 18th century, and around the middle of the century the modern operation for the extraction of cataracts was devised.

The leading surgeons of the capital cities of Europe were skilled in most, and often all, of these procedures, but they were still a relatively small group, numbering perhaps between 50 and 100 in Paris, the leading center. The expansion of the hospitals, both in number and size, stimulated the growth of surgery. Hospitals employing the foremost surgeons increasingly became the focal points for the practice and teaching of surgery, and advanced surgical students received room and board in the hospitals. Similar developments did not occur in medicine until the early 19th century. However, most surgeons continued to practice bloodletting and to treat wounds, ulcers, abscesses, and a variety of minor medical diseases in their shops or in the patient's home.

The progress of the surgical profession in France was greatly supported by the royal government. The chief surgeons of the king—Georges Mareschal, François de la Peyronie, and Pierre de la Martinière—were also leaders of the surgical communities in Paris and the provinces. They used their influence with the government to obtain legislation and financial support. They used their influence over the surgeons to put their reforms into effect. Within a 20-year period, from 1724 through 1743, a royal college of surgery was established in Paris, educational requirements for surgeons were raised, and the surgeons were finally separated from the barbers. The formation of the Royal Academy of Surgery in Paris in 1731 profoundly influenced surgery not only in Paris but throughout France and the rest of Europe.

The leading Paris surgeon of the first half of the 18th century was Jean Louis Petit, who studied blood clotting and devised a tourniquet to control bleeding. His writings dealt with a wide range of surgically treated diseases, operations, and instruments. Toward the end of the century, French surgery was dominated by Pierre Joseph Desault, the chief surgeon of the Hôtel Dieu. Although Desault published very little, his work was made known by his students, the most famous of whom was Xavier Bichat. Desault was a conservative surgeon, who avoided amputation whenever possible and popularized bloodless methods (using elastic tubes) for removing obstructions from the urinary passages and esophagus. Desault's main contributions were in the fields of blood vessel surgery, orthopedics, and diseases of the urinary system.

William Cheselden, the outstanding London surgeon and anatomist of the first half of the 18th century, was famous for his dexterity and speed in extracting bladder stones. He was also well known for his construction of an artificial pupil that restored the sight of a blind child. Cheselden began a tradition of high quality teaching among London hospital surgeons, and he was influential in securing the separation of the surgeons from the barbers by Parliament in 1745. Percival Pott succeeded Cheselden as the most prestigious London surgeon in the second half of the century. Another London surgeon, John Hunter, was a pioneer in the experimental approach to an understanding of normal function and disease. From his studies on the circulation of the blood in animals, he devised a procedure for operating on aneurysms.

The German-speaking countries lagged behind France and England during the 18th century. While barber surgeons continued to flourish, most university professors of surgery wrote about operations that they did not personally practice. In Germany the educational gap between the physician and the surgeon persisted, though it had been eliminated by mid-century in Paris and by 1800 in London. Only a few individuals, including Lorenz Heister and August Gottlieb Richter, were outstanding teachers, authors, and practitioners.

In Italy, surgery continued to hold a respectable place in the universities. Antonio Scarpa, a professor at Pavia, published beautifully illustrated texts on surgical anatomy.

19th Century. In France, in 1794, the Revolutionary convention established new medical institutions, the Écoles de Santé, which united the teaching of medicine and surgery. All students were to receive the same theoretical and practical training, with slight variations in the final year depending on whether they wished to become physicians or surgeons. In England, medicine and surgery remained separated institutionally, but the creation of the Royal College of Surgeons in 1800 was evidence of the social and intellectual equality of the two professions. Several German teaching institutions, such as the Josephium in Vienna, combined the teaching of medicine and surgery. In the United States, rigid separation of the two professions had never developed.

Progress in surgery was gradual and unspectacular during the early 19th century. The Napoleonic Wars brought improvements in wound treatment and amputation. Pierre Percy and Dominique Larrey, distinguished French military surgeons, instituted methods of bringing prompt care to wounded soldiers. Guillaume Dupuytren, the leader of Paris surgery from 1815 to 1835, studied pathological anatomy. In London, pupils of John Hunter, including Astley Cooper and John Abernethy, carried on Hunter's tradition of experimentation, as did Philip Syng Physick in Philadelphia. Two other American surgeons, Ephraim McDowell and J. Marion Sims, were pioneers in the field of gynecological surgery.

In 1846 the first major operation with the anesthetic ether was performed in the Massachusetts General Hospital. A dentist, William Morton, had persuaded Boston surgeons to try his sleep-inducing pain-killer. Morton's success was dramatic and well published, and within a short time anesthesia was adopted by leading surgeons throughout Europe. Excruciating procedures, such as the reduction of fractures, could now be done painlessly, and organs that had rarely been operated on, particularly the abdominal organs, could now be treated surgically. The time available for operating was greatly increased, and surgeons no longer had to steel themselves to agonizing cries of patients or to worry about the patient overcoming the restraint of cords and assistants. To a considerable extent, the patient's fear of operations was also removed.

However, anesthesia was not an unmixed blessing. The time limit for an operation was restricted to about an hour, and an operation could be interrupted by too light or too heavy doses of anesthetic. Even more seriously, bolder surgical operations led to a marked increase in deaths after apparently successful operations. Those surgeons who followed relatively sanitary procedures, like the British surgeon Lawson Tait, or those who operated outside the hospitals achieved better results. Some improvement was made by using instruments, rather than the hands, for clamping severed blood vessels and by the draining of abdominal wounds. But surgeons were unaware of the relationship between microorganisms and infectious disease and were unable to deal with the alarming rise in fatal postoperative wound infections. It was unthinkable to most surgeons that they themselves were contaminating their patients' wounds.

In the 1840's the medical profession rejected the observation by Oliver Wendell Holmes that the occurrence of puerperal, or childbed, fever was related to the uncleanliness of the obstetrician. A few years later, Ignaz Philipp Semmelweis, an obstetrician in Vienna, realized that puerperal fever is a contagious disease similar to a wound infection. His statistical studies, which were published in 1861, clearly showed that women became infected during childbirth by contact with unclean material usually carried on the hands of the obstetrician. In spite of the fact that Semmelweis had been able to eliminate puerperal fever among his patients by instituting sanitary measures, chief of which was the washing of his hands in a disinfectant solution, the medical community actively opposed his conclusions.

The work of the French chemist Louis Pasteur in the 1850's and later led to the eventual widespread adoption of the germ theory of disease. Joseph Lister, professor of surgery at Glasgow, learned of Pasteur's studies of fermentation in 1864 and realized that microorganisms might also cause tissue breakdown and pus formation, just as microbial ferments brought about the decomposition studied by Pasteur. This would explain why compound fractures, which were exposed to the air and thus exposed to harmful germs, became infected, whereas simple, or closed, fractures did not. Lister reasoned that the elimination of germs from a surgical wound would stop infection, and he attempted to achieve this antiseptic effect by placing dressings soaked in a solution of carbolic acid (phenol) over the wound. Later, Lister applied the carbolic acid to sutures and instruments and even sprayed the operating room with it. Lister's first paper on antisepsis, published in 1867, reported the successful treatment of open fractures without the pus formation that most surgeons had come to accept as unavoidable or necessary. Despite Lister's increasing success, many of his fellow surgeons were opposed to his ideas. German surgeons were among the first to adopt his method of antisepsis, and finally, by about 1875, it was generally accepted.

Antisepsis was unquestionably one of the most important advances in the history of surgery. The use of carbolic acid, however, was somewhat unsatisfactory because of the acid's caustic nature. In 1878, Pasteur suggested the sterilization of surgical instruments and other materials by heating them. This method is known as asepsis. In antiseptic surgery, germs in a wound are destroyed by chemical agents. In aseptic surgery, the aim is to remove germs from everything contacting the patient's skin or wound. Asepsis was adopted in the mid-1880's by the French surgeons Terrilon and Terrier and by the German surgeon Ernst von Bergmann. By 1890 it was generally preferred to antisepsis. The introduction of sterile rubber gloves by the American surgeon William S. Halsted in 1885 and the later introduction of the sterile cap, mask, and sheets furthered the development of aseptic surgery.

By the last quarter of the 19th century, Germanic cities, particularly Berlin and Vienna, had become the world's leading centers for surgery. In Vienna, Theodor Billroth and his colleagues and students performed the first operations for cancer of various gastrointestinal organs. The Billroth clinic also expanded experimental surgery and the microscopic study of diseased tissue. Theodor Kocher, a Swiss surgeon, operated on the thyroid gland as a treatment of goiter in the 1880's. He also discovered the nature of the thyroid gland and many of its various functions.

Eduardo Bassini, at Pavia, Italy, devised the modern operation for the repair of an inguinal hernia in the late 1880's, and in London, Victor Horsley pioneered in the field of surgery on the nervous system. In the United States, Halsted contributed to thyroid, breast, hernia, and blood vessel operations. He devised new surgical instruments, suture materials, and techniques of hemostasis (control of bleeding) and tissue handling during operations.

20th Century. To a large extent, 20th century surgery has been concerned with making the operations developed during the 19th century safer. This progress has been aided by the close cooperation between surgery and the rapidly developing fields of physiology, biochemistry, genetics, immunochemistry, and other branches of science.

The discovery of X-rays by the German physicist Wilhelm Konrad Roentgen in 1895 soon led to the use of X-rays as invaluable diagnostic tools for both medicine and surgery. In 1900 the Austrian pathologist Karl Landsteiner distinguished the basic blood groups in man, and blood transfusions, which had been attempted sporadically since the 17th century, often with disastrous results, became feasible. Improvements in blood storage and transfusion made after World War I permitted the routine performance of operations that had previously been avoided because of the high risk of the patient hemorrhaging and going into shock.

World War I turned the surgeon's attention from spectacular new operations back to the fundamental problems of wound treatment. Despite antisepsis, the mortality rates from wound infections were appalling. Although the antibiotic penicillin was discovered by the British bacteriologist Alexander Fleming in 1929, his work was at first ignored and it was not until the beginning of World War II that penicillin was produced on a large scale. Meanwhile, army surgeons learned that the removal of dead tissue and foreign material, followed by the open treatment of wounds, achieved better results than the immediate closing of the wound.

Much was learned in the field of neurosurgery from the injuries suffered by soldiers in World War I. Harvey Cushing of Boston was the leader in brain surgery and surgery of the endocrine glands. Cushing's laboratory studies on animals enabled him to correlate experimentally induced disorders with many conditions in his patients.

During the period between the two world wars, improvements in anesthesia permitted much longer operations, and anesthesiology became a medical specialty, not simply a task relegated to junior surgeons or hospital attendants. Many other specialties became well defined during this period. Scientific as well as economic world leadership passed from Germany to the United States, where many physicians returned from military service with experience in surgery and the desire to pursue a specialty. In 1937 the American Board of Surgery was formed to set standards for training and practice. Residency programs modeled on Halsted's at Johns Hopkins University were established at many universities.

The period following World War II has seen the increasing development of surgical clinics with facilities for all specialties. Laboratories in which surgical techniques are tested and physiological problems are studied have become prominent features of university surgical departments.

Perhaps the most rapidly expanding field has been cardiovascular surgery. The heart-lung machine, introduced in the early 1950's has permitted extensive surgery of the heart itself, including the correction of congenital heart defects, the repair or replacement of impaired heart valves, and heart transplantation.

TOBY GELFAND
Johns Hopkins University Institute of the History of Medicine

Bibliography

Allbutt, T. Clifford, *The Historical Relations of Medicine and Surgery to the End of the 16th century* (London 1905).
Davis, Loyal, ed., *Christopher's Textbook of Surgery,* 9th ed. (Philadelphia 1968).
Garrison, Fielding H., *An Introduction to the History of Medicine,* 4th ed. (Philadelphia 1929).
Leonardo, Richard A., *History of Surgery* (New York 1943).
Meade, Richard Hardaway, *An Introduction to the History of General Surgery* (Philadelphia 1968).
Thorwald, Jürgen, *The Century of the Surgeon* (New York 1957).
Zimmerman, Leo M., and Vieth, Ilza, *Great Ideas in the History of Surgery,* 2d ed. (New York 1967).

SURICATE, sŏŏr′ə-kāt, a small mongoose (*Suricata suricatta*), also called the meerkat, found in southwestern Africa. It grows to about 1 foot (30 cm) in length, with a slender tail about 8 inches (20 cm) long. Its color is grayish, with dark eye patches, black ears, and several dark bands across the back.

Suricates are found mainly in dry, open country and are believed to require no drinking water. They live in colonies of 20 individuals or more, sometimes in association with yellow mongooses (*Cynictis*) and ground squirrels (*Geosciurus*). Suricates bask in the sun outside their burrows, sitting up on their haunches, and disappear below ground when alarmed. Diet consists mainly of small animals, such as insects and lizards. Two to four young are born in a litter.

W. F. H. ANSELL, *Department of Wildlife, Fisheries and National Parks, Zambia*

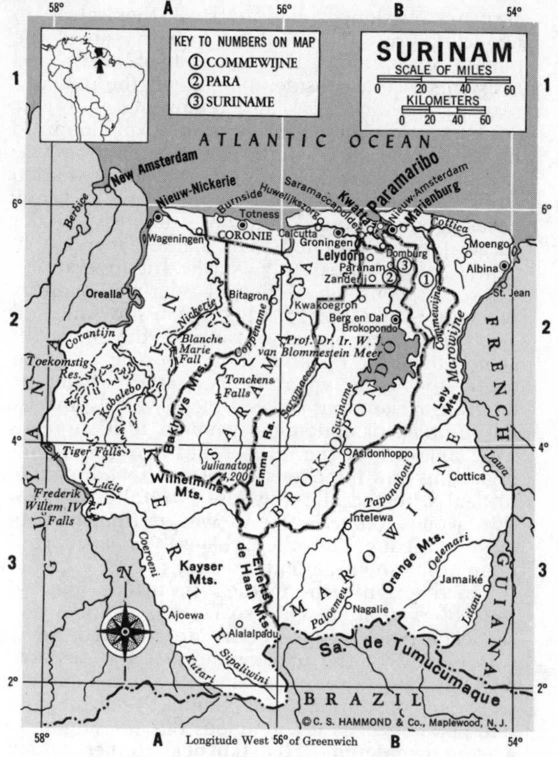

SURINAM Map Index

Place	Grid	Place	Grid
Corantijn River	A-2	Paramaribo	B-1
Marienburg	B-2	Paranam	B-2
Marowijne (Maroni) River	B-2	Suriname River	B-2
Moengo	B-2	Wilhelmina Mountains	A-3
Nieuw Nickerie	A-1	Totness	A-2

SURINAM, sŏŏ′rə-nam, is an autonomous part of the Kingdom of the Netherlands, situated on the northeastern coast of South America. It is a former Dutch colony with a relatively small population (1968 est. 375,000). Its present name (officially, Suriname) was adopted in 1948. Before that time it had been known as Netherlands Guiana or Dutch Guiana.

The topography of Surinam is that of an unevenly sloping surface, descending gradually from the Guiana Highlands plateau in the south to an almost featureless coastal plain in the north. About 90% of the population is concentrated within the coastal band, which extends less than 50 miles (80 km) inland and is 230 miles (370 km) long. A narrow zone of scattered savanna grasslands lies behind the coastal plain.

The forested, hilly interior region covers at least four fifths of Surinam's total land area of 55,000 square miles (145,000 sq km), reaching its highest elevation (4,200 feet, or 1,280 meters) in the Wilhelmina Mountains. Several rivers rise in these mountains, some of them flowing directly to the Atlantic Ocean and some draining either into the Marowijne (Maroni) River, which constitutes the eastern boundary with French Guiana, or the Corantijn River, which forms the western boundary with Guyana (formerly British Guiana).

The climate is that of a tropical rain forest, with temperatures constantly in the 75°–90° F (24°–32° C) range and humidity uncomfortably high. These enervating conditions are occasionally relieved on the coast by onshore easterly winds. Rainfall is heavy, averaging over 80 inches (2,000 mm) a year, and is fairly evenly distributed.

Along the coast, the brackish seawater allows various kinds of mangrove vegetation to flourish. The undrained coastal areas, or wet savannas, support coarse tropical grasses and many kinds of trees. A dense equatorial rain forest covers most of the interior.

The capital and only major city is Paramaribo, a port situated about 15 miles (24 km) from the mouth of the Suriname River. Residents of the capital (1968 estimate, 123,000) make up over 30% of Surinam's total population.

The People. More than a third of the population are Creoles, a term that, in Surinam, refers to those of mixed Negro and other ancestry. Another third are people from India, called "East Indians." Some 16% are Indonesians, mainly Javanese. These two latter groups are made up of descendants of plantation workers who arrived in the late 19th and early 20th centuries. Somewhat less than 10% of the population are Bush Negroes, or full-blooded descendants of African slaves who escaped to the interior before the mid-19th century, and about 2% are American Indians. Bush Negroes and American Indians make up almost all of the population of the interior. Finally, there are small communities of Europeans and Chinese in the coastal cities.

Of the larger ethnic groups, the Creoles are dominant economically. Many East Indians have entered trade, but most remain farmers and plantation laborers. Aside from the isolated Bush Negroes and Amerindians, the least assimilated people are the Javanese, who have remained almost entirely in agriculture. The total population of Surinam, though still small, increased more than fivefold between 1900 and 1970, with the rate of growth especially rapid among the East Indians.

Spoken languages reflect the diversity of backgrounds. Although Dutch is the official language, English, Hindi, Javanese, and Chinese may be heard, as may a vernacular called Sranan Tonga, or Surinamese, which is a blend of Dutch, English, Spanish, and Portuguese.

Religion and Education. Religious freedom is complete, and religious affiliations are varied. In the late 1960's there were over 90,000 Hindus, about 75,000 Roman Catholics, 65,000 Muslims, and at least 20,000 Protestants, principally of the Reformed and Lutheran denominations. There were also some Confucians and Jews.

There are a few private denominational schools operated by Roman Catholic and Protestant missions, but primary education is provided principally by the government in free public schools. All children between the ages of 6 and 12 are required to attend school. In 1970 there were three institutions of higher learning.

The Economy. The principal economic resource of Surinam is bauxite, the ore of aluminum, which accounts for about 70% of the value of exports. However, the great majority of the population is engaged in the production of foodstuffs.

Rice, the chief crop and main food staple, is grown on about half of the cultivated land. Some sugarcane, once the principal product of Surinam, is grown, as are bananas, oranges, grapefruit, corn, and coconuts, all mainly for export. Cattle, sheep, goats, pigs, and poultry are raised. Agricultural activities are confined almost entirely to the coastal zone. The most productive soils occur in polder lands—formerly inundated lands reclaimed by diking and draining.

The principal centers of bauxite mining, which began after 1922, are Moengo, in the northeast, and the Paranam area on the Suriname River, where hydroelectric power facilities have been developed. Some of the ore is processed into alumina in Surinam, but most is shipped in raw form to the United States. Gold mining was once important but has declined, and deposits of iron ore and other minerals are yet to be exploited.

There is some lumbering, but manufacturing is confined mainly to the processing of the bauxite ore. Among the few other industries are

CARL FRANK, FROM PHOTO RESEARCHERS

BUSH NEGRO village of Djuka on the Marowijne River, the border between Surinam and French Guiana.

GOVERNOR'S RESIDENCE in Paramaribo, the capital and largest city of Surinam.

EDITORIAL PHOTOCOLOR ARCHIVES

sugar and rice milling, shrimp freezing, and the production of fruit juices, paints, and plywood.

The main exports are bauxite and alumina, rice, oranges, grapefruits, and timber. Imported goods include fuels and lubricants, construction material, industrial equipment, and automobiles. The United States absorbs about 75% of Surinam's exports and, together with the Netherlands, supplies most of its imports. The balance of trade in Surinam has long been unfavorable.

Transportation and Communications. The surface transportation system is limited and serves the coastal area almost exclusively. There were no more than 800 miles (1,300 km) of good roads in 1970, although a highway was under construction to link the two frontier rivers. Numerous streams are navigable by shallow-draft vessels but generally only within the coastal zone. Air services are more highly developed, and some 2,000 commercial landings are recorded each year at the main airport near Paramaribo.

Four daily and two weekly newspapers claimed a circulation of 40,000 in the late 1960's. Surinam has only a handful of broadcasting stations. Telephone service is adequate in Paramaribo and in most of the coastal zone.

Government. After centuries of colonial rule, Surinam achieved partial autonomy as an integral part of the Kingdom of the Netherlands in 1948. Two years later it became virtually self-governing in matters not related to foreign affairs or defense. The head of government is the governor, who is appointed by the Dutch sovereign. A 9-member council of ministers is appointed by the governor but is responsible to a 39-member Legislative Council elected every four years by universal adult suffrage. Some half dozen political parties are represented in the Legislative Council.

History. In 1499 the Spaniard Alonso de Ojeda discovered the coast of Surinam, but Spanish attempts at settlement were short-lived. The first major imprint in the Guianas was made by the English after 1651, when experienced colonists were brought in from nearby Barbados to raise sugar and established many successful plantations. In 1667, after a war in which a Dutch fleet captured Paramaribo, the British traded what is now Surinam for New Netherlands (New York). England held Surinam again in 1799–1815, during the era of the Napoleonic Wars.

African slaves were imported from the 1680's to make sugar planting profitable, but Dutch attention to Surinam declined as their interest in the East Indies grew. The sugar economy never recovered from the effects of the emancipation of the slaves in 1863. Plantation labor began to be recruited in India in the 1870's and in Java after 1890, but by this time sugar was giving way to rice and other crops.

As in neighboring Guyana, the principal developments in the 20th century have been the birth of a bauxite-mining industry and the social and political diversification of the population. Since World War II, particularly, the more disadvantaged Far Eastern groups have become increasingly insistent in their demands for a greater share of Surinam's meager resources. Politics has come to reflect the bitter rivalry between East Indian Hindus, the most active of these groups, and the more prosperous Creole class, which dominates commercial life in the capital city.

KEMPTON E. WEBB
Columbia University

T. H. EVERETT

Surinam cherry (*Eugenia uniflora*)

SURINAM CHERRY, soŏor′ə-nam, a tropical South American large shrub or small tree with small, edible, reddish-orange fruits that are eaten fresh or made into jelly or sherbet. The Surinam cherry (*Eugenia uniflora* or *E. michelii*) is a member of the myrtle family (Myrtaceae) and is not related to the true cherry, which belongs to the rose family (Rosaceae).

The Surinam cherry has opposite, smooth-edged leaves about 2 or 2.5 inches (50–63 mm) long. The white flowers, about half an inch (13 mm) in diameter, differ from those of related species in that they are borne singly. The rounded fruits range from 1 to 1.5 inches (25–38 mm) in diameter and are fluted with 8 deep longitudinal grooves. The flesh is juicy and aromatic with a slightly acid flavor. In warm regions, two crops of fruits may ripen each year, one in the early spring and one in the late summer. Surinam cherries are also grown as ornamentals and hedges. Propagation is usually by seed.

RICHARD A. CRILEY
University of Hawaii

SURINAM TOAD, soŏor′ə-nam, an unusual, highly aquatic frog found only in South America, ranging through the entire eastern region, and Trinidad. The Surinam toad is rather large for a frog, with a body length of 4 to 5 inches (10–12.5 cm). Its head and body are flattened so that it looks as if it had been stepped on. It has tiny, lidless, beadlike black eyes. It also has long, muscular hind legs with large webbed feet that it uses for swimming. The forelimbs, in contrast, are slender and have long, tapering webless "fingers" tipped with glandular filaments that add to the toad's tactile surface. The Surinam toad is generally light brown and usually has large blotches of darker brown on the back.

The Surinam toad probably never leaves the water voluntarily. It eats a variety of aquatic animals, including worms, insects, crustaceans,

G. B. RABB, CHICAGO ZOOLOGICAL PARK

Surinam toad. Its eggs are embedded in its skin.

and even small fishes. It uses its slender forelimbs with its sensitive fingers to search for food on the muddy bottoms of jungle pools and to stuff food animals into its cavernous mouth.

Unlike most frogs, the Surinam toad does not lay its eggs directly into the water. The breeding is a complicated loop-the-loop movement. The male encircles the female with his forelimbs, fertilizes the eggs as they are extruded, and then presses them onto the female's back with his belly. Her softened skin swells and grows up over the eggs to provide individual brooding chambers. There, the eggs hatch and go through their entire larval stage, emerging as miniature replicas of adults about 16 weeks later.

The Surinam toad, *Pipa pipa,* is a member of the family Pipidae, a group of tongueless aquatic frogs, found only in Africa and South America. The family is classified in the order Salientia.

HERNDON G. DOWLING
The American Museum of Natural History

SURMULLET, a term sometimes applied to goatfishes. See GOATFISH.

SURRA, sŏŏr′ə, is a disease that can occur in all domestic animals and some wild animals. Camels, horses, and dogs are highly susceptible. Cattle, pigs, and buffaloes are often only carriers of the disease and do not have any symptoms when infected. Sheep and goats are rarely affected.

The infective agent, a protozoan parasite, *Trypanosoma evansi,* is transmitted primarily by the bites of flies, but it may also be spread through the bite of a vampire bat or by the eating of meat of a freshly killed infected animal. Once an animal is infected, it may have varying degrees of remittent fever, anemia, loss of appetite, and dropsy (swelling caused by the accumulation of fluid). Sometimes there are eye lesions and the loss of some hair. Most animals eventually develop extreme weakness of the hind legs. They also become emaciated and die within several months if not treated.

Adequate treatment of surra with quinapyramine sulfate and other drugs is generally successful. There is no known way of preventing the disease.

KEITH WAYT, D. V. M.
Colorado State University

SURREALISM, sə-rē′ə-liz-əm, an artistic movement of the early 20th century that stressed fantasy and the subconscious mind. The surrealists were an organized group of artists and writers who gathered about the poet André Breton in 1924 in Paris and who later became active throughout Europe, the United States, and Japan. They sought to revolutionize art so that both subject matter and stylistic coherence were violently antitraditional if not actually fantastic.

There is no one surrealist style in painting. Some artists, such as André Masson and Joan Miró, produced abstract works employing an automatism generated by inner impulses. Others, such as Salvador Dali, preferred a kind of fantastic but illusionistic realism.

Surrealism in the broadest philosophical sense is one of the poles toward which art and thought in all periods may be drawn—the world of dreams and fantasy. In this sense, Bosch in the 15th century, Salvator Rosa in the 17th, and Goya in the 19th may be considered surrealists. Unlike 20th century surrealists, however, they made the unconventional, fantastic element in their painting secondary to the traditional form of a work of art.

Sources. The ideological origins of surrealism are found principally in Freud's methods of psychological investigation, which gave the artists a model for their own experiments and revealed to them a new world of fantastic images drawn from the subconscious and from dreams. The literary precursors of the movement were Baudelaire and Poe among the romantics, Rimbaud and Mallarmé among the symbolists, and, later, Apollinaire. In the visual arts the surrealists looked back not only to the great painters of imaginary subjects but also to the sculpture of primitive peoples, especially the fantastic figures and masks of Oceania.

Precursers of the surrealists in European painting were Francis Picabia, whose works with nonsense titles were among the first abstract paintings, and Marcel Duchamp, whose *Nude Descending a Staircase* caused a sensation in the art world. Both men exhibited at the Armory Show in New York in 1913. Man Ray produced collages in 1916 that were already surrealist in spirit.

The Dadaists, a group founded in 1916, were painters who worked toward insurrection against whatever was pompous, conventional, or just boring in art. After Dadaism degenerated into public demonstrations, violent arguments, and riots, many of its members became surrealists.

The Surrealist Group. In 1924 appeared André Breton's *Manifeste du surréalisme,* which encouraged the expression of "the real process of thought . . . free from any control by the reason. . . ." The first group exhibition of surrealist work was held in 1925 at the Galerie Pierre. Artists represented included Jean Arp and Max Ernst, both former Dadaists, Giorgio de Chirico, Paul Klee, André Masson, Joan Miró, Pablo Picasso, Man Ray, and Pierre Roy. Yves Tanguy joined the group in 1927, Salvador Dali in 1929, and Echaurren Matta in 1937.

The surrealists shared with the Dadaists the desire to break with the past. Unlike the anarchistic Dadaists, however, the surrealists were a closed group obedient to the doctrinaire theories of Breton. They were more concerned with the revolutionary aspects of a new view of life than with creating an art style. This new view

THE MUSEUM OF MODERN ART, NEW YORK CITY

André Masson's *Battle of Fishes* (1927)

attempted to fuse the real and the irrational into, as Breton later put it, "a sort of absolute reality, a *surreality.*"

One of the many original forms of expression the surrealists developed is Ernst's method of *frottage,* or rubbings taken from wood or other rough surfaces capable of producing evocative shapes. Frottage stemmed from experiments in "automatic" drawing, which Ernst had conducted with Breton about 1922, and from Breton's theories about inducing hallucinations by exciting the sensibilities. Another form of expression was *corps exquis,* a process in which each of several persons contributed portions of a common drawing without having seen what the others had done. The surrealists also continued experimenting with collage.

The year 1929 saw the rise of severe internal conflicts over some of the surrealists' support of the Communist party in France. Breton's second surrealist manifesto (1930) attempted to redefine surrealism in terms sympathetic to communist ideology but not to its practice in Stalinist Russia. Although he continued to stress that artistic action arose from social and political revolution and had no aesthetic value in itself, surrealist painters often freely explored the unconscious. In 1939, however, Freud labeled the surrealists "complete fools."

Influence. Surrealism had already spread outside France, and with the advent of World War II, many European surrealists fled to the United States. These were attacked by artists and writers remaining in France, such as Camus and Sartre, for nihilism and inaction, for contriving their little "games" instead of resisting the enemy. Following the war there was a surrealist exhibit in Paris in 1947, but after that the movement as an ideological and artistic force ceased to exist.

In the United States, however, abstract forms of surrealism influenced American painters. Arshile Gorky's early work reflects the biomorphism of Miró and Matta. The free improvisation of Jackson Pollock's drip style is based on the surrealist methodology of automatism. Surrealist influence, by releasing the unconscious, freed Americans from the socially oriented realism of the 1930's and opened up the new expressive and dynamic potentialities of abstract expressionism, which became the first internationally recognized American painting style.

HERSCHEL B. CHIPP, *Author of "The Theories of Modern Art"*

Bibliography

Barr, Alfred H., Jr., *Fantastic Art, Dada, Surrealism* (New York 1936).

Jean, Marcel, *History of Surrealist Painting* (New York 1960).

Levy, Julien, *Surrealism* (New York 1936).

Nadeau, Maurice, *History of Surrealism* (New York 1965).

Rubin, William, *Dada, Surrealism, and Their Heritage* (New York 1968).

Waldberg, Patrick, *Surrealism* (Lausanne 1965).

Salvador Dali's *Giraffe on Fire* (1935)

KUNSTMUSEUM, BASEL: COLLECTION, EMANUEL HOFFMAN

SURREALISM, sə-rē′ə-liz-əm, a major literary movement in France in the 1920's and 1930's Reacting against established aesthetic tradition and against the sterility of Dada, the surrealists sought to create a superreality that would blend the perceptions of the unconscious mind with the external realities of the phenomenal world. The stylistic innovations of the movement have exercised a wide influence on modern art, poetry, fiction, drama, and the cinema.

Origins. The word "surrealism" was coined by the poet Guillaume Apollinaire, whose autobiographical novelette *Le poete assassiné* (1916) was very popular with the surrealists. The hallucinatory imagery of the Comte de Lautréamont's prose poetry, notably *Les chants de Maldoror* (1868), was another direct antecedent of surrealist writing, which also has roots reaching back to Baudelaire and Rimbaud.

André Breton led the movement, and his *Manifeste de surréalisme* (1924) formally announced its beginning. Although the surrealists rejected Dada, they had learned from its methods—as they had from Cubism's erosion of conventional concepts of art. Breton urged writers to substitute irrational for rational vision and to search the "unknown mind" in an effort to express "the real process of thought." Breton and his followers had great respect for Sigmund Freud and his extensive probings of the human unconscious. There, the surrealists felt, rests the ideal reality—available to man in the innocence of childhood and in dreams. All the surrealists recorded their dreams, and many practiced "automatic writing" in an attempt to liberate the imagination from the prison of rationalism.

Theories. The surrealists wished to create an art free of all "aesthetic or moral preoccupations." They often employed grotesque themes, dreams, hallucinations, and subconscious visions in their writing. A recurrent device was the placing of familiar objects in new or illogical relationships to stress the superficiality of conventional visions of reality. They also tried to rediscover what the critic Arpad Mezei called the "multidimensional" qualities of words.

Major Figures. The leading surrealist writers published in the movement's two major journals, *La révolution surréaliste* and *Le surréalisme au service de la révolution* (both 1924–1933). These writers included the poets Breton, Paul Éluard, René Char, Antonin Artaud, and Louis Aragon. Among authors of surrealist novels, in addition to Breton, were Maurice Fourré, Joyce Mansour, and Alain Jouffroy.

In the 1930's painters took predominance in the movement. This was partly because in the late 1920's many writers, including Aragon and Éluard, broke away in the belief that more radical forms of "revolution" were necessary.

Influence. By about 1940, surrealism ceased to enjoy the authority of an organized movement. However, in opening up for the artist the rich realm of unconscious thought and in cutting across established disciplines and forms, it was symptomatic of some of the most fruitful attitudes in modern thinking. Major authors that reveal a surrealist heritage are Nathanael West, James Purdy, Nathalie Sarraute, and Michel Butor.

DAVID D. GALLOWAY
Case Western Reserve University

Further Reading: Balakian, Anna E., *Surrealism: The Road to the Absolute* (New York 1959); Fowlie, Wallace, *The Age of Surrealism* (Bloomington, Ind., 1960).

SURREY, Earl of (?1517–1547), English poet and soldier, who helped develop the English sonnet and introduced blank verse into English poetry. Henry Howard, the son of Thomas, 3d Duke of Norfolk, was known by the courtesy title of Earl of Surrey. He was educated with the Duke of Richmond, the illegitimate son of Henry VIII. Thereafter he alternated between a military career and a career at court. A controversial figure, Surrey was often involved in political and court intrigues and was several times imprisoned. In 1546 the Seymour family plotted his downfall. He was executed in London on Jan. 19, 1547.

Surrey's short poems were first printed in *Tottel's Miscellany* (1557), together with poems by his older contemporary, Sir Thomas Wyatt. Wyatt, who probably had more originality and passion than Surrey, was less polished and mellifluous than the younger man. While Wyatt preferred the Petrarchan sonnet rhyming abba abba cdecde, Surrey preferred the so-called "Shakespearean" form, abab cdcd efef gg. Among Surrey's outstanding poems are his elegies on Wyatt and Richmond. His translation of Books II and IV of the *Aeneid* marked the first appearance of blank verse in English poetry.

DAVID F. C. COLDWELL
Southern Methodist University

SURREY, a county in southeastern England, immediately south of London, extends 35 miles (56 km) west from Kent to Hampshire and about 25 miles (40 km) south to Sussex. The average north-south depth is much less, because many areas are within the boundary of Greater London.

Its main physical features include a chalk range, the North Downs, 882 feet (269 meters) high at the Kent border, extending west across the county to Guildford. The chalk range continues almost to Farnham along the narrow ridge known as the Hog's Back. Greensand Hills, a parallel range, rise at Leith Hill to 965 feet (295 meters) and at Hindhead to 895 feet (275 meters). Both ridges are beautifully wooded and are popular resort areas for Londoners. Two rivers, the Mole and the Wey, cut through the chalk at Dorking and Guildford, respectively, and continue on a northerly course to the River Thames.

Dairying and livestock are the main agricultural enterprises, although there is much poultry farming. Grain is grown in the south, in the Weald, and hops in the west, near Farnham. There are chalk- and lime-workings along the North Downs and large beds of fuller's earth near Redhill.

A track along the North Downs is popularly known as "The Pilgrims' Way," although it long antedates Chaucer's pilgrims and is part of an ancient route from Winchester into Kent. Runnymede, a Thames-side meadow about 20 miles (32 km) west of London, is the probable site of the signing of Magna Carta in 1215. Here, too, is a memorial to U. S. President John F. Kennedy.

The principal town in Surrey is Guildford, where the University of Surrey and an Anglican cathedral concentrated in 1962 are situated. Epsom is famed for its racecourse, but the magnesian salts to which it gave its name are no longer produced there. Camberley is an important military center. Population of the county: (1963) 950,000.

GORDON STOKES
Author of "English Place-Names"

U. S. NATIONAL MUSEUM, SMITHSONIAN INSTITUTION

Canopied two-seater was the most popular surrey.

SURREY, a 4-wheeled American carriage generally designed with two seats to carry a total of four passengers. However, some early types had only one seat. Most surreys were equipped with either canopies or folding tops. The surrey was adapted from the English Whitechapel cart and introduced in 1872 by James B. Brewster and Co. of New York. Surreys were very popular until the end of the carriage era.

DON H. BERKEBILE, *Smithsonian Institution*

SURROGATE, sur'ə-gāt, a deputy, or person appointed to act for another. In English law, a surrogate serves as the deputy of a bishop or chancellor, and issues marriage licenses without banns. He also may substitute for a judge in an admiralty or probate proceeding. In many jurisdictions in the United States, a surrogate is a judge who presides in probate court or surrogates' court over the settlement of estates, guardianships, and adoptions.

SURROGATES' COURT. See PROBATE COURT; SURROGATE; WILL.

SURTEES, sûr'tēz, **Robert Smith** (1805–1864), English writer of humorous sporting novels, who created the character Jorrocks, a fox-hunting Cockney grocer. Surtees was born in Northumberland, England, on May 17, 1805. He became a solicitor but gave up law for journalism. In 1831 he helped found and became editor of the *New Sporting Magazine*. The Jorrocks sketches that he created for it were later worked into novels. After inheriting the family estate in 1838, Surtees became a county magistrate. He died in Brighton on March 16, 1864.

Surtees' novels are valued for their portrayal of English hunting life. They were published anonymously, and some were illustrated by John Leech. Jorrocks figures in *Jorrocks's Jaunts and Jollities* (1838), *Handley Cross* (1843, 1854), and *Hillingdon Hall* (1854).

SURTSEY, sûrt'sē, is a volcanic island that erupted from the sea floor off Iceland's southwest coast, near the Vestmannaeyjar Islands, on Nov. 14, 1963. Its permanence assured by a lava flow that started in 1964, the island began to be colonized by plant life as early as 1965. Named for the Norse god of fire, Surtsey is about 1 square mile (3 sq km) and is over 500 feet (150 meters) high.

VINCENT H. MALMSTRÖM
Middlebury College

SURVEYING is the art of using scientific principles to make comparatively large measurements to a required accuracy. Surveying has two basic functions: (1) to measure what exists, to determine where it is located, and usually to prepare a map to show the results of these data from which a plan or a boundary description can be made; and (2) to establish marks to guide construction according to a plan or to show the boundaries according to a description or other data.

Since no project of importance can be efficiently designed or constructed without a map and survey control, surveying is an essential part of nearly every field operation. Its use extends from measuring property boundaries and making a plot plan for a house to great construction projects like canals, railroads, and highways. Even the placement of tracking devices for space vehicles must be accurately located by surveys. The principles of precision surveying are also used in optical tooling to control the construction and alignment of large products like airplanes, rockets, and turbines.

SURVEYING MEASUREMENTS

The direction of gravity is used as a reference in all measurements. "Vertical" measurements are those made in the direction of gravity, and "horizontal" measurements are those made perpendicular to gravity.

Only four types of measurements are made: horizontal lengths, vertical heights, horizontal angles, and vertical angles.

A level surface is everywhere perpendicular to gravity, like the surface of still water. It is slightly curved, since it follows the curvature of the earth. Thus a *horizontal length* is horizontal throughout its length, even though it is slightly curved.

A *vertical height* is the distance between two level surfaces.

A *horizontal angle* is an angle in a plane perpendicular to gravity at the point of measurement.

A *vertical angle* is an angle in a plane vertical at the point of measurement. Sometimes a *zenith angle* is measured: it is the angle from a vertical line down to a given point.

For surveys that have a width of 12 miles (19 km) or less, no correction for earth curvature is required. These are called *plane* surveys. For larger surveys, exactly the same types of measurements are made in the field, but in computing results the shape of the earth is taken into account. These are called *geodetic* surveys.

In the United States all distances, both horizontal and vertical, are usually measured in feet and decimal parts of a foot, never in inches. Throughout most of the rest of the world, and sometimes in the United States, meters and decimal parts of a meter are used.

In the United States all angles are usually measured in degrees, minutes, and sometimes seconds of arc. There are 360 degrees to a full circle, 60 minutes to 1 degree, and 60 seconds to 1 minute. Another form of angular measurement is based on units of 100's, with 100 grads to a right angle and 400 grads to a full circle (or 360 degrees). There are 100 minutes to 1 grad, and 100 seconds to 1 minute.

Horizontal Positions. The horizontal position of a point is almost invariably specified by *rectangular coordinates*. These are the distances from the point to a pair of previously chosen lines positioned at right angles to each other. The choice of the positions and orientation of these lines establishes the coordinate system set up for each particular survey. These coordinates are computed from traverses and triangulation measured in the field.

A *traverse* is a series of straight lines connecting a number of points known as *traverse stations.* The lengths of these lines and the angles between these lines are measured, and usually the lines are arranged to return to the place of beginning, so that the extent of the errors can be computed. The sum of the angles must be equal to $(n - 2)180°$, where n is the number of angles. If there are five angles, $n = 5$ and $(n - 2)180° = 3 \times 180° = 540°$. If the measured value is 540°10′, the error is +10′. If this error is allowable within the desired accuracy, it is usually eliminated by correcting each angle equally—subtracting 2′ from each—resulting in "adjusted" angles.

The *bearing* of each line of the traverse must be computed. A bearing is the angle from the north or south, whichever is nearest. If one side of an enclosed area has the measured or assumed bearing N18°53′E—that is, it lies in a NE direction at an angle of 18°53′ measured in a clockwise direction from the north—those of the other sides can be computed through the adjusted angles. A side lying in a northwesterly direction at a clockwise angle of 96°03′ from the side whose bearing is N18°53′E would itself have a bearing of N65°04′W, which is the difference between 114°56′ (the sum of 96°03′ and 18°53′) and 180° (true north). Sometimes *azimuths* are used. An azimuth is the clockwise angle from the north, or sometimes from the south. An azimuth of 100° from north is the same as bearing S80° E. Similarly, 230° equals S50° W.

The *latitude* of a line is the distance it extends north. South is minus. The *departure* is the distance east. West is minus. These are computed by means of two trigonometric functions: cosine $\theta = a/h$ and sine $\theta = b/h$, where a = latitude, θ = bearing, and b = departure. For a traverse that returns to the place of beginning, the sum of the latitudes must equal zero, and so must the sum of the departures.

The total error, E, is computed by using the formula $E = \sqrt{L^2 + D^2}$, where L is the error in latitude, and D is the error in departure. The error in latitude is proportionally distributed among the latitudes of the sides, and the error in departure is proportionally distributed among the departures. One point is then given a y (north) coordinate and an x (east) coordinate, and the coordinates of the other points are computed from the adjusted latitudes and departures.

Triangulation is used for large distances and areas, where it is usually cheaper, or where traverses cannot be employed. It consists basically of a series of triangles, either in the form of a chain or a broad network. The triangles are formed by interconnecting triangulation stations, with each triangle having at least one side in common with each adjacent triangle. The initial side, or base line, of the first triangle is measured, as are all the angles. All other side lengths are computed by the formula

$$\frac{a}{\sin A} = \frac{b}{\sin B} = \frac{c}{\sin C}$$

The angles are adjusted according to the theory of least squares to comply with geometric requirements. Coordinates of triangulation stations are computed from the adjusted results.

Vertical Positions. The vertical position of a point is given by its *elevation,* which often is based on an assumed or a local system. Permanent points called *bench marks* (B. M.'s) are established and connected by lines of levels. The differences are adjusted by the theory of least squares so that the same elevations result by whatever route they are computed.

Vertical Heights. The vertical heights of the ground are shown by *contour lines.* A contour line is a line connecting points of equal elevation. The vertical interval used between contour lines is small on large-scale maps, large on small-scale maps. In the United States, contour lines usually are drawn at even elevations at intervals of 1, 2, 5, 10, 20, 50, and 100 feet.

SURVEYING MEASUREMENTS

Horizontal length

Vertical height

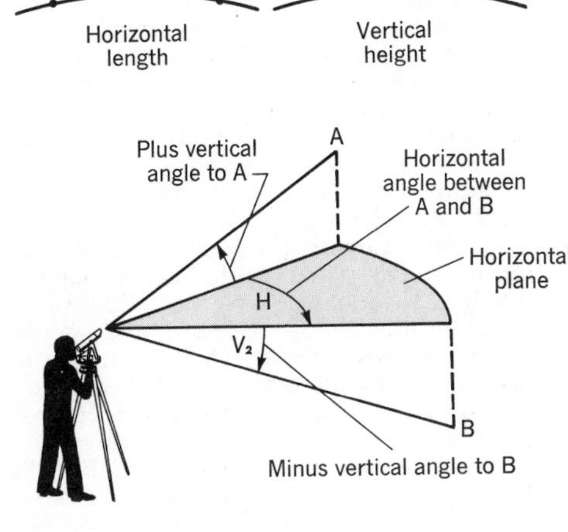

Horizontal plane

Zenith angle

Minus vertical angle

SURVEYING METHODS

Surveys are designated as first order, second order, third order, or fourth order. "First order" indicates maximum precision, "second order" and "third order" progressively less precision, and "fourth order" mimimum precision, according to established criteria.

Since the cost of a survey increases with accuracy, *control surveys,* consisting of comparatively few but highly accurate measurements, are made. Then less accurate surveys or measurements are connected, or tied, to them to locate the required numerous surveying lines at a lower cost.

For example, a triangulation system might be the superior control. Traverses would be run from one triangulation station to another, and each traverse would be adjusted so that bearings and coordinates would fit those of the triangulation. Further ties to detail might be made by transit stadia, plane table, cloth tape, or photogrammetry.

Vertical control is handled similarly. Superior control would be an accurate level net—a series of adjusted interconnected bench marks. Less accurate leveling might be run between bench marks on this net and adjusted to them. Side observations could be made to detail by photogrammetry, transit stadia, or plane table.

SURVEYING INSTRUMENTS

Angular Measurements. According to current American terminology, there are basically two kinds of surveying instruments used to measure horizontal and vertical angles, the *American transit* and the *theodolite*.

The *American transit* is essentially a telescope and is usually equipped with a level and stadia hairs (two additional cross hairs). With its 24 to 30 power, it is possible to point the telescopic

TRAVERSE COMPUTATION

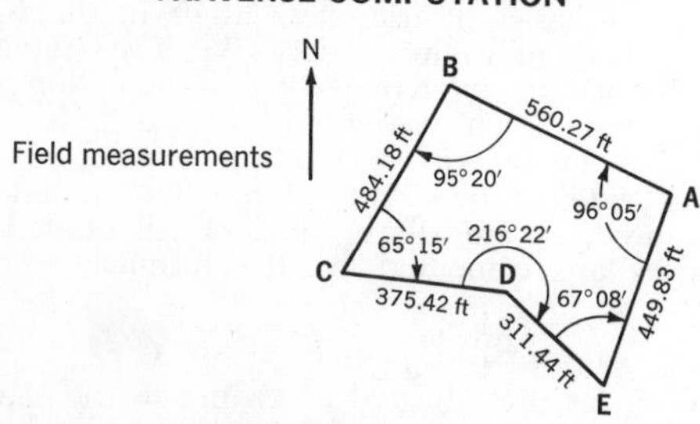

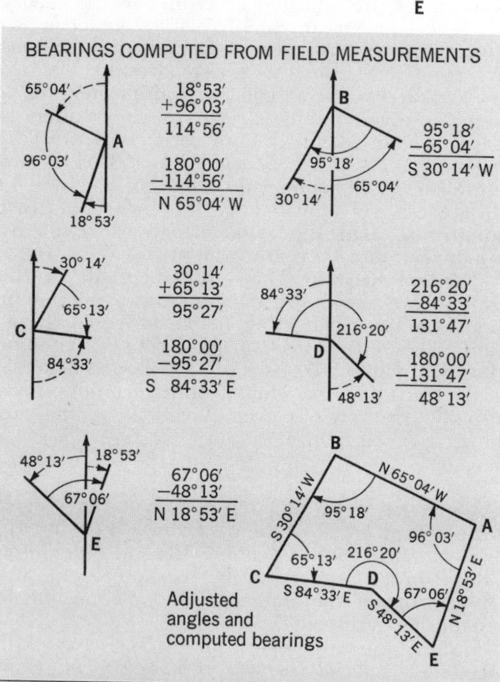

COMPUTATION OF ERROR

Course	Length	Bearing	Cosine	Sine	Latitude	Departure
AB	560.27	N65°04′ W	.42156	.90680	+236.19	−508.05
BC	484.18	S30°14′ W	.86398	.50352	−418.32	−243.79
CD	375.42	S84°33′ E	.09498	.99548	− 35.66	+373.72
DE	311.44	S48°13′ E	.66632	.74567	−207.52	+232.23
EA	449.83	N18°53′ E	.94618	.32364	+425.62	+145.58
Sums	2181.14				+ 0.31	− 0.31

End −0.31 +0.31 Error Start

$$\text{Error} = \sqrt{(.31)^2 + (.31)^2} = 0.44$$

$$\frac{0.44}{2181} = 1{:}5000 \text{ Accuracy}$$

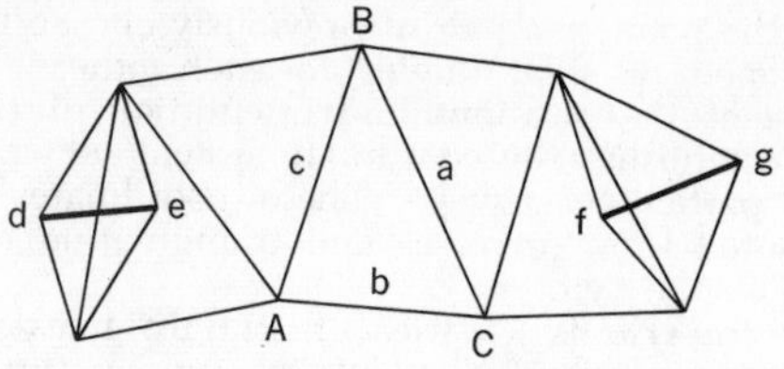

A simple triangulation system. All angles are measured, as are the base, *de*, and the check base, *fg*.

sight within one second—that is, to within 5/16 inch (8 mm) of the target at one mile.

The telescope can be rotated in elevation and turned completely over, from direct to reversed. The aim in a vertical plane is controlled by the "elevation motion," a clamp with a tangent screw. Two spirit levels on the "upper plate" indicate when the instrument is leveled (the azimuth axis made vertical). "A" and "B" verniers, 180° apart, are used to read a horizontal plate called the horizontal circle. The entire assembly, called an *alidade*, is mounted on a conical spindle.

The horizontal circle provides for rotation, called "lower motion," between itself and the leveling head resting on the tripod. The horizontal circle is mounted on a conical tube into which the conical spindle of the alidade fits. This arrangement of spindle-within-tube is the "double center," an excellent device found only in American transits. Rotation between the alidade and the horizontal circle is called "upper motion," and the ability to utilize both upper and lower motion enables the American Transit to accumulate the angle (make repeated measurements of the same angle), once for each time it is turned. The angle valve is obtained by dividing the final valve by the number of turns.

To center the transit over a specified point, either a plumb bob, suspended from the vertical axis, or an optical plummet is used. The latter is an optical vertical sighting device. A special parallel-shift tripod head prevents the instrument from turning when shifted and thus from going out of level, since the tripod head is seldom level. With it the instrument can be shifted 2 inches (5 cm).

The word *theodolite* means simply an angle-measuring instrument. In the United States, however, it is used to mean a precise angle-measuring instrument. In the theodolite the alidade and the horizontal circle turn in separate bearings in the leveling head, so that the computation of angles requires the subtraction of one reading from another. Thus a theodolite is often called a direction instrument, as opposed to a transit, which is a repeating instrument.

Modern theodolites have an optical plummet, a parallel-shift plate, and a gravity-controlled zenith angle index, so that the zenith reading is independent of the accuracy of leveling. The objective lens has a very short focal length, which makes possible a short telescope, short standards (upright supports), and hence a smaller, lighter instrument. The circles are often read with micrometer microscopes. Some microscopes automatically give the average of the two sides of the circle, 180° apart.

In an effort to match the advantageous double center of the American transit, may theodolites now have a snap clamp that joins the horizontal circle to the alidade. This makes it possible to repeat angles and to start an angle at zero reading, as in the American transit.

Targets. Transits and theodolites are usually aimed at plumb bob cords or range poles. For long sights, many special devices may be used.

Compasses. A magnetic compass is frequently used in wooded country to measure the magnetic bearings of a line or to run a reasonably straight line through the woods. A compass is frequently part of a transit and sometimes an attachment for a theodolite. An independent compass is usually mounted on a jacob's staff (a pointed rod) or a light tripod.

Distance Measurements. Devices used to measure distances vary from simple woven tapes marked off in units of length to complex electronic transmitters.

Gunter's chain, developed by the Englishman Edmund Gunter in 1620, was used in the United States for distance measurements until almost the end of the 19th century. It still appears in land descriptions and is the unit in the U. S. Public Land System. Even when a steel tape is used, the operation is still usually called "chaining." Based on decimal units, the chain is 1/10 of a furlong (66 feet, or 20.3 meters) in length and is made up of 100 links. Ten square chains equal one acre (24.7 chains equal 1 hectare), and 80 chains equal one mile (49.7 chains equal 1 km). A quarter of a chain is a rod, 16½ feet (5 meters) long.

In the United States most measurements now are made with a *steel tape* 100 feet (30.48 meters) long and graduated to 0.01 foot (3 mm). Metric steel tapes are usually 25, 30, or 50 meters (82, 98.4, and 164 feet) in length. Side measurements for mapping are made with woven tapes. For precise measurements, as for triangulation base lines, an invar tape is used. Invar, an iron-nickel alloy, has a very low coefficient of thermal expansion, and it can be used in very bright sunlight without the heat significantly distorting its length.

Stadia is a method for determining approximately horizontal distances and differences in height by merely sighting a graduated rod through a transit or a theodolite. Two extra horizontal cross hairs, called stadia hairs, are placed on the cross-hair plane, equidistant from the central hair and spaced so that their lines of sight separate at a rate of 1:100. The distance and difference in height between the transit or theodolite and the graduated stadia rod is determined from the length of the rod visible between the stadia hairs and is computed from the measured vertical angle. A stadia slide rule or a table is used to handle the formulas. This makes it possible to run, simultaneously, traverses to an accuracy of about one part in 300 to 500, and levels to about 0.005 feet $\sqrt{F}$, where F is the length of the traverse in feet.

Stadia is invaluable for topographic mapping and for tying topographic detail and photo-control points to control.

The *plane table* is a drawing board, and an alidade, mounted on a tripod for field use. The alidade's telescope is equipped with stadia hairs. Directions from stations are ruled on a map and marked off with the reduced stadia distance, and the elevation is computed in the field. The method is slightly less accurate than transit stadia, but the topographer can draw contours while viewing the ground, so fewer points need to be located. It is excellent for mapping but has now been superseded by photogrammetry. It is used to fill in where the ground does not show in the photographs or for small maps.

Electronic Instruments. Radar, loran, shoran, hiran, and many other navigational devices measure distances by electronics—using the length of time it takes an outgoing signal to return from a distant point as the measuring method—but not to the accuracy required for surveying. Extreme accuracy, however, is attained by "phase-shift" electronic distance measurement. The mean square error is ±1 to 3 mm plus 1 to 5 parts in 1,000,000. It can measure up to 40 miles (64 km) across water or between hilltops.

Several phase-shift devices have been developed. All depend on the same fundamental principle. Like radio, they use a main frequency (the carrier frequency), which is modified, or modulated, by the message (voice, music) it is carrying. The carrier frequency of these instruments, however, is very much higher than that of radio. The *Geodimeter* uses light, generated by a small searchlight or laser. The *Tellurometer* and other similar instruments use microwaves. In both types the carrier frequency is modulated by a precise crystal-controlled lower frequency.

In operation the transmitter is placed at the near end of a distance, and its output is beamed

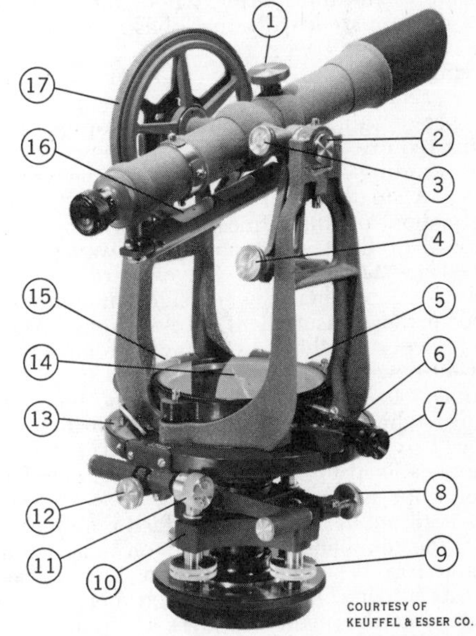

COURTESY OF KEUFFEL & ESSER CO.

An American transit: (1) Focusing knob. (2) Elevation axis. (3) Elevation clamp. (4) Elevation tangent screw. (5) Plate level. (6) B vernier. (7) Eyepiece of optical plummet. (8) Lower motion tangent screw. (9) Leveling screw. (10) Leveling head. (11) Two-speed upper motion tangent screw. (12) Upper motion clamp. (13) A vernier. (14) Compass needle. (15) Plate level. (16) Telescope level. (17) Vertical circle.

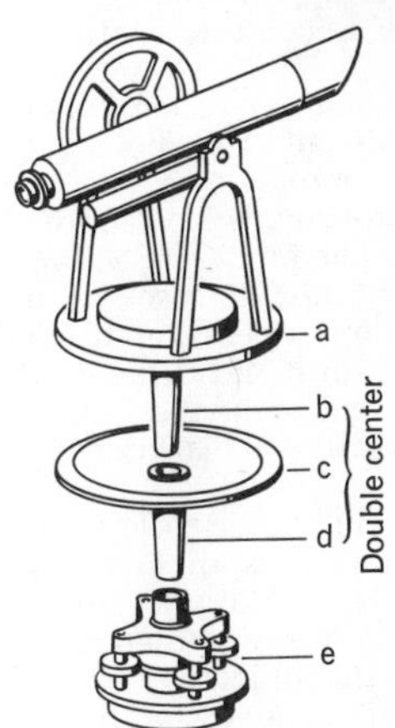

Transit disassembled: (a) Alidade. (b) Inner center. (c) Horizontal circle. (d) Outer center. (e) Leveling head.

COURTESY OF KEUFFEL & ESSER CO.

Zeiss theodolite

to a set of corner mirrors or a retransmitter at the remote end of the distance. These return the beam to the transmitter, where the incoming phase is compared with the phase of the outgoing beam.

Using light for a carrier frequency gives greater accuracy. Microwaves penetrate fog, haze, heavy rain, dust, and sand storms. Both systems require correction for the known delays in the sending instruments and in the remote devices. A small correction is made for the index of refraction of the atmosphere, which affects the speed of light waves and microwaves.

Leveling Measurements. Levels are used to establish a horizontal line of sight and are employed in the measurement of elevations. A surveying level usually consists of a telescope of about 40 power with a very sensitive spirit level attachment to the telescope tube. The telescopic line of sight is level when the spirit level's bubble is centered. In the *dumpy level* the telescope is fixed to its supports. In the *wye level* the telescope is removable.

In a *tilting level*, which is faster and easier to use, the telescope is mounted on a horizontal axis and can be tilted through a few degrees. The tilt is controlled by a micrometer screw. Mounted on the main frame is a circular level used to level the spindle approximately, and thereafter the main bubble is centered with the tilting screw.

Automatic levels are becoming more and more popular. When the instrument has been approximately leveled with a circular level, the line of sight is made precisely level by an optical part controlled by pendulum action. These levels are very accurate and very fast to use, as no time is lost in the meticulous operation of exactly centering a tubular spirit level, and all shots can be taken without checking the bubble.

Rods. A specially marked rod is used for readings with all levels.

Planoparallels. Usually in precise leveling, the smallest division on the rod is divided into 10 points by estimation. To avoid estimations, a lens with flat parallel sides is mounted on a horizontal axis in front of the objective lens of the level. When it is slanted, it moves the line of sight up or down parallel to itself. A control knob is graduated to read the extent of this movement, thus measuring the exact value.

PHOTOGRAMMETRY

Photogrammetry is a method of locating contour lines and other details to be mapped from control surveys by means of photographs, usually aerial photographs aimed nearly vertically downward. The airplane is flown along "flight strips" arranged so the strips of photographs overlap each other about 10%. The camera is regulated so that the photographs within a flight strip overlap each other about 60%. The overlap of any two adjacent photographs forms a "stereo pair." Maps are drawn from successive stereo pairs in one of many types of "plotters."

All plotters operate on three principal elements: (1) a projection system for projecting photographs stereoscopically; (2) a viewing system that presents the viewer with a miniature 3-dimensional model of the mapped area; and (3) a measuring system for determining horizontal and vertical distances of the model. In their simplest form, these elements are best demonstrated by the multiplex plotter.

Objects on the ground that can be identified on the photographs, called photo control points, are tied to survey control, usually by transit stadia or plane table, and then are plotted on the future map. A transparent positive (diapositive) of each photograph is projected toward the map, over which is positioned a disc, or "tracing table." The tracing table consists of a white plate, 6 inches (15 cm) in diameter, mounted on a movable stand and adjustable in height. At its center is a tiny white light, which serves as a "floating dot," or marker. A pointer, which can be replaced with a pencil lead, is situated directly below the light. The tracing table is placed over each control point and set at the scale height of the desired contour line. The projector is adjusted so that the image of each control point falls on the white light of the tracing table.

The two projectors, together projecting a stereo pair, have complementary color filters. One has a green filter, and its projected image is seen with the left eye through a green glass. The other has a red filter, and its image is seen with the right eye through a red glass. The result is an anaglyph—a 3-dimensional, or stereoscopic, view of the projected image.

Both eyes see the white light, which is used as a guide for the movements of the tracing table. With the white light set at ground level in the stereo model, the tracing table is moved along, following and drawing the contour lines of the projected image.

KINDS OF SURVEYS

Geodetic control surveys in the United States are made by the U. S. Coast and Geodetic Survey. Horizontal control consists of a system of chains and areas of triangulation and some precise traverses, which covers the entire United States, except Alaska and Hawaii. It is adjusted to be consistent throughout, as well as with Canadian triangulation. Positions are given in geodetic latitude and longitude based on Clark's spheroid of 1866 and astronomical observations at many stations.

Vertical control in the United States is also a function of the U. S. Coast and Geodetic

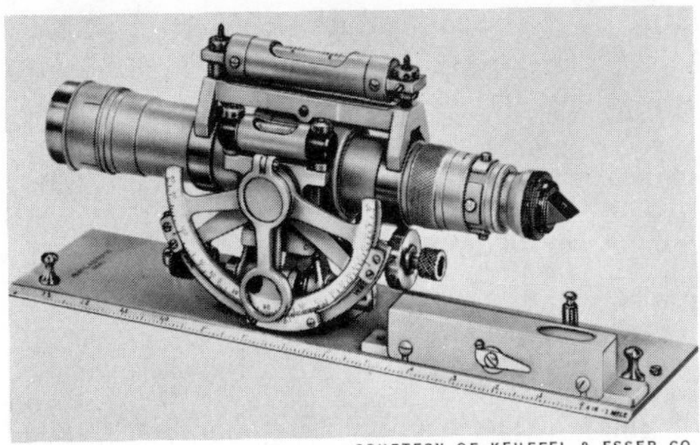

COURTESY OF KEUFFEL & ESSER CO.

Small plane-table alidade

Survey. It consists of many thousands of bench marks interconnected with lines of levels and adjusted to be consistent throughout and to agree with mean sea level determined by many gauges along the coastlines. The net covers the entire United States, except Alaska and Hawaii, and is connected with Canadian leveling.

State Plane Coordinate Systems were designed by the U. S. Coast and Geodetic Survey to eliminate the need to use laborious geodetic computation in order to tie to geodetic horizontal control. Each state was fitted with one or more map projections, representing the spherical surface of the earth, in zones 128 miles (206 km) wide. The projections used were the Lambert conformal conic projection, which can be extended indefinitely east and west, or the transverse Mercator projection, which is also conformal (its depicted areas changed very little from the true representation) and can be extended indefinitely north and south. The difference between a distance computed from these projection coordinates and the true distance is never greater than 1:10,000. The coordinates have been or can be easily computed from the latitude and longitude of any triangulation station so that a surveyor can run a survey from one to the other and check his work by ordinary computation.

Topographic Surveys are for maps that include contour lines. Based on horizontal and vertical control, the details are surveyed by photogrammetry, transit or plane table stadia, or woven tape measurements, or by levels, taken at the corners of 25- to 50-foot (7.5- to 15-meter) squares or along lines perpendicular to traverse lines. The contours are sketched in from these data.

Hydrographic Surveys are made chiefly for charts for navigation. First, control surveys are established on land. Then, depending on the methods used, transit stations and targets visible from the water are tied in to determine their positions. Tide gauges are tied in to determine their elevations.

Soundings are made in certain patterns by measuring the depth of water with poles, lead lines, and fathometers, the last by measuring the time it takes a sound made underwater from shipboard to return as an echo from the bottom. Because of tides, the time as well as the location of each sounding must be recorded.

Property surveys are of great importance and should be made by a surveyor familiar with the territory. He makes what is known as a "survey" or a "resurvey." A survey provides the information for writing a description of the boundaries, and a resurvey is made according to a description already existing. Frequently it is a combination of both.

Public land surveys are a systematic method of marking out great areas of the United States in approximately square parcels 40 acres (16 hectares) in area. It also makes it possible to describe any one of the parcels with great simplicity. This system extends over 30 states, excluding the 13 original states and Hawaii, Kentucky, Maine, Texas, Tennessee, Vermont, West Virginia, and the District of Columbia.

Engineering surveys provide topographic maps used in planning engineering projects. Small-scale maps are used for reconnaissance, large-scale maps for detailed planning. The scale used in detailed planning depends on the type of project. For buildings, 4 feet, 8 feet, and 16 feet to the inch are used; for larger projects, 20 feet, 40 feet, and 50 feet to the inch. Railways, highways, and canals require route surveys, long strip maps on which the rights-of-way are laid out and the construction details are planned. Aerial photography and photogrammetry are used extensively both for topographic maps and for estimating real estate costs. Maps of areas must be available for highway interchanges, railway yards and terminals, canal locks, and other appurtenances.

The elevations are of supreme importance for canals, as are the rates of grade (slope) and curvature for railroads and highways. The length of a train is controlled by the rate of grade (the ruling grade), and the purpose of the highway limits the rate of grade and curvature that can be used.

HISTORY OF SURVEYING

The Great Pyramid of Khufu at Giza, built about 2700 B. C., is so accurately square and so perfectly oriented to the cardinal points of the compass that it is evident that the Egyptians used surveying as means of controlling construction, just as we do today. Surveying also was used to determine property lines, as Sumerian clay tablets (1400 B. C.) show records of land measurement and plans of cities and nearby agricultural areas. Boundary stones marking property corners have been preserved, and there is representation of land measurement of the Menna at Thebes (1400 B. C.) showing two men chaining a wheat field with what appears to be a cord with knots at regular intervals. The head chainman carries an extra length of cord, and the rear chainman has gathered up the rear end.

The Egyptians used an instrument called a *gromma* to establish right angles. It was a wooden cross with a plumb bob hanging from the end of each of the four arms. It was supported by a cord at its center. The Egyptians also had a level—an A-frame with a plumb bob supported by a cord at the peak of the A, the plumb bob hanging past an index marked on the bar of the A. With these instruments the ancient Egyptians were able to measure land areas, record the positions of boundary markers, and build the huge pyramids to very exact dimensions.

The Romans, who were in Egypt from 30 B. C. to 642 A. D., slightly improved the Egyptian devices and added a water level and a plane table with a crude alidade to the list of instruments available for surveying. The water level was either a wooden trough filled with water, or it was a tube with its ends turned up. It must have been quite accurate, since a level would be essential in building the Roman aqueducts.

A crude odometer for distance measurements was introduced in 30 B. C. by the Roman architect Vitruvius. It consisted of a device like a wheelbarrow, with a wheel of known circumference that automatically dropped a pebble into a container at each revolution.

The Greek astronomer and mathematician Hipparchus is credited with the development of trigonometry about 130 B. C. When the Scottish mathematician John Napier invented logarithms about 1614, 17 centuries later, and logarithmic tables were published in 1620, portable angle-measuring instruments became important and surveying took a long step forward. These instruments were called "topographicall" instruments or "theodolites." They had a hand-divided circle and a pivoted arm for sighting and were capable of measuring horizontal and vertical angles. Some may have had magnetic compasses, which had been developed about 1511 by Martin Waldseemüller.

Distances were measured with wooden rods or by cords called "lines." A line was 66 feet (20.3 meters) long, and four rods equaled one line. Ten square lines equaled one acre.

Levels basically were improved Roman water levels, but about 1704 Rowley built a spirit level. Lacking telescopic sights, he used a sighting device about 1 meter long to gain accuracy.

Edmund Gunter introduced his famous chain, 66 feet (20.3 meters) long and composed of 100 links, in 1620.

The development of the circle-dividing engine by the British instrument maker Jesse Ramsden about 1775 produced one of the greatest advances in surveying methods. Heretofore it had been impossible to measure angles accurately with a portable instrument.

The vernier, developed by the French mathematician Pierre Vernier in 1631, the micrometer microscope developed by William Gascoigne in 1638, the telescopic sight probably developed by the French astronomer Jean Picard in 1669, and the spirit level were all available to be incorporated in the theodolite of Jonathan Sisson about 1720. Stadia hairs were first applied by James Watt in 1771. Spirit levels were equipped with telescopic sights about this time.

These instruments make up a large part of the surveyor's equipment today. Modern instruments are smaller, lighter, and much more accurate, but nearly the same in principle. The major changes are the shorter telescope that will transit (reverse vertically), the American double center, the steel tape, the gyroscopic compass, electronic distance measurement, and, of course, photogrammetry.

PHILIP KISSAM
Author of "Surveying Practice"

Bibliography

Breed, Charles B., and others, *Principles and Practice of Surveying,* vol. 1, 9th ed. (New York 1958); vol. 2, 8th ed. (New York 1962).

Ives, Howard C., and Kissam, Philip, *Highway Curves,* 4th ed. (New York 1952).

Kissam, Philip, *Optical Tooling* (New York 1962).

Kissam, Philip, *Surveying for Civil Engineers* (New York 1956).

Kissam, Philip, *Surveying: Instruments and Methods,* 2d ed. (New York 1956).

Kissam, Philip, *Surveying Practice,* 2d ed. (New York 1971).

Mitchell, H. C., "Definitions of Terms Used in Geodetic and Other Surveys," U. S. Coast and Geodetic Survey *Special Publication* 242, 1948.

SURVEYOR. See SPACE EXPLORATION—*Recent Unmanned Space Flights.*

SUSA, sōō′sə, was a city in ancient Elam. The site, in modern Khuzistan, southwest Iran, is marked by an enormous mound representing successive building periods. Beside it, the village of Shush preserves the ancient city's name.

The earliest written documents of the Sumerians and Akkadians in Mesopotamia (Iraq) refer to the peoples of Susa and Elam as enemies or as conquered subjects. The city was overcome by kings of Akkad (about 2370–2230 B. C.) and of the 3d Dynasty of Ur (about 2100–2000 B. C.). But the last ruler of Ur, Ibbi-Suen, was captured by Elamite sovereigns who, as "Viceroys of Elam, Shimash, and Susa," had become independent. Cuneiform texts in Akkadian from the immediately succeeding period (ending about 1600 B. C.) testify to Mesopotamian influences on Susa and Elam. The history of the city is then obscured for over 300 years.

Shortly after 1300 B. C. monarchs calling themselves "Kings of Anshan and Susa" interfered repeatedly in Babylonian and Assyrian affairs and made extensive conquests in Mesopotamia and Iran. Most of their records were written in the Elamite language, which has been only partially deciphered and has no known relationship with any other tongue. After Nebuchadnezzar I of Babylon defeated their army about 1140 B. C., Susa's history again becomes obscure. The city came into prominence once more during the late Assyrian period, after 750 B. C., but it was sacked and devastated by Ashurbanipal in 636.

Under Persian rule, Susa was rebuilt by Darius I (reigned 521–486 B. C.) and his heirs, and it served as one of the three major capitals. As "Shushan the palace" it was the setting for the Biblical story of Esther. Captured by Alexander the Great in 331 B. C., Susa became an important center of Greek influence under his immediate successors and remained so under the Parthians after 140 B. C. The Sassanian Shapur II (reigned 309–379 A. D.) wreaked havoc upon it because it was believed to be a Christian center. Thereafter it was only sporadically occupied.

French excavations at Susa since the 1880's have recovered such masterpieces of culture as the "Victory Stele" of Naram-Sin, king of Akkad, and the "Law Code" of Hammurabi. Both had been taken as booty from Mesopotamia.

GEORGE G. CAMERON
Author of "History of Early Iran"

SUSANNA, The Story of, in the Bible, an account of a Jewish woman who, through the assistance of the prophet Daniel, is exonerated of adultery. The story is included as part of the Book of Daniel by the Roman Catholic and Eastern Orthodox churches and is placed among the Old Testament Apocrypha by Protestants, Anglicans, and Jews. It survives only in Greek, but many scholars think it had a Hebrew original.

When Susanna refuses the advances of two elders, they charge her with adultery with another. She is convicted, but Daniel interrupts the proceedings and, by cleverly questioning the two elders, exposes their lies. It is not a historical account but a story illustrating the belief that the righteous will prevail.

SUSIANA. See ELAM.

SUSLOV, sōōs′lôf, **Mikhail Andreyevich** (1902–), Soviet Communist party official. This quiet, gaunt man devoted his career to perpetuating strict party control at home and Soviet leadership of world communism abroad.

Born in Shakhovskoye, Russia, on Nov. 21, 1902, of peasant stock, he joined the Communist party in 1921 and completed his secondary schooling with a crash course in 1924. Obviously able, he spent the next six years studying Communist social and political theory at the Plekhanov Institute of National Economy in Moscow. A capable ideological watchdog, he worked for the party's security agencies from 1931 to 1936, purging party members. After more advanced study at the party's Institute of Red Professors, he became a party functionary in 1937 and reached the post of territorial first secretary in 1939.

During World War II he carried out important assignments involving the reconquest of the Caucasus and the political integration of Lithuania into the USSR. In 1947, after serving for one year as head of the party's department of Agitation and Propaganda (Agitprop), he became a party secretary with special responsibility for ideological matters. In 1947 he helped to form the Cominform. His work in that area was the first of many assignments relating to international communism. As chief Soviet delegate to the Cominform (1948–1953) and as editor of *Pravda* (1949–1950), he led the Soviet campaign against Tito's Yugoslavia. He also undertook a number of other ideological missions for Stalin prior to the latter's death in March 1953.

Suslov was elected to the party's Presidium in 1955, and he played a prominent role in the suppression of the Hungarian revolution in 1956. He was also influential both in the defeat of Khrushchev's opponents in 1957 and in the ouster of Khrushchev himself in 1964. An ideological "purist," he was an uncompromising opponent of the demands for intellectual freedom in the 1960's. In general, he is opposed to change—an attitude that is the result of a lifetime spent in the service of Stalinist orthodoxy.

George W. Simmonds
Wayne State University

SUSPENSION, a liquid medium containing small solid particles that are at least 1 micron (0.00004 inch) in diameter and do not pass through filter paper. On standing, the particles of a suspension settle to the bottom of the liquid. Mixtures containing solid particles that are small enough to pass through filter paper and that do not settle out on standing are called colloidal suspensions or sols. See Colloid.

SUSPENSION, Automobile. See Automobile.

SUSPENSION BRIDGE. See Bridge.

SUSQUEHANNA RIVER, sus-kwə-ha′nə, rises in Lake Otsego in southern New York, where it is known as the North Branch. The river flows generally south for 440 miles (708 km) in an irregular course across Pennsylvania to the head of Chesapeake Bay in Maryland. It is the longest U. S. river flowing into the Atlantic Ocean, and it drains an area of 27,500 square miles (72,225 sq km).

Its two principal tributaries, the West Branch and Juniata, are entrenched into the Appalachian Plateau, which is rich in bituminous coal. With steep gradients, many gorges, and large volume, the Susquehanna has the greatest power potential of any Eastern Seaboard river.

In the Appalachian Ridge and Valley Province the Susquehanna and its tributaries have cut through alternating northeastward trending ridges and valleys to provide classic examples for geologic study. This area is the foremost producer of anthracite coal. Scranton and Wilkes-Barre, Pa., are leading mining and manufacturing centers.

Early settlement proceeded upstream from Chesapeake Bay to exploit fertile lands of the Piedmont and Great Valley to Harrisburg, Pa. Later, in 1779, removal of the Indian threat encouraged settlers into the upper Susquehanna. Frontier type agriculture dominated the region until about 1840, when anthracite and its use in smelting iron were discovered. This, in turn, encouraged lumbering, mining, and industry.

Clark I. Cross, *University of Florida*

SUSQUEHANNAH COMPANY, sus-kwə-han′ə, a company of land speculators and emigrants chartered by the colony of Connecticut in 1753 to settle the Wyoming Valley along the Susquehanna River in Pennsylvania. The valley supposedly fell within the sea-to-sea boundaries of Connecticut's charter, but it was also claimed by Pennsylvania and by the Six Nations, the Iroquois Indian confederation.

Both Pennsylvania and the Six Nations urged the Wyoming Indians to resist the Susquehannah Company settlers. The company contrived the assassination of Chief Teedyuscung and the burning of his village on April 19, 1763, after which his son massacred settlers at Mill Creek. In 1768, the Six Nations ceded the Wyoming Valley to Pennsylvania, but the Connecticut company continued operations. Pennsylvania speculators organized a competitive settlement resulting in the Yankee-Pennamite Wars of 1769–1799.

In 1782, Congress awarded the valley to Pennsylvania, but the strife continued. Dissenting settlers were persuaded to accept Pennsylvania's jurisdiction 1799 in return for Pennsylvania's promise of confirmation of their titles. See also Pennamite Wars; Wyoming Valley.

Francis Jennings, *Cedar Crest College*

SUSSEX, a county in southeastern England, extends about 90 miles (145 km) along the coast of the English Channel, and inland to a depth of about 27 miles (43 km). Sussex is mainly agricultural, but towns along the coast are popular as holiday and residential areas. More than half of the county's population is concentrated in this coastal strip.

The coastline is generally low-lying except at two points—east of Hastings and west of Eastbourne, where Beachy Head on the Channel rises to 565 feet (472 meters). These points mark the eastern end of the South Downs, a chalk range that crosses the county from northwest to southeast. North and east of the South Downs are the rich farmlands of the agricultural area called the Weald. Also to the north is the Forest Ridge, the source of the rivers Arun, Adur, and Ouse whose mouths make the harbors of the small Channel seaports of Littlehampton, Shoreham, and Newhaven. Sheep graze the Downs and there are large grain-growing farms.

Chichester has a number of Roman remains and a cathedral dating from the 12th and 13th centuries. Sompting church has a noted Saxon tower, and there are remains of Norman castles at Bramber, Lewes, Hastings, and Pevensey. Battle Abbey, now a ruin at the site of the Battle of Hastings (1066), was built by William the Conqueror to commemorate the first victory in his invasion of England. Architecturally important are the modern Gothic chapel of Lancing College, the University of Sussex at Brighton, and the famous Oriental Royal Pavilion at Brighton built by George IV when Prince of Wales. Goodwood and Petworth mansions have noted art collections. The Royal Observatory, long associated with Greenwich, is now at Herstmonceux. Gatwick Airport is the second most important serving London.

For administrative purposes the county is divided into East Sussex and West Sussex. Population: (1961) East Sussex, 665,904; West Sussex, 411,613; total, 1,077,517.

GORDON STOKES
Author of "English Place-Names"

DR. E. RICKARDS

Sussex spaniel

SUSSEX SPANIEL, a heavily built dog, longer in body than in height, that moves with a rolling gait unlike that of any other spaniel. The Sussex spaniel averages from 15 to 16 inches (38–41 cm) in height at the shoulders and between 35 and 45 pounds (16–20.5 kg) in weight. It has a broad, slightly domed head, with wide nostrils, a deep muzzle, and low-set, drooping ears. The eyes are dark hazel and deeply set. The tail, docked to about one fourth its length, is carried slightly below the level of the back. The Sussex spaniel's coat is characteristically silky and flat, with a good undercoat. It is a rich golden liver in color, each hair having a golden tip.

The Sussex spaniel was developed in England, particularly in Sussex, in the early 1800's. It originated primarily as a gun dog for those hunting on foot in rough brushy areas.

Easily trained, the Sussex spaniel is a relatively slow-moving but determined hunter, with an excellent nose. It can hunt a wide variety of upland game but tends to "give tongue" on the trail. It is a fine devoted companion.

ESTHER RICKARDS
European Spaniel Congress, Oxford, England

SUTHERLAND, George (1862–1942), American judge, ablest of a bloc of conservative members of the U.S. Supreme Court who in the 1920's and 1930's voted to hold unconstitutional a number of social welfare laws, particularly such laws enacted by Congress during the presidency of Franklin D. Roosevelt. Sutherland voted to invalidate laws regulating business, protecting labor unions, setting minimum wages and maximum hours for labor, and providing social security and retirement benefits for workers.

He was born at Stony Stratford, Buckinghamshire, England, on March 25, 1862, and two years later was taken to the United States, where his family settled in Utah. After graduating from Brigham Young University, he attended the University of Michigan law school. In 1896 he became a member of the first Utah state legislature. He served in the U.S. House of Representatives (1901–1903) and the Senate, (1905–1917). In 1922, President Harding appointed him associate justice of the Supreme Court, where he served until 1938. He died in Stockbridge, Mass., on July 18, 1942.

LEO PFEFFER
Author, "This Honorable Court"

SUTHERLAND, Graham Vivian (1903–), English painter, whose works present disquieting parallels between man and nature. In his view, human parallels and correspondences can be read into the forms of landscape, natural growths, insects, and animals. His studies of thorns suggest the agonies of a crucifixion. Mystery and violence are central themes in Sutherland's work.

Sutherland was born in London on Aug. 24, 1903. He attended Goldsmiths' College School of Art in London from 1921 to 1926. He first established a reputation as an engraver of picturesque landscapes in the tradition of Thomas Bewick, Samuel Palmer, and Jean François Millet. When the market for engravings collapsed around 1929, Sutherland turned to the decorative arts and to painting. Between 1935 and 1940 he lived in Wales, where he nurtured his

Graham Sutherland's *Thorn Trees* (1945)

ALBRIGHT-KNOX ART GALLERY, BUFFALO, N. Y.

visual imagination on the wild Welsh landscape. During this period he painted romantically expressive pictures that had resonant contrasts of black against a few sharp, luminous colors. For these paintings, Sutherland evolved a simple, loose style that was both very personal and very English.

During World War II, Sutherland was employed as an official war artist, painting bombed buildings, wrecked machinery, arsenals, flaming structures, and other subjects related to the war. This involvement in human tragedy hastened his artistic maturity, extended his emotional range, and sharpened his vision. During this time he also profited from his first contacts with the work of contemporary European artists.

By 1945, Sutherland was recognized as an original and important artist. Paintings characteristic of his mature style include *Head of Thorns* (1946) and *Three Standing Forms in a Garden* (1952). He also painted portraits of Somerset Maugham (1949), Sir Winston Churchill (1954), Prince Fürstenberg (1959), and Konrad Adenauer (1963). His religious works include *Crucifixion* (1946), in St. Matthew's Church, Northampton, and a gigantic tapestry, *Christ in Majesty* (1957–1962), in Coventry Cathedral.

DOUGLAS COOPER
Author of "The Work of Graham Sutherland"

SUTHERLAND, Joan (1926–), Australian singer, one of the leading 20th century coloratura sopranos and a specialist in the early 19th century bel canto repertory. She was born in Sydney on Nov. 7, 1926. After leaving school, she studied singing in her spare time and in 1950 won the *Sun* aria competition.

She went to London and made her debut at Covent Garden in 1952 as First Lady in Mozart's *Magic Flute.* In 1954, Miss Sutherland married the Australian pianist and aspiring conductor Richard Bonynge, who coached her and persuaded her to specialize in the bel canto repertory. She sang the title role in Handel's *Alcina* for London's Handel Opera Society in 1957.

After studying with the Italian conductor Tullio Serafin, Miss Sutherland scored a triumph at Covent Garden in 1959 in Donizetti's *Lucia di Lammermoor*, then sang regularly at La Scala in Milan, the Metropolitan in New York, and other leading opera houses. Her repertory includes Bellini's *Norma*, Rossini's *Semiramide*, and Verdi's *La Traviata.* She made many recordings, generally with her husband conducting. Although sometimes criticized for faulty diction and a lack of dramatic intensity, she has won wide acclaim for the beauty of her voice and her impeccable technique.

HAROLD ROSENTHAL, *Author of "Great Singers of Today"*

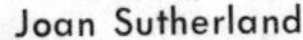

Joan Sutherland

HORST TAPPE-PIX

SUTHERLAND is a county in northwest Scotland, the most desolate and least populated part of Britain. Mostly mountainous or hilly moorland country, Sutherland has great scenic beauty. The coast is sharply indented with sea lochs (inlets), impressive cliffs, and sandy bays. Only 1.5% of its 2,000 square miles (5,260 sq km) is suitable for farming, mostly near the coast. Sheep farming is the main economic activity, with some effort devoted to root crops, cattle, and fishing. There is small-scale production of whiskey, woolens, and bricks. Kinlochbervie is a fishing port; Dornoch, Lochinver, and Brora are small tourist centers. Its climate is variable. It is good country for deer and grouse hunting and for salmon and trout fishing.

Prehistoric remains in Sutherland include unusual Neolithic horned, chambered cairns. Some 80 brochs—circular wall structures with cell complexes within the walls—have been identified, especially near Dornoch Firth in the southeast, striking evidence of flourishing societies after the 1st century A. D. Sutherland experienced temporary Norse occupation in the 11th century. The 13th century cathedral in Dornoch, much rebuilt, is now the parish church. Between 1810 and 1820 the Marquess of Stafford, the future Duke of Sutherland, evicted thousands of tenants to introduce sheep farming. Driven to the coast, these people were further impoverished by the potato famine of 1846. Migration has continued since that time. Population: (1961) 13,507.

C. J. BARTLETT, *University of Dundee*

SUTLEJ RIVER, sut'lej, in Asia, the easternmost and longest tributary of the Indus river. It rises in Tibet and flows northwest to India, where it travels generally westward through the Zaskar, Great and Lesser Himalaya, and Siwalik ranges and onto the Punjab plain, there receiving the Beas River. It then turns southwest, forming part of the border between India and West Pakistan and finally flowing through West Pakistan into the Indus river. Its total course is over 900 miles (1,400 km). Its lowermost section, after it receives the Chenab River, is called the Panjnad, or Five Rivers, because it carries the waters of the Sutlej, Beas, Chenab, Ravi, and Jhelum.

The Sutlej is important both for irrigation and for hydroelectric power. The use of its water was long a cause of dispute between India and Pakistan, especially because of India's construction of the huge Bhakrā-Nangal project to divert water for irrigation and hydroelectric power. The dispute was resolved by treaty in 1960. See also INDUS—*Water Management.*

JOSEPH E. SCHWARTZBERG
University of Minnesota

SŪTRA, sōō′trə, in Hinduism, a collection of brief rules pertaining to ritual, law, or custom. The term was used originally in the Brahmanic literature of the 2d millennium B.C. to designate aphoristic rules describing details of the Vedic sacrifice. The Sanskrit word *sūtra* means "thread" or "cord" and is derived from the root *siv*, "sew." The word probably refers to the aim of "sewing" together the separate parts of the ritual—in their proper sequence—with accompanying Vedic stanzas. The Pali and Prakrit form of the word Sūtra is "Sutta."

Brevity of statement was an aim of the Sūtras, and the aphorisms would frequently be unintelligible without the commentary that has long accompanied them. The Sūtra style was also used for manuals to teach grammar and philosophy. Later the use of the term Sūtra was relaxed, and it was applied to original textbooks (as distinguished from explanatory works) on those subjects and to expositions of household religious ceremonies and codes of behavior.

In Buddhism and Jainism a Sūtra, or Sutta, is a Sanskrit, Pali, or Prakrit work that teaches doctrine, preaches sermons, or narrates the lives or deeds of persons who have been prominent in the faith.

W. NORMAN BROWN
Author of "Man in the Universe: Some Continuities in Indian Thought"

SUTTEE, sə-tē′, was a custom, formerly practiced in India, in which a widow sacrificed her own life after the death of her husband. The Sanskrit word *satī* means "virtuous woman," or "faithful and devoted wife." Since the self-immolation of a widow on her husband's funeral pyre came to be regarded in India as the supreme demonstration of wifely devotion, early British officials and missionaries erroneously used the word *satī* (suttee) to designate the practice itself, as well as the devoted wife.

Legal actions in 1829 and 1830 effectively killed the custom of suttee in the parts of India that were under British rule at that time. It survived longer in other areas of India, however, and rare instances of suttee have been reported even in the 20th century.

The origin of widow-burning in India is unknown. It is not mentioned in early Brahmanical literature, although a passage in a funeral hymn in the Rig Veda admonishing a woman to rise from beside her dead husband's body as it lies on the funeral pyre has sometimes been taken as evidence that at some still earlier time widow-burning must have been practiced.

The first recorded instance of the practice in India appears in Greek accounts of Alexander the Great's invasion in the 4th century B.C. By the 6th century A.D., memorial *satī* stones were being erected. Some tribes in central Asia practiced widow-burning, and their members may have helped spread the practice when they entered India.

The custom is first reported chiefly among Kshatriya (princely or noble) families. In later centuries, it also appears among Brahman families. By such self-immolation a woman won happiness for herself and her husband in a future existence and brought fame to her family in this one.

W. NORMAN BROWN
Author of "Man in the Universe: Some Continuities in Indian Thought"

SUTTER, John Augustus (1803–1880), American pioneer. Wily and visionary, Sutter established a personal empire in the California wilderness. However, when gold was discovered at his sawmill in the Sacramento Valley in 1848, his land was overrun by squatters, and he lost his fortune in the gold rush that followed.

Sutter, originally Johann August Suter, was born in Kandern, Baden, Germany, on Feb. 15, 1803. Little is known about his youth except that he lived for some time in Switzerland. He emigrated to the United States in 1834, supposedly to escape imprisonment for debt and the anger of his wife. Arriving in New York, he traveled across the United States to Santa Fe and Oregon and then to Hawaii and Alaska before settling in California in 1839.

California at the time was a territory of Mexico, and Sutter obtained permission from the Mexican governor to occupy a 50,000-acre (20,000-hectare) tract in the Sacramento Valley near the junction of the Sacramento and American rivers. He became a Mexican citizen and served as a semiofficial representative of the Mexican government.

Sutter's Fort. In 1840, with the help of Hawaiian and Indian laborers, Sutter began to construct an adobe fort to guard his holdings. His colony, which he named "New Helvetia," grew into a kind of barony, with irrigated fields, orchards, and large numbers of sheep, cattle, horses, and hogs. It became a trade center and rendezvous for newcomers winding down the trails over the Sierra Nevada, all of whom received a hearty welcome. General Sutter, as he was called, became a trapper, farmer, stock raiser, merchant, and military ruler. He had authority to administer justice, prevent robberies, repel Indian attacks, and to check illegal trapping and fishing.

In 1844, Sutter's son, John, arrived from Germany to share in his father's prosperity. The rest of the family followed within a few years. By this time Sutter had become interested in the movement toward statehood, and his friendliness toward Americans irritated local Mexicans. Sutter might have become a California political leader but for an odd turn of fortune.

The Gold Rush. On Jan. 24, 1848, a carpenter employed by Sutter, James W. Marshall, discovered gold while building a sawmill on Sutter's property. Nine days later, Mexico signed the Treaty of Guadalupe Hidalgo, ceding California to the United States. Sutter's title to his land under American law was questioned, and he was unable to protect his property from the stream of squatters that swarmed over it in search of gold. By 1852 he was bankrupt. He spent most of the rest of his life appealing in vain to the state and federal governments for compensation of his losses. From 1864 to 1878 he received a pension of $250 a month from the state of California. Bills for his relief were introduced in Congress in 1876 and 1880, but no action was taken.

In 1873, Sutter moved to the Moravian village of Lititz, Pa. He was seeking redress in Washington, D.C., when he died on June 18, 1880. See also FORTY-NINERS; SACRAMENTO.

ANDREW F. ROLLE, *Occidental College*

Further Reading: Gudde, Erwin G., *Sutter's Own Story* (New York 1936); Sutter, J. A., *The Diary of Johann Augustus Sutter* (San Francisco 1932); Zollinger, J. P., *Sutter: The Man and His Empire* (New York 1939).

SUTTNER, zo͞ot′nər, **Bertha von** (1843–1914), Austrian novelist and pacifist who won the 1905 Nobel Peace Prize. Born in Prague on July 9, 1843, she was the daughter of Count Franz Joseph Kinsky, a retired officer in the Austrian army. In 1874 she became the governess to the children of Baron Arthur von Suttner, whose son Arthur she married two years later.

Baroness von Suttner published more than a dozen novels on social issues. Her most compelling work, *Die Waffen nieder!* (1889; Eng. tr., *Lay Down Your Arms!*, 1892), recounts the tribulations of a fictional noblewoman, Martha von Tilling, during four contemporary wars. Its huge popular success aroused initially enthusiastic support for her Austrian Peace Society (1891). She maintained a correspondence with Alfred Nobel during the last 20 years of his life, and her ideas may have influenced the founding of the Nobel Peace Prize. In 1905 she became the first woman to win that honor.

Baroness von Suttner edited the pacifist journal *Die Waffen nieder!* (1892–1899), and she attended most of the congresses on world peace. She died in Vienna on June 21, 1914.

MICHAEL WINKLER
Rice University

SUTTON HOO SHIP BURIAL, sut′ən ho͞o, an archaeological find made in Suffolk, England, in 1939. It consists of the remains of an ancient wooden ship, laden with treasure, which was apparently the grave of a 7th century king of East Anglia. To make a tomb the ship had been lowered into a trench and then covered with a mound of earth. Coins found among the grave goods make it possible to date the burial between 650 and 670 A. D.

The ship was 86 feet (25 meters) long—longer even than later Viking vessels. The wooden parts of the ship had rotted away, but the shape of the vessel could be traced in the sand. The burial find is remarkable for the artistic value of the objects contained in it, no less than for the costliness of the treasure. The rich contents of the grave provide an excellent insight into the skilled crafts of the period and into the contacts that East Anglia maintained with parts of Europe. Among the finds were gold coins, splendid jewelry, a highly ornamented iron helmet with face mask, remains of a harp, and numerous objects of gold, silver, bronze, bone, leather, wood, horn, and stone.

ERIKA BOURGUIGNON
The Ohio State University

SUTTON HOO SHIP outlined in earth. Its timbers had rotted away long before burial mound was discovered.

THE BRITISH MUSEUM

SUVA, so͞o′vä, is the capital and chief port of Fiji in the southwestern Pacific Ocean. It is situated on the southeastern coast of Viti Levu, the largest of the Fiji Islands. Suva's reef-fringed harbor is a major stop for passenger and cargo ships en route between Australia and North America and is a focus of South Pacific inter-island shipping.

The city's population includes Europeans, Indians, Chinese, and Polynesians as well as Fijians. The major economic activities are food processing, coconut oil extraction, the manufacture of clothing and souvenirs, and tourism. The University of the South Pacific was established at nearby Laucala Bay in 1967. Suva has been the capital of Fiji since 1882. Population: (1966) 54,157.

HOWARD J. CRITCHFIELD
Western Washington State College

SUVOROV, so͞o-vô′rəf, **Count Aleksandr Vasilievich** (1729–1800), Russian field marshal and one of the greatest generals in Russian history. He was born in Moscow on Nov. 24, 1729. Suvorov began his military career as a private in the czarist army. After participating in lengthy campaigns against Sweden and Prussia, he achieved the rank of colonel in 1762. During the Russian-Polish war of 1768–1772, he was promoted to major general. In the Russian-Turkish war of 1773–1774, Suvorov distinguished himself and began to achieve national fame.

He fought the Turks again during the war of 1787–1792, and his victory at Rymnik (1788) won him the official Russian title of Count Rymniksky. During the same war, after his capture of the Bessarabian city of Izmail (1790), his troops massacred much of the city's civilian population. He was promoted in 1794 to the rank of field marshal after a successful campaign against Poland, during which his troops conducted another massacre in Praga, a suburb of Warsaw. In 1796, however, Suvorov's military career almost ended when the new Russian emperor, Paul I, dismissed him for objecting to the introduction of Prussian uniforms and drill into the Russian army.

Paul was forced to recall Suvorov to active duty in 1799, to lead Russian troops against the French revolutionary forces controlling northern Italy. Suvorov quickly drove the French out of Italy, thus earning a new official title, Prince Italisky. Then in one of the most famous marches in military history, he took his army over Saint Gotthard Pass into central Switzerland, despite snow, fog, bitter cold, and avalanches. But the second Russian army, which Suvorov had planned to support, had already been defeated by the French at Zürich. So Suvorov retreated eastward from the Swiss mountains, saving most of his troops. Again he was dismissed, and he died in disgrace in St. Petersburg (now Leningrad) on May 18, 1800. However, a year after Suvorov's death, a monument to his memory was erected in St. Petersburg by Alexander I, the new Russian emperor.

FLORIDA NEWS BUREAU DEPARTMENT OF COMMERCE

SUWANNEE RIVER, made famous by the songwriter Stephen Foster, flows through wild country in Florida.

From the 1917 Bolshevik Revolution until the mid-1930's, Soviet historians condemned Suvorov as a brutal czarist imperialist. Thereafter he was praised as a Russian patriot. Since 1943, the order of Suvorov has been the highest Soviet military decoration, and the army cadet schools (training children from 8 to 18 years of age) have been named Suvorov schools.

ELLSWORTH RAYMOND
New York University

SUWANNEE RIVER, sə-wän′ē, in southeast Georgia and northwest Florida, made famous in a song by the 19th century American songwriter Stephen Foster, who never saw the river. It drains part of Georgia, including most of Okeefenokee Swamp, enters a scenic limestone gorge near White Springs, Fla., and for most of its twisting middle course is spring-fed. The Suwannee empties into the Gulf of Mexico about 55 miles (90 km) southwest of Gainesville, Fla. It drains about 9,830 square miles (3,735 sq km) and is about 240 miles (386 km) long.

The river and its streamside springs, together with an almost primitive riverine strip of cypress and bottom hardwoods, have a high recreation potential. The proposal has been made that the Suwannee be protected as part of the U. S. wild and scenic rivers system under the Wild Rivers Act.

The Suwannee has never been important for transport and has no significant hydropower potential. Its headwaters are in a low unproductive swamp only 120 feet (36 meters) above sea level, its central portion is entrenched in a relatively infertile limestone surface, and it traverses coastal swamps and marshes before emptying into shallow Suwannee Sound.

CLARK I. CROSS, *University of Florida*

SUZDAL, sōōz′dəl, was a medieval Russian principality, combined at different periods with Rostov, Vladimir, and Nizhni Novgorod. It is regarded by many historians as the nucleus of the future Muscovite state.

Suzdal's location between the upper Volga and Oka rivers contributed to its growth and prosperity. Its forests gave it military security, and the trade routes that passed through it, connecting Novgorod with the east and south, stimulated its economy.

Its rulers were an even more important factor in Suzdal's rise in the 12th and 13th centuries. In 1095 young Yuri Dolgoruky was appointed by his father, the future grand prince of Kiev, to rule as the first prince of Suzdal. Yuri strengthened the principality and defended it against the Bulgars. Under his two sons and successors, Andrew and Vsevolod, princely power was greatly increased and was stronger in Suzdal than in any other part of Russia.

To escape boyar (noble) interference with his authority, Andrew changed his residence from the town of Suzdal to Vladimir, and then to the nearby village of Bogolyubov, after which he became known as Andrew Bogolyubsky. In 1169 he sacked Kiev and assumed the title of grand prince, but he continued to reside in the principality of Suzdal. His power struggle with the boyars led to a boyar conspiracy and his murder in 1174. Suzdal gradually declined as its lands were subdivided within the princely family, and after it was overrun by the Tatars in 1238. It was absorbed in the 15th century by Moscow. The town of Suzdal is now only a village.

CHARLES MORLEY, *Ohio State University*

SUZERAINTY, sōō′zə-rən-tē, in international law, means control or guardianship by one state of another state's foreign affairs. It is derived from a medieval term used to describe the relationship between lord, or suzerain, and vassal in feudalism.

In principle, suzerainty implies loss by the vassal state of capacity to act internationally but retention of its separate territorial existence and of autonomy in domestic affairs. The vassal state is thus reduced to half-sovereignty and dependence. In return the suzerain protects it and is, in principle, internationally responsible for it. In practice, the exact international legal position of the vassal depends on the relevant legal instruments and usage.

Formerly Korea was a vassal of China, as were Egypt of Ottoman Turkey and Indian princely states of Britain. Andorra is still formally under the joint suzerainty of France and Spain. In general, however, both in theory and in practice, suzerainty is an institution of the past.

GEORGE MANNER, *University of Illinois*

SUZUKA, sōō-zōō-kä, a city in Japan, is an agricultural and industrial center in Mie prefecture, southern Honshu. It is situated on the western shore of Ise Bay, about 30 miles (48 km) southwest of Nagoya. Suzuka was formed in the early 1940's when the cities of Shiroko and Kambe were merged.

Suzuka is noted for its kimono dyeing industry. The city is also a summer resort. Among the places of interest in the area are several shrines and the Suzuka Circuit, an auto raceway that can accommodate 200,000 spectators. Population: (1965) 100,594.

SVALBARD, sfäl'bär, Norwegian Arctic islands including the Spitsbergen archipelago, Bear Island, Hope Island, and some smaller islands in the Norwegian and Barents seas 200 to 400 miles (320–645 km) north of Norway. Spitsbergen, the main group of large islands, includes West Spitsbergen and Prince Charles Foreland off its west coast, North East Land, Barents Island, and Edge Island. The Spitsbergen archipelago covers about 23,700 square miles (62,370 sq km) and the total Svalbard land area is about 24,000 square miles (63,158 sq km).

Much of the archipelago is underlain by strongly folded, upturned, and overthrust sandstones, slates, and limestones called the Hecla Hoek system. Younger sedimentary rocks are widely distributed, and many contain coal. Basalt sills have been intruded at several places and there are some small volcanic cones and hot springs. The Arctic climate is stormy and relatively mild on the west coast but much colder and quieter on the eastern side. The islands are intensely glaciated, although many peaks pierce the snow fields in the west and numerous valleys there are ice-free.

The islands are first mentioned in Icelandic annals of 1194 A.D. The group was rediscovered by the Dutch navigator Willem Barents in 1596. Whaling became important in Spitsbergen waters in the 17th century, and small catches have been continued to the present day. During the 18th and 19th centuries Russians and Scandinavians trapped game on the islands. Later, coal was discovered there. The principal mining activity has centered at Longyearbyen, the islands' administrative center on Isfjorden.

In 1920 the League of Nations placed Svalbard under Norwegian control. During World War II, Spitsbergen suffered severely from successive occupation by the British, the Germans, and the Norwegians. In 1944 the German navy destroyed nearly all the settlements.

At the beginning of the 1970's the number of Norwegians wintering at Spitsbergen was about 1,200 and their annual export of coal between 300,000 and 400,000 tons. The Russians, with a winter population of about 2,500, may export 300,000 tons.

J. Brian Bird, *McGill University*

SVEDBERG, svād'bar-yə, **Theodor** (1884–1971), Swedish physical chemist, who won the Nobel Prize in chemistry in 1926 for his invention of the ultracentrifuge and related accomplishments. He was born in Valbo, Gastrikland, on Aug. 30, 1884. He studied at Uppsala University, where he taught from 1912 to 1949, when he founded the Gustaf Wenners Institute for Nuclear Chemistry at Uppsala, of which he became director. He died in Stockholm on Feb. 26, 1971.

As early as 1909, several years before the term "isotope" was coined, Svedberg and D. Strömholm demonstrated, apparently for the first time, the existence of elements with identical chemical properties but different atomic weights. Svedberg was one of the first to verify experimentally the theory worked out by Einstein and others that the Brownian motion of colloidal solutions obeys exactly the molecular kinetic theory of gases and the laws of ideal solutions.

While a visiting professor at the University of Wisconsin in 1923 he built, with the assistance of J. B. Nichols, the first optical centrifuge. Svedberg then developed and improved this instrument at Uppsala, to provide the ultracentrifuge and with it, a group of methods, now widely used, for determining molecular weight and molecular weight distribution of molecules of intermediate and large sizes. He showed that globular, soluble proteins are molecules in the chemical sense, having definite molecular weights in solution. These studies were of enormous significance in making the techniques of physical chemistry useful to biology and medicine.

J. W. Williams
University of Wisconsin

SVENGALI, sfen-gä'lē, is a character in George du Maurier's novel *Trilby* (1894), who through hypnotic power transforms the heroine, Trilby, into a great singer. See Trilby.

SVERDLOV, svyerd-lôf', **Yakov Mikhailovich** (1885–1919), Russian Communist revolutionary and first head of the Soviet state. He was born on June 4, 1885, in Nizhni Novgorod (now Gorky) and joined the Russian Social Democratic Workers' party at the age of 15. He sided with Lenin's Bolsheviks when the party split in 1903. Sverdlov headed the Bolshevik underground in the Urals from 1905 to 1907, and then was imprisoned.

Sverdlov rejoined the underground in 1909 but was rearrested and exiled to Siberia. He fled twice but was recaptured. He was finally released after the fall of the czar in the winter of 1917. Sverdlov was appointed chairman of the All-Russian Central Executive Committee, becoming titular head of state when the Bolsheviks seized power in the fall of 1917. He died of pneumonia on March 16, 1919, in Moscow.

Theodore Shabad
Editor of "Soviet Geography"

SVERDLOVSK, svyerd-lôfsk', a city in the USSR, is the capital of Sverdlovsk oblast, in the Ural Mountains. The largest city and industrial center of the Urals economic region, Sverdlovsk is situated on the Iset River at the junction of several rail lines and a network of highways. The city is an important manufacturing center, with heavy machinery, electric turbines, and chemical equipment accounting for half of the industrial production. The city's Uralmash plant is one of the principal Soviet producers of machinery for the iron and steel and petroleum industries.

Sverdlovsk has a dozen institutions of higher learning, including the Urals A. M. Gorky State University and the Urals Polytechnic Institute. As the seat of the Urals branch of the Soviet Academy of Sciences, the city is a research center for the region's industries. Most of the Urals' administrative agencies have their headquarters here.

The city arose in 1723 as the center of the old Urals copper- and ironworking district. It was named Yekaterinburg, for Catherine (Yekaterina) I, Peter the Great's wife. It acquired a mint in 1735 for copper coinage and a jewel-cutting factory in 1765. An early 18th century route to Siberia led through the town. After the Bolshevik Revolution of 1917, the last Russian czar, Nicholas II, and his family were executed here. In 1924 the city was renamed for Yakov M. Sverdlov, the first Soviet president.

Sverdlovsk oblast, an administrative division of the Russian republic, is situated on the eastern slopes of the Ural Mountains. It is drained by the Tavda, Tura, and Iset rivers, western tributaries of the Tobol. The region's forests limit farming opportunities. The economy is based largely on rich mineral resources, which include iron ore, bauxite (for aluminum), copper, gold, platinum, and asbestos. The principal cities, aside from Sverdlovsk, are the iron and steel centers of Nizhni Tagil and Serov and the aluminum centers of Kamensk-Uralski and Krasnoturinsk. The oblast has an area of 75,200 square miles (194,800 sq km). Population: (1970) of the city, 1,026,000; of the oblast, 4,319,000.

THEODORE SHABAD, *Editor, "Soviet Geography"*

SVERDRUP, svar′drəp, **Otto Neumann** (1854–1930), Norwegian Arctic explorer. He was born in Bindal, Helgeland district, Norway, on Oct. 31, 1854, and went to sea at the age of 17. In 1888, with the Norwegian explorer Fridtjof Nansen, he made the first crossing of the Greenland ice cap. From 1893 to 1896 he was with Nansen on his first attempt to reach the North Pole, in the specially constructed ship, the *Fram*. He was left in command of the *Fram* in 1895 when Nansen tried, unsuccessfully, to sledge to the pole.

In 1898, Sverdrup took the *Fram* on a 4-year exploration of the northern islands of the Canadian Arctic Archipelago. The island group southwest of Ellesmere Island is now known as the Sverdrup Islands. His discoveries formed the basis for Norway's claims to part of the Canadian Arctic. These were not relinquished until shortly before Sverdrup's death, when the Canadian government paid him $67,000.

In 1914, Sverdrup directed a search for a Russian ship lost in the Kara Sea. He returned to the waters north of Siberia in 1921, leading five ships in a pioneering exploration of the Russian northern sea route. Sverdrup died in Copenhagen on Nov. 26, 1930.

J. BRIAN BIRD, *McGill University*

SVERDRUP ISLANDS, sfer′drəp, in northern Canada, in the Arctic Ocean west of Ellesmere Island. The group includes Axel Heiberg and the Ringnes Islands. They were named for Otto Neumann Sverdrup, a Norwegian explorer. Norway claimed sovereignty over the islands, but shortly before Sverdrup's death in 1930 this claim was relinquished to Canada.

SVERRE, sver′ə (1152?–1202), was king of Norway. He was born of a Norwegian mother in the Faerøe Islands about 1152 and was ordained a priest while very young. He attempted to justify his claim to the Norwegian throne through an alleged statement by his mother that he had been fathered by a Norwegian king.

Sverre left the Faerøes for Norway about 1174. He soon emerged as the head of a group called the Birchlegs and led them against Ersling and his son Magnus IV of Norway. Sverre inflicted a crushing defeat on his enemies in 1179 and killed Magnus at Fimreite in 1184. Sverre's reign was marked by his struggle with the Church, in which he successfully asserted his belief in the divine right of kings despite his excommunication by Innocent III. Sverre's ability to control the landed aristocracy laid the foundations of Norway's strong medieval state. He died in Bergen on March 9, 1202.

SVEVO, zvä′vō, **Italo** (1861–1928), Italian novelist. He was born Ettore Schmitz in Trieste on Dec. 19, 1861. After pursuing commercial studies at the wish of his father, who was a businessman, Svevo worked for many years as a bank employee and later as the manager of a paint factory. He did most of his writing in his spare time and was almost totally unknown to Italian literary circles for much of his life. However, he early won the admiration and friendship of James Joyce, whose acquaintance he made in Trieste in 1903. Svevo died in Motta di Livenza on Sept. 13, 1928.

Svevo's first two novels, *Una vita* (1892; Eng. tr., *A Life*, 1963) and *Senilità* (1898; Eng. tr., *As a Man Grows Older*, 1932) were unsuccessful when first published. After the appearance of his third novel, *La coscienza di Zeno* (1923; Eng. tr., *The Confessions of Zeno*, 1930), he was belatedly recognized as a major Italian author of fiction. His novels, characterized by fine introspective analyses and vivid stream-of-consciousness narration, have been compared to those of Proust and Joyce.

JOHN CHARLES NELSON, *Columbia University*

SVOBODA, svô′bô-də, **Ludvík** (1895–), Czechoslovak government official and military leader. He was born in Hroznatín, Moravia, on Nov. 25, 1895. He fought with the Czech legion in Russia in World War I and became a career army officer. In World War II he commanded a Czechoslovak corps in the Soviet Union.

After the war Svoboda became Czechoslovak defense minister and a deputy premier, throwing the army's support behind the Communist coup in February 1948. In 1948 he also joined the Communist party, but during the Stalinist purges of the early 1950's he was imprisoned. He was "rehabilitated" in 1956 and made commandant of the Klement Gottwald Military Academy, retiring in 1959. He succeeded the Stalinist Antonín Novotný as president in 1968. As president and a member of the Presidium of the party's Central Committee he supported the liberalization of communism in Czechoslovakia.

JOSEPH F. ZACEK
State University of New York at Albany

SVYATOSLAV I, svyə-tə-sláf′ (reigned 945–972) was grand prince of Kiev. He attempted to extend the boundaries of Kievan Russia to include the valleys of the Dnieper, lower Volga, and lower Danube rivers. Svyatoslav assumed the title of grand prince on the death of his father, Igor, in 945. His mother, Olga, was regent until he reached maturity. Thereafter he allowed Olga to administer internal affairs while he devoted his energies to military campaigns.

A skillful and indefatigable leader, he began his military expeditions in 963 with an attack on the Khazars, whose empire between the Don and the Volga he destroyed. Being of restless character, he readily responded to the Byzantine emperor's request for assistance against the Bulgars. He defeated them on the Danube in 967 and took up residence at Preslavets near the mouth of the Danube. Later, however, he was attacked by his former Byzantine allies and was defeated by them in 971. Under the peace terms, Svyatoslav had to abandon Bulgaria. In 972, on his way back to Kiev, Svyatoslav was ambushed by the Pechenegs and killed.

CHARLES MORLEY, *Ohio State University*

SWABIA, swā'bē-ə, is an indefinite area in southern Germany, bounded by the Rhine in the west, by the Lech River in the east, by Vorarlberg and Switzerland on the south, and by the Palatinate on the north. Swabia or Suabia is called Schwaben in German.

In the 1st century B.C., the ancient Celts of the area were replaced by the Germanic Suevi. The Suevi amalgamated with the Alamanni, who arrived about the 3d century A.D., to form the Swabians, one of the historic German ethnic groups. They developed a distinct dialect and a kinship, which, to their pride, distinguishes them from other Germans.

The Duchy. The Swabian lands were conquered by the Frankish king Clovis in 496, after which Swabian dukes, who acknowledged formal Frankish suzerainty, administered the territory with increasing independence. In the 7th century the Swabians were converted by Irish monks with the aid of the bishops of Constance and Augsburg. Charles Martel and Charlemagne again asserted Frankish suzerainty in the 8th century, but the dukes maintained their independent rule. In the early Middle Ages the Roman name Alamannia was still often used for the duchy, but by the 11th century the term Swabia was finally established.

Henry IV of Germany gave the duchy to his son-in-law, Frederick I of Hohenstaufen, in 1079, and the Hohenstaufens enlarged its territory. On the death of Conradin, the last of the Hohenstaufen dynasty, in 1268, the duchy ceased to exist. He had enfeoffed most of the land to the duke of Württemberg, and the rest was now partitioned among other lords.

Later History. In 1488 some of the region's independent cities and lesser principalities, seeking mutual protection and a voice in their affairs, formed the Swabian League, which maintained a precarious existence until 1534, when religious squabbles brought its dissolution. When the empire was divided into 10 administrative circles in the 16th century, one was called the Swabian Circle. Much of the region became Protestant at the time of the Reformation. In the final territorial reorganization of the Napoleonic period, the Swabian lands were divided among several neighboring states.

ERNST C. HELMREICH, *Bowdoin College*

SWAHILI, swä-hē'lē, is the language of the coastal population of East Africa, roughly from southern Somalia to Mozambique, and including Zanzibar and the Comoro Islands. It is spoken by about 1.5 million people as a first language. In addition, several million people in East Africa and Congo (Kinshasa) are fluent in Swahili and use it constantly as the language of wider communication outside the context of family and tribe. In the mid-20th century, Swahili (*kiSwahili*) became the symbol of national unity in Tanzania and was one of the tools of political action leading to independence in Kenya as well. This probably accounts for its symbolic value as the language of "black power" and "liberation" among Afro-Americans.

Swahili actually consists of a number of strongly differentiated dialects, some of which are mutually unintelligible. The dialect of Lamu in northeastern Kenya gained particular prestige as a model for usage in traditional Swahili poetry, but *kiUnguja*, the dialect of the city of Zanzibar, was ultimately recognized as "standard" Swahili.

The linguistic diversity within the Swahili-speaking area is due to Swahili's origin as a language of wider communication among closely related Bantu tribal groups under the influence of Arab trade. The Arabs, sailing down the coast of the Indian Ocean, developed close commercial relations with eastern Africa, and as Arab caravan routes and settlements penetrated deeper inland, Swahili spread as a lingua franca. In the second half of the 19th century, Swahili was used by missionaries and colonial administrators among populations having extremely diversified vernaculars.

Linguistic Features. Swahili is a Bantu language with a rather simple sound system. Nouns are grouped by class as denoted by characteristic prefixes for the singular and plural: *m-ti*, "tree," "wood," plural *mi-ti*; *ki-ti*, "wooden stool," "chair," plural *vi-ti*. This class system entails agreement between the noun and adjectives, verbs, and other words that it governs: *wa-toto w-angu wa-le wa-dogo wa-naimba*, "those little children of mine are singing." Verb forms consist of an agglutination of various components. Thus *hayapatikani*, "they [eggs] are not obtainable," is composed of the negative prefix *ha-*, the subject prefix *ya-* (corresponding to the class of mayai, "eggs"), the verbal root *pat-* ("get"), the complex suffix *-ik-an-* (indicating what can be done), and the final suffix *-i* (marking a negative present). Several suffixes can be appended to the root of a verb to add special semantic connotations to its basic meaning: *penda*, "love"; *pendwa*, "be loved"; *pendeka*, "be lovable"; *pendekeza*, "cause to be loved"; "*pendeza*," "please"; *pendezesha*, "cause to please," "make popular"; *pendezana*, "be mutually agreeable."

Swahili's vocabulary is basically Bantu but contains many Arabic loanwords. There are also numerous words from Persian, Indian languages, and Portuguese. English is now the main source of loanwords, although a deliberate effort is made to coin specifically Swahili words to cover the fields of modern technical knowledge.

Literature. Swahili has a rich traditional literature consisting mainly of poetry of Islamic inspiration. Nonreligious epic poetry celebrates the heroes of the past. Some didactic poems provide interesting data on Swahili everyday life or on historical events of the 19th century. The composition of poetry according to classical patterns is still highly regarded in the Swahili homeland along the coast. The best pieces are usually published in the newspapers.

One of the best known Swahili writers is Shaaban Robert (1909–1962) of Tanzania, who played a prominent part in the renewal of Swahili writing. An excellent Swahili version of the Koran was produced in 1969 by Abdullah Saleh el-Farsy. The Christian missions published a considerable amount of religious literature, some of it in beautiful Swahili prose.

EDGAR C. POLOMÉ, *University of Texas, Austin*

Bibliography

Harries, Lyndon, ed. and tr., *Swahili Poetry* (New York and London 1962).
Knappert, Jan, *Traditional Swahili Poetry* (Leiden, Netherlands, 1967).
Polomé, Edgar C., *Swahili Language Handbook* (Washington 1967).
Rechenbach, Charles, *Swahili-English Dictionary* (Washington 1968).
Stevick, E., and others, *Swahili Basic Course* (Washington 1963).
Whitely, Wilfred, *Swahili: The Rise of a National Language* (London 1969).
Wilson, Peter, *Simplified Swahili* (Nairobi 1970).

SWALLOW, any of a large family of small insect-eating birds that feed on the wing. Swallows are found throughout the world except for the polar areas, New Zealand, and some oceanic islands. Certain species of swallows are sometimes known as *martins*, and some confusion sometimes results from the interchangeable use of the two names. For example, the bank swallow (*Riparia riparia*) of North America is also found in Europe, where it is known as the sand martin. In North America, the term martin is reserved for a large species of swallow—the purple martin (*Progne subis*). The best known swallow is the cosmopolitan *Hirundo rustica*, called the swallow by the British, the chimney swallow by the Germans and French, and the barn swallow in the United States and Canada.

Swallows are well liked for their friendly, twittering song. They figure in many legends and are often considered to herald spring. Their insect-eating habits also benefit man.

Description. Swallows are 3¾ to 9 inches (10–23 cm) long. The body is slender and sleek, with a short neck, the tail often long and forked, and the wings long and pointed. The bill is small and triangular, but the mouth is large and has bristles that help form an effective aerial insect scoop. Their plumage is compact and often has a metallic sheen. Swallows may be black or shades of brown, chestnut, metallic greens, and blues, and they often have patches of white. The sexes look alike in most species.

Behavior. Swallows spend most of their time on the wing, and although they are graceful and fast in flight they are no match for the faster swifts, with which they are often confused but are not related. They perch readily but seldom walk, as their legs are very short. They are migratory. They feed entirely on insects, and are dependent on the presence of insects in the air, which is, in turn, dependent on a warm temperature. When swallows are caught by unexpected cold weather, they eat bayberries.

Reproduction. Most swallow species are colonial, with large nesting colonies often numbering hundreds of pairs. Some are semicolonial, and still others are solitary. Swallows differ widely in the types of nests they construct. The most elaborate nests are intricately engineered structures made of hundreds of small mud balls plastered together. The female alone usually constructs the nest, but the male forms the small mud balls with his bill and carries them to the nest site in his mouth. The nest may consist of an open cup attached to a vertical surface or an elaborate retort-shaped nest attached to both a vertical and an overhead horizontal surface. The nest entrance is usually just large enough to permit the bird to enter. The mud shell of the nest is reinforced with grass, and the nest is lined with fine grasses and feathers.

Other swallows, such as the tree swallow (*Iridoprocne bicolor*) of North America, are cavity-nesters, using natural cavities in trees or abandoned woodpecker holes. They usually line the cavities with grass and feathers. A third type of nest builder is the burrow-nester, such as the bank swallow (*Riparia riparia*) which excavates nest holes 24 to 48 inches (61–122 cm) deep into sand banks. A crude nest of grass stems is made at the inner end of the burrow, and feathers are added as the eggs are laid.

Swallow eggs, three to six in number, are pure white or lightly speckled with brown. The female alone incubates the eggs, but the male assists in feeding the young. Some species, such as the barn swallow, raise up to three broods a year, and the young of the earlier broods often aid in feeding the young of later broods.

Classification. There are about 75 species of swallows classified in many genera making up the family Hirundinidae, order Passeriformes.

KENNETH E. STAGER
Los Angeles County Museum of Natural History

SWALLOW TANAGER, tan′ə-jər, a brilliant blue-green bird found in humid lowlands from Panama to Argentina and on the island of Trinidad. It is about 6 inches (15 cm) long with long wings, short legs, and a wide flat bill. The wings and tail are black, and the flanks are heavily barred with black. Males have a black facial mask that covers the throat. Females have a gray mask and are generally greener.

The swallow tanager lives in treetops. It feeds on insects captured in flight and on small

HUGH HALLIDAY FROM NATIONAL AUDUBON SOCIETY

PARENT CLIFF SWALLOWS (*left*) look out from mud nest, usually built under eaves.
BARN SWALLOW (*below*) in flight, showing characteristic long primary flight feathers.

LEONARD LEE RUE FROM ANNAN PHOTO

PAUL SCHWARTZ, FROM PHOTO RESEARCHERS

Swallow tanager

fruits. After using its bill to scrape off the fruit pulp, the bird often discards the pits and stores the pulp in its unusual distensible throat pouch. Once the breeding season starts, the swallow tanager moves to mountain forests, and the males become strongly territorial. Mating pairs nest in earthen burrows, tree hollows, and crevices. The female alone incubates the three eggs, but the male helps feed the young.

The swallow tanager, *Tersina viridis*, is classified alone in the family Tersinidae of the order Passeriformes.

JOSEPH BELL
New York Zoological Park

SWALLOWING is the complex act for moving food or other substances from the mouth into the upper portion of the esophagus. When eating, swallowing begins as a voluntary act. At other times, swallowing is involuntary and may occur as often as two or three times a minute, even during sleep.

Swallowing is initiated by the contraction of the muscles of the cheek and tongue. This contraction forces the food from the front of the mouth toward the pharynx (throat). By means of a series of sequential muscular movements, the soft palate rises to close off the opening into the nasal cavities as the base of the tongue and faucial pillars (the two arches at the back of the mouth) propel the food into the throat. A squeezing action of the pharyngeal constrictor muscles then forces the food downward into the upper esophagus where a series of peristaltic waves carries it into the stomach. The epiglottis, a thin leaflike structure of cartilage, serves as a lid for the larynx (voicebox) so that food does not enter the larynx. Also during swallowing the opening of the larynx constricts, further preventing the entry of food.

JAMES R. CHANDLER, M. D.
University of Miami School of Medicine

SWALLOWTAIL BUTTERFLY, any of a large, worldwide family of butterflies that commonly have tail-like projections extending from the hind wings. Swallowtails and their relatives make up the family Papilionidae. Most of the more than 600 known species are tropical; only about 30 species inhabit North America.

Most swallowtails are beautifully colored, often with yellow, red, green, or blue markings on a black background. Sometimes the sexes vary greatly in color, and in some species there may be more than one color form for the same sex. The oriental swallowtail (*Papilio memnon*) has three distinct color forms for each sex. In some species there may also be marked variations among different broods. For example, in the North American zebra swallowtail (*P. marcellus*) there are three distinct forms: a small, pale, early spring form; a medium-sized, darker, late spring form; and a larger, darker, late summer form.

Swallowtail larvae feed on a wide variety of trees and nonwoody plants. The black swallowtail (*P. polyxenes*) feeds on parsnips and other members of the parsley family.

DON DAVIS
Smithsonian Institution

SWAMMERDAM, sväm'ər-däm, **Jan** (1637–1680), Dutch scientist who was among the first to use the microscope effectively to discover minute animal and plant structures and functions.

Swammerdam was born in Amsterdam on Feb. 12, 1637. After studying at Leiden University and in France, he received a degree in medicine from Leiden in 1667 with a dissertation on the mechanics of human respiration. From then until 1673 he devoted himself chiefly to microscopic studies of various animals. He invented micropipettes and devised techniques for microdissection that enabled him to observe and describe many minute structures. For example, after injecting blood vessels with wax, he observed the delicate valves of the lymphatic system. He also observed capillaries and red corpuscles in the blood system and cell division and development in frogs, and he showed that muscles alter in shape but not in size during contraction.

Swammerdam also described and illustrated minute parts of crustacea, mollusks, worms, frogs, mammals, plants, and especially insects. His main contributions were descriptions of the minute anatomy of the mayfly and the bee. After studying their life histories, he classified insects according to their type of metamorphosis. His work on metamorphosis led him to favor the theory of preformation rather than the theory of epigenesis—as an explanation of how embryos develop into new individuals.

In 1673, in ill health and under the influence of Antoinette Bourignon, a popular religious mystic, Swammerdam abandoned scientific work. He died in Amsterdam on Feb. 17, 1680.

ELDON J. GARDNER
Utah State University

Tiger swallowtail butterfly (*Papilio glaucus*)

A. W. AMBLER, FROM NATIONAL AUDUBON SOCIETY

FRED K. PARRISH

In the Okefenokee swamp, cypress trees grow on masses of peat lifted to the water surface by bubbles of gas.

SWAMP, a soggy tract of land formed by the filling in of a lake or by water running slowly over a flat, low-lying area. Swamps range in size from small mountain bogs to extensive coastal-plain or river swamps such as the Sudd of southern Sudan, the Everglades of Florida, and the Okefenokee of Florida and Georgia.

Different terms are used to connote stages in the evolution of such areas into dry land. Thus *bog* implies an aquatic condition with a thick layer of peat and mats of floating vegetation. *Marsh* implies large areas of low vegetation such as grasses and sedges. *Swamp* indicates the dominance of trees and high shrubs. However, these distinctions are not sharply drawn, and there are many local names for the many different kinds of swamps.

Formation. When landmasses are lifted or the oceans recede, water leaches minerals into low areas and forms standing or slowly moving ponds or lakes. Organisms then take the minerals and incorporate them into organic compounds. If the water is shallow enough, vegetation such as cattails, water lilies, marchgrass, and cypress appears and a swamp is produced quickly.

If the water is deeper it is filled by dead organic matter sinking to the bottom, while at the same time floating mats of vegetation grow out from the shore. Fermentation in bottom sediments often produce gases that may float masses of peat to the surface, and in time these will be covered by plants. If the peat builds high enough to become dry, hardwood trees will appear.

Characteristics. Water temperatures in the swamps of Europe and the southern United States often fluctuate by 27° F (15° C) in a single day. More northerly bogs generally do not show such extreme variations. The water is usually clear but has the color of coffee or tea because of the presence of more than 20 humus-derived organic acids in a colloidal state. Light cannot penetrate more than approximately 3 feet (1 meter) into the water.

The water's oxygen content usually fluctuates widely, because at night no oxygen is produced by photosynthesis, and plants and animals use up much of the gas. There may be as many as 8 to 10 parts per million of oxygen in the afternoon and only 0.25 part per million at night. An inverse cycle for the water's carbon dioxide content has been observed. The water may also range from slightly alkaline to strongly acidic in some swamps, on a daily or seasonal basis. Concentrations of dissolved minerals are usually not very large, but sometimes there are relatively large amounts of iron and magnesium, which may be detrimental to some species.

Plant and Animal Life. The submerged vegetation in swamps often includes sphagnum moss, various algae, and vascular plants. The latter two provide abundant food for organisms such as copepods, water fleas, and insect larvae. These, in turn, are captured by insectivorous plants.

This "supermarket" of plants and invertebrates is a ready source of food for many kinds of fish, reptiles, mammals, amphibians, and birds. The last two groups are overwhelmingly abundant. For example, 203 bird species occur in the Okefenokee, and adaptations for swimming, wading, and all kinds of feeding are observed. At night the 32 species of amphibians take over, with squeals, grunts, and other calls. There are 48 reptile species, but the amphibians are far more evident and numerous.

Importance. Some people still think of swamps as unproductive "wastelands," but in fact they serve essential ecological functions. Rivers flowing from highlands have a series of swamps and other wetlands along their courses that act as successive nutrient traps, delaying the journey of minerals to the ocean. River and creek swamps appear to be natural flood controls, impeding the flow of water and absorbing large amounts for later release. This tends to reduce the size of floods and to produce a higher water table.

River swamps are also important in removing pollutants from water. Their deposits of debris provide both mechanical filtration and adequate surfaces to which organisms that remove pollutants biologically can attach themselves.

Finally, swamps are important preserves of animal life, including economically significant game. Many rare species of fish, salamanders, frogs, birds, and invertebrates live exclusively in wetlands and would quickly become extinct if such areas were destroyed. See also Bog.

Fred K. Parrish
Georgia State University

SWAMP DEER, a large Asiatic deer (*Cervus duvauceli*) resembling the red deer and American elk (wapiti). The marsh deer (*Blastocerus dichotomus*) of South America is sometimes also called the swamp deer. *Cervus duvauceli,* also called the barasingha, stands 44 to 46 inches (112–117 cm) high at the shoulders and may weigh more than 500 pounds (227 kg). In summer its coat is a rich chestnut brown, lighter below, with a dark band bordered by white spots running down the back. The band is not seen in the winter coat, which in mature stags is a very dark brown, with a prominent neck ruff. Once common on marshy grasslands in the Indo-Gangetic Basin, today the swamp deer is found only in a few localities in central and northern India and western Nepal. In central India the animals congregate at the beginning of the mating season (December) but become essentially solitary in September. Hinds (females) begin breeding at three years of age, bearing a single fawn after a gestation period of about 8 months.

The total swamp deer population is estimated at 3,500. Prospects for survival in India are poor, except in the Kaziranga Sanctuary in Assam and on private land in Uttar Pradesh. Loss of habitat, disease, and intensive illegal hunting are responsible for the decline.

NOEL SIMON
Compiler "Red Data Book," Vol. I (Mammalia)

SWAMP HICKORY, a name commonly applied to two types of hickory trees, the bitternut (*Carya cordiformis*) and the water hickory (*C. aquatica*). See HICKORY.

SWAMP LILY. See CRINUM.

SWAMP LOCUST, an ornamental tree more commonly known as *water locust.* See WATER LOCUST.

SWAMP MAPLE is a name sometimes applied to several types of maple trees, including the silver maple and the red maple. See MAPLE.

SWAMPSCOTT, swamp′skət, is a town in northeastern Massachusetts, in Essex county, on Nahant Bay of the Atlantic Ocean. It is 13 miles (20 km) northeast of Boston, of which it is a residential suburb. The town is a popular summer resort. Of interest is the Mary Baker Eddy house, where the founder of Christian Science began her career in 1866. The Humphrey house (1640), the home of John Humphrey, deputy governor of the Massachusetts Bay Colony, houses the collections of the Swampscott Historical Society. Swampscott was settled in 1629 and incorporated as a town in 1852. Population: 13,578.

SWAN, Sir Joseph Wilson (1828–1914), English chemist and inventor, who made basic contributions to photography and electric lighting. He was born in Sunderland, Durham, on Oct. 31, 1828. Apprenticed to a local druggist, he later became a partner in a chemical firm.

Swan was granted his first patent in 1864 for a perfected "carbon process" for printing photographs with permanent pigments. He then adapted this process for printing from electrotypes. In 1877, soon after his firm began to make dry plates, Swan discovered an effect unnoticed until then—that the sensitivity of a photographic emulsion could be greatly increased or otherwise altered by controlling the temperature and duration of the heat applied in preparing it. General knowledge of this effect of ripening by heat was a key factor in the subsequent rapid improvement in plates, films, and papers. In 1879 he patented the first bromide paper.

Swan was the foremost rival of Edison in the development of the incandescent lamp. From 1848 to 1860, Swan made experimental lamps that lit dimly but burned out quickly for lack of a good vacuum. In 1877, using a better vacuum pump, he began the development of new lamps embodying features that were soon widely adopted. Among these were an all-glass, hermetically sealed bulb (1879) and a durable filament of carbonized cotton thread that had first been treated with sulfuric acid (1880). Swan formed a company to make his lamps, and in 1881 he amazed Londoners by lighting the Savoy Theatre with 1,200 of them. He was knighted in 1904. He died in Warlingham, Surrey, on May 27, 1914.

KENNETH M. SWEZEY
Author of "Science Shows You How"

SWAN, any of a group of graceful, long-necked waterfowl related to geese and ducks. Like other waterfowl, swans have heavy bodies, short legs, and large webbed feet. They generally are larger than geese and usually have predominantly white plumage. The sex of both geese and swans, unlike ducks, is almost impossible to distinguish.

Swans are good swimmers and graceful in the air, often flying in "V" patterns. They extend their long necks under water to reach aquatic plant materials. Swans normally form lifelong pair bonds and generally nest in marshy areas. In most species the female alone incubates the four to six white eggs, but both parents guard the nest and care for the young.

There are eight species of swans. Along with geese and ducks they are classified in the family Anatidae of the order Anseriformes. Five species are found in the Northern Hemisphere. As juveniles, all have grayish plumage, which becomes entirely white in their adult stage. The mute swan (*Cygnus olor*), seen in city parks and zoos, has a black knob at the base of its orange bill. Actually, it is not entirely mute but has a hoarse, wheezing voice. Two other species, the

MUTE SWAN (female) incubating her eggs on nest in marshy area. Some males help in rearing young.

HAMPSON, FROM ANNAN PHOTO

LYN, FROM ANNAN PHOTO

TRUMPETER SWANS taking part in courtship display before mating. Swans often form lifelong bonds.

fairly common whistling swan (*Olor columbianus*) and the much larger and rarer trumpeter swan (*O. buccinator*)—perhaps the heaviest flying bird—are found in North America. The trumpeter at one time was threatened with extinction, but it now numbers more than 4,000. Most of those found south of Canada are in the Red Rock National Wildlife Refuge near Yellowstone Park. The Eurasian counterparts of these species are the small Bewick's swan (*O. bewickii*) and the slightly larger whooping swan (*O. cygnus*). The Northern Hemisphere species nest in the northern parts of North America and Eurasia and commonly migrate south in winter.

Three species of swans are found in the Southern Hemisphere. These include two relatively small swans—the blacknecked swan (*C. melanocoryphus*), which is white except for a black head and neck, and the unusual Coscoroba swan (*Coscoroba coscoroba*), known for its distinctive "cos-cor-oo-ba" call. The smallest of all swans, the coscoroba weighs only 7 to 8 pounds (3–3.5 kg) at maturity. The third Southern Hemisphere swan is the unique black swan (*C. atratus*) of Australia. It differs from all other swans in having all black plumage except for all white wing tips.

PAUL A. JOHNSGAARD, *University of Nebraska*

SWAN LAKE is a ballet in three acts and four scenes, with music by Peter Ilich Tchaikovsky and choreography by Marius Petipa and Lev Ivanov. It was first performed at the Maryinsky Theater in St. Petersburg on Jan. 27, 1895. The work is sometimes presented in four acts.

As *Swan Lake* opens, Prince Siegfried, who is celebrating his 21st birthday, is told by his mother that he must choose a bride at a ball the next evening. Saddened at having to lose his freedom, he goes off to hunt wild swans. As he takes aim, they become lovely maidens. He falls in love with their queen, Odette, and a tender pas de deux ensues. Suddenly Odette is spirited away by the evil magician Rothbart, but she had already told Siegfried that his fidelity could save her. At the ball, Siegfried thinks only of Odette. Then Rothbart enters with his daughter Odile, whom witchcraft has made to resemble Odette. Siegfried, overjoyed, promises to marry her, thus unwittingly breaking his vow to Odette. When Siegfried realizes what he has done, pandemonium erupts. He dashes out to find Odette and beg forgiveness. Together they plunge into the Lake of Tears and are seen united after death.

Swan Lake is one of the finest and most popular of the ballets that are romantic in theme. With its dual role of Odette-Odile, it is considered a great touchstone for the ballerina.

DORIS HERING, *"Dance Magazine"*

SWAN MAIDEN, the heroine of a folktale found throughout the world. The legend centers on a beautiful maiden who can change from human form to swan form with the aid of a magical object, such as a feather robe, a ring, or a chain. A young man discovers the magical object and hides it. He marries the swan maiden, but she eventually finds the object and returns to swan form. In a variation, the swan maiden and her lover are under a taboo. When he breaks it, she goes back to her swan form.

The swan maiden tale is found in Asia and Europe, in Australia and Polynesia, in North and South America and in parts of Africa. It is believed to have originated in early Sanskrit writings. Stories based on this theme are found in the Indian *Śatapatha-Brāhmana* and the Arabian *Thousand and One Nights.* The old Irish tale *Angus Og and Caer* is a version of the swan maiden legend.

SWANBERG, swän′bərg, **W. A.** (1907–), American author. William Andrew Swanberg was born in St. Paul, Minn., on Nov. 23, 1907. He was a graduate of the University of Minnesota (B. A., 1930) and an editor with the Dell Publishing Company from 1935 to 1944. After serving a year with the Office of War Information, he became a free-lance writer.

First Blood (1957) is a dramatic narrative of the opening shots of the Civil War. His biographies include *Sickles The Incredible* (1956); *Jim Fisk* (1959); and *Citizen Hearst* (1961). *Dreiser* (1965) is his most ambitious and most carefully researched biography. Critics agreed that Swanberg had illuminated many obscure aspects of Dreiser's turbulent personal life, but some discerned a distaste for the novelist's failings. *Pulitzer* (1967) was generally acclaimed an outstanding example of popular biography. The reviewer Gerald Johnson wryly suggested that it ought to have won the author the prize that his subject had founded.

BERTRAM WYATT-BROWN
Case Western Reserve University

SWANEE RIVER. See SUWANNEE RIVER.

SWANN'S WAY. See REMEMBRANCE OF THINGS PAST.

SWANSCOMBE MAN. See MAN, PREHISTORIC TYPES OF—*Homo Sapiens.*

SWANSEA, swän'sē, a town in southeastern Massachusetts, in Bristol county, is on Mount Hope Bay, about 5 miles (8 km) northeast of Fall River. It is a residential community in a farming region. A small mill dyes and finishes cloth.

Settlers occupied the site as early as 1623. Swansea was set off from Rehoboth as a township in 1667. The first battle of King Philip's War between the colonists and the Indians was fought here in 1675. Swansea was incorporated in 1785. Government is by a board of selectmen and a town meeting. Population: 12,640.

SWANSEA, swän'zē, a city of south central Wales, is at the head of a large bay on the north shore of the Bristol Channel about 35 miles (56 km) northwest of Cardiff. It is situated at the mouth of the River Tawe, from which it derives its Welsh name, *Aber Tawe.* Some of the bays and beaches of the peninsula of Gower are in the southwestern part of the city. Next to Cardiff, Swansea is the largest city in Wales.

There are important metallurgical industries in Swansea, and large quantities of anthracite coal are exported. The port was heavily bombed during World War II, and much of the city is now modern in style. The Civic Centre includes the council chamber and assize courts and the Guildhall with its conspicuous 160-foot (48-meter) tower.

The Glynn Vivian Art Gallery in Swansea has excellent collections of paintings, porcelain, and pottery. Brangwyn Hall contains a series of panels painted by Frank Brangwyn and intended for the British House of Lords, but they were purchased and presented to Swansea. The Royal Institution of South Wales displays archaeological and natural history collections. Swansea University College is part of the University of Wales. Swansea's so-called "castle," actually a fortified manor house, has stood here since the 14th century. Population: (1961) 167,322.

GORDON STOKES, *Author of "English Place-Names"*

SWARTHMORE COLLEGE, swôrth'môr, is a private coeducational institution of higher education in Swarthmore, Pa. Founded in 1864 by members of the Society of Friends, it became nonsectarian in control at the beginning of the 20th century.

Swarthmore's undergraduate program includes the natural and social sciences, classical and modern languages, astronomy, art history, anthropology, engineering, history, religion, mathematics, and music. Special programs in black studies, linguistics, Far Eastern studies, and studio arts have been introduced. Cooperative arrangements with Bryn Mawr and Haverford colleges and with the University of Pennsylvania permit students to enroll in specialized courses in those institutions. The honors program offers selected upperclassmen a series of six seminars in a major and a minor subject.

Facilities include a student theater, an observatory, and a studio and gallery for the fine arts. The Friends Historical Library, containing the Swarthmore College Peace Collection, provides rich resources in the history of Quakerism and peace.

Enrollment is limited by college policy to 1,200, divided almost evenly between men and women.

JAMES F. GOVAN
Librarian, Swarthmore College

SWARTHOUT, swôr'thout, **Gladys** (1904–1969), American mezzo-soprano. She was born in Deepwater, Mo., on Dec. 25, 1904, studied at the Bush Conservatory in Chicago, and received her operatic training with the Italian conductor Leopoldo Mugnone. In 1924 she began singing in Chicago with the Civic Opera and later sang with the Ravinia summer opera. She made her debut at the Metropolitan Opera in New York City in 1929, in the contralto role of La Cieca in *La Gioconda.* At the Metropolitan, where she remained until 1945, she sang mezzo-soprano parts principally, of which the best known was her Carmen.

Miss Swarthout starred in several films and appeared frequently on radio and television. She gave what many critics consider her best performance in the celebrated 1947 radio broadcast of the uncut version of Berlioz' *Roméo et Juliette,* conducted by Arturo Toscanini. Her autobiography, *Come Soon, Tomorrow: The Story of a Young Singer,* was published in 1943. She died in Florence, Italy, on July 7, 1969.

SWASTIKA, swäs'ti-kə, a figure in the form of a Greek cross with the arms bent at right angles, which became the symbol of the Nazi regime in Germany. The swastika has been found as an ornamental pattern in Europe since the Bronze Age and in Asia since the 3d millenium B.C. The word is Sanskrit in origin. It was also used by Polynesians and North American Indians, but was unknown in Australia and was rare in Africa and Central America. It is usually interpreted as a sun or fire symbol, but in Norse mythology it may have symbolized the hammer of the god Thor.

The belief that the swastika was an Aryan symbol led to its use in Austria and Germany as the sign of anti-Semitism. Because of this association, Adolph Hitler placed a black swastika in a white circle on red cloth when he created a banner for the National Socialist party in 1919. In September 1935, this banner became the official flag of the Third Reich. The swastika was displayed in all the other official emblems of the Nazi state and party.

HAJO HOLBORN
Author of "A History of Modern Germany"

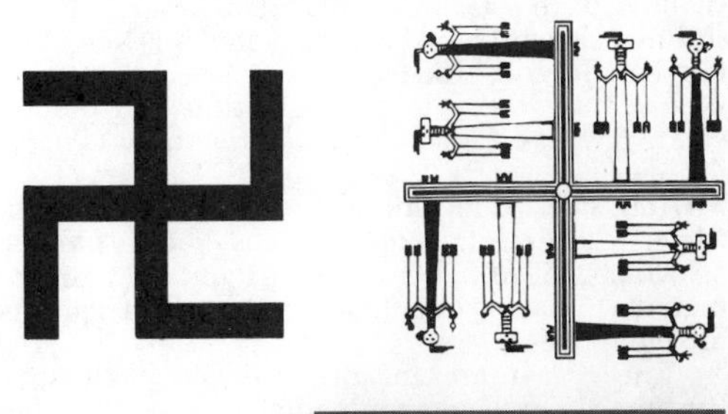

SWASTIKAS in three forms: ancient sun symbol *(above left);* Navajo Indian sign, with gods of wind and rain *(above right);* and German Nazi party emblem *(right).*

SWATOW, swä'tou', in southern China, is the third-largest city in Kwangtung province. Situated on the Han River delta, it was originally a fishing village, but after it was opened to Western commerce in 1858 it developed into a trading center for the Han valley. The city's hinterland, extending into Fukien and Kiangsi provinces, contains a population of over 12 million. The harbor, sheltered by Tahao Island, is over 30 feet (9 meters) deep and can accommodate large ocean-going vessels.

Swatow's industries include fishing, sugar milling, fruit canning, and ship repairing. The city is noted for its embroidered lace mats. Swatow (officially Shan-t'ou) was a major embarkation port for Chinese emigrants to Southeast Asia in the late 19th and early 20th centuries. Population: (1967) 300,000.

SEN-DOU CHANG, *University of Hawaii*

SWAYBACK, or *lordosis,* is an abnormal spinal curvature. See CURVATURE OF THE SPINE.

SWAYNE, swān, **Noah Haynes** (1804–1884), American Supreme Court justice, who was known for his support of federal power, including that of the judiciary. Swayne was born in Frederick County, Va., on Dec. 7, 1804. Because of his antislavery beliefs he moved to Ohio shortly after his admission to the bar in 1823. Except for service as U.S. attorney for the District of Ohio from 1830 to 1839, he achieved eminence solely in private practice, so that his appointment by Lincoln to the Supreme Court in 1862 caused some surprise. Competent but undistinguished, he served as an associate justice for nearly 20 years.

In *Gelpcke* v. *Dubuque* (1864), Swayne wrote the majority opinion rejecting the proposition that federal courts must follow state courts on issues of state law. He voted to sustain the government's power to make paper money legal tender first in *Knox* v. *Lee* (1871), which overruled the negative decision on wartime power of Congress rendered in *Hepburn* v. *Griswold* (1870), and again, in *Juilliard* v. *Greenman* (1884), which confirmed similar federal powers in peacetime. In the Slaughter-House Cases (1873), a ruling in favor of a state's police power over the meat-packing industry, his dissent foreshadowed the Court's later dedication to substantive due process. Swayne died in New York City on June 8, 1884.

PHILIP B. KURLAND
The Law School, University of Chicago

SWAZI, swä'zē, an ethnic group of southeastern Africa. Their total population is about 400,000, of which 360,000 live in Swaziland and the remainder in the Republic of South Africa and Mozambique.

The Swazi are racially Negroid with some Bushman and Caucasoid admixture. Their language, Siswati, is a click language of the Nguni group within the Bantu subfamily of the Niger-Congo group. Swazis are primarily farmers, producing corn (maize) and millet as staple foods. Livestock raising confers higher prestige, with cattle serving as an index of wealth and status.

Although never conquered, the kingdom of Swaziland was a British protectorate, later called a High Commission territory, from 1903 until it achieved independence in 1968.

ROBERT A. LYSTAD, *Johns Hopkins University*

SWAZILAND, swäz'ē-land, is a kingdom in southeastern Africa that attained its independence from Britain on Sept. 5, 1968. It is surrounded on three sides by the Republic of South Africa, to which it is economically tied in a customs union and whose currency it uses.

Although rich in natural resources and enjoying an excellent climate, Swaziland has one of the highest illiteracy and infant mortality rates in Africa. Most of its population derives a livelihood from subsistence agriculture or is forced by economic circumstances to seek employment in South Africa. Until the 1960's few Swazi benefited from the country's mineral and agricultural wealth.

The Land. Swaziland is a small, landlocked country, covering 6,705 square miles (17,366 sq km). The maximum distance from north to south is less than 120 miles (193 km) and from east to west less than 90 miles (145 km).

Surface Features. Despite its smallness, Swaziland has great geographical contrasts. Four distinct regions each extend north and south. Farthest west is the Highveld, a continuation of the Drakensberg range of South Africa. Occupying about 2,000 square miles (5,200 sq km), the Highveld is a wide belt of rugged country with an average height of 3,500 to 4,500 (1,100–1,400 meters). The highest elevation is 6,100 feet (1,859 meters). Since 1945 afforestation has made great progress and the region now boasts more than 100,000 acres (40,000 hectares) of pine and eucalyptus—the largest man-made forest in Africa.

The next region to the east, the Middleveld, covers some 1,900 square miles (4,900 sq km) and has an average altitude of 2,000 to 2,500 feet (600–750 meters). Although it is hilly in parts, good soil and plentiful rainfall permit farmers to grow a variety of crops.

The Lowveld, father east and covering more than 2,200 square miles (5,700 sq km), is gently undulating lowland, mainly between 500 and 1,000 (150–300 meters) in elevation. The bush vegetation of the region is highly suited to cattle ranching. Fertile soil in its eastern section makes

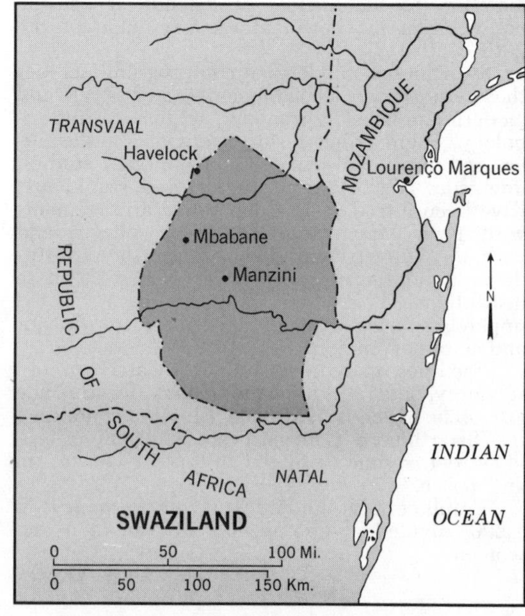

DE WYS

SWAZILAND'S beautiful scenery is evident in the Highveld, the site of a large man-made forest.

farming—with the help of irrigation—possible.

On the eastern border of Swaziland, overlooking the whole length of the eastern Lowveld, is the Lubombo plateau. It occupies nearly 600 square miles (1,550 sq km) and has about the same altitude as the Middleveld. Although mainly cattle country, the Lubombo is also an area where varied crops are raised.

Swaziland is one of the best-watered parts of southern Africa. Its major rivers traverse all four regions, flowing across the country from the Highveld toward the Indian Ocean.

Climate. The Highveld has a humid, nearly temperate climate with an average annual rainfall of 40 to 90 inches (1,000–2,300 mm). The Middleveld and Lubombo plateau are subtropical and drier. The Lowveld is almost tropical and receives between 20 and 30 inches (500–750 mm) of rain annually. Most of Swaziland's rain falls between October and March, but total rainfall varies widely from year to year. The mean annual temperature on the Highveld is just over 60° F (16° C), and on the Lowveld it is about 72° F (22° C).

Plants and Animals. The range of altitude in Swaziland is so great that there is a wide variety of plant life, including no less than 2,600 types of flowering plants and ferns. Although the total amount of wild game has been greatly reduced by hunting and poaching, hippopotamus and several types of antelope can still be found. Lions, baboons and other monkeys, and bush babies are occasionally seen. Some crocodiles are found in the rivers of the Lowveld.

The People. Swaziland had a population of 395,264 in the 1966 census. This included 9,176 whites, about half of whom were born in South Africa, and some 4,400 Eurafricans (persons of mixed European and African descent). Of the Africans, who comprise 96.8% of the population, all but 20,000 are Swazi. Continuance of the annual birthrate of 47 or 48 per 1,000 persons and death rate of about 22 per thousand would double the population by 1985.

Swaziland's population is unevenly distributed according to the pattern of land tenure. Population density varies from 27 per square mile (10 per sq km) on freehold farms to 572 (221) in part of the Ezulwine Valley (between Mbabane and Manzini) and to 741 (286) in the urban areas. By international standards the urbanization rate is very small. Mbabane, the capital city, had a population of 13,803 in 1966. The largest city, Manzini, had 16,106 inhabitants.

About 57% of the people of Swaziland are Christians. The rest adhere to animist beliefs. The Swazi language, Siswati, is spoken by most of the Africans as well as by many whites and Eurafricans. English is the official language of the country.

The pioneer work in the development of health and education services in Swaziland was done by the Christian missionary societies. Only in the 1930's did the British government begin to finance social services from the Swaziland budget and to provide grants. After 1940, Commonwealth development and welfare funds made it possible to extend social services.

Although just outside the tropics and enjoying a healthful climate, Swaziland has had a serious tuberculosis problem. Malaria was almost completely eradicated after 1958, but typhoid and paratyphoid fevers are still prevalent. Malnutrition is a major cause of disease and mortality among children. Because of the increase in the use of river water for irrigation, bilharzia has

INFORMATION HIGHLIGHTS

Official Name: Kingdom of Swaziland.
Head of State: Ngwenyama (king).
Head of Government: Prime Minister.
Area: 6,705 square miles (17,366 sq km).
Boundaries: *North, west, and south,* South Africa; *east,* South Africa and Mozambique.
Population: 395,264 (1966 census).
Capital: Mbabane (1966 population, 13,803).
Major Languages: English (official), Siswati.
Major Religions: Christianity, animism.
Monetary Unit: South African rand.
Weights and Measures: Metric system.
Flag: Blue and gold horizontal stripes on either side of a wide red stripe with a tribal shield and spears. (See also FLAG.)

DIANE RAWSON, FROM PHOTO RESEARCHERS

TRADITIONAL TRIBAL DRESS of vividly colored design is worn by Swazi men and women at a festival.

become a major health hazard. There is one practicing physician per 8,000 persons.

Swaziland has a literacy rate of about 25%. Most schools are operated by Christian missions, although usually with assistance of substantial government grants. Total school enrollment rose from over 15,000 in the early 1950's to over 67,000 in the late 1960's. Despite the vast expansion of secondary education, the country's secondary schools have places for only about two thirds of the eligible students. Most university students attend the University of Botswana, Lesotho, and Swaziland, in Roma, Lesotho. It is maintained jointly by the three countries.

Economy. Since 1950, Swaziland has undergone a remarkable economic expansion and diversification, particularly in agriculture. The once largely subsistence economy has been transformed into a fast-growing, semi-industrialized one. With an annual per capita income of about $180, Swaziland ranks among the most viable new states in Africa. The per capita income is not, however, an accurate reflection of the income of the Swazi, since most high-level economic activity is in the hands of the whites.

Some 56% of the country, covering 4,290,944 acres (1,737,224 hectares), is reserved for occupation by the Swazi and vested in the king as "Swazi nation land." The remainder of the land is owned by people of other races and by missions. The area owned by individual Swazi totals 23,700 acres (9,595 hectares). On Swazi nation land a system of communal ownership is practiced. Chiefs allocate grazing and plowing land according to need. Large parts of Swazi nation land consist of pastures and unimproved grassland.

Although cattle traditionally have been valued by the Swazi for their own sake and as evidence of wealth, slaughter stock and hides and skins have become increasingly important exports. Dairying is also growing in importance. Although most Swazi are still subsistence farmers, the number acquiring skilled or unskilled jobs in the industrial sector is steadily increasing. Most of Swaziland's industrial development is connected with the processing of its agricultural, forest, and mineral products.

Corn (maize) is the staple food crop of the country. The main export crops are sugar, cotton, citrus fruits, and rice. The sugar industry, which is based on irrigated cane, has transformed large parts of formerly useless bushveld. Sugar and forest products are the major agricultural exports.

Besides its agricultural wealth, Swaziland possesses workable deposits of such important minerals as iron ore, asbestos, and coal. Asbestos was the mainstay of the economy after the opening of the mine at Havelock in 1939, but by the end of the 1960's it had fallen from first to fourth place in export trade. The development of the Ngwenya iron ore mine, which began production in 1964, has been a major cause of the country's recent economic expansion. A 10-year contract to deliver ore to Japan provided the economic justification for the construction of a railroad across Swaziland from Ngwenya to the head of a line in Mozambique. The opening of the railroad led to the development of Swaziland's first industrial estate, at Matsapa in the central region of the country.

Swaziland's good transportation facilities have made possible its economic growth. Besides the railroad there are about 1,400 miles (2,250 km) of graveled or earth roads and a bituminized cross-country highway completed in 1964. Air service from Matsapa connects the country with South Africa, Rhodesia, and Mozambique. Over 20 grass landing strips have made all of Swaziland accessible.

History and Government. The Swazi appear to have broken away in the middle of the 18th century from the main body of Bantu migrants who had moved southward some two centuries earlier from central Africa. Originally a number of clans, the Swazi emerged as a distinct tribal group at the beginning of the 19th century. They were in constant conflict with the Zulu as well as in occasional conflict with the British, Boers, and Portuguese. In the 1840's, the Swazi ruler Mswati, from whom the Swazi are thought to have taken their name, applied to the British agent general in Natal for help against the Zulu. It was during this period that the first Europeans settled in Swaziland.

The independence of Swaziland was guaranteed by the British and Transvaal governments in 1881 and 1884. However, because of the chaotic situation arising from the many concessions granted to Europeans by King Mbandzeni, a provisional government was established in 1890 representative of the Swazi, the British, and the South African Republic (Transvaal). In 1894, under a convention between the British and South African governments, the latter was given power of protection and administration over Swaziland. At the end of the South African (Boer) War in 1902 all rights and powers over the territory passed to the British government.

The British administration took steps to settle the concessions question by defining the boundaries of the land concessions and by returning one third of the concessions to the Swazi. The boundaries of the mineral concessions were also defined and all monopoly concessions were appropriated. In 1907 control of Swaziland was vested in the British high commissioner for South Africa, who was also responsible for the administration of Basutoland (now Lesotho) and Bechuanaland (now Botswana).

An advisory council, consisting of elected representatives of the Europeans in Swaziland, was established in 1921 to advise the administration on purely European affairs. In 1944, Britain recognized the ngwenyama ("lion"), or head of the Swazi nation, as the African authority for the territory, with power to issue legally enforceable orders to Africans. But the terms of recognition never had the support of the paramount chief, Sobhuza II, until they were revised in 1950. Sobhuza also challenged the legality of the land and minerals settlement, which he had opposed from the time he became ngwenyama in 1921.

Swaziland did not receive much attention from the British government before World War II, because it was expected eventually to be incorporated into South Africa. In the early 1960's a modernist local political party, rooted in the small but articulate urban elite and working class, prompted King Sobhuza and the Swazi National Council to form their own political party, the Imbokodvo. In the 1964 elections the Imbokodvo, together with its European allies, won all 24 elective seats on the newly established Legislative Council. Having solidified its political base, the Imbokodvo then adopted many of the demands of the more radical parties, especially that of immediate independence. Following agreement on a preindependence constitution, parliamentary elections were held in 1967. All of the seats in the Assembly and the Senate were won by the Imbokodvo, which led the country to independence in September 1968.

Under the constitution of 1968 the king is the head of state. Executive authority is exercised by a cabinet presided over by a prime minister, whom the king appoints from among the members of parliament.

Parliament is composed of two chambers, the House of Assembly and the Senate. The House of Assembly has 30 members, of whom 24 are elected from 8 electoral districts and 6 are appointed by the king. Six of the Senate's 12 members are elected by the Assembly and 6 are appointed by the king. Parliament is elected at least once every 5 years and has the power to enact all laws except those affecting Swazi law and customs, which are decided by the Swazi National Council, the king's traditional advisory body. This body also advises the king on the control of mineral resources, and, together with the queen mother, decides on the royal succession.

Although Swaziland has no formal diplomatic relations with South Africa, there is close contact between the two governments through what is called "telephone diplomacy." Forced by economic and geographic circumstances to maintain cordial relations with South Africa, Swaziland has conspicuously refrained from joining other African states in condemning South Africa for its racial policies, although Swaziland does reject them. As Swaziland develops its economic potential it is expected to have a greater degree of flexibility in dealing with South Africa.

RICHARD P. STEVENS
Lincoln University

Bibliography

Barker, Dudley, *Swaziland* (London 1965).
Hailey, Lord, *An African Survey* (London 1957).
Halpern, Jack, *South Africa's Hostages* (Baltimore 1965).
Kuper, Hilda, *The Swazi* (London 1952).
Stevens, Richard P., *Lesotho, Botswana, and Swaziland* (London 1967).

SWEAT is the clear liquid produced by the sweat glands. Sweating is a vital body function, serving to eliminate certain body wastes and acting as a temperature regulating mechanism. As sweat evaporates it cools the skin and the blood vessels near the skin surface.

There are two types of sweat glands: *apocrine* and *eccrine.* The apocrine are larger than the eccrine and are located only in the armpits, ears, nipples, and sex organs. These are the glands primarily associated with body odor. There are many more eccrine glands than apocrine. It is estimated that each person has about a million eccrine glands. They occur throughout the body but are most numerous on the palms of the hands and soles of the feet. During childhood the eccrine glands begin to produce sweat. The apocrine glands become active in adolescence and gradually diminish in activity with advancing age.

As it is produced, sweat is odorless and contains about 98% water and 2% chemicals. These chemicals are sodium chloride (salt), fatty acids, urea, sulfates, albumin, and skatole. The characteristic odor of sweat is caused by the breakdown, or decompostion, of the sweat by bacteria. To eliminate the sweaty odor, frequent bathing is important, preferably with a soap containing hexachlorophene. This chemical acts as an antiseptic to prevent the decomposition of sweat. Some individuals use an antiperspirant, a preparation containing a 25% concentration of the astringent aluminum chlorhydrate. This chemical constricts the opening of the sweat glands, preventing the free flow of sweat.

The rate of sweating is related to several factors. It is increased by strenuous physical activity or by nervous or emotional tension. An abnormally low production of sweat occurs in certain congenital skin diseases, including ichthyosis and atopic dermatosis.

IRWIN LUBOWE, M. D.
Metropolitan Hospital Center, N. Y.

SWEATSHOP is a term now loosely used to characterize an establishment that employs workers at substandard wages, hours, and working conditions. The original sweatshops were the tenement-house shops that manufactured garments, artificial flowers, millinery ornaments, cigars and cigarettes, and other cheap handmade articles. Child labor and unsanitary health conditions were also prominent features.

There were two basic types of sweatshops: (1) homes in which individuals worked with the help of family members only, and (2) homes converted into factories by bringing in nonfamily members. The employer saved on rent and paid low piece rates for completed work. Large numbers of unemployed provided a ready labor market.

The state laws enacted in the 1880's and 1890's to regulate conditions in these shops were called "anti-sweating" laws. But regulation proved unsuccessful, and a movement to abolish homework by law began in the early 1900's.

Industrial homework began to decline as a serious problem in the post-New Deal period because of the substitution of power-driven machines for handwork; the rise of unionism; the rise of minimum wage, sanitation, child-labor, and anti-homework laws; improved employment opportunities; and a public opinion more sensitive toward conditions of work.

JACK BARBASH, *University of Wisconsin*

K. W. GULLERS, FROM RAPHO GUILLUMETTE

Turbulent streams in the forest country serve as roadways to carry timber to the mills of the lowlands.

SWEDEN

Coat of Arms of Sweden

CONTENTS

SWEDEN is the fourth-largest country in Europe. It occupies the eastern part of the Scandinavian Peninsula and two large islands in the Baltic Sea—Gotland and Öland.

Sweden is one of the world's northernmost countries. Its southern end is about on a line with the southern tip of Alaska, and one seventh of its total area is above the Arctic Circle. Sweden's great length of nearly 1,000 miles (1,600 km) is more than one seventh of the distance from the North Pole to the equator. For about two thirds of its length, Sweden is bounded on the west by high mountains. In spite of the country's northerly position, south and central Sweden enjoy a favorable climate because of the Gulf Stream and the prevailing westerly winds. The seasons vary between the long, haunting, opalescent summer nights and the dark, bitterly cold winter months. In the extreme north, the sun never rises above the horizon during the winter months, whereas during June and half of July the sun never sets.

Lakes, of which there are over 100,000, and rivers make up nearly one third of the country's area. Forests, primarily of pine, cover more than half of the land area and constitute, with iron ore and other metallic ores, such as lead and copper, one of the country's most important natural resources.

The native Swedish population is quite homogeneous, except for a small minority of about 10,000 Lapps in the far north. The Swedes are

INFORMATION HIGHLIGHTS

Official Name: Konungariket Sverige (Kingdom of Sweden).
Head of State: King.
Head of Government: Prime Minister.
Legislature: Riksdag (Parliament).
Area: 173,665 square miles (449,792 sq km).
Boundaries: *West and northwest,* Norway; *northeast and east,* Finland; *east and south,* Baltic Sea; *south and southwest,* Øresund, Kattegat, Skagerrak.
Elevation: *Highest point*—Kebnekaise 6,946 feet (2,117 meters).
Population: (1968 est.) 7,803,425.
Capital: Stockholm.
Major Language: Swedish (official language).
Major Religious Group: Swedish Lutheran.
Monetary Unit: Krona = 100 öre.
Weights and Measures: Metric system.
Flag: Extended yellow cross on a blue field. See also FLAG.
National Anthem: *Du gamla, du fria* (*Thou Ancient, Thou Freeborn*).

overwhelmingly Protestant, and membership in the state church, the Church of Sweden, is every Swedish child's birthright.

The impact of the Industrial Revolution was not felt in Sweden until the latter half of the 19th century. Until 1900, most Swedes were independent farmers, farm workers, or fishermen. Thereafter there was a great migration to the cities, which transformed the nation from a rural to an urban society. Today about 45% of the Swedish people earn their living from manufacturing, construction, mining, and forestry.

The vigor of Sweden's economy and the broad social welfare program of the Social Democratic party, which has governed Sweden since 1932, have brought the ordinary comforts of life within the reach of virtually everyone in modern Sweden, and the standard of living is, in general, comparatively high. Swedes sometimes refer to their system as "planned democracy."

The ancestors of the present Swedes have lived in Sweden for at least 5,000 years. Following the Viking period, which lasted from about 800 to 1050, Sweden was Christianized. In the 15th century it was at times ruled from Denmark, but with the advent of Gustav I (reigned 1523–1560), the modern independent state of Sweden emerged. It was this king who permitted the development of the Lutheran Church, which eventually became the Church of Sweden. In the next century Sweden became one of the great powers in Europe when Gustavus Adolphus (Gustav II) successfully opposed the Habsburgs in the Thirty Years' War. At its greatest extent, in the 17th century, Sweden controlled Finland, Estonia, Latvia, and other parts of the Baltic coast.

In 1809, Sweden received a constitution that is essentially the one it has today. It apportioned the executive power between the king and the Riksdag, or parliament. Gradually the Riksdag evolved into the real governing power, and today the king's authority is only formal.

MAC LINDAHL, *Associate Editor "Swedish North Star"*

1. The Land

Sweden is bordered by Norway on the west and north and by Finland on the east. Sweden's southwest coast faces the Skagerrak and the Kattegat, both arms of the North Sea. The narrow Øresund in the south separates Denmark and Sweden and links the North Sea to the Baltic Sea. The Baltic and one of its arms, the Gulf of Bothnia, are on Sweden's east coast.

Historically, Sweden was composed of three major regions—Norrland, Svealand, and Götaland—symbolized in the three crowns of the national emblem. Norrland, "the northland," makes up the vast northern frontier region. Topographically, Svealand, "the land of the Svear," the tribe from which Sweden takes its name, corresponds essentially to the Central Lowland. Götaland, "the land of the Goths," is largely coincident with the Southern Highland. Modern Sweden, however, also embraces both the region of Skåne in the far south beyond Götaland, and the islands of Öland and Gotland in the Baltic.

Norrland. By far the most extensive region in Sweden is Norrland, which occupies the northern two thirds of the country. The region's western border follows the international boundary with Norway, which largely corresponds with the drainage divide of the Scandinavian Peninsula. Apart from a break in the Jämtland district in central Norrland, the region's mountains tend to rise toward the north. Kebnekaise, Sweden's highest peak at 6,946 feet (2,117 meters), is near the 68th parallel. Through most of their length, the Scandinavian mountains have a pronounced weather-divide effect, separating a relatively mild, moist maritime climate on the Norwegian side from a drier, more severely continental climate on the eastern, or Swedish, side. As a result, Norrland experiences long and rather cold winters, while summers are short but intense. Because of the region's high latitude, there is a pronounced contrast between the depressing darkness of midwinter and the exhilarating sunshine of midsummer.

Norrland drains eastward to the Gulf of Bothnia through a dozen of Sweden's largest rivers. Two of these, the Muonio and the Torne (Tornio), mark Sweden's boundary with Finland. Most of Norrland's rivers have their sources in

LIMESTONE CLIFFS of Gotland, in the Baltic off Sweden's east coast, protected the island from invaders in the Middle Ages when it was a key trade center.

SVEN SAMELIUS

SWEDISH INFORMATION SERVICE

MÖLNLYCKE'S quiet lake and forested hills are characteristic of Sweden's terrain southeast of Göteborg.

deep, glacially scoured lakes at the foot of the mountains and plunge rapidly to the sea. As a consequence, Norrland possesses 80% of Sweden's hydroelectric power potential, and it has the country's largest power stations.

For the most part, the region is covered by forests, which are dominated by solid stands of spruce and pine with a small intermixture of birch. Norrland is Sweden's main source of forest products, with most of the processing done at mills near the rivers' mouths.

Norrland's short, cool growing season and poor, morainic soils have offered little attraction to farmers, and only about 1% of the region is cultivated. Farming is concentrated on the better clay soils of the coastal strip and in the limestone soils of the Jämtland district. Here hay, potatoes, and hardy vegetables, such as turnips and cabbages, are the main crops.

The subsoil of Norrland is very rich in metallic minerals, of which the high-grade iron ore of Lappland in the extreme north is by far the most important. Here mining is carried on chiefly at Kiruna and Gällivare. Sweden's second most important iron ore district is Bergslagen, at Norrland's southern edge, about 100 miles (160 km) northwest of Stockholm. This district was formerly a major producer of copper and silver as well, but their production, together with that of lead, zinc, and gold, is now concentrated along the Skellefte River to the north.

Norrland's principal city is Gävle, a seaport 100 miles (160 km) north of Stockholm. Because of its southerly location, Gävle serves as Norrland's leading port for imports, but even so its traffic is hampered by ice for one or two months a year. Sundsvall is not only the region's second-largest city, but it also ranks as one of the two largest wood-processing centers in the world. Skellefteå and Luleå, Norrland's third and fourth cities, are both specialized mineral-exporting ports, but their harbors are blocked by ice for six or seven months a year.

Central Lowland. Sweden's Central Lowland contrasts sharply with the rolling, forested hills of neighboring Norrland. Topographically it consists of a series of clay plains that have supported a relatively dense agriculture since before the Viking era. Stretching from east to west across the region are numerous fault-block hills that stand as islands of forest in the more extensive clearings that characterize the landscape. In early post-glacial times, the Central Lowland formed a temporary channel between the North and Baltic seas, and it is occupied today by four of Sweden's largest lakes. Vänern, in the west, was formed chiefly through the inundation of the plain, while Vättern, in the center, is the product of faulting. Hjälmaren and Mälaren, near the eastern end, are the result of a combination of geological factors.

With over 40% of its total area under cultivation, the populous Central Lowland is Sweden's second most important agricultural region and its center of commerce and industry. In the moister western half of the lowland the agricultural emphasis is largely on hay and dairying, while in the warmer and drier eastern plains the cultivation of cereals and of oilseeds, such as rapeseed, is more strongly represented.

The eastern plains, centered on Lake Mälaren, constituted the historic core of the country, Svealand. The region's towns grew rapidly through trade and industry during the country's emergence as a European power in the late Middle Ages. Today, Sweden's two largest cities bracket the Central Lowlands. Stockholm, the capital, is on the east, and Göteborg, the principal seaport, is on the west. Dotted between them are several cities with populations between 50,000 and 100,000, including Västerås, Uppsala, Norrköping, Linköping, Örebro, and Eskilstuna.

Southern Highland. The Southern Highland largely coincides with the historic region of Götaland, also called Småland. Topographically it can be thought of as a detached outlier of Norrland, for its ancient crystalline hills are thinly veneered with poor, morainic soils and studded with lakes and swamps. The region is cooler and damper than the lowlands that lie to the north and south, and is thus much less suitable for agriculture. Less than 15% of its area is under cultivation, and most of its surface is forested. Consequently, industries based on wood, including the making of furniture, paper, and matches, are scattered throughout the region. Glass making, including the production of world-renowned Orrefors crystal, is concentrated in the southeast. Like Norrland, the Southern Highland boasts few large cities. Borås, a textile manufacturing center, is in the west, while Jönköping, once the match capital of the world, is at the southern end of Lake Vättern.

Skåne. At the southernmost tip of the Swedish mainland lies the region of Skåne. It is separated from Denmark by the Øresund, the narrowest of the waterways linking the North and Baltic seas. Geologically, Skåne forms a "bridge" between the younger, flat-lying sedimentary

SWEDEN

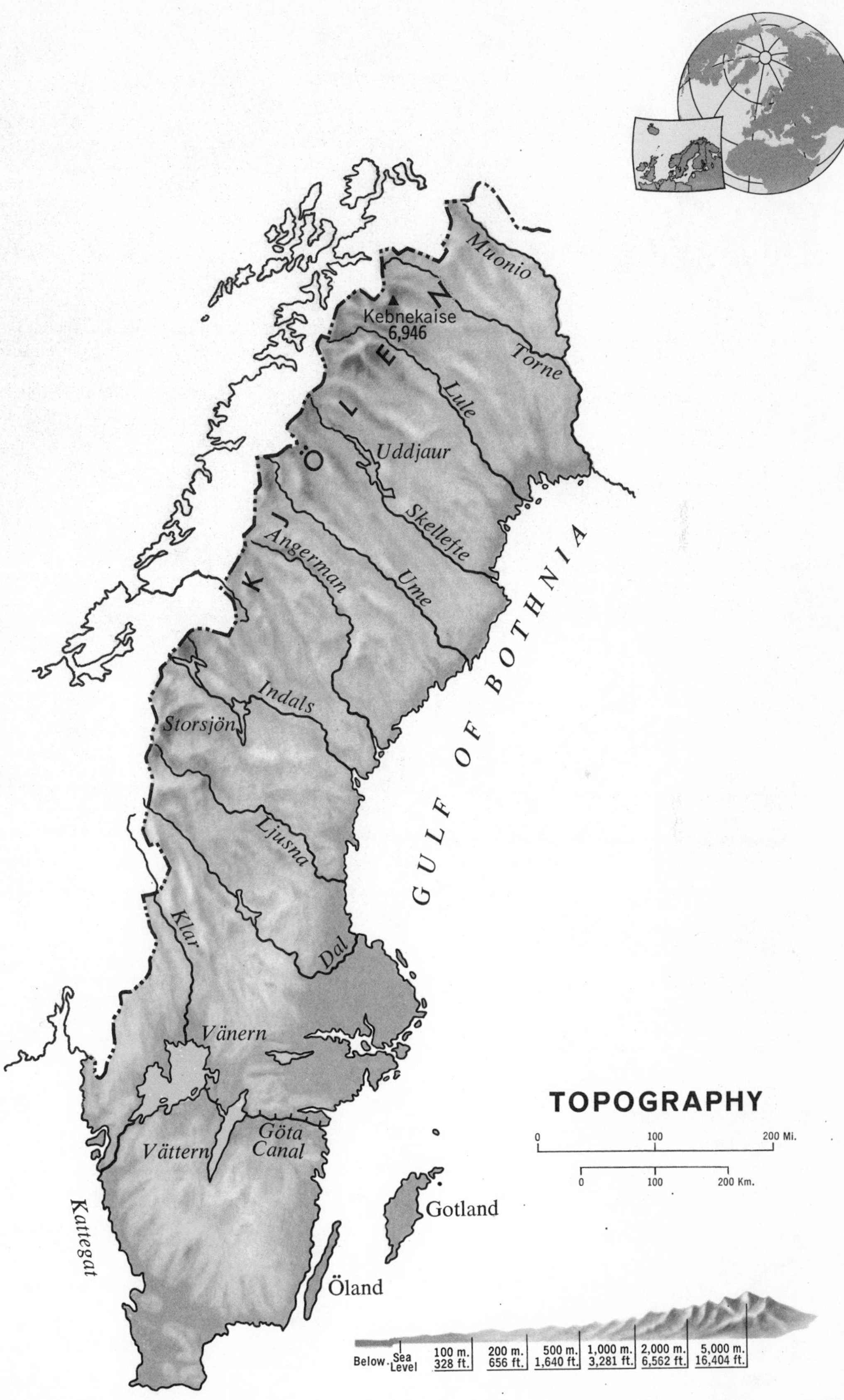

Muonio
Kebnekaise
6,946
KJÖLEN
Torne
Lule
Uddjaur
Skellefte
Angerman
Ume
GULF OF BOTHNIA
Indals
Storsjön
Ljusna
Klar
Dal
Vänern
Göta
Canal
Vättern
Kattegat
Gotland
Öland
TOPOGRAPHY
0
100
200 Mi.
0
100
200 Km.
Below
Sea Level
100 m. 328 ft.
200 m. 656 ft.
500 m. 1,640 ft.
1,000 m. 3,281 ft.
2,000 m. 6,562 ft.
5,000 m. 16,404 ft.

SWEDEN

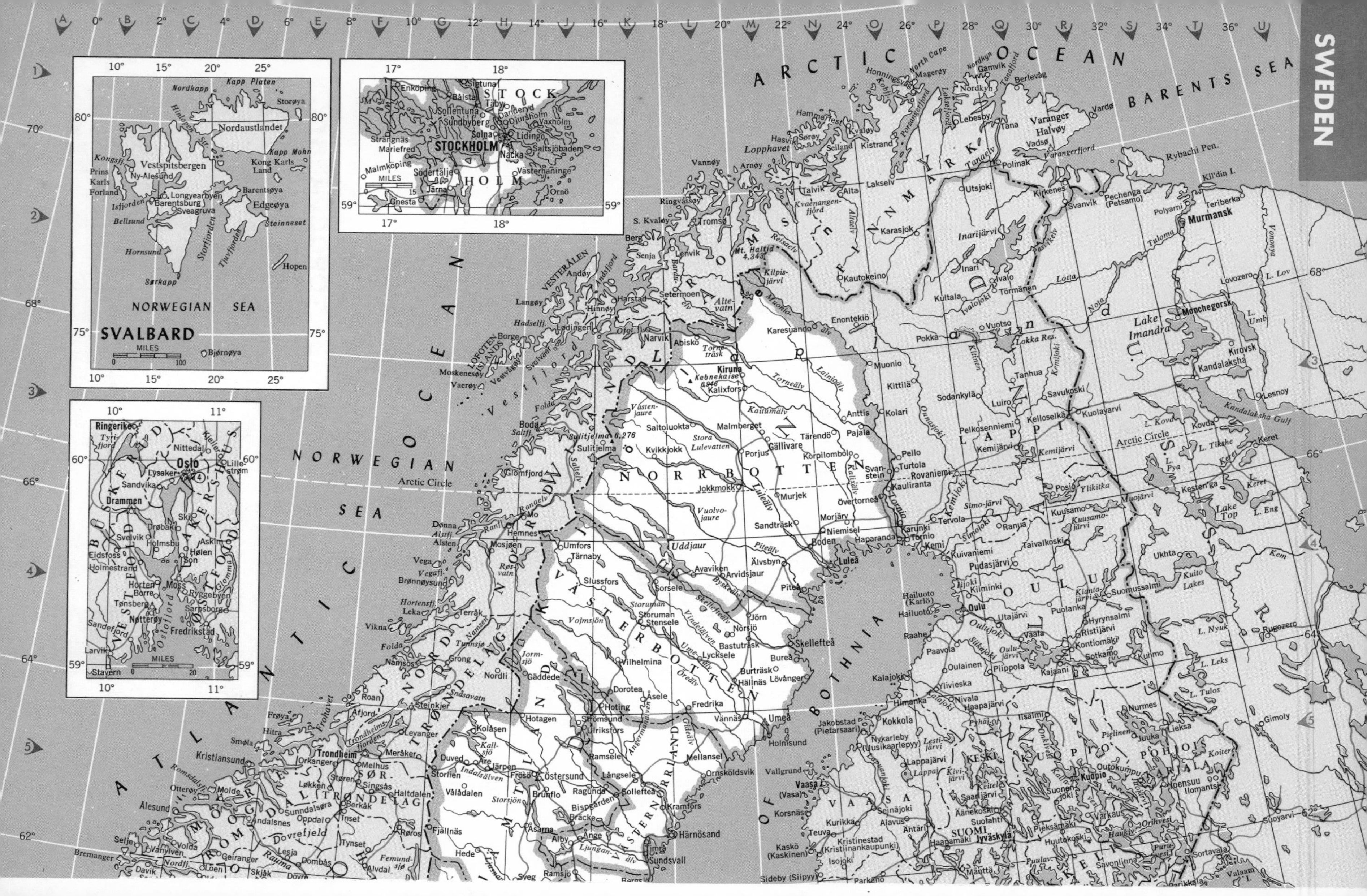

SWEDEN
ARCTIC OCEAN
BARENTS SEA
NORWEGIAN SEA
ATLANTIC OCEAN
GULF OF BOTHNIA
Arctic Circle
NORRBOTTEN
VÄSTERBOTTEN
LAPPI
OULU
FINNMARK
TROMS
NORDLAND
NORD-TRØNDELAG
SØR-TRØNDELAG
JÄMTLAND
VÄSTERNORRLAND
Murmansk
Kiruna
Kebnekaise
Luleå
Umeå
Skellefteå
Piteå
Narvik
Tromsø
Bodø
Trondheim
Östersund
Sundsvall
Härnösand
Oulu
Kemi
Tornio
Rovaniemi
Vaasa
Kokkola
Hammerfest
Vardø
Kirkenes
Lofoten Islands
Vesterålen
SVALBARD
Nordaustlandet
Vestspitsbergen
Longyearbyen
Barentsburg
Edgeøya
Bjørnøya
STOCKHOLM
Solna
Sundbyberg
Lidingö
Nacka
Södertälje
Oslo
Drammen
Moss
Fredrikstad
Sarpsborg
Tønsberg
Oslofjord
Lake Imandra
Mt. Haltia

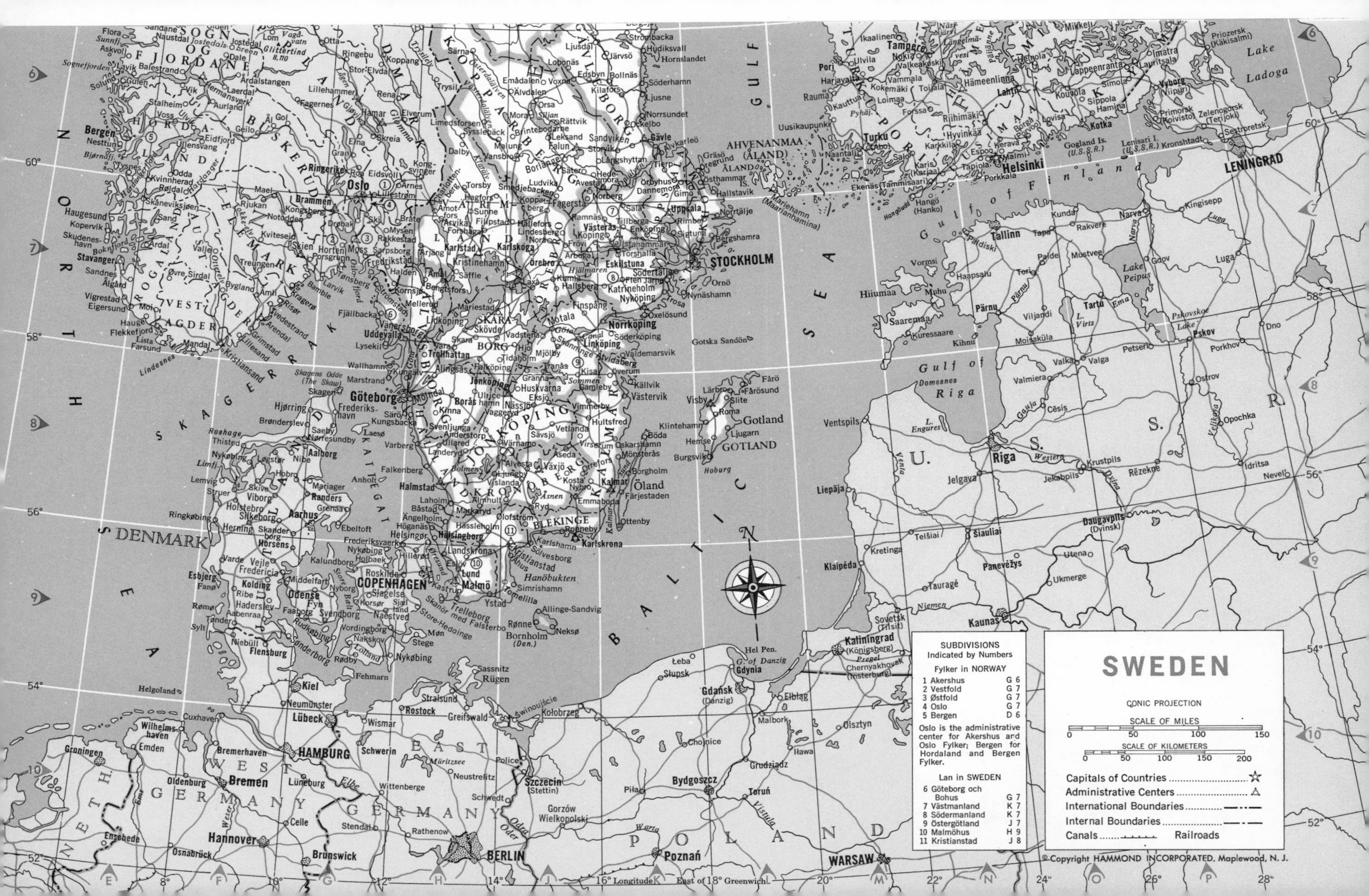

SWEDEN
CONIC PROJECTION
SCALE OF MILES
0 50 100 150
SCALE OF KILOMETERS
0 50 100 150 200
Capitals of Countries
Administrative Centers
International Boundaries
Internal Boundaries
Canals
Railroads
SUBDIVISIONS
Indicated by Numbers
Fylker in NORWAY
1 Akershus G 6
2 Vestfold G 7
3 Østfold G 7
4 Oslo G 7
5 Bergen D 6
Oslo is the administrative center for Akershus and Oslo Fylker; Bergen for Hordaland and Bergen Fylker.
Lan in SWEDEN
6 Göteborg och Bohus G 7
7 Västmanland K 7
8 Södermanland K 7
9 Östergötland J 7
10 Malmöhus H 9
11 Kristianstad J 8
16° Longitude East of 18° Greenwich

SWEDEN

Total Population, 7,969,000

COUNTIES

Älvsborg, 391,851 H 7
Blekinge, 150,901 J 8
Gävleborg, 294,916 K 6
Göteborg och Bohus, 685,449 G 7
Gotland, 50,438 L 8
Halland, 185,810 H 8
Jämtland, 121,552 J 5
Jönköping, 292,303 H 8
Kalmar, 234,175 K 8
Kopparberg, 270,971 J 6
Kristianstad, 258,295 J 8
Kronoberg, 164,309 J 8
Malmöhus, 683,752 H 9
Norrbotten, 261,410 L 3
Örebro, 259,794 J 7
Östergötland, 369,374 J 7
Skaraborg, 248,970 H 7
Södermanland, 239,451 K 7
Stockholm, 1,406,580 L 7
Uppsala, 191,821 K 6
Värmland, 273,139 H 7
Västerbotten, 235,307 K 4
Västernorrland, 277,715 K 5
Västmanland, 255,142 K 7

CITIES and TOWNS

Abisko L 2
Åhus, 4,758 J 9
Alby, †3,366 J 5
Alingsås, 19,810 H 7
Älmhult, 6,023 H 8
Älvdalen, 4,573 J 6
Alvesta, 8,957 J 8
Älvkarleö, †3,126 K 6
Älvsbyn, 4,343 M 4
Åmål, 9,397 H 7
Åmotfors, †3,026 H 7
Anderstorp, 3,960 H 8
Ånge, 4,000 J 5
Ängelholm, 13,985 H 8
Anttis N 3
Arboga, 12,266 J 7
Åre, †2,531 H 5
Årjäng, 2,893 H 7
Arvidsjaur, 7,767 L 4
Arvika, 15,901 H 7
Åsarna, †977 J 5
Åseda, 3,629 J 8
Åsele, 4,727 K 4
Åtvidaberg, 9,010 K 7
Avaviken L 4
Avesta, 29,232 J 6
Bålsta, †1,757 G 1
Båstad, 2,201 H 8
Bastuträsk, 1,665 L 4
Bengtsfors, 3,411 H 7
Bergshamra, †578 L 7
Bergsjö, †3,088 K 5
Bispgården, †2,737 K 5
Böda, †1,211 K 8
Boden, 24,912 N 4
Bollnäs, 17,123 K 6
Borås, 70,238 H 8
Borgholm, 2,443 K 8
Borlänge, 29,097 J 6
Bräcke, †2,658 J 5
Brintebodarne, †444 J 6
Brunflo, †3,700 J 5
Bureå, †4,583 M 4
Burgsvik, †584 K 8
Burträsk, †6,747 M 4
Charlottenberg, †3,112 H 6
Dalby, †2,972 H 6
Danderyd, 15,657 H 1
Dannemora, †732 K 6
Djursholm, 12,697 H 1
Dorotea, †3,964 K 4
Duved H 5
Edsbyn, †7,132 J 6
Eksjö, 9,897 J 8
Emådalen J 6
Emmaboda, 3,697 J 8
Enköping, 17,684 G 1
Eskilstuna, 65,580 K 7
Eslöv, 14,737 H 9
Fagersta, 16,609 J 6
Falkenberg, 12,920 H 8
Falköping, 16,032 H 7
Falun, 33,840 J 6
Färjestaden, †1,996 K 8
Fårösund, †1,328 L 8
Filipstad, 7,559 H 7
Finspång, 17,616 J 7
Fjällbacka, 770 G 7
Fjällnäs, †472 H 5
Flen, 9,112 K 7
Forshaga, 4,655 H 7
Fredrika, †1,386 L 4
Frösö, 9,520 J 5
Frövi, 3,082 J 7
Gäddede, †2,136 J 4
Gällivare, 9,718 M 3
Gamleby, †3,949 J 8
Gävle, 60,868 K 6
Gimo, †1,875 K 6
Gnesta, 3,275 G 2
Göteborg, 446,447 G 8
Gränna, 3,195 J 8
Hagfors, 8,964 H 6
Hällefors, 12,011 J 7
Hällnäs, †6,976 L 4
Hallsberg, 12,121 J 7
Hallstahammar, 14,099 K 7
Hallstavik, †5,880 L 6
Halmstad, 46,655 H 8
Hälsingborg, 80,801 H 8
Haparanda, 9,429 N 4
Härnösand, 16,637 L 5
Hässleholm, 16,031 H 8
Hede, †1,776 H 5
Hedemora, 17,744 K 6
Hemse, †1,159 L 8
Hjo, 4,783 J 7
Höganäs, 13,846 H 8
Holmsund, 5,778 M 5
Hotagen, †782 J 5
Hoting, †3,544 K 4
Hudiksvall, 16,057 K 6
Hultsfred, 4,979 K 8
Huskvarna, 18,198 J 8
Järna, †4,591 G 2
Järpen, †2,962 H 5
Järvsö, †4,995 K 6
Jokkmokk, 4,869 L 3
Jönköping, 53,774 H 8
Jörn, †4,275 M 4
Kalixfors L 3
Källvik, †1,116 K 8
Kalmar, 37,938 K 8
Karesuando, †1,442 M 2
Karlshamn, 30,581 J 8
Karlskoga, 38,284 J 7
Karlskrona, 37,358 K 8
Karlstad, 54,321 H 7
Katrineholm, 21,660 K 7
Kilafors, †3,408 K 6
Kinna, 6,386 H 8
Kiruna, 29,210 L 3
Kisa, †4,353 J 8
Klintehamn, †1,466 K 8
Kolåsen, †1,095 H 5
Köping, 20,807 J 7
Kopparberg, 7,985 J 7
Korpilombolo, †3,357 N 3
Kosta, †1,573 J 8
Kramfors, 11,729 K 5
Kristianstad, 42,249 J 9
Kristinehamn, 21,925 H 7
Kumla, 15,039 J 7
Kungälv, 11,213 G 8
Kungsbacka, 7,205 G 8
Kvikkjokk, 354 K 3
Laholm, 3,853 H 8
Landeryd, †1,931 H 8
Landskrona, 32,079 H 9
Långsele, †3,755 K 5
Långshyttan, 3,124 K 6
Lärbro, †1,265 L 8
Laxå, 9,498 J 7
Leksand, †7,828 J 6
Lidingö, 35,400 H 1
Lidköping, 19,700 H 7
Limedsforsen, †1,862 H 6
Lindesberg, 6,863 J 7
Linköping, 77,881 K 7
Ljugarn, †479 L 8
Ljungby, 11,930 J 8
Ljusdal, 10,630 J 6
Ljusne, †4,808 K 6
Lobonäs J 6
Lövånger, †3,671 M 4
Ludvika, 21,989 J 6
Luleå, 36,428 N 4
Lund, 50,494 H 9
Lycksele, 6,333 L 4
Lysekil, 8,000 G 7
Malmberget, †12,384 M 3
Malmköping, 3,450 F 1
Malmö, 254,990 H 9
Malung, †8,478 H 6
Mariefred, 2,502 F 1
Mariestad, 15,700 H 7
Markaryd, 5,980 H 8
Marstrand, 1,112 G 8
Mellansel, 1,422 L 5
Mellerud, 4,317 H 7
Mjölby, 12,790 J 7
Mölndal, 31,072 H 8
Mönsterås, 6,687 K 8
Mora, 13,307 J 6
Morjärv, 1,402 N 3
Motala, 27,907 J 7
Murjek, †3,089 M 3
Nacka, 25,798 H 1
Nässjö, 20,000 J 8
Niemisel, †1,676 N 3
Nora, 9,215 J 7
Norberg, 6,160 J 6
Norrköping, 94,296 K 7
Norrsundet, †4,575 K 6
Norrtälje, 11,803 L 7
Norsjö, 5,171 L 4
Nybro, 10,956 J 8
Nyköping, 31,195 K 7
Nynäshamn, 10,676 L 7
Ockelbo, †5,819 K 6
Olofström, 16,218 J 8
Örbyhus, †2,266 K 6
Örebro, 86,977 J 7
Öregrund, 2,026 L 6
Örnsköldsvik, 16,539 L 5
Orrefors, †2,121 J 8
Orsa, †6,629 J 6
Oskarshamn, 24,873 K 8
Östersund, 26,600 J 5
Östhammar, 8,858 L 6
Ottenby, †187 K 8
Övertorneå, †3,589 N 3
Överum, †2,533 K 7
Oxelösund, 14,835 K 7
Pajala, 3,871 N 3
Piteå, 32,287 M 4
Porjus, †1,015 M 3
Ragunda, †4,237 J 5
Ramnäs, †4,092 J 7
Ramsele, †3,337 K 5
Ramsjö, †1,224 J 5
Rättvik, †7,551 J 6
Rimbo, †3,426 L 7
Roma, †863 L 8
Ronneby, 29,325 J 8
Ryd, 4,013 J 8
Säffle, 12,599 H 7
Sala, 11,800 K 7
Saltoluokta L 3
Saltsjöbaden, 6,507 J 1
Sandträsk, †3,079 M 3
Sandviken, 25,476 K 6
Särna, †1,928 H 6
Särö, †2,386 G 8
Säter, 4,629 J 6
Sävsjö, 5,547 J 8
Sigtuna, 3,970 H 1
Simrishamn, 7,966 J 9
Skänninge, 4,482 J 7
Skanör med Falsterbo, 2,269 H 9
Skara, 10,376 H 7
Skellefteå, 61,880 M 4
Skövde, 27,976 H 7
Slite, 2,489 L 8
Slussfors, 1,154 K 4
Smedjebacken, 10,504 J 6
Söderhamn, 13,778 K 6
Söderköping, 5,954 K 7
Södertälje, 52,601 G 1
Sollefteå, 9,715 K 5
Sollentuna, 35,038 H 1
Solna, 57,707 H 1
Sölvesborg, 6,782 J 9
Sorsele, †3,550 K 4
Stensele, 6,343 K 4
Stockholm (cap.), 773,210 G 1
Stockholm, *1,247,234 G 1
Storlien H 5
Storuman K 4
Storvik, 2,432 K 6
Strängnäs, 9,506 F 1
Strömbacka, †3,075 K 6
Strömstad, 9,817 G 7
Strömsund, 6,058 K 5
Sundbyberg, 28,773 G 1
Sundsvall, 62,222 K 5
Sunne, 10,749 H 7
Svanstein, †2,960 N 3
Sveg, 4,975 J 5
Sysslebäck, †1,068 H 6
Täby, 33,694 H 1
Tärendö, †2,023 N 3
Tärnaby, †2,187 J 4
Tidaholm, 7,250 J 7
Tierp, 4,303 K 6
Tillberga, †270 K 7
Timrå, 12,800 K 5
Tomelilla, 6,349 J 9
Torsby, †6,796 H 6
Torshälla, 7,939 K 7
Tranås, 18,845 J 7
Trelleborg, 35,249 H 9
Trollhättan, 40,945 H 7
Trosa, 1,806 K 7
Uddevalla, 36,510 G 7
Ullared, †798 H 8
Ulricehamn, 8,504 H 8
Ulriksfors K 5
Umeå, 51,955 M 5
Umfors J 4
Uppsala, 97,315 L 7
Vadstena, 6,893 J 7
Vaggeryd, 4,840 J 8
Vålådalen H 5
Valdemarsvik, 3,590 K 7
Vänersborg, 19,975 G 7
Vännäs, 4,045 L 5
Vansbro, 2,941 H 6
Vara, 11,056 H 7
Varberg, 18,451 G 8
Värnamo, 15,939 J 8
Västerås, 108,823 J 7
Västerhaninge, †9,814 H 1
Västervik, 23,014 K 8
Vaxholm, 4,484 J 1
Växjö, 32,760 J 8
Vetlanda, 10,780 J 8
Vilhelmina, 9,426 K 4
Vimmerby, 7,257 J 8
Virserum, 4,650 J 8
Visby, 18,338 L 8
Vislanda, †2,594 H 8
Voxna, †960 J 6
Wallhamn G 7
Ystad, 14,002 H 9

OTHER FEATURES

Angerman (riv.) K 5
Åsnen (lake) J 8
Baltic (sea) K 9
Bolmen (lake) H 8
Bothnia (gulf) N 4
Byske (riv.) L 4
Dal (riv.) K 6
Fårö (isl.), 790 L 8
Gide (riv.) L 5
Göta (canal) J 7
Göta (riv.) H 7
Gotland (island), 52,952 L 8
Gotska Sandön (island) L 7
Gräsö (isl.), 706 L 6
Hanö (bay) J 9
Hjälmaren (lake) J 7
Hoburg (point) L 8
Hornslandet (peninsula) K 6
Indals (riv.) H 5
Jorm (lake) J 4
Kaitum (riv.) M 3
Kalix (riv.) N 3
Kall (lake) H 5
Kalmar (sound) K 8
Kattegat (strait) G 8
Kebnekaise (mt.) L 3
Kilpis (lake) M 2
Kjölen (mts.) K 3
Klar (riv.) H 6
Lainio (riv.) N 3
Lapland (region) M 2
Ljungan (riv.) K 5
Ljusnan (riv.) H 5
Lule (riv.) M 3
Mälaren (lake) G 1
Muonio (riv.) M 2
Öland (isl.), 20,416 K 8
Öre (riv.) L 4
Öresund (sound) H 9
Ornö (isl.), 224 J 2
Österdal (riv.) H 6
Pite (riv.) M 4
Siljan (lake) J 6
Skagerrak (strait) F 8
Skellefte (riv.) L 4
Sommen (lake) J 7
Stor (lake) J 5
Stora Lulevatten (lake) L 3
Storuman (lake) K 4
Sulitjelma (mountain) K 3
Torne (lake) L 2
Torne (riv.) M 3
Uddjaur (lake) L 4
Ume (riv.) L 4
Vänern (lake) H 7
Vasten (lake) K 3
Västerdal (riv.) H 6
Vättern (lake) J 7
Vindel (riv.) L 4
Vojmsjön (lake) K 4
Vuolvo (lake) L 3

*City and suburbs. †Population of rural parish or commune.

SWEDEN: Total pop.—1969 off. est.; counties & urban cities—1968 off. est.; capital (with suburbs)—1966 off. est.; other pops—1966 off. est.

ROLLING PLAINS of Skåne, the southernmost region, are the most fertile in Sweden. The town's whitewashed houses emphasize its similarity to Denmark, which ruled the area for centuries.

SWEDISH INFORMATION SERVICE

structures that underlie Denmark and most of the North European Plain and the ancient crystalline rocks that make up the core of the Fenno-scandian Shield in Sweden.

Southwestern Skåne is a low rolling plain, with deep, lime-rich glacial till and post-glacial clays. Its fertile soil and open terrain, combined with the longest and warmest growing season of any Swedish region, make Skåne the country's premium agricultural area. Northeastern Skåne is dominated by a series of fault-block ridges that stretch from the northwest to the southeast. The highest are forested, chiefly with beech and oak. Nevertheless, over 70% of the region is under cultivation, a fact that emphasizes Skåne's similarity to Denmark and its striking dissimilarity to the remainder of Sweden and Scandinavia. Skåne's agricultural preeminence is shown by the fact that it has nearly 25% of Sweden's wheat acreage, about 33% of its potato acreage, almost 50% of its oilseed acreage, and fully 75% of its sugar beet acreage.

Skåne's similarity to Denmark is not limited to its physical landscape and economic character, for its culture also has a Danish stamp. This is because Skåne was part of the Danish realm until the 17th century. The architectural style of its churches and of its whitewashed, half-timbered farmhouses contrasts sharply with the wooden frame buildings typical of the rest of rural Sweden.

Malmö is the largest city of the region and the third largest in Sweden. It is not only the leading commercial and industrial center of Skåne but also an important communications hub. Hälsingborg is on the Øresund opposite Helsingør, Denmark, and is the country's busiest ferry port. Lund, near Malmö, has the country's greatest cathedral and second-oldest university.

Baltic Islands. Off the southeast coast of Sweden are two low islands. Öland is near the Swedish mainland, and Gotland is near the middle of the Baltic. Both islands are composed of extremely porous limestones and sandstones. This fact, combined with the lowest precipitation of any region in Sweden, has resulted in the virtual absence of surface drainage on either island and a native vegetation that is almost steppelike. Gotland's dryness gives it the sunniest climate of any area north of the Alps.

Because of their strategic location, both islands were much contested by the Swedes and Danes during the Middle Ages. Gotland in particular occupied a critical position in the Baltic, and its west coast port of Visby became a key outpost of the Hanseatic League. But Visby never recovered after it was sacked by the Danes in 1361, and today it is a quiet tourist town. In addition to their tourist attractions, Öland and Gotland are among the country's most favored areas for cereal, oilseed, and sugar beet production.

VINCENT H. MALMSTRÖM
Middlebury College

2. The People

Geographically remote from most of the rest of Europe, isolated by mountains and the sea, Sweden has developed a remarkable homogeneity in its people, language, and religion.

The Swedes have been subject to relatively little intermixture with non-Swedish peoples, and, as a result, a general physical type has evolved: tall, fair, and blue-eyed. However, there have been occasional immigrations, of Germans in the Middle Ages and succeeding centuries, and also of Dutch, Walloons, Jews, Scots, and Finns. These have left definite traces in the population, and as a result, dark hair and brown eyes are by no means exceptional.

Linguistic and Religious Groups. The Swedish language is closely related to Danish and Norwegian. They all developed from a common

LAPLANDERS of the far north still maintain their nomadic life, depending on reindeer for food and clothes.

SWEDISH INFORMATION SERVICE

SWEDISH NATIONAL TRAVEL OFFICE

Apartment clusters, such as this imaginatively designed development near Göteborg, help ease housing shortage.

Scandinavian tongue of the Viking age. Spoken Swedish includes several regional and class dialects. Two non-Swedish languages spoken in northern Sweden are of regional importance. One is the language spoken by the Lapps of northern Sweden. The other is Finnish, spoken by a small minority living near the Finnish border. See also Section 8. *Language*.

Sweden is overwhelmingly Protestant. The Church of Sweden and the state have been linked by history and tradition since the reign of Gustav I in the 16th century. The established state church, headed by the archbishop of Uppsala, is Lutheran. Every Swedish child is born into the Church of Sweden and remains a member unless he notifies the church that he wishes to withdraw.

Family Life. Historically, Swedes have tended to marry later in life than the people of many other European countries. Partly because they marry late, Swedes have developed an unusually tolerant attitude toward premarital sexual relations and out-of-wedlock pregnancies. It has been estimated that 40% of all first-born babies are conceived before marriage. Some of these pregnancies, however, may be attributed to the continuing existence of an ancient rural tradition of delaying marriage until a child is conceived.

Although family unity has remained a key factor in Swedish life, large families are rare, and the birth rate is one of the lowest in the world. Before Sweden became industrialized, families were larger. But when it was agriculturally oriented the country could not support them all, and many young people emigrated. Modern families, many of whom live in urban areas where housing is in short supply, tend to be small, with an emphasis on shared educational, cultural, and recreational experiences.

Despite Sweden's tradition of family unity, the Swedish divorce rate is one of the highest in Europe, although not so great as that in some other highly developed nations, such as the United States. Among the reasons generally cited for the high divorce rate are the relative ease of obtaining a divorce, the declining influence of the Church of Sweden, and the emancipation of Swedish women. There are few legal obstacles to divorce, but the government makes every effort to keep families together. Compulsory mediation is required before legal separation can be granted, and the partners must be separated for a year before the divorce becomes final.

One reason for the emancipation of Swedish women has been their growing participation in the economy. As more women entered the work force, child care became a problem. Labor legislation finally divided the responsibility for child care and family support equally between the mother and the father. The establishment of numerous and inexpensive state-supported child care centers has been accelerated since World War II and has permitted many women who were previously tied to the home to enter the labor market.

Housing. Rising income levels, population movement toward the cities, and low, state-regulated rents have led to a rise in the demand for housing. The demand has outdistanced the capabilities of the highly mechanized and automated building industry. The housing shortage has created long waiting lists for rent-controlled accommodations and has led to a black market in rental contracts. New dwellings are distributed to those who have been on the waiting lists longest or to those who have special claims for preferential treatment.

The enormous heating expenses in Sweden's frigid winters have made apartments the most economical method of housing, even though there is more than enough land for individual houses. In the bigger cities a large proportion of the people, 90% in Stockholm, live in apartment houses, many with balconies.

Food and Drink. The mainstay of the Swedish diet is seafood, which is in abundant supply. Tiny fresh shrimp are brought to market daily. The Baltic herring, a fish similar to a California sardine, is cooked in many ways, often with dill. A favorite method of preparation is to dip them

K. W. GULLERS, FROM RAPHO GUILLUMETTE

Dalarna's annual cross-country race, the largest in the world, attests to skiing's continued popularity in Sweden.

in rye flour, spread mustard and clipped dill on the inside surfaces, and then sauté them in butter.

The famous Swedish smörgåsbord has its origin in pagan harvest feasts. *Smörgåsbord* means, essentially, "sandwich table." A great many of the dishes in a smörgåsbord are made up of preserved foods, such as pickled, jellied, or brine-soaked herring, and cheeses, hams, legs of lamb, sausage, and other cold meats. Salads also play an important role in it. The hot main courses are often meatballs, stuffed cabbage, and omelets. One advantage of this kind of meal is that much of it can be prepared long before the guests arrive.

The abundance of wild game, including fowl, in Sweden adds variety to the diet, as does the availability of reindeer meat, either smoked or as a roast or steak. There is, however, a noticeable shortage in the average diet of vegetables and fruit, many varieties of which must be imported. The juice of wild rose hips, extremely rich in vitamins, has become popular in recent years. It is served as a fruit juice or made into hot or cold soups. Wild lingonberries, blueberries, and many edible varieties of mushrooms are an essential part of the Swedish cuisine. The native drinks are aquavit, which is similar to vodka, and beer.

Recreation and Sports. Love of recreation is a Swedish characteristic that becomes obvious to any visitor to Sweden. Since it is an uncrowded country with much unspoiled land, Sweden has an abundance of recreational opportunities and a wide choice of outdoor activities. Strict conservation laws and a ban on roadside advertising help preserve the country's beauty. Camping and hiking in the vast Swedish woodlands and boating along the coast and on the numerous lakes are exceptionally popular pastimes. Sweden's many islands are open to all, and there are thousands of country cottages available for vacationers to rent.

Soccer, ice hockey, skiing, and skating are a few of the sports in which Swedish people of all ages participate. *Orienteering*, a grueling form of exercise combining cross-country running and the use of a compass, is also popular. Gymnastics are obligatory in school and in the military service, and many businesses have voluntary gymnastic programs. Since most Swedes are entitled to four weeks paid vacation a year, they have ample opportunities to indulge their passion for recreation.

Holidays. Most holidays in Sweden are connected with the changing of the seasons, and those that indicate a turn toward more daylight are especially festive. The birthday of the king, celebrated on November 11, is an exception. Walpurgis Night, the last day of April, signifies the long-awaited arrival of spring after seven months of darkness and cold. Midsummer's Eve

LUCIA GIRL symbolizes returning light on St. Lucia's Day, a pre-Christmas religious holiday.

SWEDISH INFORMATION SERVICE

SWEDISH NATIONAL TRAVEL OFFICE

Stockholm's Old City, which houses the Royal Palace, guards the passage between Baltic Sea and Lake Mälaren.

is marked during the week of June 19–25, the height of the brilliant northern summer. The central symbol is the maypole, a tall, flower-bedecked mast. Doors and verandas, ships, pleasure boats, buses, and taxis are all decorated with fresh green birch twigs.

The greatest family festival is Christmas. Traditionally, the Christmas season begins on December 13, when a young girl in each house assumes the role of St. Lucia (known as St. Lucy in English-speaking countries), donning a white robe and a crown of lighted candles. The custom goes back to Viking times when, under the old calendar, the night of December 12–13 was the longest of the year. The Lucia girl symbolizes returning light. During Christmas, people do their utmost to revive the old customs of rural households. The overflowing Christmas table is basically a relic of pagan times, when thanks were offered to the gods for a good harvest. The Christmas tree, introduced from Germany near the end of the 19th century, occupies the central position in Swedish homes.

STANDARDS OF LIVING AND POPULATION

Sweden has developed and maintained a superior standard of living during the 20th century, particularly since World War II. Swedish standards have continuously improved despite the problems inherent in a society whose population is changing from rural to urban, from farming to industrial.

Standard of Living and Social Welfare. Sweden has the highest standard of living in Europe and one of the highest in the world. This may be attributed to the country's vigorous economy, greatly aided by uninterrupted peace since the early 19th century, and the government's broad social welfare program, which guarantees the basic necessities of life to every citizen.

Sweden's remarkable system of social services is designed to provide financial security whenever an individual needs help, whatever the circumstances. Services range from medical care to family benefits and old age pensions. The social welfare program, to which more than 15% of the national income is devoted, is the outgrowth of an ancient Swedish commitment to mutual help. The state has assumed increasing responsibility for the various services, but the municipalities and the county councils also make contributions. Since the end of World War II the program has undergone spectacular expansion, which, while increasing benefits, has led to increased taxes.

For its older citizens, Sweden provides generous pensions. All people over 67 receive the basic pension, which includes adjustments for increases in the cost of living. In addition, former workers receive another pension, which is based on wages received before retirement. The two pensions amount to well over 50% of the income received during a worker's most productive years. Old age benefits are covered in the government's budget and by the employers' and the still-active workers' contributions.

Medical care is all-inclusive, ranging from workmen's compensation and general health coverage to maternity and child care benefits. All Swedes have been covered by compulsory health insurance since 1955. Its provisions include the cost of hospital treatment, a major portion of the costs of medicines and doctors, and daily sick-leave benefits to compensate for a high percentage of lost income. All employees are covered by workmen's compensation insurance that preserves the living standard of the injured and his family. For injuries not connected with employment, the compensation is comparable to the amount received in old-age pensions.

Sweden's far-reaching maternity and child care system has given Sweden one of the lowest infant mortality rates in the world. Every expectant mother is entitled to free prenatal and delivery care and to a cash payment when the child is born. A tax-free yearly allowance is provided for all children under 16. Pregnant women who have been employed at the same job for over a year are entitled to a six-month leave of absence; during that time they receive cash benefits equal to two thirds of their normal earnings. Low-cost government loans are available to parents, even if there is only an unwed mother or father, to establish a home for the child. Low-income families receive housing subsidies and free vacation travel for mothers and children. There are also day nurseries for the children of working mothers, and many large corporations provide extensive social services for their employees.

Population. In the early 1970's, Sweden had a population of slightly over 8 million. Since the mid-19th century, when it had about 3.5 million people, Sweden has changed from a country in which large numbers of people emigrated to new lands to a country with net immigration. During this same period it has shifted from an overwhelmingly rural society to an increasingly urban one.

Like the people in many other highly industrialized nations, the Swedes have shown a marked tendency during the 20th century to migrate to urban areas. In the mid-19th century about 10% of the people lived in urban areas; by the early 1970's the percentage had risen to over 50%. Although the average population density is slightly over 43 people per square mile (17 per sq km), there are wide variations within the country, ranging from under 10 per square mile (4 per sk km) in the extreme north to over 300 per square mile (115 per sq km) in parts of the Skåne region in the extreme south. Over 80% of the people are concentrated in the southern third of the country.

During the late 19th and early 20th centuries large numbers of Swedes emigrated, with over one million settling in the United States. By World War I, however, economic and social conditions in Sweden had improved, and emigration slowed drastically. Since World War II, people entering Sweden have greatly outnumbered those leaving the country. Immigrants are responsible for a sizable part of the increase in Sweden's population since World War II.

Although Sweden's birth rate remains one of the lowest not only in Europe but the world, it is still greater than the death rate. In addition, better standards of health permit people to live much longer than they did in the 19th century. The combination of longer life and low birth rates has produced a society with a large percentage of older people. Life expectancy is about 71 years for men and approximately 76 years for women.

3. The Culture

Sweden has an unusually varied and distinguished cultural record, expressed in both the creative arts and in science. Its culture has retained its distinctive Swedish features, but in modern times it has also acquired a strong international flavor. Throughout the country, the basic acceptance of culture and art is visible in the abundance of paintings, sculpture, industrial art objects, and handicrafts that embellish Swedish homes as well as schools, offices, and municipal buildings. Sweden has acquired added luster through its association with the world-famous Nobel Prizes.

Its cultural life is enhanced by the more than 400 private foundations, such as the Nobel Foundation, that give patronage to the arts and science and by the government's extensive program of support. State patronage embraces not only grants to schools and cultural institutions but also a system of payments to artists, actors, writers, dancers, film makers, designers, and craftsmen. Swedes are avid readers, which benefits Swedish writers, who since 1955 have received library royalties based on the number of times their books are borrowed.

Literature. Swedish literature has at times been creative and original, at other times merely reflective of current European cultural forces. For long periods it was chiefly distinguished for its poetry and nonepic literature. Only since the end of the 19th century has the country produced novelists and dramatists of eminence.

The oldest known Swedish writing is found on some 2,500 rune stones, most of which date from the 11th century and which show Sweden within the orbit of Old Norse traditions. Later, chronicles and ballads expressed Sweden's Scandinavian heritage. During the Middle Ages, much Swedish literature was devoted to religious and political-historical writings.

In 1541, some 50 years after the introduction of the printing press in Sweden, the first complete translation of the Bible gave the Swedish language a new standard of clarity and form. Olaus Petri, the chief translator of the Bible, also wrote the first critical history of Sweden. The purification and standardization of the language continued through the 17th century, notably in the work of the poet Georg Stiernhielm.

During the 18th century, Swedish literature was greatly influenced by France and by the court of Gustav III. Olof von Dalin's works reflected the influence of the 18th century rationalism, while Thomas Thorild passionately defended Jean Jacques Rousseau's idealism. The outstanding literary figure at Gustav's court was Carl Michael Bellman, a poet and composer of unique artistic skill. Linnaeus, the great naturalist, is now recognized as an early prose master. Another 18th century giant was Emmanuel Swedenborg, whose writing embraced the physical and natural sciences, religion, and philosophy.

During the first half of the 19th century, Swedish literature passed through an era of romanticism. One of this period's aspects was an interest in the past and its traditions. Esaias Tegnér was one exponent of classic tradition and also defended Platonic idealism. Later in the century Viktor Rydberg refined Tegnér's idealism and grappled with the problems of emerging industrialism.

In the late 19th century, Swedish literature was revolutionized by August Strindberg, a dramatist, novelist, poet, and painter who is now regarded as the greatest author Sweden has yet produced. Selma Lagerlöf's early work, romantic interpretations of Swedish tales, was part of the reaction against Strindberg's naturalism. She was the first Swede to receive the Nobel Prize for literature, in 1909. Gustaf Fröding, another great lyric poet, often wrote about his native Värmland. Verner von Heidenstam and Erik Axel Karlfeldt, who were also part of the neoromantic reaction against Strindberg, were both awarded the Nobel Prize for literature.

As in earlier times, much of Sweden's finest production in the 20th century has been in the field of lyric poetry, which had figures like Gunnar Ekelöf and Erik Lindegren. A group known as the Young Five, whose work was characterized by vivid imagery and a kinship with nature, emerged in the 1930's. The 20th century authors best known outside Sweden are Pär Lagerkvist, who won the Nobel Prize for literature in 1951, Vilhelm Moberg, and, with the publication of *Markings* in 1964, Dag Hammarskjöld. Among the contemporary writers who are widely admired in Sweden but unfamiliar to most foreign readers are Eyvind Johnson, Ivar Lo-Johansson, Jan Fridegård, Per Olof Sundman, and Harry Martinson, a novelist who was also one of the Young Five poets.

Theater and Motion Pictures. Both theater and motion pictures thrive in Sweden. The leading theater is the Royal Dramatic Theater in Stockholm, founded in 1788 by Gustav III. The Drottningholm Court Theater just outside Stockholm is used mainly in the summer. In addition, many communities have municipal playhouses. Radio and television programs play an important part in familiarizing the public with both classic and modern drama and comedy. Touring drama companies give thousands of performances each year in parks, hospitals, and other institutions.

The Swedish theater is decidedly international, presenting numerous foreign plays each season. The U. S. playwright Eugene O'Neill became a particular favorite of Swedish audiences. Strindberg has long been recognized as Sweden's greatest dramatist. Other noted dramatists include the 20th century playwrights Hjalmar Bergman, also a well-known novelist; Pär Lagerkvist; and Stig Dagerman.

Swedish films, highlighted by names such as Greta Garbo, Victor Sjöström, and Mauritz Stiller, enjoyed a golden age from 1916 to 1923. After a period of decline new heights were reached, primarily through the efforts of such directors as Alf Sjöberg, Ingmar Bergman, Arne Sucksdorff, Bo Widerberg, Vilgot Sjöman, and later, Jan Troell. Ingrid Bergman, who became a star in her native Sweden, made her best-known films in English. In 1963 the Swedish Film Institute, which runs training programs and awards film prizes, was established.

The Visual Arts. Swedish art dates back to the dawn of civilization. Artifacts from the Bronze Age reveal an independent style, and ornaments in gold from the 5th and 6th centuries A.D. also show remarkable artistic skill. A high degree of craftsmanship was achieved in the Middle Ages. Particularly notable are the combinations of wood, stone, and bronze in such figures as Bernt Notke's *St. George and the Dragon*, in Stockholm's Great Church.

The 18th century produced several eminent painters and a great sculptor, Johan T. Sergel, who won fame in Rome. Gustavus Hesselius, one of the fathers of American painting, and Adolph Ulrich Wertmüller were among the artists who emigrated to North America. Three 20th century Swedish artists, the painters Anders Zorn and Ernst Josephson and the sculptor Carl Milles have been accorded international recognition.

Swedish architecture has a tradition of harmonizing structures with their landscape. The medieval log cabin, a variation of which was introduced into North America by Swedish colonists; the castles of the 16th century; the classical Royalist Palace in Stockholm; and graceful manor houses all reflect this principle. Simplicity of design, a striving for light, and closeness to surrounding scenery are the main characteristics of contemporary Swedish architecture and town planning. Among distinguished Swedish architects are Ragnar Östberg, who designed Stockholm's romantic City Hall, and Sven Markelius.

The Swedes are very conscious of design. The main objectives in the applied arts are simplicity and functional utility. Swedish progress in industrial art and design has been promoted by the Society for Industrial Design, founded in 1845, which has worked to cultivate the national taste by educating the public to appreciate beautiful objects, and by cooperating with the manufacturers of furniture, textiles, and all other household equipment. In the 1930's the Swedish style of home interiors and household articles became known as "Swedish modern."

Music. Music flourished at Gustav III's court. The Academy of Music was founded in 1771 at his initiative, and the Stockholm Opera, including the Royal Ballet, was set up in 1773. The classical period of the 19th century produced one of Sweden's few composers of international significance, the symphonist Franz Berwald. Inspiration has often flowed from the nation's store of folk music, as it does in Hugo Alfvén's *Midsummer Vigil*, often known as *Swedish Rhapsody*. Several cities have their own symphony orchestras, and chamber music is also popular.

Many singers have become widely known outside Sweden. In 1850–1852, Jenny Lind, called "the Swedish Nightingale," made epochal tours in the United States. Three decades later, Christine Nilsson helped dedicate the Metropolitan Opera House in New York. She has been followed by the tenors Jussi Björling and Nicolai Gedda, and the soprano Birgit Nilsson, whose debut at the Metropolitan in 1960 was a historic success.

Science and Invention. Swedes have fashioned an enviable record in both the theoretical and the applied sciences. Jöns Berzelius, in addition to his many practical experiment's, brought organization to the field of chemistry. Carl Linnaeus, whose systems are still in use, introduced botanical classifications in the 18th century. Noted inventors have included Alfred Nobel, who developed high explosives, and John Ericsson, who devised the screw propellor and built ironclad ships during the U. S. Civil War.

Cultural Institutions. Sweden's cultural heritage is attractively preserved in its many museums. Among the museums in Stockholm are the National Gallery, the Museum of Musical History, the Skansen outdoor museum, and the Historic Museum, all of which chronicle Sweden's rich history. The Skansen exhibitions include examples of characteristic farmhouses, churches, furniture, and other objects that were common before Sweden became industrialized.

INGMAR BERGMAN (*left*) internationally acclaimed film director, sets a scene for his film *Persona*.

SWEDISH INFORMATION SERVICE

In Växjö, in the south of Sweden, there is the Glass Museum, devoted solely to the nation's world-famous glass industry, while in Luleå, in the extreme north, the Norrbottens Läns Museum reminds the modern world of the pagan history and culture of the Lapps. Architectually challenging museums are found in practically every city. One is the Emigrants' Museum in Växjö, commemorating the more than 1.5 million Swedes who sailed for North America in the 19th century.

Press, Radio, and Television. Sweden's constitution forbids censorship, and the media operate within self-imposed disciplines. The combined daily newspaper circulation is more than 4 million copies, and Stockholm dailies are quickly distributed by air all over the country. Newspapers cover the domestic and international political and cultural scenes in depth.

"Radio Sweden" sends out several simultaneous programs, including news reports, music, and educational features. Swedish television has developed very rapidly. No advertising is permitted on either radio or television.

KIT ROBBINS, FROM RAPHO GUILLUMETTE

YOUNG GIRLS in traditional regional costumes arrange bunches of wild flowers for a spring festival.

4. Education

Sweden's concern to educate all its citizens dates back to the 19th century. Primary education has been compulsory since 1842, and by the second half of the 20th century the illiteracy rate had been reduced to about 1%. The basic objective of the modern Swedish system is to give every child the opportunity to rise educationally as far as he is mentally able. Compulsory education has been extended to nine years, during the last years of which students are directed towards various forms of higher education, such as gymnasiums leading to the universities, and vocational schools. Adult interest in education is maintained through adult education courses, the "folk" high schools, and numerous study circles.

Comprehensive School System. Early in the 1960's, a nationwide, 9-year comprehensive school system was established, and a new basic curriculum was adopted in 1968. During the first six years under this system, pupils are taught all subjects by their classroom teachers, while in the last three years they are instructed by subject teachers. Classes are limited to 25 pupils in the first three years and to 30 pupils thereafter.

The teaching of English begins in grade 3, and from grade 7, when the natural sciences are introduced, either German or French may be added as a second language. Vocational guidance is also offered in grade 7 and continues through grade 8, when all pupils, regardless of their field of study, are required to complete three weeks of some kind of job training under actual working conditions. Elective subjects are introduced in grades 7 and 8, and by grade 9 the student is oriented toward one of nine different fields, five of which are academic and four of which are vocational.

The Upper Schools. The schooling that follows the first nine years is divided into three categories: the gymnasiums, the continuation schools, and the vocational institutes. After completion of their compulsory schooling, about half of the students elect to continue their education in one of these three types of schools.

Admission to the gymnasiums, through which university-bound students pass, is based upon the final marks received in the ninth grade. The gymnasiums offer three years of study in five separate areas: liberal arts, social sciences, economics, natural sciences, and technical arts. All except technical arts students are required to study three foreign languages for at least one year each.

The 2-year continuation schools, which also use ninth grade marks as entrance criteria, offer social studies, business, and technical courses. The continuation schools are designed to give pupils job-oriented educations. The vocational schools, some of which are run by private companies, have technical courses of up to four years.

Higher Education. Sweden's first university, Uppsala, was founded in 1477. There are four other universities: Lund, Göteborg, Stockholm, and Umeå, the last established in 1963. The universities grant degrees in the humanities, social sciences, and natural sciences. The four older universities each have a branch in a smaller city. There are numerous institutes of technology and medical schools, most of which are scheduled for expansion in the 1970's.

Adult Education. Sweden's educational network includes many thousands of adults as students. In the local adult education courses, the curriculums of the upper level of the comprehensive school system, the gymnasium, and the vocational school are followed. The distinctively Scandinavian folk high schools, which try to stimulate interest in social and cultural questions, are run by civic, social, political, and religious organizations and play an important part in adult education. Another form of adult education is provided by the study circles, which are run by the popular educational societies and focus on subjects of common interest to a group. The adult education system is subsidized by the national government.

An important new phase of adult education was begun in 1967 with experimental educational programs produced by the Swedish Broadcasting Corporation and transmitted over radio. People in rural districts and the remote areas of the north,

K. W. GULLERS, FROM RAPHO GUILLUMETTE

Modern farm equipment is used in Skåne's southern plains, where Swedish farms are largest and most productive.

previously cut off from more organized education courses, may choose among a wide variety of programs. The broadcasts are financed by the government.

Government Aid. Sweden has a highly developed student-aid system aimed at allowing all students, whatever their financial status, to obtain as much schooling as they need. All younger pupils receive a flat grant that is supplemented according to need. Pupils in the 9-year comprehensive school system receive free textbooks, free educational materials, and free lunches. Grants and scholarships are available for students at a more advanced level, and all students in need of further economic assistance are entitled to loans.

MAC LINDAHL, *Associate Editor*
"Swedish North Star"

5. The Economy

In the last decades of the 19th century, Sweden ranked as one of the poorest countries in western Europe. Its day as a great political power was long since past. Its rural, agrarian society was barely able to feed itself. In addition, a massive wave of emigration to North America was beginning, a wave that took almost 20% of its population before World War I virtually stopped emigration.

Today, in contrast, Sweden ranks as the wealthiest country per capita in Europe. Its urban-industrial society enjoys what is probably the most uniformly high standard of living of any nation in the world. Sweden has become a goal for many thousands of economically, socially, and politically disadvantaged persons from other European countries as well as a model for developing nations in all parts of the globe. This near-miraculous transformation of Swedish society can in large measure be attributed to the dramatic changes that have taken place in the economy since World War I.

Agriculture, Forestry, and Fishing. In the early 1970's less than one Swede in eight earned his livelihood in the primary occupations of farming, forestry, and fishing, compared with nearly three out of four at the turn of the century.

Agriculture. In the agricultural sector this transformation has manifested itself not only in an absolute and a relative decline in the number of persons living and working on farms but also in a steady decrease in the number of farms. The number of farms has fallen from more than 300,000 in the 1920's to about 180,000. At the same time the average farm's size has grown through consolidation to about 35 acres (14 hectares).

Mechanization has proceeded to the point where agricultural economists feel that many farms are actually over-capitalized in equipment. This is especially so on the larger and more prosperous holdings in the south and central regions, where nearly 90% of the tractors are found. The improvement of plant and animal strains, together with the extensive use of fertilizers, has steadily boosted the output of both crops and livestock products, and estimates place the increase in productivity of farm labor in the 1960's at 5% to 6% per year.

Only 8% of Sweden's land area is in agricultural use—7.5% under cultivation and 0.5% in permanent pasture. The distribution of arable land is extremely uneven, ranging from about 70% of the area of the Skåne lowland to about 0.5% in the interior of heavily-forested Norrland. The largest farms are found on the more extensive plains of Skåne, the Central Lowland (Svealand), and Sweden's Baltic islands. Small farms predominate in the forests and valleys of the Southern Highland (Götaland) and Norrland.

The economic returns of Swedish farms correlate very closely with their size and geographic location: those in the plains regions of the south and center earn half again as much as the national average. In contrast, farms in the forest and valley regions of the south and center are only half as profitable as the larger farms in the plains, and those in Norrland earn less than one third as much.

The average farmer derives 60% of his income from animal products, with dairy products exceeding meat in importance. Though vegetable products contribute about 25% to the average farmer's income, they vary in importance from over one third of the total income of the larger farms in the plains regions to less than 4% on the marginal farms of Norrland. The reverse is true of the contribution made to farm income by forest products, which average about 9% for the country as a whole. In the plains forest products yield less than 4% of farm income, but in Norrland they contribute almost 30% of the total.

Of Sweden's arable land, nearly 80% is used for the cultivation of fodder crops such as hay, oats, and barley. Winter wheat, the most important bread grain, occupies 10% of the cultivated land, and potatoes, root crops, and oilseeds, such as rapeseeds, occupy most of the remainder.

Cattle, Sweden's most important form of livestock, are fairly evenly distributed over the country. In the 1960's, the number of milk cows decreased by one third, but because the yield per cow increased, the actual volume of milk sold rose steadily. Almost all dairy production and distribution is handled by cooperatives. The number of sheep nearly doubled between 1960 and 1970, with one third of the total raised on the islands. Pigs also increased slightly but were almost totally restricted to Skåne and Halland in the far south.

Sweden's farms are capable of supplying all of the dairy products, meat, potatoes, and sugar beets consumed in the country, as well as over 80% of the bread grains. Tropical and subtropical foodstuffs constitute a sizable import item for the affluent Swedish market.

Forestry. Forestry, on the other hand, is primarily an export-oriented occupation. Although lumber has represented a major item in foreign trade for over 300 years, the discovery in Sweden in the mid-19th century of a process for making paper from wood pulp greatly spurred the country's wood industries. Over half the annual cut is now used for pulpwood and a further 40% is harvested as lumber.

To maintain a sustained yield, the annual cut is kept to a rate of only about two thirds the annual regrowth. Because growth is slower in the more northern latitudes, Norrland, which has nearly half the forest resources, contributes only about 40% of the annual regrowth. Svealand and Götaland contain about 25% of forest resources each, but, because of their faster growth rates, they contribute some 60% of the annual forest regrowth.

More than half of the woodlands are owned by individual farmers, especially in Svealand and Götaland. The largest corporate holdings are in the more accessible and productive areas of southern Norrland. State holdings are primarily concentrated in the more marginal northern and mountain districts of Norrland, where strictly supervised harvesting insures the forests' preservation.

Accessibility is a primary factor in the economic value of any forest area, and in Sweden this has chiefly meant access to rivers down which timber could be floated. Some 7,100 miles (11,425 km) of timber floatways are in use, principally along the larger rivers of Norrland. But because their utility is restricted to the high-water period of late spring and early summer, a steadily increasing proportion of the timber harvest is taken to processing centers by rail and road transport.

Fishing. In fishing, as in farming, there has been a definite trend since World War II toward fewer, but larger and more efficient, operating units, with a consequent reduction in the number of persons employed. There are fewer than 7,500 full-time fishermen, a reduction of nearly 25% in the 1960's. Sweden's west coast fishermen make up more than 60% of the fishing labor force. Modernization of the fishing fleet after 1960 resulted in a 50% increase in the annual catch. Most fishing takes place in the North Sea and the adjacent Skagerrak and Kattegat, and the bulk of the processing is done in Bohuslän, north of Göteborg. The principal species caught in Swedish waters are herring, cod, *strömming* (Baltic herring), and mackerel.

Mining. Sweden's subsoil is the richest in mineral resources in northern Europe, and mining has made an important contribution to the economy since Sweden's emergence as a state in the 13th century. By far the greatest mineral resource is iron ore, of which there are vast high-grade deposits both in Lappland, in the far north of Norrland, and in Bergslagen (literally, "the mining district"), at the southern edge of Norrland.

There are about 300 iron mines within these two districts, employing about 7,000 miners and producing more than 28 million tons (25 million metric tons) of iron ore annually. Most of the ore, which accounts for 75% of the annual value of minerals, is exported through the ports of Narvik, in Norway, and Luleå in the north and through Oxelösund, south of Stockholm.

There are also some 120 other mines, most of which produce such metallic ores as copper, lead, zinc, silver, and gold. By far the largest concentration is found in the Skellefte district of Norrland, centered on the town of Boliden. There a large flotation works separates about half a dozen metals from a polymetallic ore, one of whose impurities is arsenic, making Sweden the world's largest producer of this poison. In the Central Lowland near Örebro, uranium is extracted from oil shale deposits, and in northwestern Skåne, near Bjuv, there is some production of low-grade coal.

Manufacturing. In the early 1970's about 35% of the labor force earned its living in industry. The most important branch of manufacturing is metal products and engineering, which employs

DRIED FISH, a staple of the Swedish diet, are processed in the west country of Bohuslän. Most fishing is done in the nearby Skagerrak and Kattegat.

SWEDISH NATIONAL TRAVEL OFFICE

nearly 50% of the industrial labor force. One measure of the international reputation of the Swedish engineering industries is the fact that one third of all their production is done under foreign contract.

Among the leading metal products of these industries are transportation equipment, electrical machinery, iron and steel, and ships. The transportation equipment industry is dominated by the production of cars, trucks, and buses, but also includes aircraft and railway rolling stock. Some of the internationally known firms working in this field include Volvo, with its headquarters in Göteborg, and SAAB, centered in Linköping. SAAB is also Sweden's principal builder of military aircraft.

The electrotechnical industry specializes in items such as high-voltage equipment, including electric locomotives and telecommunications equipment. Among a host of other well-known Swedish electrical and nonelectrical machinery products are household appliances, computers, and office equipment.

The iron and steel industry is also noted for the quality rather than the quantity of its products. By specializing in stainless, alloy, and high-carbon steels and by continuing technological innovation, the steel industry finds a ready market both at home and abroad, though it cannot at present meet Sweden's own demand for ordinary commercial steels. Thus, Sweden is a net importer of iron and steel by volume, but it has a substantial export surplus by value.

Most steel mills are located in or near the Bergslagen. In the 1960's, however, two of the largest mills were built near the coast, one by private interests at Oxelösund, the main shipping port for Bergslagen ores, and one at Luleå, constructed by the government. Luleå's was built to help diversify the economy of Lappland and to help fill the nation's needs for structural steel.

In shipbuilding, Sweden has edged ahead of both Britain and West Germany to become second only to Japan. Unlike Japan, which capitalizes on its relatively low wage rates, Sweden, with the highest hourly wages in Europe, has stressed automated building techniques. The country's largest shipyards are on the west coast near Göteborg and Malmö. More than 75% of their work is carried out under foreign contract, with Norway the largest single buyer.

The wood-using industries, drawing their raw materials from Sweden's forests, are the second most important branch of manufacturing. Paper and cardboard, cellulose, sawmill products, and furniture are the main products. Because these industries chiefly make use of raw materials, they are concentrated at river mouths along the coast of Norrland, on the shores of Lake Vänern, and in the Southern Highland. The furniture and car-

Göteborg, Sweden's largest port, serves both commercial and passenger vessels and has extensive shipyards.

K. W. GULLERS, FROM RAPHO GUILLUMETTE

SWEDISH INFORMATION SERVICE

KIRUNA'S iron mines in Lapland are among the richest in the world. Government housing and high wages are provided in order to lure workers to this barren region.

pentry goods industries are primarily in the Southern Highland, where both hardwoods and softwoods are found.

Unlike the metal, engineering, and wood-using industries, most other branches of manufacturing are domestically oriented. The textile and clothing industry is chiefly centered around Göteborg and Borås in the west and around Stockholm and Norrköping in the east. Food processing is widely scattered over the center and south and is locally concentrated in Skåne. There are also chemical, earth and stone, and graphics industries, the last primarily localized in Stockholm.

Labor Force. About 95% of all Swedish workers are members of one of the 37 unions associated with the Landsorganisationen i Sverige (LO), or Confederation of Trade Unions. About 20% of the members are women. Since the LO's founding in 1898, Swedish workers have been organized by branches of industry rather than by specialized crafts. As a consequence all collective bargaining is at once industry-wide and nationwide, so Sweden has enjoyed protracted periods of labor peace. Salaried workers also have strong organizations. Early in 1970 a separate organization representing workers in the various state-owned industries was created after their representation had become a major issue in a wildcat strike in the Lappland iron mines. On the management side, negotiations are handled by the Svenska Arbetsgivareföreningen (SAF), or Swedish Employers' Confederation, which represents 43 branch associations.

Sweden's major post–World War II labor problem has been a scarcity of skilled workers. High wages have drawn increasing numbers of married women and foreign emigrants into the labor market. Rather than instituting unemployment insurance, the Swedish government has adopted a policy of full employment by maintaining a job service, by providing moving expenses, by assisting the unemployed with grants until they are reemployed, and by retraining workers displaced by automation.

Power and Transportation. Although Sweden is notably deficient in fossil fuels, it is bountifully supplied with hydroelectric energy. The country is estimated to have a developable potential of some 20 million kilowatts, of which only half was harnessed in the early 1970's. Because over 80% of its waterpower reserves are in Norrland, Sweden has been obliged to construct some of the longest high-tension transmission lines in the world to bring power to the cities and factories in the south. There are also auxiliary thermoelectric stations near the three largest cities, and two nuclear-powered plants are scheduled for construction on the east coast south of Stockholm whenever such power becomes economically competitive. The Swedish power grid is linked to those of Norway, Finland, and Denmark.

Sweden's first venture in the field of "modern" transportation was undertaken in 1832 with the construction of the Göta canal system linking the east and west coasts through Lakes Vänern and Vättern. The canal's utility was restricted by ice from the outset and in modern times its small locks have limited its use to small steamers and pleasure craft, except in the section between Göteborg and Lake Vänern. The railway age dawned in Sweden in 1856, and construction proceeded rapidly until World War II. Since the end of the war, however, railway mileage has gradually decreased. About 95% of the railroads are owned by the state, and nearly 60% of the mileage is electrified. Passenger traffic declined in the 1960's, but freight traffic increased by about 50% during the same period. Domestic air transportation links all major provincial towns and even such outlying areas as Gotland and Lappland with Stockholm and other large cities. The country's two busiest airports are Arlanda and Bromma, which serve Stockholm, followed by those at Göteborg, Malmö, and Visby.

No country in Europe has reoriented its transportation system toward the automobile more than Sweden. From an average of one passenger car for every 125 Swedes in 1945, the proportion rose by the early 1970's to more than one for every four persons. In the interests of safety and of conforming with other continental countries, Sweden switched from left-hand to right-hand driving in 1967 and has embarked on an ambitious program of highway improvement, especially near large cities. Of the more than 60,000 miles (96,550 km) of highways, some 8,000 miles (12,800 km) are maintained as national roads.

Since Sweden depends heavily on both exports and imports, shipping is a key factor in commerce. About 75 million tons (68 million metric tons) of goods move through Swedish ports each year, with Göteborg accounting for nearly 20% of the total. Not only does Göteborg serve as the country's principal import port, but it also handles sizable transshipments to second-ranking Stockholm. Luleå and Oxelösund both specialize in iron ore export, but in all other major ports the inbound traffic exceeds outbound traffic by a substantial margin.

Trade and Banking. About 15% of the labor force earns its living in commerce. Almost 20% of the country's retail sales take place in consumer cooperatives. The Kooperativa Förbundet, originally active in food distribution, is now engaged in numerous sectors of the economy.

In foreign trade, Sweden maintains a slight imbalance of imports over exports. The principal imports are crude oil and petroleum products, automobiles, clothing, finished steel, fresh fruit, and coffee. The countries of the European Free Trade Association (EFTA) and the European Economic Community (EEC), or Common Market, each contribute just over one third of the total. West Germany is Sweden's biggest single supplier, followed by Britain, the United States, and Norway. Sweden's principal exports are pulp and paper, finished steel, automobiles, lumber, iron ore, telecommunications equipment, and office machines, with more than 40% destined for countries of the EFTA and just over 25% to the EEC. The largest buyers of Swedish goods are Britain, West Germany, Norway, and Denmark.

The Bank of Sweden, which shapes the nation's economic policies, is controlled by the Riksdag and works closely with the government. It serves as a central bank and as the clearinghouse for commercial banks.

VINCENT H. MALMSTRÖM
Middlebury College

6. Government

Sweden is a constitutional monarchy. The king is chief of state, but his functions are mainly ceremonial. Political power is divided between the executive branch and the legislative branch, as provided in the written constitution. Although Sweden has a multiparty system, it has enjoyed stable government since the 1930's. Adult suffrage is universal. Swedish government has been built upon an ancient respect for the rule of law, and life, liberty, and property are rigorously protected.

National Government. The Swedish constitution has four fundamental laws. The basic Instrument of Government of 1809 outlines the national government's essential organization, powers, and responsibilities. The Succession Act, passed in 1810 when Marshal Jean Baptiste Bernadotte became crown prince, provides for inheritance of the crown by male primogeniture in the Bernadotte family. The other two basic laws are the Parliament Act and the Freedom of the Press Act. Formal amendments to the constitution are effective only when approved by the executive branch —called the "government"—speaking through the king, and when adopted by two successive sessions of the Riksdag, or parliament.

The prime minister is the head of the government. He presides over the cabinet, which is composed of approximately 20 ministers. All but five or six of these have portfolios, which means that they head a government department. A unique feature of Swedish government is that, except for the minister of foreign affairs, the ministers are not responsible for routine administrative work, which is handled by central boards. The ministers and their immediate staffs are therefore free to spend their energies on questions of policy, instead of dissipating them on minute supervision.

To gain office and to remain in office the cabinet must enjoy the confidence of the Riksdag, although they need not be members of it. If the Riksdag expresses a loss of confidence by defeating a key government proposal, the government may either resign or dissolve the Riksdag and hold new elections.

In 1971 the Riksdag became unicameral, with 350 members elected for 3-year terms by proportional representation. Candidates for public office are nominated by their respective parties. The main functions of the Riksdag are to accept, revise, or reject government proposals for new laws, to pass a budget, to impose taxes, and to control the administration. Powerful standing committees examine what the government has done and what it proposes to do. On any particular issue, it is possible to solicit the views of the electorate directly through a consultative referendum.

Political Parties and Pressure Groups. Political parties in Sweden are marked by consensus and stability. The largest party is the Social Democratic party, which normally gains about half the vote and half the seats in the Riksdag elections. It has dominated Swedish governments for decades. The Communist Left party has the smallest representation in the Riksdag, drawing about 5% of the vote. The remaining 45% of the votes and the corresponding seats are divided more or less equally among the three bourgeois parties: the Center party, which has a strong agrarian base; the Liberal, or People's, party; and the Moderate Unity party, formerly the Conservative party. Each party in the Riksdag receives a state subsidy of 60,000 kronor per seat.

There is a general consensus in the population and among the four large parties on the most basic issues of political and economic policy, as well as foreign policy. The governing Social Democrats are moderate socialists, dedicated to parliamentary democracy. The use of private property is restricted by taxation and government regulation, but the underlying basis of the economy is private ownership. The social welfare system guarantees that no one need be hungry or homeless, and it assures the sick of medical care, but it does not remove the incentive to work for material rewards beyond these bare necessities.

Since there is a consensus on basic issues, political rivalry concerns itself with the allocation of marginal resources among competing groups. The parties in the Riksdag are paralleled by outside pressure groups, such as the Confederation of Trade Unions (L.O.), the Federation of Swedish Farmers' Associations, the Central Organization of Salaried Employees, the Federation of Swedish Industries, and the Swedish Employers' Confederation (S.A.F.). Nationwide collective labor agreements are negotiated by the

L.O. and the S.A.F. The very powerful cooperative movement is exemplified by the Kooperativa Förbundet, or K.F., which is at once manufacturer, importer, wholesaler, and retailer on behalf of its more than 1 million consumer members. Voluntary associations are widespread and very influential in Swedish political life.

The genius of the Swedish political system is found in the highly developed art of engendering compromise. No important bill is introduced into the Riksdag without advance consultation by the government with all interested groups. More serious matters may be referred to a royal commission for exhaustive investigation before a program is outlined. The goal, often attained, is to reach a pragmatic unanimity in which differences have been reconciled, bargained away, or simply transcended.

Administrative System. Central administration is carried out by independent administrative boards. Although subordinate to the government ministries, the boards work independently. The agencies that are included within the purview of a particular ministry are headed by a director general, who makes decisions in consultation with his bureau chiefs. The director general does not take orders directly from a minister, but applies the law (Riksdag statutes and governmental regulations) on his own responsibility. Among the duties of a central board is supervising the implementation of the laws by subordinate agencies, including those of local government.

Civil servants have job security, and they may not be dismissed arbitrarily. A number of devices are used to ensure that government employees themselves do not act arbitrarily. One of these is the unique requirement that official documents be open to the public, including the press, to read and copy.

In addition to scrutiny by the public and the Riksdag, administrative officials are subject to investigation and censure or prosecution by the chancellor of justice and by the three ombudsmen who are appointed by the Riksdag to receive the public's complaints of bureaucratic abuse. The Swedish institution of ombudsman has spread to Finland, Denmark, Norway, New Zealand, several Canadian provinces, Hawaii, and, slightly modified, to Britain.

Local Government. Sweden is divided into 25 län, or counties, including Stockholm, which is a distinct unit under a special law. Each county has a crown-appointed governor and an elected council. Some of the larger municipalities have autonomy from the county councils. In addition to administering national laws, the county administrations supervise local government units, which are responsible for primary and secondary education, social and public services, hygiene and sanitary conditions, and local taxes.

The main units of local self-government are the urban and rural districts, which are governed by city councils or rural councils elected by proportional representation. For greater efficiency, the number of districts is being reduced, on the principle that each should have a population of at least 8,000. Depending upon the size of the district, the number of councilmen varies from 15 to 80, except for Stockholm, which has 100. The Stockholm city council chooses 12 of its own members to serve as an executive committee and 9 others, some of whom may not be councilmen, to serve as full-time, salaried administrative commissioners.

Legal System. Judicial independence is well established in Sweden. Supreme judicial power rests in a supreme court and a supreme administrative court. The courts do not normally test the constitutionality of laws passed by the Riksdag, but the government obtains an advance opinion on their constitutionality and on other technical questions from the law council, composed of selected members of the two supreme courts. Under the supreme court are six courts of appeal and urban and rural district courts. In rural district courts, elected laymen serve as assistants to the judge and, if they unanimously disagree with his decision, can overrule him. Otherwise, Sweden does not use juries, except in cases involving freedom of the press. There are also special courts, such as the labor court, which hears disputes arising from collective bargaining agreements.

Defense. Sweden has not fought in any war, either local or international, since 1815. When wars have broken out, Sweden has announced its neutrality. To buttress its nonalignment, Sweden strives towards military self-sufficiency and belongs to no military alliances. The Swedish arms industry is substantial. A strong army, navy, and air force are maintained through universal military service.

Within the limits of nonalignment, Sweden pursues an active foreign policy directed toward the maintenance of international peace and the application of humanitarian principles. This policy is expressed through membership in Nordic, European, and world organizations. Sweden supports arms limitations. The government speaks out against what it considers to be unlawful or unjust acts by other states. The goal for aid to developing nations has been set at 1% of Sweden's gross national product.

STANLEY V. ANDERSON
University of California, Santa Barbara

7. History

The first signs of human habitation in Sweden date from between 10,000 and 8000 B. C., following the last glacial period. The earliest inhabitants were hunters and gatherers. Settled agriculture and livestock raising appeared around 3000 B. C. Bronze was used in Scandinavia by about 1500 B. C. and iron after about 500 B. C. With the development of the iron ax, new farmland could be cleared and more elaborate boats built. A rude democracy of armed peasant freemen came into being, and the characteristic peasant commune evolved. Early place-names reveal no pre- or non-Nordic settlement, except by the Lapps in the far north.

Native historical records are notably lacking for Sweden before the 14th century. Occasional references in foreign sources, from the 1st century A. D. on, indicate that central Sweden, around Lake Mälaren, was inhabited by the Svear, or Swedes. These people, perhaps by the 9th century A. D., dominated the Götar, who lived around Lakes Vättern and Vänern. The Goths who had invaded the Roman Empire were very likely related to the Götar. The southern and western coastal districts belonged to Denmark and Norway until the 17th century.

By the 7th century, population pressure seems to have driven the Swedes to the eastern Baltic in search of land and trade. During the Viking age, after about 800, the Danes and Norwegians led the way in westward ventures, though Swedes took part in them. The Swedes, meanwhile, concentrated mainly on eastern trade. By the early 9th century, Swedes had penetrated to the Black and Caspian seas and were trading with Byzantium and the Baghdad caliphate via the Russian rivers. Tradition has it that the first Russian monarchy was established in the 9th century by a Swede, Rurik. Swedes also made up the Byzantine Varangian guard.

Christianity and Kingship. As early as 500 A. D., Old Uppsala was a leading heathen cult center. St. Ansgar (Anskar), a Frankish monk, undertook a mission to the Swedes in 829, with some success. Around 1000, Olof Skötkonung became Sweden's first Christian king. He was converted to Christianity, evidently in the hope of strengthening his authority, since he also adopted western administrative and fiscal ideas. However, heathen tradition proved more tenacious in Sweden than elsewhere in Scandinavia and it was only rooted out by around 1100, though even then vestiges long survived. In 1164, Sweden obtained its own archbishop at Uppsala. Meanwhile, Cistercian monks established themselves, contributing much to the civilizing of the country. Having become Christians, the Swedes vented their warlike energies by crusading against the heathen of the eastern Baltic.

Sweden's early kings were elected and were primarily war leaders. Their powers were limited by custom, self-governing peasant communes, and the old provinces, whose assemblies of freemen, the *things* or *tings*, could accept or reject the monarch in their own regions. In the 12th century, however, a complex struggle for the throne between and within rival dynasties favored the emergence of a landed warrior nobility of the European type. A shadowy figure of this period is St. Eric, Sweden's king and patron saint, who died about 1160.

Folkung Dynasty. By around 1200 the family of Birger Brosa rose to prominence in the office of jarl, that is, commander of the royal levies on land and sea and the king's right-hand man. The family's most illustrious member was Birger Jarl, who dominated Sweden from 1248 to 1266. He established Stockholm to guard the entrance to Lake Mälaren, invited German merchants and artisans into Sweden to develop the economy, and Christianized much of Finland, incorporating it into the Swedish realm.

Birger Jarl's eldest son, Waldemar, who was elected king in 1250, was the first member of the Folkung royal dynasty. He ruled in the shadow of his father, however, and was overthrown by his younger brother, Magnus Ladulås, soon after Birger Jarl's death in 1266. In 1279, Magnus Ladulås became king. Though he granted tax immunity to the new military aristocracy, Magnus protected the peasants and townsmen. Under his rule the medieval Swedish monarchy attained its greatest power, prosperity, and prestige.

Sweden was again rent by dynastic struggles among his sons and grandsons. Reigning kings were compelled to grant their brothers extensive, semiautonomous duchies, which threatened the country with feudal disintegration. Sweden meanwhile suffered from a general European economic stagnation, German commercial domination, and, in 1349–1350, the devastation of the Black Death. A notable 14th century figure was the mystic St. Bridget (Birgitta).

In 1319, Magnus Ericsson, a grandson of Magnus Ladulås, who had already succeeded his maternal grandfather as king of Norway, was elected king in Sweden as Magnus II, subject to a coronation oath limiting his power. In 1350, Magnus II promulgated his Land Law, Sweden's first common law code, which maintained the elective monarchy, secured the rights of subjects, and required the king to rule with the advice of a council of noblemen.

Magnus was involved during most of his reign in a bitter struggle with Waldemar IV of Denmark, even though Magnus' son Haakon, who became king of Norway as Haakon VI in 1343, married Margaret, daughter of Waldemar, in 1363. In that year the Swedish nobility, encouraged by Waldemar, deposed Magnus, the last Folkung, and elected Albrecht of Mecklenburg, Magnus' nephew, as King Albert.

The Union of Kalmar. At the start of his reign, Albert seemed a tool of the magnates, but in time he attempted to strengthen his position. The Swedish nobility rebelled and in 1388 offered the throne to Margaret, Haakon VI's widow, who had been elected to the Danish and Norwegian thrones after the death of her son Olaf (Olav) in 1387. In 1397 the councils of the three Scandinavian kingdoms met with Margaret at Kalmar in Sweden, where they elected Eric of Pomerania, her grandnephew, their common sovereign. Although each land was to retain its laws and administration, Margaret ruled as regent until her death in 1412, skillfully concentrating power in her own hands.

Eric continued Margaret's centralizing policies, largely to free Scandinavia from economic exploitation by the German trading cities of the Hanseatic League. He lacked her tact, however, and his conflict with the Hanse ruined Sweden's overseas trade. Discontent came to a head among the hard-hit miners of the Bergslagen district, who in 1434 rebelled under

RUNIC WRITING borders entwined serpents and various other symbols. Rune stones frequently recorded heroic deeds such as the Viking expeditions.

SWEDISH INFORMATION SERVICE

Engelbrekt Engelbrektsson. The uprising attracted wide support not only among the peasantry, but among the townsmen, clergy, and nobility as well. In 1435, representatives of these four estates of the realm convened in what is considered Sweden's first Riksdag, or parliament. The representation of the peasantry is unique among medieval European parliaments. The Swedish and Finnish peasants never lost this right and were never reduced to serfdom, as were the peasants in most of Europe. In 1436, Engelbrekt was assassinated, but King Eric, confronted with uprisings in Norway and Denmark, withdrew to Gotland as a pirate.

Karl Knutsson, a powerful noble, was made regent by the Swedish council, which deposed Eric in 1439. Eric's nephew, Christopher of Bavaria, was elected king of Denmark in 1440, of Sweden in 1441, and of Norway in 1442, subject to provisions that left the real power with the separate councils.

Upon Christopher's death in 1448, the Swedes elected Karl Knutsson king as Charles VIII, hoping that the Danes and Norwegians would follow suit. But Denmark and Norway chose Christian of Oldenburg instead. This did not yet imply the formal dissolution of the Union of Kalmar, for it was agreed that the surviving king should inherit the other's domains. The Swedish nobility was by now divided by family feuds into unionist and nationalist factions. Charles VIII was deposed first by Christian I, later by noble opponents. Following a final, brief restoration, Charles died in 1470.

Regency of the Stures. Christian I and his Swedish supporters now sought to reestablish his personal rule in Sweden. The nationalist party, led by Sten Sture, however, defeated Christian's forces at Brunkeberg, outside Stockholm, in 1471. Sten Sture was elected regent by the council of nobles. Christian I's successor, John (Hans), was not prepared to relinquish control over Sweden, and he formed an alliance with Ivan III, grand prince of Moscow. The alliance helped establish his authority in Sweden briefly and became the first of repeated Danish-Russian alliances that were to plague Sweden until the early 19th century. Sten Sture managed to restore his regency and was followed in 1503 by Svante Sture. (The two Stures were not related.)

Svante was succeeded in 1512 by his son, Sten Sture the Younger, who, while still in his teens, exhibited unusual energy in consolidating power. Undoubtedly his aim was to become king. In this he was opposed not only by much of the nobility, ever fearful of strong monarchy, but by the young and equally ambitious King of Denmark and Norway, Christian II. Christian aspired to rule a unified Scandinavian state, based on lower-class support and powerful enough to break the Hanseatic League's economic stranglehold.

The leader of Sture's aristocratic unionist opponents was Gustav Trolle, the new Archbishop of Uppsala. In 1517, Sture convened a Riksdag that deposed and imprisoned the archbishop. Sture and his supporters were excommunicated and Christian II seized this opportunity to intervene with an army in 1520. Sten Sture was killed, and Stockholm surrendered after a hard siege. Christian was accepted as hereditary monarch by the Swedish nobility and set about strengthening his authority. Though Christian had granted a general amnesty, Archbishop Trolle, now reinstated, demanded that he try for heresy those who had deposed him. The result was the Stockholm Bloodbath, in which 82 leading nobles, churchmen, and burghers were executed.

THE VASA DYNASTY

Christian had overreached himself. By the end of 1520, Gustav Vasa, a young nobleman and the son of a victim of the Bloodbath, raised the standard of revolt among the peasants of the Dalarna region. Though the peasantry were not unsympathetic toward Christian's antiaristocratic stance, they were alienated by his high-handedness. Nobles, townsmen, and clergy joined the revolt. In 1521, Gustav Vasa gained support from Lübeck, which was anxious to foil Christian's anti-Hanseatic designs, in return for a virtual monopoly of Sweden's foreign trade. In 1523 the estates elected Gustav king as Gustav I. That same year, Christian II was deposed by uprisings in Denmark and Norway, which ended the immediate threat of restoration of the Union.

Early Vasas. Gustav's problem was to subordinate those very elements that had helped him gain power, for he was no less ambitious than the Stures or Christian II to concentrate power. Gustav put down repeated noble conspiracies and peasant revolts. In 1527, faced with financial difficulties, he persuaded the Riksdag to sequester the property of the Roman Catholic Church. He thereby replenished the state's coffers and gained the means to buy off noble opponents. Lutheran reformers were meanwhile active with the King's support. By 1531 Sweden had broken with the papacy, and in 1540 the church was reorganized under strict state control. Further peasant uprisings, partly in favor of the old faith, followed, and Gustav suppressed them with difficulty.

Meanwhile, from 1534 to 1536, he joined Christian III of Denmark and Norway in a war against Lübeck, which now supported the deposed Christian II. The war enabled Gustav to break Lübeck's control over Sweden's foreign trade. The King devoted himself with skill and energy to improving the country's economy. In 1544, at Gustav's urging, the Riksdag declared the monarchy hereditary in the Vasa family. When he died in 1560, Gustav left a strong government and a well-filled treasury.

He was succeeded by his son, Eric XIV, whose younger half-brothers, Dukes Johan, Magnus, and Karl, were left large, semiautonomous duchies. Eric was immediately faced with the collapse of the power of the Livonian Knights in the Baltic provinces, causing a conflict of interest among Denmark, Sweden, Poland, and Russia, all of whom made claims in the area. Eric seized the initiative and proclaimed a Swedish protectorate over the trading port of Reval in northern Estonia. This involved Sweden from 1563 to 1570 in the ruinous Seven Years' War of the North with Denmark, whose king, Frederick II, sought to reestablish the Union of Kalmar by force.

The brilliant but erratic Eric meanwhile alienated the nobility by his autocratic behavior. He imprisoned one brother, Duke Johan of Finland, and numerous suspects, one of whom, a Sture, he murdered with his own hands. By this time he was plainly insane. In 1568 he was deposed and imprisoned by his brothers.

The principle of strict hereditary succession was already broken. In 1569, the Riksdag recognized Duke Johan as King John III, but in return considerable concessions were made to the nobility. Though he made peace with Denmark, John became involved in the Livonian War, a struggle with Ivan IV of Russia over the Estonian port of Narva. Sweden's expansionist policy for the next 150 years had now evolved. Sweden was to try to dominate the eastern shores of the Baltic in order to control and tax the trade of the hinterland and to deny potential enemies access to the sea. Narva fell to the Swedes in 1581, and Sweden's possession of Estonia was acknowledged by Russia in 1595.

John III too was an autocrat by nature. Friction developed with the nobility. The King's interest in reconciliation with Rome and his marriage to a Catholic Polish princess created conflicts, not least with his brother, Duke Karl of Södermanland. In 1587, John's son Sigismund was elected king of Poland.

Sigismund and Charles IX. In 1592, Sigismund succeeded his father in Sweden. Most Swedes feared the new monarch's Catholicism, while the nobility, led by the council, was determined to impose constitutional restraints on his authority. In 1593, Duke Karl seized the opportunity to summon a church convocation at Uppsala, which officially adopted the Augsburg Confession, the basic profession of Lutheran beliefs. Sigismund was compelled to guarantee the religious settlement and the powers of the council. Sigismund soon returned to Poland, and in 1595 Karl convened a Riksdag that proclaimed him regent.

Thus far, Duke Karl had profited by his alliance with the aristocratic council. It posed, however, an obstacle to his own authority, as it had to Sigismund's. He thus turned increasingly for support to the lower classes, skillfully exploiting their antiaristocratic sentiments. Some nobles turned for protection to Sigismund, who arrived in Sweden with an army in 1598. Checked in his first encounter, however, Sigismund lost heart and sailed home. His own and his successors' claims to the Swedish throne were to embroil Sweden and Poland in repeated conflicts until 1660. Karl was now, however, free to square accounts with his opponents and in the Linköping Bloodbath of 1600 he executed the council's leading proponents of aristocratic constitutionalism.

The Duke, who ruled with an iron hand, was proclaimed King Charles IX in 1604. He sought unsuccessfully to pry loose the region of Livonia from Poland. When Russia was torn by internal strife in the Time of Troubles, Poland and Sweden backed rival factions, and in 1610 a Swedish force briefly occupied Moscow. Charles hoped to gain strategic territories, which would bar Russia from both the Gulf of Finland and the White Sea, thus allowing Sweden to control Russia's trade with western Europe. His ambitions clashed with those of Christian IV of Denmark and Norway, who likewise hoped to profit from the Russian White Sea trade and aspired to restore the Union of Kalmar. Taking advantage of Charles' involvements to the east, Christian declared war in 1611. The same year, Charles died, bequeathing to Gustav II, his 16-year-old son, a restive nobility and war with Denmark, Poland, and Russia.

Gustavus Adolphus and Christina. The young King, better known as Gustavus Adolphus, revealed unusual talents as a statesman and soldier and has remained Sweden's most popular monarch. He first ended the war with Denmark and Poland. He then concentrated on Russia and in 1617 won the Peace of Stolbova, by which Russia was cut off from the Baltic. At his accession, he was compelled to make great concessions to the nobility, led by his chancellor, Axel Oxenstierna, which gave the nobles a virtual monopoly on state service. But the King was a natural conciliator, which permitted smooth cooperation between the crown, the chancellor, and the nobility. Important military, administrative, and economic reforms were undertaken, including a constitution, approved in 1634, after his death, that apportioned power among the crown, the council, and the four estates.

In 1621, Gustavus Adolphus attacked the Poles in Livonia, which he conquered by 1629. The King was then drawn into the Thirty Years' War in Germany to bolster the Protestant cause and to bar Habsburg power from the Baltic. In 1630 he landed in Pomerania with the best-trained army of the time. The following year he soundly defeated the forces of Holy Roman Emperor Ferdinand II at Breitenfeld. After a far-ranging campaign in southern Germany, Gustavus Adolphus was killed at Lützen in 1632.

Gustavus' goals had included a permanent Protestant German alliance under his own leadership and a territorial bridgehead on the German Baltic coast. These goals were ably advanced by Chancellor Oxenstierna, who served as regent for Christina, Gustavus Adolphus' daughter. In 1643, Swedish forces in Germany were turned against Denmark, and by the Peace of Brömsebro of 1645, Denmark ceded to Sweden the Baltic islands of Gotland and Ösel (Saaremaa) and the Norwegian border provinces of Jämtland and Härjedalen. The Peace of Westphalia, which ended the Thirty Years' War in 1648, awarded Sweden western Pomerania; Wismar, a port; and the ecclesiastical sees of Bremen and Verden. These territories gave Sweden control over the mouths of the Oder, Elbe, and Weser rivers and made Sweden a threat to Denmark from the land. Sweden briefly entered the competition for overseas colonies by founding New Sweden in America in 1638 and a slaving station on Africa's Gold Coast in 1650.

Christina, who came of age in 1644, had strong intellectual interests but little aptitude for routine state affairs. She granted extensive crown lands to favorites and creditors among the nobility, which aroused resentment among the nonnoble estates. In 1650, Christina manipulated class antagonisms in the Riksdag to secure the succession of her cousin, Karl Gustav, who became king as Charles X Gustav in 1654 when Christina abdicated. She then turned Roman Catholic and spent her later years in Rome.

Charles X Gustav and Charles XI. At the Riksdag of 1655, the question of crown lands lost to the nobility (alienated lands) became acute. Charles X Gustav, backed by the non-nobles, put through a measure for their recovery. The King's interest was, however, diverted by the opportunity to attack Poland, then at war with Russia, in the hope of seizing the Polish coast and closing the gap between Swedish Livonia and Pomerania. Charles' Polish campaign of 1655–1657 was brilliant but inconclusive, and incurred the enmity of the Holy Roman Empire, Brandenburg, Denmark, and Russia. When Denmark declared war in 1657, Charles made a forced march from Poland and overran Jutland.

KALMAR CASTLE, a vast fortress on the southeast coast, was a citadel for medieval kings. In 1397 the Union of Kalmar, linking Denmark, Norway, and Sweden is believed to have been signed here.

SVEN SAMELIUS

Taking advantage of an unusual freeze, the Swedes crossed the ice to Zealand (Sjælland), forcing the Danes to sue for peace. In the Treaty of Roskilde of 1658, Denmark ceded to Sweden the provinces of Skåne, Blekinge, Halland, Bohuslän, and Trondheim, and the island of Bornholm.

Only a few months later, Charles mounted a second, surprise attack on Denmark, this time to annex all of Denmark and Norway to Sweden, forming a single Scandinavian state. Copenhagen withstood his siege, however, and in 1660 the King suddenly died, leaving a minor, Charles XI, as his heir.

The Swedes concluded the Peace of Copenhagen of 1660, returning Bornholm and Trondheim, but retaining the other gains of 1658. Thus Sweden was now rounded out to its present natural frontiers on the south and west and, while dominating the inner reaches of the Baltic, had broken Danish control over its entrance. Peace was also concluded with Poland in 1660.

Charles XI's minority, like Christina's, saw a strong aristocratic resurgence. In 1674, Sweden, as France's ally, was drawn into war with Brandenburg, which inflicted a humiliating defeat on the Swedes at Fehrbellin in 1675. Denmark invaded Skåne, supported by local uprisings. The King, who came of age in 1672, expelled the Danes, and his ally, Louis XIV, secured peace for Sweden in 1679 with only minor concessions to Brandenburg in Pomerania.

Charles now took advantage of popular resentment against the high nobility, who were blamed for mismanagement during the regency and for the recent war. The Riksdag of 1680 demanded the return by the nobles of all alienated crown lands and gave the King virtually unlimited power. The recovery of crown lands restored state finances, weakened the nobility, and secured the peasantry against the loss of ancient liberties. For the rest of his reign, Charles devoted himself to financial and administrative reforms, primarily with the aim of improving the economic support for the army.

Charles XII, 1697–1718. Charles XI was succeeded in 1697 by his 15-year-old son, Charles XII, whom the council, to avoid another regency, immediately declared of age. To Sweden's Baltic rivals, this appeared a welcome opportunity. Augustus II of Poland (and as Frederick Augustus I, elector of Saxony), Peter the Great of Russia, and Frederick IV of Denmark and Norway formed an alliance, and in 1700 they attacked Sweden to begin the Great Northern War. They misjudged their opponent. In a lightning attack on Zealand, Charles forced Denmark out of the war and then, hastening to Estonia, soundly defeated the invading Russians at Narva. He next moved south against Poland, campaigning brilliantly. He gained a following in the Polish diet, which in 1704 deposed Augustus and as Sweden's ally declared war on Russia. In 1706, Charles invaded Saxony and compelled Augustus to make peace.

Charles now turned on Russia. His march on Moscow in 1708 was deflected to the Ukraine by scorched-earth tactics and the approach of winter. In the spring of 1709 his weakened army was disastrously defeated by the Russians at Poltava. Charles and a few other survivors escaped to Turkey. He now hoped to persuade the Turks to attack Russia from the south, while the Swedes and Poles mounted a new offensive from the west. Although Turkey did briefly go to war with Russia three times in 1710–1712, a renewed Swedish offensive failed to materialize.

After Poltava, the coalition of 1700 reformed. Augustus recovered Poland, and the Danes attacked Skåne. Having taken the Baltic provinces, Russia occupied Finland. In 1714, Charles crossed Europe incognito to Sweden. The country's economy was now ingeniously reorganized for the war, and the last manpower resources mobilized. Charles sought to break the unstable alliance against him, concentrating first on Denmark through an attack on Norway. In 1718 he was killed besieging the Norwegian fortress of Fredrikssten.

The Era of Freedom, 1718–1772. As Charles died without direct heirs, the throne was disputed between his sister Ulrika Eleonora and his nephew, Duke Charles Frederick of Holstein-Gottorp, which permitted the estates to reassert themselves. When Ulrika renounced the royal absolutism of 1680 the estates recognized her as queen, and in 1720 they accepted her husband as King Frederick I, under a new constitution establishing the supremacy of the estates.

The new government liquidated the war at a heavy cost. Prussia took part of Pomerania, and Hannover acquired Bremen and Verden. At the Peace of Nystad of 1721, Sweden ceded Livonia, Estonia, Ingria, and eastern Karelia to Russia, which now became the dominant Baltic power.

The following "Era of Freedom" was nonetheless a period of economic and cultural advance, which spread abroad the names of such eminent Swedes as Linnaeus, Karl Scheele, and Emanuel Swedenborg. The estates developed a promising form of parliamentary government, with the council as a basically executive cabinet, two parties ("Hats" and "Caps"), electioneering, and political propaganda.

Russia, however, sought to dominate Swedish policy through bribery and threats. Administratively and militarily weakened under the constitution of 1720, Sweden found it difficult to resist. The situation worsened when Sweden tried to attack Russia in 1741 and was badly defeated. The Russians occupied Finland and only returned most of it in 1743 on the condition that Sweden accept their nominee, Adolf Friedrich of Holstein-Gottorp, as Frederick I's successor. This defeated the candidature of Crown Prince Frederik of Denmark, under whom Scandinavia might have been reunified. Adolf Friedrich acceded to the Swedish throne as Adolf Frederick in 1751. From 1757 to 1762, Sweden played a minor role in the Seven Years' War against Prussia.

Meanwhile, there was growing friction between the ascendant aristocracy and the other social classes, resulting by 1771 in an assault on privilege in the Riksdag. Many feared civil strife leading to a partition of Sweden by stronger powers. In 1772, Gustav III, who had succeeded his father, Adolf Frederick, in 1771, took advantage of Russia's involvement in a war with Turkey to carry off a coup d'etat to strengthen royal power.

The Gustavian Period, 1771–1809. Largely to satisfy the nobility, which had generally backed him, Gustav III granted a new constitution with somewhat ambiguous checks on his prerogative. The King was, however, an enlightened despot at heart. In his earlier years he carried out numerous practical reforms. Gustav was also keenly interested in the arts and literature, which flourished under his reign. In time, however, he aroused increasing opposition among the nobility by his disregard of the constitution and among the commoners by his favoritism toward the nobility.

Gustav soon turned toward ambitious foreign projects. Russia and Denmark hoped to weaken Sweden by reimposing the constitution of 1720 and intrigued with the King's opponents. In 1788, Gustav seized the opportunity provided by Catherine II's second Turkish war by attempting to attack St. Petersburg, to end Russian interference in Swedish politics and to regain the Baltic provinces. The attack failed, and Denmark joined Russia. A large part of the aristocratic Swedish officer corps mutinied and plotted with Catherine to reduce Gustav's powers. Gustav skillfully manipulated the antiaristocratic passions of the non-nobles, put down the mutiny, and at the Riksdag of 1789 put through an Act of Union and Security that granted him almost absolute powers in return for suppressing most noble privileges.

In 1790 the King himself commanded at Sweden's last great military victory, the sea battle at Svensksund. He was thus able to end the Russian war without loss, and turned to plans to lead a monarchical crusade against revolutionary France. The nobility remained resentful, however, and in 1792, through an aristocratic conspiracy, Gustav was assassinated.

He was followed by his son, Gustav IV Adolf, a minor, whose uncle, Duke Karl of Södermanland served as regent until 1796. Although there were some useful reforms during his reign, notably agricultural enclosures, the young King was autocratic and narrow-minded. Having encountered opposition in 1800 at his first Riksdag, he never called another. In 1805 he joined Britain, Russia, and Austria in the Third Coalition against Napoleon and ineptly commanded the Swedish forces in the war that followed. In 1807, Russia and France made both peace and an alliance, which was joined by Denmark. Russia demanded that Sweden join Napoleon's Continental System, but the King, by now fanatically anti-French, refused to abandon Britain. Early in 1808, Russia and Denmark attacked. By November the Russians had occupied Finland and threatened Sweden.

Dissatisfaction with the King's autocracy and military incompetence reached a peak, and in March 1809, Gustav was deposed by a conspiracy of officers and bureaucrats. His uncle was made King Charles XIII, subject to a new, liberalized constitution, which with modifications is still in effect. In September the new regime made peace with Russia at Fredrikshamn, at the sacrifice of Finland and the Åland Islands, which together contained a third of Sweden's territory and population. Peace with Denmark and France followed, and Sweden entered the Continental System. A Danish prince, Christian August of Augustenborg was elected successor to the childless Charles XIII.

The death of the new crown prince in 1810 touched off a new crisis over the succession, the main contenders being Frederick VI of Denmark, who hoped to reunite Scandinavia, and a French field marshal, Jean Baptiste Bernadotte. The Riksdag, believing the Marshal to enjoy Napoleon's favor elected him crown prince.

THE BERNADOTTE DYNASTY

Foreseeing war between France and Russia, the Swedes expected Bernadotte to regain Finland by supporting Napoleon. In 1812, however, Bernadotte joined Russia and its allies in order to acquire Norway from France's ally, Denmark. After campaigning in Germany in 1813, Bernadotte turned north against the Danes. At the Treaty of Kiel in 1814, Denmark was forced to cede Norway in return for Swedish Pomerania. When the Norwegians themselves rejected the settlement, Bernadotte invaded Norway. In the Convention of Moss in August 1814, Norway accepted union with Sweden, but under its own constitution and government.

SWEDISH NATIONAL TRAVEL OFFICE

GÖTA CANAL, which links Sweden's east and west coasts, was first proposed in 1516. Finally built in early 19th century, it became a key to economic development.

Bernadotte, Sweden's real ruler since 1810, became King Charles XIV John in 1818. The old Jacobin proved strongly conservative and authoritarian. Fearful of a restoration of the Vasa dynasty, he put his faith in close relations with Russia. In his later years, however, the Riksdag became less subservient, and strong liberal opposition developed.

The liberals put their hopes in Charles XIV's son, who succeeded as Oscar I in 1844. The new King had liberal sympathies, at least until 1848, when a wave of revolution in Europe produced violent repercussions in Stockholm. He freed the press from his father's restrictions and the economy from outworn guild and government restraints. From 1848 to 1850 he joined Russia in backing Denmark in the first Schleswig–Holstein crisis.

The Crimean War (1854–1856), however, provided Sweden with a chance to lessen Russian power in the north and to regain Finland. Oscar negotiated with Britain and France and was preparing to enter the war when it ended. At the Treaty of Paris in 1856, Russia was compelled to demilitarize the Åland Islands, but Sweden was left diplomatically isolated. Oscar thus turned to Pan-Scandinavianism, which had aroused much enthusiasm in intellectual circles since the 1830's, in the hope of gaining an alliance with Denmark or even a dynastic settlement leading to the union of the Scandinavian countries.

Oscar's son, Charles XV, who succeeded him in 1859, was an enthusiastic Scandinavianist. In 1863, Charles personally promised Swedish-Norwegian military support to Frederick VII of Denmark if the Germans should attack Schleswig. When the Schleswig-Holstein problem led Prussia and Austria to attack Denmark in 1864, Charles' ministers refused to back his promise, thereby crushing the hopes of the Scandinavianists. Though strongly conservative, the King was unable to withstand pressure for representational reform in the Riksdag. The constitution of 1809 had preserved the traditional organization of the Riksdag into four estates, though certain previously unrepresented groups had since been added to them. The noble estate at last joined the others in voting for reform, and in 1865 the Riksdag became bicameral.

The reform mirrors the growing importance of the bourgeoisie and the more prosperous farmers. Population increased rapidly, doubling between 1800 and 1900. This caused a growing agrarian crisis, despite increased agricultural production. By mid-century some new employment was provided by new industrial developments. The use of steam led to railroad building in the 1850's and opened large, previously inaccessible areas to settlement. Steam saws created a boom in the northern lumber industry. New techniques allowed increased exploitation of Sweden's vast supply of iron ore.

Before large-scale industrialization was properly underway, however, the greatest outlet for population pressure was emigration, mainly to North America. From the 1840's, growing numbers of Swedes left, impelled by poverty at home, the attraction of free land, and, to an extent, religious freedom. The movement reached its peak in the 1880's and was essentially over by

1914. This drain of about 20% of the population aroused much anxiety but eventually encouraged economic development and political democratization at home to compete with the attractions of America. The technology and religious life of modern Sweden were also much influenced by American examples.

Beginning of the Modern Era. Industrialization and its social consequences were the principal problems faced by Oscar II (reigned 1872–1907) and in his first years by Gustav V (reigned 1907–1950). Following recessions in the 1870's and 1880's, Sweden experienced vigorous economic growth between 1890 and 1914. Cheap foreign grain forced agriculture to reorient itself largely to dairying. The paper and pulp, electrical, and engineering industries played an increasingly important role.

The growing industrial proletariat, though still unenfranchised, was by now literate and became increasingly involved in public affairs through popular movements such as Free Church revivalism, temperance, women's rights, adult education, cooperative societies, and trade unions. A movement for universal manhood suffrage got under way, greatly stimulated by the introduction in 1901 of universal military service.

These developments were interrupted by the breakup of the Swedish-Norwegian Union in 1905. The Norwegians had long resented their junior status in the Union and had gradually loosened their ties. A crisis over the joint consular service caused the Norwegian parliament to declare the union dissolved. Despite much tension, the separation was negotiated, and the frontier demilitarized.

The first years of the century were filled with serious labor disputes. In 1907, however, the Riksdag enacted universal manhood suffrage. This gave labor its own political representation, particularly through the Social Democratic party, established in 1889, and labor thenceforth advanced its objectives by parliamentary means. The democratization of government was completed with the final establishment, between 1907 and 1917, of the principle of collective responsibility of the ministry to the majority in the Riksdag and with the extension of the franchise to women in 1921.

Though Swedish symphathies were divided during World War I, the nation as a whole supported neutrality, in common with Norway and Denmark. This led to close collaboration in foreign policy, of lasting significance for later Nordic cooperation. The war disrupted Sweden's foreign trade, causing shortages of traditional imports. In response, the government imposed strict controls on the economy, providing precedents for later social measures. In 1921, Sweden demonstrated its faith in the League of Nations, when it abided by the League's decision to uphold Finland's claim to the Åland Islands, whose Swedish-speaking population wanted to join Sweden. The electoral reforms resulted in a large increase in the Social Democrats' strength. Its leader, Hjalmar Branting, headed three ministries from 1920 to 1925. Largely under his influence, the party abandoned orthodox Marxism in favor of a gradualist, parliamentary approach to social reform and was prepared to cooperate with the bourgeois parties. An extreme faction broke away in 1921 to form the Communist party. After Branting's death in 1925, Sweden was ruled by predominantly conservative ministries as prosperity returned after a postwar economic slump.

By 1931, however, Sweden was overtaken by the Depression, which caused widespread unemployment. The 1932 elections returned the Social Democrats to power, where they have remained almost without interruption. By public works and bold financing, the new government soon stabilized the economy. It then initiated an ambitious program of social welfare. Sweden's unique "middle way," combining private enterprise with state economic planning for social purposes, aroused international interest. The Social Democrats, meanwhile, rarely had a clear majority and thus generally ruled through coalitions,

SWEDISH INFORMATION SERVICE

KING GUSTAV VI, wearing his ceremonial robes of office, formally opens the Riksdag by reading the Speech from the Throne.

notably with the Center (Farmers') party. Since the earliest social legislation was passed under conservative ministries around the turn of the century, all parties have indeed contributed to the Swedish "People's Home."

During World War II, Sweden was the only Scandinavian country to succeed in remaining neutral, despite sympathy for its neighbors and for Germany's opponents. Sweden was obliged to continue exports to Germany and, from 1940 to 1943, to allow the transportation of German troops over its railroads to Norway and Finland. Much of the Swedish merchant marine was meanwhile leased to Germany's opponents and suffered heavy losses. Sweden was more self-sufficient economically and better organized than in World War I. It took in many foreign refugees and gave much aid to war-ravaged countries during and after the war.

Post-World War II. Sweden has been a strong supporter of the United Nations, headed in 1953–1961 by a Swedish secretary-general, Dag Hammarskjöld. Swedish troops have played a leading part in UN peace-keeping operations, and Sweden has given much assistance to developing nations. Sweden has also participated since its inception in 1952 in the Nordic Council, a unique experiment in Scandinavian cooperation. A Swedish effort in 1948–1950 to organize a nonaligned Scandinavian defense pact failed, however, when Denmark and Norway chose to enter the North Atlantic Treaty Organization. Sweden maintains strict neutrality, backed by powerful defenses. Because it escaped damage in World War II, Swedish industry was in a strongly competitive position when the war ended. Swedes now enjoy one of the world's highest living standards. At the same time, the state's social welfare program has developed into the world's most advanced. In 1950, Gustav VI Adolf succeeded to the throne.

H. ARNOLD BARTON
University of California, Santa Barbara

Bibliography

Land and Economy

Hoffman, George W., ed., *A Geography of Europe*, 3d ed. (New York 1969).
Johnston, Thomas L., *Collective Bargaining in Sweden* (Cambridge, Mass., 1962).
Mead, William R., *An Economic Geography of the Scandinavian States and Finland* (London 1959).
Sømme, Axel, ed., *A Geography of Norden* (Oslo 1960).

People, Culture, and Education

Austin, Paul B., *On Being Swedish* (Miami, Fla., 1969).
Fleisher, Frederic, *New Sweden* (New York 1967).
Gustafson, Alrik, *A History of Swedish Literature* (Minneapolis 1961).
Jenkins, David, *The High Cost of Progress* (New York 1968).
Lorenzen, Lilli, *Of Swedish Ways* (Minneapolis 1964).
Paulsson, Thomas, *Scandinavian Architecture* (Newton, Mass., 1959).
Scott, George W., *Swedes* (New York 1967).
Strode, Hudson, *Sweden: Model for a World* (New York 1949).
Swedish Board of Education, *The New School in Sweden* (Stockholm 1963).

Government and History

Andersson, Ingvar, *A History of Sweden* (New York 1956).
Andrén, Nils, *Modern Swedish Government* (Stockholm 1961).
Childs, Marquis, *Sweden: The Middle Way*, rev. ed. (New Haven 1947).
Heckscher, Eli F., *An Economic History of Sweden*, tr. by Gören Ohlin (Cambridge, Mass., 1954).
Oakley, Stewart, *A Short History of Sweden* (New York 1966).
Wizelius, Ingemar, ed., *Sweden in the Sixties* (Stockholm 1967).

8. Language

Swedish is the official language of Sweden and one of two official languages of Finland, where it is spoken by about 8% of the people. Swedish is a Scandinavian language, intelligible also to people who speak Norwegian and Danish. All three languages developed from Common Scandinavian, the northern branch of Germanic. Swedish is therefore cognate with English and German and more remotely related to all the other Indo-European languages. See also INDO-EUROPEAN LANGUAGES.

Development. The earliest known Swedish writing is in the old runic alphabet and consists of inscriptions dating from about 200 A.D. and later. They were written in a form of late Germanic or very early Scandinavian; later inscriptions reflect the gradual splitting off of Scandinavian from Germanic and the eventual emergence of Swedish as a distinct dialect around 1000. The old diphthongs were simplified (*ei* became *ē*, *au* and *öy* became *ȫ*); *ē* became long *ǟ*; *h* was lost before consonants; and *fn* became *mn*.

Even after Christianity came to the region in the 11th century, the runes continued to be used for inscriptions in the native language, but by 1250, the date of the earliest preserved Swedish manuscripts (laws, religious writings, translations), it had become usual to write Swedish in Latin letters. The language written from about 1000 to about 1500 is called Old Swedish, which had its classical period from 1225 to 1375. The chief centers of Old Swedish writing were Vadstena Monastery (Östergötland), Uppsala (the archbishop's seat), and Stockholm (the royal chancery). The writings from these centers show some dialectal differences, but common forms were established by the early 16th century.

Sweden's political independence from Denmark, achieved in 1523 under King Gustavus I (Gustavus Vasa), led to a deliberate cultivation of the national Swedish language, and the Lutheran translation of the Bible (1541) became a model for all kinds of writing. In 1786, King Gustavus III established the Swedish Academy to promote the "purity, strength, and sublimity" of the language. The development of an extensive literary and scientific tradition in the 17th and 18th centuries contributed to the establishment of a linguistic norm. A trend toward a livelier style developed in the 20th century.

Spoken Swedish, however, still varies according to community and social class. The centuries-long isolation of the rural population is reflected in the numerous local and regional dialects, not all of which are mutually intelligible. The dialects may be grouped into South Swedish (spoken in the old Danish provinces), Göta dialects, Dalecarlian, Svea dialects (spoken especially in the Uppsala-Stockholm area), North Swedish, East Swedish (spoken in Finland and Estonia), and Gotlandish. The grammar and pronunciation of standard Swedish are based on the written norm and are used by educated people. While considerable regional variation is tolerated, the Svea dialect tends to be normative.

Vocabulary. The basic word stock of Swedish is Germanic, with a number of early borrowings from Latin and Greek for ecclesiastical concepts. A major impact on the language came in the late Middle Ages (about 1250–1450) from traders and immigrants speaking Low German. Their prestige left its mark on Swedish in the form of thousands of Low German words used in commercial, military, technical, and governmental affairs. Words like *herr* ("sir") and *fru* ("lady") entered the language, as did new prefixes and suffixes. Later influences have been comparatively minor; they include High German (through the Lutheran Church), French (especially in the 18th century), and English (from the 19th century on).

Pronunciation. Swedish spelling is a good guide to its pronunciation, with some exceptions. The alphabet (of 29 letters) includes three extra vowels at the end (*å, ä,* and *ö*), which, with *a, e, i, o, u,* and *y,* make a total of nine vowels. The consonants include a set of palatalized (soft) sounds spelled *k, g,* and *sk* before front vowels; before back vowels, such as *a, å, o,* and *u,* they are spelled, respectively, *kj* or *tj, gj* or *j,* and *skj, sj,* or *stj.*

The language employs two distinct musical pitch patterns (word tones), so that a word like *buren* can be read to mean either "the cage" or "borne." The resulting musical or sing-song intonation is typical of standard Swedish but is not found in Finland.

Grammar. The typical Germanic inflections of Old Swedish were greatly simplified in Modern Swedish. There are two genders—neuter and nonneuter, the masculine having combined with the feminine into the nonneuter. The definite articles (*den,* nonneuter; *det,* neuter; *de,* plural for both) are separate words before adjectives, as in *den gamla mannen* ("the old man"), but are suffixes (*-en, -et, -na*) on nouns without adjectives, as in *mannen* ("the man"). Plurals are formed by adding *-ar, -er, -or, -r,* or *-n* (in some cases there is also umlaut of the vowel in the stem). The only case ending is the possessive *-s.* Adjectives agree with nouns in number and gender except after the definite article, when they always end in *-a.* Adverbs derived from adjectives have the neuter suffix (usually *-t*). Comparatives are formed by adding *-are* and *-ast.*

Pronouns have nominative and accusative forms and derived possessives. The informal word for "you" is *du;* the formal form *Ni* is used mostly with strangers. In particularly respectful address a third-person title or a passive is used. Verbs have typically Germanic strong and weak conjugations, but without personal endings.

Sentence order is similar to that of English, but when part of the predicate comes first, the subject follows the verb (as in German). In subordinate clauses, certain adverbs, like *inte* ("not"), usually precede the verb. Complex numerals are ordered as in English: *sjuttiofem* ("seventy-five"), for example.

Style. The cleavage between written and spoken Swedish has diminished greatly, but there are still considerable differences between the often slangy and informal style of everyday speech and the prose of legal and parliamentary documents. The latter reflect the old chancery style of Latin and German, with long and complex sentences. In everyday speech final consonants often are dropped, as in *huse(t)* ("the house") or *kalla(de)* ("called"), and the old dative *dom* ("they") takes the place of *de.*

EINAR HAUGEN, *Harvard University*

Further Reading: Bergman, Gösta, *A Short History of the Swedish Language* (Stockholm 1947); Björkhagen, Immanuel, *Modern Swedish Grammar,* 9th ed. (San Francisco 1962); Harlock, W. E., and Kaerre, Karl, eds., *Swedish-English and English-Swedish Dictionary,* 2 vols. (New York 1964–1967); Higelin, Siv, *Swedish: A Beginners Course* (Totowa, N. J., 1969).

SWEDENBORG, swē′dən-bôrg, **Emanuel** (1688–1772). Swedish scholar who is best known as a Biblical theologian but who also made important contributions to science and philosophy. He was born in Stockholm, Sweden, on Jan. 29, 1688. When the family was ennobled the name was changed from Swedberg to Swedenborg.

Upon finishing his formal education at Uppsala University (1699–1709), Emanuel went to England and studied physics and astronomy. He also traveled to Holland, France, and Germany (1710–1714). He enjoyed mechanics and learned watchmaking, bookbinding, engraving, and lens grinding. Later studies included cosmology, mathematics, anatomy, economics, metallurgy, geology, and chemistry. He also became thoroughly versed in the Bible.

Scientific Contributions. Swedenborg's learning led to appointment as an assessor for the Swedish Board of Mines in 1716. His career also included extended service in the upper house of the Swedish national legislature. His inventive genius produced a dry dock of new design, machinery for working salt springs, and a system for moving large boats overland.

In metallurgy his conclusions regarding treatment of iron, copper, and brass advanced both the science and the technology involved. In biology, he supplied the first accurate understanding of the importance of the cerebral cortex.

Theology. Swedenborg's central philosophic interests, cosmology and the nature of the human soul, occupied him for years. In early 1745 he underwent a transcendent experience and entered a period of spiritual crisis. Swedenborg believed God commissioned him to present a new revelation to the world. For the remainder of his life he added theological writings to his already lengthy list of scientific and philosophic works.

His longest theological study, the 8-volume *Arcana coelestia* (1749–1756), explicates Genesis and Exodus. He also wrote on the book of Revelation and on divine providence and love and wisdom. His spiritual experiences are detailed in *Heaven and Hell* (1758).

Swedenborg rejected traditional doctrines of the Trinity, original sin, the vicarious atonement, a chief devil, and eternal punishment as an expression of divine vengeance. He proclaimed that God was forever manifest in Christ, and he taught man's spiritual freedom and responsibility. He also taught that eternal life was an inner condition beginning with earthly life, that gradual redemption occurs through personal regulation of spiritual states, and that practical love is a necessity in every relationship.

While Swedenborg never sought to found a sect, small adherent groups sprang up after his death and exist in many countries (see SWEDENBORGIANS). He is recognized as having had a liberalizing influence on traditional religious dogma. He sorted out what he regarded as the polytheistic tangle of orthodox concepts of God and the process by which Christ's humanity was made divine. He indicated that heaven and hell are not places but states, saw a causal relationship between the spiritual and natural worlds, and discussed the Bible in terms of both its surface and deeper meanings. Swedenborg died in London on March 29, 1772.

SIG SYNNESTVEDT
State University of New York, Brockport

Further Reading: Sigstedt, Cyriel O., *The Swedenborg Epic* (New York 1952).

SWEDENBORGIANS, swēd-ən-bôr′jē-ənz, are followers of the teachings of Emanuel Swedenborg (1688–1772), who published some 30 volumes of theological reasoning. Although he made no attempt to organize a sect, he spoke in favor of a "new Christianity" that would eventually spread over the earth. While venerating the Bible, Swedenborg insisted that he had been commissioned to bring a further divine revelation to men.

Shortly after his death, a Londoner named Robert Hindmarsh happened upon a copy of Swedenborg's *Heaven and Hell.* Swedenborg's description of the spirit world so impressed Hindmarsh that he organized the first group of Swedenborgians. In 1784, James Glen formed a Swedenborgian reading circle in Philadelphia. Johan Rosén and Gabriel A. Beyer, two noted Swedish intellectuals, formed a group in the theologian's native land.

Swedenborgians have three major bodies: the General Conference, headquartered in England; the General Convention of the New Jerusalem in the United States; and the General Church of the New Jerusalem, also in the United States. They differ somewhat in their understanding of the precise nature of Swedenborg's theological writings. The Conference and Convention, with a congregational form of church organization, tend to view the writings as inspired Biblical commentaries. The General Church, using the episcopal form of government, tends to assign divine authority to the writing. The Conference and Convention favor widespread missionary activity, while the General Church conducts schools and advocates the philosophy of "growth from within."

During the 19th century Swedenborgians, although never a very large group, had considerable vogue. In the 20th century there has been a lessening of interest.

Sig Synnestvedt
State University of New York, Brockport

SWEDISH LITERATURE. See Sweden—*Culture.*

SWEELINCK, svā′lingk, **Jan Pieterszoon** (1562–1621), Dutch musician, who was the last of the great Dutch composers and the first important baroque organist. He was born in Deventer in 1562 but lived in Amsterdam from 1564. He adopted Sweling, the surname of his mother, instead of Swybertszoon, that of his father, who was organist at the Old Church in Amsterdam for many years. Sweelinck assumed the post in 1580 and held it for the rest of his life. He died in Amsterdam on Oct. 16, 1621.

Sweelinck's only published works during his lifetime were vocal—psalms, motets, and chansons—essentially late Renaissance in style and of high quality. His greatest achievement, however, lay in his keyboard works for organ, first published in 1895–1903. His toccatas, fantasias, and particularly his variations influenced not only his many pupils, including Samuel Scheidt, Heinrich Scheidemann, and Jan Reinken, but were also the principal foundation of German baroque organ music, which culminated in the work of Johann Sebastian Bach.

R. Alec Harman, *Coauthor of "Man and His Music"*

SWEEP GENERATOR. See Television—*Television Transmitters.*

SWEEPSTAKES are a form of lottery. Originally, one or a few winners took all the stakes. By the 17th century the term was used almost exclusively for schemes based upon horse races. This form of gambling apparently began in medieval times as entertainment for tavern patrons. Shakespeare, in *Hamlet,* called them "swoopstakes."

Sweepstakes differ from other lotteries in that players contribute to a pool; a drawing decides who will be "given" horses, and race results determine how much of the "pot" or prize money each of these receives. The largest and most famous is the Irish Sweepstakes, organized in 1930 to benefit hospitals. As many as 10 million people have bought chances in a single pool.

In 1963 and 1966, respectively, the states of New Hampshire and New York legalized such lotteries to support public schools. In a typical contest New Hampshire pays prizes of $50,000, $25,000, and $12,500 to those holding its $3 tickets on the first three horses in a race, plus numerous smaller sums. New York, with chances at $1 each, offers 500 prizes for each million tickets sold. Between 30% and 35% of the money collected is normally paid out in awards.

Many other types of contests are called sweepstakes, but are not legally defined as such.

John S. Ezell, *University of Oklahoma*
Author of "Fortune's Merry Wheel"

SWEET ACACIA, ə-kā′shə, is an ornamental shrub with small round heads of fragrant, deep yellow flowers. It grows from 6 to 10 feet (1.8–3 meters) tall, and has leaves made up of 10 to 25 pairs of short thin leaflets. The sweet acacia is native to Africa, Asia, Australia, Mexico, and Texas. It is known botanically as *Acacia farnesiana.* See also Acacia.

SWEET ALYSSUM, ə-lis′əm, a popular garden annual with flat-topped clusters of small, fragrant white or purplish flowers. The sweet alyssum, *Lobularia maritima,* belongs to the mustard family (Cruciferae) and is native to the Mediterranean region of Europe and western Asia. It is also called madwort.

The sweet alyssum grows about a foot (30 cm) tall, and its flowers have four petals in the form of a cross. Dwarf forms, such as Tiny Tim, Little Gem, Violet King, Royal Carpet,

Sweet alyssum (*Lobularia maritima*)

T. H. EVERETT

and carpet of snow, range in height from 3 to 6 inches (7.5–15 cm) and are sometimes grown in rock gardens and borders. Propagation is by direct seeding in the late fall or early spring, and weeding may be a problem before the plants are established. Flowering is most abundant in cool weather, and the plants will survive the winter in mild climates.

A related species, *L. saxatile,* is a perennial with golden yellow flowers and gray green leaves. Dwarf varieties are used for low borders and rock gardens.

ANTON KOFRANEK
University of California, Davis

SWEET BASIL. See BASIL.

SWEET BAY is a name commonly applied to two different trees, the bay laurel and a magnolia. See LAUREL; MAGNOLIA.

SWEET CHERVIL. See SWEET CICELY.

SWEET CICELY, swēt cis′ə-lē, a name commonly applied to several fragrant plants of the parsley family (Umbelliferae). One plant, *Myrrhis odorata,* also known as myrrh, is widespread in Europe, ranging from Great Britain to the Caucasus. It is a branching plant from 2 to 3 feet (0.6–0.9 meters) tall. It has a carrotlike root, hollow stems, and hairy or downy leaves made up of toothed or cut segments. The white flowers are borne in compound umbels (flat-topped clusters). *M. odorata* is sometimes cultivated for its pleasing aroma. It is propagated by seed or division and thrives in almost any soil. It is particularly well suited to the wild garden.

Other plants known as sweet cicely are members of the genus *Osmorhiza,* a small North American genus closely related to *Myrrhis.* Their leaves are anise-scented and are sometimes used for flavoring. The small white flowers of these plants are borne in few-rayed umbels. Two species native to the northeastern United States are *O. claytoni* and *O. longistylis.* Both of these species grow in woodlands and along moist roadsides.

ANDREW LEISER
University of California, Davis

Sweet cicely (*Myrrhis odorata*)

ROCHE

SWEET CLOVER, any of a small group of short, fragrant clovers widely grown for forage and soil improvement. Because of their deep and extensive root systems and their ability to fix large amounts of nitrogen, they are among the most widely grown plants used as cover crops and soil enrichers. Sometimes they grow as weeds in cultivated fields and along roadsides.

Sweet clovers make up the genus *Melilotus* of the legume family (Leguminosae). Only three species are important in North America: the white sweet clover (*M. alba*), a coarse, white-flowered, erect annual or biennial; the yellow

JOHN H. GERARD, FROM NATIONAL AUDUBON SOCIETY

White sweet clover (*Melilotus alba*)

sweet clover (*M. officinalis*), a more branching, less erect, yellow-flowered annual or biennial; and the bitter, or sour, clover (*M. indica*), a yellow-flowered annual that grows in more arid areas. Biennial white clover reaches a height of 4 to 5 feet (1.2–1.5 meters) in fertile soil. The other species are shorter. All sweet clovers have leaves made up of three leaflets, and their florets are borne in elongated terminal clusters. When the plants are crushed or dried they give off a fragrance similar to that of coumarin.

H. A. MACDONALD
Cornell University

SWEET CORN. See CORN—*Types of Corn.*

SWEET FERN, a small aromatic North American shrub found in eastern Canada and in the United States from Maine westward to Michigan and Indiana and southward to North Carolina. The sweet fern grows from 1.5 to 5 feet (0.5–1.5 meters) tall. The slender, scalloped leaves, from 2 to about 5 inches (5–12 cm) long, have resin dots on the under surface. The leaves are arranged alternately and because of their scalloped margins they make the branches resemble fern fronds. The tiny male flowers appear in slender spikes (catkins) about 3/5 of an inch (15 mm) long. The round female flowers may be as much as an inch (25 mm) in diameter.

The sweet fern, known botanically as *Comptonia peregrina,* belongs to the wax myrtle family (Myricaceae). One variety, *C. peregrina asplenifolia,* has smaller leaves and larger fruits.

PETER R. HANNAH
University of Vermont

DOROTHY COMPTON, FROM NATIONAL AUDUBON SOCIETY

Sweet flag (*Acorus calamus*)

SWEET FLAG, a tall perennial plant with stout aromatic underground rootstocks. In eastern Russia, northern Europe, and parts of the United States, the rootstalks are sometimes dried and used as a flavoring agent, a chewing material, a breath sweetener, and an aid to digestion. Calamus oil, which is extracted from the rootstocks, is used as a flavoring in snuff and a number of alcoholic beverages, including beer and gin. It is also used as an ingredient in perfume and as a moth repellent and insecticide.

The sweet flag (*Acorus calamus*) belongs to the arum family (Araceae) and is also commonly known as calamus or sweetroot. It is found in temperate regions throughout the world and grows in marshes and swamps and along the margins of ponds and streams. It reaches a height of 2 to 4 feet (60–120 cm) and bears long, slender, sword-shaped leaves sometimes marked with longitudinal yellow stripes. The tiny yellowish flowers form a pattern of diamonds on the slender spadix (spike), which is 2 to 4 inches (50–100 mm) long. The spadix emerges at an angle from a long spathe that looks very much like the leaves.

H. A. MACDONALD, *Cornell University*

SWEET GALE is a small deciduous North American shrub sometimes raised as an ornamental. Also known as the meadow fern and piment royal, it reaches a height of 6½ feet (2 meters) and has slender leaves that are dark green and smooth on top and hairy underneath. The leaves are widest near the tip and have smooth edges that become toothed near the tip. They are spotted with dots of aromatic yellowish resin.

The male flowers are borne in slender spikes (catkins) about 0.4 inch (10 mm) long. The female flowers are borne in similar spikes and are clustered near the ends of ascending (not drooping) branches. At maturity, they appear cone-like and bear two-winged, resin-dotted nuts.

The sweet gale is usually found in swamps and bogs and along streams from Alaska to Labrador and Newfoundland, in Oregon, from the Great Lakes to New England, and south to North Carolina and Tennessee. It also grows in Europe and northeastern Asia. It is known botanically as *Myrica gale*.

PETER R. HANNAH, *University of Vermont*

SWEET GRASS is a common name for any grass that smells or tastes sweet. One of the best known is sweet vernal grass. See SWEET VERNAL GRASS.

SWEET GUM, an important timber tree native to the eastern United States and the mountains from Mexico to Nicaragua. The sweet gum, *Liquidambar styraciflua,* also known as the red gum, sap gum, starleaf gum, and bilsted, belongs to the witch hazel family (*Hamamelidaceae*).

The mature trees reach a height of 120 feet (36.5 meters) and have a straight trunk sometimes 5 feet (1.5 meters) in diameter. The gray bark is deeply furrowed. The star-shaped, long-stalked aromatic leaves are from 3 to 7 inches (76–178 mm) long and wide, usually with five or seven long, pointed, finely toothed lobes. Round heads of male flowers are borne in terminal clusters and the female heads are single. The fruit is a long-stalked brownish ball about 1 inch (25 mm) in diameter. It has hornlike projections and contains several narrow, winged seeds.

The fine-textured wood is moderately heavy and hard. Easily worked, it is used for furniture, plywood veneer, boxes, cabinets, barrels, and other items. The gum, or resin, known as storax, has been used in perfumes and drugs.

ELBERT L. LITTLE, JR., *Forest Service U. S. Department of Agriculture*

Sweet gum tree. Inset details leaves and fruit.

TREE: GRANT HEILMAN; INSET: T. H. EVERETT

SWEET MARJORAM. See MARJORAM.

SWEET PEA, a widely cultivated annual raised for its attractive, highly fragrant flowers. The sweet pea (*Lathyrus odoratus*) belongs to the legume family (Leguminosae). It has winged stems and well-developed tendrils that aid in climbing. Its leaves are usually composed of two leaflets, and the flowers, which are an inch (25 mm) or more long, may be various colors, including white, pink, red, and blue.

There are two distinct horticultural forms of sweet peas. One is a summer-flowering plant that must be sown as early as possible in the spring, as soon as the ground can be worked. The other, a winter-flowering plant, is raised chiefly in greenhouses for cut flowers. This type of sweet pea can be grown outdoors in the southern part of the United States.

T. H. EVERETT

Sweet pea (*Lathyrus odoratus*)

A nonclimbing variety of sweet pea, *L. odoratus nanellus*, forms low compact plants suitable for use in garden beds and borders. It blooms from June until late summer, and the flowers may be striped, mottled, or solid colors with plain or ruffled petals.

J. A. YOUNG
U. S. Department of Agriculture

SWEET POTATO, a creeping perennial plant cultivated for its fleshy underground roots. Probably native to tropical America, it was introduced into Spain from the West Indies in 1526. It was then disseminated to other parts of Europe, and is believed to have been first grown in the United States in 1648.

The sweet potato has prostrate stems containing a milky latex-like sap. Its leaves may be rounded, heart-shaped, or lobed, and are often 2 to 6 inches (50–150 mm) long. The pink or violet flowers are about 2 inches (50 mm) long and resemble those of the morning glory. The tuberous roots are usually several inches long, and their flesh may be white, yellow, or orange. The varieties used for food are classified into soft-fleshed and hard-fleshed varieties. The former are sweeter and softer when cooked. The nonfood varieties are used for flour, livestock feed, and several chemical processes.

Sweet potatoes are susceptible to injury by frost and require a long, warm growing season. Although they are more drought resistant than most other vegetables, they are generally grown in regions where the annual rainfall is 40 inches (100 cm) or more. In the United States, the leading producers are Louisiana, North Carolina, Texas, and Virginia.

A sandy loam soil and a clay loam subsoil are preferred for growing sweet potatoes. A very sandy soil without a fairly compact subsoil usually results in long, slender roots, while heavy clay soils produce rough, irregularly shaped roots. Sweet potatoes are grown from plants or sprouts produced by roots of the previous crop. If the season is long enough, vine cuttings may be used for propagation. Roots for growing new plants are placed in beds and covered with a few inches of sand. Planting in the field should be delayed until the danger of frost is past. The usual distance between rows is from 3 to 3½ feet (90–105 cm) and within a row the plants may be from 1 to 1½ feet (30–45 cm) apart. Shallow cultivation to control weeds may be continued until the vines occupy the spaces between the rows.

Maturity in sweet potatoes is characterized by a high starch content and is indicated by the drying of a freshly cut surface when exposed to air. If the roots are to be stored they should be mature at harvest and cured for a few weeks at temperatures of 80° to 90° F (about 27° to 32° C) and a relative humidity of 85%. Low temperature storage should be avoided.

The sweet potato (*Ipomea batatas*) belongs to the morning glory family (Convolvulaceae). Although it is sometimes called a yam, the true yam belongs to the family Dioscoreaceae.

JOHN P. MCCOLLUM
College of Agriculture, University of Illinois

SWEET POTATO WEEVIL, a shiny blue-black beetle that attacks sweet potato plants and other members of the morning glory family. The weevil has a bright red thorax and legs, and its body is shaped somewhat like an ant's. It is about ¼ of an inch (6 mm) in length.

The adult sweet potato weevils feed on the stems and leaves of the plants, while the cylindrical, legless grubs bore into the tubers. It is believed that the beetle was imported into the United States from Asia, and it is now an important pest in the Gulf states. Effective control is possible only by treating the soil around the plants with chemical insecticides.

The female beetles deposit their eggs on or in the stems of plants or in the tubers. Breeding is continuous throughout the winter, and there are several generations a year. The larval (grub) stage lasts two or three weeks and the pupal stage, which takes place inside the tuber, lasts a week.

The sweet potato weevil (*Cylas formicarius elegantulus*) belongs to the family Curculionidae.

R. H. ARNETT, JR., *Purdue University*

SWEET SULTAN is a plant of the genus Centaurea. See CENTAUREA.

SWEET VERNAL GRASS is a relatively small, tufted, perennial grass with a vanilla-like fragrance. Sweet vernal grass (*Anthoxanthum odoratum*) was originally native to Europe and northern Asia but now occurs as a naturalized species in moist regions of Canada and the northern half of the United States.

Sweet vernal grass forms dense tufts and has slender, straight culms (stems) that usually range in height from 1 to 2 feet (0.3–0.6 meters). At the tip of each culm is a somewhat open, spike-like cluster of brownish green or golden spikelets. Sweet vernal grass is one of the earliest spring grasses to appear. It is not good forage grass and is rarely cultivated. If the plants are eaten by cattle, the meat and milk may have a vanilla-like flavor. Sometimes the plants are dried and used to scent pillows, decorative baskets, and other items.

H. A. MacDonald, *Cornell University*

SWEET WILLIAM, a widely cultivated pink of the carnation family (Caryophyllaceae). The sweet William (*Dianthus barbatus*) is originally native to Europe and Asia but has become naturalized in the eastern United States.

The sweet William grows from 18 to 24 inches (45–60 cm) tall and has erect stems with

T. H. EVERETT

Sweet William (*Dianthus barbatus*)

bulging nodes. The leaf has a prominent midrib and may be 3 inches (76 mm) long. The flowers, which are ¼ to ½ inch (6–13 mm) wide, are borne in dense, flat-topped clusters. They may be white, pink, red, purplish, or striped and may be fragrant or not. Dwarf varieties with single or double flowers are in various colors.

Sweet William is propagated from seed and may bloom the first year, although it is considered a biennial. It grows best in sunny locations and is most effective in mass plantings.

Anton Kofranek
University of California, Davis

SWEETBREAD, the thymus or pancreas of a young animal, usually a calf, but sometimes a lamb or pig. Sweetbreads, considered a delicacy, are relatively low in nutritional value.

After being blanched until firm and white they are trimmed and cut into pieces to be fried or served in a sauce. Sometimes they are combined with other ingredients in a pie or rice dish.

Betty Wason
Author, "The Everything Cook Book"

SWEETBRIER. See Eglantine.

SWEETENER, Artificial, any of several sweet-tasting compounds used by diabetics and others who restrict their intake of cane sugar, beet sugar, and dextrose. Artificial sweeteners are available in powder, granulated, liquid, and tablet form. They are used to sweeten many dietetic foods and beverages as well as tobacco, toothpaste, chewing gum, and pharmaceutical preparations. They have no nutritive value and are also known as nonnutritive sweeteners.

Saccharin. Saccharin (2, 3-dihydro-3-oxobenzisosulfonazole) was discovered in 1879 by Ira Remsen and Constantine Fahlberg of Johns Hopkins University. The most widely used sweetener in the United States, saccharin is 300 to 500 times as sweet as sugar but in some individuals leaves a bitter aftertaste. Saccharin and its calcium and sodium salts are available as a crystalline powder and as small tablets containing one fourth of a grain to one grain (0.0005 to 0.002 oz) of sweetener.

Cyclamates. The cyclamates (N-cyclohexylsulfamic acid and its sodium and calcium salts) are 30 to 80 times as sweet as sugar and, unlike saccharin, leave no bitter aftertaste. They were discovered in 1944 by Ludwig Audrieth and Michael Sveda of the University of Illinois. Cyclamates were widely used in the United States until October 1969, when they were removed from the list of approved additives because it was found that bladder tumors formed in rats that were fed extremely large quantities of cyclamates for nearly two years. The ban was mandatory because an amendment to the Food, Drug and Cosmetic Act provides that "no additive shall be deemed safe if it is found to induce cancer when ingested by man or animal."

Other Compounds. Dulcin (4-ethoxyphenylurea) is 100 to 300 times as sweet as sugar but is not approved for use in the United States because of its toxicity. It is gradually being banned in other countries as well. Perillartine (the antioxime of 1-perillaldehyde) is 2,000 times as sweet as sugar and is used on a small scale in Japan. It is not used elsewhere because adequate safety tests have not been performed. 5-Nitro-2-propoxyaniline is about 4,000 times as sweet as sugar and is probably the sweetest substance known. It is used in some European countries but not in the United States because of its possible carcinogenic effects.

There have been several developments in the search for new sweeteners. Robert Horowitz of the U. S. Department of Agriculture found that naringin, the bitter principle in the rind of the grapefruit, can be used to make naringin dihydrochalcone, which is 300 times as sweet as sugar. He also found that neohesperidin, the bitter principle in the Seville, or bitter, orange, can be used to make neohesperidin dihydrochalcone, which is 2,000 times as sweet as sugar. Naringin is more readily available than neohesperidin, and scientists have found a way of converting naringin into neohesperidin dihydrochalcone.

Another potential sweetener, L-aspartyl-L-phenylalanine methyl ester, is thought to be 100 to 150 times as sweet as sugar, and the artificial amino acid D-tryptophane is 10 times as sweet as sugar. However, the naturally occurring L-tryptophane, which differs from the D form only in spatial configuration, is bitter. See also Taste.

F. B. Zienty
Research and Development, Monsanto Company

ROCHE

Sweetleaf (*Symplocos paniculata*)

SWEETLEAF, any of a group of trees and shrubs often grown for their attractive flowers and fruits. Sweetleafs make up the genus *Symplocos* of the sweetleaf family (Symplocaceae). They are distributed throughout warm regions of North and South America, Asia, and Australia. They have alternate, simple, pointed oval leaves and clusters of small flowers consisting of 3 to 11 petals. All sweetleafs prefer a moist soil and shady location. Propagation is by seeds, cuttings, and layering.

One species, the horse sugar or yellowwood (*S. tinctoria*), is a large shrub or small tree found in the United States from Delaware to Texas. Its thick, almost evergreen leaves are sweet and are eagerly eaten by cattle. Another species, the Asiatic sweetleaf (*S. paniculata*) has an abundance of white flowers, which appear in the spring.

J. A. YOUNG
U. S. Department of Agriculture

SWEETSOP, a tropical American tree with somewhat heart-shaped edible fruits. The fruits have a very fragrant white pulp but are so perishable that they are difficult to ship to northern markets. The sweetsop ranges in height from 15 to 20 feet (4.5–6 meters) and bears alternate leaves and solitary greenish-yellow flowers with two rows of three petals each.

A member of the custard apple family (Annonaceae), the sweetsop is classified as *Annona squamosa*. It is closely related to the cherimoya (*A. cherimola*) and the soursop (*A. muricata*). Another member of the same family is the papaw (*Asimina triloba*).

J. A. YOUNG
U. S. Department of Agriculture

SWEETWATER, a city in west central Texas, the seat of Nolan county, is about 185 miles (296 km) west of Fort Worth. It is a center of a farm and ranch region and ships livestock, grain and feed, wool, and mohair. Sweetwater has railroad shops, an oil refinery, cotton gins and compressors, cottonseed-oil mills, and meat-packing and dairy products plants. The community was settled about 1876. Government is by council and manager. Population: 12,020.

SWELLING is a puffiness caused by the accumulation of fluid in the extracellular spaces of the body tissues. Swelling is known in medicine as *edema* and it is often an important symptom of an underlying disorder. "Swollen glands" are actually enlarged lymph nodes and are not at all related to true swelling.

The more serious forms of swelling occur in the legs and are most noticeable around the ankles. They are sometimes caused by the depletion of protein, as occurs in kidney disease and liver cell destruction. They may also be caused by seepage of fluid from the veins, as occurs in heart failure and diseases of the leg veins, primarily varicosities.

Allergic reactions are a common cause of localized swelling. Among the allergens that may cause swelling are bee venom and certain foods and drugs. A condition known as angioedema may result from acute allergic reactions. It is characterized by swelling of the eyelids, lips, genitalia, and mucous membranes of the mouth, tongue, or respiratory tract.

REAUMUR S. DONNALLY, M. D.
Washington Hospital Center, Washington, D. C.

SWEYN I, sve'in (died 1014), king of Denmark and England, whose long reign, marked by great national expansion, climaxed the Viking era. The son of Harold Bluetooth, Sweyn, called Forkbeard, revolted against his father and succeeded him about 985.

Sweyn intensified the Viking attacks on England in 994, exacting large sums called the Danegeld from King Æthelred II. In 1002, Æthelred massacred many of the Danes who had settled in England, and in response, Sweyn's forces stepped up their attacks. By the end of 1013, after a brilliant campaign by Sweyn, England was conquered. Sweyn died at Gainsborough on Feb. 13, 1014, soon after he had been declared king of England.

SWIFT, Gustavus Franklin (1839–1903), American meat-packer, who revolutionized the meat industry by opening a national market for dressed beef shipped in railroad refrigerator cars. He was born near Sandwich, Mass., on June 24, 1839, and by the time he was 21 was a cattle dealer and meat market operator there. In 1875 he established in Chicago what later became Swift & Co.

At that time, beef for Eastern markets was shipped from Chicago as livestock and slaughtered in the East. Swift decided to ship dressed beef by rail. He dispatched his first carload to Boston late in 1877. For shipping in warm weather, Swift hired an engineer to design a refrigerator car, cooled by ice. Swift made important contributions to its development and built the cars at his own expense. His plan met with resistance from Eastern butchers and from railroads, but he was able to introduce his dressed beef by forming partnerships with butchers throughout New England and inducing the Grand Trunk Railway, which had no stockyards or large traffic in cattle, to carry his shipments. In 1902 he joined with the packing houses of Armour and Morris to form the National Packing Company, but this "Beef Trust" was broken up by judicial decree. Swift died in Chicago on March 29, 1903.

WILLIAM GREENLEAF
University of New Hampshire

SWIFT, Jonathan (1667–1745), Anglo-Irish churchman, political writer, and poet, who was one of the greatest satirists in world literature.

Swift's writing, while it is frequently tied to the political concerns of his day, transcends the limitations of time and place. Works like *Gulliver's Travels* have been read in all nations, and there is reason to believe that Swift intentionally wrote for such an international audience, for his satire concerns itself with the largest issues of human nature and culture. Swift is constantly raising the question of whether the achievements of civilization—its advancing technology, its august institutions, its refinement of manners—cannot be seen as complex and decadent forms of barbarism.

Swift is always ready to tear away the cloak of social habit and the comforting masks of stereotype that men assume to hide their savagery and inhumanity, even from themselves. He is not, however, a primitivist, for he has no trust in mere spontaneity. For him, as for Alexander Pope and others of their age, the "natural" is something to be earned through vigilance and self-discipline. It is the proper realization of humanity rather than the easiest expression of appetite or passion. Therefore, Swift's satires are often puzzling, mocking both unthinking adherence to social and religious forms on the one hand and self-indulgent individualism on the other. Because of the very puzzlement they create, Swift's works have sometimes been attacked as pessimistic, misanthropic, or even nihilistic.

Critics since 1930, however, have done much to uncover the implicit standard of sanity that Swift teases us into recognizing. And so after bitter and often uncomprehending attacks upon him by a number of earlier critics, including Dr. Samuel Johnson and William Makepeace Thackeray, Swift has been read with increasing sympathy in the 20th century, and this sympathy has extended even to his puzzling but remarkable personality.

Jonathan Swift, from a portrait by Charles Jervas.

NATIONAL PORTRAIT GALLERY

Swift is one of the great masters of English prose. The force and energy of his style come from a conciseness that achieves at once great clarity of surface and great depth through parody, understatement, and other devices of irony. He is consistently the critic as well as the reporter, the examiner as well as the narrator, the moral judge as well as the meticulous observer. His contempt for folly and knavery is most vividly expressed through his biting parodies of their deceptive language. His satires often present themselves as the work of an impercipient, morally obtuse author, and the reader is challenged to supply the awareness the fictitious author signally lacks.

Swift's achievement as a poet is also considerable, ranging from early travesties of the sublime, like *Baucis and Philemon* (1709) or the *Description of a City Shower* (1710), to the tender and self-mocking poems to Stella or *Cadenus and Vanessa* (1713). Among his finest poems were several late works, especially the *Verses on the Death of Dr. Swift* (1731), in which the poet anticipates what people will say about him after his death.

Swift also wrote histories and tracts on contemporary events. Although his contribution to political thought was negligible, these works are of great value to the historian of Swift's age and to the student of rhetoric.

Early Years. Swift was born in Dublin, Ireland, on Nov. 30, 1667, to Abigail Erick Swift, a few months after the death of his father, Jonathan. Through the help of his uncle, Godwin Swift, he was educated first at Kilkenny School and then, from 1682, at Trinity College, Dublin. There his record was undistinguished, except in classics, and his degree was awarded, "in a manner little to his credit," in 1686. Swift continued at Trinity, almost completing his master's degree, when the outbreak of political violence in Ireland in 1688 forced him to join his mother in England. He spent most of the next 10 years in the household of his mother's distant relative, Sir William Temple, who had retired from a diplomatic career to live at Moor Park, near London. Although Swift's position there was often difficult because of his uncertain status and prospects, it grew in importance until, in his last 3-year stay before Temple's death in 1699, he became a literary executor, preparing Temple's papers for publication. In the intervals of his work for Temple, Swift took an M. A. in 1692 after brief residence at Oxford, and, following his ordination in 1694 in the Church of Ireland (Anglican), he held the prebend of Kilroot in Ulster, where he was in residence for about a year.

Meanwhile, Swift began to write extensively, beginning with a series of Pindaric odes much influenced by the work of the poet Abraham Cowley. They reveal many of Swift's mature attitudes in a form more direct and impassioned than he was later to allow himself. John Dryden, upon seeing these odes, is said to have urged, "Cousin Swift, turn your thoughts another way, for nature has never formed you for a Pindaric poet." Swift did turn from the sublime to more colloquial forms, and by 1700 he had attained the style that was to characterize his work for the rest of his career. What gives these later poems their importance are Swift's masterful concise-

CULVER PICTURES

Illustration from Swift's *Gulliver's Travels.*

ness and dryness, by which he achieves great intensity of feeling in a seemingly artless idiomatic style.

Swift's principal literary work in the years with Temple was, however, the extensive reading for, and the early versions of, his first great satires, *A Tale of a Tub, The Battle of the Books,* and *The Mechanical Operation of the Spirit,* published together in 1704. This volume shows Swift at his most dazzling. It is full of brilliant parody and extravagant wit, at times carried to the point of risking accusations of religious skepticism. Indeed, such accusations were not long in coming, and Swift wittily annotated the 1710 edition of these works with quotations from his hostile commentators.

Churchman and Statesman. After Temple's death Swift returned to Dublin as vicar of Laracor and as chaplain to the 2d Earl of Berkeley, a lord justice of Ireland. He took the degree of doctor of divinity at Trinity College in 1701, after becoming a prebendary at St. Patrick's Cathedral in Dublin. But his hopes for higher church office were not yet to be realized. With the advent of a new Tory government in England and the impeachment by the House of Commons of Whig leaders responsible for King William III's second Partition Treaty—which attempted to settle the question of the Spanish succession—Swift used historical examples to frame an attack upon the tyranny of the "many" and to defend a balance of power in *A Discourse of the Contests and Dissensions between the Nobles and Commons in Athens and Rome* (1701).

By the time *A Tale of a Tub* was published, Swift had come to know the circle of Whig writers that included Joseph Addison and Richard Steele—later editors of *The Spectator*—and Swift's school friend William Congreve. Swift's commitment to the Whig cause was, however, tempered by his primary loyalty to the church. His political views, although they were based upon acceptance of the Revolution of 1688, were influenced by the fear that the Whigs' concessions to dissenting sects might undermine a firm church establishment.

As a churchman Swift went to England in 1707 to gain financial benefits from Queen Anne for the Irish clergy. He remained in England and in the next two years wrote a series of brilliant political pamphlets, whose titles show their concern, including *A Letter Concerning the Sacramental Test, The Sentiments of a Church of England Man,* and *A Project for the Advancement of Religion.* Perhaps the most witty of these tracts, the *Argument Against Abolishing Christianity,* is an ironic defense of an expedient "nominal" Christianity that exposes such a doctrine as mere accommodation of religion to "schemes of wealth and power."

Persuaded of the Whigs' reluctance to help his church cause, Swift turned in 1710 to the new Tory ministers and became for the next four years the foremost pamphleteer and journalist on the side of Robert Harley, Earl of Oxford, and Henry St. John, Viscount Bolingbroke. This was the period of Swift's greatest political power in England. Harley, although he could never confide fully in anyone, showed great esteem for Swift and became part of the Scriblerus Club, for which Swift, Pope, John Arbuthnot, and John Gay undertook a series of satiric projects.

Swift wrote for *The Examiner* from Nov. 2, 1710, to June 7, 1711, and in these weekly papers he undermined the reputation of Whig leaders and their popular hero, the Duke of Marlborough. Swift's most influential work of that period, *The Conduct of the Allies* (1711), was widely read and helped to prepare the nation for the settlement of its costly war with France.

Unable to end growing differences between Harley and Bolingbroke, Swift left London in 1714, only to learn afterward of the death of Queen Anne and the fall of the Tory government. With no prospects of a further career in England, he returned to Dublin, where, in 1713, he had been appointed dean of St. Patrick's Cathedral.

Irish Patriot and Satirist. During his years at Moor Park, Swift had taken as a pupil Esther (or Hester) Johnson, a young girl who lived in Sir William Temple's household. Later, when Esther moved to Dublin to eke out her small income, she kept up a correspondence with her former teacher, and Swift's remarkable letters to her from England form *The Journal to Stella* (published posthumously in 1768). His friendship with Stella (Swift's name for Esther) lasted through her lifetime and inspired some of his finest poems. It was rumored during Swift's lifetime that he and Stella were married in 1716, but the evidence is inconclusive and no marriage was ever acknowledged. What seems clear is that if marriage took place at all, it was never consummated. Stella died in 1728.

During his stays in London, Swift had come to know the Vanhomrigh family, whose daughter Esther—Vanessa, as Swift called her—fell in love with Swift. Esther followed Swift to Ireland, hoping that he would marry her, but she died there unhappily in 1723.

Political events once more made Swift a public figure in 1724–1725. King George I's grant to William Wood in 1722, empowering him to coin copper halfpence in great quantities for Ireland, threatened to produce inflation by draining off gold and silver. This measure only emphasized the desperate plight of the country, which was without manufactures, limited in exports by British mercantilist policy, and kept poor by absentee landlords. Swift, writing as "M. B.," a linen draper, published six pamphlets known as *The Drapier's Letters.* They reached a pitch of defiance in the fourth, *A Letter to the Whole People of Ireland.* The letter was proclaimed seditious, but, although Swift was known to be the author, no one wished to charge him. When the coinage was withdrawn in 1725, he became an Irish hero.

In 1729, Swift wrote his best-known and most powerful tract on the plight of the Irish, *A Modest Proposal.* This brief ironic work proposed to cure Ireland's overpopulation and lack of exports by the sale of babies as delicacies for gentlemen's dinner tables. Cannibalism becomes Swift's symbol for inhumanity, and the tract is a fine parody of the impersonal style of the social scientist.

As early as 1720, Swift had begun to compose his great satire, *Gulliver's Travels.* Published six years later as Lemuel Gulliver's *Travels into Several Remote Nations of the World,* the book was immediately acclaimed, and it has been widely read ever since as both a fantasy for children and a bitter satire for their elders. In it Swift compressed the central themes of his work, with one exception: he makes little direct reference to revealed religion. Instead, he concentrates on the moral nature of man, showing the grotesque misuse man has made of his rational capacities and the foolish complacency by which he mistakes mere ingenuity or complexity for rational achievement.

During this period Swift's influence upon two major contemporaries was marked. It was from his suggestion that John Gay developed *The Beggar's Opera* (1728), and it was to Swift that Alexander Pope dedicated his scathing satire *The Dunciad* (1728). These works, with *Gulliver's Travels,* dominated London's literary world for years.

Declining Years. Much of the remainder of Swift's active life was dedicated to church concerns—the recovery and improvement of church incomes and the defense of the Irish interest against control by English bishops in the Church of Ireland. His fight was carried on despite pessimism about its outcome. Among his weapons were such striking poems as *The Legion Club* (1736), but equally important for his cause were his example of dutiful service and his great charities.

Swift's melancholy deepened steadily with a growing sense of isolation and of failing powers. Alternately indolent and violent, he was cared for by a cousin, Martha Whiteway, and finally his affairs were put into the hands of guardians. Swift died in Dublin on Oct. 19, 1745, and was buried in St. Patrick's, where, in the words of his own great epitaph, "savage indignation can tear his heart no more." See also GULLIVER'S TRAVELS; TALE OF A TUB.

MARTIN PRICE, *Yale University*

Bibliography

Editions of Swift's works include: *Prose Works,* ed. by Temple Scott, with annotations, 12 vols. (London 1897–1908); *Prose Writings,* ed. by Herbert Davis, the best text, with valuable introductions, 14 vols. (London 1939–1968); *Poems,* ed. by Harold Williams, 2d ed., 3 vols. (New York and London 1958); *Correspondence,* ed. by Harold Williams, 5 vols. (New York and London 1963–1965).

Biographical Studies

Ehrenpreis, Irvin, *Personality of Jonathan Swift* (Cambridge, Mass., 1958).
Ehrenpreis, Irvin, *Swift: The Man, His Works, and the Age,* 3 vols. (Cambridge, Mass., 1962–).
Landa, Louis A., *Swift and the Church of Ireland* (New York and London 1954).
Murry, John M., *Jonathan Swift: A Critical Biography* (New York 1955).

Critical Studies

Bullitt, John M., *Jonathan Swift and the Anatomy of Satire* (Cambridge, Mass., 1953).
Davis, Herbert J., *Jonathan Swift: Essays on His Satire and Other Studies* (New York and London 1964).
Donoghue, Denis, *Jonathan Swift: A Critical Introduction* (New York and London 1969).
Ewald, William B., *Masks of Jonathan Swift* (Cambridge, Mass., 1954).
Price, Martin, *Swift's Rhetorical Art: A Study in Structure and Meaning* (New Haven, Conn., 1953).
Quintana, Ricardo, *Mind and Art of Jonathan Swift* (New York 1936).
Quintana, Ricardo, *Swift: An Introduction* (New York 1955).
Rosenheim, Edward W., *Swift and the Satirist's Art* (Chicago 1963).
Voigt, Milton, *Swift and the Twentieth Century* (Detroit 1964).
Williams, Kathleen, *Jonathan Swift and the Age of Compromise* (Lawrence, Kans., 1958).

SWIFT, the common name for any of 68 species of rapidly flying, insectivorous birds found throughout the entire world, except the polar regions, New Zealand, most of Australia, and some isolated oceanic islands. Most swifts live in the tropics or subtropics, but some species inhabit mountains up to the snowline, and others spend the breeding season in the temperate zones, migrating to the tropics in winter.

Although they superficially resemble swallows in form and flight, swifts are more closely related to hummingbirds and are classified with them

Chimney swifts, courting

LYNWOOD M. CHACE, FROM NATIONAL AUDUBON SOCIETY

in the order Apodiformes. There are two families of swifts—the Apodidae, or true swifts, and the Hemiprocnidae, or crested swifts.

Description. Swifts vary in size from the 3½ inch (9 cm) cave swiftlet (*Collocalia*) of the East Indies to the giant collared swift (*Streptoprocne*) of South America with its 18-inch (45 cm) wingspan. Swifts have powerfully built, streamlined bodies; flattened heads with small, short, slightly hooked beaks; and enormous mouths that extend laterally to beneath the eyes. The legs are very short but possess powerful clinging toes. In color, the swifts are mostly dull brown or gray-black, although a few species display white or gray patches or, rarely, other hues. In the true swifts, the sexes are alike in coloring.

Swifts are the most aerial of all birds, and their wings show corresponding adaptations. Externally, the wings are large, narrow, long, and with little curvature. The specialized structure of the wings coupled with powerful breast muscles make possible rapid, sustained, highly maneuverable flight. Swifts have been credited with air speeds of over 100 miles (160 km) per hour.

True Swifts. There are 65 species of true swifts. Most (subfamily Chaeturinae) have spiny-tipped tail feathers that serve as props when the birds cling to vertical surfaces. Included in this group is the common chimney swift (*Chaetura pelagica*) of eastern North America. Other true swifts (subfamily Apodinae) lack the spiny tail feathers but have all four toes directed forward to make an effective wall-gripping mechanism. This group includes the common swift (*Apus apus*) of Europe.

True swifts not only feed on the wing, but also collect nesting materials and mate while airborne. They cling to walls, trees, chimneys, and other vertical surfaces and often spend the night in flight. True swifts never alight on the ground, and in fact, if placed on the ground, they can take flight only with difficulty.

True swifts are strict insectivores. They eat voraciously to meet their high energy requirements for nearly continuous flight. Since insects on the wing can be caught only in fine, warm weather, flocks of true swifts may travel hundreds of miles to avoid a meteorological low with its adverse stormy weather. When nestling swifts, still unable to fly, are threatened with starvation by inclement weather, their body temperatures drop more than 50° F (28° C), and they become torpid. With their metabolism thus reduced, they can survive up to 10 days without food.

The nests of true swifts may be built with twigs, plant fibers, seeds, moss, lichens, or feathers, but in all cases, the materials are cemented together with the bird's mucilaginous saliva. The nests may be glued to the vertical walls of caves, cliff crevices, chimneys, hollow trees, belfries, palm fronds, and even cliffs behind waterfalls. The eggs are oblong or cylindrical in shape and invariably white. There may be only one or, rarely, as many as six in a clutch. Both parents share the unusually long incubation period, lasting from 16 to 20 days, depending on the weather. The young require five to eight weeks to fledge.

One group of true swifts—the cave swiftlets (*Collocalia*) of southeast Asia—construct their nests entirely of salivary mucus. These nests were once highly prized for making bird's-nest soup. Millions of cave swiftlets nest deep in caves and find their way by means of echolocation.

Crested Swifts. There are three species of crested, or tree, swifts, making up the genus *Hemiprocne*. They are found along the edges of tropical forests in India, Malaya, and the East Indies. Crested swifts are colorful birds with erectile crests on the forehead and blackish facial masks. They also have deeply forked tails. The sexes are different in plumage, with the male more elaborately dressed. A single crested swift makes a cuplike nest by gluing strips of bark to the side of a tree limb. The one grayish-white egg is cemented to the bottom of the nest.

CARL WELTY
Beloit College

HAL M. HARRISON, FROM NATIONAL AUDUBON SOCIETY

Southern fence lizard, or swift

SWIFT, any of several spiny lizards (genus *Sceloporus*) found in many parts of North America. Some species are also called "fence lizards." The *Sceloporus* lizards are neither burrowing nor water-loving. They prefer warm, dry regions and frequently climb rocks and trees. They are active and bold, especially during the day, and are easily observed.

SWIFT CURRENT is a city in southwestern Saskatchewan, Canada, on Swiftcurrent Creek, about 140 miles (205 km) west of Regina. It is the retail and service center for a large agricultural area where wheat is the principal crop. Oil wells in the region have been producing since the early 1950's. Swift Current was incorporated as a village in 1904, as a town in 1907, and as a city in 1914. Population: 15,415.

SWIM BLADDER, a gas-filled sac in bony fishes. It is primarily a hydrostatic organ but may also function in respiration and sense perception. See FISH—*Anatomy and Physiology*.

SWIMMER'S ITCH is an itchy rash caused by larvae of the parasitic fluke *Schistosoma*. The microscopic larvae, called *cercariae*, swim about in still bodies of fresh water. As they penetrate the skin, the swimmer feels a pricking sensation. About an hour later each site of entry becomes a red spot that soon fades. Itchy papules develop 10 to 15 hours later and last for about a week.

Because the *Schistosoma* species that cause swimmer's itch are not parasites of man, the larvae soon die. Other species, however, cause a serious illness known as *schistosomiasis*. See also SCHISTOSOMIASIS.

STEPHEN E. SILVER, M. D.
Montefiore Hospital, New York

LEE PILLSBURY

The Santa Clara Aquamaids, a team of synchronized swimmers, execute a float pattern from a championship routine.

CONTENTS

SWIMMING is popular throughout the world, both for recreation and as a competitive sport. It ranks as one of man's oldest physical activities. Diving is a related activity (see DIVING).

Early pictographs, bas-reliefs, and sculptures establish that man has swum for a least 2,000 years. For example, in the Nimrud Galleries of the British Museum in London, bas-reliefs dated about 880 B. C. show Assyrian soldiers swimming. Low-relief art from the Olmec, Toltec, and Zapotec cultures in the National Museum of Anthropology in Mexico City also show men swimming. But little is known of the exact strokes swimmers used before the 19th century.

The modern sport of swimming was developed by the English. The first bath, or pool, was opened in Liverpool in 1828. The first contests, using the breaststroke, were conducted in London in 1837, where about six pools were available. In 1844 in London some North American Indians won a 100-yard contest with an overarm stroke, a style familiar to the aborigines in the Americas and the South Pacific Islands. The English, however, not concerned then with speed over short distances, were unimpressed.

In the 1860's swimming clubs in London began to hold interclub competitions. In 1869 the Metropolitan Swimming Association (later called the London Swimming Association) was formed to govern the contests, and the rivalry among the clubs created a desire for a faster style of swimming. The sidestroke, then, began to replace the breaststroke. In 1873, J. Arthur Trudgen developed a double overarm stroke, later to be called the *trudgen crawl,* and achieved greater speed than competitors using the sidestroke. In 1902, Richard Cavill, a champion Australian swimmer, went to England and won the 100-yard event in a record 58.6 seconds. His *Australian crawl* combined the double overarm with an up-and-down leg action. Charles M. Daniels, of the New York Athletic Club, speeded up the kicks and in 1906 swam 100 yards in 56 seconds, establishing a world record with the *American crawl.* Instructors soon adopted the American crawl as the fastest stroke for competition.

Today, competitive swimmers throughout the world are controlled by local, regional, national, and international swimming organizations. The world governing body, formed in 1908, is the Fédération Internationale de Natation Amateur (FINA), which comprises all national controlling bodies. In the United States the Amateur Athletic Union (AAU) is the national controlling body. The National Collegiate Athletic Association (NCAA) establishes rules governing intercollegiate competition, while the National Interscholastic Swimming Coaches Association (NISCA) governs high school competition.

The program with the greatest number of yearly participants in the United States is the AAU age-group swimming competitions, begun

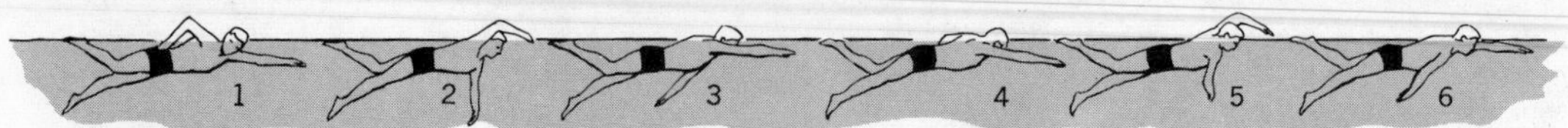

IN THE SIX-BEAT CRAWL the swimmer alternates three kicks as the left arm pulls (1, 2, 3) and three kicks as the right arm pulls (4, 5, 6). He takes in air through his mouth on one arm stroke and exhales through his nose and mouth on the other arm stroke. The arm strokes are the main source of propulsion.

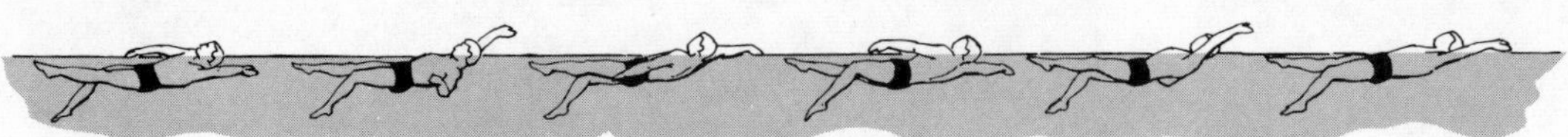

IN THE BACKSTROKE the arm and leg cycle ratio is 1 to 6 as in the crawl, but the feet do not break the surface of the water. The elbow bends in the arm pull (1, 2, 3,) but remains straight in the recovery (4, 5, 6). The swimmer keeps the back of his head in the water and inhales once and exhales once per arm cycle.

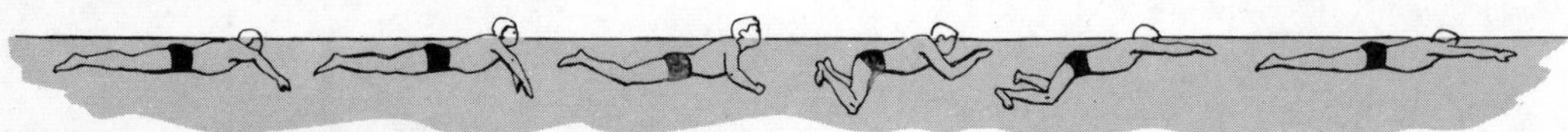

IN THE BREASTSTROKE the propulsive phases of the arms and legs are alternated. Up-and-down leg action is prohibited. The swimmer begins the arm pull while the legs are fully extended (1, 2). After the leg recovery (3, 4, 5) and thrust, the completely extended body remains briefly in a prone glide (6).

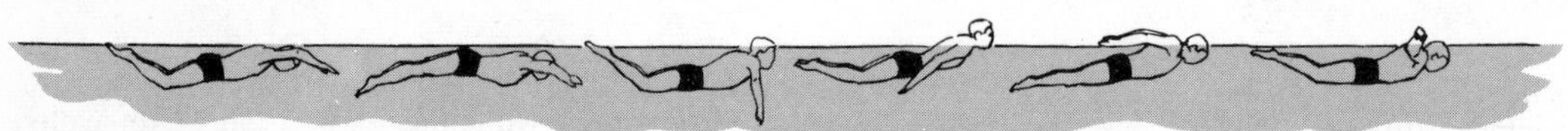

IN THE BUTTERFLY the arms and legs move together in unison, and the kick dominates the stroke. The legs complete one kick (1, 2, 3), and the swimmer exhales before the arms finish the pull. On the second downbeat (4), the swimmer inhales. The arms recover forward and over the water on the upbeat of the second kick (5, 6).

THE SIDESTROKE is swum with the body in a side horizontal position, nose above the water's surface (1). With the pull of the underarm and the forward action of the upper arm, the knees begin to bend for the kick (2, 3). Propulsion comes from the drive of the scissors kick and the pull of the upper arm (4, 5, 6).

in 1952. Since then supervised classes and annual meets—local, sectional, and national—have been held for boys and girls 10 years of age and under; 11 and 12 years old; 13 and 14; and 15, 16, and 17.

An International Swimming Hall of Fame was established at Fort Lauderdale, Fla., in 1964 to recognize achievements in swimming and other aquatic sports throughout the world.

SWIMMING STROKES

The common strokes used in swimming are the crawl, backstroke, breaststroke, and sidestroke. Variations of these, such as the trudgen crawl, inverted breaststroke, and single overarm sidestroke, are valuable for recreational swimming, long-distance swimming, and lifesaving. The butterfly stroke is used mostly in racing.

The Crawl. The crawl, or freestyle, is the fastest of all strokes. Performed with the body prone on the surface of the water, it combines an alternate pull and recovery arm cycle, alternate leg beats, and rhythmic breathing. The arm strokes are the main source of propulsion. The kick serves primarily as a stabilizer and keeps the feet high in the water.

In the arm cycle, one arm makes a zigzag backward pull underwater, as the other reaches upward and forward over the water. The pulling arm is almost straight when the hand enters the water. Midway through the pull, the elbow bends to form a 90° angle, and at the completion of the stroke, the arm is straightened again. When the hand leaves the water to start the recovery to the original position in front of the shoulder, the arm is almost straight. During the recovery, the elbow is held high, with the hand almost touching the water. The two arm strokes are timed so that one arm finishes its drive just before the other is replaced in the water at the end of the recovery.

The most common kick is a *flutter kick,* a series of six beats, three alternating on each arm stroke. It is performed with the knees slightly bent and close together and the feet stretched backward. With each beat the feet separate on the vertical plane between 10 and 16 inches. Distance swimmers often use one beat on each arm stroke.

To breathe, the swimmer rotates his head to one side as his pulling arm finishes the stroke and sucks air in through his mouth as the arm makes its recovery. Before the hand reaches the water ahead, he returns his face to the water and exhales through both nose and mouth. Breathing is done on only one of the two arm strokes.

In the trudgen crawl, the kick is a scissors-like action. As the swimmer takes a breath he flexes his knees, draws his heels backward, and then moves the under leg backward and the upper leg forward. He reaches out his legs and forcefully executes a whip motion with the upper leg and a kicking action with the under leg, which bring both legs together fully extended.

The Backstroke. The backstroke is swum on the back, with an alternate pull and recovery arm action and a 6-beat kick. The arm enters the water in a line directly over the shoulder, little finger of the hand first. The pull begins with the arm straight. It bends at the elbow progressively until the backward pull is about half completed. At this point the arm begins to extend, and the swimmer finishes the pull by pushing downward with a straight arm, palm down. The recovery is made out of the water in a vertical plane, with no bend in the elbow. The primary force of the kick, an inverted flutter, occurs on the upbeat as the knees bend. The knees are almost straight on the downbeat. The swimmer keeps the back of his head in the water and inhales once and exhales once with each arm cycle.

The Breaststroke. The propulsive phases of the arms and legs are alternated in the breaststroke. From a prone position, legs and arms fully extended and palms of the hands facing outward, the swimmer starts this stroke with a lateral arm pull. As both hands press downward and outward, he exhales through the nose and mouth. He inhales as the mouth breaks the surface of the water when the arms reach their maximum spread, elbows bent. Before completing the arm pull, he starts the leg recovery by bending his knees. Then he lowers his head back into the water as he brings his heels up toward the buttocks. He turns his hands inward, extends his arms forward, and thrusts his feet outward, backward, and inward in a semicircular action. The kick, described as a frog kick, derives its power from pushing backward with the soles of the feet. After the swimmer completes the kick, he holds his body briefly in a prone glide.

When performed on the back with the frog kick, the stroke is called an *inverted breaststroke.* It is used in rescue methods in lifesaving.

The Butterfly. The pull of the arms and hands propels the swimmer forward in the butterfly, but the kick, which resembles the tail movement of a dolphin, dominates the stroke. Both arms pull backward at each side of the body under the water and recover forward over the water as the legs make two kicks.

On the first kick, as the extended arms begin the pull and the swimmer exhales, the legs beat downward vigorously. This elevates the hips and keeps the submerged body almost horizontal. The second kick starts downward during the last part of the arm pull, at which point the swimmer's head rises above the water, and he inhales. Arm recovery begins with a slight bend in the elbows. The palms of the hands face up as they leave the water and face down as the arms rotate laterally to move forward ahead of the shoulders.

The Sidestroke. The sidestroke, an important adjunct to methods of rescue in lifesaving, is swum with the body in a side horizontal position, nose above the surface of the water, and eyes directed toward the rear. It begins with the under arm extended forward directly under the head, palm facing down, and the top arm extended rearward, palm on the upper leg.

The arm cycle involves a downward pull of the under arm and a forward recovery of the top arm, with hands crossing just under the head; and a forward recovery of the under arm and downward and backward pull of the top arm. A scissors kick is used. During the propulsive phase of the kick, the top arm pulls and the lower arm is fully extended. The swimmer holds the resulting glide until he slows down. The top arm may recover out of the water. In this case, the stroke is called a *single overarm sidestroke.*

COMPETITIVE SWIMMING

National governing bodies require adherence to specific rules and regulations at sanctioned meets. These include methods for starts and

THE SIMPLEST CRAWL TURN is made from a hand touch under water. Simultaneously with the touch (1) the swimmer tucks his feet under his body and spins around laterally (2) to hit the wall with his feet (3). He pushes off vigorously and stretches into a glide (4).

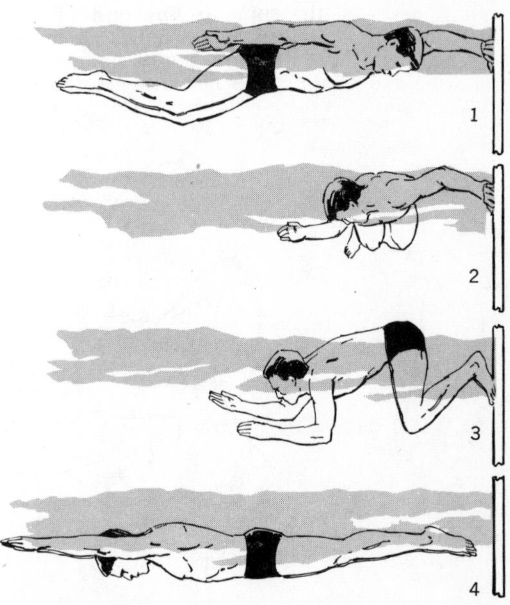

turns, standards for swimming pools, and specifications for the events.

Starts. In all races except the backstroke, the start is made from the starting blocks and facing the course. At the starter's command "Take your marks," the swimmer steps forward, wraps his toes around the forward edge of the block, and bends forward. On the starter's pistol shot, the swimmer swings his arms in a large circular movement first to the rear and then downward and forward almost to eye level. He thrusts himself forward and slightly upward with his legs to get maximum distance in the air and enters the water on a somewhat horizontal plane.

The backstroke start is made from within the water. At the command "Take your marks," the swimmer grasps the starting grip with both hands, places his feet high against the side of the wall, and pulls his chest up against the backs of his hands. At the start he throws his head backward, swings his arms sideward and over his head, and pushes himself up and over the water. On entry, he submerges and immediately pulls one arm and starts to kick, the motion of which brings him to the surface.

Turns. In crawl events, some part of the body must touch the wall of the pool in the turn. In the backstroke, breaststroke, and butterfly, a touch by hand is required.

The simplest crawl turn is made from a hand touch under water. Simultaneously with this touch, the swimmer tucks his feet under his body and spins around laterally. He whips his free hand around, touches the wall with his feet, extends his arms and thrusts his body forward, legs close together. A short glide brings him out from under the water, and he starts stroking.

The backstroke turn is similar in that a tuck of the body occurs as one hand, inverted, hits the wall, and this throws the knees over the shoulder of the contact arm. The body spins on its back while in the tuck position, the feet touch the wall, and the legs push off vigorously as the body extends for the glide to the surface.

In the breaststroke, the swimmer lowers his head just before both hands touch the wall. He tucks his legs as he bends his elbows and makes a lateral turn with his hips. One arm leaves the wall to assist in the spin. In the push-off, the knees and ankles extend as the hands are thrust forward. The first arm pull begins immediately following the thrust. The head breaks the surface of the water on the second arm pull. The turn for dolphin butterfly is almost the same as for the breaststroke. If the push-off is shallow, the body can be driven to the surface on the initial arm stroke.

Pool Standards. Swimming meets are conducted in both long- and short-course pools, but for FINA approval, the record must be made in a long-course pool. Preferred measurements for an 8-lane long-course pool are 55 yards by 75 feet, with two outside lanes 10½ feet wide and six inside lanes 9 feet wide. Short-course pools should measure 25 yards by 60 feet, with two outside lanes 9 feet wide and six inside lanes 7 feet wide. Floating markers outline the lateral limits of the lanes, which are numbered, with 1 starting from the right facing the course. Starting platforms, similarly numbered and flush with the end of the pool, stand 30 inches above the water. Hand grips for backstroke events are 18 to 30 inches above the water. Depth of pools is between 4 and 6 feet. Outdoor championships are generally held in long-course pools; indoor contests, in short-course pools.

Swimming Events. Contests are classified according to whether the race is an individual or a team event, to stroke, and to distance required. In the United States, distances are measured in both yards and meters, but world records are approved in meters only. International competitions, such as the Olympic Games, are conducted in meters only.

The major categories of events for individuals are freestyle, butterfly, backstroke, and breaststroke. AAU-recognized distances for freestyle include 110, 220, 440, 880, 1,650, and 1,760 yards (1 mile) and 100, 200, 400, 800, and 1,500 meters. Butterfly, backstroke, and breaststroke distances are 110–220 yards and 100–200 meters. In addition, there is an individual medley, in which each contestant swims one quarter of the race with the butterfly, one quarter with the backstroke, one quarter with the breaststroke, and the fourth quarter with some other stroke, generally the crawl. Individual medley distances are 220 and 440 yards and 200 and 400 meters.

Four swimmers generally constitute a team. In a medley relay the first individual swims backstroke, the second breaststroke, the third butterfly, and the fourth freestyle. Distances for the medley relay are the same as for the individual medley. In a freestyle relay, each team

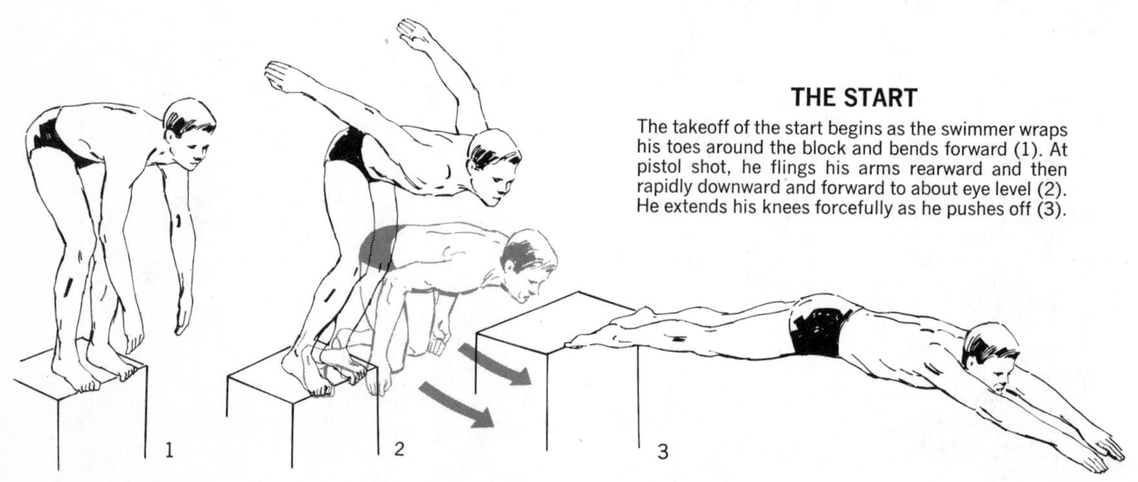

THE START

The takeoff of the start begins as the swimmer wraps his toes around the block and bends forward (1). At pistol shot, he flings his arms rearward and then rapidly downward and forward to about eye level (2). He extends his knees forcefully as he pushes off (3).

MEN'S WORLD RECORDS

(records in minutes and seconds)

Distance	Record	Holder	Country	Date
FREESTYLE				
100 meters	51.22	Mark Spitz	United States	Sept. 3, 1972
200 meters	1:52.78	Mark Spitz	United States	Aug. 29, 1972
400 meters	3:58.18	Rick DeMont	United States	Sept. 6, 1973
800 meters	8:16.27	Stephen Holland	Australia	Sept. 8, 1973
1,500 meters	15:31.85	Stephen Holland	Australia	Sept. 8, 1973
BREASTSTROKE				
100 meters	1:04.02	John Hencken	United States	Sept. 4, 1973
200 meters	2:19.28	David Wilkie	Great Britain	Sept. 6, 1973
BUTTERFLY				
100 meters	54.27	Mark Spitz	United States	Aug. 31, 1972
200 meters	2:00.70	Mark Spitz	United States	Aug. 28, 1972
BACKSTROKE				
100 meters	56.30	Roland Matthes	East Germany	Sept. 4, 1972
200 meters	2:01.87	Roland Matthes	East Germany	Sept. 6, 1973
INDIVIDUAL MEDLEY				
200 meters	2:07.17	Gunnar Larsson	Sweden	Sept. 3, 1972
400 meters	4:30.81	Gary Hall	United States	Aug. 3, 1972
FREESTYLE RELAY				
400 meters	3:26.42	United States National Team (David Edgar, John Murphy, Jerry Heidenreich, Mark Spitz)		Aug. 28, 1972
800 meters	7:33.22	United States National Team (Kurt Krumpholz, Robin Backhaus, Rick Klatt, Jim Montgomery)		Sept. 7, 1973
MEDLEY RELAY				
400 meters	3:48.16	United States National Team (Mike Stamm, Tom Bruce, Mark Spitz, Jerry Heidenreich)		Sept. 4, 1972

WOMEN'S WORLD RECORDS

Distance	Record	Holder	Country	Date
FREESTYLE				
100 meters	57.54	Kornelia Ender	East Germany	Sept. 9, 1973
200 meters	2:03.56	Shane Gould	Australia	Sept. 1, 1972
400 meters	4:18.07	Keena Rothhammer	United States	Aug. 22, 1973
800 meters	8:52.97	Novella Calligaris	Italy	Sept. 9, 1973
1,500 meters	16:54.14	Jo Harshbarger	United States	Aug. 25, 1973
BREASTSTROKE				
100 meters	1:13.58	Catherine Carr	United States	Sept. 2, 1972
200 meters	2:38.50	Catherine Ball	United States	Aug. 26, 1968
BUTTERFLY				
100 meters	1:02.31	Kornelia Ender	East Germany	July 14, 1973
200 meters	2:13.76	Rosemarie Kother	East Germany	Sept. 8, 1973
BACKSTROKE				
100 meters	1:04.99	Ulrike Richter	East Germany	Sept. 4, 1973
200 meters	2:19.19	Melissa Belote	United States	Sept. 4, 1972
INDIVIDUAL MEDLEY				
200 meters	2:20.51	Andrea Huebner	East Germany	Sept. 4, 1973
400 meters	4:57.51	Gudrun Wegner	East Germany	Sept. 6, 1973
FREESTYLE RELAY				
400 meters	3:52.45	East German National Team (Kornelia Ender, Andrea Eife, Andrea Huebner, S. Eickner)		Sept. 8, 1973
MEDLEY RELAY				
400 meters	4:16.84	East German National Team (Ulrike Richter, Renata Vogel, Rosemarie Kother, Kornelia Ender)		Sept. 4, 1973

Source: Fédération Internationale de Natation Amateur, as of Sept. 30, 1973.

member swims a quarter of the distance freestyle. Distances include 220, 440, and 880 yards and 200, 400, and 800 meters.

Distance swimming embraces an annual men's 4-mile (6.4-km) individual and team championship event. These are separate championships but are combined in one swimming race. Women have a comparable 3-mile (4.8-km) event.

Dual or triangular meets—that is, contests between two or three teams—are often part of college and high school swimming programs. Events are generally chosen from the following: 50, 100, 200, and 500 yards in freestyle; 100 or 200 yards in backstroke, breaststroke, and butterfly; 200 or 400 yards in individual medley, medley relay, and freestyle relay. In these meets, a group can enter only two of its members in each event, except relays, and no swimmer may compete in more than three events.

OPEN-WATER ENDURANCE SWIMMING

Endurance swimming in open waters is conducted on both amateur and professional bases. Those who take part in long, grueling swims display an almost fanatical devotion to the sport.

English Channel Swims. Interest in marathon swimming was highlighted when Matthew Webb, an Englishman, successfully swam the

English Channel, one of the most treacherous small stretches of water. The first person to perform this feat, he swam breaststroke from Dover, England, to Cape Gris-Nez, France, on Aug. 25–26, 1875, covering the 20-mile distance in 21 hours and 45 minutes. In 1926, Gertrude Ederle of the United States became the first woman to swim the channel. She completed the 35-mile swim from Gris-Nez to Kingsdown, England, in 14 hours and 31 minutes. The next year the Channel Swimming Association was founded. It is the official body that sets the rules and approves the records of channel swimmers.

Edward H. Temme of England was the first swimmer to cross the English Channel twice: in 1927 from France to England and in 1934 from England to France. The U. S. swimmer Florence Chadwick became the first woman to swim both ways, once in 1951 and the return in 1952. In 1965, Ted Erikson of the United States made a nonstop round trip in 30 hours and 3 minutes.

Other Endurance Swims. Open waters other than the English Channel have challenged endurance swimmers. In 1927, George Young of Toronto made the first swim across the 21-mile-wide Catalina Channel, swimming from Catalina to Los Angeles in 15 hours and 48 minutes. Florence Chadwick broke his record in 1952. In 1947, Thomas Blower of Nottingham, England, became the first to swim the North Channel between Ireland and Scotland. Daniel Carpio of Peru made the first swim of the Strait of Gibraltar in 1948.

The greatest long-distance swimmer of record was Pedro A. Candiotti of Argentina. He made some 15 unsuccessful attempts to swim the Río de la Plata from Rosario to Buenos Aires, a distance of about 205 miles. In 1935 he successfully swam the Paraná River from Santa Fe to Zárate, covering the 281 miles in 84 hours. In 1940, John V. Sigmund of the United States made a 292-mile swim down the Mississippi River from St. Louis in 89 hours 48 minutes, the world's longest officially recorded swim.

JAMES E. COUNSILMAN
Swimming Coach, Indiana University

SYNCHRONIZED SWIMMING

Swimming is said to be "synchronized" when one or more swimmers perform aquatic techniques or movements to music in a planned pattern. Rhythmic swimming to music was first undertaken by professionals. It was called *water ballet* because the swimmers "danced" in patterns much as dancers perform on a stage. Synchronized swimming was popularized by the Modern Mermaids show at the 1933–1934 Century of Progress Exposition in Chicago. The popularity of the activity was enhanced by the Aquacade, an elaborate rhythmic spectacle presented at the 1939–1940 World's Fair in New York. The next year Katherine Curtis, a physical education instructor at the University of Wisconsin, founded the first amateur synchronized swimming group. Since that time the sport has become an integral part of girls' swimming programs in the United States, Canada, and most other nations of the world.

In 1948 the AAU approved synchronized swimming as a competitive sport. This organization conducts indoor and outdoor championships annually and sanctions international competition. In 1963 the AAU began annual age-group synchronized swimming competition.

After exhibition teams from the United States and Canada performed at the 1951 Pan American Games in Buenos Aires, Argentina, the Amateur Swimming Union of the Americas (ASUA), founded in London in 1948, approved the sport for future Pan American Games. The rules adopted by FINA govern all international competition.

Strokes. Fundamental to synchronized swimmers is a knowledge of the standard strokes. The strokes can be varied to interpret the mood of the music or the theme of the composition. Any change of angle, direction, or timing of the movements of hands, arms, or legs modifies a standard stroke. Also, parts of two or more strokes can be combined to form a "hybrid" stroke. A chief difference between a standard stroke and its variation is that in the latter the

The International Swimming Hall of Fame complex includes a shrine building, Olympic-size pool, and diving well.

SWIMMING HALL OF FAME, FORT LAUDERDALE, FLORIDA

SYNCHRONIZED SWIMMING STUNTS

BARRACUDA, BACK PIKE SOMERSAULT. From a back layout the swimmer starts a back somersault. As the feet rise above the water, the body moves to a 90-degree angle. The trunk drops vertically as the legs thrust upward and then submerge completely.

KIP. From a back layout position the swimmer tucks the body and rotates backward. When the legs from knees to toes are perpendicular to the water, the trunk straightens. The legs extend vertically upward and then the body submerges.

swimmer carries the head higher for grace and showmanship and the feet lower to cut splash.

Stunts. Stunts form an integral part of a synchronized swimmer's repertoire. In performing stunts, the swimmer uses many of the basic body positions and movements familiar to divers, dancers, and gymnasts. Among these are the back and front layout positions, with the body horizontal and fully extended; the ballet leg position, with the body in back layout and one or both legs raised to the perpendicular; the front tuck, with the knees drawn close to the head, chin on chest, and heels close to the buttocks; the front pike, with the body bent at the hips to form a 90° angle, head in line with the trunk; and the back pike, with the body bent at the hips, legs straight, and feet extended over the head. Basic movements include sculling, or moving the hands back and forth; twisting, or revolving, the body, head down; and spinning, or rapidly rotating, the body, head down.

Stunts are classified according to types of skills: (1) *ballet leg,* in which the ballet leg position is dominant in a combination of a variety of movements; (2) *dolphin, head first* and (3) *dolphin, foot first,* in which the body describes a circle underwater as arm and leg movements vary; (4) *somersault, front and back,* in which the tucked body makes a complete revolution in combination with other skills; and (5) *diverse,* in which different skills are highlighted.

An example of a stunt in group 4 is the *barracuda, back pike somersault.* In its execution from a back layout, the swimmer assumes a back pike and starts a back somersault. As the feet rise to the water level, the body moves to a 90° angle, the legs vertical. The trunk drops to the vertical as the swimmer thrusts the legs upward. The stunt is completed when the feet submerge.

The *kip,* a basic stunt, falls in group 5. The swimmer begins from a back layout. He tucks his body and completes a back somersault. Then, when the legs from knees to toes are perpendicular to the surface of the water, the swimmer straightens the trunk to the vertical and extends the legs upward. The body descends vertically, and the kip is completed with the submergence of the feet.

Routines. In developing a theme for a routine, the choice of music is of paramount importance. Familiar tunes, simply orchestrated in 3/4 (waltz), 2/4, and 4/4 time are best.

How to express and stage the theme in a unified manner tests the creative abilities of the swimming choreographer. Basic points to consider in planning a routine follow:

(1) Number and skills of participants: for one swimmer alone, two swimmers, or a team.

(2) Pool pattern: lines, circles, diagonals.

(3) Transition: continuous action from one skill to another.

(4) Variety: in design, tempo, and skill combinations.

(5) Staging: lighting, sound effects, costumes and properties, and setting.

Swimming skills and interpretive talents are of equal significance in the production.

Competition. Competition is in solo, duet, and team events, the teams being composed of 4 to 8 participants. Each competitor performs and is scored in both stunt and routine presentations. Judges score these from 0 (failure) to 10 (perfect).

In stunt competition, a swimmer must perform 3 required stunts (those that must be done under certain circumstances) and 3 optionals (stunts the competitor chooses). Each is rated, from 1.0 for the easiest stunt to 2.2 for the most difficult. A final stunt score is arrived at by multiplying the degree of difficulty of the stunt by the total points of three judges. The AAU recognizes more than 100 stunts. Tables listing the difficulty ratings are published annually by the national governing organizations.

A maximum of 4 minutes for a solo and duet routine and 5 minutes for a team routine is permitted. Following the routine, the judges score the performer or performers on (1) execution of the stunts and strokes and (2) style, which includes originality, synchronization, difficulty, and spectator appeal.

JOY NELL CUSHMAN, *Chairman, U. S. Olympic Synchronized Swimming Committee*

Bibliography

Amateur Athletic Union, *Swimming, Diving, Water Polo Official Handbook* (New York, current ed.).

Amateur Athletic Union, *Synchronized Swimming Handbook* (New York, current ed.).

American Association for Health, Physical Education, and Recreation, *Aquatics Guide* (Washington, biennially).

Armbruster, David A., Allen, Robert H., and Billingsley, Hobart S., *Swimming and Diving,* 5th ed. (St. Louis 1968).

Counsilman, James E., *The Science of Swimming* (Englewood Cliffs, N. J., 1968).

Harriss, Marjorie M., *Basic Swimming Analyzed* (Boston 1969).

Meyers, Carlton R., and Sanford, W. H., *Swimming and Diving Officiating,* rev. ed. (Palo Alto, Calif., 1966).

National Collegiate Athletic Association, *Official Swimming Guide* (Phoenix, Ariz., current ed.).

E. L. WAGNER COMPANY

SWIMMING POOL with aluminum diving board at deep end. The pool was built with Gunite concrete sprayed under pressure from a specially adapted hose.

SWIMMING POOL, a tank constructed of cement, wood, steel, plastic, fiber glass, or other material and used for swimming or pleasure bathing. Swimming pools may be built above ground or in the ground or as a combination of the two.

Aboveground and On-Ground Pools. Aboveground pools range from the simplest circular model, 6 feet (1.8 meters) in diameter, with a uniform depth throughout, to more elaborate pools with an around-the-edge deck and either a sloping bottom or a bottom with a sudden drop at one end to form a "hopper."

The on-ground pool is a variation of the aboveground pool but requires an excavation at one end or in the center for a deep hopper. This allows the pool to be deepened to a maximum depth of 8 to 10 feet (2.4–3 meters) for diving.

ABOVEGROUND POOL is generally of uniform depth but may have a deep "hopper" for diving at one end. Entry ladder swings up as a gate to keep infants out.

BILNOR CORPORATION

Portability and ease of assembly are two features of aboveground pools. These models can be assembled in a day or less, and when winter arrives they can be easily packed or stored for the season.

Typical aboveground pools are constructed of wood, steel, aluminum, or fiber glass. A vinyl liner about ¾ inch (20 mm) thick is usually placed inside the pool to retain the water and protect the pool walls. Large pools are usually reinforced with trusses that support the weight of the water on the walls. Decking, if present, ranges from a top rim just wide enough for sitting to a fully fenced-in area wide enough for sun bathing or patio furniture.

For most purposes, the pool should provide at least 36 square feet (3.3 sq meters) of water for each swimmer and 100 square feet (9.3 sq meters) of 8-foot (2.4-meters) deep water for each diver.

In-Ground Pools. The in-ground pool, built of concrete, steel, aluminum, or fiber glass, is nearly always installed by professional pool contractors. The first and most important step in the installation of an in-ground pool is the excavation. Pool strength and shape depend mainly on the excavation. The most popular in-ground pool shapes are circles, rectangles, teardrops, kidney forms, and free forms.

Gunned Construction. Poured concrete was previously used extensively in in-ground pool construction but has been replaced to a large extent by Gunite concrete. Gunite is a dry mixture of cement and sand that is mixed with water and forced by a compressor through the nozzle of a hose. Gunite construction eliminates the expense and labor involved in forming the walls and in putting in and removing the wooden forms needed for poured concrete construction. The pool is excavated by machine, and then steel reinforcing rods are placed along the sides and bottom to resist pressure. The Gunite mix is then hosed over and under the steel reinforcing rods. When applied at an even consistency, the Gunite forms a one-piece shell with no weak or thin spots where cracks may form. The concrete is given a week to harden, and the surface is plastered or painted.

Dropped Construction. Metal pools have a much shorter installation time, but the cost is a little higher. Even though these pools are constructed to hold water, most of them have a vinyl-lined interior similar to the aboveground pool to protect the pool shell from the reaction to chemicals and water.

These pools are usually constructed in straight or curved panels at the plant and arrive at the pool site ready to be bolted or welded together and dropped into the excavation. This method cuts the on-site construction time in half.

One-piece fiber glass pools are molded at the plant and delivered to the site ready to drop into the excavation. Sectioned fiber glass pools consist of panels, molded together at the pool site. The base of the wall is anchored in a concrete slab, and the sections are bolted and fiberglassed together. Standard fittings and a vinyl coping are installed. The final touch involves the pouring of a deck.

Filters and Pumps. The recirculating system of filter and pump is the most important pool accessory. By filtering and serving as a mixing site for added chemicals, the recirculating system makes it possible for the same water to be utilized over a long period of time. With a good system, one filling with fresh water should suffice for the complete season, with only small amounts of water added to make up for evaporation.

A skimmer can also be a timesaving addition to any pool. It is attached to the filter line to direct the top few inches of the water surface to the filter. The skimmer cleans off foreign matter that tends to float on the pool surface and consequently helps remove it from the pool before it sinks to the bottom where it may be missed or harder to reach.

Heating and Enclosing. Heating a pool is not a necessity from an operational standpoint, but it can extend the pool season by one or more months depending on the climate. The swimming season may be extended to a year-round basis by the installation of a pool enclosure. These vary from small inflatable models to large glass-enclosed types with sliding panels.

Chlorination. All pools need regular maintenance to remain in sanitary condition. The most important task involves keeping the water chlorinated to eliminate bacteria and algae that endanger the swimmers' health or make swimming unpleasant. A chlorine test kit is essential. Testing involves filling a small tube with water and adding a few drops of test solution. The treated water is then compared with color standards to determine the chlorine content. The water should be tested on a daily basis and chlorine added if required, to bring the chlorine content to within the proper range.

Cleaning. The pool should also receive a thorough vacuuming at least once a week to keep it clean and attractive and to remove debris that has settled at the bottom of the pool. If the pool is equipped with a surface skimmer, which is in constant use, vacuuming can be a simple procedure involving 10 or 15 minutes a week.

PORTLAND CEMENT ASSOCIATION

FREE-FORM POOLS of concrete may be built to fit landscape features or to conform to the house design.

Both the vacuum and the skimmer pull foreign matter from the pool and direct the water through the filter. Vacuums usually include a cloth bag in which heavier particles are trapped to make the filter load lighter.

Also available are automatic pool cleaning systems that partially eliminate weekly cleaning. These systems force clean water from the filter through a floating head that churns up debris to be filtered out, while heavier particles are forced out through the main drain. During the off-season, permanent pools may be cleaned only every few weeks.

DAVID KAISER
Hoffman Publications, Inc.

ALUMINUM POOL resists freezing, thawing, ground-swelling, and corrosion, and needs little maintenance. It is factory-fabricated and assembled in place.

ALUMINUM COMPANY OF AMERICA

SWINBURNE, swin′bərn, **Algernon Charles** (1837–1909), English poet and critic, who was probably the most accomplished metrist in the history of English poetry. He is remembered for his bold experiments in verse, especially for his anapestic rhythms. His influence was so great that it can best be measured by the intensity of the reaction against him, even before his death. Swinburne's lifetime spanned Queen Victoria's reign, but he was the least Victorian of the major poets of that era.

Life. Swinburne was born in London on April 5, 1837, the son of Adm. Charles Henry Swinburne and his wife, Lady Jane Henrietta, the daughter of the 3d Earl of Ashburnham. He attended Eton and Balliol College, Oxford. After leaving college in 1859, he settled in London and lived there, except for enforced absences, for 20 years.

BY PERMISSION OF THE SYNDICS OF THE FITZWILLIAM MUSEUM, CAMBRIDGE, ENG.

ALGERNON CHARLES SWINBURNE, from a portrait painted in 1862 by his friend D. G. Rossetti.

Of his inner life in the 1860's and 1870's little is known, but from hints in his writings, some vague contemporary reports, and a few clues in his letters it seems certain that he was blighted, emotionally and philosophically, by an unhappy love affair. He drank excessively, and neither his close associates nor his idol, Giuseppe Mazzini, the Italian patriot, whom he met in 1867, seemed able to reform him. Finally, in 1879, his friend and legal confidant, Theodore Watts (later Watts-Dunton), an influential critic, acting with the approval of the Swinburne family, took the poet into his own house in Putney. There they lived together until Swinburne's death at Putney on April 10, 1909. There is little doubt that Watts' dramatic action effectively saved Swinburne's life and that his firm tact thereafter preserved it.

Prose. Swinburne published one novel, *A Year's Letters* (1877; later retitled *Love's Cross-Currents*), written in his most condensed, evocative prose, and he began another, *Lesbia Brandon,* of which the fragments were first published in 1952.

In criticism Swinburne was practical rather than theoretical, aesthetic rather than moral—an appreciative, expert amateur rather than a professional. He wrote more than a dozen volumes, principally dealing with the Elizabethan and Jacobean dramatists, Victor Hugo, and English writers of the 19th century.

Never in any sense a temperate man, Swinburne was given to such extremes of denunciation and praise in his criticism that his learned, illuminating, fastidious comparisons and distinctions are sometimes overlooked. No other critic of his time, however, so consistently focused attention on his fellow poets and novelists, and no other critic was equipped, as he was, to compare them with their French contemporaries.

Verse. In verse Swinburne was even more prolific than in prose. His two dozen volumes include 12 poetic dramas. Although his plays, like those of all the other 19th century poets, are better in print than on the stage, no other apology need be made for the finest of them. *Atalanta in Calydon* (1865) and *Erechtheus* (1876) are equaled only by Milton's *Samson Agonistes* (1671) as English dramas on the Greek model. The best of his other dramas are *The Queen-Mother* and *Rosamond,* two plays that made up his first published volume (1860), and *Chastelard* (1865), *Bothwell* (1874), and *Mary Stuart* (1881), a trilogy on Mary, Queen of Scots.

The astonishing range of Swinburne's nondramatic verse can best be seen if it is classified according to genre, subject matter, or source of inspiration. *Poems and Ballads* (1866) deals explicitly with the psychology of sexual passion. *Songs Before Sunrise* (1871) and *Songs of Two Nations* (1875) are of political inspiration. *Poems and Ballads, Second Series* (1878) and *Astrophel and Other Poems* (1894) are in the elegiac mode, and *The Heptalogia* (1880) is a collection of parodies. *A Century of Roundels* (1883), *Poems and Ballads, Third Series* (1889), and *A Dark Month* in *Tristram of Lyonesse and Other Poems* (1882) celebrate babyhood. The poem *A Midsummer Holiday* (1884) is topographical, and *Tristram of Lyonesse* and *The Tale of Balen* (1896) are narrative. *The Commonweal* and *The Armada* in *Poems and Ballads, Third Series* are nationalistic. The classification could be extended to include satires, poems on literary figures, and translations, ballads, and metrical exercises, as well as works reflecting the deep autobiographical strain that was long unobserved by critics of Swinburne's work.

CECIL Y. LANG
University of Virginia
Editor of "The Swinburne Letters" and "New Writings by Swinburne"

Bibliography

Gosse, Edmund, *Life of Algernon Charles Swinburne* (London 1917).

Hyder, Clyde K., ed., *Swinburne Replies* (Syracuse, N. Y., 1966).

Hyder, Clyde K., *Swinburne's Literary Career and Fame* (Durham, N. C., 1933).

Lafourcade, Georges, *La jeunesse de Swinburne, 1837–1867,* 2 vols. (Paris 1928).

Lang, Cecil Y., ed., *New Writings by Swinburne . . ., Being a Medley of Poems, Critical Essays, Hoaxes and Burlesques* (Syracuse, N. Y., 1964).

Lang, Cecil Y., ed., *The Swinburne Letters,* 6 vols. (New Haven, Conn., 1959–1962).

SWINE, or pig, a general term for the stout-bodied, long-snouted mammals of the family Suidae. American farmers commonly refer to the domestic animals as "swine," young swine as "pigs," and mature swine as "hogs." See PIG.

SWINE FEVER, also called hog cholera, is an acute virus disease that affects pigs in North America. It is transmitted by direct contact or by contact with contaminated objects, and it can spread through a herd within one or two weeks. The infected pig suddenly becomes ill and develops high fever, loss of appetite, and weakness of the hind legs. The mortality rate is high, and treatment is successful only in the early stages. Prevention is by vaccination.

The name "swine fever" is also applied to another disease, African swine fever, a virus disease of pigs in Africa and western Europe.

KEITH WAYT, D. V. M.
Colorado State University

SWING, in music, is a term applied to jazz in two different ways: to designate a rhythmic element that is essential to all genuine jazz and to characterize the big-band dance music of the 1930's and 1940's. The first meaning defies definition, because swing is not a rhythmic formula but a manner of performance that involves accurate timing and a feeling for inflection and accentuation peculiar to jazz. Gunther Schuller's *Early Jazz* (1968) mentions the "forward-propelling" quality of swing that is vital in genuine jazz.

Louis Armstrong's innovations in jazz rhythm and accentuation during the 1920's superbly illustrate what is meant by swing as a stylistic term. In his book *Swing That Music* (1936), Armstrong made the point that the old New Orleans jazz bands had been "swinging" long before the rise of the big New York bands that made the term widely familiar. According to Armstrong—and in the words of a popular song—"It don't mean a thing if it ain't got that swing."

A pioneer in the trend to the big dance bands of the Swing Era (1934–1945) was Fletcher Henderson, who had his own band and also became the chief arranger for Benny Goodman's orchestra. Goodman became known as "The King of Swing" after his radio program *Let's Dance* began in 1934 and gained immediate success. Other band leaders rose to fame on the tide of swing's popularity—among them, Tommy and Jimmy Dorsey, Artie Shaw, Glenn Miller, and the great Duke Ellington. Historically the Swing Era was important because it brought jazz into the main current of American popular music. See also JAZZ.

GILBERT CHASE
Author of "America's Music"

SWINGS, swaN, **Pol** (1906–), Belgian astrophysicist, known for his applications of laboratory and theoretical spectroscopy to the study of cosmic objects and events. He was born in Ransart, Belgium, on Sept. 24, 1906. He took his doctor's degree at the University of Liège in 1927 and a special doctorate in physics there four years later. In 1936, the university made him a full professor.

Swings' major contributions were in the physics of comets. Alone and in collaboration with others, he discovered the presence of the free radicals OH, NH, NH_2, CO_2^+, CH^+, and OH^+ in comets by examining their spectra. He also discovered the excitation mechanism, now known as the "Swings effect," that leads to the formation of the radicals.

Swings did important work in many areas of astrophysics. Between 1940 and 1945 alone, he and Otto Struve published 35 papers on planetary nebulae, interstellar matter, novae, symbiotic objects, bright-line stars, Wolf-Rayet and Of–stars, and stellar molecular bands.

Besides winning Belgium's highest prizes in science—the Francqui Prize in 1947 and the Decennial Prize in Physics for 1949–1958—Swings received the Solvay Prize in 1970. He was president of the International Astronomical Union from 1964 to 1967.

M. MIGEOTTE
University of Liège

SWISS, in textiles, is a sheer cotton fabric made in Switzerland. All leading cotton textile nations now produce similar fabrics. Swiss is a plain-weave cloth, made by a simple over-and-under process to form a checkerboard weave.

Swiss has many variations. *Batiste,* a sheer, opaque fabric with a high luster, is made of long-staple cotton and is mercerized (chemically treated for a silken luster). *Voile,* a limp cloth, is made of ply yarn (yarn consisting of two or more threads twisted together) throughout and may have woven motifs or printed patterns. *Mock voile* is made from single, or unplied, yarn. *Muslin* is a thin semitransparent cloth, bleached pure white and given considerable dressing (applications of sizing) in finishing. Closely set dots or sprigs (floral patterns) often adorn this fabric. *Organdy* is a muslin made transparent by chemical finishing. It has a crisp finish, which can be restored by ironing after washing or dry cleaning. *Curtain Swiss,* coarser and less crisp than organdy, is used in window drapes. *Mull* is a fine, crisp Swiss, highly dressed in finishing.

GEORGE E. LINTON
Author of "The Modern Textile Dictionary"

SWISS CHARD is a variety of the common beet. It has large leaves that are often eaten as a vegetable. See BEET—*Swiss Chard.*

SWISS FAMILY ROBINSON, an adventure novel for young people, usually credited to the Swiss author Johann Rudolf Wyss and published originally in German as *Der schweizerische Robinson* (4 vols., 1812–1827). The story, modeled after Defoe's *Robinson Crusoe,* concerns the experiences of a Swiss family on a remote island in the Pacific Ocean after surviving a shipwreck. It was written mainly by Johann David Wyss, a clergyman, for the entertainment of his family and was completed and edited by his son, J. R. Wyss. The story has been translated into many languages and has remained widely popular.

SWISS GUARDS, bodyguard troops of Swiss mercenaries, celebrated for their bravery and fidelity. They were employed by the kings of France from the late 15th century until 1830 and are still the principal honor guards of the pope in Vatican City.

Swiss troops first entered French service under Louis XI. A select group was assigned in 1497 to bodyguard duty by Charles VIII under the name of *Cent Suisses,* or "Hundred Swiss." Around this nucleus grew a force of guards that

RALPH CRANE, FROM BLACK STAR

SWISS GUARD at Vatican wears colorful Renaissance uniform said to have been designed by Michelangelo.

increased to more than 14,000 by 1790. The Swiss Guards remained faithful to the royal family during the French Revolution, and many were massacred during the attack on the Tuileries on Aug. 10, 1792. The guard was reorganized after the Restoration of 1814 but was finally disbanded during the Revolution of 1830.

The Papal State's Swiss Guards, who now number about 80, were organized by Julius II in 1506, took heavy losses in the sack of Rome in 1527, and were reestablished by Paul III in 1548. Dissolved during the French revolutionary conquest of Rome, they were revived in 1825. They continue to serve as the pope's personal bodyguard and to perform other protective duties. Their colorful uniforms have changed little since the guards were founded.

HERBERT H. ROWEN
Rutgers—The State University

SWISS LITERATURE. See SWITZERLAND—*Culture*.

SWISSVALE is a borough in southwestern Pennsylvania, in Allegheny county, on the Monongahela River, about 6 miles (9 km) east of the center of Pittsburgh. The community manufactures railway communications and control equipment, safety equipment for industry, heat-resistant materials, and glassware.

Swissvale was settled about 1760 and incorporated in 1898. It has a mayor-council form of government. Population: 13,821.

SWITCH, Electric, a device that passes or interrupts the current in an electric circuit. Manually operated switches are commonly used in homes to turn lights on and off. Automatically operated switches are commonly used in highway and railway signaling, telephone switching networks, computers, and many other applications.

Knife Switch. The knife switch (Fig. 1), which is still in use, was one of the first manually operated mechanical switches. It is simple to construct and is useful where only manual operation is required.

Relay. In the mid-19th century, a need developed for an electrically operated mechanical switch to serve as a repeater in long telegraph lines. This need was fulfilled by the relay (Fig. 2). In its operation, a small current i passes through winding W, thereby producing a magnetic field in gap G. The magnetic field causes the iron armature A to rotate clockwise around pivot P. As a result, the contacts at S close, and a large current I flows through S. If current i is removed, the armature rotates counterclockwise, the contacts open, and current I is interrupted. The relay repeater functions by accepting a small current i from a previous repeater and controlling a large current I for operation of the next repeater down the line. The relay, which was perfected for use in telephone switching networks during the 1920's and 1930's, also was used in experimental relay computers in the late 1930's and early 1940's. However, the relay's switching action takes 1 to 10 milliseconds because the armature is a moving mechanical part.

Vacuum Tube. The vacuum tube also can be used as an electrically operated switch. Its switching action is much faster (0.1 to 1 microsecond) than the relay because it has no moving mechanical parts. The development of reliable

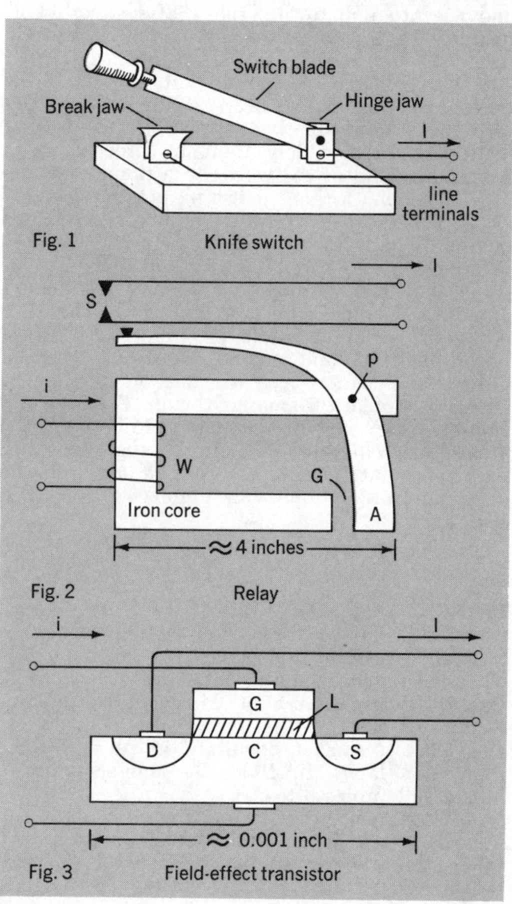

vacuum tubes during World War II led to their use in the late 1940's in a number of experimental vacuum-tube computers, including Eniac and Edsac. The vacuum tube also was used as the principal switching element in the commercial computers of the 1950's, starting with Univac I.

Transistor. The transistor, invented in the late 1940's, improved in many ways on the vacuum tube. In particular, the switching action of a transistor is much faster (1 to 10 nanoseconds) than a vacuum tube because of its smaller size. The field-effect transistor (Fig. 3) operates very much like a relay. A small current i at the gate G is sufficient to control a large current I flowing from source S to drain D through the channel C. The channel current is controlled by an electric field across the insulating layer L. See also COMPUTERS—*History*; SWITCHING THEORY.

PAUL E. WOOD, JR.
Honeywell Information Sciences Center

SWITCHBOARD. See TELEPHONE–*Telephone Circuits and Equipment.*

SWITCHING THEORY deals with the analysis, synthesis, and simplification of switching networks. It was first developed in the late 1930's for the design and analysis of complex telephone switching networks. In the following decades, the theory was modified to encompass a wide variety of switching networks used in scientific computation, business data processing, communication switching, and industrial process control. Once switching theory was well established, it served as a foundation for the understanding of digital computers and other digital systems.

A switching network is a collection of switches with inputs $X_1, \ldots, X_n$ and outputs $Z_1, \ldots, Z_m$. All switching networks can be divided into two classes—combinational networks and sequential networks. In a combinational network, the present output of the network is determined solely by the present input to the network. In a sequential network, the present output of the network is determined by the present input and one or more past inputs to the network. The sequential network is said to have memory because it must "remember" past inputs, whereas a combinational network is memoryless.

Gates. If electronic switches such as vacuum tubes or transistors are used, it is convenient to think of a switching network as being composed of gates. A gate is a simple combinational network. It has one output and one or more inputs, and the present output is determined solely by the present input. The gate input and output are almost always restricted to two values—a high voltage and a low voltage. By convention, the high voltage is assigned the symbol 1, and the low voltage is assigned the symbol 0. A common

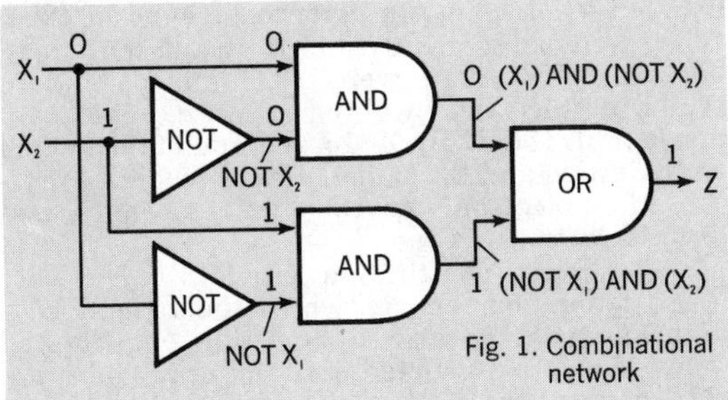

Fig. 1. Combinational network

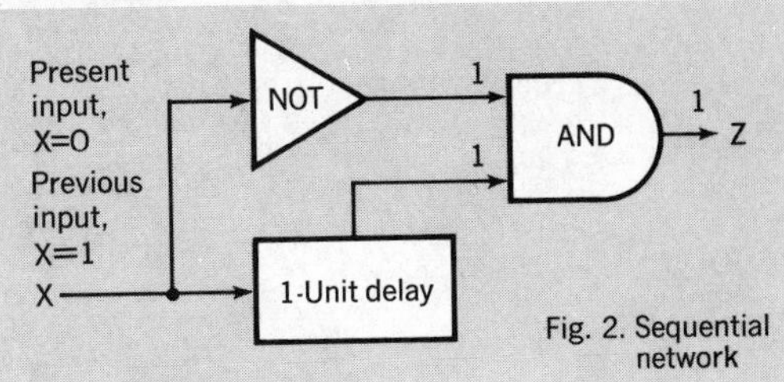

Fig. 2. Sequential network

set of gates is the AND gate, the OR gate, and the NOT gate. The set of gates AND, OR, and NOT is convenient because the input-output behavior of any combinational network can be realized by a network of only these gate types.

Combinational Network. As an example of combinational network synthesis, consider the problem of constructing a combinational network with two inputs X_1 and X_2 and one output Z such that Z is 1 if and only if X_1 and X_2 differ. This can be expressed as $Z=[(X_1) \text{ AND } (\text{NOT } X_2)] \text{ OR } [(\text{NOT } X_1) \text{ AND } (X_2)]$. The corresponding combinational network can be synthesized directly from this notation by using AND, OR, and NOT gates as shown in Fig. 1.

Sequential Network. In describing the combinational network, we implicitly assume that a change in gate input value immediately produces its corresponding change in the output value; that is, there is no delay in the propagation of a signal through a gate. However, if a delay is introduced, sequential behavior may result. Consider a network with a one-unit unit delay as shown in Fig. 2. The present output value of unit delay D is the value of the X input exactly one unit of time ago. The present output value of the NOT gate is 1 if the present value of X is 0. The output Z of the network is 1 if and only if the present input value of X is 0 and the previous input value of X was 1. Since Z partly depends on the previous value of X, the network shown in Fig. 2 is a sequential network. In effect, the unit delay D serves as a memory that "remembers" the value of the previous X input. See also COMPUTERS–*Computer Software and Hardware.*

PAUL E. WOOD, JR.
Honeywell Information Sciences Center

Further Reading: McCluskey, Edward J., *Introduction to the Theory of Switching Circuits* (New York 1965); Wood, Paul E., Jr., *Switching Theory* (New York 1968).

SWITHIN, swith'in, **Saint** (c. 800–862), English ecclesiastic. Swithin or Swithun was born in Wessex, England, educated at Winchester, and ordained a priest. He became chaplain to King Egbert of the West Saxons and tutor to his son Aethelwulf. When the latter became king in 839, he kept Swithin as his spiritual and ecclesiastical adviser. Made bishop of Winchester in 852, Swithin became renowned for his humility, his zeal, and his charity to the poor. He died in Winchester on July 2, 862, and at his own request was buried in the cathedral yard so that his grave would be walked and rained on. He was reburied within the church on July 15, 971, and his shrine was moved in 1093 to the new cathedral of Winchester.

A familiar tradition claims that, rain or shine, the weather on St. Swithin's Day, July 15, determines the weather for the next 40 days.

JOHN K. RYAN
The Catholic University of America

SWISS NATIONAL TOURIST OFFICE

SWITZERLAND'S CHISELED PEAKS entice visitors from all over the world. Sheep and cattle graze on the lush high pastures during the summer months.

SWITZERLAND

National Emblem of Switzerland

Switzerland is a republic in Europe, noted for the striking beauty of its Alpine scenery. It is an important manufacturing center, specializing in precision engineering products and other quality goods. It is also a center for international banking.

Switzerland is a focal point of Europe in both a geographic and a linguistic sense. Lying astride the Alpine range, it is drained to the North Sea by the Rhine, to the western Mediterranean by way of the Rhône, and to the Adriatic via the Ticino, which flows into the Po. The country is also a meeting place of three major language groups of western Europe, with German, French, and Italian all official languages. About 70% of the population speaks German, 19% French, and less than 10% Italian. The indigenous language Romansch, one of four national languages, is spoken by a very small minority.

The early history of Switzerland was marked by the piecemeal revolt of its future cantons from neighboring states and by the union of these territories to form the embryo of the present confederation. The earliest cantons, the so-called Forest Cantons of Schwyz, Uri, and Unterwalden, banded together into a defensive league in 1291. They were subsequently joined by adjacent areas, and in 1513 there were 13 formal members. Much of this area was not organized into cantons until 1803. By 1815 the present cantonal organization and the boundaries of modern Switzerland, subject only to very minor changes, had been achieved.

The Swiss constitution provides for a very loose federation, one in which the federal government, with its seat in Bern, has only limited powers and a restricted jurisdiction. There are 22 cantons, three of which are subdivided so

CONTENTS

that there are 25 local government units. The subdivided cantons are Appenzell, Basel, and Unterwalden. The cantons are relatively powerful, and their sovereignty is restricted only by the powers they have delegated to the federal government.

Swiss Neutrality. In 1815, Switzerland adopted a policy of neutrality. It became unconsititutional for the federal government to enter into political alliances or to make war except in self-defense. In accordance with this policy, Switzerland has not joined the United Nations, though it does participate in the activities of a number of its specialized agencies. Switzerland has contacts with various European political and economic associations, but these are limited.

Switzerland's neutrality has led numerous international organizations to establish their headquarters in the country. The League of Nations chose Geneva as its center. The European headquarters of the United Nations are in Geneva. Switzerland is also the headquarters of the International Red Cross. Neutrality and political independence have enabled Switzerland to play an important role in international banking and finance and permit Swiss diplomats, who often act as intermediaries, to play a key role in relieving international tensions.

1. The Land

Switzerland is small and mountainous. Very little of its area is less than 1,000 feet (300 meters) above sea level, and more than half the total area is over 3,000 feet (900 meters). The country contains several peaks that rise above 14,000 feet (4,200 meters).

The topography of Switzerland tends to form a series of belts that run approximately southwest-northeast. The three major regions—the Jura, the Swiss Plateau, and the Alps—follow the same general southwest-northeast direction. The drainage pattern also follows this directional trend, but it is altered by those rivers that cut across the mountains. The greater part of the country is in the Rhine Basin, but the southwest is drained by the Rhône and a small area in the south by the Ticino.

SWISS NATIONAL TOURIST OFFICE

LE LANDERON, on Lake Biel, is one of numerous medieval villages to be found in the Swiss Plateau.

The Jura. The most northwesterly of the three regions is the Jura, a relatively small area on the French border. It is made up of a series of ridges, generally limestone. They are commonly steep-sided, and many of their summits are forested. Altitudes are not particularly high—between 3,000 and 4,000 feet (900–1,200 meters)—but the ridges have few gaps and present a barrier to human movement. This is a region of few resources and a sparse population. The only city of importance, Basel, is on the Rhine, where the river cuts across the northeastern Jura.

The Swiss Plateau. Toward the southeast, the Jura ends in a straight, continuous, and steep front that looks out across the Swiss Plateau toward the Alps. The Swiss Plateau, despite its name, is a very hilly region drained by Rhine tributaries. There are numerous lakes, most of them produced after glacial deposits dammed the valleys. The largest lakes, Geneva and Constance, lie, respectively, at the southwestern and northeastern limits of the region and form part of the French and German frontiers. Other well-known lakes, such as Zürich, Lucerne, and Thun, are primarily within the Alps, but they extend at their lower ends into the Plateau region. Lakes Neuchâtel and Biel are at the foot of the Jura scarp.

INFORMATION HIGHLIGHTS

Official Name: Swiss Confederation.
Head of Government: President.
Legislature: Vereinigte Bundesversammlung (Federal Assembly)—Upper chamber, Ständerat (Council of States); lower chamber, Nationalrat (National Council).
Area: 15,941 square miles (41,288 sq km).
Boundaries: *North,* West Germany; *east,* Austria and Liechtenstein; *south,* Italy; *west,* France.
Elevation: *Highest point*—Monte Rosa (Dufourspitze), 15,203 feet (4,633 meters).
Population: (1970 est.) 6,300,000.
Capital: Bern.
Major Languages: German, French, Italian, and Romansch.
Major Religious Groups: Protestant, Roman Catholic.
Monetary Unit: Swiss franc = 100 centimes.
Weights and Measures: Metric system.
Flag: White cross on a red field. See FLAG.
National Anthem: *Trittst in Morgenrot daher* (*On the mountains when the sun proclaims a beautiful morn*).

LAKE LUGANO is in the extreme south of Switzerland. Its warm climate and attractive setting make it popular with both Swiss and foreign vacationers.

SWISS NATIONAL TOURIST OFFICE

The Swiss Plateau, which covers about 30% of the country, is not a region of high fertility. Much of it is under grass, and the dominant form of farming is dairying. But because of its more favorable terrain, it is by far the most densely populated Swiss region and contains most of the large cities. These include Geneva, where the Rhône leaves Lake Geneva, and Lausanne, on the lake's northern shore. Bern, the Swiss capital, is picturesquely situated in the middle of the region within a meander of the Aare River. Lucerne and Zürich lie at the lower ends of lakes of the same name. The manufacturing cities of Winterthur and St. Gallen are close to the mountains in the extreme northeast of the plateau. There are also a number of smaller cities, including Solothurn, Neuchâtel, Fribourg, and Schaffhausen. Many of the small towns are quaint and picturesque, some retaining their medieval walls and gates.

The Alps. The Swiss Alps cover more than half the country and make up its most familiar region. The most southerly canton, Ticino, extends to the edge of the Italian plain and contains part of Lake Lugano and part of Lake Maggiore.

ZÜRICH, at the head of Lake Zürich, is Switzerland's largest city. It is primarily German-speaking.

SWISS NATIONAL TOURIST OFFICE

The Alps form two parallel mountain ranges. The northern chain is made up of the Bernese Alps (Bernese Oberland) and their northeastward continuation, the Alps of Uri and Glarus. The Bernese Alps rise to 14,022 and 13,642 feet (4,273 and 4,158 meters) in the Finsteraarhorn and the Jungfrau, their highest peaks. In a 110-mile (177-km) stretch there are only two crossings of this range, the steep and difficult Grimsel Pass and the easier valley of the Reuss, which makes a very deep and narrow cut.

The southern ranges, including the lofty Pennine Alps, are separated from the Bernese Alps by the almost straight, longitudinal trench formed by the valleys of the upper Rhône and Rhine. These two valleys, whose rivers discharge in opposite directions, are linked by passes at their heads. They contain, at least in their lower parts, most of the Alps' population, as well as its few towns, such as Martigny and Sion in the Rhône Valley and Chur in the Rhine.

The southern mountain chain enters Switzerland from France and continues eastward into Austria and Italy. It contains the highest mountains in Europe, including the Matterhorn, and widens, especially on the border of Switzerland and Italy and again in Graubünden Canton in eastern Switzerland, into a broad mass of trackless mountain, much of which is under perpetual snow. Monte Rosa, Switzerland's highest mountain group (15,203 feet; 4,633 meters), is on the Italian border.

The southern range is interrupted by a large number of passes. None of these is easy, and all are closed or rendered extremely hazardous by snow in winter. The Great St. Bernard, the Simplon, St. Gotthard, and a number of closely spaced passes that thread the ranges in Graubünden are used the most. A road tunnel runs under the Great St. Bernard Pass, and one under the San Bernardino Pass is being built.

Population is quite sparse throughout the mountain areas. Agriculture is of slight importance, and cultivated land is restricted to small areas along the valley floors. Dairy farming is the main occupation. The cattle are grazed on the high alpine meadows during the summer and are brought down to the valleys for winter. The chief economic resources of the region are its hydroelectric power, generated by the turbulent mountain streams, and its scenery and ski slopes, which attract tourists. The many towns are designed primarily for tourists. See also ALPS.

SWITZERLAND

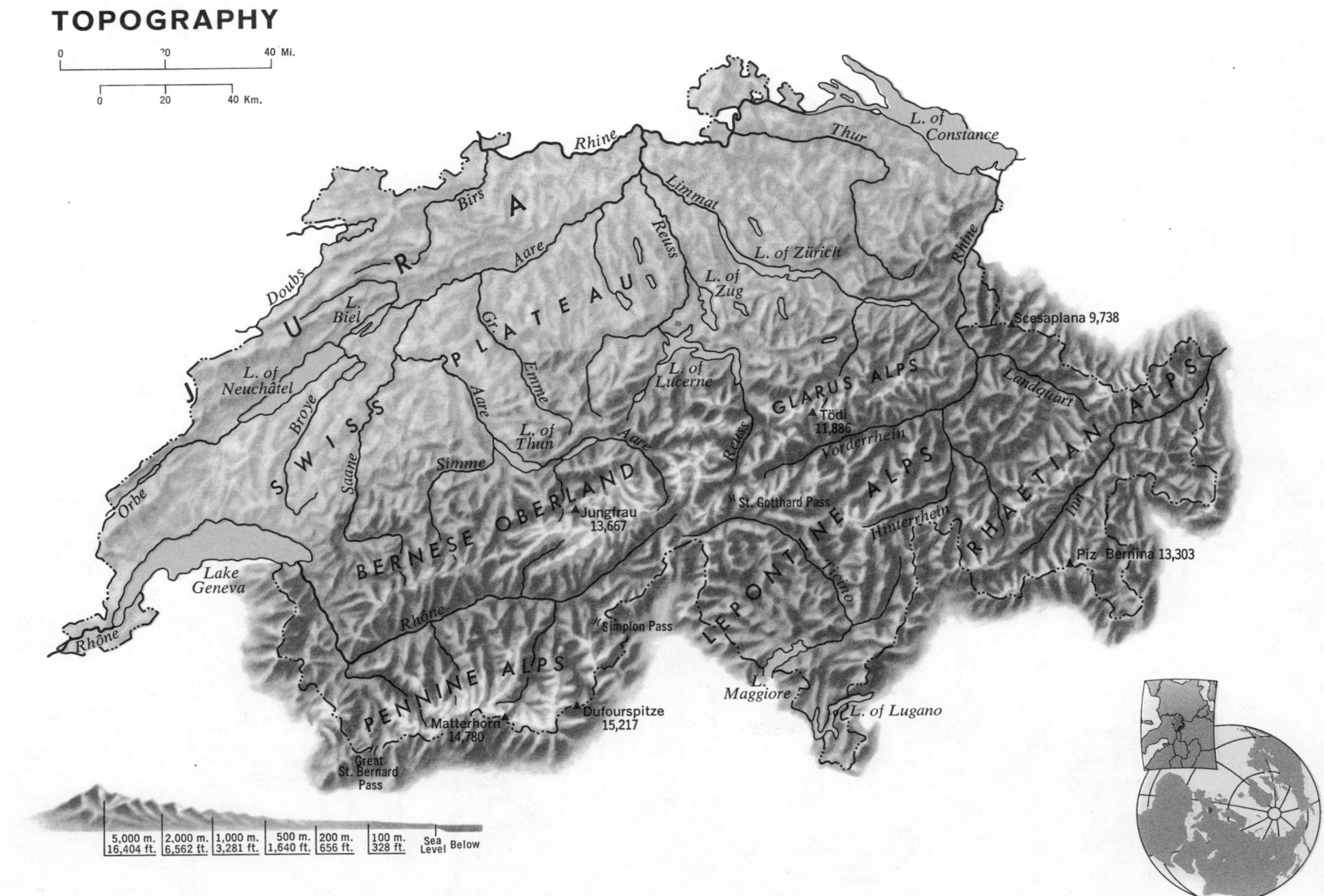

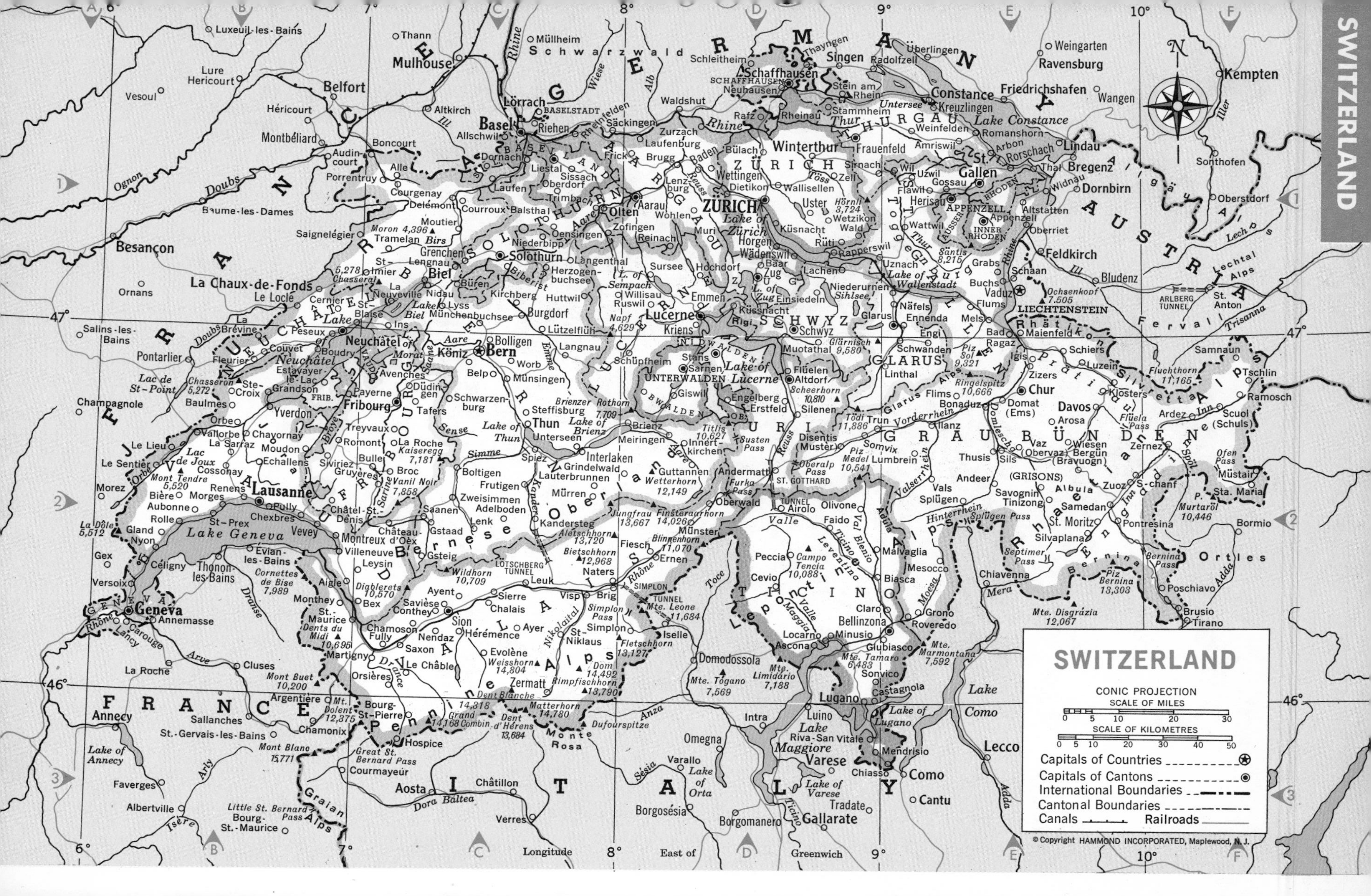

SWITZERLAND
SWITZERLAND
CONIC PROJECTION
SCALE OF MILES
SCALE OF KILOMETRES
Capitals of Countries
Capitals of Cantons
International Boundaries
Cantonal Boundaries
Canals
Railroads
© Copyright HAMMOND INCORPORATED, Maplewood, N.J.

SWITZERLAND

Total Population, 6,115,000

CANTONS

Aargau, 397,000 D 1
Appenzell, Ausser-Rhoden (half-canton), 50,000 E 1
Appenzell, Inner-Rhoden (half-canton), 13,500 E 1
Basel-Land (half-canton), 177,900 C 1
Basel-Stadt (half-canton), 237,300 C 1
Bern, 958,000 C 2
Fribourg, 163,000 C 2
Geneva, 304,400 B 2
Glarus, 42,000 E 2
Graubünden (Grisons), 155,000 E 2
Lucerne, 274,000 D 1
Neuchâtel, 161,000 B 2
Nidwalden (half-canton), 25,000 D 2
Obwalden (half-canton), 25,000 D 2
Sankt Gallen, 363,000 E 1
Schaffhausen, 72,000 D 1
Schwyz, 84,800 D 1
Solothurn, 220,000 C 1
Thurgau, 183,000 E 1
Ticino, 220,000 D 2
Unterwalden, 50,000 D 2
Uri, 33,000 D 2
Valais, 191,000 C 2
Vaud, 486,000 B 2
Zug, 61,000 D 1
Zürich, 1,048,000 D 1

CITIES and TOWNS

Aarau, 17,400 D 1
Adelboden, 2,881 C 2
Aigle, 4,381 B 2
Airolo, 2,023 D 2
Allschwil, 15,500 C 1
Altdorf, 7,477 D 2
Altstätten, 8,751 E 1
Amriswil, 6,752 E 1
Andermatt, 1,523 D 2
Appenzell, 5,082 E 1
Arbon, 13,100 E 1
Arosa, 2,600 E 2
Ascona, 3,053 D 2
Ayent, 2,402 C 2
Baar, 9,114 D 1
Baden, 14,900 D 1
Bad Ragaz, 2,699 E 1
Balsthal, 5,735 C 1
Basel, 212,100 C 1
Basel, *358,700 C 1
Bellinzona, 14,900 D 2
Belp, 4,922 C 2
Bern (capital), 166,800 C 2
Bern, *254,900 C 2
Bex, 4,667 C 2
Biasca, 3,349 E 2
Biberist, 7,188 C 1
Biel, 67,800 C 1
Bière, 1,166 B 2
Bolligen, 19,400 C 2
Boudry, 3,086 B 2
Brienz, 2,864 D 2
Brig, 4,647 C 2
Brugg, 6,683 D 1
Buchs, 6,345 E 1
Bülach, 8,188 D 1
Bulle, 5,983 C 2
Buren, 2,432 C 1
Burgdorf, 15,600 C 1
Carouge, 15,600 B 2
Castagnola, 3,775 E 2
Chamoson, 2,088 C 2
Château-d'Oex, 3,378 C 2
Châtel-Saint-Denis, 2,666 B 2
Chexbres, 1,449 B 2
Chiasso, 7,377 D 3
Chur, 29,100 E 2
Conthey, 3,563 C 2
Couvet, 3,450 B 2
Davos, 9,588 E 2
Delémont, 9,542 C 1
Dietikon, 20,600 D 1
Disentis (Mustèr), 2,376 D 2
Domat (Ems), 3,469 E 2
Dornach, 4,260 C 1
Düdingen, 4,248 C 2
Einsiedeln, 8,792 D 1
Emmen, 21,400 D 1
Engelberg, 2,646 D 2
Erstfeld, 4,126 D 2
Estavayer-le-Lac, 2,583 B 2
Flawil, 7,256 E 1
Fleurier, 3,814 B 2
Flums, 4,462 E 1
Frauenfeld, 16,800 D 1
Fribourg, 38,500 C 2
Frick, 2,123 C 1
Frutigen, 5,565 C 2
Fully, 3,419 C 2
Geneva, 170,500 B 2
Geneva, *301,000 B 2
Giswil, 2,656 D 2
Giubiasco, 4,281 E 2
Glarus, 5,852 D 1
Gossau, 9,731 E 1
Grabs, 4,218 E 1
Grandson, 2,091 B 2
Grenchen, 19,800 C 1
Grindelwald, 3,244 C 2
Gruyères, 1,349 B 2
Herisau, 15,500 E 1
Herzogenbuchsee, 4,641 C 1
Hochdorf, 4,452 D 1
Horgen, 15,300 D 1
Huttwil, 4,664 C 1
Igis, 3,902 E 2
Innertkirchen, 1,230 D 2
Ins, 2,486 C 1
Interlaken, 4,738 C 2
Kirchberg, 5,554 C 1
Klosters, 3,181 E 2
Köniz, 30,600 C 2
Kreuzlingen, 14,900 E 1
Kriens, 17,200 D 1
Küsnacht, 12,800 D 1
Küssnacht, 6,287 D 1
La Chaux-de-Fonds, 42,800 B 1
Lachen, 3,913 D 1
Lancy, 6,967 B 2
La Neuveville, 3,216 C 1
Langenthal, 12,400 C 1
Langnau, 9,201 C 2
Laufen, 3,955 C 1
Lausanne, 136,600 B 2
Lausanne, *210,900 B 2
Lauterbrunnen, 3,216 C 2
Le Châble, 4,237 C 2
Le Locle, 15,100 B 1
Lenzburg, 6,378 D 1
Leuk, 2,546 C 2
Leysin, 2,241 C 2
Liestal, 11,300 C 1
Linthal, 2,645 E 2
Locarno, 12,200 D 2
Lucerne, 73,700 D 1
Lucerne, *146,700 D 1
Lugano, 21,100 D 2
Lützelflüh, 3,960 C 1
Lyss, 5,616 C 1
Martigny, 5,239 B 2
Meiringen, 3,749 D 2
Mels, 5,254 E 1
Mendrisio, 5,100 E 3
Monthey, 6,834 B 2
Montreux, 20,100 C 2
Morges, 8,420 B 2
Moudon, 2,806 B 2
Moutier, 7,472 C 1
Münchenbuchsee, 3,652 C 1
Münsingen, 6,051 C 2
Muotathal, 2,592 D 2
Muri, 3,957 D 1
Näfels, 3,617 E 1
Naters, 3,797 C 2
Nendaz, 3,838 C 2
Neuchâtel, 36,300 C 2
Neuhausen, 11,800 D 1
Nidau, 4,371 C 1
Niederbipp, 3,141 C 1
Niederurnen, 3,347 D 1
Nyon, 7,643 B 2
Oberriet, 5,498 E 1
Oensingen, 2,907 C 1
Olten, 21,900 C 1
Orbe, 3,824 B 2
Orsières, 2,281 C 2
Payerne, 6,024 C 2
Peseux, 4,933 B 2
Pontresina, 1,067 E 2
Porrentruy, 7,095 B 1
Poschiavo, 3,743 F 2
Pully, 15,900 B 2
Rapperswil, 7,585 D 1
Reinach, 5,174 D 1
Renens, 15,200 B 2
Rheinau, 2,363 D 1
Rheinfelden, 5,197 C 1
Riehen, 20,100 C 1
Rolle, 2,942 B 2
Romanshorn, 7,755 E 1
Romont, 2,982 C 2
Rorschach, 13,400 E 1
Ruswil, 4,657 D 1
Rüti, 8,282 D 1
Saanen, 5,649 C 2
Saint-Blaise, 2,412 C 1
Sainte-Croix, 6,925 B 2
Saint-Imier, 6,704 C 1
Saint-Maurice, 3,196 B 2
Saint-Moritz, 3,751 E 2
Samedan, 2,106 E 2
Sankt Gallen, 78,900 E 1
Sarnen, 6,554 D 2
Savièse, 3,203 C 2
Saxon, 2,305 C 2
Schaffhausen, 37,400 D 1
Schiers, 2,363 E 2
Schupfheim, 3,771 D 2
Schwanden, 3,020 E 2
Schwyz, 12,200 D 1
Sierre, 8,690 C 2
Sion, 18,900 C 2
Sirnach, 3,075 D 1
Sissach, 4,574 C 1
Solothurn, 18,900 C 1
Spiez, 8,168 C 2
Stans, 4,337 D 2
Steffisburg, 12,100 C 2
Stein am Rhein, 2,588 D 1
Sursee, 5,324 D 1
Thal, 4,459 E 1
Thayngen, 3,013 D 1
Thun, 33,700 C 2
Tramelan, 5,567 C 1
Unterseen, 3,783 C 2
Uster, 20,800 D 1
Uznach, 3,173 E 1
Uzwil, 7,828 E 1
Vallorbe, 3,990 B 2
Versoix, 3,426 B 2
Vevey, 18,000 B 2
Villeneuve, 2,366 C 2
Visp, 3,658 C 2
Wädenswil, 14,300 D 1
Wald, 7,778 D 1
Wallisellen, 8,601 D 1
Wattwil, 7,480 E 1
Weinfelden, 6,954 E 1
Wettingen, 19,700 D 1
Wetzikon, 12,600 D 1
Widnau, 4,309 E 1
Wil, 12,900 E 1
Willisau, 2,508 D 1
Winterthur, 91,000 D 1
Winterthur, *103,100 D 1
Wohlen, 8,636 D 1
Worb, 5,885 C 2
Yverdon, 19,200 B 2
Zermatt, 2,731 C 2
Zofingen, 8,779 D 1
Zug, 22,300 D 1
Zürich, 432,500 D 1
Zürich, *663,900 D 1
Zurzach, 2,694 D 1
Zweisimmen, 2,676 C 2

OTHER FEATURES

Aare (river) C 1
Aletschhorn (mt.) C 2
Bernese Alps (mts.) C 2
Bernina (pass) F 2
Bernina Alps (mts.) E 2
Biel (lake) C 1
Bietschhorn (mt.) C 2
Birs (river) C 1
Blinnenhorn (mt.) D 2
Brienz (lake) C 2
Brienzer-Rothorn (mt.) C 2
Broye (river) B 2
Chasseron (mt.) B 2
Constance (lake) E 1
Dent Blanche (mt.) C 2
Dents du Midi (mt.) B 2
Dolent (mt.) B 3
Dom (mt.) C 2
Domleschg (valley) E 2
Doubs (river) B 2
Drance (river) C 2
Dufourspitze (mt.) C 3
Emme (river) C 2
Engadine (valley) E 2
Finsteraarhorn (mt.) D 2
Fletschhorn (mt.) D 2
Fluchthorn (mt.) F 2
Flüela (pass) E 2
Furka (pass) D 2
Geneva (lake) B 2
Glärnisch (mt.) D 2
Glarus Alps (mts.) E 2
Grand Combin (mt.) C 3
Great Saint Bernard (pass) C 3
Hinterrhein (river) E 2
Hörnli (mt.) D 1
Inn (river) E 2
Jorat (mt.) B 2
Joux (lake) B 2
Jungfrau (mt.) D 2
Jura (mts.) B 2
Kander (river) C 2
La Dôle (mt.) B 2
Lepontine Alps (mts.) D 2
Lötschberg (tunnel) C 2
Lucerne (lake) D 2
Lugano (lake) E 3
Maggiore (lake) D 3
Matterhorn (mt.) C 3
Medel (mt.) D 2
Mera (river) E 2
Moësa (river) E 2
Mont Blanc (tunnel) B 3
Moron (mt.) C 1
Murten (lake) C 2
Napf (mt.) C 1
Neuchâtel (lake) B 2
Oberalp (pass) D 2
Ofen (pass) F 2
Pennine Alps (mts.) C 3
Prätigau (valley) E 2
Reuss (river) D 1
Rhaetian Alps (mts.) E 2
Rhätikon (mts.) E 2
Rhine (river) D 1
Rhône (river) D 2
Rimpfischhorn (mt.) C 2
Ringelspitz (mt.) E 2
Rosa (mt.) C 3
Saane (Sarine) (river) C 2
Saint Gotthard (tunnel) D 2
Säntis (mt.) E 1
Sarine (Saane) (river) C 2
Scherhorn (mt.) D 2
Sempach (lake) D 1
Sense (river) C 2
Septimer (pass) E 2
Silvretta (mt.) F 2
Simme (river) C 2
Simplon (pass) C 2
Splügen (pass) E 2
Spöl (river) F 2
Susten (pass) D 2
Tamaro (mt.) D 2
Tendre (mt.) B 2
Thun (lake) C 2
Thur (river) D 1
Ticino (river) D 2
Titlis (mt.) D 2
Tödi (mt.) D 2
Töss (river) D 1
Unter (lake) E 1
Vorderrhein (river) E 2
Walen (lake) E 1
Weisshorn (mt.) C 2
Wetterhorn (mt.) D 2
Wildhorn (mt.) C 2
Zug (lake) D 1
Zürich (lake) D 1

*City and suburbs.

Total pop.—1969 off. est.; cantons—1965 off. est.; cities (& with suburbs) (Bern, Basel, Geneva, Lausanne, Lucerne, Winterthur & Zürich)—1968 off. est.; other cities (over 10,000)—1965 off. est.; other pops—1960 final census.

LOUIS GOLDMAN, FROM RAPHO GUILLUMETTE

CLIMBERS 10,000 feet high in the Pennines look out across a glacier-studded and barren alpine landscape to the majestic, knife-like ridges of the Matterhorn.

Climate. Switzerland generally experiences cold winters and mild summers, but the great range of altitude causes extreme variations. Rain falls in all four seasons. It is heavy in most areas and very heavy in the mountains, where it falls as snow for much of the year. Rainfall is usually greatest in summer. There is prolonged sunshine in both summer and winter, but in winter fogs often persist in the valleys, whereas the higher mountain slopes, enjoyed by the skiers, bask in brilliant sunshine.

NORMAN J. G. POUNDS
Indiana University

2. The People

Next to its striking geography, the best-known aspect of Switzerland is the harmony in which people of diverse linguistic and cultural origins coexist. But Swiss history demonstrates clearly that this harmony was not achieved easily or quickly. It resulted ultimately not from a "melting pot" effect but from a conscious policy of maintaining cultural, linguistic, and religious differences.

The Swiss do, of course, share many characteristics. They are generally known as orderly and industrious, and Swiss cleanliness is renowned. Their thrift and business acumen are also legendary. Although often conservative in thought and action, the Swiss lighten their lives through their love of good food and drink.

Ethnic and Linguistic Groups. Ethnically, most Swiss are descendants of four basic groups. The Celts and Rhaetians inhabited the territory prior to the Roman conquest in the 1st century B. C. The Burgundians and the Alamanni were Germanic tribes who conquered the land in the 5th and 6th centuries A. D. Subsequent immigration and the extensive migration among the cantons have blurred these lines considerably.

Linguistic differences are far more important in modern Switzerland than ancient ethnic ties. There are four recognized national languages: German, Italian, French, and Romansch, a tongue of ancient Latin origin spoken only by a minority of the residents of Graubunden canton. About 70% of the population speaks German, 19% French, 10% Italian, and less than 1% Romansch. Foreign residents account for more than half of the Italian-speaking population.

The French- and German-speaking districts tend to reflect the division between the early Burgundian (French) and Alamanni (German) territories. The Italian-speaking citizens of Ticino Canton represent lands and peoples conquered by the Swiss Confederation after the 14th century. German, French, and Italian are all official languages. Legal and governmental business may be carried on in any of them, and government publications must be issued in all three.

The languages spoken in the five French- and one Italian-speaking cantons are generally similar to those spoken in France and Italy. The languages of the 16 German-speaking cantons, however, may be one or several of the many Swiss-German dialects. There are, of course, recognizable minorities in each canton who speak other than the dominant language in that canton. In some cantons it is possible to find neighboring villages, one totally German speaking, the other thoroughly French.

Standard of Living and Social Welfare. Switzerland's prosperous economy, benefiting from advanced industrial development and Swiss avoidance of war for 150 years, has established a relatively high standard of living for the vast majority of the Swiss people. Since its educational system is designed to train workers for available jobs, unemployment is virtually nonexistent.

In general, sickness, unemployment, and accident insurance is administered under a complex system of federal, cantonal, and communal jurisdiction and through a mixture of public and private insurance organizations. Old age, invalid, and widows' or widowers' insurance is compulsory for the entire population. The government also protects all families from hardship caused by military training, an important consideration in a country with military reserve obligations for all men up to the age of 50.

Role of Women. As a rule Swiss women have been slow to move into areas of life outside the family, which remains a strong and highly structured unit. While single and newly married women often work in low-income industrial positions, they generally cease outside work as soon as family responsibilities increase.

Although women were long excluded from all elections, during the late 1960's and early 1970's a number of cantons and municipalities

J. ALLAN CASH, FROM RAPHO GUILLUMETTE

WINTER RESORTS, often nestled in small valleys among towering mountains, bring thousands of skiing and other sports enthusiasts to Switzerland each year.

changed their laws to permit women to vote in local elections. A major breakthrough for women's political liberation occurred in 1968, when Mrs. Lise Girardin was elected mayor of Geneva and became the first woman in Swiss history to hold a major elective post.

In 1971, Swiss males solidly supported a proposal to grant women the vote in federal elections and referenda, reversing the stand they had taken in 1959, the last time the issue was put to a vote. Resistance to granting women the franchise was highest in rural German-speaking cantons in central and eastern Switzerland. In these areas, efforts to secure local voting rights for women were intensified.

Religion. The Swiss enjoy freedom of religious worship. There is no established national church, but cantons may designate one or more denominations as established churches, which may then be supported at least in part by cantonal funds. At the same time, no citizen is required to pay taxes specifically designated for support of a denomination other than his own. The Swiss constitution, reflecting concern over possible outside religious influence, prohibits the establishment of new bishoprics without federal consent, forbids the foundation of new religious orders or convents, outlaws the Society of Jesus (Jesuits) within its borders, and forbids all active clergy from holding seats in the National Council. Protestants outnumber Roman Catholics by about 52% to 45%. There are small minorities of Old Catholics, a group found mainly in Switzerland and Germany that split from the Roman Catholic church in the 19th century, and of Jews.

Population. Switzerland's population of more than 6 million is spread very unevenly across the country. Zürich, the only canton with more than 1 million people, and the cantons of Bern, Vaud, Aargau, St. Gallen, and Geneva account for almost 4 million inhabitants. None of the other cantons has a population over 300,000. Zürich's metropolitan area has over 750,000 people, and Basel's exceeds 500,000. Geneva, Bern, Lausanne, Lucerne, Wintherthur, and St. Gallen have metropolitan populations between 100,000 and 400,000.

During the 1960's the live birthrate was approximately twice the death rate, producing an annual population increase through births of between eight and nine persons per thousand (0.8%–0.9%). The overall population increase, including immigrants, averaged 1.1% annually. About 160,000 Swiss citizens resided in other countries around the world.

Foreign Residents and Workers. Foreigners have always regarded Switzerland as a good place to live. This fact, coupled with a surplus of jobs, attracted vast numbers to Switzerland during the 1960's. In 1960 there were fewer than 600,000 foreign nationals residing in Switzerland. By 1970 they totaled almost 1 million, their numbers rising much faster than the natural population increase. The foreign population includes a labor force of approximately 600,000, most of whom are from Italy, France, and Spain.

Rising antiforeign sentiment among many Swiss resulted in unsuccessful government efforts in the late 1960's to impose restrictive guidelines on industries regarding the percentage of foreign workers to be employed. Ultimately, the government was forced to restrict the immigration of resident foreign workers and to limit seasonal permits for foreign laborers.

3. Culture

The multiplicity of Switzerland's ethnic and linguistic divisions has prevented the development of a distinctive national culture. Partly in response to a desire to preserve remnants of ancient peasant customs and folklore and partly to serve as attractions for Switzerland's booming tourist industry, many national and regional folk festivals are held each year. The emphasis is on traditional costuming, folk music, yodeling, folk dances, and a wide variety of athletic competitions. Ultimately, however, it is the old sections of cities such as Basel, Bern, Fribourg, Lucerne, and Schaffhausen, carefully maintained and reflecting styles from the Middle Ages onward, that provide the greatest cultural attractions in Switzerland.

Libraries and Museums. In addition to the resources of the seven cantonal universities, most of the major cities have libraries and museums that display items concerning Switzerland's heritage. The National Museum is in Zürich, while historical museums also are found in Basel, Bern, and Geneva. The Basel Museum of Fine Arts is noted for its collection of 15th and 16th century

German painting, the Museum of Fine Arts in Bern specializes in Swiss Renaissance art, and the Zürich Art Museum contains 17th century Dutch and Flemish paintings and the work of modern Swiss painters. There is an ethnographic museum in Neuchâtel.

Intellectual and Artistic Movements. The very diversity of cultures has prevented the development of a cohesive, full-fledged national culture. There is no national theater or film center. Swiss born artists such as the architect Le Corbusier, the painter Paul Klee, and the sculptor Alberto Giacometti have become identified with neighboring countries. In the same way, many Swiss writers have tended to associate themselves with literary movements in France, Italy, or Germany, depending on their native tongue. On the other hand, Switzerland's domestic tranquillity and rigid neutrality in international affairs have made it a haven for creative persons, with the result that the Swiss intellectual and artistic community has been at the forefront of almost every major European cultural development of the past century.

Numerous Swiss authors, usually writing in French or German, have established worldwide reputations. Johann Wyss' *Swiss Family Robinson* and Johanna Spyri's *Heidi* are internationally popular. Jeremias Gotthelf and Gottfried Keller were outstanding novelists of the 19th century. Conrad Meyer made the history of other countries the subject matter of his epic poems. Jakob Burckhardt presented an original interpretation of the Italian Renaissance that is still acclaimed. Twentieth century Swiss luminaries include Friedrich Dürrenmatt and Max Frisch, two influential playwrights who wrote in German.

The Swiss are a nation of avid readers. There are over 125 daily newspapers, plus numerous weeklies and a thriving popular magazine industry. The government-owned radio and television system reaches almost every Swiss home.

FRESH FLOWERS and vegetables attract shoppers to weekly market in Morges, on Lake Geneva.

SWISS NATIONAL TOURIST OFFICE

4. Education

Switzerland has long been known for its excellent and varied education system. Its educational facilities successfully meet both the vocational and academic needs of its citizens and of Swiss society. To a great extent, this is the outcome of reforms instituted in the 19th century.

Johann Pestalozzi. The work of Johann Pestalozzi, an ardent Swiss nationalist and educational reformer of the late 18th and early 19th centuries, was particularly important in the development of Swiss education. He believed that the individual must not be regarded as merely part of a collective group that can find its only definition and meaning in a centralized, depersonalized government. Rather, he believed the state existed only to aid and encourage the greater development of man as a free individual.

Thus Pestalozzi encouraged the perpetuation of cultural differentiation and individual initiative as the best basis for true national loyalty. He therefore emphasized the development of a public education system that would pay particular attention to the poor, who must be educated so that they could assume roles as responsible individual citizens and not be the unwitting or passive tools of demagogues or centralized bureaucratic authority. To aid in this process he introduced simplified techniques of instruction aimed at reducing primary learning to basic components involving number, shape, and name. His theories of education stressed the necessity of a rich and varied background, with real knowledge gained through actual observations, as on field trips.

Curriculums. Inspired in part by Pestalozzi's theories, most of the cantons had established primary school systems even before the Federation of 1848. In 1874 primary education was made compulsory for the entire country, and as a result illiteracy has been eradicated. Though financial aid is provided by the federal government, administration and jurisdiction over the school system remains in cantonal hands. Attendance is required for eight or nine years, depending on the canton, and the primary system is buttressed by a free secondary school system and by a wide variety of vocational, agricultural, commercial, and teacher-training institutions. A system of higher middle schools prepares students for admission to the universities. Students between 15 and 19 who become industrial apprentices must continue to attend vocational schools part of the time.

There are seven cantonal universities in Switzerland. Basel, Zürich, Bern, Geneva, Lausanne, Fribourg, and Neuchâtel had an enrollment of about 30,000 Swiss students in the late 1960's. Basel, founded in 1460, is the oldest. In addition, the Federal Institute of Technology in Zürich, the School of Technology in Lausanne, and the St. Gallen College of Economics and Social Sciences have been accorded status equivalent to the major universities.

Switzerland has always enrolled a considerable number of foreign students, attracted by the quality of its universities and the progressive diversity of its many private schools as well as by Switzerland's beauty and recreational opportunities.

PAUL HELMREICH
Wheaton College, Mass.

FARMERS harvest summer hay crop in a meadow high in the Alps. The hay will be used to feed livestock during the winter months.

DORKA RAYNOR, FROM NANCY PALMER AGENCY

5. The Economy

Switzerland has long been one of the most prosperous and, in income per capita, one of the wealthiest countries in the world. Its prosperity is due in part to uninterrupted peace for over 150 years, in part to the effective exploitation of its natural resources, and in part to the advantages derived from its central position on the European continent.

Commerce has been at the center of the Swiss economy since the Middle Ages, when the main overland routes crossed the alpine passes, and the Swiss provided services for Italian and German merchants. The deep involvement in European commerce led naturally to banking, and Switzerland's modern policy of neutrality has made it a safe haven for foreign investments. In addition, the banks' legendary secrecy about their accounts has attracted foreign investors.

Swiss manufacturing evolved gradually from its traditional crafts. During the long winters, when outdoor work was impossible, the peasants used to carve wood and make mechanical devices, such as clocks. Although cottage manufactures are of only minor modern importance, the manipulative skills acquired in this way encouraged the growth of industries such as watch and clock making, electrical engineering, the preparation of dyestuffs and pharmaceuticals, and the weaving of fine fabrics. Industry depends heavily on the export of its specialized products.

Banking, commerce, and tourism all employ large numbers of Swiss and earn considerable amounts of foreign currencies. Tourism is a major industry in this "nation of hotel keepers," and the foreign visitors sometimes outnumber the Swiss citizens. Both the winter and summer seasons are popular. Visitors support not only large numbers of hotel and restaurant employees but also many engaged in transportation and other services.

Agriculture and Forestry. About 75% of the total area has some value for agriculture or forestry. Of this acreage only about 8% is devoted to crops, of which potatoes and coarse grains are the most important. A small area is under vineyards, producing some wine of good quality. Of the productive land, 40% is used for grazing, either as improved meadowland or as rough pasture.

Dairy farming is by far the most important branch of agriculture, and dairy products such as butter, the famous Swiss cheeses, and other milk products account for the bulk of the farm exports. Most of the extensive forests, which cover 24% of the total area, are publicly owned. Native timber satisfies most domestic needs for softwoods. About 9% of the labor force is engaged in agriculture and forestry.

Manufacturing. Manufacturing employs the largest part of the labor force, about 57%, and contributes most to the national income. The engineering, textile, and chemical industries are the most important.

The growth of manufacturing has faced a number of difficulties. The country is almost totally lacking in mineral fuels, and large-scale factory industries had to await the development of Switzerland's abundant hydroelectric power. Coal is imported, however—mainly from Germany—and thermal electric power is used to supplement hydroelectricity.

The basic iron industries are lacking, but there is some production of high-quality steel, made from scrap metal and imported pig iron. The engineering industries, concentrated primarily around Zürich and Basel, are engaged mainly in electrical and precision engineering. The manufacture of turbines and generators has been encouraged by domestic demand. Optical and precision instruments are also important, and there has long been a major clock and watch industry.

Textile production is second in importance to the engineering industry and, like engineering, is concerned mainly with quality manufactures. Textile manufactures, carried on primarily in northeastern Switzerland, in and around the cities of Zürich, Winterthur, and St. Gallen, is dominated by cotton and mixed fabrics and by the spinning and weaving of synthetic fibers.

ROBERT MOTTAR, FROM PHOTO RESEARCHERS

SWISS NATIONAL TOURIST OFFICE

A CRAFTSMAN (*above*) carefully inspects a giant cheese, which must be watched constantly as it ripens.

A SKILLED MACHINIST (*left*) makes precise measurements to ensure the high quality of his work.

There is also a small but important manufacture of woolen cloth, linen, and silk.

The chemical industries, which are located mainly in Basel, concentrate more on the production of dyestuffs, drugs, and pharmaceutical goods than on basic chemicals and fertilizers. There is a large export of the more refined chemical products.

Other industries include food processing, notably milk products and chocolate, printing, and the manufacture of footwear, leather goods, glass, ceramics, and furniture.

Labor. The Swiss labor force in general is technically trained and highly skilled. In manufacturing, female employment is high only in the textile branch. There is a serious shortage of unskilled labor, which has led to a large number of temporary immigrants, most of them Italian. In the late 1960's and early 1970's, foreign workers made up 15% to 20% of the work force. Their presence has created social tensions, and attempts have been made to pass legislation limiting the number of foreign workers.

Transportation. Despite the rugged terrain, Switzerland has developed a network of excellent, all-weather roads. The electrified railroad system provides fast and frequent service. Domestic air transportation is negligible, but Switzerland has important international airports, from which there are regular flights to most parts of the world. Switzerland has a large Rhine River port at Basel and a small fleet of merchant marine vessels.

Trade. Switzerland's policy of neutrality has kept it out of the European Economic Community (Common Market), but the Swiss have joined the European Free Trade Association (EFTA). About half of Switzerland's total trade is with the countries of the European Economic Community. Trade with the members of the EFTA increased sharply during the early 1970's. Trade with the rest of the world is not extensive. The United States is the most important non-European trading partner.

Switzerland's foreign trade is normally unbalanced, imports exceeding exports in value. The difference is made up by the revenue earned from tourism and by the services of Swiss financial and commercial institutions. The leading imports are manufactured goods, food, and industrial raw materials. In value the largest group of exports consists of the products of the engineering industries, followed by chemicals and textiles.

NORMAN J. G. POUNDS
Indiana University

6. Government

Switzerland is a republic, a confederation of 22 cantons. Three cantons—Appenzell, Basel, and Unterwalden—have been divided into half cantons that govern themselves as autonomous units. For many years residents of seven French-speaking communes in the Jura region of German-speaking Bern Canton have sought the creation of a separate canton for themselves.

The executive branch of the government is headed by the Federal Council, and the republic's president and vice president are chosen from among the council's seven members. Switzerland has a bicameral legislature. There are both federal and cantonal court systems. Since the cantons retain a great deal of autonomy, Switzerland's federal government is less powerful in some areas than the federal governments of more centralized states.

Federal Government. The central government of the Swiss Confederation controls matters relating to peace, war, treaties, army regulations, and national resources and public works such as rivers, forests, highways, railroads, atomic energy development, and petroleum pipelines. The government also regulates and controls public communications and is responsible for coining money, issuing banknotes, running the Swiss National Bank, and regulating the systems of customs duties and weights and measures. The government holds a monopoly over the manufacture and sale of gunpowder and alcoholic beverages. In addition, the government has authority in the area of common law and in the enforcement of the uniform penal code of 1942.

The structure of the legislature is bicameral. The Council of States (Ständerat) has 44 members, 2 from each canton and 1 from each half canton. The methods of choosing the members as well as the length of their term in office is left to the cantons. The 200 members of the National Council (Nationalrat) are elected on the basis of proportional representation, with each canton or half canton guaranteed at least one seat. Citizens over 20 are eligible to vote.

Federal Council. The combined membership of the two representative bodies, meeting together as the Federal Assembly (Bundesversammlung), elects every four years a 7-member Federal Council (Bundesrat) that serves as the basic administrative element of the government. Each council member must come from a different canton, and tradition decrees that at least two seats shall be held by persons from French- or Italian-speaking cantons. Each member of the council holds one of the seven governmental portfolios: foreign affairs, interior, justice and police, military affairs, finance, agriculture and industry, and transportation, communication, and energy.

Every year the Federal Assembly elects two members of the Federal Council to serve one-year terms as president and vice president of the confederation. The president of the confederation, who is also president of the Federal Council, may not succeed himself and is normally succeeded by the vice president.

Initiative and Referenda. The Swiss government places an unusually heavy reliance upon popular referenda and upon popular initiative. All constitutional amendments are subject to popular approval and must receive a majority both in total votes and in votes within a majority of the cantons. In this way the influence of the less populous cantons on constitutional amendments is greatly enhanced. Public initiation of a constitutional amendment may be obtained through a petition signed by 50,000 voters. The amendment is then submitted to the electorate. In 1970, for example, the voters narrowly rejected a proposed constitutional amendment, originally brought forward by popular initiative, that would have limited foreign residents to 10% of the population in each canton.

Any law or international treaty must be submitted to a referendum if such a step is requested by 30,000 voters or by the governments of at least eight cantons. In 1969, for example, Zürich engineering students, upset by the government's failure to grant them a role in their school's administration, led a successful referendum campaign to repeal a law regulating the administration of the state's engineering schools.

Local Government. Although the specific organization and structure of government vary from canton to canton, there are basic similarities. All cantons have an administrative council and some form of legislative assembly, although the method of election to both varies widely. Most cantons make heavy use of the techniques of referendum and popular initiative. Three cantons—Appenzell, Glarus, and Unterwalden—continue to use the ancient custom of the Landsgemeinde, and annual open-air assembly of all male citizens of voting age. The Landsgemeinde retains the power of legislation in that it must approve all laws and regulations drafted by the cantonal legislative body.

The cantons are entrusted with powers in all matters not specifically reserved to the federal government. Thus the cantonal governments retain control over the areas of education, health, and sanitation, but cantonal standards often must conform to those set by the central government in Bern. The cantons also administer federal laws in such areas as military training and weights and measures. The cantons control the police and organize and direct all elements of the judicial system with the exception of the federal court, the nation's highest tribunal.

Many cantons are divided into districts composed of several communes, each headed by a prefect who oversees and administers cantonal regulations. The commune is the smallest organizational unit in the governmental structure. The more than 3,000 communes serve as local municipal governments. To qualify for cantonal or national citizenship, people must first become citizens of a commune.

Political Parties. There are three major and several minor political parties in Switzerland. The Catholic Conservatives seek to protect the interests of Roman Catholics and tend to defend cantonal rights. The Radical Democrats represent the liberal middle, or left of center, of the political spectrum. The Social Democrats are moderate socialists, who support female suffrage and favor greater federal action in social reform. In addition to these three major parties there are two relatively important minor parties, the Farmers' party and the Independents. There are also miniscule Liberal (Protestant Conservative) and Communist parties.

Courts. Switzerland's highest tribunal, the federal court, meets in Lausanne. It does not have the power of judicial review of federal legislation. Its main function is to serve as a court of appeal for the cantonal court systems, which are responsible for trying cases at the lower level. The federal court also serves as the first court in trials for revolution and treason and for suits between the confederation and the cantons or between two cantons. In rare cases it becomes the trial court for suits involving individuals or corporations if large sums of money are at stake.

Defense. Geared exclusively to fighting a defensive war, the Swiss have developed plans for destroying every tunnel, bridge, and pass leading into Switzerland and have implemented a program of universal military service for all men between the ages of 20 and 50. Conscientious objectors and those physically unqualified for active training are liable for noncombative duties or for terms of alternate service in hospitals or in public-service projects. Many who receive exemptions from any form of service, including those living outside Switzerland, are subject to a special tax in lieu of military service.

The Swiss military structure is based upon

the concept of a national militia. The militia includes highly mobile and well-equipped armored units along with several specially trained alpine divisions. The Swiss also maintain an excellent air force with almost 400 planes. Since defense is rooted in the militia, the army retains only a small force of approximately 400 officers and 200 noncommissioned officers on a full-time basis. This cadre is used to train the national militia, which can number more than 600,000 when fully mobilized.

Military training is divided into three periods, with duties becoming successively less demanding. All draftees undergo four months of basic training, then serve 12 years in the Élite reserve, with a minimum of eight 20-day training periods. Ten years are spent in the Landwehr, which has biennial 13-day training sessions. Finally, there are eight years of service in the Landsturm, which has one 13-day training period. Infantrymen traditionally keep their rifles, uniforms, and ammunition at home.

The cantons, which are responsible for administering and training the militia, may promote officers to the rank of captain. The federal government controls subsequent promotions up to colonel, the highest peacetime rank. Only in a national emergency does the federal assembly elect one man to the temporary rank of general. This has occurred only five times since 1848.

7. History

The history of Switzerland from the beginning has been dominated by its geography. Surrounded by peoples of different languages and cultures, the Swiss state emerged as an admixture of all of them. At the same time, Switzerland's rugged terrain gave its people a sense of unity and provided the means by which they could defend their independence against much more powerful neighbors.

The area that now constitutes Switzerland was ruled by several powers before it began to emerge as a distinct entity. The Romans conquered the Helvetii, a Celtic tribe living in the western part of the area, in the 1st century B. C. The Helvetii continued to live there under Roman protection until two German groups, the Alamanni and the Burgundians, invaded the area in the 5th century A. D. The Franks absorbed it in the 6th century.

Switzerland became a western outpost of the Holy Roman Empire in the 11th century. Various feudal families ruled it thereafter within the empire, including the rising house of Habsburg.

League of Forest Cantons. The history of the Swiss Confederation began in 1291 when three forest cantons, Uri, Schwyz, and Unterwalden, banded together in a league for mutual defense. The Holy Roman emperor, Frederick II, a Hohenstaufen, had already granted to both Uri (1231) and Schwyz (1240) charters of independence within the empire. The charters specifically released them from previous feudal obligations to the Habsburg family, a change that the Habsburgs refused to recognize. Unterwalden had for some time been under direct Habsburg rule.

When Rudolf of Habsburg was elected Holy Roman emperor as Rudolf I in 1273, he was able to assert the Habsburg rights with imperial authority, and Uri and Schwyz had no one to whom they could appeal for protection. The death of Rudolf in July 1291, therefore, constituted a signal for action, and in August the three cantons formed an alliance. The Swiss have celebrated August 1 as their national day of independence ever since. It was in connection with the alliance that the popular legend of William Tell later appeared, a legend that, however dramatic, seems to have no factual foundation.

While the three cantons did not claim independence from the empire in the pact of 1291, they did renounce direct family rule by the Habsburgs. Thus it was hardly surprising that in 1315, Duke Leopold of Habsburg tried to reassert family authority over Schwyz and Unterwalden. However, his army was ignominiously routed by an inferior force of Swiss foot soldiers at the Battle of Morgarten (1315).

Growth of the Confederation. During the 14th and 15th centuries Swiss history was dominated by the territorial expansion of the confederation and by a series of military conflicts with outside powers. Between 1332 and 1353 five new cantons came into the confederation. Lucerne entered it in 1332, Zürich in 1351, Glarus and Zug in 1352, and Bern in 1353. These additions included several major urban centers and gave the confederation a new commercial and population base. This continued territorial expansion in turn led the Habsburgs to try to assert their authority again, but after decisive Swiss victories at Sempach in 1386 and Näfels in 1388, the Habsburg threat was greatly reduced.

During the 15th century the confederation was beset by internal problems and external threats. These arose, at least partially, from a lack of cohesiveness among the cantons. The confederation was little more than a series of interlocking alliances created for military purposes and tied together by the three forest cantons' membership in all the alliances. Symptomatic of the divisions was the war between Zürich and its neighboring cantons, which raged spasmodically between 1436 and 1450.

The growing military reputation of the Swiss was enhanced by a series of victories in 1476 and 1477 against Charles the Bold of Burgundy, whose territorial ambitions in Alsace were regarded as a threat to the confederation. This was followed by a victory in the south over Milan. A final military triumph came in 1499 when Swiss armies, with financial support from France, defeated Emperor Maximilian I and forced the signing of the Treaty of Basel. The treaty recognized Swiss independence and the removal, in fact if not in theory, of imperial obligations.

Meanwhile, the confederation continued to grow. The cantons of Fribourg and Solothurn were admitted in 1481. Basel and Schaffhausen joined in 1501, and Appenzell was admitted in 1513. This brought the total to 13, where it remained for nearly two centuries.

The Reformation. By the time the Protestant Reformation of the 16th century began, Switzerland's status as an independent confederation was firmly established. This was fortunate, for religious strife within the confederation became so severe that it could never have survived had it not been left to its own devices during the 16th, 17th, and 18th centuries.

The Reformation in Switzerland is usually considered to have begun in Zürich in 1519 under the leadership of Ulrich Zwingli, a former Roman Catholic priest. The teachings of Zwingli ultimately spread and were accepted by Schaffhausen, Appenzell, Glarus, Bern, and Basel. In response, the cantons of Lucerne, Uri, Schwyz,

Kodachrome by Willard R. Culver © N.G.S. Reproduced by Special Permission from "National Geographic Magazine"

Vineyards flourish in the vicinity of Vevey. These vines are on the shores of the Lake of Geneva in the Canton of Vaud.

SWITZERLAND

Above: **Villas and hotels dot the hillside across lovely Lake of Lugano, seen from the Swiss resort town of the same name.**

SWITZERLAND

Left: **The remarkably impressive International Monument of the Reformation in Geneva's Promenade des Bastions, commemorating great Protestant leaders, was erected in 1917.**

Below: **Bern is famous for its many ornamental fountains. This one, the Bagpiper Fountain, dates from the 16th century.**

(Bottom right) Josef Muench; (others) Swiss National Tourist Office

Below: **A Swiss watchmaker checks the movement of a watch before placing it in its case.**

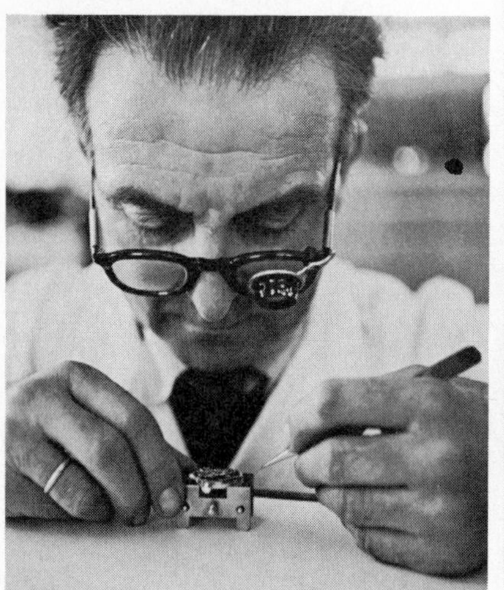

Unterwalden, Zug, Fribourg, and Solothurn banded together to oppose Zürich and in 1531 defeated it at the Battle of Kappel, in which Zwingli was killed. The religious division of the confederation was complete.

From 1531 to 1798 the cantons avoided direct involvement in the many European conflicts that occurred. But it would be a mistake to view this period as a time of peace and prosperity. The conflict between the Catholic and Protestant cantons flared periodically, most notably in the two Villmergen wars of 1656 and 1712. In addition, Swiss soldiers by the thousands fought as mercenaries on both sides in many European wars. Until the 1690's the Catholic cantons supplied troops to the Habsburgs and their allies, whereas the Protestants found no alternative but to enlist the support of France and to pay for it by providing troops to help the French monarchs in their frantic attempts to ward off Habsburg encirclement. In 1693 the sides reversed. The Protestants agreed to provide troops to help the Dutch and British fight Louis XIV, while the Catholic cantons supplied men for Spain, which ultimately allied itself with France in the War of the Spanish Succession.

Structure of the Confederation. Despite the great weakness of the confederation, in 1648 the nations of Europe formally recognized its independence from the Holy Roman Empire in the Peace of Westphalia following the Thirty Years' War. This was little more than official confirmation of what had existed in fact since 1499.

Technically speaking, a federal diet consisting of two delegates from each canton existed throughout this period. However, all decisions required not only unanimity within the diet but also subsequent cantonal ratifications. Such a system would have guaranteed the ineffectiveness of central authority under the best of circumstances; given the deep religious split, it was worse than useless. So completely did the federal concept disappear that the diet did not meet at all between 1663 and 1776.

Local government developed in a wide variety of ways. Six of the older rural cantons governed themselves through annual assemblies of free citizens, known as the Landsgemeinde. The urban cantons of Bern, Fribourg, Lucerne, and Solothurn were controlled by a legislative body of representatives from a closed group of leading aristocratic families. Zürich, Basel, and Schaffhausen had similar governments, except that the leading families were the commercially powerful. Tied to the confederation through alliances with one or more of its members were a number of cities and states. The most important were Graubünden (Grisons), the abbey and town of St. Gallen, the principality of Neuchâtel, and the Free Republic of Geneva.

Calvin's Geneva. Despite the fact that Geneva was not a member of the Swiss Confederation, no account of Swiss history during the Reformation would be complete without mention of the city and the work of its great religious and political leader, John Calvin. Throughout the 16th, 17th, and 18th centuries Geneva made common cause with the Protestant cantons on many issues and was regarded by most of Europe as politically and diplomatically part of Switzerland.

Calvin's success lay in his ability to combine strong religious convictions with great persuasive and administrative talents. Arriving in Geneva in 1536, he was forced to leave the city in 1538 but was recalled in 1541 when Geneva's governing council collapsed into squabbling factions. Calvin proceeded immediately to organize a government that made Geneva world famous as a great bastion of Protestant strength. While the governance of the city was left primarily in the hands of a lay council, the council was expected to administer according to the wishes and teachings of the church, which was completely dominated by Calvin's precepts. Often, the result was drastic legislation regarding morals as they related to men's outward behavior.

Calvin's religious doctrines spread rapidly, particularly to Scotland, the Netherlands, and southern France, and Calvinist scholars from all over Europe went to study in Geneva. The city also became a center for refugees from Catholic persecution, though Calvin himself did not hesitate to prosecute heretics, the best known of whom was Michael Servetus, the Spanish scholar and Unitarian.

Economic and Cultural Revival. During the latter part of the 18th century, the Swiss cantons experienced growing economic prosperity. A flourishing textile industry in wool, cotton, linen, and silk goods developed in Zürich, St. Gallen, and Basel. Because most of the work was done by hand, textiles provided work for peasants in the outlying districts during the winter months. The famed Swiss talent for embroidery stems from this period. It was also during these years that Geneva began to gain an international reputation for the production of clocks, a reputation that helped spur the later development of the Swiss watch industry.

The Swiss cantons were also greatly influenced by the intellectual flowering of the 18th century Enlightenment, which was the culmination of two centuries of great scientific and intellectual activity dedicated to the rationalistic pursuit of knowledge. Zürich became a center for German literature and thought, while Geneva provided a counterpart for French thinkers, among whom the most notable were Jean Jacques Rousseau, a native Genevan, and Voltaire, who spent much time there after 1755.

The French Revolution and Napoleon. The impact on the confederation of the French Revolution was swift and direct. In 1798 a French army invaded Switzerland and forced the cantons to accept the formation of the Helvetic Republic under French supervision. For all practical purposes local autonomy was abolished, and a system of prefects responsible only to a highly centralized authority was established. At the same time, the constitution abolished all hereditary distinctions and established equality before the law. This effectively broke the power of the old oligarchical elites, which had dominated the urban cantons for so long.

While many Swiss greeted the new constitution with enthusiasm, they did not wish continued supervision by their French overlords. Moreover, many Swiss, particularly in the rural cantons, became increasingly restive over loss of local rights. The basic problem the Helvetic Republic faced was the creation of a uniform centralized state in an area with severe linguistic, cultural, and religious diversification.

Recognizing these problems, Bonaparte called Swiss delegates to Paris in 1802 and set them to drafting a new governing document. This compromise settlement, issued in 1803 as the Act of Mediation, was primarily the result of Bona-

SWISS NATIONAL TOURIST OFFICE

LANDSGEMEINDE, or open-air parliament, in Glarus Canton allows all adult males to voice their opinions on the canton's laws and regulations.

parte's own views, and its moderation and subsequent success is one of the best testimonies to his talents and skills.

The Act of Mediation substituted a federalist system for the centralized structure of the Helvetic Republic. A federal diet was to have power in the areas of war and peace, currency regulation, military forces, and international relations. All other powers were restored to the cantons, of which an additional six, St. Gallen, Graubünden, Aargau, Thurgau, Ticino, and Vaud, were created out of territories formerly subject to the old cantons. The new constitution retained the abolition of special privileges before the law and guaranteed citizens freedom of movement and the right of each to choose his occupation. Finally the act gave France the right to recruit Swiss soldiers. In time the Swiss government was obliged to provide 14,000 to 15,000 men for Napoleon's international army.

Reaction and Reform. With the fall of Napoleon, the settlement created by him also disappeared, and the Swiss were forced, under pressure from the great powers of Europe, to draft a new constitution. This document, the Pact of 1815, clearly reflected the triumphant European conservative reaction against the ideals of the revolutionary period.

The Pact of 1815 constituted a return to the total decentralization of the old confederation. The only powers left to the federal diet related to military affairs, questions of war and peace, and treaties with other countries, though cantons were also free to conclude treaties as they related to special cantonal interests. The concept of Swiss citizenship and national guarantees concerning freedom of movement, worship, and occupation were all abolished. While the earlier regulations that had ended the political rights of specific classes were not terminated, the cantons were encouraged to establish their old forms of government, with the result that the old privileged groups soon reasserted their authority and power. The 1815 settlement also created the final three Swiss cantons—Valais, Neuchâtel, and Geneva.

Most important, however, for the future of Switzerland was the formal recognition by the powers of Europe on March 20, 1815: "that the neutrality and integrity of Switzerland and its independence from any foreign influence are in the true interests of European policy as a whole." This statement has remained the basis for Switzerland's unswerving commitment to neutrality.

A period of relative quiet was disrupted in 1830 when the first wave of liberal nationalism swept across Europe. Between 1830 and 1833, 10 cantons liberalized their laws in the direction of universal male suffrage, direct election of representatives, freedom of the press, and greater equality before the law. Events reached crisis proportions in 1834 when the delegates of the liberal cantons in the federal diet adopted a program designed to give the central government the power to tax church property, to exclude the Jesuits, to establish a system of secular education, and to provide freedom of worship within each canton. This action led seven Catholic cantons, Lucerne, Uri, Schwyz, Unterwalden, Zug, Fribourg, and Valais, to form a separate league within the confederation known as the Sonderbund. When this group refused to disband upon order of the federal diet, the other cantons sent an army into the field and in a brief but bloody civil war routed the forces of the Sonderbund in November 1847. In 1848 the liberal cantons proceeded to draft a new constitution that provided for a careful balance between cantonal and federal powers. With minor alterations in 1874 and a few subsequent amendments, it has remained the law of Switzerland.

The federated centralized state that emerged from the Constitution of 1848 was the result of various forces at work in Switzerland. Many Swiss recognized that if they were to make their policy of neutrality and freedom from foreign intervention viable, a stronger, centralized defense system was necessary. Secondly, it was clear that continual internal disruptions and the lack of a uniform system of weights, measures, customs, and currency were hurting the economic development of all the cantons. Finally, Switzerland was not immune to the liberal political fervor that swept Europe in 1848.

Modern Switzerland. Switzerland's history since 1848 has been remarkably peaceful and prosperous. The religious and cantonal differences that had created 350 years of internal friction were at last resolved. The federal-cantonal system of government provided the democratic means for maintaining local prerogative while at the same time adjusting to meet the perpetual changes of an increasingly industrial society. During the late 19th century Switzerland benefited from the general free trade policy of the era and established a world market for its products, while its standard of living rose rapidly.

Much of Switzerland's advance was achieved through its successful pursuit of neutrality. In 1859 the use of Swiss soldiers as recruited mercenaries was outlawed. In 1927, Swiss were forbidden to enlist in any foreign army. At the same time, the Swiss periodically modernized and strengthened their own military establishment, ultimately evolving the present system of extensive service in a national militia.

In both World Wars I and II, though it had hostile powers as neighbors, the Swiss were able to assert and preserve their neutrality. At times this meant arriving at economic and transportation arrangements with belligerents with whom the Swiss government and people did not agree, particularly with Nazi Germany. Its neutral position, however, enabled Switzerland to exercise a role of extreme importance as a center for refugees and for international humanitarian organizations such as the Red Cross and as a channel for communications between belligerent powers with respect to prisoners of war.

Center for International Activities. Switzerland's policy of neutrality and its central location led it to become one of the major centers for international organizations. The International Red Cross was organized by Genevan Swiss with the support of the Federal Council in 1864. The League of Nations, founded after World War I, was located at Geneva, and by the 1970's over 150 international organizations had their headquarters there.

Although the Swiss have always taken steps to make sure that their rights of permanent neutrality were specifically recognized, they have often joined in international agreements and worked in organizations whose aims and techniques they considered pacific, progressive, and essentially nonpolitical. Thus Switzerland became a member of the League of Nations. Though it subsequently refused to join the United Nations, it does belong to many of the United Nations' subsidiary organizations. Since World War II, Switzerland has participated in the Marshall Plan for European economic recovery, has joined the Council of Europe and the European Free Trade Association, and has filed an application for associate membership in the European Economic Community (Common Market).

PAUL HELMREICH
Wheaton College, Mass.

Bibliography

Bonjour, Edgar; Offler, H. S.; and Potter, G. R., *A Short History of Switzerland* (New York 1952).
Codding, George A., *The Federal Government of Switzerland* (Boston 1965).
Herold, J. Christopher, *The Swiss Without Halos* (New York 1948).
Kohn, Hans, *Nationalism and Liberty: The Swiss Example* (London 1956).
New Helvetic Society, *Switzerland, Present and Future* (Bern 1963).
Postan, Michael M., *Economic History of Western Europe* (New York 1967).
Pounds, Norman J. G., *Europe and the Soviet Union*, 2d ed. (New York 1966).
Rappard, William E., *The Government of Switzerland* (New York 1936).
Siegfried, André, *Switzerland, A Democratic Way of Life* (New York 1950).

SWORD

SWORD, a short-handled, long-bladed weapon, akin to a dagger but larger. It is carried in a scabbard, usually wood-lined, normally strapped to the left side of the body.

Blade Types. The numerous types of blade can be broken down into four main groups: (1) straight cutting blades sharp on one or both edges; (2) straight, stiff blades solely for thrusting; (3) curved cutting blades usually sharp on the convex edge; (4) recurved, or S-shaped, blades, in which the cutting edge curves forward from the hilt and then backward toward the point—this type usually widens near the point to place the maximum weight at the point of percussion.

Straight Cutting Blades. Early swords were of bronze, cast in one piece in a stone mold, and normally had two-edged, leaf-shaped blades intended primarily for cutting. They were replaced by forged iron swords of similar form, developed in central Europe about the 10th century B.C. Iron was at first too soft to produce a thrusting blade, and early examples were two-edged with an obtuse point.

Straight Thrusting Blades. Improved techniques —pattern welding in the Dark Ages and the introduction of spring tempering about 900 A.D.— made it possible to produce blades tapering to a point and capable of giving a lethal thrust. These were developed alongside broader, two-edged blades intended purely for slashing, such as the 18th century Scottish broadsword and the Indian *khanda.*

Single-edged straight swords were uncommon in Europe before the 16th century but thereafter became popular, particularly in military circles, in the forms known as the backsword and the lighter spadroon. Most of these blades have a shallow gutter (the fuller) along each face—to reduce their weight without weakening them.

Narrow, stiff thrusting blades had been used in the 16th century B.C. and reappeared as more efficient body armor developed in the 14th century A.D. Called tucks, they became increasingly popular in the 17th century, particularly among east European cavalry, who used them in addition to sabers. The thrust is more difficult to parry than the cut and tends to be more lethal. The dueling sword of the late 17th and the 18th centuries was a purely thrusting weapon.

Curved Cutting Blades. Curved, single-edged iron swords have been used in Japan since the 7th century A.D. They were forged by a complicated system of pattern-welding under carefully regulated conditions.

Similar blades also developed, apparently independently, during the 9th century in the area between the Caucasus and the Carpathian Mountains. They differ from Japanese swords in frequently having a sharp step in the spine and a sharpened forward section of the spine (the chamfer). By the 14th century this sword was replacing straight two-edged blades throughout the Middle East.

The Persian sword (*shamshir*) became increasingly curved during the 16th and 17th centuries, and the chamfer disappeared. This type was introduced by the Moguls from Persia into India, where it was imitated by native smiths. During the 18th century a heavier curved blade was also adopted in India, possibly under European influence.

From the 16th century similar swords became popular in western Europe, particularly for

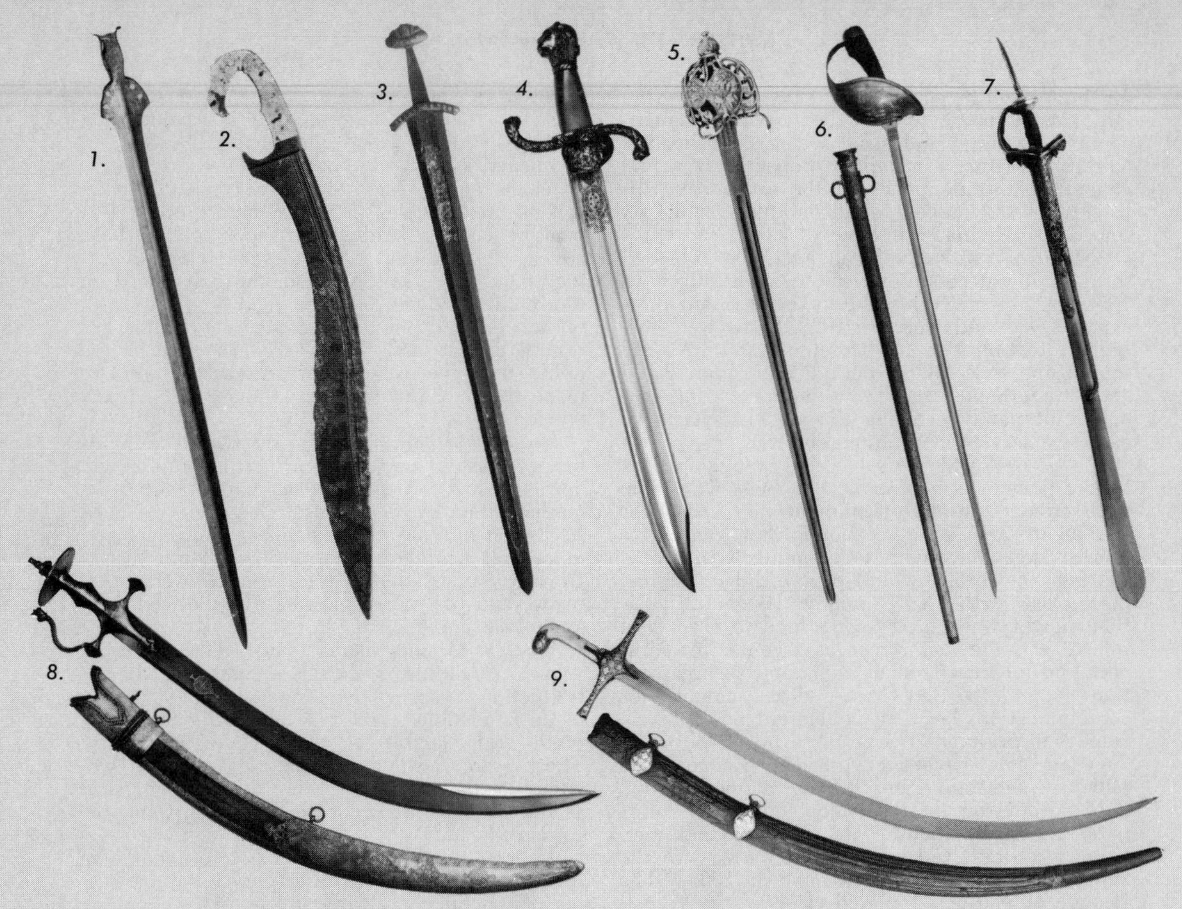

Shown here are: 1. Danish bronze thrusting sword of about 1000 B.C.; 2. 5th century B.C. Greek cutting sword; 3. two-edged Viking sword of about 900 A.D.; 4. late 15th century European sword; 5. mid-18th century British cavalry sword; 6. British cavalry sword of 1908; 7. 18th century Indian sword with encrusted hilt; 8. late 18th century Indian sword with steel blade; 9. 18th century Persian sword with encrusted hilt.

1, NATIONAL MUSEUM, COPENHAGEN; 2 AND 3, THE BRITISH MUSEUM; 4, 7, 8, 9, CROWN COPYRIGHT, THE WALLACE COLLECTION; 5 AND 6, CROWN COPYRIGHT, THE ARMOURIES, H.M. TOWER.

light cavalry. This fashion also was stimulated by contacts with heavily curved Oriental swords during the period of European expansion around 1800. During the 19th century, attempts were made by European armies to improve the curved blade so that it could also be used for thrusting. Some used such devices as forging it with a stiff rib down the spine. All such attempts were unsuccessful, however, and resulted only in reducing the capacity to cut. The ideal cavalry weapon did not appear until 1908, when the British introduced a long narrow thrusting blade with a very effective solid handguard.

Recurved Blades. The recurved blade that appeared in Greece in the 6th century B. C. (the *machaira*) is presumably the ancestor of the yataghan blade found throughout the Balkans and the Middle East, and also of similar and sometimes very exaggerated forms in India. A simple serviceable form—the *kukri*—is still used by Gurkha troops.

Joining of Hilt and Blade. Five main types of junction of hilt and blade exist. (1) The blade is simply fixed to the forward edges of the hilt by transverse rivets, as on early Bronze Age swords. (2) The base (tang) of the blade is cast or forged to the outline of the grip, and plates of some material, such as ivory, are riveted onto each face of it, as on the Persian *shamshir*. (3) A very narrow tang passes through the guard and the grip, and is then hammered over on top of the pommel to hold the whole complex together, as on most European swords. (4) The flat tang passes through the guard and is secured within the grip by a transverse wooden peg, as on Japanese swords. (5) The tang is merely cemented into a one-piece metal hilt, as on many Indian swords.

Handguards. Sword guards outside Europe are rarely more than a simple cross guard or a shaped plate in front of the hand. In Europe the simple cross guard sufficed from the Dark Ages to the 15th century, but from about 1350 some hilts began to have extra bars added to the cross to protect the hand from an opposing blade. By the 16th century a wide variety of combinations of guards surrounded the hand, some found all over Europe, others of purely local distribution. From the late 17th century the patterns used by specific regiments were stipulated by their colonels and later by the higher command. In India the influence of European swords seems to have led to the addition of knuckle guards to hilts of native type.

See also FENCING.

A. V. B. NORMAN
Author of "Arms and Armour" and "History of War and Weapons, 449–1660"

SWORD DANCE, a folk dance for men, who hold swords, sticks, flails, or similar implements. Found throughout the world, sword dances derive from ancient fertility rituals, such as the Dionysian rites of Greece and the Roman Saturnalia. They often involve a death and resurrection theme and combat between the forces of life and death. Generally there are two groups of dancers, one with blackened faces, as in English Morris dances and Spanish morescos, symbolizing possibly evil or the Moors. There may be various characters, such as a leader or fool, recalling the dying vegetation god of ancient Mediterranean peoples, and a woman (actually a man).

The dancers make high leaps and move in rings or opposing or interweaving lines, forming such figures as the wheel, waves, and the nut, lock, or rose. In this last spectacular, often climactic figure, a network of swords is held aloft. The figures and swords nowadays may symbolize fertility, battle, or the beating of swords into plowshares, or be merely the means to display the dancers' acrobatic skill or grace.

Sword dances vary from region to region. Tacitus described naked Germanic youths of the 1st century A. D. leaping and hurling themselves in a "lascivious" dance amid the points of swords. In the Turkish sword dance, two men armed with scimitars progress from a slow, ceremonial start to a climax of flashing steel, dexterity, and danger. The Javanese *kris* dance is martial. In the Cameroons, the swords are carried in orderly procession. The sword dances of England, Ireland, and Germany have been especially well studied. English dances are often associated with mummers' plays and other ritual folk dramas, such as those at Ampleforth and Revesby. They are distinct from the Scottish sword dance performed over swords laid on the ground.

FRANCIS LEE UTLEY, *Ohio State University*

BELL & STANTON, INC.

BALINESE SWORD DANCERS, whose state of trance prevents injury from their daggers.

SWORD FERN, any of a large group of widely distributed ferns with sword-shaped leaves. Sword ferns make up the genus *Polystichum* of the family Polypodiaceae. More than 100 species are known. They are found in temperate regions throughout the world and are common in the woods and mountains of the western and northeastern United States. The plants are evergreen, with leaves growing in tufts from a short scaly underground stem, or rhizome. The sori, or fruiting bodies, are borne along the leaf veins.

Sword fern (*Polystichum adiantiforme*)

PAUL E. GENEREUX

The most common sword fern in the Pacific Northwest is *P. munitum,* which has leathery leaves 1 to 4 feet (30–120 cm) long. It thrives in almost any garden situation. Two other species, *P. lonchitis* and *P. scopulinum,* have smaller leaves and prefer dry, well-drained soil. These ferns make excellent rock garden plants.

The Boston fern (*Nephrolepis exaltata*), a widely grown house plant, is sometimes also called "sword fern."

J. A. YOUNG, *U. S. Department of Agriculture*

SWORDFISH, a game fish found in tropical and temperate seas around the world. The fish's upper jaw and snout are prolonged into a formidable, broad, swordlike structure that may be one third the length of the fish. Swordfish also have two short-based dorsal fins, but, unlike their relatives the marlins, they lack ventral fins. They are lightly colored along the belly and blue to dark purple on the back. The skin is smooth and scaleless in all fish larger than 30 inches (75 cm). Swordfish are pugnacious and have been known to attack dories and schooners.

Swordfish measuring 7 to 10 feet (2–3 meters) and weighing from 120 to 250 pounds (55–115 kg) are most often caught. The largest swordfish taken on a hook and line was a 15-foot (4.6 meters) specimen weighing 1,182 pounds (537 kg) caught off Chile. Swordfish have been caught at depths to 200 fathoms (1,200 feet, or 365 meters), where they were apparently feeding on the bottom. They are commonly taken, however, on long lines fished in midwater or at the surface or are harpooned at the surface.

WIDE WORLD

Broadbill swordfish weighing over 400 pounds (180 kg)

Swordfish have long been prized as food fish, but in May 1971 the U. S. Food and Drug Administration advised the public to stop eating swordfish because more than 90% of the swordfish samples that they tested contained excessive amounts of mercury. Excessive mercury levels in the body are dangerous to health and may even cause death.

The swordfish, *Xiphias gladius,* is the only member of the family Xiphiidae of the order Perciformes.

DANIEL M. COHEN
U. S. Fish and Wildlife Service

SWORDTAIL, name given to several species of livebearers that are found in freshwater from northeastern Mexico to Honduras. They are called "swordtails" because the males have long, pointed, swordlike extensions of the lower part of the tail fin. The largest male swordtail is about 6 inches (15 cm) long, with the tail comprising about one half of this length.

Swordtails and closely related platyfish make up the genus *Xiphophorus* of the viviparous topminnow family Poeciliidae. Although they live in overlapping geographic areas, swordtails and platyfish do not hybridize in nature because they rarely inhabit the same microenvironment, or niche. Some prefer deep pools of headwater streams and others the centers of small streams and pools. Swordtails and platyfish are regularly crossed in captivity, however, to produce beautifully colored hybrids, prized by the aquarist. This crossing has also revealed information about inheritable cancers, thus contributing to medical and genetics research.

Swordtail (*Xiphophorus helleri*)

TROPICAL FISH HOBBYIST PUBLICATIONS

DONALD ZUMWALT
John G. Shedd Aquarium, Chicago

SYBARIS, sib′ə-rəs, was the earliest Greek colony on the Gulf of Taranto, in Italy. It was founded about 720 B.C. by settlers from Achaea and Troezen. The site in the plain between the rivers Crathis (Crati) and Sybaris (Coscile) was then ideal for agriculture and viticulture, while the hinterland provided timber, silver, and pasture for cattle and sheep.

Sybaris soon planted colonies on the west coast of southern Italy at Posidonia (Paestum), Scidrus, Laus, and elsewhere, and it later gained control of the intervening territory and native peoples. Its small empire contained a two-day route overland for the portage of goods, which suited merchants better than the sea passage. The terminals of this route, Sybaris and Laus, became fantastically rich by taxing goods in transit and by offering markets of exchange to merchants from East and West, especially Milesians from Asia Minor and Etruscans from Campania.

In an age of expanding commerce Sybaris became a Greek El Dorado. The Sybarites reputedly lived in such luxury that their name has come to denote any person devoted to luxurious living. Its history exemplified the Greek belief that excess incurs divine retribution. First, the Achaeans expelled the Troezenian settlers, breaking an oath and bringing the gods' wrath on the city. Then by liberal grants of citizenship they became a large state, gained vast wealth, and aroused the enmity of their neighbors, Siris and Croton. Within Sybaris party strife ended in the democrats expelling the oligarchs, who invoked the aid of Croton.

In 510 B.C., Sybaris was razed by Croton. Attempts by survivors and their descendants to refound Sybaris succeeded only for five years (about 453–448 B.C.). Efforts to find the ruins failed until the late 1960's, when magnetometers and drilling provided some clues.

N. G. L. HAMMOND, *University of Bristol*

SYCAMORE, sik′ə-môr, any of several medium to large deciduous trees native to North America, Europe, and Asia. Sycamores belong to the genus *Platanus* of the plane tree family (Platanaceae). They have alternate, palmate veined leaves with three to seven lobes and long leaf stalks that are enlarged at the base to enclose the next year's bud. The male and female flowers are borne separately on the same tree. The male flowers are very tiny, but the female ones are borne in round heads about an inch (25 mm) in diameter. Mature flowers develop into ball-shaped heads of small, single-seeded nuts with fine brown hairs at the base.

Three species of sycamore are native to the United States. Most common is the American sycamore (*P. occidentalis*), also called button-

ANNAN PHOTO

AMERICAN SYCAMORE, right, is widely grown as an ornamental. Its leaves and nuts are shown above.

L. L. RUE III, FROM NATIONAL AUDUBON SOCIETY

wood and American plane tree. It grows throughout the eastern United States and west to Nebraska and Texas. It is commonly over 100 feet (30 meters) tall with a trunk 8 feet (2.5 meters) in diameter. The bark on the young branches and trunk base is brown and scaly, while that on the large branches and upper stems has large mottled green and white bark plates. The American sycamore is popular as an ornamental tree. Its wood is used for lumber, crates, and paper.

The other two sycamores native to the United States are the Arizona sycamore (*P. wrightii*) and the California sycamore (*P. racemosa*). The Arizona sycamore is found along stream banks and canyon walls of southern Arizona and southwestern New Mexico. The California sycamore occurs along streams in coastal ranges and on the western slopes of the Sierra Nevada.

The London plane (*P. acerifolia*) is an important ornamental regarded as a hybrid of the American sycamore and the Oriental plane (*P. orientalis*). It is used as a shade tree throughout Europe and in warmer parts of the United States.

PETER R. HANNAH, *University of Vermont*

SYCOSIS, sī-kō′səs, is a bacterial infection of the hair follicles that affects the beard. See BARBER'S ITCH.

SYDENHAM, sid′ən-əm, **1st Baron** (1799–1841), governor-general of Canada, whose prime task was to pacify and unite the Canadas and implement such parts of the Durham Report of 1839 as were acceptable to the British government.

Charles Poulett Thomson was born in Wimbledon, England, on Sept. 13, 1799, and educated in private schools. After spending some years in his father's business in St. Petersburg, Russia, he returned to Britain, where he was elected to the House of Commons in 1826. He became president of the Board of Trade in 1834.

Appointed governor general of Canada in 1839, Thomson worked ceaselessly to restore the economy and discourage emigration. His business and administrative background prompted him to stress order and prosperity while avoiding any decision on the principle of responsible government. As governor general, he effected a union of Upper and Lower Canada and was able to promise an imperial loan to reduce the debt and facilitate public works. He reorganized the executive government but did not allow his ministers to dominate him. He maintained a majority in parliament but failed to conciliate the French Canadians.

Created 1st Baron Sydenham in 1840, he died in Kingston, Ontario, on Sept. 19, 1841.

G. DE T. GLAZEBROOK, *Author of "A History of Canadian Political Thought"*

SYDENHAM, sid′ən-əm, **Thomas** (1624–1689), English physician, one of the few early physicians to put observation before theory. Not much concrete evidence is available on Sydenham's life before he became a doctor. He was born in Dorset on Sept. 10, 1624. At the outbreak of the English civil war, he was 18 and had just entered Oxford. He fought in the civil wars, returned to Oxford for a time, studied medicine briefly in France, and then, apparently in 1655, began practice in London. But he had no license to practice medicine until 1661 and no M. D. until he was 52.

His wish was to serve mankind, and as a doctor he did all he could for his patients without making a mystery of it. "There were cases," he wrote, "where I have consulted my patient's safety and my own reputation by doing nothing." Rather than recommend the virtually useless medical books of the time, he suggested reading *Don Quixote*. He believed that acute symptoms, such as fevers and inflammations, were the body's efforts to fight off outside attacks. Chronic diseases he attributed to diet and habit. With respect to the description of diseases, he compared himself to a botanist, saying "that botanist would have but little conscience who contented himself with a general description of a thistle and overlooked the special and peculiar characteristics in each species."

Sydenham described the type of chorea that bears his name, as well as malaria, hysteria, and gout. He did the first real work in epidemiology after Hippocrates, recording every available fact, including weather conditions, time, and place. He died in London on Dec. 29, 1689, liked by patients, disliked by many doctors.

SYDENHAM'S CHOREA. See CHOREA.

J. ALLEN CASH, FROM RAPHO GUILLUMETTE

Sydney Harbour Bridge from the harbor's north shore.

SYDNEY, sid'nē, is the largest city and port in Australia and is the capital of New South Wales. It is located in the southeastern part of the continent, on the Pacific Ocean. Spreading out from the shores of scenic Port Jackson, one of Australia's finest harbors, the Sydney metropolitan complex covers some 670 square miles (1,730 sq km), including the city proper and 38 adjoining municipalities.

Sydney is Australia's main international gateway as well as the financial, commercial, industrial, cultural, and communications center of New South Wales. Backed by a flourishing foreign trade and a wide range of industrial output, the city ranks as a major supply base and distribution center not only for Australia but also for the South Pacific area. Sydney sets the pace for the economic expansion of the burgeoning continent and reflects its prosperity. It underwent rapid development in the 1960's to emerge as one of the world's most dynamic cities. A spectacular new skyline took shape as high-rise office blocks in striking architectural styles replaced older buildings in the downtown area and along the harbor.

A great influx of new settlers and visitors from abroad has helped transform Sydney into a sophisticated tourist center with excellent restaurants, nightclubs, hotels, and motor inns. Intellectual activities have gained a new significance in the life of its citizens. Sailing, surfing, sunbathing, and competitive sports such as tennis are very popular, and the average Sydneysider, influenced by the subtropical climate and drawn to open-air pursuits by a delightful natural environment, spends most of his leisure hours outdoors.

Description. Sydney has grown up around the many arms of Port Jackson. The harbor's main arm penetrates 15 miles (24 km) inland from the Pacific Ocean, dividing the metropolis into northern and southern segments. Sydney Harbour Bridge, opened in 1932, links the northern and southern shores of the city.

Sydney's chief business and commercial area is on the southern shore. Many of the professional and business activities are localized. For example, Macquarie Street is largely occupied by doctors and dentists; many of the shipping companies have offices on or close to Bridge Street; and stockbrokers are concentrated on O'Connell Street near the Stock Exchange. A cosmopolitan section known as the Cross (from its center, King's Cross) has developed along the lines of London's Soho or New York's Greenwich Village. The industrial areas are largely south and west of the urban center.

Clusters of apartment buildings and fine residences hug the inlets along both the northern and southern shores. Since the 1950's the principal housing developments have been in the outer suburbs. Many new suburban areas extend along the ocean front north and south of Sydney Heads, the harbor entrance. The built-up area extends for as much as 20 miles (30 km) from the central part of Sydney.

An Australian flavor is imparted to most residential suburbs by the predominantly red-roofed, bungalow-style dwellings, each with a flower garden. Closer to the heart of the city, in the older sections, the visitor may see in one street some of the characteristics of London and in another reminders of San Francisco.

There are several spacious parks in the heart

of Sydney, and three large natural reserves within 15 miles (24 km) of the center are maintained as wildlife sanctuaries. Many fine beaches for bathing and surfing attract vacationers from all over the country.

One of Sydney's oldest landmarks is an obelisk, erected in 1819, from which distances along Australia's early roads were marked. Buildings dating from the early 19th century include St. James' Church, the Hyde Park Barracks (now the law courts), and Parliament House, the central portion of which was built as a hospital. In the inner suburbs, terraces of town houses—many with balconies and wrought-iron trimmings—date from the second half of the 19th century. Among the newer buildings is the opera house, which overlooks the harbor. Its glistening white, sail-like roof structures are thematic reminders of the yachts that dot the harbor.

Sydney contains three universities: the University of Sydney, inaugurated in 1852; the University of New South Wales, chartered in 1949; and Macquarie University, which began classes in 1964. The city has Anglican and Roman Catholic cathedrals.

The Public Library of New South Wales, opened in 1869, houses a general reference library and has an extensive collection of Australiana. The National Art Gallery has an extensive collection, including the works of most of Australia's leading painters.

Economic Life. Sydney's economic development is related to its role as the capital and chief port of Australia's oldest state. It is the natural focal point for rail, road, and air services, and it provides the commercial, financial, and other services needed for the development of an extensive hinterland. The city is Australia's busiest port, clearing more than 4,000 ships a year. Chief exports are wool, wheat, and meat.

Sydney is an important livestock market and the world's leading wool-selling center. It is also a major industrial city, with foundries, oil refineries, automobile plants, woolen and cotton textile mills, and food packaging and processing plants. Building materials, household goods, chemicals, rubber, glass, plastics, and paper are produced.

Sydney is an important naval base. Its port has major repair facilities, floating docks, and slipways. The city is served by international and domestic airlines. As a result of the active development of local and international tourism, transportation services have been augmented.

History. The first European settlement in Australia, Sydney was founded in 1788 as a British penal outpost. Capt. Arthur Phillip, the first governor of New South Wales, chose the site on Port Jackson in preference to Botany Bay, the original choice, and named the settlement in honor of Lord Sydney, the British home secretary. The introduction of the wool industry in the interior attracted many free settlers in the 1820's.

Sydney was incorporated as a municipality in 1842. The office of lord mayor was established in 1902. Sydney grew rapidly after the federation of the Australian colonies in 1901, and has become the second-largest English-speaking city in the Commonwealth of Nations, after London. Population: (1966) of the city, 158,801; of the metropolitan area, 2,444,735.

R. M. YOUNGER
Author of "Australia and the Australians"

SYDNEY, in northeastern Nova Scotia, Canada, is an industrial city and port on Cape Breton Island. It is on the south arm of Sydney Harbor, about 190 miles (304 km) northeast of Halifax. The city is the commercial center for a coastal coal-mining area. Its chief industrial establishments are a steel mill and a coke plant. The Canadian Coast Guard College, the Eastern Institute of Technology, and Xavier College are in Sydney. The Fortress of Louisbourg National Historic Park is on the coast about 25 miles (40 km) to the southeast.

Sydney was founded in 1785 as the seat of government for the colony of Cape Breton by Joseph F. W. DesBarres, the colony's first lieutenant governor. The advantages of the site were well known to DesBarres from his experience as an officer at the siege of Louisbourg in 1758 and from his work in preparing the *Atlantic Neptune,* a series of charts, plans, and views of the eastern coast of North America.

Sydney was settled by United Empire Loyalists after the American Revolution. It was incorporated as a town in 1886 and as a city in 1904. Population: 33,230.

MARY L. FRASER
Cape Breton Regional Library

SYDNEY, University of, a public, nonsectarian university located in Sydney, Australia. Incorporated in 1850, it is the oldest university in Australia. Classes were first held in 1852.

Bachelor's and master's degrees are offered in 10 fields: agriculture, architecture, dentistry, economics, engineering, law, liberal arts, medicine, science, and veterinary science. The doctorate is awarded in these fields and also in divinity and music. Diplomas are available in more than 30 subjects. Enrollment, which increased rapidly in the years after World War II, was stabilized by 1970 at 15,000 to 16,000 men and women.

The university conducts research in the natural, physical, and medical sciences, and in engineering and allied areas, using experimental and observational facilities throughout the state of New South Wales. A special joint research center in radio astronomy has been established with Cornell University. The university library of about one million volumes is the largest among those of Australian universities.

HARRISON BRYAN
University of Sydney

SYDNEY MINES is a town in northeastern Nova Scotia, Canada, on Cape Breton Island, near the mouth of Sydney Harbor, 10 miles (16 km) north of Sydney. It has been an important coal-mining center since 1830. The coal is shipped through the port of North Sydney, 3 miles (5 km) away. Sydney Mines was incorporated in 1889. Population: 8,991.

SYENE. See ASWAN.

SYENITE, sī′ə-nīt, is a granular igneous rock that consists predominantly of orthoclase, a potash feldspar, with lesser amounts of oligoclase, a soda-lime feldspar. If the ratio is about equal, the rock is called a *monzonite.*

Syenite is light colored, like granite, but has little quartz. It typically contains some hornblende and mica and usually some magnetite, zircon, and apatite. It is named "syenite" after a stone quarried at Syene (now Aswan), Egypt.

SYLACAUGA, sil-ə-kô′gə, is a city in east-central Alabama, in Talladega county, about 40 miles (64 km) southeast of Birmingham. Cotton, timber, and livestock are raised in the area, and the city has textile and woodworking plants. Quarries near the city produce a fine quality marble, which has been used in important buildings throughout the United States. Talladega national forest is east of the city. Sylacauga was incorporated in 1886 and is governed by mayor and council. Population: 12,255.

SYLLOGISM, sil′ə-jiz-əm, a form of argument consisting of three propositions, in which the third, called the *conclusion,* follows necessarily from the other two, called the *premises.* The following is an example:

All organisms are mortal;
All men are organisms;
Therefore, all men are mortal.

The argument has three terms—"men," "organisms," and "mortal." The subject term of the conclusion ("men") is called the *minor term,* usually symbolized by S; the predicate term of the conclusion ("mortal") is the *major term,* symbolized by P; the remaining term ("organisms") is the *middle term,* symbolized by M.

It is clear that if this argument is valid, any other argument of the same form—"All M is P; all S is M; therefore, all S is P"—will be valid also, whatever terms are substituted for those here used. Hence, in general, the syllogism is an argument that shows the relation of two terms (S and P) to each other by showing their relation to a third term (M).

There are many forms of syllogism, some valid and some invalid. For the rules of its valid construction, see LOGIC.

The theory of the syllogism was first worked out by Aristotle, and logicians long considered it the main and even the only form of reasoning. It is no doubt exceedingly common; some logicians have held that we use it implicitly whenever we recognize anything—for example, that soldier (S) must be a sergeant (P), since he wears three stripes on his arm (M). But there are many forms of the mental process known as reasoning, of which the syllogism, although very important, is only one.

BRAND BLANSHARD
Author of "The Nature of Thought"

SYLPH, in folklore and mythology, an elemental spirit that lived in the air and served as a link between material and immaterial beings. The concept of the sylph was originated by Paracelsus, a 16th century Swiss physician and alchemist. He devised a system of cosmogony that combined supernatural mysteries with the scientific knowledge of his time. According to his theory, the four elements thought to make up the physical world were inhabited by beings that had magical powers but no souls. Sylphs dwelt in the air; salamanders in fire; undines in water; and gnomes or dwarfs in earth.

SYLPHIDES, sil-fēd′, **Les,** a classical ballet in one act, with choreography by Michel Fokine to music by Frédéric Chopin. The ballet was originally given as *Chopiniana,* the title of the suite of Chopin piano pieces orchestrated by Aleksandr Glazunov, which serves as the score for the ballet. The early version was given in St. Petersburg in 1908. The following year, Sergei Diaghilev presented a revised version in Paris, renaming it *Les Sylphides.*

The scene is a wooded area near the ruins of a monastery. There is no story, only pure dance, performed by three female soloists, a male soloist, and a corps de ballet. The ballet opens and closes with a pas de deux and ensembles, and the solos are linked by ensembles. The male dancer wears a black velvet doublet and white tights, and the females are in long, full white skirts. A serene mood predominates.

SYLT. See FRISIAN ISLANDS.

SYLVANITE, sil′və-nīt, a rare telluride of gold and silver, is used as a source of the two precious metals. It is usually found in a granular, massive form in veins. The brittle, opaque crystals of sylvanite are silvery white and have a metallic luster. Leading deposits are found in Rumania, Australia, and Colorado.

Composition, $(Au,Ag)Te_2$; hardness, 1.5–2.0; specific gravity, 8.0–8.2; crystal system, monoclinic.

SYLVANUS, sil-vān′əs, in Roman mythology, a god of woods and open fields. Sylvanus (or Silvanus) is often confused with Faunus or Pan.

SYLVESTER I, Saint (died 335), pope from 314 to 335. Sylvester was a Roman by birth. His long reign was overshadowed by Emperor Constantine, who dominated both the political and ecclesiastical world. It was Constantine who called the Council of Arles in 314, which condemned Donatism. In 325 he also summoned the Council of Nicaea, which condemned Arianism. A legend dating from about 500 claimed that Constantine, cured of leprosy when baptized by Sylvester, gave Rome and the western empire to the Pope. This legend represents an attempt to give legal standing to the growing political and ecclesiastical independence of the papacy. Sylvester's feast is celebrated on December 31.

ALFRED C. RUSH, C. SS. R.
The Catholic University of America

SYLVESTER II (c. 945–1003) was pope from 999 to 1003. He was the first French pope. His original name was Gerbert, and he was born near Aurillac, France. From 967 to 870 he was a student in Spain. From there he went to Rome and then to the court of Emperor Otto I. Returning to France in 972, Gerbert taught in the cathedral school of Reims and was ordained there. Otto II named him abbot of Bobbio, but because he was not welcome there, Gerbert resumed his teaching in Reims. Hugh Capet, king of France, chose him to take the place of the deposed Archbishop Arnulf of Reims. However, two popes refused to give their approval.

Gerbert became the teacher of the youthful Otto III, and in 998 he was appointed archbishop of Ravenna. With the support of Otto III, Gerbert was consecrated Pope Sylvester II on April 2, 999. He carried out his duties with great earnestness, sought to eliminate simony and nepotism, and demanded celibacy of the clergy. In 1000 he gave Poland its first archbishop, and also recognized Stephen I as the first king of Hungary. Sylvester died in Rome on May 12, 1003.

MARION A. HABIG, O. F. M.
St. Augustine Friary, Chicago

SYLVESTER, James Joseph (1814–1897), English mathematician, who was the founder and first editor of the *American Journal of Mathematics*. He was born in London on Sept. 3, 1814, and educated at Cambridge University. He did not take his degree there, however, because his Jewish faith prevented him from subscribing to the Thirty-nine Articles of the Anglican Church. On leaving Cambridge in 1837, he was appointed professor of physics at London University. In 1840 he resigned to teach at the University of Virginia, but six months later his antislavery views forced him to return to England. For the next 14 years he worked as an insurance actuary and lawyer. At the same time he published innumerable mathematical papers, particularly on invariants, which established him as one of the best mathematicians of the day.

In 1855, Sylvester became professor of mathematics at the Royal Military Academy, Woolwich, where he remained until 1870. Among the papers he published in this period were ones on determinants, the theory of numbers, invariants, and a proof for the discovery of imaginary roots for algebraical equations up to and including the fifth power.

In 1877, Sylvester went to the United States again, this time as the first professor of mathematics at Johns Hopkins University. Besides his part in starting the *American Journal of Mathematics,* he was instrumental in the growth of the study of higher mathematics in the United States. In 1883 he returned to England to teach mathematics at Oxford University. He died in London on March 15, 1897.

SYLVITE, sil′vīt, is mineral potassium chloride. It is an important ore of potassium and the chief source of potassium compounds, which are extensively used as fertilizers.

Sylvite is usually found in granular crystalline masses. The crystals are transparent and colorless when pure but may show shades of blue, yellow, or red when impurities are present. The mineral has a salty taste but is more bitter than halite, or common salt ($NaCl$).

Sylvite is formed in the same way and occurs in the same places as halite, but is much rarer. It is found with halite in extensive salt beds that were formed by the gradual evaporation and ultimate drying up of landlocked bodies of salt water. The beds thus produced are often covered by other sedimentary deposits and have been found at great depths. Similar deposits are being formed in Utah's Great Salt Lake and in the Dead Sea.

The mineral is found in important amounts in salt deposits of Germany and Poland. In the United States there are sylvite deposits in New Mexico and western Texas.

Composition: KCl; hardness, 2; specific gravity, 1.99; crystal system, isometric.

GEORGE SWITZER, *Smithsonian Institution*

SYLVIUS, sil′vē-əs, **Franciscus** (1614–1672), German physician and teacher, whose ideas in anatomy, physiology, chemistry, and therapeutics were pivotal in 17th century medicine.

Sylvius, also known as François de la Boe, or Dubois, was born in Hanau, Prussia (now Hannover, Germany), on March 15, 1614, of Dutch parents. He received his medical degree in Basel, Switzerland, in 1637. In 1658 he joined Leiden University, first in the chair of the practice of medicine and later as rector of the university. He died in Leiden on Nov. 16, 1672.

Sylvius was an early supporter of William Harvey's theory of the circulation of the blood. He also developed a theory of the interaction between acid and alkalies that he used to explain physiological and chemical phenomena. He described the nature and functions of the body fluids, especially blood, lymph, pancreatic juice, and saliva according to anatomical and mechanical principles, but erroneously concluded that all these fluids were either acids or alkalies. This view led to the concept of disease as an excess of either acid or alkali body fluid and to treatment based on restoring the correct chemical balance. Although this idea was later proved wrong, Sylvius stirred the medical community of his time.

AUDREY B. DAVIS
Smithsonian Institution

SYMBIOSIS, sim-bī-ō′səs, is any close association of two dissimilar types of organisms. There are three broad categories of symbiosis based on whether the individual organisms are benefited or harmed by the association: *commensalism, parasitism,* and *mutualism.*

In commensalism, one member of this association is benefited while the other is apparently unaffected. Most cases of commensalism involve small plants or animals living in or on larger ones, perhaps receiving protection or sharing food but in no way interfering with the host's physiological processes. If the symbiotic relationship is in any way detrimental to the host, the association is called parasitism. If both members of the association are benefited by their living together, the relationship is often called mutualism, and many biologists apply the term symbiosis only to this type of cooperative partnership. In many cases, however, the exact physiological roles played by the partners of an association are unknown, and thus the distinctions among commensal, parasitic, and symbiotic, or mutualistic, relationships are often arbitrary and indistinct. Intermediate and evolving, or changing, relationships also exist.

Examples of Symbiosis. Close mutualistic relationships have evolved in many different kinds of organisms. One of the first such relationships recognized was the partnership between the algae and the fungus that form a lichen. The fungus maintains the water supply and provides support for the system, and the algae manufactures food through the process of photosynthesis.

An interesting and widespread mutualistic association is that of microorganisms, such as bacteria and protozoa, that live in the digestive tracts of large animals. The hosts typically lack the enzymes necessary to digest certain complex molecules in their food, and the microorganisms function to break down the food and synthesize vitamins and other compounds needed by the host, at the same time receiving from the host food and a suitable environment in which to live. For example, all large grazing ruminants, including cattle, goats, and camels, harbor symbiotic bacteria in their digestive tracts. These bacteria digest cellulose in the ruminant's diet, and through their metabolism supply vitamins and proteins to the host's milk products. Similarly, flagellate protozoa live in the gut cavity of wood-eating termites, breaking down the cellulose in the wood.

Symbiosis on a Population Level. An association may be deleterious on an individual level but beneficial at the population level. For example, a well-integrated predator-prey system may involve the preferential destruction of weak or sickly prey so that the prey population as a whole benefits. In one case, when the wolves in an area were killed off, the local moose population grew explosively, overate their food supply, and began to fail in reproduction. Individual moose became weak and infested with parasites. When the wolves were allowed to reestablish new populations, the weak and sick moose were preferentially taken and the total number of moose decreased, but the moose herd again became well-fed and healthy. On a population level, such a predator-prey system results in a mutualistic symbiosis.

DONALD E. LANDENBERGER
University of California, Los Angeles

SYMBOL, something associated with something else that it signifies or represents. Symbolic relationships may be entirely provisional, as when an unknown quantity in mathematics is represented by *x*, or they may be so firmly established through custom as to approximate identity. Thus the idea of unity is represented by the number 1, and duality by the number 2, and these symbols serve the purpose of calculation just as if they were the actual quantities involved instead of symbols representing quantities. In the sciences, symbolic systems have been developed that are far more precise than language. Words used in ordinary speech have wider associations than scientific symbols. Language, consequently, is a form of symbolism that not only accepts ambiguity but in some measure employs it effectively. The use of words to suggest or to intimate, rather than to convey specific meaning, is an essential characteristic of poetry.

Origins. While simple signification appears to be a mechanism operating on even the lowest biologic levels, symbols become complex in proportion to the development of intellect. Man has been called a symbolizing animal. It seems clear that at some point in its evolution—perhaps in Neolithic times—the human species distinguished itself by forming conceptions of the cosmos that made the environment in some degree comprehensible. Such conceptions, normally based on human patterns of behavior, served to order the external world in terms of symbols that functioned as reality until they were superseded by symbols of greater cogency and were consigned to the fantasy world of myth.

The mechanisms of myth, however, are by no means insubstantial. Myth is woven into the very texture of human life, and the patterns of myth, together with the symbolism of dreams, indicate the intense figural activity that underlies the rational faculty at every stage of its evolution and, in some sense, directs it.

Images. Although images are visual symbols produced through the imitation of perceived objects, pictorial representation is never purely imitative. It necessarily involves both abstraction and creation. Consequently, the outer world may be considered a projection of the symbols through which it is perceived and by means of which it is pictured. As a rule, these symbols are generalizations. The reduction of 3-dimensional reality to 2-dimensional figures, as in painting, illustrates the principle of analogy that is basic in all symbolic representation. Doubtless imitation had a practical purpose originally. From a primitive viewpoint, the connection between image and object would certainly be sufficiently intimate to warrant an attempt to control the object by manipulating its symbols. To this day we burn people in effigy.

The transition from pictograph to ideograph, which took place at the dawn of history, illustrates the continuous process of abstraction that resulted in the development of language and the use of symbols to denote general ideas. A consequence—at a highly advanced stage of civilization—was the philosophic system based on a hierarchy of ideal forms, or archetypes, associated with Plato and transmitted to the Christian era by such influential authorities as Philo Judaeus, Dionysius the Areopagite, Porphyry, and St. Paul. On this basis was founded the vast system of symbolism that gave direction to the medieval arts and sciences and is still dynamically effective as a force in art and literature.

Signs and Signals. Signs, distinguishable from symbols mainly on the basis of simplicity, serve chiefly to identify and to direct attention to the things they designate. Many signs, such as insignia of rank or function, are designations conventionally agreed upon. But it is common to devise signs on the basis of a real or fancied analogy. Thus arrows are used to point direction, and traffic signals make use of colored lights associated with danger and safety. The letters of the alphabet are signs mainly of phonetic significance, although they may be given all sorts of special associations. In combination these signs make words, which are complex symbols having phonic, visual, and conceptual reference. Words, nevertheless, may function solely as signs. The word "Shoes" displayed outside a shop serves the same purpose as the image of a shoe. Personal marks were used in early times to authenticate the documents to which they were affixed. Such signs were generally superseded after 1300 by seals and later still by autograph signatures, often accompanied by a seal or its equivalent.

Analogy in Symbolism. Whereas signs are often arbitrary in character, symbols frequently are based on a likeness. The lion represents courage because lions are said to be brave. The lily symbolizes purity because it is white. Such symbols often have the force of metaphor or comparison. When they embody or imply a moral statement, proverb, or motto, they are called emblems or, if they are personal devices, impresas. Of this sort is the symbol of the cherry blossom, which in Japan represents the professional warrior, the samurai, because it is beautiful, blooms early, and dies soon.

Symbolic identifications, if apt, have a certain persistence, but symbols are detachable and in time may find other affinities. The eagle of Jupiter, a heavenly messenger, became identified in Christian times with St. John, but in alchemy the eagle became the symbol of volatilization. In a somewhat stranger fashion, red—the color of Christian *caritas* (charity) because love was considered a fiery spirit—became associated for quite other reasons with communism and class conflict.

Figural Interpretation. In late classical times, Stoic and neo-Platonic scholars attempted to rationalize the Greek myths by interpreting them allegorically. At the dawn of the Christian era such methods were employed in the interpretation of Scripture. In the 3d century, Origen concluded that the sacred writings had a threefold meaning and that the literal sense of the Old Testament was mainly significant as a symbolic guide to the truths it concealed. The way then was open not only for an interpretation of the Hebrew Bible in terms of the person and work of Christ but for the figural interpretation in similar terms of the whole of classic literature.

In the Renaissance all epic poetry was thought to be composed, accordingly, in the sibylline style and was subject to allegorical interpretation. The final step was the allegorization of nature. From this viewpoint the world, created by the Word, was a book of symbols to be deciphered by the discerning.

Symbol and Allegory. Rhetoric books of the 16th century make no distinction between symbol and allegory. Both are classified as tropes, or figures. The disparagement of allegory in later times results from the literary reaction associated with romanticism, which regarded allegory as an illustrative device of no great value, while symbolism was held to have profound philosophic connotations. In allegory it is customary to personify abstractions. Wrath is represented as an angry man bearing a club. In such terms, an obvious one-to-one correspondence may be set up between symbol and concept. The result is often a sermon-like discourse in narrative form. Bunyan's *Pilgrim's Progress* employs symbols in this manner.

Correspondences. The theory of correspondences, attributable to Hugh of St. Victor (12th century), involved the idea that all parts of creation are related through analogy, so that to every material manifestation there corresponds a reality of a higher order. Thus the hermetic motto "As above, so below; as below; so above" furnished a guide for the ascent of the soul to wisdom. In this manner, *figura*—similitude or metaphor—served as a bridge connecting the visible with the invisible, and poetic symbolism became a means of revealing the hidden correspondences of the universe.

Modern Symbolism. These early ideas of the function of symbols in poetry were renewed vigorously in the 19th century, but by this time it had become necessary to interpret reality in terms of symbols less precise than those of Christian allegory. In *The Tyger,* Blake suggests the dual aspect of God as creator and destroyer, but the symbol remains enigmatic. For the modern symbolist, mystery is the special province of art. Unlike Renaissance symbolism—which, however abstruse, is meant to be understood—modern symbolism is essentially an intimation that bypasses logic but is intended through reverie and association to probe the mystery of consciousness.

Meanwhile, the Freudian exploration of the unconscious mind has resulted, among other things, in a glossary of symbols that serve both to exhibit and to conceal the inner life. Jung considered these symbols to have universal validity as clues to the psychic configuration of all humanity. Symbolism thus became a means of psychic exploration on a general plane, and it has lately opened the way for the special techniques of cultural and structural anthropology. See also the Index entry SYMBOL.

MAURICE VALENCY
Columbia University

Bibliography

Balakian, Anna, *The Symbolist Movement* (New York 1967).
Bevan, Edwyn R., *Symbolism and Belief* (Boston 1957).
Bowra, Cecil M., *The Heritage of Symbolism* (London 1943).
Cassirer, Ernst, *The Philosophy of Symbolic Forms,* tr. by R. Manheim, 3 vols. (New Haven 1953–1957).
Dunbar, Helen F., *Symbolism in Medieval Thought* (New Haven 1929).
Eliade, Mircea, *Images and Symbols,* tr. by Philip Mairet (New York 1961).
Freud, Sigmund, *The Interpretation of Dreams,* vols. 4 and 5 of the Standard Edition of the Complete Psychological Works (London and New York 1953).
Goldsmith, Elizabeth E., *Sacred Symbols in Art* (London 1912).
Hopper, Vincent Foster, *Medieval Number Symbolism* (New York 1938).
Jung, Carl Gustav, and Kerényi, K. (Carl), *Introduction to a Science of Mythology,* tr. by R. F. C. Hull (London 1951).
Lévi-Strauss, Claude, *The Raw and the Cooked,* tr. by J. and D. Weightman (New York 1969).
Urban, Wilbur M., *Language and Reality* (New York 1939).
Whitehead, Alfred N., *Symbolism: Its Meaning and Effect* (New York 1927).
Wilson, Edmund, *Axel's Castle* (New York 1931).

SYMBOLIC LOGIC. See LOGIC, SYMBOLIC.

SYMBOLISTS, a group of French and Belgian writers of the late 19th century, who rebelled against what they regarded as the excessively rigid, rhetorical principles of traditional French poetry. Like the impressionist painters, they abandoned inherited concepts of art in an effort to transmit directly the essential qualities of the individual's unique emotional experience. They sought in the external world symbols of the inner world of reality and beauty.

Origins. The symbolist movement stemmed from a general admiration of Charles Baudelaire's *Les fleurs du mal* (1857). It was also influenced by the critical theories and poetic practice of Edgar Allen Poe. Arthur Rimbaud and Paul Verlaine were among its earliest practitioners.

The symbolist manifesto that Jean Moréas published in *Le Figaro* in 1886 declared war on the descriptive realism and the impersonal, didactic methods of Parnassian poetry. In the following years, little magazines, new manifestos, and the publications of hostile critics created an atmosphere of great conflict and creative fervor.

Theories. The symbolists believed in the supremacy of art over all other forms of expression and had an intense concern with the nature of individual experience. Their goal was to create an art that would convey the poet's own "inner dream." Poetry was freed from traditional metrical forms so that it could utilize various rhythms and develop thematic motifs in an uninhibited manner. Paul Valéry asserted that poetry should borrow from the principles of musical composition, and music was a common guide in the search for ways "to express the inexpressible."

Practices. The tonal qualities and the evocative power of language were stressed, images were often presented in startling ways, and the device of synesthesia, the suggestion of several sensations simultaneously, was employed to evoke what Baudelaire had called the "dark and confused unity" of the unseen world. The prose poem was a form frequently used by symbolist poets, who also popularized *vers libre* (free verse).

Major Figures. In addition to Rimbaud, Verlaine, and Valéry, important symbolists included Stéphane Mallarmé, Jules Laforgue, Henri de Régnier, and René Ghil. Symbolist theories were successfully applied to the theater by Maurice Maeterlinck, to criticism by Remy de Gourmont, and to the novel by Joris-Karl Huysmans. Paul Claudel is often seen as a direct heir to the movement, and the novels of Marcel Proust are generally regarded as a grand finale to the life style and aesthetic ideals of the symbolists.

Decline and Subsequent Influence. Symbolism fell into disfavor after 1900 as a decadent, excessively ornamental art form. Many symbolists had once called themselves "decadent," with its overtones of an overly refined civilization, to express scorn for materialistic society. However, critics often use the word as a term of derision. Nonetheless, the technical innovations of the symbolists are of major significance. William Butler Yeats, T. S. Eliot, and James Joyce were particularly responsive to the movement, and through their work symbolism has influenced a broad spectrum of modern literary thought. See also DECADENTS.

DAVID D. GALLOWAY
Case Western Reserve University

Further Reading: Balakian, A. E., *The Symbolist Movement: A Critical Appraisal* (New York 1967); Cornell, Kenneth, *The Symbolist Movement* (New Haven 1951).

SYMINGTON, sī′ming-tən, **Stuart** (1901–), American government official and business executive. William Stuart Symington was born in Amherst, Mass., on June 26, 1901. After graduating from Yale in 1923, he worked for a railroad equipment company operated by his family. In succeeding years, on his own initiative, he successfully pioneered in numerous business ventures. He was then president of the Rustless Iron and Steel Company in Baltimore (1935–1937) and chairman of the board and president of the Emerson Electric Manufacturing Company in St. Louis, Mo. (1938–1945).

In 1945, President Harry S Truman named Symington chairman of the Surplus Property Board, and he directed the disposal of billions of dollars worth of government property. He was the assistant secretary of war for air (1946–1947) and secretary of the air force (1947–1950). Arguing that a military threat from the USSR required the United States to increase the size of its air force, Secretary Symington resigned in protest against budgetary restrictions. After briefly heading the National Security Resources Board and then the Reconstruction Finance Corporation, Symington entered the U. S. Senate in 1953, representing Missouri as a Democrat. In domestic affairs he was a moderate liberal. In the late 1960's he was critical of U. S. involvement in Vietnam and alleged waste and extravagance in the defense budget.

Stuart Symington

U. S. SENATE

SYMINGTON, sī′ming-tən, **William** (1763–1831), Scottish engineer and inventor of the first successful steamboat. Born in Leadhills, Scotland, in October 1763, Symington studied for the ministry at the universities of Edinburgh and Glasgow. However, his interest in science led him to become a civil engineer.

In 1786, with his brother, he constructed a model of a steam road carriage. An improved model of the carriage's engine was used to power Symington's first steamboat, which was tried out in October 1788 and was only a partial success. In March 1802 he completed another vessel, the *Charlotte Dundas,* which had a successful maiden run. Her engine used a piston rod guided in a straight line by rollers. A connecting rod joined it to a crank that was attached to the paddle-wheel shaft. This system for driving the shaft became standard on all paddle-wheel craft.

Although the importance of what Symington did was not immediately recognized in Scotland, Robert Fulton's *Clermont* was modeled on Symington's boat. Symington died in obscurity in London on March 22, 1831.

SYMMACHUS, sim′ə-kəs, **Saint** (died 514), pope from 498 to 514. A Sardinian by birth, Symmachus was a deacon at the Lateran when elected pope on Nov. 22, 498. An influential minority of clergy chose the archpriest Laurentius as pope. Theodoric the Great, king of the Ostrogoths and ruler of Italy, at first recognized Symmachus as the rightful pope. A synod held in Rome on March 1, 499, declared that a majority vote should stand. Laurentius submitted, but not his supporters, who soon resorted to criticism, calumny, and violence.

When Pope Symmachus, fearing violence, refused to appear before a synod of bishops called in 501 to hear charges against him, Theodoric gave his support to Laurentius. The schism continued until 506, when Theodoric was persuaded to acknowledge Symmachus as pope. The controversy also produced the Symmachan Forgeries, spurious documents that tried to give historical precedence for the belief that no earthly power can sit in judgment over the pope. Pope Symmachus died on July 19, 514. His feast day is July 19.

MARION A. HABIG, O. F. M.
St. Augustine Friary, Chicago

SYMMETRODONTA, si-met′rō-dän-tə, an extinct group of primitive mouse-sized mammals of the order Pantotheria. Symmetrodonts, known only from fossilized jaws and teeth, are the earliest therian mammals—that is, mammals whose young undergo early development in the uterus—a group that excludes only the egg-laying platypus and echidnas and the extinct multituberculates, docodonts, and triconodonts. Symmetrodonts lived from the latest Triassic to the middle Cretaceous, about 190 to 100 million years ago, in Asia, Europe, and North America. The presumably insectivorous symmetrodonts gave rise to other Pantotheria before the middle of the Jurassic, about 160 million years ago.

The symmetrodont's lower jaw is thin and lacks an angular process, a projection at the lower rear end characteristic of therian mammals. The most primitive lower jaws consist of several bones, and these are gradually reduced to one, as in all recent mammals. Each tooth has three main cusps arranged roughly in a symmetrical triangle, hence the name Symmetrodonta. In the family Amphidontidae, including *Tinodon* and those sometimes classed as the family Kuehneotheriidae, there are only about four lower molars, and the triangle is broad, or obtuse. In the family Spalacotheriidae there are six lower molars, and the triangle is sharp, or acute.

LEIGH VAN VALEN, *University of Chicago*

SYMMETRY is a word that carries many meanings. Synonyms offered by a dictionary—"proportion," "harmony," "balance"—appropriate the word to aesthetics. In Anna Wickham's apostrophe, "God, Thou great symmetry," it connotes perfection. In William Blake's darker reference,

Tiger, tiger, burning bright
In the forests of the night,
What immortal hand or eye
Could frame thy fearful symmetry?

• • • • • •

When the stars threw down their spears,
And watered heaven with their tears,
Did he smile his work to see?
Did he who made the lamb make thee?

lamb and tiger become good and evil, and the duality is asserted as a symmetry relation, like that between positive and negative or an object and its mirror image.

Duality is inherent in man. He is good and bad, beautiful and ugly, profound and shallow. Of his many dualities, the one that can be made precise is the geometric: the geometric duality in his external appearance can be specified precisely by a single plane of symmetry—a plane dividing his body vertically in half. His left and right halves look alike, in the sense that each, when reflected through that plane, becomes the other. The reflection consists in the transfer of each part of his body through the plane at right angles to it and out the other side to an equal distance. His right hand becomes his left and his left hand his right (Fig. 1) in that necessarily imaginary transformation. Such symmetry, called bilateral symmetry, is characteristic of most forms of life: in this respect Blake's lamb and his tiger are alike.

Fig. 1. By an imaginary operation of reflection, a man's right hand can be transformed into his left hand, and his left into his right.

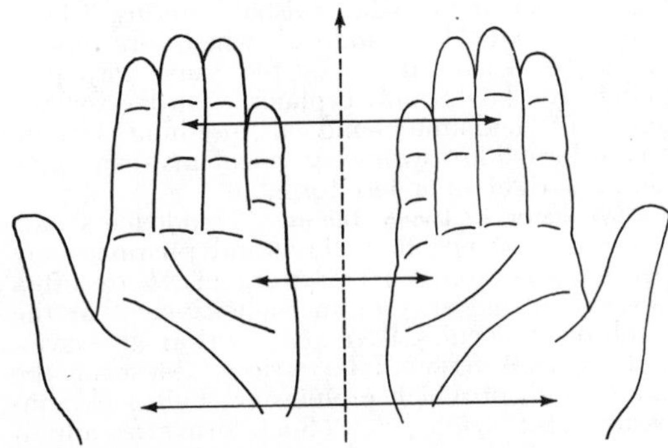

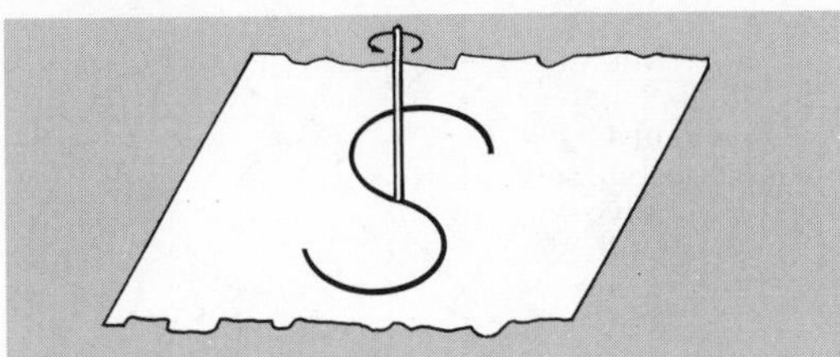

Fig. 2. The letter S has an axis of 2-fold rotational symmetry perpendicular to its center.

Geometric Symmetry. The imagined act of transferring the ingredients of an object through a plane is an example of a "symmetry operation," and the plane to which the transfer is related is an example of a "symmetry element." In this case the operation is called *reflection* and the element is called a *plane of reflection.* A symmetry operation can be defined as any transformation that leaves an object wholly unchanged or unchanged in certain important respects. The reflected man, for example, looks like the real man: the same height, the same build, the same appearance, in the same place. If you met a reflected friend on the street, nothing about him would startle you, except that you might notice that he used to part his hair on one side and has now decided to part it on the other. If the word "symmetry" is written in capital letters—SYMMETRY—each of the letters Y, M, and T, like a man, has a plane of reflection passing vertically down its middle, and the letter E has a plane of reflection cutting it horizontally.

The letter S introduces a different kind of symmetry. The letter is transformed into itself not by reflection but by rotation. Turning it clockwise or counterclockwise about a line perpendicular to and passing through its center, brings it into correspondence with itself when it has accomplished half a complete turn (Fig. 2). The symmetry element related to this rotation is called an "axis of twofold symmetry" because rotation about that line brings the letter into correspondence twice—first after a half turn and again after a full turn. Thus of the upper case forms of the letters in the word "symmetry," only the letter R lacks both planes and axes of symmetry.

The letter H has both a horizontal and a vertical plane of reflection, and an axis of twofold symmetry as well. Indeed many familiar shapes have several symmetry elements. A complete specification of the symmetry of a cube (Fig. 3) would enumerate three fourfold axes, four threefold axes, six twofold axes, and nine planes of reflection. A cone has an axis of universal rotation—an infinite-fold axis—and all planes containing that axis are planes of reflection (Fig. 4). A cylinder also has these symmetry elements, and in addition it has a plane of reflection perpendicular to the axis, and all lines lying in that plane and passing through that axis are axes of twofold symmetry (Fig. 5). In a sphere, the most symmetrical of all objects, all lines passing through its center are axes of universal rotation, and all planes passing through its center are reflection planes.

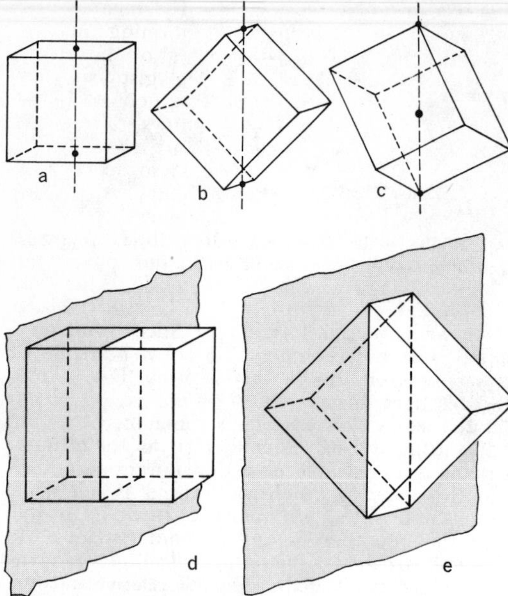

Fig. 3. A cube has (a) three 4-fold, (b) six 2-fold, (c) four 3-fold axes of symmetry, (d) three planes of reflection parallel to its faces, and (e) six planes of reflection through pairs of opposite edges.

A sphere is the only object with that symmetry, and any sphere can be defined by naming that symmetry and its size. In contrast there are many objects having each of the other symmetries mentioned. For example a regular octahedron (Fig. 6), made of eight equilateral triangles, has the same symmetry as a cube. The earth, if regarded as a sphere slightly flattened at two opposite poles, has the symmetry of a cylinder.

Notice that there must always be an internal consistency in the combinations of symmetry elements possessed by an object. By internal consistency is meant that the symmetry elements must not conflict with one another. In the cube, for example, a quarter turn around any fourfold axis not only brings the cube into correspondence with itself, but also moves each threefold axis to the position of one of the others. This can be seen by considering the top face of the cube in Fig. 3a. A threefold axis sticks out and upward from each corner of the top face, and a quarter rotation about the vertical fourfold axis simply moves each corner, with its threefold axis, to the next corner. Moreover, each reflection plane converts rotation axes and other mirrors either into themselves or into another of their kind.

Fig. 4. The symmetry of a cone (sometimes called polar symmetry) consists of an infinite-fold rotation axis and an infinity of planes containing that axis. (b) The geometric symmetry of an hourglass partly filled with sand is conical, but its functional symmetry is cylindrical.

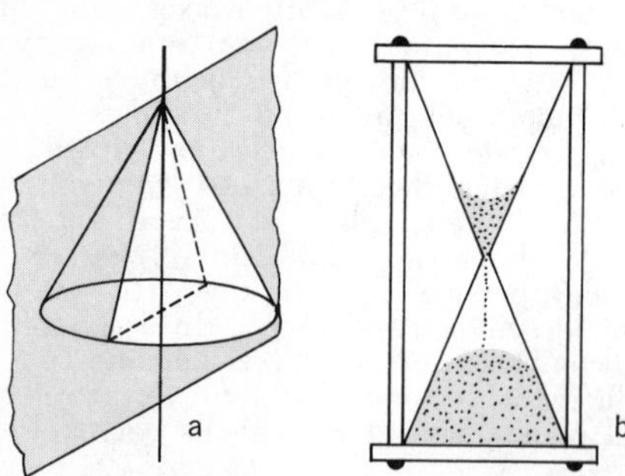

If the internal consistency described here did not exist, the repetition of one symmetry operation might yield infinitely many of the other symmetry elements. The sets of symmetry operations that may be contemplated simultaneously—that is, that do not conflict with one another—can be shown to form "groups" in the mathematicians' sense (see GROUP THEORY). One of the group properties is that the result of any symmetry operation within a group can be accomplished by a combination of some of the other operations in the group.

Between the symmetries of rotation and reflection there is a deep-lying distinction: a rotation can be physically accomplished by turning an object, whereas a reflection can be accomplished only by an optical trick such as the use of a mirror. The pentagram illustrates the importance of this distinction between "performable" and "nonperformable" operations. The symmetry of the pentagram in Fig. 7a consists of a fivefold axis of rotation and five planes of reflection. When the pentagram is "woven," as in Fig. 7b, it loses the planes of reflection and can then appear in two distinguishable forms, "right-handed" and "left-handed," which are mirror images of each other. In the same way propellers for boats and airplanes, "birds" for the game of badminton—indeed anything lacking nonperformable symmetry elements—can take either a right or a left form.

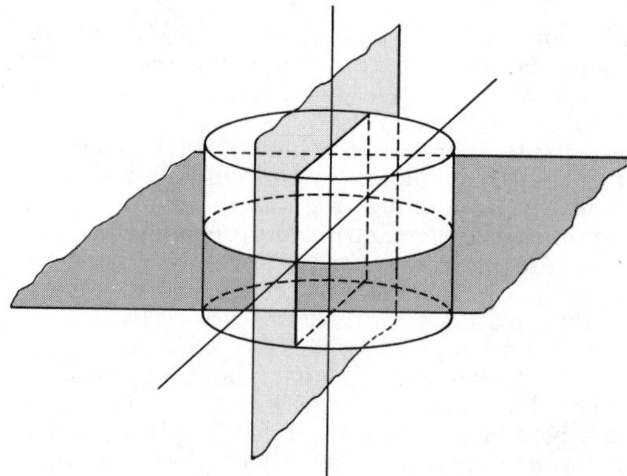

Fig. 5. Cylindrical symmetry includes the symmetry elements of the cone, a plane of reflection perpendicular to the principal axis, and 2-fold axes of rotation in that plane.

Symmetry in Living Things. "Handedness" acquires importance in biology and pharmacology because the atoms in living organisms are often bonded to one another in such a way that the resulting molecules have only performable symmetries (see STEREOCHEMISTRY). Most of the amino acids of which proteins are built lack nonperformable symmetries. Such drugs as adren-

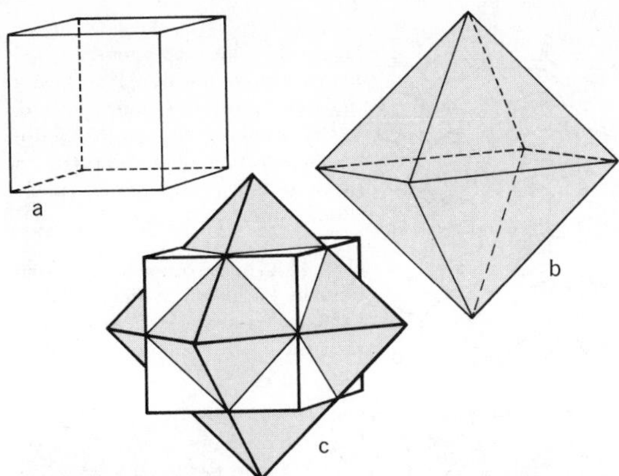

Fig. 6. A model in which a regular octahedron and a cube interpenetrate shows especially clearly that the symmetries of the two figures are the same.

aline, used to contract the blood vessels, are effective in one form and ineffective in its mirror image. Some accident determined these forms when life originated. Had the accident occurred otherwise, all life might have proceeded in the mirror image of its present forms, probably just as successfully.

To the biologist, symmetry of function is more important than symmetry of shape. His idea can be illustrated by an hourglass charged with sand (Fig. 4). From the geometric viewpoint, the hourglass has the symmetry of the cone (Fig. 4). It does not have the symmetry of the cylinder (Fig. 5), because the sand inside would not be symmetrical about the plane passing through its neck. From the functional viewpoint, however, the hourglass does have the symmetry of the cylinder, for when it has been used once for timing it can be turned upside down and used again for the same purpose. The two ends are functionally the same, though at any particular moment one end is serving one function—for example, letting sand out—and the other end the other function—collecting sand. Similarly, when a biologist speaks of the "bilateral symmetry" of the higher animals, he is not referring to the fact that the organism can be so placed that it has geometric symmetry about a reflection plane, which is a rather rigid attitude, suggesting a soldier at attention, which most organisms rarely adopt. He means that both sides are capable of performing in the same way, one as the mirror image of the other.

In functional terms, the biologist can account for the evolutionary development of bilateral symmetry somewhat as follows. Protozoa, floating weightlessly and without motility in water, are indifferent to direction in space and exhibit spherical symmetry. Somewhat higher forms of life, such as sea anemones and other polyps, sink, attach themselves to the ocean floor, and exhibit the symmetry of the cone (Fig. 4). The axis of a creature of this kind, as one would expect, is determined by the direction of gravity. When phylogenetic progress brings motility, the organism responds to two directions, up and down and forward and back. The plane determined by these two directions is the plane of bilateral symmetry. It is easy to see why higher organisms—higher, that is, in the phylogenetic sense—have developed bilateral symmetry. Without it, the organism would tend to fall sideways—for example, if its left legs were longer than its right legs—and would tend to travel in circles.

Operations with Indistinguishable Elements. The word "symmetry" calls attention to another sort of symmetry operation besides reflection and rotation. If the two *m*'s were plucked from the page, interchanged, and put back, no one would notice. The ability to interchange indistinguishable objects is one of the most pervasive symmetries in technology, in nature, and in thought. Basic to chemistry, for example, is the belief that the world is made of about a hundred species of atoms, and within each species one atom behaves chemically like any other. In other words, things are symmetric to the interchange

Fig. 7. When a pentagram is woven, it loses its five planes of symmetry and can take either a right-handed or a left-handed form.

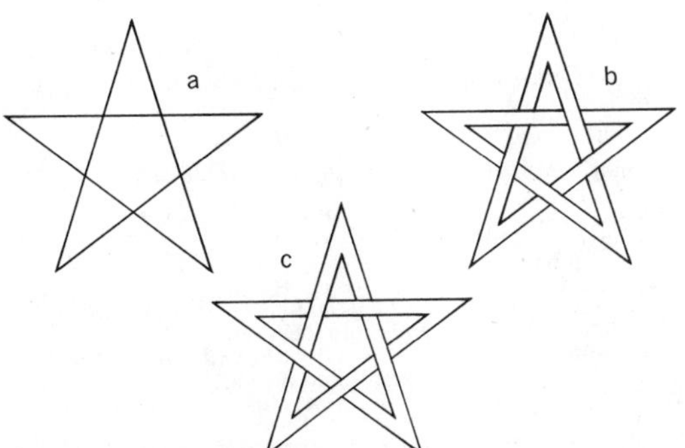

Fig. 8. The tesselation (a) by squares and equilateral triangles is called semiregular because its components are regular polygons and its corners are all alike. A tesselation can take either a right-handed or a left-handed form (b) when it lacks performable symmetries.

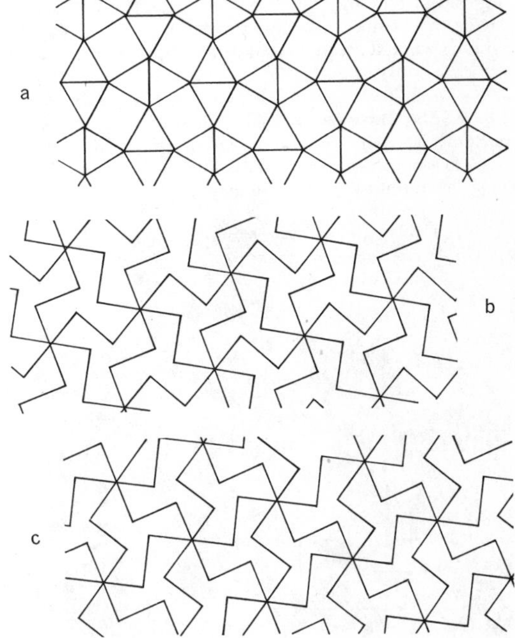

of atoms of any one species. More deeply, the present understanding of matter rests on the belief that it is composed of a few types of fundamental particles such as electrons and protons. If one example of a type cannot be distinguished from another, then no physical law implying their distinguishability can be valid.

Where many indistinguishable objects are placed in line in a regular repetitive array, a new geometric symmetry operation arises, called *translation.* If a row of bricks, for example, is pushed along its line for a distance equal to the length of one brick, the row looks as if nothing has happened to it, except perhaps the removal of one brick from one end of the row to the other. The row is "symmetric to translation" by the length of a brick or any whole number of bricks. The man-made world shows many examples of translatory symmetries, from picket fences to row housing. Translatory symmetry abounds in art, with especial splendor in Moorish tiles and certain Greek friezes.

The complexities of translatory symmetry are enriched in tiling by extension in two dimensions: the row of bricks becomes a brick wall. Such "plane tesselations" as those in Fig. 8 can be discovered in great variety. The modern Dutch engraver M. C. Escher has taken a special interest in tesselations that represent the interlocking of birds, fish, and animals (Fig. 9).

The further extension of tesselations into three dimensions has an especially important application in describing the arrangements of the atoms in solid matter. Most solids are composed of a jumble of crystals, little and big, and within each crystal the atomic arrangement has repetitive order. In a few crystalline species the only symmetry operation is translation, but most crystals have also axes of rotation and planes of reflection. Since the structure is repetitive, so are the symmetry elements. See CRYSTAL.

Mathematical study shows that there are just 230 internally consistent, or possible self-consistent, combinations of the repeated symmetry elements. The symmetry of each of the great variety of crystal structures must therefore be obedient to one or another of these "space groups." Since all the properties of a crystal flow from its atomic structure, the symmetry of its external appearance must reflect the symmetry of its structure when it grows without interference. Thus the fact that crystals never exhibit fivefold symmetry axes follows from the fact that no space group includes such an axis.

Fivefold axes are conspicuous, however, in many living things, such as buttercups and starfish. Translatory symmetries appear in the shoots of plants and in the segmented animals (Fig. 10). More often, the translatory operation in the organic world is accompanied by a dilatation (growth), so that the repeated parts are geometrically similar rather than congruent, producing "growth forms." A beautiful example is the shell of *Nautilus pompilius,* whose section has the shape of a logarithmic spiral (Fig. 11).

The foregoing examples, diverse as they may seem, all fall under the mathematicians' embracing definition of symmetry as "invariance under a transformation." (See SYMMETRY PRINCIPLES.) Squeezing a lump of putty is accordingly a symmetry operation inasmuch as the lump remains putty, continues to occupy three dimensions, and retains the same volume. Similarly, were good and evil of comparable moment, and were the operation of interchanging them definable, William Blake's poetic use of "symmetry" could also be precise.

ALAN HOLDEN
Coauthor, "Crystals and Crystal Growing"

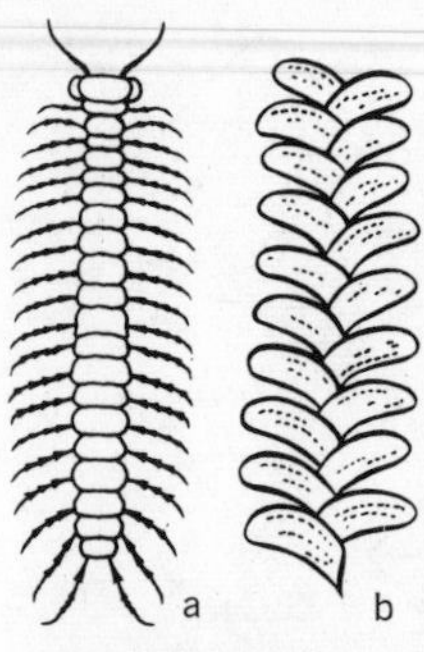

Fig. 10. The scolopendrid (a) shows fairly regular translatory symmetry and a plane of reflection symmetry. In the shoot of *Angraecum distichum* (b), a glide plane replaces the reflection plane.

Fig. 11. The sequence of chambers in the shell of the Nautilus exhibits a regular expanding sequence of similar shapes.

AMERICAN MUSEUM OF NATURAL HISTORY

Fig. 9. The inversion of light and dark is often an important symmetry operation. (Figure is reproduced from *Symmetry Aspects of M. C. Escher's Periodic Drawings,* by Caroline M. MacGillavry.)

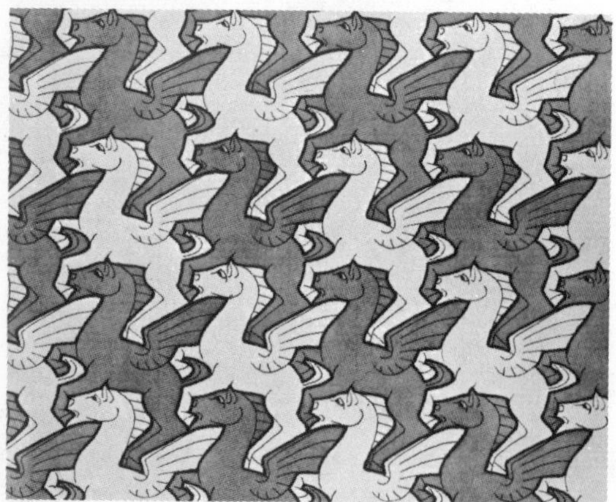

Bibliography

Gardner, Martin, *The Ambidextrous Universe* (New York 1964).
Holden, Alan, and Singer, Phylis, *Crystals and Crystal Growing* (Garden City, N. Y., 1960).
Kepler, Johannes, *A New Year's Gift, or On the Six-cornered Snowflake,* tr. by C. Hardie (London 1966).
MacGillavry, Caroline M., *Symmetry Aspects of M. C. Escher's Periodic Drawings* (Utrecht 1955).
Thompson, Sir D'Arcy, *On Growth and Form,* abridged by John Tyler Bonner (London 1961).
Wells, Alexander F., *The Third Dimension in Chemistry* (London 1956).
Weyl, Hermann, *Symmetry* (Princeton, N. J., 1952).

SYMMETRY PRINCIPLES, in physics, a general term for principles in physical phenomena resulting from symmetry considerations. A symmetry principle usually states that some natural laws or phenomena are invariant, that is, unchanged, under a certain transformation of coordinates. For example, all properties of the atomic structure of a crystal are unchanged by a displacement of one lattice length. This symmetry is called *crystalline symmetry*. A sphere is unchanged by any rotation of the observer around it, exhibiting a symmetry called *isotropy*, or independence of orientation. Symmetry principles as applied to these two cases refer to specific objects—a crystal or a sphere. More important symmetry principles refer to natural laws. For example, the magnitude of the Coulomb force between two charges is dependent only on the distance between them. It is invariant under a rotation of the two charges around each other by any angle, provided the distance is unchanged. Physicists thus say that the Coulomb law of force exhibits isotropy.

EARLY HISTORY

Symmetry in ordinary usage means balanced proportions. The existence of symmetry principles in natural phenomena was noticed in early human civilization. The bilateral symmetry—the symmetry of the left and the right sides—of the human body found its way into ancient art forms. Circular symmetry and repetitive translatory symmetry, both natural and man-made, found their ways into ancient handicraft and architectural motifs.

Indeed, throughout history, symmetry and its antithesis *asymmetry* formed essential ingredients in many aspects of human activity, such as poetry and music. It is only natural that, in contemplating physical phenomena, philosophers and scientists introduced concepts based on symmetry or harmony. For example, Johannes Kepler in his *Mysterium cosmographicum* (1595) tried to reduce the distances in the planetary system to the distances within a sequence of regular polyhedrons alternatingly inscribed and circumscribed to spheres.

Up to the end of the 19th century, the use of symmetry principles in physics was largely confined to fluid mechanics and to crystal physics. In the first 20 years of the 20th century, Albert Einstein introduced profound concepts into physics based on symmetry principles (see below). However, the pervading importance of symmetry principles in physics really began later with the development of modern quantum physics in 1925. It was recognized soon afterward that symmetry considerations lead to quantum numbers and to selection rules. Quantum numbers designate the states of an atomic system. Selection rules govern transitions between them. Since quantum numbers and selection rules are indispensable in the experimental and theoretical description of atomic, nuclear, and subnuclear phenomena, symmetry principles assume great importance in contemporary physics.

One type of important consequence of symmetry principles in physics is the conservation laws. For example, it can be shown that invariance of physical laws under a space displacement implies the conservation of momentum for a system under no external influence. Similarly, the invariance of physical laws under a rotation implies the conservation of angular momentum for a system under no external influence. Conservation laws are, of course, fundamental in classical physics as well as quantum physics. The fact that they are related to invariance principles was not fully appreciated and utilized until the 20th century. In classical mechanics discrete symmetry principles such as space reflection symmetry (see below) do not lead to conservation laws. In quantum mechanics they do, leading consequently to increased usefulness of symmetry considerations.

SYMMETRY IN CONTEMPORARY PHYSICS

The symmetry principles discussed in atomic, nuclear and subnuclear physics can be classified into the following categories:

1. Geometrical symmetries:
   a. Relativistic symmetry L.
   b. Reflection symmetry P and time reversal invariance T.
2. Algebraic symmetry: Charge conjugation invariance C.
3. Others: Isotopic spin invariance I, $SU(3)$, and so on.

The geometrical symmetries concern invariances under a transformation, that is change, of the coordinate system x, y, z and the time coordinate t. There are five types of coordinate system transformations:

1. Translation, or displacement of the origin of the coordinate system and of the starting time $t = 0$.
2. Rotation of the coordinate axes x, y and z.
3. Lorentz transformation, that is,

$$x' = \frac{x + vt}{\sqrt{1 - \frac{v^2}{c^2}}}$$

$$y' = y$$

$$z' = z$$

$$t' = \frac{t + \frac{v}{c^2}}{\sqrt{1 - \frac{v^2}{c^2}}}$$

where c is the velocity of light and v is a positive or negative velocity less than c in magnitude.

4. Space reflection, or reflection of the coordinate system with respect to the xy plane.
5. Time inversion, or the transformation $t' = -t$.

Geometrical Symmetry L. This is also called relativistic invariance. This symmetry principle is a generalization to four dimensions of the easily acceptable principle that space is homogeneous and isotropic. More precisely, it states that all physical laws governing atomic, nuclear, and subnuclear phenomena are unchanged under any translation, space rotation, or relativistic transformations.

Relativistic symmetry was first clearly enunciated by Einstein as the principle of special relativity. Because of the slight violations of other symmetries discovered since 1957 (see below), relativistic symmetry has been given increasingly more stringent tests in recent years. No violations have been found. It is thus usually taken as one basic cornerstone of microscopic—atomic, nuclear, and subnuclear—physics.

Geometrical Symmetry P. Symmetry P (parity) is space reflection symmetry. It states that the laws of microscopic physics are unchanged under

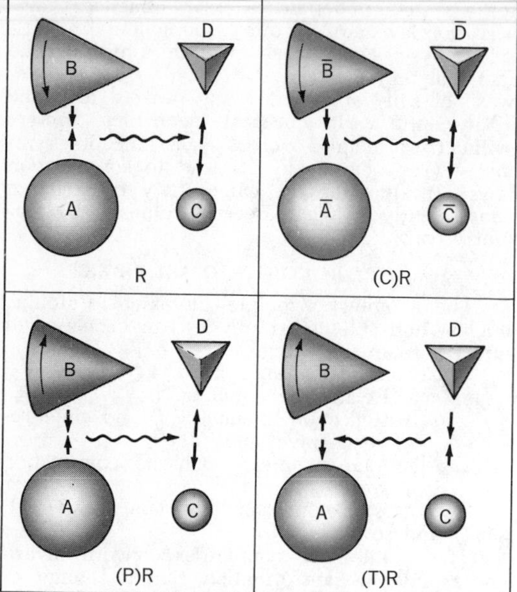

FROM C. N. YANG, BROOKHAVEN NATIONAL LABORATORY LECTURES IN SCIENCE 3, GORDON AND BREACH, 1968.

Fig. 1. This sequence of drawings illustrates the operations *C*, *P*, and *T* by means of a hypothetical reaction *R*, which transforms particles *A* and *B* into particles C and *D* ($A + B \rightarrow C + D$). *A* and *B*, represented schematically by a large sphere and a spinning cone, are oppositely charged and therefore attract each other; C and *D*, represented by a small sphere and a tetrahedron, have like charges and therefore repel each other. The reaction *(P)R* is *R* reflected in the plane of the drawing. Notice the reversed spin of *B* and the reflection of the tetrahedron *D*. *(T)R* is the time-reversed version of *R*, describing $C + D \rightarrow A + B$. It is what one would see if a movie of *R* were run backward. Notice the spin direction of *B*. The charge conjugate reaction (C)*R* is the same as *R* but with all the particles replaced by antiparticles.

the transformation of coordinates 4 above. An equivalent way of describing this symmetry is that two experimental arrangements that are mirror images of each other always give the same readings, if each of them is isolated from all outside influence. Still another way of describing this symmetry is that any reaction *R*, such as

$$A + B \rightarrow C + D$$

illustrated in Fig. 1, proceeds at the same rate as the reaction $(P)R$ in the same figure.

The principle of reflection symmetry was found, up to 1956, to be well observed in atomic and nuclear phenomena to great accuracies. In analyzing some puzzling new experimental findings, however, C. N. Yang and T. D. Lee of Columbia University found in that year that, contrary to accepted opinion, there was in fact no evidence that in the weak interactions among nuclei and elementary particles reflection symmetry was observed. The weak interactions are one of the four types of interactions between nuclei and subnuclear particles. They suggested a number of experiments to test the principle of reflection symmetry in the weak interactions. The weak interactions are one of the two types of forces involved in nuclear processes. The first test was made later that year by C. S. Wu of Columbia and a group from the National Bureau of Standards. The test demonstrated that the principle of reflection symmetry was *not* observed in β-radioactivity, the best known type of weak interactions (Fig. 2), in which an electron or positron is emitted from the nucleus of a radioactive isotope. Shortly thereafter it was found that the violation of reflection symmetry was in fact a general characteristic of all weak interactions.

Algebraic Symmetries. These are symmetries whose origin lies in the algebraic properties of the number system used in the theoretical formulation of physical laws. There is today only one known symmetry of this type, called charge conjugation symmetry, or symmetry *C*. This concept originated in the work of P. A. M. Dirac in the early 1930's. Dirac introduced the idea of "holes in an infinite sea," later renamed "antiparticles." According to this idea, every particle has an antiparticle with equal but opposite electric charge. For example, the positron (e^+) is the antiparticle of the electron (e^-), the antiproton is the antiparticle of the proton, and so forth. The discoveries of these antiparticles and a number of other experiments led to the belief, held up to 1956, that charge conjugation symmetry is observed in all atomic, nuclear, and subnuclear phenomena. This symmetry implies that any reaction *R* and its charge conjugate reaction $(C)R$ (Fig. 1) proceed at the same rate. The charge conjugate reaction is the reaction with all particles replaced by their antiparticles—that is, each particle is replaced by its antiparticle, and each antiparticle is replaced by the corresponding particle.

The decisive experiment of C. S. Wu, E. Ambler, R. W. Hayward, D. D. Hopper, and R. P. Hudson schematically illustrated in Fig. 2 that proved the violation of reflection symmetry in the weak interactions also proved that charge conjugation symmetry is violated in the weak interactions. This conclusion was based on some complicated theoretical reasoning. Some months later more direct evidence for the violations of charge conjugation symmetry in the weak interactions was found in the reactions

$$\mu^+ \rightarrow e^+ + \text{neutral particles} \quad (1)$$
$$\mu^- \rightarrow e^- + \text{neutral particles} \quad (2)$$

where it was determined that the e^+ in (1) are almost all spinning like a right-handed rifle bullet while the e^- in (2) are almost all spinning like a left-handed bullet. The symbols μ^+ and μ^- stand for antimuon and muon, respectively. If one takes (1) to be reaction *R*, the reaction $(C)R$, as defined in Fig. 1, is then (2) but with right-handed spinning e^-. Thus the rate for $(C)R$ is practically zero and is not the same as that of *R*, illustrating explicitly the violation of charge conjugation symmetry in the weak interactions (1) and (2).

Combined Symmetry *CP*. The violation of the symmetries *C* and *P* in the weak interactions led several workers to propose independently that perhaps the combined symmetry *CP* is observed in the weak interactions. Indeed, if reaction (1) above is taken to be *R*, the reaction $(CP)R$—obtained by first constructing $R' = (P)R$ according to Fig. 1, and then constructing $(C)R'$ according to the same figure—turns out to be precisely (2). Notice that the operation *CP* has changed a right-handed spinning e^+ into a left-handed spinning e^-. Now (1) and (2) do proceed at the same rate, providing an example of *CP* symmetry.

Between 1957 and 1964 it had seemed that the hypothesis of *CP* symmetry was valid for all interactions. However, in an experiment published in 1964 by J. H. Christenson, J. W. Cronin, and R. Turlay it was found that in one weak interaction, the decay of K^0 (a kaön), *CP* symmetry is violated. The exact manner in which this symmetry is violated has been a subject of many experiments in recent years. A full clarification has not yet resulted.

Geometrical Symmetry T. This is time reversal symmetry. It states that if the motion of any atomic, nuclear, or subatomic particles were reversed, it would precisely retrace its steps. Or, equivalently, any reaction *R* and its time-reversed reaction $(T)R$ shown in Fig. 2 have a definite ratio for their rates. This symmetry was found to be very precisely observed when the motion or reaction studied is under the influence of strong electric and magnetic forces. It is now known that for motions and reactions involving weak interactions, time inversion symmetry is not in general observed.

CPT Theorem. In the mid-1950's J. S. Schwinger, Gerhart Lüders, and Wolfgang Pauli in their independent studies of field theory, a fundamental branch of theoretical physics, formulated a theorem now known as the *CPT* theorem. According to this theorem the rates of any reaction *R* and its *CPT* conjugate, $(CPT)R$, are proportional (Fig. 3). This is a general theorem the validity of which is accepted by all physicists today. We write this theorem symbolically as

$$(CPT)R \cong R$$

for any *R*. Similarly we write for the *CP*-symmetry-violating reaction R_0 (for example K^0 decay):

$$(CP)R_0 \not\cong R_0.$$

Now it is clear from the construction illustrated in Fig. 1 that

Fig. 2. Schematic diagram of the experiment showing violation of reflection symmetry *P*. The experiment concerned the beta-decay rate of cobalt-60, which was polarized by a current-carrying loop as indicated in the diagram. The two experimental setups shown, one the mirror image of the other, gave different counting rates.

DIAGRAM FROM C. N. YANG, SCIENCE, VOL. 127, P. 565 (1958)

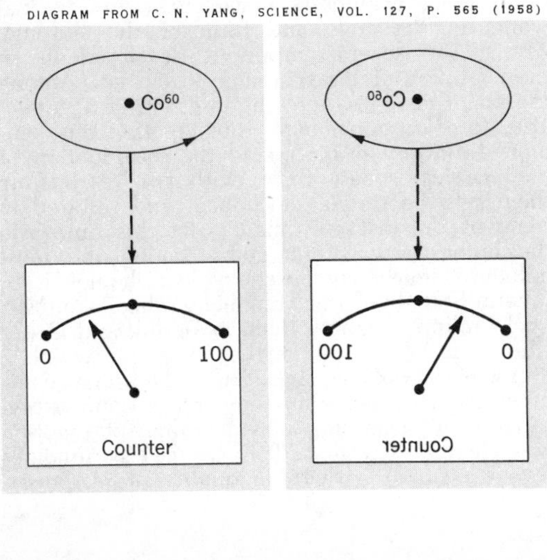

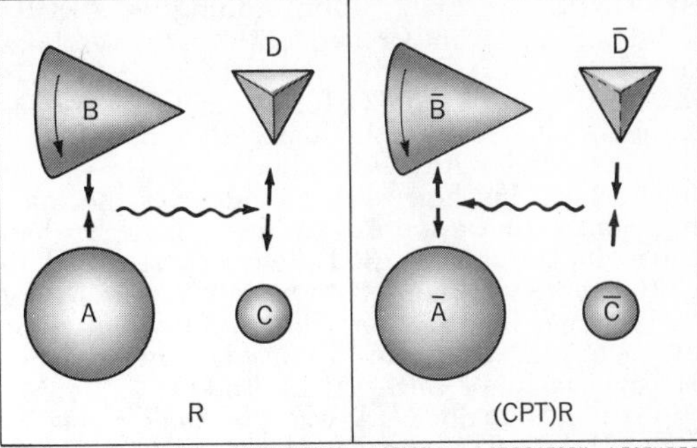

(FROM C. N. YANG, BROOKHAVEN NATIONAL LABORATORY LECTURES IN SCIENCE 3, GORDON AND BREACH, 1968, P. 188.)

Fig. 3. The *CPT* theorem. The reaction $(CPT)R$ is obtained by applying to *R* the operations *T*, *P*, and *C* in succession. The *CPT* theorem states that the rates of *R* and of $(CPT)R$ are proportional.

$$(T^2)R_0 = R_0,$$

where the symbol (T^2) stands for time reversal performed twice. Thus

$$R_0 \not\cong (CP)R_0 = (CPT^2)R_0 = (CPT)\ (T)R_0.$$

The last expression is, by the *CPT* theorem, equal to $(T)R_0$. Hence

$$R_0 \not\cong (T)R_0$$

demonstrating that time reversal symmetry is also violated in the decay of K^0, a decay caused by a weak interaction.

Other Symmetries. There are a number of other symmetries that play important roles in contemporary physics. The most important of these symmetries are isotopic spin invariance *I* and $SU(3)$.

Isotopic spin invariance is basically the symmetry describing the experimental knowledge that the proton and the neutron, except for the difference in their electric charges, are exactly the same in their interactions with each other. The physical basis for isotopic spin invariance was first recognized in 1936 by Gregory Breit, Edward U. Condon, and Richard D. Present. The mathematical formulation of the symmetry had been given earlier by Werner Heisenberg in 1932.

$SU(3)$ symmetry, a method of grouping elementary particles, was first put forward in 1961 independently by Murray Gell-Mann and Yuval Ne'eman. It is only an approximate symmetry which is related mathematically to the algebraic group called $SU(3)$, or the special unitary group in three dimensions. Experimentally, the existence of this symmetry requires the grouping of elementary particles into sets of 1, 8, 10, and of higher order, called multiplets. Such grouping is indeed experimentally verified. Because of the existence of the multiplet of 8, $SU(3)$ symmetry is sometimes called the eightfold way, a phrase taken from a saying of Buddha.

CHEN NING YANG
Nobel Prize Winner in Physics
State University of New York at Stony Brook

Further Reading: Chew, G. F., Gell-Mann, M., Rosenfeld, A. H., "Strongly Interacting Particles," *Scientific American,* February 1964; Weyl, Hermann, *Symmetry* (Princeton 1952); Yang, C. N., "Elementary Particles," *A Short History of Some Discoveries in Atomic Physics* (Princeton 1962); id., "Law of Parity Conservation and Other Symmetry Laws," *Science,* vol. 127, p. 565, 1958.

SYMONDS, sĭm'əndz, **John Addington** (1840–1893), English author and critic. He was born in Clifton, near Bristol, on Oct. 5, 1840. He attended Harrow and Oxford and, to please his father, studied law in London, but illness forced him to make lengthy visits abroad. In 1864, hoping to curb his homosexual tendencies, he married Janet Catherine North, by whom he had three daughters. In 1869, Symonds returned to Clifton to devote himself to literature, but a lung hemorrhage in 1877 forced him to spend most of each year thereafter in Davos, Switzerland. He died in Rome on April 19, 1893.

Symonds' major work was *The Renaissance in Italy* (1875–1886), an aesthetic and critical history, in which he called the Renaissance "the resurgence of personality in the realm of thought." But the homosexual's problems were an absorbing concern to Symonds. He made the first complete English translation of Michelangelo's sonnets—many of which are homosexual in content—and wrote a two-volume biography of Michelangelo. He also wrote a critical study of Walt Whitman and collaborated with Havelock Ellis on the pioneer study *Sexual Inversion* (1897). Symonds' other works, besides some poetry, include *Studies of the Greek Poets* (1873 and 1876), biographies of Sydney and Shelley, and studies of Dante and the Elizabethan poets. His flamboyant style and love of art and the classics made him popular, but his works are now dated.

GEORGIA DUNBAR, *Hofstra University*

SYMONS, sĭm'ənz, **Arthur** (1865–1945), English critic and poet. He was born in Milford-Haven, Wales, on Feb. 28, 1865, and grew up in the south and west of England, where his father was a Methodist preacher "on circuit." As a youth, Symons went to London, where he frequented music halls and supported himself by translating, editing, and writing for literary journals. In 1896, assisted by the artist Aubrey Beardsley, he edited the short-lived literary periodical *The Savoy*. A mental breakdown in 1908 caused Symons to be hospitalized for over a year, after which he wrote nothing comparable to his earlier work. He died in Wittersham, Kent, on Jan. 22, 1945.

Symons' importance in the development of English literature at the end of the 19th century began to be recognized only after his death. His criticism and translations introduced English readers to Baudelaire, Verlaine, and French Symbolist poetry. T. S. Eliot admitted the influence on his early works of Symons' poems, which combined a conversational tone with symbolism. Intensely interested in the dance, Symons saw it as a perfect symbol for the poet's struggle to find meaning and beauty in life, and he may have inspired the symbolic use of the dance in the poetry of Yeats. Symons' most important work, *The Symbolist Movement in Literature* (1899), defines Symbolist literature and attempts to create a general aesthetic from the unsystematized sense impressions that Walter Pater had called the only true form of communication.

GEORGIA DUNBAR, *Hofstra University*

SYMPATHETIC NERVOUS SYSTEM, one of the two subdivisions of the autonomic nervous system. With the other division, called the *parasympathetic nervous system*, it helps control involuntary activities. See NERVOUS SYSTEM.

SYMPHONIC POEM, or tone poem, a type of orchestral composition, usually in one movement, that describes or suggests a specific person or thing, such as a literary or historical figure, a literary or art work, or a place, event, or idea. The subject is indicated in the work's title. Certain compositions, such as Tchaikovsky's *Romeo and Juliet* and *The Tempest*, though called overtures, are essentially symphonic poems.

The term "symphonic poem" was introduced by Franz Liszt for 12 orchestral works written about 1850–1860. Among the subjects that inspired him were a great poet, in *Tasso;* patriotism, in *Hungaria;* and part of a poetic work, Alphonse Lamartine's *Méditations poétiques,* in *Les Préludes*. These, like later symphonic poems, consist of one movement, divided into contrasting sections and unified by a motive or theme that is suitably modified in each section.

Many subsequent 19th century and early 20th century composers wrote symphonic poems. Bedrich Smetana's set of six pieces, collectively titled *My Country,* was inspired by Czech legend, history, and landscape. French symphonic poems include César Franck's *The Mad Hunter* and Paul Dukas' *The Sorcerer's Apprentice*. The greatest German composer of symphonic poems was Richard Strauss, who wrote such works as *Don Juan, Till Eulenspiegel's Merry Pranks,* and *A Hero's Life*. The Italian composer Ottorino Respighi wrote *The Pines of Rome*. In the 20th century, increasing interest in objective composition led to the decline of the symphonic poem.

HOMER ULRICH, *Coauthor of "A History of Music and Musical Style"*

SYMPHONY, sĭm'fə-nē, an extended musical composition, usually divided into three or four parts, or movements, and written for full orchestra. It is one of the major forms of Western music. Within its prescribed form, it allows for infinite variation in mood and style, and it has been used to convey a wide range of emotion by great composers, among them Haydn, Mozart, Beethoven, Brahms, and Mahler.

Origins. The immediate ancestor of the modern symphony was a new form of the 17th century Italian operatic overture, the *sinfonia,* introduced by Alessandro Scarlatti in Naples in the late 1690's. Sinfonias, which consisted of three movements—fast, slow, and fast—were light and pleasing works. By the mid-18th century they were often performed in concert independently of the operas they originally preceded. At the same time, composers began to write original works in the style and form of the sinfonia. After 1750 several important developments in the evolution of the symphony occurred. Among the major changes were the insertion of a *minuet* after the slow movement, thus creating the common 4-movement form, and the introduction of the classical sonata form, with two contrasting themes to be stated, developed, and restated in some of the fast movements. At this time also the orchestra was enlarged. Among the most influential early composers of symphonies were Johann Stamitz of the Mannheim school of music, Carl Philipp Emanuel Bach in Berlin, and Georg Christoph Wagenseil of the Viennese school.

Emergence of the Symphony. The first composer to make the symphony into a composition capable of expressing a wide range of emotion was Haydn. The first 70 of his 104 symphonies reveal a steady growth in quality of workmanship and depth of expression. His most important contribution thereafter was the establishment of the principle of thematic development. His later works reveal the variety of expression, the dramatic contrasts, and the balance between form and content that characterize classicism.

The first 30 or so of the almost 50 symphonies by Mozart reflect successively the influences of Johann Christian Bach in London, of the Viennese school, and of the stylistic mixture that prevailed in France and Italy. By the 1770's, the influence of Haydn, along with that of the Mannheim composers, became strong. As a result, Mozart's later symphonies reveal an assimilation of Haydn's method of thematic development and an ever-increasing refinement of expressive means and fine proportions. At the same time, Haydn was influenced by Mozart's accomplishments, and the older master's last 20 symphonies, especially Nos. 93–104, reflect many of Mozart's stylistic devices. It was Mozart, however, who in his last three symphonies, Nos. 39, 40, and 41, carried the classical symphony to its finest expression.

Early 19th Century. The first two of the nine symphonies of Beethoven take their point of departure from Haydn, but even here Beethoven's powerful individuality is felt. A new type of third movement, the *scherzo,* often with humorous overtones, replaces the minuet. The Symphony No. 3, known as the *Eroica,* is a monumental work with a range of emotion not found in any earlier symphony. The relaxed, cheerful, and melodious Symphony No. 4 is distinguished by the expanded role given to the woodwind instruments.

Symphony No. 5, terse, concentrated, and intense, is characterized by emotional and rhythmic drive, serious expression, and a jubilant climax. No. 6, known as the *Pastoral,* is a leisurely work. Its movements have titles that reflect Beethoven's responses to the countryside. Symphony No. 7 depends on rhythmic drive and power for much of its effect, while No. 8 is a humorous work that confines its energy to the last movement. Vocal resources were added to the symphony for the first time in the finale of Beethoven's great Symphony No. 9, in which the composer used a chorus and four soloists to sing a text adapted from Schiller's *Ode to Joy.*

With the turn into the romantic period, initiated by Beethoven, in content if not in form, the symphony underwent many changes. The last two of the nine symphonies of Franz Schubert—No. 8, the *Unfinished,* and the C major, known variously as No. 7, 9, or 10—retain the classical forms, as do his other symphonies. However, their lyricism, colorful harmonies, and, in the C major, rhythmic drive and concentration are completely romantic in feeling.

Hector Berlioz added a detailed program to his *Symphonie fantastique.* The work's subtitle, "Episodes in the life of an artist," refers to the fantasies of a love-sick musician who has taken opium. Even more important, Berlioz introduces an *idée fixe,* a fixed melody that appears throughout, either in whole or in part, with appropriate changes in each movement to unify the work.

Felix Mendelssohn adhered closely to the classical forms in his five symphonies. However, he added elements of nervous excitement and breathless speed, especially in his duple-meter scherzos. The four symphonies of Robert Schumann are highly romantic, characterized by lyricism, eloquence, drama, and varied instrumental colors. His Symphony No. 4 in D Minor was the first in which all four thematically related movements were played without a pause between them.

Mid-19th Century. More changes occurred in the symphony from the middle of the 19th century. The four symphonies of Johannes Brahms retain the classical balance between form and content, but the influence of romanticism is felt in their emotional power and in the varieties of instrumental sound found in them.

The nine numbered symphonies, the last unfinished, by Anton Bruckner, are monumental works. Highly individual in style, they are characterized by sonorous writing—with brass instruments having a prominent role—wide-ranging themes that carry an air of proclamation, and greatly expanded forms in which themes are repeated or ornamented rather than developed. The single symphony of César Franck is composed in cyclical form in which successive movements are thematically related, a concept similar to the *idée fixe* in the *Symphonie fantastique.*

Late 19th Century. In the late 19th century, with the emergence of nationalist composers, various folk idioms became sources of thematic material. Tchaikovsky, though not an avowed nationalist composer, occasionally quoted Russian folk songs in his early symphonies. In all seven of his symphonies, he revealed a great melodic gift, a sense for dramatic climaxes, and a feeling for instrumental color unmatched by his contemporaries. Symphonies 4, 5, and 6 are especially noteworthy for their beautiful melodies, variety of mood, and power.

The nine symphonies of Antonín Dvořák are in a sense the Czech counterparts of Tchaikovsky's works. Dvořák's symphonies are marked by an occasional use of dance forms, a moodiness coupled with exuberance, and fine workmanship. Another nationalist composer was the Finn, Jean Sibelius, who wrote seven symphonies.

The symphony found one of its foremost romantic exponents in the Austrian composer Gustav Mahler. Mahler, who wrote 10 symphonies, expanded his forms beyond all previous dimensions and greatly enlarged the orchestra. Occasionally he added texts, ranging from Gregorian hymns to adaptations of Chinese poetry, which were sung by vocal soloists and choruses with enormous dramatic effect.

20th Century. In the 20th century new technical approaches to composition resulted in a wide variety of individual styles. Romanticism declined, and objective writing became fashionable again. The grandiose aspects of the symphony were abandoned, and dissonance prevailed. The three symphonies of Igor Stravinsky written between 1930 and 1945 are marked by strong rhythmic elements and by the use of angular, wide-ranging melodies.

Some composers, however, retained elements of romanticism in their symphonies. Sergei Prokofiev combined warm expression with contemporary techniques, especially in the fifth of his seven symphonies. Dmitri Shostakovich, who wrote 14 symphonies, became essentially a post-romantic composer with a strong admixture of pungent and humorous writing. The six symphonies of the English composer Ralph Vaughan Williams are strongly individualistic.

The serial technique, derived from the 12-tone writing of the Austrian Arnold Schoenberg, is best seen in the short Symphony by his countryman Anton von Webern. Serial composition has become the dominant style of the present day and has influenced the writing of many composers. Chief among the American composers whose works reveal this influence, although not exclusively, are Walter Piston, Roy Harris, Aaron Copland, and William Schuman.

HOMER ULRICH, *Coauthor of "A History of Music and Musical Styles"*

Further Reading: Lang, Paul H., ed., *Symphony, 1800–1900* (New York 1969); Ulrich, Homer, *Symphonic Music* (New York 1952); Young, Percy M., *Symphony* (Boston 1968).

SYMPLOCOS. See SWEETLEAF.

SYMPOSIUM, The, sim-pō′zē-əm, a dialogue of Plato in the form of a conversation that is supposed to have taken place at a banquet given by the tragic poet Agathon to celebrate his victory in a drama contest. Instead of drinking—in Greek, *symposion* literally means "drinking together"—the guests decide to discuss love.

In their speeches, in which Love is praised as a mighty god, ideas are introduced that are later corrected and expanded by Socrates. In the most interesting speech, Aristophanes tells a parable of how human beings were originally round, with four arms and four legs, but Zeus, offended at the race's presumption, split them in half. Love, therefore, is the desire of each half to find its counterpart and reunite.

Socrates expounds what he claims to be the teachings of the wise woman Diotima. Love is not a great god, he says, but the yearning of the ever-perishing individual to circumvent death, on the lowest level by physical reproduction, on a higher level by the attainment of fame, and on the highest level by intellectual union with the absolute beauty that transcends all the realities of space and time. At this point the drunken Alcibiades comes in and sings Socrates' praises, and the entrance of more revelers leads to general confusion and ends the dialogue.

RICHMOND Y. HATHORN *Author of "Tragedy, Myth, and Mystery"*

SYNAGOGUE, sin′ə-gog, a Jewish house of worship. The term "temple" is sometimes used as a synonym, particularly by Reform Jews. In Yiddish the synagogue is called "shul."

Organization and Practices. Membership in a synagogue is voluntary. Each synagogue is an independent institution erected and maintained by a local Jewish community. The congregation elects such officials as the president (*parnas*), treasurer (*gabbai*), and the other unpaid members of the council. Since the 19th century, and only in Western lands, these men have employed the rabbi, or the spiritual leader. The cantor (*hazzan*) and the sexton (*shammash*) have functioned in synagogues at least since Talmudic times (3d–5th centuries A. D.).

Traditionally, services in synagogues were held twice a day—in the morning for the recitation of morning prayers (shaharith) and at dusk for the saying of afternoon (minhah) and evening (*maarib*) prayers. In modern times, services are held in many synagogues only on the Sabbath and holidays. Emphasis increasingly is placed on the social and cultural aspects of congregational activities.

History. The first synagogues were built in Babylonia and Egypt in the 3d century B. C. and in Palestine in the 2d century B. C. The existence of synagogues in Palestine can be inferred from the reference in Psalm 74:8 to the burning "of all the meeting places of God in the land." This is taken as an allusion to the Syrian persecution of the Hebrews in 168–165 B. C.

By the 1st century A. D. there were hundreds of synagogues in Palestine, many of them in Jerusalem. Several of these were in communities of Alexandrian, Cyrenian, and Cilician Jews who had settled in the city. The custom of immigrant groups establishing and maintaining separate synagogues survived in the Jewish Diaspora (the dispersion of Jews outside Palestine) and down to the present time in countries with large Jewish immigrant populations, such as the United States.

After the destruction of the Jerusalem Temple (70 A. D.), synagogues became more important and were built in Syria, Asia Minor, Cyprus, mainland Greece, Cyrenaica, and Italy as well as Palestine. Ruins of synagogues have been found in Dura-Europos in Syria, dating from the 3d century A. D., at Capernaum in Galilee, dating from the 1st to the 4th century, and many other sites. The great synagogue of Alexandria, Egypt, with its separate sections for each trade guild, is described in the Talmud. This synagogue was built in or before the 1st century A. D.

Purpose. In contrast to the Jerusalem Temple, the synagogue has no sacrificial or sacramental ritual and it does not require a specially chosen, hereditary priesthood. The Hebrew term for synagogue is *bet haknesset,* "house of assembly." The English term synagogue comes from a Greek word meaning "assembly." This derivation indicates that originally the synagogue served not only as a place of prayer and worship, but as a gathering place for many kinds of communal functions. This broader application has been retained by the traditional synagogue to the present day. Those gathering in it were, and remain, a fellowship of worshipers. The atmosphere pervading it is characterized by a thorough at-home feeling and emotional warmth. In addition to being a house of worship, the synagogue also serves as a place of study and public assembly, and for marriage ceremonies. In the past, lawsuits were settled in the synagogue.

Architecture. Continuing an architectural feature first introduced into the Jerusalem Temple, the synagogues had separate sections for women. From the 3d century A. D. on this was in the form of a gallery.

In the Middle Ages it became general to place the Ark containing handwritten scrolls of the Torah against the wall facing Jerusalem. The worshipers face in this direction during their prayers. An important feature of every synagogue is the Eternal Light burning in front of the Ark, in memory of the perpetual fire on the altar of the Tabernacle (Leviticus 6:6) and symbolizing the permanence of faith.

In architecture, design, and decoration the synagogue buildings showed the influence of the non-Jewish environment. In Alexandria they had the prevailing basilica form, in North Africa and Spain they showed Moorish influence, in Christian medieval Europe, Romanesque and Gothic styles prevailed, and in Poland the stone or wood architecture of the country was utilized. The ritual bath (*miqveh*) frequently adjoined the synagogue. In modern times the synagogue com-

THE SYNAGOGUE'S center of reverence is the Ark containing the scrolls of the Torah. The Ark may vary in design from that in a small synagogue to the magnificence of this Ark in New York City's Temple Emanu-el.

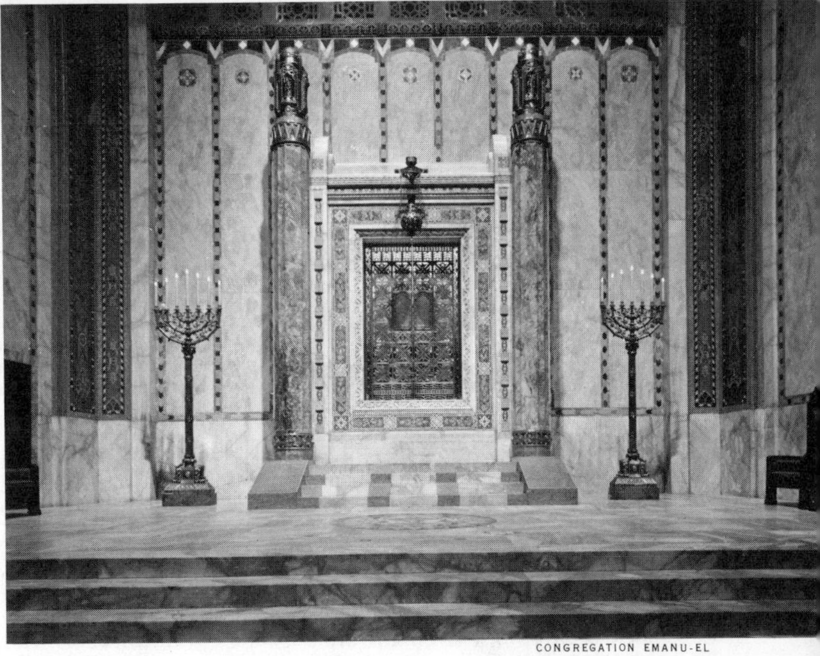

CONGREGATION EMANU-EL

plex often includes classrooms, a library, a social hall, and athletic facilities.

As a mark of mourning for the Jerusalem Temple, all instrumental music was traditionally banned from the synagogues. The Jewish Reform movement introduced the organ in the 19th century. In Reform temples the reader's platform (almemar or bema) has been moved from the center to the front, and men and women worship together.

RAPHAEL PATAI
Theodor Herzl Institute

Further Reading: Abrahams, Israel, *Jewish Life in the Middle Ages* (New York 1958).

SYNAPSE, sin'aps, the point at which a nerve impulse passes from one nerve cell to another. The mechanism of transmission is not fully known, but special transmitter substances, such as acetylcholine, have been isolated.

SYNCHRO, sin'krō, an electromechanical machine that has a shaft-mounted part termed a *rotor,* which is free to rotate, and a stationary part termed a *stator.* The rotor carries the primary winding, and the stator carries the secondary windings in skewed slots distributed around its periphery. In a synchro system, three wires from the stator of one synchro are connected to three wires from the stator of a second synchro. Each of the rotors of the two synchros usually has two wire leads that serve as the input or output terminals of the system.

Synchro systems are used to transmit small torques over a distance, for instance to convey angular shaft position information from one location to another without using a rigid mechanical connection. For example, large synchros (5 inches, or 13 cm, in diameter) were used to repeat the compass heading at several places on a ship during World War II. In this case, a master synchro was connected to the ship's main compass and several repeater synchros were connected to repeater compasses. This synchro system caused the cards of the repeater compasses to take the same angular position as that of the card of the master compass.

A synchro system is especially useful as an error detector in a servomechanism. Synchros used as precision error detectors are only about 1 inch (2.5 cm) in diameter and are used only as indicators of shaft angular displacement. In this case, one synchro is coupled to the command shaft, and a second synchro is coupled to the controlled shaft. The rotor of the command synchro is excited by an alternating voltage, which causes a voltage to occur at the rotor of the second synchro. This voltage signal, which is proportional to the difference in angular position between the controlled shaft and the command shaft, can then be used to position the controlled shaft in correspondence with the command shaft.

C. J. SAVANT, JR.
MCA Technology, Inc.

SYNCHROCYCLOTRON, a particle accelerator used to produce particle energies greater than 20 or 30 Mev. See PARTICLE ACCELERATOR.

SYNCHRONIZED SWIMMING. See SWIMMING—*Synchronized Swimming.*

SYNCHRONOUS MOTOR. See ELECTRIC MOTORS—*Alternating-Current Motors.*

SYNCHROTRON, a particle accelerator for producing particle energies from 1.0 to more than 200 Gev. See PARTICLE ACCELERATOR.

SYNCLINE, sin'klīn, a downward fold in sedimentary rocks. It is the opposite of an *anticline,* or upfold. Synclines alternate with anticlines when compressive stresses in the crust of the earth cause the folding of crustal rocks. Such folds may range in size from mountainous to microscopic. See also FOLD.

In a symmetrical syncline the rock layers on the *limbs,* or flanks, of the fold are inclined downward at equal angles from opposite directions toward the horizontal *axis,* or center line, of the fold. In asymmetrical synclines, the angles of inclination of the two limbs are not equal. The limbs of an *overturned syncline* are squeezed together until they are parallel, and the fold leans over from the vertical.

Fold axes are rarely horizontal over long distances. Instead they are inclined to be horizontal, giving rise to *plunging synclines.* The alternation of plunging synclines and anticlines yields zigzag mountain ridges. If both ends of the axis of a syncline are inclined toward each other, the resulting formation is an oval-shaped topographic basin.

WARREN E. YASSO
Teachers College, Columbia University

SYNCRETISM, sing'krə-tiz-əm, in philosophy and religion, is an attempted reconciliation or synthesis of opposing principles or practices. On the unconscious level philosophies and religions are syncretistic to the extent that they have absorbed elements from a culture not completely consistent with a core of beliefs. For example, Christianity affirmed at one time certain concepts of the mother-goddess derived from paganism. These were not consistent with the professed belief in Christ as sole mediator and redeemer. However, syncretism usually refers to the conscious effort to select from various sources. To this extent it is similar in meaning to eclecticism.

In religion an attempt at syncretism can lead to a reduction of beliefs of diverse groups to a common core, such as "response in feeling to the infinite," a feeling of goodwill, or a simple ethical code. However, this becomes reductionism and not syncretism. Most attempts at syncretism fail because a religion is related to a culture, and this fact is in part the secret of its success, the "price of its existence." If justice is done to the particularities, diversity remains. If the particularities are denied, what emerges has no roots and evokes no commitment. Sikhism is called a syncretistic religion because it was founded to reconcile Hinduism and Islam. However, it flourished where most of the people were either Hindus or Muslims, and the beliefs and practices advocated were not completely alien or without roots.

LEE A. BELFORD, *New York University*

SYNDICALISM is an anticapitalist, working-class ideology and movement with revolutionary and anarchist elements. The term is derived from the French *syndicat,* meaning labor union. The movement developed in France toward the end of the 19th century and then spread mainly to the Latin nations in Europe and America. Its most important intellectual source is to be found in the writing of Georges Sorel (1847–1922).

Syndicalist Concepts. Syndicalism concurs with Marxism in analyzing capitalist society as split between the exploiting capitalists and the exploited workers and in maintaining that this split must be ended by revolutionary action of the workers. Parting with the Marxists, however, the syndicalists reject the use of political means for destroying the capitalist economy and the capitalist state. Like the anarchists, they reject the concept of the state entirely. A syndicalist society would have the labor union as its key institution. Each enterprise would be managed as a cooperative association of production and distribution, and the industrial unions would be linked in loose federative groupings.

To win power, the syndicalists believe in direct action against the employer—striking, working at a slow pace, sabotaging machinery, and turning out faulty products—to paralyze the productive process. Syndicalists hold that the main purpose of strikes is not to wrest concessions from employers but to sharpen the workers' class consciousness. Ultimately a general strike would destroy the capitalist system.

Syndicalists look upon the democratic process in a capitalist society with skepticism and even contempt. They have no use for voting, which deflects workers from revolutionary commitment. Consequently, they stress the crucial role of an elite "active minority" that can mobilize the inert masses to revolutionary action.

Syndicalist Movements. Syndicalism reached its peak in France around 1905, dominating the Confédération Générale du Travail (CGT). In 1906, however, the workers did not support a CGT-called general strike, and in 1910 the government thwarted a CGT railroad strike by drafting strikers into the armed forces. Finally, when France entered World War I, the workers unhesitatingly put defense of nation above syndicalist class considerations.

Strong syndicalist currents also existed in the Italian labor movement before World War I. In Spain syndicalism survived longest. Supported by the anarchists, the syndicalists were prominent during the early phases of the Spanish civil war. The weakening of syndicalism in Spain in the late 1930's led to a similar decline in several Latin American countries where it had been important among the newly developing unions. In the United States the syndicalist-oriented Industrial Workers of the World (IWW) was influential before World War I, but its opposition to American entry into the war and its use of violence aroused hostility, which resulted in its disintegration in the 1920's.

The syndicalist movement heightened the awareness of the dangers of bureaucratism and massive political power. On the other hand, syndicalism provided strength for antidemocratic movements by emphasizing violence and elitism.

WILLIAM EBENSTEIN
University of California, Santa Barbara

Further Reading: Cole, George D. H., *A History of Socialist Thought,* 5 vols. (New York 1953–1960).

SYNGE, sing, **John Millington** (1871–1909), Irish dramatist, whose masterpieces, *The Playboy of the Western World* and *Riders to the Sea,* classics of the English-speaking stage. With W. B. Yeats and Lady Gregory, Synge was codirector of the Abbey Theatre in Dublin.

Life. Edmund John Millington Synge was born in Rathfarnham, near Dublin, on April 16, 1871. His father, a barrister, died in 1872, leaving Synge's mother to bring up five children on an annual income of £400. Synge received his early education mainly at home with private tutors. He then entered Trinity College, Dublin, where he took his B. A. degree in 1892. In 1893 he went to Germany to study the violin. By the following year he had settled in Paris, where he wrote literary articles and reviews for British and European periodicals.

In Paris, in 1896, Synge met W. B. Yeats, who said to him, "Give up Paris, you will never create anything by reading Racine, and Arthur Symons will always be a better critic of French literature. Go to the Aran Islands. Live there as if you were one of the people themselves; express a life that has never found expression."

IRISH TOURIST BOARD

John Millington Synge, 1905 portrait by John B. Yeats

Synge did not respond to Yeats' advice until the summer of 1898, when he made the first of five extended visits to the Aran Islands, off the coast of Galway. The experience was decisive in that it converted a man of undefined talent into a writer of genius.

Synge never married. He was engaged to the actress Maire O'Neill at the time of his death, in Dublin on March 24, 1909.

Works. *The Aran Islands* (1907), Synge's account of his observations in the islands, reveals how the life and folklore of the people there inspired his three most important dramas. These were his first play, the one-act *In the Shadow of the Glen* (1903); *Riders to the Sea* (1904), believed by many to be the best one-act play in English; and his greatest work, *The Playboy of the Western World* (1907). Because of its astringent satire of contemporary Irish attitudes, *Playboy* inspired riots at its first performances in Dublin and demonstrations by Irish-Americans when it was performed in the United States by the Abbey players during their first American tour in 1911. Synge's last play, the unfinished *Deirdre of the Sorrows,* which deals with heroic figures from ancient Irish saga, was produced posthumously in Dublin in 1910.

Synge's *The Aran Islands* not only reveals the inspiration for his subject matter but also identifies the source of the highly rhythmic and colorful dialect that became his hallmark. Based on the English used by the Gaelic-speaking peasants of western Ireland, it has been called synthetic by some critics. This view, however, ignores the fact that Synge's language embodies a strong substratum of Gaelic syntax, laced with English archaisms from the language taken to Ireland by the Cromwellian conquerors in the 17th century.

Synge gave a frank yet sympathetic portrayal of the traditional life of Ireland and captured the cadences of Anglo-Irish dialect. His work epitomized the ideals of the Irish literary revival.

DAVID H. GREENE
Editor of "An Anthology of Irish Literature"

Further Reading: Greene, David H., and Stephens, Edward M., *J. M. Synge, 1871–1909* (New York 1959); Price, Alan, *Synge and Anglo-Irish Drama* (London 1961).

SYNGE, sing, **Richard Laurence Millington** (1914–), English chemist, who shared the 1952 Nobel Prize in chemistry with another English chemist, Archer J. P. Martin, for their work on partition chromatography as a technique for separating closely related chemical compounds in complex mixtures.

Contributions to Science. Working in the laboratory of the Wool Industries Research Association (1939–1941), Synge and Martin sought an effective method for the separation of acetylated amino acids in wool fibers. Attempting to partition the amino acids between immiscible solvents, such as water and chloroform, they hit upon the suspension of the water phase on a column of silica gel while passing the organic solvent chloroform with the amino acids dissolved in it through the column. This procedure led to the successful separation of the amino acids.

Extending the technique of partition chromatography, they next used filter paper as a suspending medium, and using a third solvent obtained 2-dimensional separations. Synge and Martin then sprayed the paper with the chemical ninhydrin to reveal the position of individual amino acids on the paper. The technique of paper chromatography has become an important tool in the analysis of proteins, which are made up of amino acid sequences. Using the technique, Synge was able to work out the amino acid sequence of the antibiotic substance gramicidin S, and other workers have studied other proteins. See CHROMATOGRAPHY.

Life. Synge was born in Liverpool on Oct. 28, 1914. He received his Ph. D. from Cambridge University in 1941. Two years later he joined the Lister Institute. In 1948 he became head of the department of protein chemistry at the Rowett Research Institute at Bucksburn, Aberdeen, Scotland.

AARON J. IHDE, *University of Wisconsin*

SYNOD, sin'əd, an official Christian ecclesiastical council or assembly of bishops and clergy. A synod meets for the purpose of defining doctrine, enacting canons or other disciplinary regulations, making pronouncements on social or moral issues, or furthering programs of evangelistic work or church renewal. Frequent and regular synodical activity has always been characteristic of the Christian church in its periods of greatest influence.

It has become customary to employ the word "synod" for meetings that are local or regional in character. A diocesan synod, for example, is a meeting of a bishop and the clergy of his diocese. A provincial synod is an assembly of the bishops and representative clergy of the several dioceses that form an archbishop's ecclesiastical province. The synonymous term "council" is usually used for assemblies that are ecumenical or representative of the whole church. Thus, the Synod of Arles (314) was an assembly of representatives of the western portion of Christendom, while the Council of Nicaea (325) was a general council of the whole church.

Modern official use of the term synod is largely restricted to the Roman Catholic Church, Eastern Orthodox churches, and the Anglican churches. See also COUNCIL.

POWEL MILLS DAWLEY
The General Theological Seminary, New York

SYNODICAL MONTH. See MONTH.

SYNONYMS AND ANTONYMS. A *synonym* is a word that has the same or nearly the same meaning as another word in the same language. For example, "bony," "emaciated," "gaunt," "skeletal," and "wasted" are synonyms when used in the same context, but as used in "a bony fish" and "wasted time," the words "bony" and "wasted" are not synonyms. An *antonym* is a word entirely opposed in meaning to another word, so that if one in asserted, the other is negated. "Plump," "chubby," and "well-fed" are antonyms of the synonyms listed above.

The kind of meaning involved is denotation (dictionary meaning), for both synonyms and antonyms can vary in other kinds of meaning. "Inebriated" and "plastered," for example, are synonyms, but they differ in connotative and stylistic meaning and hence would not be readily interchangeable in a sentence. For this reason and others, exact synonyms are quite rare.

Semanticists and logicians are interested in the abstract relations that constitute the "sameness" of synonyms and the "oppositeness" of antonyms, and they disagree about these. On the more practical plane, synonym dictionaries and the handling of synonyms in general dictionaries are chiefly concerned with difference rather than sameness. They aim to help the user in discriminating among words that are synonymous (or "related" or "analogous"), so that his choice of words may precisely express his thought and feeling. They also serve as memory-joggers in case the exact word has not leaped to mind.

Few books are as useful for jogging the memory or providing a wide range of choice as Roget's *Thesaurus of English Words and Phrases,* first published in 1852. The *Thesaurus,* or "treasury of works," is not strictly a synonym book and not a dictionary. It is a huge compilation of words and phrases grouped by various kinds of association under many "heads of signification." The user locates clusters of helpful words by looking up a word in the index, and he may be led to several heads in different parts of the book. The words under a given head go well beyond any admissible range of synonymy, and the user who unwarily treats them as synonyms will use a strange language indeed.

The *Thesaurus* is available in several good modern editions, including *Roget's International Thesaurus* (3d ed., 1962). The best synonym dictionary is *Webster's New Dictionary of Synonyms* (1968), which includes as its introduction a superb essay on synonyms and antonyms by Rose F. Egan. March's *Thesaurus-Dictionary* (1958) is the best book combining the thesaurus with the dictionary format.

ROBERT L. CHAPMAN, *Drew University*

SYNOPTIC GOSPELS, sə-näp′tik, the Gospels of Matthew, Mark, and Luke, which can be arranged side by side because these three New Testament books give parallel accounts of the life of Jesus. The word "synoptic" refers to this parallel arrangement and is derived from the Greek, meaning "to take in at a glance." The Gospel of John, the last of the four Gospels to be written, is arranged differently and is less concerned with the historical details of life of Jesus. Therefore it is not placed in this arrangement. The literary interrelationship of the synoptic Gospels is called the "Synoptic Problem." See also GOSPELS; LUKE, GOSPEL OF; MARK, GOSPEL OF; and MATTHEW, GOSPEL OF.

SYNOVIAL FLUID, sə-nō′vē-əl, is the clear thick fluid between the adjacent bones of a movable joint. The fluid, which resembles egg white, lubricates the ends of the bones, allowing free movement. See JOINT.

SYNOVIAL MEMBRANE, sə-nō′vē-əl, the thin membrane that forms a sac between the ends of the bones at a movable joint. The synovial membrane has special cells that secrete synovial fluid, which allows the bones to move freely. See JOINT.

SYNOVITIS, sin-ə-vī′təs, is an inflammation of the synovial membrane, the inner lining of the fibrous capsule that surrounds and enfolds the bone ends at a joint. The cells of the synovial membrane secrete synovial fluid. When the joint is inflamed the cells produce excess fluid, causing the joint to appear swollen. The joint is also somewhat painful and feels warm to the touch.

Synovitis may be caused by injury or chronic strain on a joint. It is also associated with many diseases. Arthritic diseases, particularly rheumatoid arthritis, degenerative arthritis, and gout, may cause synovitis. Most crippling deformities of rheumatoid arthritis are directly related to synovitis. Infection within a joint may cause severe synovitis and result in the ultimate destruction of the functioning of the joint.

In treating synovitis the cause of the inflammation should be identified and removed before permanent damage occurs. It is important to seek medical attention promptly. Often the excess fluid has to be drawn out with a needle so that it can be studied.

JOHN J. GARTLAND, M. D.
Jefferson Medical College, Philadelphia

SYNTAX, sin′taks, is the part of grammar, or the subsystem of a grammar, that deals with the position, order, and function of words and larger units in sentences, clauses, and phrases. The "rules" of English syntax are so numerous and complex that they will never be fully codified. They control our verbal expression over a vast range of free choices and choices required by the rules of grammar—from the construction of complex sentences, to the precise patterns required for questions and passive constructions, to the very subtle ordering of modifiers and nouns. The terms "subject," "predicate," "object," and the like are syntactic designations.

Where our choices have to do not so much with "correctness" as with beauty and force of expression, syntax merges with stylistics. It also merges with morphology. The use of a possessive, as in "the *girl's* hat," involves not only the choice of a distinctive form, which is the province of morphology, but also a syntactic choice, since the possessive form shows the relation between "hat" and "girl." Linguists find it difficult to define the exact limits of syntax, but the meaning of the Greek *syntassein* (to arrange; to put in order), from which "syntax" derives, provides a good basis of understanding.

ROBERT L. CHAPMAN
Drew University

SYNTHETIC FIBER. See FIBER—*Man-Made Fibers.*

SYNTHETIC RUBBER. See RUBBER, SYNTHETIC.

SYPHILIS, sif'ə-ləs, is a systemic disease caused by the spirochete *Treponema pallidum.* Most often this microorganism is spread through sexual contact, and syphilis therefore is considered to be a venereal disease. Although syphilis is not as prevalent as gonorrhea, it is generally much more serious. In the United States, a blood test for detecting the presence of the syphilis spirochete is required by most states before marriage licenses can be granted.

Incidence. Syphilis is widespread throughout the world. In warm areas with poor sanitation and crowded conditions it assumes a less virulent form. There are no precise data on worldwide incidence, but it is estimated that there are about 20 million new cases a year. In the United States the incidence of syphilis reached its peak in 1945, when 106,500 new cases were reported. Ten years later, a low was reached, with only 6,500 new cases reported. After 1955, however, the federal government withdrew much of its support from eradication programs, and the incidence of syphilis once again surged upward. Eradication programs were established under the Kennedy administration in the early 1960's, and the increase was halted by 1966. However, these measures gradually lost ground to other programs, and the number of cases again began to rise. By the early 1970's, there were approximately 21,000 new cases reported in the United States each year.

HISTORY

The origins of syphilis are not completely known. Some of the earliest evidence of the disease has been found in skeletons of pre-Columbian South American Indians. Many historians believe that syphilis did not exist elsewhere in the world until it appeared in Naples shortly after the return of Christopher Columbus from his first voyage to the New World. In 1494 many Spanish sailors who had sailed with Columbus and had contracted syphilis in the West Indies joined the army of the French king Charles VIII for the invasion of Naples. These men transmitted the disease to the many camp followers as well as residents of the city. It was, in fact, the ravages of syphilis that finally dispersed the French army.

After the fall of Naples in 1495 the disease was carried throughout the known world over the next 15 years. Medical historians estimate that it claimed 10 million victims during that time. In France the disease was first known as "the Neapolitan disease," whereas in Naples it was called "the French sickness." It came to be called "syphilis" in 1530 when the Italian physician, historian, and poet Girolamo Fracastoro wrote his epic poem *Syphilis sive Morbus Gallicus.* The central character in this poem is an infected shepherd lad named Syphilus.

Although syphilis could be diagnosed through its symptoms, its causative organism was not discovered until 1905, when it was first observed by the German bacteriologists Fritz Schaudinn and Erich Hoffmann. This discovery of the spirochete had to wait until the development of the dark-field microscope. This microscope sidelights the organism against a dark background so that it can be seen in much the same way as dust particles are seen in a sunbeam against a dark background.

In 1907 the German bacteriologist August von Wassermann developed the first blood test for detecting syphilis, and in 1910 the German scientist Paul Ehrlich introduced salvarsan, or 606, an arsenic compound hailed as the first drug for curing syphilis. Although salvarsan was found to have its shortcomings, in 1931 it was learned that the drug could be more effective when used in conjunction with bismuth. Even so, this method of treatment required 30 bimonthly injections of salvarsan interspersed with 40 injections of bismuth. Many patients died of the disease because they did not want to complete this grueling regimen.

Penicillin, the first specific cure for syphilis, was discovered in 1928 by the British bacteriologist Alexander Fleming. However, it was not used for treating syphilis until 1943, when John Mahoney and the staff of the U. S. Public Health Service Hospital on Staten Island, N. Y., were seeking an answer to the growing problem of syphilis control. Through research and experimentation, penicillin treatment of syphilis reached a high level of effectiveness in the early 1950's. Other antibiotics, notably the tetracyclines, have also been found effective, but penicillin remains the drug most often used.

CAUSE

The syphilis-causing organism, *Treponema pallidum,* is a pale, slender spirochete with evenly spaced spirals. It ranges in length from about 5 to 20 microns. (One micron is about 1/25,000 of an inch.) Humans are the only animal naturally infected by the spirochete, although syphilis has been artificially induced in apes and rabbits by inoculation with *T. pallidum.*

The spirochete is readily destroyed by exposure to disinfectants, soap, and heat. However, it is resistant to very low temperatures and can be kept frozen for long periods of time. Like other anaerobic organisms, the spirochete thrives only in places where there is no air.

COURSE OF THE DISEASE

The syphilis-causing organisms can enter the body through any mucous membrane or skin abrasion, but most often they are introduced in the anogenital or oral region during sexual contact. Following inoculation, there is usually an incubation period of about 21 days but sometimes as long as 90 days. During this period there are no signs or symptoms of the disease, but the organisms are being carried deep into the body tissues and organs by the circulating blood and lymph.

Primary Syphilis. Early signs of the disease can usually be seen first between 10 and 90 days after infection. Commonly, the first sign is a single lesion, called a *chancre,* the appearance of which marks the beginning of the stage known as primary syphilis. Many persons, however, fail to develop a lesion. In others who do, the lesion does not always resemble the typical chancre of syphilis.

The chancre appears at the organism's site of entry, which most frequently is in the anogenital area but may also be on the tongue, larynx, tonsil, lip, breast, finger, toe, or other part of the body. The chancre is almost always painless, hardened, and ulcerated, and its surface is highly infectious. Often it is concealed, particularly in women, where it occurs most commonly in the vagina or on the cervix. The chancre is often concealed in homosexual men, where it occurs most commonly in the rectum. Consequently, the infected person, although highly infectious, is seldom aware of the chancre, the earliest sign of the disease. If a chancre does not become infected with bacteria or other organisms it will disappear spontaneously in a matter of days or weeks.

Secondary Syphilis. The signs and symptoms of the secondary stage of syphilis usually appear several weeks after the disappearance of the chancre. This stage is marked by a wide variety of signs and symptoms. Most patients have a low fever and suffer malaise. Frequently there is also a painless swelling of various lymph nodes.

The most common lesions characteristic of the secondary stage appear on the skin and mucous membranes. These lesions may be few or many, large or small, and may include blotches, bumps, and scales. Usually they are dry, but moist-looking welts and bumps frequently occur around the genitals. They also may occur in chafed or rubbed areas, as the armpits and between the toes. Whitish patches in the mouth and throat and on other mucous membranes may also signal secondary syphilis, as may patchy falling hair and inflammations of the eyes and throat.

As with the initial chancre, these secondary skin and mucous membrane lesions—especially the moist ones—are teeming with *T. pallidum* organisms. Also like the chancre, these lesions will disappear in time, even without treatment. However, they may reappear from time to time during the next weeks and months, sometimes up to the second year of infection.

Latent Period. The period following the second stage of syphilis or between secondary stages is known as the latent period. This period may extend over several years and is characterized by the absence of any signs or symptoms of disease. Throughout the latent period the disease can be diagnosed only by tests of the blood.

Late Symptomatic Syphilis. After a period of time symptoms may reappear, marking the beginning of the stage called late symptomatic syphilis. This stage is characterized by two types of damage: chronic, highly destructive, but localized damage to the skin, bones, and visceral organs, and generalized damage to the heart or central nervous system (brain and spinal cord). With the exception of pregnant women, who can transmit the disease to their unborn babies, most patients are not infectious after the last appearance of the secondary lesions. In contrast to the lesions of primary and secondary syphilis, the skin lesions of late syphilis are not infectious.

Involvement of the heart, known as *cardiovascular syphilis,* may become increasingly serious anytime after the fifth or sixth year of infection. Often it results in death. Inflammation of the central nervous system by *T. pallidum,* called *neurosyphilis,* may result in crippling, paralysis, and mental disorders. One form of neurosyphilis, *tabes dorsalis* (also called locomotor ataxia), commonly occurs 20 to 30 years after infection. It is associated with severe pains in the legs, visual disturbances, and urinary difficulties.

CONGENITAL SYPHILIS

When a woman with syphilis becomes pregnant, her baby will be infected unless the mother is treated before the 18th week of pregnancy. After that time the spirochetes will pass through the placenta to the developing fetus. However, if the mother's infection has lasted four years or more, there is no more than an even chance of the fetus being infected.

In the United States most states require that physicians and midwives perform a blood test for syphilis on every pregnant woman at the time of her first visit. Public health authorities, however, strongly urge that blood tests be performed in both the first and third trimester of pregnancy because a single test early in pregnancy is not useful if the woman is in the incubation period. Also, the woman may not contract syphilis until later in pregnancy and the disease might not be detected.

Treatment of the pregnant woman almost always cures the baby while it is in the uterus. However, if treatment is started very late in pregnancy the baby may be near death and not respond to treatment.

Early congenital syphilis—that is, syphilis in children under the age of two—often causes blistery skin or mucous membrane lesions, damage to the bones, enlargement of the liver and spleen, and kidney disease. It also often causes anemia, pneumonia, and meningitis.

Late congenital syphilis—that is, syphilis that has progressed after the age of two—may cause serious eye disease, and the child on reaching adolescence may become blind. Syphilitic damage to tooth buds may also affect the development of the permanent teeth, causing conditions known as Hutchinson's teeth (widely spaced or pegged upper incisors notched along the biting edge) and mulberry molars (first molars with a small cusp and a shoulder of enamel bulging around the crown). In rare cases congenital syphilis may cause deafness, neurosyphilis, and destructive lesions of the skin, bones, and visceral organs. The most noticeable of these are the bone lesions that produce a saddle nose (nose with a sunken bridge), a perforation of the nasal septum or palate, and painless swellings of the knees.

DIAGNOSIS

In diagnosing syphilis, the physician considers the patient's history. He asks whether the patient has noticed any signs or symptoms of the disease and whether he knows of having been exposed to the disease. The physician then performs a physical examination, looking for characteristic lesions and other signs. If he finds a lesion, he uses a dark-field microscope to look for *T. pallidum* organisms in the ooze from the lesion's surface. Finally, the physician orders laboratory tests on the patient's blood.

Blood tests for syphilis are generally of two types. One type, of which the Venereal Disease Research Laboratory (VDRL) test is the most popular and dependable, tests only for the presence of an antibodylike chemical complex known as *reagin.* This substance is manufactured by the body in response to a number of pathological conditions. Although this test is extremely useful, a positive result does not always indicate syphilis. Nor does a negative result always indicate that the patient does not have the disease. The original Wassermann test is no longer used, although a few states may still use the name. In most areas of the United States the VDRL test is used more than any other.

Newer types of blood tests use a fluorescent substance that relates in a specific way to the spirochete. One of these tests is the fluorescent treponemal antibody (FTA) test. This test indicates only that the patient has or had syphilis, but a negative FTA test rules out syphilis completely. Although this type of test is more difficult to perform than the VDRL test, it is useful in ruling out syphilis in questionable cases. However, it cannot indicate whether the person who has had syphilis received adequate treatment, which the VDRL test can do within certain limits.

After the physician has weighed all the evidence and determined the probable extent of the disease, he must decide on a course of treatment. He must also decide how long to observe the patient after treatment and what tests should later be used to see if he has been cured. The physician also inquires into the patient's recent sexual contacts. This is extremely important in helping to reduce the spread of the disease. Generally, the patient is reluctant to discuss his sexual contacts. Even when he names many individuals, he frequently omits his more regular partners in the mistaken belief that he is protecting them. These are the people most likely to be infected. Because the disease may be hidden during the first few months, all persons known to have been exposed to infectious syphilis should be treated immediately not only for their own protection but also for that of the community.

TREATMENT

Acquired syphilis can be cured by the administration of proper amounts of penicillin, but any tissue damage remains. Generally, a single injection of benzathine penicillin G is effective. For persons who are allergic to penicillin, other antibiotics, notably the tetracyclines, can be substituted. Congenital syphilis is also treated with penicillin or other antibiotics.

There is no vaccine against syphilis. Once a person is infected, immunity to the disease is generally slow to develop and seldom affords lasting protection against reinfection.

William J. Brown, M. D.
Chief, Venereal Disease Branch
State and Community Services Division
U. S. Public Health Service

Further Reading: Catterall, R. D., *Short Textbook of Venereology: The Sexually Transmitted Disease* (Philadelphia 1967); Dennie, Charles C., *History of Syphilis* (Springfield, Ill., 1962); Luger, Anton, ed., *Antibiotic Treatment of Venereal Diseases* (White Plains, N. Y., 1968); Wilcox, Richard R., *Textbook of Venereal Disease and Treponematoses* (Springfield, Ill., 1964).

SYR DARYA, sir där′yə, the longest river in Soviet Central Asia. It was called the *Jaxartes* in ancient times. As the Naryn River, it rises in the central Tien Shan mountain system south of lake Issyk-Kul and cuts through the Fergana Range. As the Syr Darya, it then flows through the Fergana Valley. At the valley entrance it bends around a spur of mountains and, beyond the rapids at Begovat, emerges on the desert plain to flow in a northwesterly direction to the Aral Sea. The Naryn-Syr Darya is 1,780 miles (2,865 km) long.

Averaging 16 to 23 feet (4.8–7 meters) in depth, the Syr Darya floods during spring and summer. The first high water follows the melting of the snow in the mountains; the second, the swift thawing of glacial ice. Its lower course is frozen from December to early April. The Syr Darya is a source of irrigation water, and it is navigable by small vessels.

SYRACUSE, sir′ə-kūs, capital of Italy's Syracuse province, is on the Ionian Sea in southeastern Sicily. Its name in Italian is Siracusa. The city is built on the island of Ortygia and, across a causeway, on the coast itself. It has two superb harbors, the Little Harbor east of the causeway and the Great Harbor to the southwest. The plateau of Epipolae lies to the north.

A busy fishing center, Syracuse is known especially for its oysters and mussels. It also has saltworks, vegetable-oil refineries, wineries, and cement and soap plants.

Points of Interest. On Ortygia are the spring of Arethusa, a site associated with a famous legend; a Greek temple of the 6th century B. C. alongside the cathedral of 640 A. D.; another Greek temple of the 5th century B. C.; and, in the Archaeological Museum, fine terra-cotta decorative elements and other objects. The island's narrow streets contain fine medieval buildings.

The ancient market (*agora*) lay across the causeway on the coast, where there are now Roman remains, including a colonnade. To the northeast is Lower Achradina, with remains of Roman houses and Christian catacombs near the 12th century church of San Giovanni. To the northwest are the Greek theater, rock-cut and overlooking the Great Harbor; the great altar of Hieron II; and the amphitheater of Augustus. West of the Great Harbor two monolithic columns mark the 6th century B. C. temple of Olympian Zeus. The city's newer quarters are on the mainland. Population: (1961) 74,783.

The Rise of Syracuse. Greek colonists from Corinth occupied Ortygia and the coast about 733 B. C., expelling the native Sicels. An oligarchy of aristocratic landholders, using the Sicels as serfs, ruled Syracuse and built the early temples. Trade by land and sea brought prosperity, and Syracusan colonies planted in southeastern Sicily hedged in a considerable domain. A causeway linking Ortygia to the coast was completed about 525 B. C. Commercial and artistic ties with Corinth were close, and Syracuse entered the 5th century as the greatest state in Sicily.

The collapse of oligarchies in Sicily was followed by a number of able tyrants, or dictators. One of these, Hippocrates of Gela, captured Camarina and defeated the Syracusans, but he came to terms with them when Corinth and Corcyra (Corfu) mediated. In 485 B. C. his successor, Gelon, seized Syracuse while it was being rent by factions. Gelon made it his capital as a better base from which to expel the Carthaginians from western Sicily. He enlarged its population by transplanting people from other cities, and he increased his armed forces, maintaining a navy of 200 warships, a citizen infantry of 20,000, a great body of cavalry, and large numbers of specialist mercenaries. He built a new causeway and extended the city walls toward Epipolae. When the Carthaginians counterattacked in 480 B. C., Gelon met them at Himera and won a decisive victory.

Gelon and his brother Hieron I made Syracuse the wealthiest state in Sicily. The court attracted Simonides, Pindar, and Aeschylus, and its splendor was unparalleled in the Greek homeland. But in 466 B. C. the people expelled the alien elements and established a democracy.

Victory over Athens. Democratic Syracuse led the Sicilian states to further successes against the Etruscans and the Sicels, whose leader Ducetius gave himself up at Syracuse and was sent to Corinth. But in trying to dominate its neighbors by force, Syracuse became involved in rivalries that led to intervention by Athens.

In 424 B. C. a Syracusan statesman, Hermocrates, united Sicily and excluded Athens, but war broke out again, and in 415 B. C. an Athenian expedition of unprecedented size sailed against Syracuse. After twice defeating the Syracusan infantry, the Athenians tried to blockade the city by land and sea. The courageous Syracusans, however, were gaining on land and sea when a second Athenian expedition arrived.

With their combined forces the Athenians made a night attack on Epipolae, but the Syracusans rallied and drove the Athenians back to the unhealthy swamps by the Great Harbor. After making repeated attacks by sea and land, the Syracusans forced the enemy, some 40,000 strong, to retreat overland, destroyed them piecemeal, and herded the 7,000 survivors into quarries (413 B. C.).

Tyrants and Democrats. But victory was followed by factionalism. An extreme democrat Diocles, came to power, banished the war leader, Hermocrates, who was operating in the Aegean, and became embroiled with Carthage. In 406–405 B. C., huge Carthaginian forces destroyed city after city until they reached the walls of Syracuse. There democracy had been overthrown by Dionysius I, a young man who established himself as tyrant by the use of mercenary troops. An opportune plague struck the Carthaginian army, saving Syracuse and Dionysius from disaster.

For nearly two centuries Syracuse had a succession of dictators and liberators. The greatest tyrant, Dionysius I (ruled 405–367 B. C.), included Epipolae in his fortifications, converted Ortygia into a citadel for his mercenaries, and enlarged the population by bringing people from conquered cities. He failed to expel the Carthaginians from western Sicily, but he created an empire that covered most of Sicily, southernmost Italy, and some islands in the Adriatic Sea. The wealth and the power of Syracuse were unrivaled in the Greek world.

His son and successor, Dionysius II, however, lacked his father's ruthlessness and ability. Plato tried without success to make him a philosopher-king. The empire crumbled, Dionysius was under attack, and in 343 B. C., a Carthaginian fleet occupied the Great Harbor.

This time an idealistic statesman from Corinth, Timoleon, saved Syracuse and the rest of Sicily and established a constitution that was intended to arrest the constant swing from democracy to dictatorship. In 317 B. C., Agathocles became tyrant. He attacked the Greek cities, fell foul of Carthage, and was defeated. When the Carthaginians besieged Syracuse from 311 B. C. onward, he boldly invaded Africa and obtained a favorable peace in 306 B. C.

Decline of Syracuse. On Agathocles' death in 289 B. C., civil war raged in Syracuse. It was again besieged by Carthage. This time Pyrrhus of Epirus was the city's savior. Soon a new tyrant emerged, Hieron II, who ruled as king from 269 to 215 B. C. He was forced into alliance with Rome against Carthage, became a supporter of Rome in the First Punic War, and was left independent when Rome made the rest of Sicily a province. In the Second Punic War, Syracuse sided with Carthage and was attacked by Rome in 213 B. C. After a siege of two years, the city fell by treachery and was looted, Archimedes the inventor being among the casualties.

Stripped of its possessions and its independence but retaining its commercial importance, Syracuse was colonized by Emperor Augustus, but it did not regain its earlier prosperity. In 665–668 A. D. it was the capital of the Byzantine Emperor Constans II. Its population was annihilated in 878 by the Arab conquerors. Thereafter its history followed that of Sicily.

N. G. L. HAMMOND, *University of Bristol*

Further Reading: Finley, Moses I., *Ancient Sicily to the Arab Conquest* (London 1968); Mack Smith, Denis, *A History of Sicily*, 2 vols. (London 1968).

EDITORIAL PHOTOCOLOR ARCHIVES

SYRACUSE'S PONTE NUOVO joins the island of Ortygia to the mainland. This small island in the harbor contains elements of both the old and the new city.

NEWS BUREAU, SYRACUSE UNIVERSITY

SYRACUSE UNIVERSITY campus is located in southern Syracuse. Hendricks Chapel, on the campus, is a neoclassic structure built in the shape of a Greek cross.

SYRACUSE, sir'ə-kūs, a city in central New York, the seat of Onondaga county, is situated at the eastern end of Onondaga Lake about 140 miles (225 km) east of Buffalo. The city is an important industrial, commercial, and cultural center. Its industries are highly diversified. They make air conditioning units, radio and television sets, telephone equipment, tool steel, automobile gears, machine shop products, and farm implements. They also produce electronic equipment, furniture, pharmaceuticals, pottery, clothing, shoes, handbags, candles, soda ash, caustic soda, and other chemicals.

The city is the seat of Syracuse University and LeMoyne College, both four-year institutions, and of Onondaga Community College and Maria Regina College, which have two-year programs. The College of Forestry and the Upstate Medical Center, both of the State University of New York (SUNY), are also there.

Cultural facilities include the Everson Museum of Art, noted for its ceramics collection and its bold design by I. M. Pei, and the Lowe Art Center at Syracuse University, which sponsors many art exhibits. The Canal Museum, housed in an original "weigh-lock" building, specializes in memorabilia of the Erie Canal. Syracuse has a symphony orchestra and was once a thriving tryout city for pre-Broadway legitimate theater productions.

The city is a religious center for the state. It is the state headquarters for several churches and is also a Roman Catholic see and the seat of an Episcopal diocese.

The New York State Fair Grounds, 4 miles (6 km) west of the city, is the scene of yearly exhibits of livestock, dairy and fruit produce, and such homemade articles as ceramics and handicrafts.

Before its settlement by white men, the area around Syracuse was the home of the Onondaga Indians, the chief tribe of the Iroquois Confederacy. In 1656, French Jesuits built a mission and fort on the shores of Onondaga Lake but soon abandoned it because of Indian hostilities. The mission, known as Fort Ste.-Marie de Gannentaha, was later reestablished, and one of its members, Father Simon LeMoyne, discovered the salt springs whose commercial value led to the forming of the city. For many years most of the nation's salt came from Syracuse, and it was known as the "Salt City" for its leading industry until about 1900, when the salt brines were depleted and production declined.

The community was settled in 1805. It had a succession of names, including Webster's Landing, Bogardus Corners, Milan, Salt Salina, Cossit's Corners, and Corinth. In 1820, at the suggestion of its first postmaster, it was named Syracuse for the ancient Sicilian city. Syracuse was incorporated as a village in 1825 and as a city in 1848. The opening of the Erie Canal here in 1819 and the arrival of the first railroads in the late 1830's spurred the growth of the city.

Syracuse has lost many of its residents to the suburbs, but, by 1970, renewal programs and the building of new stores, offices, and parking areas had begun to revitalize the central city. Syracuse has a mayor-council form of government. Population: 197,297.

REID A. HOEY
Onondaga Library System

SYRACUSE UNIVERSITY, sir'ə-kūs, is a private, nondenominational institution in Syracuse, N. Y. It was chartered in 1870 under the auspices of the Methodist Episcopal Church with the help of citizens of Syracuse. The first classes were held in 1871, and the main campus was opened in 1873.

The oldest and largest division of the university is the college of liberal arts. In addition there are colleges and schools of architecture, art, business administration, citizenship and public affairs, education, engineering, graduate studies, home economics, journalism, law, library science, music, nursing, social work, and speech and dramatic arts. Total enrollment exceeds 24,000 men and women, about half of whom are from out of state. Nearly one third are graduate students. The library of 1.4 million volumes ranks 13th in size in the United States among those of private institutions.

The university also operates or participates in many other educational centers, including Utica College, a 4-year affiliated liberal arts college in Utica, N. Y., and University College for extension teaching and adult education. The State University College of Forestry is on the Syracuse campus.

WARREN N. BOES
Syracuse University

JIM HUBBARD, FROM PHOTO RESEARCHERS

Imposing main mosque in Homs testifies to importance of Islam to Syrians, most of whom are Sunnite Muslims.

SYRIA

National Emblem of Syria

CONTENTS

SYRIA, sir'ē-ə, is an Arab republic of southwest Asia. Its population is primarily Muslim. Syria (Arabic, Suriya) has been an independent nation in modern times only since the end of World War II. But Syria's history is as long as that of any country in the world, and in the past the nation embraced an area significantly larger than it covers today.

Syria possesses a varied land surface, extending from the coastal plain along the Mediterranean in the west, across mountains, to the vast desert in the east that is traversed by the Euphrates River. Syria's economy is primarily agricultural. The country is poor in natural resources. Nonetheless it has attracted migrants throughout history. Some of its diverse minority peoples, including Druzes, Alawites, and Kurds, still retain a recognizable identity, chiefly because they have lived in natural geographical enclaves.

Central to Syrian history has been the country's domination over centuries by powerful neighbors, although it has had brief periods of self-rule and of high cultural achievement. Important remains of Syria's past that can be seen today include traces of a Bronze Age township at Ras Shamra, of Hittite settlements on the Euphrates at Jerablus and Kadesh, and of Assyrian (and much earlier) habitation at Tel Ahmar. There are Phoenician ruins on the Mediterranean coast at Amrit and imposing Roman buildings at mid-desert Palmyra. Important examples of Muslim architecture are found in Damascus, Aleppo, and elsewhere, and the Christian tradition in Syria is represented by the cathedral at Tartus and by many Christian monuments elsewhere. Finally, there are the splendid Crusader castles, including the remarkable Krak des Chevaliers, and those at Markab and Sahyun.

Contemporary Syria, since its independence, has experienced a number of military coups and government changes. Successive governments have attempted to balance pan-Arabism and Syrian nationalism, in a socialist context. Major domestic goals have included economic improvement and the welding together of diverse elements in the population to achieve a cohesive na-

INFORMATION HIGHLIGHTS

Official Name: The Syrian Arab Republic.
Head of State: President.
Head of Government: Prime minister.
Legislature: The People's Assembly.
Area: 71,665 square miles (185,180 sq km).
Boundaries: *North,* Turkey; *east,* Iraq; *south,* Jordan; *west,* Israel, Lebanon, Mediterranean Sea, and Turkey.
Elevation: From sea level to 9,232 feet (2,814 meters) at Mount Hermon.
Population: (1970 estimate) 5,900,000.
Capital: Damascus.
Main Languages: Arabic (official), Armenian, Kurdish, Syriac, and Turkish.
Major Religious Group: Sunnite Muslims.
Monetary Unit: Syrian pound (S£), divided into 100 piastres.
Weights and Measures: Metric, but with some traditional local survivals.
Flag: Three horizontal stripes—red on the top, white with three green pentagonal stars in the center, and black on the bottom. See also FLAG.

tional outlook. Syria's relations with its Arab neighbors have often been less than amicable, and its hostility to neighboring Israel is unremitting.

1. The Land and Natural Resources

Syria is a land of variety and contrast. About one third of the country is desert or barren mountain, one third scanty and unreliable pasture, and one third potentially cultivable land. Skirting the Mediterranean is a narrow, flat coastal strip. To the east of this strip are mountains and valleys. The mountain zone is extended southward, after a fertile gap, by the Anti-Lebanon (Jebel esh-Sharqi) range, the crest of which forms the Lebanese frontier. To the east of the mountain zone is the main cultivable area, in which are found Syria's major cities and the bulk of its population. Still farther to the east is the Syrian Desert, traversed in a southeasterly direction by the great Euphrates River. Each region has distinctive scenery, climate, and resources.

Coastal Plain. The Mediterranean forms about one fourth of Syria's western border. Extending inland from the coast for 5 to 20 miles (8–32 km) is a populous and cultivated plain. Its climate, though humid in summer, is never excessively hot. Winter frost is rare, and rainfall is adequate.

From the coastal plain's small ports of Tartus and Baniyas and the important city of Latakia the immemorial fishing fleets ply. Latakia has a good harbor but poor inland communications.

The Mountains. To the east of the plain, and extending far south of it, are discontinuous mountain ranges. The northern range, the internally complex Jebel Ansariya, reaches 5,200 feet (1,585 meters). The ridge is broken and irregular. In the northern part of the range is Syria's nearest approach to woodland. The lower western slopes are heavily terraced to avoid soil denudation by rains of some 40 inches (100 cm) a year. The Ansariya range affords sites for dozens of villages but no major town. There is good cultivation around the villages, and summer conditions at the higher levels are pleasant, though the area is among those least known to foreigners.

South of the Ansariya range is a fertile gap west of Homs. The mountains resume with the Anti-Lebanon range. These are authentic mountains often approaching 7,000 feet (2,135 meters) and snowcapped for half the year, but the terrain is generally barren and offers poor grazing. There are a few sizable villages, wherever a spring makes habitation possible, with limited cultivation at the infrequent favorable sites. Most of the heavy winter rains are quickly absorbed, and the rain-fed streams descend eastward. The Hermon range forms, almost continuously, the southern section of the Anti-Lebanon Mountains. At Mt. Hermon it reaches 9,232 feet (2,814 meters), a snowcapped landmark visible from afar. The region is mostly barren and uncultivated.

Cities and Cultivable Zone. Syria's major cities—from north to south, Aleppo, Hama, Homs, and Damascus—lie to the east of the mountains. These cities are located within Syria's most productive agricultural areas, which are interspersed with steppe-desert land.

Aleppo (Haleb), Syria's second-largest city with more than 500,000 inhabitants, is of legendary antiquity and crowned with an imposing medieval fortress. The city below agreeably mingles old and new building styles. For centuries it has been a political nucleus and a great trading and communications center for northern Syria. The mainly flat or undulating region around Aleppo enjoys a favorable climate, though winter frost is common and August temperatures can exceed 100° F (38° C). Rainfall ranges from 15 to 20 inches (380–510 mm), and the humidity is low.

Southwestward lies the great marsh of the Ghab, fed by the Orontes River and by mountain streams. Having been drained, it affords a valuable irrigation source. The Orontes rises in Lebanon and passes northward to the sea by way of the cities of Homs, Hama, and (in Turkey)

WESTERN DRESS of village leaders at traditional meal contrasts sharply with desert garb of followers.

E. BOUBAT, FROM PHOTO RESEARCHERS

Antioch. Homs and Hama are important cities central to Syrian political and social life, and they dominate their provinces as administrative and economic centers. This west-central Syrian countryside is flattish and often monotonous. Like that of Aleppo, it supports considerable agriculture but has much more steppe-desert, though all existing means of irrigation are in use and the rainfall suffices in average years for good or fair crops.

Damascus, the capital and largest city of Syria, reflects modern developments in building and planning as well as medieval structures and quarters of great picturesqueness. Well watered by its carefully fostered streams, the city lies on the edge of the famous Ghuta oasis, rich in shady fruit gardens. Today historic Damascus teems with governmental, academic, and commercial life. The climate, like that of all Syria east of the mountains, is continental, with great day-to-night variations, low rainfall, and dry atmosphere.

To the southeast, between Damascus and the Jordan border, the Jebel Druze rises from a base surrounded by wide areas of lava-strewn desert. An elevated plateau rather than a single mountain, the Jebel Druze attains some 5,500 feet (1,675 meters). It is formed of basalt capped by volcanic cones and presents a grim yet attractively romantic aspect. There is little agriculture here. Good roads and some railroad communication with the outside world exist.

West of the Jebel Druze lies the fertile Hauran district, partly occupied (the "Golan Heights") by Israel in 1967.

The Syrian Desert. East of the main cultivable zone lies the wide Syrian Desert, which is hilly in the center and northeast. Here are half a dozen isolated villages, including the magnificent ruins of ancient Palmyra (Tadmor). There is cultivation mainly in a belt along the Turkish border, flourishing most in the northeast.

Along the ever-impressive Euphrates lie scores of riverain villages—and also along its major tributaries, the Khabur and Balikh. The only significant, though isolated, city in this wide area is Deir ez-Zor, an attractive place with pleasant gardens. Summer heat in the desert is intense and oppressive.

The natural resources of the desert and steppe areas are scanty. There is, after good spring rains, some short-lived grazing for sheep and goats but otherwise only the barest living, from scrub and thorn, for the camel herds. There are mid-desert gazelle, jerboa, and bustard, but little else of economic value—except for oil discovered in the northeast.

Natural Resources. As a whole, Syrian natural resources are minimal. Except for oil in the northeast and plentiful gypsum and basalt—and unconfirmed hopes of phosphates, lead, and copper—exploitable minerals and timber are almost completely lacking. Only in Latakia province are a small outcrop of bitumen and some chrome being worked.

2. The People

The almost total predominance of the Arabic language in Syria indicates that the main migrations to Syria over the centuries have been those of Semitic-speaking peoples from Arabia. However, from prehistoric times people from other parts of Asia have flowed into this area as well. The amalgam of all of these migrants, with very small additions from Europe, have produced the present-day Syrian tribesman, villager, and city dweller.

Today there is no more uniformity in physical type in Syria than in any other modern nation. If an Arab physical type truly exists at all, it is confined to the desert tribes, who have, also, a darker skin pigmentation than other Syrians.

The Arabic spoken in Syria is remarkably uniform, though there are slight variations from

Barren desert, whose fringes can be used for livestock grazing, makes much of Syria uninhabitable.

E. BOUBAT, FROM PHOTO RESEARCHERS

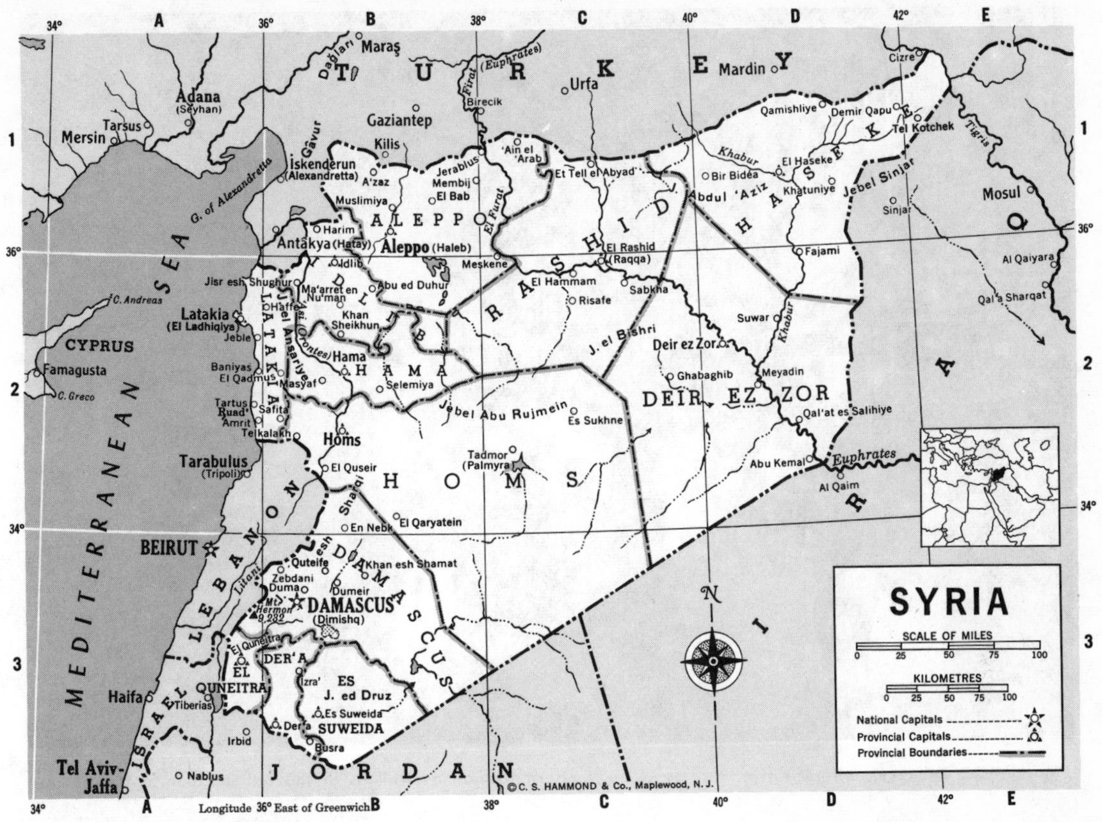

SYRIA Map Index

area to area and between Muslims and Christians. In most cases members of the small non-Arabic-speaking communities can understand Arabic.

Variations in Way of Life. Although 80% of the Syrian population are Sunnite Muslims and nearly all Syrians speak Arabic, there are significant differences in Syrian life patterns. The way of life of the city dwellers differs substantially from that of the country people. It also varies between those who have received a modern education and those who have received a traditional education or who are almost without education. The generations also differ in their life styles, and even party affiliations sometimes affect the mode of living.

Until the end of the 19th century, the prevailing way of life in Syria was Islamic, unambitious, traditional, non-European, and almost static. Today, in perhaps a half of the whole population—including two thirds of the tribesmen and villagers—it remains substantially the same. This was and is a life of great simplicity, of devotion to local and habitual interests. It focuses on traditional housing, clothing, food, amusements, and outlook—and is especially characterized by the complete, deeply Islamic subjection of women.

But this pattern of life has been modified or abandoned during the past century, and with acceleration since World War I, by an increasing minority that today claims to stand for Syria and holds all public power—civil, military, and industrial. This dominant element in the population, the great majority of whom live in the cities or towns, controls the nation's life. Its members —and their wives—play bridge and tennis, read, listen and dance to music, and practice modern professions and occupations. This element is the creation of rapid East-West communications, two world wars, and a keen desire to "catch up" with the West.

Thus, "a Syrian" today may be an ill-fed, ill-clad, totally uneducated—though highly picturesque—camel-tending, migratory tribesman of the great Aniza or Shammar groups; or he may be a cultivator or peddler or donkey-driver in his native village; or he may be a polished lawyer, doctor, professor, or politician in Aleppo or Damascus—or at the United Nations. And within the elite there is room both for the left-wing revolutionaries, who came to power in the 1960's, and for the representatives of old, conservative, and now dispossessed families. There is room also for those in militant student movements or

PICTORIAL PARADE

Market in Damascus offers wares displayed in modern fashion as well as in the old manner of the bazaar.

in military or ideological cliques critical of the established regime, and for many more who seek only security and continuity.

Religious Minorities. The differences or strata that are found among Syria's majority Muslim population also exist, though to a lesser degree, within the important minority communities, both Christian and Islamic.

Of these, the Christian sects, which total some 500,000 to 600,000 persons but are widely dispersed and disunited, have tended to favor the more modern ways. They retain a keen sense of community and revere their own bishop, archimandrite, or cardinal. Generally they have a sense of being less than full Syrian-Arab citizens and sometimes possess less nationalistic fervor than other Syrians.

The Catholic communities, mostly Eastern rite, consist of 65,000 Catholic Melchites, 20,000 each of Armenian and Syrian Catholics, 17,000 Maronites, 6,000 Catholic Chaldeans, and 5,000 Latin-rite Roman Catholics. The large congregations are in the cities or among northeastern farmers. This is also true of the Orthodox Eastern, the Monophysite, and Protestant communities. The Syrian Orthodox number some 175,000. Among the Monophysite communities there are about 100,000 Syrian Jacobites and about 115,000 Armenian Church members. There are also about 10,000 Assyrian Christians (Nestorians).

In addition to the Sunnite Muslims, there are various sects belonging to the Shiite branch of Islam. Among these are the doctrinally heterodox Ismailis, located chiefly in Hama. They are followers of the Aga Khan. There are Kurdish Sunnite groups in the northeast and in Damascus, and also the Yazidis, a "devil worshiping" group in the northeast and around Aleppo.

The Alawites of Latakia and Tartus provinces, whose ethnic admixtures are unknown but who profess a unique form of Islam mixed with paganism and elements of Christianity, form about 70% of the population of these provinces and are well represented also in those of Homs and Hama. They may number 400,000. They are men of strong, dour character, shaped through centuries of self-sufficiency and near-autonomy. A remarkably high proportion of them are found in senior central government and military posts.

The Druzes, not dissimilar in type although dominated by two or three noble but quarrelsome families, have for the last century tried hard to isolate themselves and to live untroubled in the Jebel Druze in the south. Such a policy of isolation has no future now, however, and gradual assimilation probably awaits them. Their religion, since it broke off from true Islam in the 11th century, has been kept jealously secret. It venerates the strange 6th Fatimid caliph, al-Hakim, and incorporates non-Islamic elements.

A few hundred Jews in Syria have survived emigration or expulsion, out of a total of 30,000 living in Syria at the end of World War II.

Education and Communications as a Unifying Force. Since World War I, Syria's leaders have sought to weld together a score of disparate communities. The means they have chosen to form a homogeneous nation have included close control of the Christian community's schools, education of more of the young and through this education a broadening of the Syrian's outlook, and also government propaganda.

The strictly educational effort of successive Syrian governments since 1920 has been very considerable. There are learned societies, libraries, and museums in the biggest cities, and universities at Damascus and Aleppo, with an Arab academy and an institute of music and the arts, also in Damascus. Teachers' training colleges, high schools, primary schools, and preprimary schools are widespread, employing in all some 25,000 teachers.

The work of unifying and modernizing the country has been abetted by the development of a government-controlled press, as well as by broadcasting, the cinema, and the spread of paperback literature. As Syria has been shaped by these forces, it has at the same time lost some of its tribal, family, and township loyalties, and it may be that the force of Islam itself has been weakened.

Population Growth. The overall population of Syria, approaching 6,000,000 in 1970, had at least doubled in the preceding quarter century. Syrian population figures, except those for cities, are incomplete and unreliable. This holds true for data concerning birthrates and life expectancy, both of which are doubtlessly increasing.

3. The Economy

The natural economic assets of Syria are severely limited. It is primarily an agricultural country. About 40% of its land is arable, and there is a fair if insufficient supply of water. Oil, discovered in 1959, is the leading mineral resource. But Syria's deficiency in natural resources is the most important factor hindering the nation's economic development.

A sound economic substructure for Syria has failed to materialize. This is partly due to the low level of personal income, which has limited purchasing power and the accumulation of savings for investment in the nation's enterprises. Syria therefore must seek from abroad financial aid and help in developing industrial skills and experience. Another economically inhibiting factor is that the citizenry expects the economy to support a full range of social, military, bureaucratic, diplomatic, and other services that meet modern Western standards.

Successive governments, also, have shaped their economic policies more often than not according to their own political ideologies rather than purely economic considerations. Much governmental action in the economic field—agricultural, industrial, and commercial—has flowed from the prescriptions of state socialism. For ideological reasons private property has been expropriated wholesale, and private enterprise has been discouraged.

Agriculture. Agriculture is still by far the largest-scale activity in Syria, even though a bare sixth or less of the country is under cultivation. Cotton, from improved seed, is the most important export, Syrian output rivaling that of the Sudan. Export of grain—wheat, barley, millet, and maize—is on a small scale and annually variable. In some years, a net import of grain is necessary. Fruit, except for grapes, and vegetables are mostly consumed locally. Little has been done to increase, or to create, a forest-timber output. The small but valuable tobacco crop is largely exported. Sugar-beet growing is increasing.

The Ghab Valley, through which the Orontes flows, has been drained and canalized to increase the land under cultivation. A huge dam on the Euphrates River was begun in 1968, partly financed by Soviet loans. It is intended to irrigate 1.5 million acres (6.07 million hectares) of land.

The government has expropriated all privately owned agricultural land above a certain limited acreage. This massive expropriation and redistribution among the peasants has had the effect of diminishing agricultural output in those cases where large-scale farming is potentially more productive.

Stockbreeding, the occupation of thousands of desert tribesmen and villagers, is essentially unchanged from earlier years. It supplies subsistence needs with a small potential for export both on the hoof and as products such as wool, hair, and hides. It also utilizes land that would otherwise be valueless.

Industry. Great hopes have been placed on industrial development in Syria as a source of pride and wealth and as the hallmark of a truly modern state. And in this field much has been done. Syria claims to be, after Egypt, the leading state in the Arab world in manufacturing, which provides almost half as much revenue to the treasury as does agriculture. The government has acquired almost all privately owned factories or has major shares in them.

Syrian workshops produce cotton yarn, cotton and silk textiles—the largest in scale of local industries—woolen fabrics, cement, asphalt, glass, soap, sugar, canned foods, edible oils, tobacco, beer, wine, and arrack, a liquor of high alcoholic content. The traditional silverwork and the inlaid furniture of Damascus and Aleppo are still produced and valued, and some minor cottage industries contribute to the national wealth.

Oil. Petroleum resources are significant. Russians operate small oil fields in the northeast, and a Yugoslav-built pipeline from these to Tartus crosses Syria. Production of crude oil in 1969 amounted to 3.5 million tons, all exported by sea except for the supply to the small Czech-built refinery at Homs. Oil pipelines from Iraq and Saudi Arabia cross parts of Syria and are a source of effortless, but vulnerable, income for the Syrian treasury.

Labor Force. The labor force is sufficiently large for Syrian agriculture and industrial activities. Syrians readily acquire new skills, and Western technology is taking root. Underemployment exists chiefly in white-collar occupa-

SKEPTICAL FARMERS, who still use animals in the fields, examine village's first tractor-driven plow.

GEORGE RODGER, FROM MAGNUM

tions and on the fringes of the bureaucracy. Women are employed widely in clerical and the lighter technical occupations, as well as in medicine, the civil service, commerce, and communications. The Islamic public quickly forgets how revolutionary this innovation is. Trade unions are not unknown but are ill-organized, markedly political, and in any case closely controlled by the government.

Transportation and Power. Transport facilities in Syria have been improved. Roads, both dirt and hard surfaced, have been greatly extended. Telegraph and telephone services are countrywide, adequate, and in part automated. The port of Latakia, transformed by Yugoslav engineers, is busy with ocean shipping. The state-owned railways are still as the Syrian government inherited them. The rail system is linked with lines in Turkey, Iraq, Jordan, and Lebanon. A British company has operated a transdesert Damascus-Baghdad bus service since 1923. Internal civil aviation is developed, and foreign lines use the modern facilities of the international airport at Damascus.

All these means of transport foster the growing tourist industry, for which the country's many ancient sites and remains form the basis. Hotels are generally adequate and improving.

Trade and Finance. Domestic marketing is partly conducted by amicable bargaining in the bazaars and partly along Western lines in modern shops. Banking and insurance are widely developed but have been under state control since the expropriation of all foreign institutions in these fields. The state's Central Bank manages the currency. Loans to agriculture and industry are made by government banks.

Syria's foreign trading partners are mainly the Communist countries—including Cuba and China—Arab neighbors, Italy, France, Turkey, West Germany, and Japan. Its main exports are crude oil, raw cotton, textiles, cereals, and live animals and animal products. Its principal imports are textiles, solid fuels, cement, oil seeds and other plants and foods, machinery, building materials, metals, chemicals, vehicles, and tobacco. The visible balance of payments is clearly adverse, causing the Syrian economy to depend, especially for all capital works and munitions, on foreign sources.

4. History and Government

The geography of Syria, which in the ancient world comprised roughly the territories of present-day Syria, Lebanon, Israel, Jordan, and part of Turkey, has been a determining factor in Syria's political and cultural history. At the crossroads of historic military and trade routes between the Mediterranean and Mesopotamia, Syria was the object of invasion and occupation by powerful neighbors from earliest times.

Archaeological finds from the Stone Age confirm that Syria was one of the areas in which early man lived and developed. Later, but still in prehistoric times, Semitic-speaking peoples moved into the territories of the original inhabitants. One such invasion was that of the Amorites in the 3d millenium B. C. Later there were those of the Canaanites (Phoenicians), Aramaeans, Hebrews, and similar tribes of the same Arabian origin.

The earliest Syrian historical period was in the 2d millenium B. C., during the incursions of the Hittites from Asia Minor, who achieved dominance in northern Syria. Egyptians conducted similar raids and temporary occupations. Although it was the prey of both these neighbors for centuries in the 2d millenium, Syria retained its identity, Semitic dialects, and local autonomy in sizable areas.

As Hittite power declined, its place was assumed by the Assyrians of northern Iraq. Assyrian monarchs, from the mid-8th century B. C., repeatedly occupied the more attractive Syrian areas, levied tribute, and seized hostages. In the face of these and Egyptian invasions the population centers of Syria could not maintain their independence as city-states. Then, in the 6th century, the Persian empire intervened and held hegemony over Syria for two centuries.

Persian domination ended in 332 B. C. with the conquest of Syria by Alexander the Great. It was followed by three centuries of vigorous Hellenization and the founding of important Greek cities. Under Pompey in 64–63 B. C. the Roman occupation began. Rome administered Syria as a Roman province but normally tolerated some local self-rule. The language and traditions of the Syrian cities and tribes survived, and most were spared the rigors inflicted on Palestine, the cradle of a new religion, Christianity.

In 330 A. D., when the administrative center of the Roman world shifted from Rome to Byzantium (Constantinople), Syria was little affected, except for a greater spread of Christianity. Frequent incursions and partial occupations by the Sassanian Persians concerned the Syrians from the 4th to 7th centuries.

The Arab Conquest. From all its passively endured foreign invasions and occupations, Syria had gained new experience of community life, politics, culture, and ideas. Yet the Syrians were unprepared for the crucial event of 635—the invasion of their territory by Arabs from Arabia, suddenly militant as fanatical converts to Islam, the new religion of Mohammed.

Within a quarter century Damascus had become the capital of the first imperial Islamic caliphate, the Umayyad (661–750). Massive conversion of town and tribe alike to Islam occurred, the Arabic language began to prevail over all others, and Arab culture was everywhere in evidence. This Islamization and Arabization continued after the Abbasid caliphate of Baghdad superseded the Umayyad in the mid-8th century.

In succeeding centuries, as the caliphate lost its hold, Syria and other Muslim lands paid mere lip service to the enfeebled caliph. Turkish elements entered the Fertile Crescent as mercenary troops and stayed on as masters and finally as dynasts. At times Syria maintained a fitful, fragmented autonomy, while at other times it suffered the short-lived rule of the partially revived Abbasids or that of the Tulunids and Ikhshidids, based in Egypt, of the northern Iraqi Hamdanids—a brief cultural "golden age"—and of Seljuk and Zangid rulers from northern Iraq and Turkey.

From the mid-10th to mid-12th centuries petty local dynasties rose and fell within Syria, but the country was mostly under the uninspiring sway of the Shiite Fatimids of Egypt. During the latter period the European Crusaders were able, against feeble resistance, to establish military states in Syria, at Edessa (Urfa), Antioch, Tripoli, and Jerusalem. The effect of these Crusading states within Syria was local and limited. However, the 200-year stay of the Crusaders in

Palmyra, or Tadmor, an ancient, once-powerful oasis city, stands in impressive ruins in the Syrian Desert.

the Levant did much to increase familiarity between West and East, Christianity and Islam.

The virile Ayyubids, whose greatest ruler was Saladin, evicted the Fatimids from Egypt in about 1160, effectively ruled Egypt and Syria, and expelled most of the Crusaders. Declining morally and militarily, the Ayyubids were in turn (1249) succeeded in Egypt, and thereby as de facto rulers of most of Syria, by the Mamluks. These were a remarkable corps of mainly Turkish and Circassian former slaves who had evolved into an oligarchic military elite. Mamluk commanders succeeded in repelling invasions by the Mongol hordes—the brutal scourge of western Asia in the 13th and 14th centuries—from Genghis Khan to Timur (Tamerlane). Even so, Mongols devastated the land and committed mass slaughter in 1260, 1270, and 1300. In the period from 1250 to 1515, Syria was an unhappy country, as it suffered the ambitions of its local dynasties and resisted non-Arab rule from outside.

Ottoman Rule. An event as sudden as that of the Arab conquest, though less unexpected, now settled Syria's fate for four centuries: the invasion and occupation of the country by the Ottoman Turkish Sultan Selim I in 1517. For the next 400 years Ottoman rulers, who were Muslim but non-Arab and unsympathetic toward or contemptuous of all Arabs, permitted Syria some limited regional autonomy, granted intra-community self-rule to the Christian sects, and allowed some privileged foreign trade. But they ignored local social conditions, which were backward and impoverished. For Syria, the Ottoman period was in the main one of nonprogressive passivity until about 1800.

From roughly 1800, Syria was emerging from Ottoman stagnation. The territory today known as Syria was edging toward its future as a revitalized, ambitious state, in control of its own destiny as it had rarely been in the past. This movement resulted in part from reforms in the central Turkish government—reforms that were greatly accelerated early in the 20th century under the revolutionary Young Turks.

Also contributing to Syrian emergence was the increasing Arab-Islamic pride of Syrians and Lebanese, who were then indistinguishable, and indeed of Arabs everywhere. Other factors included a remarkable Arab literary revival in modern styles, improved communication with Europe through trade, books, and newspapers, better schools, and the fast evolution of the upper social strata from ancient ways. Direct French, American, and British educational and philanthropic work also contributed. Syria also drew lessons from the national self-liberation efforts of long-suppressed communities in East Europe, Latin America, and elsewhere.

Also educative, in terms of broadening Syrian perspectives, was the 10-year Egyptian occupation of Syria-Lebanon by Ibrahim Pasha from 1831 to 1840. French intervention in Druze-Maronite quarrels in 1860–1861 had a similar effect. It was at this point that half the Druze community moved from their Lebanese home to their present Jebel Druze abode in southern Syria.

By 1914 tribal and village life was actually little changed from that of earlier centuries, except for higher standards of law and order and a habituation to better organized government. But members of the Syrian elite, with increased numbers and greater aspirations, were attending universities, forming social and political clubs, and formulating, with like-minded Arabs elsewhere, a political program. Their program was intended to lead to "decentralization" in the Ottoman Empire, to a greater share of power for Arabs in, or against, Turkish officialdom, and finally, though not yet specifically, to an Arab state or states.

During the period 1900–1914 this movement—in Paris as well as in Cairo, Beirut, Damascus, and elsewhere in the eastern Arab world—attained a strength alarming to the Turkish authorities. In fact, however, Arab reformers had achieved nothing practical before the outbreak of World War I in 1914. And during the war the brutal execution by the Turks of dozens of the Arab ideological leaders as traitors, the army's firm grip on the entire country, and sheer hunger paralyzed all reforming effort.

The French Mandate. The movement revived, however, after British forces entered Syria in October 1918 and evicted the Turks. The League of Nations bestowed on France a mandate for Syria-Lebanon in 1920, and the local Christian, especially the Catholic communities, hailed the move with delight. But the great majority strongly opposed the mandate and the French presence, which was to last 25 years. They objected to the detachment by France of considerable Muslim areas of Syria to form the separate Greater Lebanon—which later (1926) became a republic—and to the pervasive closeness of French control and the French policy of "divide and rule" in a Syria now diminished territorially.

Syrian nationalists, eager for self-determination and power, were not placated by French excellence in the techniques of administration, justice, the social services, and communications. Their chronic discontent took the form in 1925 of a sizable, though partial and ill-organized, uprising, the so-called "Druze rebellion." To crush it, the French were compelled to devote increased forces over a two-year period.

By 1939, successive Syrian ministers and French high commissioners had still not solved the conflicts between mandatory and mandated in the constitutional, political, and administrative fields. Feeling was further embittered by the enforced cession of the Antioch-Alexandretta province, which Syrians claimed was strictly Arab, to Turkey in 1939. France consented to the transfer of this area, the present-day Turkish province of Hatay, because of its desire for Turkish goodwill.

Nevertheless, by 1939, Syria was better organized and equipped and its elite better trained and experienced than ever before. And the nationalists' goal, that of complete independence, was within reach.

During World War II, in 1941, British forces expelled from Syria French troops of the Vichy government. Their Free French successors still withheld independence from Syria. They refused to admit the termination of the hated mandate, although in 1941 they had promised this to the country, and the British favored the move. The French did allow elections in 1943, and in August, Shukri el-Kuwatli of the National party was elected president of the republic.

As the war ended, discontent was acute among all political elements, and disorders broke out in urban centers. Only British intervention cut short a French bombardment of Damascus. The mandate, never officially abrogated, in fact faded and disappeared in 1945–1946, and the last foreign troops withdrew, leaving a number of Syro-French problems still unsolved. But Syria, having become a sovereign member of the United Nations in 1945, was now an independent, constitutional republic.

Independent Syria. In the first years of independence the government, ministerial and parliamentary in form, strove to settle its outstanding disputes with France and Lebanon. Unlike Lebanon, it left the franc currency bloc. It tried to achieve economies and necessary reforms, permitted political parties to revive, endured student demonstrations, and sustained frequent cabinet changes. But Syria's relations with its neighbors were mostly suspicious or hostile, and the shock of the foundation of Israel in 1948 and the failure of the Arab armies' campaign—in which Syria played little part—was traumatic and lasting. The elder "founding fathers" of the country's independence soon lost their prestige, hoped-for progress seemed unattainable, and disillusion spread.

Early in 1949 the government was overthrown and President Kuwatli deposed in a military coup. The next four years saw two short-lived military dictatorships and one longer, but less absolute, regime, all sullenly resented by most politicians. A new constitution was proclaimed in 1950 and another in 1953. Elections were held but widely boycotted. Street demonstrations increased, inevitably to be suppressed by the army, while the army itself was "purged." Frontier incidents with Israel multiplied. The third dictator, Col. Adib el-Shishakli, was forced by mounting opposition to leave the country early in 1954.

Political discord persisted, and Syria's relations with its neighbors were as unstable as ever. Syria rejected the Iraqi-Turkish Baghdad defense pact of 1955 (later to be known as the Central Treaty Organization) and viewed with indignation the Franco-British assault on the Suez Canal in 1956. Following Egypt's lead, Syria acquired arms from the USSR. The latter power became widely popular, and the Syrian Communist party flourished. Partly in reaction against these developments, the newly created Baathist party, which advocated pan-Arab nationalism abroad and a socialist regime at home, led the country into an unexpected union with Egypt. The United Arab Republic (UAR), composed of Egypt and Syria, was formally established in February 1958.

Syria's 43 months in the UAR were unhappy ones. Free political life was not allowed, and the Baathist party, unpopular with the Egyptian leader Gamal Abdel Nasser, president of the UAR, was eclipsed. Under a dualistic constitutional structure Egyptian officialdom was too obviously dominant in Syria. The UAR's relations with Iraq and Jordan were hostile, and the reported infiltration of armed Syrians into Lebanon created an alarming crisis and led to U. S. intervention in Lebanon in 1958. Soviet aid to Syria increased visibly. Wholesale land expropriation by the government alienated landowners, and foreign trade was disrupted by rigid controls. In September 1961 the now unpopular union was abruptly dissolved by a military coup in Syria, and Syria regained its independence.

Elections were held in December 1961, and a new constitution was drafted. Political parties re-formed, the revived Baathist group splitting into extreme and less extreme factions.

But in the following years military coups occurred almost annually, with changes of cabinets and of the military revolutionary councils. Syria concluded various pacts with its neighbors, but in practice these agreements were largely ignored. Arab League meetings and "summits" were sometimes attended, sometimes boycotted. Reformation of the union with Egypt was proposed, pressed, resisted—and refused outright by Nasser. Violent border episodes with Israel were frequent.

Domestically, large-scale nationalization of lands, properties, and businesses continued. Massive street demonstrations and smaller armed uprisings occurred in Damascus, Hama, Aleppo, and elsewhere, and offenders were tried by "special courts." Another constitution was promulgated in April 1964 and still another in January 1965.

Delegations revisited Egypt, and further agreements were reached, only to remain inoperative. Syria signed a pact with Iraq, but little constructive action followed, and their relations again deteriorated. Government in Damascus was conducted by successive groups of officers, supported by varying civilian elements and led by "revolutionary councils." Such conditions necessarily impaired the continuity and efficiency of the administration. Meanwhile, the Baath party —no other party had been permitted since 1963 —and partisans of the USSR gained ground, as had the USSR itself through its aid to Syria. The coup of February 1966 was the country's ninth in postindependence years. By this time many formerly leading families and statesmen had left the country.

Syria took a minor part in the Israeli-Arab War of June 1967, which resulted in a debacle for the Arabs and Israeli occupation of Syria's southwestern fringe territory, the Golan Heights. Subsequently Syria outdid the other Arab states in its uncompromising attitude toward Israel. Most of the other Arab states accepted a UN peace formula (November 1967), but Syria rejected it. Israel proceeded to colonize the occupied territory. Syria's relations with the USSR, its main supporter, were variable. It broke off diplomatic relations with the United States and Britain in 1967.

Quarrels between Baathist factions continued throughout 1968 and 1969, colonels and civilian ideologists waging bitter if largely invisible war. In May 1969 another provisional constitution was promulgated, the cabinet reinstated, and elections—the first in seven years—were promised. Syro-Israeli clashes multiplied, culminating in all-day battles in April and June 1970. And more Lebanese-Syrian friction arose from the former's objection to the provocation of Israel by Syrian guerrillas operating from Lebanese bases.

On October 6, 1973, the war was renewed as Syrian troops invaded the Israeli-held Golan Heights on the north and Egypt simultaneously struck across the Suez Canal at the Israeli-held Sinai Peninsula on the south. Initial Syrian advances were reversed, and on October 23, when Syria conditionally accepted the ceasefire, Israel occupied more of Syria than before the war.

Through the mediation efforts of U. S. Secretary of State Henry Kissinger in May 1974, an Israeli-Syrian troop-separation agreement was concluded, with Syria recovering land lost in October and a strip of the Golan Heights lost in 1967. But Syria expressed determination to regain all the Golan area. When President Nixon visited President Hafez al-Assad in June 1974, they resumed U. S.–Syrian diplomatic relations.

STEPHEN H. LONGRIGG*
Author of "Syria and Lebanon under French Mandate"

Bibliography

Europa Publications, Ltd., *The Middle East and North Africa* (London, annually).
Fedden, Henry R., *Syria and Lebanon,* 3d ed. (London 1966).
Fisher, William B., *The Middle East, a Physical, Social and Regional Geography,* 5th ed. (London 1966).
Glubb, John B., *Syria and Lebanon* (London 1966).
Hitti, Philip K., *History of Syria,* 2d ed. (London 1957).
Hourani, Albert H., *Syria and Lebanon,* 2d ed. (London 1954).
Longrigg, Stephen H., *Syria and Lebanon under French Mandate* (London 1958).
Seale, Patrick, *The Strugg'e for Syria* (London 1965).
Tibawi, A. C., *A Modern History of Syria* (London 1969).
Torrey, Gordon H., *Syrian Politics and the Military, 1945–1958* (Columbus, Ohio, 1964).
Ziadeh, Nicola A., *Syria and Lebanon* (New York 1957).

SYRIAC LANGUAGE AND LITERATURE, sir'ē-ak. Syriac is a language in the Northern Branch of the Semitic languages and is closely related to Aramaic. Syriac was used in Christian writings starting in the 2d century, including a version of the Bible. See ARAMAIC LANGUAGE; SEMITIC LANGUAGES.

SYRIAN CHURCHES, sir'ē-ən, in the broadest sense, are those Christian churches that trace their origins to the ancient church of Antioch, Syria. Some of the churches have remained Orthodox in doctrine while others have embraced Monophysitism or Nestorianism (see MONOPHYSITES; NESTORIANISM).

East Syrian Churches. The church centered in Edessa, Turkey, became Nestorian after the condemnation of Nestorius in 431 and established a separate Persian church. It evangelized parts of Persia, Mongolia, China, and India. A movement developed among these Nestorian Christians in 1553 to unite with Rome and resulted in the formation of the Chaldean Catholic Church. The daughter Nestorian church in India, the Malabar Nestorians, split over the issue of union with Rome later in the 16th century. One group united with Rome, ultimately becoming the Malabar Indian Church. Another group united with the Syrian Jacobites—who were Monophysite—and became the Indian Jacobite Church. Part of this last group joined with Rome in 1930 and are known as Syro-Malankara Rite Catholics.

Western Syrian Churches. Many of the west Syrian churches embraced Monophysitism after the Council of Chalcedon (451). The majority became known as Jacobites (see JACOBITES). Another group remained orthodox, and in the 18th century some of them united with Rome to form the Catholic Melchite Church of Antioch.

The Maronite Church, centered in Lebanon, was formed in the 8th century, primarily because of jurisdictional difficulties. It reestablished ties with Rome in the 12th century.

Membership. The approximate membership of the Syrian churches is: Nestorian Church, mainly in Iraq, 70,000, with 5,000 in India called Mellusians; Chaldean Catholic Church, 190,000; Syro-Malabar Catholic Church, 1,400,000; Syrian Jacobite Church of Antioch, 130,000; Jacobites of India, 700,000; Syro-Malankara Rite Catholics, 125,000; Syrian Catholic Church of Antioch, 80,-000; Syrian Orthodox (Melchite) Church of Antioch, 605,000, with 115,000 in North America; Catholic Melchite Church of Antioch, 400,000, with a diocese in Boston, Mass., of 55,000; Maronite Church of Antioch, 850,000, with a diocese in Detroit, Mich., 125,000.

GEORGE A. MALONEY, S. J.
John XXIII Center, Fordham University

SYRIAN DESERT, sir'ē-ən, in the northern Arabian Peninsula, between the cultivated Mediterranean coast and the fruitful area once called Mesopotamia. This large, arid region includes central and southeastern Syria, western Iraq, eastern Jordan, and northern Saudi Arabia.

SYRINGA, sə-ring'gə, is a common name for the mock orange, an ornamental shrub with fragrant flowers. *Syringa* is also the scientific name for the lilac genus. See LILAC; MOCK ORANGE.

SYSTEMATICS is the study of the classification of living things. See TAXONOMY.

SYSTEMIC LUPUS ERYTHEMATOSUS. See LUPUS.

SYSTEMS ANALYSIS is the study of the structure and behavior of sets of interacting elements. The elements and the interactions among them may be purely abstract, as in a mathematical representation, or concrete, as in the solar system, a communication system, or a business management system. The distinguishing feature of systems analysis is the concept of treating problems as a whole rather than piecemeal, as in the more traditional specialized approaches to problem solving. This feature necessitates consideration of all the major variables and their interactions. In this way it is usually possible to achieve better overall solutions and avoid unexpected and often detrimental effects.

Systems problems, although long encountered in the physical sciences, are largely an outgrowth of advanced technology. The underlying reasons for the growing interest in systems problems and systems methods are the increase of knowledge in science, engineering, and allied fields; the growth of large-scale industrial and government enterprises; the rapid development of defense and space technology; and the demands of society for more effective solutions of complex environmental, production, and transportation problems. In modern society, systems problems are increasingly critical because of imbalances created by the differences in the rates of technological and social change.

The breadth of meaning of the term "system" and looseness of its use have caused some confusion about the scope of the term "systems analysis." For instance, "systems analysis" sometimes is used narrowly in connection with data-processing systems or as a synonym for cost-effectiveness analysis, and sometimes it is used to denote almost any kind of process. As used here, "systems analysis" means the study and use of systems based on scientific and mathematical methods. Related terms such as systems methods, systems approach, systems engineering, and systems science imply similar procedures and therefore are sometimes used interchangeably with systems analysis.

The most advanced applications of systems analysis are in the physical sciences and associated technologies because there are precise general laws and well-developed mathematical methods for dealing with these fields. Systems analysis is more advanced in dealing with economics and business management than in other behavioral and social fields because the former are better structured. In the biological sciences, systems methods have a tremendous potential, but they are still in the early stages of development. Barriers to development have been the lack of general theories, insufficiently developed mathematical methods applicable to complex biological systems, and a dearth of mathematically trained scientists in biological fields. Areas where systems concepts and methods already have attained major importance include computers; electric power systems; on-line process and production control in oil refineries, steel mills, and paper mills; transportation; space exploration; air and water pollution; public health; management and decision making; information handling; urban planning; and architectural planning and construction.

Historical Background. Systems science has its roots in classical mathematics, physics, and astronomy. The first system analysis was accomplished by Newton in his mathematical analysis of the solar system set forth in *Principia* (1687). Here the elements are the sun, planets, moons, and comets, and the interactions are the gravitational forces between these bodies. The analysis is based on Newton's three laws of motion plus his law of universal gravitation. The mathematics is geometry and calculus, and the results are quantitative and precise. This work has served as a model for subsequent studies of various systems.

The development of the generalized methods of dynamics by Joseph L. Lagrange, William R. Hamilton, and others in the 18th and 19th centuries constitutes one of the most advanced and elegant models of systems analysis even to this day. In 1864, James Clerk Maxwell enlarged the scope of generalized dynamics to include systems of electric currents and their interactions with mechanical elements. Maxwell's work provided a basis for the systematic analysis of electromechanical systems and for much of modern electric network theory.

The development of systems methods in the 20th century mainly stems from the massive scientific and technical work carried on during World War II. The outstanding accomplishments during the war years were the development of radar systems, electronic digital computers, and advanced feedback control systems, as well as the application of sophisticated mathematical methods to military operations (called *operations research* by the military to distinguish it from the more familiar laboratory research).

In the postwar years, mathematical methods were developed for dealing with management and decision problems. These methods included linear programming, game theory, queuing theory, decision theory, and various production scheduling techniques such as PERT (program evaluation and review technique) and CPM (critical path method). Also, advances in high-capacity, high-speed digital computers and computer programs have continued to be essential factors in coping with systems problems, which typically have hundreds or thousands of variables and involve millions of calculations.

Two notable developments in the 1960's were the broadened application of the systems approach for military and space systems, and the use of the systems approach in long-range planning by government and industry. Also, systems methods were put to use at the state and city levels in dealing with public and social problems such as urban planning, mass transportation, waste management, budgeting, crime, and fire prevention.

Steps in the Systems Approach. The typical steps in the systems approach are: (1) formulate the problem; (2) identify and describe the components of the system and their interrelationships; (3) develop mathematical or logical models; (4) analyze system performance and study alternative means for accomplishing objectives in terms of criteria such as cost, size, effectiveness, and risk; (5) select the best system on the basis of the specific criteria; and (6) build or implement the physical or abstract system that has been selected. These steps are interrelated and therefore are under constant review until a project is completed successfully.

Problem formulation requires deep understanding of the overall system and the environment in which the system will be put to use. It is the province of the generalist rather than the specialist because goals and policies are dominant factors. For some technical areas, the goals and policies may be relatively simple. For management and public problems, they are likely to be complex. The air-pollution problem is an example of an increasingly common situation in which both technical and public aspects are important.

In the next step in the systems approach, the system is subdivided into increasingly smaller subsystems until the basic components are identified. The behavior and interactions of the components are described mathematically, graphically, or verbally. A mathematical or logical model is constructed. This often requires a delicate balance in order to retain the most significant features of the system without introducing undue complications.

Analysis and optimization of the system are done on the basis of the model. Analytical techniques and computer simulation are used for these steps. The former are more general and provide deeper insight into the workings of the system, whereas the latter, along with numerical methods, is necessary for specific designs. In some cases, only computer simulation can be used because of the lack of applicable analytic methods.

In the last step in the systems approach, the results determined from the model are translated into practical action. For example, the action might be the design, construction, and operation of an electronic device or an electric power distribution system, or the establishment of a regional system for air quality control.

Techniques of Systems Analysis. Mathematical methods derived mainly from applications in physics and astronomy in the 17th, 18th, and 19th centuries are still fundamental in the analysis of technical systems. However, systems problems have led to the development of many new mathematical optimization techniques.

Prominent among these newer methods are various mathematical programming methods such as linear programming, nonlinear programming, and dynamic programming. Linear programming, the most widely used, has been applied to numerous problems involving resource allocation, production scheduling, and economic models. Probability and statistical theory are applied extensively to stochastic system problems, which involve probabilistic rather than deterministic variables. For example, forecasting, decision making, and equipment reliability problems involve probabilistic variables.

Computer methods dominate much of systems analysis because only very small systems application problems can be solved without the use of computers. Traditional engineering design methods for many kinds of systems were revolutionized by the introduction of computer methods. For instance, computers aid in the design of highway systems, mechanical feedback control systems, and electrical and electronic systems. In addition, computer simulation plays an essential role in dealing with complex management, economic, and biological systems.

HARRY J. WHITE
Portland State University

Further Reading: Martens, Hinrich, and Allen, Don, *Introduction to Systems Theory* (Columbus, Ohio, 1969); Porter, William A., *Modern Foundations of Systems Engineering* (New York 1966); Ramo, Simon, *Cure for Chaos* (New York 1969); White, Harry J., and Tauber, Selmo, *Systems Analysis* (Philadelphia 1969).

SYSTEMS ENGINEERING deals with methods for selecting the most appropriate combination of workers and machines to accomplish specified objectives. Although these methods were practiced by engineers many years ago, they became much more important during World War II and the postwar years when man-machine interactions and desired objectives became more and more complex. Concurrently, scientists and engineers became increasingly concerned with how technology should be used to meet the needs of society, and this trend further highlighted the need for systems engineering methods in achieving complex objectives.

Systems engineering activities include the conception, definition, design, construction, operation, and test of a system. In this context, a system can be defined as a collection of interacting diverse human and machine elements integrated to achieve a desired objective by the manipulation and control of workers, materials, information, and energy.

A systems engineer deals with the overall design of a complete system, and this is a unique activity. In contrast, an engineering design specialist deals with the detailed design of individual parts of a system. The systems engineers and the engineering design specialists play complementary roles in achieving a complete system, and the interplay between the systems engineers and the specialists requires close coordination by engineering management.

Historical Background. Modern systems engineering arose partly from the development of large-scale electric power systems. The steam-electric power plant built by Thomas Edison in New York City in 1882 was the first of numerous electric power systems that spread over many miles. To meet the constantly growing demand for electricity, engineers had to design, build, and operate large-scale electrical systems and devise new ways of making and using electrical equipment.

Most importantly, however, the engineers had to consider the integrated operation of all the parts of a complex system, not just each part by itself. All of the stages in the production and use of electricity—energy conversion, power generation, power transmission, power distribution, and final use in homes and industries—were considered in relation to each other to realize an integrated system that would provide cheap, efficient, and readily controllable energy for man's use. This approach represents an application of systems engineering as it is known today.

Similar considerations arose as electrical communications systems, particularly the telephone system, grew from small-scale local interconnections to gigantic intracontinental networks. Commercial service for Alexander Bell's telephone began in New Haven, Conn., in 1878, when the first telephone switchboard was opened. It served 21 subscribers, who were interconnected by manual switching. In the following years, as the number of telephones, calls, switching centers, and miles of telephone lines increased, telephone engineers made constant efforts to integrate the operation of all parts of the system so that efficient communications would be maintained. An integrated and highly automated system containing more than 115 million telephones is now in operation in the United States, partly as a result of systems engineering guidance provided by Bell Telephone Laboratories.

The need for better military weapons systems was another reason for the rise in the importance of systems engineering. During the 1930's and 1940's, for instance, it became apparent that systems engineering was needed to develop gunfire-control systems for warships. This goal was achieved through a team effort. Engineering specialists designed individual parts such as target locating devices, computers, and gun drives, and systems engineers played a key role in developing the overall system.

The development of computer information systems and aerospace systems during the 1950's and 1960's further highlighted the need for increased skills in systems engineering. In fact, systems engineering became indispensable in coping with the challenges posed by such projects as building an information storage and retrieval system or making a round-trip flight to the moon.

Although systems engineering mainly has been identified with technical projects and enterprises, its scope has gradually broadened to include deliberate attempts to use technology to bring about distinct changes in the way man lives in his natural and social environment. From this point of view, technological work is done not only for technical reasons but also for economic, social, or political ends. Air pollution control, health service, and law enforcement programs, for example, are not strictly within the province of systems engineering, but the systems approach is providing a useful influence on these programs and many others in which technical activities have a direct impact on community interests and social relations.

Concepts of Systems Engineering. Systems engineering focuses attention on both the ends being sought and the means being used to achieve them. In doing so, it provides a generalized approach to the solution of many different problems. Systems engineers thus are guided by certain fundamental concepts in solving problems.

One fundamental concept is that changes take place in time. For instance, a system may undergo many start-operate-stop cycles, and it may wear out in a few months or in many years. All such changes in time must be identified, anticipated, and accounted for in the design and specifications of the system.

A second fundamental concept is that there are alternative ways to realize a particular system. In building an aircraft, for instance, there may be a choice between using aluminum or titanium and between one metalworking technique or another. Also, a considerable amount of detailed information may be needed to accomplish a task in one way, whereas less detail may be needed in an alternative way. Such considerations must be identified and evaluated in order to realize a system in the most appropriate way.

A third fundamental concept is that there are commonly accepted criteria for judging the value of a system. Each particular system can be evaluated, for instance, on the basis of performance, cost, reliability, maintainability, and life expectancy. For each system, the relative and absolute weighing of these criteria must be established quantitatively, even though subjective judgments do enter into the procedure. In all cases, the weighing of the criteria should be influenced by the needs of the users of the system.

A fourth fundamental concept is that each system has its own environment. Environmental factors that may affect system performance include temperature, pressure, humidity, mechanical shock, vibration, and damaging radiation. The skills of manufacturing personnel and the quality of the machines used in building a system also are considered environmental factors that affect system performance. Each environmental factor to which a system may be exposed must be identified, anticipated, and evaluated.

A fifth fundamental concept is that computational and experimental techniques can be used to facilitate the systems engineering effort. Typically, this effort is aided by the use of computers, mathematical models, simulation techniques, or actual tests of parts of the system rather than the complete system. Such procedures reduce the time, expense, and uncertainty associated with accomplishing the desired result.

General Approach. In a characteristic systems engineering problem, the exact nature of the results sought may not be known in detail. Consequently, the successful solution of systems engineering problems tends to depend on certain steps that constitute a general approach. The major steps are: (1) formulate or define the problem; (2) evaluate system requirements and objectives and tentatively establish the capabilities the system must have to meet them; (3) make a tentative design of the overall system; (4) determine the capabilities of the tentative design quantitatively and compare these capabilities with the system requirements and objectives; (5) enumerate errors determined from this comparison and make the necessary corrections for refinements of steps 2, 3, and 4; (6) repeat steps 2, 3, and 4, taking account of the corrections determined in step 5; and (7) repeat steps 5, 2, 3, and 4 until a satisfactory final design is established. During the repetitive procedure, consideration may also be given to the possibility that changes in the formulation and definition of the problem (step 1) may also be required to bring the overall system solution within an acceptable bound.

In this procedure, an iterative method is used to refine, further refine, and still further refine the overall system design. This procedure characterizes the approach used in solving systems engineering problems.

Another way of looking at the systems engineering approach is to consider the series of activities that take place. The first activity is to define and specify the different parts of the system, their functions, and their interrelationships. The second is to design the parts of the system in conjunction with reviews of the progress of the overall system design. The third is to make or buy the individual parts. The fourth is to assemble the parts into subsystems and test them. In the fifth, all the subsystems are integrated to form the overall system. Finally, the system is put into operation to produce the results for which the system was proposed. Even a completed system may later be modified and improved to produce even more effective results by using the iterative method previously described.

HAROLD CHESTNUT, *General Electric Company*

Bibliography

Chestnut, Harold, *Systems Engineering Methods* (New York 1967).

Chestnut, Harold, *Systems Engineering Tools* (New York 1965).

Gosling, William, *The Design of Engineering Systems* (New York 1962).

Hall, Arthur D., *A Methodology for Systems Engineering* (Princeton 1962).

SYZRAN, siz'rȧn, a city in the USSR, is on the Volga River 70 miles (113 km) west of Kuibyshev in the Russian republic. The city, a railroad hub and industrial center, produces heavy machinery and harvester combines. An oil refinery dates from 1942 and a carbon-black plant from 1963. An oil shale mine, in operation since 1918, is on its southern outskirts. The shale is burned in a steam-electric station and partly converted into pharmaceuticals. Northeast of Syzran is the timber transfer port of Oktyabrsk, formerly called Batraki.

One of the oldest Russian towns on the Volga, Syzran was founded in 1683 and served as a fortress guarding Russian lands against nomads beyond the Volga. Industrialization began in the 1930's and was greatly stimulated by World War II. Population: (1970) 174,000.

THEODORE SHABAD
Editor of "Soviet Geography"

SZCZECIN, shchet'sēn, is a city in northwestern Poland, 285 miles (360 km) northwest of Warsaw and only 80 miles (130 km) northeast of Berlin. Until World War II it was known by its German name of Stettin. After the war, the area was transferred to Poland because much of the city's natural hinterland now lay in Poland, and because Poland needed a port at the river's mouth. Szczecin is the capital of the *województwo,* or province, of the same name that is bordered by East Germany on the west and the Baltic Sea to the north.

Szczecin lies on the steep, western bank of the Oder River, about 40 miles (65 km) from the sea. The city is Poland's second port and serves the highly industrialized Oder basin. It specializes in bulky commodities, particularly the export of coal from upper Silesia and the import of iron ore. Szczecin is also an important manufacturing center, with metallurgical and chemical factories.

History. A settlement existed at Szczecin in the 10th century, when the area was under Polish jurisdiction. It then passed to Pomerania and was gradually Germanized by large numbers of German settlers. It was a member of the Hanseatic League in the 14th century and became Protestant during the 16th. Sweden gained control of the area at the end of the Thirty Years' War but ceded it to Prussia in 1720. Under German rule it prospered as a port until the 19th century. Szczecin was almost wholly destroyed in 1945, and except for its Renaissance castle, little remains of the picturesque churches and other buildings that formerly existed. The city was rebuilt, however, and its docks extended.

The Province. The województwo of Szczecin covers an area of 4,896 square miles (12,675 sq km). Even though much of its soil is poor, it is mainly an agricultural region, with few towns. The province is studded with glacial lakes and has extensive forests. Between the city and the Baltic lies a large lagoon, Zalew Szczecinski, and the island of Uznam, across which a navigation channel has been cut. At the mouth of the channel is Świnoujście (Swinemünde), a small port and resort. Population: (1967 est.) the city, 320,000; the province, 872,000.

NORMAN J. G. POUNDS, *Indiana University*

EASTFOTO

SZCZECIN'S RENAISSANCE CASTLE, built by the dukes of Pomerania, overlooks the Chrobry Ramparts.

SZECHWAN, su'chwän', is the most populous province in China, with an estimated 70 million inhabitants in 1967. Situated in the southwest, it has an area of 220,000 square miles (569,000 sq km).

The province consists of two natural regions. In its western third, composed of high plateaus and mountains, live most of Szechwan's non-Chinese minorities—about 3% of the provincial population, grouped mainly in the Ahpa–Tibetan, Kantse–Tibetan, and Liangshan–Yi autonomous districts. Most of this area, which was the eastern half of former Sikang province until 1955, is over 10,000 feet (3,000 meters) above sea level. Its highest point, Minya Konka, reaches 24,900 feet (7,590 meters). The eastern two thirds of the province is occupied by the Szechwan Basin, also known as the Red Basin. Nearly surrounded by lofty mountains, it is drained by the Yangtze River and its tributaries. The basin includes the extensive, fertile, and densely populated Chengtu Plain.

While temperatures in the west vary widely according to altitude, the east generally has a mild, foggy winter and a warm, moist summer, with a growing season of 11 months. Szechwan leads the nation in output of tung oil and rapeseed and food crops such as rice, wheat, maize, barley, sweet potatoes, millet, and kaoliang. Other crops are sugarcane, cotton, tea, tobacco, sugar beets, and citrus fruits. The province is a major silk producer. Pigs, goats, sheep, and yaks are raised, and the province is noted for its hog bristles.

Szechwan's abundant mineral resources include coal, mined near Chungking, and salt, taken mainly from Tzukung. Oil and gas, iron, copper, phosphorus, and placer gold are also found in the province.

Szechwan contains two large industrial centers. Chungking, the national capital during World War II, is the biggest city in southwestern China, with more than 2 million people. It has large chemical, machinery, and iron and steel plants. Chengtu, the provincial capital, supports a population of over 1 million. Its industries include textile and engineering plants and railroad workshops. Neikiang is a sugar-milling center; Tzukung manufactures salt; and Yaan processes tea.

Formerly, Szechwan was accessible mainly through the Yangtze gorges from Hupei, on the eastern border. In 1952, Szechwan's first railroad was opened, between Chengtu and Chungking. Later it was linked with the national rail system in Shensi to the north and Kweichow to the south. The Chengtu–Ahpa and Szechwan–Tibet highways provide transportation to the west.

DAVID CHUEN-YAN LAI
University of Victoria, British Columbia

SZEGED, seg'ed, is a city in southeastern Hungary, about 100 miles (160 km) south of Budapest. It is on the west bank of the Tisza River, near its confluence with the Maros. The city was largely rebuilt following a disastrous flood of the Tisza in 1879. Since then the river has been regulated so that there is less danger of flooding. The city center, characterized by dull, late 19th century architecture, lies close to the river. Away from the river, the buildings are more typical of Hungarian Plain villages. Farm-type structures are close together, and although many are no longer farms, some peasants still till distant fields.

The city, which is a separate administrative unit, or *megye*, in the county of Csongrád, is becoming increasingly important as a manufacturing center. The manufactures are based mainly upon local agricultural production, but cotton textiles have been intensively developed since World War II. József Attila University was founded in 1921. Population: (1967 est.) 120,000.

NORMAN J. G. POUNDS
Indiana University

SZEKLERS, sek'lûrz, a people inhabiting eastern Transylvania, now in Rumania. The origins of the Szeklers (Magyar, Székely) have been sought among the Huns, Avars, Pechenegs, Khazars, and other early peoples. They are probably true Magyars or descendants of a Magyarized Turki people who were settled in Transylvania in the Middle Ages as frontier guards.

The Szeklers, the Magyars, and the Saxons were the three privileged nations of Transylvania. The Szeklers enjoyed autonomy under the Hungarian crown, were exempt from taxation, and regularly supplied some of Hungary's best soldiers. Their privileges, however, were gradually lost under the Habsburgs. For resisting their duties as border militia, many were massacred. Many others fled. The last remnants of their autonomy were suppressed after the revolution in 1848. Today they are essentially Magyar in speech and culture. Numbering about 500,000, they are officially recognized as a national minority by Rumania and occupy most of its Magyar Autonomous Region.

JOSEPH F. ZACEK
State University of New York at Albany

SZELL, sel, **George** (1897–1970), American conductor, who developed the Cleveland Orchestra into one of the foremost symphonic organizations in the United States. Szell was born to Czech parents in Budapest, Hungary, on June 7, 1897. He made his debut as a pianist with the Vienna Symphony at the age of 10, and was appointed conductor of the Strasbourg Opera in 1917. From 1924 to 1929 he was principal conductor of the Berlin State Opera.

Szell made his American debut in St. Louis in 1930. He was musical director of the German Opera in Prague from 1930 to 1933, and then divided his conducting between opera and symphony orchestras. He conducted at the Metropolitan Opera House in New York, 1942–1945, and in 1946 became principal conductor of the Cleveland Orchestra. Szell became a U. S. citizen in 1946. He died in Cleveland on July 30, 1970.

SZENT-GYÖRGYI, sent-jûr'jē, **Albert** (1893–), Hungarian-American biochemist, who was awarded the 1937 Nobel Prize in physiology or medicine "for his discoveries in connection with the biological combustion processes with special reference to vitamin C and the catalysis of fumaric acid." In later years, Szent-Györgyi studied the chemistry of muscles and did research on the thymus gland and its relation to cancer.

Contributions to Science. While studying oxidation-reduction systems in the 1930's, Szent-Györgyi succeeded in isolating a crystalline compound from orange juice, cabbage juice, and the adrenal cortex. This compound, first called hexuronic acid, was later named ascorbic acid and identified as vitamin C. After the isolation of ascorbic acid, Szent-Györgyi determined its molecular structure.

Szent-Györgyi next turned his attention to the study of muscles and discovered actin, a protein found in muscle fiber. Taking actin and myosin, a previously discovered protein constituent of muscle fiber, he succeeded in making an artificial muscle fiber that contracted when he added the energy source ATP. This work provided an important basis for later more detailed biochemical studies of muscle. Szent-Györgyi then made extensive studies of the thymus gland

Albert Szent-Györgyi

UPI

and its relation to growth, muscle function, fertility, and cancer. He also studied the process of cell division in an attempt to learn about cancer.

The extent of Szent-Györgyi's studies is reflected in his numerous publications, including the books *Chemistry of Muscular Contraction* (1947), *The Nature of Life* (1947), *Chemical Physiology of Contraction in Body and Heart Muscles* (1953), *Bioenergetics* (1957), *Submolecular Biology* (1960), and *Science, Ethics, and Politics* (1963). *The Crazy Ape* (1970) reveals his concern over man's fate on the earth.

Life. Szent-Györgyi was born in Budapest, Hungary, on Sept. 16, 1893. He received his M. D. from the University of Budapest in 1917. After studying in Germany and Holland, he went to England as a Rockefeller fellow at Cambridge University, where he received his Ph. D. in chemistry in 1927. After some work at the Mayo Clinic in Minnesota, he returned to his native country, joining the faculty at Szeged University. He served as professor of medical chemistry from 1931 until 1945 and as professor of biochemistry until 1947. In that year, he returned to the United States, where he established and became director of research at the Institute for Muscle Research at the Marine Biological Laboratories in Woods Hole, Mass.

KARL FOLKERS
University of Texas at Austin

SZIGETI, si'gə-tē, **Joseph** (1892–1973), American violinist, who specialized in playing ambitious, difficult works by contemporary composers. He was born in Budapest, Hungary, on Sept. 5, 1892. He received his early training in Budapest, studying with Jenő Hubay, and made his concert debut at the age of 13. By 1915 he was famous as a concert violinist in England and on the Continent. He performed with impressive vitality and virtuosity, using an unconventional playing stance—with his bow-arm held very close to his body.

Szigeti taught at the Conservatory of Geneva from 1917 to 1924. He made his American debut in Philadelphia in 1925, settled in the United States, and became a U. S. citizen in 1951. He published an autobiography, *With Strings Attached* (1947; rev. ed., 1967). He died in Lucerne, Switzerland, on Feb. 19, 1973.

SZILARD, zē-lärd', **Leo** (1898–1964), Hungarian-American physicist, and one of a small group of nuclear physicists responsible for developing the atomic bomb. Szilard was born in Budapest, Hungary, on Feb. 11, 1898. He studied at the University of Berlin and was a member of the physics department from 1922 to 1932. With the rise of Hitler, Szilard went to England, where he and T. A. Chalmers evolved a new principle of isotope separation of artificially radioactive elements. In 1937, Szilard emigrated to the United States. He became a U. S. citizen in 1943.

Szilard was instrumental in interesting the American government in the military potential of uranium fission. He and Enrico Fermi directed the experiments at Chicago that on Dec. 2, 1942, produced the first controlled nuclear chain reaction. In 1945, Szilard was one of the first scientists to oppose using the atomic bomb, and he later led the successful fight for civilian control of the U. S. atomic energy program.

In 1946, Szilard turned his energies to molecular biology and accepted a research post at the University of Chicago. He did much experimental work in this field, producing several theories on mutations as well as on the aging process and other biophysical phenomena. More remarkable, perhaps, was the catalytic effect of his inventive imagination on the work of scientists whose fields were very different from his own. Animated by a restless, wide-ranging curiosity, he inspired new approaches to a great variety of problems, often leaving to others not only the hard work of testing but any credit that might come from the results. He died in La Jolla, Calif., on May 30, 1964.

SZOLD, zōld, **Henrietta** (1860–1945), Jewish-American educator, author, and social worker, who was active in Zionist causes. The daughter of a prominent rabbi and Hebrew scholar, she was born in Baltimore, Md., on Dec. 21, 1860, and received a thorough Jewish education. At the age of 19 she began to write articles for the Anglo-Jewish press. In 1893 she became literary secretary of the Jewish Publication Society of America. In this post, which she held until 1916, she translated into English, rewrote, and revised a number of important Jewish scholarly works. In 1903 she moved to New York City, where she studied at the Jewish Theological Seminary.

Following a visit to Palestine in 1909, she evinced increasing interest in the health problems there. In 1912 she had a central role in founding Hadassah, the Women's Zionist Organization of America, and in 1917 organized the American Zionist Medical Unit, which went to Palestine in 1918. In 1920 she moved to Palestine, although she continued to visit America frequently. In 1927 she became the first woman member of the Executive of the World Zionist Organization and in 1930 became a member of the National Council of the Jews of Palestine, heading its department of social welfare.

One of her outstanding achievements was Youth Aliya, which she took charge of in 1934 and greatly expanded. This organization rescued tens of thousands of Jewish teenagers from Nazi-dominated Europe. Miss Szold died in Jerusalem on Feb. 13, 1945.

RAPHAEL PATAI
Theodor Herzl Institute, New York City

SZYMANOWSKI, shi-mä-nôf'skē, **Karol** (1882–1937), Polish composer. He was born on Oct. 6, 1882, on the family estate near Yelizavetgrad (now Kirovograd), the Ukraine, and went to Warsaw in 1901 to study with the composer Zygmunt Noskowski. Szymanowski's first composition, *Nine Preludes for Piano*, was published in 1906. In Berlin (1906 to 1908) he came under the influence of Richard Strauss. In 1908, Szymanowski returned to Warsaw, where his First Symphony was performed that year. His second Symphony (1911) showed the influence of the Russian composer Scriabin.

Szymanowski's music later underwent a stylistic change in the direction of French impressionism, as in his String Quartet No. 1 (1917). By 1920 he was considered Poland's most important composer, and in 1926 he was appointed director of the Warsaw Conservatory. His other important works include two violin concertos and a string quartet. He died in Lausanne, Switzerland, on March 28, 1937.

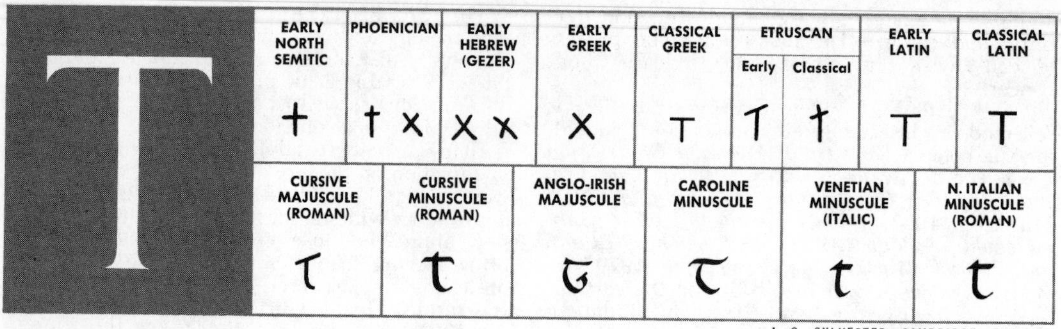

T	EARLY NORTH SEMITIC	PHOENICIAN	EARLY HEBREW (GEZER)	EARLY GREEK	CLASSICAL GREEK	ETRUSCAN Early	ETRUSCAN Classical	EARLY LATIN	CLASSICAL LATIN
	+	t ×	X X	X	T	T	T	T	T

CURSIVE MAJUSCULE (ROMAN)	CURSIVE MINUSCULE (ROMAN)	ANGLO-IRISH MAJUSCULE	CAROLINE MINUSCULE	VENETIAN MINUSCULE (ITALIC)	N. ITALIAN MINUSCULE (ROMAN)
t	t	t	t	t	t

A. C. SYLVESTER, CAMBRIDGE, ENGLAND

DEVELOPMENT OF THE LETTER T is illustrated in the above chart, beginning with the early North Semitic letter. The evolution of the majuscule (capital) T is shown at top; that of the minuscule (lower-case) at bottom.

T is the 20th letter and the 16th consonant of the English alphabet and of other European alphabets derived from Latin. It was the 19th letter of the Greek and Latin alphabets but the 22d and last letter of the original North Semitic alphabet, as it is in modern Hebrew. Its earliest known form was X or +, and the Semitic name for it is *taw*, which simply means "mark" or "sign" (as in Ezekiel 9:4). The Greeks called the letter *tau* and regularized its form. In early Greek manuscripts the letter is written +, which in time came to be written T, its final form. The minuscule (lower case) *t* is only a slight variant of the capital T.

Pronunciation. The letter *t* represents a voiceless dental explosive—a sharp mute consonant—to which *d* answers as a sonant. In English pronunciation the *t* might be classed with the cerebrals (speech sounds made with the tongue on the hard palate), but on the Continent it is a true dental because in its pronunciation the tongue comes in contact with the teeth. Its normal sound, as in "table," is generally modified by the accent. Before long *u* and after an accented vowel, it has the sound of *ch*, as in "creature," whereas before *ia* and *io*—unless the *t* is preceded by an *s*—it sounds like an *sh*, as in "palatial" or "nation." Between two consonant sounds, the *t* is mute, as in "listen."

In combination with *h*, the *t* forms two different sounds—the voiceless dental fricative sound, as in "think," and the voiced dental fricative sound, as in "the" or "than." Indeed, the Anglo-Saxon alphabet had two different letters for these two sounds, although in Old English manuscripts there was little consistency in the employment of these letters. In some words, *th* sounds like a simple *t*, as in "Thomas."

In spelling (but not in sound value) the English *th* corresponds in some German words to *d*, as in *Dank* ("thanks") and *Bruder* ("brother"). It might also be added that in some German words the English *t* is a *z*, as in *zehn* ("ten") and *Zeit* ("time").

Development of Shape. The chart above shows the development of the external form of the letter T in its 3,500 years.

Other Uses of T. T is used to refer to something shaped like the letter, such as T square and T-shirt. The expression "to a T," in which T is short for "tittle," means "to perfection."

See also ALPHABET.

DAVID DIRINGER
Author of "The Alphabet"

Further Reading: See the bibliography for ALPHABET.

TAAFFE, tä'fə, **Count Eduard von** (1833–1895), Austrian government official. During his long prime ministership from 1879 to 1893, Austria was beset by rising conflicts among its diverse nationalities that Taaffe managed to allay.

Taaffe was born in Vienna on Feb. 24, 1833. In his youth he was chosen as a companion for the future emperor Francis Joseph, and they remained lifelong friends. Taaffe entered the Austrian civil service in 1852 and became governor of Upper Austria in 1867. In the same year he was made interior minister and helped implement the constitutional changes after the Austro-Hungarian Compromise, or *Ausgleich*, of 1867. He was appointed prime minister in 1868. Taaffe wanted a more federal state organization and resigned in January 1870 when the German liberals, who favored centralism, refused their support. He returned later in 1870 as interior minister and became governor of Tyrol in 1871.

Taaffe returned to Vienna as interior minister in February 1879. He again became prime minister in August, when liberal opposition to Austrian occupation of Bosnia-Herzegovina forced Francis Joseph to make governmental changes. Taaffe's government was based on a coalition, called the Iron Ring, of Czechs, Poles, the Clerical party, and German conservatives. He made concessions to Czech demands for increased official use of their language in administration, in the courts, and in education. The University of Prague was separated into German and Czech teaching institutions. Economic legislation was also enacted. Taaffe extended the franchise, but his plans for a wider electoral reform brought defeat and retirement in 1893. Although not a great orator, he had a knack for getting along with individuals and was a skillful politician. He died in Ellischau, Bohemia, on Nov. 29, 1895.

ERNST C. HELMREICH, *Bowdoin College*

TABARI, al-, tä'bə-rē (839–923), the first great compiler of a "universal" Islamic history. Born in Amul, northern Persia, he studied in various parts of the Middle East before settling in Baghdad, when he was nearly 40, as a teacher and scholar. All his known writing is in Arabic.

Tabari's major work, *The History of Prophets and Kings*, though uneven, is an indispensable source for Islamic history prior to about 900 and for the general Islamic world view of ancient times. Most earlier sources incorporated by him have vanished. While his inspiration is religious, his scholarly citation of multiple accounts and long chains of authority for each statement is uniquely valuable—even if prejudicial to the narrative flow. This work was subsequently much abridged and adapted and also summarized in Persian and Turkish. In 1879–1901 it was restored to its original form by a team of European scholars, but only fragments of this text have been translated into Western languages.

Tabari also published a great *tafsir*, or commentary on the Koran, as well as works on Islamic law and Tradition.

G. M. Wickens
University of Toronto

TABASCO, tə-bas′kō, is a state of southeastern Mexico, on the Gulf of Mexico, bordered by Guatemala to the southeast. Its low, flat terrain slopes gently from the Chiapas Highlands to the coast. Tabasco is the Indian word for "damp earth," and the state's area of 9,783 square miles (25,337 sq km) is covered with swamps, lakes, and dense tropical forests. Heavy rains and alluvial soils make the area ideal for raising tropical products. It ranks first among the states in banana production, second in cacao, and fourth in pineapples. Chicle, rubber, and various woods are extracted from its forests. Minerals are scarce.

Communications are difficult. A main highway and a railroad cross the state from east to west. The Usumacinta and the Grijalva rivers are the main north-south arteries of communication. Both are navigable, and they have a common mouth on the Gulf of Mexico at the port city of Álvaro Obregón, sometimes called Frontera. The sparsely settled state is highly rural, and most of its residents live along the transportation routes.

Villahermosa, the capital, is on the Grijalva River and is the state's political and economic center. From 1938 to 1946 evidence of the ancient Olmec civilization was unearthed at La Venta, an island in the coastal swamps, and the archaeological treasures from the site were transferred to a museum and park in Villahermosa.

Juan de Grijalva explored the region in 1518. In 1519, Cortés founded Santa Maria de la Victoria, the first settlement on the continent, on its coast. Population: (1960) 493,340.

Reynaldo Ayala
San Diego State College

TABBY, the striped coat pattern of the domestic cat. A "tabby cat" is a striped cat, but the term is often loosely used. See Cat.

TABERNACLE, the portable sanctuary built by the Israelites when they were encamped in the desert. The description of the tabernacle is found primarily in Exodus 25–31 and 35–40. In these accounts the tabernacle is placed in the middle of the camp. A shorter account in Exodus 33:7–10 describes the tabernacle as being placed outside of the camp.

According to the longer accounts the tabernacle was a tent constructed by the architect Bezalel (Exodus 36:2) under the direction of Moses. It had an outer court where the priests offered sacrifices. The structure itself was made of various textiles and had a framework of acacia wood. Inside the tabernacle and behind a curtain was the Holy of Holies, which contained the Ark of the Covenant (see Ark). Also in the tabernacle was a seven-branched golden candelabra (Menorah) and an altar on which incense was burned. The metals used on the altar on other fittings were gold, silver, and brass. The high priest entered the Holy of Holies only once a year on Yom Kippur (the Day of Atonement).

Some scholars feel that as it is described the tabernacle would have been too elaborate a structure for a transient people. These scholars believe that the Exodus accounts reflect the period of Solomon's temple rather than Moses' times.

In Old Testament accounts the tabernacle moved with the Israelites through the desert on the way to the promised land of Canaan. It is last mentioned in II Chronicles 1:5.

"Tabernacle" in Roman Catholic usage refers to the receptacle in which the hosts (bread) consecrated at Mass are kept. The tabernacle is normally placed on the main altar of the church.

Edward T. Sandrow
Rabbi, Temple Beth El, Cedarhurst, N.Y.

TABERNACLES, Feast of, a Jewish festival celebrated in the fall. Called *Sukkot* in Hebrew, it begins five days after the Day of Atonement, on the 15th day of the Hebrew month of Tishri. It is mentioned in Exodus 23:16 as the "feast of the harvest" and in Leviticus 23:37 as the "feast of Tabernacles."

The harvest symbols of the holiday described in Scripture are retained to this day. In the synagogue and in the home, blessings are recited over the palm branch (*lulav*), citron (*etrog*), myrtle (*hadassah*), and willow twigs (*shannat*)—all held together and gently swayed. It is traditional to build and take meals in a *Sukkah* or tabernacle—a tentlike structure—in commemoration of the period when the Israelites wandered in the desert and lived in tents (*Sukkot*). The Bible indicates that the festival lasted 8 days, the eighth being the "Feast of Conclusion" (*Shemini Atzeret*). Later a ninth day was added, called *Simhat Torah* or "Rejoicing of the Torah." In the United States, Orthodox and Conservative Jews observe the full nine days, but Reform Jews keep eight days.

Edward T. Sandrow
Rabbi, Temple Beth El, Cedarhurst, N. Y.

FEAST OF TABERNACLES is observed by Orthodox Jews bearing bound palms, myrtle, willow, and a citron.

LOUIS GOLDMAN, FROM RAPHO GUILLUMETTE

METROPOLITAN MUSEUM OF ART

TILT-TOP TABLE of carved walnut, in an Italian design of the 16th century.

TAYLOR AND DULL

LOUIS XV WRITING TABLE, of 18th century French design.

KNOLL INTERNATIONAL

PEDESTAL TABLE of molded plastic, by Eero Saarinen.

TABLE, a piece of furniture generally composed of a horizontal top with vertical supports or legs to raise it from the floor. Although some primitive societies never developed the table, among most peoples it has been one of the basic types of furniture. Table styles differ considerably from region to region and period to period, but the fundamental form is unchanged.

Early Forms. Surviving Egyptian tables, dating from about 1600 to 1500 B. C., are small wooden rectangles with four legs connected by stretchers, or rungs. Greek and Roman tables, with extant examples in marble and bronze, were round or rectangular and stood on three or four legs, a pedestal, or two slabs. In the Middle East and Japan, areas where it was customary to sit on the ground, wooden tables were low and portable. Chinese tables, used with chairs or stools, were larger, carefully proportioned wooden rectangles.

In the medieval West most tables were crude series of boards placed on trestles and dismantled after use. The long, narrow refectory table found in monasteries was permanently fixed on trestles. In the Renaissance the refectory table continued for secular use, supported by fat balusters, heavy slabs, or four legs connected by stretchers. There was also a return to classic Greek and Roman forms and ornament. These early tables were used principally for dining, although they might serve as altars or for writing.

Later Forms. In the 16th and 17th centuries, European tables showed baroque influence. Elaborately carved pedestals and legs, sometimes representing human forms, gave a feeling of solidity and a sculpturesque quality. In the 18th century, tables were decorated with delicate curved ornament in the rococo style, then with light rectilinear designs derived from the classical.

During these centuries, as domestic life became more complex, a variety of table forms developed. A common 16th century form was the draw table. Just under the top was a second top in two sections, which could be drawn out to increase the size of the table. Another form was the drop leaf table composed of a fixed center section with two suspended leaves that could be raised and supported by brackets or slides or by a swinging leg. The latter type was called a gatelegged table. English 18th century dining tables could be pulled apart in the middle and extra leaves inserted.

There were also tables for different purposes. Console tables for display were fastened directly to the wall or placed against it resting on a bracket, pedestal, or legs and were decorated on one side only. A related form was the side table, for the service of food, from which the sideboard developed. The writing table, or library table, was created by placing drawers below a table top. There were also small tables for sewing, reading, playing cards and other games, and serving tea. Some had hinged tops that tilted vertically. Dressing tables, for both men and women, were closely related to cabinets and had intricate arrangements of mirrors and drawers.

In the 20th century, tables continued to be made in traditional forms and styles. New materials and techniques, however, made possible new kinds of tables in glass, metal, or plastic. Some incorporate supports and top in one solid geometric shape.

JOSEPH T. BUTLER
Author of "American Antiques, 1800–1900"

TABLE TENNIS is an indoor game for two or four players, who use a small wooden racket to hit a hollow celluloid ball over a net stretched across a table. When two persons play, the game is called singles. When four play, with two on each side, the version is known as doubles. Played throughout the world by persons of varying skills and ages, table tennis is also a highly competitive international sport.

Under the trademark Ping-Pong the game became a parlor craze in Europe and the United States early in the 20th century. After World War I, with its name changed to table tennis and equipment standardized, the game became international. The Middle Europeans were dominant until 1952 when, at the Bombay World Championships, the Japanese took the lead. In 1959 at Dortmund, West Germany, China took the men's singles title and remained dominant for eight years. In 1967, with internal turmoil disrupting China, Japanese players regained ascendancy.

The International Table Tennis Federation (ITTF) was founded in 1926 by seven European countries—Germany, Austria, Hungary, England, Wales, Sweden, and Czechoslovakia. From 1927 to 1957 the ITTF held annual championships in men's and women's singles and doubles, and in mixed doubles. Since 1957 championships have been held biennially. Emblematic of world team supremacy since 1927 is the Swaythling Cup for men and, since 1934, the Marcel Corbillon Cup for women. By the 1970's the ITTF had a membership of nearly 100 nations, having become one of the largest sports federations in the world. The American affiliate is the U. S. Table Tennis Association, organized in 1933.

THE NEW YORK TIMES

TABLE TENNIS world champion, Shigeo Ito of Japan, uses a penholder grip and an unusually small bat.

Equipment. The playing area is a rectangular table 9 feet (2.74 meters) long and 5 feet (1.5 meters) wide. The playing surface is 2 feet 6 inches (76.2 cm) from the ground. The surface is edged with ¾-inch (1.9 cm) white end and side lines. A white line the length of the table divides it into four sections, or courts. These are used only in doubles. A 6-foot long (2-meter) and 6-inch high (15.24 cm) net across the center, parallel to the end lines, divides the table in half.

The racket must be of wood and may be of any weight, size, or shape. Pimpled rubber or a layer of cellular rubber surfaced by pimpled rubber may cover the blade. The white ball is about 1½ inches (37.2 mm) in diameter and weighs about 1/10 ounce (2.40 grams).

Basic Rules. To begin, the server, determined by toss, stands behind the end of the table and hits the ball after projecting it upward from the open palm of the free hand. The ball must strike first the server's court and then, passing over the net, strike the receiver's court. The receiver returns the ball directly into the service court. Thereafter, server and receiver alternately endeavor to make a good return. When one fails to do so, the opponent scores a point. Volleying, that is, striking the ball before it bounces once, is not permitted. Service alternates after each 5 points. A serve that touches the net and drops on the receiver's court is a "let" and does not count.

A game is won by the first player or team with 21 points. If both reach 20 points, play continues with service alternating after each point until one side gains a 2-point margin. A match is the best of three or of five games.

In doubles, the ball must be struck alternately by each partner, and the service must always be from the server's right-hand court to the receiver's right-hand court. The order of service in a game between AB and XY is A to X, X to B, B to Y, and Y to A, and so on.

Techniques. There are two basic grips: the "shakehands" and the Asian "penholder" grip. By far the greatest number of players use the shakehands grip. In this grip the player holds the racket so that the blade rests in the "Y"

SHAKEHANDS GRIP OF BAT

Both front (left) and back sides are used in play.

PENHOLDER GRIP OF BAT

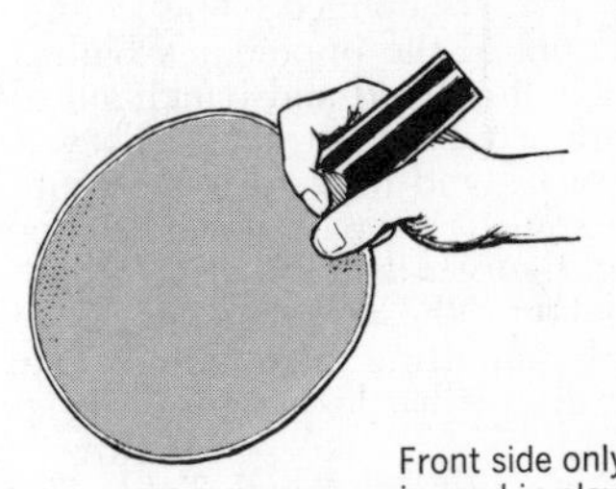

Front side only is used in play.

IMPARTING SPIN TO THE BALL

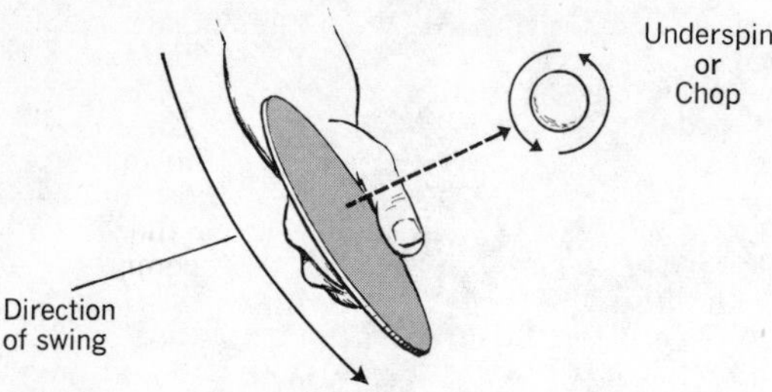

With underspin the ball rotates toward the hitter. The ball will not come through to the opponent. It checks on bounce. When it hits the receiver's bat, the ball shoots downward. Offset underspin by aiming high.

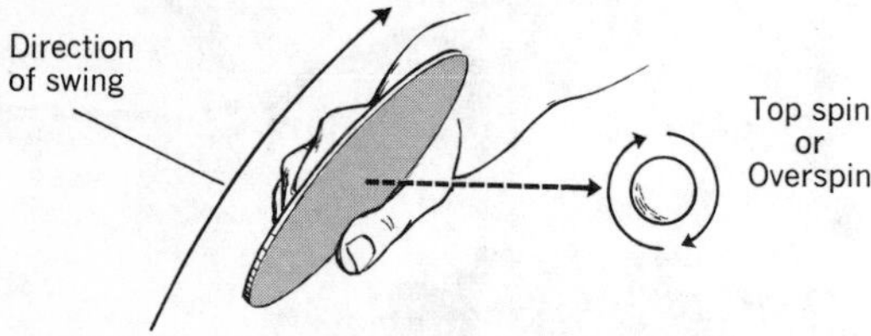

Top spin imparts a dipping flight to the ball, which accelerates forward on bounce. With top spin the ball bounds forward to the opponent and "climbs up on his bat." Offset top spin by aiming down.

formed by the thumb and forefinger, the thumb resting on the front side of the blade and the forefinger along the back. Thus both sides of the racket can be used. In the penholder grip, the racket is held between the thumb and forefinger like a pen, the blade downward and the remaining fingers spread against the back. Only one side of the racket can thus be used.

The basic strokes are the half volley, block, forehand and backhand drives, and forehand and backhand chops. Control of the ball at any speed is accomplished by imparting spin to the ball. With top spin, or overspin, the ball rotates toward the opponent and shoots forward on bounce. With underspin, or chop, the ball rotates away from the opponent and checks on bounce. As each shot is played, the player turns to face the ball, using short shuffling steps forward or backward to bring the ball within striking distance.

In the half volley, the player meets the ball at the height of its bounce with a forward and downward movement of the racket and, with underspin, literally pushes the ball across the net. He accomplishes a block shot by angling the face of the racket directly in the path of the ball just after its bounce. This counteracts the speed and spin of the opponent's ball.

The forehand and backhand drives are fundamental attacking strokes. They are played with a forward and upward movement of the racket as top spin is imparted. The player moves his weight forward at impact. Chop shots are used in defense, the racket moving forward and downward, imparting underspin. The ball is played late, after it has lost much of its speed.

H. Roy Evans, *President*
International Table Tennis Federation

TABLETS OF THE LAW. See Ten Commandments.

TABOO, a prohibition applying to something that is forbidden or set apart because it is sacred, consecrated, or unclean—and therefore is considered dangerous. A person, a place, an object, or an act can be taboo. A taboo is enforced by supernatural sanctions. That is, those who believe in the taboo expect that anyone who breaks it will automatically suffer death, illness, or some other misfortune. The taboo may also be enforced by social sanctions. In 19th century Hawaii, for example, a man who broke a taboo could be put to death by his fellows.

The term is Polynesian in origin and is also spelled tabu, tapu, or kapu. It was introduced into English in the late 18th century by Capt. James Cook.

The South Pacific. In the South Pacific taboos were highly developed. Polynesians believed that tribal chiefs had so much supernatural power that commoners were endangered by contact with the person or possessions of the chief. The chief, therefore, was taboo, and on many islands a "talking chief" was required to act for him in dealing with the people. Certain places were also taboo. The forests of New Zealand were normally taboo, although the taboo could be lifted temporarily by suitable ritual to permit lumbering or hunting. When a chief wished to assure a supply of food for a feast or other occasion, he placed a taboo on certain trees, land, or fishing grounds until the food was needed. A commoner protected his fruit trees or gardens from theft by placing a taboo on them. Individuals were subject to taboos at certain times. A pregnant woman was restricted by a number of food taboos, the breaking of which would result in deformities in the offspring. On the death of a chief the whole community became taboo, and its members were forbidden to engage in normal activities such as cooking, gardening, fishing, or singing.

Scholarly Studies. In the late 19th century scholars became interested in the nature of taboo and studied it in other cultures. William Robertson Smith in *The Religion of the Semites* (1889) gave special attention to Jewish and Muslim taboos, and Sir James Frazer devoted a whole volume in *The Golden Bough* (1911–1915) to taboos among primitive and ancient peoples. While anthropologists were studying taboos in primitive societies, psychologists became interested through reading the works of Smith and Frazer. Wilhelm Wundt saw the origin of taboos in a primitive fear of demonic powers, which in a later stage of social evolution split into dual feelings of veneration and horror.

Sigmund Freud, stimulated by Wundt and Frazer, sought in his *Totem and Taboo* (1913) to relate primitive taboos to modern psychoneuroses. He was particularly concerned with incest taboos, the almost universal prohibition on sexual relations between close kin. Developing Wundt's theory that taboos are based on both veneration and horror, Freud introduced the concept of ambivalence, in which both primitive taboos and modern phobias are explained as repulsions from objects, persons, or acts that are subconsciously desired or venerated. Although Freud's use of data on primitive peoples was often naive, his concept of ambivalence had considerable impact on psychoanalytic theory.

In addition to its special usage in anthropology and other social sciences, the word *taboo* has become a part of the general vocabulary of English and other western European languages, in the meaning of "forbidden by tradition or social usage."

ELIZABETH E. BACON
Michigan State University

Further Reading: Steiner, Franz, *Taboo* (Baltimore, Md., 1968).

TABOR, tā′bər, **Horace Austin Warner** (1830–1899), American mining magnate, who led in developing bonanza silver mining in Colorado. He was born in Holland, Vt., on Nov. 26, 1830, worked there as a stonecutter, and farmed in Kansas.

Tabor joined the Pike's Peak gold rush in 1859. The next year, he went to the headwaters of the Arkansas River, where he was a miner and maintained a store. He also grubstaked prospectors. In 1878 two of them, George Hook and August Rische, discovered the silver lode that became the Little Pittsburgh Mine. For a $17 grubstake, Tabor received one third of this immensely productive find. Valuable mining enterprises, notably the Matchless Mine, were developed on land he acquired nearby. Soon Tabor had a fortune estimated at $9 million.

He became a lavish and ostentatious spender. He gave an opera house to Leadville and became that city's first mayor and postmaster in 1878. Tabor was lieutenant governor of Colorado (1879–1883) and sat for 30 days in the U. S. Senate to fill an unexpired term in 1883. He divorced his wife and in 1882 was secretly married to Elizabeth McCourt (Baby) Doe, a young divorcée whom he remarried publicly at the Willard Hotel in Washington on March 1, 1883, with President Chester A. Arthur as the guest of honor.

The panic of 1893 left Tabor bankrupt. In 1898, poor and broken, he was made postmaster of Denver. He died there in April 10, 1899. "Baby" Doe spent her last years in poverty in a shack near the Matchless Mine, where she was found frozen to death on March 7, 1935. See also BALLAD OF BABY DOE.

WILLIAM GREENLEAF
University of New Hampshire

TABOR, tā′bər, **Mount,** a mountain in Israel frequently mentioned in the Old Testament and traditionally held by Christians to be the site of the transfiguration of Jesus. Tabor is situated about 5 miles (8 km) southeast of Nazareth in the northeast corner of the Plain of Jezreel. Composed of limestone, its steep sides rise to a domelike top approximately 1,875 feet (571.5 meters) above sea level. In Biblical times it was surrounded by forests and woods.

In Psalm 89:12 the mountain is referred to as a symbol of God's "might." In Jeremiah 46:18, Tabor is used as a sign of God's constancy. According to Judges 4:6–14 the battle Deborah and Barak waged against Sisera took place in the vicinity of Tabor. The mountain was fortified under King Antiochus III of Syria in 218 B. C.

Mt. Tabor is not specifically mentioned in the New Testament, but it is traditionally believed to be the place where Jesus appeared with Moses and Elijah before three of His disciples. (Matthew 17:1–8; Mark 9:2–8; Luke 9:28–36).

EDWARD T. SANDROW
Rabbi, Temple Beth El, Cedarhurst, N.Y.

TABORITES, tā′bə-rīts, the name of the radical faction of the 15th century Hussites. The designation was derived from Mt. Tabor, their stronghold in Bohemia near Prague. After the burning of Bohemia's national and religious hero, Jan Hus, by the Council of Constance in 1415, the country burst into revolt against the pope, the emperor, and the council. The Taborites, most militant and violent of the rebels, were under the leadership of General Žižka, a brilliant commander. They defended themselves for some time against the forces of Emperor Sigismund as well as the armies of the Calixtines, the moderate and more orthodox followers of Hus. For a short time the Taborites carried their crusade into some of the eastern provinces of Germany. The Taborites soon split into factions, and their dissolution was accelerated by the defeat of the more radical of them at the Battle of Lipany in 1434. See HUSSITES.

Taborites repudiated all traditional Catholic theology and sacramental practice, advocating a Christian life of fanatical simplicity. Their religious ideas were combined with leveling social and political doctrines. The Taborites in many ways resembled the radical Anabaptists of a century later, who may have been influenced by this Hussite faction.

POWEL MILLS DAWLEY
General Theological Seminary

TABRIZ, ta-brīz′, a city in Iran, is situated in the extreme northwest of the country close to both Turkey and the USSR, some 390 miles (628 km) by road from Teheran, the national capital. Long the chief center of the region of Azerbaijan, Tabriz is now the capital of East Azerbaijan ostan (province).

It is located within a natural amphitheater, about 4,900 feet (1,495 meters) above sea level, with hills on three sides and an extensive plain on the fourth. The meager Aji River runs through the city, some 40 miles (65 km) above its entrance into salty Lake Urmia (Rizaiyeh). Tabriz has wide, paved avenues and modern public utility facilities. The University of Tabriz is located on the outskirts of the city. Many of the inhabitants of Azerbaijan are of old Turkish stock, and both Turkish and Persian are currently spoken in Tabriz.

A broad (Russian) gauge rail line joins Tabriz with Dzhulfa (Julfa) on the Soviet frontier and ties into the Soviet rail system, while a standard gauge line runs from Tabriz to Teheran. The province is a rich agricultural region, and much of its wheat, fruit, and grapes is handled in the bazaars of Tabriz. The city is noted for the production of carpets, silverware, and leather.

History. Tabriz long lay on a major trade route between the West and the Orient, and for many centuries it was a flourishing center of commerce and trade. Near the end of the 13th century it became the capital of the Mongol Il-Khan empire, and Marco Polo, who visited it, called Tabriz a great and noble city. Timur (Tamerlane) sacked it in 1392. In the very beginning of the 16th century, it was briefly the capital of the new Safavid dynasty of Iran. The city, however, lay directly in the path of the warring armies of Iran and of the Ottoman empire. Ottoman Turks seized it after the Battle of Chaldiran in 1514 and held it for long periods until the first half of the 18th century. The city failed to regain its early prosperity,

WORLD WIDE PHOTOS

BLUE MOSQUE, built in the 15th century and now in ruins, is one of the few remaining monuments in Tabriz.

although during the 19th and early 20th centuries it was traditional for the crown princes of the Kajar dynasty to live at Tabriz.

The city lies within an active earthquake belt, and it has suffered severely over the centuries. Its older walls have completely vanished, and there are few surviving monuments of major historical periods. The towering brick walls of the so-called Ark, or citadel, are actually the remains of the 14th century mosque of Ali Shah. The badly battered Blue Mosque, built in the 1400's, still displays splendid panels of carved alabaster and surfaces clad with light and dark blue faience mosaic. Population: (1963) 404,855.

DONALD N. WILBER
Author of "Iran Past and Present"

TACHÉ, tȧ-shā′, **Sir Étienne Paschal** (1795–1865), Canadian political leader, who was a prime mover in Confederation. He was born on Sept. 5, 1795, at St.-Thomas-de-Montmagny, Lower Canada. Educated at Quebec Seminary, he served in the British forces in the War of 1812. Thereafter, he studied medicine at Laval University and practiced in his native parish. From 1841 to 1846 he represented L'Islet constituency in the legislative assembly of the United Canadas. From 1846 to 1848 he was deputy adjutant general of militia for Canada East. He became receiver general in five successive ministries and was also a member of the legislative council from 1848 to 1864, and speaker of its upper house from 1856 to 1858. In the latter year he was knighted, and in 1860 was named aide-de-camp of Queen Victoria and honorary colonel in the British Army. During the militia crisis of 1863, he wrote *Quelques réflexions sur l'organisation des volontaires et de la milice,* in which he criticized the proposed reorganization.

In 1864 he was called from retirement to become prime minister in the coalition ministry that had been formed to achieve Confederation, and he presided at the Quebec Conference of 1865. But before the federal union for which he had labored was achieved, Taché died at his birthplace on July 30, 1865.

CORNELIUS J. JAENEN, *University of Ottawa*

TACHINA FLY, tak′ə-nə, any fly of the family Tachinidae, the largest family of flies in North America, with more than 1,300 species. Most species are beneficial to man because they parasitize a number of important insect pests, particularly the destructive caterpillars and pupae of moths, butterflies, some sawflies, and the adults of a few Orthoptera (chiefly locusts) and Hemiptera (bugs).

Tachina flies have robust, bristly bodies and range in length from about 1/10 to 7/10 of an inch (3–18 mm). They attack their hosts in various ways. Some attach their eggs to the host, others place their eggs in or over the host's food, and still others deposit living larvae in or on the host. A host that is invaded by tachina larvae usually dies.

Many kinds of tachina flies have been used in the biological control of such pests as the European corn borer, gypsy moth, and browntailed moth. One of the best-known species, the red-tailed tachina (*Winthemia quadripustulata*) attacks more than 50 types of caterpillars.

RALPH H. DAVIDSON, *Ohio State University*

TACHISTOSCOPE, tə-kis′tə-skōp, an instrument that provides a brief, timed exposure of visual stimuli. It is used in experimental psychology to study visual perception. The stimuli—words, symbols, or pictures—can be exposed for 1/10 to 1/100 of a second, regulated either by interrupted lighting, a falling screen, or a camera shutter. With the falling screen, the stimuli are viewed through an aperture as the screen moves rapidly across it. In a projection tachistoscope two slide projectors, containing camera shutters, alternate in momentarily projecting stimuli on a screen. Experiments have involved the effect of suggestion, of interest of the individual, and of type of stimuli on the accuracy of perception.

TACHOMETER, ta-kä′mə-tûr, an instrument that indicates the revolutions per minute (rpm) of a rotating shaft, such as an automobile or airplane engine crankshaft, or of other machinery. Most tachometers have a pointer that moves over a dial to provide a direct reading of rpm.

Hand tachometers, either mechanical or electrical in operation, are brought into contact with the rotating end of a shaft so that the tachometer rotates at the shaft speed. In mechanical tachometers, weights attached to a rotating spindle swing out by centrifugal force against the action of a spring and move the indicating pointer over a dial. In electric types, a rotating armature generates a current that is indicated as rpm on the dial. Such a tachometer is really a millameter or a voltmeter, indicating the output of a small generator turning at shaft speed.

A vibrating-reed tachometer is used when it is impossible for instrumentation to reach a rotating shaft. This tachometer has a number of metallic strips (reeds), each attuned to vibrate at a frequency in the normal operating range of a machine. The rotational speed of the machine is thus shown by the visible vibration of a reed in resonance with the speed of rotation. In other instances in which instrumentation cannot reach the rotating shaft, belt drive or gearing is used to drive a tachometer, usually of the electric type.

The strobotac and similar instruments are also used as tachometers. In a strobotac, an electronically controlled light, the frequency of which can be changed, flashes on a rotating part of the machine. When the flashes reach synchronization with the machine, the machine appears to be standing still; a calibrated dial then indicates the speed of rotation or frequency of oscillation.

In another device a magnetic or mechanical pickup coupled to the shaft transmits a series of impulses which are integrated by a timing device, such as an electric clock, to provide a direct reading of rpm. Still another arrangement incorporates a so-called Arago's disk—a metal plate that, rotating in a magnetic field, creates a torque. This torque, when resisted by spring action, can be calibrated to indicate the speed of the shaft that drives the disk.

BURGESS H. JENNINGS
Northwestern University

TACHYCARDIA, tak-i-kärd'ē-ə, is a rapid beating of the heart, usually more than 100 beats per minute. It may be caused by strenuous exercise, emotional stress, or disease.

TACHYLYTE, tak'ə-līt, is a black volcanic rock consisting of basalt in a glassy form. Such glassy basalt is produced when lava cools rapidly at the earth's surface as it flows from an erupting volcano. Tachylite may also be found as a lining material in some dikes, probably because the intruding volcanic material lost heat very rapidly where it came in contact with the surrounding rocks and cooled before any crystals could form. See also BASALT.

TACHYON, tak'ə-on, a hypothetical subatomic particle that travels faster than the speed of light in free space, which is about 300,000 kilometers per second, or 186,000 mph. Its name is derived from the Greek word *tachys* meaning "swift." While it has often been stated that the special theory of relativity implies that nothing can travel faster than light, in reality that theory rules out only the possibility of accelerating a particle from a speed below that of light to a speed greater than that of light. Such acceleration is not required in the theory of tachyons, which is consistent with relativity, because these particles always travel faster than light and hence need not be accelerated through the "light barrier."

If tachyons indeed exist, their energy and momentum would be real quantities and could be measured by their interactions with ordinary objects. One unusual property that tachyons would have is that their kinetic energy would decrease as their speed increases. Hence, a tachyon that radiates away some of its energy would speed up, eventually reaching infinite speed as its energy approached zero. On the other hand, a tachyon that gains energy from some outside source would slow down, and its speed would come closer to the speed of light but never go below it.

Several experiments have been performed in an effort to create and detect tachyons. These experiments are based on the hypothesis that if tachyons exist, then, like other subatomic particles, it should be possible to create them in reactions between known particles, even if no tachyons were present at the beginning of the experiment. As of 1970, none of the experiments succeeded in creating and detecting tachyons. Whether this means that tachyons do not in fact exist, or whether future experiments of a different type will reveal them, remains uncertain.

GERALD FEINBERG
Columbia University

TACITUS, tas'ə-təs, **Cornelius** (c.55–c.118 A. D.), one of the greatest Roman historians. Little is known of his life. Roughly accurate guesses can be made about the years of his birth and death, but his parents are unknown. He was a Roman senator who began his official career under Emperor Vespasian (reigned 69–79 A. D.). He reached the consulship under Emperor Nerva in 97 and was proconsul of Asia, probably in 112–113, under Emperor Trajan.

Although Tacitus' political career was relatively distinguished and his reputation as an orator and a lawyer was very high in his day, it is as a writer and particularly as a historian that he is famous today. Five of his literary works survive, two of them—the *Annals* and the *Histories*—only in part.

Works. Tacitus' earliest work was the *Dialogue on Oratory*, probably written about the year 80, in which he discusses the decline of oratory in Rome after the days of Cicero. His next work, published in 98, was a biography of his father-in-law, *The Life of Gnaeus Julius Agricola.* Agricola, a Roman senator and general, had been instrumental in the conquest of Britain. In the same year Tacitus published a book on the tribes of Germany, *De origine et situ Germanorum*, also known as the *Germania.* It is one of the major sources of information about the German tribes before the barbarian invasions of Rome. All three of these early works are short—fewer than 50 pages each in most editions.

Tacitus' greatest works are two long histories covering the 1st century A. D., the period of the Julio-Claudian and Flavian emperors from Tiberius through Domitian (14–96). The first to be written, the *Histories*, covered the last third of the century, the period of the Flavian emperors from 69 to 96. Unfortunately most of the *Histories* is lost. All that survive are the first four books and a few chapters of the fifth dealing with the years 69 and 70. The *Histories* must have been very long because the fragments that exist today total more than 200 pages in most editions.

Tacitus' last and most impressive work was the *Annals*, covering the history of the Julio-Claudian Rome (14–68) year by year. Only part of the *Annals* has survived, but the existing books amount to about 400 pages in most editions. The *Annals* is particularly famous for the opening books on the reign of Emperor Tiberius, in which Tacitus sets forth in powerful, cryptic Latin prose his personal view of Tiberius and his general view of the Roman emperorship.

Tacitus' Views and Approach. Tacitus believed that the Roman emperors of the 1st century were evil and capricious men who stifled republican freedoms, practiced arbitrary despotism while hypocritically claiming to champion free institutions, and indulged themselves in moral degeneracy. Under such emperors, according to Tacitus, the Roman Senate was transformed into a body of sycophants who "rushed into slavery." Tacitus blamed the first Roman emperor, Augustus, for creating the despotism, but directed most of his venom at Augustus' successor Tiberius, an emperor who "plunged into every wickedness and disgrace."

Tacitus' extremely critical view of most of the emperors of the 1st century and his rancorous, virulent prose style have combined to make him the most controversial of all the major Roman historians. In other respects he is very much like his contemporaries. He made no significant methodological contribution to ancient historiography. He was a didactic annalist who saw the gods occasionally at work in the course of human affairs, although he was usually content with secular rather than divine explanations of causation.

In general, Tacitus was a careful researcher, and even his severest critics ordinarily concede that his facts are accurate. There are mistakes in his works, but no more than in the works of other major historians of antiquity.

He differs from other ancient historians only in his unrelieved pessimism. He was even gloomier than Thucydides. In a famous aside in the *Annals* he wrote: "So now, after a revolution, when Rome is nothing but the realm of a single despot, there must be good in carefully noting and recording this period. . . . Still, though this is instructive, it gives very little pleasure. . . . I have to present in succession the merciless biddings of a tyrant, incessant persecutions, faithless friendships, and the ruin of innocence, the same causes issuing in the same results, and I am everywhere confronted by a wearisome monotony in my subject matter."

Evaluations of Tacitus. Modern scholars have generally been rather critical of Tacitus. Tacitus began his *Annals* by saying that he was going to write the history of the Julio-Claudian dynasty "without either bitterness or partiality," a claim that seems unjustified by the acrimonious account that follows. Tacitus obviously had a partisan, senatorial bias against the emperors, and some modern historians have argued that Tacitus' bias was so strong that he deliberately misinterpreted the facts. At several points in his narrative Tacitus relates apparently decent and responsible actions or statements by Emperor Tiberius and then through skillful use of innuendo imputes mean and petty motives. Tacitus also accused Tiberius and other emperors of conducting reigns of terror by arbitrary use of the treason laws against senators. Modern historians have argued that many senators were actually guilty of conspiring against the emperors, as Tacitus' own facts show.

After World War II, however, Tacitus' reputation as a historian improved. Modern scholars more readily admit the arbitrary and absolute nature of the Julio-Claudian and Flavian dynasties. Many senators were executed or exiled in the 1st century A. D. Although these senators were frequently guilty of treason, having conspired against the emperors, some historians now argue, in general agreement with Tacitus, that the conspiracies were justified by the repressive nature of the imperial regimes. There are enough documented cases of innocent victims to lend some credence to Tacitus' sense of outrage.

Tacitus, nevertheless, remains a controversial historian, and he probably always will be. No one who reads him can fail to be impressed by the power of his narration. But some readers, in sympathy with Tacitus, will react strongly against the emperors, and others will cast his historical works aside as embittered, partisan diatribes.

ARTHER FERRILL
University of Washington

Further Reading: Syme, Ronald, *Tacitus,* 2 vols. (London 1958); Tacitus, Cornelius, *Complete Works,* tr. by A. J. Church and W. J. Brodribb (New York 1942); Walker, Bessie, *The Annals of Tacitus* (New York 1952).

TACITUS, tas′ət-əs, **Marcus Claudius** (died 276 A. D.), Roman emperor. After the death of Emperor Aurelian, the Roman armies asked the Senate to select the next emperor, and Tacitus, an elderly and respected senator, was finally chosen. His reign was brief—from September 275 to about March 276—but he did win a victory over the Goths in Asia Minor before he was apparently murdered by his own troops at Tyana in Cappadocia. He attempted but failed to reestablish senatorial control over the army.

ARTHER FERRILL
University of Washington

TACKLE, a device used for lifting. See BLOCK AND TACKLE.

TACNA-ARICA QUESTION, täk′nä ä-rē′kä, a long dispute between Peru and Chile over the border districts of Tacna and Arica. Chile, victorious in the War of the Pacific against Peru and Bolivia, controlled the Peruvian south coastal territories of Tacna, Arica, and Tarapacá. By the terms of the Treaty of Ancón, ratified by Peru and Chile in 1884, Peru ceded the province of Tarapacá to Chile. But the final possession of Tacna and Arica was to be determined by a plebiscite to be held after 10 years of Chilean occupation and administration. (See also WAR OF THE PACIFIC.) The two countries could not agree on the conditions and procedures of the plebiscite, and it was never held. The dispute festered, leading to a break in diplomatic relations in 1910 and to the verge of renewed open warfare in 1919.

Chilean President Arturo Alessandri Palma recognized that his nation's ultranationalist posture was depriving Chile of hemispheric leadership, and he reestablished communication with Peru in 1922. Attempts by the United States to mediate the dispute between 1922 and 1926 failed. In 1928 representatives of Chile and Peru agreed to abandon the plebiscitary approach and to assign Tacna to Peru and Arica to Chile. Fearing outraged reactions from chauvinists of both countries to this compromise solution, the governments asked Frank B. Kellogg, U. S. secretary of state, to make the proposal, thus allowing both governments to placate domestic opposition by alleging pressure from the United States. Under the terms of the final agreement, signed on July 28, 1929, Chile paid an indemnity of $6,000,000 to Peru, promised to build a rail link between the oasis city of Tacna and the sea port at Arica, and to provide a free port for the passage of Peruvian goods.

JOHN N. PLANK, *The Brookings Institution*

WASHINGTON STATE DEPARTMENT OF COMMERCE AND ECONOMIC DEVELOPMENT

Tacoma Narrows Bridge over an inlet of Puget Sound is a major traffic artery. The city is in the background.

TACOMA, tə-kō′mə, a city in southwestern Washington, the seat of Pierce county, is situated on Puget Sound, 30 miles (48 km) south of Seattle. It is the third-largest city in the state, a leading port, and an industrial and wholesale center.

Tacoma has a fine natural setting. The city's residential districts have sweeping mountain and marine vistas. The Olympic Mountains are visible to the northwest, and snow-capped Mount Rainier in the Cascade Range rises in the east. The suburban areas are dotted with many lakes. There are many kinds of recreational opportunities, including mountain climbing and skiing at Mount Rainier National Park, about 40 miles (64 km) to the southeast. Tacoma's climate is equable, with mild winters and cool summers.

The port of Tacoma in Commencement Bay, a fine natural harbor, is a thriving industrial complex, comprising more than 4,000 acres (1,620 hectares), and has easy access to transcontinental railways, airports, and major highways. Wheat, flour, and lumber account for a substantial share of the cargo moved from the port's 23 deepwater berths, but other products such as raw rubber from Malaysia and meat from Australia are also handled.

Tacoma's major industries, many of them located within or near the port, include shipbuilding, copper smelting and refining, aluminum reduction, and the manufacture of ferroalloys and of iron, steel, and bronze castings. Other establishments produce electrochemicals, mineral wool, furniture, men's clothing, and a variety of forest products including doors, lumber and millwork, plywood, pulp, and paper. Tacoma is also a major chemical center, making ammonia, plastics, explosives, paints, and adhesives.

The educational facilities of Tacoma include the University of Puget Sound and Tacoma Community College in the city, Pacific Lutheran University in nearby Parkland, and Fort Steilacoom Community College, situated in the suburban lakes district.

The city has an extensive park system. Point Defiance Park offers large areas of wilderness, an aquarium, a zoo, a boathouse, a special park for children, a replica of a logging camp, and a restoration of Fort Nisqually, which was a trading post of the Hudson's Bay Company established in 1833. There are additional park areas outside the city limits.

Tacoma's points of interest include the Washington State Historical Museum, featuring exhibits on the state's development and artifacts of the Pacific Northwest, and the Tacoma Art Museum. The Tacoma Narrows Bridge, spanning a narrow arm of Puget Sound between the city and the Gig Harbor peninsula, was completed in 1950 and is one of the nation's longest suspension bridges. A number of military installations, including McChord Air Force Base, Camp Murray, and Fort Lewis, a U. S. military reservation, are south of the city.

Tacoma was settled in 1852, but actual development of the site was not begun until 1868 when Gen. Morton M. McCarver established a town on the west shore and called it Commencement Bay. The name was later changed to Tacoma, the Indian word for Mount Rainier. The arrival of the Northern Pacific Railway in 1887 gave impetus to growth of the community. Tacoma was incorporated as a city in 1884. It adopted the council-manager form of government in 1953. Population: 154,581.

CAROLYN J. ELSE
Pierce County Library

TACONITE, tak′ə-nīt, a low-grade iron ore, is a sedimentary rock containing hematite and magnetite. With the steady depletion of high-grade iron ores, taconite has become an important source of iron; following World War II, magnetic and gravity processes were developed to concentrate the ore for industrial use. The name "taconite" was first applied to deposits in the Lake Superior region of the United States. See also IRON—*Kinds of Iron Ore.*

TACTICS, in military science, is the art of using troops, weapons, and equipment in combat. The relationship of tactics to strategy was aptly expressed by the Prussian military philosopher Karl von Clausewitz: "The decision by arms (combat) is to all operations in war, great and small, what cash settlement is in business." *Strategy* seeks to place and maneuver one's forces in a theater of operations so as to bring them into combat under the most advantageous conditions possible. When that is accomplished, defeating the enemy in battle is a matter of tactics, and a tactical failure can nullify the most brilliant strategy.

At the start of the Chancellorsville campaign (1863) of the American Civil War, Maj. Gen. Joseph Hooker's strategy outwitted Gen. Robert E. Lee, forcing him to fight at a serious disadvantage. Once the fighting began, however, Hooker's irresolute tactics enabled Lee to seize the initiative and gain a spectacular victory.

Tactics of smaller units, or of a single combat arm, is called *minor tactics*. Tactics of large forces is termed *grand tactics*. *Tactical mobility* is the ability to move rapidly from one part of a battlefield to another. Airmobile, armored, and mechanized units normally possess this capability, but in very difficult terrain or weather only lightly equipped infantry may be capable of fast movement.

The general principles governing the conduct of tactical operations are the same principles of war that govern strategy.

Essentially commonsensical concepts, embodying generations of military experience, these principles have remained largely unchanged, but continuous technological development has required corresponding modifications in their tactical application—usually from the introduction of new weapons. During the Civil War, for example, the "rifled musket," with its greater range and accuracy, forced major changes in both grand and minor tactics.

The development of new forms of transportation and communication also makes new tactics possible. World War II "blitzkrieg" operations would have been impossible during World War I because the tanks, aircraft, and radios of 1917–1918 lacked the requisite power, range, and mechanical reliability. More recently, the helicopter has permitted the development of "airmobile" tactics.

In any particular military operation the choice of tactics will be influenced by a number of factors. These include the commander's mission, the forces and weapons available to him, the terrain over which he must operate, the enemy's strength and dispositions, and the weather. The overall military situation likewise exerts great influence. A commander defending or attacking a continuous established front, as in the Korean War or the Western Front in World War I, usually has fewer tactical options than one operating in an area where both sides hold vital bases which must be protected but neither side holds a fixed line, as in Vietnam or on the Eastern Front in World War I.

The commander's choice of tactics may be further influenced by national policy. He may be required to reduce his offensive operations in the hope of inducing the enemy to negotiate, or to assuage domestic popular opinion by reducing casualties and expenditures. Conversely, a government may adopt a policy of terrorization to cow an enemy into submission.

Modern tactics, as exemplified by combat in Southeast Asia and the Middle East, are those of mobile warfare. Their objective is the destruction of the enemy. Captured territory may be abandoned if it has no tactical or strategic value because the troops that would be required to hold it can be more effectively employed on offensive missions. The cumulative effect of such operations, however, increases the territory controlled by the victor.

TACTICAL OFFENSIVE THEORY

The object of military operations is to defeat the enemy's armed forces and destroy his will to fight. This can be accomplished only by offensive operations. The offensive also gives the attacker the initiative. He strikes at the time and place of his own choosing and thereby forces the defender to concentrate on attempting to counter his maneuvers.

Terminology. Offensive tactical operations fall into six categories: envelopments, turning movements, penetrations, frontal attacks, defensive-offensives, and pursuits. These offensive operations may be used by units of any size. In clashes between two platoon-size patrols, each usually attempts to envelop one of the other's flanks.

An offensive action is *coordinated* when the various units of the attacking command are so used as to give each other maximum assistance. These units may attack at different times to confuse the enemy. Unity of effort, rather than simultaneous actions, is the desired result. An attack in which units are used as they become available, or in which their planned coordination breaks down, is a *piecemeal attack*. Because it lets the enemy deal separately with each attacking unit, it should be avoided unless the attacker has overwhelming strength.

In offensive operations the attacker normally organizes his forces into three groupings: main attack, secondary attack, and reserve. The *main attack* is the decisive effort, which seeks to destroy the enemy. It is assigned the greatest possible proportion of troops and supporting fires. The *secondary attack* is designed to confuse the enemy, force him to commit his reserves prematurely, or otherwise reduce his capability to react effectively against the main attack. The *reserve* usually consists of mobile forces. These are committed at the decisive time and place to maintain the momentum of the main attack and to exploit its successes. Should the secondary attack achieve unexpected success that promises decisive results, the reserve may be shifted to it instead. The reserve is the attacking commander's principal means of influencing the action once his offensive is fully launched.

Enveloping Maneuvers. Envelopments are further classified as single, double, vertical, and amphibious.

Single Envelopment. In a single envelopment, which is also called simply an envelopment, the attacker attempts to fix the enemy in position by a secondary attack while his main attack overlaps one of the enemy's flanks and drives into the enemy's rear. This maneuver enables the attacker to threaten the defender's communications and overrun his supporting weapons, forcing the defender to fight in two or more directions as the main and secondary attacks converge. The main and secondary attack forces remain within mutual supporting distance, and the enemy is destroyed in and around his original position. An excellent example is Lee's attack on Hooker's right flank at Chancellorsville (1863).

Double Envelopment. This differs from the single envelopment in that there are main attacks against both of the enemy's flanks, while a secondary attack between them attempts to hold the enemy in position. A successful double envelopment can surround much of the hostile force. It is a difficult maneuver. The attacker must have considerable combat superiority, either in numbers or in the greater mobility and quality of troops, and must himself be a commander of superior skill and resolution.

The Battle of Cowpens (1781) during the Revolutionary War and the Falaise-Argentan "pocket" (1944) are outstanding examples. During World War II, the terms "encirclement" and "pincers movement" were applied to large-scale double envelopments, as by the Germans in their invasion of the USSR (1941) and by Soviet armies at Stalingrad (1942–1943).

Vertical Envelopment. In this relatively new tactical concept, airborne or airmobile troops are landed behind the enemy to cut his communications or block his efforts to withdraw. It should be combined with offensive operations against the enemy's front or flanks. Developed from World War II airborne operations, it was attempted at Sukchon-Sunchon, North Korea (1950), but achieved little success because of the limited tactical mobility of airborne troops once they had landed. The introduction of airmobile units, which have their own organic helicopters, made such operations far more effective, as in the Ia Drang campaign in South Vietnam (1965).

Amphibious Envelopment. This is a single envelopment, in which the enveloping force moves by water. It normally is more difficult to prepare and carry out successfully but can be more demoralizing because of its unexpectedness. Small-scale amphibious envelopments were used by Allied forces with limited success during the liberation of Sicily (1943). Japan used them against Filipino-American forces defending Bataan Peninsula (1942), but the enveloping forces were too weak for their mission and so were destroyed.

Turning Movements. Whereas the envelopment seeks to destroy the enemy in his position, the turning movement swings wide around one of the enemy's flanks to threaten his communications and rear-area installations. Because such a threat cannot be ignored, the enemy must move to counter it, even if this forces him to retire from an advantageous position or break off a promising offensive. A disadvantage of this maneuver is that the main attack force, which executes the turning movement, and the secondary attack force, which must fix the enemy, usually will be too widely separated for mutual support. Both therefore must be strong enough or mobile enough to avoid defeat in detail.

Penetration. A penetration is an offensive maneuver in which the main attack strikes directly at the front of the enemy position, attempting to break completely through it. One or more secondary attacks confuse the enemy as to which is the main attack and attract as many of the enemy's reserves as possible.

Once the breakthrough is achieved, the enemy line on either side of it is rolled back and enveloped, thus widening the gap. Meanwhile, mobile forces pass through to strike at objectives —reserves, communications, supply depots, air or missile bases—deep in the enemy rear. This last phase, which is called *exploitation,* must be pressed rigorously to prevent the enemy from rallying and reestablishing his front. It may be combined with vertical envelopments. A penetration is the only large-scale maneuver possible against an enemy whose flanks can be neither enveloped nor turned.

In mobile warfare a penetration is useful against an overextended enemy, or one caught attempting to establish a position. Under such conditions a penetration often can be organized and executed more rapidly than an envelopment. The Meuse-Argonne offensive (1918) of World War I is an example of a successful penetration. In fighting in jungles or other difficult terrain, a penetration may be achieved by *infiltration*—individuals or small units seep through the enemy line to regroup under cover behind his positions.

Frontal Attacks. Here, the attacker advances all along his front without grouping his forces into main and secondary efforts. The obvious disadvantage of this type of attack is that it is unlikely to be strong enough anywhere to achieve a decisive success. But it can overrun a much weaker enemy and is sometimes appropriate for a secondary attack, since it engages a wide portion of the enemy's line and initially gives the impression of greater strength than it actually possesses.

Defensive-Offensive Operations. A commander with an offensive mission may decide to stand on the defensive initially, either because of temporary combat inferiority or because he deliberately plans to trap enemy troops by luring them to attack in a certain area. By inducing enemy troops to attack first, the commander hopes to fix and wear them down and, when they are fully committed, launch a decisive counterattack with strong reserves that he holds concealed.

This operation requires great tactical skill and first-class troops. The commander must be able to conceal his intentions and lead the enemy to underestimate his strength. It remains a risky maneuver, for he must begin by surrendering the initiative, and his final success depends on the enemy reacting as he desires. Napoleon's victory at Austerlitz (1805) is the classic tactical defensive-offensive.

Pursuit. Pursuit is an offensive action against a retreating enemy—the final phase of a successful attack. Its object is the destruction of the enemy, who must be pushed unsparingly and given no opportunity to rally. Pursuit usually is conducted by two elements: a *direct-pressure force,* which continuously attacks the enemy's rear; and one or more *encircling forces,* which move swiftly around his flanks to intercept his retreat. Airborne or airmobile forces may play the latter role. Air support is particularly effective during a pursuit. Lt. Gen. Ulysses S. Grant's pursuit of Robert E. Lee from Petersburg to Appomattox remains a perfect example of pursuit.

TACTICAL DEFENSIVE THEORY

Defensive action is negative in that it cannot produce decisive results, except in such rare instances as the Battle of New Orleans (1815), where the attacker obligingly ruins his army in futile attacks against a static defense. At best, it only staves off defeat.

The defensive should be adopted only under two circumstances: (1) when sufficient forces for an offensive are not available, and the enemy must be held off while the necessary strength is built up; (2) the defensive may be assumed on one part of the front in order to concentrate maximum strength for an offensive in another sector. The defender normally has the advantage in being able to choose favorable terrain for his stand and to fortify his position, but he surrenders the initiative to the attacker.

Terminology. In practice, one command may use several types of defensive tactics, depending on its mission, the terrain, and the composition of its own and enemy forces. The principal types of tactical defensive action are *area defense* and *mobile defense*. *Cordon defense* is seldom used. If the defending force is defeated, or too weak to fight a sustained defensive battle, it must make some form of *retrograde movement*.

Another tactic is *perimeter defense*, the establishment of an all-around defensive position. In mobile warfare, as in the Vietnam War, both sides build strong perimeter defenses around their bases. To guard against surprise, units on the offensive form defensive perimeters at every halt.

Modern defense is organized in depth. Mobile *covering forces* patrol the approaches to the main defensive position, which may consist of an *outpost line* and one or more *battle positions*. Reserves, supporting artillery, and supply and service units are in the *rear area*. Normally these form defensive perimeters to guard against attacks by enemy airborne, airmobile, or guerrilla forces.

Area Defense. This type of defense is used when a specific position must be held and sufficient troops are available to man it. The greater part of the defending force is stationed in the battle position, consisting of a deep belt of fortified unit positions, each organized for all-around (perimeter) defense and sited so as to be mutually supporting. See also FORTIFICATIONS—*Field Fortifications*.

The covering forces and the troops in the outpost line attempt to inflict maximum delay and casualties on the enemy, forcing him to deploy prematurely. Forces holding the battle position rely on their firepower, and that of supporting artillery and air forces, to halt the enemy. The reserve is committed to wipe out any penetrations the enemy may make, to reinforce a threatened sector, or to deliver a limited spoiling attack to disrupt enemy preparations. Because the largest part of the defending force occupies fixed positions, it is relatively vulnerable to attacks by nuclear weapons. Against such weapons, the terrain must be organized with particular care without, however, dispersing the defensive forces so thinly that they can be easily penetrated or infiltrated by conventional (non-nuclear) offensives. This general type of defense was used by the United Nations forces during much of the Korean War (1950–1953).

Mobile Defense. This type of defensive action is suited to armored, mechanized, and airmobile forces. It is used when the terrain is unsuited to area defense, or the defending force is too small to establish an area defense in its assigned sector but has mobility equal or superior to the enemy's.

The greater part of the defending force is assigned to the reserve, the rest to the covering force and to the forward portion of the battle position. After the covering force has delayed the enemy as long as possible, the troops in the battle position oppose him by a combination of delaying tactics, the defense of key terrain features, and local counterattacks. When any unit is in danger of being overwhelmed, it withdraws to a predesignated alternate position.

These tactics slow, confuse, and weaken the enemy and "canalize" his advance into areas where he will be vulnerable to a decisive counterattack by the defender's reserves. Because of its greater dispersion and freedom of maneuver, the mobile defense is favored for a major war in which nuclear weapons may be used.

Cordon Defense. This form of defense seeks to hold a position by spreading out the available forces equally along its front. Such a defense lacks flexibility. Once it is enveloped or penetrated, the defending commander can only fall back, or attempt to shift troops from other sectors of his line to counter the attack. This further weakens his defenses, and the troops so detached seldom arrive on time. The cordon defense may be forced on a commander who must defend a wide front, as in the final Serbian stand (1915) in World War I.

Retrograde Movements. These are movements away from the enemy, either voluntary or forced by enemy action. Such movement has become increasingly dangerous with the development of air, airmobile, and armored forces that are especially adapted for pursuit. The defender therefore should have mobile reserves to counter pursuers. Retrograde movements are classified as *withdrawals, retirements, and delaying actions*.

Withdrawals. These are the operations by which a force breaks off an action and disengages itself from the enemy in order to regain, or preserve, its freedom of action. A withdrawal may be followed by a retirement, a delaying action, a defensive action in a new position, or even offensive action. Against an aggressive enemy, it is a critical operation that must be carefully controlled. Consequently, unless the terrain will conceal their movements, large units normally attempt to hold out until nightfall and withdraw under cover of darkness.

Retirements. A retirement (frequently termed a *retreat*) is a maneuver by which a force moves away from the enemy, either during preliminary maneuvering before any serious contact has been established or following a successful withdrawal. Security detachments give all-around protection to the movement. The most masterly withdrawal and retirement in recent military history was that of the United Nations forces from the Changjin reservoir to Hungnam (1950) during the Korean War.

Delaying Actions. These tactics are employed by a defending force that seeks to slow the advance of a superior enemy by trading space for time and to inflict the maximum possible punishment without becoming seriously engaged. Usually the defender accomplishes this by occupying a good defensive position and offering enough resistance to force the enemy to reconnoiter, deploy, and prepare a coordinated attack. He then withdraws to another position and repeats the process. Delaying operations require mobility and great firepower.

SPECIAL OPERATIONS

Certain types of military operations require special tactics for particular requirements.

Airborne Operations. These involve the movement of combat forces and their logistic support into the objective area by air. There are two principal types: the *link-up,* in which friendly ground forces are expected to reach the airborne forces soon, and the *independent,* in which the airborne forces are expected to operate alone for a considerable period, receiving supplies by air.

Tactical airborne operations are usually small-scale, link-up vertical envelopments. Since airborne troops and their supplies are transported by Air Force planes, considerable advance planning and coordination are necessary.

The initial landings usually are by paratroopers, followed by troops in assault aircraft that can land on short, rough fields. If airfields can be seized or longer airstrips cleared, reinforcements and supplies can be landed in larger transport aircraft. Airborne forces are extremely vulnerable while landing and immediately thereafter. They must immediately reorganize and seize their initial objectives before the enemy recovers from his surprise.

They next move out to seize an *airhead line*—a perimeter around the airstrip—large enough to prevent direct enemy fire on the airstrip. Meanwhile the buildup of troops and supplies continues. When sufficient forces are available, the commander begins the offensive operations required by his mission.

Because of weight limitations, airborne forces lack the heavier weapons, vehicles, and armor of comparable infantry units. They therefore are vulnerable to counterattacks by enemy armored forces, and their freedom of maneuver is further restricted by the need to protect their airheads. Adequate air support and effective antitank weapons and tactics are essential. The capture of key bridges in the Netherlands by American airborne troops to clear the way for British armor in Operation Market–Garden (1944) was a typical tactical link-up airborne operation.

Airmobile Operations. These are the movements of combat forces and their weapons and equipment about a battlefield in aircraft, under the control of a ground force commander to engage in ground operations. In such operations, army aviation units can move and support reconnaissance, infantry, and artillery units across almost any type of terrain, shifting them rapidly from one area to another. Since airmobile units have their own organic air vehicles, airmobile operations present fewer command and control problems and can be organized and launched more rapidly than airborne operations. They are particularly suited for mobile warfare, including counterguerrilla operations.

Amphibious Operations. These are attacks launched from the sea, involving a landing on hostile shores. They probably are the most difficult of military operations, since their success depends on precise coordination of the sea, land, and air forces involved. Typical tactical amphibious operations include amphibious envelopments, the seizure of minor offshore islands, raids, reconnaissance, or amphibious withdrawal of endangered forces. Depending on the degree of secrecy desired, the landing may be supported by naval and air bombardment. The landing must be as rapid as possible, using landing craft, amphibious tracked vehicles, or helicopters, and prompt measures taken to secure a beachhead to serve as a base for the forces ashore.

Operations at River Lines. Unfordable and comparatively wide rivers are serious obstacles to offensive operations, and they form natural lines for defensive action. On occasion an attacker can make a *crossing of opportunity,* by surprising an inadequately defended ford or bridge. If the far bank is not too strongly defended, the attacker attempts a *hasty crossing,* coming up to the river on a broad front and attacking across it at once. Such a crossing may be spearheaded by airmobile or airborne units that seize commanding terrain on the far bank.

Reconnaissance units, mechanized infantry, and self-propelled artillery "swim" the river—a large variety of modern tracked military vehicles are amphibious—with air and artillery fire support. Tanks and heavy artillery are floated across on rafts or large special vehicles that can be used as powered ferries. Bridge construction begins as soon as possible. Amphibious vehicles are supplemented by heavy cargo helicopters, assault boats, captured river craft—even improvised rafts. Once across, the attacking troops continue forward to clear a bridgehead area large enough to ensure that the crossing sites are relatively secure from enemy ground action. Such a crossing is "hasty" only in the speed with which it is executed. It requires thorough planning to select the most promising crossing sites and to ensure that the necessary equipment is immediately available.

A *deliberate crossing* in the face of a determined defender remains a difficult operation, requiring special preparations. In execution, it resembles a penetration. One or more secondary crossings are attempted prior to or simultaneously with the main crossing. Feints are made elsewhere to confuse the enemy. The secondary crossings are located sufficiently near the main one so that reserves can be switched rapidly to exploit any success.

Surprise is gained through secrecy in preparations and deception as to the time and place of the main crossing. The means used in crossing are the same, but much heavier fire support is necessary. If the opposite bank is fortified in depth, several successive assaults may be necessary to secure a sufficiently large bridgehead.

Defense of a river line will vary with the defender's strength and the tactical situation. Security forces remain on the far bank of the river as long as possible to delay the enemy's advance and determine his probable crossing sites. All bridges, boats, and ferries are removed or destroyed, and obstacles are created or strengthened to block possible landing sites. The defender may use either an area or mobile defense, or a combination of the two. In the first, he uses the river as a major obstacle directly in front of a position fortified in depth. In the second, the river line is defended by small units at possible crossing sites, while the greater part of the forces is held in reserve. Once the attacker forces his way across the river, the defender counterattacks the flanks of the crossing forces.

The Allied crossings of the Rhine in 1945 are examples of operations at river lines. The seizure of the Remagen bridge was a crossing of opportunity. Lt. Gen. George S. Patton made two hasty crossings at Oppenheim and Boppard. Sir Bernard L. Montgomery carried out a deliberate crossing at Wesel.

Operations at Defiles. A defile is a terrain feature that canalizes an advance by restricting the width of its front. The meaning of the term is relative; for example, a small unit may have plenty of maneuver room in terrain that forms a defile for a larger unit. Typical defiles are mountain passes, towns, and roads through heavy woods, jungle, swampy areas, or lake regions. In such terrain a small force may ambush or at least check a larger force, since the latter cannot readily use its superior strength to envelop the defenders. An attack through a defile is a risky and often costly action. Whenever possible, defiles should be avoided or enveloped. Airmobile forces may seize them before the enemy can organize his defenses. If caught in a defile, the attacker must move quickly to seize any dominating terrain on his flanks and to infiltrate forces through the obstacles creating the defile to outflank the defender.

Operations in Towns. As noted, a town is essentially a defile and so restricts the movements of the attacker. Heavily constructed towns are extremely resistant to air and artillery bombardment. Though upper stories may be destroyed, the lower floors, basements, subways, and sewers remain intact, and falling rubble blocks the streets. The capture of such a labyrinth becomes a slow, careful infantry and combat-engineer operation, house by house, and room by room, using demolition charges, grenades, flamethrowers, and automatic weapons. Whenever possible, the town should be enveloped to cut the defenders off from resupply and water. Operations at Cassino (1944) and Stalingrad are good examples.

Operations in Woods. Large woods are good defenses, restricting enemy movement and concealing the defenders. Small woods offer easy targets for massed bombardment, and can be easily surrounded. Since the edge of a forest offers a clearly defined target, defenders normally organize their positions well back, leaving only observation posts and security detachments at its edge. Underbrush is cleared carefully to give the defenders good fields of fire, without revealing their location. Attacking a large wooded area is much like attacking a town. If possible, it should be surrounded, and its actual reduction should be methodical. Fighting in Hürtgen Forest (1944) was typical.

Jungle Warfare. Tropical jungle imposes even greater limitations on combat. Movement may be restricted to narrow paths. Visibility from the air and on the ground is reduced. Small-scale operations are best carried out by specially trained, conditioned, and equipped troops. For large-scale offensives the American technique of "removing the jungle" in critical areas by firepower, engineer operations, and defoliation makes it possible to use armor, artillery, and other conventional forces with surprising success. World War II jungle operations largely involved the attack on or defense of fortified positions. U. S. operations in South Vietnam tended to more mobile warfare.

Attack on a Fortified Position. Fortified positions may be either isolated strongpoints or major defensive zones such as the German West Wall (Siegfried Line) of World War II. Massively built of reinforced concrete and steel, largely subterranean, well camouflaged, protected by minefields and other obstacles, they present a difficult problem to the attacker. Behind them, mobile reserves are held under shelter for counterattacks.

Such fortifications should be enveloped whenever possible. Otherwise, as in town fighting, infantry and engineer assault teams, supported by tanks and preceded by massive air and artillery bombardments, infiltrate the defenses and open gaps by the methodical reduction of interlocking groups of bunkers and emplacements.

The German capture of Fort Eben Emael in Belgium (1940) is an example of the reduction of an isolated fortification. The Allied attacks on the West Wall in 1944 represent the penetration of a fortified frontier. Operations in Iwo Jima and Okinawa in 1945 involved the reduction of Japanese cave fortifications—less strong, but far more difficult to locate.

Mountain Warfare. Operations in mountains tend to become battles to control defiles. High altitudes, uncertain weather, and poor road nets slow movements, make resupply difficult, and limit the types of weapons and equipment that can be used. Pack animals or human porters may be necessary. Even helicopters are unreliable at extreme heights. Direct assaults on mountain positions usually are costly. Consequently the attacker attempts to envelop or turn them. Failing that, he may infiltrate them at night. Skilled mountain troops are worth several times their number of ordinary infantry. Operations in Italy in World War II and in Korea during 1950–1951 are examples.

Operations in Cold Regions. Arctic operations are influenced by the basic consideration that troops, weapons, and equipment must all undergo special preparations simply to remain in functional, not to mention fighting, condition. Special clothing and equipment are required. Aircraft, vehicles, and weapons require special care. Atmospheric conditions and sudden weather changes hamper reconnaissance. Muskeg, deep snow, and rough terrain make cross-country movement difficult. Properly trained and conditioned troops are essential. The Soviet-Finnish War (1939–1940) is an example.

Desert Warfare. Deserts permit wide freedom of maneuver and are particularly suitable for the combined action of armored and air forces. However, the lack of natural concealment makes it difficult to hide forces from an aggressive enemy. Air superiority is almost essential to successful offensive action. Supply, particularly of water, is always an acute problem, especially when both armies are moving. The defender nearly always uses a mobile defense. The best examples of desert warfare are the operations in Egypt and Libya (1940–1942) and the Arab-Israeli Wars of 1956 and 1967.

See GUERRILLA WARFARE.

IMPLICATIONS OF NUCLEAR WEAPONS

The creation of nuclear weapons has been the most important technological advance of recent times, but the effect of nuclear weapons on warfare can only be surmised. Experience since World War II indicates that future wars may be fought without recourse to nuclear weapons, but that military forces must be organized, trained, and equipped to fight either nuclear or nonnuclear wars.

Low-yield "tactical" nuclear weapons may be delivered by guided missiles and artillery or used as demolition to block defiles. They provide greatly increased combat power, and render all troops and installations increasingly vulnerable. To reduce their vulnerability, units must have increased mobility and be capable of greater dispersion. These requirements, in turn, make more effective command systems and communications systems necessary.

The increased destructiveness of nuclear firepower and the greater mobility of combat units will increase the tempo of operations. In a nuclear war, engagements will tend to be short and extremely violent. Small and self-sufficient armored, airmobile, and tactical air units will maneuver over battlefields extending 100 miles (160 km) in depth. The attacker will mass rapidly, strike, and then disperse before his forces become the target for a nuclear counterattack. The defender will dispose his units in great depth.

Because of their dispersion, both attacker and defender may be vulnerable to infiltration by enemy units too small and two swift to be targets for nuclear weapons. Every effort will be made to identify and destroy the enemy's "nuclear capability"—his reserves of nuclear weapons, the units that launch them, and the command systems that direct their use.

The logistical support of combat units will be extremely demanding. Large supply installations are excellent targets and so must be replaced by numbers of small ones, well dug in and garrisoned against attack. Supply convoys must be able to move rapidly across country, rendezvous with combat units, and then return to base —if necessary, fighting off enemy detachments en route. Reserves will be held in concealed, fortified positions, their immediate mission being to survive until needed. Command and communications systems must be carefully protected and provided with alternate installations.

At the crisis of the action many units will be isolated and out of communication with their higher headquarters. Under such conditions their commanders must act on their own initiative. Any large-scale engagement probably will leave both sides disorganized and badly hurt—the one that can regroup first and seize the initiative undoubtedly will be the winner.

Nuclear weapons will make impossible the World War II style of major amphibious operations, with their immense concentrations of shipping. Similarly, old-style airborne operations would be dangerous because of the relative immobility of airborne forces once they had established their airhead. Future amphibious landings may be made by airmobile troops launched from fast aircraft carriers at various points along the hostile coastline. Technological developments in matériel for nonnuclear warfare, such as improved air vehicles, protective devices, simplified vehicular fuels, and more reliable communication and control systems, may greatly simplify the problems of nuclear wafare.

These changes probably will be more evolutionary than revolutionary. Terrain, weather, and the human spirit will continue to exert their ancient authority.

JOHN R. ELTING, *Colonel, USA (Retired)*
Coauthor of "A Military History and Atlas of the Napoleonic Wars"

Further Reading: Esposito, Vincent J., and Elting, John R., *A Military History and Atlas of the Napoleonic Wars* (New York 1965); Fuller, John F. C., *The Conduct of War, 1789–1961* (New York 1968); Merglen, Albert, *Surprise Warfare: Subversive, Airborne, and Amphibious Operations* (London 1968); Weller, Jac, *Weapons and Tactics: Hastings to Berlin* (New York 1966).

TACTICS, Naval. See NAVAL STRATEGY AND TACTICS.

TADEMA, Sir Lawrence Alma. See ALMA-TADEMA, SIR LAWRENCE.

TADOUSSAC, tad'ə-sak, a village in eastern Quebec, at the confluence of the Saguenay and St. Lawrence rivers, about 130 miles (208 km) northeast of the city of Quebec. The site was visited in 1535 by Jacques Cartier, and there, in 1600, Pierre Chauvin built the first house erected in Canada by a white man. A mission for the Indians was begun there in 1615, and the first stone church in Canada was built in 1646. It was replaced in 1747 by a wooden structure. Tadoussac was a port for deepsea craft in the early 17th century and was a major fur-trading post for 200 years until the mid-19th century, when settlement of the community began. Tourism contributes importantly to the economy. Population: 1,010.

TADPOLE, a larval amphibian. More specifically the term refers to a frog or toad larva. See FROG; TOAD.

TADZHIK SOVIET SOCIALIST REPUBLIC, tä'jik, one of the 15 constituent republics of the USSR, in the southeast of Soviet Central Asia. Also called Tadzhikistan, it adjoins Afghanistan and China on the south and east, and the Uzbek and Kirghiz SSR's on the west and north. The name is also transliterated Tajik.

The People. The Tadzhiks, an Iranian people with an admixture of Mongoloid and Turkish blood, make up about 53% of the population. There are also sizable Tadzhik minorities in Uzbek SSR and in Afghanistan. The Uzbeks make up about 23% of the republic's population and the Russians about 13%. The balance are Tatars, Ukrainians, and Kirghiz.

Tadzhik, closely related to Persian but written with a Cyrillic alphabet, and Russian are the official languages. Most of the Tadzhiks are Sunni Muslims, though many of their beliefs are pre-Muslim in origin. Religious practice, however, has declined due to the opposition of the state and changing social and economic conditions.

Under Soviet rule there has been a steady drive on illiteracy. The Tadzhik State University was established in 1948 and a Tadzhik Academy of Sciences in 1951. There are native-language newspapers, books, and theater performances. Russification is well advanced in the towns, but in rural areas there is still resistance to new ways. Although women have been emancipated officially since the 1920's, there are still cases of bride purchase and child marriage, and most native girls leave school early.

The Land. The Tadzhik SSR has an area of 55,000 square miles (142,500 sq km). Its population and agriculture are concentrated in the Fergana Valley in the north and the Gissar and Vakhsh valleys in the south. The remainder of the republic is mountainous, consisting mainly of the sparsely settled Gorno-Badakhshan Autonomous Oblast in the east in the Pamirs. This area is a 12,000-foot (3,650–meter) plateau, culminating in Mount Communism (formerly Mount Stalin), at 24,590 feet (7,495 meters), the highest peak in the USSR. The parallel Turkestan, Zeravshan, and Gissar ranges, running east-west, dominate western Tadzhikistan.

The main river is the Amu Darya (the ancient Oxus), called the Pyandzh in its upper course. It forms the frontier between Tadzhikistan

TASS FROM SOVFOTO

MOUNT LENIN, second-highest peak in the USSR, is on the Tadzhik SSR's border with the Kirghiz SSR.

and Afghanistan. Its main tributaries are the Vakhsh, the Kafirnigan, and the Surkhan Darya. The northern part of the country takes in part of the Syr Darya River basin. There are many glaciers in the Pamirs, and the 50-mile (80-km) Fedchenko Glacier is one of the world's longest.

The climate is sharply continental: hot in summer and severely cold in winter. Annual precipitation varies from 10 to 15 inches (255–380 mm) in the higher altitudes to about 6 inches (210 mm) in the western semidesert. The republic's collective and state farms obtain 80% of their output from irrigated land. There are virtually no wooded areas.

Dushanbe, the capital and largest city, formerly called Stalinabad, has a population of about 340,000. Other important towns are Leninabad, Khorog, Garm, and Kurgan Tyube.

The Economy. No agriculture is possible in most of the mountain regions. But under irrigation, which has been practiced since antiquity, the gray desert soils in the valleys in the southwest and northwest produce heavy yields. Cotton is the main crop in the lowlands, along with rice and fruits; orchard fruits are grown on the lower mountain slopes; and mulberry trees are grown for silk culture. Increased irrigation has greatly expanded the amount of land under cultivation.

Tadzhik industry involves mainly food processing, textiles, and mining. The country is rich in minerals, especially in the mountains bordering the Fergana Valley. Coal is mined at Shurab and in the Zeravshan Valley, and crude oil is produced at Nefteabad. There is limited extraction of precious and other nonferrous metals. Rich, but inaccessible, deposits of other minerals remain untapped.

History. Tadzhiks are a remnant of the Iranian stock once predominant throughout western Central Asia. There are archaeological indications of settled societies in the region from about 3000 B.C. The local kingdoms of Bactria and Sogdiana became tributaries of the Persian Empire. From 329 B.C., Alexander the Great and his successors made the region an important east-west link. From the 2d century B.C. to the 7th century A.D. the area underwent successive invasions by Iranians and Turkic peoples.

In the 7th century the Arabs invaded the region and converted the population to Islam. The Arabs and the native dynasty of the Samanids brought unity and prosperity to the region, and cultural life flourished. Further invasions, including those of the Mongols in 1221, followed. In the 15th century, the Tadzhiks were conquered by the nomadic Uzbeks. In the 18th century the Afghans took over the Tadzhiks living south of the Amu Darya. Russia took part of the remainder in 1868. British concern over Russian penetration of the region caused tension between the two powers until 1895, when a joint commission fixed the Afghan frontier on the Pyandzh River and separated the Russian Empire and India by a narrow Afghan corridor.

After the October Revolution of 1917, part of Tadzhikistan was included in the Turkestan Autonomous Soviet Socialist Republic and part in the Bukharan People's Soviet Republic. In 1924 both parts were included in the Tadzhik ASSR, within the Uzbek SSR. The Tadzhik SSR was proclaimed in 1929. Population: (1968 est.) 2,736,000.

RICHARD A. PIERCE, *Queen's University*

TAEGU, tī-gōō, South Korea's third-largest city, is the capital of North Kyongsang province. It is situated about 60 miles (100 km) northwest of Pusan on the Seoul–Pusan railroad and highway. An important textile center, it has several modern mills and small-scale factories. Rice, cotton, and silk cocoons are among the chief agricultural products of the area, and the Taegu apple is renowned as Korea's finest. Kyungpuk National University is located in the city.

Although many centuries old, Taegu remained a minor administrative seat until 1895, when it became the provincial capital. In 1950, during the Korean War, the city was a bastion of the "Pusan perimeter," the southeast corner of Korea that UN forces successfully defended against Communist attacks. Population: (1966 est.) 845,073.

TAENIODONTA, tē′nē-ə-dän-tə, an extinct order of mammals that inhabited North America during the Paleocene and Eocene, some 65 million to 40 million years ago. The taeniodonts, descended from insectivores, were presumably insectivorous initially, but later forms became herbivorous. The teeth became high crowned, extending far into the skull, and tooth enamel became reduced, being limited to bands along the sides of the teeth.

The single known family, the Stylinodontidae, is divided into two subfamilies. Members of the subfamily Conoryctinae increased through time from the size of a hedgehog to that of a small bear, with a massive skull. In the subfamily Stylinodontinae the skull also became more massive, the canine teeth became specialized for gnawing, and the limbs became short and powerful, with large claws for grasping or digging.

LEIGH VAN VALEN
University of Chicago

TAFFETA, taf′ə-tə, is a rather crisp cloth made of silk or man-made fibers such as rayon or nylon. The cloth probably originated in Iran, its name coming from a Persian word meaning "twisted" or "woven." Taffeta has a compact structure and is plain woven. The filling yarns are slightly heavier or bulkier than the warp yarns.

Taffeta may be solid, plaid, or printed. It is often given a moiré, or watermarked, effect. *Faille taffeta* has a plain or twill weave that gives it a cross-ribbed effect. *Paper taffeta* is lightweight and is given a paperlike finish. *Tissue taffeta* is very lightweight and is transparent.

The crunching or rustling sound produced when taffeta is worn or handled is due to *weighting*, a process in which a fabric is impregnated with metallic salts. Weighting has a detrimental effect on the durability of fabrics; hence silk taffeta does not wear as well as other fabrics made of silk.

Taffeta is used for a wide variety of articles, including dresses, slips, linings, draperies, bedspreads, umbrellas, and ribbons.

George E. Linton
Author of "The Modern Textile Dictionary"

TAFT, Lorado (1860–1936), American sculptor, lecturer, and author. He was born in Elmwood, Ill., on April 29, 1860. After graduating from the University of Illinois in 1879, he studied at the École des Beaux-Arts in Paris. In 1886 he opened a studio in Chicago and began a long teaching career at the Art Institute. He became widely known in 1893 with his decorative groups for the Horticultural Building at the Columbian Exposition in Chicago. Taft's monuments and fountains were often inspired by allegorical themes. His best-known work, the cast concrete *Fountain of Time* (1922; Midway Park, Chicago), depicts Time, mantled, gazing majestically down at an endless and idealized procession of humanity. Among Taft's other major works are *Solitude of the Soul* (1901; Chicago Art Institute) and *Black Hawk* (1911; Oregon, Ill.).

Deeply concerned with stimulating popular interest in art, Taft lectured widely in the Middle West, encouraging young artists and campaigning for more and better museums. His *History of American Sculpture* appeared in 1903. Taft died in Chicago on Oct. 30, 1936.

Katherine G. Kline
"Art News" Magazine

TAFT, Robert Alphonso (1889–1953), American political leader. The son of President William Howard Taft, he served as a U. S. senator from Ohio from 1939 until his death. An important leader of the Republican party, he was a serious but unsuccessful contender for the presidential nomination three times.

Born in Cincinnati, Ohio, on Sept. 8, 1889, Taft lived there until 1900, when he accompanied his parents to the Philippine Islands, where his father shortly became governor. In 1903, Taft entered the Taft School in Watertown, Conn., founded and headed by his uncle, Horace D. Taft. Consistently encouraged by his parents and uncle, he led his classes at Taft, at Yale University, and at the Harvard Law School. Friends found him reserved and anxious to compete and excel. The example of his father spurred his ambitions and his sense of duty.

Taft practiced law in Cincinnati (1913–1917), served as assistant consul for the U. S. Food Administration during World War I, and helped handle American relief activities in Europe after the war. These experiences left him critical of federal regulatory activities and of the apparent selfishness of European nations. From 1919 to 1939 he was a successful attorney and an active Republican in Cincinnati. A member of the Ohio House of Representatives from 1921 to 1926, he was the majority leader in 1925 and speaker in 1926. He served in the state Senate in 1931 and 1932.

UPI

Sen. Robert A. Taft

U. S. Senator. As a senator, Taft's greatest influence was on domestic policy. Thoroughly prepared and courageously consistent, he earned his colleagues' respect. From 1946 to 1952 he dominated the powerful Republican policy committee, and in 1953 he served as the majority leader. His struggle against what he considered the excesses of labor unions culminated in legislation passed in 1947. (See Taft-Hartley Act.) Carelessly labeled a right-wing conservative, Taft assailed unbalanced budgets but also supported federal aid to education and cosponsored the public housing law of 1949. Believing in equality of opportunity, he favored welfare programs but opposed legislation that in his view impeded individual liberty, curbed business incentive, or surrendered to pressure groups.

Taft had less influence on foreign policy. Opposing American participation in World War II before Pearl Harbor was attacked, he reluctantly approved postwar foreign aid. During President Harry Truman's administrations Taft opposed major commitments of American ground forces in Europe, U. S. membership in the North Atlantic Treaty Organization, and U.. S. policies in East Asia. Critics branded him a partisan isolationist, but Taft in fact was a nationalist who doubted America's ability to become involved effectively in problems around the globe.

Presidential Candidate. Taft's presidential ambitions were not fulfilled. At Republican conventions he lost to Wendell Willkie in 1940, to Thomas E. Dewey in 1948, and to Gen. Dwight D. Eisenhower on one close roll call in 1952. As a presidential aspirant, Taft suffered from an exaggerated image as a conservative and isolationist. Critics also stressed his heavy style of public speaking and his unexciting personality. Republican delegates admired his integrity and intelligence, but many of them consistently doubted his ability to win in November.

At the peak of his influence Taft died of cancer in New York City on July 31, 1953.

James T. Patterson, *Indiana University*
Author, "The New Deal and the States"

LIBRARY OF CONGRESS

WILLIAM HOWARD TAFT

27th PRESIDENT OF THE UNITED STATES
IN OFFICE FROM 1909 TO 1913

BORN	Sept. 5, 1857, in Cincinnati, Ohio.
HIGHER EDUCATION	Yale College, B. A., 1878; Cincinnati Law School, LL. B., 1880.
RELIGION	Unitarian.
OCCUPATIONS	Lawyer, judge, public official.
MARRIAGE	June 19, 1886, to Helen Herron.
CHILDREN	Robert Alphonso Taft (1889–1953); Helen Herron Taft (1891–); Charles Phelps Taft (1897–).
POLITICAL PARTY	Republican.
LEGAL RESIDENCE WHEN ELECTED	Ohio.
POSITION WHEN ELECTED	Secretary of War.
PRINCIPAL WRITINGS	*The Anti-Trust Act and the Supreme Court* (1914); *The United States and Peace* (1914); *Our Chief Magistrate and His Powers* (1916).
DIED	March 8, 1930, in Washington, D.C.
BURIAL PLACE	Arlington National Cemetery, Arlington, Va.

Wm H Taft

TAFT, William Howard (1857–1930), 27th president of the United States and 10th chief justice of the United States. He was the only man in American history to hold both offices. He esteemed his service on the Supreme Court (1921–1930) more highly than the presidency, having aspired to a judicial career from his youth. He recoiled from active participation in politics and had small talent for its vicissitudes, being too easygoing and not enough of a fighter for the political arenas. Taft was not an innovator, either in the White House or on the bench. His record as chief executive was not without distinction, though it was beclouded by the bitter political factional quarrel that ended his presidency after one term (1909–1913). He is chiefly remembered as the friend and then the political antagonist of the Progressive Republican President Theodore Roosevelt, with the effect that Taft is often supposed to have been more conservative than in fact he was.

Early Career. Taft was born in Cincinnati, Ohio, on Sept. 5, 1857. His father, Alphonso Taft (1810–1891), was a lawyer who later served as secretary of war and as attorney general in President Ulysses S. Grant's cabinet and then as ambassador to Austria-Hungary and Russia. Alphonso Taft's wife, the former Louise Torrey, wrote of her son William a few weeks after he was born: "He is very large of his age and grows fat every day." The words were prophetic, for Taft as an adult weighed 300 pounds or more, the heaviest of any president.

William grew up in Cincinnati, which was the political base for the Taft family through several generations. He graduated with distinction from Yale in 1878. In 1880 he graduated from Cincinnati Law School and was admitted to the bar. His first public office was as assistant prosecuting attorney of Hamilton county from 1881 to 1883. He was briefly the collector of internal revenue for Cincinnati in 1882. He practiced law in Cincinnati from 1883 to 1887, but already yearned for a judicial post. That goal was realized when he was appointed to an Ohio superior court vacancy in 1887. The next year he was elected to a term of his own, and this was the only office other than the presidency that he ever won by election.

In 1890, President Benjamin Harrison called Taft to Washington to the post of solicitor general. Two years later Harrison named him to the U.S. circuit court for the 6th district. Taft's record as a state and federal judge was honest and competent, and he was receptive to the problems of labor in a nation that was just beginning to emerge from the influence of the laissez faire philosophy.

Taft's attractive wife, the former Helen Herron of Cincinnati, whom he had married in 1886, was ambitious for her husband and a principal influence in persuading him to leave the law and the bench. But a larger opportunity did not come until the turn of the century.

The Philippines. Taft began to gain national stature in 1900, when President McKinley appointed him head of a commission to terminate U.S. military rule in the Philippine Islands, which had become an American possession after the Spanish-American War. The appointment gave Taft his first opportunity to demonstrate ability as an administrator.

In 1901, McKinley named Taft the first civil governor of the Philippines. Taft's governorship of the islands (1901–1904) was a high mark in colonial administration for any nation. Taft had, in marked contrast to the military, no trace of racial prejudice. He was warmly sympathetic to the problems of the Filipinos. He believed in giving them the widest possible degree of self-government and constantly worked toward that end. On the other hand, Taft was never deceived by the extremists among them. He recognized that the first steps toward the ultimate goal of independence was public education in the islands and the end of ownership of land by the Roman Catholic friars. Taft negotiated an agreement with the Vatican in 1903 whereby, with American financial assistance, the lands were sold in small parcels to the Filipinos.

Secretary of War. Theodore Roosevelt succeeded the assassinated McKinley as president in 1901. Roosevelt had known Taft in Washington during the latter's service as solicitor general. Though different in temperament—Roosevelt was dynamic and impulsive, Taft restrained and judicial—they became close personal friends and political allies. Roosevelt twice offered Governor Taft a place on the U.S. Supreme Court, but Taft declined, pleading that his work in the Philippines was not finished.

But Roosevelt had come to regard Taft as his eventual successor and became convinced that he needed him in his cabinet. Taft accepted the post of secretary of war with the understanding that he could continue to oversee Philippine affairs from Washington.

Taft observed with some accuracy that he had "no aptitude for managing an army," but the generals took care of that matter. The next four years were crowded and, all in all, successful. The secretary of war became the administration's "trouble shooter" at home and abroad. Between 1904 and 1908 he had direct charge of the construction of the Panama Canal. In 1906, when revolution threatened Cuba, he brought a degree of peace through negotiations. In Tokyo in 1907, he improved Japanese-American relations strained by the abuse of Japanese immigrants in California.

President. "Politics, when I am in it, makes me sick," Taft wrote to his wife in 1906. The secretary of war initially had no desire to run for president, but on Roosevelt's demand and with the urging of his wife and brothers, he accepted the Republican nomination in 1908. Benefiting from the popularity of the Roosevelt administration, Taft defeated William Jennings Bryan, the Democratic candidate, by an electoral vote of 321 to 162 and a popular vote of 7,679,114 to 6,410,665. His inauguration on a storm-tossed March day in 1909 presaged four unhappy years in the White House.

The new President inherited widespread demands for a lower tariff. He accepted the compromise Payne-Aldrich Act (1909), a truly downward revision that satisfied neither big business nor the Progressive Republicans. Taft, with an ineptitude that so often marked his public utterances, called it the best tariff in history. The President negotiated with Canada an agreement that promised relatively free trade between the two countries, only to have Canada ultimately reject it.

Vigorously enforcing the Sherman Antitrust Act, Taft's attorney general, George Wickersham, initiated twice as many antitrust suits against big corporations as had the previous administration, but Roosevelt, not Taft, is remembered as the "trustbuster."

Conservation had a friend in Taft. Yet he properly supported his secretary of the interior, Richard Ballinger, against the somewhat fanatical Gifford Pinchot, chief of the Forest Service and loyal to Roosevelt. Pinchot had accused Ballinger of favoring private interests. Taft dismissed Pinchot. Ballinger, unable to recoup his reputation though unjustly charged, resigned.

Taft further alienated the Progressives by declining to side openly with the congressional insurgents opposing the dictatorial rule of the speaker of the House, Joseph G. Cannon. But, then, neither did Roosevelt.

On the plus side, the Taft administration saw the creation of the postal savings system and the parcel post, the establishment of a separate Department of Labor, and the admission of Arizona and New Mexico, the last of the 48 contiguous states. Constitutional amendments providing for the direct election of senators and for a federal income tax passed Congress and went to the states for ratification.

The Democrats captured control of the House in 1910, and Progressive Republicans looked to Roosevelt for their presidential candidate in 1912. Roosevelt, swinging farther to the left while Taft watched with alarm, was soon opposing the man whose nomination he had effected four years earlier. Taft felt heartbreak and despair when Roosevelt entered the contest for the 1912 presidential nomination. Taft did win renomination, but by "steamroller" methods. Roosevelt, loudly declaring that the nomination had been stolen from him, ran as an independent candidate for president. The result was the election of the Democratic candidate, Woodrow Wilson. Taft

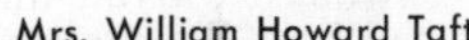

Mrs. William Howard Taft

CULVER PICTURES

LIBRARY OF CONGRESS

PRESIDENT TAFT AND HIS FAMILY in 1911. Charles, Helen, and Robert stand behind their parents.

ran third in the election, carrying only Utah and Vermont. He left office without due recognition for much that had been accomplished.

Chief Justice. Taft retired to serve as Kent professor of law at Yale University with dignity and grace. He was then joint chairman of the National War Labor Board during World War I. The board had little power to settle labor disputes, but Taft's 14 months in the post were an important educational experience. He came into closer contact with organized labor than ever before. It is possible that the knowledge he gained influenced some of his opinions as chief justice.

When Chief Justice Edward D. White died in 1921, President Warren G. Harding elevated Taft to the office he had long coveted. The court was badly divided when the new chief justice took his place on it. Taft's greatest service lay in bringing more harmony and greater efficiency to the court rather than in outstanding contributions to judicial knowledge. He helped effect passage of an act of Congress permitting the Supreme Court greater discretion over the cases that came before it.

The chief justice never permitted personal opinions to influence him. Although he had not favored prohibition, he stood for strict enforcement of the 18th Amendment and the Volstead Act, which enforced prohibition. For Taft, law was law, whether it worked or not.

In other decisions, Chief Justice Taft rejected congressional efforts to impose controls on child labor through taxation; declared that the stockyards industry was national in scope and open to federal regulation; and sustained the president's right to remove executive appointees without the concurrence of the Senate.

But Taft's principal interest was in accelerating the work of the courts. To this end his contributions were major. Dissenting opinions were a possible cause of delay, and he shrank from all of them, including his own. "I would not think of opposing the views of my brethren," he declared in 1927, "if there is a majority against my own." The remark well sums up Taft's philosophy regarding courts and judges.

Heart disease forced Taft to retire from the court on Feb. 3, 1930, and a month later, almost as if this surrender of the work he loved had sapped his remaining strength, he died in Washington, D.C., on March 8, 1930.

In addition to his father, members of Taft's family who achieved distinction included his stepbrother, Charles Phelps Taft (1843–1929)—the son of his father's first wife—who was the successful publisher of the Cincinnati *Times-Star*; and his older son, Robert (1889–1953), a leader of the Republican party and elected three times to the U. S. Senate.

HENRY F. PRINGLE
Author of "The Life and Times of William Howard Taft"

Bibliography

The William Howard Taft papers, a huge collection of more than 1,000 portfolios, is housed in the Library of Congress.

Manners, William, *TR and Will: A Friendship That Split the Republican Party* (New York 1969).

Mowry, George E., *The Era of Theodore Roosevelt, 1900–1912* (New York 1958).

Pringle, Henry F., *The Life and Times of William Howard Taft*, 2 vols. (New York 1939).

Ragan, Allen E., *Chief Justice Taft* (Columbus, Ohio, 1938).

Ross, Ishbel, *American Family: The Tafts, 1678–1964* (New York 1964).

Taft rides Roosevelt's shoulder in *Puck* cartoon.

TAFT-HARTLEY ACT, known officially as the Labor-Management Relations Act, 1947. It amended the Wagner Act, known formally as the National Labor Relations Act of 1935. The Taft-Hartley Act was enacted to correct what, in the opinion of the public and a majority of the Congress, were union abuses that had emerged under the Wagner Act. The Taft-Hartley Act continues, with changes, the Wagner Act protection of the right of workers to organize in unions of their own choosing and to bargain collectively with employers. But, unlike the Wagner Act, it also specifies protections for the employer in collective bargaining.

The Taft-Hartley Act deals with four main subjects: (1) unfair labor practices by employers against unions and workers—practices whose definitions were carried over, with changes, from the Wagner Act; (2) unfair labor practices by unions against employers and workers, which constitute a major addition; (3) a mechanism for employee selection of representatives for collective bargaining; and (4) regulation of union practices with respect to strikes creating national emergencies, contributions to health and welfare funds, violations of contracts, and political contributions—none of which was covered by the Wagner Act. The Taft-Hartley Act also provided for reorganization of the National Labor Relations Board to enforce the first three provisions. The Taft-Hartley Act applies only to labor disputes that affect interstate commerce.

The Landrum-Griffin Law, formally the Labor-Management Reporting and Disclosure Act of 1959, amended certain sections of the Taft-Hartley Act.

JACK BARBASH, *University of Wisconsin*

TAGALOGS, tə-gäl′əgz, the cultural-linguistic group inhabiting the fertile plains of central Luzon and the Mindoro coast of the Philippines. This group, once known as the Tagals, makes up slightly more than one fifth of the population of the Republic of the Philippines.

The Tagalogs are concentrated in metropolitan Manila, which includes the national capital, Quezon City, and are preeminent in Philippine commerce, industry, transportation, health, education, and the arts. They have provided such revolutionary leaders as Jose Rizal, Andres Bonifacio, Emilio Aguinaldo, and Apolinario Mabini, and such statesmen as Manuel Luis Quezon, Ramon Magsaysay, Claro Recto, and Jose Laurel.

The concentration of the Tagalogs around Manila, a crossroads of international trade and cultural exchange, has affected the people both physically and socially. Typical Filipinos have a slender build, brown skin, straight black hair, and a flat face with a wide nose and thick lips. These features have been modified in the Tagalogs by their openness to intermarriage with Chinese, Europeans, and Americans. Similarly, their urban orientation and the gradual growth of a middle class among them has included many Tagalogs to adapt local customs to cosmopolitan influences.

On Dec. 30, 1937, it was proclaimed that Tagalog would be the core of a composite national language, which was named Pilipino in 1954. Until late in the 1960's, literature in school was restricted largely to Tagalog classics, and national literary prizes were awarded only to writers in Tagalog.

LEONARD CASPER, *Boston College*

TAGANROG, tȧ-gən-rôk′, a port in the USSR, is on the Gulf of Taganrog in the Sea of Azov, which is an extension of the Black Sea. It lies 45 miles (72 km) west of Rostov-on-Don. Its metallurgical and engineering industries make it a major industrial city. It is connected by rail with Rostov and with the Donets industrial area. The harbor is icebound for part of the winter.

Taganrog was founded in 1698 by Peter the Great. It was destroyed in 1712 and then rebuilt between 1769 and 1774. In the 19th century it was the principal port in the Black Sea area until it was overtaken by Odessa. It was occupied by the Germans in World Wars I and II. Population: (1959) 201,000.

TAGLIONI, tä-lyō′nē, **Marie** (1804–1884), Italian ballerina, who, more than any other dancer, typified the romantic era in ballet. Marie (or Maria) Taglioni was born in Stockholm on April 23, 1804. Her mother was Swedish, and her father Filippo was one of a family of Italian dancers. Small and dark, with sloping shoulders and long, softly rounded arms, she was a highly disciplined technician who avoided the tendency of her time to emphasize virtuosity above all else. When she rose to the tips, or pointes, of her soft satin shoes it was not to impress but to enhance the dramatic context. When she executed a pirouette, her soft muslin gown with its bell-shaped skirt flowed delicately about her calves, contributing to her ethereal quality.

Following her debut in Vienna in 1822, Taglioni danced in various European cities for the next 10 years. In 1832 she had a sensational success at the Paris Opéra in *La Sylphide*, a ballet devised for her by her father, in which she danced a forest sprite in love with a young Scotsman. It set the tone for many later romantic ballets. Her interpretation was so exquisite that she remained the embodiment of every poet's dream of the enticing yet incorporeal female. She died in Marseille, France, in 1884.

DORIS HERING
"Dance Magazine"

TAGORE, tə-gôr′, **Rabindranath** (1861–1941), Indian poet, philosopher, social reformer, and dramatist from Bengal. He was awarded the Nobel Prize for literature in 1913.

Life and Thought. Rabindranath was born in Calcutta on May 7, 1861, into a family that owned extensive estates in what is now East Pakistan. His family, though Brahmin, was not considered ritually "pure," but it was wealthy and brilliant. His grandfather Dwarkanath Tagore was a financier, and his father, Debendranath (1818–1905), was a learned and deeply religious man, one of the founders of the Brahmo Samaj religious reform movement. Rabindranath grew up in a very large and intellectually stimulating household. It included among his relatives the painters Abinindranath and Gaganendranath Tagore and, among his own 11 elder brothers and sisters, the writer-philosopher Dvijendranath, the musician Jyotirindranath, and Bengal's first woman novelist, Svarnakumari Devi. Rabindranath's early life, however, was dominated by servants and schoolmasters who confined him strictly, and his longing for freedom never left him in later life.

As a boy Rabindranath showed poetic talent and was urged by his brothers and sisters to express himself in poetry. He gave the first public reading of his poetry when he was 14, at a Bengali cultural and nationalistic festival, and his poem contrasting India's great past with its current servitude was widely acclaimed. When he was 17 his brother Satyendranath, the first Indian admitted to the upper echelons of the Indian civil service, took him on the first of his many trips to England.

Despite his nationalistic pride, Rabindranath stood aloof from the radical nationalistic movements that swept India throughout his life. He chose to express his love of freedom in personal ways. In 1901 he founded at Shantiniketan a school that embodied his ideals of education: freedom from traditional restrictions, classes held in the open air, students of all countries participating in common experience. It grew into Visva-Bharati, the "World University." He also founded an experimental village, Shriniketan, which has been a model of the Indian village as a viable social and economic unit.

Rabindranath was knighted by the British crown in 1913 but resigned his knighthood six years later. His action protested the massacre of Indians who were demonstrating at Amritsar against the British regime in India. Rabindranath died in Calcutta on Aug. 7, 1941.

Works. On a trip to London in 1912, Rabindranath read to W. B. Yeats and Ezra Pound some of his own translations into English of works from his Bengali collection of religious poems called *Gitanjali* (*Song Offerings*). Pound immediately sent some of the poems to Harriet Monroe's *Poetry* magazine for publication. Soon after they appeared the collection as a whole was published with an introduction by Yeats. In 1913 came the Nobel Prize. The resultant fame brought a disruption of the quiet life he longed for, and thereafter he made frequent trips to China, Japan, Europe, and the United States, lecturing and reading his poetry. Tall, robed, and bearded, he made a profound physical impression in the West.

The West often bases its opinion of Tagore on the religious poetry of *Gitanjali*, but that book and the spate of similar ones that followed its enthusiastic reception show only one facet of a long and varied literary career. Moreover, they show nothing of the humor or intellectual rigor of which he was capable. Rabindranath's short stories range from humor to satire and to meditation. His novels, such as *Gora*, *Seser kavita* (*Farewell My Friend*), and *Ghare baire* (*The Home and the World*), brought many innovations to Bengali prose. His collections of essays, such as *The Religion of Man* and *Sadhana*, have prompted some thinkers to consider him a philosopher. He was a social and political theorist, and dramas like *The King of the Dark Chamber* show, through their fantasy, complex social commentary.

It would be a mistake to consider Rabindranath only as a writer, as many in the West do. Late in life he took up brush and ink, and his moody and sometimes whimsical wash drawings are unique. Not least, he was a musician—a singer as well as a composer—and the *rabindrasangit*, the style of music he created, was named after him. Like all his other work, his music is a mixture of the classical with the modes of expression of the common people, such as the songs of boatmen and wandering mendicants.

Tagore's musical ear caught the natural rhythms of the Bengali language. Free in spirit, he paid scant attention to the classical rules of poetry, and the new forms he created account as much as anything for his continued popularity in Bengal. His literary work is incompletely contained in 26 large volumes, most of which have not yet been translated into English.

EDWARD C. DIMOCK, JR., *University of Chicago*

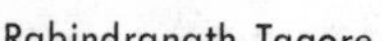

Rabindranath Tagore

PICTORIAL PARADE

Bibliography

Bhattacarya, Bhabani, ed., *Towards Universal Man* (Bombay 1961).

Chakravarty, Amiya, ed., *A Tagore Reader* (New York 1961).

Kripalani, Krishna, *Rabindranath Tagore: A Biography* (New York 1962).

Tagore, Rabindranath, *Collected Poems and Plays* (New York 1958).

Tagore, Rabindranath, *The Religion of Man* (London 1931).

TAGUS, tä′gəs, the longest river in the Iberian Peninsula. It rises in Spain's Albarracín mountains and flows west to enter the Atlantic at Lisbon. The Spanish form is Tajo, the Portuguese, Tejo. It is about 625 miles (1,005 km) long, and at one point it forms the Spanish-Portuguese border.

Although rapids restrict its use for large-scale navigation, it is used extensively for local traffic. The main Spanish city on its banks is Toledo. Near its mouth, the Tagus broadens to form Lisbon's excellent harbor.

TAHITI, tə-hē′tē, is the largest and most important island of French Polynesia in the South Pacific Ocean. It is 35 miles (55 km) long and has an area of 402 square miles (1,042 sq km). The island is well known for its beautiful scenery and pleasant climate.

The Land. Tahiti, one of the Society Islands, consists of two volcanic domes that merge at the narrow Isthmus of Taravao to give the island a figure-8 shape. The larger section is called Tahiti-Nui, and the smaller forms the Taiarapu Peninsula, or Tahiti-Iti. Rugged mountains of the interior, rising to 7,339 feet (2,238

FISHNETS drying on trees are a common sight in the villages on Tahitian shores. Coconut palms provide both food and roofing.

FRED LYON, FROM RAPHO GUILLUMETTE

meters) at the summit of Mt. Orohena, are etched by precipitous valleys. A narrow plain along the entire coast has the island's best soils and most of the residential land. Passages through a coral reef that nearly surrounds the island give access to a protected coastal lagoon.

Tahiti's tropical climate is moderated by the southeast trade winds. Mean monthly temperatures range from about 75° F (24° C) in August to 80° F (27° C) in March. Rainfall averages 70 inches (1,800 mm) annually in the lowlands and is greater on the windward slopes, where the vegetation is tropical rain forest.

The People. The population of Tahiti was 61,519 at the time of the 1967 census. The Tahitian people are primarily Polynesian, but most of them have some European or Oriental ancestry. The Chinese are the most numerous minority. There are also French, British, and American inhabitants.

The major concentration of people is in Papeete, which is the capital of French Polynesia as well as the administrative center of Tahiti. Papeete had a population of 22,278 in 1967. The rural population is dispersed in settlements along the coastal plain.

The Tahitian language is a Polynesian dialect, but French is common in business and government, and English is increasing as a language of tourism. Christianity is the main religion, but many Chinese are Buddhists or Confucians.

Economy. The economy of Tahiti is based on fishing and farming. The principal crops are coconuts, taro, breadfruit, yams, and various other fruits and vegetables. Copra, vanilla, and handicrafts are the leading exports.

Transpacific cargo and passenger ships and interisland vessels make regular calls at Papeete, which is the chief port of French Polynesia. The jet airport at Faa is about 3 miles (5 km) southwest of Papeete. Hotel construction and the expansion of tourism have been significant elements of the Tahitian economy since 1960.

History. The European discovery of Tahiti was made in 1767 by the British navigator Samuel Wallis, who named it King George III Island. The next year the French explorer Louis de Bougainville visited it and named it New Cythera, although he recorded the local name as "Taiti." In 1769, at Point Venus east of Papeete, the British explorer James Cook observed the transit of Venus for the Royal Society, London; a monument marks the spot. The French painter Paul Gauguin lived on Tahiti in the 1890's.

The British established a Protestant mission on the island in 1797 and the French a Catholic one in 1836. Tahiti has been under French control since 1842.

HOWARD J. CRITCHFIELD
Western Washington State College

TAHOE, Lake, tä'hō, on the California-Nevada border, about 23 miles (37 km) southwest of Reno, Nev., at an elevation of 6,225 feet (1,898 meters) above sea level in the northern Sierra Nevada. The Carson Range, a spur of the Sierra, runs along the lake's eastern shore. The Sierra Nevada, a single colossal block with a granitic core, has been subject to faulting along its eastern front, and Lake Tahoe lies in a fault basin. The lake, at its northwestern end, empties into the Truckee River.

Tahoe is about 22 miles (35 km) from north to south and 12 miles (20 km) across at its widest. Its great depth—over 1,600 feet (490 meters)—tends to keep it from freezing over in winter. About two thirds of the lake is in California.

Tahoe has been called one of the most beautiful lakes in the world. It is part of the Eldorado National Forest. Tahoe National Forest, nearby, was the site of the 1960 Winter Olympics. Snow-capped peaks of the Sierras frame its lovely setting. As a summer and winter resort, Tahoe offers water sports and winter skiing.

The lake was discovered in 1844 by John C. Frémont, while on a government surveying mission. It was called by several names before it was finally given the name Tahoe, an Indian word meaning "much water." In the 20th century it developed rapidly as a vacation resort. Highways, towns, and villages encircle the lake.

MAURICE E. LANDRE, FROM NATIONAL AUDUBON SOCIETY

Himalayan tahr

TAHR, tär, or *thar,* a goatlike Asiatic mammal typically inhabiting tree-covered hills or mountain slopes. Tahrs reach 40 inches (1 meter) in height at the shoulders and 200 pounds (90 kg) in weight.

The Himalayan tahr (*Hemitragus jemlahicus*) is found from Bhutan to Kashmir and has been introduced into New Zealand. It is covered with long, shaggy, usually deep reddish brown hair. The hair becomes manelike on the neck and shoulders but is extremely short on the head and lower legs. Both sexes have rather short, somewhat flattened horns.

The Nilgiri tahr (*H. hylocrius*), found in southern India, has a short, crisp, dark yellowish to brownish coat. The Arabian tahr (*H. jayakari*), found in Oman, is the smallest of the tahrs. It has a relatively short but shaggy, grayish to tawny brown coat.

B. C. MAHENDRA, *President*
The Academy of Zoology, Agra, India

TAI CHEN, dī jun (1723–1777), also known as Tai Tung-yüan, was a Chinese philosopher and scholar. He was born in Hsiuning, Anhwei, to a poor family. Although Tai taught school for two years and did some tutoring, he spent most of his life writing, editing, and compiling works on a wide range of subjects. In 1773, by imperial command, he was appointed a compiler of the *Four Libraries,* and he retained that post until his death.

Tai was an expert in mathematics, astronomy, waterworks, phonetics, the collation of texts, and textual criticism. He advocated the scientific method, demanding objective evidence to support conclusions. Reflecting the generally practical spirit of his time, he strongly attacked rationalistic Neo-Confucianism, which had dominated Chinese thought since the 12th century.

Tai's best works are the *Commentary on the Meaning of Terms in the Book of Mencius* and *An Inquiry on Goodness.* Although he had no large following, Tai Chen was the outstanding Chinese thinker of the 18th century. See also CHINA—*Philosophy and Religion.*

WING-TSIT CHAN
Compiler and Translator of "A Source Book in Chinese Philosophy"

TAI SHAN, tī shän, the highest peak in the uplands of central Shantung province, is revered by Buddhists and Taoists as China's most sacred mountain. A road extending 15 miles (24 km) north from Taian city ends in a flight of 6,300 steps leading to the summit, about 5,060 feet (1,542 meters) above sea level. Along the ascent are shrines and temples dedicated to the Tai Shan god—giver and protector of life—and other deities.

T'AI TSUNG. See T'ANG T'AI TSUNG.

TAICHUNG, tī-jo͝ong, the principal city of central Taiwan, China, lies about 85 miles (135 km) southwest of Taipei. It is located in a fertile paddy-field basin between the island's low west coast hills and the central mountains. Taichung is served by the north-south railroad.

The city was developed by the Japanese during their administration of Taiwan, which lasted from 1895 to 1945. During that period it was primarily a trading center for the rice, sugar, and bananas of the island's central plain. Since 1949, when the Nationalist government of China was established on Taiwan, food processing and chemical industries have been developed in Taichung and the city's population has doubled. Population: (1967) 391,625.

A few miles south of Taichung is Chunghsing-hsintsun, or Chunghsing New Village, the seat of the Taiwan provincial government. It includes modern office buildings for government departments, an auditorium, in addition to living quarters for government workers and their families.

SEN-DOU CHANG
University of Hawaii

TAIGA, tī-gä′, is a northern woodland or forest of coniferous trees, such as spruces and firs. The term is used somewhat loosely, even by the Russians, who coined it. It denotes either the open woodland that lies south of the tundra and north of the dense forest, or more broadly, the entire area dominated by coniferous trees, whether scattered or bunched or formed into dense stands.

In the narrower sense, taiga, as differentiated from forest, is generally open woodland characterized by an upland growth of coniferous evergreen trees, between which extend more or less continuous carpets of reindeer lichens and scattered small trees (birches and alders, for instance) and ericaceous (heath family) shrubs. The river edges, especially toward the south, sometimes harbor denser stands or continuous strips of forest. The bare rock and abrupt outcrops frequently support low tundra vegetation. Extensive areas (the muskegs) remain undrained and accumulate peat continuously.

The woodland caribou is probably the most typical animal of this region, which has been variously subdivided according to particular vegetational characteristics, animal populations, and climatic fluctuations.

The Russian taiga has boundaries of contact with the steppe (plains) as well as the forest, and in the driest part of Siberia it occurs with larch, a conifer that sheds its leaves annually, as the dominant plant—a feature that is almost absent in America.

PIERRE DANSEREAU
Université de Montréal

LOKE WAN THO

Longtailed Indian tailorbird

TAILORBIRD, any of a genus of Old World warblers that stitch leaves together to make containers for their nests. Tailorbirds frequent gardens and settled lands from India through Southeast Asia and the East Indies to the Philippines.

Tailorbirds are 4 to 6 inches (10–15 cm) long and have sharp, slender bills, olive-green backs, reddish crowns, and light-gray breasts. The tail, which is longer in males, is frequently carried erect over the back. In their search for insects, tailorbirds are energetic and noisy, calling persistently in a harsh voice.

The tailorbird nest is usually placed in dense vegetation. The Indian tailorbird (*Orthotomus sutorius*) uses its sharp beak to stab holes along the margins of one or two broad leaves. With a series of stitches, it draws cottony plant down or spider webbing through the holes to bring leaf margins together to make an open-topped pouch. The bird lines the nest with plant down, fine grass, or hair. The two or three pale eggs are heavily spotted with brown.

Tailorbirds make up the genus *Orthotomus* of the family Sylviidae, order Passeriformes.

CARL WELTY, *Beloit College*

TAINAN, tī'nän', is an industrial and marketing city in southwestern Taiwan, China. The island's oldest city, it was founded by the Chinese in 1590's. In the 17th century it was the Dutch headquarters on Taiwan for nearly four decades. Then from 1662, after the island had come under Chinese rule, it was the capital of Taiwan for more than 200 years.

In the early days the city's center was near its port, Anping, 3 miles (5 km) west of the present center. A city wall was constructed in the early 18th century but was pulled down during the Japanese occupation of Taiwan (1895–1945) to facilitate the building of a railroad and highways. During the Japanese period, the railroad station, on the east side of the city, became the business center. The city has many places of historical interest, and Anping contains the site of the old Dutch Fort Zeelandia. Population: (1967) 429,024.

SEN-DOU CHANG
University of Hawaii

TAINE, ten, **Hippolyte Adolphe** (1828–1893), French historian, critic, and philosopher, whose naturalistic, scientific approach to the study of society and art exerted a deep influence on French thought in the late 19th century. He was born in Vouziers in the Ardennes on April 21, 1828. He attended the prestigious École Normale and quickly distinguished himself as one of its most brilliant students.

But Taine failed to advance rapidly in French academic life because his philosophical materialism and his disapproval of Louis Napoléon's regime offended his superiors. When Taine's doctoral thesis on *The Sensations* was rejected for ideological reasons in 1852, he undertook a new thesis on the fables of La Fontaine and received his doctorate in the following year. He then began an extremely successful career as a professional man of letters, reentering academic life only in 1864 as professor of art history at the École des Beaux-Arts in Paris.

Taine was a prolific, forceful, and controversial writer. In the decade before he assumed his professorship he established himself as a leader of the positivist school, which emphasized a scientific approach to philosophy. In 1855 the French Academy gave a prize to Taine for an essay on the Roman historian Livy, *Essai sur Tite-Live,* despite the essay's aggressive materialism. In 1857 he published *Les philosophes français du XIX siècle,* an energetic attack on the reigning philosophical school in France and an early statement of his positivist view that man's history, art, and literature must be studied in the manner of the natural sciences. He expounded the same doctrine in 1863 in the introduction to his greatest work of literary criticism, the *Histoire de la littérature anglaise.* He asserted that all human phenomena were products of three factors: race, environment, and historical moment.

Later Work and Influence. Taine was profoundly troubled by the defeat of France by Prussia in 1870–1871 and by the savage suppression, later in 1871, of the Commune of Paris by the French government. Fearing that violence menaced the social order, Taine resolved to devote his life to seeking the causes of France's instability. The study that resulted, *Les origines de la France contemporaine,* was still unfinished when he died. This was Taine's most controversial work. He asserted that the French propensity for revolutionary upheaval was largely the work of the 18th century *philosophes* and their revolutionary disciples who had undermined the social and religious institutions that alone checked man's evil passions. Powerful, though violently partisan and polemical, the work inspired a generation of conservative writers.

Taine was his generation's foremost exponent of positivism. Throughout his life he attempted to apply the methods of natural science to the study of human society. History, he asserted, was "a mechanical problem," susceptible to precise analysis. His famous dictum epitomized 19th century materialism: "Virtue and vice are products, like sugar and vitriol." Taine did not achieve his ambitious goals, and positivism was increasingly attacked during the 1890's for its rigidity and sterility. Taine's aspirations, however, remain those of 20th century social science. He died in Paris on March 5, 1893.

RICHARD T. BIENVENU
University of Missouri

TAINO INDIANS. See Arawak Indians.

TAINTER, tān'tər, **Charles Sumner** (1854–1940), American inventor. He was born in Watertown, Mass., on April 25, 1854, and was trained as a technician and instrument maker. In 1880 he began work in Washington, D. C., in a laboratory established by Alexander Graham Bell for research in acoustics. One of Tainter's jobs was to try to improve the crude tinfoil phonograph Edison had patented and then abandoned in 1878.

In 1886, Tainter and Chichester A. Bell were granted a patent on an improved phonograph. It featured a disk or cylinder of cardboard coated with wax in place of tinfoil, and a flexibly mounted stylus instead of Edison's rigidly mounted one. Fluctuation of pitch was reduced by replacing the hand crank with a foot-treadle mechanism or an electric motor. Public acclaim for this better-sounding "graphophone" aroused Edison and others to make further improvements in phonographic instruments.

Tainter later invented the dictaphone, for taking and repeating dictation. He died at San Diego, Calif., on April 20, 1940.

Kenneth M. Swezey
Author of "Science Shows You How"

TAIPEI, tī'bā', the largest city and capital of Taiwan, is the political, economic, and cultural center of Nationalist China. It is situated near the northern end of the island, on the east bank of the Tansui River, about 16 miles (26 km) southwest of Keelung (Chilung), its port. Taipei is the site of National Taiwan University. The National Palace Museum, which houses much of the collection from the National Palace Museum of Peking, is in a suburb of the city. Industries are located mainly in the suburban areas, and they include textiles, chemicals, printing, transportation equipment, food processing, and machinery.

TAIPEI'S CHUNG CHAN MARKET houses hundreds of shops and restaurants serving Taiwan's largest city.

UPI

Taipei developed in the early 1700's as a small market town where Chinese from the mainland bartered food and clothes with the Taiwan aborigines. It became the seat of Taipei prefecture in 1879, and when Taiwan was made a province in 1886, the governor general built his official residence within the city walls. In 1891, Taipei was officially designated the capital of Taiwan.

After Taiwan was ceded to Japan in 1895, Taipei was the seat of the Japanese governor general. Its name was changed to Taihoku. Within 10 years the Japanese had reconstructed much of the city, tearing down its walls and laying out new streets. When Taiwan was returned to China in 1945, Taipei again became the provincial capital.

In 1949 the Nationalist government of China moved to Taiwan and selected the city as its provisional seat. With the influx of refugees from mainland China, Taipei's population increased from 271,754 in 1946 to 562,756 in 1951. As part of a policy of urban decentralization, the provincial government was moved in 1958 from Taipei to Chunghsing-hsintsun in central Taiwan. In 1968, Taipei was made a national municipality under the direct jurisdiction of the central government, and its area increased from 26 square miles (67 sq km) to 105 square miles (272 sq km). Population: (1968) 1,560,088.

Sen-dou Chang, *University of Hawaii*

T'AI-P'ING REBELLION, tī'ping', the greatest rebel movement of 19th century China and one of the most destructive civil disturbances in recorded history. Lasting from 1851 to 1864, it spread to 17 provinces and caused 20 to 30 million deaths. The T'ai-p'ings strove to overthrow the Ch'ing (Manchu) dynasty and establish a theocracy based on their own militant brand of Christianity. They endeavored to create a more egalitarian society, which, like their movement, featured religious brotherhood, primitive communism, and puritanical fervor and discipline. Fanatical in their faith, they waged a massive civil and religious war against the Manchus, idolatry and ancestor worship, and the Confucian state and society.

The leader of the T'ai-p'ing movement was a frustrated scholar, Hung Hsiu-ch'üan (1814–1864), a Hakka from Kwangtung province. After repeatedly failing the civil service examinations, Hung fell ill and had visions of entering heaven. By 1843, through Christian tracts he had picked up in Canton, Hung came to believe that he was a son of God and the younger brother of Jesus, and that he was destined to play a messianic role in history. With a few converts, he moved to Kwangsi province, where his followers founded the God Worshipers Society in 1844.

In 1850 the God Worshipers clashed with government troops for the first time. In January 1851 they made a formal declaration of revolution and proclaimed a new dynasty, the "Heavenly Kingdom of Great Peace" (*T'ai-p'ing t'ien-kuo*). Hung was declared "Heavenly King," and later the senior leaders received subordinate kingly titles. Beginning in April 1852, the T'ai-p'ings advanced rapidly northward from Kwangsi and then down the Yangtze. By the time they took Nanking in March 1853, their forces totaled well over a million. Afterward, the T'ai-p'ings attempted to take Peking and Shanghai. Gradually, however, they were hemmed in by the newly created provincial armies. These forces were supported in part by the Western-trained "Ever Victorious Army," commanded by Charles George Gordon.

Hung, who had left the direction of the T'ai-p'ing movement to incompetent relatives, committed suicide in June 1864, just before the fall of his capital, Nanking. The city's capture in July by the Hunanese army, trained by Tseng Kuo-fan and led by his brother, Tseng Kuo-ch'üan, virtually ended the rebellion. However, the T'ai-p'ing movement had already deteriorated. Through intrigue, two of its best generals had lost their lives in 1856, and eventually its intolerance and harsh regimentation caused the movement to lose popular support.

HARRY J. LAMLEY
University of Hawaii

Further Reading: Boardman, Eugene P., *Christian Influence upon the Ideology of the Taiping Rebellion, 1851–1864* (Madison, Wis., 1952); Hail, William James, *Tseng Kuo-fan and the Taiping Rebellion*, 2d ed. (New York 1964); Michael, Franz, *The Taiping Rebellion: History and Documents* (Seattle and London 1966); Shih, Vincent Y. C., *The Taiping Ideology: Its Sources, Interpretations, and Influences* (Seattle and London 1967).

TAIRA, tī'rä, a great Japanese warrior clan that emerged in the 10th century. Like their rivals, the Minamoto, the Taira were descendants of members of the imperial family who had gone out to the provinces as officials and had chosen to remain there after their terms of office expired. Because of the failure of the imperial court at Kyoto to maintain effective control over the provinces, a class of professional warriors had developed. By the late 12th century this class, led by the Taira and Minamoto, had replaced the Kyoto courtiers as rulers of Japan.

In 1156 the Taira and Minamoto became involved in an armed struggle in Kyoto over succession to the throne. Another conflict erupted in 1159, and was essentially a clash between the Taira and Minamoto for military supremacy. The victory of Taira-no-Kiyomori gave the Taira a national preeminence that they held for more than 20 years.

Once in power the Taira devoted more attention to court politics than to consolidating their control over the provinces, and in 1180 the Minamoto revolted. Within five years they had overthrown the Taira and established at Kamakura, in the east, Japan's first true warrior government.

See also Japan—*Medieval History*.

H. PAUL VARLEY
Author of "The Samurai"

TAISHO, tī-shō (1879–1926), 123d emperor of Japan. Taisho ("Great Righteousness") is the reign name of Yoshihito, third son of Emperor Meiji (Mutsuhito).

Yoshihito was born in Tokyo on Aug. 31, 1879, and was educated at the Peers' School. In 1900 he married Princess Setsuko, daughter of Prince Kujo Michitaka. Yoshihito ascended the throne on his father's death on July 30, 1912, but retired in 1921 because of ill health. Hirohito, his eldest son, then became prince regent and on Yoshihito's death succeeded him as emperor. Yoshihito was not active in politics. He died at Hayama on Dec. 25, 1926.

TAIT, tāt, **Archibald Campbell** (1811–1882), archbishop of Canterbury. Tait was born in Edinburgh on Dec. 21, 1811. He joined the Church of England at Oxford University, where he graduated in 1833. Ordained in 1836, he was fellow and tutor at Balliol College (1834–1842) and headmaster of Rugby School (1842–1848). While dean of Carlisle Cathedral (1848–1856) five of his six children died tragically of smallpox in 1856. An early broad churchman, he joined the protest against Newman's Tract XC in 1841, but on liberal principles returned to Oxford to vote against the proposed censure on Newman in 1845 (see NEWMAN, JOHN HENRY).

In 1856, Tait became bishop of London and in 1869 archbishop of Canterbury. As administrator and pastor he endeavored to moderate controversies in the church. As archbishop he developed the worldwide responsibilities of the office. He had been a leader at the first Lambeth Conference of Anglican Bishops in 1867, and by calling another in 1878 made the conference into an institution. He guided the church in adjusting to Gladstone's reforms, in particular the disestablishment of the Irish church, and helped secure a more adequate settlement for the Irish clergy. In 1874 he hesitantly accepted Disraeli's Public Worship Regulation Act, which was designed in Disraeli's phrase "to put down ritualism." However, he insisted upon the inclusion of an episcopal veto on prosecutions of any clergy. He and other bishops generally employed the veto after 1881. Archbishop Tait died in Addington, Surrey, on Dec. 3, 1882.

EDWARD R. HARDY, *Cambridge University*

TAIT, tāt, **Peter Guthrie** (1831–1901), Scottish mathematician and physicist, who was among the first scientists to recognize the applicability of quaternions to physics.

Tait was born on April 28, 1831, at Dalkeith, Scotland. After attending Edinburgh Academy and spending one year at the University of Edinburgh, he went to Cambridge, where he graduated with highest honors in mathematics. He remained at Cambridge as a fellow and lecturer at Peterhouse College until 1854, when he became professor of mathematics at Queens College, Belfast. Six years later Tait returned to Edinburgh as professor of natural philosophy. He held this post until his death in Edinburgh on July 4, 1901.

Soon after arriving in Belfast, Tait became acquainted with Sir William Hamilton and his *Lectures on Quaternions*, which had appeared a year earlier. Tait immediately adopted Hamilton's new mathematical method and showed the fertility of quaternions when applied to problems of mathematical physics. However, he withheld publication of his *Elementary Treatise on Quaternions* (1866) until the posthumous publication of Hamilton's *The Elements of Quaternions*. In 1873, Tait published *An Introduction to Quaternions* with Philip Kelland, which was influential in bringing the theory of quaternions to the attention of physicists. Tait is also known for his work in thermodynamics. His first important work in this field appeared in 1864.

With Lord Kelvin, Tait is the author of the *Treatise on Natural Philosophy* (1867), a classic textbook in mathematical physics, which helped educate a whole generation of British physicists.

L. PEARCE WILLIAMS, *Cornell University*

CHINESE INFORMATION SERVICE

TAIPEI CELEBRATES the Chinese New Year with a huge dragon borne through the streets on the shoulders of young men.

TAIWAN, tī-wän′, is a Chinese island in the western Pacific Ocean, between the East and South China seas. It is separated from the mainland of China by the Taiwan Strait, 80 miles (130 km) wide at its narrowest point. As the bastion of the Nationalist government of China since 1949, Taiwan has more than doubled in population and has shown impressive economic growth. By 1970 it had slightly over 14 million people and one of Asia's highest per capita incomes.

The island has an area of 13,803 square miles (35,760 sq km) extending about 244 miles (393 km) from north to south and up to 90 miles (165 km) from west to east. It constitutes a province of China, along with the 13 small adjacent islands of the Taiwan group and 64 lesser islands in the Penghu (Pescadores) group. The total land area of the province is 13,885 square miles (35,961 sq km). The largest city and seat of the Nationalist government is Taipei. The seat of the provincial government is Chunghsinghsintsun.

Taiwan is known for its rugged terrain and the majestic beauty of its mountain ranges. Its name means "Terraced Bay" in Chinese. The island got its Western name, Formosa, from the Portuguese, who called it Ilha Formosa ("Beautiful Isle") when they sailed past in the late 1500's.

The Land. The surface of Taiwan slopes steeply eastward and more gradually to the west. The massive Central Range (Chungyang Shanmo) occupies about half the total area and includes four lofty ranges extending north and south for almost three fourths of the island's length. More than a dozen of the mountain peaks are over 3,500 meters (11,480 feet) in elevation. The highest, Yü Shan (Mt. Morrison), is 13,113 feet (3,997 meters). Along the east coast between Suao and Hualien, mountains of the Central Range drop abruptly into the Pacific, forming some of the world's highest sea cliffs. The Central Range is also the source of the island's largest rivers. Another major range, the Taitung, is on the east coast. There are volcanic mountains in the Tatun group in the north.

A narrow zone of foothills, from 300 to 1,600 feet (100–500 meters) in elevation, surrounds much of the Central Range. From these foothills the terrain descends gradually to the lowlands. The coastal plain and river basins are quite level. The western coastline contains tidal flats formed by heavy erosion of the mountains and by frequent flooding in the lowland areas.

The climate of Taiwan is influenced by its topography and its location astride the Tropic of Cancer, as well as by the warm Japan, or Black Stream, ocean current that surrounds the island. The northeast (winter) monsoon brings rain to the northern part. During the southwest (summer) monsoon, southern Taiwan receives rain, while the north has relatively dry weather. The annual rainfall averages 40 to 60 inches (1,000–1,500 mm) on the west coast and exceeds 200 inches (5,000 mm) in some mountainous areas. The mean temperature varies from 80° to 90° F (27°–32° C) in summer and 50° to 60° F (10°–15° C) during the winter.

Natural Resources. Taiwan's landscape features a profusion of vegetation, ranging from tropical to alpine varieties. The forests, which cover about 55% of the island, mainly in the central and eastern mountain ranges, are well preserved. Stands of bamboo and acacia occupy moist sites at lower elevations. Subtropical and temperate hardwoods are found at levels of 650 to 3,300 feet (200–1,000 meters), and conifers are more common at higher elevations. There are nearly 200 species of trees of commercial value, including types of cypress, oak, hemlock, spruce, pine, and bamboo. Tree ferns, banyans, and mangroves flourish in the dense forests that cover the foothills and lower mountain slopes, along with such flowering plants as azaleas, lilies, rhododendrons, and orchids.

The animal life also varies with the change in altitude. Deer, goats, and wild pigs frequent the mountainous areas, while bands of monkeys inhabit the humid forests in the south. Domesticated animals include the water buffalo and yellow ox. Less evident are the 37 species of snakes, of which 12 are poisonous. Taiwan also has some rich offshore fishing grounds.

More than 70 minerals are found in Taiwan, but only coal is comparatively abundant. The Central Range, with its heavy rainfall, offers abundant water for irrigation and the generation of hydroelectric power. More than 75% of the total cultivated land is irrigated.

The People. Taiwan's location along natural sea lanes made it accessible to many cultural influences and peoples. Archaeological evidence shows that the late Neolithic Lungshanoid culture of North China eventually spread to the island, as did elements of early cultures from South China. Megaliths along Taiwan's east coast suggest influences from Luzon in the Philippines.

The island's diverse aboriginal population indicates that further migrations occurred at later periods. Eight aboriginal tribes still inhabit the mountainous areas, and another, the Yami, lives on nearby Lan Hsü island. Differing in language and customs, these ethnic groups are thought to be of Indonesian and Malayan extraction, and, in some cases, possibly of East China origin. The aborigines number over 200,000.

Most of Taiwan's population is Chinese. However, there are distinctions between those who are native to Taiwan and more recent arrivals from the mainland. The native Taiwanese are descendants of immigrants from southern Fukien and eastern Kwangtung provinces, who settled on the island from the 16th through the 19th century. The speech and habits of the Fukienese, or Hoklos, differed from those of the Kwangtungese, who were mostly Hakkas. Since the Hoklos outnumber the Hakkas four to one, their Min-nan, or Amoy, language remains prevalent among the Taiwanese. Under Japanese rule (1895–1945), the Taiwanese were cut off from the mainland, and many acquired the language, education, and mannerisms of the Japanese. The rural majority, however, retained their Chinese ways for the most part. Their village communities remained intact, as did their religion—a mixture of popular Buddhism, Taoism, ancestor worship, and veneration of local deities.

Most of the mainlanders crossed over to Taiwan in 1949 during the Communist take-over of the rest of China. These Chinese, who fled from all parts of the mainland, originally numbered over two million. They have not readily assimilated with the Taiwanese. Mainland civilians live principally in the Taipei area and other urban centers. The common use of the national vernacular (Kuo Yü), intermarriage, and joint schooling for the young are factors tending gradually to merge the two groups.

Taiwan province has one of the world's fastest-growing and densest populations. Augmented by the mainlander influx, the population soared to 13,383,357 by the census of 1966, or twice what it had been in 1946. From 1963 to 1968 the annual rate of increase averaged 2.9%. Since 1968 the density has exceeded 969 persons per square mile (374 per sq km). About 60% of the inhabitants live in cities and towns.

Economy. Taiwan's economy suffered during World War II and the transitional period that followed. Recovery to prewar levels was not effected until 1952, after which there were steady increases in agricultural and industrial output. In 1969, under the fifth Four-Year Economic Plan, the gross domestic product rose to over $4.7 billion, and per capita income reached $257.

Agriculture remains the island's main economic activity. About one fourth of the total area is under cultivation. Rice is grown as the major crop on over half this farmland. Secondary crops include sweet potatoes, wheat, peanuts, soybeans, and maize. Grown for export as well as domestic consumption are sugarcane, tea, tobacco, tropical fruits, and mushrooms.

From 1953 until about 1967, Taiwan's agricultural production recorded an average annual growth rate of over 7%. This increase was due partly to the technical and financial assistance rendered by the Sino-American Joint Commission on Rural Reconstruction (JCRR). Also, a series of rural land reforms were initiated, including a farm rent reduction program (1949), government sale of public land (1951), and the resale of tenant-cultivated farmlands to those who tilled them (1953). Later, to stimulate farm production, a new economic policy, announced in 1970, shifted official emphasis from the small cultivator to large agricultural enterprises using modern, efficient methods of farming.

Manufacturing has advanced even more rapidly than agriculture. The fastest development has been in textiles, chemicals, canning, and the wood-processing industries. A dozen major industries operate as state enterprises under the supervision of the ministry of economic affairs. Structured as corporations, these enterprises include sugar, petroleum, coal, aluminum, fertilizer, alkali, machinery, textiles, electric power, fisheries, shipbuilding, and metal mining.

The expansion of manufacturing spurred commercial growth. Since 1957, exports of light industrial products have increased at a marked rate, and imports of raw materials and capital goods have been steady. Banks and insurance companies have expanded their operations, indicating increases in savings and in the money supply. In 1962 the Taiwan Stock Exchange was established to channel savings into investment.

CHINESE INFORMATION SERVICE

TAROKO GORGE, an area of great scenic beauty in eastern Taiwan, is a favorite viewing spot for visitors.

Transportation facilities on the island include over 10,370 miles (16,700 km) of highways and roads and over 2,297 miles (3,700 km) of railroads. Partly to promote tourism, two new scenic cross-island highways have been constructed and a third undertaken. Besides the international air service offered by several lines, local airlines provide regular domestic service.

Local Government. Since Nationalist rule is confined almost entirely to the province of Taiwan, central and local governments overlap in many fields. Nevertheless, considerable local authority is exercised over domestic affairs through a system of self-government.

Local government extends from the provincial level down to the 16 counties (*hsien*), including Penghu, and the five municipalities (*shih*). In turn, each county exercises jurisdiction over rural districts (*hsiang*), townships (*chen*), and the smaller cities, while the municipalities do so over urban districts (*ch'ü*). The rural districts are further divided into villages (*ts'un*), and the townships, cities, and urban districts into subunits known as *li*.

The highest organ of self-government is the provincial assembly, which is an elected body. Self-government prevails on all lower levels. The county and municipal councils, magistrates and mayors, along with heads and representatives of rural and urban divisions, are elected by direct suffrage and secret ballot.

History. For centuries Taiwan was not clearly identified in Chinese annals. Not until the Ming dynasty (1368–1644) was its exact location established and the name "Taiwan" used in official sources.

Taiwan's recorded history began in the latter part of the 16th century, when immigrants from Fukien joined the few Chinese and Japanese already there. Although Taiwan had been sighted by the Portuguese, the Dutch were the first Westerners to set foot on the island. After establishing a trading station in the Taiwan area in 1624, they built forts and churches, encouraged Chinese immigration, and taxed the inhabitants. Missionaries of the Dutch Reformed Church sought to convert the aborigines. In 1641 the Dutch succeeded in driving out the Spanish, who had founded small communities in the north. Twenty years later the Dutch, in turn, were forced to leave by the Chinese patriot Cheng Ch'eng-kung (Koxinga), who was loyal to the overthrown Ming dynasty. Under Cheng family rule, Taiwan became a base of operations against mainland Manchu rule and a flourishing center of trade.

Cheng Ch'eng-kung's grandson surrendered to the Manchus in 1683, and Taiwan was made a prefecture of Fukien in 1684. During the early Ch'ing (Manchu) period severe regulations restricting emigration and shipping to Taiwan hindered the island's development. Subsequently, local government was ineffective, and conditions were chaotic. Still, large numbers of Chinese emigrated to Taiwan. By 1895 the Chinese inhabitants totaled over 2.5 million.

In the 1860's, as provided by the Tientsin treaties, the ports of Tamsui, Keelung, Anping, and Takao (Kaohsiung) were opened to Western trading companies and missionaries. A Japanese expeditionary force was sent to the southernmost part of the island in 1874, prompting the Chinese authorities to increase the effectiveness of their administration. French forces landed in the Keelung area a decade later but were checked by Liu Ming-ch'uan, who became the first governor. After Taiwan was made a separate province of China in 1886, he initiated reforms.

In 1895, Taiwan was ceded to Japan after China's defeat in the first Sino-Japanese War. The Japanese encountered local resistance, and expressions of anti-Japanese sentiment occurred over the next several decades. Nevertheless, Japan was able to impose order and improve the economy through effective government based on Western colonial precedents. In October 1945, following Japan's defeat in World War II, Taiwan was returned to China.

The first years of restored Chinese rule proved disappointing. Provoked by the corrupt practices of Governor Ch'en Yi, the Taiwanese staged a widespread uprising in February 1947. Tension continued, particularly when large numbers of mainland Chinese arrived during 1949. After the Nationalist government retreated to Taiwan late in that year and Chiang Kai-shek resumed the presidency in March 1950, more constructive rule was forthcoming. With the outbreak of the Korean War in 1950, the U. S. 7th Fleet began to operate in the Taiwan Strait to protect the island. A few months later the United States initiated a program of military and economic assistance to the Nationalists, and in 1954 a Chinese-U. S. mutual defense treaty was signed. Since then, Taiwan has continued to serve as the redoubt of the Nationalist regime. See also CHINA.

HARRY J. LAMLEY
University of Hawaii

Further Reading: Chen Cheng-siang, *Taiwan: An Economic and Social Geography*, 2 vols. (Taipei 1963); Davidson, James W., *The Island of Formosa Past and Present* (London and New York 1903); Gallin, Bernard, *Hsin Hsing, Taiwan: A Chinese Village in Change* (Berkeley 1966); Hsieh Chiao-min, *Taiwan—Ilha Formosa: A Geography in Perspective* (London 1964).

TAIWAN STRAIT, tī'wän', a body of water connecting the East and South China seas and separating the Chinese island of Taiwan from the Chinese mainland province of Fukien. The strait, 80 to 120 miles (130–190 km) wide, contains the Penghu (Pescadores) islands, which, like Taiwan, are controlled by the Nationalist government of China.

The Taiwan (Formosa) Strait is important to international politics because of the U. S. commitment, dating from 1954, to defend Taiwan and the Penghu group from attack by the mainland (Communist) Chinese. This commitment does not extend to the Nationalist-held islands of Quemoy and Matsu, which are just off the coast of Fukien.

TAIWAN UNIVERSITY, National, tī'wän', a coeducational institution in Taipei, supported and operated by the ministry of education of the Republic of China. The university was founded in 1928 by the Japanese during their occupation of Taiwan and was named Taihoku Imperial University. In 1945 the Chinese government took over the university and named it the National Taiwan University.

The university has colleges of liberal arts, science, law, medicine, engineering, and agriculture. In addition, the university operates the Taiwan Agricultural Research Center.

The university library contains almost 900,000 volumes. Enrollment increased from about 8,000 men and women in 1960 to about 10,000 by 1970.

TAIYÜAN, tī'yü-än', the capital of Shansi province in northern China, is situated in the center of the province, on the Fen River, a tributary of the Hwang Ho. It has been the political, economic, and cultural heart of Shansi for centuries.

Taiyüan is the trading and processing center of Shansi's central agricultural basin. It is also a key industrial city. Modern industries were started in 1930 by Yen Hsi-shan, the warlord of Shansi from 1912 to 1947. During that period the city was called *Yangkü* and the name "Taiyüan" referred to the small city of Chinyüan to the southwest. After 1949, Taiyüan's iron and steel plant was expanded into one of the largest metallurgical enterprises in North China, and several machine-building plants were established. Taiyüan contains Shansi University and technical colleges. Population: (1957) 1,020,000.

DAVID CHUEN-YAN LAI
University of Victoria, British Columbia

TAIZ, ta'iz, is the principal town in the southern part of the Yemen Arab Republic. Situated at an altitude of 4,500 feet (1,372 meters), Taiz (also Taizz) is watered by mountain streams and surrounded by verdant gardens. It is considered the most beautiful town in Yemen. Long a center of Islamic learning, Taiz has at times served as the capital of the country. In the past its external trade was routed through Aden, but in the 1960's the United States built a road from Taiz to Yemen's southern port of Mocha and the USSR built another to Yemen's northern port of Hodeida. Population: (1963 est.) 80,000.

GEORGE RENTZ
Hoover Institution, Stanford University

TAJ MAHAL, täj mə-hul', a mausoleum on the outskirts of Agra, India. The authorship of its design is uncertain.

The building derives its name from the title Mum*taz Mahal* (Chosen of the Palace), given to Arjumand Banu Begum, the favorite wife of the Mughul Emperor Shah Jahan. Arjumand Banu died at Burhanpur in 1631, while giving birth to her 14th child. Her remains were moved six months later to Agra, where the grief-stricken Emperor determined to build a tomb of the utmost magnificence. The structure was completed in 1648.

J. ALLAN CASH, FROM RAPHO GUILLUMETTE

THE TAJ MAHAL, at Agra, India, is considered one of the finest examples of Muslim architecture.

The Taj Mahal is on the bank of the Yamuna (Jumna) River, where it can be seen across a bend in the river from Shah Jahan's palace in Agra fort. The tomb stands on a square platform with the Yamuna flowing past its northern side. This platform and the tomb itself are faced with white marble from Makrana in Rajasthan, but other buildings in the complex are of local red sandstone with marble details. The tomb is approached from the south through a formal garden, divided by paths and ornamental pools and entered by an imposing gateway. This in turn is approached from the west through a rectangular court, which is flanked by a row of shops.

In its ground plan, the mausoleum occupies a square measuring 186 feet (57 meters) on each side, with its corners chamfered off. The exterior elevations are broken up by arched recesses containing screened openings through which the interior is lit, and the spandrels of these arches and other sections of the surface are elegantly inlaid with decorative motifs in semiprecious stones. Above the central chamber is a dome of excellent proportions supported by a drum and topped by a metal pinnacle. The dome is surrounded by 4 open kiosks and also by 16 slender pinnacles situated around the perimeter of the roof. The composition is completed by 4 marble-faced minarets, one at each corner of the platform. On either side of the tomb, at a lower level, are placed a mosque on the west and a matching assembly hall on the east.

Inside the tomb are five chambers, of which the large central one is joined to the rest by radiating passages. Within this central chamber a pierced marble screen, of later date than the tomb itself, surrounds the inlaid marble sarcophagi of Arjumand Banu and Shah Jahan, who are buried in a crypt below.

Originally the Emperor intended to build a replica of the Taj Mahal in black marble for his own burial. It was to be on the other bank of the river and connected with the Taj Mahal by a bridge. Before Shah Jahan could realize this ambition, however, he was deposed.

ROBERT W. SKELTON
Victoria and Albert Museum, London

TAJIK. See TADZHIK SOVIET SOCIALIST REPUBLIC.

TAKAMATSU, tä-kä-mä-tsōō, a city in Japan on the Inland Sea, is the island of Shikoku's chief port for trade with Honshu and for travel between the two islands. The city is the capital of Kagawa prefecture.

Takamatsu's Ritsurin Park is an outstanding example of Japanese landscape gardening. In Tamamo Park stand remains of a 16th century castle. Near the city are the scenic peninsula of Yashima, which was once an island, and the island of Megi. In a popular fairy tale, Megi contained the den of demons subjugated by Momotaro and his followers—a monkey, a pheasant, and a dog. Population: (1965) 243,444.

TAKAMINE JOKICHI, tä-kä-mē-ne jō-kē-chē (1854–1922), Japanese chemist, who in 1901 isolated adrenalin. This first isolation of a hormone in crystalline form marked a breakthrough for the chemistry of hormones as well as for hormonal therapy.

Takamine was born in Takaoka, Japan, on Nov. 3, 1854. He graduated from the University of Tokyo in 1879 and studied in Scotland for two years. In 1883 he became a Japanese government chemist but left the government in 1887 to develop the first superphosphate works in Japan. In this period he also isolated a potent starch-digesting enzyme, called Takadiastase. In 1890 he moved to the United States and introduced this enzyme into the distilling industry. Ultimately, it was taken over for medicinal use by Parke, Davis & Co., with whom Takamine remained associated throughout his professional life.

From the United States, Takamine continued to serve Japanese industry. He contributed to the development in Japan of dyes, aluminum fabrication, Bakelite, the electric furnace, and nitrogen fixation. Through his influence, the Imperial Research Institute was established in 1913. He died in New York City on July 22, 1922.

J. F. BENNETT, *Stanford University*

TAKAOKA, tä-kä-ō-kä, a city in Japan, is situated in west central Honshu, in Toyama prefecture, 165 miles (265 km) northwest of Tokyo. The city is a commercial and manufacturing center with metalware, lacquerware, cotton-spinning, and textile-print dyeing industries. Steel and plastics industries were developed after World War II.

The city's growth dates from 1609, when Maeda Toshinaga built a castle there. Only the moats remain in the handsome park that occupies the castle site. Zuiryuji Temple in Takaoka contains many old treasures, including autographed letters of Emperor Goyozei (reigned 1586–1611). Population: (1965) 139,502.

TAKASAKI, tä-kä-sä-kē, a city in Japan, is situated in Gumma prefecture on central Honshu, 60 miles (100 km) northwest of Tokyo. It is an important railroad junction and has textile and food industries. Takasaki is noted for its colossal statue of Kannon, goddess of mercy, which stands 42 meters (138 feet) high. Population: (1965) 173,887.

TAKAYAMA, tä-kä-yä-mä, is a city in Japan that is noted for its festivals and folk arts. It is situated in Gifu prefecture, central Honshu, about 70 miles (110 km) north of Nagoya. Takayama has a fine view of the Hida Mountains, which form the western end of the Japan Alps, and is near Chubu Sangaku National Park.

Visitors are attracted to the city by the park and by the festivals of the Hie and Hachiman shrines. The festivals feature music and dancing and parades with colorful, elaborately decorated floats. Many old houses have been preserved in the city. One of these is a folkcraft museum, and there are remains of a castle and a feudal lord's house. Takayama's many craftsmen produce lacquerware and woodcarvings, but there is little modern industry. Population: (1965) 53,399.

PRUE DEMPSTER, *Author of "Japan Advances"*

TAKIN, tä'kēn, a heavy, clumsy-looking mammal (*Budorcas taxicolor*) most closely related to the musk ox. It is found in the mountainous regions of Bhutan Himalaya, northeastern India (Mishmi Hills of Assam), eastern Tibet, the Burma-Assam frontier, and west-central China (Tsinling Mountains of Shensi). The takin is about 3½ feet (1 meter) high at the shoulders and 4 feet (1.2 meters) in length, plus a 4-inch (10-cm) tail. Adults range in weight from about 500 to 600 pounds (227–272 kg). The takin has an immense, bulbous face, a heavy mouth, and a tremendously thick neck. The horns, borne by both males and females, bend sharply outward from the midline of the head, then turn backwards and upward. The coat is shaggy and commonly brownish, but the Chinese takin is golden yellow in color.

The takin's preferred habitat is dense thickets or woods on steep mountain slopes, at about 3,000 to 10,000 feet (900–3,000 meters) elevation. In summer, takins congregate about their drinking places in herds of 30 or more, but in winter they live in bands of up to 12 animals. Old bulls may be solitary. Mating in west-central China takes place in July and August, and usually a single young is born after about 9 months' gestation. The calf is weaned at 1 month.

ARTHUR AMBLER, FROM NATIONAL AUDUBON SOCIETY

TAKINS, such as this young male calf and adult female, are native to Bhutan, India, Burma, Tibet, and China.

B. C. MAHENDRA, *President*
The Academy of Zoology, Agra, India

TAKLA MAKAN. See TARIM BASIN.

TAKOMA PARK, tə-kō'mə, is a town in central Maryland, in Montgomery and Prince Georges counties. It is just northeast of Washington, D. C., of which it is a residential suburb. It is the home of Columbia Union College, a Seventh-day Adventist coeducational institution founded in 1904, and of Montgomery College. Takoma Park was chartered in 1890. It is governed by a mayor and council. Population: 18,455.

TAKORADI, a seaport town in Ghana, was united with Sekondi in 1946 to form the municipality of Sekondi-Takoradi. Population: (1960) 40,937.

TAKRAW, tə-krô', a throw and catch game for 2 to 12 players, is played within or without defined boundaries. Each participant uses a lightweight bat with a cone-shaped "trap" and a curved tip, or extension, to maneuver a hollow plastic ball in such a manner that the opposing side cannot retrieve it. Speed and dexterity are needed to play the game well, but all ages can enjoy it in a strictly informal manner.

The game originated in Malaya, where players catch and pass a rattan ball, or *takraw*, with their feet. The use of a bat is an American invention. In the modern game, players use the bat to hook the ball in flight and then throw it.

The game may be played with a net and on a badminton-size court, which is 44 feet (about 13 meters) long and 20 feet (6 meters) wide. The space between the two short service lines on the badminton court, however, is an out-of-bounds space in takraw. Players on each side may position themselves anywhere within the inbounds area.

One player, determined by toss, starts the game by throwing (serving) the ball over the net so that it hits inbounds on the opposite court. Any opponent may try to catch and return the ball or catch and pass it to a teammate who volleys it over the net. An out-of-bounds throw or a missed catch scores a point for the opponent. The side winning the point serves the next ball. Game is 21 points.

The game also may be played without a net or boundary lines. The players keep about 25 feet (7.6 meters) apart and a throw must be one that the receiver can reach with the bat without taking more than one step or leaving the ground with both feet before the ball hits the surface. In this version each catch scores one point, and a bad throw or failure to catch a proper throw results in loss of a point.

With practice a player learns how to let the ball strike the curve of the bat in order to trap it and then how to throw it accurately. The easiest way of throwing is by raising the bat overhead and, with a quick wrist snap, flipping the ball upward (out of the cone) and forward. To make a sidearm throw the player must keep the ball moving along the curved extension of the bat. The fastest throws are from shoulder height. However, in takraw, accuracy is more important than speed. To practice the techniques a player can throw the ball against a wall and try to catch it before it touches the ground.

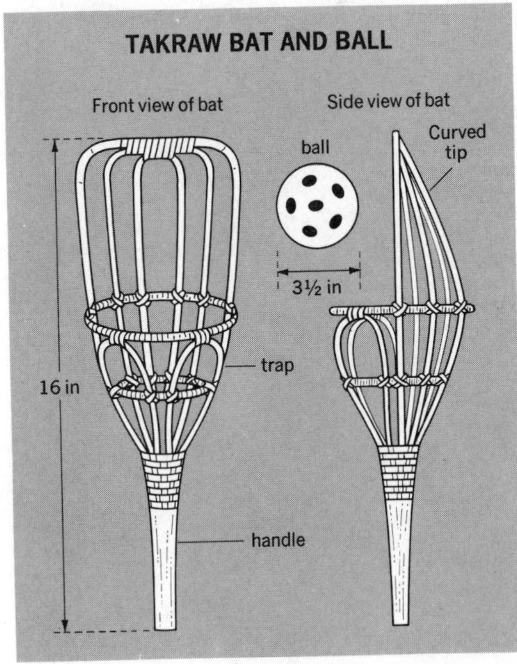

TALBERT, Billy (1918–), American tennis player, who won the U.S. men's doubles title four times and captained the Davis Cup team from 1952 to 1957. William Franklin Talbert, III, was born in Cincinnati, Ohio, on Sept. 4, 1918. He became a tennis star after his graduation from the University of Cincinnati in 1940.

Talbert was an outstanding doubles player whose singles play was often overlooked. His game was sound and dependable and free from flourish. With Gardnar Mulloy he shared the national doubles title in 1942, 1945, 1946, and 1948. With Margaret Osborne, he shared the mixed doubles crown from 1943 to 1946. He took the men's indoor singles title in 1948 and 1951, and shared the indoor mixed doubles title in 1947 and 1948 and the men's doubles crown from 1949 to 1952 and in 1954. He wrote several books on tennis strategy, including *The Game of Doubles in Tennis* (1956).

NEIL L. AMDUR, *New York "Times"*

TALBOT, John (1388?–1453), English soldier, who fought in about 40 battles of the Hundred Years' War between England and France. He was born about 1388, the second son of the 4th Baron Talbot. He was lord lieutenant of Ireland three times (1414–1419, 1424–1427, and 1445–1447), but after 1419 he served principally in the English army in France.

After Joan of Arc had raised the Siege of Orléans on May 8, 1429, the English withdrew to Patay, where they were defeated on June 18 and Talbot was captured. After his release in 1433, he won several victories. He was created 1st Earl of Shrewsbury in 1442.

In 1452 he was sent to Gascony, France, in response to an appeal by the people for help against the French. Talbot occupied Bordeaux, but was persuaded against his judgment to attack a superior French force at Castillon, 30 miles (48 km) to the east, on July 17, 1453. His army was routed, and Talbot was killed. This was the last battle of the Hundred Years' War.

TALBOT, Mary Anne (1778–1808), English adventuress, who was purported to have served four years in the British Army and on ships at sea posing as a man. She was born in London on Feb. 2, 1778. At the age of 13 she eloped with a Captain Bowen to Santo Domingo, where she posed as a serving boy, taking the name of John Taylor. She accompanied Bowen in 1792 as a drummer boy with the British Army in Flanders.

On Bowen's death, she became a beggar until September 1793, when she shipped as cabin boy on a French lugger, which was captured by a British man-of-war. Mary Anne was enlisted on the British ship as a powder monkey, and in the Battle of the First of June (1794) she was wounded in the ankle. After recovering, she rejoined the navy but was captured by the French and imprisoned for 18 months. Returning to London, she was seized by a press-gang, and only then, it was said, was it discovered that she was a woman.

Mary Anne became a servant in the home of Robert S. Kirby, a publisher, who told her story in the second volume of his *Wonderful Museum*, published in 1804. She died in Shropshire on Feb. 4, 1808.

TALBOT, Richard. See TYRCONNEL, EARL OF.

TALBOT, Thomas (1771–1853), Canadian colonizer and administrator. He was born on July 17, 1771, at Castle Malahide, County Dublin, Ireland. As a young officer in the British Army, he went to Quebec in 1790 and became secretary to the first lieutenant-governor of Upper Canada, and was able to visit the rich unoccupied lands in the western part of the province.

After serving in England's continental wars against France from 1794 to 1800, Talbot returned to Upper Canada in 1801. He obtained a grant of 5,000 acres of land on the north shore of Lake Erie and founded the Talbot Settlement, centered on the village of St. Thomas. In 1809 this grant was extended, enabling Talbot to build roads and to settle, in 30 years' time, some 6,000 settlers in 28 townships.

For almost 50 years Talbot governed his extensive domain, becoming more patriarchal and eccentric as he grew older. Finally, settlers' complaints obliged the government to relieve him of executive authority in the settlements. He died on Feb. 6, 1853, in London, Canada.

D. M. L. FARR, *Carleton University*

TALBOT, William Henry Fox (1800–1877), English scientist and inventor of the negative-positive system on which most of modern photography is based. He was born in Lacock, Wiltshire, England, on Feb. 11, 1800, and educated at Harrow and Cambridge. Noted for his pioneering work in photography and photomechanics, he also contributed to the fields of mathematics, botany, optics, electricity, chemistry, English etymology, and to linguistics with his translations of Assyrian cuneiform inscriptions.

In 1840, five years after inventing the negative-positive system, Talbot discovered that exposure of silver halide materials produced a latent image that could be developed. His *The Pencil of Nature*, the first commercially produced book to be illustrated with photographs, was issued in six parts between 1844 and 1846. It contained 24 photographs.

At a June 1851 meeting of the Royal Institution, Talbot made the first high-speed photograph. It was the picture of a newspaper page, which had been fastened to a disk, rotated rapidly, and illuminated by the spark of a discharging Leyden battery. The first practical photomechanical system of halftone image reproduction was patented by Talbot in 1852, forming the basis for modern contact cross-line photogravure techniques. He died at Lacock Abbey on Sept. 17, 1877.

EUGENE OSTROFF, *Smithsonian Institution*

TALC, talk, is a hydrous magnesium silicate mineral used for a large number of commercial products. Its extreme softness when pure—it is at the bottom of the Mohs scale of hardness—led to its use as talcum powder and face powder. However, most talc is used in ceramics and roofing because it resists fire well and is a poor conductor of heat and electricity. It is also used as a filler in rubber, paint, and paper.

The impure form of talc rock is *steatite*, or *soapstone*. In this form it is made into acid-proof laboratory sinks and table tops, laundry tubs, and slabs for electrical switchboards. American Indians used steatite for making bowls, pots, and stoves.

Talc is a metamorphic rock closely related to serpentine. The masses in which it occurs may be very large, making talc a major rock-forming mineral. It is usually pale green but may be white or gray, and the presence of iron turns it reddish or brown.

The mineral is found largely in mountainous regions. The United States is the chief source, followed by Japan and the Soviet Union. Another source, the Pyrenees mountains, contributed to the start of the French cosmetics industry.

Composition, $Mg_3Si_4O_{10}(OH)_2$; hardness, 1; specific gravity, 2.82; crystal system, monoclinic.

RICHARD M. PEARL
Colorado College

TALCA, täl'kə, a city in Chile, is situated in the fertile Central Valley, about 150 miles (240 km) south of Santiago and 40 miles (65 km) east of the Pacific Ocean. It is the capital of Talca province, the nation's principal wine-producing area and a major source of wheat, livestock, and vegetables. The city is an important manufacturing center, with foundries, paper mills, distilleries, and shoe factories. Founded in 1692, Talca was destroyed by earthquakes in 1742 and 1928. It was rebuilt after 1928 and now has a modern aspect, enhanced by spacious parks and avenues. Population: (1960) 68,148.

TALCAHUANO, täl-kə-hwän'ō, a city in south-central Chile, situated on a small peninsula that extends into the Pacific Ocean about 9 miles (13 km) north of Concepción. Its natural harbor, considered the best in Chile, has made it an important commercial port and the site of the nation's principal naval base. In the vicinity are metallurgical plants, petroleum refineries, fish canneries, flour mills, and glass factories. Talcahuano became the port for Concepción after that city was destroyed by an earthquake in 1730. The port city itself was severely damaged by a series of earthquakes in the 1960's. Population: (1968) 108,668.

TALE OF A TUB, Jonathan Swift's first great satire, composed in large part by 1697 and first published in 1704. *A Tale of a Tub* presents parallel corruptions in religion and learning through an allegorical tale and interspersed digressions—which are actually essential parts of the design—dealing with the world of letters.

The tale concerns Peter, Martin, and Jack, three brothers who stand for the modern churches of divided Christianity—Roman, Anglican (or Lutheran), and Calvinist. Their father wills each of them a coat that will last a lifetime and always fit if it is kept clean. The will instructs the brothers in the proper use of their coats. After a period of obedience to this testament, the brothers go to a fashionable town—the churches, that is, become worldly—where they can pursue wealth and prestige only by adorning their coats in the current fashion. Led by Peter, they subject the will's restrictions to ingenious and increasingly tortured interpretation until it serves their own desires. Jack later "reforms" his coat by tearing off all its ornament and reducing it to shreds. Martin, more cautious, patiently removes what he can from his coat without destroying the fabric—his is the humble middle way of the Anglican church, which has recovered primitive Christian teachings in as pure a form as is possible after 17 centuries. In the digressions, evils similar to those in the tale are revealed among writers and critics, who deny the wisdom of the past only to spin helplessly in the whirl of fashion.

The work incorporates parody of religious dogma, scientific jargon, and the smug self-celebration of Swift's contemporaries. Its deliberately elaborate form looks back with mockery to an age of baroque rhetoric and intense doctrinal controversy.

MARTIN PRICE, *Yale University*
Author of "Swift's Rhetorical Art"

Further Reading: Harth, Phillip, *Swift and Anglican Rationalism* (Chicago 1961); Paulson, Ronald, *Theme and Structure in Swift's Tale of a Tub* (New Haven, Conn., 1960); Starkman, Miriam K., *Swift's Satire of Learning in A Tale of a Tub* (Princeton, N. J., 1950).

TALE OF GENJI, gen-jē, an early 11th century romance that is generally recognized as the supreme masterpiece of Japanese prose literature. The author of most if not all of it was a court lady known today as Murasaki Shikibu. Her dates are unknown and her real name is widely debated, but it seems clear that she belonged to the powerful Fujiwara clan and was in the service of an empress.

The *Tale of Genji* (*Genji monogatari*) consists of 54 chapters and, in Arthur Waley's very free and somewhat abridged English translation (1925–1933), comes to more than 1,100 closely printed pages. It tells of the life and loves of an idealized Lord Genji, the son of an emperor by a concubine; of his early successes and the clouds that gather over his later years; and of the altogether gloomier and less robust activities of the generation of his grandchildren after his death.

Richly symbolic, the book spins a Buddhist web of retribution in Genji's own affairs and relates a Buddhist parable of decline as it moves on to the affairs of his grandchildren. It reviews the varieties of courtly love and achieves increasingly impressive psychological depths as it recounts the quest for a lost parent in both generations. Because of the variety and power of the characterization and the book's remarkable success in re-creating a whole aristocratic way of life, it has justifiably been called the first great novel in the literature of the world.

The *Genji* was written over an unknown period of years in the early 11th century, quite possibly with later additions, revisions, and corruptions. Scholars debate spiritedly over how long it was in the writing, whether it is the work of a single hand or is an accretion, and whether the standard sequence of chapters follows the original order. These problems are greatly complicated by the absence of a text from earlier than two centuries after the period of major composition. Modern research seems to have answered the last question conclusively. The chapters were composed in an order considerably different from that in which they were later assembled. There is persuasive but inconclusive evidence that the work is substantially from a single hand and that the composition covered a very extensive portion of the author's life. One sees not an agglomeration but the maturing of a single talent. Thus "Murasaki Shikibu" becomes the greatest literary genius Japan has produced.

EDWARD SEIDENSTICKER
University of Michigan

TALE OF THE HEIKE. See JAPAN–*Literature* (The Kamakura Period).

TALE OF TWO CITIES, a novel by the English author Charles Dickens, first published serially in 1859 in his magazine *All the Year Round.* A tale of action and adventure, set in London and Paris at the time of the French Revolution, it has always been popular, although it lacks the fullness of characterization, social panorama, and humor of Dickens' best work.

A Tale of Two Cities deals with the fates of a small group of characters who are drawn into the events of the Revolution. The French physician, Dr. Manette, broken by 18 years of unjust imprisonment in the Bastille, settles in London with his beautiful daughter Lucie. She falls in love with and marries Charles Darnay, an exiled French aristocrat, innocent heir of the evil Evrémonde family. Returning to Paris, Darnay is seized by the revolutionaries and escapes death on the guillotine only through the self-sacrifice of Sydney Carton, a dissolute English lawyer with a great and pure passion for Lucie. Carton, the novel's real hero, bears a strong resemblance to Darnay, which he uses to substitute himself for the doomed man shortly before his execution. Around this central intrigue is the seething life of revolutionary Paris, epitomized in the citizen Defarge and his formidable wife.

The tale is held together, as a work of art and a vision of history, more by its dominant tone of revolutionary unrest and its symbolism than by its skillful but melodramatic plot and rather flat characters. The somber image of the prison overshadows the whole, while Madame Defarge's knitting is figuratively the working of fate. Dickens shows the cruelty of the *ancien régime* as well as the bloodthirstiness of the mob. His achievement lies in making the Revolution into a symbol of the destruction that threatens any oppressive and unjust social system.

INGA-STINA EWBANK, *University of Liverpool*

TALENT, a unit of weight and value used widely by the ancient Greeks. The talent was the heaviest of the four Greek units of weight, and was divided into 60 minas or 6,000 drachmas. It had a monetary value equal to its weight in silver. There were a number of standards for the talent, which ranged from about 57 pounds (26 kg) for the Greek Attic silver standard to 83 pounds (41 kg) for the Aeginetian standard. Used as early as the 8th century B.C. by the Babylonians, the talent was also employed by the Hebrews, Egyptians, and Romans.

TALES OF A WAYSIDE INN is a collection of narrative poems by the American writer Henry Wadsworth Longfellow, published in three parts (1863, 1872, and 1873) and collected in 1886. It presents a series of stories told by a group of friends. Many of the stories were derived from European legends and a few from American sources. The stories are linked by interludes that introduce the narrators, who can be identified with actual people from Longfellow's characterizations of them. Among them are the violinist Ole Bull and the poet T. W. Parsons.

Tales of a Wayside Inn is not among Longfellow's most distinguished works, but a few of the tales are renowned, including *Paul Revere's Ride,* told by the landlord of the inn, and *King Robert of Sicily.*

The Wayside Inn was really the old Red Horse Inn at Sudbury, Mass. The inn, which burned down in 1955, was fully restored in 1958.

TALES OF HOFFMANN, an opera in three acts, prologue, and epilogue, by the French composer Jacques Offenbach. Its French title is *Les Contes d'Hoffmann.* The libretto, by Jules Barbier and Michel Carré, is based on three stories by E. T. A. Hoffmann. *The Tales of Hoffmann* was the last work and the only serious opera by Offenbach, who was famous for his comic works. It had its first performance, in Paris, on Feb. 10, 1881, several months after the composer's death. It has become a staple of the French opera repertory.

In the prologue, the poet Hoffmann describes to his friends his three great love affairs, all of which ended disastrously. Each act portrays one of these affairs. The first is with Olympia, a mechanical doll that Hoffmann thinks is human. The second is with Giulietta, a Venetian courtesan. The third is with Antonia, a girl dying of consumption. The two most celebrated musical passages in the opera are Olympia's *Doll Song* (*Les oiseaux dans la charmille*) in Act I and the popular *Barcarolle* in Act II.

DAVID EWEN, *Author of "Encyclopedia of the Opera"*

TALIEN, dä'lē'en', a city in the Chinese northeastern province of Liaoning, is the chief port of Manchuria. It lies near the tip of the Liaoning Peninsula. Talien was a small fishing village in 1898, when the Russians began to develop it as a rail terminus and modern port. In 1905 it passed to the Japanese. The Russians called it *Dalny;* the Japanese, *Dairen.* Talien, the Chinese form, is also spelled *Dalian.* In 1945, Talien and nearby Lüshun (Port Arthur) were constituted a joint Sino-Soviet naval base area, which the Soviets vacated in 1955. They now make up the municipality of Lüta (from the first syllables of Lüshun and Talien). Talien is the seat of the Lüta municipal government and for that reason is sometimes itself designated as Lüta.

With its deep, ice-free harbor and its position as the southern terminus of the South Manchurian Railroad, Talien is an outlet for the products of Manchuria. It exports grain, soybean products, and coal and imports oil, textiles, machinery, and tobacco. Talien is Manchuria's chief soybean-processing center and rivals Mukden as a manufacturer of machinery. Its products include construction, mining, and transportation equipment; machine tools; boilers; chemicals; and textile, glass, and ceramic products. There are also large shipyards and an oil refinery. Population: (1953) 766,400.

DAVID CHUEN-YAN LAI
University of Victoria, British Columbia

TALIESIN, tal-i-es'in, was a Welsh bard, who lived, according to tradition, in the 6th century A.D. A 14th century manuscript, the *Book of Taliesin,* has been ascribed to him, but the 56 poems included in it may have been written at different times and by different persons. One modern view is that he wrote during the Middle Ages and was narrating contemporary events disguised as earlier happenings. According to another view he was not an actual person but a mythical Celtic character whose name was traditionally associated with the poems. See also CELTIC LITERATURES—*Welsh Literature.*

The American architect Frank Lloyd Wright named two of homes "Taliesin"—one in Wisconsin, the other in Arizona.

RICHARD L. CARLTON, FROM NATIONAL AUDUBON SOCIETY

A talipot in flower

TALIPOT, tal'ə-pät, a massive palm tree with huge fan-shaped leaves. The talipot, *Corypha umbraculifera,* is a member of the palm family (Palmaceae). It is found in Ceylon, the Philippines, and the Malabar coast of India, and is sometimes grown in Florida and southern California.

The talipot's trunk reaches a height of 80 feet (24 meters) and a thickness of 2 or 3 feet (60–90 cm). The leaf-blades are 8 to 16 feet (2.4–4.8 meters) wide and supported on stalks 6 to 10 feet (1.8–3 meters) long. The terminal flower cluster, which develops after 50 to 70 years, may be 15 to 20 feet (4.5–6 meters) high and 30 to 40 feet (9–12 meters) across. Each flower ripens into a small nut about 1½ inch (38 mm) wide. The fruits require 13 months to develop to maturity.

J. A. YOUNG
U. S. Department of Agriculture

TALISMAN, tal'ə-smən, an object believed to be endowed with magical properties and thus capable of transforming ill fortune into good and of influencing human actions and feelings in an extraordinary way. As with amulets, the power of a talisman is thought to derive from a connection with physical forces, from religious associations, or from being made in a ritual manner out of special material. The capacity of a talisman to change events is what differentiates it from an amulet, the function of which is chiefly protective. See also AMULET.

Talismans were common in ancient Egypt and Babylon, where they were thought to alter the forces of nature. Folktales, from ancient to modern, relate the miraculous powers of talismans such as fairies' wands, seven-league boots, and magic swords that defeat all enemies.

JANET CHERNELA
American Museum of Natural History

TALL OIL, a byproduct of kraft paper manufacture, is a clear yellow oily liquid consisting mainly of fatty acids and rosin acids. It is of great industrial importance as one of the cheapest sources of certain organic acids. One of the most important uses of tall oil is in the manufacture of alkyd resins. It is also used in other synthetic resins, adhesives, cutting oils, disinfectants, emulsifiers, flotation agents, greases, linoleum, paint dryers, concrete additives, soaps, and waterproofing agents.

Tall oil consists of about 45% to 50% fatty acids (mostly oleic and linoleic acids), 42% to 48% rosin acids, and 6% to 9% sterols. It also contains high molecular weight alcohols and other materials. It is obtained by acidifying the skimmings of the waste liquor residue of the kraft paper process. The product is then fractionated under high vacuum.

OTTO W. NITZ
Stout State University, Menomonie, Wis.

TALLADEGA, tal-ə-dē'gə, a city in eastern Alabama, the seat of Talladega county, is about 40 miles (64 km) east of Birmingham. The city is a trading and processing center for cotton, corn, and hay. It manufactures cotton and elastic yarn, pipe fittings, sawmill machinery, textile machinery parts, lumber, and boxes. Marble is quarried and iron ore and talc are mined nearby. The Alabama International Motor Speedway is in Talladega.

The city is the home of Talladega College and of a state school for the deaf and blind. Talladega National Forest is in the area.

On the site of Talladega, Andrew Jackson defeated a band of Creek Indians on Nov. 8, 1813. Talladega was settled in the early 1830's and incorporated in 1835. It is governed by a commission. Population: 17,662.

TALLAHASSEE, tal-ə-has'ē, a city in northwestern Florida, is the state capital and the seat of Leon county. It is situated 160 miles (257 km) west of Jacksonville and 25 miles (40 km) north of the Gulf of Mexico. It is the commercial center of northwest Florida and is an educational and administrative center. Built on seven hills, the city is famous for its beautiful live oaks, gardens, flowering shrubs, and historic homes and nearby plantations, many of them built before the Civil War. The principal agricultural activities of the area are cattle raising and truck farming. There are 6 million acres (2,430,000 hectares) of commercial forest in the city's trade area. The only important industries are the manufacture of mobile homes and of wooden crates and boxes.

Tallahassee is the seat of two state universities, Florida State University and Florida Agricultural and Mechanical University, and of Tallahassee Junior College. Among the city's cultural organizations are the Little Theater, Historical Society, Junior Museum, and LeMoyne Art Foundation. Its libraries include the State Library, the Leon County Public Library, and the David Walker Memorial Library.

An annual 6-week spring festival includes tours of Tallahassee's homes and plantations. Two notable colonial mansions are Goodwood, completed in 1843, and the Grove, built around 1830 by Richard Keith Call, who was twice Florida's territorial governor. The First Presbyterian Church, the city's oldest church building, was

FLORIDA NEWS BUREAU DEPARTMENT OF COMMERCE

Tallahassee has many fine homes built before the Civil War. Goodwood Plantation is an outstanding example.

completed in 1838. Later remodeled, it still contains the slave gallery of the original building. Tallahassee's many public buildings include the state capitol (1845), built in a cruciform design and featuring a massive dome. The exterior of the modern governor's mansion is modeled after the Hermitage, Andrew Jackson's home in Nashville, Tenn.

History. The original inhabitants of the Tallahassee region were the Apalachee, an Indian tribe that is now extinct. After the destruction of the Apalachee towns by Englishmen and Creek Indians, the area was occupied by the Seminole, who still lived here when the site of Tallahassee was chosen as the territorial capital in 1823. Selected for its location between Pensacola and St. Augustine, Florida's two principal towns at that time, the site was called "Tallahassee," a word of Creek origin meaning "old friend" or "old town."

The first town lots were sold in 1825 and the city of Tallahassee was incorporated later that year. The city developed rapidly. The fertile lands attracted settlers from other southern states who opened plantations, and the capital became the trade center of the area. Prince Achille Murat, Napoleon's eccentric nephew who opened a plantation near Tallahassee in 1825, was an early resident.

During the Civil War, Tallahassee was the only Southern capital east of the Mississippi River not captured by Union troops. Citizens, young cadets from West Florida Seminary, and a few regular troops turned back a march on the capital in 1865 at the Battle of Natural Bridge, 16 miles (26 km) south of the city. Tallahassee's importance as a trade center had declined by 1900 with growth of other parts of the state, but its rising importance as a cultural and administrative center was shown by the 49.2% population gain during the 1960's. Government is by commission and manager. Population: 71,897.

CODY H. ALLEN
Leon County Public Library

TALLAHATCHIE RIVER, tal-ə-hach'ē, in Mississippi, rising in Tippah county in the northeastern part of the state. It flows west and south about 300 miles (480 km) to join the Yalobusha, just north of Greenwood, and form the Yazoo River. Sardis Dam, in Panola county in northern Mississippi, was built on the river in 1940 as a flood control project. The dam impounds the waters of Sardis Lake, which is approximately 30 miles (48 km) long.

TALLCHIEF, tôl'chēf, **Maria** (1925–), American ballerina, known especially as an interpreter of the works of George Balanchine. She was born in Fairfax, Okla., on Jan. 24, 1925, of an Osage Indian father. At an early age she moved with her family to Los Angeles, where she studied dancing. From 1942 to 1947 she was with the Ballet Russe de Monte Carlo. She married Balanchine in 1946 and the next year joined the Ballet Society, of which he was director. This group became the New York City Ballet, and she was its prima ballerina in 1954–1955.

Her marriage to Balanchine was annulled, but she remained with the company except briefly in 1960, when she was prima ballerina of the American Ballet Theater. Her sister, Marjorie Tallchief (1927–), also a ballerina, achieved success in Europe, first with the de Cuevas company and then with the Paris Opéra ballet.

TALLEMANT DES RÉAUX, tä-lə-mäɴ' dē rā-ō, **Gédéon** (1619–1692), French author of *Historiettes,* short anecdotal biographies of members of the French court and Parisian society of the first half of the 17th century. Tallemant was born in La Rochelle on Oct. 2, 1619, into a wealthy Huguenot family. He went to Paris in 1634 to work in the family bank. In Paris he associated with academicians and frequented the fashionable salons. There he met many of the subjects of his *Historiettes,* which he wrote mainly

1657 and 1659. He died in Paris on Nov. 10, 1692.

The "little histories" are colorful portraits, written in informal style, that emphasize intimate details of daily behavior. The manuscript, long forgotten, was rediscovered in the 19th century and published in 1834–1835. It was translated into English as *Miniature Portraits* (1926).

TALLEYRAND, tȧ-lā-räɴ′, but pronounced by the family as tȧl-räɴ′, **Prince de** (1754–1838), French diplomat, who survived many changes of government to emerge as the most influential French politician of his era. His masterful maneuvering at the Congress of Vienna in 1814–1815 permitted a defeated France to maintain its status as a major European power.

Charles Maurice de Talleyrand-Périgord was born in Paris on Feb. 2, 1754. He was the second son of an undistinguished noble family and became the eldest after the death of another brother. An accident in infancy left him with an obvious limp and disqualified him for the young nobleman's usual commission in the army.

The Church was the next obvious source of financial security and, in its higher offices, social esteem. Charles Maurice was therefore stripped of his rights of primogeniture in favor of a younger brother and sent to prepare for the priesthood. Though temperamentally most ill-fitted to be a priest, he soon acquired several benefices, the title of abbé, and eventually, in 1788, the post of bishop of Autun.

Talleyrand and the Revolutionary Era. By 1789 he had already made his mark in society as an *abbé de salon*—clever, charming, worldly, and most attractive to women. But he had also shown himself, as agent general of the clergy of France, to be a skilled administrator and financier. He was quite naturally chosen to represent the clergy of the diocese of Autun in the Estates General of 1789. When this body transformed itself into the revolutionary National Assembly and set about remaking France, Talleyrand quickly—but, characteristically, not too quickly—went over to the popular side of the commoners.

In this National Assembly he played an important role as a moderate reformer. He made an admirable report on public education, following a form he was to use in much of his later work. Much of the report was prepared by his staff, indeed partly ghostwritten. But he himself worked hard on it and put his stamp on it. In all his varied posts in later life he displayed this great administrative gift.

Talleyrand's most important act in the National Assembly was a successful motion in October 1789 to transfer all ecclesiastical property to the French state. The property was to be the basis for solving the financial problems of the bankrupt French treasury. The state would assume the costs of maintaining the clergy. Although it was a sensible and almost inevitable measure, the proposal seemed especially scandalous coming from a bishop and in this respect was characteristic of what his enemies have always called his many treasons. In the ensuing schism between the clergy who refused to abide by the reformed Civil Constitution of the Clergy of 1790 and the constitutional clergy who accepted it, Talleyrand took the schismatic side and performed the ceremony of consecrating three bishops in the new Church. This act brought about his excommunication by the Vatican in April 1791 and his complete abandonment of a clerical career.

Talleyrand had nothing of the extremist or the terrorist in him, and he was wise, or lucky, enough to get sent to Britain on a mission in 1792, just before the September massacres in which the Jacobin Commune killed over 1,000 royalists, priests, and others being held in prison. Considered a dangerous radical in Britain, he was obliged to go on to the United States, where he waited for the end of the Reign of Terror.

Minister for Foreign Affairs. He returned to France in 1796 and became minister for foreign affairs in 1797 in the moderate government of the Directory. While foreign minister, he was a moving spirit in an unsuccessful attempt to secure bribes from U. S. negotiators in the famous XYZ Affair. See XYZ Correspondence.

Talleyrand's diplomatic ventures were usually much more successful than the XYZ Affair. He proved a good foreign minister for the Directory, and later for Bonaparte when Bonaparte was first consul. But after his coronation as emperor, Napoleon showed more and more signs of megalomania, taking seriously the goal of "world conquest." Talleyrand, always keenly aware of international as well as national politics as the "art of the possible," began to try to restrain his master. After several violent quarrels, Talleyrand, who had been made prince and duke de Bénévent in 1806, went into voluntary retirement on his estates in 1807.

Restoration and July Monarchy. Talleyrand's withdrawal from Napoleon's government put him in a position to take advantage of Napoleon's defeat and abdication in 1814 by assuming the leadership of the provisional government that returned the Bourbon dynasty. Once more he was sworn in as minister for foreign affairs, this

Prince de Talleyrand

THE BETTMANN ARCHIVE

time to Louis XVIII. Having made out his own instructions, Talleyrand set out for the Congress of Vienna, which was to be the scene of his greatest triumph and his greatest service to France.

At Vienna, Talleyrand took advantage of a quarrel among the victors, Britain and Austria on the one hand and Russia and Prussia on the other. Talleyrand was able to insinuate himself, representative of a badly defeated state though he was, into the circle of the great powers and to secure a very good treaty for France. His argument was that the war had not been against France, and certainly not against the Bourbons. Rather, it had been against Napoleon, and Louis XVIII as rightful monarch should be supported and not penalized. At a time when Europe was championing "legitimate" rulers, the victors found it difficult to resist Talleyrand's argument. In spite of this great service, Talleyrand's identification with the Revolution and his status as an unfrocked priest made it impossible for Louis to retain him in office. In 1815 he was dismissed and retired to his château.

Fifteen years later, at the age of 76, the old gentleman emerged to gain office and prominence in still another regime. Talleyrand had little to do with preparing the July Revolution of 1830 that overthrew Charles X, the last of the direct Bourbon line. He did, however, have much to do with fending off a republican regime and securing the establishment of a bourgeois monarchy, called the July Monarchy, under the Orléanist Louis Philippe. Talleyrand was rewarded with a major diplomatic mission from 1830 to 1834 as ambassador to London, where he allayed British alarm at the prospect of a French prince on the throne of newly created Belgium.

Last Years. Now over 80, Talleyrand was, in spite of his immoral past, an almost beloved grand old man. His last years were spent as a kind of living legend. Just before his death he was taken back into the Church. As he was about to receive extreme unction he held out his hands closed, palms down, as a bishop should, saying, "Don't forget I am a bishop." He died in Paris on May 17, 1838.

Talleyrand served some seven regimes, most of them established by revolution, defeat, or coup d'etat. His private life was enjoyable and not very proper. He made a great deal of money, some of it disreputably. In the eyes of Frenchmen, especially, he had betrayed their great national hero, Napoleon, and therefore France itself. He was certainly not a man of high moral principle. Yet he liked to call himself, and indeed was, a "good European." He disliked chauvinism and unprincipled idealism, was a superb technician in diplomacy, and managed, clearly, to do a great deal of good in a harsh world.

CRANE BRINTON
Author of "The Lives of Talleyrand"

Further Reading: Brinton, Crane, *The Lives of Talleyrand* (New York 1963); Cooper, Duff, *Talleyrand* (New York 1932); Lacour-Gayet, Georges, *Talleyrand*, 4 vols. (Paris 1928–1934).

TALLIEN, tà-lyaN, **Jean Lambert** (1767–1820), radical French revolutionary who played a prominent role in the conspiracy that overthrew Maximilien Robespierre. Tallien was born in Paris on Jan. 23, 1767. An enthusiastic supporter of the Revolution, he took an active part in the antimonarchical insurrection of Aug. 10, 1792, and was rewarded with the post of secretary of the Commune of Paris.

In 1792, Tallien was elected to the National Convention, where he distinguished himself by his republican zeal. He voted for Louis XVI's death. In October 1793 he was sent to repress counterrevolution in Bordeaux. His ruthless policies, based more on intimidation than bloodshed, were successful. But when he fell in love with Thérésa Cabarrus, one of his prisoners, he was suspected of political moderation and profligate behavior and was recalled to Paris.

Fearing for his life, Tallien helped overthrow Robespierre on July 27, 1794. He emerged as a leader of the moderate Thermidorean Reaction and married Thérésa. Although he was a member of the Council of Five Hundred during the Directory, his influence soon ended. He served as a consul in Spain until he contracted yellow fever. He spent his last years ill, poor, and alone. Thérésa had deserted him in 1801. He died in Paris on Nov. 16, 1820.

RICHARD T. BIENVENU
University of Missouri

TALLIN, tal'ən, a Soviet city, is the capital and economic and cultural center of the Estonian SSR. It is situated on the south coast of the Gulf of Finland, opposite Helsinki, about 200 miles (320 km) west of Leningrad. Tallin, or Tallinn, was formerly known as Revel (Russian) or Reval (German).

Tallin has large and varied manufacturing plants, producing electrical and mechanical equipment. There are also shipbuilding, woodworking, printing, textile, and food-processing industries. Tallin's harbor is good, and there are rail connections with other cities.

The city consists essentially of three parts. The old city is situated on a plateau above the sea. Its castle dates from the 13th–14th centuries. A newer city grew up below the old city. It has remains from the 14th to 16th centuries. The most recent sections of Tallin were built outside the lower city's walls.

History. In 1219 the Danes founded a town on this site. Subsequently a member of the Hanseatic League, Tallin in 1346 fell under the control of the Teutonic Knights. In 1561 it became Swedish, gaining a measure of autonomy in 1675. After the Northern War (1700–1721), Tallin became a Russian naval base and provincial capital. It remained in Russian hands until the Russian Revolution. Occupied by the Germans in 1918, Tallin later was the capital of independent Estonia until 1940, when the USSR annexed Estonia. Population: (1967 est.) 340,000.

W. A. D. JACKSON
University of Washington

TALLIS, tal'is, **Thomas** (c. 1505–1585), English composer and organist, often referred to as "the Father of English church music" because he was the first important composer to write substantially for the Anglican rite. Nothing is known of Tallis' early life except that he was employed at Waltham Abbey, Essex, sometime before its dissolution in 1540. In 1542 he was appointed one of the gentlemen of the Chapel Royal. Later, but before 1575, he became joint organist of the Royal Chapel with William Byrd. In 1575, Elizabeth I granted Tallis and Byrd the monopoly of printing music and music paper in England, and in the same year they published jointly a book of motets dedicated to the Queen. Tallis died in Greenwich on Nov. 23, 1585.

Tallis wrote over 20 keyboard pieces and a few secular songs, but the bulk of his output was sacred vocal music. That for the Catholic service comprises about 60 compositions, including over 50 motets. His Anglican music consists of nearly 50 works, including 18 anthems, but excluding 9 anthems adapted from motets. The style of the Latin music ranges from elaborate polyphony to simple homophony. His music to English words, however, is basically chordal, designed to achieve the clarity desired by the Anglican Church at that time.

R. ALEC HARMAN, *Coauthor of "Man and His Music"*

TALLMADGE, tal'mij, a city in northeastern Ohio, in Summit county, is immediately east of Akron. It is a residential community, founded in 1807 by the Rev. David Bacon of Connecticut. The township was laid out in the shape of a wheel. Eight roads converge at the Circle, where the Congregational Church stands. Government is by mayor and council. Population: 15,274.

TALLOW is a solid fat extracted from the tissues of cattle and sheep. It is principally used in soap. The tallow is rendered by digesting the fat with steam under pressure. The liquid is drained off and cooled, and the tallow layer is then removed from the water. Pure tallow is creamy, white, tasteless, and odorless. In soap making, it is usually mixed with plant oils, such as coconut oil, and heated with alkali in a kettle or hydrolyzed under pressure to form fatty acids and glycerine. The fatty acids are separated and treated with caustic soda to produce soap.

Tallow consists of the glyceryl esters of long-chain organic acids, such as oleic, palmitic, stearic, linoleic, and palmitoleic acids. Oleic and stearic acids, hydrolysis products of tallow which are industrially useful, are separated from the other fatty acids by running the molten mixture into pans. The contents are then chilled and pressed. A liquid, which is mainly oleic acid, is separated from the solid, which consists principally of stearic acid. Vacuum distillation can be used to separate other acids.

OTTO W. NITZ
Stout State University, Menomonie, Wis.

TALLULAH, tə-lōō'lə, a village in northeastern Louisiana, the seat of Madison parish, is about 135 miles (215 km) north of Baton Rouge. Cotton, soybeans, oats, wheat, and hay are raised in the area. Tallulah is also an important center for beef cattle. Hunting and fishing attract visitors. The village is governed by a mayor and council. Population: 9,643.

TALMADGE, tal'mij, **Eugene** (1884–1946), American political leader, who as governor of Georgia represented the Southern agrarian philosophy of fiscal and racial conservatism. Talmadge was born in Forsyth, Ga., on Sept. 23, 1884. He graduated from the University of Georgia law school and practiced law. Called a demagogue by many, he used flamboyant campaign tactics to win three terms as Georgia's commissioner of agriculture (1926, 1928, and 1930) and four as governor (1932, 1934, 1940, and 1946). He died before the beginning of his fourth term.

WIDE WORLD

Eugene Talmadge addresses a political rally in 1935.

Though devoid of a statesmanlike program, Talmadge loved a good political fight. Not very tall and of wiry build, he was filled with energy and possessed a magnetic personality and a great talent for leadership. When campaigning, he would "shuck off" his coat revealing red suspenders, flip a lock of hair down into his eyes, and "set the crowd afire." As commissioner of agriculture, he attacked fertilizer trusts and "slick fellows from the city." As governor he paid out funds under an 1821 law when the legislature failed to enact an appropriation measure, and he ordered that state treasurer George Hamilton be carried bodily from his office. He used the National Guard to break textile mill strikes and interfered with the University of Georgia to the extent that its accreditation was suspended. In 1936, Talmadge led an abortive movement against the reelection of President Franklin Roosevelt, and he also failed in his 1936 and 1938 bids for a U. S. Senate seat.

Governor-elect Talmadge's death in Atlanta, Ga., on Dec. 21, 1946, precipitated a protracted controversy over the succession (See GEORGIA—*Government*). His son, Herman Talmadge, served as governor (1947 and 1951–1955) and in the U. S. Senate from 1957.

SARAH M. LEMMON, *Meredith College*

TALMAGE, tal'mij, **Thomas De Witt** (1832–1902), American Presbyterian clergyman, preacher, and writer. He was born in Bound Brook, N. J., on Jan. 7, 1832, and educated at the University of the City of New York (now New York University) and the New Brunswick Theological Seminary. Ordained in 1856, he served pastorates in Belleville, N. J., Syracuse, N. Y., and Brooklyn, N. Y., and as a chaplain in the Civil War.

Talmage's sermons and other religious articles were printed weekly in a large number of newspapers. In 1873 he became editor of *The Christian at Work,* a New York religious weekly, and devoted so much attention to his writing that he resigned his pastorate. He was successively editor of *The Advance, Frank Leslie's Sunday Magazine,* and *The Christian Herald.* Talmage died in Washington, D. C., on April 12, 1902.

POWEL MILLS DAWLEY
The General Theological Seminary, New York

TALMUD, täl′mōōd, the most important work of religious law in post-Biblical Judaism. The basic text of the Talmud is the Mishnah (Mishna), a codification of oral law. The other part of the Talmud is called the Gemara, which contains discussions of the Mishnah. The Gemara exists in two major forms, the Babylonian and the Palestinian, but the Mishnah is the same for both.

Role of the Talmud in Judaism. The laws of the Talmud were binding on every Jew. Post-Talmudic rabbis could interpret these laws and hand down rulings on new problems on their basis, but they were not authorized to abolish any.

Until the 18th century, when many Jews discarded certain religious beliefs and practices, the Talmud regulated every aspect of Jewish life, private or public. Until then, individuals or groups who did not recognize the authority of the Talmud found themselves excluded from the Jewish community. In modern times a significant segment of the Jewish people still adheres strictly to the laws of the Talmud. Others observe them to a lesser degree or not at all.

The Talmud was studied by laymen as well as rabbis. The constant study of the Law, which primarily meant the Talmud, was a religious commandment incumbent upon all. No male Jew, whatever his age or status, was free from that obligation. Every young Jew received instruction in the Talmud in the Jewish primary school, and many continued their studies in yeshivot, higher institutions of Talmudic learning.

Over the centuries a large rabbinic literature has been composed on the Talmud. It may be divided into two groups. The first contains works on the practical application of the Talmudic laws, including post-Talmudic regulations and customs, in addition to codes, commentaries on codes, and rabbinic responses. The second is concerned primarily with theoretical study and includes commentaries, supercommentaries, and novelle. The Babylonian Talmud was studied much more than the Palestinian Talmud. Consequently, a much larger literature has grown up around it. See also JEWISH HISTORY AND SOCIETY—*World of the Talmud*.

Until modern times the attitude of the Christian church to the Talmud was determined by a hostile attitude toward the Jewish religion. The Talmud was attacked, defamed, and censored.

The Mishnah. Judaism distinguishes between two chief sources of Jewish law. The first is the Written Law—the Torah, or Pentateuch. The second is the Oral Law, or ancient traditions, which contains additions to and explanations of the Written Law, transmitted over generations by word of mouth. Both Written and Oral laws are held to be of divine origin and of equal binding force.

The Mishnah (Hebrew for "repetition") was the first systematic codification of the Oral Law. Its origins go back to the period of the Second Jewish Commonwealth (538 B.C. to 70 A.D.). In time the original Mishnah came to include new customs and legal institutions as well as the individual views of teachers on disputed matters. From the 1st century A.D., a number of teachers evolved different versions of the Mishnah reflecting their particular points of view. About 200 A.D., Rabbi Judah ha-Nasi, called *the Prince*, the spiritual leader of Palestinian Jewry, made a final edition of the Mishnah, incorporating in it parts of earlier versions. Those parts that were not incorporated into Judah's edition became known as *Baraithot* (Baraita), Aramaic for "external." Some of these parts were later collected into a separate work called *Tosephta* (Tosefta), Aramaic for "addition."

The language of the Mishnah is Hebrew. It is simpler than that of the Bible and different in vocabulary and syntax. The laws are set forth in the form of general rules and of concrete examples. Occasionally, actual cases are cited. Generally, no reference is made to the Biblical texts on which the laws are based.

The Mishnah is divided into six orders: (1) *Zeraim* ("seeds"), laws on agricultural work and on the share of the priests, Levites, and poor in the agricultural harvest; (2) *Moed* ("appointed seasons"), laws regarding the observance of the Sabbath, the festivals, and fast days; (3) *Nashim* ("women"), laws for marriage and divorce; (4) *Nezikin* ("damages"), civil and criminal law; (5) *Kodashim* ("holy things"), laws relating to the Temple and the sacrificial service; and (6) *Tohorot* ("purities"), regulations on ritual purity of persons and objects. Each order is divided into treatises, which are subdivided into chapters.

With the destruction of the Second Temple (70 A.D.), a considerable part of the laws lost their practical value. They were retained in the Mishnah in the hope that the Temple would be rebuilt in the not too distant future.

Rabbis of the 1st and 2d centuries whose views are cited in the earlier or final versions of the Mishnah are referred to as *Tannaim*, Aramaic for "teachers." They begin with the disciples of Hillel and Shammai, the founders of two schools of rabbinic interpretation. Among the important Tannaim were the rabbis Gamaliel, Gamaliel II, Eliezer ben Hyrcanus, Johanan ben Zakkai, Eleazar ben Azariah, Joshua, Ishmael, Tarphon, Akiva, Meir, Simeon ben Gamaliel II, Jose ben Halaphta, and Judah ben Ilai.

Judah ha-Nasi and his contemporaries were the last generation of Tannaim. Subsequent teachers became known as *Amoraim*, Aramaic for "interpreters." The Amoraim were not permitted to dispute the opinions of the Tannaim, merely to interpret them.

The Tannaim were also the authors of halakic Midrashim, expositions of Scripture in the light of the Oral Law. The origins of the halakic Midrashim antedate the beginnings of the Mishnah. The rabbis explained the laws of the Pentateuch in conformity with traditional practice, even if it did not agree with the straightforward meaning of the text.

Extant works of halakic Midrashim are chiefly the products of the schools of Rabbi Ishmael and Rabbi Akiva, who were exponents of different rules of Biblical interpretation.

The Gemara. The word "Gemara" is Aramaic for "learning." Rabbi Judah's edition of the Mishnah became established as the authoritative code of the Oral Law, and, like its predecessors, was taught and studied orally. It became the main subject of study and discussion in the academies of Palestine and Babylonia.

The Amoraim devoted themselves to expounding the Mishnah—clarifying its meaning, reconciling seeming contradictions, tracing the sources of the law and its underlying principles—and finding solutions to new problems, actual or theoretical. In the pursuit of these objectives they made use of the Baraithot and halakic Midrashim. They also established principles for interpreting the language of the Mishnah and evolved new legal concepts.

The main academies in Palestine in the era of the Amoraim were those of Tiberias, Sepphoris, and Caesarea; in Babylonia, Nehardea, Sura, and Pumbeditha. There was a steady exchange of scholars between the countries.

The discussions of the academies of Palestine and Babylonia were collected separately. Hence, there are two versions of the Talmud—the Palestinian and the Babylonian. The older of the two is the Palestinian Talmud. A minor part of it was compiled about the middle of the 4th century A. D. in Caesarea. The major part was compiled two generations later in Tiberias.

The compilation of the discussions of the Babylonian academies also was begun in the 4th century, but their redaction took a much longer time. It was completed only in the 5th century by Rav Ashi, longtime head of the academy of Sura, in cooperation with members of his academy, and by Rabina II, the last of the Amoraim. Subsequently, in the 6th century, the Babylonian Talmud underwent final editing by the *Saboraim*, Aramaic for "expounders," the successors of the Babylonian Amoraim.

Many hundreds of Amoraim are mentioned in the Talmud. The deliberations of the Amoraim concentrated on all the treatises of the Mishnah, regardless of whether the laws they contained were operative at that time. However, discussions have not been compiled for every treatise.

In addition to the discussions on the laws of the Mishnah, the Talmud also contains homiletic comments on Scriptural texts, ethical maxims, narratives, theological and cosmological views, popular medicine and beliefs, folklore, and a variety of other nonlegal matter. The nonlegal contents of the Talmud form only a small part of the Babylonian Talmud and a still smaller part of the Palestinian. It is called *Haggadah* ("narrative"), a term originally applied only to homiletic exposition of Scripture. The strictly legal matter is known as *Halakha* (Halaka; "rule").

The non-Hebrew parts of the Palestinian and Babylonian Talmud are in Western Aramaic and Eastern Aramaic respectively. The former was current in Palestine; the latter, in Babylonia. The two versions of the Talmud differ also in methods employed to interpret the Mishnah and in legal concepts.

Because the Babylonian Talmud was completed later than the Palestinian Talmud, and Babylonian Jewry emerged as the major center of world Jewry, superseding that of Palestine, the Babylonian Talmud came to be recognized as the more authoritative of the two.

Editions and Translations. Handwritten fragments of the Talmud dating from the 8th and 9th centuries are extant. The oldest complete manuscript of the Palestinian Talmud dates from the 13th century, and that of the Babylonian Talmud from the 14th century. The first complete printed editions of the Babylonian (1520–1522) and Palestinian Talmud (1523) were published in Venice. The entire Babylonian Talmud has been translated into German and English, and the Palestinian Talmud into French.

TOVIA PRESCHEL
Jewish Theological Seminary of America

Further Reading: Lieberman, Saul, *Hellenism in Jewish Palestine* (New York 1950); Strack, Hermann L., *Introduction to the Talmud and Midrash* (Philadelphia 1931).

TALON, tȧ'lôɴ, **Jean** (1626–1694), French administrator and first intendant of New France. He was born in Châlons-sur-Marne, France, where he was baptized on Jan. 8, 1626. With administrative experience gained in the French army and in 10 years as intendant of Hainault, he arrived in Quebec for his first term, 1665–1668, a symbol of royal interest in building up the weak, disorganized colony of New France. He encouraged immigration and settlement, and during his administration, the population more than doubled to about 7,500 people. Attempting to shift the colony away from sole reliance on the fur trade, he encouraged grain and vegetable cultivation, also hemp, flax, hops, and the raising of livestock. Talon labored to develop industry, introducing looms, a tannery, and hat factory, and also obtained subsidies for fisheries and promoted forestry.

During his second term, 1670–1672, Talon became more wary of the English and more aware of the need for the French to control the western American continent. He advocated French expansion, sending expeditions to Hudson Bay, Acadia, the Great Lakes, and the upper Mississippi. His domestic and imperial activities have won him the appellation "great," but New France lost direction without his encouragement. Talon died in Paris on Nov. 24, 1694.

JAMES S. PRITCHARD
Queen's University, Kingston Ontario

TALUS, tā'ləs, in geology, a large sloping pile or cone of rocks at the foot of a steep mountainside or cliff. Talus slopes, the accumulation of fallen rocks, are always about 35° to the horizontal. Breccia is formed when such piles consolidate into a rock.

TAMALE, tə-mäl'ē, a Mexican dish consisting of highly spiced minced meat and other ingredients inside a layer of cornmeal dough that is, in turn, wrapped in corn husks. It is then either baked or steamed in a kettle. The exact origin of tamales is not known, but they were eaten by the Aztecs long before the arrival of the Spanish conquistadores.

BETTY WASON
Author of "The Art of Spanish Cooking"

TAMANDUA, tə-man-də-wä', a small, tree-dwelling anteater (*Tamandua tetradactyla*), also called the collared anteater, found in forested areas from southern Mexico to southern Brazil and Bolivia. Tamanduas grow to 23 inches (58 cm) in length, plus a 22-inch (56-cm) tail. The short, coarse, dense hair is usually colored cream, tan, or bay, with a "vest" of black extending from between the hind and front legs to around the neck. All-white and all-black animals are common.

Tamanduas are solitary animals and are usually active at any hour of the day. They spend much of their time in trees, using their prehensile tails as aids in climbing. The middle finger of the hand is armed with a large powerful claw, requiring the animals to walk on the outside of their hands. The claws are used to rip open the nests of termites and bees. The tamandua's toothless, elongated snout and mouth form a narrow down-curving tube from which the sticky tongue is protruded.

FERNANDO DIAS DE AVILA-PIRES, *Museu de Historia Natural Minas Gerais, Brazil*

TAMAQUA, tə-mä'kwə, is a borough in northeastern Pennsylvania, in Schuylkill county, on the Little Schuylkill River, about 75 miles (120 km) northwest of Philadelphia. It is a coal-mining center and also manufactures explosives, foundry and machine shop products, and underwear. A sawmill was built on the site in 1799 by Berkhard Moser. Part of his home, built of logs in 1801, is preserved. Mining began when anthracite was discovered in 1817.

Tamaqua was laid out in 1829 and incorporated as a borough in 1832. The name derives from an American Indian word for "beaver." Government is by burgess and council. Population: 9,246.

TAMARACK. See LARCH.

TAMARAW, tam-ə-rou', a small, stockily built, cowlike mammal (*Anoa mindorensis*) found only on the island of Mindoro in the Philippines. The tamaraw, or tamarau, stands about 3½ feet (1 meter) high at the shoulders and is blackish, with short, thick, slightly upswept horns. Little is known about tamaraws because of their secretive ways and secluded habitats. They apparently live in small groups and feed mainly at night. Newborn calves have been sighted in December and January.

In the recent past, tamaraws were particularly plentiful in and around the lowland swamps and marshlands. After World War II a successful malaria eradication program opened these previously uninhabitable areas to human settlement, and tamaraws no longer exist in the lowlands. The surviving animals inhabit the highlands, where they are subjected to increasing pressures from lumbering and ranching operations and from illegal hunting.

Tamaraws inhabit three principal areas: Mt. Calavite Reserve, Mt. Iglit Game Refuge, and the hinterland of the Sablayon Penal Settlement, where hunter's fear of escaped convicts provides fortuitous, but effective, protection. The three small, but probably viable, populations total approximately 100 animals.

NOEL SIMON
Compiler, "Red Data Book," Vol. 1 (Mammalia)

Tamaraw

PHILIPPINE TOURIST AND TRAVEL ASSOCIATION

SAN DIEGO ZOO PHOTO

Tamarins, or cottontop marmosets (*Saguinus oedipus*)

TAMARIN, tam'ə-rən, a small monkeylike primate of the marmoset family (Callithricidae), native to forested areas in Panama and South America. The true tamarins (*Saguinus*) comprise 21 to 22 species found from eastern Panama and northern South America south through the Amazon region. The three species of golden lion tamarins (*Leontideus*) are restricted to southeastern Brazil.

True tamarins range from about 7 to 12 inches (18–30 cm) in head and body length, plus a somewhat longer tail. Golden lion tamarins range from 6½ to 14 inches (16.5–35.5 cm) or more in head and body length, plus a tail of approximately the same length. Body weights commonly vary between ½ and 1¼ pounds (225–570 grams).

True tamarins are black, brown, or dark red; or dark brown above and white below; or with yellowish brown hindquarters and white forequarters. A moustache, crest, or contrasting color marking may be present. Golden lion tamarins have long silky coats, which form a lionlike mane around the head and shoulders. Their coat color may be either a uniform reddish gold, or it may be black, with gold markings on the head, limbs, and tail.

The tamarin's diet may include fruit, insects, and lizards. Laboratory studies indicate that the family group is the basic social unit. Gestation lasts about 5 months (140–150 days); the female bears one, usually two, or occasionally three young. The male parent plays a major role in rearing the young. Tamarins have lived to more than 10 years of age in captivity.

LEONARD A. ROSENBLUM, *Director*
Primate Laboratory, State University of New York

TAMARIND, tam'ə-rənd, a tall evergreen tree believed to be native to tropical Africa and possibly to southern Asia. It has been cultivated throughout the tropics and is sometimes also grown in southern Florida. The tamarind is cultivated for its attractive appearance and its acidic pulpy fruits, which are widely used in the Orient for making chutney and curries.

CARL FRANK

TAMAULIPAS is one of the most prosperous states in Mexico. This scene shows a village square.

Mature tamarinds attain a height of about 80 feet (24 meters) with a trunk diameter of 6 to 8 feet (1.8–2.4 meters). The bark is brownish gray and somewhat shaggy in appearance. The alternate, pinnate leaves of the tamarind are composed of 20 to 40 small leaflets. The flowers are borne in long narrow clusters at the ends of the branches. Each flower has three superior petals that are pale yellow with red veins. The pod that develops from the flower is cinnamon brown in color and ranges in length from 3 to 8 inches (76–203 mm). Inside the pod the brown pulp encloses from 1 to 12 seeds.

The tamarind, *Tamarindus indica,* belongs to the legume family (Leguminosae). The wild tamarind, or lead tree (*Leucaena glanca*), is a small tropical tree.

J. A. YOUNG
U. S. Department of Agriculture

TAMARISK, tam'ə-risk, any of a genus (*Tamarix*) of graceful deciduous trees and shrubs with long slender branches and heath-like leaves. The small pinkish flowers are freely borne in loose clusters, giving the plants a feathery appearance.

Tamarisks are native to Europe and Asia but also grow wild in North America. There are about 75 species, and they belong to the family Tamaricaceae. The three hardiest species are *T. parviflora,* which has reddish bark and flowers that bloom in the spring; *T. odessana,* which has upright slender branches and flowers that blossom in midsummer; and *T. pentandra,* which has purple branches and flowers that bloom in late summer. The English tamarisk (*T. anglica*) has white flowers tinged with pink. It is similar to the French tamarisk (*T. gallica*).

J. A. YOUNG
U. S. Department of Agriculture

TAMATAVE, täm-ä-täv,' is the major seaport and second-largest city of the Malagasy Republic. It is situated in the eastern part of Madagascar, on the coast of the Indian Ocean and the Canal des Pangalanes, a chain of navigable lagoons.

Tamatave is connected by rail, road, and air with the capital city of Tananarive. Its chief exports are coffee, sugar, rice, bananas, essential oils, spices, and some graphite and chromium ore. Imports include crude petroleum supplies for the city's oil refinery. Metal containers are manufactured and a variety of agricultural products are processed. Tamatave was almost wholly rebuilt after it was devastated by a tropical storm in 1927. Population: (1969) 49,400.

IRENE S. VAN DONGEN
California State College, Pennsylvania

TAMAULIPAS, tä-mou-lē'päs, is a state in northeastern Mexico, on the Gulf of Mexico, bordered on the north by Texas. The state's area is 30,734 square miles (79,600 sq km). It comprises an extensive plain that slopes gently to the coast, but its central and southwestern sections are crossed by the Sierra Madre Oriental. The coastline is broken by lagoons, swamps, and barrier beaches. There is a tropical savanna climate in the south, while a steppe climate prevails in the north and west.

The river valleys of Tamaulipas are irrigated. Cotton is grown on the lower Río Grande and sugarcane and citrus fruits around El Mante. Henequen fields are scattered throughout the south. Cattle are raised in the Huasteca and Tampico regions. Tamaulipas is the oldest petroleum-producing area in Mexico, and oil is its greatest source of wealth. The state is served by an excellent communications network.

The prosperity of Tamaulipas is reflected in its dynamic population growth. The population is concentrated along mountain slopes and in economic centers. Ciudad Victoria, its capital, is an important agricultural, commercial, and communications center in central Tamaulipas. Tampico is the second-largest port and oil refining center in Mexico. The border cities of Nuevo Laredo, Reynosa, and Matamoros are growing faster than their Texan counterparts.

Tamaulipas, once inhabited by Tamaulipan Indians, was colonized late (1746) by the Spaniards and remained a backward area until petroleum was discovered about 1900 and irrigation introduced. Population: (1960) 1,024,182.

REYNALDO AYALA, *San Diego State College*

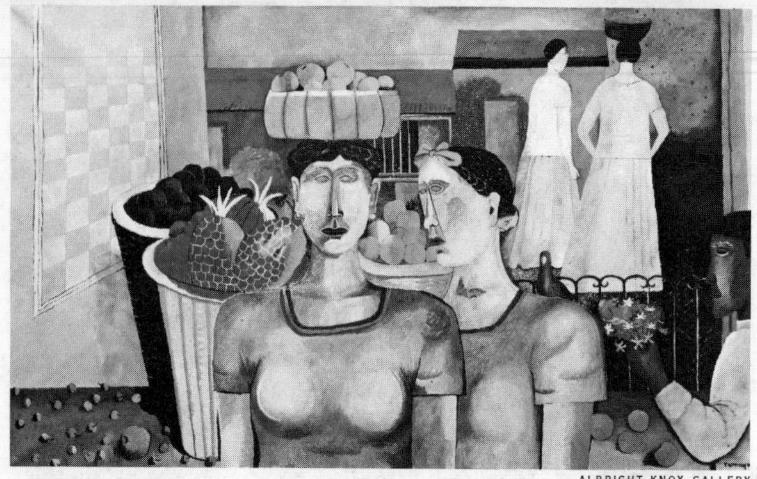

ALBRIGHT-KNOX GALLERY

RUFINO TAMAYO'S *Women of Tehuantepec,* painted in 1939, shows this Mexican artist's concern with his national heritage and the influence of French cubism on his work after about 1925.

TAMAYO, tə-mä'yō, **Rufino** (1899–), Mexican painter, whose works combine modern international art forms with aspects of pre-Columbian art. He was born in Oaxaca, Mexico, on Aug. 26, 1899, and, after being orphaned in boyhood, lived with an uncle in Mexico City. In 1917 he entered the National School of Fine Arts but soon left to paint independently. Searching for inspiration, he turned first to the popular arts of Mexico, where he found a vigorous style that served as an antidote to academic refinement. His knowledge of native pre-Columbian art developed after he became head of the department of ethnographic drawing at the National Museum of Archaeology in 1921.

During the 1920's, Tamayo also became increasingly interested in modern French painting, especially cubism. This interest was later reflected in both his style and his artistic position and separated him from contemporary Mexican artists such as Rivera, Orozco, and Siqueiros, who favored a more native style and more pointed—often political—content. To be closer to the European art he admired, Tamayo went to New York City in 1925 and thereafter exhibited, worked, and taught in both Mexico and the United States. He made his first visit to Europe in 1949.

Although best known as an easel painter of figures and still lifes, Tamayo executed many murals both in Mexico and abroad. Among his easel paintings are *Women of Tehuantepec* (1939), *Homage to the Indian Race* (1952), and *The Sleep Walker* (1954).

NICOLAI CIKOVSKY, JR.
University of Texas

TAMBOURINE, tam-bə-rēn', a musical instrument in the percussion family. It consists of a skin stretched across one edge of a shallow ring; the player strikes it with his fingers or hand. Sometimes little bells (or metal disks called "jingles") are attached to the frame, and the instrument is shaken as well as struck. The tambourine is used in the orchestra for Spanish or gypsy effects, or by itself to accompany a dance.

TAMBOV, təm-bôf', is a city and oblast in the USSR, in the Russian republic. Tambov, the oblast capital, is on the Tsna River, 260 miles (418 km) southeast of Moscow. Tambov was founded in 1636 as a fortified outpost against the marauding Crimean Tatars. Industrial expansion under the Soviet regime has contributed to its rapid growth. It is primarily a railroad transportation center and a processing center for the surrounding farm area. Among the city's industries are large railroad shops and factories producing automobile parts and industrial equipment.

Tambov oblast, with an area of 13,240 square miles (34,300 sq km), lies in a low, level region between the central Russian uplands and the Volga hills. Its rich black earth makes it an important agricultural district, growing grains, potatoes, sugar beets, and tobacco. Beef cattle and hogs are raised. Industries, based mainly on local farm output, include flour mills, distilleries, and meat-packing plants. Population: (1969 est.) of the oblast, 1,494,000; of the city, 220,000.

THEODORE SHABAD
Editor of "Soviet Geography"

TAMBURLAINE THE GREAT, tam'bər-lān, is a two-part tragic history in blank verse by Christopher Marlowe, published in 1590 after being staged to great acclaim in 1587. The play, recognized as the first great tragedy in English literature, tells of the rise of its hero, the historical Timur (or Tamerlane), from brigand to monarch of all Asia and challenger of heaven. Early in Part I, he reveals his thirst for the "sole felicity of an earthly crown." After ruthless conquests he proclaims himself also a "Scourge of God" and, as Part I ends, celebrates his triumphs by marrying the "divine" Zenocrate. Part II opens with her fatal illness, after which he becomes increasingly savage and deranged. Eventually Tamburlaine orders a march "against the powers of heaven" but has to resign himself to failure and death.

Romantic critics have tended to equate Tamburlaine's fervor with Marlowe's supposed beliefs. Such an interpretation is unjustified. Rather, Marlowe was dramatizing in his hero's ambition a tragic error potential in Everyman.

ROY W. BATTENHOUSE
Author of "Marlowe's Tamburlaine"

TAMERLANE. See TIMUR.

TAMIL, tam'il, an important language of the Dravidian group, is spoken by over 32 million people, chiefly in southeastern India and northern Ceylon. It is the principal language of the Indian state of Tamil Nadu (formerly Madras) and of major cities in that state such as Madras, Thanjavur, and Madurai.

Available evidence indicates that Dravidian speakers were already in India when the Aryans arrived and that they once occupied much more territory than they now hold. They have been subjected to a continuous process of Aryanization over a long period. Because of the remoteness of their territory from the Aryan centers of northern India and their ancient literary heritage in a dialect that was as highly cultivated as Sanskrit, Tamil has been less Aryanized in vocabulary than the other Dravidian languages. This fact has become politically significant in the conflict between south India and north India and between the Dravidian Tamil culture and the Aryan Sanskrit.

The earliest known works of Tamil literature perhaps can be assigned to the centuries just before Christ. They arose only after cultural contact with the Aryans. Although classical Tamil literature is no rival to Sanskrit literature in richness and its content is largely derived from Sanskrit writings, it includes some works that embody an independent tradition of poetic art. The language of this art is, like Sanskrit, a highly artificial dialect, cultivated exclusively for literary purposes. It differs sufficiently in grammar and vocabulary to be scarcely intelligible to the Tamil speaker without special training. However, the spoken dialects peculiar to different areas and social groups differ only slightly from one another. In the 20th century a "standard" spoken Tamil has emerged as the language of formal address, periodicals, and newspapers, and a popular literature has developed. See also DRAVIDIAN; INDIA—*Literature*.

LEIGH LISKER
University of Pennsylvania

TAMIL NADU, tum'il nä'dōō, is the southernmost state of India, occupying the southeastern portion of the peninsula, between the Western Ghats and the Bay of Bengal. The dominant language is Tamil, an old Dravidian tongue with a well-developed literature. The state was formerly called Madras, and the city of Madras is its capital and chief port.

The Land. Tamil Nadu occupies an area of roughly 50,000 square miles (130,000 sq km) with a great diversity of topography, climate, and vegetation. The land slopes abruptly from the Western Ghats, on the western border, to the lower plateau and plains region bordering the Bay of Bengal on the east.

Most of Tamil Nadu's rivers flow from west to east. They rise with the onset of the summer monsoon rains (June–September) and dwindle to a trickle as the hot season approaches (February–May). The heaviest rainfall is in the Western Ghats. The eastern portion of the state receives additional precipitation from October through January, when winds blow onto the land from the northeast across the Bay of Bengal.

Natural vegetation reflects the distribution of rainfall, ranging from lush forests in the western hills to scrub bush and drought-resistant palmyra in the southern and interior lowland. Agriculture depends on careful storage and redistribution of the limited water supply. Numerous dams, irrigation channels, and tanks (storage ponds) have been constructed to ensure a stable water supply. Earth-embanked tanks, many over 1 mile (1.6 km) in diameter, dot the surface, chiefly in the southern districts.

The People. Tamil Nadu had an estimated 38 million inhabitants in 1970. The population is predominantly Hindu, but Christians and Muslims constitute roughly 10% of the total. The growth of population has been relatively slow, controlled in the past partly by migration and since the late 1960's partly by family planning. Tamil Nadu is a leader in the adoption of birth control techniques in India. However, population growth is a problem, because the state's density is nearly double the average for India, and unemployment is increasing.

Agriculture is the predominant economic activity, with rice the preferred food and major crop. The chief rice-producing area is the delta of the Cauvery River. Tea and coffee are important crops in the western hills, and cotton in the southern lowlands. Manufactures include textiles, foodstuffs, and leather goods. Engineering activities are concentrated in the vicinity of Madras.

History. In ancient and medieval times the Pandyas, Cholas, and Pallavas established powerful Hindu states in what is now Tamil Nadu. The Dravidian culture, of which the area was a center, produced the architectural monuments of such cities as Thanjavur, Madurai, and Kanchipuram, and was spread to Southeast Asia.

The region came under Muslim rule in 1565. European penetration also began in the 16th century, and by 1801 the entire region was under British administration, which lasted until 1947. The present boundaries were fixed by the partition of Madras state on linguistic lines in 1953 and 1956. The Tamil-speaking state retained the name Madras until 1968, when it adopted the traditional name Tamil Nadu ("Land of the Tamils").

GEORGE E. STONER, JR.
Bradley University

TAMING OF THE SHREW, a comedy by William Shakespeare, printed in the Folio of 1623. The date and circumstances of its composition are controversial. The controversy centers on the play's relationship to a similar but anonymous play, *The Taming of a Shrew*, published in 1594. Some scholars hold that *A Shrew* is the basis of *The Shrew*, others that both derive from a common source, and still others that *A Shrew* is a reconstruction of *The Shrew*. Depending upon which case they favor, authorities date the play some time between 1592 and 1596. Despite the stylistic unevenness of *The Taming of the Shrew*, no really sound evidence has been offered that it is not entirely by Shakespeare.

The story of *The Taming of the Shrew* has three sections. The plot of the drunkard persuaded of his nobility, which appeared as early as the *Arabian Nights*, is abandoned by Shakespeare in the first act. The other two plots, which are closely interwoven, start as a play presented before the drunken countryman Christopher Sly but become the central action. The more interesting one, about the subduing of a termagant, is found in English balladry. The other—adapted from George Gascoigne's *The Supposes* (1556), a prose translation of Ludovico Ariosto's *I suppositi* (1509)—deals with the wooing of the shrew's sister by a suitor who changes identity with his servant.

The play is less attractive for its poetry than for its vigor. The courtship of the gentle Bianca is colorless, and the characters involved in this section of the play are conventional. It is far otherwise with Katharina and Petruchio, the participants in the battle of the sexes. To see the play as a mere breaking of a woman's will is a mistake. The taming of the shrew is not primarily a physical taming. By behaving outrageously on the pretense of being kind to his bride, Petruchio makes Kate see herself as others see her, recognize the absurdity of her ill-tempered obstinacy, and thus achieve a basis for social and marital harmony. The corrective is laughter.

This laughter has been popular with audiences. The play was reprinted in 1631 and acted at court in 1633. John Fletcher wrote a sequel, *The Woman's Prize: or, The Tamer Tamed* (printed in 1647). Shakespeare's play was adapted in the Restoration and 18th century and condensed by David Garrick in *Catherine and Petruchio* (1754). The true version returned in the 19th century, the most notable revival being Augustin Daly's in 1887 with John Drew and Ada Rehan. Among the many performances since, those by Alfred Lunt and Lynn Fontanne in 1935–1936 were especially spirited. Cole Porter wrote the music and Sam and Bella Spewack the book for *Kiss Me, Kate,* a musical version of *The Taming of the Shrew,* which was a Broadway success in 1948.

ROBERT HAMILTON BALL
Queens College, City University of New York

Further Reading: Charlton, Henry B., *Shakespearian Comedy,* 4th ed. (London 1949); Parrott, Thomas Marc, *Shakespearean Comedy* (New York 1949); Tillyard, Eustace M. W., *Shakespeare's Early Comedies* (New York 1965); Traversi, Derek, *Shakespeare: The Early Comedies* (London 1960).

TAMIYA HIROSHI, tä-mē-yä hēr-ō-shē (1903–), Japanese biologist and biochemist who made several important contributions to biochemistry. He is perhaps best known for developing a technique for the mass culture of algae.

In 1951, interested in more efficient bases for world food supply, Tamiya started culturing unicellular algae. He and his collaborators used an "open circulation method" in which growing cultures of the green alga *Chlorella* were cropped intermittently. Given 12 hours of light and 12 hours of dark, the *Chlorella* cells grew in the light and divided in the dark with a high degree of synchrony. Thus the method produced unexpected dividends for pure science. Refinements of the technique facilitated varied studies of cellular events at specific stages of the life cycle of cells.

Tamiya worked on other fundamental problems in biochemistry, including heat production from respiration in the mold *Aspergillus oryzae* and oxygen origin in algal photosynthesis. He also studied hemoglobin in paramecia and the functioning of respiratory enzymes in acetic acid bacteria.

Tamiya was born in Osaka, on Jan. 5, 1903. He received his Sc. D. from the University of Tokyo in 1932 and was professor there from 1939 until his retirement in 1963.

JOHN F. BENNETT, *Stanford University*

TAMM, täm, **Igor Yevgenievich** (1895–1971), Soviet scientist and one of the world's leading theoretical physicists. He shared the 1958 Nobel Prize in physics with his countryman I. M. Frank "for the discovery and interpretation of the Cherenkov effect"—the radiation emitted by electrons moving faster than the speed of light in an optically transparent medium. This theory led to the development of the Cherenkov counter, which has played an important part in the detection and measurement of elementary particles, including the antiproton.

Tamm was born in Vladivostok on July 8, 1895. He studied briefly at the University of Edinburgh and graduated from Moscow State University in 1918. In 1927, he was made a full professor at Moscow State, and in 1934 he took charge of the theoretical division of Lebedev's Physical Institute of the Soviet Academy of Sciences. From 1953 he was an Academy member. He died in Moscow on April 12, 1971.

Much of Tamm's scientific work was concerned with the application of quantum mechanics to solid-state physics, but he also made valuable contributions to the study of elementary particles, nuclear forces, and the theory of nuclear synthesis.

L. PEARCE WILLIAMS, *Cornell University*

TAMMANY HALL, tam′ə-nē, the popular name for the Democratic party organization in New York County, whose leaders influenced city and state politics during the 19th century and first half of the 20th. Because of the number of scandals and exposés of corruption linked to the organization, the name Tammany bears an onus of evil in politics.

The Society of St. Tammany, or Columbian Order, was founded in New York City on May 12, 1789, by William Mooney, a former Continental soldier. The name derived from Tamanend, the legendary chief of the Delaware Indians, known for his wisdom and love of liberty. The founding of Tammany and other patriotic societies was a manifestation of resistance to the apparent fostering of a hereditary aristocracy by patrician organizations such as the Society of the Cincinnati.

In satirical contrast to the elegance of the patrician groups, Tammany affected Indian titles and usages. The 13 trustees, commemorating the 13 original states, were called sachems, and the president was the grand sachem. The title Great Grand Sachem was conferred upon presidents of the United States, and Andrew Jackson was the last president thus honored. A master of ceremonies was a sagamore, a secretary was a scribe, a doorkeeper was a *wiskinskie,* and a meeting place was a wigwam.

By the early 1800's Tammany members were involved in politics, with the democratization of the ballot box a major goal. With the removal of the property qualifications for voting in 1821, Tammany won a greater following in New York City. Soon the society established a pattern of corruption, election, dictation, and cover-up.

Tammany Hall politics flourished in the 1850's when Fernando Wood, the Democratic mayor of New York City, ruled in an era of gang fights and flagrant political abuses. The most infamous sachem, William M. "Boss" Tweed, built the most predatory band of looters in American urban history. Boss Tweed's Ring had nearly secured control of the state government by 1868. Before prominent citizens were aroused to concerted action against Tammany, the theft by the Tweed Ring reached tens of millions of dollars.

Corruption continued under bosses such as "Honest John" Kelly, Richard F. Croker, and

Charles F. Murphy. Murphy ruled from 1902 until his death in 1924. In 1930 and 1931 an investigation of the city magistrates' courts, headed by Samuel Seabury, discredited Tammany Hall and ultimately brought about the resignation in 1932 of Mayor James J. Walker. During the administration of Mayor Fiorello H. La Guardia, elected by an anti-Tammany Fusion party in 1933, Tammany declined greatly. In the 1950's it revived under the leadership of Carmine DeSapio, who helped elect Robert F. Wagner, Jr., as mayor in 1953. Later, as leader of an anti-Tammany movement, Wagner succeeded in winning a third mayoral term in 1961. In the new era of reform politics in the Democratic party, the big city machines have declined in importance. But in presidential elections the regular politicians are still courted—in New York and nationally.

HERBERT MITGANG
Author of "The Man Who Rode the Tiger"

TAMMERFORS. See TAMPERE.

TAMMUZ, tăm′o͝oz, a Middle Eastern underworld god of vegetation. Tammuz is the Aramaic and Hebrew form of the Sumerian name Dumuzi ("rightful son"). His cult existed in Sumer early in the 3d millennium B.C. and later became widespread in the ancient Middle East, particularly in Babylonia. His cult is mentioned in Ezekiel 8:14. The Syrian worship of Adonis is related to the same mythical tradition. Dumuzi, the shepherd-king of Uruk, became an underworld god of vegetation and had an important role in the fertility cult. In a Sumerian myth he is condemned to the underworld for having slighted the goddess Inanna (Ishtar).

TAMPA, tam′pə, a city in western Florida, the seat of Hillsborough county, is 170 miles (2.2 km) southwest of Jacksonville. Situated at the mouth of the Hillsborough River on Tampa Bay, an inlet of the Gulf of Mexico, Tampa is a port of entry, the trade center for Florida's west coast, and one of the most industrialized cities in the state. Citrus canning and the shrimp industry are important, and the city is a leading phosphate-shipping port. Its manufactured products include fabricated steel, electronic equipment, cigars, beer, paint, and fertilizers.

Tampa is the seat of MacDill Air Force Base. Educational facilities include two 4-year coeducational institutions, the University of South Florida and the University of Tampa.

Ponce de Léon visited the site of Tampa in 1521, followed by Pánfilo de Narváez in 1528 and Hernando de Soto in 1539. The earliest settlement was made in 1823. The military post of Fort Brooke, established on the site in 1832, played a prominent role in the Second Seminole War. The settlement that grew up around the post was also known as Fort Brooke, but the Indian name of Tampa was later revived. The city was captured by the Union Navy in the Civil War. During the Spanish-American War, Col. Theodore Roosevelt made a Tampa hotel his headquarters in 1898, when the city was the chief port of embarkation for troops to Cuba.

Tampa was chartered by the state legislature in 1885. It is governed by a mayor and council. Population: 277,767.

CECIL P. BEACH, *Director of Libraries Tampa and Hillsborough Counties*

TAMPERE, tam′pə-rā, is Finland's second-largest city and its principal industrial center. In southwestern Finland, it is about 100 miles (160 km) northwest of Helsinki. Tampere (Swedish, *Tammerfors*) is in an area that was long under Swedish domination. It is on the banks of the Tammer Falls, from which it takes its name, between lakes Näsijärvi and Pyhäjärvi. It is an attractive, well-planned city and a cultural center. Among its many notable examples of contemporary architecture are the Institute of Social Sciences and an open-air theater.

Chartered in 1779, it began to grow in 1820 when James Finlayson, a Scot, built a machine shop near the falls. Russia's Czar Nicholas I recognized the industrial potential of the site's waterpower and in 1821 made Tampere a free city, permitting free importation of machinery and raw materials. Steady industrialization followed. Modern Tampere has the largest textile and knit-goods mills in northern Europe, and its diversified industries produce steel castings, turbines, shoes, and rubber and wood products. Population: (1968 est.) 150,000.

VINCENT H. MALMSTRÖM, *Middlebury College*

TAMPICO, tam-pē′kō, a city in northeastern Mexico, is the second-ranking seaport in the country. The largest city in Tamaulipas state, it is situated some 210 miles (338 km) northeast of Mexico, on the Pánuco River 5 miles (8 km) inland from its mouth on the Gulf of Mexico. Dredging of the river's mouth, excellent loading facilities, and good communications make the port the most modern in Mexico. Situated in the tropics, Tampico often experiences hurricanes.

The discovery of petroleum nearby in 1901 was a great boon to the city's development. Although Tampico's growth slowed after 1938, when Mexico expropriated foreign-owned property, the city continued to process a third of Mexico's oil. The developing cattle industry and the processing and export of hemp, chicle, and various woods make Tampico, together with neighboring Ciudad Madero to the north, an important economic and commercial center.

Tampico was an Aztec village before a monastery was founded here in 1532. The French occupied the city in 1862. The arrest of American sailors in Tampico in 1914 triggered the occupation of Veracruz by the U. S. Navy. Population: (1960) 122,535.

REYNALDO AYALA, *San Diego State College*

TANA, Lake, tä′nä, the largest lake in Ethiopia, with an area of about 1,400 square miles (3,625 sq km). Lake Tana is in the northwestern part of the country at an elevation of 6,000 feet (1,830 meters). It drains into the Abbia (Blue Nile) River, which plunges over the high Tisisat Falls, just south of the lake. At the falls is a hydroelectric station. The islands of Dega and Dek in Lake Tana are the sites of historic monasteries.

TANAGER, tan′i-jər, any of a large family of over 200 species of birds native mainly to tropical and subtropical regions of North and South America. Although some species are somberly colored, tanagers are generally among the most brilliantly plumaged birds in the world. Their name, in fact, is derived from the Brazilian Tupi Indian word *tangara,* which means a brightly colored bird. One species—the scarlet tanager

HAL H. HARRISON, FROM NATIONAL AUDUBON SOCIETY

Male summer tanager, with young in the nest.

(*Piranga olivacea*)—is beneficial because it eats insects that are detrimental to trees.

Tanagers range from 4 to 12 inches (10 to 31 cm) in length and vary in shape and coloring. Most, however, are plump, short-necked birds with rounded wings and short-to-medium length tails. A few are crested. The typical tanager bill is conical and toothed near the tip. In most species, the males and females are alike in coloring, but in a few species they are markedly different. In the tiny euphonias (genus *Tanagra*), for example, the males are glossy bluish to greenish black on the upper surface and bright yellow below, while the females are dull green.

A few tanagers are ground-dwelling, but the majority live in treetops. Some species are gregarious, while others are solitary. They feed on fruits and insects. Although tanagers are basically nonmigratory, a few tropical forms make seasonal moves from humid lowlands to drier, cooler mountain regions.

Tanagers vary in nesting behavior. Some nest in trees, while others nest in shrubs, hollows, and crevices. The clutch size varies from two eggs in the smaller species to five in the larger species. The female alone incubates the eggs, but the males help in rearing the young.

Tanagers, classified in several genera, make up the family Thraupidae of the order Passeriformes.

JOSEPH BELL, *New York Zoological Park*

TANAKA GIICHI, tä-nä-kä gē-ē-chē (1863–1929), Japanese general and premier, was born in Hagi, Yamaguchi prefecture (formerly Choshu), on June 22, 1863. Trained as a professional soldier, he served in the wars with China in 1894–1895 and Russia in 1904–1905. He was minister of the army in 1918–1921 and 1923–1924, a baron from 1920, and a full general from 1921.

In 1922, Tanaka became head of the powerful Choshu faction of the army. President of the Seiyukai political party from 1925, he took office as premier in April 1927. His ministry, lasting until July 1929, was marked by political and economic unrest at home and by tension abroad. Tanaka died in Tokyo on Sept. 29, 1929.

The authenticity of his supposed memorandum to the emperor in 1927, known as the Tanaka Memorial, is extremely doubtful. The document urged the Japanese takeover of China as a prelude to world conquest. Tanaka did advocate a stronger policy in China, but the chief cause of his political downfall was his failure to persuade the army to punish extremist officers who had murdered the Chinese warlord Chang Tso-lin.

HYMAN KUBLIN, *Brooklyn College*

TANAKA KAKUEI, tä-nä-kä kä-kōō-e (1918–), Japanese political leader, who in 1972 became Japan's youngest prime minister since the end of World War II. Tanaka was born in Nishiyama, Niigata prefecture, on May 4, 1918. He left school at the age of 15 to become a construction worker, and eventually he set up his own construction company. After serving two years in the army during World War II he returned to his business, which by 1945 had become one of Japan's largest construction firms.

Tanaka was first elected to the House of Representatives in 1947. He was named deputy minister of justice in 1949 but soon after was jailed briefly on charges of accepting bribes—charges of which he later was acquitted.

In 1957, Tanaka became minister of communications. He later served as finance minister in three cabinets and as secretary general of the Liberal Democratic party. Premier Sato Eisaku appointed him minister of international trade and industry in 1971. In July 1972, Tanaka succeeded Sato as prime minister. Among Tanaka's first acts as prime minister was to establish diplomatic relations with the People's Republic of China. He attended a summit meeting with Chou En-lai in China in September 1972.

TANANARIVE, tə-nan'ə-rēv, is the capital and largest city of the Malagasy Republic. Situated at an elevation of 4,815 feet (1,476 meters) in the temperate central highlands of Madagascar island, the city is spread spectacularly on hilltops overlooking a fertile plain.

Tananarive (Antananarivo) is the commercial and manufacturing center of the Malagasy Republic. Its large colorful market, the Zoma, sells a wide variety of products. Industries include food processing, tanning, woodworking, printing,

TANANARIVE is the capital of the Malagasy Republic.

PICOU, FROM DE WYS

automobile assembly, and the production of clothing, chemicals, pharmaceuticals, construction materials, and handicrafts. The city is connected by rail with the seaport of Tamatave, about 135 miles (215 km) northeast.

Tananarive was the capital of the Merina kingdom, which ruled most of Madagascar in the 18th and 19th centuries. After Madagascar's occupation by France in the late 19th century, the city became the administrative center of the French government and the hub of road and rail communications.

Tananarive has a university, an observatory, technical schools, and research institutes. The relics of the Merina monarchy are housed within the Rova, the former royal estate atop a rock dominating the city. Sacred Lake Anosy, several baroque palaces, and numerous old churches grace various sections of Tananarive. Population: (1966) 335,149.

IRENE S. VAN DONGAN
California State College, Pennsylvania

TANBARK OAK, an evergreen hardwood tree of the Pacific Coast region of California and southwestern Oregon. The tanbark, or tanoak, *Lithocarpus densiflora,* belongs to the beech family (Fagaceae) and is the only New World member of its genus. More than 200 other species are native to southeastern Asia.

Mature trees are often 150 feet (45.5 meters) tall with a trunk diameter of 4 feet (1.2 meters). The trees reach maturity after about 100 years, and some are more than 250 years old. The alternate, short-stalked, oblong leaves are 3 to 5 inches (76–127 mm) long with toothed edges. As in chestnut trees, the upright spikes of minute yellowish male flowers often bear a few greenish female flowers at the base. The acorns are 1 inch (25 mm) long, with a shallow cup covered by long hairy scales.

The reddish brown wood is hard, heavy, tough, and strong but difficult to season, or dry out. It has been used for fuel, furniture, mine timbers, and pulpwood. The thick red-brown furrowed bark is rich in tannin.

ELBERT L. LITTLE, JR., *Forest Service*
U. S. Department of Agriculture

TANCRED, tang'krəd (c. 1076–1112), Norman soldier, who was a leader of the First Crusade. On his mother's side, he was a grandson of Robert Guiscard, the first Norman ruler of southern Italy. Of his father, Odo, nothing is known. In 1096, Tancred joined his uncle Bohemund on the Crusade, fought gallantly at the Battle of Dorylaeum and the siege of Antioch, and took part in the capture of Jerusalem in 1099. The massacre that took place on the fall of the Holy City angered him because the victims included some to whom he had promised safety.

Tancred had already taken steps to carve out a principality for himself in Cilicia. When Bohemund, who had become prince of Antioch, was captured by the Turks in 1100, Tancred acted as regent for him and continued to do so after Bohemund's release and return to Italy. Similarly, when Baldwin of Edessa was taken prisoner in 1104, Tancred was invited to rule his territory as well, which he did by deputy. He vigorously defended Antioch against the Muslim emirs, led by Ridwan of Aleppo, and the Byzantines, who claimed it was an imperial city. He died, probably of typhoid, in 1112.

Brave but self-seeking, Tancred seemed at times prepared to endanger the whole Crusading enterprise in order to achieve his personal ambitions. He was a typical Norman warrior-prince, and the picture drawn of him by the Renaissance poet Tasso in his *Jerusalem Delivered* as a Christian hero-knight is scarcely historical.

JOHN J. SAUNDERS, *University of Canterbury*
Christchurch, New Zealand

TANDY, tan'dē, **Napper** (1740–1803), Irish revolutionary and hero of the ballad, *The Wearing of the Green.* James Napper Tandy was born in 1740 in Dublin, to a family of middle-class Protestant shopkeepers. In 1791, Tandy cofounded the United Irishmen, a group inspired by the French Revolution, to advocate democracy and Catholic Emancipation. Exiled in 1793, he moved to America and then to France. In September 1798, with a small French force, he invaded and briefly occupied the island of Rutland, off Donegal. He escaped to Hamburg, where the authorities surrendered him to the British. Tandy was tried in Ireland in 1800 and sentenced to death, but Napoleon's intervention saved him. In 1802 he was released from Wicklow jail and went to France. He died in Bordeaux on Aug. 24, 1803.

LAWRENCE J. MCCAFFREY
Loyola University, Chicago

TANEGASHIMA, tä-nā-gä-shē-mä, is one of the Osumi (Satsunan) Islands of Japan, just south of Kyushu across the Osumi Strait. Tanegashima, which is flat and has many bays, stretches some 35 miles (55 km) north-south and is about 7 miles (11 km) wide. The inhabitants depend chiefly on farming and fishing for their livelihood. The chief city and port, Nishinoomote, is on the northwest coast.

Tanegashima is famous as the place where the first guns reached Japan from Europe. After their introduction by the Portuguese in 1543, firearms were long called *tanegashima* in Japanese. The government now has a space satellite center on the island. Population: (1965) 60,130.

PRUE DEMPSTER
Author of "Japan Advances"

TANEY, tô'nē, **Roger Brooke** (1777–1864), fifth chief justice of the United States. Although vigilant in maintaining federal judicial supremacy, he also believed that "the object and end of all government is to promote the happiness and prosperity of the community by which it is established," and that this purpose could best be served by strengthening local, as distinguished from national, legislative authority. Thus he gave greater scope than had John Marshall to the exercise of state and other local powers.

Taney was born on March 17, 1777, on an ancestral plantation in Calvert county, Md. He graduated from Dickinson College in 1795 and studied law in Annapolis, in the office of Judge Jeremiah T. Chase.

After serving for a year in the Maryland legislature Taney began private practice in 1801 in Frederick, Md. There, five years later, he married Anne Key, the sister of Francis Scott Key, author of the words of *The Star Spangled Banner.* Taney was a Roman Catholic and Anne a Protestant. Their six daughters were reared as Protestants. Taney served (1816–1821) in the state senate. Moving to Baltimore, he rose rapidly to the top of his profession, and became attorney general of Maryland in 1827.

Four years later, Taney became U. S. attorney general and in 1833 secretary of the treasury in President Jackson's cabinet. He played a leading part in the contest over the second Bank of the United States.

The Bank War. The bank's control over public funds gave it immense economic power, free of governmental restraint. Believing its power excessive, Jackson proposed to let its charter expire in 1836. But in 1832, hoping to defeat Jackson in the election of that year, Henry Clay made the bank an immediate issue by securing the passage of a bill for recharter. Jackson vetoed the bill in a message prepared by Taney. He was overwhelmingly reelected and adopted a plan, devised by Taney, that led ultimately to the bank's extinction.

Jackson had named Taney secretary of the treasury in 1833, by recess appointment. However, the bank's supporters blocked Senate confirmation and also blocked confirmation of his appointment in 1835 as associate justice of the Supreme Court. In 1836, after John Marshall's death, Jackson made Taney chief justice, and the new Senate confirmed him.

Taney and Marshall. Taney was as concerned as Marshall for the independence and power of the court. Under Marshall, admiralty jurisdiction had been limited to tidal waters, but in the case of *The Genesee Chief* v. *Fitzhugh* (1852) Taney extended the exclusive admiralty jurisdiction of the federal judiciary to the Great Lakes and inland waterways.

Subsequently, in *Ableman* v. *Booth* (1859), a fugitive slave case, he asserted the supremacy of the U. S. Supreme Court in constitutional matters, and in an opinion unsurpassed in strength and clarity, held that the state courts had no power to interfere with the enforcement of federal statutes by federal courts.

Marshall had extended the contract clause of the U. S. Constitution to legislative charters, in effect permitting one legislature to tie the hands of its successors. Taney accepted Marshall's decision but altered its thrust, limiting it to the strict wording of the charters. In *Charles River Bridge Co.* v. *Warren Bridge Co.* (1837), where a toll bridge had been chartered without specifying that its rights were exclusive, he permitted a later legislature to authorize another bridge next to it.

Marshall considered the power of Congress over interstate commerce to be exclusive. In *Cooley* v. *Board of Port Wardens* (1852) the Taney court limited such power to matters of national concern, leaving the states free to regulate interstate commerce in matters of local concern where Congress had not acted.

Taney and Marshall diverged in their attitudes on political questions. Marshall's decisions establishing the power of the court had been acts of statesmanship that necessarily involved politics. Taney sought to withdraw the court from political involvement. Except for his opinion in the Dred Scott case he was the leading apostle of judicial restraint.

Dred Scott. The year 1855 brought tragedy. Vacationing in Virginia, Taney's wife and youngest daughter died of yellow fever. He was spared, but was stunned by grief. Then, in December 1855 the Dred Scott case, formally *Scott* v. *Sandford*, came before the Supreme Court.

HARVARD UNIVERSITY, LAW SCHOOL COLLECTION

Roger Brooke Taney, from a portrait by Henry Inman.

Taney was opposed to slavery. He had freed the slaves that he inherited and supported them in need. In 1819, in the trial of Jacob Gruber for inciting slaves to revolt, he had said, "A hard necessity compels us to endure the evil of slavery for a time. Yet while it continues it is a blot on our national character, and every real lover of freedom confidently hopes that it will be effectually, though it must be gradually, wiped away." But as a judge he felt bound by the Constitution's recognition of slavery in Article I, sections 2 and 9, and Article IV, section 2.

Taney had refused to pass upon the controversial issue of Congress' right to bar slavery from the territories. When abolitionists sought to force this issue upon the court again in the Dred Scott case, he resisted. On the court's first vote a majority agreed to sidestep. But the pressure mounted. Two justices proposed to cover the issue in dissenting opinions. President Pierce, President-elect Buchanan, and Attorney General Caleb Cushing requested a decision, hoping that it would set the matter at rest. Finally, a majority of the nondissenting justices voted that Taney should write an opinion covering all the controversial points. Against his better judgment, Taney, then turning 80, yielded. He held that Congress had no power to bar slavery from the territories, and that Negroes were ineligible for citizenship. See also DRED SCOTT CASE.

Later, Taney made a magnificent stand for wartime civil liberty, holding in *Ex Parte Merryman* (1861) that President Lincoln could not suspend the writ of habeas corpus. But his reputation never recovered from the Dred Scott case. Charles Evans Hughes, a leading chief justice, said that Taney "thought he was rendering a national service. There was a fundamental error in the supposition that the imperious question which underlay the controversy could be put at rest by a judicial pronouncement." But, said Hughes, "He was a great chief justice." Taney died in Washington, D. C., on Oct. 12, 1864.

WALKER LEWIS
Author of "Without Fear or Favor: A Biography of Chief Justice Roger Brooke Taney"

TANEYEV, tu-nyā′yəf, **Sergei Ivanovich** (1856–1915), Russian composer and teacher. Taneyev was born in Vladimir district, Russia, on Nov. 25, 1856. He began studying piano at the Moscow Conservatory at the age of 10 and later studied composition with Tchaikovsky, whose close friend he became. In 1878 he succeeded Tchaikovsky as professor of harmony and orchestration at the Moscow Conservatory and in 1881 became chief professor of piano there. Taneyev was director of the conservatory from 1885 to 1889 but resigned to teach counterpoint and composition, until 1906. His important treatise *Convertible Counterpoint in the Strict Style* (1909) was translated into English in 1962. Taneyev died in Moscow on June 19, 1915.

Among Taneyev's most important compositions are the opera *Oresteia* (1895) and the Symphony in C Minor (1896–1897). He wrote choral works, songs, and chamber music.

T'ANG DYNASTY, täng, the dynasty that ruled China from 618 to 906. It established Chinese power from Korea to Afghanistan and Vietnam, and its political structure and arts profoundly influenced civilization in Japan and Vietnam. Among the remarkable figures of the age were Empress Wu (reigned 690–704), the only woman to rule China in her own name; the Buddhist scholar Hsüan-tsang (596–664), who crossed the deserts of Central Asia alone on a journey to India; and Emperor Hsüan Tsung (reigned 712–756), who neglected his realm for the love of a concubine.

The T'ang dynasty was founded by Li Yüan and his son Li Shih-min (see also T'ANG T'AI TSUNG). T'ang power was based partly on an effective military system and on a land distribution system that worked well through the 7th century. Important changes were made in the tax structure, and recruitment of officials by examinations became basic to Chinese government. These and other developments were related to profound socioeconomic changes accompanying urbanization and commercial growth. Technological innovations included the invention of printing.

Among the achievements in the arts were the high development of Buddhist sculpture and the attainment of new heights in painting and ceramics. Chinese poetry reached its peak, and fiction first appeared, in the short story form. Although Buddhism continued to flourish, with the Ch'an (Zen) sect as its most notable development, Confucian thought began its revival, especially in the works of Han Yü (768–824).

T'ang power collapsed in the 750's with major military defeats abroad and a rebellion led by An Lu-shan at home. After the rebellion was suppressed, T'ang emperors retained the throne for another 150 years, their powers greatly restricted by regional warlords. Discontent grew, and in the late 9th century a peasant rebellion laid waste to large areas. The last T'ang emperor was murdered in 907. See also CHINA–*Art and Architecture; History; Literature.*

JAMES R. SHIRLEY, *Northern Illinois University*

T'ANG T'AI TSUNG, täng tī dzo͝ong (599–649), was the second emperor of the T'ang dynasty of China. His reign (626–649) is considered the first high point in T'ang history.

T'ai Tsung, whose personal name was Li Shih-min, was the second son of Li Yüan, a military official of the Sui dynasty. Brilliant and ambitious, Li Shih-min early demonstrated military ability and charismatic qualities. As the Sui government collapsed in civil war, he encouraged his father to rebel. Forming an alliance with Turkish invaders, they captured the city of Ch'ang-an (now Sian), where Li Yüan was declared first emperor of the T'ang dynasty in 618.

Li Shih-min is often given major credit for directing the rebellion and for suppressing competing forces during the next decade. In 626 he killed his two brothers, who may have been plotting to kill him, and forced his father to abdicate in his favor.

As emperor, posthumously titled T'ai Tsung ("Great Exemplar"), Li forged a powerful military force and established Chinese authority throughout the northern frontier area and central Asia as far as modern Afghanistan. At the same time he placed the dynasty on a firm foundation, resolving serious problems of inflation and encouraging construction work.

JAMES R. SHIRLEY, *Northern Illinois University*

TANGANYIKA, an East African territory that became independent in 1961 and united with Zanzibar in 1964 to form Tanzania. See TANZANIA.

TANGANYIKA, Lake, tan-gən-yē′kə, in east central Africa. It is the largest lake in Africa after Lake Victoria and the deepest in the world after Lake Baikal in the USSR.

Lake Tanganyika lies within the deep western trough of the Great Rift Valley but has a surface elevation of about 2,500 feet (760 meters). Extending some 400 miles (650 km) north and south and 25 to 40 miles 40–65 km) across, it covers 12,700 square miles (32,900 sq km). Its waters, which are fresh, plunge to a depth of 4,710 feet (1,436 meters).

Lake Tanganyika separates Tanzania on the east from Congo (Kinshasa) on the west. It is also bordered by Burundi on the northeast and Zambia on the south. Its only outlet, the Lukuga River, is often silted up, causing changes in the level of the lake.

Lake Tanganyika is navigable throughout and is known for its many varieties of fish. Its principal ports are Albertville in Congo, Bujumbura in Burundi, and Kigoma in Tanzania.

Arab slave traders operated on the coasts of Lake Tanganyika during most of the 19th century. In 1858, John Speke and Richard Burton became the first Europeans to reach the lake. The encounter between Stanley and Livingstone in 1871 took place at Ujiji on the east coast.

IRENE S. VAN DONGEN
California State College, Pennsylvania

TANGE KENZO, tän-ge ken-zō (1913–), is Japan's leading modern architect. He made his name when his design for the Peace Museum in Hiroshima won the open competition in 1949.

Tange specializes in public buildings. Among those he has designed are the Kanagawa Prefectural Office, the Roman Catholic Cathedral in Tokyo, and the Tokyo City Hall. His two National Gymnasiums for the 1964 Olympics in Tokyo are his most striking work—imaginative and bold.

Most of Tange's buildings are of concrete. Ferroconcrete is the logical material for major buildings in Japan because the country's frequent earthquakes limit the use of glass and brick.

CONSULATE GENERAL OF JAPAN, N. Y.

TANGE KENZO designed this starkly modern Roman Catholic cathedral in Tokyo. Completed in 1965, it has four stainless steel roofs. Each covers an entire side.

Thus glass walls in the Mies van der Rohe manner are impractical, and Tange and other modern Japanese architects have been influenced by Le Corbusier, who pioneered the use of rough, unadorned concrete.

Tange was born in Osake on Sept. 4, 1913. He studied architecture at Tokyo University in 1935–1938 and 1942–1945, becoming a professor there in 1946. Although he prefers architectural practice to teaching and writing, he is an active theorist. Some of his writings, which include many books, articles, and lectures, have been translated into English.

ROBERT MOES, *Denver Art Museum*

TANGELO, tan′jə-lō, a citrus fruit produced by crossing a tangerine with a grapefruit, or pomelo. The tangelo looks very much like an orange and has a sweet flavor. It is sold primarily as a novelty fruit.

The first tangelo was produced in 1897 by Walter T. Swingle and his colleagues at the U. S. Department of Agriculture. Among their early varieties were Sampson and Thornton. Later varieties include Orlando, Minneola, and Seminole.

By the 1970's about 15,000 acres (6,000 hectares), mainly of Orlando, were under production in Florida. About 2.5 million boxes of fruit were being produced annually. Orlando and Minneola had also become commercially important in California.

LOUIS W. ZIEGLER, *University of Florida*

TANGENT, tan′jənt. In geometry, a tangent is a straight line that touches a curve at only one point. See CIRCLE: *Geometry—Euclidean geometry.* In trigonometry, the tangent of an acute angle A in a right triangle is the ratio of the side opposite A to the side adjacent to A. See TRIGONOMETRY—*Elementary Trigonometry and the Right Triangle.* In calculus, the tangent to a curve at point P is defined as the line in the limiting position of the secant line PQ as point Q approaches P along the curve. See CALCULUS—*The Derivative.*

TANGERINE, tan-jə-rēn′, or *mandarin orange,* a small, yellow to orange or orange-red citrus fruit with a loose rind and loosely adhering segments. The fruit first gained commercial importance in India and Japan and is now widely cultivated in Florida.

At one time all tangerines were considered to belong to a single species, *Citrus reticulata,* but now several distinct species are recognized. The variety most widely marketed for home use is the Dancy tangerine (*C. tangerina*), which was developed about 1871 at Orange Mills, Fla. In the mid-1950's production of Dancy tangerines in Florida reached 5 million boxes annually. However, the fruits are difficult to grow and market satisfactorily and have met competition from such hybrids as the Temple orange and tangelo.

The Ponkan (*C. reticulata*), which is larger than the Dancy, is grown only in small quantities. The Cleopatra (*C. reshni*) is too small and acidic for home use. It is used as a rootstock.

Tangerines are used to produce some hybrid fruits, such as the tangelo, a cross between a tangerine and a grapefruit, and the tangor, a cross between a tangerine and a sweet orange. These hybrids are gradually replacing the Dancy as specialty citrus fruits.

LOUIS W. ZIEGLER
University of Florida

TANGIER, tan-jēr′, is a seaport in northern Morocco at the entrance to the Strait of Gibraltar. It is situated at the northwestern tip of Africa, 36 miles (58 km) southwest of Gibraltar. Tangier's strategic location, political history, and former international status have made it a busy port of call as well as a cosmopolitan center of commerce, diplomacy, banking, and tourism. The subtropical climate, with dry summers and mild winter rainfall, appeals to retired Europeans. In its three principal languages the city is known as Tanger (French), Tánger (Spanish), and Tanja (Arabic).

Layout of the City. Tangier spreads over the slopes of a natural amphitheater, which overlooks the port, protected on the north and west by a curved breakwater. The downtown European sector has boulevards with hotels, restaurants, and travel agencies serving the tourist trade, as well as shops, offices of corporations and shipping companies, and a number of banks.

The adjoining walled Medina, the old Arab city, is noted for its white buildings, mosques, many-colored minarets, and labyrinth of crooked, narrow streets. The northwestern part of the Medina is the site of the old palace of the sultan, the Museum of Antiquities, the Museum of Modern Moroccan Art, and, at the highest point, the casbah, or old fort. The Great Mosque is in the southeastern corner of the Medina. Nearby is the Petit Socco (little market), with its European cafés, peddlers, and money changers. Streets radiating from it are lined with small shops that sell Moroccan and imported jewelry, leather goods, luggage, pottery, clothing, and novelties. The Grand Socco (Great Market) lies to the southwest, just outside the walled Medina. Here, in shops, stalls, and open squares, are sold fruits, vegetables, poultry, and grain, while jugglers and snake charmers offer entertainment. On special market days rural Moroccans mounted on donkeys, mules, or horses add to the local pedestrian traffic. These traditional features contrast with scattered modern buildings and American-built taxicabs.

Beyond the Medina and the Grand Socco are modern residential streets, foreign schools, hospitals, European villas, and the luxurious quarters of foreign diplomatic missions.

Economic Life. Tangier exports goatskins, canary seed, cork, almonds, and Moroccan leather from the interior, but these are commercially less important than passenger traffic and the entrepôt trade in imported goods that are exchanged in the city. Small handicraft industries in the older sections produce leather goods, brassware, copperware, furniture, pottery, and textiles for sale to tourists and the local population. There is a small modern industrial district with machine shops, flour mills, fish canneries, soap factories, and soft drink bottling works.

The Tangier-Fez Railway links the port with the Moroccan rail system. There are highways to Rabat and Tétouan. An international airport is 8 miles (13 km) southwest of Tangier.

History. Tangier was probably founded by the Phoenicians. The Carthaginian navigator Hanno recorded a visit to Tingis, at the site of Tangier, in 530 B. C. During the Roman period Tingis became a free city and gave its name to Mauretania Tingitana, the large region in northwestern Africa that it served. Later, the city was occupied by the Vandals (429 A. D.), Byzantines (541), and Visigoths (621). In 682 it was seized by the Arabs, who massacred the men and took the other inhabitants as captives. Resettled, the city was again taken by the Arabs in 707, and a Moorish garrison installed. From the 10th to the 13th century, control of Tangier was disputed among Moorish leaders from Spain, Morocco, and Tunisia, and the city changed hands several times.

The Portuguese captured Tangier in 1471 and the city became the capital of Portuguese possessions in Morocco. Spain ruled Tangier from 1578 until 1640, when the city reverted to Portuguese control. In 1661, through a royal marriage, Tangier was ceded to Britain. After building new fortifications, and withstanding a siege in 1680, Britain abandoned Tangier to the Moors in 1684. The city was rebuilt, acquiring the palace and several mosques and schools. But later it declined, and by 1810 it had only about 5,000 inhabitants.

In the mid-19th century, Tangier became the main gateway to Morocco, and developed as a modern port and center for foreign and Moroccan diplomats. A threat of German interference in 1905 led to the Algeciras Conference in 1906 under which European powers took control of customs duties at Tangier. The partition of Morocco between France and Spain in 1912 excluded Tangier, and final agreement on its status was delayed by World War I. Agreements among European powers in 1923 and 1928, however, gave the Tangier zone a neutral international status with a government in which representatives from nine European powers, as well as from Morocco, shared control. Spain occupied Tangier during World War II, from 1940 to 1945, when the city was placed under interim international control. It was absorbed by Morocco in 1956. Population: (1968) 150,000.

BENJAMIN E. THOMAS
University of California at Los Angeles

TANGLEWOOD FESTIVAL, a name sometimes applied to the Berkshire Festival, an annual summer music festival at Lenox, Mass. See BERKSHIRE FESTIVAL.

TANGLEWOOD TALES, by the American writer Nathaniel Hawthorne, was published in 1853 as a sequel to *The Wonder Book* (1852). Like its predecessor, it contains six Greek myths retold for children. The myths are *The Minotaur, The Pygmies, The Dragon's Teeth, Circe's Palace, The Pomegranate Seed,* and *The Golden Fleece.*

The young collegian Eustace Bright is again the narrator, and through him Hawthorne defends himself for "purifying" the legends—a process that sometimes invokes drastic bowdlerizing. At times, Hawthorne is annoyingly arch, but he generally redeems himself with touches of dry humor.

TANGO, tang'gō, a slow, graceful ballroom dance, characterized by frequent deep bendings of the knees and quick changes of direction on the balls of the feet. The accompanying music, generally in duple meter, is syncopated.

TANGIER'S MEDINA, or old Arab city, is a walled district rising directly above the city's harbor.

BERNARD G. SILBERSTEIN, FROM RAPHO GUILLUMETTE

The tango emerged near Buenos Aires in Argentina late in the 19th century. It developed from the *habanera* and the *milonga* and is therefore derived in part from West Indian Negro dance forms. The tango quickly became popular in Latin America and by the early 1920's was a ballroom favorite in Europe and the United States. Later, composers incorporated original tango melodies into some of their orchestral suites.

TANGOR, tan'jôr, a citrus tree produced as a hybrid by crossing a sweet orange with a tangerine. The two most important commercial varieties are the King orange and the temple orange. Like other tangors, they have deep orange fruits with easily peeled skins. See also ORANGE; TANGERINE.

TANGSHAN, täng'shän', a city in northeastern China, is a center of mining and heavy industry. It is situated in Hopei province, about 65 miles (100 km) northeast of Tientsin, on the Tientsin–Mukden (Shenyang) railroad.

Tangshan is in the Kailan coal-mining district, one of China's major fuel-producing areas. The city grew up as a mining center after exploitation of the Kailan deposits began in 1878. Following World War II, other industries were developed, especially iron and steel. Tangshan also produces machinery, reinforced concrete, and textiles, and it supplies distant areas with electricity from its thermal power plants. Population: (1957) 800,000.

TANGUT. See HSI-HSIA.

TANGUY, täN-gē', **Yves** (1900–1955), French-American surrealist painter, who was entirely self-taught. He was born in Paris on Jan. 5, 1900. Although familiar with surrealist literature, he had no thought of painting as a career until inspired in 1923 by a work of Giorgio de Chirico. In the mid-1920's he met André Breton, began to contribute paintings to the magazine *La Révolution surréaliste,* and became a member of the surrealist group in Paris. He went to the United States in 1939, married the American surrealist painter Kay Sage in 1940, and settled on a farm in Connecticut. Tanguy became a U.S. citizen in 1948. He died in Woodbury, Conn., on Jan. 15, 1955.

Yves Tanguy's *Slowly Toward the North* (1942).

MUSEUM OF MODERN ART, NEW YORK; GIFT OF PHILIP JOHNSON

Tanguy's style reflects the deep space and enigmatic stillness of Chirico, the biomorphic forms of Miró, and the dreamlike states of surrealist art and literature, but it is also highly personal. His works—such as *Mama, Papa Is Wounded!* (1927), *Slowly Toward the North* (1942), and *Multiplication of the Arcs* (1954)—are among the best examples of surrealist painting.

NICOLAI CIKOVSKY, JR., *University of Texas*

TANIMBAR ISLANDS, tə-nim'bär, a group of 66 fairly low islands in eastern Indonesia, between the Banda and Arafura seas. Once known as the Timorlaut Islands, the group is part of the province of Maluku (Moluccas). Its largest island is Jamdena, about 70 miles (110 km) long by 28 miles (45 km) wide.

The Tanimbars are covered by forests, savannas, and swamps. The major products are corn (maize), rice, sago, yams, coconuts, fruits, pigs, fish, tortoiseshell, and trepang. The people are Alfurs. Most are animists, but some are Christians or Muslims. Population: (1970) 588,000.

WILLIAM Y. DESSAINT
The New University of Ulster

TANIS, tā'nəs, was an ancient Egyptian city, the seat of the 21st dynasty. In Egyptian it appears as *Ḏ'nt,* in the Bible as *Zoan.* Situated on the northeastern edge of the Nile delta at the junction of an ancient branch of the river and an early east-west waterway, Tanis flourished as a port for over a millennium. It was abandoned after erosion of the south coast of Lake Manzala and the incursion of the sea in about the 4th century A. D.

The origins of Tanis are bitterly debated. Inscribed monuments of the Old and Middle Kingdoms have been found there, but no buildings can be dated before the reign of Rameses II (about 1290–1223 B. C.), and even the Ramesside stonework is believed by some to have been stolen from elsewhere for reuse. Either at Tanis or at a site nearby were located Avaris, the capital of the Hyksos kings, and Pi-Rameses, the delta residence built by Rameses II and used by his successors. Temples to the Egyptian god Amon and the Syrian goddess Anat are still standing, and the burials of five kings of the 21st and 22d dynasties have been discovered.

CAROLINE NESTMANN PECK, *Brown University*

TANIZAKI JUNICHIRO, tä-nē-zä-kē jo͝on-ē-chē-rō (1886–1965), was a Japanese novelist, admired for a traditionalism that was increasingly apparent in his later years. He was born in Tokyo on July 24, 1886. It is commonly said that his removal to a town in the Osaka region, occasioned by the earthquake of 1923 that destroyed Tokyo, brought him a new awareness of Japan's traditional values and marked the maturing of his literary powers.

In *Some Prefer Nettles* (1929; Eng. tr., 1955), Tokyo and Osaka are made symbols of the conflict between Westernized and traditional culture in Japan. Tanizaki's admiration for old Osaka is nowhere more obvious than in his re-creation of

ALLISON DIVISION, GENERAL MOTORS

Tank prototype of the 1970's, MBT70/XM803 of the U. S. Army, fires a guided missile or 152-mm artillery shell.

Osaka family life in the 1930's, *The Makioka Sisters* (1946–1948; Eng. tr., 1957). Through a career of a half-century he remained true to a single, rather traditional theme: absolute submission to a mother figure. The influence of the Japanese classics is overt in his writings from the 1930's on, as in the discursive, lyrical novel *A Portrait of Shunkin* (1933; Eng. tr., 1963).

Tanizaki died in Yugawara, south of Tokyo, on July 30, 1965. He had become one of the most honored figures in Japanese literature.

EDWARD SEIDENSTICKER, *University of Michigan Translator of "Some Prefer Nettles" and "The Makioka Sisters"*

TANJORE. See THANJAVUR.

TANK, a heavily armored combat vehicle moving on caterpillar treads and mounting guns, missiles, or both. Tanks are the principal assault weapons of armored infantry troops, and, because they combine firepower, mobility, and armor protection, the most formidable nonnuclear ground weapons of modern armies. Tanks are also used in limited-war combat and in shows of force.

Description. Tanks are of two categories, main battle tanks (MBT's) and light tanks. MBT's range from 52 to 37 tons. Their primary armament consists of guns of 120–mm to 90–mm. Light tanks of 25 tons to 9 tons have main guns of 90–mm to 76–mm, except for the U. S. Sheridan, which has a 152–mm combination missile launcher and gun. Tanks also have machine guns. They attack swiftly, using all guns, either as independent units or with infantry.

Tanks differ from armored cars, reconnaissance vehicles, personnel carriers, or self-propelled artillery. None of these specialized vehicles has all the tank's capabilities. Tanks are modified for special functions such as bridge laying, bulldozing, antiaircraft fire, missile launching, and recovery of disabled tanks.

Snorkel and Amphibious Tanks. One big challenge to tanks is river-crossing ability. Most modern MBT's have snorkel devices enabling them to submerge and cross on the bottoms of shallow rivers. MBT's are not amphibious —that is, they are unable to float. Two MBT's, however, the British Vickers and the Swedish STRV103, can be equipped with flotation shields, which enable them to cross inland waters. For light tanks, flotation with shields is the main means of crossing inland waters. The USSR's light tank, the PT76, is amphibious.

The U. S. Marine Corps pioneered and has long used amphibious armored vehicles in ocean waters. These craft, called LVT's (landing vehicle, tracked), mount 50–caliber machine guns or 105–mm howitzers, or both. Some of them are amphibious tanks, but most are gun-firing armored personnel carriers. They operate from ship to shore as spearheads of amphibious landings. Marines also use Army M48 tanks, some of which have special flame throwers.

Airborne Tanks. Airborne tanks are lightest. The British Scorpion (8.7 tons) is the first all-aluminum tank and the most easily transported by air. The French AMX13 (14.6 tons) and the Soviet PT76 (15.4 tons) are next lightest. The Sheridan M551 (16.8 tons) is the main reconnaissance vehicle for U. S. infantry and the principal assault weapon of airborne troops.

Tank Equipment. Tanks also mount searchlights, night-seeing devices, and fire-control radar. Some have map-reading devices. Tank guns are gyrostabilized, like those on a warship. They have automatic range finders, including the laser type, and automatic gun loaders. Great improvements were achieved after 1945 in armor plating, in the penetrating power of the guns, and in tank cruising ranges. The U. S. M60 can operate continuously for up to 48 hours.

Tanks and Nuclear Weapons. Tanks can operate near nuclear explosions because their armor protects against blasts and radioactivity. Tactical nuclear weapons call for thinning out the battlefield. Here tanks are the best nonatomic weapons because they can disperse or concentrate rapidly. Quick concentration and mobile exploitation of nuclear blasts are vital.

International competition in tank development is intensive, with technology and cost factors significant and limiting. Major problems include increasing protection against other tanks, land mines, and antitank and nuclear weapons; improving gun and missile penetration; and reducing tank weight while increasing range, mobility, and versatility. Ammunition is so greatly improved that gun calibers can be reduced.

Tanks of Major Nations. The chief MBT's are: *United States:* the 52–ton Patton M48 with 90–mm gun, being replaced by the 51–ton M60, with 105–mm gun. Under development is the MBT70/XM803. *USSR:* The 40–ton T54 (100–

IMPERIAL WAR MUSEUM

BRITISH TANK, the "Chieftain," has stabilizer to keep its gun on target as it lumbers over rough ground.

mm gun) and the 40.8–ton T62 (115–mm gun). *West Germany:* The 43–ton Leopard (105–mm gun). This is also sold to other non-Communist European nations. *Britain:* The 56.6–ton Chieftain (102–mm gun) and the Vickers MBT of 38 tons (105–mm gun and possible missiles). *France:* The AMX30 of 37 tons (105–mm gun), the lightest of the MBT's. *Sweden:* the STRV103 of 41 tons (105–mm gun), the most radically designed MBT, with low profile and no turret.

The main light tanks are: *United States:* 16.8–ton Sheridan (152–mm missile launcher and gun); 25.4–ton M41 (76–mm gun). *USSR:* 15.4–ton PT76 (76–mm gun)—amphibious. *Britain:* 8.7–ton Scorpion (76–mm gun)—the first aluminum tank. *France:* 14.6–ton AMX13 (90–mm gun, also the SS11 guided missile).

History. Tanks evolved from war chariots. Against fortifications men developed war carts armored with wood. In 1482, Leonardo da Vinci invented a covered chariot propelled by men inside. In 1901 the French placed an armored tub and machine gun on an automobile. By 1911 the idea of a military tracklaying vehicle was developed in Europe, but it found no acceptance.

World War I. The trench warfare, machine guns, and artillery duels of World War I brought military mobility to a standstill. Frontal infantry assaults and heavy artillery fire cost great losses for small territorial gains. In this stalemate, the British in 1915 created the first tank, a motor-powered armor-plated vehicle with caterpillar treads that could cross trenches. Withstanding machine-gun fire and mounting guns of its own, it eventually overcame the power of German defenses. The original idea is credited to Lt. Col. (later Maj. Gen.) Ernest Dunlop Swinton, who received support from Winston Churchill, then first lord of the admiralty. British development of the new machines was a well-kept secret. The name "tank" stuck after the vehicles were shipped to France in crates labeled "Tank" to deceive German agents.

Some 49 tanks fought for the first time in the battle of the Somme, attacking on Sept. 15, 1916, but major success was not achieved until Nov. 20, 1917, when 400 tanks under Brig. Gen. Hugh J. Elles made a surprise attack at Cambrai, breaking through 10 miles (16 km) of the Hindenburg Line. Elles took 8,000 prisoners and 100 heavy guns, and routed the rest.

Tanks were developed about the same time by the French, at first by Col. (later Gen.) Jean B. Estienne. French tanks consisted of metal boxes and guns placed on Holt caterpillar tractors. In 1916 the British and French agreed that Britain would produce heavy models, France, light ones. The Renault interests developed small, light tanks used by France. The United States built heavy tanks on the British model, but they never saw action. The U. S. Tank Corps was created on Jan. 26, 1917. It entered combat on Sept. 12, 1918, and fought in 27 more engagements, but it used British and French tanks. The Germans salvaged captured tanks and fought in them.

World War II Sherman tanks and infantry of the U. S. Seventh Army, camouflaged for snow, near Heidelberg.

U.S. ARMY

Between the Wars. After World War I the major nations developed various new tanks and concepts for their use. Arguments polarized as to whether tanks should augment infantry or fight independently. Pioneers of "independence" were two British officers, Gen. J. F. C. Fuller and Capt. B. H. Liddell Hart, whose ideas influenced the German development of tank divisions and blitzkrieg techniques. U. S. Army officers—Gens. Adna Chaffee, George S. Patton, and others—also fought for independent armor. Charles de Gaulle's creative ideas on tank warfare were ignored.

The Spanish Civil War (1936–1939) was a proving ground for German and Russian tanks, demonstrating the deadliness of concentrated tank attacks. The Germans used this method later.

Tank development concentrated on better guns, improved armor, and mobility. There was controversy over light versus heavy tanks.

World War II. In 1939, Germany defeated Poland with tanks and dive bombers in blitzkrieg warfare. Similarly, in 1940, Hitler's tank, mechanized infantry, and air forces invaded Belgium, the Netherlands, and France. French and British tanks outnumbered the German, but they were widely dispersed in accordance with the French doctrine that tanks must support infantry closely. German armor prevailed.

In North Africa, Gen. (later Field Marshal) Erwin Rommel conducted brilliant desert warfare against the British. His tanks were near Cairo when Marshal Montgomery's Eighth Army forced Rommel into retreat and defeated him. Quick repair of tanks was as vital as tactics in desert campaigns, which were similar to the long-range maneuver tactics originally envisaged by Fuller as being like those of warships at sea.

Hitler's tank-heavy Panzer armies attacked the USSR in mid–1941 with about 3,500 tanks against 24,000 Soviet tanks that were too widely deployed. In three months the USSR lost 17,500 tanks and the Germans about 550. Hitler's Panzer forces destroyed many of the USSR's armies. By December 1941, Hitler's tanks were close to Moscow. Germany had all but defeated the USSR, when winter and Soviet resistance halted Hitler's blitz. The Germans advanced slowly, using tank units as main striking forces. Meanwhile, the USSR built up tank and mechanized armies.

In the Pacific campaign, both Japan and the United States used tanks. The U. S. Marine Corps and Army employed amphibious self-propelled artillery and tanks to spearhead ship-to-shore invasions.

The largest tank battle in history was fought around Kursk, USSR, in 1943, with nearly 3,000 tanks. Here the USSR changed from defense to offense. Massive Soviet tank and mechanized armies swept the Germans back to Berlin. This gigantic campaign was one of three climactic strategic tank operations of World War II.

The second great tank campaign followed the Allied invasion of Normandy in June 1944. The United States landed 16 armored divisions and numerous tank units. British and French tank formations participated. The main thrust was by U. S. Gen. George S. Patton's Third Army. The third major armored campaign came in the summer of 1945 in Manchuria: Soviet tanks and mechanized forces defeated Japanese forces in three weeks.

Heavy tanks were used by the USSR and Germany in World War II but were tactically and logistically cumbersome. The United States abandoned its heavies for medium and light tanks.

LIBRARY OF CONGRESS

WORLD WAR I French Renault tanks, manned by U. S. doughboys. The Allies used 4,000 of these 7-ton tanks.

Since 1945. In the Korean War (1950–1953), North Korea's Soviet-built tanks were dominant until U. S. tanks changed the balance. Tank warfare thereafter was not truly mobile because of terrain, road, and defense limitations. It was realized that tanks are best used in masses and in open terrain, as the Israelis used them against the Arabs in the brief 1956 and 1967 wars.

In the 1965 Kashmir war, Indians and Pakistanis decimated each other in a standoff at Sialkot, the most wasteful tank battle since 1945.

In the Vietnam War, U. S. and South Vietnamese troops used tanks (including airborne) successfully, but mainly in limited tactical sweeps.

ROBERT B. RIGG
Colonel, U. S. Army, Ret.
Author of "War–1974"

Further Reading: Institute of Strategic Studies, *The Military Balance–1969–70* (London 1969); Ogorkiewicz, R. M., *The Design and Development of Fighting Vehicles* (New York 1968); von Mellenthin, F. W., *Panzer Battles* (Norman, Okla., 1956).

TANK CIRCUIT, an electric circuit consisting of a coil and a capacitor connected in parallel. This inductor-capacitor (*L-C*) combination, also called a parallel resonant or parallel tuned circuit, is commonly used in radio transmitters and receivers. It is especially useful in oscillator circuits that generate a specific frequency in the range from several thousand hertz (cycles per second) to hundreds of megahertz and in transmitter and receiver circuits that efficiently amplify specific frequencies in the same range.

The chief characteristic of a tank circuit is that it is electrically resonant at a single frequency. Resonance is initiated by a pulse applied to the tank circuit, which creates an ac voltage at the natural frequency of the inductor-capacitor combination. The particular frequency at which resonance occurs depends on the amount of inductance of the coil and the capacitance of the capacitor. In equation form the relationship can be expressed as $f = 1/2\pi\sqrt{LC}$, where f is the frequency in hertz, L is the inductance in henrys, and C is the capacitance in farads.

The use of *L-C* tuned circuits began in 1886–1888 when Heinrich Hertz in effect used an *L-C* combination in first demonstrating the transmission and reception of radio waves.

MARVIN BIERMAN, *RCA Institutes Inc.*

CENTRAL PRESS

GIGANTIC OIL TANKER, *Universe Ireland*, carrying over 300,000 tons of crude petroleum, is eased toward a dock in Bantry Bay, Ireland, by five tugboats. Tankers of this huge size, built in increasing numbers, are most economical in the competition of the world's petroleum trade.

TANKER, or *tank ship,* is an oceangoing vessel designed to carry bulk cargo, usually liquid, and primarily petroleum. Small tankers carry oil in coastal and river traffic, and large ones move it from the main petroleum-producing areas—Middle East, North Africa, Venezuela—to the main consuming areas—United States, western Europe, Japan. The economics of this highly competitive business has brought successive enlargement in the size of tankers. The newest are three times the size of the nuclear aircraft carrier U. S. S. *Enterprise.* The larger a tanker is, the less it costs to deliver each ton of oil, because requirements for engine power and crew do not increase as rapidly as does its oil-carrying capacity.

Giant Tankers. The Universe class of tankers, of which the first, *Universe Ireland,* was completed in Japan for an American company in 1968, have a carrying capacity of 312,000 deadweight tons (DWT) each. The length is 1,133 feet (345 meters), beam 175 feet (53 meters), and draft 79 feet (24 meters). Cruising speed is 14.6 knots. The total crew is 51 persons.

Cargo space comprises a tank in the bow, 8 center tanks down the length of the ship, and 16 wing tanks beside them. Three small tanks near the engine room in the stern hold the ship's own fuel. An array of large piping above the deck permits all tanks to be loaded or unloaded through nozzles at a central point either on the port or the starboard side of the ship. Loading, by means of strong pumps, takes 24 to 36 hours, and discharging takes 36 to 40 hours. As on most tankers, all navigation and living space are at the stern, situated in a large superstructure over the engine.

Maximum tanker size is determined by depths of water in ports and critical waterways. The limiting load displacement for the Suez Canal is 70,000 tons, and so larger tankers were carrying Middle East oil all the way around Africa to Europe even before the canal was closed by the Israeli–Arab War of 1967. The size of tankers delivering oil from the Persian Gulf to Japan is limited by the 60-foot (18-meter) depth of Malacca Strait. The largest on this run is *Idemitsu Maru* of 206,000 DWT. Universe-class tankers transport crude oil from Kuwait via the Cape of Good Hope to Bantry Bay, Ireland, where the 120-foot (37-meter) depth can accommodate even larger tankers. Oil is reshipped from there to refineries throughout Europe.

Development of Tankers. Petroleum originally was transported in wooden kegs stowed in the holds of sailing ships. The first bulk tanker was *Glückauf,* built in England for a German company in 1886. Her design of large tanks built into the hull, with the engine room aft, has remained basically the same. The first major use of tankers was to transport bunker fuel for oil-burning warships. World War I increased the use of gasoline for internal-combustion engines and of fuel oil for merchantmen.

The sea movement of petroleum began in earnest after World War I and had become extensive by 1939. A steady stream of U. S.-flag tankers steamed between refineries in Texas and the industrial Northeast, carrying gasoline and fuel for ships. In the late 1930's oil began replacing coal for heating U. S. homes, much of the oil coming from Venezuela. Other petroleum sea routes were from California to Japan and to fleets in the Pacific, and from refineries in Curaçao and Aruba to Europe.

Because of the many tankers built in World War I, few new ones were needed. Design changed little until the late 1930's, when the U. S. Navy forced oil companies to accept an improved tanker design. This became the famous T-2 of World War II. These ships, of which over 500 were built, were of 16,600 DWT.

Tanker Revolution. Tankers bearing oil from the Middle East were the key to the postwar recovery of western Europe and Japan. This movement increased world tanker tonnage from 16.5 million in 1938 to 120 million in 1968. By 1969 more than 80% of all tankers exceeded 45,000 tons, and 280 exceeded 160,000 DWT. This tanker revolution produced two other phenomena: the rise of Japan's shipbuilding industry and the use of "flag-of-convenience" registry.

Japanese Shipbuilding. An American, Daniel K. Ludwig, builder of the Universe-class tankers, started Japan's shipbuilding rise. In 1951, just after the Japanese peace treaty was signed, he leased the former Kure navy yard where the world's largest warship, *Yamato,* had been built. He introduced assembly-line and prefabrication methods for the building of supertankers. Other companies followed suit, so that by 1968 Japan was producing 8.5 million tons of new ships annually, more than 55% of the world's new tonnage. Over 5 million tons was for export.

Flags of Convenience. Ships can be built in Japan for American companies and operated under foreign registry with foreign crews at about one third the cost of operating under the American flag. They can thus compete with traditional maritime countries.

The use of flags of convenience for U. S.-owned tankers began under Panama registry before World War II. Liberian registry was used after 1948, and by 1969 the "Liberian fleet" had reached 27 million tons or 15% of the world tonnage, of which 45% was American-owned. See also FLAG OF CONVENIENCE.

Problems. Giant tankers have had their difficulties. In 1967 the Union Oil Company tanker *Torrey Canyon* was wrecked near Lands End, England. Her 120,000 tons of oil fouled British and French beaches and made the world conscious of the hazards of moving vast quantities of oil across the seas. In 1969 heavy explosions took place in three newly built tankers, all ships of over 200,000 tons, and one of them sank. Vapor ignited during tank cleaning while the ships were returning without cargo to the Persian Gulf.

Northwest Passage. The discovery of rich oil deposits on the Arctic Slope of Alaska may change the pattern of tanker trade and the design of the ships. The feasibility of transporting oil from Alaska to the eastern U. S. seaboard via the Northwest Passage was tested in the late summer of 1969 when the Humble Oil Company, with British Petroleum and Atlantic Richfield, sent the tanker *Manhattan* through the passage. The ship, of 112,000 DWT, largest under the American flag, and equipped with an icebreaking bow, reached Alaska's north shore via Prince of Wales Strait after failing to navigate the more direct McClure Strait. The voyage indicated the need for ships of at least 250,000 tons, with twin or triple screws and 100,000 shaft horsepower (SHP), compared with the 37,500 SHP of *Universe Ireland.*

On the return voyage, ice tore a large hole in the *Manhattan*'s side. No oil leaked, but Canada took measures to prevent pollution by possible future leaks, ignoring the U. S. claim that the Northwest Passage constitutes international waters. A second survey trip was made by *Manhattan* in the summer of 1970, Humble Oil agreeing to abide by Canadian regulations.

Dry-Cargo Tankers. Since the first tanker was built, the distinction between tankers and dry-cargo ships has been marked. However, with the development of machinery for fast handling of dry bulk such as grain and coal, improved tank-cleaning methods, and the economic need to eliminate long, profitless voyages without cargo, this separation of types is ending. Old tankers now carry grain. New ones are equipped to carry either liquid or dry bulk in the same hold, so that they can, for example, carry oil in one direction and grain in the other.

JOHN D. HAYES
Rear Admiral, United States Navy (Retired)

Further Reading: Sawyer, T. A., and Mitchell, W. H., *Merchant Ships of the World: Tankers* (New York 1967); Dunn, Laurence, *The World's Tankers* (London 1967).

TANNENBERG, Battle of, tan′ən-bûrg, in World War I, a decisive victory of the Germans over the Ru sians in East Prussia on Aug. 25–30, 1914. Tannenberg, now Stębark, Poland, is 95 miles (155 km) northwest of Warsaw. The German plan of Gen. Alfred von Schlieffen, prepared before World War I, was to encircle and annihilate Russia's armies near the Masurian Lakes in case of a two-front war with Russia and France.

On August 17, two Russian army groups under Generals Rennenkampf and Samsonov invaded East Prussia to ease the German pressure against the French at the western front. After a clash at Gumbinnen (now Gusev, USSR) on August 20, Gen. Max von Prittwitz of Germany, favoring withdrawal to the Vistula River, was dismissed by Marshal von Moltke. Meanwhile Col. Max Hoffmann, in charge of operations, began moving most of the German troops facing Rennenkampf for an attack on the right wing of the Samsonov armies separated from Rennenkampf's by the lakes.

The newly appointed German commander, von Hindenburg, and his chief of staff, Ludendorff, used the same strategy. Their calculation that Rennenkampf would not try to relieve Samsonov, partly because of personal enmity, was confirmed by intercepted uncoded Russian radio messages. The Germans triumphed after their corps commander, General von François, disregarding orders, lured Samsonov's troops into a trap, encircled, and annihilated them—90,000 Russians were taken prisoner, and Samsonov committed suicide.

Moltke sent two corps from the western front. Too late for Tannenberg, they joined the attacks against Rennenkampf that forced his retreat from East Prussia in disarray. The Russian sacrifices slowed the German advance in the west, helping the French to withstand the German assault at the most critical moment of the war.

VOJTECH MASTNY, *Columbia University*

TANNER, Benjamin Tucker (1835–1923), American bishop of the African Methodist Episcopal Church. Tanner was born in Pittsburgh on Dec. 25, 1835, and educated at Avery College, where he became a licensed Methodist preacher. He continued his studies at the Presbyterian Western Theological Seminary until 1860 and served as a preacher in a Presbyterian church in Washington, D. C. Returning to Methodism, he was licensed to preach in the Baltimore Conference in 1862.

Tanner defended black separatism, for the sake of developing black independence, in *An Apology for African Methodism* (1867), and black dignity in *The Negro's Origin; and Is He Cursed of God?* (1869). He was elected bishop in 1881 and moved to Philadelphia. Tanner died in Philadelphia on Jan. 15, 1923.

JAMES H. SMYLIE
Union Theological Seminary, Richmond, Va.

TANNER, Henry Ossawa (1859–1937), American painter, whose major works were on religious themes. Tanner, a Negro, was born in Pittsburgh, Pa., on June 21, 1859. His father, Benjamin Tucker Tanner, was an author and a bishop of the African Methodist Episcopal Church. Henry Tanner studied at the Pennsylvania Academy of Fine Arts under Thomas Eakins and in Paris under J. P. Laurens and Benjamin Constant. He toured Palestine a number of times to obtain authentic backgrounds for his religious paintings.

ATLANTA UNIVERSITY NEGRO COLLECTION

HENRY TANNER showed his concern with religious themes in such works as *Disciples Healing the Sick,* painted about 1924.

Among Tanner's well-known paintings are *Destruction of Sodom and Gomorrah* (Metropolitan Museum, New York City), *Two Disciples at the Tomb* (Chicago Art Institute), *Christ and Nicodemas* (Pennsylvania Academy of Fine Arts), the *Raising of Lazarus* (Luxembourg Museum, Paris), and *Banjo Lesson* (Hampton Institute). He also painted landscapes and scenes of Breton peasants. Tanner died in Paris on May 25, 1937.

TANNER, Henry Schenck (1786–1858), American map maker and the first American to make a map using a scale expressed in terms of the size of the earth. His training as an engraver and his interest in science enabled him to become the leading map maker of his day.

Tanner's most successful work, *A New American Atlas,* appeared in 1823. Consisting of maps of the various states, or of groups of states, and a scale of 17⅓ miles per inch, it was based on careful research and painstaking study of source materials. In scientific thoroughness it compares favorably with most modern atlases. A native of New York City, Tanner died there in 1858.

TANNHÄUSER, tän′hoi-zər (c.1200–c.1270), German minnesinger. He probably was born in Franconia and may have served Emperor Frederick II on the Crusade of 1228. Among his patrons was Duke Frederick of Austria, whose death in 1266 he mourned in an elegy. Of Tannhäuser's poems, only 6 *Leiche,* or nonstrophic love lyrics, 10 songs, and some didactic verse have survived. A master of the conventional imagery of 13th century love poetry, he also incorporated fabulous stories of adventure into his verse. Some of his more ironic poetry anticipated 14th century parodies of courtly love lyrics.

Probably as a result of the fabulous elements in his work, Tannhäuser became the hero of a legend of the Venusberg, an enchanted land of sensual pleasure. After a long stay he is driven by a guilty conscience to seek Christian absolution. When rejected he disappears forever in the Venusberg. A ballad about the legend appeared in the 15th century, and the story was subsequently treated by the poets Heine and Tieck. Wagner also used it for his opera *Tannhäuser.*

W. T. H. JACKSON
Author of "Medieval Literature"

TANNHÄUSER, tän′hoi-zər, an opera in three acts by Richard Wagner, first produced at Dresden in 1845. A revised version with an extended ballet was given at the Paris Opéra in 1861. The libretto of *Tannhäuser,* by the composer, is based on a legend, dating from the Middle Ages, about a singers' contest at the Wartburg castle in Thuringia.

In the Venusberg, a mountain inhabited by the goddess of love, the knight Tannhäuser sings the praises of Venus but longs to return to the world. At his mention of the Virgin, the Venusberg disappears, and Tannhäuser finds himself in the Valley of the Wartburg. He is greeted by his friend Wolfram, who tells him of the sadness experienced by Elisabeth, the Landgrave's niece, since his departure.

At a music tournament, Wolfram sings of pure, selfless love, but Tannhäuser sings in praise of Venus and is banished to seek absolution from the pope in Rome. Elisabeth prays that Tannhäuser may be forgiven, and when the pope refuses absolution, she dies of a broken heart. Pilgrims then arrive from Rome, bearing the pope's staff, which has sprouted leaves—a symbol that God has forgiven Tannhäuser.

Popular segments of the opera are the overture and the Venusberg music, Elisabeth's Greeting and Prayer, Wolfram's song to the evening star, and the Pilgrims' chorus. These are often heard as separate pieces.

HAROLD ROSENTHAL
Editor of "Opera" Magazine

TANNIC ACID, a complex mixture of materials extracted from the wood, bark, or leaves of certain plants. Other names for tannic acid are tannin, gallotannin, and gallotannic acid. Tannic acid forms insoluble products with proteins and thus turns animal skins into leather. It has been used for this purpose for centuries. It is also used in the manufacture of permanent ink, the sizing of paper and fabrics, as a mordant in dyeing, to clarify wine, in photography, and as a source material for the manufacture of pyrogallol and gallic acid. In the past tannic acid was used medicinally. However, since it was found to be damaging to the liver, it is no longer prescribed.

Tannic acid is a yellowish amorphous powdery or flaky material that slowly darkens when exposed to light and air. It is slightly soluble in water and very soluble in alcohol and acetone. Tannic acid is not uniform in composition. One group of tannins consists primarily of hydrolyzable esters of glucose and gallic acid or other hydroxybenzoic acids. Another group, which cannot be hydrolyzed, consists of flavanols.

One commercial source of tannic acid has been galls, which are growths formed on twigs of young oak trees by certain parasitic insects. Most tannic acid is now obtained from the South American quebracho tree, which gives a high yield of the acid. A form of tannic acid is found in both green and black tea. Tannic acid is extracted with warm water from the ground or shredded plant material, and the dilute solution is evaporated.

OTTO W. NITZ, *Stout State University*

TANNIN. See TANNIC ACID.

TANNING. See LEATHER.

TANNU-TUVA. See TUVA AUTONOMOUS SOVIET SOCIALIST REPUBLIC.

TANOAN, tän′ə-wən, a linguistic family of North American Indians, including four subgroups of Rio Grande Pueblo Indians. Members of the Tewa group live in the communities of Nambe, Tesuque, San Ildefonso, San Juan, Santa Clara, and Pojoaque in New Mexico, and Hano, in Arizona. Communities of the Tiwa group are Isleta, Sandia, Taos, and Picuris in New Mexico and Isleta del Sur, a small community at El Paso, Texas. The Jemez group consists of the single pueblo of Jemez in New Mexico and the Piro group of very small Mexicanized communities near El Paso.

Most Tanoan villages are built of adobe, situated on ancient sites, and surrounded by fields and gardens. The New Mexico pueblos —Taos is the best known—are extremely picturesque. Tanoan people, with the exception of some in the vicinity of El Paso, are known for conservatism in religion and social organization.

STEPHEN E. FERACA
Bureau of Indian Affairs

TANSY, tan′zē, any of a group of annual and perennial plants with aromatic leaves and terminal clusters of small buttonlike heads of yellow disk flowers. A few types of tansies are grown as garden flowers and occasionally their bitter-tasting leaves are used as a flavoring in cooking. At one time tansies were raised as medicinal herbs, used for treating bruises, sprains, and rheumatism.

Tansies make up the genus *Tanacetum* of the composite family (Compositae). The common tansy (*T. vulgare*) is native to Europe and Asia but also grows as a weed in waste places and along roadsides in North America. It is an erect, strongly scented perennial plant from 1½ to 3 feet (45–90 cm) tall. Its leaves are alternate and either pinnately divided or deeply cut. The leaves at the base of the plant are often as long as a foot (30 cm). The variety *T. vulgare crispum* has much more finely cut foliage.

Another species, *T. huronense*, is a perennial with hairy leaves and fewer flower heads than the common tansy. It grows throughout the northern United States.

J. A. YOUNG
U. S. Department of Agriculture

TANTA, tän′tä, is a city in Egypt, in the Nile delta, 60 miles (95 km) north of Cairo. It is the capital of Gharbiya province. The city has cotton gins as well as cottonseed-oil extraction plants.

Among the places of interest in Tanta are several old mosques and a palace that was used by the royal family when Egypt was a kingdom. Tanta also has an educational institute, al-Gami al-Ahmady, founded in 1276. It is a branch of Cairo's al-Azhar University. Population: (1970 est.) 254,000.

TANTALITE. See COLUMBITE.

TANTALUM, tant′əl-əm, symbol Ta, is a hard, ductile metallic element. It was discovered in 1802 by the Swedish chemist Anders G. Ekeberg. Tantalum is used extensively in the construction of acid-resistant equipment for chemical processes. It is also used in electrolytic capacitor anodes and as a getter in vacuum tubes. Because it is inert to body fluids and tissues, tantalum is used in surgical implants and in suture wire and wire gauze. Tantalum lithium oxide, $LiTaO_3$, is used for laser radiation modulation, and tantalum carbide, TaC, is used to produce hard cutting tools.

Tantalum, which is one of the transition metals, is located in Group VA of the periodic table. Its atomic number is 73, its atomic weight is 180.948, and it has a valence of +5. The element has a high melting point of 2996° C (5425° F) and a boiling point of 6100° C (11,012° F). It is very ductile and can be cold-worked. Below 150° C (302° F) it is one of the most inert of all metals, but at high temperatures it becomes chemically reactive.

Tantalum makes up 0.00021% of the igneous rock of the earth's crust. It is usually found associated with niobium in the form of a ferrous-manganese tantalite-columbite mineral $(Fe,Mn)(Ta,Nb)_2O_6$. Pure tantalum is obtained by separation of the metal from niobium through a complex series of reactions, using liquid-liquid extraction, electrolysis, and other methods. This produces a powdered metal, which is compacted and then sintered by passage of an electric current.

HERBERT LIEBESKIND, *The Cooper Union*

TANTALUS, tant′əl-əs, in Greek mythology, a figure whose punishment by the gods is the origin of the word "tantalize." For an offense against the Olympians, Tantalus was condemned to eternal torment. Homer represents him as standing up to his throat in water with delicious fruits hanging over his head. Each time he tries to drink, the water recedes. When he tries to eat the fruit, it moves up out of his reach. According to Pindar, a great rock suspended over Tantalus' head is ever on the verge of falling.

Tantalus was the son of Zeus—or, in another story, of Tmolus—and the father of Pelops and Niobe. There are different versions of the crime for which the gods made him a type of the great sinner. In one legend he cooked his son Pelops and served him to the gods. According to other ancient authors Tantalus was punished because he, like Prometheus, revealed secrets of the gods to mankind.

TANTRISM. See BUDDHA AND BUDDHISM; JAPAN —*Religion and Philosophy* (Buddhism): The Shingon Sect.

YLLA, FROM RAPHO GUILLUMETTE

Giraffes roam a plain within sight of snow-capped Mt. Kilimanjaro, Africa's highest peak.

TANZANIA, tan-zə-nē'ə, is a country in East Africa. Officially the United Republic of Tanzania, it was created in April 1964 by the union of two independent African states, Tanganyika and Zanzibar. Tanganyika, the largest country in eastern Africa, had become independent in 1961 after being successively under Arab, German, and British control. Zanzibar, composed of the two small offshore islands of Zanzibar and Pemba, was a British protectorate governed by an Arab sultan before it gained independence in 1963.

INFORMATION HIGHLIGHTS

Official Name: United Republic of Tanzania.
Head of State: President.
Head of Government: President.
Area: 362,820 square miles, or 939,698 sq km (Tanganyika: 361,800 square miles, or 937,062 sq km; Zanzibar: 1,020 square miles, or 2,636 sq km).
Population: (1967 census) 12,313,469 (Tanganyika: 11,958,654; Zanzibar: 354,815).
Capital: Dar es Salaam (1967 population, 272,821).
Major Languages: Swahili, English, tribal languages.
Monetary Unit: Tanzania shilling.
Major Religions: Islam, Christianity, animism.
Flag: Black diagonal stripe running from lower left corner to upper right corner and flanked by two gold stripes. Diagonal stripes separate two triangular areas—green at upper left and blue at lower right. See also FLAG.
National Anthem: Tanzanian National Anthem, set to new words of the hymn *Mungu Ibariki Afrika* (*God Bless Africa*).

The population of the two areas is overwhelmingly African, with Arab, Indian, and European minorities. Close cultural and political ties between Zanzibar and the Tanganyikan coast are of long standing, and both areas are largely agricultural. The national capital is Dar es Salaam on the coast of Tanganyika.

The two countries united after the overthrow of the sultan of Zanzibar by revolution in January 1964, and the rise to power of the Afro-Shirazi party, which had close ties with the Tanganyika African National Union, the governing party on the mainland. The union gave Zanzibar a home-rule status and was regarded by both parties as a step toward pan-African unity. In practice, Zanzibar has remained largely autonomous, and most official policies and reports deal only with the mainland, which continues to be referred to as Tanganyika. Tanzania has been a leader among African states in both foreign and domestic matters, developing a pragmatic socialist economy and following a policy of nonalignment that is also vigorously anticolonial.

1. The Land

Geography and Climate. The mainland area, Tanganyika, consists of three major regions: a warm and tropical coastal belt, a low eastern plateau, and a higher central plateau broken by the geological fault known as the Great Rift Valley. Zanzibar and Pemba are primarily coral islands but share many of the climatic features of the neighboring coast.

The average elevation of the mainland is 3,000 feet (900 meters) above sea level. Isolated mountain areas are found primarily on the borders of the country. Mt. Kilimanjaro in the north, which rises to an altitude of 19,340 feet (5,894 meters), is the highest point in Africa. In the west lie the three great lakes of Malawi (Nyasa), Tanganyika, and Victoria.

Rainfall is heavy along the Tanganyikan coast, averaging about 60 inches (1,500 mm) annually in the north. The coastal area is subject to monsoon winds that blow northeast from December to March and southwest from May to October. Although two rainy seasons occur in most of the interior, rainfall is not heavy except in mountain areas such as Tukuyu in the south, which receives 100 inches (2,500 mm) yearly. Drought is common in most of the central plateau region, where rainfall is below 30 inches (760 mm) and is unreliable.

The low eastern plateau is characterized by scrub woodland and by tsetse fly infestation, while on the higher central plateau the soils are poor except in parts of the valleys. Agricultural and even pastoral activities are therefore difficult to pursue. As a result, the population clusters in favored highland areas, in the Lake Victoria basin, and along the rivers.

Animals and Plants. Tanganyika, like other areas in East Africa, is known for its magnificent plant, animal, and bird life. The Serengeti plains, in the northwestern part of the country, are one of the major preserves of wildlife in Africa. Each year thousands of gazelles, zebras, buffaloes, and other animals migrate across these broad plains.

The Tanzanian government has established an extensive system of national parks and reserves and has created a college of wildlife management to train game guards and conservators. Control and conservation are difficult but urgently necessary. Wild animals are carriers of trypanosomiasis (sleeping sickness) and must be kept away from populated regions. Elephants and baboons are extremely destructive of crops. In turn, poachers seeking meat and ivory have killed many animals and have endangered the survival of such species as the rhinoceros.

Conservation areas are centered on the plains, where most of the animals live. Provision must be made, however, for water animals, such as the hippopotamus and crocodile, and for mountain dwellers like the colobus monkey.

The different climatic regions produce many types of plants, including mangrove and palm on the coast, thornbush and baobab on the central plateau, and alpine flora on Kilimanjaro. The familiar African violet came originally from the Usambara mountains in the northeast.

2. The People

The majority of Tanzania's 12 million inhabitants are Africans known as Bantu, a linguistic classification that includes many African peoples. In Tanzania the Bantu, who are primarily farmers, were divided in the past into some 120 tribal societies. In the northern mainland areas live groups of pastoralists who speak Erythraic languages. There are also other non-Bantu peoples, who speak languages believed to be of Khoisan (Bushman) origin.

The non-African population in 1966 included about 26,000 Arabs, 85,000 Indians and Pakistanis, and 15,000 Europeans. The Arabs live mainly on Zanzibar and in the mainland coastal towns. The Europeans, most of whom are not permanent residents, are mainly civil servants, missionaries, and businessmen.

Nearly 95% of Tanzania's people live in rural areas, although a very gradual movement to the towns has quickened since independence. Dar es Salaam had a population of 272,821 in 1967 and Zanzibar city had 83,313 residents, but no other large towns exist. About a third of the people on the mainland live on one tenth of the land, and overcrowding in fertile areas has produced land hunger.

Way of Life. In the past, the peoples of both the mainland and Zanzibar lived in tribal groups, each of which possessed a distinct territorial area and a common culture, language, and religion. Some tribes were led by chiefs, while others were governed by elders or clan leaders. There were many differences in tribal law, family structure, and economic activities, although basic similarities existed among the Bantu peoples who spoke related languages. The largest tribal group, the Sukuma of the Lake Victoria area, was agricultural and pastoral. It had many chiefs, a characteristic shared by many of Tanzania's larger tribal groups—the Nyamwezi, Haya, Makonde, Ha, Chagga, Gogo, and Nyakyusa. The Hehe of the southern highlands had developed a single paramount chief. The best known Erythraic-speaking tribe, the Masai, were pastoralists who moved seasonally with their cattle, following water and grazing, and had no central leadership. Today the Sukuma number more than 1 million, other tribes mentioned have 200,000 to 300,000 members, and remaining groups are much smaller.

Politically, Tanzania's tribal groups changed greatly under colonial and national rule and have retained little or no power. Tribal solidarity was affected after the beginning of the 20th century by the introduction of Western education, by the modern economic structure with its migrant labor outside the tribal area and export crop production within it, by the development of modern communications, and by the arrival of Christian-

THREE MASAI talk in a marketplace. The Masai, a pastoral people, were once known as fierce warriors.

CARL FRANK, FROM PHOTO RESEARCHERS

TANZANIA Map Index

Arusha	C2	Pemba	D3
Dar es Salaam	C3	Serengeti Nat'l Park	C2
Kigoma-Ujiji	A2	Tanga	C2
Kilimanjaro, Mt	C2	Ujiji	see Kigoma-Ujiji
Kilwa Kivinje	C3	Zanzibar	C3

ity and Islam. In areas without roads, however, changes in daily life were minor until well after independence. Traditional ways were followed still. There was little economic differentiation, and family relationships, religion, and custom were dominant. By the late 1960's, however, government policies aimed at rural development had begun to change this picture.

The towns, except Zanzibar city, are creations of the colonial period. Africans moving to towns for work or for education leave many tribal habits behind them, but the extent to which complete detribalization occurs should not be exaggerated. In the towns new patterns of conduct are worked out. Intertribal marriage makes new family law necessary, and Africans going into trade or wage labor need far more comprehensive support than tribal custom provides. New problems occur, and slums, unemployment, delinquency, and prostitution have become major urban concerns. On the other hand, many Africans retain links with their areas of origin, and family and land ties are particularly close.

Town life produces major economic differences. In the colonial period Tanganyika and Zanzibar had social and economic class systems based mainly on race, with Europeans in the top rank, Asian groups in the middle, and Africans at the bottom. This class-race structure was a major African grievance. It changed rapidly after independence, and elite groups of Africans arose on the basis of education and political status. In Zanzibar, where the Arab and Indian minorities controlled much land, race-class conflicts were a major factor in the 1964 revolution.

Religion. The peoples of Tanzania were traditionally animist, most tribes having a religious system centering on the ancestors, the land, and various ritual objects. The powers of chiefs were frequently priestly or rainmaking in character.

Since the 1840's the major European religions have maintained missions in what is now Tanzania. The Christian churches are mainly self-governing and self-financed. One fourth of the population is believed to be Christian. Church influence has been particularly important in the fields of education and health, and a large percentage of the leaders of contemporary Tanzania were trained in mission schools.

Islamic influence has been even more widespread. Islam reached Zanzibar and the Tanganyika coast centuries ago. It spread inland in the 19th century and is powerful in many areas. Probably more than half the people of Tanzania are Muslims. Many sects are represented.

Education. During the colonial period both Tanganyika and Zanzibar had an educational structure based on British models. Control was centralized in the ministry of education, and there were country-wide examinations. Primary schooling was generally for eight years, with instruction in Swahili, a Bantu language widely used in East Africa. This was followed by four years of secondary schooling, generally in English, with two additional years required to prepare a student for university entrance. Until 1960, schools were racially segregated, and the caliber of education varied according to whether the students were Europeans, Asians, or Africans. Many students did not finish the primary course, while at the secondary level they tended to concentrate on such subjects as English and history. Scientific and technical education was neglected.

This pattern began to change just before independence, when schools were integrated. Throughout the 1960's attempts were made to expand the schools to reach more children as well as to make the education offered more appropriate for African students. In 1967 major changes to modify the syllabus and the whole spirit of the schools were announced. Emphasis was placed on civic education, the role of the school in the community, and preparation of students for nation-building tasks. Curricular changes were designed to present more material pertinent to Africa, to include practical training such as agricultural work, and to lessen the tendency of students to seek white-collar training and white-collar jobs. Increasing emphasis was put on Swahili instruction. The primary course was shortened to seven years.

By 1970, 47% of the children of appropriate age were in the first grade. The government hoped for universal primary education in 20 years. About 800,000 children were enrolled in primary schools and 29,000 in secondary schools. Some 3,500 students were receiving higher education at University College in Dar es Salaam, at the University of East Africa in Uganda, at technical colleges, or overseas.

Expansion of the school system has been limited primarily by the shortage of funds and of teachers. Tanzania spends 20% of its national budget on education, and it is still dependent on foreign teachers in the secondary schools and the university. Government planning for educational development put major stress on reducing this figure.

Mission schools, which were very important in Tanganyika's history, were absorbed by the government in 1970. There are a few private schools and, for Muslims, a large number of Koranic schools on the coast and in Zanzibar.

Expansion of the school system has not had a material impact on the major problem of adult illiteracy. But adult education and community development programs are spreading.

3. The Economy

Tanzania's economy has traditionally been based on subsistence agriculture, and the subsistence sector still accounts for nearly 40% of the gross national product. Cotton, coffee, sisal, and cloves are widely planted and exported in substantial quantities, along with a few mineral products such as diamonds and gold. Industrial production is small.

Tanzania's stated economic and social objective is the achievement of socialism. In the Arusha Declaration on Feb. 5, 1967, President Nyerere announced sweeping changes designed to replace earlier capitalist policies and attitudes. This was followed by a series of laws and regulations that nationalized some important sectors of the economy, such as banks, and gave the government a majority holding in major industries. In the countryside, cooperative endeavor was stressed, and the second five-year development plan, introduced in 1969, laid major emphasis on rural development. A general improvement in the standard of living was hoped for, together with a considerable increase in the number of Tanzanians able to fill the technical and managerial posts necessary for modernization of the country. Nationalization of the export-import trade was announced in 1970.

Tanzania is a member of the East African Community, an economic organization that also includes Kenya and Uganda. It was created in 1967 as a successor to several interterritorial groupings of the colonial period. Railroad, harbor, air, postal, and tax collection systems of the member nations are operated in common. A common market is being created. The treaty establishing the community envisaged considerable interterritorial economic collaboration through a conference of the national presidents, supported by various ministerial committees. But there have been many divisive tendencies because of differences in the level of economic development and of outlook in the three countries. In 1966 the East African Currency Board, a colonial creation, was disbanded and each country created its own currency and central bank. The Tanzanian shilling remained at par with the currencies of Uganda and Kenya. In 1968 interterritorial cooperation was tested when Britain devalued the pound. The three East African countries decided together not to maintain previous parity with the pound and did not devalue their currencies.

Agriculture. Major subsistence crops raised on the central plateau are millet, cassava, and yams, which need little moisture, and maize (corn). Plantains form the staple diet in the wetter regions, and rice is grown on the coast and in Zanzibar.

Most commercially grown crops were introduced during the colonial period, although cotton and coffee were established earlier. The principal export crop is sisal. Zanzibar is the world's principal source of cloves. Other major exports are cotton, coffee, pyrethrum, tea, hides and skins, and beeswax.

LYNN MCLAREN, FROM RAPHO GUILLUMETTE

ZANZIBAR'S MAIN BAZAAR attracts customers to its stalls with offerings of clothing and hardware.

The value of export crops rose slowly during the 1960's, but by the end of the decade increased use of synthetics seriously affected sisal prices and production drastically declined. Drought and lack of transportation have limited the increase of other crops. Inadequate knowledge of modern production techniques and local apathy in trying new products or in improving others have been other limiting factors. The major crops (except sisal, which demands large-scale capital) are largely produced on small farms. Grading and marketing are carried out by cooperatives united in the Cooperative Union of Tanzania, and a major campaign of agricultural extension and improvement is being carried out by the government through their auspices.

The clove industry in Zanzibar, which was based on a plantation system using labor from the mainland, was nationalized in 1964. Attempts are being made to diversify the single-crop economy of the islands.

Mining. No extensive mineral deposits have been found in Tanzania, although small amounts have been exploited. Gold is found in the west and south, and there is a large diamond mine in the northwest at Mwadui. Rubies and sapphires have been found, and a new gem stone, now called tanzanite, was discovered near Kilimanjaro in 1968. Deposits of mica, tin, and meerschaum are being worked. Coal deposits near Lake Malawi are large but of poor grade.

Manufacturing and Trade. Manufacturing is largely confined to processing and other secondary industries. Production includes textiles, soap, shoes, razor blades, tires, wheat products, and powdered coffee. There is an oil refinery.

Manufacturing and trade, previously carried on principally by the Asian and European communities, have increasingly come under government control. Many marketing and producing activities are now undertaken by government bodies, such as the National Development Corporation. Their interests range from cattle ranching and sisal marketing to building tourist hotels. The second five-year plan, while retaining major economic development in government hands, envisaged a private sector constituting about 25% of the economy, and the encouragement of private overseas investment in some fields. Consumer cooperative societies are encouraged.

Transportation. Public transportation and communication services are controlled by a series of autonomous corporations acting within the structure of the East African Community. Tanzania earmarked for this sector of the economy one third of the funds to be spent under its second five-year plan.

The central railroad line of Tanzania extends from Dar es Salaam northwest to Kigoma-Ujiji on Lake Tanganyika. A branch line runs to Mwanza on Lake Victoria. Another main line extends from the port of Tanga northwest to Arusha, and is connected with both the Tanganyikan central line and other railroads in Kenya. Planned railroad expansion includes a line in the south to Zambia, for which financial guarantees were obtained from the People's Republic of China in 1970.

In its program of road building and improvement the government has concentrated on the construction of feeder roads to encourage agricultural production in isolated areas. Communication with many points is easier by East African Airways than by road.

4. Government

The constitution adopted in July 1965 provided for a strong presidency and a parliament and included semifederal arrangements that gave Zanzibar local autonomy. It accorded legal recognition to a single party, and established a close relationship between the party and governmental organization, policies, and elections. The two existing parties—the Tanganyika African National Union (TANU) on the mainland and the Afro-Shirazi party in Zanzibar—were expected to amalgamate but did not do so. No other parties are permitted.

The head of state and government is the president, who is nominated by the TANU national party conference and is elected by the people. Only one candidate is nominated for this office, but two or more may be nominated for any parliamentary seat. There are two vice presidents, the first of whom is also president of Zanzibar. Cabinet ministers are chosen from the National Assembly.

The unicameral National Assembly consists of: (a) 120 constituency members elected by popular vote from candidates nominated through TANU; (b) 20 members who are regional commissioners; (c) 15 national members elected by the assembly itself to represent interest groups such as cooperatives, trade unions, and the university; (d) up to 30 members appointed by the president for similar purposes; and (e) up to 32 members of the Zanzibar Revolutionary Council.

The National Assembly is the forum for discussion of policies and public questioning of the government. Major decisions, however, are made by the TANU National Executive Committee, a group of about 70 members chosen each year by the party conference. The constitution gives the National Executive Committee certain legal powers, such as the right to call for information or witnesses. Its proceedings are private. Annual party conferences are attended by members chosen from districts and regions by a system of indirect elections in which all TANU members may participate. Party membership is open to all citizens who accept its major objectives.

Governmental administrative structure recognizes the fusion between party and state. Tanzania has 20 regions, 17 on the mainland and 3 in Zanzibar, which are in turn divided into areas. In each region, a commissioner represents the central government, serves as chief political and administrative officer, and performs important party functions. The civil service is not an independent entity. Civil servants may participate in party affairs, and party and administration are therefore largely interchangeable.

Party and government leaders are not allowed to have major outside sources of income. The 1965 constitution created a national commission of inquiry, which operates as an ombudsman to deal with corruption and maladministration.

Elected local government councils exist in all areas, and town councils are found in the larger towns. Their relationship with TANU is close, and the chairman of each council is usually the district chairman of the party. Councils have some powers of local taxation, but most of them are heavily dependent on financial support from the central government, to which they are distinctly subordinate.

The administrative structure utilizes many foreign civil servants. When the united republic was formed in 1964, more than 40% of the higher-ranking civil servants were non-Tanzanians. The largest number of these were in such technical departments as geological survey, health, and civil aviation. Other departments have been largely Africanized, and the government hopes to have Tanzanians in most major positions by 1980. Substantial progress toward this objective has been made.

Local legislation for Tanganyika is formulated by the National Assembly of Tanzania. Tanganyika has an independent judiciary appointed by the president. Before independence, there were separate and parallel courts enforcing British and African customary law, and the basis of court procedure and of the civil and criminal law remains British. Unification of law is proceeding, and there are new codes dealing with such subjects as marriage and inheritance.

The chief executive of the Zanzibar region is the president of Zanzibar, who is first vice president of the union. He has his own cabinet for local affairs, including such matters as education, agriculture, and roads. External affairs and defense are controlled by the union government. The Zanzibar Revolutionary Council formulates local legislation. The court system, formerly similar to Tanganyika's, has been abolished. Some cases are considered by military and revolutionary peoples' courts.

SHARON INC., FROM BLACK STAR

The business center of Dar es Salaam, Tanzania's capital and major seaport. The harbor is at right.

The 1965 constitution marked a major change from earlier political structures, which had been based on the British parliamentary model. Although it recognizes only one party, its provisions on membership, elections, and other organizational problems aim to make democracy possible within the party itself and to lead the country toward the concept of *ujamaa* (Swahili for "familyhood"), formulated by President Nyerere.

5. History

Tanzanian history has only recently been investigated, and there are still many gaps in the knowledge of Tanzania's past. Since 1959, at Olduvai Gorge in Tanganyika, hominid remains of greatest antiquity have been found in association with very primitive stone tools. Little archaeological work has been done, however, except on the coast, and even there only a few of more than 150 known sites have been excavated.

The ancient Greeks knew of the Tanganyikan coast, which they called *Azania.* From linguistic and other evidence it is believed that the Bantu peoples of the Tanganyika interior arrived there about the 1st century A. D. Many tribal groups have legends of a people preceding them, and these may refer to the Khoisan-speaking peoples who probably arrived much earlier.

Early History. After the 10th century A. D., Arabic writers began to mention a series of coastal city-states with independent ruling dynasties. Tradition maintains that they were founded by Muslim refugees from Arabia. For many years the most important town was Kilwa, a trading community in southern Tanganyika that controlled an ancient gold route into the interior. The traveler Ibn Battuta visited the town in 1331 and described its mosques and the personality of its reigning sultan. In early records there is evidence of the development of the Swahili language, and some authorities speak of a Swahili civilization. Kilwa had wide contacts across the Indian Ocean with Arabia, India, Persia, and at least indirectly with China, but there is little evidence of contact inland. The city was challenged in later years by other coastal powers, including Zanzibar and Mombasa.

When the Portuguese appeared in the Indian Ocean—Vasco da Gama reached Zanzibar in 1499—they easily defeated the local sultans. The Portuguese controlled the coast in rather spasmodic fashion, concentrating their efforts on Zanzibar and Mombasa. East Africa was secondary to their interests in India, and in Tanganyika their influence was minimal.

Rule by the Arabs. Early in the 18th century the Arab sultanate of Oman sent expeditions to the coast and seized Pemba and Kilwa. After a long contest with the Mazrui dynasty of Mombasa, the Omanis emerged in control, and in 1840 the ruler of Oman, Sayyid Said Ibn Sultan, moved his court to Zanzibar. During a subsequent period of prosperity, based partly on clove cultivation and partly on development of the inland trade in slaves and ivory, Zanzibari influence spread widely. By the 1850's trading caravans reached into the Congo.

In the late 1700's the Masai invaded Tanganyika from the north, pushing other tribal groups before them until defeated themselves by the Hehe. In the south appeared several Ngoni groups from southern Africa, who seized land, cattle, and tributary populations. The slave trade created much unrest and dislocation of life. Several African leaders, among them Kimweri of the Shambala and Mirambo of the Nyamwezi, took the opportunity to carve out kingdoms for themselves. These leaders negotiated with and sometimes paid tribute to the sultan in Zanzibar.

Sayyid Said signed treaties with the United States in 1833 and with Britain in 1839. U. S. traders were active in Zanzibar during the clipper ship era, trading principally in cotton cloth. The British undertook a long campaign to abolish the slave trade in the sultan's dominions, and British influence became predominant in Zanzibar, especially during the long consulship of Sir John Kirk, which began in 1867.

European influence led to the establishment of Christian missions and to the exploration of the Tanganyikan interior. The Anglican Church Missionary Society began work in Zanzibar in 1844, and in 1848 one of its missionaries, Johannes Rebmann, became the first European to see Kilimanjaro. In 1858, Richard Francis Burton and John Hanning Speke visited Lakes Tanganyika and Victoria. David Livingstone explored the southern areas of Tanganyika in the 1850's and 1860's, and the famous search for him took Henry Morton Stanley across central Tanganyika to Ujiji in 1871.

Colonial Control. Zanzibar's hegemony was soon challenged from Europe. In 1873 the sultan prohibited the export of slaves from his African lands, but Tippu Tip, a powerful slave trader, maintained an independent empire in the western interior until the 1880's. In 1884 the German explorer and adventurer Karl Peters signed treaties with inland chiefs that led eventually to the creation of a German chartered company and, in 1890, to the establishment of the German East Africa protectorate. Britain and France joined the complicated diplomatic negotiations that permitted this annexation, and Zanzibar itself was declared a British protectorate in 1890. The sultan retained his throne, but a British resident was installed and British courts established.

The mainland area remained part of German East Africa until the end of World War I, during which it was the site of major fighting. The German commander, Paul von Lettow-Vorbeck, fought a brilliant guerrilla campaign against British and Belgian troops, surrendering only after the signing of the European armistice. In Tanganyika the war caused large-scale tribal dispersions and a serious famine in 1919. It is estimated that the war brought death to 250,000 Africans in Tanganyika.

By the Versailles Treaty in 1919, German East Africa was divided and placed under mandate to the League of Nations. Tanganyika was assigned for administration to Britain. The mandate agreement outlined general standards of administration and required annual reports to the League.

British administration in Tanganyika had two principal characteristics. The first was financial stringency. Until World War II the territory's meager financial resources could barely begin to deal with problems of education, health, and economic development. Second, the British stressed the policy known as indirect rule, or native administration, by which African tribal groups were encouraged to run their own affairs in their own way, although under British influence. This policy worked reasonably well and was acceptable to the African peoples, but it did not allow for rapid change and was later criticized by nationalists as encouraging tribalism. Under the mandate, settlers from various European countries were allowed to enter Tanganyika. The largest groups were Greeks and Germans. The Germans became a problem in the 1930's when a Nazi movement flourished in Tanganyika.

Although 80,000 Tanganyikans served in the British forces in World War II, the war did not have great effect on the territory. At its end, Tanganyika became a trust territory of the United Nations, and Britain pursued more vigorous policies. In both Tanganyika and Zanzibar, legislative councils made up of officials had been created in 1926. Their scope and membership were now widened, the first Africans being appointed to the Tanganyikan council in 1945. More local residents, including Arabs and Indians as well as Africans, were brought into the civil service. The first elections were allowed in local governments, and plans were worked out for economic and educational development.

The 1950's were a period of political and economic experimentation for both countries. In Tanganyika change was encouraged by the Groundnut Scheme, a plan to develop large areas of land for the mechanical cultivation of peanuts, but the project failed despite large British investment. Pressures from the United Nations also encouraged change, as did the unification of the East African railways and other economic services in 1948.

Independence for Tanganyika. The nationalist movement in Tanganyika began with the formation in 1954 of the Tanganyika African National Union (TANU). This political party was the creation of Julius K. Nyerere, who was then a schoolteacher, and a small group of associates. TANU sought to create an independent African nation with participation of all local groups. Its economic program was moderately socialist. Membership in TANU was exclusively African, and the party was regarded by the British administration as both radical and subversive. Despite some difficulties posed by legal requirements on registration and finance, party membership increased rapidly after 1957. TANU decisively won the first national elections in 1958, although multiracial franchise requirements forced it to support non-African candidates and to appeal to non-African voters.

TANU proved able to work with Europeans and Asians, and the march toward independence was rapid and smooth. There were few internal dissensions. The British were anxious to withdraw and were urged to do so by the United Nations. Nyerere's leadership was also decisive. He was the major architect of party policy, although most party decisions were taken by the TANU national executive committee and he was sometimes overruled. On Dec. 9, 1961, Tanganyika became independent, declaring itself a republic one year later. Nyerere was elected as the first president in 1962. He was able to convince non-African Tanganyikans that they had a place in a primarily African state. Membership in TANU was opened to non-Africans in 1963.

Independence for Zanzibar. In Zanzibar the independence movement was not unified. The Zanzibar Nationalist party (ZNP), representing primarily Arab groups, was first regarded as highly radical. It was opposed by a more moderate grouping of resident Africans, known as Shirazi because of their reputed Persian descent, and newly arrived African laborers from the mainland. The Shirazi group was successful in the first elections in 1957, but it later split into the Afro-Shirazi party and the Zanzibar and Pemba People's party (ZPPP).

Subsequently personal antagonisms became bitter. Elections conducted in January 1961 resulted in an absolutely even split among the parties, one parliamentary seat being won by a single vote. Second elections in the same year ended in rioting and the death of 68 persons. A coalition ZNP-ZPPP government was formed, although the Afro-Shirazi party had received the largest number of votes. New elections in 1963 had similar results, and the coalition government remained in office. Zanzibar became independent on Dec. 10, 1963.

Union. In January 1964, a month after Zanzibar had achieved independence, a revolution occurred. The immediate events were precipitated by a self-styled field marshal, an adventurer from Uganda named John Okello. The revolution was chaotic, and several thousand Arabs were killed in a few days. The Zanzibar Revolutionary Council, headed by Abeid Karume of the Afro-Shirazi party, formed a government and asked Tanganyika to help maintain law and order.

The example of Zanzibar and the dispatch of some 300 Tanganyikan police to the island in turn encouraged an army mutiny in Tanganyika in February 1964. Local grievances over wages and the government's failure to Africanize officer cadres prompted the mutiny. It was not designed to overthrow the government, but its effects were serious, and President Nyerere called in British troops to maintain order.

In April 1964, at President Karume's request, Zanzibar and Tanganyika were united. Popular support for the union seemed widespread, but attempts to coordinate policies in the two regions were not markedly successful. Zanzibar remained largely in control of its own affairs. President Karume (who became first vice president of Tanzania and who was assassinated in 1972) assumed an increasingly intractable position in support of the nationalization of major sectors of the islands' economy and complete control of policy by the Revolutionary Council and the Afro-Shirazi party. Opposition to the regime was not permitted, and the president declared that there would be no elections. A rigid line in race relations was also established, Indian and Arab groups being told that they must integrate into the African community.

In Tanganyika, elections were held in 1965. President Nyerere was reelected for a 5-year term, and a new National Assembly was chosen. Since then, government policy has been concentrated on economic development and Africanization. TANU remained the mobilizing group for change within the country. Using the party structures and especially the *kumi-kumi*, local wards or cells of ten families each, the national leadership attempted to explain national policies and also to obtain popular participation both in deciding on development programs and in carrying them out. With increased emphasis on rural development and agriculture under the second five-year plan, party officials were instrumental in establishing *ujamaa* cooperative villages and state farms. President Nyerere occupied an increasingly important and prestigious position within the country and continued to be the major spokesman of party policy. At Arusha, on Feb. 5, 1967, he delivered a historic speech on the development of a socialist and egalitarian country. This statement, now known as the Arusha Declaration, together with later ones on education for self-reliance and on rural development, established the main outlines of Tanzanian policy.

Opposition to the single-party state and to specific policies appeared in the late 1960's. In 1966, President Nyerere dismissed some 400 students from University College, Dar es Salaam, for protesting against the imposition of national service. The next year Oscar Kambona, formerly organizing secretary of TANU and a cabinet minister, fled the country and denounced the government. There was also concern about the status and attitudes of the army. Tight control of recruitment was achieved by enrolling only those young men who had proved themselves in the TANU Youth League and the national service. Trade unions were also placed under close government control.

Tanzania has played a major role in Pan-African affairs, particularly in connection with the African Liberation Committee of the Organization of African Unity, which has worked closely with liberation movements in white-ruled southern Africa. Support was particularly strong for FRELIMO, the independence movement of Mozambique, which was permitted to maintain headquarters in Dar es Salaam and training camps elsewhere in Tanzania. Tanzania broke diplomatic relations with Britain in 1966 because of British failure to prevent Rhodesia's white-dominated government from making itself independent. Tanzania worked particularly closely with Zambia to help that country to establish its economic independence of southern Africa. Links between the two were expected to be strengthened by the Tanzania-Zambia railroad.

In foreign policy generally, Tanzania has maintained a position of nonalignment with any major power bloc. Its trading relations with Peking were greatly expanded in the late 1960's, and China became a major aid supplier, especially for the railroad to Zambia.

MARGARET L. BATES, *Smith College*

Bibliography

Bates, Margaret L., "Tanganyika," in *African One-Party States,* ed. by Gwendolen M. Carter (Ithaca, N. Y., 1962).

Bienen, Henry, *Tanzania: Party Transformation and Economic Development* (Princeton 1970).

Ingrams, William H., *Zanzibar: Its History and Its Peoples* (London 1931).

Lofchie, Michael, *Zanzibar: Background to Revolution* (Princeton 1965).

Middleton, John, and Campbell, Jane, *Zanzibar: Its Society and Its Politics* (London 1965).

Nyerere, Julius K., *Freedom and Socialism* (Dar es Salaam 1968).

Oliver, Roland, and others, eds., *History of East Africa,* 2 vols. (London 1963, 1965).

DAR ES SALAAM MUSLIMS are seated outside a mosque on an important religious holiday.

LYNN MCLAREN, FROM RAPHO GUILLUMETTE

TANZANITE, tan′zə-nīt, is a blue variety of zoisite. Named for Tanzania, where it was found, it is used as a gem. See ZOISITE.

T'AO CH'IEN, tou chē-en′ (365–427), was a Chinese poet, popularly regarded as the epitome of the poet-recluse. His real name was *T'ao Yüan-ming.* He held a few minor government posts but soon retired from public life. Styling himself T'ao Ch'ien ("T'ao, the hidden one"), he wrote poems celebrating the virtues of rustic life.

His descriptions of nature are unrivaled in their combination of precise observation and associative power. His engaging simplicity of taste is best revealed through his favorite images of wine and chrysanthemums, as in this vignette:

I pluck chrysanthemums by the eastern hedge,
Far in the distance loom the southern hills.

T'ao Ch'ien is by turns introspective, carefree, and involved with everyday matters like children, farming, friends, and daily cares. However, he is not insensitive to political turmoil.

Writing in an age when poetic taste increasingly required a florid style and abstruse themes, T'ao Ch'ien did not initially receive the high critical acclaim later accorded him in the T'ang and Sung dynasties. The Wordsworthian simplicity of his poetic diction and perhaps the very accessibility of his thought provoked the charge of a too "unadorned simplicity." But this presumed lack of elegance came to be regarded as an admirable "fidelity" to experience.

RONALD C. MIAO, *University of Michigan*

TAOISM, dou′iz-əm, is a philosophical and religious system of China, where it has been second only to Confucianism in importance. As a philosophy its influence has been tremendous. It has supplemented and enriched Confucianism and contributed to the growth of Buddhism. It has provided spiritual inspiration and moral standards for the Chinese, while imbuing Chinese poetry, landscape painting, and other art forms with its love of nature and sense of serenity. As both a philosophy and a religion Taoism has supplied strength and refuge to the old, the poor, and the oppressed, and also to rebels and secret societies.

PHILOSOPHY

Theory. Taoism is named after its central idea, *Tao,* or "the Way," which is the basic principle of the universe. Tao is all-inclusive, everlasting, and good, but indescribable. It is not a thing but a creative process.

A person who grasps the meaning of Tao, the underlying principle and governor of all life, follows the doctrine of *wu-wei,* or "doing nothing." This means not interfering with Nature. It is the nature of a fish to swim, and it is the destiny of a mushroom to live for a day and a pine for 500 years. Man is happy and free when he preserves his own nature and fulfills his own destiny, which he does by avoiding anxiety about life and death, rising above gain and loss, and living a simple and spontaneous life, like a child. The Taoist ruler shuns pomp and ceremony, warfare, and interference in his subjects' lives. Through gentleness, humility, and nonstruggle, man gains nobility of soul, serenity of mind, harmony of emotions, and freedom of spirit.

History. Taoist philosophy is traditionally traced back to Lao Tzu (6th century B. C.), a custodian of government archives whom Confucius consulted about ceremonies but about whom little is known. Tradition attributes to Lao Tzu the 5,000-word *Tao-te ching,* or *Classic of Tao and Its Virtue,* also called the *Lao Tzu.* This work, which contains the basic Taoist teachings, has been the most influential book in China next to the *Analects* of Confucius. The *Tao-te ching* was actually not written until after Lao Tzu's time, but some of its fundamental principles may well have been his.

The philosopher Chuang Tzu (4th–3d century B. C.) raised Taoism to new heights with his doctrines of the equality of all things, the spontaneous transformation of Tao, and man's mystical union with the universe. The Taoists of the 3d and 4th centuries A. D., who were called Neo-Taoists, developed the concept of nonbeing as pure, absolute reality. See also LAO TZU; CHUANG TZU; CHINA—*Philosophy and Religion.*

RELIGION

While the Taoist philosophy was unfolding, priest-magicians were offering formulas to increase physical and mental power, restore youth, achieve superhuman ability, and obtain everlasting life on earth. By the 1st century B. C. the movement came to be known as the Way of Huang-Lao—after Huang-ti, the legendary Yellow Emperor who was said to have achieved immortality, and Lao Tzu, possibly because he had taught that man could achieve immortality.

The historical founder of the Taoist religion was Chang Ling, a popular religious leader and rebel. He urged his followers to read the *Tao-te ching* and in 143 A. D. organized them into the Way of Five Bushels (or Pecks) of Rice, so called because he collected that amount of grain from members. His followers called him "Heavenly Teacher" (*T'ien Shih*). The last holder of this title died in Taiwan in 1969.

Cult of Immortals. After the founding of the Taoist religion, two movements developed. One was the cult of immortals, which sought immortality through meditation, breathing exercises, bathing, gymnastics, sexual arts, medicines, chemistry, and other means. A measure of systemization was brought to this school of Taoism by Wei Po-yang (2d century A. D.), who in his *Ts'an-t'ung-ch'i,* or *The Three Ways Unified and Harmonized,* attempted to synthesize Taoist techniques for achieving immortality and teachings of the occult *I ching* (*Book of Changes*). He believed that all elements of the universe could be so concentrated and harmonized in one's body that life would be everlasting. Ko Hung (284–363) in his *Pao-p'u Tzu,* or *The Master Who Embraces Simplicity,* combined Taoist occultism with Confucian ethics and formulated a merit system whereby the number of days in a life are increased or decreased by one's deeds. Later Taoists abandoned the search for immortality and accepted the Buddhist promise of Paradise. They turned their attention to seeking earthly blessings like health and happiness.

Way of the Heavenly Teacher. The other Taoist movement, the Way of the Heavenly Teacher, was made into a highly organized religion by K'ou Ch'ien-chih (died 432), who regulated Taoist ceremonies, fixed the names of deities, and formulated a theology. This school has an enormous pantheon of gods of every description and many heroes and saints. It borrowed heavily from Buddhism, especially in its trinity of the Three Pure Ones, its belief in heavens and hells,

TAOS PUEBLO, an ancient Indian dwelling near Taos, N. Mex., has changed little since Spanish explorers saw it in 1540. Access still is by outside ladders.

JOSEF MUENCH

and its clergy, monasticism, and canon. Its practices include temple worship, offerings to the dead, geomancy and other forms of divination, plus witchcraft and the use of charms—all for driving away evil spirits and obtaining earthly blessings.

The clergy divided into two schools. The Southern, or True Unity, School relies on charms and magic to preserve man's spirit, or true self. Its priests marry, live at home, and accept the Heavenly Teacher as their head. Priests of the Northern, or Complete Unity, School live in temples, are vegetarians, and rely on medicine and diet to prolong life.

History. Taoism was the state religion of China for a while during the 5th and 6th centuries and under the T'ang dynasty (618–906). Afterward it existed primarily as a religion of the illiterate masses. In modern times it has steadily declined.

In mainland China, most, if not all, priests have been ordered back to lay life and most temples are used for other purposes. There the religion is practically dormant, although many of its teachings—patience, simplicity, contentment, harmony—have enduring appeal. There has been some revival of Taoism in Taiwan and Hong Kong, where new temples have been built.

WING-TSIT CHAN
Editor and Translator of "The Way of Lao Tzu"

Further Reading: Chan, Wing-tsit, *Religious Trends in Modern China* (New York 1969); id., comp. and tr., *A Source Book in Chinese Philosophy* (Princeton 1963); id., and others, *The Great Asian Religions: An Anthology* (New York 1969); Thompson, Laurence G., *Chinese Religion: An Introduction* (Belmont, Calif., 1969).

TAORMINA, tä-ôr-mē′nə, an ancient Italian town, is on the east coast of Sicily, 30 miles (48 km) south of Messina. It lies near the summit of a very steep hill and commands magnificent views of the Sicilian coast and Mount Etna. Noted for its mild climate, it is now important chiefly as a winter resort.

Taormina was settled in early classical times and had a troubled history until its conquest by the Romans in the 2d century B.C. It then enjoyed a period of prosperity, when its existing Greek theater was rebuilt. In the Middle Ages a castle was built above the town. Today Taormina is picturesque and colorful, with narrow, winding streets, many of them closed to motor traffic, and the architectural remains of its Roman and medieval past. Population: (1970 est.) 7,000.

NORMAN J. G. POUNDS, *Indiana University*

TAOS, tous, a village in northern New Mexico, the seat of Taos county, is situated at the foot of the Sangre de Cristo Mountains, 69 miles (110 km) northeast of Santa Fe. It is a residential community at the heart of a tight cluster of small villages. Its culture is Indian, Spanish, and "Anglo." Taos is a trade and tourist center and, since the late 19th century, has been a noted colony for artists and writers. Farming, lumbering, ranching, mining, and the ski industry are the main sources of income in the area.

Each summer the Taos School of Music and several universities offer courses here. The Kit Carson Home and Museum, the Millicent A. Rogers Museum featuring Spanish-Colonial and Indian articles, and the St. Francis of Assisi Mission, one of the oldest churches in the Southwest, are of interest. Taos Pueblo, the nation's largest and, probably, oldest pueblo, is 3 miles (5 km) to the northeast. The 5-story adobe buildings house over 1,000 Indians whose colorful ceremonies draw many visitors. The beauty of the area has attracted many writers and painters, including Willa Cather, Robinson Jeffers, D. H. Lawrence, Dorothy Brett, and Maurice Sterne, all of whom lived here for a time.

Established in 1615 as Don Fernando de Taos, the site is one of the oldest white settlements in the United States. The Indian revolt against the Spanish in 1680 was planned at Taos Pueblo. Taos was incorporated in 1934. It is governed by a mayor and council. Population: 2,475.

MABEL M. KUYKENDALL
"Taos News"

TAP DANCE, an indigenous American step dance form, usually in complex, syncopated rhythms and executed audibly with the toes and heels of the feet in specially designed shoes.

The form was born of adversity. After the Stono slave insurrection of 1739, American Negro slaves were prohibited from "beating drums, blowing horns or the like." They substituted handclaps and footbeats.

Gradually, the footbeats became a form of entertainment. By the late 1830's, Negro step dancers like Juba (William Henry Lane) were on the stage. At about this time Irish and Lancashire clog dances, performed on stiff wooden soles, became popular in the United States. By the end of the 19th century, the static clog dance, sometimes done on a pedestal, had virtually disappeared.

CULVER PICTURES

TAP DANCE ROUTINES of great intricacy were performed by dancers Eleanor Powell and Fred Astaire.

In 1902, Ned Wayburn, a producer, introduced his "Minstrel Misses" in blackface. They wore clogs with split wooden soles and their work was for the first time called "tap and step dancing." In 1912, tap dancers began to wear metal cleats on the heels and toes of their shoes.

Vaudeville tap dancers, like the great Bill "Bojangles" Robinson (1878–1949), tended to keep the upper body relaxed and emphasize rhythmic syncopation in the feet. The art was given a new direction by Fred Astaire, Ray Bolger, Gene Kelly, and Paul Draper, who included the tapping as part of a total artistic expression.

DORIS HERING, *"Dance Magazine"*

TAPACOLO, ta-pə-ko'lo, any of a family of small to medium-sized ground-dwelling birds found from Costa Rica to Tierra del Fuego and the Falkland Islands. The more than 25 species of tapacolos, or tapaculos, are variously known as *huet-huets, gallitos,* and *crescent-crests.*

Tapacolos are stocky birds 4½ to 10 inches (11–25 cm) long with short rounded wings and powerful legs and feet. Some are crested. The plumage is soft, loose, and dark. Some species are almost black, while others are spotted with chestnut or white. A fleshy movable flap on the nostrils may serve to keep out dust. They rarely fly but walk and run with the tail erect. Tapacolos are secretive birds. Alone or in small groups, they forage for seeds and insects. Both parents incubate the two to five eggs and care for the young. Tapacolos make up the family Rhinocryptidae of the order Passeriformes.

JOSEPH BELL, *New York Zoological Park*

TAPAJÓS RIVER, täp-ə-zhôs', a tributary of the Amazon River in north-central Brazil. It flows northeast in the State of Pará, emptying into the Amazon near Santarém. The river is formed by the confluence of the Teles Pires and Juruena rivers, both of which rise on the Mato Grosso plateau. The Tapajós is over 1,100 miles (1,800 km) long and, in its lower course, broadens to a width of about 12 miles (19 km). There are large rubber plantations along its banks.

TAPE RECORDING, a technique for storing information on the magnetic surface of a tape. The recording surface consists of magnetic particles uniformly distributed in a thin film of nonmagnetic material. Although plastic tape is the most commonly used base, magnetic surface films may also be applied to wires, discs, and drums. Any form of information that can be transformed into an electrical signal can be stored magnetically. For example, music is transformed to electrical signals by means of a microphone. Similarly, pictures may be electrically scanned by means of a television camera and converted into a serial stream of electrical impulses. In data processing, binary "ones" and "zeros" may be represented by voltage or current levels. Thus, all of these forms of information can be transformed and stored magnetically.

TAPE RECORDING PRINCIPLES

Magnetic recording depends upon the existence of two phenomena. The first is that a magnetic field is associated with every electric current. The second is that ferromagnetic (highly magnetizable) materials retain magnetization after being exposed to a magnetic field.

The Recording Head. A special device, a *recording head,* is used to transform electric current into a magnetic field. It consists of a circular or rectangular iron core wound with wire and having a small opening, or gap, at one end. The recording head is thus an electromagnet. When current, produced by the electrical signal of a microphone, television camera, or other transducer flows through the wire, the core becomes magnetized. Within limits, the greater the current flow, the greater the magnetization. When current ceases to flow, the core loses its magnetism. Therefore, a varying magnetic field will surround the windings when current flows.

Since the iron core of the recording head has a lower resistance to magnetic lines of force than does air, the magnetic lines of force, or flux, will flow preferentially through the magnetic structure. The flux is forced to flow through the air in the region of the gap, however, because no magnetic material exists there. Since lines of magnetic flux repel each other, many are forced to bulge out in the vicinity of the gap, creating a "fringing field." If a tape is placed next to the gap, it will experience a fringing magnetic field that varies in magnitude with the incoming electrical signal. If the input signal is shut off, the tape will retain a magnetization that is determined by the magnitude of the last current that flowed through the windings.

A stationary recording head and tape are satisfactory only for taking a "snapshot" of an electrical signal. Actually, the snapshot is that of the last electrical signal present. However, if the tape is moved with respect to the head, if the head is moved with respect to the tape, or if both the head and tape are moved, one can record a series of time-varying electrical signals.

Magnetic Tape. Magnetic tape consists of a large assemblage of magnetic particles, each of which can be considered a bar magnet with a north and south pole. When the polarity of the input signal changes and the strength of the fringing field increases to a certain necessary level, the north-to-south magnetization of the particle will reverse. As the magnitude of the input signal changes, the pole strength will increase or decrease accordingly.

Since magnetic flux must form a completely closed path, the lines of magnetic force flowing from the north to south poles of the magnetized particles in the tape create fringing flux fields in the air above the tape.

Reproduce Head. If a magnetic structure is placed in such a flux path, and if the structure offers a path with less magnetic resistance than air, the flux will pass preferentially through the magnetic structure instead of through the air. Just as electric current produces a magnetic field, a magnetic field can produce an electric current. If the magnetic structure placed in the flux path is surrounded by a coil of wire, forming a reproduce head, changes of flux in the head will result in a voltage being produced at the terminations of the wire. The electrical signal has now gone full cycle. It originated with an input transducer and created a magnetic field in the record head. The magnetic field was then recorded on tape. The residual magnetic field on the tape has now produced a time-varying electrical signal in the reproduce head.

Erasing. Erasure is accomplished by randomizing the orientation of north and south poles in such a way that they cancel each other's effects and thus no external field is present. This is done by means of an erase head, which impresses a decreasing alternating field upon the tape. The net result is very much like a community that has voted 50% "yes" and 50% "no." To the outside world, the net result is zero.

Recording Formats. In order to accommodate different types of information, various recording formats are used. The most common one is the longitudinal format. In this, the record and reproduce heads are held stationary while tape is moved past them. The result is a magnetic track recorded in the direction of tape travel. Different tape and track widths may be used. Each variation is dictated by efficiency and convenience for the specific application. For example, digital recorders for data processing use 7- and 9-track formats on ½-inch (13-mm) tape. Audio recorders generally use tape that is ¼-inch (6 mm) wide. The recorded track may occupy the full width of a ¼-inch tape or some submultiple of the width according to the type of application. Full track recording may be used in a mastering

Current, produced by the electrical signal from a microphone, flows through the core wiring, magnetizing the core and inducing the flow of magnetic flux across the gap. The variations in this flux, or fringing field, are transferred to the tape.

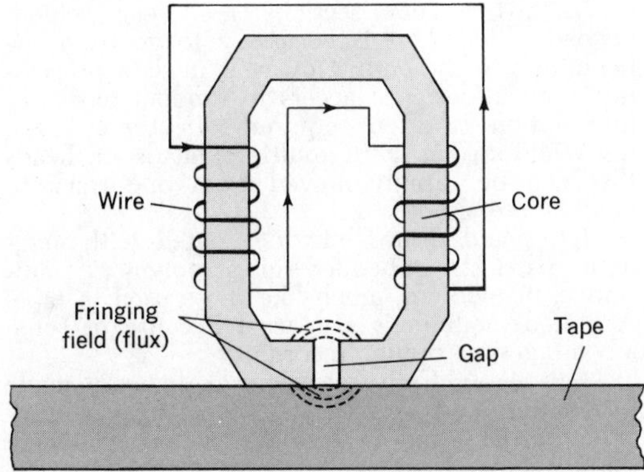

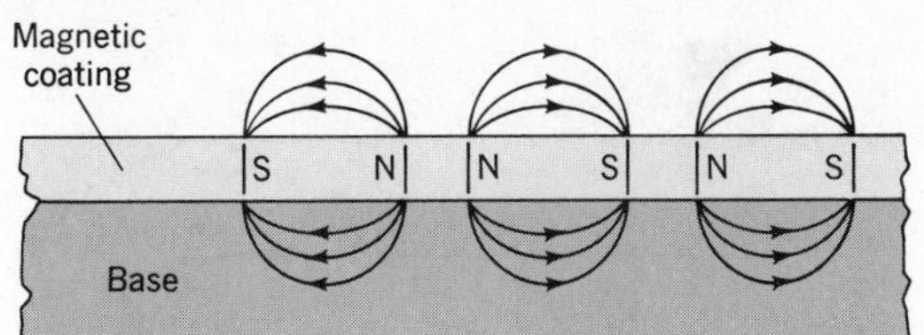

The magnetic particles of the tape, arrayed by the recording process, act like tiny bar magnets and produce fringing fields above the tape. In playback, the fringing fields induce changes in the flux of the reproduce head, causing current to flow in the wiring. This current is amplified and fed to a loudspeaker.

(recording) studio where the highest possible fidelity of recording is a prime objective. Cassette tapes, which are narrow in themselves, use narrow tracks, convenience and size being important considerations.

The shortest segment of information on tape (the wavelength of the information) is limited by mechanical and electrical considerations. It is necessary to increase the relative speed between the head and the tape in order to increase the frequency of information to be stored. Typical home or professional audio recorders operating at 7½ inches (190.5 mm) and 15 inches (381 mm) per second have frequency ranges of 10 cycles per second to 15,000, 18,000, and even 20,000 cycles per second. Cassette recorders, which operate at 1⅞ inches (47.6 mm) per second, will not record frequencies higher than 10,000 or 12,000 cycles. Longitudinal instrumentation recorders, which are used for telemetry and recording of data from satellites and rockets, may operate with tape velocities as high as 120 inches (3,048 mm) per second. Instrumentation recorders with upper frequency limits of 2 million cycles per second are commercially available.

Speeds in excess of 120 inches per second introduce mechanical problems. In addition, the amount of tape that can be stored on reels of convenient size becomes a consideration. In order to record the higher frequencies that are necessary for broadcast-quality television recording, a transverse format was invented. In this format, the recording and reproduce heads are mounted on a drum that rotates at high speed in the direction perpendicular to the direction of tape motion. The tape is formed into an arc by appropriate mechanical guides so that the heads may engage the tape through 90° of travel. This permits very high head-to-tape speeds—broadcast video recorders operate at a head-to-tape speed of 1,560 inches (39,624 mm) per second —with relatively slow longitudinal tape speed. For broadcast video recorders, longitudinal tape speed is 15 inches (381 mm) per second.

A helical format has also been used. Here the head or heads are mounted on a drum and engage the tape in a diagonal fashion. This system requires less complex equipment than the transverse format does, but the recordings are somewhat poorer in quality.

Linearity. Magnetization is inherently a nonlinear process. A doubling of the magnetic field impressed on a material does not result in a doubling of the residual magnetism left in the material after the magnetizing field is removed. However, in high-fidelity recording of music or

RECORDING FORMATS

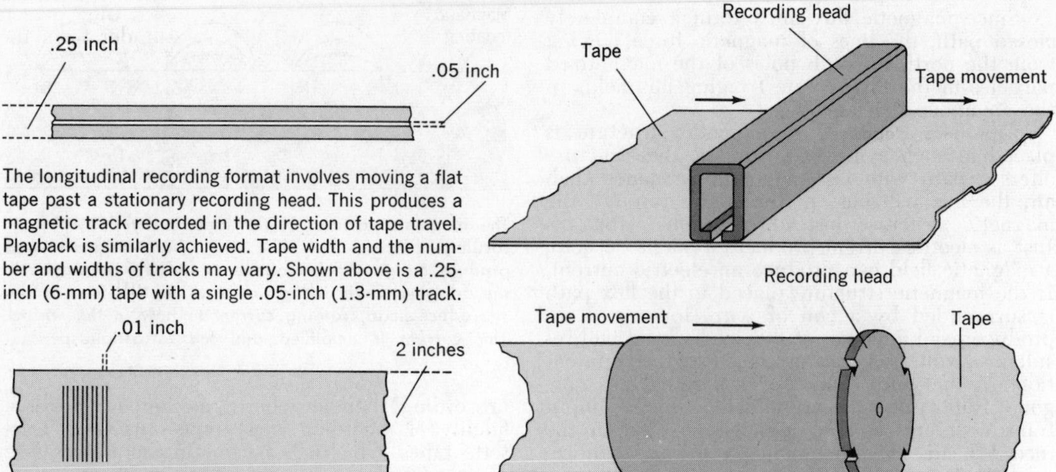

The longitudinal recording format involves moving a flat tape past a stationary recording head. This produces a magnetic track recorded in the direction of tape travel. Playback is similarly achieved. Tape width and the number and widths of tracks may vary. Shown above is a .25-inch (6-mm) tape with a single .05-inch (1.3-mm) track.

Transverse recording entails the use of a drum-shaped recording head that revolves at high speed, producing magnetic tracks across the entire width of the tape. To achieve head-tape engagement through 90 degrees, it is necessary to form the tape into an arc as it passes the head. In the accompanying figure is illustrated a 2-inch (50-mm) tape with .01-inch (.2-mm) tracks.

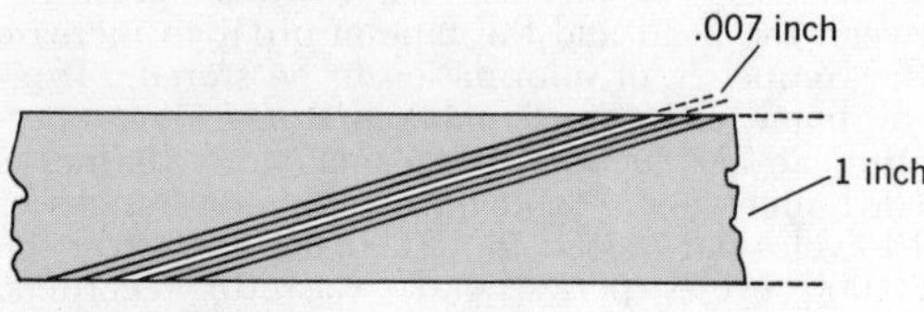

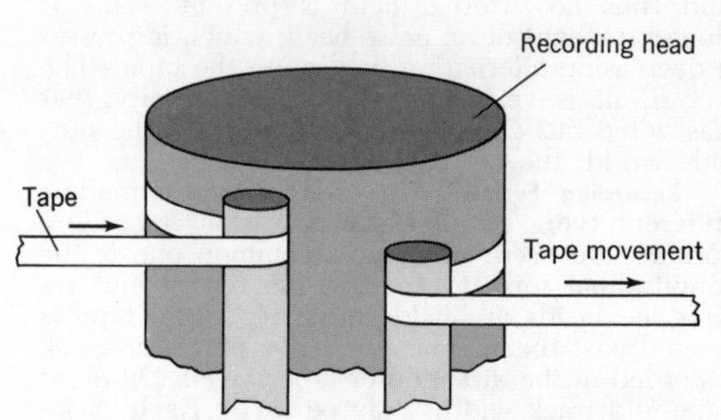

The helical format also employs a drum, but the tape engages the drum in a helical fashion, producing magnetic tracks diagonally across the tape. This system requires less complex equipment than does the transverse format, but the recordings are of lesser quality. Shown above is a 1-inch (25-mm) tape with .007-inch (.18-mm) tracks.

scientific data, it is essential that linearity be maintained. If the music being recorded doubles in volume, the recorded playback should also double in volume. For high fidelity, it is necessary to know not only the time variation of signal but also the magnitude of the variation in time to a high degree of accuracy. Magnetic recording may be linearized, within limits, by mixing a high-frequency, high-amplitude signal known as a *bias signal* into the signal to be recorded. This has the effect of subjecting the magnetic particles in the tape to many cycles of current, thereby increasing the likelihood of their proper response while maintaining the relative variations of the original input.

Linearity is not required in some kinds of recording. In digital recording, it is only necessary to be able to distinguish between two states. Such binary changes may be recorded in terms of changes in magnetization level, changes of magnetic polarity, frequency changes, and many other variations. It is also possible to use schemes other than the amplitude modulation that is commonly used for sound recording. Frequency modulation, pulse code modulation, pulse duration modulation, and many other schemes have been used for special applications.

MAGNETIC TAPE

Magnetic recording can be accomplished on any ferromagnetic surface or substrate. In principle, it is possible to record on wires, thick sheets, bars, or other geometries. However, since the magnetic fringing fields emanating from a record head extend only fractions of a thousandth of an inch (microns) away from the surface of the head, economy of material and efficiency of storage dictate the use of thin magnetic coatings on a substrate that provides mechanical strength. Thin magnetic surfaces coated on tapes, discs, drums, and belts have been used.

Tape is efficient in a volumetric sense in that it is a surface wrapped on itself to provide compact storage. Its disadvantage, however, is that information at the very end of the tape can only be reached, or accessed, by traveling the complete length of tape. It is awkward for rapid searches. For recording programmatic material such as music or a television production, access to random sections are very seldom needed. Indeed, it is necessary to go from the beginning to the end. However, in data processing applications, fast access to random blocks of information is often required. In these cases, discs and drums with multiple heads or heads that can be rapidly moved from one track to another are used.

Discs and drums may be coated with magnetic particles imbedded in a polymeric substance, or medium, much like those used in tape. A plated medium is also used because of some advantages in digital recording.

Tape Base. Early magnetic tapes were made by coating a paper base with a mixture of iron-oxide particles and an adhesive. Such tapes were unsatisfactory from the mechanical point of view.

Nonmagnetic metal bases were tried, as were plastic films. Most tapes today use polyester, generally known by trade names such as Mylar or Celenar, for the base material. It has a good combination of chemical resistance, mechanical strength, surface smoothness, and low cost, which has led to its selection as the preferred material.

Various thicknesses of base film may be used, ranging from a half-thousandth of an inch (0.013 mm) to 1½ thousandth of an inch (0.038 mm). Thicker base films have more mechanical rigidity and are easier to handle. Thin-base films permit higher volume-storage efficiency and are used in applications such as cassettes.

Magnetic Coating. Oxide-coated magnetic tape is used in more than 90% of all applications. Although a variety of materials have been used for experimental purposes, and some have been commercially introduced, most tapes today use the gamma form of iron oxide (γFe_2O_3) as the magnetic particle. The particles are needle shaped, with a long dimension ranging from 8 to 32 millionths of an inch (0.2–0.8 microns). Length-to-breadth ratios are in the range of 2:1 to 6:1. The starting material is the hydrated form of αFe_2O_3. This material is nonmagnetic. It is converted to the magnetic gamma form by reducing dehydrated αFe_2O_3 to Fe_3O_4 and then oxidizing the Fe_3O_4 under carefully controlled conditions.

It is important that the particles be uniformly distributed throughout the binder, that the surface presented to the heads be smooth, and that the binder adhere firmly to the base material. The particles are dispersed in the binder by ball milling. In this process a mixture of particles and binder is placed in a cylindrical can, and the can is partially filled with stainless steel balls. As the can rotates in a specially designed mechanism, the balls break up agglomerates and thoroughly mix the constituents.

The mixture of particles and binder is applied to the base material by any of several techniques. In knife coating, a layer of the mixture is deposited on the web of base material, and a knife edge is used to spread the coating to the desired thickness. In the gravure process the mixture is applied to an incised, or engraved, cylindrical metal roll, and the excess is scraped off with a blade. The web of base material is then passed over the roll, where it picks up binder from the spaces, or interstices, of the roll.

Magnetic alignment of the particles is required to ensure optimum performance of the tape. While the binder is still wet, a magnetic field is applied to the web, and the particles are oriented either in the direction of the motion of the web or in a transverse direction. The latter is required for tapes that are to be used for transverse video recorders. After passing through the drying oven, the tape is buffed and calendered in order to provide as smooth a surface as possible. After calendering, the tape is slit to the desired width and wound on reels.

TAPE RECORDING EQUIPMENT

For each application of tape recording, special equipment has been developed. In some cases the principal constraints have been technical. In others, economic considerations have played a major role.

Reel to Reel. Reel-to-reel machines are used in recording studios, and are also used in the home when the highest fidelity of reproduction is desired. In reel-to-reel record or playback, tape is moved from reel A to reel B or from reel B to reel A at the design speed, which may be 3¾, 7, 15, or 30 inches per second. Tape motion in the vicinity of the heads is controlled by a capstan and pinch roller, which maintain tape speed near the heads and eliminate undesirable variations in signal output. Low frequency signal variations are called "wow," and higher frequency variations are called "flutter."

During the record process, an input signal is amplified, mixed with a high-frequency bias signal, and recorded on the tape by means of a record head. The record level may be adjusted by adjusting the amplifier gain. In some home equipment, automatic gain control is provided, and no adjustment of the record amplifier is required.

During playback the signal picked up by the reproduce head is amplified. The signal level is adjusted by the playback volume control. Base and treble may be adjusted by built-in filter networks that emphasize or attenuate high- or low-frequency output.

In the typical home tape recorder, tape is moved from a supply reel to a take-up reel. A pinch roller is employed to press the tape against a rotating capstan, forcing the tape to move at the controlled capstan speed.

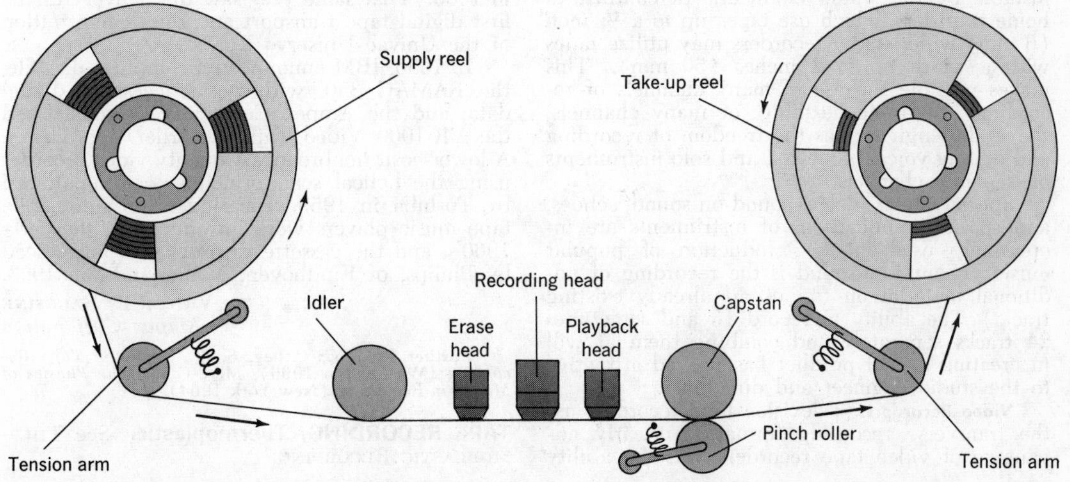

In monaural systems, only a single sound track is recorded, although many microphones may be switched in and out at the discretion of the recording engineer. On playback, only a single speaker is required. The speaker may have sections optimized for base and treble, but these act as a single source. In stereo recording, two tracks are recorded and two speaker systems are required. The speakers should be separated by at least several feet. The arrangement of microphones in recording is such that on playback the two speaker systems provide a directional effect and recreate the depth of sound experienced in a concert hall. A balance control adjusts the level of sound produced by each speaker system. Four-channel recordings have been produced. On playback, four speaker systems are required, producing the illusion of being surrounded by sound.

Reel-to-reel systems are optimum for the high-fidelity enthusiast. The reel sizes are such that playing times of one and two hours can be achieved at tape speeds that make possible outstanding musical fidelity. A large catalog of prerecorded musical selections ranging from popular music to opera is available.

Cartridges and Cassettes. Reel-to-reel machines suffer the inconvenience of requiring that the tape be correctly threaded through a prescribed path and engaged to the takeup reel. While this degree of complexity is perfectly acceptable to the music enthusiast, it is not appealing to the more casual user. Cartridge and cassette recorder/reproducers have become extremely popular. In a tape cartridge, tape is wound on a single reel. An endless tape loop is formed by pulling the tape from the center of the roll, passing it over the heads, and winding it on the outside of the roll. When the cartridge is inserted into a receptacle in the tape recorder/reproducer, the tape loop engages the record and reproduce heads. Specially lubricated tape is required to permit the slippage that is necessary to extract the tape from the inner diameter without damage to the tape pack.

A cassette is a reel-to-reel tape arrangement in a convenient package. When placed in the tape recorder/reproducer, the heads can be made to engage the tape while the reel hubs are driven by shafts.

Studio Recorders. Studio recorders are machines that have been built to withstand constant usage and to provide precise control of tape motion combined with electronic assemblies that are adjustable by the studio engineer. In contrast to home recorders, which use tapes up to a ¼ inch (6 mm) wide, studio recorders may utilize tapes with a width up to 2 inches (50 mm). This makes possible the use of many channels of recording. With the flexibility of many channels, the studio engineer has the freedom of recording and editing voice, orchestra, and solo instruments on separate channels.

Special effects such as sound-on-sound, echoes, and special combinations of instruments are increasingly used in the production of popular music. (Sound-on-sound is the recording of additional material on top of an already existing track.) The ability to record 16 and sometimes 24 tracks separately and combine them at will in creating a final product has proved attractive to the studio engineer and director.

Video Recorders. Television tape recorders use the transverse recording format. An early advantage of video tape recorders was the ability to record off-the-air for playback at a later time in order to accommodate time zone differences. For example, network evening news programs are generally heard at 6 or 6:30 P.M. local time, whether they are viewed in New York or in San Francisco. This is accomplished by the San Francisco station's recording the program at 3 P.M. Pacific Time and playing it back three hours later.

In recent years, disc recorders have been developed that have made possible slow-motion and stop-action playback, frame-by-frame editing, and special effects. Video recorders have therefore become powerful production tools, which can create animation, change color with the twist of a knob, or provide slowdown, speedup, dissolves, multiple images, and other special effects.

Contact printing of video tapes is now possible. Many organizations are working to develop machines that will provide inexpensive and rapid duplication of magnetic tapes. Such duplication will remove a serious economic disadvantage of tape with respect to film, for which contact printing has been used for many years. See also TELEVISION—*Development of Television Equipment* (Television Recording).

HISTORY OF TAPE RECORDING

The first experiments in magnetic recording were performed in the latter part of the 19th century. A patent describing a method of recording and reproducing sounds or signals on magnetic wire was granted to Valdemar Poulsen by the U. S. Patent Office on Nov. 13, 1900.

Although this established a technical basis for magnetic recording, many advances in both materials and electronics were required before magnetic recording could become practical. The first widespread application occurred during World War II when speeches by Hitler and other prominent Nazi leaders were broadcast at times and places calculated to confuse Allied intelligence. When news of this device reached the United States, the Ampex Corporation in California undertook the development of an audio recorder patterned after the German machine. The first recorder was delivered to the American Broadcasting Company in April 1948 and was used for the delayed broadcast of the Bing Crosby Show.

With the realization that scientific data could be recorded on tape, an audio machine was modified and delivered to the U. S. government in 1950. That same year saw the delivery of the first digital tape transport and the demonstration of the Univac Uniservo I.

In 1956, IBM announced a computer disk file, the RAMAC 350, with rapid access to digital data, and the Ampex Corporation demonstrated the VR-1000 Video Tape Recorder/Reproducer. A lower-cost, nonbroadcast quality video recorder using the helical scan principle was announced by Toshiba in 1959. Cartridges for automobile tape music players were introduced in the early 1960's, and the cassette recorder was introduced by Philips, of Eindhoven, Netherlands, in 1963.

VICTOR E. RAGOSINE
Ampex Corporation

Further Reading: Athey, S. W., *Magnetic Tape Recording* (Washington 1966); Mee, C. D., *The Physics of Magnetic Recording* (New York 1964).

TAPE RECORDING, Thermoplastic. See THERMOPLASTIC RECORDING.

FRENCH EMBASSY PRESS AND INFORMATION DIVISION

Modern French tapestry, *Mandoline*, by the French artist Jean Lurçat, was made in 1955.

TAPESTRY, tap′ə-strē, is a handwoven patterned fabric. The weft consists of numbers of different colored threads, each interlaced with the warp, not across the whole width of the fabric but only in the areas where its particular color is required. The weaver, passing a weft thread forward and backward (right to left and back) through part of the warp, shapes one area of color at a time until eventually, when the whole warp is entirely covered, the fabric and its pattern are complete.

Tapestry weaving is basically a simple, even primitive, technique, which has been practiced since early antiquity. Through the skill and artistry of the weaver, great beauty and refinement can be achieved. The most spectacular examples of tapestry are large pictorial wall hangings, but it has been used for many other purposes, including covers, cushions, and upholstery for furniture, carpets, and articles of dress.

Although the term "tapestry" is often applied to needlework, machine-woven textiles, or other fabrics resembling true tapestry or used for similar purposes, this article is concerned only with tapestry as defined above.

TECHNIQUE

Materials. Tapestry may be woven from any textile fiber. Warp threads, which are hardly seen in the finished fabric, must be strong. Weft threads must be easy to dye. The fiber most extensively used for both warp and weft is wool, which produces a robust, hard-wearing fabric and takes color well. For subtler or more luxurious effects, woolen tapestries sometimes include details woven with weft threads of silk, or even of gold or silver. Very fine and delicate tapestries have been woven entirely in silk, which is fairly easy to dye. Vegetable fibers, such as cotton, linen, and hemp, are more difficult to dye and are chiefly used for the warp.

The art of the dyer, who dyes the threads before weaving, is essential to tapestry. French 18th and 19th century tapestry, which sought to emulate all the coloristic effects of painting, used threads in thousands of different shades. But tapestries in periods and places that cultivated the bolder effects more congenial to the medium were in a limited range of fine colors with maximum resistance to fading.

Weaving. Tapestry weaving depends largely on the hand and eye of the weaver, not on any mechanical device. Hence tapestries have been produced on primitive looms in various parts of the world. To this day they are woven on quite simple versions of the prehistoric vertical loom (high-warp weaving) and horizontal loom (low-warp weaving). In both, the warp is held in ten-

PERUVIAN TAPESTRY of pre-Columbian era, made of cotton and wool, has stylized religious motifs.

AMERICAN MUSEUM OF NATURAL HISTORY

ROYAL NORWEGIAN EMBASSY

NORWEGIAN TAPESTRY (detail), of about 1800, depicts ***The Five Wise and the Five Foolish Virgins.***

sion between two beams or rollers. In weaving, the odd-numbered warp threads must be raised above the even-numbered threads, and vice versa, so that each time a weft thread can be passed between them. These openings of the warp are effected by systems of rods and cords, which in high-warp weaving are operated by hand and in low-warp weaving generally by foot treadles. The weaver passes bobbins wound with different colored weft threads forward and backward through the openings in the warp to weave the separate patches of color that eventually make up the pattern.

When there is a straight vertical junction between two patches of different colors—that is, one parallel to the warp threads—a slit occurs in the tapestry because adjacent warp threads are not bound together. A slit can be avoided if the junction is made slightly serrated instead of straight. Otherwise, the slit can be sewn up after weaving. But small slits are often left open, especially in pictorial tapestries, since a series of them, little bigger than pinholes, is a particularly effective means of rendering facial features and other fine details.

To protect the front of the fabric from accidental damage, the weaver works from the back. In high-warp weaving he can inspect the front of his work either directly or through a mirror, but in low-warp weaving he could not do so until swinging looms were introduced in 18th century France.

Pictorial Tapestries. Where geometric and other nonpictorial tapestries are woven by one individual, large pictorial tapestries generally require a team of weavers. Those who specialize in faces are the most skillful and highly paid. Although weavers may reproduce simple traditional patterns without referring to a visible design, for more elaborate pictorial work they require a full-size cartoon prepared by a professional designer. The outlines of the cartoon are traced upon the warp and the cartoon itself is then hung behind the high-warp weaver or placed under the warp of the low-warp weaver. In low-warp weaving the composition will appear in reverse on the front of the tapestry, and the designer must take this into account.

Large pictorial tapestries are accommodated on looms of reasonable width by being woven on their sides. Lines that will be vertical in the finished composition are actually woven as horizontal lines. The warp, vertical while weaving, will run horizontally in the completed tapestry.

Although the distinction between high-warp and low-warp weaving is extremely important in the tapestry workshop, it has very little effect on the finished product. It is often difficult or impossible to decide by which of the two methods a particular tapestry has been woven.

NONEUROPEAN TAPESTRY

Ancient World. Tapestry probably was woven for some thousands of years over a wide area of the Middle East, but knowledge of its early history is based chiefly on finds from the dry soil of Egypt. Various cloths and articles of dress from the tombs of Thutmose IV and Tutankhamen (15th–14th century B. C.) have patterns of hieroglyphs, lotus flowers, and other ornament woven in linen thread of various colors. Bands of woolen tapestry of about the 4th century B. C. found at Pazyryk in central Asia show human figures and lions in a Persian style. They suggest that some of the decorated costumes and textiles represented in Assyrian and Persian reliefs probably were based on tapestry-woven originals.

A duck-patterned fragment of woolen tapestry of about the same period, found in the Crimea, may be of Greek or Middle Eastern origin. Greek vase painting, Greek and Latin literature, and other sources provide abundant evidence for the use of hangings and other patterned textiles in classical times. Although the technique is rarely defined, it is reasonably certain that many of them must have been of tapestry.

From the 3d century A. D., remains of tapestry have been found in great abundance in Coptic graves in Egypt and in smaller numbers at various Middle Eastern and central Asian sites. They are chiefly of wool but also sometimes of silk and gold thread. Most are ornamental bands and panels from articles of dress, but there are also some large-scale pictorial hangings, such as one depicting Nereids and another showing the Virgin and Child with saints. From the 4th century, fine silk tapestry hangings and church vestments were produced in Byzantium.

In many of the earlier examples of Coptic, Middle Eastern, central Asian, and Byzantine work the dominant style is that of Hellenistic naturalism, whereas later pieces show increasing Oriental stylization. The shift reflects the decline of Roman political power and religion and the rise of the Byzantine and Sassanian Persian states concomitantly with Christianity and Oriental religions.

Islamic World. The Arab forces of Islam, which about 640 A. D. overran the whole of the Sassanian and much of the Byzantine empires, including Egypt, had few artistic traditions of their own. Generally they adopted those they found in the conquered areas. Thus the early Islamic tapestries found in Egypt, chiefly decorative panels from costumes, are virtually indistinguishable in style from earlier pieces. Gradually, however, Oriental stylization became more pronounced, and animal designs inherited from the Sassanian period in Persia gradually replaced human figures.

In the later Middle Ages, as increasing wealth brought greater material luxury, tapestries were generally woven in silk rather than wool. Patterns, on the other hand, were affected by puritanical movements in Islamic thought. Animal forms were excluded in favor of religious inscriptions, interlacing, and geometrical and stylized plant ornaments (arabesques). Besides the Egyptian finds, a number of tapestries of silk and gold (gilt metal strip wound on silk) woven in Islamic Spain and Morocco show a similar evolution. They range from the 10th century veil of Hisham II to large military banners of the later Middle Ages.

In the postmedieval period, Islamic tapestry was chiefly rugs. Fine examples in silk and gold thread were woven in Persia during the 16th and 17th centuries. Less ambitious pieces, often called *kilim* rugs, woven in wool, continue to be produced in many parts of the Islamic world and in areas of eastern Europe that were formerly under Turkish rule.

Far East. There is no very early evidence of tapestry in the silk-weaving areas of the Far East, and it may well be that the technique was introduced from the wool-weaving areas of central and western Asia at a comparatively late date. Nevertheless, examples found in central Asia and Japan indicate that by the T'ang period (618–906 A. D.) the weaving of silk tapestry, called *k'o-ssu,* often with gold thread (gilt paper), was well established. A number of Chinese tapestry panels with delicately naturalistic pictorial and floral subjects are thought, because of their analogies with paintings, to have been woven during the Sung and Yüan periods (960–1368). Larger pieces with similar subjects in bolder styles are assigned to the Ming period (1368–1644).

Most surviving examples of Chinese tapestry were produced under the Ch'ing dynasty (1644–1911). They comprise formal robes woven with dragons and other symbols indicating rank, informal robes with elegant designs of flowers, birds, and butterflies, and various types of hangings and pictures. The weaving is often very fine, but in examples of the 18th and 19th centuries many small details are added in paint. Similar work, often of more robust quality, was done in Japan.

Pre-Columbian America. Numerous examples of tapestry, chiefly articles of dress, have been found in the early burial grounds of Peru. It is probable that the technique was practiced there for at least 1,500 years before the arrival of the Spanish in the 16th century. The tapestries, generally with woolen weft and cotton warp, show stylized human figures or deities, animals, birds, and geometrical ornaments.

From the 16th century, Peruvian tapestry weavers found a new market among the Spanish settlers, for whom they produced hangings and covers in European Renaissance or Chinese styles. Tapestry-woven garments and articles produced by the Indians of Latin America in later times may be surviving traces of a widespread pre-Columbian tradition.

EUROPEAN TAPESTRY

Romanesque. Representations of patterned hangings in the Ravenna mosaics and elsewhere, together with many references to wall hangings in northern Europe from the Merovingian period and later, suggest that tapestries were perhaps not unfamiliar to Europeans during the Dark Ages that followed the decline of Rome. By the Romanesque period (about 1050 to 1150), western Europe was certainly acquainted with the silk tapestries of Byzantium and the Islamic world. A fine Byzantine hanging was recovered from an 11th century tomb at Bamberg Cathedral. Smaller Islamic silk-and-gold pieces were found in France and northern Spain. Similar silk-and-gold tapestries, probably woven in Palermo, formed part of the coronation mantle of the Norman kings of Sicily. No doubt the Crusades and the growing volume of East-West trade made such things increasingly familiar.

Excluding the Bayeux tapestry, which was embroidered, the earliest wool tapestries found in western Europe date from about the 12th to the 13th century. They include a hanging found in Cologne with a pattern of beasts in circles imitated from a Byzantine silk textile, pictorial hangings at Halberstadt Cathedral with Scriptural and philosophical subjects, and a hanging in Oslo with representations of the months. It is likely that all were woven in western Europe, probably in Germany or Norway.

Gothic. In both the Romanesque and Gothic periods, tapestries gave warmth and color to

MODERN ENGLISH TAPESTRY by Graham Sutherland hangs behind the altar of Coventry Cathedral.

THOMPSON, COVENTRY, FROM ART REFERENCE BUREAU

stark stone medieval interiors. They were also an easily movable form of furnishing in a society whose members traveled continually from one residence to another.

Paris. The Book of Trades, a collection of guild regulations dating from about 1263, indicates the existence of professional tapestry weavers in Paris in that period. The earliest surviving product of the Paris workshops is also one of the best known and best documented in the whole history of tapestry—the great set of hangings known as the *Apocalypse of Angers* (Musée des Tapisseries, Angers). It consisted originally of 6 or 7 huge pieces, each displaying 14 scenes from the Apocalypse in 2 tiers of 7 compartments. The set was designed by the Flemish painter Jean Bondolf between 1375 and 1379 and executed by the Paris contractor Nicolas Bataille, to the order of Louis II, Duke of Anjou.

Numerous other tapestries supplied to the court by Bataille and his competitors Jacques Dourdin and Pierre de Beaumetz are known only from documentary references, but two other works of the same period have survived—a fragmentary set of *Nine Heroes* (The Cloisters, New York) and the *Presentation of Christ in the Temple* (Musée du Cinquantenaire, Brussels).

All these tapestries reflect the charming style, combining refinement with simplicity, that characterized Franco-Flemish painting and book illumination in the late 14th century. Their tiered compositions and their backgrounds powdered with initials or flowers are derived from the same source. Tapestry weaving in Paris ended abruptly with the crushing defeat of the French at Agincourt in 1415 and the ensuing English occupation of northern France.

Arras. The lavish patronage of the dukes of Burgundy in the late 14th and early 15th centuries brought Arras such success and reputation as a center of tapestry weaving that the name became a synonym for tapestry. Besides the *Story of St. Piat and St. Eleuthère* (Tournai Cathedral), which is known to have been woven in Arras in 1402, other tapestries attributed to Arras include the late 14th century hanging the *Romance of Jourdain de Blaye* (Museo Civico, Padua) and, from the early 15th century, several hangings with courtly and religious subjects in the international Gothic style and four large tapestries with hunting scenes. All these works are notable for the elegance of their figures and their large decorative compositions, in which the various groups are disposed, without perspective, in green landscapes full of flowers. Production in Arras virtually came to an end when the town was sacked by the French in 1477.

Tournai. Tournai was already weaving tapestries in the late 14th century, but its great period began in the mid-15th century under the patronage of the dukes of Burgundy. Two hangings of the *Story of Alexander* (Palazzo Doria, Rome) and two fragments of the *Knight of the Swan* correspond to tapestries known to have been delivered to Duke Philip the Good by Pasquier Grenier of Tournai in 1459 and 1462. Various tapestries of the *Story of Troy* correspond to a set of 11 large hangings made for Duke Charles the Bold by the Grenier workshop in 1472 and repeated for Henry VII of England in 1486, for Charles VIII of France about 1490, and for other clients.

The figure style of these Tournai productions is comparable to that of contemporary Flemish painters such as Rogier van der Weyden and Dirk Bouts. The compositions, however, packed from top to bottom with figures and with rich ornamental detail, show that the designers continued to regard tapestries primarily as wall decoration. They deliberately avoided the perspective illusionism favored by the painters, which, enlarged to a scale suitable for a wall, must inevitably compromise the wall's visual unity and solidity. Many other tapestries with scenes of sacred and profane history, and of courtly and peasant life, are attributed to the workshops of Tournai. In the 16th century, as the town suffered heavily from plague, siege, and religious persecution, its production of tapestries became insignificant.

Brussels. Another tapestry weaving center patronized by the house of Burgundy in the late 14th and early 15th centuries was Brussels. Its earliest known product is a heraldic tapestry of the *millefleur* type, one of a set supplied to Philip the Good by Jean de Haze of Brussels in 1466.

From the late 15th century, the Brussels weavers, particularly Pieter van Aelst, enjoyed the patronage of the Habsburgs, heirs of the dukes of Burgundy. The only fully documented example of Brussels weaving in this period is the *Justice of Archambault* (1513; Musée du Cinquantenaire), designed by Jan van Roome. Others were almost certainly made in Brussels—for example, the set of *Notre Dame du Sablon* (1518; Musée du Cinquantenaire), probably designed by Bernard van Orley.

By analogy with these pieces, many tapestries are attributed to Brussels. They frequently have erudite theological or allegorical subjects. The compositions remain densely packed with figures, but the latter are more elegant than those of Tournai. The human types are gentle and reflective, influenced by the style of such painters as Gerard David and Quentin Massys. The decorative details of the costumes, jewelry, and other features of the designs are more elaborate than ever before, and for the first time many of the tapestries are framed in floral borders. The weaving is of outstanding skill and regularity, and in the finest examples there is lavish use of silk, silver, and gold.

During the late 15th and early 16th centuries numerous tapestries were woven for French clients. They include church hangings with sacred stories, as well as secular hangings with court, hunting, or pastoral scenes—for example, the set depicting the *Hunt of the Unicorn* (The Cloisters, New York). Some of them belong to a particularly charming class of tapestry showing small groups or single figures against *millefleur* backgrounds, as in the famous set of the *Lady with the Unicorn* (Musée de Cluny, Paris). Although these tapestries often seem to exhibit characteristically French styles, different from those of Tournai and Brussels, there is little documentary evidence of French tapestry weaving in this period. Hence it remains uncertain whether they were produced in unknown French workshops or in Tournai, Brussels, and other Flemish centers for the French market.

Other Centers. Most countries of western Europe obtained their tapestries from Flanders. Henry VIII of England owned some 2,000 Flemish hangings, and rulers of Spain, Portugal, and Italy also had Flemish collections. Some countries also imported Flemish tapestry weavers from

TAPESTRY

Top row: St. Paul receives the Veil from Plantilla **(Franco-Flemish, 15th century);** ***Martyrdom of St. Paul*** **(Franco-Flemish, c. 1460);** ***Winter*** **(French, 1781), Gobelin.** ***Left:*** **Fragment, Trojan War series (Flemish, c. 1475).** ***Right: Adoration of the Magi*** **(French, 1480).** ***Bottom row, left and right:*** **Third and seventh panels of** ***Victory Tapestry*** **depicting Battle of Britain (British, 1941–1946) by Janet Barrow.**

Courtesy (1) National Gallery of Art, Washington, D.C.; (2–5) Museum of Fine Arts, Boston; (6, 7) British Information Services

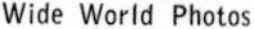

Wide World Photos

The Start of the Hunt, first in the series of Unicorn Tapestries at The Cloisters, The Museum of Medieval Art of The Metropolitan Museum of Art.

The Metropolitan Museum of Art

Detail of a 16th century German tapestry, showing the Virgin and Child.

Wide World Photos

The Earth, a French contemporary tapestry, by Marcel Gromaire.

time to time. A set of Passion tapestries of about 1400 in San Marco, Venice, was evidently woven by northern craftsmen after Italian designs. In the mid-15th century Flemish weavers were active in Ferrara and Mantua.

Germany and Switzerland from the 14th to the 16th century possessed many tapestry workshops—for example, at Basel, Nuremberg, and Strasbourg. However, they were never favored with the lavish support that enabled the Flemish weavers to work not only on a vast scale but also with the utmost refinement of technique. German and Swiss tapestries, produced for local patrons, are small and unpretentious, but lively drawing and vivid color often give their religious and romantic subjects great decorative charm.

Renaissance. Tapestries in the Renaissance manner were first produced in Italy—for example, a *Deposition* after Cosimo Tura, doubtless woven at Ferrara (Cleveland Museum of Art) and a set of *Months* (1503; Castello Sforzesco, Milan) woven at Vigevano after designs by Il Bramantino. The decisive irruption of the Renaissance style into the mainstream of tapestry tradition was the set of *Acts of the Apostles* (Vatican) designed by Raphael and woven for Pope Leo X between 1516 and 1519 in the Brussels workshop of Pieter van Aelst. Raphael's cartoons (Victoria and Albert Museum, London), the most famous and influential in the history of tapestry, are conceived in the manner of High Renaissance fresco painting. Monumental figures are dynamically grouped and interlinked by powerful psychological tensions within an extensive three-dimensional picture space. They make no concession to the long-standing tradition of tapestry as an ornamental wall surface but subjugate it to the painter's laws, breaking through the wall into an imaginary space beyond.

Raphael's designs were enormously admired and repeatedly rewoven throughout the 16th and 17th centuries. Several of his pupils, such as Giulio Romano and Giovanni da Udine, were also called upon to provide designs for the Brussels weavers. Flemish designers, too, were wholeheartedly converted to the Raphaelesque conception of tapestry. Among their outstanding designs in this vein are those of the *Hunts of Maximilian* (Louvre, Paris) and the *Battle of Pavia* (Museo di Capodimonte, Naples), both attributed to Bernard van Orley; the *Virtues* (Kunsthistorisches Museum, Vienna), attributed to Michiel Coxcie; the *Seven Deadly Sins* (Royal Palace, Madrid), attributed to Pieter Coecke; and the *Conquest of Tunis* and the *Story of Vertumnus and Pomona* (both Royal Palace, Madrid), attributed to Jan Vermeyen. These and other fine sets, often enriched with gold and silver, were woven about 1525–1550 by leading Brussels workshops, such as those of the Geubels and Pannemaker families, for the Emperor Charles V and other princes.

Splendid sets continued to be woven in Brussels during the second half of the 16th century—for example, the *Grotesque Months*, so called for its grotesques, a fanciful type of classical ornament popularized by Raphael and his school. The bitter political and religious struggles of this period, coupled with the fact that various foreign princes set up their own tapestry workshops manned by immigrant Flemish weavers, tended to reduce the demand for Brussels work of the highest quality. Nevertheless, the industry was sufficiently well organized and broadly based to adapt itself to changing conditions. Besides Brussels, it was established at Aalst (Alost), Antwerp, Ath, Bruges, Enghien, Gramont, Liège, Lille, Oudenarde, and Tournai. From 1528 the appropriate town mark was woven into each tapestry (for example, a red shield with BB for Brussels, Brabant), and individual workshops often added their own cipher. Many of these Flemish workshops catered to the growing international demand for tapestries of cheaper grades, especially verdures (with leafy designs) and landscapes. There were also Dutch workshops, such as that of the Spierincx family, which made fine tapestries in Delft.

In Italy a group of Flemish weavers set up workshops for the ducal families of Ferrara, Mantua, and Florence in the 1530's and 1540's. The Ferrara and Mantua workshops, which wove tapestries after Giulio Romano, Giovanni da Udine, and others, were short-lived. The Medici workshop, which wove grotesques after Il Bacchiacca and figure-scenes after Florentine Mannerist painters such as Jacopo da Pontormo, Francesco Salviati, and Il Bronzino, continued until the 18th century.

The most important French workshop was an ephemeral royal enterprise of the 1540's at Fontainebleau, which produced one very handsome set after Italian designs. Flemish weavers were also active in Germany and in short-lived workshops set up by the kings of Denmark and Sweden in the later 16th century. A workshop organized by an English country gentleman, William Sheldon, wove tapestries of a somewhat rustic character in the late 16th and early 17th centuries. Work of similar quality was produced in Norway.

17th Century. Despite mounting competition from foreign enterprises, the flourishing family workshops of Brussels, Oudenarde, and other Flemish centers still retained a major share of the European market, including such clients as the Habsburgs and other wealthy princes. Besides inherited skills, Flemish assets included new designs by Rubens for such sets as the *Story of Decius Mus*, the *Triumph of the Eucharist*, and the *Story of Achilles*. The exuberant baroque style of these designs, with bulky figures engaged in actions so vigorous that they seem about to burst out of the hangings, was very influential. The painter Jacob Jordaens produced designs in a similar, though quieter, vein for sets of *Country Life*, *Proverbs*, the *Riding School*, and several more.

In 17th century France there was a sustained and highly successful effort to develop the tapestry weaving industry. In 1601, Henry IV prohibited imports of foreign tapestry. In 1607 he gave extensive privileges to the workshop set up in Paris at the Gobelins dyeworks by the Flemish weavers Marc de Comans and François de La Planche, and in 1608 he established another workshop in the Louvre. These workshops wove tapestries of excellent quality. A set of designs for the *Story of Constantine* (Philadelphia Museum of Art) was commissioned from Rubens in 1622, and good designs were produced later by Simon Vouet and Philippe de Champaigne.

In 1662 the Paris workshops and others were combined to form the royal factory of the Gobelins (see GOBELINS). It then embarked on a period of intense activity under Charles Le Brun, whose admirable designs were widely admired and imitated. In 1664 another royal workshop was set up at Beauvais, which, among other work, wove many repetitions of an immensely successful set of *Grotesques*, designed by Jean Bérain about 1689. Various independent workshops at Aubusson were active throughout the century producing tapestries of cheaper grades, including both verdures and scenes with figures.

Between 1604 and 1615 a workshop of Flemish weavers established by the Duke of Bavaria at Munich produced some fine sets after designs by Pieter Candid. At the end of the 17th century several small workshops in Germany and Switzerland were manned by Protestant weavers from Aubusson, who left France as a consequence of the revocation of the Edict of Nantes in 1685. The Medici workshop remained active in Florence, and the Barberini workshop, established in Rome in 1635, wove designs by Pietro da Cortona and Romanelli. In England, James I in 1619 set up the Mortlake factory, where some fine sets were woven, including repetitions of Raphael's *Acts of the Apostles*. Production slackened during the Civil War and ended later in the century.

18th Century. During the 18th century, as European taste moved toward lighter, more delicate rococo and neoclassical styles of decoration, tapestries gradually lost favor. Nevertheless, some work of high quality was produced.

Brussels continued its tradition of excellence in the early years of the century. Most Flemish workshops, however, concentrated on cheaper landscape tapestries with small figures in the manner of David Teniers the Younger.

The French industry was better able to defend itself against changing fashion thanks to royal patronage, good organization, and excellent designers. Many fine sets were produced at the Gobelins factory. Beauvais likewise remained active, weaving, for example, six different sets designed by J. B. Oudry and six more by François Boucher. Some of these sets, such as Boucher's *Story of Psyche* and *Noble Pastoral*, with their graceful figures and delicate coloring, are among the most attractive of rococo tapestry designs and were repeatedly copied. Tapestry with designs of similar type, but of cheaper quality, were woven in great numbers at Aubusson and Felletin. Besides hangings, all these centers wove chair covers and other small pieces.

English 18th century tapestry woven in London included chinoiserie hangings from the workshop of John Vanderbank and hangings with floral ornament from that of Joshua Morris. Workshops were set up or encouraged by various princes at Berlin, Dresden, Erlangen, Munich, Schwabach, Würzburg, Copenhagen, Stockholm, St. Petersburg, Warsaw, Naples, Rome, Turin, Madrid, and Tavira. Most followed French styles, but the Madrid factory wove a fine series from designs by Goya.

19th and 20th Centuries. During the 19th century the art of tapestry was at a low point. Some of the state workshops, such as the Gobelins, Beauvais, and that of Madrid, continued to operate, as did a few independent workshops in Aubusson, and elsewhere. The main private demand was for reproductions or pastiches of 18th century hangings and chair covers. The few new works, commissioned generally for public buildings, aimed at exact reproduction of academic paintings.

In significant reaction against this worn-out style were the tapestries woven from 1881 by the workshop of William Morris in England. The designs, by Morris, Sir Edward Burne-Jones, and others, inspired by late medieval work, reject the illusion of perspective space in favor of strongly patterned surfaces. This characteristic was still more apparent in tapestries woven at Scherrebek in Germany from 1896 with designs in a genuine modern style—that of art nouveau.

These late-19th century productions foreshadowed a renaissance of tapestry in the 20th century. The immense development of mass production and the use of synthetic fabrics have led to a recognition of the value of handcraftsmanship in natural materials. Meanwhile, modern painting has rejected the pictorial illusionism that reigned from the Renaissance and has adopted idioms of abstraction and surface-pattern, which are readily translated into tapestry. In addition, modern architecture, like medieval architecture, produces buildings in stark, hard styles in which the color and softness of wall hangings are welcome. Coventry Cathedral in England was actually designed to receive the gigantic tapestry of *Christ in Majesty,* after Graham Sutherland.

The new creativity in tapestry has taken two forms of production. One, characteristic of the 20th century, as of primitive cultures, is that of the artist-weaver, who both designs and weaves the tapestry, so that the processes of design and execution are not dissociated but interact continuously upon one another. Work of this kind generally must be small in scale. The other form is that of the traditional European workshop, in which a design is first produced by a professional artist and then woven by groups of professional weavers. Both forms now flourish in many parts of the world, and a wide selection of the resulting tapestries has been exhibited at the Biennales Internationales de la Tapisserie held at Lausanne from 1962.

In regard to tapestries made by workshops, France enjoys the immense advantage of having preserved traditional skills and organization, as was strikingly demonstrated by the great exhibition of French tapestry that toured the world from 1946. The state factories of the Gobelins and Beauvais still function, now side by side in Paris, and a number of independent workshops flourish at Aubusson and Felletin. Since the 1930's the most influential French designer has been Jean Lurçat, who, like Morris, was strongly influenced by medieval work. In later years, artists such as Marcel Gromaire and Marc Saint-Saëns have produced designs in a variety of modern styles. Tapestry, which appeared moribund in the 19th century, appears in the late 20th century to have much to offer the future.

DONALD KING
Victoria and Albert Museum, London
MONIQUE KING
Musées Nationaux, Paris

Bibliography

Ackerman, Phyllis, *Tapestry the Mirror of Civilization* (New York 1933).
Cavallo, Adolph S., *Tapestries . . . in the Museum of Fine Arts, Boston* (Boston 1967).
Hunter, George Leland, *The Practical Book of Tapestries* (Philadelphia 1925).
Jarry, Madeleine, *World Tapestry* (New York 1969).
Thomson, William George, *A History of Tapestry* (London 1930).
Thomson, William George, *Tapestry Weaving in England* (London 1914).
Verlet, Pierre, and others, *Great Tapestries* (Lausanne 1965).
Weigert, Roger Armand, *French Tapestry* (London 1962).

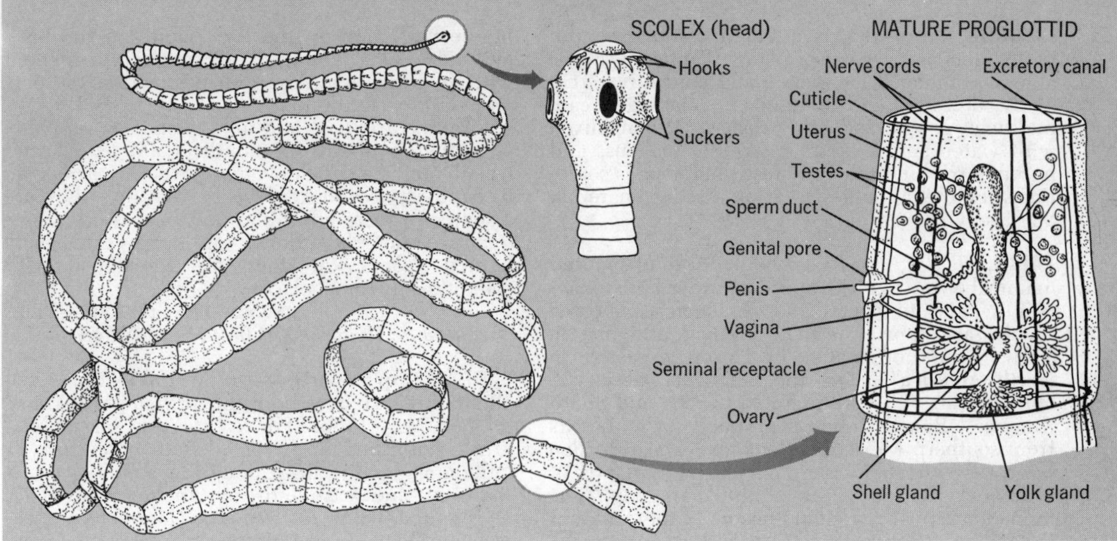

TAPEWORM, any of a large class of parasitic flatworms that infest man and other animals. Although they are often large in size, they produce surprisingly little physical disturbance in the infected individual. They may cause anemia, but contrary to popular belief, they do not cause increased appetite or weight loss.

Tapeworms make up the class Cestoda of the phylum Platyhelminthes (flatworms). The most common large worm that infects man is the beef tapeworm (*Taenia saginata*), which is found in all parts of the world. The two other large species that infect man—the pork tapeworm (*T. solium*) and the fish tapeworm (*Diphyllobothrium latum*)—are slightly more limited in their geographic distribution. The pork tapeworm is found in Central and South America, Africa, and Asia. The fish tapeworm is found in Europe, central Africa, and parts of North America, Asia, and South America. The dwarf tapeworm (*Hymenolepis nana*), about 2 inches (50 mm) long, is found in all temperate and tropical regions. Unlike other species it can be transmitted directly from one person to another. Other tapeworms require at least one intermediate host.

Beef Tapeworm. The adult beef tapeworm usually ranges in length from 10 to 15 feet (3–4.5 meters). Like all other tapeworms it consists of a head, or *scolex*, and a chain of segments, or *proglottids*, each of which is actually a separate individual with both male and female reproductive organs.

The scolex, the smallest part of the tapeworm, is a tubular structure about 1 inch (25 mm) long and .04 to .08 inch (1–2 mm) in diameter. When viewed under a microscope or magnifying lens it is seen to have four muscular suckers by which it holds onto the lining of the host's intestine. The proglottids are produced one after another at the hind end of the scolex. As they move further away from the scolex they grow and mature. By the time the proglottids reach the end of the worm they are about ¾ of an inch (19 mm) long, and inside each one the uterus is full of fertilized eggs. When fully mature, the end proglottids break off and pass out of the host's body. If deposited on the ground they move about and in so doing cause the uterus to rupture. The hundreds of eggs are then squeezed out onto the ground where they may be eaten by cattle.

If an egg is eaten by a cow or steer, the embryo inside the egg is freed when it gets to the host's stomach. It then travels to a muscle where it forms a cyst. Each cyst contains a scolex, and the person who eats uncooked beef containing a cyst then becomes infected. When the scolex reaches the intestine it attaches itself and within two or three months becomes an entire tapeworm that may live for 10 years or more. A diagnosis of beef tapeworm infestation is confirmed by identifying the proglottids in the person's stool.

Pork Tapeworm. The pork tapeworm has a life cycle similar to that of the beef tapeworm except that the intermediate host is a pig. It closely resembles the beef tapeworm except that the scolex has a circle of tiny hooks in addition to the four suckers. An important feature of this tapeworm is that the cyst stage may occur in humans as well as pigs. When cysts form in a person's muscle tissue they cause little trouble but when they form in the eye or brain they may cause serious damage, and the person may die. The diagnosis of pork tapeworm infestation is made by examining the person's stool.

Fish Tapeworm. This species, which may reach a length of 30 feet (9 meters), is acquired by eating raw freshwater fish, such as pike. The scolex is olive-shaped and has no hooks or suckers. The proglottids are very small and do not break off individually. Each one produces scores of eggs every day, and they are discharged into the intestine in large numbers. The life cycle of the fish tapeworm requires two intermediate hosts: a tiny crustacean (copepod) and a fish. A frequent complication of fish tapeworm infestation is pernicious anemia, caused by the worm's absorbing the vitamin B_{12} eaten by the person.

Treatment of Tapeworm Infestation. The most effective and least toxic remedy is niclosamide (Yomesan). Other effective remedies include extracts of the male fern (*Dryopteris filix-mas*) and the synthetic drug quinacrine (Atabrine).

HOWARD B. SHOOKHOFF, M. D.
Columbia University College of Physicians and Surgeons

TAPIOCA, tap-ē-ō′kə, is a starch made from the fleshy roots of the cassava plant. Tapioca is available in granular, flake, pellet, and flour form. It is easily digested and is used in making bread, puddings, soups, and other dishes. When mixed with water and heated, it swells, thickens, and becomes translucent. In industry, tapioca is sometimes used as an adhesive or as a sizing material. See also CASSAVA.

TAPIR, tā′pər, a heavy-bodied, long-snouted mammal of the family Tapiridae, order Perissodactyla, related to horses and rhinoceroses. Three species are known in the Americas and one in Asia. Tapirs originated in Europe, existed in North America during the Oligocene about 35 million years ago, and migrated to Asia and South America. Baird's tapir (*Tapirus bairdi*) occurs from southern Mexico to Ecuador. The Brazilian tapir (*T. terrestris*) is found in the lowlands of Colombia, Venezuela, Brazil, and Paraguay. The mountain tapir (*T. roulini*) occurs in the Andes of Colombia, northern Peru, and western Venezuela. And the Malayan tapir (*T. indicus*) is native to Burma, Thailand, Vietnam, Malaysia, and Sumatra.

The tapir has a massive body supported by short legs, a stump of tail, and small eyes set in a thick skull. It is rather sparsely haired, except for the mountain tapir, which is sometimes called the *woolly tapir*. Its snout and upper lip are formed into a short trunk, shorter in the Asiatic species, which it uses to browse the vegetation that grows on the riverbanks and in shallow water. The tapir is nocturnal and lives in dense forests, where it tunnels a path that invariably leads to a stream or lake. It has poor sight but good hearing.

Tapirs attain 6 to 8 feet (1.8–2.5 meters) in length, plus a short tail 2 to 4 inches (5–10 cm) long, and stand 29 to 40½ inches (0.7–1 meter) at the shoulder. They weigh from 500 to 650 pounds (225–300 kg). The American species are reddish brown to black above and lighter below. The Malayan tapir is black on the front half of the body and on the legs, white on the back and sides. The young of all species are marked with yellowish lengthwise stripes or rows of spots on a dark background.

Tapirs are shy and live alone or in pairs. Gestation is about 13 months (400 days), and usually only a single young is born. Life-span in captivity is about 30 years. Because they are a source of meat and hides and because they frequently raid plantations, tapirs are extensively hunted. Tapirs, in fact, are threatened with extinction in some places.

FERNANDO DIAS DE AVILA-PIRES
Museu de Historia Natural, Minas Gerais, Brazil

BAIRD'S TAPIR (*Tapirus bairdi*) (*top*) from Central and South America. Malayan tapir (*T. indicus*) (*below*).

A. W. AMBLER, FROM NATIONAL AUDUBON SOCIETY

BUCKY REEVES, FROM NATIONAL AUDUBON SOCIETY

TAPPAN, tap′ən, **Arthur** (1786–1865), American abolitionist. He was born in Northampton, Mass., on May 22, 1786. His New York silk-jobbing firm, established in 1816, grossed more than $1 million a year in sales through an innovative low mark-up and cash-and-carry policy. In 1827, he founded the *N. Y. Journal of Commerce*, an experiment to combine religious and economic news. He supported civic efforts to suppress prostitution, and devoted funds to help found Lane Seminary and Oberlin College. In 1833 he became a cofounder, chief financial supporter, and first president (until 1840) of the American Anti-Slavery Society. He lost his fortune in speculative investments, and died in New Haven, Conn., on July 23, 1865.

BERTRAM WYATT-BROWN
Case Western Reserve University

TAPPAN, tap′ən, **Lewis** (1788–1873), American businessman and abolitionist. He was born in Northampton, Mass., on May 23, 1788. He became a Boston merchant, but business reverses forced him to relocate in New York City, where he joined his brother Arthur's silk firm. In 1833, Lewis helped to form the American Anti-Slavery Society, but he broke with the increasingly radical William Lloyd Garrison in 1840 and formed a rival abolitionist organization. In 1841 he founded the first national credit-rating agency, later Dun & Bradstreet. His greatest contributions were his antislavery publishing efforts, particularly the *National Era;* his unheralded labors to free the *Amistad* black mutineers (see AMISTAD CASE); and his founding in 1846 of the American Missionary Association. Tappan died in Brooklyn, N. Y., on June 21, 1873.

BERTRAM WYATT-BROWN, *Author, "Lewis Tappan and the Evangelical War Against Slavery"*

TAPPAN ZEE, tap′ən zē, in southeastern New York, is a broad portion of the Hudson River between Westchester county on the east bank and Rockland county on the west. It is about 6 miles (9 km) long and about 2½ miles (4 km) wide. The Tappan Zee Bridge crosses from Tarrytown to Nyack. "Tappan" means "cold spring" in Indian and "Zee" means "sea" in Dutch.

TAPTI RIVER, tap′tē, in peninsular India. Approximately 450 miles long, the Tapti rises near the eastern end of the Satpura Range in Madhya Pradesh. It flows in an often narrow trough between the Satpuras and the Deccan Lava Plateau, through the fertile cotton-growing Khandesh region of Maharashtra. After entering the narrow coastal plain in Gujarat, it empties into the Gulf of Cambay, an arm of the Arabian Sea. It is navigable only for the last 20 miles (30 km).

TAR, a dark brown to black substance formed from the destructive distillation of organic materials, such as wood, coal, and petroleum. Most tars are liquid or semiliquid and have a characteristic odor. Pitch is the residue remaining after the distillation of tars. Coal tar has the greatest economic importance.

Most coal tar is obtained as a by-product of the coking of coal for blast furnaces. The tar is separated by fractional distillation into fractions. The exact composition of these fractions varies, depending on the coal used and production conditions. More than 200 compounds have been separted from coal tar. These compounds are used in the manufacture of such diverse products as dyes, explosives, flavorings, disinfectants, and wood preservatives. Some coal tar is still used for waterproofing, as fuel for steel furnaces, and as road building and roofing material. See COAL TAR.

Wood tars are obtained both from hardwoods and from resinous woods, such as pine. Wood-tar creosote is obtained from the heavy oil fraction of hardwood tar. Pine oil is used in zinc and lead ore flotation, in industrial detergents, and as disinfectants.

OTTO W. NITZ
Stout State University, Menomonie, Wis.

TARA, tar'ə, a hill in County Meath, Ireland, 23 miles (37 km) northwest of Dublin, on which once stood the cultural and religious capital of ancient Ireland. Thomas Moore immortalized it in one of his best-known early 19th century *Irish Melodies,* "The harp that once through Tara's halls."

Archaeological excavations at Tara have revealed a "passage grave" dating from before 2000 B.C., when immigrants from the vicinity of Brittany settled there. However, the Gaelic Celts came to the country from Europe and Spain about the middle of the 4th century B.C., and in the pre-Christian era Tara became a place of great importance. It was then the scene of the great triennial assembly, or *feis.* Later it became the seat of kings who ruled the northern half of Ireland. But by the end of the 6th century A.D., Tara had lost its importance.

Earthworks, which appear as mounds on the low hill, may show the site of structures mentioned in a 12th century manuscript: King Cormac's house (3d century A.D.), the Banqueting Hall, the Fort of the Kings, and the Mound of the Hostages. A pillar stone at the site of Cormac's house is said to be the Lia Fáil, or Stone of Destiny, on which the kings of Ireland were traditionally crowned.

Amateurs have dug on Tara in the belief that they would find the Ark of the Covenant, which was last located in Solomon's temple.

THOMAS FITZGERALD
Department of Education, Dublin

TARABULUS. See TRIPOLI, Lebanon; TRIPOLI, Libya.

TARANTELLA, tar-ən-tel'ə, a swift, whirling Italian dance. It is executed by two people, either a man and woman or two women, to music in 6/8 time.

The dance is believed to have acquired its name from either the town of Taranto in southern Italy or from the tarantula, a kind of wolf spider that thrives in that region. The tarantella was at one time popularly thought to be a remedy against tarantism, a disease believed caused by the spider's bite, which, however, is relatively harmless.

TARANTO, tär'ən-tō, is an industrial city and port in southern Italy. It is the capital of Taranto province, in the region of Apulia. Called Tarentum by the Romans, it was one of the chief cities of southern Italy in ancient times.

Province and City. Much of Taranto province lies in the low-lying Apulian coastal plain, but the northeast is hilly. The province covers an area of 940 square miles (2,436 sq. km). Wheat, wine, olive oil, and fruit are the main crops.

The old city, or Città Vecchia, is on a small island, formerly a peninsula, that almost closes the waterway between a lagoon, the Mare Piccolo (Little Sea), and the Gulf of Taranto. The island is a congested area of narrow, picturesque streets. The "new town" to the east is modern and regularly laid out.

Little remains of the ancient city, but its medieval buildings are better represented. The small cathedral of San Cataldo, dedicated to an Irish saint who settled in Taranto in the 7th century, is basically of the 11th century but has been much overlaid by baroque ornament. At the southeastern angle of the island is the Byzantine fortress, rebuilt in the 15th century, that is the city's most considerable medieval monument. When the fortress was rebuilt, a canal was cut beside it to give it greater protection.

Taranto has long been an important Italian naval base and has shipbuilding and food-processing industries. In the early 1960's a large iron and steel works was established to the north of the old city. The

TARANTO, long an Italian naval base, became increasingly industrialized after World War II.

EDITORIAL PHOTOCOLOR ARCHIVES

History. As the colony of Taras, Taranto was founded by the Spartans at the end of the 8th century B. C. The island formed the fortress of the mainland to the east. Taras became one of the wealthiest and most prosperous cities in Magna Graecia—the Greek-occupied south of Italy. In the 3d century B. C., Taranto was threatened by the expanding power of Rome, and called in the aid of King Pyrrhus of Epirus. In the course of the war that followed the city was captured and was forced to ally itself with Rome after 272 B. C. The Greek tradition remained very strong in Taranto and was reinforced during the early Middle Ages, when Taranto was part of the Byzantine Empire.

The city survived the barbarian invasions of Italy, but it was completely destroyed by the Moors in 927 A. D. It remained a battleground between Muslims and Christians until it was eventually recaptured and rebuilt by the Byzantine emperors. In 1063 it fell into the hands of the Normans, who had invaded southern Italy in the 11th century. From the Normans it passed, along with southern Italy, to the Hohenstaufen emperors of Germany and, after their extinction, to the French dukes of Anjou. It was finally absorbed into the Kingdom of the Two Sicilies. In 1860 the city became part of the Italian state. In World War II a British aerial attack on Italian naval facilities inflicted severe damage on the city. Population: (1967) the city, 214,705; the province, 468,713.

NORMAN J. G. POUNDS
Indiana University

TARANTULA, tə-ranch′ə-lə, any of a family of dark, silky-haired, long-legged spiders. Most tarantulas live in semitropical and tropical regions, but some are occasionally found in cooler regions, having been carried there in shipments of produce. In the United States there are nearly 30 known species. Most of these species are found in the Southern and Southwestern regions of the country.

Characteristics. Tarantulas vary considerably in size. North American species usually range in body length from 1.2 to 2.75 inches (3–7 cm) and have a leg span of about 5 inches (13 cm). A large South American species found in the Amazon Basin has a body almost 3.5 inches (9 cm) long and a leg span of nearly 10 inches (25 cm).

Desert tarantula (*Aphonopelma*)

ROBERT H. WRIGHT, NATIONAL AUDUBON SOCIETY

Like other spiders, tarantulas are carnivorous. They catch the victim with their chelicerae, or jaws, inject it with venom, macerate the tissues, and suck up the liquids. Usually tarantulas prey on invertebrates, small snakes, lizards, toads, and mice. Some of the larger species, often called "bird spiders," prey on nestling birds.

All tarantulas have poison glands that empty through narrow ducts in the chelicerae. The venom is used for paralyzing prey, and it is relatively harmless to man. A tarantula, even when handled, will seldom bite a human being.

Life Cycle. Tarantulas mate several times a year, usually from August to October. The following summer the female constructs a silken cocoon in which it deposits 1,000 or more eggs. The eggs hatch about six weeks later, and the spiderlings leave the cocoon. During the next two years they molt, or shed their outer covering, four times each year. In the following three or four years they molt about twice a year. Appendages that are lost are regenerated between molts if there is an interval of at least 30 days between the loss of the appendage and the next molt.

The life-span of a tarantula is much longer than that of other spiders. Females, which are much longer-lived than males, are known to have lived 20 years. Tarantulas are capable of withstanding extremely unfavorable conditions. In laboratory tests females lived 2⅓ years without food. They lived 80 days without water in the summer, and when water was withheld at other times of the year, they survived as long as 7 months.

Classification. Tarantulas make up the family Theraphosidae of the suborder Orthognatha, order Araneida, class Arachnida. Close relatives often called tarantulas are the trap-door spiders (family Ctenizidae), the funnel-web mygalomorphs (family Dipluridae), and the purse-web spiders (family Atipidae).

RALPH H. DAVIDSON
Ohio State University

TARANTULA HAWK, tə-ranch′ə-lə, any of several large, long-legged, solitary wasps with a blue-black body and smoky blue to orange-red wings. Using its venomous stinger, the tarantula hawk paralyzes a tarantula or other spider and carries it back to a prepared nest where it lays an egg on the victim. The nest is sealed, and the tarantula hawk begins to prepare another nest. When the egg hatches, the young larvae feed on the paralyzed prey. *Pepsis formosa,* a tarantula hawk common in the southwestern United States, often is more than 2.75 inches (7 cm) long, including the leg span.

See also WASP.

RALPH H. DAVIDSON
Ohio State University

TARASCANS, tä-räs′kanz, an Indian group living in the State of Michoacán, Mexico. The name is also spelled Tarascos. The early history of Michoacán is imperfectly known and offers no clues as to the origins of the Tarascans. It was once customary to label all archaeological remains in western Mexico (Michoacán, Jalisco, Colima, and Nayarit) as "Tarascan," but this practice is now generally avoided.

According to tradition, the Tarascan nation came into being when the Chichimecs ("barbarians") of Zacapu, in north central Michoacán, conquered the peoples of the Lake Pátzcuaro area in the 12th to 14th centuries. A powerful Tarascan state was founded during the reign of Tariácuri (about 1400), and expanded by conquest until it comprised most of present-day Michoacán and the adjacent regions to the north, west, and south.

On their eastern frontier during the 15th century the Tarascans came in conflict with the expanding Aztec Empire. They were successful in repelling the invasions of this foe, but in 1522, unable to organize effective resistance against the far more formidable Spaniards, the Tarascan king, Tangaxoan Zincicha, gave up after a brief struggle. Disease and the effects of forced labor in the mines diminished the Tarascan population during the rest of the 16th century. Simultaneously the work of missionaries and the establishment of Spanish settlements began the process of acculturation.

As a result of Spanish acculturation, the area in which Tarascan is spoken has contracted steadily since about 1750. The Tarascan area now measures about 1,350 square miles (3,500 sq km), consisting mainly of the core region around Lake Pátzcuaro and the sierra to the west. Even within this area, mestizos speaking Spanish exclusively form nearly 25% of the population. The Tarascans are losing their identity as an ethnic group and are becoming a regional variant of the Mexican peasantry.

PEDRO ARMILLAS
State University of New York, Stony Brook

TARASCON, ta-ras-kôN′, is a French town in Bouches-du-Rhône department. It is on the east bank of the Rhône River, 14 miles (23 km) south of Avignon. The walls of Tarascon's 14th-15th century Castle of King René rise abruptly from the Rhône. They once guarded the river crossing to the twin fortress town of Beaucaire, where medieval merchants assembled for one of Europe's great trading fairs. The historic church of Ste. Marthe, the town's patron saint, was badly damaged in World War II.

Modern Tarascon is a market town. Completion in 1970 of the Vallabrègues power dam upstream created new opportunities for irrigation, flood control, and navigation. Tourism is of increasing importance in a town made widely known by Alphonse Daudet's novel *Tartarin de Tarascon,* which satirized the Provençal native. Population: (1962) 6,475.

T. H. ELKINS, *University of Sussex*

TARAWA, tä-rä-wä, is an atoll of the Gilbert Islands in the western Pacific. It has an area of 8 square miles (20 sq km) and is the capital and commercial center of Britain's Gilbert and Ellice Islands colony.

The urban area is divided into three parts: Betio, with commercial and trading facilities; Bairiki, 2 miles (3 km) along the reef, with administrative offices and the commissioner's residence; and Bikenibeu, connected by causeway to Bairiki, with facilities of the departments of education, health, and agriculture.

During World War II, Tarawa was occupied by the Japanese in 1941 and recaptured by the U.S. Marines after a bloody battle in 1943. Population: (1963) 4,772.

TARBELA DAM, tär-bā′lä, an earth-embankment dam under construction in West Pakistan on the upper reach of the Indus River, about 40 miles (65 km) northwest of Rawalpindi. Tarbela Dam will be the world's largest earth dam when completed in 1976. The dam will contain 159 million cubic yards (121.6 million cu meters) of earth. The present world's record of 125 million cubic yards (95.6 million cu meters) is held by Fort Peck Dam in Montana. Tarbela Dam will be 470 feet (143 meters) high and will have a crest 1.7 miles (2.7 km) long.

The reservoir created by the dam will have a capacity of 11 million acre feet (13.6 billion cubic meters), or roughly 3.5 trillion gallons (13.6 trillion liters). The hydroelectric installations ultimately will consist of 12 hydroelectric units of 175,000 kilowatts each, making a total capacity of 2.1 million kilowatts. Two spillways will be provided with a total discharge capacity of 1.5 million cubic feet per second (673.25 million gallons per minute, or 6.1 million liters per second).

T. W. MERMEL
Chairman, World Register of Dams

TARBELL, tar′bel, **Ida Minerva** (1857–1944), American editor and author. Her *History of the Standard Oil Company* (1904), which exposed ruthless competitive practices and misuse of natural resources, was a landmark in business history and reform. She was born in Erie county, Pa., on Nov. 5, 1857. Her father was an oil producer beset by resourceful oil-refiners, though she denied that this fact influenced her work. She joined *McClure's Magazine* in 1894. Miss Tarbell wrote lives of Napoleon and Madame Roland, then the first of her nine books on Abraham Lincoln (1900). Its serialization in *McClure's* helped establish the publication. In 1906, dissatisfied with Samuel S. McClure's management, she, Lincoln Steffens, and others left to establish the *American Magazine.*

Muckraking was an incident in her career.

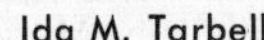
Ida M. Tarbell

CULVER PICTURES

A liberal, rather than a radical, she sought to present both sides of public issues, as in *The Tariff in Our Times* (1911) and *The Business of Being a Woman* (1913). Her biography of the steel magnate Elbert H. Gary (1925) was laudatory. Her own memoirs, *All in the Day's Work* (1939), illuminate her era, as well as herself. She died on Jan. 6, 1944, in Bridgeport, Conn.

LOUIS FILLER, *Antioch College*

TARDE, tȧrd, **Gabriel** (1843–1904), French sociologist. He was born in Sarlat, France, on March 12, 1843. He became a judge in Paris in 1869 and director of the bureau of criminal statistics of the ministry of justice in 1893. In 1900, Tarde was elected to the Institute of France and became a professor of philosophy at the Collège de France. He died in Paris on May 13, 1904.

Tarde's theories focus on society in terms of the individual minds that make it up. He saw sociology as the study of beliefs and desires as they determine social relationships and collective behavior. The key processes of social change are repetition (imitation), opposition (war, competition, discussion), and adaptation (through invention). Oppositions in society create tensions to which adaptations are made. Adaptation is the creative act of an individual mind and represents a societal advancement. Tarde held that only one man in a hundred is creative. The others are imitators who spread the innovation throughout the society. This diffusion generates new tensions and the whole process is repeated.

While Tarde's work on imitation has been criticized by Émile Durkheim and others, his stress on statistical research methods, his work concerning the effects of the environment on crime, and his studies on the diffusion of innovation have been valuable contributions to sociological research.

PHILIP J. LEONHARD, *City College, New York*

TARDENOISIAN, tär-də-noi′zhən, in archaeology, a cultural epoch of the Mesolithic period, or Middle Stone Age, from about 7000 to 4000 B.C. Centered mainly in France, Germany, and England, the culture of the epoch is characterized by geometrically shaped microliths—small stone tools or weapon points—which are believed to have been introduced from North Africa. The name is derived from a site at Fère-en-Tardenois, Aisne, France.

TARDIEU, tär-dyû′, **André** (1876–1945), three-time premier of France and staunch supporter of Georges Clemenceau's policies. He was born in Paris on Sept. 22, 1876. Prodigiously talented, he entered the civil service but then switched to journalism. Before World War I his political connections and his acute newspaper analyses made him a power in diplomatic circles.

With one interruption, Tardieu served in the Chamber of Deputies from 1914 to 1936. In 1917 he was appointed high commissioner for France in the United States. As a close associate of Clemenceau, Tardieu drafted important clauses of the Treaty of Versailles. In the ensuing years he assumed cabinet posts and served three times as premier. Lack of major party support to back his right-of-center politics, which borrowed some moderate-left proposals, hindered his effectiveness. A technocratic bent and his criticism of parliamentary mores made him increasingly unpopular. Some of the constitutional reforms that he proposed before World War II were adopted by the Fifth Republic. In retirement after 1936, Tardieu died in Menton on Sept. 15, 1945.

HENRY W. EHRMANN, *Dartmouth College*

TARDIGRADE, tärd′ə-grād, any of a large group of minute animals found in fresh and salt water, sand, mosses, algae, and lichens. One species is known to live as a parasite on sea cucumbers. Tardigrades, also called "water bears," are usually less than 1/25 of an inch (1 mm) long. They have segmented bodies and eight legs tipped with claws. Some, called *heterotardigrades,* have skeletal plates and head appendages. Others, the *eutardigrades,* lack them.

Tardigrades have an unusual ability to withstand drying. When water is not available they enter an anabiotic state, marked by a very low rate of metabolism. They can survive long periods, even years, in this state. When water is again available, they revive and become active.

Because the tardigrades in some ways resemble arachnids, such as spiders and mites, they are sometimes classified as a class of the phylum Arthropoda. However, they are also sometimes considered a separate phylum, the Tardigrada.

PAUL A. MEGLITSCH, *Drake University*

TARE is a name for the common vetch or the wild vetch. The tare mentioned in the Bible is believed to be a type of ryegrass, *Lolium temulentum.* See RYEGRASS; VETCH.

TAREE, tä-rē′, is a town in New South Wales, Australia, on the Manning River, about 160 miles (255 km) northeast of Sydney. Dairying, lumbering, and mixed farming are the main economic activities of the region. Taree was settled in 1851 and incorporated as a municipality in 1885. Population: (1966) 10,559.

TARENTUM. See TARANTO.

TARGUM, tär′gōōm, is a word meaning translation of a text into any language. When capitalized it refers specifically to the Aramaic translation of part of the Hebrew Bible. A few such translations were already in existence at the beginning of the Christian era. The best known is the Targum Onkelos (2d century A. D.), the Aramaic translation of the Five Books of Moses, or Pentateuch, by Onkelos. There is a theory that the Targum became an essential part of the study of the Pentateuch when Aramaic replaced Hebrew as the spoken language of the Jewish people.

The translations are usually literal, but often homiletical allusions as well as legal and theological nuances have been inserted. Also, some sentences or expressions in the Torah are paraphrased and clarified in the Targum. It became common for the reader to recite a verse from the Torah in the synagogue and the interpreter to render it at once into Aramaic from the Targum. Targums of other books of the Old Testament appeared from the 5th to the 9th centuries.

EDWARD T. SANDROW
Rabbi, Temple Beth El, Cedarhurst, N.Y.

TARIFF. A tariff is a tax levied on imported goods or, in rare cases, on exported goods, payable when goods cross the customs boundary of the levying country. It is sometimes called a customs duty.

Tariffs increase the costs of international trade, and they figure prominently in debates over national economic policy. For the last 200-odd years these debates have centered on the pros and cons of a policy of free trade—that is, zero tariffs.

Since 1947 the General Agreement on Tariffs and Trade (GATT) has made rules governing most international trade between non-Communist countries. GATT also has promoted the reduction of tariffs and, since 1965, has sought ways to improve trading conditions for less-developed countries.

BACKGROUND AND HISTORY

Tariffs may be *specific* or *ad valorem* or a combination of the two. A specific tariff, in the United States, is a fixed number of cents or dollars per pound, ton, or other physical unit of measure. An ad valorem tariff is a fixed percentage of the value of an imported article. Examples are a specific tariff on ground pepper, 2.1 cents per pound; an ad valorem tax on motorcycles, 7%; and a compound tariff on fountain pens, 2.8 cents per pen plus 18.5% ad valorem.

Purposes. *Revenue* tariffs are levied for the money they supply to governments. In contrast, protective tariffs are designed to protect domestic producers against competition from imports. Debates over tariff policy usually center on protective tariffs. Historically, revenue tariffs have been a more important source of government income for the economically advanced countries than they are today. As late as 1910 tariffs brought in about half of the U. S. government's tax revenue.

A good revenue tariff should be levied on "necessities" that are not produced domestically and, to be effective, it should be low so as not to discourage their importation. A protective tariff is levied on imports that compete with similar domestically produced goods, and it should be high enough to keep them out of the country. An implication, therefore, is that a good revenue tariff provides little or no protection, and a good protective tariff provides little or no revenue.

Protective tariffs by one country often lead to the enactment of retaliatory tariffs by other countries. Also, the subsidizing of exports by one country may lead an importing country to enact a *countervailing* tariff to offset the price-reducing effect of the subsidy.

Economic Significance. A protective tariff raises the prices of imported goods and unquestionably benefits domestic producers of "import substitute" goods. Economic debate turns on whether or not this is in the interest of the tariff-levying country. At least since Adam Smith published *The Wealth of Nations* in 1776, most English-speaking economists have opposed protective tariffs. They point out that a country's consumers benefit from purchasing foreign goods less expensively than they could be produced domestically. Moreover, if all countries adopted a free trade policy, efficiency in the allocation of the world's resources would be promoted because each country would produce and export those goods it was most suited to produce.

Most non-English-speaking economists, however, assert that the free trade doctrine ignores the dynamics of economic development. In the developing countries "infant" industries usually have high costs, and they need tariffs to protect them from established lower-cost industries in mature countries.

Politically, the free trade doctrine has been charged with ignoring purely nationalistic considerations. Protective tariffs may: (1) increase employment in one country; (2) promote a better national balance between agriculture and manufacturing; (3) improve a country's terms of trade with the rest of the world, and (4) protect industries that have military significance.

Early Tariffs. Revenue tariffs existed in Greece and Rome as well as in medieval Europe. In late medieval times export tariffs were used, along with export prohibitions, to keep adequate supplies of food and raw materials at home in an age of occasionally extreme scarcities. Before the rise of national states in Europe, transit duties and tolls were levied on trade at important market towns, bridges, or harbors, often to assure protection and safe conduct for the trader and his wares. As national gevernments began to assert authority in Europe these local tolls and tariffs were reduced or eliminated.

In the 16th, 17th, and 18th centuries national governments followed mercantilist trade policies, which called for the accumulation of national hoards of gold and silver. Since these precious metals would flow into a country whose exports exceeded its imports, the mercantilists turned to import prohibitions and tariffs as a way of promoting export surpluses for their countries.

The British government, influenced by the philosophy of individualism and the growing political power of its commercial and manufacturing classes, adopted free trade in the 1840's. The British maintained free trade for almost 100 years, but during most of this period the other large trading nations—the United States, Germany, France, and later Japan—were protectionist for the most part. Only for a brief period in the 1860's did it appear possible that free trade policies might take hold in other major European countries. Thereafter, in an increasingly nationalist environment, countries other than Britain used variations of the infant-industry argument to justify protective tariffs.

Twentieth Century Developments. Four events dominated tariff history in the 20th century: (1) the rise of neo-mercantilism in the 1930's; (2) the abandonment of the philosophy of protectionism by the U. S. government and its sponsorship of international tariff-cutting agreements; (3) the revival of customs unions in Europe and elsewhere; and (4) the plea by the less-developed countries for preferential tariffs.

Protective tariffs reached their high point in the American Smoot-Hawley tariff of 1929–1930, which was followed by Britain's abandonment of free trade in 1931. In the Great Depression of the 1930's, most countries raised protective tariffs in the hope—often a disappointed one—of larger employment. Other forms of economic nationalism became more important than tariffs—quota restrictions on imports, bilateral trade agreements, competitive currency devaluations, controls over foreign exchange, and state trading. When the state is the foreign trader, as in the USSR, tariffs lose their meaning.

Partly because of the forceful leadership of

Secretary of State Cordell Hull, the U. S. government adopted the Reciprocal Trade Agreements Act in 1934 and became a champion of reducing tariffs through intergovernmental tariff bargaining. Congress granted the U. S. president power to bargain U. S. tariffs down by 50% in exchange for equivalent tariff concessions from its trading partners. When coupled with the use of the unconditional "most-favored-nation" clause in trade agreements—a clause guaranteeing equality of trading opportunities to all signatory countries —this action became a powerful weapon for lowering world tariffs. American experience with tariff-reducing trade agreements in the 1930's led to the postwar General Agreement on Tariffs and Trade.

American policy long opposed preferential tariffs—those that discriminate among different countries. After World War II, however, such tariffs became increasingly important outside the United States. Six countries formed the European Common Market in 1957 as a customs union with zero tariffs among the members and a common external tariff. Seven countries formed the European Free Trade Area, establishing zero tariffs among the members but no common external tariff. Similar regional preferential tariff agreements arose elsewhere.

In 1964 and again in 1968 at UN Conferences on trade and development, the less-developed countries proposed drastic changes in world trading rules because the expansion of world trade had passed them by. One principal demand was that the rich industrialized countries grant them preferential tariffs, and a beginning was made toward acceding to this demand. See also the Index entry, *Tariff*.

ROBERT W. STEVENS, *Indiana University*

GENERAL AGREEMENT ON TARIFFS AND TRADE

The General Agreement on Tariffs and Trade, signed initially by representatives of 23 countries in Geneva in 1947, has contributed materially to the reduction of tariff and nontariff restrictions on world trade. The agreement incorporated a code of international-trade rules, made provisions for multilateral trade negotiations, established a procedure for adjusting trade grievances among members, and provided for the continuing review of actions by member countries. The recurring deliberations of the GATT have germinated ideas for resolving world trade problems.

Organization. The membership of the GATT, referred to as the contracting parties, increased from 23 original signatories in 1947 to 77 at the start of the 1970's. A permanent staff of about 100, under a director general, serves the GATT. Its offices are in Geneva. Most of the work in negotiations, consultations, complaints, and reviews is carried on either by the Council of Representatives or by selected groups composed of representatives of member countries.

Early Negotiations. After World War II, various circumstances combined to obstruct world trade. A large part of the world's productive facilities needed rehabilitation. High tariff barriers, inherited from the 1930's, hampered the international exchange of goods. So did the quantitative import controls that many countries imposed, mainly to save scarce foreign exchange.

In 1947 the United States, in collaboration with other major trading countries, initiated comprehensive multilateral negotiations in efforts to prevent a postwar contraction of world trade similar to the contraction that occurred in the 1930's. The negotiations resulted in the formation of the GATT.

An initial concern of founders of the GATT was to reduce tariffs. They were also determined that the benefits of tariff concessions thus negotiated should not be nullified either by resort to nontariff barriers—mainly restrictions on the quantities of imports—or by the discriminatory application of the concessions.

In a series of six multilateral tariff negotiations, the contracting parties exchanged significant reductions in tariffs and other trade barriers. In the first negotiation, conducted at Geneva simultaneously with the formulation of the general agreement itself, concessions were exchanged on trade estimated at about $10 billion annually. The second and third rounds of negotiations were held in Annecy, France (1949), and Torquay, England (1951). The fourth and fifth rounds (1956 and 1960–1962) took place in Geneva. Between the third and fourth rounds Japan became a new contracting party.

In the fifth round (known as the Dillon Round for C. Douglas Dillon, then U. S. secretary of the treasury), the European Economic Community began to participate as a unit and negotiated reductions in its common external tariff. By 1963, 50 countries, accounting for more than 50% of free-world trade, had joined the GATT, and more than 65,000 concessions had been exchanged.

Kennedy (Sixth) Round. The sixth round, which became known as the Kennedy Round for U. S. President John F. Kennedy, began in Geneva in 1964 and closed there in 1967. In this round more than 50 countries agreed to reduce import duties by from 20% to 50% in stages over a 5–year period beginning in 1968. The reductions covered a wide range of products estimated to account for about $40 billion worth of trade annually.

Import duties on a broad range of industrial products were reduced by half, and duty reductions of from 35% to 50% were made on even more products. Articles on which the principal negotiating countries, including the United States, made reductions averaging more than 35% included machinery, photographic equipment, automobiles, optical and scientific instruments, books, fabricated metal products, and wood products.

The negotiations on steel resulted in closer harmonization of tariffs among the major steel-producing countries. Significant tariff concessions on aluminum were made by the United States, the European Economic Community, some other northern European countries, the United Kingdom, Canada, and Japan. The negotiating countries agreed on a system of minimum and maximum world export grain prices and on a world food-aid program. Negotiations on textiles resulted in extension of the Long-Term Cotton Textile Arrangement (LTA) and more liberal access to import markets protected by the LTA.

Agreements on nontariff barriers provided for an international code on antidumping practices (which curtail sales abroad at prices less than those prevailing at home), for the reduction or elimination of internal taxes affecting imported commodities, and for the simplification of customs administrative procedures.

To expand the exports of the less-developed countries, tariffs on many tropical products and on some other articles were either reduced or eliminated by a number of developed countries.

Problems in the Kennedy Round. Several problems impeded the progress of the negotiations. One was the so-called *tariff disparities.* The duty rates in the tariff schedules of some countries differ more widely from one another than do the rates in other countries. At the negotiations the EEC held that most rates in its common external tariff ranged between 10% and 20% ad valorem (based on the value at the port of entry). In contrast, it noted that many U. S. rates exceeded 50%. So the EEC pressed for special duty-reduction rules, since across-the-board reductions would not eliminate such disparities.

Other problems included the *exception lists,* made up of products to be withheld from full negotiation because of overriding national interests. Nations negotiating with the EEC considered its exceptions list too large in comparison with those submitted by other countries.

Negotiations on agricultural products were difficult because most industrialized countries were allocating a part of their national resources to price support for farm products and consequently were reluctant to permit unlimited import competition in such products. Moreover, the EEC countries were in the process of combining their separate farm policies into a single system, a process essentially completed by 1968, but not without some dissension. The differences within the EEC concerned mainly the support prices for certain products and the share of support funds to be supplied by each member country. During 1969, the common agricultural arrangements were strained by the relative weakness of the franc and strength of the mark. After adjustment of currency values, difficulties in administering the price controls persisted.

The American selling price (ASP) system of customs valuation, employed by the United States in assessing duties on benzenoid chemicals and a few other products, was viewed by several countries as a heavy burden on their exports. They wanted rates based on selling price in the country of origin. In the agreement on chemicals, part of the concessions by the EEC were made conditional on repeal by the United States of the ASP system of valuation.

Consultations, Complaints, and Reviews. Besides the negotiations and plenary deliberations, consultations are held among parties that differ on adherence to the rules or on the equity of various permitted actions. Dissatisfied parties can request consultations with the alleged offender or with the entire membership. Many trade disputes have been amicably adjusted in this manner. Others, although not settled, have been subjected to study and discussion. The agreement itself requires the contracting parties to consult regularly with those member countries that maintain quantitative import restrictions because of a persistently unfavorable balance of payments. The contracting parties, by group action, have also required periodic reports from those members that follow certain policies—such as subsidizing exports or restricting agriculture and from those that have been granted waivers to pursue programs, presumably temporary, that deviate from one rule or another.

For an overall view of international commerce, see TRADE. For other aspects, see COMMERCIAL TREATIES; FREE TRADE; UNITED STATES —*Foreign Trade.* For recent developments in tariffs, see THE AMERICANA ANNUAL.

GLENN W. SUTTON, *U. S. Tariff Commission*

TARIM BASIN, dä′rēm′, a depression occupying more than half of the Sinkiang-Uigur Autonomous Region of northwestern China. It extends some 900 miles (1,500 km) from east to west and up to 300 miles (500 km) from north to south. The Tarim Basin is nearly surrounded by lofty mountains—the Tien Shan, Kunlun, and Pamirs—but this rampart is breached on the east by a low gap that links the region with the Kansu Corridor. The basin plain has a general elevation of 4,600 to 2,600 feet (1,400–800 meters), sloping downward toward the northeast. There it descends to its low point of 2,560 feet (780 meters) in the Lop Nor depression.

Along the foot of the mountains is a belt of gravel. Beneath it, groundwater is formed from the seepage of surface waters fed by melting snow from the mountains. At a lower elevation is a concentric belt of finer deposits. There the groundwater is near enough to the surface, or is forced up to the surface, to irrigate a string of oases that have been inhabited since ancient times by farmers and nomads. The main cities of the Tarim Basin—such as Kashgar, Yarkand (Soche), and Hotien (Khotan)—are located in this zone.

The interior and largest part of the basin is occupied by the Takla Makan, a huge desert of shifting sands interrupted only by patches of clay. It is one of the driest regions on earth. Along the northern edge of the desert the basin's main stream, the Tarim River, flows eastward for 1,300 miles (2,100 km). It is joined on the south by the Hotien (Khotan) River, which crosses the Takla Makan and divides the desert into two parts—the Taklan Makan proper to the west and the somewhat smaller Desert of Cherchen to the east.

The Tarim River flows into the Lop Nor, a large, shallow salt lake without a clearly defined shoreline or even a permanent location. In periods of water surplus the lake spreads across the neighboring salt marshes, which also change their outlines constantly. The extent of the marshes depends on the influx of water and its evaporation rate, which changes seasonally. Since October 1964, Chinese scientists and engineers have carried out nuclear and thermonuclear tests near Lop Nor.

FREDERICK HUNG
University of Guelph

TARIQ, tä′rik, Muslim general, who was mainly responsible for conquering most of Spain in the 8th century. Probably a Berber, Tariq Ibn Ziyad was a subordinate of Musa Ibn Nusayr, the Arab governor of North Africa. After Musa's conquest of Morocco, Tariq was left in charge of Tangier. In about May 711, on Musa's order, he invaded Spain with 7,000 men, mostly Berbers. Landing near Gibraltar, he first took up a position on the rock and thereby gave his name to it. Gibraltar is a corruption of *jebel Tariq,* "Tariq's mountain."

In July 711, near Trafalgar, Tariq defeated Roderick, the Visigothic king of Spain. Tariq then pushed forward and occupied the Spanish capital, Toledo, without resistance. Musa, jealous of Tariq's success, crossed to Spain with 18,000 Arabs in 712, and the two generals occupied most of Spain. In 714, Tariq accompanied Musa to Damascus and disappeared into obscurity.

W. MONTGOMERY WATT
University of Edinburgh

TARKINGTON, Booth (1869–1946), American novelist and playwright, who is known for his studies of middle-class life in small Midwestern cities. Newton Booth Tarkington was born in Indianapolis on July 29, 1869. His Indiana boyhood was a rich source for his fiction, and his education—including study at Princeton University, where he founded the Triangle Club—broadened his horizons. His interest in politics inspired *The Gentleman from Indiana* (1899), a novel about a crusading newspaper editor, and led to a term in the Indiana House of Representatives (1902–1903). However, he was made famous by his historical romance *Monsieur Beaucaire* (1900). Thereafter he wrote many novels and plays, collaborating on some of the latter with Harry Leon Wilson. Tarkington died in Indianapolis on May 19, 1946.

Two of his novels won Pulitzer Prizes—*The Magnificent Ambersons* (1918), which tells of the rise and fall of an Indiana family, and *Alice Adams* (1921), the story of a girl's futile attempts to rise in society. The former, together with *The Turmoil* (1915) and *The Midlander* (1923), formed the trilogy *Growth* (1927). His stories of boyhood and adolescence, notably *Penrod* (1914) and *Seventeen* (1916), became young people's classics. Tarkington was extremely popular, but his conservative values and his indulgence in sentimental melodrama soon dated his works. The best of these, however, reflect the tradition of William Dean Howells and the French realists. See also MAGNIFICENT AMBERSONS; PENROD.

JEROME H. STERN, *Florida State University*

TARLETON, Sir Banastre (1754–1833), English army officer, who was an outstanding cavalry leader during the American Revolution. He was born on Aug. 21, 1754, in Liverpool, and educated at Oxford University. He purchased an army commission in April 1775 and upon the outbreak of the revolution volunteered to serve with Lord Cornwallis in America. Tarleton directed a number of brilliant actions in the northern campaign and was made lieutenant colonel of loyalist troops—the British Legion.

In the 1780's, Tarleton served with Sir Henry Clinton and Cornwallis in the Carolinas. The skillful operations of his legion, both cavalry and foot soldiers, continued to add to his reputation. On Jan. 17, 1781, with some 1,000 men, he attacked Gen. Daniel Morgan at Cowpens, about 40 miles (65 km) west of Charlotte, N. C. The Americans, about equally strong, soundly defeated Tarleton. His reputation never regained its luster—although eventually he became a general and baronet. He died at Leintwardine, Shropshire, on Jan. 25, 1833.

Tarleton had a reputation for barbaric cruelty that may not have been entirely justified. His troops—not well disciplined—were exiled Loyalists and were bitter at the Americans.

EDWARD P. HAMILTON
Director, Fort Ticonderoga

TARN, tärn, is a department of southern France, located on the southern flank of the Massif Central. It is drained by the Tarn River and its tributaries. Tarn's chief industries are coal mining and textiles. Agriculture is also important. Albi is the departmental capital. The area of the department is 2,232 square miles (5,780 sq km). Population: (1962) 319,560.

TARN-ET-GARONNE, tärn ā gə-rän′, is a department of southwestern France. Primarily agricultural, the department is drained by the Garonne, Tarn, and Aveyron rivers. Montauban is the departmental capital. The area of Tarn-et-Garonne is 1,441 square miles (3,732 sq km). Population: (1962) 175,847.

TARN RIVER, tärn, a tributary of the Garonne in southern France. It rises in the Cévennes range and follows a westerly course through the departments of Lozère, Aveyron, Tarn, and Tarn-et-Garonne, joining the Garonne near Moissac. Its length is 235 miles (377 km).

In the plateau region known as the Causses, the Tarn flows through gorges that contribute to the area's scenic beauty. These gorges are a well-known French tourist attraction.

TARNISH is the film coating caused by the reaction of a metal and nonmetal. Tarnish is considered "dry corrosion." In this process there is a direct combination of the metal, which acts as the anode, with a nonmetallic element, such as oxygen or sulfur, serving as the cathode. Oxide films may be invisible or dulling, while sulfide films may have many colors. The film may protect the metal against more corrosion.

The metals and their alloys that are subject to tarnish are aluminum, copper, gold (below 14 carat), magnesium, iron, nickel, chromium, zinc, cadmium, and silver.

The tarnish film that forms on silver is composed of silver sulfide. The sulfur may come from the burning of industrial fuels or from common foods such as onions and eggs.

The simplest method of preventing tarnish on silver is to keep it from coming into contact with air. Any covering that will maintain a stagnant air or an airless atmosphere will do. Once tarnish does form, it can be removed by abrasive polishing, electrolytic reduction, or chemical reagents. Abrasive polishing is risky because it can, for example, eventually remove the entire silver surface from a plated article.

ALVIN S. COHAN
Scientific Design Company, Inc.

TARNISHED PLANT BUG, a small destructive bug that attacks more than 50 types of plants, including cotton, tobacco, vegetables, fruits and other crops. It is found throughout the United States and in many other parts of the world. The adult has a flattened oval body about 1/4 inch (6 mm) long and half as wide. It is brownish mottled with white, yellow, reddish brown, and black.

The bugs feed on plant sap and during feeding they apparently introduce a toxic substance into the plant tissue. The leaves become deformed, the stems scarred and discolored, and the buds and fruits dwarfed and pitted.

The adult bugs spend the winter under stones, tree bark, and leaves and in other sheltered places. In the spring the female inserts her eggs into the stems, petioles, leaf midribs, buds, or developing flowers of plants. Yellowish green nymphs hatch from the eggs and start feeding on the host plant. Both nymphs and adults are controlled with insecticides.

The tarnished plant bug, *Lygus lineolaris,* belongs to the family Miridae, order Hemiptera.

ARLO M. VANCE, *Entomologist (Retired)*
U. S. Department of Agriculture

USDA PHOTO

G. R. ROBERTS

TARO LEAVES (*right*), large enough to shelter this Fiji Islander, illustrate the size to which this plant grows. (*Left*) Edible taro tubers grown in Trinidad.

TARNÓW, tär′nuf, is a city in southern Poland, 45 miles (72 km) east of Cracow and 155 miles (250 km) south of Warsaw. The city lies in a belt of open, fertile country that extends across southern Poland. It was a medieval route and market center and, despite the damage of two world wars, retains its late medieval churches. A Renaissance city hall stands in the middle of the picturesque market square.

On the western edge of the city is a large chemical manufacturing complex that dominates Tarnów's economy and is one of Poland's main fertilizer and basic chemical manufacturing centers. The city also has important engineering and ceramic manufactures. Population: (1967 est.) 80,000.

NORMAN J. G. POUNDS
Indiana University

TARO, tär′ō, is a large-leaved tropical plant that has been grown as a staple food crop in the Orient for more than 2,000 years. Although all parts of the plant are edible, it is grown mostly for its fleshy underground corms and tubers, which are rich in starch and portein and are usually either eaten as a potato-like vegetable or used to make flour. Hawaiian poi is made with cooked taro that is pounded into a pasty mass and sometimes allowed to ferment. Taros are richer than potatoes in carbohydrates and most vitamins and minerals.

The corms and tubers, as well as the other plant parts, contain needle-like crystals of calcium oxalate that give the plant a bitter taste but that can be destroyed by cooking. The leaves and leafstalks are rich in vitamin C and are eaten as green vegetables. The young blanched shoots obtained by growing the corms in the dark have a delicate flavor similar to that of mushrooms. A variety of taro called dasheen (probably from the French *de la Chine*, meaning "from China") is less bitter.

Taro is an erect plant that ranges in height from 3 to 7 feet (0.9–2.1 meters) under favorable growing conditions. Its whorled leaves are attached near the center of the blades to the long thick leafstalks, which range in color from green to deep purplish maroon. The leaf blade is heart-shaped and dark velvety green on the upper surface. The flower of the taro is similar to that of the jack-in-the-pulpit. The fleshy central spike, or spadex, is enclosed by a pale yellow rolled bract, or spathe, which may be 6 to 15 inches (15–38 cm) long. Because of its attractive leaves and flowers, it is sometimes grown as an ornamental.

It is believed that the taro is originally native to Malaysia and Indonesia. It is widely grown in the warmer parts of the Orient and on the islands of the Pacific. It was introduced into the southern United States in 1905 and has been cultivated there on a small scale since 1913.

Taro is a long-season crop that requires a warm, frost-free period of at least seven months. It does best in a rich, loamy soil with abundant ground water and good drainage. Yields range from 200 to 350 bushels per acre (175–300 hectoliters per hectare).

The taro is known botanically as *Colocasia esculenta.* It is a member of the arum family (Araceae).

JOHN C. MCCOLLUM
College of Agriculture, University of Illinois

TAROT CARDS, ta-rō′, are the oldest surviving playing cards. They are also used in telling fortunes. Tarot cards were introduced into Italy in the last quarter of the 14th century by returning Crusaders or wandering Gypsies. Although the origins of Tarot cards are not known, connections have been suggested with Hebrew and Oriental mysticism and Egyptian mythology. Similarities to the circular cards used in the Far East in the 9th century to teach philosophy and religion have also been noted.

In its most elaborate form the Tarot pack consisted of 78 cards, 56 of which were called the Minor Arcana. These were divided into four suits, comparable to modern playing cards—wands or batons (clubs), cups (hearts), swords (spades), and pentacles or money (diamonds). Each suit was made up of 10 numbered cards (ace to 10) and four court cards (king, queen, knight, and page).

The remaining 22 cards, called the Major Arcana or trumps (also *atouts*), were numbered 1 to 21 and decorated with figures representing natural laws, elements, virtues, and vices. The 22d card, the fool or madman (joker), was unnumbered. See also CARDS, PLAYING.

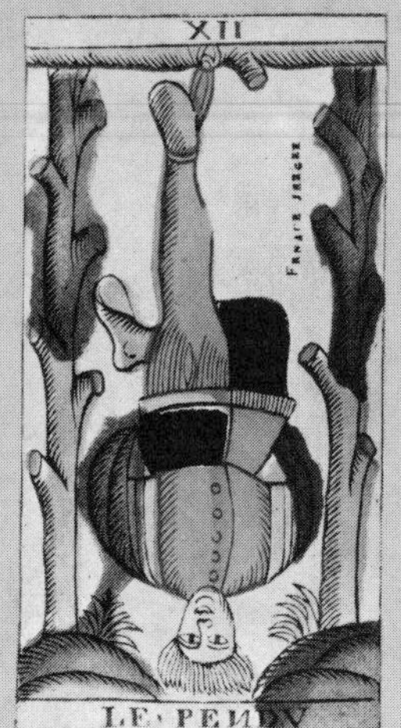

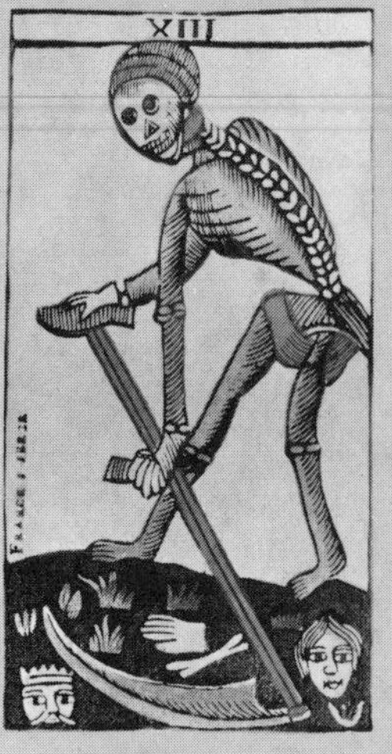

TAROT CARDS. At left is the hanged man and at center is justice, from an early 19th century Italian series. At right is the king of batons (clubs), from an 18th century Italian deck.

CINCINNATI ART MUSEUM U. S. PLAYING CARD COMPANY

Spiritualists still use Tarot cards, especially the Major Arcana, in their attempts to foretell the future. In literature, T. S. Eliot used an *atout*, called the Hanged Man, in his poem *The Waste Land*.

BERNARD MANDELBAUM
Bronx Community College

TARPAN, tär-pan′, or *European wild horse,* a coarse-looking, typically small horse, standing about 13 hands (4 feet 4 inches, or 1.32 meters) high at the withers (shoulders). It has a long head, a short thick neck, and an upright mane.

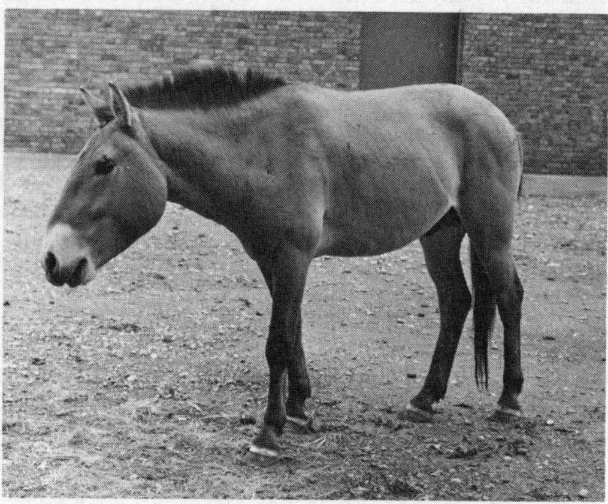

ZOOLOGICAL SOCIETY OF LONDON

Tarpan-type wild horse.

Coat color is mouse gray, sometimes varying to brownish, with intermingled whitish hairs. A dark stripe runs the length of the back.

The tarpan is best known from southern Russia and Poland, where the last wild specimens survived into the mid-1800's or possibly later. The tarpan had crossed extensively with domestic stock, and the most tarpanlike descendants of these hybrids have been reintroduced in the Bialowieza Forest of Poland and elsewhere.

The classification of the tarpan is much confused. The two most widely held views are that the tarpan is either the European branch of the Mongolian wild horse (*Equus przewalskii*) or that both the tarpan and the Mongolian wild horse are races of *E. caballus,* the same species as the domestic horse.

TARPEIA, tär-pē′ə, a Roman maiden prominent in the legendary tale of the Sabine war. According to tradition, the Sabines under Titus Tatius attacked Rome's citadel on the Capitoline Hill. Tarpeia, daughter of the commander of Rome's garrison, opened the gates to them. Some versions report that she aided the enemy for a promised reward of golden ornaments, others that she intended to deceive them. On entering, the Sabines, who suspected Tarpeia of double-dealing, crushed her to death with their shields. A portion of the Capitol was then renamed the Tarpeian Rock, and from it Roman criminals were thrown to their death.

ERICH S. GRUEN
University of California, Berkeley

TARPON, tär′pən, a large fish found in the western Atlantic from Nova Scotia to southern Brazil, but most often in tropical areas, and in the eastern Atlantic off tropical western Africa. The tarpon, a popular gamefish, is noted for its spectacular leaps when hooked.

The tarpon has a compressed body covered with large smooth scales. It has a projecting lower jaw, a large forked tail, and a dorsal fin whose last ray is greatly elongated. The back is blue, the sides and the belly usually silvery. The largest tarpon on record, caught in Florida, weighed about 350 pounds (157.5 kg) and measured more than 8 feet (2.4 meters) in length. Specimens about 6 feet (1.8 meters) long and weighing about 100 pounds (45 kg) are not at all uncommon.

Tarpons live close to the shore and may be found in brackish and fresh waters as well as in

Tarpon

ANNAN PHOTOS

seawater. Spawning probably occurs in the tropics. A large female may lay more than 12 million eggs. The young are transparent and resemble the ribbonlike larvae of eels. They reach sexual maturity when about 4 feet (1.2 meters) long.

The scientific name of the tarpon is *Tarpon atlanticus,* and, along with the ten-pounder, it belongs in the family Elopidae.

DANIEL M. COHEN
U. S. Fish and Wildlife Service

TARQUINII, tär-kwin'ē-ī, was an ancient Etruscan city, situated in the Tuscan hills 5 miles (8 km) from the Tyrrhenian Sea and about 60 miles (97 km) north of Rome. Iron age cremation urns show settlements at Tarquinii as early as about 800 B. C. Etruscan occupation of the site probably took place about a half century later, when burial in the ground first appears. Archaeological findings seem to bear out the tradition that Tarquinii was head of the Etruscan League and possessed cultural and commercial connections with Greece.

Tarquinii flourished in the 7th and 6th centuries as a chief center of the bronze industry but declined thereafter, eclipsed by other commercial towns like Caere and Vulci. Wars with Rome in the 4th century further weakened its influence. The city's independence ceased in 90 B. C., when its inhabitants observed Roman citizenship. The culture of Tarquinii is preserved in brilliant tomb paintings that depict scenes of banquets, athletics, festivals, and religious ceremonies.

ERICH S. GRUEN
University of California, Berkeley

TARQUINIUS PRISCUS, tär-kwin'ē-əs pris'kəs, **Lucius,** 5th king of Rome (reigned 616–579 B. C.). According to Livy's history, Tarquinius came from the Etruscan town of Tarquinii. His wife Tanaquil nagged him into moving to Rome, where he won the favor of Rome's king, Ancus Marcius. On Ancus' death, Tarquinius removed the king's two sons from the city and gained the throne. Tradition records important military successes against Latins and Sabines during his reign. Tarquinius is also credited with building Rome's walls, draining the site of the Forum, and beginning work on the Circus Maximus and the temple of Jupiter. Ancus' sons eventually arranged Tarquinius' assassination.

Much of this story is dubious. His birth in Tarquinii may simply have been conjectured because of his name. The public works ascribed to Priscus are also ascribed to the later king, Tarquinius Superbus. But archaeological findings show the beginning of Etruscan influence in Rome about 600–575 B. C. and demonstrate a historical foundation for Livy's tale.

ERICH S. GRUEN
University of California, Berkeley

TARQUINIUS SUPERBUS, tär-kwin'ē-əs sū-pûr'-bəs, **Lucius** (reigned 534–510 B. C.), last king of Rome. The historian Livy reports that he was a son or grandson of Tarquinius Priscus, Rome's 5th king, and son-in-law of Priscus' successor Servius Tullius. Tarquinius Superbus, according to tradition, was prodded by his wife into engineering Servius' assassination and taking the throne himself. As ruler he allegedly executed Rome's leading senators, instituted a reign of terror, and governed by arbitrary whim—whence the name Superbus (the haughty).

Tarquinius markedly extended Rome's power over its neighbors. At home he used conscripted labor to complete the Circus Maximus, the Roman sewage system, and the temple of Jupiter on the Capitol. But his tyrannical activities alienated the nobility. A revolt led by Lucius Brutus resulted in the King's expulsion and the institution of republican government. Tarquinius later made unsuccessful efforts to recover his power, and he eventually perished at Cumae. His historicity is undeniable. Archaeological findings, for example, confirm Tarquinius' role in the building of the Capitol and the sewage system. But other details in Livy's account, influenced by stories of Greek tyrants, remain suspect.

ERICH S. GRUEN
University of California, Berkeley

TARRAGON, tar'ə-gän, is a perennial plant whose fresh leaves are used in salads and for flavoring pickles and vinegar. The dried leaves are used in meat and egg dishes, soups, sauces, mustard, and mayonnaise.

The tarragon plant (*Artemisia dracunculus*) belongs to the composite family (Compositae) and is native to the Soviet Union, from the Caspian Sea area through southern Siberia. It is cultivated in Europe, especially in France. It grows 3 feet (90 cm) tall and has erect, many branched stems, the basal portions of which are often woody. The narrow, somewhat twisted leaves are 1 to 4 inches (25–100 mm) long, usually with smooth edges, and are attached spirally along the stems. The small greenish white flower heads are borne in loose branching clusters. The plant thrives in sunny, rather dry locations and is propagated by stem cuttings or root division.

LAWRENCE ERBE
University of Southwestern Louisiana

TARRAGONA, târ-ə-gō'nə, is a seaport in northeastern Spain, about 50 air miles (80 km) southwest of Barcelona. Situated near the mouth of the Francolí River, Tarragona is composed of two distinct parts. The old city overlooks the Mediterranean from a low, rocky hill and is enclosed on three sides by massive walls, while the new city spreads along the harbor toward the southwest and is protected by a breakwater. Tarragona is the capital of the province of the same name.

Remains from the Roman era include the cyclopean city walls, the palace of Augustus, and portions of a great aqueduct, 2.5 miles (4 km) to the northwest. The city's 12th-13th century cathedral was built on the site of an earlier temple of Jupiter and a mosque. There is an archaeological museum. Industries include food processing, distilling, and the manufacture of tobacco products. The province's agricultural products, such as wine, olives, and almonds, are exported from the city.

Captured from the Iberians by Publius Scipio in 218 B. C., Tarraco, as it was known to the Romans, was later made the capital of the province of Tarraconensis. The city fell to the Visigoths in 469 A. D. and was made an archiepiscopal see while under their control. It was held by the Muslims from 714 until 1085 and suffered from attacks by the French in 1640 and 1811. Population: the city (1960), 35,689; the province (1965 est.), 364,000.

VINCENT MALMSTRÖM, *Middlebury College*

TARRYTOWN, a village in southeastern New York, in Westchester county, is on the east bank of the Tappan Zee, the widest part of the Hudson River, about 25 miles (40 km) north of New York City. It is a residential community with rich historical and literary associations. Its industries include a large automobile assembly plant. The Tappan Zee Bridge crosses the river.

Dutch traders from New Amsterdam settled the site about 1645. The building of a mill and a manor house by Frederick Philipse on land granted to him in 1680 encouraged settlement. Philipse built the Old Dutch Church, which with its Old Dutch Burying Ground is a landmark today.

During the American Revolution, allegiances in the area were divided between the American and British causes. Major John André, the British spy, was captured in Tarrytown. A monument commemorating the event was erected in 1853.

Washington Irving wrote of the region in his *Sketch Book* (1819–1820). In the late 1800's, several large estates were created in the village, such as those of Jay Gould, William and John D. Rockefeller, and Gen. John C. Frémont. Marymount College for girls and the Westchester Art Society are in the village.

Tarrytown was incorporated in 1870. Population: 11,115.

EUGENE A. PRINGLE, *Warner Library*

TARSHISH, tar'shish, a seaport of uncertain location, frequently mentioned in the Old Testament. It has been variously identified with Tarsus in Cilicia, the ancient Tartessus in Spain at the mouth of the Guadalquivir River, and other places.

TARSIA. See INTARSIA.

TARSIER, tär'sē-ā, an arboreal, rat-size primate related to the lemur but considered as representative of an intermediate stage between lemurs and the higher primates (monkeys, apes, and man). The three species of tarsier are found in rain forests, dense bamboo thickets, or secondary jungle growth, usually at low altitudes. They occur in the Philippines (*Tarsius syrichta*), on Sumatra, Borneo, and adjacent smaller islands (*T. bancanus*), and on Celebes and adjacent smaller islands (*T. spectrum*).

The tarsier has a rather squat body with long hind legs and a long, nearly hairless, nonprehensile tail. The tips of the fingers and toes are expanded into soft, flat pads, enabling the tarsier to cling to almost any surface. All but the second and third toes, which have claws used in grooming, bear flat nails. The head is broad and rounded and can be turned through 180 degrees, permitting the tarsier to look straight backward. The ears are large and hairless. The eyes are enormous, in proportion to total body size being three times larger than those of any other primate. Tarsiers range from 3⅓ to 6¼ inches (85–160 mm) in total body length, plus a tail 5⅓ to 10¾ inches (135–274 mm) long, and from 3 to 6 ounces (80–165 grams) in weight. The coat is short, dense, and silky and gray-brown in color.

Tarsiers are nocturnal, spending the day hidden in dense vegetation and emerging at night to feed on insects, spiders, and lizards. Though rather clumsy when walking on all fours,

A. W. AMBLER, FROM NATIONAL AUDUBON SOCIETY

Philippine tarsier (*Tarsius syrichta*)

tarsiers can leap about with great agility. They can jump as far as 6 feet (1.8 meters) from tree trunk to tree trunk and nearly this distance in froglike hops on the ground.

Tarsiers are usually seen in pairs and rarely singly or in groups of three or four. Breeding occurs throughout the year. Gestation is believed to be about 6 months, after which a single young is born. A tarsier is known to have lived 12 years in captivity.

LEONARD A. ROSENBLUM
Director Primate Laboratory
State University of New York

TARSUS, tar'səs, a southern Turkish city, is located toward the western end of the fertile Cilician plain near the Mediterranean in İçel province. Although today secondary to the neighboring port of Mersin, Tarsus is one of the most ancient cities in Asia Minor. It was the natural terminus of the route leading from the central plateau through the Cilician Gates, a defile in the Taurus Mountains, to the sea. It is situated on the banks of the Tarsus (ancient Cydnus) River, and alluvium buries much of its early history. Its former sea channel is blocked.

Excavations in the vicinity attest to an early Neolithic culture (5th millennium B.C.). A Hittite occupation (14th century B.C.) gave way to the Assyrians (8th century B.C.). Alexander the Great went through Tarsus in 333 B.C., and during the Seleucid period it was renowned as a center of learning. In 64 B.C. it passed to the Romans, and it was here that St. Paul was born.

Under the Byzantines, Tarsus was the seat of an archbishop, but in 787 A.D. it was taken by the Muslim Arabs. Although recovered again by the Byzantine emperor in 965, in 1084 it was captured by the Seljuk Turks, who, in turn, were driven from Tarsus by the Crusaders in 1097. Until 1375 it formed part of Lesser Armenia, although most of the time effective control was in the hands of nomadic Turkomans, who toward the middle of the 14th century held it as a dependency of the Egyptian Mamluks. When the latter were defeated by Sultan Selim I in 1518, it became Ottoman territory and has remained Turkish.

Modern Tarsus, a pleasant, prosperous city, is the marketing center for the numerous citrus groves and cotton and other farms in its vicinity. Population: (1965) 57,737.

JOHN R. WALSH, *University of Edinburgh*

TARSUS, the seven bones that form the ankle. See FOOT.

TARTAGLIA, tär-täl'yə, **Niccolò** (1500?–1557), Italian mathematician and scientist. He was born in Brescia, Italy. Largely self-educated, he excelled in mathematics, which he taught at Verona and Venice. His *Nova scientia* (1537) was the first attempt at a mathematical treatment of ballistics. He also succeeded in solving certain cubic equations by a formula which he imparted, under vows of secrecy, to Girolamo Cardano. Cardano developed it further and published it in 1545, causing a bitter quarrel between the two men.

In 1543, Tartaglia published the first Italian translation of Euclid and an old Latin translation of works by Archimedes relating to mechanics. In 1546 he published in Italian the most important medieval treatise on statics and in 1551, a practical treatise on the raising of sunken vessels. His publications made available the mathematical foundations of mechanical science, then neglected in the universities. Publication of his treatise on number and measure began in 1556 and was completed after his death, in Venice, on Dec. 13, 1557.

STILLMAN DRAKE, *University of Toronto*

TARTAN, tärt'ən, is the checkered fabric characteristic of the Highlands of Scotland. The word "tartan" is Lowland Scots. The Gaelic equivalent is *breacan,* from *braec* ("checkered"). Tartan is distinct from the checkered fabric of such countries as Portugal and Thailand. It is composed of threads of unbroken color, in which the pattern of the weft is identical with that of the warp, through which it is woven. The twill weave (two over, two under) of tartan gives it diagonal rib lines, and the squares of the same color lie diagonally across the fabric.

Contrasted to the somber dress of commoners in the ancient Mediterranean world, Celtic dress was described by Vergil as "virgatis lucent" ("striped and bright"). By the Middle Ages the Celts of western Europe had been driven into the inhospitable corners of their lands, such as the Highlands and islands of northwestern Scotland. There each clan (from the Gaelic for "offspring") was isolated by mountains or the sea. Clansmen colored their cloth with vegetable dyes—black from alder tree bark, blue from whortleberries, green from broom and whin (furze) bark, red from lichens, yellow from ash trees and bracken roots. Since the weaver's choice was limited by local flora, different colors were preponderant in different districts. The pattern ("sett") of the chief's tartan was copied by his followers so that, according to Martin Martin's *Western Islands of Scotland* (1703), "they who have seen those places, are able at first view of a man's plad [tartan worn over the left shoulder] to guess the place of his residence."

The account books of the Lord of the Isles in 1355 include "unus caligarum braccatarum de tiretatana," or trews (trousers), of tartan. For the marriage of James V in 1538, his treasurer's accounts record "iii elnis of heland tertaine." *Vestiarium Scoticum* (1842) by the Sobieski-Stuart brothers depicts 75 tartans.

As a reprisal for the Jacobite rising of 1745, the use of tartan was banned by Parliament in 1746. However, the very illegality of tartan merely whetted interest in it. On the repeal of the act in 1782, tartan appeared everywhere. Enthusiasm was enflamed by the exploits of Scots regiments abroad and by the poetry and novels of Sir Walter Scott. The wearing of tartan was further encouraged by the visit to Edinburgh of George IV, who wore full Highland dress. Portraits of him in that costume have adorned myriad whiskey bottles. Queen Victoria's interest in things Scottish further glamorized tartan and has made it almost obligatory for Scots at Highland Games. New tartans have been designed, such as that for Bruce county, Canada, and texts now record almost 300.

LT. COL. H. A. B. LAWSON, M. V. O.
Rothesay Herald, Scotland

TARTAR. See TATAR.

TARTAR, Cream of. See CREAM OF TARTAR.

TARTAR, Dental, the dense chalky material that sometimes forms on the teeth. It is made up of calcium carbonate, calcium phosphate, saliva, and organic materials from food. See DENTAL HYGIENE; DENTISTRY; TEETH.

TARTARIC ACID, tär-tar'ik, any of three isomeric organic acids of the formula $C_4O_6H_6$. These isomers are called mesotartaric or (+) or (−) tartaric acid, depending on whether and in which direction they rotate a plane of polarized light. The (+) tartaric acid is found in many plants. It is used in soft drinks and foods, in photography, and in the preparation of esters for lacquers and textile printing. Neither of the other forms of tartaric acid is commercially important. Cream of tartar, which is a salt of tartaric acid, is used in baking powder.

The tartaric acids differ in the spatial arrangements of some of their substituent groups.

(+) tartaric acid	(−) tartaric acid	mesotartaric acid
COOH	COOH	COOH
H–C–OH	HO–C–H	H–C–OH
HO–C–H	H–C–OH	H–C–OH
COOH	COOH	COOH

Mesotartaric acid is not optically active—that is, it does not rotate the plane of polarized light. The (+) and (−) tartaric acids are mirror images of each other and rotate the plane of polarized light 12° to the right and to the left, respectively. See ISOMERISM.

OTTO W. NITZ
Stout State University, Menomonie, Wis.

TARTARUS, tär′tə-rəs, in Greek legend was the lowest region of the afterworld, or Hades, where offenders of the gods were eternally tormented. In contrast were Elysium, the region of paradise, and the Plain of Asphodel, a region of neutral existence. Later, the regions lost their distinctive characters, and Tartarus and Hades became synonyms for the afterworld. In early writings Tartarus represented all of the area beneath the earth—as Heaven was everything above the earth—and was a prison of the gods to which the Titans and Cronus were banished. As a personification, Tartarus was the son of Aether (Air) and Gaea (Earth).

TARTARY was the name in common use after the 13th century for an extensive but generally indeterminate area in Europe and Asia that was under the domination of the Tatars, or Tartars. See TATAR.

TARTINI, tär-tē′nē, **Giuseppe** (1692–1770), Italian violinist, composer, and music theorist, who developed a style of bowing that is still considered the model. He was born in Pirano, near Trieste, on April 8, 1692. While studying for the priesthood, he took violin lessons and became passionately devoted to music. He left the seminary and studied the violin.

Tartini was appointed solo violinist and conductor of the orchestra at the Basilica of St. Anthony in Padua in 1721. In 1728 he established a violin school in Padua, where he trained a number of distinguished violinists. He died in Padua on Feb. 28, 1770.

Tartini's compositions include some 180 violin concertos and about 100 violin sonatas. Among his works on music theory are *Trattato di musica secondo la vera scienza dell'armonia* (1754) and *De' principi dell'armonia musicale contenuta nel diatonico genere* (1767).

TARTU, tär′to͞o, is a city in the USSR, in Estonia, on the Emaigi River, 100 miles (160 km) southeast of Tallin. Formerly known by the German name of "Dorpat" or the Russian name of "Yuriev," it was named for the Estonian god Tar, or Taara, after Estonia achieved independence in 1918. Tartu is chiefly a cultural center, but it also has important food-processing, textile, manufacturing, and sawmilling industries.

Founded by Yaroslav the Wise of Kiev in 1030, the city was captured by the Teutonic Knights in 1224. It later enjoyed great prosperity as a member of the Hanseatic League. Captured by the Russians in the mid-16th century, it was overrun in succession by the Poles, the Swedes, and again, early in the 18th century, by the Russians. Tartu was briefly occupied by Germans in 1918. The Russian-Estonian treaty acknowledging Estonian independence was signed at Tartu in 1920. Tartu was annexed with the rest of Estonia to the USSR in 1940 but fell under Nazi control from 1941 to 1944.

Swedish King Gustavus Adolphus chartered Tartu's historic university in 1632. Tartu's library, which dates from 1802, is the largest in the Baltic area. In addition there are five art schools and six museums. Many of the city's buildings are in the classical style and date from the late 18th and early 19th centuries. Population: (1967 est.) 85,000.

W. A. DOUGLAS JACKSON
University of Washington

TARTUFFE, tär-tüf′, is one of the greatest plays of the French dramatist Molière. It was first performed in 1664, but it offended the pious and was banned, as was a 1667 version entitled *L'Imposteur* (*The Imposter*). The text we know today was first performed in 1669. *Tartuffe* is a comedy, with a happy ending and the intention to provoke laughter, but it is also a serious denunciation of hypocrisy and religious bigotry and a flattering eulogy of Molière's protector, King Louis XIV.

Tartuffe, pretending religious devoutness, dupes the credulous Orgon, a wealthy Parisian bourgeois. After deeding Tartuffe his property and offering Tartuffe his daughter in marriage, Orgon comes to his senses when his wife compels him to witness Tartuffe's attempt to seduce her. Although unmasked, Tartuffe is legally able to order Orgon from his house, and only the benevolent and almost divine intervention of the monarch saves Orgon at the end of the play.

The work is a serious, almost tragic, comedy. It portrays the helplessness of a good man victimized by a clever scoundrel. Were he not a scoundrel, Tartuffe might be a tragic hero, for it is his pride and unbridled appetite that lead him to excess and folly. But we are pleased by his downfall, which represents a defeat for religious pretense. See also MOLIÈRE.

RAYMOND GIRAUD, *Stanford University*

TARWEED, any of a small group of sticky, strong-smelling annual or perennial plants with yellow daisylike flower heads that open in the evening and close before noon the next day. Tarweeds make up the genus *Madia* of the composite family (Compositae) and are native to the Western Hemisphere.

The common tarweed (*M. elegans*) is found on dry hills and in waste places from Oregon to Lower California. It reaches a height of 2 feet (0.6 meter) and has narrow leaves 3 to 5 inches (76–127 mm) long. Its flower heads are about ¾ inch (19 mm) wide and are borne on long stalks. *M. sativa,* a species found in the eastern United States, is a stout annual that reaches a height of 4 feet (1.2 meters) and has ½-inch-wide (13-mm) flower heads.

J. A. YOUNG
U. S. Department of Agriculture

TASCHEREAU, tash-rō′, **Sir Henri Elzéar** (1836–1911), Canadian legislator and chief justice of the supreme court of Canada. He was born on Oct. 7, 1836, at Ste.-Marie-de-la-Beauce, Lower Canada. He attended the Seminary of Quebec, studied law, and was called to the bar of Lower Canada in 1857. He practiced in the city of Quebec and in 1867 was named queen's counsel. From 1861 to 1867 he represented Beauce county as a conservative in the legislative assembly of Canada. He was appointed a judge of the superior court of the province of Quebec in 1878, and was chief justice of the supreme court of Canada from 1902 to 1906. He died in Ottawa on April 14, 1911.

CORNELIUS J. JAENEN, *University of Ottawa*

TASCHEREAU, tash-rō′, **Louis Alexandre** (1867–1952), Canadian political leader and premier of Quebec. He was born in Quebec city on March 5, 1867. Educated at Laval University, he was called to the bar in 1889 and named king's counsel in 1903. From 1900 to 1903 he was a member of the legislative assembly. He served as minister of public works and as attorney general, retaining the latter post when he became Liberal party leader and premier in 1920. As premier, Taschereau promoted the industrial prosperity of Quebec but retarded both social legislation to protect workers and national regulation of provincial commerce. From 1930 to 1932 he was also treasurer. After a public accounts investigation involving members of his cabinet in 1936, he resigned as premier and retired from politics. He died in Quebec on July 6, 1952. His son Robert was chief justice of Canada from 1963 to 1967.

CORNELIUS J. JAENEN, *University of Ottawa*

TASHKENT, tash-kent′, is the capital of the Uzbek republic of the USSR, in Central Asia, and also the capital of Tashkent oblast. The city lies in a loess oasis, watered by the Chirchik River, a tributary of the Syr Darya, between the Tien Shan range on the north and east and the Golodnaya Steppe to the south and west.

In the 20th century, Tashkent expanded greatly, and many of the narrow, twisting streets and clay dwellings of the old part of the city were replaced by broad boulevards, parks, imposing buildings, and apartment houses. Few ancient architectural monuments survive. A severe earthquake in April 1966 devastated a large part of the city, leaving 70,000 families homeless. As part of the reconstruction of the city, work was begun in 1970 on a subway system.

Tashkent's population is multinational. Although Uzbeks are in the majority, there are Russians, Tatars, Kazakhs, Tadzhiks, and several other groups. The city's many cultural and research establishments include Tashkent University and the Uzbek Academy of Sciences, as well as museums and theaters.

The Economy. A rail and air transport center, Tashkent is also an important industrial city. Its heavy industrial enterprises produce excavators, cranes, and mining equipment. Its many light industries process food, cotton, and tobacco, and manufacture chemical products, furniture, and textiles. Tashkent's cotton mills form the heart of the Uzbek cotton industry.

History. Chinese sources mention a settlement on the site as early as the 2d century B.C. By the 8th century A.D. the Muslims ruled the town, which became an important trading center. After a succession of other rulers, it fell to the Mongols in 1220. Timur (Tamerlane) and his successors occupied it from 1361 to the end of the 15th century. After being contested by the Uzbeks and Kazakhs for some four centuries, Tashkent was conquered by the Russians in 1865 and made the capital of the governor generalship of Turkestan in 1867. The capital of the Turkestan ASSR from 1922 to 1924, it became the center of the newly formed Uzbek SSR in 1930.

The Oblast. Tashkent oblast, formed in 1938, covers 9,690 square miles (25,100 sq km). Its agriculture centers on cotton, for which extensive reclamation projects have been undertaken. Population: (1970) of the city, 1,300,000; (1961 est.) of the oblast, 2,402,000.

RICHARD A. PIERCE, *Queen's University*

TASK FORCE, a grouping of personnel and resources to accomplish a single objective or a series of related objectives. The term was coined by the U.S. Navy to denote a grouping capable of large-scale combat or support operations. A Navy *task organization* assigns a task, personnel, and matériel to a task force under a responsible commander. The task force may be subdivided into *task groups, task elements*, and *task units*, their size varying with the size of the task force. A *task fleet* is a mobile command of ships and aircraft assigned to a specific, major continuing task.

The U.S. Army and Air Force use the terms "task force" and "air task force" for temporary groupings to accomplish specific objectives, but the Navy's task forces may be semipermanent. The Navy numbers its task forces and the Army names them.

"Task force" also applies to civilian committees organized to accomplish specific objectives in politics, industry, or public service.

TASMAN, taz′mən, **Abel Janszoon** (1603–1659), Dutch navigator, who discovered Tasmania and New Zealand. He was born in the Dutch village of Lutjegast. In 1633 he went to Batavia (Djakarta), Java, where he entered the service of the Dutch East India Company. Six years later he was second in command of an expedition to search for legendary islands east of Japan. He commanded his own voyages to Japan in 1640, to Cambodia in 1641, and to Sumatra early in 1642.

The East India Company then gave Tasman the command of an expedition to determine the southern extent of the "Great South Land" (Australia). He left Batavia with two ships, *Heemskerck* and *Zeehaen*, on Aug. 14, 1642. After visiting Mauritius in the Indian Ocean, he sailed south of Australia. On November 24 he discovered the island now known as Tasmania, which he named Van Diemen's Land for Anton Van Diemen, governor general of the Dutch East Indies.

Sailing eastward across the sea that now bears his name, Tasman sighted the South Island of New Zealand on Dec. 13, 1642. Four of his men were killed by Maoris on December 19 when they attempted to land at Golden Bay, which Tasman named Massacre Bay. The ships then continued along the west coast of North Island. Tasman called New Zealand Staten Land after the States of Holland. Continuing in a northerly direction he discovered islands in the Tonga and Fiji groups and then turned northwest and visited New Guinea before returning to Batavia on June 15, 1643. Although he did not see the Australian mainland, Tasman's passage between it and Antarctica proved that Australia was not part of the southern polar continent.

Tasman commanded an expedition in 1644 to the southwest coast of New Guinea and the north coast of Australia, where he mapped the Gulf of Carpentaria. He later led trading voyages to Sumatra and Thailand and commanded a fleet against the Spanish in the Philippines. Tasman died in Batavia in 1659.

HOWARD J. CRITCHFIELD
Western Washington State College

TASMAN SEA, taz′mən, part of the Pacific Ocean separating the Australian continent and Tasmania on the west from New Zealand on the east. Its width is about 1,200 miles (1,900 km). On the north it merges with the Coral Sea and on the southwest with the Indian Ocean. The sea was named for Abel Janszoon Tasman, who in 1642 discovered Tasmania, crossed the Tasman Sea, and discovered New Zealand.

AUSTRALIAN NEWS AND INFORMATION BUREAU

The Derwent, one of Tasmania's major rivers, flows through fertile countryside near New Norfolk.

TASMANIA, taz-mā'nē-ə, is an island state in Australia, lying 150 miles (240 km) off the southeastern coast of the Australian continent. Its area totals 26,363 square miles (68,280 sq km), of which 26,215 square miles (67,892 sq km) are accounted for by the heart-shaped main island. Numerous smaller islands make up the balance, including King, Flinders, Bruny, and subantarctic Macquarie.

The Land. Tasmania is a detached part of the eastern highlands of Australia, separated by the relatively shallow Bass Strait. A dominant feature is the lake-studded Central Plateau, which exceeds 4,000 feet (1,220 meters). It terminates abruptly northward and eastward in a 2,000-foot (600-meter) escarpment and is drained southeastward by the Derwent River. Westward lie a series of peaks and ridges parallel to the west coast. Here the highest mountain in Tasmania, Mt. Ossa, reaches 5,305 feet (1,617 meters). Southward lie the uninhabited, little-explored southern highlands, and northward a plateau that slopes gently to a cliff coast.

Northeastern Tasmania consists mainly of the uplifted remnants of old mountains, with small basins. Its highest area is the 5,000-foot (1,520-meter) mesa Ben Lomond, separated from the Central Plateau by a rift valley drained by the Esk River. The rest of eastern Tasmania is a low dissected plateau, ending on the southeast in a "drowned" coastline.

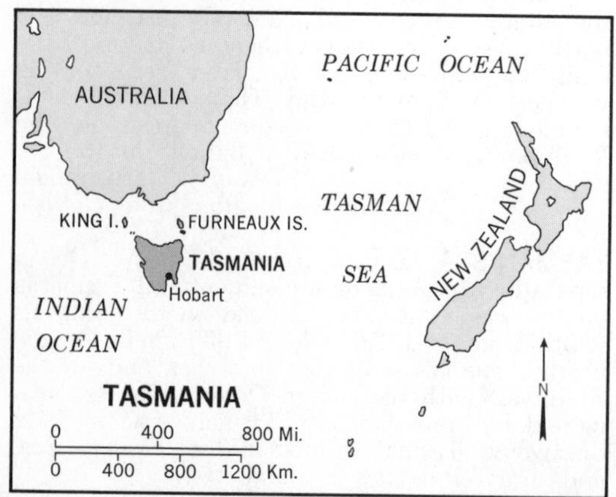

Tasmania's location in the westerly wind belt of the mid-latitudes ensures a moist equable climate, with mild to warm summers, mild winters in most settled areas, and rain in all seasons. Yet cloud cover rarely persists for long, summers are often dry, the daily range of temperature is considerable, and there is abundant sunshine. Occasionally in summer, hot winds penetrate from the mainland.

Annual rainfall exceeds 100 inches (2,500 mm) in the west and decreases eastward to 30 to 20 inches (750–500 mm); the north has 50 to 30 inches (1,300–750 mm). In general, the wettest areas have temperate rain forest, intermediate areas good-quality eucalyptus forest, and the drier areas poor-quality eucalyptus forest or savanna woodland. There are many areas of heathland and moorland.

Tasmania has large numbers of ground-dwelling animals, but not as many species—especially bird species—as continental Australia. Distinctive animals are the common Tasmanian devil and the rare Tasmanian tiger.

The People. With an estimated 392,000 inhabitants in 1970, Tasmania is the least populous Australian state. It also has the smallest population growth rate (1.2% annually). Yet among the states Tasmania has the highest birthrate and the highest proportion of its population in the youngest age groups (32% aged 0–14). Its slow growth has been due to long-continued and substantial emigration to the mainland, particularly by young people of working age, and to a low rate of immigration. Tasmania has the smallest proportion of British immigrants in its population (5%), the smallest proportion of persons born in Europe (3%), and the highest ratio of Australian born (90%).

No other state has so even a balance of population among capital city, other towns, and countryside. Hobart, the capital, on the Derwent estuary in the southeast, had 119,469 inhabitants in the 1966 census. Other towns, including

Launceston (60,456) in the north and Burnie (15,806) and Devonport (14,875) in the northwest, totaled 141,520. Rural areas, including centers of less than 1,000 persons, contained 109,772 persons.

The Economy. Tasmania has a diversified economy. Of the net value of all primary and secondary production, manufacturing contributes about 65%, farming 21%, forestry 5%, mining 8%, and fishing 1%.

Manufacturing is dominated by electrometallurgical and electrochemical specialties, notably electrolytic zinc refining at Risdon, aluminum and ferromanganese manufacture at Bell Bay, and carbide production at Snug. About 40% of the newsprint used in Australia is manufactured at Boyer. Other major manufactures are fine paper at Burnie, pulp and paper at Wesley Vale, wood pulp at Port Huon, cement at Railton, chocolate at Claremont, textiles at Launceston, Devonport, and Hobart, and carpets at Devonport.

Hydroelectric power development has been closely associated with the growth of manufacturing. In 1970 the installed capacity of the hydroelectric system was 1,046,200 kw.

Farming diversity derives from the varied relief, soils, and local climates. Dairying for butter production characterizes the north; sheep grazing for wool, the midlands; and specialized horticulture (fruit and hops), the valleys of the southeast. Important subsidiary enterprises in the north are green peas, potatoes, pigs, fat stock, and fruit; in the midlands, beef cattle and cereals; and in the southwest, milk and fat stock. The principal agricultural exports, in order of importance, are wool, fruit, meat, butter, potatoes, and hops.

Sawmilling is widespread but centered mainly in the northwest. Fishing on a small scale, chiefly for crayfish, takes place in all coastal waters. The chief minerals are copper from Queenstown, lead and zinc from Rosebery, and iron ore from Savage River, made into pellets for export to Japan. Small quantities of tin, tungsten, and coal are produced in the northeast.

Tasmania has 571 miles (919 km) of railroad, four major seaports (Hobart, Burnie, Launceston, Devonport), and four main airports. Most exports go to mainland Australia.

Government. Tasmania is represented in Australia's Parliament at Canberra by 5 members of the House of Representatives and 10 members of the Senate. The governor is appointed by the British sovereign. The Tasmanian Parliament consists of a House of Assembly with 35 members and a legislative Council with 19 members. The 5 constituencies for the House of Assembly are identical with the 5 electoral divisions for the federal House of Representatives.

Local government areas comprise 3 cities (Hobart, suburban Glenorchy, and Launceston) and 46 municipalities, of which 42 are administered by elected municipal councils, 3 (Clarence, Kingborough, and Zeehan) by multiple-member commissions that the governor appoints, and one (St. Leonard's) by an administrator.

History. Tasmania was discovered in 1642 by the Dutch navigator Abel Janszoon Tasman, who named it Van Diemen's Land. White occupation began in 1803 with the establishment of a British penal settlement at Risdon, administered from New South Wales. Tasmania became a separate colony in 1825.

Until the 1850's settlement was largely confined to the pastoral woodlands of the midlands and the east. In 1850 the population was estimated at 68,870. Transportation of prisoners to Tasmania ceased in 1852. The aboriginal population was extinct by 1876.

Responsible government dates from 1856, and in that year the island was renamed Tasmania. The period 1850–1900 saw the beginnings of dairying, fruit growing, mining, and railroad building. In 1901, with a population of 172,475, Tasmania became a state of Australia.

Since 1914, when the pattern of land settlement was virtually completed, the major trends have been toward denser rural settlement and the development of hydroelectric power, secondary industry, and tourism.

PETER SCOTT
University of Tasmania

TASMANIAN DEVIL, taz-mā′nē-ən, a carnivorous marsupial (*Sarcophilus harrisii*) of the family Dasyuridae. The Tasmanian devil is found only in Tasmania, where it is still common. Fossil and subfossil materials, 500 to 4,000 years old, indicate that it was once widely distributed on the Australian mainland.

AUSTRALIAN NEWS AND INFORMATION BUREAU

The Tasmanian devil, an animal unique to Tasmania.

Tasmanian devils are heavily built animals with broad and powerful heads and shoulders and large and very strong jaws. Adult males have a head and body length of about two feet (60 cm), a tail length of about one foot (30 cm), and a body weight of up to 26 pounds (12 kg). Females average somewhat smaller. Both sexes are black in color and usually have minor white markings on the chest and rump.

The Tasmanian devil's bite is capable of inflecting a severe wound, but the animal's rather slow movements render it less dangerous than its appearance suggests. Although mainly a ground-dweller, the Tasmanian devil is a competent climber. It is nocturnal and hides by day in any available cover. It feeds mainly on medium-sized mammals and birds. A feature of its feeding is that all of the prey is eaten, including the skin and bones. Breeding is most common in the autumn, and up to 4 young are carried in a pouch for about 3½ months.

A. G. LYNE, *Author of "Marsupials and Monotremes of Australia"*

AUSTRALIAN NEWS AND INFORMATION BUREAU

TASMANIAN TIGER, or thylacine, a nearly extinct wolflike marsupial. This photo, taken in 1933, is one of the very few showing the living animal.

TASMANIAN TIGER, taz-mā'nē-ən, a carnivorous marsupial (*Thylacinus cynocephalus*) of the family Dasyuridae, now usually known as the thylacine. It is also called the Tasmanian wolf. The thylacine, now confined to Tasmania, once ranged widely on the Australian mainland. The most recent record is provided by an almost complete skeleton, estimated to be 3,300 years old, collected from a cave on the Nullarbor Plain, Western Australia. Fossil remains have also been found in New Guinea. Formerly common in Tasmania, the thylacine was very rare by 1914. The last specimen was collected in 1930, but recent reports indicate that it is not yet extinct.

The thylacine is the largest living flesh-eating marsupial known, being about 5 feet (1.5 meters) in overall length, of which the tail makes up 1¾ feet (0.5 meter). It is doglike in appearance, with a tawny yellow-brown coat marked with 16 to 18 distinctive dark brown bars on the back, rump, and base of the tail. The thylacine is mainly nocturnal and is usually a solitary animal. There are usually 3 or 4 young in a litter, and the period of pouch life is probably about 4 months.

A. G. LYNE, *Author of "Marsupials and Monotremes of Australia"*

TASS, tas, is the news agency of the Soviet Union. The name is an acronym of the Russian name for Telegraphic Agency of the Soviet Union. It is a monopolistic state agency, handling official propaganda on national and international levels.

Tass has been called a "gatekeeper" in controlling and censoring the news reaching the Russian people as well as that sent to the rest of the world. Through its worldwide network of correspondents, Tass is also a major part of the Soviet Union's intelligence system. It has a sealed confidential information service available only to metropolitan editors and high officials of the Communist party.

Tass was organized in 1925 to succeed Rosta, the Russian Telegraph Agency. Rosta had been formed by Lenin in 1918 by merging competing agencies in Petrograd and Moscow.

JOHN TEBBEL, *New York University*

TASSELFISH. See THREADFIN.

TASSO, täs'sō, **Torquato** (1544–1595), Italian poet, who was the most important poet in Italy in the second half of the 16th century. His masterpiece, *La Gerusalemme liberata,* known in English as *Jerusalem Delivered,* is the greatest epic poem in Italian literature.

Life.—Early Years. Tasso was born in Sorrento on March 11, 1544, the son of the poet-courtier Bernardo Tasso. He attended a Jesuit school in Naples and was also educated at home by his mother. Bernardo, who had been exiled from Naples for political reasons in 1552, leaving his family behind, was joined by Torquato in Rome in 1554. In 1556, Torquato's mother, to whom he was very attached, died prematurely. These tragic events deeply affected the youth. His education was continued in various Italian cities, notably in Urbino, where he studied at the court of Duke Guidobaldo II delle Rovere.

In Venice, in 1559, Tasso helped his father revise his epic poem the *Amadigi.* The youth's own first major work was the narrative poem *Rinaldo,* published when he was 18 to considerable critical acclaim. Tasso studied first law and then philosophy at the universities of Padua and Bologna. In Padua, he joined a literary society, the Accademia degli Eterei, sponsored by his friend, Prince Scipione Gonzaga. Another Paduan friend, the philosopher Sperone Speroni, introduced him to classical poetic theory. In 1565, Tasso went to Ferrara, where he entered the service of Cardinal Luigi d'Este and in 1571 of the Cardinal's brother, Duke Alfonso II. There, Tasso wrote his fine pastoral drama, *Aminta* (1573), and *La Gerusalemme liberata* (1575).

Later Years. The completion of the *Gerusalemme* marked a tragic turning point in Tasso's life. He began to show signs of extreme nervousness and paranoia, brought on by fear that the poem contained elements and ideas that conflicted with the teachings of the Roman Catholic Church. The Counter-Reformation was then reaching its height, and church strictures on literature and the arts were being strongly enforced. Obsessed with doubt and guilt, Tasso gave excessive credence to caviling charges by critical friends that the poem put too much emphasis on romance and included elements of magic, and he insisted on being examined for heresy by the Inquisition. He began to have various kinds of delusions, and when, in 1579, he indulged in a furious outburst against his patron Alfonso, he was declared insane and confined to a hospital for seven years. The romantic myth that he was imprisoned for daring to love the Duke's sister Leonora, immortalized in Goethe's play *Torquato Tasso* (1790), was exploded in 1895 by Angelo Solerti's exhaustive biography of the poet.

Tasso's release was followed by years of impoverished wandering in Italy. He continued to be haunted by doubts about *Gerusalemme* and finally, after constant rewriting, produced a sequel, *La Gerusalemme conquistata* (1593), a mediocre, emasculated work read only by scholars. Late in 1594, he was invited to Rome by Pope Clement VIII to be crowned poet laureate. Before the ceremony, however, Tasso became seriously ill. He died in Rome on April 25, 1595.

Works.—"Aminta." The pastoral drama *Aminta* is one of the finest works of its genre. An elegant idealization of court life, it projects the values of love and of *gentilezza,* or nobility, kindness, and courtesy, into a world of rustic myth. Musical,

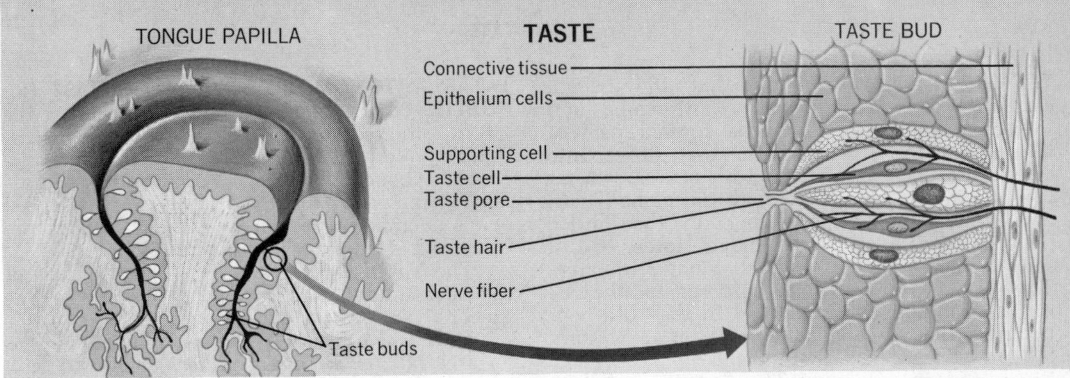

idyllic, hedonistic—more lyrical than dramatic—it presents a series of exquisite vignettes involving the shepherd Aminta and his Silvia, who are blissfully united at the conclusion.

"La Gerusalemme liberata." In *Aminta,* Tasso had been able to indulge his hedonistic tendencies freely. However, in *Gerusalemme,* based on an important religious event in history, he had to come to terms with medieval history, Aristotelian poetics, and Roman Catholic morality. The work is about the First Crusade and the liberation of the Holy Sepulcher from the Saracens by Godfrey of Bouillon in 1099. However, the most interesting characters are those invented by Tasso: the Christian heroes Rinaldo and Tancredi and their Saracen ladies Armida and Clorinda. The seduction of Rinaldo by Armida influenced the "Bower of Bliss" canto in Book 2 of Edmund Spenser's *The Faerie Queen.* The scene in which Tancredi unwittingly kills his beloved Clorinda in battle is still one of the most poignant in literature.

Despite the work's tight epic structure, its chief charm lies in its amorous and idyllic interludes. This apparent paradox has led to the description of the *Gerusalemme* as a great poem with flawed architecture. For all his desire to sing the faith of the age, to "profit men with the example of human actions," and to adhere to historical fact, Tasso ended by celebrating his own credo, pleasure. See JERUSALEM DELIVERED.

Other Works. Tasso wrote about 2,000 short poems, including sonnets and madrigals, as well as the tragedy *Re Torrismondo* (1587). Among his prose works are an extensive and lively collection of letters and 31 erudite *Dialoghi.* His theoretical writings include *Discorsi del poema eroico* (1594), a restatement of ancient theories of poetry.

JOHN CHARLES NELSON, *Columbia University*

Further Reading: Bowra, Cecil Maurice, *From Virgil to Milton* (London 1945); Tasso, Torquato, *Jerusalem Delivered,* tr. by Edward Fairfax, with introduction by John Charles Nelson (New York 1963).

TASTE is a special sense closely related to smell. Taste conveys information about fairly high concentrations of chemicals dissolved in liquids, while smell detects lower concentrations of chemicals in gaseous form. Often, smell plays an important role in the perception of many sensations considered to be tastes. For example, when the nasal passages are blocked, as when one has a cold, it is difficult to distinguish between bland foods.

In man and other mammals the taste receptor cells are located in the fungiform papillae at the front of the tongue and in the foliate and circumvallate papillae at the back of the tongue. (See diagram accompanying the article TONGUE.) Among insects and other invertebrate animals, taste receptors are located in specialized hairs on the feet, legs, or body surface. Because of the accessibility of taste receptors in some insects, much of the fundamental research on taste mechanisms has been conducted on these animals. The first recordings of electrical impulses from taste cells were obtained in 1955 from a receptor of a fly. In mammals, it is customary to study the electrical activity of the chorda tympani nerve, which supplies the fungiform papillae.

The idea that there are four different types of taste receptors, each giving rise to a single sensation—sweet, salt, sour (acid), and bitter—is a popular oversimplification. A single taste receptor cell may alter its output of electrical impulses in response to any three or four of these so-called taste modalities. It is generally assumed that the cell membrane of a receptor cell has various sites that combine with different chemicals. The sensations perceived in the brain evidently result from a complex coding of the electrical impulses transmitted by the receptor cells. A preference for sugar, the so-called "sweet tooth," is common among many animals, and taste cravings to compensate for dietary or hormonal imbalances are well known. These generally result from the brain's processing of incoming taste impulses rather than from changes in the receptors themselves.

The stimulation of taste receptors by salts is mainly a function of the positively charged ions (cations) of the chemicals. No single type of chemical stimulant appears to account for sensations of sweetness, although relatively small sugar molecules with a ring configuration are especially stimulating. Saccharin has a different structure and yet it is confused with sugar by man and other primates. Other mammals, however, can tell them apart.

The delicate relationships between the molecular structure of a stimulus, the receptor response, and the sensation perceived have been well illustrated by studies on the chemical phenylthiocarbamide (PTC). For people who have inherited a dominant "Taster" gene, PTC evokes an unpleasant bitter taste. For others it is mildly sweet or tasteless. The bitter taste is evoked by a very small part of the PTC molecule, and if a minor change is made in that part the molecule becomes several hundred times sweeter than sugar.

EDWARD S. HODGSON, *Tufts University*

Further Reading: Hayashi, Takashi, ed. *Olfaction and Taste* (Elsford, N.Y. 1967); Kare, Morley R., and Maller, O., *The Chemical Sense and Nutrition* (Baltimore 1967).

TATAR, tä'tər, a Mongol tribe that after the 5th century A.D. settled in eastern Mongolia and western Manchuria. The tribe formed part of the hordes of Genghis Khan that drove into eastern Europe early in the 13th century. After the breakup of Genghis' empire the name Tatar, or Tartar, became identified with the Turkic peoples that made up the Golden Horde, one of the remnants of the original Mongol domain. The Golden Horde, which bordered on the rising Russian state, disintegrated in the 15th century into the Tatar khanates of Sibir in western Siberia, Kazan and Astrakhan on the Volga River, and the Crimea. The first three fell to the Russians in the 16th century. The Crimea, after 300 years under Turkish rule, passed to Russia in 1783.

The Volga Tatar culture, the most developed of the Tatar cultures, was suppressed after Ivan IV the Terrible conquered Kazan in 1552. Its eclipse lasted until the 19th century, when a literary revival occurred under the czars. The Soviet regime, after 1917, recognized the Tatars as one of the major ethnic groups inhabiting the Soviet Union and fostered Tatar culture within the bounds of Communist ideology.

Tatar is one of the Turkic languages of the Altaic language family. It has a number of dialects coinciding with the various historical-geographic groups of Tatars. Volga Tatar, the language of the Kazan Tatars, is considered the standard literary language. In religion, the Tatars are Sunnite Muslims.

Distribution of the Tatars. Out of a total Tatar population of more than 5 million in the Soviet Union, about 25% live in the Tatar republic, the only ethnic political division associated with the Tatar nationality. The other Tatars are widely distributed through the Soviet Union, with 600,000 in the Volga Valley outside the Tatar ASSR; 1,600,000 in the Urals; 150,000 in western Siberia; and 800,000 in Kazakhstan and Central Asia. These figures do not include some 50,000 Altaian Tatars, known officially simply as Altaians, who live in the Gorno-Altai autonomous oblast.

The Soviet Union's Tatar population is about evenly divided between rural and urban areas. Most of the urban centers of European Russia have significant Tatar minorities. Few Tatars live outside the Soviet Union.

Fate of the Crimean Tatars. The Crimean Tatars, who numbered about 200,000 in 1939, formed the basis of the Crimean ASSR, set up in 1921. In World War II they were accused of collaborating with the German occupation force in the Crimea. As punishment the Crimean Tatars were exiled to Central Asia, mainly the Uzbek republic, and were deprived of their civil rights, including the right to foster their language and culture. The Crimean republic was abolished in 1945 and made a nonethnic oblast of the Russian SFSR.

During the de-Stalinization program under Premier Nikita Khrushchev, the exiled Crimean Tatars regained their civil rights in Uzbekistan in 1956, but they were not permitted to return to the Crimea, which had been incorporated into the Ukrainian SSR in 1954. Protest demonstrations by Crimean Tatars in the Uzbek SSR were repressed in the late 1960's, and some of their leaders were tried as political dissidents.

THEODORE SHABAD
Editor of "Soviet Geography"

TATAR AUTONOMOUS SOVIET SOCIALIST REPUBLIC, tä'tər, an ethnic political division of the USSR, situated in the Russian republic on the middle Volga River and its eastern tributary, the Kama. About 45% of the population is indigenous Tatar and about 45% Russian, the rest being neighboring minority groups, such as the Chuvash, Mordvinians, Udmurt, and Mari.

The Tatar ASSR, set up in 1920, was one of the first autonomous areas established by the Soviet regime along ethnic lines.

Regions and Economy. The republic, which has an area of 26,200 square miles (68,000 sq km) can be divided into three natural regions: (1) the uplands on the west bank of the Volga, with gully erosion, black-earth soils, and deciduous forest; (2) the north bank of the Kama, low-lying, marshy, and wooded with coniferous forest on podzolic soils; and (3) the south bank of the Kama, a lowland with grassy steppe vegetation on black earth.

Agriculture in the moister northwestern section stresses the cultivation of fodder crops, potatoes, hemp, and sugar beets; hog and poultry farming; and dairying. In the drier southeast the accent is on hard-grained wheat, sunflowers, beef cattle, and sheep.

Manufacturing is concentrated in the northwest around Kazan, the republic's capital, which produces chemicals, leather, furs, and machinery; Zelenodolsk, which makes wood products and glass; and Chistopol, which turns out clocks and watches. One of the Soviet Union's largest truck-manufacturing complexes is being located at Naberezhnye Chelny, at the site of a new hydroelectric station on the Kama River. After the discovery of large petroleum deposits, the Tatar ASSR in the 1950's became the Soviet Union's largest oil producer. The oil fields, centered on the city of Almetievsk, supply refineries in European Russia and in eastern Europe via the Friendship pipeline system. The oil industry gave rise to a major petrochemical center at the new city of Nizhnekamsk, on the Kama River north of Almetievsk. Population: (1970) 3,131,000.

THEODORE SHABAD
Editor of "Soviet Geography"

TATE, Allen (1899–), American writer, best known as a poet and literary critic. He was born John Orley Allen Tate in Winchester, Ky., on Nov. 19, 1899. A graduate of Vanderbilt University (1922), Tate taught at several institutions, including the University of Minnesota (1951–1966). He published some 20 books and received numerous literary honors—among them, the Bollingen Prize for poetry in 1956. His marriages to the novelist Caroline Gordon, in 1924, and to the poet Isabella Stewart Gardner, in 1959, ended in divorce.

Tate was identified with the "Fugitive group" at Vanderbilt—John Crowe Ransom, Robert Penn Warren, and others, who initiated the Southern literary renaissance—and with the "new criticism" and the ironic style of modernist poetry. Of his poems, *Ode to the Confederate Dead* (1927), an exercise in sustained irony, seems most likely to outlast changing fashions. *Reactionary Essays on Poetry and Ideas* (1936) influenced a generation of college teachers. *Essays of Four Decades* appeared in 1969.

HYATT H. WAGGONER, *Author of "American Poets, from the Puritans to the Present"*

TATE, Nahum (1652–1715), English poet and dramatist, who was a typical Restoration literary hack. He was born in Dublin on Aug. 12, 1652. After graduating from Trinity College in 1672, he went to London, where he became an active literary figure. As a dramatist he is best remembered for his adaptation (1681) of Shakespeare's *King Lear,* in which Cordelia survives and a happy ending is imposed on the tragedy. In 1682, Tate collaborated with John Dryden on Part II of *Absalom and Achitophel,* writing the larger—and less distinguished—part of that anti-Whig satire. Tate was made poet laureate in 1692. He died in London on Aug. 12, 1715.

Tate was a prolific but undistinguished writer. None of his dramatic work has proven durable, and only antiquarians find his poems of interest. His libretto for the opera *Dido and Aeneas* (about 1690) survives by virtue of Henry Purcell's great music, and not because of Tate's verses. Tate's best poetry is found in the *New Version of the Psalms* (1696), written with Nicholas Brady, and in *Panacea: a Poem on Tea* (1700).

FRANK J. WARNKE, *Coeditor of "Seventeenth Century Prose and Poetry"*

TATE GALLERY, an art museum in London. It was founded and financed by the sugar refining magnate and philanthropist Sir Henry Tate (1819–1899).

The Tate Gallery, originally called the National Gallery of British Art, was opened on Aug. 16, 1897. The building is in a free classic style, with a portico supporting a statue of Britannia and galleries grouped around a central hall. Its collection is mainly of paintings of the British school from the 18th century on and from foreign schools after 1850. It also includes some modern sculpture.

Sir Henry Tate, the museum's donor, started as a grocer's assistant, later held the lucrative patent for cube sugar, and was ultimately created a baronet. An avid art collector, he gave 65 of the paintings in the original collection and paid for the building. The British government subsequently added to both the collection and the building.

TATIAN, tā'shən, a 2d century Syrian Christian apologist and teacher. A native of the Assyrian country between the Tigris and Euphrates rivers, he was schooled in Greek philosophy. He became a Christian about the year 150, apparently drawn to Christianity by his admiration for the monotheism of the Old Testament and the teachings of the Hebrew prophets. Unlike Justin Martyr—under whom he studied—and most apologists who accepted Greek philosophy as preparative for Christianity, Tatian was violently hostile to Hellenic culture. His only work to survive in complete form is the *Address to the Greeks* (about 160), which contains a harsh and unrestrained diatribe against Greek thought.

Tatian left Rome about 175 to establish a school in Syria. His most famous work is the *Diatessaron,* a harmony of the four Gospels with every verse worked into a continuous narrative of the life of Christ. Probably compiled for Sunday liturgical readings, it was used in Syrian churches until the 5th century.

POWEL MILLS DAWLEY
The General Theological Seminary, New York

TATIUS, Achilles. See ACHILLES TATIUS.

TATLER, a periodical published by Richard Steele from April 12, 1709, to Jan. 2, 1711. After *The Spectator,* its illustrious successor, *The Tatler* was the best of the 18th century English periodicals. Of the 271 papers (issues), Steele wrote 188 and Joseph Addison wrote 41 or 42. The purpose of *The Tatler* was "to expose the false arts of life, to pull off the disguises of cunning vanity, and affectation, and to recommend general simplicity in our dress, our discourse, and our behaviour."

The early papers of *The Tatler* were devoted to items of social and literary gossip that were purportedly gleaned by agents in coffeehouses. By mid-1710, however, the papers were in the form of single essays. In his papers, Steele assumed the character—borrowed from Jonathan Swift—of the gossiping "Tatler," Isaac Bickerstaff. Steele's warm, colloquially intimate style and his praise of family life and the simple virtues were a novelty at that time. Addison's papers foreshadowed the polished, good-natured, but detached satires perfected in *The Spectator.*

See also SPECTATOR, THE.

GEORGIA DUNBAR
Hofstra University

TATLIN, tät-lyēn', **Vladimir Yevgrafovich** (1885?–?1956), Soviet sculptor, who founded the Constructivist movement. Tatlin studied at the School of Painting and Sculpture in Moscow. A still life model seen in Picasso's Paris studio inspired Tatlin to make "relief constructions" in 1913–1914. They consisted of geometric shapes of wood, sheet metal, and cardboard coated with plaster, glaze, and broken glass. In a similar vein were his "counter-reliefs," or "corner constructions," which hung from the corners of rooms. Both kinds of sculpture were concerned with showing motion in space.

After the Russian Revolution, Tatlin applied Constructivist principles to practical uses. He built an 80-foot model of a *Monument for the Third International* (1919), consisting of a revolving cylinder, cube, and cone inside a tilted iron spiral. He also taught in Moscow and Leningrad and designed theatrical sets.

TATRA MOUNTAINS, tä'trə, two ranges in the western part of the Carpathians. The High Tatra mountains lie along the Czechoslovak-Polish border. The Low Tatra mountains are to the south. See CARPATHIAN MOUNTAINS.

TATTING is a delicate handmade lace, or the process of making such lace by using a small hand shuttle usually to knot and loop a single cotton thread into various circular designs. Known for centuries, tatting became popular in the early 1700's, before the advent of textile machinery. Appenzell and St. Gallen, Switzerland, and Plauen, Germany, were centers for its manufacture.

Although delicate in appearance, tatting is quite strong. Each stitch is a unit by itself and does not rely on a neighboring stitch for strength. The stitch is a minute knot over a single running thread, and two stitches, reversed to each other, form the base of the work. A break or a mis-stitch does not cause the fabric to ravel—a new piece fills the gap. Shuttles are of bone, plastic, steel, or tortoiseshell. Experienced tatters use a hook at one end. The best thread is a tightly twisted, mercerized cotton of 20s or 30s yarn count.

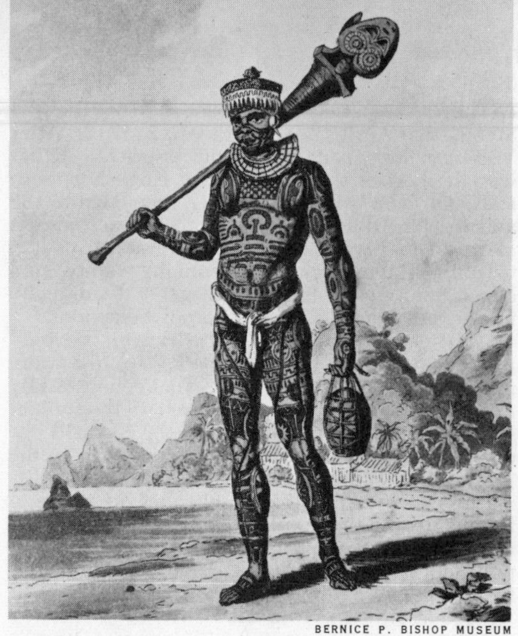

BERNICE P. BISHOP MUSEUM

In tatting, stitches are worked over a thread on the left hand. A foot (30 cm) or so of thread is unwound from the back of the shuttle, which is held in the right hand. The thread end is placed between the first finger and thumb of the left hand so that the idle portion of thread is below the thumb. The thread is then passed around the left hand and brought back to lie to the right of the thread already held, thus forming a loop of thread around the hand.

The single stitch is a half stitch. The second half of the stitch, which is called a double stitch, completes the stitch binding making the loop secure.

Picots, which are small decorative loops, are most popular, for they provide the lacelike effect that makes it possible to join the rings together as work progresses. The use of a second thread makes the chain formation possible, increasing embellishment. Picot-edgings are very popular. Other uses of picots include collar and cuff sets, doilies, matting, and "narrow-work" of several types.

GEORGE E. LINTON
Author of "The Modern Textile Dictionary"

TATTING, which is done by hand with a single small shuttle, can produce delicate and intricate designs, but it nevertheless is quite strong.

MC CALL'S NEEDLEWORK AND CRAFTS MAGAZINE

WIDE WORLD

TATTOOING, as practiced by a London artist (*above*), is done with vegetable dyes applied with a high-speed needle. (*Left*) Elaborate tattooing of the entire body of a Marquesan islander, done in the 19th century.

TATTOO, ta-tōō′. Tattooing is the production of patterns on the face and body by inserting dye under the skin. Some anthropologists think the practice developed from painting the face and body. It may be done for decoration, as an indication of status, or as a means of obtaining magical protection.

Methods. There are several methods of tattooing. In the Pacific islands, tattooers use a dark pigment made of soot mixed with water or oil and sometimes vegetable juice. The tattooer follows an outline traced on the skin, tapping the back of a comblike arrangement of thorns or bone to force the row of points repeatedly through the skin. The comb may be dipped into the dye before tapping, or the coloring matter may be rubbed into the freshly made wounds. Since the points do not penetrate deeply, the pain caused is not severe. Once applied, the designs are permanent, and mistakes cannot be corrected.

The operation is sometimes performed to the accompaniment of group chanting and dancing, which are intended to encourage the patient. An experienced tattooer is usually a man of high rank and is well paid for his skill.

In New Zealand a unique process was formerly used in tattooing Maori warriors. Special artists, called *tohunga*, marked the warriors' faces with individual combinations of curves and spirals, with the dye laid into grooved lines cut into the skin rather than into punctures. The design became an important mark of a man's identity.

Eskimo women of the Canadian Arctic used a kind of sewing as a method of tattooing. Lines on the chin to denote marriageable age were produced by drawing a blackened thread through the skin with a bone needle. Similar effects—though produced by other methods—have been observed in members of the Yakut tribe of Siberia. Two young people of this tribe were shown to the Russian court in 1733 and were described as having "sewn faces," because the designs resembled stitching.

In 20th century Europe and the United States, tattooers used an electrically powered needle. This device has been banned in some places—New York City, for one—for fear that the use of the needle may spread infections.

Worldwide Extent of the Custom. Tattooing is an old custom that is distributed around the world. It was practiced in Egypt before 1300 B. C., evidence of tattooing was found in burial remains in Siberia dating from 300 B. C., and Julius Caesar reported that the natives of Britain were tattooed when he invaded their island in 54 B. C.

The most complex decorations were made on the Marquesas islands in Polynesia. In fact, the word "tattoo" comes from the Tahitian *tatu.* Both men and women were tattooed, especially those of high social status. Sometimes a man's entire body was covered with a network of designs. Even the scalp, eyelids, and the inside of the lips might be ornamented. Marquesan designs were abstractions based on the human figure and objects in everyday use.

Some tribes of South America use an arrow or a tooth in their designs in the belief that man can intimidate evil spirits with the picture of a sharp implement. Burmese males were once tattooed from the waist to the knee with repeated inidvdual figures in patterns. Demon figures were expected to protect against snake bites, and cats were believed to increase the wearer's agility. All the non-Muslim tribes in Borneo used tattoos, with different decorations for men and women. One of the men's tattoo devices showed that the individual had taken a head and was therefore mature and entitled to marry. Up to the middle of the 20th century many people in Iran were tattooed to beautify themselves, to cure sickness, or to protect against the evil eye.

Tattoo decoration has never been really popular in American or European society. Studies have suggested that the practice has been found more frequently among criminals than in the population at large. On the other hand, merchant seamen and members of the armed forces have experimented with it, especially in foreign ports. "Tattooed ladies"—or men—used to be sideshow attractions at fairs and circuses.

In some parts of Africa, Australia, and New Guinea, where the people's skin is too dark to contrast effectively with the pigments used in tattooing, a permanent patterning is achieved by producing artificially raised scars, or keloids. In some cases these marks are used for clan or tribal identification. They are a feature of some types of initiation and are sometimes considered to enhance a person's beauty.

PHILIP C. GIFFORD, JR.
American Museum of Natural History

TATUM, tā'təm, **Art** (1910–1956), American jazz pianist. Arthur Tatum, a Negro, was born in Toledo, Ohio, on Oct. 13, 1910. From birth he was totally blind in one eye and had only slight vision in the other, but he studied violin and piano. After playing the piano in a Toledo radio station and in local night clubs for three years, he went to New York City in 1932 to accompany the singer Adelaide Hall and made recordings with her and as a soloist. He then led his own band in Chicago for two years.

By the mid-1930's, Tatum's delicacy of technique and originality in improvisation had brought him international fame. His best-known recordings as a piano soloist were *Tea for Two, Sweet Lorraine,* and *Get Happy.* From 1943 he worked chiefly as part of a trio. He received the *Esquire* magazine Gold Award (1944) and won the *Down Beat* critics' poll (1954). He died in Los Angeles, Calif., on Nov. 5, 1956.

TATUM, tā'təm, **Edward Lawrie** (1909–), American geneticist and biochemist, who shared the 1958 Nobel Prize in physiology or medicine with two other American geneticists, George W. Beadle and Joshua Lederberg. Tatum helped to establish some of the basic principles of chemical genetics. He and Beadle were honored for "their discovery that genes act by regulating specific chemical processes."

Contributions to Science. In his early work, Tatum studied the nutritional requirements and metabolic activity of insects, especially the fruit fly *Drosophila melanogaster.* These studies later led to his and Beadle's isolation and identification of kynurenine as an eye color hormone in *D. melanogaster.*

In the early 1940's, Tatum and Beadle began joint research on the pink bread mold *Neurospora crassa.* By irradiating the mold with X-rays, they hoped to modify the mold's genes and thus obtain a *Neurospora* strain chemically different from the normal mold. They succeeded in identifying an X-ray damaged, or mutant, gene and the biochemical process it impaired, thus showing that genes regulate specific chemical processes. Tatum later showed that similar mutations could be produced in the common intestinal bacterium *Escherichia coli.* Using mutant *E. coli* strains, he and Lederberg demonstrated genetic recombination in the bacteria, indicating their sexual reproduction.

Tatum next turned to the problem of gene activity at the molecular level and how it determined the characteristics of an organism. He also studied cytoplasmic inheritance, nucleic acid metabolism, and antibiotic biosynthesis.

Life. Tatum was born in Boulder, Colo., on Dec. 14, 1909. He studied at the University of Wisconsin, receiving his A. B. in chemistry in 1931, an M. S. in microbiology in 1932, and a Ph. D. in biochemistry in 1934. Three years later he joined the faculty of Stanford University, where he was first a research associate and later an assistant professor of biology. From 1945 to 1948 he taught at Yale University and then returned to Stanford as professor of biology. In 1957 he joined the Rockefeller Institute of Medical Research in New York.

WILLIAM D. MCELROY
Johns Hopkins University

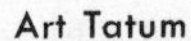

Art Tatum

DOWN BEAT

TATUNG, dä'to͝ong', is an industrial city in northern Shansi province, China, lying on the west bank of the Yü River, a tributary of the Sangkan. Strategically located between the northern and southern stretches of the Great Wall, Tatung (Datong) was for centuries an important garrison town guarding China's northern frontier. It was the capital of the Northern Wei dynasty from 398 to 494, and during that period most of the sculptures in the nearby Buddhist cave temples of Yünkang were carved.

The city is a trading center for the Tatung Basin, where wheat, millet, kaoliang, and beans are grown and sheep are raised. It stands at the junction of two main railroads and is connected with the Trans-Mongolia line. Because of its transportation advantages and the presence of good coking coal nearby, Tatung has become a manufacturing and coal-mining center. Its products include locomotives, mining machinery, and cement. Population: (1953) 228,500.

David Chuen-yan Lai
University of Victoria, British Columbia

TAULER, tou'lər, **Johannes** (c. 1300–1361), German mystic and preacher. Tauler entered the Dominican order in his native city of Strasbourg about 1315. After studying at Strasbourg, he went to the Dominican house of studies at Cologne, where he came under the influence of Meister Eckhart. Tauler was also influenced by Neoplatonism and the teachings of Thomas Aquinas. In Cologne, Strasbourg, and Basel, Tauler carried out pastoral duties and became especially esteemed for his sermons, usually preached to the nuns of the Dominican houses of the Rhineland. He died in Strasbourg on June 16, 1361.

Tauler's theology survives only in his sermons. The condemnation of many of the reputed doctrines of Eckhart by Pope John XXII in 1329 made Tauler sensitive to the possibility of misunderstanding, and he was careful to express himself in a clearly orthodox style.

John W. O'Malley, S. J.
University of Detroit

TAUNTON, tôn'tən, a borough in southwest England, the county seat of Somerset, is on the River Tone about 36 miles (58 km) southwest of Bristol. It is an attractive market town situated amid some of the loveliest scenery in the west of England. Men's shirts and precision instruments are among the borough's diverse products.

The Saxon king Ine founded Taunton and built the first castle there early in the 8th century. Architecturally the most noteworthy building is the Perpendicular Gothic St. Mary's Church, which has one of the finest towers in England's west country. The Somerset County Museum is contained in a 13th century castle.

Two pretenders to the English throne were based in Taunton: Perkin Warbeck in 1497 and the Duke of Monmouth in 1685. During the English Civil War, Taunton was held by the Parliamentarians. Population: (1961) 35,192.

Gordon Stokes
Author of "English Place-Names"

TAUNTON, tôn'tən, an industrial city in southeastern Massachusetts, is the seat of Bristol county, on the Taunton River, 32 miles south of Boston. Its principal products are silverware, electronic components, textiles, and clothing.

The community's founder was Elizabeth Pole, an Englishwoman who moved to Massachusetts in 1633, bought land from the Wampanoag Indians, and established the plantation of Cohannet. In 1640 the settlement was named Taunton in honor of Taunton, England. The city seal bears the motto *Dux Femina Facti,* meaning: "A woman was leader of that which was done."

A gristmill was begun in 1640, an ironworks in 1656, a sawmill about 1660, shipbuilding and brickmaking in the early 1700's, and stove casting in 1825. Isaac Babbitt, the inventor of babbitt metal, began manufacturing britannia ware utensils in Taunton in 1824. His firm was the forerunner of the modern silver industry.

Taunton became a town in 1639 and a city in 1864. It is governed by a mayor and council. Population: 43,756.

TAUNUS, tou'nəs, a mountain range in West Germany. Geologically part of the Rhenish Slate Mountains, the Taunus range extends eastward from the Rhine, north of the Main River. The highest point, the Grosser Feldberg, is 2,887 feet (880 meters).

The Taunus district is well-wooded and has mineral springs. Its most famous spas include Wiesbaden, Bad Nauheim, and Bad Homburg. On the southern slopes of the Rheingau Mountains, the western section of the Taunus, outstanding wine grapes are grown. The district has numerous ruins of medieval castles, as well as remains of fortifications from Roman times.

TAURANGA, tou-rang'gə, is a port city in New Zealand, on the north coast of North Island, 95 miles (150 km) southeast of Auckland. The city is on the long bay called Tauranga Harbour, near the Bay of Plenty. A major port for overseas shipping, Tauranga exports pulp and paper, pine logs, dairy products, and meat. Population: (1966) 31,606.

TAURUS, tôr'əs, is a winter constellation of the Northern Hemisphere. One of the 12 signs of the zodiac, it lies across the ecliptic immediately north of the constellation Orion on the celestial sphere. In Greek mythology, the constellation represented the white bull into which Zeus

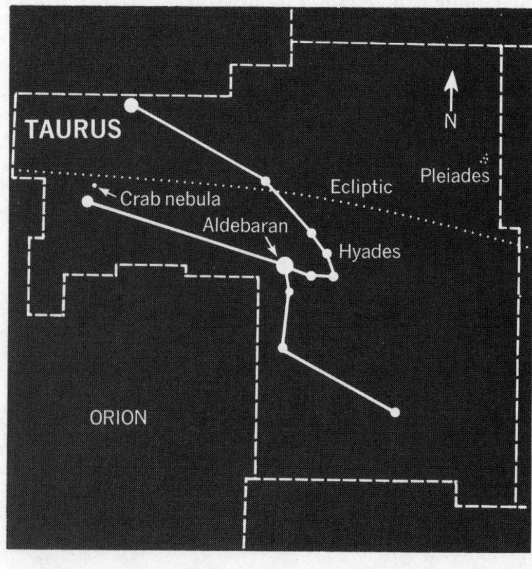

transformed himself when he carried off Europa, Princess of Phoenicia. Taurus (from Greek *tauros*) means "*bull*" in Latin.

The constellation is primarily in the shape of an elongated V, constituting the head and horns of the bull. The brightest object in the constellation is Aldebaran, a reddish star with an apparent magnitude of about 0.8—one of the 20 brightest stars in the sky (see ALDEBARAN). Near Aldebaran are the Hyades, an open star cluster, a few members of which can be observed with the naked eye (see HYADES). Some distance away in the constellation is an even more striking star cluster, the Pleiades, of which several members can be seen (see PLEIADES).

Taurus is of interest also as the sector of the sky that contains the famous Crab Nebula, the remnant of a supernova observed in 1054 A. D.

TAURUS MOUNTAINS, tôr'əs, in south central Turkey, forming the southern edge of the central Anatolian plateau, between Antalya on the west and the delta of the Seyhan River to the east. They are composed of a series of folded sediments of irregular trend, with deep valleys between the ridges. There are mineral deposits. Forests cover the more remote inner slopes, and the higher elevations, ranging well above 9,000 feet (2,740 meters), are covered with snow in the winter.

The famous pass known as the Cilician Gates, a route used since antiquity, leads through the eastern part of the mountains from the plateau to the delta of the Seyhan near Adana.

GARY L. FOWLER, *University of Kentucky*

TAUSSIG, tou'sig, **Frank William** (1859–1940), American economic theorist, historian, and sociologist, who was regarded as his country's greatest teacher of economics of the first three decades of the 20th century. He was also the leading U. S. authority on international trade, particularly the tariff, and he set up the U. S. Tariff Commission as its first chairman, serving from 1917 to 1919. He was born in St. Louis, Mo., on Dec. 28, 1859, and was educated at Harvard. He taught at Harvard from 1885 and was chairman of its economics department for 40 years.

Taussig was the ablest spokesman of his time for conservative and orthodox economic theory, and his textbook, *Principles of Economics* (1911), was a leader in its field. He offered a rounded system of economics: to the classical fundamentals of David Ricardo and J. S. Mill he added the perceptions of Eugen von Böhm-Bawerk, Alfred Marshall, and the German historical school. He was a master at combining factual and theoretical analysis. His powerful and sustained influence was directed toward understanding the strengths and potential of American capitalism. In another leading textbook, *International Trade* (1927), Taussig clarified classical principles and demonstrated their use. He died in Cambridge, Mass., on Nov. 11, 1940.

SHERMAN E. GUNDERSON
Wisconsin State University, Oshkosh

TAUSSIG, tou'sig, **Helen Brooke** (1898–), American physician, best known for her work with Alfred Blalock in developing an operation to save "blue babies." She developed the theory that so-called "blue babies" suffered from insufficient circulation to the lungs caused by stenosis, or constriction, of the artery carrying the blood to the lungs. In 1941 she started work with Blalock at Johns Hopkins University to develop an artificial arterial duct to carry the blood past the constricted area in the pulmonary artery. The procedure was tested on dogs and then, starting in 1944, successfully used on thousands of babies suffering from this defect. Dr. Taussig's book *Congenital Malformation of the Heart* (1947) is standard in the field. She also did research on rheumatic fever and helped alert American physicians to the danger of thalidomide.

Helen Taussig was born in Cambridge, Mass., on May 24, 1898. From 1930 to 1963, she was physician-in charge of the Children's Heart Clinic of the Harriet Lane pediatric unit of the Johns Hopkins Hospital. She became an associate professor of pediatrics at Johns Hopkins in 1946 and in 1959 became the first woman to hold a full professorship there.

JOHN C. BURNHAM, *Ohio State University*

TAUTOG, tô'tôg, a marine fish that inhabits inshore waters along the Atlantic coast of North America from Nova Scotia to South Carolina. It is particularly abundant between Cape Cod and Delaware Bay, and it occasionally enters brackish water. Sometimes known as the "blackfish," the tautog is popular as a game fish. Commercially, it is taken incidentally with other fishes. The white flesh has a good flavor, but its quality is not widely known.

A stout, slablike fish, the tautog may grow to a length of 3 feet (90 cm) and a weight of 22 pounds (10 kg), although specimens over 10 pounds (4.5 kg) are rare. The dorsal fin is long, and the caudal fin is rounded. Scales cover the body and extend onto the head. Large specimens are blackish with irregular darker blotches; the blotches are more noticeable on smaller fish. The coloring pales on the sides.

Tautogs usually remain close to the coast, lying along rocky ledges, around submerged wrecks, piers, or docks, or sometimes on a smooth bottom. They eat a variety of invertebrates, including mussels, crabs, shrimps, and lobsters. Spawning takes place in June near Cape Cod, a little later farther north. The eggs, about 1 mm in diameter, hatch in 1½ to 2½ days.

The tautog, *Tautoga onitis*, is in the wrasse family (Labridae) of the order Perciformes.

WILLIAM B. SCOTT, *University of Toronto*

TAUTOMERISM, tô-tom'ə-riz-əm, is the phenomenon by which two isomeric forms of an organic substance exist in equilibrium and are spontaneously interconvertible. The word was coined by the chemist Conrad Laar in 1885 to indicate isomeric structures that are instantly converted from one form into the other. In modern chemistry the word refers merely to the concurrent existence of interconvertible forms, not to the rate of conversion.

In 1911 the German chemist Ludwig Knorr succeeded in isolating two forms of acetoacetic ester and studying their properties. He identified them as an *enol* form, referring to an alcohol with a double bond, and a *keto,* or ketone form.

$$CH_3-\overset{\overset{\displaystyle OH}{|}}{C}=\overset{\overset{\displaystyle H}{|}}{C}-COOC_2H_5 \qquad CH_3-\overset{\overset{\displaystyle O}{\|}}{C}-\underset{\underset{\displaystyle H}{|}}{\overset{\overset{\displaystyle H}{|}}{C}}-COOC_2H_5$$

enol form keto form

The pure keto form separated as crystals when an

ether or hexane solution of acetoacetic ester was cooled to $-80°$ C ($-112°$ F). The pure enol form was obtained by treating a suspension of sodioacetoacetate with acid at $-80°$ C. The two pure isomers can be stored for several weeks at room temperature if kept in quartz vessels. Interconversion is catalyzed by traces of acid or base, and even the minute basicity of a glass surface can produce tautomerization. It was later found that the two pure forms can be separated by distillation in a quartz apparatus, since the enol form is slightly more volatile than the keto form. At room temperature the equilibrium mixture of acetoacetic ester contains about 7% of the enol form and 93% of the keto form. Theoretically, any compound containing the atomic grouping

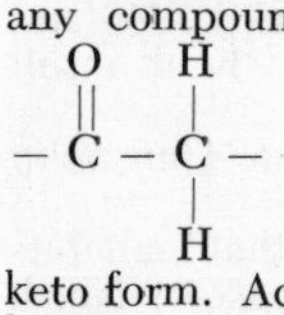

$$-\overset{\overset{\displaystyle O}{\|}}{C}-\overset{\overset{\displaystyle H}{|}}{\underset{\underset{\displaystyle H}{|}}{C}}-$$

should exist in both an enol and a keto form. Actually, simple aldehydes, esters, and ketones contain essentially no enol form.

Examples of tautomerism involving nitrogen compounds are (a) nitroethane and (b) cyanic acid.

(a) $$\mathrm{CH_3\overset{H}{\overset{|}{C}}{=}\overset{OH}{\overset{/}{N}}\underset{\diagdown O}{}} \rightleftarrows \mathrm{CH_3CH_2{-}\overset{O}{\overset{/\!/}{N}}\underset{\diagdown O}{}}$$

(b) $$\mathrm{HOC{\equiv}N} \rightleftarrows \mathrm{HN{=}C{=}O}$$

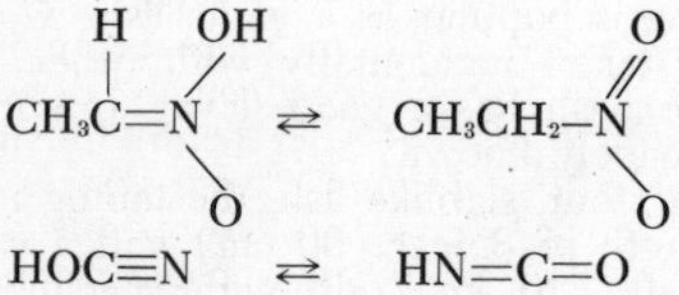

OTTO W. NITZ
Stout State University, Menomonie, Wis.

TAWNEY, tô'nē, **Richard Henry** (1880–1962), English economic historian, known for a moral fervor unique among scholars of his day. He was born in Calcutta, India, on Nov. 30, 1880, the son of a British civil servant, and was educated at Oxford, where he spent many years teaching and writing. In 1919 he moved to the University of London as a reader in economics, and in 1931 he was appointed professor of economic history, serving as well on many government commissions. He died in London on Jan. 16, 1962.

R. H. Tawney showed great interest in the plight of the workingman, an interest aroused early in his career when he studied slum conditions in the East End of London. A believer in more education for workers, he lectured to them on economics and related subjects in adult education programs. He urged greater equality—a sentiment that led him to refuse his M. A. degree at Oxford because a fee was required.

A compelling figure on the lecture platform, Tawney was likely to put a still-lit pipe into his pocket as he talked. His philosophy of reform markedly influenced the British labor movement in the early part of the 20th century. Although his methods of historical investigation are often rejected now because he did not stress the use of statistical data, he did draw attention to the ethical basis of social science. His book *Religion and the Rise of Capitalism* (1926) sought to show how religious beliefs affect the economy.

Tawney's specialty was 16th century economic conditions, on which he stimulated much research. He was a brilliant writer for whom the construction of a new society was not merely an economic and political task but a moral one as well.

BEN B. SELIGMAN
University of Massachusetts

TAX. Taxes and taxation are generally regarded as unpleasant subjects. Justice John Marshall's oft-quoted dictum that "the power to tax is the power to destroy" is representative of the overtones of this area, as is the historic linkage of death and taxes—both are inevitable. But against this aura of unpleasantness must be set the statement of Justice Oliver Wendell Holmes, Jr., that "taxes are the price we pay for civilization."

Taxes are the most important source of government revenue. Governments may secure a command over resources by borrowing and spending the proceeds, or by creating money. Governments may also secure resources by profit from enterprises such as pu licly owned electric power facilities or the sale of timber from public lands. Occasionally governments may secure funds from reparations or from gifts. But the major source of government revenue consists of taxes—compulsory payments by persons or organizations. Thus taxes involve a transfer of control over resources from persons or organizations to the state. Taxes become the major means for financing the government's activity.

Taxes are themselves burdensome since they reduce the economic power that would otherwise be possessed by individuals or organizations. But the activities that are financed from the tax proceeds will presumably bring benefits to individuals and organizations. The net burden of taxes, then, must take the nature of government expenditures into account. It follows that an examination of the impact of taxation should extend to an examination of the whole of a government's budget to ascertain the burdens and benefits for individuals or for groups or classes of individuals. This examination is a complex undertaking.

In underdeveloped or nonmarket economies taxes may be collected in terms of commodities, but in a market economy they are collected in terms of money. The base of the tax and its rate will be specified in law, together with a designation of the classes of persons or organizations that are legally liable for the payment. The tax liability is the product of the base and the rate of tax.

Most taxes are levied on income, on commodity transactions, or on wealth, and are clearly understood to fall within the category of taxes. There are, however, a great many borderline cases that are not as clearly taxes and partake, instead, of the character of payment for specific governmental services. Fees paid for government documents, such as passports or marriage licenses, fall into this category. Motor vehicle licenses are sometimes regarded as fees and not as taxes. The same is true of special property assessments used to finance specific improvements, such as street lighting or sewerage facilities. In the United States social security contributions by employers and employees are regarded as taxes, but in western European countries they are more commonly regarded as payments to secure future benefits.

TAX CLASSIFICATION

Economic activity, in a modern market economy, is variegated and complex, and governments have exercised great ingenuity in devising instrumentalities of taxation to match the complexities. As a result there is no simplified classification of taxes that is considered satisfactory for all purposes.

Who Pays? One important distinction is between taxes on persons and on business organizations. Individuals may be subject to an income tax and liable for property taxes on their ownership of land and buildings. Corporations may be subject to an income tax, but with a different base and rate structure than that applicable to individuals. All business firms, including corporations, partnerships, and proprietorships, may be subject to special taxation in the form of licenses or perhaps in the form of a value-added tax. In the latter the tax base is measured as the difference between the value of sales and the value of purchases of raw materials and other inputs from business firms.

Which Base? Taxes may also be classified in accordance with whether their base is income, wealth, or a commodity transaction. Income is the most important of all tax bases in developed countries. Wealth is subject to taxation under the property tax, particularly in the English-speaking countries, and is also subject to taxation under the death tax—commonly known as an estate or inheritance tax. Commodity transactions are subject to impositions of sales or excise taxes. Here the form of the tax may be either specific (such as a gasoline tax of 10 cents a gallon) or ad valorem (such as a state sales tax of 5% of the value of the sale).

Direct or Indirect? A traditional distinction in taxation is that between direct and indirect levies. It is intended, by this distinction, to classify those taxes that are not shifted—the direct taxes—from those that are shifted to someone else who pays. In this classification income taxes on individuals and estate or inheritance taxes are treated as direct taxes. The property tax on a homeowner is also put in this category. Indirect taxes will include property taxes on business firms, the corporation income tax, and other business taxes that may be shifted in whole or in part and all excise and commodity taxes that are usually assumed to be shifted forward to the consumer.

Progressive, Proportional, or Regressive? Taxes may also be classified in accordance with the relationship between the base and rate. If the rate of tax increases as the base increases, the tax is said to be *progressive*. If the rate remains the same as the base increases, the tax is *proportional*. A tax is *regressive* if, as the base increases, the rate is reduced.

In descriptions of specific taxes or of tax systems the terms progressive, proportional, or regressive are usually applied in relation to family income, which is treated as the implicit base out of which taxes are paid. Thus a sales tax is regressive, since family expenditures subject to tax do not, on the average, increase as rapidly as family income. Because the sales tax is levied at a flat rate, it exacts a larger proportion of income from low-income families than from middle- and upper-income families. A property tax on owned homes is similarly regressive. It is imposed at a flat rate on the value of the residence, and since families, on the average, spend proportionately less on housing as their income increases, the impact of the tax is more severe on lower-income families than on families in higher-income brackets. A property tax on rental housing is also regressive.

The one tax that contributes importantly to progressivity in the tax system as a whole is the personal income tax. Here the progressivity is attributable to the rate structure, which, for most national governments that employ this levy, rises rapidly as income increases. Similarly, estate and inheritance taxes are also progressive in impact.

The progressive, proportional, or regressive nature of a tax may be very much modified by changes in the base. Although a general sales tax is regressive, a sales tax with a food exemption is very nearly proportional over the range of family income. Even if an income tax were levied at constant rates, the exemption of the lowest incomes would distribute the total income tax burden progressively.

A number of studies have attempted to estimate the aggregate burden of the U. S. tax system for all income classes and for all levels of government—federal, state, and local. Richard A. Musgrave of Harvard University, who constructed a number of these estimates, found the burden of taxes in the United States regressive in the lowest brackets, roughly proportional through the middle-income range, and progressive only at the top. State and local tax systems tend to be regressive throughout their entire range, while the federal system tends to be progressive throughout. When the benefits of government expenditures are taken into account—although these are extremely difficult to estimate with accuracy—the picture changes markedly. Then the tax-expenditure system, for the nation as a whole, appears to operate progressively—that is, to redistribute income from middle and upper brackets to lower-income brackets.

Who Benefits? A final tax classification would attempt to separate those levies that are intended for the support of general government activities from those that are intended to support a specific class of beneficiaries. Social security taxes would fall in the latter category, as would taxes on motor vehicles and gasoline. In many governments the motor vehicle and gasoline taxes are segregated into a special fund and the proceeds are devoted to the construction and maintenance of highways, thus precluding their use for general government purposes.

For general government levies, on the other hand, there is no *quid pro quo* relationship. It is not possible to establish a specific linkage between the tax payment and the benefit of the government activity. Indeed, this is a major economic characteristic of general government operations: persons cannot be excluded from participating in the benefits provided by public goods. The national defense establishment protects all citizens, although perhaps in varying degree, depending on where they live. The space program adds to a national prestige that all may enjoy.

THE PRINCIPLES OF TAXATION

The utilization of various taxes is as old as organized society, but the attempt to develop a body of doctrine or principles about taxation is of much more recent vintage. Ancient Rome, for example, employed both death taxes and excise taxes. In the 14th century, Spain introduced the *alcabala*, a form of general sales tax. The decline of the Spanish empire is sometimes attributed, although with doubtful validity, to the repressive nature of this levy. In feudal times and during the period of mercantilism all manner of excise taxes were intermittently imposed. Often, revenue from customs duties and income from crown lands relieved much of the need for governmental tax revenue.

It was not until the decline of mercantilism and the beginnings of the Industrial Revolution that the need for a regularization of governmental revenue became apparent. This need gave rise to efforts to theorize about the role of government in the economy and the relationship of taxation to private economic activity. Adam Smith's canons of taxation, published in 1776 in *The Wealth of Nations,* attempt to construct a theory of taxation. These canons, or maxims, as he termed them, are as follows:

(1) "The subjects of every state ought to contribute towards the support of the government, as nearly as possible, in proportion to their respective abilities; that is, in proportion to the revenue which they respectively enjoy under the protection of the state."

(2) "The tax which each individual is bound to pay ought to be certain and not arbitrary."

(3) "Every tax ought to be levied at the time, or in the manner, in which it is most likely to be convenient for the contributor to pay it."

(4) "Every tax ought to be contrived as both to take out and to keep out of the pockets of the people as little as possible, over and above what it brings into the public treasury of the state."

These four canons are usually described as equality, certainty, convenience, and economy. Two of them—certainty and convenience—are administrative prescriptions that are all too seldom attained even by contemporary governments, and they continue to be important in tax administration in all governments. The search for equality in taxation is never ending and has been the subject of major policy concern among many governments.

The prescription for economy was one that Smith interpreted broadly. Not only should there be a minimum of tax-gatherers, but in addition he warned that a tax ". . . may obstruct the industry of the people, and discourage them from applying to certain branches of business which might give maintenance and employment to great multitudes." Such a tax, Smith pointed out, would not only restrict economic activity but also restrict the future growth of tax revenues. In contemporary discussion the concern with economy in terms of "obstruction" of industry is usually subdivided into an examination of the effect of taxation on incentives to work and invest and on the efficient allocation of resources in the market sector.

The major canon of taxation that has been added since Adam Smith's time is that taxation should contribute to economic stabilization. This objective is a product of the Keynesian revolution and may be interpreted to mean that taxation should be so ordered as to promote full employment, and, if possible, a stable price level. The stabilization of the balance of payments may be a subsidiary objective of a well-ordered tax system.

From time to time, governments also have used the tax system to promote social objectives that are deemed worthwhile. Alcoholic beverages and tobacco may be subject to heavy taxation, presumably to discourage their use. Conversely, home ownership may be encouraged by special exemptions for homeowners. The use of taxation to achieve social objectives was relatively unknown in Adam Smith's time. Today it is an important rationale for a great many features of modern tax systems.

Most of the contemporary discussion of the principles of taxation within a system of public finance centers on four major concepts: equality, economic stabilization, the effect of the tax system on the allocation—that is, the efficient use—of resources, and the use of taxation for purposes of social control. Many governments must also be concerned with the adequacy of their revenues.

Equality in Taxation. No subject in the field of taxation has been more warmly debated than that of equality. The economists in the 19th century generally argued that equality should be interpreted in terms of benefits derived from the state. Since these benefits were thought to be proportional to income, it followed that the appropriate basis for taxation should be proportionality. In the latter part of the century, with the rise of marginal utility economics, it came to be argued that there was a diminishing marginal utility of income—that is, as income increases the utility or satisfaction derived from additional increments decreases. This justified a progressive tax system, and some economists went so far as to argue that income should be taxed from the top down—the top brackets should be leveled down to the middle before the middle brackets were taxed. Only in this way, it was contended, would there be a minimum aggregate sacrifice for the whole body of taxpayers. The major practical difficulty with this approach, which would achieve maximum progressivity in the tax system, is the resulting adverse consequences on incentives to save and invest in a system of private property ownership.

Few students of taxation today would accept a minimum-aggregate-sacrifice approach, partly because of their concern with possible disincentive effects but also because of a reluctance to undertake comparisons of the marginal utility of income among different persons. Clearly, no one person can judge the satisfactions derived from the income that his neighbor receives.

The case for progressivity in taxation must therefore rest on grounds other than utility comparisons. Most generally the argument for progressivity is couched in terms of broad social policy. It is contended that it is desirable to modify the distribution of income that emerges from the functioning of the market and thus prevent an undue accumulation of wealth and income in a few hands. A progressive tax system will contribute to such modification. It is also argued that the concept of ability to pay is built into the social ethic—the more affluent members of a family are expected to contribute more heavily to its support, and the more affluent members of the community are expected to contribute more heavily to the support of churches and private charities. Sometimes the case for progressivity in taxation rests on aesthetic grounds, and it is argued that undue concentration of income and wealth is simply "unlovely."

Whatever the justification, there is certainly a general ethic, in developed and underdeveloped countries alike, holding that the distribution of income should be modified in favor of the poor and that the tax system should contribute to this end. It follows that the personal income tax should exempt minimum incomes, that the rate structure should be progressive, and that corporate income should be taxed. Luxury goods may appropriately be subject to heavy excises. The degree of progressivity will always be a matter for controversy at any particular time. There is no "scientific" way by which it can be decided how much more the rich ought to pay as compared with the poor.

The attainment of an appropriate degree of progressivity in the tax system is a search for vertical equity, and this will always be a controversial matter. There is much more consensus that a tax system should attempt to achieve horizontal equity. This concept can be defined simply as the equal treatment of equals and, as Carl S. Shoup of Columbia University has put it, "the almost equal treatment of those almost equally circumstanced." Shoup points out that the concept of horizontal equity has a number of facets. All taxpayers must be subject to the same degree of certainty with respect to their tax liabilities. There should be continuity—small changes in income, for example, should not give rise to large changes in tax liability. There should be uniform costs of compliance. Tax laws should be impersonal and not individualized for small and specialized groups.

The equal treatment of equals is thus partially determined by the way in which tax laws are written. It is also determined by the way in which they are administered. John and Richard who live on the same street and occupy similar houses should pay equal property taxes. This can be assured only if property tax assessors are properly trained and adequately paid. Similarly, the equal treatment of equals under the income tax will be assured only if the auditing staff of the tax collection agency is adequate for its task.

Economic Stabilization. A tax system should contribute to the stabilization of levels of income and employment. Stabilization may occur automatically—that is, the tax system may be a built-in stabilizer. This will be the case if there are a progressive personal income tax and a corporation tax as significant components of the aggregate system. Then, as economic activity increases, tax revenues increase more than proportionately. This excess revenue, in turn, serves as a depressant on levels of economic activity and reduces inflationary pressure. Conversely, a decline in economic activity brings a more than proportionate decline in tax revenue, which serves to cushion the decline.

The tax system may also be altered to cope with specific stabilization considerations, such as the encouragement or discouragement of private expenditure on investment or on consumer goods. The general rule is that increases in taxation will depress private economic activity, and reductions in taxation will increase private economic activity. Western European nations and the United States have usually followed this Keynesian rule since World War II.

National governments commonly employ tax increases to combat inflation. Such increases may be very general, in the form of increased rates of personal and corporate income taxes, or they may take the form of additional excise taxes to discourage consumer expenditure. Economic forecasting is by no means precise, but it is usually possible to predict with reasonable accuracy the aggregate economic effects of tax increases or reductions.

The use of taxation as an instrument of economic stabilization is reserved wholly to national governments. In a federal system, state and local governments do not undertake compensatory fiscal actions. Also, taxation as an instrumentality in economic stabilization must be meshed with other instrumentalities of control, particularly with monetary policy as practiced by the central bank.

Resource Allocation. Since taxation transfers resources from private control to public control, it is highly desirable that this transfer be effected with a minimum of disruptive effects on the private sector. Thus taxation should be neutral in not imposing excess burdens on the private sector.

With this generalization as a starting point, economists have devised a number of prescriptions that are intended to serve as guides to tax policy. A general sales tax is preferable to a pattern of selective excises, even if the yield were the same. A general income tax is to be preferred to the taxation of specific types of income.

These prescriptions rest on the assumed behavior of households and business firms as they attempt to improve or optimize their economic position. For example, if a household must pay a selective excise tax on bread it will alter the family expenditure pattern to consume less bread and more of other commodities. Thus the tax on bread distorts the consumer expenditure pattern of the household. It follows that a general sales tax on all items of family consumption is to be preferred to a specific excise tax on one commodity for which there are ready substitutes. It also follows that an income tax imposed on the family will be neutral with respect to preferences for consumer goods and neutral in the choice between consumer expenditures and savings. The tax burden may remain the same, but there are no additional distorting effects.

Attempts to analyze the effect of specific tax measures in terms of consequences for resource allocation are inherently difficult because there may be little prior knowledge of the degree to which substitution among factors of production by business firms or among commodities by households will, in fact, occur. Attempts to avoid adverse allocational consequences may also run afoul of other considerations. For example, a tax that is neutral with respect to personal choices between work and leisure is the head tax, also known as a poll tax or per capita tax. But a head tax is seriously regressive and thus conflicts with equity criteria.

Social Control. Since taxes, in and of themselves and without reference to expenditure benefits that they may finance, are an impediment to economic activity, it is not surprising that governments have attempted to discourage some kinds of economic activities by heavy taxation thereon and to encourage other kinds of activities by tax exemption. As noted, the exceptionally heavy taxation to which liquor and tobacco are subject is usually justified on grounds of social control. On the other hand, a great many activities that are thought to be socially useful are encouraged by tax exemption. The statutes of all states exempt from taxation the property that is owned by religious, educational, and charitable institutions. Many states, in addition, exempt from property taxes a part or all of the value of owned homes. Under the federal personal income tax there is an extra exemption for those over 65 and for persons who are blind.

Tax exemptions, however laudable their objectives, create a favored class of taxpayers. In some cases the legislative consensus under which they are obtained is thinly based, and the favorable treatment that they accord is highly controversial. This is the case, for example, with the preferential treatment that has been historically extended to the owners of gas and oil properties. Percentage depletion permits, under the federal income tax, the annual deduction of a flat percentage of the gross revenue derived from the property. In some cases this allows a total deduction over time of amounts that substantially exceed the original cost of the property.

The use of taxation as an instrument of social control is certainly a legitimate exercise of public authority, even though it may be subject to abuse. The majority of students of taxation, unlike the majority of legislators, would undoubtedly favor a widespread elimination of many of the tax concessions that have eroded the tax base. Such elimination would expand the tax base and permit lower rates of taxation.

Revenue Adequacy. Some governments may legitimately be more concerned with the adequacy of their revenues than with considerations such as equity or neutrality. For national governments the adequacy of revenue is not a problem. Within the limits that are set by the need to control inflation, revenues can be secured by borrowing or by credit creation. But this is not the case with subnational governments. In the United States, state and local governments live in a perpetual state of revenue crisis. Their borrowing capacity is typically limited by rigid constitutional provisions and they have no credit-creating authority. In the face of rising citizen expectations for improved public services, state and local governments engage in a continued search for new sources of revenue. Governments are always limited, however, by a concern that economic activity may be driven outside their borders if tax burdens are increased.

TAX SHIFTING AND INCIDENCE

The person or organization with legal liability for paying a tax may not suffer the final burden of the levy. In the United States, cigarette manufacturers are legally liable for the payment of the federal excise tax on their product. But it it reasonable to conclude that the manufacturers are successful in shifting a substantial proportion of their excise tax payments forward to the consumer. Thus it becomes possible to distinguish the impact of the tax—on the manufacturers—from the process of shifting the tax as the cigarettes are sold.

The incidence of the tax is defined as the ultimate burden—on the consumers, in the case of cigarettes. This burden may be measured in monetary terms, as a percentage of household income. In addition, there may be other economic effects of the tax that must be taken into account. In the examination of allocational consequences, there may be substitution effects that are important. In short, the entire complex of economic effects stemming from the imposition of a tax properly belongs within the examination of incidence. This is a difficult and complex area in which economists have not been particularly successful.

The traditional way of looking at tax incidence may be described as the partial equilibrium approach. This method of analysis, which dominated economic thinking about taxation until the 1950's, assumes that government expenditures are unchanged and then explores the consequences of changes in tax instruments or tax rates or some combination thereof that would produce equivalent revenues. It is then possible, with a knowledge of the conditions of supply, demand, and market structure, for a given industry to reach at least tentative conclusions as to whether a tax will be shifted forward to consumers, backward to the factors of production—such as wage earners—or remain where it is imposed.

Unfortunately, a partial equilibrium approach is most limited. There may be side effects on other industries as commodities or factors are substituted one for another. There may be income effects that alter the economic position of firms or households and that lead to further shifts in demand and supply relationships. And, perhaps most important of all, it is necessary to analyze the consequences not only of a specific change in the tax structure but the consequences of any accompanying changes in government expenditure. Thus a very broad general equilibrium analysis of tax-expenditure combinations is required for a complete knowledge of incidence. The complexities of such analysis are beyond the reach of the tools now possessed by economists.

Nevertheless a series of generalizations have emerged about the shifting and incidence of specific taxes. These would appear to be reasonably adequate generalizations, even though they cannot be supported by precise analysis. They include the following: the property tax on homeowners is not shifted, but rests on the homeowner. The property tax on rental property is usually shifted forward to the tenant, unless there is an excess supply of rental property. The property tax on business firms is shifted forward in the price of the firm's product and thus has an effect comparable to that of a sales tax. Sales and excise taxes tend to be forward-shifted. If the demand for the taxed commodity is generally inelastic—that is, unresponsive to changes in price, as would be the case with a tax on salt—the quantity purchased will be little affected. In these circumstances, the excise tax has about the same effect as a lump-sum tax on income.

For income taxes it is usually concluded that the personal tax cannot be shifted—the burden remains where it is imposed. The incidence of the corporation income tax is much more complicated. There appear to be no useful generalizations here. The tax may, depending on a number of market conditions, rest on the stockholders, be shifted forward in the form of higher prices, or be shifted backward in the form of reduced wage payments.

One of the most critical aspects of incidence is the impact of taxes on incentives to work and to invest. Again, unfortunately, too little is known about such relationships. It might be expected, for example, that the corporation income tax, at rates around 50% in the United States since the beginning of World War II, would have had serious adverse effects on the volume of corporate investment. This, however, appears not to have been the case. The ratio of corporate investment to total investment and to gross national product was about the same in the 1950's and 1960's as it was in the 1920's when tax rates were much lower.

There are frequent complaints, particularly among upper-income professionals, that the personal income tax is a serious disincentive to work effort. The hard evidence to support this contention is very much lacking. Personal income taxes may encourage some persons to substitute leisure for work, but there may be a positive incentive effect for other persons. A higher tax rate may encourage additional work effort on the part of taxpayers who are anxious to retain their former, pre-tax net income.

Similarly, it would be most uneconomic to devise a tax system that discourages individuals from undertaking new and risky investments. The economy would lose important sources of innovation. But here again it is very difficult to untangle complex economic considerations and trace through the effects of specific tax measures on risk-taking incentives.

TAXATION IN A FEDERAL SYSTEM

In a federal system, such as that of the United States, Canada, India, or Brazil, taxes are imposed by multiple levels of government—the national government, the states or provinces, and local governments. In the United States, there is no single system of taxation, but rather there are 51 systems, one for each state, plus the District of Columbia, and a great many subsystems, derived from local variations in tax measures. In consequence, there is an infinite variety in these systems and subsystems, the more so when differing expenditure patterns are taken into account.

There appears to be an inescapable tendency in a federal system for fiscal authority to shift to the national government over a period of time. The national government inevitably acquires the most productive sources of revenue—personal and corporate income taxes—and the states and local governments are left with less productive and less flexible sources of revenue. This has certainly occurred in the United States, where the personal income tax accounts for almost half of federal budget receipts and the corporation income tax for 15% to 20% more. Increases in economic activity will generate more than proportionate increases in personal and corporate income tax revenue. This puts the federal government in a relatively favorable revenue position.

State government tax structures depend on less elastic revenue sources. The income tax is less heavily utilized. Sales taxes are important sources of revenue for the states, together with excises on tobacco, motor vehicles, gasoline, and alcoholic beverages.

Local government fiscal structures are dominated by the property tax, which provides more than 80% of locally raised revenue. The property tax has turned out to be a surprisingly resilient source of revenue in the years since World War II, but this has required sharp increases in the rate of tax. The growth of the property tax base itself has not kept up with the pressure of local needs for revenue.

In a federal system, the fiscal disparities that emerge among the different levels of government can be importantly remedied by increased grants-in-aid from the national governments. This trend is very much in evidence in the United States. Federal grants to states and local governments increased from $2.5 billion in 1950 to more than $20 billion in 1970. This trend is not likely to be abated. The public service requirements for an increasingly urbanized economy, the demands for increased public expenditures for environmental improvement, and the inadequacy of state and local revenue bases will tend to lead to significant further increases in federal grants. See also BUDGET, GOVERNMENT; INCOME TAX; PUBLIC FINANCE; UNITED STATES—*Public Finance*.

THE FUTURE OF TAXATION

The relative growth of the public sector appears to be characteristic of all nations, whether developed or developing. As a society becomes more urbanized and specialized, public service requirements increase, and higher levels of per capita income make it possible to finance such increases in demand. There is no reason to believe that this historic pattern of taxation will soon be altered.

In developing countries the ratio of taxes to national income ranges from 10% to 20%. In developed countries the ratio exceeds 20%. In the United States the ratio is 25%, and this is exceeded by some countries in western Europe. Since economic development and high taxes have been so strongly associated in times past, there is every reason to believe that this association will continue.

JESSE BURKHEAD, *Syracuse University*
Author of "State and Local Taxes for Public Education"

Bibliography

Burkhead, Jesse, *State and Local Taxes for Public Education* (Syracuse 1963).
Due, John F., *Government Finance*, 4th ed. (Homewood, Ill., 1968).
Goode, Richard B., *The Corporation Income Tax* (New York 1951).
Goode, Richard B., *The Individual Income Tax* (Washington 1964).
Harvard University, International Program in Taxation, *Taxation in the United States* (Chicago 1963).
Musgrave, Richard A., *The Theory of Public Finance* (New York 1959).
Netzer, Dick, *Economics of the Property Tax* (Washington 1966).
Pechman, Joseph A., *Federal Tax Policy* (Washington 1966).
Prest, Alan R., *Public Finance in Theory and Practice* (Chicago 1960).
Shoup, Carl S., *Public Finance* (Chicago 1969).

TAXCO, täs'kō, a city in southwestern Mexico, is in Guerrero state, about 70 miles (112 km) southwest of Mexico City. The picturesque colonial settlement, famous as a silver mining center, is carved out of the green mountainsides from which the silver is extracted. Steep cobblestone streets all converge on the Plaza Borga. The white colonial houses, with their red-tile roofs, have wrought-iron balconies decorated with a profusion of colorful plants and flowers. The city is officially called Taxco de Alarcón.

The economic activity of Taxco revolves around tourism and the silver industry. The city was founded in 1529 by Spaniards, who discovered the silver mines soon after. In 1745, José de la Borda, a French miner, ordered the construction of the church of Santa Prisca, which, with its exquisite rose-colored towers, is among the most famous baroque buildings in Mexico. In 1930, William Spratling, an American, revitalized the silver industry so that today the city is crowded with shops producing Mexico's finest silverwork. Taxco has been declared a national monument by the government and, to preserve intact its colonial architecture, the construction of buildings in a modern style is prohibited. Population: (1960) 14,773.

REYNALDO AYALA, *San Diego State College*

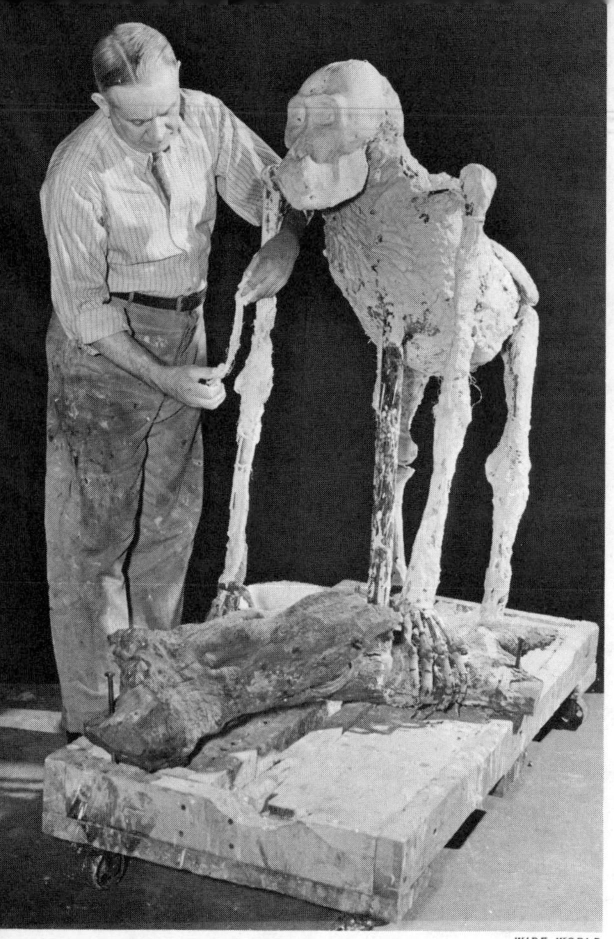

WIDE WORLD

TAXIDERMIST begins to form a clay model of a gorilla over a framework made from the animal's skeleton.

WIDE WORLD

FINISHED CLAY MODEL will be copied by molding to make a hollow burlap-and-glue model of the gorilla.

TAXIDERMY, tak-sə-dər′mē, is the art of preserving the skins of birds, mammals, fish, and reptiles and stretching them over artificial body forms to represent the living animal in a lifelike and characteristic attitude. These mounted animals are used for study purposes and exhibited in museums.

Formerly, specimens were filled with excelsior or any kind of available material and then stuffed into shape. In every instance, the completed specimen looked stuffed. In modern taxidermy, careful notes are taken of the color of the specimen's eyes and skin and fleshy parts—and of its bill and feet in the case of a bird—and each part of the specimen is measured, drawn, and, very often, photographed as well. For large mammals, plaster of Paris casts are made of important parts such as the nose, eyes, and ears before the animal is skinned.

History. The first modern attempt to mount birds was made in the Netherlands in the 17th century, and the Sloane collection, which formed the nucleus of the British Museum in 1753, shows that a form of taxidermy was practiced in England before that date. The oldest specimen in existence today is a rhinoceros, still preserved in the Zoological Museum in Florence, Italy. During the middle of the 19th century many examples of British taxidermy were shown at the great exhibitions held in England, and a special taxidermy section was prepared by Edwin Ward for the Paris Exhibition in 1865.

Associated with the beginnings of taxidermy in the United States was John Scudder, who succeeded to the proprietorship of Gardner Baker's American Museum, which had been founded in New York by the Tammany Society in 1791. The museum was later acquired by P. T. Barnum, and reestablished as Barnum's Museum in 1842. Titian Peale, who was appointed assistant manager of the Philadelphia Museum in 1821, made important contributions to its natural history exhibits.

In 1861, Henry Augustus Ward's Natural Science Establishment was founded at Rochester, N. Y. To this establishment can be given credit for placing taxidermy on a level with other allied arts and beginning a new era in museum exhibitions. Many later taxidermists, whose work was among the best exhibited, could credit their careers to Ward's Establishment, and many museums have exhibit collections built around these early Ward specimens.

It was at Ward's that the Society of American Taxidermists was founded on March 24, 1880. This society, the first of its kind in the United States, held three competitive exhibitions. Terminated after the last exhibit in 1883, the society in three short years had done more for taxidermy and the natural history museum in general in the United States than had ever been accomplished previously.

One of the earliest published works on taxidermy is R. A. F. de Réaumur's *Treatise* (1749). Today museums publish books and pamphlets giving advice on collecting and mounting natural history specimens. In general, however, these publications are specialized studies intended primarily for the benefit of the trained collector and scientist.

Techniques. The processes involved in the mounting of natural history specimens can most easily be discussed under the subdivisions—birds, mammals, fish, and reptiles.

WIDE WORLD

THE GORILLA'S SKIN has been tanned and is here being pulled over the burlap model and carefully fitted.

WIDE WORLD

RESTORING FADED SPOTS WITH OIL COLORS is the final step in preparing a mammal for exhibition.

Birds. After a bird is skinned, an artificial body is made of balsa wood and a neck of fine tow, wrapped on a wire to simulate the natural dimensions. Cotton is placed in the eye sockets. Wings, legs, and tail are now wired, and tow or fine cotton is wrapped around the wing and leg bones to replace the flesh that was cut away. Then the artificial body is put in the skin. The wings, legs, and tail are anchored in their proper positions, and the incision is sewed together. Glass eyes are inserted in the eye sockets and held in place with paste and cotton. The feathers are arranged in their feather pattern. When the mounted bird is dry, all thread and wires are removed, and the faded parts restored with oil colors.

Mammals. The proper mounting of large animals requires years of study and more years of actual work. Using the skeleton as a foundation, a framework is constructed. Modeling clay is applied over the framework, and plaster of Paris over the clay form. When the plaster mold has hardened, it is removed, and several layers of burlap are glued into it to form a manikin. After several days the plaster mold is soaked in water, which allows it to be broken away from the manikin. An exact copy of the clay form of the animal is thus left in this light, strong, hollow burlap manikin. It is covered with a paste and the tanned skin of the animal is pulled over it, fitted, and adjusted. Faded parts are restored with oil colors.

Fish. Many methods are employed today in fish taxidermy, but the most important step is to give the mounted fish the coloring it had in life. Two methods of fish mounting are common: in one, the fish skin is fitted over a modeled form; in the other, the fish is reproduced as a cast in plastic, which preserves the true colors of the fish.

Reptiles. The greatest advance in taxidermy has been made in the mounting of reptiles. A thin mixture of plaster of Paris is poured over the reptile and allowed to harden. A heavier layer is then added. When the mold has set, the reptile is removed. The mold now has the impression of the reptile as it was in life. The work of making the reproduction takes place inside this plaster mold. The reproduction is made of plastic, often clear celluloid. Oil pigments are mixed into it to match the many colors on the reptile's skin. Following carefully the color notes and observing the preserved body of the reptile, the taxidermist applies celluloid of each color in its proper place inside the plaster mold. The colored celluloid assumes exactly the shape, pattern, and details of the mold.

After the colors are painted in, a backing of several different materials—plaster, cloth, wax, wire—is worked into the mold on top of the celluloid. This strengthens the mold, which is now allowed to dry. After drying, the mold, with the celluloid reptile still inside it, is immersed in water, and the plaster is broken away. The reproduction is carefully cleaned of any small particles of the plaster mold; the eyes are set in; and it is lightly oiled to give it a gloss and placed on its base.

JOHN W. MOYER
Author of "Practical Taxidermy"

Further Reading: Moyer, John W., *Practical Taxidermy* (New York 1953); Pray, Leon L., *Taxidermy* (New York 1943); Rowley, John, *Taxidermy and Museum Exhibition* (New York 1925).

TAXIS, tak′səs, is the movement by which an animal orients its body in response to particular stimuli. Taxis is contrasted with kinesis, which is undirected animal movement or response without bodily orientation and includes such activities as changes in speed of movement or in rates of turning.

Organisms regulate their movements and position according to environmental stimuli. For example, animals must move in specific ways in order to find food, shelter, and mates. Their prey-catching and courtship movements must be such as to achieve the proper goals. How the appropriate orientations and locomotions are made has long been a puzzling question, and the main effort of animal behaviorists has been to categorize rather simple sorts of movement and orientation of lower animals. In this way, behavior that appears quite complicated can frequently be explained in terms of simple taxes and kineses.

Types of Taxes. Several categories of taxes have been defined according to whether the animal orients to achieve a balance in the intensities of stimulation on each side of its body or whether it orients to only one of several stimuli. A common example of the first sort of balancing orientation is that of fly maggots to light. As they crawl, they swing their heads from side to side, successively comparing the intensities of light on both sides of their bodies. They continue to turn until the two sides are equally stimulated. They then stop swinging and crawl in a straight line oriented directly away from the light source. This type of orientation is called *klinotaxis*. In a similar orientation, called *tropotaxis*, the comparison of intensities is not successive but simultaneous, and the swinging movement is absent. In *telotaxis* the orientation is toward just one of several stimuli, with the animal reacting as if all stimuli but one were inhibited.

A special type of orientation, *menotaxis*, is one in which the animal orients at a constant angle with respect to the direction of a source of stimulation. The light-compass movement of bees and ants is a menotactic orientation with respect to the direction of the sun's rays.

Taxes are also often classified according to the type of stimuli they respond to. *Phototaxis* thus refers to response to light, *geotaxis* to gravity, *rheotaxis* to currents, and *chemotaxis* to chemical substances. If the animal orients towards the stimulus, his response is termed positive, but if he orients away from the stimulus, his response is negative. Thus, a moth that flies toward a light shows positive phototaxis, while an insect climbing up a tree shows negative geotaxis.

Recent Findings. The system of classification of movement according to taxes and kineses is most useful when applied to lower organisms under highly simplified laboratory conditions. It considers only cases that involve isolated sources of stimuli. However, evidence is accumulating that the orientational movements of certain insects in their complex natural habitats may involve appreciable integration of complex sets of stimuli. In these situations the orientations are not readily classifiable and the categories tend to flow together. Several theories of orientation based on systems theory may eventually be elaborated to cover these more complex kinds of orientation.

Donald E. Landenberger
University of California, Los Angeles

TAXONOMY, tak-son′ə-mē, is the theory and practice of classifying organisms. More than a million species of animals and half a million species of plants have already been described and classified, and estimates on the number of still undescribed living species range up to 10 million. The number of extinct species, represented only by fossils, is many times larger. It would be impossible to study this enormous diversity of the living world if it were not ordered and classified. Two branches of biology—systematics and taxonomy—cover this area. *Systematics* is concerned with the entire diversity of organisms in all its aspects and includes taxonomy.

The term "classification" has two meanings. It is the process of ordering organisms into groups on the basis of their relationship, and it is also the product of such ordering. Classification should not be confused with *identification*. In classification, the ordering of populations and groups of populations at all levels of relationship is undertaken, using inductive procedures, whereas in identification deductive reasoning is used to place an individual organism into a previously established class—for example, the determination that a particular tree is a red oak (*Quercus rubra*).

The classification of a group of organisms has the qualities of a scientific theory. First, it has *explanatory* value, designating the members of a particular group as derived from a common ancestor. A good classification also has high *predictive* value with respect to previously unstudied characters or newly discovered species. Finally, classification has *heuristic* value in that it may suggest previously overlooked connections and relationships.

Units of Classification. The taxonomist deals with natural objects, such as thrushes, oaks, and mosses, and assigns to them a rank in a hierarchy of categories. Terms like "thrushes," "oaks," or "mosses" refer to groups of organisms. Any such group of populations if worthy of distinction is called a *taxon*. A taxon is a group of organisms of any rank that is sufficiently distinct from other groups of organisms to be worthy of being assigned to a definite category. A taxon always denotes a concrete group of animals or plants.

A *category*, on the other hand, designates rank or level in a hierarchic classification. It is a class, the members of which are all the taxa assigned a given rank. For instance, the species category is a class, the members of which are the species taxa. Thus category is an abstract term, a class name, whereas the taxa placed in these categories are concrete zoological or botanical groups.

The most important units, or categories, used in classification are the species, genus, family, order, class, phylum, and kingdom. The categories above the species category are called the "higher" categories. These basic categories are often supplemented by auxiliary categories, such as superfamily, subfamily or subclass, providing for greater flexibility in groups that are particularly rich in species. Insects, for example, have over 750,000 species.

Scientific Name. In describing and classifying all living things, taxonomists give each organism a scientific name. The modern system of scientific names is the Latin binomial nomenclature in which each organism is given a two-word Latin name, which is always printed in italics. The first word is the genus name, always capitalized. The second word is the species name, which is not capitalized. For example, the red oak is *Quercus rubra* and the white oak *Quercus alba*, *Quercus* being the genus name and *rubra* and *alba* the species names.

The practice of giving scientific names is useful for several reasons. First, it provides scientists of all nations with a method of communicating. Second, it eliminates the confusion often caused by the common names of plants or animals since the same plant or animal may be known under various common names in different parts of its range. In addition, many common names are very misleading. For example, the glass snake is not a snake at all but a legless lizard. Third, the scientific name often gives some information about the plant or animal being described. For example, the adjective *viridis* in the scientific name tells us that the plant or animal is green, *alba* white, and so on.

Importance. Taxonomy plays an important role in biology. It provides organisms with a scientific name. It functions as an information storage and retrieval system, organizing a vast amount of information about plants and animals. The organization of various organisms into a cohesive framework also permits a reconstruction of the phylogeny, or natural relationships, of living things and provides evidence on which inferences about the trends and rates of evolution can be based. Taxonomy also supplies virtually all the information on which entire branches of biology, such as biogeography, are based. It also serves an important function in helping with the identification of organisms. This is particularly valuable when a specific disease vector or a specific insect pest must be identified in public health or agricultural work.

SPECIES CATEGORY

The species category occupies a unique position in the taxonomic categories. It is the one we have foremost in mind when we speak of "kinds" of plants and animals.

Species Concepts. From the first attempts at classification by the ancient Greeks until the present day, there have been varying concepts of species. Two of the main concepts—the typological and the nominalist—have been abandoned in favor of the biological species concept.

Typological Species Concept. According to this concept, the observed diversity of the universe reflects the existence of a limited number of underlying universals, essences, or types. This species concept, held by Linnaeus and other early naturalists, was based on the theory of *essentialism*, which in turn was derived from the philosophies of Plato and Aristotle.

Essentialism held that all members of a taxon reflect the same essential nature and thus conform to the same type. This ideology therefore is sometimes referred to as *typology*. To the essentialist, the natural system reflects the plan of creation. The constancy of taxa and sharpness of the gaps separating them are exaggerated. Variation is considered irrelevant and tends to be ignored. There is no method by which the essential nature of an organism can be established, so adherence to essentialism leads to arbitrariness. Since the degree of difference is the only criterion to be used in delimiting species, the essentialist or typologist is stumped by a natural phenomenon such as sexual dimorphism (male and female of the same species appear very different and mistakenly may be identified as belonging to different species), age differences in which the same species looks different at different stages of its life cycle, polymorphism (a single species has more than one form), and by all other forms of discontinuous variation. For all these reasons, the typological species concept was later rejected. Not only does it lack a sound philosophical basis, but using degree of difference as the chief criteria of species status, it fails in the numerous cases where the degree of morphological difference does not parallel evolutionary divergence.

Nominalist Species Concept. This concept denies the existence of universals and asserts that only individuals exist and that species are man-made abstractions. This concept was based on the philosophy of nominalism expounded by William of Occam and his followers. The nominalists held that all classes are human inventions. This basic tenet of nominalism and the nominalist species concept is invalidated by universal fact, observed by both primitive naturalists of the past and ecologists of today, namely, that natural groups of organisms—whether birds, bats, or butterflies—do exist, and that at any given locality most species are well defined and are clearly delimited. Groups of organisms are products of evolution and not of the human mind, and therefore the concept of a species is not merely a human invention.

The method of numerical phenetics is in part based on the principles of nominalism. This method consists in the computer analysis of a large number (at least 100) of unweighted characters of the taxa to be classified. In poorly known groups without sound classifications, this method has achieved useful results. In most cases, the phenetic classifications have only confirmed the traditional classifications, but the development of appropriate methods for weighting characters may increase the usefulness of the phenetic approach.

Biological Species Concept. The third and now prevailing species concept defines species as *groups of interbreeding natural populations that are reproductively isolated from other such groups*. This concept considers the species as a reproductive community, as an ecological unit, and as a genetic unit consisting of a single gene pool protected from mixing with other gene pools by reproductive isolating mechanisms. A species is not defined by intrinsic properties but by its relation to other species—the relation of reproductive isolation.

Difficulties with the Biological Species Concept. Certain difficulties arise when the biological species concept is applied to naturally occurring organisms. This is true particularly in cases of variation, asexual reproduction, and incipient species.

Some types of variation, such as sexual dimorphism, age differences, and polymorphism, that occur naturally among groups of organisms often lead to the erroneous recognition of a variant as a separate species. Usually only subsequent biological research establishes that the variant is not a species but simply a variant, or unusual, member of a previously described species.

Uniparental, or asexual, reproducing organisms present a serious difficulty to the biological species concept. This concept, which is based on the presence or absence of interbreeding between populations, is meaningless for asexually reproducing organisms. Self-fertilization, parthenogenesis, or other types of asexual reproduction may result in separate strains or phyletic lines. Species recognition in these cases must depend on analogy, with the degree of morphological difference and discontinuity between lines accepted as species criteria.

The fact that evolution produces many populations that constitute incipient species presents a third difficulty for the biological species concept. A careful analysis of such situations usually reveals whether or not the doubtful population should be included in the parental species. Hybridization between species, polyploidy (chromosome doubling), and sibling species also create difficulties.

Sibling Species. During the process of speciation, incipient species diverge genetically, acquire isolating mechanisms, and usually become different in many ways. A few species, however, fail to acquire conspicuous morphological differences. Such very similar hard-to-distinguish species are called *sibling species*. Sibling species are widespread in the animal kingdom and are particularly common among host specific, plant-feeding insects.

Sibling species are usually recognized only when additional detailed characters of the organism, such as chromosomes, cross-fertility, food preferences, or sounds are investigated. In former times some sibling species were designated as biological races, but since they are reproductively isolated from one another, it is better to consider them species. The question whether the members of polyploid plant species, particularly autopolyploids, which are hardly or not at all distinguishable morphologically, should be considered species is not yet resolved.

Subspecies and Ecotypes. Most species are not uniform throughout their entire geographic range but form well-defined local races or geographic isolates. When sufficiently distinct, such geographic races are formally designated as *subspecies*. A subspecies is an aggregate of phenotypically similar populations of a species, inhabiting a geographic subdivision of the range of the species, and differing from other populations of the species. Species that consist of several subspecies, or geographic races, are characterized as *polytypic*.

In botany another subdivision of species, the *ecotype*, is recognized. An ecotype is a local population whose characteristics are determined by the nature of their substrate, habitat, or exposure. For instance, sand dune, meadow, seashore, and forest ecotypes of some plants may be recognized.

The term *variety*, formerly widely used in taxonomy, has been largely abandoned because it created confusion and was used ambiguously to refer to individual variants within populations as well as geographic races and ecotypes.

HIGHER CATEGORIES

The higher categories cannot be defined nonarbitrarily. Yet they have an objective basis because taxa placed in a higher category are descended from a common ancestor, and all are more closely related to one another than to other taxa in different categories.

Genus. Groups of related species can be combined into a genus, the lowest of the higher categories. For example, various species of wolves and jackals and the domestic dog are grouped in the genus *Canis*. Species included in a genus or still higher taxon generally share a certain number of taxonomic characters. A genus taxon is a phylogenetic unit of which the included species are postulated to be descended from a common ancestor. In most cases the genus is also an ecological unit, consisting of species adapted for a particular mode of life. The genus is especially important because its name is included in the scientific name of an organism.

Other Higher Categories. Groups of related genera are grouped into families, families into orders, orders into classes, and classes into phyla (or divisions in botany). The phyla of the many-celled higher organisms readily fall into two kingdoms—the plant kingdom and the animal kingdom. The single-celled organisms and microorganisms were formerly combined in the kingdom of the protists, a heterogeneous assemblage that is now subdivided into *eucaryotes*—organisms with a well-defined cell nucleus—and procaryotes —organisms lacking a discrete nucleus.

CONSTRUCTING A CLASSIFICATION SYSTEM

Biological classification is the arrangement of organisms into groups of species derived from a common ancestor. The delimitation and ranking of these groups—that is, the construction of a classification system—involve several steps. The first step is the evaluation of similarities among organisms. The comparison is based on taxonomic characters—that is, the attributes of a member of a taxon that differentiate it from a member of another taxon. The second step is the recognition of species. The third step is the assembling of related species into groups and the delimitation of these groups by the recognition of gaps between them. In the final step these groups are arranged according to appropriate hierarchic rank.

Taxonomic Characters. Almost any characteristic or an organism can be useful as a taxonomic character provided it differs from the equivalent feature in members of other taxa. Classical taxonomy relied almost exclusively on structural characters, although Aristotle realized that groups of animals might be characterized by "their way of living, their actions, and their habits."

The structural characteristics most useful in taxonomy differ from one type of organism to another. Mammals, fishes, insects, jellyfish, flowering plants, mosses, fungi, and bacteria all have their special taxonomic characters. In mammals, the skull, particularly the teeth, together with the fur are most useful characteristics. In birds the color of the plumage is especially valuable. In fishes the dimensions, number of fin rays and vertebrae, and various skull characteristics are important. In all vertebrates internal characteristics are useful, particularly for the classification of higher taxa. The genitalia of many animals, particularly insects, show a great deal of structural detail that differs from species to species. In many groups of insects and spiders it is virtually impossible to identify the species without a study of the genitalia. This is further complicated because in some groups the distinguishing characteristics of the genitalia appear in only one sex.

The morphological characters discovered and relied upon by classical taxonomy are still useful, although they have been supplemented increasingly by a large array of nonmorphological characters. Taxonomists realize that many other factors, including the stages in the life cycle of an organism, various physiological features, the number and structure of chromosomes, biochemical characters such as the structure of macromolecules, antigenic interactions, and DNA matching, as well as behavioral patterns are valuable in distinguishing species. Closely related species of animals often are more different in behavior than in morphology, and many previously overlooked species have been identified on the basis of observed differences in habitats, host preferences (in cases of host specific insects, parasites, or symbionts), or other behavioral patterns. Analyses of distribution patterns have also served as valuable tools in delimiting species.

Weighting Characters. Different taxonomic characters have different degrees of usefulness. Those characters that serve as reproductive isolating mechanisms serve to distinguish species and are most useful. Characters that evolve slowly are useful in ranking higher categories. On the other hand, the reduction or loss of certain characters, such as eyes, wings, toes, or scales, can happen repeatedly in unrelated evolutionary lines as a result of parallel evolution and is not very useful in taxonomy. Thus, there are no characters that unequivocally designate categorical rank.

The combining of species into a higher taxon is based on a careful evaluation of weighted similarity. A dolphin (porpoise) may look like a shark, but such superficial resemblance is due to convergence—that is, evolution that produces increasingly similar characteristics in organisms whose ancestors were different. The art of taxonomy consists in being able to see through superficial similarities and single out among hundreds of taxonomic characters those that are indicative of common descent.

The process of weighting characters is one of the most important procedures in taxonomy. For example, it has been known since the time of Linnaeus that the structure of the flower has "high weight" in the classification of plants. Other attributes, such as climatic adaptations in animals, are of "low weight" and not particularly helpful in delimiting taxa and ranking categories.

"High Weight" Characters. On the basis of experience, taxonomists believe that the following kinds of characters have particularly high weight in classification: (1) complex characters—the joint possession by two organisms of a character that differs from that of the common ancestor; (2) constant characters—characters that are consistently present in most or all members of a higher taxon and consistently absent in related taxa; (3) characters that are not correlated with a highly specialized mode of life; (4) characters that are not affected by ecological shift; and (5) correlated characters in which the correlation is due to function.

Delimiting and Ranking Taxa. In the recognition of taxa the relative merits of five criteria must be considered: (1) the size of the gap that separates one cluster of species from the next cluster; (2) the degree of difference between the two groups; (3) the evolutionary and ecological role each group plays in nature; (4) the size of the taxon—the larger a group of species the better justification for its formal recognition as a taxon; and (5) the criteria of ranking related groups.

In all these operations, it must be kept in mind that since a classification system is an information storage and retrieval system, the taxa should be neither too large nor too small. In addition, no experimental departures from existing classification should be undertaken unless fully substantiated by available information.

HISTORY OF CLASSIFICATION

Attempts at classifying living things have been made since primitive times, when man began to recognize similarities and differences among organisms and to group organisms under collective terms such as birds, fishes, grasses, and so on. The first attempts at a comprehensive classification started with the ancient Greeks, and efforts have continued to the present day.

Greek Efforts. The Greek philosopher Aristotle (384–322 B.C.) was the first to propose a comprehensive classification. Concentrating mainly on animals, he designated groups by alternate characters. For example, he grouped all warm-blooded animals apart from cold-blooded animals. Many of the groups proposed by Aristotle are still recognized today. Many others, however, were highly artificial and have been abandoned. Aristotle's pupil Theophrastus (371–287 B.C.) concentrated on the ordering of plants and is often considered the father of plant taxonomy. He tried to group all plants according to their uses and the methods by which they were cultivated.

16th and 17th Centuries. There were no significant advances in taxonomy for about 2,000 years after the work of Aristotle and Theophrastus. A few writers, notably the Roman Pliny (23–79 A.D.), the Swiss naturalist Konrad Gesner (1516–1565), and the Italian naturalist Ulisse Aldrovandi (1522–1605) made some original observations of plants and animals but no really new attempts at classification.

In the 16th century the German botanists Otto Brunfels and Leonhard Fuchs attempted to describe all the plants then known, paying particular attention to their medicinal value. The Italian physician-botanist Andrea Cesalpino, influenced by Aristotle, was probably the first to study plants comparatively. The first attempt to compile a list of the names and descriptions of plants was probably that of the Swiss physician-botanist Caspar Bauhin. Subsequent advances were made by the German botanist Joachim Jung and the French botanist Joseph Pitton de Tournefort. One important finding of this period was that of the sexuality of plants, discovered by Rudolph Camerarius.

These naturalists together described not only thousands of plants that had been unknown to the ancients but also utilized different attributes to classify them, such as growth form, roots, leaves, flowers, and fruits. They also experimented with various systems of naming plants. The most important taxonomic work of this period undoubtedly was that of the 17th century English botanist John Ray. In his *Methodus plantarum* (1682), Ray systematized and summarized all that was then known of plants, describing both species and genus. He and Francis Willoughby also worked on zoological classification, but not extensively.

Linnaeus. The many-sided and often contradictory efforts of the 16th and 17th centuries were brought to a climax in the *Systema naturae* of Carolus Linnaeus, the great 18th century Swedish naturalist. In his later writings, Linnaeus consistently applied the binomial nomenclature to animals and plants, provided a rigid hierarchy of categories, and supplied unambiguous diagnoses and extensive synonymies. Different portions of the Linnaean system were of unequal value. For instance, his arrangement of insects was very good, but his classification of the cold-blooded vertebrates and of the lower invertebrates was very poor. Linnaeus' methods were artificial. He often chose conspicuous but biologically unimportant characters on which to base his classification. He also ill-advisedly attempted to provide simultaneously a classification and an identification scheme. Nevertheless, the Linnaeus classification and methods have provided the basis for all subsequent classifications.

The century following the publication of the 10th edition of *Systema naturae* in 1758 was characterized by enormous activity in taxonomy. Specialists revised single taxons such as birds, beetles, mosses, or some other group, and an increasing number of taxonomic characters were evaluated to delimit taxa.

Charles Darwin. Charles Darwin ushered in a new period in the history of taxonomy with the publication of *Origin of Species* in 1859. He and his followers recognized that it was the task of classification to establish groups that had descended from a common ancestor. They thought that only this guiding principle could lead to the recognition of "natural" groups. The ensuing period was characterized by attempts to establish phylogenetic trees and to find "missing links" between higher taxa, such as the fossil *Archaeopteryx* between reptiles and birds.

Early 20th Century. Another new period of taxonomy began in the 1920's and reached its height in the 1930's and 1940's. This movement, often designated as the *new systematics*, or as *population systematics*, was characterized by the detailed study of intraspecific populations and their comparison with one another and led to a reevaluation of the species concept. The population systematist recognizes that all organisms occur in nature as members of populations and that specimens cannot be understood and properly classified unless they are treated as samples of natural populations.

Two other developments characterized early 20th century taxonomy. One was an increasing emphasis on nonmorphological characters, and the other was the wide-ranging introduction of experimental methods and of a genetic analysis of wild populations, particularly in botany. All these developments were responsible for the adoption of the biological species concept, of polytypic species taxa, and a recognition of the adaptive nature of species characters.

MODERN TAXONOMY

The contemporary period in taxonomy is characterized by three trends: the increasing use of computers to sort taxonomic characters and specimens and generate classifications; a vigorous search for biochemical characters, particularly those that would help establish relationships between higher taxa; and a very active interest in taxonomic theory.

Since the publication of Darwin's *Origin of Species* (1859), there have been only two taxonomic theories, both based on the principle of common descent. One theory, *cladism*, was established by the German taxonomist Willy Hennig in 1950. Cladism recognizes only genealogical relationship and only one phylogenetic process—the branching of the phylogenetic tree. Consequently, it bases all taxonomic groupings on the nearest common branching point, or "recency of common ancestry." For example, since crocodilians branch off the phylogenetic tree closer to birds than to other reptiles, the cladist groups crocodilians with birds in one taxonomic group.

The other and more widely accepted modern theory of taxonomy is that of *evolutionary taxonomy*, established by Darwin himself. This theory gives equal weight to two processes—the branching of the phylogenetic tree and evolutionary change after the branching. The evolutionary taxonomist would group the crocodilians with other reptiles and not with birds. This is because birds have evolved and changed so drastically, adopting an aerial mode of life, since their branching from the phylogenetic tree.

The basic principle of evolutionary taxonomy is to establish taxa and rank them in categories on the basis of their inferred genetic similarity. The most recent branching of the phylogenetic tree is only part of the evidence studied.

STABILITY OF CLASSIFICATION AND NOMENCLATURE

As new information about a particular plant or animal is collected, existing classifications may have to be revised. Some revisions are minor, like the shifting of a genus to a different family, but sometimes entirely new classifying criteria are discovered, and a completely new classification scheme is worked out. For example, the classifications of sponges, turbellarians, and fishes have been drastically revised.

In some fields, specialists organize committees that publish official lists or classifications of the plants or animals in that field. They do this to reduce arbitrariness and to provide a uniform sequence of taxa to all the workers in a field. Such lists are revised at irregular intervals as new information accumulates. On the whole, however, the principle of "taxonomic freedom," whereby each specialist adopts the particular classification he thinks best, is generally recognized.

There is even less arbitrariness in nomenclature than there is in classification. Zoologists, botanists, and bacteriologists obey International Codes of Nomenclature that are authoritative in their respective fields. The objectives of such codes are well stated in the Preamble to the Code of Zoological Nomenclature: "The object of the Code is to promote stability and universality in the scientific names of animals and to ensure that each name is unique and distinct." Each name is based on a concrete specimen ("type") and when there is a conflict between names, the earlier name usually prevails ("priority") unless a later name has long been adopted ("statute of limitation").

ERNST MAYR
Author of "Principles of Systematic Zoology"

Bibliography

Crowson, Roy A., *Classification and Biology* (London 1970).
Hennig, Willy, *Phylogenetic Systematics* (Urbana, Ill., 1966).
Mayr, Ernst, *Principles of Systematic Zoology* (New York 1969).
Simpson, George G., *Principles of Animal Taxonomy* (New York 1961).

TAY RIVER, tā, is the longest river in Scotland. It is about 118 miles (188 km) long, and its volume of water ranks it with any river in the United Kingdom. The river rises in the mountains of central Scotland and flows northeast until it enters Loch Tay in Perthshire. After issuing from the lake, it turns east and then southeast, flowing past the city of Perth into the Firth of Tay. The firth extends northeast past Dundee, a major port, into the North Sea. Salmon fishing in Loch Tay is famous among sportsmen.

TAY-SACHS DISEASE, tā′saks′, is a rare, hereditary disease of infants caused by the abnormal metabolism of fats. It is an amaurotic family idiocy and is characterized by progressive mental deterioration, blindness, and paralysis.

The baby, born at full term, appears normal until the first symptoms occur between the third and sixth month. Listlessness and apathy first occur. Weakness of the neck, back, and limbs is soon noted, and the infant's vision does not seem normal. As the disease progresses, blindness occurs and the eyes, while wide open, roll in a jerky fashion. Atrophy of the muscles and paralysis are followed by muscular contraction. Physical and mental degeneration reduces the child to a level of blind idiocy punctuated by epileptic seizures and general paralysis.

The diagnosis of Tay-Sachs disease depends largely on a microscopic examination of the brain cells. There is no treatment for the disease.

RAYMOND L. OSBORNE, M. D.
Mount Sinai Hospital, New York City

TAYLOR, A. J. P. (1906–), English historian. Alan John Percivale Taylor was born in Birkdale, Lancashire, on March 25, 1906. He was educated at Quaker schools and at Oriel College, Oxford, where he took first class honors in modern history in 1927. Taylor studied in Vienna before being appointed by Lewis B. Namier as a lecturer at Manchester University in 1930. He became a fellow of Magdalen College, Oxford, in 1938.

Taylor has written major works in both European and English history. His earliest publications were detailed analyses of *The Italian Problem in European Diplomacy, 1847–49* (1934) and *Germany's First Bid for Colonies, 1884–85* (1938). He published *The Habsburg Monarchy, 1815–1918* (1941) and *The Course of German History* (1945).

Other books and hundreds of academic and popular articles and reviews displayed his wide interests and expository skill. But perhaps his most enduring contributions to scholarship and to education are *The Struggle for Mastery in Europe, 1848–1918* (1954) and *English History 1914–1945* (1965). Written with characteristic flair, both volumes reveal a mastery of published sources.

Taylor has often been admonished for paradoxical and opinionated expression, especially in his study *The Origins of the Second World War* (1961)—"a story without heroes; and perhaps even without villains." Although he was never appointed to the professorships for which he was amply qualified, Taylor's influence on British historical writing and teaching in the 20th century is unrivaled.

CAMERON HAZLEHURST
The Queen's College
Oxford University

TAYLOR, Bayard (1825–1878), American travel writer and poet. James Bayard Taylor was born in Kennett Square, Pa., on Jan. 11, 1825. His volume of poetry *Ximena* (1844) brought him the chance to write travel articles. The resulting best seller, *Views Afoot; or, Europe Seen with Knapsack and Staff* (1846), made his reputation. In *Eldorado* (1850) he told of his trip to the California goldfields.

Taylor's many books about his travels to Africa, Europe, and the Middle and the Far East made him known as "the American Marco Polo." His ambition, however, was to establish himself as a writer of serious literature. He wrote three novels—*Hannah Thurston* (1863), *John Godfrey's Fortunes* (1864), and *The Story of Kennett* (1866)—and more than a dozen volumes of poetry, including *Poems of the Orient* (1854) and *Home Pastorals* (1875). But he is now remembered for the poem *Bedouin Song* and his translation of Goethe's *Faust* (1870–1871), in the original meters. The latter won for him academic recognition and in 1878 the post of U. S. minister to Germany. He died in Berlin on Dec. 19, 1878.

JEROME H. STERN, *Florida State University*

TAYLOR, Brook (1685–1731), English mathematician, who is best known for his discovery of Taylor's series (see TAYLOR'S THEOREM). He was born in Edmonton, Middlesex, on Aug. 18, 1685, and died in London on Dec. 29, 1731.

In his book *Methodus Incrementorum Directa et Inversa,* published in 1715, Taylor presented an approach to the infinitesimal calculus using finite increments that marked the beginning of the calculus of finite differences. He developed an interpolation formula from which his series was derived. Other original contributions contained in the book were formulas for the interchange of dependent and independent variables in differentiation and applications of the calculus to the problems of the vibrating string, free hanging and loaded strings, capillary action, and centers of percussion.

Taylor also wrote two works on linear perspective in which he gave a theory for perspective drawing and generalized the concept of vanishing points.

PHILLIPS S. JONES
University of Michigan

TAYLOR, Deems (1885–1966), American composer and music critic. Joseph Deems Taylor was born in New York City on Dec. 22, 1885. He graduated from New York University in 1906 and then studied harmony and counterpoint privately. He was music critic for several newspapers and magazines between 1917 and 1932, meanwhile composing such works as the suite for chamber ensemble *Through the Looking Glass* (1919; rescored for full orchestra, 1923) and the opera *The King's Henchman,* with book by Edna St. Vincent Millay, which the Metropolitan Opera Company had commissioned and which it produced in 1927. The Metropolitan also commissioned and produced his *Peter Ibbetson* (1931; libretto by Constance Collier from the novel by George du Maurier).

Taylor became well known as a radio commentator from 1936 to 1943, on the broadcasts of the New York Philharmonic. He wrote *The Well-Tempered Listener* (1940) and *Some Enchanted Evenings* (1953). He died in New York City on July 3, 1966.

TAYLOR, Edward (c. 1642–1729), Puritan minister and poet, whose works, unpublished until 1939, give him rank as the finest poet of colonial America. The stylistic resemblances of his work to that of the English metaphysical poets—George Herbert especially—have led critics to call Taylor "the American metaphysical."

Life. Little is known of Taylor's early life. He was born near Coventry, England, about 1642 and probably attended Cambridge University briefly. He taught school until his Puritan conscience made him refuse to take the oath required by the Act of Uniformity of 1662. In 1668 he went to New England, entered Harvard, and graduated in 1671. He then became minister of the church at Westfield, Mass. The death of his first wife in 1689 was the occasion for one of his most moving poems, *Meditation 33, First Series.* He died in Westfield on June 24, 1729.

Works. All of Taylor's poems concern religious subjects. Taylor requested that his heirs not publish them, and in 1883 a descendant gave the manuscripts to Yale University. None of the poems was published until the collection *The Poetical Works of Edward Taylor,* edited by Thomas H. Johnson, appeared in 1939. If Taylor had published his works, they presumably would have appeared in five sizable volumes entitled *Preparatory Meditations; Preparatory Meditations, Second Series; God's Determinations Touching His Elect; A Metrical History of Christianity;* and *Miscellaneous Poems.*

The *Meditations* series were written as devotional exercises to be used before Communion. The preface to *God's Determinations,* celebrating God's power in homely imagery, is one of Taylor's best, and best-known, poems. The work itself is a defense of the Puritan doctrines of election and reprobation—a subject treated in Wigglesworth's more famous but less readable *Day of Doom* (1662). Many of the poems of strongest interest today—such as *Upon a Spider Catching a Fly, Huswifery,* and *Upon Wedlock, and Death of Children*—belong to the *Miscellaneous* group.

HYATT H. WAGGONER, *Author of "American Poets, from the Puritans to the Present"*

Further Reading: Grabo, Norman S., *Edward Taylor* (New York 1962); Stanford, Donald E., *Edward Taylor* (Minneapolis, Minn., 1965); id., ed., *The Poems of Edward Taylor* (New Haven, Conn., 1960).

TAYLOR, Elizabeth (1932–), American motion picture actress. She was born of American parents in London, England, on Feb. 27, 1932, and at the outbreak of World War II went to live with her grandparents in Pasadena, Calif. She made her motion picture debut in *Lassie Come Home* (1943) and became a star in *National Velvet* (1944). She survived the "awkward age" and a series of mediocre films to become a superstar.

Miss Taylor matured as an actress and scored a critical triumph in *A Place in the Sun* (1951). She later appeared in *Giant* (1956), *Raintree County* (1957), and *Cat on a Hot Tin Roof* (1958) and won the 1961 Academy Award for the best performance by an actress for her work in *Butterfield 8* (1960). She costarred with her fifth husband, Richard Burton, in *Cleopatra* (1963); *Who's Afraid of Virginia Woolf?* (1966), winning her second Academy Award; and *The Taming of the Shrew* (1967). She also starred in *The Only Game in Town* (1970).

TAYLOR, Frederick Winslow (1856–1915), American engineer, inventor, and efficiency expert, who pioneered the principles of "scientific management" in industry and business. He was born in Germantown, Pa., on March 20, 1856. He was educated in France and Germany and at Phillips Exeter Academy and in 1874 was graduated from Harvard Law School. Poor eyesight compelled him to give up a law career, and from 1874 to 1878 he was apprenticed as a pattern maker and machinist in a Philadelphia pump manufacturing company.

In 1878, at his own insistence, Taylor became a manual laborer for the Midvale Steel Company in Philadelphia. He rose rapidly through the ranks to become chief engineer in 1884. Meanwhile he studied at night and in 1883 received a mechanical engineering degree from the Stevens Institute of Technology. During his lifetime he obtained about 100 patents.

Taylor systematically studied and measured shop operating methods at Midvale. He began to formulate the principles of manufacturing organization, classification, and analysis that later would be called scientific management, or the "Taylor system" of time-and-motion study.

He established an independent practice as a shop management consultant in Philadelphia in 1891 but from 1898 to 1901 served exclusively as a consultant to the Bethlehem Steel Company. His book *Principles of Scientific Management* was published in 1911. He died in Philadelphia on March 21, 1915.

WILLIAM GREENLEAF
University of New Hampshire

TAYLOR, George (1716–1781), American patriot, political leader, and signer of the Declaration of Independence. Born in Ireland in 1716, he arrived in Philadelphia as a redemptioner in 1736 and became a successful iron manufacturer in Easton, Pa. From 1764 to 1770 he served in the provincial assembly for Northampton county. In 1774 and 1775 he was a member of the county committee of correspondence and committee of safety, and in 1775 he was reelected to the assembly.

When the 1776 Pennsylvania convention made new appointments to the Continental Congress,

Elizabeth Taylor in *Taming of the Shrew.*

CULVER PICTURES

Taylor was among them. He took his seat on July 20 and signed the Declaration of Independence on August 2. Not reelected to Congress in 1777, he returned to Easton. He died there on Feb. 23, 1781.

JOHN J. ZIMMERMAN
Kansas State Teachers College

TAYLOR, Jeremy (1613–1667), English scholar and bishop, an important figure among the 17th century Anglican churchmen and theologians known as the "Caroline Divines." Born in Cambridge in 1613 and educated at Caius College, Cambridge, he was elected a fellow of his college in 1633, the year of his ordination. In the bitter controversy between Anglicans and Puritans he allied himself with the followers of Archbishop Laud, who made him a fellow of All Souls', Oxford, in 1635. Like nearly all the high churchmen of the time, Taylor was an ardent Royalist. In 1638, he became one of the chaplains to King Charles I. In 1642, when the King's forces were ranged against the Parliamentary army, Taylor left his parish at Uppingham to serve as a chaplain with the Royalist army. The victory that overthrew both church and monarchy temporarily drove him into retirement in southern Wales, where he spent a number of years as chaplain to Lord Carbery at Golden Grove, near Llanfihangel Aberbythych.

During the years at Golden Grove, Taylor produced most of his best-known works. In 1647 he published his *Liberty of Prophesying,* a plea for tolerance and charity. In 1650 appeared the first of the two books upon which so much of his later fame was to rest. *The Rule and Exercise of Holy Living.* It was followed within a year by its companion, *The Rule and Exercise of Holy Dying.* Classic expositions of Anglican spirituality, these devotional handbooks are as valuable for their beauty and force of language as for their spiritual insights. Taylor sought to explore the principles of moral theology from a distinctively Anglican standpoint. His *Unam necessarium* (1660) was a treatise on sin and repentance, and his lengthy compendium *Ductor dubitantium* (1660) was a manual of moral theology, intended to guide the clergy as confessors.

In 1660, with the restoration of the monarchy and the reestablishment of Anglicanism, Taylor was made bishop of Down and Connor in Ireland, serving until his death in Lisburn, Ireland, on Aug. 3, 1667. His episcopate was a stormy one, troubled by the hostility of both Presbyterians and Roman Catholics.

POWEL MILLS DAWLEY
General Theological Seminary

TAYLOR, John (1753–1824), American statesman and agrarian philosopher, known as John Taylor of Caroline after the Virginia county in which his plantation, "Hazlewood," was situated. He was born probably in Mill Hill, Va., on Dec. 19, 1753. Orphaned at an early age, he was reared by his uncle, Edmund Pendleton, and educated by tutors. He entered the College of William and Mary in 1770 but left to read law, receiving a license to practice law in 1774.

During the American Revolution, Taylor served in the Continental Army and as a lieutenant colonel in the Virginia militia. A member of the Virginia House of Delegates for seven years between 1782 and 1800, he introduced the Virginia resolutions of 1798, celebrated statements of the states' rights theory of government. He was a United States senator on three occasions–1792 to 1794, 1803, and 1822–until his death. A purist disliking compromises necessary in politics, he preferred to live on his plantation conducting agricultural experiments and writing.

In pamphlets published in 1794, Taylor attacked Alexander Hamilton's fiscal program as an unconstitutional measure favoring business interests. An ardent Jeffersonian Republican, he saw the party as a strict constructionist bulwark against federal centralization.

Taylor's contemporary fame rested on his major political writings: *An Inquiry into the Principles and Policy of the Government of the United States* (1814) and *Construction Construed and Constitutions Vindicated* (1820). He advanced an agrarian theory of government, arguing that free institutions could be preserved only in a nation of independent landowners. He also believed that the only protection of individual rights against the federal government, which was dominated by business interests, lay in the augmentation of the power of the states. In *The Arator* (1813), a collection of essays on agriculture, he urged Virginians to cease planting tobacco, which depleted the soil, and to turn to grain crops with regular rotation. Taylor died at Hazlewood on Aug. 21, 1824.

HARRY AMMON, *Southern Illinois University*

Further Reading: Simms, Henry Harrison, *Life of John Taylor* (Richmond, Va., 1932); Mudge, Eugene T., *Social Philosophy of John Taylor of Caroline* (New York 1939); Risjord, Norman K., *The Old Republicans* (New York 1965).

TAYLOR, John (1808–1887), 3d president of the Utah Mormons. Taylor was born in Milnthorpe, England, on Nov. 1, 1808. Showing religious insights at an early age, he was appointed a lay preacher of Methodism before his family settled in Canada in 1832. Not satisfied with Methodism he turned first to the Irvingites and then was baptized a Mormon in 1836.

Taylor rose in the Mormon ranks as elder, missioner, and then apostle, defending the Mormon cause in Ohio, Missouri, and Illinois. He was a prominent member of the Nauvoo (Ill.) community and was seriously wounded by the same mob that martyred Joseph Smith at Carthage, Ill., in 1844. As one of the 12 Mormon Apostles he supported the presidency of Brigham Young and participated in the epic migration to Utah. Before and after colonization in the American West, Taylor introduced Mormonism to England, Scotland, and Ireland (1840–1841), to France (1849), and later to Germany. He translated *The Book of Mormon* into French and German.

Working in the eastern part of the United States, in 1854 he attempted to spread Mormonism through a newspaper, *The Mormon,* published in New York City. Because of mounting hostility he returned to Utah in 1857. There he distinguished himself as legislator (1857–1876), as judge (1868–1870), and as the territorial superintendent of schools (1877). After the death of Young in 1877, Taylor assumed leadership of the church and was made president in 1880. In 1882 he published one of his most interesting theological works, *An Examination into and an Elucidation of the Great Principles of the Mediation and Atonement of Our Lord and Savior Jesus Christ.*

Taylor was a Mormon "fundamentalist." He accepted the revelation to Smith about polygamy, and had seven wives. After plural marriages were outlawed by the Edmunds-Tucker act of 1882, Taylor went into seclusion and exile, but he continued to administer the church until his death on July 25, 1887, in Kaysville, Utah. See also MORMONS.

JAMES H. SMYLIE
Union Theological Seminary, Richmond, Va.

TAYLOR, John (1580–1653) minor English poet and comic writer, who called himself the "Water Poet." He was born in Gloucester on Aug. 24, 1580. After serving in the navy, Taylor became a London waterman, ferrying passengers across the Thames. When ferrying declined, he educated himself to become a poet and, beginning with *Laugh and Be Fat* (1612), produced scores of prose and verse pamphlets. He died in London in December 1653.

A staunch Anglican, a Royalist, and a simple moralist, Taylor denounced cursing, drunkenness, Puritans, papists, debt defaulters, and court parasites. His attacks on fellow poets and his accounts of his ridiculous journeys—including trips to Edinburgh on foot with no money (1618) and to Queenborough in a brown-paper boat, with two stockfish tied to canes as oars (1619)—brought welcome notoriety. Taylor described his adventures and the hospitality given him with blunt humor, many puns and classical allusions, poor meter, amusing rhymes, and fantastic titles. His early poems were published in 1630, and his extant works in 1869–1878.

GEORGIA DUNBAR, *Hofstra University*

TAYLOR, Laurette (1884–1946), American actress. She was born Helen Laurette Cooney in New York City on April 1, 1884, and began her career as a child performer in vaudeville. In 1900 she married Charles Taylor and during the next few years starred in plays written by him. She divorced Taylor in 1908 and married the playwright J. Hartley Manners in 1911. Her first outstanding success was in Manners' *Peg o' My Heart* (1912), a play with which she was long identified.

After Manners died in 1928, she acted only rarely, though in 1938 she won new fame as Mrs. Midgit in a revival of Sutton Vane's *Outward Bound*. She ended her career triumphantly in the 1940's as Amanda Wingfield in Tennessee Williams' *The Glass Menagerie,* often considered one of the outstanding performances of the 20th century. She died in New York City on Dec. 7, 1946.

OSCAR G. BROCKETT, *Indiana University*

TAYLOR, Maxwell Davenport (1901–), American general and ambassador to Vietnam. He was born in Keytesville, Mo., on Aug. 26, 1901, and graduated from the U. S. Military Academy in 1922. In World War II he pioneered airborne warfare in Sicily and Italy. Taylor made a daring but futile trip into German-dominated Rome in 1943 to meet Italian authorities who sought to deliver the city to the Allies. He led the 101st Airborne Division on D-Day in Normandy, and later in the Netherlands, the Ardennes, and Germany.

After the war Taylor was superintendent of the Military Academy. He commanded the U. S. Eighth Army late in the Korean War. He was chief of staff of the U. S. Army from 1955 to his retirement in 1959. President Kennedy appointed him special presidential military adviser, and chairman of the Joint Chiefs from 1962 to 1964. He was among those who recommended increased U. S. commitment in Vietnam. President Johnson appointed him ambassador to South Vietnam in 1964. After his resignation in 1966 he continued to serve as special adviser to the president.

Taylor wrote *The Uncertain Trumpet* (1960) and *Responsibility and Response* (1967). His colleagues knew him as a man of exemplary integrity, a scholar commanding eight languages, and an inveterate tennis player.

CHARLES B. MACDONALD
Author of "The Mighty Endeavor"

TAYLOR, Myron Charles (1874–1959), American industrialist and diplomat. He was born in Lyons, N. Y., on Jan. 18, 1874. He received A. B. and LL. B. degrees from Cornell University and practiced law briefly in New York City. He then became the manager of a group of textile mills in New England and in 1927 joined the U. S. Steel Corporation as finance committee chairman. From 1932 to 1938 he was its chairman of the board and chief executive officer. He reorganized U. S. Steel's finances and averted a strike in 1936 by signing the industry's first collective-bargaining agreement with the Congress of Industrial Organizations (CIO).

In 1938, Taylor was appointed U. S. delegate and chairman of the Conference on Political Refugees at Evian, France, and in 1939 he was named President Franklin D. Roosevelt's personal representative to the Vatican, with the rank of ambassador without portfolio. Continuing to serve in that capacity under President Truman until 1950, he then went on special diplomatic missions for the president until his retirement in 1953. Taylor's *Wartime Correspondence Between President Roosevelt and Pope Pius XII* appeared in 1947. He died in New York City on May 6, 1959.

TAYLOR, Richard (1826–1879), American Confederate general, who was the only son of President Zachary Taylor. He was a brother-in-law of Jefferson Davis, president of the Confederate States of America. Taylor was born on Jan. 27, 1826, in Jefferson county, Ky., and passed his early life on Western army posts with his father, then an officer. He graduated from Yale in 1845 and become a sugar planter in Louisiana. In 1845–1861 he served in the Louisiana Senate.

Soon after the Civil War began, Taylor was named colonel of the 9th Louisiana infantry regiment. Valorous service in Virginia brought him promotions to the rank of major general by 1862. For the next two years Taylor commanded the district of West Louisiana. His most noted achievement there was the repulse of Gen. N. P. Banks' Red River expedition in 1864. Later Taylor was promoted to lieutenant general and assigned to the department of Alabama and Mississippi. He surrendered the last Confederate army on May 8, 1865.

Rendered destitute by the war, Taylor worked tirelessly for leniency toward the vanquished South. He was an accomplished writer. His delightful memoirs, *Destruction and Reconstruction,* were published shortly before he died in New York City on April 12, 1879.

JAMES I. ROBERTSON, JR.
Virginia Polytechnic Institute

ZACHARY TAYLOR

12th PRESIDENT OF THE UNITED STATES IN OFFICE FROM 1849 TO 1850

BORN	Nov. 24, 1784, in Orange county, Va.
RELIGION	Episcopalian.
OCCUPATION	Soldier.
MARRIAGE	June 21, 1810 to Margaret Mackall Smith (1788–1852).
CHILDREN	Ann Mackall Taylor (1811–1875), married Robert C. Wood; Sarah Knox Taylor (1814–1835), married Jefferson Davis; Mary Elizabeth Taylor (1824–1909), married 1st William W. S. Bliss, 2d Philip P. Dandridge; Richard Taylor (1826–1879), married Myrthé Bringier; two daughters died in infancy.
NICKNAME	"Old Rough and Ready."
POLITICAL PARTY	Whig.
POSITION WHEN ELECTED	Major general, U.S. Army.
DIED	July 9, 1850, in the White House, Washington, D.C., at age 65.
BURIAL PLACE	Zachary Taylor National Cemetery, Jefferson county, Ky.

CHICAGO HISTORICAL SOCIETY

Z. Taylor.

TAYLOR, Zachary (1784–1850), 12th president of the United States. A career soldier who never voted, he served fewer than 500 days in the White House. Yet he significantly influenced political developments during the first half of 1850, when there was a domestic crisis and a grave possibility of civil war. Although long a slaveholder, Taylor was as much a Westerner as a Southerner. He was nationalistic in his orientation, seeking, above all, to preserve the Union.

Ancestry and Early Life. Taylor was a member of several prominent families. One forebear was William Brewster, a *Mayflower* pilgrim. James Madison was Taylor's second cousin, and Robert E. Lee also was a kinsman. The 12th president's father was Lt. Col. Richard Taylor of the Revolutionary Army. His mother was Sarah Dabney Strother Taylor.

Zachary Taylor was born in Orange county, Va., on Nov. 24, 1784. A third child and third son, he had six younger brothers and sisters. As an infant he was taken to what became Jefferson county, Ky., and he grew to manhood on a farm near Louisville. His formal schooling was slight.

Early Military Career. In 1808, Taylor was commissioned a first lieutenant of infantry. Two years later he married Margaret Mackall Smith of Calvert county, Md. As a captain he won distinction in September 1812 for his defense of Fort Harrison in Indiana Territory against an Indian attack. For this achievement the young officer became the first brevet major in the U. S. Army. In 1814, Taylor led U. S. troops against British and Indians at Credit Island in Illinois Territory. Outnumbered three to one, he scored temporary successes before withdrawing. In 1815 he was promoted to the lineal grade of major.

After a year as a civilian, Taylor reentered the army in 1816. At various times he served in the states or future states of Wisconsin, Minnesota, Missouri, Mississippi, Louisiana, Arkansas, and Oklahoma. Commissioned a colonel in 1832, he fought in the Black Hawk War that year, participating in the Battle of Bad Axe. Taylor acquired his nickname, "Old Rough and Ready," fighting the Seminole Indians in Florida Territory from 1837 to 1840. His victory at the Battle of Okeechobee in 1837 was the single most successful U. S. effort of the protracted Second Seminole War. Breveted a brigadier general in 1838, he commanded all U. S. troops in Florida. He emerged from the struggle with the reputation of a determined, resourceful leader.

There followed five placid years, 1840–1845, during which Taylor remained in the army, but also gave careful attention to his plantation in Mississippi. The annexation of Texas, however, enabled him to receive his most important military assignment. In August 1845 he was in command of a small army of regulars near the mouth of the Nueces River at Corpus Christi, Texas. Both the United States and Mexico claimed the region between this river and the Rio Grande, and because Mexican military activity was rumored, Taylor augmented his troops and awaited specific instructions before moving through the disputed region.

Mexican War. Early in 1846 the order came. Advancing to his new supply base at Point Isabel, General Taylor ordered the construction of Fort Texas (later Fort Brown, site of Brownsville, Texas) on the American side of the Rio Grande opposite Matamoros. Nearby on April 25 about 1,600 Mexican soldiers, who had crossed the river, surrounded an American detachment and killed or captured its members. This was the unofficial start of the Mexican War. Taylor set out for Point Isabel to secure his base and, after several days devoted to strengthening its defenses, began a return march to relieve Fort Texas, which had come under Mexican bombardment.

The American force of 2,228 found its route blocked by a Mexican army more than twice its size. On May 8 at Palo Alto, 12 miles (19 km) northeast of Fort Texas, Mexican Gen. Mariano Arista opened cannon fire, and Taylor retaliated. Palo Alto was the war's first battle. It was a minor U. S. victory, which demonstrated the superiority of American artillery.

The next day told a more dramatic story. Arista fell back 5 miles (8 km) to terrain where embankments, underbrush, and chaparral offset the effectiveness of Taylor's cannon. The fight at Resaca de la Palma that afternoon was especially bloody. Little headway could be made against the strong Mexican right flank by the greatly outnumbered Americans. But before the insistent hammering of Taylor's infantrymen, Arista's left flank was turned, and his army crumbled. The Mexicans retreated hastily across the Rio Grande. Fort Texas was safe and the American army triumphant. The Mexicans suffered three times as many casualties as the Americans.

THE BETTMANN ARCHIVE

Mary Taylor Bliss Dandridge, daughter of President Zachary Taylor.

The two May victories resulted in Taylor's becoming not only a major general but also a national hero. Then, Congress having declared war, volunteer regiments made it possible for "Old Rough and Ready" to have 6,641 troops when he launched his attack on Monterrey on Sept. 21, 1846. Northern Mexico's largest community proved to be well defended. Gen. Pedro de Ampudia's army of 7,303 held many advantages behind fortified hills and adjacent strongpoints. Much of the fighting was house-to-house as sharpshooters fired from doorways, windows, and roofs while artillery controlled the streets and plazas. For three days the combat raged. Finally, Ampudia broached an eight-week armistice, stipulating his willingness to surrender the city if Taylor would permit withdrawal of the Mexican troops. Because his supply lines were extended and this seemed the best result he could obtain, Taylor accepted Ampudia's proposal.

Despite the indecisive outcome and the numerous U. S. casualties, many Americans at home regarded Monterrey as a third Taylor success. Not so President James K. Polk. Losing confidence in Taylor, Polk transferred most of the seasoned soldiers to Gen. Winfield Scott. Polk himself, however, made a serious mistake. He gave the exiled Mexican dictator Antonio López de Santa Anna a safe-conduct through the U. S. naval blockade in the belief that the opportunistic firebrand would arrange peace negotiations. Instead, Santa Anna attacked Taylor.

The Battle of Buena Vista on Feb. 22–23, 1847, marked the climax of Taylor's Mexican War service. With fewer than 500 regulars in his force of 4,760, he was outnumbered by Santa Anna four to one. Amid crags and gullies near Saltillo, the doughty commander halted waves of mounted and dismounted assailants and turned the tide in counterassaults. After two days of struggle, Santa Anna retreated from the rugged terrain. The field and the victory were Taylor's.

Election of 1848. Buena Vista, more than anything else, elevated Taylor to the presidency. His unassuming personality, earthiness, and courage contributed substantially to his appeal. The Whig party, trying to repeat its one great success with William Henry Harrison in 1840, nominated this second old soldier as its presidential candidate in June 1848. Taylor was a military hero whose views on the crucial issues of the day were not well enough known to be damaging. His ownership of blacks and a cotton plantation helped in the South.

Taylor's opponents in the campaign were Democrat Lewis Cass and Free Soil standard-bearer Martin Van Buren. The main issue was the extension of slavery into the vast regions ceded by Mexico to the United States in the Treaty of Guadalupe Hidalgo, which ended the Mexican War. While Van Buren explicitly opposed extension, neither major-party aspirant took a clear position. Van Buren, a former Democrat, split the Democratic vote in pivotal New York. Taylor defeated Cass 163 to 127 in the electoral college. Taylor carried half the states, seven in the North and eight in the South. His popular vote was 1,362,101; Cass', 1,222,674; Van Buren's, 291,616.

President. Zachary Taylor was president from March 5, 1849, to July 9, 1850. The Thirty-first Congress, which did not assemble until December 1849, had a Democratic plurality in the House and a Democratic majority in the Senate. Its members were far from agreement on the burning issues of the times.

Many Southern senators and representatives favored projecting the Missouri Compromise line of 36° 30′ to the Pacific Ocean, with slavery legal south of the line. Other senators, notably Henry Clay and Stephen A. Douglas, supported mutual concessions, including the application of popular sovereignty to two western territories they wished to create. Taylor rejected those schemes, the "President's Plan" being limited to the admission of California and New Mexico as states.

Because California had applied to enter the Union as a free state, and it was thought that New Mexico would follow suit, Taylor's stand was clearly anti-extension. His congressional backing consisted almost wholly of free-state Whigs. With two exceptions, every Northern Whig senator explicitly or implicitly sided with the president.

Thus Taylor's role is vital to an understanding of the memorable debates of 1850, during which some congressmen carried firearms, and prominent politicians were involved in fist-fights. There was fear and danger of civil war and a possibility that the Texas militiamen would attempt to drive the U. S. Army out of Santa Fe before the year was over. A Unionist in the Jacksonian tradition, President Taylor made it clear that he would not hesitate to employ the full authority of his office to quell rebellion in any form. See also COMPROMISE OF 1850.

Taylor died in Washington, D. C., on July 9, 1850, when the national crisis was particularly acute. Except for the dramatic congressional speeches over the extension of slavery—some among the most famous in American history—the sole major event associated with the Taylor administration is the signing of the Clayton-Bulwer Treaty with Britain, which provided for control over a future canal or other route across Central America. See CLAYTON-BULWER TREATY.

Assessment. Taylor was a conscientious military officer, popular with his subordinates, considerate, and brave, although not one of the truly great commanders. Stocky, sturdy, of medium height, with furrowed face and graying hair, he habitually wore civilian garb during the Mexican War—preferring a wide-brimmed straw hat and unmatched trousers and coat. When reviewing his troops on Old Whitey, he liked to sit sidesaddle with one leg casually thrown over the pommel. Afoot he was often taken for a farmer. In Washington, dressed more formally but with his top hat perched on the back of his head, the President frequently went about unrecognized. Simplicity, in its best sense, is the word most accurately characterizing Taylor both before and after he became famous.

Devoted to his invalid wife, his children, and grandchildren, Taylor valued family life and played host to countless relatives. He became fully reconciled to his son-in-law, Jefferson Davis, who had married Sarah Knox Taylor in 1835 against her father's wishes only to become a widower three months later. Another Taylor daughter, Mary Elizabeth ("Betty"), then married to Col. William Bliss, acted as White House hostess during her father's presidency.

A cotton planter, Taylor took an abiding interest not only in land and crops but particularly in his Negroes, who were well treated. Owning 118 slaves when elected president, he acquired 64 more and a sugar plantation several weeks before he died. Yet he adamantly opposed the extension of slavery. From Taylor's point of view this was not inconsistent. He respected slaveholders' rights in the 15 states where the institution was legal. At the same time, he did not wish to jeopardize the Union because of the extension issue.

In some Southern eyes, Taylor, politically, was a doughface in reverse—a Southern man with Northern principles. Fundamentally he was a dedicated Unionist, a son of the West, a product of the frontier, a patriot who placed the highest value on what he conceived to be national interests and national welfare.

HOLMAN HAMILTON
University of Kentucky

Further Reading: Dyer, Brainerd, *Zachary Taylor* (New York 1967); Hamilton, Holman, *Zachary Taylor*, 2 vols. (Hamden, Conn., 1966); id., *Prologue to Conflict* (Lexington, Ky., 1964); Samson, William H., ed., *Letters of Zachary Taylor from the Battlefields of the Mexican War* (Rochester, N. Y., 1908; reprinted New York 1969).

TAYLOR, a city in southeastern Michigan, in Wayne county, is 20 miles (23 km) southwest of Detroit, of which it is a residential suburb. Its principal industries manufacture machinery, wood products, concrete, concrete pipe, and glass. The production of sand and gravel is important.

Taylor was founded in 1847 as a township and named after Gen. Zachary Taylor, a hero of the Mexican War, who became the 12th president of the United States (1849–1850). It was incorporated as a city in 1968 and has a mayor and council form of government. Population: 70,020.

TAYLOR, a city in south central Texas, is in Williamson county, about 32 miles (51 km) northeast of Austin. It is the center of an area that raises cotton, grain, cattle, sheep, and goats and has resources of oil, lime, sand, and gravel. Taylor's industries include woodworking, food processing, and the manufacture of bedding, furniture, and clothing. Government is by council and manager. Population: 9,616.

TAYLOR'S THEOREM, a basic principle of calculus, is used to represent a complex mathematical function by a simpler expression, thus making it possible to deduce conclusions about complex functions more readily. The theorem was first published by the English mathematician Brook Taylor in 1715. He was one of the immediate successors of Isaac Newton and Gottfried Wilhelm von Leibniz, who were two of the founders of the calculus.

If we denote a function of x by $f(x)$, then Taylor's theorem can be stated as

$$f(x) = f(a) + f'(a)(x-a) + f''(a)\frac{(x-a)^2}{2!} + \dots + f^n(a)\frac{(x-a)^n}{n!} + f^{n+1}(\bar{x})\frac{(x-a)^{n+1}}{(n+1)!}$$

where a is an arbitrarily chosen fixed value of x, $f'(a)$ is the value of the first derivative of $f(x)$ at $x = a$, $f''(a)$ is the value of the second derivative of $f(x)$ at $x = a$, and $f^n(a)$ is the value of the nth derivative of $f(x)$ at $x = a$. The symbol $n!$ means the product $1.2.3 \dots n$. In the last term, called the *remainder term*, $\bar{x}$ is some value of x between a and x. Except for the last term in the equation, the right side is a polynomial because the quantities $f'(a)$, $f''(a)$, and the higher derivatives of $f(x)$ at $x = a$ are constants. There may be two, three, or more terms on the right side because the value of n is arbitrary. For large n, $(n + 1)!$ is very large, and thus the remainder term is small. If this term is neglected, then $f(x)$ is represented very closely by a polynomial.

If the remainder term approaches zero as n approaches an infinite value, then the function $f(x)$ is represented by an infinite series called the Taylor series. This series, which is obtained by extending the polynomials given by Taylor's theorem to infinitely many terms, has the form

$$f(x) = f(a) + f'(a)(x-a) + f''(a)\frac{(x-a)^2}{2!} + \dots$$

Taylor series can be used to calculate functions such as $\sin x$, $\log(1 + x)$, and e^x. The successive terms in such series become smaller and smaller in value, so the accuracy to which one wants to calculate $f(x)$ depends on the number of terms used.

MORRIS KLINE
New York University

NOVOSTI, FROM SOVFOTO

TBILISI'S statue of Vakhtang Gorgaslani, 5th century liberator of Georgia, stands high above the city and its river, the Kura.

TAYLORVILLE is a city in central Illinois, the seat of Christian county, on the south fork of the Sangamon River. It is situated 26 miles (41 km) southeast of Springfield. Taylorville's chief industries are coal mining, paper making, garment manufacturing, and the production of animal feeds. Abraham Lincoln practiced in the old county courthouse. The community was settled in 1839 and was incorporated in 1882. It has a mayor-council form of government. Population: 10,644.

TAYRA, tī′rə, also known locally as the *eira* or *irara, a* weasel-like carnivore (*Eira barbara*) found from southern Mexico to northern Argentina. It is blackish or brownish, with a brownish or gray head and a broad yellowish patch on the neck and breast. The tayra grows to 27 inches (68 cm) in head and body length, plus a tail 18½ inches (47 cm) long, and weighs about 10 pounds (4.5 kg). It is a good climber and preys on squirrels and other small mammals, birds, and eggs, but also takes fruits and honey. The tayra lives in pairs or small family groups. Females are believed to average three young per litter.

R. VAN NOSTRAND, FROM NATIONAL AUDUBON SOCIETY

Tayra

FERNANDO DIAS DE AVILA PIRES, *Director*
Museu de Historia Natural, Minas Gerais, Brazil

TB. See TUBERCULOSIS.

TBILISI, tə-bē-lē′sē, is the capital and the cultural center of the Georgian republic in the USSR. The city is situated on the Kura River, at the junction of railroads and highways and at the southern end of the Georgian Military Highway across the Greater Caucasus range. Tbilisi is a manufacturing city, producing machine tools, electric locomotives, electrical equipment, and instruments. Its satellite city to the southeast, Rustavi, is an iron and steel center and the site of chemical plants.

The Georgian Academy of Sciences is located in Tbilisi. The city also has Tbilisi University, a music conservatory, and an art academy. Halfway up Mtatsminda Mountain, which rises 1,000 feet (305 meters) above Tbilisi, is St. David's Monastery, a pantheon where the famous dead of Georgia are buried. Other ancient memorials are the 13th century Metekhi castle, former palace of Georgian kings, and Zion Cathedral, which was originally built in 575 and which is now the seat of the catholicos (head) of the Georgian Church.

One of the oldest cities of the Soviet Union, Tbilisi stands on a site where archaeologists have found traces of settlement dating from the 4th millennium B.C. Tbilisi was first mentioned in chronicles of the 4th century A.D. The name, derived from the Georgian word *tbili,* meaning "warm," refers to the area's hot sulfur springs. The town was successively under Persian, Byzantine, and Arab rule before it flourished as the capital of an independent Georgia in the 12th and 13th centuries. After further invasions it passed in 1801 to Russia and was known by the Russianized name of *Tiflis.*

During the Russian Revolution of 1917 the city was the capital of the anti-Bolshevik Transcaucasian Federation. Its Georgian name was officially restored in 1936. Population: (1970) 889,000.

THEODORE SHABAD
Editor of "Soviet Geography"

TCHAD. See CHAD.

TCHAIKOVSKY, chī-kôf′skē, **Peter Ilich** (1840–1893), Russian composer, who is generally regarded as one of the greatest musicians his country has produced and who is ranked among the outstanding composers of the world. His music, written with immense technical skill and marked by emotional warmth, lyrical melody, and colorful orchestration, has long had wide appeal for the general public. A versatile composer, he wrote operas, symphonies, concertos, chamber works, solo songs, piano compositions, and liturgical music, and he succeeded brilliantly in several spheres. At least one of his operas, *Eugene Onegin,* is an acknowledged masterpiece. His *Swan Lake, Sleeping Beauty,* and *Nutcracker* helped to reestablish, as an important art form, the full-length ballet, which had suffered a decline in the mid-19th century. Among his orchestral works, his symphonies, particularly the Fourth, Fifth, and Sixth (the *Pathétique*), his Piano Concerto No. 1, and his Violin Concerto are among the most popular world classics.

LIFE

Early Years. Tchaikovsky was born at Votkinsk on May 7, 1840. His father, an inspector of mines, was Russian, but his mother was half-French. Peter showed signs of exceptional musical ability at an early age, but his parents did not encourage his interest, and he had only piano lessons from indifferent teachers. In 1852 he enrolled in the St. Petersburg School of Jurisprudence, and following his graduation in 1859, he became a clerk in the ministry of justice. He began to study music seriously in 1861, when he started to take harmony lessons with Nikolai Zaremba, at first privately and in the next year at the St. Petersburg Conservatory. In 1863 he resigned from the civil service and broadened his musical studies, including instrumentation from Anton Rubinstein.

Middle Years. After graduating from the Conservatory in 1865, Tchaikovsky accepted the post of professor of harmony at the Moscow Conservatory of Music. He composed his first symphony, the Symphony in G Minor (*Winter Daydreams*), in 1866 and his first opera *The Voyevoda* in 1868. During rehearsals of the opera he met a French soprano, Désirée Artôt, with whom he fleetingly contemplated marriage, presumably in an effort to conquer his homosexual tendencies.

The Voyevoda had only five performances. Tchaikovsky's next opera, *Undine* (1869), was never produced, and the two that followed, *The Oprichnik* (1872) and *Vakula the Smith* (1874), were unsuccessful. It was his instrumental works that earned him his early triumphs. These included the Second Symphony in C Minor (1872) and Third Symphony in D Major (1875), the overture-fantasia *Romeo and Juliet* (1869), the symphonic fantasias *The Tempest* (1873) and *Francesca da Rimini* (1876), the Piano Concerto No. 1 in B-Flat Minor (1875), the 3-act ballet *Swan Lake* (1876), and his three string quartets (1871, 1874, 1876).

Later Years. The year 1877 was one of shattering crisis for Tchaikovsky. In July 1877 he made a last desperate attempt to conquer, or at least conceal, his homosexuality by marrying Antonina Milyukova, a 28-year-old ex-student from the Conservatory who had declared her love for him. The marriage collapsed almost immediately. Tchaikovsky tried to commit suicide by walking into the Moskva River in an unsuccessful attempt to contract pneumonia. After fleeing to St. Petersburg, he was taken abroad for several months by one of his brothers. Yet in this same year he wrote two masterpieces, *Eugene Onegin* and the Fourth Symphony.

Earlier in 1877, Nadezhda von Meck, a wealthy and eccentric widow, who admired his music, communicated with Tchaikovsky. Mme. von Meck, who insisted on never meeting Tchaikovsky personally, settled on him a handsome annuity that enabled him, in 1878, to resign from the Conservatory. His new financial independence enabled him to spend his winters abroad, usually in Italy or France, and his summers in the country. Although he continued to write operas, including *The Maid of Orleans* (1879), *Mazeppa* (1883), *The Little Shoes* (a much-revised version of *Vakula;* 1885), and *The Sorceress* (1887), his fame was enhanced, as before, by his orchestral works. Among these were the Violin Concerto in D Major (1878), the overture *The Year 1812* (1880), the *Manfred* Symphony (1885), and the Fifth Symphony in E Minor (1888).

In 1887–1888, Tchaikovsky embarked on his first conducting tour of western Europe. He met with great success, notably in England, and made a second tour in 1889. In 1890 he suffered another personal crisis when Mme. von Meck arbitrarily terminated both his annuity and their long epistolary friendship. Despite this blow, which deeply affected Tchaikovsky's neurotic, self-torturing ego, he composed in that year two of his finest scores, the 3-act ballet *Sleeping Beauty* and the opera *The Queen of Spades.*

In April and May of 1891, Tchaikovsky was in the United States, conducting in New York, Baltimore, and Philadelphia before highly enthusiastic audiences. On his return to Russia, he completed a one-act opera, *Iolanta* (1891), and the two-act ballet, *Nutcracker* (1892), and started to compose the *Pathétique.* Although his work on the symphony was interrupted by a last visit to England in June 1893, it was finished in August and had its first performance in St. Petersburg on Oct. 28, 1893. A few days later,

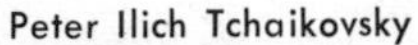

Peter Ilich Tchaikovsky

BROWN BROTHERS

in St. Petersburg, Tchaikovsky knowingly drank a glass of unboiled water and was stricken with cholera. He died on Nov. 6, 1893.

WORKS

Tchaikovsky criticized Wagner for never writing a "broad, complete melody," and Brahms because "a melodic phrase is no sooner hinted at [in his work] than it is smothered in all sorts of harmonic ingenuities." Neither criticism can be aimed at Tchaikovsky. His custom of "working like a cobbler, day in, day out, and often to order," as he put it, sometimes drained dry even his reservoir of melodic inspiration. When the current flowed, however, he presented and fitted together his broad, complete melodies with superbly effective craftsmanship.

The quintessence of Tchaikovsky's best music lies in its intensely personal melody, which ranges from the grace of a waltz tune like that in the *Serenade* for string orchestra (1880) to the expression of anguish of the *Pathétique* symphony and owes nothing to contrivance or to folk music. It does owe something to Bellini and to Bizet, but its *morbidezza* (softness) is Russian, not Italian, and its emotional unrestraint is very un-French.

Tchaikovsky's orchestration is effective not merely because it is highly colored but because it is based on beautifully fluent harmony; a melody is shown now in one light, now in another, by counter subjects and subordinate melodic strands or novel and fascinating patterns of accompaniment. His natural flair for colorful scoring was rather crude at first, but he went on refining it all his life.

One curious trait gave Tchaikovsky a special inducement to refine his style: his love of the 18th century idioms. Perhaps the earliest example of his pseudo-18th century style is the minuet in the court scene of *Vakula*, and it surfaces again and again, notably in the long "pastoral interlude" in *The Queen of Spades*.

Instrumental Music. Tchaikovsky excelled in instrumental music, particularly when he was unhampered by the limitations of chamber music or of the piano, for to produce his best work, he needed a range of tone color and the semihuman quality of string sound. Even the elements to which the Piano Concerto No. 1 owes its popularity are orchestral rather than pianistic, and the three string quartets, despite beautiful movements, are too orchestral in feeling to be good chamber music.

Given his mastery of the orchestra, Tchaikovsky had no difficulty in representing the warring families in *Romeo and Juliet;* Ariel, Caliban, and the sea in *The Tempest;* the whirlwind of the Inferno in *Francesca da Rimini;* and the Alpine waterfall in the *Manfred* Symphony. These pictorial representations, however, are clever contrivances, the exercise of technical skill.

Tchaikovsky's strength lay in the expression of powerful emotion. His seven symphonies, ranging from 1866 to 1893, reveal an evolution from objective to intensely subjective content. The First Symphony, after the impressions of a winter landscape in the first two movements, gives way to a rehash of student work in the scherzo. The Second, preoccupied with folk song, has a march movement salvaged from the lost opera, *Undine*. The Third, in five movements, including a *Ländler* and a polonaise, is almost in the nature of a suite. In the Fourth Symphony, however, as Tchaikovsky confided to Mme. von Meck, the first three movements project his own moods, and the finale is an attempt to escape from them. The unnumbered *Manfred* Symphony, based on Byron's poem, is frankly programmatic, and the second, third, and fourth movements are pictorial music. But the first movement is a subjective self-portrait, since the guilt-laden composer could identify with Byron's guilt-laden hero. The Fifth Symphony is an obviously subjective, frankly emotional work, and the last symphony, the *Pathétique*, is one of the most unrestrainedly emotional pieces of musical autobiography ever written.

Operas. Tchaikovsky's relative failure as an opera composer is due not to musical deficiencies but to a psychological deficiency—his general inability to identify with characters. He recognized the importance of having characters who were "people, not dolls," but he was able to bring them to musical life only when they corresponded to something in himself, as did the chief characters of *Eugene Onegin* and the hero of *The Queen of Spades*. Both these masterworks also benefited from the influence of *Carmen*, which deeply impressed Tchaikovsky when he heard it in 1876. Bizet's work opened for Tchaikovsky a way of escape from the type of "grand opera" he had written till then, to a more intimate style in which he was far more successful.

Tchaikovsky longed all his life for success in opera, the medium that he felt "alone gives the means to communicate with the masses of the public.... Opera, and opera alone, makes your music familiar to the real public." Yet he admitted on another occasion, "Despite all the seductions of opera, I write a symphony, sonata, or quartet with infinitely greater pleasure." Ironically, his operas have contributed little to his popularity, while those works written "with infinitely greater pleasure" have made him "familiar to the real public" all over the world.

GERALD ABRAHAM
Author of "Tchaikovsky: A Short Biography"

Bibliography

Abraham, Gerald, ed., *The Music of Tchaikovsky* (New York 1946).
Blom, Eric, *Tchaikovsky: Orchestral Works* (London 1927).
Evans, Edwin, *Tchaikovsky*, rev. by Gerald Abraham (New York 1963).
Tchaikovsky, Peter I., *Diaries*, tr. by Vladimir Lakond (New York 1945).
Warrack, John, *Tchaikovsky: Symphonies and Concertos* (London 1969).
Weinstock, Herbert, *Tchaikovsky* (New York 1943).

TCHELITCHEW, chel-ə-chef′, **Pavel** (1898–1957), Russian-American painter and stage designer. He was born on his father's estate near Moscow on Sept. 21, 1898. He studied at the University of Moscow and the Kiev Academy of Art and after the Revolution went to Berlin, where he received his first commissions for stage designs. There he designed ballets for Diaghilev and became associated with a group of "neoromantic" painters in revolt against abstract art. He went to the U.S. in 1934 and became a citizen in 1954. He died in Rome on July 31, 1957.

Tchelitchew is known for his attempts to create motion in his paintings by applying two or three perspectives, or points of view, to various objects on the same canvas. Among his best-known works are *Still Life Clown* (1930) and the monumental *Hide-and-Seek* (1940–1942). His portraits include several of the poet Edith Sitwell.

J. ALLAN CASH FROM RAPHO GUILLUMETTE

A tea estate, or plantation, near Kericho, Kenya. Kenya is one of the ten largest tea-producing nations.

TEA, a small tree or shrub, *Camellia sinensis,* a preparation of its dried and cured leaves and other plant parts, and a beverage made from these parts. Beverages similar to tea made from other plants are also called "tea" but are almost always preceded by a modifying term, as in sassafras tea, Labrador tea, and sage tea.

The Beverage. Tea has three important ingredients: caffeine, tea tannins, and an aromatic principle. In black tea the aromatic principle is attributed to one of the plant's essential oils. In freshly picked tea leaves the solid materials—cellulose, fiber, and pure protein—constitute only about 25% by volume of the total leaf. The bulk of the fresh leaf consists of water, in which various substances are dissolved. The water-soluble substances are tea tannins, caffeine, protein bodies, gummy matter, and sugars. The caffeine content, to which tea owes its utility as a stimulant, averages about 3%. Like ordinary tannins, tea tannins combine with proteins in tea. Tea tannins have a bitter taste, contrasting with the astringent taste of other tannins.

In preparing tea, to obtain its full flavor and body, bring freshly drawn water to a bubbling boil. Pour the water on the tea leaves in a previously scalded pot, and allow it to remain covered for five minutes. Then strain the tea from the leaves. The leaves should not be used again. One teaspoon (35 grains) of tea for each cup is standard. Tea bags may be treated similarly. But because the tea is generally small in size, it should only be steeped for four minutes, especially if it is to be taken with milk or cream or used for iced tea.

The Plant. The plant *Camellia sinensis,* from which the young and tender leaves are plucked and used for making commercial tea, is a small evergreen tree of the family Theaceae. Although originally named *Thea sinensis* by Linnaeus, it is closely related to *Camelia japonica.* In its natural state it grows to a height of 15 to 30 feet (4.5–9 meters), but under cultivation it is restricted by pruning and plucking to a bushlike plant 2 to 5 feet (0.6–1.5 meters) tall. The tea plant's spearhead-shaped (lanceolate to oblong lanceolate), serrated leaves are borne on short stalks and are arranged alternately on the stem. They vary in length from 1½ to 10 inches (4–25.5 cm) and in width from ½ to 4 inches (1.3–10 cm). Mature leaves are rather thick, smooth, and leathery. The fragrant flowers, single or in groups of two or three, are located in the axils of the leaves. They consist of five white petals surrounding a showy group of yellow stamens. The fruit consists of one to three hard-

BRIAN BRAKE FROM RAPHO GUILLUMETTE

HARVESTING TEA IN CEYLON. In Ceylon, India, and Africa, tea plants are plucked every 7 to 15 days.

shelled, dark brown capsules resembling hazelnuts.

Cultivation. Although not all varieties of tea thrive equally well in all localities, few major crop plants appear to have a wider range of adaptability. Tea-producing countries include China, Japan, India, Pakistan, Ceylon, Taiwan (Formosa), Indonesia, a number of countries in Africa, the Georgian republic of the USSR, Malaysia, Turkey, Brazil, and Argentina.

Tea does best in a warm climate where rainfall averages 90 to 200 inches (2,286–5,080 mm) a year and where the soil is a deep, fertile, well-drained loam or clay-loam containing a substantial amount of well-decomposed organic matter. The tea plant thrives from sea level to elevations of 7,000 feet (2,100 meters). Other factors being equal, the higher the elevation, the better the quality of the tea.

In tea plantations (called estates or gardens) in India, Ceylon, Indonesia, or East Africa, the plants generally are set 4½ feet (1.4 meters) apart and arranged in lines forming squares (checks) or with an additional plant in the center of each square (quincunxes). The latter arrangement permits better cultivation if the alleyways are kept clean. When tea is planted on terraces or hillsides, however, this method cannot strictly be followed. In Japan most of the planting is done in hedgerows 4 to 5 feet (1.2–1.5 meters) apart, the plants being set 2 to 3 feet (0.6–0.9 meter) apart in the rows.

The tea plant is produced from seed in all tea-growing countries except Taiwan, where propagation generally is by branch layering (bending down a branch and buying the tip in the soil). When the branch layers are well rooted, they are pruned away from the parent plant and transplanted in new fields. In most other countries seeds are planted in nursery beds, and then the seedlings are transplanted. In India, however, the seeds are often planted at stake—that is, a new clearing is staked off, and four or five seeds are planted at the foot of each stake—and the plants are thinned out after the seedlings begin to grow.

The tea plant is pruned to a height of 2 to 5 feet (0.6–1.5 meters) for convenience in plucking and, more importantly, to induce the plant to bring forth more tender young leaves.

Plucking or Harvesting. The tea plant produces a *flush* (full complement) of leaves on an average of every 40 days. In China, Taiwan, and Japan the crop is plucked when most of the leaves in a flush have reached the proper stage of growth. In Ceylon, India, Java, Sumatra, and elsewhere, the leaves are plucked every 7 to 15 days. This results in a larger yield of good, uniform tea, since nearly all the leaves in a flush are gathered at the best time.

Beginning at the top, the leaves on a shoot that has a full complement of leaves are known as follows: pekoe tip or flowery pekoe, orange pekoe, pekoe, first souchong, second souchong, first congou, and second congou (bohea). In fine plucking, only the first two leaves (the pekoe tip) and sometimes the third leaf are taken.

Manufacture. There are three primary types of tea: black (fully fermented), oolong (partially fermented), and green (unfermented). Though any of the varieties of tea can be used to produce the three types, certain varieties are better suited for making one or more of them.

Black Tea. There are four important steps in the most common method of manufacturing black tea: withering, rolling, fermenting, and drying.

Withering removes much of the leaf's water content, making the leaf soft and pliable and suitable for rolling. In factories, it is generally accomplished by spreading the leaves very thinly on trays and allowing them to wither naturally for 12 to 24 hours. Sometimes it is done artificially by heating the leaves in machines in a current of air at a temperature of about 140° F (60° C).

Rolling, usually done in special machines, turns and spindles the leaves, breaking the leaf cells. The liberated juices and enzymes then spread over the surface of the leaves, initiating the fermentation (oxidation) process. The juices that dry on the leaves, contributing to the flavor of the tea, are easily dissolved in hot water. Rolling also reduces the surface of the leaf, imparting to it the familiar twist of most commercial teas.

The leaves are then fermented (oxidized) to the desired degree by spreading them on tables or cement floors and allowing them to absorb oxygen for two to four hours. The best results are obtained when the oxidizing room is kept as damp as possible, a humidity of 95% being ideal. The finest flavors in East Indian black teas develop when the temperature is maintained between 75° and 84° F (24°–29° C). For China black teas, oxidation is carried out at a higher temperature by spreading the rolled leaves in the sun or by forming them into balls that are kept overnight in a warm moist place. During fermentation the leaf changes from a dark green to a bright coppery color, and the leafy odor is converted into a characteristic fruity one.

When the desired characteristics appear, the fermentation is checked by drying, or firing, in a current of hot air. East Indian and African teas are dried at a temperature of 190° to 200° F (88°–93° C), the whole process taking about 20 minutes.

China black teas are dried in baskets over charcoal fires at a very low temperature. The process requires six to eight hours because the baskets are removed at intervals from the fires, and the tea is stirred. The most important of the China black teas are the North China black leaf congous and the South China red leaf congous.

In some districts of India, Malawi, and Ceylon, black tea is made by an entirely different process, which omits the withering stage. In the manufacture of nonwither tea, the fresh leaf is put through cutters adjusted to give a cut of about 1/32 of an inch (0.8 mm). The cut leaf is rolled slowly in either standard or modified tea rollers. The tea is then cooled, given a second rolling and cooling, and placed in the fermenting room. After fermentation, the tea is dried at a high temperature, which reduces the moisture content to about 10%. This rapid, high-temperature firing seals the flavor and essential oil into the leaf. The leaf is then passed through a second drier at a lower temperature, which removes all traces of moisture and ensures exceptional keeping qualities.

Oolong Tea. In the manufacture of oolong tea, fermentation (oxidation) is permitted to proceed only part way. This is accomplished by allowing the leaves to wilt partially in the natural way, either by spreading them on trays in the factory or in the sun, or by stirring them in shallow baskets placed in the sun. After this partial fermentation has been carried out, the oxidizing properties are destroyed by stirring the leaves in pans heated to about 250° F (121° C). The leaves are then rolled and fired immediately in hourglass-shaped baskets over charcoal fires at a low temperature.

Oolong teas come from both mainland China and Taiwan. The former, known as Foochow, Amoy, and Canton oolongs, have been superseded to some extent by Taiwan oolongs. Both kinds are often scented with flowers.

Green Tea. When green tea is made, the leaves are first either sterilized in live steam, as is done in Japan, Ceylon, and India, or heated in hot pans over charcoal fires at 250° F (121° C), as is done in China, in order to inhibit the oxidizing, or fermenting, enzymes as completely as possible. The treated leaves are then rolled and fired, or dried, immediately at a temperature of about 200° F (93° C). In India, Ceylon, and Java, green tea is generally made by machinery. Steam is used as a sterilizing agent, and excess water is removed by centrifuging.

Grading. After manufacturing, teas are graded—some for quality (cup test), some for style (size and age of leaf), and some for both quality and style.

The simplest form of grading classifies whole leaves according to age and size, ranging from the tenderest orange pekoe, through pekoe and pekoe souchong, to souchong. Fannings, or broken leaves, are graded as broken orange pekoe, broken pekoe, broken pekoe souchong, and broken souchong. Most of these grades are separated by means of a series of oscillating sieves or revolving cylindrical sieves. Grading is only for style classification. The market value of the tea must be determined by the teataster.

Teatasters sampling tea. A federal board of teatasters sets standards for teas imported into the United States.

WIDE WORLD PHOTOS

The style grades of China green teas, established by passing the finished tea through sieves, include young hyson, hyson, gunpowder, imperial, and pea leaf. In Japanese teas, quality grades are indicated by district names such as Yamashiro and Enshu.

Production. The average world production of tea during the mid-1960's was 2.52 billion pounds (1.26 million tons, or 1,144 million kg) per year. India was the leading tea producer, followed by Ceylon, China (mainland), Japan, and the USSR. Tea production has continued to rise throughout the world, with African and South American nations showing the most marked increase. Countries such as New Guinea, Ecuador, and South Africa, which had not previously grown tea on a significant scale, are now seriously involved in tea production.

Consumption. World consumption of tea continues to absorb the entire output of the producing countries. The producing nations themselves have shown a definite increase in consumption, particularly those developing nations in which there has been a rise in the purchasing power of the working class. Important countries, on the other hand, have tended to stabilize their imports at a much lower rate of increase.

The leading tea-consuming nations are Britain, India, Japan, the USSR, and the United States. Britain also consumes the most tea per person, followed by Ireland, Libya, New Zealand, Australia, and Iraq.

INVENTORY OF TEA STORES. After processing is completed, the teas are packed into bags for shipping.
J. ALLAN CASH FROM RAPHO GUILLUMETTE

The well-known Lapsang souchong, a large leaf congou (lower leaf) with a smoky or tarry flavor, is highly prized among connoisseurs in Britain and the United States. Black teas of the East Indian type (cold-fermented) constitute about 95% of all of the teas that are used in the United States.

Tea packaged in tea bags accounts for the largest share of the tea sold for home consumption in the United States. At the start of the 1970's, tea bags accounted for approximately 52% of the tea sold, instant tea for 28%, loose tea in packages for 14%, and tea used in ice tea mixes for 6%.

This distribution represents a considerable change in the pattern of consumption. The quantity of tea used in instant tea and in iced tea mixes has increased substantially, chiefly at the expense of loose tea in packages. Instant tea is manufactured in the tea-producing countries for distribution in all countries of the world.

History. The Chinese provide the earliest written record of tea. There are several references to a shrub supposed to have been tea in a work edited by Confucius (c. 551–479 B.C.), but the first authentic citation occurs in a biography of a Chinese official who died in 273 A.D. Tea was unknown to Europeans until 1559, when Giovanni Battista Ramusio mentioned it in *Delle navigationi et viaggi.* The first English-language reference to tea was by R. Wickman, an agent of the English East India Company, in a letter from Japan in 1615. In 1767 a considerable quantity of tea was purchased by Thomas Garway, proprietor of a London coffeehouse later known as Garraway's.

The U.S. tea trade began in 1784, when the first American vessel sailed for China to pick up a cargo of tea. By 1787 the American tea trade amounted to over 1 million pounds (0.4 million kg) a year. Soon tea merchants and shipbuilders cooperated in launching fast clipper ships, a development that culminated in the celebrated Yankee clippers.

In 1826 the Dutch succeeded in establishing tea plantations in Java, and in 1836 the East India Company introduced tea cultivation into India. After the loss of its coffee estates due to the rust fungus *Hemileia vastatrix* in the 1870's, Ceylon also became a tea-growing country.

Many attempts have been made to cultivate and manufacture tea in the United States. The most noteworthy was that of C. U. Shepard, undertaken in cooperation with the Department of Agriculture in 1890. His experiments were conducted on an estate near Summerville, S.C., where he installed a fully equipped factory using many laborsaving methods and machines. The tea produced was of excellent quality, but labor costs proved too high to meet Asian competition, and the experiment was ended in 1916.

GEORGE F. MITCHELL, *Tea Consultant*

Bibliography

Bald, Claud, *Indian Tea,* 6th ed., rev. by Christopher J. Harrison (Calcutta 1953).

"Forty Years of Tea Legislation," *Tea and Coffee Trade Journal,* vol. 81, pp. 50–52, November, 1941.

Harler, Cambell R., *The Culture and Marketing of Tea,* 3d ed. (New York and London 1964).

Ukers, William H., *All About Tea,* 2 vols. (New York 1935).

THE TEA CEREMONY of Japan is performed in its traditional setting. Following the strictest code of etiquette, the hostess and principal guest bow to each other before the alcove of honor.

JAPAN NATIONAL TOURIST ORGANIZATION

TEA CEREMONY, a centuries-old ritual that was developed in Japan and is still a part of Japanese cultural life. *Cha-no-yu,* its name in Japanese, means "the way of tea."

History. In ancient China, tea was a precious commodity. Poets called it the froth of the liquid jade, and Taoists considered it the elixir of life. Buddhist monks of the Ch'an school (Zen in Japanese) eulogized tea for its medicinal properties and drank it to prevent drowsiness during their long hours of meditation. When the Japanese adopted Chinese customs and manners, they ennobled the drinking of tea into a religious and aesthetic ritual.

The Japanese tea ceremony, based on Zen philosophy, has its roots in the 12th century. At that time Zen was reintroduced from China, and tea drinking became customary in Zen monasteries. The ceremony took shape during the 15th century, when Zen culture was dominant in Japan. Early votaries of the *cha-no-yu* included not only Buddhist monks but powerful rulers, artists, and poets. In the 16th century, Sen-no Rikyu, the greatest of the tea masters, applied the four fundamental principles of Zen to the "way of tea." They are harmony (*wa*), respect (*kei*), purity (*sei*), and tranquillity (*jaku*).

Setting. *Cha-no-yu* can hardly be considered apart from the tea garden. There, plants, an arbor (covered waiting bench), a stone basin for purification, and a path of irregular stones leading to the tea house are designed to foster a calm withdrawal from earthly cares and induce awareness.

The tea house (*sukiya*) consists of a tea room and a service room. The entrance is an aperture about 3 feet (1 meter) high, made low purposely to inculcate humility. The tea room accommodates five guests. Its atmosphere of tranquillity and mellowness is suggested by the earth-color wash on the walls and by the lighting, diffused through small paper-covered windows.

The Ceremony. There are different ways of performing the *cha-no-yu,* but they have a basic similarity. The most formal ceremony lasts about four hours. Two types of tea are served: *koicha,* a thick tea, and *usucha,* a thin tea.

Guests and host conduct themselves according to the strictest code of etiquette. On entering the sparsely decorated tea room, each guest kneels in front of the *tokonoma,* the alcove of honor. With his folding fan placed before him, he admires the simple flower arrangement or the hanging scroll, and the incense, which emits a delicate fragrance. Then, after an exquisite repast, the guests retire to the garden.

A gong is sounded by the host to signal the beginning of the main ceremony. The principal guest is given the honored seat, next to the host and nearest the *tokonoma.* The host prepares the tea, following a precise and intricate sequence of movements. Only the sound of boiling water, called the "soughing of the wind in the pines," breaks the silence of the room. The principal guest receives the freshly brewed tea from the host, takes a sip, and compliments him on the flavor and consistency of the tea. After a few more sips he wipes the rim of the bowl and passes it to the next guest. This ritual is repeated by all present. Utensils used in preparing the tea are also passed around for scrutiny and praise. The atmosphere is one of great spiritual discipline and harmony.

RACHEL E. CARR
Author of "Japanese Floral Art"

TEA ROSE, a climbing, nearly evergreen shrub with fragrant white, yellow, or pink flowers that are borne singly or in groups of three. The tea rose (*Rosa odorata*) is an important species used in the development of the hybrid tea rose. Originally native to western China, it is now grown in many parts of the world.

The tea rose shrub usually ranges in height from 5 to 10 feet (1.5–3.0 meters) and its branches are armed with hooked thorns. The leaves are made up of 5 to 7 elliptical to oblong-ovate leaflets with sharply toothed edges. They range in length from 1 to 3 inches (25–75 mm) and are shiny on the upper surface. The double flowers, which are borne on short stalks, bloom during the summer.

The tea rose has been used successfully as stock for the budding of other greenhouse and garden roses. The hybrid tea rose itself is sometimes grafted onto stocks of other roses.

ANTON KOFRANEK
University of California, Davis

TEABERRY is a name for the wintergreen and for the partridgeberry. See PARTRIDGEBERRY; WINTERGREEN.

TEACH, Edward. See BLACKBEARD.

BETTMANN ARCHIVE

In 1900 the teacher was a strict disciplinarian, supervising pupils sitting at desks set in fixed rows.

TEACHING. The task of teachers is central to education. Teachers must transmit to new generations the cultural heritage of a society—the knowledge, skills, customs, and attitudes acquired over the years. They must also try to develop in their students the ability to adjust to a rapidly changing world. Much teaching is done informally, as in the home, but in the course of history, teaching has achieved the status of a professional specialty. The focus of this article is on formal teaching in schools and colleges. The article surveys the history of teaching, careers in teaching, the education of teachers, and professional organizations of teachers.

HISTORY OF TEACHING

In primitive societies much of the teaching was done in the family. Children learned by observation and imitation, by sharing in the work and other activities of the family, and by direct instruction from parents in matters of conduct and belief regarded as important.

Even in the most primitive tribes, however, rituals and customs developed. The task of passing them on to new generations was generally assigned to the elders of the group. Rites associated with puberty were highly educational, dealing not only with proficiencies in skills such as hunting and fighting but also with ideas and beliefs concerning religion, morals, magic, and health.

As civilization developed and education became more formal, parents, elders, and priests instructed the young. In ancient Egypt, as in other early civilizations, education took place in the home, in temple schools, and under the guidance of scribes. The temple was the university of the time, and the religiously trained elders were the scholars and the teachers of the more privileged classes.

Ancient Greece and Rome. In ancient Greece the pedagogue played a unique role as an educational agent. Usually an old and trusted slave, he was assigned the task of supervising the schooling of the boys of a family. He saw that they studied their lessons, helped them recall what they had learned, corrected their speech, and trained them in manners, morals, and deportment.

Toward the end of the 5th century B. C., the Sophists emerged as the first professional teachers. Small in number and wandering from city to city, the Sophists experimented with organizing knowledge so that it could be better taught. They are regarded as the first exponents of liberal education. Protagoras, the most distinguished of their number, is credited with preparing the first grammar, distinguishing parts of speech, tenses, and moods.

Socrates was the most famous of the ancient teachers. Primarily a philosopher, he held that reason was all-powerful and that society flourishes only as men learn to seek truth, think rationally, and expand their knowledge and wisdom. To accomplish his objectives, Socrates used a method of questioning and analysis still known as the Socratic method.

Early Roman education was primarily a family affair. As Greek influences began to be felt, schools were formed. The *ludus,* an elementary school emphasizing the three R's, was taught by men who were primarily disciplinarians. Punishments were severe, with flogging employed to subdue rebellious pupils.

The grammar school and the school of rhetoric were the next two stages. Teachers were better educated, though discipline was still harsh. Lectures, note-taking, memorizing, and recitation predominated. The school of rhetoric involved reading both Greek and Latin literature. Training for oratory was stressed.

The Early Church. Fathers in the early Christian church were also teachers. In the 4th century, St. Jerome, translator of the Bible into Latin (the Vulgate), established a school for boys at his monastery in Bethlehem, where he taught for 34 years. Other schools began to develop in monasteries and cathedrals as the religious motive became predominant. By the 6th century the priests and monks had become the custodians of education.

The Middle Ages and the Renaissance. During the Middle Ages the great masses of people received only the rudiments of education, usually

ZIMBEL, FROM MONKMEYER

By 1970 many teachers were working with small groups in informal settings, utilizing movable furniture.

at the hands of the parish priests. However, a minority studied the seven liberal arts in the universities. The medieval universities were originally associations of students. They congregated in a center of learning such as Bologna or Paris for the purpose of learning, and hired professors of the disciplines in which they were interested. Because books were rare, lecturing was the primary means of instruction. Teachers were the employees of the students and could be fined for failure to meet classes or for poor preparation of lectures. Thus students rather than faculty members or administrators made decisions about what to study and who should teach.

As time went by, particularly well-informed and eloquent lecturers attracted crowds of students. These able teachers gained prestige and influence, and the universities began to develop a faculty organization. The European universities played a major role in teaching philosophy and theology, in the preparation of men for professions such as law and medicine, in the rise of scientific inquiry, and in the general revival of learning in the late Middle Ages.

Other teaching opportunities opened up as grammar schools were organized to prepare young men for the universities. During the Renaissance Latin grammar schools became increasingly important because classical languages were considered essential parts of education. These secondary schools developed in England and on the Continent and, in the early 17th century, were transplanted to America.

Meanwhile, after the division of Christendom at the Reformation, the Roman Catholic Church began a new educational system through the Society of Jesus. Jesuit schools presented a rigorous curriculum, leading to higher studies in theology to train priests and in philosophy to train teachers. Instructors were highly trained, and the Jesuit schools attracted an élite group of students. Such famous thinkers as Molière, Voltaire, and Descartes got their early training from Jesuit teachers.

One outgrowth of the Reformation in predominantly Protestant countries was the interest in providing education that would enable a man to read the Bible himself. This involved the establishment of primary schools for the masses and a demand for teachers to staff them.

The 17th to 20th Centuries. In colonial America the rudiments of education were often provided in "dame schools," where, for a small fee, women in their own homes taught neighborhood children. Reading, writing, some arithmetic, and the catechism were usually taught.

Later, as public education became more general and more necessary, the district school developed as the most important primary institution. Teachers were still predominantly women, and their level of preparation was not high. On the frontier of America it was often the rule that anyone who had been to school could be a schoolteacher. This same rule may still apply in developing nations, where there is a shortage of teachers and of colleges to train them. It may be necessary to use men and women with little more than high school education to teach in the lower grades.

In the 17th and 18th centuries the Latin grammar school continued as a leading form of secondary school. The Latin grammar school offered instruction beyond the 3 R's, preparing the student for college primarily through the study of classical languages. Its teachers were men—often ministers in the early days—and the best educated men of their community. Their instruction was exacting, and they enforced strict discipline. As the academy became the dominant secondary school, the tradition of men teachers continued until the first seminaries for girls began to attract women teachers.

Public high schools began to increase in numbers and in enrollments in the second half of the 19th century, and after 1890 this growth accelerated. There were 3,526 U. S. high schools in 1890, 6,005 in 1900, and 23,930 in 1930. This large number of new schools meant a demand for teachers with the competence to handle secondary subjects. While the tradition of using men teachers at this level was initially strong, women began to join high school staffs—particularly as more and more girls enrolled in public education. To meet the need for teachers, more teacher training institutions opened. In addition, more specific qualifications for teaching became common.

Meanwhile, universities grew in number and enrollments, and university professors became a prestigious class. In Germany, for example, professors not only were leaders in scholarship but also had the high social standing accorded to army officers. In the United States, university scholars often became public figures. Some, for example, moved into government service as consultants or as officials.

In many countries, the 20th century saw teaching established as a major profession. In the United States, for example, education has been described as the largest single enterprise, involving 30% of the population as students or teachers. The teachers included nearly 2,250,000 men and women in elementary and secondary schools and 830,000 in colleges and universities. These teachers made up by far the largest professional group in the country.

See also EDUCATION—*History of Education.*

TEACHING AS A CAREER

Teaching has been described as a social service profession. The profession includes a great range of duties, from lecturing in person or on TV to halls full of students to working intensively with a single pupil. In most teaching, however, serving others is an important part of the job. Many of the most successful teachers are motivated by the personal satisfactions of aiding students to realize their potential.

Characteristics of the Effective Teacher. The teacher must be a many-sided person. Above all, he must be interested in individuals as persons, whether they be children in the kindergarten and primary grades or undergraduate and graduate students in the university. Unless he can enjoy associating with children and youth, be patient with them in their efforts or lack of effort to learn, take pride in their accomplishments, and give generously of himself in the day-to-day life of his students, teaching becomes a chore rather than an exhilarating experience.

The effective teacher is capable of creating a desire to learn. He must be able to sense the interests of students, recognize their needs, and make learning purposeful not only in relation to course objectives but in the minds of his students.

The successful teacher has a basic knowledge of how students learn. He is no longer a hearer of lessons but a director of learning. He recognizes subject matter not as an end in itself but as a means to the development of human personality. He is willing to work with students as they are, rather than as they are expected to be.

The task of the teacher has increased in complexity. Not only are many more students enrolled, but they also represent a broader range of ability, backgrounds, and interests. School and college curriculums have become increasingly specialized, placing new demands upon the competency of teachers. They often need intensive preparation in a subject field. After they have begun teaching, they must try to keep up with the "knowledge explosion," which may make familiar textbooks and course materials suddenly obsolete.

Teachers may have to adapt to different methods of assignment to classes. Some schools follow the traditional pattern of one teacher to one roomful of students. Newer plans include team teaching, in which four teachers, for example, might be responsible for the whole program for a group of 100 students. Such plans require flexibility and cooperativeness in the teacher.

Another problem for teachers is learning to work with new communications media such as television. Audiovisual aids and teaching machines are used in many schools at all levels. Some teachers have felt that such "hardware" is a threat to the role of the teacher as a personal force in education. Most educators, however, see technological aids as means to extend the teacher's work rather than as a device to diminish his importance. See also EDUCATION—*Instructional Technology;* TEXTBOOK.

Still another concern for teachers is that they are "instruments of society" with responsibilities to the community. Their contacts usually extend to the parents of their students and to the neighborhood or town. In the ghetto areas of large cities, for example, the task of the teacher is especially challenging. Students from deprived areas may not only lack adequate food, clothing, and shelter but also the incentive to learn. The successful teacher finds ways to build the self-image of such children so that they can develop in themselves a strong interest in learning.

Exceptional demands and opportunities await the teacher who has the interests and the skills to work with other kinds of handicapped children. Patience and special training are important for teaching blind, deaf, or retarded students or children with emotional handicaps. See also EDUCATION—*Education of Exceptional Children.*

The Status of Teachers. In the 19th and early 20th centuries schoolteachers in the United States, especially in rural areas, led rather restricted lives. Their conduct was expected to set an example of rigorous morality for their students. Their personal lives were subject to close community scrutiny. The use of alcohol or tobacco was often expressly forbidden in school board contracts. Participation in political activity was frowned upon. They were expected to avoid teaching anything that might be regarded as immoral or unpatriotic. Women teachers were frequently caricatured as frustrated old maids.

Teachers now enjoy much more normal lives. They are in general free to lead their own lives as long as they exercise reasonable judgment. They can, for example, be active in local politics. Their freedom to teach is not likely to be restricted as long as they do not use their classrooms as forums for propaganda. Many women teachers are married, and it is not uncommon for mothers to resume teaching after their children have grown up.

Another sign of the improved status of teachers is the effort by public school administrators to relieve them of nonteaching chores. Teachers have often felt that supervising playgrounds and shepherding children onto buses interfered with their primary work with children. Many schools employ teacher aides to handle such nonteaching routines.

In America more than 70% of the elementary teachers are women, but the number of men is increasing, especially as uniform salary schedules eliminate the differential between elementary and high school teaching. At the secondary level, the sexes are about equally divided. In higher education, the proportion of men is still very large, especially in institutions favoring the employment of Ph. D. holders, since only about 11% of the doctoral recipients are women.

Salaries and Benefits. On the average, salaries for teachers are below those of other professional groups. On the other hand, salaries of U. S. public school teachers increased by almost 50% in the decade of the 1960's. There is a wide range in the pay of teachers from one region of the country to another and from elementary to university-level education. The top salaries of public school and college teachers compare favorably with those of other men and women with the same amount of training.

Many teachers supplement their basic salaries by teaching or writing during summer vacations. College teachers particularly can advance their professional standing by using free time for research and writing.

Numerous fringe benefits add to the attractiveness of teaching careers. Most school systems and colleges have retirement benefit plans. Many provide funds for advanced study to enable the teacher or professor to improve his academic or professional standing. A number offer leaves of absence, with or without part pay, for advanced study. Sick leaves, group insurance plans, reduced travel rates, and other benefits are usually available to members of the teaching profession. See also EDUCATION–*Careers in Education.*

TEACHER EDUCATION

Knowledge of the subject is still the primary qualification of those who would teach others, whether formally or informally. On the other hand, history shows a trend to require teachers to be trained in pedagogical methods. Obviously, some men and women are more successful than others in imparting knowledge and developing skills. Their relationships with students, the materials they use, and the procedures they follow can be observed and used to advantage to improve the teaching-learning process.

Historical Background. What is probably the earliest manual for teachers was written by Quintilian in the 1st century A. D. His *Institutes of Oratory* influenced not only contemporary practices in Rome but also the procedures employed by teachers elsewhere and in later generations.

In medieval times a university degree conferred the right to teach (see DEGREE). During the Renaissance and after, universities supplied reasonably competent teachers for higher and professional branches of learning. With the rise of schools at the secondary level, they contributed teachers prepared as academic specialists but with no formal training in methodology.

One major teacher-training effort grew out of the educational activities of the Society of Jesus. The Jesuits made a deliberate effort to select, train, and supervise the very best teachers. They gave thorough instruction in methodology and required students to teach demonstration lessons. In the 16th to 18th centuries the Jesuits founded 612 colleges and 157 normal schools (specialized teacher-training institutes) throughout Europe.

Jean Baptiste de la Salle, a member of another Catholic order, organized a school at Reims in 1685 to prepare members of the Society of the Brothers of the Christian Schools to teach children of the poor. As the society grew and spread, it established other normal schools where de la Salle's *The Conduct of the Schools* was used as a textbook of methodology.

MONKMEYER PRESS PHOTO SERVICE

ELEMENTARY TEACHER uses audiovisual equipment to stimulate the students' interest in learning.

John Amos Comenius, a Moravian, produced both a treatise on teaching, *The Great Didactic Setting Forth the Whole Art of Teaching All Things to All Men* (1632) and a series of textbooks for schools. Later, men like Johann Pestalozzi and Friedrich Froebel sought to extend and improve the education of teachers, stressing the importance of direct experience in learning, understanding of children, and appropriate methods of teaching.

In 1794 the first government-sponsored normal school was established in France. Rousseau's theories led to emphasis upon child psychology as the basic subject.

Early in the 19th century, Prussia was the first country to establish a state-controlled system for the training of teachers. Methodology was based upon the educational theories of Pestalozzi and, later, of Johann Herbart.

Development of Professional Standards in the United States. In the United States educational leaders such as Horace Mann and Henry Barnard realized that the success of the common school movement depended upon an adequate supply of trained teachers. Institutes for the training of teachers were held, and some academies introduced special departments.

The first publicly supported normal school opened in Lexington, Mass., in 1839. The course was two years in length. By the end of the 19th century, normal schools were the chief source of elementary teachers in the United States. Standards were low academically compared with those of liberal arts colleges. Methodology and professional content were emphasized. Much instruction was on the level of today's secondary school.

As secondary education became more popular and states extended the period of compulsory education to include at least some high school attendance for youth, the demand for teachers at that level grew rapidly. At the turn of the century the movement to require professional training for prospective high school teachers began to gain momentum. Men like John Dewey and Edward Lee Thorndike insisted that a knowledge of how and why students learn was necessary. Normal schools became 4-year teachers colleges with curriculums for the preparation of high school teachers. Universities established departments of education offering professional courses for teachers. In time, state certification laws made professional courses compulsory for other than temporary licenses to teach.

Standards increased accordingly. No longer were methodology and subject matter sufficient. All teachers were expected to have a broad background of knowledge.

For elementary teachers, academic course requirements were set to ensure adequate familiarity with the subject fields ordinarily included in the elementary curriculum. Prospective teachers were given general or survey courses treating the discipline as a field of organized knowledge, with emphasis on aspects most relevant for teaching.

Professional courses for elementary teachers now stress an understanding of children, a knowledge of their interests and capacity for learning at various stages of maturity, their social, physical, and emotional needs, and ways of selecting and presenting subject matter to facilitate learning. Many programs also require the elementary teacher to study one field in depth.

For high school teachers the standard requirement is not only general education but also the intensive study of at least one academic discipline as a major subject. A typical 4-year curriculum devotes about 40% of the program to general education, 40% to the academic major and related fields, and 20% to professional education. However, great diversity exists, and these percentages are only approximations.

The professional training seeks to provide a knowledge of the high school pupil and how he learns, a familiarity with materials and methods in the major subject field, and supervised teaching experience in a typical classroom. Courses such as those dealing with educational psychology, the foundations of education, the secondary school and its curriculum, and the history and philosophy of education are typical.

Student teaching, a relatively recent requirement for high school teacher training, is regarded as highly important. Most states now stipulate student teaching for anything other than temporary certification. Some states consider all certification as temporary until the student has completed a specified probationary period in a public school system.

Since World War II most teachers colleges have been upgraded into multipurpose state colleges. Many are now state universities, with enrollments of 10,000 or more and with teacher education as only one of the programs offered.

Controversies over the education of teachers have developed, centering about charges of overprofessionalization. Critics have asserted that state departments of education and professional educators emphasize credits in education courses at the expense of thorough scholarship in the academic disciplines. They claim that such emphasis fosters the "miseducation" of American teachers.

Organizations such as the American Council on Education, through its Commission on Teacher Education, and the National Education Association's National Commission on Teacher Education and Professional Standards (TEPS) have sought to arrive at a realistic rationale for teacher education. They plan to develop a program that will provide both academic and professional competencies.

Certification in the United States. The certification of teachers is the means by which the standards of preparation are set. At one time the examination and appointment of teachers was a major function of local boards of education. However, toward the end of the 19th century the licensing or certifying of public school teachers became a responsibility of the state. Now each of the 50 states sets its requirements for teaching certificates. No two are exactly the same. A teacher must hold a valid certificate issued by the state in which he teaches.

All states now specify at least a bachelor's degree for high school teachers. Three states require five years of college work. All but three states require a college degree for elementary teachers.

Certificates are issued for a specific period of time, usually 5 to 10 years. For renewal, the teacher may be required to complete six or more additional credit hours in academic or professional courses through evening or summer study. Other methods of continuing and in-service education are teachers workshops and institutes, refresher courses, interschool visitation, work on professional journals and publications, supervisory services, provisions for leaves of absences for advanced study or travel, and programs offered at local, state, and national meetings of professional associations and departmental organizations.

New Practices in the United States. New ideas about the education of teachers are constantly influencing practices in the United States. Conspicuous developments are the introduction of the master of arts in teaching and the accreditation of teacher-education programs within individual institutions to simplify certification.

The master of arts in teaching (M. A. T.) was designed originally for liberal arts graduates to encourage and qualify them to become teachers. The program involves both advanced academic courses in the major subject and professional courses such as the learning process, adolescent psychology, the curriculum, and principles of teaching. A feature of the M. A. T. program is internship. The student becomes a full-time staff member of a cooperating school system and teaches under supervision for a full semester. The salary earned helps the intern to finance his graduate program.

The National Council for the Accreditation of Teacher Education (NCATE) has developed a plan of institutional evaluation that, through the cooperation of regional associations and state departments of education, accredits the teacher education programs of individual colleges and universities. Visiting committees analyze the quality of faculty, curriculums, facilities, and services for teacher education. Graduates of approved programs are then certified as teachers upon the recommendation of the institution. Freedom and experimentation are encouraged. Many states have adopted the NCATE accreditation system in teacher certification.

Other trends in teacher education include the extension of internships to replace conventional student teaching, greater participation by academic departments in teacher preparation, more reliance on public school staffs in training centers for the supervision of student teachers, and introduction of independent study and honors programs for able students in professional courses. Finally, there is a growing conception of teacher education as a "process of becoming," in which the development of beliefs, values, and personal meaning is given high priority.

Teacher Education in Other Countries. A survey of 50 nations conducted by UNESCO revealed that normal schools designed especially to prepare teachers for elementary education are still the typical pattern in most countries. However, teachers colleges or education departments of universities are playing an increasing role, especially in Europe. Normal schools ordinarily provide free tuition, although in several countries students must agree to teach for a certain length of time after finishing their course. Most governments provide some type of scholarship aid.

In general, training courses are the same for men and women. In some instances men students receive special training in industrial and technical or agricultural subjects, whereas women have courses in home economics and child care. A few normal schools include premilitary training for men students.

In some Middle Eastern countries the normal school course is at the secondary school level, with students admitted at the age of 15 when they have completed the equivalent of an elementary school education. Such institutions usually have a mixed curriculum, giving both general and professional education.

In other nations the normal school course may be (1) entirely at the higher education level, as in the United States and in most of Europe, (2) divided into a secondary level of general education and a higher cycle of professional studies, or (3) begun at the secondary level and extended into the level of higher education without any sharp distinction between general and professional education.

Professional training invariably includes courses in methods of teaching, general and special; psychology, usually child and educational psychology; and observation and practice teaching either in an institutional practice school or in adjacent cooperating schools.

Ideas about the proper preparation of secondary teachers depend upon the concept of the nature and function of secondary education. Some leaders assert that the chief function of the secondary school teacher is to train the minds of his students by seeing that they learn a given body of knowledge. Therefore he needs above all a thorough knowledge of his subject. Teaching is regarded as a skill that a bright young university graduate can learn on the job from experienced colleagues and without the necessity of professional training.

The academic tradition continues to influence the training of secondary teachers in many parts of the world. University graduation in a program of academic specialization is the widely accepted pattern, particularly in countries where secondary education is highly selective and designed to prepare students for further education at the university or professional level.

Since teacher education reflects national attitudes and varies from country to country, it is difficult to generalize. A brief description of programs in England and in France may afford a basis of comparison with those in the United States and also indicate current practices in those two countries.

England. In England teacher education is centered in training colleges and university departments of education. The training colleges, about 150 in number, developed late in the 19th century to prepare teachers for the new state-supported elementary schools. They also prepare teachers for the "secondary modern school," a coeducational institution modeled after the American comprehensive high school and offering both academic and vocational courses.

Teachers for the grammar schools, the traditional secondary schools, are university graduates who may or may not have had a year of professional training. The ministry of education encourages such training through grants to students but does not require it.

Graduates who enter a department of education for this training have had a long and thorough secondary education and a highly specialized university course. They have been screened both by examinations at several levels and by high academic standards. The course is entirely professional, including lectures on educational theory and methodology and practice teaching.

France. In France there is a teacher training college for men and women (École Normale) in each of the country's departments. Students are admitted by competitive examination, and all their expenses are paid by the state. The baccalaureate is awarded in two or three years, depending upon the length of secondary school preparation, and is followed by a vocational training class of one or two years.

Professional training for secondary teachers is provided in the higher normal schools (Écoles Normales Supérieures), again on a highly selective basis. Universities also offer teacher preparation to baccalaureate holders, leading to advanced certificates—the *licence d'enseignement* or the *diplôme d'études supérieures.*

Graduates of these advanced programs may, through intensive academic study and rigorous examinations, qualify for the highly prized *agrégation.* This professional distinction carries high status and leads to teaching appointments in select *lycées* and *collèges.*

TEACHER ORGANIZATIONS

Professional organizations have played a major role in improving standards of teacher preparation, advocating better salaries for teachers, and furthering public understanding and support of education in the United States. Teachers have worked through professional groups and unions to improve their salaries and advance their rights. By the early 1970's it was a common practice in many school districts for teacher representatives to negotiate with school administrators about salaries and working conditions. The image of the "militant teacher" was widely accepted.

National Education Association. The National Education Association of the United States (NEA) enrolls over a million teachers, principals, supervisors, superintendents, and other members of the education profession. It was organized in Philadelphia, Pa., in 1857 as the National Teachers' Association with the stated purpose of elevating the character and advancing the interests of the profession of teaching and promoting the cause of popular education in the United States. In 1870 it merged with the National Association of School Superintendents and the American Normal School Association, to form the National Education Association, which in 1906 was chartered by Congress and assumed its present name. Policies of the association are determined by an assembly of delegates chosen by over 500 state and local educational associations affiliated with the NEA.

The NEA organizational structure is complex, encompassing many facets of education. There are 4 commissions, some 15 committees, several joint committees to cooperate with other organizations having mutual interests, and 35 departments, national affiliates, and associated organizations. Prominent among the latter group are the American Association of School Administrators, the National Association of Secondary School Principals, the American Association for Higher Education, and the Association of Classroom Teachers.

The NEA seeks to promote the cause of education at all levels, local, state, and national. For many years it championed the cause of federal aid to education, which has amounted to several billions of dollars annually in various types of programs. At the state and local levels efforts to improve education are made through the affiliated state and local associations, often with materials supplied by the national office.

In 1968 the NEA withdrew from its longstanding position against strikes by teachers when it backed a three-week "walk-out" in Florida, the first statewide strike of teachers. It continues to engage in activities involving teachers' rights and teachers' salaries in widely scattered areas.

American Federation of Teachers. The American Federation of Teachers (AFT) is an autonomous national union of preschool, elementary, secondary, and college classroom teachers affiliated with the American Federation of Labor-Congress of Industrial Organizations (AFL-CIO). Organized in Chicago in 1916, the AFT comprises more than 850 local unions of teachers in the United States and its territories, with a national headquarters in Washington. Its policies are determined by delegates to an annual convention elected by local union members.

The AFT and its local federations have championed the right of teachers to organize, negotiate, and bargain collectively. Essentially a teachers' organization, the AFT has sought to improve salaries and working conditions, especially in the larger cities where its membership is most numerous.

National attention centered on the AFT, when in the fall of 1968 a strike by the 49,000-member United Federation of Teachers (the New York City AFT affiliate) delayed the opening of schools for three weeks and ended with the ratification of a new contract providing increased wages and benefits. Education in the nation's largest public school system was practically suspended for the first 36 school days during a UFT-led controversy over school board decentralization and community control of local schools.

The tactics of the AFT have been criticized by school boards and administrators. However, strikes and the threat of strikes produced results, and AFT membership increased to over 200,000 by 1970. Collective bargaining agreements with AFT locals were put into effect in New York City, Philadelphia, Washington, Chicago, Boston, and other large cities.

American Association of University Professors. The establishment of the American Association of University Professors (AAUP) in 1915 was the result of a growing professional self-consciousness among American educators as well as increasing evidence of the need of an organization that would serve to protect the academic freedom of the university faculty member.

The AAUP explicitly banned college and university presidents and deans from membership. Its first (1915) report, dealing with academic freedom and tenure, was hailed as a landmark in the development of the teaching profession, but it also provoked antagonism from college administrators and even from professors, many of whom opposed in principle any national organization of their colleagues.

Within a few years, however, college administrators took a kindlier attitude towards the AAUP. The 1940 Statement of Principles on Academic Freedom and Tenure, formulated jointly with the Association of American Colleges, has been endorsed by many colleges and universities and by more than 60 national organizations.

The association's Committee A, on academic freedom and tenure, has been vigilant in defending and promoting the rights of teachers. See also ACADEMIC FREEDOM. Reports by Committee Z, on the economic status of the profession, have helped to increase faculty compensation, especially in the lower-rated institutions.

The association has continually emphasized the responsibilities of members of the profession, as in the 1966 *Statement on Professional Ethics.* Other activities of the AAUP are reflected in the 1966 *Statement on College and University Government* and a 1969 *Joint Statement on Rights and Freedoms of Students,* formulated in cooperation with the U. S. National Student Association and organizations of administrators.

EDWARD ALVEY, JR.
Mary Washington College of the University of Virginia

Bibliography

Adams, Sam, and Garrett, J. L., Jr., *To Be a Teacher: An Introduction to Education* (New York 1969).
Beggs, Walter K., *The Education of Teachers* (New York 1965).
Cole, Luella B., *A History of Education: Socrates to Montessori* (New York 1950).
Combs, Arthur W., *The Professional Education of Teachers* (New York 1965).
Conant, James B., *The Education of American Teachers* (New York 1963).
Dikshit, S. S., *Teacher Education in Modern Democracies* (Delhi, India, 1969).
Dreeben, Robert, *The Nature of Teaching* (New York 1970).
Ely, Frederick, and Arrowood, Charles F., *The History and Philosophy of Education, Ancient to Medieval* (New York 1940).
Majault, Joseph, *Education in Europe: Teacher Training* (Strasbourg, France, 1965).
Stabler, Ernest, *The Education of the Secondary School Teacher* (Middletown, Conn., 1962).
Stiles, Lindley J., and others, *Teacher Education in the United States* (New York 1960).
Stinnett, Timothy M., *A Manual on Certification Requirements for School Personnel in the United States* (Washington, triennially).
Stone, James C., *Breakthrough in Teacher Education* (San Francisco 1968).
UNESCO, *Primary Teacher Training* (Geneva 1950).

TEACHING MACHINE, a device that arranges conditions needed for efficient learning. It presents pictorial, printed, or auditory material to a student and records his response. For example, the student reads a sentence and supplies a missing word, or listens to a spoken question and supplies the answer. He may do so by operating a typewriter keyboard, writing on a strip of paper exposed in the machine, indicating a choice among printed words or visual patterns, and so on. The machine then tells the student whether or not his response is correct.

Over a period of time a teaching machine guides the student through a carefully prepared "program," consisting of many thousands of steps arranged in a convenient order of development, each step being so small that it can almost always be correctly taken. The material is designed so that the student can usually respond correctly because of the preparation he has already received. Teaching machines thus differ from self-testing machines, which examine the student on previously learned material. In contrast with much classroom instruction where the slow student gradually falls farther and farther behind, the teaching machine permits each student to move at his own rate. The fast learner is not held back by the slow, and the slow finds time to become fully competent. See also EDUCATION—*Educational Psychology* (Applications to Instruction); *Instructional Technology.*

Machines have been designed and used experimentally at age levels between nursery school and professional industrial training. They have been adapted to a variety of verbal subject matters, such as mathematics, languages, literature, and the sciences. In a broader sense, the term also covers devices that teach manual skills, as well as combinations of verbal and manual skills, as in the arts and trades. With appropriate modifications, they are particularly valuable for the handicapped.

B. F. SKINNER
Harvard University

TEAGARDEN, Jack (1905–1964), American jazz trombonist and singer, who was one of the first white musicians to rank as a top blues player. Weldon John Teagarden was born in Vernon, Texas, on July 20, 1905. He was largely self-taught as a trombonist. In 1927 he went to New York City, where he played in Ben Pollack's band from 1928 to 1933 and in Paul Whiteman's orchestra from 1934 to 1938. Teagarden led his own band from 1939 to 1947, played in Louis Armstrong's band from 1947 to 1951, and thereafter led a small "combo." He also appeared in several motion pictures. Teagarden died in New Orleans on Jan. 15, 1964.

Jack Teagarden's style, both as a trombonist and as singer, was relaxed, though the sound he made on the trombone was rather harsh. He was celebrated for his interpretations of *St. James Infirmary, I've Got a Right to Sing the Blues,* and *Beale Street Blues.*

TEAK, a tall tropical deciduous tree cultivated for its hard, durable, and decay-resistant wood. Teakwood is also easily worked. It is used for ships, piers, furniture, and carvings.

The teak tree is native to India, Indonesia, and parts of the Malay Archipelago. Extensive forests of teak trees are found on Burma and Thailand. The trees reach a height of 100 feet (30 meters) and have whorls of branches with large opposite or whorled leaves and four-sided twigs. The tiny white flowers are borne in large branching clusters at the ends of the branches. They ripen into small cherry-like fruits containing oily seeds.

Teakwood sinks in water unless it is thoroughly dried. Before a tree is cut, it is girdled—that is, a ring of bark and sapwood is cut out. The tree then dies and is left standing for about two years to make sure it dries out.

The teak tree, *Tectona grandis,* belongs to the vervain family (Vervenaceae).

J. A. YOUNG
U. S. Department of Agriculture

TEAL, a river, or dabbling, duck. See DUCK—*River Ducks.*

TEAMSTERS UNION. The International Brotherhood of Teamsters, Chauffeurs, Warehousemen and Helpers of America, known as the Teamsters, is the largest labor union in the United States. Its economic strength has improved the wages and working conditions of its members and has partially stabilized the trucking industry. Because of its strategic importance in transportation, the Teamsters Union has also provided great assistance to other unions.

Founded in 1899 to organize drivers of horse-pulled vehicles, the organization was first called the Team Drivers International Union. It changed its name to the International Brotherhood of Teamsters in 1903. Daniel J. Tobin served as president from 1907 to 1952, building the Teamsters from a membership of 40,000 in 1907 to 1,100,000 in 1952. In the early days Tobin took a craft-union approach, which concentrated the membership in the "delivery crafts"—ice, coal, bread, and milk. But this approach was swept away by the depression of the 1930's, the New Deal, and the great industrial union drives of the CIO. By the time Tobin retired, intercity drivers and warehousemen were the largest Teamster groups.

Dave Beck, who succeeded Tobin as president, combined the weak joint councils of locals into five regional conferences. These conferences took over organizing and political functions, but the negotiation and administration of contracts—the most significant union activity—remained a local-union responsibility. Beck ran afoul of the U. S. Senate Select Committee on Improper Activities in the Labor-Management Field—the McClellan committee—and eventually went to jail for embezzlement.

James Hoffa, who became president in 1957, converted the Teamsters into a strongly centralized union. By bargaining on a regional and national basis instead of locally, the union improved contracts considerably. But Hoffa, in turn, soon became the main target of the McClellan committee. In 1957 the Teamsters were expelled from the AFL-CIO. In 1964, Hoffa was found guilty of tampering with a jury, and in 1967 he began serving a term in a federal penitentiary. Some of the power that had been centralized by Hoffa then returned to the local unions and joint councils.

In 1968 the Teamsters joined with the Auto Workers to form the Alliance for Labor Action, a new labor federation.

HARVEY L. FRIEDMAN
University of Massachusetts

TEANECK, tē′nek, is a township in northeastern New Jersey, in Bergen county, about 4 miles (6 km) northwest of the George Washington Bridge. It is primarily a residential community. Many of its people commute to work in New York. There is some light industry. A branch of Fairleigh Dickinson University is in Teaneck.

Teaneck was settled by the Dutch in the mid-17th century. It was incorporated in 1895. Government is by mayor and council and city manager. Population: 42,355.

TEAPOT DOME is the popular name for a scandal during the administration of U. S. President Warren G. Harding. The scandal, which involved the secret leasing of naval oil reserve lands to private companies, was first revealed to the general public in 1924 after sensational findings by a committee of the U. S. Senate. One cabinet member eventually went to prison for his part in the affair, and a number of Washington officials were implicated, threatening to destroy confidence in Republican leaders of the period. But Calvin Coolidge, who had acceded to the presidency on Harding's death in 1923, handled the problem skillfully and averted damage to his own administration.

Origins of the scandal went back to the growth of federal conservation policy in the presidencies of Theodore Roosevelt, Taft, and Wilson, specifically to the creation of naval petroleum reserves in Wyoming and California. These reserves were tracts of public land in which it was intended that oil should be kept in its natural reservoirs, or domes, for the future use of the Navy. Teapot Dome, near Casper, Wyo., acquired its name from a rock resembling a teapot that rose from the oil-bearing land.

Leaders of both parties supported the petroleum reserve policy. That it would be a continuing one seemed certain, with the passage of new statutory provisions in 1920. Actually, however, private oil interests and many politicians had always been opposed, claiming that the reserves were unnecessary, that American oil companies could provide for the needs of U. S. naval vessels. One of these politicians, a longtime foe of federal conservation programs, was Sen. Albert B. Fall of New Mexico. In 1921, Fall became Harding's secretary of the interior and quickly moved to open the reserves to private exploitation. Though he attempted to keep his actions secret he could not, and the Senate authorized an investigation by the committee on public lands. The driving force in this difficult assignment was Thomas J. Walsh, a Montana Democrat respected for his legal prowess and incorruptibility. Most responsible for initiating the probe were Sen. Robert M. LaFollette of Wisconsin and the conservationist "watchdogs" who advised and supported him.

The Senate committee held extended hearings and soon set in motion a whole chain of occurrences. Secretary Fall, they found, had convinced Secretary of the Navy Edwin Denby and others that the administration of the reserves should be turned over to him. Fall had then leased Teapot Dome to Harry F. Sinclair's Mammoth Oil Company and the rich Elk Hills reserve in California to Edward L. Doheny's Pan-American Petroleum and Transport Company, meanwhile receiving from these oilmen gifts and "loans" amounting to some $400,000. The leases Fall had made were technically complicated and could be defended, but the money was his undoing. For a time, Fall had the protection of powerful friends in the government, including Attorney General Harry M. Daugherty, but widespread distrust of the Department of Justice and of Daugherty (who resigned in 1924) forced President Coolidge to appoint special prosecutors under presidential direction to protect the interests of the government.

Civil and criminal suits, lasting through the 1920's, then followed. The Supreme Court, finding that the oil leases had been corruptly obtained, invalidated the Elk Hills lease in February 1927 and the Teapot Dome lease in October of the same year. The reserves, as a result, were restored to government control. Albert Fall was found guilty of bribery in 1929. He was fined $100,000 and sentenced to one year in prison. The lessees were assessed for damages, but it is ironic that the oilmen and their associates escaped conviction on a conspiracy charge, whereas the official who took their money was convicted. Sinclair did not escape entirely. A second Senate investigation in 1928 gave additional, damning evidence of his payments to Secretary Fall and of corporate malpractices that had provided Sinclair with his "slush fund." After refusing to cooperate with government investigators, Sinclair was charged with contempt and eventually received a short sentence for tampering with the jury, or criminal contempt.

The legacy of Teapot Dome is an ambiguous one, although the scandal in its final outcome was a victory for honest government. Neither party could take full credit for the disclosures, and when the Democrats tried in 1924 and 1928 they were defeated. The policy of conservation made some gains; yet the petroleum reserves, as such, did not prove to have the importance earlier attributed to them. All in all, this controversy illustrates the complexity of natural resource problems and the difficulty of planning successfully for the public interest and for generations yet to come.

J. LEONARD BATES
University of Illinois

Further Reading: Bates, J. Leonard, *The Origins of Teapot Dome* (Urbana, Ill., 1966); Nash, Gerald D., *United States Oil Policy, 1890–1964* (Pittsburgh 1968); Noggle, Burl, *Teapot Dome: Oil and Politics in the 1920's* (Baton Rouge, La., 1962); Stratton, David H., ed., *The Memoirs of Albert B. Fall* (El Paso, Texas, 1966).

TEAR or **TEARS,** the clear fluid that constantly flows over the eyeball to lubricate and protect it. Tears are composed of mucoprotein oils suspended in a watery layer containing sodium chloride, sodium bicarbonate, and other substances. The continuous flow of this fluid removes dust particles, bacteria, air pollutant debris, and other foreign bodies from the eye. Because tears contain lysozome, an enzyme that destroys certain microorganisms, they also help keep the eye free of infection.

Tears are produced by the lacrimal glands and, after flowing over the eye, empty through the tear duct and nasolacrimal duct into the nasal cavity. The rate of flow is increased by bright lights, wind, foreign bodies, emotional stimuli, and infections and inflammations of the cornea and conjunctiva. When the flow is greatly increased, as in crying, or when the tear duct is obstructed, the tears flow over the eyelid onto the cheek. Obstructions of the tear duct can sometimes be corrected surgically.

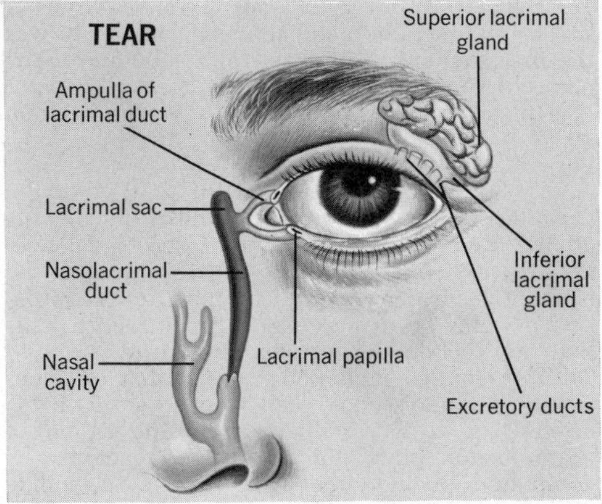

In xerophthalmia the flow of tears is not sufficient, and the eye becomes too dry. This disorder is associated with a deficiency of vitamin A, and symptomatic relief may be achieved by using eye drops containing 1% methyl cellulose.

IRWIN LUBOWE, M. D.
Metropolitan Hospital Center, N. Y.

TEAR GAS is an agent that initiates eye pains and the excessive flow of tears. It is used as the effective charge of grenades or shells and is released on explosion of the projectiles. Respiratory masks containing filter pads, with ground activated carbon serving as the adsorbent, afford protection against tear gas.

Tear gas was introduced as a chemical warfare agent during World War I by the Germans, who used shells containing shrapnel mixed with the irritant dianisidine chlorosulfonate. Because the effects of tear gas are not long-lasting and usually produce relatively mild incapacitation, tear gas is not considered effective as a real chemical warfare agent. However, tear gas has been used frequently by law enforcement agencies to control mobs and riots or to flush armed suspects out of hiding places.

The ability to irritate the lacrimal, or tear, glands is a characteristic of many compounds, including acid halides, anhydrides, and compounds containing both an allyl group ($CH_2 = CH -$) and a halogen atom. To be effective in riot control, a tear gas must produce symptoms when present in very low concentrations; it must initiate symptoms within a short time after exposure; and it must be equally effective by absorption through different pathways to the body, such as eyes, skin, and respiratory tract. It must be stable during storage for long periods of time and easily incorporated into grenades and shells.

Some of the earliest tear gas compounds were ortho-chlorobenzylidene malononitrile, ethyl bromoacetone, bromoacetone, benzyl bromide, and α-bromobenzyl cyanide.

Alpha-chloroacetophenone ($C_6H_5COCH_2Cl$), which is known by the U. S. Army code name of CN, is widely used in riot control. This compound is phenacylchloride, or phenylchloromethylketone, and is prepared by the actions of chloroacetylchloride on benzene in the presence of aluminum chloride. Only 10 mg of α-chloroacetophenome per cubic meter (0.0044 grains/cu ft) of air is effective in acting as an irritant. There are two forms of CN—the omega and para forms. They are both white and crystalline and soluble in alcohol and ether but insoluble in water. The para form melts at 20° C (68° F) and boils at 236° C (456° F), while the omega form melts at 59° C (138° F) and boils at 245° C (473° F).

Alpha-bromobenzyl cyanide is a tear gas that is effective in concentration as low as 5 mg per cubic meter (0.0022 grains/cu ft).

Another tear gas developed by the U. S. Army, with the code name CS, produces almost immediate incapacitation upon inhalation. More rapidly acting than α-chloroacetophenone, it causes severe burning of upper respiratory passages, pain, and involuntary inability to open the eyes. It also causes excessive tearing of the eyes and burning sensations in the nose and mouth. However, only 5 to 10 minutes after the victim begins to breathe fresh air, the symptoms disappear. Thus the effects of tear gas are reversible and temporary.

Sternutators, or irritants of the nose, are also used in riot control. For example, inhalation of solid diphenylchloroarsine disseminated in the form of a cloud of fine particles by an explosive charge causes sneezing, coughing, excessive tearing of the eyes, headache, nausea, vomiting, and temporary incapacitation.

HERBERT LIEBESKIND
The Cooper Union, New York

TEASDALE, tēz′dal, **Sara** (1884–1933), American poet, who wrote of personal suffering and 20th century alienation. Her style was traditional, but she seemed to many to be a spokesman for her generation. She was born in St. Louis, Mo., on Aug. 8, 1884, was educated privately, and spent some time in travel abroad. The poet Vachel Lindsay courted her, but she finally married a much older man, from whom she was divorced in 1929. Her life ended in suicide in New York City on Jan. 29, 1933.

Miss Teasdale wrote eight volumes of verse, which won many admiring readers. *Rivers to the Sea* (1915), *Love Songs* (1917), *Flame and Shadow* (1920), and *Dark of the Moon* (1926) —treating the evanescence of love and beauty and the oncoming nothingness of death—may strike today's readers as rather shrill and self-pitying. But in her final volume, *Strange Victory* (1933), she achieved a new control of feeling and tone. Many of these poems are beautifully achieved expressions of the poet's renunciations. Her *Collected Poems* appeared in 1937.

HYATT H. WAGGONER, *Author of "American Poets, from the Puritans to the Present"*

TEASEL, tē′zəl, any of a small group of biennial and perennial plants native to Europe, Asia, and northern Africa. Teasels make up the genus *Dipsacus* of the family Dipsacaceae.

Fuller's teasel (*D. fullonum*) has dense pale lilac flower heads with hooked bracts extending between the florets. When dried, the heads have been used for raising ("teasing") the nap of woolen cloth. The plant ranges in height from 4 to 6 feet (1.2–1.8 meters) and has prickly stems. The opposite leaves are lance-shaped and may be 12 inches (30 cm) long. The bases of the leaves are cup-shaped and collect water after a rainfall. The flower heads are rounded or egg-shaped and may be 4 inches (10 cm) long. Fuller's teasel grows well from seed and has become naturalized in the northeastern United States from plantings that were once grown commercially for the heads.

The common teasel (*D. sylvestris*) differs from the Fuller's teasel in that the bracts on the flower heads are not hooked but may extend beyond the heads. Sometimes the heads are used in dried flower arrangements.

ANTON KOFRANEK
University of California, Davis

TEBALDI, tə-bäl'dē, **Renata** (1922–), Italian lyric-dramatic soprano. She was born in Pesaro on Feb. 1, 1922. After studying singing in Parma, she made her debut in 1944 at Rovigo, as Elena in Boito's *Mefistofele*. In 1946 she was invited by Arturo Toscanini to sing at the reopening, after World War II, of La Scala, in Milan.

Miss Tebaldi made her British debut in 1950, singing in Verdi's Requiem at the Edinburgh Festival. A few weeks later she made her American debut in San Francisco. In 1955 she first appeared at the Metropolitan in New York, where she sang regularly thereafter in the Verdi and the Puccini repertory, in Ponchielli's *La Gioconda,* Giordano's *Andrea Chénier,* and Cilèa's *Adriana Lecouvreur.* After attracting a large American following, she rarely sang outside the United States.

A temporary vocal crisis in the early 1960's caused Miss Tebaldi to lose some of her steadiness, but after a period of rest and study her voice regained much of its former beauty.

HAROLD ROSENTHAL, *Author of "Great Singers of Today"*

RENATA TEBALDI in costume and makeup for the title role in Puccini's opera *Madama Butterfly*.

WIDE WORLD PHOTOS

TECHNETIUM, tek-nē'shē-əm, symbol Tc, is a silver-gray metallic radioactive element. It was the first element synthesized in a laboratory. Its name derives from the Greek word *technētos* ("artificial"). Technetium was synthesized in 1937 by the physicists Emilio Segré and C. Perrier.

Technetium is located in Group VIIA of the periodic table. Its atomic number is 43, its atomic weight is 98.913, and it shows valences of +4, +6, and +7. At least 13 isotopes of the element have been identified; they are all radioactive. However, because of their short half-lives, no technetium is found in nature.

The element is a spongy metal that tarnishes slowly in moist air and melts at 2140° C (3884° F). It is produced from the fission of uranium and plutonium in nuclear reactors. Its compounds include the oxide Tc_2O_7; the sulfide TcS_2; and salts of pertechnic acid, $HTcO_4$. Five parts of technetium per million will protect carbon steels from corrosion at room temperature.

HERBERT LIEBESKIND, *The Cooper Union*

TECHNICAL EDUCATION prepares students for jobs in the many fields of modern technology. Technicians are usually classed as semiprofessionals or paraprofessionals. For example, a mechanical technician falls between the levels of the skilled mechanic and the mechanical engineer. His work may involve helping the engineer design and test new equipment, thus increasing the amount of research the engineer can accomplish. A technician needs more formal education than a craftsman but less than a professional engineer. Technical education in the United States typically requires two years of study beyond high school. Two-year programs are offered in colleges and universities, junior colleges, technical institutes, area vocational schools, and other kinds of institutions.

Technical Occupations. Schools giving technical education face the problem of providing courses for growing numbers of students in an increasing variety of fields. By 1970 more than one million Americans—predominantly men but with an increasing proportion of women—were working as technicians. The range of areas in which they worked can be shown by a partial list of technologies: aeronautical, aerospace, automotive-diesel, agribusiness, agricultural engineering, architectural engineering, air-conditioning, building construction, chemical engineering, commercial design, computer, data processing, dental, electrical, electronics, electromechanical, engineering science, forest, fire protection, food processing, graphic art, highway, hydraulic, machine tool, mechanical, medical laboratory, optical, surveying, structural engineering and design, soils, textile engineering, and X-ray.

In addition to these established fields, others were expected to develop increasing importance during the 1970's. Among these are: systems engineering; automation engineering technology; instrumentation technology, including hydraulic and electronic control; materials engineering; biomedical engineering; oceanographic technology; water use and treatment, including pollution prevention and control as well as desalinization; conservation of natural and human resources; government and municipal services, including law enforcement; food science; and traffic control.

Programs that combine skills and knowledges from two or more traditional technical areas have been introduced. Examples of these are electro-mechanical technology, bio-medical equipment technology, and electro-optics technology.

Programs. The objective of programs in technical education is to give students a broadly based competence in a field of applied science. The student should have enough background knowledge so that he can start a job with a brief orientation period and quickly take on full responsibilities. It is also essential that the training be broad and deep enough to allow the graduate to work in a cluster of related occupations. The requirements of jobs and the demand for trained men and women change. For example, shifts in government priorities and budgets may mean less emphasis on aerospace engineering and technology and more on conservation of resources and on urban problems. Workers at all levels have an advantage if they are not limited by their training to one highly specific skill but can apply basic knowledge in several ways.

The curriculum in technical education normally includes courses in four classifications: basic science and related mathematics, technical specialty courses, communications courses, and human relations and social studies. Science and mathematics courses show the student principles governing work in his field of technology. Other courses require the student to make practical applications of concepts by working with tools and machines and giving specific services to people. Still other courses teach skills such as report writing and introduce the student to fields such as psychology and sociology. The whole program typically follows graduation from high school and requires full-time attendance for two years. Frequently the program leads to an associates degree—for example, associate in science (A. S.).

A typical curriculum is that offered by the Miami-Dade Junior College, Miami, Fla., in a 2-year aerotechnology program leading to the A. S. degree. During his freshman year the student takes aeronautical science and engineering laboratory, expository writing, technical drawing, technical mathematics and manufacturing processes, aerophysics, aeronautical science, including engine and structure theory, algebra and trigonometry with applications, and a study of the slide rule. His sophomore courses include aeronautical science and engineering laboratory, aeronautical science in electricity and electronics, hydraulics and pneumatics, technical report writing, social science, aerodynamics, aeronautical science systems, and aircraft instruments. In addition, the student is required to have 30–40 hours of materials testing or internship per week during the spring term of his last year.

A competent instructional staff is the most important element of a technical program. Securing qualified teachers was a problem in the 1960's and was expected to persist as technical education programs expanded. The initial preparation of an instructor for technical subjects demands a balance of general, technical, and professional teacher education courses combined with work experience closely related to the field in which the teacher will instruct.

Institutions Offering Technical Education Programs. During the 1960's, technical education grew from a relatively small program in a few private schools to a significant segment of public education. As the demand for technicians increased, young men and women sought out technical education programs as alternatives to four-year college courses or professional school courses. For example, young people with an interest in medicine, but unable to complete 9 or more years of training beyond high school, have found careers as laboratory or X-ray technicians. Federal laws—notably the Vocational Education Act of 1963 and the 1968 amendments to this act—served as a powerful stimulus by providing funds for technical education programs. Technical education programs are provided by nearly every type of educational institution, both public and private, in the 50 states. The *Technician Education Yearbook, 1969–1970,* lists 1,168 schools, colleges, and other institutions in the United States that report offering some form of technician training.

As already noted, the majority of technicians are trained in institutions above the high school level. It is true that high schools offer excellent technical courses, but the increasing complexity of modern technology makes training beyond the 12th grade more and more essential. Institutions educating students for technical occupations include the following.

Area Vocational-Technical Schools. The area vocational-technical schools are public schools normally oriented to prepare youths and adults for occupations in the region the school serves. These schools are usually designed for high school graduates, but many have some arrangement for accepting high school students from the surrounding areas. The area vocational-technical school also provides opportunities for those who have dropped out of high school or for those who wish additional specialized occupational training. The area vocational-technical school allows several neighboring communities or counties to pool their resources and bring high quality technical program to the area.

Junior Colleges. The junior or community college is the most rapidly growing segment of higher education in the United States. The phenomenal growth of junior colleges has aided the development of the technical education movement. Junior colleges are ideally designed to offer technical education for several reasons. They specialize in 2-year curriculums. They offer the necessary general education courses that parallel and enrich technical education programs. They provide courses at a level between high school and a 4-year college. This level fits the concept of semiprofessional and technical occupations.

Colleges and Universities. Colleges and universities have provided some types of 2-year technical education for many years. Certain engineering and agricultural technologies and paramedical specialties, such as dental technology, have had widespread acceptance in the 4-year institutions. Normally some type of specialized diploma or certificate is awarded following the 2-year sequences of study. Associate degrees are often granted.

Technical Institutes. Technical education in the United States began in the technical institutes. The Ohio Mechanics Institute, founded in 1828 in Cincinnati, is usually credited with starting the first formalized program of technical education in the United States, and other private institutions led the way in the early development of technical education. Technical institutes, both public and private, continue to offer excellent programs in technical education.

Private Industry. Most large industrial corporations provide technician training programs for their employees. Courses range from highly specific and technical work in areas directly related to the employee's current job to a study of management and communication techniques that will allow an employee a greater opportunity for advancement.

The Armed Forces. The armed services have maintained technical schools for military personnel for many years. The military technical schools focus on specific skills such as electronics repair or data processing. Many methods and techniques pioneered in the military services have been adopted by civilian technical education institutions, and many technical education teachers received their initial training during their military careers.

See also CAREER PLANNING; JUNIOR COLLEGE; VOCATIONAL EDUCATION.

Technical Education in Other Countries. All industrialized countries need to train technicians. Programs in other leading nations differ considerably from the pattern established in the United States.

Soviet Union. In the Soviet Union technical education begins in the "technicum," which is a combination of secondary and higher education. Students who complete the 8-year school—equivalent to the elementary school in the United States—may enter the technicum at age 15 and remain for five years. Those who have had two years of secondary work and have graduated from the 10-year school may enroll in the technicum for two or three years.

The technicum is the major source of technical workers for Soviet industry. In the late 1960's there were approximately 3,500 technicums in the Soviet Union and they were training nearly 2 million students.

Germany. The technical universities in Germany have the status of institutions of higher education, and their curriculums include general theoretical subjects from the natural sciences and the humanities. All technical universities have faculties of civil and mechanical engineering, and in some cases also a faculty of electrical engineering.

The general prerequisite for admission to the technical universities is the leaving certificate from the gymnasium, which is obtained after 13 years of schooling and some practical work experience. For some subjects at the technical universities, the required period of practical work is half a year. However, the work period varies, and students of agriculture must have had a year and a half of practical experience.

Britain. Technical education in Britain is offered at several levels, each having a different objective. Twenty-five regional colleges of technology form the basis for a post-secondary level of instruction called the polytechnic. They overlap into university level work.

An additional level of post-secondary education, which still includes some university work, is given in the 500 technical colleges. Of these, about 350 offer full-time study for 120,000 students. They also provide courses for 565,000 part-time day students and for nearly 700,000 evening students.

One popular method of obtaining technical training is through "sandwich" courses. The term "sandwich" refers to periods alternately spent in the college and in industry. The periods vary in length, but one form is to spend a preparatory year in industry, follow this with a full-time college course, and move back to industry for an additional year. The student is able to gain experience, earn a living, and receive a diploma.

JAMES W. HENSEL
University of Florida

Bibliography

Emerson, Lynn A., "Education for a Changing World of Work," in *Technical Training in the United States* (Washington 1963).

Harris, Norman C., *Technical Education in the Junior College. New Programs for New Jobs* (Washington 1964).

King, Edmund J., *Other Schools and Ours*, 3d ed. (New York 1967).

Phillips, Donald S., and Briggs, Lloyd D., *Review and Synthesis of Research in Technical Education* (Columbus, Ohio, 1969).

Technician Education Yearbook, 1969–1970 (Ann Arbor, Mich., annually).

U. S. Department of Labor, *Occupational Outlook Handbook* (Washington, new edition every two years).

U. S. Office of Education, Division of Vocational and Technical Education, *Criteria for Technician Education* (Washington 1966).

TECHNICOLOR. See FILM; MOTION PICTURES—*The History of Motion Pictures.*

TECHNION, tek'nē-on, a privately controlled institute of university rank located in Haifa, Israel. The full name is Technion—Israel Institute of Technology. The institute was founded in 1908, but instruction did not begin until 1924.

Technion has faculties or departments of general studies, education, mathematics, physics, chemistry, chemical engineering, mechanics, mechanical engineering, electrical engineering, materials engineering, civil engineering, architecture and town planning, agricultural engineering, aeronautical engineering, industrial and management engineering, nuclear science, and computer science. Courses leading to the bachelor's degree are offered in the sciences, engineering, and architecture and town planning. Graduate studies lead to the master of science and doctor of science degrees. Enrollment reached about 6,000 men and women by 1970.

TECHNOCRACY was a radical social movement and philosophy that exploded into prominence in the United States in the early 1930's. It was an indictment of both capitalism and the money system of exchange. It emphasized and even glorified the machine process and technical skills and knowledge. It proposed that engineers and scientists direct economic life. A new unit—productive energy—was to replace monetary standards

Technocracy had a false start in 1918 under Howard Scott, an engineer, who formed the Technical Alliance. The chief intellectual source of Technocracy was Thorstein Veblen, who wrote *The Engineers and the Price System* (1921). Veblen saw capitalism as dominated by conflict between the destructive force of business and the benign force of technology. The movement emerged under the name of Technocracy in 1932, with headquarters at Columbia University. Technocracy's highest vogue was in early 1933. It faded rapidly because of its extremism and disdain for political action and because of the rapid reforms made by the New Deal.

SHERMAN E. GUNDERSON
Wisconsin State University, Oshkosh

TECHNOLOGY refers to ways of making or doing things. The term "technology" is derived from the Greek *technē,* meaning "art" or "craft," but it is generally used in either of two more restricted senses. In the narrower sense, "technology" refers only to the industrial processes that succeeded craft operations. In the broader sense in which the term is used in the present article, "technology" refers to all processes dealing with materials. Technology always has to be learned, whether in the form of manual dexterity or as an applied science.

It is impossible to prove that primitive men were any more rational technologists than are beavers. However, since primitive man's technological aptitudes were so various—painting, modeling, firemaking, toolmaking—without any concomitant biological specialization, as occurs in animals, it is natural to suppose that thought, training, and discipline were prerequisites for man's technological achievements. But the mentality of the technologist in the long stretch of human history through which man began to be a toolmaker and, much later, a reshaper of the natural environment through farming, are lost. Without written records the historian can say what problems were mastered, such as the breeding of plants and animals, the smelting of metals, the making of glass, and the constructing of building, but little or nothing can be said about how such mastery was won.

The earliest technical methods are known essentially through reconstruction. An expert can make a very good estimate of the temperature at which a metal casting was poured, for example, or a clay pot was baked. Hence, even without other archaeological evidence, he can have a good idea of the kind of furnace that was used. But it is only with the beginning of written history that some relationship between craft and idea can be followed. It is a mistake to suppose that early craftsmen lacked principles and theories or that they blindly did what their predecessors had done.

On the contrary, principles and theories were distilled from the successes and failures occurring throughout the millennia. For example, it was learned that in laying timber below ground, elm should be used because it will not rot. There were firm theories insisting that if temples or ships were built according to different proportions they would be ugly or unseaworthy. Such theories ultimately generated design procedures worked out with considerable geometric sophistication, as with the medieval master mason-architect. Yet the methods of the mason had nothing to do with science in the modern sense. He had no idea where a line of stress went or what it was.

The transition of technology from the principles and theories of the crafts to the theory and principles of science was slow and complex. In many cases the crafts died out as applied science replaced them. Furthermore, a distinction must be made between the indirect and the direct influence of science on technology. The former began at least as far back as the 13th century and continued until about the middle of the 19th century. The whole history of steam power is a good example of such indirect indebtedness. The concepts underlying the Newcomen atmospheric steam engine were certainly scientific, but their realization in practical form was wholly due to a group of artisans.

From one point of view the whole Industrial Revolution (c. 1750 to 1840 or 1850) is an example of the indirect application of science—physics, mechanics, chemistry, and other disciplines. The distinguishing feature of this stage of the relations of science and technology is that science was adequate to suggest an idea but powerless to prescribe the manner of implementation. Implementation was the inventor's business. In the direct application of science to technology, on the other hand, how an object may be achieved is often as clear from the basic science as the object itself; the problem is to make the method practical and economic in commercial production.

This article is a general survey of the history of technology from the Stone Age to the present, discussing major technological innovations and their impact on society. For a more thorough treatment of a specific topic, see the individual article. For example, for a detailed discussion of computers and their use, see the article *Computer*.

CONTENTS

STONE AGES

The oldest technology of which anything is known is that of fabricating stone implements. Products of other technologies disintegrated, but the stone survived. The long era of stone tools is divided into two major periods, early and late. In the earlier and much longer period, known as the Paleolithic, men lived chiefly by hunting and gathering food. In the later, or Neolithic, period agriculture and domesticated animals became the

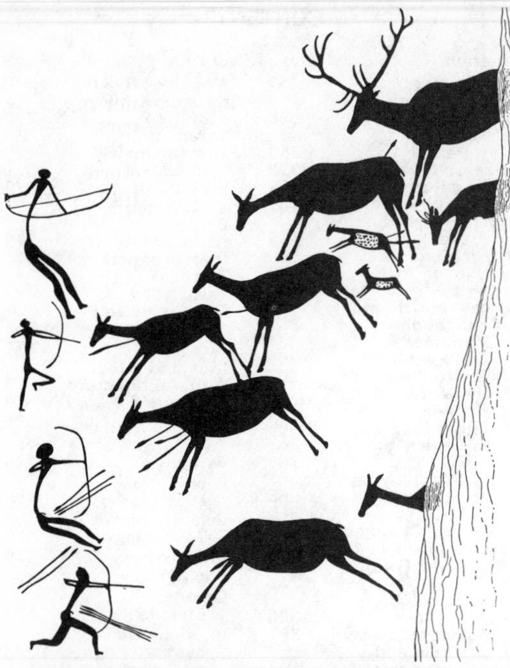

COURTESY OF THE AMERICAN MUSEUM OF NATURAL HISTORY

CAVE PAINTING of archers hunting stags. From Upper Paleolithic period, Albocácer, Castellón, Spain.

chief food supply. In northern Eurasia a long intermediate period called the Mesolithic provided a transition between the Paleolithic and Neolithic periods.

Paleolithic Period. The oldest chipped pebble tools, products not of *Homo sapiens* but of *Pithecanthropus*, an older, separate, and more primitive hominid genus, have been assigned to the early Pleistocene period of about half a million years ago. A conservative estimate would put the oldest (Abbevillian epoch) tools associated with the Paleolithic cultures of *H. sapiens* about 100,000 or 200,000 years later. From then on the sequence is unbroken through the Acheulian, Levalloisian, and other prehistoric cultures down to the beginnings of the Neolithic period approximately 6000 to 5000 B. C. It is not known whether the earliest stoneworkers had mastered other techniques, such as the control of fire.

The various prehistoric cultures are distinguished by the methods they used to produce stone implements. In making the earliest tools, moderate-sized pieces of relatively homogeneous stone, such as flint or obsidian, were chosen. A waterworn pebble might be used as a hammer, and fragments of the stone were removed by striking with proper force and angle. The core that remained was the implement. Later, larger masses of stone were struck against an anvil to produce big flakes that could themselves be shaped into implements. In the Acheulian culture, finer control of the tool's shape and of the sharpness of its edge was obtained by striking blows in a different way with a rather soft hammer of wood or bone. In another technique, small fragments were forced off the flakes by applying pressure with a bone shaper.

Even in the Lower Paleolithic there was a diversification among stone tools. Besides hand axes there were various forms of scrapers and piercers. In the Upper Paleolithic of Europe, beginning about 75,000 years ago when *H. sapiens* alone survived of the hominid species, progress was made in the diversification and perfection of stone tools and the introduction of others made of bone and wood. Tools were definitely hafted—that is, set on handles. The bow and the spear-thrower were used, and specialized fishing implements were made of bone and shell. Sewing with needle and sinew made possible the protection of the body with animal skin clothing. Apart from the artifacts themselves, such as arrowheads, needles, fishhooks, and awls, this technological mastery is actually illustrated in the magnificent cave paintings that survive from the Magdalenian period, particularly in the southwestern part of France. These cave paintings belong to the last stages of the Paleolithic cultures, which occurred from about 25,000 to 15,000 years ago.

In the replacement of one technology by another, the succession, or sequence, of changes is more significant than the actual lapse of time between them. For example, Indians in North America were still making stone arrowheads in the 17th century A. D. and were thus living in what was essentially a Stone Age culture. Where the replacement of one technology by another occurs late in a given region, it is likely to have been effected by diffusion rather than by native invention. Thus, in the northern parts of the Old World the intermediate Mesolithic culture persisted long after the cultures of the Middle East had passed from an Upper Paleolithic technology to the quite different technology of the Neolithic period, which had begun by 6000 to 5000 B. C. From the Middle East, Neolithic technology spread to other regions and eventually displaced the Mesolithic technology.

Neolithic Period. The Neolithic Period is marked by the transition from food gathering to farming. This transition is not complete today, when fish farming is still insignificant compared with the "gathering" of fish from the oceans by fishermen. Neolithic man may well have obtained most of his meat by hunting. Nevertheless, while the domestication of animals is consistent with nomadism, as in the steppes of the Old World or in Arabia, agriculture necessarily enforced settlement or encouraged village life if, for other reasons, it had already begun. Technologically, the Neolithic period is distinguished from the Paleolithic by the use of stone tools ground smooth by abrasives and bored for the attachment of handles.

This "Neolithic revolution" possibly first occurred in western Iran, a region in which the history of village life can be traced back to about 7000 B. C. It required not only immaterial techniques—the domestication and care of animals—but a new material technology involving agricultural implements such as sickles. These tools were made by setting small flakes of flint in a wooden handle to form a long curved blade. Food technology, such as the drying and salting of meat, as well as roasting, may well be much older than agriculture, but with the development of farming and the first harvesting of grain, additional food technologies were introduced. It became necessary, for example, to store food and prepare it for eating.

Basketry and pottery are two ways of making containers for agricultural crops. They may be associated with each other, particularly if the first pot was a clay-daubed basket. In pottery fire was used for the first time to effect a chemical change and form a material that does not exist in nature.

The making of ropes and lines of some sort goes back to the Upper Paleolithic. The northern Mesolithic yields nets made of vegetable fiber. Mats as well as baskets are known to have existed in the ancient Neolithic settlement of Jarmo (in modern Iraq). Textiles are also linked with the Egyptian Neolithic. Hence primitive spinning was probably a Neolithic innovation, although looms have not been traced beyond 3000 B.C. Neolithic man also had boats or rafts made from dug-out logs, skins, or bundles of reed.

RISE OF CITIES

The word "civilization" generally denotes an urban way of life rather than the appearance of any easily definable technical step—unless the use of mud-brick is so considered. The growth of cities was possible only after the beginning of the Neolithic period, when the development of agriculture allowed the accumulation of food surpluses to feed the urban populations. In historical evolution, urban life was closely linked with metallurgy, the wheel, and the transport animal; it was also associated with writing. However, the origin of these developments is no clearer than that of other major technological steps. It is not even certain that they were unique discoveries that diffused from a single center, although it is usually supposed that this was the case.

Urban life seems to have developed independently from a number of focuses in the Old World as well as in the New World, and its history and regional variation are explained by social rather than technological factors. The countryside, containing the mass of humanity, was the seat of primary production—animal breeding, farming, mining and quarrying, probably smelting, and fishing—while the development of craftsmanship proceeded in the towns and was particularly stimulated by the temples and courts in which writing and numeration were practiced extensively. Just as the initial practice of agriculture provided greater security of food supply, so improved farming on the rich irrigated lands of river valleys provided the surplus that made possible both civilization and the specialization of crafts.

Metallurgy. The earliest metalworking involved deposits of native metal that were worked by conventional "stone age" techniques of hammering and cutting with stone tools. Cooper awls made in this way and thought to date from before 7000 B.C. have been found at Cayonu Tepesi in Turkey. About 4000 B.C. native copper was annealed in fire to overcome work hardening. About this time the smelting of ores and other metal-working techniques based on the use of fire began to be practiced, progressing from gold through copper to iron and steel.

Even before 3000 B.C. copper oxide ores were smelted, and the molten metal was cast into the shapes of tools, such as axes. Bronze was made by smelting cassiterite, a tin ore, with the copper. The distinction between pure metals and alloys was not recognized until much later. Before 2000 B.C. both silver and lead were obtained from galena, a sulfide ore, and not long afterwards the technique of roasting copper sulfide ores was mastered.

Iron effectively came into use for tools and weapons about 1200 B.C., quickly replacing bronze in edge tools and weapons, although bronze remained important for armor and other uses. Hence bronze remained the chief metal of war and craft for well over 2,000 years.

There is no direct knowledge of the earliest technology of metals. It must be inferred from surviving remains—most commonly from the European Bronze Age—from the later evidence of art, beginning about 3000 B.C., and from the practices of modern primitive cultures. For example, works of art found at ancient Ur and elsewhere demonstrate that more than one type of soldering was practiced in ancient Mesopotamia. Similarly, Chinese bronze vessels of about 1500 B.C. are known to have been cast in piece molds, of which burned fragments have been found.

Fragments from Mesopotamia of objects covered in metal, particularly gold, prove that ingots were beaten out into thin sheets. But information is lacking about the smelting of metal earlier than shown in Egyptian pictures beginning about 2500 B.C. These pictures show that the Egyptians used blowpipes and pot-bellows with a skin diaphragm worked by foot to provide a blast for the fire. Crucibles of molten metal were carried by withy (green wood) "tongs." Although the furnace hearth was very simple, large works such as gates could be cast. Moreover, despite the seeming crudity of the means available, smiths were able to produce jewelry, raised bowls, and other fine metalwork of great beauty.

For the separation of metals, such as silver from lead and gold from silver and copper, cupellation was used. The changes in color and other properties in a metal brought about by alloying with other metals or by chemical reactions were recognized very early. This recognition was the practical foundation of alchemy. In the New World, for example, copper-gold alloys were heat-treated to expose a surface that appeared to be pure gold.

Iron Working. Until about 1400 A.D. iron was invariably smelted by the direct, or bloomery, process. Ore was reduced by charcoal, which was the regular fuel of all early metallurgy, at a temperature considerably less than the melting point of iron. This process yielded a spongy mass, or bloom, weighing at most a few pounds. The bloom contained slag, fuel, and unreduced ore. It was consolidated, purified, and strengthened by prolonged hammering while hot. Since it had not fused, this wrought iron contained only a little dissolved carbon and was malleable. Tools, weapons, and later armor fabricated from wrought iron were therefore submitted to further carburizing processes before quenching and tempering. Such processes were the most secret feature of the smith's art. Although in ancient times there was no clear distinction between iron and steel, in practice a smith could derive by inspection a very useful understanding of the properties of different pieces of metal.

The Horse and the Wheel. Before the advent of iron, warfare had already been transformed by the introduction of the horse as a draft animal, about 2000 B.C. Vehicles with solid wooden wheels pulled by a pair of animals, one on each side of the draft pole, had been used for at least a thousand years before that. They were drawn by oxen and onagers (wild asses). The light, horse-drawn, two-wheeled war chariot carried a driver and a warrior, who was either an archer or a foot soldier who sprang out to attack. The riding of horses came long after the chariot.

In Egypt by 1500 B. C., beautifully carpentered wheels were made with separate hubs, fellies, and four spokes. Egyptian paintings do not show any use of the wheel for throwing pottery. However, intermittent rotary motion was employed in other devices, such as the bow drill and pump drill and the primitive ground lathe, from about 1000 B. C.

Architecture. The outstanding symbols of urban power are great buildings, such as the pyramids of Egypt, the granaries of the Indus Valley, and the ziggurats of Mesopotamia.

All the ancient peoples used both sun-dried and fired brick, and some excelled in stone. In Asia, brick was strengthened and made waterproof with bitumen. Sewers and larger open spaces were roofed over with barrel vaults of brick. Egypt excelled in the working of building blocks and columns from quarries. Long before iron was available this work was done with tools of hard rock because bronze was too soft to be useful. In their temples the Egyptians employed a trabeated (post-and-lintel) form of construction similar in principle to the later Greek architecture.

While the life of the craftsmen in Egyptian cities, as is known from papyri, was hard and brutish, the rich enjoyed well-planned, cool, and comfortable city mansions. A consequence of this was that the furniture design improved considerably. Navigation by large sailing boats on the Nile and the Mediterranean Sea and the opening of a canal to the Red Sea brought luxuries from remote parts of the world to wealthy Egyptians.

Uses of Rivers. All the rivers around which ancient civilizations thrived required management. The Indus River changed its course and produced destructive floods. The periodic inundations of the Nile brought fertility to the land. However, the flooding could be turned to best advantage by the digging of canals to lead the floodwater over the country and by forming basins in which the water could be stored when the river level fell. In Mesopotamia the problem was different; water was brought to the land by the digging of canals from the upper reaches of one river to lower levels of the same or another river.

In all these countries the final stage of irrigation involved the raising of water from a ditch to the fields. The *shadūf*, or swipe, which was used for this purpose is an ancient instance of the lever principle. Much of the earliest development of machinery was associated with raising water levels. Whether such machines were used in Egypt before classical times is doubtful.

Writing. It is supposed that the invention of writing was intimately related to the needs of government and institutionalized religion and was another essential element of urban technology. The oldest evidence of writing is in the form of Sumerian pictographs on clay tablets, 4000 to 3000 B. C. These pictographs became conventionalized and simplified into the cuneiform syllabary, which were impressed into the clay with a reed stylus. The cuneiform syllabary in turn became the vehicle for recording many distinct languages. The emergence of Egyptian hieroglyphs can be seen on the palette of King Narmer, about 3000 B. C.

The oldest known Chinese writing is the set of about 3,000 archaic characters inscribed on the "oracle bones" used in divination by the rich Bronze Age culture of Honan about 1300 B. C. By this time the origins of the Latin alphabet were already taking shape in Phoenicia. Both the Roman and Cyrillic scripts were derived from Greek. Medical and astrological tablets from Babylonia and similar papyri from Egypt attest to uses of writing other than record keeping before 2000 B. C.

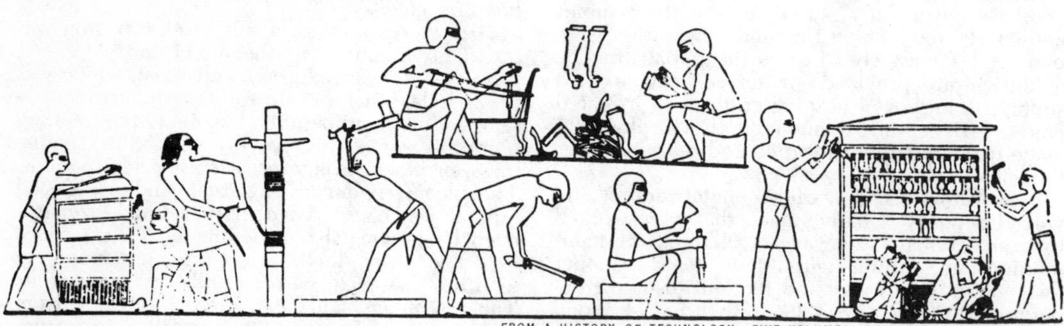

FROM A HISTORY OF TECHNOLOGY, FIVE VOLUMES, BY CHARLES SINGER, ET AL.

Craftsmen working on various stages of furniture production. From a tomb at Thebes from about 1400 B. C.

Netting and curing fish and netting birds. From a tomb at Beni Hasan, Egypt, from about 1000 B. C.

A HISTORY OF TECHNOLOGY

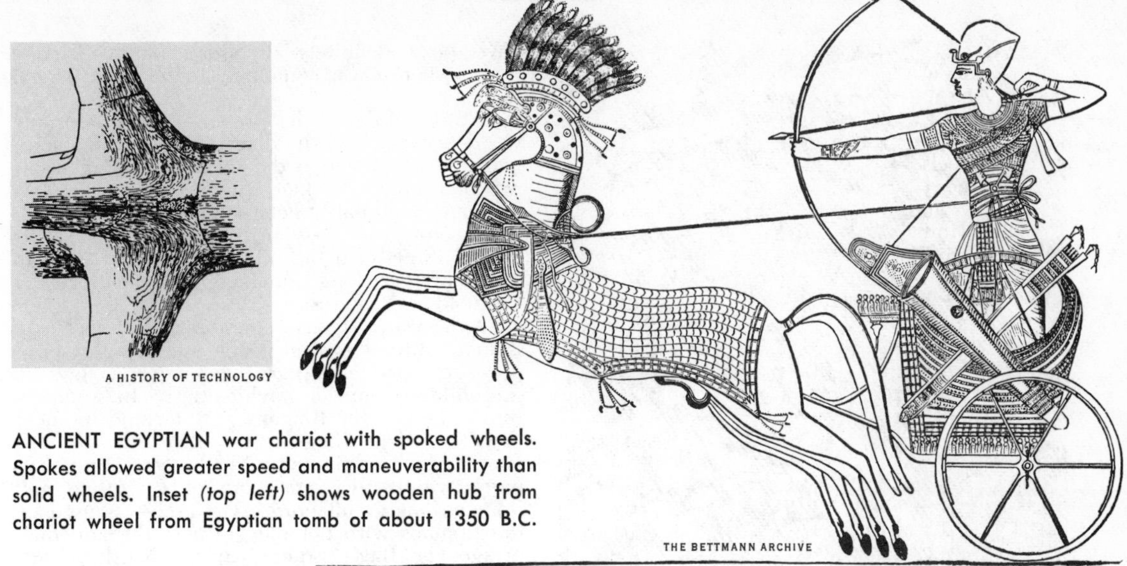

ANCIENT EGYPTIAN war chariot with spoked wheels. Spokes allowed greater speed and maneuverability than solid wheels. Inset *(top left)* shows wooden hub from chariot wheel from Egyptian tomb of about 1350 B.C.

GREEK AND ROMAN CIVILIZATIONS

Most of the basic elements of technology were pre-Greek, and only a few fundamental contributions can be traced to Greek inventiveness. However, one Greek discovery, the use and study of machines, was fundamental, and this in turn gave rise to the concept of natural power. The Greeks were great improvers. For example, in pottery they developed a delicate control of the atmosphere within a kiln, thus producing brilliant effects of color from carefully applied clays. They made transparent goblets of glass instead of using it only as a vivid glaze. They also understood the full aesthetic and technical potentialities of post-and-lintel architecture and learned to reinforce their stone with iron. The Greeks rendered the oared ship the most formidable fighting vessel the world was to know—outside Chinese waters—before the 15th century.

The Greek texture of civilization was appropriated and extended by the Romans. The outstanding fact about the Roman world is that over a period of a thousand years it transferred the improved techniques of the Middle East to northwestern Europe. Roman water mills reached western Germany and Hadrian's Wall. Roman coins were carried to India in the south and to Sweden in the north. Under the Romans, iron became a far more common metal. Thousands of pounds of iron smelted in the forests of southern Poland were sold to Rome. From Provence and the Mediterranean shore of Spain, Romanization only slightly diminished to southern Britain. The Mediterranean civilization extended around the Black Sea and up to the Danube to Rumania. Despite the "barbarian invasions" and the "fall" of the Roman Empire, most of the technological innovations that were imported from the Middle East were retained by the West, if only in monastic houses.

Machines. With the spread of Middle Eastern technology went a concomitant rationalism, which was never wholly lost in the West although its resurgence was long delayed. The systematic, mathematical, logical spirit of inquiry among the Greeks produced not only pure science, such as Aristotle's embryology and Archimedes' statics, but also a series of technological treatises. The writers on machines were all Greeks, except Vitruvius, whereas the writers on agriculture, architecture, and hydraulics were mostly Romans, who were heavily influenced by the Greeks.

The mechanical treatises fall into two groups—those dealing with war machines and those dealing with pneumatic and automatic devices intended for amusement or mystification rather than actual work. The Greeks had a clear intuitive, but not logical, grasp of mechanical advantage (what is gained in ease is lost in time) and knew of the screw, windlass, pulley, and inclined plane. The simple pulley existed among the Assyrians in the 9th century B.C., while the Greeks of the 5th century B.C. had the compound pulley and windlass. The water screw is associated with Archimedes, who may or may not have invented it. The screw press was described approximately 200 years later (about 65 A.D.) by Hero of Alexandria.

Reaping grain (above). Grain is thrown into large net by harvesters and then taken to be threshed. From tomb about 1420 B.C. (Below) Shaduf for irrigation of palm garden. From tomb about 1500 B.C.

A HISTORY OF TECHNOLOGY

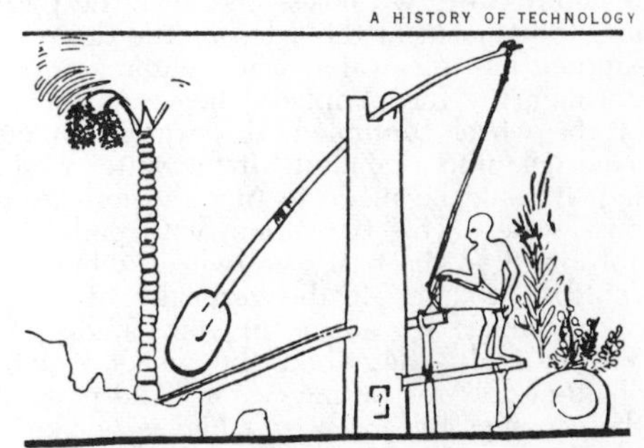

A HISTORY OF TECHNOLOGY

COPPER MINE in the Alps, with rock face being broken up by fire. From about 1600–800 B. C.

The early Greeks were acquainted with several forms of gearing, although they did not employ gears for power transmission. They understood the piston-and-cylinder combination. They knew how to make force pumps and that air expands when heated to fill "empty" spaces. They introduced machines into warfare on a large scale, using movable devices for attacking fortifications and catapults for projecting stones or heavy arrows. These catapults, or ballistae, derived their elastic force from twisted webs of hair or sinew. The Romans made these ballistae regular components of their armies.

The Roman architect Vitruvius wrote on water-raising devices essential to irrigation. Among them he described a drum (tympanum) mounted on a horizontal axle and turned by men treading it around. This drum was divided radially into compartments, each of which was penetrated by two holes—one near the periphery and the other near the axle. As the drum turned, dipping into the water, water entered each compartment by the peripheral hole. As the motion of the wheel continued, this water ran out the axial hole into a conduit. If the water were flowing, it could be made to turn the mill itself and raise water. This tympanum with paddles probably inspired the true waterwheel, which in turn could be coupled to the vertical shaft of a pair of millstones by means of right-angle gearing. Vitruvius also described the wheel-of-pots and chain-of-pots for raising water. The powering of these pumps by a geared whim is not known to have been definitely described before Islamic times, when it was commonly found from Bengal to Spain.

At the close of the pre-Christian era simple wooden gears were used in power transmissions, and natural power in the form of flowing water was mastered. In fact, the mastery of waterpower had probably been achieved about a century before, in the horizontal waterwheel attached directly to the mill shaft. The Vitruvian mill, however, long remained the chief focus of technological interest,

Architecture. The inseparability of Greek and Roman cultures is seen in the use of ballistae, of pressure pipelines to carry water over valleys, in shipbuilding, and in architecture. In architecture, however, the Romans were technically more inventive than the Greeks. The idea of the dome, which originated with the crossing of two barrel vaults, was the core of Byzantine and Romanesque architecture. The arch was used by the Romans with notable grace in the aqueduct bridges of Italy, France, Spain, North Africa, and Asia. Some of these bridges had large, accurately squared stone blocks with unmortared joints, while others had brick.

Concrete, a new construction material discovered by the Romans, was made possible by volcanic ash from Pozzuoli, near Naples, which formed a hydraulic cement when burned. Sometimes, in order to lighten the fabric of a concrete dome, clay tiles or hollow clay pots were used. Concrete was also used occasionally in the construction of Roman roads as well as in arch bridges.

Written Records. Compared to their predecessors, the Romans governed through a relatively large literate bureaucracy. Detailed army records were kept, and maps were made. Provincial governors corresponded with Rome, and private friends exchanged letters. Besides the postal service, the Romans, like the Greeks and the Egyptians, had the advantage of papyrus as a writing material. The most common form of book or record was the roll, but at the close of the Roman era, the codex, the modern type of book, came into use. Literacy was not again so widespread for a long period.

With the fall of Rome, the technology of urban life—water supply, sewerage, street paving and lighting—which had begun long before in the great cities of Mesopotamia and the Indus, fell into long neglect.

EARLY MIDDLE AGES

Massive vestiges of Roman technology were still obvious and useful in the first centuries after the collapse of the empire. The barbarian invaders—the Huns, Vandals, and others—had been slightly influenced by Roman technology. Thus glassworking continued in the forest of Germany, and Anglo-Saxon kings struck simulacra of Roman coins. The water mill flourished, the Domesday Book recording nearly 6,000 such mills. Some may have been horizontal-wheel, or Norse mills, which were representative of a tradition different from that described by Vitruvius. Nevertheless, many had geared vertical wheels. The use of iron was never lost. New influences were strong during the Early Middle Ages, particularly from the Islamic world, extending from Iran to Spain, which introduced many new crops to Europe. These crops included rice, cotton, sugar, dates, and oranges.

Horses. The Romans and all Mediterranean peoples used horses primarily to draw chariots or light carts. The horses were attached to the cart by a narrow strap passing high around the animal's neck. The strap, by throttling the horse, limited its pull. By the 9th century A. D. the strap had been replaced by a padded collar against which the animal could thrust without ill effect. The horseshoe has never been definitely shown to precede early medieval times. The use of the improved harness and the horseshoe led to the breeding of large horses capable of pulling heavy wagons. The bit used to control the horse by its mouth has been used since the domestication of the animal.

Early riders sat bareback. The shaped saddle with a solid frame first appeared in the 1st century A. D. Stirrups probably originated in central Asia. They were adopted by Muslim cavalry in the 7th century and by western Europeans possibly early in the 8th century. They may have been brought into Europe by the Avars, who drove the Lombards into Italy. Early cavalrymen were archers. Later, the stirrup enabled them to adopt shock tactics—that is, to charge with lances fixed at rest.

Agriculture. During the Early Middle Ages there were also changes in agriculture. The large, open, communal fields of the medieval village were plowed by teams of eight oxen. Although a strong plow fitted with wheels was already in use in late Roman times, the Germanic people of northern Europe do not seem to have adopted the characteristic heavy plow with colter, moldboard, and wheels before the 6th century. This type of plow was more efficient than earlier models. When pulled by a powerful team, it could break the heavier and moister soils, thus stimulating the clearing of the forests that then covered much of Europe. In the long run, it made possible the accumulation of surplus food and in turn the growth of urban areas.

Influence of the Far East. The end of early medieval history is marked technologically by evidence of migration of ideas from the Far East. By the 11th century, western Europe was well set on an expansionist course. Although both the Islamic and Byzantine cultures were technologically in advance of the West and enjoyed a high standard of urban life, at this time they began their long decline.

China's technological advancement excelled that of Europe, Islam, and Byzantium. In many techniques Chinese invention and practice long preceded those of Europe—from the manufacture of porcelain to the making of iron suspension bridges. Some of this Chinese skill entered Europe through Islam or Byzantium along channels that are still obscure. The best documented case is that of papermaking, a secret that spread from Samarkand (751) to Baghdad (794) and Cairo (c. 810) and then to Spain (before 1150). Shortly thereafter, the first paper mill on the French side of the Pyrenees began manufacture. The remote origins of the magnetic compass lie in China about the beginning of the Christian era. Possibly by the 5th century A. D. the Chinese used suspended, floating, or pivoted magnets for divination. By the 10th or 11th century they knew of the magnetized, pivoted steel needle, and soon thereafter applied its south-pointing property to navigation. In the West the magnetic needle was first described in 1179. Its use in navigation is untraceable before the 1200's. The sternpost rudder, as distinct from a steering oar hanging in a sling over the side of the vessel, may have come from China at the same time. In Europe it was first illustrated on the seal of the city of Elbing (now Elbląg, Poland) about 1242.

LATE MIDDLE AGES

The zenith of medieval technology in Europe, preparing the way for the modern period, was marked by a number of significant developments, such as the casting of iron, the perfection of oceangoing sailing ships, and most important of all, the multiplication and diversification of machines. During this period Europe continued to profit from the diffusion of ideas from the Far and Middle East.

A HISTORY OF TECHNOLOGY

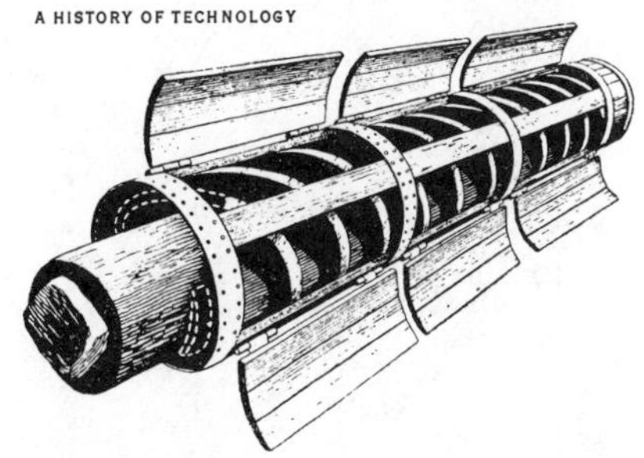

ARCHIMEDES SCREW ***(left)*** **from mine at Sotiel, Spain. It is made of oak, and axle is 24 inches in diameter.** ***(Below)*** **Hero's device for opening temple doors. When fire is lighted on altar, hot air forces water from container to bucket, which drops, turning door spindles and raising counterweights.**

A HISTORY OF TECHNOLOGY

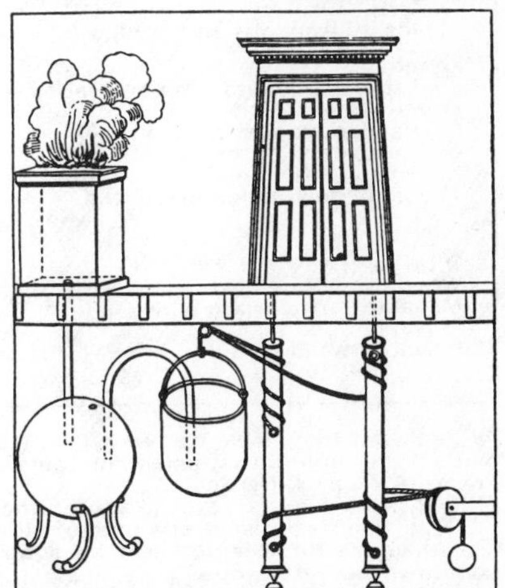

A HISTORY OF TECHNOLOGY

WATER-LIFTING DEVICES described by Vitruvius are, from left to right, a chain of buckets, a scoop wheel, and a tympanum.

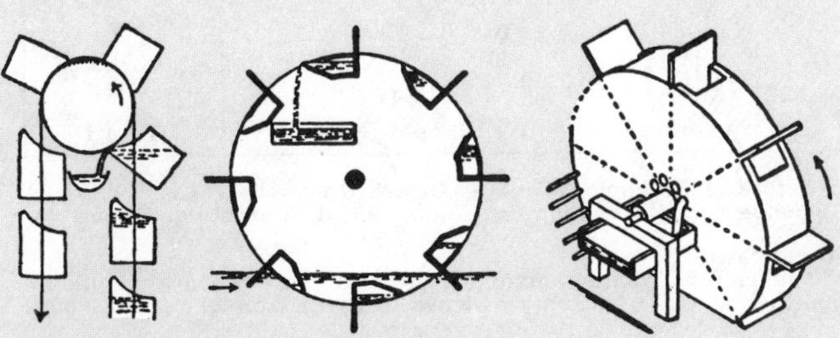

TRANSMISSION OF TECHNOLOGY FROM CHINA TO THE WEST[1]

Invention or Discovery	First confirmed use in China[2]	First confirmed use in Europe[2]	Approximate minimum time lag in centuries[3]
Square-pallet chain pump	189	1672	15
Edge-runner mill	170	1607	13
Water powered	400	1607	11
Trip-hammer mill	4th century B. C.	...	...
Water powered	20	1607	14
Rotary winnowing machine with crank handle	40 B.C.	Late 18th century	14
Rotary fan for ventilation	180	1556	12
Blowing engines for furnaces and forges with waterpower	31	13th century	11
Blowing engines with crank drive	1310	1757	4
Piston bellows, for continuous blast	4th century B. C.	16th century	14
Drawloom for figured weaves	about 100 B. C.	4th–5th century	4
Silk-reeling machine	1st century B. C.	end of 13th century	3–13
Waterpower applied	1310	14th century	...
Wheelbarrow	231	about 1200	9–10
Sailing carriage (first high land speeds)	552	1600	10–11
Wagon mill, grinding during travel	340	1580	12
Efficient draught harness for horses:			
Breast strap	2d century B. C.	about 1130	8
Collar	3d to 7th century	about 920	6
Crossbow (individual weapon)	3d century B. C.	11th century	13
Kite	about 400 B. C.	1589	12
Helicopter top (spun by cord)	320	18th century	14
Zoetrope (lamp cover revolved by ascending hot air)	180	17th century	10
Deep drilling (for water, brine, and natural gas)	1st century	1126	11
Iron casting	2d century B. C.	13th century	10–12
Concave curved iron moldboard of plow	9th century	about 1700	25
Seed-drill plow, with hopper	85 B. C.	about 1700	14
Gimbals	180	about 1200	8–9
Segmental arch bridges	610	1345	7
Cable suspension bridges	1st century B. C.	...	...
Iron chain suspension bridges	580	1741	10–13
Canals and rivers controlled by series of gates	3d century B. C.	1220	17
True lock gates and chambers	825	1452	7
Shipbuilding:			
Sternpost rudder	8th century	1180	3
Watertight compartments	5th century	1790	12
Rig:			
Efficient sails (mat-and-batten principle)	1st century B. C.	19th century	18
Fore-and-aft rig	3d century	9th century	6
Gunpowder:	about 850	13th century	4
Rockets and fire lances	about 1100	15th century	3–4
Projectile artillery	about 1200	about 1320	1
Explosive grenades and bombs	about 1000	16th century	4–5
Magnetism:			
Lodestone spoon rotating on bronze plate	83	...	...
Floating magnet	1020	1190	4
Suspended magnetic needle	1086	...	...
Compass used for navigation	1117	...	2
Knowledge of magnetic declination	1030	about 1450	4
Theory of declination discussed	1174	about 1600	4
Paper	105	1150	10
Printing:			
Wood or metal blocks	740	about 1400	6
Movable earthenware type	1045	...	...
Movable wood type	1314	...	...
Movable metal type	1302 (Korea)	1440	1
Porcelain	3d–7th century	18th century	11–13

[1]Adapted from table on pp. 770–771 of *A History of Technology,* vol. 2 (Oxford University Press, 1956), ed. by C. Singer and others; and from Table 8 in *Science and Civilisation in China,* vol. 1 (Cambridge University Press, 1954), by J. Needham.

[2]All dates are A. D. except where otherwise indicated.

[3]The time lags listed attempt to allow for considerable doubt and obscurity and therefore are frequently less than the number obtained by subtracting the date of first confirmed use in China from the date of first confirmed use in Europe.

THE BETTMANN ARCHIVE

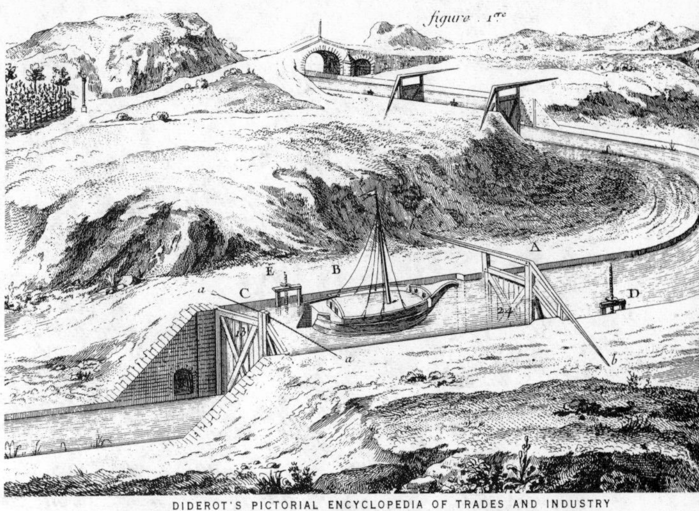

DIDEROT'S PICTORIAL ENCYCLOPEDIA OF TRADES AND INDUSTRY

SUCTION PUMP (*above, left*) for drainage of mine is powered by waterwheel. From Agricola, 1556.

PLATE (*above, right*) shows canal that carries water across rising ground instead of through a tunnel.

PEASANTS doing farm chores, including plowing, planting, and harvesting. From 15th century French painting.

THE BETTMANN ARCHIVE

Gunpowder was introduced at this time. The use of gunpowder in artillery gave the Europeans global mastery in war from the 16th century onward. Gunpowder was a Chinese invention, but it seems likely that guns, which the Chinese had failed to develop, were an independent European invention.

The silk industry, originally imported from China into the western Mediterranean in the 5th century A. D., settled in southern Europe. The manufacture of cotton textiles, by techniques that had originated in India, followed the importation of the silk industry.

Printing. Printing was another imported technique. In China the printing of books from engraved wooden blocks, a technique well suited to Chinese calligraphy, had begun about 700 A. D. and by 900 had reached Egypt. Before 1400, block printing of playing cards and religious images was practiced in Europe. The alphabetization of European writing suggested the use of separate letter types rather than the engraving of a separate block for each page. Letter type was devised by the German inventor Johann Gutenberg about 1445. This invention had been anticipated a few generations earlier in Korea and attempted previously by the Chinese.

Ceramics. Europeans obtained knowledge of many branches of chemical technology from the Islamic world, particularly the art of distillation and the making of high-quality glass. Syria, Egypt, and Mesopotamia excelled in the production of pottery in the 9th and 10th centuries, while in the 12th and 13th centuries Persia was dominant and even influenced China. In the West these transferred techniques gave rise to the majolica ware that was brilliantly painted in tin-glaze pictures or, especially in Spain, with the metallic lusters that were imitated from Islamic works.

Social Changes. The thrust of technological development during this period was not solely—as it was so often from the Sumerians onward—toward the satisfaction of an aristocratic minority in life and their commemoration in death. There was a drive in northern Europe toward the mass production of rather coarse goods.

There was also a shift toward mechanical power in place of muscle. From about 1200, heavy, rough woolen clothes were fulled by waterpowered machines rather than by man. For the first time, laborsaving iron tools were used by peasants. By 1500, coal was being used as a domestic fuel in manors in northern England.

THE BETTMANN ARCHIVE

COLLIERY (*above*) at Staffordshire, England, using Watt's double-acting rotative steam engine to draw coal from the mines.

THE BETTMANN ARCHIVE

COAL (*right*) was carried in carts from mines to surface by young children in English mines.

Before the end of the Middle Ages waterpower was used not only to grind grain and full cloth but also to work hammers and bellows in ironworks, saw lumber, polish armor and weapons, and pump mines dry. From the late 12th century, windmills were used to grind corn and drain land. Although there were windmills in the Far East and elsewhere, the two types used in Europe were developed independently of these models.

Toward the end of the Middle Ages the techniques of shipbuilding and navigation were perfected, and Europeans began to travel all over the world.

RENAISSANCE AND BAROQUE PERIODS

Following the Middle Ages, during the Renaissance and baroque periods, there were fewer major innovations in the crafts. It was a period of great artistic eminence, of the birth of great cities, and of scientific revolution. It was an age of north-to-south and transatlantic movement of techniques and ideas—of printing to England, Mexico, and Massachusetts, of Majolica ware to France, and of the related Delft faience to England. Mastery of mining and metallurgy spread north from Italy and southern Germany, aided by the publication of the first technological literature describing these crafts, chief among which were Vannoccio Biringuccio's *De la Pirotechnia* (1540) and Georgius Agricola's *De re metallica* (1556).

Canals. An example of gradual technical development in civil engineering is afforded by the canal, starting from early efforts to improve river navigation. The key invention was that of the pound-lock in the mid-15th century. Shortly thereafter, the first extensive system of canals was built to connect Milan with its neighboring rivers—a project in which Leonardo da Vinci was engaged.

A century later Brussels was connected to the English Channel, and other canals were cut in England, Germany, and the Netherlands. Between 1604 and 1646 the Briare Canal was constructed to connect the Loire and the Seine rivers. Finally, the Languedoc Canal of France, begun in 1666 and completed in 1692, shows great mastery of all major canal-building techniques, including surveying and leveling, the construction of locks, the provision of reservoirs, and the supply of water.

Introduction of Coke. The development of coal-fuel technology in this period was an important stimulus to economic growth. It also prepared the way for the first great technical achievement of the following age—the smelting of iron with coke. This new metallurgical technique, developed by Abraham Darby at Coalbrookdale, Shropshire, England, in 1709, was one of the prime contributors to the industrial revolution in Britain. Soap boilers, salt panners, brewers, and even blacksmiths were forced to substitute coal for wood in areas, such as northern Britain and the southern Low Countries, where coal was abundant and lumber scarce. Often raw coal could be used, but where, as in smithing, malting, or glassmaking, there was a danger of contamination from sulfurous and smoky coal, the coal was first "charked" in heaps and then burned as coke. When coal was first converted to coke is not known, but there had been a series of 17th century patents for its application to iron smelting when Darby succeeded in using it for smelting iron.

Agriculture. During the 17th century the economic development of northwestern Europe, which offered opportunities for technological innovation, was accompanied by an increase in population in the Netherlands, England, Wales, and Sweden. In contrast, there was a decline in Spain, France, Italy, and Germany. The basic cause of these changes was the incidence of famine, disease, and war. But to some extent before about 1650 and increasingly thereafter, the maintenance of a larger European population —notably larger everywhere by 1800—depended on improvements in agricultural technology. Such improvements had their origins in the 16th century in improved crop rotation and the production of fodder for animals. These techniques resulted in a more efficient use of land and improved the raising of food animals to meet Europe's pressing need for an abundant and reliable food supply.

Science and Technology. The relation of science to technology became a little better established in the 17th century. Science generated new crafts. One example is the making of optical instruments, which in turn made possible important progress in surveying and navigation. Also, several physicists and astronomers, including the Italian Galileo and the Dutchman Christiaan Huygens, attempted to solve the problem of determining longitude at sea, which could be done either chronometrically or by various types of astronomical observation. Thirdly, from Galileo's time onward, a few mathematicians sought to develop a theory of structures, though what was done had no real application to building. Finally, science evolved the idea of the atmospheric engine.

By the late 1640's it was understood that the mass of the air exerts a pressure at sea level of 14.7 pounds per square inch (10.33 kg/cm^2). If the atmosphere could be brought to bear on one side of a piston, with reduced pressure on the other, the movement of the piston would do work. In Huygens' heat engine, gunpowder was used to heat and rarify air in a cylinder below a piston. In the French physicist Denis Papin's improved engine a little water was heated externally to make steam. Finally, the British engineer Thomas Newcomen's atmospheric engine, developed in 1712, was a workable realization of the idea. The steam was produced in a separate boiler and then condensed by a jet in the cylinder to form a partial vacuum. The conversion of heat into mechanical energy was accomplished, and a new era of technology was opened.

In this instance only the basic idea came from science. The successful implementation and application of the idea came from artisans. Moreover, the steam engine would have been much harder to introduce had there not been coal mines to be drained of water. These mines also provided very cheap fuel for the boilers of the engines. At this time science was a source of technological ideas for the craft inventor, but it was not as yet a guiding or even stimulating force for technological change. Solutions to the actual problems of technological evolution had to come from the technologists themselves. This was true throughout the Industrial Revolution.

THE INDUSTRIAL REVOLUTION IN BRITAIN

The Industrial Revolution of the 18th century was in part a vast expansion of manufacture (as compared with agriculture, the traditional occupation of the people), in part a change in the character of manufacture (from the domestic or craft to the factory system), and in part a great demographic upheaval. It also involved the application of new techniques. However, industrial change is not necessarily founded on technological change. Some historians maintain that virtually no technological revolution occurred in the late 18th century: they claim that the basic technical ideas were all available before 1750 and some before 1650.

CULVER PICTURES

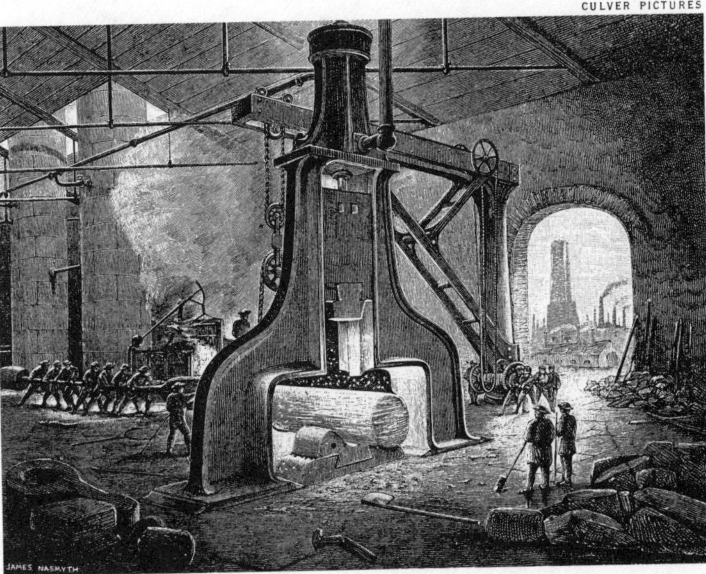

STEAM HAMMER, developed by James Nasmyth, used steam to lift the hammer and give it added power on the downstroke.

For many years technical progress gradually had prepared the way for the economic and social changes that became dramatically obvious in Britain after about 1770. All parts of Europe were fertile in inventions designed to improve shipbuilding, mining, agricultural implements, textile manufacture, metallurgical industries, glass- and pottery-making—indeed every form of manufacture and transport. Some of the early inventions preceding the Industrial Revolution were horse-drawn tramways (1556), the screw-cutting lathe (1578), Dud Dudley's coke furnace (1619), and the automatic loom (1678). A vast reservoir of technical expertise was ready to play a revolutionary role when the time was ripe. Skills of instrument maker and clockmaker were put to quite different uses, such as the making of spinning machinery. The millwright and the blacksmith became builders of steam engines. The machines that had drilled gun barrels could turn steam engine cylinders.

Although there had been many important technological innovations earlier, the rapidity of technical change was certainly greater after about 1770 than before, as was the rate of industrial development. Although many steam pumps were working in England and Europe before the Scottish engineer James Watt's patent of 1769, the transformation of industry by steam and the application of the engine to various forms of rotary motion, metallurgy, and transportation occurred only after 1770. Similarly, a number of technical inventions essential to the mechanization of textile manufacture, such as roller drafting (Lewis Paul, 1738) and the flying shuttle (John Kay, 1733) were made a generation or so before the Industrial Revolution proper. Again, however, the critical period of changeover to new textile machines that really worked came only after 1760 or 1770.

New technical ideas are not always fully operative at their inception. Paul's spinning machine, for example, was ineffective—unlike Sir Richard Arkwright's water frame and James Hargreaves' jenny, both about 1770. The Coalbrookdale Company took half a century to develop the coke blast furnace to the point where it was far more productive than the charcoal furnace and yielded metal of not much lower quality that could be converted into wrought-iron bars. Consequently, it was only about 1780 that the whole British iron industry began to swing over to coke and to expand greatly. The first great achievement of the cast-iron era was the Coalbrookdale Bridge completed in 1779.

Many new inventions were so imperfect or so hard to introduce on the industrial scale that many of the innovators went bankrupt.

What made the time ripe in the late 18th century for the extension and exploitation of half-developed ideas such as the Newcomen steam pump? The factors were economic and social. Population growth offered a greater market and a larger, more mobile, labor force. Low interest rates made promising though risky industrial ventures attractive. The circulation of capital was accelerated somewhat. Above all, was the expansion of Britain's empire and trade. British products, particularly textiles, were in great demand. Where technical advances made the lowering of prices feasible—as happened fantastically with iron and with cotton goods—the demand seemed insatiable. Finally, war that was almost continuous and, on the whole, profitable to Britain from 1756 to 1815 fanned the fires of the economy.

From many branches of technology it is possible to show not only that there was a demand, but that there was a rapid succession of developments leading to radical changes in the technology during no more than 50 years.

Textiles. The phenomenon of rapid, successive change is well known in the history of textile manufacture, where the initial difficulty of securing a sufficient supply of spun thread for weaving led to the introduction of a hand-operated multispindle machine. The next step was the introduction of power—first as waterpower, then as steam—and the extension of machine spinning to the finer counts of thread, so that finally machines were spinning thread as fine as that of the famed handworkers of India. Then there was the multiplication of spindles in the machine, the introduction of fresh methods, such as cap spinning and ring spinning, and the application of many relatively minor improvements. Fur-

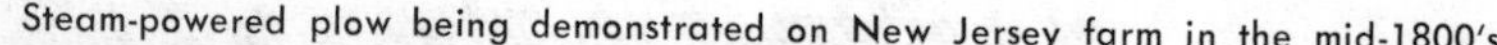

Steam-powered plow being demonstrated on New Jersey farm in the mid-1800's.

CULVER PICTURES

Dynamo room of the first Edison electric lighting station in New York.

thermore, the mechanization of spinning acted as a stimulant on the preparation of the fibers and on the weaving operation.

After the American inventor Eli Whitney's production of the cotton gin in 1793, every stage after the picking of the cotton—ginning, opening, carding, and slubbing—was mechanized. The machines often used cheap child labor rather than skilled adults, because children could take the product off one machine and feed it onto the next. Similar developments also occurred in the processing of wool and flax.

In weaving, the first working, though unsatisfactory, power looms of Edmund Cartwright and Jeffrey of Paisley (1785) were improved by Robert Miller (1796) and William Horrocks (1813), so that between 1813 and 1820 the number of such looms increased sevenfold. Richard Roberts' power loom, about 1822, was the first to have a long life. Power weaving demanded ancillary equipment, such as warping machines and sizing machines. Furthermore, the greatly increased output of cloth forced changes on the finishing trades—shearing, calendering, fulling, bleaching, and dyeing—so that the textile revolution merged into the chemical revolution.

Development of the Steam Engine. Sustained industrial growth combined with continual technological evolution is an endlessly ramifying and interdependent process. A fossilization of technique at any level immediately imperils the whole process. This can be shown in the development of the steam engine. Watt's separate-condenser invention of 1769 was still a pump. Only after the introduction of sun-and-planet gear about 1780 was rotative power available. This type of gearing was devised by the Scottish inventor William Murdock and was put into use in 1781. In principle, though not in fact, steam could now be applied to land and sea transport as well as to manufacture.

The separate condenser was not so much an accomplishment in itself as a key to future achievement. Moreover, this great invention, in turn, became superfluous when the atmospheric engine was replaced by the high-pressure engine, which worked at steam pressures that imposed far greater demands on the boiler. James Watt resisted this development, fearing accidents from boiler failure, thus casting his influence against technological progress. Such failures, however, were not unfrequent in later years and led to legislative control.

Development of the Locomotive. The British inventor Richard Trevithick led the way in high-pressure engines from about 1800. His Coalbrookdale engine of 1802 worked at 145 pounds per square inch (25 kg/cm^2). The power-to-weight ratio of the high-pressure engine was enormously better, and Trevithick at once showed that it could be used for transportation. In 1801 he made a road carriage, in 1804 a tramway engine that hauled 25 tons, and the following year an engine for a colliery.

Trevithick's work had been preceded by the experimental "automobiles" of Joseph Cugnot in France (1769), William Murdock (1784), and Oliver Evans in the United States (1797). Evans also introduced high-pressure stationary engines at about the same time. The Stockton and Darlington Railway, the first public railroad, opened in 1825. The famous Liverpool and Manchester Railway trials from which the *Rocket* emerged victorious, took place in 1829. The first locomotive built in the United States was the *Tom Thumb* (1830).

Development of the Steamboat. At this time the Atlantic Ocean had been crossed several times by vessels equipped with steam, as well as sails, beginning with the *Savannah* in 1819. Following earlier experiments, a working steamboat had navigated the Saône River upstream in 1783. William Symington introduced steam to the Forth-Clyde area with the *Charlotte Dundas,* a paddlewheel tug in 1802, and the American inventor Robert Fulton sent the *Clermont* up the Hudson River in 1807, following earlier attempts in France. The first of the great Atlantic passenger steamers was Isambard K. Brunel's *Great Britain* (1843). The hull, which is still extant, was made of iron. Iron barges preceded by some years oceangoing iron vessels, such as the *Aaron*

A. T. & T. CO.

Telephone exchange, central office. Men and boys were used as telephone operators in the first exchanges.

Manby (1821) and the *Garry Owen* (1834), which in a storm first showed the superior strength of wrought-iron ribs and plates. The first armored vessels for naval use were not laid down until 1858. Beginning in 1839, when the first two steamers using the new principle were independently constructed, the screw began its gradual replacement of the paddlewheel. Brunel made the change in the *Great Britain*.

The early iron steamship of about 1840 was the product of many interlocking aspects of technological evolution. Mechanical advances had created the engines, pumps, stearing gear, and derrick, as well as the machine tools by which the machinery and hull were formed. Improvements in materials and techniques for working them made possible the forming, shaping, and assembling of the wrought-iron for the hull.

Machine Tools. The Industrial Revolution marked the transition from the use of timber to that of coal and iron. Iron, though it had the advantage of relative cheapness and ease of casting, was difficult to cut, drill, and shape. Wrought iron, the most commonly used material of the engineer, was prepared from pig by the "puddling" process invented by Henry Cort in 1784 and improved by Joseph Hall in about 1830. It was then rolled into bars, rods, rails, angles, and plates for actual use. The engineer worked on it with tools originating in the carpenter's and blacksmith's shop. Such shops changed their character when the steam engine and textile machinery made it necessary to machine large parts accurately.

The fundamental invention among machine tools was that of the screw-cutting lathe, which was pioneered by the Frenchman Jacques de Vaucanson (1745) and perfected at nearly the same time by Senot in France, David Wilkinson in the United States, and Henry Maudslay in England. Maudslay had worked for Joseph Bramah, inventor of the hydraulic press, an improved toilet, and a famous patent lock. Maudslay's workshop in turn was the training ground for some of the great British mechanics of the next generation—Richard Roberts, Joseph Whitworth, and James Nasmyth. All these men helped develop effective shapers, lathes, planers, and milling machines for facilitating machine-shop work and making it more accurate. This British tradition reached its zenith about 1840. Thereafter, leadership passed to the United States.

Specialized Production Machines. Another type of machine tool was the specialized production machine. The earliest examples of this type of machine are the bench machines used by clockmakers for cutting gear teeth. Apart from Bramah's shop, the most famous early example was the Portsmouth (England) blockmaking machinery designed by Marc Isambard Brunel and built by Maudslay (1801–1808). By this technique the making of three sizes of ship's blocks was reduced to a series of steps, each performed by a specialized semiautomatic machine. Some of the machines were capable of shaping several work pieces at once. Jigs and templates obviated the need for skill in the machine operators. The whole assembly was driven by steam.

Interchangeable Parts. Brunel's machinery used the principle of manufacture with interchangeable parts, which Thomas Jefferson had already described to Congress in 1785. In Paris, Jefferson had visited an inventive gunsmith named Le Blanc who used this idea in the manufacture of gun locks. In the United States, Eli Whitney set up a factory to make muskets upon this plan in 1798. Simeon North made weapons on this principle beginning in 1799, as did Samuel Colt from 1835. Colt's plant in Hartford, Conn., contained 1,400 machine tools. The interchangeable system was more successfully developed in the United States than elsewhere, and it was applied to the manufacture of rotary pumps, sewing machines, bicycles, and other machines.

Ironworking Machines. Development of circular saws, bandsaws, machine planes, and morticing machines for working timber on a factory scale was relatively light industry compared with the development of steam blowing engines, hot rolling stands, and huge hammers required for forging large masses of metal, such as the propeller shafts of ships. Nasmyth's invention of the steam drop hammer in 1839 was regarded as a triumph of such heavy engineering. Almost as massive machinery was later used in shipyards for cutting and bending ships' plates and drilling rivet holes.

Structural Uses of Iron. Other cast-iron bridges followed the bridge at Coalbrookdale, including Thomas Telford's bridge at Buildwas (1795) and Rowland Burdon's at Sunderland (1796). Telford also used cast-iron aqueducts for canals. The use of wrought iron for suspension bridges was first attempted in the United States. James Finley of Pennsylvania invented (1808) the modern type of suspension bridge, with the road suspended horizontally by rods, as in the 244-foot (75-meter) bridge across the Merrimac River. This bridge used normal chains. The chain-link construction was adopted for the Tweed Bridge (1820; 300 feet, or 90 meters) and the Menai Bridge (1826; 580 feet, or 175 meters). Wire cable construction was developed in France by the Seguins and was used in Joseph Chailey's 876-foot (292-meter) bridge at Fribourg in 1834.

Small iron beams and chains had long served to give tensile strength to masonry. Cast-iron pillars and beams were introduced about 1792 to make textile mills fireproof. Iron beams supported on pillars spanned the interior space between the walls, while the floors were completed by building shallow arches of bricks, sometimes hollow, between the beams. Many builders sought to make a flat floor reinforced by iron rods, but not until the introduction of Portland cement about 1855 was this type of construction possible. As the technique of rolling wrought iron bars improved, rolled sections replaced cast beams. However, cast iron was used increasingly in architecture in window and door frames, capitals, screens, and lamps.

Ceramics. Progress in modern ceramics began with the making of "soft-paste" porcelain (St. Cloud, 1693; Chantilly and Vincennes, 1738). The achievement of true hard porcelain was made by Johann F. Böttger at Meissen in 1713. The Sèvres hard porcelain came much later (1768). English potteries at Chelsea, Bow, and Worcester made only soft-paste ware. Later, bone ash was added to the material to make "bone china." The design of English china, except Wedgwood's, was much influenced by Continental ware. Josiah Wedgwood's potteries became famous for original kinds of ware of high quality and unusual design.

The Chemical Industry. The development of the chemical industry was closely linked with innovations in metallurgy and textiles. The large-scale manufacture of sulfuric acid began near London in 1736. It was extended by John Roebuck and Samuel Garbett in Birmingham in 1746 by the use of lead containers (in place of glass vessels) in which sulfur, and later pyrites, was burned. The perfected lead-chamber process was begun by Charles Tennant near Glasgow in 1803.

In the early 19th century chlorine was used as the starting chemical for bleaching powder. Its bleaching action had been discovered by the French chemist Claude Louis Berthollet in 1785. The French absorbed chlorine in a fluid ("eau de Javel"), whereas Tennant absorbed it in slaked lime to form a solid bleach. This chemical agent enormously accelerated the bleaching of cloth, especially linen, which formerly depended on a combination of buttermilk and sunlight.

At about this time many workers were attempting to produce soda (sodium carbonate) synthetically. This substance, which was essential as a textile detergent and as an ingredient of glass, was obtained mostly from the ashes of plants, including seaweed. The process that was ultimately successful was that of the Frenchman Nicolas Leblanc (1787). Use of the Leblanc process was started by James Muspratt in Liverpool in 1823 and by Tennant in Glasgow in 1825. The Leblanc process was of basic importance to the heavy chemical industry for about a century.

During this period there were relatively few changes in dyeing processes, which were little understood as yet. In France, P. J. Macquer introduced the dye Prussian blue, and in Scotland Charles MacIntosh made a good Turkey red. There was also an increase in the production of dyes and mordants, especially alum.

New chemical products were being obtained from coal. Coal tar was made by Lord Dundonald beginning in 1781, primarily for nautical use. Gas evolved from coal was used experimentally as an illuminant by J. P. Minkelers at Louvain in 1785 and by William Murdock at Redruth, Cornwall, in 1792. Mills were being lit by gas before 1805, and Frederic A. Winsor founded the Gas Light and Coke Company for the public supply of gas in 1812. The use of by-products of the gasworks, notably ammonia, did not develop quickly, but by 1819, MacIntosh was using by-product tar and ammonia, and thence derived the first solvent (naphtha) for rubber, which made possible the development of waterproof fabrics.

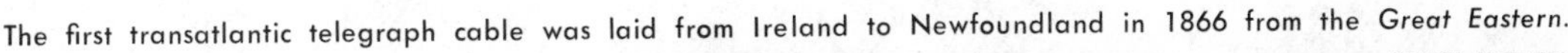

The first transatlantic telegraph cable was laid from Ireland to Newfoundland in 1866 from the *Great Eastern.*

CULVER PICTURES

Social Effects. The Industrial Revolution had already begun to affect the lives of the people of Britain. During the 18th century the population of England not only increased considerably but altered its distribution toward the north. New industries developed everywhere. Only expanding industry and trade permitted the growth of population to proceed unchecked. As in all countries where urbanization and industrialization has proceeded rapidly—the United States after the Civil War, Russia after 1922, China after 1945—the social and economic strains were intense. Moreover, Britain enjoyed no inflow of external capital. Capital and plants were accumulated out of profits. Mills, factories, and houses were built in large numbers, and much of the building was bad. No one knew or cared about the planning of new communities, the provision of public services, or the exercise of controls. Local government collapsed as houses swamped the fields.

There was total inexperience concerning new industrial hazards—the chlorine in bleaching powder works, the poisonous nature of the lead used in glazes or phosphorus in matches, and the emission of hydrochloric acid gas from the soda plants. New food adulterants or pigments, such as Paris green, were equally dangerous. There were also the dangers from heavy moving machinery and deep mines. The prevailing philosophy was the opposite of paternalistic. Reacting against the restrictive social and economic legislation of the previous period, the philosophy of the late-18th century was marked by the retreat of state activity and the complete freedom of commerce.

THE NINETEENTH CENTURY

Britain moved into a new phase of technological expansion when the long wars ended in 1815, but France was far behind and the rest of Europe was virtually untouched. In Britain and elsewhere the new technology was localized. In the United States it was in New England and Pennsylvania. In France it was in the northeast, and in the Rhineland it was in the north. By the time of the Great Exhibition of 1851, British technology still seemed supreme. Thereafter its eclipse was rapid. After some early unsuccessful attempts to resist export of its skilled workmen and engineers, Britain supported the growth of other countries by the export of machinery. The markets won by building up the industrial potential of other countries were tremendous. For example, Britain in 1871 exported over 500,000 tons of iron rails to the United States.

Railroads. Britain's technological feats were not always sources of profit. In general, Britain paid a high price for the early development of high technical standards. For example, British railroads were the most expensive in the world. However, the high initial costs were partially offset by low repair costs, whereas repairing and rebuilding cheap railroads, particularly in the United States, was very expensive. By 1840, Britain had 1,331 miles (2130 km) of track; France, 264 miles (422 km); and the United States, 2,816 (4506 km). By 1860, Britain had reached 10,400 miles (16,640 km) of track, which was nearly half its total eventual mileage, whereas in France, Germany, the Netherlands, and the United States the big growth of railroads occurred after 1860. In the United States there was a more than sixfold increase before 1900, and in Germany a nearly equal increase within the same period.

Iron Production. The first coke iron-smelting furnace in France was put in blast in 1785 and in Prussia in 1802. In Europe and in the United States, where lumber was abundant, it was only after 1850 that the amount of iron produced with coke became greater than the amount produced with charcoal. When coke was widely adopted outside Britain, it was with the latest improvements. The size of the furnace and the blast pressure had increased by 1800. More important was James B. Neilson's introduction of the hot blast, effective by 1832. Regenerative working—

THE BETTMANN ARCHIVE

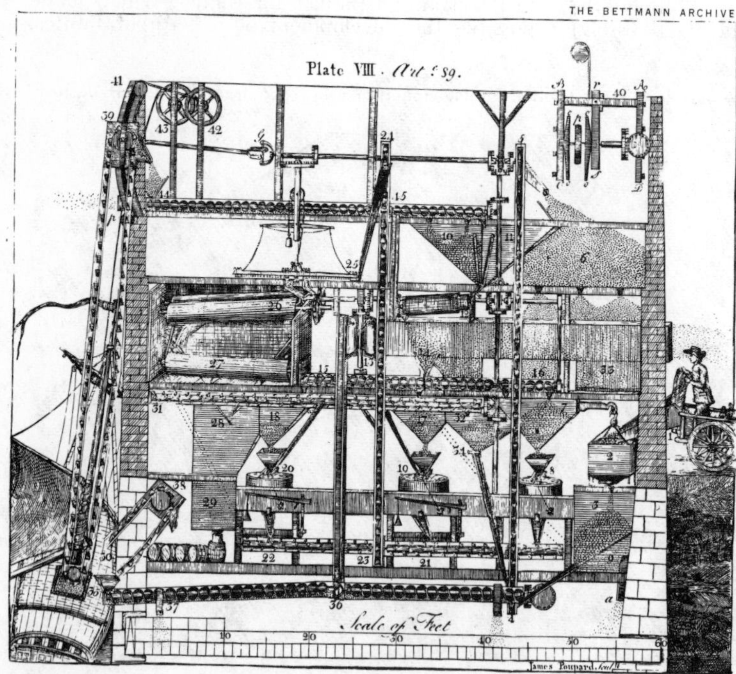

GRIST MILL designed by Oliver Evans in 1785 was first attempt at fully automatic factory. Screw conveyors and bucket elevators were used to connect various operations.

BROWN BROTHERS

Assembly line for Model "T" Fords, which were produced from 1908 to 1927 with no major changes in design.

the use of the hot gases of the furnace to heat the blast—was achieved in several centers in the early 1830's. It resulted in a threefold or greater increase in the economy of the operation and opened the possibility of using raw coal or anthracite without coking. In Britain the production of pig iron multiplied about twelve times between 1800 and 1840, when it exceeded 2 million tons.

Textiles. Inventions in the English textile industry were diffused much more rapidly than those of iron technology. The new spinning machines had reached France and Poland before 1780 and the United States, German, Hungary, and Russia before 1800. While the self-acting mule, about 1820, was a British development, other inventions, such as ring spinning, came from the United States and other textiles areas. However, the displacement of hand weaving by power looms proceeded more slowly and was incomplete by 1850. The Jacquard drawloom for figured weaving in silk was invented in France in 1801 but did not reach England until about 1820. In woolen manufacture the key machine was the Knowles power loom (1863), developed in America but widely adopted in Yorkshire. The first successful automatic loom, the Northrop, was also American (1895). Each weaver could mind 20 of these looms. By this time the lead in the manufacture of textile machinery of all kinds had decisively passed to the United States. Textile manufacture was also progressing in both France and Germany, even though in almost all textile areas antiquated equipment remained in use.

Telegraphy. In a new technology, such as electrical communication, the pattern of diffusion is very different. Electric telegraphy was developed in a number of centers, springing from the original discovery of electromagnetism by the Danish physicist Hans Christian Oersted in 1820. Two German scientists, the mathematician Johann Karl Gauss and the physicist Wilhelm Eduard Weber, the German-Russian Paul Schilling and Alsatian Karl von Steinheil first worked out the elementary principles. These principles were used in the development of the earliest commercial telegraph by William F. Cooke and the English physicist Sir Charles Wheatstone (1837). Although Cooke appreciated the immense value of the telegraph to the railway companies, the public and strategic significance of the telegraph came later.

Meanwhile, the American inventor Samuel Morse planned an alternative method, improved by Alfred Vail, that was used for a line constructed between Washington and Baltimore (1842–1844). Expansion of this line was rapid, and the Western Union Company was founded in 1856. A successful cross-channel cable linking England and France was completed in 1851. A transatlantic telegraph was first attempted in 1857, but success did not come until 1866. Morse not only developed the code that is named for him, but he was also the inventor of the essential relay.

Later technical improvement of the telegraph was effected by American, British, and European engineers. The range of signaling was increased, and the rate of working was speeded up. Greater economy in the cables was accomplished by duplex and multiplex working, and automatic apparatus was invented for sending and receiving messages. Ultimately, it was possible to signal directly from London to San Francisco.

Telephone and Phonograph. In the late-19th century development of telegraphy, several important contributions came from the American inventor Thomas Alva Edison, who had begun his career as a newsboy and telegraph operator. The telegraph stimulated other areas of invention. Its most obvious derivative was the telephone, though Alexander Graham Bell's original experiments were based upon Helmholtz's study of sound. Bell's system was patented in 1876, and three years later the first telephone exchange was established in London. Meanwhile, Edison had almost at once devised the carbon microphone as a substitute for Bell's electrodynamic speech transmitter, and his interest in sound led him almost

CULVER PICTURES

WRIGHT BROTHERS' BIPLANE, made for U. S Army, in test flight at Fort Myer, Va., in 1909.

simultaneously to the phonograph (1877). Development of telephone systems required even more sophisticated inventions, such as the introduction of the line-loading coil, envisaged already by the English physicist and electrical engineer Oliver Heaviside in 1887 and introduced by G. A. Campbell of the American Bell Telephone Company (1899).

By this time there was, at the international level, both a similarity and diversification in technological progress. The similarity may have arisen from common British origins, whereas diversification arose from local needs or opportunities. Technological opportunity prompted simultaneity of invention, as with Edison and the English physicist and chemist Sir Joseph Swan in the development of the incandescent electric lamp (1880–1881).

Steel. In the 1740's the Englishman Benjamin Huntsman developed a process in which steel was melted in a crucible and the slag skimmed off in order to produce a more homogeneous metal. Crucible steel was later replaced by bulk steel produced by the Bessemer converter and the open-hearth process. It was not until the late-18th century that the crucial importance of carbon in iron and steel began to be understood and not until the 1860's that Henry C. Sorby began metallographic studies of the two materials. Steel alloys effectively began with the tungsten-manganese tool steel of Robert F. Mushet (1868), although he had been anticipated by Franz Koller in Austria.

In 1847, William Kelly, a Kentucky iron founder, began experiments on the direct decarburization of plastic, rather than fluid, pig iron by an air blast. By 1851 he had developed a "converter" but took out no patent until 1857. By this time he had been overtaken by the English metallurgist Sir Henry Bessemer, who in 1856 had publicly described his converter in which the oxidation of the carbon in the iron brought the metal to a very high temperature.

At almost exactly the same time Frederick and Karl Wilhelm Siemens began the development of the open-hearth steelmaking process using regenerative heating for greater economy. This was also applied to the blast furnace from about 1860. Ultimately the open hearth was to prove an even better process than the converter, but the full exploitation of both new methods required many years so that the maximum production of wrought iron in most countries was only attained by about 1890. From then on its decline in favor of steel was rapid. The chief difficulty—as Bessemer's early licensees discovered to their chagrin—was that the new processes succeeded only with ores that contained no phosphorus. Britain could obtain such ores from Cumberland and northern Spain, while in the United States they were mined near Lake Superior. France and Germany had ready access only to phosphoric ores. As a result, steel production first increased rapidly in the United States and Britain, with the United States exceeding Britain's production by 1890. In comparison, Germany and France lagged behind, with Germany producing less than half Britain's output in 1879, and France only one third.

From that time on, however, the position was greatly altered by the extensive exploitation in Germany of the Englishman Sidney G. Thomas'

DIFFERENCE ENGINE, shown in part, is a computing machine that Charles Babbage began to build in 1823.

IBM

UNIVERSITY OF PENNSYLVANIA

ENIAC, the first all-electronic digital computer, was developed at the University of Pennsylvania by Dr. John Mauchly

invention of "basic" steel. A limestone lining and flux, applicable to either the converter or the open hearth, absorbed the phosphorus and formed a slag that could be sold as fertilizer. The phosphoric ores of Lorraine and Sweden were now suitable for modern steelmaking, and Germany went ahead with the development of larger and more efficient units of manufacture. By 1898, Germany made more steel than Britain, exported more, and sold it at a cheaper price. By 1903, Germany also made more pig iron.

Iron and Steel in Architecture. The original incentive for producing large quantities of steel arose not only from the high price of crucible steel but from the need for massive castings to make cannon. However, steel was of great value to machine constructors and to railway engineers. It also replaced wrought and cast iron in ship, bridge, and building construction.

Arches, domes, columns, tracery, window frames, ornamental wall panels, and even complete office blocks—some of which still survive—made of cast iron were commonly erected in the 1850's in London, New York, Glasgow, and other cities. This material was used freely in the new Houses of Parliament (1840–1857) and for the 485-foot (148-meter) spire of the Rouen Cathedral (1823–1876). Wrought iron was mainly employed in the form of joists built up from plate or, later, rolled directly into I-beams. The very large spans of railroad stations were obtained by forming wrought-iron trusses. The one, for example, at St. Pancras, London (1865), has a span of 240 feet (73 meters). The Eiffel Tower (985 feet, or 300 meters) was built from wrought iron as late as 1889, although at that time steel was chosen for the Forth Bridge. A few buildings used wrought-iron framing, the Menier chocolate factory at Noisel-sur-Marne, France, being a famous example.

Elevators. The rolling of steel joists began in the 1879's. Already the high price of city land had created the need for tall buildings, which had been made practicable by the introduction of mechanical elevators from about 1850 to 1860 by such engineers as the American Elisha Otis. It was essential to strengthen such buildings with metal if they were to exceed 15 floors. The Home Insurance Building (1883) in Chicago, though less high, used wrought and cast iron, as well as much steel. The Rand McNally Building in Chicago had the first completely steel frame. This form of construction extended to New York and many other cities of the United States. The resulting change in the character of city architecture is still taking place elsewhere.

Cement. After centuries of stagnation there was fresh progress in the manufacture of building cement at the end of the 18th century. The essential feature, which was found in Portland cement from about 1850, was the burning of a mixture of clay and chalk to form tricalcium silicate. These English manufacturing methods were adopted in France and Germany in 1853 and 1855, respectively. Later, in Germany, more exact chemical controls led to the still further strengthening of the product. A possibility for mass-concrete construction now existed. Improvements in kiln design and mining methods made the new material cheap as well as strong.

Since concrete, like masonry, is weak in tensile strength, iron tie bars were used to strengthen it. Embedded in the concrete, the bars would not rust, and the two materials expand and contract similarly. At the Paris Exposition of 1855 there was a reinforced concrete rowboat. A Frenchman, Joseph Monier, took out several patents for reinforcement and its applications. Two Germans, G. A. Wayss and Mathias Koenen, worked out the theory of reinforced concrete construction (1887).

The most dramatic ventures occurred in the United States, where experimental structures had been attempted by William E. Ward and Thaddeus Hyatt. The immigrant English architect Ernest L. Ransome used reinforced concrete for a number of large buildings beginning in 1888, among them the Leland Stanford Jr. Museum in Palo Alto, Calif. (1892). The first high-rise structure in reinforced concrete was the 16-floor Ingalls Building in Cincinnati (210 feet, or 64 meters), which was built in 1902–1903.

In bridge building the full aesthetic and structural potentialities of reinforced concrete were first realized in the 1930's. Many early concrete structures resemble masonry bridges in finish and decoration—for example, the Pont de la Tournelle near Notre Dame in Paris. François Hennebique, who as early as 1893 had built a concrete girder bridge, constructed in the Pont de Châtellerault in 1898 the first large concrete arch (172 feet, or 52 meters). The Sando Bridge in Sweden (1938–1943) attained a span of 866 feet (264 meters).

Water. While the most dramatic use of hydraulic resources, through the creation of dams and other plants, is the generation of electric power, other industrial and human uses of water are of wide significance and pose greater problems. Though the percentage of the world's available energy coming from water is small, large quantities of water are required by metallurgical and other manufacturing industries, mainly for cooling. Large cities require huge volumes of tap water. Sewage disposal, even after purification, imposes heavy demands on the water of rivers and lakes. All these problems of supply and disposal were tackled by civil engineers in the late-19th century, and many of their works are still functioning. Before 1900 the importance of unpolluted drinking water had been recognized, and major outbreaks of cholera in Western cities became rare or nonexistent.

Farming. The growth of population, largely in industrial cities, forced great changes in food technology. In advanced countries the production of food per farm worker increased tremendously after 1850 through use of agricultural machinery, fertilizers, improvement of crops and animals through breeding, and control of predators.

Machinery. Machinery came to the farm first. The first threshers were working soon after 1800. All-metal and multiple-share plows followed along with the seed drill. Patrick Bell developed the first effective reaper (1826), but Cyrus McCormick's reaper of 1831 was far better known and was widely used on the prairies. From about 1850 the steam engine began to appear in the countryside, and after 1900 the internal-combustion engine was also present.

FIRST NUCLEAR REACTOR used for generation of electricity for civilian needs, Shippingport, Pa., 1957.

WESTINGHOUSE ELECTRIC CORPORATION

New Crops. In other areas of the world European enterprise created new monocultures: coffee in Brazil and Kenya; tea in northern India and Ceylon (after the earlier failure of coffee there); cocoa, groundnuts, and other oil plants in West Africa; rubber in Malay; and copra in Polynesia.

Food Industries. By the end of the 19th century the manufacture of foodstuffs gave rise to important industries, such as the factory milling of grain, meatpacking and preservation, sugar refining, and the preparation of edible fats. Railways and steamships provided the means of transporting these enormous quantities of food over great distances.

Special techniques of preservation were needed to supplement ancient methods of dehydration. First came canning, which arose from the original methods of the Frenchman Nicolas Appert and the Englishman Peter Durand. Canning became a factory process well before 1850. Shipments of refrigerated meat to Britain, either frozen or chilled, were made from both Argentina and Australia starting about 1877. Ships were specially fitted out for the purpose. Factory dehydrated foods, which were used very early for military purposes in both the American Civil and the Boer wars, did not come into general use until much later.

Science and Technology. Before 1900 the inception and much of the development of most of the new technologies was empirical. The role of the individual inventor and entrepreneur was a critical one. However, by 1900 the scope of pure science had widened. In the 20th century the effects of applied science on technology have been decisive. Scientific knowledge has stimulated technical invention. For example, Marconi's invention of radiotelegraphy was suggested by laboratory experiments on electromagnetic waves. Scientific knowledge permits accurate design studies to be made, and it makes possible the use of instrumentation for the control of manufacturing processes. Of these three effects, the first two were already of limited value in the 19th century.

Electricity. Virtually every branch of electrical engineering developed from scientific discoveries. For a few years after 1830 it was hoped that the chemical energy of batteries, which could be used for driving electric motors, would provide cheap and convenient power. When this hope was frustrated, half a century elapsed before pioneers like the English engineer S. Z. Ferranti, the American engineer George Westinghouse, and the American inventor Thomas Alva Edison realized that the great merit of electricity was in its ease of distribution for use at many distant points. From about 1887, the modern pattern of high-voltage power lines radiating from large central generating stations began to take shape. The Niagara Falls hydroelectric scheme was begun in 1893. By this time the design of generators and motors for either direct or alternating current had progressed considerably. From about this time electric motors were applied to traction—streetcars and urban railways—elevators, and machine tools.

Much earlier the discovery of the arc lamp, made possible by the battery, suggested specialized applications in electric lighting—lighthouses, theaters, street lights. Also, the problems of the arc lamp promoted the search for an alternative lamp appropriate to domestic use. At this time homes were still lighted by improved oil lamps

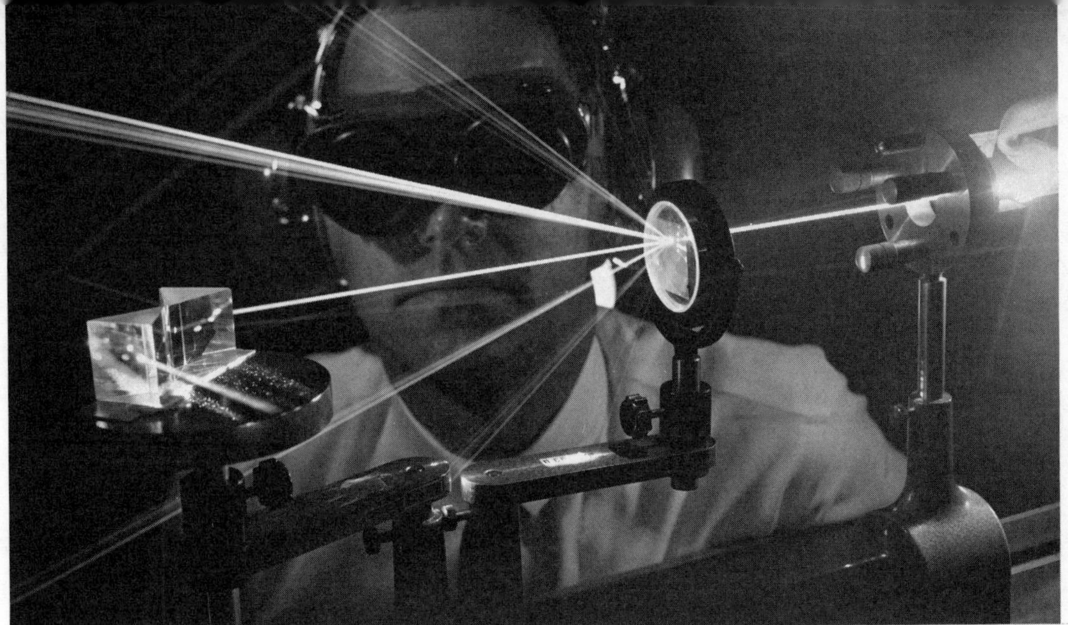
HUGHES AIRCRAFT COMPANY

Argon ion laser may be used for communications for future space missions and for carrying television signals.

and naked gas flames, as well as by candles. Both the English physicist and chemist Sir Joseph Swan and Edison were led to the invention of the incandescent electric filament lamp in an exhausted (vacuum) bulb about 1878. The perfection of this device occupied many years and ultimately led to the distinct innovation of the vacuum tube—the Fleming diode in 1904.

Apart from telegraphy, the other principal early use of electricity was for plating metals. Later came such electrolytic processes as those yielding copper (Elkington, 1865), sodium (Castner, 1888; Castner-Kellner, 1894), and nickel (Thompson, 1893). Electrolysis made aluminum, which had been an expensive curiosity of chemists, the most important of the new metals. However, the Hall-Héroult process (1886), by which aluminum is produced, consumes up to 20 megawatt hours of electricity for each ton of aluminum produced.

Photography. Scientific interest in photochemical effects, particularly the darkening of silver chloride on exposure to light, led to the discovery of photography as a means of obtaining permanent record. The experiments of the Frenchmen Joseph N. Niepce and Louis J. M. Daguerre (1826–1837) and the English inventor William H. F. Talbot (1835) and others led to the first widely practical glass-plate "collodion" process of F. Scott Archer (1851). This technique was supplanted in the 1870's by the use of a gelatin emulsion. Film came into use in 1889, a year after the introduction of the Eastman Kodak.

The production of seemingly moving images had already begun, but with the introduction of film, true cinematography became possible. Although E. J. Marey had tried it with sensitized paper in 1887, commercial cinematography was initiated by the Lumière brothers in 1895. The addition of electronic techniques to film took about 20 years, and the first "talkie," *The Jazz Singer*, was made in 1927.

Organic Chemicals. Another great area of technology deriving from science in the 19th century is the organic chemical industry, which was initiated by the accidental discovery of the dye mauve by the English chemist Sir William Henry Perkin in 1856. After this discovery intense research was devoted to the synthesis of new dyestuffs, mostly from coal tar derivatives. This research was facilitated by increased knowledge of the structure of complex molecules. Success in this research and its exploitation created the powerful German chemical industry and made obsolete the use of vegetable dyes, such as madder and indigo. Many other types of chemicals, particularly pharmaceuticals, were later obtained from coal tar.

Internal Combustion Engine. The establishment of the new science of thermodynamics in the 1850's taught engineers how to think correctly about the conversion of heat from fuel into mechanical energy. Such thinking was particularly important for the development of the internal-combustion engine. The first workable internal-combustion engine was developed by the Belgian-French inventor Jean Joseph Étienne Lenoir in 1859. Lenoir used this engine to power an automobile and a boat. The German inventor Nikolaus August Otto developed the first internal-combustion engine using the 4-stroke cycle. It was this type of engine that made possible the development of the automobile and the airplane. Gottlieb Daimler, who began as Otto's assistant, developed a small, relatively fast-running engine that burned gasoline. This engine contained the first carburetor. The German inventor Rudolf Diesel developed the diesel engine during the 1890's. This engine could use petroleum fractions heavier than gasoline.

In another direction the search for lightness and thermodynamic efficiency led the British engineer Sir Charles Algernon Parsons to the successful development of the marine steam turbine in 1884. Subsequently the diesel engine and the turbine replaced the reciprocating steam engine, and the turbine has almost entirely taken over electric power generation.

THE TWENTIETH CENTURY

Although some dramatic phenomena of contemporary technology, such as aerial bombardment and space travel, were already envisioned in 1900, the detailed changes that have occurred within living memory, and their multiple effects, were unimaginable then. There has been no equal revolution in technology since the beginning of city life. The basic factor is obviously the great quantity of mechanical energy available to advanced societies, derived not only from water, coal, and oil but also from natural gas and nuclear reactions. The civil exploitation of nuclear power has proceeded more slowly than had been predicted, yet its ultimate predominance seems certain. Power is not only available for transport, manufacture, and scientific research but is diffused into the dozen or more small electric motors found in many homes.

The earliest machines for mass consumption—the bicycle, sewing machine, and typewriter—were late-19th century inventions. In advanced societies automobiles, color television, and various automatic machines take their place. Similarly, in offices, the manual typewriter and adding machine have made room for complex devices such as electrostatic copiers and many types of computers.

This is one major aspect of the electronics revolution, which in one generation has achieved the greatest change in the recording and ciphering activities of man since the Babylonians began to bake clay tablets. Though office routine and accountancy had been increasingly mechanized since at least 1880, it had been affected by no really new idea since the introduction of double-entry bookkeeping in the late Middle Ages. Electronic information systems are not only applicable to personal and business affairs but can equally be employed to control manufacturing processes.

The principle of automated manufacture is not new. It was used in the Jacquard loom, whose punched cards were a "memory" telling the machine how to form a pattern. The punched tape of a Wheatstone telegraph transmitter, the pins on the drum of a music box, and the grooves on Edison's phonograph were all crude mechanical memories. The great virtue of modern systems is that they can store very complex instructions and can also be made self-correcting.

Electronic Communications. The older aspect of the electronics revolution is concerned not with processing and storing information but with communicating it. The origins of modern communications technology—the radio of the Italian electrical engineer Guglielmo Marconi in 1896—coincided very closely in time with the beginnings of modern atomic physics, which was to transform Marconi's invention in a way he could never have imagined. Radio communication began and was developed commercially for over a decade without any electronic sophistication. It was achieved with enormous wire coils and glass plates, oil engines, alternators, sparks, and arcs, together with a multitude of ingenious mechanical gadgets. World War I accelerated the shift to electron tubes and circuitry, diverging in the 1920's into the cathode-ray tube that made television possible. After World War II, which stimulated the rapid development of still more advanced techniques for radar and communications purposes, the development of the transistor permitted a complexity of electronic circuitry hitherto impractical with electron tubes.

Printing. Developments using both electronics and photography have begun to supplant the mechanical printing techniques that had evolved in slow succession since about 1450. Gutenberg's invention was a triumph of mass production, which nevertheless created its own craftsmanship. The industrialization of printing in the early 19th century followed by the mechanization of typesetting with the Linotype machine (1884) and its successors rendered craftsmanship obsolete. These developments, together with the introduction of wood-pulp paper, made possible the enormous proliferation of printed matter that characterized the 20th century.

Airplanes. The internal-combustion engine has effected two revolutions in transportation—the urban and the aerial. By about 1900 the power-to-weight ratio of this type of engine was sufficient to make powered flight possible. Earlier experiments in heavier-than-air flying inevitably were confined to gliding, although the American astronomer and physicist Samuel Langley achieved some success with model steam airplanes as early as 1896. However, these machines could not carry a pilot. The first successful powered flight was made by the American inventor Orville Wright in 1903. Between 1903 and 1910 many improvements were made in the design of airplanes. Thousands of military planes were built in World War I, the largest ones capable of carrying heavy loads. In 1919 two members of the Royal Air Force, John Alcock and Arthur Whitten Brown, crossed the Atlantic in the first nonstop flight from Newfoundland to Ireland. By 1930 all-metal construction was becoming established. Commercial air transport was beginning. The first jet passenger service was inaugurated in 1952.

Materials. The chemical products of the 19th and early 20th centuries were mainly produced from natural substances, such as alcohol, rubber, or coal. Since the mid-20th century, much of the chemical industry has been based on the production of plastics and other polymers from petroleum and natural gas. Many other types of new materials have been introduced, including special ceramics, such as cermets, and fiber-reinforced materials.

EFFECTS OF TECHNOLOGY

If man's immediate needs for energy and food become the only determinant of the surface character and atmosphere of this planet, then it is clear that "nature" as it has been known will cease to exist. This is not to say that all birds and predators will necessarily vanish, or that the whole surface of the globe will become as devastated as those regions completely dominated by technological priorities in the 19th century. But the total application of technology seems incompatible with the maintenance of natural ecosystems. It is comparable to a worldwide and dramatic change of climate. No one can foresee its consequences.

A. Rupert Hall
Imperial College of Science and Technology
London, England

Bibliography

Buchanan, Robert A., *Technology and Social Progress* (New York 1965).

Colborn, Robert, ed., *Modern Science and Technology* (New York 1965).

Derry, T. K., and Williams, Trevor, I., *A Short History of Technology* (New York 1961).

Klemm, Friedrich, *History of Western Technology* (Cambridge, Mass., 1964).

Kranzberg, Melvin, and Pursell, Carroll W., Jr., *Technology in Western Civilization* (New York 1967).

Singer, Charles, and others, eds., *A History of Technology* (New York 1958).

Walker, Charles, *Modern Technology and Civilization* (New York 1962).

White, Lynn R., *Medieval Technology and Social Change* (New York 1962).

TECTONOPHYSICS, tek-ton'ə-fiz-iks, is the branch of geology that applies concepts of physics, particularly mechanics and thermodynamics, to tectonic studies. Tectonics is concerned with the larger structures of the earth's surface and crust—continents, ocean basins, mountain ranges, plains, and plateaus—and with problems of their origin and relationships. Because these features are produced by forces that deform the crust, tectonophysics is also concerned with the ongoing stresses and fractures that cause earthquakes.

Work in tectonophysics now is largely concerned with the geological evidence that suggests the mid-ocean underwater ridges are rifting apart and that ocean floors are spreading away from the ridges. This discovery has renewed scientific interest in the theory of continental drift. The fact that earthquakes occur primarily in narrow belts also suggests that large plates of the earth's crust are moving horizontally relative to one another.

Thus oceanic ridges of volcanoes are located where the crustal plates drift apart, as in Iceland. Island-arc mountain belts, as in Japan, form where the plates override, and major fractures, such as California's San Andreas fault, form at the slipping edges of the plates. The apparent rates of movement are only an inch or so per year, but this amounts to hundreds of miles over periods of geological time.

The major problem of tectonophysics is to determine how such movements take place. What are the forces involved, and how are they generated? On what kind of surface does the bottom of the earth's crust move? Tectonophysicists work out complex mathematical models of the convection patterns in very viscous rock material that may exist at depths of about 100 miles (160 km), and they experiment with the strength of rocks subjected to the high temperatures and pressures of this region. They also consider why some faults slip continuously, while the sides of other faults lock together until the accumulating strains are released in catastrophic earthquakes. Thus tectonophysics offers an approach to understanding earthquakes and perhaps partially controlling the forces involved.

ROBERT W. DECKER, *Dartmouth College*

TECTORIAL MEMBRANE, tek-tôr'ē-əl, a thick jellylike membrane in the inner ear. It plays an important role in hearing. See EAR—*Structure of the Human Ear;* HEARING.

TECUMSEH, tə-kum'sə (1768?–1813), American Indian chief, who sought to organize a confederacy of Midwestern tribes against the encroaching whites. A Shawnee, he was born near the Mad River in Ohio. He fought the Americans as a young man, but achieved general fame only after 1805. In that year his brother Tenskwatawa, known as "The Prophet," began to preach an Indian religious revival at Greenville, Ohio. Tecumseh made use of this movement in an attempt to create an Indian political alliance.

In 1808 the brothers moved their village to the Tippecanoe River in Indiana. From there Tecumseh traveled widely, urging resistance to the Americans. He argued that because the land belonged to the Indians in common no one tribe could legally make cessions to the U. S. government. From 1808 the brothers received advice and supplies from the British in Upper Canada.

SMITHSONIAN INSTITUTION

Tecumseh, about 1808, from a copy of a sketch.

Hopes for an effective confederacy were soon dashed, however. While Tecumseh was traveling to recruit southern tribes, Indians led by the Prophet clashed with troops commanded by Gen. William Henry Harrison at the Battle of Tippecanoe on Nov. 7, 1811, and the forces of the confederacy were dispersed.

In the War of 1812, Tecumseh fought for the British on the Detroit frontier, and recruited Indians for the British cause. He was killed at the Battle of the Thames in Upper Canada on Oct. 5, 1813.

REGINALD HORSMAN
University of Wisconsin, Milwaukee

Further Reading: Tucker, Glenn, *Tecumseh: Vision of Glory* (Indianapolis 1956).

TEDDER, Arthur William (1890–1967), British air marshal, who was deputy supreme commander to Gen. Dwight D. Eisenhower in World War II. He was born in Glenguin, Scotland, on July 11, 1890, and was educated at the University of Cambridge. He fought in World War I with the Royal Flying Corps. Between wars he became a strong champion of a separate air force.

Tedder became commander of the Royal Air Force for the Middle East in 1940. He subsequently headed the Mediterranean Air Command, under Eisenhower. When Eisenhower was named supreme commander, Tedder accompanied him to Britain to plan the invasion of Europe. Tedder represented Eisenhower in Moscow early in 1945 to coordinate the approaching juncture of Russian and Allied armies. As Eisenhower's deputy, he signed the documents in the second German surrender ceremony staged for the benefit of the Russians in Berlin.

Tedder was promoted to air marshal in 1945 and created 1st Baron Tedder of Glenguin in 1946. In the postwar years he served as air chief and chairman of the joint staff, a position analogous to that of the chairman of the U. S. Joint Chiefs of Staff. Tedder died at Banstead, Surrey, on June 3, 1967.

CHARLES B. MACDONALD
Author of "The Mighty Endeavor"

TEENAGERS. See ADOLESCENCE and Index entry *Adolescence.*

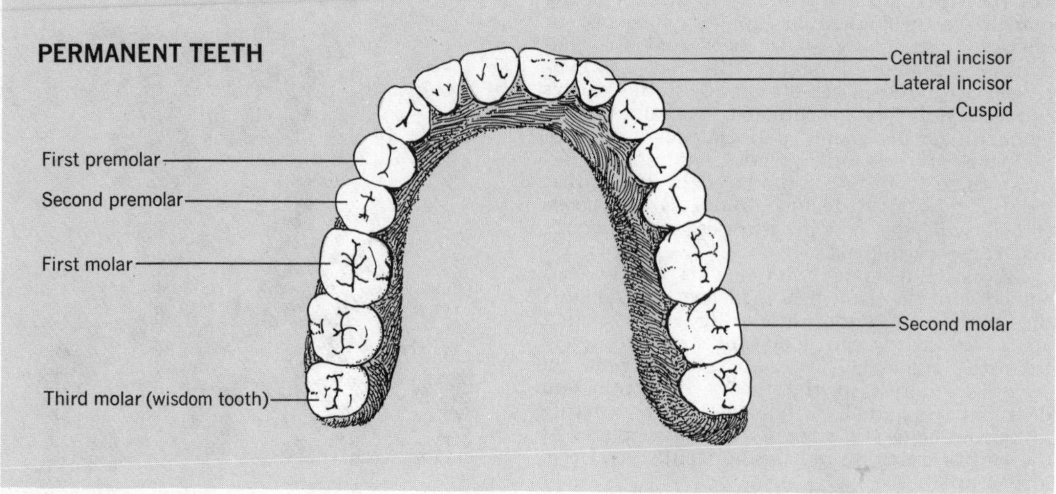

TEETH are the highly specialized, hardened structures in the jaws of man and most other vertebrate animals. Teeth are used primarily for biting, tearing, crushing, and grinding food. In some animals they are used also for defense and capturing prey. Elephants and wild boars, for example, use their tusks as weapons of defense, and some snakes have hollow fangs through which they inject venom into their attackers or prey. In man, the teeth play an important role in speech.

HUMAN TEETH

During his lifetime, man has two sets of teeth. The first set is called the *primary dentition,* and it consists of 20 teeth, 10 in each jaw. In either half of each jaw there are 2 primary incisors, 1 cuspid, and 2 molars. This arrangement is expressed by the dental formula $\frac{\text{I2 C1 M2}}{\text{I2 C1 M2}}$.

The second set of teeth, known as the *permanent dentition,* consists of 32 teeth, 16 in each jaw. In one half of each jaw there are 2 permanent incisors, 1 cuspid, 2 premolars, and 3 molars. The dental formula for the permanent dentition is $\frac{\text{I2 C1 P2 M3}}{\text{I2 C1 P2 M3}}$. The permanent teeth are generally larger and yellower than the primary teeth.

The permanent teeth that replace similar primary teeth, such as the incisors, are known as *succedaneous* teeth. Those that have no similar predecessors are called *accessional* teeth.

Types of Teeth. Human teeth generally are divided into two portions: an upper part, or *crown,* and a lower part, or *root.* Man has four different types of teeth, and they vary in the size and shape of the crown and the number of roots.

Incisors. Incisor teeth have wide flattened crowns and, as in other mammals, are used primarily for biting and grasping. The incisors in the upper jaw are larger than those in the lower jaw, and the central, or middle, incisors of the upper jaw are larger than the lateral, or side, ones. Each incisor has a single root, and all primary incisors are replaced by permanent ones.

Cuspids. The four cuspids have somewhat fang-shaped crowns and are sometimes called *canine teeth.* Like the incisors, they are used for biting and grasping. Each cuspid has a single root, and each primary cuspid is replaced by a permanent cuspid.

Premolars. The premolars are wider than the incisors or cuspids and are used for grinding and crushing. They are also known as *bicuspids* because the crown of each one generally has two tapered projections called *cusps.* Sometimes the second premolar in the lower jaw has a small third cusp. The number of roots varies among the premolars. The first premolar in the upper jaw usually has two roots but may have only one. The second upper premolar usually has one root but may have two. The lower premolars usually have only one root. The premolars are found only in the permanent dentition and replace the two molars of the primary dentition.

Molars. The molars are the largest teeth and, like the premolars, are used for grinding and crushing. The first molars are the largest ones. The third molars, the *wisdom teeth,* are the smallest ones. The crown of a molar may be rectangular, square, or trapezoidal (4-sided with only two parallel sides). The upper molars have four cusps, the lower ones have five. Upper molars have three roots, and the lower ones have two.

Parts of a Tooth. The four basic parts of a tooth are the enamel, dentin (or dentine), cementum, and pulp. Other tissues attach each tooth to the surrounding gum and underlying bone.

Enamel. Enamel, the hardest substance in the body, covers the entire crown and is thickest at the tips of the cusps. It contains 96% inorganic matter, mostly calcium phosphate, and 4% organic matter and water. Structurally, it consists of elongated columns, called *rods* or *prisms,* that extend outward at right angles from the underlying dentin. Between the prisms is *interprismatic* substance, which acts as a cementing material.

Dentin. Dentin is a hard, yellowish material that forms the bulk of the tooth and provides support and nourishment to the enamel and cementum. Dentin is a highly sensitive tissue but has not been found to contain any nerves. Its sensitivity may be due to an enzyme system within the tissue.

Dentin contains 70% inorganic matter and 30% organic matter and water. Structurally, it is made up of extensions of the cell bodies of special cells (odontoblasts) that line the pulp cavity.

Cementum. Cementum is the thin covering of the roots. It consists of about 45% inorganic matter and 55% organic matter and is darker yellow than the dentin. Its primary function is to provide attachment for tissues surrounding the tooth.

Pulp. The dental pulp occupies the central cavity of the tooth, and its function is to provide nourishment for the enamel, dentin, and cementum. It is made up of connective tissue cells and fibers, intercellular substances, arteries, veins, lymphatic vessels, and nerves. The blood and lymphatic vessels and nerves enter and leave the tooth through a small opening at the root tip. These openings are called *apical foramina*. Because primary teeth have fewer nerves than permanent teeth, they are not so sensitive to drilling.

The cellular content of the pulp of young primary teeth is relatively high while the fiber content is low. As the teeth grow older the cells decrease in number and the fiber content increases.

Attachment Tissues. Each tooth is attached to its bony socket, or *alveolus*, by a *periodontal ligament*. This ligament is composed largely of connective tissue fibers that are embedded at one end in the tooth cementum and at the other end in the wall of the tooth socket, in the cementum of the adjacent tooth, or in the connective tissue core of the gum. The *alveolar process* is the part of the jawbone that supports the tooth socket. It develops in response to tooth growth and use. It gradually disappears when a tooth is removed. The alveolar process consists of two parts. One is a thin layer of compact dense bone that lines the alveolus and to which the periodontal ligament is attached. The second part is a spongy type of bone that underlies the compact bone.

The *gum*, or *gingiva*, is the soft pinkish tissue that surrounds each tooth. *Attached gingiva* is the tissue that is attached to the tooth or bone. *Free gingiva* is the tissue that surrounds the neck of the tooth but is separated from it by a narrow furrow called the *gingival sulcus*. The triangular portions of gingiva that lie between the teeth are known as the *interdental papillae*. Adjacent to the attached gingiva is a soft darker colored tissue called the *alveolar mucosa*.

Growth and Development. Approximately five weeks after conception, certain cells lining the embryo's oral cavity begin to multiply rapidly and form a ridge, the *dental lamina*, along the free margin of each jaw. One week later, 10 swellings appear on each dental lamina. These swellings, called *buds*, represent the precursors of the 10 primary teeth. The cells in these buds multiply and become differentiated into the cells that will give rise to the different tooth tissues. Calcification of the primary teeth begins between the fourth and sixth month of development and continues until root growth is complete. Once the crowns of the teeth are developed, they move toward the oral cavity until their crowns pierce the gum.

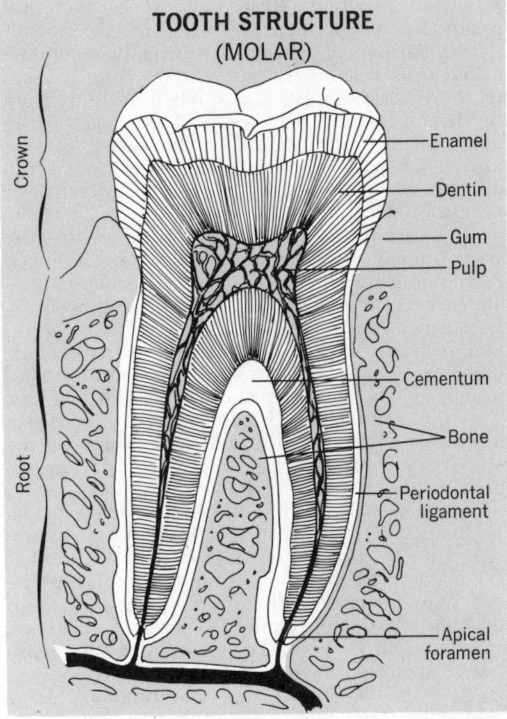

Succedaneous permanent teeth are formed in a way similar to that of the primary teeth, developing from buds on the dental lamina. Accessional permanent teeth, the three molars, are formed by the dental lamina growing beyond the primary second molars.

The first primary tooth emerges, or erupts, when the infant is about six months old. The primary dentition is usually completed by the age of two and lasts in its entirety until about the age of six. The first permanent tooth usually erupts when the child is six or seven. Until the age of 12 he has a mixture of both primary and permanent teeth. This combination is called

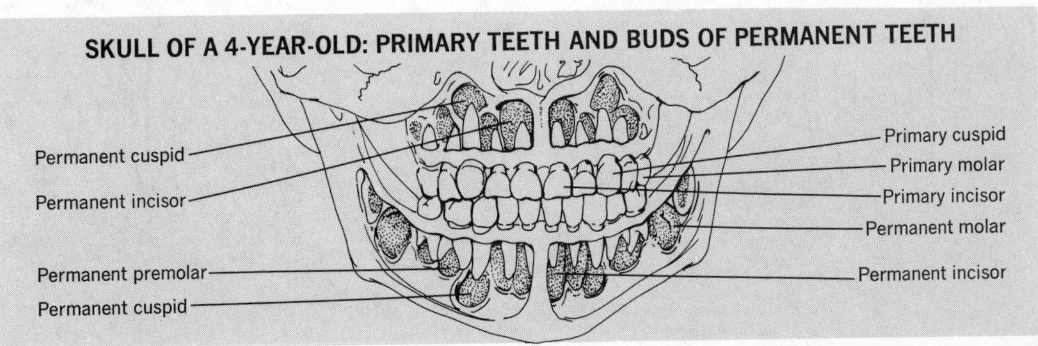

the *mixed dentition.* By the age of 12, the child usually has 28 permanent teeth. By the age of 21, his permanent dentition is usually complete.

There is much variability in the time it takes for the teeth to erupt, and small deviations from the average timetable are not serious. More important are deviations in the order, or sequence, of tooth eruption. Such deviations often indicate future problems in the alignment, or occlusion, of the teeth.

The first primary teeth to appear are usually the two lower central incisors. They are followed by the four upper incisors and the two lateral ones. Next, the first molars erupt, followed by the cuspids and second molars. The first permanent teeth to appear are often the first molars, followed by the incisors, the first and second premolars, the cuspids, and the second molars. The third molars, or wisdom teeth, erupt last. Sometimes, there is not sufficient room in the jaws for the third molars to erupt and they remain beneath the alveolar bone.

Effects of Aging. Like other parts of the body, the teeth are affected by aging. As a person ages, the teeth erupt further so that the crowns of the teeth become longer and portions of the root may become visible above the surface of the gum. Also, the enamel covering the chewing and biting surfaces of the crowns becomes worn down, and the underlying dentin may be exposed. As the dentin ages, additional layers form within the tooth, decreasing the space occupied by the pulp. The pulp also undergoes changes, becoming more fibrous. Somtimes calcified masses, called *pulp stones,* develop. These stones may press on nerves or blood vessels, causing pain and reducing the flow of blood to the tissues of the tooth.

Another effect of aging is the receding of the gum, so that the spaces between the teeth are no longer filled with the interdental papillae. The alveolar bone also recedes, and the teeth may become loose. Recession of the alveolar bone is greatly increased if a tooth is lost or removed.

Diseases and Disorders. Among the major diseases and disorders of the teeth and their supporting tissues are decay of the enamel and dentin, inflammation and destruction of the gums, and malocclusion, or faulty tooth alignment.

Dental Decay. Dental decay, or dental caries, results from a series of events. First, a yellowish white material, called *dental plaque,* forms on the teeth. Next, bacteria become enmeshed in the plaque and convert fermentable carbohydrates, such as sugars, into acids. These acids destroy the enamel and dentin by removing the minerals, mostly calcium and phosphorus, from them. The destroyed area is called a *cavity.*

Dental decay should be treated before it spreads and affects the entire tooth. The dentist, after removing the decayed area, fills the cavity with silver amalgam or other filling materials. The best defense against dental decay is prevention. Fluorides in the drinking water and in toothpaste are effective in reducing dental cavities, and proper toothbrushing and use of dental floss to remove dental plaque is essential. Reducing the intake of sweets is another preventive measure.

Periodontal Disease. Diseases of the gums and other supporting tissues progress slowly and result often from irritation of the tissues. Pyorrhea, or advanced gum disorder, is a major cause of tooth loss in adults.

Periodontal disease most often results from the accumulation of dental plaque on the teeth. Unless dental plaque is removed, it hardens into a calcified material known as *dental tartar,* which causes gum irritation. Dental tartar can be removed only by a dentist or oral hygienist.

Malocclusion. An improper alignment of the teeth may be inherited. Other factors that may cause malocclusion are loss of teeth and direct pressure on the teeth, which may occur in a child who sucks his thumb. In many cases it is best to treat a malocclusion early. Treatment usually entails the use of braces or other appliances.

Others. The size, shape, number, and structure of the teeth may be affected by a variety

PROGRESS OF TOOTH DECAY: *Left:* the enamel of the tooth's crown has been penetrated. *Middle:* The soft dentin underlying the enamel has been attacked, and the decay has spread to the adjoining tooth. *Right:* the pulp has been killed, and an abscess has formed at the root base. Pulp of next tooth is also attacked.

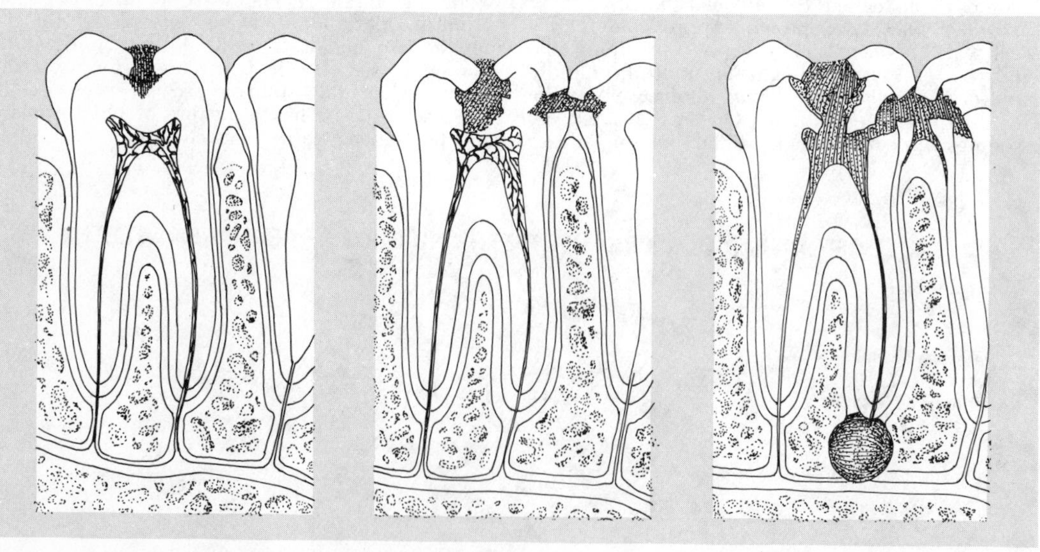

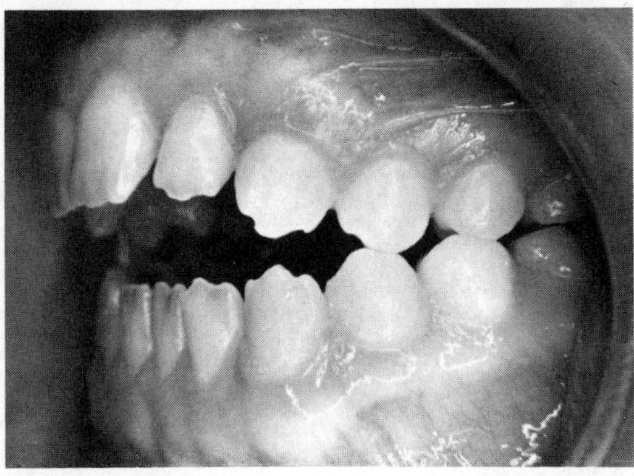

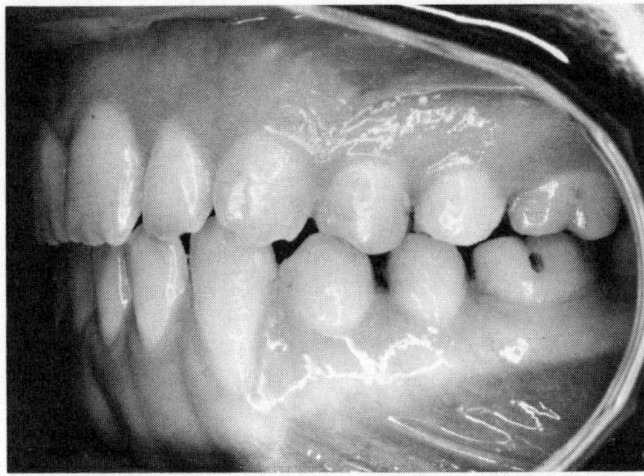

AMERICAN ASSOCIATION OF ORTHODONTICS

MALOCCLUSION, or improper bite, can usually be corrected through the wearing of braces and other types of appliances. The photo on the right was taken after the patient had undergone orthodontic treatment.

of diseases and disorders. Genetic factors as well as factors affecting the development of the embryo may cause the development of too many or too few teeth. Unusual molar and incisor shapes may be associated with congenital syphilis. A deficiency of vitamin D may result in abnormal enamel development. Fluorosis is a mottling of the enamel that results from the ingestion of unusually large amounts of fluorides. Although the teeth are somewhat brittle, they are more resistant to decay.

TEETH IN OTHER ANIMALS

There are two basic types of vertebrate teeth: ectodermal teeth and true teeth. The only major group of vertebrates that lack teeth are the birds, although some fossil birds did have them.

Ectodermal Teeth. These teeth are in no way homologous with true teeth. Each tooth is derived from the epidermis and is simply a horny hardened outgrowth of the skin. The only vertebrates that have ectodermal teeth are the cyclostomes (lampreys and hagfishes), the larvae (tadpoles) of frogs and toads, and the adult platypus.

True Teeth. Enamel, cementum, and dentin are not present in all true teeth. Sharks, rays, and skates have only dentin. Mammals, reptiles, amphibians, and bony fishes have both enamel and dentin. Mammals generally are the only living animals that have cementum, although some fossil reptiles also had it. The cementum normally covers the roots, but in horses and donkeys it is located between the structural folds of the crown enamel.

Only mammals have a distinguishable pulp cavity, crown, and root. The root may be open-ended or closed. Teeth with open-ended roots continue to grow throughout the lifetime of the animal and are never completely worn down. Such roots are found in rodent incisors, boar and elephant tusks, and rabbit incisors. Teeth with closed roots do not grow continuously. All human teeth have closed roots.

Animals whose teeth are similar in size, shape, and function are said to be *homodonts*. Animals with different types of teeth are said to be *heterodonts*. Heterodonty is often described in dental formulas. The dental formula for a dog, for example, is $\frac{\text{I3 C1 P4 M2}}{\text{I3 C1 P4 M3}}$. A cat's dental formula is $\frac{\text{I3 C1 P3 M1}}{\text{I3 C1 P2 M1}}$. The dental formula for the house rat and house mouse is $\frac{\text{I1 C0 P0 M3}}{\text{I1 C0 P0 M3}}$. These animals have no cuspids or premolars.

Humans, dogs, and the domestic cat have two sets of teeth during their lifetime, and are said to be *diphyodonts*. Mice and rats have a single set of teeth, and are said to be *monophyodonts*. Reptiles, amphibians, and fishes generally have many sets of teeth and are said to be *polyphyodonts*.

ROBERT RAPP, D. D. S. and JAMES T. WALLACE
University of Pittsburgh

CROSS SECTION OF ECTODERMAL TOOTH (LAMPREY)

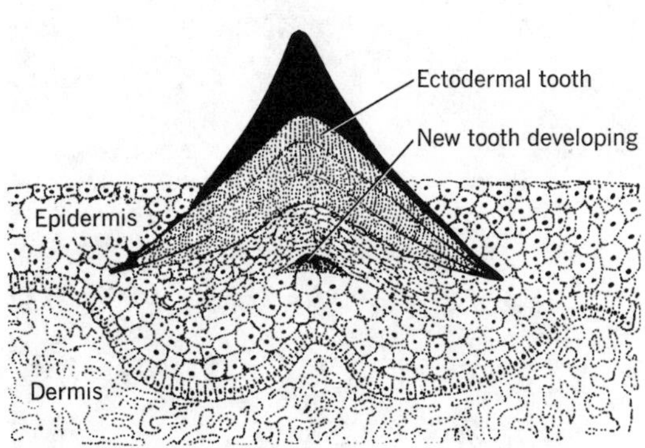

Bibliography

Massler, Maury, and Schour, Isaac, *Atlas of the Mouth,* 2d ed. (Chicago 1958).
Moyers, Robert E., *Handbook of Orthodontics* (Chicago 1963).
Shapiro, Max, ed., *The Scientific Bases of Dentistry* (Philadelphia 1966).
Sicher, Harry, ed., *Orban's Oral Histology and Embryology* (St. Louis 1966).
Watson, Ernest H., and Lowrey, George H., *Growth and Development of Children,* 5th ed. (Chicago 1967).
Wheeler, Russell, *Textbook of Dental Anatomy and Physiology* (Philadelphia 1965).

TEETHING is the eruption of the teeth. For a number of weeks before eruption the gums may be red and swollen, and the baby may salivate, lose his appetite, and be fretful.

TEFLON, tef′lon, is the trade name of an extremely stable plastic material. It is a polymer made up of completely fluorinated carbon chains. Teflon, first marketed in 1944, is widely used because of its high chemical stability and its resistance to adhesion.

In the chemical industry Teflon is used for tubing, stopcocks, valve packing and lining, and gaskets. It is also formed into rollers, bearings, conveyor belt coatings, and chemical-resistant work surfaces. In the electrical industry Teflon is used for insulation, coaxial cable parts, sockets, plugs, and bases. Tough, heavy-duty Teflon coatings can be used on all kinds of cooking utensils to prevent food from sticking. Because the Teflon coating reduces friction and protects against corrosion, it is also applied to handsaw and power-saw blades.

Teflon is a soft, waxy, opaque material that is nearly white in color. It is about 90% crystalline and has a molecular weight between 500,000 and 2,000,000. The monomer from which it is polymerized is tetrafluoroethylene, $CF_2{=}CF_2$, which is produced through a series of reactions from chloroform.

Teflon is inert to all solvents and chemical reagents except molten alkali metals and hot fluorine gas. It will stand continuous exposure to temperatures ranging from near absolute zero (−273° C, or −459.7° F) to 250° C and gets rubbery about 325° C (617° F). Although it does not char, it begins to depolymerize above 600° C (1112° F). It is nonflammable and is very stable to weathering. Although it cannot be extruded or injection-molded by the usual methods, it can be shaped by sintering or by pressing in simple dies. It can be cut or drilled easily and machined to obtain more exact dimensions.

OTTO W. NITZ
Stout State University, Menomonie, Wis.

TEGEA, tē′jē-ə, is an ancient Greek city in the southeastern plain of Arcadia in the Peloponnesus. Since it lay on the main route north from Sparta, Tegea was often a meeting place for Spartans and their allies on military marches. In legend, King Echemus of Tegea defeated the Heraclid Hyllus in single combat at the Corinthian Isthmus and so saved the Peloponnesus from immediate invasion.

Tegea was a close ally of Sparta from the founding of the Peloponnesian League in the 6th century B.C. until the Battle of Leuctra in 371 B.C. There were 500 Tegeans at Thermopylae (480 B.C.), and 1,500 Tegeans fought next to the Spartans at Plataea (479). Tegea was one of the founding states of the Arcadian League in 370. Scopas was both architect of and chief sculptor for a new temple of Athena Alea after fire destroyed the earlier temple in 395 B.C.

JAMES R. WISEMAN, *University of Texas*

TEGNÉR, teng-nār′, **Esaias** (1782–1846), Swedish poet, whose major work, *Frithjof's Saga* (1825), is a classic of Swedish literature. He was born at Kyrkerud, in Värmland, on Nov. 13, 1782. He graduated from the University of Lund in 1802 and later became a professor of Greek at Lund and the bishop of Växjö.

Tegnér's writing was influenced by the romantic movement, especially its Gothic phase. His poetry is characterized by flashing wit and rich, lively feeling. His first popular work, *Svea* (1811), was a patriotic poem. *Frithjof's Saga* is an epic poem adapted from an old Icelandic saga. Translated into a number of languages, it was the first Swedish poem to win international fame.

Tegnér died near Växjö on Nov. 2, 1846. His works were collected and published in 1847–1850 by Carl W. Böttiger, his biographer. See also FRITHJOF'S SAGA.

TEGUCIGALPA, tə-gōō-sə-gal′pə, is the capital of Honduras. It is the only Central American city not located on the Inter-American Highway, nor on any railway, being situated in an isolated mountain basin, at an altitude of about 3,200 feet (975 meters). The city includes two townships: Tegucigalpa, which lies at the foot of Mt. El Picacho and extends up its slopes; and Comayagüela, which is on level ground, separated from Tegucigalpa proper by the Choluteca River. Together, Tegucigalpa and Comayagüela are governed as the Distrito Central.

The city was founded in 1524 close to silver mines discovered by the Spaniards. The area also produced gold and marble during the colonial era, and still yields some silver and gold. Tegucigalpa did not become the Honduran capital until 1880, succeeding Comayagua. Although it is the largest city of one of the larger Central American countries, its remoteness from the main currents of national commerce has robbed it of the dynamism of most Latin American capitals and even of that of some other Honduran cities. There is no heavy industry and only a small amount of light industry. Population of city and suburbs (1965 estimate): 170,535.

KEMPTON E. WEBB, *Columbia University*

TEGUCIGALPA is linked to the Comayagüela area by the Mallol Bridge, which crosses the Choluteca River.

CARL FRANK

STERN MAGAZINE, FROM BLACK STAR

Teheran, lying in the shadow of the Elburz Range, is Iran's modern capital and the nation's leading city.

TEHERAN, tā-ə-rän′, the capital and largest city of Iran, is located in north-central Iran, at the juncture of the Trans-Iranian rail network. Teheran (also Tehran) is the capital of Teheran ostan (province). About 65 miles (105 km) south of the Caspian Sea, the city lies on a broad alluvial plateau that slopes south from the Elburz Mountains. The older part of the city lies lower down the slope than the modern center. The elevation of the latter is about 4,000 feet (1,220 meters). Modern residential suburbs, such as Shimran, are at the base of the mountains. Numerous *qanats* (tunnel-wells) terminate in the city, and irrigation ditches flow down many streets, providing water for gardens inside courtyard walls.

Places of Interest and City Plan. Maydan Sepah (formerly Topkhaneh) is the focal point of the city. A large and beautiful square, it is surrounded by modern government buildings, including the ministry of post and telegraph, the radio station and police headquarters, and offices of the municipality. The Museum of Iranian Ethnology and the Museum of Iranian Art and Archaeology, also on the square, have outstanding collections of national cultural artifacts.

The historic citadel, or *arg,* and main bazaar are nearby. The classical Muslim city of Teheran, with its mosques, religious schools, baths, teahouses, and sporting clubs, centers on this area. Most of the major mosques are near the bazaar, including the Shah mosque, which was the center of revolutionary activity leading to the establishment of constitutional government in Iran in 1906. The Gulistan (Rose garden) Palace, which dates from 1786, houses the marble throne of Karim Khan Zand and the jeweled Peacock Throne of Fath Ali Shah. The crown jewels of Iran and the Grand Mughul (Mogul) throne are kept in the National Bank.

New Teheran stands in striking contrast to the old city. The layout of the streets and residential areas is reminiscent of European capitals, especially Paris. Reza Shah adopted a grid-pattern for Teheran in 1926. The rectangular plan was partially superimposed over the old city and completely dominates the business and residential areas north of Shah Reza Avenue and west of Pahlavi Avenue.

The pattern of urban life is influenced by Western models. Middle-class residential areas have developed in the central city, near the new centers of business and administration, as well as around the apartment complexes in the northwest and southwest. Although their numbers have decreased, traditional minorities, such as Jews and Armenians, have moved north to the Doulat quarter and beyond. Near the base of the mountains, the new suburbs have luxury hotels, the summer seats of foreign legations, and residences of the rich and elite. Elsewhere on the periphery of the city, the new residential areas include slum villages that house new immigrants and workers in the adjacent industries.

Many of the modern businesses are located near Shah Reza Avenue and Maydan Sepah. The Iranian Oil Company headquarters building is the focus of a new commercial area, which includes the Plasko Shopping Center and the Firdausi Department Store. Most of the banks and dealers in antiques, modern handicrafts, and Persian carpets are on Firdausi Street. Jewelers, cloth merchants, tailors, lawyers, physicians, and real estate brokers are on Lalehzar Street. To the west, Shah Reza Avenue leads to the House of Parliament, in the modern center of government and administration. The city's educational institutions include the University of Teheran and Teheran Teachers College.

The Economy. Industry, commerce, and services dominate the city's economy. Although traditionally concentrated in the bazaar, the shops and offices, especially the newer ones, are scattered throughout greater Teheran. Less than half of the more than 30,000 industrial and manufacturing establishments are in the central part of the city. They include a wide variety of traditional, small-scale handicraft industries such as textiles, paper products, printing and publishing, and leather and leatherworking.

Most of the medium and large modern firms are located on the main transportation routes near the periphery of the city. Textile mills, chemical industries, and oil storage facilities are in the southwestern sector. Brick furnaces and plants producing construction materials are in the south, and transport equipment manufacturers are in the west, along the highway to Karaj. Other industries, such as food processing and metal assembly, are found in all sectors of the city.

History. Teheran is located 6 miles (10 km) north of the ruins of the ancient city of Ray. After the Mongols destroyed Ray in 1220, many of the people were attracted to the village of Teheran by its rich soil and good climate. The village grew, and by the mid-16th century it was a prominent center of agriculture, trade, and commerce. The first wall was built in 1553–1554. It was 3 miles (5 km) in length, with 114 towers and 4 gates. A chapter of the Koran was buried under each tower.

In 1788 the founder of the Kajar (Qajar) dynasty, Aga Muhammad Khan, moved the capital from Shiraz to Teheran. A century later, a second wall was built by Nasir al-Din Shah. Patterned after the wall of Paris, it was octagonal in shape, with a circumference of 10 miles (16 km), and had 12 gates and 58 towers. This wall determined the form of Teheran until 1926, when it was destroyed as part of Reza Shah's plan of urban development. During the 1950's and 1960's the city grew to more than six times the size of Isfahan, the next largest city in Iran.

The Province. Teheran province, with an area of 60,000 square miles (154,000 sq km), is one of the major agricultural and industrial regions in Iran. The *qanats* and streams that flow from the Elburz across the piedmont fans provide the water necessary to irrigate large areas for a variety of fruits, vegetables, and grains. More than one quarter of Iran's industries are located in the province. These include textile, chemical, and mining concerns as well as a number of assemblage and food processing plants. A dam and reservoir near Karaj, an industrial center 30 miles (48 km) west of Teheran, provides hydroelectric power and water to the capital. Population: (1966) of the city, 2,719,730; (1960) of the province, 2,989,100.

GARY L. FOWLER
University of Kentucky

TEHERAN, University of, te-ə-ran′, a state institution of higher learning in Iran's capital city, Teheran. Established in 1934 by the national government, it has since become the largest university in Iran. The institution offers a widely varied educational program covering 16 disciplines. These include letters and literature, fine arts, law, education, agriculture, science, medicine, dentistry, technology, pharmacy, engineering, forestry, public health, veterinary medicine, theology, and business administration. An attached institute founded in 1958—the Teheran Nuclear Research Center—does research in nuclear sciences and offers training and advice on peaceful applications of atomic energy.

By 1970 the university's student body totaled more than 18,000. The faculty included many members educated in Europe or in the United States.

TEHERAN CONFERENCE, te-ə-ran′, a meeting of U. S. President Franklin Roosevelt, British Prime Minister Winston Churchill, and Soviet Premier Joseph Stalin in Teheran, Iran, from Nov. 28 to Dec. 1, 1943. It was the first of the Big Three summit conferences (Teheran, Yalta, Potsdam) of World War II.

With the war still far from won, the conference gave priority to questions of military strategy. Churchill, anxious to drain off more of Germany's strength before undertaking the projected cross-Channel invasion ("Overlord"), argued for an expansion of military operations in the Mediterranean area. But Stalin, who wanted to ensure Soviet control of eastern Europe, vigorously opposed such a campaign and called for concentration on the buildup for Overlord. He was supported by Roosevelt, and it was agreed that the United States and Britain would invade France in May or June 1944. Stalin reaffirmed his promise that the USSR would enter the war against Japan soon after the defeat of Germany, and the Allies agreed to respect Iran's independence and territorial integrity after the war.

CARL H. PEGG
University of North Carolina

TEHUANTEPEC, Isthmus of, tə-wän′tə-pek, the narrowest section of Mexico, where only 125 miles (200 km) of land separate the Gulf of Tehuantepec, an inlet of the Pacific Ocean, and the Gulf of Campeche, a part of the Gulf of Mexico. It includes parts of the states of Veracruz and Oaxaca.

The isthmus, a lowland area east of the southern highlands, comprises two distinctive regions. The area near the Gulf of Mexico is tropical, wet, hot, and humid, and has no dry season. It was covered with tropical rain forest before unsystematic and destructive cutting depleted the forest of its valuable cabinet woods. A fast-growing region, it represents an important frontier of Mexico, with irrigated agriculture around the Coatzalcoalcos River and fertilizer and petrochemical industries around Coatzalcoalcos and Minatitlán.

The Pacific Ocean area has a drier climate. Vegetation varies from tropical deciduous to semideciduous forest. Completion of the Benito Juárez Dam on the Tehuantepec River permitted the opening of irrigated land where sugarcane, corn, and sorghum are cultivated. Stockraising is important. Culturally this area is part of Oaxaca, where Zapotec matriarchal traditions have persisted.

Railroad, highway, and pipeline facilities cross the isthmus from Salina Cruz to Coatzalcoalcas, carrying oil and other products for shipment. The isthmus has been considered a possible site for an interoceanic canal, but estimated costs have so far proved prohibitive.

REYNALDO AYALA, *San Diego State College*

TEHUELCHE INDIANS, tə-wel′chē, a Patagonian people. Judging from scanty archaeological evidence, they numbered about 4,000 at the time of the Spanish conquest. They dwindled to under 100 by the mid-20th century. They were a migratory people of the southern South American plains who obtained all their food by hunting and gathering. Their only domesticated animal was the dog, used in hunting. They wore scant clothing and had few material possessions. They were one of the few South American peoples to have a belief in a supreme being prior to European contact. Their main weapon was the bow and arrow until the mid-19th century.

After they stole and learned to ride horses, introduced by the Spaniards, the Tehuelche underwent a transformation. They formed predatory bands, larger than aboriginal social groups, and organized themselves under military chiefs.

LOUIS C. FARON
State University of New York, Stony Brook

TEIKA, tä-kä (1162–1241), Japanese poet and critic, whose full name was Fujiwara Teika, or Fujiwara Sadaie. He was the son of the poet Shunzei. As Teika's art developed, his style evolved from the ornate to the artfully plain. In his youth he advocated a new style of poetic composition embodying the concept of *yōen,* or ethereal charm. *Yōen* was the ideal of the 8th imperial anthology of poems, the *Shinkokinshū,* of which Teika was one of five distinguished editors. However, he clashed over the work with its sponsor, Emperor Gotoba, who was himself a poet and critic.

After the Jokyu War (1221), which resulted in the Emperor's exile, Teika rose to high rank at court and was recognized as the leading poet. His new poetic ideal was *ushin,* or intense feeling with elegance and refinement. In his most important critical work, *Maigetsushō* (1219; *Monthly Notes*), he distinguishes 10 styles of poetic diction but stresses the concept of *ushin* as an essential element in all 10. In later years he helped compile the 9th imperial anthology, the *Shinchokusenshū.*

DANIEL PFEIFER, *Georgia State University*

TEILHARD DE CHARDIN, tā-yår′ də shår-daN′, **Pierre** (1881–1955), Roman Catholic priest, paleontologist, and exponent of a synthesis of science and Christianity. Teilhard was born in Sarcenat, Orcines, Puy de Dôme, France, on May 1, 1881. He entered the Society of Jesus (Jesuits) in 1899 and was ordained a priest in 1911. The following year he began higher studies in paleontology and received his doctorate at the Sorbonne in 1922. From 1923 to 1946 he worked largely in China, participating in the discovery of the fossil human remains called "Peking Man." Following this, until his death in New York on April 10, 1955, his main research was conducted in Paris and New York.

The major importance of Teilhard is probably not so much in pure science as in his constant effort to create a synthesis between his Christian vision and the evolutionary perspectives of contemporary science. A paleontologist, he nevertheless insisted that his true interest lay in the future rather than in the past.

His best-known volume, *The Phenomenon of Man,* was finished in 1947 but was not published until after his death. It was translated into many languages and made Teilhard a popular world figure. In this volume Teilhard describes the evolution of man as he sees it and then moves on to attempt an explanation of the evolutionary process. He sees matter passing from an undifferentiated state to that of organized forms of more and more complex structure. He finds man as "the ascending arrow of the great biological synthesis." The universe becomes increasingly "hominized," humanity increasingly converging or moving toward the "superior pole" of all evolution, which Teilhard calls the "omega point."

As a Christian, he identifies the omega point with the risen Christ. "For the Christian," Teilhard wrote, "the final biological success of man on earth is not a simple probability but a certitude: for Christ (and in him, virtually, the world) is already risen."

This intuitive, indeed mystical, effort at seeing reality in terms of the "cosmic Christ" is further developed in other works, notably *The Divine Milieu* (Eng. tr., 1960). In its optimism and synthetic sweep, it exercised wide appeal. In ecclesiastical circles, Teilhard's work was for a short time under a cloud, though never condemned by the church. Teilhard has been admired by non-Christian humanists and Marxists, who find in him a point of dialogue.

C. J. MCNASPY, S. J.
Associate Editor of "America"

TEISSERENC DE BORT, tes-räN′ də bôr, **Léon Philippe** (1855–1913), French meteorologist, who discovered the stratosphere and pioneered the use of balloons to gather meteorological data. He was born in Paris on Nov. 5, 1855. In 1880 he became a meteorologist with the French central bureau of meteorology and studied the worldwide distribution of atmospheric pressure. He introduced the concept of action centers, which he elaborated in *Les Bases de la météorologie dynamique* (2 vols., 1898–1907), written jointly with H. H. Hildebrandssohn.

In 1892, Teisserenc de Bort left full-time service with the bureau, and in 1896 he founded his own observatory at Trappes. That year and the next he took part in an international study of clouds. He and the American meteorologist A. L. Rotch then investigated the upper atmosphere with instrument-carrying kites. Later Teisserenc used sounding balloons and by 1906 he found, independently of Richard Assmann, the German meteorologist, that atmospheric temperature fell until about 7 or 8 miles (11–13 km) and then became constant in a region that he named the stratosphere. He had begun to examine the chemical composition of the stratosphere before his death, in Cannes, on Jan. 2, 1913.

W. A. SMEATON, *University College, London*

TEJO RIVER. See TAGUS.

TEJU, tə-zhōō, any of a genus of large, fast-moving lizards found in the American tropics. It is also spelled *tegu.* Tejus are mainly ground-dwellers. This, plus their size and daytime activity, makes them among the most conspicuous reptiles of the region. They are wary and shy, however, and are well-named "jungle runners."

Adult tejus are usually 2 to 3 feet (60–90 cm) long, but old males may be larger, exceeding 4 feet (1.2 meters) in length and weighing more than 2 pounds (0.9 kg). The common teju (*Tupinambis teguixin*) is black with rows of small white spots extending across the body. The golden teju (*T. nigropunctatus*) is similar, but has rows of yellow spots. The red teju (*T. rufescens*) is reddish-brown with broad black crossbands.

Around 9 or 10 A.M. tejus move out from their burrows to bask in the sun on a sandbank or other exposed spot to raise their body temperature from the nighttime low to 100° F (38° C). They then run about the jungle floor, actively and noisily scratching among the leaves and nosing under rocks and logs in search of

JOHN MARKHAM

Great teju (*Tupinambis tegunin*)

food. They feed on almost anything available. They eat leaves, flowers, and fruits as well as insects, frogs, other lizards, and small snakes. A favorite food is birds' eggs, and tejus are often blamed for raiding chicken yards and eating the eggs and chicks. Tejus themselves are often hunted and eaten by the people of their region.

Tejus often lay their eggs in termite nests located in trees 4 to 5 feet (1.2–1.5 meters) above the ground. The eggs are cream colored and about 2 inches (5 cm) long. There are usually four to six eggs in a clutch.

Tejus make up the genus *Tupinambis* of the family Teiidae, order Sauria.

H. G. DOWLING
The American Museum of Natural History

TEKAKWITHA, CATHERINE. See CATHERINE TEKAKWITHA.

TEKRUR, tek'roo̅r, was a West African kingdom from the 10th to the 15th centuries. It was situated along the middle Senegal River, but many medieval Arabic chroniclers incorrectly applied the name Tekrur to the entire Western Sudan (modern Mali, Niger, and Upper Volta).

During its first two centuries Tekrur (Takrur) was at times a rival and at other times an appendage of the empires of ancient Ghana and Mali. It supplied gold and slaves for the trans-Saharan trade to North Africa and imported salt from the Saharan oases. Its inhabitants wove a coarse cloth. From the 11th century, Tekrur was the home of the Tukulor, a Senegalese people who much later established Islamic states on the high plateaus of Senegal, Guinea, and Mali.

ROBERT ROTBERG, *Author of "A Political History of Tropical Africa"*

TEKTITE, tek'tīt, one of the naturally occurring glassy objects found in various locations around the earth. Tektites vary in size from microscopic to grapefruit-size or larger, and in color from black to translucent green. They have been objects of intensive study and controversy for almost 200 years, primarily because of the possibility that they had an extraterrestrial origin.

Origin. Almost all scientists now agree that tektites were formed by the impacts of giant meteorites or comets. The enormous temperatures and pressures thus generated melted the rocks at the impact sites, and liquid droplets were splashed great distances. The droplets cooled rapidly to a glass during flight. The question is whether the impacts took place on earth or on the moon, with the tektites flying through space and reaching the earth. Radioactivity measurements indicate that the tektites could not have come from beyond the earth-moon system.

The theory of a terrestrial origin is supported primarily by the general similarity between the compositions of tektites and that of some widespread terrestrial rocks. In addition, several tektite-strewn areas correlate with the location of meteor-impact craters. The theory of a lunar origin is supported by aerodynamic considerations suggesting that the tektites passed through the earth's atmosphere at very high velocities. Studies of Apollo lunar samples do not support a lunar origin of tektites.

Occurrence and Age. Tektites have been found in the United States, Czechoslovakia, the Ivory Coast, and the southwestern Pacific Ocean region. In addition, "microtektites" less than 0.04 inch (1 mm) in diameter have been found in ocean cores taken off the Ivory Coast and in the southwestern Pacific and Indian oceans. Tektites are most abundant in the Australasian area, their total mass there being estimated as 150 million tons (about 135 billion kg).

Radioactivity measurements show that the North American tektites formed—that is, melted—about 32 million years ago, the Czechoslovakian tektites about 15 million years ago, the Ivory Coast samples about 1 million years ago, and those of Australasia about 700,000 years ago.

C. C. SCHNETZLER
Goddard Space Flight Center, NASA

TEL AVIV-JAFFA, tel-ə-vēv'jäf'ə, the largest city in Israel, is located on the Plain of Sharon, 34 miles (56 km) northwest of Jesusalem. It was founded in 1909 as a Jewish suburb on the sand dunes north of Jaffa. The two cities were officially joined in 1949.

Tel Aviv-Jaffa is the hub of the national transport and communication systems and the center of an urban area of nearly a million people. Tel Aviv-Jaffa merges with a series of satellite towns into a built-up urban area that accounts for 31% of the population of Israel on less than 1% of the land area. Ramat Gan, Holon, Bene Beraq, Bat Yam, Givatayim, and Herzeliyya are the major centers in the Greater Tel Aviv region. They are residential suburbs for workers in Tel Aviv as well as sites for many industrial firms.

Beyond the built-up area is an outer ring of medium-sized towns that are becoming economically more dependent on Tel Aviv. Petah Tiqwa, Rehovot, Rishon Le Ziyyon, Ramla, and smaller centers such as Kefar Sava and Raanana are in this ring. With the Greater Tel Aviv region, this area contains about 40% of Israel's population on only 3% of the land area. Continued urban expansion is at the expense of the rich agricultural land in the Plain of Sharon.

Economy and Culture of the City. Commercial and cultural activities dominate the city's economy. The major banks and other national institutions are located there, as is the ministry of defense and the Histadrut (labor federation) headquarters. The offices of the Hebrew daily newspaper and of most publishing houses are in

Tel Aviv. Cultural attractions include the Habima Theater, the Mann Concert Hall and the Israel Philharmonic Orchestra, the Municipal Museum and Art Gallery, and the Haaretz Museum. Tel Aviv University is one of Israel's leading higher institutions, and the Maccabiah games, an international athletic competition, are held there.

Before Israel became independent in 1948, the commercial and cultural institutions were concentrated in south Tel Aviv, on Herzl Street and Allenby Road. They since have shifted northeastward to Dizengoff Square and Dizengoff Road. The Jaffa quarter of Manshiye was transformed in the 1970's into a banking and commercial center extending south to Jaffa Hill. The waterfront on ha-Yarqon Street, with its hotels, is the chief center of tourism in Israel.

About a third of the labor force of Tel Aviv is employed in industry and manufacturing. Most of the industrial workers, however, work in small, highly specialized firms. The Tel Aviv port, which opened in 1936, was closed in 1965 upon completion of the new port at Ashdod.

History. The British established Tel Aviv as a separate, all-Jewish town in 1921, when it had about 30,000 people. The largest city in Palestine, it contained the majority of the Jewish population in the Mandate Territory.

Tel Aviv grew rapidly during the British mandate (1923–1948). It was the principal destination for new immigrants, many of whom were small merchants from eastern Europe and Jews from Jaffa. By 1935, Tel Aviv was the cultural, commercial, and administrative center of the Jewish community in Palestine. Physical expansion, however, was limited to a narrow coastal strip until the barriers to expansion inland were removed during the Israeli-Arab War of 1948.

Tel Aviv was the seat of the transitional government and the Knesset (legislature) from 1948 to 1949, when Jerusalem became the capital of Israel. Tel Aviv continued to grow, however, and in 1961 new immigrants, more than two thirds of whom were from European countries, accounted for over half of the city's population. Population: (1968 est.) 388,000. See also JAFFA.

GARY L. FOWLER, *University of Kentucky*

TELAMON, tel'ə-mən, in Greek legend, was the King of Salamis and the father of Ajax the Telamonian. When Telamon and his brother Peleus murdered their half-brother Phocus, they were expelled from Aegina by their father Aeacus. Telamon was received by King Cychreus of Salamis, whose daughter, Glauce, he married. He succeeded to the throne of Salamis, and by his second wife, Periboea, or Eriboea, became the father of Ajax, a hero of the Trojan War. Telamon went on the expedition of the Argonauts and was the first to scale the walls of Troy. Hercules gave him the king's daughter Hesione as part of the spoils.

TELAUTOGRAPH, tel-ôt'ə-graf, an electromechanical device for sending and receiving handwritten messages by wire. Each movement of the sender's stylus is converted to electric signals that actuate a distant receiving stylus, which duplicates the movement of the sending stylus. It was invented by Elisha Gray in 1888.

TELEDU, tel'ə-do͞o, or Malay stink badger, a small, short-tailed mammal (*Mydaus javanensis*) of the weasel family found in Sumatra, Java, and Borneo. It is blackish brown, with a white stripe running down its back. Like a skunk, the teledu can eject a foul-smelling liquid.

TELEGONUS, tə-leg'ə-nəs, in Greek legend, was the son of Odysseus and Circe. At his mother's order he sailed to Ithaca to find Odysseus. Not recognizing his father, Telegonus killed him in a struggle. He then carried the body home, accompanied by his half-brother Telemachus and Penelope, whom he later married.

Tel Aviv (*foreground*) was officially linked with Jaffa (*background*) after Israel achieved independence.

A. L. GOLDMAN, FROM RAPHO GUILLUMETTE

EWING GALLOWAY

TELEGRAPHER sends Morse code messages by means of a key. A sounder (top) clicks out incoming messages.

TELEGRAPH, tel'ə-graf, an apparatus for sending messages over a distance by using a code of some kind. The word "telegraph" was first used to describe a visual signaling system invented by Claude Chappe in France in 1792. The word now almost always denotes the electric telegraph in all its forms.

The first practical electric telegraphs were invented in England and the United States in the 1830's. Each consisted of a transmitter and receiver connected by one or more wires that carried electric current from a battery. At the transmitter, an operator caused current to flow in a particular pattern. At the receiver, an incoming current caused the deflection of needles or a pencil. When needles were used, they pointed to a particular letter of the alphabet. When a pencil was used, it marked a piece of paper with a code representation of a particular letter of the alphabet.

Similar but improved electric telegraphs provided the only means of fast communication over long distances until the 1890's, when some long-distance telephone lines were installed. Over the next 40 years or so, the telephone grew in importance while the telegraph declined. However, since about 1930 the telegraph has regained importance, chiefly because of the increased use of teletypewriters. With these machines, messages can be transmitted between offices by an unskilled operator as easily as making a telephone call. Teletypewriters also provide a printed record, which is often needed in business and government.

In the late 1960's the development of communications satellites and advanced electronic techniques further improved the flexibility of telegraph systems. In the future, it may even be possible to deliver business letters immediately via a telegraph satellite at a cost no higher than for much slower postal service.

GROWTH OF TELEGRAPH NETWORKS

Landline and Underground Cable. The first practical electric telegraph was introduced in 1838, linking Paddington Station, London, with West Drayton station, 13 miles (21 km) away. The first long-distance line was opened in 1844 by Samuel F. B. Morse. It ran from Washington to Baltimore, a distance of 40 miles (64 km).

In 1856, Hiram Sibley, an American businessman, consolidated many fledgling telegraph companies into the Western Union Telegraph Company. As a result of his foresight, a transcontinental line was completed by 1861. Under Sibley's direction, the number of Western Union offices increased from 132 in 1856 to 4,000 in 1866. During this period the telegraph also played an important part in the Civil War.

As the wires of the electric telegraph stretched farther and farther across the land surface of the earth in the late 19th and early 20th centuries, various forms of transmission paths were developed. These are still being used. In open country, signals usually are sent over bare copper wires supported on insulators mounted on wooden, steel, or concrete poles. On busy routes, it is common practice to enclose a large number of individually insulated wires in a protective sheath, thereby forming a cable. Within city limits such cables are usually placed in wood, tile, or iron pipes for protection and buried in the ground. In open country, cables can be buried without such protection.

Each telegraph office cannot be connected directly to all other telegraph offices because construction costs would be too expensive. Therefore, they are usually linked via one or more central telegraph offices. For example, a message from an office in suburban New York to an office in suburban Baltimore is transmitted to a central message-switching center in New York City, sent to a switching center in Baltimore, and then to a suburban office. A transcontinental message may go through as many as nine message-switching centers before reaching its final destination. At each station the message is automatically recorded on a magnetic drum or on paper tape by a machine called a *reperforator* and held for transmission until the line to the next office is free.

Teletypewriters also are connected via switching centers, but there is no intermediate recording of the message. Instead, a continuous connection is set up between two teletypewriters, as is done between two telephones. Although less effective use is made of telegraph line traffic capacity than in intermediate recording, the convenience of a continuous connection more than compensates for this in some circumstances.

Line costs are very high, so methods of sending a number of messages over a single line at the same time have been widely used. Mechanical methods early in the 20th century enabled five or six teletypewriters to share a single wire. These methods have largely been replaced by electronic systems that simultaneously send signals from as many as 24 teletypewriters over a single channel of an ordinary telephone network.

Submarine Cable. At first, telegraph lines came to an abrupt halt when they reached the sea. Although Morse had laid some short lines in New York harbor in 1842, the first cable in the open sea was not laid until 1850. This cable ran under the English Channel between Cap Gris Nez in France and Cape Sutherland in England. Other narrow sea areas were bridged shortly thereafter, but by far the most important gap in the telegraph network was the one separating Europe and North America. The laying of a cable to close this gap was an epic of courage, enterprise, and perseverance. It took the untiring efforts of Cyrus W. Field to keep the project going until Aug. 5, 1858, when the first telegraph message was sent across the Atlantic. Although this cable soon failed, more reliable cables were developed and laid.

Submarine telegraph cable networks now run under every ocean. They carry international and intercontinental traffic and link large islands with an adjacent mainland. A telegraph message between any two major cities of the world can be sent along a route that includes both submarine cables and landlines.

On long transoceanic routes, signals travel vast distances and become very weak and distorted, causing errors in transmission and reducing the maximum signaling speed. One way of avoiding these difficulties is to split long routes into sections. Transpacific routes, for example, hop from island to island. On each island, a repeater station completely restores the strength of the signals and sends them to the next station.

The introduction of submerged telegraph repeaters by Western Union in 1950 was a major advance in submarine telegraphy. These repeaters, which consist of electronic amplifiers and signal-shaping networks fitted into a watertight steel case, are connected into the cable in deep water 60 to 300 miles (97 to 483 km) from shore, where the continental shelf ends. Incoming signals are given a boost by the repeater just before they reach the shallower shelf water where they may be affected by interference due to changes in the earth's electric and magnetic fields and by electric storms associated with sunspot activity. By reducing the effects of interference in this way, the signaling speed can be increased to about 1,000 characters per minute, which is three or four times faster than the signaling speed in repeaterless cables of the same type.

Submarine telephone cables using carrier-frequency techniques also handle transoceanic telegraph traffic, supplementing the older submarine cables used exclusively for telegraphy.

Radiotelegraph Links. Telegraph signals are sent by radio over land where the terrain is too rugged to build telegraph lines, over seas and oceans lacking sufficient traffic to justify the high cost of laying a submarine cable, and over some very long-distance routes where a direct radio link is cheaper than a landline route.

Round-the-world communication links are provided by low- and very-low frequency radio signals, but stations transmitting on such frequencies are extremely bulky and expensive and have a low traffic capacity. Smaller, less costly stations are possible in the medium-frequency part of the spectrum around 500 kilohertz, which is used for radiotelegraph traffic between shore stations and ships within a few hundred miles.

By far the greatest part of worldwide radiotelegraph traffic is transmitted in the high-frequency part of the spectrum, which provides round-the-world service for point-to-point links between fixed stations and for communication with ships and aircraft thousands of miles from a sending station. High-frequency radio links tend to be unreliable over distances shorter than a few hundred miles, and some have been replaced by tropospheric scatter systems operating on ultrahigh frequencies around 900 megahertz. These systems provide a reliable, high-capacity link over the shorter distances.

Microwave relay systems use signals beamed from hilltop to hilltop by a series of antennas mounted on towers. These systems have come into use where telegraph links between large cities have to traverse rugged terrain, where the origin-to-destination distances are great, and where the traffic is too heavy for a high-frequency radio link.

Telegraph traffic also is sent via communications satellites. Each satellite provides a service complementing that provided by submarine telegraph cables, transcontinental cables, and microwave radio links. In addition, each satellite can relay signals to any ground station within an area extending over one third of the earth's surface. Satellites thus can provide small countries with direct links far more cheaply and reliably than any other method.

TELEGRAPH SERVICES

Public Services. Probably the best-known public telegraph service is the telegram service. Telegrams are messages sent between two points in one country. The message is written by the sender, who either submits it to a local telegraph office or dictates it over the telephone to the office. It is sent on to its destination by an operator using a teletypewriter. At the receiving station, the message is printed on a form and delivered by hand to the person to whom it is addressed, or it is read over the telephone.

A Mailgram is sent by telephoning the message to Western Union, which uses a computer to transmit the message to a post office near the addressee. The message then is delivered by the local letter carrier, usually on the next business day. This service is provided in the United States, except Alaska and Hawaii.

Cablegrams are international telegrams that are usually, but not necessarily, sent over a submarine telegraph cable. The message is handed in at a telegraph office and is delivered to the addressee in the same way as a telegram.

Radiotelegrams are telegraph messages sent by radio, commonly to someone traveling on board a ship. They are presented to a local telegraph office in the usual way and then sent to a radiotelegraph station that is in communication with the ship.

Customer-to-Customer Services. Teletypewriter services provide a direct link between one customer's office and another. A teletypewriter operator connects her machine to the wanted teletypewriter by dialing over a network similar to that of the public telephone network. She types out the message on a typewriterlike keyboard, and it is printed out immediately by the receiving teletypewriter. In the United States the teletypewriter network is known as the TWX system, in Europe as Telex. See also TELETYPEWRITER EXCHANGE SERVICE; TELEX.

Pictures can be sent from one office to another by means of facsimile equipment. In one technique, a picture is divided up into about 250,000 elemental areas, and the light values of these areas are sequentially transmitted as electric signals to the receiving equipment. At the

INTERNATIONAL MORSE CODE

A	•—	N	—•
B	—•••	O	———
C	—•—•	P	•——•
D	—••	Q	——•—
E	•	R	•—•
F	••—•	S	•••
G	——•	T	—
H	••••	U	••—
I	••	V	•••—
J	•———	W	•——
K	—•—	X	—••—
L	•—••	Y	—•——
M	——	Z	——••

1	•————	Period	•—•—•—
2	••———	Comma	——••——
3	•••——	Interrogation	••——••
4	••••—	Colon	———•••
5	•••••	Semicolon	—•—•—•
6	—••••	Quotation marks	•—••—•
7	——•••		
8	———••		
9	————•		
0	—————		

receiving end, the electric signals are converted into light signals that build up the picture on photographic film.

Private-Wire Services. Large organizations often find it convenient to have sole use of a telegraph circuit to send information between their offices. The press, industrial organizations such as oil companies, military services, and government agencies have extensive private-wire networks. Usually, the telegraph circuit is built and maintained by the telegraph company and leased to the user. A well-known private-wire service carries news of the continually changing prices of stocks from the stock exchanges of the world to brokers' offices.

THEORY AND TECHNOLOGY

Telegraph Codes. Morse code is undoubtedly the best known of the telegraph codes (see table). It consists of short and long electric pulses (code elements) known as dots and dashes. The particular patterns of dots or dashes that make up letters were chosen by Morse and his assistant Alfred Vail. The more frequently used letters in the English language, such as *e* and *t,* are represented by more simple patterns. Morse and Vail determined this after visiting a local printer, who showed them how many of each letter of the alphabet was needed in his type cases.

On early submarine cables the dots and dashes became so distorted as to be indistinguishable, so a modified form of the Morse code was introduced for use on submarine cables. In this code, the dot is a positive current pulse, the dash is a negative current pulse, and both pulses have the same length.

Once telegraphy was shown to be practical, inventors quickly turned their attention to devising machines that would send and receive telegraph signals automatically. They soon found that the different letter lengths in the Morse code made it difficult for a machine to distinguish successive letters. They also found that the transmitting and receiving machines had to be synchronized with a precision that is costly and difficult to maintain.

The first problem was solved by replacing the Morse code and using a 5-unit code for machine operation. In such a code, there are two equal-length signal elements—a mark and a space—and all letters and other characters are of equal length. One 5-unit code was invented in 1874 by Émile Baudot, an officer of the French telegraph service. Another 5-unit code was devised by the British inventor Donald Murray about 1901 (see table).

The second problem was solved by the use of the Murray code with a "start" signal element at the beginning of each letter and a "stop" signal element at the end of each letter. This technique effectively provided synchronization letter by letter for teletypewriter transmissions, and it eliminated the problem of maintaining precise synchronization of transmitting and receiving machines throughout the transmission of a message.

One drawback of a 5-unit code is that there are 32 possible combinations of marks or spaces, all of which are put to use. Consequently, if signals are mutilated in transmission, converting a mark into a space or vice versa, the receiving equipment will print out a wrong letter. To overcome this, a 7-unit error detecting code has come into use on noisy circuits with high error rates. This code has 128 different permutations, but only the 35 permutations in which there are three marks and four spaces are used. An error produced in transmission alters this balance, and so it can be detected.

How Telegraph Machines Work. The teletypewriter is the commonest telegraph machine now in use. It is used both for transmitting and receiving. To send a message, the operator simply types it on a keyboard. Each time she depresses a key, five long bars are released and arrange themselves according to the 5-unit Murray code for the particular letter (see figure). For spaces, the appropriate bars are held in place by tabs on the letter keybar. For marks, the appropriate bars move to the left and protrude beyond the space bars. The protruding bars close electrical

MURRAY FIVE-UNIT CODE

Figures	Letters	1	2	3	4	5	Figures	Letters	1	2	3	4	5
·	A	●	●				1	Q	●	●	●		●
?	B	●			●	●	4	R		●		●	
:	C		●	●	●		'	S	●		●		
WRU	D	●			●		5	T					●
3	E	●					7	U	●	●	●		
%	F	●		●	●		—	V		●	●	●	●
0	G		●		●	●	2	W	●	●			●
£	H			●		●	/	X	●		●	●	●
8	I		●	●			6	Y	●		●		●
Bell	J	●	●		●		+	Z	●				●
(	K	●	●	●	●		Carr. ret.					●	
)	L		●			●	Line feed			●			
.	M			●	●	●	Fig. shift		●	●		●	●
,	N			●	●		Let. shift		●	●	●	●	●
9	O				●	●	Space				●		
ϕ	P		●	●		●	Unp. tape						

switches, which send current along the line when a rotating cam connects a battery to each of the bars in turn. At the receiving teletypewriter, the reception of each mark causes an electromagnet to depress one of five bars and thereby set up a 5-unit code combination representing a particular letter. The depressed bars for marks and the unmoved bars for spaces allow a correspondingly cut latch to fall and stop a rotating typehead when that particular letter is at the top of the typehead. The back of the letter is then struck with a hammer, printing the letter on paper.

A teletypewriter operator cannot type continuously and so cannot make full use of an expensive telegraph line. Much better use can be made of lines if the operator first punches out the message in 5-unit code in the form of holes (marks) and no holes (spaces) in a paper tape. On the tape, each letter of the Murray code is represented by a vertical line of holes and no holes. The tape is fed continuously into a device known as an *autotransmitter*, where it is probed by five metal fingers. Where a mark has been punched, a finger rises up through the hole and operates a contact that sends a mark signal along the line. Where a finger is blocked by the tape, the contact remains open and a space signal is sent. The tape is advanced during the transmission of the stop pulse, so no time is lost between the transmission of two letters.

At message switching centers the incoming signals usually operate a *reperforator*, which punches out the message on paper tape. Reading machines that convert punched tape into a typed message on a strip or sheet of paper also are used at switching centers.

Telegraph Switching. In a message center using a semiautomatic switching system, the paper tape is fed automatically from the receiving reperforator to an adjacent autotransmitter. The destination address, as soon as it is received, is printed out on a teletypewriter at a central operating position, where it is read by an operator who positions switches to connect the autotransmitter to the desired outgoing line.

In the newer electronically controlled switching centers, messages are stored on a magnetic drum, read out from it when the desired outgoing line is free, and sent along to the next switching center without human intervention.

Transmission Methods—*Direct-Current Signaling*. For 100 years or so all telegraph systems used direct-current signaling. Very early, the high cost of telegraph lines led to the development of methods for increasing the number of messages that could be sent over a single line at the same time. The duplex system, which sends two messages in opposite directions simultaneously over the same line, was proposed by Wilhelm Gintel of Vienna as early as 1853. The quadruplex system, which sends two messages simultaneously in each direction, was invented in 1874 by Thomas Edison, who once earned his living as a telegraph operator. Brilliant though his quadruplex system was, it was soon surpassed by simpler and even more effective time-division multiplex systems. In these systems several operators (usually four but as many as six) shared a single line by sending in a specified sequence for a specified short length of time, such as the time taken to transmit one letter. Baudot introduced the first successful time-division multiplex system and his 5-unit code for manual multiplex operation in 1874. Improved versions of his

TELEPRINTER SENDING MECHANISM

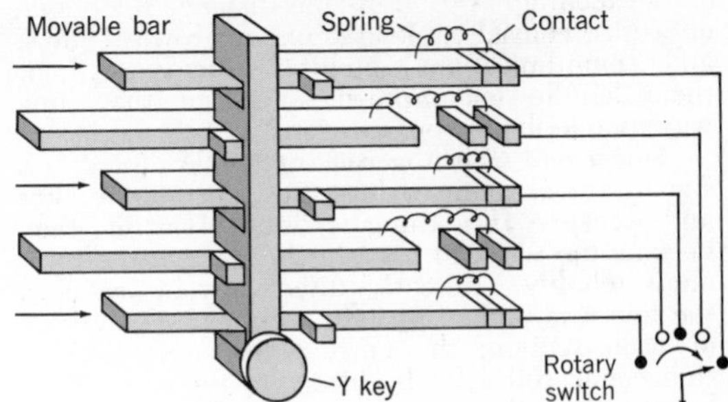

A TELEPRINTER "Y" KEY with its associated movable bars and its electrical contacts.

multiplex system, which was a mechanical one, were used extensively on landlines until the late 1930's. All such time-division multiplex systems operate by automatically dividing transmission time among the several operators.

The Baudot multiplex system and all other direct-current telegraph signaling systems now survive only for use on submarine telegraph cables and on landlines over distances up to 100 miles (160 km), but they are obsolescent.

***Alternating-Current Signaling*.** The development of long-distance telephone landlines, submarine telephone cables, and telephone lines terminal equipment has led to the use of alternating-current signaling for the great bulk of telegraph traffic. A major advantage of alternating-current signaling is that both telegraph and telephone traffic can be sent simultaneously over the same line by using frequency-division multiplexing.

In alternating-current signaling using a frequency-division multiplex system, a different carrier frequency is used for each telegraph channel, which occupies a narrow band of frequencies centered about the carrier frequency. In this way, the channels can be easily separated out at the receiving end by tuned band-pass filters. Thus, telegraph messages are separated by intervals of frequency in a frequency-division multiplex system, in contrast to being separated by intervals of time in a time-division multiplex system.

Telegraph message information is impressed on a carrier wave in one of three ways: amplitude modulation, frequency modulation, or phase modulation. In amplitude modulation, the alternating current of the carrier wave is switched on and off to represent marks and spaces, respectively. In frequency modulation, the carrier frequency is switched backward and forward between two narrowly spaced frequencies, one of which represents a mark and the other a space. In phase modulation, the phase, or timing, of the alternating-current waveform is switched backward and forward to represent marks and spaces.

In the United States it is common practice to use 16 carrier frequencies. In other parts of the world 12, 18, or 24 carrier frequencies normally are used. Whichever number is used, the carrier frequencies and their associated telegraph channels can all be accommodated within the band of frequencies used for a single telephone conversation. Because of this, 12 to 24 telegraph messages can be sent simultaneously over a single telephone circuit, using a voice-frequency band from 300 to 3,300 hertz. Groups of telegraph channels also can be handled by higher frequency carrier techniques used in long-distance telephone networks, coaxial cable systems, microwave links, and communications satellite systems. All of them handle telegraph messages in the same way as telephone conversations.

Strong and Clear Communications. As telegraph signals travel along a line they become weaker and weaker. If nothing is done about it, they become too weak to operate the receiving equipment reliably. In early direct-current systems, the line was broken up into sections. At the end of each section, the current operated a relay that connected a fresh battery to the line. To a large extent, the simple relay has been replaced by an electromechanical or electronic device known as a *regenerative repeater,* which completely restores weak and distorted signals on long telegraph lines.

On high-frequency radiotelegraph circuits the rapid fading to which such radio waves are subject is reduced by the use of frequency modulation. The knowledge that fading tends to occur at only one place and on only one frequency at any single time also helps in reducing its effects. A *space-diversity* system picks up the best signal from two or three antennas spaced far apart. A *frequency-diversity* system selects the best of two signals sent on two different frequencies at the same time. In a *time-diversity* system, the best of two signals sent at different times is used. The start and stop elements of teletypewriter transmissions are very vulnerable to fading, and so 5-unit code signals without start-stop elements, high-speed Morse signals, or 7-unit error detecting codes are used.

DEVELOPMENT OF TELEGRAPH EQUIPMENT

The French engineer Claude Chappe built the world's first modern telegraphic communications link in 1794. He was inspired by the ideas of the English physicist and chemist Robert Hooke, who in 1684 had described visual telegraph systems using the telescope, then recently invented. Chappe's visual telegraph system had a series of towers along a 143-mile (230-km) route between Paris and Lille. A vertical wooden pole fitted with a pivoted beam and arms was mounted on the roof of each tower on the route. The letters of the alphabet were represented by different configurations of the arms and beam. These configurations were read by a man with a telescope on the next tower, who relayed the message by positioning the beam and arms at his tower.

Although Chappe's system was slow compared with modern electric telegraphs, it made a tremendous impression in his time. It played an important part in the success of the French armies in the French Revolutionary wars. Because of Chappe's telegraph, the French government was able to deploy its forces much more speedily and with greater certainty of sending them to the right place than the allied enemy forces, which had no high-speed communication system.

The first visual telegraph system in the United States was built by Jonathan Grout in 1800 and was used principally to carry shipping news from Martha's Vineyard to Boston.

Interest in the potentially much quicker and cheaper electric telegraph began about 1750, but no practical system was established in the 18th century because only static electricity was available, which was elusive and capricious. It was not until the Italian physicist Alessandro Volta produced the first battery in 1800 that an abundant and controllable supply of direct current needed for electric telegraphy became available. Even then, progress was slow because there still was no practical way of detecting the arrival of electric current at a receiving station.

The next breakthrough came in 1832 when the Russian diplomat Paul Schilling showed that the deflection of a compass needle, when electric current flowed in a coil of wire around it, could form the basis of a telegraph detector. Karl F. Gauss and Wilhelm Weber made significant experiments in the following year, but it was a young Englishman, William Fothergill Cooke, who quickly followed up on the work of Schilling. After failing to overcome early difficulties, Cooke enlisted the help of Charles Wheatstone, a professor of natural philosophy at King's College, London. These two men constructed the first practical electric telegraph system.

Cooke-Wheatstone Telegraph. In the version of the Cooke-Wheatstone telegraph built in 1837, a letter was sent by passing currents through two of five wires laid between a transmitter and a receiver. The currents deflected two of five compass needles in the receiver, and the two needles together pointed toward the selected letter (see figure). In 1838 they reduced the number of wires and needles to two of each, thus saving a great deal of the cost of building a telegraph connection. Letters were transmitted using a code based on the number of deflections of each of the two needles. Cooke-Wheatstone telegraphs were widely used in England but eventually were superseded by the telegraph invented by Morse in the United States.

Morse Telegraph. As early as 1837, Morse detected the arrival of current by passing it through an electromagnet that deflected a pencil, which in turn marked a moving strip of paper passed beneath it (see illustration, p. 395). His system had a number of advantages, chiefly that it required only one wire between two stations.

Morse had the ideas, the ability, and the connections for putting his ideas into practice, but he lacked mechanical ability. This was provided by Alfred Vail, who began helping Morse in 1837. Vail invented the telegraph key by 1840, and he refined their signal code to what became known as the Morse code by 1845. Morse also en-

TELEGRAPH RECEIVER perfected by Cooke and Wheatstone in 1837 used needles to point to letters.

listed the help of the American scientist Joseph Henry, who had invented a relay that could restore weak telegraph signals on long lines. After much lobbying in Congress, Morse in 1843 received $30,000, which he used to build a telegraph line between Baltimore and Washington. Miss Ellsworth sent the first message over the line on May 24, 1844. The message, received by Vail in Baltimore, was the Biblical verse "What hath God wrought" (Numbers 23:23).

Morse thought that an inked-paper recorder was essential because he did not realize that his code signals could be interpreted by ear. Once the early telegraph operators found they could interpret the signals by ear from the sound of the movements of the electromagnet armature, messages were written directly by human operators, and the inked-paper recorder went out of use. It was reintroduced to receive signals sent at 70 words per minute by automatic Morse transmitting equipment invented in the late 1850's.

Morse's telegraph, with or without a recorder, was a huge success in the 19th century, but by the early 1900's the development of machines capable of dealing more effectively with increased traffic made it obsolescent. Perhaps its most important drawback was its unsuitability for use with a receiving letter-printing machine. As a consequence, the dots and dashes had to be translated by a Morse operator before a message could be handed to the person to whom it was addressed. This was true whether the message was received by ear or inked on a recorder.

As early as 1850 many inventors were working to perfect a machine that could print out messages in plain language. One plain-language telegraph was invented in 1855 by David E. Hughes, who was a professor at New York University, as was Morse. At the receiving end, Hughes used a typewheel driven through an electromechanical clutch. At the sending end, he provided the operator with a pianolike keyboard for sending electrical pulses that released the clutch and brought the typewheel to rest when the desired letter was over a moving strip of paper. Although Hughes' equipment was much improved by his French partner, Paul Gustave Froment, it was rather complex and often broke down.

A much more practical plain-language printing telegraph was introduced by Émile Baudot in 1874. In this system, the sending operator was provided with a special keyboard of five keys on which the Baudot 5-unit code of any particular letter was set up. The receiving equipment was similar in principle to that of the modern teletypewriter. In the Baudot multiplex system, a number of operators sent messages over the line, switching it rapidly between them by means of a rotating switch. A block of five code elements from each sending operator's machine was sent down the line one after the other. At the receiving end, the line was connected to each appropriate receiving machine in turn by another rotating switch synchronized with the one at the transmitting end.

Around 1900, printing-machine telegraphs could not be widely used because the sending and receiving apparatus had to be synchronized with great accuracy, and the cost of employing highly skilled operators was not justified on lines carrying little traffic. This problem was overcome by introducing a start element at the beginning of each 5-unit code letter and a stop at the end of each letter. The first start-stop instrument was introduced in the United States by Charles L. Krum in 1907. Beginning about 1920, his idea was developed and perfected for modern teletypewriter transmissions by Siemens and Halske in Germany, by Creed & Company in England, and by the Morkrum Company in the United States. Start-stop elements added to the 5-unit Murray code are now used on almost all teletypewriter routes.

THE WESTERN UNION COMPANY

TELEGRAPH built by Morse in 1837 penciled a code on a paper ribbon moved by clock gears. (Replica shown.)

Frequency-division multiplex systems are now used on almost all busy telegraph routes. Experimental systems using alternating-current tones were described as early as 1878 by the American inventor Elisha Gray and were produced by the French physicist Ernest Mercadier in 1897, but satisfactory systems could not be made with the equipment available to them. Frequency-division multiplex systems made rapid progress only after the development of improved electronic amplifiers in the late 1920's.

The development of message switching centers got under way in the 1930's. Reperforators for receiving messages in the form of perforated tape at a switching center were developed in the late 1930's. Fully automatic message switching centers using tape were in use by the mid-1950's, and fully automatic message switching centers using electronic controls were introduced in the 1960's.

See also CABLE; RADIO; TELEPHONE; TELETYPEWRITER.

RONALD BROWN
Author of "Telecommunications"

Bibliography

Biswas, N. N., *Principles of Telegraphy* (New York 1964).
Brown, Ronald, *Telecommunications* (New York 1970).
Freebody, J. W., *Telegraphy* (London 1958).
Harlow, Alvin F., *Old Wires and New Waves* (New York 1936).
International Telecommunications Union, *From Semaphore to Satellite* (Geneva 1965).
Perkins, W. T., *Modern Telegraph Systems and Equipment* (London 1946).
Thompson, Robert L., *Wiring a Continent* (Princeton 1947).

TELEGRAPH PLANT, a name commonly applied to two unrelated plants. *Desmodium gyrans* is a purple-flowered, Asian perennial tick trefoil of the legume family (Leguminosae). It is sometimes grown as a greenhouse curiosity because of the peculiar jerking movements of its leaflets. *Heterotheca grandiflora,* is a tall, shaggy, annual of the composite family (Compositae), native to the Western United States and abundant in coastal southern California. Its yellow daisylike flower heads are borne in a flat-topped cluster.

J. A. YOUNG
U. S. Department of Agriculture

TELEGRAPHONE, tə-leg′rə-fōn, an early electromechanical device for recording and reproducing sound. In recording by telegraphone, a microphone converted sounds to electric currents, the currents passed through the windings of an electromagnet, and the electromagnet produced a magnetic field that varied the magnetization of a moving steel wire in proportion to the current strength. In reproducing sounds, the magnetized wire was run past the electromagnet, producing currents in its windings; these currents were converted by earphones to the sounds of the original message.

The telegraphone, invented by the Danish engineer Valdemar Poulsen in 1898, was the first commercial magnetic recorder. It was made in the United States for use as a dictating machine.

TELEMACHUS, te-lem′ə-kus, in the Homeric Trojan War cycle, was a son of Odysseus (Ulysses) and Penelope. He was a baby when Odysseus left home to take part in the Trojan War. When Odysseus had been absent from home for about 20 years, Telemachus was urged by Athena (Minerva) in the guise of Mentor, a friend of Odysseus, to search for his father. At Athena's suggestion he sought news of Odysseus at the courts of Nestor and Menelaus. Telemachus next sailed back to Ithaca, where his mother's many suitors, whom he had denounced (because his father was still alive), planned to ambush his ship and murder him, but he escaped their plan. Again with Athena's help he met his father, who was disguised as a beggar. Telemachus later assisted his father in overcoming the suitors. After Odysseus' death he married Circe, and by her he became the father of Latinus. See also ODYSSEUS.

TELEMANN, tä′lə-män, **Georg Philipp** (1681–1767), German composer, who was the most versatile and influential musician of his day in Germany. He was born in Magdeburg on March 14, 1681. Musically, he was largely self-taught, but his aptitude was so great that he began to compose at a very early age and continued to do so after entering Leipzig University in 1701 to study law and philosophy. In 1704 he became organist at the New Church in Leipzig, but left shortly to become court composer at Sorau. From 1708 to 1712 he was court composer at Eisenach and from 1712 to 1721 was music director at the churches of the "Barefooted Friars" and St. Catherine in Frankfurt. In 1721 he moved to Hamburg, where he was appointed cantor of the Johanneum and music director of the five major churches there. In 1737 he went to Paris, where he was enthusiastically received and was in turn greatly impressed by French musical ideas. He died in Hamburg on June 25, 1767.

The bulk of Telemann's output was church music, including 44 Passions and numerous services, oratorios, and cantatas. However, he also composed much chamber, orchestral, and secular vocal music and over 40 operas. He had the highest regard of his contemporaries, including Bach, whose eldest son was Telemann's godchild.

R. ALEC HARMAN, *Coauthor of "Man and His Music"*

TELEMETRY, tə-lem′ə-trē, is the branch of engineering that deals with the detection and measurement of physical quantities at one location, the transmission of the measurement data to a distant receiving station, and the recording, display, or interpretation there of the data. The distance between the point of measurement and the receiving station may be only a few inches, as in ground tests of engines, or it may be many millions of miles, as in the transmission of data from deep-space probes. Sometimes the transmission link is used exclusively for telemetry and sometimes for telemetry and other purposes such as human communications or flight commands to a spacecraft.

Historical Background. Long-distance telemetry was first used in 1874, when electrical signals representing meteorological data were transmitted by wire from the slopes of Mont Blanc to Paris, a distance of about 300 miles (485 km). Wire-link telemetry also was used in 1913–1914 to report the water level in the locks of the Panama Canal and the position and movement of the lock gates, and to display to measured quantities at a central control board. In the 1920's telemetry became more widely used, including the reporting of load conditions in electrical power transmission systems and of pressure conditions in long petroleum pipelines.

An early use of radio telemetry was in France in 1931, when small unmanned balloons sent weather data, such as temperature, pressure, and humidity measurements, to ground stations. Soon after 1940, the first radio telemetry systems for flight tests of aircraft were designed and used for measuring structural strains and flight characteristics. This occurred in response to the need for more complete and reliable measurements than could be provided by on-board recorders or pilots' observations during experimental flights of military aircraft. By 1945 radio telemetry was used for flight measurements taken during tests of small rockets. About the same time rockets were provided with telemetry equipment for exploration of the upper atmosphere at altitudes far above those reached by balloons.

By 1955 large and complex rocket-propelled vehicles were being designed and built in the United States, spurring the development of radio telemetry systems that could transmit hundreds of measurements for subsequent data processing. By 1970 the development of unmanned satellites for space research, communications, meteorology, and earth resources evaluations, of unmanned space probes for investigating the solar system, and of programs for manned space flight had led to even more advanced telemetry systems. These made use of computer control and data processing before transmission. Telemetry also became increasingly useful in biomedical research.

How a Telemetry System Works. In the operation of a telemetry system the major steps are those that: (1) make a measurement; (2) originate a signal that represents a measured quantity needed for eventual interpretation or decision; (3) encode, or modulate, this signal to give it greater immunity to errors that may arise during its passage over the transmission link; (4) transmit the encoded signal over the link, generally by wire or radio; (5) receive the encoded signal; (6) decode, or demodulate, the received signal to obtain the wanted measurement data; and (7) record, display, store, or interpret the data that have been obtained.

In most uses of telemetry systems, it is necessary to send signals representing many measurements over the same channel. This is accomplished by the use of some form of multiplexing. In one technique, called *frequency-division multiplexing*, each measurement signal is assigned to a frequency band that does not overlap any of the other frequency bands to which signals are assigned. In another technique, called *time-division multiplexing*, each measurement signal is assigned to a time interval that does not overlap any of the other time intervals to which signals are assigned.

The coding techniques that are used include pulse-amplitude modulation (PAM), pulse-duration modulation (PDM), and pulse-code modulation (PCM). In the 1960's, PCM was used increasingly in all areas of telemetry as a result of the development of complex microelectronic circuits, digital computers for data processing, and improved coding methods. See also RADIO—*Principles of Radio*.

APPLICATIONS

Telemetry has two major applications: as a permanent part of a fully developed operational system and as a temporary part of a system being tested. When part of an operational system, as for industrial control or for space probes, the telemeter must be compatible with the rest of the system with respect to cost, reliability, maintainability, and other factors. When part of a system being tested, as in rocket vehicle tests or in biomedical research experiments, the telemeter need not be fully compatible with the rest of the system.

Industrial Control. A telemetry system for supervisory control of a gas pipeline may extend over 2,000 miles (3,220 km), often using wire circuits for much of the basic transmission link. At a typical compressor station on the pipeline route, the telemetry system makes measurements to determine station status, pressure set points, actual pressures, and gas flow, and converts the data to digital form by using pulse-code modulation. On demand, the system transmits the data to a central office, where they are evaluated by a computer. Based on this evaluation, appropriate control signals are sent to various compressor stations along the route.

Rocket Vehicle Tests. A radio telemetry system for flight tests of the Saturn rocket launch vehicle made as many as 1,000 measurements and transmitted all the data by the time-division multiplex method. The rocket was so large that the time-division multiplexer was divided into subunits distributed throughout the rocket in order to reduce the excessive amount of signal circuit wiring that would otherwise be needed.

Dental Research. A telemeter placed inside the human mouth can transmit as many as 10 measurements, including some on the forces and motions of the teeth. The entire telemeter, including a battery and a radio transmitter, fits in the space of the crown of a molar tooth. In this application time-division multiplexing and pulse-amplitude modulation are used in transmitting the data to a radio receiver.

LAWRENCE L. RAUCH, *University of Michigan*

Further Reading: Golomb, Solomon W., and others, *Digital Communications* (Englewood Cliffs, N. J., 1964); Nichols, Myron H., and Rauch, Lawrence L., *Radio Telemetry* (New York 1956); Stiltz, Harry L., ed., *Aerospace Telemetry*, vols. 1 and 2 (Englewood Cliffs, N. J., 1961, 1966).

TELEOLOGY, tēl-ē-ol′ə-jē, from the Greek *telos*, "end," is the explanation of a thing or event by its purpose, aim, or end—that is, by what it is for. Thus one might say that animals have eyes in order to detect distant enemies or prey—eyes, therefore, exist as a means to that end. Eyes are the "efficient cause" (in Aristotle's term) of detection—or simply its cause, as we normally say (see CAUSE); but detection is their "final cause" (from Latin *finis*, "end")—the reason for them, as we might say.

Purposes indisputably yield at least provisional explanations of conscious human acts. Teleology, or "finalism," as a philosophy emphasizes or magnifies this principle in either or both of two ways. It extends its scope to analogous but nonconscious processes in men, animals, and plants or, indeed, beyond all apparent analogy to inanimate objects. And it asserts the independence or irreducibility of teleology by denying, for instance, that a purpose itself can be explained away as just another efficient cause with causes of its own. This philosophy is supported in part by whatever successes it meets and whatever failures befall nonteleological accounts, but mostly it is supported by examination of what is involved in existence and explanation themselves. Only reasons, it argues, are truly antithetical to "mere chance" and can really explain or "make sense" of things.

Primitive peoples and persons are natural teleologists, ascribing vague purposes to everything. This idea received highly sophisticated expression in Aristotle's doctrine that the essence of anything is the final cause it strives to realize. Such "internal" teleology contrasts but does not conflict with the "external" teleology of the belief, sublimated in Judaism and Christianity, that the world as a whole was designed by a deity. The teleological argument for God—that the order and beauty of nature prove his existence —is thus also a theological argument for teleology (see GOD). Medieval Scholasticism, combining Aristotelian essences with divine creation, was the acme of teleology.

The causalist, or mechanist, retorts that the charm of finalistic explanation is more sentimental than logical (see MECHANISM). Finalism, he says, is not only unclear but paradoxical, since it alleges that a present actuality is due to the mere value of a mere future possibility. He may add that, historically, finalism has been either quite unproductive—"a barren virgin," said Francis Bacon—or prone to excesses, as in Voltaire's parody that man's nose was provided to support his spectacles. Causal determinism, on the other hand, is comparatively clear and has succeeded so often in application that it can reasonably be expected to cope with even the most obviously purposive phenomena. The first philosophers of Greece were valiant causalists. Their considerable achievements were not enough to discourage the teleological reaction, as expressed in Socrates, Plato, Aristotle, and Christian theism, but their antiteleology was vigorously reaffirmed as the program of the sciences so triumphant since the Renaissance.

Teleology, nevertheless, does not lack common-sense uses or metaphysical advocates. So-called analytic philosophies are generally hostile to it, but every form of idealism, pragmatism, and existentialism—and even such scientifically oriented systems as those of Samuel Alexander and A. N. Whitehead—finds the universe alive with will, nisus (striving), or "concern." And recent physics, limiting the incidence of causation, cannot complain if teleologists fill the gaps with "reasons." Biologists, who bear the main brunt, mostly reject the special finalistic agencies proposed by vitalism (see VITALISM), but they commonly doubt that organic wholes are explicable by the physicochemistry of their parts. Meantime, they face the task of formulating exactly the observable "goal-directedness" of organisms and organs—the coordination of functions by which they survive and flourish—without either asserting or denying that these can eventually be traced to physical causes.

Teleological ethics looks to ends not to explain acts but to define their rightness or wrongness. An act is the right one if it involves, in itself and all its effects, the greatest sum of good that is possible in the circumstances—for example, the most happiness (see UTILITARIANISM)—rather than because of any inherent trait such as conformity with an abstract rule of duty ("formalism" or "deontologism"). See also Index entry TELEOLOGY.

DONALD C. WILLIAMS
Author of "Principles of Empirical Realism"

TELEOSTEI, a subclass of ray-finned bony fishes containing many of the world's fishes. See FISH—*Classification of Fishes.*

TELEPATHY, tə-lep'ə-thē, is direct communication from mind to mind by some means other than the usual senses. Telepathy is considered one of the subclasses of extrasensory perception (ESP). Psychologists carry out research on telepathy by analyzing reports of spontaneous cases and by experimenting under laboratory conditions.

Reports of Spontaneous Cases. Records of what seem to be instances of telepathy vary strikingly. Telepathic impressions may be vague or clear, simple or detailed. They may be over in a flash or last for minutes. Sometimes the experience comes as a visual image and sometimes as a sound, perhaps of a voice. Sometimes the report is of knowledge without sensory imagery—for example, one says, "When the telephone rang I knew it was John, though I hadn't heard from him in months." Such experiences resemble hallucinations or delusions, and the mentally ill often mistakenly think their hallucinations are telepathic.

Investigators of such reports try to find if the experience was described before there was other information about the event, and also if the event took place as reported. Many accounts have been authenticated, some of important or crisis situations. Other cases involve trivial matters, as when a woman in Scotland believed she saw a friend wearing a purple dress. She was astonished because she thought the friend was in England and she believed the friend never wore purple. Later the woman learned that her friend had indeed been in London at that time and had been trying on a new purple dress, the first she had ever bought.

After authenticated cases are collected, two critical questions must be raised about them. Could the experience be explained by normal associations of ideas? For example, might the woman in Scotland have suspected her friend was ready to buy something daringly different? Might the apparent telepathy be only coincidence? If, for example, a mother "hears" her son calling her when he is in a distant accident, consider how often she and other mothers have had a similar experience when nothing was wrong.

Laboratory Experiments. Laboratory investigations seem to confirm that telepathy can occur. They also show that it is a weak ability in most people, and that it is hard or perhaps impossible for a person to be sure that a particular impression is telepathic. Experiments are conducted under tightly controlled conditions, in which the telepathic "messages" follow a random order, the sender and receiver are separated so that there can be no sensory cues, and there is independent recording of what is sent and what is received. Results indicate that telepathy is more likely to be successful between two people who know and trust each other than between strangers, between two who have a good deal in common than two whose attitudes are dissimilar, and between warm, outgoing people than between hostile or reserved ones. It is also more likely to be successful with vivid, emotionally toned stimuli than neutral ones.

In most cases of what is called telepathy, the person may be responding to some object or event rather than to anyone's thoughts about it, as in the case of a father away from home who had a sudden vivid image of his young son falling out of bed. He wrote his wife and learned the child had fallen out of bed at just about the time of his image. If this is more than coincidence, it might represent a response to the event (clairvoyance) instead of to his wife's or child's thoughts (telepathy). Experiments have therefore been conducted in which there was no objective record of the message. The sender translated the digits of a random number table into a private code, never written or spoken, and then "sent" the message in code. These experiments have given results that cannot be explained by chance, thus indicating the existence of "pure telepathy."

Conclusions. There is no good theory of how telepathy occurs. It is sometimes suggested that brain waves from one person or animal may be picked up by another. This seems unlikely for several reasons. Brain waves of sufficient energy to give detailed information over long distances are not found by even the most sensitive instruments. Changes in distance have little effect upon telepathic accuracy. And such brain waves do not account for other forms of ESP that closely resemble telepathy. All types of ESP seem to function intermittently, are difficult to control or identify, show systematic, predictable errors, and have more success with warmth, cooperative interest, and good rapport than with a mood of negativism, hostility, or apathy. See also CLAIRVOYANCE; PSYCHICAL RESEARCH.

GERTRUDE SCHMEIDLER
The City College, New York

Further Reading: Schmeidler, Gertrude, *Extrasensory Perception* (New York 1969).

TELEPHONE. In its most basic form, a telephone system is a pair of wires connecting two telephones. This simple arrangement enables two persons separated by some distance to talk to each other. The fundamental idea in telephony is to convert a speaker's sound waves into analogous electric waves, transmit these waves over a distance, and then use them to re-create sound waves for the listener.

Alexander Graham Bell patented the telephone in 1876, and soon thereafter telephone systems began a steady growth in size and complexity. Local networks grew into regional networks, regional networks grew into national networks, and national networks eventually had interconnections forming a global network.

Telephone systems now are very large and almost incredibly complex. For instance, a caller in the United States can dial a few numbers and reach any one of the 110 million telephones in the country. He also can reach more than 209 other countries and more than 96% of the telephones in the world.

Telephone systems provide an array of services besides person-to-person voice communications, although the fundamental service is handling local, long-distance, and overseas calls.

The television and radio broadcast industry is furnished with suitable circuits for transmitting television and radio programs to various stations in the country to facilitate network operations.

Many kinds of data circuits are provided to interconnect different types of data processing facilities, and telephone networks have been handling a growing volume of computer data. Private-line data channels also are available with line capacities to suit various data speed requirements. The Bell System's Data-Phone service provides a convenient way to send digital data over the regular telephone network.

The Bell System's visual telephone service, called Picturephone, was introduced into commercial service in Pittsburgh, Pa., on June 30, 1970. The initial subscribers included a department store, a radio station, an accounting firm, and several manufacturing companies. Picturephone service is expected to be offered in many localities in subsequent years.

AMERICAN TELEPHONE AND TELEGRAPH CO.

PICTUREPHONE service, introduced in 1970, enables caller and called party to see and hear each other.

1. Growth of Telephone Systems

The telephone provided two important advantages over the telegraph, its initial competitor. It eliminated the need for a telegraph operator, and it provided person-to-person voice communication. These advantages caused the rapid growth of telephone systems.

In Boston in May 1877, the first telephone exchange started as an adjunct to a burglar alarm system. In August 1877, there were 700 telephones in service in the United States. The first commercial exchange was opened in New Haven, Conn., in January 1878. It provided 8 lines and served 21 telephones. After a few years, there were many local exchanges, each providing service to its subscribers.

National Network. The initial link between New York and Boston was put into service on March 27, 1884. Within a few years, there were lines from New York to Philadelphia and Washington, and from New York to Albany. The long-distance network gradually was extended until it reached Denver in 1911. At that time, the line could not be increased in length because the telephone signal became weaker as the line became longer and audibility eventually became marginal.

Increasing the size of the wires helped, but the wires on the Denver link were almost the size of small bars. What was needed was a method to amplify the signals. The invention of the triode vacuum tube by Lee De Forest in 1906 and its improvement by others in 1912 provided the means for making a suitable amplifier, or "repeater" as it is called in telephone work.

Such a repeater was soon produced, and the line was extended from Denver to San Francisco, using vacuum-tube repeaters installed at Philadelphia, Pittsburgh, Chicago, Omaha, Denver, Salt Lake City, and Winnemucca, Nev. On Jan. 25, 1915, the first official transcontinental call was made between Alexander Graham Bell in New York and Thomas A. Watson in San Francisco. Using a replica of the first telephone, Bell said "Mr. Watson—come here. I want you!" He had transmitted this message over the first telephone on March 10, 1876.

Worldwide Network. The next big challenge was to span the oceans. This was first accom-

CONTENTS

plished by means of a powerful radio transmitter at Arlington, Va., and a radio receiver in Paris, France. The first transatlantic radiotelephone transmission was achieved on Oct. 21, 1915, when H. R. Shreeve, at the Eiffel Tower in Paris, heard the words, "and now, Shreeve, good night," addressed to him by B. B. Webb from the transmitter at Arlington. However, this conversation between two Bell System engineers occurred more than 10 years before the radiotelephone was ready for commercial use. Commercial radiotelephone service was opened between New York and London on Jan. 7, 1927. The following year, radiotelephone service was extended to Brussels, Amsterdam, Berlin, Paris, Stockholm, Madrid, Vienna, Prague, and other cities in Europe. Soon thereafter, radiotelephone service was extended to other continents.

The first round-the-world telephone call was made on April 25, 1935. Walter S. Gifford, president of the American Telephone and Telegraph Company, and T. G. Miller were in the same building in New York City. Gifford talked to Miller over a 23,000-mile (37,000-km) circuit of wire and radio channels.

Although worldwide telephony had arrived, serious problems remained. The radiotelephone links were subject to severe ionospheric disturbances, making them unusable for days at a time. Furthermore, the demand for transatlantic telephone service was so great that sometimes one had to wait several hours to place a call. The atmospheric disturbances can be avoided by using submarine telephone cables, but their development was a formidable task.

Submarine Telephone Cables. Transoceanic submarine telegraph cables have been used successfully since 1866. The first successful transoceanic submarine telephone cable came into use 90 years later because the technical requirements for a telephone cable are much more exacting than those for a telegraph cable. For satisfactory transmission, a telephone cable must carry a much wider band of frequencies than a telegraph cable. Furthermore, amplifiers are necessary in submarine telephone cables, just as they are on long land lines. The formidable problem was to develop a very reliable, long-life amplifier that could withstand the stresses of cable laying and the pressures at the ocean bottom. Also, the power for the amplifiers had to be supplied from a land station, sometimes more than 1,000 miles (1,610 km) away.

The first major step was taken in 1950 when two cables, one for each direction of transmission, were laid between Key West, Fla., and Havana. Each submarine telephone cable had three amplifiers to boost the signal strength at intervals along the 115-mile (185-km) route. Building on this success, the first transatlantic telephone cable was put into commercial service on Sept. 25, 1956. It provides 29 telephone circuits between London to New York and 6 between London and Montreal. The deep-sea portion from Oban, Scotland, to Clarenville, Newfoundland, is 1,950 miles (3,140 km) long. Other submarine telephone cables, including some from North America to Europe and one from Hawaii to Japan, were laid soon thereafter. Some of these telephone cables have a considerably greater circuit capacity than that of the 1956 cable.

Although very successful, transoceanic telephone cables have been expensive to install, and they have provided a relatively small number of channels. Furthermore, these telephone cables were not designed to transmit television signals, which require a much wider frequency band than telephone channels. See also CABLE.

Communications Satellites. Communication by satellite filled the need for a facility capable of carrying television or many telephone channels. The era of transmission via satellite started in August 1960 when radiotelephone signals were successfully transmitted between Holmdel, N. J., and Goldstone, Calif., using radio waves reflected off the Echo 1 satellite. Echo 1, a balloon with a 100-foot (30-meter) diameter, had an aluminized surface to reflect the radio waves transmitted from the ground transmitting station to the distant ground receiving station.

Telstar 1, Telstar 2, and many later communications satellites have shown conclusively that satellites will have an important place in global telephony. The high quality and low cost of satellite and submarine telephone circuits have encouraged their use, and overseas telephone calls have been increasing at the rate of 25% per year. See also COMMUNICATIONS SATELLITE.

WORLDWIDE SURVEY OF TELEPHONE SYSTEMS

The key features of telephone systems are similar in most countries, although the details differ. This similarity results from patent licensing, interchange of scientific ideas, the sale of telephone components and systems in a worldwide market, and the standardization encouraged by the need for interconnection.

International Telephone Standards. Just as railroad companies must use accepted standards for such items as the width between rails, telephone companies must agree on standards in order to interconnect and operate properly. The agency responsible for these standards is the International Telecommunications Union (I T U). About 138 countries are members of the I T U. It is the United Nations' specialized agency for telecommunications. This organization promotes the advancement of international telecommunications by means of international agreements that are based on the prepared standards. Experts from many countries work together to develop and prepare these standards. At first this work was done mainly at international conferences, but the expanding scope of the work soon required a more organized approach. Consequently, the following International Consultative Committees (CCI's) were formed: the International Telephone Consultative Committee (CCIF) in 1923, the International Telegraph Consultative Committee (CCIT) in 1925, and the International Radio Consultative Committee (CCIR) in 1927. The first two committees were combined in 1956 to form the International Telegraph and Telephone Consultative Committee (CCITT).

TELEPHONES BY CONTINENTAL AREA[1]

Continental area	Number of phones, Jan. 1, 1969	Percent of world	Per 100 population
North America	117,686,000	49.5	52.7
Central America[2]	2,224,000	0.9	2.5
South America	4,924,000	2.1	2.7
Europe	77,359,000	32.5	12.0
Africa	2,961,000	1.2	0.9
Asia	27,628,000	11.6	1.4
Australia and Oceania	5,118,000	2.2	26.5
World	*237,900,000*	*100.0*	6.8

[1]Source: American Telephone and Telegraph Co.
[2]Includes Mexico, Caribbean islands, and Bermuda.

Private Versus National Ownership. Countries in which most telephone systems are operated by private companies include Canada, United States, Mexico, Brazil, Peru, Venezuela, Denmark, Finland, and Spain. Countries in which most telephone systems are operated by the government include Cuba, Argentina, Colombia, Uruguay, Austria, Belgium, Czechoslovakia, France, East Germany, West Germany, Netherlands, Norway, Poland, Sweden, Switzerland, and South Africa. In some cases, as in Italy, Japan, and the United Kingdom, government-controlled systems are operated as public corporations.

Number of Telephones. Since 1955 the number of telephones in the world has been increasing at a rate of about 6% per year. By 1969 there were 237,900,000 telephones in the world. The number of telephones in various continental areas and in various countries are given in the two accompanying tables. The United States ranks first, with 109,256,000 telephones; Japan is second, with 20,525,000 telephones; and the United Kingdom is third, with 12,910,000 telephones. The United States has 45.9% of the world's telephones, and it has the highest ratio of phones to population—54 per 100 population. In contrast, India has about 1 million phones and a ratio of 0.2 phone per 100 population. As for cities, New York leads with 5.7 million telephones, Tokyo is second with 3.6 million, and London ranks third with 3.2 million.

COUNTRIES THAT HAVE MORE THAN 500,000 TELEPHONES[1]

Total Telephones in Service

Country	*1969*	*1959*	*Per 100 pop. (1969)*
Argentina	1,599,861	1,223,509	6.72
Australia	3,392,436	2,056,000	28.20
Austria	1,242,785	615,328	16.88
Belgium	1,847,363	1,036,305	19.18
Brazil	1,560,701	949,306	1.74
Canada	8,820,770	5,118,293	42.12
Colombia	574,700[2]	243,986	2.85
Czechoslovakia	1,789,373	889,684	12.44
Denmark	1,516,802	976,667	30.88
Finland	1,009,336	545,338	21.50
France	7,503,491	3,703,578	14.98
Germany, East	1,896,151	1,175,131	11.10
Germany, West	11,248,979	5,090,102	18.65
Greece	761,550	168,993	8.63
Hungary	684,389	400,972	6.66
India	1,057,193	378,496	0.20
Italy	7,752,042	3,182,455	14.37
Japan	20,525,211	5,096,296	20.12
Mexico	1,174,943	447,984	2.44
Netherlands	2,917,384	1,402,155	22.80
New Zealand	1,155,465	641,342	41.56
Norway	1,036,027	683,075	27.02
Poland	1,650,896	732,682	5.08
Portugal	653,407	332,309	6.87
Rumania	596,000[2]	261,700	2.99
South Africa	1,397,725	887,601	7.29
Spain	3,723,239	1,490,151	11.44
Sweden	4,110,579	2,526,424	51.76
Switzerland	2,685,800	1,475,003	43.42
United Kingdom	12,901,000	7,525,000	23.26
USSR	9,900,000[2]	3,810,000	4.14
United States	109,256,000	66,645,000	54.02
Yugoslavia	549,019	217,542	2.70

[1] Source: American Telephone and Telegraph Co.
[2] Estimated

2. How a Telephone System Works

A telephone system performs three major functions. It transmits the voice signals between the two telephones; it switches circuits to set up a unique path for the call; and it uses signaling circuits to handle tasks such as ringing, busy tone, and dialing.

SENDING AND RECEIVING

A telephone set consists of a transmitter, a receiver, a dial mechanism or push-button facility, and a switch hook.

The transmitter or microphone converts sound waves into electrical waves. In a typical transmitter, specially processed carbon granules do this job efficiently and cheaply. The carbon granules are placed in a box in such a way that pressure is exerted on the granules by a thin diaphragm. When a caller takes the telephone off the switch hook, an electric current flows through the carbon granules. When he speaks, the sound waves force the diaphragm to increase or decrease the pressure on the granules. These pressure changes result in similar increases or decreases in the intensity of the current through the granules.

The receiver converts the varying currents sent by the distant transmitter into sound waves, which the called party hears as speech. This is done by means of a thin steel disk or diaphragm, which is acted upon by an electromagnet. The electromagnet is energized by the varying electrical current. The varying electric current alters the magnetic strength of the electromagnet, which changes the position of the steel diaphragm. The back-and-forth movement of the diaphragm reproduces the sound waves originated by the caller.

The telephone set provides the signals that enable the switches at the central office to set up the wanted connection. This is commonly done by a dial mechanism, which sends out the number of the desired party. As noted previously, when the telephone is taken off the switch hook, a current flows through the transmitter. This current is supplied by a battery in the central office. When a digit such as 6 is dialed, the dial mechanism operates a switch that interrupts the current six times. These current interruptions, or pulses, are counted by a circuit in the central office. In order to make properly timed pulses, the dial is controlled by a mechanical governor.

A newer method of signaling makes use of pushbuttons to send out the number of the desired party. Push-button (Touch-Tone) signaling works by sending out a unique pair of tones for each digit or push button. The tones are generated by transistor tone oscillators, which are energized when the buttons are pushed. A receiver in the local office recognizes each pair of tones and indicates the digit being sent.

How a Call is Made. To place a call, the telephone set is taken off the hook. This operation closes a switch in the telephone set, and current from a battery at the central office flows through a pair of wires to the telephone. The flow of current energizes the carbon transmitter and also indicates to the central office that this line is calling for service. When the switching machine is ready to provide service, a source of dial tone is connected to this line. The calling party, by dialing or by push button, sends the digits of the telephone number of the desired party to the switching machine. The called number is checked for a busy condition. If busy, the calling line is connected to a busy tone.

If the called party is not busy, then ringing is applied to the called party. Simultaneously, a ringback tone is sent to the calling party to indicate that ringing is in process. When the called party answers, this is indicated by current flow in his telephone. The ringing and ringback circuits are disconnected, and the two parties are connected for their conversation.

Two basic jobs must be performed by the switching machine. The state of every call in progress must be watched, and the machine must be prepared to take appropriate action when signaling information, such as that given by dialing, is received. The machine must be capable of rapidly setting up connections between the two parties as well as connections for dialing, busy tone, and ringing. This job is done in different ways by various switching facilities.

SWITCHING

Although about 99% of the telephones in the United States are served by automatic switching systems, manual switchboards for operator-assisted calls still are in use in some communities. A manual switchboard includes sockets, or jacks, each connected to a line, and a set of flexible wires, or cords, with plugs on both ends. A connection is set up by plugging the ends of a cord into the two jacks associated with the correct lines. Auxiliary circuits provide the means for ringing the called telephone, indicating when a line wants service, or when a call is completed.

The growth of manual switchboards made it necessary to establish permanent connections, called trunks, between nonadjacent switchboards. Trunking is a simple but very important technique in telephone switching. In a small and simple switching facility, each jack leads to an individual telephone, and there is only one path between two telephones. With trunking, a number of different connections are available between switchboards. For example, either a direct trunk between two switchboards or an alternative path via another switchboard may be selected.

Automatic Electromechanical Switching—*Step-by-Step Systems.* The development of automatic switching began in 1889, when Almon B. Strowger, an American businessman, invented a rotary stepping switch. It still forms the basis for a substantial amount of step-by-step switching equipment. A version of the Strowger switch now in use has an array of 10 rows of 10 sets of fixed contacts. Each row is arranged in a circle, as shown in Fig. 1. The contact arm has two independent directions of motion. One direction is provided by a vertical motion to any desired row, and the other direction is provided by a rotary motion to any contact in that row. Thus the contact arm can connect one telephone to any one of 99 other telephones.

Fig. 1. Strowger switch shown here has 10 rows of 10 contacts. When the number 23 is dialed, for instance, the vertical and rotary drive fingers move the contact arm to the second row and the third contact in that row. This contact provides a connection to phone 23.

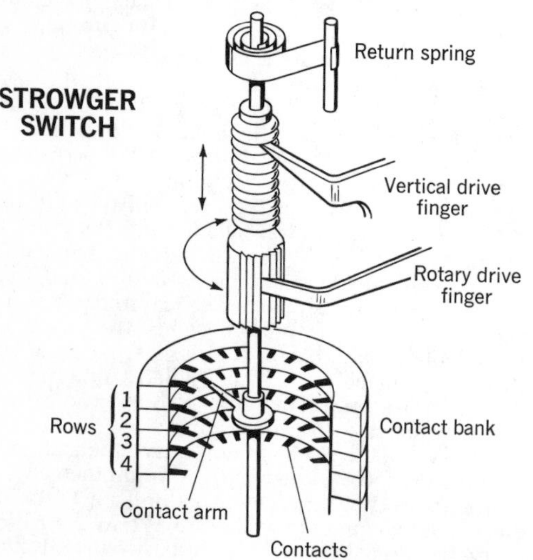

The switch is activated by electromagnets and a ratchet mechanism. For example, two pulses of current in one electromagnet cause the contact arm to move to the second row, and three pulses in another electromagnet cause the contact arm to step around to the third contact in that row. Afterward, the arm is released by a third electromagnet, which allows it to go back to its starting point.

This switch is used to build a step-by-step system. The key idea is that each step in the operation of the switch is under the control of the customer's dial. The dial control and switching functions are closely related. A simple example with several telephones is shown in Fig. 2. In this figure, only the principle of using successive banks of contacts is represented. For actual large systems, it is necessary to introduce trunks and a technique called hunting.

In hunting, a switch automatically searches a series of contacts until the first desired (nonbusy) contact is found. This can be done by connecting two contact arms so that they move in unison, each over its own bank of contacts. One bank is used for the connection, and the second bank is used to carry a signal indicating busy or idle. If a contact is busy, a pulse is automatically given to an electromagnet to make the arm step to the next position. As a result, the switch hunts contacts until it finds the first idle contact.

In a large step-by-step system, each telephone starting a call is connected to the moving arm of a first switch, called a selector. The contacts of this switch are not connected to other telephones but to trunk groups. The switch, under control of the dial, moves to a particular row of contacts and then hunts an idle trunk. This process continues until the customer reachs a switch that can connect to a group of telephones including the called party. The last digits dialed cause that switch to make the connections to the called party.

The number of switches required to build a system can be reduced by using the hunting concept to search over a group of lines for the purpose of finding the one that is requesting service. This line-finder switch then connects the selector switch to the line wanting service. Thus switches can be provided in smaller numbers appropriate to the traffic rather than on a basis of one selector switch per telephone. Step-by-step systems, many with improvements not described here, are still widely used. Although they do not represent the most advanced technology, they are reliable workhorses.

Crossbar Systems. Crossbar systems are perhaps the most modern electromechanical switching systems. Two basic changes distinguish crossbar systems from step-by-step systems. One change is that in step-by-step systems, the switching and control functions are related, whereas in modern crossbar systems these functions are com-

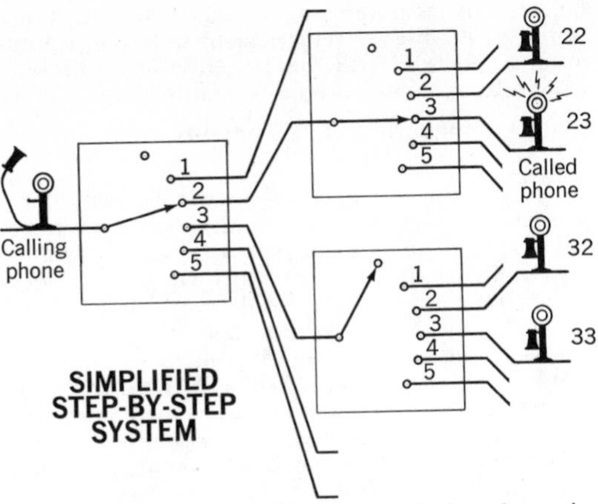

Fig. 2. Step-by-step switching system is based on the use of successive banks of contacts called selectors. In the two-step system shown here, the ten's selector moves to position 2 and the unit selector moves to position 3 when number 23 is dialed. This completes the connection from the calling phone to phone 23.

pletely separated. The crossbar switching network has the sole function of setting up connections. These connections are set up under the centralized and separate control of circuits called markers, which mark a path through the network.

The second basic change is the arrangement and operation of the switch. The switch consists of a grid of 10 horizontal wires and 10 vertical wires, with a small separation between the horizontal and vertical wires (see Fig. 3). A contact at each intersection enables up to 10 separate paths to be closed. The 100 contacts are opened and closed by 5 horizontal bars and 10 vertical bars. Two electromagnets are required for each horizontal bar and one for each vertical bar, making a total of 20.

The advantages of the crossbar switch are its small rapid motions and its adaptability for setting up connections. The separation of the control and switching functions not only provides substantial advantages in speed and flexibility but also certain new features.

One new feature is that the system makes a second trial if the first attempt to set up a call is unsuccessful. A second feature is alternative routing. If all the trunks to a particular central office are busy, the marker selects a route via another office. A third feature is that the system can detect failures in its own equipment and report them on punched cards.

Electronic Switching Systems. Electronic switching systems have the greatest promise for future advances. They provide great versatility, new features, and small size. The key elements that make electronic switching possible are transistors and semiconductor diodes. The important advantages of transistors are that they operate in a millionth of a second or less, and they are extremely small. Several transistor circuits can be made on a tiny wafer that is barely visible to the naked eye.

The development of electronic switching has clarified the role played by logic and memory. The earliest Strowger switching system used logic and memory, but these functions were obscured by mechanical detail. These two functions stand out very clearly in electronic systems. Furthermore, when the logic, memory, and network switching functions are separated, they are particularly adapted to the efficient use of electronic circuits.

When processing a call, a switching system essentially makes a series of simple logical decisions. The control action taken each time there is a change in the state of a call depends entirely on the information received from switch hook, the dial or push buttons, and the present state of the call. Logic can be built into a control system in two ways. In one method called wired logic, a tailor-made circuit is built to perform a particular logic function. Almost all decisions made in electromechanical switching systems use wired-logic circuits. They are built to take advantage of multiple-contact relays and other types of switches. These wired-logic circuits function very well, but changes are difficult because rewiring is required.

Stored-Program Systems. An alternative method using a special-purpose computer is called stored program. In one system, two memories are used. One is a semipermanent memory in which the call-handling procedures (or programs) are stored. These programs are written or magnetically encoded on plug-in cards. Changes or additions to the call-handling procedures are made by inserting different cards. Short-term information, such as the status of the calls in process, is stored in a second memory, which acts as an electronic scratch pad. Information received from telephone hooks and dials is also stored in the short-term memory. The information in the short-term memory is continually being changed as calls are processed.

The processing of a telephone call is analyzed into a number of discrete states. There may be several hundred such states, and each is assigned a number. This state number and instructions as to the different actions that may be required, depending on information from switch hook and dial, are stored in the semipermanent memory.

The processing of a call proceeds as follows. A call is started when a customer takes his telephone off the hook. Assume this situation is labeled state 1. The calling telephone number and state 1 are written in the scratch-pad memory in a space now assigned to this call. This memory is interrogated frequently. At the next interrogation, state 1 is read out and the semipermanent memory is checked for instructions associated with state 1. These instructions are

Fig. 3. Crossbar switch shown here can handle ten simultaneous calls. Paths for three calls are shown.

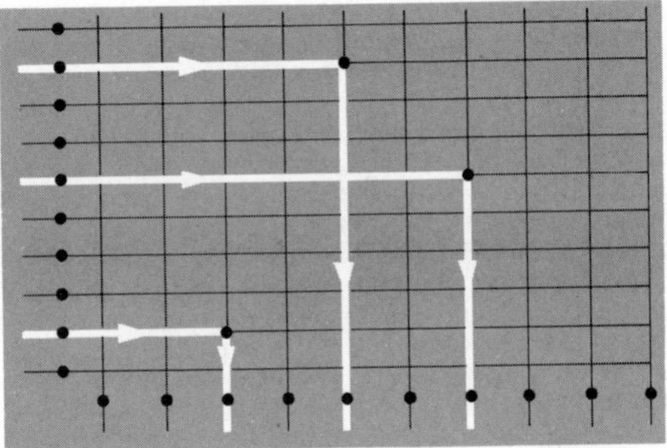

to determine whether the telephone is answering a call or originating one. In this example, the scratch-pad memory shows that the off-hook telephone is not connected to another telephone or to dial tone. Therefore this is a call origination, and the program instructs the network to connect the telephone to a register that supplies dial tone. When this is done, the scratch-pad memory is revised to list the call as being in state 2.

When received, the dialed digits are recorded in the scratch-pad memory. When all the digits are available, they are read out, and the stored program chooses a path through the network. As each call is acted on, the scratch pad is changed to read state 3, state 4, or whatever is appropriate. The scratch-pad memory has a space for each call in process. The information in the various spaces is examined sequentially; however, the sequence is so rapid that the calls seem to be handled at the same time rather than one after the other.

A stored program control has the advantage of great flexibility. New routines and features can always be introduced by changing the program instructions. The only limitation is the size of the memory. Stored program control also permits greater use of self-checking and automatic diagnosis than previous systems.

Many stored-program electronic switching systems (ESS-1 systems) have been placed in service in various cities in the United States.

Time-Division Switching Systems. Transistors have made possible still another major innovation in switching networks. The previous networks were known as space-division networks because the calls were separated from each other in space —that is, each call traveled over a different path. In a new approach, calls travel over the same path but are separated from each other in time. This is known as time-division switching.

In this method each telephone is connected to a common path by a switch. To set up a connection, the switches associated with two telephone are closed and opened synchronously at a rapid rate. Typically, they are closed for one microsecond out of every 100 microseconds. During the brief closures, a series of pulses is transmitted from the sending end of the connection. These pulses are samples of the electric wave from the sending telephone. Each sample represents a small slice of this electric wave, which was formed by speaking into the telephone. In order to reconstruct the electric wave from the pulses samples at the receiving end of the connection, a filter is used between the switch and the telephone at the receiving end. This filter converts the pulses into an electric wave that is a replica of the one formed by the sending telephone. This reconstructed wave is fed to the receiving telephone, which converts it to a replica of the sound originated by the speaking party.

A second connection between two other telephones is made over the common path in a similar manner, except that the switch closures for this conversation occur at microsecond instants different from those for the first connection. Connections between other pairs of telephones are made over the common path in a similar manner, with each connection using microsecond instants for switch closures that differ from those for any other connection. Although only samples of electric waves are transmitted, any required fidelity in reproducing speech can be obtained by proper design. Electronic switching systems using both the stored-program method and the time-division switching (ESS-101 systems) are now used in many places.

3. Interconnection of Telephones and Telephone Offices

The telephone network in the United States consists of exchange (local) networks and intertoll (long-distance) networks. Each exchange area network is concerned primarily with local calls (see Fig. 4). The local central office interconnects local subscribers and has interoffice trunks to other local central offices. It also has trunks to at least one toll office. This toll office is the gateway to the long-distance network. Large metropolitan areas have tandem offices that function solely as switching points for trunks between local central offices.

When toll circuits were switched manually by operators, very few circuits could be connected in tandem. Long-distance service was comparatively slow, and trunks were often used inefficiently. Automatic switching of toll circuits increased the speed of service. It also provided for alternate routing, which is a very efficient way of using costly long-distance circuits. This efficiency results from the fact that it is only necessary to provide sufficient trunks between two locations to take care of normal traffic. Any unusual traffic loads are handled by the alternate routes.

Fig. 4. Exchange area network primarily handles local calls. Toll office is gateway to long-distance network. Tandem office provides switching points for trunks between local central offices.

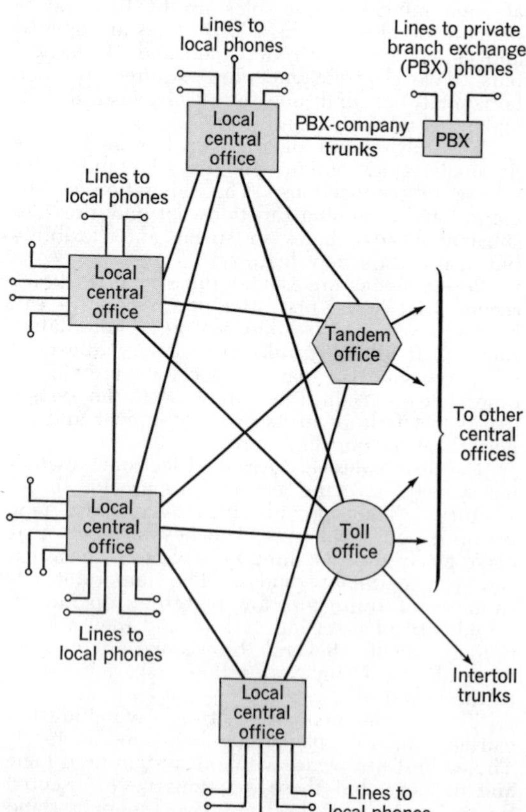

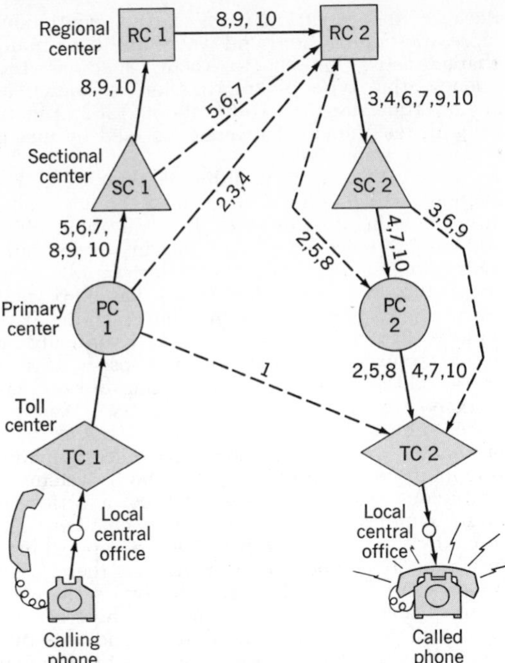

Fig. 5. Ten possible routes for a long-distance call are shown. The shortest route free for a call is preferred. Thus route 1—the shortest route—is the first choice, route 2 is the second choice, and route 10—the longest route—is the tenth choice.

The present Bell System toll switching plan provides for five ranks of switching centers. The highest rank is the regional center, and the lowest rank is the local central office. The chain of switching centers and the routing of a call are shown in Fig. 5. As shown, there are 10 possible routes for the call. Of course, the shortest route free for a call is preferred. A longer route is only used when others are full of traffic.

Interconnections for International Calls. In the case of international calls, it is necessary to take into account the substantial differences between signaling arrangements, dials, and equipment in various countries. Therefore, international connections are switched to a transit center, where equipment and operators are available to provide compatible switching and operation with the different national networks. Transit centers are located in White Plains, N. Y., New York City, Jacksonville, Fla., and Oakland, Calif. Operator dialing of overseas calls, which began in 1963, is in use between the Bell System and 23 countries. Direct customer dialing of overseas numbers is available on a limited basis. To facilitate future expansion of international dialing, the world has been divided into numbered zones. These zones are analogous to the numbered zones used in the United States to facilitate direct distance dialing.

4. Transmission Methods

Telephone transmission systems are designed to enable two persons to converse over a distance with about the same ease as in talking face to face. Experience has shown that certain quality standards must be applied to the voice signals in order to achieve this goal. For good fidelity, it is desirable to transmit voice signals in the frequency range from 200 to 3,500 hertz (cycles per second) with about equal strength. The listener must be provided with adequate volume, and noise and distortion must be minimized.

Long-distance calls present special problems, such as delay and delayed echo. Delayed echo occurs when the speaker hears his own voice returned to his ear speaker a small fraction of a second after he has spoken. If this echo is not controlled, it can be very annoying. A delay called round-trip delay occurs when the time taken for the other party's signal to return is so long that two-way talks become difficult.

Local Transmission Methods. For distances up to several miles, satisfactory service can be obtained by stringing a pair of wires on poles. However, the increased use of telephones led to unsightly mazes of telephone poles and wires. This situation was largely eliminated by the use of telephone cables, both on poles and underground, which have largely replaced open wire. The cables are made of a large number of twisted wire pairs.

Most wires are made of copper, but aluminum wires have been used increasingly. The wire insulation may be paper pulp or plastic. Wrappers of plastic, lead, or other metals are used around the outside of the cable to provide protection and mechanical strength and to prevent the entry of water. The wire-pair sizes typically range from 19 to 26 gauge. Cables with as many as 2,700 pairs of 26-gauge wire are used in urban areas.

The performance of cables can be improved by loading. Cable is loaded by inserting inductance coils in series with each cable pair at fixed intervals. A typical arrangement is 88 millihenrys of inductance at 6,000-foot (1,830-meter) intervals.

For local transmission, a single pair of wires carries the signals going in both directions. This is called 2-wire transmission. On longer calls where amplifiers are necessary, it is convenient to use two pair of wires for each circuit. This is called 4-wire transmission. One pair of wires is used for transmission in one direction, and the second pair for transmission in the other direction. Four-wire transmission makes it possible to use amplifiers, which are inherently one-way devices. Two-wire circuits can be changed to 4-wire (or vice versa) by the use of special devices called hybrids.

Long-Distance Transmission Methods. A big achievement has been the design of circuits that can transmit thousands of telephone conversations over very long distances. This is done by means of high-frequency waves and carrier circuits. The basic idea is simple. A telephone circuit or any other communication channel must be allotted a certain range of frequencies—a frequency band. The greater the width of the band, the greater is the amount of information that can be transmitted. A telephone conversation typically requires a band of frequencies from 200 hertz to 3,500 hertz, but it is often assigned to a band 4,000 hertz wide to allow a margin against interferences. A television picture requires a band about 4.2 million hertz wide because of its greater information content. The controlling factor is bandwidth rather than the particular range of frequencies. For instance, a single telephone conversation can be allocated to a frequency band from zero to 4,000 hertz, or it can be allocated to a frequency band from 1,000,000 to 1,004,000 hertz.

By the use of circuits called modulators and demodulators, a conversation can be shifted from one frequency band to another. In using this way, for example, 12 zero-to-4,000 hertz channels carried by wire pairs from a local cable can be shifted up to 12 consecutive 4000-hertz slots from 1,000,000 to 1,048,000 hertz occupying a single high-frequency channel. Thus the 12 channels originally in a band of low frequencies carried by spatially separated wire pairs are placed on a single high-frequency circuit where they are separated in frequency. This is called frequency-division multiplexing. Except for circuits in a local exchange area, most telephone conversations are transmitted over carrier circuits using frequency-division multiplexing.

For example, the L-4 coaxial cable system, which is a long-haul carrier system for underground use, has a bundle of 10 pairs of coaxial cables, with each pair having a capacity of 3,600 voice channels. Two coaxial cables are spares, so the bundle actually provides 32,400 voice channels. Each cable uses a frequency band 17 million hertz wide.

Undersea Transmission Methods. Submarine cables operate on the same basic carrier principles as land cables, although there are important differences. For instance, a submarine cable must withstand the deep-sea cable-laying process and the rigors of the deep-sea or shore-end environment. The transmission part of the link consists of a coaxial cable that is about 1 inch in diameter and has polyethylene insulation. The repeaters inserted in the cable are powered from the land, and they are spaced about 10 or 20 nautical miles (20 or 40 km) apart. The newest cables have a capacity of more than 720 voice channels.

Submarine cables are very costly and the traffic is so great that a special method is used to increase the effective number of channels. This method is called time assignment speech interpolation (TASI). TASI comes into operation when all the circuits in a cable are in use. To provide additional circuits, the TASI system finds pauses in the conversations already in process. (One half of a 2-way channel is idle when one person is talking and the other person listens.) During those pauses, the circuit is assigned to a waiting caller. By this means, the overall capacity of the cable is about doubled.

Microwave Relay Systems for Overland Transmissions. Microwave radio relay systems are carrier systems that consist of a series of towers separated by 20 to 30 miles (32 to 48 km). A directional antenna atop each tower receives the weak signal from the previous tower and, after amplification, transmits it to the next tower. Very high frequency radio waves (microwaves) are used. A typical band allocated for this service is from 3,700 to 4 200 million hertz. A system such as the TD-3 provides 12 radio channels in this band with 1 200 two-way telephone circuits in each channel. Microwave radio relay systems are reliable and economical.

DIGITAL TRANSMISSION METHODS

Although present telephone transmission systems are very complex, they basically do the same job that was first done in 1876. This job is to convert a speaker's sound waves into analogous electric waves, transmit these electric waves over a distance, and then convert the electric waves to sound waves for the listener. Because the electric waves are a continuous representation of the sound waves and have many characteristics similar to them, such as frequency, this type of transmission is known as analog transmission. Until about 1962, practically all telephone calls were processed by means of analog transmission.

Since 1962 a very different type of transmission, called digital transmission, has come into increasing prominence. In 1969 about 500,000 digital voice channels were in service, and their number has been increasing rapidly. Because this type of transmission has important advantages, digital transmission facilities are rapidly expanding nationwide. Eventually a digital transmission network perhaps will rival or exceed the nationwide analog transmission network now in use.

A digital transmission system is the twin brother to the time-division electronic switching system discussed previously. In both systems a continuous wave is represented by a series of pulse samples, and the different channels are separated by their relative order of appearance in a repetitive time frame. However, there is an important difference between the two systems.

In a time-division electronic switching system each sample pulse is transmitted, and the different heights of the pulses represent the original sound wave. In a typical digital transmission system each sample pulse height is represented by a code of pulses, and this code of pulses is transmitted as a sequence of on-off, or binary, pulses. This type of digital transmission is called pulse-code modulation (PCM). For example, in a 3-bit pulse code, a pulse height of 7 units is represented by 3 pulses, which corresponds to the binary number 111, which corresponds to the decimal number 7. (See also BINARY NOTATION; RADIO—*Principles of Radio*.) The received binary pulses are used to regenerate a series of pulses whose heights correspond to the heights of the initial pulse samples. These regenerated pulses then are sent through a filter, which converts the pulses to an electric wave. This wave is fed to a receiving telephone, which converts it to a replica of the original voice wave at the sending end.

Digital transmission has a tremendous advantage: when the pulses are weakened and distorted by transmission, they are regenerated. A pulse generator sends out a new stream of pulses that correspond to the received pattern. In this way, all the distortion introduced by the line is completely eliminated, and there is a fresh start each time. From a practical standpoint this means that digital messages are received without significant loss or distortion. In comparison, analog transmission is always limited by the unavoidable noise and distortion introduced by transmission and amplification.

The disadvantage of digital transmission for telephone service is the costly conversion from the initial electrical wave to digital form and back again. However, it is expected that new technology will reduce this cost substantially in the future.

HERBERT S. FEDER
Bell Telephone Laboratories

Further Reading: Hilder, S., *From Smoke Signals to Telstar* (Hemel Hempted, England, 1966); Michaelis, A. R., *From Semaphore to Satellite* (Geneva 1965); Talley, David, *Basic Carrier Telephony* (New York 1966); Talley, David, *Basic Telephone Switching Systems* (New York 1969).

5. Development of Telephone Technology

Practically all the 19th century inventions associated with the telephone were made in the United States, even though many of the preconditions for its development were first established in Europe. As has so frequently occurred in the history of technology, the telephone was simultaneously invented by several men. Before its invention in 1876, each had been working on the problem of increasing the number of telegraph messages that could be simultaneously transmitted over a single circuit. Their work on this problem led directly to the invention of a number of electrical instruments of varying design for the transmission and reception of the human voice.

Some earlier efforts to transmit sound over a distance were based on mechanical methods rather than electrical means. For example, the English scientist Charles Wheatstone studied the transmission of sound through wooden rods in the 1830's, and the American inventor Elisha Gray devised a "lover's telegraph" in 1875. Gray's device consisted of two tin cans, with the center of each bottom side connected by a taut string for carrying vibrations. When a person spoke into the open end of one can, vibrations traveled along the string and the speech could be heard in the other can.

However, the German schoolteacher Philipp Reis, as early as 1861, had invented an experimental electrical device that could be used to send musical notes. Whether it could transmit speech has never been ascertained. In the 1880's a few scientists claimed that Reis' instrument could transmit and reproduce the human voice, but no one sought to develop it for this purpose. Accordingly, the Reis instrument lies outside the line of development leading to the invention of the telephone.

INVENTION OF THE TELEPHONE

In the mid-1870's several men became aware that it might be possible to transmit the human voice by electrical means. They were Elisha Gray, Alexander Graham Bell, and, slightly later, Thomas Alva Edison. Gray was a telegraph-line superintendent for the Western Electric Company in Chicago and was already a well-known telegraph inventor. Bell was a speech teacher of deaf persons in Boston and a spare-time telegraph inventor. Edison, who previously had worked for the Western Union Telegraph Company, was a free-lance electrical inventor at Menlo Park, N. J. Another inventor with some claim to independent discovery of a telephone was Amos E. Dolbear, a professor at Tufts University, who devised an electrostatic telephone in 1879.

In the 1870's the rapidly growing telegraph industry urgently required a greater message-carrying capability. One alternative was to construct more telegraph lines, but this was expensive. Another alternative was to *multiplex* the already existing lines—that is, to increase the number of messages that could be sent over a single line. Gray's approach to multiplexing was to replace the on-off keying of a direct current for producing the familiar telegraph dots and dashes. Instead, he used the transmission or nontransmission of a current oscillating at an audio frequency. At the receiving end, only a properly tuned reed responded to this frequency.

AMERICAN TELEPHONE AND TELEGRAPH CO.

ALEXANDER GRAHAM BELL opened first telephone line from New York to Chicago on Oct. 18, 1892.

This formed the basis of the harmonic telegraph in which the number of messages that could be transmitted simultaneously was determined by the number of audio frequencies being used.

At first, Gray used a separate transmitter and a separate receiver for each audio-frequency channel, but he sent the various audio frequencies over a common circuit. Then he contrived a single receiver that responded to a broad range of frequencies and thereby reproduced musical chords. Gray was aware that the human voice is made up of notes of various frequencies. He saw that if he could devise a suitable transmitter, he would be able to change the sounds of the human voice into electrical signals that could be converted into a facsimile of the human voice at the other end of the line by means of a receiver, which he had already invented.

Bell, like Gray, started with the same problem of multiplexing, and he came to the same solution of devising a harmonic telegraph. Indeed, Bell had worked out a harmonic telegraph similar in principle to Gray's telegraph, and he also had recognized that if many frequencies could be transmitted, so too could the many components of the human voice. Then, in March 1875, Bell visited the noted scientist Joseph Henry at the Smithsonian Institution in Washington, and Henry urged Bell to continue with his experiments. In June 1875, Bell and Thomas A. Watson, who had joined him as an assistant in 1874, devised a transmitter for all the various voice frequencies by placing a magnetized reed in the center of a circular diaphragm that was set in vibration by the human voice. The vibrating reed induced varying electrical oscillations in an associated electromagnet. The same device at the distant end of the circuit functioned as a receiver (see photo A on page 408).

On Feb. 14, 1876, Bell applied for a patent on his invention. Patent 174,465, which was issued to Bell on March 7, 1876, became one of the most profitable and one of the most contested of all 19th century electrical patents. Legal diffi-

EARLY TELEPHONE EQUIPMENT underwent rapid development. (A) Bell's first transmitter sent sound tones. (B) Bell's cone-shaped telephone was first to transmit speech. (C) Bell's box telephone used Watson's thumper, which hit diaphragm to signal the called party. (D) Improved "butter-stamp" telephone had transmitter and receiver combined in a portable wooden handset; it was developed at Brown University. (Photos courtesy of A. T. & T.)

culties began on the day of his application, for that was also the day that Gray applied for a caveat on the invention of an electrical telephone. (The caveat was a legal notice that he had already begun work on such an invention.) At that time, neither Bell nor Gray had transmitted speech by his invention. Bell did not do so until March 10, 1876, when he uttered and transmitted the famous words to his assistant, "Mr. Watson, come here, I want you" (photo B). It was not until the summer of 1876, after Gray had seen Bell's telephone in operation at the Philadelphia Centennial Exposition, that Gray is said to have tested his own device.

Having found a telephone that at least worked between two rooms, Bell and Watson devoted their efforts to making it work over greater distances, first over a few miles and then between nearby cities. Bell's patent on this second phase of the evolution of his telephone was granted on Jan. 30, 1877.

However, the telephone as it had evolved so far, the so-called box telephone, was a large bulky object, and one had to speak loudly or shout into it (see photo C). In 1876–1877 a group of professors at Brown University created a portable and more efficient device (photo D). At first, in June 1877, these handsets were individually made to order and rented. The following month, the Bell Telephone Company was formed to provide an adequate financial basis for developing the telephone business.

COMPETITION WITH THE TELEGRAPH

At first, the telephone began to compete successfully with the district telegraph already in use in the major cities. The district telegraph primarily was a private-line system in which each home or office was connected only to a central telegraph office. Half a dozen coded messages, such as "send a messenger," "send for a doctor," and "send for the police," could be sent over it by using the right combination of dots and dashes. The telephone was potentially a much more useful instrument than the telegraph for sending such messages because voice communication eliminates the need for a special code, such as the Morse code.

To meet this unexpected competition, the Western Union Telegraph Company, which until then had dominated the field of electrical communications, hired Edison in 1876 to invent a transmitter different from Bell's so it would not have to pay for the use of Bell's invention. In the following year, Western Union formed the American Speaking Telephone Company. The new company purchased the patents of Gray and Dolbear, and added them to Edison's telephone patents.

Edison had been working on the problem of multiplexing as early as 1873. He had patented, in 1875, a harmonic telegraph with a receiver similar to that of Gray and Bell. By the spring of 1876, Edison was able to transmit complete sentences. By 1877, Edison had completed his development of a telephone transmitter that was based on a new principle. It used carbon contacts to control the flow of current. Edison's carbon transmitter was much more efficient than the Bell transmitter. After further development by Edison and others, it replaced the Bell transmitter.

In London, the British-American inventor David E. Hughes worked on a carbon transmitter independently of Edison. In the spring of 1878,

Hughes showed that hard carbon contacts could be used to amplify sounds electrically, thereby making a device he called a microphone. Because of its uncertain action, Hughes did not take out a patent on his discovery. However, during the winter of 1878, Henry Hunnings, an English clergyman, used Hughes' work to patent a telephone transmitter that had loose carbon granules.

In the United States, Emile Berliner invented a transmitter with two metallic contacts in 1877, and the next year Francis Blake devised a successful transmitter that made use of the contact between a platinum bead and a carbon block.

In the face of Edison's work and the strengthened position of Western Union, the Bell Telephone Company bought Berliner's patent rights, and it subsequently obtained the patent rights to the Blake and the Hunnings instruments. The inventions of Edison, Hunnings, Blake, and Berliner were similar in principle, but they used different physical means to control the current. The two competing telephone companies finally solved the question of their overlapping patents and of which company was to have the telephone business in 1879. The Bell Company agreed it would not become involved in the telegraph business, and Western Union agreed it would not become involved in the telephone business. Western Union agreed to transfer its telephone patent rights and telephone system to the Bell company in return for certain sums to be paid over the 17-year life of the patents.

DEVELOPMENT OF THE TELEPHONE SYSTEM

As the telephone system began to grow, new problems arose—interconnecting all the possible subscribers, increasing the efficiency of the interconnections, and extending the length of the telephone lines.

The first solutions to these problems derived from techniques already in use in the telegraph industry. For example, some district telegraph systems had a central office, or exchange, in which the telegraphs of various subscribers could be interconnected. The new telephone industry simply adapted such exchanges to its own needs. Additions were also made. In 1878, Watson added the magneto ringer, whereby a subscriber could signal the central exchange and the latter could signal the individual subscriber. In 1879, Hilborne L. Roosevelt introduced the hook switch, which automatically made the necessary connections to place the telephone in service when it was picked up or out of service when it was hung up.

Switching. The first telephone operators in the exchange were young boys. When they proved unreliable, the telephone company began hiring women, thereby contributing to women's growing economic independence. Not everyone was happy with operators. Almon B. Strowger had difficulties in getting the right number, and he concluded that the solution was to eliminate the operator by substituting an automatic electromechanical switching system. In 1891, Strowger patented a step-by-step process by which an electrical contact was moved first vertically and then horizontally over a rectangular grid of contacts on the inside of a cylindrical box until it finally reached the proper one (see Fig. 1). A dial placed on the sending transmitter actuated the Strowger electromechanical switch in the central exchange. During the next decade the Strowger switch slowly spread in use. However, the greater efficiency and lower cost of mechanical switching were not fully realized until the early 1920's, when the Bell System introduced a modified version of the Strowger switch in its exchanges.

A further development of electromechanical switching was the crossbar switching system, which was first put into service in 1938 at a central office in Brooklyn, N.Y. The crossbar switch and the marker method of switching control associated with it provided great flexibility and speed. These features still constitute the fundamental elements of electromechanical switching systems now in use.

Since its invention in 1948, the transistor has increasingly replaced the electron tube in communications circuits, and it has increasingly taken over many of the functions performed by electromechanical relays and other mechanical devices. For example, Touch-Tone calling, which was first tested in 1960, uses audio frequencies generated by transistors rather than the successive impulses from a mechanical dial in order to initiate switching. Moreover, computer technology, logic circuits, and transistors and semiconductor diodes have been used to create a completely electronic switching system. The first experimental test of an electronic switching system was completed by the Bell System at Morris, Ill., in 1955, and the first commercial test of the system was made there in 1960. The first large electronic switching exchange was put into service at Succasunna, N.J., in 1965.

Transmission. Associated with the problem of interconnecting an ever-increasing number of subscribers was the related problem of transmitting over ever-longer lines. As the lines reached out further and further, signals became weaker and weaker, partly because of the increased resistance of the longer line. The first telephone circuits consisted of an iron line and a ground return, as did the telegraph circuits. Although such circuits were cheap, they were very noisy and could not be used over any distance. Copper is a better conductor than iron, but the copper wire of that time lacked the tensile strength necessary for stringing it over long distances.

A hard-drawn copper wire, produced by Thomas B. Doolittle on an experimental basis, was used in 1877 for the first successful long-distance telephone conversation, which took place between Bell in New York and Watson in Boston. However, a number of years passed before the new process was reliable, and it was not until 1884 that all-copper long-distance circuits were opened for commercial service. For a while the number and the length of lines grew rapidly. In 1892, a 950-mile (1,530-km) line was opened between New York and Chicago, with Bell participating in the opening ceremony in New York City. In 1893 a line was opened between Boston and Chicago, in 1896 between New York and St. Louis, and in 1897 between New York and Omaha.

Such long lines were expensive to build, maintain, and use. Consequently, the earlier problem of sending many telegraph messages over a single circuit (multiplexing), which originally led to the invention of the telephone, became more and more important in sending telephone messages. One of the first methods of increasing the message-handling capacity was devised by John J. Carty in 1886. In his phan-

AMERICAN TELEPHONE AND TELEGRAPH CO.; AUTOMATIC ELECTRIC COMPANY

TELEPHONE became more convenient to use as it underwent development after 1900. Desk set introduced in 1950 is commonest phone in the United States. Phones with push buttons instead of dials were introduced in 1963.

tom circuit, four wires (two circuits) could be used for three telephone messages and one telegraph message. However, his method was very difficult to apply in practice, and it came into limited commercial use only after 1900.

In 1900, Michael I. Pupin of Columbia University and George A. Campbell of the Bell System independently found that increased capacitance as well as increased resistance caused signals to become weaker as the telephone lines became longer. Each also found that if loading coils (inductances) of the proper value were placed at regular intervals along the line, the signal would lose strength more slowly. Once proper methods of doing this were worked out, long-distance lines again began increasing in length. In 1911 a New York to Denver line was completed. In January 1915 the first transcontinental line was opened—from New York to San Francisco. A month later a line from Philadelphia to San Francisco was opened.

Repeaters. All-copper circuits and loading coils helped greatly to extend long-distance communications, but neither solved the more fundamental problem of amplifying a weakened signal and doing so without introducing distortion. As early as 1904, a first step was taken by H. E. Shreeve of the Bell System, who devised a mechanical repeater. However, there were major obstacles to the use of the mechanical repeater. It introduced and multiplied unwanted distortions, and it was unusable on loaded lines.

A solution was finally attained when Lee De Forest's 3-element electron tube was converted into a high-vacuum electron tube by Harold D. Arnold of the Bell System and by Irving Langmuir of the General Electric Laboratory independently of each other in 1912. In the following year, the first vacuum-tube repeaters were installed at Philadelphia on the New York–Baltimore telephone line. The success of these repeaters soon led to their use on all major long-distance circuits. In 1927, Harold S. Black of Bell Telephone Laboratories conceived the negative-feedback amplifier, which provided amplification characteristics that were greatly superior to previous results. It came into increasingly wider use after 1930.

Radio-Frequency Carrier Systems. The high-vacuum electron tube can be used not only as an amplifier but also as an oscillator or a modulator. These multiple uses and the invention of the electrical band-pass by George A. Campbell of the Bell System in 1917 made possible a new approach to sending more messages over a single telephone circuit (multiplexing). Radio-frequency carriers were provided, as many in number as the number of voice channels desired. Each of the carriers was modulated by a separate voice message at the transmitter. The resulting modulated carriers then were sent simultaneously over long-distance lines, and the signals were strengthened by repeaters 100 to 200 miles (160 to 320 km) apart. At the receiving end the modulated carriers were separated out by band-pass filters, and then the separated modulated carriers were demodulated to recover the original voice messages.

The first radio-frequency carrier system went into service on the Pittsburg–Baltimore line in 1918. In a few years, its use rapidly spread to all long-distance circuits. The first telephone carrier system provided four voice channels, and the number jumped to 12 in 1938 by increasing the frequency of the carriers.

With the success of the telephone carrier system, another phase in the development of long-distance communications was completed. The succeeding step, which provided thousands of channels instead of only a dozen or so, required the use of microwaves, which have much higher frequencies than the earlier carrier frequencies.

Microwave Carrier Systems. The introduction of microwave carrier systems required a completely new radio technology—entirely new oscillators, amplifiers, modulators, and transmission lines. An ordinary pair of wires is impractical for microwave transmissions because too much energy can be lost by radiation from the wires. However, a coaxial cable can transmit microwaves successfully because its configuration greatly reduces losses due to radiation. The transmission of microwaves by coaxial cable was first described in a 1931 patent granted to Lloyd Espenschied and Herman A. Affel of the Bell Telephone Laboratories.

The promise of greatly increasing the number of voice channels per telephone circuit led to systematic research on a completely redesigned carrier system using coaxial cable. By 1936 such a system was in experimental use for both telephone and television transmission. The first commercial coaxial-cable carrier system began operating in 1941. It was the L-1 sy tem, with 480 voice channels between Stevens Point, Wis., and Minneapolis, Minn. More widespread use of coaxial cable systems was delayed until after World War II, but by 1948 they had spanned the continent. The signal attenuation along the cables was considerable, so compact auxiliary repeaters were placed at intervals of about 5 miles (8 km) and main repeater stations at intervals of about 100 miles (160 km).

The efficiency of the coaxial cable telephone systems increased rapidly. The L-3 coaxial cable system, introduced in 1953, provided 1,860 telephone channels. The L-4 system, introduced in 1969, provided 3 600 telephone channels, with main repeater stations about 300 miles (485 km) apart and auxiliary repeaters about 2 miles (3.2 km) apart.

Shortly after World War II, a competitor to coaxial cable systems began to appear. It was the microwave radio relay link, in which microwaves were transmitted through the air over a line-of-sight path from one station to another rather than over a cable. The growth of network television made it necessary to transmit TV programs to distant cities throughout the country. Unlike radio programs, this could not be done over ordinary telephone circuits, but only over means of transmission appropriate to the higher frequencies used in television. In theory, coaxial cable telephone systems could be used, but the many amplifiers in the cable routes introduced distortions that were negligible for telephone conversation but were intolerable for television signals.

Consequently, the alternative to coaxial cable was the use of a microwave radio relay system. Such a system was completed from New York to Chicago in 1950. In the following year it reached the West Coast and was in regular use for coast-to-coast television as well as for telephone communications.

The TD-2 microwave radio relay link system, introduced in 1954 and used for heavy short-haul or interurban traffic, has a capacity of 6,000 telephone circuits. The TH system, introduced in 1961 and used for long-haul traffic, carries 10,800 telephone circuits or 6 television channels. The TD-3 system, introduced in 1968 to supplement the TD-2 and provide additional routes, carries 12,000 telephone circuits.

Satellite Communications. Although the telephone network has been extended overseas by cable and radio, the most spectacular link for transoceanic communications undoubtedly is a communications satellite. The British writer Arthur C. Clarke first suggested such a device in 1945. John R. Pierce of the Bell Telephone Laboratories developed the major scientific and engineering requirements in 1955, and the U. S. Air Force launched an experimental communications satellite in 1959. In 1962 and 1963, Telstar 1, Relay 1, and Telstar 2 were placed in orbit. Since then, communication satellites have been in constant use for the transmission of telephone, telegraph, and television signals. See also COMMUNICATIONS SATELLITE.

W. JAMES KING
Henry Ford Museum, Dearborn, Mich.

Bibliography

Albert, Arthur L., *Electrical Communications* (New York 1950).
American Telephone and Telegraph Company, *Events in Telephone History* (New York 1958, with subsequent additions).
Casson, Herbert N., *The History of the Telephone* (Chicago 1910).
Crowley, Thomas H., and others, *Modern Communications* (New York 1962).
Harlow, Alvin, *Old Wires and New Waves* (New York 1936).
Hunt, Frederick V., *Electroacoustics* (New York 1954).
Josephson, Matthew, *Edison* (New York 1959).
King, W. James, *Development of Electrical Technology in the 19th Century: The Telegraph and the Telephone,* U. S. National Museum, Bulletin 228 (Washington 1962).
MacKenzie, Catherine, *Alexander Graham Bell* (New York 1928).
Miller, Kempster B., *American Telephone Practice* (New York 1905).
Page, Arthur W., *The Bell Telephone System* (New York 1941).
Prescott, George B., *The Speaking Telephone* (New York 1878).
Rhodes, Frederick L., *Beginnings of Telephony* (New York 1929).
Robertson, J. H., *The Story of the Telephone* (London 1947).
Taylor, Lloyd W., "The Untold Story of the Telephone," *American Journal of Physics,* vol. 5, no. 6, pp. 243–251, December 1937.
Watson, Thomas A., *The Birth and Babyhood of the Telephone* (Chicago 1926).
Webb, H. L., *The Development of the Telephone in Europe* (London 1911?).
Wile, F. W., *Emile Berliner* (Indianapolis 1926).

MOUNT WILSON AND PALOMAR OBSERVATORIES

The 200-inch Hale reflecting telescope at Mt. Palomar, California

TELESCOPE. Almost all of man's information about the universe beyond the earth has arrived at the earth's surface in the form of electromagnetic radiation—visible light and ultraviolet light, infrared radiation, X-rays, and radio waves. The instruments that astronomers use to gather this radiation and to produce images are called telescopes. This article is concerned with the most commonly used of these instruments, the optical telescope and the radio telescope.

DEVELOPMENT OF THE OPTICAL TELESCOPE

The optical properties of mirrors and lenses were known to Arab scientists in the Middle Ages and were being studied in Europe as early as the 13th century. The first known telescope is generally credited to Hans Lippershey, a Dutch lens grinder, who tried to patent such a device in 1608. However, it was Galileo who in 1609 first applied a telescope to astronomical observations. From the early instruments, which were no more than single-tube opera glasses, magnificent precision devices weighing hundreds of tons have evolved.

Despite changes in form and size, all optical telescopes have two basic elements. These are the *objective,* which intercepts and focuses incoming radiation, and the *mounting,* by which the objective is supported and aimed. The objective may be a lens or combination of lenses, as in *refracting telescopes;* a mirror, as in *reflecting telescopes;* or a combination of lenses and mirrors, as in *catadioptric* systems. An *eyepiece* is used for viewing the image formed by the objective.

Early Models and Improvements. The earliest telescopes were very simple, small refracting telescopes consisting of an objective lens and an eyepiece mounted in a tube. However, it was quickly realized that the light-gathering power of telescopes had to be increased if faint astronomical objects were to be observed. Isaac Newton developed the first crude model of a reflecting telescope in 1668, and by the late 17th century several large reflecting telescopes were built.

These telescopes were only modestly successful because clumsy mechanisms were used to drive and point them, and the highly polished metal used to form the objective tarnished easily. The same clumsy drive mechanisms limited the success of the very long telescopes built in the 18th century. Such telescopes were constructed when it was realized that in order to view planetary and other details a very long focal length was required to obtain a large-scale image. Lenses with focal lengths of 200 feet (60 meters) or more were constructed, but they were unwieldly.

The art of making good-quality optical glass in larger and larger discs developed slowly in the late 18th and 19th centuries. As this art developed, the apertures of telescopes were increased. At the same time, steady advances were made in the development of mechanisms for mounting, moving, and pointing the larger telescopes. In the 20th century, progress continued in the field of precision optics, especially in the testing of large optical components.

Telescopes Today. At the present state of development in optics, and with the development of low-expansion materials (discussed later), the limits on the performance of ground-based telescopes are set only by engineering problems and the earth's atmosphere. To overcome some of these problems, astronomers are turning to special-purpose telescopes.

Because telescopes are expensive instruments, all major telescopes in the past were designed for general-purpose use. They could be used to observe the planets, stars, nebulae, and galaxies, and could collect radiation over a wide region of the electromagnetic spectrum. But telescopes today are designed for such specific tasks as the study of infrared radiation, the measurement of light intensities of stars and galaxies, and the study of special objects.

The limits on image quality imposed by the earth's atmosphere have plagued astronomers ever since telescopes with apertures larger than 12 inches (30 cm) were built. Locations were sought where visibility was least impaired. This process gradually led to the location of observatories on high mountaintops in areas where the absolute humidity was low.

As early as the 1920's, however, it was clear that the ultimate way to overcome the problem of the earth's atmosphere was to place a telescope on the moon or in orbit around the earth. This step was first realized in the 1960's, when both the United States and the Soviet Union placed telescopes in earth orbit.

Another way of possibly surmounting the difficulties introduced by the atmosphere is to reconstruct a radiation wave front as it existed before it enters the atmosphere by sampling the wave front when it reaches the ground. The problem is a familiar one to the communications engineer. A familiar example is listening to a telephone conversation against a noisy background. If only one word out of three is heard, the entire conversation may conceivably be reconstructed. A similar reconstruction of a radiation wave front may be possible.

FUNCTIONS OF A TELESCOPE

The primary function of a telescope for professional astronomers is to gather light. The other major function is to provide resolution—that is, to separate the images of objects that appear close together in the sky. Magnification of the image is ordinarily provided by the eyepiece of a telescope.

Light Gathering. The light-gathering power of a telescope can be understood by picturing the incoming photons of light as a steady rain. Obviously, a large tub will collect more rainwater than a small bucket, and the ability of both to collect water is proportional to the areas of their openings. Similarly, the light-gathering power of a telescope increases directly as the square of the surface diameter, or aperture, of its objective. For example, if a telescope objective is 2 inches in diameter and the pupil of a person's eye is 0.2 inch in diameter, the telescope collects $(2/0.2)^2$, or $(10)^2$—or 100 times more light than the eye does. The assumption is made here that there are no losses in the optical system, but actually there are small reflection losses amounting to about 2% at each surface and some transmission losses caused by scattering in the glass. Such losses amount to about 10% on each reflection for freshly coated mirrors and much more when the coatings are old.

Astronomers give brightness differences in magnitudes, which are on a logarithmic scale. Thus a difference in brightness of 100 is a difference of 5 magnitudes on this scale. The human eye can easily see stars of the 5th magnitude on a dark night. A 2-inch (5-cm) telescope reveals stars of the 10th magnitude, since it can observe stars 100 times less bright than the human eye can see readily. The 200-inch (500-cm) Hale telescope on Mt. Palomar in California collects $200/0.2)^2$ or 1 million times more light than the eye. This means that the Hale telescope can observe stars 15 magnitudes fainter than the eye can readily see—that is, it can observe stars of about the 20th magnitude. With photographic film the telescope can record images of stars of the 23d magnitude because film can integrate the incoming light and build up a record of it. Image intensifier tubes and other accessories can also enhance the light-gathering power of telescopes. See also IMAGE TUBE.

Resolution. The sharpness of the images is limited by the disturbing effect of the atmosphere. The limit of resolution imposed is normally about 2 seconds of arc on the celestial sphere. At some sites, due to atmospheric conditions, the limit is as low as 0.25 seconds of arc. This applies to point sources of light such as stars rather than to extended images such as neighboring planets.

A simple formula gives the least resolvable element seen by a telescope as

$$\text{degree of arc} = 2.5 \times 10^5 \lambda / a$$

where λ is the wavelength of the radiation and a is the aperture, both being given in the same units. If its optical surfaces are good, a telescope with an aperture of 3 inches (10.5 cm) can achieve a resolution of 2 seconds of arc at visible wavelengths. A 24-inch (60-cm) telescope

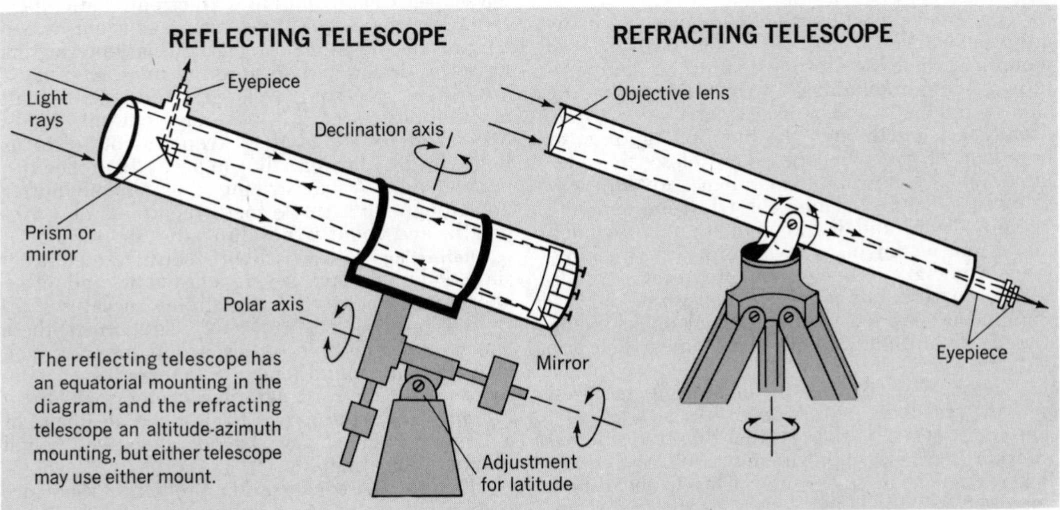

The reflecting telescope has an equatorial mounting in the diagram, and the refracting telescope an altitude-azimuth mounting, but either telescope may use either mount.

can achieve a resolution of 0.25 second of arc. Thus if resolution were the only important requirement for astronomers, very large telescopes would be much rarer than they actually are, since their increased resolution would largely be nullified by atmospheric conditions.

Magnification and Eyepieces. Persons who are not astronomers often confuse magnification with light-gathering power. The magnifying power of telescopes as normally used by astronomers is unity. One degree on the sky projects unaltered as one degree on the plate at the telescope's focal plane. To enlarge what is seen at the focal plane, an eyepiece is used. The magnifying power of the telescope, then, is the ratio of the focal length of the telescope to the focal length of the eyepiece. For example, a telescope with a focal length of 50 inches and an eyepiece with a focal length of 1 inch provides a total magnification of 50. The magnifying power can be whatever the astronomer chooses, within the optical limits determined by resolution and light-gathering power. All that is required for a given magnification is an eyepiece of the proper focal length.

A good eyepiece has an angular field of view of about 40°. This limit is imposed in order to avoid objectionable distortions. The field of view of the telescope seen by this eyepiece, sometimes called the *true field,* is determined by dividing the field of view of the eyepiece by the magnification of the system. Thus a 1-inch focal length eyepiece used with a 400-inch focal length objective has a magnification of 400. If the eyepiece field of view is 40°, the true field of view is then 0.1° or 6 minutes of arc.

Tracking. To produce good images on a photographic plate, a telescope must track astronomical objects as the earth rotates on its axis. A mounting that has two axes of rotation can point a telescope in any desired direction toward the celestial hemisphere above it. If one of these axes is parallel to the earth's axis of rotation, it becomes the only axis that requires driving motion for tracking. This is because celestial bodies appear to circle the earth in paths parallel to the equator, and the telescope on its north-south axis and pointed toward a given celestial object can readily follow the object's east-west motion. Such a mounting is called an *equatorial mounting,* and almost all large telescopes use it.

However, special-purpose telescopes and many very large radio telescopes may have special mountings such as altitude mountings and altitude-azimuth mountings. An *altitude mounting* cannot track. It has a fixed plane of rotation, usually passing through the line of longitude, or *meridian,* of the telescope. The telescope is rotated up and down the meridian. An *altitude-azimuth mounting* enables the telescope to swing up and down, and it has a rotating base much like a gun mount on a naval ship. For tracking, the altitude-azimuth mounting requires a small, special-purpose computer to transform the instantaneous position of the celestial object being studied to altitude-azimuth coordinates. See also Azimuth.

An accurate driving mechanism is required for an excellent performance by a telescope. The rate of the drive is that of the sidereal rotation—that is, approximately 366/365 times faster than mean solar time. This is the difference between the sidereal day and the solar day (see Day). Thus the drive must turn the telescope a little more than 15 seconds of arc during each second of time, which amounts to a full rotation around the polar axis in a little less than one day. Very good drives even allow for the small change in the theoretical drive rate caused by atmospheric refraction.

Until the early 20th century, telescopes were driven by falling weights, but these cumbersome —although excellent and reliable—systems have been replaced by electronic mechanisms and electric motors. Electronic drives are much more versatile and respond to automatic tracking requirements instantaneously. Furthermore, they can be computer-controlled, as in the special-purpose mountings mentioned above.

REFRACTORS AND REFLECTORS

Until the end of the 19th century the great telescopes of the world were refracting telescopes, which use lenses as their objective. When it became possible to coat large glass surfaces with silver it became feasible to make large reflecting telescopes. Silver coatings tarnish rather quickly and have since been replaced with aluminum coatings that last three to ten years before recoatings are necessary. In the 20th century the largest telescopes are reflectors, which use curved mirrors to bring incoming radiation to a focus. The relative advantages and disadvantages of reflectors versus refractors have to do with the aberrations observed in the different optical systems, as well as the variations in flexibility of the instruments.

Aberrations. All telescopes have certain image defects away from the central axis of the objective. Lenses, however carefully designed, have chromatic aberration—that is, different colors do not come to a focus at the same focal plane. Even if monochromatic light is used, the lenses show other aberrations such as spherical aberration, coma, astigmatism, and distortion. Mirrors do not have chromatic aberration but suffer from all of the other defects. It is the task of the optical designer to minimize these defects in order to achieve the given purpose of the telescope. Sometimes a solution is achieved by a combination of mirrors and lenses. See also Aberration, Optical.

By combining two lenses of different refractive indexes for the objective of a refracting telescope, it is possible to correct chromatic aberration to the extent that many adjacent wavelengths are put in good focus. All large refractors have this design and are referred to as *achromatic doublets.* Even so, wavelengths toward the limit of visibility are still severely out of focus. Special filters are used to keep this out-of-focus light from blurring the image. In reflectors, parallel light waves striking a paraboloid mirror are brought to a single focus regardless of wavelength, and there is no chromatic aberration.

Refracting Systems. Short-focus refractors of simple design have severe chromatic and other aberrations because of the strong curvatures required on the lens surfaces. To correct these aberrations, multiple lenses are required, much as in the compound lens of a camera. Such telescopes are called astrographic cameras, or *astrographs.* Their purpose is to produce an image of a large portion of the sky on a relatively small photographic plate.

Despite these aberration problems, there are certain advantages to refracting telescopes. First, there is no central "stop" or other diffraction-causing member in the path of the incoming light, as in reflecting telescopes. Second, the light losses caused by reflection and transmission in the telescope are essentially constant over long periods of time. Third, refractors are stable and retain their alignment over long periods. It is the latter factor that makes long-focus refractors ideal instruments for precise astrometric work.

Reflecting Systems. Reflecting telescopes have a variety of configurations for achieving a specified optical performance and for placing the focal plane where desired. If a single concave mirror is used, the focus is called the *prime focus*. However, the prime focus is inside the tube of the telescope and is inaccessible except in the largest telescopes. Therefore a diagonal flat mirror may be placed in front of the focal plane in order to reflect the focus to the side of the tube, where it is accessible. This focus is called the *Newtonian focus*, after Isaac Newton who first proposed and used it.

If a mirror is placed in front of the focal plane to reflect the focus back through a hole in the primary mirror, the system is called a "folded" prime focus system, and the focus is referred to as the *Cassegrain focus*, after its 17th century French designer. The advantage of this system is that the incoming beam is "folded" back on itself and does not have to converge so quickly. The telescope may have a very large effective focal length, even though the physical length of the telescope is fairly small.

If the effective focal length of a reflector is very large, the incoming beam of light can be reflected out of the telescope and down the polar axis to a focus in a room below the telescope. This is called the *coudé focus* (from French "coudé," meaning "bent like an elbow"). The coudé focus enables the astronomer to set large, heavy instruments at the focus of the telescope without having to move or rotate them as the telescope tracks the desired object.

Most large reflectors are designed to be general-purpose telescopes. They can be used at several of the focuses mentioned as well as for photography, photometry, or spectroscopy. The most popular optical system for general-purpose reflectors is the Ritchy-Chrétien two-mirror system. This gives a larger aberration-free field than does the Cassegrain system. The field is curved, however, and if the large field is to be used it is necessary to insert a system of additional lenses referred to as a "field flattener."

Advantages and Disadvantages of Reflectors. Reflecting telescopes have numerous advantages besides circumventing chromatic aberration. First, they can be kept fairly short in physical length by "folding" the focus and hence can be housed in relatively small domes for their effective size. Second, the objective mirrors can be made very large from nontransparent glass because the mirrors can be supported from their entire rear surface, with only the front surface requiring an optical finish. All of the great telescopes of the 20th century have been reflecting telescopes, and all intermediate-sized telescopes built since 1920 have been reflectors as well.

Reflectors have some undesirable features, however. If images of optimum quality are to be obtained, the telescope's mirrors must be precisely aligned. Therefore elaborate devices are built into the telescope for adjusting the lateral position and tilt of the mirrors. The secondary

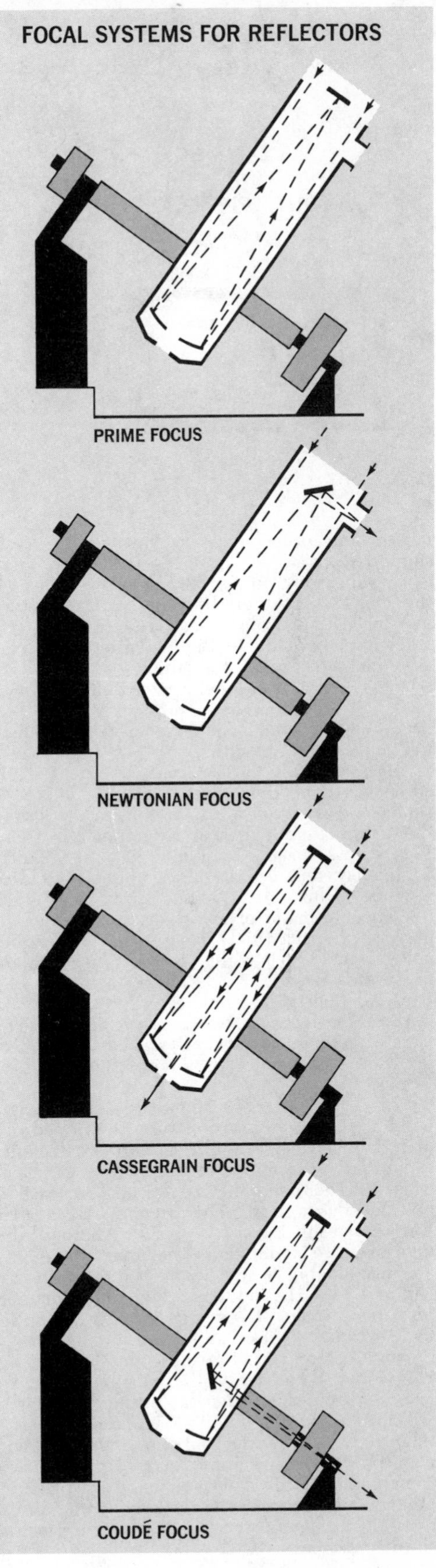

FOCAL SYSTEMS FOR REFLECTORS

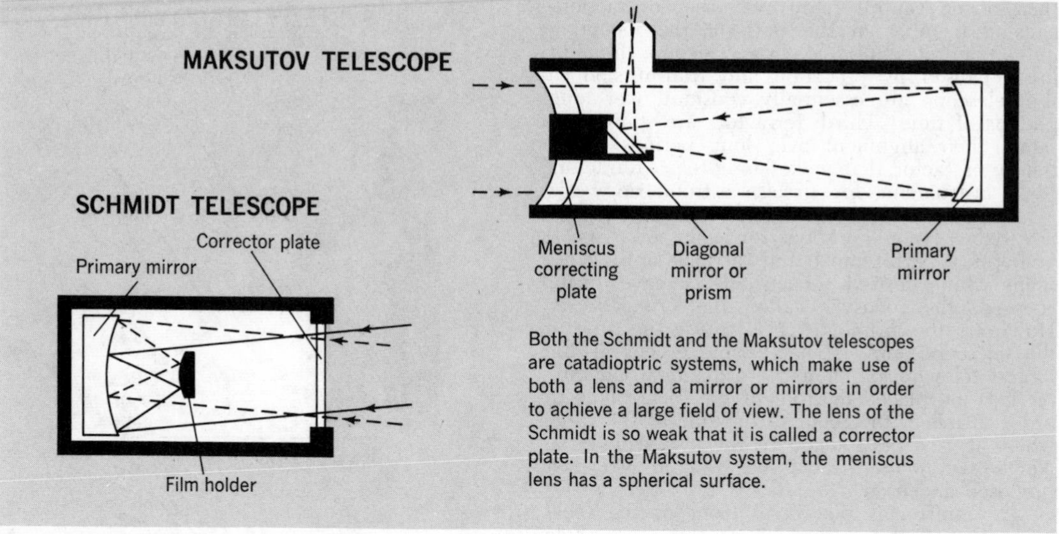

Both the Schmidt and the Maksutov telescopes are catadioptric systems, which make use of both a lens and a mirror or mirrors in order to achieve a large field of view. The lens of the Schmidt is so weak that it is called a corrector plate. In the Maksutov system, the meniscus lens has a spherical surface.

mirror—and other auxiliary mirrors, if used—is supported by a set of vanes called a "spider." The vanes introduce diffraction spikes into the images. Another difficulty with reflectors is that reflection is a linear function. A small change in the angle of the incoming beam causes an equal change in the angle of the outgoing beam, the net result being twice the change in angle. Thus the mirror surfaces must be very accurately ground. They are also very sensitive to changes in temperature.

New Materials for Reflectors. A great deal of effort has gone into making glass having a low coefficient of expansion to minimize or eliminate the temperature effect in reflectors. As soon as Pyrex glass became available in large units, it completely replaced ordinary glass for telescope mirrors. Thus the 200-inch mirror of the Hale telescope is made of Pyrex, as are the auxiliary mirrors. In the 1950's progress in quartz technology made it possible to cast large "blanks" of quartz. Because of its lower coefficient of expansion, quartz has replaced Pyrex for making mirrors for large telescopes. Because quartz is very expensive, however, Pyrex has continued to be used for mirrors in intermediate-sized telescopes.

In the 1960's two remarkable materials for making telescope mirrors were developed. The materials have essentially a zero coefficient of expansion with temperature. The first, CerVit, is a vitreous ceramic that can be cast and polished like glass. The second, ULE (Ultra Low Expansion), is a true glass. Another advantage of these materials is that even though they are unavoidably heated while being polished and "figured" by the optician, he can immediately test the surface. Even with Pyrex, an optician had to allow weeks and even months for the mirror to stabilize before he could test his work. He would then polish the mirror again, wait, test, and polish further as needed. Thus the "pacing" factor in building a telescope was the time required by the optician, most of which was spent simply waiting for the mirror to cool. CerVit and ULE have virtually displaced all other materials for new large mirrors and are rapidly displacing them for new intermediate-sized telescopes as well.

SPECIAL-PURPOSE TELESCOPES

Although the cost of a telescope makes general-purpose telescopes desirable, special telescopes play an important role in astronomy.

Catadioptric Systems. Reflectors having very large fields have been replacing astrographs. The large field is achieved by using both a correcting lens and a mirror or mirrors. Telescopes in which this combination of lens and mirror is used are known as *catadioptric systems.*

One such system is the Schmidt telescope. This design has a very weak lens, so weak that it is referred to as the "corrector plate." The lens is coupled with a spherical mirror and can produce images of fields as large as 10 degrees on a side. Its focal surface is curved, and there is still a small amount of residual chromatic aberration because of the correcting plate.

Another system is the Maksutov-Bouwers design, composed of a spherical mirror and a meniscus lens having spherical surfaces. In the Cassegrain configuration this system can have a very long effective focal length. Hence it is popular as a "small" telescope and is widely used as a telephoto lens for cameras.

The limitation on the size of catadioptric systems is the optical quality of the glass and the tendency of large, thin pieces of glass to sag and deform under their own weight. Telescopes with corrector plates or meniscus lenses larger than 60 inches (150 cm) in diameter are very unlikely. However, a catadioptric system that may achieve large sizes—although it has not yet been used even for intermediate-sized telescopes—is one in which both the front and the back surface of a mirror are ground, the back surface being aluminized for internal reflection. When light enters the front surface of the glass, it is refracted. It passes through to the back surface, is reflected, and passes back through the glass, being refracted again as it leaves the front surface. Such a system is called a "thick" mirror, or *Mangin mirror.*

Special-Observation Systems. Other special-purpose telescopes incorporate mechanical or optical features by means of which the telescope serves a particular function or is used to observe a particular celestial object.

For example, a *coronograph* is a telescope designed to observe the sun's corona. By carefully placing an occulting disk to block out the sun and using a series of light baffles to cut down on scattered light, an observer can photograph the corona in daylight on any clear day.

A *heliostat* is a telescope used to observe the sun. By means of a moving flat mirror the sun's light can be fed to the fixed telescope, thus keeping the focal plane fixed and accessible for large equipment. A similar installation used for observing stars is called a *siderostat*.

Zenith telescopes contain a fixed lens that looks directly overhead, toward the zenith. Incoming light is reflected off a mercury pool onto a photographic plate at the focus. Such telescopes, incorporating photographic recording, are excellent for precise determinations of time.

RADIO TELESCOPES

All the telescopes discussed thus far are themselves special-purpose telescopes, in the very broad sense that they are designed for collecting light. Telescopes can be designed for other regions of the electromagnetic spectrum as well. The most widely used of these nonoptical systems are radio telescopes.

The energy available in a radio photon is so small that very large collectors and extremely sensitive receivers must be used in radio astronomy. The paraboloidal telescopes serve to collect and focus the radiation exactly as reflecting telescopes collect and focus light. Radio telescopes also must be large in order to get resolving power because the radio wavelengths involved —from about 0.4 inch to 130 feet (1 cm—40 meters)—are much longer than light waves.

Many radio telescopes are exactly analogous to their optical counterparts, some being built in a fashion similar to zenith tubes, others similar to siderostats, and so forth. Still others, however, have no optical analog. For example, common helical and dipole antennas can be arranged for receiving radio signals directly from outer space. Such antennas are more like optical photocells than telescopes in the ordinary sense. Actually, dipole antennas often are set at the focus of large paraboloidal reflectors, and in this configuration the telescope and antenna function exactly like an optical telescope that has a photocell at its focus.

Mountings. Many radio telescopes have an altitude-azimuth mounting in order to reduce the engineering problems involved in precisely pointing and driving such large structures. Radio telescopes often are 260 to 330 feet (80–100 meters) in diameter and tend to flex and sag.

Nevertheless radio astronomers have found it convenient to use equatorial mountings for large radio telescopes with very precise reflecting surfaces. This is because the telescopes need to remain focused for long intervals on very faint radio sources and the sources need to keep the same orientation at the focus. In an altitude-azimuth mounting the sky appears to rotate as it moves from horizon to horizon.

Resolution Techniques. Several ingenious ways have been devised to get around the resolving-power problem at radio wavelengths. If two telescopes are coupled together by feeding their signals to a common receiver, they become an *interferometer* and thus have the resolving power of a theoretical telescope as large as the distance between them. The telescopes need not be physically connected. Two tape recorders synchronized by means of a precise atomic clock can record the signals, which are then mixed together at a convenient location. Couplings that have spanned continents and even the oceans have been used successfully. Resolutions of 0.001 second of arc have been achieved in this way.

In order to obtain higher sensitivity as well as higher resolution, a technique called *aperture synthesis* is used. Any interferometer is an aperture synthesis instrument, but nonsteerable devices may be used as well. Rows of fixed antennas may be set up so that their beams cross

LARGE OPTICAL TELESCOPES

Diameter (in inches)[1]	Observatory	Location
REFLECTORS[2]		
200	Mt. Wilson and Palomar	Mt. Palomar, Calif.
120	Lick	Mt. Hamilton, Calif.
107	McDonald	Fort Davis, Texas
102	Crimean Astrophysical	Simferopol, USSR
100	Mt. Wilson and Palomar	Mt. Wilson, Calif.
98	Royal Greenwich	Hailsham, England
84	Kitt Peak National	Tucson, Ariz.
82	McDonald	Fort Davis, Texas
80	Schwarzschild	Jena, East Germany
76	Haute-Provence	Near Forcalquier, France
74	Dunlap	Richmond Hill, Ontario
74	Radcliffe	Pretoria, South Africa
74	Mount Stromlo	Canberra, Australia
74	Tokyo Astronomical	Mitaka, Japan
74	Helwan	Helwan, Egypt
72	Dominion Astrophysical	Royal Oak, British Columbia
69	Perkins	Flagstaff, Ariz.
61	Agassiz Station, Harvard	Harvard, Mass.
60	Bosque Alegre, Cordoba	Bosque Alegre, Argentina
60	Boyden	Mazelspoort, South Africa
60	Arizona University	Tucson, Ariz.
60	Mt. Wilson and Palomar	Mt. Wilson, Calif.
REFRACTORS		
40	Yerkes	Williams Bay, Wisc.
36	Lick	Mt. Hamilton, Calif.
33	Astrophysical Section, Paris	Meudon, France
32	Astrophysical	Potsdam, East Germany
30	Allegheny	Pittsburgh, Pa.
30	Bischoffsheim	Mont Gros, Nice, France
28	Royal Greenwich	Hailsham, England
27	Union	Johannesburg, South Africa
27	Vienna University	Vienna, Austria
26	Royal Greenwich	Hailsham, England
26	Mount Stromlo	Canberra, Australia
26	Leander McCormick	Charlottesville, Va.
26	Naval	Washington, D.C.
26	Berlin-Babelsberg	Babelsberg, East Germany
26	Tokyo Astronomical	Mitaka, Japan
26	Astronomical	Belgrade, Yugoslavia
26	Pulkovo	Pulkovo, USSR

[1] Diameter of mirror, for reflectors, and of lens, for refractors. Diameters sometimes approximate. 1 inch equals 2.54 centimeters.

[2] Several very large reflecting telescopes are under construction. Included are a 236-inch reflector in the USSR, a 158-inch reflector for Cerro Tololo Inter-American Observatory in Chile, and a 150-inch reflector to be installed at Siding Spring Observatory in Australia.

and define a very narrow common beam. The Mills Cross in Australia is such an instrument. This system is limited by natural and man-made radio noises that come into the instrument in its so-called "side lobes"—regions of sensitivity off to the side of the main pattern. By observing with the antenna array in phase, when the main beam and all the side lobes are recorded, and then out of phase, when just the side lobes are recorded, the out-of-phase signal can be subtracted from the in-phase signal, leaving the signal from the main beam. Such techniques applied to interferometer arrays are called *aperture supersynthesis*.

CONSTRUCTING A TELESCOPE

The construction of a large telescope is a major undertaking. A "large" telescope is one having an aperture of 60 inches (150 cm) or greater. Even the construction of an intermediate-size telescope—24 inches (60 cm) to 60 inches —involves much detailed planning if an effective instrument is to be achieved. Optically, there are no theoretical obstacles to the size of a reflecting telescope, but the lens of a refracting telescope would tend to distort under its own weight if it were too large.

It is relatively simple for the average person to build his own telescope and make his own mirrors. The cost of making even a 10-inch (25-cm) reflector is not prohibitive. All that is required is patience.

See also ASTRONOMY; OBSERVATORY.

LAURENCE W. FREDRICK
University of Virginia

Bibliography

Howard, Neale E., *The Telescope Handbook and Star Atlas* (New York 1967).
Jennison, Roger C., *Introduction to Radio Astronomy* (New York 1967).
King, Henry C., *The History of the Telescope* (Cambridge, Mass., 1955).
Kuiper, Gerard P., and Middlehurst, Barbara M., eds., *Telescopes* (Chicago 1960).
Miczaika, G. R., and Sinton, W. M., *Tools of the Astronomer* (Cambridge, Mass., 1961).
Texereau, Jean, *How to Make a Telescope* (New York 1957).

TELESCOPIUM. See CONSTELLATION.

TELESIO, te-le′zyō, **Bernardino** (1509–1588), Italian philosopher, who was the first major proponent of scientific naturalism during the Renaissance. He was born in Cosenza and studied at Padua. He spent some years in monastic retreat, then wrote his major work, *De rerum natura* (1565; revised and completed in 1586).

Called "the first of the moderns" by Francis Bacon, Telesio deserved this title for his resolute attempt to found natural philosophy upon observation and inductive reasoning alone. His basic assumption is that nature is a unified system of causal connections. In natural philosophy one can only observe how this system operates and make inferences about the ultimate principles by analogy. Thus Telesio eliminated formal and final causes—except for the universal tendency towards self-preservation in all things—and constructed a physical theory using only material and efficient causes. He believed that the primitive causes of natural events were heat, the life principle, and cold—qualitative concepts rather than quantitative like Galileo's matter and motion.

H. S. HARRIS, *York University, Toronto*

TELESPHORUS, tə-les′fərəs, **Saint** (died c. 136), early pope and martyr. Historical sources agree that Telesphorus was a Greek and that he was pope for 11 years, but they disagree on the exact dates. Most probably he reigned from 125 to 136. It is certain that he was a martyr, probably during the reign of Emperor Hadrian. The tradition that he was buried in the Vatican has not been supported by modern excavations.

His feast is celebrated by Western Christians on January 5 and by Eastern Christians on February 22.

PHILIP F. MULHERN, O. P.
St. Mary's Priory, New Haven, Conn.

TELETYPESETTER, an electromechanical system for operating typesetting machines automatically. The teletypesetter (TTS) consists of a perforator that has a typewriterlike keyboard for punching holes in a paper tape, and a paper-tape reader that is attached to the keyboard of a linecasting machine.

Each key stroke made by a perforator keyboard operator is encoded in the form of a 6-unit TTS code consisting of a vertical line of holes or no holes in the paper tape. They represent upper or lower case letters, numbers, punctuation marks, or special instructions for the linecasting machine.

In one mode of operation the perforator is adjacent to the paper-tape reader, and the perforated tape is fed to it directly. As the tape runs through the reader, a sensing mechanism reads the character code perforations and translates them into movements of the linecasting-machine keys, which in turn cause the release of character matrices from the magazine of the machine. Under automatic tape control it casts a justified solid line (slug) of characters at rates up to 15 lines per minute, about twice as fast as the speed attainable with a manually operated keyboard of a linecasting machine.

In a second mode of operation the perforated tape is fed into a teletype sender that converts the perforations into electrical impulses and transmits them over special long-distance wire circuits to receiving stations at many different locations. In this case, the original punched tape is reproduced by a reperforator at each receiving station, and this reproduced tape is then fed to a paper-tape reader controlling a linecasting machine.

Uses. The first mode of TTS operation is used in many commercial printing shops for automatically setting type for books, law briefs, greeting cards, personalized checks, and business and telephone directories.

The second mode of TTS operation is widely used for the transmission of news stories. For this purpose, news associations and syndicates in the United States and other countries make use of teletype transmission facilities to provide teletypesetter service to newspapers. Some news agencies also mail feature material in justified tape form for automatic typesetting.

History. The development of the teletypesetter was first suggested in 1926 by Walter W. Morey, a West Orange, N. J., printer. This enterprise was financially backed by the newspaper publisher Frank E. Gannett. The teletypesetter was first tested successfully in 1927, and the system was perfected in the early 1930's by Sterling Morton, Howard Krum, and Edward Kleinschmidt. The first commercial use of the equipment was made at the Newburgh (N. Y.) *News* and the Beacon (N. Y.) *News* in 1932.

At first, trade-union opposition to the time- and labor-saving teletypesetter limited its use, and later World War II hampered further commercial development. As a result it was not until 1951 that the United Press (later United Press International) and the Associated Press began transmitting news in justified tape form for automatic typesetting. By 1970, about 1,600 daily newspapers and 400 weeklies in the United States and about 2,000 newspapers in other countries were using teletypesetter equipment. See also PRINTING; TELETYPEWRITER.

THOMAS CORPORA
United Press International

TELETYPEWRITER, an electromechanical device for transmitting and receiving printed messages. It was perfected in the early 1900's as a result of the work of several men, notably the American inventors Sterling and Joy Morton, Charles C. Krum, and Edward E. Kleinschmidt. After their work, the teletypewriter machine began to replace the Morse telegraph operator.

The teletypewriter combines the mechanical functions of the typewriter with the electrical functions of the telegraph key and sounder to form a unique interface between man and a telegraph circuit. At the transmitting location, a teletypewriter converts a key-stroke input to electrical impulses, encodes these impulses, and transmits them serially to the telegraph circuit. At the receiving location, another teletypewriter detects and decodes the electrical impulses and prints a letter, number, or punctuation mark on a roll of paper. Each encoded character consists of a start pulse, several equal-length information pulses, and a stop pulse.

The two basic coding schemes in current use are the Murray code, adopted by Donald Murray from the original Baudot code, and the newer American Standard Code for Information Interchange (ASCII). In the Murray code, each character is represented by five information pulses (5-unit code). In the ASCII code, each character is represented by eight information pulses (8-unit code). Teletypewriters that use one of these coding schemes are available with various operational features to facilitate message handling.

The line facility that connects two teletypewriter stations is a telegraph circuit consisting of a local channel, an intercity carrier circuit, and another local channel. Each local channel generally consists of a cable circuit between a teletypewriter sending or receiving station and a central office. The intercity portion of the circuit consists of a telegraph channel derived from a standard telephone channel on a frequency-division multiplex basis; that is, messages ride on different carrier frequencies sent simultaneously along a single line.

Services. Private-line, or leased-line, teletypewriter service is designed specifically for the transmission of records or written messages. In this service, two or more teletypewriter stations are connected by a telegraph circuit that is available full time to the user. This service is offered throughout the United States and internationally where transmission facilities are available. Messages commonly are sent at speeds of 60, 75, and 100 words per minute (wpm) in the United States and at 67 wpm between the United States and other countries. For a description of other services, see TELETYPEWRITER EXCHANGE SERVICE; TELEX.

History. Experimental teletypewriter service was first furnished to the press in 1915, and service rates were introduced by the American Telephone and Telegraph Company in June 1917. In the same month, the United Press signed the first contract for three private-line teletypewriter services. From this meager beginning, the service came into widespread use by industry and various government agencies. Typical users include the press, airlines, trucklines, and fuel companies. Information such as news reports, administrative messages, and business orders and records is sent. Many users now have large networks consisting of several multistation telegraph circuits radiating from a central computer. In this time-shared service, the computer sequentially polls each station, stores and edits its message, and delivers it to the destination.

L. E. ROYSE
American Telephone and Telegraph Company

TELETYPEWRITER EXCHANGE SERVICE, often called TWX service, provides two-way printed communications between two or more subscribers' machines temporarily connected by lines and switching equipment. TWX service is provided in the United States and Canada. Messages are sent and received by teletypewriters at speeds of 60 or 100 words per minute (wpm) in the United States and 100 wpm in Canada. A similar service is known as Telex. See TELEX.

Station equipment for TWX service consists of a teletypewriter, a data set, and a dial. The 60-wpm machines use the 5-unit Murray code to represent letters and numbers by direct-current pulses, and the 100-wpm machines use the 8-unit ASCII code (see TELETYPEWRITER). The data set, which serves as an interface between the teletypewriter and the subscriber's line, converts the direct-current pulses to tones suitable for transmission over a switched network. The dial permits access to the switched network from the subscriber's station, and it provides the signaling and supervisory functions to establish a station-to-station connection.

A subscriber using a 60-wpm machine is served from a telephone central office, and his message is switched over the telephone network in a manner similar to that for a telephone call. A subscriber using a 100-wpm machine is served from a specially equipped central office, and his message is switched over a separate TWX network. Communication between 60- and 100-wpm machines is possible by means of speed and code conversion units in telephone company offices.

TWX service is best suited for subscribers with low- or medium-traffic volumes to widely scattered locations, whereas heavy traffic volumes between restricted locations are more economically handled by private-line service. Typical uses for TWX include the transmission of payroll and inventory data and the handling of ordering and shipping invoices.

History. TWX service was first inaugurated by the American Telephone and Telegraph Company on Nov. 21, 1931, using subscriber connections manually established by operators. The service was converted to automatic dial operation on Aug. 31, 1962. TWX is now available with either rotary-dial or Touch-tone signaling.

L. E. ROYSE
American Telephone and Telegraph Company

TELEVISION PRODUCTION of a play. Performers are limited to a small area of acting space because of the size and amount of mobile and stationary equipment.

PICTORIAL PARADE

TELEVISION, a medium of communication primarily used for broadcasting visual impressions of reality through space, is the most effective means of mass communication known to mankind. After about 80 years of development, television made it possible for millions of people to share a single experience. For instance, about 750 million people witnessed the funeral of President John F. Kennedy in 1963, and about 600 million people saw man first set foot on the moon in 1969.

Scientists in Britain, Germany, France, the USSR, and the United States contributed to early experiments in television, but it was Britain, the United States, and Japan that solved the problems leading to a full television service. Britain started regular TV broadcasts in 1937. Japan pressed its research in the hope of telecasting the Olympic Games from Tokyo in 1940, but this hope was dashed by World War II. The United States began full-scale television immediately after the war and developed its television service more rapidly than any other country.

Other nations soon recognized that the new medium was a tremendous force for political persuasion, for education and enculturation, and for selling goods. By 1970, 118 countries—all nations in the Western Hemisphere, all nations in Europe, about half of the nations in Africa, and most of the nations in Asia—had a privately, publicly, or governmentally owned television service. In the United States in 1970 a total of 880 television stations were on the air—509 commercial VHF, 181 commercial UHF, 82 public VHF, and 108 public UHF stations. About 59.4 million homes were equipped with one or more TV receivers, and 25.3 million homes had color TV. Network television alone sold a record $1.7 billion worth of time to advertisers in 1969.

The average American has his set turned on for about 6.5 hours each day. In fact, television has become the American's eyes and ears on the world.

CONTENTS

1. History of TV Broadcasting

The dream of extending human vision, as the telegraph and the telephone had extended communication by signals for words, began to be realized in 1883. In that year Paul Nipkow, a German scientist, invented a scanning device that could break down an image into a sequence of tiny pictorial elements. His scanning device was a spirally perforated rotating disk. This crude mechanical scanner was used with a photoelectric cell that converted light into electrical impulses.

Experiments with mechanical scanning devices were pursued in the 1920's, particularly in the laboratories of three men. The American inventor Charles Francis Jenkins, who became interested in the possibility of television as early as 1890, used elaborations of the Nipkow disk to broadcast silhouette pictures from his workshop in Washington, D. C., in 1925.

The Scottish inventor John Logie Baird, following similar lines of investigation, made a public demonstration of television in 1926, but he also produced only shadow pictures. By 1928 he had broadcast television pictures in color, outdoor scenes, and stereoscopic scenes. Baird also televised motion pictures.

Ernst F. W. Alexanderson, who worked at the General Electric (GE) laboratories in Schenectady, N. Y., began daily TV tests on the experimental station W2XAD in 1928. On Sept. 11, 1928, GE presented the first dramatic production on television. It was *The Queen's Messenger,* with the sound carried on radio station WGY. Three motionless cameras were used, and the image for the viewer was seen on a 3-by-4-inch screen. In 1931 the Radio Corporation of America (RCA) made experimental tests over station 2XBS in New York, and David L. Sarnoff, president of RCA, predicted that within five years television would become "as much a part of our life" as radio.

Despite these early successes, mechanical scanning had inherent drawbacks. In particular, it did not provide sharpness of detail. Consequently, further advances depended on the development of electronic scanning. Its roots go back to experiments by Heinrich Hertz and Wilhelm Hallwachs (in the 1800's), to Einstein's publication of the theory of photoelectric effect (1905), and to Karl Braun's discovery that he could change the course of electrons in a cathode-ray tube by subjecting them to a magnetic field (1906). In 1907 the English scientist Alan Campbell Swinton proposed a television system using a cathode-ray tube at the receiving end, and the Russian scientist Boris Rosing, following Campbell Swinton's ideas, patented such a system in that year.

World War I put an end to all but theoretical work, but its aftermath brought to America one of the outstanding scientists in the development of television. He was Vladimir K. Zworykin, a student of Rosing. He developed a crude, but workable, partly electronic TV system in 1923. He evolved the principles of the iconoscope, the basic tube of the television system that was demonstrated at the New York World's Fair in 1939.

Philo T. Farnsworth, an Idaho farm boy born in 1906, was 14 before he knew of the existence of electricity, but he grasped its principles rapidly. Within two years, he rejected the idea of mechanical scanning and worked out an electronic television system. In 1930 he developed a new electronic scanning system that made TV pictures suitable for the home.

Allen B. Du Mont, an electrical engineering graduate from Rensselaer Polytechnic Institute, also made significant contributions to television —notably, improvements in the cathode-ray picture tube. His DuMont Laboratories, which he organized in 1931 with an investment of $500, made the first television sets for the public in 1939.

Television fever mounted in the 1930's and nowhere more than in David Sarnoff, president of RCA. The National Broadcasting Company (NBC), a subsidiary of RCA, began experimental telecasts from the Empire State Building in 1932, and Sarnoff in 1935 announced that the parent company was ready to invest $1 million in television program demonstrations. It was essential for the growth of television that broadcasters and set manufacturers accept uniform standards, and hearings by the Federal Communications Commission (FCC) began a year later.

On Nov. 6, 1935, Edwin H. Armstrong announced his development of frequency modulation (FM) broadcasting, which was adopted for the transmission of sound for television in 1941.

Significant experimental work also was accomplished in Britain. In 1935 the British Broadcasting Corporation (BBC) was authorized to take over control of television, and Baird Television, Ltd., and Marconi-EMI Television Company, Ltd., made experiments at a London station. At this stage of development Baird was working on 240-line picture transmission and Marconi-EMI on a 405-line system. French engineers began work on a 1,000-line system, which eventually resulted in France's 819-line standard.

The tempo of development quickened in 1936. RCA began field tests of an all-electronic system from the Empire State Building, broadcasting 343-line pictures at a rate of 30 complete pictures (frames) per second. Studio 3H in Radio City was converted for TV and began to feed programs to the Empire State transmitter on a twice-a-week schedule. The Columbia Broadcasting System (CBS) ordered a television system from RCA and began to install it in the Chrysler Building, near its studios in the Grand Central Terminal Building. On the West Coast the Don Lee Broadcasting System began public demonstrations.

In Britain the BBC began a regular television service with a 405-line picture transmitted from its new Alexandria Palace Station. This was the Marconi-EMI standard, whose victory over the Baird system was made official early in 1937. By this time, British TV was able to broadcast the coronation procession of George VI over a broad area.

NBC began a regular television service in 1939, starting off with the opening ceremonies at the New York World's Fair. On this occasion, President Roosevelt became the first president to be televised. There were other "firsts" that year —the first broadcast of a major league baseball game and the first broadcast of a college football game.

The first official network television broadcast in the United States took place on Feb. 1, 1940, when a program from NBC in New York City was picked up and rebroadcast by General Electric's station WRGB in Schenectady, N. Y. At about the same time the Zenith Corporation began a regular program service in Chicago. Parts of the 1940 Republican National Convention in Philadelphia were televised after transmission to New York via coaxial cable, and films of the Democratic Convention in Chicago were flown to New York for telecasting. Late in the year Peter Goldmark of CBS Laboratories made a successful color television broadcast from New York City.

The FCC authorized commercial TV beginning on July 1, 1941. WNBT, New York, became the first commercial station, offering 15 hours a week of programs. The FCC transferred television sound from AM to FM and raised the standard for the picture from 441 to 525 lines, where it has since remained. In England, Baird demonstrated color and stereoscopic television. CBS presented the first television newscast, on Dec. 7, 1941, reporting the events at Pearl Harbor.

Pearl Harbor greatly slowed the development of television. In April 1942 the Defense Communications Board ordered an end to the con-

CULVER PICTURES

CULVER PICTURES

POPULAR FAVORITES on early television programs included Milton Berle, who starred in his own variety show, and Jackie Gleason (*right*), who bickered with his television wife, Audrey Meadows, in *The Honeymooners*.

struction of radio and television stations. What television broadcasting remained began to be used for such purposes as civil defense and air-raid warden training, Red Cross instruction, and war bond sales.

And yet work went on, so that NBC in 1945 was able to begin network television, tying together Philadelphia, New York, and Schenectady. DuMont readied its direct-view 20-inch screen for home use. RCA announced the image orthicon camera, still the standard for black-and-white TV. Television covered the events of VE and VJ days—for instance, WNBT broadcast films of the Japanese surrender.

By 1948 there were 36 television stations on the air, about 70 under construction, and about 1 million sets in use. Problems began to appear, chiefly the interference of one station's signal with another's. On Sept. 30, 1948, the FCC declared a freeze on the licensing of any new TV stations in order to have time to study frequency allocations and to consider problems posed by color television. At that time, two cities, New York and Los Angeles, had seven stations; 22 cities including Boston, Chicago, and Philadelphia, had two or more stations; many major cities, such as Houston, Pittsburgh, and St. Louis had only one station; and a number of cities, among them Denver, Austin, and the two Portlands, had no station.

This situation continued for three and a half years, prolonged by the Korean War and a consequent shortage of critical materials. The FCC lifted the freeze in April 1952 with its Sixth Report and Order. This document supplemented the existing channels (channels 2 through 13) in the VHF (very high frequency) band with 70 new channels (channels 14 to 83) in the UHF (ultrahigh frequency) band. Within a few months the FCC processed a backlog of 700 applications for new stations and granted 175 licenses. Within a year, there were 377 stations on the air, and by the middle of 1954, almost 90% of the country had television coverage. The boom was on. Television had become the most important mass medium of all time.

American television began with four networks, but in 1955 it settled down to three—NBC, CBS, and the American Broadcasting Company (ABC)—when DuMont was unable to support its small network operation. Since then, every attempt to establish a fourth national commercial network has met with failure. As of May 1970 there were 650 network-affiliated stations on the air.

TV Channels. In 1945 the FCC authorized black-and-white television on 13 channels in the VHF band between 44 and 216 megahertz (MHz). Channels 1 through 6 were assigned frequencies within the band from 44 to 88 MHz, and channels 7 through 13 were assigned frequencies in the band from 174 to 216 MHz. There was also to be some sharing of the TV channels where it could be established that no interference would result. In addition, the FCC made channels from 480 to 920 MHz in the UHF band available for experimental purposes. At the time the commission clearly recognized that in the long run these allocations would not be sufficient for a truly competitive nationwide service. Somewhat later the FCC took channel 1 from TV and assigned its 6-MHz frequency band to land mobile radio, which has had a great need for more space in the radio-frequency spectrum.

When the FCC lifted its freeze in 1952 it allocated channels in the VHF band for more than 500 stations and channels in the UHF band for

CULVER PICTURES

YOUR SHOW OF SHOWS introduced comedian Sid Caesar (*left*) to millions of viewers.

more than 1,400 stations. The decisions to locate these stations in 1,300 communities were made on the basis of population density, the nature of the terrain, and the requirement that city-based stations be able to serve surrounding rural areas.

Many of the VHF channels were quickly put to use by new stations, but UHF channels were introduced more slowly because receivers and antennas had to be modified to accept UHF signals. UHF television got a lift with the passage of a law requiring that all sets manufactured after 1964 must be capable of receiving both VHF and UHF signals. The law was successful in its intent. By 1970 more than 60% of the TV sets in the United States were equipped to receive UHF signals.

Color Television. After the FCC's freeze in 1948, the role of color television and its relationship to the standard black-and-white broadcasts remained unresolved. CBS, RCA, and Color Television, Inc., each presented a color television system for judgment by the FCC. The CBS system was not compatible—that is, its color broadcasts could not be picked up in black and white by existing receivers—whereas the other two companies claimed their systems were compatible. There were demonstrations, tests, and testimony. In September 1950 the FCC found that the CBS system met its standards for color. As a result, the FCC selected this system for broadcasting, although it kept the door open for the development of a better system. CBS began limited broadcasting in color in June 1951 but seemed to lose interest after November, when the National Production Authority prohibited the manufacture of color TV sets because of a shortage of certain materials essential in the Korean War.

In January 1953 the National Television Systems Committee (NTSC) adopted specifications for a compatible color TV system supported by most of the major manufacturers. Toward the end of the year the FCC issued rules for the use of this fully electronic, fully compatible system. It has been in use in the United States ever since.

In most respects this system was developed by RCA. The rest of the industry left it to RCA and its subsidiary NBC to develop and promote color television. Alone of the three networks, NBC built color facilities and began to try out its major programs in color. Ten years after the adoption of the system, NBC was broadcasting as much as 40 hours a week of color programs. CBS had done little color programming, and ABC virtually none. Despite the cost of color receivers, the public appetite had begun to be whetted, and color became an increasingly important element in program costs and set sales.

CBS did not abandon its color system. In fact, it was used by Apollo astronauts to send back to earth their remarkable color pictures of the moon and the earth.

Early Programs and Celebrities. Faced initially with filling the evening hours, television in the late 1940's transferred from radio about two dozen popular programs, such as *Talent Scouts* with Arthur Godfrey, *Studio One, Big Story,* and *Suspense.* There were also wrestling matches, quiz and panel shows, roller derbies, and so on, but the first real smash was NBC's *Texaco Star Theater,* a variety show starring comedian Milton Berle. It had much the same wildly enthusiastic reception from audiences as *Amos 'n' Andy* had in radio 20 years earlier and was a major stimulus to the purchase of sets in 1948 and 1949. The variety format proved well suited to television, resulting in short order in *Your Show of Shows,* starring Sid Caesar and Imogene Coca, *Toast of the Town,* the original title of what has long since been *The Ed Sullivan Show,* and *Garroway At Large,* a Chicago-produced variety show that was attractively low key and casual. *I Love Lucy,* starring Lucille Ball, also came along. It was produced on film and thereby served notice that filmed programs could be distributed to other stations, and thereby bypass the lack of transcontinental facilities for broadcasting. Burr Tillstrom and his *Kukla, Fran, and Ollie* were early favorites who gave real distinction to the new medium, as did Ed Murrow in 1951 with the CBS weekly documentary *See It Now,* the outgrowth of radio's *Hear it Now.* Drama was well served by *Philco Playhouse* and *Goodyear Playhouse,* with Fred Coe as producer, and by *Robert Montgomery Presents.* These and other early dramatic programs, some of a highly melodramatic nature, like the Sidney Lumet-directed *Tales of Adventure,* developed numerous writers, directors, and producers who have since contributed greatly to theater and films. Audiences were electrified in 1951 by the televised Senate committee hearings on organized crime and in 1952 by television's first opera, *Amahl and the Night Visitors,* composed by Gian-Carlo Menotti.

The presidential election campaign in 1952 made a really big show, pitting the military hero Dwight Eisenhower against the witty Adlai Stevenson. Because of the coaxial link with New York, both conventions were held in Philadelphia. Westinghouse paid NBC \$3.5 million to sponsor them, and Americans came to know Betty Furness as a saleswoman for refrigerators. The Eisenhower campaign, with the advertising agency of Batten, Barton, Durstine, & Osborn much in evidence, wrote the script for future elections—widespread use of spot announcements, mostly 20 seconds long, and emphasis on the image of the candidate, in this case as "hero."

The "special," first known as the "spectacular," came to television in 1953 with the memorable 2-hour Ford show starring Mary Martin and Ethel Merman. Credit for the concept and its development mainly belongs to Sylvester Weaver, who joined NBC in 1949 as vice president in charge of television and went on to become president and chairman of the board. Weaver was the originator of many of TV's newest concepts in programming: the *Today* show, *Tonight*, the *Home Show*, *Wide Wide World*, and others.

JOHN M. GUNN
State University of New York at Albany

Further Reading: Barnouw, Eric, *A History of Broadcasting in the United States*, vols. 1–3 (New York 1966–1970); Briggs, Asa, *The Birth of Broadcasting: The History of Broadcasting in the United Kingdom* (New York 1961); Kendrick, Alexander, *Prime Time: The Life of Edward R. Murrow* (Boston 1969).

2. Broadcasting in the United States

The reasons for producing a television program may vary from station to station, but everywhere the broadcasting techniques are basically the same.

Program Origination. Television programs originate in one of four ways: as live programs broadcast from a studio as they are happening; as live programs covering events outside the studio as they are happening; as programs originally recorded on film and as programs originally recorded on magnetic tape (videotape). Any given program may use a mix of some or all of these kinds of program origination.

From 1948 to 1958 most TV programming was live. Variety shows, dramas, and quiz and panel programs originated in the studio, and programs covering sports and news events originated where they occurred. If a delayed broadcast of a live program was necessary, the program was "kinescoped"—that is, it was first photographed on film from the images presented live on a TV picture tube and then was rebroadcast by using this film. Exceptions to these practices were the broadcasts of old movies, notably Westerns, and *I Love Lucy*, one of the industry's first hits. This program, which started in 1951, was photographed on film by three 35-mm cameras before a studio audience and then edited to its half-hour format. The production flexibility and the possibility of endless replays provided by this technique gradually led to an emphasis on filmed television in the United States. In contrast, emphasis is still placed on live programming in Britain.

The use of videotape—magnetic tape for recording TV programs—began in 1956, and problems of compatibility between recording and playback units were solved by 1959. Videotape provides instant replay, an enormous advantage over film, which must first be processed. It also provides excellent storage of program material and has a form that can be edited readily.

Remote broadcasts or remote pickups—programs that have not been staged in the studio—have become commonplace in television. Programs covering sports, political events, and space exploration are examples. Here the world becomes the studio, and the control room is often a large truck or van. The van basically is a small TV station, equipped with everything required to put a program on the air. The van may use a line-of-sight microwave link to the master control room or the transmitter, or it may be connected to them by coaxial cable. Sometimes the van carries its own videotape recorder.

Studio Program Production. Every television studio should have an open, level, uncluttered floor space to allow for the erection of scenery and the free movement of cameras around the sets and performers. In addition, every studio should have a ceiling height of at least 12 feet (3.6 meters) to allow for the hanging of lights.

Early television studios were converted radio studios or office building space. Both often had the drawbacks of small doorways and low ceilings, making set handling and lighting difficult. However stations and networks soon found more adequate premises. In New York, CBS acquired a large creamery and turned it into a complete production center. NBC supplemented its converted studios in Radio City with motion picture stages in Brooklyn and made them into its first color studios. ABC bought a large stable and riding ring on Manhattan's West Side, and converted them for its TV operations. All three networks also bought movie and legitimate theaters for studio space. In San Francisco, KQED began programming from a garage, and other stations took over armories, nightclubs, or any space that was large, open, and high-ceilinged. On the West Coast in the mid-1950's, the networks built their "television cities"—complexes of office spaces, vast studios, scene shops, and storage areas.

The control room for any studio houses a variety of equipment for producing programs. Monitors (television screens) give the director a view of what any camera is shooting and what is being fed to the transmitter or a videotape recorder. A switcher gives the technical director control over transition from camera to camera or transitions from camera to slides or film or videotape inserts. A shader gives an operator electronic control of the quality of the picture. The audio console gives one control of the sound. The equipment and the personnel to man it generally are divided into areas of program control, video (picture) control, and audio (sound) control. The television director must be able to preview all pictures, hear the sound, give directions to the technical director and to his associate director, and talk by phone line with his cameraman, floor manager, and lighting director.

The master control room, which contains switching control for programs coming from studios, vans, or the network, feeds the program to the transmitter. In addition, it normally houses the film chain—the TV camera and the projectors through which any slides are fed into the program sequence; the sync (synchronization) generators, whose electronic pulses synchronize picture transmission and reception in order to produce a stable picture on the home screen; and the videotape recorders.

Putting a show on the air may involve only a single performer, a single camera, and a minimum crew, or many persons and much equipment. For a series such as *Star Trek* or *Ironside* or *Mission Impossible*, 26 or more feature films are made each year. Their production staffs consist of an executive producer, producers, directors, writers, set designers and decorators, sound effects men, music scorers, post-production per-

SESAME STREET, a program for preschool children, uses cartoons and puppets to teach letters and numbers, and problem-solving to teach rudimentary logic.

THE CHILDREN'S TELEVISION WORKSHOP INC.

sonnel, editors, cameramen and lighting men, stagehands, scene shifters, electricians, carpenters, painters, script girls, secretaries, and other personnel.

Normally, a producer provides the basic idea for a program, and a writer develops the idea into script form. A director and set designer are called in, and all confer on the physical appearance of the program. When agreement has been reached, the set designer creates the set from stock units or from newly built and painted elements. As these matters are settled, the producer chooses and contracts for the performers. In all of these considerations the producer keeps a wary eye on costs, usually on the basis of a budget for the program prepared by a budget officer or someone else skilled in costs. The producer also orders graphic materials such as slides or film or off-set pictures, as called for in the script.

As the time for broadcast nears, the program goes into rehearsal. At this point, the director takes responsibility for the program. When the program does not involve much movement of the performers, it is rehearsed immediately on camera. When considerable movement is involved, the program is blocked in a rehearsal room, with the floor taped to delineate playing areas within the set. Eventually the program moves to the studio, where the stage is set by the studio crew of stagehands, decorated by the prop men, and lighted by the electricians under the guidance of the lighting director. In addition to the crew, the studio holds the cameramen, performers, and the floor manager, who conveys the director's orders to the performers and the stage crew.

In the control room are the director; his associate director, whose function is to keep a timing on the program and to ready upcoming shots; the technical director, who does the switching from camera to camera and is responsible for all technical operations; the audio man, who controls all sound elements of the program; and the video man, who controls the quality of the picture being fed to the transmitter or videotape recorder. There also may be a backseat for the producer, whose sole function at this point is to catch any slips not noticed by the director or associate director.

Network and Local Stations. There are 650 network-affiliated stations and a total of 690 commercial stations. Thus 94% of the commercial stations have network affiliations.

The program logs of representative network-affiliated stations across the country show a fair amount of coverage of local news, often well done; occasional panel or discussion shows on matters of community interest; some small coverage of local sports events; small attention to local religious broadcasting; and large amounts of locally purchased old movies, sometimes following the late news but occasionally supplanting network offerings in prime time because the financial returns for the locally originated movie are greater. Independent stations have often followed the road of endless reruns of network programs.

A common criticism of local commercial broadcasting is that the local station has abdicated its responsibility to serve its community's needs and in return for guaranteed, risk-free profits has "sold" itself to the network. It was not always so. In general, early television provided local programming in the daytime and network programming at night. Then the networks—following a path that had been charted years before by national radio—found there was gold in the daytime, and so they began an endless stream of game shows, soap operas, and weekend sports events.

Aware of the drift toward network domination of both day and night TV, the FCC in 1960 listed 14 program areas in which to judge a station's performance at license renewal time and then apparently ignored its own strictures for a decade. Prompted by the Westinghouse group of stations, the FCC finally proposed a rule limiting network programming in the top 50 markets to three hours of prime time, effective Sept. 1, 1971. This move may open prime time to new and perhaps fresher sources of programming. Within the industry there is agreement only that local news may benefit from the order.

Cable TV. Cable TV, or CATV (community antenna television), systems provide good TV signals in areas distant from transmitters or in areas where mountains, tall buildings, or other obstructions impede signal reception. The first community antenna TV service began in Lansford, Pa., in 1950. Soon thereafter, other small communities with no TV station of their own erected a tall master antenna and connected individual sets to it by cable. For this service subscribers paid a monthly fee. Cable TV rapidly turned into an extensive and fast-growing business, partly because transmission by cable provided up to 12 VHF channels and partly because microwave relay systems in some cases were used with the master antenna to provide for the importing of distant signals.

Beginning in 1964, cable TV came to large cities, where tall buildings are as great an obstacle to good reception as mountains are elsewhere. There is no precise source of information about the extent of cable TV because it is not licensed by the FCC. By 1965 an estimated 1.7 million homes were served by about 1,600 cable TV systems, and by 1970 an estimated 4.5 million homes were served by 2,385 cable TV systems. About 7% of all TV homes had cable service by 1970, and it continued to grow.

Cable TV does not broadcast programs through the air to home sets, and it normally is not engaged in interstate commerce. Consequently, the FCC at first felt it had no jurisdiction under the Communications Act of 1934. In fact, it said so specifically in 1959. By 1965, however, the FCC became concerned about the effects of cable TV on the economic well-being of stations providing the only local service in small communities. The FCC therefore adopted rules governing cable systems served by microwave relay links, feeling itself on safe ground because these links use a form of radio transmission. The rules required cable systems served by microwave links to carry the signals of local TV stations on request and to refrain from duplicating local commercial-station programs within 15 days after their broadcast.

In 1966 the FCC asserted its jurisdiction over all cable TV systems and adopted rules to fit them into the overall television transmission system. It also changed the 15-day ban to a ban only on the day of broadcast, and it asked Congress for legislation that would clarify its rights and duties with regard to cable TV. Its right to regulate cable TV was upheld by the Supreme Court in 1968.

After that decision, the FCC made rules aimed at equalizing the competition between broadcasters and cable TV owners. Under these rules a cable system within 35 miles of a major city in the top 100 markets can not pick up the signals of a station more than 35 miles away unless that station gives permission. In effect, the rule eliminated what was considered to be unfair competition with stations serving the top 100 markets. The rules also protected stations in smaller markets by putting limitations on what signals the cable system could pick up from a distant station. The FCC also passed a rule, effective Jan. 1, 1971, that required cable systems with more than 3,500 subscribers to originate programs on their own. It gave them the right to sell advertising, but only if the commercials were inserted in the "natural breaks" in the programs.

A cable TV system obtains its franchise from a city government or a state public service commission, whereas a station that uses the airwaves is licensed by the FCC. This situation presents problems to cable systems owners, so their industry association, the National Cable TV Association, seeks single jurisdiction by the FCC. Other problems have to do with copyrights—the question of who own what rights to what programs. Copyright problems will be answered only when Congress passes a long-awaited revision of the Copyright Act of 1909.

Commercial broadcasters foresee that a cable system originating its own programs may become the competitor of a TV station and that an interconnection of cable TV systems may become a competitor of the established networks. They are concerned about tendency toward mergers, such as that of Teleprompter Corporation and H. B. American Corporation, which created a single cable TV system with 350,000 subscribers.

The future of cable television is not clear. It might continue to operate chiefly as an extension of regular television, or it might offer its subscribers regular television service plus a host of information services. These services might provide descriptions of data needed in marketing and shopping, business communications, information retrieval, and so on—all the services that its most enthusiastic proponents have foreseen. Indeed, the possibilities inherent in cable TV have led some visionaries to predict a future in which all American homes will receive television by cable, with the airwaves left free for radio broadcasting and land mobile radio. See also COMMUNITY ANTENNA TELEVISION.

Pay TV. Pay TV, also known as toll TV or subscription TV, differs from cable TV in two important respects. Pay TV entirely originates its own programs and charges a fee for viewing each program. Two transmission methods are used. In closed-circuit pay TV, signals are transmitted by cable. In broadcast pay TV, a scrambled signal is transmitted through the air to receivers equipped with decoding and billing devices specially made for this kind of service.

In the 1950's the FCC said that trials of pay TV should be made, but there was opposition from theater owners, who already were suffering from the competition of free television. Proponents of pay TV promised high-quality programming, including first-run movies, opera, ballet, and major sports events. In 1962 experimental pay TV broadcasting on a UHF channel began under FCC authorization in Hartford, Conn. A trial of closed-circuit pay TV was made in a suburb of Toronto, Canada, and still another pay-TV experiment was conducted in California.

Data from the Hartford test were submitted to the FCC in 1965, and in December 1968 it authorized pay TV under careful controls protecting free television. The rules, which took effect in June 1969, provided for pay TV only in major markets. Under these rules the time given to movies and sports could take up a maximum of 90% of the program time, and the system would have to supply 28 hours a week of free television. The movies could not be more than two years old, and there were other similar restrictions. Even so, the National Association of Theater Owners and the Joint Committee Against Toll TV challenged the FCC action in court.

Theater television, an operation somewhat similar to pay TV, has been far more successful.

TELEVISION PERFORMERS often rely on "cue cards," on which are printed the words to be sung or spoken. Also within view is a monitor (*far left*) that permits them to see their own performances.

PICTORIAL PARADE

It has shown major sports events, notably championship boxing matches, on large screens in theaters. In such cases, the signals are transmitted by coaxial cable or microwave link from the site of the event to the theater. Admission prices have been fairly high, and promoters have often made more from these showings than from the admissions to the events themselves.

Educational TV. During the FCC freeze on TV expansion from 1948 to 1952, about 108 television stations were on the air, but only one resembled an educational TV (ETV) station. That was WOI-TV, owned by Iowa State College (now Iowa State University) in Ames, Iowa. When the FCC lifted the freeze, it allocated 80 VHF and 162 UHF channels for "noncommercial educational purposes." The assignments of these channels for education were a triumph for Frieda Hennock, an FCC commissioner who organized a campaign that prompted the commission to make the allocations. Since 1952 the number of channels reserved for educational TV has increased from 242 to 309.

The first new educational station on the air was KUHT in Houston, which started broadcasting on May 25, 1953. The first state ETV network was established in Alabama on April 28, 1955. There were hopes that ETV might solve some of the problems of coping with the ever-increasing numbers of students, who were filling colleges and universities faster than they could build classrooms and recruit faculties. However, educators showed none of the rush businessmen have shown to get on the air. There were only two ETV stations in 1953, 15 in 1955, and 34 in 1958. Costs were high, and similar efforts to establish educational radio had had a discouraging history.

From the beginning, educational television had a dual purpose—to supply programs for in-school use as a supplement to the teacher during the day, and to supply programs of community interest and cultural enrichment at night. Early studies showed that teaching by television generally was about as effective as normal classroom procedure, and therefore ETV was promising. As for cultural programming, the need for it increased as commercial TV became less and less a service and more and more a business.

From the beginning, funding for educational and cultural programs was the major problem. Funds came from state taxes for state-supported systems, from public subscription, from local businesses, from commercial broadcasters who often made generous gifts of equipment, and from foundations. Without the continuous support of the Ford Foundation since 1952, it is doubtful whether educational TV, or public television, as it is now known, could have become a workable alternative to commercial television. The Ford Foundation began its support in 1952 by providing funds for the National Educational Television and Radio Center (NET), which became an association of noncommercial educational TV stations. These funds were used to produce a limited amount of educational and cultural programs on tape or film for noncommercial stations and to supply grants for the construction of new noncommercial stations. From 1953 to 1962, NET made grants to member stations to assist them in the production of programs suitable for showing on all stations, and it handled the distribution of programs. NET also procured a limited number of programs from the BBC and other outside sources.

Hoping for even better programming, the Ford Foundation increased its annual subsidy to NET to $6 million in 1963. Programs seemingly became better, but not enough to satisfy the Ford Foundation. This led it to abandon its previously passive role and to originate and underwrite specific programs, such as *Public Broadcast Laboratory* (1967) and *Hollywood Television Theater* (1970). In the meantime the Ford Foundation continued to support NET and to assist new stations with construction grants.

Educational television got a boost in 1958 from the passage of the National Defense Education Act, which provided up to $100 million a year over a 3-year period for the encouragement and improvement of the teaching of mathematics, the sciences, and foreign languages. Four years later Congress passed a measure providing $32 million for the construction of ETV stations, with the federal funds to be matched by state or local sources. The most hopeful congressional action in this area was the passage of the Public Broadcasting Act, signed into law on Nov. 7, 1967. Based on a recommendation of a commission set up by the Carnegie Foundation, the act established a 15-man Corporation for Public Broadcasting to dispense federal and private funds. President Johnson asked Congress for an initial appropriation of $20 million. Congress settled on $9 million but has not yet worked out a system of long-term financing.

The interconnection of public television stations soon became desirable to increase their effectiveness. Interconnection was achieved in the northeast in 1962 with the creation of the Eastern Education Network, tying together stations from Maine to Washington, D. C. National interconnection became a reality with the debut on Nov. 5, 1967, of *Public Broadcasting Laboratory,* the brainchild of Fred W. Friendly, a television consultant to the Ford Foundation and formerly president of CBS News. It was a 2-hour program fed to 126 stations on Sunday, with $10 million support from the Ford Foundation for a 2-year period. Although often brilliant, it failed to live up to its ambitions and faltered to an end in 1969. At about the same time, the Corporation for Public Broadcasting instituted an interconnection of two to three hours per night, Sundays through Thursdays. To manage the interconnection of stations and the distribution of programs, the corporation in 1969 created the Public Broadcasting System (PBS). It may remain a limited operation or become a full network operation.

NET Festival has brought viewers many events from the concert, opera, and dance worlds that the commercial networks have ignored. *NET Playhouse* not only has presented theater classics, such as the BBC's masterly production of the Shakespearean chronicle plays as *The Age of Kings,* but also has kept alive the idea of original drama for television at a time when the commercial networks had virtually abandoned the form. NET has kept pace with the best the networks offer in public affairs programs and has done considerably better in children's programs. *Sesame Street* turned out to be an unqualified success—a breakthrough in children's programming—after being given $8 million by the Carnegie Corporation, the Department of Health, Education and Welfare, and others for preparation (a year's study) and production. *Misterrogers* and *What's New,* two other NET children's programs, have kept to a high standard for years.

In the fall of 1969 public television came up with another success, the superb BBC dramatization of the John Galsworthy novels *The Forsyte Saga.* Its 26 hour-long episodes probably drew a larger and more faithful audience than any other program offered on public television.

Role of Public Television. By 1970 public television had achieved a status only dreamed of at the beginning of the 1960's. The ratio of public television stations to commercial stations was greater than 1 to 4, and public television was in a position to become the second service that American television has so long needed. Many public television stations are underfinanced and held together by the dedication of their staffs. Some stations pay salaries comparable to those in commercial television, thereby holding personnel who might be tempted to greener fields and attracting talented persons from commercial television who are looking for greater artistic freedom.

At first, few Hollywood or Broadway stars appeared on public television. In the spring of 1970, this situation was changed by two remarkable dramatic productions. *They,* a dramatization of the Marya Mannes novel, had five stars, and *The Andersonville Trial,* directed for television by George C. Scott, had a large cast of name players.

Public television still plays to relatively small audiences rather than attempting to reach the mass audience with every program. A Lou Harris and Associates report in 1969 showed that 4 out of every 10 households watch some public television regularly and that its audience is composed of all age groups and economic and educational backgrounds. Public television is available in 74% of all TV homes, but the viewing is highly selective. The median for all TV viewing in the United States is 11.9 hours per week, whereas for public television it is 1.4 hours per week.

Broadcasting via Domestic Satellites. The relaying of television signals via a domestic satellite system was first suggested by the American Broadcasting Company in 1965. This idea began to receive serious attention in the 1969–1970 season after the American Telephone and Telegraph Company (AT&T) raised its rates for network interconnections by $20 million a year.

AT&T charges about $65 million a year for network interconnections, which could become obsolescent if a domestic satellite system for TV broadcasting were established.

Governmental Regulations. The Communications Act of 1934 set up the Federal Communications Commission as an independent regulatory agency charged with the general supervision of broadcasting. The commission consists of seven members, each appointed for a 7-year term. No member may have a financial interest in broadcasting operations or the manufacture of equipment, and no more than four members may belong to one political party. The commission holds regulatory power over virtually all forms of electronic communications engaged in interstate commerce. For instance, it allocates frequencies for television broadcasting services in order to carry out the intent of international agreements, the Communications Act of 1934, and other laws having to do with radio and television broadcasting.

The FCC issues licenses for radio and TV broadcast services, amateur radio, and land mobile radio. It has the power to renew or revoke them and to approve transfers of ownership. With regard to radio and television stations, it determines the station location, assigns the frequency, power, and operating time, designates the call letters, keeps checks on the equipment, regulates to prevent interference on the air, and monitors the airwaves to ensure there are no violations of its rules.

Although the commission does not directly regulate networks, it maintains a degree of control over them through its regulation of stations owned and operated by networks. The Communications Act gives it the right to refuse a license to any station having a contract with a network that is violating the law in some way.

The Communications Act sets certain basic requirements for the licensing of stations. Applicants must be qualified legally, technically, and financially, and they must be citizens of the United States. Under the act stations are licensed to operate "in the public interest, convenience, and necessity" because the air belongs to the public. Therefore, an applicant must demonstrate his willingness and ability to operate in the public interest.

The FCC exercises control largely through its power to grant or withhold licenses. It also may issue cease and desist orders against violators and may impose fines up to $10,000. However its powers are poorly defined by law, leaving it subject to industry or congressional pressures that sometimes seem to compromise its status as an independent agency.

The FCC conducts an enormous amount of business. It deals annually with millions of licenses of many kinds with a small budget and a small staff. This partly explains its slowness to come to grips with problems that have faced it. The 1948–1952 freeze lasted more than three years, and studies of cable TV and pay TV lasted more than five years. Also, there have been delays because many of the commission's powers have to be validated by the courts, which is often a slow process.

The FCC may not censor programs, nor may it control the form or content of programs. Therefore, it has no control of the quality of television or of the quality or quantity of TV advertising. However, it may insist on fairness in dealing with issues of public concern, and it may refuse to renew a license if it is satisfied that the licensee has failed to operate in the public interest.

As the 1970's began, the major issue troubling the FCC was the concentration of control of the communications media. At present no single group may own more than five VHF and two UHF TV stations. However, the commission has proposed a rule for limiting a single ownership to one AM station, one FM station, one TV station, or one newspaper in one market—a condition that does not exist in many major markets in the United States.

Broadcasting Today. Problems that confront the FCC include the application of the fairness doctrine, the concentration of media control, network domination of prime time, the challenges to license renewals, the framing of policy for a domestic satellite system, the insatiable demands of land mobile radio for more frequency allocations, and the status of cable TV and pay TV. All of these problems also confront the radio-wave broadcaster in the conduct of his enterprise. In addition, he must contend with the public outcry against advertising clutter and sterile programming, the loss of cigarette advertising revenue, the increase in network line charges, the possibility of decreasing audiences, and the development of the home videotape recorder. As a result the broadcaster faces an uncertain future. See also RADIO.

JOHN M. GUNN
State University of New York at Albany

Further Reading: Emery, Walter B., *Broadcasting and Government: Responsibilities and Regulations* (East Lansing, Mich., 1961); Friendly, Fred, *Due to Circumstances Beyond Our Control* (New York 1967).

3. Broadcasting in Other Countries

Television got a modest start in several countries in the 1930's. Canada, England, and the USSR conducted experiments as early as 1936, and by 1938 the USSR was telecasting some programs regularly. It was not until after World War II, however, that significant progress was made in television.

By 1970 more than 100 countries had television, and there were more than 250 million TV sets in the world. Some countries, such as India and Ethiopia, had only one or two TV stations and fewer than 10,000 TV receivers. Other countries, such as Japan, the USSR, Britain, and West Germany had more than 100 stations and more than 15 million receivers.

In organization and control, television abroad follows much the same pattern as radio. There is government ownership and operation, as in China, the USSR, and the eastern countries of Europe. There is control by public corporations or statutory authorities, as in England, Belgium, Germany, and New Zealand. In Sweden and Portugal there are corporate monopolies in which government and private interests share control. Other countries such as Canada, Australia, and Japan have public and private systems. Private commercial operation with strict government regulation is the pattern in Mexico, most of the other countries in Central America, and countries in South America.

CANADA

Canadian television has made marked progress despite Canada's rugged and varied terrain, comparatively limited resources, high population density in a few eastern cities, and deep-seated and long-standing communal and cultural differences (one third of the population is French).

Canadians began experimenting with television during the early 1930's, but it was not until 1951 that the Canadian Broadcasting Corporation (CBC), a public body created in 1936, initiated regular programs in Montreal and Toronto. At about the same time, some private commercial stations started broadcasting.

Ten stations now make up the CBC's basic network for broadcasts in English, and more than 30 privately owned commercial stations are linked to this network. CBC's network for broadcasts in French consists of six main stations that are connected with nine privately owned affiliated stations.

The CTV television network, a commercial network financed by advertising, spans the nation. Also, as in the United States, there has been a large growth in cable TV systems, which transmit TV programs to subscribers who pay a fee.

CBC offers a variety of programs with emphasis on news, documentaries, and film features. On its English-language network it broadcasts numerous American productions such as *Bonanza* and the *Ed Sullivan Show*. The CTV commercial network features light entertainment, including a sizable number of American shows. Both CBC and CTV broadcast some programs in color.

There are no license fees for receivers, although there is a sales tax on sets and spare parts. CBC operations are financed with advertising revenue and parliamentary grants.

All broadcasting, including cable systems, is regulated by the Canadian Radio-Television Commission (CRTC), which was established in 1968.

EUROPE AND THE USSR

Britain. The British Broadcasting Corporation (BBC) operates under a royal charter and is licensed by the postmaster general. It provides two noncommercial television services, which are financed by license fees on receivers. BBC-1 began operations in 1936, but its service was interrupted by World War II. Since then it has developed a nationwide service, providing a 405-line picture for viewers. BBC-2, which was established in 1964, covers most of the country. It provides a 625-line picture on UHF channels, and it makes color transmissions. The greater number of lines provides a finer picture structure for the viewer.

In 1954, Parliament established the Independent Television Authority (ITA) to provide commercial TV. ITA telecasts, with advertisements, are produced by contracting companies in 14 areas. ITA itself is empowered to include program material when "necessary to achieve a proper balance" in the overall program structure.

BBC programming includes varied entertainment plus news, informational broadcasts, and instruction for the classroom. About 45% of ITA programs consists of news, documentaries, and light entertainment. Sports and educational programs make up a large part of the rest.

France. All television in France is provided by the Office of Radio and Television (ORTF), which is controlled by an administrative council. Half of the council members are government officials and the other half are citizens selected from nomination lists submitted by private organizations.

ORTF operates two national TV networks. Programs on the first network, which provides an 819-line picture, are varied in content and designed for wide appeal. The second network, which uses the SECAM color transmission system developed in France, offers a diversified schedule and attempts to give viewers a wider choice of programs. Most programs on both networks emanate from studios in Paris, although some are produced at the regional and local levels. Operations are financed largely by license fees for receivers. Some revenue is derived from advertising, which was first authorized by the government in 1968.

Germany and Italy. West Germany began experimental television broadcasts in 1948, and by 1952 stations in Cologne and Hannover were making broadcasts regularly. TV in West Germany is financed by license fees and advertising and is provided by nine autonomous corporations in the various states (Länder) of the country. These organizations and their TV stations are loosely bound together in the Association of Broadcasting Corporations (ARD). Acting jointly, they provide two network services, one of which presents programs in color. Some stations have added a third service for regional telecasts.

The two networks devote much time to news, discussion, sports, and light entertainment. The third service, which is available on a few stations, emphasizes programs with high aesthetic and intellectual appeal.

Broadcasting in Italy is financed by license fees and advertising and is provided by a joint stock company, Radiotelevisione Italiana (RAI). Government and private investors share ownership of RAI, with the former exercising majority control.

After some experimentation, RAI began television in Italy in 1953, operating three stations in Turin, Milan, and Rome. Two networks now span the nation, and both use a 625-line picture. Telescuola, a unit in RAI's program department, uses more than a fourth of the time on one network to broadcast classroom instruction.

Other Western European Countries. In Austria, Spain, and Portugal, television is mainly under state control, although some private commercial operation is permitted in the Iberian countries. In Belgium, public establishments operate separate TV services. One broadcasts in Flemish and uses a 625-line picture. The other broadcasts in French and uses an 819-line picture, the standard in France. In the Netherlands, private groups (mainly religious groups) and a public foundation do all the telecasting.

Broadcasting systems in Denmark, Norway, and Sweden enjoy monopolistic privilege and are subject to a minimum of state control. There is wide participation of citizens in the councils of administration. While entertainment is not neglected, educational and cultural programs receive comparatively heavy emphasis. Finland began television broadcasts in 1957. Unlike its Scandinavian neighbors, it has both a government and a private system and derives considerable income from television advertising.

Eastern European Countries. All television services in eastern European countries are owned by the governments and controlled by the Communist party. A few countries, notably Czechoslovakia, Hungary, and Yugoslavia, permit a limited amount of advertising, but the main source of revenue is an annual license fee for receivers. In Yugoslavia, unlike other eastern countries, control is exercised at regional and local levels. Some organizational unity is achieved by the Yugoslav Radio and Television Association (JRT), which serves as a national planning and coordinating agency for the broadcast media. Television service in Yugoslavia began in 1958.

The USSR. Television in the USSR is provided by the State Committee for Radio and Television. Central TV facilities are located in Moscow, and four separate broadcast services are provided. The first service is designed for broad appeal, and the second is mainly directed to viewers in the Moscow area. Some advertising is carried on the first and second services. The third service consists mostly of school programs. Some telecasts on the fourth service, which is largely informational, are transmitted in color.

In the USSR, 126 regional TV centers provide programs on at least one channel. An acceptable signal has been transmitted by satellite to a wide area, and nationwide coverage via a satellite system is contemplated.

ASIA

Except for Japan, television in Asian countries is in the early stages of development. About 23 million TV sets are in use in 24 Asian countries. Japan has about 21 million sets, more than 90% of the total for Asian countries. The Philippines ranks second with 350.000 sets, and India ranks last with less than 10,000 sets.

Most Asian television is governmentally operated and financed. In some cases costs are borne by license fees for receivers. A few countries, such as Pakistan and Turkey, have granted monopolies to public corporations. In three countries, television is provided by commercial in-

Above: **The colorful pageantry of a New York Thanksgiving Day parade is captured by a television camera perched high atop a mobile boom.**

Above: **In a TV musical revue an old song, *Up In A Balloon*, is gaily launched, with a miniature barn as a prop to give an illusion of height.**

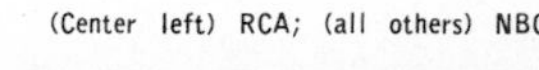
(Center left) RCA; (all others) NBC

Above: **Color adds a new dimension of enjoyment to home television.**

TELEVISION

Right: **Under the glaring lights of a spacious studio, a faithfully simulated snow scene from a Christmas play is being televised in black-and-white and color.**

Scene being televised

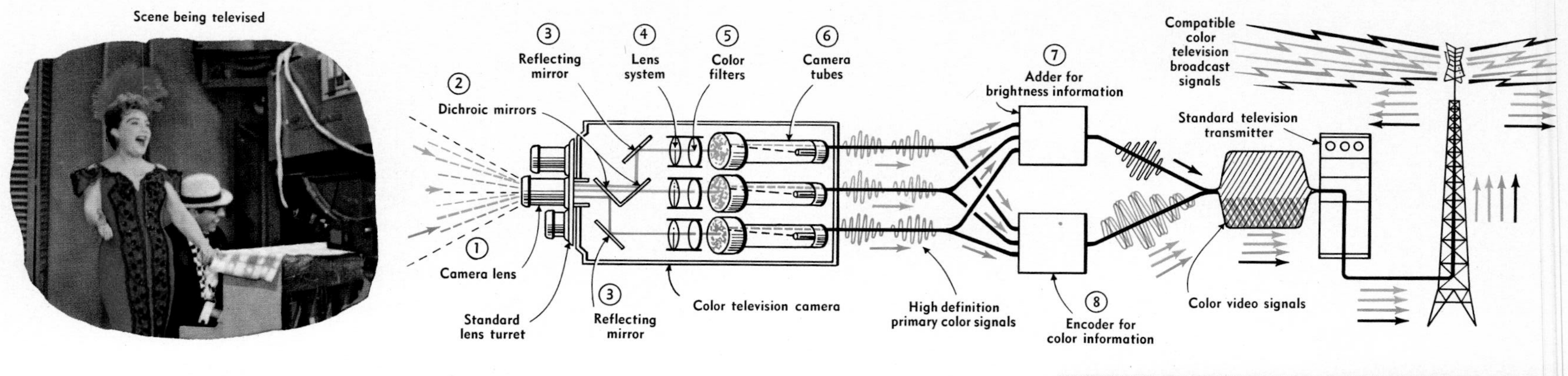

Above: **PICKUP AND TRANSMISSION OF COLOR TELEVISION.** The lens (1) of the color television camera collects light rays in full color from the scene being televised, and the image is focused into a series of mirrors. In the center are two dichroic mirrors (2). The first mirror reflects red light, while blue and green pass through; the second mirror reflects blue but passes green. Thus one image in each primary color is created. Reflecting mirrors (3) and a lens system (4) focus these images on the faces of three camera tubes (6). Color filters (5) assure that the color quality of each primary image has the right value for the system. The electron beam in each camera tube scans the image pattern formed in the tube screen, thereby producing a primary color signal. The three signals are then processed for transmission. Samples of these signals, in proper proportions, go to an electronic adder (7), which combines them to make the brightness, or black-and-white, signal. At the same time, samples of the three primary signals are fed to a unit (8) which combines them into a signal carrying hue and saturation information. This color signal is then combined with the brightness signal to form complete color television signal.

Below: **RECEPTION OF COLOR TELEVISION.** When the color broadcast signals reach a black-and-white receiver, the electronic data for hue and saturation are ignored by the receiver's circuits; only the brightness signal remains effective. When the color broadcast signals flow down a standard antenna lead-in and through standard amplifying circuits (1), the receiver separates (2) the color signal from the brightness signal. Next the color information is decoded (3) so that when it is recombined with the brightness information, a series of high-definition primary color signals is produced, ready to be applied to the color tube (4).

Right: **Televised scene as it appears on a color television receiver.**

Diagrams courtesy RCA

IN BLACK AND WHITE

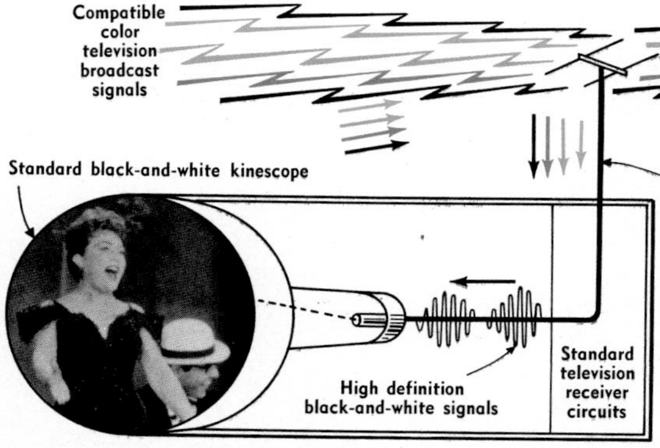

IN COLOR

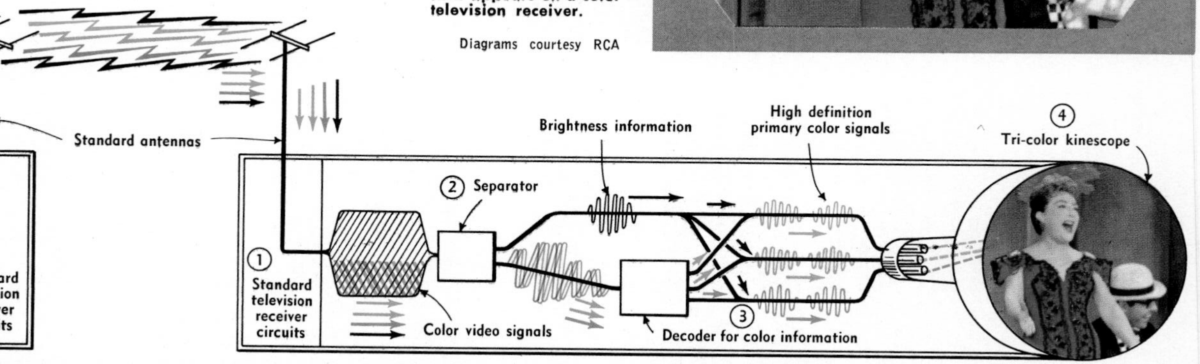

Compatible color television broadcast signals

Standard black-and-white kinescope

Standard antennas

High definition black-and-white signals

Standard television receiver circuits

① Standard television receiver circuits

Color video signals

② Separator

Brightness information

High definition primary color signals

③ Decoder for color information

④ Tri-color kinescope

terests only. In eight countries, including Japan, the Philippines, and Thailand, government and commercial interests operate separate broadcasting systems.

Japan. The first television station for regular broadcasting in Japan was put into operation by the Japanese Broadcasting Corporation (NHK) in 1953. By 1970, Japan had more than 160 stations, half of which are NHK stations and half are commercial. NHK, a quasi-governmental organization, operates a large number of stations that are strictly educational in character.

Japanese viewing patterns seem to be much like those in the West. The general audience consistently seems to prefer entertainment—sports, comedy, mystery drama, and Westerns. Some American programs, dubbed in Japanese, are carried regularly on network shows. Both the NHK and the privately owned stations use a 525-line picture, the standard in the United States, and transmit some programs in color, using the American color transmission system.

AFRICA

Only about half the African countries have any television at all. The United Arab Republic has the largest number of stations (23) and the most receivers (about 500,000). Television in Africa generally is governmentally owned and operated and is financed by license fees. In a few cases, advertising provides some revenue.

Broadcast schedules feature light entertainment, including American, British, and French programs. In some countries such as Ghana, the Ivory Coast, Nigeria, and Zambia, television has been used effectively to provide classroom instruction and to overcome illiteracy.

CENTRAL AMERICA

TV facilities are comparatively limited in the countries of Central America. Most stations are privately owned and are financed by advertising, but the government generally plays an important participatory and regulatory role.

Mexico. Television service in Mexico started in 1950. Twenty years later, Mexico had more TV receivers than any other country in Central America. It has transmitting facilities in a number of its larger cities. Telesistema Mexicano, a privately owned network of 26 stations, supplies program service to a wide area.

Mexican TV offers a variety of programs—news, sports, feature films, variety shows, and educational seminars. Some of the programs that have received high ratings are American productions such as *Bonanza* and *The Untouchables.*

Television expanded considerably in Puerto Rico and Cuba in the 1950's and 1960's. By 1970, Cuba had 575,000 TV sets, giving it a ratio of one set to nine persons. Puerto Rico had 400,000 TV sets, one set to six persons. In contrast, Mexico had a ratio of one set to 22 persons.

AUSTRALIA

Australian TV began in 1956. It uses a 625-line picture, as do some European countries. In 1970, Australia had a ratio of about one set to four persons, giving it a high rank among the nations of the world in terms of this indicator of TV's importance in the country.

The Australian Broadcasting Commission (ABC) provides a national network service financed largely by license fees. Its network has about 40 stations, including some located in the state capitals. There are 40 commercial stations supported wholly by advertising.

Australia has commercial and noncommercial broadcasting. As a result, viewers get a wide variety of programs—sports, drama (adventure, mystery, Westerns), and discussion programs. About 15% of the broadcast time is devoted to instructional programs. Commercial programs consist mainly of drama, variety shows, and music, and more than half of the offerings consist of filmed material produced in the United States.

WALTER B. EMERY
The Ohio State University

Further Reading: Dizard, Wilson, *Television: A World View* (Syracuse, N.Y., 1966); Emery, Walter B., *National and International Systems of Broadcasting: Their History, Operation and Control* (East Lansing, Mich., 1969); Paulu, Burton, *Radio and TV Broadcasting on the European Continent* (Minneapolis, Minn., 1967); World Radio–Television Handbook Company, Ltd., *World Radio TV Handbook 1971* (Hellerup, Denmark, 1971).

4. International TV Broadcasting

International TV broadcasting is the transmission of live or prerecorded television programs beyond the boundaries of a country. This is accomplished by the use of communications satellites and earth stations to relay programs over long distances. Receiving countries use their established television networks to present these programs to their peoples.

Intelsat 3 System. International TV broadcasting on a global basis was first established in mid-1969 by a global system of Intelsat 3 satellites. Early in 1970, four Intelsat 3 (third generation) satellites—two over the Atlantic, one over the Pacific, and one over the Indian Ocean—were working with earth stations in 25 countries. About 50 countries were expected to have their own earth stations by 1973.

In addition to transmitting television, telephone, telegraph, digital data, and facsimile signals simultaneously, the Intelsat 3 satellites have a multipoint communications capability that is particularly useful for distributing TV programs. For instance, a TV program produced in the United States can be broadcast for simultaneous viewing in many countries in Latin America, Europe, and Africa via an Atlantic Intelsat 3 satellite at the same time that it is broadcast to countries in the Far East and Middle East via the Pacific and Indian Ocean Intelsat 3 satellites.

There are now more TV sets in the world than telephones, and "Live via Satellite" has become a familiar household phrase around the globe. People have seen news events as they were taking place in other countries and even in outer space. Some of the major events that have been widely viewed via satellite include the Apollo lunar missions, World Series and All-Star baseball games, the Olympic Games and other sports events, and political activities and elections in the United States and France.

In July 1969, when Neil Armstrong and Edwin Aldrin made the first manned landing on the lunar surface, an estimated 600 million people in some 50 countries on six continents witnessed this event as it was happening.

Plans. Even as the Intelsat 3 satellites were being launched, construction was well advanced on the giant Intelsat 4 satellites planned for launch beginning in 1971. These satellites will be able to transmit 12 TV programs simulta-

WIDE WORLD

"LIVE" PRESS CONFERENCES from the White House were introduced by President Kennedy.

neously, or about 6,000 telephone calls simultaneously, or various combinations of programs and calls. They will have about five times the capacity of the Intelsat 3 satellites, adding a new dimension to international broadcasting.

TV broadcasting via satellite also has a vast potential for educational purposes. India, for example, is participating in an experiment in which a NASA satellite would distribute educational programs to perhaps as many as 5,000 communities throughout the country by the mid-1970's.

Historical Background. The transmission of commercial television across an ocean first became possible in April 1965, when Early Bird (Intelsat 1), the first commercial communications satellite, was placed over the Atlantic.

Three Intelsat 2 satellites were launched in 1967. One was placed over the Atlantic and two over the Pacific. These satellites extended coverage to more than two thirds of the world. Three Intelsat 3 satellites, launched in 1968–1969, established the first global system. During the latter part of the 1960's, the growth in TV transmission via satellite was dramatic. Total hours of TV carried per year grew from 78 hours in 1966 to 779 hours in 1969.

In February 1969, the Communications Satellite Corporation (Comsat) reduced its rates by 40%, thereby lowering the cost of a one-hour color TV program to 19% of the cost in 1967. See also COMMUNICATIONS SATELLITE.

JOSEPH V. CHARYK
Communications Satellite Corporation

5. Social Significance of Television

Since World War II, television has become the most popular mass communications medium in history—perhaps the first mass medium to reach all segments and groups in a society. Next to sleeping and working, Americans spend the greatest part of their time watching television, and TV viewing clearly is a pervasive social activity in some other countries as well.

The extent of television's impact on society is yet to be fully documented, and it is difficult to pinpoint its effects in any specific instance. Nevertheless, the outline of some factors seems clear. Within a little more than one generation, television has raised hopes for a higher standard of living; it has become a significant agent in the rearing of children; it has served as a major source of news and entertainment; and it has provided a medium of communications that has altered election campaigns and the role of political parties.

George Gerbner, an American scholar in mass communications, has said, "Television has profoundly affected what we call the process of socialization, the process by which members of our species become human." It is anticipated that the influence of television on social patterns probably will become stronger as succeeding generations are transmitted a culture via this medium. Nevertheless, it would be wrong to think of a viewer merely as an apathetic body sitting passively in front of his set each day. Each person selects the programs he wants to see, perceives the content of the program in his own way, and later remembers only the part that is meaningful to his life-style.

Influence on Material Expectations. Perhaps unwittingly, commercial television in the United States has been a factor in social change through its constant advertisements of products. The programs and the advertisements are aimed at the entire community and are viewed both by the white majority and by the nonwhite minority groups. As a result, slum dwellers, mostly black, are shown what they are missing—things that other Americans take for granted.

A survey in a large east coast city in 1968 revealed that 100% of the slum homes had television sets, whereas only 14% of these homes took newspapers. Day after day an unemployed Negro, Puerto Rican, or Mexican-American sits in front of his television receiver and is shown the rewards of living in an affluent society. When he contrasts this picture with conditions in his home, however, frustration sets in and his despair with rhetoric becomes more acute. One can only speculate whether television viewing was a strong factor in the widespread riots by blacks in Newark, Detroit, Cincinnati, and other cities in 1967, although the Kerner Commission on Civil Disorders said that television viewing in the ghetto areas definitely exacerbated the despair within these communities.

As television flourishes in all parts of the world, it serves as a catalyst for viewers' images of other countries. For example, in the city of Quito, Ecuador, there were no less than six television stations in 1970, and most of them relied on programs from the United States for the bulk of their transmissions. The programs sold to Ecuador generally were very popular American shows, such as *The Beverly Hillbillies,* which are dubbed in Spanish. The overwhelming material wealth of the United States becomes evident in almost all of its television entertainment fare, and it may be as resented by poor Ecuadorans as by the people in the ghettos of Detroit or Newark.

As television transmissions via satellites become more and more widely used, the men and women in small villages all over the world will gather around the community color television set and learn about the world outside their communities. They may be offered commercial television fare, or they may be offered a balance of cultural and educational television fare, perhaps under the auspices of the United Nations.

Influence on Children. From the earliest days of the medium, adults have expressed concern about television's influence on children. Parents have shown anxiety about the influence of violence on TV programs and have worried about the effects of television on the taste of their children. Various studies of children's viewing behavior indicate that the patterns of their taste are fairly well set by the time they are 10 or 11 years old. Also, there is little evidence that television has a harmful effect on the social adjustment or mental health of a child who enjoys warm and secure relationships at home or with his peers and who has no background of mental illness.

Nevertheless, various parents groups in the United States blame television as a causal agent in the malaise of their children and have formed organizations such as the National Association for Better Broadcasting. By 1970 the clamor for better programs for young viewers had achieved substantial results. There were such shows as the widely acclaimed *Sesame Street* for the preschool viewer, and each of the major networks had appointed senior personnel to be in charge of programs for children.

Violence on TV. One of the most debated aspects of television is the extent to which violence on TV influences social behavior. One researcher projected that the average American child, in growing from a 5-year old to a 14-year old, would witness the violent death of 13,000 human beings on television, but it has been difficult to draw definite conclusions from such statistics. Wilbur Schramm, an American researcher on the way children use television, has suggested one viewpoint. He said, "We are taking a needless chance with our children's welfare by permitting them to see such a parade of violence across our picture tubes. It is a chance we need not take. It is a danger to which we need not expose our children any more than we need expose them to tetanus or bacteria from unpasteurized milk."

The average American appears to be concerned about the amount of violence on TV. A national survey (1968) by Louis Harris pollsters for the National Commission on the Causes and Prevention of Violence showed that 59% of male adults and 63% of female adults felt there was too much violence on television; 32% of the population felt it likely that television makes people insenstive to actual acts of violence; and 52% felt it likely that television triggered violent acts from persons who are socially maladjusted or mentally unstable.

There has been scant scientific evidence to prove causal relationships such as one between violence on television and an increasing crime rate in the United States. However, a major study under the auspices of the National Institute of Health was undertaken in 1970 to ascertain scientifically whether the public's concern over violence on TV was justifiable.

Effects on Other Communications Media. Television viewing in the United States quickly dominated all other forms of leisure activity. As a result, there was considerable concern that radio, movies, and other communications media might face extinction. This has not occurred, although there has been a definite readjustment in magazine reading. Many mass-circulation general magazines failed when their readers essentially turned to television. In contrast, surviving successful magazines have aimed at specialized audiences for the most part.

Newspaper readership has kept pace with population growth, but there are fewer daily newspapers than when television began to be a force in American society. In the period from 1945 to 1970 nearly 700 commercial and 175 educational television stations began operation, whereas from 1940 to 1970 the number of daily newspapers decreased from 1,878 to 1,752. Book publishing has not been adversely affected by television. More and more titles have been published each year both in hard-cover and paperback editions. Moreover, book circulation in public libraries has increased dramatically since 1945.

Television has become the most credible of the mass media, although the reasons for this are not entirely clear. It also has become the major source of news. Roper Research has conducted a national survey of public attitudes toward the mass media every two years since 1959. The same key questions have been asked each time, and the results appear to have substantial validity. In its 1968 study, respondents were asked, "Which medium would you believe if you got conflicting reports?" In reply, 44% said television as opposed to only 21% for newspapers. In the 1968 study, respondents were asked, "Where do you get most of the news about what's going on in the world?" In reply, 59% said television, 49% said newspapers, 25% said radio, and 7% said magazines. (The figures add up to more than 100% because multiple answers were permitted.)

Influence in Politics. One of the most conspicuous ways that television has affected life in the United States has been in politics. Television played a part in the presidential elections in 1948, but its nationwide influence was limited because only 35,000 sets were in use and only 37 stations were on the air. Four years later, television substantially influenced voter turnout for the first Eisenhower-Stevenson election, when

CBS TELEVISION NETWORK

TELEVISION NEWS teams go to the scene of the action, in this case a national political convention.

there were more than 15 million homes with television receivers. The election year of 1960 saw television put to a spectacular political use in the debates between John F. Kennedy and Richard M. Nixon. These confrontations gave the candidates an opportunity to discuss differences on issues and party positions and to have the chance for immediate rebuttal. In addition, the viewer had an unprecedented chance to see and hear the presidential candidates. Four debates took place during September and October of 1960. Although they informed the electorate of some issues, the main results of the debates were essentially image making and image unmaking. A study by the Mass Communications Research Center at the University of Wisconsin summarized these debates: "Kennedy did not necessarily win them, but Nixon lost them."

The television industry claims that it has significantly raised the percentage of eligible voters who finally go to the polls. However, the interaction of various communications media must be considered in assessing television's effects on voter turnout. A study by William A. Glaser of Columbia University indicated that at first glance television seemed to have superior impact because more people recalled televised reminders to vote than those from other media. This study showed, however, that reminders through the mail and in the press proved to be more effective in actually getting people to vote.

There can be no doubt, however, that television gives the politician a huge audience. In 1968, for example, twice as many people saw Nixon on a single political advertisement on television as had seen him in person in 1960 when he visited all 50 states. According to Joe McGinnis, an adviser on the TV coverage, the credo of the 1968 Nixon campaign was "the response is to the image, not to the man." Insofar as this is true, future national elections in which a combination of salesmen, cameramen, and speechwriters adjust the candidate's image through skillful use and manipulation of television can be anticipated.

This phenomenon is not restricted to the United States. Candidates for public office wherever television has become a mass medium are becoming increasingly sensitive to the way they are physically perceived by their audience. For instance, a candidate for president in a South American country in 1970 shaved off his moustache when his public relations advisers conducted a survey and found that the public perceived him as too austere.

Essentially, however, television serves to reinforce a viewer's allegiance to a candidate rather than to change his voting preference. Research studies repeatedly have indicated that viewers who are interested in politics tend to watch candidates for office much more than those who are politically apathetic.

DAVID MANNING WHITE
Boston University

Further Reading: Cole, Barry, ed., *Television* (New York 1970); Green, Maury, *Television News: Anatomy and Process* (Belmont, Calif., 1970); Small, William, *To Kill a Messenger* (New York 1970); White, David M., and Averson, Richard, eds., *Sight, Sound and Society* (Boston 1968).

6. Careers in Broadcasting

A career in broadcasting may suggest a vision of glamour, of bright lights and glitter, of big money earned without drudgery in a constant flurry of excitement. It is understandable that this view has been commonly held. Show business in all its forms—from carnivals to opera—has always maintained this facade. Television has seldom showed any more of its enterprise than what was taking place under the lights or an occasional brief view of the intense and ordered concentration of the control room, but the realities of careers in TV broadcasting belie that picture.

There is drudgery and routine work in broadcasting, as there is in almost any kind of endeavor. There are low-salaried jobs, and there are many of them. The big money goes to the star performers on camera, in management, or in sales, and the road to such eminence generally is long and hilly. Nevertheless, television is rewarding in ways that transcend the hard work and the routine. For instance, there is great satisfaction in being involved in a field that puts a premium on the use of the creative imagination.

There are four main departments for careers in broadcasting: program, production, engineering, and management. Each has requirements peculiar to it, but the departments are not mutually exclusive. In fact, certain positions are expressly designed for liaison between departments, an indication that the broadcasting field is tightly knit.

Program. Here one first lists the performers who are on-camera personnel. There are announcers, interviewers, narrators, demonstrators, and models for commercials, as well as entertainers, actors, singers, dancers, comedians, and variety performers such as magicians and acrobats. With few exceptions, all on-camera personnel are members of one or both of two closely affiliated unions—the American Federation of Television and Radio Artists (AFTRA) and the

Screen Actors Guild (SAG). Almost all on-camera personnel have a background in some aspect of show business.

Television newsmen and sports announcers are a special class of program personnel. Newsmen must not only be good reporters but also good or acceptable on-camera personalities. Early television recruited them from newspapers, but it later became possible for the neophyte to gain the necessary experience in TV newsrooms. The television newsman must be skilled in the use of an audiotape recorder and a film camera, and he must know the principles of good film editing.

Sports announcers and commentators also are specialists. Just as a newsman needs a broad general background in liberal arts and the sciences to understand and report stories intelligently, so does a sports announcer need some understanding of the whole world of sports, as well as a thorough knowledge of his specialties. Increasingly, retired athletes have been used as sports broadcasters.

To present the on-camera performer, there is a chain of production personnel. Of them, producers and writers function under the program department, and directors under the production department. A writer's duties may be as simple as writing continuity or outlining an interview, or as complex as writing commercials, film scripts, or drama. In any case he must be able to write for the ear and eye under the pressure of a time schedule. A background in music and theater is helpful. Writers, producers, and directors benefit from a liberal arts education, a general knowledge of the sciences, and some first-hand knowledge of show business. Directors and producers often belong to the Directors Guild of America, and writers to the Writers Guild of America.

Production. In addition to providing directors and associate directors, the production department assigns floor managers, set designers, graphics artists, studios, and their supporting scenery shops. In production, especially, there are positions for women. The way from secretary to script girl or production assistant is not long, although there still are not many women in important positions in the industry.

The television studio, it seems fair to say, is purely the province of the stagehands, property men, and electricians, especially at those stations where they are members of the powerful International Alliance of Theatrical Stage Employees and Motion Picture Machine Operators, commonly written IATSE and pronounced "Yatsee." Makeup artists and wardrobe handlers are also members of IATSE.

Engineering. The chain of engineering services begins in the studio, with the cameramen and the microphone boom operator; moves on into the control room, with its technical director, video man, and audio man; continues on into the master control room, with one or two engineers on duty during all of the broadcasting day; and ends at the transmitter location, where an engineer may or may not always be on duty, depending on the station's degree of automation.

FCC regulations generally require that engineers have a first-class radiotelephone operator's license, and the demands of the job often call for a thorough grounding in electrical engineering and physics. Engineers usually belong to the International Brotherhood of Electrical Workers (IBEW), the National Association of Broadcast Engineers and Technicians (NABET), or the engineering section of IATSE.

Management. The management personnel handle the daily business of the station. They include the general manager, program manager, production manager, sales manager (or director) and his time salesmen, traffic manager, promotion and publicity director, and the unit manager. Many of these personnel come to their positions after having had more active roles in the programming process.

In the world of television, the walls between departments are often breached. Thus a set designer may become a producer, an actor may become a director, a producer may become a program manager, and so on. At a small station, each person must handle a variety of tasks—the director may do his own camera switching, the announcer may sell time, the technical director may handle the audio or video controls, and all may take part in promotion. The small station offers the newcomer more opportunity to test his talents in several directions and to find his proper place in the enterprise than does a large station.

Career Opportunities. The growth rate of commercial television has slowed, and so employment opportunities more frequently are limited to replacements. Public television seems to be in greater need of personnel in virtually all positions. It also has been willing to give women more important and challenging work. Once cable TV begins to originate its own programs, it too will offer new opportunities. Because television is the major advertising medium in the United States, the advertising agencies employ TV production personnel, as do companies producing programs for television syndication.

College degrees in broadcasting are seldom a requirement for employment in television, but they often are a decided advantage.

JOHN M. GUNN
State University of New York at Albany

7. Special Applications of Television

Television has a wide range of special-purpose applications in industry, business and commerce, medicine, and government. In each of these, a nonbroadcast system called a closed-circuit television (CCTV) system is used, and CCTV has been firmly established as a versatile technique in modern communications.

A TV broadcast over the airwaves requires costly and complex studios and transmitters to send program signals to millions of home TV sets. A cable TV system generally picks up and relays these program signals to home TV sets via cable. In contrast, a CCTV system has only small cameras linked by cables to TV sets, or monitors. The pictures are presented to meet special needs and are viewed by a relatively small number of persons.

CCTV essentially is private television tailored to meet specific purposes. For instance, airports use TV cameras and monitors to display information on arrivals, departures, and flight and gate numbers, and thereby reduce the number of inquiry desks and personnel. Also, congested major cities use CCTV cameras and monitors to assist police and transport authorities in diverting and controlling motor vehicle traffic flow.

Equipment. After some early attempts to use broadcast equipment for special applications of TV, it was quickly realized that the costs were

WIDE WORLD

IN A LABORATORY, a television camera looks into a microscope, then feeds information to a computer.

far too high and the equipment far too complex for unskilled users to operate. Therefore, special equipment was developed to provide cheapness, small size, flexibility, and ease of operation and maintenance.

The basic component of almost all nonbroadcast systems is a TV camera that weighs about 8 pounds (3.6 kg) and is small enough to be held in the hand. Such a camera usually has a 16-mm cine lens and generates good-quality picture signals that are sent via coaxial cable to one or more picture monitors. Sometimes the monitors are simplified home TV receivers, but there is a wide range of monitors with picture screen sizes ranging from 5 to 25 inches (12.7 to 63.5 cm). In the simplest application inside a building, one fixed camera views the scene to be transmitted and the picture is displayed at some remote point on a monitor.

The TV camera and monitor vary in design and performance to suit the application. For recording, especially for industrial and commercial training applications, low-cost, portable videotape recorders are used. Pictures and sound are then immediately available for playback.

In all special applications where protective housings or special attachments are used, complete control of the TV camera is possible from a location that may be several miles distant from the camera. In these cases the camera is commanded to move up or down and left or right, as required to point at the scene, by means of electrical signals sent by wire to reversible motors at the camera location. Electrical signals also are sent to the camera to regulate the aperture of the lens or control focus or zoom.

Industry—Security *Applications*. Factories and plants often need to provide surveillance over parking lots, openings in gates and fences, strongrooms, warehouses, and areas where classified data are handled. In such cases TV cameras for indoor and outdoor use and appropriate lighting are installed to send continuous pictures to locations where security personnel view monitors.

***Production*.** Plants that have manufacturing and assembly lines or many stages for processing raw materials often have employed personnel solely for watching over these operations. Such tasks can be accomplished much more effectively by using a CCTV system that displays pictures so that instant corrective or shutdown action can be taken. Applications include surveillance of operations in mines and factories, steel mills, oil refineries, gas and chemical plants, nuclear-electric and other power stations, and food-processing plants. CCTV also has been used increasingly to speed up industrial training.

Business and Commerce. In business and commerce, CCTV systems principally are used for security in supermarkets, shops, stores, banks, casinos, and offices; for advertising and sales promotion; for data transmission, sometimes in conjunction with computers; and for training personnel. Sales promotion can be effected by using films or slides viewed by TV cameras and displaying the pictures on several monitors.

Data transmission by CCTV is used by stock exchanges, banks, insurance companies, sporting establishments, and similar business organizations. The camera views stock prices, statements, record cards, Telex messages, and any other data that need to be viewed at one or more remote locations.

Medicine. TV cameras and monitors are used in hospitals to show trainees how medical operations are performed. They also are used to watch over individual patients or wards or to view X-ray plates and patients' records from a central location. For pathology laboratories, forensic medicine, and for research or training, the camera may be coupled to a microscope so that pictures are seen on large screen monitors for group viewing. Color cameras, color monitors, and video recorders are used where needed.

Government. Governments make use of CCTV systems for surveillance in defense establishments to prevent unauthorized access and for speeding up the training of military and other personnel. In national and local government establishments, CCTV is used for data transmission to avoid undue movement of classified information or a waste of personnel time in moving around large office complexes. Cameras coupled to telephone systems provide for personal identification when requests are made in security areas. In prisons, large-scale use is made of CCTV to aid security and discipline and to prevent breakouts.

F. J. LUBBOCK
Pye TVT Limited, Cambridge, England

8. Principles of Television

To ordinary persons, the notion that anything significant can happen in one millionth of a second seems unfamiliar. Yet each element of the TV pictures that he watches is created in ⅛ of one millionth of a second. This ability to control rapid events accounts for much of the fascination and triumph of electrical engineering.

BLACK-AND-WHITE TELEVISION

Transmission and Reception. The signal of a live television broadcast originates in a television camera. In this circumstance, the scene being televised is optically focused on the photo-

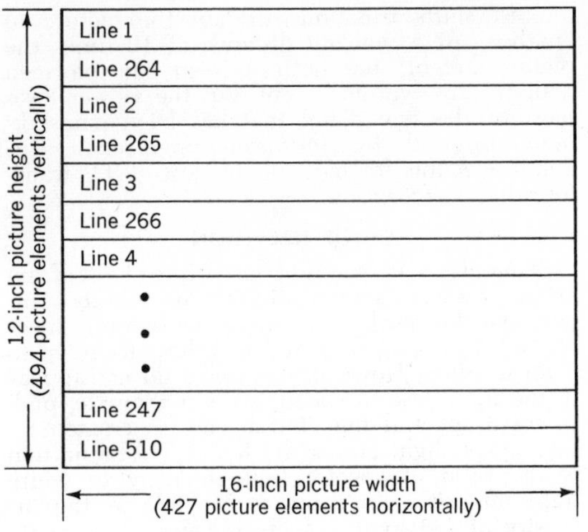

Fig. 1. INTERLACED line scanning method forms a complete picture on 20-inch TV screen in 1/30 second.

cathode of a camera tube. Each element of the photocathode generates an electrical current in accordance with the luminance that it receives. The resulting charges are sequentially sampled by an electron beam to create the picture (video) signal. This signal is enormously amplified and is eventually transmitted as the modulation of a radio-frequency (r-f) carrier. The accompanying sound (audio) is transmitted on a separate radio-frequency carrier that is 4.5 MHz (megahertz) above the frequency of the picture carrier. (Numerical values given in this section are valid only for television in the United States.) In the receiver, the picture and the sound signals initially are amplified together. Later they are individually processed. The audio signal is fed to a loudspeaker, and the video signal goes to a picture tube.

Scanning Technique. A TV picture is in effect broken up into dots. It is similar to a newspaper photograph, which is reproduced as a mosaic of black dots of varying diameters. Each TV picture is made up of about 211,000 elements, although far less than this number may be visible if the receiver is improperly adjusted.

The size of a TV picture is designated by the diagonal length of the picture. For example, a

Fig. 2. SAWTOOTH wave used for vertical scanning is shown. Wave used for horizontal scanning is similar in shape, but it rises and falls in only 1/15,750 second. A voltage sawtooth is used if the scanning beam is electrostatically deflected, and a current sawtooth is used if the beam is magnetically deflected.

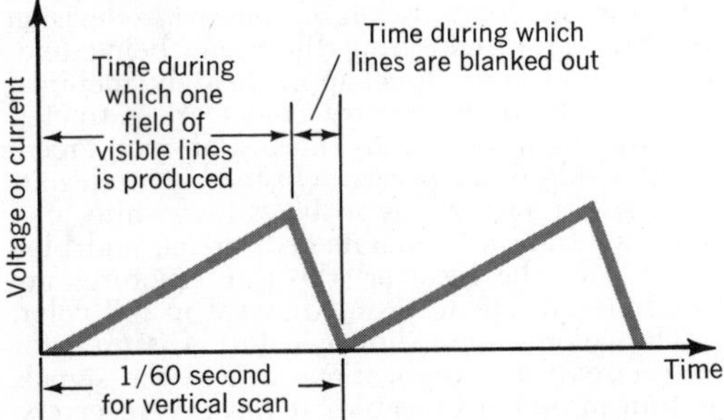

20-inch picture is depicted in Fig. 1. As transmitted, this picture should have a height of 12 inches and a width of 16 inches. A single picture element is 0.038 inch wide by 0.024 inch high. Thus, there are approximately 494 elements (lines) vertically and 427 elements horizontally. The product of 427 and 494 yields approximately 211,000 visible elements. (The effective vertical resolution will be less than 494 elements if the camera beam has appreciable diameter because it can then straddle two adjacent objects.)

The elements of the picture are transmitted one at a time. In the camera tube at the transmitter, an electron beam sequentially scans the elements representing the scene to be televised by moving rapidly from left to right and more slowly downwards, much as our eyes do in reading a page of text. In the picture tube at the receiver, another electron beam recreates the elements in synchronism with those at the transmitter. Necessarily, the elements displayed by the receiver are delayed by the brief time taken for the video signal to travel through the equipment and through the air.

The line scanning process also is indicated in Fig. 1. In order to reduce picture flicker that is objectionable to the human eye, an interlaced line-scanning method is used. In this method, the first field of alternate lines is formed by the line sequence 1, 2, 3, 4, and so on—as shown in Fig. 1. The last visible line in the first *field* is number 247. Lines numbered 248 through 263 normally are not visible because the time period for them is used to return the electron beam to the top of the screen for the next sequence of lines.

The second *field* starts with lines 264, 265, 266, and so on, which are interlaced between lines 1, 2, 3, and so on, as shown in Fig. 1. The last visible line in the second field is number 510. Lines numbered 511 through 525 are blanked out for the return of the electron beam to the top of the screen. If the receiver brightness control is excessively advanced, however, lines 248 to 263 and lines 511 to 525 will become visible. Thus, there is a total of 525 lines, of which 494 are visible. A complete scan consisting of 525 lines is called a single *frame*.

The voltage or current wave form that is used to deflect the electron beam vertically has the *sawtooth* shape shown in Fig. 2. The beam produces 60 fields per second. Two fields equal one frame, so there are 30 frames per second. (In commercial motion picture practice, there are 48 fields per second and 24 frames per second. In televising movies, the discrepancy between movie and television standards is overcome by means of specially designed TV studio equipment.)

The horizontal scanning motion also is supplied by a sawtooth similar to that shown in Fig. 2. The horizontal scan rate is 15,750 lines per second, and thus 63.5 microseconds are allocated to a line. However, the 427 visible horizontal elements in a line only require 53.3 microseconds (427 times ⅛ microsecond). During the remaining 10.2 microseconds, the beam is blanked out as it rapidly retraces from right to left. It then is in a position to begin the next line scan.

The left-to-right motion of the electron beam across a 20-inch tube face is accomplished at a speed of almost 5 miles per second, and the beam returns from the right to the left at a speed of 25 miles per second. These high speeds are required in order to display 30 complete pictures per second.

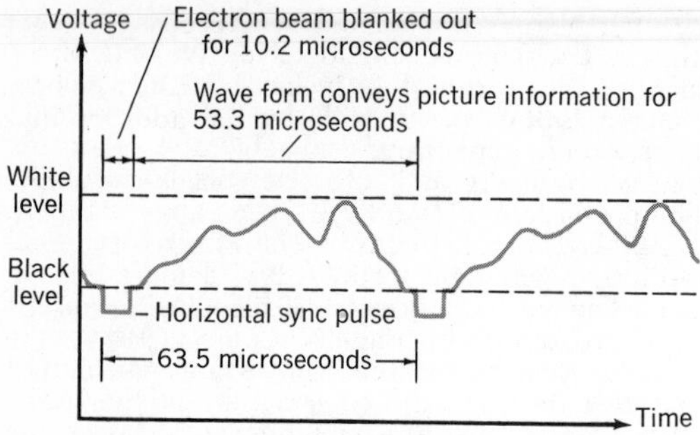

Fig. 3. VIDEO signal for one line of horizontal scan is shown. A sync pulse blanks out beam each time it retraces from right to left to begin next line scan.

Synchronization. Synchronization between the electron-beam motion in the camera tube and the electron-beam motion in the picture tube is maintained with the aid of *sync pulses.* Vertical sync pulses are inserted while the beam is returning from the bottom of the picture to the top, and horizontal sync pulses are inserted while it is returning from right to left. The video signal, including horizontal sync pulses, is shown in Fig. 3. Because the sync pulses extend below the black level, they are not normally visible.

When the receiver fails to synchronize horizontally, the picture becomes torn with diagonal lines. When it fails to sync vertically, the picture rolls in a vertical direction.

Role of the TV Viewer. The TV viewer experiences an optical illusion. A single spot of light (0.024 inch in diameter for a 20-inch tube) moves over the entire screen so rapidly that a visual impression of a single, unified whole is created. Because 60 fields per second are produced, the light from each region of the screen is replenished 60 times per second. This is somewhat above the 48-cycle-per-second rate at which, at a reasonable luminance level, the eye begins to perceive flicker. Interlaced scanning is a trick to prevent flicker despite the fact that only 30 complete TV pictures are generated per second. The same trick is especially important in home movies. They use only 16 frames per second, but the shutter opens 3 times during each frame to create the flickerless illusion of 48 pictures per second.

What is the correct viewing distance from a TV screen? When a person with normal vision looks at a mosaic display such as a newspaper halftone, the individual dots vanish at a viewing distance equal to 1,500 times the spacing between adjacent dot centers. As the viewing distance is increased beyond this length, picture information is lost. On a 20-inch picture tube, the average spacing between adjacent element centers is 0.03 inch. By applying the "1,500 rule," we get a viewing distance of approximately 4 feet, which is four times the 12-inch picture height. As a general rule, then, the TV viewing distance should be four times the picture height, but it may not be the most comfortable distance.

The central portion of each eye—the region that is involved with the analysis of visual patterns—contains only 30,000 cones. Consequently, at a viewing distance of four times the picture height, we can concentrate on only 15% of the 211,000-element picture at any given time. Considerable eye motion is entailed as the center of interest shifts from one side of the picture to another. At a viewing distance of 10 times the picture height, the entire screen can be seen without any eye movement, but the viewer loses most of the fine detail that has been painstakingly inserted by television engineers. This detail accounts for most of the cost of TV transmission and reception.

COLOR TELEVISION

Principles. If sunlight or white light from an incandescent source is broken up into its components, the result is a continuous band of spectral hues ranging from red to yellow to green to cyan to blue. However, all colors do not appear in the incandescent spectrum. For example, pink is not a spectral hue, but it can be created by mixing red light and white light. The saturation is the ratio of spectral hue intensity to white light intensity. In the case of pink, as the intensity of red light is increased, we go from 0% saturation ("pure" white) to 50% saturation (equal red and white) to 100% saturation ("pure" red). Another color that is not a spectral hue is magenta, which can be created by mixing red light and blue light.

Color television, as well as many of the other human uses of color, depends on an optical illusion. Almost any naturally occurring color can be reproduced by the proper mixture of only red, green, and blue light. These colors are therefore called *primary* colors. Some of the colors visually created by mixing various amounts of the primary hues are shown in the table. For example, white results from a mixture of equal amounts of all three primary colors. Pink is equivalent to 50% red plus 50% white, but since 50% white is equivalent to 16% red + 17% green + 17% blue, we get total percentages of 66% red, 17% green, and 17% blue.

SOME OF THE COLORS CREATED BY MIXING PRIMARY HUES

Red (percent)	Green (percent)	Blue (percent)	Resulting Color
50	50	0	Yellow
0	50	50	Cyan
50	0	50	Magenta
33	34	33	White
66	17	17	Pink
17	66	17	Pale green
17	17	66	Pale blue

In color TV the faithful reproduction of color also requires proper *luminance,* or brightness values. In scientific work, luminance is the actual value of light intensity, whereas brightness refers to the subjective sensation of intensity. As equal red, green, and blue intensities are decreased, for example, we go from white to gray to black (the absence of light).

Transmission and Reception. The foregoing color principles are the basis of a simple technique for the transmission of color via television (see Fig. 4). Light from the scene being televised is split into three approximately identical beams. The three primary colors are extracted from the light beams by means of red, green, and blue filters, as shown. Instead of transmitting a single picture, as in black-and-white television, we transmit separate red, green, and blue pictures. In the receiver, the three pictures are recombined to create a single image in full color.

The color system shown in Fig. 4 is used for closed-circuit TV applications, where the signals are transmitted over cables to nearby receivers.

However, this system is not used for broadcasting over the airwaves because it is too wasteful of precious channel space. If it were used, we would have to restrict color broadcasts to the UHF region (channels 14 through 69), where it is possible to assign two channels for the three pictures and sound needed for a single color program.

In the color system for broadcasting, approved by the FCC in 1953, three color signals are simultaneously sent over the same channel that is used for a black-and-white broadcast. Each television station can broadcast either black-and-white or color pictures. Furthermore, a black-and-white receiver can pick up a color broadcast (the colors are seen as various shades of gray), and a color receiver can pick up a black-and-white broadcast. The success in squeezing three color signals into a single channel formerly occupied by a single black-and-white signal was a major triumph of electrical engineering. It was the work of many ingenious persons who took advantage of every possible trick.

The video signals for a color TV broadcast start out as shown in Fig. 4, but they are not transmitted as red (R), green (G), and blue (B) signals. The basic solution to the problem of squeezing three color signals (R, G, and B) into a channel formerly occupied by a single white (W) signal is to derive three new signals, designated W, I, and Q, from the R, G, and B signals. This is done because the W, I, and Q signals are better able to meet the requirements of the compatible black-and-white and color broadcasting system.

It is possible to transform simply and reliably from one set of signals to another at the transmitter and then transform back to the original set at the receiver for final viewing. The transformations at the transmitter are described by three equations: $W = 0.30R + 0.59G + 0.11B$; $I = 0.60R - 0.28G - 0.32B$; and $Q = 0.21R - 0.52G + 0.31B$. Solving these three simultaneous equations for the relationships needed to recover the R, G, and B signals at the receiver, we get $R = W + 0.95I + 0.62Q$; $G = W - 0.28I - 0.64Q$; and $B = W - 1.11I + 1.73Q$. These transformation equations entail the addition and subtraction of electrical signals.

The White (W) Signal. A black-and-white (monochrome) receiver tuned to a color broadcast should show a reasonably good black-and-white picture. One could use the G camera output for this purpose, but a red dress or a blue sky would then appear to be black. Instead, the W signal is used for monochrome reception. The W signal is always positive, thus satisfying the requirement that every color on a televised scene should result in some shade of gray on a monochrome receiver.

In accordance with the equation for the W signal, a red dress is seen as gray with a luminosity of 30%, a green landscape is seen with a relative "whiteness" or luminosity of 59%, and a blue sky appears as dark gray with a luminosity of 11%. A white sheet of paper, which excites the R, G, and B cameras equally, is seen with a luminosity of 100%.

The 30–59–11 percentages agree with the relative sensitivity of the eye as the hue of the object is varied. That is, a green sheet of paper appears to be 59% as bright as a white sheet of paper under similar circumstances, and so forth. The W signal yields the most natural rendition of color broadcasts as viewed on a black-and-white receiver.

In a black-and-white TV broadcast, the W signal is transmitted, and the I and Q signals are absent. When the I and the Q signals are zero, the transformation equations show that a color receiver tuned in to this program will get $R = W$, $G = W$, and $B = W$. Because R, G, and B are equally excited, only various shades of gray are produced if the set is properly adjusted. In fact, this is one of the main criteria that the serviceman must satisfy in fixing a color receiver.

In-Phase (I) and Quadrature (Q) Signals. To maximize information content, the I signal and

Fig. 4. COLOR TV CAMERA includes lens, mirrors, filters, and camera tubes. Dichroic mirrors split light from scene being televised into red, green, and blue beams. Each beam is directed through a filter onto a camera tube. Each camera tube converts a primary color image of the scene into an electrical signal.

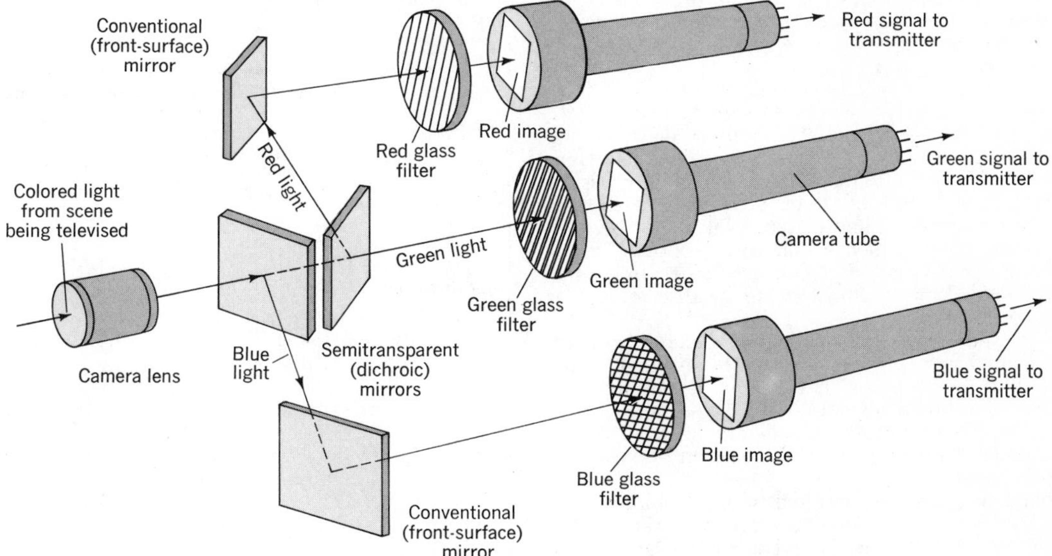

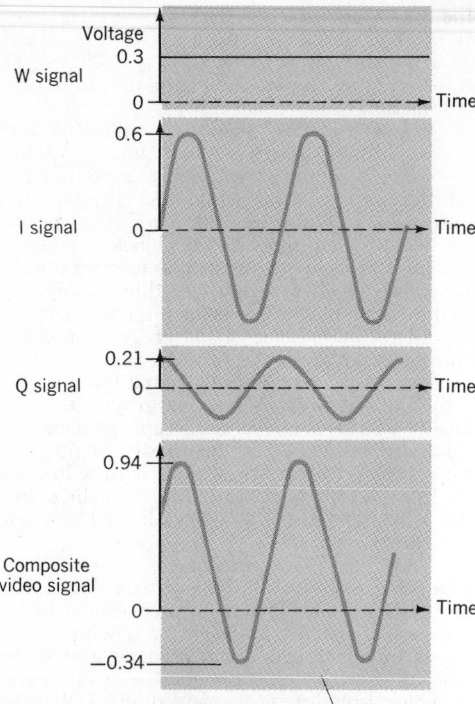

Fig. 5. COMPOSITE VIDEO signal, shown here for a red hue, is the algebraic summation of the W signal and the I and Q signals. The I and Q signals are shown after they have modulated the color subcarrier.

the Q signal (called the in-phase signal and the quadrature signal, respectively) should differ as much as possible from the W signal and from each other. Also, the transformation equations show that a white object, which equally excites each camera with a relative value of 1, results in zero I and Q outputs, and the same result holds true for any shade of gray. This is one of the main advantages of using the I and Q signals rather than the original R, G, and B signals. The I and the Q signals produce interference dots in the black-and-white reception of a color broadcast. However, where the scene being televised contains white or gray, there are no interference dots because the I and Q signals are zero.

The Composite Video Signal. Thus far we have generated the W, I, and Q signals from the R, G, and B signals, but the problem of squeezing three signals into a single channel remains. Here the solution is to use the I and Q signals to modulate the amplitude of a 3.579545-MHz sine-wave subcarrier. It is called a subcarrier because the composite video signal will eventually modulate the r-f carrier. The subcarrier frequency is rounded off to 3.6 MHz in the discussion that follows.

A positive I signal is sent as a sine wave with an amplitude proportional to the I-signal value, and a negative I signal is sent as an inverted sine wave with an amplitude proportional to its value. Similarly, Q signals are sent as cosine waves. This is why Q signals are known as quadrature (90° out-of-phase) components, whereas I signals are called in-phase components. The phase is measured relative to a short burst (8 cycles) of the 3.6-MHz subcarrier that is sent after each horizontal sync pulse. The burst is not visible in the receiver picture because it occurs while the cathode-ray tube (picture tube) beam is blanked out on its rapid return from right to left.

The composite video signal is the algebraic summation of the W signal and the I and Q signals. This composite signal is shown in Fig. 5 for a red spectral hue, for which W = 0.3, I = 0.6, and Q = 0.21. The result of combining the I and Q signals is a modulated 3.6-MHz wave that has a peak amplitude of $\sqrt{0.6^2 + 0.21^2}$ or 0.64. When this wave is added to the W = 0.3 signal, a composite video signal that swings from a minimum of − 0.34 to a maximum of 0.94 is obtained.

In the color TV receiver, the received burst is used to generate a 3.6-MHz sine wave and a cosine wave. The sine wave extracts the I signal from the composite video signal and ignores the Q signal. Similarly, the cosine wave extracts the Q signal and ignores the I signal.

The wave shape of a typical horizontal line of a color broadcast is shown in Fig. 6. This wave shape is taken from a scene that includes red, green, blue, white, and black areas.

The Color Subcarrier. The 3.6-MHz color subcarrier is not visible on a color receiver because a filter is used to limit the upper band to 3.5 MHz. This results in somewhat lower resolution than that of a black-and-white receiver, where a 4-MHz band is used.

The 3.6-MHz color subcarrier is visible on a monochrome receiver because colored areas of the original scene produce fine black-and-white interference dashes. (These dashes are commonly called dots.) The actual frequency of the 3.6-MHz subcarrier—3.579545 MHz—is chosen so as to minimize this dot interference. The technique here is to produce a black dot at a particular point on the TV screen, and then produce a white dot when the beam returns to the same point one frame period later on. Because of the persistence of vision, our eyes tend to see a steady, average tone when black and white dots are rapidly alternated.

Resolution. Suppose that a scene being televised consists of an array of differently colored poles gradually carried closer to the TV camera. If the colored poles are held horizontally as they

Fig. 6. WAVE SHAPE shown is a composite video signal for a typical horizontal line of a color broadcast.

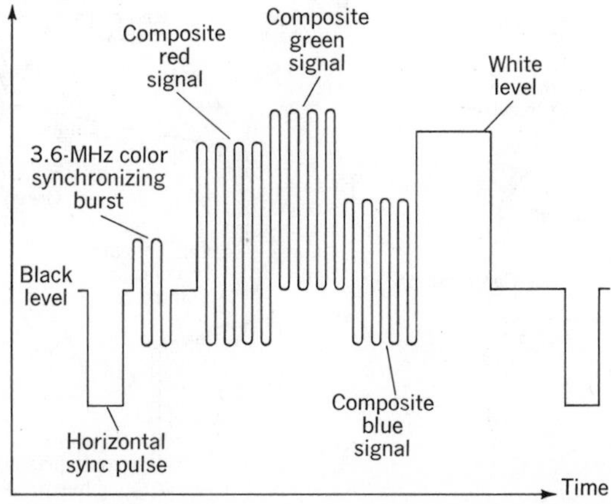

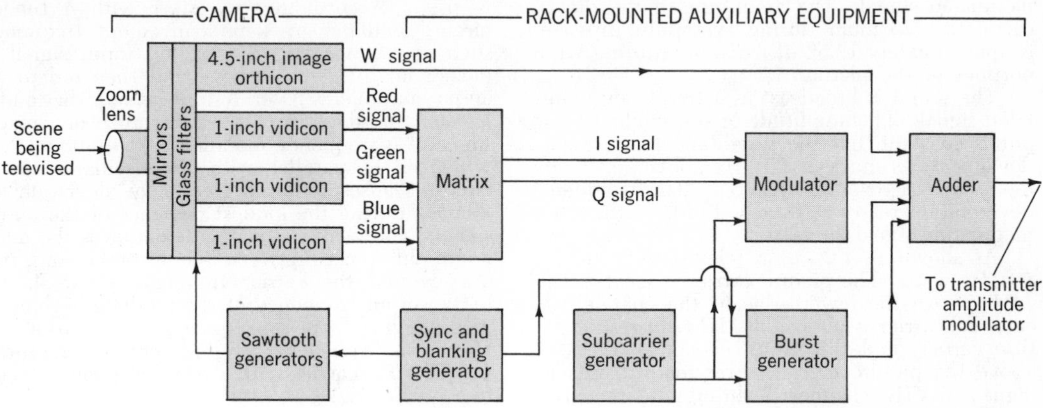

Fig. 7. Color TV camera and auxiliary equipment for broadcasting is represented by simplified block diagram.

are brought closer to the TV cameras, they will become visible in full color on the receiver when each pole subtends a height of 0.024 inch. (Numerical values here are for a 20-inch tube.) If they are held vertically, however, they will first be seen as various shades of gray when they subtend a width of 0.043 inch. As the poles are moved closer to the cameras, orange and cyan poles will be seen in true color when they subtend a width of 0.1 inch, but red, yellow, and magenta poles will appear to be orange, and green and blue poles will appear to be cyan. Finally, when the poles are near enough to subtend a width of 0.3 inch, all of the poles will appear in true color. It will come as a surprise to most color TV viewers to learn that, in general, objects have to be at least 0.3 inch wide on a 20-inch tube before they are seen in correct color rendition.

Role of the TV Viewer. For black-and-white TV, we have mentioned that the viewer experiences an optical illusion. This is even more so for color TV, where the viewer's eye and mind must re-create almost all naturally occurring colors given only red, green, and blue hues.

The color picture tube screen usually consists of small red, green, and blue phosphor dots. If the image is white, one can actually see the individual colored dots from a close viewing distance. As the viewing distance is increased to the normal value of four times the picture height, the individual dots merge to produce the illusion of a homogeneous white surface.

SID DEUTSCH
Polytechnic Institute of Brooklyn

Further Reading: Buchsbaum, Walter H., *Fundamentals of Television* (New York 1964); Fink, Donald G., and Lutyens, David G., *The Physics of Television* (New York 1960).

9. Television Transmitters

Live TV broadcasts typically are in color, so it is assumed in this section that the camera and associated transmitter equipment are designed for color work. It is not necessary to consider monochrome equipment by itself because a typical color camera supplies a black-and-white or luminance (W signal) output equivalent to that of a monochrome camera. The numerical values given here are valid only for television in the United States.

TV CAMERA

A simplified block diagram of a representative color television camera and its auxiliary equipment, RCA type TK-42, is shown in Fig. 7. The unit has a high-quality, 4.5-inch-diameter image orthicon camera tube that generates the black-and-white (W) signal. Because the resolution requirements for the chrominance (I and Q color) signals are considerably less than that for the W signal, the camera uses three relatively simple and inexpensive 1-inch-diameter vidicon camera tubes to generate the color signals. The unit also includes an 8-inch color picture tube monitor that the cameraman uses as a viewfinder.

As shown in Fig. 4, the light from the scene being televised is split into three approximately identical beams by a group of dichroic (semitransparent) and conventional (front-surface) mirrors. The three primary colors are then extracted by the red (R), green (G), and blue (B) filters.

The camera operates in conjunction with rack-mounted auxiliary equipment, which is connected to the camera by a multiconductor cable. As indicated in Fig. 9, synchronizing and blanking signals are generated in the auxiliary equipment. These signals are fed back to the camera section, which includes sweep generators that produce sawtooth wave forms (see Fig. 2) for controlling the deflection of the camera tube beams.

The remaining components indicated by blocks in Fig. 7 are used for the production of the composite color video signal. We start with the R, G, and B signals from the camera and then transform them into I and Q signals in accordance with the equations $I = 0.60R - 0.28G - 0.32B$, and $Q = 0.21R - 0.52G + 0.31B$. These transformations are accomplished in the matrix unit. Next, the I and Q signals modulate the 3.579545-MHz subcarrier. Finally, the composite video signal shown in Fig. 6 is produced by adding together the W signal, the I and Q signals, the horizontal and vertical synchronizing pulses, and the subcarrier burst.

TV TRANSMITTER

Transmitter Exciter. The picture carrier and the sound carrier are generated by a radio-frequency transmitter in a section of it called the transmitter exciter.

The picture is broadcast as an amplitude-modulated signal. The amplitude of the picture carrier is maximum during sync-pulse tips and is approximately 12.5% of maximum during white portions of the picture.

The sound is broadcast as a frequency modulated signal. The amplitude of the sound r-f output is constant, but the instantaneous frequency deviates by as much as 25 kHz above and below the sound carrier frequency. The frequency deviation decreases as the amplitude of the audio modulating signal decreases.

As shown in Fig. 8, a television channel is 6 MHz wide. The picture carrier is located 1.25 MHz above the lower edge of the channel, the color subcarrier is about 3.6 MHz above the picture carrier, and the sound carrier is 4.5 MHz above the picture carrier. Frequency bands assigned to VHF channels 2 through 13 are given in the accompanying table. Channels 14 through 69 are in the UHF range. Each of the 56 UHF channels occupies a 6-MHz band of frequencies, starting at 470 and ending at 806 MHz.

VHF TV CHANNELS

Channel number	Allocated frequency band (megahertz)	Channel number	Allocated frequency band (megahertz)
2	54 to 60	8	180 to 186
3	60 to 66	9	186 to 192
4	66 to 72	10	192 to 198
5	76 to 82	11	198 to 204
6	82 to 88	12	204 to 210
7	174 to 180	13	210 to 216

As a typical example, consider the RCA type TT-25EH transmitter adjusted for broadcasting on channel 7. The picture carrier frequency is 175.25 MHz, and the sound carrier frequency is 179.75 MHz. The picture carrier frequency must be accurate to within 0.0005%, so a crystal oscillator must be used. Because the crystal vibrates mechanically, it is necessary to start at a relatively low frequency, such as 4.868 MHz. This frequency is then multiplied by 36 to yield the desired 175.25-MHz carrier frequency.

A crystal oscillator cannot be used for the FM sound because it is necessary to vary the oscillator frequency when frequency modulation is used. Accordingly, we start with a tuned-circuit oscillator at some convenient frequency such as 4.993 MHz. The sound input signal is picked up by a microphone and then fed to an audio amplifier. After amplification, the audio signal is used to vary the inductance or capacitance of a frequency modulator. The modulator, which is in parallel with the oscillator tuned circuit, causes a peak frequency deviation of 694 Hz during the loudest passages of the audio signal. The peak frequency deviation is the maximum difference between the instantaneous frequency and the carrier frequency. The 4.993-MHz output frequency of the oscillator, which is modulated by a peak frequency deviation of 694 Hz, is multiplied by 36 to yield the required 179.75-MHz carrier with a peak frequency deviation of 25 kHz.

The instantaneous frequency, which represents the sound information, is almost always increasing or decreasing with respect to 179.75 MHz, but its average value must be accurately maintained at 4.5 MHz above the picture carrier within ± 0.001%. This is accomplished by generating a correcting voltage to restore the tuned-oscillator frequency to its correct average value of 4.993 MHz whenever it starts to change from this average frequency.

Transmitter Power Amplifier Section. The transmitter exciter supplies relatively low-power picture carrier and FM sound signals to the transmitter power amplifier section, as shown in Fig. 9. The picture carrier and the composite video signal from the TV camera and auxiliary equipment are fed to an amplitude modulator, where the composite video signal is used to modulate the amplitude of the picture carrier. In the next stage, the modulated signal is amplified by high-power amplifiers. The frequency spectrum of the signal out of the power amplifier stage consists of the picture carrier plus sidebands extending about 4 MHz above and below the picture carrier. The vestigial sideband filter removes the lower sideband portion that extends more than 1.25 MHz below the picture carrier,

Fig. 8. A TELEVISION CHANNEL occupies a band of frequencies that is 6 megahertz (MHz) wide. For example, the allocated frequency band for channel 7 is 174 to 180 MHz. For broadcasting on this channel, the picture carrier is at 175.25 MHz, the color subcarrier is about 3.6 MHz above the picture carrier, and the sound carrier is 4.5 MHz above the picture carrier. Each of the other television channels makes use of a 6-MHz band of frequencies in a similar way to that shown for channel 7.

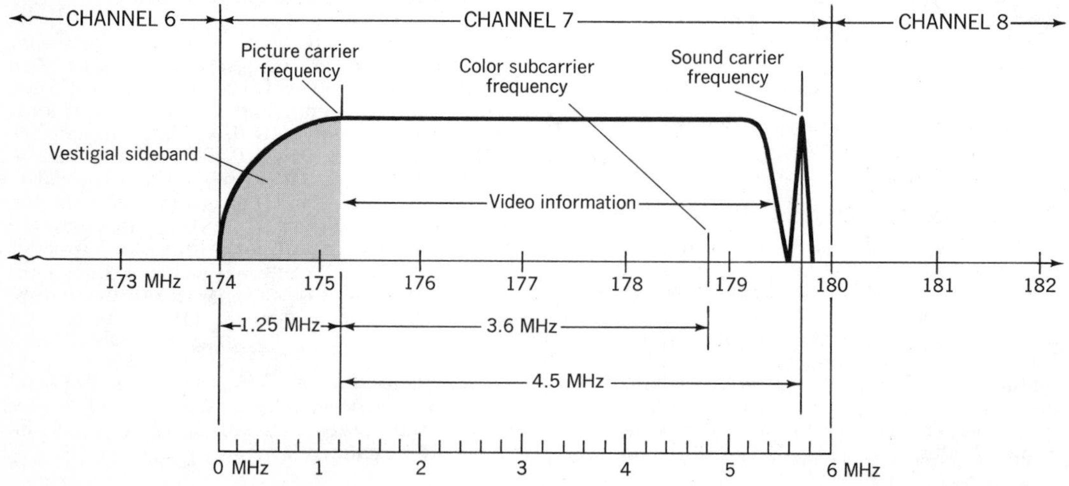

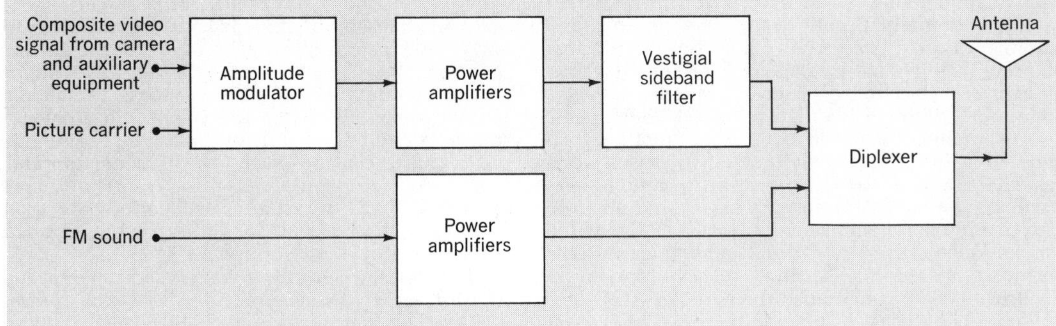

Fig. 9. TV TRANSMITTER power amplifier section, represented by block diagram, processes video and sound signals so that they are ready for broadcasting. Incoming composite video signal was obtained as shown in Fig. 7.

leaving the vestigial lower sideband shown shaded in Fig. 8. The upper sideband, shown as the area extending above the picture carrier frequency in Fig. 8, carries the color information as well as the black-and-white information.

Meanwhile, the FM sound signal is amplified in separate high-power stages, as indicated in Fig. 9. At this point, the picture and sound r-f signals are ready for broadcasting. It is frequently advantageous to use a single antenna for both signals. In that event, they must be combined in a diplexer, as indicated in Fig. 9. The diplexer consists of transmission line sections that are arranged so that the picture and sound counterparts of the TV signal can be fed to the same antenna without "crosstalk"—that is, without either counterpart feeding back and disturbing the other counterpart of the signal.

SID DEUTSCH
Polytechnic Institute of Brooklyn

Further Reading: Hansen, Gerald L., *Introduction to Solid-State Television Systems* (New York 1969); Wentworth, John W., *Color Television Engineering* (New York 1955).

10. Television Receivers

Color TV has become increasingly popular, but there still are a substantial number of monochrome (black-and-white) receivers because they are relatively inexpensive to purchase and maintain. Accordingly, both monochrome and color TV receivers will be described in this section. The numerical values given here are valid only for television in the United States.

BLACK-AND-WHITE RECEIVERS

For discussion of a black-and-white receiver, we consider the Zenith 22AB55, which is a typical fully transistorized model except for the picture tube.

Tuners—*VHF Tuner*. The VHF tuner has a different set of coils for each channel in the range 2 through 13. When the station selector switch is set at channel 7, for instance, one set of coils is switched in to tune the receiver to this channel.

The tuner includes a VHF r-f transistor amplifier, which amplifies the signal picked up by the antenna. The amplified r-f signal is mixed with a local oscillator frequency to shift the signal to an intermediate frequency that is more convenient for further signal processing. If the tuner is set on channel 7, for example, the local oscillator frequency is 221 MHz. This beats with the 175.25-MHz r-f picture carrier to produce a difference frequency of 45.75 MHz, which is the intermediate-frequency (i-f) picture carrier. Similarly, the local oscillator frequency beats with the 179.75-MHz r-f sound carrier to produce a difference frequency of 41.25 MHz, which is the i-f sound carrier. These i-f signals are amplified in a single tuner stage.

***UHF Tuner*.** When the station selector switch is set to UHF, the UHF tuner and its local oscillator come into use. Because there are 56 UHF channels, it is not practical to use a separate set of coils for tuning the receiver to each channel. Instead, variable capacitors are used to tune continuously over the UHF range. Two capacitors tune the r-f circuits from 473 MHz (channel 14) to 803 MHz (channel 69). A third capacitor correspondingly increases the local oscillator frequency from 517 to 847 MHz.

In the UHF mode, r-f amplification is not used because the frequencies are too high to obtain useful transistor gain. Instead, the incoming signal is beat with the local oscillator sine wave in a diode mixer, and the i-f output then goes to the VHF tuner. In the UHF mode, the r-f amplifier and mixer portions of the VHF tuner become tuned to 44 MHz, which is the center of the intermediate frequency band. Thus the VHF tuner is made to serve as an i-f amplifier that plays a very useful role in UHF reception.

Picture Signal Amplifiers. After the tuner stage, there are three additional i-f stages. At the input to the first i-f stage, three trap circuits are used to remove some sources of picture interference. The traps, which form series-resonant short circuits to ground, are tuned to the picture carrier and sound carrier intermediate frequencies in adjacent channels and to the associated sound i-f carrier.

The signal that emerges from the third i-f amplifier stage normally has a peak-to-peak amplitude of more than 9 volts and is ready for AM detection. This operation, which is accomplished by a germanium diode, yields the composite video signal shown in Fig. 6. This detected signal is used at five different points in the receiver.

A video driver supplies the energy needed to feed these various loads. One of the loads is a video amplifier that supplies the cathode of the picture tube with an 80-volt peak-to-peak inverted version of the signal shown in Fig. 6.

The video driver also feeds an AGC (automatic gain control) amplifier. This circuit automatically adjusts the gain of the first i-f amplifier stage to keep the AM detector output constant at approximately 2 volts from sync tip to maximum white. The AGC amplifier minimizes flutter, such as that caused by a broadcast signal that is reflected from a nearby airplane, and also minimizes manual gain (contrast) adjustments when tuning from one station to another. To guard against the danger that noise pulses, such as those caused by some nearby automobile, will result in an inaccurate AGC output, the AGC amplifier is allowed to "look at" the video signal only during horizontal sync pulses. This is done by feeding "gating" pulses from an H (horizontal) output transformer to the AGC amplifier. These pulses coincide with the horizontal sync pulses.

As the AM detector output becomes larger than 2 volts peak to peak, the AGC amplifier feeds an increasingly negative bias to the first intermediate-frequency amplifier stage. When a relatively strong signal is tuned in, the AGC output voltage becomes sufficiently negative to activate an AGC delay stage. As the AM detector output becomes larger, the AGC delay stage feeds an increasingly negative bias to the VHF tuner r-f amplifier. In combination with the bias fed to the first i-f amplifier, this system guards against overload due to unusually strong r-f input signals.

Horizontal Sweep Section. In order to synchronize the horizontal (H) and vertical (V) scanning in the receiver picture tube with that of the transmitter camera, one must discard the varying part of the composite video signal shown in Fig. 6. This is done in a sync limiter, a transistor that is biased so that only the sync pulses appear in its output.

If a strong noise pulse occurs during a sync pulse, it may be passed along by the sync limiter, causing faulty synchronization. A noise gate is therefore used to cut off the sync limiter when a strong noise pulse is present. This produces a hole in the sync limiter output, but a hole that lasts only a few microseconds is less damaging to synchronization than a strong pulse of noise.

Despite these precautions, the sync limiter output may contain appreciable noise, especially if a weak signal is being received. The noise may cause a momentary displacement of horizontal picture lines to the right or left of their correct position, so additional noise-reduction techniques are needed.

The solution is to use an H (horizontal) oscillator that is isolated from the incoming signal. Its frequency is slowly increased or decreased by means of a slowly varying correcting voltage. The incoming sync pulses and the sawteeth supplied by an H output transformer are compared in an H APC (horizontal automatic phase control) stage. If the H oscillator frequency starts to change, the H output transformer sawteeth start to move to the left or right relative to the incoming sync pulses. The H APC stage then develops a correcting voltage that restores the proper H oscillator frequency.

The sine wave that is generated by the H oscillator is shaped into huge voltage pulses by an H amplifier. These pulses, which are 1,000 volts high, rapidly return the scanning beam from right to left during the 10.2-microsecond period for horizontal retrace. During the remainder of the 63.5-microsecond period for a horizontal line scan, the pulses are at zero voltage, and the scanning beam sweeps relatively slowly from left to right. For a variety of technical reasons, magnetic coils are used for H and V deflection of the electron beam in the picture tube. The output voltage wave shape of the H amplifier yields a sawtooth of current (as shown in Fig. 2) in the H deflection coil. A special switching transistor is used to generate the H pulses that are fed to the H deflection coil. During the retrace period, the transistor is an open circuit. During the sweep period, the transistor is a short circuit, and the current through it rises to a peak value of 3 amperes.

The H amplifier output also is fed to a step-up transformer that converts the 1,000-volt pulses in its primary winding into 20,000-volt pulses in its secondary winding. The 20,000-volt pulses are rectified by selenium high-voltage diodes to provide 20,000 volts for the anode of the picture tube.

Vertical Sweep Section. The vertical sweep section is much less complex than the horizontal sweep section because the vertical sweep rate is much slower than the horizontal sweep rate. High-frequency components of the incoming sync signal—along with practically all of the noise—are removed in a V integrator. The remaining V sync signal is used to synchronize the V oscillator, which generates a sawtooth. This wave is shaped in a V amplifier, which produces an 800-volt peak-to-peak signal whose shape is a mixture of a pulse and a sawtooth. This shape, known as a trapezoid, yields a sawtooth of current in the V deflection coil. The V amplifier output feeds into a stepdown transformer that reduces voltage and correspondingly increases current fed to the V deflection coil. The V and H transformers also block direct current from reaching the V and H deflection coils. This is done to keep the picture from being thrown off center.

Sound Signal Amplifiers. The output of the AM detector includes a 4.5-MHz component created by mixing the i-f sound and picture carriers. This intercarrier beat is unusual in that it is both frequency and amplitude modulated—that is, it carries the frequency changes of the FM sound signal and the amplitude changes of the AM picture signal. If the amplitude changes are not removed, we hear components of the picture signal in the loudspeaker. The most prominent audio contribution is a sharp 60-Hz buzz caused by V sync pulses.

The video driver feeds the 4.5-MHz intercarrier signal to a sound i-f amplifier. The amplitude changes of the video signal are removed in a sound i-f limiter, a following stage that yields a 4.5-MHz sound carrier with a peak frequency deviation of 25 kHz. In the next stage, an FM detector converts changes in instantaneous frequency to changes in audio output voltage. The output of the detector is amplified until it has sufficient power to drive the loudspeaker.

COLOR RECEIVERS

The devices and methods previously described for black-and-white receivers form the basis for color TV reception, but they must be supplemented by color signal processing circuits.

In a color TV receiver, the wave shape of the composite video signal from the video driver is as shown in Fig. 6. To extract the W (black-and-white) component, the video driver output is passed through a 3.5-MHz low-pass filter. This process removes the 3.579545-MHz color subcarrier variations shown in Fig. 6. In their place, we get a voltage corresponding to their average value. (In the text that follows, 3.579545 MHz is rounded off to 3.6 MHz.)

To extract the I (in-phase) and Q (quadrature) color information from the composite video signal, we first pass the video driver output through a 2- to 4.1-MHz filter. This process yields the modulated I and Q frequency components. All of the low-frequency video signals, including horizontal and vertical sync pulses, are rejected by this filter. However, the 3.6-MHz burst is retained. The H output transformer supplies a gating pulse that turns on a burst amplifier only during the burst. The burst is only 2.2 microseconds long out of a total of 63.5 microseconds per horizontal period.

Demodulation of the I and Q signals requires continuous 3.6-MHz sine and cosine waves that have a fixed phase relationship to the burst reference signal. In order to do this, a continuous wave generated by a subcarrier oscillator and the output of the burst amplifier are compared in a subcarrier APC (automatic phase control) stage. If the subcarrier oscillator frequency starts to change, its cycles start to move to the left or right relative to the incoming burst cycles. The APC stage then generates a voltage that restores the proper subcarrier oscillator frequency. An accurate 3.579545-MHz crystal oscillator is used so that normally only small changes in phase occur. Large errors in phase, which can develop when the receiver is tuned to a weak station, result in incorrect hues.

The subcarrier oscillator output is fed to a phase shifter that supplies the 3.6-MHz sine and cosine waves. The sine wave is in phase with the I-signal modulation, and the cosine wave is in phase with the Q signal modulation. Each wave extracts its in-phase component in a synchronous detector. The output of the I detector is cleaned up by means of a 1.5-MHz low-pass filter to yield the I signal, and the output of the Q detector is cleaned up by an 0.5-MHz low-pass filter to yield the Q signal.

Instead of directly generating red (R), green (G), and blue (B) signals from the W, I, and Q signals in accordance with the transformation equations given in Section 8, we first generate R-W (red minus white), G-W, and B-W signals in a matrix unit. The transformation equations are $R\text{-}W = 0.95I + 0.62Q$; $G\text{-}W = -0.28I - 0.64Q$; and $B\text{-}W = -1.11I + 1.73Q$. The W component subsequently is added to the R-W, G-W, and B-W signals to generate the R, G, and B signals for the picture tube.

The reason for this strategy is that there are circumstances—during a monochromatic transmission, for example—when any colors that appear are bound to be incorrect and distracting. In such circumstances, the three outputs from the matrix unit can be simultaneously reduced to zero, leaving only a single black-and-white W signal for the picture tube. The circuit that disables the color signals is called the "color killer."

The picture tube contains three separate electron guns that produce three different scanning beams simultaneously. The beam from the electron gun that receives the red signal strikes a red phosphor dot on the face of the picture tube. This dot glows red. Similarly, the beams from the guns that receive the green and blue signals strike nearby phosphor dots that glow green and blue, respectively. The viewer sees a single color that is a combination of red, green, and blue. The color he sees depends on the relative intensities of the red, green, and blue signals.

SID DEUTSCH
Polytechnic Institute of Brooklyn

Further Reading: Buchsbaum, Walter H., *Color TV Servicing*, 2d ed. (New York 1968); Deutsch, Sid, *Theory and Design of Television Receivers* (New York 1951).

11. Development of Television Equipment

As compared with other systems for transmitting information, the distinctive elements of a television system are the television camera at the sending point and the picture tube at the receiving point. The television camera generates electrical signals that correspond to the light intensity and color distribution of the scene being televised. These electrical signals are processed and amplified so that they can be transmitted over long distances to the receiver, where they are recovered and applied to the picture tube. It displays an image reproducing the original scene.

The television camera must contain a photoelectric device that changes a current or voltage in response to a change in incident light intensity. The television picture tube must contain a device that alters the brightness of any one spot or picture element of the image field in response to a current or voltage change.

Two photoelectric effects are used in the television camera: the photoemissive effect, and the photoconductive effect.

Photoemissive Effect. In the photoemissive effect, light falling on a photoemissive surface, or photocathode, ejects electrons from it. The electrons are drawn toward a more positive electrode (anode) in the same vacuum envelope as the photocathode. As a result a current proportional to the incident light flows in an external circuit connecting the photocathode and the anode. Enclosure in a vacuum is essential since all good photoemitters contain a highly reactive alkali metal, such as cesium.

The photoemissive effect was discovered by Heinrich Hertz in 1887, but practical photoemissive cells (phototubes) did not become available until 1913. One of the important properties of the photoemissive effect is the extremely rapid current and voltage changes in the external circuit in response to changes in light intensity. This response is essentially limited only by the time it takes for the electrons to go from the photocathode to the anode—about one hundred-millionth of a second for an electrode spacing of one inch and an applied voltage of 100 volts.

Photoconductive Effect. The photoconductive effect is the change of the electrical resistance of a photoconductive element when it is exposed to light. When such an element is connected in series with a battery in an electric circuit, current and voltage changes corresponding to the incident light are produced, just as with a phototube. The photoconductive current changes in response to light intensity changes occur no more quickly than about one hundredth of a second, which is much slower than the response time of a phototube. However, for a given light input, a photoconductive element commonly produces a much larger current change than the change produced by a photoemissive element.

The photoconductive effect in gray crystalline selenium was discovered by the British cable engineer Willoughby Smith and his assistant Louis

NIPKOW DISK TV

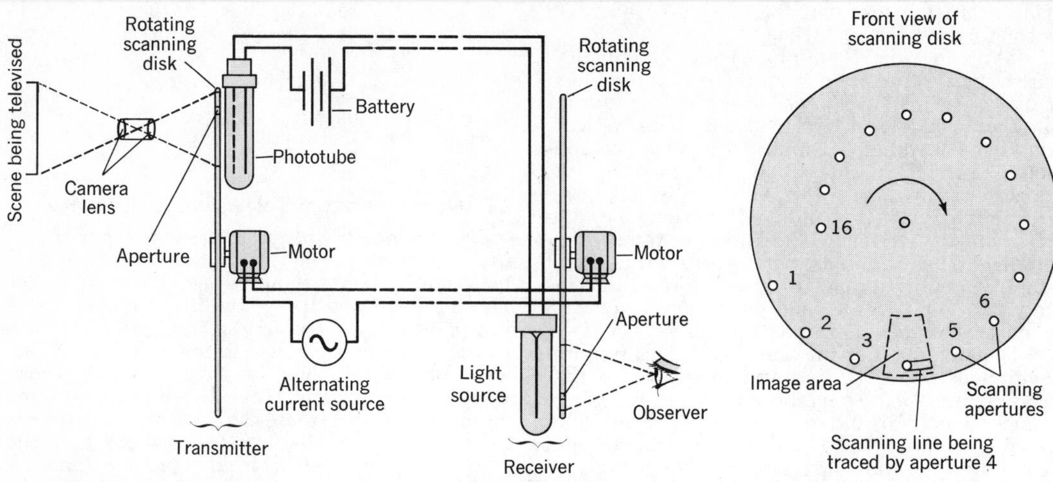

ADAPTED FROM V. K. ZWORYKIN AND E. G. RAMBERG, PHOTOELECTRICITY (WILEY 1949)

Fig. 10. **TELEVISION SYSTEM** shown uses mechanical scanning. At transmitter, the picture is focused on image area of Nipkow disk. As disk rotates, its apertures traverse the image area in a sequence of lines. Each aperture passes light in proportion to light and shade along a strip of the image area. Phototube converts sequence of light signals into a sequence of electric currents. At receiver, brightness of a light source varies in accordance with these currents. Light source is viewed through second Nipkow disk rotating in synchronism with first disk. As apertures sequentially traverse the image area rapidly, an observer sees crude representation of original scene.

May in 1873. Even though the photoconductive current from selenium may persist undesirably for minutes after exposure to light, practically all television inventions up to 1908 were based on the use of this material.

Parallel Signal Transmission. The selenium cell came closest to being practical in television systems that were simplest in concept, such as one proposed, but not translated into practice, by George R. Carey in Boston in 1875. In his system, light-sensitive elements arranged in an array in the image plane of a camera were individually coupled to light sources in a geometrically similar array at the receiver. With this arrangement even selenium cells would be adequate for picturing still objects and objects in slow motion. However, the system required as many transmission lines as there were picture elements, so it was completely impractical for modern high-definition television, which uses as many as 300,000 picture elements.

Scanning. Instead of transmitting electrical signals corresponding to the brightness of individual picture elements in parallel over a large number of transmission lines, the brightness signals can be transmitted one after another over a single transmission line. A system of this sort requires one scanner at the camera and a second scanner at the receiver. The first scanner transfers the individual picture element to the transmission line. The second scanner, which is synchronized with the first one, connects the transmission line with the corresponding element in the reconstituted picture at the receiver. Both mechanical and electronic scanners have played important roles in the history of television.

Mechanical Scanners. The Nipkow disk is a mechanical scanner that was patented by the German inventor Paul Nipkow in 1884. It came into practical use for television in the 1920's and remained in use for television transmission in the United States, Britain, the Netherlands, and Germany until about 1940.

The Nipkow disk is perforated with a series of apertures placed along a spiral path close to the disk edge (see Fig. 10). At the camera, a picture of the scene is projected on the disk. The picture width that is transmitted is equal to the distance separating two successive apertures, and the picture height corresponds to the radial distance between the beginning and the end of the spiral series of apertures. A phototube is placed so that it collects the light transmitted by the apertures as they traverse the picture field. As the disk rotates at uniform speed, the disk apertures describe a sequence of scanning lines across the image field. At any single moment, one aperture transmits light from a single picture element, which has an area equal to that of an aperture. After the phototube receives the light the resulting photocurrent is amplified and used to modulate the brightness of a large-area light source, such as a neon glow lamp, at the receiver. This is viewed through a second Nipkow disk, rotated in synchronism with the first (see Fig. 10). A crude representation of the original scene can be seen in this way.

In 1889 the French engineer Lazare Weiller devised a mechanical scanner consisting of a

ICONOSCOPE, a TV camera tube, was developed by Vladimir Zworykin and co-workers in the early 1930's.

RCA CORP.

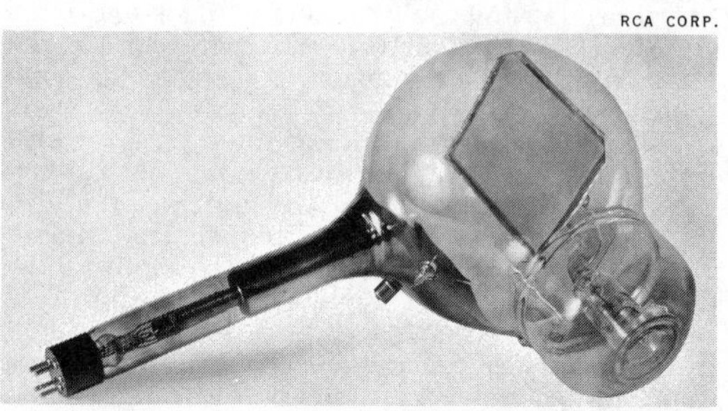

mirror drum. It had a number of mirrors, each tilted with respect to its predecessor so as to produce the desired vertical line displacement. Thus there were as many mirrors as there were scanning lines in the picture.

In these mechanical systems the light intensity required at the transmitter for the reproduction of a satisfactory picture quickly becomes very large because the required intensity depends on the fourth or a higher power of the number of scanning lines. For a television system using 525 scanning lines and a picture frequency of 30 per second, the illumination required becomes so great that a mechanical scanning system is impracticable.

The more essential devices for television—the photo-tube, the vacuum-tube amplifier, and the modulated light source—became readily available only after World War I. As a result, numerous television demonstrations using mechanical scanning for transmitting and reproducing pictures with 24 to 60 scanning lines were given in the United States, Britain, and Germany in the late 1920's.

Electronic Scanning. The possibility of using electronic scanning for television reception was demonstrated by Max Dieckmann in Munich as early as 1906 and was proposed by the Russian inventor Boris Rosing in St. Petersburg in the following year. Electronic scanning makes use of the fact that an electron beam is deflected by transverse electric or magnetic fields through an angle proportional to the field strength.

The absence of moving parts and the low power requirements for beam deflection gave electronic scanning important advantages over mechanical scanning. On the other hand, the early cathode-ray tubes had low deflection speeds, small operating voltages, and relatively dim and unsharp pictures.

Kinescope. The shortcomings of the early picture tubes were overcome by Vladimir K. Zworykin, a former student of Rosing, after Zworykin went to the United States in 1919. At Westinghouse in Pittsburgh, Zworykin demonstrated the first all-electronic television system by transmitting crude patterns in late 1923. After further research work on the picture tube, Zworykin in 1929 demonstrated a television receiver with a kinescope. This kinescope was a cathode-ray tube that had the principal features of all modern picture tubes. It had a high vacuum, permitting high voltages and rapid beam deflection; beam focusing by electric fields between coaxial electrodes, in accord with the new science of electron optics; and beam modulation by applying the picture signal to a negatively biased aperture disk in front of the electron emitter, which was an oxide-coated thermionic cathode.

Iconoscope. After joining RCA in 1930, Zworykin undertook the improvement of the camera tube. The primitive device used in the 1923 demonstrations contained an aluminum target that was oxidized on one side. The light image was projected through a collector grill onto the photosensitized insulating oxide surface, producing an electrical charge image on it by photoemission. The metal side of the target was scanned by an electron beam. The beam penetrated the insulating surface, producing a momentary conducting path that permitted the discharge of the charge stored on the insulator. As a result, a corresponding signal pulse was produced in the circuit connected to the grill.

By 1931, Zworykin and his co-workers had perfected a practical camera tube, the iconoscope (see photo). The target was a mica plate coated on the back with a conducting film called a signal plate. A mosaic of minute mutually insulated silver globules, oxidized and photosensitized with cesium, covered the front of the target. Both the light image and the high-velocity scanning beam impinged on this front side. Between successive scans, photoemission from the mosaic built up a charge distribution on the globules corresponding to the image. The brighter portions of the image were represented by more positive charges than those representing the darker portions of the image. At the point of scan, the beam returned a globule to its equilibrium potential. As a result, a current was produced in a circuit connected to the signal plate, and its magnitude was determined by the charge deposited on the globule. This process was repeated as the beam passed over each globule in the mosaic.

Image Dissector. In the meantime another American inventor, Philo T. Farnsworth, was working in San Francisco on a different camera tube. It was the image dissector, which he patented in 1927. In this tube, the image was projected on a large-area photocathode. Its photoemission electrons were accelerated and focused by superposed electric and magnetic fields into an electron image in the anode plane. At its center there was a fine aperture backed by an electron collector. Magnetic deflecting fields swept the electron image across the aperture so that at any single moment photoemission from a single picture element entered the electron collector.

At sufficiently high light levels, the image dissector proved capable of transmitting excellent pictures. However, it could not match the iconoscope in sensitivity. The image dissector can use only the photoemission during the period of coincidence of the picture element with the collector aperture. In contrast, the iconoscope stores charge for signal generation throughout the period between successive scans. The sensitivity of an ideal camera system with charge storage divided by the sensitivity of an ideal camera system with nonstorage is simply the number of picture elements—several hundred thousand for present television standards.

Flying-Spot Scanner. Even with such a disadvantage, one other camera system with nonstorage has played a role in broadcast television. The flying-spot scanner was suggested in a Zworykin patent filed in 1923, and this idea was translated into practice by the German inventor Manfred von Ardenne in 1930. In a flying-spot scanner, the unmodulated scanning raster on the

TV CAMERA TUBES are image orthicon (top), standard 1-inch-diameter vidicon (center), and 0.5-inch-diameter vidicon (bottom), which is about 3 inches long.

RCA CORP.

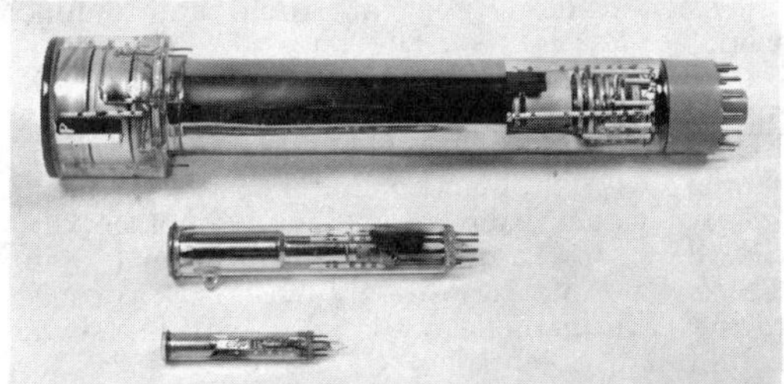

screen of a cathode-ray tube is optically projected on a film transparency. The light transmitted through the film is directed by a lens so that it strikes the photocathode of a phototube.

The phototube generates the picture signal used in televising film transparencies. To prevent horizontal smear in the reproduced image, the persistence of the phosphors at the face of the flying-spot cathode-ray tube should be a small fraction of a microsecond. This was not realized until the late 1940's, when the flying-spot scanner became a convenient signal generator for color transparencies.

Image Iconoscope, Orthicon, and Image Orthicon. In the iconoscope, the high-velocity beam scanning the target ejects many low-velocity secondary electrons for every incident beam electron. Thus the bombarded globule under the beam assumes an equilibrium potential slightly positive with respect to the adjoining collector electrode. As a result all but one secondary electron per beam electron are returned to the bombarded globule. Many of the electrons that do leave the globule are redistributed to the remainder of the target instead of being collected and contributing to the output signal.

The collection of photoemission electrons is similarly inefficient, making the sensitivity of the iconoscope about 1/20 that of a tube with perfect collection of photoelectrons and secondary electrons. Furthermore, the redistribution of the electrons produces spurious shading in the picture, which must be compensated by special shading signals.

Having recognized these shortcomings of the iconoscope, Zworykin and his co-workers set about devising camera tubes free of its deficiencies. As a first step, Harley Iams, George Morton, and Zworykin described the image iconoscope in 1939. In this tube the light image is projected on a more efficient photocathode, and the photoemission is imaged on the iconoscope target with secondary-emission gain. As a result the stored-charge image was improved by a factor of about 10. Tubes of this general type, developed elsewhere, came to be widely used outside the United States.

Next, Albert Rose and Iams described the orthicon in 1939. This tube used low-velocity scanning instead of high-velocity scanning, resulting in complete collection of photoelectrons and secondary electrons. The focus of the low-velocity beam at the target was maintained by introducing an axially symmetric structure with a transparent target and new methods of focusing and deflection by extended superposed magnetic fields.

Finally, Rose, Paul Weimer, and Harold Law described the image orthicon in 1945. This tube features an initial electron-imaging stage, low-velocity scan, and internal signal amplification in a secondary-emission multiplier. Since World War II, the image orthicon has been the principal television camera tube for studio and outdoor work.

Vidicon. The vidicon was developed by Weimer, Stanley Forgue, and Robert Goodrich at RCA in 1949. It is a small, compact camera tube, similar in structure and operation to the orthicon. In the vidicon the target is a photoconductive layer on a transparent metal signal plate. The signal plate is positively biased with respect to the beam cathode potential, which is also the equilibrium potential of the scanned target surface under the beam. In darkness, the photoconductive layer is essentially an insulator, and a fixed potential is maintained between its two surfaces. Under illumination, the scanned surface of the layer acquires positive charge by conduction throughout the period between scans. This stored charge is neutralized by the scanning beam, giving rise to a corresponding signal current in a circuit connected to the signal plate.

The vidicon thus takes full advantage of the storage effect. The high sensitivity of the photoconductive layer makes it a practical camera tube without the complication of an electron image stage or internal signal amplification. (See photo.)

A vidicon with an antimony trisulfide target is generally used as the camera tube for nonbroadcast applications. This tube is inferior to the image orthicon in that it has poorer sensitivity and greater lag, resulting in a smear of moving objects transmitted at low light levels. A vidicon-type tube with a lead-oxide target, called a Plumbicon, was introduced by the Philips company in the Netherlands in the early 1960's. This tube exhibits adequate freedom from lag and has a linear response, making it particularly suitable for color broadcast cameras.

In another variation of the vidicon, the target has a thin silicon wafer containing about 600,000 individual silicon diodes per square centimeter. The diodes, which are formed by integrated-circuit techniques, provide a broad spectral response and immunity to damage by overexposure. This version of the vidicon serves as the camera tube in the Picturephone service of the Bell System.

High-resolution vidicons used in conjunction with color gratings superposed on the image field have made possible single-tube color cameras, resulting in freedom from color registration difficulties, compactness, and simplicity of operation.

Black-and-White Picture Tubes. Modifications of the monochrome picture tube since Zworykin introduced the kinescope in 1929 were minor in comparison with those of the camera tube. They consisted in changes in the electron gun and operating voltages to improve the spot sharpness and brightness; more efficient white (zinc sulfide) screens to replace the original green willemite phosphor; the deposition of a thin aluminum layer on the back of the screen to increase the brightness and contrast of the picture; the addition of a filter face plate to reduce the adverse effect of ambient illumination; and the development of deflection yokes and associated circuits to produce beam deflection angles up to 110°, permitting the use of large-screen tubes in thinner receivers. See also CATHODE-RAY TUBE.

Color Picture Tubes—*Shadow-Mask Kinescope*. An intensive exploration of different approaches to color reproduction at the picture tube was undertaken at the RCA laboratories in Princeton, N. J., in the late 1940's and early 1950's. It resulted in the selection of the 3-beam shadow-mask tube, originally proposed by Alfred N. Goldsmith and Alfred C. Schroeder and perfected by Harold Law, as the most promising design.

Phosphors. After its commercial introduction in 1953, the shadow-mask tube was continuously improved by advances in manufacturing technique and design. Special attention was given to the phosphors to realize higher light output and better color balance. RCA soon replaced the original combination of a group of phosphate, silicate, and sulfide phosphors with a more efficient all-sulfide group of phosphors. In both groups the conversion efficiency of the red phosphor was the limiting factor. This limitation was overcome by highly efficient red rare-earth phosphors announced by Sylvania in 1964. A further improvement in screen brightness was achieved by surrounding the phospher dots by a black matrix. It absorbed incident ambient light and permitted use of a lower-density filter faceplate. See also PHOSPHOR.

Other Color Picture Tubes. The only other color picture tube to reach the commerical market by 1970 is the Sony Corporation's 3-beam Chromatron. In the Chromatron the color-selection element is a grill of fine wires, and the phosphor dot screen is replaced by a phosphor line screen. A large potential difference applied between the grill and the screen causes beam electrons incident on the space between adjoining wires to be focused into a narrow line element centered on a phosphor line of the appropriate color. Since the fine-wire grill intercepts a much smaller fraction of the incident beam electrons than the conventional shadow mask, the Chromatron utilizes the available beam power more efficiently.

Many color picture tubes with a single electron-beam gun have been devised and constructed, but none has achieved practical importance. In such tubes the beam is modulated by the color signal and is switched periodically from one phosphor to the next. This process leads to intrinsically lower screen brightness.

Projection Television. There has always been a limited demand for projection television for theater use. For this purpose RCA designed special kinescopes with relatively small screens—up to 7 inches (17.7 cm) in diameter—to be operated at high currents and voltages. High-efficiency optical systems resembling an inverted Schmidt reflector telescope projected the kinescope image on the viewing screen, providing images 15 by 20 feet (4.5 by 6 meters) in size as early as 1941. Since 1949, projection systems incorporating three smaller units of this type have been widely used for projecting color television pictures on medium-sized screens.

A quite different and much more complex theater television system is the Eidophor system. This highly successful system originally was developed by Fritz Fischer in Switzerland in the early 1940's. In place of the usual phosphor screen, the Eidophor system uses a thin oil film, illuminated by collimated light from an intense arc source. The scanning beam modulates the surface of the oil film so that it scatters a portion of the incident light proportional to the picture signal. Only the scattered light is used for forming the projected picture. The remainder is intercepted by appropriately placed stops in the optical system.

Television Recording. With the advent of television broadcasting, it became apparent that there was a need for recording video programs, for rebroadcasting them at a later time, and for distributing recorded programs to other stations. In the United States, cameras for recording kinescope pictures on 16-mm film were introduced by Eastman Kodak in 1948. Such cameras came into general use in broadcast studios. They were not too satisfactory for recording color programs because of the high cost of color film and the difficulties and long delays in color-film processing. Color separation film and embossed-film processes were developed to circumvent some of these difficulties, but their solution rested on the use of magnetic-tape recording.

In magnetic-tape recording, the electrical signal is recorded as a variation of the magnetization in a thin film of iron oxide which is deposited on a plastic tape base. In playback, the magnetic fields accompanying the magnetization stored in the tape induce an electrical signal in an external circuit as the tape moves past the reading head. Magnetic tape has an important advantage over film in that it can be played back immediately without any processing delay. Also, the tape record can be erased for reuse and the tape material is cheaper than photographic film, taking into consideration processing costs.

A key difficulty in video recording, as compared with sound recording, is that the signal bandwidth (the information to be recorded in a second) in video recording is several hundred times greater than that in sound recording. Consequently, corresponding increases in the relative speed between the recording head and the tape, and the reading head and the tape, are needed.

Black-and-white video recording on magnetic tape was first demonstrated by Bing Crosby Enterprises in late 1951. The frequency bandwidth was limited to less than half that of the standard video channel, which has a bandwidth of 4 megahertz. Ten parallel tracks, with two tracks added for synchronization and sound, were recorded in parallel on 1-inch tape to reduce the tape speed to 100 inches per second. Two years later, RCA demonstrated video recording for both black-and-white and color transmissions on ¼-inch tape moving at 30 feet per second. A single video track was used for black-and-white transmission, and separate red, blue, and green signal tracks were used for color transmissions. The transmission bandwidth was close to that of a standard video channel, and the picture quality was good. Because of the high recording speed, a 17-inch reel of tape was required for a recording period of only 4 minutes.

Helical scanning, introduced by the Ampex Corporation in 1956, is now the preferred method for recording on magnetic tape for use in television broadcasts. In this method, four magnetic heads are mounted on a rapidly rotating drum. The heads scan 2-inch tape, which is fitted to a cylindrical surface, in parallel tracks transverse to the direction of tape motion. This made it possible to reduce the tape speed to 15 inches per second and to provide a playing time of 64 minutes, using a 12-inch reel of 0.001-inch-thick tape. The first Ampex recorders were designed only for black-and-white transmissions. In 1959, RCA and Ampex introduced helical-scanning video recorders that provided color recording. See also TAPE RECORDING.

EDWARD G. RAMBERG
RCA Corporation

Bibliography

Fink, Donald G., *Television Engineering* (New York 1952).

Fink, Donald G., *Television Engineering Handbook* (New York 1957).

Settel, Irving, and **Lass, William,** *Pictorial History of Television* (New York 1969).

Wentworth, John W., *Color Television Engineering* (New York 1955).

Zworykin, Vladimir K., and **Morton, George A.,** *Television,* 2d ed. (New York 1954).

TELEX, tel'eks, is a telegraph exchange service that enables subscribers to communicate directly with one another by means of teletypewriters (teleprinters) temporarily connected by lines and switching equipment. Telex, which started on a national basis in Europe in the early 1930's, became an international service by the mid–1930's. It expanded rapidly, mainly after World War II, and is now available in almost every country in the world.

Telex service is analogous to the public telephone service except that machine-printed messages replace speech. The printed record makes Telex particularly useful in the business world, which requires the authority of the written word. Another advantage is that a call can be made and a message left at an unattended machine, which is very useful where there are time differences.

The teletypewriter, which has a typewriterlike keyboard, produces electrical signals that are transmitted to a distant point, where another teletypewriter produces a printed copy from the electrical signals transmitted to it. Messages are sent in a 5-unit code at 67 words per minute. Calls can be made automatically, semiautomatically, or manually. In automatic calling, no operator is required. In semiautomatic calling, an operator is required at the district of origin. In manual calling, an operator is required at the district of origin and the district of destination. Calls are charged according to the distance between subscribers and the time the circuit is available.

See also TELETYPEWRITER; TELETYPEWRITER EXCHANGE SERVICE.

B. J. BONNICK
Cable and Wireless Limited

TELFORD, tel'fərd, **Thomas** (1757–1834), Scottish engineer, who designed the Menai Suspension Bridge in Wales, the longest such construction of its day.

Telford was born in Eskdale, Dumfriesshire, Scotland, on Aug. 9, 1757. He was apprenticed to a mason, quickly learned the trade, and moved in 1782 to London. Largely self-educated, he was knowledgeable in many areas and was made surveyor of public works in Shropshire. In 1793 he was appointed chief engineer for the construction of the Ellesmere Canal, the first of the many canals, roads, bridges, and harbor facilities he built. In 1808 he laid out and constructed a system of waterways for Sweden.

Besides the Menai Bridge, with its span of 579 feet (176 meters), Telford planned the great mail road from London to Holyhead—one of a number of roads and bridges he built in Scotland. He developed an excellent broken-stone surface for roads similar to the macadam surface that later was popularized by John McAdam. He died in London on Sept. 2, 1834.

ROBERT S. WOODBURY
Georgia Institute of Technology

TELL, William, legendary hero of the Swiss struggle for freedom from Austrian domination during the early part of the 14th century. According to various folk tales, Gessler, the tyrannical Austrian bailiff of the Swiss canton of Uri, ordered the citizens to pay homage to a cap hung in the square of Altdorf as a sign of their acceptance of Austrian domination. Tell, a native of Bürglen and a leader of the dissident Swiss in Uri, refused, and Gessler forced him to shoot an apple from the head of Tell's son. Tell succeeded, but because he had threatened Gessler, he was seized and taken by boat across Lake Lucerne. A violent storm prevented the boat from landing, and Gessler permitted Tell, who was known for his strength and skill, to take the rudder. Tell brought the boat to shore, escaped, and later killed Gessler from ambush at "Hohle Gasse" (Hollow Way) near Küssnacht. On his return to Uri, Tell helped to organize the Swiss forces that vowed to expel the Austrians. Tell supposedly fought at the Battle of Morganten in 1315 and died in a flood in 1350.

The earliest versions of the Tell story appear in 15th century ballads and in the tales told in the *Chronicle* of 1482 by Melchior Russ of Lucerne, and the *Weisse Buch von Sarnen* (*White Book of Sarnen*) of about 1470. The tale is also found in later works such as Gilg Tschudi's *Chronicon Helveticum* (1734–1736) and Johannes von Müller's *History of the Confederation* (1780). Despite the many efforts to substantiate these accounts, there is still no proof of a real William Tell in Uri in the 14th century. However, Tell's exploits and the Swiss ideal of liberty continue to live in Friedrich Schiller's drama, *Wilhelm Tell* (1805) and in Rossini's opera (1829).

BERNARD MANDELBAUM
Bronx Community College

TELL, a hill-shaped site containing the remains of human habitations. Tell is the Arabic word for "mound." Tells are characteristic of Palestine, Syria, Iraq, and Anatolia, parts of Iran, where mounds grew up over the remains of ancient towns. Towns in these regions were built near a source of water, frequently on high ground as protection from storms and attack.

A tell is made up of superimposed layers—new cities were built on the rubble of others destroyed earlier by fire, earthquake, or enemy attack. The buildings, usually of mud-brick, were leveled and new structures erected above them. Tells are important in archaeology. Each level is carefully excavated in turn, tracing walls, foundations, and floors from the topmost city down to its earliest constructions. Some tells contain the rebuilding efforts of 9,000 years. Analysis of the layers suggests settlement patterns, means of subsistence, and character of life, as well as the extent of trade and contact the area had with other cultures at various times in its history.

PHILIP C. GIFFORD, JR.
American Museum of Natural History

TELL EL-AMARNA, tel el-ə-mär'nə, is the modern name commonly given to the ruins of the ancient Egyptian city Akhetaton on the east bank of the Nile, 190 miles (300 km) south of Cairo. This city was founded about 1360 B.C. by Amenhotep IV (Akhenaton).

In an area marked off by huge stelae, Akhetaton took shape along three roughly parallel north-south thoroughfares. Near the river the largest building (official palace or great temple?) extended more than 1,900 feet (580 meters). Across the main road was the King's private residence. South of this residence stood a small temple for use by the royal family, and to the north was an unroofed structure containing emplacements for more than 700 altars. Like the city itself, the temples were dedicated to the Aton, or Divine Sundisk.

HIRMER FOTOARCHIV

AKHENATON and his family worship the sun in this fragment from a temple at Tell el-Amarna.

One of the buildings in the central city was the "Bureau for the Correspondence of Pharaoh," in which were found clay tablets from the diplomatic exchanges of the Egyptian court with rulers of Mitanni, Assyria, Babylonia, Khatti, Tyre, and lesser Asian kingdoms. On high ground near the desert were quarters for the military police, complete with stables and a parade ground. Elsewhere were walled estates.

The language of documents from el-Amarna differs in grammar and spelling from that of preceding reigns, apparently substituting the contemporary spoken idiom for the antiquated forms of the schools. Startling changes appear also in sculpture and painting. Tomb scenes are devoted almost entirely to the activities of the royal family. The plastered floors and walls of buildings are covered with scenes or designs of flowers, birds, and small animals. Columns and ceiling beams are often gaily painted. Greater freedom is permitted in rendering movement and emotion, and there is an almost unrestrained use of curves.

Akhenaton's reasons for moving to Akhetaton are not certainly known, although they were probably connected with his fervent worship of the sun disk and apparent neglect of other deities. Early in the reign of Tutankhamon the court returned to Thebes, and Akhetaton was abandoned to the ravages of time and later builders, who used it as a quarry.

See also AMENHOTEP.

CAROLINE NESTMANN PECK
Brown University

TELLER, Edward (1908–), Hungarian-born American physicist, sometimes called "the father of the hydrogen bomb." He was born in Budapest on Jan. 15, 1908. His doctoral thesis, written under the direction of Werner Heisenberg at the University of Leipzig in 1930, was on the theory of the hydrogen molecular ion. As a Rockefeller fellow at the Niels Bohr Institute in Copenhagen, he soon extended his interests to nuclear physics. In 1935 he went to the United States and became a U. S. citizen six years later.

While professor of physics at George Washington University, Teller collaborated with George Gamow in strengthening U. S. capabilities in theoretical physics. In 1941 he joined Fermi and others on the Manhattan Engineer District at Columbia University, to work on the problem of nuclear fission as it related to national defense. The following year he assisted Robert Oppenheimer in establishing the Los Alamos Scientific Laboratory. In 1951 he and Ernest Lawrence set up a branch of the Radiation Laboratory at Livermore, Calif., to further U. S. research on thermonuclear weapons.

Teller's work on the hydrogen-fusion, or H-bomb, is still secret. It is known that he was one of the discoverers of the method by which it could be made to work, so that the first bomb of this type could be tested in the Pacific in 1952.

In theoretical physics Teller made prominent contributions to many fields, including molecular structure, nuclear reactions, cosmology, solid state, and cosmic rays. He became particularly well known for the generalization of the selection rule in beta radioactivity—proposed jointly with George Gamow—and for giant nuclear resonances, which he worked out with Maurice Goldhaber. Among other innovations, Teller introduced the concepts of strong coupling and separable potentials in the field theory of nuclear physics. In 1962 he became professor at large at the University of California.

CHARLES L. CRITCHFIELD
Los Alamos Scientific Laboratory

TELLER, Henry Moore (1830–1914), American senator, who was known for his legislative efforts on behalf of the remonetization of silver. He was born in Granger, N. Y., on May 23, 1830. He attended Alfred University and was admitted to the bar in 1858. He practiced law in Illinois and, after 1861, in Central City, Colo.

When Colorado achieved statehood, Teller was elected as a Republican to the U. S. Senate, serving from 1876 to 1882, when he became secretary of the interior in President Chester A. Arthur's cabinet. Reelected to the Senate as a Republican in 1885, he served there continuously until 1909. In 1896 he bolted the Republican convention and helped form the Independent Silver Republican party, supporting the Democratic nominee for president. He was reelected to the Senate as a Silver Republican in 1897 and as a Democrat in 1903. On the eve of the outbreak of the Spanish-American War in 1898, he helped secure adoption of the Teller Resolution pledging the United States to an independent Cuba. From 1908 to 1912 he was a member of the National Monetary Commission. He died in Denver on Feb. 23, 1914.

TÉLLEZ, Gabriel. See TIRSO DE MOLINA.

TELLOH. See LAGASH.

TELLURIUM, tə-lo͝or'ē-əm, symbol Te, is a silvery white, semimetallic element. It was discovered in 1782 by the Austrian chemist Franz Joseph Müller. Its name comes from the Latin word *tellus*, meaning "earth."

Tellurium is added to steel and copper to improve their machinability, and to lead to increase its strength and hardness. It is also used in the production of semiconductors and thermoelectric alloys. In the form of tellurium diethyldithiocarbamate $[(C_2H_5)_2NCSS]_4Te$, and in conjunction with mercaptobenzothiazole, it is the fastest known accelerator for butyl rubber manufacture.

Tellurium, which is located in Group VIB of the periodic table, is associated with the oxygen family of elements. Although it is more metallic than oxygen, sulfur, and selenium, tellurium is a metalloid—that is, a semimetal and a semiconductor. Its atomic number is 52, and its atomic weight is 127.61. There are eight stable isotopes of tellurium, ranging in mass from ^{120}Te to ^{130}Te. Its melting point is 450° C (842° F), and its boiling point is 1390° C (2534° F). It exhibits oxidation states of -2, $+4$, and $+6$. Tellurium is insoluble in all liquids except those with which it undergoes chemical reaction.

Tellurium is a moderately reactive element. It burns in air to form the oxide TeO_2 and combines directly with halogens and numerous metals and nonmetals. It reacts with concentrated sulfuric and nitric acids on heating.

There are no important ores of tellurium. It is found mainly as an impurity in metal sulfide ores. Commercially, tellurium is recovered from the slimes produced by the electrolytic refining of copper. These slimes contain tellurium in concentrations ranging from traces to about 8%. The tellurium is dissolved during removal of the copper from the slime and is subsequently recovered by precipitating tellurous acid, H_2TeO_3. The tellurous acid then is dissolved in caustic soda, from which the metal is obtained by electrolysis. Tellurium is also recovered from flue dusts resulting from combustion of silver and gold sulfide ores and from the lead chambers used in the manufacture of sulfuric acid.

HERBERT LIEBESKIND
The Cooper Union, New York

TELLUS is the Roman name of the earth goddess Gaea. See GAEA.

TELSTAR. See COMMUNICATIONS SATELLITE.

TELUGU, tel'ə-go͞o, is a major language of south India, belonging to the Dravidian group. Its speakers, about 38 million at the 1961 census, are concentrated chiefly in Andhra Pradesh, a state formed as Andhra in 1953 from northern Madras and enlarged in 1956 by the addition of part of the former state of Hyderabad. The creation of the new state on linguistic lines was the result of political agitation by the Telugu speakers, or Andhras.

Although the Andhras speak a language cognate with Tamil, they prefer generally to emphasize the Aryan elements in their speech, even to the point of denying its Dravidian affinities. Politically, they have been in conflict with the Tamils rather than with north India, where Aryan languages are spoken. Telugu, much more than Tamil, has been strongly influenced by Sanskrit and related Aryan languages, but its essential structure is undeniably non-Aryan.

Telugu literature, going back to the 11th century A. D., consists mainly of translations from Sanskrit. Under the influence of English literature, a popular literature has developed, written in a language based on the colloquial dialect. See also DRAVIDIAN; INDIA—*Literature* (Dravidian Literature).

LEIGH LISKER
Author of "Introduction of Spoken Telugu"

TEMESVÁR. See TIMIŞOARA.

TEMPE, tem-pē', a city in south-central Arizona, in Maricopa county, is on the Salt River, 9 miles (14 km) east of Phoenix. The river is usually dry. Tempe's climate attracts health-seekers and retired persons. The city has steel and electronics industries.

Tempe is the home of Arizona State University, which was established in 1885 as the Territorial Normal School. The Grady Gammage Auditorium, designed by Frank Lloyd Wright, is a center of cultural activity.

The community grew up around a flour mill built there by Charles Trumbull Hayden in 1871. Hayden's son, Carl T. Hayden, who was a U. S. senator from 1927 to 1968, was born in Tempe.

Tempe, named for the Vale of Tempe, Greece, was incorporated in 1894. Government is by council and manager. The community grew rapidly in the 1960's, with the population more than doubling in that period. Population: 62,907.

TEMPE, Vale of, tem'pē, in Greece, the valley between the Olympus and Ossa mountains through which the Peneus River reaches the Aegean Sea from the central plain of Thessaly. The first temple of Apollo at Delphi was said to have been made of laurel from Tempe, and every ninth year there was a sacred procession from the vale to Delphi. The valley, only about 5 miles (8 km) long, is strategically important as the chief pass into central Greece from Macedonia.

JAMES R. WISEMAN, *University of Texas*

TEMPERA PAINTING, tem'pə-rə, uses a medium in which dry pigments are "tempered" (mixed) with water and a fatty binder. The simplest, most commonly used binder is egg yolk, which is a natural emulsion of fat and water. It is separated from the egg white and combined with an equal amount of water, often distilled, to produce a mixture with the consistency of light cream. Other kinds of binders include egg white, gum arabic, and wax. Egg white, however, is brittle when dry and tends to crack. In the field of commercial art the term "tempera" has erroneously been extended to cover any opaque water-based paint.

Technique. Tempera is applied in thin films, or glazes, which dry to the touch in seconds and become very brittle. Because of the danger of cracking they cannot safely be used on flexible canvas. Instead, they are applied to rigid panels of wood or masonite covered with several thin layers of gesso (a mixture of chalk, whiting, or plaster of Paris and glue, gelatin, or casein), which are usually sandpapered. Much of the brilliance in tone comes from the interaction of the light gesso ground and the many layers of tempera glazes over it. Historically, the boards that were glued together to form the traditional wood

METROPOLITAN MUSEUM OF ART, JULES S. BACHE COLECTION

METROPOLITAN MUSEUM OF ART

TEMPERA TECHNIQUE, seen in detail of a 15th century madonna (*left*) by Carlo Crivelli, is crisp and sharp, as compared with loose, rich oil technique seen in detail from Frans Hals' *Malle Babbe* (*right*), 17th century.

panel eventually warped, and the cracks where they were joined showed through. The masonite panels of the 20th century free the painter from that problem.

Because tempera dries quickly, colors cannot easily be blended to show modeling. Traditionally the medium has required minute cross-hatching and carefully planned underpainting, a time-consuming process that many artists are unwilling to follow. The paint surface can be worked over indefinitely, unlike transparent watercolor, without "picking up" or washing away the underlayers. Thick impasto should be avoided because the paint tends to crack and fall off. Sometimes, however, many thin layers of paint can be safely built up. Tempera colors are lighter when dry than when wet. Characteristically mat (unshiny), they have little of the depth and transparency of oil.

For the first few years after its completion, a tempera painting is soft and easily scratched. It does not crack in the large, weblike patterns of oil paint but may in time develop an almost indiscernible crackle.

Attempts have been made, with varying success, to combine the oil and egg tempera techniques. Stand oil, sun-thickened oil, Venice turpentine, and linseed oil have been added to egg yolk or whole egg to produce modified egg emulsions or "mixed media." Oil glazes may be used over tempera underpainting.

History. Tempera was used in the ancient world: for example, in Egyptian portrait panels from the Faiyum in Roman times and in Roman murals. Byzantine and European panel painters worked in tempera in the Middle Ages. The technique was carried to a high point by such late medieval and early Renaissance painters as Giotto, Fra Angelico, and Botticelli.

Many painters from the 14th to the 16th century, such as Giovanni Bellini in Italy and Jan Van Eyck, Bruegel, and Bosch in the north, probably used oil glazes over tempera or added oil to the tempera. A milestone in this gradual transition to the softer, more fluid, rapid, richer oil technique is Verrocchio's *Baptism of Christ* (15th century; Uffizi, Florence). The major part of the work is in traditional tempera, but the head of the angel in the lower left, attributed to his pupil Leonardo, is in oil. Soon afterward, tempera was abandoned almost completely.

In the 20th century, especially in the United States, there has been an amazing reawakening of interest in tempera. Such artists as Reginald Marsh, Paul Cadmus, Andrew Wyeth, Bernard Perlin, and Ben Shahn found new ways to use the medium. Tempera can be splattered onto the panel from a distance, dropped from above, or applied with a sponge. Because the surface dries almost immediately, the artist need not wait to apply new layers and can create unusual textures and patterns by such means as scraping the paint with a razor blade or sandpaper. Although the acrylic (rubber-based) paints can achieve some of these effects, tempera remains unique.

ROBERT VICKREY, *Painter*

TEMPERANCE MOVEMENT, an organized drive for total abstinence from alcoholic beverages. Such a movement gained ascendancy in the United States in the 19th century and reached its zenith with the ratification of the Prohibition Amendment to the Constitution in 1919.

Rise of the Movement. Most Americans of the 17th and 18th centuries viewed moderate drinking as a pleasure, even a necessity. In the 18th century, Quakers began to warn against spirits, and they were joined in this by a Pennsylvania physician, Benjamin Rush.

Rush's writings stirred New Englanders concerned about the breakdown of social control, which they believed stemmed from the Revolution and democracy. In the early 19th century, one of them, the Rev. Lyman Beecher, denounced spirit-drinking as a social evil and proposed the creation of voluntary reform societies to replace the weakening legal enforcement of morality. As a result, the American Temperance Society was formed in 1826 in Boston. Its missionaries persuaded thousands to sign a pledge against spirit-drinking. In 1836, when reorganizing as the American Temperance Union, the reformers redefined "temperance" to include abstinence from fermented beverages.

LIBRARY OF CONGRESS

Temperance wins out in Currier's 1851 lithograph.

After 1840 the Washington Temperance Societies, which appealed to drinkers to become abstainers, took up such emotional devices as revivalistic meetings featuring the confessions of "reformed drunkards." Similar temperance movements occurred in Europe, especially in the British Isles. In Ireland, Father Theobald Mathew led a successful crusade for temperance (1838–1842). He visited the United States to recruit Catholics (1849–1851), but the movement remained overwhelmingly Protestant, native American, and nonurban.

To reduce drinking by the unconverted, many temperance men turned to statewide prohibition. In the 1840's and 1850's, led by Neal Dow, they won victories, but popular opposition and then the Civil War caused setbacks. Subsequently the movement gained strength from the Woman's Christian Temperance Union (WCTU), headed by Frances E. Willard, and from the Anti-Saloon League.

Prohibition and Repeal. To the people of the small towns and countryside, abstinence from alcohol, drugs, and often from tobacco became a badge of middle-class respectability. Their last great victory over the emerging cities was the adoption in 1919 of the 18th (Prohibition) Amendment. As problems of nationwide enforcement became more apparent, abstinence became less fashionable. After the repeal of prohibition in 1933 the WCTU continued its struggle.

FRANK L. BYRNE
Kent State University

Further Reading: Byrne, Frank L., *Prophet of Prohibition: Neal Dow and His Crusade* (Madison, Wis., 1961); Gusfield, Joseph R., *Symbolic Crusade: Status Politics and the American Temperance Movement* (Champaign, Ill., 1963).

TEMPERATE ZONE, an old geographical term for the areas between the Tropic of Cancer and the Arctic Circle and between the Tropic of Capricorn and the Antarctic Circle. More meaningful temperature zones are defined on maps by isotherms or by climatic types. See CLIMATE.

TEMPERATURE. Although there is an intimate connection between heat and temperature, the relationship is not as direct as that, for example, between mass and weight. Heat is a sensation that is the product, at the macroscopic level, of the activity, or thermal energy, of atoms. The temperature of a body is not a measure of its quantity of thermal energy (heat content), which is always dependent on the nature of the substance being measured. Because of this the specific heat, or heat capacity, of a unit of matter at a specific temperature is defined as the amount of heat, or thermal energy, that must be transferred in order to raise the temperature of the material one degree. Therefore, the transference of equal amounts of heat to two different materials will not, in general, raise the temperatures of the materials by equal amounts. Temperature is a quantitative value of the degree or intensity of heat and is independent of the nature of the substance. Nevertheless, because temperature is in practice obtained by instruments (see THERMOMETER) that depend upon the particular properties of a specific substance—for example, expansion coefficient, specific heat, resistance—it is necessary to distinguish the practical from the theoretical scale of temperature.

This division corresponds historically to the separation between the evolution of heat theory and of temperature measurements. Thermometers and scales of temperature were in use for over a century before the establishment of thermodynamics in the 1860's. Though considerable effort has since been directed toward fusing the scientific concepts of temperature with the older practice of thermometry, there are still two different and complementary ways of arriving at an understanding of the meaning of temperature, the theoretical and the practical.

Theoretical Scales. The thermodynamic scale is based upon the work of Sadi Carnot, James P. Joule, Rudolf Clausius, William Rankine, and Lord Kelvin (William Thomson). It postulates the existence of an absolute scale of temperature, known either as the Kelvin scale (°K) or the Rankine scale (°R), which has a lower limit of 0° (absolute zero) corresponding to a lack of almost all atomic and molecular motion. According to the thermodynamic formulation, the ratio of two absolute temperatures is defined by the ratio of the amount of heat added to, and that subtracted from, an ideal reversible Carnot engine operating between these two temperatures. If Q represents the quantity of heat and T the absolute temperature, one writes $T_1/T_2 = Q_1/Q_2$.

These definitions are purposely independent of any particular substance. They neither imply the use of a particular scale nor define the size of intervals or degrees of temperature. Rankine chose to align his scale with the Farenheit system (see below) by fixing the ice-steam interval at 180°, while Lord Kelvin selected 100° for the same interval to fit with the Celsius, or centigrade, scale. Though each system, therefore, produces different numerical values for the fixed points generally used in practical thermometry, they are equivalent. Scientists have come to prefer the Kelvin scale.

Although the thermodynamic, or absolute, scale is independent of the properties of any particular substance, it is possible to fix the absolute temperature scale by means of the properties of gases. In particular, the numerical value for absolute zero was first approximated by a consideration of the behavior of ideal gases, that is, gases that obey the ideal gas law of Boyle and Charles (see GAS): $PV = RT$, where P is the pressure, V the volume, T the absolute temperature, and R the universal gas constant.

According to this law, a gas at constant pressure loses about 1/273 of its volume for each degree Celsius that its temperature is lowered. Similarly, at constant volume it loses 1/273 of its pressure. This suggests that at about −273° C an ideal gas will lose all its volume or pressure, thereby reaching the point of no thermal energy. The value now accepted for absolute zero (−273.15° C), defined by convention in 1948, is used chiefly for practical thermometry.

Practical Scales. There are two practical scales of temperature in use today: the Celsius, or centigrade, scale (C) and the Fahrenheit scale (F).

The thermodynamic scales discussed above and the practical scale were reconciled by agreements reached at the General International Conferences on Weights and Measures in 1927, 1948, 1954, and 1968, which permit the present-day scientist to convert easily from one scale to another. Since the degrees of the scales K and C are of equal size, conversion is obtained solely by addition or subtraction. The equations are:

$$°C = °K - 273.15$$
$$°K = °C + 273.15$$

In some English-speaking countries another set of scales, the R and F scales, are in common usage. Conversion is obtained simply by use of the following formulae:

$$°F = °R - 459.67$$
$$°R = °F + 459.67$$

The size of the degree in each set of scales being different, conversion between the C and F scales is obtained by the following:

$$°C = 5/9\,(°F - 32)$$
$$°F = 9/5° C + 32$$

Calibration of Scales. The same General International Conferences devised procedures to standardize the measurement of temperatures. Periodically these standards, which have been adopted for calibration throughout the world, are reviewed and revised. The present international practical temperature scale is based on 11 primary fixed and reproducible temperatures that have been assigned values (see Table 1).

Table 1. PRIMARY POINTS

Equilibrium state[1]	Assigned value of International Practical Temperature °K	°C
Triple point of equilibrium hydrogen	13.81	−259.34
Boiling point of equilibrium hydrogen[2]	17.042	−256.108
Boiling point of equilibrium hydrogen	20.28	−252.87
Boiling point of neon	27.102	−246.048
Triple point of oxygen	54.361	−218.789
Boiling point of oxygen	90.188	−182.962
Triple point of water	273.16	0.01
Boiling point of water	373.15	100
Freezing point of zinc	692.73	419.58
Freezing point of silver	1235.08	961.93
Freezing point of gold	1337.58	1064.43

[1] Boiling and freezing points are obtained at a pressure of one atmosphere.

[2] At a pressure of 25/76 atmosphere. Adapted from Metrologia, vol. 5, pp. 35–44, 1969.

Determination of the temperature in the intervals between the fixed points is done with the aid of several types of thermometers. More than one type of thermometer must be used because no one type, except the gas thermometer, can give sufficiently accurate readings over the whole temperature range. Gas thermometers, unfortunately, are too impractical to be suitable for general use—it can take weeks to make an exact measurement—and therefore other types of thermometers are relied upon.

Thus, to construct the international practical temperature scale, the General International Conference divided the scale into three parts, each of which is calibrated by the use of a particular type of thermometer. The standard instrument used from −259.34° C (13.81° K) to 630.74° C is the platinum resistance thermometer. From 630.74° C to 1064.43° C, it is the platinum-platinum/10% rhodium thermocouple. Above 1064.43° C the optical pyrometer is the standard instrument. Below 13.81° K no instruments have yet been designated as international standards.

The thermometric properties of each type of thermometer, for example, resistance, electromotive force, or radiant energy, are related to the temperature by definition at the primary points. To find the temperatures between these points we use interpolation equations. The interpolation equations covering the range of the resistance thermometer have been broken up into temperature stages: 13.81° K to 20.28° K; 20.28° K to 54.361° K; 54.361° K to 90.188° K; 90.188° K to 273.15° K (0° C); and 0° C to 630.74° C. These equations are binomial equations of the general family:

$$R_t = R_0\,(1 + At + Bt^2 + Ct^3 + \ldots)$$

where R_t is the resistance of the standard thermometer at the temperature (t), R_0 the resistance at 0° C, and the constants A, B, C, and so on are derived from the primary temperature points between 13.81° K and 630.74° C.

Between 630.74° C and 1064.43° C the interpolation equation using the thermocouple is:

$$E = a + bt + ct^2$$

where E is the electromotive force (volts) of the standard thermocouple when one junction is at 0° C and the other is at the temperature t (° C). The constants a, b, and c are calculated from the values of E at 630.74° C ± 0.02° C and at the freezing points of silver and gold.

For temperatures above 1064° C the primary instrument used is the optical pyrometer. This instrument contains a lamp that can be adjusted to match the brightness of gold at its freezing point. To measure higher temperatures one could, in principle, either increase the brightness of the lamp to match the increased brightness of the source, or decrease the amount of radiation from the source to match the brightness of the lamp in such a way that the temperature of the source, or object to be measured, is readily calculable. It is the latter method that is used in practice. A rotating wheel with adjustable sectors that decreases the amount of radiation is placed between the lamp and the lens system through which light is admitted from the source. The amount of light received from the source is reduced by a ratio determined by the size of the sectors. A rather complex formula based on the Planck radiation equation (see THERMODYNAMICS) and the sector wheel ratio are used in the extrapolation equation.

Table 2. SECONDARY POINTS

Equilibrium state	International Practical Temperature °K	°C
Triple point of normal hydrogen	13.956	−259.194
Boiling point of normal hydrogen	20.397	−252.753
Triple point of neon	24.555	−248.595
Triple point of nitrogen	63.148	−210.002
Boiling point of nitrogen	77.348	−195.802
Sublimation point of carbon dioxide	194.674	−78.476
Freezing point of mercury	234.288	−38.862
Ice point (water)	273.15	0
Triple point of phenoxy-benzene	300.02	26.87
Triple point of benzoic acid	395.52	122.37
Freezing point of indium	429.784	156.634
Freezing point of bismuth	544.592	271.442
Freezing point of cadmium	594.258	321.108
Freezing point of lead	600.652	327.502
Boiling point of mercury	629.81	356.66
Boiling point of sulfur	717.824	444.674
Freezing point of the copper-aluminum eutectic	821.38	548.23
Freezing point of antimony	903.89	630.74
Freezing point of aluminum	933.52	660.37
Freezing point of copper	1357.6	1084.5
Freezing point of nickel	1728	1455
Freezing point of cobalt	1767	1494
Freezing point of palladium	1827	1554
Freezing point of platinum	2045	1772
Freezing point of rhodium	2236	1963
Freezing point of iridium	2720	2447
Temperature of melting tungsten	3660	3387

Adapted from Metrologia, vol. 5, pp. 35–44, 1969.

Below 13.81° K there is no international scale. The U. S. National Bureau of Standards has devised and maintains a National Scale for the United States using various instruments. Between 20° K and 2° K a resistance thermometer, using a semiconductor material (doped germanium) as the resistor, is the accepted standard. Between 5° K and 1° K the vapor pressure of helium with a mass of 3 (^{3}He) or 4 (^{4}He) is used as the standard thermometer. Below 1° K to about 10 millidegree K (0.010° K) the magnetic susceptibility of cerium-magnesium-nitrate (CMN) is the accepted thermometric method. The susceptibility of CMN is the ratio of its magnetization to the magnetic field imposed.

The National Bureau of Standards, along with other calibration laboratories, uses a number of secondary calibration points (Table 2). These reproducible temperatures are adequate for most industrial and laboratory processes and allow calibration of thermometers in an easier and less expensive manner. Further refinements will undoubtedly be made in years to come to suit changing practical needs and the increasingly more secure understanding of the nature of heat.

Roger Hahn
University of California, Berkeley
Pierre M. Hahn
University of California, Los Angeles

Bibliography

Belcher, W. E., Jr., and others, *Temperature Measurement* (Metals Park, Ohio, 1956).
Comptes Rendues Neuvième Conférence Générale des Poids et Mesures (Paris 1948).
Hall, John A., *The Measurement of Temperature* (London 1966).
Herzfeld, Charles M., ed., *Temperature: Its Measurement and Control in Science and Industry,* vol. 3, part 1 (New York 1962).
"The International Practical Temperature Scale of 1968," *Metrologia,* vol. 5, pp. 35–44, 1969.
King, Allen L., *Thermophysics* (San Francisco 1962)
Weber, Robert L., *Temperature Measurement and Control* (1941).

TEMPERATURE, Body. Animals can be divided into two groups based on how their body temperature is regulated. The *poikilotherms,* or cold-blooded animals, such as insects, snakes, and fish, have essentially the same temperature as their surroundings. The *homeotherms,* or warm-blooded animals—the birds and mammals—have automatic physiological mechanisms that regulate their body temperature, maintaining it at a precise set point. In cats, dogs, and many farm animals the set point ranges from 100° to 103° F (37.8°–39.4° C), and in horses, elephants, and monkeys from 96° to 101° F (35.6°–38.3° C). In humans it lies between 98° and 99° F (36.7°–37.2° C), the average being 98.6° F (37° C). In women, normal fluctuations reflect different stages of the menstrual cycle.

Man's body temperature is maintained by very precise, powerful, and complex mechanisms that are dominated by a small sensory structure—the "human thermostat"—in the front portion of the brain's hypothalamus. Temperatures taken in the mouth or rectum have been used as indicators of disease for more than a century. Now, the temperature of the thermostat itself can be obtained from the eardrum.

Cooling Mechanisms. When the thermostat's temperature rises above the set point, special heat-sensitive neurons in it send impulses to the skin's sweat glands and blood vessels. The sweat glands, when stimulated, produce more sweat, which evaporates and cools the body surface. When the blood vessels are stimulated, they widen and carry larger amounts of blood from the internal organs to the skin surface. As the blood passes near the skin surface it becomes cooler. The frequency at which the heat-sensitive neurons fire is directly related to the temperature of the thermostat (proportional control). The higher the temperature over the set point, the faster the firing of the neurons. When the body temperature starts to fall, the rate of firing decreases.

Warming Mechanisms. When the temperature falls below the set point, the body responds by shivering, a muscular activity that increases the production of body heat. This response is triggered by cold-sensitive neurons in the skin, firing impulses to another brain center. From this center, which is in the back portion of the hypothalamus, impulses are sent to the muscles responsible for shivering. This action is strictly controlled by the thermostat, which continuously fires inhibiting impulses to the second center as long as the body temperature remains above the set point. Only when the temperature falls below the set point do these inhibiting impulses stop, allowing the second center to induce shivering.

When the body temperature is very low or when the body is exposed to low temperatures over long periods of time, special cold-sensitive neurons in the thermostat may produce mild shivering or stimulate the pituitary, adrenal, and thyroid glands. These glands are capable of increasing the body's metabolic rate.

Fever. When a person has a fever, his normal set point has been shifted upward by the action of certain substances (pyrogens) on the heat-sensitive neurons of the thermostat. Antipyretic drugs, such as aspirin, restore the action of the neurons.

T. H. Benzinger, M. D.
Director, Bioenergetics Laboratory
Naval Medical Research Institute, Bethesda, Md.

TEMPERATURE-HUMIDITY INDEX (THI), formerly known as the "discomfort index," is a measure of the discomfort experienced in hot weather. People begin to feel discomfort when the THI goes above 70, and the majority are uncomfortable when it exceeds 75. THI values in the 80's bring a risk of heat exhaustion.

The index is based on the air temperature and the temperature of a wet-bulb thermometer—a well-ventilated thermometer that has a moistened cloth on its bulb. The latter temperature, which depends on both air temperature and relative humidity, represents the lowest temperature to which the skin can be cooled by evaporation of perspiration. The sum of the two temperatures, in degrees Fahrenheit, is multiplied by 0.4, and the number 15 is added to the product. For example, a temperature of 90° F (32.2° C) and a wet-bulb temperature of 80° F (26.7° C), corresponding to a relative humidity of 65%, give a THI of 83.

The THI is reported daily in summer by local offices of the U. S. Weather Bureau. Forecasts enable power companies to anticipate the demand for electric power to run air conditioners.

JAMES E. MILLER
New York University

TEMPERATURE INVERSION. See AIR POLLUTION; INVERSION.

TEMPERATURE SENSE. See TOUCH.

TEMPERING. See GLASS—*Glassmaking* (Tempering); STEEL—*Steel Technology* (Heat Treatment).

TEMPEST, The, a dramatic romance by William Shakespeare, first published in the Folio of 1623. There was a court performance at Whitehall on Nov. 1, 1611, and it was among the entertainments for the betrothal and marriage of James I's daughter Elizabeth in the winter of 1612–1613. Since *The Tempest* as it stands is relatively short and contains a masque suitable for such festivities, it may well be that the Folio form represents the text as arranged for court production.

No direct source for the play has been discovered, but for details of the storm and the island Shakespeare went to a recent event, the Bermuda shipwreck of the *Sea Adventure* in 1609, accounts of which had reached England in 1610. The dramatist's use of these materials provides a link with the New World for *The Tempest,* though his "uninhabited island" is not Bermuda but fancifully Mediterranean. The play therefore must have been written in 1610–1611.

The plot is a simple, romantic story of events arranged by a magician to further a revenge that better thoughts convert into a reconciliation. It is a story of love at first sight, only temporarily crossed, and of spirits and a monster and of connivers, sober and comic. The play is enlivened by music and song, dance, and spectacle. After the apparently authentic shipwreck that opens the play, the action, which takes place on an island, is fantasy.

Most of the characters tend to be types, but Caliban and Ariel are remarkable creations. Caliban is a complex embodiment of earth and water. Ariel is an embodiment of air and fire. Both are altogether believable in our willing suspension of disbelief.

There has long been a tendency to interpret the play as allegory. Certainly Shakespeare's characters raise questions about the treatment of aborigines, the nature of ideal government, the viability of the "brave new world" of innocent wonder—questions of responsibility and forgiveness and freedom. There are suggestive images, symbols, and concepts in profusion, enough to provide various responses. But *The Tempest* stands on its own feet as a romantic tragicomedy, and critics who try to make it something vast and momentous or, on the other hand, autobiographic and personal succeed only in distorting or destroying its artistic beauty and poetic charm.

Until the 20th century the stage history of *The Tempest* had been one of alteration. It was imitated by John Fletcher and Philip Massinger in *The Sea Voyage* (1622), adapted by John Dryden and Sir William Davenant (1667), and made into operas by Thomas Shadwell (1674) and Henry Purcell (1695). William Charles Macready restored the play in 1838 at Covent Garden. Charles Kean (1857) and Sir Herbert Beerbohm Tree (1904) emphasized spectacle. Modern productions have demonstrated that what was once thought a play so undramatic as to require adaptation or embellishment is delightful in the theater in its own right.

ROBERT HAMILTON BALL
Queens College,
City University of New York

Further Reading: James, David Gwilym, *The Dream of Prospero* (New York 1967); Wilson, John Dover, *The Meaning of the Tempest* (Newcastle-upon-Tyne, England, 1936).

TEMPLAR, Knights. See KNIGHTS TEMPLAR.

TEMPLE, Frederick (1821–1902), English archbishop of Canterbury from 1896 to 1902. Temple was born on Nov. 30, 1821, in Santa Maura in the Ionian Islands, where his father, an army officer, was stationed. He graduated from Oxford University with high honors in 1842, and was ordained in 1846. From 1842 to 1848 he was a fellow and tutor of Balliol College Oxford, and from 1848 to 1858 was involved in the training of teachers. He served as headmaster of Rugby School from 1858 to 1869. His paper *The Education of the World* in the volume *Essays and Reviews* (1860) caused him to be attacked for his liberal theology.

Temple's formal election after nomination to the bishopric of Exeter in 1869 was opposed, but the cathedral chapter accepted him by a vote of 13 to 6. At Exeter he devoted himself to the pastoral work of the diocese, and he secured a separate bishopric for Cornwall in 1875. In 1876 he married Beatrice Lascelles. Among their children was William Temple, who became archbishop of Canterbury.

In 1885, Frederick Temple was translated to the diocese of London, and in 1896 became archbishop of Canterbury. He organized the Fourth Lambeth Conference of Anglican Bishops in 1897, marking the 1,300th anniversary of St. Augustine's coming to England. His published works include the Bampton Lectures at Oxford in 1884, which were entitled *The Relations Between Religion and Science.* Temple died in London, Dec. 23, 1902.

EDWARD R. HARDY
Cambridge University

SHIRLEY TEMPLE BLACK

SHIRLEY TEMPLE in the 1934 film *Baby Take a Bow*, at the height of her career as a leading child star.

TEMPLE, Shirley (1928–), American film actress and political figure, who as a child star was one of motion pictures' greatest money-makers and an international celebrity. Shirley Jane Temple was born in Santa Monica, Calif., on April 23, 1928, and began her motion picture career at the age of 4. In her first feature starring role, in *Stand Up and Cheer* (1934), she sang *Baby, Take a Bow,* which immediately made her famous. In *Bright Eyes* (also 1934), for which she received a special Academy Award, she introduced her best-known song, *On The Good Ship Lollipop.*

Her 54 curls and her dimples, gay brown eyes, and vivacious personality seemed to be what Depression-ridden America needed. From 1934 to 1938 she was rushed into a series of enormously successful films, including *Little Miss Marker, The Little Colonel, Captain January, Heidi,* and *Little Miss Broadway. The Little Princess* (1939) is considered by many to be her best film. As she grew up, Miss Temple found it increasingly difficult to obtain suitable roles, and she retired from the screen at 21.

As Mrs. Charles A. Black, the wife of a California businessman, she became active in local Republican politics and in 1967 ran unsuccessfully for the U.S. House of Representatives. In 1969 she was appointed as a U.S. delegate to the UN General Assembly.

HOWARD SUBER
University of California, Los Angeles

TEMPLE, Sir William (1628–1699), English diplomat and author. He was born in London and educated at Emmanuel College, Cambridge University. In 1648, en route to France, he met Dorothy Osborne, whose witty letters, written to him from 1652 to 1654, became famous. They were married in 1655.

Temple's first diplomatic mission was to the bishop of Münster, the ally of England in the Second Dutch War. Temple is best known as the architect of the Triple Alliance (1668) between England, Holland, and Sweden. Later he was posted both to Brussels and The Hague and had the deep trust of William III of Orange. Temple wrote many books of essays and memoirs and was the patron of Jonathan Swift. He died at Moor Park, Surrey, on Jan. 27, 1699.

MAURICE ASHLEY
University of Loughborough, England

TEMPLE, William (1881–1944), English theologian and philosopher and archbishop of Canterbury from 1942 to 1944. The son of Frederick Temple, William Temple was born in Exeter, Devonshire, on Oct. 15, 1881. He graduated from Oxford University in 1902. While a fellow and lecturer at Queens College he developed what was to be a lifetime interest in social reform. He was ordained in 1906. In 1910 he became headmaster of Repton School and in 1914 rector of St. James', Piccadilly, London. In 1917 he resigned his parish to work for the Life and Liberty Movement, which sought greater freedom for the Church of England and led to the establishment of the Church Assembly in 1919. Temple was successively a canon of Westminster Abbey (1919–1920), bishop of Manchester (1921–1928), and archbishop of York (1929–1942).

He continued his work in philosophical theology with *Mens Creatrix* (1917), *Christus Veritas* (1924), and the Gifford Lectures, *Nature, Man, and God* (1934). His genius in guiding conferences was manifested in the Conference on Politics, Economics, and Citizenship at Birmingham in 1924 and in many gatherings of the ecumenical movement. In 1937, at Edinburgh, he presided at the Second World Conference on Faith and Order, one of the chief sources of the World Council of Churches.

In 1942, Temple became archbishop of Canterbury. As primate of England he opened communication between the Church of England and the Vatican. Archbishop Temple died in Westgate-on-Sea, Kent, on Oct. 26, 1944.

EDWARD R. HARDY, *Cambridge University*

TEMPLE is a city in central Texas, in Bell county, 35 miles (56 km) south of Waco. Temple's industries include railroad shops and the manufacture of steel and aluminum products, farm machinery, precision tools, plastic building materials, furniture, leather goods, clothing, and cottonseed products. Situated in a cotton and grain area, Temple is the seat of the Texas Soil Conservation Service and the Blackland Experiment Station and is the Texas headquarters of the Farmers Home Administration (FHA).

Temple's excellent climate has made it a hospital center that includes Scott and White Hospital, King's Daughters' Hospital, Veterans Administration Hospital, and Santa Fe Hospital.

Temple Junior College and the locally organized cultural activities center are in the city. The city was founded in 1881 by the Gulf, Colorado and Santa Fe Railroad and named for B. M. Temple, its chief construction engineer. It was incorporated in 1882 and adopted the city-manager form of government in 1922. Population: 33,431.

HALLIE MILLER, *Temple Public Library*

LAWRENCE L. SMITH, FROM PHOTO RESEARCHERS

INDIAN TEMPLE of Kandāriya Mahādeo at Khajurāho, Northern Hindu style, set on a terrace with clustered towers and bands of carved divinities, about 1000 A. D.

TEMPLE, a structure made sacred by the presence of a deity or holy symbol. The Latin *templum*, from which the word "temple" is derived, merely signifies a sacred enclosure; the essential element of sanctity is there but not the idea of edifice. Yet the word "temple" instantly conjures up an image of a building at once splendid, monumental, and holy, preeminently the Temple of Jerusalem, described in the Bible as the dwelling place of the Lord. A full definition must take account not only of a society's religious institutions but also of cultural, political, and economic factors.

Although Christian houses of God might be considered temples, the word is not usually applied to them, except for Mormon temples. Muslim mosques are not dwellings of the divinity but places of prayer. See CATHEDRALS AND CHURCHES; ISLAMIC ART AND ARCHITECTURE.

In time the word "temple" has gone far beyond its original meaning. In the Middle Ages a Christian military order, the Knights Templar, derived their name from the fact that their headquarters were next to the site of the Temple of Jerusalem. Two English legal societies, the Middle Temple and the Inner Temple, were so called from their original location in the house of the English branch of the Knights Templar, or Temple. The word "temple" also came to be appropriated for secular buildings of size, splendor, and lofty purpose; for example, Masonic temples and temples of science and knowledge. By analogy, St. Paul considered the human body a temple of the Holy Spirit (I Corinthians 6:19), and Shakespeare, in *Macbeth*, likened the king's body to the Lord's temple.

Freestanding Temples. The great majority of the world's temples are freestanding structures, as distinguished from the few cut out of rock. In the New World, pre-Columbian temples have not been sufficiently studied to permit a general discussion of their structures and purposes. In the Old World, however, temples have been extensively analyzed. They seem to have incorporated six architectural elements considered characteristic of a sacred edifice—elements that, however varied or disguised, remain constant from region to region.

Basic Architectural Elements. (1) The *enclosure* is a wall or other clear marker separating sacred from secular space. Within it is the area sufficiently sacred for processions and circumambulations around the holy of holies and yet not too sacred for laymen, the audience essential for religious festivals. (2) The *gate* is the defined approach, the portal permitting movement between secular and sacred space. (3) The *altar* is the raised platform for ritual sacrifices. Monumentally increased in size, it becomes the terrace on which the temple itself is built. (4) The *tower* is a structure representing the mountain on whose summit gods and humans met, as in ancient Mesopotamian belief, or a specific mountain of cosmological meaning, such as Mt. Sinai or the Buddhist Mt. Meru. (5) The *pillar* is a column standing within the enclosure, either singly or in numbers. According to Buddhist and Hindu belief, for example, the pillar keeps heaven and earth apart to provide space in which humans can live. (6) The *cella* is the holy of holies—the most sacred place contained within the sanctuary, or temple proper, where the image of the deity or his symbol is kept.

These elements are described with special clarity in accounts of the Hebrew Temple in Jerusalem.

Temple of Jerusalem. King Solomon built the first Temple of Jerusalem to house the Ark holding the sacred Tablets of the Law, which the Lord had given to Moses. Solomon chose for a site Mt. Moriah, where his father, David, had offered sacrifice. He obtained timber and skilled Canaanite workmen from Hiram, King of Tyre, and stone from local quarries. The construction took seven years (967–960 B. C.).

Interpretations of Biblical accounts vary. All agree, however, that the temple proper, of dressed stone, was about 100 feet (30 meters) long, 35 feet (11 meters) wide, and 50 feet (15 meters) high and that the Temple faced east. The exterior wall was divided into three tiers of chambers used for storing the Temple treasure and ceremonial equipment and as working space.

Within this ring of rooms was a building divided into two sections. At the rear was the Holy of Holies (cella), a windowless cube containing the Ark. Over the Ark two cherubim of olive wood stretched their wings from wall to wall. According to some authorities, the room contained an altar for burning incense, a table for the 12 loaves of shewbread, 10 candlesticks, and other ritual items, all of solid gold. Olive-wood doors, gold chains, and a multicolored linen curtain separated the Holy of Holies from the front section of the Temple, the rectangular Holy Place. The Holy Place was lined with cedar, and the floor, doorposts, and doors were overlaid or inlaid with gold. Every surface was carved with cherubim, palms, or flowers, creating an Edenlike garden for the abode of God. The room was entered from a porch, which, in the view of some scholars, soared to a high tower.

Like a casket for this mighty jewel, the Court of the Priests surrounded the sanctuary. Before the porch stood two pillars, 38 feet (12 meters) high. A little to the southeast was the "molten sea," an enormous bronze basin of water for ritual cleansing, borne on 12 bronze oxen. Near the porch stood a brazen altar for burnt offerings. Outside the Court of the Priests was the walled Great Court containing a complex of buildings including the royal palace.

This joining of temple-complex and palace inside one enclosure expresses the Biblical use of the word "house" to mean both temple and palace. Nevertheless, sacred space was sharply demarcated from secular. Indeed, degrees of sanctity were clearly marked off. Only the High Priest could enter the Holy of Holies, and only ritually clean priests and their assistants could enter the Holy Place. Although worshipers might bring their offerings into the Court of the Priests, they generally remained in the Great Court, where the adult male population gathered on each of the three annual pilgrimage festivals. Solomon's Temple occupied a unique place in the life as well as the religion of the Hebrews. It was at once the House of the Lord and in close proximity to the seat of secular power, the visible symbol of Hebrew social and national unity.

The Temple was destroyed by the Babylonian ruler Nebuchadnezzar in 587 B. C., later rebuilt twice, and then utterly demolished in 70 A. D. by the Romans, who also exiled the Jews. At a time when they had lost both the Temple and Jerusalem as physical entities, the idea of Temple and Jerusalem took tenacious hold in their memories and hopes. As exiles they would erect no temple, because they believed that, although God was everywhere, only Jerusalem was pure enough for His house. Out of this situation evolved the synagogue for the public reading of His word. Therefore, personal worship in present-day synagogues, even where some more liberal ones call themselves "temples," differs radically in character from the formalized sacrifices once conducted in the Temple.

The Temple of Jerusalem also survived as an allegory in the Christian mind. Jesus spoke of destroying and rebuilding the Temple in reference to his own death and resurrection. Medieval Christian theologians spoke of Solomon's Temple as a prefiguration of the Heavenly City, the Celestial Jerusalem. The creators of the Gothic cathedrals conceived of the Temple as the prototype of their soaring sanctuaries.

Rock-cut Temples. Distinguished from the shrines of Paleolithic man in natural caves are the architecturally planned temples of historic man hewn from living rock. The earliest example is Egyptian—the temple cut by Rameses II in the imposing cliffs at Abu Simbel in the 13th century B. C. India has the greatest number (2d century B. C.–7th century A. D.), serving Buddhism, Jainism, and Hinduism. China has Buddhist rock-cut temples, such as those of Yünkang and Lungmen, dating from the 5th and 6th centuries A. D. Christian rock-cut chapels in Gorëme, Turkey, were made between the 9th and the 11th century A. D. There are also many Coptic rock-cut churches in Ethiopia—that at Beta Medhane is the largest and noblest of the Lalibela group (13th century).

A characteristic feature of rock-cut temples is that although they are carved out of living rock and are thus freed from all the constructional elements essential to freestanding buildings, these elements are faithfully reproduced. For example, in the Karli cave-temple in western India (about 50 B. C.), the columns are carefully carved to resemble the local wooden house-posts set in pots filled with water to prevent white ants from attacking the wood. Similarly the ribbed, vaulted ceiling recalls a bamboo house roof sloped to shed the monsoon rains. Such embellishments have no structural function.

Some rock-cut temples may have relatively small, plain interiors, like Abu Simbel's. Others may be large and richly ornamented and include the six essential elements of freestanding temples. Thus the Hindu temple-complex Kailasanatha at Ellora covers an area equal to that of the Parthenon and took 200 years (about 770–970) to build. In such sanctuaries the work is done from the top down. First, rock cutters rough out the contours. Then the sculptors refine, carve, and smooth. Everything is precisely planned to make the several parts a unified whole.

ANCIENT WORLD

Mesopotamia. The city-states of Mesopotamia were the earliest communities to develop the temple-complex. In addition to its characteristic religious components, such as a cella containing a divinity on a plinth, there were also scores of storerooms and workrooms to accommodate the economic, social, and literary activities in which the temple was involved. Our knowledge of these buildings is derived from archaeological sites and written data. Ritual texts, myths, and prayers give the names, powers, and histories of the deities housed in these early temples, but they fall short of explaining the beliefs expressed in liturgical action or the ambiguities of oracular and augural pronouncements. The faith held by the Mesopotamians is as dead and remote from our understanding as the ruins of their deserted temples. Analogies from living religions with roots in a Mesopotamian past, such as Judaism, are worthless or suspect because the spiritual climate has changed.

Socioeconomic Function. Legal and financial records kept by the temples, however, indicate that they were economic institutions, which played a vital role in an emerging urban economy. The temple—like its mirror image, the palace—owned large estates, including grainfields, date palm groves, river land for irrigation and fishing, and outlying pasture. The temple accumulated both the products of its own estates and offerings from worshipers. This wealth was disposed of in three ways: (1) the finest produce was reserved for the care and feeding of the god's image in a daily ceremony and was then sent to the palace for royal consumption; (2) rations were issued to all those engaged in the temple's business; (3) staples were stored.

In addition, the temple was a redistribution center, ritualizing interchange among specialized production groups. This relation is suggested by the list of 100 herdsmen in one temple inventory and a huge pile of fishbones found in another temple, indicating that herdsmen and fishermen, through the temple, exchanged their products for goods they lacked. The temple was also a manufacturing center, where female slaves wove cloth for local use and foreign trade. Officials called accountants or priests oversaw these activities, and scribes kept careful records of receipts and payments.

Architecture. In a land lacking both wood and stone, Mesopotamian builders created splendid temples out of the earth and clay available. Originally, the walls were of rammed earth, and the long, flat, drab surfaces were brightly painted. Then the Mesopotamians invented baked clay brick, molded to standard sizes, which enabled them to build higher, lighter walls and gain interior space. They gave rhythm and interest to the long, monotonous, horizontal lines by building terraces, intricate recesses, and massive buttresses, often studded with painted clay cones. Eventually they sheathed the walls with mosaics of glazed bricks arranged in stylized designs. The magnificence of this architecture enhanced the stirring religious rituals performed before it. The ground plan in some temple-complexes heightened the sense of divine mystery. Avoiding axial symmetry, the architects placed the doorways of various courts and rooms so as to keep the image of the god invisible until at last, after a sharp right-angle turn, the worshiper saw the divinity in the cella.

Dominating the flat river valley of Mesopotamia were the *ziggurats* (towers). Their presence distinguished the temple-complex from the palace. A ziggurat was a man-made, multiterraced mountain of earth faced with painted plaster or glazed brick. Steep stairs or ramps laced the exterior and led, according to most authorities, to a small shrine for the god on top. The Hebrews, influenced by Mesopotamian temple design, remembered the ziggurat with consternation in the Biblical account of the Tower of Babel.

Egypt. About the same time that the Mesopotamian city-states were building temples of earth and clay, which have long since eroded away, Egypt was creating mighty temples of stone that have been victorious over time and abuse. Almost all the temples that remain from the period before about 1500 B. C. are mortuary buildings dedicated to individual divine pharaohs. Many from after that date are dedicated to gods. The development of Egyptian temples can be divided into three periods: the Old Kingdom, or Age of the Pyramids (2664–2155 B. C.), when the civilization was brilliant and exuberant; the Middle Kingdom (2052–1786 B. C.), a renascence after a time of troubles, when the first temple at Deir el-Bahari was built; and the New Kingdom, or Empire (1554–1075 B. C.), an age of expansion that produced the Temple of Amon at Karnak and the colossal statues at Abu Simbel.

JULIEN BRYAN, FROM PHOTO RESEARCHERS

EGYPTIAN TEMPLE: The Ramesseum, at Thebes, hypostyle hall and statues of Osiris, about 1250 B. C.

All the temples proclaim the same faith: that the god-king, the pharaoh, was the only contact between men and the gods. Death did not affect him. He who had ensured order, security, and prosperity while ruling this world would continue, after death, as sun-god to watch over his land from the next world. The lavish provision for his well-being in earthly life was extended to include his afterlife. Although changes in temple architecture expressed a practical shift of political and economic power from the central control of the pharaoh to the hands of a bureaucracy of priests and officials, theological dogma did not change. Virtually everything in official Egyptian life continued to serve the mortuary cult of the pharaoh.

Architecture. As brick architecture was the invention of the Mesopotamians, stone architecture was that of the Egyptians. Excellent stone was available in quarries along the Nile. Stonemasons, encouraged by a long tradition of small-scale work in stone, quickly learned to create monumental stone pyramids and temples, cutting, dressing, polishing, and handling blocks many tons in weight.

For a model, builders had the desert cliffs along the Nile, with their familiar and aesthetically satisfying sloping line. They were also influenced by the traditional dwellings, which, flat-topped for a rainless climate, were fashioned out of bundles of reeds, tied top and bottom, and smeared with mud to make them rigid. Out of such native forms and materials came the charac-

HERBERT LANKS, FROM BLACK STAR

Greek temple in the Doric style, the Theseum, Athens, with porches and colonnade, 5th century B. C.

teristic slope of the pyramids, pylons (gates formed by two truncated pyramids), and walls. The reed bundles were translated into stone columns, and their tufted and flowered heads were reproduced as floral capitals—the origin of the classical orders of columns. To preserve the mystery of the hidden cella and bring light into the enclosed interiors, the Egyptians devised the clerestory.

Stone architecture, associated with ideas of permanence and glory, spread from Egypt. It influenced the Canaanites, who built Solomon's Temple, and later the Greeks. Christian crypt burial may have derived from Egyptian burial chambers. It is important to note both the continuity of ideas and their modification to suit cultural and environmental needs.

Pyramids and Related Mortuary Temples. The Egyptians of the Old Kingdom built the pyramids, massive tombs to safeguard the body of the pharaoh and his grave furnishings, and mortuary temples for the elaborate ceremonials essential to his well-being in the next world. They also built the temple to the sun god, Re, at Heliopolis. Its cella contained the *benben,* a small pyramidal granite stone on which Re was believed to have appeared in the form of a phoenix.

Of the some 80 pyramids known to have been built, the largest, finest, and most famous are the three at Giza (near Cairo), on the west bank of the Nile. All are oriented to the four points of the compass and are built with an extraordinary precision, considering the contemporary level of mathematics and technology. All terminated in a benben, symbol that the dead pharaoh was indeed the sun-god. The Great Pyramid of Krufu (Cheops) had a square base, 756 feet (230 meters) on each side, and originally rose 481 feet (146 meters). It was built of solid blocks of stone with a narrow entrance corridor leading to a small, cunningly concealed, granite-lined burial chamber.

Each pyramid dominated a complex of buildings for handling the lengthy funeral rites. The complex included the "Purification Tent," where the royal corpse was washed; the "House of Embalmment," where it was mummified; and the "Valley Building," where the dead king was magically enabled to "eat" and "see." Lastly, connected by a causeway to the other buildings, was the mortuary temple itself, a kind of commodious anteroom to the pyramid. It contained five areas for five cultic practices: (1) an entrance hall; (2) an open court beyond which only priests could advance; (3) a room with five niches holding five statues for the pharaoh; (4) five storerooms stocked with reserve food, in case the priests neglected their daily offerings; and (5) at the very end, closest to the pyramid, a cella.

This complex of ancillary buildings led in a straight line to the pyramid itself, symbol of the supremacy of the pharaoh. As the broad base of the pyramid carried on high the benben as its capstone, so the masses of peasants composing Egyptian society supported the pharaoh at their head.

Deir el-Bahari. Egypt's second notable style of mortuary temple is embodied in the terraced temple built by Mentuhotep II (Nebhepetre) in the 21st century B. C. For a site he chose a deep bay in the cliffs at Deir el-Bahari on the west bank of the Nile, opposite Thebes. The earlier elements of a temple-complex were used—including the Valley Building, causeway, mortuary temple, and pyramid—but so arranged and subordinated to fresh designs as to revolutionize the style. Thus, for example, the causeway became an avenue almost ¾ mile (1 km) long, lined with hundreds of statues of the king in the guise of the mummy of the god Osiris. It led from the river across the desert to a vast enclosure planted in rows of trees. Beyond that it became a ramp leading up to a terrace supported on a stately colonnade partly hewn out of the cliff. From the terrace rose a large, square building, whose colonnaded sides echoed those below and on which, mounted on a high podium, a modest pyramid was built. The pyramid still symbolized the soaring supremacy of the god-king, but now there were the colonnades, equally evident and symbolizing the hierarchy of bureaucrats supporting the pharaoh.

About 600 years later, in the 15th century B. C., Queen Hatshepsut took this temple as the noble model for her larger, strikingly beautiful mortuary temple, which she placed nearby. The Queen was a great builder and, with Senmut, her architect and minister of public works, revitalized architecture. She was the first to have a sarcophagus carved out of stone, although it faithfully reproduced the traditional wooden model. She added to the Temple of Amon at Karnak two obelisks (mammoth pillars topped by a benben), a shrine, and the Eighth Pylon.

Karnak and Other Temples. The Temple of Amon at Karnak (Thebes) has been called "the most massive temple of all time." In addition, it is connected to the temple complex at Luxor—the destination of the god's annual ritual outing—by an avenue 2 miles (3 km) long, lined by ram-headed sphinxes. Amon ("Hidden One") began as an invisible Theban air deity and emerged out of obscurity when his city became the capital of a reunited nation during the Middle Kingdom. He was joined to Re, the sun-god, and as Amon-Re became the supreme deity during the empire. His temple was 20 centuries in building. By Hellenistic times it was a crowded, rambling conglomeration of buildings stretching over many acres.

Like other temples of the period, that of Amon was entered by pylon gates, before which stood obelisks and statues. Among the immense ruins is a series of hypostyle (column-filled) halls, including the spectacular and awe-inspiring Great Hypostyle Hall completed by Rameses II in the 13th century B. C. Its dense grove of soaring, 80-foot (24 meter) columns carried 60-ton architrave blocks above their capitals of papyrus buds and flowers. Beyond lay the cella, holding the sacred boat that carried the image of Amon in processions. In the wall was a smaller room containing the image itself.

Rameses II had the imperial instinct for creating larger-than-life forms. The Ramesseum, his mortuary temple west of Thebes, had a 1,000-ton colossus of the pharaoh in the first court. His temple to the sun-god at Abu Simbel, far up the Nile, had four 63-foot (19-meter) figures of Rameses seated in front of the facade. Unlike the hidden burial chambers in the pyramids, this temple was a series of pillared halls extending into the cliff about 185 feet (56 meters).

The innovation of colossi spread far and wide. The Roman conquerors of Egypt adopted the idea to portray their emperors, who proclaimed themselves divine. From Rome the idea was carried eastward to the Greco-Roman settlements in northwest India, where, later, under the Kushana empire, the Buddha was first carved in human form. In Asian countries the Buddha, not the ruler, was portrayed monumentally—for example, the figure carved from a cliff at Bamian in Afghanistan; the statues in the rock-cut temples at Yünkang and Lungmen in China; the stone Buddha at Sawankhalok in Thailand; and the gilded bronze Great Buddha (Daibutsu) at Nara, Japan.

Greece. The earliest known Greek temples, simple buildings made of wattle-covered split tree trunks or sun-dried brick and wood, date from the 8th century B. C. Probably from Egyptian artisans and examples the Greeks adopted basic structural forms and learned to use the fine marble with which their country was well supplied. By the 7th century B. C., they had established the characteristics of their temples.

Generally the Greek temple faced east. Its heart was the *naos* (cella), a windowless rectangular room housing the image of the god. It was entered and dimly lighted by a single door that opened from the *pronaos* (porch). The *opisthodome* (another porch, back to back with the cella), sometimes harbored another room that held the temple treasure. Both porches were supported by columns. Sometimes a *peristyle* (colonnade) surrounded the cella and porches to provide a covered space for circumambulations. The entire structure stood on a *stylobate* (a low, three-stepped terrace), which lifted it above the ground level and made the columned ambulatory accessible from all sides. Outside the temple, on a line with the door of the cella, stood the altar. Altar and temple lay within a sacred precinct in which other shrines and votive images were placed—all enclosed and entered by a portal.

Thus, except for the pillar and tower, all the elements found in the Mesopotamian and Egyptian temples were present. The fact that Greek temples were not part of a complex is, perhaps, a reflection of the difference in the Greeks' attitude toward the gods. For although the Greek temple borrowed Egyptian forms and techniques, the Greek genius used them to state Greek values and attitudes. The flat-topped Egyptian temples suited the hot, rainless Nile Valley, and the huge complexes are evidence of a society that eventually became spent, static, and priest-dominated. In like manner, the pitch-roofed Greek temples were adapted to the rainy, hilly, wooded land, as their isolation suited priest-free citizens possessing an eager, questioning spirit.

The Parthenon captures the high moment in Greek life, thought, and artistic accomplishment that followed the Greek victory over the Persians. On the Acropolis, a hill in Athens, the architects Ictinus and Callicrates and the sculptor Phidias created a temple that a scholar has called the most perfect example of beauty embodied in architecture. Greek temples are to be found all over the Greek world. Those in Sicily and in southern Italy at Syracuse, Segesta, Agrigentum, and Paestum, as well as the superb Theseum (the Temple of Hephaestus in Athens) and the Par-

INDIAN CAVE TEMPLE at Ajanta, carved out of living rock; Buddhist, 2d century B. C.–7th century A. D.

VAN BUCHER, FROM PHOTO RESEARCHERS

GOVERNMENT OF INDIA TOURIST OFFICE

INDIAN STUPA: The Great Stupa at Sanchi, with gate, terrace, mound, and umbrella; about 250 B. C. It is one of the most famous Buddhist monuments.

thenon, have powerful, upthrusting Doric columns with simple round capitals. In Asia Minor, Greek colonists built temples of great size, especially that to Artemis at Ephesus, which had elegantly graceful Ionic columns with volutes (spirals) on the capitals. There were a few round temples, the most famous of which was the Doric temple to Apollo at Delphi.

Rome. The Romans borrowed temple forms from the Greeks, and, like the Greeks, changed their borrowings to suit their own circumstances. The simple domestic altar of early Rome, centered on the hearth and household gods, was gradually magnified to imperial proportions to suit Rome's political expansion. In the process the Roman temple was placed within the forum, the focus of Roman civic life, as though the gods were involved in daily secular transactions. Generally, the major temple was the focal point of the forum, as was the temple to the Deified Caesar in the Roman Forum. Its role was to serve as a background for obligatory official rituals.

The resulting changes seem slight but are significant. No longer was the east-facing temple set apart in a sacred precinct. Rather, its orientation depended on its position in the forum, a position planned to sanctify civic ceremonies. No longer did the low, three-stepped terrace invite the citizen to enter the ambulatory around the cella at any point. Instead, the temple was set on a high podium approached by one flight of steps. The back porch was eliminated to make the cella longer as well as wider, and the portico in front was accented. The columns that had ringed the stylobate were reduced to pilasters along the cella walls. Usually they were of the floridly splendid Corinthian order, which best set off imperial ceremonies.

The temples in Rome itself are either in ruins or altered for Christian worship. Of those that Rome planted throughout its vast empire, one of the most famous and best preserved is the Maison Carrée at Nîmes, France. Others are the spectacular Temple of Bacchus at Baalbek, Lebanon, with its high-soaring columns, and the Temple of the Sun at Palmyra, Syria, each tinged with western Asian influences.

The Roman discovery of concrete (volcanic sand mixed with lime) revolutionized temple architecture by making possible large domes, which freed it from the tyranny of the rectangular box form of post-and-lintel construction. The emperor Hadrian encouraged his architects to explore the potential versatility and strength of concrete in building the Pantheon, completed about 125 A. D. This remarkable structure, dedicated to the myriad deities of Rome, rested on a round podium, 142.5 feet (43.4 meters) in diameter, while its dome soared to an equal, dizzying height and admitted light at the apex through an opening 28 feet (8 meters) in diameter. The Pantheon's glory is not its rich interior of colored stone sheathing, but its breathtakingly large interior space uncluttered by supporting columns—a space created by a framework of sturdy concrete vaults arranged in graduated tiers of diminishing size that carry the dome to its height. The Pantheon is a triumphant development of the form stated in the small round Greek Temple of Apollo at Delphi. It was copied many times, for the new religions of Christianity and Islam, with their congregational worship, required large interior spaces to hold multitudes of the faithful.

INDIA

Indian temples include those of several religions: Hinduism, which accounts for by far the greatest number; Buddhism and Jainism, which were originally reform movements of an early stage of Hinduism; and Sikhism, a relatively recent faith, which draws on Hinduism and Islam. Early temples were probably freestanding structures of wood, but the oldest remaining ones are rock-cut shrines. Buddhist and Jain monks, seeking isolation, carved temples and living quarters out of rock cliffs, as at Bhaja, Karli, and Ajanta (2d century B. C.–7th century A. D.).

Hinduism recovered ground from Buddhism and Jainism from about the 6th century A. D. on. It too produced rock-cut temples, such as those at Badami (6th century) and the Kailasanatha at Ellora (8th–10th centuries). Freestanding stone structures became important when royal patrons wished to build Hindu temples at sites of their own choosing, not at those attractive to monastic communities.

Buddhist. Even earlier than the rock-cut temples are the first *stupas*, or *dagobas*, reliquary structures favored by both Buddhists and Jains. As the ancient Indian grave mound, from which the stupa takes its form, covers the body, so the stupa holds buried in its center a holy relic. The oldest and most famous is the Great Stupa at Sanchi, a huge hemispherical mound of solid masonry begun by Emperor Ashoka (Asoka) about 250 B. C., upon his conversion to Buddhism.

The Great Stupa incorporates the six architectural elements of temples, but they are fused together and endowed with special Indian metaphysical symbolism. A stone railing encircles a space 120 feet (36 meters) in diameter, which serves as a lower ambulatory and recalls the Wheel of Doctrine. Four high *torana* (gateways) outside the railing are oriented to the four points of the compass and represent the Four Noble Truths. Inside the railing a *sopana* (double staircase) leads to a 16-foot-high (5-meter) altar-terrace, which forms an upper ambulatory.

From the terrace rises the 54-foot-high (16-meter) mound, or dome (*anda*, "egg"), corresponding to the sanctuary, which represents the egg-shaped cosmos and also Mt. Meru, home of the gods and central mountain of the universe. Its flattened crest supports a 3-tiered *chatravalis* (umbrella), a mark of royalty, which is here considered an abbreviated tower. The umbrella shaft alone corresponds to the pillar and symbolizes the vertical axis of the cosmos. It is imagined as continuing down to the small reliquary in the cella in the middle of the mound, although actually it does not. Terrace and mound together symbolize Nirvana, the transcendent reality. The total effect is monumental and, except for the intricately carved gates, austere.

As Indian Buddhism expanded outside India, the stupa—symbol and reliquary—changed in size and outline to accommodate alien influences and styles. As a small bas-relief it became the sacred focal point within rock-cut temples. It was also the center of freestanding temples. The Ruanweli dagoba, built by Ashoka's son at Anuradhapura, Ceylon, gives greater mass to the umbrella shaft. A little later, in the larger temples of the Kushana empire, the altar-terrace was taller, and the stupa was repeated in a series of diminishing drums topped by an umbrella of as many as 13 tiers. These were the stupas that Chinese pilgrims described as pagodas.

In the Shwe Dagon at Rangoon, Burma, the spherical mound is stretched into a slim, tapering 370-foot (112-meter) spire. Borobudur ("Many Buddhas") in Java accentuates the flat, horizontal line by a series of superimposed terraces diminishing in size: first five square ones, and then three circular ones with 72 small stupas spaced evenly around them. Finally, 100 feet (30 meters) above the ground, almost like an umbrella shaft, a plain stupa rises.

Jain. Jain temples resemble other Indian temples, except for the four-faced temples, which uniquely express the Jain faith. The images they house are not gods but the Tīrthankaras, 24 men who, in the successive ages of the world, became saints and prophets. They appear as individuals, known, named, and with distinct iconography. The cella of the four-faced temple has four images—either four different Tīrthankaras or four images of the same one—placed back to back. This multiplication necessitates changes in the temple. Instead of a single opening on the dark, mysterious cella, there are four openings from the sunlit courtyard that clearly reveal the four images in their well-lit niches.

The Jains also have extraordinary *tirthas* (places of pilgrimage), temple-cities that are perched on the summits of what they regard as "mountains of immortality." Among the holiest tirthas is Mt. Girnar, on whose summit are more than 100 temples. No human beings live there, and at nightfall, when the pilgrims leave, only the Tīrthankaras remain in their shrines high on the sacred hill.

Sikh. The principal Sikh *gurdwara* (temple) is the Harimandar, the Golden Temple at Amritsar. Built in the 16th century by Ram Das, the fourth of the 10 revered gurus (teachers) of the Sikhs, it was rebuilt by Ranjit Singh, their outstanding political leader, in 1802. This monotheistic faith has no priests, and the temples have no images. They are the hallowed place where the Granth, or "Book," the Sikh scripture, is kept. It is a collection of hymns written or compiled by Arjan, the fifth guru, and may be read in the temple by any believer, man or woman. The Sikhs celebrate the birthdays of the gurus by carrying the Granth through the streets in a great procession.

Hindu. India's Hindu temples reflect a wide spectrum of beliefs and practices, ranging from simple offerings and prayers made to personal

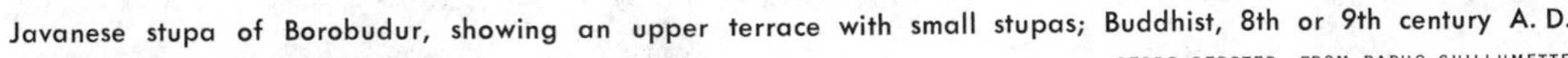

Javanese stupa of Borobudur, showing an upper terrace with small stupas; Buddhist, 8th or 9th century A. D.

GEORG GERSTER, FROM RAPHO GUILLUMETTE

deities to a highly developed system of meditation on abstract principles. Thus each individual seeks his own way to spiritual freedom. The temples, regardless of size, are essentially sanctuaries that enclose the divine image or symbol in a cella. Ritual ablutions make water necessary in the temple—whether it is the holy Ganges used by temples at Varanasi (Benares), a large tank inside the sacred enclosure, or a jar filled with water at the entrance.

The lavishly sculptured and painted mural decorations are meant to be looked at, in the belief that sculpture is the silent voice of theology, teaching the power of the gods. The gods and their spouses, shown as the divine counterparts of ideal human beauty, act out sacred dramas to instruct the heart of the worshiper.

Hindu temples have been divided into two major architectural styles—the Northern, or Indo-Aryan, and the Southern, or Dravidian—though the differences are neither religious nor regional. Temples have also been classified according to the dynasties under which they were built. All, however, have the six prescribed elements.

The enclosure can be a wall, railing, or passageway. The gate can expand into vestibules, galleries, halls, pavilions, and balconies on an altar-terrace. Inevitably all lead to the *vimāna* (sanctuary) and to the door in the east side of the *garbhagṛha* ("womb house," or cella), the small dark cavity within the *vimāna* where the image of the god is. The *vimāna* terminates in a *śikhara* (spire). Sometimes the altar-terrace and the *vimāna* make one unit, which, in truncated form, may be repeated in diminishing size to create a towering structure. The enclosure can be repeated on these levels to mark off degrees of sanctity or to provide a series of ambulatories for worshipers.

Sometimes the pillar or pole is visible in the temple enclosure. Sometimes it is transmuted through the Indian genius for metaphysics into an imaginary pillar, thought of as rising from the ground through the image in the cella and the solid masonry tower above it to the finial. The finial, the supreme point, represents the moment of Release into Nirvana. In the temples dedicated to Shiva, the finial is a trident. In those to Vishnu, it is a disk or wheel.

Northern Style. An outstanding example of the Northern style is the Temple of Kandāriya Mahādeo, the largest and most perfectly realized of the group of temples at Khajurāho in central India, built about 1000 A. D. A high masonry terrace forms its unusual enclosure and frames the temple with ample space on all sides. It is reached by a single flight of steps. The altar-terrace of the temple raises the floor of the sanctuary 28 feet (8 meters) above the secular ground level. A second flight of steep steps leads to an *ardhamaṇḍapa* (entrance portico) and thence into a *maṇḍapa* (assembly hall), to an *antarāla* (vestibule), and finally to the *garbhagrha* (cella). The distinctive feature of this Northern temple is the *śikhara* (spire). That of Kandāriya Mahādeo is 88 feet (27 meters) high. Taut and tenuous, it is given a luxuriant rhythm of the design and distribution of subsidiary towers superimposed on all sides to break the unrelieved mass.

Perhaps the temples at Khajurāho are most famous for their sculptured friezes, which, in parallel lines, follow the alternate projections and recesses of the exterior walls around the entire building. The figures, 650 in number, half life-size and carved in high relief, form an animated, unending procession of delectable divinities, shapely in appearance, exquisite in workmanship, and of inexhaustible interest.

Southern Style. The immense 17th century temple at Madurai, one of the famous, still functioning temples of the Southern style, covers an area 850 feet (259 meters) long and 725 feet (221 meters) wide. It is a kind of double temple with two cellas, one enshrining Shiva, the other his consort. The temple expanded when its ritual became enormously elaborated as Shiva assumed a temporal as well as a spiritual role. This

AMERICAN PHOTOS, FROM BLACK STAR

CHINESE TEMPLE: The Temple of Heaven (rebuilt 1890's), on three circular terraces, from the Temple of Heaven complex, Peking.

JAPANESE TEMPLE: The Great Shrine at Ise to the Shinto goddess Amaterasu, a thatched wooden house periodically rebuilt in ancient Japanese style.

CONSULATE GENERAL OF JAPAN

secular-sacred duality determined the temple's plan. The god and goddess dwell in separate apartments in the innermost precinct, accessible only to priests. But, like royalty emerging from the palace at official festivals, the couple's images are carried through the public sections of the temple complex when they annually celebrate their wedding anniversary, a union signifying cosmic harmony and ensuring the earthly well-being of believers.

Architecturally, the two distinctive features of the Southern style temple are their monumental *gopurams* (gateways) and the profusion of pillars carved with deities and dragons and other grotesque forms. The Madurai temple has 11 extravagantly carved *gopurams*. The four largest are skyscrapers 150 feet (45 meters) high and are placed at the four outside walls. The others, in diminishing height, mark the approaches to the different parts of the interior. The temple also has 2,000 pillars, almost half of them in a huge hypostyle hall. The other half, used to support flat roofs, create vistas of unending colonnades in the vast courts, corridors, and halls. Within the enclosure and visible above the flat roofs, a small *śikhara*, marking Shiva's cella, rises like a golden sceptor.

THE FAR EAST

China. China differs fundamentally from the civilizations of ancient Mesopotamia and the Mediterranean in that it never produced a comprehensive cosmology and dogma to structure religious thought and institutions: neither Confucianism nor Taoism is a religion. Buddhism was an import from India. Underlying these markedly intellectual approaches were the ancient Chinese beliefs in nature gods and ancestor worship. Early ancestral temples, as seen in a site from the Shang dynasty (about 1523–1028 B.C.), were laid out in rows running north and south and focusing on an earthen altar at the north. This arrangement reveals the Chinese instinct for symmetry along an axis, a plan generally continued in their later building.

Confucian. Confucianism was essentially a sociopolitical system. It extended ancestor worship, which gave supernatural sanction to obedience within the partriarchal family, to include worship of the emperor, the "father" of the state. A Confucian "temple," where teachers rather than priests carried out ceremonies in honor of the Great Teacher of the 6th to 5th century B.C., was different from imperial and other secular structures. Within a walled enclosure, on stone terraces, buildings were laid out along a central axis. Their wooden columns and brackets supporting overhanging roofs were often richly carved, painted, and gilded. The secular quality of the well-known "temple" at Choüfu, Shantung, supposed to be Confucius' birthplace, is unmistakable. The principal building is a library. Two little enclosures where offerings were made were mundanely dedicated to "kitchen gods."

Taoist. Taoism has been described as a "unique and extremely interesting combination of philosophy and religion incorporating also 'proto'-science and magic." A reaction against the rigid order of Confucian society, it advocated a return to nature. Instead of imposing the axial symmetry of Confucian temples on their buildings, the Taoists placed them so as not to intrude on the natural setting, an arrangement that influenced Chinese and Japanese gardens.

Buddhist. China's Buddhist temples belong to the past and to a religion that was alien to the Chinese worldview. Buddhism flourished when it had official protection but finally declined and disappeared, leaving behind architectural memorabilia revered for their beauty but not for their sanctity.

Chinese Buddhists adopted Indian architectural forms but stamped them with their own style. The temple complex was dominated by the tower-like pagoda, arranged on an axis with halls for worship and study, although it sometimes stood alone. The pagoda, developed in the 4th to 6th centuries, resulted when the Indian stupa and tiered finial was merged with the *lou*, the multi-storied watchtower used in Han times (202 B.C.–220 A.D.). The oldest pagoda, which is also the oldest brick building in China, is the pagoda of Sung-yüeh Ssŭ, built in 520. It is one of 15 that belonged to the temple monastery complex on Mt. Sung in Honan. The pagoda shows its Chinese ancestry in its many sides and 15 stories and its Indian ancestry in its overall moundlike shape and finial on top. The Chinese also rephrased the Indian *torana*, which became the tall Chinese *p'ai-lou* (gate building).

Temple of Heaven. The Chinese temple that is a true temple and wholly Chinese is the complex in Peking, called the T'ien T'an (Temple of

Heaven). Its name is that of its principal building, which is also known as the Hall of Prayer for Good Harvests (Hall of Annual Prayers). In the Temple of Heaven the emperor, holding the "mandate from Heaven," performed ancient sacrificial ceremonies on behalf of his people. The Temple of Heaven has been called one of the "most remarkable architectural compositions in the world," achieving "an overwhelming effect with an extraordinary economy of elements." It was begun in the 14th century and rebuilt in the 19th. The main enclosure, about a mile (1.6 km) square, is crossed on a north-south axis by a causeway from the north gate. An inner enclosure on the west contains the Palace for Fasting, where the emperor stayed while preparing for the ceremony.

The causeway joins the Hall of Prayer for Good Harvests at the north end to the Altar of Heaven at the south end. The Hall has a three-tiered roof of blue tiles, supported by pillars of the customary red, and walls paneled in red, blue, green, and gold. Hall and Altar, both circular, each stand on a series of three concentric circular terraces faced with carved balustrades of dazzling white marble. The lowest terraces are, in turn, each set in a square enclosure. Seen from the Altar, the effect of a round terrace precisely contained in a square enclosure expresses the Chinese saying "The earth is square and the sky is round." This succession of varied spaces in a related sequence is the idiom of a people more intent on social relationships than on transcendent awakening.

Japan. The two chief faiths of Japan are Shinto, which has existed since ancient times, and Buddhism, which was imported from China by way of Korea in the 6th century A. D. Buddhism did not replace Shinto but assimilated many of its elements, and the two exist together.

Shinto. Shinto, "the Way of the Gods," involved worship of *Kami* (nature deities) and *ujigami* (tutelary clan spirits). Believers offered obeisance, prayers, and offerings at a public shrine, which was usually in a place of natural beauty and consisted of a simple wooden sanctuary containing a prayer room and a cella with a holy object. In larger shrines the sanctuary and additional buildings were in an enclosure entered by *torii* (plain wooden gateposts, derived from the Indian *torana*). Shinto gods were also worshiped at miniature shrines in private homes. Ritual defilement, not moral sin, was the main cultic preoccupation, and purification rites were the principal cultic activities. Because the sun-goddess, Amaterasu, was the deity of the imperial clan, she assumed greater and greater importance. The goddess herself is said to have revealed that the sun and the Buddha were the same, thus sanctioning their peaceful coexistence. It is common for a house that has a *kami-dana* (Shinto shrine) also to have a *butsu-dan* (Buddhist family altar.).

The Great Shrine at Ise, dedicated to Amaterasu, has as its holy relic the Yata mirror, given by the goddess to her grandson as proof that she had given him rule over Japan. It is one of the great pilgrimage sites, and its two annual "purification" festivals cleanse the pilgrim of all defilement for six months.

The Great Shrine is great in holiness, not size. In form it is a simple rectangular wooden house, with a floor raised above the ground and a thatched roof. The whole is just large enough for an altar and a priest. The worshiper stands outside, bowing deeply or clapping his hands, saying a simple formulaic prayer, and presenting his offerings. The Ise Shrine is honorably ancient in its form, which dates from the 5th or 6th century. But it is new in its material. The present structure, the 59th, was built in 1953, in obedience to a command of the emperor in 686 that the shrine be rebuilt every 20 years in exactly the same form as before. Thus the shrine is symbolic of the country itself, faithfully adhering to tradition, yet constantly new.

Buddhist. Japanese Buddhists derived their art, architecture, sects, and ceremonials from Chinese models observed by Japanese priests who went to China for study. In time the Japanese advanced from imitation to creation. Buddhist temples, like other cultural imports, were adapted to the Japanese scene and style. Of the six Buddhist sects introduced during the Nara period (710-794) the Ritsu sect, which insisted on the legitimate descent of authority in the ordination of monks and nuns and on submission to discipline, became, in effect, the official sect. At Nara, the imperial capital, the Todai-ji Monastery was built. Its *kaidan*, the special platform where ordination took place, was faithfully copied from its Chinese model, as that had been from its original Indian form. The *kaidan* was placed in the *kondo* (great hall) of the monastery, about 288 feet (88 meters) long, 171 feet (52 meters) wide, and 154 feet (47 meters) high, where the newly made Daibutsu (statue of the Buddha) was housed. The present hall was rebuilt in smaller size in 1705. Very little remains of the original temple-complex—large lecture hall, gigantic main gate, and smaller inner gate with two 328-foot (100-meter) high pagodas between.

The Todai-ji, following contemporary Chinese temple-complexes, expresses the Japanese rulers' attempt to transplant the power and brilliance of T'ang China. It was also the center of a network of Buddhist temples located throughout the realm to support the centralized administration. There are many temples throughout Japan belonging to other Buddhist sects, other periods, other styles. But the Todai-ji stands as a noble monument to that transforming moment when Buddhism provided a political unity and motivating force in the formative Nara period and seeded Japanese culture with the spiritual, intellectual, and artistic achievements of the high civilizations of India and China.

JEANNETTE MIRSKY
Author of "Houses of God"

Bibliography

Adams, Robert M., *The Evolution of Urban Society* (Chicago 1966).
Boyd, Andrew, *Chinese Architecture and Town Planning, 1500 B.C.–1911 A.D.* (Chicago 1962).
Brown, Percy, *Indian Architecture* (Bombay 1956).
Dinsmoor, William B., *Architecture of Ancient Greece* (London 1950).
Frankfort, Henri, and others, *Before Philosophy* (New Orleans 1959).
Kramer, Samuel Noah, *The Sumerians* (Chicago 1963).
McKendrick, Paul, *Mute Stones Speak: Story of Archaeology in Italy* (New York 1960).
Mirsky, Jeannette, *Houses of God* (New York 1965).
Oppenheim, Leo, *Ancient Mesopotamia* (Chicago 1964).
Rowland, Benjamin, *The Art and Architecture of India* (Baltimore 1953).
Sansom, Sir George B., *Japan: A Short Cultural History* (New York 1943).
Willetts, William, *Chinese Art,* vol. 2, *Architecture* (Baltimore 1958).
Wilson, John, *The Culture of Ancient Egypt* (Chicago 1956).

TEMPLE BAR, a point in central London, just north of the river Thames, where the Strand and Fleet Street meet. Since the 12th century some kind of bar or gate, or the present memorial, has existed there to mark the western boundary of the City of London, dividing it from the borough of Westminster. When English monarchs visit the city on state occasions, they still observe the ancient custom of securing permission from London's lord mayor "to pass Temple Bar."

Originally a wooden structure, Temple Bar was used as a prison. A stone gate, erected by Sir Christopher Wren in 1672, was surmounted by iron spikes on which were exhibited the heads of criminals. The present memorial, which replaced it in 1880, honors Queen Victoria and Edward VII, as Prince of Wales.

TEMPLE CITY, a city in southwestern California, in Los Angeles county, is 11 miles east of the center of Los Angeles, of which it is a residential suburb. Formerly it was farming community that raised citrus fruits, walnuts, and poultry. It was founded in 1827 but was not incorporated as a city until 1960. Government is by council and manager. Population: 29,673.

TEMPLE MOUNDS. See MOUND BUILDERS AND MOUNDS.

TEMPLE UNIVERSITY is a nonsectarian, coeducational university, with its main campus in Philadelphia, Pa. Temple College was chartered in 1888, under the leadership of a Baptist minister, Russell Conwell. By 1907, the addition of professional schools and hospitals justified the change of name to Temple University. In 1965 an act of the state legislature made the university, though still privately controlled, "state-related" as a unit of the commonwealth system of higher education.

Undergraduate degrees are offered in liberal arts, business administration, education, fine arts, music, social welfare, communications and theater, and engineering technology. Graduate programs lead to masters and doctors degrees. Professional degrees are granted in law, medicine, dentistry, pharmacy, and allied health professions. Many programs utilize separate locations, as far apart as the Ambler campus in the suburbs of Philadelphia and the Tyler School of Art in Rome, Italy. The Samuel Paley Library, opened in 1966, has a capacity of 1,000,000 volumes.

The student body reached 35,000 by 1970, including a large number of part-time and evening students. Special attention is given to students with inadequate early training.

MIRIAM I. CRAWFORD
Samuel Paley Library, Temple University

TEMPO, tem'pō, the Italian word for time, is employed as a musical term to refer to the speed at which a composition or its parts are to be performed. The choice and variation of tempos constitute an important element of musical interpretation.

Until about 1600, musical notation implied proper speed through the use of notes with nearly fixed duration values. During the next 50 years, however, composers began to add indicative words to their scores to request faster and slower tempos. The words used in Italy, then the musical center of Europe, became the accepted terms for all countries to indicate tempo. These words include *largo, grave, lento,* and *adagio* for slow tempos, *allegro* and *presto* for fast tempos, and *ritardando* for a slowing down and *accelerando* for a speeding up.

After the metronome was invented in 1816 and became widely accepted, the Italian words were used in combination with metronomic figures that show the part of a minute during which a note of indicated value should endure. See also METRONOME; RHYTHM.

TEMÜJIN. See GENGHIS KHAN.

TEN COMMANDMENTS. The Ten Commandments are the most terse, inclusive, and celebrated abridgment of a code of ethical conduct in all of mankind's written tradition. Judeo-Christian tradition believes them to have the highest possible authority for man because, as related in the Bible, they were revealed by God to Moses. They are often referred to as the *Decalogue,* a term that comes from Greek and means the "ten words." They are the basic moral component of God's covenant with Israel. Although they consist mainly of prohibitions, they have the widest positive implications for human responsibility toward God, other people, and things. The Christian law of love does not abrogate the Ten Commandments, but the Christian believes that faith in Christ gives an entirely new meaning to ethical conduct, based on a new relationship between him and God.

Versions in Exodus and Deuteronomy. The Ten Commandments appear in two different places in the Old Testament (Exodus 20:1–17; Deuteronomy 5:6–21). The phrasing is similar but not identical (see text of both versions given on page 470).

Very likely the additional words that embellish some of the commandments in both versions are accretions from the time when Exodus and Deuteronomy were written down, long after the actual revelation of the Decalogue. The versions often employed in teaching the commandments are paraphrases of the Biblical texts. The number ten, as well as the allocation into two "tables" of the law, does not appear clearly in either of the two listings of commandments, but both appear in other parts of Exodus and Deuteronomy (Exodus 24:12; 31:18; Deuteronomy 4:13; 10:4).

Most Protestant, Anglican, and Orthodox Christians enumerate the commandments differently from Roman Catholics and Lutherans. Mainly following the Exodus text and Palestinian and Greek tradition, they make the prohibition against "other gods" the first commandment, after the introductory words, "I am the Lord. . . ." The prohibition against idolatry forms the second commandment, reverence for the name of God the third, and keeping the Lord's day the fourth. The prohibition against "coveting," whether of a neighbor's wife or of his property, constitutes the tenth.

Lutherans and Roman Catholics follow the Deuteronomic version and the enumeration of St. Augustine and the Western Church. The prohibition against "other gods" and idolatry are combined to make the first commandment, reverence for the name of God is the second, and observance of the Lord's day is the third. The precept against coveting a neighbor's wife forms the ninth commandment, and that against coveting a neighbor's goods is the tenth.

Jewish tradition considers the introduction, "I am the Lord . . ." to be the first commandment and makes the prohibition against "other gods" and idolatry the second. The remainder follows the Exodus version.

Abridged Text of the Ten Commandments in Exodus 20:1–17 (R. S. V.)

I. I am the Lord your God, who brought you out of the land of Egypt, out of the house of bondage. You shall have no other gods before me (vs. 2a, 3).
II. You shall not make for yourself a graven image (vs. 4). You shall not bow down to them or serve them (vs. 5a).
III. You shall not take the name of the Lord your God in vain (vs. 7).
IV. Remember the sabbath day, to keep it holy (vs. 8).
V. Honor your father and your mother (vs. 12a).
VI. You shall not kill (vs. 13).
VII. You shall not commit adultery (vs. 14).
VIII. You shall not steal (vs. 15).
IX. You shall not bear false witness against your neighbor (vs. 16).
X. You shall not covet (vs. 17a).

Abridged Text of the Ten Commandments in Deuteronomy 5:6–21 (R. S. V.)

I. I am the Lord your God, who brought you out of the land of Egypt, out of the house of bondage. You shall have no other gods before me. You shall not make for yourself a graven image; you shall not bow down to them or serve them (vs. 6, 7, 8a, 9).
II. You shall not take the name of the Lord your God in vain (vs. 11a).
III. Observe the sabbath day, to keep it holy (vs. 12a).
IV. Honor your father and your mother (vs. 16).
V. You shall not kill (vs. 17).
VI. Neither shall you commit adultery (vs. 18).
VII. Neither shall you steal (vs. 19).
VIII. Neither shall you bear false witness against your neighbor (vs. 20).
IX. Neither shall you covet your neighbor's wife (vs. 21).
X. You shall not desire your neighbor's house, his field, or anything that is your neighbor's (vs. 21).

Mosaic Origin. Some 19th and early 20th century Biblical scholars denied the traditional attribution of the Ten Commandments to Moses or the Mosaic era. They generally believed the concepts too advanced for that period and preferred a later date, such as the age of the prophets, in the 7th century B. C. More recent scholarship has tended to reinstate the tradition, since the prophets betray knowledge of the commandments, and since similar ethical codes existed in ancient times, though lacking the religious purity of the decalogue. The Mosaic origin can be upheld at least in the sense that the commandments transformed known ethical imperatives into the most solemn signs of a covenant, or treaty, between God and His people. The tradition concerning stone tablets is suggestive of a treaty, as is the writing "by the finger of God" (Exodus 31:18) and the mediation by Moses.

Ethical Precepts. The precept against having "other gods" and idols meant that no rival gods were permitted in opposition to the one true God. Idols and the use of the name of a god indicated some knowledge of the inner nature of the god, and hence some control over him. In the commandments of the first "table" (1 to 4) Israel was taught its obligation to obey and serve God, not to attempt to control Him or to coerce His favor. The commandment about the observance of the Lord's day has been important in the social life and thought of man; one day's rest out of seven for man and beast, and one day for public worship in the week. The precepts of the second "table" (5 to 10) demand respect for basic human rights and require social responsibility, both in outward act and inward desire. For example, the honoring of parents implies a whole ethic of family life, and includes the obligation of parents to command justly as well as that of children to obey. They also aim at the integrity and wholeness of God's people as a society. The commandments are profoundly positive and enlarging. They give no warrant for legalistic religious interpretations. They are often cited in the New Testament (Matthew 19:18f; Mark 10:19; Luke 8:20; Romans 13:9; James 2:11), and they are revered in common by Christians and Jews.

CHARLES E. SHEEDY, C. S. C.
University of Notre Dame

Further Reading: Stamm, J. F., and Andrew, M. E., *The Ten Commandments in Recent Research* (Naperville, Ill., 1967).

TEN LOST TRIBES, the subject of a popular legend about the fate of those northern Israelites who were carried into exile by the Assyrians in the 8th century B. C. In 721 B. C. the armies of Sargon II decisively defeated Samaria (northern Israel) and reportedly took more than 27,000 Israelites into exile.

The legend of the Ten Lost Tribes assumes, inaccurately, that northern Israel was populated in the 8th century B. C. only by the 10 distinct tribes that separated from Judah and Benjamin after the death of Solomon (933 B. C.) and formed the kingdom of Israel. According to legend these "lost tribes" reappeared throughout the world at various times and places. In all probability a majority of the captives were assimilated into societies where they were settled or formed isolated Jewish communities.

RONALD B. SOBEL
Rabbi, Temple Emanu-El, New York City

TEN YEARS' WAR (1868–1878), the bloody first stage of Cuba's 30-year struggle for independence from Spain. After most of Spanish America won independence in the 1820's, Spanish rule in Cuba became more oppressive. Failure of the Cuban creoles to win reforms led to rebellion. The Ten Years' War began in October 1868, when a small group of creole planters in Oriente province issued the "Grito," or proclamation of Yara, demanding an independent republic and gradual abolition of slavery. A constitution was drafted, and Carlos Manuel de Céspedes was elected president by a rebel assembly.

Warfare was centered in this eastern region, which suffered heavy property damage and loss of life. In the western half of the island, many creole slave-holding planters supported Spain, partly because of fear of abolition and "Africanization." Indeed, the conflict had characteristics of a civil war, for creoles fought on both sides. It was also racial, with rebel forces being heavily black and mestizo (mulatto), because slaves who enlisted usually were freed. Regular Spanish forces were outnumbered by the Spanish militia, composed mainly of Spanish civilians resident in Cuba.

The Cuban forces, resorting increasingly to guerrilla warfare and despite prepetual supply problems, fought the Spanish to a stalemate. The Pact of Zanjón (February 1878) provided for amnesty, reform, and a guarantee of the freedom of former slaves in the rebel forces. The war, in which 200,000 persons died, doomed slavery in Cuba, but the peace was only a prelude to further conflict. See CUBA–*History*.

DAVID D. BURKS, *Indiana University*

TENAFLY, ten′ə-flī, is a borough in northeastern New Jersey, in Bergen county, about 5 miles (8 km) north of the George Washington Bridge. Many of its residents commute to New York. There is some light industry. The Lamb Studios, makers of stained glass, are in Tenafly.

The first settlers were Dutch, who went from New Amsterdam (New York) to the district between the Hudson and Hackensack rivers about 1640. The name of the district was originally Tene Vlay, which can mean either "Willow Meadow" or "Little Valley." Tenafly became a borough in 1894. Government is by mayor and council. Population: 14,827.

TENANCY is a term used in real estate law and practice to refer to the occupancy of realty. Because it has more than one meaning, it must be used with care. The word is derived ultimately from the Latin *tenere,* meaning "to hold." Accordingly, anyone using or occupying real estate, whether he owns or leases the premises, is technically a tenant. In one use of the term, "tenancy" refers to the period of time over which the tenant may legally occupy the premises. It can also mean the rights in realty that one holds as a tenant.

The most common use of "tenancy," however, is to describe the form that a landlord-tenant relationship takes when realty is leased. The party to whom the realty is leased is the lessee, or tenant. While the lease is in effect, the tenant has certain rights of occupancy, exclusion, and disposition that vary with the nature of the lease agreement. Basically, the conditions and length of a tenancy under a lease are determined by a combination of prevailing law and private contract. Tenancy by an owner is similarly defined and prescribed by law and by the specific provisions of the deed or other instrument.

See also JOINT TENANCY; LANDLORD AND TENANT; LEASE; RENT, LAW OF.

WILLIAM N. KINNARD, JR.
University of Connecticut

TENCH, a slow-moving sluggish fish of the carp family. It is found in mud bottom ponds and shallow, quiet, weedy waters of rivers in Europe and Asia, excepting the Arctic regions of these continents. It sometimes occurs in brackish water. In England and Europe it is an important sport fish and in Europe it is raised in ponds for food. A golden variety is bred to decorate ornamental ponds. The tench has been introduced into some parts of North America.

The tench is a deep-bodied, laterally compressed fish with thick lips, a pair of prominent barbels at the corners of the mouth, and small orange eyes. The fins are rounded and uniformly dark, and the tail is only slightly forked. The scales are small and imbedded in thick skin that is often heavily coated with mucus. The tench is generally olive-green to brown or almost black. Its sides show a golden iridescence when the fish is out of water. It feeds on insect larvae, crustaceans, and snails. It spawns from April to August, maturing in about four years at a length of 9 to 10 inches (23–25.4 cm). Some European tench grow to 28 inches (71 cm) and 17 pounds (7.7 kg).

The tench, *Tinca tinca,* is classified in the family Cyprinidae of the order Cypriniformes.

EDWIN J. CROSSMAN
Royal Ontario Museum, Toronto

TENDAI, ten-dī, is the Japanese name of a Mahāyāna Buddhist sect that originated in China. Its Chinese name is *T'ien-t'ai.* See JAPAN—*Religion and Philosophy* (Buddhism).

TENDON, a fibrous cord or narrow band of specialized connective tissue. Tendons attach muscles to bones. At one end the tendon fibers are firmly attached to muscle cells, and at the other end they connect with fibers in the bone. In some parts of the body, such as the arms and legs, they stretch several inches between these two points of attachment.

Among the tendons in the human body are the Achilles tendon of the heel and the hamstrings at the back of the knee. These and other tendons sometimes rupture from injury or disease.

JOHN J. GARTLAND, M.D.
Jefferson Medical College, Philadelphia

TENDRIL, a slender, spirally coiled plant structure by which a vine or other climbing plant clings to an object. Tendrils are actually modified leaves, stems, or leaf parts. In some plants, such as the Boston ivy, each tendril has an expanded adhesive disk at the tip. See LEAF; STEM.

TENERIFE is the largest island of the Canary Islands, which are located off the northwest coast of Africa and belong to Spain. See CANARY ISLANDS.

TENIERS, ten′yûrz, **David, the Younger** (1610–1690), Flemish painter, who excelled in peasant genre scenes, still lifes, and landscapes.

Life. David Teniers the Younger was born in Antwerp and baptized on Dec. 15, 1610. He came from a family of painters, including his father, David the Elder (1582–1649), with whom he studied, and his son David (1638–1685). David the Younger became a master in the Antwerp painters' guild about 1632 and dean in 1645. He married the daughter of Jan Bruegel the Elder in 1636. In 1651, David was called to Brussels to the court of Archduke Leopold William, regent of the Spanish Netherlands, to be court painter and keeper of the ducal art collection. David ran a busy workshop, but his work became less assured in later years. He died in Brussels on April 25, 1690.

Work. David the Younger carried on the realistic, "low life" tradition of Adriaen Brouwer, in his peasant and drinking scenes, such as *The Card Players* (Royal Museum, Brussels), *Inn Scene* (Mauritshuis, The Hague), and *The Dentist* (Gemäldegalerie, Dresden), but with greater restraint and delicacy. His scenes of peasants dancing recall Rubens' kermesses (festivals) in subject but are generally simpler in composition and more subdued in color. David the Younger also painted mythological and religious subjects, such as the *Temptation of St. Anthony* (one version, Gemäldegalerie), and satire, as in *A Party of Monkeys* (Alte Pinakothek, Munich).

His landscapes, such as *Landscape with Rainbow* (Museum Dahlem, Berlin) and *River Landscape* (Gemäldegalerie), and still lifes, for example *Study of Accessories* (Royal Museum), rival those of the Dutch masters in their clarity of treatment and their tonal and atmospheric effects. He included in the backgrounds of his later landscapes his country house near Brussels. David the Younger also recorded contemporary civic and historical scenes and portrayed his patron's *Picture Gallery* (one version, Prado, Madrid.

LOLA B. GELLMAN, *Queen's College, New York*

TENNANT, ten'ənt, **Smithson** (1761–1815), English chemist and discoverer of osmium and iridium. Born near Wensleydale, Yorkshire, on Nov. 30, 1761, Tennant received his early education at home. He showed a particular interest in science, and in 1781 he became a student of Joseph Black in Edinburgh. The next year he studied chemistry and botany at Cambridge. Although he took two degrees in medicine at Cambridge (1788 and 1796), he never practiced. By then much of his time was spent in managing his rural estates in Lincolnshire and Chester. He also traveled extensively in Europe and spent long periods in London.

In an early paper (1791), Tennant provided the analytic proof for the composition of carbon dioxide. In 1797 he showed that diamond is composed entirely of carbon. In 1804 he and his assistant, W. H. Wollaston, isolated osmium and iridium from platinum minerals.

Tennant was appointed professor of chemistry at Cambridge in 1813. He was killed in a riding accident near Boulogne, France, on Feb. 22, 1815.

AARON J. IHDE, *University of Wisconsin*

TENNANTITE, ten'ən-tīt, is an arsenic sulfide of copper, iron, zinc, and silver. It is harder and denser than tetrahedrite, the corresponding antimony sulfide, and forms a series with that mineral. See also TETRAHEDRITE.

TENNENT, ten'ənt, **Gilbert** (1703–1764), American Presbyterian minister. A son of William Tennent, he was born in County Armagh, Ireland, Feb. 5, 1703. He emigrated to America and was trained in his father's "Log College." He was licensed to preach by the Presbytery of Philadelphia in 1725. While a pastor at New Brunswick, N.J., he was influenced by Theodore Frelinghuysen, an early leader of the revival movement called the Great Awakening.

In 1740, Tennent preached his abusive sermon *The Dangers of Unconverted Ministry,* in which he attacked ministers who resisted the Awakening ferment. In turn he was accused of "censoriousness," and "itineracy," and he helped to bring on the bitter New Side and Old Side division (1741–1758) in American Presbyterianism.

In 1743, Tennent was called to the Second Presbyterian Church in Philadelphia, where he grew increasingly unhappy over this division. He published a tract *Irenicum Ecclesiasticum* (1749) in which he urged reconciliation. With Samuel Davies he visited England in 1753 to raise funds for the College of New Jersey (now Princeton), and in 1758 participated in the reunion of the denomination. He died in Philadelphia on July 23, 1764.

JAMES H. SMYLIE
Union Theological Seminary, Richmond, Va.

TENNENT, ten'ənt, **William** (1673–1746), American Presbyterian minister. Born in Ireland and educated at the University of Edinburgh, Tennent was ordained by the Church of Ireland in 1706. He moved to America in 1716 or 1717 and was admitted to the Presbyterian ministry. About 1727 he began to educate young men for the ministry in his own home at Neshaminy, Pa., and in 1735 he built a log house in which to teach his students. From this "Log College" 21 trained young men went out, including his own sons, Gilbert, Charles, John, and William.

A Calvinist, Tennent taught what has been called an evangelical federal theology because of his emphasis upon the covenants of the Old and New Testaments and the experimental knowledge of religion. Tennent filled his students with a zeal for learning as well as for religion, and they, in turn, established other academies throughout the colonies. Tennent died in Neshaminy on May 6, 1746.

JAMES H. SMYLIE
Union Theological Seminary, Richmond, Va.

THE METROPOLITAN MUSEUM OF ART

DAVID TENIERS THE YOUNGER is known for his studies of ordinary people in a festive mood, as in this painting, *A Marriage Festival.*

FRANK J. MILLER

Farmlands occupy about 60% of the area of Tennessee. These tidy farms nestle in a valley of Carter county.

TENNESSEE

Great Seal of Tennessee

INFORMATION HIGHLIGHTS

Location: In east south central United States, bordered north by Kentucky and Virginia, east by North Carolina, south by Georgia, Alabama, Mississippi, west by Arkansas and Missouri.
Elevation: *Highest point*—Clingmans Dome, 6,643 feet (2,025 meters); *lowest point*—on Mississippi River, 182 feet (55 meters); *approximate mean elevation,* 900 feet (274 meters).
Area: 42,244 square miles (109,412 sq km); rank, 34th.
Population: 1970 census, 3,924,164; rank, 17th. Increase, 1960–1970: 10.0%.
Climate: Generally mild winters; hot, humid summers; abundant rainfall.
Statehood: June 1, 1796; order of admission, 16th.
Origin of Name: From *Tanasi,* a Cherokee village.
Capital: Nashville.
Largest City: Memphis.
Number of Counties: 95.
Principal Products: *Manufactures*—chemicals and allied products, food and kindred products, apparel and related products, electrical machinery; *farm products*—tobacco, cotton, soybeans, cattle, dairy products; *minerals*—stone, zinc, coal.
State Motto: *Agriculture and Commerce.*
State Song (adopted April 10, 1926): *My Homeland Tennessee.*
State Nickname: Volunteer State.
State Bird (adopted April 19, 1933): Mockingbird.
State Flower (adopted April 19, 1933): Iris.
State Tree (adopted March 13, 1947): Tulip Poplar.
State Flag: A red field with three white stars in a blue circle, centered and bordered in white; narrow white and blue stripes at right edge of field. See also FLAG—*Flags of the States.*

CONTENTS

TENNESSEE, one of the South Central states of the United States, is situated between the Mississippi River on the west and the Unaka range of the Appalachian Mountains on the east. Lying between the border state of Kentucky and the Deep South states of Mississippi, Alabama, and Georgia, Tennessee itself is often regarded as a border state. Its character, as reflected in its political, social, and economic life, has both a Northern and a Southern flavor.

Tennessee has an unusually varied landscape, ranging from rugged mountain country along the North Carolina border in the east, to plateaus and uplands in the center, and to low plains and swamps along the Mississippi River. Spruce and fir forests grow in the Great Smoky Mountains and cypress in the swamps in the west.

TENNESSEE CONSERVATION DEPARTMENT

COTTON CARNIVAL is held each year in Memphis, the state's largest city. Decorative floats are featured in the parade.

These geographical contrasts helped shape Tennessee's character. The division of the state into East, Middle, and West Tennessee, indirectly recognized in the state constitution, underlines the sectionalism that has defined so much of its history. The conflicting interests of the wealthy cotton planters in the west and the independent farmers and mountain men in the east divided Tennessee in the Civil War. Many East Tennesseans remained loyal to the Union even after the state had joined the Confederacy. East Tennessee affiliated with the Northern branches of the Methodist and Baptist churches, while the rest of the state joined the Southern branches. Traditionally the east is Republican, whereas much of the remainder of the state is overwhelmingly Democratic.

Tennessee is favored with fertile soil, plentiful rain, and a mild climate. However, aided by its central location and the diversity of its natural resources, the state shifted from an agricultural to an industrial economy after World War II. Memphis, by far the largest city, produces a variety of goods while maintaining its position as the nation's leading cotton market.

In Great Smoky Mountains National Park the wilderness is preserved as it looked to the first white settlers. Numerous Civil War battlegrounds across the state are grim reminders of that conflict. There is much interest in pioneering crafts, and in some remote areas of the mountains old English ballads are still sung in their original form.

But Tennessee has emerged from its historic past into the atomic age. The scientific community at Oak Ridge, drawing on the vast power supply of the Tennessee Valley Authority (TVA), explores the applications and potentials of the peaceful uses of atomic energy. The Tennessee River, once untamed and flood-prone, was converted by the TVA into a series of flood-control dams and reservoirs used for power and recreation. Tennessee is the national center of country music, with its capital city, Nashville, the home of a thriving music industry.

POPULATION SINCE 1790

Year	Population	Year	Population
1790	35,691	1920	2,337,885
1820	422,823	1940	2,915,841
1850	1,002,717	1950	3,291,718
1880	1,542,359	1960	3,567,089
1900	2,020,616	1970	3,924,164

Gain, 1960–1970: 10.1% (U. S. gain, 13.3%). **Density** (1970): 92.9 persons per square mile (U. S. density, 56.2).

URBAN-RURAL DISTRIBUTION

Year	Percent urban	Percent rural
1920	26.1 (U.S., 51.2)	73.9
1930	34.3 (U.S., 56.2)	65.7
1940	35.2 (U.S., 56.5)	64.8
1950	44.1 (U.S., 64.0)	55.9
1960	52.3 (U.S., 69.9)	47.7
1970	58.7 (U.S., 73.5)	41.3

LARGEST CENTERS OF POPULATION

City or Metropolitan area[1]	1970	1960	1950
Memphis (city)	623,530	497,524	396,000
Metropolitan area (Tenn. portion)	722,014		
Nashville-Davidson (city)	448,003	170,874	174,307
Metropolitan area	541,108	463,628	321,758
Knoxville (city)	174,587	111,827	124,769
Metropolitan area	400,337	368,080	337,105
Chattanooga (city)	119,082	130,009	131,041
Metropolitan area (Tenn. portion)	254,236	....	....
Jackson	39,996	34,376	30,207
Johnson City	33,770	31,187	27,864
Kingsport	31,938	26,314	19,571
Clarksville	31,719	22,021	16,246
Oak Ridge	28,319	27,169	30,229
Murfreesboro	26,360	18,991	13,052
East Ridge	21,799	19,570	9,645
Columbia	21,471	17,624	10,911
Millington	21,106	6,059	4,696

[1] Standard metropolitan statistical area.

1. The People

Tennessee's Indian inhabitants were largely Cherokee, though a few Chickasaw lived in West Tennessee along the Mississippi River. The early settlers of the colonial period were predominantly English, but there were considerable numbers of Scots, Irish, and Germans as well as smaller numbers of Dutch and French.

From 1790 to 1830, as Indian lands in Tennessee were opened to settlement, the population of the state grew much faster than that of the United States as a whole. For the next 100 years, however, Tennessee's growth was considerably slower than that of the nation. In the 1930's it was again somewhat greater, but from 1940 to 1950 it was a bit less, and from 1950 to 1960 much smaller. The slower rate of growth from 1830 to 1930 was due largely to emigration to other states. The 1970 population of 3,924,164 represented an increase of 357,075, or 10%, from the 3,567,089 inhabitants of the state in 1960.

Characteristics of the Population. Most Tennesseans are native-born. The state census of 1870 revealed that less than 2% of the population was foreign-born, and in 1970 foreign-born whites comprised less than 1% of the total. The census of 1790 recorded that almost 10% of the population was Negro, a larger percentage than any other non-English group except the Scots. Negroes made up about 15% of the population in 1970, as compared with a peak of 26% in 1880. Most Negroes, originally brought to the state to work the cotton fields of West Tennessee, live in that part of the state or in the larger cities.

Protestants have the largest church membership in Tennessee. The most numerous denominations are the United Methodists and Southern Baptists. There are smaller numbers of Roman Catholics and Jews.

Way of Life. While Tennessee's population was long predominantly rural (56% as late as 1950), a marked urban trend was apparent by the mid-20th century. By 1960 the urban population exceeded half of the total population. About a third of the people lived in the state's four largest cities. Because of the growth of the suburbs, almost half of the population of Tennessee is concentrated in the four standard metropolitan areas.

Largest Centers of Population. Tennessee has four cities of 100,000 or more inhabitants. Memphis, the largest city and a thriving river port, is strategically situated on the Mississippi River in West Tennessee. Located in rich cotton and lumber producing areas, it is a major cotton and hardwood market. Nashville, on the Cumberland River in Middle Tennessee, is Tennessee's capital and second-largest city. Its central location makes it a significant distribution point. Knoxville and Chattanooga are the state's third- and fourth-largest cities in the 1970 census. Both on the Tennessee River, they are the chief cities and industrial centers of East Tennessee. Smaller cities are Jackson, Johnson City, Kingsport, and the "atomic" community of Oak Ridge.

2. The Land

In general the surface of the state slopes from east to west, with peaks rising to more than 6,000 feet (1,900 meters) in the Unaka Mountains, to some elevations in the Mississippi Flood Plain of less than 300 feet (90 meters) above sea level.

Major Physical Divisions. From east to west there are six well defined physiographic regions: the Unaka Mountains (sometimes erroneously called the Alleghenies); the Ridge and Valley region, or Great Valley of East Tennessee; the Cumberland Plateau; the Highland Rim; the Central or Nashville Basin; and the Gulf Coastal Plain. There are also two minor geographic subdivisions: the western valley of the Tennessee and the Mississippi Flood Plain. The latter is sometimes called a seventh physiographic region.

The Unaka Mountains constitute the rugged western front of the Blue Ridge physiographic province, with the crest extending along the North Carolina border. The Unakas, a heavily forested and sparsely populated region, are composed of several separate ranges. The most notable of these is the Great Smoky Mountains, of which the highest section has been set aside as Great Smoky Mountains National Park. In the park is Clingmans Dome which, at 6,643 feet (2,025 meters), is the highest point in the state.

A segment of the Appalachian Valley, the Ridge and Valley region in East Tennessee extends from northwestern Georgia to southwestern Virginia. The region, from 35 to 55 miles (56 to 88 km) wide, is made up of a series of parallel low, forested ridges rising above long, intervening valleys. The valleys have some of Tennessee's richest farmland.

The Cumberland Plateau, a section of the much longer Appalachian Plateau, extends across the state from Alabama to Kentucky. Its eastern edge is Walden Ridge, a steep escarpment rising about 1,000 feet (300 meters) above the Great Valley of East Tennessee. While the average elevation of the undulating plateau is about 2,000 feet (600 meters) above sea level, the northeastern section is rugged and mountainous. The beautiful Sequatchie Valley extends from Alabama in a northeasterly direction halfway across the state.

The Highland Rim division in Middle Tennessee forms a rim around the Central Basin. Its eastern section, a gently rolling plain, borders the Cumberland Plateau, from which it runs westward to the relatively high land along the western valley of the Tennessee River. With an area of about 10,650 square miles (27,583 sq km), it is the largest physiographic region of the state and is extremely rugged in some of its sections. The Central Basin, from 400 to 600 feet (120–150 meters) below the Highland Rim, is shaped like an oval dish, with the surrounding highlands constituting a broad, flat brim. The surface is from rolling to hilly. Many of the state's most productive farms are in the basin.

HIKERS on the Alum Cave trail to Mount Leconte in the Great Smoky Mountains, an alluring wilderness.

EARL PALMER, FROM MONKMEYER

The Gulf, or West Tennessee Coastal Plain, which lies between the western valley of the Tennessee River and the Mississippi River, is an area of rolling hills and flat lowlands. From its highest section just west of the Tennessee River it slopes gently westward to bluffs on the bank of the Mississippi or overlooking the Mississippi Flood Plain. This narrow strip of swampy land is also known as the Mississippi Bottoms. Much of it may be covered with water when the river is at flood stage. The plain, 10 miles (16 km) wide in the north, vanishes at some points in the south where the Mississippi flows past the Chickasaw Bluffs.

Rivers and Lakes. The state's chief river, the Tennessee, is formed just east of Knoxville at the junction of the Holston and the French Broad. Its tributaries include the Little Tennessee, Clinch, Duck, and Hiwassee rivers. The Mississippi River system drains all of Tennessee except a small area east of Chattanooga that is drained by the Alabama River system. For the most part, the Gulf Coastal Plain is drained directly into the Mississippi, but almost all the rest of the state is drained by the Tennessee and Cumberland river systems, which flow into the Ohio River short distances from the Mississippi.

With the exception of Reelfoot Lake, in the extreme northwest corner of the state, which was formed by the New Madrid earthquakes of 1811–1812, Tennessee has no natural lakes of consequence. There are several large and beautiful artificial lakes formed by the dams of TVA and the U. S. Army Corps of Engineers. Among the larger reservoirs are Kentucky, Pickwick Landing, Chickamauga, Watts Bar, and Fort Loudoun on the Tennessee River, and Barkley Lake on the Cumberland, which like Kentucky Lake is partly in Kentucky. Many of the dams create electric power and play a role in flood control. The reservoirs are popular recreation areas.

Climate. Tennessee has a climate midway between that of the continental climate of the North and the humid subtropical climate of the South. While not directly in any major storm track, Tennessee comes under the influence of storms that pass along the Gulf of Mexico and up the Atlantic coast as well as those that move from Oklahoma to the Great Lakes. The climate is therefore mild and relatively free from extremes or sudden changes. However, there is a wide annual range of temperatures, and seasons are pronounced. Precipitation is ample for agricultural needs, averaging 50 inches (1,270 mm) a year. The heaviest rains fall in late winter or early spring. The driest season is mid-autumn. Annual snowfall is light.

Summers are relatively long and warm, while winters are usually mild and short. Temperatures, which reflect the state's varying topography, are warmest in the extreme southwest and coolest in the mountains. Summer temperatures average 77.1° F (25° C) and the coldest winters average 40° F and (5° C). Zero temperatures occur about once or twice a year in low areas, but temperatures fall considerably below zero in the mountains. The growing season varies from 150 days in the mountains to about 220 days, or nearly 8 frost-free months, in the west.

Plant Life. The plant life of Tennessee is predominantly deciduous. Small trees and shrubs provide a dense undergrowth. Many of these, such as the mountain laurel, azalea, and dogwood, are renowned for their beautiful flowers. The great variety of trees and shrubs shows a marked degree of adjustment to climate, topography, and soil. Plant life in the Great Smokies is especially varied and luxuriant.

Tennessee was originally almost completely covered with trees. Although less than half of the state is wooded today, forests are still among the more important of the state's resources. Every county contains some commercial timber, but the most productive areas are in the Unaka Mountains, the Cumberland Plateau, and the lowlands of West Tennessee. Important varieties are ash, beech, maple, chestnut, cypress, cedar, cottonwood, yellow pine, hemlock, tulip or yellow poplar, and oak.

Animal Life. When white settlers arrived in the area, they found a wildlife that generally was characteristic of the forest. With the removal of the great forests and development of agriculture, some mammals, such as the bison and panther, became extinct, while the quail and many other birds became more numerous. About the only remaining large mammals are the black bear and the white-tailed deer. There are still many small mammals such as the red and gray fox, mink, raccoon, striped skunk, and weasel. Game fish found in Tennessee waters include trout, bass, catfish, crappie, and pike.

Minerals. Tennessee's diverse geographic provinces possess a variety of mineral resources. Among the major mineral deposits are stone, zinc, coal, phosphate rock, sand and gravel, copper, and clays. Bituminous coal occurs widely in the Cumberland Plateau, and its availability as a cheap fuel has been vital to the state's industrial growth. Phosphate occurs commercially in Middle Tennessee. The Ducktown basin in the southeast corner of the state contains large deposits of copper and iron sulfide minerals. Sphalerite, an important zinc ore, and marble occur in East Tennessee.

Conservation. For many years widespread soil erosion, floods, and forest mismanagement were the state's chief conservation problems, and the TVA played a vital role in the efforts toward their solution. Eroded areas were reforested with seedlings, cover crops were planted to hold the soil, and contour plowing was introduced. After almost 30 years of effort, combined state and federal agencies have revitalized thousands of square miles of land. By 1970 the TVA was devoting increased attention to the growing problems of air and water pollution.

The state's department of conservation is made up of four divisions devoted to forestry, geology, water resources, and state parks.

3. The Economy

The economic pattern of life in Tennessee has vastly changed since the 1930's, spurred by the rise of industry as a primary base of the state's economy. The rapid shift to an industrial economy is due in large part to increased electric power at low rates in the region served by the TVA, the stimulus to industrial development provided by World War II, an improved transportation network, and the state's central location in relation to markets. Industry, which has become increasingly complex, is characterized by an ever greater division of labor, while mechanization has significantly affected agriculture.

Less than a twelfth of Tennessee's labor force is engaged in agriculture. Manufacturing is the state's largest single source of employment, ac-

TENNESSEE

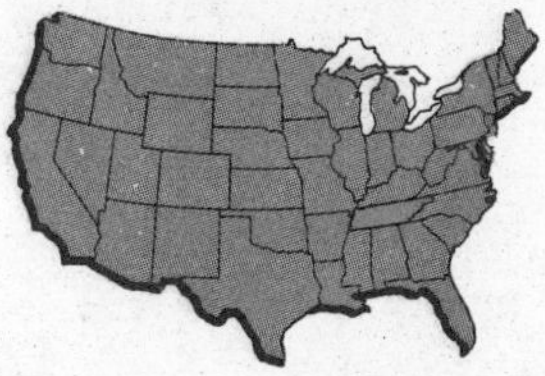

TOPOGRAPHY

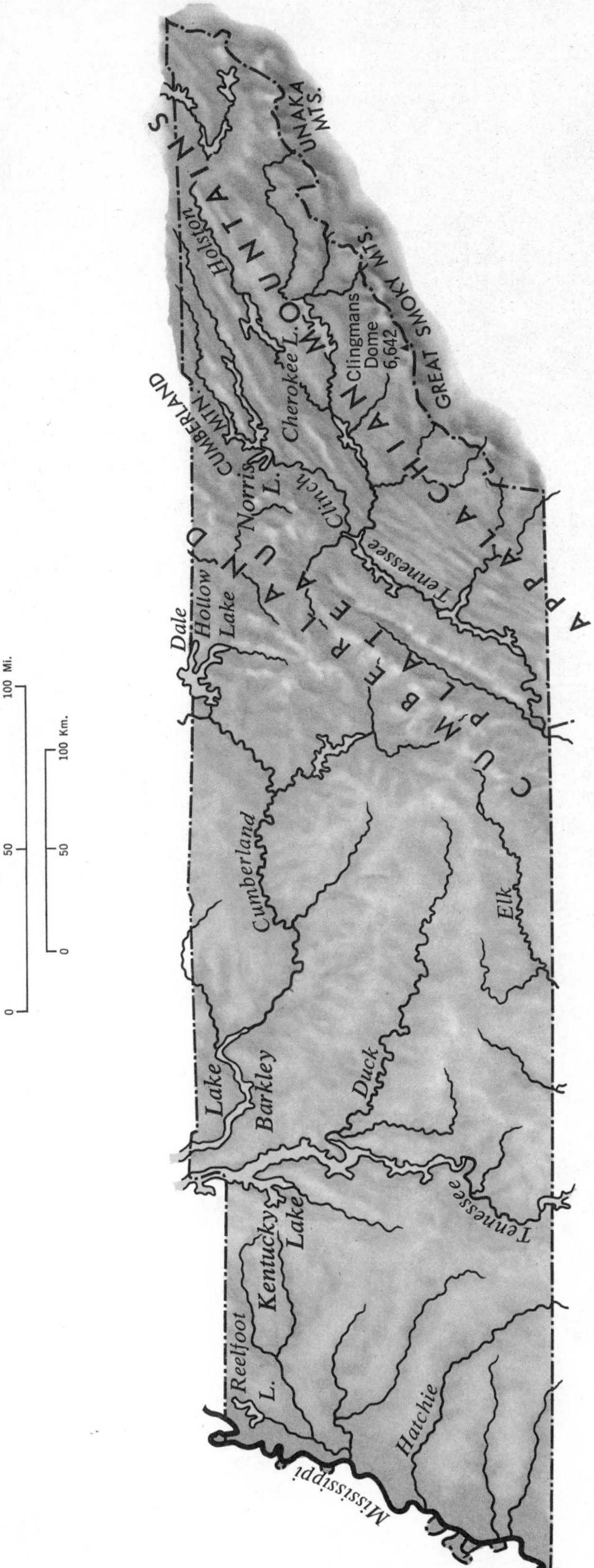

APPALACHIAN MOUNTAINS
UNAKA MTS.
GREAT SMOKY MTS.
Clingmans Dome 6,642
Holston
Cherokee L.
CUMBERLAND MTN.
Norris L.
Clinch
Tennessee
CUMBERLAND PLATEAU
Dale Hollow Lake
Cumberland
Elk
Duck
Lake Barkley
Kentucky Lake
Tennessee
Reelfoot L.
Hatchie
Mississippi
0 50 100 Mi.
0 50 100 Km.

Below Sea Level
100 m. 328 ft.
200 m. 656 ft.
500 m. 1,640 ft.
1,000 m. 3,281 ft.
2,000 m. 6,562 ft.
5,000 m. 16,404 ft.

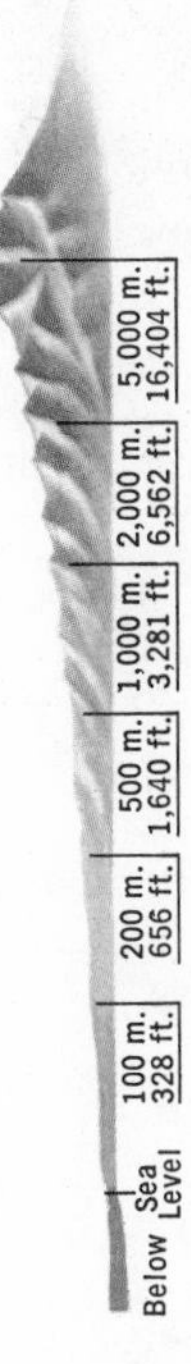

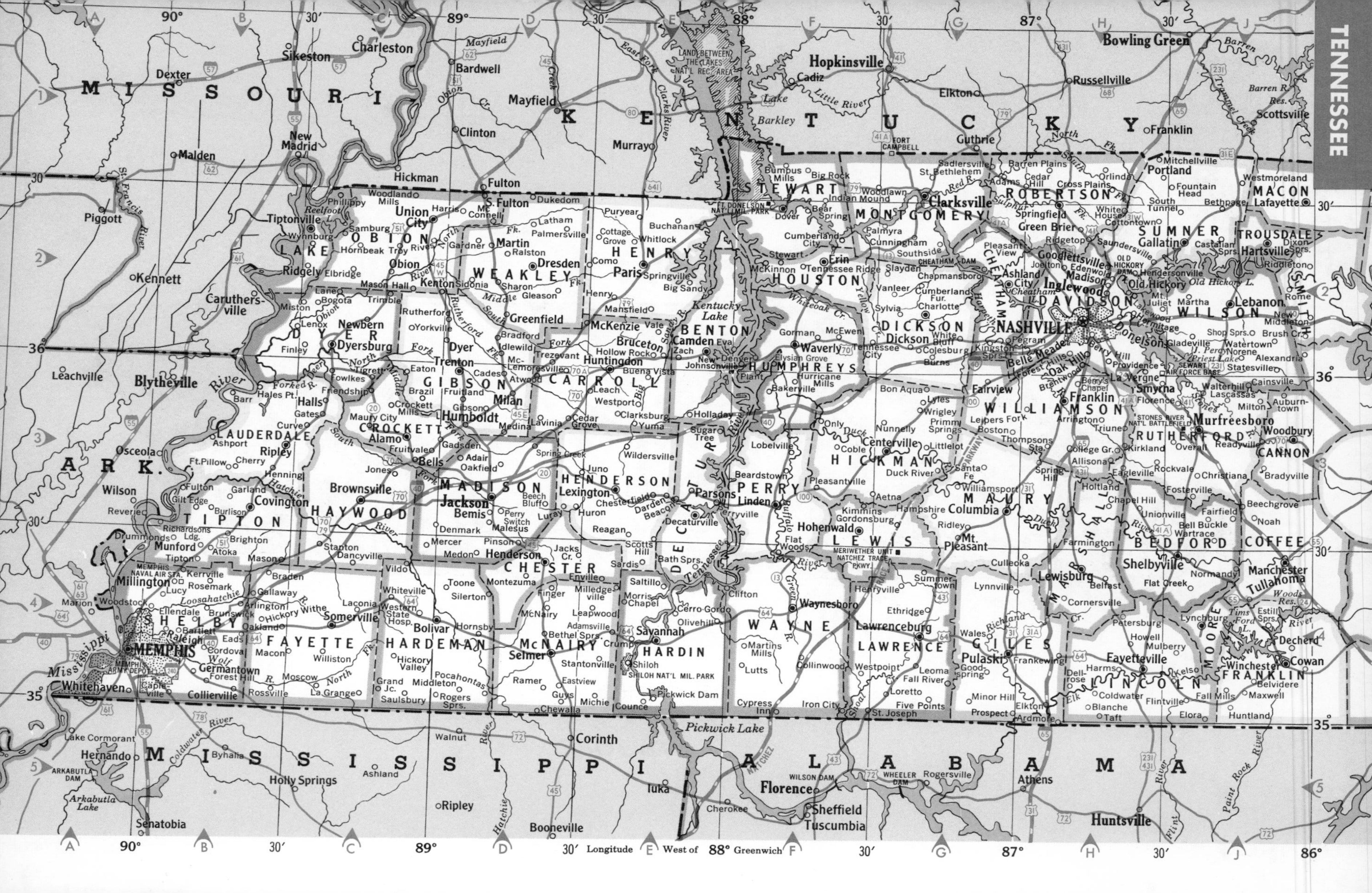

MISSOURI
KENTUCKY
ARK.
MISSISSIPPI
ALABAMA
NASHVILLE
MEMPHIS
Jackson
Clarksville
Murfreesboro
Columbia
Franklin
Bowling Green
Hopkinsville
Florence
Sheffield
Tuscumbia
Huntsville
Corinth
Blytheville
Kentucky Lake
Pickwick Lake
LAND BETWEEN THE LAKES NAT'L REC. AREA
FORT CAMPBELL
SHILOH NAT'L MIL. PARK
FT. DONELSON NAT'L MIL. PARK
STONES RIVER NAT'L BATTLEFIELD
MEMPHIS NAVAL AIR STA.
OBION
WEAKLEY
HENRY
STEWART
MONTGOMERY
ROBERTSON
SUMNER
MACON
TROUSDALE
WILSON
DAVIDSON
CHEATHAM
DICKSON
HOUSTON
HUMPHREYS
BENTON
CARROLL
GIBSON
DYER
LAKE
CROCKETT
LAUDERDALE
TIPTON
SHELBY
FAYETTE
HAYWOOD
MADISON
HARDEMAN
CHESTER
HENDERSON
McNAIRY
HARDIN
DECATUR
PERRY
WAYNE
LEWIS
HICKMAN
MAURY
WILLIAMSON
RUTHERFORD
CANNON
COFFEE
BEDFORD
MARSHALL
GILES
LAWRENCE
LINCOLN
MOORE
FRANKLIN
90°
89°
88°
87°
86°
36°
35°
30′
Longitude West of 88° Greenwich

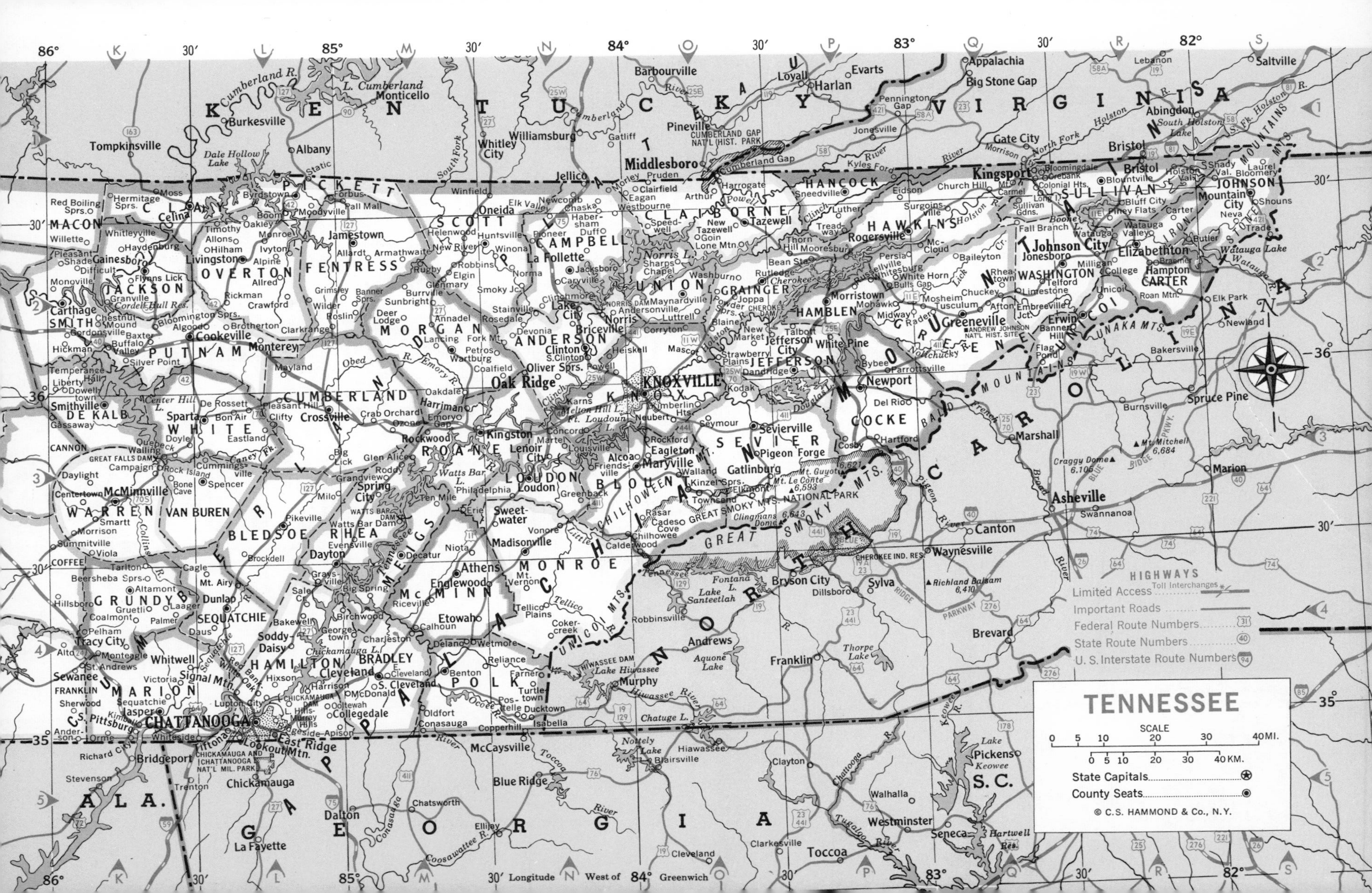

TENNESSEE
SCALE
0 5 10 20 30 40 MI.
0 5 10 20 30 40 KM.
State Capitals
County Seats
© C.S. HAMMOND & Co., N.Y.
HIGHWAYS
Limited Access
Toll Interchanges
Important Roads
Federal Route Numbers
State Route Numbers
U. S. Interstate Route Numbers
KENTUCKY
VIRGINIA
NORTH CAROLINA
S.C.
GEORGIA
ALA.
KNOXVILLE
CHATTANOOGA
Oak Ridge
Johnson City
Kingsport
Bristol
Asheville
Middlesboro
Cookeville
Crossville
Cleveland
Greeneville
Morristown
Maryville
Gatlinburg
Sevierville
Newport
Elizabethton
GREAT SMOKY MTS. NATIONAL PARK
CUMBERLAND GAP NAT'L HIST. PARK
CHICKAMAUGA AND CHATTANOOGA NAT'L MIL. PARK
30′ Longitude West of 84° Greenwich

TENNESSEE

COUNTIES

Anderson, 60,300 ... N 2
Bedford, 25,039 ... J 3
Benton, 12,126 ... E 2
Bledsoe, 7,643 ... L 3
Blout, 63,744 ... O 3
Bradley, 50,686 ... M 4
Campbell, 26,045 ... N 2
Cannon, 8,467 ... J 3
Carroll, 25,741 ... E 3
Carter, 42,575 ... R 2
Cheatham, 13,199 ... G 2
Chester, 9,927 ... D 4
Claiborne, 19,420 ... O 2
Clay, 6,624 ... K 1
Cocke, 25,283 ... P 3
Coffee, 32,572 ... J 3
Crockett, 14,402 ... C 3
Cumberland, 20,733 ... L 3
Davidson, 447,877 ... H 2
Decatur, 9,457 ... E 3
DeKalb, 11,151 ... K 3
Dickson, 21,977 ... G 2
Dyer, 30,427 ... C 2
Fayette, 22,692 ... C 4
Fentress, 12,593 ... M 2
Franklin, 27,244 ... J 4
Gibson, 47,871 ... D 3
Giles, 22,138 ... G 4
Grainger, 13,948 ... O 2
Greene, 47,630 ... Q 2
Grundy, 10,631 ... K 4
Hamblen, 38,696 ... P 2
Hamilton, 254,236 ... L 4
Hancock, 6,719 ... P 1
Hardeman, 22,435 ... C 4
Hardin, 18,212 ... E 4
Hawkins, 33,726 ... P 2
Haywood, 19,596 ... C 3
Henderson, 17,291 ... E 3
Henry, 23,749 ... E 2
Hickman, 12,096 ... G 3
Houston, 5,845 ... F 2
Humphreys, 13,560 ... F 2
Jackson, 8,141 ... K 2
Jefferson, 24,940 ... P 2
Johnson, 11,569 ... S 2
Knox, 276,293 ... O 3
Lake, 7,896 ... B 2
Lauderdale, 20,271 ... B 3
Lawrence, 29,097 ... G 4
Lewis, 6,761 ... F 3
Lincoln, 24,318 ... H 4
Loudon, 24,266 ... N 3
Macon, 12,315 ... J 1
Madison, 65,727 ... D 3
Marion, 20,577 ... K 4
Marshall, 17,319 ... H 4
Maury, 43,376 ... G 3
McMinn, 35,462 ... M 4
McNairy, 18,369 ... D 4
Meigs, 5,219 ... M 3
Monroe, 23,475 ... N 4
Montgomery, 62,721 ... G 2
Moore, 3,568 ... J 4
Morgan, 13,619 ... M 2
Obion, 29,936 ... C 2
Overton, 14,866 ... L 2
Perry, 5,238 ... F 3
Pickett, 3,774 ... L 1
Polk, 11,669 ... N 4
Putnam, 35,487 ... K 2
Rhea, 17,202 ... M 3
Roane, 38,881 ... M 3
Robertson, 29,102 ... H 1
Rutherford, 59,428 ... J 3
Scott, 14,762 ... M 2
Sequatchie, 6,331 ... L 4
Sevier, 28,241 ... O 3
Shelby, 722,014 ... B 4
Smith, 12,509 ... K 2
Stewart, 7,319 ... F 1
Sullivan, 127,329 ... R 1
Sumner, 56,106 ... J 2
Tipton, 28,001 ... B 3
Trousdale, 5,155 ... J 2
Unicoi, 15,254 ... R 2
Union, 9,072 ... O 2
Van Buren, 3,758 ... L 3
Warren, 26,972 ... K 3
Washington, 73,924 ... Q 2
Wayne, 12,365 ... F 4
Weakley, 28,827 ... D 2
White, 17,088 ... L 3
Williamson, 34,330 ... H 3
Wilson, 36,999 ... J 2

CITIES and TOWNS

Adair, 4 ... D 3
Adams, 458 ... G 1
Adamsville, 1,344 ... E 4
Aetna, 50 ... G 3
Afton, 550 ... Q 2
Alamo⊙, 2,499 ... C 3
Alcoa, 7,739 ... N 3
Alexandria, 680 ... J 2
Algood, 1,808 ... K 2
Allardt, 610 ... M 2
Allisona, 35 ... H 3
Allons, 600 ... L 2
Alpine, 400 ... L 2
Altamont⊙, 546 ... K 4
Alto, 250 ... K 4
Anderson, 90 ... K 4
Andersonville, 425 ... O 2
Annadel, 50 ... M 2
Apison, 435 ... L 4
Ardmore, 601 ... H 4
Arlington, 1,349 ... B 4
Armathwaite, 625 ... M 2
Arrington, 185 ... H 3
Arthur, 500 ... O 1
Ashland City⊙, 2,027 ... G 2
Ashport, 100 ... B 3
Athens⊙, 11,790 ... M 4
Atoka, 446 ... B 4
Atwood, 937 ... D 3
Auburntown, 213 ... J 3
Baileyton, 258 ... Q 2
Bakerville, 45 ... F 3
Bakewell, 600 ... L 4
Banner Hill, 2,517 ... Q 2
Banner Springs, 350 ... M 2
Barr, 75 ... B 3
Barren Plains, 200 ... H 1
Bartlett, 1,150 ... B 4
Bath Springs, 725 ... E 4
Baxter, 1,229 ... K 2
Beacon, 200 ... E 3
Bean Station, 500 ... P 2
Beardstown, 61 ... F 3
Bear Spring, 200 ... F 2
Beech Bluff, 140 ... D 3
Beechgrove, 600 ... J 3
Beersheba Springs, 560 ... K 4
Belfast, 250 ... H 4
Bell Buckle, 393 ... J 3
Belle Meade, 2,933 ... H 2
Bells, 1,474 ... C 3
Belvidere, 230 ... J 4
Bemis, 1,883 ... D 3
Benton⊙, 749 ... M 4
Berry Hill, 1,517 ... H 2
Berry's Chapel, 1,345 ... H 3
Bethel Springs, 781 ... D 4
Bethpage, 305 ... J 1
Big Lick, 263 ... L 3
Big Rock, 400 ... F 1
Big Sandy, 539 ... E 2
Big Spring, 72 ... M 4
Birchwood, 900 ... M 4
Blaine, 650 ... O 2
Blanche, 300 ... H 4
Bloomingdale, 3,120 ... Q 1
Bloomington Springs, 800 ... K 2
Blountville⊙, 900 ... R 1
Bluff City, 947 ... R 2
Bogota, 300 ... C 2
Bolivar⊙, 6,674 ... C 4
Bon Air, 240 ... L 3
Bon Aqua, 400 ... G 3
Bone Cave, 65 ... L 3
Boom, 25 ... L 1
Boston, 40 ... G 3
Braden, 400 ... B 4
Bradford, 968 ... D 2
Bradyville, 75 ... J 3
Braemar-Hampton, 1,100 ... R 2
Brazil, 250 ... C 3
Brentwood, 4,099 ... H 3
Briceville, 850 ... N 2
Brighton, 952 ... B 4
Bristol, 20,064 ... R 1
Brockdell, 150 ... L 3
Brotherton, 200 ... L 2
Brownsville⊙, 7,011 ... C 3
Bruceton, 1,450 ... E 2
Brunswick, 500 ... B 4
Brush Creek, 228 ... J 2
Buchanan, 100 ... E 2
Buena Vista, 500 ... E 3
Buffalo Valley, 150 ... K 2
Bulls Gap, 774 ... P 2
Bumpus Mills, 425 ... F 1
Burlison, 397 ... B 3
Burns, 257 ... G 2
Burrville, 200 ... M 2
Butler, 500 ... S 2
Bybee, 150 ... P 2
Byrdstown⊙, 582 ... L 1
Cades, 94 ... D 3
Cades Cove, 50 ... O 3
Cagle, 150 ... L 4
Cainsville, 65 ... J 3
Calderwood, 50 ... N 3
Calhoun, 624 ... M 4
Camden⊙, 3,052 ... E 2
Campaign, 300 ... K 3
Capleville, 450 ... B 4
Carter, 300 ... R 2
Carthage⊙, 2,491 ... K 2
Caryville, 648 ... N 2
Castalian Springs, 200 ... J 2
Cedar Grove, 250 ... D 3
Cedar Hill, 355 ... H 1
Celina⊙, 1,370 ... K 1
Centertown, 181 ... K 3
Centerville⊙, 2,592 ... G 3
Cerro Gordo, 30 ... E 4
Chapel Hill, 752 ... H 3
Chapmansboro, 300 ... G 2
Charleston, 792 ... M 4
Charlotte⊙, 610 ... G 2
Chaska, 25 ... N 1
Chattanooga⊙, 119,082 ... K 4
Chattanooga, ‡304,927 ... K 4
Cherry, 30 ... B 3
Chesterfield, 150 ... E 3
Chestnut Mound, 190 ... K 2
Chewalla, 155 ... D 4
Chilhowee, 150 ... O 3
Christiana, 350 ... J 3
Chuckey, 250 ... Q 2
Church Hill, 2,822 ... Q 1
Clairfield, 650 ... O 1
Clarkrange, 675 ... L 2
Clarksburg, 349 ... E 3
Clarksville⊙, 31,719 ... G 1
Cleveland⊙, 20,651 ... M 4
Clifton, 737 ... F 4
Clifty, 63 ... L 3
Clinchmore, 200 ... N 2
Clinton⊙, 4,794 ... N 2
Coalfield, 712 ... N 2
Coalmont, 518 ... K 4
Coble, 100 ... F 3
Cokercreek, 500 ... N 4
Coldwater, 15 ... H 4
Colesburg, 150 ... G 2
Collegedale, 3,031 ... M 4
College Grove, 290 ... H 3
Collierville, 3,625 ... B 4
Collinwood, 922 ... F 4
Colonial Heights, 3,027 ... Q 1
Columbia⊙, 21,471 ... G 3
Como, 140 ... E 2
Conasauga, 150 ... M 4
Concord, 500 ... N 3
Cookeville⊙, 14,270 ... L 2
Copperhill, 563 ... N 4
Cordova, 600 ... B 4
Cornersville, 655 ... H 4
Corryton, 500 ... O 2
Cosby, 100 ... P 3
Cottage Grove, 119 ... E 2
Cottontown, 400 ... H 2
Counce, 975 ... E 4
Covington⊙, 5,801 ... B 3
Cowan, 1,772 ... J 4
Crab Orchard, 900 ... M 3
Crawford, 75 ... L 2
Crockett Mills, 170 ... C 3
Cross Plains, 200 ... H 1
Crossville⊙, 5,381 ... L 3
Crump, 392 ... E 4
Culleoka, 300 ... G 4
Cumberland City, 416 ... F 2
Cumberland Furnace, 800 ... G 2
Cumberland Gap, 231 ... O 1
Cummingsville, 25 ... L 3
Cunningham, 170 ... G 2
Curve, 205 ... B 3
Cypress Inn, 500 ... F 4
Dancyville, 125 ... C 4
Dandridge⊙, 1,270 ... O 2
Darden, 111 ... E 3
Daus, 311 ... L 4
Daylight, 150 ... K 3
Dayton⊙, 4,361 ... L 3
Decatur⊙, 698 ... M 3
Decaturville⊙, 958 ... E 3
Decherd, 2,148 ... J 4
Deer Lodge, 300 ... M 2
Delano, 128 ... M 4
Dellrose, 170 ... H 4
Del Rio, 115 ... P 3
Denmark, 61 ... D 3
Denver, 175 ... F 2
De Rossett, 196 ... L 3
Devonia, 250 ... N 2
Dickson, 5,665 ... G 2
Difficult, 100 ... K 2
Dixon Springs, 56 ... J 2
Dover⊙, 1,179 ... F 2
Dowelltown, 329 ... K 2
Doyle, 472 ... K 3
Dresden⊙, 1,939 ... D 2
Drummonds, 700 ... A 4
Duck River, 140 ... G 3
Ducktown, 562 ... N 4
Duff, 190 ... N 2
Dukedom, 150 ... D 2
Dunlap⊙, 1,672 ... L 4
Dyer, 2,501 ... D 2
Dyersburg⊙, 14,523 ... C 2
Eads, 325 ... B 4
Eagan, 300 ... O 1
Eagleton, 5,345 ... O 3
Eagleville, 437 ... H 3
East Cleveland, 1,870 ... M 4
Eastland, 55 ... L 3
East Ridge, 21,799 ... L 5
Eastview, 423 ... D 4
Eaton, 142 ... C 3
Eidson, 101 ... P 1
Elbridge, 150 ... C 2
Elgin, 500 ... M 2
Elizabethton⊙, 12,269 ... R 2
Elkmont, 10 ... O 3
Elkton, 341 ... H 4
Elk Valley, 750 ... N 1
Ellendale, 1,500 ... B 4
Elora, 300 ... J 4
Elysian Grove, 25 ... F 2
Embreeville Junction, 1,293 ... Q 2
Emory Gap, 500 ... M 3
Englewood, 1,878 ... M 4
Enville, 228 ... E 4
Erie, 113 ... M 3
Erin⊙, 1,157 ... F 2
Erwin⊙, 4,715 ... R 2
Estill Springs, 919 ... J 4
Ethridge, 600 ... G 4
Etowah, 3,736 ... M 4
Eva, 250 ... E 2
Evensville, 475 ... M 3
Fairfield, 75 ... J 3
Fairview, 1,630 ... G 3
Fall Branch, 825 ... Q 2
Fall Mills, 100 ... J 4
Fall River, 200 ... G 4
Farmington, 185 ... H 3
Farner, 300 ... N 4
Fayetteville⊙, 7,030 ... H 4
Finger, 267 ... D 4
Finley, 950 ... B 2
Five Points, 125 ... G 4
Flag Pond, 160 ... Q 2
Flat Creek, 130 ... J 4
Flat Woods, 311 ... F 4
Flintville, 500 ... J 4
Florence, 250 ... H 3
Flynns Lick, 50 ... K 2
Forbus, 250 ... M 1
Forest Hill, 850 ... B 4
Forest Hills, 4,255 ... H 2
Fork Mountain, 150 ... N 2
Fort Pillow, 700 ... B 3
Fosterville, 180 ... J 3
Fountain Head, 130 ... J 1
Fowlkes, 200 ... C 3
Frankewing, 75 ... H 4
Franklin⊙, 9,404 ... H 3
Friendship, 441 ... C 3
Friendsville, 575 ... N 3
Fruitland, 175 ... D 3
Fruitvale, 175 ... C 3
Fulton, 88 ... B 3
Gadsden, 523 ... D 3
Gainesboro⊙, 1,101 ... K 2
Gallatin⊙, 13,093 ... H 2
Gallaway, 304 ... B 4
Gardner, 300 ... D 2
Garland, 292 ... B 3
Gassaway, 40 ... K 3
Gates, 523 ... C 3
Gatlinburg, 2,329 ... O 3
Georgetown, 400 ... L 4
Germantown, 3,474 ... B 4
Gibson, 302 ... D 3
Gladeville, 500 ... J 2
Gleason, 1,314 ... D 2
Glen Alice, 150 ... M 3
Glenmary, 250 ... M 2
Gilt Edge, 406 ... B 3
Goin, 50 ... O 2
Goodlettsville, 6,168 ... H 2
Goodspring, 29 ... G 4
Gordonsburg, 10 ... F 3
Gordonsville, 601 ... K 2
Gorman, 150 ... F 2
Grand Junction, 427 ... C 4
Grandview, 1,250 ... M 3
Granville, 80 ... K 2
Graysville, 951 ... L 4
Greenback, 318 ... N 3
Green Brier, 2,279 ... H 2
Greeneville⊙, 13,722 ... Q 2
Greenfield, 2,050 ... D 2
Grimsley, 500 ... L 2
Gruetli, 910 ... K 4
Guys, 425 ... D 4
Habersham, 800 ... N 2
Hales Point, 50 ... B 3
Halls, 2,323 ... C 3
Hampshire, 500 ... G 3
Hampton-Braemar, 1,100 ... R 2
Harms, 45 ... H 4
Harriman, 8,734 ... M 3
Harris, 200 ... C 2
Harrison, 500 ... L 4
Harrogate, 950 ... O 1
Hartford, 336 ... P 3
Hartsville⊙, 2,243 ... J 2
Haydenburg, 75 ... K 2
Heiskell, 350 ... N 2
Helenwood, 675 ... M 2
Henderson⊙, 3,581 ... D 4
Hendersonville, 262 ... H 2
Henning, 605 ... B 3
Henry, 302 ... E 2
Henryville, 125 ... G 4
Hermitage Springs, 175 ... K 1
Hickman, 225 ... K 2
Hickory Valley, 180 ... C 4
Hickory Withe, 200 ... B 4
Hilham, 100 ... L 2
Hillsboro, 223 ... K 4
Hixson, 6,188 ... L 4
Hohenwald⊙, 3,385 ... F 3
Holladay, 175 ... E 3
Hollow Rock, 722 ... E 2
Holston Valley, 200 ... R 1
Holtland, 250 ... H 3
Hornbeak, 418 ... C 2
Hornsby, 212 ... D 4
Howell, 175 ... H 4
Humboldt, 10,066 ... D 3
Huntingdon⊙, 3,661 ... E 2
Huntland, 849 ... J 4
Huntsville⊙, 337 ... N 2
Huron, 40 ... E 3
Hurricane Mills, 400 ... F 3
Idlewild, 280 ... D 2
Indian Mound, 600 ... F 1
Iron City, 504 ... F 4
Isabella, 400 ... N 4
Ivyton, 100 ... L 2
Jacksboro⊙, 689 ... N 2
Jacks Creek, 250 ... D 4
Jackson⊙, 39,996 ... D 3
Jamestown⊙, 1,899 ... M 2
Jasper⊙, 1,811 ... K 4
Jefferson City, 5,124 ... P 2
Jellico, 2,235 ... N 1
Johnson City, 33,770 ... R 2
Jones, 50 ... C 3
Jonesboro⊙, 1,510 ... Q 2
Joppa, 80 ... O 2
Juno, 50 ... E 3
Karns, 1,105 ... N 3
Kelso, 150 ... J 4
Kenton, 1,439 ... C 2
Kerrville, 200 ... B 4
Kimball, 807 ... K 4
Kimberlin Heights, 332 ... O 3
Kimmins, 59 ... F 3
Kingsport, 31,938 ... Q 1
Kingston⊙, 4,142 ... N 3
Kingston Springs, 312 ... G 2
Kinzel Springs, 175 ... O 3
Kirkland, 30 ... H 3
Knoxville⊙, 174,587 ... O 3
Knoxville, ‡400,337 ... O 3
Kodak, 250 ... O 3
Kyles Ford, 60 ... P 1
Laager, 675 ... K 4
Laconia, 50 ... C 4
Lafayette⊙, 2,583 ... J 1
La Follette, 6,902 ... N 2

⊙ County seat. ‡ Population of metropolitan area. ■ Name not shown on map.

All figures available from 1970 final census are supplemented by local official estimates.

La Grange, 213 C 4
Lake City, 1,923 N 2
Lake Hills-Murray Hills, 7,806 L 4
Lakewood, 2,500 H 2
Lancing, 250 M 2
Lane, 150 C 2
Lascassas, 287 J 3
Latham, 85 D 2
Laurel Bloomery, 300 S 1
La Vergne, 2,825 H 3
Lavinia, 150 D 3
Lawrenceburg⊙, 8,889 G 4
Leach, 87 E 3
Leapwood, 100 E 4
Lebanon⊙, 12,492 J 2
Leipers Fork, 350 G 3
Lenoir City, 5,324 N 3
Lenox, 300 C 2
Leoma, 400 G 4
Lewisburg⊙, 7,207 H 4
Lexington⊙, 4,955 E 3
Liberty, 332 K 2
Limestone, 500 Q 2
Linden⊙, 1,062 F 3
Littlelot, 120 G 3
Livingston⊙, 3,050 L 2
Lobelville, 773 F 3
Lone Mountain, 200 O 2
Long Island, 1,352 Q 2
Lookout Mountain, 1,741 L 5
Loretto, 1,375 G 4
Loudon⊙, 3,728 N 3
Louisville, 500 N 3
Lucy, 250 B 4
Lupton City, 750 L 4
Luray, 150 D 3
Luther, 100 P 2
Luttrell, 819 O 2
Lutts, 850 F 4
Lyles, 285 G 3
Lynchburg⊙, 361 J 4
Lynnville, 327 G 4
Macon, 300 B 4
Madison, 13,583 H 2
Madisonville⊙, 2,614 N 3
Malesus, 600 D 3
Manchester⊙, 6,208 J 4
Mansfield, 75 E 2
Martel, 500 N 3
Martha, 5 J 2
Martin, 7,781 D 2
Martins Mills, 440 F 4
Maryville⊙, 13,808 O 3
Mascot, 1,050 O 2
Mason, 443 B 4
Mason Hall, 200 C 2
Maury City, 813 C 3
Maxwell, 160 J 4
Mayland, 400 L 2
Maynardville⊙, 702 O 2
McCloud, 100 Q 2
McConnell, 200 D 2
McDonald, 500 M 4
McEwen, 1,237 F 2
McKenzie, 4,873 E 2
McKinnon, 150 F 2
McLemoresville, 328 D 3
McMinnville⊙, 10,662 K 3
McNairy, 250 D 4
Medina, 755 D 3
Medon, 136 D 4
Memphis⊙, 623,530 B 4
Memphis, ‡770,120 B 4
Mercer, 340 D 4
Michie, 377 E 4
Middleton, 654 D 4
Midway, 400 P 2
Milan, 7,313 D 3
Milledgeville, 349 E 4
Milligan College, 1,170 R 2
Millington, 21,106 B 4
Milo, 95 L 3
Milton, 200 J 3
Minor Hill, 315 G 4
Miston, 205 B 2
Mitchellville, 177 J 1
Mohawk, 100 P 2
Monoville, 150 K 2
Monroe, 40 L 2
Monteagle, 934 K 4
Monterey, 2,351 L 2
Montezuma, 100 D 4
Moodyville, 225 L 1
Mooresburg, 200 P 2
Morley, 400 O 1
Morris Chapel, 225 E 4
Morrison, 379 K 3
Morrison City, 2,178 Q 1
Morristown⊙, 20,318 P 2

Moscow, 448 C 4
Mosheim, 450 Q 2
Moss, 237 K 1
Mount Airy, 100 L 4
Mountain City⊙, 1,883 S 2
Mount Carmel, 2,821 Q 2
Mount Juliet, 800 H 2
Mount Pleasant, 3,530 G 3
Mount Vernon, 350 N 4
Mulberry, 225 H 4
Munford, 1,281 B 4
Murfreesboro⊙, 26,360 J 3
Nashville (cap.)⊙, 447,877 H 2
Nashville, ‡540,982 H 2
Neubert, 1,500 O 3
Neva, 35 S 2
Newbern, 2,124 C 2
Newcomb, 550 N 1
New Johnsonville, 970 E 2
New Market, 950 O 2
New Middleton, 200 J 2
Newport⊙, 7,328 P 3
New River, 250 M 2
New Tazewell, 1,192 O 2
Niota, 629 M 3
Noah, 130 J 3
Norene, 30 J 2
Norma, 150 N 2
Normandy, 122 J 4
Norris, 1,359 N 2
Nunnelly, 375 G 3
Oakdale, 376 M 3
Oakfield, 150 D 3
Oak Hill, 4,490 H 2
Oakland, 353 B 4
Oakley, 400 L 2
Oak Ridge, 28,319 N 2
Obion, 1,010 C 2
Oldfort, 125 M 4
Old Hickory, 7,500 H 2
Olivehill, 125 E 4
Oliver Springs, 3,405 N 2
Oneida, 2,602 N 1
Only, 125 F 3
Ooltewah, 1,200 M 4
Orebank, 1,111 Q 1
Orlinda, 347 H 1
Orme, 122 K 4
Overall, 120 J 3
Ozone, 250 M 3
Pall Mall, 500 M 1
Palmer, 898 K 4
Palmersville, 132 D 2
Palmyra, 125 G 2
Paris⊙, 9,892 E 2
Parrottsville, 115 P 2
Parsons, 2,167 E 3
Pegram, 850 H 2
Pelham, 200 K 4
Perry Switch, 20 D 3
Perryville, 250 F 3
Persia, 200 P 2
Petersburg, 463 H 4
Petros, 800 M 2
Philadelphia, 554 M 3
Phillippy, 20 C 2
Pickwick Dam, 150 E 4
Pigeon Forge, 1,361 O 3
Pikeville⊙, 1,454 L 3
Piney Flats, 325 R 2
Pinson, 236 D 4
Pioneer, 154 N 2
Plant, 250 F 3
Pleasant Hill, 293 L 3
Pleasant Shade, 150 K 2
Pleasant View, 150 G 2
Pleasantville, 80 F 3
Pocahontas, 250 D 4
Portland, 2,872 H 1
Postelle, 150 N 4
Powder Springs, 250 O 2
Powell, 1,200 N 2
Primm Springs, 150 G 3
Prospect, 350 G 4
Providence, 3,830 H 2
Pruden, 60 O 1
Pulaski⊙, 6,989 G 4
Puryear, 458 E 2
Quebeck, 250 K 3
Rader, 150 Q 2
Raleigh, 2,500 B 4
Ralston, 15 D 2
Ramer, 347 D 4
Rasar, 200 O 3
Readyville, 218 J 3
Reagan, 100 E 3
Red Bank, 12,715 L 4
Red Boiling Springs, 726 K 1
Reliance, 400 N 4

Reverie, 82 A 3
Rheatown, 156 Q 2
Riceville, 500 M 4
Richard City, 132 K 5
Richardsons Landing, 50 B 4
Rickman, 500 L 2
Riddleton, 150 J 2
Ridgely, 1,657 B 2
Ridgeside, 458 L 4
Ridgetop, 810 H 2
Ridley, 200 G 3
Ripley⊙, 4,794 B 3
Rives, 385 C 2
Roan Mountain, 950 R 2
Robbins, 200 M 2
Rockford, 950 O 3
Rock Island, 125 K 3
Rockvale, 300 J 3
Rockwood, 5,259 M 3
Roddy, 250 M 3
Rogers Springs, 100 D 4
Rogersville⊙, 4,045 P 2
Rosedale, 100 N 2
Rosemark, 950 B 4
Roslin, 250 M 2
Rossville, 410 B 4
Rugby, 115 M 2
Russellville, 850 P 2
Rutherford, 1,385 C 2
Rutledge⊙, 863 P 2
Sadlersville, 50 G 1
Saint Andrews, 225 K 4
Saint Bethlehem, 200 G 1
Saint Joseph, 637 G 4
Sale Creek, 900 L 4
Saltillo, 423 E 4
Samburg, 463 C 2
Santa Fe, 300 G 3
Sardis, 350 E 4
Saulsbury, 156 C 4
Saundersville, 150 H 2
Savannah⊙, 5,576 E 4
Scotts Hill, 476 E 4
Selmer⊙, 3,495 D 4
Sequatchie, 450 K 4
Sevierville⊙, 2,661 P 3
Sewanee, 1,886 K 4
Seymour, 500 O 3
Shady Valley, 126 S 1
Sharon, 1,188 D 2
Sharps Chapel, 325 O 2
Shelbyville⊙, 12,262 H 4
Sherwood, 350 K 4
Shiloh, 60 E 4
Shop Springs, 190 J 2
Shouns, 427 S 2
Sidonia, 210 D 2
Signal Mountain, 4,839 L 4
Silerton, 88 D 4
Silver Point, 200 K 2
Slayden, 95 G 2
Smartt, 250 K 3
Smithville⊙, 2,997 K 3
Smoky Junction, 100 N 2
Smyrna, 5,698 H 3
Sneedville⊙, 874 P 1
Soddy-Daisy, 7,569 L 4
Somerville⊙, 1,816 C 4
South Carthage■, 859 K 2
South Cleveland, 5,070 M 4
South Clinton, 1,484 N 2
South Fulton, 3,122 D 2
South Pittsburg, 3,613 K 4
Southside, 800 G 2
South Tunnel, 400 H 2
Sparta⊙, 4,930 K 3
Speedwell, 395 O 2
Spencer⊙, 1,179 L 3
Spring City, 1,756 M 3
Spring Creek, 500 D 3
Springfield⊙, 9,720 H 2
Spring Hill, 685 H 3
Springville, 60 E 2
Stainville, 200 N 2
Stanton, 372 C 4
Stantonville, 296 E 4
Statesville, 150 J 2
Static, 135 L 1
Stewart, 200 F 2
Strawberry Plains, 680 O 2
Sugar Tree, 109 E 3
Sullivan Gardens, 950 Q 1
Summertown, 700 G 4
Summitville, 500 K 3
Sunbright, 500 M 2
Surgoinsville, 1,285 Q 2
Sweetwater, 4,340 N 3
Sylvia, 74 G 2
Taft, 300 H 4
Talbott, 975 P 2

Tarlton, 90 K 3
Tazewell⊙, 1,860 P 2
Telford, 300 R 2
Tellico Plains, 773 N 4
Temperance Hall, 150 K 2
Tennessee City, 150 F 2
Tennessee Ridge, 664 F 2
Ten Mile, 700 M 3
Thompsons Station, 300 H 3
Thorn Hill, 200 P 2
Tiftona, 1,750 L 5
Tigrett, 300 C 3
Timothy, 75 L 2
Tipton, 150 B 4
Tiptonville⊙, 2,229 B 2
Toone, 200 D 4
Townsend, 267 O 3
Tracy City, 1,388 K 4
Trade, 425 S 2
Treadway, 712 P 2
Trenton⊙, 4,226 D 3
Trezevant, 877 D 2
Trimble, 675 C 2
Triune, 65 H 3
Troy, 826 C 2
Tullahoma, 15,311 J 4
Turtletown, 212 N 4
Tusculum, 1,157 Q 2
Unicoi, 500 R 2
Union City⊙, 11,925 C 2
Unionville, 150 H 3
Vale, 75 E 2
Vanleer, 320 G 2
Victoria, 800 K 4
Vildo, 100 C 4
Viola, 193 K 3
Vonore, 524 N 3
Wales, 100 G 4
Walland, 200 O 3
Walling, 300 K 3
Walterhill, 350 J 3
Wartburg⊙, 541 M 2
Wartrace, 616 J 3
Washburn, 425 O 2
Watauga, 314 R 2
Watauga Valley, 300 R 2
Watertown, 1,061 J 2
Watts Bar Dam, 20 M 3
Waverly⊙, 3,794 F 2
Waynesboro⊙, 1,983 F 4
Westbourne, 200 O 1
Western State Hospital, 2,900 C 4
Westmoreland, 1,423 J 1
Westpoint, 400 G 4
Westport, 200 E 3
Wetmore, 120 N 4
White Bluff, 516 G 2
Whitehaven, 19,000 A 4
White Horn, 200 Q 2
White House, 650 H 2
White Pine, 1,532 P 2
Whitesburg, 500 P 2
Whiteside, 523 K 5
Whiteville, 992 C 4
Whitleyville, 100 K 2
Whitlock, 75 E 2
Whitwell, 1,669 K 4
Wilder, 250 L 2
Wildersville, 340 E 3
Willette, 150 K 2
Williamsport, 200 G 3
Williston, 282 C 4
Winchester⊙, 5,211 J 4
Winfield, 950 M 1
Winona, 125 N 2
Woodbury⊙, 1,725 J 3
Woodland Mills, 250 C 2
Woodlawn, 500 F 1
Woodstock, 500 A 4
Wrigley, 294 G 3
Wynnburg, 300 C 2
Yorkville, 243 C 2
Yuma, 142 E 3
Zach, 200 E 2

OTHER FEATURES

Andrew Johnson Nat'l Hist. Site Q 2
Appalachian (mts.) N 4
Bald (mts.) Q 3
Barkley (lake) F 1
Big Sandy (riv.) E 2
Boone (lake) R 2
Buffalo (riv.) F 3
Caney Fork (riv.) L 3
Center Hill (lake) K 3
Cheatham (dam) G 2
Cheatham (lake) H 2

Cherokee (dam) O 2
Cherokee (lake) P 2
Chickamauga (dam) L 4
Chickamauga (lake) L 4
Chilhowee (mt.) N 3
Clinch (riv.) N 3
Clingmans Dome (mt.) O 3
Collins (riv.) K 3
Conasauga (riv.) M 5
Cordell Hull (res.) K 2
Cumberland (plat.) L 3
Cumberland (riv.) F 1
Cumberland Gap Nat'l Hist. Park O 1
Dale Hollow (lake) L 1
Douglas (lake) P 3
Duck (riv.) F 3
Elk (riv.) H 4
Emory (riv.) M 2
Flint (riv.) J 5
Forked Deer (riv.) C 3
Fort Campbell, 9,279 G 1
Fort Donelson Nat'l Mil. Park F 2
Fort Loudon (lake) N 3
French Broad (riv.) Q 3
Great Falls (dam) K 3
Great Smoky (mts.) P 3
Great Smoky Mts. Nat'l Park O 3
Green (riv.) F 4
Guyot (mt.) P 3
Harpeth (riv.) G 2
Hatchie (riv.) B 3
Hiwassee (riv.) O 4
Holston (riv.) O 2
Iron (mts.) R 2
J. Percy Priest (lake) J 2
Kentucky (lake) E 2
Le Conte (mt.) P 3
Lick (creek) Q 2
Little Tennessee (riv.) O 4
Loosahatchie (riv.) B 4
Melton Hill (lake) N 3
Memphis Army Depot A 4
Memphis N.A.S. B 4
Meriwether Unit, Natchez Trace Pkwy. F 4
Middle Fork, Forked Deer (riv.) C 3
Middle Fork, Obion (riv.) D 2
Mississippi (riv.) A 4
Nolichucky (riv.) Q 2
Norris (dam) O 2
Norris (lake) O 2
North Fork, Forked Deer (riv.) C 3
North Fork, Obion (riv.) C 2
North Fork, Wolf (riv.) C 4
Obed (riv.) M 2
Obion (riv.) C 2
Ocoee (riv.) M 4
Old Hickory (dam) H 2
Old Hickory (lake) J 2
Paint Rock (riv.) J 5
Pickwick (lake) E 5
Pigeon (riv.) Q 3
Powell (riv.) O 1
Red (riv.) G 1
Reelfoot (lake) C 2
Richland (creek) G 4
Rutherford Fork, Obion (riv.) D 2
Sequatchie (riv.) L 4
Sewart A.F.B. J 2
Shiloh Nat'l Mil. Park E 4
Shoal (creek) F 4
South Fork, Forked Deer (riv.) C 3
South Fork, Holston (riv.) S 1
South Fork, Obion (riv.) D 2
South Holston (lake) R 1
Stone (mts.) S 2
Stones (riv.) J 3
Stones River Nat'l Battlefield H 3
Sulphur Fork, Red (riv.) G 2
Tellico (riv.) N 4
Tennessee (riv.) E 4
Tims Ford (lake) J 4
Unaka (mts.) R 2
Unicoi (mts.) N 4
Watauga (lake) S 2
Watauga (riv.) S 2
Watts Bar (dam) M 3
Watts Bar (lake) M 3
Whiteoak (creek) F 2
Wolf (riv.) B 4
Woods (res.) J 4
Yellow (creek) F 2

TENNESSEE CONSERVATION DEPARTMENT

TOBACCO is a major cash crop. This field in Davidson county grows tobacco that will be fire-cured.

PERSONAL INCOME IN TENNESSEE

Source of wage and salary disbursements	1968	1960	1950
	(Millions of dollars)		
Farms	291	273	338
Mining	45	33	39
Contract construction	490	246	182
Manufacturing	2,804	1,398	693
Wholesale and retail trade	1,423	846	512
Finance, insurance, and real estate	377	200	94
Transportation, communications, and public utilities	486	309	212
Services	1,131	595	297
Government	1,185	580	281
Other industries	16	10	5
	(Dollars)		
Per capita personal income	2,043	1,543	994
Per capita income, U.S	2,746	2,215	1,496

Source: U. S. Dept. of Commerce, *Survey of Current Business.*

VALUE OF FACTORY, FARM, AND MINE PRODUCTION

	1965	1960	1950
	(Millions of dollars)		
Value added by manufacture	4,096	2,586	1,174
Cash farm income	623	526	437
Value of mineral production	183	146	90

Sources: U. S. Dept. of Commerce, *Census of Manufactures;* U. S. Dept. of Agriculture, *The Farm Income Situation;* U. S. Dept. of the Interior, *Minerals Yearbook.*

counting for about 35% of the nonagricultural labor force.

Manufacturing. The diversification of manufacturing in Tennessee is unequaled elsewhere in the South. The production of chemicals is the principal industry, accounting for almost a fourth of the total value added by manufacture. Other leading industrial groups are processed foods, clothing, electrical machinery, textile mill products, primary metals, and stone, clay, and glass products. Paper and allied products, printing and publishing, fabricated metal products, and nonelectrical machinery are also important.

With the exception of Shelby county in West Tennessee and Davidson county in Middle Tennessee, manufacturing is concentrated in the eastern part of the state, where raw materials, low-cost electric power, and coal are plentiful. In addition to the four largest cities, leading industrial centers include Alcoa, site of a large aluminum smelting and rolling plant, and Kingsport, home of one of the nation's largest book-printing plants. Elizabethton has textile mills, and Johnson City processes hardwoods.

The state's industrial development division has been active in locating new industries in smaller cities. Plants that make air-conditioning equipment have been located in Fayetteville and McMinnville. New industries in Jackson produce cereal foods and fiberglas, and one in Union City makes tires.

Agriculture. Tennessee's mild climate and long growing season are conducive to diversified farming, and there is enough rain for temperate-zone crops. Soils are most fertile in the Gulf Coastal Plain and Central Basin. Farmland covers about 60% of the state's area.

Tobacco, cotton, soybeans, hay, and corn account for most of the cash-crop income. In the late 1960's tobacco displaced cotton as the leading cash crop. Other crops include wheat, white and sweet potatoes, apples, strawberries, and truck products. Tobacco raising is concentrated in the eastern, central, and north central parts of the state. Cotton is grown mainly in the fertile lowlands of West Tennessee. Corn, used mainly to feed livestock, is grown in every county of the state. Market gardens flourish near the four major cities, but truck farming as an industry is principally concentrated in the area around Humboldt.

Almost half of Tennessee's farm income is derived from the sale of livestock and livestock products. With an abundance of pasture and water resources, the state is an excellent place to raise both dairy and beef cattle. It leads the South in dairying and is also the national center for the raising of Jersey cattle. Hogs, sheep, and mules are also raised. The Tennessee Walking Horse, noted for its distinctive gait, is bred in the region around Shelbyville and Lewisburg. Poultry are raised in all areas.

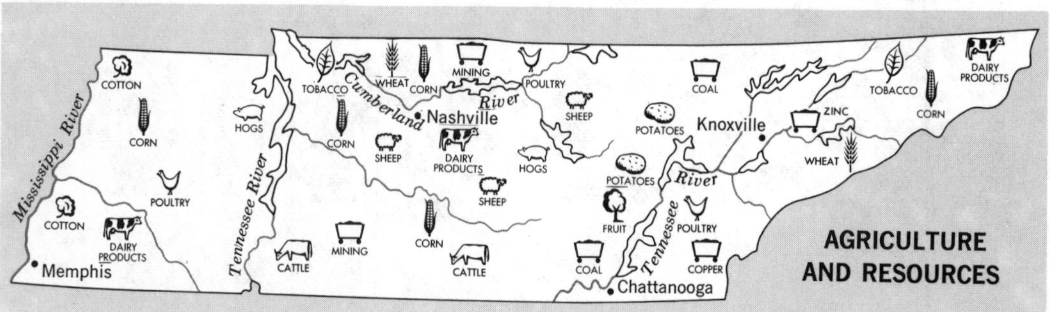

GRANT HEILMAN

BLACK ANGUS cattle graze in eastern Tennessee. Abundant pastureland and water resources favor the raising of both dairy and beef cattle in the state.

Mining. Stone, made up primarily of limestone, marble, and sandstone, is produced in many counties of Middle and East Tennessee, and is the state's leading mineral. Tennessee ranks high among the states in quarrying of marble, much of which has gone into the construction of public buildings. The state leads the nation in zinc production, centered in Knox and Jefferson counties, and it is also the leading producer of pyrite and ball clay. Tennessee ranks third in the output of phosphate rock, produced mainly in the Central Basin. Bituminous coal, mined chiefly in the Cumberland Plateau, is a major economic resource of the state. Blister copper and sulfuric acid are produced in the Ducktown basin.

Power. Almost all of Tennessee is served by the TVA power system. About a fourth of the state's electricity is generated by hydroelectric power and the remainder by large thermal plants fueled by coal.

Transportation. Its central geographic position gives Tennessee definite advantages in the field of transportation. All the major markets of the South are accessible through its water, road, rail, and air systems, and more than half of the population of the United States lives within 24 hours' shipping time.

Despite navigational hazards, the Mississippi, Tennessee, and Cumberland rivers were used from early times as highways of commerce and travel. Together the three rivers have a total of about 1,000 miles (1,610 km) of navigable channel within the state.

The first roads usually followed buffalo and Indian trails. One such trail became the famous Natchez Trace, a pioneer highway between Nashville and Natchez, Miss. Maintenance of through highways was usually turned over to chartered turnpike companies. The modern highway system, maintained by state and federal funds, consisted in the late 1960's of about 77,000 miles (131,000 km) of surfaced roads.

Although Tennesseans became interested in railroad construction in the 1830's, it was not until 1854 that the first railroad line, between Nashville and Chattanooga, was completed. In 1920 the state had more than 4,000 miles (6,440 km) of track, but by the end of the 1960's the number of railroads and track miles in operation were declining. As a result of the competition of automobiles and airplanes, rail passenger traffic declined even more significantly.

Air service is provided by several major airlines. The largest municipal airports serve Memphis, Knoxville, Chattanooga, and Nashville. A fifth major airport serves the tri-city area of Bristol, Johnson City, and Kingsport.

Research and Development. Research programs in both industry and agriculture have been carried on by the TVA since its inception. Research activities in Oak Ridge are also significant. Oak Ridge was built during World War II to produce material for the atomic bomb. Today the Oak Ridge facilities, administered by the U. S. Atomic Energy Commission (AEC), are a center of scientific research vital to the nation's nuclear energy program. Development of reactors for the power industry and research in the use of isotopes are among the areas under study.

Research activities of the University of Tennessee and of other institutions of higher learning continue to be of assistance to both agricultural and industrial development.

4. Government and Politics

The government of Tennessee is organized under a constitution that has been revised several times. First adopted in 1796 before the state was admitted to the Union, it was revised by a convention in 1834 that reflected the spirit of Jacksonian democracy by removing property-holding qualifications for office holding and by democratizing county government and the tax system. But it disfranchised free Negroes. After the Civil War and Reconstruction, a convention of 1870 confirmed the abolition of slavery and enfranchisement of Negroes, but added a poll tax requirement for voters.

The next change came in 1953, when a limited constitutional convention proposed eight changes, which were approved by the required majority of the number of votes cast for legis-

TENNESSEE CONSERVATION DEPARTMENT

Capitol at Nashville, designed by William Strickland.

lators. Among the changes was a provision for the calling of future limited conventions not oftener than once in six years, subject to the approval in a popular referendum by a majority vote; each change proposed by the convention must be approved by a majority vote in a subsequent election. Individual amendments are still legal, but require approval by two General Assemblies, the second by a two-thirds vote, and

GOVERNORS

TERRITORIAL		
William Blount		1790–1796
STATE		
John Sevier	Dem.-Rep.	1796–1801
Archibald Roane	Dem.-Rep.	1801–1803
John Sevier	Dem.-Rep.	1803–1809
Willie Blount	Dem.-Rep.	1809–1815
Joseph McMinn	Dem.-Rep.	1815–1821
William Carroll	Dem.-Rep.	1821–1827
Sam Houston	Dem.-Rep.	1827–1829
William Hall (acting)	Dem.-Rep.	1829–
William Carroll	Democrat	1829–1835
Newton Cannon	Whig	1835–1839
James K. Polk	Democrat	1839–1841
James C. Jones	Whig	1841–1845
Aaron V. Brown	Democrat	1845–1847
Neill S. Brown	Whig	1847–1849
William Trousdale	Democrat	1849–1851
William B. Campbell	Whig	1851–1853
Andrew Johnson	Democrat	1853–1857
Isham G. Harris	Democrat	1857–1862
Andrew Johnson	Military	1862–1865
William G. Brownlow	Republican	1865–1869
DeWitt C. Senter	Conservative-Rep.	1869–1871
John C. Brown	Democrat	1871–1875
James D. Porter	Democrat	1875–1879
Albert S. Marks	Democrat	1879–1881
Alvin Hawkins	Republican	1881–1883
William B. Bate	Democrat	1883–1887
Robert L. Taylor	Democrat	1887–1891
John P. Buchanan	Democrat	1891–1893
Peter Turney	Democrat	1893–1897
Robert L. Taylor	Democrat	1897–1899
Benton McMillin	Democrat	1899–1903
James B. Frazier	Democrat	1903–1905
John I. Cox	Democrat	1905–1907
Malcolm R. Patterson	Democrat	1907–1911
Ben W. Hooper	Republican	1911–1915
Thomas C. Rye	Democrat	1915–1919
Albert H. Roberts	Democrat	1919–1921
Alfred A. Taylor	Republican	1921–1923
Austin Peay	Democrat	1923–1927
Henry H. Horton	Democrat	1927–1933
Hill McAlister	Democrat	1933–1937
Gordon Browning	Democrat	1937–1939
Prentice Cooper	Democrat	1939–1945
Jim Nance McCord	Democrat	1945–1949
Gordon Browning	Democrat	1949–1953
Frank G. Clement	Democrat	1953–1959
Buford Ellington	Democrat	1959–1963
Frank G. Clement	Democrat	1963–1967
Buford Ellington	Democrat	1967–1971
Winfield Dunn	Republican	1971–

GOVERNMENT HIGHLIGHTS

Electoral Vote—10. **Representation in Congress**—U. S. senators, 2; U. S. representatives, 8. **General Assembly**—Senate, 33 members, 4-year terms; House of Representatives, 99 members, 2-year terms. **Governor**—4-year term; may not succeed himself. **Voting Qualifications**—Age 18; residence in state, 1 year; in county, 3 months. **Elections**—General, Tuesday after first Monday in November of even years; primary, first Thursday in August.

approval by the voters in a general election by a majority of the number of votes cast for governor.

Other significant changes by the 1953 convention increased the governor's term from two to four years, increased the pay of legislators, and ended the poll tax requirement for voting. Limited conventions were held in 1959 and 1965. Since 1953, 19 amendments have been approved.

The most important changes of 1965 required the apportionment of both houses of the legislature according to population, unless the U. S. Constitution should be amended to permit some other basis, and the subdivision of urban counties in legislative apportionment for both houses. The latter changes, with the influence of U. S. Supreme Court decisions and court action, have increased greatly the urban influence in the legislature and increased the number of Negro members. A. W. Willis, Jr., of Memphis, elected in 1964, became the first Negro seated in the lower house since 1887, and in each of the elections of 1966 and 1968 six Negroes were elected to the House of Representatives. In 1968, two Negroes were elected to the state Senate, the first in Tennessee's history.

Structure of Government. Tennessee's chief executive, the governor, is elected for a term of 4 years and cannot immediately succeed himself. The governor's cabinet, exclusive of staff agencies, consists of 13 appointed commissioners and the adjutant general.

The General Assembly is composed of a Senate and a House of Representatives. Senators are elected for four years and representatives for two years. The legislature meets in organizational session on the first Tuesday in January of odd-numbered years and on the fourth Tuesday of each February for legislation. It may be called into special session of up to 30 days by the governor. Any bill vetoed by the governor may still become a law if it is again passed by each house of the legislature by a majority of the number of members to which each house is entitled.

The state judiciary consists of a supreme court of five judges, of whom not more than two may reside in any one grand division of the state; a court of appeals, a court of criminal appeals, as well as chancery, circuit, and criminal courts. In addition to a county court for each county, there are justice of the peace and special, city, and general sessions courts.

Public Finance. The state levies a general sales tax, a corporate income tax, a personal income tax on dividends and interest only, taxes on motor fuels, tobacco, and alcoholic beverages, and various privilege taxes. It also receives a considerable amount of revenue from the federal government for highways, education, public welfare, and other purposes.

Social Services. The Tennessee departments of public health and mental health are responsible for health needs. Health policies are set by the public health council. The state has mental hospitals near Knoxville, Nashville, Bolivar, Chattanooga, and Memphis. Donelson and Greeneville have homes for retarded children. The mental health department also sponsors the establishment of community mental health clinics.

The department of public welfare supervises public assistance, child welfare, and services for the blind. The department of correction administers several adult correctional institutions, including the Tennessee State Penitentiary at Nashville and the Brushy Mountain Penitentiary, a maximum security prison at Petros.

Political Parties. The Democratic party has dominated state politics since 1869. Only three Republicans have been elected governor since the Reconstruction period. The Republicans, however, have been able to carry Tennessee in six presidential elections, and in 1966, Howard H. Baker, Jr., became the first popularly elected Republican senator from Tennessee. With the more equitable apportionment of the state's congressional and legislative districts following the historic Supreme Court decision in the "Tennessee case," *Baker* v. *Carr*, of 1962, the Republicans have increased their representation in Congress, and in 1969 they gained control of the lower house of the state legislature for the first time in the modern era. See BAKER V. CARR.

When Tennessee became a state in 1769 it was overwhelmingly devoted to the Democratic-Republican party of Thomas Jefferson, because the Federalists had opposed its admission to the Union. The party later split into factions, and Andrew Jackson, the leader of one faction (later Democrats), was elected to the presidency in 1828, ushering in the era of Jacksonian democracy. A revolt against his leadership led to the rise of the Whig party. The Whigs held a slight edge in the state until the rise of the slavery issue which caused the end of the party and of its successor, the American, or Know-Nothing party. The Democrats dominated Tennessee politics until 1860, when a Tennessean, John Bell, of the Constitutional Union party, carried the state. After the Civil War the Radical Unionists, who later affiliated with the Republicans, completely disfranchised ex-Confederates and remained in power until the Democrats regained control in 1869.

5. Education and Culture

A law of 1873, similar to an act passed by the Radicals in 1867 but repealed in 1870, establishing a statewide system of free public education for whites and Negroes, became known as the parent act of Tennessee's modern educational system. Enrollment in the state's public schools totaled about 892,000 in the late 1960's, whereas enrollment in private and parochial schools exceeded 35,000. More than a third of the state's annual spending is earmarked for public education.

In addition to its many public and private institutions of higher learning, Tennessee has a rich assortment of museums, research facilities, and libraries. The University of Tennessee is one of the fastest-growing centers of higher learning in the South.

Elementary and Secondary Education. Before the Civil War, opportunities for elementary and secondary education were provided largely by academies and other private schools. There was a system of public or common schools free to pupils whose parents could not pay, but it was highly decentralized and handicapped by the stigma of pauperism. In 1838 a common school fund, consisting largely of land revenue, was made a part of the capital of a state bank. The fund was later supplemented by state and local taxes. Nashville and Memphis established city school systems before the Civil War.

Modifications of the 1873 school law included the creation of a state board of education in 1875, provision for a secondary school system in 1891, and the creation of a general education fund in 1909. In 1923 the state superintendent of public instruction became the commissioner of education. Revenue from the general sales tax, of which a major portion is earmarked for education, has greatly benefited the schools.

Following the U. S. Supreme Court decision of 1954 barring racial segregation in the public schools, much progress was made in integrating Tennessee schools. There was some violence in Clinton and Nashville, but as a result of speeding up the grade-a-year plan first used in Nashville in 1957, the public schools in the state were largely integrated by the late 1960's.

Higher Education. The state university and land-grant college of Tennessee is the University of Tennessee, first chartered in 1794 as Blount College (see TENNESSEE, UNIVERSITY OF). The

PERFORMERS on Nashville's *Grand Ole Opry* television show, which has popularized country music.

WSM PHOTO BY LES LEVERETT

main campus of the university is in Knoxville, and it has divisions in Memphis, Martin, Nashville, Tullahoma, Oak Ridge, and Chattanooga. Other state-supported institutions are East Tennessee State University at Johnson City, Middle Tennessee State University at Murfreesboro, Memphis State University, Austin Peay State University at Clarksville, Tennessee Technological University at Cookeville, and the Tennessee Agricultural and Industrial State University, predominantly Negro, at Nashville. In public higher education all formerly white-only colleges were integrated by 1961. There are also several state-supported junior, or community, colleges and several vocational-technical schools. The higher education commission, a coordinating agency, was created in 1968.

There are more than 30 privately supported 4-year colleges and universities in the state. The two largest, Vanderbilt University and George Peabody College for Teachers, are both at Nashville. Fisk University, at Nashville, welcomes all students but is best known as a distinguished school for Negroes. Meharry Medical College at Nashville, Lane College at Jackson, and six private junior colleges are other institutions primarily for Negroes

Historical and Scientific Research Centers. The Tennessee Historical Society has published the *Tennessee Historical Quarterly* since 1942 with the aid of the Tennessee historical commission. The East Tennessee Historical Society, founded in 1925, has published at Knoxville an annual *Publications* since 1929, and the West Tennessee Historical Society has published at Memphis an annual *Papers* since 1947. The Tennessee Historical Commission has collaborated with the University of Tennessee and Vanderbilt University in collecting and publishing the correspondence of Andrew Johnson and James K. Polk.

The University of Tennessee Memorial Research Center and Hospital is a center for medical research with radioactive isotopes. While nuclear research is carried on at Oak Ridge, the Arnold Engineering Development Center at Tullahoma, in conjunction with the University of Tennessee Space Institute, conducts research in missile production.

OAK RIDGE scientist tries experimental device at the laboratory, which does vital nuclear research.

USAEC OAK RIDGE OPERATIONS OFFICE

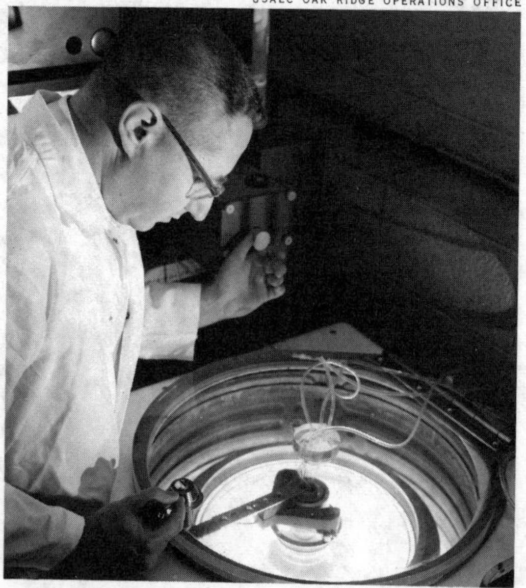

Libraries. The largest public libraries are those of the cities of Memphis, Nashville, Knoxville, and Chattanooga, and the Tennessee State Library at Nashville. Many of the smaller public libraries share the facilities of the state's 11 regional libraries. Major university libraries include those of the University of Tennessee at Knoxville and Memphis and the School of Medicine Library of Vanderbilt University at Nashville.

The Technical Library of the TVA at Knoxville has collections on such subjects as engineering and Southeastern natural resources. The Oak Ridge Institute of Nuclear Studies and the University of Tennessee Space Institute at Tullahoma both have important scientific libraries.

Museums. Tennessee's fine arts galleries include the Brooks Memorial Art Gallery in Memphis; the Dulin Gallery of Art in Knoxville; the George Thomas Hunter Gallery of Art in Chattanooga; and the Tennessee Botanical Gardens and Fine Arts Center and the Parthenon, both in Nashville. The Parthenon is a full-size replica of the Parthenon in Athens. The Memphis Museum and the Tennessee State Museum in Nashville are general museums. The unique American Museum of Atomic Energy at Oak Ridge features nuclear science exhibits. The Frank H. McClung Museum of the University of Tennessee in Knoxville and the Thruston Collection at Vanderbilt University have fine archaeological collections. The collections on the Civil War and Abraham Lincoln at Lincoln Memorial University at Harrogate are excellent.

Music and Theater. The vogue of mountain or country music in the modern era had a considerable part of its origin in Tennessee. The Nashville radio and television program *Grand Ole Opry* contributed greatly to the popularity of this "country and western" music. Nashville is also one of the nation's leading recording centers. W. C. Handy, often called the "father of the blues," began composing in Memphis. The Fisk Jubilee Singers have done much to preserve Negro spirituals. Several popular radio and television artists, including Ernie Ford, Dinah Shore, Chet Atkins, and Minnie Pearl, came from Tennessee. The four large cities support symphony orchestras and little theater groups. Oak Ridge and other smaller towns have significant activities in music and theater.

Folk Arts. At about the beginning of the 20th century the mountainous areas, especially the Great Smokies, saw a significant revival of folk arts and crafts. The Pi Beta Phi Settlement School at Gatlinburg and the Southern Highland Handicraft Guild have helped to maintain the traditional crafts.

Newspapers, Television, and Radio. About 160 newspapers are published in Tennessee, of which about 30 are dailies. The Clarksville *Leaf-Chronicle,* founded in 1808, is the oldest newspaper in continuous publication. Major newspapers are the Memphis *Commercial Appeal,* the Nashville *Banner* and *Tennessean,* the Memphis *Press-Scimitar,* the Knoxville *Journal* and *News-Sentinel,* and the Chattanooga *News-Free Press* and *Times.* The *Times* was published after 1878 by Adolph S. Ochs, who later owned and developed the New York *Times.*

The first radio station in Tennessee, WKN at Memphis, was licensed in 1922. The state now has more than 200 AM and FM radio stations and nearly 30 television stations.

6. Recreation

Tennessee is an extremely popular vacation land. It offers the spectacular beauty of its mountains and lakes as well as many historic sites, including famous battlefields and the homes of three U. S. presidents. Tourist spending is about 6% of the state's retail business.

National Areas. The state's largest and best known park is Great Smoky Mountains National Park of Tennessee and North Carolina. The park contains the loftiest range east of the Mississippi. Cumberland Gap National Historic Park, which Tennessee shares with Kentucky and Virginia, features the famous mountain pass on the Wilderness Road. The Natchez Trace Parkway, partly in Alabama and Mississippi, follows the general route of the old Indian trail and pioneer road. Stones River National Battlefield commemorates the Battle of Stones River, or Murfreesboro. The national military parks of Chickamauga and Chattanooga (partly in Georgia), Shiloh, and Fort Donelson memorialize Civil War battles.

Cherokee National Forest is located almost entirely in Tennessee. Reelfoot National Wildlife Refuge, in the western part of the state, attracts more than 250 species of birds.

State Areas. The state administers 21 parks in Tennessee. Among them are Pickett State Park and Forest in Cumberland Plateau, where rushing streams, tall magnolias, and caves make a wilderness refuge; Fall Creek Falls State Park in the Cumberlands; and David Crockett State Park, near Lawrenceburg, which preserves one of the frontiersman's homes. In West Tennessee are Shelby Forest State Park in the Mississippi Bottom lands and Natchez Trace State Park.

Privately administered caverns with beautiful rock formations include the Tuckaleechee and the Craighead Caverns, and Jewel, Dunbar, and Lookout Mountain caves.

Historic Sites. The National Park Service maintains the Andrew Johnson National Historic Site at Greeneville, which includes the restored home of the 17th president, his tailor shop, and his grave. Two other homes of presidents are preserved as museums. The Hermitage, Andrew Jackson's stately home, is near Nashville, and the ancestral home of James K. Polk is at Columbia. Other historic houses include the homes of William Blount, Tennessee's first territorial governor, at Knoxville; John Sevier, first governor of the state, near Knoxville; Sam Davis, the young Confederate soldier and spy, at Smyrna; and Gen. Nathan Bedford Forrest, near Camden. The Sam Houston Schoolhouse near Maryville and Fort Loudoun, a British colonial fort near Vonore, are also of interest.

Annual Events. Smyrna has a Sam Davis pageant, *Son of This House,* each October, and the *Davy Crockett Pageant* at Rogersville and *The Melungeon Story* at Sneedville are presented each summer. The Tennessee State Fair is held in Nashville in September. Tennessee's annual festivals include the Dogwood Arts Festival at Knoxville, the Cotton Carnival at Memphis, the Craftsman's Fair at Gatlinburg, the Ramp Festival at Cosby, and the Hillbilly Homecoming at Maryville.

GRANT HEILMAN

REELFOOT LAKE is a wildlife refuge with 250 kinds of birds. Bald cypress trees stand in the water.

7. History

In many parts of the state artificial mounds and other remains give evidence of prehistoric inhabitants of the Tennessee region long before the coming of the white man.

Indians. Among the prehistoric natives who lived in Tennessee were groups called Paleo-Indians, who arrived in the area perhaps as many as 15,000 years ago. These were followed by Archaic, Woodland, and Mississippian Indians.

When the English and French began exploring Tennessee, the principal Indian tribes occupying the region were the Cherokee, Chickasaw, Shawnee, Creek, and Yuchi (Uchean). The tribe that had the closest relationship to Tennessee history was the Cherokee, who had some of their towns in what is now southeastern Tennessee. To the west of the Cherokee, near the Mississippi River, lived the small but warlike Chickasaw tribe. Their towns were in north central Mississippi, but they claimed all of West Tennessee and disputed the title to much of Middle Tennessee with the Cherokee. Around 1714, the Shawnee, who inhabited the Cumberland Valley, were driven north of the Ohio by the Cherokee and the Chickasaw. At about the same time, the Creek and the Yuchi were driven southward into the Georgia and Alabama country, and other small tribes also departed. Thereafter the country between the Tennessee and Ohio rivers was a hunting ground for many tribes, but the home of none.

Exploration and Settlement. The first white men to set foot in Tennessee are believed to have been Spaniards in the Hernando de Soto expedition that passed through southeastern Tennessee in 1540 and reached the Mississippi in 1541. In 1566–1567 another Spaniard, Juan Pardo, led two expeditions into southeastern Tennessee and built a fort, later abandoned, near the site of Chattanooga. Englishmen and Frenchmen arrived al-

BRUCE ROBERTS, FROM RAPHO GUILLUMETTE

PRESIDENT POLK'S home at Columbia was built about 1839. It is maintained as a museum.

most simultaneously in Tennessee in 1673. James Needham and Gabriel Arthur, two Virginia traders, entered eastern Tennessee, and the missionary Father Jacques Marquette and the fur trader Louis Jolliet (or Joliet) sailed down the Mississippi as far as the mouth of the Arkansas River. In 1682 the famous French explorer René-Robert Cavelier, Sieur de La Salle, built Fort Prud'homme near the mouth of the Natchez River.

In the struggle between the English and French for control of the Cherokee Indians during the French and Indian War, an expedition from South Carolina built Fort Loudoun in 1756–1757 on the Little Tennessee River. Despite the presence of Fort Loudoun, the Cherokee eventually went over to the French. The construction of the fort had, however, postponed the defection of the Cherokee until it was too late to influence the general result of the war. By the terms of the Treaty of Paris (1763), British title to the area was assured.

The members of the garrison of Fort Loudoun and of the expeditions sent to subdue the Cherokee became aware of the appeal of the Tennessee country for settlement. So-called "long hunters," such as Daniel Boone, Kasper Mansker, and Isaac Bledsoe, returned with glowing reports of the richness of the land, and companies were organized to exploit the region. The English, Scotch-Irish, and German inhabitants of the backcountry of Virginia and the Carolinas, dissatisfied with their political and economic status, looked to the west for a haven from their oppressors. Although the British government, by the Proclamation of 1763, had prohibited any settlement west of the Appalachians, the pioneers ignored the ban.

The first permanent settlement in Tennessee was probably made by William Bean, who brought settlers from Pittsylvania county, Virginia, to the Watauga River about 1769. Other prominent early settlers were James Robertson of North Carolina and John Sevier of Virginia. By 1772 there were four areas of settlement in the northeastern corner of what is now Tennessee. Only one community was on land legally belonging to whites. The other three groups were ordered to move by the British superintendent of Indian affairs. To rectify the situation the settlers leased their lands from the Cherokee in 1772 for 10 years. They then established their own democratic, independent government, called the Watauga Association.

The Revolutionary Period. When the American Revolution broke out in 1775, these pioneers supported the colonies' cause. Faced with the danger of an Indian attack in 1776, they appealed to North Carolina, within whose western claim they were located, and were annexed by that state. The next year, North Carolina created Washington county, to include almost all of present-day Tennessee. The Wataugans not only repulsed the Indian attacks in 1776, they also organized the expedition that marched across the mountains into South Carolina and defeated the British at King's Mountain on Oct. 7, 1780.

It was during the Revolution that the first organized settlement of the Cumberland Valley occurred. In 1775, Richard Henderson, a North Carolina jurist, and the Transylvania Company met the Cherokee Indians at Sycamore Shoals of the Watauga River and purchased from them, for £10,000, a tract including the northern half of Middle Tennessee and a large part of Kentucky. At the same time, the Wataugans took advantage of the opportunity to convert the lease of their land into an outright purchase.

After Virginia had nullified the Transylvania Company's title to the Kentucky part of the Transylvania purchase, Henderson turned to the portion within the bounds of North Carolina. He chose as his agent James Robertson, who selected the site of Nashville as the place of settlement. The settlers moved into the area by two routes during the winter of 1779–1780 and organized a temporary government under the Cumberland Compact. Sheer determination carried the future Nashville through its first years. Indian raids were numerous, and only the spirited leadership of Robertson prevented abandoment of the settlement. In 1783, however, North Carolina created Davidson county, and after the war other settlements arose in the Central Basin to assure the white settlement of Middle Tennessee.

Formation of the State. North Carolina ceded its Tennessee territory to the United States in 1784, and Congress passed an ordinance authorizing the formation of new states in the federal territories. The residents of eastern Tennessee organized a new state and named it Franklin in honor of Benjamin Franklin. Although North Carolina repealed the cession, this did not check the Franklin movement. The Franklinites adopted a constitution, elected John Sevier governor, and continued their efforts to become the 14th state.

For four years the State of Franklin maintained a precarious existence, characterized by Indian troubles, intrigues with the Spanish, internal dissension, and repeated but ineffectual efforts to obtain recognition by Congress and North Carolina. By 1789, North Carolina had succeeded in reestablishing its jurisdiction. In that year, North Carolina again ceded its western claim to the United States, and in 1790 Congress organized the whole Tennessee area into the Territory of the United States South of the River

Ohio, familiarly known as the Southwest Territory. (See FRANKLIN, STATE OF.)

The new territory was governed in accordance with the provisions of the Northwest Ordinance of 1787, except that slavery was not prohibited. William Blount, a North Carolina political leader, was appointed governor by President Washington. Agitation in favor of statehood continued to grow, however, and when a census of 1795 revealed that the population had exceeded the required 60,000 residents, a consitutional convention assembled in Knoxville, the capital. It soon completed the drafting of the state's first constitution and, without waiting for congressional approval, provided for the immediate organization of a state government. In an election in March 1796 members of the General Assembly were chosen, and Sevier was selected as governor. Finally, on June 1, Tennessee gained admission to the Union as the 16th state.

Early Statehood. By 1796 only a little more than half of the valley of East Tennessee and the region watered by the Cumberland and its tributaries had been cleared of the Indian title. One of the chief demands of the new state upon the federal government was that title to the remainder be quickly disposed of. Through treaties with the Cherokee (1798–1819) and the purchase of West Tennessee from the Chickasaw (1818), all of Tennessee was cleared except for the southeastern corner. This area was finally opened to settlement in 1838, when the Cherokee were forcibly removed to the West. Meanwhile, in 1806, a triangular land dispute with North Carolina and the United States was adjusted.

The War of 1812 was popular in Tennessee, and large numbers of Tennesseans volunteered for service. Their activities, however, were confined mainly to the crushing of the Creek Indians and to participation in the battles of Pensacola and New Orleans. Later, when Tennessee supplied many soldiers in the Mexican War, the readiness of Tennesseans to volunteer helped confirm for Tennessee the nickname "Volunteer State."

The Civil War Period. Following the withdrawal of South Carolina and other Southern states from the Union, the people of Tennessee refused to call a convention to consider secession. With the beginning of hostilities at Fort Sumter in April 1861, however, a strong secessionist sentiment swept the state. Gov. Isham G. Harris refused to respond to President Lincoln's call for troops, and on June 8, the state as a whole voted overwhelmingly for separation from the Union. East Tennessee, where there were relatively few slaves, remained opposed to this action.

Next to Virginia, Tennessee was the leading battleground of the war. More than 400 battles or skirmishes were fought within its borders. The most important were the battles of Fort Henry and Fort Donelson, Shiloh, Stones River or Murfreesboro, Chickamauga, Chattanooga, Franklin, and Nashville. Tennessee sent more troops to the Civil War than any other Southern state. Of a total of 145,000 soldiers, 30,000 were in the Union Army, mostly from East Tennessee.

When Federal troops occupied Middle and West Tennessee in the spring of 1862, Andrew Johnson took office as military governor of the state. East Tennessee was cleared of Confederates by the end of 1863. The Union Convention to provide for reestablishment of civil government convened in Nashville on Jan. 9, 1865. This meeting proposed amending the state constitution to abolish slavery. The measure, which was approved by popular vote on February 22, became

FAMOUS RESIDENTS OF TENNESSEE

Agee, James (1909–1955), writer; winner of Pulitzer Prize for novel *A Death in the Family*, 1957.

Anderson, William R. (1920–), commander of *Nautilus*, first atomic submarine, in voyage under North Pole; U. S. representative.

Baker, Howard H., Jr. (1925–), U. S. senator.

Barnard, Edward Emerson (1857–1923), astronomer, who discovered the fifth satellite of Jupiter.

Bell, John (1797–1869), U. S. representative and senator; Constitutional Union presidential nominee, 1860.

Blount, William (1749–1800), governor of Southwest Territory, 1790–1796; U. S. senator.

Bradford, Roark (1896–1948), author of *Ol' Man Adam an' His Chillun*, known for his depiction of Negro life.

Brownlow, William Gannaway (1805–1877), newspaper editor, state governor and U. S. senator.

Brush, George de Forest (1855–1941), portrait painter.

Campbell, Sir Francis Joseph (1832–1941), educator of the blind.

Carmack, Edward Ward (1832–1914), editor and prohibitionist; U. S. representative and senator.

Carroll, William (1788–1844), officer in War of 1812; reform governor, who served longer than any other Tennessee governor.

Claxton, Philander P. (1862–1957), crusader for public education; U. S. commissioner of education.

Crockett, David (1786–1836), frontiersman, state legislator, and U. S. representative.

Crump, Edward Hull (1874–1954), despotic political leader; mayor of Memphis and U. S. representative.

Farragut, David Glasgow (1801–1870), naval officer in Civil War and first full admiral in U. S. Navy.

Forrest, Nathan Bedford (1821–1877), Confederate cavalry general known for his use of mounted infantry.

Gore, Albert Arnold (1907–), U. S. representative and senator.

Halliburton, Richard (1900–1939), writer and explorer.

Harris, George Washington (1814–1869), humorist, known for homespun tales collected as *Sut Lovingood Yarns.*

Harris, Isham Green (1818–1897), state governor, 1857–1862; U. S. representative and senator.

Houston, Sam (1793–1863), governor of Tennessee; later, a founder of Texas and U. S. senator from Texas.

Hull, Cordell (1871–1955), U. S. secretary of state, 1933–1944; winner of Nobel Peace Prize, 1945.

Jackson, Andrew, 1767–1845; 7th president of the United States, U. S. senator, and hero of War of 1812.

Johnson, Andrew (1808–1875), 17th president of the United States; state governor and U. S. senator.

Kefauver, Carey Estes (1903–1963) U. S. representative and senator; Democratic vice presidential nominee, 1956.

McKellar, Kenneth Douglas (1869–1957), U. S. representative, senator, president pro tempore of U. S. Senate.

Moore, Grace (1901–1947), opera and concert singer.

Naegele, Charles Frederick (1857–1944), portrait painter.

Peay, Austin (1876–1927), legislator and governor, who reorganized state administration.

Polk, James Knox (1795–1849), 11th president of the United States, who guided nation through Mexican War.

Robertson, James (1742–1814), pioneer settler in Watauga region and founder of Nashville.

Sequoya (1770?–1843), Cherokee Indian scholar and educator.

Sevier, John (1745–1815), pioneer settler; first and only governor of State of Franklin; first governor of Tennessee.

Stribling, Thomas Sigismund (1881–1965), writer; winner of Pulitzer Prize for novel *The Store.*

Walker, William (1824–1860), adventurer and filibuster; president of Nicaragua, 1856–1857.

White, Hugh Lawson (1773–1840), legislator, jurist, and U. S. senator; Whig presidential candidate, 1836.

York, Alvin C. (1887–1964), World War I hero.

HISTORICAL HIGHLIGHTS

1540 Hernando de Soto entered Tennessee region.
1566 Spaniards under Juan Pedro built fort near site of Chattanooga.
1673 First English (Needham and Arthur) and French (Marquette and Jolliet) explorers visited Tennessee area.
1682 La Salle and party built Fort Prud'homme near mouth of Hatchie River.
1757 Fort Loudoun, westernmost English fort, completed by expedition from South Carolina.
1769 First permanent white settlement established in Watauga Valley.
1772 Tennessee settlers formed homespun government called Watauga Association.
1779 Organized settlement of Middle Tennessee began with founding of Nashville.
1780 Tennesseans helped defeat British at King's Mountain, S. C.
1784 Settlers in eastern Tennessee formed short-lived State of Franklin.
1790 Tennessee country organized as Southwest Territory.
1794 University of Tennessee chartered as Blount College.
1796 Tennessee joined Union as 16th state (June 6).
1818 West Tennessee acquired from Chickasaw by Jackson Purchase.
1835 New state constitution replaced charter of 1796.
1838 Cherokee removed to the West on "Trail of Tears."
1843 Nashville selected as permanent state capital.
1854 Tennessee's first railroad completed between Nashville and Chattanooga.
1861 Tennessee seceded from Union to join Confederacy.
1865 Civil government restored and slavery abolished.
1866 Tennessee readmitted to Union.
1867 Negroes given right to vote by legislative act.
1870 New state constitution framed and adopted.
1925 Famous Scopes "monkey trial" held at Dayton.
1933 Tennessee Valley Authority created by Congress.
1942 Manhattan Project for creation of atomic bomb established at Oak Ridge.
1954 First amendments to constitution of 1870 approved.
1962 U. S. Supreme Court ruled, in historic "Tennessee case," that federal courts could require reapportionment of legislative seats.
1964 Tennessee Space Institute established at Tullahoma.
1967 Howard H. Baker, Jr. became first popularly elected Republican senator from Tennessee.

the first state action prohibiting slavery in an area exempted from the application of the Emancipation Proclamation. The convention also nominated William G. Brownlow for the governorship and candidates for all seats in the legislature. These candidates were elected by a total vote of more than the necessary 10% of the presidential votes cast in 1860. With the inauguration of Brownlow on April 6, 1865, civil government returned to Tennessee.

Postwar Developments. During the Brownlow regime the state was controlled by the Radical Unionist party, dominated by East Tennesseans, which eventually affiliated with the Republican party. Since ex-Confederates were disfranchised, the small number of Conservative Unionists could not prevent ratification of the 14th Amendment on July 19, 1866. Five days later, the state was readmitted to the Union, thereby escaping the harsh program of Reconstruction applied to the other 10 states of the Confederacy. Negroes were enfranchised in 1867, and in the following year were granted the privilege of holding office. However, the Radicals were overthrown in 1869 in an election that was preceded by considerable activity by the Ku Klux Klan.

Recovery from the war was slow, and social and economic problems caused considerable hardship. At the close of Reconstruction the state faced the divisive issue of a large debt. After several attempts at settlement had failed, the bondholders, with few exceptions, were forced to accept in 1883 new bonds ranging from 50 to 80 cents on the dollar. In the 1870's and 1880's the economic distress of the farmers, who were organized by the Grange and the Farmers' Alliances, was another disruptive influence. Coal miners, angered by the use of convicts as strikebreakers under the convict lease system, rose in revolt in 1891 and 1892 in the so-called "Coal Miner's War," an uprising that led to the abandonment of the lease system. The prohibition and women's rights movements both caused controversy.

Since 1900. The Scopes "monkey trial" was held at Dayton in 1925. The famous trial of John T. Scopes, a Tennessee high school teacher, served to draw attention to the religious fundamentalism in the state. (See Scopes Case.) The antievolution law was finally repealed in 1967.

Tennesseans, who more than filled the state's troop quota in the Spanish-American War, volunteered in great numbers in World War I. In World War II more than 315,000 Tennesseans entered the armed forces. Large areas of the state were given over to training maneuvers and to war industry, and the atomic bomb was developed at Oak Ridge.

Tennessee suffered acutely during the Depression, and the plight of farmers was heightened by severe drought. The economy was materially aided by the creation of the TVA in 1933, and industry supplanted agriculture as the chief source of wealth in the decades after the war. The urbanization of the state was reflected in the legislature that convened in 1967, the first to be apportioned under the Supreme Court's one-man, one-vote rule. Over half of the lawmakers were from urban or semiurban counties. In 1968 the assassination in Memphis of Dr. Martin Luther King, Jr., the nonviolent leader, set off serious racial disorders in that city and Chattanooga and Nashville.

Stanley J. Folmsbee
University of Tennessee

Bibliography

Abernethy, Thomas P., *From Frontier to Plantation in Tennessee,* reprinted (University, Ala., 1967).
American Guide Series, *Tennessee: A Guide to the State,* rev. ed. (New York 1949).
Folmsbee, Stanley J., Corlew, Robert E., and Mitchell, Enoch L., *History of Tennessee,* 2 vols. (New York 1960).
Folmsbee, Stanley, J., Corlew, Robert E., and Mitchell, Enoch L., *Tennessee: A Short History* (Knoxville 1969).
Folmsbee, Stanley J., *Sectionalism and Internal Improvements in Tennessee, 1796–1845* (Knoxville 1939).
Govan, Gilbert E., and Livingood, James W., *The Chattanooga Country,* rev. ed. (Chapel Hill, N. C., 1963).
Greene, Lee S., and Avery, Robert S., *Government in Tennessee,* rev. ed. (Knoxville 1966).
Hamer, Philip M., *Tennessee: A History, 1763–1932,* 4 vols. (New York 1933).
Law, Henry L., *Tennessee Geography,* rev. ed. (Norman, Okla., 1967).
Lewis, Thomas M. N., and Kneberg, Madeline, *Tribes That Slumber: Indians of the Tennessee Region,* reprinted (Knoxville 1966).
Parks, Joseph H., and Folmsbee, Stanley J., *The Story of Tennessee,* 5th ed. (Norman, Okla., 1968).
Rothrock, Mary U., *This is Tennessee* (Knoxville 1963).

TENNESSEE, The University of, a state university with its administrative center located in Knoxville. It was established there in 1794 as Blount College, a private, nonsectarian school, one of the first two colleges west of the Blue Ridge Mountains and the first in America to admit women. It became a public institution in 1807, the state land-grant college in 1869, and the state university in 1879.

The president and four vice presidents of the university administer a statewide system of higher education. Chancellors supervise campuses at Knoxville, Martin, Chattanooga, and Nashville and medical units at Memphis. The Space Institute is located at Tullahoma, the Graduate School of Biomedical Sciences is at Oak Ridge, and there are university centers in Memphis and Kingsport. Agricultural experiment stations, extension service offices, and agricultural and home demonstration agents are distributed throughout the state.

The divisions of the university offer programs of study leading to the bachelor's degree in 120 fields, the master's in 141, and the doctorate in 50. Enrollment grew from 12,500 in 1960 to more than 35,500 in 1970, including about 5,000 graduate students. The combined libraries have more than a million volumes.

WILLIAM H. JESSE
University of Tennessee, Knoxville

TENNESSEE RIVER, a stream that, with its tributaries, drains a 7-state area. Half of this area is within Tennessee, but portions of Virginia, North Carolina, Georgia, Alabama, Mississippi, and Kentucky are also drained by the river system.

The Tennessee River is formed by the confluence of the Holston and French Broad rivers just north of Knoxville, Tenn. From there it follows a circuitous course of 652 miles (1,043 km) southwestward into Alabama and northward through Tennessee and Kentucky to its junction with the Ohio River near the southern tip of Illinois. Since the source waters of the Tennessee originate on the eastern slopes of the Cumberland Mountains of Virginia and in the Great Smoky Mountains of Tennessee and North Carolina, some of the water in the river system falls from an elevation of more than 3,000 feet (915 meters) to a level of 300 feet at the junction of the Tennessee with the Ohio.

The people in the river basin once lived in constant dread of floods, but the Tennessee Valley Authority, established in 1933, eliminated the hazard by building a series of dams. See also TENNESSEE VALLEY AUTHORITY.

MALCOLM A. MURRAY
Georgia State University

TENNESSEE STATE UNIVERSITY is a state-supported, land-grant institution located in Nashville. It opened as the Tennessee Agricultural and Industrial State Normal School in 1912, and the first college-level instruction was given in 1922. In 1927 the name was changed to Tennessee Agricultural and Industrial State College. A graduate program was started in 1941. In 1951 the college became a university, and in 1958 it attained land-grant status. In 1969 the present name was adopted.

The university consists of 5 schools and 24 departments. The schools include agriculture and home economics, arts and sciences, education, engineering, and the graduate school, which offers programs leading to the master's degree in arts and sciences, agriculture, and education. The enrollment exceeds 5,000 men and women, with about 180 graduate students. Agriculture is a major field of research at Tennessee State.

TENNESSEE TECHNOLOGICAL UNIVERSITY is a state-supported university in Cookeville. It was established by an act of the general assembly in 1915 as Tennessee Polytechnic Institute, and it opened in 1916. In 1958 a graduate program was started, and in 1965 university status was granted by the general assembly.

The university is composed of six colleges and schools that are divided into some 30 departments offering over 1,100 courses. They include arts and sciences, agriculture and home economics, business administration, education, engineering, and the graduate school, which offers M. A. or M. S. degree programs in arts and sciences, education, and engineering. Tennessee Tech has a faculty of over 300 and a student body of about 6,000 men and women, including about 240 graduate students.

C. P. SNELGROVE
Tennessee Technological University

TENNESSEE VALLEY AUTHORITY, a federal agency created by the U. S. Congress in 1933 to develop the Tennessee River and its tributaries. The TVA applied the concept of overall planning to a river basin comprising 40,000 square miles (about 104,000 sq km) and covering parts of seven states.

The TVA is the most ambitious and far-reaching attempt by the U. S. government to bring about the coordinated, integrated, and long-range development of the resources of a large area. Its experience has demonstrated the feasibility of a multiple-purpose approach (flood control, navigation, and hydroelectric power) to stream development. It has tested such concepts as the integration of activities, decentralized administration and centralized authority, and education as a means of achieving program objectives.

Although the TVA has done a great deal to change the mores of the Tennessee Valley, it has never fulfilled its early promise as an economic and social experiment in regional planning. Yet its impact in the United States and abroad has been enormous. As a symbol and model, it has attracted attention and emulation all over the world.

Origins. The Tennesseee, fourth-largest river in streamflow in the United States, was subject to periodic floods before the TVA was created. Navigation of its middle passage was obstructed by a series of impassable shoals. And the basin it drained, though rich in natural resources, was a region of exhausted soil and depressed economy. No significant development of the river had taken place until World War I when, in 1918, the federal government built two nitrate plants and began the construction of a dam at Muscle Shoals, Ala., the most important water-power site on the river.

The disposition of the Muscle Shoals facilities became one of the major political issues of the 1920's, involving conflicting hopes concerning the river's vast hydroelectric potential, the production of cheap fertilizer, the industrialization of the Tennessee Valley, and the desirability of public management of natural resources. The Republican administrations in Washington sought

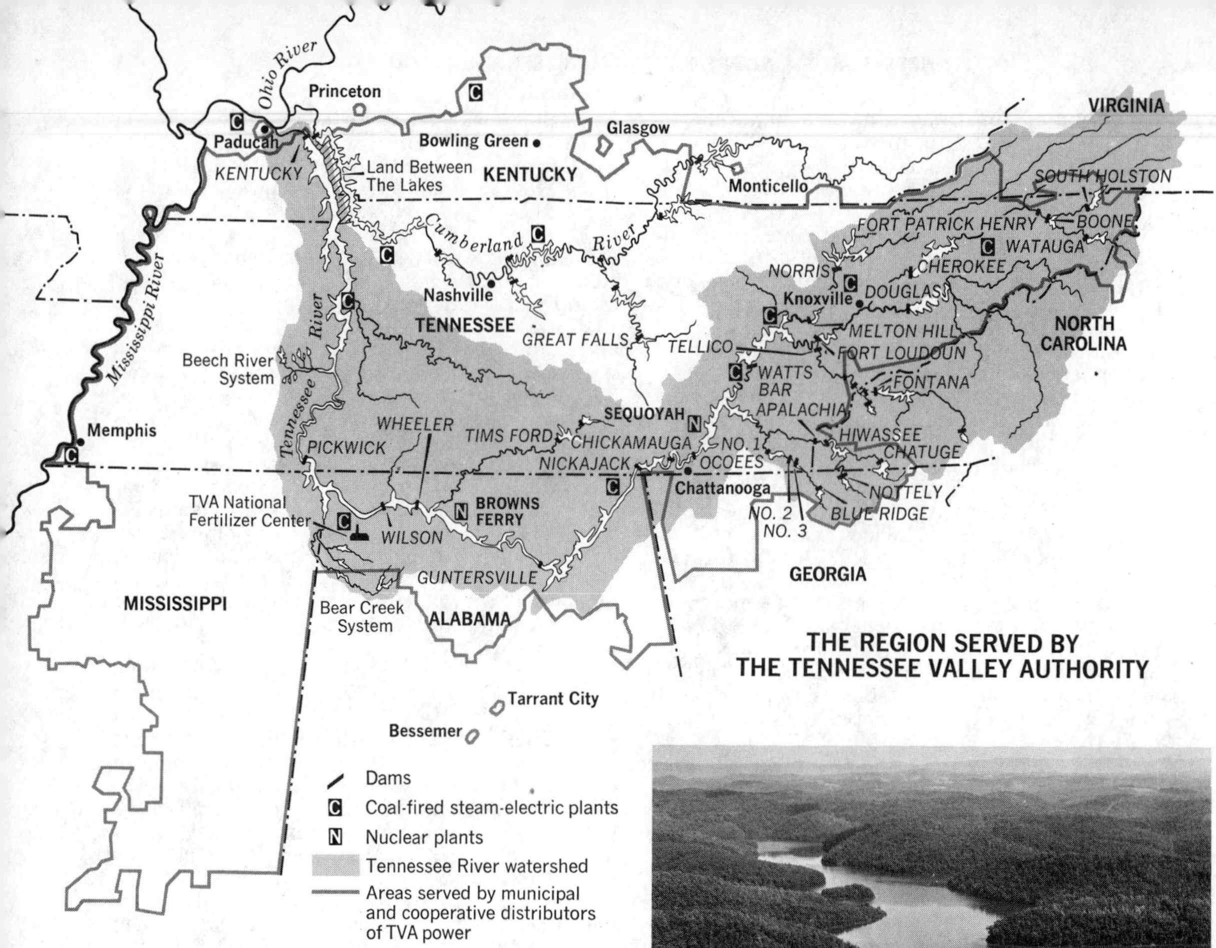

THE REGION SERVED BY THE TENNESSEE VALLEY AUTHORITY

Dams
Coal-fired steam-electric plants
Nuclear plants
Tennessee River watershed
Areas served by municipal and cooperative distributors of TVA power

to lease the facilities to a private concern, but these efforts were defeated by a group of congressmen led by Sen. George W. Norris of Nebraska. Norris managed to obtain congressional approval of bills providing for government operation, but they were vetoed by President Calvin Coolidge in 1928 and by President Herbert Hoover in 1931. In the presidential campaign of 1932, Franklin D. Roosevelt endorsed the Norris approach, and his interest in forests, land, and water led him as president to recommend an even broader plan to Congress in 1933.

The result was the Tennessee Valley Authority Act of 1933, which created a government corporation under the control of a 3-man board, endowed with sweeping authority subject to the general supervision of the president and Congress. The purposes of the act included flood control, navigation, the generating of electric power, reforestration, the proper use of marginal lands, and "the economic and social well-being" of the people living in the river basin.

During the 1930's the new agency survived an attack on its constitutionality, a conflict within its board of directors, and a congressional investigation. In 1939 it purchased the facilities of the private power companies in the valley for $78.5 million. Meanwhile, the authority, using funds appropriated by Congress, proceeded to construct its great multipurpose dams, completing the last of the nine main river structures in 1944.

Programs. The TVA's greatest success has been as a producer and distributor of cheap, plentiful electric power. But its accomplishments in controlling floods and improving river navigation have also been notable. Its physical plant represents an impressive engineering and architectural achievement. The authority has been the chief regionwide stimulus in the area since 1933. It has contributed substantially to the industrialization and strengthening of the regional economy.

TENNESSEE VALLEY AUTHORITY

NORRIS DAM on the Clinch River, completed in 1936, was the first dam to be built by the TVA.

Flood Control and Navigation. The TVA dams and reservoirs created an almost perfect system of water control. The authority could hold back or release water as needed to perform its varied functions. No major floods have occurred in the valley since the completion of the main dams, and hundreds of millions of dollars in cumulative flood damage have been averted. A system of high-lift locks now connects the lakes created by the dams, providing a great inland waterway with a 9-foot channel 650 miles in length.

Electric Power. The TVA built an integrated power system, pioneered in the use of promotional rates, and gave its region the lowest-cost electricity and highest per capita use in the nation. It distributes power at wholesale rates to about 160 municipalities and cooperatives, as well as to the Atomic Energy Commission and other government agencies. Increased demand after World War II led the authority to expand its power system by adding coal-fired steam plants, which eventually produced more than 75% of the total power output. In the 1960's the agency also began constructing nuclear-fueled generating plants. By 1970 its total generating capacity was 19 million kilowatts, and facilities being built or planned were to add 13 million kw.

Sponsors of the TVA argued that it would serve as a "yardstick" for the regulation of private power rates, but critics insisted that the "yardstick" theory was unfair. In practice the problems of allocating costs among navigation, flood control, and other purposes made it impossible to use TVA rates as a precise measuring device. The agency's rates, however, were unquestionably a decisive factor in the reduction of electric charges all over the country. In 1959, Congress authorized the TVA to sell its own bonds to finance the expansion of its power program, but at the same time the corporation was forbidden to expand beyond its existing operating territory.

Agriculture and Forestry. The TVA cooperated with local authorities and citizen groups in promoting better farming methods, conservation techniques, and reforestration. The agency has emphasized fertilizer research and production, especially of phosphates. It has encouraged scientific agriculture on thousands of demonstration farms in the region. It has helped reforest more than 1 million acres (405,000 hectares) of gullied land and vulnerable watersheds.

Other Activities. Among the auxiliary programs of the TVA was the creation of opportunities for boating, fishing, and camping on the "Great Lakes of the South." In the 1960's the authority launched an ambitious project for a national outdoor recreation center, Land Between the Lakes, situated in western Kentucky and Tennessee.

In earlier years the TVA carried out a successful program of mosquito control and cooperated with other agencies in promoting better health services. It established libraries, sponsored adult education programs, and conducted many kinds of research. From the beginning, the TVA made a practice of working through the valley's existing governmental units and of enlisting the cooperation of quasi-public bodies and private groups in advancing its programs.

DEWEY W. GRANTHAM, *Vanderbilt University*
Author of "The Democratic South"

Bibliography

Clapp, Gordon R., *The TVA: An Approach to the Development of a Region* (Chicago 1955).
Droze, Wilmon Henry, *High Dams and Slack Waters: TVA Rebuilds a River* (Baton Rouge, La., 1965).
Hubbard, Preston J., *Origins of the TVA: The Muscle Shoals Controversy, 1920–1932* (Nashville, Tenn., 1961).
Kyle, John H., *The Building of TVA: An Illustrated History* (Baton Rouge 1958).
Lilienthal, David E., *TVA: Democracy on the March,* rev. ed. (New York 1953).
Martin, Roscoe C., ed., *TVA, the First Twenty Years: A Staff Report* (Knoxville, Tenn., 1956).
Moore, John R., ed., *The Economic Impact of TVA* (Knoxville 1967).

TENNESSEE WALKING HORSE, a breed of light horse developed in the central basin of Tennessee about 1790. Its foundation stock includes early representatives of the Morgan, American saddle horse, thoroughbred, and other breeds present in the area at that time. Originally a utility and work animal of the Tennessee settlers, it is now a pleasure and show horse. It averages 15½ hands (5 feet 2 inches, or 1.57 meters) high and 1,000 to 1,200 pounds (450–545 kg) in weight. Coat colors are sorrel, chestnut, black, roan, white, bay, brown, gray, and yellow.

The Tennessee walking horse is the only breed capable of naturally overstriding—that is, placing the back hoof in front of the fore hoofprint. It has three gaits: the flat-foot walk, the running walk, and the canter, with particular emphasis placed on the running walk.

PETE YOKLEY, *Tennessee Walking Horse Breeders' Association of America*

TENNIEL, ten'yəl, **Sir John** (1820–1914), English cartoonist and illustrator. He was born in London on Feb. 28, 1820. He received his first art training at the Royal Academy but also studied under the illustrator Charles Keene and carried on special studies at the British Museum. One of his first commissions, for the House of Lords in 1845, was a fresco illustrating Dryden's *St. Cecilia.* He joined the staff of *Punch* magazine in 1850 and remained with *Punch* until his retirement in 1901 (see CARTOON—*Political Cartoons*). He was knighted in 1893 and died in London on Feb. 25, 1914.

Tenniel illustrated some 30 books and produced over 2,000 *Punch* cartoons. In his own time his greatest achievement was thought to be his illustrations for an 1861 edition of Thomas Moore's *Lalla Rookh,* but he is most affectionately remembered as the illustrator of Lewis Carroll's *Alice's Adventures in Wonderland* and *Through the Looking Glass.* See also ALICE'S ADVENTURES IN WONDERLAND; LITERATURE FOR CHILDREN.

COLTA FELLER IVES
Metropolitan Museum of Art, New York

Tenniel drawing for Carroll's *Through the Looking Glass.*
NEW YORK PUBLIC LIBRARY

FOREHAND DRIVE. The player swings his racket back on a line with the flight of the oncoming ball. He meets the ball about mid-point of his body as he transfers his weight from rear to front foot. His racket moves forward and upward in the follow-through.

BACKHAND DRIVE. The player keeps one shoulder facing the net and one hand bracing the throat of the racket until just before he swings forward to hit the ball opposite his front foot. He hits it at arm's length and follows through in a full swing.

TENNIS is an outdoor or indoor game, played on a rectangular court by two persons (singles) or by four persons (doubles), who use rackets to hit a ball back and forth across a net. The object is to score points by striking the ball in such a way that an opponent cannot return it successfully. The game originated in England and was first played on grass. It was called *lawn tennis* to distinguish it from *court tennis,* the ancient parent game (see also COURT TENNIS). Today, however, the game is referred to as tennis.

Tennis is popular among persons of all ages, both male and female. When played solely for recreation, the game attracts millions of participants. Only a few hundred players enter international tournaments, most of whom are professionals who compete for prize money. Governing all play are the rules established by the International Lawn Tennis Federation (ILTF), founded in 1913. The federation embraces more than 70 national organizations, among them the U. S. Lawn Tennis Association (USLTA).

The four major championships on the international circuit are the British, Australian, French, and the United States, together known as the Big Four. Other important tournaments include the Italian, West German, and South African. The premier title is the British, popularly called Wimbledon. The richest is the U. S. Open, held at Forest Hills, N. Y., offering more than $150,000 in prize money.

The most coveted team trophy in men's international play is the International Lawn Tennis Challenge Trophy donated in 1900 by an American, Dwight F. Davis, and known as the Davis Cup. More than 50 countries, organized by geographical zones, enter the annual competition. Since its inception, only four countries have ever won the trophy—Australia and the United States, which have dominated play, and Britain and France.

In 1963, in observance of its 50th anniversary, the ILTF inaugurated the Federation Cup for the world women's team championship. More than 20 countries compete for the trophy. British and American women's teams play annually for the Wightman Cup. Hazel Hotchkiss Wightman of California presented the cup to the USLTA in 1919; competition began in 1923.

The National Lawn Tennis Hall of Fame and Tennis Museum opened in Newport, R. I., in 1954. Distinguished players and officials are selected for membership in the Hall of Fame on the basis of sportsmanship, skill, and contributions to the game.

The Court and Equipment. The court measures 78 feet (23.77 meters) long at the *sidelines* and, for the singles game, 27 feet (8.2 meters) wide at the *base lines.* For doubles, the court is made 9 feet (2.7 meters) wider by extending the base lines 4½ feet (1.37 meters) in each direction. The extensions, enclosed by added sidelines, are called *alleys.*

A net parallel to the base lines divides the court at the center. The net, which is of natural or synthetic cord, is strung between two posts. It is 3 feet (0.91 meter) high at the center and 3½ feet (about 1 meter) at the sideline posts. On either side of the net, 21 feet (6.4 meters) from it and parallel to it, are the *service lines.* A *center line* between the service lines and parallel to the sidelines creates two service courts, each 13½ feet (about 4 meters) wide. These service courts are used in serving for both singles and doubles.

Any of several surfaces may be used on the court, including grass, clay, cement, wood, and synthetic fibers. The size, shape, and markings, however, are standard.

The ball is a cloth-covered rubber sphere that is white or yellow in color, approximately 2½ inches (6.35 cm) in diameter and 2 ounces (56.69 grams) in weight. It is pressurized so that it will bounce at least 53 inches (134.62 cm) and not more than 58 inches (147.32 cm) when dropped 100 inches (254 cm) onto a concrete base. The livelier, high-pressure ball is more common in the United States than in other countries, favoring the hard-driving "power game." The lower pressure ball is easier to control, and an exchange back and forth over the net usually lasts longer. This applies especially to a clay surface, which is generally considered "slow" because the ball takes a higher, more leisurely bounce. Grass is considered a "fast" surface because the ball takes a low, uncertain, and skidding bounce.

Traditionally the leading titles—Wimbledon, United States, and Australia—have been contested on grass. The grass court is being replaced in the United States by synthetic turf. The French championship is considered the world's foremost clay-court event, with the Italian and West German championships gaining stature. The South African championship is played on a slow cement, although cement is usually a fast surface. The top indoor events in the United States are conducted on a variety of synthetic surfaces, fast and slow.

Rackets of laminated wood predominate as the implement for striking the ball. Steel, aluminum, fiber glass, and plastic are also used for racket material. There are no limitations on racket size or weight. However, the weight usually averages between 13 and 15 ounces (368.5–425 grams), and the length is about 28 inches (71 cm). An open oval frame, or head, is attached to a straight handle, which measures about 4½ inches in circumference at the grip. The frame, about 9 inches (22.8 cm) wide, is crossed horizontally and vertically with gut or nylon strings.

Scoring. Units of scoring are points, games, sets, and matches. Scoring is the same in singles and in doubles. A player or team scores a *point* when the opposition fails to return the ball properly. A side must score at least four points to win a *game.* The first point made is called *15;* the second, *30;* the third, *40;* and the fourth, *game.* If both sides score 3 points—that is, if the score is 40–40, or 40 all—it is a *deuce,* or tie, game. To win a deuce game, one side must score two consecutive points from deuce. The first point is called *advantage,* or *ad.* If the player holding advantage wins the next point, he wins the game. Otherwise, the score reverts to deuce. The term *love* means zero. Thus a score of 30–love is 30–0.

The side winning six games wins a *set.* If each side wins five games—that is, if the score is 5 all—it is a deuce set, which can be won only by the player or team that wins two games in a row. The deuce principle may result in prolonged matches.

A *match* consists of winning two of three sets (women and men) or three of five sets (men only).

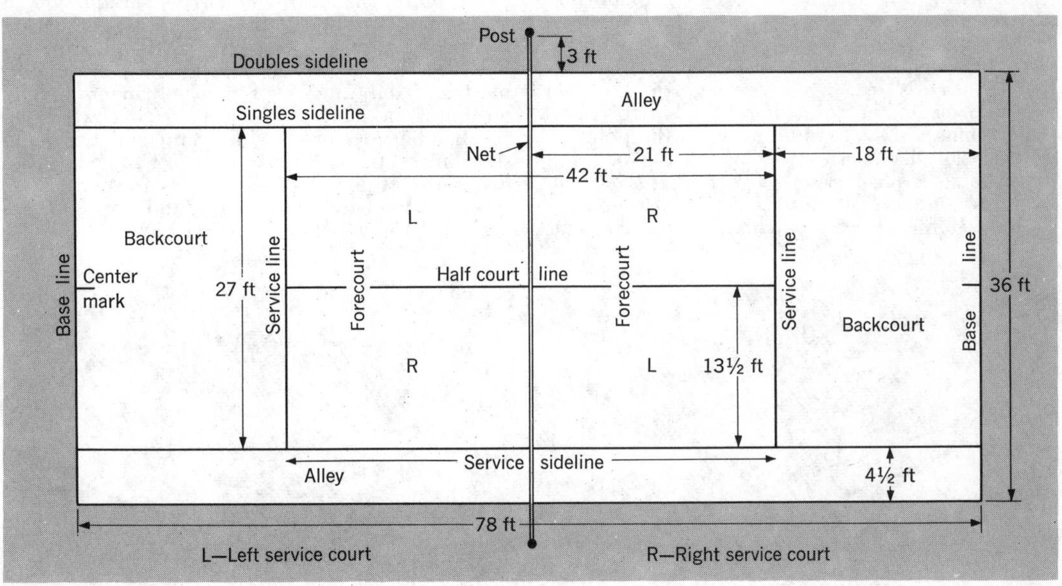

The most famous comeback on record is that of Henri Cochet of France, who defeated Bill Tilden of the United States at Wimbledon in 1927. Although Cochet trailed, seemingly hopelessly, by two sets and by 1–5 in the third, he won the match 2–6, 4–6, 7–5, 6–4, 6–3.

The longest singles match was played in Warsaw in 1966 in the King's Cup tournament. A total of 126 games were played before Roger Taylor of Britain defeated Wieslaw Gasiorek of Poland 27–29, 31–29, 6–4. In a doubles match in the Newport (R. I.) Casino Invitation in 1967, Richard Leach and Richard Dell defeated Leonard Schloss and Thomas Mozur 3–6, 49–47, 22–20, a total of 147 games.

To avoid such tennis marathons and to permit a match to be completed within a predictable amount of time, a sudden-death tie-breaker system augmented the traditional tennis scoring in 1970. With the tie-breaker method, if a set reaches 6 all in games, the players alternate serves in a best-of-nine points sequence. For example, the first server (A) serves points 1 and 2. The second server (B) serves points 3 and 4. A serves points 5 and 6, and B serves points 7, 8, and 9, if necessary. The first player to score five points in the playoff wins the set or match. The set is scored 7–6.

In 1958, James Van Alen of the United States, the inventor of the sudden-death tie-breaker system, introduced the Van Alen Streamlined Scoring System (VASSS), which uses single points. The first player to reach 31 points wins the set, and the 31-point set must be won by at least two points. Serve changes every five points. Another feature of VASSS is No-ad, eliminating deuce. The first player to win four points wins a game. The first to win six games wins a set, unless games are 5 all. In this case a sudden-death tie-breaker is played.

Play Procedures. Before a match the choice of sides on the court and the right to serve or receive service are decided by toss of a coin. The server begins play for the first point of a game from behind the base line in the right half of the court. He tosses the ball into the air and hits it with the racket diagonally across the net into the right service court of his opponent. If he drives the ball into the net, or if the ball goes beyond the receiver's service court, it is a *fault,* and he must serve again. The server can also commit a fault by touching the base line or any part of his court with his feet while serving. He has two serves to begin the point. If he faults both times he commits a *double fault* and loses the point. A served ball that strikes the top of the net and drops into the receiver's service court is a *let ball.* A let does not count, and the server gets another try. After the serve, a ball that touches the net and lands fair is a *net-cord ball* and remains in play. A good serve that the receiver cannot hit with his racket is called an *ace.*

Once the first point is made, the server delivers the ball for the second point from behind the base line in the left half of the court and to the left service court of the receiver. Services in succeeding points are alternated behind the halves of the base line. After each game, the contestants alternate the service. Players change sides of the court after odd-numbered games beginning with game one.

The receiver must return a served ball on the first bounce. Then an exchange, or *rally,* continues until a player either wins the point outright by striking a ball that the opponent is unable to return or loses the point by an *error*—for example, missing the ball, stroking the ball into the net, or sending the ball out of bounds. During a rally for a point, players may strike the ball before it bounces (on the *volley*), or on its first bounce. The player who permits a ball to bounce twice loses the point.

Doubles play is similar to singles, but partners must alternate in serving complete games when it is their team's turn to serve. Partners receive the service alternately throughout each game. During a rally, either member of the team may make a return.

Fundamentals of Play. There are five basic tennis strokes: the *service,* an overhead stroke, used to begin play for a point; the forehand and backhand *drives,* strokes made after the ball bounces; the *volley,* a short stroke made before the ball touches the ground; and the *smash,* a hard overhead stroke. (A *lob* is a ball lofted high.) How a player holds the racket to make these strokes is an individual matter. He must find the most comfortable and effective position for the hand.

Of the three types of grips—Eastern, Continental, and Western—the Eastern is the norm from which most players make slight adjustments and adaptations in playing the ball. The forehand grip is taken by standing the racket on the edge of the frame and then "shaking hands" with it. As the fingers close around the handle, the "V" formed by the fingers and thumb rests over the plane of the handle, which is a continuation of the frame. The line of the arm, wrist, and racket is straight. For the Eastern backhand grip, the handle is held with the back of the hand uppermost and the knuckle of the first finger directly on top of the handle. The thumb may extend up the handle as a brace. Forehand and backhand shots are made on different faces of the racket. In the course of play, a person makes a quick change from the forehand to the backhand grip by turning the hand slightly counterclockwise.

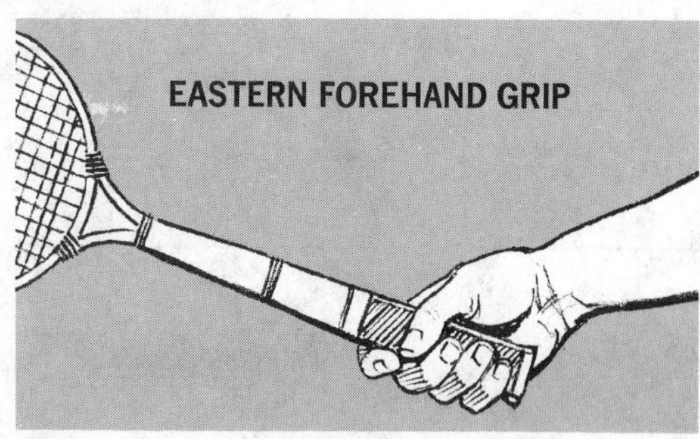

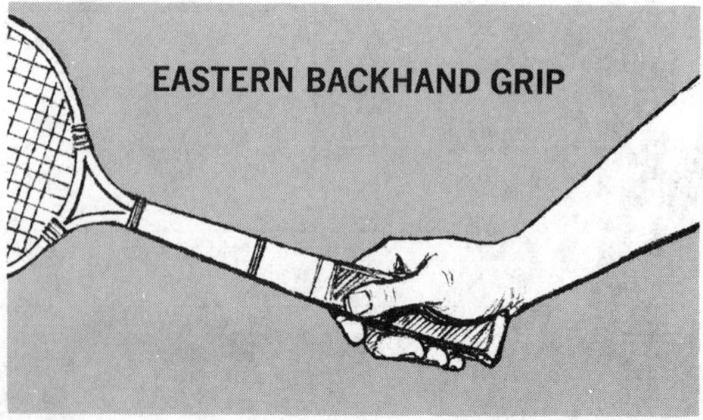

The Continental grip is halfway between the Eastern forehand and backhand. The "V" formed by the thumb joining the hand rests directly on the top of the handle. A player makes the forehand and backhand shots on opposite sides of the racket face but does not change his grip.

To take the Western grip a player places the racket with its face parallel to the ground and then drops his hand on top of the handle. For the forehand drive the hand is almost underneath the handle. The same racket face is used for the forehand and the backhand strokes. With the Western grip, it is difficult to handle low bouncing balls. This grip puts strain on the wrist and it is seldom used. Bill Johnston, U. S. title holder in 1915 and 1919 and a member of the Davis Cup team, was an exponent of the Western grip.

A beginning player should try to hit the ball *flat*, that is, his racket at impact should meet the ball squarely. The flatter the hit the greater the ball's speed through the air and the swifter its bounce. Knowledge of the effects of *spin* on the ball helps a player's overall game. Spin means control. The more spin on the ball the less pace. Hitting over the top of the ball imparts top spin, which tends to make the ball drop and bounce high, and an opponent has trouble volleying it. To *slice* the ball, the player passes the racket under the ball. A slice results in a low bounce. With a *chop*, the ball receives its rotation from a downward glancing blow from the racket. The backspin or underspin thus imparted causes the ball to bounce abruptly and low, with no speed.

The Service. The Eastern backhand grip is the one most often used in the service. To serve, the player stands perpendicular to the net, with his front shoulder in line with the spot where he wants the ball to land. For a flat service, he tosses the ball well above his head and slightly in advance of it. He swings the racket back, up, and forward and meets the ball over the head squarely, as he transfers the weight to the ball of his front foot. He hits the ball down into the opponent's court from the highest point of the raised racket. After contact with the ball, the player continues the swing in a follow-through down and across the body. It is advisable to stand about six inches behind the base line in serving to avoid stepping on the line. This breach of the rules is called a *foot fault*.

Players usually impart spin to the service, and the Continental grip is popular for those who impart top spin or slice the ball. A right-handed player tosses the ball up and over his left shoulder and then imparts top spin by hitting over the ball. The ball will bounce high and to the right of the server. To cause the ball to skid off to the opponent's right, he slices the ball after tossing it slightly to his right.

Forehand and Backhand Drives. For the forehand and backhand strokes, a level swing with the arm fully extended at the moment of impact is the ideal for which to strive. In the forehand, the palm (fore) of the racket hand leads in the direction in which the hand is moving. With the backhand, the racket strikes the ball with the back of the hand leading. Both strokes begin with the body perpendicular to the net.

A righthanded player hits a forehand by pivoting on his right foot and pointing his left shoulder toward the ball. As his body turns, he carries his racket back to the right on a line with the flight of the oncoming ball. He keeps his knees bent and, if playing a low ball, bends them even more to permit a level swing. A ball coming over the net high probably will bounce high. If it just clears the net the bounce may be low. As he swings the racket forward to meet the ball, the player transfers the body weight from the rear to the front foot. After the hit, the follow-through carries the racket in the direction the ball has taken. On a flat drive, the racket movement ends in front of the body. On a forehand with topspin, the racket head ends toward the far shoulder.

The principles of the backhand stroke are the same as for the forehand. However, the position of the feet and hitting arm and the body movement are reversed. The right-hander keeps the right shoulder facing the net from the backswing until the start of the follow-through. The techniques discussed should be reversed for a left-handed player.

The Volley and Smash. The *volley* is made facing the net. Using a short backswing, the player punches the ball with the racket instead of swinging at it. The *smash* is made with the body sideways to the net. The player hits the ball overhead with much the same motion as for the serve. The smash is often used to return a lobbed ball. With a particularly high lob, a player may let the ball bounce before he makes the smash.

Origin and Beginnings of Tennis. Tennis is of comparatively recent development. The game dates from 1873, when a British army officer, Walter C. Wingfield, adapted the rules and techniques of court tennis to devise a game to be played on grass. He introduced his invention at a garden party in Nantclwyd, Wales. The original court resembled an hourglass, measuring 60 feet (18.2 meters) in length, with 30-foot (6.4-meter) base lines and a 21-foot (6.4-meter) center line. The net was 7 feet (2.1 meters) high at the ends and sagged to about 5 feet (1.5 meters) high at the middle. Contestants played with a rubber ball and an oval-shaped racket. The game was considered a gentle pastime for those who wished a change from croquet.

In 1874, Wingfield patented his invention under the name of Sphairistiké. Because the name was ponderous and difficult to pronounce, he soon settled on lawn tennis. Within a year the hourglass shape was replaced by a rectangle with the present court dimensions, and the Marylebone Cricket Club of London issued a set of rules that have remained essentially unchanged. The height of the net was changed several times and finally standardized at 3 feet in 1884.

In June 1877 the first championship tournament was held at the All-England Croquet Club, soon thereafter to be named the All-England Lawn Tennis and Croquet Club, at Wimbledon, a suburb of London. Spencer W. Gore, a London racquets star, won the men's singles, the only event. From the start the All-England club had a decisive influence on the game, and the annual tournament, most often called Wimbledon, became the tournament for the world championships. Until 1907, winners of the matches were natives of the British Isles. Men's doubles were added to the Wimbledon program in 1879, women's singles in 1884, and women's doubles and mixed doubles in 1913. The British governing body, the Lawn Tennis Association, was founded in 1888.

BRITISH (Wimbledon) CHAMPIONS

Men's Singles

1877–Spencer W. Gore
1878–P. Frank Hadow
1879–80–J. T. Hartley
1881–86–William Renshaw
1887–Herbert F. Lawford
1888–Ernest Renshaw
1889–William Renshaw
1890–Willoughby J. Hamilton
1891–92–Wilfred Baddeley
1893–94–Joshua L. Pim
1895–Wilfred Baddeley
1896–Harold S. Mahony
1897–1900–Reginald Doherty
1901–Arthur W. Gore
1902–06–Hugh L. Doherty
1907–Norman Brookes (Austr.)
1908–09–Arthur W. Gore
1910–13–Anthony F. Wilding (N. Z.)
1914–Norman Brookes (Austr.)
1915–1918–No competition
1919–Gerald Patterson (Austr.)
1920–21–William T. Tilden (U. S.)
1922–Gerald Patterson (Austr.)
1923–William Johnston (U. S.)
1924–Jean Borotra (Fr.)
1925–René Lacoste (Fr.)
1926–Jean Borotra (Fr.)
1927–Henri Cochet (Fr.)
1928–René Lacoste (Fr.)
1929–Henri Cochet (Fr.)
1930–William T. Tilden (U. S.)
1931–Sidney B. Wood (U. S.)
1932–Ellsworth Vines (U. S.)
1933–John Crawford (Austr.)
1934–36–Fred J. Perry
1937–38–J. Donald Budge (U. S.)
1939–Robert L. Riggs (U. S.)
1940–1945–No competition
1946–Yvon Petra (Fr.)
1947–John A. Kramer (U. S.)
1948–Robert Falkenburg (U. S.)
1949–Fred R. Schroeder (U. S.)
1950–J. Edward Patty (U. S.)
1951–Richard Savitt (U. S.)
1952–Frank Sedgman (Austr.)
1953–E. Victor Seixas (U. S.)
1954–Jaroslav Drobny (Czech.)
1955–Tony Trabert (U. S.)
1956–57–Lewis Hoad (Austr.)
1958–Ashley Cooper (Austr.)
1959–Alejandro Olmedo (Peru)
1960–Neale Fraser (Austr.)
1961–62–Rodney Laver (Austr.)
1963–Charles McKinley (U. S.)
1964–65–Roy Emerson (Austr.)
1966–Manuel Santana (Spain)
1967–John Newcombe (Austr.)
1968–69–Rodney Laver (Austr.)
1970–John Newcombe (Austr.)
1971–John Newcombe (Austr.)
1972–Stan Smith (U. S.)
1973–Jan Kodes (Czech.)
1974–Jimmy Connors (U. S.)

Women's Singles

1884–85–Maud Watson
1886–Blanche Bingley
1887–88–Lottie Dod
1889–Blanche Bingley Hillyard
1890–L. Rice
1891–92–Lottie Dod
1894–Blanche Bingley Hillyard
1895–96–Charlotte Cooper
1897–Blanche Bingley Hillyard
1898–Charlotte Cooper
1899–1900–Blanche B. Hillyard
1901–Charlotte Cooper Sterry
1902–M. E. Robb
1903–04–Dorothy K. Douglass
1905–May G. Sutton (U. S.)
1906–Dorothy K. Douglass
1907–May G. Sutton (U. S.)
1908–Charlotte Cooper Sterry
1909–Dorothea P. Boothby
1910–11–Dorothy D. Chambers
1912–Ethel W. Larcombe
1913–14–Dorothy D. Chambers
1915–1918–No competition
1919–23–Suzanne Lenglen (Fr.)
1924–Kathleen McKane
1925–Suzanne Lenglen (Fr.)
1926–Kathleen McKane Godfree
1927–29–Helen N. Wills (U. S.)
1930–Helen Wills Moody (U. S.)
1931–Cecil Aussem (Ger.)
1932–33–Helen Wills Moody (U. S.)
1934–Dorothy E. Round
1935–Helen Wills Moody (U. S.)
1936–Helen H. Jacobs (U. S.)
1937–Dorothy E. Round
1938–Helen Wills Moody (U. S.)
1939–Alice Marble (U. S.)
1940–1945–No competition
1946–Pauline Betz (U. S.)
1947–Margaret Osborne (U. S.)
1948–50–Louise Brough (U. S.)
1951–Doris J. Hart (U. S.)
1952–54–Maureen Connolly (U. S.)
1955–Louise Brough (U. S.)
1956–Shirley J. Fry (U. S.)
1957–58–Althea Gibson (U. S.)
1959–60–Maria Bueno (Brazil)
1961–Angela Mortimer
1962–Karen H. Susman (U. S.)
1963–Margaret Smith (Austr.)
1964–Maria Bueno (Brazil)
1965–Margaret Smith (Austr.)
1966–68–Billie Jean King (U. S.)
1969–Ann Haydon Jones
1970–Margaret S. Court (Austr.)
1971–Evonne Goolagong (Austr.)
1972–73–Billie Jean King (U. S.)
1974–Chris Evert (U. S.)

U. S. OPEN (Forest Hills) CHAMPIONS

Men's Singles

1881–87–Richard D. Sears
1888–89–Henry W. Slocum
1890–92–Oliver S. Campbell
1893–94–Robert D. Wrenn
1895–Fred H. Hovey
1896–97–Robert D. Wrenn
1898–1900–Malcolm Whitman
1901–02–William A. Larned
1903–Hugh L. Doherty (U. K.)
1904–Holcombe Ward
1905–Beals C. Wright
1906–William J. Clothier
1907–11–William A. Larned
1912–13–Maurice E. McLoughlin
1914–R. Norris Williams
1915–William Johnston
1916–R. Norris Williams
1917–18–R. Lindley Murray
1919–William Johnston
1920–25–William T. Tilden
1926–27–René Lacoste (Fr.)
1928–Henri Cochet (Fr.)
1929–William T. Tilden
1930–John H. Doeg
1931–32–Ellsworth Vines
1933–34–Fred J. Perry (U. K.)
1935–Wilmer L. Allison
1936–Fred J. Perry (U. K.)
1937–38–J. Donald Budge
1939–Robert L. Riggs
1940–W. Donald McNeill
1941–Robert L. Riggs
1942–Fred R. Schroeder
1943–Joseph R. Hunt
1944–45–Frank A. Parker
1946–47–John A. Kramer
1948–49–Richard A. Gonzales
1950–Arthur D. Larsen
1951–52–Frank Sedgman (Austr.)
1953–Tony Trabert
1954–E. Victor Seixas
1955–Tony Trabert
1956–Kenneth Rosewall (Austr.)
1957–Malcolm Anderson (Austr.)
1958–Ashley Cooper (Austr.)
1959–60–Neale Fraser (Austr.)
1961–Roy Emerson (Austr.)
1962–Rodney Laver (Austr.)
1963–Rafael Osuna (Mexico)
1964–Roy Emerson (Austr.)
1965–Manuel Santana (Spain)
1966–Fred S. Stolle (Austr.)
1967–John Newcombe (Austr.)
1968–Arthur R. Ashe
1969–Rodney Laver (Austr.)
1970–Kenneth Rosewall (Austr.)
1971–Stan Smith
1972–Ilie Nastase (Rum.)
1973–John Newcombe (Austr.)
1974–Jimmy Connors

Women's Singles

1887–Ellen F. Hansell
1888–89–Bertha L. Townsend
1890–Ellen C. Roosevelt
1891–92–Mabel E. Cahill
1893–Aline M. Terry
1894–Helen R. Helwig
1895–Juliette P. Atkinson
1896–Elisabeth H. Moore
1897–98–Juliette P. Atkinson
1899–Marion Jones
1900–Myrtle McAteer
1901–Elisabeth H. Moore
1902–Marion Jones
1903–Elisabeth H. Moore
1904–May G. Sutton
1905–Elisabeth H. Moore
1906–Helen Homans
1907–Evelyn Sears
1915–18–Molla Bjurstedt
1908–Maud Bargar-Wallach
1909–11–Hazel V. Hotchkiss
1912–14–Mary K. Browne
1915–18–Molla Bjurstedt
1919–Hazel H. Wightman
1920–22–Molla B. Mallory
1923–25–Helen N. Wills
1926–Molla B. Mallory
1927–29–Helen N. Wills
1930–Betty Nuthall (U. K.)
1931–Helen Wills Moody
1932–35–Helen H. Jacobs
1936–Alice Marble
1937–Anita Lizana (Chile)
1938–40–Alice Marble
1941–Sarah Palfrey Cooke
1942–44–Pauline Betz
1945–Sarah Palfrey Cooke
1946–Pauline Betz
1947–Louise Brough
1948–50–Margaret O. duPont
1951–53–Maureen Connolly
1954–55–Doris J. Hart
1956–Shirley J. Fry
1957–58–Althea Gibson
1959–Maria Bueno (Brazil)
1960–61–Darlene R. Hard
1962–Margaret Smith (Austr.)
1963–64–Maria Bueno (Brazil)
1965–Margaret Smith (Austr.)
1966–Maria Bueno (Brazil)
1967–Billie Jean King
1968–Virginia Wade (U. K.)
1969–70–Margaret Smith Court (Austr.)
1971–72–Billie Jean King
1973–Margaret S. Court (Austr.)
1974–Billie Jean King

Tennis was first played in the United States in 1874. In March of that year an American, Mary E. Outerbridge, after observing Englishmen playing the game in Bermuda, brought rackets, balls, and a net home with her to Staten Island, N. Y. She introduced tennis to her friends, and the Staten Island Cricket and Baseball Club permitted her to mark out an hourglass-shaped court on its grounds at St. George. That year James Dwight and F. R. Sears, Jr., laid out a similar court at Nahant, Mass. The first U. S. tournament took place at Nahant in 1876.

Confusion and controversy over the size of the ball, height of the net, and other inconsistencies led to demands for standardization of the game. This was accomplished in 1881 in New York, when tennis leaders from Eastern clubs organized the U. S. National Lawn Tennis Association, later called the USLTA. From then on the organization administered the tournaments and amateur developments in the United States.

In 1881 the first National Championship was held at Newport, R. I. A Bostonian, Richard D. Sears, won the singles title and retained it through 1887, a record that has never been equaled. The U. S. Nationals, since 1968 called the U. S. Open, moved to Forest Hills in 1915 where it has remained since, except for the years 1921 through 1923 when the matches were conducted in Philadelphia.

UPI

Suzanne Lenglen

UPI

Bill Tilden

WIDE WORLD

Helen Wills Moody

WIDE WORLD

Don Budge

WIDE WORLD

Maureen Connolly

WIDE WORLD

Pancho Gonzalez

CENTRAL PRESS

Rod Laver

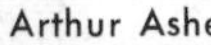
Arthur Ashe

UPI

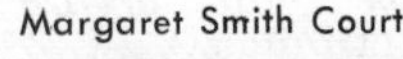
Margaret Smith Court

S & G, FROM PICTORIAL PARADE

Tennis was introduced to Canada about 1874 and to Australia in 1879. But not until 1900 was there a serious attempt at international play. That year Dwight F. Davis, then a student at Harvard College, donated a trophy for international team competition, to include four singles matches and one doubles. British players challenged the Americans and were defeated in Boston by a score of 3–0 (one match was not played, and one was left unfinished), thus launching the best-known annual worldwide competition, known simply as the Davis Cup. Up to World War I the United States, Britain, and Australasia (Australia and New Zealand) monopolized the trophy.

Early Champions. The first foreigners to win the U. S. men's and women's singles titles were Hugh L. Doherty of Britain in 1903 and Molla Bjurstedt Mallory of Norway in 1915. The first foreigners to claim the Wimbledon singles crown were May G. Sutton of the United States in 1905 and Norman E. Brookes of Australia in 1907. Not until 1920 was the Wimbledon men's singles title won by an American. It was claimed by Bill Tilden, considered the finest player of all time. That year he began a run of six U. S. championships during a period that also marked the United States' greatest Davis Cup successes.

The French players began to reign in 1924, the year Jean Borotra won at Wimbledon. They reached world superiority in 1927, when Borotra, Henri Cochet, J. René Lacoste, and Jacques Brugnon, called the "Four Musketeers," took the Davis Cup from the United States and held it until 1933. The British regained supremacy with the ascendancy of Fred Perry, the first man to win all of the Big Four titles. With the arrival of Don Budge, a challenger to Tilden in the list of all-time greats, the United States regained the Davis Cup in 1937. Budge in 1938 scored a historic "grand slam" in tennis, winning all Big Four titles in the same year. The American Maureen Connolly performed the same feat in 1953, the Australian Rod Laver in 1962 and 1969, and the Australian Margaret Smith Court in 1970.

An important influence on the game for women was Suzanne Lenglen of France, whose brilliant play permitted her to conquer Wimbledon from 1919 through 1923 and again in 1925. A worthy successor, the American Helen Wills Moody, won the first of her seven U. S. titles in 1923 and the first of her eight Wimbledon titles in 1927. Her greatest rival was Helen Jacobs, who took the U. S. singles crown four years in succession (1932–1935) and who won the Wimbledon crown in 1936.

Tennis was first played professionally in 1926, when promoter C. C. Pyle organized a surprisingly successful tour of the United States. The prime attraction was Suzanne Lenglen. Others on the tour included Mary K. Browne, Vincent Richards, Harvey Snodgrass, and Howard O. Kinsey of the United States and Paul Feret of France.

The biggest advance in professional tennis came when Tilden turned professional in 1931. Other great players then joined the professional ranks. They included Ellsworth Vines, Don Budge, and Alice Marble of the United States and Fred Perry of Britain.

After World War II. U. S. players were supreme in the early postwar years, with Jack Kramer, Fred Schroeder, Frank Parker, and Pancho Gonzales winning four straight Davis Cup championships. After 1950, Australia controlled the game, with the strongest continuous line of players in history—Frank Sedgman, Ken McGregor, Lew Hoad, Ken Rosewall, Ashley Cooper, Neale Fraser, Roy Emerson, John Newcombe, Tony Roche, and Rod Laver—to name the most prominent. A few players from Latin America won titles for the first time. Alex Olmedo of Peru won the Wimbledon title in 1959, and Rafael Osuna of Mexico took the U. S. championship in 1963. In 1965, Manuel Santana became the first Spaniard and the first continental European since Cochet of France in 1928 to win the U. S. title. Santana also won at Wimbledon in 1966.

American women captured all Wimbledon and U. S. titles until 1959, with such stars as Pauline Betz, Louise Brough, Doris Hart, Margaret Osborne du Pont, Maureen Connolly, and Althea Gibson. In 1959, María Bueno of Brazil took over, winning three Wimbledon and four U. S. titles, among others. Between 1960 and 1970 an Australian, Margaret Smith Court, won 52 Big Four titles in singles, doubles, and mixed doubles, more than any other player.

Two U. S. champions—Bobby Riggs and Jack Kramer—revived professional tennis in 1947 and began tours with such stars as Budge, Gonzales, Sedgman, and Francisco Segura. From 1954 to 1963, Kramer achieved considerable success promoting his own world tours with top international champions. Between 1963 and 1968 Rod Laver was the only amateur champion to turn professional, and the professional game languished until Lamar Hunt of Dallas, Texas, signed five leading amateurs for tournament play: John Newcombe and Tony Roche of Australia; Cliff Drysdale of South Africa; Nikki Pilic of Yugoslavia; and Roger Taylor of Britain. Hunt's promotion of professional tennis was influential in hastening the acceptance of open tennis by the public. Now the professional game is well established.

The abuses of amateurism, in the form of overly indulgent payments of expense money, fomented a demand for open tennis—that is, for tournaments accepting both amateurs and professionals and offering prize money rather than "expenses." This principle was accepted in 1968 by the ILTF after Wimbledon rebelliously declared itself "open." Quickly prize-money tournaments came into vogue, the first being the British Hard Court Championship at Bournemouth in 1968, which Rosewall, a professional, won.

Leading tournaments fall into three categories: (1) open, for all players, professional or amateur; (2) contract professional, for professional players contracted to a promoter only; and (3) independent professional, for professional players under control of a national amateur association only. Few important tournaments are exclusively for amateurs. Independent professionals remain eligible for Davis, Federation, and Wightman Cup play. In 1969, Laver completed the first open "grand slam," earning acclaim as the greatest player of the post-World War II era. He broke his money record in 1970, winning $201,453.

Bud Collins, *Boston "Globe"*

INTERNATIONAL LAWN TENNIS CHALLENGE TROPHY—THE DAVIS CUP

Australasia (Australia and New Zealand)—1907–1909, 1911, 1914, 1919; Australia—1939, 1950–1953, 1955–1957, 1959–1962, 1964–1967, 1973
British Isles (including Ireland)—1903–1906, 1912; United Kingdom—1933–1936
France—1927–1932
United States—1900, 1902, 1913, 1920–1926, 1937–1938, 1946–1949, 1954, 1958, 1963, 1968–1972
No matches in 1901, 1910, 1915–1918, 1940–1945

Bibliography

Barbaby, John M., *Racket Work: The Key to Tennis* (Rockleigh, N. J., 1969).
Brady, Maurice, *Lawn Tennis Encyclopedia* (New York 1969).
Davidson, Owen, and Jones, C. J., *The Great Ones* (London 1970).
Gensemer, Robert E., *Tennis* (Philadelphia 1969).
Grimsley, Will, *Tennis: Its History, People and Events* (Englewood Cliffs, N. J., 1971).
King, Billie Jean, and Chapin, Kim, *Tennis to Win* (New York 1970).
Lardner, Rex, *Complete Beginners' Guide to Tennis* (New York 1967).
Laver, Rodney, and Collins, Bud, *The Education of a Tennis Player* (New York 1971).
Pollard, Jack, *Lawn Tennis the Australian Way* (London 1964).
Talbert, William F., and Old, Bruce S., *Game of Doubles in Tennis*, 3d ed. (Philadelphia 1968).
Talbert, William F., and Old, Bruce S., *Game of Singles in Tennis* (Philadelphia 1962).
United States Lawn Tennis Association, *The Official Yearbook and Tennis Guide* (New York, current edition).

BROWN BROTHERS

Alfred Tennyson

TENNYSON, ten′ə-sən, **Alfred** (1809–1892), English poet, who was the most influential poet of the Victorian era. He served as poet laureate for 42 years and in that capacity was the poetic spokesman of the Queen and her subjects, who looked to him to give artistic expression to their moral and intellectual concerns.

Life. Tennyson was born in Somersby, Lincolnshire, on Aug. 6, 1809, the third of 11 children. His father, a clergyman, was subject to manic depression, and the family's life was frequently unhappy. The elder Tennyson was able, however, to undertake personally the education of his children, largely at home. Alfred began to write verse at an early age. His first published works appeared in the inaccurately titled *Poems by Two Brothers* (1827), which also included verse by his brothers Frederick and Charles.

In 1827, Tennyson matriculated at Trinity College, Cambridge. There he met Arthur Hallam, who became his closest friend. Though morbidly shy, Tennyson was encouraged by Hallam to enter into the society of the university and was accepted into a literary club, "The Apostles," whose members warmly praised his poetry. In 1829, Tennyson won the Chancellor's Medal for his poem *Timbuctoo* and in the following year published his first volume, *Poems, Chiefly Lyrical.* In 1831 his father died, and he was forced to leave Cambridge without a degree and return home to Somersby.

The next few years were difficult for Tennyson. His volume *Poems,* published in 1833, received unfavorable reviews. In the same year, Hallam, who had been engaged to Tennyson's sister Emily, died suddenly, and his death proved a staggering blow to the poet. Although Tennyson continued to write, he practically ceased publication for almost 10 years. He reworked early poems and composed new ones, finally publishing the two-volume *Poems* in 1842. This collection, which included the *Morte d'Arthur,* later to be incorporated into *Idylls of the King,* and *Ulysses,* established Tennyson as the chief poet of his generation. His preeminence was confirmed in 1850 with the publication of *In Memoriam,* dedicated to Hallam's memory. In the same year, Tennyson was named poet laureate.

Tennyson married Emily Sellwood, his love of many years, in 1850. He had met and fallen in love with her in 1836, but her father had forbidden a match at the time because of Tennyson's financial insecurity. The couple settled in Farringford, a house in Freshwater on the Isle of Wight in 1853. His years there with his wife and two sons, Hallam and Lionel, were the happiest of Tennyson's life. The family remained in Freshwater until 1869, when they moved to Aldworth, a house built for them in Surrey.

Tennyson's later years were uneventful but his creativity continued unabated. His great work of these years was the *Idylls of the King* (1859–1885). From the 1860's he decided seriously to try his hand at poetic drama, but none of his plays became successful. In 1884, almost universally revered and admired, he accepted a peerage, becoming Baron Tennyson of Aldworth and Farringford—the first Englishman to be elevated to such high rank for literary distinction alone. Lord Tennyson died at Aldworth on Oct. 6, 1892, and was buried in the Poets' Corner in Westminster Abbey.

Works. Tennyson's career may be divided into two parts—before *In Memoriam* and after. Prior to 1850 he was a young poet seeking to define his role in society. Thereafter he developed into a Victorian sage, who addressed himself to the problems of his time. His very earliest verses, unpublished in his own lifetime, are imitative and full of undigested learning. However, they are bursting with vitality and reveal hints of both the visionary and melancholy qualities associated with his mature poetry. Tennyson's unfinished play, *The Devil and the Lady,* written when he was 14, but first published in 1930, shows his early facility with blank verse. His contributions to the *Poems by Two Brothers* are written in a Byronic vein and have isolation and loss as their themes. The melodic inventiveness and descriptive power that characterize some of his best work are first seen in the *Poems, Chiefly Lyrical.* The finest poem of this collection, *Mariana,* shows how he was able to depict inner states of feeling in terms of outward objects.

Poems (1833), containing *The Lady of Shalott, Oenone, The Lotos-Eaters,* and *The Palace of Art,* marks an advance over the earlier volume, manifesting a lyric sensuousness unparalleled by any modern poet save Keats. The dreamy atmosphere surrounding most of the poems in the volume reflects the poet's own distance at this time from the world of reality, from social responsibility. His people live apart from society, sustained by aesthetic pleasures, but vaguely apprehensive that such an existence is wrong. When they try to enter society, however, they find it almost impossible to do so. The Lady of Shalott, for example, is destroyed in her attempt to partake of the life of the world. In nearly all these poems, Tennyson was exploring the role of the poet, carefully weighing self-indulgence against social responsibility.

The verses, both new and revised, in *Poems* (1842) were written during Tennyson's period of intense grief for Hallam. Many of them lament the loss of a happy past and the absence of value and meaning in the present. This contrast is treated in the *English Idylls—Dora* and

The Gardener's Daughter—as well as in *Break, Break, Break,* one of his finest lyrics. Other poems in the collection, including *Ulysses* and *Locksley Hall,* which are among the first dramatic monologues in English literature, are concerned with the necessity of carrying on and looking for hope in the future. Underlying almost all these poems is the sense of Tennyson's continuing evaluation of the poet's purpose and function in society, his growing concern with the poet's relation to his audience, as interpreter, critic, teacher, and sage.

Tennyson's great work, *In Memoriam* (1850), a long elegy on the death of Hallam, begun in 1833 and completed in 1849, explored his personal thoughts on God, Christ, immortality, and the meaning of loss. Because it gave voice to both the doubts and the aspirations of his generation and because of its lyric beauty, it was almost universally acclaimed as a masterpiece. By 1850, Tennyson had worked out his ideas on the function of the poet in the modern world, and in his elegy he indicated his willingness to don the bardic mantle and reorient his poetry toward more ambitious goals.

The work of Tennyson's later years is consequently of a more public nature. He took his duties as laureate seriously and complied often with official requests for poems in commemoration of important occasions. His odes are triumphs of metrical brilliance. The *Ode on the Death of the Duke of Wellington* (1852) examines how an individual personality became a public symbol, and the *Ode Sung at the Opening of the International Exhibition* (1862) captured the excitement of a large exposition. *A Welcome to Alexandra* (1863) gracefully offers greetings to the Danish princess, who was soon to marry the Prince of Wales. The patriotic poems, such as *The Charge of the Light Brigade* (1854) and *The Charge of the Heavy Brigade* (1882), express his country's appreciation of heroic action.

Tennyson also responded to the demands for a poetry of the living present, of the problems of daily life, made by such critics as Ruskin. As early as 1847, he had written *The Princess,* his first long poem, on the position of women and their rights. In the 1860's he wrote domestic narratives, including *Sea Dreams* (1860) and *Enoch Arden* (1864), which attempted to render in verse of a rather ornate style the homely subject matter of certain Victorian novels. Some critics, pointing out the sentimentality of his domestic idylls and the jingoism of his patriotic verses, have charged that Tennyson compromised his art in the 1850's and 1860's to accommodate Victorian middle-class morality. In any case, these poems apparently did not engage his deeper sensibilities, although they give every evidence of superb workmanship.

It should be noted, however, that during this same period, Tennyson was also writing poems rejecting many of the banal assumptions and values of his time and presenting his own strictures on the frivolities of the modern world. *Maud* (1855) shows the devastation wrought on an individual's personality by the pressures and evils of a totally materialistic society. The *Idylls of the King,* on which Tennyson was engaged for the greater part of his laureate years, present the recalcitrance of the world to truth, order, and other human ideals. *Locksley Hall Sixty Years After* (1886), a companion piece to the earlier poem, while expressing great hope for the future, nonetheless evinces the poet's deep-rooted pessimism.

Despite Tennyson's pessimism about the human condition, he did not waver in his belief in God and the power of love. *The Ancient Sage* (1885) and *Akbar's Dream* (1892) testify to his faith in life after death and in the redemption offered by love. Even those poems like *Maud* and *Idylls of the King,* in which he appears to put the least favorable construction on human actions, bear witness to his belief that God is Love and that human love is the means not only of glorifying the Creator but also of personal salvation.

There was no diminution of Tennyson's poetic energies. During the last 20 years of his life he wrote seven poetic dramas, the best known of which are *Queen Mary* (1875), *Harold* (1876), and *Becket* (1884). He also published five major collections of verse. These are *Ballads and Other Poems* (1880), including the ballad *The Revenge* and the dramatic monologue *Rizpah; Tiresias and Other Poems* (1885); *Locksley Hall Sixty Years After; Demeter and Other Poems* (1889), including *Demeter and Persephone,* as well as the famous *Crossing the Bar,* which Tennyson requested be placed at the end of all editions of his poetry; and *The Death of Oenone and Other Poems* (1892).

Evaluation. Tennyson has been prized in the 20th century chiefly as a lyric poet whose genius lay in his ability to render various moods in song. T. S. Eliot said that Tennyson possessed the finest ear of any English poet since Milton. Other critics view him as the greatest English poet between Wordsworth and Yeats. Until recently, Tennyson's poetry to 1850 was more highly valued than his later work. Gradually, however, Tennyson has been given his due as a thinker, and his later poems are now held in high regard as well.

CLYDE DE L. RYALS, *Author of "Theme and Symbol in Tennyson's Poetry to 1850"*

Bibliography

Editions of Tennyson's works include the "Eversley Edition," ed. by Hallam Tennyson, with notes by the poet, 9 vols. (London 1907–1908) and *The Poems of Tennyson,* ed. by Christopher Ricks (London 1969).

Buckley, Jerome H., *Tennyson: The Growth of a Poet* (Cambridge, Mass., 1960).

Nicolson, Harold, *Tennyson: Aspects of His Life, Character, and Poetry* (Boston 1923).

Pitt, Valerie, *Tennyson Laureate* (London 1962).

Ryals, Clyde de L., *From the Great Deep: Essays on "Idylls of the King"* (Athens, Ohio, 1967).

Smith, Elton E., *The Two Voices: A Tennyson Study* (Lincoln, Neb., 1964).

Tennyson, Sir Charles, *Alfred Tennyson* (London 1949).

TENOCHTITLÁN, tā-näch-tē-tlän, was the capital of the Aztec Empire. Mexico City now includes the site of the ancient city. It was located on an island in the western part of what was then Lake Texcoco. The city was founded about 1325 and eventually grew to support a population of several hundred thousand. Surrounded by "floating gardens"—artificially created islands where produce was grown—the city was joined to the mainland by three causeways. An aqueduct supplied fresh water from Chapultepec. Besides the many palaces and marketplaces of the city, a central plaza, the Tecpan, contained the two chief temples, built on a huge terraced pyramid. The famous Calendar Stone of the Aztecs was found in the Tecpan. The Spanish destroyed Tenochtitlán in 1521, building Mexico City on the Aztec ruins.

TENOR, ten′ər, is a musical term derived from the Latin *tenere,* meaning "to hold." It has several meanings. Most familiarly, it labels the highest natural range of the male voice, usually covering one octave on either side of the A on the top line of the bass clef. The word is also applied to instruments having a similar range.

In Gregorian chants and other modal music, the tenor or repercussion is the pivotal or reciting note, typically the dominant of the mode being used. In polyphonic music earlier than the 16th century, the tenor is the vocal melody to which the other voices are conceived as being added. With reference to part singing in later contrapuntal terminology, the tenor—also called *cantus firmus* or *canto firmo*—came to be the part or melodic line next above the lowest. See also COUNTERTENOR.

TENORITE, ten′ə-rīt, is mineral cupric oxide. It is rarely found in the form of crystals and usually occurs in massive and earthy deposits. Its color ranges from steel gray to iron gray and black.

The massive variety of tenorite is called *melaconite.* It is a common mineral in copper deposits, where it is usually associated with cuprite, limonite, and other secondary minerals. There are important occurrences of this massive form in Chile, France, South West Africa, Spain, and some of the western United States. Tenorite is found as crystals in lavas at Mt. Vesuvius and Mt. Etna, Italy.

Composition: CuO; hardness, 3.5; specific gravity, 5.8–6.4; crystal system, monoclinic.

GEORGE SWITZER, *Smithsonian Institution*

TENPOUNDER, a slender marine fish closely related to tarpons and found throughout the world, mostly in warm seas. Some of the seven species are sometimes called *ladyfish.* Schools of tenpounders often occur in bays and brackish water estuaries. They give a spirited fight when caught; they are edible, but opinions about their taste vary.

Most tenpounders are less than 20 inches (50 cm) long. They have deeply forked tails, a single dorsal fin set in the middle of the back, and scaly sheaths on the bases of the dorsal and anal fins. The back is blue or blue-green and the sides a bright silvery color.

Tenpounders (genus *Elops*) and tarpons make up the family Elopidae of the order Elopiformes.

DANIEL M. COHEN
U. S. Fish and Wildlife Service

TENREC, ten′rek, a rabbit-sized insectivorous mammal *Tenrec ecaudatus* or, more broadly, any member of the family Tenrecidae. *T. ecaudatus,* found on Madagascar and nearby smaller islands, is a hedgehoglike animal with a long snout and a grayish brown to reddish brown coat of mixed hairs and spines. It reaches about 15 inches (390 mm) in head and body length, with a very short, ⅝-inch (16-mm) tail. It is nocturnal, spending the day in hollow logs or under rocks and emerging at night to feed on insects, worms, and some plant material. *T. ecaudatus* hibernates during the cold, dry season (April-October) and probably mates soon after emerging from hibernation. *T. ecaudatus* is among the most prolific of mammals. Females have been found to contain up to 32 embryos, and 12 to 16 living young are not uncommon.

RON GARRISON, SAN DIEGO ZOO

Streaked tenrec (*Hemicentetes semispinosus*)

The family Tenrecidae, of the order Insectivora, consists of 9 or 10 genera and 20 to 30 species. Two other genera, *Potamogale* and *Micropotagale,* the otter shrews of West Africa, are sometimes also placed in this family. The Tenrecidae, largely restricted to Madagascar, are quite varied in form and habits. Some resemble hedgehogs (*Tenrec, Setifer, Echinops*), and others appear superficially similar to moles (*Oryzorictes*), shrews (*Microgale*), or muskrats (*Limnogale*).

TENSE is the grammatical capability of verbs to show by distinctive forms or arrangements the time when the action of the verb occurs, occurred, or will occur. "Tense" is derived from Latin *tempus* (time). Any set of forms or structures signaling a particular time relation is called a tense of the language (as, present tense, past tense).

Among grammatical categories, tense is one of the most complex and controversial because (1) time as such is an abstruse philosophical notion; (2) grammarians cannot agree on a way of analyzing the linguistic markers of time relation; (3) known languages present a bewildering array of time patternings; and (4) tense merges with mood or mode in analyzing verbs.

Recognizing the commonsense division of time into "now," "before now," and "after now," traditional grammarians say that a modern English finite verb has six tenses: the present (he *walks*), the past or preterit (he *walked*), the future (he *will walk*), the present perfect (he *has walked*), the past perfect or pluperfect (he *had walked*), and the future perfect (he *will have walked*). They also identify a "progressive tense" (he *is walking, was walking*) and an "emphatic" conjugation (he *does walk, did walk*).

Structural-descriptive grammarians prefer to restrict the term "tense" to cases in which the form (sound and spelling) of the base verb actually changes to signal a time relation. Hence, for them, modern English has only two tenses—the present or common tense and the past or preterit. They deal with the other traditional tenses as phrasal verbs varying in aspect, phase, and mood or mode. Aspect and phase deal not with the now, before now, and after now but with the state of the action—is it beginning, going on, or finished? The durative aspect, for example, signals an action in process (he *is walking*); the perfect phase signals an action completed (he *has walked*). The "future tense" employs a modal auxiliary ("shall" or "will"), which is grammatically analogous to "can," "may," "must," and the like. This analysis not only stresses the formal characteristics of English but also recognizes the historical development of the English tense system from the combination of base forms with various auxiliaries.

ROBERT L. CHAPMAN, *Drew University*

TENSILE STRENGTH, ten'səl, is the inherent capability of a material to resist the stress put on it by tensile loading. Under tensile loading a structural element is subjected to a pulling action. Unit stress, *s*, is the magnitude of the force *F* in pounds that acts on the element, divided by the cross-sectional area *A*, in square inches, at the point of stress. Thus, $s = F/A$, the conventional units of *s* being in pounds per square inch, or psi. The same member can have both tensile and compressive stresses. For example, when a load is placed on a beam supported at its ends, the beam deflects under the load, and the lower fibers of the beam are stretched and put under tension, while the upper fibers of the beam are under compression.

The internal strength of materials varies a good deal. For ordinary steels, tensile strengths range from 30,000 to 60,000 psi. Alloyed steels and certain heat-treated steels develop tensile strengths as great as 200,000 psi. On the other hand, cast iron, which is very strong in compression, is very weak in tensile strength, having a range of 6,000 to 15,000 psi. Brass and bronzes range from 10,000 to 25,000 psi.

In using structural material the designer must be careful that the tensile stress that the material will have to bear does not exceed its ultimate tensile strength. To ensure that this does not happen, he usually employs a safety factor, making parts from two to five times larger than the minimum calculations based on the presumed strength of the material.

BURGESS H. JENNINGS
Northwestern University

TENSKWATAWA, Shawnee Indian warrior, brother of Tecumseh. See TECUMSEH.

TENT, a portable shelter, usually made of flexible materials stretched over poles.

Nomadic Dwellings. Primitive nomads have no means of transporting tents and so set up fresh shelters at each campsite. Peoples who have canoes or domestic animals can carry all or part of their dwelling from camp to camp. Indians of Tierra del Fuego abandoned the brush skeleton of their windbreak but packed the skin covers in their canoes. Similarly the Ojibwa of the Western Great Lakes region usually transported the mat or hide coverings of their wigwams, but not the poles.

The Plains Indians arranged the tentpoles of their tepees to form a travois on which the hide covers were loaded. When there were only dogs to drag the travois, the tepees were necessarily small. They became much larger after the horse was introduced. In the forested Sayan Mountains of southern Siberia, the Uriankhai also lived in

THE AMERICAN MUSEUM OF NATURAL HISTORY

TENT at left is a summer tepee of reeds and brush of the Salish Indians in British Columbia. Below is a skin-covered summer tent of a Chukchi or Eskimo family in Siberia in 1899. Sealskin floats hang from the top.

BUREAU OF AMERICAN ETHNOLOGY, SMITHSONIAN INSTITUTION

ARABIAN-AMERICAN OIL COMPANY

tepees but did not transport them even when they had domesticated reindeer. Instead, they built permanent frames at various campsites, covering these with fresh birchbark each season. Other reindeer breeders, such as the Lapps of Scandinavia and the Chukchi and Koryak of northeastern Siberia, transported on sleds the poles and skin coverings of their tents.

The classic portable dwellings are those still used by the pastoral nomads of Asia and North Africa. The central Asian *yurt* has a skeleton of wood. The walls are formed of sections of lattice, which is expanded when the yurt is set up and is collapsed for packing. Four or more such sections are arranged in a circle, with a space for the door. The roof consists of rods tied to the wall at one end, at the other end fitted into holes in a large wooden circle at the top. The yurt is covered with pieces of heavy felt held by horsehair rope, and felt rugs lie on the floor. The walls are felt-lined in winter and lined with reed mats in summer for ventilation and privacy.

The "black tent," which is found from Mauretania in North Africa to Afghanistan and Tibet, is made of cloth woven of black goat hair (yak hair in Tibet) stretched over poles and held by guy ropes fastened to stakes. The black cloth is water repellent, and the draped form allows ample ventilation. The tent is suited to the hot arid climate of the Middle East, but not to the chill winds of the Tibetan highlands. Early Arabs lived in skin-covered tents like those still used by the Sleb of Arabia and some Berber tribes in North Africa. Hebrew pastoralists of Old Testament times also lived in such tents.

Temporary Shelters. Tents are also utilized by town dwellers as temporary shelters. In the late Middle Ages and the Renaissance, fair ladies in the shade of silken pavilions watched knights jousting. Sumptuous tents were used for entertaining guests not only in Europe but in Iran. In the early 8th century, Charlemagne received a magnificent tent from Harun al-Rashid, Caliph of Baghdad.

Clavijo, Spanish ambassador to Tamerlane in 1404, described tents at the royal court in Samarkand. One tent had "walls of crimson tapestry, with insets of white embroidery." Another was of red silk "adorned with rows of silver gilt spangles." He waited in the shade of an awning of "white linen stuff overset and let in with colored embroidery" before being taken to the vast reception pavilion. Here the tall tent poles were painted blue and gold. The inner walls were hung with crimson tapestry, the outer walls with silk cloth woven in white, black, and yellow stripes, and the whole pavilion was surrounded by a wall of many-colored silk cloth.

The silk tents shown in miniatures or described in old manuscripts were of several shapes: the awning or canopy, open in front and held taut by guy ropes in the back; the round "parasol," with a single center pole and the oval "double parasol" with two poles; the tent with a ridgepole; and the "saddleback," in which the fabric dips between two end poles. These same forms are found today covered with canvas rather than silk, at circuses, fairs, garden parties, and other such events. See also CAMPING.

LANDAU, FROM RAPHO GUILLUMETTE

TENTS are adapted to varied environments. The black tent of the Bedouins of North Africa (*top*), woven of goat hair, is well ventilated for the hot climate. The Mongolian yurt (*bottom*), on a lattice frame,ı is lined with felt in winter and with reed mats in summer.

ELIZABETH E. BACON
Michigan State University

TENT CATERPILLAR, the name commonly applied to the larva, or caterpillar, of any moth of the genus *Malacosoma.* There are about six species in Europe and Asia and about six in North America. They are of great economic importance because they defoliate many trees and shrubs, especially members of the rose, oak, and willow families.

In early summer the female deposits her eggs, usually from 150 to 200, on the twigs of the host plant. As they are laid, the female usually covers them with a frothy secretion. The eggs hatch about the time the first new leaves appear in the spring, and the larvae soon begin feeding on the leaves and buds. Most species also construct a conspicuous silken nest, or tent, in a fork of the tree or shrub. They do not feed within the tent but move to nearby branches, spinning a strand of silk wherever they go and then following it back to the tent after feeding.

After about four to eight weeks, the larvae reach maturity and pupate underneath the bark,

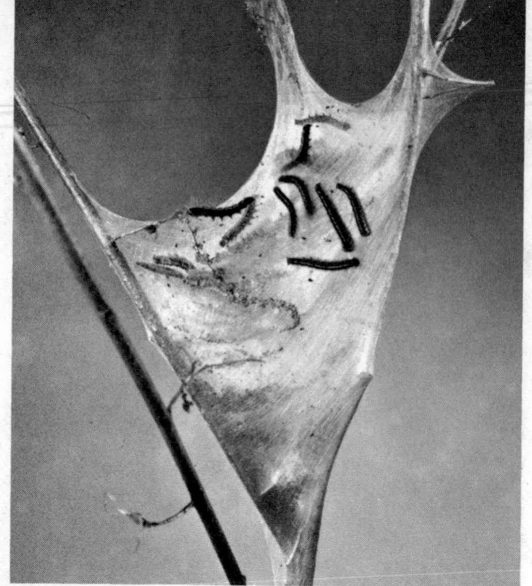

ROCHE, FROM NATIONAL AUDUBON SOCIETY

Tent caterpillars

between leaves, or in various other places in and around the tent. The mature larvae are about 3 inches (5 mm) long, rather hairy, and have bright spots or streaks of blue or yellow on a dark background. The adult moths usually emerge in the middle or toward the end of summer. They are usually brown and have a wingspan ranging from 1 to 2 inches (25–50 mm). Tent caterpillars belong to the family Lasiocampidae. A common North American species is the eastern tent caterpillar (*Malacosoma americanum*).

DON DAVIS, *Smithsonian Institution*

TENT SHOW, a dramatic performance under canvas, or the touring repertory company giving it. Tent shows played summer one-week engagements, with a different show every night, in the rural Midwestern and Southern United States from the early 1900's until World War II. They traveled at first by train and later by truck. Among the first "tent reps" or "rag operas" in the Midwestern were Case-Lister Shows and Jesse Colton Shows. Many stars of films and television began in tent shows.

The tent show's week in town was the one exciting event in many rural communities. The performers were professionals, and the shows were often well equipped. The Harley Sadler Show, touring Texas, had a tent seating 1,500, a 25-piece cowboy band and an orchestra, an elevated auditorium floor, carpeted aisles, uniformed ushers, and standard theater lighting. Well-known vaudevillians from the Orpheum and Pantages circuits performed between the acts.

A small company had about 10 people, each playing several roles. Each played a band instrument and helped with the tent and properties.

Tent shows were also called "Toby" shows. Toby Wilson was a favorite tent-show comedian, and perhaps because of him the comedy hero was always named Toby. Toby was a freckle-faced country lout in baggy pants who always routed the city-slicker villain and won the girl.

The popularity of tent shows waned with the coming of radio and sound films. World War II travel restrictions ended most of them. But at least one was still playing in the 1970's—the Jimmy Davis Show, in Missouri, Iowa, and Texas.

ZACHARY BALL, *Author of "Tent Show"*

TENTH CENTURY. In the 10th century, the young civilization of Western Europe was pushing its frontiers to the north and east by the conversion of pagan rulers to Christianity, while to the south the most advanced outposts of Islam in southern France and peninsular Italy were eliminated. During this period two mature civilizations on the borders of Western Europe reached high points of their development. In the lands of Eastern Christendom, the Byzantine Empire, under its Basilid rulers, recovered much of its former territory, crushing the first empire of Bulgaria and thrusting the Muslims back in the Middle East. The period in Byzantine art is known as the Second Golden Age. Islamic civilization, although it suffered territorial losses and remained politically fragmented, enjoyed a period of cultural brilliance, with centers at Córdoba in Spain, at the newly founded city of Cairo, and at Baghdad.

Thousands of miles to the east the magnificent T'ang dynasty in China collapsed in 907. After years of turmoil, imperial unity was to some extent restored in 960 by the politically less glamorous but culturally scintillating Sung dynasty. In South Asia, much of the political confusion in the southern portion of the Indian subcontinent was eliminated with the rise of the Chola empire, while in Southeast Asia, the great Indianized empires of Angkor and Srivijaya were prominent. The pre-Islamic West African empire of Ghana was at its height at the end of the 10th century. In America, the classic Mayan civilization had ended, but the Mexican cities of Chotollan flourished farther north.

HYMAN KUBLIN, *Brooklyn College*

1. Europe

The main achievement of the 10th century in Europe was the turning of the tide of external invasion that had run so strongly and disastrously during the previous century. Before the end of the 9th century the Viking attacks had been brought under control, and with the establishment of the duchy of Normandy, which took place in stages between 911 and 933, they practically ceased for two generations. There remained only the task of absorbing the alien populations that the Viking invasions had left in France and England, and this task was performed in the course of the 10th century—in France by a process of quiet absorption, and in England as a result of the heroic efforts of the short-lived but brilliant descendants of King Alfred the Great. The other frontiers of European civilization saw a similar process of stabilization and enlargement. The victories of Otto I the Great—over the Hungarians on the Lechfeld plain south of Augsburg in 955, and later against the Wends east of the Elbe River—marked the start of a period of Christian expansion under German leadership.

EXPANSION OF CHRISTIANITY

By the end of the 10th century the rulers of Norway, Denmark, Poland, and Hungary had all been converted to Christianity. The foundation of new episcopal sees under the archbishops of Hamburg and Magdeburg consolidated the expansion of Christianity into the lands north and east of the Elbe River. The foundation of the bishoprics of Poznań in Poland in 968 and of Prague in Bohemia in 975 continued this process. The conversion of Stephen I of Hungary and the establishment of the Christian kingdom of

Hungary in the year 1000 made that country part of western Europe. The victory of Otto I in 955 also brought a cessation of Hungarian raids in Italy.

The Saracens, who until 915 had a base on the Garigliano River between Naples and Rome, were expelled from the Italian mainland before the close of the 10th century, although their domination of Sicily did not finally end until 1091. The Saracen stronghold at La Garde-Freinet (Fraxinetum), in Provence, maintained itself until 972, when a concerted attack put an end to a menace that had seriously threatened communications between Italy and France.

By the year 1000 it was only in Spain and in England that the battle against the enemies of Christendom appeared doubtful. In Spain the military activity of the Muslim leader al-Mansur (Almanzor), who captured Barcelona in 985, threatened to overwhelm the Christian kingdoms and counties south of the Pyrenees. In England the Viking attacks that began in 991 under Olaf Tryggveson temporarily ruined the kingdom, which had been painfully consolidated in the course of the century. These attacks, destructive and victorious though they were, turned out to be the last spasms of a dying energy. Before the expansive energy of the Vikings waned, however, it had brought them to the threshold of a new world—to Greenland and probably also to America.

ECONOMIC AND CULTURAL CONTACTS

Trade. The hostility between western Europe and its neighbors did not make all peaceful communication impossible. If trading with the Muslims was a crime—as most men in the West thought—then Venice, which traded with Alexandria, was guilty. The wars on the eastern frontiers of Germany, moreover, were made to serve the needs of trade with the caliphate of Córdoba. There was a regular caravan route along which slaves, who in most cases probably were captured Slavs, were taken down into Spain. Trade, too, was as much engrained in the Viking way of life as piracy and war, and the long trade route that had been opened up in the 9th century, joining Ireland, Scotland, and northern England with the Baltic, Novgorod, Kiev, and Constantinople, lost nothing of its importance in the 10th century. But by far the most important contacts between Latin Christendom and the world beyond were its direct links with Constantinople and the Byzantine Empire. Venice played the leading part in maintaining these openings to the East.

Byzantine Influence. For the Byzantine Empire, the late 10th century was a period of outstanding military success under Emperors Nicephorus II Phocas (reigned 963–969), John I Tzimisces (reigned 969–976), and Basil II (reigned 976–1025). The empire pushed back the Muslims in the south, regaining Antioch, Aleppo, and the island of Cyprus. In the north a long struggle with the Bulgars ended in the reduction of Bulgaria to the status of a Byzantine province in 1018. In the midst of these military achievements the Byzantine church, about 988, obtained its greatest and historically most important extension of territory and authority by the conversion of Vladimir I, prince of Kiev, and his marriage to a Byzantine princess. Russia thus lay open to Byzantine influence, and its long association with Orthodox Christianity began.

Of all this the West knew little and cared less. Although a spirit of disrespect for the rulers of the Byzantine Empire became dominant in Western minds and remained so until the fall of Constantinople, the West was receptive to Greek influence in art. The fine illuminated manuscripts of Germany and England in particular show the strong influence of Greek models in their technique of illustration and choice of subjects.

In a limited way, the West was influenced by the Byzantine Empire in political matters. The elaborate ceremonial of the Byzantine court expressed supremely well the majesty and sacred dignity of the secular ruler, and its influence on the ceremonial of the German emperors must be reckoned a contribution to the political thought and outlook of the West. This influence was especially strong during the reign (983–1002) of Otto III, who had a Greek mother. It was all the more important because the stability of the Ottonian system of government depended greatly on the ruler's control of ecclesiastical appointments, and his control was strengthened and justified by the quasi-sacerdotal character of the ruler, expressed in court ceremony.

POLITICAL DEVELOPMENTS

The most significant political developments in Europe in the 10th century were the disappearance of the last vestiges of Carolingian rule and the rise of a local territorial aristocracy maintaining itself by force of arms and assuming most of the functions of government over a limited area. The importance of the first of these events was perhaps more symbolic than real, for the disintegration of the Carolingian empire had been going on since the death of its founder, Charlemagne, in 814. The extinction of the Carolingian house in its various branches throughout Europe announced the triumph of the local dynasties that had grown up under its shadow. But it was in the nature of things that while these dynasties pulled the Carolingian empire to pieces, a few of them would have sufficient strength and confidence in themselves to assume, in an attenuated form, the inheritance of Carolingian authority. The most important and successful of these in the 10th century was the Saxon house in Germany.

Holy Roman Empire. When Otto I the Great, who had been king of Germany since 936, entered Rome on Feb. 2, 962, and was crowned emperor by the Pope on the same day, he renewed a tradition that had almost died out. There had been no emperor in the West since 924, and no even tolerably effective emperor since the middle of the 9th century. Otto I could not, after the divisions of a hundred years, renew the European-wide empire of Charlemagne, but he presented a formidable challenge to the process of local disintegration and the wearing down of central government and royal authority that had been going on for a century or more. The vast area that he and his successors attempted to control, from the Baltic to the south of Italy and from the Meuse almost to the Oder, was far beyond the scope of the military science or resources of the day. For the cohesion of this realm the emperors had to depend on the loyalty of men, only loosely attached to their service, whose military duties could neither be exactly assessed nor consistently enforced.

Inevitably the emperors depended very largely on the bishops whom they had appointed and who had both the power and the will to provide the support and counsel that they required. Control over episcopal elections was one of the foundations of the Ottonian system of government, and control over papal elections was a logical and necessary extension of this authority. It was no accident that one of Otto I's earliest acts as emperor was to procure, in 963, the deposition of John XII, the pope who had crowned him. John XII was a representative of the local Roman aristocracy, and for the next century—as long as the system of government inaugurated by Otto I remained reasonably intact—imperial nomination to the papal chair was the main check to the submersion of the papacy in the crosscurrents of local politics.

On the whole this imperial control was acceptable to thoughtful men who appreciated the difficulties of orderly government and accepted the strict interdependence of secular and spiritual affairs as a necessary condition of peace and order. The government of Otto I and his successors depended for its survival on the continuance of this state of mind. It was not destined to last, but the change of temper belongs to the 11th and not the 10th century. Apart, however, from doubts about the legality of the interference of the lay ruler in ecclesiastical affairs, the imposing facade of imperial government suffered from another serious weakness. It masked, but it could not reverse, the process of disintegration into local governmental units that was going on in Germany and Italy as well as elsewhere. Indeed, by arresting the process in its early stages, the Saxon emperors seem only to have ensured that it would continue longer and go deeper than anywhere else in Europe, and that Germany would become a byword for local particularism.

France. In France, where the process of disintegration was least disguised in the 10th century, the story was different. Here, as in Germany, the descendants of Charlemagne went down before a local dynasty—in this case, the Capetian. But the death agonies were more protracted, and there was little royal authority left to be transferred to Hugh Capet, duke of the Franks, when he became king in 987. All over France local counts and dukes had been consolidating their power. These men had emerged from the distresses of the 9th century as the effective rulers of France. With their military vassals, with their stone castles (of which the earliest surviving examples belong to the late 10th century), and above all with their primitive tenacity of purpose, they imposed a certain stability and order on the countryside, but were themselves the chief agents of anarchy in the body politic at large.

OTTO III ENTHRONED, from an illuminated manuscript produced at Reichenau, Germany, in the 990's.

HIRMER FOTOARCHIV

The early Capetian kings, though maintaining the forms and pretensions of their Carolingian predecessors, had no power to control the Frankish aristocracy. Their ability to survive lay in their capacity to accept things as they were, and, being men of few ideas, they found this limitation less irksome than it would otherwise have been. From such unpromising beginnings no one in the 10th century could have foreseen that the Capetian dynasty, in the course of nearly 350 years of uninterrupted male succession, by steady perseverance, craft, and occasional genius, was to become the greatest royal house in Europe.

INTELLECTUAL AND RELIGIOUS LIFE

Literature and Learning. In Germany, the unsure foundations of imperial rule were hidden from contemporaries, and scholars gave evidence of their enthusiasm for the Ottonian cause in many works of literature and art. The literature and learning of the period belonged in spirit and equipment to the Carolingian age. Like the emperors, scholars were engaged in recapturing the glories and techniques of a past age; and, since most of the distinguished centers of learning were in Germany—in monasteries like St. Gall, Reichenau, Corvey (Korvei), and Gandersheim—it was natural that the achievements of the emperors should strike a responsive note in the literature of the time.

Much of this literature smacks of the schoolroom, and both in bulk and importance it falls below the literature of the 9th century. But the efforts of the scholars of this period are not to be judged so much by their literary productions as by the impetus that they gave to scholastic disciplines. This is well illustrated by the career of one of the most notable of 10th century scholars, Gerbert, who became pope in 999 as Sylvester II. Apart from his letters, which are mostly political in content, and one or two reported speeches, his writings are dry, difficult, and technical. But although they contain nothing to attract a reader or to satisfy a thinker, they laid foundations in the study of mathematics and logic that were built upon by the teachers of the next century.

Monastic Activity. Perhaps the most far-reaching of all the 10th century contributions to the internal formation of Europe lay in the sphere of religious life. The middle years of the century in particular saw an enthusiasm and activity in the foundation of new monasteries, and in the reform of old ones, that has seldom been paralleled. The main centers of this activity were in Upper and Lower Lorraine and in Burgundy, stemming from the monasteries of Gorze, Brogne, and Cluny, but very quickly the influence of these houses reached Flanders, central and southern France, Italy, and England. The speed of the movement was astonishing. In England alone during the reign (959–975) of King Edgar the Peaceful it has been reckoned that over 30 and possibly as many as 40 monasteries were either founded or reformed. It was a characteristic of the time that the reform spread with great rapidity not only from the main centers, which have already been mentioned, but also from secondary centers like Fleury and St. Peter's (at Ghent), as soon as they had been reformed by the abbots of Cluny and Brogne respectively.

The leaders and instigators of the monastic activity of the 10th century concentrated on the elaboration of an ornate and absorbing liturgical routine marked by the strictest attention to detail and to uniformity of observance. They threw their whole energy into the preparation and execution of the corporate services of the day, but to manual labor they appear to have been comparatively indifferent. The community had too many skilled and exacting tasks on its hands to have much time for the rough work of field or garden. There were differences in detail between the aims of the reform in Lorraine and at Cluny, but the general direction was the same everywhere. In England the reformers, working in the closest harmony with the king, drew their ideas from both main currents of Continental reform. The document known as the *Regularis concordia Anglicae nationis*, which describes their plan in detail, is one of the most precious witnesses to the spirit of the reform. In Germany, on the other hand, except in Lorraine, the reform made little impact. The hardening against new ideas that this fact suggests brought German leadership in Europe to an end in the course of the next century.

R. W. SOUTHERN
Author of "The Making of the Middle Ages"

2. The Islamic World

The 10th century has justly been characterized as marking the zenith of classical Islamic civilization. Territorially, the Islamic lands embraced essentially the Arab and Iranian worlds from Spain and Morocco on the west to Afghanistan and Transoxiana (roughly modern Uzbekistan) on the east. The Muslims had bridgeheads against the Christians in Sicily and Crete and open frontiers with the Byzantines along the Taurus Mountains and with the Turks in Central Asia.

POLITICAL DEVELOPMENTS

Spain. The Umayyad caliphs of Córdoba, who ruled the greater part of Spain, reached the apogee of their power under Abd ar-Rahman III (reigned 912–961). But they never managed to dislodge the Christians from the mountains of Asturias and Cantabria, and these inaccessible regions formed a base for the Christian reconquest, which began in the next century after the collapse of the Umayyad Caliphate.

North Africa. In North Africa, the local Muslim dynasties all went down during the 10th century in the face of the dynamic Fatimids, who traced their descent back to the Prophet Mohammed's family. The Fatimids utilized this claim to attract followers and build up a powerful state. With their Berber armies, they conquered Egypt in 969, built Cairo as their capital, and expanded eastward as far as southern Syria. The Sahara stood as a great natural barrier to Muslim penetration to the south. The Christian kingdoms in Nubia and Ethiopia prevented the spread of Islam up the Nile Valley.

Middle East. The Abbasid caliphs in Baghdad lost much of their prestige because of the rise of the Fatimids. The moral and spiritual influence of the Abbasids was reduced to the central and eastern lands of Islam. Their direct political authority was ever more circumscribed by the Iranian Buwayhid (Buyid) dynasty, which controlled Iraq and western Persia. The expansion of the Buwayhids from the region of the Elburz Mountains in the 10th and 11th centuries is a historical phenomenon as yet unexplained. Their coming undoubtedly brought social as well as politcal changes, for it hastened the spread of a system of land grants for supporting military and civil officials of the ruling class. That system, though sometimes called "feudal," presents distinct differences from the European feudal system.

The Islamic world had fluid frontiers in northern Syria, where it bordered the Byzantine empire, and along northeastern fringes, beyond which lay the Central Asian steppes and the Indian cultural world. The Arabs were thrown back on the defensive in northern Syria in the mid-10th century, when the Byzantine Greeks launched a counterattack that at one point threatened Damascus and Jerusalem. But this setback was balanced by an outburst of Muslim expansion into the plains of India.

The Muslims had been static in their outpost of Sind (now in Pakistan) for more than two centuries. But after 977, Sabuktigin, Turkish slave-governor of Ghazni (in eastern Afghanistan) for the Saminid rulers of Transoxiana, began a policy of raids into the Punjab. These were brilliantly continued by his son, Sultan Mahmud of Ghazni (reigned 998–1030). As a result of the campaigns, large numbers of Indian slaves were brought back, and bullion from the Hindu temples stimulated the economy of eastern Islam.

The foundations for the wholesale conversion of the Turkish peoples of the Central Asian steppes were laid in this period by the conversion about 950 of the Qarluq tribe, followed by that of the Oghuz Turks. From Transoxiana, fighters for the Islamic faith went into the steppes to work among the pagans, so that over the succeeding centuries almost all the Turks, except those in northeast Siberia, became Muslim.

CULTURAL LIFE

Despite symptoms of political decay at the center of the Caliphate, the rise of rival dynasties in outlying regions, and the assumption of autonomy by provincial governors, Islamic civilization has never been so splendid as in the 10th century. Cities like Córdoba, Cairo, and Baghdad provided a refinement of life and a cultured environment that totally outshone that of the shrunken towns of Europe, with their closed economies and localized outlooks.

Arabic remained the culturally dominant language, and it was during the middle years of the 10th century that the greatest of Arabic poets, al-Mutanabbi, flourished. Arabic had reduced other indigenous languages of the Islamic lands, such as Syriac, Coptic, and Berber, to the status of vernaculars. Only at the two extremities of the Islamic world, in Spain and Persia, did local tongues flourish. This period is in fact notable as witnessing a renaissance of New Persian language and literature. Soon after the end of the century Firdausi completed his version of the Iranian national epic, the *Book of Kings* (see also SHAH NAMEH).

Although Arabic lineage still conferred social prestige, the Arab ruling class had lost political control in many of the Islamic lands. In Persia, local Iranian elements reemerged after their eclipse following the Arab conquest. Even in an ethnically Arab land like Iraq, real power was in the hands of Iranian or Turkish military leaders. This situation was one result of the abandonment of the old free Arab army for a mercenary force composed mostly of Turkish slaves.

The Islamic ethos still accorded the highest prestige to the scholar and civilian, but politically the Muslim world was becoming a network of military autocracies, whose fighting forces lived off land grants rather than salaries. The agrarian consequences of this were inevitably the depression of the small landowners and peasantry. In the realm of government the despotic "power state" became the ideal for many rulers. On the other hand, industry and commerce flourished to a remarkable degree. It was based on the small-scale production of urban craftsmen and the existence of a system of land and water communications for bringing products to centers of consumption like Baghdad.

The Islamic world was largely a self-sufficient economic unit. Its chief imports were slaves and luxury articles, and it was to pay for these imports that coins from the eastern Islamic world found their way in vast numbers as far afield as the Baltic and Iceland. Moreover, the high standard of general prosperity provided a stable level of prices and enabled rulers like the Fatimids and Ghaznavids to mint coinages with a high bullion content.

C. E. BOSWORTH
Author of "Islamic Dynasties"

3. India and Southeast Asia

The political history of the 10th century in South and Southeast Asia is essentially a chronicle of four great states—the Rashtrakuta and Chola empires of India, Srivijaya in Indonesia, and the Khmer empire in Cambodia. These states fought numerous wars and left brilliant monuments for posterity. There was also an impressive development of new forms of Hinduism and Buddhism. Both religions were intimately connected with statecraft and political ideas and stimulated the growth of literatures in a number of Asian languages.

India. Through the 8th and 9th centuries successive Rashtrakuta monarchs had extended their influence from Kanchipuram in the south to Kanauj in the north. Until the collapse of their power in the 10th century they repeatedly defeated the Gurjara-Pratiharas of northern India and from time to time controlled their imperial capital, Kanauj. The Rashtrakutas gained complete mastery over south India by 965, but within a decade their empire crumbled. The Gurjara-Pratiharas then attempted to expand at the cost of the Palas of Bengal, who in the 10th century were clearly in decline.

The fall of the Rashtrakutas gave the Cholas a free hand in south India. The greatness of the Cholas began with the reign (907–953) of Parantaka I, who conquered the city of Madurai from the Pandyas. The real builder of the Chola empire, however, was Rajaraja I the Great (reigned 985–1014), who again took Madurai, annexed what are now Tamil Nadu and areas in Andhra Pradesh, and conquered the northern half of Ceylon. During his reign and that of his successor, Rajendra I (reigned 1014–1044), the Chola empire extended over the whole of southern India as far north as the Tungabhadra River, and included the Maldive Islands as well as northern Ceylon. The Cholas' formidable navy enabled them to control an extensive commerce in the Bay of Bengal and challenge the supremacy of the Indonesian kings of Srivijaya. The Cholas were great builders, and their structures have a massive grandeur.

Cambodia. The Khmer kingdom, founded in the early 9th century, controlled what are now Cambodia and part of South Vietnam. Its prosperity was based largely on extensive irrigation works. The Khmer kings fought against the Chams in the north and extended their rule westward. They also conducted a vast building program that culminated in succeeding centuries in one of the world's most magnificent temples, the Angkor Wat. Yashovarman I built the first city of Angkor in the late 9th century. A moat 700 feet (200 meters) wide enclosed an area of some 16 square miles (41 sq km).

The 10th century Khmer kings were responsible for the development of the cult of the *devaraja* (god-king), established in the 9th century, in which the ruling king was regarded as sacred during his lifetime and identified with the Hindu gods Vishnu or Shiva after his death. The great Angkor monuments were built as shrines of this cult. Vishnu worship, Shiva worship, and Buddhism all flourished in the Khmer kingdom and influenced one another there.

Vietnam. Events to the north and east of Cambodia assumed a very different character during the 10th century. After the fall of the great T'ang Dynasty of China in 907, the Vietnamese achieved their independence from Chinese rule with the establishment of the kingdom of Dai-co-viet (northern and central Vietnam) in 939. This almost inevitably led to a protracted conflict between the rising power of the Vietnamese and their southern neighbors, the Chams, whose kingdom of Champa was culturally oriented toward India.

Indonesia. In Indonesia, the 10th century saw the golden period of the Srivijaya kingdom based on Sumatra and parts of Java. Its control of the waterways through which trade between India and China passed enabled it to become one of the greatest powers in the history of Indonesia. Arab chroniclers described in some detail the great wealth and power of the Srivijaya kingdom, and the Chinese annals frequently mentioned sustained contacts between China and Srivijaya during the 10th century. But the rising power of the south Indian Cholas was fast becoming a challenge to Srivijaya, which by 1025 had been dealt a crippling blow through a daring Chola naval raid.

B. G. GOKHALE, *Wake Forest University*

4. China and Korea

In China, the 10th century marked a political transition from the moribund T'ang dynasty to renewed prosperity and power under the Sung emperors. For more than a century the T'ang government had been gradually undermined until only a semblance of its authority remained after the Huang Ch'ao Rebellion (875–884). By 901 the emperor was a puppet of Gen. Chu Wen, who had been one of Huang Ch'ao's officers. Chu usurped the throne in 907, becoming one of three peasants who have been recognized as emperor of China, and founded the short-lived Later Liang dynasty (907–923).

Political Changes in China. Political order could not easily be restored from the chaos created by the T'ang policy of giving unbridled power to military governors. Four short dynasties followed the Later Liang: the Later T'ang (923–936), Later Chin (936–947), Later Han (947–950), and Later Chou (951–960). The years 907–960 are therefore generally known as the Five Dynasties period. The partly military, partly political struggles reflected in these changes were largely restricted to North China, while the south enjoyed a more stable order under independent regional authorities.

The successive governments in the north struggled with the problem of restoring central authority over the provinces. Therefore when the throne was usurped in 960 by Gen. Chao K'uang-yin (Sung T'ai Tsu), who established the Sung dynasty, institutional arrangements appropriate to a revived central order had already been established. Before his death in 976, Sung T'ai Tsu had largely reunited China. What remained of this work was accomplished by his brother and successor Sung T'ai Tsung, who failed only in his attempts to restore the Peking region to Chinese control. This area had fallen to the Khitan Mongol Liao dynasty (947–1125), and the Sung never recovered it.

Cultural Developments in China. Culturally, the 10th century in China saw the development of trends established in the T'ang period that were to culminate in the Sung. Except about Changan (modern Sian), the military conflicts of the 900's did not seriously disrupt the social order, and there was considerable continuity despite the succession of governments. This fact is exemplified by the career of Feng Tao (882–954), who served as chief administrative officer under 11 emperors of four dynasties.

The decline of the old "aristocratic" elite in Chinese society, a tendency that had appeared in the T'ang period, was accelerated during the 10th century. It is estimated that half the elite at the end of the century were "new men." Also, military technology developed rapidly under the stress of the times. The first known use of gunpowder for military purposes—as the igniter in a flame thrower—was described in 919, and grenades and bombs were in use by 1000.

The peaceful arts likewise advanced, especially printing. The first complete printing of the Confucian classics was ordered by a Later T'ang emperor in 932 and completed under the Later Chou in 953. Between 971 and 983 the complete Buddhist canon of sacred writings, the Tripitaka, was printed for the first time. As it did later in Europe, the reduction of the cost of books brought a widening of educational horizons. Another development was that the use of chairs became widespread in Chinese houses. Many fine examples of the flourishing art and literature of the 10th century were preserved when the Buddhist cave temples at Tunhwang were sealed in 1035, to be rediscovered in 1900.

There were important religious changes as well. Islam spread rapidly in the northwest to become a permanent part of Chinese life there, while Buddhist thought tended toward the Amitabha cult, which preached salvation through faith. Buddhist dominance over Chinese thought was being undermined by a continuation of the T'ang Confucian revival that was to culminate in Sung Neo-Confucianism. A major attack on Buddhism was carried out by the Later Chou government in 955 with the suppression of over 30,000 temples and monasteries and with new regulations that brought Buddhist institutions and clergy under state licensing control.

NATIONAL PALACE MUSEUM, TAIPEI

MOUNTAIN SCENE in ink on silk is by Kuan T'ung, one of many 10th century Chinese landscape masters.

Korea. In Korea, the 10th century saw events superficially similar to those in China. The state of Silla declined after peasant rebellions broke out in 880. Wang Kon (T'aejo; died 943), founded the state of Koryo (918–1392) and reunified Korea in 936. In imitation of Chinese models, he created a magnificent capital at Kaesong (Songdo) and a Chinese-style administration. The heavy hand of this state and the harsh class lines on which it was based seem to have restricted Korean development.

JAMES R. SHIRLEY
Northern Illinois University

5. Japan

During the 10th century Japan's ancient courtier society reached its highest level of perfection and cultural brilliance at the imperial court in Kyoto. After centuries of cultural borrowing from China and the creation of a centralized state on the Chinese model, Japanese court society in the 9th century had terminated its official contacts with China. It also had begun to mold its institutions and culture into forms quite distinct from Chinese.

Political and Economic Changes. During the 10th century the ministerial family of Fujiwara finally consolidated its position next to the throne and assumed virtually dictatorial power at court as imperial regents. The Fujiwara married their daughters into the imperial family and, through the practice of forcing emperors to abdicate, sought to keep the occupants of the throne young and politically impotent.

The system of allotment of public land to peasants, adopted from China in the mid-7th century, had been in decay from at least the 8th century because courtier families and Buddhist and Shinto religious institutions had steadily gathered lands into private holdings. By the 10th century the public domain that had provided the allotments was completely supplanted by these private estates.

Courtier Society. During the 9th and 10th centuries the Kyoto courtiers, who probably constituted less than 1% of the population, became a rigidly exclusive and highly inbred society. Besides ending foreign relationships, they withdrew from all but the most essential contacts with the provincial administrations. To the 10th century courtier, even a brief trip outside the environs of the capital was likely to be viewed with distaste and apprehension.

Japanese court society in its most mature stage of development, at the end of the 10th century, was one of the most interpersonally exacting and aesthetically oriented in world history. The courtiers were obsessed with the smallest matters of social protocol and with observance of the hierarchical privileges of birth. They were also passionately devoted to the appreciation of beauty in all forms, both natural and artificial.

The Arts. The visual arts, strongly influenced by Buddhism, flourished under the patronage of the courtiers. But it was on literature, especially poetry, that they lavished their greatest love.

Poetizing skill in the brief, evocative *waka* form, which had become dominant at court, was virtually essential to social success. Anthologies of the finest poetic compositions were compiled under imperial auspices. The 10th century also saw important developments in Japanese prose literature, culminating in *The Tale of Genji*. Written by Lady Murasaki Shikibu, probably at the beginning of the 11th century, it is an idealized depiction of court society about 1000 A. D. and an incomparable commentary on the styles and behavior of the time.

H. PAUL VARLEY, *Columbia University*

6. Subsaharan Africa

The 10th century in Subsaharan Africa saw a notable continuation of Iron Age developments that had begun more than 1,000 years before. Metal-using agricultural settlements had spread throughout western, eastern, and central Africa, while early Bantu settlement had already reached south of the Limpopo River, in the northerly parts of modern South Africa.

Many communities had grown large enough to require more sophisticated forms of government. The 10th century brought the first clear evidence of substantial African kingdoms. Writing of a voyage far down the east coast of Africa in 915, the Arab geographer al-Masudi reported a large "Kingdom of Zanj" (that is, of the Blacks), which conducted regular gold trade with the interior.

Just over 150 years later the Andalusian Arab geographer Abu Ubayd al-Bakri completed an important collection of travelers' reports on parts of Africa, including the empire of ancient Ghana in the Western Sudan. From his report it is clear that Ghana reached the zenith of its power shortly before the year 1000. Ghana dominated all the main caravan trails across the western and possibly the central Sahara and, through its trade in gold, greatly stimulated the further evolution of kingdoms in the Maghreb (modern Algeria, Morocco, and Tunisia).

BRONZE dated about 1000 A. D. was found at Tada, Nigeria, near the early bronze-casting center of Ife.

PHOTO COURTESY BROOKLYN MUSEUM

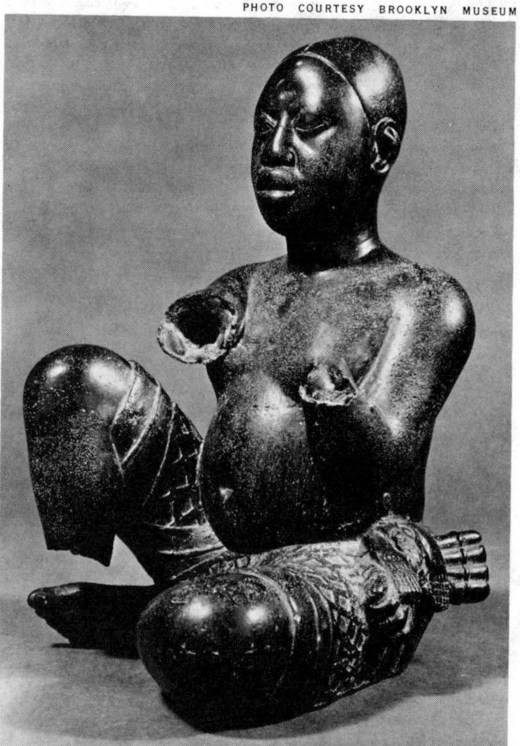

EVENTS OF THE TENTH CENTURY

c. 905 The *Kokinshu*, first imperial anthology of poetry in Japanese, was completed.
907 T'ang dynasty in China fell, beginning a period of disunity.
910 Benedictine abbey of Cluny, influential center of monastic reform, was founded in France.
911 Norse chieftain Rollo was ceded lands by Charles III of France in Normandy.
912 Abd ar-Rahman III, greatest of the Umayyad rulers in Spain, ascended the throne.
915 Arab poet Mutanabbi was born (died 965).
925 Lorraine, under French suzerainty since 911, was restored to Germany.
936 Koryo dynasty, founded in 918, unified Korea.
939 Vietnamese achieved independence from Chinese.
c. 940 Persian poet Firdausi was born (died 1020).
945 Muizz ad-Daula of the Iranian Buwayhid dynasty entered Baghdad and established control there.
953 First complete printing of the Confucian classics was finished.
955 Germans decisively defeated Hungarians at the Lechfeld in Bavaria.
955 Buddhism was suppressed in China by the Later Chou dynasty.
959 Peaceful and prosperous reign of Edgar I began in England.
962 King Otto I the Great of Germany was crowned emperor in Rome.
972 Muslim base at Fraxinetum (Garde-Freinet) in southern France was eliminated.
970 Al-Azhar, oldest university in the Islamic world, was founded in Cairo.
973 Rashtrakuta dynasty in south India was overthrown.
979 Reunification of China was completed by the Sung dynasty, founded in 960.
985 Rajaraja I the Great, builder of formidable Chola empire in south India, ascended the throne.
c. 985 Norsemen colonized Greenland.
987 Hugh Capet ascended the throne in France after death of the last Carolingian king, Louis V.
c.987 Chichén Itzá, Mayan city in Yucatán, was occupied by the Itzá, possibly led by Toltecs.
c. 988 Vladimir I the Great, Prince of Kiev, was converted to eastern Christianity.
991 Vikings renewed their attacks on England.
996 Basil II began last phase of Byzantine conquest of the Bulgarian Empire.
997 Stephen I (St. Stephen) became king of Hungary.
998 Mahmud of Ghazni, who continued destructive Turkish raids on north India, ascended the throne.

During the 10th century there were parallel developments in the forest lands of West Africa, although probably not associated with the stimulus of long-distance trade. Some of the famous terra-cotta sculptures of the Yoruba civilization, centered at Ife in western Nigeria, have been shown to date from this century, thus confirming oral traditions that trace the foundation of the earliest Yoruba kingdom to shortly before 900. To the 10th century also belongs the origin of the Benin state on the western side of the lower Niger River. Archaeological evidence suggests that other major peoples of the West African forest land, including the Akan, were going through the early phases of state formation in relatively large settled communities.

By 1000, earlier developments in the domestication of cattle, farming, metal using, and long-distance trade had led to the firm foundation of many African cultures. Thus, throughout most of Subsaharan Africa, the basis for social, economic, and political growth had been achieved.

BASIL DAVIDSON, *Author of "Africa in History"*

7. The Americas

In the central Andes the 10th century was a period of decline in town life and revival of regional art styles—the outcome of political disintegration. The former highland cultural centers of Taihuanaco and Huari were in eclipse, and the Inca Empire had not begun its rise. Pachacamac, a political and religious center on the coast of Peru, appears to have remained prosperous to the end of the century.

In the tropical rain forest area of northern Central America and adjacent sections of Mexico, the classic Mayan civilization disintegrated after six centuries of splendor. Although the causes of this failure are not known, ecological factors may have been operative, for the decline did not affect the northern Mayan centers in the less humid parts of Yucatán.

Through the 10th century and longer, Cholollan (Cholula) had widespread in the Mexican sphere of civilization. Long a center of high culture, it had become the metropolis of the central Mexican plateau after the fall of Teotihuacán in the 7th or 8th century. Cholollan's power may have been linked to the ascendancy of the semihistorical dynasty of the Olmec-Xicalanca people. Civilization continued to push northward with the advance of agriculture. The rise of the northerly Toltec state, around Tollan (Tula), may have been due to its position near the new frontier of Mexican civilization.

During this period, aboriginal cultural development in the middle Mississippi basin reached its climax. With the introduction of improved strains of corn (maize), subsistence became based on intensified agriculture. Large settlements, including palisaded towns and flat-topped earth mounds to support temples and chiefs' houses, attest to an expanded civil and ceremonial life.

In the far north, where the Norsemen settled in southern Greenland in the 980's, the upswing of a warming cycle favored the spread of Eskimo whale hunters. They carried the distinctive Thule culture across the Canadian Arctic to the northwest coast of Greenland.

PEDRO ARMILLAS, *Author of "The Native Period in the History of the New World"*

Bibliography

Barraclough, Geoffrey, *The Origins of Modern Germany*, 2d ed. (New York 1947).
Brockelmann, Carl, *History of the Islamic Peoples* (New York 1949).
Cambridge University Press, *Cambridge Medieval History*, vols. 3–4 (New York and London 1922–1923).
Davidson, Basil, *A History of East and Central Africa* (Garden City, N. Y., 1969).
Duckett, Eleanor S., *Death and Life in the Tenth Century* (Ann Arbor, Mich., 1967).
Dvorník, František, *The Making of Central and Eastern Europe* (London 1949).
Fage, John D., *A History of West Africa*, 4th ed. (New York and London 1969).
Hall, Daniel G. E., *A History of South-East Asia*, 3d ed. (New York 1968).
Majumdar, Ramesh C., ed., *The History and Culture of the Indian People*, vol. 5 (Bombay 1957).
Mez, Adam, *Renaissance of Islam* (London 1937).
Morris, Ivan, *The World of the Shining Prince: Court Life in Ancient Japan* (New York 1964).
Murasaki Shikibu, *The Tale of Genji*, tr. by Arthur Waley (Boston 1925–1933).
Reischauer, Edwin O., and Fairbank, John K., *East Asia: The Great Tradition* (Boston 1960).
Runciman, Steven, *A History of the First Bulgarian Empire* (London 1930).
Sansom, George B., *Japan: A Short Cultural History*, 2d ed. (New York 1962).
Saunders, John J., *A History of Mediaeval Islam* (New York 1965).
Southern, Richard W., *The Making of the Middle Ages* (New Haven, Conn., 1953).
Symons, Thomas D., ed. and tr., *Regularis Concordia* (Edinburgh 1953).
Thapar, Romila, *A History of India*, vol. 1 (Baltimore 1966).
Vasiliev, Alexander A., *A History of the Byzantine Empire*, 2d Eng. ed. (Madison, Wis., 1952).
Vernadsky, George, *Kievan Russia* (New Haven, Conn., 1948).

TENURE OF OFFICE ACT, a law passed on March 2, 1867 that prohibited the president of the United States from removing without senatorial approval any official who had been appointed with the Senate's consent. It was one of the laws intended to reestablish the traditional domination of the federal government by Congress, but more specifically, it was designed to restrict the power of the inept and unpopular President Andrew Johnson during the Reconstruction period following the Civil War. Many of the act's Radical Republican backers were anxious to protect the secretary of war, Edwin M. Stanton, the only cabinet member who favored the Radicals and their Reconstruction program.

President Johnson's subsequent attempt to oust Stanton led the House of Representatives to impeach him in 1868; the House stressed the President's violation of the Tenure of Office Act. But the vote in the Senate was one short of the two-thirds majority necessary for conviction. This controversial law was repealed in 1887.

F. N. BONEY, *University of Georgia*

TENZING NORKAY, ten'sing nôr'gā (1914–), Sherpa mountaineer. He won fame in 1953 when he and Sir Edmund Hillary became the first climbers to reach the summit of Mt. Everest, the world's highest peak.

Tenzing Norkay (or Norgay) was born in Nepal and at 18 moved to Darjeeling, India. In 1935, as a porter, he went on his first expedition to Everest. He accompanied other Himalayan expeditions almost annually, and in 1947 became a *sirdar* (head porter).

In 1951, with a French expedition, Tenzing climbed the east peak of Nanda Devi. He participated in two Swiss expeditions to Everest in 1952 before reaching the summit the following year with Hillary, a New Zealander. In 1964 he became director of field training at the Himalayan Mountaineering Institute, Darjeeling.

Tenzing's autobiography, *Tiger of the Snows,* in collaboration with James Ullman, appeared in 1955.

DAVID ROBERTSON, *Barnard College*

TEOSINTE, tā-ə-sint'ē, is a tall annual grass considered by many authorities to be an ancestor of corn. Teosinte (*Euchlaina mexicana*) is native to Mexico and Central America and is cultivated to a limited extent in Central and South America for forage. Sometimes it is grown as an ornamental.

The plant grows to a height of 8 to 12 feet (2.4–3.6 meters) and has large, broad leaves from 3 to 4 feet (0.9–1.2 meters) long. The flowers and seeds (kernels) are very similar to those of the corn plant.

H. A. MACDONALD, *Cornell University*

TEOTIHUACÁN, tā-ō-tē-wä-kän', was the first city of the pre-Columbian civilizations in Middle America. It is located 25 miles (40 km) northeast of Mexico City between the Valley of Mexico and the Valley of Pueblo. Teotihuacán first arose in the late pre-Classical period, about 100 B. C., and the city flourished through most of the Classical period, until about 750 A. D., as a major religious, political, and commercial center. Little is known of the people of the city. But their culture was Olmec-based, and they strongly influenced the succeeding Toltec and Aztec cultures. At the peak of its development, about 500 A. D., Teotihuacán had an area of 8 square miles (21 sq km) and supported a population of more than 50,000.

Evidently, the city was built to conform to a grid pattern. There is a main north-south axis, the Street of the Dead, traversed by an east-west axis at the city center. The center consists of the Citadel on the east side and the Great Compound on the west side. Inside the Citadel is the Temple of Quetzalcoatl, which is the best evidence of the skill achieved in stone sculpture. The Great Compound lacks significant religious structures and may have been an administrative or economic center. The city's largest structure, the truncated Pyramid of the Sun, was built during the first period of growth. The smaller Pyramid of the Moon is at the north end of the Street of the Dead.

There are also smaller temples and over 4,000 apartment buildings—one-story, lime-plastered complexes of connected rooms and passages. Religious murals have been found on many temple walls, and a distinctive pottery style, based on the champlevé technique, has been identified.

PYRAMID OF THE SUN in Teotihuacán, near Mexico City, is more than 200 feet (61 m) high. A stairway leads up five concentric terraces to the top platform, where religious rites were held.

MARILU PEASE, FROM MONKMEYER

TEPEE, tē′pē, a type of tent primarily associated with the Plains Indian tribes of North America. The tepee (or tipi) also became popular with Plateau groups living in the Columbia River area. Originally the tepee was a small, conical shelter, made of skins, supported by slender poles, and transported by dogs or human beings. After the Indians acquired horses for transport, it became a large tent of buffalo hide—later replaced by canvas—requiring as many as 22 poles. Often 25 feet (9.6 meters) in length, the poles protruded some distance above the covering. The Crow had perhaps the tallest tepees, and the Cheyenne had relatively low, squat types.

Unique among the tents of nomadic peoples was the development of adjustable flaps on either side of the top or smoke hole to keep the wind or rain from getting into the hole.

STEPHEN E. FERACA
Bureau of Indian Affairs

MUSEUM OF THE AMERICAN INDIAN, HEYE FOUNDATION

NEZ PERCÉ COUPLE BEFORE TEPEE, which is made of hides stretched over a pole framework.

TEPHRA, tef′rə, are the loose fragments of lava ejected by an erupting volcano. Such fragments are produced in a wide range of sizes, from fine volcanic ash and lumps of cinder and pumice to massive volcanic "bombs." The term "tephra" was introduced by an Icelandic geologist, Sigurdur Thorarinsson, in 1954 as a collective term for these unconsolidated lava fragments, as distinguished from ejected material that derived from earlier lava flows or from crustal rocks in the volcano.

TEQUILA, tə-kē′lə, is an alcoholic beverage distilled from hearts of the agave, which is known also as the century plant, American aloe, maguey, or mescal. Tequila is a strong spirit, clear or amber in color, made in or near the Mexican city of Tequila. It is closely related to the Mexican drinks pulque and mescal.

To make tequila, agave hearts are split and steamed to remove the sap, which is then distilled. A traditional way of drinking tequila is to squeeze lime or lemon juice onto the tongue, add salt to it, and then swallow the liquor.

MUSEUM DAHLEM, BERLIN

***The Concert,* a familiar Ter Borch theme.**

TER BORCH, tər bôrkh′, **Gerard** (1617–1681), Dutch painter, who specialized in domestic genre scenes and portraits. Ter Borch (also Terborch or Terburg) was born in Zwolle and studied with his father and in Amsterdam and Haarlem. He was in London by 1635, in Rome about 1640, and then in Spain, where he painted Philip IV. From 1654, Ter Borch lived in Deventer, Netherlands. He died there on Dec. 8, 1681.

Ter Borch's earliest works, barrack scenes of soldiers, show his fine feeling for color and restrained atmosphere. Later he did small portraits and miniatures. His group portrait of delegates signing the *Peace of Münster* (National Gallery, London) closing the Thirty Years' War in 1648 is a rare historical document.

Ter Borch is best known for interior genre scenes ranging from simple subjects such as *Flea Hunt* (Alte Pinakothek, Munich) to more elaborate groups of elegant people, in which are subtly depicted social situations and psychological relationships. He painted intimate scenes with such delicacy that their true subject is not immediately apparent. For example, the painting known as *The Parental Admonition* (Museum Dahlem, Berlin) is actually a brothel scene. Cool silvery light brings out the figures in rooms of airy semidarkness.

LOLA B. GELLMAN, *Queens College, New York*

TERBIUM, tûr′bē-əm, symbol Tb, is a soft, ductile metallic element. It is classified as one of the rare-earth, or lanthanide, elements. Terbium was discovered in 1843 by the Swedish chemist Carl Gustav Mosander. Found mainly in the form of the mineral monazite, it makes up only about 9 parts per million of the earth's crust. Terbium is used to dope calcium fluoride and other compounds used in solid-state devices. Terbium compounds are used as phosphor activators.

The atomic number of terbium is 65, and its atomic weight is 158.924. There are 18 isotopes of the element with atomic masses ranging from ^{147}Tb to ^{164}Tb. When freshly cut, the metal has a bright luster. It melts at 1356° C (2473° F) and boils at 2800° C (5072° F). In most of its compounds terbium forms pale pink +3 ions, but a +4 state is also known.

Terbium compounds are separated from other rare earths by ion-exchange or solvent extraction techniques. The anhydrous chloride of fluoride is then reduced with calcium to yield the metal. Aqueous solutions of terbium salts are also reduced to the metal by electrolytic processes.

HERBERT LIEBESKIND
The Cooper Union, New York

TERBORCH, Gerard. See TER BORCH, GERARD.

TERCEIRA. See AZORES.

TEREDO, tə-rēd′ō, a large genus of highly specialized wormlike clams that burrow into wood. These so-called "termites of the sea" or "shipworms" leave few external marks on the wood but honeycomb it internally so that it collapses. A few teredos are found in fresh water, but most live only in marine or brackish water, attacking wharfs, pilings, and wooden ships. Despite the use of concrete and steel for construction and of metal, plastic, and fiber glass for ship hulls, teredos still cause great damage.

Teredos pass through a free-swimming juvenile stage at the end of which they die if they do not bore into wood. The clam's foot glands secrete attachment threads, and as its shell develops, the animal scrapes together a protective cone of wood fibers. The shell and body then undergo many changes. The shell becomes ridged and notched so that it becomes an effective rasping structure. Powerful adductor muscles develop to manipulate the shell. The foot becomes a suction cup to hold the animal in place while it bores, and the body elongates so that the shell covers only a small part of it.

A great deal of research has been directed toward the control of teredos. Creosote-treated wood, if properly prepared, interferes mechanically with the boring action of the shell. Special paints and coating materials containing heavy metals such as copper are effective in protecting wooden hulls. Untreated wood is infested by teredos very rapidly.

PAUL A. MEGLITSCH, *Drake University*

Teredos bore into wharf pilings, causing serious damage.

DR. DOUGLAS P. WILSON

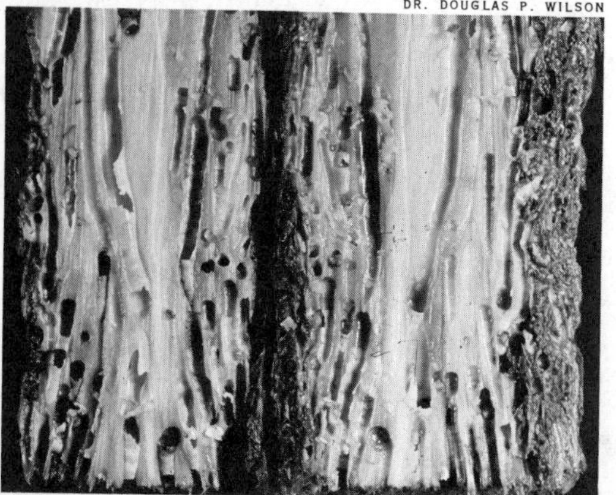

TERENCE, târ′ənts (195?–159 B.C.), Roman writer of comic drama. His full name in Latin is Publius Terentius Afer. Information about his life is sketchy and unreliable and must be pieced together from his prologues, from the *didascaliae* (prefaces) to his plays, and from an account found in the commentaries of Donatus (4th century A.D.) that is attributed to Suetonius (2d century A.D.).

The traditional story obtained from such sources is that Terence was born in Carthage and taken to Rome as a slave, where he was educated and set free by his owner, the senator Terentius Lucanus. Terence later became acquainted with the general, consul, and literary patron Scipio Africanus the Younger and perhaps was a member of the Scipionic Circle. It was to the learned and noble members of that circle that Terence submitted his plays for criticism. After the production of his sixth play, he went to Greece in search of manuscripts of Greek plays and never returned. He either drowned at sea or lost the manuscripts in a storm and died from the shock.

Works. Terence wrote only six plays, all of which are extant. Their order of composition is the subject of scholarly debate, but a possible order is: *Andria* (*Woman of Andros*), 166; *Hecyra* (*Mother-in-Law*), 165; *Heauton Timorumenos* (*Self-Tormentor*), 163; *Eunuchus* (*Eunuch*), 161; *Phormio*, 161; and *Adelphi* (*Brothers*), 160. In each play, Terence used the prologue to answer his detractors, rather than to explain the story as was customary. Thus the denouements of his plays are often a surprise.

Terence's plays may be called comedies of manners. Interest centers on the characters and their reactions to the situation. The humor is quiet and the action restrained. There is "nothing in excess." His characters are types—the courtesan, the wayward son, and the stern father—but each representative of a type has individual traits. The scene of all the plays is Athens, and the customs, dress, and manners of the characters are Greek. The tone of the plays is aristocratic, and for that reason they held little appeal for the Roman populace, as we learn from remarks in the prefaces.

Hecyra and *Phormio* were based on earlier Greek plays by Apollodorus of Carystus. Each of the other plays was drawn from one or two comedies by the Greek playwright Menander. Until the discovery in 1957 of a manuscript of Menander's *Dyscolos*, much of our understanding of that author was derived from Terence's adaptations of his plays.

Influence. Terence's simplicity and charm of language, as well as his moralizing precepts expressed in memorable phrases, made him a favorite with later Roman authors. The early church fathers denounced him for making attractive the world of lust and intrigue, but through the Middle Ages and the Renaissance and into modern times he has been admired by many writers. Although his influence as a dramatist has been slight, his language and thoughts have been used by such men as Erasmus, Melanchthon, Molière,

George Chapman. In more recent times the American writer Thornton Wilder's *Woman of Andros* made extensive use of Terence's *Andria*.

EDWARD N. O'NEIL
University of Southern California

Further Reading: Beare, William, *The Roman Stage*, 3d ed. (New York 1965); Duckworth, George E., *The Nature of Roman Comedy* (Princeton, N. J., 1952).

TERESA OF ÁVILA, tə-rē'sə ä'vē-lə, **Saint** (1515–1582), Spanish religious reformer and author of works on the spiritual life. She was one of the first two women to be named Doctors of the Church, the other being St. Catherine of Siena. Teresa de Cepeda was born in Ávila, Spain, on March 28, 1515, of a noble family. At the age of 15 she was sent to a convent school and five years later entered the Carmelite monastery of the Annunciation at Ávila. She left the monastery for a time because of poor health and was partially paralyzed for three years.

After 19 years as a Carmelite nun Teresa experienced "a conversion." She became conscious of God's presence within her and experienced the physical nearness of Jesus Christ. She suffered from contradictory advice about these experiences from her spiritual directors, but learned men such as St. Francis Borgia, St. Peter of Alcántara, and Domingo Bañez encouraged her.

In 1560, with the approval of Roman ecclesiastical authorities, she founded the first of her monasteries on an ancient and more rigorous Carmelite rule. In the same period, in obedience to her confessor, she wrote the *Vida* (*Life*), an account of her spiritual experiences. Despite continuing local opposition she went on, with Rome's approval, to establish several more reformed Carmelite monasteries. The opening of the second one in 1563 was accompanied by near riots, by the townspeople, who opposed her innovations—a vigorously enforced rule and the establishment of convents without an endowment. Five years of comparative peace followed this outbreak.

During this period Teresa wrote for the nuns of her monasteries *The Way of Perfection,* an instruction on the methods of prayer and the means of achieving virtue. In 1567, through her friendship with St. John of the Cross, she began to influence the setting up of reformed Carmelite monasteries for men.

In the midst of these cares she continued to mature spiritually and, in 1572, according to her own account, she was raised to "spiritual marriage," the highest stage of the spiritual life, through which the soul remains absorbed in God. In 1575 her ecclesiastical superiors in Rome, on the basis of biased accounts of her work, ordered her to return to her convent and desist from founding new monasteries. Through the intervention of King Philip II of Spain the order was reversed four years later.

Teresa carried on a large correspondence throughout her life. Her collected letters show a woman of remarkable intelligence and common sense, with a sense of humor. Among her other works are the *Book of Foundations,* which relates her efforts in creating new monasteries, and her greatest spiritual work *The Interior Castle.*

Teresa died in Alba on Oct. 4, 1582. Canonized in 1662, she was declared a Doctor of the Church in 1870. Her feast day is October 15.

PHILIP F. MULHERN, O. P.
St. Mary's Priory, New Haven, Conn.

LONDON DAILY EXPRESS

Valentina V. Tereshkova, first woman in space.

TERESHKOVA NIKOLAYEVA, tyə-rəsh-kō'və nyi-ku-lä'yə-və, **Valentina Vladimirovna** (1937–), Russian cosmonaut and first woman to fly in space. Tereshkova was born near Yaroslavl, USSR, on March 6, 1937. When Yuri Gagarin made the first manned space flight in 1961, she was working in a textile mill. A Communist party member and an expert parachutist, Tereshkova volunteered and became a member of the second group of Soviet cosmonauts.

On June 16, 1963, Vostok 6 was launched with Tereshkova as pilot, and she flew it for 70.8 hours and 48 orbits of the earth. She was honored with the title of Hero of the Soviet Union. In the same year she married Col. Andrian Grigorievich Nikolayev, commander of the cosmonaut unit and pilot of the Vostok 3 flight.

F. C. DURANT, III, *National Air and Space Museum, Smithsonian Institution*

TERHUNE, tər-hūn', **Albert Payson** (1872–1942), American author and journalist, who is remembered chiefly as a writer of dog stories. He was born in Newark, N. J., on Dec. 21, 1872. After graduation from Columbia University in 1893, he worked on the New York *Evening World* from 1894 to 1920. His books include *The Years of the Locust* (1915), *Lad: A Dog* (1919), *Bruce* (1920), *Lad of Sunnybank* (1928), and his autobiography, *Now That I'm Fifty* (1924). Terhune died at his farm, "Sunnybank," near Pompton Lakes, N. J., on Feb. 18, 1942.

TERLINGUAITE, tər-ling'gwə-īt, is a mercury mineral, found near Terlingua, Texas. It has transparent yellow crystals with a glassy luster. Composition, Hg_2C1O; hardness, 2-3; specific gravity, 8.7; crystal system, monoclinic.

TERMAN, tər'mən, **Lewis Madison** (1877–1956), American psychologist, who pioneered in measuring intelligence and achievement. He was born in Johnson county, Ind., on Jan. 15, 1877, was associated with Stanford University throughout his career, and died in Palo Alto, Calif., on Dec. 21, 1956.

After a decade of research, Terman in 1916 published the Stanford Revision of the Binet-Simon intelligence scale and *The Measurement of Intelligence,* a guide for the use of the scale. He also contributed to the Army Alpha group intelligence test used during World War I. He published the Terman Group Test of Mental Ability (1920) and was a coauthor of the Stanford Achievement Test (1923). See also INTELLIGENCE.

Terman carried on researches that were extensive in scope and time. His most significant contribution came in *Genetic Studies of Genius*. The first volume, *Mental and Physical Traits of One Thousand Gifted Children* (1925), was followed by four volumes reporting studies of the same subjects at later times in childhood and adulthood. The studies showed that the gifted children continued to have high IQ's and were usually well adjusted as adults.

RICHARD MADDEN, *San Diego State College*

TERMINAL MORAINE. See MORAINE.

TERMITE, tûr'mīt, any of a large order, Isoptera, of social insects that live in highly integrated colonies. Termites superficially resemble ants in their habits and appearance, and they are sometimes called "white ants." However, termites have no close affinities with ants; actually, they are closely related to cockroaches.

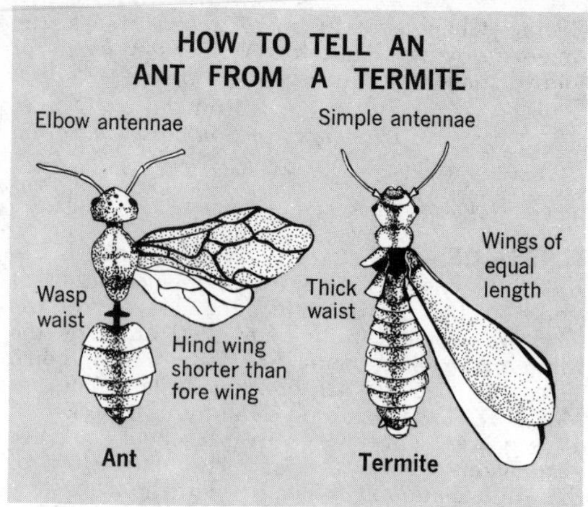

COURTESY OF THE AMERICAN MUSEUM OF NATURAL HISTORY

Feeding Habits. The primary food of all termites is cellulose, a carbohydrate found in plants. Although termites are best known for their destruction of timber in houses and other structures, many species obtain their cellulose from grass, humus in the soil, and decaying wood. It is of interest that termites themselves cannot digest cellulose. They rely on special organisms living in their intestinal tract to do it for them.

Some termites, such as *Hodotermes* in southern Africa, forage in the open in full sunlight, cutting grass stalks to take to their nest. In Australia, *Drepanotermes* has similar habits but forage at night. Some, such as *Cornitermes* in Panama, burrow through the soil and feed on humus. Some species of *Nasutitermes*, a pantropical genus, build nests in trees and forage under arcades they construct of chewed wood, debris, and their feces. Some, such as *Zootermopsis* in California, spend their lives in decaying logs. The best-known termite pest in the United States, *Reticulitermes*, is subterranean and destroys sound timber in houses and other structures.

Nests. The habitations of termites range from simple cavities in logs to complicated nests, or termitaria, of tropical species. Some termitaria are very large. In Australia, some are 20 feet (6 meters) high. An interesting type of nest is that of *Amitermes meridionialis,* the so-called magnetic termite found around Darwin, Australia. The long axis of the nest, which may be 10 feet (3 meters) long, points north and south, and the shorter axis runs east to west.

Life History. In the typical life history of a termite colony, winged adults, called alates, are formed in the nest. These individuals leave the nest in a swarm and after they disperse and settle, both males and females break off their wings. In many species the females then assume a characteristic "calling" attitude, with the tip of the abdomen pointing upward. This position probably exposes a gland that produces a chemical attractant, a type of pheromone. When a male touches a female, she lowers her abdomen and runs off, the male following close behind. The female finds a crevice and excavates a nuptial chamber, sometimes aided by the male. Once the chamber is completed, the male and female copulate, and she lays her eggs.

The first nymphs that hatch from the eggs molt several times to become workers and soldiers.

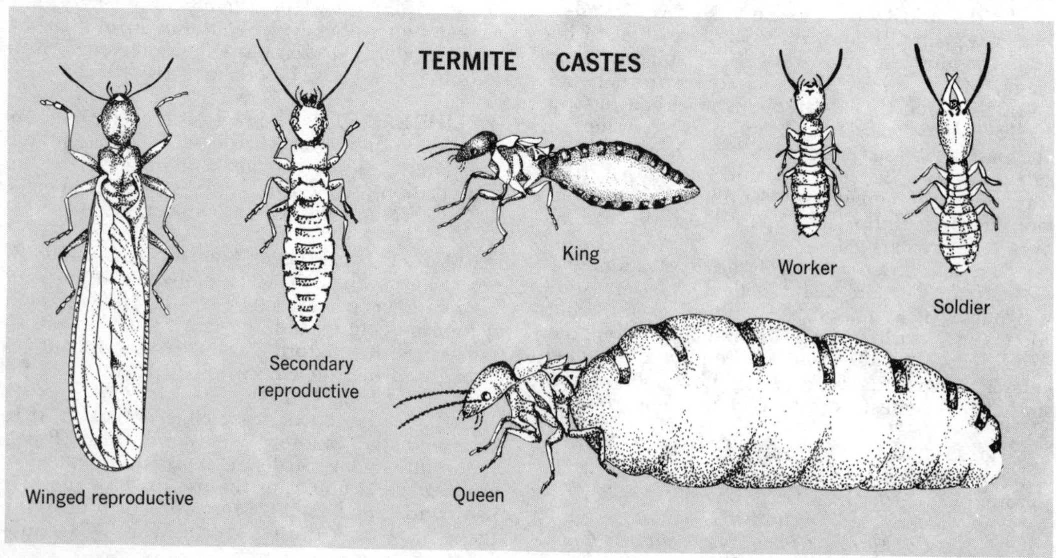

As more eggs are laid, the colony grows and the various tasks are performed by the new progeny. Once the colony has reached a certain size, new alates are produced. They ultimately leave the nest and found new colonies.

Social Organization. In many species the loss of the original king and queen, the *primary reproductives,* does not end the colony. Certain individuals in the nest will undergo changes, notably the development of their reproductive organs, and will take the place of the original reproductives. These new forms are considered to be members of a special caste, called the *secondary,* or *replacement, reproductives.*

Usually, three other castes are present in a termite colony: the *soldiers,* which are adapted to defend the colony; the *alates,* which will form new colonies; and the *workers,* which forage for food, build the nest, look after the eggs and feed the soldiers, the young, and the reproductives. The number of members of each caste varies according to species. Sometimes certain castes may be entirely absent.

The determination of castes is complicated. In general, the numbers and formation of the different forms are controlled by the presence or absence of inhibitory pheromones produced by individuals already formed. For example, the reproductives produce a pheromone that prevents the young from becoming reproductives. If the reproductives are removed from the colony, the pheromone is also lost, and the development of new reproductives, the secondary forms, begins.

Communication. To achieve the high level of integration observed in a termite colony, the individual members must be able to communicate with each other. It is known that they communicate by mechanical contact and through the production of pheromones. Chemical trails communicate the direction of food sources or other sources of excitation, such as the entrance of an intruder into the nest. It is also likely that some species may use sound, usually produced by banging the head against an object, or they communicate visually.

Control Measures. The most common method of termite control is aimed at killing them directly with insecticides. The exact method varies according to the species being exterminated. In the case of the *Reticulitermes,* a poisonous chemical, such as dieldrin or chlordane, is injected into the soil surrounding a dwelling and into the cavities of basement walls. Also, all the damaged wood is removed. Preventive measures, however, are the best means of control and require good building techniques. There should be ample ventilation in the basement, timbers should not be in contact with the soil, and termite barriers, mechanical or chemical, should be introduced.

The insecticides used in termite control are persistent and hazardous. Other control methods using biologically active substances such as pheromones and hormones, are being developed.

Classification. Many authorities divide the order Isoptera into seven families: Mastotermitidae, Kalotermitidae, Termopsidae, Hodotermitidae, Rhinotermitidae, Serritermitidae, and Termitidae. One leading taxonomist includes the Termopsidae in the Hodotermitidae. The most advanced and highly specialized family is the Termitidae, and the most structurally primitive is the Mastotermitidae.

ALASTAIR M. STUART
North Carolina State University

ALLAN D. CRUICKSHANK, FROM NATIONAL AUDUBON SOCIETY

Sooty tern sitting on its egg in sand nest.

TERN, tûrn, any of a group of slender, graceful seabirds with long pointed wings, forked tails, and sharp pointed bills. They are found in all oceans from the tropics to the polar regions as well as on inland lakes, marshes, and rivers. Most species are coastal, seldom straying far from land, but others are at home in mid-ocean.

Terns vary in size from the dainty 8-inch (20-cm) least tern (*Sterna albifrons*) to the heavy-bodied 23-inch (58-cm) Caspian tern (*Hydroprogne caspia*). Most terns are white, with the wings and back gray, the feet red or black, and the bill red, black, yellow, or a combination of these colors. Many species have a black cap during the breeding season, with some of the larger forms also having shaggy crests. Other species, such as the marsh terns (genus *Chlidonias*) have black and gray bellies. A distinctive group of terns—the noddies—all have black bills and feet, though they vary in plumage coloring from black through light gray to all white.

Although terns have webbed or partly webbed feet, they are not notable swimmers. Most plunge into water for small fish and crustaceans. Terns are highly social in feeding and breeding, and breeding colonies may include millions of birds. Their calls are sharp and rasping and consist of a combination of short notes and drawn-out cries. Most terns are migrants. In fact, the Arctic tern (*Sterna paradi aea*), which breeds in the Arctic tundra and winters south of the Antarctic Circle, probably migrates the longest distance of any bird.

Most terns nest on the ground, but the noddies nest in trees. The eggs—usually two or three, rarely one—are gray or brown, speckled and spotted with lavender and black. Both parents incubate the eggs and feed and defend the downy young.

Terns make up the subfamily Sterninae of the gull and tern family Laridae of the order Charadriiformes.

GEORGE WATSON, *Smithsonian Institution*

TERNATE, ter-nä′tā, is one of the Moluccas, or Spice Islands, of eastern Indonesia. The small, circular island, which has an area of 25 square miles (65 sq km), is an active volcano. It has a dense population composed mainly of Muslim and Christian Alfurs, who speak Ternatese. The island has luxuriant vegetation. Its chief cash crops are nutmeg, pepper, coconuts, and coffee.

In 1513, when a Portuguese expedition reached

Ternate, the island's sultan largely controlled the Molucca spice trade. The Portuguese gained special trading privileges by helping him against the sultan of Tidore but were expelled from Ternate in 1574. The Spaniards made a series of attacks on the island from 1582 to 1606.

In return for help against both the Portuguese and Spaniards, the Dutch then received special trading rights. They destroyed many of Ternate's spice plantations in order to restrict production to a few islands. In 1683 they imposed direct rule, and except for short interludes Ternate remained under Dutch control for over 250 years. Population: (1957) 33,964.

WILLIAM Y. DESSAINT
The New University of Ulster

TERNEPLATE. See STEEL–*Steel Technology*.

TERNI, ter'nē, an Italian city, lies in the Nera valley in the central Apennines, 50 miles (80 km) north of Rome. The capital of Terni province, it is situated on the edge of a small fertile basin, for which it has served as a market center since classical times. Its modern importance, however, is chiefly as a center of metallurgical and chemical manufactures, based upon hydroelectric power from the famous waterfalls, Cascata delle Marmore, to the east, and of food processing industries.

Terni, a prosperous town in Roman times, was the birthplace of the Latin historian Tacitus. It suffered severely during the barbarian invasions and subsequently during the wars of the Guelphs and Ghibellines. Then it passed to the Papal States. Terni retains few monuments from its eventful past, but there are remains of an amphitheater. Population: (1967) 103,936.

NORMAN J. G. POUNDS, *Indiana University*

TERPANDER, tûr-pan'dər (c.700–650 B.C.), Greek musician and poet, who is often called the father of Greek classical music. He was born at Antissa in Lesbos. He was reputed to have gone to Sparta at the command of the Delphic Oracle. Despite his reputation, only a few lines of his work and very little writing about him remain. He is credited with developing the first Greek school of music and with increasing the number of strings on the lyre from three or four to seven. However, evidence indicates an earlier date for the change on the lyre. In 676 B.C. he was awarded the music prize at the feast of Apollo Carneius. Terpander also wrote lyric poetry, some intended to be sung in chorus to his lyre and flute music. He is believed to have died in Sparta.

TERPENE, tûr'pēn, group of isomeric hydrocarbons with the formula $C_{10}H_{16}$, which are found in turpentine and other essential oils. The term terpene is also used to include compounds with 15 or more carbon atoms that are based on the isoprene unit, C_5H_8. Natural rubber latex is mostly a polyterpene. Some plant extracts of the terpene group are used for food flavoring and in perfume.

A few of the terpenes with high molecular weights are solid, but most are colorless liquids that boil between 155° and 185°C (311–365°F). They have characteristic, often pleasant, odors. They may be open-chain or cyclic compounds, or a mixture of the two. They are chemically active.

TERPSICHORE, tûrp-sik'ə-rē, in Greek legend, was one of the nine Muses, the daughters of Zeus and Mnemosyne. She was thought to be the originator and patroness of the art of dancing and of the accompanying singing or recitation of lyric poetry. Her name is translated as "she that rejoices in the dance." Some have also credited her with the invention of the cithara. She is usually represented in a mirthful attitude, crowned with laurel and holding a lyre.

TERRA, târ'ə, **Gabriel** (1873–1942), Uruguayan public official, who was president of Uruguay from 1931 to 1938. Born in Montevideo, he received his law degree in 1895 from the University of Montevideo, where he later taught law. After several years' service in the Uruguayan National Congress as a leading member of the conservative wing of the ruling Colorado party, he became president in 1931. On March 31, 1933, in the face of severe economic depression caused mainly by the lack of foreign demand for wool and other export products, Terra dissolved the National Congress and national administrative council and set up a dictatorship. He thus interrupted Uruguay's impressive record of democratic stability.

A new constitution, drafted by a constitutional assembly and adopted in 1934, provided that executive powers be discharged by the president, assisted by a council of ministers. Terra was elected for a second term and took office on May 19, 1934. A dam for harnessing the Río Negro for hydroelectric power was completed while he was president. He died in Montevideo in 1942.

JOHN J. FINAN, *The American University*

TERRA COTTA, ter'ə kät'ə, is fired earthenware, usually unglazed. The term "terra cotta" is Italian for "baked earth." After firing, terra cotta ranges in color from gray through buff to reddish brown or red. It may be left its natural color, painted, or, sometimes, glazed. Unglazed terra cotta, which remains porous despite firing, is used chiefly for decorative work such as sculpture, ornamental vases, and architectural ornament. In warm regions, however, unglazed terra cotta vessels serve as water coolers because the process of moisture percolating the walls of the vessel and evaporating on the outer surface cools the remaining liquid. Terra cotta, glazed or unglazed, is also used for bricks, tile, structural materials, and fireproofing.

In its widest definition, derived from its meaning in Italian, "terra cotta" refers to all kinds of fired clay. In its most restricted sense the term is used for small sculptures of red, lightly fired, unglazed earthenware popular since the Renaissance.

Techniques. Terra cotta can be handled in many ways. Large sculpture of solid terra cotta is rare because during the firing the thicker parts of the figure absorb and lose heat more slowly than the thinner parts, thus creating unequal stresses that usually cause firecracks. To avoid firecracks, a large figure is often first modeled in solid form and then cut in half vertically. The two interiors are hollowed out, and the front and back shells, now of uniform thickness, are rejoined and fired.

A large hollow figure may also be made by handpressing a layer of damp clay into two halves of a plaster or fireclay press mold. Solid

ANDERSON-ART REFERENCE BUREAU

MUSEUM OF PRIMITIVE ART, NEW YORK

TERRACOTTA PIECES

ALINARI-ART REFERENCE BUREAU

FREER GALLERY OF ART, WASHINGTON, D. C.

Greek gorgon with her child, the winged Pegasus, painted relief, possibly from an altar at Syracuse, late 7th century B. C. (*upper left*); Huari style painted bowl, possibly from central coast of Peru, about 900 to 1200 A. D. (*lower left*); Etruscan Apollo from roof of the temple at Veii, about 500 B. C. (*center*); Chinese glazed funerary figurine of a woman on horseback, T'ang dynasty (*above*).

figurines, too small to split in firing, may be formed by filling a press mold with clay. Frequently the component parts of a figure are made in separate press molds and then joined together before firing. Some parts may be interchangeable, allowing a large variety of figures to be made from a limited variety of parts.

Small hollow sculpture may be made by slip casting; that is, by pouring slip, a creamy mixture of clay and water, into a drain mold of plaster, which absorbs the water and leaves a firm clay coating on the mold. The surplus slip is poured off and the mold removed. Both press molds and drain molds allow production in large quantities.

Large terra cotta vessels can be made by press mold, smaller ones by slip casting. Frequently, circular vessels are made by throwing the clay on a potter's wheel. Larger vessels are usually thrown in two or more parts. When the clay has dried to a leatherlike hardness, the vessel is frequently turned on a lathe and may be incised with designs.

History. Terra cotta has been made over wide areas since Neolithic times. Much early work was painted but unglazed. Especially noteworthy are Chinese tomb figures of dancers and horses from the T'ang period (7th–8th centuries A. D.), the glazed ones more finely modeled than the unglazed. Tanagra and other parts of the ancient Greek world produced many funerary and votive figurines in solid painted terra cotta by press mold with interchangeable parts.

The Etruscans developed the technique of firing extremely large press-molded objects, such as sarcophagi surmounted by reclining figures and inch-thick wall slabs as large as five feet (1.5 meters) by two feet (0.6 meter), painted or molded in relief, for lining stone tombs. Both the Etruscans and the Romans used unglazed terra cotta for molded architectural ornament, such as antefixes, which are plaques concealing the joints of roof tiles, and for other decorative reliefs because, unlike stone objects, they could be reproduced cheaply. Roman factories also mass-produced quantities of molded red Samian ware with delicate raised designs.

Terra cotta fell out of favor during the Middle Ages, except for pottery. It returned to popularity during the Renaissance, especially for architectural ornament on brick palaces and cathedrals, for sculpture, and for maquettes, models for sculpture. The reliefs of Luca della Robbia, covered with tin enamel glaze, and his painted, unglazed portrait busts are fine examples of Renaissance terra cotta. Small, modeled terra cotta figurines and groups, often of classical or pastoral subjects, were made in France from the 16th to the 18th century, as exemplified in the work of the 18th century sculptor Clodion. In the 19th century, terra cotta was used for sculpture and for molded architectural ornament.

In the pre-Columbian period in the Americas the more advanced Indians produced a variety of terra cotta pottery and figurines, mostly unglazed. The Hohokam Indians of southern Arizona made crudely modeled figurines in buff clay decorated with iron-red slip. Striking, sophisticated painted figures and vessels were fashioned by the Indians of Mexico and Central America. The Zapotec made urns in the form of gods, and the Mixtec painted pottery with religious motifs. The Mochica of northern Peru were noted for jars modeled in the form of human heads, which are thought to be portraits, or painted with lifelike birds and animals in red on buff. The Chimu, who succeeded the Mochica, produced similar wares in black or gray, but molded and of poorer quality. The ancient tradition died out under Spanish domination.

GEORGE SAVAGE, *Author of "Pottery Through the Ages"*

TERRA NOVA NATIONAL PARK, ter′ə nō′və, in southeastern Newfoundland, Canada, is on Bonavista Bay, 162 miles (259 km) north of St. John's, the provincial capital. Its varied wilderness scenery includes a rugged, rocky coastline, deep bays and fjords, and rolling forested inland hills interspersed with lakes, ponds, and marshes. Wildlife is abundant, notably moose and black bear, and there are many species of seabirds, including some that are native to the subarctic zone. Icebergs are commonly visible from the coast.

Terra Nova park was established in 1957 and comprises an area of 153 square miles (396 sq km).

TERRACING, a series of steplike benches or broadbase embankments and channels constructed across a hill to divide its slope into relatively level areas. Each level area slows the rate of water runoff, thereby reducing erosion.

The steep embankments of bench terraces are built of sod or masonry. Bench terraces have been used for centuries in Europe, Asia, and the Philippines but are seldom constructed today because they are very costly and ill-suited for heavy farm machinery.

The broadbase terrace consists of a wide, shallow channel dug uphill from a wide, gradually sloping embankment. Both channel and embankment are planted to crops with the rest of the field. The first such terrace was built in North Carolina in 1885 by P. H. Mangum.

Broadbase terraces are of two types. Level (absorption) terraces are designed to retain water until it is absorbed. They are extensively used on the Great Plains of the United States and in other semiarid areas. Graded (diversion) terraces are used in the southeastern United States to reduce erosion by slowing runoff water and diverting it into outlet channels. Both types are constructed along contours and are designed for mechanical farming.

LAWRENCE ERBE
University of Southwestern Louisiana

BENCH TERRACES used for growing rice on steep, otherwise untillable valley slopes in the Philippines.

AUTHENTICATED NEWS INTERNATIONAL

TERRAMYCIN, a brand name for oxytetracycline, one of a group of six tetracycline antibiotics. See TETRACYCLINE.

TERRAPIN, ter′ə-pən, any of several North American turtles found in fresh or brackish water. The name is most often applied to the diamondback terrapin of the genus *Malaclemys* and to the cooter, or slider, of the genus *Pseudemys*. In Great Britain, the term refers to a much larger group of land-dwelling turtles. See COOTER; DIAMONDBACK TERRAPIN.

TERRARIUM, tə-rar′ē-əm, an enclosure for keeping and raising live plants and animals indoors. Thus it is the counterpart of the aquarium, in which living fish are kept. A terrarium may house plants alone, animals alone, or both together. It may be of almost any size or shape, depending on the type of plants or animals to be kept and the space available to keep them in. The terrarium is most often set up in a small glass tank or jar. A glass and metal aquarium tank makes an ideal terrarium container and can be obtained readily in any pet shop or department store.

A terrarium can be set up in any of a number of ways, simulating different natural settings, or habitats, according to the type of animals or plants to be kept. It is important to recognize that each species of animal or plant life has a particular habitat to which it is adjusted and that, for instance, a desert plant or animal should not be kept in a terrarium set up as a bog or swamp habitat. It is therefore necessary to determine the requirements of the plants and the living habits of the animals before the terrarium is set up to house them.

Preliminary Preparation. The general types of terrarium containing plant life are the semiaquatic terrarium, the bog or swamp terrarium, the field or woods terrarium, and the desert terrarium. They differ primarily in moisture content, type of material on the bottom, and, sometimes, in temperature.

The *semiaquatic terrarium,* as the name indicates, is half water and half land. It can be set up by laying a line of flat stones across the middle of the tank to serve as a retaining wall for the land area. The remainder of the land section is covered with coarse gravel to a depth almost equal to the desired depth of water. Then a soil mixture is placed on top of the gravel, forming a layer 1 to 2 inches (2.5–5 cm) deep. For the semiaquatic and bog terrarium the best soil mixture is one composed of equal parts of sphagnum moss and acid soil.

The *bog or swamp terrarium* is set up in a similar fashion except that its water area is smaller and generally shallower than that of the semiaquatic terrarium. Sometimes a mat of sphagnum moss one or two inches thick is substituted for the soil mixture used in the semiaquatic terrarium.

The *field or woods terrarium* is set up without an area of water, though a small dish containing water may be placed in the soil. Coarse gravel is again used as the foundation material.

ROCHE

A WOODLAND TERRARIUM, including some rattlesnake plantain, reindeer moss, hepatica, spotted wintergreen, ground pine, ground cedar, and partridgeberry.

It is laid on in a layer at least one inch deep. It is generally covered with a mixture made up of equal parts of sand and humus to a depth of 2 or 3 inches (5 or 7.6 cm).

In the *desert terrarium,* the bottom is covered uniformly with two or three inches of coarse building sand. If desert sand is available, a thin layer of it may be used to top the coarse layer of building sand. Rocks and pieces of wood may be added for decorative material. A small water dish can be sunk in the sand of the desert terrarium.

Drainage and Ventilation. In every terrarium good soil drainage and ventilation is important. Without them, the soil mixture will become sour or get too damp, with the result that mold will appear and kill both plants and animals. One method for ensuring good drainage and ventilation in terrariums that require medium moisture is to make a false bottom for the tank itself. This can be done with a hardware cloth of 0.25- or 0.5-inch (0.64- or 1.3-cm) mesh. A section of this wire mesh, slightly wider and longer than the tank, is cut; the edges are then turned down in such a way as to support the mesh at a height of about 1.5 inches (3.8 cm) along the back, and about 0.5 inch (1.3 cm) along the front edge. Thus the false bottom slopes from back to front. Coarse gravel or crushed stone is then placed on the wire, and the desired soil mixture is put on top of that.

Stocking the Terrarium. Once the basic terrarium setup is established, suitable plants and animals can be introduced. In a semiaquatic terrarium common aquarium plants, such as *Vallisneria, Elodea,* or *Cabomba,* can be put in the water section. Mosses, ferns, lichens, and decorative fungi should be planted on the land area. Larvae of aquatic insects, crayfish, snails, aquatic salamanders, tadpoles, fish, or small turtles are suitable for this type of terrarium. Care should be exercised to select animals that will not eat the plants and will be too small to damage them by digging.

A bog or swamp terrarium can be planted attractively with some of the interesting insect-eating plants that live on wet, acid soils. Pitcher plants, Venus's-flytraps, sundews, and butterworts are well suited to this setting, as are some of the larger species of swamp mosses. Because of the desirability of insect-eating plants and the high moisture requirements of this type of terrarium, the best forms of animal life are small amphibians, such as red-spotted newts, swamp tree frogs, small wood frogs, and spring peepers.

A field or woods terrarium offers the greatest latitude for introducing variety in plant and animal life. The basic setup, as described above, can be used to grow plants requiring fair amounts of moisture, such as mosses, liverworts, and ferns; or, by decreasing the moisture content, it can be made into a somewhat drier habitat, with grasses and field plants. Moisture can be regulated quite easily by controlling the amount of water added to the soil mixture, by covering the terrarium with either glass or a screen top, and by either using or not using an artificial light. Adding small quantities of water and using a screen top and a small incandescent light will give a warm, rather dry habitat. Using a larger amount of water, adding a glass top, and using either no light or a very weak one will give a damper setting.

The use of the glass cover is important in terrariums where bog, swamp, or damp woodland plants and certain amphibians are kept. Many of these delicate organisms will thrive only where the air is moist. On the other hand, in cases where excess moisture is harmful, only a screen top should be used over the terrarium, and if only plants are kept in such a terrarium, no top is necessary.

Many species of cactus, small yuccas, and other succulent desert plants can make the desert terrarium one of the most attractive types. It is also the easiest to maintain. Many people like to have a desert terrarium for the sake of the plants alone, but others like to include one or more of the colorful, sometimes bizarre, small desert reptiles, such as collared lizards, desert swifts, and the lizards called horned toads. If any of these little reptiles are included, extra light and warmth must be provided. That is easily done by placing a 60-watt incandescent light over one end of the terrarium.

Selection of Animals. The animal life of the terrarium adds greatly to its interest and charm. Just a few snails, a crayfish or two, some insects, a frog, a salamander, a lizard, a turtle, or a snake may make all the difference in the world. They should be selected according to the type of habitat reproduced in the terrarium, the interests of the owner, and the availability of the animals. Many of these creatures can be purchased from pet shops or biological supply houses. However, owners often prefer to collect the animals and plants personally. Diligent search will reveal numbers of animals suitable for terrariums in all parts of the United States.

The most popular terrarium animals are salamanders, frogs and toads, lizards, small turtles, and occasionally small snakes. Species can be selected for any of the basic types of terrariums discussed above. However, the choice must be one that will fit into the setup already created. Or, if the animal is the primary interest, the terrarium should be adapted to its needs. Small turtles are better kept in an aquarium or in a sparsely planted terrarium because they will dig up small plants. Small salamanders do little damage to plants, but the larger ones may dig. The same is true of lizards. When larger reptiles are kept indoors, it is usually impossible to keep living plants in the same enclosure. Here the living plants can be replaced by attractive pieces of driftwood, interestingly shaped rocks, or other nonliving, decorative materials.

Care of Terrarium Animals. Feeding the animals in a terrarium is sometimes a problem since many of them will eat only live insects, worms, or spiders. Tubifex worms and "mealworms"—actually larval flour beetles—can be purchased in pet shops for feeding purposes. A globule or tiny strip of meat moved enticingly on the end of a broom straw may lure a reluctant animal. Sometimes it is desirable to remove the pet from the terrarium and feed it in a separate smaller dish or container; this adds to the routine of feeding and helps keep the terrarium clean by keeping it free of uneaten food. Most amphibians and reptiles thrive on a schedule of one to three feedings a week. It is possible to feed these animals too much, and overfeeding should be guarded against. If the feeding is conducted in the terrarium itself, the owner should periodically remove particles of food left decaying and uneaten by the terrarium animals.

The water supply should be kept fresh. This is particularly important if amphibians are being raised, because they readily absorb moisture through their skins and can be poisoned by impurities in it. Some owners change the water in their terrariums at each feeding.

A shallow aquarium setup is better for freshwater turtles and alligators than is a semiaquatic or swamp terrarium. These animals spend most of their time in the water and come out primarily to bask. The water should be deep enough to cover the animals completely—usually 2 to 4 inches (5–10 cm) is enough—and overstocking of the tank should be avoided. One or two low, flat rocks should be set at one end of the tank so that the turtles or alligators can climb out easily to bask. As is the case in caring for all cold-blooded animals, temperature is an important factor. A gooseneck or table lamp should be placed over the rocks, with the light at the level of the top of the tank. A 60-watt bulb is sufficient for all but very large tanks. The light should be kept on all day and can be used on cool nights to raise the temperature.

Semiaquatic turtles such as wood turtles and box turtles can be kept in a semiaquatic terrarium without any living plants. The water area should be large enough to allow the turtles to submerge. If there are large turtles, the edge of the land area must be firmly reinforced to prevent crumbling. For turtles, in fact, it is advantageous to use a large plastic or glass dish for the water area, since it keeps the land area firm and uncontaminated by soiled water and also makes it easier to change the water.

Large lizards and snakes can be kept in a glass tank set up as a field, woods, or desert terrarium but, again, without living plants. The decorative pieces of rock and wood should be arranged to provide a shelter area into which the reptiles can retire. This area should be constructed in such a way that the animals can be removed from it easily when their removal is desirable. Like the turtles and alligators, most of these animals should be provided with a light at one end of the terrarium. The top of the tank should be covered with a screen and have a light frame around it to prevent escape.

Sometimes, if the terrarium is large enough, a few interesting live plants can be included. They should be such plants as will not be damaged if the reptiles climb on them, or, if possible, they should be placed where the animals cannot get at them.

The Wooden Terrarium. In keeping some large lizards and most snakes, it is desirable to provide a terrarium of the simplest sort. Sometimes more ventilation is necessary than is possible in a glass and metal tank. A terrarium in the form of a wooden cage is usually preferable for the large land reptiles. Such a terrarium should have a glass front and ventilation holes or screens at the sides and top. The degree to which a natural setting can be provided depends in part on the kind of reptile kept and the time available for care. With large reptiles, the more natural the setting, the more time is required for care of the terrarium.

The barest essential furnishings are a dry cover for the bottom of the cage, a water dish large enough to permit the animal to submerge completely, and a small sheltered retreat. These can be provided in the simplest way by covering the bottom with newspapers folded to the size of the cage, and by providing a plastic refrigerator dish for water and a cardboard box with a small hole for the shelter. Such a setup, while not very attractive, is highly practical. Really attractive cages, however, can be set up with natural materials if sufficient time and ingenuity are brought to bear.

JAMES A. OLIVER, *Director*
The Aquarium of the City of New York

Further Reading: Leavitt, Jerome, and Huntsberger, John, *Fun Time Terrariums and Aquariums* (Chicago 1961); Gilbert, Miriam, *Science-Hobby Book of Terrariums*, rev. ed. (Minneapolis 1968); Roberts, Mervin, Jr., *Your Terrariums* (New York 1963); Wong, Herbert, and Vessel, Matthew, *Our Terrariums* (Reading, Mass., 1969).

TERRE HAUTE, ter′ə hōt, a city in west central Indiana, the seat of Vigo county, is situated on the east bank of the Wabash River, 5 miles (8 km) east of the Illinois state line and 70 miles (112 km) west of Indianapolis.

It is the trade center for a rich agricultural and coal strip-mining area. The city's wide variety of manufactured goods includes fabricated metals, industrial and agricultural chemicals, medicines, phonograph records and tapes, packaging materials, processed foods, and paint products.

Indiana State University, a 4-year coeducational institution, is in Terre Haute. Rose Polytechnic for men and St. Mary-of-the-woods College for women are near the city. The city has a symphony orchestra and a community theater. A federal penitentiary is 4 miles (6 km) southwest.

Points of interest include the Early Wheels Museum, which displays early automobiles; the Sheldon Swope Art Gallery featuring 19th and 20th century painting and sculpture; and the Historical Museum of the Vigo County Historical Society. The birthplace of Paul Dresser, author and composer of the state song, *On the Banks of the Wabash,* and the home of Eugene V. Debs, a Socialist labor leader and presidential candidate who was born in Terre Haute, are open to the public.

French traders called the site *terre haute,* or "high land." A military fort was established there in 1811 by Gen. William Henry Harrison, Indiana's first territorial governor. The community was incorporated as a town in 1816 and became a city in 1853. Terre Haute has the mayor-council form of government. Population: 70,286.

EDWARD N. HOWARD
Vigo County Public Library

TERRELL, ter′əl, **Mary Church** (1863–1954), American Negro lecturer and civic leader. Mary Church was born in Memphis, Tenn., on Sept. 23, 1863. She graduated from Oberlin College in 1884 and taught at Wilberforce University in Ohio, and then at the High School for Colored Youth in Washington, D. C. In 1891 she married Robert H. Terrell. In 1895 she was one of the first two women, and the first Negro, named to the Washington school board. She was also active in the woman's suffrage movement.

Mrs. Terrell was in demand as a lecturer. She spoke at the International Congress of Women in Berlin (1904), the International League for Peace in Zürich (1919), and at the World Fellowship of Faiths in London (1937).

Throughout her career Mrs. Terrell led campaigns to open doors for Negroes in professional associations. One of her victories was her drive to integrate the Washington branch of the American Association of University Women. She also demonstrated against segregated facilities in Washington. Her autobiography, *A Colored Woman in a White World,* appeared in 1940. Mrs. Terrell died in Annapolis, Md., on July 24, 1954.

LUTHER H. FOSTER
Tuskegee Institute

TERRELL, ter′əl, a city in eastern Texas, is in Kaufman county, about 30 miles (48 km) east of Dallas. It is the distribution center for a diversified farming area where cotton, beef cattle, small grains, and vetch are raised and dairying is an important activity. The city's industries produce ice cream, athletic uniforms, dresses, livestock feeds, aluminum doors, steel shelving, and school supplies. Terrell State Hospital contributes to the economy by providing employment for a large staff. Southwestern Christian College, a predominantly Negro school sponsored by the Church of Christ, is in Terrell.

The site was settled in 1872 by Robert A. Terrell. His home stands on the college campus. The city was incorporated in 1875. It has a home-rule charter and the city manager form of government. Population: 14,182.

TERRESTRIAL MAGNETISM. See EARTH; GEOMAGNETISM.

TERRIER, a dog originally developed to hunt and destroy small mammals, such as rats and foxes, often by pursuing the quarry into underground dens. The name "terrier" comes from Latin *terra,* meaning "earth." Terriers were derived from basic hound stock modified to obtain specific abilities, ranging from hunting otters to fighting in pits.

The terrier type and its utility are first mentioned in Gace de la Bigne's *Poème sur la chasse* (about 1359). A more detailed description is given in the *Boke of St. Albans* (1486) and *De canibus Britannicis* (1570). The section on quadrupeds (1755–1767) of Buffon's *Histoire naturelle* was the first book to recognize long- and short-legged varieties.

By about 1800, terriers in Scotland and England had been bred into reproducible types, the progenitors of today's breeds. The old Scotch terrier, for example, a rough-coated, long- and low-bodied dog, gave rise to the cairn, Scottish, Dandie Dinmont, Skye, and West Highland white terriers. The old English terriers were of two coat types, rough and smooth, and occurred in varying colors. Crossed with small hounds and the bulldog, the English terriers produced the fox terrier. The Airedale resulted from crosses with the otter hound. The Bedlington terrier came from crosses with a coursing hound.

Terriers have a recognized place in the official classification of several national kennel clubs. The American Kennel Club recognizes more than 20 terriers (counting varieties). The Kennel Club of England has a comparable grouping. A number of breeds not classified as terriers by these kennel groups are of terrier descent, often indicated by the inclusion of the term "terrier" in the breed name: Boston terrier, standard schnauzer, Lhasa apso, schipperke, silky terrier, Yorkshire terrier.

Terriers range in size from 23 inches (48.5 cm) in height at the withers (shoulders) and 50 pounds (23 kg) in weight for the Airedale to 10 inches (25 cm) and 11 pounds (5 kg) for the Norwich terrier. Coats vary from harsh (Irish, Welsh, Scottish terriers) to soft (Kerry blue, Bedlington terriers) or smooth (Staffordshire, Manchester, bull terriers). Most terriers have small eyes. All have large teeth and strong, tough feet. Ears range from upright to drop or button.

JOHN T. MARVIN
Author of "The Book of All Terriers"

TERRITORIAL EXPANSION. See WESTWARD MOVEMENT.

TERRITORIAL WATERS, also known as territorial seas or maritime belts, are seaward extensions of a country's sovereignty in conformity with international law. Subject only to the right of innocent passage by foreign ships, a sovereign state exercises over its territorial waters and their seabed, their subsoil, and the air above them the same absolute and exclusive jurisdiction as over its territory and inland waters. These maritime belts, established mainly for economic and security reasons, thus abridge the freedom of the seas.

Territorial waters were once generally fixed at cannon range, or 3 miles (5 km) out from low-water or straight coastal baselines. But the width of the maritime zone has become controversial, some states claiming up to 200 miles (300 km). Nations with large merchant fleets, like Britain and the United States, maintain the 3-mile limit. Communist and developing countries generally claim 12 miles (19 km). Accelerated exploration and exploitation of the sea's resources have supported the trend toward greater seaward extension of national territory.

GEORGE MANNER
University of Illinois

TERRITORY, in biology, is a specific physical area occupied by an individual animal (or occasionally by a small group of animals) and defended against others of the same species or occasionally of different species. The phenomenon of an animal appropriating a territory is especially widespread among the vertebrate animals, where it is frequently associated with courtship, mating, and the raising of young. It also occurs in some invertebrates.

In those animals that breed only during a certain season of the year, the process of establishing a territory takes place each year at the start of the breeding season. The size of a particular territory and the length of time that the animal holds it vary considerably.

Establishing a Territory. In the early stages of establishment, the territory is not well defined, and an animal's attacks on other animals are not tied to a particular locality. As time goes on, however, an animal sets up boundaries of his territory, and his attacks begin to be restricted to those animals that cross the boundaries. The boundaries are often marked by such objects as rocks and trees. In many cases, the intruder's proximity to such objects seems to determine whether or not he is attacked. The tendency of the territory's holder to attack or retreat is itself dependent on his location within the boundaries. It has been suggested that the boundary areas are those areas in which the tendency to attack and the tendency to retreat are more or less balanced. The holder of a territory within which conflicts with other animals occur is almost always victorious.

The result of territorial competition is that each individual or pair in the breeding population uniquely occupies and holds its own bit of space. Territorial neighbors are often hostile, but once they have established a territory they rarely kill a neighbor or try to gain more territory. Within its area, the occupant dominates other individuals, and usually excludes them. Most often, this is accomplished by active defense, but other kinds of interactions, such as threatening visual or vocal displays or mutual avoidance have evolved in some species so that physical conflict may be minimal or absent. Where attacks do occur, the stimuli eliciting them are typically quite general. A male robin, for example, will attack a bunch of red feathers or a stuffed red robin as readily as he will a live red robin. Similarly a stickleback fish reacts to a simple model with a red belly as readily as he will to a red-bellied stickleback.

The establishment of a territory allows animals to carry out particular aspects of their behavior in suitable surroundings and in comparative safety. For many of the higher vertebrate animals, particularly those in which reproduction is a seasonal phenomenon, the establishment of a territory is a prerequisite to reproduction. When reproduction and territoriality are intimately linked, fighting is usually limited to those periods during which the sex hormones are being released. At this time males often develop bright colors that not only stimulate attack and consequent defense but also stimulate sexual reception by the females of the species. In fact, in some animals the hormonal activity that brings about changes in color and behavior has been shown to be related to a stimulus from the territory itself. Thus, the complex of behavioral and morphological changes taking place in reproduction and territoriality is one phenomenon in which simple cause-and-effect relations do not seem to apply.

Territoriality is not necessarily strictly associated with competition for mates, however. Particularly in some invertebrates, defense of a specific physical space, or territory, is often related to other requirements, such as food or shelter. In these cases too, however, territorial behavior and aggressive behavior are intimately linked.

Aggressiveness and Territoriality. Territoriality and aggressive behavior seem to be so closely related that some biologists consider them a single phenomenon. This may be misleading, however, for aggressive behavior is not unique to territorial animals. Aggressive behavior toward one's own species is essential in holding a territory, but even in territorial animals, fighting seems more than just a stereotyped response to territorial intrusion. Once territorial rights have been established, an intrusion is not always necessary to provoke aggression. On the contrary, territorial animals often seem actively to seek out an aggressive encounter. A territorial male may show an inclination toward behavior that brings him into conflict with another male. For example, mice rapidly learn to make a response that will get them into a situation in which they can attack another mouse.

Adaptive Advantages of Territoriality. The widespread occurrence of territorial behavior among vertebrates suggests that the phenomenon has evolved independently many times. It is useful to consider the selective advantage conferred by this behavior. The spacing that results from territoriality may have several ecological consequences. Most importantly, population densities are held below levels at which food becomes scarce. In some species of higher vertebrates, the physical dimensions of each year's territories seem to be directly or indirectly related to the abundance of food available to that year's offspring. This flexibility appears to constitute a mechanism whereby the densities of populations are regulated according to the favorability of the environment. For example, population densities of temperate song birds, which frequently show such flexibility, fluctuate less than do the population densities of other kinds of organisms. This fact may be related to their reproductive and territorial behavior.

Another adaptive advantage of territorial spacing may be a freedom from disturbance by predators while mating and feeding the young. Spacing would also seem to confer some protection from disease and parasites that thrive best in crowded conditions. Territoriality may also be important in the evolution of social groups. The social aggregations that have evolved in higher mammals often exhibit a group defense of territory. It has been suggested that such behavior may be an evolutionary step in the development of internally cooperative complex societies.

DONALD E. LANDENBERGER
University of California, Los Angeles

Further Reading: Ardrey, Robert, *The Territorial Imperative* (New York 1969); Lorenz, Konrad, *On Aggression*, tr. by Marjorie K. Wilson (New York 1966); Klopfer, Peter H., *Habitats and Territories: A Study of the Use of Space by Animals* (New York 1969); Tinbergen, Nikolaas, "On War and Peace in Animals and Man," *Science*, vol. 160, pp. 1411–1418 (Washington 1968).

TERRITORY, in political science, is a broad term with several meanings. Only a few will be treated here. Although examples are drawn exclusively from the United States, any major power could provide equivalent illustrations.

Territory is always an attribute of sovereignty, but the converse is not so. The citizens and government of a state may control extensive territory that they do not own. On the other hand, a nation that is recognized as sovereign and independent may be controlled by others and may in fact not be sovereign.

Types of Territories. Perhaps the most elementary distinction between types of territories is that between the territory of a national domain and a public domain. The national domain is ordinarily the total land and water area under the jurisdiction of a government. The public domain is only that portion of the national domain that the national government owns itself. In 1781 the public domain of the United States consisted of only the present five-state area of Ohio, Indiana, Illinois, Michigan, and Wisconsin, and the eastern portion of Minnesota—an area called the Northwest Territory. The national domain in 1781 included the area between Florida and Canada from the Atlantic Ocean to the Mississippi River. In time both the national and the public domain greatly increased, as the country gained territory through land cessions, purchases, and conquest. The U. S. government has disposed of more than one billion acres of the public domain but continues to retain title to nearly half a billion other acres.

Territories also may be classified in at least five broad categories on the basis of legal characteristics of ownership. First are the outright possessions of a nation under its own jurisdiction. Such possessions of the United States include Puerto Rico and the Virgin Islands. Second are the leased territories, including the Panama Canal Zone and many military and naval bases around the world.

The Trust Territory of the Pacific Islands represents a third category. Administered by the United States since 1945, but under United Nations authority since 1947, the Trust Territory consists of some 2,100 islands and islets and covers about 3 million square miles (7.8 million sq km) of ocean.

Claimed territories constitute a fourth category. They may be land areas disputed by two nations or territorial waters beyond the 3-mile (4.8 km) international limit. The fifth category, foreign territories, is illustrated by Okinawa and other islands belonging to Japan but administered by the United States after World War II.

In a sixth category, one might list a major power's "informal colonies"—technically independent states over which the major power exerts great economic or political influence.

Status of U. S. Territorial Residents. The constitutional status of persons living in territories under U. S. jurisdiction is complex. The issue has been debated since the Constitutional Convention of 1787. In the popular view that long prevailed, citizenship and the Constitution and laws of the United States followed the flag, at least insofar as white settlers were concerned. Congress treated all contiguous territories as incorporated, and the constitutional status in incorporated territories was not in question in any case.

The acquisition of Alaska and a number of islands during the 1850's and 1860's significantly changed things because the idea of incorporating these new areas was less generally acceptable. The U. S. occupation and annexation of other islands—during and after the Spanish-American War in 1898—with large nonwhite populations brought a solution to the problem. It was fortunate for the contiguous territories that the solution had not come earlier. In 1901 the Supreme Court in effect declared in the insular cases that territories are colonies and that their inhabitants have no rights except those specifically granted by Congress. In a series of decisions that articulated the apparent primary intent of Article IV, Section 3, of the Constitution when it was drafted, the court ruled that the Constitution, citizenship, and the laws of the United States do not automatically extend to newly acquired territories. Thus Congress was free to legislate or not, and no promise of eventual statehood or any other guarantees could be assumed or held inviolate.

See also INSULAR CASES; NORTHWEST TERRITORY; PUBLIC LANDS; TIDELAND; TRUSTEESHIP SYSTEM.

JACK ERICSON EBLEN, *Author of "The First and Second United States Empires"*

TERROR, Reign of. See REIGN OF TERROR; FRANCE—*The Revolution, Consulate, and Empire;* FRENCH REVOLUTION.

TERRY, Bill (1898–   ), American baseball player and manager, who in 1930 won the National League's most valuable player award, tied the league record for most hits in a season with 254, and led the league with a .401 batting average.

William Harold Terry was born in Atlanta, Ga., on Oct. 30, 1898. He signed with the New York Giants in 1922, was sent to Toledo in the American Association, and was brought up to the Giants late in 1923. He compiled a lifetime batting average of .341 during 14 years as first baseman with the Giants, the last 5 years of which he also served as manager. He was then a nonplaying manager from 1937 to

1941. Terry led the Giants to National League pennants in 1933, 1936, and 1937. In 1954 he was elected to the Baseball Hall of Fame. He was president of the South Atlantic (Sally) League from October 1954 to 1957.

CLIFFORD KACHLINE, *Historian*
National Baseball Hall of Fame and Museum

TERRY, Dame Ellen (1847–1928), English actress noted for her performances in Shakespearean roles, especially as Beatrice in *Much Ado About Nothing.* Alice Ellen Terry was born in Coventry, into a theatrical family, on Feb. 27, 1847. She began her career as a child in Charles Kean's company in 1856 and made her adult debut in 1862 in Bristol. Achieving only indifferent success, she left the stage in 1868. During her retirement she had two children by the architect Edward Godwin, to whom she was not married. Their children were Edward Gordon Craig, director and designer, who became one of the major influences in the modern theater, and Edith Craig, who became an actress and director.

Ellen Terry returned to the stage in 1874 and won her first major success in 1875 as Portia in *The Merchant of Venice.* In 1878 she became Henry Irving's leading lady and remained with him until 1902. They were considered the leading acting team in the English-speaking theater. In addition to appearing regularly at the Lyceum Theatre, London, they traveled widely, making eight tours of the United States between 1883 and 1901.

With Irving's company, Miss Terry played in Shakespearean dramas, traditional comedies, and modern romantic plays. After leaving Irving's group, she performed occasionally in such plays as Ibsen's *The Vikings at Helgeland,* Barrie's *Alice Sit-by-the-Fire,* and Shaw's *Captain Brassbound's Conversion,* which Shaw had written for her. After 1907 she acted only rarely, although she undertook several lecture tours. Her last appearance as an actress was in 1925. That year she became the first actress to be named a Dame Grand Cross of the Order of the British Empire. She died at Small Hythe, Tenterden, Kent, on July 21, 1928.

OSCAR G. BROCKETT, *Indiana University*

Further Reading: Craig, Edward Gordon, *Ellen Terry and Her Secret Self* (New York 1932); Manvell, Roger, *Ellen Terry* (New York 1968).

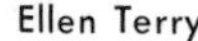

Ellen Terry

CULVER PICTURES

TERRY CLOTH is a cotton fabric with uncut loops forming a pile on both sides of the cloth. Terry cloth with a pile effect on only one side is called Turkish toweling.

Terry cloth is made either on dobby or Jacquard looms, which are capable of weaving various designs. Two sets of warp (lengthwise) yarns are used—one to form the base and the other, kept very slack in the loom, to give the uncut pile effect. A number of picks (crosswise yarns) are woven into the warp, some loosely, others tightly. As the tight picks are drawn into the material, they cause the loose yarn to bunch up into pile.

GEORGE E. LINTON
Author of "The Modern Textile Dictionary"

TERTIARIES, tûr′shē-er-ēz, are lay associates of religious orders chiefly in the Roman Catholic Church. Lay persons, while continuing their secular occupations, may enroll in one of several associations known as Third Orders Secular. Third Order rules generally stipulate practices of prayer, a life of moderation, and works of Christian charity and social action. The idea originated in the 13th century with the Franciscans. Third Orders were established by other orders, including the Dominicans, Augustinians, and Carmelites.

TERTIARY PERIOD, tûr′shē-er-ē, the period of geological time extending from about 65 million to about 2.5 million years ago, and including almost all of the time in which mammals have been the dominant animals on land.

The name "Tertiary" derives from an early hypothesis of German geologists that the rocks of the earth's crust were precipitated out of the primal oceans in four great phases. The terms "Primary" and "Secondary" dropped out of use when they were found to represent several thousand million years of geological time, but the terms "Tertiary" and "Quaternary"—the latter including the Pleistocene and Recent epochs—are still in use. The Tertiary and Quaternary together make up the Cenozoic era. The six epochs of the Tertiary are as follows:

Epoch	Began	Ended	Duration
	(Millions of years ago)		
Paleocene	65	59	6
Eocene	59	34	25
Oligocene	34	25	9
Miocene	25	12	13
Pliocene	12	2.5	9.5

The lengths of the epochs vary greatly because they were all of unknown duration when named by 19th century geologists. Thus it was long thought that the Paleocene might be one of the longest epochs because of the striking degrees of evolutionary change seen in successive samples of fossil mammals from Paleocene rocks. Today it is realized that the Paleocene was a shorter period of relatively rapid evolutionary experimentation.

CLIMATES AND CONTINENTS

It has been learned from the study of fossil pollens and plants that at the beginning of the Tertiary, climates were considerably warmer than they are today. Later there was a gradual trend toward a cooler climate, and at least by Miocene times cycles of glacial activity had begun near the poles. By the end of the Pliocene, temperatures were considerably lower than today. This

FIELD MUSEUM OF NATURAL HISTORY, ARTIST CHARLES R. KNIGHT

Tertiary mammals included the small, four-toed Eocene horse, Orohippus, and the rhino-size Uintatherium.

ERA	PERIOD	
CENOZOIC		QUATERNARY
		TERTIARY
MESOZOIC		CRETACEOUS
		JURASSIC
		TRIASSIC
PALEOZOIC		PERMIAN
	CARBON-IFEROUS	PENNSYLVANIAN
		MISSISSIPPIAN
		DEVONIAN
		SILURIAN
		ORDOVICIAN
		CAMBRIAN
PRE-CAMBRIAN TIME		

BASILOSAURUS, AN EARLY WHALE, was widespread and common 45 million years ago. The body of the primitive, toothed whale was more than 50 feet (15 meters) long. Basilosaurus did not survive the Eocene.

FIELD MUSEUM OF NATURAL HISTORY, ARTIST CHARLES R. KNIGHT

led to the Pleistocene glaciations that covered large parts of the northern continents with ice sheets. Many theories have been advanced to account for these changes, but none has been confirmed. See also ICE AGE.

Continents and Land Bridges. In Tertiary times the continents had shapes rather like those they have now, but there were differences. For example, there were north-south seaways across eastern and western Asia in the early Tertiary, and most of present Arabia, Iraq, Persia, and parts of Pakistan and India were submerged.

Throughout the Tertiary, Madagascar and Australia remained islands. However, Eurasia and North America were at times connected by an Alaskan-Siberian land bridge, which was crossed by many groups of mammals. As a result, during most of the Tertiary the animals of the northern continents maintained a greater degree of similarity than those of the southern continents. Although South America and Africa did have some sort of imperfect faunal contact with the northern continents in the early Tertiary, land bridges allowing many kinds of mammals to move in and out were not reestablished until the end of Miocene times. There is also increasingly good evidence that rifting and spreading of the northern Atlantic Ocean was still in progress in the early Tertiary. See also CONTINENT.

The size and shape of the Mediterranean Sea fluctuated during the period. Mountain ranges such as the Himalaya, Pyrenees, Alps, and others appeared across the western two thirds of Eurasia, and the rift valley system developed in Africa. All of these changes had their effect on the distribution of mammals and birds of the areas. In addition, expansion of the deserts of the American west, central Asia, and northern and southern Africa in later Tertiary times also affected land life radically.

EVOLUTION IN THE TERTIARY

In general, the larger and more central continental masses of Eurasia and North America seem to have been the places where the most durable groups of Tertiary mammals differentiated. The two continents are the ancestral homes of cats, dogs, bears, deer, horses, rhinoceroses, cattle, tapirs, and many other groups. Africa produced the elephants and probably the apes and man as well. No mammalian stock of worldwide significance—with the possible exception of porcupines

—had its origin in South America.

Unlike the slowly evolving plants, many mammal groups have very broad environmental tolerances. The more climate-dependent primates are the only group whose distribution reflects the Tertiary climate changes. Widely distributed in the northern continents in early Tertiary times, they were relatively rare in those continents after the mid-Tertiary.

Paleocene. Knowledge of Paleocene land life is relatively limited, because rocks containing continental faunas of the epoch are scarce. No Paleocene site is known in Africa or eastern North America, and in Europe the total exposure of such rock is only a few square miles. However, rather larger exposures exist in Wyoming and adjacent states, Asia, and South America.

Of the 35 principal known orders of mammals, 20 of which still exist, few had come into being by the time of the Paleocene. There was one holdover group of archaic mammals from the era of the dinosaurs still thriving, the multituberculates. Another order, the marsupials or pouched mammals, was already on the decline during the Paleocene, apparently through competition with the placental mammals. The primates and carnivores had also differentiated by the Paleocene, but these animals were very primitive and almost certainly would not have looked or acted much like their modern relatives. In addition, by the end of the epoch a variety of large plant-feeding mammals had evolved.

Eocene. Much more is known of mammal evolution in the Eocene. At the beginning of the period several dozen kinds of mammals appeared to be nearly the same if not identical in the Eastern and Western hemispheres—the greatest faunal community ever to exist between the two regions in the Tertiary. Many orders such as whales, bats, odd- and even-toed ungulates, rodents, hares, and allied forms first appeared or became abundant in the epoch. Among them were the ancestral "dawn horse" and ancestors of the rhinoceros.

A few advanced forms of primates appeared in the Eocene. These primates had already evolved two nearly distinctive features of modern primates: hands and feet suitable for grasping and leaping among branches, and a brain-body volume ratio closer to that of modern man than to that of most other Eocene mammals.

Oligocene. With the spread of grasslands in Oligocene times, a great variety of plant-eating mammals evolved in addition to earlier forest-browsing forms. The odd-toed ungulates were the most diversified and in fact were at the peak of their radiation into various adaptive zones. The largest land mammal ever to exist appeared in central Asia at this time—*Indracotherium,* a long-necked rhinoceros with a height at the shoulder of about 15 feet (5 meters).

Fossils of the "dawn apes" and the earliest monkeys have been found in abundance among Eocene rocks of Egypt's Fayum region, in association with the earliest ancestors of the elephants.

Miocene. Much of Eurasia was forested in the Miocene. Toward the end of the epoch a land bridge between Africa and Eurasia enabled apes and monkeys, such as the extinct great ape species of genus *Dryopithecus,* to spread through the northern continent. The earliest hominids—of genus *Ramapithecus*—later differentiated, presumably through the adoption of terrestrial feeding habits and locomotion. Other kinds of mammals came to resemble their modern descendants more closely, while in South America many exotic mammal groups became extinct through competition with other mammals that had crossed a land bridge from North America.

Pliocene. Near the beginning of the last Tertiary epoch, climates became cooler and drier through much of the world. Horses and various bovids were diversified, and primates either had to adapt to more open country or be confined to restricted ranges where the forests remained. In the middle and late Pliocene, ancestors of man such as *Australopithecus,* as well as the giant ape *Gigantopithecus,* were associated with open-country faunas. By the end of the epoch, *Australopithecus* species had invented toolmaking and were well on the way toward the full development of man in the Pleistocene epoch, or Quaternary.

ELWYN L. SIMONS, *Yale University*

Further Reading: Pearson, Ronald, *Animals and Plants of the Cenozoic Era* (London 1964); Stirton, Ruben A., *Time, Life and Man* (New York 1963).

TERTULLIAN, tər-tul'yən (c. 160–c. 230), was a North African ecclesiastical writer, and the first Christian theologian to write in Latin. Quintus Septimus Florens Tertullianus was born in Carthage. The son of a Roman centurion, he was educated in law and rhetoric and knew Greek as well as Latin. He practiced law in Rome and is probably to be identified with the jurist Tertullianus who is quoted in the Digest, or Pandects, a collection of writings by the Roman jurists.

Tertullian was converted to Christianity about 195. In that year he returned to Carthage, where he became an instructor of catechumens and was soon launched on a literary career. The evidence shows that he was married, but it is disputed whether he was ordained a priest, as St. Jerome claimed. About 207, Tertullian joined the Montanists, an apocalyptic heretical group advocating rigorous asceticism. Within a short time he became a leader of his own party, called the Tertullianists. According to St. Jerome, Tertullian survived to an advanced age. His last work appeared in 220.

Character and Style. Tertullian tended to be an extremist. Of his days in Rome he later wrote that he had "drained the cup of lust to its dregs." Just as he had engaged in vice to the full before his conversion, so, as the years went on, he became more and more a rigorous moralist. His writings reflect his impatient and sometimes acerbic personality. They contain frequent sharp barbs, sarcasm, and irony. His Latin style was difficult and often obscure, but his works are filled with short, highly quotable sections. It has become axiomatic that Tertullian is always quoted but never at length.

As the first Christian theologian to write in Latin, Tertullian had considerable influence in the formation of the Latin vocabulary of Christian theology, particularly because of his own precise Latin style. An innovator in both style and content, he coined over 900 new words. Although he eventually adhered to the heterodox rigorism of Montanism, Tertullian's works, except for his ascetical treatises, are on the whole doctrinally orthodox. Some 31 of his treatises survive, and at least 12 others have been lost. His works show a wide knowledge of both secular and religious literature.

Works. Tertullian's works may be divided into three categories: (1) apologetical, (2) polemical, (3) disciplinary and ascetical. The most famous of his apologetical works is the *Apologeticum* (about 197). Directed to the provincial governors of the Roman Empire, it refutes several political charges against the Christians, including the claim that they opposed the state and committed sacrilege. It is significant for being the first apologetical work to refute anti-Christian charges on the basis of Roman juridical concepts.

The principal polemical works of Tertullian are the *De praescriptione hereticorum, Adversus Marcion,* and *Adversus Praxean.* In the *De praescriptione hereticorum* (about 200) he made use of the Roman legal concept of *praescriptio,* by which a litigant challenged crucial parts of his opponent's case in an attempt to have it thrown out of court before it ever came to trial. He thus challenged the right of the heretics to use Sacred Scripture as part of their argument. He maintained that the Scriptures were the possession of the apostolic churches, to whom they had been entrusted by the Apostles.

Adversus Marcion (about 207) is an extremely clear exposition of the unity of God and the identity of Christ with the Messiah prophesied in the Old Testament. The *Adversus Praxean* (about 213) marks the first time that the word *trinitas* (trinity) was applied to the three persons of the Godhead—Father, Son, and Holy Spirit.

In Tertullian's ascetical works his tendency toward rigorism is most apparent. *De pudicitia* (after 212) rejects the idea that the bishop has the power to forgive all sins. Tertullian claims that there are some sins that can only be forgiven by God directly, for example, adultery, murder, and apostasy.

Tertullian was a brilliant and original thinker. His influence on the development of ecclesiastical Latin and of doctrine was real, although it is sometimes exaggerated. However, because of his heretical views he is not numbered among the Fathers of the Church, where he would otherwise have had a prominent position.

Bibliography

The Works of Tertullian may be found in Migne, J., ed., *Patrologia Latina* (Paris 1879), vols. 1 and 2. Translations are in the *Ante-Nicene Christian Library* (Edinburgh 1869–1870), vols. 7, 11, 15, and 18.

Altaner, Berthold, *Patrology* (New York 1961), pp. 166–182.

Quasten, Johannes, *Patrology,* vol. 2 (Westminster, Md., 1950), pp. 246–340.

TERZA RIMA, tert'sə rē'mə, is a verse form composed of three-line groups, or tercets, that have an interlinking rhyme scheme. Usually the meter is iambic pentameter (see IAMB), and the first and third lines of a tercet rhyme. After the first tercet, the second line of the preceding group supplies the rhyme for the group that follows, giving the rhyme scheme *aba, bcb, cdc, ded,* and so on. The last group generally has an extra line that rhymes with the middle line of that tercet, giving the scheme *yzy z.* The best-known example of the form is Dante's *Divine Comedy.* With some variations in meter and rhyme, terza rima has been popular among English poets.

TESCHEN, tesh'ən, is a region in southeastern Silesia, now divided between Poland and Czechoslovakia. The Czech form of the name is Těšín, and the Polish is Cieszyn. It is important for its industry, its rail connections, and its iron and coal deposits.

From 1109 to 1625 it was a principality ruled by a branch of the Polish Piasts. As a fief of Bohemia, Teschen passed under Habsburg control in 1526. Poles, Czechs, and Germans intermingled in Teschen, and when the Habsburg monarchy fell in 1918, Poland and Czechoslovakia both claimed it. In 1920, Poland was awarded the eastern part, while the larger and more valuable west went to Czechoslovakia. In 1938, after the Munich Conference, Czechoslovakia was forced to cede its share to Poland. In 1945, Soviet pressure forced a return to the 1920 boundary.

JOSEPH F. ZACEK
State University of New York at Albany

TESLA, tes'lə, **Nikola** (1856–1943), Yugoslav-American inventor, who pioneered in radio and invented the alternating-current motor and system that made the universal transmission and distribution of electricity practicable. He was born in Smiljan, Croatia, on July 10, 1856. His father was a clergyman of the Serbian Orthodox Church and his mother an expert needleworker and an inventor of home implements. Tesla received a technical training at the polytechnic school in Graz and the University of Prague. In 1881 he began work for the newly founded telephone company in Budapest, and in late 1882 he joined the Continental Edison Company in Paris.

Unable to interest European engineers in a new alternating-current motor he had conceived, Tesla went to the United States in 1884. For nearly a year he redesigned dynamos for Thomas Edison in New York City. Establishing his own laboratory in 1887, he began a spectacular career of research and invention. He became a U. S. citizen in 1891. By the turn of the century his accomplishments had made the name of Tesla as world famous as that of Edison.

Electric Power Transmission. Tesla's first and probably greatest achievement was his discovery of the rotating magnetic field (a magnetic whirlwind produced in a motor winding by the interaction of two or more alternating currents) and his brilliant adaptation of it to his induction motor and polyphase system for the generation, transmission, and distribution of electric power (see ELECTRIC MOTORS—*Alternating-Current Motors*). The combination of this motor and this system (patented 1888–1896) provided the first practical means for generating large quantities of electricity of a single kind in one place and transmitting it economically over long distances for use at another place. It made possible the original large-scale harnessing of Niagara Falls (1895–1903) and furnished the key that soon changed the era of local electric lighting in large cities to one of electric light and power wherever needed.

Today practically all the electricity used in the world is generated and transmitted by means of the 3-phase form of the Tesla polyphase system and is turned back into mechanical power by updated models of 3-phase and split-phase motors originally covered by his patents.

Tesla Coil. Hoping to develop a light more efficient than the incandescent lamp, Tesla began researches with alternating currents of high frequency and high potential in 1889. At first he produced these currents with high-frequency alternators of his own design. Desiring still higher voltages, he invented the "Tesla coil" (1891), an air-core transformer that had its primary and secondary tuned to resonance. For operation on these high voltages, he created many gas-filled, phosphor-coated, tubular lights without filaments—prototypes of modern neon and fluorescent lights. While investigating currents from his coil, Tesla also made pioneer contributions to the then unborn fields of high-frequency induction heating, diathermy, and radio. One of his discoveries was that alternating current at tremendously high voltage could be harmless if the frequency were high enough.

Tesla's lectures in America and Europe (1891–1893) aroused widespread interest in currents of high frequency and potential. They became known as "Tesla currents," and by 1900 probably every university laboratory in the world had acquired a Tesla coil to demonstrate them.

Radio and Wireless Power. Tesla predicted wireless communication (1893) and devised basic circuits and apparatus that were later adapted by himself and others for actual wireless transmission. At Colorado Springs (1899–1900) he built the largest Tesla coil ever constructed—a 12-million-volt machine that gave sparks up to 135 feet long—in an attempt, partially successful, to send electric power without wires. As early as 1900, Tesla proposed a "world wireless" plant that would send not only ordinary messages but many other services. These included facsimiles of pictures and a program of time, weather, and other reports that was later introduced as "broadcasting." In 1898, anticipating radio-guided missiles and aircraft, Tesla developed torpedoes and ships guided by radio, and in 1917 he accurately forecast radar.

Honors. Among many honors, Tesla received degrees from Columbia and Yale Universities, the Elliott Cresson Medal of the Franklin Institute, and the Edison Medal of the American Institute of Electrical Engineers. In 1956, as part of international commemorations of the centennial of his birth, the term "tesla" (T) was adopted as the unit of magnetic flux density in the mksa system (see ELECTRICAL AND MAGNETIC UNITS—*Mksa Units*). He died in New York City on Jan. 7, 1943.

KENNETH M. SWEZEY, *Author of "Nikola Tesla," in "Science"*

Bibliography

Hunt, Inez, and Draper, Wanetta W., *Lightning in His Hand–The Life Story of Nikola Tesla* (Denver 1964).
Nikola Tesla Museum, *Nikola Tesla–Lectures, Patents, Articles* (Belgrade 1956).
Nikola Tesla Museum, *A Tribute to Nikola Tesla–Letters, Articles, Documents* (Belgrade 1961).
O'Neill, John J., *Prodigal Genius–The Life of Nikola Tesla* (New York 1944).
Pratt, Haraden, "Nikola Tesla, 1856–1943," *Proceedings of the Institute of Radio Engineers,* vol. 44, pp. 1106–1108, September 1956.
Swezey, Kenneth M., "Nikola Tesla," *Science,* vol. 127, pp. 1147–1159, May 16, 1958.

TESS OF THE D'URBERVILLES, a novel by Thomas Hardy, published in 1891, tells the story of Tess Durbeyfield, the daughter of an improvident father who learns that he is descended from the ancient, titled d'Urbervilles. To claim kin with a wealthy family that had assumed this name, the Durbeyfields send Tess to serve in this household. She repulses the son Alec but is overcome. She returns home, bears a child that dies, and then goes as a milkmaid to a distant farm, where she falls in love with Angel Clare, a clergyman's son. After their marriage, Angel's confession of sexual sins leads Tess to reveal her past. Shocked, he leaves her, and she becomes a field worker. Hopeless of Angel's return, she is forced eventually to become Alec's mistress to help provide for her destitute family. When Angel does return and Alec speaks insultingly of him, Tess kills Alec and is hanged.

Subtitled *A Pure Woman Faithfully Presented,* the novel develops with realism and compassion the theme that a woman who is forced by circumstances to accept a lover may be pure in heart and intention. Victorian reviewers were shocked, but the depth and fidelity of Hardy's portrayal of Tess and his factually based scenes of rural life in southwestern England have made the novel a classic.

J. O. BAILEY
Author of "The Poetry of Thomas Hardy"

TESSIN. See TICINO.

TEST ACTS, former English laws requiring the reception of Holy Communion in the Church of England as a qualification for officeholding. The principle first appeared in the Corporation Act of 1661, which required members of municipal councils to have received Anglican communion.

The Test Act proper was passed in 1673 as part of the reaction to the conversion to Roman Catholicism of Charles II's brother and heir presumptive, who became James II. It required members of Parliament and officeholders, to make a declaration against transsubstantiation on taking office, and to receive the Sacrament at an Anglican service within three months.

After long debate the Schism Act, extending the Test Act to schoolmasters, and the Occasional Conformity Act, against those who followed the requirements of the Test Act but then returned to dissenting meetings, were passed in 1713. Under George I these two acts were repealed in 1718. Beginning in 1727, Protestant Dissenters were allowed to take office and then by Indemnity Acts excused from the sacramental test on the disingenuous ground that they had neglected or forgotten it. Roman Catholics remained excluded.

One of the first steps in 19th century reform was the repeal of the Test and Corporation acts in 1828. Catholic Emancipation, restoring civil rights to Roman Catholics, followed in 1829. The parliamentary oath still effectively excluded Jews and conscientious unbelievers. The former were admitted by the Jews Act in 1858, and the latter were exempted from the oath in 1886. Quakers had been allowed to substitute an affirmation for an oath since 1836.

EDWARD R. HARDY, *Cambridge University*

TESTACY, the state or circumstances created when there exists a valid will for a deceased person. See INTESTACY; WILL.

TESTAMENT, a term applied to Jewish and Christian sacred writings, originally meaning a covenant rather than a document. See BIBLE.

TESTICLE. See TESTIS.

TESTIMONY is the evidence a person gives under oath when he is being questioned in a legal proceeding. See EVIDENCE.

TESTING. In education and psychology testing is a systematic way of studying the ability of an individual or a group to solve problems or perform tasks under controlled conditions. The problems may be presented orally or in writing. The test taker may be asked to mark an answer sheet or complete a work sample. The work sample may be a simple repetitive task under stress of time or a production of a completed object of some complexity.

A task performed becomes a test only when the product is judged as to quality against a previously determined standard. This standard may be 100% mastery—a perfect product—or it may be a response judged to be good or not good by comparison with the performance of a reference group.

The term "test" is used loosely to include everything from brief school examinations to complex inventories of personality traits. Some of these tests yield numerical grades, whereas others result in a report of the examiner's impressions. Many psychologists use the terms *measurement* or *evaluation* rather than testing as a way to suggest the scope of the field.

This article surveys testing in the broad sense. For more specific discussion of measurement in the schools, see also EDUCATION—*Educational Measurement*. For measurement of intelligence, see also INTELLIGENCE.

WHY TESTS ARE USED

All U. S. schoolchildren and many adults are tested at various times in their lives. Tests are used by schoolteachers to judge their students' progress, by college admissions officers as an indicator for selecting or rejecting applicants, by personnel experts as a basis for hiring employees or promoting executives, and by psychiatrists as a help in diagnosing personality problems and mental illness. In these and many additional uses the purpose of testing is the same—to see how one individual or group stands in relation to others.

Uses in Education. Perhaps the best-known kind of test is that used to measure achievement in school. An arithmetic test, for example, is a means of judging whether students have learned facts and procedures that have been presented to them. The results may be used to give students grades ranging from 100 to 0 or from A to F. An additional use of the results might be to determine that one student is ready to go on to the next lesson, whereas another needs to review subtraction. In either case the test results distribute pupils along a continuum or scale from good performance to poor.

Reading tests measure a skill rather than a specific body of information that has just been studied. But again the tests spread students out along a continuum from highly literate to illiterate, or from those who are ready to advance to those who need remedial help.

Millions of American high school students have taken College Entrance Examination Board tests, particularly the Scholastic Aptitude Test. This test yields a numerical score, and many colleges pick all or most of their freshmen from applicants who score above 500.

Another extensive testing project in the United States is the National Assessment program, a government-supported effort to measure the achievement and attitudes of schoolchildren and adults across the country. Here the results are given for groups rather than individuals, but the intention is to see how well members of several age groups measure up to a set of criteria.

Uses in Personnel Work. School guidance counselors use tests to help young people choose careers. In business and industry, tests are used to screen job applicants and candidates for promotion. For these purposes the so-called intelligence tests are widely used. These devices enable the tester to rate an individual's mental ability against that of others who have taken the test. Personnel experts in the armed forces give intelligence measures as a means of assigning recruits or drafted men to specialties. In fact, the first group intelligence scales were developed for the U. S. Army during World War I.

Personnel workers often use devices to measure interests and personality. These are not tests in the sense of instruments that yield objective scores. Instead they are inventories that help evaluate a subject's likes and traits. If one subject shows strongly outgoing or extraverted characteristics, he may be evaluated as a better prospect for a sales job than a man who focuses more on his inner life.

Clinical Uses. Clinical psychologists and psychiatrists use a variety of tests and inventories. One frequent problem is making a diagnosis that will differentiate a patient as neurotic or psychotic. There is no single test that will settle this question by a simple score. However, measuring techniques help the clinician reach a judgment. The techniques are based on concepts of what is normal behavior, what is neurotic, and what is more seriously mentally ill behavior. Thus an inventory helps place a patient along the continuum from normal to abnormal.

VARIETIES OF TESTS

For convenience in discussion, the various instruments used in educational and psychological measurement can be grouped under headings according to what is being tested.

Achievement Tests. Tests to measure achievement in schoolwork include the simplest teacher-made quizzes—for example, asking the students to spell 25 words or do 10 subtraction examples. Since students need to know subtraction before they start division, the teacher aims for 100% success on these tests. Another traditional form of teacher-made test involves essay answers to questions—for example, about books studied in literature courses or events covered in history classes.

Teacher-made tests have disadvantages. To begin with, the grades on anything but the simplest tests often are influenced by the teacher's general estimate of students. Investigators of grading once asked a number of teachers to grade one mathematics paper. They gave it marks ranging from 92 down to 28. Essay tests are particularly difficult to grade with objectivity. Another problem is that, if each teacher makes her own tests, grades for one class cannot be compared with those of another. Nor can the achievement of one school be matched against that of other schools.

A major development in 20th century education and psychology has been an effort to improve measurement by constructing standardized tests. Standardized achievemest tests are developed and produced by publishers and are intended for wide use by schools. Test questions originate in a study of the current curriculum as embodied in textbooks, courses of study, and statements of the objectives of instruction. Questions are then studied to try to ensure that each one is a valid measure of whether a student has learned what the course aims to teach. Then experimental forms of the test are given to large numbers of students, a representative sample of the group for which the test is designed.

The standardization program for one test involved giving it to more than 200,000 students in 100 school systems distributed across the 50 states. On the basis of the results from the sample group, standard scores are computed. Any individual's score can then be interpreted by its relation to the standard results.

When a test has been completed, it is ready for sale to schools. They can buy question booklets, answer sheets, and directions for scoring and interpreting. All students can then be tested and graded by the same procedure.

Achievement tests for use in schools are often organized in batteries—groups of tests constructed to determine the educational status of individual students, classes within a grade, grades within a school, grades in all the schools of a community or larger geographic area. The Stanford Achievement Tests, the Metropolitan Achievement Tests, and the California Achievement Tests are examples of batteries that have been extensively used in U. S. schools. One form of the high school battery of the Metropolitan Achievement Tests includes the following separate tests: reading, spelling, language, language study skills, social studies study skills, social studies vocabulary, social studies information, mathematical computation and concepts, mathematical analysis and problem solving, scientific concepts and understanding, and science information. Multiple-choice questions are used, so that answer sheets are easily scored. See also EDUCATION—*Educational Measurement*.

Mental Ability Tests. Mental ability tests differ from general achievement tests largely because their content is not based strictly on what is taught in school but is drawn from the total body of knowledge in the individual's environment. The intent of these tests is to measure general problem-solving ability. A test item might say: "Hat is to head as shoe is to what?—arm, leg, foot, head?" The purpose is to find out whether the subject has grasped the notion of analagous relationships. Most children learn from general experience that a hat goes on the head and the shoe goes on the foot.

Mental ability tests—commonly called intelligence tests—have been extensively used in schools and in personnel work, starting with Alfred Binet's scale for evaluating children in 1905. Scores on these measures have been shown to have a high correlation with achievement in school and college. Such tests also have the great advantage of allowing a person who has had difficulty with specific school-taught material to show that he has benefited by the total experience of living. His achievement scores may be relatively low, but his ability test results may demonstrate that he has acquired important skills and knowledge. Thus he might be considered a good risk for promotion in school or acceptance as an employee.

At one time it was believed that an intelligence quotient (IQ), based on test results, was an index of inherited ability. It was also held that intelligence was a quality that remained more or less constant throughout life. However, psychologists have moved away from this idea to the position that what is measured by ability tests is native ability overlaid and modified by the effects of environment. What happens to a person in home, in school, on the street, or on the job can push test scores up or down. Test scores must be used with these facts in mind.

Particular caution is needed when mental ability tests are given to children whose environment is depressing, as in a city slum or remote country area. Attempts have been made to construct tests that are "culture free" or "culture fair"—that is, they do not require familiarity with relatively affluent, middle-class life. However, test scores still tend to reflect the debilitating effects of life under substandard conditions. See also INTELLIGENCE.

Aptitude Tests. In *Aptitude Testing* (1928), Clark L. Hull, a pioneer in this field, wrote: "The conception of specialized aptitudes and the desirability of having tests of behavior which will indicate in advance latent capacity, is very ancient. It appears repeatedly, for example, in Plato's *Republic*." Following this, Hull quoted from Plato: ". . . in the first place, no two persons are born exactly alike, but each differs from each in natural endowments, one being suited for one occupation and another for another." Nothing has happened in the centuries since Plato wrote to change the basic truth of this assumption, despite the fact that arguments have waxed and waned concerning the relative contribution of heredity and environment to the actual life-style of an individual. The 20th century consensus seems to be that the argument is futile and incapable of being settled on rational grounds since there is no clear way in which the contributions of heredity and of environment can be separated. See also APTITUDE TEST.

It is possible, however, to differentiate functionally between the aptitude test and the mental ability measure. In an aptitude test the test maker is concerned specifically with the prediction of success in a restricted and defined sphere of activity—a clerical occupation, for example, or more specifically, success in operating a telephone switchboard. On the other hand, developers of tests of intelligence or mental ability generally are interested in measuring an overall characteristic of the individual that places him somewhere on a continuum in terms of the characteristic called, for lack of a better term, intelligence. Job-oriented tests are extensively used in government, especially in the armed forces, in industry, by the U. S. Employment Service, and in schools.

One widely used instrument is the General Aptitude Test Battery, developed over decades of experimentation by the U. S. Employment Service. The battery of 12 tests yields scores for each test that are combined to give scores on nine factors or components involved in aptitudes for jobs. The majority of the tests are of the paper-and-pencil variety, but two require apparatus—a manual dexterity test and a finger dexterity test.

The General Aptitude Test Battery is administered by the U. S. Employment Service to job applicants seeking help in locating suitable work. It is also given as a general aptitude battery to students in the 11th or 12th grades of the senior high school who are not college oriented and who may go to the U. S. Employment Service as a step in obtaining a job.

DISTRIBUTION OF SCORES ON A STATEWIDE TESTING PROGRAM

On this chart each dot represents 11 cases

SCORE	PERCENTILE	STANINE	FREQUENCY
2	1	1	8
3	1	1	13
4	1	1	15
5	1	1	28
6	1	1	51
7	1	1	68
8	2	1	80
9	3	1	116
10	4	1	174
11	6	2	220
12	8	2	266
13	10	2	305
14	13	3	295
15	15	3	343
16	18	3	380
17	22	3	423
18	25	4	435
19	29	4	490
20	32	4	465
21	36	4	515
22	40	4	551
23	45	5	566
24	49	5	485
25	53	5	560
26	57	5	493
27	61	5	497
28	64	6	498
29	68	6	527
30	72	6	437
31	75	6	453
32	79	6	421
33	82	7	409
34	85	7	401
35	87	7	304
36	89	7	296
37	92	8	285
38	93	8	233
39	95	8	227
40	96	8	163
41	98	9	137
42	98	9	116
43	99	9	70
44	99	9	57
45	99	9	34
46	99	9	31
47	99	9	9
48	99	9	2

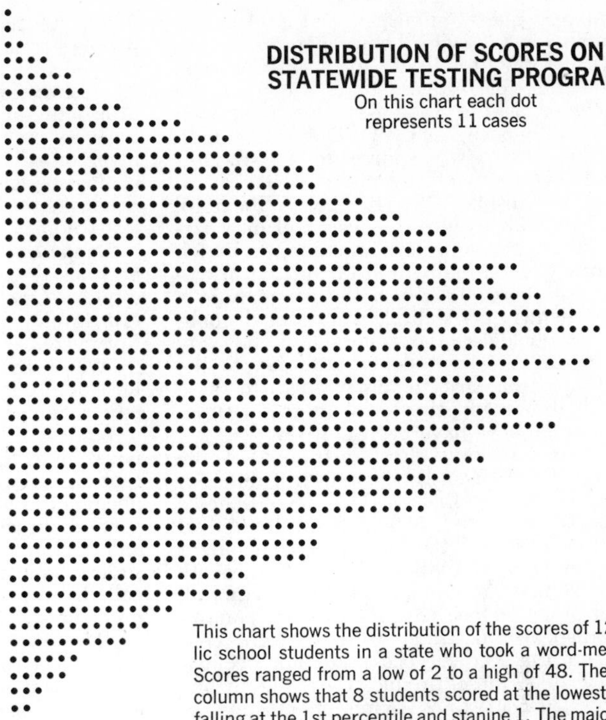

This chart shows the distribution of the scores of 12,952 public school students in a state who took a word-meaning test. Scores ranged from a low of 2 to a high of 48. The frequency column shows that 8 students scored at the lowest level, thus falling at the 1st percentile and stanine 1. The majority scored in the middle range, falling between the 40th and 60th percentiles and in stanines 4 to 6. A few ranked in the 98th and 99th percentiles and in stanine 9. The scores happened to make a pattern close to a normal curve of distribution.

Also widely used is the Differential Aptitude Test. This test is intended for younger persons as far down as the 8th grade.

Tests of Developed Abilities. During the 1960's the term "test of developed abilities" became popular. Educational Testing Service, a private corporation, developed such a test, which it called the School and College Ability Test. It is intended to be neither an intelligence test in the conventional sense nor an achievement test. Instead, it attempts to measure abilities of a quantitative and verbal nature that seem to be prerequisite to success in school at levels from 4th grade through college.

The Analysis of Learning Potential, a more comprehensive series of measures intended to predict success in school, was constructed on somewhat the same position. The premise is that success in school is best predicted by measures clearly related to specific environmental learning as contrasted to specific in-school learning. However, careful attention must be paid to those mental abilities that seem to be important for success in school at each successive grade.

For these tests of developed abilities, the criterion has been the correlation between the test scores and school achievement as measured by standardized achievement tests. This criterion raises a question about the validity of the tests. If this correlation is high, it may indicate only that the so-called predictive measures are merely alternative forms of the achievement test. Since the criterion for validity is that the test measures what it is intended to measure, the predictive test could not be called valid.

School Readiness Tests. Another very widely used type of test is the school readiness test. This is a specific test of aptitude for learning at the 1st grade level. It contains material somewhat similar to that found in some mental ability tests for this level plus material obviously related to specific in-school instruction.

It is characteristic of U. S. society that parents and relatives of children in middle-class homes put a high value on success in school. They encourage children to develop school-like learnings prior to entering the public schools. Such children may learn to recognize the letters of the alphabet and even to read fairly efficiently prior to kindergarten. They also may learn some basic number skills. This type of instruction gives them an edge over children from disadvantaged homes when they begin formal in-school work. It is obvious that only children with average or better than average mental ability will respond to such informal opportunities to learn. Thus readiness tests do indeed identify children with better than average learning potential.

Other types of instruments are used to determine whether a child is sufficiently mature socially and physically as well as intellectually to enter kindergarten. In some school systems these tests are used as a basis for permitting or denying entrance to school.

Prognosis Tests. Prognosis tests are used at the secondary school level to measure an individual's readiness and talent for learning in specific areas of the curriculum where a course-oriented plan is in effect. For example, it is important to admit students to courses such as Algebra I and II, which are intended mainly for college-going students, only if they have the potential for success in this subject.

Interest Inventories. Some instruments, widely used in schools, business, and government, are not tests in the strict sense. The Strong Vocational Interest Blank, published first in 1927, is an example. It is a very comprehensive instrument with forms for both men and women. While a variety of response types are used, the most common is the LID response, signifying "Like," "Indifference," and "Dislike." The individual taking the test responds to a stimulus word such as "architect" by circling "like," "indifferent," or "dislike." On the basis of careful studies of individuals already successful in a particular field of endeavor, keys are set up to match the responses of the individual taking the instrument against those already in the occupation.

In the hands of a skillful, well-trained counselor or psychologist, the results may be very helpful in directing a student's attention to the similarity or dissimilarity of his interests to those of individuals already successful in the occupations for which keys have been derived.

The second major interest instrument is the Kuder Preference Record, which uses a different approach to the problem. The forced-choice technique is introduced, in which the individual chooses the most and the least preferred out of a cluster of three activities. The activities are generally similar in amount of time required, cost, and other factors. By a somewhat complicated statistical procedure, 10 keys were constructed for the Kuder. These are not occupational keys like those produced by the Strong inventory. Instead they represent clusters of preferred activities, such as those associated with outdoor work, mechanical work, computational work, or scientific work.

The following item, of the type used on the Kuder record, may illustrate how these instruments work. In this hypothetical test the directions might say:

> Read each group of activities. Select the one which you most prefer and mark it by crossing out the "M"; then select the one you least prefer and mark it by crossing out the "L."
>
> 1. work outdoors in the garden M L
> 2. repair or tune up your automobile M L
> 3. stay in the house and read a *popular science* magazine M L

Responses to such an item would be assigned weights derived by relating the percent choosing each to responses by people whose interests are known. See also INTERESTS AND THEIR MEASUREMENT.

Personality Measures. Devices for appraising human personality also should be called instruments rather than tests. They vary widely in their approach to the problem. Many are devised for use with cross-sectional groups of individuals with the idea of differentiating among those individuals on traits considered to be within the normal range. Others were devised to be used with those who were mentally ill or suspected of being so, with the intent of further delineating the nature of their difficulties. Many are group tests of a rather simple paper and pencil type, in which the individual responds to questions such as "Do you feel self-conscious about speaking out in a group?" Yes-No-?. The individual responding to the item marks "yes" or "no," or if his feeling is not clear in the matter, he marks the "?."

Other instruments have been devised to study disabling psychological abnormalities. The outstanding example is the Minnesota Multiphasic Personality Inventory, which provides scores on nine clinical scales. In this instrument the individual reacts to questions such as "I believe people should express themselves no matter who gets hurt."

The use of instruments of this sort is inappropriate in normal school situations or in business or industry as a selection device. Such inventories are properly used by clinical psychologists and psychiatrists. Interpreting the results requires an extensive background of clinical studies.

Projective Techniques. Other devices used in personality appraisal are called projective techniques. One example is the Rorschach inkblot test developed by the Swiss psychiatrist Hermann Rorschach and put into use in 1921. The projective technique is distinguished chiefly by its unstructured approach. That is, it presents a task that permits an almost unlimited variety of responses by the subject. On the Rorschach he is asked to tell what he sees in each of 10 inkblots. This allows free play on the subject's imagination, limited only by very simple and general directions. He can project his thoughts and feelings as he talks about the blots. The subject taking the "test," as it is inappropriately called, may not be aware of the intent of the procedure.

The interpretation of the responses made by the subject cannot be considered objective. This can be said in spite of the fact that tremendous effort has been made to record and evaluate typical responses by many types of individuals.

In other instruments of this sort, the stimuli represented by symmetrical inkblots are replaced by pictures, as in the Thematic Apperception Test or the Blacky Test. In all instances, the devices are suitable for use only by experts intensively trained in the use and interpretation of the particular instrument.

SPECIAL TESTING PROGRAMS

In the United States the greatest amount of educational testing is done within public, private, and parochial school systems. They are responsible for selecting the tests and making arrangements about the administration and method of scoring and interpretation. The tests are bought from the publishers. Thereafter, all responsibility for the use of the tests, their administration and interpretation, rests with the local groups.

Tests may be scored by teachers in the schools where they are administered. On the other hand, the school or school system may choose to use some kind of outside scoring service. The test publisher may not only score the tests but also make various summaries according to an agreed schedule. These services also provide comprehensive reports, including analyses of scores and records showing pupil and class standings. Teachers insist on being freed of much of the clerical work associated with teaching school. Thus the use of such centralized scoring services has increased.

However, there is another kind of testing program that falls outside the "local option" type. This is the so-called secure testing program—"secure" because the test administration and scoring are handled entirely by the organization that produces the test. The best-known example is the program of the College Entrance Examination Board (CEEB).

College Board Tests. College Boards, as they are commonly called, are administered in the junior or senior year of high school, or sometimes in both school years. The express purpose is to provide a basis for appraising the ability of a student to succeed in college. A large number of well-established colleges and universities subscribe to the College Entrance Examination Board service and require applicants to submit one or more test scores, along with high school records. Applicants are most often required to take the Scholastic Aptitude Test (SAT), which yields scores on mathematical and verbal sections. The average scaled score is theoretically 500.

Chances for admission to college are much greater for applicants who score well above 500. This is particularly true with colleges that set highly selective standards for admission. Here the average SAT score of a new freshman class may be well over 600. In moderately selective colleges and universities the average is often nearer 500.

Some colleges require applicants to take College Board achievement tests in addition to the Scholastic Aptitude Test. For example, a prospective mathematics or science major may have to submit a score on a math achievement measure.

College Entrance Board Examinations are constructed and administered by the Educational Testing Service (ETS), a nonprofit organization, founded by the joint action of the American Council on Education, the Carnegie Foundation for the Advancement of Teaching, and the College Entrance Examination Board. ETS more than any other organization is known for the number of similar secure examination programs it sponsors. These include the Graduate Records Examination, the Advanced Placement Examination, and more than 20 others.

Some of these are qualifying examinations for business enterprises and for professional fields of endeavor, such as the Chartered Life Underwriters examinations and the licensing examination of the American Board of Obstetrics and Gynecology. In tests of this sort, the attrition rate may be far greater than it is on the college examination. However, it must be made clear that these standards are set by the group or institution served and not by Educational Testing Service itself.

Another evaluating device used to screen college applicants is produced by the American College Testing Program (ACT). This is an organization of colleges and universities founded in 1959. Numbers of colleges with moderately selective admissions policies—state universities, for example—require ACT results. Some institutions will accept either ACT or CEEB scores. The ACT battery includes English, social studies, mathematics, and natural science tests. The ACT tests are less expensive to take than the CEEB —an important factor in view of the fact that the student has to pay for the cost of college-qualifying examinations.

National Assessment. In 1968 a major nationwide testing program was instituted under the name National Assessment. The program was supported by federal funds and initiated by the Carnegie Corporation through a Committee on Assessing the Progress of Education. Later, the program came under the direction of the Education Commission of the States, an organization of educators and political leaders. The stated purpose was to conduct "a systematic census-like survey of knowledges and skills, understandings and attitudes, designed to sample four age levels in ten different subject areas." The initial testing was done in science, citizenship, and composition, comparing young people in the 9, 13, and 17-year age groups and young adults aged 26 to 35.

National Assessment of Educational Progress (NAEP) is concerned with group results and not with reporting on individual pupils. Results are reported for age groups rather than for school grades. Age, rather than grade, was selected as the basis for grouping for two reasons. First, it was felt that age was easier than grade for lay persons to understand. Second, there are substantial differences around the country in the legal school entrance age and in promotional policy, so that being a "third-grader," for example, is not a clear enough description of the group for research purposes.

INTERPRETING TEST RESULTS

Test results have to be interpreted—that is, translated into a set of scores that have some intrinsic meaning for those receiving the information. The only exceptions to this are instruments of the inventory type that do not completely satisfy the definition of a test. They do not yield scores as such but rather patterns of responses to be analyzed with clinical insight. This section is concerned with tests in the strict sense, particularly mental ability and achievement tests.

Norms. Tests that are thus interpreted are called "norm-referenced" tests. More explicitly, such tests are interpreted by a comparison of the earned score with the scores made by some clearly defined group of individuals representative of the group for whom the test was made. The precision of the definition of the norm group and its consistency from one level to another are all-important requirements for norm-referenced interpretation.

Group mental ability tests were the first instruments to use norm-reference interpretation extensively. Test scores were distributed by successive age samples, and attempts were made to ensure that the groups were representative at each age level. The average score for any month of age was said to represent a mental-age equivalent to the naming month. For example, the average score earned by children who were 8 years and 6 months of age at the time of testing was said to have an age equivalent of 8 years and 6 months. This is sometimes called a "mental age."

In an effort to get an index of brightness independent of age, the intelligence quotient (IQ) was devised. This was the ratio of mental age to chronological age. For example, a child receiving a score equal to that of an average 12-year-old would have a mental age of 12 years or 144 months. If his chronological age was 10 years 6 months or 126 months, his IQ would equal 144/126 or 1.14. For convenience sake, the convention of dropping the decimal soon became established practice. Thus this IQ is recorded as 114. Misunderstanding of the IQ might have been reduced if psychologists had retained the decimal point and dropped the second place of the decimal. For example, it used to be said that an individual with an IQ of 120 would be a better prospect for college work than one with an IQ of 110. If these IQ's had been expressed as 1.2 and 1.1, more caution might have been shown in claiming that one was superior to the other.

Intelligence testers found that mental ages became more and more difficult to assign as they dealt with older individuals. Eventually this problem resulted in the abandonment of the ratio IQ and the substitution for it of the so-called deviation IQ. This expresses the degree of an atypical performance in terms of the amount by which the individual differs from the average for his age. The deviation IQ is now used almost universally in place of the ratio IQ for tests for which such a measure of brightness is appropriate. See also INTELLIGENCE.

For achievement tests, a norm based on average scores by grade is used. Grade equivalents are substituted for age equivalents, but no quotient similar to the IQ is used. The process is complicated because it is increasingly difficult to obtain comparable populations at successive grade levels, even from grade 1 through the upper elementary grades. Retardation—keeping children in one grade for a second year—as an administrative practice has somewhat fallen out of favor. However, from 15% to 25% of children in grade 8 will be a year or more older than the typical age for the grade. These largely will be slow learners for whom the retardation is one method of adapting instruction to their individual needs.

It becomes impossible to obtain comparable populations in junior high school and senior high school grades since there is little or no continuity for instruction from grade level to grade level. Students are not "promoted" or "held back" at the junior and senior high school level. Instead they pass or fail a specific course, which can then be made up by repeating the course or substituting another in order to satisfy the requirements for graduation.

More and more the deviation approach is being used in the interpretation of achievement tests as well as mental ability or aptitude tests. Once a norm group is clearly defined—for example, grade 4 tested in October of the school year—the scores for all children tested at this time are distributed. Raw scores, usually number of items answered correctly, are interpreted by indicating how far above or below the average for this defined group of fourth graders an individual stands. The norm group can be a local group, a regional group, a group with some other defined characteristic such as children of a certain socioeconomic level within a defined geographic area, or even a national group. Most standardized achievement tests are published with national norms, presumably based upon carefully derived representative national samples.

Percentiles. Perhaps the type of norm most widely used to place the individual with respect to his standing in a group of his peers is the percentile rank system. According to this system, each score (percentile) is interpreted by assigning to it a percentage indicating the proportion of the total group having reached or exceeded the given score. A score with a percentile rank of 10 means that the individual has reached or exceeded the performance of 10% of the group. A percentile rank of 90 characterizes the score that has been earned or exceeded by 90% of the group in question. For example, if 100 individuals were arranged in order of height, the individual whose height was equal to or greater than 90% of the individuals involved would be said to have a percentile rank of 90.

Unfortunately, percentile ranks are not equal units because heights, or weight, or foot size, or test scores do not arrange themselves in rectangular distributions. That is, a graph showing how many people there are at heights from 4 feet to 7 feet will not be a rectangular shape. Instead, the curve will be bell-shaped because there are far more cases toward the center of the range of heights than toward either extreme. This bell-shaped line is called the "normal curve of distribution."

Test scores are not always normally distributed because not all tests include items of sufficient difficulty to measure the most able while also having items sufficiently easy to provide some nonchance score for the least able individuals tested. Lack of normality in the distribution of test scores does not indicate that the underlying trait being measured is not normally distributed. It simply means that the items comprising the test have not been selected to permit this truth to be demonstrated. Some tests are deliberately constructed so that they will not produce normally distributed scores. For example, a test designed to select a small, highly qualified group may include many questions that only a minority can answer correctly.

Stanines. Most standardized tests provide stanines as a basic interpretive device. The word *stanine* is an abbreviation of "standard score on a nine point scale." Scores are distributed on a scale from 1 to 9. Typically, the majority of scores cluster toward the center—about 54% fall in steps 4, 5, and 6. Only about 4% fall at the highest step (9) or the lowest (1). Any student's score can be interpreted by telling which step it belongs on.

If a series of tests is given to the same group, stanines can be computed to compare results on mental-ability tests with scores on other measures such as achievement tests.

MEASUREMENT PROGRAMS AROUND THE WORLD

Educational and psychological testing has been used throughout the world for many decades. German, French, and British psychologists made notable contributions to the development of testing in the modern sense from the very beginning. Hermann Ebbinghaus and Wilhelm Wundt in Germany, Alfred Binet in France, Charles Spearman in England—these are only a few of the eminent psychologists from these countries who contributed to testing. It is undoubtedly true that testing developed more rapidly and penetrated more areas of private and public life in the United States than in any other country. However, the systematic use of tests, especially as entrance examinations to higher education has been very extensive in Germany, France, Britain, and many other countries.

After World War II, American foreign aid assisted in spreading the use of standardized testing around the world. There is hardly a country visited by American educators as consultants where testing has not followed. Testing by American methods has been introduced, for example, to Afghanistan, Republic of the Congo, Ethiopia, India, Turkey, and many countries in Latin America.

The translation of American-made tests has been widespread. As one example, the Otis Self-Administering Test and Quick-Scoring Tests—both mental ability measures—have been translated into more than a dozen languages. However, the simple translation of a test from one language to another has not proved successful.

In 1966, Educational Testing Service began to publish an international newsletter on educational evaluation and research. Within a few years, at least 30 countries made contributions to the newsletter, describing efforts made in the development and use of tests. The list runs alphabetically from Australia to Yugoslavia, with particularly strong activity reported by Australia, Canada, Britain, Germany, Japan, and Sweden.

The United Nations through UNESCO has provided the framework for many international studies of measurement. The International Association for the Evaluation of Educational Achievement—a nongovernmental, nonprofit, scientific association—was founded to foster such international studies.

Phase I of the activities of this group was a cross-national study in the area of mathematics. This study involved testing 13-year-olds and pre-university students. In all, 133,000 pupils from 5,450 schools were tested. Approximately 50 million separate pieces of information were recorded and stored on magnetic tape at the University of Chicago Computation Center, where the analyses were carried out. Phase II of this major international investigation includes the development of tests in six subject matter areas: science, civic education, French as a foreign language, English as a foreign language, reading comprehension, and literature.

The activities of this association are especially important because they illustrate both the comprehensiveness of the international effort and the universality of the problems investigated by means of tests.

College Entrance Examination Board testing has also penetrated the foreign field. College Board tests are administered in 91 countries outside the United States. The increased movement of students from nation to nation after World War II has accentuated international testing.

A Spanish Language Scholastic Aptitude Test was developed for the board in Puerto Rico and administered there as well as in selected Latin American countries. The board has also developed a special version of the Scholastic Aptitude Test for the African scholarship program in American universities. The College Entrance Examination Board has cooperated in the development of a test of English as a foreign language. This examination is offered four times a year in test centers overseas as well as within the continental United States.

WALTER N. DUROST
University of New Hampshire

Bibliography

Adams, Georgia S., and Torgerson, Theodore L., *Measurement and Evaluation in Education, Psychology, and Guidance* (New York 1964).
Cronbach, Lee J., *Essentials of Psychological Testing*, 3d ed. (New York 1969).
Downie, Norville M., *The Fundamentals of Measurement: Techniques and Practices*, 2d ed. (New York 1967).
Durost, Walter N., and Prescott, George A., *Essentials of Measurement for Teachers* (New York 1962).
Ebele, Robert L., *Measuring Educational Achievement* (New York 1965).
Freeman, Frank S., *The Theory and Practice of Psychological Testing*, 3d ed. (New York 1962).
Harrower, Molly, *Appraising Personality: An Introduction to Projective Techniques* (New York 1968).
Noll, Victor H., *Introduction to Educational Measurement*, 2d ed. (Boston 1965).
Remmers, Hermann H., and others, *Practical Introduction to Measurement and Evaluation*, 2d ed. (New York 1965).
Thorndike, Robert L., and Hagen, Elizabeth P., *Measurement and Evaluation in Psychology and Education*, 2d ed. (New York 1961).

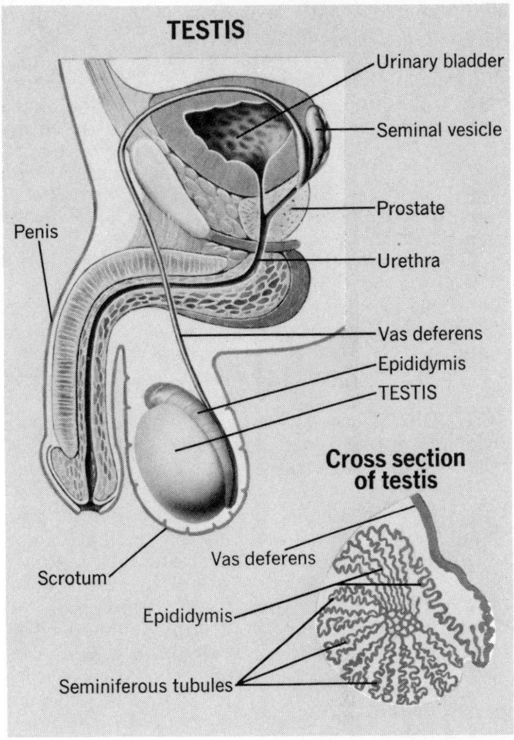

TESTIS, the male gonad, or reproductive organ, which produces both sperm cells and male sex hormones (androgens). Testes are found in all animals that reproduce sexually. Some lower animals, such as earthworms, have both male and female gonads.

In humans, the testes descend from the abdominal cavity into the scrotum before birth. This prenatal descent also occurs in monkeys, goats, pigs, sheep, horses, and bulls. In other mammals, such as rats, the testes descend right after birth, and in elephants, stags, and some rodents they descend at the mating season. In fish, amphibians, reptiles, and birds, the testes are normally located in the abdominal cavity.

The human testis is composed of *seminiferous tubules*, whose development during adolescence is stimulated by a hormone from the anterior pituitary gland, and *interstitial*, or *Leydig, cells*, which when stimulated by another pituitary hormone produce androgens, the most important of which is probably testosterone. Spermatogenesis, the formation of sperm cells, occurs in the seminiferous tubules. The mature sperm are stored in the epididymis and are discharged along with other substances through the ureter during ejaculation. See also COITUS; HUMAN REPRODUCTION; SPERMATOZOON; TESTOSTERONE.

JUDITH C. HOPKINS
T. F. HOPKINS
University of Connecticut

TESTOSTERONE, tes-tos′tə-rōn, is a male sex hormone, or androgen, that is produced throughout life by the testes. It is the most abundant androgen and probably the most active. Its secretion by the *interstitial*, or *Leydig, cells* is regulated by a pituitary hormone known as *luteinizing hormone* or *interstitial cell stimulating hormone* (ICSH). Because it has a steroid nucleus and 19 carbon (C) atoms, it is classified as a C-19 steroid.

Testosterone promotes protein synthesis and the development and activity of the accessory male reproductive structures, such as the penis and seminal vesicle. Secondary sex characteristics are also influenced by the action of testosterone. In humans, it lowers the pitch of the voice, regulates the distribution and growth of hair, and stimulates skeletal growth and development of the male body structure.

Testosterone is also antiestrogenic, blocking or suppressing the action of estrogen, an important female hormone. Women who receive testosterone as a drug may develop masculine features.

T. F. Hopkins, *University of Connecticut*

TESTUDINATA, te-stōō'də-nä-tə, or Chelonia, an order of reptiles. See Tortoise; Turtles; Tortoises, and Terrapins.

TESTUDO, tes-tōō'dō, a cover of overlapping shields used by the soldiers of ancient Rome to protect themselves against missiles, boiling oil, or molten lead while attacking the bottom of a wall of a city or fort. A heavy roof, on wheels or rollers, to protect army engineers trying to batter through or undermine a wall was also called a testudo.

TET is the name commonly given by the Vietnamese to their New Year festival, Tet Nguyen-dan. The festival is celebrated during the first seven days of the first month of the lunar calendar. Thus it may begin on any day from January 21 to February 19. Whatever occurs during it supposedly portends the year's happenings to come. Other Vietnamese festivals include Tet Doang-ngo (summer solstice), Tet Trung-thu (women and children's festival), Tet Trung-cu'u (chrysanthemum festival), and Tet Song-thap (when good and bad actions are reviewed).

During the Vietnam War, a major Vietcong action—the Tet offensive—was timed to coincide with the New Year festival of 1968.

William Y. Dessaint
The New University of Ulster

TETANUS, tet'ən-əs, is a disease produced by tetanospasmin, a component of the toxin secreted by the bacterium *Clostridium tetani*. Tetanospasmin is an extremely strong poison that affects the nervous system. A single milligram of it can kill about 20 million white mice.

Epidemiology. *Clostridium tetani* bacteria can enter the body through any wound, but perforated wounds of the feet and wounds containing foreign bodies are the ones most often infected. Although tetanus exists throughout the world it is particularly prevalent in tropical areas with poor sanitation. In India, for example, tetanus causes several hundred thousand deaths a year, but in Sweden it causes less than ten. About 80% of the people in the United States who get tetanus are addicted to injectable drugs.

Course of the Disease. The incubation period ranges from 2 to 60 days. The dominant early symptoms are headache, toothache, and profuse sweating. The patient may also be anxious and overexcited. Soon there are muscular contractions, or spasms. The intensity, frequency, and sites of these contractions vary considerably. In mild cases they are limited to the head and neck, a condition commonly known as *lockjaw*. In severe cases the spasms are generalized, occurring in the back, extremities, diaphragm, and respiratory muscles.

There are many complications of tetanus, including intestinal ulcers, blood clot formation, and respiratory disorders. The complications most often responsible for death are respiratory disorders and cardiac arrest. Only in mild cases of tetanus is the prognosis favorable. The overall fatality rate is more than 40%.

Treatment. There is no known treatment for tetanus. In young patients the prognosis can be improved with artificial respiration in a respirator and the administration of such muscle-relaxing drugs as curarines or diazepam. Contracting tetanus once does not provide future immunity, and all tetanus patients should be immunized after they recover.

Prevention. Active immunization against tetanus is totally safe and effective. The substance used for immunization is tetanus toxoid, toxin that has been deprived of its harmful properties but not its ability to provoke the body's formation of antibodies. For children, three intramuscular injections of toxoid, usually combined with other vaccines, should be given after the third month of life. Adults should receive two or three injections. There is fair evidence that such immunization, enhanced by a booster injection later on, provides immunity for life.

After an injury has occurred, completely immunized patients should receive a toxoid booster unless they have had one during the past year. Patients only partly immunized or not immunized should receive active immunization. However, such a measure cannot guarantee protection against the disease in nonimmunized people. Additional prophylaxis may be afforded by the administration of tetanus antitoxin (antibodies).

Leo Eckmann, M. D., *Author of "Tetanus"*

TETANY, tet'ə-nē, is a condition characterized by spasms of the wrist and ankles, muscle twitches, painful muscle cramps, and convulsions. Tetany results when the alkalinity of the blood is too high or the calcium content too low. It occurs with such conditions as alkali ingestion, hyperventilation, vitamin D deficiency, parathyroid deficiency, kidney failure, and obstruction of the opening between the stomach and the small intestine. The characteristic symptoms make the diagnosis of tetany unmistakable. The treatment and prognosis are determined by the underlying cause.

Raymond E. Osborne, M. D.
Mount Sinai Hospital, N. Y.

TETHER BALL is an outdoor game for two players. First called "English Tether Ball," the game originated in Britain in 1896. Players use an inflated ball enclosed in a net casing and secured to the top of a tapered 10-foot pole by a 7½-foot cord or rope. A white stripe marks the pole at a height of 6 feet, and a circle, or neutral area, 6 feet in diameter, surrounds the pole. A line 20 feet long passes through and bisects the circle. A service spot is marked on each side of the line, perpendicular to the line and 6 feet from the pole. Players keep on their own side of the line and outside the neutral area as they bat the ball, trying to wind the cord around the pole above the 6-foot mark.

The winner of a toss for serve selects the direction he intends to wind the cord. Standing on his service spot, he throws the ball in the air and hits it. The opponent tries to return the ball in the opposite direction. After the serve, either may bat the ball as often as possible. When the ball rests against the pole above the winding mark, the player in whose direction the cord is wound scores a point. Game is four points.

A player fouls if he holds or catches the ball, touches the pole or cord, or steps into the circle or out of his own court. After a foul the opponent gets a free hit. He may not unwind the cord more than a half turn to take the hit.

Variations occur in type of equipment and in layout of the court. Many play tetherball with paddles or rackets, and tennis balls may be used.

FRANK K. PERKINS
Boston "Herald"

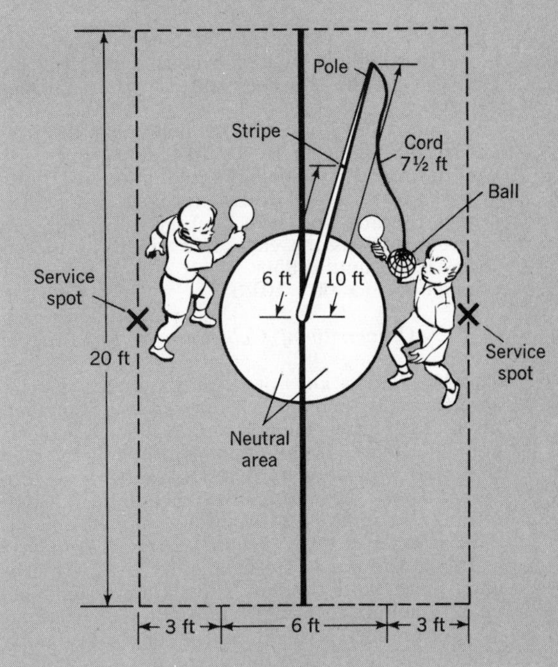

TETHYS, tē'thəs, in Greek mythology, was one of the Titan daughters of Uranus and Gaea. With her husband and brother, Oceanus, she ruled the waters of the earth. The offspring of Tethys and Oceanus included the rivers of the earth and 3,000 ocean nymphs, the Oceanides. The name Tethys is believed to mean "nurse" or "rearer" and probably refers to her role as a primeval sea mother. When the Titans were overthrown, Neptune and Amphitrite became the new powers of the waters.

TETHYS, tē'thəs, or *Thetys,* was a great ocean that, according to theory, existed in pre-Tertiary time, more than 100 million years ago. In Greek mythology, Tethys was the wife of Oceanus, god of the sea before Poseidon.

The ancient sea was given the name "Tethys" by the Austrian geologist Eduard Suess. He postulated that it occupied the region now compressed to form the mountain ranges of the Alps and the Himalayas, lying across southern Eurasia from the East Indian Ocean coast to the Atlantic Ocean coast, and perhaps as far west as the West Indies. He believed that in late Paleozoic time, about 300 million years ago, the sea acted as a barrier separating Gondwanaland, the supercontinent to the south, from Laurasia, the supercontinent to the north. The two supercontinents had quite distinctive floras, indicating their separation, while similarities in marine faunas in oceans of that period also support the existence of the Tethys ocean channel.

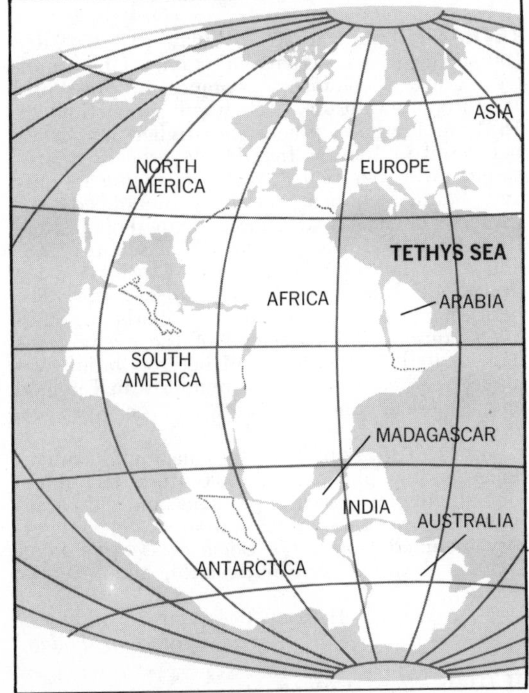

Present scientific opinion supports the view that, in Tertiary time, continental drift brought fragments of the ancient supercontinents together to close the Tethys ocean, whose sedimentary strata were converted into folded mountains.

J. T. WILSON
University of Toronto

TETON INDIANS. See DAKOTA INDIANS.

TETON RANGE, tē'ton, in northwestern Wyoming and southeastern Idaho, just south of Yellowstone National Park. It is a rugged mountain massif with several peaks over 13,000 feet (about 3,960 meters). Grand Teton (13,766 feet) is the highest. The summits rise only about 7,000 feet (about 2,130 meters) above the floor of Jackson Hole, the valley on the east side. Much of the range lies within Grand Teton National Park. Its precipitous side are a challenge to expert mountain climbers.

TÉTOUAN, tā-twän', is a city in northern Morocco. It is situated on a plateau overlooking the Wadi Martin, about 10 miles (16 km) from the Mediterranean Sea and 60 miles (96 km) southeast of Tangier. Formerly the capital of Spanish Morocco, Tétouan (Tetuán) is now mainly a market center with some light industry.

The medieval section of Tétouan has narrow streets, some 70 mosques, and shops specializing in leather goods, jewelry, and copperware.

It includes a Jewish quarter, the Mellah. The newer area, built by the Spanish, contains two Roman Catholic churches and a modern business district.

There were Roman settlements near the present site of Tétouan. In the 14th century the city was destroyed by Spain in retaliation for pirate attacks. Muslim and Jewish refugees from Spain settled there in the 16th century.

Tétouan was the capital of Spanish Morocco from 1912 until 1956, when Spain withdrew. Population: (1960) 101,352.

BENJAMIN E. THOMAS
University of California at Los Angeles

TETRA, te'trə, any of several small, glasslike colorful fishes popular with aquarists. Some representative tetras include the brilliantly colored glowlight tetra (*Hemigrammus gracilis*), the neon tetra (*Hyphessobrycon innesi*), the cardinal tetra (*Cheirodon axelrodi*), the head-and-tail-light tetra (*Hemigrammus ocellifer*), and the South American jewel tetra (*Hyphessobrycon callistus*). Tetras are found in freshwater in South America and Africa, and thousands are transported each year to aquarists in many parts of the world.

Tetras are classified in the characin family, Characidae, and have the characin characteristics —teeth in the jaws and an adipose fin between the dorsal and caudal fins. In nature, tetras are constantly on the move and live peacefully with one another. Most prefer the lime-free, peaty waters common to the tropical Amazon rivers. They are largely omnivorous. Tetras are egg-layers, dropping adhesive or semiadhesive eggs.

DONALD ZUMWALT
John G. Shedd Aquarium, Chicago

TETRACYCLINE, te-trə-sī'klēn, any of six clinically useful antibiotics that exert their anti-infective effects by inhibiting protein synthesis in sensitive organisms. They are "broad-spectrum" antibiotics, active against many species of bacteria as well as nonbacterial forms such as *Rickettsiae,* amebae, *Mycoplasma pneumoniae, Leptospira,* the spirochetes of syphilis, and the agents responsible for trachoma, lymphogranuloma venereum, psittacosis, and inclusion conjunctivitis. The six tetracyclines in order of decreasing level of activity are doxycycline (Vibramycin); methacycline (Rondomycin); chlortetracycline (Aureomycin) and demethylchlortetracycline (Declomycin); tetracycline (Achromycin, Panmycin, Polycycline, Steclin, Tetracyn) and oxytetracycline (Terramycin).

All the tetracyclines are absorbed from the gastrointestinal tract. Their absorption is impaired by the ingestion of milk or milk products and particularly by the concomitant administration of aluminum hydroxide gels and calcium and magnesium salts. Chlortetracycline, oxytetracycline, and tetracycline are usually taken by mouth but in certain forms may be given intravenously. However, intramuscular injection of these agents causes considerable pain. All the tetracyclines are removed from the blood by the liver where they are concentrated and passed, by way of the bile, into the intestine. From there they are absorbed into the blood and excreted in the urine.

Reactions to the tetracyclines include skin rashes, brown or black coating of the tongue, pruritus ani, vaginitis, fever, abdominal distress, nausea, vomiting, diarrhea, phototoxic skin reactions, liver injury, and suprainfections. The tetracyclines are especially dangerous and may cause death in pregnant patients, especially when kidney function is decreased. These drugs must be given with great care to any patient with impaired kidney function. Children receiving tetracyclines and babies born to women treated with these agents from midpregnancy on may develop brown discoloration of the teeth. Increased intracranial pressure may result from the use of tetracyclines in young babies.

LOUIS WEINSTEIN, M. D.
Tufts University School of Medicine

TETRAETHYL LEAD, te-trə-eth'əl, an organometallic compound with the formula $(C_2H_5)_4Pb$. It is used as a gasoline additive to reduce ignition knock and increase the octane number of the fuel. See GASOLINE.

TETRAHEDRITE, te-trə-hē'drīt, is an abundant mineral consisting of a double sulfide of antimony and several metals. It sometimes contains enough silver to be an important ore of that metal and occasionally is an ore of copper. Iron and mercury also are found in tetrahedrite, and arsenic may occur instead of antimony to form a mineral series that grades into tennantite.

The mineral is called tetrahedrite because it occurs in tetrahedral-shaped crystals, but it is much better known as "gray copper ore." In its massive, granular to compact form, there is nothing distinctive about its appearance except a metallic luster; it is gray to black in color.

Formed mostly at low to moderate temperatures, tetrahedrite occurs in veins with other sulfides and sulfosalts. Exceptionally fine crystals have been found in mines in Germany, Rumania, France, England, and a number of western mining districts of the United States.

Composition, $Cu_{12}Sb_4S_{13}$; hardness, 3.0–4.5; specific gravity, 4.6–5.1; crystal system, isometric.

RICHARD M. PEARL, *Colorado College*

TETRAHEDRON. See POLYHEDRON.

TETRAZZINI, tā-trät-tsē'nē, **Luisa** (1871–1940), Italian singer, who is known as one of her country's greatest coloratura sopranos in pre-World War I operatic history. She was born on June 29, 1871, in Florence, where she studied and made her debut in 1890 as Inez in Meyerbeer's *L'Africaine.* After nearly 13 years of singing in Italy and South America, relatively unnoticed, she gained her first real successes in Poland and Russia in 1903 and in San Francisco in 1904. She made her London debut at Covent Garden in 1907 as Violetta in Verdi's *La Traviata.* The performance began before an apathetic, half-filled house, but by the end of the evening she had created a sensation, and her reputation was made. Thereafter she sang regularly in England and America. She died in Milan on April 28, 1940.

Luisa Tetrazzini had an amazingly brilliant voice and a phenomenal coloratura technique. Her singing of staccato passages and her ornamentation were especially admired. Her repertory included Donizetti's *Lucia di Lammermoor,* Delibes' *Lakmé,* Verdi's *Rigoletto,* and Thomas' *Hamlet.*

HAROLD ROSENTHAL, *Author of "Great Singers of Today"*

TETUÁN. See TÉTOUAN.

TETZEL, tet′səl, **Johann** (1465–1519), German friar, who was a famous Roman Catholic preacher of indulgences at the time of Martin Luther. Tetzel was born in Pirna, Germany. He received his bachelor's degree at the University of Leipzig in 1487 and soon afterward joined the Dominican order in that city.

After rather extensive experience as a preacher and inquisitor, he became in 1516 a preacher of the indulgence—remission of punishment for sin —granted to those who contributed to the construction of the new basilica of St. Peter in Rome. In January 1517 he began promulgating this indulgence in the territory of Archbishop Albrecht of Brandenburg. Tetzel's enthusiastic rhetoric at Jüterbog in April attracted the attention of the inhabitants of nearby Wittenberg, where Luther was teaching theology.

Luther had already begun to evolve his doctrine of justification by faith alone. He was repelled by what he heard about Tetzel's sermons, and he was thus led to the publication of his famous 95 theses later that same year. On Jan. 20, 1518, Tetzel replied with 122 theses of his own, which were written by Konrad Wimpina. In April, Tetzel showed he grasped the radical implications of the debate by writing *Vorlegung*, a defense of the authority of the Roman Catholic Church.

Many who strenuously opposed Luther were equally critical of Tetzel's teachings. In particular they objected to the ideas that contribution was not required to obtain a plenary indulgence for the dead and that such an indulgence could be applied to some specific soul in purgatory. See also INDULGENCE.

In the remaining months of his life Tetzel suffered slanderous attacks on his character and morals. He has since been absolved of these personal charges. Worn out and disheartened by the controversies his preaching had ignited, Tetzel died in Leipzig on Aug. 11, 1519.

JOHN W. O'MALLEY, S. J.
University of Detroit

TEUCER, tū′sər, in Greek legend, was the son of Telamon, king of Salamis, and Hesione, a daughter of Laomedon, king of Troy. Teucer was a major hero among the Greeks in the Trojan War, where he had a reputation as the best archer. When Teucer returned to Salamis, Telamon refused to receive him because he had not avenged the death of his half brother Ajax. Teucer settled on Cyprus, where he founded a city that he named Salamis. See also AJAX.

Teucer was also the name of the son of the river god Scamander and the nymph Idaea. He became the first king of Troy, and the Trojans were sometimes called *Teucri* after him.

TEUTOBURGER WALD, Battle of the, toi′tō-bo͞or-gər vält, a battle in 9 A. D. in which German tribesmen inflicted a disastrous defeat on the Romans. At that time Publius Quinctilius Varus, one of Emperor Augustus' relatives, commanded the Roman army in Germany. Late in the summer of 9, Varus led three legions to meet an army of rebellious Germans under the command of Arminius, a Cherusci chief. As Varus' army marched through the difficult terrain of the Teutoburg Forest, Arminius ambushed and annihilated the Romans. Varus committed suicide. The exact location of the battle is unknown, but it was probably between Osnabrück and Detmold.

The Battle of Teutoburger Wald was the greatest defeat suffered by the Roman Army during the early Roman Empire, and many historians believe that it is one of history's most significant battles. It has been claimed that the defeat put an end to Roman plans for the conquest of Germany because Augustus could not replace the men that were lost. When he heard about the defeat, he is reported to have lamented, "Quinctilius Varus, give me back my legions."

ARTHER FERRILL
University of Washington

TEUTON, tū′tən. The Teutons were one of the tribes that comprised the Germanic peoples. Allied with the Cimbri, the Teutons (or Teutones) invaded northern Italy in 102–101 B. C., but were decisively defeated by the Romans.

In adjectival form, *Teutonic* is used to refer to all Germanic peoples. Teutonic also refers to the family of Indo-European languages that includes German. See GERMAN LANGUAGES; GERMANIC PEOPLES.

TEUTONIC KNIGHTS, one of several military-religious orders founded in the 12th century during the Crusades. The Teutonic Knights came to play an important role in the settlement of eastern Europe during the late Middle Ages.

The Knights, also known as the Order of the Germans of the Hospital of St. Mary and as the Teutonic Order, originated in 1190 during the Third Crusade, when citizens of Lübeck and Bremen founded a hospital for the besiegers of Acre. In 1198 the foundation became an order of knights devoted to fighting for the Christian faith. The Knights quickly acquired much property in the Holy Land, Greece, southern Italy, and Germany. With the waning of crusading zeal in the Holy Land in the early 13th century, their assistance was sought for the conversion of heathens in eastern Europe.

Activities in Europe. Beginning in 1211, under Grand Master Hermann von Salza, they undertook, in order to protect Hungary, conquests and conversions in neighboring Transylvania. When the Knights demanded too many lands for themselves, they were expelled but were soon summoned by Conrad, the Polish Prince of Masovia, to lend a hand against the heathen Prussians to the northeast. Empowered in 1226 by Holy Roman Emperor Frederick II to become overlords of Prussia, the Knights established themselves in Thorn (Toruń) and Kulm (Chełmno). Their ranks were swelled by increasing numbers of crusaders seeking new fields of action, and to consolidate their holdings they invited German peasants and nobles to settle in Prussia. In 1237 the Knights advanced into Livonia (modern Estonia and Latvia), but a further advance against the Orthodox Christians of Russia was stopped by the forces of Alexander Nevsky at Lake Peipus in 1242. Thus the sovereignty of the order came to be confined to the Baltic coastlands, stretching from Courland (now part of Latvia) to Pomerelia, an area west of the Vistula River.

The order was governed by a grand master, selected for life, who resided first in Venice, then in Marienburg, and from 1466 in Königsberg. The grand master owed allegiance to the Holy Roman emperor, although he was neither an imperial prince nor enfeoffed by the emperor. Assisted by five "grand lords," the grand master controlled the provincial governors. Membership was shared between knights and priests. They wore a uniform of a white coat with a black cross.

The invasion of Prussia by the order and the oppression of the native heathen Slavs resulted in the Germanization and Christianization of the area. The territory of the order had its greatest cultural and economic flowering under the administration (1351–1382) of Grand Master Winrich von Kniprode. It developed a remarkable architecture in its many castles and a characteristic religious-historical literature. The most flourishing cities, such as Danzig, Thorn, Elbing, and Königsberg, belonged to the Hanseatic League. The Knights' original tasks of conquest and conversion gave way to peaceful administration and trade. But the aristocratic and alien nature of the conquest was a source of discontent in Prussia, even though the German colonists tended to merge with the native population.

As the order promoted Christianization it helped to create a situation in which the existence of the order itself tended to become superfluous. By the time Christian Lithuania and Christian Poland united in 1386, the state of the order had become a German outpost against another Christian group, the Orthodox Slavs. An originally religious crusade had become a racial conflict, with Christians on both sides.

Decline of the Knights. In an attempt at self-assertion, the Knights went to war, but they were decisively beaten by a Polish-Lithuanian army at Tannenberg in 1410. At the same time there was growing discontent in the Prussian cities with the rule of the Knights. After an abortive attempt to reform the order by Grand Master Heinrich von Plauen, the secular nobility and the towns formed the Prussian Union in 1440 to seek assistance from Poland against the order. As a result, the Knights were forced in 1466 to surrender much land to Poland and accept Polish sovereignty for the remainder.

After unsuccessful requests for help from the Holy Roman Empire in the 16th century, Grand Master Albert of Brandenburg, following the secularizing trend of the Reformation, transformed Prussia into a hereditary dukedom and as Duke of Prussia became the vassal of the king of Poland. The provincial masters of Livonia vainly tried to maintain the independence of the order there. In 1530, Emperor Charles V made the provincial master of Germany the grand master and charged him with the administration of the far-flung properties. Even so it became almost impossible for the Knights to follow the general trend and to acquire territorial sovereignty for their possessions within the empire. The Teutonic Knights were dissolved by Napoleon but were refounded as a religious order by Emperor Francis I.

PETER MUNZ
Victoria University of Wellington, New Zealand

Further Reading: Carsten, Francis L., *The Origins of Prussia*, chapter 5 (London 1954).

TEUTONIC LANGUAGES. See GERMAN LANGUAGE.

TEUTONIC ORDER. See TEUTONIC KNIGHTS.

TEVETH, tā-vāth', is the tenth month of the Jewish ecclesiastical year and the fourth month of the Jewish civil year. It corresponds to the December-January period. See JEWISH CALENDAR.

TEWFIK PASHA, tou-fēk' pä'shä, **Mohammed** (1852–1892), khedive of Egypt. He was born on April 30, 1852, a son of Khedive Ismail Pasha. He became khedive in 1879 after his father was deposed for refusing to cooperate with the British and the French.

In 1880, Tewfik was forced to accept increased British-French control over Egypt's finances. The following year the army rebelled under the leadership of Col. Ahmed Arabi Pasha, and Tewfik was forced to flee from Cairo to Alexandria. British troops invaded Egypt in 1882 to reestablish order and restore Tewfik to the throne. Under British rule Tewfik lost considerable power to the British consul general, Sir Evelyn Baring (later Lord Cromer). By the time of Tewfik's unexpected death at Helwan on Jan. 7, 1892, British rule was established in Egypt.

ROBERT L. TIGNOR, *Princeton University*

TEWKESBURY, tūks'bə-rē, is a municipal borough in southwest England, 10 miles (16 km) northeast of Gloucester, near the junction of the Avon and Severn rivers. Its principal industries are flour milling and the manufacture of airplane parts. A Benedictine monastery was founded there in 715. The abbey church, dating from 1123, was restored in the late 19th century. The town was incorporated in 1574. It has some fine old houses and inns. To the south is the site of the final battle of the Wars of the Roses, in which the Yorkists, led by Edward IV, decisively defeated the Lancastrians on May 4, 1471. Population: (1961) 5,184.

TEWKSBURY, tūks'ber-ē, a town in northeastern Massachusetts, is in Middlesex county, about 20 miles (32 km) northwest of Boston. It is primarily residential but has nurseries and printing and woodworking plants. It was settled in 1637 as a part of Billerica and became a separate town in 1734. Government is by town meeting. Population: 22,755.

TEXARKANA, tek-sär-kan'ə, is the name of twin cities, one the seat of Miller county in southwestern Arkansas and the other in Bowie county, northeastern Texas. They are situated 150 miles (240 km) southwest of Little Rock, Ark., and 185 miles (296 km) northeast of Dallas, Texas. The state line runs through the middle of the post office, which serves both cities. The name is derived from syllables in the names of Texas, Arkansas, and Louisiana.

The two cities are a trading center for parts of these states and of Oklahoma. Their diversified industries include creosoting the production of sand, gravel, and lumber, and the making of tank cars, rock wool, sewer tile, tires, mobile homes, and pickles. A federal ammunition plant, an army depot, and a federal correctional institution are in the Texas city.

Lake Texarkana, 12 miles (19 km) southwest of the cities, provides recreation facilities. The Four States Fair and Rodeo is held in Texarkana annually in September.

The Texas city was incorporated in 1874 and the Arkansas city in 1880. Each city has a city manager and a separate school system and police and fire departments. Some municipal services are shared. Population: Texarkana, Ark., 21,682. Texarkana, Texas, 30,497.

ANNE L. CAPSHAW
Texarkana Public Library

JOSEF MUENCH

The Alamo in San Antonio, "Cradle of Texas Liberty," was defended by 184 Texans against 6,000 Mexicans in 1836.

TEXAS

State Seal

TEXAS, tek′səs, one of the west south central states of the United States, is the second largest in the Union. It is the only one that was an independent republic before its admission to the Union. Texas is known as the Lone Star State in honor of the single star that marks the state flag.

Texas was one of the 11 states of the Confederacy—a slave-owning, cotton-growing state—and it can properly be described as Southern. But it is also Southwestern: it has arid and semiarid locales, and the Texan way of life preserves many characteristics of the state's frontier past when Indians roamed the plains and wild longhorn cattle grazed the open range.

These contrasts stem in part from the state's vast size. One can travel in a straight line for more than 800 miles (1,290 km) within its borders. Four great physiographic regions of the United States extend into the state, and its terrain, soils, climate, and plant and animal life display tremendous variety. Its area embraces magnificent pine and hardwood forests, coastal swamplands, sweeping grassy plains, sun-baked deserts, and jagged mountains. The climate ranges from subtropical to northern temperate.

Diversity also marks the people and their culture. The population is predominantly native, of European stock, but Negroes and Mexican-Americans are more than a fourth of the total.

The large-scale discovery of oil in Texas early in the 20th century recast the state's economy. Its storehouse of natural resources has made Texas rich. And, although oil, cotton, cattle, and grain are still important, they have been overshadowed by commerce and industry.

The state's political tradition is conservative, although populism, the Progressive movement, and the New Deal have been influential countertendencies. Texas is the only one of the nation's most populous states with a one-party system. Most political battles have been fought out within the Democratic party, although Republicans are challenging the long reign of the Democrats.

The embattled past of Texas has helped shape the character of its people. Texas has existed under six flags—of Spain, France, Mexico, the Republic of Texas, the Confederate States of America, and the United States. Texans fought

CONTENTS

for their own independence and established their own nation. Citizens of the state have carried from that experience a fierce pride in all things Texan and an exaggerated confidence in their own capacities. Life on the raw frontier was another shaping factor, for the Indian wars were long and bloody and, even when the Indians had gone, the frontier was a violent place where only the fittest survived. Texas has always held out the prospect of great wealth. It has lured Southern planters who brought their slaves and cotton, cattlemen drawn by the seemingly endless plains of grass, modern-day prospectors searching for black, liquid gold, and ambitious entrepreneurs willing to invade the marketplace.

The state has produced a unique breed of men. The Texan is traditionally bold, aggressive, and bombastic, believing with fervor in the doctrines of individualism and self-help, willing to rule but reluctant to be governed, spurred on by materialism but constrained by a strong sense of duty and honor. Of course, not all Texans fit this description and, as the state's colorful past recedes and immigration continues to increase, the proportion who do fit it will steadily diminish.

Texas folkways also reflect the agrarian past, but they are rapidly changing as a result of the state's broad urbanization. Houston and Dallas are among the nation's fastest growing cities. By 1970, when the population of the nation as a whole was inching toward warmer latitudes, Texas was the fourth most populous state in the Union. The dynamic economic development that began in the state in 1940 is still under way. The presence in the state of the Manned Spacecraft Center, nerve center for the nation's efforts in space and home of the astronauts, brings all Texans especially close to the future.

1. The Land

Texas constitutes one twelfth of the continental land mass of the United States and varies considerably in topography and climate. It sprawls from the level, treeless plains in the northwest, past the vast open spaces of the central plains, to the fertile, semitropical lower Rio Grande Valley in the south. To the east are coastal marshes and dense pine forests. To the west is the dramatic mountain and desert area of the Trans-Pecos region. The land rises from sea level to elevations of more than 8,700 feet (2,650 meters) in the west.

Major Physical Divisions. Four major physiographical regions of the North American continent extend into Texas: the Coastal Plain, ranging from the Atlantic seaboard to Mexico; the Central Lowland, stretching from the midwestern United States southward through Kansas and Oklahoma into north central Texas; the High Plains section of the Great Plains, sloping gently from western Nebraska and eastern Colorado into the Panhandle and central Texas; and the Rocky Mountains, whose eastern ranges traverse the Trans-Pecos region in west Texas.

The Gulf Coastal Plain, a subdivision of the Coastal Plain, covers the eastern and southern portions of the state and is composed of several regions, each with distinctive soils, plants, and climate: the low-lying, flat Coastal Prairie of the upper Gulf Coast; the drier Rio Grande Plain of south and southwestern Texas; the dense Pine Belt that covers east Texas; the Post Oak Belt that ranges through the east-central portion of the state almost from Oklahoma to Mexico; and the fertile Blackland Prairie between the east Texas timberlands and the Balcones Escarpment, which marks the inland perimeter of the Coastal Plain in Texas. The escarpment, a line of cliffs formed by faulting and erosion, arcs gently from the Red River near Denison southeastward to the Colorado River near Austin and then to the Mexican border near Del Rio. Elevations in the Texas portion of the Gulf Coastal Plain range from sea level to about 1,000 feet (305 meters) at a few points on the fault line.

The portions of the Central Lowland that make up much of north-central Texas also have a varied terrain. Elevations rise gradually from 600 to 1,000 feet (188 to 305 meters) in the east and south to 2,000 to 3,000 feet (610 to 915 meters) in the west. Low, rolling prairies cover most of the land. They extend in a broad belt from the eastern edge of the Panhandle to Wichita Falls and then south to the San Angelo area. The sandy loams and reddish clays of the prairies support considerable ranching and farming. The rugged Llano Basin, or Central Mineral Region, in central Texas has a wide variety of igneous and metamorphic rocks.

INFORMATION HIGHLIGHTS

Location: In west south central United States, bordered north by Oklahoma, east by Arkansas and Louisiana, south by Mexico and the Gulf of Mexico, west by New Mexico.
Elevation: *Highest point*—Guadalupe Peak, 8,751 feet (2,667 meters); *lowest point*—Gulf of Mexico (sea level); *approximate mean elevation*—1,700 feet (518 meters).
Area: 267,339 square miles (692,408 sq km); rank, 2nd.
Population: 1970 census, 11,196,730; rank, 4th. Increase from 1960 to 1970: 16.9% (U.S. increase, 13.3%).
Climate: Hot summers; mild winters in the south, cold in the north; abundant rainfall in the east, dry in the west.
Statehood: Dec. 29, 1845; order of admission, 28th.
Origin of Name: From the Indian *Techas* or *Taychas*, meaning "allies."
Capital: Austin.
Largest City: Houston.
Number of Counties: 254.
Principal Products: *Manufactures*—chemicals and allied products, petroleum and coal products, food and kindred products, transportation equipment; *farm products*—cattle, grain sorghums, cotton lint and seed, wheat, rice, dairy products; *minerals*—petroleum, natural gas, natural gas liquids.
State Motto: *Friendship.*
State Song (adopted May 28, 1929): *Texas, Our Texas.*
State Nickname: Lone Star State.
State Bird (adopted Jan. 31, 1927): Mockingbird.
State Flower (adopted March 7, 1901): Bluebonnet.
State Tree (adopted March 20, 1919): Pecan.
State Flag: On the left, a broad vertical bar of blue, with a single white star in the center; on the right, horizontal bars of white (above) and red (below). See also FLAG.

SANTA ELENA CANYON is a spectacular feature of Big Bend National Park. The Rio Grande, which flows through it, is the national boundary. As seen here, the right bank is in the United States, the left bank in Mexico.

JOSEF MUENCH

A second distinctive escarpment known as the Cap Rock rises several hundred feet above the prairie. Sometimes called the Break of the Plains, it marks the western limit of the Central Lowland and the beginning of the grassy, treeless, and semiarid High Plains, known south of the Canadian River as the Llano Estacado or Staked Plain. The plains extend from the Panhandle south to the Midland-Odessa area and west to New Mexico. Originally the Llano Estacado was thought fit only for cattle raising, but dry-land farming efforts on the flat land gradually opened considerable acreage to the production of cotton, wheat, and corn. The large underground water supplies of the area have been exploited for irrigated farming.

The Edwards Plateau in south central Texas is a southeastern extension of the High Plains. An area of low, angular hills, narrow valleys, and thin, rocky soil, it is used primarily for sheep, goat, and cattle raising. In its eastern part is the rugged area popularly known as the Hill Country. The High Plains rise gradually from about 2,500 to 3,000 feet (760 to 915 meters) on the east to more than 4,500 feet (1,235 meters) in the northwestern Panhandle.

The wild Trans-Pecos region is the only truly mountainous portion of Texas. It is characterized by broad valleys and high plateaus, mountain peaks rising to 8,000 feet (2,440 meters), sparse vegetation, and an arid climate.

Rivers and Lakes. The rivers of Texas were the focal points for its early exploration and settlement, and they have shaped its patterns of urbanization. The Red, Brazos, and Colorado rivers and the Rio Grande are each more than 600 miles (965 km) long, and each drains an area of about 40,000 square miles (103,600 sq km). The Red River rises in New Mexico, flows eastward across the lower Panhandle, and forms most of the Texas-Oklahoma boundary before emptying into the Mississippi. The Brazos River stretches almost across Texas on a southeasterly course to the Gulf of Mexico at Freeport. The Colorado River drains the High Plains farther to the south. The Rio Grande defines the international boundary in its course between El Paso and the Gulf of Mexico. It flows from headwaters in the mountains of southern Colorado to the Gulf. Extensive irrigation projects in New Mexico have reduced the river to a trickle between El Paso and the point near Presidio where confluence with the Rio Conchos, a major Mexican river, restores some of its momentum.

The Sabine, Neches, and Trinity rivers, all in east Texas where rainfall is heavy, are notable for the volume of water they carry. The Nueces, San Antonio, and Guadalupe rivers rise in the center of the state and flow across the Coastal Plain to the Gulf. The Canadian River rises in New Mexico and veers northeastward across the Panhandle to its junction with the Arkansas River.

Texas has few natural lakes. Sharp increases in the amount of water required for municipal and agricultural purposes, as well as long-standing problems of flood control, necessitated the construction of numerous dams and the rapid expansion of storage capacity after World War II. With more than 100 major reservoirs and an even larger number of smaller ones, the state is now generously dotted with lakes.

Texas obtains a little more than a third of its annual water supply from underground sources. Two of the largest and most important of these are the Ogallala Formation, which furnishes water for the intensive agriculture of the High Plains, and the Gulf Coast Sands, whose supply aids agriculture and municipal purposes.

Climate. The continental type of climate predominates in Texas, although the state's great size and range of elevation allow for considerable variation from one region to another. The state has mild winters, hot summers, and enjoyable but short autumns and springs. The erratic interaction of major climatic influences such as warm winds from the Gulf and cold fronts from the north or west produces sudden and dramatic changes in temperature.

East Texas has hot, humid summers and mild winters. Summer temperatures of about 95°F (35°C) are common. Greater humidity and heavier rainfall prevail along the Gulf coast, but coastal breezes reduce summer temperatures, and winter readings seldom drop below the freezing point. The growing season reaches 330 days or more a year in the lower Rio Grande Valley. At the other extreme, the Panhandle has a growing

GRANT HEILMAN

A combine harvests wheat on the Great Plains of Texas. Irrigation has opened vast areas to cultivation.

season of fewer than 200 days. Summers are hot, but winter temperatures are often well below freezing, and sub-zero readings are not uncommon. The south High Plains and Trans-Pecos areas are somewhat warmer in all seasons.

The climatic extremes in Texas are not confined to temperature. Tornadoes often strike north and south Texas, and hurricanes have occasionally devastated the Gulf coast. Although most of the state has moderate precipitation, the rains are unevenly distributed, varying from 50 to 55 inches (1,270 to 1,397 mm) a year in the east to under 10 inches (254 mm) in some areas of the west. In almost all areas of the state the combination of high temperatures and scanty rainfall make the summers difficult for plants and wildlife. Snowfall varies from as much as 25 inches (635 mm) in the High Plains to small amounts or none elsewhere in the state.

Plant Life. The variations in soil, topography, and climate in Texas have produced in turn a varied natural cover. There are more than 500 grasses and 200 trees native to the state. Although ten distinct vegetational zones have been identified, plant life may be divided into forest resources, grass resources, and arid-land vegetation. Tall forests are mostly confined to the Pine Belt of east Texas, where favorable conditions have produced vast stands of pines and hardwoods (oaks, hickory, and gum). Low forests are found in the Post Oak Belt, where post and blackjack oaks predominate, and in portions of the Cross Timbers in the western Coastal Plain and the Edwards Plateau (oak, mesquite, and cedar). A sizable part of the state is covered by grassy prairies important for grazing. In the semiarid and arid regions of southwest Texas and the Trans-Pecos, plant life ranges from brushy mesquite, huisache, and chapparal to desert cacti and greasewood.

Pecan, walnut, and hickory trees provide plentiful nut crops in central and east Texas. Massive live oaks range from the Edwards Plateau to the Louisiana border, and bald cypress grow in the east Texas lowlands. Stately palms tower over the lower valley of the Rio Grande. In the mountainous Trans-Pecos there are interesting remnants of Pacific species of fir, pine, and juniper. The mesquite, with its delicate flowers, is found almost everywhere, sometimes as a sizable tree, sometimes as brush.

Of the more than 4,000 species of Texas wildflowers, the bluebonnet is perhaps the most celebrated, for it dominates the spring landscape in central and south Texas. In arid regions, yuccas, century plants, and 100 or more varieties of cacti provide a backdrop for the more delicate desert wildflowers.

Animal Life. Like the plant life, the animal life in Texas is varied. Almost 150 species of mammals are native to Texas, although quite a few are now rare or extinct, including the black bear, otter, beaver, panther, bison, bighorn sheep, gray wolf, and prairie dog. White-tailed and mule deer, rabbits, squirrels, fox, and raccoons are still abundant. Bats are found in great numbers in some areas, and the armor-plated armadillo is widely distributed.

Almost 600 different species of birds are present in Texas. Many of the nation's major flyways for migratory birds cross the state, and ducks and geese fill the autumn skies as they head for their winter homes in the marshes along the coast. Although only a few golden and bald eagles remain in Texas, other predators such as hawks and owls abound. Wild turkeys, quail, and mourning dove are prized game birds. The rare whooping crane winters in a small colony in the Aransas Wildlife Refuge on the Gulf coast.

Reptiles are perhaps more common in Texas than in any other state. More than 100 species have been recorded. Four of the major types of poisonous snakes are present—rattlesnake, copperhead, water moccasin, and coral snake. Alligators still can be found in east Texas waters.

Commercial fishing is a major industry along the Gulf of Mexico, with shrimp the leading market item. Oyster, crab, sea trout, red snapper, and drum are also harvested. Sport fishing, quite important in the coastal area, dominates the inland waters.

Minerals. By far the most important mineral resource in Texas is petroleum. Texas has almost half the known domestic petroleum and natural gas reserves. Oil and natural gas are found, sometimes together and sometimes singly, in almost all parts of the state. Much of the nation's helium reserves are found in the Panhandle. Texas is one of the world's leading sulfur-producing areas. Much of the sulfur is found in the Permian Basin of west Texas and along the Gulf coast. Large quantities of salt are also found in

TEXAS

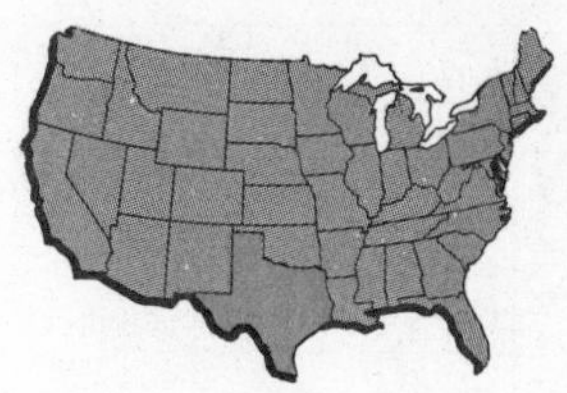

TOPOGRAPHY

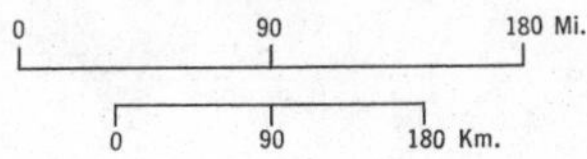

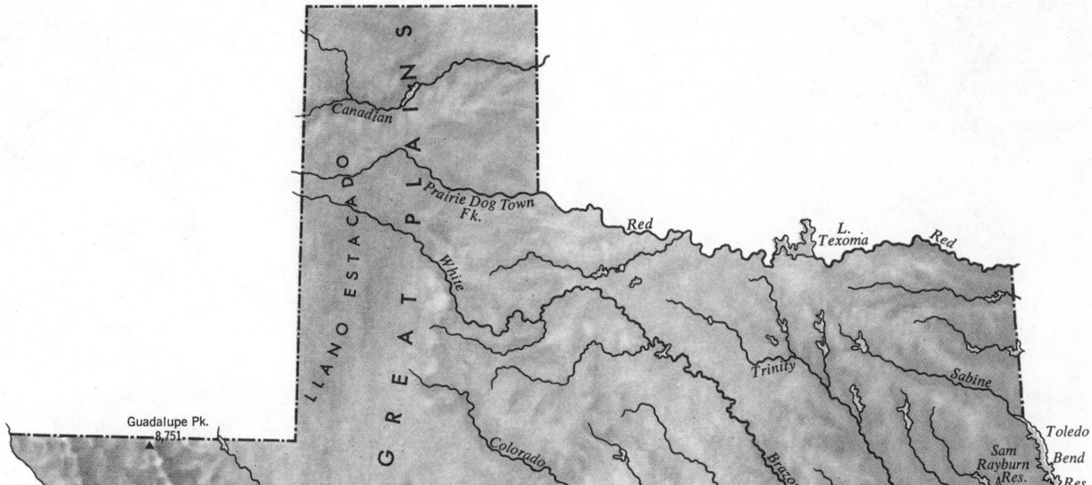

0
90
180 Mi.
0
90
180 Km.

LLANO ESTACADO
GREAT PLAINS
Canadian
Prairie Dog Town Fk.
Red
L. Texoma
Red
White
Trinity
Sabine
Guadalupe Pk. 8,751
Colorado
Brazos
Toledo Bend Res.
Sam Rayburn Res.
Pecos
EDWARDS PLATEAU
DAVIS MTS.
STOCKTON PLATEAU
Rio Grande
Lake Livingston
Neches
Sabine
Trinity
BALCONES ESCARPMENT
Colorado
Galveston Bay
Waterway
Intracoastal
CHISOS MTS.
Emory Pk. 7,835
Amistad Res.
Guadalupe
San Antonio
COASTAL PLAIN
Nueces
Matagorda I.
Rio Grande
Padre Island
Falcon Res.
Laguna Madre

5,000 m. 16,404 ft.
2,000 m. 6,562 ft.
1,000 m. 3,281 ft.
500 m. 1,640 ft.
200 m. 656 ft.
100 m. 328 ft.
Sea Level
Below

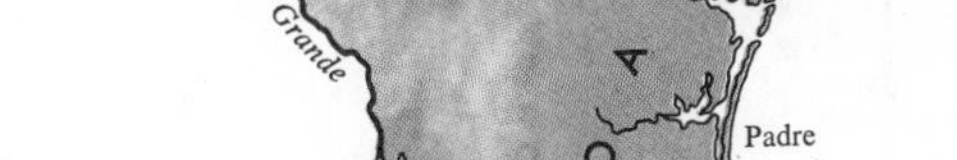

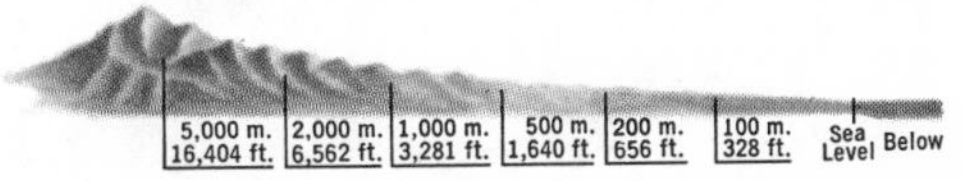

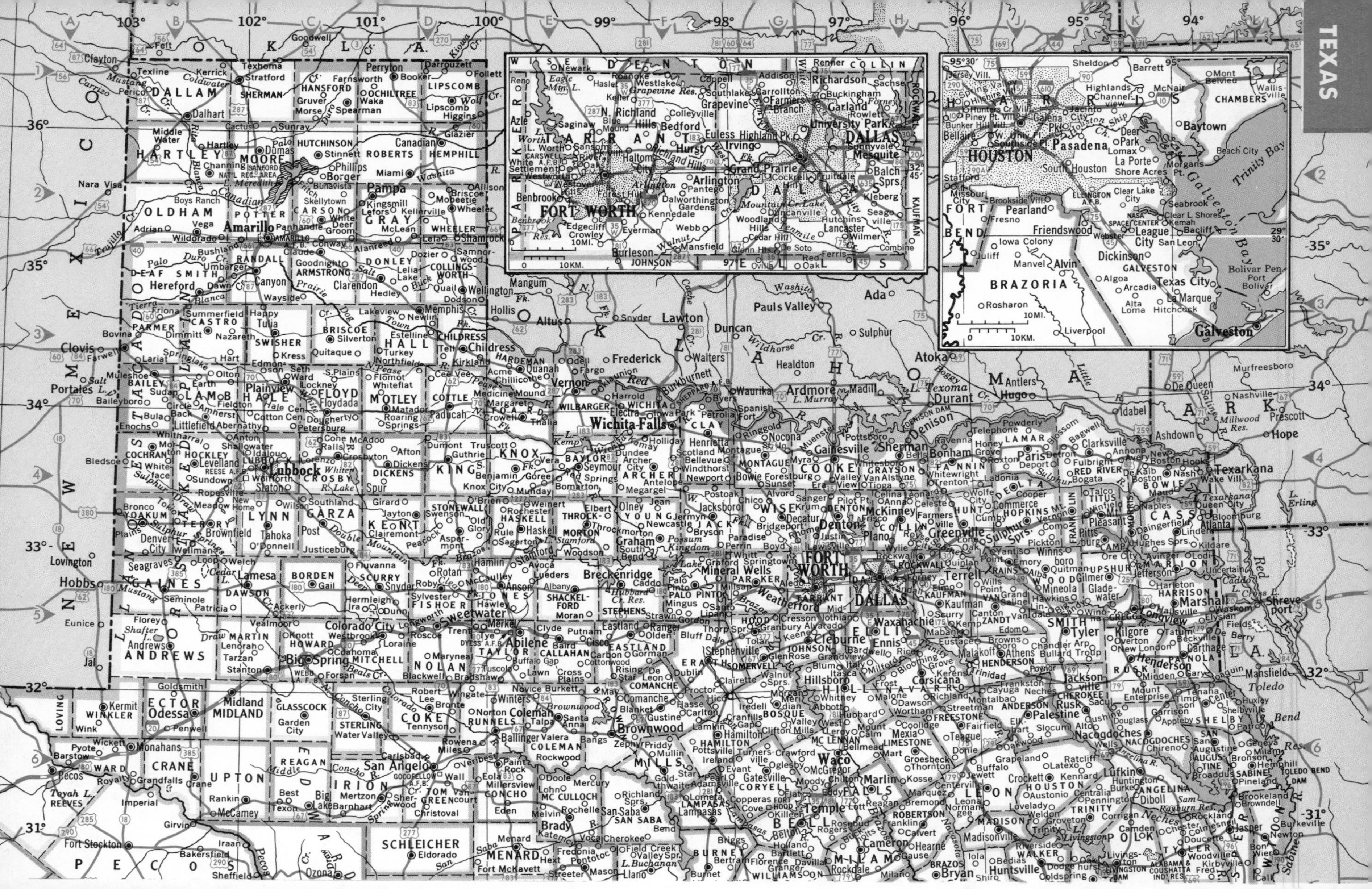

HOUSTON
Pasadena
Baytown
Galveston
Galveston Bay
Trinity Bay
Texas City
League City
Dickinson
Friendswood
Pearland
Alvin
BRAZORIA
GALVESTON
CHAMBERS
FORT WORTH
DALLAS
Arlington
Irving
Grand Prairie
Garland
Mesquite
Richardson
TARRANT
DENTON
COLLIN
ROCKWALL
KAUFMAN
Amarillo
Lubbock
Wichita Falls
Abilene
San Angelo
Midland
Odessa
Big Spring
Waco
Temple
Bryan
Tyler
Longview
Texarkana
Shreveport
Lawton
Clovis
Hobbs

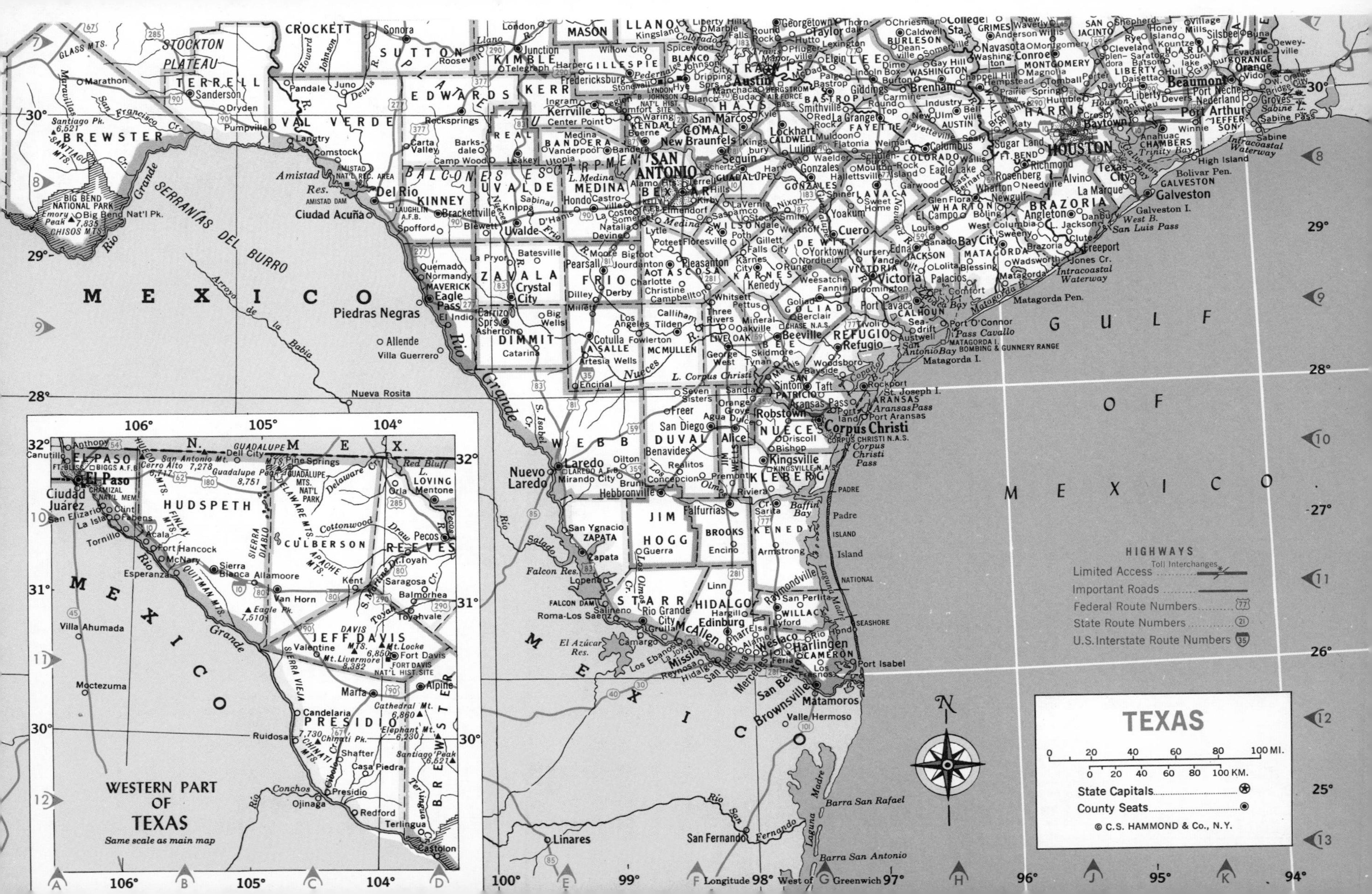
TEXAS
0 20 40 60 80 100 MI.
0 20 40 60 80 100 KM.
State Capitals
County Seats
© C.S. HAMMOND & Co., N.Y.
HIGHWAYS
Limited Access
Toll Interchanges
Important Roads
Federal Route Numbers
State Route Numbers
U.S. Interstate Route Numbers
G U L F
O F
M E X I C O
M E X I C O
WESTERN PART OF TEXAS
Same scale as main map
Longitude 98° West of Greenwich 97°
HOUSTON
Austin
SAN ANTONIO
Corpus Christi
Galveston
Beaumont
Laredo
Brownsville
El Paso
Rio Grande

TEXAS

COUNTIES

Anderson, 27,789 J 6
Andrews, 10,372 B 5
Angelina, 49,349 K 6
Aransas, 8,902 H 10
Archer, 5,759 F 4
Armstrong, 1,895 C 3
Atascosa, 18,696 F 9
Austin, 13,831 H 8
Bailey, 8,487 B 3
Bandera, 4,747 E 8
Bastrop, 17,297 G 7
Baylor, 5,221 E 4
Bee, 22,737 G 9
Bell, 124,483 G 6
Bexar, 830,460 F 8
Blanco, 3,567 F 7
Borden, 888 C 5
Bosque, 10,966 G 6
Bowie, 67,813 K 4
Brazoria, 108,312 J 8
Brazos, 57,978 H 7
Brewster, 7,780 A 8
Briscoe, 2,794 C 3
Brooks, 8,005 F 11
Brown, 25,877 F 6
Burleson, 9,999 H 7
Burnet, 11,420 F 7
Caldwell, 21,178 G 8
Calhoun, 17,831 H 9
Callahan, 8,205 E 5
Cameron, 140,368 G 11
Camp, 8,005 K 5
Carson, 6,358 C 2
Cass, 24,133 K 4
Castro, 10,394 B 3
Chambers, 12,187 K 8
Cherokee, 32,008 J 6
Childress, 6,605 D 3
Clay, 8,079 F 4
Cochran, 5,326 B 4
Coke, 3,087 D 6
Coleman, 10,288 E 6
Collin, 66,920 H 4
Collingsworth, 4,755 D 3
Colorado, 17,638 H 8
Comal, 24,165 F 8
Comanche, 11,898 F 5
Concho, 2,937 E 6
Cooke, 23,471 G 4
Coryell, 35,311 G 6
Cottle, 3,204 D 3
Crane, 4,172 B 6
Crockett, 3,885 C 7
Crosby, 9,085 C 4
Culberson, 3,429 C 11
Dallam, 6,012 B 1
Dallas, 1,327,321 H 5
Dawson, 16,604 C 5
Deaf Smith, 18,999 B 3
Delta, 4,927 J 4
Denton, 75,633 G 4
De Witt, 18,660 G 9
Dickens, 3,737 D 4
Dimmit, 9,039 E 9
Donley, 3,641 D 2
Duval, 11,722 F 10
Eastland, 18,092 F 5
Ector, 91,805 B 6
Edwards, 2,107 D 7
Ellis, 46,638 H 5
El Paso, 359,291 A 10
Erath, 18,141 F 5
Falls, 17,300 H 6
Fannin, 22,705 H 4
Fayette, 17,650 H 8
Fisher, 6,344 D 5
Floyd, 11,044 C 3
Foard, 2,211 E 3
Fort Bend, 52,314 J 8
Franklin, 5,291 J 4
Freestone, 11,116 H 6
Frio, 11,159 E 9
Gaines, 11,593 B 5
Galveston, 169,812 K 8
Garza, 5,289 C 4
Gillespie, 10,553 F 7
Glasscock, 1,155 C 6
Goliad, 4,869 G 9
Gonzales, 16,375 G 8
Gray, 26,949 D 2
Grayson, 83,225 H 4
Gregg, 75,929 K 5
Grimes, 11,855 J 7
Guadalupe, 33,554 G 8
Hale, 34,137 C 3
Hall, 6,015 D 3
Hamilton, 7,198 F 6
Hansford, 6,351 C 1
Hardeman, 6,795 E 3
Hardin, 29,996 K 7
Harris, 1,741,912 J 8
Harrison, 44,841 K 5
Hartley, 2,782 B 2
Haskell, 8,512 E 4
Hays, 27,642 F 7
Hemphill, 3,084 D 2
Henderson, 26,466 J 5
Hidalgo, 181,535 F 11
Hill, 22,596 G 5
Hockley, 20,396 B 4
Hood, 6,368 G 5
Hopkins, 20,710 J 4
Houston, 17,855 J 6
Howard, 37,796 C 5
Hudspeth, 2,392 B 10
Hunt, 47,948 H 4
Hutchinson, 24,443 C 2
Irion, 1,070 C 6
Jack, 6,711 F 4
Jackson, 12,975 H 9
Jasper, 24,692 K 7
Jeff Davis, 1,527 C 11
Jefferson, 244,773 K 8
Jim Hogg, 4,654 F 11
Jim Wells, 33,032 F 10
Johnson, 45,769 G 5
Jones, 16,106 E 5
Karnes, 13,462 G 9
Kaufman, 32,392 H 5
Kendall, 6,964 F 8
Kenedy, 678 G 11
Kent, 1,434 D 4
Kerr, 19,454 E 7
Kimble, 3,904 E 7
King, 464 D 4
Kinney, 2,006 D 8
Kleberg, 33,166 G 10
Knox, 5,972 E 4
Lamar, 36,062 J 4
Lamb, 17,770 B 3
Lampasas, 9,323 F 6
La Salle, 5,014 E 9
Lavaca, 17,903 H 8
Lee, 8,048 H 7
Leon, 8,738 J 6
Liberty, 33,014 K 7
Limestone, 18,100 H 6
Lipscomb, 3,486 D 1
Live Oak, 6,697 F 9
Llano, 6,979 F 7
Loving, 164 D 10
Lubbock, 179,295 C 4
Lynn, 9,107 C 4
Madison, 7,693 J 6
Marion, 8,517 K 5
Martin, 4,774 C 5
Mason, 3,356 E 7
Matagorda, 27,913 H 9
Maverick, 18,093 D 9
McCulloch, 8,571 E 6
McLennan, 147,553 G 6
McMullen, 1,095 F 9
Medina, 20,249 E 8
Menard, 2,646 E 7
Midland, 65,433 B 6
Milam, 20,028 H 7
Mills, 4,212 F 6
Mitchell, 9,073 D 5
Montague, 15,326 G 4
Montgomery, 49,479 J 7
Moore, 14,060 C 2
Morris, 12,310 K 4
Motley, 2,178 D 3
Nacogdoches, 36,362 K 6
Navarro, 31,150 H 5
Newton, 11,657 L 7
Nolan, 16,220 D 5
Nueces, 237,544 G 10
Ochiltree, 9,704 D 1
Oldham, 2,258 B 2
Orange, 71,170 L 7
Palo Pinto, 28,962 F 5
Panola, 15,894 K 5
Parker, 33,888 G 5
Parmer, 10,509 B 3
Pecos, 13,748 B 7
Polk, 14,457 K 7
Potter, 90,511 C 2
Presidio, 4,842 C 12
Rains, 3,752 J 5
Randall, 53,885 C 2
Reagan, 3,239 C 6
Real, 2,013 E 8
Red River, 14,298 J 4
Reeves, 16,526 D 11
Refugio, 9,494 G 9
Roberts, 967 D 2
Robertson, 14,389 H 6
Rockwall, 7,046 H 5
Runnels, 12,108 E 6
Rusk, 34,102 K 5
Sabine, 7,187 L 6
San Augustine, 7,858 K 6
San Jacinto, 6,702 J 7
San Patricio, 47,288 G 10
San Saba, 5,540 F 6
Schleicher, 2,277 D 7
Scurry, 15,760 D 5
Shackelford, 3,323 E 5
Shelby, 19,672 K 6
Sherman, 3,657 C 1
Smith, 97,096 J 5
Somervell, 2,793 G 5
Starr, 17,707 F 11
Stephens, 8,414 F 5
Sterling, 1,056 C 6
Stonewall, 2,397 D 4
Sutton, 3,175 D 7
Swisher, 10,373 C 3
Tarrant, 716,317 G 5
Taylor, 97,853 E 5
Terrell, 1,940 B 7
Terry, 14,118 B 4
Throckmorton, 2,205 E 4
Titus, 16,702 K 4
Tom Green, 71,047 D 6
Travis, 295,516 G 7
Trinity, 7,628 J 6
Tyler, 12,417 K 7
Upshur, 20,976 K 5
Upton, 4,697 B 6
Uvalde, 17,348 E 8
Val Verde, 27,471 C 8
Van Zandt, 22,155 J 5
Victoria, 53,766 H 9
Walker, 27,680 J 7
Waller, 14,285 J 8
Ward, 13,019 A 6
Washington, 18,842 H 7
Webb, 72,859 E 10
Wharton, 36,729 H 8
Wheeler, 6,434 D 2
Wichita, 121,862 F 3
Wilbarger, 15,355 E 3
Willacy, 15,570 G 11
Williamson, 37,305 G 7
Wilson, 13,041 F 8
Winkler, 9,640 A 6
Wise, 19,687 G 4
Wood, 18,589 J 5
Yoakum, 7,344 B 4
Young, 15,400 F 4
Zapata, 4,352 E 11
Zavala, 11,370 E 9

CITIES and TOWNS

Abernathy, 2,625 B 4
Abilene⊙, 89,653 E 5
Abilene, ‡113,959 E 5
Alamo, 4,291 F 11
Alamo Heights, 6,933 F 8
Albany⊙, 1,978 E 5
Alice⊙, 20,121 F 10
Allen■, 1,940 H 4
Alpine⊙, 5,971 D 11
Alvarado, 2,129 G 5
Alvin, 10,671 J 3
Amarillo⊙, 127,010 C 2
Amarillo, ‡144,396 C 2
Anahuac⊙, 1,881 K 8
Anderson⊙, 500 J 7
Andrews⊙, 8,625 B 5
Angleton⊙, 9,770 J 8
Anson⊙, 2,615 E 5
Anthony, 2,154 A 10
Aransas Pass, 5,813 G 10
Archer City⊙, 1,722 F 4
Arlington, 90,643 F 2
Aspermont⊙, 1,198 D 4
Athens⊙, 9,582 J 5
Atlanta, 5,007 K 4
Austin (cap.)⊙, 251,808 G 7
Austin, ‡295,516 G 7
Azle, 4,493 E 1
Bacliff, 1,900 K 2
Baird⊙, 1,538 E 5
Balch Springs, 10,464 H 2
Balcones Heights■, 2,504 F 8
Ballinger⊙, 4,203 E 6
Bandera⊙, 891 E 8
Barrett, 2,750 K 1
Bastrop⊙, 3,112 G 7
Bay City⊙, 11,733 H 9
Baytown, 43,980 L 2
Beaumont⊙, 115,919 K 7
Beaumont-Port Arthur
Orange, ‡315,943 K 7
Bedford, 10,049 F 2
Beeville⊙, 13,506 G 9
Bellaire, 19,009 J 2
Bellmead, 7,698 H 6
Bellville⊙, 2,371 H 8
Belton⊙, 8,696 G 7
Benavides, 2,112 F 10
Benbrook, 8,169 E 2
Benjamin⊙, 308 E 4
Beverly Hills■, 2,289 G 6
Big Lake⊙, 2,489 C 6
Big Spring⊙, 28,735 C 5
Bishop, 3,466 G 10
Boerne⊙, 2,432 F 8
Bonham⊙, 7,698 H 4
Borger, 14,195 C 2
Boston⊙, 500 K 4
Bowie, 5,185 G 4
Brackettville⊙, 1,539 D 8
Brady⊙, 5,557 E 6
Breckenridge⊙, 5,944 F 5
Brenham⊙, 8,922 H 7
Bridge City, 8,164 L 7
Bridgeport, 3,614 G 4
Brownfield⊙, 9,647 B 4
Brownsville⊙, 52,522 G 12
Brownsville-Harlingen-
San Benito, ‡140,368 G 12
Brownwood⊙, 17,368 F 6
Bryan⊙, 33,719 H 7
Bryan-College Station,
‡57,978 H 7
Bunker Hill Village, 3,977 J 1
Burkburnett, 9,230 F 3
Burleson, 7,713 F 2
Burnet⊙, 2,864 F 7
Caldwell⊙, 2,308 H 7
Calvert, 2,072 H 7
Cameron⊙, 5,546 H 7
Canadian⊙, 2,292 D 2
Canton⊙, 2,283 J 5
Canyon⊙, 8,333 C 3
Carrizo Springs⊙, 5,374 E 9
Carrollton, 13,855 G 1
Carthage⊙, 5,392 K 5
Castle Hills■, 5,311 F 8
Castroville, 1,893 E 8
Cedar Hill, 2,610 G 2
Center⊙, 4,989 K 6
Centerville⊙, 831 H 6
Channelview, 9,000 K 1
Channing⊙, 336 B 2
Childress⊙, 5,408 D 3
Cisco, 4,160 E 5
Clarendon⊙, 1,974 C 3
Clarksville⊙, 3,346 K 4
Claude⊙, 992 C 2
Clear Lake Shores, 500 K 2
Cleburne⊙, 16,015 G 5
Cleveland, 5,627 K 7
Clifton, 2,578 G 6
Clute, 6,023 J 9
Cockrell Hill, 3,515 G 2
Coldspring⊙, 500 J 7
Coleman⊙, 5,608 E 6
College Station, 17,676 H 7
Colleyville, 3,368 F 1
Colorado City⊙, 5,227 C 5
Columbus⊙, 3,342 H 8
Comanche⊙, 3,933 F 6
Commerce, 9,534 J 4
Conroe⊙, 11,969 J 7
Cooper⊙, 2,258 J 4
Coppell, 1,728 F 1
Copperas Cove, 10,818 G 6
Corpus Christi⊙, 204,525 G 10
Corpus Christi, ‡284,832 G 10
Corsicana⊙, 19,972 H 5
Cotulla⊙, 3,415 E 9
Crane⊙, 3,427 B 6
Crockett⊙, 6,616 J 6
Crosbyton⊙, 2,251 C 4
Crowell⊙, 1,399 E 4
Crowley, 2,662 E 2
Crystal City⊙, 8,104 E 9
Cuero⊙, 6,956 G 8
Daingerfield⊙, 2,630 K 4
Dalhart⊙, 5,705 B 1
Dallas⊙, 844,401 H 2
Dallas, ‡1,555,950 H 2
Dayton, 3,804 J 7
Decatur⊙, 3,240 G 4
Deer Park, 12,773 K 2
De Kalb, 2,197 K 4
De Leon, 2,170 F 5
Del Rio⊙, 21,330 D 8
Denison, 24,923 H 4
Denton⊙, 39,874 G 4
Denver City, 4,133 B 4
De Soto, 6,617 G 2
Devine, 3,311 E 8
Diboll, 3,557 K 6
Dickens⊙, 295 D 4
Dickinson, 10,776 K 3
Dilley, 2,362 E 9
Dimmitt⊙, 4,327 B 3
Donna, 7,365 F 11
Dublin, 2,810 F 5
Dumas⊙, 9,771 C 2
Duncanville, 14,105 G 2
Eagle Lake, 3,587 H 8
Eagle Pass⊙, 15,364 D 9
Eastland⊙, 3,178 F 5
Edcouch■, 2,656 G 11
Edinburg⊙, 17,163 F 11
Edna⊙, 5,332 H 9
El Campo, 8,563 H 8
Eldorado⊙, 1,446 D 7
Electra, 3,895 F 4
Elgin, 3,832 G 7
El Paso⊙, 322,261 A 10
El Paso, ‡359,291 A 10
Elsa, 4,400 G 11
Emory⊙, 693 J 5
Ennis, 11,046 H 5
Euless, 19,316 F 2
Everman, 4,570 F 2
Fabens, 3,241 B 10
Fairfield⊙, 2,074 H 6
Falfurrias⊙, 6,355 F 10
Farmers Branch, 27,492 G 1
Farmersville, 2,311 H 4
Farwell⊙, 1,185 A 3
Ferris, 2,180 H 2
Floresville⊙, 3,707 F 8
Floydada⊙, 4,109 C 3
Forest Hill, 8,236 F 2
Forney, 1,745 H 5
Fort Davis⊙, 900 D 11
Fort Stockton⊙, 8,283 A 7
Fort Worth⊙, 393,476 E 2
Fort Worth, ‡762,086 E 2
Franklin⊙, 1,063 H 7
Fredericksburg⊙, 5,326 E 7
Fredonia, 50 E 7
Freeport, 11,997 J 9
Freer, 2,804 F 10
Friendswood, 5,675 J 2
Friona, 3,111 B 3
Frisco, 1,845 H 4
Fritch, 1,778 C 2
Gail⊙, 150 C 5
Gainesville⊙, 13,830 G 4
Galena Park, 10,479 J 1
Galveston⊙, 61,809 L 3
Galveston-Texas City,
‡169,812 L 3
Garden City⊙, 300 C 6
Garland, 81,437 H 1
Gatesville⊙, 4,683 G 6
Georgetown⊙, 6,395 G 7
George West⊙, 2,022 F 9
Giddings⊙, 2,783 H 7
Gilmer⊙, 4,196 J 5
Gladewater, 5,574 K 5
Glen Rose⊙, 1,554 G 5
Goldthwaite⊙, 1,693 F 6
Goliad⊙, 1,709 G 9
Gonzales⊙, 5,854 G 8
Graham⊙, 7,477 F 4
Granbury⊙, 2,473 G 5
Grand Prairie, 50,904 G 2
Grand Saline, 2,257 J 5
Grapevine, 7,023 F 1
Greenville⊙, 22,043 H 4
Gregory■, 2,246 G 10
Griffing Park■, 2,075 L 8
Groesbeck⊙, 2,396 H 6
Groves, 18,067 L 8
Groveton⊙, 1,219 J 7
Guthrie⊙, 150 D 4
Hale Center, 1,964 C 3
Hallettsville⊙, 2,712 G 8
Haltom City, 28,127 F 2
Hamilton⊙, 2,760 G 6
Hamlin, 3,325 E 5
Harker Heights■, 4,216 G 7
Harlingen, 33,503 G 11
Haskell⊙, 3,655 E 4
Hearne, 4,982 H 7
Hebbronville⊙, 4,079 F 10
Hedwig Village■, 3,255 J 1
Hemphill⊙, 1,005 L 6
Hempstead⊙, 1,891 J 7
Henderson⊙, 10,187 K 5
Henrietta⊙, 2,897 F 4
Hereford⊙, 13,414 B 3
Highland Park, 10,133 G 2
Highlands, 3,462 K 1
Hillsboro⊙, 7,224 G 5
Hitchcock, 5,565 K 3
Hollywood Park■, 2,299 F 8
Hondo⊙, 5,487 E 8
Honey Grove, 1,853 J 4
Hooks, 2,545 K 4
Houston⊙, 1,232,802 J 2
Houston, ‡1,985,031 J 2
Humble, 3,278 J 7
Hunters Creek Village,
3,959 J 1

⊙ County seat. ‡ Population of metropolitan area. ■ Name not shown on map.

All figures available from 1970 final census are supplemented by local official estimates.

OTHER FEATURES

SAN ANTONIO'S River Walk is a quiet promenade that winds for miles through the heart of the city. It lies one level below the traffic of the streets.

TEXAS HIGHWAY DEPARTMENT

these locales. There are uranium beds in several south Texas counties and in the geologically distinct areas of the Llano Basin and the Trans-Pecos. Vast, unexploited deposits of coal are in parts of north central, west, and southwest Texas. Lignite is plentiful in central and east Texas. Iron ore occurs in the east, and smaller quantities are found in the Trans-Pecos region.

Among the nonmetallic resources of significance are such building stones as limestone, marble, and granite. Gypsum and clay are quite common throughout the state, and there are extensive sand and gravel deposits. Potash is a major mineral in the Permian Basin.

Small quantities of silver, copper, mercury, molybdenum, feldspar, fluorspar, manganese, lead, and zinc are known to exist in the Trans-Pecos and the Llano Basin.

Conservation. Like most Americans, Texans have been prodigal with their natural resources. Millions of acres of land that never should have been taken out of timber or grassland were put to the plow, and millions more were subjected to destructive lumbering and grazing practices. Soil erosion has been a major problem. The abuse of the land probably reached its peak in the 1930's. Since that time the state has sought to improve the handling of land resources.

The rapid depletion of underground water sources with slow recharge rates increases the likelihood of a water crisis in parts of Texas before the end of the 20th century. While west Texas is a dry region where water is a scarce and valuable commodity, east Texas is a water surplus area, and much remains to be done to make water available when and where it is needed. An ambitious plan was proposed in the late 1960's to help solve this problem.

The pollution of surface and underground water by unsound municipal and industrial waste disposal practices reached crisis proportions in some areas by the late 1960's. Air pollution began to be a serious problem in the larger cities. The state is attempting to improve the quality of its air and water.

2. The People

Before the arrival of the Europeans, Texas was inhabited by Indians—Apache and Comanche in the west, Tonkawa in the central region, Karankawa along the Gulf coast, and, in the east, Caddo and later arriving Cherokee, Alabama, and Coushatta refugees from Southern states. The Spanish came to stay in the late 17th and early 18th centuries, looking alternately for treasure and for religious converts and hoping to forestall French and American expansion into the territory. In the early 19th century, Anglo-Americans, mostly from the southern states, began to arrive in numbers. Some landed along the upper Gulf coast and pushed up the rivers, others came across Louisiana, and still others made their way across Arkansas and eastern Oklahoma into northeast Texas. Drawn by the prospect of cheap and fertile land, they brought with them many Negro slaves.

A variety of European immigrants began to enter the state in the mid-19th century. The Germans came in the greatest numbers, but there were also many eastern Europeans and Scandinavians. The late 19th and early 20th centuries saw a great influx of Mexicans.

Components of the Population. About three fourths of all present-day residents of Texas were born in the state. Most of the remainder were born elsewhere in the United States and emigrated to Texas. Only 3% of the population is foreign-born. The foreign stock, including those born abroad and another 8% who are native-born but one or both of whose parents were born abroad, is overwhelmingly from Mexico (61%), with Germany, the United Kingdom, Czechoslovakia, and a dozen other countries contributing the remainder.

Death or removal has virtually eliminated the native Indian population. The Tigua Indian Missions in the El Paso area and the Alabama-Coushatta reservation in east Texas are the only visible remnants of Indian culture. As a result, the Texas population falls naturally into three groups: Negroes, Mexican-Americans, and Anglos. While the Negro population has slowly increased over the years, it has declined in relative strength from approximately one fourth of the total population to a little over one tenth. Most Negroes live in the eastern half of the state and in the major metropolitan areas. Mexican-Americans have not been regularly identified in the decennial censuses, but counts of residents with Spanish surnames indicate that they constitute about 15% of the population. They are concentrated in south and west Texas, but have spread broadly since World War II.

The rest of the population is commonly lumped together as Anglo, although a great many of those included are obviously not of Anglo-Saxon stock. Most of the European immigrant groups, including Germans, Swedes, Czechs, Poles, and Italians, have seen their language and culture all but disappear since coming to the state. The assimilation of the Mexican-Americans has proceeded at a much slower rate.

The Protestant denominations are preponderant in Texas; Baptists and Methodists are the largest church groups. Roman Catholics account for almost a third of the state's church membership and are in the majority in some communities.

Way of Life. Before the Civil War, life in Texas was characterized by the conflict between the culture and values of the old South and those of the western frontier. In the post–Civil War period, cultural tensions arose between ranchers and the state's growing legion of small farmers. By the 20th century agrarian interests were forced to compete with those associated with urbanization and industrialization.

Viewed from a different perspective, the life style of Texans has traditionally reflected several dominant subcultures, such as those of the Negroes, Mexican-Americans, and Germans. In addition, life in Texas has been shaped by religious differences. The Puritan ethic and fundamentalist theology of Protestantism have long held sway, although Catholicism and liberal Protestant groups provide alternative codes.

Traces of all these cultural elements are still apparent. The frontier tradition survives not only in Texans' fondness for boots, guns, wide-brimmed hats, and horses but also in their pervasive belief in human equality and the fluidity of class distinctions. From the legacy of the old South there survive racial prejudice and discrimination as well as the hospitality and friendliness that never fail to impress Northerners. The Puritan ethic underlies the Texans' firm belief in hard work and self-help and in their lingering hostility to labor unions on the one hand and the frivolities of the rich on the other. Religious fundamentalism is one element in the state ban on open saloons.

But the ties to the past are being increasingly strained and broken. Urbanization is perhaps the leading cause of the change. In the 20th century, and particularly since the 1930's, the large-scale shift of the population to cities has virtually stripped the countryside of its residents. As late as 1900, more than 80% of the population was rural, and only one city, San Antonio, had more than 50,000 inhabitants. In 1960, however, 4 out of every 5 Texans lived in one of the state's 23 standard metropolitan statistical areas, and, according to the preliminary estimates of the 1970 census, there were five cities with more than a quarter million residents. Texans are increasingly losing their distinctive way of life and coming to resemble urban dwellers across the nation.

Largest Centers of Population. Houston, the state's biggest city and the sixth-biggest in the nation, is a boomtown of more than 1.2 million

POPULATION SINCE 1850

Year	Population	Year	Population
1850	212,592	1920	4,663,228
1870	818,579	1940	6,414,824
1880	1,591,749	1950	7,711,194
1890	2,235,527	1960	9,579,677
1900	3,048,710	1970	11,196,730

Gain, 1960–1970: 16.9% (U. S. gain, 13.3%). **Density** (1970): 41.8 persons per square mile (U. S. density, 56.2).

URBAN-RURAL DISTRIBUTION

Year	Percent urban	Percent rural
1920	32.4 (U. S., 51.2)	67.6
1930	41.0 (U. S., 56.2)	59.0
1940	45.4 (U. S., 56.5)	54.6
1950	62.7 (U. S., 64.0)	37.3
1960	75.0 (U. S., 69.9)	25.0
1970	79.7 (U. S., 73.5)	20.3

LARGEST CENTERS OF POPULATION

City or metropolitan area[1]	1970	1960	1950
Houston (city)	1,232,802	938,219	596,163
Metropolitan area	1,985,031	1,418,323	806,701
Dallas (city)	844,401	679,684	434,462
Metropolitan area	1,555,950	1,083,601	743,501
San Antonio (city)	654,153	587,718	408,442
Metropolitan area	864,014	716,168	500,360
Fort Worth (city)	393,476	356,268	278,778
Metropolitan area	762,086	573,215	392,643
El Paso (city)	322,261	276,687	130,485
Metropolitan area	359,291	314,070	194,968
Beaumont-Port Arthur-Orange (metropolitan area)	315,943	306,016	235,650
Austin (city)	251,808	186,545	132,459
Metropolitan area	295,516	212,136	160,980
Corpus Christi (city)	204,525	167,690	108,287
Metropolitan area	284,832	266,594	165,471
McAllen-Pharr-Edinburg (metropolitan area)	181,535	180,904	....
Galveston-Texas City (metropolitan area)	169,812	140,364	113,066
Lubbock (city)	149,101	128,691	71,747
Metropolitan area	179,295	156,271	101,048
Amarillo (city)	127,010	137,969	74,246
Metropolitan area	144,396	149,493	87,140
Beaumont	115,919	119,175	94,104
Wichita Falls (city)	97,564	101,724	68,042
Metropolitan area	127,621	129,638	105,309
Irving	97,260	45,985	2,621
Tyler (metropolitan area)	97,096	86,350	74,701
Waco (city)	95,326	97,808	84,706
Metropolitan area	147,553	150,091	130,194
Odessa (metropolitan area)	91,805	90,995	42,102
Arlington	90,643	44,775	7,692
Abilene (city)	89,653	90,368	45,570
Metropolitan area	113,959	120,377	85,517
Pasadena	89,277	58,737	22,483
Sherman-Denison (metropolitan area)	83,225	73,043	....

[1] Standard metropolitan statistical area.

HOUSTON is Texas' largest city. The Albert Thomas Convention and Exhibit Center is in the foreground.

BERT BRANDT

TEXAS HIGHWAY DEPARTMENT

BEEF CATTLE on a Texas ranch are tended by cowboys on horseback. Ranching has been famous here for a century, but the modern era is changing its character.

people. Situated about 50 miles (80 km) from the Gulf of Mexico, the city owes much of its expansion to its deep-water port connected to the Gulf by the Houston Ship Channel and to its oil refineries and petro-chemical plants.

The second-largest city is Dallas, in north central Texas. Dallas is distinguished from Houston by its higher proportion of white-collar, Anglo residents and its dependence for economic growth on wholesale and retail trade, light industry, and banking.

San Antonio, which ranks third in size among the cities of Texas, is one of the oldest settlements in the state and is of great historical interest. The unofficial capital for much of south Texas, it has a sizable—and poor—Mexican-American population. A mild climate and low living costs bring many here for retirement.

Fort Worth, the fourth-largest city, a close neighbor of Dallas, is predominantly Anglo. However, it is much more a blue-collar, working-class city.

El Paso, in far west Texas, ranking fifth in size, is an old historical city with a high proportion of Mexican-Americans. Besides being a major center for mining and smelting, El Paso is a tourist resort and a gateway to Mexico. Austin, the state capital, is an attractive city in south central Texas. A cultural and education center, it is the seat of the largest unit of the huge University of Texas System.

3. The Economy

The Texas economy, once based almost entirely on cotton, cattle, and oil, is today highly diversified. While the growth of manufacturing in Texas since World War II has been remarkable, the end of agriculture's domination of the economy is perhaps the most significant postwar development. As late as 1940, 30% of all Texans were involved in agricultural production, which generated much more income than industrial or commercial activity. By the late 1960's, however, agricultural employment had dipped to 8% of the labor force, and both manufacturing and mining produced far more revenue.

Texas traditionally leads the nation in production of livestock, cotton, and grain sorghum. The quality of its beef cattle is renowned. The state has ranked first among the states in value of mineral production since 1935, and its petroleum-related industries continue to grow. The establishment in the state of some of the federal government's major installations, such as the National Aeronautics and Space Administration's Manned Spacecraft Center near Houston, has been a special boon to the Texas economy, particularly its electronics and aerospace industries.

Agriculture. Texas has for several decades ranked third or fourth in the nation in total farm income—a ranking undoubtedly related to the state's great size. Almost 85% of the land is in farms and ranches. Agricultural income is almost evenly divided between crop production and livestock and poultry raising.

Cotton was king in Texas until well into the 20th century, and it still accounts for about 30%

PERSONAL INCOME IN TEXAS

Source of wage and salary disbursements	1968	1960	1950
	(Millions of dollars)		
Farms	1,320	1,092	1,229
Mining	1,023	903	584
Contract construction	1,741	869	616
Manufacturing	5,556	2,755	1,226
Wholesale and retail trade	4,836	2,902	1,760
Finance, insurance, and real estate	1,423	774	349
Transportation, communications, and public utilities	1,924	1,273	763
Services	3,700	1,886	931
Government	3,631	1,764	754
Other industries	74	38	23
	(Dollars)		
Per capita personal income	3,029	1,925	1,349
Per capita income, U. S.	3,421	2,215	1,496

Source: U. S. Dept. of Commerce, *Survey of Current Business.*

VALUE OF FACTORY, FARM, AND MINE PRODUCTION

	1965	1960	1950
	(Millions of dollars)		
Value added by manufacture	8,612	5,817	2,269
Cash farm income	2,470	2,350	2,172
Value of mineral production	4,719	4,126	2,674

Sources: U. S. Dept. of Commerce, *Census of Manufactures;* U. S. Dept. of Agriculture, *The Farm Income Situation;* U. S. Dept. of the Interior, *Minerals Yearbook.*

COTTON, once dominant in Texas agriculture, still is a major contributor to the total production value.

PETROCHEMICAL plant near Pasadena is a unit of the huge industrial complex in the Houston region.

of the value of agricultural production. Grain sorghums and such food grains as wheat and rice are also important. The corn, oat, peanut, and barley crops are valuable. Although vegetables, fruits, and nuts account for only about 5% of farm production, they are the leading commodities in some areas of the state. The increasing mechanization of farming has resulted in sharply reduced employment, greater capital investment, and larger scales of operation. The average farm more than doubled in size between 1940 and 1970. About a third of all planted acreage is irrigated. The growth of irrigated farming in the High Plains, west Texas, and portions of south Texas has been accompanied by a decline in crop production in older farming areas of east and central Texas.

Ranching is as vital a part of the economy as it is of the state's history and image. The beef cattle industry—a mainstay of the Texas economy since the post–Civil War era—continues to grow, but there have been many changes since the fabled cattle drives over the Chisholm and Dodge City trails. The open range is now fenced, most of the cattle baronies have been broken up, the Texas longhorn has been replaced by other breeds, and the cowboy's way of life has all but disappeared. Nevertheless, the number, quality, and economic importance of beef cattle continue to rise, and Texas retains its position as the leading cattle state by a wide margin. Cattle raising is now widespread over the entire state, and a notable decentralization of cattle markets has resulted.

Mining. Petroleum is not the whole story of mining in Texas but it is certainly most of it. The fabulous oil wealth of some Texans is a vital part of the state's legend. More than 90% of the total value of the state's mineral production is from mineral fuels. Texas has led the nation in their production for many years, contributing a third of domestic crude oil and an even greater percentage of natural gas. Its natural gas liquids are also valuable.

The petroleum industry in Texas began to come of age at the turn of the century. The discovery of the great Spindletop field near Beaumont in 1901 was followed by discoveries of other fields, large and small, in almost every area of the state. Finally, the opening of the giant east Texas field in the early 1930's produced such a flood of oil that the Texas legislature eventually adopted a policy of limiting production to protect the market and to conserve the state's most valuable natural resource.

Texas is one of the leading states in the production of sulfur, helium, salt, and cement. Other commercially important nonmetallic minerals are gypsum, clays, stone, and sand and gravel. Of the metals, iron ore, uranium, and magnesium are produced in significant amounts.

Manufacturing. Texas ranks among the leading ten states in manufacturing. Much of its industrial output is in bulk form from the processing of natural resources and agricultural products, but there is increasing production of consumer goods as well. Texas' manufactures are richly varied. The oil refining and petrochemical industries lead the state in value added by manufacture. Most refineries and petrochemical plants are concentrated along the Gulf coast in the Houston, Beaumont–Port Arthur, and Corpus Christi areas. Another major industry is the manufacture of transportation equipment, of which aircraft and aerospace equipment are the principal products, but automobile assembly, ship and boat building, and the production of mobile homes and trailers are also important.

The state's giant food processing industry features grain milling, meat packing, and fruit, vegetable, poultry, and dairy processing. Machinery manufacturing is another major activity. Nonelectrical machinery includes oil field, construction, and agricultural equipment, while electronic and electrical goods include communications equipment, air conditioners, and other appliances. The primary metals industry turns out large quantities of steel and iron, aluminum, and magnesium. Textile and clothing manufactures, the processing of timber, and the making of stone, clay, and glass products, also contribute significantly to the economy.

Manufacturing began in Texas primarily as a means of developing the raw products of the land. Grist mills, cotton gins, ice plants, and tanneries were typical early manufacturing estab-

TEXAS HIGHWAY DEPARTMENT

GRAPEFRUIT are loaded in the lower Rio Grande valley, where fruit-raising is a principal enterprise.

lishments. Economic growth broadened the range and increased the size of Texas' enterprises, but industrialization was still not very far advanced at the beginning of World War II. The war and the technological changes that followed it greatly accelerated industrial development.

Power. Almost all electric power is generated at steam plants, most of which use natural gas for fuel. Rivers in Texas lack sufficient momentum to generate much hydroelectric power and the state's hydroelectric potential is relatively low.

Labor Force. The civilian labor force in Texas totaled about 4.5 million persons by the early 1970's. The work force is dominated by professional, managerial, and clerical employees, whereas the number of operators, craftsmen, laborers and other industrial workers is relatively small. Negroes and Mexican-Americans are grossly underrepresented in the higher paying and higher status occupations, with almost a third of the males in these minority groups being employed as laborers. In the 1960's, Negro and Mexican-American unemployment rates were generally more than twice as high as the rates of the state as a whole.

Wholesale and retail trade, the largest category of employment, accounts for almost one fourth of all jobs. Manufacturing, the next largest category, employs about 20% of the labor force. Employment in personal services and government is also high. Agriculture, construction, and public utilities each employ from 5% to 10% of the work force.

Most of the major labor unions have locals in Texas. Union strength is concentrated in the Gulf coast area around Houston, Beaumont, and Corpus Christi, and in the Dallas–Fort Worth area. However, the state's rural heritage and its high proportion of hard-to-organize white-collar workers make unionization difficult. State policy regulating labor-management relations has generally had an anti-union cast.

Tourism. Although Texas boasts a superior highway system, a long coastline, numerous outdoor recreational facilities, and proximity to the attractions of Mexico, it was slow to promote tourism. In the mid-1960's the state began to make serious efforts to attract visitors. A state tourist development agency was created and funded by the legislature, convention facilities in Texas cities were upgraded, the state park system was expanded, and historical sites were developed. By the early 1970's, Texas had more than 20 million visitors annually, and tourism accounted for as many jobs or as much income as some of the major industries.

Transportation. Because of the great size of the state, Texans are especially dependent on

BERT BRANDT

OIL WORKERS operating a rig offshore in the Gulf of Mexico, where the rich deposits attract exploration and drilling.

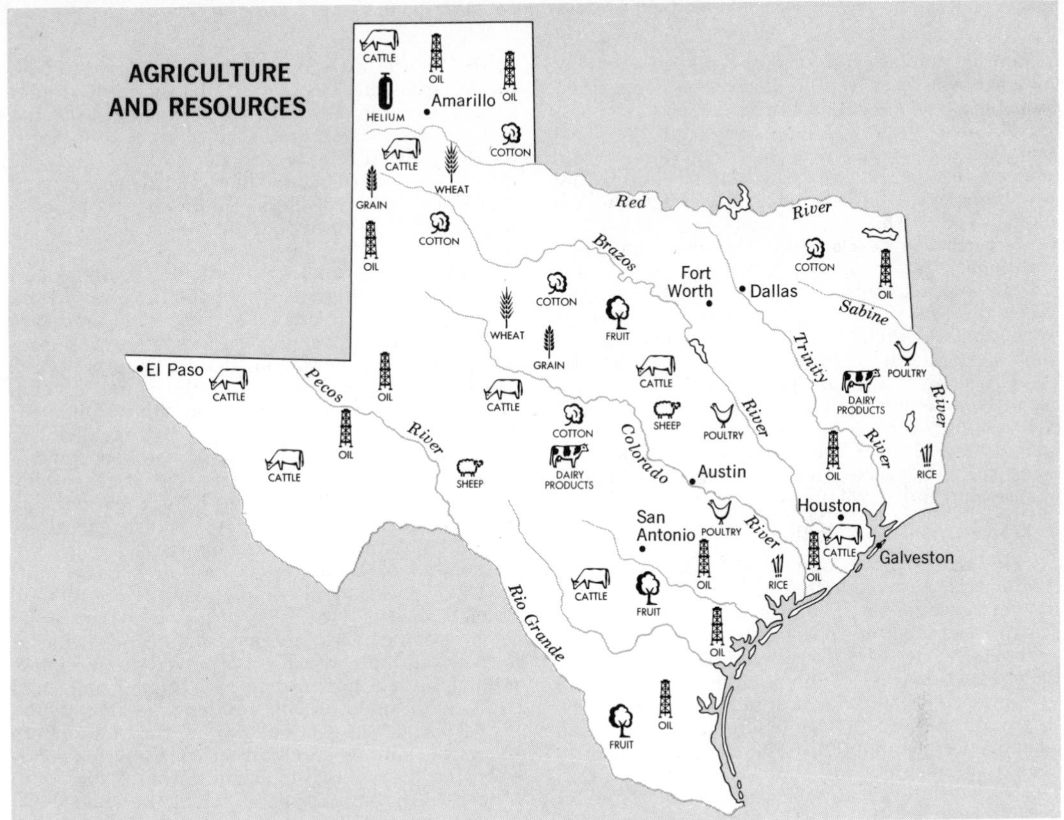

their transportation facilities. All the major forms of transportation play vital roles in the Texas economy.

Waterborne shipping has been important since the early days, bringing immigrants to the state and providing outlets to national and international markets for cotton and, later, for other agricultural and mineral products. The state's seaports are well distributed along the coast and provide deepwater harbor for large numbers of oceangoing vessels. Several of the ports are connected to the Gulf by ship channels. Houston, the busiest port, is one of the nation's top four ports in total tonnage moved each year. Other major ports are Beaumont–Port Arthur, Galveston–Texas City, Corpus Christi, and Brownsville. Major exports are petroleum, chemical products, sulfur, fertilizer, grain sorghums, rice, and wheat. Leading incoming cargoes are crude oil, iron and aluminum ore, iron products, and nonferrous metals.

Rivers are not used for shipping as they were in the first half of the 19th century, but there is heavy inland marine traffic on the Intracoastal Waterway that extends along the entire Texas coastline.

Major rail centers include Houston, Dallas, Fort Worth, and Amarillo. Texas has about 14,000 miles (20,900 km) of main-line track. The first railroad in Texas was built in 1853, but extensive rail development was postponed by the Civil War. Railroad building, aided by state subsidies, picked up quickly after the war, and, for the next 50 years, the inland movement of people and goods was handled largely by the railroads. The coming of highways and motor vehicles brought stiff competition for passengers and freight. The railroads eventually abandoned the fight for passengers, and by the early 1970's passenger trains had almost disappeared from Texas tracks. However, the railroads were able to strengthen their position as movers of freight.

The state's highway system, the largest in the nation, is one of its greatest assets. The construction of public roads was left to county governments until the early 1920's, and progress tended to be spasmodic. The Texas highway department was created in 1917 to take advantage of federal grants-in-aid for highways, and by the late 1930's the state had assumed exclusive responsibility for highways. Bolstered by revenues from motor fuel taxes and substantial federal grants, and strongly supported by the legislature, the highway department built an outstanding system, contributing more than 65,000 miles (104,600 km) to the state's network.

The growing concentration of automobiles in the large cities has necessitated greater and greater spending for urban freeways, and the end is not in sight. Highway safety and the air pollution produced by the automobiles are serious and growing problems.

Texans rely heavily on commercial air travel. The largest cities are served by a number of the nation's scheduled airlines and by several foreign airlines. The Dallas–Forth Worth area is one of the nation's major centers of air traffic, and Houston, with its large modern airport, is becoming another leading center. San Antonio is the chief point of departure for international travelers. The great distances to be traveled and the generally good flying weather encourage the use of private planes for business and pleasure.

Military aviation in the United States was launched at Fort Sam Houston in San Antonio in 1910, and Texas figured prominently in its development. Kelly Field at San Antonio was a major training center for World War I pilots.

Favorable climate and terrain—and the political influence of Texas representatives in Congress—contributed to the establishment of a great number of military air bases in Texas during World War II. After the war some of these were retained as permanent installations and other new bases were built, so that the state now has about 15 U. S. Air Force bases.

Research and Development. The older and more traditional sectors of the Texas economy have not always recognized the need for research. When they have done so, they have preferred to leave the research to educational institutions. Most agricultural research has been carried on by Texas A&M, Texas Tech, and other state-supported universities. But petroleum and chemical firms have long maintained their own laboratories. Newer industries, such as aircraft, aerospace, and electronics, have invested heavily in research and development.

4. Government and Politics

The Texas constitution, the fifth in the history of the state, was adopted in 1876, succeeding the constitutions of 1845, 1861, 1866, and 1869. The present charter reflects the conservative reaction to what were considered the excesses of Reconstruction. Its highly detailed and restrictive character had made frequent revision necessary, and almost 200 amendments have been passed since its adoption. The same resistance to change permeates the state government itself. Texas legislators, administrators, and judges seldom lead reform efforts, and, in some ways, the political and governmental processes of the state are the least progressive aspect of Texas society.

Structure of Government. The head of the executive branch is nominally the governor. However, his formal position as chief executive is largely without meaning. The heads of several important state agencies are themselves directly elected and owe little or nothing to the governor. In addition, there are a large number of administrative agencies headed by policy-making boards and commissions and, while most of the board members are appointed by the governor, they serve staggered terms, hire and fire the agencies' administrative personnel, and cannot be removed from office by the governor. With rare exceptions, he is not permitted to dismiss or issue orders to any administrative personnel outside his own staff. Almost all of his appointments require Senate confirmation by a two-thirds vote.

As a result of these limitations on the governor's power, administration in Texas is fragmented and decentralized, and this undoubtedly has retarded the adoption of progressive policies on personnel and administrative procedures. The governor's influence is heavily dependent on his political strength, his ability to lead public opinion, and his effectiveness as a leader of the legislature, a capacity in which he is aided by strong veto powers.

The bicameral state legislature meets biennially, in odd-numbered years, starting the second Tuesday in January for a maximum of 140 days, although special sessions may be called by the governor. The lieutenant governor, the Senate's presiding officer, is chosen by the voters on a statewide basis. The speaker of the House of Representatives is elected by the members. Both officers have great power and influence in the legislative process. Until reapportionment of the legislature was ordered in the mid-1960's, urban areas in Texas were badly under-represented. Historically, the Republican party has had scant representation, and consequently legislative decision making is marked by factional rather than partisan conflict. Partly because it retains an effective role in the budgetary process, the Texas legislature has an unusual degree of influence in state affairs.

Texas has a dual court system, criminal and civil, in the higher appellate levels. Minor criminal and civil cases are first tried in justice of the peace or county courts. More serious cases are first heard in district courts. Civil cases go on appeal to one of the courts of civil appeals and, if appropriate, to the 9-member supreme court. Criminal cases, if appealed, are heard by the 5-member court of criminal appeals, which has final jurisdiction in the state system. Judges are formally chosen by direct election, but the governor's power to fill vacancies by initial appointment is quite important.

Political Divisions. Texas has three basic units of local government—municipality, county, and special district. Municipalities of more than 5,000 people may adopt a home-rule charter and choose their own form of government. Those municipalities not opting for home rule and those with under 5,000 residents must be governed under the general laws of the state. Both home-rule and general-law cities show a preference for the council-manager form of city government. In general, the status of the almost 900 Texas municipalities is that of semi-independent governmental corporations limited by the constitution and the general laws of the state but possessing considerable latitude in the management of affairs within their jurisdiction.

The 254 Texas counties, in contrast, legally are administrative subdivisions of the state, created to carry out certain state policies and limited to activities authorized by state law, such as law enforcement and the administration of minor cases of justice. Some of these activities are conducted on a countywide basis, while others are confined to unincorporated areas by informal agreements with city governments. Each county is divided into 4 precincts and is governed by a commissioners court composed of the county judge, elected at large, and four commissioners, one elected from each precinct. The state defines most county roles and powers, but leaves the administration, including the selection of personnel and the overseeing of their performance, to local voters. Consequently, the system is often inefficient.

Within the areas covered by the general purpose municipal and county governments, Texas has more than 2,000 special districts organized for specific purposes, for which they may collect taxes. Some districts are created specifically by

GOVERNMENT HIGHLIGHTS

Electoral Vote—26. **Representation in Congress**—U. S. senators, 2; U. S. representatives, 24. **State Legislature**—Senate, 31 members, 4-year terms; House of Representatives, 150 members, 2-year terms. **Governor**—2-year term; may succeed himself. **Voting Qualifications**—Age, 18; residence in state 1 year, in county 6 months, in district 6 months. **Elections**—General and state, Tuesday after first Monday in November of even years; primary, first Saturday in May.

the legislature and others are created in accordance with general statutory or constitutional provisions. The more than 1,000 independent school districts are by far the most important districts since they provide almost all public education at the primary and secondary levels.

Public Finance. Until the early 1960's Texas held down its spending in order to avoid a state income tax or a general sales tax, relying instead on a variety of other levies. However, revenue needs became so pressing that, after an extremely bitter fight, the legislature enacted a general sales tax law in 1961. Sharply increased expenditure in the 1960's necessitated raising the sales tax rate to 3¼%.

Three categories of expenditure account for some 85% of the state's spending. Education needs claim as much as 45% of the budget, highways account for about 25%, and welfare programs more than 15%. The general sales tax and taxes on the sale of motor fuels, tobacco, and alcoholic beverages provide more than a third of all state revenues. Other important sources of revenue include federal grants-in-aid; severance and production taxes on oil, gas, sulfur, and cement; motor vehicle registration fees; and taxes on corporate franchises, personal and real property, insurance companies and utilities, and inheritances. Non-tax sources such as royalties, land sales, and rentals are also significant.

Social Services. When the states of the Union are ranked on the basis of the per capita payments made under the major welfare programs, Texas consistently falls in the lower half, and often it falls in the lowest quarter. A pervasive skepticism among Texas voters concerning the merits of welfare programs operates to limit the financial support they are willing to give. Texas also faces problems in the provision of health services. Mental hospitals and special schools are overcrowded, and community mental health centers are not sufficiently numerous. Other health services are usually in the hands of local authorities, and the health care provided is generally below the needs of the community, especially its poorer citizens.

The state's correctional system stands out in sharp contrast. So great are the improvements made since World War II that some observers rate the Texas prisons among the best in the nation. Great stress is put on training and rehabilitation.

State Politics. Texas politics since World War II has been shaped by a wracking factionalism between liberals and conservatives in the Democratic party and the rise of the Republican party to a competitive position in presidential elections and some state and local contests. In the factional battles within the Democratic party, the conservatives usually have prevailed, although liberals have often had a sizable minority in the state legislature.

The Republican revival in Texas began when conservative Democrats, dissatisfied with the liberal stance of the national Democratic party and its presidential nominees, defected to the Republican party in presidential elections. Such support enabled Dwight D. Eisenhower to carry Texas twice. Richard Nixon lost narrowly in 1960 and 1968 but won Texas easily in 1972. Barry Goldwater, the defeated Republican nominee in 1964, did as well in Texas against Lyndon Johnson, a Texan, as he did in the nation.

The organization, status, and support gained

JOSEF MUENCH

Texas state capitol at Austin

in presidential campaigns were used by Republicans in other elections. John G. Tower was elected to Johnson's vacated Senate seat in 1961 and reelected in 1966, becoming the first Republican Senator from Texas since the Reconstruction period. Republican representation in the state legislature remains small, but the party's candidates have gained a few local offices. The Republicans have benefited greatly from the conflict within the Democratic party by effectively appealing to the losing faction.

Such partisan conflict was unknown from 1900 until after World War II. During that period, Texas was a one-party state, with political battles always fought out in the Democratic

GOVERNORS

J. Pinckney Henderson	Democrat	1846–1847
George T. Wood	Democrat	1847–1849
P. Hansborough Bell	Democrat	1849–1853
James W. Henderson (acting)		1853
Elisha M. Pease	Democrat	1853–1857
Hardin R. Runnels	Democrat	1857–1859
Sam Houston	Independent and Unionist	1859–1861
Edward Clark (acting)	Democrat	1861
Francis R. Lubbock	Democrat	1861–1863
Pendleton Murrah	Democrat	1863–1865
Interregnum		1865
Andrew J. Hamilton (appointed)	Conservative	1865–1866
James W. Throckmorton	Conservative	1866–1867
Elisha M. Pease (appointed)	Republican	1867–1869
Interregnaum		1869–1870
Edmund J. Davis	Republican	1870–1874
Richard Coke	Democrat	1874–1876
Richard B. Hubbard	Democrat	1876–1879
Oran M. Roberts	Democrat	1879–1883
John Ireland	Democrat	1883–1887
Lawrence S. Ross	Democrat	1887–1891
James S. Hogg	Democrat	1891–1895
Charles A. Culberson	Democrat	1895–1899
Joseph D. Sayers	Democrat	1899–1903
S. W. T. Lanham	Democrat	1903–1907
Thomas M. Campbell	Democrat	1907–1911
Oscar B. Colquitt	Democrat	1911–1915
James E. Ferguson	Democrat	1915–1917
William P. Hobby	Democrat	1917–1921
Pat M. Neff	Democrat	1921–1925
Miriam A. Ferguson	Democrat	1925–1927
Dan Moody	Democrat	1927–1931
Ross Sterling	Democrat	1931–1933
Miriam A. Ferguson	Democrat	1933–1935
James V. Allred	Democrat	1935–1939
W. Lee O'Daniel	Democrat	1939–1941
Coke R. Stevenson	Democrat	1941–1947
Beauford H. Jester	Democrat	1947–1949
Allan Shivers	Democrat	1949–1957
Price Daniel	Democrat	1957–1963
John B. Connally	Democrat	1963–1969
Preston Smith	Democrat	1969–1973
Dolph Briscoe	Democrat	1973–

primary elections. After Reconstruction the Republicans had seen their officials swept from office and their base of support narrowed principally to Negroes, and no Republican was elected governor of Texas after 1874. Some competition had been offered in the 1890's by the People's (Populist) party, which originated in Texas.

The conservative Democratic grip on state politics in the 20th century was strengthened by two controversial electoral devices. Until 1944 when the "white primary" was finally outlawed by federal courts, Negroes were barred from the Democratic primary, where for half a century the only real contest took place. A restrictive approach to suffrage and voter qualification also prevailed. From 1902 until it was invalidated in 1966 by federal courts, payment of a poll tax was a prerequisite to voting. Furthermore, the poll tax had to be paid before February 1 of the election year—long before campaigns began to generate voter interest. A very low voter turnout, particularly among minority groups and lower-class Anglos, was the result. With the end of these practices and with increased party competition, there has been a slow but steady gain in voter participation.

5. Education and Culture

Education in Texas is characterized at all levels by a reliance on public rather than private institutions. While the system is quite sound in many respects, it has rarely achieved distinction and has neglected the needs of the state's Negro and Mexican-American minorities for more than a century. Rising concern for the shortcomings of education in Texas led in the 1960's to efforts to reform and revitalize it. The results were mixed. Spending for education was increased, there were some administrative reforms, and some significant innovations were introduced, such as a bilingual education program for young Mexican-American pupils. Generally, however, the movement to upgrade education failed to effect a major transformation.

Elementary and Secondary Education. Education at the elementary and secondary level is almost entirely the responsibility of the more than 1,000 local public school districts, although there is a leavening of private schools. The compulsory school attendance law, in effect since 1915, calls for 12 years of free schooling for each child, but it is frequently violated. The result is a distressingly high dropout rate, particularly among members of minority groups. The state treasury provides about half the funds for public education and the local districts supply most of the remainder. The federal government's share has been increasing. The state defines curricula and educational policy. The local districts concentrate on personnel, facilities, and day-to-day administration.

The Gilmer-Aiken Law, enacted by the legislature in 1949, established the Minimum Foundation School Program to ensure the maintenance of minimum standards in the educational program of each local district. Wealthier districts must pay their own way, but the poorer ones are allocated additional state funds on the basis of an economic index. Another important set of changes in state policy was made in the World War I period, when educational financing was improved, free textbooks authorized, and compulsory attendance inaugurated.

Much of the state's 20th century legislation was aimed at overcoming the ills visited upon the public school system in the 1870's and 1880's. The state voted to establish a uniform school system in 1854, but the most farsighted and progressive steps were taken during Reconstruction, including compulsory attendance and state financial aid. In the 1870's conservative Democrats, determined to undo the work of Reconstruction, dismantled much of the educational program that had been developed.

The policy of segregating blacks in the schools was written into the state constitution of 1876, and with few exceptions the education for blacks has proved markedly inferior to the education available to Anglos. Mexican-Americans have also suffered from neglect and discrimination in the public schools. While the worst forms of racial and ethnic discrimination in the educational system were reduced in the 1950's and 1960's, Negroes and Mexican-Americans still receive neither the quantity nor the quality of education available to Anglos.

Higher Education. Texans' strong commitment to higher education is evident in the large number of colleges and universities in the state. There were about 120 in 1970, half of which were senior colleges and universities. The great number of institutions, their geographic dispersion and relatively low admission standards, compounded with the very low tuition rates of the public institutions, have made higher education available to a very large part of the population.

The stress on quantity has had an adverse effect on quality, but there are several institutions whose programs have earned recognition. Of the public universities, the University of Texas System with its main campus at Austin is preeminent for reasons relating to its size, the scope of its programs, and the quality of its faculty and students. Texas A&M University at College Station has traditionally emphasized engineering and scientific studies, and the University of Houston typifies the modern urban university, with its commuting student body, diversity, and great size. The state supports more than a dozen other universities and colleges, including Texas Tech University in Lubbock and North Texas State University in Denton.

Some of the senior institutions are grouped for administrative purposes into one of three major systems: the University of Texas System, the Texas A&M System, and the Senior College System. Each system is headed by a board of regents appointed by the governor. The remaining senior institutions have their own similarly appointed governing boards. Most of the junior colleges are organized as independent districts, with locally chosen policy-making boards. The state's technical institutes were largely developed in the late 1960's.

The Coordinating Board of the Texas College and University System was created in 1965 in an effort to solve the problem of administrative fragmentation. Unfortunately, the board was not given very ample powers, and consequently its effectiveness has been limited. Inadequate financing is another long-standing problem. The most intractable problem of all has been the unwillingness of many administrators, regents, and state officials to promote and defend academic freedom for faculty and students.

The state's more than 30 private institutions offer an interesting diversity. Rice University at

THE KALITA HUMPHREYS THEATER in Dallas is one of the state's modern arts centers.

SHEL HERSHORN FROM BLACK STAR

Houston, with a small, select student body, has emphasized science and engineering. Southern Methodist University in Dallas has a much larger student body and offers a wider range of undergraduate and graduate programs. Austin College in Sherman stresses the liberal arts tradition.

The state's first colleges, established before the Civil War, were all privately supported. Even when the state began to create its own institutions, the private sector remained a fully equal partner in higher education. There was a slow shift toward public education before World War II, but it was in the postwar period that private institutions clearly began to be eclipsed. The demand for low-cost higher education was so great that many new state colleges and universities had to be created to relieve the overcrowding in existing institutions.

Scientific and Historical Research. The highly regarded Texas Medical Center at Houston is a complex of hospitals, medical schools, and research institutes. The U. S. Army and Air Force training, treatment, and research centers in the San Antonio area have won recognition. The Southwest Center for Advanced Studies, in the Dallas area, originally planned as a scientific research institute, has become the nucleus of a new University of Texas at Dallas. NASA's Manned Spacecraft Center near Houston has given a major boost to science and technology in the area. The Lunar Scientific Institute was founded nearby in 1968. The Southwest Research Center in San Antonio houses three important research organizations.

The study of Texas history is kept alive by the Texas State Historical Association, which

FAMOUS RESIDENTS OF TEXAS

Adams, Andy (1859–1935), cowboy and writer, known for *Log of a Cowboy*.

Austin, Stephen F. (1793–1836), known as the Father of Texas; *empresario* and leader in Texas struggle for independence.

Biggers, John (1924–), Negro painter and sculptor.

Borden, Gail (1801–1874), colonial surveyor, publisher, and pioneer in American dairy industry.

Carter, Amon G. (1879–1955), publisher of Fort Worth *Star-Telegram*, civic leader, and philanthropist.

Clark, Tom C. (1899–) U. S. attorney-general, 1945–1949; U. S. Supreme Court justice, 1949–1967.

Cliburn, Van (1934–) concert pianist, who won 1958 International Tchaikovsky Piano Competition in Moscow.

Connally, John B. (1917–) popular governor, 1963–1969.

Connally, Thomas T. (1877–1963), U. S. representative; U. S. senator, 1929–1953.

Cooley, Denton (1920–), medical researcher and pioneer in open-heart surgery.

Davis, Edmund J. (1827–1883), Reconstruction governor and influential Texas Republican.

De Bakey, Michael E. (1908–), surgeon, heart specialist, and medical researcher and administrator.

Dobie, J. Frank (1888–1964), writer, educator, folklorist, and Texas man of letters.

Eisenhower, Dwight D. (1890–1969), 34th president of the United States.

Ferguson, James E. (1871–1944), governor of Texas and controversial political leader.

Ferguson, Miriam A. (1875–1961), first and only woman governor of Texas, 1925–1927; wife of James E. Ferguson.

Garner, John Nance (1868–1967), vice-president of the United States, 1933–1941; speaker of the U. S. House of Representatives, 1931–1933.

Gonzalez, Henry B. (1916–), Mexican-American political leader; U. S. representative.

Hobby, Oveta Culp (1905–), newspaper publisher and first U. S. secretary of health, education, and welfare.

Hogg, James S. (1851–1906), reform governor, 1891–1895; lawyer and state attorney general.

House, Edward M. (1858–1938), known as Colonel House; Texas political leader, diplomat, and close friend and adviser to President Woodrow Wilson.

Houston, Sam (1793–1863), hero of the battle of San Jacinto; first president of the Republic of Texas; U. S. senator; governor of Texas.

Hunt, H. L. (1889–), petroleum executive, known for his crusades for conservatism.

Johnson, Jack (1878–1946), heavyweight boxing champion.

Johnson, Lyndon B. (1908–1973), 36th president of the United States; U. S. vice-president, 1961–1963.

Jones, Jesse H. (1874–1956), publisher, financier, and public official; U. S. secretary of commerce, 1940–1945.

Lamar, Mirabeau B. (1798–1859), president of the Republic of Texas; educator, who helped found Texas public education system.

Lea, Tom (1907–), painter, illustrator, and novelist.

Ledbetter, Huddie (1888?–1949), known as Leadbelly; Negro folksinger discovered in a Texas prison.

Lomax, John A. (1867–1948), early student of folk music, author of *Cowboy Songs and Other Frontier Ballads*, 1910.

Martin, Mary (1913–), popular singer and actress.

Ney, Elisabet (1883–1907), German-born sculptress, who helped bring fine arts to Texas.

Nimitz, Chester W. (1885–1966), U. S. naval officer; commander-in-chief of the Pacific Fleet, World War II.

Owens, William A. (1905–), author, whose works include *This Stubborn Soil*, 1966.

Parker, Quanah (1845?–1911), half-breed Comanche warrior and chief.

Porter, Katherine Anne (1890–), writer, whose *Collected Stories* won the Pulitzer Prize, 1966.

Rayburn, Samuel T. (1882–1961), speaker of the U. S. House of Representatives from 1940 to 1961, except for two terms.

Shivers, Allan (1907–), governor of Texas for three consecutive terms, business leader.

Travis, William B. (1809–1836), joint commander, with James Bowie, of Texas force at the Alamo.

Umlauf, Charles (1911–), artist and sculptor.

Webb, Walter Prescott (1888–1963), historian and writer, whose works deal extensively with Texas.

publishes the *Texas Historical Quarterly,* and by regional and county historical associations.

Libraries. Much of the library service available to Texans is provided by local public libraries. Some are financed and administered by the cities, some by county governments, and a few are privately supported. Many units were established in the 1960's, so that by the end of the decade there were more than 350 local public libraries, many of them in rural counties previously without library service. Nevertheless, many communities are still without libraries, and many of those in existence are quite rudimentary. Even in the larger cities such as Houston and Dallas the library system is overloaded and insufficiently financed. The State Library and Historical Commission operates the State Library in Austin.

There are, in addition, about 150 libraries in the state's junior and senior colleges. The Mirabeau B. Lamar Library of the University of Texas at Austin is the state's largest library.

Museums. Given the legendary pride of most Texans in their state, it is not surprising that many of the museums are devoted to Texas and western themes. The Institute for Texan Cultures in San Antonio effectively illustrates the racial and ethnic contributions to the development of Texas. The Texas Memorial Museum in Austin has collections on natural and cultural history. Both of these museums are administered by the University of Texas System. The two major shrines of Texas history also have museums. The Alamo Museum in San Antonio is managed by the Daughters of the Republic of Texas. The San Jacinto Museum is on the battlefield of that name near Houston. Texas history is also the focus of the Panhandle-Plains Historical Museum in Canyon and the Daughters of the Republic of Texas Museum on the state capitol grounds in Austin.

The Museum of Natural Science in Houston and the Museum of Natural History in Dallas are excellent in their fields. These cities also have art museums with noteworthy general collections. The Amon Carter Museum of Western Art in Fort Worth and the holdings of the Contemporary Arts Association in Houston feature more specialized material.

Music and Theater. The Houston Symphony Orchestra is the best known of Texas' more than 20 orchestras. Dallas and San Antonio also have major orchestras. The theater, like other arts, in Texas has flourished best in Houston and Dallas. Houston's rise to preeminence in the fine arts was underscored by the completion in the late 1960's of the Jesse H. Jones Center for the Performing Arts, an outstanding complex of theaters and halls. Houston's Alley Theater has earned a national reputation for the quality of its productions. The state's four largest cities have opera companies.

Architecture. While Texas has not developed a distinctive architectural style, geography and history have sometimes combined to produce interesting designs. Semiarid conditions and the Spanish-Mexican heritage have influenced styles in south and far west Texas, while the Southern legacy has shaped design in east Texas and the upper Gulf coast.

Communications. The vast area of Texas makes the mass media especially important to its communications system. The same factor, however, has made it difficult for any single publishing or broadcasting enterprise to develop a statewide following. Instead, there tend to be overlapping spheres of influence, each based in one of the state's major population centers.

In 1970 there were about 100 daily newspapers and about 550 weeklies. The Houston *Chronicle* has the largest circulation in the state. The state's first newspaper began publication at Nacogdoches in 1813 during the last years of Spanish domination. In the 50 years after statehood, the newspaper industry entered a dynamic and exciting period. Although there has been less room for personal journalism as the industry matured, many of the better newspapers have a history of personal or family commitment.

Radio broadcasting began in Texas in 1920. There are now more than 400 AM and FM stations in operation. Texas has more than 70 television stations.

6. Recreation

Texas is rich in opportunities for sportsmen and sightseers. Its recreational resources can accommodate almost the entire spectrum of outdoor sports. Boating, swimming, and fishing are especially popular along the 600-mile (965-km) Gulf coast and on the many inland lakes. Hunting is a major pastime. For fans of professional sports, there are major league baseball, football, and basketball teams in Dallas and Houston. The Astrodome, Houston's domed stadium, draws millions each year for sports and entertainment.

Its highly varied climate and topography make Texas exciting for naturalists as well as tourists, and the restored forts and Spanish missions that dot the state are a delight for students of history. In addition, several of the larger cities have amusement centers built around historical or contemporary themes.

National Areas. The terms of the state's annexation by the Union allowed Texas to retain title to all of its public lands. As a result, all federally administered lands had to be acquired by purchase or donation.

Both of the state's national parks are in the Trans-Pecos region. Big Bend National Park covers about 1,100 square miles (2,850 sq km) along the great bend of the Rio Grande. It combines the stark but delicate beauty of the desert with the rugged scenery of the Chisos Mountains. Guadalupe Mountains National Park, authorized in 1966, features Guadalupe Peak, which, at 8,751 feet (2,667 meters), is the highest point in Texas. Establishment of a national park in the heavily forested Big Thicket area of southeast Texas is under consideration.

A different setting is provided by Padre Island National Seashore. Its 80 miles (129 km) of beaches and dunes along the Gulf coast can be enjoyed year round. Armistad and Sanford National Recreation Areas have large reservoirs.

Texas' four national forests—Angelina, Davy Crockett, Sabine, and Sam Houston—cover about 940 square miles (2,435 sq km) in east Texas. The Forest Service also administers the Panhandle National Grasslands.

Fort Davis, a careful restoration of an important military post in west Texas established in 1854, and San José Mission at San Antonio, an important example of Spanish mission architecture, are national historic sites. The mission is administered by the Roman Catholic Church and the state. Alibates Flint Quarries in the Panhandle, a major source of flint for Indians for thousands of years, is a national monument. The

National Aransas Wildlife Refuge, a marshy reserve along the Gulf of Mexico, is the winter home for many wildfowl species.

State Areas. Texas lagged behind some states in providing recreational services until the 1960's, when it began expanding its programs. It now administers a growing number of recreational and scenic parks and historical sites and monuments. The state parks and historical sites are administered by the Texas Parks and Wildlife Department. The Texas Tourist Development Agency publicizes existing facilities and encourages the development of others.

The state's more than 40 parks are widely distributed and have a great variety of settings, including desert sand dunes at Monahans Sandhills Park, beaches at Goose Island and Velasco parks, deep canyons at Palo Duro Canyon Park, bayou country at Caddo Lake Park, and a large cave at Longhorn Cavern Park. Among the notable historical sites are the battleship U.S.S. *Texas* and San Jacinto Battleground along the Houston Ship Channel and Lyndon B. Johnson Park at Stonewall near the LBJ Ranch.

An important, although sometimes uncounted, recreational asset to the recreation system are the hundreds of roadside parks provided by the state highway department. All beaches in Texas are state property and are open to the public.

Other Points of Interest. Tourists are drawn by the mild winter climates to Texas' coastal and southern areas, notably Galveston, Corpus Christi, and the lower Rio Grande Valley. The presidency of Lyndon Johnson stirred tourist interest in the Hill Country north and west of San Antonio. The city itself is popular with tourists, featuring such sites as the Spanish Governor's Palace, several interesting missions, and the Alamo, the shrine of Texas freedom. The home of Sam Houston in Huntsville and the birthplace of Dwight D. Eisenhower in Denison are preserved as historical houses. Six Flags over Texas, situated midway between Dallas and Fort Worth, and Astroworld in Houston are popular amusement centers.

Annual Events. There is hardly a city in Texas without its annual fair, livestock show, or rodeo. Houston, Fort Worth, and San Antonio each has major events of this kind. The State Fair of Texas is held in Dallas in October. One of the most exciting rodeos is the Texas Prison Rodeo staged by inmates at Huntsville on successive weekends in the fall.

Many cities offer festivals that reflect aspects of their economy or local history. Residents of the Mexican cities across the Rio Grande join freely in Charro Days in Brownsville and the Washington's Birthday Celebration in Laredo. The Sun Carnival in El Paso and the Cotton Carnival in Dallas are climaxed by the Sun Bowl and Cotton Bowl football games. The Fiesta de San Antonio, held in San Antonio in the spring, and Buccaneer Days, in Corpus Christi in May, are other special celebrations.

7. History

Very little is known of prehistoric Texas, although the existence of ancient peoples in the area about 10,000 B.C. is firmly documented. In 5,000 B.C. another distinctive culture emerged, possibly derived from later and racially distinct arrivals on the continent. Much later, the agricultural revolution and modest technological advances, such as the bow and arrow, ushered in a

BERT BRANDT

RODEOS feature such events as calf-roping. After being secured, the animal is branded.

Neo–American Indian culture. In the Texas Panhandle and the Trans-Pecos there are remains of Pueblo dwellings similar to those found in New Mexico. The Mississippi Mound Builders penetrated east Texas.

Indians of Texas. When the Europeans first ventured into the area, Texas was occupied by Indians of four different cultures. The Caddo tribes in east Texas were the most highly developed. They lived in permanent wooden buildings in sizable villages and had a defined social and political structure. The Coahuitecan and Karankawa in the coastal areas and south Texas were the most primitive Indians, with little in the way of agriculture or social organization.

The nomadic Plains Indians were represented by the Tonkawa in central Texas, the Lipan Apache to the northwest, and, later, by the Comanche, Kiowa, and Kiowa Apache after their arrival in west Texas about 1700. The Wichita, usually considered Plains Indians, arrived at about the same time in north Texas and the Red River Valley. In far west Texas, peripheral Pueblo tribes eked out a precarious existence for a time before disappearing.

Exploration and Early Settlement. The first Europeans to explore Texas were Spaniards. Alonso de Pineda skirted the Gulf coast from Florida to Mexico in 1519, claiming the land for Spain. The first knowledge of the interior was gained from Álvar Núñez Cabeza de Vaca's experiences after he was shipwrecked on the coast in 1528 and forced to make his way across Texas to western Mexico. In the early 1540's, Francisco Vásquez de Coronado wandered into west Texas, and Hernando de Soto's party penetrated east and central Texas.

Discouraging reports from the Coronado and de Soto expeditions stifled interest in Texas for half a century. After 1598 far west Texas felt the side effects of Spain's colonization of northern New Mexico. Not until René-Robert Cavelier, Sieur de La Salle, claimed the Texas area for France in 1682 and established Fort St. Louis on Matagorda Bay in 1685 were the Spanish moved to take possession of their Texas province.

Misfortune and hostile Indians ended the French invasion, but the Spanish were alarmed by the incursion and in 1690 established two missions, later abandoned, among the Caddo in east Texas. In time the fear of French encroachment again stirred the Spanish authorities, and in 1716 they founded a string of five missions across east Texas. In the next 50 years Spain's efforts in Texas waxed and waned, depending on Spanish-French relations.

After the ceding of Louisiana to Spain in 1762, the Spaniards shifted their attention to the coastal and southwestern portions of Texas. But at the end of the 18th century, San Antonio, Goliad, and Nacogdoches were the only permanent Spanish settlements in the state. The Spanish presidio and mission system of colonization simply would not work in most of Texas; the Indians were too hostile and the environment was unsuitable. In 1800, France regained title to Louisiana, and, three years later, Napoleon sold it to the United States. Since no official boundary had ever been set between the Spanish and French territories, the Americans held a shadowy claim to Texas that was not relinquished until the Florida Purchase Treaty of 1819.

Spain's empire, undermined by internal unrest, was in decline. The revolt against Spain led by Father Miguel Hidalgo y Costilla in 1810 spread into Texas, and, although it was soon suppressed, a decade of disturbance followed, nourished by several filibustering expeditions headed by American adventurers convinced that the province could be seized.

Anglo-American Settlement. In its twilight hours the Spanish empire decided to allow orderly colonization of its Texas lands, and in 1821 Moses Austin of Missouri was given a permit to settle 300 families in Texas. After his death, his son, Stephen F. Austin, persuaded the newly independent Mexican government to continue the policy, and in the autumn of 1821 the first colonists began arriving in Texas. Attracted by the generous grants of land, other land agents (called *empresarios*) began colonization efforts. By 1835 they had brought in about 20,000 settlers and 4,000 slaves. Most of the colonists were from the United States, and others arrived from Mexico and Europe. The flood of Anglo-American immigrants, the persistent efforts by the United States to purchase Texas, and the abortive Fredonia Rebellion of 1827 convinced many Mexican authorities that there were American designs on Texas. Efforts by the Mexicans to check immigration were unsuccessful, and new colonists kept coming.

SAN JOSÉ MISSION at San Antonio, founded in 1720, is noted for its baroque architecture.

RALPH KRUBNER FROM BLACK STAR

Independence. The Texas Revolution was brought about by social, religious, economic, and political differences between Mexico and the Anglo-American colonists. Specific conflicts included the collection of customs duties, Mexican attempts to limit the institution of slavery, and violations of the Mexican constitution by the central government under the military dictator Antonio López de Santa Anna.

The formation of a small "war party" by the colonists provoked military retaliation by Mexico. When armed conflict commenced in October 1835, the Texas leaders declared that they were fighting for the preservation of the Mexican Republic and the Mexican constitution of 1824. Texans meanwhile laid siege to the Mexican stronghold of San Antonio and captured it. Santa Anna mobilized a large army and marched into Texas. On March 2, 1836, the insurgents met in convention, issued a declaration of independence, drafted a constitution, and set up a provisional government. At about the same time the advancing Mexican army defeated and massacred a Texas force at Goliad and recaptured San Antonio, killing all the defenders of the Alamo by March 6 (See ALAMO).

Santa Anna then moved his army east in pursuit of the fleeing and demoralized remnants of the Texas army. The two forces met on April 21 at San Jacinto near present-day Houston, where the Texans won a decisive victory. The independence of Texas became an established fact after the victory, but the central Mexican government refused to recognize the new Republic of Texas. A permanent government, with Sam Houston as president, was inaugurated in October.

Statehood. The fledgling republic faced many problems, including internal rivalries, an unstable currency, and an empty treasury, and it was with great relief that annexation by the United States was effected on Dec. 29, 1845. The ensuing war between the United States and Mexico made the Rio Grande an international boundary. However, the war left open the Texas claim to the portion of New Mexico and Colorado east of the Rio Grande. The troublesome issue was finally resolved by the Compromise of 1850, which fixed the state's present western boundary. Texas was paid $10 million for its lost territory.

The period between annexation and the Civil War was one of tremendous population growth. Slowly a social and political system was institutionalized. Land was made available, towns began to spring up, roads were built, schools established, and law and order imposed after a

JOSEF MUENCH

Fort Davis, an army post in west Texas (1854–1891), has been restored. Officers' homes face the parade ground.

fashion. Although immigrants arrived from many states, most were from the deep South, and their cotton-and-slave culture predominated. The western half of the state was tentatively explored and a string of army posts established, but there was much Indian resistance and the western line of settlement moved slowly.

The Civil War. Like the rest of the nation, Texas was gripped by the slavery issue in the late 1850's. Soon the state's extreme proslavery element was in control. Old Sam Houston, twice president of the Republic of Texas and U. S. senator between 1846 and 1859, sided with the Union. Although he managed to win the Texas governorship in 1859, his Unionist sentiments were soon overridden and in early 1861 the secessionists withdrew the state from the Union, joined the Confederacy, and deposed Houston.

Although Texas contributed men and supplies to the Confederate cause, there was little fighting in the state. At the outbreak of the war, federal troops and equipment in Texas were surrendered to the Confederates by sympathetic commanders. Unionists in north Texas and in the German counties of central Texas were persecuted throughout the war, and many were forced to flee the state. Texas troops invaded Arizona and New Mexico but, after a few months, were defeated and forced to retreat. The federal blockade shut most Texas ports, although Union forces were beaten at Galveston and Sabine Pass. Ironically, the Confederates won the war's last battle near Brownsville, almost a month after Robert E. Lee's surrender at Appomattox.

The Post–Civil War Era. After the war Union troops occupied the state. The Reconstruction period in Texas lasted until 1874. Efforts by conservatives to retain control of state government and to hold the newly freed Negroes in a condition of peonage were thwarted by Congress and the military authorities. In 1870, Radical Republican Edmund J. Davis took office as governor and Texas was readmitted to the Union. The dismantling of Reconstruction began when conservative Democrats regained control of the state in 1874. In the late 1880's there began a brief era of reform but, by the end of the 1890's, Negroes had been effectively shut out of Texas politics and racial segregation imposed.

The Indians' resistance to the settlers and their attacks on the western frontier had intensified during the Civil War. In the early 1870's federal troops launched a major campaign of harassment. By 1875, Indian resistance on the High Plains was broken and the few survivors relocated on reservations in the Indian Territory. Far west Texas was secure by 1880 and only a handful of Indians remained in the state. Unsettled areas began to fill rapidly, and, at the end of the 19th century, the frontier had vanished forever.

The post–Civil War era presented tremendous problems of law enforcement. From its earliest days Texas had attracted more than its share of adventurers, criminals, and social misfits. Law enforcement was made difficult by the vast expanses of the state and by conditions on the frontier. The Texas Rangers, first organized under the Republic and well known for their lack of concern for legal niceties, were very active in this period and public order was eventually restored to most areas.

In the rebuilding of the shattered Texas economy after the war, land and cattle were the state's greatest assets. Ranching commenced on an unparalleled scale, and a cowboy culture soon developed and spread. Huge herds of cattle were driven north to Kansas and Nebraska markets. The state subsidized the building of many railroads in an effort to stimulate the economy.

The population kept rising, with a fourfold increase between the end of the Civil War and 1900. Because most of the newcomers were farmers and small farmers were the hardest hit by the unstable economic conditions, a vigorous agrarian protest movement developed. In the 1880's the Farmers' Alliance became the movement's chief vehicle. In 1892 its members helped organize the People's (Populist) party, which soon spread into other states. The Populists were able to elect a number of legislators and local officials and helped effect some significant reforms in state government. Through their attacks on banks, corporations, and the financial community, they infused Texas politics with a strain of agrarian radicalism that still persists.

The Early 20th Century. Texas entered the 20th century with a reasonably sound economy. The cotton market made a strong comeback, and agricultural development of the Rio Grande Valley proceeded rapidly. The large-scale discovery of oil in 1901 and the subsequent oil boom changed the complexion of the economy. The oil industry brought great wealth to a few

HISTORICAL HIGHLIGHTS

1519 Alonso de Pineda explored coast of Gulf of Mexico and claimed Texas area for Spain.
1528 Álvar Núñez Cabeza de Vaca penetrated Texas interior after shipwreck on Texas coast.
1541 Vásquez Francisco de Coronado led expedition across west Texas.
1542 Survivors of de Soto expedition reached central Texas.
1682 Spaniards founded first permanent settlement at Ysleta near present-day El Paso.
1685 La Salle built Fort St. Louis near Matagorda Bay.
1690 First Spanish missions established in east Texas.
1716 Spaniards revived mission settlements.
1718 Mission San Antonio de Valero, later known as Alamo, founded on site of San Antonio.
1813 First Texas newspaper began publication at Nacogdoches.
1821 Texas became part of new nation of Mexico; Stephen F. Austin brought first Anglo-American colonists to Texas under *empresario* system.
1835 Texas Revolution began.
1836 Texas declared independence from Mexico and formed provisional government for Republic of Texas; Alamo fell to Mexicans under Santa Anna; Texans defeat Santa Anna at San Jacinto, April 21.
1837 United States recognized Republic of Texas.
1845 Texas annexed as 28th state of Union, December 29.
1861 Texas seceded from Union to join Confederacy.
1866 First major cattle drive to Kansas opened era of long trail drives.
1870 Texas readmitted to Union.
1876 Present state constitution adopted.
1883 Instruction began at University of Texas at Austin.
1900 Disastrous storm struck Galveston, killing 6,000 persons.
1901 Discovery of Spindletop oilfield launched oil boom.
1910 First U. S. Army airplane flown at Fort Sam Houston.
1915 Compulsory school attendance law passed.
1917 Gov. James E. Ferguson impeached.
1931 East Texas oilfield discovered.
1944 U. S. Supreme Court invalidated state's "white primary" voting law.
1947 Explosion at Texas City Refinery dock killed 460 persons, injured 4,000.
1950 U. S. Supreme Court ended racial segregation in University of Texas Law School.
1953 Texas offshore tidal oil lands restored to state.
1961 Hurricane heavily damaged Texas coast; Houston selected as site for Manned Spacecraft Center.
1963 President John F. Kennedy assassinated in Dallas.
1965 State legislature reapportioned to conform to one-man, one-vote principle.
1966 Federal courts invalidated state law requiring payment of poll tax as prerequisite to voting.
1968 International exposition HemisFair '68 held in San Antonio to mark city's 250th anniversary.
1970 Hurricane devastated Corpus Christi and surrounding area.

Texans and employment to many others. Commerce and industry picked up and its cities grew.

In the decade before World War I, the reforming spirit of the 1890's was rekindled, and the Progressive movement won a number of legislative and political victories. The issue of prohibition was prominent in every campaign from 1908 until 1918, when the state ratified the national prohibition amendment.

Fergusonism, a new force in Texas politics, emerged in 1914 when James E. Ferguson won the governorship by appealing directly to poor farmers. Although his opponents accused him of demagoguery, Ferguson had a constructive first term. During the second term he was charged with misuse of state funds and became embroiled in a vicious dispute with the University of Texas. In 1917 he was impeached by the legislature, removed from the governorship, and barred from holding that office again. For the next 17 years he and his wife, Miriam Ferguson, carried their case at intervals to the voters. She won the governorship in 1924 and again in 1932. Although the Fergusons lost their reforming zeal, they fought and defeated the Ku Klux Klan, which had become a real political and social threat in the early 1920's.

The depression was as traumatic in Texas as in the rest of the nation. Business and industrial activity dropped sharply and the rate of population increase hit a record low. Farmers and ranchers, notoriously slow to adopt proper conservation practices, found that years of soil erosion and severe drought in some areas endangered their economic survival. The progressive leadership of Gov. James V. Allred in the late 1930's helped introduce many New Deal programs.

World War II and Later. World War II brought an economic upturn and a resurgence of conservatism in Texas politics. New Deal reforms were undone or delayed whenever possible, and several statutes were passed to restrict organized labor activity. The University of Texas came under attack for the liberalism of its faculty.

The Texas economy was notably strong and dynamic in the 1950's and 1960's, surviving without difficulty a decline in the oil industry in the mid-1950's. The U. S. Supreme Court ruled against all racial segregation in public schools in 1954, but it was almost 10 years before segregation of public facilities was legally ended in Texas, and *de facto* segregation continues. There has been slow progress in race relations.

On Nov. 22, 1963, Texans saw the assassination of President John F. Kennedy in Dallas. The legislature was forced to reapportion to conform to the one-man, one-vote principle in 1965.

The pace of economic development in Texas has been rapid and steady since 1940. The state's natural resources are well suited for modern industrial technology, and, if certain emergent problems such as strained race relations, pollution, and water shortage can be met, the vigorous development can be expected to continue.

CLIFTON MCCLESKEY
The University of Texas at Austin

Bibliography

American Guide Series, *Texas: A Guide to the Lone Star State,* rev. ed. (New York 1969).
Bainbridge, John, *The Super-Americans* (New York 1961).
Dallas Morning News, *Texas Almanac* (Dallas, biennially).
Douglas, William O., *Farewell to Texas: A Vanishing Wilderness* (New York 1967).
Fehrenbach, T. R., *Lone Star: A History of Texas and the Texans* (New York 1968).
Goodwyn, Frank, *Lone-Star Land* (New York 1955).
Johnson, Elmer H., *Natural Regions of Texas* (Austin 1931).
McCleskey, Clifton, *The Government and Politics of Texas,* 3d ed. (Boston 1961).
Newcomb, W. W., Jr., *The Indians of Texas: From Prehistoric to Modern Times* (Austin 1969).
Olmsted, Frederick Law, *Journey Through Texas* (New York 1857).
Owens, William A., *This Stubborn Soil* (New York 1966).
Richardson, Rupert N., *Texas: The Lone Star State,* 2d ed. (Englewood Cliffs, N. J., 1958).
Texas State Historical Association, *Handbook of Texas,* 2 vols. (Austin 1952).
Webb, Walter P., *The Texas Rangers,* rev. ed. (Austin 1965).

TEXAS, University of. See TEXAS SYSTEM, THE UNIVERSITY OF.

TEXAS A&I UNIVERSITY is a state-supported university in Kingsville, Texas. It was established as South Texas Normal School in 1917. It was known as the Texas College of Arts and Industries from 1929 to 1967, when the present name was adopted.

The schools of the university are arts and sciences, agriculture, business administration, engineering, and teacher education. The graduate school offers master's degrees in 17 fields. The university also maintains the Citrus and Vegetable Training Center at Weslaco for research and instruction. Enrollment in the late 1960's was close to 5,000 men and women.

TEXAS A&M UNIVERSITY, the oldest public institution of higher education in Texas, is a land-grant university situated at College Station. It was founded by act of the Texas legislature in 1871 as the Agricultural and Mechanical College of Texas, and instruction began in 1876. It adopted its present name in 1963. Its enrollment grew from about 7,000 men in 1960 to about 15,000 men and women in the early 1970's.

The University comprises the colleges of agriculture, architecture and environmental design, business administration, education, engineering, geosciences, liberal arts, and science and veterinary medicine, and a graduate college. Largest graduate enrollments are in the areas of agriculture, education, engineering, and the sciences.

Texas A&M is the central unit of the Texas A&M University System. Research and service units of the system include the Texas Agricultural Experiment Station, the Texas Agricultural Extension Service, the Texas Engineering Experiment Station, the Texas Engineering Extension Service, and the Texas Transportation Institute. Representative of the major research facilities on campus are a $6 million cyclotron, a computer center, and a veterinary diagnostic center. The University also operates the Texas Maritime Academy at Galveston.

The system also includes two colleges. Prairie View A&M College, at Prairie View, offers 2-year, 4-year, and master's degree programs. Tarleton State College, at Stephenville, offers 2-year and 4-year programs.

JOHN B. SMITH
Texas A&M University

TEXAS CHRISTIAN UNIVERSITY is a private institution located in Fort Worth, Texas. Enrollment reached about 6,500 men and women by 1970. The university is church related, but the enrollment is nonsectarian.

The university was founded as the AddRan Male and Female College at Thorp Spring, Texas, in 1873 under the leadership of two brothers, Addison and Randolph Clark. In 1889 the school became affiliated with the Christian Churches of Texas and was renamed AddRan Christian College. The present name was adopted in 1902.

The university is composed of eight divisions: AddRan College of Arts and Sciences, M. J. Neeley School of Business, Brite Divinity School, School of Fine Arts, School of Education, Harris College of Nursing, The Evening College, and the Graduate School.

PAUL PARHAM
Texas Christian University

TEXAS CITY, in eastern Texas, is in Galveston county, on Galveston Bay, about 35 miles (56 km) southeast of Houston. It is a major industrial center and an important port of oceangoing shipping. The city has chemical plants, oil refineries, and a large tin smelter. The port ships petroleum and petroleum products, sulfur, chemicals, metals, cotton, and grain.

Texas City was incorporated in 1912. It expanded greatly during and after World War II. In 1947 a ship explosion followed by fires in the city took many lives and caused great damage, but the city was rebuilt. The city has a commission government. Population: 38,908.

TEXAS FEVER is a protozoan disease that occurs in cattle, buffalo, and zebras in warm climates throughout most of the world. It was a major disease of cattle in the southern United States during the 19th century.

The parasite that causes Texas fever is transmitted by certain ticks of the genus *Boophilus*. Once the parasites enter the bloodstream they invade and destroy the red blood cells. A sick animal has a high fever, anemia, jaundice, weakness, and red-colored urine. Mature animals are severely affected, while young animals develop only a mild infection.

Affected animals can be successfully treated, but often they remain permanent carriers of the disease. Immunization of young animals and the use of pesticides to kill the ticks are the most common methods of controlling the disease.

KEITH WAYT, D. V. M.
Colorado State University

TEXAS RANGERS, the oldest state law enforcement agency in the United States. No other group of American fighting men has earned so great a reputation nor as eminent a place in Western lore. In gaining this distinction, the Rangers brought law to a violent land.

Stephen F. Austin, the first Anglo-American impresario in the Texas portion of Mexico, hired 10 men in 1823 to "range" around his settlement to keep track of hostile Indians. Comanche, Apache, and other tribes posed such a threat that even during the war for Texas independence the task of the enlarged Ranger force remained that of protecting settlers against the Indians, not Mexicans. In 1836 their success led the new republic to organize a battalion of mounted Rangers, rather than an army, for frontier protection. In 1881 the Frontier Battalion of the Texas Rangers defeated the last of the renegade Indians in the Diablo Mountains of West Texas.

The Rangers produced many notable leaders, including Ben McCulloch, W. A. A. (Big Foot) Wallace, and John Coffee Hays. Hays commanded a Texas regiment of 500 men that distinguished itself under both Zachary Taylor and Winfield Scott during the Mexican War—the only time that the Rangers have operated as a unit in the U. S. Army. Although they proved indomitable fighters, General Taylor complained about their poor discipline.

During the lawlessness spawned by Reconstruction, the Frontier Battalion of the Rangers broke up feuds, private wars, train-robbing gangs, and El Paso's Salt War—an 1877 dispute over the ownership of salt deposits. The Special Force under a 130-pound consumptive, Capt. L. H. McNelly, invaded Mexico against all rules of neutrality to bring back a large herd of stolen cattle. Desperadoes such as John Wesley Hardin, King Fisher, and Sam Bass submitted to Ranger justice. Later, Mexican revolutions that spilled across the Rio Grande, oil booms, and prohibition placed demands on the Rangers that they could not meet as their leaders became political appointees who added little to the esteem and effectiveness of the force.

The modern Texas Ranger force evolved in 1935, when it became a division of the Department of Public Safety. Its four major functions are to protect life and property, suppress riots and insurrection, investigate major crimes, and apprehend fugitives. It has full access to a statewide communications network, crime laboratory, and criminal records. The automobile and the airplane have supplanted the horse as transportation.

Fewer than 100 men remain as heirs to the Ranger tradition. Under law each Ranger still carries his saddle and horse gear in his car, and he wears a circled star, a replica of the original badge carved from a silver dollar by some early Ranger.

In their modern role the Rangers have suppressed strikes in labor-management disputes and controlled violence during civil rights confrontations. As a result they have been accused of being defenders of the status quo, and citizen groups and some political leaders have called for abolishing the force.

JOE B. FRANTZ, *The University of Texas*

TEXAS SYSTEM, The University of, a state-supported system of general academic and professional schools and hospitals distributed throughout the state. The system, which is headed by a chancellor who reports to a board of regents, has its headquarters in the state capital.

The university was authorized by the state legislature in 1876, and a campus was founded at Austin in 1883. In the 1950's, as additional institutions were established as parts of the state university, the statewide educational complex was renamed The University of Texas System. The Austin campus, in addition to being the oldest unit in the system, is the largest. It includes thirteen academic and professional colleges and schools, a graduate school, McDonald Observatory at Mount Locke in west Texas, and the Marine Science Institute on the Gulf of Mexico. The library has over 2 million volumes.

The Systemwide Nursing School has its headquarters on the Austin campus and branches in Galveston, San Antonio, and El Paso.

The University of Texas at Houston comprises a medical school authorized in 1969; a dental branch; M. D. Anderson Hospital and Tumor Institute for cancer research and treatment, authorized in 1941; the graduate school of biomedical sciences, established in 1963; and the school of public health, activated in 1967.

In San Antonio, university institutions include a medical school authorized in 1959 and a 4-year college and a dental school, both authorized in 1969.

In north Texas are the Southwestern Medical School at Dallas, which was founded in 1943 and became state-supported in 1949, and two general academic institutions, The University of Texas at Arlington, which joined the state university in 1965, and the University of Texas at Dallas, acquired by gift in 1969 and limited to graduate enrollment until 1975.

At Galveston, the university operates a medical school and associated hospitals.

In far-west Texas, The University of Texas at El Paso, founded in 1913, became part of the state university in 1919. It is a general academic institution.

In 1969, the system was authorized to establish The University of Texas of the Permian Basin, with authority to enroll only juniors, seniors, and graduate students.

By 1970 the total enrollment in the general academic institutions of the university system was about 65,000 men and women, more than 40,000 of them on the Austin campus. Enrollment in the health-related units throughout the state was about 2,500.

HENRIETTA JACOBSEN
The University of Texas System

TEXAS TECH UNIVERSITY is a state-supported university in Lubbock, Texas, chartered on Feb. 10, 1923, as Texas Technological College. Instruction began in 1925. The present name became effective in September 1969.

Texas Tech consists of the colleges of arts and sciences, agriculture, business administration, education, engineering, and home economics, with a school of law, a graduate school, and an allied school of medicine. Research facilities include a computer center, a seismological observatory, the Southwest Collection (archives and history), the International Center for Arid and Semi-Arid Land Studies, and a library of more than a million volumes. Texas Tech enrolled 20,000 men and women, including about 3,000 graduate students, in the early 1970's.

R. C. JANEWAY
Texas Tech University

TEXAS v. WHITE was a landmark decision of the U. S. Supreme Court in 1869 that decreed by law what the Union's victory in the Civil War had established by force: namely, that the United States is an indestructible union from which no state can secede.

In 1850 the state of Texas had received $10 million in federal bonds in settlement of boundary claims. In 1862 these bonds, which lacked the signature of the governor, as required by law were transferred by the secession state government to pay for Confederate supplies. At the war's end, the Reconstruction government of Texas brought a suit in the Supreme Court, against citizens of several states, to recover the bonds. Although the U. S. Constitution provides that a state may bring an original suit in the Supreme Court, the defendants claimed that because Texas had seceded from the Union at the outbreak of the Civil War, it could not sue.

The court, in an opinion by Chief Justice Salmon P. Chase, upheld the right of Texas to sue and to recover the bonds. "The Consitution, in all its provisions," the opinion said, "looks to an indestructible Union, composed of indestructible States." The unsuccessful effort of Texas to secede may temporarily have lost the state the rights and privileges of membership but not membership itself.

LEO PFEFFER
Long Island University

TEXEL, tek'səl, one of the West Frisian Islands, in the North Sea, belonging to the Netherlands. See FRISIAN ISLANDS.

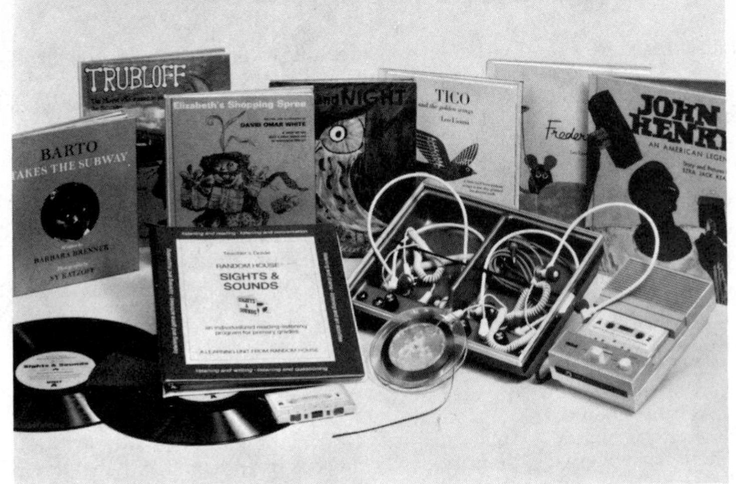

COURTESY, RANDOM HOUSE

SCHOOL BOOKS have changed in format and use since the 1840's, when the English grammar shown below served as a textbook. Many classes now use learning units instead of a single book. The reading-listening unit at left allows students to read stories in books and listen to them on records, cassettes, or tapes.

TEXTBOOK. In the strict sense of the term, a textbook is a book that presents a body of knowledge in an organized and usually simplified manner for purposes of learning. The textbook is frequently the most important teaching tool because it can determine not only what will be taught but also how it will be taught. Although television and other new media are rivalling printed materials of communication, textbooks remain major resources in schools and colleges. About half the books produced in the world are textbooks. In the United States, which leads the world in educational publishing, about 215 million textbooks were sold in 1970.

The Nature and Use of Textbooks. "Textbook" can mean several different kinds of printed materials. A general work can fill the role of a textbook. The ancient Greeks, for example, used Homer's poetry for the study of language and literature. In Islamic countries the Koran was the basic book in traditional schools and even in the great Muslim university of al-Azhar at Cairo well into the 20th century. Typically, however, textbooks are written specifically for use in school or college courses.

"Textbook" may mean one volume, as in the case of an introductory survey of psychology for college freshmen. In elementary and secondary schools, on the other hand, textbooks often are constructed and sold in series—for example, arithmetics for grades 1 through 6 or science books for grades 7 through 9. Basic texts are often supplemented by workbooks, which provide drill and practice on topics introduced in the textbook. Publishers also furnish tests and frequently provide teachers' manuals or teachers' editions that give suggestions on ways in which the subject matter should be taught and supplementary materials worked in. Each complete set of a series of arithmetic or reading books for grades 1 through 6, for example, include 24 or more printed items.

Printed materials are frequently accompanied by audiovisual aids such as tapes, recordings, slides, filmstrips, models, or maps. Some U. S. firms that used to call themselves textbook publishers now refer to themselves as publishers of educational materials and to their products as packages of instructional materials. Still, the package is typically built around a book.

In the move away from the single textbook toward a series of related materials, the paperback revolution has played an important role. College courses frequently require the use of series of readings that are available in paperbacks at less cost than hardbound books. For secondary school history and literature, for example, publishers often prepare paperbound books of readings from primary sources.

Textbooks are used in many ways. It used to be a common practice for teachers to follow the book, covering a set number of pages or units each week. The text materials provided the content of the course and even controlled the teaching schedule for the year. Some educators object to too much dependence on textbooks, arguing that the teacher should be free to create his or her own teaching plan and to use whatever sources of information may be appropriate. It has long been standard practice for teachers to have students use reference books, magazines, and newspapers and to draw on other sources such as radio and TV programs and interviews with parents, friends, and others outside the school.

THE INFANT'S GRAMMAR 8

VERBS ACTIVE AND PASSIVE.

The company, laughing, now stood up in ranks,
Whilst the ACTIVE VERBS play'd on the PASSIVE their pranks.
But some were so lazy they SLEPT on the floor,
And some were so stupid they STOOD by the door.
In short, all the actions that mortals can DO,
Were DONE by these VERBS, and ENDUR'D by them too.

CULVER PICTURES

The increasing popularity of individualized instruction and independent study in U.S. schools leads teachers to encourage wider use of the library and other resources, with correspondingly less reliance on single textbooks.

In many cases the individual teacher has little or no choice about using a textbook. Some countries control the content of education by prescribing which books are to be used. In Hungary, for example, courses of study are planned and books are written under the direction of government officials. Even in countries such as the United States, where there is no federal control of education, teachers may find that local or state authorities govern—or set limits on—the planning of teaching programs and the selection of textbooks.

The Production of Textbooks. As just noted, textbooks in some countries are written under government direction and published by government bureaus. In other countries—the United States, Canada, and Britain are examples—textbooks are produced by the private enterprise of authors and publishers. Some publishers specialize in educational materials, while others issue both trade and educational books. In the United States nearly 100 educational publishers are members of the Association of American Publishers. By 1970 the total annual cost of textbooks and related printed materials sold to schools and colleges was more than $790 million.

Authors and publishers work in many ways, but the production of a textbook typically follows certain steps. The idea for a new book or series may originate with an author or with the publisher. Once the idea has taken shape, the next step is an analysis of the potential market, to make sure that the proposed book will sell. A major series of school books may require the publisher to invest several million dollars, so bad planning can be costly. On the other hand, a successful book may go through many editions and return handsome profits. The market analysis entails such steps as reviewing courses of study used in the schools, seeing what books are currently available, and trying to find out what competing publishers are doing or planning to do. Once the publisher has decided to go ahead, he may enlist coauthors—for instance, classroom teachers may be teamed with subject specialists. The authors share the royalty payments.

At almost every stage of planning, outlining, and actual writing, consultants may be brought in to advise authors and editors. They are usually experts in the specific field of the text or in the methodology of teaching. The writing of the text by a group of authors usually requires extensive editorial coordination by the publisher. The editors usually oversee the development of the text rather closely. With elementary materials, for example, they are particularly concerned that the vocabulary be appropriate for the age and grade level for which the text is intended.

Editors and authors also must consider the point of view expressed in the text. In a book that is to be used by millions of students in all or most states, it is difficult to treat controversial topics without offending someone at some time. U. S. school books have been attacked from various sides. In the 1930's, 1940's, and 1950's there were complaints that texts failed to present American history and society in a sufficiently patriotic light. In the 1960's critics began to charge that history books, for example, gave an unrealistically favorable view of the U. S. past, particularly neglecting to portray the problems of minority groups. Such criticisms have to be weighed while a manuscript is being outlined and written. Publishers have made an effort to have all textbooks take account of the roles of ethnic groups.

After the manuscript has been completed, the publisher's editors do the final editing and styling. The publisher also obtains photographs, has art work created if maps, drawings, or diagrams are needed, and designs the page layout and selects the type style. Copy is then sent to a typesetter. Proofs must then be read and the type and illustrations assembled into pages. Finally, the printer takes over for the printing and binding stages.

College textbooks usually follow a less involved course of development. The author or authors typically have a freer hand, and the stamp of the authors' personality is more evident in the completed book.

The next stage of the textbook publisher's efforts is marketing his books. Major publishers employ numerous salesmen—often former teachers or school administrators—to sell text materials to schools and colleges.

Adoption Procedures. In the United States primary and secondary education is basically the responsibility of state and local governments. Therefore, practices governing the adoption of texts differ according to laws and policies of the states and school districts. Of the 50 states, 22 follow what is called the multiple adoption policy for elementary schools, and 18 have multiple adoptions for secondary schools. The state makes up a list of approved books for each area of study. Committees are usually appointed by the state office of education to screen new texts. The local school districts, the schools, or even individual teachers, pick books from the state list of approved titles. California has what is called a basal adoption system for elementary school textbooks. That is, only one or two books are approved, and they must be used throughout the state.

The remaining states use a variety of means in adopting textbooks on a local level. The most typical of these is to assign responsibility to a committee that is representative of the interests involved. For example, different grade levels of language arts teachers, or all teachers of single grade level, may be involved in the consideration and adoption of textbooks.

The majority of states provide textbooks to students free of charge to be used during the school years. The average life of a textbook in the United States is three to five years. For the country as a whole, the average per-pupil expenditure for textbooks is about $6 a year for elementary schools and $11 for secondary schools.

Other Influences on the Development of the Textbook. Several professional organizations are influential in the improvement and utilization of textbooks in the United States. For example, the National Education Association and its several departments, such as the National Science Teachers Association, the National Council for the Social Studies, and the Department of Elementary School Principals, work through committees and consultants to improve textbook quality.

The federal government has had increasing influence through grants for curriculum development projects. For example, the National Science Foundation made grants beginning in 1959 to the Physical Science Study Committee to help develop a new curriculum for the teaching of physical sciences in high schools. Through the U. S. Office of Education, curriculum projects in mathematics, social studies, foreign languages, and other fields have been initiated. These projects establish new goals and teaching methods and thus require new texts and teaching aids. Curriculum projects in physics, biology, and anthropology, for example, resulted in the issuing of experimental text materials. Some of these were turned over to commercial publishers. Thus, federal funds have stimulated the development of new text materials.

Textbooks in Canada. In Canada, as in the United States, textbooks are largely produced by commercial publishers. Each province has a department of education that has the responsibility of selecting the textbooks to be used in the schools of the province. The provincial minister of education, acting on the recommendation of the director of curriculum, makes the selection. The director of curriculum bases his recommendation on the reports of several committees of professional educators and laymen.

In eight of the ten provinces textbooks are provided free of charge. In the other two provinces students rent their textbooks for a nominal sum. Textbooks in French are provided for the French-language schools of Quebec.

Japan. In Japan the ministry of education must authorize all textbooks before they can be used. Only those that conform to the purposes of the Fundamental Law of Education and the School Education Law receive the authorization. Thus, textbooks generally conform to the established course content rather than create new courses. In 1967 a Japanese professor began a lengthy court case challenging the right of the government to require changes in his history texts.

The average period of use for a text varies but usually is from three to five years. Textbooks in Japan are purchased by the students.

Soviet Union. All textbooks in the USSR are published at the expense of the state in the publishing offices of each of the republics. The language used is that of the republic in which it is published. All textbooks must be approved by the ministry of education, which receives lists of books from the screening done by the ministry's council for systematic teaching. It is the stated purpose of the government to have textbooks present the doctrines of the regime.

The average life for a textbook, at least in the first eight grades, is about ten years.

England. In contrast to the practice in many other countries, textbooks in England are not written to fit a prescribed syllabus or course of study. Too much variability in content and method exists to make uniformity in texts feasible to any degree. The responsibility for selecting textbooks rests with the teachers and headmasters.

Because the personnel of each school or area have the freedom to decide when to replace a text with a new or revised edition, there is great variability in the life of a textbook. Textbooks are lent free to students, and the cost is borne by the local education authorities.

The Developing Nations. Countries that are striving to expand their economies and at the same time to educate more of their people face the problem of obtaining teaching materials. Commercial publishing may not be profitable enough in a small country to justify the founding of textbook firms. Translation of books published in other countries is one possible solution to the problem. Production of texts by the government may be necessary.

Famous Old Textbooks. Some textbooks have important places in the history of education because they influenced the way generations of young people were taught in school. For example, *The Visible World*, written in Latin by John Comenius in 1658, became so popular that it was translated into 14 languages. This book used both pictures and text to teach lessons, and it was a pioneering effort to give pupils material suited to their own level of ability.

A famous elementary schoolbook in colonial America was the *New England Primer*, a beginning reading textbook. The inculcation of religious ideals and beliefs as well as the teaching of reading and writing were of central importance. For example, the beginning lines of the *New England Primer* are "In Adam's fall, We sinned all."

Noah Webster is a central figure in the development of specifically American textbooks. His first speller, published in 1783, and especially the edition revised to correspond to his *American Dictionary* (1828), led the way to the Americanization of textbooks. Later editions of the speller called *The Elementary Spelling Book* (1829) had a blue binding and became popularly known as the "Blue-backed Spellers." More than 35 million copies were sold, and they were used in American schools for over a century.

McGuffey's Eclectic Readers were the most common textbooks in the United States in the 19th century. First published in 1836, the readers had sold over 120 million copies by 1920. They were prepared by William H. McGuffey, a professor at the University of Virginia, for the firm of Truman and Smith. This firm was one of the first American publishing companies to devote itself entirely to the production of textbooks. The readers were a major influence not only in American education but on American morals as well. There were seven readers in all, and each had a pervasive and insistent sense of morality. Later editions of the readers included selections from works by Dickens, Shakespeare, Longfellow, and Emerson. As the historian Henry Steele Commager remarked, "They [the *Readers*] gave to the American child of the nineteenth century what he so conspicuously lacks today—a common body of allusions, a sense of common experience and of common possession." On the other hand, 19th century textbooks have been charged with presenting an ideal world rather than the real world.

See also CURRICULUM; AUDIOVISUAL EDUCATION; EDUCATION—*Instructional Technology*.

MICHAEL LANGENBACH
University of Oklahoma

Bibliography

Bereday, George Z. F., and Lauwerys, J. A., eds., *Communications Media and the Schools: The Year Book of Education 1960* (New York 1960).

Cronbach, Lee J., *Text Materials in Modern Education* (Urbana, Ill., 1955).

Elson,, Ruth M., *Guardians of Tradition* (Lincoln, Nebr., 1964).

International Bureau of Education, *Primary School Textbooks* (Geneva 1961).

Nietz, John, *Old Textbooks* (Pittsburgh 1961).

Smith, Karl U., and Smith, Margaret F., *Cybernetic Principles of Learning and Educational Design* (New York 1966).

TEXTILE, a fabric made by weaving, knitting, netting, or braiding. The term is also applied to the component fibers, such as silk, wool, cotton, linen, rayon, and nylon, of such fabrics. Beautiful fabrics have been made in many lands since antiquity. Equipment and methods have altered, but the basic processes of spinning and weaving have not changed since the 14th century. See SPINNING; WEAVING.

CONTENTS

1. History of Textiles

In the broadest sense, a history of textiles would be a history of man since the Neolithic period. In most parts of the world, clothing is as basic a human need as food and shelter, and when fabrics replaced the animal skins of the earliest men, textiles became a main factor in economic history. They have affected, and been affected by, political, cultural, military, and even religious history. To give a few examples of their importance: a textile, wool, was the basis for the prosperity of the most important medieval city-states in Italy and Flanders, for the trading activities of the Hanseatic League, and for the rise of England as a commercial nation. Some of the earliest guilds were organized to fabricate and market it, but in England the making of wool cloth was the first manufacture to break loose from their restrictions and to be produced under the "domestic system." More recently, wool has been the mainstay of the Australian economy.

Silks have ranked with jewels and spices as the most coveted imports from the East since the days of the Roman Empire. Placing silk manufacture on a firm basis was one of Jean Baptiste Colbert's main achievements in his thoroughgoing reorganization of the French economy. The revocation of the Edict of Nantes, in 1685, which drove Protestant weavers out of France, greatly increased the prosperity of many other European countries. Silk also played an important part in the transformation of Japan from a feudal to a modern nation.

Cotton was such an irresistible import in 18th century Europe that it contributed to the downfall of the mercantile system. When it became really cheap, pretty dresses and draperies were brought within the reach of the poorer classes, and the gap between them and the wealthy was narrowed. In the southern United States the replacement of tobacco with cotton as the chief crop served to perpetuate the slave system, and so perhaps made the Civil War inevitable.

The first factories were built to make textiles, the first processes of mechanization were applied to them, and their production and distribution were the first to be organized on a capitalistic basis. The desire to produce textiles quickly, cheaply, and in enormous quantities was one of

NUNS made cloth in about 1400 by using reel, loom, and a horizontal loom with foot treadles (*far left*). At monastery (*near left*), imperfections were removed and the cloth was stretched on a frame.

WINDOW at Semur-en-Auxois cathedral (1460) in southern France shows fuller trampling cloth in a vat (*bottom left*); the raising of the cloth before shearing (*bottom center*); and the shearing of the cloth (*bottom right*).

FROM CHAPTER 6 OF A HISTORY OF TECHNOLOGY, VOL. 2, ED. BY C. SINGER AND OTHERS, OXFORD 1956

the main causes of the Industrial Revolution. In the 20th century the replacement of natural fibers by synthetics may have equally far-reaching consequences. All these aspects of the history of textiles can be fully studied in written records, without reference to the fabrics themselves.

On the other hand, the history of actual textiles, based on existing examples and supplemented by documentary and pictorial evidence, is full of gaps. Textiles are among the most perishable of major artifacts. This characteristic is most important for the prehistoric period, since, like wooden implements, textiles cannot survive burial unless the soil is very dry or very wet. Even in later ages the complete disintegration of most discarded fabrics has caused historical distortions, for almost always only the most precious textiles were not thrown away. A hundred white satin wedding dresses of the 1870's have survived for one set of long woolen underwear.

Generally speaking, it may be said that surviving fabrics are those made with much mental and physical labor, that is, those intended to be works of art. All embroidery and lace fall into this category, but, of woolen goods, only tapestries and carpets; of cotton, only painted and printed cloths; of linen, apart from lace, only elaborate damasks. Silk, on the other hand, was less used for purely utilitarian purposes. Consequently, a written account of its history, illustrated by actual specimens of material, is far more possible than for wool. This is so, even though in most countries much more wool than silk must always have been woven, and its economic importance was at least equally great. The rarity of ancient specimens of wool is also due to the fact that of all fabrics it is the most liable to destruction by insects.

The study of fine textiles, like that of other decorative works of art such as ceramics, glass, or furniture, can be that of a branch of the history of art. Owing, however, to the extreme difficulty of the craft of cloth making, and the consequent conservatism of its masters, there is often a time lag between the introduction of a new style by artists and its acceptance by weavers. Gothic velvets, for example, were still being woven in Italy during the High Renaissance. The written and pictorial evidence of the historical period, of course, adds greatly to our knowledge, but it is not always easy to interpret correctly. Names of fabrics are notoriously vague and frequently change their meanings. Thus, *dimity,* now the name of a thin, sheer cotton fabric, was used for a heavy cotton in the 18th century. Cotton itself, in the 16th century, meant a lightweight wool made in Manchester, England, later the center of the true cotton industry. Classical and medieval terms such as *staurax, blatta, baldachin, nacco,* frequently derived from place-names, are often unintelligible today.

Pictorial evidence, though it provides fairly reliable information about the patterns used at different periods, and, more rarely, about the types of looms and other tools, seldom shows how the pattern was placed on, or incorporated into, the cloth. When a fabric in a painted representation has an elaborate design, it is often not possible to determine whether that design was produced on the drawloom, by tapestry weaving, by embroidery, by knotting (as in rugs), or even by painting or printing.

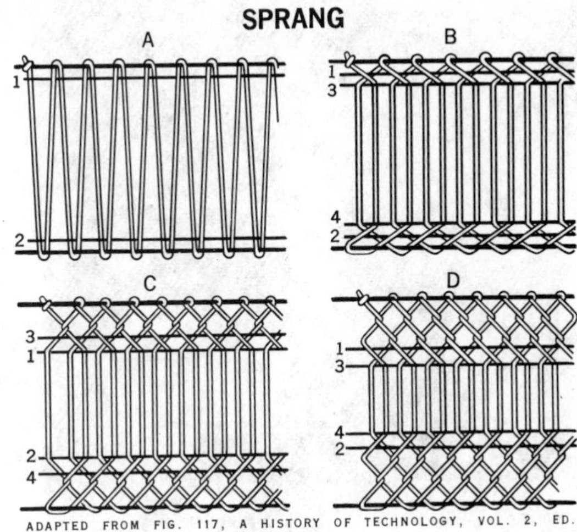

ADAPTED FROM FIG. 117, A HISTORY OF TECHNOLOGY, VOL. 2, ED. BY C. SINGER AND OTHERS, OXFORD 1956

SPRANG, a meshed fabric, which probably originated between 1500 and 1000 B. C., is more elastic than woven material. In one method for making sprang a single continuous warp thread was formed into a plaited mesh on a rectangular frame by inserting, removing, and reinserting rods in loops in a series of steps—A,B,C,D—moving nearer and nearer toward the center.

Prehistoric Period. Despite the paucity of evidence, however, it is clear that textiles, like pottery, were invented by Neolithic man. Fragments of woven linen and wool have been excavated from Swiss lake villages and other very damp prehistoric sites. Even when the actual textiles have disappeared, traces of them occasionally have been found on pottery and metal. The presence of stone or pottery spindles and loom weights provides incontrovertible proof of spinning and weaving. The work of peoples living today in a Stone Age culture can also reasonably be studied as evidence for the development of the earliest textiles. Among these people a great variety of techniques are found that are used for basketry as well as for flexible fabrics. Many of these techniques undoubtedly antedate the loom—for example, coiling, a one-thread technique known in Tasmania, Peru, and Scandinavia. Spinning, to hold the fibers together, is often considered a necessary preliminary to weaving, but there are tribes that weave with knotted threads.

With the invention of the warp beam—a bar that holds taut the far ends of the warps, or lengthwise yarns—the loom can be said to have been invented. However, there are many widespread primitive techniques using stretched threads that are not actually weaving—for example, sprang, which interlaces stretched warps without wefts (crosswise yarns), and which was known in Egypt, South America, and some European peasant cultures. Only when mechanical methods of forming the shed (separation of warps), using the sword and heddle rods, were added to the loom can true weaving be said to have begun. Felt is also probably older than woven fabrics, and it is especially frequent among nomadic tribes. The tapa cloth of Polynesia, which is made from bark, is another successful substitute material for woven fabric, produced by people who had no fibers suitable for weaving.

AMERICAN MUSEUM OF NATURAL HISTORY, NEW YORK

PERUVIAN PONCHO, a strongly patterned fabric similar to textiles of pre-Columbian Peru, is woven of llama wool.

Early Civilizations. By the time men began to live in cities, all the natural fibers were in use, and textile production was certainly extensive. Unfortunately, there are only two early civilizations, those of Egypt and Peru, from which large amounts of actual fabrics have been preserved. Woven linen, between 6,000 and 7,000 years old, has been found in Egypt, as have patterned designs, in tapestry technique, dating from the 15th century B. C. In Peru, cotton and the wool of the llama and similar animals were used, and fabrics woven from them have been found in the earliest culture levels. Elsewhere, the existence of textiles must be inferred, but cotton is believed to have been woven in India from at least 2000 B. C., and silk in China from perhaps 500 years earlier. Minute fragments of woven and embroidered silk have been found embedded in the patina of bronzes of the Shang dynasty (1523–1028 B. C.).

Classical Antiquity. Very few textiles have survived from the period of the Roman Empire in the West and the Han Dynasty (202 B. C.–220 A. D.) in the East, but there are enough to illustrate the written accounts of the important trade in silk that had sprung up between these two centers. Silk fragments have been found in excavations at the Chinese frontier station of Loulan, on the 3,000-mile (4,800-km) Silk Road across Asia, at Palmyra in Syria, and at Noin-Ula in Siberia. They show that the Chinese were using an elaborate loom in the 1st century B. C. The revolutionary drawloom, which employed a special type of harness that made possible the weaving of designs in both the width and length of the fabric, has been described as an invention equal in economic importance to the printing press. It may have been invented in China early in the Christian era, though some authorities believe it was first used in Syria. It enabled elaborately patterned fabrics to be made in great quantities, instead of by the slow method of tapestry weaving. The importation of cotton cloth from India to the West is mentioned by classical authors but has not yet been confirmed by excavated specimens. It was as precious as silk by the time it reached Rome.

The only extensive extant group of Old World fabrics of this period are the "Coptic" textiles found in the graves of Roman Egypt. Many complete garments and thousands of fragments,

METROPOLITAN MUSEUM OF ART

COPTIC FABRIC of the third to fourth century A. D.

dating from the 1st to the 7th century A. D., are scattered through the museums of the world. The Christians of Egypt were known as Copts, and some of these textiles show Christian subjects, but the great majority have classical patterns or figures. The textiles are of wool and linen, usually in tapestry weave, and are coarse in design and technique. The few silk fragments that have been found in Egypt are drawloom fabrics and are believed to have been woven in Syria. The remarkable textiles excavated from ice-filled tombs in Siberia in the second quarter of the 20th century are thought to date from about 400 B. C., though some authorities place them much earlier. They include knotted rugs, tapestries, and much appliqué embroidery in felt.

Middle Ages. The Persian textiles from the Sassanid era (224–642 A. D.) are known from the writings of European contemporaries, from the costumes of the figures on huge rock carvings

TAPA CLOTH is a coarse fabric used for centuries in the Pacific islands. Tapa is made of the pounded bark of breadfruit, paper mulberry, and other trees.

AMERICAN MUSEUM OF NATURAL HISTORY

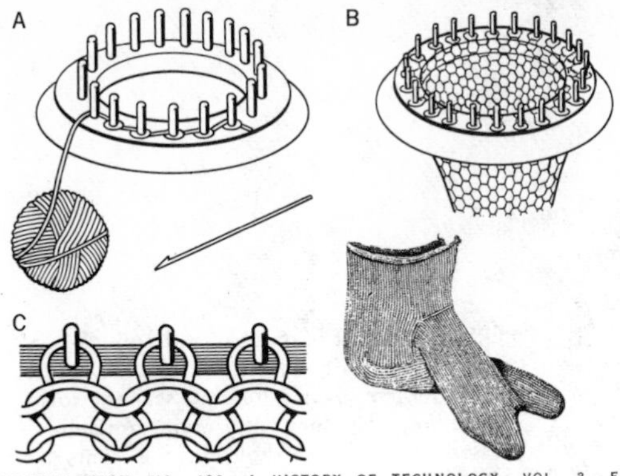

ADAPTED FROM FIG. 120, A HISTORY OF TECHNOLOGY, VOL. 3, ED. BY C. SINGER AND OTHERS, OXFORD 1957

KNITTING ON A CIRCULAR FRAME such as those used by Arabs for making sandal socks (*lower right*), caps, etc. (A) Casting on. (B) Formation of the fabric. (C) Detail of the yarn loops on the knitting frame.

in Persia, and from fragments of silks that came to Europe and were preserved as wrappings for relics, endpapers for bookbindings, and other uses. These are among the earliest textiles that have never been buried, comparable to those of the Shoso-in collection at Nara, Japan, which includes thousands of Chinese silks of the T'ang dynasty (618–906 A. D.). Some of the latter are strongly influenced by Sassanid designs, which also greatly affected the silk weavers of the Byzantine Empire. In 552, silkworm eggs were smuggled into Constantinople, and the West no longer had to depend on the importation of raw silk. There are Byzantine silk fabrics of the 8th century, but the finest known were made from the 10th to the 12th. This is the period of some of the first great Islamic silks, made in Baghdad, Syria, Persia, Egypt, and Spain.

Sicily was also an Islamic center until it fell to the Normans in the 11th century. The cultivation and weaving of silk continued there for 200 years, the fabrics showing a mixture of Muslim and Byzantine motifs. Some superlative 12th century Sicilian embroideries have also been preserved. It is customary to attribute the rise of the silk industry on the Italian mainland to the decline of Sicilian weaving in the mid-13th century. But there is documentary evidence that 100 years before that decline set in, the silk industry was already flourishing at Lucca, though the earliest silks recognizably from there date from the 14th century. They are remarkable works. The Mongol conquests of the 13th century temporarily reopened the overland silk routes, which had been closed by the Muslims for 600 years. It will be remembered that Marco Polo reached the court of the Great Khan in 1275. Chinese silks once more entered Europe in quantities, causing extraordinary changes in Italian textile design.

Unfortunately, only a few of the actual imports have survived, and no silks of the period have been identified in China, but their influence on the weavers of Lucca is unmistakable. The lively, fantastic creatures of the asymmetrical Chinese designs replaced the stiff, heraldic Romanesque animals and, when treated with typical Late Gothic spirit and naturalism, produced fabrics like illustrations to fairy tales. The 14th century in Europe, in fact, gave us three types of textiles that have never been surpassed: the woven silks of Lucca, the woolen tapestries of France, and the silk embroideries, *opus anglicanum*, of England.

From this period the history of luxury fabrics in Europe can be followed in paintings, and many complete vestments, altar frontals, and other church furnishings have survived. Italy and Spain were the centers for silk weaving throughout the Middle Ages. In 15th century fabrics most of the designs are based on the so-called pomegranate—which may be derived ultimately from the Egyptian lotus, as transformed by Chinese and Persian weavers—and most of the extant fabrics are silk velvets. Velvet was the last weave to be invented, perhaps in Italy or Persia in the 12th century. Wool is found in

MUSEUM OF FINE ARTS, BOSTON

BYZANTINE SILK fabric, a twill-weave textile of the 11th century, when the workshops of Byzantium led the world.

SILK BROCADE of 14th century Italy. Textiles such as this product of Lucca in Tuscany have never been surpassed.

COOPER–HEWITT MUSEUM OF DESIGN, SMITHSONIAN INSTITUTION

MUSEUM OF FINE ARTS, BOSTON

PERSIAN VELVET of the mid-16th century. This intricately patterned fabric, which depicts several hunting scenes, was the ceiling of a tent. The main tent pole passed through the hole in the center.

FRENCH PRESS & INFORMATION SERVICE

DETAIL from one of several tapestries making up "La Vie Seigneuriale" ("The Lordly Life"), a great 16th century series now at Ochier Museum in Cluny.

ITALIAN FABRIC with the distinctive pomegranate design typical of fine costume materials of the early 16th century, when Italy was the chief European silk-weaving center.

METROPOLITAN MUSEUM OF ART

the tapestries of northern Europe. Some linen pieces of the period are still in existence, the most notable being the towels made in Perugia, ornamented with Gothic designs in blue cotton.

16th to 18th Century. The discovery of the New World and the opening of the sea routes to the Far East brought about immense changes in textile production, distribution, and design. The Spanish invasion of Peru ended 1,000 years of textile making there. Great numbers of fabrics of amazing technical elaboration and perfection, worked on very primitive equipment, have been preserved from pre-Conquest Peru, thanks to the dryness of the soil.

Silks and cottons from China and India, after an interval of some 200 years, began to reach Europe in ever-increasing quantities. The 16th and early 17th centuries were the golden age of Persian textiles. Polychrome silk velvets of incredible complexity vied with the finely knotted rugs, often in silk, too. Both frequently included human and animal figures in their designs. The Ottoman Empire reached its height at about the same time, and the velvets of Bursa, though never as subtle as the Persian, are magnificent products. However, that quality declined at the end of the 17th century. Among European fabrics of the 17th century, it is possible to distinguish fine fabrics intended solely for use as costume material from those primarily designed as wall coverings. The latter have characteristic baroque large-scale motifs. For the former, a scattered pattern of little branches and leaves, very commonly in giselé velvet, is as typical of the period around 1600 as the "pomegranate" was a hundred years earlier.

Italy remained the chief European center for silk manufacture until about 1700, and humble linen was surprisingly converted into two types of luxury goods—the elaborate pictorial damasks of the Low Countries and lace. Though forerunners of this amazing fabric, lace, have been found among primitive tribes and in ancient Egypt and Peru, its appearance in Italy and Flanders in the 16th century and its rise to the status of a great decorative art form by 1650 is one of the most astonishing episodes in the history of textiles.

The late 17th century saw the decline of Italy and the rise of France, thanks largely to the genius of Jean Baptiste Colbert. Lyon became, as it has since remained, the chief silk center of Europe. Tapestry making, which had been concentrated in Brussels, flourished in the French royal manufactories, and Venetian lace was driven off the market by the products of Alençon and Argentan. A threat to the silk business, however, was the growing amount of imported printed cotton. Most European countries banned its use, but the edicts, like all sumptuary laws, were unenforceable. Later in the 18th century a wiser course was taken, permitting domestic manufacture to compete with the imported articles. The English permissive law dates from 1736, the French from 1759. The French designs were the more successful, the most famous being those made at the factory of Christophe Philippe Oberkampf at Jouy-en-Josas.

COOPER–HEWITT MUSEUM OF DESIGN, SMITHSONIAN INSTITUTION

TURKISH VELVET (fragment) of the 16th century, made in workshops of Bursa, capital of the Ottoman Empire.

19th and 20th Centuries. Improvements in the tools of spinning, weaving, and cloth printing had been accumulating slowly through the centuries, but in the late 18th and early 19th centuries such far-reaching ones were introduced that they revolutionized the whole industry. From the point of view of the art historian, the

LACE: Four examples of lace from its 18th century heyday in Europe. *Far left,* Flemish; *Left center,* Venetian needlepoint in relief; *Right center,* French needlepoint; *Far right,* English, Honiton bobbin, detail of tarde.

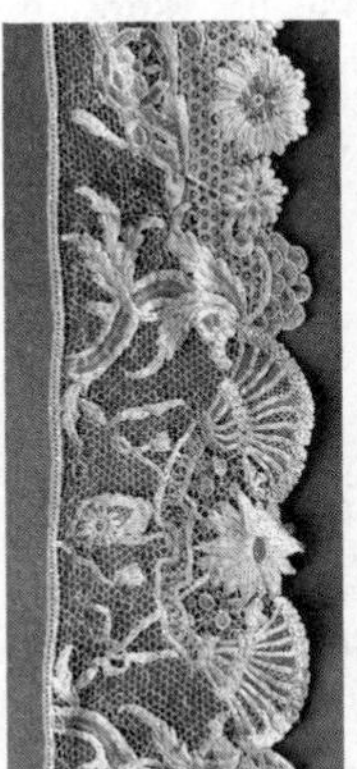

most important was the Jacquard attachment to the drawloom, which made the weaving of elaborately patterned fabrics a mechanical process. But even more destructive of artistic quality in textiles were the rising standard of living and the increase in population. Quantity production became a necessity in every branch, from lace to printed cottons. Textiles, like all other decorative arts, felt the effect of the unprecedented gulf that suddenly opened between the fine and the applied arts.

The 19th century is the first period in history for which there is no evidence of a relationship between the work of the great artists and that of the designers for the applied arts. The great artists themselves were seldom appreciated by their contemporaries. Only toward the end of the century were some types of luxury fabrics produced that testify to a normal relationship. William Morris in England designed tapestries and printed cloths in a neomedieval style related to that of the pre-Raphaelites, and founded the arts and crafts movement. Hector Guimard in France, soon after the turn of the century, designed embroideries as well as subway stations in the style called art nouveau.

COOPER—HEWITT MUSEUM OF DESIGN, SMITHSONIAN INSTITUTION

TROMPE L'OEIL TAPESTRY, depicting leaves, flowers, and vegetables, was made about 1750 in Beauvais, France.

In the first half of the 20th century a number of centers, such as the Wiener Werkstätte in Austria and the Bauhaus in pre-Hitler Germany, produced textiles in harmony with contemporary style. In France, tapestry, which had simultaneously reached a nadir of banality and a zenith of technical perfection in the 19th century, was restored to the status of an art form. By mid-century there was some evidence that the challenge of the machine had been met and that mass-produced textiles could hold their own alongside contemporary architecture, sculpture, and painting, but only the future would tell whether they would ever rank as worthy successors to the masterpieces of the past.

Collections. The chief museum specializing in textiles is the Musée Historique des Tissus in Lyon, France. Another, less comprehensive, is the Textile Museum in Washington, D. C. All museums concerned with the decorative arts include textiles: important collections are owned by the Victoria and Albert Museum in London, England; the Musée des Arts Décoratifs in Paris, France; the Textilingenieurschule in Krefeld, Germany; the Musées Royaux d'Art et d'Histoire in Brussels, Belgium; the Metropolitan Museum of Art and the museum of the Cooper Union in New York City. Many of these museums have textile study rooms as well as display galleries, where their collections can be examined.

EDITH A. STANDEN
The Metropolitan Museum of Art

COOPER—HEWITT MUSEUM OF DESIGN, SMITHSONIAN INSTITUTION

PRINTED FABRIC, made in Jouy, France, in late 18th century, is produced by copperplate printing method.

FABRIC designed by William Morris of England in late 19th century exemplifies his neomedieval style.

COOPER—HEWITT MUSEUM OF DESIGN, SMITHSONIAN INSTITUTION

Bibliography

Bunt, Cyril G. E., ed., *World's Heritage of Woven Fabrics*, 12 vols. (Metuchen, N. J.).
Clark, Leslie J., *Craftsman in Textiles* (New York 1968).
Clouzot, Henri, and Morris, Frances, *Painted and Printed Fabrics* (New York 1927).
Flemming, Ernst, *An Encyclopedia of Textiles* (New York 1927).
Fraser, Grace Lovat, *Textiles by Britain* (London 1948).
Geijer, Agnes, *Oriental Textiles in Sweden* (Copenhagen 1951).
Hunter, George Leland, *Decorative Textiles* (Philadelphia 1918).
King, Mary E., ed., *Ancient Peruvian Textiles* (Washington 1965).
Little, Frances, *Early American Textiles* (New York 1931).
Moss, A. J. E., *Textiles and Fabrics: Their Care and Preservation* (New York 1961).
Nordland, Odd, *Primitive Scandinavian Textiles in Knotless Netting* (New York 1961).
Pfister, R., and Bellinger, Louisa, *The Textiles; The Excavations at Dura-Europos* (New Haven 1945).
Priest, Alan, and Simmons, Pauline, *Chinese Textiles* (New York 1931).
Reath, Nancy Andrews, *The Weaves of Hand-Loom Fabrics* (Philadelphia 1927).
Reath, Nancy Andrews, and Sachs, Eleanor B., *Persian Textiles and their Technique* (New Haven 1927).
Riefstahl, R. A. Meyer, *Persian and Indian Textiles from the Late Sixteenth to Early Nineteenth Century* (New York 1923).
Simmons, Pauline, *Chinese Patterned Silks* (New York 1948).
Walton, Perry, *The Story of Textiles* (New York 1936).
Weibel, Adèle Coulin, *Two Thousand Years of Textiles* (New York 1952).

2. Growth of the Industry

Throughout centuries of recorded history, as improvements in basic textile-making techniques slowly evolved, textile workers grouped together. Sometimes it was because they practiced the same craft, such as dyeing or weaving, or because they worked in the same fiber: cotton in India, silk in China, wool in England, flax in the Low Countries.

During the Middle Ages the grouping of textile artisans was formalized by guilds that regulated the education and working conditions of craftsmen and set standards of quality for their products. Yet throughout this period professional craftsmen worked mainly in their own homes or individual workshops. Only a few factories—such as the Gobelins tapestry works in Paris—operated with a variety of skilled craftsmen working under the same roof, carrying out many processes and transforming raw materials into finished products.

Britain: The Beginnings of the Modern Industry. About 1760 the profound changes that began to stir the textile industry erupted into the Industrial Revolution, which in the mid-20th century was still going on in newly emerging nations throughout the world. The Industrial Revolution originated in Britain and later extended to the United States, both nations contributing a series of time- and labor-saving inventions that mechanized spinning, weaving, and other textile-making processes. It was natural that the factory system should result. Among other reasons, economy dictated that groups of the new machines be assembled near their source of power—first animals, then water, then steam, and finally electricity.

Among the factors stimulating the 18th century development of the British textile industry were (1) the increasing demand for more textiles created by active trade between Britain and her colonies; (2) the technical readiness of the various textile processes for the changeover to mechanization; (3) the availability of workers then engaged in processing textiles at home; (4) the suitability of Britain's damp climate for processing cotton, a fiber whose strength improves under moist conditions; (5) the comparative ease with which cotton fibers could be spun by mechanical means; and (6) the fact that the mechanization of one process and an increase in the speed with which it could be performed created demands for faster and more efficient machines to cary on related processes.

In the 19th century the cotton blockade resulting from the American Civil War (1861–1865) affected the British textile industry by hastening the disappearance of the handweaving of cotton and encouraging the mechanization of the linen, jute, and wool-shoddy industries. The 1873–1896 depression hastened the application of innovations that cut costs and speeded up production in Britain.

THE SCALAMANDRÉ MUSEUM OF TEXTILES

TEXTILE DESIGN by Bauhaus artist successfully combines principles of art and 20th century technology.

After the 1860's the textile industry entered a new phase, characterized by the application of science to industry. This was readily observable in the chemical industry's development of new sources and ranges of dyestuffs. Mass production techniques in industry led to specialized production.

Beginnings of the American Industry. Between 1760 and 1830 the Industrial Revolution was mainly confined to Britain. However, by forbidding the export of skilled labor, machines, and manufacturing techniques, Britain was partially responsible for the development of the American textile industry. In 1790, Samuel Slater, an Englishman experienced with the Arkwright spinning system, emigrated to America and from memory built the first cotton-spinning frame in the United States, in Pawtucket, R. I. The circumstance of its being set up in a factory that eventually processed cotton from the fiber to fabric stages proved to be a major step in the establishment of the American textile industry.

The impact of Eli Whitney's invention of the cotton gin in 1793 was felt in American agriculture as well as in its textile industry. Because it made possible the mechanical separation of cottonseed from the fiber, workers formerly employed in that time-consuming process could now work in the fields. Both the demand for cotton and its supply greatly increased and made the United States an important exporter of raw cotton.

The American invention and production of practical sewing machines around the mid–19th century also had a great impact on the textile industry. Its speed in sewing garments made possible the development of the ready-to-wear industry and created new demands for cloth.

European Textile Industries. The British were partially responsible for the early spread of the Industrial Revolution to Belgium, through their establishment of machine shops and textile factories in Liège. France, although it maintained supremacy in luxury branches of the textile trades such as silks and fine worsteds, which required highly trained workers and more time-consuming production methods, did not become an industrial power until the mid-19th century.

One of France's major contributions to the growth of the textile industry was the Jacquard mechanism, a loom attachment utilizing an endless chain of punched cards that enabled a weaver, unaided, to make complex patterned fabrics. This device, introduced about 1804 by Joseph Marie Jacquard of Lyon, successfully combined ideas previously developed by Falcon and Jacques de Vaucanson, who both tried to automate the process of weaving complex patterned silks. First used in silk manufacture, the Jacquard mechanism was applied to shawl weaving in Britain about 1818 and to the weaving of coverlets, carpets, and table linens in the United States about 1820.

Political turmoil in Germany and other European countries was a hindrance to industrial growth. Once this was resolved, Germany's textile industry grew very rapidly. Between 1870 and World War I, it developed the world's leading synthetic dye industry. Russia was exporting linen as early as the 19th century, but eastern European countries in general lagged behind until after the first 5-year-plans brought them into the circle of industrial powers.

Asian Textile Industries. Although both had long been famous for their fine textiles, China and India did not begin modernizing until the 20th century. Japan, until it opened its commerce to Western trade in the 1850's, produced cottons and silks mainly by hand methods. Even as late as the 1890's drawlooms were used for weaving complex patterned silks. After Japan recovered from the effects of World War II, its textile industries advanced so much that the United States and other big producers enacted tariffs and other measures to reduce Japanese competition.

TECHNICAL CHANGES

Mechanization of the Loom. British inventions were in the forefront of the early efforts to speed up the weaving process. John Kay's invention of the flying shuttle in 1733 was the first step leading to the mechanization of the loom. It speeded up weaving by allowing the weaver to catapult the shuttle back and forth across the web more rapidly than could be done by hand. In 1785, Samuel Cartwright was issued a patent for his first power loom, but not until the problem of warp dressing (preparation) was overcome in the early 19th century did the power loom gain acceptance in the industry. In 1813, William Horrocks, a Scot, improved the winding of woven fabric on the cloth beam and also introduced an iron loom. At this time only about 100 power looms were in operation in England.

In America, Francis Lowell began experimenting with power looms in Boston and succeeded in increasing loom speed. One of the first original American contributions to the power loom's development was Ira Draper's 1816 invention of the self-acting temple. This wooden bar with pins at either end, when inserted into each selvage (side edge of the cloth) during the weaving process, maintained uniform cloth width. Hand-manipulated temples were used in England as late as 1850.

In 1837, William Crompton, an English machinist working in Massachusetts, developed a loom for weaving Jacquardlike patterns in woolens and cottons. This loom was later greatly improved by George Crompton. A modified version was still in use in the mid-20th century.

In 1863, Lucius J. Knowles, an American inventor, developed the first open-shed loom, which in a modified form was established as the most commonly used power loom in Britain.

James Northrop of Massachusetts laid the foundations for the future development of the power loom when he patented his completely automatic loom for plain cotton weaving in 1894. Although the loom was slow, it halved the number of weavers needed to attend it. Its use

JACQUARD loom, first built in 1801, uses holes punched in a series of cards to control steps in weaving.

CULVER PICTURES

spread in the United States, where labor was scarce. It was not introduced into Britain until 1902 because of technical limitations and British labor's hostility to change.

Carpet manufacturing, one of the most complex branches of weaving, was the last to be mechanized. Britain, due to its skilled and lower priced labor, became the world's leading manufacturer of carpets. By 1830 its annual exports, measured in square yards, exceeded total American production. To compete, American mills were forced to develop more efficient manufacturing techniques. Thus Erastus Bigelow's invention, in 1841, of a power loom for making ingrain carpets was a boon to the American carpet industry. He later developed power looms suitable for weaving Wilton, Brussels, and tapestry carpets.

The power loom lowered the costs of production, enabling countries such as Belgium, France, Germany, and Canada to gain prominence in the carpet market during the first half of the 20th century. By mid-century, Britain still continued to export much carpeting, chiefly to Commonwealth countries, while the American carpet industry, the largest in the world, still sold almost exclusively to home markets. Japan's carpet industry exported most of its production.

Mechanization of Spinning. By the 1750's the flying shuttle had created a demand for more yarn, thus spurring on efforts to improve spinning methods. Again, the British led the way. Lewis Paul, in 1738, patented a system for drawing out cotton fibers through pairs of rollers, each pair operating faster than the preceding one. Sir Richard Arkwright applied Paul's system to his waterframe spinning machine, patented in 1769. This machine, with its four spindles, had the potential of spinning four times as much yarn as a single spinner working at a hand-operated wheel. The resulting yarn was strong and well twisted enough to be used for warp threads and knitted hosiery. James Hargreaves' spinning jenny, patented in 1769, was best for spinning softer yarns. This was followed by Samuel Crompton's mule, a spinning device that combined the water frame's rollers and the spinning jenny's movable carriage.

Although used and patented in Britain, an important American contribution was Charles Danforth's throstle-spinning frame for spinning warp yarn, developed in 1828.

The self-acting mule, a machine for spinning cotton, first used in England in 1830, was introduced in Alsace in 1852 and in Germany in 1860. In 1830 a similar device was applied to spinning short-staple wool in England.

All major developments in spinning were made before 1850. The last of these was the ring-spinning frame, invented in the United States in 1828. Its use continued to the mid-20th century, when it was considered a standard in the world's spinning industry. It employs spindles revolving in the middle of rings to which are attached light C-shaped clips, or travelers. As the yarn passes through the traveler on its way to the spindle, it is drawn around the ring, the traveler giving it its twist, and the vertical up-and-down movement of the ring winding it on the bobbin.

Man-made Fibers. Rayon has had important and diverse effects on the development of the textile industry throughout the world. This first manufactured fiber was once considered an artificial substitute for silk. Although the first known patent for the manufacture of rayon was issued in 1855, its development as a textile fiber began with a Frenchman, Hilaire de Chardonnet, who produced the first rayon fibers in 1884. Commercial production began in 1891. After many improvements, notably Charles F. Topham's discovery of an aging process in 1898 and his invention of a "spinning box" in 1902, the industry has continued to gain momentum.

Nylon is the other man-made fiber that has had immeasurable effects on the world's textiles. It was first produced in the United States in 1935 under the direction of Wallace H. Carothers. In 1939 the first knitted nylon hosiery were introduced. Although World War II temporarily interfered with its development for civilian uses, the war's end in 1945 not only made available a wide range of nylon fabrics but also opened up a whole new field of man-made fibers.

Mid-20th Century Trends. Constantly increasing labor costs, as well as improvements in efficiency and speed, have led to increased automation and computerization of production in the textile industry. Though modern looms must still go through the basic weaving steps of shedding, picking, and beating in, the newest shuttleless looms carry out these operations with ever-increasing speed and efficiency. In some of the latest shuttleless looms the weft (crosswise) yarn is projected directly from spools under its own momentum across the web, entering the shed (opening between lengthwise yarns) on a jet of air or water. Another important trend is toward the use of nonwoven—knitted and bonded—fabrics as substitutes for woven cloth.

RITA J. ADROSKO
Division of Textiles, Smithsonian Institution

Bibliography

Burnley, J., *The History of Wool and Wool Combing* (London 1889).
Ciba, Ltd., "The Loom," *Ciba Review*, December 1938 (Basel, Switzerland).
Duxbury, V., and Wray, G. R., eds., *Modern Developments in Weaving Machinery* (1962).
Hayes, John L., *American Textile Machinery* (Cambridge 1879).
Murphy, W. S., *The Textile Industries*, 8 vols. (London 1912).
Singer, Charles, and others, eds., *A History of Technology*, 5 vols. (London 1954–1958).

3. Fabric Construction

The making and use of textile fabrics predates recorded history. Some processes are little changed from ancient times, whereas others are among the latest developments of the modern technological age. Almost all fabrics are made from textile fibers. The few from other sources, such as paper, are relatively unimportant.

FIBERS AND YARNS

Kinds of Fibers. The hundreds of textile fibers in the world today may be placed in one or two main categories: natural or man-made. The natural fibers consist of three classes based on chemical structure: (1) protein (animal), of which wool and silk are the best known; (2) cellulosic (vegetable), of which cotton, linen, and jute are the most widely used; and (3) mineral, of which asbestos is the only fiber.

The man-made fibers may be placed in one of two categories on the basis of their sensitivity to heat. The thermoplastic fibers—for example, acetate, nylon, polyester, olefin, acrylic—soften and become pliable, or "plastic," on contact with heat of rather low temperatures. The nonthermoplastic fibers—rayon, glass, metallics—do not soften or become pliable with heat at the range of temperatures encountered in homes, institutions, businesses, or most industries. In the United States, under the definitions of the U. S. Textile Fiber Products Identification Act (1960), man-made fibers must be labeled as one of 17 different classes, as determined by their chemical base: acetate or triacetate, acrylic, anidex, azlon, glass, metallic, modacrylic, nylon, nytril, olefin, polyester, rayon, rubber, saran, spandex, vinal, and vinyon.

Making Yarns. Almost all fabric-construction processes require that fibers be made into yarns as an intermediate step. The amount and type of processing required depend on a number of fiber properties including length, diameter, strength, tenacity, surface characteristics, susceptibility to various treatments, and reaction to finishing processes. Processes may be specific for one fiber or common to a number of fibers. Preparatory processes carried out prior to those common to several fibers are termed "preprocesses."

Preprocesses. Cotton is the shortest spinnable fiber and probably could not be made into a yarn were it not for the frequent spiral twists, or convolutions, along its length. Preprocesses for cotton are picking, ginning, baling, and classifying as to grade, staple, and character.

Picking is the removal of the ripe cotton from the opened bolls and may be a hand or a machine process. *Ginning* is the process by which the fibers (lint) are removed from the cottonseed. Saw gins are used for short- and medium-length fibers, and slower roller gins for long-fiber cottons. *Baling* follows the removal of the seeds, the cotton fiber being compressed into rectangular blocks, or bales. In the United States each bale weighs about 500 pounds (227 kg) and measures 45 or 48 × 54 × 27 inches (114 or 122 × 137 × 69 cm). Bales are wrapped in burlap and banded with steel bands to protect the cotton, maintain bale shape, and facilitate handling.

Classifying according to grade is determined by a composite of three factors: color, leaf, and preparation. The U. S. Department of Agriculture has established 40 standard grades for upland cotton, which are used the world over. The whiter and more even the *color*, the better the grade. *Leaf* refers to the amount of foreign material left in the cotton after ginning, such as bits of lead, stem, bolls, and sand. *Preparation* refers to the degree of smoothness or roughness due to knots (neps), matted fibers (naps), damaged fibers, and other types of nonuniformity.

Staple classification indicates fiber length and uniformity, which are very important in processing on high-speed machines, and *character* refers to fineness, luster, body, spirality, and any other property not covered by grade or staple but that will affect yarns or fabrics.

Linen (flax) preprocessing steps are pulling, rippling, retting or decortication, breaking, and scutching. Flax plants must be *pulled* from the ground, with roots kept intact through the retting process to prevent degradation of the fiber. The plants are dried in bundles, and then the seeds are removed by rippling—pulling the seed end of the bundles against a large comblike instrument. *Retting* is the breakdown of the brittle outer layer of the stem through fermentation by bacterial action and moisture. The outer bark is sometimes scraped off instead (*decortication*). After the retted stems are dry again, they are put through fluted rollers to break up the brittle outer layer (*breaking*). The broken stems are then beaten (*scutched*) to remove the pieces of outer layer and to destroy the gums and other substances holding the long fibers together.

Wool preprocessing consists of shearing or pulling, grading, sorting, scouring, burr picking, and carbonizing. *Shearing* is the clipping of the fleece from a living animal, and *pulling* is the removal of wool from the pelt of a nonliving animal after the skin side has been chemically treated to loosen the fiber roots. *Grading* is the classification of each fleece based on fiber length, diameter, and condition in preparation for marketing. *Sorting* is a further, finer grading determined by the final uses to which the different areas of the fleece, which vary in quality, will be put. *Scouring* is the method used to remove the natural grease (lanolin), suint (salts and other minerals), dirt, and other soluble foreign materials from wool. Bits of burrs, sticks, and other vegetable matter remaining after scouring are largely removed by *burr picking*, or carrying the wool over toothed rollers and a rack where air currents remove much of the loosened material. It is sometimes necessary to *carbonize* the last bits of burrs and sticks by treatment with a weak acid and heat, which causes charring. Heavy rollers then crush the carbonized material so it can be shaken or beaten out.

Silk, a long continuous (filament) fiber, requires only reeling and degumming preprocesses. *Reeling* is the unwinding of the silk filaments from cocoons and winding into skeins. *Degumming* is removal of the gum serecin from raw silk so that the silk may be handled by machines in making fabric.

Man-made fibers do not need preprocessing, as they are manufactured clean and ready for production into yarns and fabrics.

General Processes. General processes common to many staple length fibers are opening and blending, carding, combing, drawing, spinning, and winding. Opening and blending are carried

A KEY STEP IN WEAVING is shedding (A), in which warp threads are separated to form a space ("shed") through which the shuttle passes. (B) The thread carried by the shuttle is pressed against the previously woven cloth.

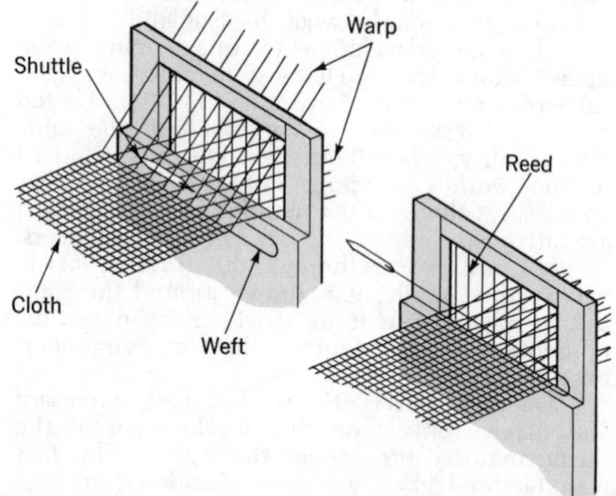

NATIONAL COTTON COUNCIL

BURLINGTON INDUSTRIES

BURLINGTON INDUSTRIES

BURLINGTON INDUSTRIES

BURLINGTON INDUSTRIES

TEXTILE MANUFACTURE

The basic steps in making textiles from natural fibers are shown here. (*Top left*) In carding, the fibers are disentangled, formed into a thin web, and gathered into a loose mass called a sliver. (*Top right*) In the next stage, drawing, several slivers are combined into one. (*Center left*) The slivers produced by drawing are passed through a roving frame to reduce their thickness. (*Center right*) Spinning machines convert the rovings into tightly twisted yarns suitable for weaving (*right*).

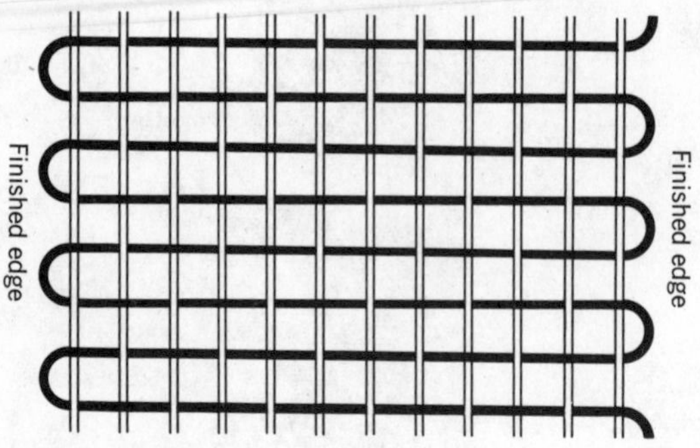

WARP yarns (white) run vertically and filling, or woof, yarns (black) run horizontally in a woven cloth design.

on simultaneously. *Opening* consists of pulling out or opening up rather large, fluffy masses of fibers from the bales, boxes, or sacks of fibers. *Blending* is the mixing of fibers from different bales, bags, or suppliers to ensure uniformity of large quantities of yarn.

Carding, combing, and drawing also contribute to blending. The object of *carding* is to separate the fibers and to place many of them parallel to each other while forming a wide, thin, gossamer sheet of fibers of uniform depth. The fibers are then gathered into strands, 1 inch (2.4 cm) thick, known as "card slivers." Long-staple fibers are sometimes put through a *combing* operation to make them thoroughly parallel and to remove all short fibers. Several of the fine combing slivers may be combined and *drawn* into a "roving," which is similar in size to a card sliver.

Drawing, spinning, and winding are carried on together. Two to six card slivers or rovings are fed into the machines together, spread, and further blended by drawing, which lengthens and thins the combined strands. It is accomplished by several sets of drums rotating at different speeds to draw the strands out, pulling some of the fibers past the others. At the end of the series of drums the desired amount of twist, necessary to hold the fibers together, is inserted in a spinning operation. The resulting yarn is wound on bobbins, spools, or other holders. Continuous, long-strand filament fibers, such as silk and many of the man-mades, do not require spinning. They need only to be given enough twist (throwing) to hold the filaments together during fabric construction. Filament yarns, however, may be given high degrees of twist for certain types of fabrics, such as crepes.

Many yarns are texturized by imparting a permanent curl, loop, crimp, or twist to the individual filaments. *Texturizing* adds bulk or stretch or reduces opacity, or provides a combination of these. The thermoplastic man-made fibers are most used for texturizing. They may be permanently heat set, then combined into various types of texturized yarns. Nonthermoplastic fibers or yarns may be given texture by resin setting in special crimping processes.

FABRIC CONSTRUCTION

Yarn Fabrics. Woven, knitted, braided, net, and lace fabrics all require yarns for their manufacture. Woven fabrics are produced on a loom, in which at least two sets of yarns—a warp (also called ends) and a filling (also called weft or picks)—are interlaced at right angles to each other. Three patterns of interlacing—plain, twill, and satin—are considered basic, since almost all other weaves are variations or combinations of these. In the plain weave the filling (crosswise yarn) is carried over one warp (lengthwise) yarn and under the next alternately across the fabric. In the twill weave at least three yarns are required. In the simplest twill weave the filling (or warp) is carried over two warp (or filling) yarns and under the third. Each successive row progresses in a predetermined manner to produce parallel diagonal ridges on the face of the fabric. In the satin weave the filling is carried over at least four warp yarns and then under one, the over-and-under progression of the following rows being adjusted to complete a balanced pattern.

Knitting consists of forming loops of yarn by means of needles, then drawing new loops through those previously formed according to a prescribed manner or pattern. In machine-knitting, a multiplicity of needles, needle holders, and yarn feeds replaces the pins, hands, and fingers of the hand knitter, but the operations are essentially the same. Machine-knitting is of two types: (1) weft, or filling, usually made on circular knitting machines, with yarns being carried around horizontally; and (2) warp knit, made on flat-bed knitting machines, primarily for wide-width fabrics. Warp knits have separate yarns for each vertical row (wale) and require special interlooping operations between rows.

Basic knitting stitches are plain, rib, and purl, with a variant of the rib stitch known as "interlock." In the *plain stitch* new loops are pulled through previously formed loops toward the face of the fabric. In the *purl stitch* new loops are all pulled toward the back of the fabric (hand knitting) or alternate courses of loops are pulled to opposite sides (machine knitting). In the *rib stitch* alternate loops of the same course are pulled to opposite sides of the fabric.

Braids are narrow fabrics made by diagonal interlacing of at least three strands of yarn or other material in such a way that individual strands form a zigzag pattern as they crisscross one another, and no two adjacent strands make complete turns about each other. Shoe laces, cord coverings, and fishing lines are typical braids, as are fancy braids that are used for trimmings.

Net is an open-mesh fabric constructed from yarns (or threads) on special bobbinet machines,

KNIT, or face, side of a plain weft-knitted fabric is shown. On reverse side, loops cross differently.

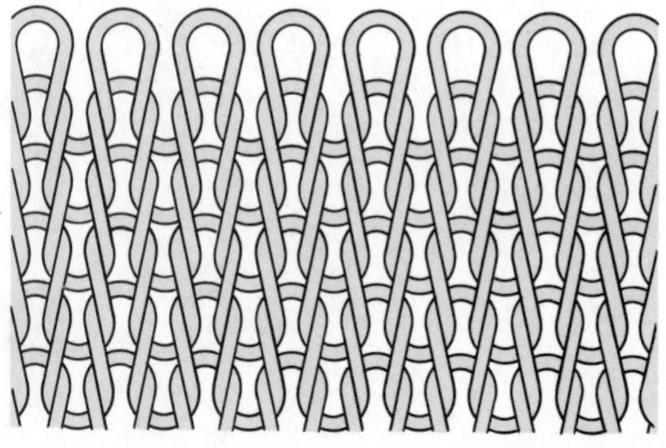

raschel knitting machines, or by hand tieing. True nets have 4- to 6-sided openings with interlacing or knotting at each corner to hold the mesh open.

Lace is characterized by a decorative design on an open mesh background. It may be made on lace or embroidery machines or it may be knitted, crocheted, tatted, or made by hand on "pillows."

Non-Yarn Fabrics. Fabrics made directly from fibers include felt, bonded nonwovens, needle-punched webs, stitch-bonded sprayed fiber, and laminates. These fabrics depend on the shrinking and matting action of wool under specific conditions, on adhesives or on heat-fusing of thermoplastic fibers, napping, or other bonding methods. Such fabrics do not have a warp or a filling and lack the "give" and usually the strength of fabrics made of yarns. Laminated fabrics are made of two previously constructed fabrics—usually woven or knitted—held together with an adhesive or by heat fusion.

FABRIC FINISHING

All fabrics go through one or more of a series of finishing processes to improve aesthetic appearance, improve service qualities, or both. The number of processes depends on the final use for which the fabric is intended. General finishing processes are cleaning, bleaching, drying, heat-setting (for thermoplastics), inspection, repair, singeing (burning off fuzzy fiber ends), shearing, brushing, softening, preshrinking, mercerizing (to add luster, strength, and absorbency), sizing (to add stiffeners), weighting and fulling (to the body), tentering (setting warp and filling at right angles), dyeing, and application of design.

The design may be given by the construction process such as the pattern of a figure weave, the stripes and checks of gingham, or the patterns resulting from the spacing or grouping of different types of yarns. Or designs may be applied after a fabric is constructed. Decorative applied designs may be attained by many types of printing, embossing, embroidery, appliqué, tie-and-dye, hand painting, moiré, or quilting.

Many fabrics are given special finishes to serve particular functions. These processes may render cloth waterproof or water-repellent, mothproof, flame-retardant or flameproof, wrinkle-resistant, and crease-recovering.

EVELYN E. STOUT, *Author of "Introduction to Textiles"*

4. Glossary

Acetate.—Generic name for cellulose acetate fibers, yarns, threads, and fabrics.

Acrylic.—A thermoplastic man-made fiber in which the fiber-forming substance is composed mostly (85% in the United States) of acrylonitile units ($-CH_2-CH(CN)-$).

Backed Cloth.—A single-woven cloth with an extra warp or filling interlaced on the back to add warmth and weight, as in Frenchback cloth.

Basket Weave.—A plain weave in which two or more yarns are handled together, as if they were one.

Batiste.—In cotton, a sheer mercerized muslin, often with stripes, woven from fine-combed yarns.

Braid.—Any narrow textile fabric used for binding or trimming. It may be woven or plaited.

Broadcloth.—Originally, a silk shirting cloth woven 29 inches (74 cm) wide and hence contrasted to narrow goods. In contemporary usage, broadcloth is a plain-weave, lustrous cotton cloth with fine crosswise ribs or a smooth woolen with a napped face and twill back. The name is also applied to comparable fabrics made of blends of several major fibers.

Broken Twill.—A weave made by running either a left-hand or right-hand twill for a desired distance and then reversing it. Herringbone is an example of a broken twill.

Buckram.—A ply-yarn scrim cloth with a stiff finish. It is also made by glueing together two open-mesh, sized cotton cloths.

Burlap.—A coarse plain-weave fabric made of cotton, hemp, or jute. It is often woven 40 inches (1 meter) wide and from 6 to 14 ounces in weight per yard (186–424 grams per meter).

Calendering.—A mechanical method, analogous to home ironing, in which heavy rollers are used to impart a regular, even finish to cloth, chiefly cotton and rayons. Variations in steam, heat, pressure, and the number and type of roller used produce a wide assortment of finished effects.

Calico.—A closely woven, plain-weave, inexpensive cloth first produced in Calcutta, India. It may be white or patterned with a printed motif.

Canvas.—A heavy, plain-weave cloth made from 2-ply to 14-ply yarns. The terms *duck* and *canvas* are often used interchangeably.

Carding.—A process in which fibers are separated, cleaned, laid parallel, and formed into small strands known as card slivers, or slivers. No twist in fibers.

Cashmere.—Cloth made from the soft, strong undercoat (pashm) of Kashmiri goats.

Cavalry Twill.—A strong, rugged, woolen cloth with a pronounced double twill on the face and the twill line running at a 63° angle.

Cellulose Acetate.—Solidified filaments of an acetic acid ester of cellulose.

Chambray.—A plain-weave, yarn-dyed, high-texture cotton usually made with a white warp and a blue filling.

Chased Finish.—A finish that imparts a temporary luster to cotton cloth by passing 4 to 16 layers of cloth through "chasing" rollers.

Cheesecloth.—A thin, loosely woven, lightweight, cotton cloth of open construction, used for teabags, surgical gauze, bedspreads, crinoline, and other purposes.

Chenille.—A cotton, wool, silk, or rayon yarn with a pile protruding all around at right angles.

Cheviot.—Originally, a rough, coarse, twill-weave suiting similar to tweed, made from the wool of sheep raised in the Cheviot Hills of Scotland. It now may be a plain or twill weave of any coarse wool yarn.

BASIC WEAVE constructions are shown below. In plain weave (left) weft thread passes under one warp thread and over next in every row. In twill weave (center), weft thread passes under and over warp threads in an under-and-over pattern repeated in each row. In satin weave (right), the under-and-over pattern varies from row to row.

Chiffon.—A plain-weave, sheer, lightweight cotton, rayon, or silk cloth made from highly twisted yarn.

Chintz.—A glazed, plain-weave cotton cloth decorated with large printed motifs.

Circular Knitting.—Cloth made on a circular-knitting machine in contrast to that made on a flat-knitting machine. In the circular knitting machine the needles are arranged in a circle, and tubular fabrics, such as socks and seamless hosiery, are produced.

Combing.—A process following carding but applied only to high-grade yarns of cotton, worsted, and certain other fibers in which all fibers below a given staple length are removed. The fibers remaining in the sliver are set in uniform, parallel order, with nearly all remaining foreign matter removed.

Corduroy.—A material usually made of one warp and two fillings, with one filling woven tightly to form the body of the cloth and the second woven with a float. The floats of the second filling are cut in the center to form a pile, creating narrow to wide wales in the warp direction.

Course.—A horizontal row of stitches in knitgoods.

Crease Resistance.—The ability of a garment to resist wrinkling by virtue of an application of synthetic resins or other chemicals to the fabric.

Crepe.—Lightweight cloth of silk, cotton, wool, or man-made fibers having a crinkled, puckered, or pebbled face. The crepe effect is achieved by hard-twist yarns, chemical treatment, special weaves, or embossing.

Crinoline.—A heavily sized, stiff, open-weave, cotton cloth, originally made of linen and horsehair.

Damask.—A firm, durable, glossy, Jacquard-patterned cloth of cotton, linen, rayon, silk, or other fibers or blends of these. It is similar to brocade but flatter and reversible.

Denim.—A rugged, heavyweight, left-hand twill cotton cloth made with a colored and a write warp and a white filling.

Denier.—Originally, a Roman coin and later a French and western European coin whose weight was used as a measure of fineness of silk yarn. In contemporary usage, denier is the weight of 9,000 meters (9,846 yards) of silk or man-made yarn in grams. Thus 9,000 meters of 150-denier silk yarn would weigh 150 grams (5.3 ounces), and 9,000 meters of 30-denier silk would weigh 30 grams (1 ounce).

Dimity.—A sheer, thin, cotton fabric made of combed yarn. Corded stripes and checks may be present in the pattern.

Donegal.—A thick, rugged, woolen homespun with colorful, thick spots of slubs woven into the fabric.

Dotted Swiss.—A sheer, high-quality cotton with a dot motif alone or in combination with other patterns. Looms with swivel-weaving attachments tie in the dots on the back of the goods; hence, the frequent reference to "tied dots" in conjunction with this cloth.

Double Twill.—A twill weave in which twill lines in one direction are intersected by uninterrupted twill lines in the opposite direction.

Doubling.—The feeding of two or more slivers, slubbings, rovings, or yarns into a textile machine to offset the effects of drafting (drawing) and redoubling and to prevent the stretched strands from collapsing.

Drawing.—Increasing the length while decreasing the diameter of card slivers by the use of rollers moving at different speeds. Six card slivers are fed into each delivery, and the drawn sliver is about the size of a single card sliver.

Drill.—A strong cotton fabric of coarse yarn and medium weight. Most drill is woven as a left-hand twill.

Duck.—A durable, closely woven cloth heavier than canvas, generally made with ply yarn warps and various sizes and weights of fillings.

Dungaree.—A coarse, usually blue denim cloth.

Dyeing.—See *Piece Dyeing; Stock Dyeing; Tie Dyeing; Yarn Dyeing.*

End-And-End Shirting.—Broadcloth, chambray, madras, or similar cloth with consecutive alternation of colored and white warps or warps of two different colors, producing a fine pin-check effect.

Face.—The right side of a cloth or the side with the more appealing surface effect.

Faille.—A semilustrous, plain-weave cloth with a crosswise rib effect produced by a wavy crepe filling.

Felt.—A fabric constructed by the interlocking of fibers, the fibers not having been spun into yarn. The fibers are made to felt, or lock together, by the use of heat, moisture, steam, and pressure. For derby hats, shellac is also used for stiffness.

Felted Fabric.—A woven fabric that is heavily fulled to cover up the spaces in the weave and present a thick, felted appearance. Melton is an example of such cloth.

Fiber.—The smallest unit in any yarn or fabric. Fibers may be made directly into fabric, as in the case of felt, or they may be spun into yarn.

Filament.—A fiber of indefinite length, such as the single strand of silk extruded by the silkworm in spinning its cocoon, or a strand of nylon or other man-made fiber, which may be several miles in length.

Filling.—Yarn running in the horizontal, or crosswise, direction in a woven fabric. It is also known as *filling picks, picks, weft,* and, sometimes, *woof.*

Filling Knit.—See *Weft Knit.*

Filling Picks.—See *Filling.*

Finish.—The surface effect given to a fabric. It includes napping, calendering, embossing, glazing, crease-retention, and others.

Finishing.—The final operation in the processing of textiles. It may include bleaching, dyeing, pressing, printing, waterproofing, and other treatments.

Flannel.—A light-weight, soft woolen cloth with a napped surface or a twill-weave, heavy cotton cloth napped on one or both sides to imitate wool flannel. A lighter cotton flannel is often called *flannelette.*

Flat Knitting.—Cloth made on a flat-knitting machine in contrast to that made on a circular-knitting machine. In the flat-knitting machine the needles are set in a straight line, and flat fabrics used for scarves or belts.

Float.—The portion of a yarn that crosses over two or more other yarns. Also, an imperfection caused by the failure of a warp yarn to weave into the fabric.

Foulard.—A light-weight, plain- or twill-weave fabric of silk, nylon, or rayon noted for its soft finish and feel. Used in dress goods and scarves.

Fulling.—A finishing process in wool in which the cloth is dampened and beaten under heat and pressure, causing shrinking, compactness, and obscuring of the weave.

Gabardine.—In wool, a durable, twill-weave worsted in medium to heavy weights, with a pronounced 45° or 63° twill line. In cotton, gabardine made with all single-ply yarn is usually a left-hand twill; if made with ply warp and single filling, it it usually a right-hand twill. Gabardine is also made in rayon and in combination of several major fibers.

Gauze.—See *Leno.*

Gingham.—A sturdy, yarn-dyed, usually plain-weave cloth of cotton or man-made fibers, commonly with a check or stripe effect produced by the use of colored yarns.

Harris Tweed.—A durable handwoven tweed made on the islands of the Outer Hebrides, Scotland. In Britain and the United States it is illegal to use the name for any other fabric.

Herringbone.—A cloth made in broken twill weave, the weave reversals perfectly balanced to produce a uniform angular effect. Widely used in apparel.

Homespun.—Originally, an undyed woolen cloth handspun and handwoven in the home. It is now identical to tweed in texture, yarn, weight, feel, and uses, except that it is made in a plain weave as contrasted with the twill weave of tweed.

Jacquard.—An intricate method of weaving to produce elaborate effects in the woven cloth, or a cloth made by this method. Each warp yarn is controlled by punched cards to regulate its raising or lowering to form the design. Examples of Jacquard cloth are brocade, brocatelle, tapestry, and damask.

Jersey.—Knitgoods made in plain stitch in weft (circular or flat) or warp knit. The name is also applied to some woven, lightweight silk or rayon broadcloth of some porosity. Any of various close-fitting garments, such as athletic pullovers, are commonly referred to as jerseys.

Knitting.—The manufacture of fabric using needles to form and interloop loops of yarn.

Lace.—An ornamental open-mesh fabric ordinarily made from thread (a specialized yarn).

Lamé.—Any fabric in which real or simulated metallic yarns are used in the warp or filling for decorative effect.

Laminated Fabric.—A fabric constructed of two or more layers of material held together by adhesives, heat fusion, or other means.

Left-Hand Twill.—See *Twill.*

Leno.—A weave used to make open-mesh cloth, such as mosquito netting, in which pairs of warp yarns cross over each other before and after each filling yarn has been woven into the cloth.

Madras.—A fine, usually plain-weave cotton shirting with woven stripes, cords, or small checks. It was originally made in Madras, India.

Melton.—A tightly woven, compact, heavyweight, smoothly napped cloth used in pea jackets and coats.

Mercerizing.—Imparting a permanent silken luster to cotton by immersing it in a cold caustic soda bath.

Moiré.—A special finish that imparts a wavy, watery appearance to fabric; also, a fabric with a moiré finish. It is produced by passing the fabric between engraved cylinders, the crushed and uncrushed parts of the fabric reflecting the light differently.

Muslin.—A plain-weave cotton cloth, varying widely from sheer to coarse but commonly a thin, semitransparent, bleached fabric. Lightweight sheeting printcloth is usually sold as "unbleached muslin."

Nap.—The fuzzy or protruding fibers on the surface of a finished material. Originally, the raised layer of naturally projecting fibers on the surface of the cloth;

now commonly obtained by artificially raising the short fibers, which are then cut and smoothed.

Nonwoven Fabric.—A fabric made of fibers held together by chemical bonding agents, or adhesives. Thermoplastic fibers are bonded by fusion under heat and pressure.

Organdy.—A plain-weave, sheer cotton with a durable stiff finish.

Oxford.—A soft, porous cotton shirting fabric made in basket weave with a fine warp and a coarse, bulky filling. It soils easily.

Percale.—A fine, close-textured, plain-weave cotton cloth with a smoother surface than muslin, often printed.

Picks.—See *Filling.*

Piece Dyeing.—Dyeing of fabrics after weaving.

Plain Weave.—One of the three basic weaves, along with twill weave and satin weave. There is only one plain weave, though with some variations, such as basket weave. The filling yarn is carried over one warp and under the next repeatedly across the width of the fabric. Most woven fabrics are made in plain weave.

Plaited Fabric.—A fabric, such as gauze, made with a single yarn interlacing freely to form the cloth or a narrow fabric made by the interlacing (braiding) of one set of at least three yarns, as in shoelaces.

Plush.—A velvet in which the pile is more than ⅛ inch (3 mm) high.

Ply Yarn.—A multiple yarn; that is, two or more single yarns twisted together.

Polished Cotton.—A cotton fabric given a luster by means of a resin finish and friction.

Poplin.—A fabric comparable to cotton broadcloth but with a slightly heavier crosswise rib yarn. The filling yarn is bulkier than the warp yarn and is particularly cylindrical to give the characteristic rounded rib line in the horizontal direction. Poplin cloth is mercerized and usually chased for high luster.

Printcloth.—A carded (uncombed) cotton cloth similar to cheesecloth but with more yarns per square inch.

Right-Hand Twill.—See *Twill.*

Roving.—The stage just prior to spinning in which the slivers are further drawn and condensed, twisted, doubled and redoubled to a diameter finer than that of slivers but greater than that of spun yarn.

Satin Weave.—One of the three basic weaves, along with plain weave and twill weave. It requires at least five yarns, with the filling yarn passing over (or under) all warps but one and then under (or over) that one warp to complete the pattern. Successive rows must follow a certain progression (the counter or base) to avoid forming a twill ridge or duplicating a previous row before it is required.

Scrim.—(1) An open-meshed, plain-weave cotton cloth, as used in buckram and curtains. (2) A bleached and sized cheesecloth. (3) A plain-weave or leno-weave sheer cloth, often with colored checks or stripes, used in curtaining.

Seersucker.—A durable, puckered cloth of cotton or man-made fibers. The vertical rows of crepelike surface are obtained by chemical treatment and uneven tensions in the warp yarn.

Serge.—A twill-weave, usually worsted fabric made with a right-hand twill at a 45° angle. Harsh in feel.

Single Woven.—A cloth made with a single set of warps and a single set of fillings.

Single Yarn.—A yarn that can be untwisted into the separate fibers from which it was made.

Sizing.—The application of starch or other stiffeners to a fabric.

Slub.—An irregularity in the diameter of yarn. It may be a defect or intentionally done to produce a desired appearance, as in shantung. The term is also applied to imperfections made by nubs or tufts of yarn in cloth.

Slubbing.—An attenuated sliver. The slubbing process follows the carding process and precedes the roving process.

Spinning.—Drawing or twisting of fiber into yarn or thread.

Stock Dyeing.—Dyeing of fibers before the spinning stage. Also known as raw stock dyeing.

S-Twist.—A clockwise twist.

Taffeta.—A smooth, plain-weave cloth with a fine crosswise rib effect. It may be plain, iridescent, or moiréd.

Terry.—A thick cotton fabric having uncut loops forming a pile on both sides of the cloth. It has excellent absorbency and is used for toweling, beach cloth, and similar purposes.

Texture.—In a technical sense, the number of warp and filling yarns per given area (1 inch is standard in the United States). An 88 x 72 cloth would have 88 warp yarns and 72 filling yarns per square inch. If the number of warps and fillings are the same, as 64 x 64, the cloth is referred to as "square" material. In sheeting, texture is given in total yarns per square inch, and a number-128 sheeting might be a 72 x 56, 68 x 60, or a 64 x 64 cloth. In a nontechnical sense, texture refers to the finish and appearance of the completed cloth.

Thread.—A highly specialized yarn used for sewing, basting, embroidery, and similar purposes. It is plied for strength, 3-ply and 6-ply being the most common.

Ticking.—A rugged, high-texture, right-hand twill cotton cloth, usually having colored and white warps and white filling to form vertical striping.

Tie Dyeing.—Dyeing fabrics tightly tied so dye does not take uniformly or at all in certain parts.

Tweed.—A rough, irregular, soft, unfinished shaggy woolen cloth named for the Tweed River in Scotland. It is identical with modern homespun except that it is a twill weave as contrasted to plain weave. Stock sold as Donegal tweed may be a plain-weave fabric. Very popular for outerwear.

Twill Weave.—One of the three basic weaves, along with plain weave and satin weave. It requires at least three yarns, with the filling (or warp) being carried over two and then under the third warp (or filling). A very popular twill weave uses four yarns, with the filling yarn passing over two warps and then under two warps. Each successive row progresses to the right or left in a predetermined manner to form a diagonal line or ridge on the cloth. The diagonals may run from the lower left to the upper right (right-hand twills) or from the upper left to the lower right (left-hand twills), usually at a 45° angle, but angles of 15°, 20°, 27°, 63°, 70°, and 75° are also used.

Unfinished Worsted.—Along with woolens and worsteds, one of the three types of cloth made from wool. Unfinished worsted may be made from a worsted warp and a woolen filling or with the warp and filling carrying a mixture of other fibers.

Velour.—A soft, thick, compact cloth with a close nap finish. Is usually of wool, but other fibers may be used.

Velvet.—A fabric with warp yarn formed into pile and with the adjacent rows of pile standing closely together to present a uniform surface. The pile may be of cut or uncut loops or a combination of both.

Velveteen.—A fabric in which an extra set of filling yarns is formed into pile of cut loops.

Voile.—A limp, plain-weave, sheer cloth with high-twist yarns for strength. It has good draping ability and is commonly used for curtains and dressgoods.

Wale.—A vertical row of stitches in knitgoods.

Warp.—Yarn running in the vertical, or lengthwise, direction in a woven fabric. Also known as *warp ends, ends,* and *woof.*

Warp Ends.—See *Warp.*

Warp Knit.—Along with weft knit, one of the two basic knitting processes. In warp knit, which often uses hundreds of yarns in the lengthwise direction to produce the cloth, there is uusually a single yarn for each needle. Each needle forms its yarn into a chain of loops that are connected by a special interlooping operation. Warp knitgoods are usually made on flat-knitting machines.

Wash-and-Wear.—A garment that can be washed by hand or by machine in warm water, drip-dried, and then worn without need of pressing.

Weaving.—The manufacture of fabric by interlacing two systems of yarn at right angles.

Weft.—See *Filling.*

Weft Knit.—Along with warp knit, one of the two basic knitting processes. In weft knit, the fabric is produced by knitting in a crosswise direction. Weft knit, of which hand knitting is an example, often uses only one yarn at a time, the yarn being carried from side to side in hand knitting and flat knitting or around and around in circular knitting. Also called *filling knit.*

Whipcord.—A compact, twill-weave cloth of wool, worsted, or other fibers. The pronounced twill lines are either right-hand or left-hand and run at a 63° angle.

Woof.—See *Warp; Filling.*

Woolens.—Along with worsteds and unfinished worsteds, one of the three types of cloth made from wool. Woolens generally have a rather fuzzy appearance and are heavier and bulkier and with less tensile strength than worsted. There is also a fewer number of interlaced yarns per given area.

Worsted.—Along with woolens and unfinished worsteds, one of the three types of fabric made from wool. Worsted is woven from choice woolen stock made of fibers of approximately the same staple length. Worsted fabric should show a clear outline of the plain- or twill-weave construction.

Yarn.—Usually, a group of fibers spun (twisted) together to form a strand suitable for weaving, knitting, or other interlacing techniques of fabric construction. Some yarns may have no twist, and some may consist of a single filament (monofilament).

Yarn Dyeing.—Dyeing of yarn before it is woven into fabrics.

Z-Twist.—A counterclockwise twist.

GEORGE E. LINTON
Author of "The Modern Textile Dictionary"

TEXTUAL CRITICISM is a method of studying literary works that aims at establishing a text as close to the author's words as the evidence of the preserved documents permits. This article will be concerned only with the general principles of textual criticism as they apply to literary study. For a discussion of the principles for dealing with manuscript texts of the Bible, see BIBLE—*Textual Criticism of the Old Testament* and *The Text of the New Testament*.

Texts are preserved in two forms: autograph and transmitted. Although "autograph" has traditionally been applied to a document in the author's handwriting, the term must be broadened for modern usage to include mechanically produced documents, such as typescripts and recordings. The important thing is that whatever form the document takes, the author himself must have produced it. A text is designated as "transmitted" when it is nonauthorial copy.

Although textual criticism is not subject to rigid rules, there are two basic processes for establishing a text: (1) the selection of the authoritative form or forms of the text after the examination of the available documentary evidence and (2) emendation, the correcting of the form of the text so arrived at in order to reconstruct the author's hypothetical fair copy. These processes differ for manuscripts and printed books and require separate treatment.

Manuscripts. No Greek or Roman classical texts have survived in copies in the authors' hands. All extant manuscripts are derived from the originals through an unknown number of intermediate copies. Before the invention of the printing press all books were copied by hand, and in the process of repeated copying, errors were introduced into the text. Whatever corruptions or alterations appeared in the immediate ancestor—the specimen from which the manuscript was being copied—were likely to be preserved, and new errors were introduced. The textual critic must first isolate these errors and alterations by a study of each manuscript individually and then determine the relationship of the various manuscripts by collating, or comparing, all known copies and recording the variations among them.

On the basis of these variations the stemma, a diagram resembling a family tree, is constructed, demonstrating the interrelationship of the manuscripts. At the head of the stemma is the archetype, which is closest to the original and from which originate the first branches. The archetype and its branches—all the extant manuscripts with the inferential manuscripts needed to explain their relationship—are called a family. Any group of manuscripts of a given work will be one of three types: ancestral, belonging to a single line of descent; collateral, belonging to different lines of descent; and mixed, neither purely ancestral nor purely collateral.

Even the best manuscripts will be partially corrupt, and even the most corrupt may provide some authoritative readings that otherwise would have been lost. Accordingly, the textual critic, after exhausting the documentary evidence, begins critical emendation, bringing his knowledge of paleography, linguistics, and literary criticism to bear on the construction of an eclectic text from the corpus of variants.

Printed Books. The transmission of texts in printed books differs from the transmission of nonauthorial manuscripts in that manuscript texts derive from the "autograph" through lost intermediaries, whereas printed texts are usually contiguous in their relationship to a preserved common ancestor. This may be the autograph manuscript itself or the first edition printed from it. Since the descent of printed texts is direct, the variations between the editions, or forms, of the texts can usually be dated and attributed with some certainty to either the author or the agent responsible for producing the edition.

The textual critic must recognize the divided authority of substantives—readings that affect the author's meaning or the essence of his expression—and accidentals, such as spelling, capitalization, punctuation, and word division, that affect mainly the formal presentation. This distinction does not exist for nonauthorial manuscript texts, because no exemplar is close enough to the autograph for its accidentals to have been reproduced with any fidelity. Hence they have no authority and are modernized. But for printed books this distinction is important, because one of the printed texts is usually derived directly from the author's manuscript. In the absence of the manuscript, the only authority for its characteristics is the edition—usually the first—printed directly from it. If the printed text carefully reproduced the accidentals of the manuscript, there would be little problem, but this is rarely the case. The textual critic must attempt to separate the author's hand from that of the compositor or in modern times that of the house editor, using the evidence provided by analytical bibliography. This is the examination of the book as artifact in order to discover the details of its manufacture and their effect on the transmission of the text. See BIBLIOGRAPHY—*Analytic Bibliography*.

The first edition is usually chosen as copy-text, or basic text, and its accidentals are retained even when it is not certain that these are the author's. Copy-text readings are emended, however, with substantive variants from later editions. If the author's revision of a later edition was demonstrably thorough enough to affect the accidentals, the texture of that edition may be considered authoritative. When the author's manuscript survives it may be chosen as copy-text. The manuscript of Hawthorne's *House of the Seven Gables*, for example, is much closer to the author's intentions than is the first printing, which introduces a number of errors. But Mark Twain's manuscripts can rarely be used as copy-text because they are essentially drafts that did not reach final form until print.

The editor-critic proceeds by collating all editions over which the author may have had control and admitting the authoritative variants—those that can be demonstrated to have been introduced by the author—from later editions. The editor cannot pick and choose among variants as did the editor of early manuscripts, assuming that he is recovering independent pure readings from multiple sources. The final establishment of a definitive text depends on the critic's ability to couple his bibliographical knowledge of the history of the text with sound critical and literary judgment.

O M BRACK, JR., *Coeditor of "Bibliography and Textual Criticism"*

Further Reading: Bowers, Fredson, *Bibliography and Textual Criticism* (New York 1964); Brack, O M, Jr., and Barnes, Warner, eds., *Bibliography and Textual Criticism: English and American Literature, 1700 to the Present* (Chicago 1969); Greg, Walter W., *The Calculus of Variants* (New York 1927); Maas, Paul, *Textual Criticism* (New York 1958).

NATIONAL PORTRAIT GALLERY

CULVER PICTURES

THACKERAY (*left*) was an illustrator as well as a novelist. The drawing above appeared in *Punch*.

THACKERAY, thak′ə-rē, **William Makepeace** (1811–1863), English novelist, whose narrative method, ironic insight, and analysis of motivation contributed greatly to the range and resources of late- and post-Victorian writers. His fiction is both typically Victorian and idiosyncratic. It discredits current ethical values, satirizes romantic idealisms, sometimes achieves, sometimes misses artistic equilibrium.

Thackeray's background and his personal life were as anomalous as his works. His grandfather and his father, men of some distinction, served in the East India Company—a career of dubious reputation. His mother, whose antecedents were semirespectable, married Thackeray's father in India in 1810, after having been forcibly separated from her lover. When her husband died in 1816, she married the man she had first loved and later returned with him to England. For Thackeray, she was both a beatific mother and a memory of maternal rejection—both a prudish, possessive woman and a heroine of romance.

Life—*1811–1845*. Thackeray was born in Calcutta on July 18, 1811, into surroundings both foreign and nationalistic. When his mother remarried, he was sent back to England. After an intensively classical training at Charterhouse in London, he entered Cambridge but left in 1830 without taking a degree. His peculiar partial alienation was expressed in conflicting tendencies to rebel and to conform. He visited Weimar and other German cities, worked at law in London, became a journalist, studied art in Paris, lost his inheritance, and in 1836 married Isabella Shawe, an Anglo-Irish girl.

Thereafter he worked more seriously as both writer and illustrator, often using pseudonyms, including Mr. M. A. Titmarsh and George Savage Fitz-Boodle. Thackeray's drawings are often central in work that ranges from reportorial to dramatic. Although his finished scenes, like the vignettes for *Vanity Fair* (1847–1848), are hardly more than competent, his personal talent appears in satiric caricatures or in the intricate allegorical miniatures that decorate initial letters in his early novels.

Until 1842, Thackeray wrote mainly for *Fraser's Magazine*, contributing to it such works as *The Yellowplush Correspondence* (1837–1838), *A Shabby Genteel Story* (1840), and *The History of Samuel Titmarsh and the Great Hoggarty Diamond* (1841). Thereafter, he contributed increasingly to *Punch*, where he published *The Snobs of England, by One of Themselves* (1846–1847), a series of his most incisive satirical essays. His work of this period typically exposes social pretense and human exploitation, and in the longer works of fiction, like *Catherine* (*Fraser's*, 1839–1840) and *The Luck of Barry Lyndon* (*Fraser's*, 1844), it satirizes popular myths—Byronic pathos, romantic promiscuity, heroic opportunism. In his independent journalism, human behavior is universalized and philosophical attitudes are developed—*The Paris Sketch Book* (1840), *The Second Funeral of Napoleon* (1841), and *Notes on a Journey from Cornhill to Grand Cairo* (1846).

Thackeray's marriage, although apparently conventional, was essentially insecure, as his earlier familial relations had been. His wife suffered mental depression following the birth in 1840 of a third daughter, Harriet (later Mrs. Leslie Stephen), and thereafter lived in institutions. A second daughter died in infancy. The oldest, Anne (later Lady Ritchie), herself a novelist, provided notes on Thackeray for the Biographical Edition of his works.

***1846–1863*.** In mid-life Thackeray once again faced an aberrant situation—married but without a wife, disestablished domestically yet with two young children. In 1846, when he acquired a house in London, his daughters came to live with him. In the following year, *Vanity Fair* established his reputation. *The History of Pendennis* (1848–1850) ensured his popularity. *The History of Henry Esmond Esq.* (1852) was less favorably received, but *The Newcomes* (1853–1855) was a further success. During its publication Thackeray's health began to fail, and with *The Virginians* (1857–1859) his fiction declined in popularity. He had other resources, however. In 1851 he delivered in London a series of lectures entitled *The English Humourists of the Eighteenth Century* (repeated in the United States in 1852–1853), polished and perceptive, though occasionally prudish, discussions of neoclassical art and wit. *The Four Georges* followed—sardonic portraits of England's Hanoverian kings, first presented in the United States in 1855–1856.

In 1859, Thackeray became editor of *The Cornhill Magazine,* where he published *Lovel the Widower* (1860) and *The Adventures of Philip on His Way Through the World* (1861–1862), versions of earlier themes, and *The Roundabout Papers* (1860–1863), perhaps his finest essays. He died in London on Dec. 24, 1863.

The Major Novels. Parody, which predominates in Thackeray's journalism, leads directly to *Vanity Fair.* Of the two earlier extended narratives, *Barry Lyndon* imitates Fielding's ironic satire, but *Catherine* is a pastiche of mannerisms mockingly borrowed from Scott, Byron, Bulwer-Lytton, and fashionable female writers. In *Catherine,* scenes presented twice in contrasting styles suggest that Thackeray's sense of the way conventions control perception, while perception determines the content of experience and objectivity, is equivocal if not illusory.

Vanity Fair, like *Catherine,* includes a scene in multiple styles and culminates in a parody of the "happy ending" of fashionable fiction. The actors, personifications of popular conventions, participate in the novel's extended metaphor—a puppet show. In their roles as martyred mother, noble rake, blooded bully, and bohemian adventuress, they ironically betray pathetic motivations—sexual repression, defensive insecurity, inarticulate aspiration, the struggle to survive. Individual identities cannot be defined, and the narrator makes the point in a final comment: "Come, children, let us shut up the box and the puppets, for our play is played out."

Such "commentary" in Thackeray's fiction—a modification of Fielding and Sterne—is a sympathetic or skeptical, ambivalent, self-questioning chorus. It reappears in *Pendennis,* where "the maternal passion," including "a sexual jealousy on the mother's part," is "symbolized" in the sinister religious image of "a bosom bleeding with love." If man's devious idealisms are Thackeray's recurrent theme, he nowhere more effectively explores them for the Victorian audience than in the image of the beatified mother.

Henry Esmond, set in the 18th century, recreates the nation's cultural past. Of it, Thackeray said, "I . . . am willing to leave it, when I go, as my card." The protagonist's chivalric heritage fuses with the satiric attitudes of his Augustan maturity and mellows into the poetic insights of a 19th century sensitivity. The "roles" of earlier novels recur as traditional idealisms. If chivalry, pastoral, and epic are often masks for corruption and brutality, they have a tenuous truth as well. Thackeray's premise of multiple "truth" (*Pendennis,* chap. 61) is akin to the "negative capability" of Keats and the "relative spirit" of Pater. It is central in *Esmond* ("turn the perspective glass, and a giant appears a pigmy"), where mythic maternal personae reveal disparate aspects of an equivocal feminine figure, with incestuous implications that offended contemporary readers.

The hero of *Esmond* is the narrator as well. An old man as he "writes," he assumes the detachment of Thackeray's earlier "commentator"; yet he is also the young man whom he describes ("Such a past is always present to a man"). A Proustian fusion of past and present is thematic in *Esmond,* and the process of writing represents, as in Proust, the hero's realization of an "identity" through art.

The *Newcomes* is diffuse and erratic. The interplay of conflicting insights that constitutes the "relative spirit" of Thackeray's best work becomes increasingly disorganized. "Commentary" is now a defensive device, a "mask," as Thackeray remarked in one of his letters. Irony fails to modify sentiment, and satire, poetic allusion, naturalism, and fable are no longer effectively integrated. But the novel profoundly influenced later writers. For Henry James, *The Newcomes* was a "large loose baggy monster"; yet James' *Wings of the Dove* alludes to it, and in *The Ambassadors*—where James' characters, the Newsomes, recall Thackeray's Newcomes—Mme. de Vionnet is apparently related to Thackeray's Mme. de Florac.

The Virginians offers a Jamesian juxtaposition of old world and new, but although the novel opens brilliantly, it eventually loses vitality. *Lovel the Widower* and *Philip* recur to themes Thackeray had already explored, and *Denis Duval* (published in 1864) was interrupted by his death.

Influence. Victorian critics often contrast Dickens and Thackeray—aptly—since their disparate talents anticipate a full range of fictional resources. Dickens' novels include mythic, fantastic, absurdist elements that play little part in Thackeray, but these Dickensian motifs, typical in modern narrative modes, were too idiosyncratic to create a novelistic convention. Thackeray's fiction—with its ironic, relativistic vision, psychological insights, and dispassionate "commentary"—offered both theme and method to later novelists. Thackeray's voice persists in the compassionate irony of George Eliot's narration, in Meredith's complexities and James' subjective "point of view," and in the thematic recurrence of feminine exploitation, of dubious masculine chivalry, of America, England, and Europe juxtaposed. Virginia Woolf and E. M. Forster extend a convention that may find its culmination in Proust's *Remembrance of Things Past,* although Proust drew directly on Eliot, Ruskin, and Pater. In the United States, Hawthorne was perhaps indebted to Thackeray, Howells certainly was, and without explicit "influence," Sinclair Lewis, Fitzgerald, and even Faulkner continued variously to develop a method that may be said to have disintegrated only with the incipient rejection of the traditional novel. See also the Index entry THACKERAY, WILLIAM MAKEPEACE.

JOHN W. LOOFBOUROW
Boston College

Bibliography

The most inclusive collections of Thackeray's works are the Biographical Edition, 13 vols. (London and New York 1898–1899) and the Oxford Thackeray, edited by George Saintsbury, 17 vols. (London 1908). Bibliographic and research sources are *A Thackeray Library,* collected by Henry S. Van Duzer (New York 1910), and *Victorian Fiction: A Guide to Research,* edited by Lionel Stevenson (Cambridge, Mass., 1964).

Loofbourow, John W., *Thackeray and the Form of Fiction* (Princeton, N. J., 1964).

Ray, Gordon N., ed., *The Letters and Private Papers of William Makepeace Thackeray,* 4 vols. (Cambridge, Mass., 1945–1946).

Ray, Gordon N., *Thackeray,* 2 vols. (New York 1955, 1958).

Saintsbury, George, *A Consideration of Thackeray* (London 1931).

THAILAND

Coat of Arms

TEMPLE OF DAWN in Bangkok is one of Buddhist Thailand's most impressive landmarks. The 240-foot central tower (*right*) and its surrounding pagodas and pavilions are richly decorated.

ACE WILLIAMS, FROM BLACK STAR

THAILAND, tī'land, is a country of Southeast Asia that was known as Siam through most of its long national existence. In the center of mainland Southeast Asia, touching on Laos, Cambodia (or the Khmer Republic), Malaysia, and Burma, it has great strategic importance. Thailand, compared with other countries in the region, has generally enjoyed stability and prosperity. But it has also endured upheavals, such as the overthrow of the military regime in 1973, and has experienced periods of economic stagnation.

As the region's only nation to have avoided the experience of colonial domination, Thailand was able to preserve much of its traditional society, its religious traditions, and its ancient India-derived conception of governmental authority. The modernization changes that Thailand has experienced since the mid-19th century have not been particularly disturbing because they were largely royally sponsored rather than imposed from the outside. A succession of able rulers recognized that accommodation to external pressure was unavoidable if the kingdom was to survive. Today's visitor to Bangkok is struck by the contrast between the modern airport, the deluxe hotels, and the heavy motorized traffic, on the one hand, and the many surviving evidences of royal tradition, the colorful Buddhist temples, and the still heavy *klong* (canal) traffic on the other. Although Western dress is increasingly in vogue in the cities, the countryside seems little changed. Within a radius of 50 miles (80 km) of Bangkok can be seen the impressive monuments of pre-Thai Mon and Khmer civilization, along with the ruins of an early Thai capital, Ayuthia (Ayutthaya). The cultural vitality of the past is very much in evidence.

CONTENTS

Thailand's national history dates from the 13th century, when Thai leaders at Sukhothai in the north assumed independence from the faltering Khmer state of Angkor. The kingdom of Siam, as Thailand was called until 1939, included only a portion of the total region inhabited by Thai-speaking peoples. The change of name to Thailand by Premier Pibun Songgram reflected his ambition to extend his country's frontiers by taking advantage of Japanese power and hostility to Western colonial rule in Asia. Border areas were annexed during World War II when Thailand was an ally of Japan. The annexed border areas in Laos and Burma were inhabited by Thai peoples, and those in Cambodia and Malaya, although not ethnically Thai, had been under

MARC AND EVELYNE BERNHEIM, FROM RAPHO GUILLUMETTE

Bangkok, Thailand's capital, combines traditional and modern. The Grand Palace compound is in the distance.

INFORMATION HIGHLIGHTS

Official Name: Prathet Thai ("Land of the Free").
Head of State: King.
Head of Government: Premier.
Legislature: National Assembly.
Area: 198,456 square miles (514,000 sq km).
Boundaries: *North,* Burma and Laos; *east,* Laos, Cambodia, and Gulf of Siam; *south,* Malaysia; *west,* Andaman Sea and Burma.
Elevations: Highest point—Doi Inthanon, 8,452 feet (2,576 meters); lowest point—sea level.
Population: (1960 census) 26,257,916; (1973 est.) 39,900,000.
Capital: Bangkok (Krung Thep).
Major Languages: Thai (official), English, Chinese, Malay, tribal languages.
Major Religions: Buddhism, Islam, Christianity, animism.
Monetary Unit: Baht (100 satang).
Weights and Measures: Metric system.
Flag: Broad blue horizontal stripe in the center, flanked above and below by narrower pairs of stripes, the inner ones white and the outer ones red. See also FLAG.
National Anthem: *Pleng Chard (National Anthem),* beginning "Thailand is the place for all Thai . . ."

Siamese control at one time. The name Thailand was abandoned in 1945 by the pro-Allied Free Thai government in order to expedite peace negotiations with Britain, but it was revived in 1948 when Pibun returned to power.

Thailand has been a constitutional monarchy since 1932. The monarchy provides a symbol of governmental authority and is respected by the population. Political power, however, long resided with the military, who shared governing duties with a permanent, nonpolitical bureaucracy, leaving the legislature with little real power. But this pattern was altered by the student uprising that overthrew the regime of Field Marshal Thanom Kittikachorn in 1973. An essentially civilian government was then installed. The government has traditionally been paternalistic toward the Thai ethnic majority; it has also been prompt to discourage overt dissent.

1. The Land

Thailand may be divided into five distinct regions. The heart of the country is the central valley, or plain, of the Chao Phraya Menam. The word *menam* means "river."

Regions. The Chao Phraya is formed by the confluence of northern tributary streams, and its flat, heavily sedimented valley is capable of extensive agricultural development through irrigation. Dams and conduit canals have done much in modern times to expand rice cultivation beyond the limits previously imposed by an inadequate rainfall of 40 inches (1,000 mm) a year. Burma's Irrawaddy delta, by comparison, receives around 115 inches (2,900 mm) annually. In the heart of the central valley is located the ancient Khmer city of Lavo (modern Lopburi). Just south is the site of Ayuthia, and near the lower (southern) end of the valley is Bangkok. A subsidiary region lies to the east and south of Bangkok, bordered by the shores of the Gulf of Siam and the mountains of Cambodia. This area enjoys an abundant summer rainfall but is mountainous and lacks extensive cultivable areas. Modern highways link its new port of Sattahip with central and northeast Thailand.

The northwestern region, one of the most interesting, is made up of the four parallel valleys of the Ping, Wang, Yom, and Nan rivers, all tributary to the central Chao Phraya River. The valleys are separated by low watersheds but the region as a whole is enclosed by a formidable horseshoe rim of mountain ranges, open to the south. The present city of Lamphun, just south of Chiengmai (Chiangmai), was the seat of the ancient Mon state of Haripunjaya. The region exhibits a cultural identity all its own.

An equally ancient Mon state, called Dvaravati, occupied a third region, located to the west of Bangkok and extending southward. Its center was Nakhon Pathom. Strongly influenced by Indian culture at an early date, the Dvaravati Mons maintained connections between the northwestern corner of the Gulf of Siam and passes that led through the mountains to ports on the Andaman Sea.

A fourth region is the Korat plateau in northeastern Thailand, extending from the limits of the Chao Phraya Valley eastward to the Mekong River boundary. Largely wooded, the Korat includes a number of parallel river valleys draining into the Mekong basin. The soil is generally infertile, often sandy and leached of mineral nutrients, so that the area of irrigated rice cultivation is severely limited. The people of the Korat are identical with Lao-Thai peoples who inhabit the

THAILAND

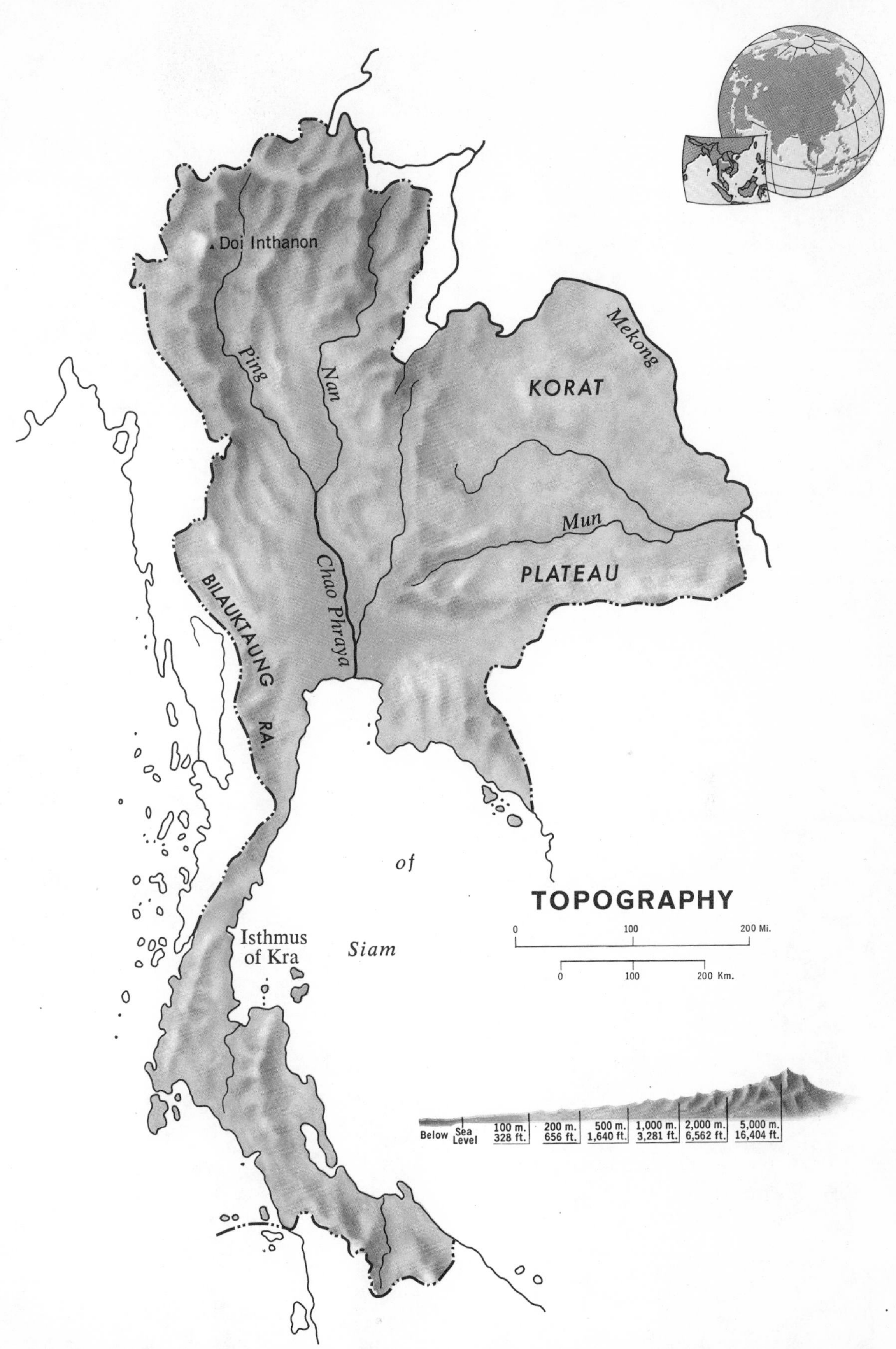

Doi Inthanon
Ping
Nan
Mekong
KORAT
Mun
PLATEAU
Chao Phraya
BILAUKTAUNG
RA.
of
Isthmus
of Kra
Siam
TOPOGRAPHY
0
100
200 Mi.
0
100
200 Km.
Below
Sea
Level
100 m.
328 ft.
200 m.
656 ft.
500 m.
1,640 ft.
1,000 m.
3,281 ft.
2,000 m.
6,562 ft.
5,000 m.
16,404 ft.

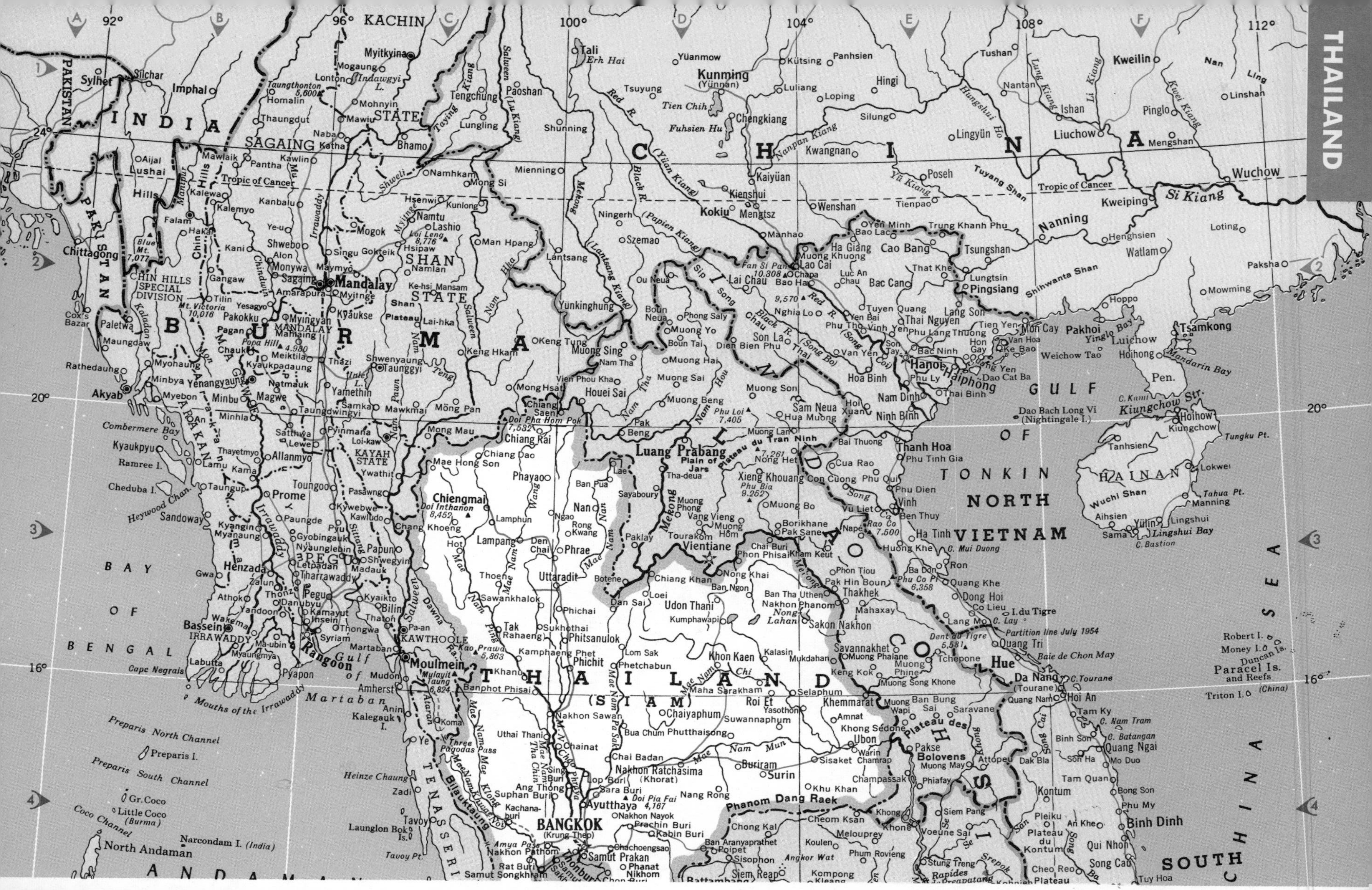

THAILAND
(SIAM)
BURMA
LAOS
CAMBODIA
NORTH VIETNAM
CHINA
INDIA
PAKISTAN
HAINAN
GULF OF TONKIN
SOUTH CHINA SEA
BAY OF BENGAL
ANDAMAN
Gulf of Martaban
BANGKOK
(Krung Thep)
Thonburi
Rangoon
Mandalay
Moulmein
Chiengmai
Vientiane
Luang Prabang
Hanoi
Haiphong
Hue
Da Nang
(Tourane)
Kunming
(Yünnan)
Nanning
Akyab
Bassein
Chittagong
Imphal
Sylhet
Lashio
Bhamo
Myitkyina
Prome
Toungoo
Pegu
Henzada
Ayutthaya
Nakhon Ratchasima
(Khorat)
Udon Thani
Khon Kaen
Ubon
Phitsanulok
Lampang
Chiang Rai
Tavoy
Pakse
Savannakhet
Thakhek
KACHIN
STATE
SHAN STATE
KAYAH STATE
KAWTHOOLE
SAGAING
MANDALAY
MAGWE
PEGU
IRRAWADDY
ARAKAN
CHIN HILLS SPECIAL DIVISION
TENASSERIM
Salween
Irrawaddy
Mekong
Chindwin
Red R.
Black R.
Si Kiang
Tropic of Cancer
Partition line July 1954
Paracel Is.
and Reefs
Preparis North Channel
Preparis South Channel
Coco Channel
North Andaman
Narcondam I. (India)
Phanom Dang Raek
Plateau du Tran Ninh
Plain of Jars
Plateau des Bolovens
Dong Hoi
Thanh Hoa
Vinh
Lai Chau
Dien Bien Phu
Sam Neua
Xieng Khouang
Kweilin
Liuchow
Wuchow
Pakhoi
Kiungchow Str.
Hoihow
Lingshui Bay
Cape Negrais
Mouths of the Irrawaddy
Combermere Bay
Ramree I.
Cheduba I.
Kyaukpyu
Sandoway
Mt. Victoria 10,016
Doi Inthanon 8,452
Fan Si Pan 10,308
Phu Bia 9,252

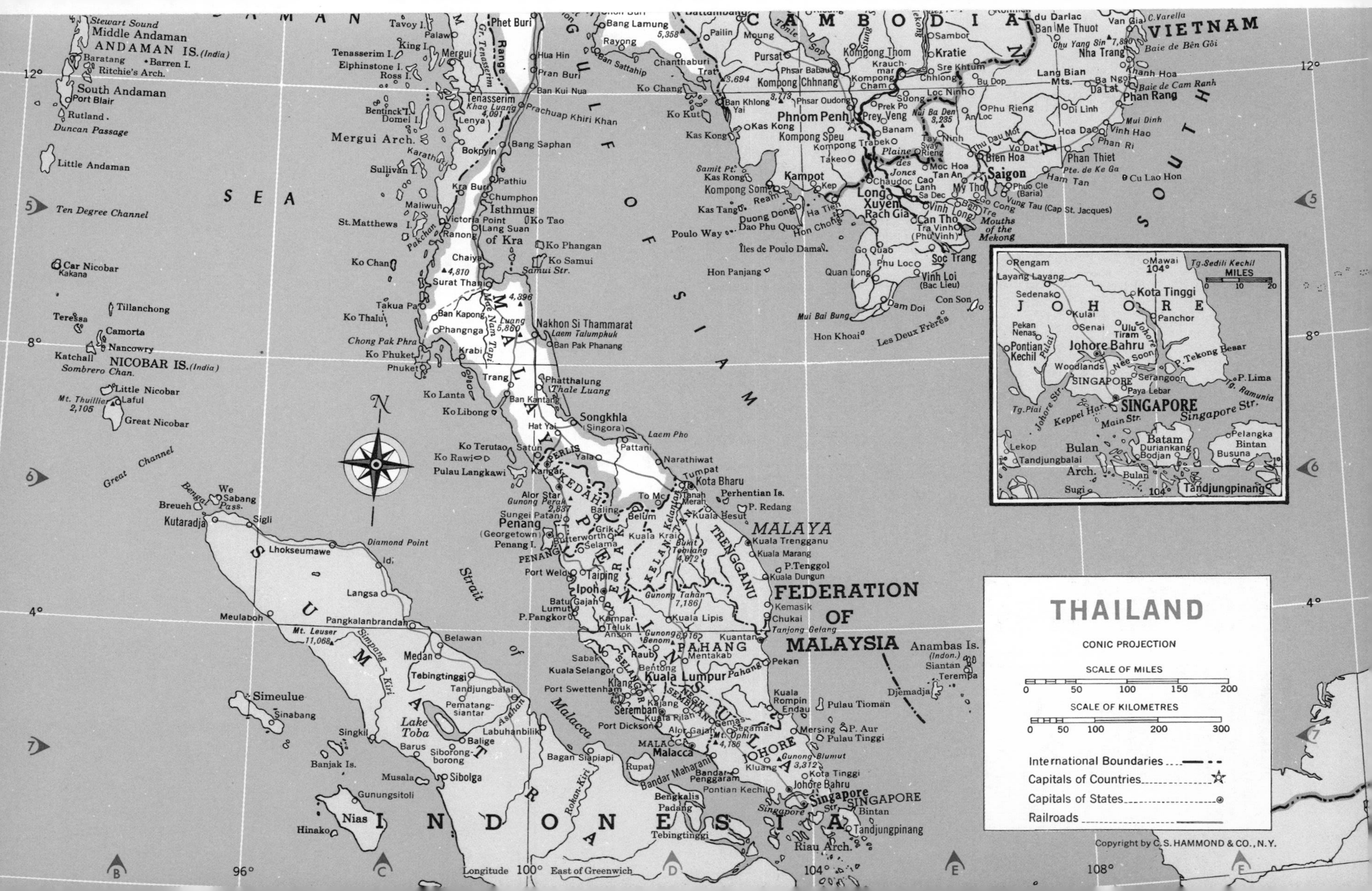
THAILAND
CONIC PROJECTION
SCALE OF MILES
0 50 100 150 200
SCALE OF KILOMETRES
0 50 100 200 300
International Boundaries
Capitals of Countries
Capitals of States
Railroads
Copyright by C. S. HAMMOND & CO., N. Y.
Longitude 100° East of Greenwich

THAILAND

Total Population, 34,738,000

CITIES and TOWNS

Amnat, 11,335 .... E 4
Ang Thong, 6,458 .... C 4
Ayutthaya, 24,597 .... D 4
Ban Aranyaprathet, 11,112 .... D 4
Bangkok (capital), 1,299,528 .... D 4
Bangkok, *2,000,000 .... D 4
Bang Lamung, 9,087 .... D 4
Bang Saphan, 6,959 .... C 5
Ban Kantang, 5,076 .... C 6
Ban Kapong, 1,300 .... C 5
Ban Khlong Yai, 3,815 .... D 5
Ban Kui Nua .... D 4
Ban Ngon .... D 3
Ban Pak Phanang, 11,963 .... D 5
Banphot Phisai, 6,036 .... C 3
Ban Pua, 12,317 .... D 3
Ban Sattahip, 22,942 .... D 4
Ban Tha Uthen, 7,297 .... D 3
Bua Chum, 12,052 .... D 4
Buriram, 12,579 .... D 4
Chachoengsao, 19,809 .... D 4
Chai Badan, 6,158 .... D 4
Chai Buri, †31,135 .... D 3
Chainat, 4,652 .... D 4
Chaiya, 3,607 .... C 5
Chaiyaphum, 9,633 .... D 4
Chang Khoeng, 6,037 .... C 3
Chanthaburi, 10,780 .... D 4
Chiang Dao, 8,017 .... C 3
Chiang Khan, 5,810 .... D 3
Chiang Rai, 11,663 .... C 3
Chiang Saen, 5,443 .... C 2
Chiengmai, 65,600 .... C 3
Chon Buri, 32,496 .... D 4
Chumphon, 9,342 .... C 5
Dan Sai, 6,710 .... D 3
Den Chai, 12,732 .... C 3
Hat Yai, 35,504 .... C 6
Hot, 3,486 .... C 3
Hua Hin, 17,078 .... D 4
Kabin Buri, 3,703 .... D 4
Kalasin, 11,043 .... D 3
Kamphaeng Phet, 7,171 .... C 3
Kanchanaburi, 12,957 .... C 4
Khanu, 1,062 .... C 3
Khemmarat, 5,426 .... E 4
Khon Kaen, 19,591 .... D 3
Khorat (Nakhon Ratchasima), 41,037 .... D 4
Khu Khan, †122,206 .... E 4
Krabi, 2,691 .... C 5
Kra Buri, 3,717 .... C 5
Krung Thep (Bangkok) (capital), 1,299,528 .... D 4
Kumphawapi, 20,759 .... D 3
Lae, 5,743 .... D 3
Lampang, 36,488 .... C 3
Lamphun, 10,602 .... C 3
Lang Suan, 4,108 .... C 5
Loei, 7,301 .... D 3
Lom Sak, 8,386 .... D 3
Lop Buri, 21,244 .... D 4
Mae Hong Son, 3,445 .... C 3
Maha Sarakham, 15,680 .... D 3
Mukdahan, 17,738 .... E 3
Nakhon Nayok, 8,048 .... D 4
Nakhon Pathom, 28,426 .... C 4
Nakhon Phanom, 14,799 .... D 3
Nakhon Ratchasima, 41,037 .... D 4
Nakhon Sawan, 34,947 .... D 4
Nakhon Si Thammarat, 25,919 .... D 5
Nan, 13,843 .... D 3
Nang Rong, 15,623 .... D 4
Narathiwat, 17,508 .... D 6
Ngao, †32,643 .... D 3
Nong Khai, 21,120 .... D 3
Pathiu, 1,343 .... C 5
Pattani, 16,804 .... D 6
Phanat Nikhom, 9,307 .... D 4
Phangnga, 4,782 .... C 5
Phatthalung, 10,420 .... C 6
Phayao, 17,959 .... C 3
Phet Buri, 24,654 .... C 4
Phetchabun, 5,947 .... D 3
Phichai, 5,258 .... D 3
Phichit, 9,258 .... D 3
Phitsanulok, 30,364 .... D 3
Phon Phisai, 6,745 .... D 3
Phrae, 16,005 .... D 3
Phuket, 28,163 .... C 6
Phutthaisong, 9,315 .... D 4
Prachin Buri, 13,420 .... D 4
Prachuap Khiri Khan, 6,303 .... D 5
Pran Buri, 7,795 .... D 4
Rahaeng (Tak), 13,274 .... C 3
Ranong, 5,993 .... C 5
Rat Buri, 20,383 .... C 4
Rayong, 9,680 .... D 4
Roi Et, 12,930 .... D 4
Rong Kwang, †39,375 .... D 3
Sakon Nakhon, 16,457 .... E 3
Samut Prakan, 21,769 .... D 4
Samut Sakhon, 27,602 .... D 4
Samut Songkhram, 12,801 .... C 4
Sara Buri, 17,572 .... D 4
Satun, 4,369 .... C 6
Sawankhalok, 7,880 .... C 3
Selaphum, 10,395 .... E 3
Sing Buri, 8,384 .... D 4
Singora (Songkhla), 31,014 .... D 6
Sisaket, 9,519 .... E 4
Songkhla, 31,014 .... D 6
Sukhothai, 8,627 .... D 3
Suphan Buri, 13,859 .... C 4
Surat Thani, 19,738 .... C 5
Surin, 13,860 .... D 4
Suwannaphum, 15,731 .... D 4
Tak, 13,274 .... C 3
Takua Pa, 6,308 .... C 5
Thoen, 17,283 .... C 3
Thonburi, 402,818 .... D 4
Thonburi, *460,000 .... D 4
Trang, 17,158 .... C 6
Trat, 3,813 .... D 4
Ubon, 27,092 .... E 4
Udon Thani, 29,965 .... D 3
Uthai Thani, 10,729 .... C 4
Uttaradit, 9,120 .... D 3
Warin Chamrap, 7,067 .... E 4
Yala, 18,083 .... D 6
Yasothon, 9,717 .... D 4

OTHER FEATURES

Amya (pass) .... C 4
Andaman (sea) .... B 4
Bilauktaung (range) .... C 4
Chan, Ko (isl.) .... C 5
Chang, Ko (isl.) .... D 4
Chao Phraya, Mae Nam (river) .... D 4
Chi, Mae Nam (river) .... D 3
Chong Pak Phra (cape) .... C 5
Dang Raek, Phanom (mts.) .... D 4
Doi Inthanon (mt.) .... C 3
Doi Pha Hom Pok (mt.) .... C 2
Doi Pia Fai (mt.) .... D 4
Inthanon, Doi (mt.) .... C 3
Kao Prawa (mt.) .... C 3
Khao Luang (mt.) .... C 5
Khwae Noi, Mae Nam (river) .... C 4
Ko Chan (isl.) .... C 5
Ko Chang (isl.) .... D 4
Ko Kut (isl.) .... D 5
Ko Lanta (isl.), 9,486 .... C 6
Ko Libong (isl.) .... C 6
Ko Phangan (isl.) .... D 5
Ko Phuket (isl.), 75,652 .... C 5
Ko Rawi (isl.) .... C 6
Ko Samui (isl.), 30,818 .... D 5
Ko Tao (isl.) .... D 5
Ko Terutao (isl.) .... C 6
Ko Thalu (isls.) .... C 5
Kra (isthmus) .... C 5
Kut, Ko (isl.) .... D 5
Laem Pho (cape) .... D 6
Laem Talumphuk (cape) .... D 5
Lahan, Nong (lake) .... D 3
Lanta, Ko (isl.), 9,486 .... C 6
Libong, Ko (isl.) .... C 6
Luang (mt.) .... C 5
Luang, Thale (lagoon) .... D 6
Mae Klong, Mae Nam (river) .... C 4
Malay (pen.) .... C 5
Mekong (river) .... E 3
Mun, Mae Nam (river) .... D 4
Nan, Mae Nam (river) .... D 3
Nong Lahan (lake) .... D 3
Pakchan (river) .... C 5
Pa Sak, Mae Nam (river) .... D 4
Pha Hom Pak, Doi (mt.) .... C 2
Phangan, Ko (isl.) .... D 5
Phanom Dang Raek (mts.) .... D 4
Phuket, Ko (isl.), 75,652 .... C 5
Pia Fai, Doi (mt.) .... D 4
Ping, Mae Nam (river) .... C 3
Rawi, Ko (isl.) .... C 6
Salween (river) .... C 3
Samui (strait) .... D 5
Samui, Ko (isl.), 30,818 .... D 5
Siam (gulf) .... D 5
Tao, Ko (isl.) .... D 5
Tapi, Mae Nam (river) .... C 5
Terutao, Ko (isl.) .... C 6
Tha Chin, Mae Nam (river) .... C 4
Thale Luang (lagoon) .... D 6
Thalu, Ko (isls.) .... C 5
Three Pagodas (pass) .... C 4
Wang, Mae Nam (river) .... C 3

*City and suburbs. †Population of district.

Total pop.—1969 off. est.; cap. (with suburbs)—1968 off. est.; Thonburi (with suburbs)—1964 off. est.; other pops—1960 final census.

east bank of the middle Mekong River. Cultural and commercial connections are largely in the direction of Thailand's central valley, however, partly because the lower reaches of the Mekong are not navigable.

In the extreme south Thailand occupies the Isthmus of Kra and the long narrow neck of the Malay Peninsula. Isthmian Thailand has tin ore deposits and prospective offshore oil resources.

Climate. Thailand's climate is hot and humid most of the year. In the central valley temperatures rarely go below 65° F (18° C) in the coolest months, December and January, and extend upward to around 100° F (38° C) in the hot season, from March to May.

The central valley lies in the "rain shadow" of the Burmese mountains, which intercept moisture-bearing winds. Burma's Tenasserim (southeastern) coast receives 220 inches (5,600 mm) of rain a year compared to 40 inches (1,000 mm) at Bangkok. Summer monsoon winds bring a rainy season from June through September.

Plants and Animals. Thailand's plant life is tropical throughout. Valuable teakwood timber is obtained from the northwestern sections adjacent to the Salween River boundary with Burma. The country produces a great variety of delicious fruits, such as mangoes, bananas, pineapples, citrus fruits, litchis, durians, and mangosteens. Among the animals is the elephant, which is used in logging and is a symbol of Thai royalty. There are also monkeys, wild and tame buffaloes, and tigers as well as smaller cats. The Siamese domestic cat is probably native to China rather than Thailand. Tropical birds are present in great variety.

2. The People and Their Culture

Except in the border mountain areas and in the extreme south, the population of Thailand is largely homogeneous. The Thai people are racially Mongoloid. Lighter complexioned than the neighboring Burmese, Cambodians, and Malays, they resemble kindred peoples of South China. The Thai people speak the Thai language, use the same script, are socially integrated, and are committed to a common Buddhist faith. The Lao of the Mekong lowlands are also culturally and ethnically Thai, and non-Buddhist Thai-speaking tribal groups extend northward through the mountains of Laos and across the border of China.

The Thai language, like Chinese, is tonal in character—that is, words which are different in meaning may be identical in sound except for the height and movement of the fundamental pitch of the voice. Thai is also similar structurally to Chinese but has a different vocabulary and different inflectional systems. Modern Thai includes many Sanskrit words, reflecting heavy literary borrowing from Indianized Mons and Khmers who preceded the Thai in Thailand.

Ethnic Minorities. The one large minority people in Thailand are the Chinese, who comprise approximately 10% of the country's total population. They concentrate in centers of trade and industry, such as Bangkok, where they dominate the world of business. Discriminated against for most of two decades (1937–1957) by Premier Pibun, the Chinese escaped such treatment after the advent of Marshal Sarit to power in 1957. Sarit expanded governmental controls over trade through designated monopolies, high customs duties, and export licenses, but otherwise encouraged private enterprise. Nevertheless Chinese firms found it expedient to name prestigious members of the Thai ruling elite to directorships and as owners of unpurchased blocks of stock. The Thai Chinese are adaptable and not politically inclined. They perform important functions in many areas of economic life.

Thailand's next largest minority are the Malays. Thai-speaking Muslims, they are mainly fishermen and rice cultivators and live in the southern provinces bordering Malaysia. This area recently has been plagued by Communist guerrillas.

The tribal peoples are less important. Those living along the Burma borders—the Lisu, Luwa, Shan, and Karen—are usually slash-and-burn cultivators, shifting their residence in accordance with the cycle of land utilization. Christianization of border Karens by American missionaries was carried over from Burma after foreigners were excluded from that country in the early 1960's.

Difficulties have arisen along the northernmost borders adjacent to Laos from alien Meo tribesmen, who are fairly recent migrants from South China. Their intrusions into the Mekong Valley are the most recent example of the age-long migration of peoples southward from China. The Meo live by subsistence agriculture and opium sales to the outside and tend to locate in

ALFRED VAN SPRANG, FROM BLACK STAR

FLOATING MARKET offers a wide variety of goods in Bangkok. The sampans also serve as living quarters for thousands of people.

BERYHAUS, FROM BLACK STAR

BUDDHIST MONKS carrying iron pots for food receive breakfast of rice and fruit from Thai women.

mountaintop areas left unoccupied by longer-resident tribal groups. Meo guerrilla activities, said by Bangkok to be Communist inspired, caused the Thai government in 1969 to begin attempts to relocate the Meo away from the Laos border.

Several thousand Vietnamese refugees who went to Thailand during the period 1945–1954 live in the Korat region. Some have been suspected of ties with Hanoi.

Religion. Adherence to Theravada Buddhism is almost universal among the Thai, and all Buddhist young men are expected to spend some time in a monastery as novices. Popular religion includes a variety of animistic and kindred beliefs. These include spirit (*phi*) propitiation, reverence for sacred images, and various forms of magic.

Thai religious tradition is conservative, nonpolitical in character, and in general not involved in a positive way with promoting or guiding social and cultural change. A few monastic leaders are reacting to change and to mounting social needs, but their following is slight and they have no political power. Thai Buddhists cherish their beautiful *wat* (temples) and continue lavish expenditures on them. But the traditional religious activities and celebrations often seem to attract less popular interest than modern diversions, like the movies.

Social System. Thai society is loosely structured, without clans or strict class lines. The monogamous family is the basic social unit. Marriages continue to be arranged by parents, although those based on personal choice are increasing.

Most Thai live in villages. These socially integrated communities respect the influence of elders and customary patron-client relationships, which function informally as agencies of social control. Government activities, by comparison, constitute an unwelcome intrusion.

Local trade and craftsmanship are in the hands of the Thai ethnic group, but the distant marketing of surplus produce is handled by itinerant Chinese traders. Thai farmers work their plots of land individually but pool their labor at harvest time. Young male villagers from outlying areas, particularly the Korat, often journey to Bangkok to make their fortunes operating *samlor* (3-wheeled taxis), or working on construction projects. They assemble in squatter hutments adjacent to drainage canals or on the edges of the city. Many such migrants return home with their savings after a few years' absence. They then acquire a home, some land, and a wife and settle more comfortably into peasant routines.

Thai men tend to aspire to civil service jobs or to police or army service rather than to business careers. Generally speaking, it is the Thai women who engage in business. They manage bazaar stalls and sometimes perform manual labor in construction projects, up to the level of carpenter and bricklayer. Educated middle class women operate real estate agencies and substantial business ventures in the cities—functions that otherwise fall to resident Chinese.

The Buddhist 8-fold path of righteous living includes high ethical principles for earning merit by conquering desire, but the prevailing social mores accommodate the traditional symbols of power. Socially potent are the demands connected with status, requiring deference and respect from below and paternal concern from above. A person's status can be measurably enhanced by educational accomplishment. In fact, university graduates prefer to receive their diplomas from the hand of the king. Other roads to status are civil service appointments, of which there are several grades, and the cultivation of useful personal and family connections.

Overseas study and degrees have carried a high premium since the beginning of the 20th century, when only princes were afforded such opportunities. Foreign-trained professional men and private engineers usually hold some status job although they derive their principal income from business or personal services. The status structure reaches its incontestable peak in royalty, which provides the divine sanction for the exercise of governmental authority.

Within the status hierarchy, criticism by a subordinate is unwelcome and is not usually offered. Silence envelops competition for power and wealth within the upper levels of Thai society. However, the maintenance of governmental stability requires that the prerequisites of power should be widely shared within the elite community in order to forestall armed coups and other expressions of rebellion. Ruling circles must also try to prevent popular grievances—such as high food prices, increased bus fares, and additional direct taxes—that might generate widespread discontent. An unscrupulous individual who has operated successfully within the hierarchical system is usually envied rather than criticized. Popular hatred is reserved for the greedy Chinese employer or merchant, who is alien to the system. Well-to-do Thai families are not averse to acquiring an educated Chinese son-in-law earning a good income, but such ethnic assimilation takes place only at the upper social levels.

Adjustment to Change. There is a growing cultural gap between village Thailand and Bangkok, a modern city of more than 2 million people. But the gap between countryside and metropolis appears to be somewhat less abrupt in Thailand than it is in the Philippines, South Vietnam, and Malaysia.

One reason for this difference between Thailand and other Southeast Asian states is the tenacity of traditional Thai social standards even under the pressure of a modern urban environment. Thailand's long experience with modernization sponsored by its own kings, rather than imposed by foreigners, contributed to its capacity for tolerating and rationalizing paradoxical situations. Reverence for royalty and the insistence that power is exercised in the king's name, plus the inertia of the vast civil service structure, respect for status, and the persistence of Thai identity as distinct from that of resident aliens, are all important factors contributing to the stability and unity of Thai society. Moreover, the country has been spared the devastation of warfare and consequent social dislocation in modern times. The vitality of the Buddhist faith also does much to bridge social gaps, such as prevail between city and countryside.

The genius of the Thai social system is that it can encompass contradictory factors within the framework of an expanding economy and culture. Economic depression, involvement in warfare, or the eventual sheer pressure of excess population could disrupt the adjustment process, as could overabuse of power and privilege at the center.

Education. The Thais have traditionally regarded education as highly important, and until the late 19th century the responsibility for educating the young rested with the temple monks. In the gradual transition to modern public instruction the educational system has remained conservative.

Since 1950 the Thai government has greatly increased the number of public schools and their pupil enrollment. However, parents who can afford to send their children to private schools often prefer to do so because they believe the standards of instruction are higher in the private schools. There are inadequacies in the training of teachers for public schools, and teachers' salaries are low. English-speaking foreigners in Thailand are inclined to notice the deficient results of English language training, which begins in the elementary grades. Substantial assistance in the expansion of elementary education has been rendered by the United Nations Children's Fund (UNICEF).

University education emphasizes lectures rather than outside reading. *Achorns* (lecturers) are traditionally regarded as fountainheads of learning, and there is little pressure on them to revise their lectures once these have been prepared. The emphasis on memorization of lecture notes is detrimental to future scholarship.

Health and Medicine. General health and standards of medical practice in Thailand have improved greatly since 1950. For example, malaria has been mostly eliminated from Bangkok and large areas elsewhere in the country. Partly because of lower infant mortality rates, the rate of population growth (over 3% a year) is exceeded in Southeast Asia only by that of the Philippines. Outside agencies such as the Rockefeller Foundation in Bangkok and the World Health Organization have substantially helped the government in improving public health.

The Arts. Thai artistic activity is at its best in wood carving, the classical dance, and religious sculpture and temple decoration. Traditional Thai art is religious, and it is based on Indian forms. The building of temples and the production of sculpture and paintings were ways of earning religious merit. The traditional theater is an interweaving of dance, literature, music, and drama. Thai craftsmen do excellent work in furniture, particularly in bamboo and rattan. Their work in textiles is much admired also, but increasingly the beautiful Thai silks are produced for the foreign market.

Much of classical Thai literature was lost beyond recovery in the Burmese destruction of Ayuthia in 1767. Surviving from the pre-1500 period were copies of the linguistically valuable *Oath of Allegiance*, a historical narrative of Ayuthia's warfare with Chiengmai, various masterpieces in the fields of ethical poetry and tragic romance, and examples of dignified Thai prose found in legal preambles. The golden age of Thai literature, during the century from King Narai's accession in 1657 to the renewal of the Burmese wars, saw an outpouring of poetry, folklore, songs, dance drama, pilgrimage ballads based on Hindu sources, and grammars, but only a fraction of this survived 1767. Recovery efforts of the new Chakri Dynasty centered at first on scriptures, legal codes, a Buddhist history of Siam, and adaptations of Hindu classics. In the 19th century, King Rama II was a poet, Rama III collected a library, and Mongkut's reign (1851–1868) saw the emergence of prose fiction.

The impact of European patterns on Thai literature has been evident since 1910. Among the notable modern writers are Dok Mai Sot and Si Burapha, novelists; Sot Kuramarohit and Kukrit Promoj, novelists and journalists; and Kukrit's brother, Seni Promoj, lawyer, politician, and journalist, and compiler of a distinguished anthology of Thai poetry.

3. The Economy

The economy of Thailand is inextricably tied to the ownership and utilization of land. Most Thai consider land to be the only form of safe investment. Long-established peasant holdings, not easily subject to mortgage alienation, still provide the essential basis of economic livelihood and social stability throughout the countryside. Mortgage holders usually prefer to keep cultivator-debtors in residence.

Another aspect of the economic importance of land relates to the large concentrations of wealth generated within expanding urban communities. New residential and business areas have been developed, so that real estate values generally have skyrocketed. Much of the surviving wealth of the royal family, for example, is currently concentrated in Bangkok real estate. Construction costs incurred during the 1960's for modern residences suitable for foreign visitors were usually retired from high rental collections within four or five years. Many high government officials own lucrative apartment-house complexes or share ownership in new hotels. Such urban wealth is often tax favored.

AN ELEPHANT helps move felled teak trees in Thailand. Teakwood is a valuable export commodity.

PAOLO KOCH, FROM BLACK STAR

Agriculture. The flat central valley, or central plain, is the agricultural heartland of Thailand, and rice is the staple crop. Land cultivation has been extended by the government's construction of irrigation dams and canals, the three major systems being located within and adjacent to the central plain. In portions of the better-drained sections of the eastern edges of the plain, corn (maize) production has been developed for sale in Japan, with kenaf and jute fibers, tapioca, and sugarcane as alternative crops. Modern highways facilitate the delivery of surplus output to Bangkok. Rice exports have long accounted for 30% to 40% of Thailand's overseas sales, but domestic demand has reduced surpluses.

The peasants own an estimated 7 million buffaloes, which provide the power for cultivation. The almost equally numerous cattle are less important economically, partly because the dairy industry is nonexistent. Poultry production has realized substantial gains since 1950.

Fishing. Fish provides the principal protein element in the national diet. The freshwater catch accounts for about one third of consumer needs for fish. A great variety of sea fish are gathered by some 4,500 offshore boats operating in the Gulf of Siam and the Andaman Sea. Cold storage facilities have improved the marketing of sea fish. The offshore catch in the south has suffered from depletion of the fish by Japanese and other fishermen farther out to sea.

Forestry. Forests cover some three fifths of Thailand's land surface. They provide not only timber, charcoal, bamboo, and rattan, but also usable lac, other resins, and gums. Bamboo is used in village home construction and, combined with rattan, in the making of furniture. Teakwood extraction along the northwestern borders of Thailand is proceeding at a wasteful pace, which threatens to exhaust the supply. Small-estate rubber production covers around 1 million acres (400,000 hectares) in the southern part of the isthmus, but capital needed for planting more productive varieties of trees is not available to smallholders under existing market prices. The government is engaged in replanting operations for evergreens, teak, and various other kinds of hardwoods, but more is needed.

Minerals. Because Thailand's mineral resources are few and badly distributed, the prospect for basic industrial development is limited. Particularly serious is the lack of good quality coal. Charcoal supplies are needed for cooking purposes. Offshore oil-drilling explorations under way in the Gulf of Siam may remedy Thailand's fuel shortage, but the outcome remains uncertain. The fading tin ore resources in the isthmus may also be substantially augmented by the discoveries of tin ore deposits underwater in the Gulf. Scattered iron ore resources are not suitable either in quality or location for commercial exploitation. Lead and tungsten are found on the isthmus in limited quantities. Salt is abundant.

Manufacturing. The very substantial industrial development that has occurred since 1960 has concentrated for the most part on the processing of agricultural products. These include rubber, timber, sugar, cotton, tobacco, silk, and plywood. Government funds have been most profitably expended on power installations, irrigation facilities, highways, and plane services. Some 140 business enterprises directly sponsored by the government are operated outside the bureaucratic framework on a semimonopoly basis. Most of the projects, including brick and cement manufacture and glass, paper, and sugar enterprises, operate at a loss.

Investment and Planning. Government investment and planning greatly improved after Marshal Sarit Thanarat took over control in 1958. He invited the assistance of agencies of the International Monetary Fund and the World Bank and followed their suggestions to deemphasize state enterprise in favor of encouraging private investment and operation.

Starting in 1960, Sarit provided tangible incentives for private firms that were prepared to invest in selected capital-intensive industries needed by the economy. These included the production of tires, chemicals, metals, electrical equipment, and truck assembly operations. Such firms could apply for exemption from all business taxes and customs dues normally payable on capital goods imports. Industries less important strategically could receive rebates of one third to one half of the amount of import dues. Small-industry sponsors were also afforded credit services by government-sponsored provincial and agricultural banks. Some 30,000 applicant borrowers were served by 1967. Positive results were measured by the 6% annual increment in gross national product realized by 1963, which increased to 8% by the late 1960's. Virtually all gains were registered in the private sector.

Foreign investment received similar stimulation under the Industrial Promotion Act of 1965. Within less than two years, more than 300 foreign firms, mainly Japanese, Taiwanese, and American, applied for preferred tax and customs privileges in the development of essential industries. Investments covered a wide range of products, from textiles to electronics and from rubber tires, fertilizers, and cement to tin smelters and oil refineries.

Thailand's second 5-year plan was prepared in 1966, again with World Bank assistance. It contemplated government emphasis on transportation and irrigation needs but with increased diversification of production, especially in agriculture. The goal of an annual output increment of 8% to 10% was approximated, despite unforeseen problems. One problem was a gradual reduction of available foreign reserves, due to the disparity between exports and increasing imports. Additional deficits were caused by the decline of U. S. expenditures on construction and by increased military costs attributable to the war in Vietnam.

The Thai meanwhile had learned to service and maintain a large variety of modern equipment. Thai labor, working often under Chinese foremen, developed into a dependable and competent construction force.

4. History and Government

Thai and related Shan-speaking peoples are widely dispersed, from Burma's Shan state and adjacent areas of China eastward to Laos and southward through Thailand to the border of Malaysia. Thai migration southward from China occurred a long time after the similar progression of Mon and Khmer peoples along many of the same routes in the early centuries A. D. It also came for the most part after the Tibeto-Burmans had reached the Irrawaddy Valley of Burma in the mid-9th century. The Shan-Thai migration probably developed some volume during the early Sung period (from 960) in China, against considerable Khmer, Mon, and Burman resistance. Although the Thai were similar ethnically to the South Chinese, they had not assimilated the sophisticated Chinese civilization by acquiring literacy, adopting of Confucianism or Buddhism, or accepting the Chinese symbols of emperorship and Mandarin rule.

Some Thai peoples were subjects of the kingdom of Nan Chao, which emerged in the 7th century in the western part of what is now the Chinese province of Yünnan, but the ruling elite at Nan Chao's capital spoke Lolo Tibetan rather than Thai. Nan Chao's eventual fall to Mongol armies in 1253 came long after the southward dispersion of Thai-speaking migrants and mercenary adventurers had begun. Late 11th century relief carvings at Angkor, capital of the Khmer kingdom of Cambodia, depict Thai mercenary troops marching with the Khmer armies. Thai entry into the upper Chao Phraya Valley of modern Thailand was long blocked by the Mon state of Haripunjaya (Lamphun). It was the decline of Cambodia in the middle of the 13th century that opened to the Thai an entryway farther east.

Sukhothai. The first independent Siamese state, centered at Sukhothai, southeast of Chiengmai and Lamphun, appeared in 1238 (some say 1219). The city was taken over by the Thai leader of its Cambodian garrison, who is known by his Hindu title, Sri Indradit. The limited extent of the arable terrain around Sukhothai, flanked as it was by mountains, was incapable of supporting the cost of expanding military activities and a large governing operation. From Sukhothai, Sri Indradit and his successor raided the long-settled communities to the south, originally Mon-ruled but under Cambodian control since the mid-11th century. Unable to capture the fortified city of Lavo, on the east bank of the Chao Phraya River, the Thai invaders proceeded southward along the west bank, overrunning the Mon state of Dvaravati and continuing into the isthmus. Cambodian control also collapsed in the Korat area along the middle Mekong.

The incomparable hero of early Siamese history was Rama Khamheng. The second son of Sri Indradit, he took over in 1275 and ruled until 1317. Siamese legend probably exaggerates his stature as a man of learning, but he was a skillful military leader and diplomat and a wise and just ruler. He reportedly challenged the rigid Khmer tradition of divine absolutism by permitting popular appeals for redress of grievances by direct application to the palace itself. The impressive palace ruins at Sukhothai reflect the strong cultural influence emanating from Khmer Angkor, including an imposing colonnaded reception hall and massive Buddhist shrines. But the laterite blocks available locally at Sukhothai were a poor substitute for the more easily sculptured sandstone of Angkor. Rama's military operations were patterned on the model of the Mongol armies of Kublai Khan, with whom Sukhothai cultivated friendly vassal relations. The resistance of Haripunjaya was crushed in 1292 by Rama's ally, King Mangrai of Chiengrai, a Thai state located to the northeast along the major route of Thai entry from the north. Mangrai then founded a new capital at Chiengmai. Other Thai communities, in the upper Mekong basin as far upstream as Luang Prabang in modern Laos, became tributary to Sukhothai. Rama Khamheng is properly acclaimed as the creator of the Siamese state.

Also vassal to Sukhothai was King Wareru of the Mon state of Pegu in southern Burma. Wareru was a mercenary leader, formerly in Rama's employ, who took over Pegu following the overthrow of the northern Burmese state of Pagan by Mongol armies in 1287. In Burma's central valley, other Shan-Thai military chiefs seized control of important irrigation centers, which they successfully defended from later attacks by the Mongols.

It is more than coincidental that Thai hegemony developed during the peak period of the Mongol impact on Southeast Asia, but the latter factor was more occasion than cause. The early Siamese borrowed from both Mons and Khmers in such cultural areas as alphabet and script, spirit propitiation and Theravada Buddhism, architecture and art forms, kingship traditions and governmental institutions. But a distinct Thai flavor was added.

Ascendancy of Ayuthia. Following Rama Khamheng's death in 1317, it became evident that the extended Thai empire required a capital centrally located in the lower Chao Phraya Valley, close to the Gulf of Siam, and adjacent both to Cambodia and to the passes leading across the isthmus to ports on the Andaman Sea. The city and kingdom of Ayuthia were accordingly founded in 1350 by Ramadhipati, a descendant of the Chiengmai line, in a move long resisted by Sukhothai. During his 20-year rule, Ramadhipati extended Ayuthia's control along the Tenasserim coast of the Bay of Bengal and promulgated a Siamese law code that combined local customs (such as trial by ordeal) with adaptations of the classical Indian Code of Manu. It was not until 1438 that Sukhothai acknowledged vassaldom to Ayuthia, and Chiengmai's resistance continued well into the next century.

GEORGE HOLTON, FROM PHOTO RESEARCHERS

WAT PRA KEO or Temple of the Emerald Buddha in Bangkok is guarded by statues of mythical giants. The temple houses Thailand's most revered image, a green jasper statue of Buddha.

Meanwhile, Ayuthia's armies under King Boromoraja II overran Angkor in 1432, eliminating it as the Cambodian capital and causing its famed irrigation facilities to be swallowed up by jungle. King Boromo Trailok (reigned 1448–1488) divided his administration into several functional departments. He also assigned fief-like estates to high officials and set up a code of palace law defining the status of princely personnel and the obligations of vassal states. The office of deputy king (*uparat*) was instituted to relieve the difficulty of selecting successors.

Ayuthia's rise owed much to the collapse of older Mon and Khmer power, to the dismemberment of the Pagan kingdom in Burma, and to the slowness of the southward movement of the Vietnamese along the east coast of Indochina in the face of tenacious Cham resistance. But Siam encountered inevitable opposition—in the 15th century from Malacca, a powerful commercial center in Malaya that the Portuguese took over in 1511, and in the 16th century from the Toungoo Dynasty of Burma.

A Burman attack upon Ayuthia came in the late 1540's, when King Tabinshweti, assisted by Portuguese gunner mercenaries, invaded Siam by way of Tenasserim. This attack ran aground partly because Ayuthia itself had enlisted the assistance of another group of Portuguese gunners. Approximately a decade later, Burma's King Bayinnaung, now in full command of Burman and Shan resources, invaded Siam through the Chiengmai corridor in the north, where support for Ayuthia was less than enthusiastic. Chiengmai became for a time vassal to Burma, as did the new Laotian state of Lan Ch'ang. Bayinnaung's first capture of Ayuthia in 1564 was promptly annulled by its rebellion. His second attempt in 1569 was devastatingly effective. A vassal king was installed, and so powerless did Ayuthia become that the Cambodians managed to return to Angkor.

The disintegration of Bayinnaung's empire after his death in 1581 saw the emergence of the heroic Phra Naret, son of Ayuthia's vassal king. He challenged the Burmese power after 1584, recaptured Angkor in 1589, and took over Ayuthia in his own right as King Naresuen in 1590. He recovered Tenasserim in 1593 and also reestablished suzerainty over Chiengmai in 1595. Naresuen and Rama Khamheng are the authentic heroes of Siam's history.

European Intervention and Renewed Burman Invasions. Throughout most of the 17th century, Siam was receptive rather than hostile to newly arrived European trading companies operating in Southeast Asia. Ayuthia welcomed Dutch traders in 1608 and the British in 1612. The British became discouraged in 1622, and Ayuthia broke with the Dutch under King Narai (reigned 1657–1688), who invited first the British and then the French to replace the Dutch. Two decades of intrigue on the part of French Jesuit missionaries and agents of the Paris government with Constantine Phaulkon, an unscrupulous Greek adventurer-interpreter in high position at Narai's court, threatened to subvert the kingdom to French control. A hostile court faction intervened in 1688, during the course of Narai's terminal illness. Phaulkon was executed, and his palatial residence of Lopburi can still be identified. After his death, the Dutch resumed commercial operations with Siam, but for more than a century and a half thereafter, other Europeans were suspect in Ayuthia.

Trouble again developed between Siam and Burma in the mid-1700's, when the vigorous new Konbaung dynasty unified Burma. A Burman attack on Ayuthia failed in 1759 when King Alaungpaya was fatally injured. His son, Hsinbyushin, was successful in 1766–1767, attacking from both Tenasserim and the north. This time Ayuthia's defenses were completely destroyed, together with its palaces and temples and its artistic and literary treasures.

Siam benefited from the invasion of Burma by Chinese armies in 1767–1770 and from internal troubles that subsequently developed there. Meanwhile, Siamese guerrilla resistance broke out in areas to the west of the lower Chao Phraya Valley. The guerrillas were led by a half-Chinese named P'ya Taksin, who repelled renewed Burmese invasions, eliminated the last heir of the Ayuthia line, and set himself up as king in 1778 with his capital at Thonburi, on the lower Chao Phraya River. Taksin was rightly acclaimed as a military hero, but he early demonstrated signs of mental derangement and was pushed aside in 1781 by a coterie of nobles. In 1782 they installed King Rama I as the first representative of the new Chakri dynasty. A new capital, Bangkok, was built directly across the river from Thonburi and was adorned with a splendid palace and temple areas.

Recovery Under the Chakri. Siam required several decades to recover from the catastrophe of 1767. Rama I repelled Burmese attacks during the 1780's and 1790's, gained control over the lower isthmus and Chiengmai, and carried through the laborious drainage operations on Bangkok's water-logged site. He also took advantage of civil strife raging in Vietnam to establish Thai hegemony in Cambodia. His successor, Rama II (reigned 1809–1824), contributed substantially to the recovery of religious, literary, and art treasures lost at Ayuthia, but he failed to recover Tenasserim from Burma.

Rama III (reigned 1821–1851) made minimal concessions in 1822 and 1826 to the British presence at Penang Island off Kedah, which was theoretically vassal to Bangkok, but failed to recover Tenasserim during and after the first Anglo-Burmese War of 1825. However, Siam's security was enhanced by the veto that British possession of Tenasserim provided against subsequent Burmese attacks. Rama III afforded little encouragement to Europeans either in terms of trade or treaty relations, and he endeavored to strengthen Siam internally. He conquered most of Laos after 1828 and subsequently agreed to share suzerainty over Cambodia with the Nguyen Dynasty of Vietnam.

Colonial Threat. At the end of Rama III's 30 years of firm rule, Siam faced expanding European colonial influences on its borders. An indefinite continuation of Bangkok's refusal to come to terms commercially and politically with developing British-Indian hegemony in Southeast Asia would have raised serious problems.

Prince Mongkut (Rama IV) lived as a Buddhist monk throughout the reign of his half-brother Rama III. He was a reformist Buddhist scholar, who had acquired a command of English and Latin from missionary friends, along with a lively interest in Western science. Mongkut (reigned 1851–1868) negotiated the Bowring Treaty with Britain in 1855, which provided a pattern for treaties with other Western powers. The treaties limited Siam's control of foreign trade, domestic taxes and customs collections, and Siamese court jurisdiction over resident foreigners. Mongkut initiated the practice of inviting a variety of Western advisers of different national origins to assist him in the modernization of government, transportation, education, and the armed services. The advent of French imperialism in southern Vietnam and Cambodia in the 1860's presented an ominous threat with which Mongkut's son and successor, King Chulalongkorn, or Rama V (reigned 1868–1910) would have to deal.

Chulalongkorn's initial caution as a reforming king, in deference to court conservatives, gave way in the face of threats of colonial intrusions. British interference in several of the Malay sultanates in 1874–1875 challenged Bangkok's traditional suzerain claims there. France moved into northern Vietnam in 1883–1885, and British Burma absorbed what was left of the Burma kingdom in 1885. In 1893–1895, France erased Siam's holdings in Cambodia and took over all of Laos east of the Mekong in a warlike gesture that found Bangkok virtually defenseless when the British refused assistance.

From 1893 to the death of Chulalongkorn in 1910, Bangkok made rigorous efforts to modernize the government, courts and legal codes, the economy, and foreign relations. The lead was taken by two princes who had been trained in Europe, Prince Damrong as interior minister and Prince Dewawongse in law and foreign relations. Siam made its final territorial concessions to France in Laos (1904) and Cambodia (1907) and to Britain when Thailand gave up its claim to suzerainty over four Malay sultanates (1909).

World War I finally dissipated the colonial threat. By the statesmanship of two rulers, Siam was thus spared the experience of colonization. The postwar period witnessed the final revision of all of Siam's unequal treaties, dating from 1855.

Limited Monarchy. Chulalongkorn's two sons, who took over successively in 1910 and 1925, were educated in Europe and fitted rather badly into the Bangkok setting. King Wachirawut (reigned 1910–1925) aspired to be a writer and actor and became a patron of rugby and polo and an extravagant entertainer. His brother Prachotipok (reigned 1925–1935) was politically more liberally inclined, but lacked the personal authority and intellectual vigor needed to carry through reforms in the face of conservative opposition at court. Forced by the post-1929 depression to curtail expenses, he offended the European-educated civilian and army elite, who regarded monarchal absolutism as a barrier to progress.

When the malcontents staged their coup in 1932, the King failed to challenge the rebels and eventually had to abdicate in favor of a youthful nephew living in Switzerland. The reformers eventually split between a somewhat leftist civilian faction, led by the lawyer Pridi Banomyong and Colonel Pibun Songgram's military group. The colonel took over power in 1937 and trimmed his sails to catch the Japanese breeze during World War II as a means of recovering territories on all of Thailand's frontiers. As the

GOLD BUDDHA weighing 5½ tons is housed in Wat Trimitr, Temple of the Golden Buddha, Bangkok.

BERNARD G. SILBERSTEIN, FROM RAPHO GUILLUMETTE

RENÉ BURRI, FROM MAGNUM

KING BHUMIBOL ADULYADEJ (Rama IX), shown with Queen Sirikit, succeeded to the throne in 1946.

war turned against Japan, Pibun gave way in 1944 to Pridi's Free Thai faction, which made peace with Britain but gave initial support to various anti-French factions in Indochina.

Pridi lost out in 1946–1947. As the royal regent, he recalled King Ananda from Europe in late 1945 in an endeavor to prepare him for his future symbolic role as ruler. When, on the eve of Ananda's return to Europe in June 1946, the King was found shot in bed under mysterious circumstances, political enemies of Pridi, with no justification, blamed him for the deed. His meager civilian and naval support was unable to withstand Pibun's mobilization of royalist and army opposition, and Pridi was obliged to flee the country in 1947, leaving the military faction in full control.

Pibun was joined by younger police and army leadership in the persons of Phao Sriyanond and Sarit Thanarat, respectively. They kept the trial of Ananda's alleged assassins going on until 1955, while pursuing an anti-Chinese policy in the domestic economic field. King Bhumibol, Ananda's younger brother, returned to Bangkok in 1950, and played a symbolic role in the government.

Marshal Sarit ousted both Pibun and Phao in 1957, assumed direct control of the government in 1958 and was vested with almost absolute powers as premier. He began an extensive economic development program that was continued, after his death in 1963, by his successor, Marshal Thanom Kittikachorn.

Early in 1964, Communist terrorists became active in the jungles of southern Thailand. By 1965, Communist insurgency was under way in the northeastern region of the country. Guerrilla activity continued in the south and the north through the 1960's and into the 1970's.

A new constitution that had undergone nine years of drafts and revisions did not become effective until 1968 because of opposition from a conservative army faction. It provided for a bicameral legislature, with a Senate appointed by the king and a House of Representatives elected by the people. Money bills had to carry the endorsement of the president of the Council of Ministers, and constitutional rights could be suspended by emergency decree. In 1969 the first general elections in 11 years marked the end of martial law. Although Thanom's United Thai People's party did not win a majority of seats, Thanom formed a government without difficulty.

In November 1971, in a bloodless coup, Thanom overthrew the constitution and returned to government by decree. To justify this action, he cited strikes, student demonstrations, Communist insurgency, and his own displeasure with the legislature. Late in 1972 the legislature was reinstituted under an interim constitution.

Ouster of Thanom. The military regime made efforts to moderate its course early in 1973—in vain, as it turned out. The economy worsened, and food shortages appeared. Mostly nonviolent student demonstrations during the summer became massive—and bloody—in mid-October. Students overwhelmed police and the army in Bangkok, demanding the ouster of Thanom. Thanom resigned and fled the country. Sanya Dharmasakti, an adviser to the king, was named premier, and an essentially civilian cabinet was installed. A new draft constitution was completed early in 1974.

Foreign Relations. Anti-Communist after Mao Tse-tung's triumph in China in 1949, Thailand sent a contingent to support UN forces during the Korean War. In 1954, Thailand joined the United States and six other nations in signing the collective defense treaty that created the Southeast Asia Treaty Organization (SEATO).

Bangkok's support of the U. S. role in South Vietnam from 1964 through the ceasefire of 1973 was encouraged by the receipt of substantial military and other aid. Accompanying Thanom's overthrow in 1973, however, was a certain amount of anti-American sentiment.

JOHN F. CADY*, *Author of "Southeast Asia: Its Historical Development"*

Bibliography

Basche, James R., *Thailand: Land of the Free* (Taplinger 1971).

Blanchard, Wendell, and others, *Thailand: Its People, Its Society, Its Culture* (Human Relations 1958).

Bowring, John, *The Kingdom and People of Siam*, 2 vols. (Oxford 1969).

Cady, John F., *Thailand, Burma, Laos, and Cambodia* (Prentice-Hall 1966).

Ingram, James C., *Economic Change in Thailand Since 1850* (Stanford Univ. Press 1955).

Landon, Kenneth P., *Siam in Transition* (reprint, Greenwood Press 1969).

Mole, Robert L., *Thai Values and Behavior Patterns* (Tuttle 1973).

Riggs, Fred W., *Thailand: The Modernization of Bureaucratic Policy* (Univ. of Hawaii Press 1966).

Sieben, Hubert, and Basche, James, *Thailand: Land of Color* (Taplinger 1969).

Siffin, William J., *Thai Bureaucracy: Institutional Change and Development* (East West Center Press 1966).

Skinner, George W., *Chinese Society in Thailand: An Analytical History* (Cornell Univ. Press 1957).

Thompson, Virginia, *Thailand: The New Siam*, 2d ed. (Paragon Bk. 1967).

Vella, Walter F., *The Impact of the West on Government in Thailand* (Univ. of Calif. Press 1955).

Weatherbee, Donald E., *United Front in Thailand: A Documentary Analysis* (Univ. of S. C. Press 1970).

Wilson, David A., *Politics in Thailand* (Cornell Univ. Press 1962).

Wood, William A. R., *A History of Siam . . . to A. D. 1781*, 2d ed. (Probsthain 1960).

THAÏS, thā'is, Greek courtesan of the 4th century B. C. She was said to have persuaded Alexander the Great to burn the city of Persepolis in 330. This story, probably untrue, was used by the English poet John Dryden in *Alexander's Feast* (1697). After Alexander's death in 323, Thaïs was probably the mistress of Ptolemy, who later became Ptolemy I Soter, king of Egypt.

Another Thaïs, an Egyptian courtesan of the 4th century A. D., was converted to sanctity by a desert monk, probably St. Paphnutius. Her story appears in the 13th century book *The Golden Legend,* and she appears in the martyrologies of the Eastern Christian churches. The French author Anatole France used her story as a basis for his ironic novel *Thaïs* (1890). The novel was, in turn, the basis for Jules Massenet's opera of the same name, first produced at the Paris Opéra in 1894. The opera is famous for its *Méditation,* often played as a separate piece.

In France's version of the story, the monk Paphnuce (Athanaël in Massenet's opera), after converting Thaïs, confesses that he lusts after her. In the final scene he collapses beside her as she lies dying in a convent garden.

THALAMUS, thal'ə-məs, a small structure in the diencephalon of the brain. Its many functions include the relaying of sensory impulses to the cerebral cortex. See BRAIN—*Major Divisions of the Brain* (Diencephalon).

THALASSEMIA is a type of anemia more commonly known as Cooley's anemia. See COOLEY'S ANEMIA.

THALES, thā'lēz (c. 634–c. 546 B. C.), was the first known Greek philosopher and scientist. Traditionally known as the father of philosophy, he also invented theoretical geometry and abstract astronomy and was the first of the Seven Sages of Greece. It is not known where Thales was born, but his parents were Greek and he was a citizen of Miletus in Asia Minor. He was educated during an early sojourn in Egypt, where he calculated the heights of various pyramids.

Although most ancient authors asserted that Thales had not committed his scientific and philosophical principles to writing, even in antiquity at least four treatises were ascribed to him: *Nautical Astronomy, On Beginnings, On the Solstice,* and *On the Equinox.* These works have been lost, however, and all that remain are their titles. Whatever Thales taught was transmitted in oral tradition until Greek scholars collected doctrines and aphorisms attributed to him and anecdotes related about him.

Scientific Achievements. In mathematics, Thales first demonstrated that a circle is bisected by its diameter, that the angles at the base of an isosceles triangle are equal, that two intersecting straight lines produce opposite and equal angles, and that the angle of a semicircle is a right angle. In astronomy Thales was the first to determine the sun's course from solstice to solstice and to estimate, with reasonable accuracy, the size of the sun and of the moon in relation, respectively, to the solar and lunar circles. His greatest achievement in this area was his prediction, within a year, of the total eclipse of the sun on May 28, 585 B. C.

Philosophic Speculation. Thales was the founder of the Ionian school of philosophy, which was chiefly concerned with understanding the physical universe. Thales himself taught that water is the universal primary substance; all comes from water and to water all returns. This proposition he supplemented with the statement that the earth is a flat disk that floats on water. No ancient explanation of his doctrine of the formation of the universe exists, but Aristotle provides a probable conjecture on how Thales selected water as the one primal kind of existence. According to Aristotle, Thales probably derived his opinion from observing that the nutriment of everything is moist, that even actual heat is generated from moisture, that water sustains animal life, that the seeds of all things have a moist nature, and that water is a first principle of all things that are humid.

Significance. It may be asked why such a crude idea should suffice to confer on Thales the title of father of philosophy. The significance is not that his teaching about water has any intrinsic value, but that his speculation is the earliest recorded attempt to explain the universe on naturalistic principles. Even more significant is that Thales not only propounded the problem of the nature of the primal principle from which all things have emanated, but that he also, in seeking to find a single ultimate principle underlying the multiplicity of natural phenomena, determined the direction as well as the character of Greek philosophy until the mid-5th century B. C. At that time the Sophists began to discard cosmological investigation and to shift the emphasis in philosophy to ethical speculation concerning man's place in the world, human life and conduct, and man's nature as a political animal.

P. R. COLEMAN-NORTON, *Princeton University*

Further Reading: Burnet, John, *Early Greek Philosophy,* 4th ed., pp. 40–50 (London 1958); Freeman, Kathleen, *The Pre-Socratic Philosophers,* 3d ed., pp. 49–55 (Oxford 1953); Kirk, Geoffrey S., and Raven, John E., *The Presocratic Philosophers,* pp. 74–98 (Cambridge, England, 1960).

THALIA, thə-lī'ə, in Greek mythology, was one of the nine Muses. Her name means "she that flourishes." As the muse of comedy and pastoral poetry, she is usually shown with a comic mask, a shepherd's staff, and an ivy wreath. She was also one of the three Charities, or Graces, and represented bloom. As goddesses of charm and beauty, the Charities were closely associated with the Muses. See also GRACES; MUSES.

THALIACEA, one of the three major groups of tunicates. See TUNICATA.

THALIDOMIDE, thə-lid'ə-mīd, is a hypnotic, or sleep-producing, drug no longer generally available because of its notorious tendency to cause congenital anomalies in infants. In laboratory studies, thalidomide showed great promise as an effective hypnotic with low toxicity. It seemed innocuous and to have such a large margin of safety between effective and dangerous dosage that it would have been difficult to commit suicide by taking it.

The apparent safety of the drug led to its widespread use in West Germany and many other countries from 1958 on. It was available only as an experimental drug in the United States because the Federal Food and Drug Administration deferred approving it for general use. From 1959 on, an increasing number of infants with deformed limbs and other abnormalities were born in Germany. The German physician Widukind Lenz established the role of thalidomide in producing these congenital defects. Subsequent studies of case histories indicate that thalidomide is most likely to cause fetal deformities when taken by the mother between the 29th and 40th days of pregnancy. The exact way thalidomide acts in producing fetal abnormalities is not understood. The human fetus has been found to be much more susceptible to the drug than are usual laboratory animals.

The thalidomide disaster had some salutary consequences. First, it made physicians more cautious about the use of drugs in pregnant women, especially during the first trimester of pregnancy when the fetus is particularly vulnerable to chemical teratogens. Second, it stimulated the adoption of strict regulations on the testing of new drugs in the United States.

In early 1970, the experimental use of thalidomide in the treatment of leprosy was reported.

Andres Goth, M. D.
University of Texas Southwestern Medical School

THALLIUM, thal′ē-əm, symbol Tl, is a soft, heavy metallic element. The metal was isolated independently by the English scientist William Crookes and the French chemist Claude Auguste Lamy in 1862. Thallium is the 58th most abundant element in the earth's crust and is found in minerals such as crookesite, $(Cu,Tl,Ag)_2Se$, and lorandite, $TlAsS_2$. It is produced commercially from flue dust and residues of processes involving the sulfide ores of heavy metals.

While there are no commercial applications of metallic thallium, a low-melting alloy of thallium and mercury has been proposed as a substitute for mercury in switches and seals used under Arctic conditions. Thallous sulfide is used in some infrared-sensitive photoelectric cells.

Thallium is located in Group III B of the periodic table. Its atomic number is 81, and its atomic weight is 204.39. Only two stable isotopes, ^{203}Tl and ^{205}Tl, occur in nature. The freshly cut metal is lustrous, but the luster disappears on exposure to air or water. Thallium melts at 304° C (579° F) and boils at 1457° C (2655° F.); its density is 11.85 g/cc (0.43 lb/cu in) at 20° C (68° F). It is fairly reactive and forms compounds in which its oxidation is +1 (thallous compounds) or +3 (thallic compounds). The +1 state is more stable and more common than the +3.

Herbert Liebeskind
The Cooper Union, New York

THALLOPHYTES, thal′ə-fīts, a collective name for algae and fungi. During the latter part of the 19th century and the early 20th century, botanists classified the algae and fungi as a division, the Thallophyta, of the plant kingdom. Today, however, algae are divided into several divisions, and fungi are classified as a separate division or even as a third kingdom, distinct from the plant and animal kingdom.

Both algae and fungi differ from other plants in that they are relatively simple in structure and lack multicellular reproductive organs. One major difference between them is their method of obtaining food. Algae contain chlorophyll and can manufacture their food by the process of photosynthesis. Fungi do not have chlorophyll and obtain their food from other organisms, either as saprophytes on dead organisms or as parasites on living organisms. See Algae; Fungi.

THALLUS, thal′əs, is the botanical term for a plant body that does not have true roots, stems, and leaves. Only algae and fungi—sometimes known collectively as the Thallophyta—are said to have a thallus. See Thallophytes.

THAMES, River, temz, in southeastern England, rising in Gloucestershire among the Cotswold Hills, flowing eastward past London, and emptying into the North Sea at The Nore, a sandbank at the mouth of the Thames estuary about 48 miles (77 km) east of London Bridge. The source or the Thames is usually said to be at Thames Head, 3 miles (5 km) southwest of Cirencester, 210 miles (338 km) from The Nore. Another source claimed for it is at Seven Springs, 4 miles (6 km) southeast of Cheltenham. Streams from these sources unite near Cricklade, where the Thames is 237 feet (72 meters) above sea level.

During the Roman occupation of Britain the Thames was named Tamesis. Joining the upper Thames just below Oxford is the tributary Thame (pronounced tame). Medieval scholars believed the Latin name Tamesis was made up of Thame and Isis. Thus the upper Thames is often called the Isis—particularly by Oxford University students

Course of the River. The Thames is not normally a fast-flowing river. The width increases gradually from 150 feet (45 meters) at Oxford, to 800 feet (245 meters) at London Bridge, 2,100 feet (640 meters) at Gravesend, near the river's mouth, and 5½ miles (9 km) at The Nore. Ancient fords and crossing places on the Thames provided sites for such historic cities and towns as Oxford, Abingdon, Wallingford, Reading, Marlow, Maidenhead, Windsor, Staines, Kingston, and, of course, London, founded at the lowest fordable point.

There are many highway and railway bridges across the Thames, especially in Greater London. The most famous one, London Bridge, was sold to an American and shipped to Arizona in 1968. It has been replaced by a concrete structure.

Above Oxford the Thames is navigable only by such craft as punts and canoes. From Oxford to London it is used by barges and small steamers and by large numbers of sailboats, motorboats, and other pleasure craft. Below London it supports a great system of docks available to vessels drawing 14 feet (4 meters) of water and, in the Royal Docks system, 34 feet (10 meters). Oceangoing liners call at Tilbury, below London, where the alongside-depth at the landing stage is 40 feet (12 meters). There are also harbor and dock facilities in the estuary of the Medway River, a branch of the Thames estuary.

The Grand Union Canal connects the lower Thames and the English Midlands, and vehicular tunnels pass under the river at Rotherhithe, Blackwall, and Dartford. East of London much of the riverside is reclaimed marshland, and there are many factories and industrial buildings. Near the river mouth, however, are such resorts as Margate and Southend-on-Sea, popular with Londoners.

The Scenic River. The Thames above London is mainly a pleasure river. Famous sporting events are the Henley Regatta and the annual boat race between the universities of Oxford and Cambridge. A succession of regattas is held at riverside towns throughout the summer. A footpath follows the river on one bank or the

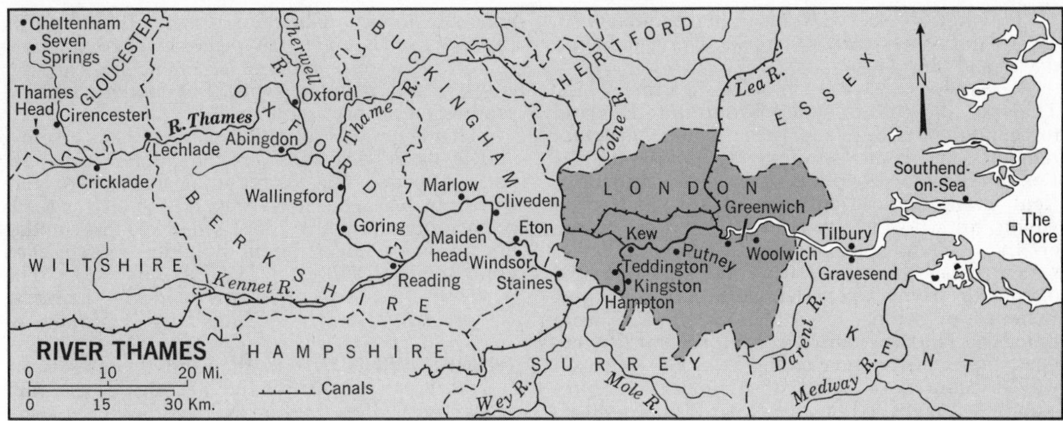

other from Putney to Lechlade, but only glimpses of the river are caught from the roads.

From its source to the outskirts of London the Thames displays some of the finest river scenery in England. Its early course is among low-lying meadows. At Oxford it offers attractive views of that lovely old city. Thence it gradually approaches the splendidly wooded escarpment by Goring, where the river has cut a gap dividing the Chiltern from the White Horse hills. An even finer tree-covered escarpment—most beautiful of all Thames reaches—is that at Cliveden, between Cookham and Maidenhead. The river continues past Windsor and Eton to Hampton Court Palace, Richmond, and the Royal Botanic Gardens at Kew—all highly popular with Londoners and their guests. A notable point below London is Greenwich, where the National Maritime Museum and the Royal Naval College are situated.

Jurisdiction and Control. The Port of London Authority (established 1909) is responsible for the conservancy and navigating safety of the river from a point just below Teddington lock to a line drawn from near Gunfleet Old Lighthouse, in Essex, to about 4 miles (6 km) northwest of the North Foreland in Kent. Above Teddington lock the river and catchment area are the responsibility of the Thames Conservancy, which was originally incorporated in 1857. It comprises 41 members elected by riparian owners, such as county councils. In addition to maintaining navigation, it is responsible for registering boats, protecting fisheries and gauging and recording the daily flow at Teddington. The normal daily rate is about 1,357 million gallons (5,020 million liters); the highest ever recorded was 15,000 million gallons (55,500 million liters) in 1894.

To offset the effects of spells of dry weather on the river level and the towns relying on it for domestic and other water supplies, government sanction was given in May 1970 for the provision of additional boreholes and pumping stations from which the upper reaches of the river can be kept filled. And to control flooding in central London due to high tides and unfavorable winds the government also sanctioned the construction of a "flood barrier" across the river in the Woolwich area.

Until the incorporation of the Thames Conservancy, the city of London had jurisdiction over the Thames as far as Staines, where a stone monument erected in 1285 marks the old limit. By arrangement with the Thames Conservancy, which is under statutory obligation to maintain a minimum daily flow at Teddington of 170 million gallons (629 million liters), water is drawn from the Thames for domestic uses at Oxford, Staines, and at Hampton for London, which is by far the biggest user. Two thirds of London's water (about 250 million gallons, or 925 million liters, per day) is drawn from the Thames.

One of the first acts of the Thames Conservancy on its incorporation in 1857 was to set about controlling pollution of the river. Today it is claimed that the Thames above Teddington lock is technically clean throughout its length and supports more angling and pleasure navigation than any other river of similar size in the world.

RIVER THAMES, between London and Windsor, is a placid stream winding through a neat rural country.

ROTKIN, P. F. I.

Pollution control has been more difficult in the tidal Thames with its creeks and canals and docks and shipping.

Archaeology. Since prehistoric times the Thames Valley has provided a route into England for immigrant tribes from Europe, and important remains have been found in the gravels of the London Basin. In 1935–1936 at Swanscombe, Kent, were found fragments of the skull of a young girl who belonged to the hand-ax culture of the mid-Acheulean period (about 200,000 B. C.). Other discoveries have included bones of mammoth, rhinoceros, elephant, and musk ox. Remains of Bronze Age canoes of oak were found at North Woolwich, and several Roman boats have been uncovered. In 1962 a causewayed camp was found at Staines. The prehistoric site yielded a rich hoard of Neolithic pottery and flints.

GORDON STOKES
Author of "English Place-Names"

Further Reading: Cracknell, Basil E., *Portrait of London River: The Tidal Thames from Teddington to the Sea* (New York 1968); Fletcher, Geoffrey, *London's River* (New York 1966); Peel, John H. B., *Portrait of the Thames from Teddington to the Source* (New York 1967).

THANATOS, than'ə-tos, in Greek mythology, was the god of death. He was the son of Night and lived in the underworld with his twin brother Hypnos, or Somnus, the god of sleep. Thanatos was the personification of death, whose mission was eventually to bring each living soul to the underworld.

In Freudian psychology the Thanatos principle, or death instinct, accounts for destructive impulses in the individual and opposes the Eros principle, or life instinct.

The name thanatology is applied to the study of the medical and psychological problems associated with dying—problems of the patient and of bereaved friends and relatives.

THANESAR, tä-nä'sər, is a city in India, in Haryana state, 90 miles (145 km) north of Delhi. An important pilgrimage center, it is situated in the first homeland of the Aryans in India, the territory known as Brahmavarta. Thanesar (Thaneswar) stands on the Plain of Kurukshetra, site of the legendary battle between the Kauravas and Pandavas, described in the Sanskrit epic *Mahābhārata.* Around the city are many holy places, notably the Kurukshetra tank, a pool regarded as particularly sacred during solar eclipses.

Thanesar, or Sthanviśvara in ancient times, became the seat of the Pushyabhuti dynasty in the late 500's A. D. Its greatest ruler, Harsha (reigned 606–647), united the kingdoms of Sthanviśvara and Kanauj and built a short-lived empire in northern India. After his reign, Thanesar lost much of its political importance. Its final decline dates from its sack by Mahmud of Ghazni in 1014. Population: (1961) 16,828.

THANJAVUR, tun-jä'vo͞or, is a city and district capital in Tamil Nadu state, southeastern India. It is located in the Cauvery (Kaveri) River delta, about 170 miles (270 km) southwest of Madras. The name is also spelled *Tanjore* and *Tanjavur.*

The city has one of the finest examples of Dravidian architecture, the Shivaite Brihadishvara Temple, built about 1010. The Great Fort houses the former palace, which has an important library, and a church built by the German Protestant missionary Christian Friedrich Schwartz (Swartz). Thanjavur is primarily a marketing center. The city produces excellent silk carpets, jewelry, and repoussé work, but modern factory production is negligible.

Thanjavur was a capital of the Chola Empire and of local Naik and Maratha rulers. Although its raja ceded the surrounding district to the British in 1799, the rajas retained the city as their private domain until 1855, when a lapse in the line of succession brought it under British rule. Population: (1968 est.) 119,531.

JOSEPH E. SCHWARTZBERG
University of Minnesota

THANKSGIVING DAY in the United States is an annual day of thanks for the blessings of the past year, observed on the fourth Thursday in November in each of the states, the District of Columbia, and Puerto Rico. It is a historical, national, and religious holiday that began with the Pilgrims. After the survival of their first colony through the bitter winter, and the gathering of the harvest, Gov. William Bradford of Plymouth Colony issued a thanksgiving proclamation in the autumn of 1621. This first thanksgiving lasted three days, during which the Pilgrims feasted on wild turkey and venison with their Indian guests.

Days of thanksgiving were celebrated sporadically until, on Nov. 26, 1789, President Washington issued a proclamation of a nationwide day of thanksgiving. He made it clear that the day should be one of prayer and giving thanks to God. It was to be celebrated by all religious denominations, a circumstance that helped to promote a spirit of common heritage.

Credit for establishing this day as a national holiday is usually given to Sarah J. Hale, editor and founder of the *Ladies' Magazine* (from 1828) in Boston. Her editorials in the magazine and letters to President Lincoln urging the formal establishment of a national holiday of thanksgiving resulted in Lincoln's proclamation in 1863, designating the last Thursday in November as the day. Succeeding presidents annually followed his example, except for President Franklin D. Roosevelt, who in 1939 proclaimed Thanksgiving Day a week earlier—on the fourth but not the last Thursday—to encourage holiday shopping. In 1941, Congress adopted a joint resolution setting the date on the fourth Thursday.

A traditional Thanksgiving dinner takes place yearly at the White House and in almost every American home. Roast turkey and pumpkin pie are among the symbols of this festival. An ancient harvest symbol, the cornucopia, or "horn of plenty," has also been attached to Thanksgiving. Schools and businesses close for this day of family reunion and national, rather than individual, giving of thanks.

In Canada a legal Thanksgiving Day is observed, usually on the second Monday in October. See also HOLIDAYS AND HOLY DAYS.

SULA BENET
Hunter College, New York

THANOM KITTIKACHORN, tä-nôm' kē-tē-kä-chôrn' (1911–   ), Thai army officer and premier. Marshal Thanom was born in Tak, Thailand, on Aug. 11, 1911. After graduating from the Thai Military Academy he rose through the ranks. In 1957 he was a key supporter of Field Marshal Sarit Thanarat when Sarit toppled Premier Phibun Songkhram in a coup d'etat.

When Sarit went abroad for medical treatment in 1958, he left Thanom in charge, but displaced him later in the year on returning to Thailand.

Sarit died in 1963, and Thanom succeeded him as premier without vote or opposition. In 1969 he permitted the first national elections in a decade for the lower house of parliament, but neither he nor any other cabinet member was a candidate in the voting, which was won by Thanom's party. Under Thanom's leadership, Thailand enjoyed impressive economic growth.

RICHARD BUTWELL, *Author of "Southeast Asia Today and Tomorrow"*

THANT, tänt, **U,** Burmese diplomat, who succeeded Dag Hammarskjöld as secretary general of the United Nations. The *U* in U Thant is a Burmese form of address meaning "uncle" and conveys somewhat more respect than "mister."

Early Career. Thant was born in Pantanaw, Burma, on Jan. 22, 1909. He was educated at University College, Rangoon, and in 1931 became headmaster of the National High School at Pantanaw. During World War II, when his country was occupied by the Japanese, he worked with committees that were trying to maintain Burmese education. He entered government service in 1947 as press director and was appointed director of broadcasting in 1948. Afterward he served in the ministry of information and in the office of the prime minister, his friend U Nu. Thant's publications include books on the League of Nations, education, and Burmese history.

Thant went to the United Nations in 1952 as an alternate member of the Burmese delegation to the General Assembly. He returned in 1957 with the title of permanent representative to the United Nations. After Hammarskjöld's death in September 1961, Thant was unanimously elected acting secretary general by the General Assembly on Nov. 3, 1961, and secretary general on Nov. 30, 1962.

Secretary General. Article 99 of the UN Charter gives the secretary general certain explicit authority and implies additional powers. The UN Preparatory Commission in 1945 stated that the manner in which the Secretariat performs its tasks "will largely determine the degree in which the objectives of the Charter will be realized." Like Trygve Lie and Dag Hammarskjöld, the first two secretaries general, Thant took this statement seriously but had to cope with increasing opposition by the great powers. On critical matters his predecessors had sought to develop "UN positions" within the Secretariat, even when these might be contrary to the desires of a permanent member of the Security Council. Thant, however, developed policy papers reflecting a consensus of the Secretariat's senior officers —Communist, non-Communist, and neutral—although he did not consider himself bound by those policies. His concept of an impartial but not necessarily neutral secretary general was demonstrated by his role in the peaceful settlement of the 1962 Cuban missile crisis.

Thant refused to be a glorified clerk when UN members such as France and the Soviet Union challenged his authority on questions of international security. A political realist, he proposed in 1964 that the General Assembly should temporarily refrain from voting on any issue, thereby avoiding a U. S.-Soviet showdown over Russia's refusal to help pay for previous UN peacekeeping operations. But when India and

UNITED NATIONS

U THANT, Burmese diplomat, became secretary general of the United Nations in 1961. Although pro-Western in his general outlook, he acted with scrupulous fairness in his official capacity as secretary general.

Pakistan in 1965 sought a peaceful settlement of a dispute between them, he did not hesitate to create a new peacekeeping unit on his own responsibility—the UN India-Pakistan Observation Mission. In 1967, Thant again acted on his own responsibility when the United Arab Republic (Egypt) asked the United Nations to withdraw its emergency force from the Gaza Strip and Sinai, territories under Egyptian administration or sovereignty. Both because lives might be lost and because he believed in the UAR's right to make such a request, he had the UN force removed but warned Cairo of dangerous consequences. A new Israeli-Arab war broke out later in the year. Thant retired as secretary general effective Jan. 1, 1972.

WALDO CHAMBERLIN, *Dartmouth College*

THAR DESERT, tär, the largest desert of the Indian subcontinent. Also known as the *Great Indian Desert,* it covers some 100,000 square miles (250,000 sq km). The Thar Desert extends from the Sutlej and Indus river valleys on the northwest to the Aravalli Range on the southeast and the Rann of Kutch on the southwest. The Thar Desert occupies much of Rajasthan and part of Haryana in India and a fringe of West Pakistan.

The Thar Desert includes large areas of shifting sand dunes, some reaching heights of 500 feet (150 meters). There are dispersed outcroppings of sandstones and other bedrock. Annual rainfall ranges from below 5 inches (120 mm) in the barren east to about 20 inches (500 mm) in the southwestern thorny scrub area. There is some fairly good grassland in the south.

Irrigation from the Sutlej River is reclaiming large areas of the desert in India. The region's two cities—Jodhpur and Bikaner, in Rajasthan—were established on caravan routes. They are now served by transdesert railroads.

JOSEPH E. SCHWARTZBERG
University of Minnesota

THASOS, thā'säs, is a small Greek island in the north Aegean Sea, with an area of 154 square miles (398 sq km). Its chief town is Thasos. Tourism is important on this mountainous, wooded island, as are agriculture and lumbering.

The island was colonized about 680 B.C. from Paros, but Phoenicians had probably opened its gold mines earlier. Thasos became the richest island in the region, even operating gold mines on the nearby Thracian coast. A dispute with Athens over mining rights led to the secession of Thasos from the Delian League in 465 B.C. Athens captured the island in 462. The physician Hippocrates lived on Thasos in the late 5th century B.C. The Spartan Lysander massacred the population in 405–404, but Thasos flourished again in the Hellenistic and Roman periods. Excavations by the French have uncovered much of the ancient city. Population: (1961 census) 15,916.

JAMES R. WISEMAN, *University of Texas*

THATCH, Edward. See BLACKBEARD.

THAYER, Abbott Handerson (1849–1921), American academic painter, who portrayed women as idealized figures. He was born in Boston on Aug. 12, 1849. In Paris he acquired a solid technical background at the École des Beaux-Arts and then in the studio of J. L. Gérôme.

Thayer specialized at first in painting animals, landscapes (*Winter Sunrise, Monadnock,* Metropolitan Museum of Art, New York), and portraits (*Self-Portrait,* Corcoran Gallery of Art, Washington, D. C.). His theory of protective coloration in animals, expounded in *Concealing-Coloration in the Animal Kingdom* (1909), written with his son, G. H. Thayer, influenced the camouflage techniques used in World War I. Gradually Thayer turned to the glorification of womanhood, seen in such graceful works as *Caritas* (Boston Museum of Fine Arts) and *The Virgin* (Freer Gallery of Art, Washington). He died in Dublin, N. H., on May 29, 1921.

THAYER, Sylvanus (1785–1872), American army engineer, who established the high standards of the U. S. Military Academy. He was born in Braintree, Mass., on June 9, 1785. He graduated from Dartmouth College in 1807 and from the Military Academy in 1808, with an engineer commission. After serving in the War of 1812, he was sent to France by the academy to study military schools and fortifications and collect books and equipment.

In 1817, finding the academy crippled by years of official neglect, President Monroe appointed Thayer superintendent. Thayer established strict discipline, developed a 4-year curriculum, and provided both theoretical and practical training. He worked to develop the cadets' sense of honor and personal responsibility. Scrupulously fair, and unbending in his performance of duty, he set them an example and made the academy one of the world's finest military schools and an outstanding technical college—the first in the United States.

U. S. MILITARY ACADEMY

SYLVANUS THAYER, a leader in development of the U. S. Military Academy in the early 19th century.

In 1831, President Jackson began undermining academy discipline. Believing himself the target, Thayer resigned as superintendent in 1833, returning to engineer duties. Retired as a colonel in 1863, he established the Thayer School of Engineering at Dartmouth in 1867. He died in South Braintree, Mass., on Sept. 7, 1872.

JOHN R. ELTING, *Colonel, USA, Retired*

THE DALLES. See DALLES, THE.

THE PAS, pä, is a town in northwestern Manitoba, Canada, at the junction of the Saskatchewan and Pasquia rivers, 470 miles (756 km) northwest of Winnipeg. It is a retail and service center for mining, lumbering, and commercial fishing operations in the area and for the fur trade, which has been important there since the late 17th century.

Beginning about 1690, a succession of trading posts was built on the site of the community. The permanent settlement was established when a railroad was completed in 1907. The Pas was incorporated in 1910; the origin of the name is uncertain. A highway was opened to the town in 1939. Population: 6,062.

THE VILLAGE, a city in central Oklahoma, in Oklahoma county, is enclosed on the west, north, and east by Oklahoma City and on the south by Nichols Hills. It is a residential community, whose area is 2.9 square miles (7.5 sq km). It was established after World War II by a group of war veterans. In 1950 the development was incorporated as a town called simply "The Village." Nine years later the citizens voted to incorporate as a city under the name "The City of the Village."

The city has a home-rule charter with a council-manager form of government. Population: 13,695.

GRAPHIC HOUSE

Showboat (1927), an American musical theater masterpiece by Jerome Kern, in a New York revival in 1946.

CONTENTS

THEATER concerns primarily the art of presentation. Derived from the Greek *theatron* (a place for seeing), the word "theater" initially described an architectural structure selected or built to house dramatic offerings, though it could also accommodate other types of presentations. As used to mean the art of presentation, the term became current in English late in the 17th century. In this article, "theater" denotes the art as a whole, of which the building is only a part. In this sense theater is one of the performing arts, the distinguishing feature of which is the public nature of their expression. The musician, singer, or actor may rehearse arduously, but not until he appears before an audience does he actually create the artistic work itself.

Some confusion exists about the relation of "theater" and "drama." Normally, "drama" refers to the literary basis of a theatrical presentation, the assumption being that the written record contains the essential elements of the human experience enacted in the theater. In this view, "theater" is merely the physical expression of the playscript. Though of long standing and satisfactory enough when applied to European theater, where the written word has normally been the basis of presentation, this formulation does not apply so readily to the Oriental theater, where gestural and musical presentation has usually taken precedence over verbal presentation. It is better, therefore, to define theater as the embracing art of presentation that includes the enactment of mimetic activity. In this view theater comprises not only drama but also circus, dance, opera, and puppetry.

1. Theatrical Elements

As a performing art, theater produces no permanent object or record. It exists only while it is occurring, and for its occurrence three elements must be brought together.

The first element is the audience. The performance exists only when an audience is present, for the performer's entire purpose is to arouse recognition and wonder in the onlooker. However long the preparation for a performance may take, theater occurs only during the time that the audience is actually witnessing the presentation.

The second element is place. The act of presentation before an audience necessitates separation of the performing area from the seeing or listening area. This isolation has two purposes: a functional purpose, which is to enable all members of the audience to witness the presentation, and an artistic purpose, which is to endow the performing area with imaginative properties calculated to stir the audience.

The third element is the performer. An individual presents himself—as an acrobat demonstrating hair-raising feats, a magician doing mystifying tricks, or an actor presenting fictional

This article provides a general definition of theater and discusses the presentational or production aspects of the subject. The article DRAMA is concerned chiefly with the literature of the theater. Other related major articles are ACTING; COSTUME, THEATRICAL; DIRECTING; LIGHTING, THEATRICAL; THEATER ARCHITECTURE. For additional articles, see the Index entry *Theater*.

events. In each instance the performer uses himself (his body, his voice, and his sensibility) as the medium through which he communicates with an audience.

Audience. One of the factors that make theater possible is the presence of an audience. Usually a theater prepares a production and then advertises for an audience to see it. But this order of events is not the only one, and, in fact, the history of the theater shows that an audience often existed before any particular piece was prepared. The Dionysian celebrations in Athens and the Christmas festivities at the court of King James I of England were occasions when the expectation of an audience created, respectively, the need for a play or a masque.

Theatergoing is a social act. In classical Athens and medieval Europe, entire communities participated in theater activity while all other business of the city or town was suspended. In modern society the theatrical occasion occurs with great frequency but involves a minute portion of the populace at any one time. Only in those localities that have developed drama festivals does the theatrical occasion dominate the affairs of a society, at least temporarily.

Historically, theatrical occasions have tended to be religious, social, or political and have been associated with periodic or irregular communal celebrations. Most periodic celebrations have had a religious basis, as did the celebration of the Feast of Corpus Christi from the 14th century through the 16th. The religious purpose, however, does not exclude civic or national purposes. The addition of theatrical performances to various Athenian celebrations, notably the Dionysia, had a civic rather than a religious end. The Athenian tyrant Pisistratus seems to have used the celebration as a device for alienating the ancient clans and strengthening the newly formed tribes. In this case, the civic purpose was enhanced by the religious character of the celebration.

Irregular celebrations have been less likely to be religious, and more usually have commemorated a victory or nuptial. Military triumphs were among the occasions honored by Roman comedy. In the Renaissance a royal or aristocratic marriage was an occasion for a theatrical presentation. Often the irregular celebration had a political purpose: it was aimed at enhancing the prestige of a triumphant general or a ruling house.

After the Renaissance the religious and commemorative purposes for gathering an audience declined. Theater became a commodity, available to all, but at a price. Whereas admission to the celebratory theater had been free, the noncelebratory theater depends on collections or on attracting a paying clientele to its door.

People attend the theater chiefly for diversion. They also may attend for prestige—the opening of a new play is often the occasion for socially prominent persons to display themselves and their fashions. In contrast to these commercial purposes, civic and artistic purposes may alter playgoing habits, and the cultivation of art festivals throughout the world has imparted a civic quality to the theater. Beginning in 1680, with the establishment of the first national theater, the Comédie Française, there have slowly developed in virtually every country of Europe national theaters intended to preserve the national dramatic heritage.

Depending upon the conditions that have brought its members together, an audience tends to be communal or random. An audience has a communal character when its members share a "mythology"—a body of knowledge in the form of legends, stories, historical events, or contemporary information that contains common values. Not all the members of an audience need hold the same beliefs, but they must be able to share in those beliefs imaginatively. Because of drama's compact form, the existence of a mythology permits the use of symbols and signs to achieve profound effects. By contrast, a random audience, from a diverse population, lacks a common memory and unifying purpose.

The theatrical occasion and the attitude of the audience provide the framework for the theatrical experience, and the experience itself is chiefly the result of the interaction between audience and performer. Though an audience often responds overtly to the performer, its most important response is covert. Entertainment leads the audience to participate imaginatively in a substitute life that is composed of wondrous and familiar aspects.

Place. The place of a presentation is the second vital element in theatrical art. It embraces not merely the circumscribed area in which the performers appear, but also the place where the audience sits or stands, and even includes the geographical site of the theater. The theater may be outdoors or indoors, temporary or permanent, intimate or public. For centuries performances were given in the open air; in Southeast Asia they still are presented in open or partially open structures.

In Europe, actors erected platforms in streets or in the halls of the nobility to transform nontheatrical areas into temporary theaters. Permanent structures, designed exclusively for theatrical performance, were open to the sky as late as the 16th century, and it was not until the end of the 16th century that indoor structures, built for theatrical purposes, began to appear. From the 15th through the 17th century indoor performances were given in halls or tennis courts (in France), converted temporarily or permanently into theaters. In the 20th century, theatrical performance is almost invariably associated with a theater building, but in the long history of the drama, the enclosed theater building is of relatively recent origin. Even now, theater groups resort to the open air (the New York Shakespeare Festival), to found space (street theaters), and to converted sites (lofts and churches).

In the early communal phase, theatrical performances were given in large open spaces: in Greece, the space was at the foot of a natural amphitheater; in medieval Europe, either within the town square or throughout the entire town. Exceptionally important to the communal use of such space and to its psychological effect was the frequent association of the theatrical presentation with religious processions. The entire community participated in or witnessed a procession honoring Dionysus (in ancient Athens) or Jesus (in medieval Europe) as a prelude to from two to five days of performances. In contemporary theatergoing, such conditions are approximated, though without the religious connotation, when large numbers of persons attend theatrical or musical festivals for two or three days at a time. In these cases, the playing area truly embraces an entire region.

LAWRENCE FRIED

SHAKESPEARE IN THE PARK—*King Richard the Third* as performed on the thrust stage of the Delacorte Theater in New York City's Central Park.

The internal arrangement of a theater defines the relationship of audience to performer. This relationship is usually determined by the historical evolution of the theater and the prevailing class conditions. Theatrical performance, which in its formative years was synonymous with dance and acrobatics, first took place in a circular area surrounded by the audience. As performance shifted from dancing to acting, the audience tended to form a semicircle about the performer. With the introduction of scenery came the need to place the audience directly in front of the presentation. Furthermore, in the semicircle of the communal theater the marks of class distinction were minimized, even though leading religious or political figures were seated in prominent positions. It was in the court theaters of the Renaissance period that the arrangement of the audience became fully subordinated to social hierarchy. King James I at Whitehall and Louis XIV at Versailles were each seated in state directly opposite the stage platform in a position for optimum viewing of the perspective settings then being introduced. All the other seating was arranged in strict order of rank from that center. Since the construction of indoor theaters was initiated by the court theaters and flourished in the highly stratified societies of the 18th and 19th centuries, most auditoriums reflect the traditional class division into mutually exclusive areas (orchestra, loge, balcony). After World War II, however, large new theaters such as the amphitheaterlike structure at Stratford, Ontario, embodied a more democratic arrangement, in which an audience of more than 2,000 persons is seated in a single bank of seats.

Set within the playing area, finally, is the stage. It may be a mere circle of stamped ground, or it may be the steps of a building. Circus employs the circle. Drama, most frequently, relies on a raised platform. The platform may be freestanding, as it would be in a street, or it may be a permanent part of a building. When it is placed behind a picture frame, as it is in a theater with a proscenium, the audience is no longer aware of the platform and sees merely the frame. Primarily a device to enable an audience to witness the presentation, the platform may assume a variety of guises, and, indeed, the history of the theater reveals that each period seems to settle on a single dominant treatment of the platform.

In much of theater the platform has a purely presentational character. The magician treats it solely as a stage, making no effort to invest it with extratheatrical significance. In drama, however, the platform has a double character. It is a playing area, and the actors are frankly performers. But it also assumes a fictional character in accord with dramatic events. Throughout theatrical history the need to preserve the platform as a stage and the need to employ it as a fictional locale have been reconciled in different ways.

One solution was the permanent stage with a fixed facade that, constructed solely for performing purposes, conveyed nothing but a theatrical association. The particular elements, however, that the actors chose to include in the facade often did have extratheatrical association and might impart a symbolic significance to the whole structure of the stage. The Japanese No stage, for example, combined a pebble path and a roof resembling a pagoda, recalling the artistic ancestry of No in temple drama, with three pine trees that symbolized the universe. Though less rigid than its Japanese counterpart, the Elizabethan public theater also conveyed an emblematic significance. The roof above the stage and the trap beneath signified respectively heaven and hell. As might be expected, stages with fixed facades tended to develop traditional conventions of presentation. Chinese actors, for example, entered the stage from the door at the audience's right and departed through the left. This purely presentational convention had a parallel in the more representational convention of Roman comedy, where one side of the stage designated entrance from the forum and the other entrance from the harbor.

Scene Design. Scenic design, as it is practiced in the contemporary theater, stems from the development of perspective settings and changeable scenery at the Italian court theater of the 16th century. A product of the Renaissance, the perspective setting provided the technical means for achieving scenic verisimilitude. At first the perspective setting was mounted behind the playing area proper, with the performer confined to the forward portion (apron) of the stage. This was necessary because the scenery decreased in size as it receded upstage. For an actor to play at the rear of the setting would be to destroy the proportion essential to the optical illusion. With the enlargement of scenery for opera, however, the setting could embrace the actor as well as the playing area without suffering distortion. In time, the performer appeared within the setting, as he largely does in the modern theater. Instead of being merely a platform for theatrical presentation, the stage became an environment for the actor.

Changeable scenery, in its turn, was intended to transform the entire stage platform for each of the perspective scenes and even for moments within each scene. To be effective, these changes required some division between audience and stage in order to mark that part of the stage to be transformed and to hide the mechanism by which it was transformed—hence, the introduction of the proscenium frame.

To produce the changeable, perspective setting, Italian designers had to solve three technical problems. They had to construct lightweight forms capable of being combined into many architectural shapes, they had to move these forms readily, and they had to achieve control over lighting. The classical theater had known how to produce stage structures by stretching cloth over wooden frames, but such structures were a minor part of the classical facade. It was in the court theaters of Renaissance Italy that the framed cloth "flat" became the fundamental unit of stage construction, a unit still in use. Initially, flats were arranged to simulate two sides of three-dimensional structures. By the 17th century, three dimensions were reduced to two, and flats were utilized as canvases upon which three-dimensional forms were painted. This change was adopted to facilitate the movement of scenery.

From the 17th to the 19th century the prevailing pattern in European theater was the wing and shutter or wing and drop setting. A wing was a narrow flat placed at one side of the stage. Sets of wings painted in perspective and overlapping each other were arranged one behind the other from the front to the rear of the stage. A shutter (cloth backdrop), painted to continue the illusion of the wings, was located behind the last set of wings. By setting the wings in grooves within the stage floor, the designer was able to pull any set of wings on or off stage rapidly. Either by pulling off shutters to reveal another set behind or by lowering a drop in front of the one already in place, the stage mechanic could make the scene change quickly and completely.

In the 19th century the wing and drop setting gave way to the box set. Utilizing the basic flat, the designer arranged his frames so that they suggested three walls of a room. At first, he continued to give the illusion of three dimensions by painting moldings, pilasters, fireplaces, and even furniture directly on the walls. With the movement toward realism, however, he increasingly introduced three-dimensional objects into the setting—furniture, doors, fireplaces, and staircases. The introduction of three-dimensional elements complicated the problem of changing the scenery. The wing and drop setting did not satisfy the later taste for realism, but it did permit rapid change from scene to scene. The box set and its elaborations were more convincing but also more difficult to alter.

Wherever playwrights wrote dramas that required a single locale, the need to change the setting was eliminated. But not all playwrights relied on the single set, and consequently additional technical means were required to shift from one setting to another. Some sets were constructed so that they could be readily dismantled and either carried off or lifted out of the way. For this latter purpose, the box set adapted the flying machinery from the wing and drop set. Sets that were too bulky to remove in such a manner or that required too rapid a change were, and still are, mounted on wheeled platforms or wagons. The wagons revolve to hide one side and display another, or they may be pulled off to one side as another is introduced from the opposite side or the rear. These methods, though still current, are on the wane, as emphasis on realistic illusion lessens.

Lighting. The designer's control over his setting increased markedly in the 19th century with successive refinements in stage lighting. With the establishment of permanent roofed theaters, stage mechanics sought to control the intensity and color of stage lighting by placing basins as reflectors behind the light source, usually a candle or torch, and glass bottles filled with colored liquid in front of the source. In principle, this basic technique has persisted to this day, but lighting could not be substantially improved until adequate control over the light source was achieved. The 19th century witnessed important changes in lighting. Gas, introduced about 1820, and limelight, introduced about 1850, allowed better control than did candles or oil lamps, but only with the invention of the incandescent lamp did true lighting control begin.

From 1880, when electric light replaced other means of illumination, there were continuous refinements in stage lighting. Reflectors of different shapes and various metals have produced a more evenly diffused light, and lens refinements have enabled the designer to control the shape of the light. Control systems now enable the lighting designer to place any amount of light anywhere on the stage. Initially, he sought to achieve greater truthfulness of environmental atmosphere. Later, influenced strongly by the ideas of the Swiss designer Adolphe Appia (1862–1928), others attempted to create visual evocations of emotional moods or dynamic approximations of dream states.

Performer. The third, and most influential, element of theater is the performer's presentation. In the early stages of theatrical history specialization in presentational skills was almost nonexistent. The performer had to be a singer, a dancer, an actor, and even an acrobat. Until the middle of the 20th century these skills were required of all members of the Peking opera, and, in general, the Oriental theater has relied on a spectrum of talents that have become separate performing arts in the West. In the West, the modern musical theater comes closest to the Oriental ideal by calling for a wide variety of performing skills from a single performer.

To supplement his own body, the performer has at his disposal the clothing in which he can drape himself. The contemporary theater tends to capitalize on the individual physique and personality of the actor, a tendency that began in the Renaissance. But during a great part of theatrical history the performer sought to change his shape. In China, Japan, and Greece, he donned elaborate and enfolding garments and hid his face with masks or paint. Like the setting, the garment and face covering were often symbolic. Masks were used in Greek drama to identify types of characters. The Chinese employed color in face painting to signify both character types and personal traits—gold denoting gods; green, demons; red, vigor and loyalty; white, treachery. In the *commedia dell'arte,* masks associated with stock types were worn by the comic but not by the romantic characters. All these theaters were alike in utilizing opulent and striking costumes and masks to heighten the theatrical effect and to project a sense of the supernatural or the nonnatural.

Where the performer secures the material for his presentation depends both on the content of that presentation and the history of the particular theater. He may inherit the material from his predecessors, he may devise new presentations, or he may rely on someone else to supply new materials. In theaters that minimize the spoken element and depend on song or dance or both, gestures and inflections are codified over a period of time and then passed down to succeeding generations of performers. Occasionally a rare individual appears. A performer, composer, or poet, he may add a playscript or a bit of stage business that will be absorbed into a theatrical tradition. Still common in Oriental theater, this pattern of accretion prevailed in Europe until the 19th century.

The Dramatist. In the European tradition, with its emphasis on the spoken word, the dramatic poet early became the principal source of theatrical material. The Athenian dramatist seems to have served as director as well as writer, instructing the performer in his role and even introducing painted scenery, as Sophocles is supposed to have done. Frequently the player and poet have been one, the writer preparing plays for the use of himself and his associates. The most famous player-poet was unquestionably the French theatrical artist Molière. Shakespeare, though not quite so noted an actor, was a member of a theater troupe throughout his career. Such close connection between writer and theater company was normal until the 17th century. Thereafter, though dramatists often have been deeply involved in the rehearsal process, usually they have not been central personages in the production end of a theatrical enterprise.

As long as the dramatist was a partner of the performer, if not the same person, he drew his materials from traditional sources. Utilizing the theatrical skills of his fellow performers, whether they were singing abilities or comic routines, he incorporated them into his scripts. More often than not, he drew his subject matter from legend or history. Conventions of performance might also dictate the general form that the subject would take. The classical Athenian tragedian, for instance, almost always selected his subject from epic sources and always followed the established pattern of alternating odes and episodes. Little is known about why one dramatic form or another comes to dominate any one theatrical period; but once a particular form becomes dominant, it is virtually impossible for a dramatist to depart from it.

The divorce of dramatist from performer after the 17th century was accompanied by several other changes. The dramatist became a free agent. Instead of writing for a specific occasion to be celebrated by a specific group of performers, he tended to write a play first and then to search for a troupe willing to purchase his product. At the same time, he ceased to rely on traditional subject matter. Slowly, in the post-Renaissance age, the dramatist came to draw his materials from his own observation and, increasingly, from his personal life. He became an independent artist, expecting the performer to serve him by a faithful rendition of his script. Many dramatists, finding this situation unsatisfactory, have repeatedly attempted to become fully involved in theatrical production, but of 20th century dramatists, only Bertolt Brecht succeeded fully in resuming the ancient role of dramatist-player by serving as director of his own company, the Berliner Ensemble, from the end of World War II to his death in 1956.

Other Specialists. During the post-Renaissance period, the theater also became increasingly specialized and the performer increasingly surrounded by supporting personnel. Where once he may have made his own costumes, composed his own music, written his own dramatic speeches, and managed his own troupe, the performer came more and more to depend on specialists to help him mount a presentation. Even the designer could no longer personally supervise all facets of the stage decor. Each aspect of production—scenery, costume, and lighting—became the responsibility of a separate individual. The modern designer turns over his plans to technicians who see that the plans are executed according to specifications. For a complicated production like a musical drama, the nonperforming supporting staff may consist of a writer, a librettist, a composer, several designers, a choreographer, a musical conductor, possibly a music arranger, and, of course, a stage director. It is because of this specialization and of the introduction of nontraditional subject matter that the director emerged as an independent theatrical artist in the 19th century.

Until then, many of the director's duties were divided among performers or dramatists. Sophocles conducted rehearsals. Shakespeare is said to have instructed the actor John Lowin in preparing the role of Henry VIII. Molière, as leading actor and head of a troupe, served as manager and director. But with the disappearance of traditional troupes, with the retreat of the actor into the environment of the setting, and with the increased specialization of stage personnel, it became necessary for one man to guide an entire presentation. At first an aid to the performer, the director has become, at times, a star in his own right.

2. History—Europe

The sources of theater art remain a mystery. Scholars theorize that theater arose from a mimetic impulse common to mankind. They also have placed considerable emphasis on the ritual

GREEK NATIONAL TOURIST OFFICE

ANCIENT GREECE—*Iphigenia in Aulis,* a tragic drama by Euripides, is given a new production in a restored theater in Athens.

basis of theater; according to this theory, performance provided a mimetic parallel to the changes of the seasons or the gathering of food. In the course of a ceremonial struggle, man enacted the death of winter and the coming of spring or, in a ritual dance, portrayed the hunt, presumably to induce a favorable result through sympathetic magic. The extrahuman character of these representations was conveyed through the costumes and masks of particular cults. Whether the members of the community witnessing the ritual were audience or participants is often difficult to know, for in some instances, as in the dance ceremonies of the Plains Indians, the presentation was offered to the gods with the entire tribe serving as a virtual chorus. For such ceremonies, primitive ritual was associated with a sacred performing area. Unfortunately, the connecting links between these ceremonies and the fully developed theatrical forms that appear in Europe and the Orient cannot be traced clearly; thus, theories of the origins of theater remain tentative and conjectural.

Greece. Although there is evidence that a rudimentary passion play was enacted at Abydos in Egypt as early as the 19th century B.C., the first evidence of a fully formed theater is found in Greece. In Athens in 534 B.C. the tyrant Pisistratus established an annual contest for tragedy as part of the principal celebration (the Great Dionysia) for the god of wine, Dionysus. Held in the latter part of March or early April, the Great Dionysia commemorated the introduction of the Dionysian cult into Attica. Its five or six days of celebration consisted of a procession re-enacting the entry of Dionysus into Athens, one or two days of dithyrambic contests, and three days of theatrical performance. In the dithyrambic contests the 10 tribes of Attica competed, each represented by a chorus of 50 men or boys. Religious and political in character, the Great Dionysia was the most significant civic celebration of the year. The municipality conducted the contest and paid for the chorus. It also designated wealthy citizens as *choragoi,* charged with paying for the actors and the costumes. Since admission to the tragedies was guaranteed by the state, any person who was too poor to pay the entrance fee received it from public funds.

The greatness of Athenian theater coincided with the expansion of the Athenian empire under Pericles in the middle of the 5th century B.C. In a remarkable display of longevity, the three tragic dramatists Aeschylus (524?–456 B.C.), Sophocles (c.496–406 B.C.), and Euripides (484? or 480?–406 B.C.) spanned the century among them, providing a sequence of major works from about 472 to 406 B.C.

In addition to the Great Dionysia, Athens also celebrated two other festivals that featured dramatic performances, the more important of which was the Lenaea, held in January. At the Lenaea, though tragedies as well as comedies were presented, the comedies were featured (just as tragedy received emphasis at the Great Dionysia). Less frequented by visitors from foreign countries or neighboring cities, the comic contests of the Lenaea afforded the writer an opportunity to deal with local matters. The only extant examples of the comic genre, the 11 plays of Aristophanes (c.450–c.385 B.C.) concentrate on political, social, and cultural issues in a caustic and farcical manner.

Performances in Athens were given in the Dionysian theater located along the southeast slope of the Acropolis, the sides of the hill forming a natural unroofed amphitheater. Initially a modest structure, it was successively embellished, the surviving fragments of seats and stage being of Roman origin. The theater consisted of three major parts: the *theatron* (seating area), accommodating about 14,000 persons; the *orchēstra* (dancing circle), in the center of which stood the *thymelē* (altar); and the *skēnē* (hut), located behind the playing area, in which the actors dressed. Though the evidence is inconclusive, it appears that during the classical period there was no raised stage. As time passed, the *skēnē* was enlarged to serve as a background for the orchestra. Its roof was used as a platform upon which "gods" appeared, and it contained a machine consisting of hooks and pulleys that enabled the performers to rise from or descend to the ground. Its central door, apparently one of three doors, could be thrown open to display the result of offstage violence. Between the *skēnē* and each side of the *theatron* was a passageway called the *parodos,* through which the chorus entered.

Though the works of the three major tragic dramatists reveal considerable variety, they all adhere to the major and rather rigid conventions of the Greek tragic theater. According to the rules of the tragic contest, each dramatist was required to supply four plays—three tragic plays to be followed by a satyr play (a type of burlesque on an epic subject). Each play ran about one and a half hours. With few exceptions, the plays dealt with subjects chosen from archaic Greek legend or myth—the history of Oedipus, the invasion of Troy, the story of Atreus and his family, or the adventures of Hercules. Although Aeschylus wrote three or four plays in continuous narrative (trilogies or tetralogies), Sophocles and Euripides treated each play as a separate piece.

Whatever the narrative material, the subject was shaped into a conventional pattern. A tragedy recited a crucial moment in one of the legends, events being arranged in a sequence of *odes* and *episodes*. A *prologue* announced the subject of the play and indicated the point in the legend where it started. The opening choral song (called the *parodos*) introduced the chorus, which might consist of citizens of the community, its slaves, or its soldiers. In a sequence of four or five alternating choral odes and episodes, the narrative was unfolded and brought to a climax. After a final lament or comment on the implications of the events, the play ended with an *exodos* (exit song), the departure of the chorus.

Among the activities that filled the episodes, the most frequent were proclamations, prayers to a god, lamentations, debates, reports of messengers, and cross-examinations. The choral odes, some of which were organically related to the narrative, were danced and sung to the accompaniment of the lyre or double flute. In performance the chorus seems to have mediated between the audience and the characters, an impression heightened by the acoustics of the amphitheater, where, judging from current evidence in the theater at Epidaurus, the audience had the illusion that the sounds of the choral odes originated in the *theatron* itself.

The performers, whether professional or amateur, were male. Each year, 500 Athenian citizens participated in the dithyrambic contests, in time producing a large number of nonprofessional but highly qualified choristers. The actors with speaking roles apparently were professionals. Initially Aeschylus utilized two actors to play all the roles in one play. Sophocles is said to have added the third actor. Roles were distributed according to the prominence of the actors, the leading actor (*protagonist*) taking the major roles, the *deuteragonist* taking the secondary roles, and the *tritagonist* taking the remainder. Clothed from head to foot in rich garments, hidden by a mask somewhat larger than life size (and so constructed that it amplified the voice), crowned by the *onkos* (headdress), possibly elevated on a *cothurnus* (raised boot), the tragic actor made an imposing and striking impression. The stature and dignity of the figure were in sharp contrast to the highly impassioned expressions of suffering and anger that filled the plays. This kind of contrast, in which the reserve and convention of external behavior set off and heighten the ferocity of inner emotion, can be found in widely separated theaters.

Rome. Roman theater derived its forms and subjects from Greek theater, but the theater never occupied the central position in Roman life that it did in Greek life. Though fragments of Roman tragedies are extant, the only complete tragedies (the 10 of Seneca) were certainly not products of a popular theater and may never have been performed in their own day. Comedy, in contrast, was the product of an active Roman theater. As in Greece, plays were performed on civic and religious holidays, but in Rome the civic rather than the religious element predominated. New holidays were continually added to the calendar until, by the 4th century A. D., more than 100 were devoted to theatrical performance.

In Rome, most of the performers were slaves, responsible to a manager who supplied their services for the many celebrations. Both male and female, the performers were called upon to sing and dance as well as portray stock types. A native form of farce called the *fabula Atellana* seems to have been popular, but the only scripts to survive are those of the *fabulae palliatae* of Plautus (c.254–c.184 B. C.) and Terence (c.190–159 B. C.). The *fabulae palliatae* (from the Greek garments, or *pallia*, worn by the characters) were Latin adaptations of Greek New Comedy. In these adaptations, Plautus, who was an actor as well as a dramatist, and Terence created enduring examples of the young lover, the crusty old man, the clever slave, the scheming courtesan, and many other types. Actors specialized in one or another of these characters.

At first, performances were presented in temporary wooden theaters erected in streets or squares; not until 55 B. C. did the Roman Senate permit a permanent stone theater to be built in the city. For the comedies the early platform stage represented a street in front of two residences, entrances being possible into the houses or at either end of the street. This conventional arrangement was later elaborated or superseded,

MEDIEVAL—*Miracle play, depicted in a painting by Jean Fouquet, shows Jesus being tried before Pilate.*

GIRAUDON

but only after the days of Plautus and Terence. From the 1st century B. C. onward, permanent open-air theaters were constructed in Rome and wherever Rome extended its sway. Presentations in these theaters, however, though they included the works of the comic writers, tended to become spectacular and, in the later days of the empire, to consist of mannered and obscene dance mimes.

Roman theaters were modifications of the Greek. Although the Romans built their theaters on flat ground rather than against the sides of hills, they retained the amphitheater arrangement. In the Roman plan the sides of the amphitheater joined the scene house so that the building was entirely enclosed. The orchestra was reduced by half, for with the elimination of the chorus in later Greek drama and in Roman drama the need for the dancing circle disappeared. The scene house was elaborated into a two-story facade (*frons scaena*) richly adorned with pillars and statuary. Several late Greek (Hellenistic) and Roman theaters have been partially restored and put to use for theatrical or music festivals.

Medieval Theater. With the fall of Rome in the 5th century A. D., the classical tradition in theater virtually disappeared. By the 10th century, signs of an independent drama had begun to appear. Principally in France, though elsewhere in Europe as well, brief theatrical scenes (*tropes*) were introduced into the Christian liturgy. The first of these tropes depicted the visit of the three Marys to the tomb of Jesus. Scholars are reconsidering how these crude first steps expanded into full-blown theatrical presentations, for though it once was thought that the progression was gradual but steady, it is now clear that the history of medieval drama is both more complicated and more elusive than was earlier believed. Nevertheless, this much is certain: from the 10th century to the 14th, the dramatization of Biblical materials and the presentation of religious drama expanded considerably throughout Europe, and by the 15th century play producing was both ambitious and widespread.

RENAISSANCE—Teatro Olimpico, Vicenza, Italy, was designed by Andrea Palladio. It was begun in 1580.

ALINARI—ART REFERENCE BUREAU

Throughout the medieval period theater remained a joint clerical and civic undertaking, open to all and participated in by most townspeople. Initially, the performers were members of the clergy, but with the growth in the number of productions and the involvement of entire communities, laymen became performers and, in later years at least, some became professional actors. Presentations fell into three main categories: scenes from the Old and New Testaments, usually called mystery plays, though sometimes termed miracle plays; scenes from the lives of saints, invariably termed miracle plays; and morality plays, in which the subject was salvation and the characters represented abstract virtues or vices. A mystery or miracle play, normally only 10 to 20 minutes in length, was usually linked with others to form a continuous narrative. In England, these narratives or cycles depicted the entire story of man, starting with the Creation of the world, passing through the Annunciation, Nativity, and Passion of Jesus, and concluding with the Day of Judgment.

On the Continent, staging methods for these extended narratives differed from those in England. On the Continent, either a series of platforms was constructed around the perimeter of the town square, or "mansions" representing the various locales in the story were arranged in a row. Either type of simultaneous staging enabled actors to move from one place to another as the action demanded. In England, the most widespread method was to place each play on a separate wheeled platform, or pageant wagon, and then pull the wagons through the town, stopping at designated points to perform the piece. So ambitious an undertaking was possible because of the joint efforts of the craft guilds and the church. Usually each play was produced by one guild responsible for building or securing a pageant wagon, supplying the costumes and scenery, providing or hiring the actors, and rehearsing the presentation. Each guild member was assessed a share of the cost. Considering that two to four dozen plays were presented, it is evident that a considerable part of the populace was engaged in theatrical production. These town-wide presentations persisted into the 16th century.

Renaissance Theater. No clear date marks the end of medieval and the beginning of Renaissance theater. From country to country the yielding of liturgical drama to secular neoclassical drama occurred at different times; thus, the last vestiges of the cycles can be found in England at the same time that Greek plays were first being revived in Italy. Nevertheless, between the 15th and 17th centuries, the character of European drama underwent a major change. On the one hand, the artistic impulses generated by the rich and widespread medieval theater, divested of religious purpose, flowered in the theater of England and Spain before passing away. On the other, the Greek and Roman theatrical tradition, rediscovered and newly appreciated, indicated lines of development that excited the imagination and stimulated fresh artistic effort.

The popular, communal audience, essentially religious in character, slowly disappeared. In its stead appeared two types of audience—the general public, consisting of artisans and burghers, to whom theater was offered as an attraction and diversion; and a select aristocracy, which cultivated the theater for the aristocrats' own glory, learning, and pleasure. In some countries the two types of audience overlapped, but for the most part the theater for each type developed in its own way. In Italy this dichotomy manifested itself in the two kinds of theater that emerged during the late 15th century: the *commedia dell'arte,* the theater of the fairs and the streets; and the *commedia erudita* and *intermezzi,* the theater of the academy and the court. The *commedia dell'arte,* the improvised comedy of the professional performer, was the product of wandering troupes, sometimes playing at the ducal courts that dotted the Italian peninsula, often appearing in the open wherever an audience could be assembled. For a stage, the *commedia dell'arte* initially employed a bare platform backed by a drape to provide entrances for the performers; in later years, as they became accepted at court, the actors adopted the scenic stage.

Concurrent with the growth and expansion of the *commedia dell'arte,* a tradition of theatrical production developed among the Italian nobility. Aristocrats as well as scholars were stimulated to revive the ancient Greek and Latin plays and to write imitations in Italian. These performances were presented at court or for academies organized to renew classical culture, such as the Olympic Academy in Vicenza, for which Andrea Palladio (1518–1580) designed a classical theater (Teatro Olimpico), which opened in 1585. The same impulse that led to the literary revival also affected scenic development. Influenced by the Roman architect Vitruvius (Marcus Vitruvius Pollio) and possessing the newly discovered science of perspective, scenic artists created stage spectacles that combined the real and the ideal. Since performances of so elaborate a character were occasional, given to celebrate a marriage or a state reception, they were presented in palace halls temporarily transformed into theaters. In addition, adopting the literary convention of the pastoral, the court artists created short theatrical pieces that combined dance, song, pageantry, and classical myths, and presented them as *intermezzi* between scenes of regular plays. By the end of the 16th century, these pieces had given way to the newly established art of opera.

Paralleling the development of opera was the expansion of theater construction. In 1619 the Teatro Farnese, a permanent court theater, was completed at Parma, and during the 17th and 18th centuries many other court theaters were built. Designed to accommodate the fashionable new scenery, which was changeable and employed perspective, these theaters provided an elongated auditorium separated from the playing area by a proscenium arch. Behind the arch were arranged the wing and drop settings. As the taste for more and more elaborate spectacle grew, the proscenium arches became wider and higher and the stage considerably deeper for the purpose of assuring convincing realism or breathtaking illusion.

Through its *commedia dell'arte* and its innovations in theater design, the Italian theater exerted considerable influence throughout Europe. In both France and England, this influence began to be felt in the early 17th century; the difference was that by then England had nearly finished a period of literary greatness and France had just embarked upon one. Both countries reveal similar lines of development with quite dissimilar historical results.

England. Although exposed to the humanistic and classical influences that had altered the Italian theater, the English stage retained its popular character for many years. School plays in Latin and English early set the example of a classically oriented drama, but it was an example that was not followed. Encouraged by the crown, English actors established a native repertory and permanent playhouses and thus became the first Europeans to operate a successful commercial theater. Until 1572, under the nominal patronage of leading noblemen, the acting troupes, composed of men and boys, wandered through England, appearing in town halls, country or city inns, or wherever they were tolerated. Appearances in London might be more frequent, yet nonetheless temporary.

In 1572, players were granted permission to perform daily in London, and in 1576 James Burbage, an actor and carpenter, erected the first building intended solely as a playhouse—an open-air structure named the Theatre. No longer were special occasions to determine when performances would be given; entertainment became available five or six days a week for an admission fee. During the course of the next 40 years, seven playhouses were constructed, each seating about 2,500 persons. The most notable of these buildings, the Globe playhouse, built in 1599, housed the Lord Chamberlain's Men (later renamed the King's Men), the company to which Shakespeare belonged and for which he wrote.

With regard to both staging methods and dramatic composition acting companies adhered to medieval habits. The stage was a large bare platform, at the rear of which rose a fixed facade containing two doors and a curtained enclosure on the first level and a balcony for playing and possibly viewing on the second. A roof partly covered the platform. The plays were extended narratives reminiscent of the religious cycles. Out of this native tradition Shakespeare and his contemporaries fashioned a theatrical style distinct from the classical one.

Throughout this period the aristocratic influence, which so dominated Italian theater, had a continuing but lesser effect in England. Under Elizabeth I, the court was content to employ professional actors rather than produce its own plays. It also maintained choruses of boys for the royal chapels. Various masters of these choruses, taking advantage of the boys' availability and training, used them as actors and formed them into companies that performed not only at court but also to a paying public in converted halls. Playing in relatively intimate indoor theaters such as the Blackfriars, the children's companies drew a more limited audience, but one of a higher social rank, than the adult companies did. In style, the children's productions reflected the classical and courtly influence, stressing music, dance, and, possibly, scenic display.

With the accession (1603) of King James I, court influence became more pronounced. The major acting troupes, having been taken under the patronage of the royal family, oriented their work toward the court, and the court itself developed its own presentation, the masque, along lines that had been suggested by Italian example. The leading theater influence at the English court was Inigo Jones (1573–1652), an architect and stage designer trained in Italy. Utilizing classical motifs and the art of perspective, Jones transformed the great chamber of Whitehall into a world of fantasy.

The evolution of the court-centered theater was interrupted by the Puritan revolution and the suppression of all theaters in 1642. But with the restoration of the monarchy under King Charles II in 1660, the earlier trend toward centralization of theater under royal command continued. The court issued patents (sole rights of performance) to two men—Thomas Killigrew (1612–1683), who headed the King's Men, and Sir William Davenant (1606–1668), who headed the Duke's Men and who was particularly interested in opera and its scenic possibilities. When playing resumed about 1661, the boy-actor disappeared, and women's roles were taken by women.

France. The same forces were at work in France, but theatrical history there was somewhat different. Theater began to flourish later in France than in England because France was beset by civil war late in the 16th century. During the first 30 years of the 17th century the identical conflict between native medieval methods of staging and the newer classical revival that had earlier faced London now occurred in Paris. In France, however, the court played a more decisive role, and under the leadership of Cardinal Richelieu imposed classical prescriptions on the theater. The final struggle centered on the reception of Pierre Corneille's *Le Cid* (1636), which, according to its critics, violated the structure and decorum of the classical theater. By referring the issue to the newly organized French Academy, Richelieu in effect invited the condemnation of *Le Cid* and set French theater on a neoclassical path.

All aspects of performing came under royal command. Permission to perform in Paris was directly granted by the king, who designated the place of performance and the number of performances permitted each week. Composed of male and female performers, the troupes played in comedies and tragedies (though particular troupes were famous for one or the other). Adhering to the example of classical drama, plays contained a limited number of characters, an unchanging locale, and little violent action.

Between 1634 and 1658, three troupes performed regularly in Paris: the French actors of the Hôtel de Bourgogne and the Théâtre du Marais, and the Italian comedians of the Petit Bourbon. In 1658, King Louis XIV granted to Molière, who for 12 years had led a troupe touring the provinces, the privilege of sharing the Petit Bourbon with the Italian comedians, each company playing three days a week. This division of theatrical presentation remained virtually unchanged until after Molière's death in 1673, after which his troupe merged with the Marais actors. In 1680 the King combined the company of tragedians at the Hôtel de Bourgogne and the Molière-Marais troupe into the first national theater, the Comédie Française.

At first, public performances had been given in converted halls or tennis courts, but later they were offered in theaters that were erected for the purpose by the courtiers. In 1641, Cardinal Richelieu introduced the first proscenium stage to France in his new theater at the Palais Royal; and in 1670 the Marquis de Sourdéac built an opera house in Rue Guénégaud. Both buildings later came to be used by professional troupes. At Versailles, in addition to regular plays, scenic spectacles commissioned especially by the king were presented in indoor and outdoor settings. The role that Inigo Jones played at the English court was filled by Giacomo Torelli (1608–1678) at the French. Torelli developed machinery for changing heavy scenery, and his methods were later used on the public stage. Since French political and cultural influence prevailed throughout the Continent during the next 150 years, French theater, with its close ties to the sovereign, its reliance on spectacle, and its widespread use of music and dance, became the model for the rest of continental Europe. French companies and styles filled the theaters of the many German principalities, and the art of ballet, a French novelty of the 17th century, was later adopted by the Russian court.

Middle-Class Theater of the 18th and 19th Centuries. In London, Paris, and many other cities the professional theater adopted the court taste for elaborate scenery. To achieve its effects, the scenic theater needed complicated machinery and extensive space—in many of the court theaters the depth of the stage exceeded the depth of the auditorium. With performance concentrated in such structures, control of theater passed from the actors to the manager, who might or might not be an actor himself but whose control stemmed from his position as head of a theatrical house.

In England this situation developed more rapidly than on the Continent, for, though the Restoration of King Charles II favored aristocratic influence, the influence was temporary, and Parliament soon reasserted itself. Commercial production, however modified by the king's privilege of designating managers for the patent theaters, came to prevail. Gradually the unified acting troupe disappeared, and the manager or actor-manager in control of a theater hired performers and mounted productions. In the course of the 18th century, London playhouses grew in size, and by the early 19th century such theaters as Drury Lane and Covent Garden accommodated as many as 3,200 persons. Although outdoor theaters in Greece and Elizabethan England had held that number or more, this capacity in a proscenium house made for an extremely large structure.

The end of the 18th century saw the growth of a new theatrical sensibility. Though the theater remained essentially the same, partly commercial, partly aristocratic, it underwent internal changes. The first discernible signs were in the German theater, which had lacked a developed tradition. In the 18th century, the critic Johann Gottsched and the actress-manager Caroline Neuber joined forces to substitute French neoclassicism for the popular "Hanswurst" farces (named for a stock clown character). A generation later, Gotthold Ephraim Lessing (1729–1781) counterattacked. As a dramatist and a critic, he favored a native tradition responsive to Shakespearean and later English middle-class example. He and actors such as Friedrich Schröder sought to encourage a literary drama that would be realistic and a style of performance that would be unified.

The writers Johann Wolfgang von Goethe (1749–1832) and Friedrich von Schiller (1759–1805) seconded these attempts; and as a theater producer at Weimar, Goethe sought a harmonious manner of acting that would do justice to the playwright's work. These men were among the first dramatists who, though neither performers themselves nor attached to theatrical troupes, nevertheless exercised a decisive influence on the course of theater. They were essentially critics and managers who approached the drama from a semiparticipatory point of view. They de-emphasized the roles of stage mechanic and designer, giving attention to the dramatic event and its satisfactory literary expression. In their own plays can be found two of the recurrent strains of later writing—the romantic evocation of individual vision and the realistic depiction of domestic incident for the purposes of social criticism.

English theater underwent stylistic rather than thematic changes. Actor-managers like John Philip Kemble (1757–1823) and Charles Kean (1811–1868) sought to create a harmonious unit of text, acting, and staging. From the days of the medieval stage, it had been customary for actors to dress richly, but in the fashion of their own time. In his productions of Shakespeare's plays, Kean stressed historical accuracy in scenery and costumes. Although in the first part of the 19th century scenic accuracy had to be rendered with paint and brush, by the end of the 19th century it was being increasingly realized in three-dimensional structures.

The movement for historical authenticity and unified production achieved its fullest expression in a minor German principality, Saxe-Meiningen. Its theater-minded ruler, Duke George II (1826–1914), maintained an acting company that developed into a well-integrated ensemble. At its best in revivals of Shakespeare and Schiller, the company was also interested in more contemporary subjects, and its influence on the Moscow Art Theater was particularly marked.

The enormous theater structure, with its grandiose scenery, continued to thrive throughout the 19th century. But theaters began to appear that were more intimate and not intended for the general public. Though every new theater movement tends to be a force for social criticism, in the last quarter of the 19th century the so-called "free theaters" were the first that overtly proclaimed social criticism as their reason for existence. Beginning with the Théâtre Libre in Paris (1887), such theaters as the Freie Bühne in Berlin (1889), the Independent Theatre in London (1891), and the Moscow Art Theater (1898) shared a number of distinctive features. They strove to depict reality—not as it is found in generalized behavior, but as it can be seen in particular expressions of concrete experiences. Not painted scenery or sketched furniture, but actual chairs and tables backed by convincing frames of solid walls were placed on stage. Advances in stage lighting made possible the illusion of natural light.

To achieve more realistic productions these theaters favored intimate playhouses whose dimensions suited the new realistic plays of Henrik Ibsen (1828–1906) and Anton Chekhov (1860–1904). These plays required settings an audience could verify from its experience. Furthermore, in order to achieve the harmonious ensemble acting required by such plays, the founders of the "free theaters," including André Antoine (1858–1943) of the Théâtre Libre and, most importantly, Konstantin Stanislavsky (1863–1938) of the Moscow Art Theater, sought to create acting troupes that were united not merely by their professional interests but also by their artistic and social ideals.

NEW YORK PUBLIC LIBRARY THEATRE COLLECTION

TWENTIETH CENTURY PLAY—William Saroyan's *The Time of Your Life* (1940), set in a San Francisco bar, starred Julie Haydon and Eddie Dowling (seated).

20th Century Theater. The 20th century has been a time of invigorating but chaotic experimentation and change. A major part of the theater remains a commercial enterprise dominated by producers or managers who purvey entertainment to the public. The ultimate expression of this entrepreneurial style is American "show business." In Europe and the United States commercial theater has undergone the vicissitudes of fortune. It has often served well enough as a means for creating outstanding theater, but usually only after having been stimulated by the noncommercial theater. Many of the "free theaters" contributed to the commercial mainstream and, in some instances, merged with it. In the English-speaking theater, George Bernard Shaw (1856–1950) and Eugene O'Neill (1888–1953) managed to create major dramatic works within the confines of a "little theater" movement turned commercial.

In the case of musical comedy, the commercial theater did develop a significant art form. But, being dominated by business managers, the commercial theater has often lacked artistic continuity, a lack that became increasingly critical in the 1920's. In the business of selling entertainment to the public, the theater could succeed only as long as it offered an interesting product at a reasonable cost. With the advent of motion pictures, and particularly of sound pictures in 1928, the competitive position of the commercial theater was seriously challenged, and though this theater continues to function (chiefly in London and New York), it does so in increasingly difficult circumstances.

Concurrently, theaters of revolt, whether of social or artistic revolt, appear, contribute to the mainstream of theater, and then, as often as not, disappear. National or civic theaters, on the other hand, steadily come into being and endure.

TWENTIETH CENTURY MUSICAL—*Hair,* "American tribal love-rock musical," which set a trend in the theatrical expression of youth in the late 1960's and the 1970's.

Supported by state subsidies (in Europe), they are considered part of the national heritage. Forms of support vary considerably, but there exist in virtually every nation theatrical companies or organizations that are nonprofit in character and public in form. Being public, these theaters are expected to assume certain social responsibilities—chiefly to offer the citizenry productions drawn from the national heritage. They are expected to represent the highest dramatic standards of the country.

The communal tendency, which has manifested itself through increased state support, has also shown itself through the cultivation of theatrical festivals throughout Europe, the Americas, and even, to some extent, in Asia and Africa. These festivals either present the combined effort of a community and its performers (the festival at Stratford, Ontario, for example) or bring together a number of companies from different parts of the globe (the festival of the Théâtre des Nations, Paris). Many festivals that initially presented plays for only a few weeks in the summer have expanded into year-round enterprises.

With these changes have come changes in the relationship of audience to theater. The idea has grown that theatergoing is a right that should be available to every citizen. This view has led to the establishment of low-priced admission (or even free admission) and to special prices for students. In addition, in the United States, the theatergoer may play a decisive role as a policy maker, for the controlling bodies of many civic theaters are boards of trustees consisting of public-spirited or socially prominent individuals.

In the main, the 20th century theater has been an eclectic theater. Among the numerous styles of presentation that it has encouraged, two that actually began in the 19th century should be noted. One stresses the portrayal of outer man and his environment. Acting skill is equated with the ability to observe and reproduce the behavior, accent, and dress of contemporary man. Antoine, Stanislavsky, the Group Theatre (in the United States), all stressed these abilities. The second style, not developed fully until the 20th century, seeks to portray the inner sensibility of man. Symbolism, impressionism, surrealism, theatricalism, expressionism, and absurdism are used to express aspects of the sensibility. The Swiss visionary, Adolphe Appia, in the designs that he did for Richard Wagner's operas, succeeded in demonstrating how three-dimensional, nonrepresentational or semirepresentational shapes and selective lighting could create impressions of timelessness and dream. The German expressionists attempted to create the phantasmagoria of both the individual and the social dream by portraying environment as the vision of the distorted mind. Responding to these tendencies, designers turned from the box set and its depiction of photographic reality to theatrical expressions of emotional and mental states.

3. History—Orient

Despite their diversity of history and style, the stages of India, China, Japan, and other parts of Asia share many common features that distinguish Oriental from Occidental theater. The origin of theater, in each of these countries, lies in religious observance, but these origins are so related to mythical and legendary sources that it is difficult to separate tradition from fact. Supposedly, Brahma himself founded the Indian theater, and in the 1st millennium B.C. sacred plays were reportedly produced in China. In Japan the No theater arose from a variety of priestly dances, the common source of which was the pantomimic dance (*kagura*) employed in Shinto worship.

Whatever its origins, by the time theater was fully developed in these countries, it was an art of the ruling class and, like the No drama, exclusively a pastime of the court. The coterie nature of theater was reinforced by the private language that was employed in performance. During the classic period of Hindu drama (320–800 A.D.), plays were composed in Sanskrit, a literary language not spoken by the mass of the people. At the imperial court in China, prior to the 13th century, Wen Li, an abstruse language of exceptional complexity, was employed in drama; and in the Japanese theater, the gestures and allusions of No required cultivated understanding in order to be appreciated. Even to the modern Japanese, the No play is alien and often incomprehensible.

The Oriental countries also share common features of staging. They present lengthy narratives composed of short plays, and a program

ORIENTAL—Japanese No plays, the traditional serious drama of Japan, are performed on a stage with a fixed setting by actors wearing expressionless masks.

JAPAN NATIONAL TOURIST ORGANIZATION

may consist of one continuous narrative or selections from several narratives. The Asian theater utilizes narrative techniques known in Europe but infrequently employed there. For instance, puppetry is more widespread in the Orient than in Europe. In another type of presentation, found in the kathakali dance of India and in the Bunraku (puppet theater) and No of Japan, a storyteller or a chorus recites the story while the performer mimes or dances it to the accompaniment of musical instruments. This type of storytelling, as well as more familiar forms of theater, uses stagehands (who, according to convention, are invisible to the audience) to hold curtains and otherwise help in the performance.

Actors, though they occupied a low position in society, needed to be highly trained. In India, women as well as men could perform; in China and Japan, at least from the 18th century to the mid-20th, only men. Since performing depended on symbolic gesture, conventional singing, and narrative signs, the actor had to learn a complex theatrical language. In addition, the Chinese theater placed tremendous emphasis on acrobatic feats, which the actor had to master. Most narratives utilized distinctive character types, and normally an actor specialized in one type of role. In China there were four main types—males in general, robust males, females in general, and slapstick comedians. In No drama there were two types—the *shite* (leading actor) and the *waki* (his foil). The profession of acting, though of dubious respectability, retained a religious or mystic aura, and the traditional Oriental actor still prepares for a performance as for a sacred act. Every aspect of preparation, including dressing the body and painting the face, is conducted ritually.

Historically, the theater seems to have moved eastward through Asia. The classic period of Hindu drama, represented by its greatest work, the *Sakuntala* of Kalidasa (c.400 A. D.), ended by 800, after which there were a few ineffective efforts to revive the theater. The beginning of Chinese drama dates from the reign of Emperor Hsüan Tsung (712–756 A. D.), who encouraged the drama and maintained a large company of actors at his court.

Japan inherited its drama from China, reportedly in the 6th century. But it was not until the 14th century that a native Japanese theater was formed with the cultivation of the No drama, whose austere recitals of tragedy were relieved by comic interludes known as Kyogen. Kabuki did not appear until the early 17th century. Unlike No, Kabuki was intended for a popular audience that had been excluded from the more refined drama. A third type of theater, the Bunraku puppet theater, rivaled the Kabuki in popularity. Primarily a theater of dance, gesture, and song, the Kabuki and the Bunraku did not produce many outstanding dramatists. The most famous writer, who composed plays for both Kabuki and the puppet theater, was Chikamatsu Monzaemon (1653–1724). In the 20th century, the traditional Oriental forms have been challenged by imported Western styles.

BERNARD BECKERMAN
Author of "Dynamics of Drama"

Bibliography

Brockett, Oscar G., *History of the Theatre* (Boston 1968).
Freedley, George, and Reeves, John A., *A History of the Theatre*, rev. ed. (New York 1955).
Gorelik, Mordecai, *New Theatres for Old* (New York 1940).
MacGowan, Kenneth, and Melnitz, William, *The Living Stage* (Englewood Cliffs, N. J., 1955).
Nicoll, Allardyce, *The Development of the Theatre*, 5th ed. (New York 1967).
Simonson, Lee, *The Stage Is Set* (New York 1932).
Southern, Richard, *The Seven Ages of the Theatre* (New York 1961).

For Specialized Study

Beare, William, *The Roman Stage*, 2d ed. (London 1955).
Beckerman, Bernard, *Shakespeare at the Globe, 1599–1609* (New York 1962).
Bowers, Faubion, *Theatre in the East: A Survey of Asian Drama* (London 1956).
Ducharte, Pierre L., *The Italian Comedy*, tr. by Randolph T. Weaver (London 1929).
Ernst, Earle, *The Kabuki Theatre* (New York 1956).
Gassner, John, *Form and Idea in the Modern Theatre* (New York 1956).
Moody, Richard, *America Takes the Stage* (Bloomington, Ind., 1955).
Nicoll, Allardyce, *History of English Drama, 1660–1900*, rev. ed., 6 vols. (London 1952–1959).
Rossiter, Arthur P., *English Drama from Early Times to the Elizabethans* (New York 1959).
Scott, Adolphe C., *The Classical Theatre of China* (London 1957).
Southern, Richard, *Changeable Scenery* (London 1952).
Webster, Thomas B. L., *Greek Theatre Production* (London 1956).
Wickham, Glynne, *Early English Stages, 1300–1660*, 2 vols. (New York 1959–1962).

Greek theater in ancient Epidaurus, a large open amphitheater built into hillside slopes.

THEATER ARCHITECTURE. A theater is a carefully considered and even more carefully built place, designed to be used by specialists for a particular purpose—entertaining an audience. How well or badly the theater may serve its purpose inevitably affects the reaction to the play produced within it. It is easy to perform well in a good theater and difficult to do so in a bad one. A "good theater," of course, need not be large and expensive, but only well designed for the kinds of productions to be given within it.

The Theater as a Special Place. Suitable designs for good theaters would seem to be a relatively simple matter, seeing that men have been building them for 2,500 years. The formula should have been learned by now. But theater people keep changing their minds about the kinds of performances they wish to give, the ways in which they may be seen most effectively, and the function of drama.

Generally speaking, theaters and productions tend to fall into two major types—those that provide a close relationship between actor and audience, so that the audience is closely engaged in the activity and emotional content of the play, and those that separate actor and audience, the audience being essentially passive, objective, or intellectually rather than emotionally stimulated. There has been considerable controversy over the years regarding the relative merits of each system, but in effect they serve different purposes and cannot be compared.

Historically, drama and theater have swung back and forth between more or less conventionalized production and "new" or "radical" means. In conventional drama, it is the actor's interpretation of a well-understood type of role that is important. In more "radical" plays it is the production method that carries the principal burden of novelty, and actors tend to project their parts in a highly stylized fashion as is done in modern "guerrilla" or "rock" theater.

It would be convenient if both production methods could operate equally effectively in the same kind of theater building. But this is not the case, principally because production cannot always be defined in such simple black-or-white terms. Many plays are uneasy mixtures of diverse elements, and therefore—since theaters are built for plays and not the other way around—the theater architect is left not with two variables but with many. In effect, there is no way to build "a theater" properly once and for all because there is no such thing as "a play." Plays differ, and so must theaters.

Ideally, a theater should be built especially to accommodate the requirements of a specific theater company with a defined program and style. It could then be tailored to a favorite production method and thus serve its purpose most efficiently. Theaters, however, take longer to build and usually last longer than production companies. For this reason theaters usually are erected without an organization in mind, and a company is found to rent or lease the structure after it is completed.

For these and other reasons a theater building is seldom thought to be perfect, or sometimes even suitable, for the particular purpose to which it is put. In spite of this difficult and frequently maddening complication, a theater is indeed a "special place," one that resembles no other exactly in form or function. Plays can be produced in barns, music halls, basements, and open fields, but such places are severely limiting. Theatrical production is a complicated business that requires a preferred arrangement of spaces and an allowance for specific materials and equipment. Throughout history such preferences and allowances have changed to conform to current tastes. No theater of the past is perfectly suited to modern production, for diverse styles from several eras are used frequently enough to make any of them too limiting. As the modern painter and musician have the entire past to call upon in order to achieve a desired effect, so do the modern theatrical producer and playwright. Modern theaters, then, must be flexible enough to accommodate several production styles rather than just one. As the theatrical producer must be familiar with past production techniques, so the theater architect must be aware of previous building styles in order that he may adapt and incorporate the best features of each.

Theaters of the Ancient World. Since the drama of the ancient Greeks was based on religion and served a civic function, theaters necessarily had to accommodate most of the local population at one sitting. There were no intimate playhouses, only large open amphitheaters. These were built into hillside slopes, exact proportions being determined by ground contour rather than by formula. The preferred plan was a portion of a circle somewhat greater than 180°, the seats partially surrounding a completely circular area within which the chorus performed. A shallow stage faced the seats, and this in turn was backed by a "scene" building in which some doors were located. This served as a general locale for all plays, and the doors—together with steps to the stage at several locations—were used for all entrances.

Since Greek theaters were altered regularly over the centuries to conform to changing tastes, it is difficult to discuss them as a single type. This is true especially in regard to the scene building. What began as a small temple to Dionysus became, in time, an elaborate architectural unit. Some Greek theaters, in fact, seem to have had stage arrangements which included painted panels as scenery. The general characteristics of the Greek theater were large capacity, some seating 10,000 to 20,000 spectators; seating in an arc greater than a semicircle, with all seats facing a dancing circle; a shallow raised stage, which was low in the earliest period and grew higher each century; and a scene building of permanent construction.

Roman theaters differed from the Greek in several ways. They were not built into the slopes of hills but were constructed as separate, free-standing units. The seating arc did not extend beyond 180°, and there was no dancing circle. The stage was deeper and higher than the Greek, and the scene building was an impressive, elaborately decorated structure of several stories. Some Roman theaters had a roof over the stage, a curtain that fell into a slot at the start of performance, and a complex *velarium,* or awning, that protected the seating area from the sun. The emphasis was on splendor, comfort, and space for elaborate production.

Theaters of the Renaissance. Roman theaters fell into ruin with the collapse of the empire. Entertainment in the Middle Ages was not given in theaters—by then there were none—but in churches, as the drama slowly revived, or upon open stages in public squares. Not until Latin manuscripts were rediscovered was there enough interest in formal drama to build playhouses to accommodate it. The discovery, in the 15th century, of a treatise by the 1st century Roman architect Marcus Vitruvius Pollio helped spur interest in theater buildings. In this work—part of his *De Architectura Libri Decem* (*Ten Books*

Roman theater in Orange (ancient Arausio), France, showing the scene building and seating arc.

FRENCH GOVERNMENT TOURIST OFFICE

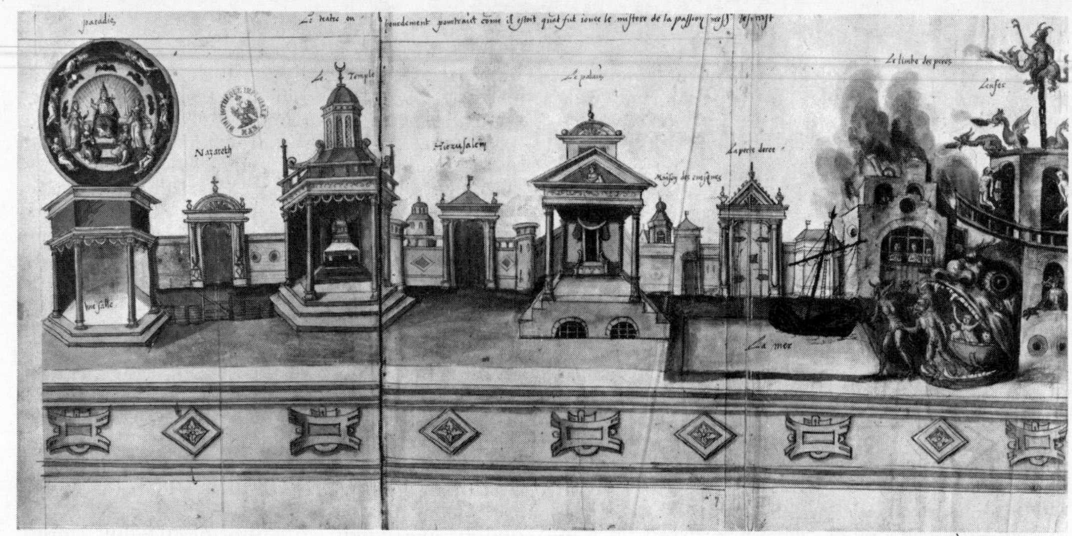

BIBLIOTHÈQUE NATIONALE

MEDIEVAL STAGE in the public square of Valenciennes (France), erected for the Passion play of 1547. Localities, from Heaven to Hell, were spread out in sequence.

on Architecture)—Vitruvius describes Greek and Roman theaters of his time and gives some instructions for building them.

No one was interested in reconstructing full Roman theaters, but the classic form had great influence upon Renaissance architects, and, as early as the 15th century, several temporary stages were built in various parts of Europe for productions of the newly discovered comedies of Terence. These rudimentary structures copied the semicircular form of the Roman playhouse as described by Vitruvius.

During the 16th and 17th centuries royal and ducal courts found new diversion in theatrical production, and ballrooms, great halls, and tiltyards—courtyards for jousting matches between knights—were converted into playing spaces. Princes vied with one another in the splendor of their new halls and in the magnificence of the productions. One of the principal types of entertainment given in the court theaters consisted of classically inspired semidramatic orations, separated by *intermezzi*—elaborate scenic displays—coupled with processions or dances that spilled out onto the main floor of the hall. Seating, therefore, was arranged in an open U shape, leaving the center free for theatrical use.

In 1548 the first permanent theater built since Roman times was opened in the Hôtel de Bourgogne, the former Paris residence of the dukes of Burgundy. The building was long and narrow, with the stage built at one end. The audience was accommodated in a gallery, divided into boxes, which was raised around three sides of the hall. The center of the room was left open and without seats—a *parterre* intended for standing patrons. The stage was prepared with scenery much like that on the temporary medieval stages. All pieces required for a production were placed on stage in the required sequence. Each was removed when no longer needed after each scene. This system produced what is called a "simultaneous setting."

A similarly shaped theater was constructed in 1576 for London audiences in the former great hall of Blackfriars, a religious enclave turned to private use. This also had galleries on three sides and a stage on the fourth, but the *parterre*—called the "pit" in England—was fitted with benches, and the stage was fixed with a permanent architectural arrangement having doors and windows that could be used for any play.

In the same year, James Burbage erected a playhouse called the Theatre outside the limits of the City of London to be free from restrictions on playing. The Theatre was unique, quite different from long and narrow playhouses like the Bourgogne and Blackfriars. Instead, it was

THE SWAN theater, London, 1590's. Drawing is only known view of the interior of an Elizabethan playhouse.

UNIVERSITY LIBRARY, UTRECHT

circular, with three galleries rising one above the other, an unroofed pit, and a platform stage jutting out into the pit area. It had much the same type of architectural setting as Blackfriars, however, and the pit patrons stood, as they did at the Bourgogne. The pattern set by the Theatre was repeated in most of the English public theaters built during the reigns of Elizabeth I and James I. The Globe was one of these, as was the Swan, of which a drawing was made by a visiting Hollander, Johannes De Witt, affording the only known view of the interior of an Elizabethan playhouse.

Effect of Scenery Innovations. Scenery received considerable attention from the Italians. Elaborate scenic effects were required in the court theater productions. The very size of the halls, however, made scenery expensive and cumbersome. Vitruvius had mentioned *periaktoi* as used by the Greeks. These were three-sided prisms with a separate scene painted on each face. Revolving several pairs of *periaktoi* at the same time would give a complete change of scene without dismantling the stage. Another method, invented by the Italians, used flat wings moving on and off the stage guided by grooves. This allowed as many changes of scene as required, and not just the three offered by the *periaktoi*. The prism system was developed by Nicola Sabbatini and Joseph Furttenbach and used in the latter's Stadttheater at Ulm, Germany, in 1641. The wing-in-groove system had been introduced in 1618 at Parma, Italy, by Giambattista Aleotti in his Teatro Farnese, which still stands. The wing system, being more flexible than the *periaktoi*, came to displace them.

Regardless of Italian developments in scenery and a trend toward multitiered auditoriums, the conservative French stuck to their intimate public theaters. The Théâtre du Marais (1671) was the second public theater in Paris, and resembled the first very closely. It, too, was long and narrow, having been constructed in a former tennis court. Two tiers of boxes, a standing *parterre*, and a small stage were part of the few arrangements thought necessary for public entertainment.

Theatricals for the French court, on the other hand, were quite a different matter. The Salle des Machines, built in Paris in 1659, capitalized on the most recent advances in scenes and machines. The stage was about 130 feet (39.6 meters) deep, and the installation of scenes was designed by Giacomo Torelli, who brought with him from Italy his new method of moving any amount of scenery quickly and easily. The Torelli system eliminated the necessity of having a stagehand handle every piece and instead introduced machinery to do the same job. Torelli's machines were located below the stage, with lines leading to the scenic pieces to be moved. Revolving a windlass would bring all pieces of scenery into motion—on or off the stage—at the same time. A similar system of machines was located above the stage for cloud and flying effects.

By the mid-17th century, playgoing was divided between two quite different kinds of drama and the different playhouses that were built to house them. Inexpensive and intimate theaters, like the Marais, rose in major European cities, catering to an audience of the middle class and lesser nobility, producing comedies and tragedies based on classic or Renaissance models. Parallel with these were the theaters built for the various courts. They were large rather than intimate, ornate rather than simple, and designed to accommodate opera, ballet, and the more grandiose neoclassic tragedy. The Marais and the Globe, although of different architectural styles, were good examples of late Renaissance public theaters. The Salle des Machines was to have an important influence on the design of court theaters throughout Europe.

The Baroque and Rococo Theater. Two of the most gorgeous theaters ever built are Germany's Bayreuth Opernhaus (1748), designed by Giuseppe Galli-Bibiena, and the Residenztheater (1752) in Munich, designed by François de Cuvilliés. Multiple tiers filled with gilt carvings, rosettes, and swags rise to elaborately painted ceilings. The prosceniums are pillared gilt picture frames, and the stages are large enough to mount the most elaborate opera filled with allegorical flights of fancy. These theaters are the finest examples of a style of ornate court playhouse that swept Europe after originating in Italy in the late 17th century.

The simple English platform stage used in the Globe and the Swan moved indoors in the 17th century and remained part of the English theater up to the 19th century. One of the earliest and best known of these indoor playhouses, the Theatre Royal, Drury Lane, built by Christopher Wren in 1674, was rebuilt by Robert and James Adam in 1775. The English playhouse had fewer tiers and boxes than its continental counterpart, and a large apron stage protruded far out into the auditorium, placing the actor in

TEATRO FARNESE in Parma, Italy, showing a section of seats and the edge of stage-left wings.

ITALIAN GOVERNMENT TOURIST OFFICE

RESIDENZTHEATER in Munich, completed in 1752, is one of the most elaborately appointed court theaters ever built.

FRITZ HENLE, FROM PHOTO RESEARCHERS

the midst of the audience. As the 18th century wore on, the apron stage increasingly was cut back, and it vanished entirely in the 19th century. Wren's Drury Lane was a modest building, approximately 58 by 112 feet (18 by 34 meters), with two tiers in the auditorium. By the time the Adam brothers and others had completed their many alterations, the theater was some 200 feet (61 meters) long and as capable as any other of mounting elaborate spectacles. Similar, though more modest, was the Little Theatre in the Haymarket, built originally in 1720, enlarged in 1766, and finally built entirely anew in 1821, to become the Theatre Royal, Haymarket.

Numerous experiments were made in the 18th century in acoustics, auditorium arrangement, and efficient stage technical apparatus. It was realized that house spaces could not be expanded indefinitely, or performers could not be heard. Pillars that held up the tiers of boxes or galleries were constantly in the way, and means were sought to reduce their number or eliminate them

Theatre Royal, Drury Lane, London, as it appeared following reworking by the Adam brothers in 1775.

BOSTON PUBLIC LIBRARY

entirely. Lobbies and foyers were not required in court theaters, since such playhouses usually were attached to palaces with numerous salons of their own. But theaters for the middle class—those without palace salons—began to offer within the playhouse some of the grandeur formerly associated only with court theaters.

A major theater of the 18th century that combines many of the best features of playhouse design up to that time is the Grand Théâtre de Bordeaux (1780), designed by Victor Louis. This civic theater-opera house is entirely freestanding, an architectural monument of a spaciousness and magnificence fit for ecclesiastic or governmental architecture. The interior is lavishly appointed. Boxes are cantilevered out from the walls so that pillars do not obstruct the view. The size of the house is determined by proper acoustics, not box-office demand, and is based upon a circle, truncated at a quarter of its diameter by the proscenium opening. This affords good sight lines from all seats. This, the first of the *grands théâtres*, was imitated widely.

Theaters in America. For many perfectly understandable reasons playhouse architecture in the Americas got off to a slow start. Not until the United States was founded were theaters of any pretension built. Colonial audiences had to make do with productions in converted barns, lofts, and warehouses. The first proper theater in North America was the Chestnut Street Theatre in Philadelphia, completed in 1793. This was a well-appointed playhouse, patterned after the Theatre Royal in Bath, England. It was followed quickly by the Newport (R. I.) Theatre (1793), converted from a handsome brick public market, and the Federal Street Theatre in Boston (1794), built by Charles Bulfinch in the style of the Théâtre de Bordeaux. The first permanent theater in New York City was the Park Street Theatre, completed in 1795 after designs by Marc Isambard Brunel.

After these first permanent theaters, others sprang up in profusion. By the 1820's every major American city had a pretentious public theater. Managements vied with one another to attract patrons, and the theaters grew larger and more magnificent. From the 2,000-seat capacity of the Chestnut Street Theatre, houses rose to 3,000 capacity in the first Bowery Street Theatre (1826) in New York City, to 4,000 in the Broadway Theatre (1847), and 4,600 in the New York Academy of Music (1854). The Boston Theatre (1854) was typical of the new plans, having vast cast-iron galleries and a few residual boxes tucked up next to the proscenium. All of these new theaters, however, were spacious and comfortable in ways unthought of in the previous century.

The 19th Century Revolution. The system of architecture and machinery that had been usual in theaters of the Western world since the 17th century began to break down in the last quarter of the 19th. Audiences were more numerous and vastly more affluent, and required more comfort and better productions. Luxuries such as upholstered chairs, common only to the court theaters, were introduced into the ordinary public playhouses. Gas lighting made greater realism possible just as public taste was turning to it. The types of plays that were economically successful had begun to change in the mid-19th century. Since the new style of play had different scenic requirements from the type that preceded it, stages had to be changed also. When scenery and stages change, auditoriums must follow suit. Scenery became more important to comprehension of increasingly realistic drama. In Booth's Theatre, New York (1869), the old wing sliding in grooves was abandoned. Instead, the scenery was held up by stage braces, an innovation that permitted flats to be mounted at any angle.

The first of the revolutionary theaters was the opera house built in 1876 in Bayreuth, especially for the music-dramas of Richard Wagner. Based

Interior of the Chestnut Street Theatre, Philadelphia, the first theater built in North America.

NEW YORK PUBLIC LIBRARY

LINCOLN CENTER FOR THE PERFORMING ARTS

MODERN AUDITORIUM: Vivian Beaumont Theater in Lincoln Center for the Performing Arts, New York.

on the designs of Gottfried Semper, the Bayreuth Festspielhaus had a steeply pitched main floor so that the entire stage could be seen from each seat. There were no side boxes, and the auditorium shape—a wedge—assured good sight lines and acoustics. This new seating plan was highly successful and has been adopted worldwide. Once the old pattern was broken, there followed almost unlimited experimentation, a search for suitable new forms for a modern theater. The requirements of realism were barely met before expressionism, epic-theater, and other production theories made continuing adjustments necessary.

The Modern Playhouse. Between the World Wars radical experiments were made in Germany and Russia, where many of the forms now considered "modern" were introduced in the 1920's. The arena style, "mass theater," simultaneous staging, fragmentary scenery, emphasis upon light, political activist "agit-prop" performances with actors in the audience, and other startling new ways of involving the audience were attempted. It was realized quickly that the formal proscenium theater was inappropriate for such new production styles, and many attempts were made to find a new architectural formula. World War II brought a temporary halt to such experiments, but they were revived by the following generation to please or plague us once more.

CONTEMPORARY INNOVATIONS in seating, stage, and stage elevator, Forum Theatre, St. Joseph, Minn.

COLLEGE OF SAINT BENEDICT

Even the most modern type of dramatic production requires scenic effects. When the old wing and drop system was found to be too inflexible, other systems were introduced to augment it—electric elevators on which large scenic pieces could be raised or lowered; large hydraulic lifts that enabled the stage to be raised, lowered, or tilted in any direction; revolving stages capable of carrying several complete settings at one time; mechanized orchestra pits that could rise and become forestages; and even seating sections that could be manipulated into several different relations with the stage. All were attempts to find appropriate solutions to modern problems. However, no single system can serve drama effectively, for contemporary theater production abides by no single formula. Modern theaters must be flexible so that several kinds of play may be done with equal ease.

The modern playhouse may have a proscenium—for that old element is too useful to abandon entirely—but usually the auditorium is capable of alteration to other forms. The Vivian Beaumont Theater in New York City's Lincoln Center for the Performing Arts is a typical modern playhouse, capable of adapting to different shapes at the push of a button. The Experimental Theatre in the National Center for the Arts, Ottawa, Canada, is frankly designed for unusual production styles, complementing the more ordinary playhouse also located in the center. The Tyrone Guthrie Theatre in Minneapolis is a modern attempt to achieve some of the effects possible in a Greco-Roman style house, in which the performer and an architectural background take the place of normal scenic display. The Forum Theatre of the Benedicta Arts Center in St. Joseph, Minn., combines a proscenium with manipulatable seat-wagons that can be turned to provide an open-center acting area, which may be used together with the regular stage. These and other experimental types present alternatives in ways that prevent the modern theater from becoming conventionalized and repetitious. Few of the forms are entirely new, but the modern architect uses the riches of the past to embellish the present.

DONALD C. MULLIN, *Author of "The Development of the Playhouse"*

Bibliography

Allen, James T., *Stage Antiquities of the Greeks and Romans and Their Influence* (New York 1963).

Baur-Heinhold, Margarete, *The Baroque Theater* (New York 1967).

Boswell, Eleanore, *The Restoration Court Stage* (Cambridge, Mass., 1932).

Chambers, E. K., *The Elizabethan Stage,* 4 vols. (New York and London 1923).

Chambers, E. K., *The Medieval Stage,* vol. 2 (New York and London 1903).

Gorelik, Mordecai, *New Theatres for Old* (New York 1940).

Wiley, William, *The Early Public Theatre in France* (Cambridge, Mass., 1960).

CHILDREN'S THEATER production of Molière's *A Doctor in Spite of Himself,* by students of the Goodman School of Drama in Chicago.

COURTESY BELLA ITKIN, PRODUCER, GOODMAN CHILDREN'S THEATRE

THEATER FOR CHILDREN refers to performances of plays and other dramatic material for children. In the United States the focus is on audiences 8 to 12 years of age, but those attending may include children of preschool through junior high school age. Actors may be amateur or professional—children, teenagers, adults, or often all three age groups in the same cast. Productions may range from improvisations to conventional scripted plays, from musicals to operas, and from classical pantomimes to contemporary satirical sketches.

Development. Although dramatic performances for children were recorded earlier, it was not until after 1900 that anything resembling a children's theater movement could be discerned. The early 20th century witnessed in both the United States and Europe the emergence of performances under all the major kinds of auspices existing today: professional companies, which in Europe have achieved dominance over the entire field; educational groups, which predominate in the United States and Canada; civic service organizations; community theaters; and programs associated with recreational activities. The practice in the United States of involving many local groups resulted in numerous uniquely American community children's theaters. The professional companies remained concentrated in metropolitan areas and were smaller and less well financed than their European counterparts. Touring was early recognized as the best way for U. S. professional groups to operate. During the period 1928–1954, Clare Tree Major toured nationwide with as many as six companies. Many nonprofessional groups toured locally or regionally.

Among other leaders in the development of theater for children in the United States were Winifred Ward, author and teacher at Northwestern University, who in 1925 founded the Children's Theatre of Evanston, Ill.; Charlotte Chorpenning, playwright and director from 1931 to 1952 of the children's theater program of the Goodman School of Drama in Chicago; Hazel G. Robertson, who founded the Palo Alto (Calif.) Children's Community Theater in 1932 and who in 1944 became the first chairman of the Children's Theatre Conference of the American Educational Theatre Association; and Sara Spencer Campbell, playwright and founder and editor of the Children's Theatre Press (at Anchorage, Ky.), who from 1935 helped determine the available repertory of plays.

Current Status. A directory of U. S. children's theaters listed some 700 projects in the late 1960's but estimated that the count included less than half the existing number. The basic kinds of children's theaters have not changed, but they have become more complex, involving more and more community groups and drawing closer to the educational centers in the cities where they exist. More plays are produced on school time, and the work is increasingly supported by foundation and government grants. An international association helps distribute the best of each country's repertory, and standards of excellence are constantly rising. See also PUPPETRY.

JED H. DAVIS, *Coauthor of "Children's Theatre"*

Bibliography

Birner, William B., ed., *Twenty Plays for Young People* (Anchorage, Ky., 1967).
Chorpenning, Charlotte B., *Twenty-one Years with Children's Theatre* (Anchorage, Ky., 1954).
Davis, Jed H., and Watkins, Mary Jane, *Children's Theatre: Play Production for the Child Audience* (New York 1960).
Siks, Geraldine B., and Dunnington, Hazel B., eds., *Children's Theatre and Creative Dramatics* (Seattle, Wash., 1961).
Ward, Winifred, *Theatre for Children*, rev. ed. (Anchorage, Ky., 1958).

THEATER-IN-THE-ROUND. See ARENA THEATER.

THÉÂTRE FRANÇAIS. See COMÉDIE FRANÇAISE.

THEATRE GUILD, a group in New York City that was organized "to produce plays of artistic merit not ordinarily produced by commercial managers." The Theatre Guild did much to elevate the artistic standards of the American theater. Because of its success, its standards were soon adopted by other producers, and the Theatre Guild branched out to include every type of theater.

The group had its beginnings as the Washington Square Players, who produced plays on a small scale from 1914 until 1917. In 1919 the Players reorganized as the Theatre Guild. Their first production was *The Bonds of Interest* by the Spanish dramatist Jacinto Benavente y Martínez. The Guild later introduced works by George Bernard Shaw, William Saroyan, Maxwell Anderson, and many others. Productions ranged in mood and style from Eugene O'Neill's *Strange Interlude* (1928) to Rodgers and Hammerstein's *Oklahoma!* (1943).

THÉÂTRE LIBRE. See ANTOINE, ANDRÉ.

GEORGE GERSTER, FROM RAPHO GUILLUMETTE

Mortuary temple of Egypt's Queen Hatshepsut at Thebes rises against a dramatic background of high cliffs.

THEBES, thēbz, was a capital of ancient Egypt and the chief city of the south (Upper Egypt). Its ruins are situated on the east bank of the Nile near the present village of Karnak, 350 miles (550 km) southeast of Cairo. However, the designation "Thebes" now commonly includes the monuments as far south as Luxor on the east bank and the cemeteries and royal mortuary temples along the west bank from Qurna in the north to Birket Habu in the south. The city proper is called *Nīwt* in Egyptian and is mentioned in the Bible as *No.* The Greeks called it *Thebai* and also used the name *Diospolis.*

History. The district of Thebes became important as a political and religious center in the 11th dynasty. It was Theban rulers of the 17th and early 18th dynasties who expelled the Hyksos kings from Lower Egypt (see also HYKSOS). During most of the 18th dynasty Thebes was the southern capital of Egypt, but it began to lose importance when the kings of the 19th dynasty made their chief residence in the Nile delta. Beginning in the 21st dynasty Egypt's kings were buried at Tanis rather than at Thebes, which became merely a provincial center. There was a revival of importance in the 25th and 26th dynasties, when the high priestesses of Amon-Re at Thebes were daughters of the kings and wielded great power. The Assyrian conqueror Ashurbanipal counted his devastation of Thebes in the 7th century B.C. as one of his greatest triumphs.

Karnak and Luxor. Of central importance in the Theban area is the temple of Amon-Re, King of the Gods, at Karnak. This temple, called "the (Most) Esteemed of Places," was the god's palace and incorporated structures built over a period of nearly 2,000 years. The earliest remaining element is an altar from the reign of Amenemhet I of the 12th dynasty, and the latest is from the reign of Philip Arrhidaeus. When completed, the temple was some 1,200 feet (370 meters) long and nearly 350 feet (100 meters) wide and consisted of a series of pylons (entrance towers), courts, and columned halls. The largest hall contained 134 columns in 16 rows, with the loftiest columns, in two central rows, measuring 78 feet (24 meters) in height and 33 feet (10 meters) in circumference.

This huge building was situated in a precinct measuring 60 acres (24 hectares) surrounded by a mud-brick wall. Inside the wall were separate smaller temples. One was dedicated to Ptah, the god of Memphis; another to Khonsu, regarded at Thebes as the son of Amon; and a third to Ipet-(Ta-)weris, a goddess who protected pregnant women. Beside the rear half of the Amon temple was a large artificial lake in which the priests performed their ritual ablutions four times a day. Outside the wall, on the north, was a separate precinct for Montu, a god of war. On the south, an avenue of ram-headed sphinxes led to the temple of Mut, Amon's consort. The main, or western, approach to the Amon precinct was provided with a quay and a canal that joined others leading to the nearby temples and the river, so that the cult-statue of the god could be taken in its ceremonial bark to "visit" the temples of other deities.

Also on the east bank, at modern Luxor, are the ruins of another great temple of Amon, the "Southern Sanctuary." Although the distance between the two temples is more than a mile, the avenue connecting them was, during the 30th dynasty, bordered for its entire length with human-headed sphinxes and plantings of flowers and trees. The Luxor temple is not as large or as old as the one at Karnak. It is 840 feet (260 meters) long, and its earliest surviving parts date from the reign of Amenhotep III of the 18th dynasty. The latest part of the temple proper is a shrine that shows Alexander the Great making offerings. One small hall was converted into a sanctuary for the imperial cult by the Romans, and on its wall there remain painted figures of two Caesars of the end of the

3d century A. D. The columned courtyard and corridor begun by Amenhotep III and the front pylon with reliefs showing Rameses II at the Battle of Kadesh are particularly famous. But many of the reliefs and inscriptions that cover the walls of the Karnak and Luxor temples provide important information concerning Egyptian history and religion.

The West Bank. The antiquities on the west bank of the Nile at Thebes are more varied. Situated closest to the river are many temples for the worship of deceased rulers. Among these the 11th dynasty temple of Mentuhotep II (Nebhepetre) and the 18th dynasty temple of Hatshepsut are especially significant because of their unusual design. The particularly beautiful Hatshepsut temple consists of a rising succession of courtyards backed by wide colonnades, with the lofty cliffs serving as a backdrop.

The mortuary temple of Rameses III at Medinet Habu is also worthy of special attention. Designed to serve as a fortress besides being a temple, it was provided with mighty walls and lofty gates. It incorporated a small palace for the use of the king and a library or archives room. Apartments for feasting and recreation were built inside the towers of the High Gate. In the 20th dynasty and the 21st dynasty, this complex became the center of the administration of western Thebes, an area that had a mayor as important as the mayor of Thebes itself. In the Christian period, a church stood in the second temple court.

The mortuary temples stood east of (below) the great cliffs that mark the edge of the high desert. In the cliffs themselves are hundreds of rock-cut tombs of nobles of the 18th, 19th, and 20th dynasties, and in several valleys farther west are the tombs of their kings and queens. Many of these tombs are decorated with paintings or painted relief-sculptures. In the nobles' tombs the scenes represent events that occurred during the lives of the owners, as well as views of an idealized funeral, feasts to be celebrated after death, and favorite pastimes to be enjoyed in the next world. In the royal tombs the scenes are most often religious in character, and many of them contain long sections of texts about the next world. A few burials of royal women have been found intact, and their beautiful jewelry and toilet implements may be seen in museums in New York and Cairo. A large cache of reburied royal mummies was discovered in 1881. But the only virtually undisturbed burial of a king found so far at Thebes was that of Tutankhamen (Tutankhamon).

On the west bank, also, are found ruins of secular buildings. South of Medinet Habu were a town and a palace of Amenhotep III, and at Deir el-Medineh was a walled village built to house the families of workmen who constructed and decorated the tombs in the Theban cemeteries. Material from these places has yielded much information concerning the social and economic history of the New Kingdom.

CAROLINE NESTMANN PECK
Brown University

Bibliography

Kess, Herman, *Ancient Egypt: A Cultural Topography* (Chicago 1961).

Lange, Kurt, and Hirmer, Max, *Egypt: Architecture, Sculpture, Painting in Three Thousand Years,* 4th ed. (New York 1968).

Nims, Charles F., *Thebes of the Pharaohs* (New York 1965).

Riefstahl, Elizabeth, *Thebes in the Time of Amenhotep III* (Norman, Okla., 1964).

COLOSSI OF MEMNON, seated statues of Amenhotep III, were originally 65 feet (20 meters) high.

HIRMER FOTOARCHIV

OBELISKS at the Temple of Amon-Re in Karnak honor Queen Hatshepsut and her father, King Thutmose I.

HIRMER FOTOARCHIV

THEBES, thēbz, a major city of ancient Greece, is located in eastern Boeotia, 30 miles northwest of Athens. The modern town of Thebes (Greek, Thevai) is an agricultural community on the site of the ancient city, with a population (1970 est.) of 16,000. Remains of the ancient city walls and of the temple of Ismenian Apollo are preserved.

Legendary Thebes. Thebes was said to have been founded by the mythological Cadmus, and the tales of his descendants were among the favorite subjects of Greek poetry and tragedy. According to some traditional accounts, both the hero Hercules (Heracles) and the god Dionysus were born in Thebes. The city was walled by the divine twins Amphion and Zethus, sons of Zeus and Antiope. One of the greatest tragedies, Sophocles' *Oedipus Rex,* tells of King Oedipus of Thebes, who unwittingly murdered his father Laius and married his own mother, Jocasta.

Extant plays by both Aeschylus and Sophocles concern events surrounding the expedition of the "Seven against Thebes," the first phase of the war that followed the departure of Oedipus from the city. The city survived the first invasion but was destroyed in the next generation when the expedition of the Epigoni was led by the Argive Alcmaeon, son of Amphiaraus.

History. The time at which Thebes was first settled has not been established, but part of the palace (about 1300 B.C.) belonging to the Theban lords of the Late Bronze Age was discovered in the early 1900's. Other important sections of the palace were uncovered during the 1960's in the heart of the modern town, and in 1970, clay tablets, incised in an early form of Greek known as Linear B, were found there.

Little is known of Thebes from the end of the Bronze Age until the 6th century B.C. when it had friendly relations with Cleisthenes, tyrant of Sicyon, and with King Croesus of Lydia. Thebes, which became the chief state of the Boeotian League in the 6th century, was also on good terms with the Pisistratid family of Athens until 519, when Athens took the part of Plataea in a dispute with Thebes.

Thebes was an ally of Persia during the invasion of Greece by Xerxes (480–479) and fought against the other Greeks at the battle of Plataea. After the Greek victory at Plataea the Greeks besieged Thebes and, when the city surrendered, put to death all those who had aided the Persians.

The Boeotian League was revived in 447 after the city of Orchomenus led the Boeotians in an important victory over the Athenians at Coronea. Thebes, as the federal capital, once again became the leading city of Boeotia. During the Peloponnesian War (431–404) the Boeotian League fought on the side of the Spartans against Athens, and at the end of the conflict Thebes joined Corinth in calling unsuccessfully for the massacre of all Athenian male adults and the enslavement of the women and children. Within a year, however, dissatisfaction over the disposal of the spoils of war by Sparta, which did not share with its allies, and with Spartan leadership generally led Thebes to assume a hostile attitude toward Sparta.

Thebes joined Athens, Argos, and Corinth against Sparta in the Corinthian War (394–386). The peace that ended the war required Thebes to give up its control of the other Boeotian cities, and the threat of Spartan force persuaded the Thebans to comply. In 382, Sparta seized the Cadmea, the acropolis of Thebes, with the help of Theban oligarchs. Sparta maintained its control until 379, when the exiled democratic party recaptured the city.

During the years following the recovery of the city, Thebes became the most powerful state in Greece. The rise of Thebes to the hegemony of Greece was due largely to the leadership of Epaminondas, one of the ablest military commanders of the ancient world. With the aid of Pelopidas he made the Boeotian army the most formidable in Greece and was in command at the Boeotian victory over the Spartans at the battle of Leuctra in 371. In the following year Epaminondas led his army into the Peloponnesus and even to Sparta itself.

After the death of Epaminondas at the battle of Mantinea in 362, Theban power began a rapid decline. Thebes came under Macedonian control in 338. When it revolted three years later, the city was razed by Alexander the Great, who spared only the temples and the houses of the poet Pindar and of the cynic philosopher Crates. Cassander refounded Thebes in 316, but it never regained its former importance. In 197 B.C. Thebes was forced by arms to join Rome. Following a later revolt in the 1st century B.C. the Roman general Sulla stormed the city and plundered the sanctuaries.

JAMES R. WISEMAN, *University of Texas*

THEFT. See EMBEZZLEMENT; LARCENY.

THEILER, tīl'ər, **Max** (1899–1972), South African physician and virologist, who was awarded the 1951 Nobel Prize in physiology or medicine "for his discoveries concerning yellow fever and how to combat it."

In 1930 he found that mice given intracerebral injections of yellow fever virus developed encephalomyelitis but did not develop heart, kidney, or liver damage, unlike monkeys and humans affected with yellow fever who did. Passing the virus through the brains of a number of mice, Theiler shortened the incubation period of the disease, finally arriving at a constant time. Subcutaneous injection of this mouse-adapted strain of yellow fever virus produced active immunity from yellow fever in monkeys but affected the kidneys in humans. Combining the viral strain with a serum made from the blood of people who had recovered from yellow fever, however, provided immunity for up to six months and produced no kidney damage. Human immune serum is difficult to obtain in sufficient quantities, however, and Theiler continued working on the problem. Working with chick embryo tissue, he finally (1937) developed a vaccine that produced yellow fever immunity in humans without requiring the addition of human serum to prevent kidney damage. Millions of people have been inoculated with this vaccine.

Theiler was born in Pretoria, South Africa, on Jan. 30, 1899. He studied medicine at the University of Capetown and in England, receiving his medical degree at St. Thomas Hospital and the London School of Tropical Medicine. In 1922 he became an instructor at Harvard Medical School. In 1930 he joined the Rockefeller Foundation, becoming director of its virus laboratories in 1951. From 1964 to 1967 he taught at Yale University. He died in New Haven, Conn., on Aug. 11, 1972.

THEISM, thē'iz-əm, is generally equated with monotheism as the belief in one God who is personal and moral, who has created and sustains the universe, and who demands an unqualified response. The primary definition is derived from the concept of God in the Biblical religions. God transcends His creation and is not dependent upon it, and yet He is immanent, acting within and upon it. In contrast, deism insists on the purely transcendent nature of God, while pantheism insists on the purely immanent nature, identifying God with the cosmos. Polytheism affirms that there are many personal gods, each expressing specific forces and functions. See DEISM; PANTHEISM; POLYTHEISM.

No arguments for the existence of God are offered in the Bible. God simply is. However, as a result of the impact of philosophy, certain arguments were developed that were effective in persuading those already convinced.

Ontological Approach. In the 11th century Anselm stated the ontological argument for the existence of God. He declared that God is a Being than which a greater cannot be conceived. Moreover, a Being that exists in fact is greater than one that exists only in thought. Therefore, God necessarily exists. In the 17th century Descartes rephrased the argument to say that since the idea of an infinite and perfect God could not have been thought of by finite man, the idea must have come from God. Therefore, God necessarily exists. However, existence is not an attribute or predicate that God either possesses or does not possess. Furthermore, the statement is contingent, since it deals with a fact and therefore can be denied without a logical contradiction.

Cosmological and Teleological Approaches. The several parts of the cosmological argument relate to motion, first cause, contingency, and gradation in values. What is fundamental in all is the assumption that all things have causes and that, if the causal process is retraced, there is a First Cause. The question about this argument is why the process should not be infinite. Furthermore, cause and effect are meaningful terms only when both can be observed, which is hardly the case in this instance.

The teleological argument is a specialized application of the cosmological approach and focuses upon order and purpose in the universe. William Paley, an English theologian of the 18th century, argued that if you found a watch in a deserted place, you would assume a watchmaker. It is a logical assumption because watches are known to be made by watchmakers. However, the universe is not a member of a class, as a watch is, and such an assumption cannot be drawn about the universe. Also, the profligacy of nature and the principle of natural selection militate against the idea of a perfect designer.

Other Approaches. All of the classic arguments are deductive, which means that the conclusion is contained in the premises. St. Thomas Aquinas recognized this in the 13th century when he declared that an argument is persuasive only if the first principles, or premises, are accepted. Late in the history of apologetics the argument from religious experience was introduced. Friedrich Schleiermacher, a German Protestant theologian, declared in the early 19th century that the belief in the divine cannot be proved by arguments. It results from an experience shared by all men even though some fail to identify it, an experience of creatureliness or absolute dependence. This argument supposes that the believer correctly identifies the source of this experience, a dubious assumption.

There is also a moral argument for the existence of God, based on the assumption that moral values are not capable of naturalistic explanation or that the recognition of moral claims points to God as their basis and source. It has also been claimed that miracles and responses to prayer and mystical experiences point to God. The difficulty with these arguments is that the experiences can be interpreted in different ways and therefore cannot be considered proofs.

Contemporary Discussions. The arguments for the existence of God have been criticized because they lead to a set of propositions. However, all beliefs are necessarily phrased in propositional terms. More significant is the contention that the arguments, even if convincing, point to a god who is Necessary Being, a Perfect Being, a First Cause, and not to the god of love and mercy. The god who is worshiped in the theistic religions is told about in the sacred scriptures—books that have been preserved and given authority by a community of faith. The primary requisite for knowing God is trust, according to the scriptures. Man is declared to be free to accept or reject God. Trust and faith in God are not coerced. In such a context the question can be asked: What sort of proof is conclusive? The answer is, none, for to ask for irrefutable proof is to ask the impossible. According to the theistic religions, a man either has trust and faith or he has neither. If he has faith, then he sees the hand of God in all of history. The arguments, although fallacious as proofs, do indicate that God is the ultimate frame of reference for those who believe in him.

Atheism has been defined as the belief that no god exists. (See ATHEISM). "Exist" has many meanings. When a reflective theist affirms that God does not exist, he is really protesting against the idea that God is a substance regardless of whether defined as Supreme Being, as Cosmic Personality, or the like. He affirms that the Creator does not exist in the same way that things exist. He adds that since God is infinite, predicates or positive assertions cannot be made without implying a limitation. For example, Paul Tillich, a 20th century theologian and philosopher, said that "God" refers to the source and ground of all being and that all other statements about him are symbolic. The picture of God constructed by men participates in ultimate reality but is not in itself ultimate.

Another approach is to limit the use of the term "God" to the picture that is constructed and to call the ultimate reality merely Being. In that case the attributes ascribed to God are tentative, and there is no allegation that they are final and complete. This posture enables one to preserve in figurative language a God "out there" who acts upon people and the world. In this sense it is proper to say that God as theistically defined exists in the minds of Jews, Christians, and Muslims. Even more, God as defined makes a significant difference in the believer's view of himself, of others, and of the world.

LEE A. BELFORD, *New York University*

Further Reading: Farrer, Austin, *Finite and Infinite* (London 1960); Macquarrie, John, *Principle of Christian Theology* (New York 1966); Tillich, Paul, *Systematic Theology*, vol. 1 (Chicago 1951).

THEMIS, thē′mis, in Greek mythology, was the guardian of divine law and order. As a daughter of Uranus and Gaea (Heaven and Earth), she was a Titaness. Possessed of the gift of prophecy, she for a time lived in the oracular temple at Delphi but left it to become consort to Zeus. By him she became the mother of the Horae (Hours) and of the Moirae (Fates). In Olympus her mission was to give counsel to Zeus and to preserve order. Her daughter Dike, the goddess of human justice, is often confused with her. In art, Themis is pictured as a stately personality holding a cornucopia and a pair of scales.

THEMISTOCLES, thə-mis′tə-klēz (c. 524 B. C.–c. 459 B. C.), was an Athenian general and public official. As a champion of the lower classes and an advocate of naval expansion, he became an archon (a magistrate) in 493–492 and began fortification of Piraeus, the port of Athens, as the Persian threat to Athens grew. He supported the anti-Persian policy of the general Miltiades, and served as a general in the battle of Marathon (490) against Persia. After Miltiades' death (489), Themistocles became the leading political figure in Athens by using ostracism to eliminate rivals. He may have been responsible for reducing the importance of the archonship by introducing election to it by lot. Thereafter, the ablest politicians sought the generalship, which was accorded annually by vote.

In 483, Themistocles convinced the Athenians that they should use the silver from a newly found rich vein at Laurium to build 100 to 200 new warships, ostensibly for protection against Aegina, which had been at war with Athens, but really in preparation for the coming invasion of the Persians under Xerxes. In 481 he persuaded the Athenians to cooperate with the other anti-Persian Greeks even to the point of giving nominal command of their fleet to the Spartans, the leaders of the Hellenic League. He also seems to have convinced the Athenians, even before the arrival of Xerxes in Greece, to trust in their ships—the "wooden walls"—and so to abandon their land and city, removing the women and children to Salamis, Troezen, and Aegina. This information is not contained in the traditional account of Herodotus, but comes from an inscription found in Troezen in 1959. After the inconclusive naval battle at Artemisium and Xerxes' forcing of the pass at Thermopylae, Themistocles urged the other Greeks to fight in the narrow bay of Salamis. The decisive naval victory there in 480, which saved Greece, was attributed to his strategic and tactical planning.

After the Persian threat was removed in 479, Themistocles incurred the enmity of the Spartans by having the walls of Athens hastily rebuilt against their advice. He vexed them also perhaps by negotiating with their disgraced general, Pausanias, in an attempt to stir up anti-Spartan feeling in the Peloponnesus. He may also have wanted to cooperate with the Persians. Although acquitted when brought to trial on the latter charge about 476, he lost his political influence and was ostracized about 473. A few years later he was condemned to death, *in absentia,* on a charge of plotting with the Persians and so fled to Asia Minor, where the Persian king gave him the city of Magnesia-on-the-Meander to rule over. He died there about 459. One account held that he committed suicide rather than help Persians against Greeks.

The ancient sources were often unfriendly to Themistocles, portraying him as vain, ambitious, and greedy. They blamed him for the radicalization of the Athenian democracy by promoting a naval policy that gave political power to the lower classes upon whom the fleet depended. In fact, this did not actually happen until more than a generation later. The historian Thucydides, however, praised his judgment and foresight. Themistocles was generally considered to have been responsible for the saving of Greece from the Persians.

DONALD W. BRADEEN
University of Cincinnati

THENARD, tā-när′, **Louis Jacques** (1777–1857), French chemist and discoverer of hydrogen peroxide. The son of a peasant, Thenard was born in Louptière, France, on May 4, 1777. At the age of 17, he went to Paris where he became laboratory assistant to Louis N. Vauquelin. Encouraged both by Vauquelin and Antoine de Fourcroy, he obtained a junior post at the École Polytechnique in 1798. In 1810 he became a full professor there. He also held chairs of chemistry at the Collège de France and the Paris Faculty of Science.

Thenard did much of his important work with J. L. Gay-Lussac. In 1808 they discovered boron, and in 1811 they devised the first general method for analyzing organic compounds by oxidation with potassium chlorate. Thenard discovered hydrogen peroxide in 1818. He also introduced a new pigment, Thenard's blue, which was made by heating together certain cobalt and aluminum compounds.

Thenard was a prominent educational administrator, becoming chancellor of the University of France in 1845. His textbook *Traité de Chimie* (*Treatise on Chemistry*) ran to six editions. He died in Paris on June 21, 1857.

W. A. SMEATON, *University College, London*

THENARDITE, thə-när′dīt, or *mineral sodium sulfate,* occurs in salt lakes. The crystals are colorless to brownish and have a glassy luster. Composition, Na_2SO_4; hardness, 2–3; specific gravity, 2.7; crystal system, orthorhombic.

THEOBALD, tiʹbəld, **Lewis** (1688–1744), English scholar, poet, and dramatist, who was subjected to a brilliantly witty but unjust attack in Alexander Pope's *Dunciad.* He was born in Sittingbourne, Kent, and was educated for the law. He practiced for a time as an attorney but soon devoted himself to literary pursuits. Although Theobald wrote some poetry and a number of dramatic works, his fame rests on his work as scholar and editor. In *Shakespeare Restor'd* (1726) he demonstrated the inadequacies of Pope's edition of Shakespeare, arousing the ire of the great satirist, and the early versions of *The Dunciad* (1728) conferred on Theobald an undeserved reputation as a pedant. (See DUNCIAD.) He died in London on Sept. 18, 1744.

Theobald's first published poem was *A Pindarick Ode on the Union* (1707). A volume of verse entitled *The Grove* appeared in 1721. His dramatic works include the pseudo-Shakespearean *Double Falsehood* (1727) and the opera *Orestes* (1731). Theobald's own edition of Shakespeare (1733) displays admirable editorial gifts.

FRANK J. WARNKE, *Coeditor of "Seventeenth Century Prose and Poetry"*

THEOCRACY, thē-ok′rə-sē, a form of government whose authority and power are ascribed to God. The term was first applied by Josephus to the type of government under which the ancient Jews lived. Rulers were considered directly responsible to God and were thought to be judged by Him. Many primitive peoples lived under a theocratic form of government in which the political structure was believed subject to the rule of a deity. The god's will was usually interpreted through a king or priests. Even in the more advanced societies of the Greeks and Romans, rulers were considered incarnations of the divine or were deified in order to establish the legitimacy of their rule. Examples of theocratic government may also be found in Buddhist, Islamic, and Christian societies.

The political challenges within the Judeo-Christian tradition have been to determine (1) the extent of God's rule, (2) the political structures through which God exercises His rule, and (3) the norm for measuring what political policies and decisions are in conformity with that rule. In the struggle over practical political arrangements a number of forms have been accepted as manifestations of theocratic rule. In the Byzantine Empire the church developed Caesaropapism, in which the emperor embodied God's rule. In medieval Roman Catholicism, the papacy claimed to have ultimate authority and power in the church and over the state. In opposition to the papal view, secular authority insisted that its power came directly from God (divine right of kings).

With the breakup of medieval Europe into nation-states there was a movement away from monarchies based on the divine right of kings concept and toward constitutional democracies in which the will of God was expressed by the will of the people. In later Western history John Calvin's Geneva, Oliver Cromwell's England, and John Winthrop's Massachusetts are often cited as examples of theocracies because Protestant preachers exercised much power over civil authorities.

Some modern theologians maintain that God manifests Himself best in that form of political structure in which men and women may participate in decision-making processes that affect their lives. They also favor the independence of the religious structures of a society in order to curb any absolute or arbitrary civil power that might claim divine sanction.

The 20th century theologian and philosopher Paul Tillich used the term "theonomous" to describe a total cultural situation, God-determined and God-directed, that has priority over any legal communal arrangements of authority and power.

JAMES H. SMYLIE
Union Theological Seminary, Richmond, Va.

THEOCRITUS, thē-ok′rə-təs, a Greek poet active in the first half of the 3d century B. C., who was the first to produce works classifiable as pastoral poetry. In his small body of writing he founded the pastoral tradition that was to influence all the arts down to the end of the 18th century.

Theocritus was born most probably at Syracuse in Sicily but spent some time on the Aegean island of Kos and in the city of Alexandria. Little more is known about his life. His poems contain evidence that he sought the patronage of Hieron II, ruler of southeastern Sicily, and Ptolemy II Philadelphus, king of Egypt, but it is uncertain whether he had any success.

"Idyls." Theocritus composed poetry in a wide variety of forms, including hymns, elegies, epigrams, short narratives, invectives, and dirges. The selection that has come down under his name comprises 30 miscellaneous poems, more than 20 epigrams, and one picture poem, *Syrinx*, which has gradually shortening lines so arranged on the page as to represent panpipes. The selection, which includes several pieces of dubious authorship, was certainly not arranged by Theocritus himself nor did he give it its traditional title *Idyls*. "Idyls" at that time seems to have meant merely "poems in different styles."

Only about 12 of the pieces can properly be called bucolic or pastoral. The others include appeals to patrons, short narratives from mythology, and tales of thwarted love. Most interesting of the nonbucolic selections are Idyl 15, *The Women at the Adonis Festival*, where we follow two gossipy matrons through the streets of Alexandria to hear the song of lament over the dead god Adonis, and Idyl 2, *The Sorceress*, in which Simaetha and her maidservant recite incantations beneath the light of the moon and turn the magic wheel to bring Simaetha's lover back to her.

The Pastoral Poems. The dozen bucolic poems form the core of the *Idyls* and constitute the basis of Theocritus' fame. The author probably did not consciously set out to found a separate literary genre. Most probably he thought of himself as composing mimes—short dramatic sketches that could have been produced on the stage. But in these mimes appear all the features that were to become traditional in pastoral poetry—the background of unspoiled countryside; shepherds, goatherds, and harvesters as characters; the names that were to acquire standard bucolic associations, such as Daphnis, and Corydon; and the themes of unrequited love and of piping or singing contests. As far as can be judged, the dialect seems to be the actual Doric Greek of rustic Sicily adapted to poetry. Such customs as the contests and the stylized exchange of insults seem to be rooted in actual rituals performed in honor of Artemis or Dionysus.

In later criticism of pastoral poetry, Theocritus was considered the prototype of the realistic pastoral, as opposed to the more artificial variety associated with Vergil. But in one poem, Idyl 7, *The Harvest Festival*, Theocritus anticipates one of the characteristic features of Vergil's *Eclogues*, that of portraying real persons under the guise of shepherds. Ancient sources tell us that the character Simichidas is Theocritus himself and that other characters are his poet-friends and rivals.

RICHMOND Y. HATHORN
Author of "Tragedy, Myth, and Mystery"

THEODORA, thē-ə-dô′rə (500?–548), was the wife of the Byzantine Emperor Justinian I. She was born probably in Constantinople. She became an actress as a child, and in 522 she married Justinian, the heir apparent to the Byzantine throne. A short time before, he had persuaded Emperor Justin I, his uncle, to set aside a law prohibiting marriage between senators and actresses.

More familiar with the life style of Constantinople's Hippodrome than the imperial court, Theodora was detested by aristocrats and was denounced by the historian Procopius in his *Secret History*. He depicted Theodora as a backstairs politician who controlled her weak husband and influenced state policy following Justinian's accession in 527. Some scholars, however, have challenged Procopius' assessment. Apparently Theodora did persuade Justinian not to abdicate during the Nika riot in 532, when rival factions, the Blues and the Greens, demanded that he dismiss a number of key ministers. She may also have influenced the choice of some officials.

But in the critical theological-political contest between Monophysites and orthodox Christians, Theodora, a Monophysite, was not able to change her husband's policies. Justinian vigorously supported the orthodox theological formula devised at the Council of Chalcedon in 451. Here, as in her campaign to enhance women's status in Byzantine society, she could offer only moral and financial support to the dissidents. When Theodora died in Constantinople on June 28, 548, both causes lost their most ardent and prestigious champion.

JOHN W. EADIE, *University of Michigan*

THEODORE I (died 649), reigned as pope from 642 to 649. Theodore was a Greek-speaking native of Palestine. His reign began on Nov. 24, 642, and was primarily concerned with the heresy of Monotheletism, which claimed that Christ had only one will (see MONOTHELITES). Pyrrhus, patriarch of Constantinople, was won over to the new doctrine, and Theodore insisted that he be deposed. Pyrrhus went to Africa, where Maximus the Confessor convinced him of his error. However, he relapsed into heresy, and Theodore excommunicated him. Emperor Constans II was induced to revoke the *Echtesis*, a decree of his predecessor, Heraclius, which approved Monotheletism. However, Constans' *Typos* imposed silence on both sides. The Council of the Lateran in 649 condemned both documents. Theodore died on May 13, 649, in Rome.

ALFRED C. RUSH, C. SS. R.
Catholic University of America

THEODORE II (died 897) reigned as pope for 20 days in November 897. Theodore was a Roman by birth. The corpse of Pope Formosus (died 896) had been degraded by order of a synod under Pope Stephen VII on the grounds that Formosus was a usurper of the papacy. Theodore in a synod vindicated Formosus and had his remains honorably reinterred.

MARION A. HABIG, O. F. M.
St. Augustine Friary, Chicago

THEODORE II (1818–1868) was emperor of Ethiopia from 1855 to 1868. He was born in Kawara, in northwestern Ethiopia. Originally named Kassa, he was the leader of a bandit group and rose to prominence by conquering the kingdoms of Begemdir, Amhara, Tigre, and Gojjam. He had himself crowned emperor of all Ethiopia by the head of the Ethiopian Church (a branch of Coptic Christianity) in 1855. Soon afterward he defeated the ruler of Shoa, the last independent kingdom in Ethiopia.

As emperor, Theodore attempted to modernize the country. He welcomed technologically skilled Europeans, attempted to abolish slavery, and initiated road-building programs. But Theodore was involved in perpetual warfare against tribal leaders, and he became increasingly cruel and despotic. When he imprisoned the British consul and other British subjects, a military expedition headed by Sir Robert Napier was sent to demand their release. In 1868, as the British neared his stronghold, Magdala, Theodore committed suicide.

PETER SCHWAB, *Adelphi University*

THEODORE. For Russian czars of this name, see FYODOR.

THEODORE OF MOPSUESTIA, mop-sū-es'chē-ə (c. 350–428), bishop and theologian, in whose writings some scholars have seen the roots of the Nestorian heresy (see NESTORIANISM). Theodore was born in Antioch (now in modern Turkey). He studied under Lebanius, a pagan rhetorician, and formed a close friendship with his fellow student St. John Chrysostom.

Theodore then began study under Diodore of Tarsus at a monastery near Antioch, where he remained about 10 years. He became a priest in 383 and bishop of Mopsuestia (modern Misis, Turkey) about 392. He died in Mopsuestia in 428.

Theodore wrote voluminously on scripture, theology, liturgy, catechesis, and ascetism. Most of his works have been lost. His commentaries on scripture stressed literal meaning and employed a method that combined science, philology, and history. In theology he stressed the humanity of Christ. Theodore's separation of Christ into two persons was contrary to what was later defined as orthodox—that Christ was one person with a divine and human nature. He was condemned as heretical by the Second Council of Constantinople (553). The heretical nature of his writings has been disputed by some scholars.

ALFRED C. RUSH, C. SS. R.
Catholic University of America

THEODORIC I, thē-äd'ə-rik (died 451), became king of the Visigoths on the death of Wallia in 418. Under Wallia, Rome had settled the Visigoths as *foederati* (allied troops) in Aquitania, but the question of Visigothic sovereignty had not been resolved. To force Roman acknowledgment of their independence, Theodoric attacked the Roman province of Gallia Narbonensis in southern Gaul.

In 449, however, when Attila and the Huns threatened both Visigothic and Roman interests, Theodoric suspended hostilities and joined with the Romans. In 451, in a decisive battle near Troyes, Attila was stopped, but Theodoric was killed. His dream of an independent Visigothic kingdom was finally realized in 475 in a peace treaty with the Romans, which legitimized Visigothic conquests in Gaul and established an independent kingdom of Toulouse.

JOHN W. EADIE, *University of Michigan*

THEODORIC THE GREAT, thē-äd'ə-rik (454?–526), king of the Ostrogoths, extended Ostrogothic rule over Italy. He became king of the Ostrogoths, who were living in Pannonia, on the death of his father, Theodemir the Amal, about 471. Having returned only recently from Constantinople, where he had been a hostage of the eastern empire for almost 10 years, Theodoric had to defend his claim against a powerful rival, Theodoric Strabo. For a decade Zeno, the eastern emperor, anxious to encourage disunity among the Ostrogoths, played one against the other. But with Strabo's death in 481, Zeno recognized Theodoric as king. Zeno settled the Ostrogoths in Lower Moesia (now northwestern Bulgaria) and in 483 appointed Theodoric master of the soldiers and consul-designate for 484.

In spite of these concessions, hostilities between Theodoric and Zeno continued until 488, when Zeno, doubtless to rid the East of a troublesome neighbor, commissioned Theodoric to expel from Italy Odoacer (Odovacar), the German ruler who had succeeded the last western Roman emperor. The Ostrogoths were victorious in a series of battles, but for more than two years Odoacer's stronghold of Ravenna resisted their siege. Finally, in 493, Theodoric entered the city, murdered Odoacer, and proclaimed the Ostrogothic kingdom of Italy. His rule was formally recognized in 497 when he received the royal insignia from the eastern emperor Anastasius I.

Reign in Italy. The keynote of Theodoric's administration in Italy was peaceful coexistence with the native Roman majority. He retained the Roman administrative system and appointed Romans to important positions. A patron of art and learning, he built a royal palace and notable churches in his capital, Ravenna, supported centers of learning, and befriended literary figures.

Theodoric attempted to secure good diplomatic relations with his Germanic neighbors by marrying his daughters and sisters to their kings. He could not restrain the ambitious Frankish king Clovis, however, who succeeded in driving the Visigoths from southern Gaul in 507. Theodoric retaliated the next year, crushed the Franks and Burgundians at Arles, and designated his grandson Amalaric as king of the Visigoths. But the delicate balance of power that Theodoric had attempted to establish among the German tribes was permanently destroyed.

Religious Controversy. Although the Ostrogoths, like most of the barbarian peoples, were Arian Christians, Theodoric for most of his reign followed a policy of toleration toward his orthodox subjects. With the theological reconciliation of the churches of Rome and Constantinople in 519 and the resumption of official persecution of Arians in the eastern empire, however, Theodoric began to fear a coup d'etat engineered by orthodox easterners and their sympathizers in Italy. To counter this threat, real or imagined, he arrested a number of prominent Romans and charged some of his own advisers with treason. Among the latter was the philosopher and theologian Boethius, who was executed in 524.

Thus, when Theodoric died in Ravenna on Aug. 30, 526, his policies of integration in Italy and friendship with his Germanic neighbors were in jeopardy. When Justinian I launched his reconquest of the West in the 530's, the Ostrogothic state created by Theodoric collapsed.

JOHN W. EADIE
University of Michigan

THEODOSIA. For Crimean city of this name, see FEODOSIA.

THEODOSIAN CODE, thē-ə-dō'shən, in Latin *Codex Theodosianus,* a legal code compiled in the reign of Theodosius II. It was published in Constantinople and in Rome and went into effect with the force of law on Jan. 1, 439 A.D. The importance of the code, which was compiled by a commission appointed by Theodosius II (reigned 408–450), Roman emperor in the East, and Valentinian III (reigned 425–455), emperor in the West, is that it was the first official collection of imperial "constitutions."

By the mid-3d century, the sophisticated and coherent opinion-law (*Responsa prudentium*) of Roman jurists had been increasingly displaced by imperial legislation. Efforts to simplify the rules of law and to state them comprehensively first took the form of unofficial compilations of imperial legislation (so-called "constitutions")—the *Codex Gregorianus* from the beginning of the 4th century, followed by the *Codex Hermogenianus.* Only fragments survive.

The *Codex Theodosianus* was a precursor of Justinian's *Corpus Juris Civilis* (533 A.D.). If the official compilation of the works of the classical jurists planned to accompany this codex had been accomplished, Theodosius and Valentinian might occupy the place in legal history assigned to Justinian, but the *Codex Theodosianus* was superseded by Justinian's great consolidation and clarification. See also ROMAN LAW.

ARTHUR T. VON MEHREN
Harvard University Law School

THEODOSIUS I, thē-ə-dō'shəs (347–395), called the Great, was the last Roman emperor to rule over a united empire. He was born in Spain about 347, the son of Theodosius the Elder, a Spanish general executed by Valentinian I in 376. After his father's death, Theodosius surrendered his military post but was summoned from retirement by Gratian, Valentinian's successor, and was proclaimed Augustus (co-ruler) of the east on Jan. 19, 379.

As the eastern emperor and commander in the campaign against the Visigoths, Theodosius concluded in October 382 an unprecedented treaty that settled the Visigoths as *foederati* (allied troops) within the empire. Unchallenged in the East, Theodosius twice was called to protect his western colleague against powerful rivals. The more serious revolt was led by Arbogast, the master of the soldiers, who murdered Valentinian II in Gaul in 392 and substituted Eugenius. After several setbacks, Theodosius decisively defeated the usurpers in September 394.

Theodosius and Christianization. Theodosius, however, received the epithet "Great" not for his military exploits but for his victory over paganism. In the early years of his reign, he followed a moderate policy toward the pagans, but in 391–392 he prohibited pagan sacrifices and closed a number of pagan temples. This new militancy may have been inspired by Bishop Ambrose of Milan, his political and spiritual adviser, and was reinforced by the revolt of Arbogast and Eugenius, who supported paganism. Pagans and pagan practices survived the revolt's suppression, but 394 marked the end of paganism and the establishment of Christianity as the official state religion. In his effort to achieve religious unity Theodosius also issued no fewer than 18 constitutions restrictive against those who rejected the theological formula enunciated at the Council of Nicaea in 325.

But Theodosius could not guarantee religious and political harmony. Heretics continued to resist orthodox emperors in the 5th and 6th centuries and, following his death in Milan on Jan. 17, 395, the empire was irrevocably divided, with his elder son Arcadius ruling in the East, his younger son Honorius in the West.

JOHN W. EADIE, *University of Michigan*

THEODOSIUS II, thē-ə-dō′shē-əs (401–450) was Roman emperor of the East. He was born in Constantinople on April 10, 401, the son of Emperor Arcadius. Theodosius was crowned Augustus in 402, and in 408 he succeeded Arcadius. Throughout much of his reign, power was exercised by advisers and relatives—Anthemius, the praetorian prefect and first regent; his sister Pulcheria, regent with the title of Augusta from 414; and Eudocia, his wife from 421.

In the Persian wars of 421–422 and 441, Theodosius was successful, but his efforts to drive the Vandals from Africa failed, and he was unable to contain the Huns under Attila. A patron of higher learning, he commissioned the Theodosian Code, a collection of imperial constitutions that was published in 438. Injured in a fall, Theodosius died on July 28, 450.

JOHN W. EADIE, *University of Michigan*

THEOLOGICAL EDUCATION is a term that has been somewhat formally confined to the professional preparation of the ministry for the Christian churches. This article, however, also discusses the training of spiritual leaders in other major religions.

Early Christian Church. The formal training of clergy in the early Christian church was dependent to a great extent on the bishop. Priests assisted the bishop in liturgical or pastoral activities and were his responsibility. When theological schools were founded in places like Alexandria and Antioch, they were not really seminaries intended for training priests. Rather than attending a school, a man learned his duties in the process of moving from minor orders to the priesthood. For many centuries training consisted of a functional apprenticeship in the reading and exposition of Scripture, the manner of preparing catechumens for baptism, and the proper administration of the sacraments.

In the 4th century St. Augustine's theories of clerical education led him to set up residential obligations for his priests and for those who were candidates for the priesthood. The dimensions of spiritual training and community life were thus added to the catechetical system. Nevertheless, at the time of the Germanic invasions and the breakup of the Roman Empire, the church had no systematic approach to the education of the clergy.

In the Middle Ages, some clergy attended monastic and cathedral schools, where they were taught some theology, rhetoric, and grammar. However, not all aspirants to the priesthood attended these schools. When the university movement began in the 12th and 13th centuries, theology was the dominant field of study. Candidates for holy orders often formed residential colleges designed to foster spiritual and moral values. But again the educational practices lacked system and continuity.

Reform by the Council of Trent. By the beginning of the 16th century the ministry was functioning with such general abandon and lack of responsible direction that it finally became apparent that the reform of the church must include provisions for the formal education of the clergy. The 23d session of the Council of Trent in 1563 declared that all metropolitan and cathedral churches should train boys in ecclesiastical discipline and religion. This directive eventually led to the creation of seminaries as the major means of clerical education.

The 16th century attempts at implementing the decrees of the Council of Trent were sporadic and largely ineffective. The French religious revival of the first half of the 17th century gave impetus and form to the Tridentine directive. Vincent de Paul, founder of the Congregation of the Mission, and Jean-Jacques Olier, founder of the Sulpicians, were among the pioneers. The French heritage of the Sulpicians and Vincentians has been a dominant influence on the history of Catholic seminaries in the United States. The oldest seminary in the United States, St. Mary's in Baltimore, was founded by the Sulpicians in 1791. The number of French priests in the colonies was augmented by those who fled France during the French Revolution. The French style of training clergy adapted itself quite easily to the new American nation. The theological style of the German *Gymnasium* and university would hardly have been appropriate, whereas seminaries under direct ecclesiastical control seemed at home in the United States, where there was no established church. By 1970 there were 149 major seminaries giving theological education. Of these, 27 were strictly diocesan and 122 were run by religious orders.

These seminaries (from the Latin *seminarium*, "seed plot") have been customarily organized into two divisions, one major and the other minor. Minor seminaries are preparatory schools providing general education for boys from 12 to 18. Traditionally, the major seminaries comprise two years of philosophy and four of theology. The 6-year program begins at a level equivalent to the third year of college. In the philosophical course the student acquires the academic skills required for the rigor of his theological program. In the theological course the candidate studies liturgy, apologetics, dogmatic, moral, and pastoral theology, canon law, church history, preaching, and the science of Scriptural interpretation. In the United States in the 1960's, this system tended to evolve into a 4-year liberal arts college course, followed by four years of theological training.

The patterns of separate seminary education derived from the mandate of the Council of Trent have not aimed at offering advanced theological studies. Their emphasis has been on training in essential ecclesiastical knowledge and in piety.

Protestant Developments. The Protestant churches that grew up after the Reformation of the 16th century inherited all of the inadequacies of clerical education that existed in the church until that time. Preaching was very important to the Reformers, who understood their mission to be the recovery and promulgation of a Gospel ("good news") they felt had been lost. The Reformers stressed the importance of such doctrines as the sovereignty of God, the self-sufficiency of the Scriptures, justification by grace through faith, and the priority of the invisible Body of Christ over the institutionalized church. These doctrines called for careful presentation and interpretation. Thus Protestant Reform ministers needed to excel in teaching and preaching. Many of the Reformation leaders were ill-prepared to train ministers in these skills. Most of them had acquired their experience in the old system of apprenticeship in the conduct of services. Until the middle of the 16th century even the theological faculty of Luther's Wittenberg University did a poor job. Moreover, men were frequently assigned to lead parishes before they had learned the little that was offered in the theological course.

In Geneva, Calvin's humanistic training and propensity for system and organization contributed to early efforts at rigorous training of the clergy. Among Geneva's four church offices of preacher, teacher, elder, and deacon, it was the teachers who were responsible for the Academy, a theological and humanistic institution.

Uniformity in training ministers was difficult to achieve, and only experience could produce the proper models. Among Lutherans the highly refined confessional theology that developed after the middle of the 16th century demanded vigorous scholastic training. However, it was the 17th century Pietistic movement of Philipp Spener and August Hermann Francke that reasserted the necessity for nurturing practical skills and a recognition of the warmth of the religious experience. Halle University, founded in 1694, provided a kind of pastoral, devotional, and Biblical education that had a strong influence on the future of theological education.

Protestant theological education acquired another dimension as a result of the Enlightenment of the 17th and 18th centuries. Textual, critical, and historical scholarship came into its own. On the one hand this kind of scholarship existed for its own sake and tended to separate theological education from the needs of churches. On the other hand, the disciplined scholarship accounted for a renaissance in religious thought that has extended well into the 20th century. The most prominent examples of this kind of university theological education are found in Germany, Switzerland, and the Scandinavian countries.

Protestant Efforts in the United States. Protestant clerical education in the United States was shaped by the continental Reformation, New England Puritanism, and by the cultural ferment of the 19th century. Virtually every church and tradition had to measure its role in society against the social, political, and religious forces that took form in the national and middle periods of American history. Revivalism, denominationalism, reformism, pietism, and the emphasis on experiential and practical religion—all these factors shaped the style of training for the ministry. The fact that the United States had no established church accounted for a style of institutional organization that placed great emphasis on the voluntary nature of membership in the Christian community.

As the 19th century progressed college courses that had catered to the preparation of candidates for the ministry seemed inadequate to the needs of the times. This fact, combined with the anxiety to compensate for the formal disestablishment of religion by seeing to its moral establishment, brought on the development of theological seminaries. The seminary movement was influenced by several factors, including the styles of education in European universities and which in many cases were founded primarily to provide an educated ministry. Other important influences were the tradition of the "log college"—a sort of one-building frontier college—and private tutoring.

Orthodox Congregationalists established a seminary at Andover, Mass., in 1807. It was partly the result of the appointment of Henry Ware, a Unitarian, to the Hollis Professorship of Divinity at Harvard. Harvard's "steady drift toward Unitarianism" occasioned the Andover Creed, to which the seminary faculty subscribed as a guard against the "liberal heresy." This fact suggests that seminary education had come to be motivated by a wish to ensure denominational orthodoxy as much as by the need for an educated ministry.

The Congregationalists established two other seminaries—Bangor Theological Seminary in Maine, founded in 1816, and Hartford Theological Seminary, founded in 1834. The Episcopal Church began replacing its older procedure of "reading for orders" under a learned clergyman by founding General Theological Seminary in New York in 1817. Another seminary was opened in 1823 at Alexandria, Va. The Presbyterians entered the seminary movement by opening Princeton in 1812, Auburn in 1818, and Union Theological Seminary at Richmond in 1824. One of the most famous of modern seminaries, Union Theological in New York, was established in 1836 by the more liberal New School Presbyterians. In 1825 the German Reformed Church founded a seminary at Carlisle, Pa., and in the following year the Lutherans opened their school at Gettysburg. The great universities of New England Puritanism, Harvard and Yale, revealed the influence of the seminary movement by establishing separate divinity schools in 1816 and 1822, respectively.

Even the denominations that, because of their emphasis on conversion, moral purity, and holiness, were suspicious of an educated ministry soon found it necessary to provide for training the clergy. Influential laity of these churches demanded clergy that measured up to the stature of the better educated ministers who lived in the same towns and cities. The Baptists founded the Hamilton Literary and Theological Institution in 1820 at Hamilton, N. Y., and Newton Theological Seminary in Massachusetts in 1825. In 1829 the Methodists established the parent of the present School of Theology at Boston University.

Concern for the frontier and the untamed nation emerging in the West demanded that educational opportunities be made available to leaders of the Christianization process. Western Theological Seminary in Pittsburgh was founded by the Presbyterians in 1827. Congregationalists and Presbyterians cooperated in setting up Lane Theological Seminary in Cincinnati in 1832.

In 1918 a group of theological educators met a Cambridge, Mass., beginning a history of cooperative efforts that raised educational standards and led to the establishment in 1936 of the American Association of Theological Schools. The 1970 statistics of this association listed a total of 178 accredited and associate schools with over 28,000 students.

Eastern Orthodox Training. Theological education in the Eastern Orthodox churches has a history similar to that of the Western churches. While it is difficult to generalize, a few of the distinctive features of Orthodox theological education may be isolated. First, ordination to the priesthood has not required rigorous education until recently. Secondly, the aesthetic character of Eastern piety and liturgy has made art a significant subject for study. A third feature is the relation of theological study to the welfare of the whole church rather than to the preparation of clergy. Graduates of theological faculties such as those at Athens and Salonika often remain laymen and function as teachers of religion in secondary schools. A majority of theological professors are laymen. The preservation of tradition and the cultivation of theological reflection may be suggested as a fourth characteristic of Orthodox theological education.

St. Vladimir's Orthodox Theological Seminary in Tuckahoe, N. Y., had Russian Orthodox origins and has an eminent faculty. The Holy Cross Greek Orthodox Theological School in Brookline, Mass., was expanded to form Hellenic College in 1967, in an attempt to provide a locus for encounter between the Orthodox tradition and American culture.

Modern Trends in Christian Churches. Since World War II the ecumenical trends that began after the turn of the century have led to numerous denominational mergers, to the formation of the National and World Councils of Churches, and finally to the Second Vatican Council. The effect upon theological education has been felt in the merger of seminaries, the clustering of Protestant-Catholic schools of theology, the beginnings of a new ecumenical theology, and the emergence of concepts of the church that permit grass-roots institutional cooperation.

A second feature in the postwar development has been the rise of "specialized" ministries. Awareness of the unique character and needs of urban America has called for a radical reformulation of traditional conceptions of the mission of the church, and for training ministers in urban sociology and in techniques for relating to the people of the inner city.

The global interrelationships of cultures and political systems that mark the second half of the 20th century have required a new understanding of the religious phenomena of mankind. This fact, together with what has been termed the explosion of knowledge, has brought a challenge to theological education to which it had only begun to respond by the 1970's. The theological renaissance of the second quarter of the century was followed by the civil rights movement and intellectual currents characterized by terms like "the death of God," "secular theology," and "the new morality." All of these factors, plus others, account for a variety of trends in theological education—trends that are too current to be evaluated.

Jewish Theological Training. Much of Judaism has had a tendency to avoid the term "theology." This was especially true of Orthodox Judaism; questions of a metaphysical or speculative nature were met by an admonition to learn by knowing and living the Torah. However, because Judaism is much concerned with the relationships between God and man and between man and man, it can be said to deal with matters of theological understanding. Insofar as training for the rabbinate must concern itself with these relationships, it is involved in theological education. The rabbi's role, however, has been essentially different from the roles of the priests and ministers of Christianity. The rabbi exists primarily as a teacher and interpreter of the Torah for the Jewish community. He is not a priest, in spite of the fact that Western culture tended to force him into a role with priestly and pastoral implications.

Judaism in America expresses itself in three basic forms: Orthodox, Conservative, and Reform Judaism. Isaac Mayer Wise was the acknowledged leader of Reform Judaism until his death in 1900. His dream of a college for the education of rabbis eventually led to the founding in 1875 of the Hebrew Union College in Cincinnati, with Rabbi Wise as president. Conservative Jews, who sympathized with Reform Judaism in some respects, retained more of Jewish tradition and the Hebrew language while making effective use of reform in doctrinal and practical matters. Jewish Theological Seminary was founded in New York in 1855 as a Conservative response to Hebrew Union. Orthodox Jewry tried to stem the tide of Americanization. Schools such as the *hadarim* were established for teaching the Bible, Hebrew, and the prayer book. In 1896, Rabbi Isaac Elchanan Theological Seminary was founded in New York; it later developed into Yeshiva University.

Jewish theological education in the 1970's faced problems similar to those of Christian theological education. Studies in the common heritage of the two religions, along with scholarly dialogue, have brought new implications into Jewish theological education. At the same time, critics of current practices called for rabbinical studies to be part of a university—a trend already present in Christian theological training.

Islam and Buddhism. Islam's religious functionaries do not constitute a priesthood in the usual sense of that term. Islam is a religio-political culture, making the distinction between religious and other functions a difficult one. Nevertheless, there are some distinguishable religious tasks to be performed. Leadership of the services of the mosque and the interpretation of Muslim law and culture both require a kind of theological education. The priestly role of the imam demands knowledge of the Koran and familiarity with theological propositions and canon law. Theological scholars are necessary in order that the will of Allah may be interpreted for the political and cultural direction of Islam. The traditions of the Prophet Mohammed, the theological systems derived from the Koran and the Prophet, early Arabic literature (involving grammatical and lexicographical studies), and canon law, as well as logic and religious thought, all serve as the basis of Muslim theological education in universities like those in Cairo, Teheran, and Ankara.

Education for Buddhist monks has existed for centuries. The study of monastic rules was often pursued by ordained monks who had learned the fundamental Pali text of the Tripitaka (Buddhist scriptures) during their service as novices. There were also professional lecturers, charged with making thorough exegetical studies and interpreting the scriptures to monks and laity. The traditional monastic education underwent considerable reformation in order to meet the cultural demands of the 20th century. A kind of seminary tradition developed. Some of these "institutes for Buddhist studies" have elementary, preparatory, research, and dharma-propagation sections.

RICHARD E. WENTZ
The Pennsylvania State University

Bibliography

Bridston, Keith R., and Culver, Dwight W., *The Making of Ministers* (Minneapolis 1964).
Niebuhr, H. Richard, and Williams, Daniel Day, eds., *The Ministry in Historical Perspectives* (New York 1956).
Niebuhr, H. Richard, Williams, Daniel D., and Gustafson, James M., *The Advancement of Theological Education* (New York 1957).
Wagoner, Walter D., *The Seminary* (New York 1966).
Welch, Homes, *The Buddhist Revival in China* (Cambridge, Mass., 1968).

THEOLOGY is an intellectual discipline that aims at setting forth in an orderly manner the content of a religious faith. This definition already indicates some of the peculiarities of the subject. Calling theology an intellectual discipline involves the claim that theology has its legitimate place in the spectrum of human knowledge and the claim that it can make true statements. Therefore it can also point to defensible intellectual procedures in support of these claims. Theology has in fact often been called a science. The very formation of the word "theology" suggests a kinship with a whole range of varied scientific enterprises designated by similarly formed words—geology, psychology, topology, and the like. However, the fact that there are also pseudo sciences like astrology with similarly formed names may give us pause. Indeed, when the definition of theology goes on to say that the subject deals with the content of a religious faith, a sharp distinction seems to be made between theology and the recognized secular sciences.

It has rarely been claimed that a religious faith is itself rationally demonstrable. Religious faith is a total human attitude, including such elements of feeling and emotion as trust and awe, and of willing, such as striving and obedience, as well as of belief. Can even a reflective attempt to give expression to the content of such a faith claim to be a science, or a genuine intellectual discipline at all? Does not the acceptance of such a faith as its starting point rule out the openness and integrity that are essential to all intellectual disciplines worthy to be counted among the branches of human knowledge? Certainly, it must at once be acknowledged that in spite of the similarity of names, theology is quite a different kind of enterprise from geology. If we substitute English roots for Greek ones, geology becomes "earth-science" and theology "God-science." This draws attention to one fundamental difference between them. Whereas the earth's crust is something visible, tangible, and accessible to the senses in general, God, however we may think of him, has none of these characteristics.

From this difference in subject matter, there immediately follows another in method. Geology can and does apply such well-tried scientific methods as measurement, chemical analysis, observation, experiment, and so on. None of these methods is open to the theologian. It would seem that he must fall back on investigating the experiences that people describe with the aid of language about God. However, we must notice that the theologian does not simply describe and analyze such experiences as an outside observer, in the way that a psychologist or even a philosopher of religion might do. Because he is interested in the claims of faith to truth, the theologian cannot rest with an empirical description of the phenomenon of faith. He must raise the question of the validity of the experience and offer an interpretation of its inner springs. This he can scarcely do without himself being a participant in the experience. Thus theology differs from the natural sciences in being a form of knowledge by participation rather than knowledge by observation.

At least since the time of the German philosopher Wilhelm Dilthey (1833–1911), it has been recognized that there are some intellectual disciplines—the so-called "human sciences," for example, history—whose subject matter can be known only from the inside, by participation. Clearly, theology has more affinity to these human sciences than it has to the natural sciences. Yet even in relation to these disciplines there is difference as well as similarity, for theology claims, finally, to be in some sense not just a human science; it also purports to be a divine science.

As St. Thomas Aquinas recognized when he discussed whether theology is a science, there are many kinds of sciences and intellectual disciplines—a fact that has also been increasingly recognized as a result of modern logical analysis. There are also many kinds of investigative procedures adapted to different kinds of subject matter. There is no single model to be laid down in advance and to which every discipline must conform. Rather, each discipline must be questioned about the sources and credibility of its data, the methods that it employs in investigating and interpreting these data, and the claims to truth that it makes for its conclusions. The definition of theology given above and the claims implicit in it cannot be judged by the fact that this discipline has peculiarities differentiating it from other disciplines. They can be judged only by a fuller discussion of the sources and procedures of theology.

SOURCES AND FORMATIVE FACTORS

Prior to theology is faith, an orientation of the whole person, or even of the whole community that shares a particular faith. Theology is *fides quaerens intellectum*—faith seeking an understanding of itself, both its content and its ground. But what creates a faith? In traditional language, faith is itself the response to revelation.

Revelation. The word "revelation" is, unfortunately, often misunderstood. A revelation is not a body of ready-made truths that are somehow made known to the recipient and placed at his disposal, as if this were some easy way to truth, in contrast with the hard-won discoveries of natural science. A revelation is rather a profound experience in which there comes about a whole new way of perceiving the world and understanding the place of human life in it. Things are perceived in new relationships and new depth, and the horizons of self-understanding are expanded. New values take the place of old ones and there is a new orientation of the self in the world. Furthermore, this new perception has a giftlike character. It is called "revelation" because it seems to come about not as a result primarily of human search but as the self-revealing of a reality to man. It must be repeated, however, that this is not to be understood as the making known of complete, ready-made propositional truths. On the contrary, any revelation places on its recipients the task of exploring, interpreting, appropriating, and applying the new perceptions that have been attained.

Revelations have been received in many forms. Mystical experiences are one such form. Although the term "revelation" belongs to Western rather than to Eastern categories of religious thought, it would be applicable to such Eastern experiences as the enlightenment of the Buddha—an experience of perceiving the world and human life in a profoundly new way. However, in this case there was lacking any sense of personal encounter such as has been characteristic of Judeo-Christian concepts of revelation. A theophany, or vision of a divine Being, either directly or under some visible symbolic form, has been another type of revelatory experience. Examples of theophanies are Moses' encounter with God in the burning bush or Arjuna's vision of the divine Krishna, as related in the *Bhagavad Gītā*. In the Jewish and Christian traditions, however, historical events or clusters of events have been taken as revelations, and this is perhaps what is most characteristic of these faiths and has earned for them the description "historical religions."

In the Jewish tradition, the Exodus of the Hebrew people from Egypt, their deliverance from slavery, and their call to be a free nation is the heart of the historical revelation. It reveals a liberating power at work in history, and this is taken to be the power of God. The historical experience of the Exodus is made interpretative for other historical situations, and it gives an identity and orientation to the community of faith that founds itself on this revelation. In the Christian tradition, the history of the life, death, and resurrection of Jesus Christ, interpreted as the coming of God among men in order to bring atonement and new life, is the heart of revelation. It becomes the foundation for an entire attitude to life among those who put their faith in the revelation.

Each of the revelations mentioned has given birth to a community of faith, and so have many other revelations that have not been mentioned. In each community there has arisen a theology—Buddhist, Hindu, Jewish, Islamic, Christian—that has taken that revelation as its primary datum, has reflected upon its meaning, and has sought to discover its implications for the life of the community. Does the fact that the theologian accepts the revelation accorded to a particular community as his primary datum imply that he begins with an assumption that is incompatible with a truly scientific or intellectually sound inquiry? That does not follow. Every investigation has its presuppositions. They cannot be avoided if the investigation is to get off the ground. What is important is that they should be recognized as presuppositions so that their plausibility or implausibility may be examined.

The theologian acknowledges revelation as his presupposition. Some theologians are prepared to leave the matter there, but others seek to develop a theory of revelation that may make the occurrence of revelatory experiences more readily credible. Some Jewish and Christian theologians and philosophers of religion have used the model of an encounter between persons to illuminate the nature of a revelatory experience. Again, the model of aesthetic experience—that is, of being grasped by a work of art as a whole—offers a parallel that helps to elucidate some forms of revelation. This is especially the case with those reported in mystical and Eastern religions.

The very use of the word "faith" indicates that accepting any revelation involves a risk, but the risk need not be taken uncritically. The fact that revelatory experiences with a broadly similar structure have been reported from so many human communities over such a long period of time is a presumption in favor of the *prima facie* validity of such experiences. To be sure, the diversity of revelations is great, and so the question of their compatibility also arises. Some theologians acknowledge only the revelations accepted in their own communities. Others, while not embracing any facile syncretism, stress what is common to the religions and believe that there are deep affinities among the many revelations.

Scripture and Tradition. The great classic revelations on which the major faiths of mankind have been founded now lie in the past and are not directly accessible. Thus, although revelation is the primary datum for theology, revelation has to be mediated in various ways. It is through these mediated forms that it enters into theology. In most communities of faith, revelation is mediated by scriptures and by tradition. Scripture itself begins as oral tradition. Even at that stage the form may be rigidly fixed, and once the words have been committed to writing the verbal form tends to remain unchanged over long periods. Scripture is not itself revelation, but it is a witness to the revelatory experience. Scripture serves as the memory of the community. Through the scriptural witness, the original classic revelation continues to come alive and to shape the life of the community.

Almost all communities of faith beyond the primitive level have developed their bodies of scripture, but different communities value them in different ways. In Eastern religions there is not the same regard for the precise literal words of scripture as there is in the Middle Eastern and Western religions of Islam, Judaism, and Christianity. It is true that several centuries of Biblical criticism have eroded the authority of the Bible in the West. Few contemporary theologians would adopt the style of theology common in the Protestant churches in the years after the Reformation, when theology was little more than a commentary on the Bible and when every doctrine had to be supported by the quotation of "proof" texts.

Yet even the more liberal attitude to the Bible prevailing in the late 20th century does not take away its normative significance for Jewish and Christian theology. It remains the authentic witness to the revelatory history on which these communities of faith have been founded. Modern theologians in the Judeo-Christian tradition handle the Bible with much more freedom than did their predecessors, but Biblical teaching still remains a foundation of their thinking. They could not relinquish it and still validly claim to represent theology within their particular communities of faith.

Alongside scripture there is tradition. As well as the written record, there is the continuing life of the community. This, too, has its origin in the classic revelation and helps to mediate it. Scripture and tradition are not to be considered rivals, though they have sometimes been so considered in disputes between the Catholic and Protestant forms of Christianity. The latter stress the exclusive authority of scripture, and the former admit tradition alongside scripture. But even the most extreme Protestant groups have not been able to exclude the influence of tradition. In Christianity some traditional interpretations of the revelation, such as the trinitarian doctrine of God and the doctrine of the two natures of Christ, have come to be accepted as having a high degree of authority. They are, of course, compatible with scripture, but they go beyond the explicit formulations of scripture and rule out some other possible interpretations.

Just as contemporary theologians may not feel themselves so closely bound by scripture as did the theologians of an earlier time, so they may also feel themselves less tied by traditional interpretations. Nevertheless, since it is the faith of a *community* to which the theologian tries to give expression, he will not recklessly set up his individual judgment against the collective wisdom of his coreligionists. To that extent his theology continues to be guided by tradition. Yet he will always be seeking new interpretations of the traditions and striving to let his theology express the tension between the continuity of the past and the novelty of the future.

Experience. In addition to revelation, as mediated through scripture and tradition, a second main source for theology is experience. It would be hard to believe in the revelations made long ago unless there were some present experiences of the divine analogous to them. Thus the theologian's own experience of participation in the life and worship of a community of faith become data for his theology. William James has given a classic description of the almost endless varieties of religious experience. This variety of individual experience contributes in turn to the variety of theology.

Not only so-called "religious" but secular experiences as well are sources of relevant data for theology. Present experience, secular and religious alike, is brought into confrontation with the revelation and interpreted in the light of it. In this process, the understanding of the revelation is enlarged and deepened or, in some instances, put in question. Conversely, the understanding of present experience is likewise deepened. No theology could be persuasive that had not been exposed to the test of experience, received some confirmation in experience, and incorporated something of the wisdom and actuality of experience.

Culture. To speak of present experience is to acknowledge still another factor that enters into the construction of a theology, namely the cultural environment in which the theologian works. Some theologians have tried hard to present a theology of revelation alone, and to exclude all cultural influences. They have represented a vain hope. All human statements, including theological statements, are to some extent historically conditioned. They employ the language and thought-categories of a given period and belong to a particular moment in time.

Because of the importance of tradition in religious faith, theological formulations tend to become absolutized. They are taken to be timeless truths and persist long after the thought-categories in which they were expressed have become obsolete. This has been a major source of trouble in the history of theology. It has not been understood that theology, as much as any other science or intellectual discipline, is a dynamic study. It must continually seek new formulations and address itself to new cultural situations. This is not simply a question of translating its dogmas from one cultural idiom to another. It implies a development and deepening of the dogmas themselves as they come to be seen within new and broader cultural horizons. The progress of theology takes place as its traditional wisdom seeks to find expression in new experiential and cultural situations.

Reason and Conscience. Related to the factors just discussed are the contributions made to theology by the reason and conscience of the theologian himself. That reason has a place in theology follows from its very definition as an intellectual discipline aiming at an ordered body of knowledge. However, the function of theology is not merely to elucidate the content of faith but to criticize it. Likewise the theologian, though spokesman for a community of faith, has a critical function in the community.

In giving the content of faith a coherent expression, theology seeks to remove inconsistencies and obscurities within the affirmations of faith itself. It also seeks to reconcile the affirmations of faith with the other beliefs—scientific, historical, philosophical, and the like—that people hold. The strict exercise of this critical function by theology, even if it sometimes leads to clashes with ecclesiastical authority, is of the highest importance if the intellectual integrity of religious faith is to be maintained.

The point about conscience is similar. Beliefs once widely held may have to be criticized by theology as ethically objectionable, sometimes in the light of cultural developments, and sometimes in the light of a better understanding of the original revelation itself.

THEOLOGICAL METHOD

The diversity of the sources and formative factors that go into the making of theology indicates that there will be a corresponding diversity of methods. In particular, there has been in the history of theology a tension between faith and reason. Some theologians have placed almost the entire emphasis upon the content of faith, the revelation transmitted through scripture and tradition. For these theologians the role of reason has been an ancillary one. Others, while by no means denying the importance of revelation, have nevertheless believed it incumbent upon them to provide some rational framework within which to exhibit and elucidate the revelation. Theologians of this second group have distinguished between "natural" and "revealed" theology.

Rationalistic Approach. Natural theology consists of those basic truths concerning the existence of God and the destiny of man that are supposed to be discoverable by reason alone. Thus they are held to be accessible to all thinking men. This rational, or natural, theology provided a basis on which was erected the traditional superstructure of revealed theology. By this means the somewhat abstract truths attained by reason might be filled out and expanded in the light of the revelation which was the foundation of the religious community.

For a long time natural theology was regarded as the indispensable prelude to revealed theology, but, although it still has its advocates, its validity has become increasingly suspect. The most important part of natural theology consisted of its proofs of the existence of God. Those proofs were of two kinds. One, the ontological, was purely rational and made no appeal to experience (see also THEISM). It claimed that all men already have the idea of God and that this idea implies the existence of a corresponding reality. The classic statement of the argument was given by St. Anselm: we have the idea of a Being than which no greater can be conceived. But if this Being did not exist, we would conceive a greater, namely, a Being who added the perfection of existence to the other perfections. Therefore, this Being exists.

Many people, even in Anselm's time, questioned whether the transition from idea to reality can be made in this manner. It is widely believed that Kant finally put his finger on the fallacy of the argument by pointing out that existence is not another predicate, nor another perfection, though Anselm treats it as if it were. Though some people still dispute over refinements of the argument, it is nowadays generally held to be discredited or, at least, highly questionable.

St. Thomas Aquinas did not accept Anselm's argument, but he brought forward his own famous "five ways" of establishing the existence of God. These arguments differed from the ontological one because they did not proceed from ideas alone but appealed to our experience of the world. In general terms, a consideration of the finite beings within the world is said to lead us to conclude the existence of an infinite Being on whom the world depends. In brief summary, the five ways lead from the observed fact of motion to a Prime Mover, from causality to a First Cause, from contingent beings to Necessary Being, from the gradations of perfection among beings to a Perfect Being, and from evidences of order and design to a Supreme Intelligence.

It would be impossibe here to indicate all the refinements and criticisms to which these arguments have been subjected. Even today they are debated. But they have ceased to carry much conviction. They may not have been entirely demolished, but at the best they would establish something so nebulous as not to have any importance for theology. The verdict of the philosopher David Hume still seems to stand: "The whole of natural theology—that the cause or causes of order in the universe probably bear some remote analogy to human intelligence—has little importance for human life."

Revelational Approach. The breakdown of traditional natural theology has been welcomed by the representatives of a different approach to theological problems. This alternative way into theology received classic expression at the time of the Reformation and has been reaffirmed in the 20th century by Karl Barth and many others. In their view, natural theology can only be misleading, and no idea of God framed by human reason can be anything but distorting. Thus, natural theology is not a gateway to revealed theology but cuts us off from a proper understanding of the revelation. The business of theology is not to provide a framework for the revelation, but rather to let the revelation create its own framework and shape the theologian's thinking. The method of theology is thus understood to be exegesis, and an exegesis that is determined by the text. This method results in a strongly Biblical type of theology.

However, if this theology escapes the problems that have befallen the exponents of natural theology, it has severe problems of its own. Natural theology, by appealing to all rational beings, tried to relate the theological endeavor to the everyday understanding of men and to common reason. A theology that omits this step tends to become an isolated pursuit, unrelated to the general intellectual life of mankind. Deprived of the substructure provided by natural theology, revelation hangs in the air, so to speak, unconnected with anything else in human life. Especially in a secular age, it may seem to be taking too much for granted just to assume the reality of God and revelation and to visualize the task of theology as the exegesis of this revelation. If natural theology of the traditional sort has failed, can it simply be abandoned, or must the theologian look for a new kind of approach that will help to bridge the gap between revelation and the secular understanding?

Humanistic Approach. A third approach, which might offer the prospect of passing beyond the shortcomings of the two already considered, is indicated by the 20th century Protestant theologian Paul Tillich in his method of correlation. This begins neither with an attempt to prove a revelation nor with one simply given, but with an analysis of the human situation. It begins not with demonstration but with description. The reality that it seeks to describe is our everyday existence, open to investigation by everyone. Thus the relation between theology and secular understanding, formerly provided by traditional natural theology and then broken by revelational theology, is restored, but in a more tenable form. Furthermore, in making the human situation the methodological starting point for theology, this approach offers a reminder that theology is not concerned with abstract speculations concerning God and the other worldly. It is concerned with God precisely in correlation with the human situation.

Theology is just as much a doctrine of man as a doctrine of God. As a descriptive approach, this third theological method has found a powerful tool in phenomenology. This philosophical method has already been widely used by philosophers for the analysis of human existence, and these results have been taken over and applied by theologians. They claim that phenomenological description of the human existence known to all shows situations in which words like "faith," "revelation," "grace," and even "God" have their meaning. They also claim that the theological exposition of the content of revelation is to be related to these situations and the questions that they raise.

Tillich himself gave most attention to situations such as guilt, death, and anxiety. These did not, so he claimed, yield a positive understanding of God, but prepared man for revelation. Other writers, especially Catholic theologians such as Joseph Maréchal, Karl Rahner, and Bernard Lonergan, employ an "anthropological" approach broadly similar to Tillich's. However, they redress the balance by placing greater stress on the affirmative elements in the human situation, such as hope, love, freedom. They see man in the process of self-transcendence. God is the "whither" of this transcendence, according to Rahner, rather than the reply to the anxiety occasioned by the awareness of finitude. The Jewish theologian Abraham Heschel teaches a doctrine of man with affinities to the views described here. See also GOD.

Methods and Their Historical Development. The three theological methods here noted and the three types of theology that they tend to produce are neither exhaustive nor clearly defined. They arise because one element rather than another has been stressed in the complex texture of theology, but there are many intermediate cases. Some theologians whom we might assign to a particular type could be shown to possess characteristics that might argue for their being assigned to a different type. But as a rough guide, the threefold classification has some usefulness. The three types, with their corresponding methods, have persisted through the history of theology.

The first, or rationalistic, type goes back to the very beginnings of theology. Theology, as its name betrays, began among the Greeks. Pre-Socratic philosophy was a kind of natural theology and already introduced terms that were to be of great importance later, such as *logos* and *nomos*. When Greek thought encountered the Biblical tradition, the rationalistic style of theology entered both the Jewish schools of thought, in the work of Philo of Alexandria, and the Christian, in that of Justin Martyr, Clement of Alexandria, Origen, and most of the patristic writers. This style of theology culminated in the Middle Ages with the work of St. Thomas Aquinas. It has persisted ever since not only in the innumerable disciples of St. Thomas but in all those forms of theology that have reckoned seriously with metaphysics and science and have tried to come to terms with the achievements of secular thought.

The second type, which may be called revelational, reflects the prophetic spirit of the Bible itself and had its earliest representatives in those theologians who protested against the encroachments of Greek philosophy. It came to maturity in the work of the great reformers Luther and Calvin. Its continuing vitality is attested by the fact that to this tradition belongs the greatest Protestant theologian of the 20th century, Karl Barth.

The third, or humanistic, type has some affinities with the first, but makes its appeal to the whole spectrum of human existence or human experience, stressing the nonrational elements alongside reason. Perhaps St. Augustine could be seen as an early representative, though he might better be regarded as a bridge between the first and third types. Friedrich Schleiermacher at the beginning of the 19th century ushered in a period of dominance of humanistic theology. Albrecht Ritschl and Adolf von Harnack continued the line, and it remains to the present.

The three methods and the three types, though often rivals of one another, have all made important contributions. It is unlikely that in the future any one theological method will establish a monopoly. Nor does it seem likely that the various methods could be synthesized without loss of integrity. A measure of pluralism and controversy makes for a vigorous and healthy state in theology. As already noted, there is always a historically conditioned element in any theological formulation, and it may well be that in changing historical circumstances, now one and now another of the historic types is most appropriate for bringing the meaning of the revelation to bear on the contemporary situation. For instance, it is commonly agreed that the prophetic stance of Karl Barth was the right theological response at the time of the dominance of the German Nazis and the only one that met the challenge of that time. But as circumstances changed, a new style of theology was required to correct the overemphases of the other.

Modern Trends. Unfortunately, the history of theology has too often seemed like the swing of a pendulum. Each newly discovered insight leads to the forgetting of another of equal validity, which must then be rediscovered later. No doubt it is impossible for all points of view to be grasped simultaneously. That would be an attempt to reach a kind of timeless truth and would neglect the concreteness of the particular situation in which one approach has an appropriateness superior to others. But the complaint can justly be made that theologies do have a tendency to become too one-sided, and this has been the cause of the many violent controversies that have occurred in the history of theology.

When a theological interpretation is pushed to an extreme of one-sidedness, it becomes known as a heresy. In such a case, a segment of teaching has been taken out of its context and is presented in isolation. Frequently, it is the fact that a particular truth has been neglected in the official theology of the community that leads the so-called heretic to present it in exaggerated form. To this extent his heresy may be justified. It has been argued by some that Marxism is a Judeo-Christian heresy, called into being by the failure of the theologians of that tradition to perceive the social implications of their theology.

However, there is a tendency in the late 20th century to drop the term "heresy" from use altogether. If there is no theological formulation that is final and holds for all situations, there is probably none that is entirely devoid of truth either. Certainly, a view that deviates from the commonly accepted norm cannot be dismissed by attaching to it the pejorative label of "heresy." It can be overcome only by showing that the accepted view has better theological credentials. The criterion of truth is not the decree of an arbitrary ecclesiastical authority but the tests of theological method. Whatever may have been the case in the past, theologians today for the most part pursue their inquiries in freedom, governed only by the integrity of their own discipline.

THEOLOGY AND OTHER DISCIPLINES

Knowledge is a unity, and especially in modern times of specialization, there has grown up an awareness of the dangers of fragmentation and the need for interdisciplinary dialogue. Theology is in special danger of isolation, particularly when it assumes a markedly revelational form. It can then become a completely esoteric knowledge, cut off from the secular disciplines. Interdisciplinary dialogue is therefore especially important for theology. Furthermore, theology has in the past been engaged in somewhat sharp controversies with other subjects. These have invaded parts of what was once recognized as the territory of theology. Has that territory been completely eroded, or are there borderline areas where mutual criticism and mutual exchange of knowledge may take place? In what follows, the borderlines between theology and a number of other disciplines standing close to it will be explored. In this way, the nature and distinctiveness of the theological enterprise will be further elucidated.

Philosophy. Of all the interdisciplinary dialogues in which theology is engaged, the dialogue with philosophy is the most important, and it is certainly the oldest. Indeed, if we think of theology as having originated among the early Greek philosophers, it was at that time scarcely distinguishable from philosophy. The close relation between the two subjects has continued ever since. Admittedly, there have been interruptions and sometimes protests against the closeness of the relation. "What has Athens to do with Jerusalem?" demanded Tertullian, an early critic of philosophical influences in theology, and he has had many successors.

However, the dialogue seems to be inescapable, and after every interruption it is resumed.

There are good reasons for this. Theology makes assertions about God, man, and the world, and these themes have also occupied philosophy during most of its history. It is natural for the theologian to compare his own pronouncements with those of the philosopher. The two approaches are different, but it would be surprising if there were not something to be gained by examining the points both of agreement and of disagreement that emerge in the two inquiries. Even if much of modern philosophy has turned away from such traditional themes as the existence of God and the destiny of the human person, there remain good reasons for promoting the dialogue between theology and philosophy. For philosophy may be regarded as the voice of that which is most typical in a culture. A cultural mood finds expression in many ways, but perhaps its most precise and subtle expression is to be found in the philosophy that it inspires. If, then, it is important for theology to relate itself to cultural factors and to interpret the traditional revealed material in a language applicable to the prevailing culture, the theologian must attend to the philosophical expression of the culture. This is the case even where the philosophy may take a secular form and may lack interest in explicitly theological questions.

Theologians of the past have sometimes made alliances with forms of philosophy that seemed to support the theistic conception of reality. Sometimes they have done battle with philosophies of a materialistic kind, as these seemed to pose a threat to the validity of religious faith. The present relationship is likely to be different, for the contemporary philosopher may have nothing to say directly about theological questions at all. This does not take away the need for dialogue and may even permit it to assume a healthier form. At a time when many philosophers have turned away from metaphysics, they cannot be suspected on their side of subservience to theology. Likewise, theologians cannot be accused on their side of adapting the faith of their communities to the current metaphysical fashion. Actually, the interest of theologians in philosophy continues to flourish, and has perhaps three main focuses.

Existentialism. A fruitful discussion has taken place between theology and existentialism. We have seen that a humanistic type of theology has been influential since the time of Schleiermacher. This type of theology, stressing as it has the doctrine of man, almost inevitably must confront existentialist philosophy as a major way in which modern man has sought to express his self-understanding. Søren Kierkegaard, the father of modern existentialism, had passionate Christian convictions. He believed that faith is more a matter of the will than of belief. His influence has been very great in drawing modern theology away from academic and speculative concerns into a much closer relation with life as it is actually lived.

At the same time. Kierkegaard stressed the otherness of God and the paradoxical character of revelation. In these matters he would probably have been less than happy about the subsequent development of the relation between theology and existentialism, which has taken the direction of a more humanistic and immanentist view of faith. This later development has appealed more to the work of secular existentialists such as Heidegger and Sartre than to Kierkegaard. These secular existentialists have offered an analysis of the structures of human existence. The terminology employed in this analysis has been taken over by existentialist theologians in order to restate fundamental doctrines concerning man and faith. Sin is understood as alienation, faith as decision and commitment, and revelation itself as a new self-understanding.

The most consistent attempt to provide an existentialist theology has been Rudolf Bultmann's program of demythologizing. He seeks to eliminate from the Biblical revelation all mythological and crudely supernatural elements, and to replace the traditional language with a language describing a form of human existence. Bultmann, however, makes it clear that he does not wish to eliminate the concept of God, though certainly this concept would itself need a radical demythologizing. Existentialist theologies have been criticized not only for their alleged minimizing or even abolishing of the transcendent dimension of revelation, but also for their individualism. To some extent, this individualistic tendency has been counteracted by the influence of such philosophers of personal being as Martin Buber and Gabriel Marcel, who have shown that human existence is fundamentally social. Their influence has also operated against the reductionist tendency in some existentialist theology, for God is understood as the "eternal Thou," the founder and enabler of interpersonal relations and genuine community.

Logical Analysis. Though it has not attracted as much attention as the exchange with existentialism, the dialogue between theology and logical analysis has been of considerable importance. Especially in the English-speaking countries, logical analysis has risen to be a dominant philosophy of modern times. According to the analysts, philosophy has no special subject matter of its own. The business of philosophy is to examine the language and logic of the particular sciences with a view to discovering the trustworthiness of their procedures and the weight that may be attached to their claims to truth.

The language of theology has not escaped this scrutiny, and in the earlier phases of logical analysis, theology came off badly. For the method of the natural sciences was taken to be the norm, and theology, as well as metaphysics, ethics, and some other subjects, manifestly did not fulfill that norm. In particular, it seemed that theological assertions were untestable. Is there any experience—and "experience" was usually understood as sense experience—that is relevant to verifying or falsifying such statements as "God exists" or "God is love"? In the later phases of logical analysis, it has generally been conceded that the model of the natural sciences was absolutized in the earlier history of the movement. It has also been admitted that there are many meaningful kinds of language that do not conform to the empirical pattern. But it still remains a challenge to theologians to show that their language has a pattern as intelligible as that to which the natural scientists can point. In particular, it is a question whether theological language is genuinely cognitive or merely expresses emotion or, perhaps, moral intention. Some advance with this problem has been made through the analysis of personal language (that is, language that reflects the individual's viewpoint as opposed to external, objective phenomena) and by taking a new look at traditional theories concerning the indirect character of religious language, especially theories of analogy and symbolism.

Metaphysics. While it has been indicated that metaphysics has gone out of fashion, it has still a few practitioners. Even if it is agreed that Hume and Kant discredited rational or speculative metaphysics, it is argued that a case can still be made out for two other kinds of metaphysics: descriptive metaphysics and existential metaphysics. The first kind, exemplified by Alfred North Whitehead, seeks, on the basis of what we learn from the empirical sciences, to offer a description of the world in the most general categories. The second kind, exemplified by Nikolai Berdyaev, seeks to develop what he calls a "metaphysic of the subject," an understanding of reality to be reached from what we know through our own total participation in it.

These subtle systems of thought cannot be explored here, but their relevance to theology is obvious. Modern metaphysics has been especially influential in theological thinking about God. The traditional idea of God as a sovereign lord completely prior to and independent of his creation has been much under fire. The new metaphysics has led rather to an understanding of God as acted upon by the world as well as acting on it. Sometimes this view is called "panentheism," to distinguish it both from traditional theism and from pantheism. It has been widely received by many theologians who believe that it accords better with the Biblical belief in a "living"—dynamic—God. It is also believed to ease the problem of evil, so intractable for traditional theism with its substantial God dwelling in immutable perfection.

History. Next to philosophy, history is perhaps the most important partner for dialogue with theology. At least, that would hold for Jewish and Christian theology, for which, as we have seen, revelation has assumed a historical form. The truths of Buddhism do not seem to be dependent on their historical origin. But if God has revealed himself in the history of a people (Israel) or of a person (Jesus Christ), then the historical circumstances under which the Jewish and Christian faiths came into being are of the greatest importance in assessing those faiths. As historical religions, it would seem that Judaism and Christianity have a kind of vulnerability that some other religions escape. Yet this vulnerability is not something to be deplored. It means that at some points at least the Jewish and Christian faiths can be subjected to some empirical criteria. One of the positivist objections to the possibility of religious knowledge has been precisely that no empirical tests seem relevant. But clearly the rigorous methods of scientific historical research are relevant to determining whether indeed the Hebrews made an exodus from Egypt or whether Jesus Christ suffered under Pontius Pilate or whether these stories are simply creations of the mythical imagination.

At least from the 18th century onward, theologians have come to accept that the so-called "sacred" history of the Bible must be critically examined by the same methods that are used in the investigation of secular history. Although this critical work has led to the erosion or reinterpretation of some particulars of the Biblical narratives, and although some surprising new evidences have come to light, such as the Dead Sea Scrolls, yet the main historical outlines of both the Old and New Testaments remain unshaken. No reputable scholars would be prepared to dismiss their contents as pure fabrication. This result is important, as far as it goes, for it is hard to see how either Judaism or Christianity could survive without some core of factual history.

This is still only the beginning of the problem of theology and history. Even if the facts are broadly established, what about the interpretation? Empirical investigation might establish the probability that Hebrew tribes migrated from Egypt around 1200 B.C. or that Jesus was crucified in the time of Pontius Pilate. However, another major step has been taken when one goes on to give a theological interpretation of these events as God's action in history. To take such a step implies a philosophy of history. Perhaps there are few theologians today who would attempt to construct a theological interpretation of history on the scale of St. Augustine's *City of God.* However, all theology seems to be committed to the view that somewhere divine agency enters into the complex tissue of the historical process. At this point the theologian finds himself in conversation with other interpreters of history—Hegelians, Marxists, evolutionists, positivists, and others.

Finally, we may notice the relativizing influence of history on theology. The tremendous increase of historical knowledge in the 19th century, and especially knowledge of the history of religions, made it possible to set the Biblical history in a much wider context of human religious experience. On the one hand, this wider context has militated against claims to exclusiveness. On the other hand, it has enhanced the probability of the validity of claims to revelation and knowledge of the divine, since these are seen to be based on universal forms of human experience.

Human Sciences. Mention must be made also of the relation of theology to the human sciences—psychology, sociology, anthropology, and the like. Psychology offers in purely naturalistic terms explanations of many things that go on in the human mind. In particular, the psychology of religion has undertaken to study by empirical methods such phenomena as conversion and mysticism. The discovery by psychology and psychoanalysis of the unconscious depths of the human mind has opened new ways toward understanding religious phenomena. Is "God" simply a projection of the human mind, and are such experiences as grace and revelation to be accounted for not in terms of divine action but in terms of forces arising in the depth of the human mind itself? The theologian welcomes the new light that psychology throws on the structure of man's inner life and accepts that religious experience is subject to the same kind of psychological laws that govern other experience. He would, however, challenge the assumption that the psychological account of religion is an exhaustive one. Psychology, so far as it is an empirical science, is necessarily abstract. It does not attempt to go beyond proximate explanations of the phenomena and, indeed, has nothing to say concerning the theological type of explanation.

Similar remarks apply in the other sciences of man. The sociology of knowledge has made it clear that supposed theological differences have often been the expression of subtle social forces of an entirely untheological nature. All beliefs, as has been noted earlier, are in part determined by social, historical, and cultural factors. But this is far from implying that once the sociology of a belief has been investigated, nothing more remains to be said. There is still the important question of its truth or falsity.

Anthropology has investigated the origins of religious beliefs and traced their histories. But, once again, to trace the history of a belief is not to determine its present status or to settle its claim to truth. Theology can learn much from the human sciences, though probably their importance has been much exaggerated in recent years. Their abstractness always misses the concrete richness of the human phenomenon, and their stress on relativism, if unchecked by any other considerations, tends to slip into a complete skepticism, which eventually engulfs the human sciences themselves.

Natural Sciences. Finally, there is the question of theology and the natural sciences. Unfortunately, the best-known chapters in this story have concerned the battles between scientists and theologians. The warfare began in ancient Greece, when the philosopher Anaxagoras taught that the sun is not a god but a mass of blazing rock, and he was exiled from Athens as a punishment. At the time of the Renaissance, Galileo and others suffered at the hands of the church for teaching that the earth is not at the center of things. Theologians and geologists later quarreled over the age of the earth. The long periods of time required by geological theories seemed to conflict with the account of history given in the Bible.

The most celebrated and most acrimonious clash between theologians and scientists came in the 19th century over the theory of evolution and the descent of man from animal ancestors. The repercussions of that debate had not quite died away in the late 20th century. To many people, it seemed that in each of these encounters, theology suffered defeat, and the sciences were vindicated. This is no doubt true with regard to the matters of fact which were at issue.

What is more important is that out of these disputes the boundaries between theology and the several sciences were more clearly defined. Theology came to understand its own task better. Revelation offers no shortcut to discovering empirical matters of fact. It is rather the basis for self-understanding in a world that is differently conceived at different stages of scientific development. The doctrine of Creation, for instance, is not a rival to scientific accounts of human or cosmic origins, but an acknowledgement of the dependent status of the world and man.

The problem of the relation between theology and the sciences is a very complex one. The two inquiries are so different that any attempt to link their results is a risky one. Many attempts have in fact been made to draw theological conclusions from scientific findings. Sometimes scientists themselves have made the attempt, sometimes theologians. Teilhard de Chardin, who combined the roles of scientist and theologian, has offered a very influential interpretation of evolution in Christian terms. But it is difficult to justify the logic of theories that proceed from empirical data to theological conclusions. The old disputes between science and theology are not likely to break out again. The theologian has learned to respect the integrity of science and seeks to show that his own interpretation of reality is compatible with the scientist's.

DIVISIONS OF THE SUBJECT

Like other subjects, theology, particularly Christian theology, has become increasingly specialized. Systematic theology is concerned with the articulation of the whole body of theological knowledge and its relation to other forms of knowledge, especially those prevailing at the present time. Dogmatics and apologetics are not so much branches of theology as specific ways of stating theological content. Dogmatics sets forth the body of doctrines accepted by the community of faith. Apologetics addresses itself to the outside world and tries to present theological teaching in ways that will meet the objections of its critics. But in an age when the secular outlook has penetrated within the community of faith itself, the distinction between dogmatics and apologetics has become academic.

Historical theology deals with the rise and development of doctrines. A special branch of this is Biblical theology, which treats of the theological concepts to be found in the Bible. The application of the insights of academic theology to the concerns of life is studied in a range of disciplines known collectively as practical theology. Moral theology brings the significance of faith and revelation to bear on ethical problems. Ascetical and mystical theology have to do with prayer, spirituality, discipleship, and the relation of the believer to God. Pastoral theology is concerned with the cure of souls, including counseling.

JOHN MACQUARRIE, *Oxford University*

Bibliography

Barth, Karl, *Church Dogmatics,* 4 vols. (Philadelphia 1950–1962).
Buber, Martin, *The Prophetic Faith* (Magnolia, Mass., 1955).
Bultmann, Rudolf, *Theology of the New Testament* (New York 1951).
Eichrodt, Walther, *Theology of the Old Testament,* tr. by J. Baker, 2 vols. (Philadelphia 1961).
Harnack, Adolph von, *History of Dogma,* tr. by Neil Buchanan, 7 vols. (London 1897–1910).
Heschel, Abraham J., *Who Is Man?* (Stanford, Calif., 1965).
Jaeger, Werner, *Theology of the Early Greek Philosophers* (London 1968).
Kelly, John N. D., *Early Christian Doctrine* (New York 1959).
Mackintosh, H. R., *Types of Modern Theology* (New York 1937).
Macquarrie, John, *Principles of Christian Theology* (New York 1965).
Martin, James A., *The New Dialogue Between Philosophy and Religion* (New York 1966).
Metz, Johannes, *Theology of the World* (New York 1969).
Moltmann, Jürgen, *Theology of Hope* (New York 1967).
Niebuhr, Reinhold, *The Nature and Destiny of Man,* 2 vols. (New York 1949).
Rahner, Karl, *Theological Investigations,* 5 vols. (New York 1961–1967).
Ramsey, Ian T., *Religious Language* (New York 1963).
Richardson, Alan, *An Introduction to the Theology of the New Testament* (New York 1959).
Roberts, David E., *Existentialism and Religious Belief* (New York 1965).
Robinson, John A. T., *Exploration into God* (Stanford, Calif., 1967).
Rust, Eric C., *Science and Faith* (New York 1967).
Schelling, S. Paul, *God in an Age of Atheism* (Nashville, Tenn., 1969).
Schlette, Heinz R., *Towards a Theology of Religions* (New York 1966).
Smart, James D., *The Divided Mind of Modern Theology: Karl Barth and Rudolf Bultmann* (Philadelphia 1967).
Smith, Ronald G., *Secular Christianity* (New York 1966).
Tillich, Paul, *Systematic Theology,* 3 vols. (Chicago 1951, 1957, 1963).
Van Buren, Paul, *The Secular Meaning of the Gospel: An Original Inquiry* (New York 1963).

THEOPHANES, thē-of′ə-nēz, **Saint** (c. 725–c. 818), Byzantine monk and historian. Theophanes was born in Constantinople (Istanbul). He married the daughter of a patrician. Shortly afterwards, without consummating the marriage, he retired from the world and established the monastery of Mt. Sigriana, on the shore of the Sea of Marmara, near Cyzicus. His wife entered a convent. Later he founded another monastery on Kalonymos Island. Because he opposed the iconoclasm of Emperor Leo V, the Armenian, he was beaten, imprisoned for two years, and then banished to the island of Samothrace, where he died shortly afterwards, about 818.

Between 810 and 814, Theophanes compiled an important chronicle of the period from 284 to 813, basing it on earlier historians. It was translated into Latin in the 870's by the papal librarian Anastasius. This chronicle and the one by Nicephorus, Patriarch of Constantinople, are the main Byzantine sources for the history of the 7th and 8th centuries. Theophanes' feast day is observed on March 12 by both Eastern Orthodox and Latin rite Christians.

MARION A. HABIG, O. F. M.
St. Augustine Friary, Chicago

THEOPHRASTUS, thē-ō-fras′təs (c. 370–c. 287 B. C.), a Greek philosopher, was a friend and disciple of Aristotle and his successor as head of the Peripatetic School, or Lyceum. Theophrastus was renowned as a teacher and apparently was tireless as a writer. The titles of many of his works are the same as those of Aristotle's—such as *Physics, Metaphysics,* and *Poetics.* Works by Theophrastus are cited in fields ranging from logic to politics. Of special influence was his *Opinions of the Physicists,* which systematically expounded the theories on natural science of earlier philosophers.

With the exception of a few fragments, all of Theophrastus' books are lost. There remain only three complete works, two of which are on botany—*History of Plants,* dealing with classification and distribution, and *Causes of Plants,* dealing with structure and physiology. These two books carried the study of botany almost as far as it was to go until the Renaissance. The third extant work is the short and curious *Characters,* which consists of 30 brief sketches of personality types, such as "The Superstitious Man." As the descriptions tend to be satirical, it is probable that the work was inspired by the limited range of comic stereotypes that were stock features of the contemporary New Comedy.

RICHMOND Y. HATHORN
Author of "Tragedy, Myth, and Mystery"

THEORELL, tā′ō-rəl, **Axel Hugo Teodor** (1903–), Swedish biochemist, who was awarded the 1955 Nobel Prize in physiology or medicine for his work on the enzymes that catalyze biological oxidations and reductions.

Theorell was born in Linköping, Sweden, on July 6, 1903. He received his M. D. degree at the Karolinska Institutet in Stockholm in 1930. While still a student, he discovered and described the lipoproteins of blood plasma. In 1932–1933 he was assistant professor of biochemistry at Uppsala, where he worked on the ultracentrifuge with The Svedberg. During this period Theorell was the first to crystallize myoglobin, the protein responsible for the red color of muscle. He described many of the properties of myoglobin and also purified, crystallized, and studied other heme-containing proteins associated with cellular respiration, such as cytochrome C.

In 1934–1935, Theorell was associated with Otto Warburg in his institute in Berlin-Dahlem. While there, he worked on the "yellow enzyme" that several investigators had discovered in yeast, heart muscle, and milk. Theorell purified the enzyme by electrophoresis and separated it into two fragments by dialysis of an acidified solution. One fragment was a colorless protein. The yellow color was associated with a substance of low molecular weight, which Theorell identified as a monophosphate of riboflavin (vitamin B_2). This substance, now known as FMN, or flavin-mono-nucleotide, was the first coenzyme clearly defined. Neither fragment showed enzyme activity by itself, but when Theorell recombined them, he obtained the yellow enzyme with its enzymatic activity fully restored.

In 1937, Theorell became director of a research institute at the Karolinska Institutet. He has continued his researches into the nature of enzyme systems.

AARON J. IHDE
University of Wisconsin

THEOREM, thē′ə-rəm, a statement that can be proved by logical deduction from a set of axioms. Once proved, it can be used to prove other theorems to build a system of theorems. The classic presentation of a system of theorems based on axioms is Euclid's Elements. A logically superior foundation for geometrical theorems was provided by the German mathematician David Hilbert in *The Foundations of Geometry* (1899). See also AXIOM; GEOMETRY.

THEOSOPHY, thē-os′ə-fē, is a synthesis of religion, philosophy, and science. It is an attempt to bring together for mutual enrichment the best thinking of the Eastern and Western worlds. It is not a religion, for it has no dogma, creed, or ritual.

Origins. The name "theosophy" was first used in Alexandria in the 3d century A. D., in connection with the teachings of the Greek mysteries concerning God. Based on its Greek derivation, the word refers to the divine wisdom as it unfolds in the human spirit, not as a set of beliefs superimposed upon man. This wisdom is considered to underlie the teachings of all religions. In its present form, the word "Theosophy" came into use in the year 1875, with the founding of the Theosophical Society. However, the concepts of Theosophy have appeared in the philosophic systems of China, India, and Egypt, and in the works of the Gnostics, Neoplatonists, and Cabalists, or medieval Jewish mystics. In particular, Theosophical thought may be found in the speculative writings of the philosophers Plato, Plotinus, Apollonius of Tyana, in such mystics as Jakob Boehme and Paracelsus, as well as in the writings of the medieval mystics.

Theosophical Principles. Theosophy postulates certain basic principles: (1) There exists an "omnipresent, eternal, boundless and immutable principle" from which the visible world arises. (2) Universes come and go, and our universe is the periodical manifestation of an immaterial reality. (3) The universe, with everything in it, is temporary compared with the eternal immutability of the One. (4) Everything in the universe, throughout all its kingdoms, is conscious of its own nature and degree. (5) The universe is not the product of chance, but is worked and guided from within. (6) The whole order of nature gives evidence of purposiveness. (7) Every individual is fundamentally identified with the universal Oversoul and evolves through cycles of reincarnation in accordance with the law of cause and effect called *karma*.

The process of cosmic manifestation is regarded as having two phases. The first is *involution*, during which billions of units of spiritual consciousness, called "monads," emerge from the One undifferentiated Source. They become more and more deeply involved in matter in the mineral, vegetable, and animal kingdoms and, through the limitations and impacts of this condition, finally attain self-consciousness in the human kingdom. The other is *evolution*, during which these now self-conscious units, as humans, gradually unfold the potentials inherent in them from the beginning of the cycle, attain freedom from attachment to matter, and eventually return to the Source from which they came, but with an incalculable increase of consciousness as a result of their aeonic pilgrimage. Theosophy denies that the human spirit can ultimately be lost, because it is intrinsically eternal and indestructible. Through successive reembodiments in physical form, with accompanying emotional, mental, and psychic responses to experience, the spirit attains mastery over its vehicles, and man reaches the expression of his godhood.

Relations to Religion, Science, and Philosophy. Theosophy examines the underlying wisdom of the various religious teachings and sees them as equally important to the whole of mankind's development. It does not seek to convert anyone from the religion he holds, but instead attempts to explain and interpret on a rational basis the inner meanings of the creeds and ceremonies of religion.

In methods of observation and experiment, organization and hypothesis, Theosophy may be considered scientific. It makes no pretense of encompassing the myriad specializations and hypotheses of the advanced sciences. However, the line between some scientific hypotheses and those of Theosophy grows finer and less distinguishable, although the two are expressed in different terms.

In its philosophical aspect, Theosophy postulates a logical explanation of the universe and its laws and of man's origin, evolution, and destiny. It offers reasons for many circumstances and processes left untouched by both the credal religions and the codified sciences. It suggests that matter is the instrument of life, that thought is the creative and molding power, and that experience of both joy and suffering is the means to the growth of character and ability and the consequent attainment of spiritual power and wisdom.

Theosophy maintains that, just as the attainment of perfection is ultimately within the reach of all, there are men who have reached that goal. Among these are the Christ, the Buddha, and other great spiritual teachers and saviors, as well as some who are less well known and who, it is said, continue to work quietly and in relative obscurity for the welfare of mankind.

The Theosophical Society. Since 1875 the concepts of Theosophy have been expounded by the Theosophical Society. The principal founders of the society were Col. Henry S. Olcott, its first president, a Civil War veteran who had a distinguished career in government, agriculture, and law; Mme. Helena P. Blavatsky, a widely traveled Russian noblewoman who became a naturalized American citizen; and William Q. Judge, a New York attorney. Following Colonel Olcott, successive international presidents were Annie Besant, G. S. Arundale, C. Jinarajadasa, and in the 1970's, N. Sri Ram. In 1882 the international headquarters of the society were established at Adyar, Madras, India. By the 1970's there were also national organizations in more than 60 countries. The headquarters of the Theosophical Society in America, with 151 branches in major cities, is at Wheaton, Ill., where there is a Reference and Lending Library. The Society publishes a monthly magazine called *The American Theosophist*.

The Theosophical Society has three objects: (1) to form a nucleus of the Universal Brotherhood of Humanity without distinction of race, creed, sex, caste, or color; (2) to encourage the study of comparative religion, philosophy, and science; (3) to investigate unexplained laws of nature and the powers latent in man. The society's policy is one of complete freedom of individual search and belief.

JOY MILLS
The Theosophical Society in America

Further Reading: Blavatsky, Helena P., *The Secret Doctrine* (Adyar, India 1938); Sri Ram, N., *An Approach to Reality* (Wheaton, Ill., 1968); Winner, Anne Kennedy, *The Basic Ideas of Occult Wisdom* (Wheaton, Ill., 1970).

THERA, thir′ə, southernmost of the Greek Cycladic Islands, is located in the Aegean Sea, 60 miles (96 km) north of Crete. The name is also spelled *Thira*, and the island is sometimes called *Santorin* or *Santorini* after its patron saint, St. Irene.

Crescent-shaped, 12 miles (19 km) long and 3 miles (4.8 km) wide, Thera is the remains of an ancient volcanic crater that lost part of its ring form in a series of earthquakes and eruptions between 1520 and 1420 B. C. Archaeologists have found evidence suggesting that the civilization on Thera was linked to the Minoan culture of Crete. Some have speculated that the catastrophic eruptions that drove the inhabitants of Thera off the island may also have accounted for the sudden disappearance of the Minoan civilization.

The island was settled again, before the 9th century B. C., by the Laconian Dorians. Together with Crete, Thera founded Cyrene in 631 B. C. Thera was important in early Aegean trade.

The island was held by Venice from 1207 until the Turks conquered it in 1537. It became independent of Turkey in 1821 and is now part of the Greek department of the Cyclades. More than 9,000 people live on Thera despite occasional volcanic activity.

Excavations over the years have turned up classical remains and evidence of prehistoric culture of the Bronze Age. In 1900 a German archaeologist dug "ancient Thera" and found an agora, houses, cisterns, barracks, and a temple. Beginning in 1966, Greek archaeologists through systematic digging made further discoveries that suggest connections with early Minoan civilizations. Some speculation identifies the island as the original of Plato's Atlantis.

PHILIP C. GIFFORD, JR.
American Museum of Natural History

THEREMIN, ther'ə-mən, an electronic musical instrument developed by the Russian scientist Léon Thérémin and demonstrated by him during the 1920's. It is a console instrument that has a rod antenna and two oscillator circuits. One circuit is coupled to the antenna, and the second circuit produces a fixed high frequency. Generation of musical tones is controlled by hand movements of the player. As he moves one hand toward or away from the antenna, his body capacitance causes an increase or decrease in the high-frequency output of the first circuit. This output is beat with the fixed frequency output of the second circuit, producing a difference frequency that is an audible tone. This tone is fed through an amplifier and a loudspeaker. Volume is varied by a switch or by movement of the player's other hand over a metal loop at the side of the instrument. The theremin was first made in the United States in 1929.

SOVFOTO

The theremin is played by moving the hand near a rod.

THERESA, SAINT. See Teresa of Avila.

THÉRÈSE OF LISIEUX, tā-rez', lē-zyû, **Saint** (1873–1897), French Carmelite nun, popularly known as the Little Flower of Jesus. The youngest of the nine children of Louis and Zélie Martin, Marie Françoise Thérèse was born at Alençon, France, on Jan. 2, 1873. Her mother died when she was four years old. In 1881 the family moved to Lisieux, and Thérèse attended the Benedictine convent school as a day scholar. At Christmas time in 1886, although she was just short of 14, Thérèse experienced a conversion. Her outlook became that of a spiritually mature person.

The following year Thérèse applied for admission into the convent of the Discalced Carmelites in Lisieux, which her two older sisters, Pauline and Marie, had already entered. She was refused admission because of her age. In 1888, after she had made a pilgrimage to Rome with her father and sister Céline, she was admitted to the convent.

She lived in the convent the rest of her life, practicing and teaching her "little way"—a truly childlike relationship with God and a holy life that, in the words of Pope Pius XI, "did not go beyond the common order of things." She taught this way to novices, of whom she was appointed acting mistress in 1893. Six months before her death, her tubercular condition forced her to retire to the convent's infirmary, where she suffered much physically. Thérèse died in Lisieux on Sept. 30, 1897. She was canonized on May 17, 1925, and became one of the most popular saints throughout the world.

Before her death, Thérèse had asked her sister Pauline (Mother Agnès of Jesus) to edit her memoirs. Published as her autobiography, the book quickly became a best seller. Her feast is celebrated on October 3.

Marion A. Habig, O. F. M.
St. Augustine Friary, Chicago

THERMAL INVERSION. See Inversion.

THERMAL POLLUTION is a form of environmental pollution caused by the release of waste heat into water or air. Electric power plants are a major source of thermal pollution. In these plants, only about one third of the energy in the fuel is converted into electricity, and the remaining energy is released as heat to the local environment—into water pumped to a river, lake, or other waterway or into the air as hot exhaust gases. The entrance of this waste heat into the environment may have serious consequences.

Effects. Heat introduced into water can make the water so hot that no living thing can survive in it. In water above 140° F (60° C) it is very unusual for algae or bacteria to live, and serious problems occur at even much lower temperature levels. Unlike warm-blooded animals, fish and other cold-blooded organisms do not have a regulatory mechanism for maintaining a fixed internal body temperature. Therefore when water temperature changes, the body temperatures of the organisms also change. The resulting thermal stress may be lethal to some species. Factors such as diet, age, previous temperature exposure, weather, season of the year, and chemical composition of the water may change the specific lethal temperature point for fishes. Under certain conditions, for example, brown trout cannot live in water at a temperature above 79° F (26° C). However, some hardy fish, often known as "rough" fish, can survive in even higher temperatures—carp, for example, can live at 95° F (35° C) water temperature.

Even comparatively small temperature increases may have serious results, affecting, for example, reproduction in aquatic organisms. For example, the natural rise in water temperature during the spring causes female oysters and clams to shed their eggs. A similar, but artificially produced, temperature rise at a different time of the year can trigger the release of immature eggs. Excessive temperature can also prevent the normal development of certain eggs. The Oregon Fish Commission has reported that a rise of only 5.4° F (3° C) in the Columbia River could be disastrous to the eggs of the chinook salmon. Increased temperature may also affect hatching time in certain species. For example, herring eggs normally hatch in 47 days at a temperature of 32° F (0.° C). When the water temperature is raised to 58° F (14.5° C) the eggs hatch in 8 days. Such an early hatching often results in smaller adult size and shortened life span.

Small water-temperature increases may increase the level of activity of certain organisms, whereas higher temperatures tend to decrease the level of activity. Lake trout, for example, cruise more rapidly as the temperature nears 61° F (16° C) but then slow down above that temperature. A water temperature of 75° F (24° C) is lethal for them. As the fish's level of activity decreases so does its ability to catch food.

Some effects of raising water temperature are indirect. Generally, a higher temperature increases oxygen consumption by fish and other organisms. At the same time, however, the higher temperature lowers the oxygen-carrying capacity of water. Thus, smaller amounts of oxygen are available just when oxygen need is increasing.

If the temperature of water is already below the temperature that is most favorable for a species, the addition of waste heat could benefit the species, but does not necessarily do so. First, the species, while adjusting to the higher temperature, might lose its resistance to lower temperatures, and if the waste heat flow is suddenly interrupted and the water returns to its previous lower temperature level, the species might suffer greatly.

Possible Long-Range Effects. If the present trends of urban growth and energy use continue, the sum of all sources of thermal pollution could result in other long-range effects on the environment. By the year 2000, thermal pollution in the winter would add an additional 50% to the heat that the sun delivers daily to large parts of the eastern coast of the United States. This increase could cause local climatic changes that could in turn have serious effects on the physical environment of the earth.

Solutions. Several engineering solutions are available to minimize thermal pollution from major industrial sources. One is a cooling pond into which heated wastewater is released before it enters a natural waterway. The cooling pond permits evaporation of some water, carrying heat into the air and thus releasing cooler water into the waterway. The evaporated water might, however, under some conditions, condense, producing fogs where none existed before. In addition, the evaporation from the cooling pond might deprive the waterway of significant amounts of water, which could be serious during summer months when the natural flow in a river is low.

Another possible solution to the problem of thermal pollution is the cooling tower—either wet or dry—which also transfers heat to the air. In both types, heated water is introduced into a tower through which air is blown, and some heat is passed to the air. In wet towers, water and air are in contact, resulting in water loss. In dry towers, a device like a car radiator carries the heated water, and less water is lost.

Several suggestions for the beneficial uses of thermal pollution have been made. Among them is the possible use of heated water under fields to lengthen the growing season for certain crops, under city streets in winter to melt snow, or in cold estuarial areas to increase growth of fish and shellfish. At the moment, these schemes are untested on a large scale. All solutions must consider the general health of the environment as well as energy use patterns, overall population growth, and other factors.

GLENN PAULSON, *The Rockefeller University*

THERMIDOR, thur′mi-dôr, was the 11th month of the Revolutionary Calendar in France. Thermidor ("having to do with heat") extended from July 19 or 20 to August 17 or 18. See FRANCE—*Revolution, Consulate, and Empire;* REVOLUTIONARY CALENDAR.

THERMIONIC EMISSION, thər-mī-on′ik, is the escape of electrons or ions from a heated solid or liquid. The escape of negative electricity from a hot solid was first observed by Thomas Edison in 1883 during experiments with his evacuated carbon-filament lamp. This discovery was used by J. A. Fleming in 1904 to make the first electron tube. Since then, electron emission from hot solids has been particularly useful in radio and television tubes.

When a metal is heated, only some of its electrons acquire velocities high enough to escape to nearby space. Most of the work in escaping involves overcoming an electrostatic image force that tends to pull electrons back into the metal. This image force is reduced by applying a strong electron-accelerating electric field at the surface of the metal, thereby increasing the emission of electrons. This effect, discovered by the German physicist Walter Schottky in 1914, is called the Schottky effect.

Thermionic emission from a refractory metal such as tungsten or tantalum is increased by depositing an atomic layer of an electropositive metal such as cesium, barium, lanthanum, or thorium on its surface. These adsorbed atoms also reduce the electrostatic image force. Useful cathodes for electron devices are made from these composite surfaces by providing a reservoir for replacing electropositive atoms lost by evaporation. The thoriated tungsten cathode, Hull dispenser cathode, Lemmens "L" cathode, and Lafferty lanthanum hexaboride cathode are examples. The most widely used thermionic emitter is the oxide-coated cathode discovered by the German physicist Artur Wehnelt in 1903. It consists of a layer of small crystallites of a solid solution of barium, strontium, and calcium oxides on a nickel base. When heated to 800° C (1,432° F), this cathode typically has a thermionic emission current density of 0.5 ampere per cm^2.

J. M. LAFFERTY
General Electric Company

THERMISTOR, thur′mis-tər, a thermally sensitive resistor that is used in various electric circuits. As the temperature of a thermistor increases, its resistance decreases rapidly. In contrast, as the temperature of a conventional resistor increases, its resistance increases slightly. The change in the temperature of a thermistor may be due to heat developed by current through the thermistor, to a change in the temperature of the air around it, or to both.

Thermistors are molded in the form of disks, rods, wafers, beads, or washers. They are made of various mixtures of oxides of nickel, manganese, cobalt, and other metals. A specific mixture gives the precise variation of the resistance with the temperature that is desired. Thermistors are used to limit the current during warm-up of vacuum tubes in TV receivers, to delay operation of a motor or relay from seconds to minutes after turn-on, and to measure temperature.

MARVIN BIERMAN
RCA Institutes Inc.

THERMITE, thûr′mīt, is a mixture of iron oxide and powdered aluminum used in welding. Thermit is the trade name for the substance, and the process is often called Thermit welding. Thermit welding is the only welding process that depends on a chemical reaction to supply both the heat and the molten metal necessary to weld or repair. Welding with thermite is used primarily for the repairs of large parts that would be difficult to weld by other methods. It is particularly useful in joining square edges of heavy materials, such as tracks, spokes of driving wheels, motor casings, connecting rods, and pipes, and for repair work or fabrication in shipyards, steel mills, and railroad repair shops. One great advantage of this process is that broken parts can usually be welded in place. Almost any kind of steel part and many cast iron parts can be thermite welded.

The thermite mixture consists of approximately one part of finely divided aluminum and three parts of powdered iron oxide. When set off at about 1540° C (2800° F), the aluminum reduces the iron oxide to a pure, superheated, molten iron or steel alloy in an exothermic (heat-releasing) reaction. It also produces an aluminum oxide slag that floats on top. The reaction is:

$$8Al + 3Fe_3O_4 = 9Fe + 4Al_2O_3$$

Once started, the reaction approaches a temperature of 2,760° C (5,000° F) in about 30 seconds.

In practice the parts to be repaired are cleaned and placed in position. A mold is prepared around the parts to hold the work in place and to contain the weld metal. The parts and mold are preheated with a torch to prevent chilling. Alloying elements such as manganese and nickel are added to the thermite to control the quality and properties of the weld metal. This mixture, which is nonexplosive and safe to store, is placed in a refractory lined crucible. The reaction is started by igniting the mixture with a highly flammable "fuse" consisting mainly of barium peroxide powder. Almost immediately the weld metal becomes molten and is tapped into the preheated mold, rapidly fusing the parts and completing the repair. The welds produced are sound and have the strength and toughness of forged steel.

Alvin S. Cohan
Scientific Design Company, Inc.

THERMOCHEMISTRY is the study of heat changes during chemical reactions or changes in state. It is part of the broader discipline of chemical thermodynamics. See Thermodynamics.

The main law of thermochemistry, Hess' law, or the principle of constant heat summation, is a special case of the first law of thermodynamics—the law of conservation of energy. Hess' law says that the total amount of heat generated or absorbed in a chemical process is independent of the intermediate steps and depends only on the starting materials and the final products. For example, carbon can be burned directly to carbon dioxide with the liberation of 94.05 kilocalories (kcal) of heat per mole (the molecular weight of a substance in grams). Or, the carbon can first be converted to carbon monoxide, liberating 26.42 kcal, and the carbon monoxide can then be burned to carbon dioxide, liberating another 67.63 kcal, for a total of 94.05 kcal. The amount of heat given off is the same in both cases. This figure of 94.05 kcal is the *heat of combustion* of carbon.

Hess' law is used to predict heat changes of reactions that are difficult to perform directly. An example is the conversion of graphite, a form of carbon, to diamond, another form of carbon. The heat of combustion of graphite is 94.05 kcal, but that of diamond is only 93.60 kcal. The difference, 0.45 kcal, is called the *heat of reaction* and is the heat that must be added to a mole of graphite to turn it into diamond. Customarily, heats of reaction are given in tables at one temperature, 25° C (77° F). This means that the starting materials and the products are both at 25° C, and the heat of reaction is the amount of heat given off or absorbed between these two points. Heats of reaction at other temperatures can be predicted if the heat capacities of the reactants and products are known.

The *heat of formation* of a compound is the amount of heat absorbed or given off when the compound is formed from its constituent elements. In reactions involving gases the amount of heat given off or absorbed is affected by changes in volume or pressure during the reaction.

Herbert Liebeskind
The Cooper Union

THERMOCLINE, thûr′mō-klīn, a relatively thin layer of water, in a lake or an ocean, in which temperatures drop rapidly from warmer above to much colder below. In the same climate, thermoclines remain very stable, but their thickness and the depth at which they occur vary with the seasons and with latitude. In the ocean there is a deep-lying permanent thermocline caused by the flow of polar waters, and a shallower seasonal one. See also Ocean.

THERMOCOUPLE, thûr′mə-kup-əl, a temperature-measuring device whose operation depends on the Seebeck effect, which was discovered in 1821. A thermocouple is formed by welding together two wires of different materials to form a junction. If this junction is heated, a voltage is developed between the free ends of the wires. This is the Seebeck effect. The temperature of the junction can be determined by measuring this voltage, which usually increases as the temperature of the junction is raised. The thermocouple is handy because it is small, and the temperature can be measured at some distance from the junction by means of long wires. Its disadvantages are that the voltage is fairly small, and corrections have to be made for the temperature of the measuring instrument when precise measurements are made.

Typical couples are made of platinum and a platinum-rhodium alloy, copper and constantan, chromel and alumel, or iron and constantan. The platinum and platinum-rhodium thermocouple is more accurate than the others, but it is more expensive. Also, it develops a voltage of only about 5 microvolts per degree F, whereas the other couples develop a voltage of 20 to 25 microvolts per degree F. The typical couples measure temperatures within the range from about −330° F to 3200° F (−200° C to 1800° C). Other couples, such as one made of silicon carbide and graphite, sometimes have been used for measuring higher temperatures. A *thermopile* is used for measuring very small temperature differences. It consists of a number of thermocouples connected in series. See also Thermoelectricity.

Roland W. Ure, Jr., *University of Utah*

THERMODYNAMICS, thûr-mə-dī-nam'iks, is the study of energy and its transformation. Most thermodynamic studies are primarily concerned with two forms of energy—heat and work. Three unifying ideas form the core of thermodynamic theory: (1) All matter has energy, and energy is never created nor destroyed; (2) events tend to move predictably toward a state of equilibrium; and (3) matter in a state, or condition, of equilibrium can be described by specifying a limited number of observable characteristics.

Thermodynamics is called a macroscopic science because it is not concerned with the individual molecules, atoms, or electrons that make up all matter. Its truth, therefore, does not rest on present or future theories that describe the microscopic state of matter. The quantities utilized by thermodynamicists can either be measured or calculated from observations made in the laboratory on pieces of matter of reasonable size.

The principles and methods of thermodynamics are used by engineers in the design of heat engines, furnaces, refrigeration equipment, and petroleum, chemical, and plastics manufacturing equipment. Heat engines are devices that transform heat into work. They include steam power plants, which produce most of the world's electricity; internal-combustion engines, which power most of the world's automobiles; and gas turbine engines, which power most of the world's passenger aircraft.

The science of physical chemistry consists largely of the applications of thermodynamic principles to chemistry. The studies made by physical chemists do not result in the design of equipment; instead, physical chemists attempt to correlate the properties of matter from laboratory observations.

KEY CONCEPTS AND DEFINITIONS

A number of familiar words and ideas take on special meanings when used in thermodynamics. This is because the successful application of thermodynamic principles depends on a set of precise definitions for its important terms.

The region or mass of matter that is to be studied thermodynamically is frequently called a *system.* In thermodynamic analysis, the system is commonly separated from the part of the world that is not to be studied by an imaginary envelope called a *boundary.* Everything outside the system is generally called the *surroundings.*

The *state,* or condition, of a system is described by specifying its thermodynamic coordinates, which are usually called the *properties.* There are two kinds of thermodynamic properties—intensive and extensive. An intensive property, such as temperature or pressure, has a value that is independent of the quantity of matter enclosed by the boundary of the system. An extensive property, such as volume, has a value that is directly proportional to the mass of the system.

Experiments have revealed that only a certain minimum number of properties of a substance can be given arbitrary values. For example, suppose a constant mass of gas is in a container, and the pressure, temperature, and volume of the gas can easily be measured. If the container is rigid so that the volume is fixed and the gas is heated to an arbitrarily selected temperature, then it is impossible to vary the pressure at all. Once the volume and temperature are fixed, the value of the pressure is fixed; that is, of the three thermodynamic coordinates—pressure, temperature, and volume—only two are independent. This implies that there is an equation that interrelates these three thermodynamic coordinates. Such an equation is called an *equation of state.* Every thermodynamic system has its own equation of state, although in some cases the relationship between the three coordinates may be so complicated that it cannot be expressed in terms of simple mathematical functions.

Because thermodynamics is based on general laws of nature, it is incapable of expressing the behavior of one material as distinct from another. An equation of state therefore is not a theoretical deduction from thermodynamics but usually an experimental addition to thermodynamics. The equation expresses the result of experiments in which the thermodynamic properties of a system were measured and therefore is only as accurate as the experiments that led to its formulation.

When a thermodynamic system changes from one state to another it is said to execute a *process.* In order for a nonchemically reacting system to change its state it must interact with its surroundings; it may do so only by exchanging heat or work.

Heat and Work. The intuitive notion of work has been inadequate for use as a definition in thermodynamics. A more useful definition is that *work* is energy transferred, without transfer of mass, across the boundary of a system during any process in which the only effect external to the system could be reduced to the raising of a weight. In this definition work is defined only with reference to the boundary of a system. If a different boundary is drawn, the work quantity calculated frequently will be different. Also, it is not necessary that a weight actually be raised in any process for work to be done by the system; it is only necessary to imagine that the raising of a weight could be the only effect external to the system (see Fig. 1).

Heat, the other way for a system to exchange energy with its surroundings, is defined as energy transferred, without transfer of mass, across the boundary of a system because of a temperature difference between the system and the surroundings. In this definition, heat is defined only with reference to the boundary of a system.

Fig. 1. Does a battery do work when it is used to power a light bulb? The light bulb could be replaced by a motor and pulley system that does work in raising a weight, so the answer is "yes."

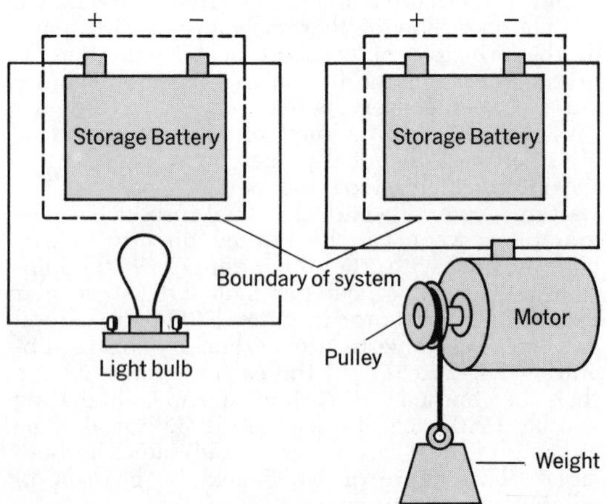

Heat and work are thermodynamic quantities that have an entirely different nature from properties like energy, pressure, or temperature. It is possible to speak of the energy or temperature of a system, but it is incorrect to speak of heat or work stored within a system. Since heat and work are forms of energy in transit across the boundary of a system, they cannot be stored within it. Heat and work are called *path functions.* Path functions are sometimes considered to be analogous to rain falling in a lake. Once the rain has fallen into the lake, it is no longer thought of as rain; it is simply water in the lake. Once heat or work has been transferred to a system, it is no longer heat or work but simply energy stored within the system.

Equilibrium. A system is said to be in equilibrium when all of its properties, such as temperature, pressure, and density, are the same throughout the system. Consider a quantity of still air in a storage tank. The tank and the air in it are in equilibrium. Now imagine that a torch is applied to one end of the tank, raising that end to a temperature much higher than that at the other end. The air in the tank now is not in equilibrium. Equilibrium is important because the properties of a system are related in a predictable way by an equation of state only when the system is in equilibrium.

Thermodynamic analyses are normally applied to processes that consist of a series of equilibrium states. In these types of processes the states of the system can be defined by virtue of their properties at each step in the series.

Reversible and Irreversible Processes. Processes made up of a series of equilibrium states are called reversible processes. A reversible process is one that can be carried out without wasting any energy in overcoming friction, electrical resistance, or any other dissipative force. It is an ideal process against which all real processes can be measured. Such a process can be thought of in the following way. If a reversible process could be done and then undone, there would be no way to discern that it ever took place.

Any process that is not reversible is said to be irreversible. All processes encountered in nature are irreversible. Thermodynamics can be applied to such processes by finding one or more reversible processes that closely follow the path believed to be followed by the irreversible process and then using correction factors in calculations to take into account the irreversible nature of the real process.

THE ZEROTH LAW OF THERMODYNAMICS

Man's first instrument for sensing hot and cold was his hand. When we touch an object, our *temperature sense* attributes a property called temperature to the object. About 1600, several scientific workers realized that man's temperature sense was inadequate. They hit on the idea of measuring temperature by means of a device somewhat similar to our ordinary weather thermometer. Their instruments were derived from an experiment by Philo of Byzantium in the 2d century B. C. Using a hollow glass globe sealed to one end of a glass tube dipped into water, he showed that air expands when heated and contracts when cooled. Galileo is usually credited with the invention of the first instrument that could be called a thermometer. Several other scientists, including Santorio Santorio (Italian), Robert Fludd (English), and Cornelis Drebbel (Dutch), worked independently on similar devices about the same time (1600).

Inventors of thermometers were trying to devise an instrument that would measure a quantity then undefined. A thermometer would indicate the same temperature for a block of wood and a block of copper even though these two blocks seemed to be of quite different coldness by the sense of touch. One concept doubtless was involved—namely, that all bodies exposed to the same cold atmosphere would ultimately attain a uniform degree of coldness, despite contrary evidence of the senses. A second concept played its part, namely, that the temperature caused some influence to pass from one body to another of unequal hotness or coldness.

The notion of temperature was finally put on firm thermodynamic grounds by the British physicist James Clerk Maxwell, who in 1871 defined the temperature of a body as "... its thermal state considered with reference to its power of communicating heat to other bodies." Expanding on this definition, he asserted that "if when two bodies are placed in thermal communication, one of the bodies loses heat, and the other gains heat, that body which gives out heat is said to have a higher temperature than that which receives heat from it." He then proceeded to state a law, which subsequently was named the zeroth law of thermodynamics by the British mathematician Ralph H. Fowler. It is commonly stated in this manner: *Two bodies, each in thermal equilibrium with a third body, are in thermal equilibrium with each other.* This law clearly turns the thermometer into a useful instrument by eliminating the need for bringing into physical contact each pair of systems whose temperatures are to be compared.

THE FIRST LAW OF THERMODYNAMICS

Pioneers.—*Joseph Black.* At the University of Glasgow in 1770, Joseph Black mixed equal masses of various pairs of liquids of different initial temperature and found that the initial temperatures of the two liquids often changed by radically different amounts. He also found that a single-phase body, such as water, would show a large temperature change when heated, whereas a two-phase body, such as a mixture of ice and water or water and steam, would show no change in temperature. He concluded that temperature was not necessarily conserved or even transmitted.

Black established the science of calorimetry, and he demonstrated in his experiments that a quantity other than temperature was conserved. This quantity was called *heat,* or *caloric.* Black's contemporaries used his work to formulate a general conservation principle known as the "caloric theory." The caloric theory had a troubled existence for about 75 years, but it never attained the dignity of a science. However, it proved to be very useful in calorimetry, and vestiges of it are found in contemporary scientific literature.

Benjamin Thompson. Caloric was thought to be an all-pervading subtle fluid that could neither be created nor destroyed. The caloric theory was not discredited until Benjamin Thompson applied his considerable talents as a scientist and inventor to the subject of caloric near the end of the 18th century. Thompson, also known as Count Rumford, showed that heat is produced by the mechanical rubbing action of a dull boring tool on a cannon, and he presented the results of his experiments to the Royal Society in 1798. See THOMPSON, BENJAMIN.

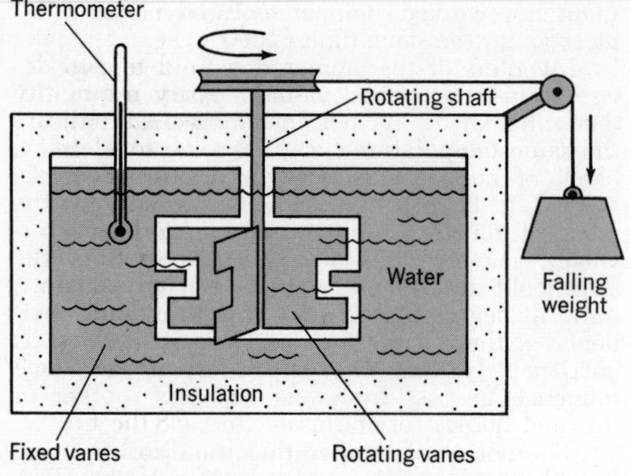

Fig. 2. Joule measured the mechanical equivalent of heat by churning water in an insulated container and noting the increase in the temperature of the water. The water is churned by a set of rotating vanes, which are set in motion by a falling weight.

Discoverers. Although Rumford dispatched the caloric theory he did not offer any comprehensive hypothesis about work, heat, and energy in its place. In the years between Rumford's experiments and 1850, a number of workers were on the verge of recognizing and verifying the grand conception of the conservation of energy that is now called the first law of *thermodynamics.* Most of the credit for discovery and confirmation of the first law as a generalization of the conservation of energy goes to Hermann von Helmholtz and Julius Robert Mayer, both German physicians, and James Prescott Joule, son of a prosperous English brewer.

Julius Mayer. In 1840, Mayer sailed to Java as a ship's doctor. While bleeding patients in the tropics, he observed that their blood was a much brighter red than that taken from veins of patients in Germany. Since it was known that the red color of venous blood was due to oxygen that had not been used for oxidation of body fuel, Mayer readily deduced that venous blood in Java was redder than venous blood in Germany because less combustion is required to supply the needed body heat in Java than in Germany. Mayer then concluded that the heat developed by oxidation of body fuel should be balanced against the body's loss of heat to the surroundings and the work the body performs. In effect, Mayer postulated that heat and work are equivalent, being merely two different manifestations of a general property called *energy.* Because he had no financial resources or laboratory equipment, he relied on laboratory data collected by the French chemist Joseph Louis Gay-Lussac in 1807, which he was able to interpret correctly by his understanding of the conservation of energy. Mayer, however, failed in getting his work accepted by the scientific community.

James Joule. Joule became interested in the possible equivalence between heat and work when he began building battery-driven electric motors. He soon realized that work could be turned into heat more simply by using mechanical equipment instead of the electrical equipment he had been working with. His early work attracted no attention, and so he decided he needed more accurate experiments. In 1845 he built a vessel containing water stirred by a set of revolving vanes that intermeshed with a set of fixed vanes (see Fig. 2). The revolving vanes were operated by a system of descending weights so that the work input could be determined precisely.

The temperature rises that were produced in the water were generally less than one degree, so Joule had to test and standardize his own thermometers. The result was that Joule's temperature measurements were the most accurate that had been made up to that time. In the end he equated the work done by the falling weights with the amount of heat that would be required to produce the same effect in the water. Joule's best value for the mechanical equivalent of heat was 772.5 foot-pounds equal to one British thermal unit (Btu) of heat. The accepted value now is 778.26 foot-pounds, which differs by less than 1% from Joule's value.

Joule came up with two conclusions: (1) heat and work are equivalent, being different forms or manifestations of energy; and (2) the numerical factors governing conversion of work to heat were accurately known from his water-stirring experiments. Most British scientists, however, were reluctant to accept these conclusions.

Hermann von Helmholtz. In 1847, Helmholtz wrote a paper in which he set forth and justified the general law of conservation of energy in more convincing and general terms than had either Mayer or Joule. He also had difficulty in getting it published. Helmholtz approached the problem of establishing the conservation of energy in a unique way. Today, we know that an effort to build a perpetual-motion machine of the first kind—a machine that attempts to create energy—is fruitless because it is contrary to the law of conservation of energy (see Fig. 3).

Helmholtz reversed this reasoning, taking as his fundamental axiom the impossibility of perpetual motion machines. Although he could not

Fig. 3. An overbalanced wheel is a perpetual motion machine of the first kind. Inventors of such machines incorrectly believed that the amount of work obtained from the falling weights is greater than the amount of work that is done in raising them.

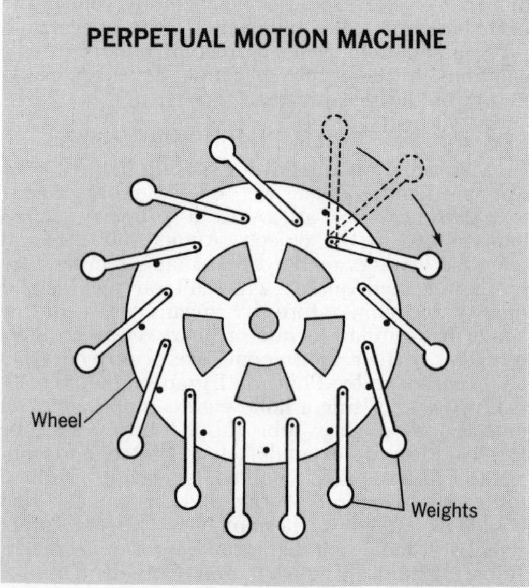

prove this axiom, he pointed out that no one had ever built a perpetual-motion machine. He then showed that the denial of perpetual-motion machines required that energy be conserved. He also showed that heat (small-scale motion) and work (large-scale motion) must both be considered as energy, and it is the total that is conserved rather than heat or work separately. Helmholtz then proceeded to show that the experiments of Joule were in general agreement with the results of calculations like those made by Mayer.

Synthesizer.—*Rudolf Clausius.* In 1850 the German physicist Clausius succeeded in combining the work of Mayer, Joule, and Helmholtz on conservation of energy with the earlier work of the French scientist Nicolas Léonard Sadi Carnot and the French engineer Benoit P. E. Clapeyron on the second law. Clausius did so in both a useful and convincing fashion, and he also originated much of the terminology in use today.

Statement of the First Law. The first law of thermodynamics can be stated concisely as follows: *Energy can be changed from one form to another, but it is neither created nor destroyed.* This statement may be expanded to say that the energy change undergone by a system is equal to the energy gained in the form of heat minus the energy lost as a result of work done on the surroundings. This statement is written symbolically as

$$E_f - E_i = Q - W, \qquad (1)$$

where E_f is the final energy of the system, E_i is the initial energy of the system, Q is the heat absorbed by the system, and W is the work done on the surroundings by the system.

Forms of Stored Energy. Energy can be stored in a system in a number of ways. The most common forms are potential energy, kinetic energy, and internal energy. *Potential energy* is stored in a body by virtue of its position in a gravitational field. If one carries a mass, such as a package, to an upper story in a building, one has increased the potential energy stored in that mass. *Kinetic energy* is stored in a body by virtue of its motion. A body moving at a velocity of 20 feet (6 meters) per second has less kinetic energy stored in it than a body moving with a velocity of 40 feet (12 meters) per second. In fact, the high-speed body has four times as much energy stored in it as the low-speed body because the kinetic energy depends on the square of the speed.

Imagine a container of water at rest. The container is insulated so that no heat transfer can take place between the water and the surroundings. Suppose the water is stirred by a paddle wheel and allowed to come to rest again. Since the elevation and velocity of the container are not changing, the potential and kinetic energy of the water do not change. But the *internal energy* of the water must have increased as a consequence of the work done on the water by the stirring process. This increase in the total internal energy of the system results in an increase in the kinetic energy of the molecules of the substance that compose the system and is usually evidenced by an increase in the temperature of the system. Chemical energy may also be stored in a system, such as a battery. A freshly charged battery obviously has greater energy stored in it than a discharged battery.

Stored Energy in a Working Fluid. In the last half of the 19th century rapid advances were made in the application of thermodynamic principles to real machines, especially heat engines. A heat engine forces a working fluid to execute a number of processes that ultimately return the working fluid to its original state. Any device that operates in this way is said to be following a cycle. Since the fluid is always returned to its original condition, it is impossible for any change to occur in the stored energy in the working fluid.

Clausius recognized this point by noting that for a cycle, $E_f = E_i$, and therefore there must be a clear proportionality between heat and work (see Equation 1). In 1851 the British scientist William Thomson (later Lord Kelvin) also emphasized the importance of this point.

Contributors.—*Henri Poincaré.* In 1908 the French physicist Poincaré used a definition and a statement of the first law to deduce the existence of a property called energy. The Poincaré method makes use of the term "heat" before stating the second law, which many thermodynamicists believe is required for a general definition of heat.

Constantin Carathéodory. In 1909, Carathéodory, a German mathematician, presented a structure of thermodynamics different from that of Poincaré but equally complete and somewhat more rigorous. It was based on the concepts of work and the adiabatic wall—a wall of perfect insulation that does not permit heat transfer. Carathéodory's treatment of the first and second laws is done without mentioning the concept of heat, but his statement of the first law, although perfectly rigorous, is restricted to simple systems.

Generalization of the First Law. The first law has now been generalized so that it may be applied to almost any type of system. It is used routinely to analyze systems that have mass crossing the boundary, to analyze systems that might be storing electrical and magnetic energy, and even to analyze systems that might be moving so rapidly that they would be subject to relativistic effects.

THE SECOND LAW OF THERMODYNAMICS

That events in the physical world will proceed spontaneously in a unique direction is the major idea on which the second law of thermodynamics rests. There are several experimental observations on which various statements of the second law have been based. One is that heat always flows spontaneously from a high-temperature body to a low-temperature one. A second observation is that two gases will mix uniformly when placed in an isolated chamber but will not separate spontaneously once mixed. (Similarly, two sets of marbles of different colors will mix thoroughly when placed in a box and shaken, but subsequent shakings will not separate them by color.) A third observation is that a battery may discharge a certain amount of energy into a resistor and thus heat it, but that same energy in the form of heat can not be added to the resistor from some external source and thereby charge the battery.

Three questions arise: why does not heat flow spontaneously from a low-temperature body to a high-temperature one; why do not gases separate spontaneously; why does not heat applied to a resistor charge a battery connected to it? Such processes do not occur because a system does not spontaneously move away from a state of equilibrium or maximum probability. The second law of thermodynamics says that such processes do not occur without external effort. Heat can be made to flow from a low-temperature body to a high-

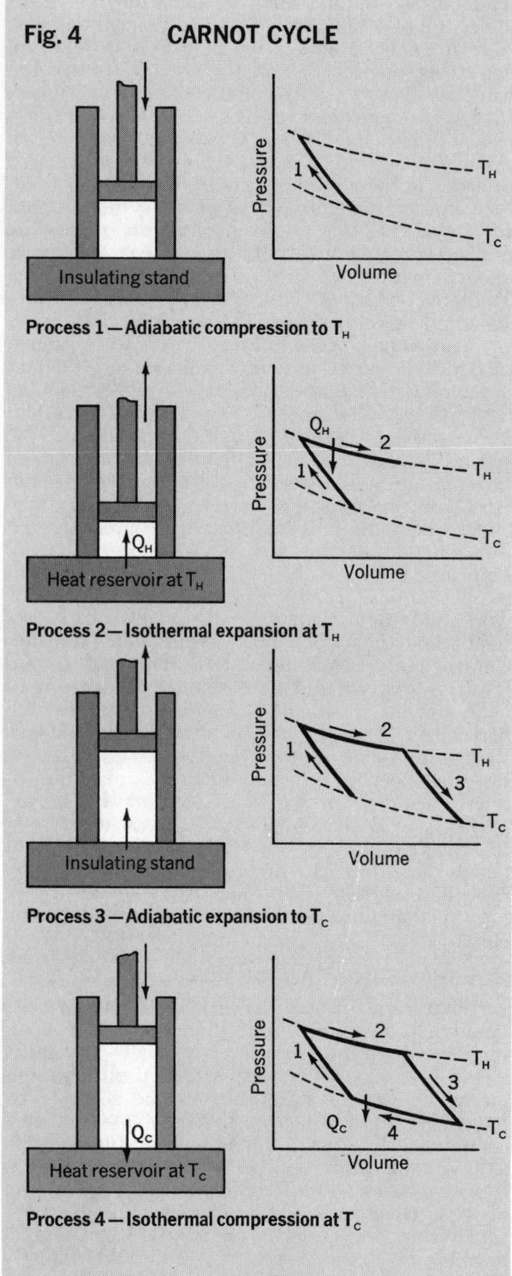

Fig. 4 CARNOT CYCLE

temperature body, but work must be done, as in a refrigerator. Gases can be separated, but work must be done on them. Batteries can be charged by using energy in the form of heat, but the heat must first be turned into electricity (with some unavoidable losses) by means of a thermally powered generator.

Discoverer.—*Sadi Carnot.* The idea that processes left to themselves would always go in one direction but not in the other was first hinted at by Carnot in 1824 in a book entitled *Reflections on the Motive Power of Fire and on the Proper Machines for Developing this Power* (*Réflexions sur la puissance motrice du feu et sur les machines propres à développer cette puissance*).

In this book Carnot introduced the concept of a cycle, set forth the notion of a reversible process that can be carried out without any kind of dissipation, and stated a new principle concerning the maximum work obtainable from a heat engine.

This principle was the first statement of the second law of thermodynamics. One of the ways he stated it was as follows: "The motive power of heat is independent of the agents employed to realize it; its quantity is fixed solely by the temperature of the bodies between which is effected, finally, the transfer of caloric."

It is ironic that Carnot discovered the second law before the first law had been established. The consequences of this situation had considerable impact on the development of thermodynamics. Carnot explained the production of work in his cyclic engine by an analogy. A water wheel depends on the fall of water from a higher to a lower level. Similarly, a heat engine depends on the flow of heat from a higher to a lower temperature region. He explained (incorrectly) that a certain quantity of heat flowed into his engine at a high temperature, and the same quantity flowed out at a low temperature. This explanation was consistent with the caloric theory, which required that the net heat interaction of the cycle be zero. Since Carnot had no other theory of heat to use, he accepted and used this misconception.

The cycle that Carnot introduced in 1824 has special significance in thermodynamics, even though no engine has ever been built that follows such a cycle. His cycle consists of four reversible (ideal) processes that are assumed to take place without any friction (see Fig. 4). Ideal engines that follow the Carnot cycle always absorb heat from a high-temperature reservoir and reject heat to a low-temperature reservoir. Carnot cycles have been imagined for engines that use gases, elastic solids, and even electric cells.

Consolidators.—*Kelvin and Clausius.* Kelvin knew and respected the work of Joule and Carnot, but in 1848 he found that he could not reconcile Carnot's water-wheel analogy with Joule's concept of the convertibility of heat and work. Two years later Clausius picked out what was relevant in their work. After reviewing the questions posed by Kelvin, he suggested that the answer lay in the kinetic (or motion) theory of heat. He pointed out that the first law could be entirely reconciled with Carnot's theory by rejecting Carnot's statement that caloric is conserved. Clausius' work crystallized the whole scheme for Kelvin. Within a year he wrote a paper, in which he attributed the first law to Joule and the second law to Carnot and Clausius.

Statement of the Second Law. One of the most widely quoted forms of the second law is the Kelvin-Planck statement: *It is impossible to construct a device that operates in a cycle and produces no other effect than the production of work and exchange of heat with a single reservoir.* This statement can be applied in a number of ways, but one of the most important was its use by Kelvin to devise a scale of absolute temperature.

Engine Efficiency. In arriving at this scale of absolute temperature, we first consider the efficiencies of two reversible (ideal) heat engines designated as engine A and engine B. The efficiency, η, of any heat engine is generally defined as

$$\eta = \frac{\text{useful work out}}{\text{heat added to engine}}.$$

Engines A and B are assumed to be obtaining the same amount of energy as heat, Q_H, from a high-temperature reservoir at T_H and rejecting energy as heat to a low-temperature reservoir at T_C. If engine A were more efficient than engine B, then engine A could drive engine B as a refrigerator. Such a combination of the two engines would result in a device capable of extracting heat from one reservoir and turning it completely into work. However, such a device would violate the Kelvin-Planck statement of the second law. Thus, we conclude that the assumption that engine A has a greater efficiency than engine B must be false. It follows that *all reversible engines operating between the same temperature limits have the same efficiency.* This efficiency may be written as

$$\eta = W/Q_H = (Q_H - Q_C)/Q_H = 1 - Q_C/Q_H. \quad (2)$$

In this statement of the efficiency, the first law has been used to evaluate the work. Since heat engines are assumed to be cyclical devices, the useful work out is equal to the net heat supplied. Since the efficiency is the same for all reversible engines operating between the same temperature limits, the ratio of heat rejected to heat absorbed, Q_C/Q_H, must be a function only of the temperatures of the two reservoirs:

$$Q_C/Q_H = \text{some function of } T_H \text{ and } T_C.$$

Kelvin suggested a very simple function:

$$Q_C/Q_H = T_C/T_H. \quad (3)$$

By using Equations (2) and (3), we find that the efficiency of any reversible heat engine operating between any two constant-temperature heat reservoirs also can be expressed as

$$\eta = 1 - T_C/T_H. \quad (4)$$

Absolute Temperature Scale. Kelvin made use of Equation (3) to define an absolute thermodynamic temperature scale. The absolute temperature scale that uses the Celsius degree was named in honor of Kelvin for this suggestion. In order to complete the derivation of the Kelvin scale, the triple point of water (that temperature and pressure where water, ice, and steam coexist in equilibrium) is arbitrarily defined to be at 273.16 Celsius degrees above absolute zero. *Two temperatures on the Kelvin scale of temperature are to each other as the absolute values of the heats absorbed and rejected by a Carnot engine operating between reservoirs at these temperatures.* The preceding derivation of the Kelvin temperature scale makes no assumption on the peculiar characteristics of any particular substance, which is what makes the scale so universal.

Consequences of the Second Law. The device made from engines A and B continuously turns energy from a low-temperature reservoir into work, and thus it is a perpetual-motion machine of the second kind. If such a device could operate, it could extract energy at no cost from seawater or atmospheric air and produce work. Such devices, although in accord with the first law, violate the second law and are impossible to construct. The second law requires all heat engines, whether they be steam power plants, automobile engines, or jet aircraft engines, to throw away as heat a part of the energy released in them.

Entropy. Scientists have found it both necessary and convenient to express themselves quantitatively when discussing heat. To do so adequately, at least two numbers must be used: one to measure the quantity of energy and the other to measure the quantity of disorder. The calorie and Btu have proved suitable for measuring the quantity of energy. The quantity of disorder is measured in terms of a property called *entropy.*

The idea of entropy is bound inextricably with all our theoretical ideas about heat and certain other phenomena. One way of defining entropy is in terms of the number of states that are possible in a system in a given situation. Entropy thus may be viewed as the number of independent degrees of freedom that a system has. A high-entropy system is free to be in many different states.

Examination of tabulated entropy values reveals that entropy is closely related to hardness. In fact, hard abrasive materials, such as diamond or silicon carbide, have small entropies because the individual atoms are bound together in 3-dimensional lattices by chemical bonds that severely limit thermal motion of the atoms. Soft substances, such as gases at room temperature, have large entropies because their molecules shoot about in every direction with a wide variety of speeds.

A change in the entropy of a system can be calculated by a number of methods. For many systems of interest to scientists and engineers, the change in entropy may be calculated from the system's heat transfer and temperature. In some cases, it is more convenient to calculate a system's change in entropy from other measurable properties. For many different kinds of substances, entropy values are tabulated as a function of pressure and temperature.

Principle of Increase. In every case it has been observed that the sum of the change of entropy of the system plus the change of entropy of the surroundings is at least zero or greater. This statement is sometimes called the *principle of increase.* The system plus the surroundings constitute the universe, and thus thermodynamicists conclude that the entropy of the universe is always increasing. This fact is sometimes regarded as a mathematical formulation of the second law.

The second law provides an answer to a question that is not within the scope of the first law—namely, in what direction does a process take place? The answer is that a process always takes place in a direction such as to cause an increase in the entropy of the universe.

THE THIRD LAW OF THERMODYNAMICS

In 1701, the French physicist Guillaume Amontons discovered that the thermal expansion of air is surprisingly uniform. He noted that if a fixed volume of air at any initial pressure is heated from room temperature to the boiling point of water, the pressure in every case will increase by about one third. He then deduced that for equal changes in temperature, the pressure of a constant volume of gas will be increased or decreased by a constant fraction of the pressure at an arbitrary point. After studying his data for some time he made a very radical suggestion. He proposed that if he kept lowering the temperature of the fixed volume of gas in his apparatus, he would eventually reach a point where the air would exert no pressure at all. In fact, he deduced that there must be an absolute zero of temperature. His contemporaries were skeptical of his conclusions, and his suggestion of an absolute thermometric scale lay dormant until the middle of the 19th century, when Lord Kelvin and Clausius set forth theories that pointed to the existence of absolute zero.

Statement of the Third Law. In the analysis of many chemical reactions, it is necessary to fix a reference state for the entropy. Walter H. Nernst, a German physical chemist, gave some attention to the problem of selecting suitable reference states. In 1906 he proposed what is now called the Nernst heat theorem, which can be regarded as the immediate forerunner of the third law. The German physicist Max Planck also worked on the problem of reference states and arrived at his statement of the third law in 1911. Although there have been a number of other statements of the third law since then, perhaps one of the least ambiguous is: *The entropy change associated with any isothermal, reversible process approaches zero as the temperature approaches zero.* Other statements of the third law indicate the impossibility of ever reducing any system's temperature to absolute zero.

The importance of the third law is now clear. It has been of immense usefulness in low-temperature research and has provided a keystone for the prediction of chemical equilibrium constants and therefore the direction of chemical reactions.

THERMODYNAMIC FUNCTIONS

Thermodynamicists use a large number of properties in their work, including temperature, pressure, specific volume, internal energy, entropy, and many others. One important question that heretofore has not been raised is which of the numerous thermodynamic properties can be experimentally measured? There are no such things as internal energy meters or entropy meters. In fact, there are only four thermodynamic properties that can be directly measured in the laboratory: pressure, temperature, volume, and mass.

This leads to a second question, namely, can values of the thermodynamic properties that cannot be measured be determined from experimental data on those properties that can be measured? The answer to this question is yes. It is possible to develop mathematical expressions called *thermodynamic functions* that interrelate the measurable and nonmeasurable properties. Then, by using experimentally determined values for the measurable properties, values for the nonmeasurable properties can be computed. Maxwell recognized the possibility of doing this, and he formulated the now well-known Maxwell relations. His equations show how changes in the pressure, temperature, and volume are related to changes in entropy in a system whose state is completely determined by its pressure, temperature, and volume.

The techniques used by Maxwell depend to a great extent on differential and integral calculus and are beyond the scope of this article. Most of the references listed in the bibliography give descriptions on the development of the Maxwell relations and other thermodynamic functions.

STATISTICAL THERMODYNAMICS

Even though classical thermodynamics deals with quantities, such as work and heat, that are directly measurable in an experiment, it fails to allay the suspicion that the observable behavior of matter basically stems from its molecular structure. The term *statistical thermodynamics* has been applied to the combination of classical thermodynamics with detailed molecular theory. The general equations of statistical thermodynamics were largely developed by Maxwell; Ludwig Boltzmann, an Austrian physicist; and Josiah Willard Gibbs, an American mathematical physicist.

Gibbs contributed extensively to many different areas of science. His greatest contribution is generally considered to be his discovery and exposition (1876–1878) of the chemical potential, a quantity that is the principal link between thermodynamics and physical chemistry. In addition, Gibbs published his *Elementary Principles of Statistical Mechanics* (1902), which is recognized as one of the cornerstones of statistical thermodynamics.

Statistical thermodynamics relies on mathematical methods, but the information it provides is always given in terms of quantities observable in a laboratory experiment. More than this, however, it affords a deeper understanding of the reasons for the laws of thermodynamics and the relationships between them. The contribution of statistical thermodynamics even extends well beyond the microscopic understanding of the laws of classical thermodynamics. Albert Einstein, the American chemists Peter Debye and William Giaque, and others made use of information provided by statistical thermodynamics to calculate thermodynamic properties of substances from knowledge of the properties of their constituent atoms and molecules.

IRREVERSIBLE THERMODYNAMICS

Much of the work now being done in thermodynamics is in an area called *nonequilibrium thermodynamics* or *irreversible thermodynamics.* The first term is appropriate because this field involves the study of systems that are not in equilibrium—the systems have temperature, pressure, or density differences across them. The second term is appropriate also because the unbalanced forces on a system cause irreversible processes to take place.

The basic principles of irreversible thermodynamics are the same as those of equilibrium thermodynamics: energy is conserved, and entropy does not decrease. However, one must further assume that these laws can be applied locally to every element of a system, and that the system is not too far displaced from equilibrium. Lars Onsager, a Norwegian-American chemist, has been a pioneer worker in this field. In 1968, he received the Nobel Prize in chemistry for his contributions to the field of irreversible thermodynamics.

STANLEY W. ANGRIST
Carnegie-Mellon University

Bibliography

Angrist, Stanley W., and Hepler, Loren G., *Order and Chaos* (New York 1967).
Callen, Herbert B., *Thermodynamics* (New York 1960).
Fay, James A., *Molecular Thermodynamics* (Reading, Mass., 1965).
Hatsopoulos, George N., and Keenan, Joseph H., *Principles of General Thermodynamics* (New York 1965).
Jones, James B., and Hawkins, George A., *Engineering Thermodynamics* (New York 1960).
Lewis, Gilbert N., and Randall, Merle, *Thermodynamics,* 2d ed. rev. by Kenneth S. Pitzer and Leo Brewer (New York 1961).
Sandfort, John F., *Heat Engines: Thermodynamics in Theory and Practice* (Garden City, N. Y., 1962).
Van Ness, Hendrick C., *Understanding Thermodynamics* (New York 1969).
Zemansky, Mark W., and Van Ness, H. C., *Engineering Thermodynamics* (New York 1966).

THERMOELECTRICITY, thûr-mō-i-lek-tris'ə-tē, is the science of the interactions of temperature differences and electric voltages in solid or liquid materials. In particular, it is concerned with the direct conversion of heat into electricity and the direct conversion of electricity into heat.

The three major thermoelectric effects are the Seebeck, Peltier, and Thomson effects. These effects have significant applications in science and engineering, particularly for measuring temperature, for heating and cooling systems, and for generating electricity from heat.

Seebeck Effect. If one end of a conductor is heated so that it is hotter than the other end, there is a tendency for an electric current to flow along the conductor. This is called the *Seebeck effect*. In order to observe the current flow or the electric voltage produced by the Seebeck effect, it is necessary to have a circuit composed of two different materials, *a* and *b*, as shown in Fig. 1. The temperature of the region around each junction is assumed to be uniform and at temperatures T_1, T_2, and T_r.

When the materials *a* and *b* are connected as shown and the temperatures T_1 and T_2 are different, a voltage V is observed. This is called the *Seebeck voltage*. For small temperature differences, the voltage is proportional to the temperature difference—that is, $V = \alpha\ (T_2 - T_1)$, where α is the Seebeck coefficient of the couple *a* and *b*.

The Seebeck voltage depends on the temperatures T_1 and T_2 at the two *a–b* junctions and on the two particular conducting materials that are used. The voltage does not change if the temperature T_r changes, nor does the voltage depend on the dimensions of the conductors *a* and *b*.

Historical Background. Thomas Johann Seebeck discovered the Seebeck effect in 1821, just one year after Hans Christian Oersted reported that a magnetic needle is deflected by a flow of electric current. Seebeck reported that when one bimetal junction in a circuit made of two different conductors was heated, a magnetic needle near the circuit was deflected. Seebeck believed that the deflection of the magnetic needle was due to the flow of heat through the conductor. He did not realize that an electric current was being produced and that it actually caused the deflection of the needle.

Peltier Effect. If an electric current is passed through a conductor, there is a tendency for one end of the conductor to become cold and for the other end to become hot. This is known as the *Peltier effect*. In order to observe the cooling or heating produced by the Peltier effect, it is necessary to have a conducting path composed of two different materials. When an electric current is passed in one direction through a junction of two different conductors *a* and *b*, heat will be absorbed at a rate that is proportional to the current. If the direction of current flow is reversed, heat will be given off instead of being absorbed (see Fig. 2). The Peltier heat is absorbed or given off only in the vicinity of a junction between two different conductors. The Peltier heat is given by $P_p = \Pi_{ab}J_{ab}$, where P_p is the rate of Peltier heat production per unit cross-sectional area of the junction. Π_{ab} is the Peltier coefficient, and J_{ab} is the current density flowing from material *a* to material *b*.

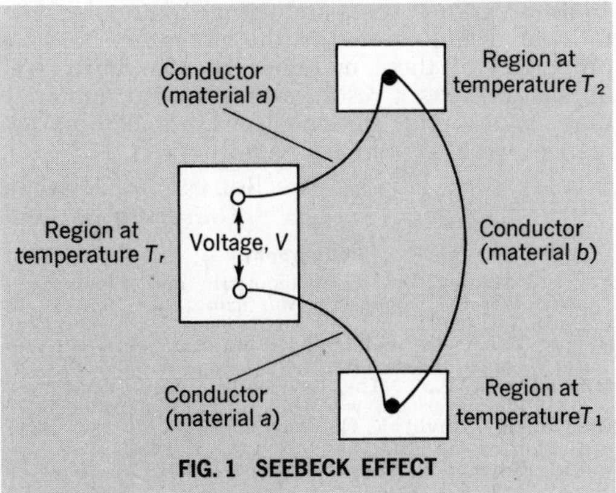

FIG. 1 SEEBECK EFFECT

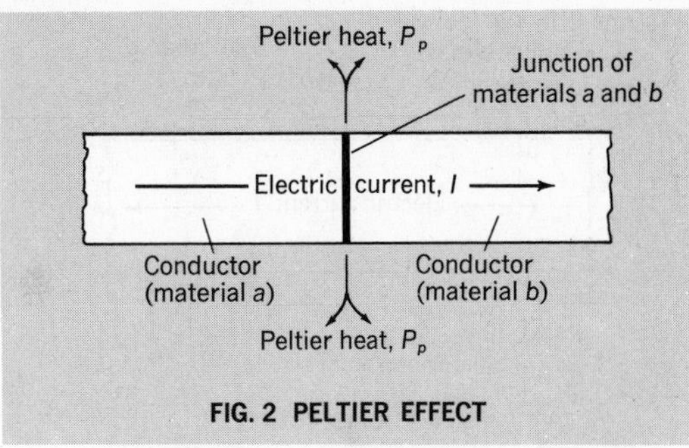

FIG. 2 PELTIER EFFECT

The Peltier heat should be distinguished from the more usual Joule heat. The Joule heat is proportional to the square of the electric current. Joule heat is always given off by a conductor regardless of the direction of current flow, and it is given off throughout the bulk of the conductor. The Joule heat, P_j, is given by $P_j = \rho J^2$, where J is the current density, and ρ is the resistivity of the material.

Historical Background. The Peltier effect was discovered in 1834 by Jean Charles Athanase Peltier, a French watchmaker who inherited a modest fortune, left business life, and pursued natural science. Like Seebeck, Peltier failed to understand his discovery. He believed it showed that Ohm's law might not hold for weak currents. The nature of Peltier's discovery was made clear by Emil Lenz, a member of the St. Petersburg Academy. In 1838 he showed that a drop of water could be frozen by passing an electric current through a bismuth-antimony junction in contact with the water.

Thomson Effect. Consider a bar of a single conducting material in which an electric current is flowing. If there is a temperature difference along the bar, as shown in Fig. 3, heat will be absorbed by the bar. The rate of heat absorption depends on the magnitude and direction of the current and on the magnitude and direction (high to low) of the temperature difference. If either the direction of current is reversed or the hot and cold ends of the bar are reversed—but not both—heat will be given off. Both the heat given off and the heat absorbed are called the *Thomson heat*. The rate of Thomson heat absorption, P_t, is $P_t = \tau J\ (T_2 - T_1)/L$, where τ is the Thomson coefficient, and $T_2 - T_1$ is the temperature difference over a distance L along the bar.

The Thomson effect can be observed using only a single material, whereas observation of the Seebeck and Peltier effects requires the use of

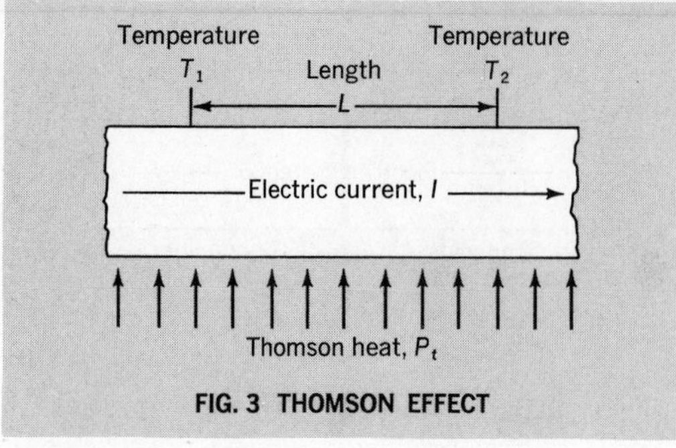

FIG. 3 THOMSON EFFECT

two different materials. It is important to distinguish between the Thomson heat and the Joule heat, even though they appear simultaneously because of the electric current flow in the conductor.

Historical Background. In 1854, William Thomson derived a relationship between the Seebeck and Peltier coefficients. Some experimental results were not in agreement with his theoretical prediction about this relationship, so Thomson concluded that there must be a third thermoelectric effect. He postulated the existence of the Thomson effect and confined its existence experimentally in 1856.

Thomson became a professor of natural philosophy at Glasgow University in 1846. He was knighted in 1866 for his part in laying the Atlantic cable, and in 1892 he was elevated to the peerage as Lord Kelvin.

Kelvin Relations. The Seebeck, Peltier, and Thomson effects are related by the Kelvin relations, which are $\Pi_{ab} = T\alpha_{ab}$, and $\tau_a - \tau_b = T(\Delta\alpha_{ab} / \Delta T)$, where T is the absolute temperature in degrees Kelvin, and $\Delta\alpha_{ab}$ is the change in the Seebeck coefficient when the temperature is raised by ΔT.

APPLICATIONS

The main applications for thermoelectric effects are measurement of temperature, refrigeration and heating, and the generation of electricity from heat. For measuring temperature the Seebeck effect is widely used. See THERMOCOUPLE.

Thermoelectric Refrigerators and Heat Pumps. The Peltier effect can be used to produce refrigeration and air conditioning. If a current is passed through a circuit formed by two different conductors, *a* and *b*, heat is absorbed at one *a-b* junction and given off at the other *a-b* junction. If the junction that gives off heat is held at a fixed temperature, the other junction will cool its surroundings as it absorbs heat. This principle can be used to run a thermoelectric refrigerator. Practical devices, such as thermoelectric refrigerators for spot cooling of electronic equipment or for cooling laboratory equipment, have a number of *a-b* junctions. The junctions that give off heat are held at a temperature close to room temperature by blowing air over them. The other junctions are placed inside a thermally insulated box. As they absorb heat, they cool the interior of the box.

The same principle can be used to make a system that functions as both an air conditioner and a heat pump. In this arrangement one set of junctions is placed outside the house, and the other set inside. During hot months, the electric current is set so that the junctions inside the house absorb heat and cool the interior of the house. During cold months, the current is reversed so that the junctions inside the house produce heat and warm the interior of the house. See also HEAT PUMP.

Thermoelectric Generators. The Seebeck effect can be used to produce electric power. One set of junctions is heated to a high temperature by a heat source, such as a hydrocarbon fuel, a radioisotope, or focused or unfocused radiation from the sun. The other set of junctions is cooled by air, water, or radiation into space. The heating of one set of junctions and the cooling of the other set produces a temperature difference, thereby causing the generation of electricity by the Seebeck effect.

Thermoelectric generators are used to supply electrical power in remote locations where maintenance is expensive. For instance, they are used to power weather-sensing stations in remote locations, radios and lights anchored in the ocean, man-made satellites, and deep-space probes.

Performance. Thermoelectric devices have a number of advantages over mechanical devices. The former are completely quiet in operation and have no moving parts. Thus, they have a long life and require very little maintenance. Thermoelectric devices have good efficiency, though not as great as large-sized mechanical systems. The efficiency of thermoelectric devices is independent of their size, whereas many mechanical devices lose efficiency when they are made in small sizes. For this reason, thermoelectric systems have usually been used at power levels less than a kilowatt, although a 5-kilowatt system has been built. However, there are no inherent reasons why larger systems could not be made.

Historical Background. In the 1820's, Seebeck investigated the thermoelectric properties of a large number of materials. Some of these materials could have converted heat to electricity with an efficiency of about 3%. This was as good as or better than the efficiency of the steam engines of that time. By about 1890, steam engines were used to drive electromechanical generators to produce electricity, but thermoelectric materials for generating electricity remained unexploited.

The basic theory of thermoelectric generators and refrigerators was derived by the German scientist Edmund Altenkirch in 1909–1911. However, serious interest in thermoelectric devices did not develop until the early 1950's. At that time, interest in semiconducting materials was stimulated by the invention of the transistor in 1948. Various semiconducting materials were fabricated and studied in the laboratory, and the properties of these materials became fairly well understood. As a result, semiconductor materials that gave better thermoelectric device performance were developed rapidly.

ROLAND W. URE, JR.
University of Utah

Bibliography

Angrist, Stanley W., "Galvanometric and Thermomagnetic Effects," *Scientific American*, vol. 205, p. 45, December 1961.

Heikes, Robert R., and Ure, Roland W., *Thermoelectricity: Science and Engineering* (New York 1961).

Joffe, Abram F., "The Revival of Thermoelectricity," *Scientific American*, vol. 199, p. 31, November 1958.

MacDonald, David K. C., *Thermoelectricity: An Introduction to the Principles* (New York 1962).

Wolfe, Raymond, "Magnetothermoelectricity," *Scientific American*, vol. 210, p. 70, June 1964.

THERMOGRAPHY, thûr-mog′rə-fē, in medicine, is a technique for measuring the amount of heat emitted through the skin. The technique evolved as an offshoot of the "snooperscope" used in World War II to detect the presence of enemy personnel and equipment at night by their emission of infrared radiation.

All objects emit infrared radiation. Man emits it continuously in the electromagnetic spectrum, with wavelengths between 3 and 20 microns. Thermographs record the radiation in the form of thermal maps, or thermograms, displaying it on Polaroid film, television monitors, or various special materials, either in a mosaic of gray halftones or in distinctive colors.

Analysis of thermograms provides valuable information for the diagnosis, prognosis, and treatment of almost all diseases. This use of thermography is based on the assumption that similar areas of the body emit nearly identical heat patterns; thus any differences noted between two similar areas are significant. For example, if a "hot spot" is noted on one breast, the doctor is alerted to the possibility of an abnormality, such as a tumor, in that area. Conversely, "cold spots" on the extremities or elsewhere may indicate the constriction or blockage of blood vessels caused by thrombosis, sclerosis, or smoking.

JACOB GERSHON-COHEN, M. D.
Temple University School of Medicine

THESE THERMOGRAMS show how smoking a single cigarette affects circulation in the hands. After 15 minutes the temperature of the fingers has dropped 6°F. It takes 1¼ hours for it to return to normal.

J. GERSHON-COHEN

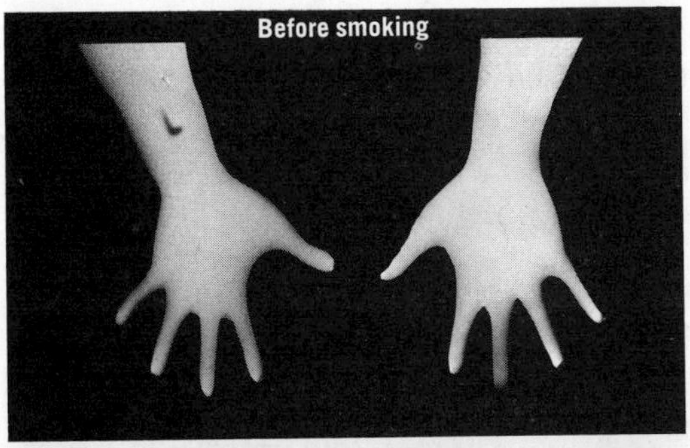

Before smoking

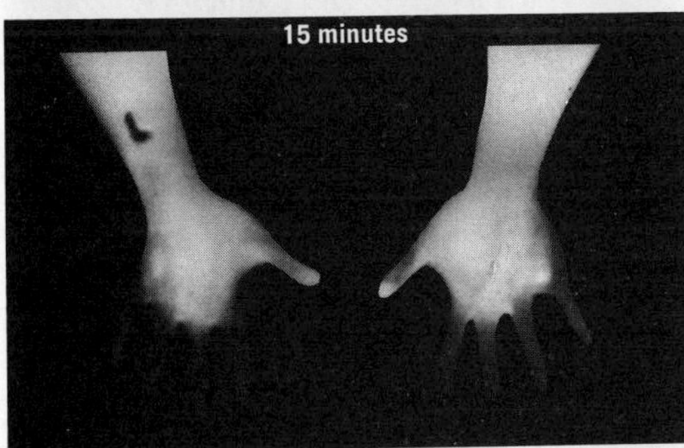

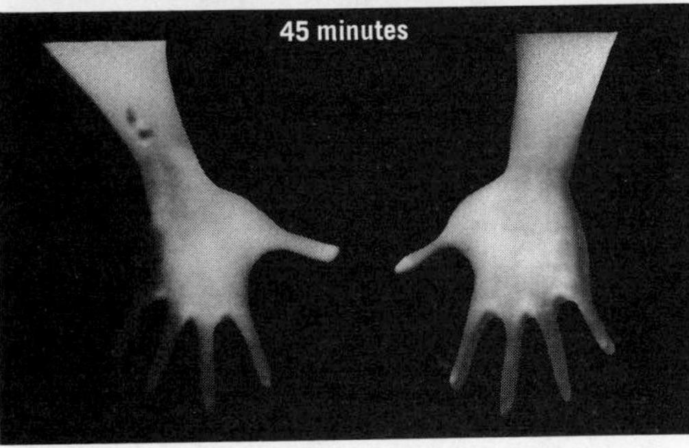

THERMOGRAPHY, thûr-mog′rə-fē, in printing, is a process that raises a printed image in simulation of steel-die or copperplate engravings. The latter are produced by an intaglio process that embosses, or raises, the paper. The thermographic image is printed by letterpress or offset. A resin powder is sprinkled over the sheet and adheres only to the sticky ink. The rest is blown or shaken off. The paper then passes under heat, from open gas flames or electric bulbs, which melts the powder. It quickly cools, and hardens into a solid raised mass that defines the printed image. The powder comes in many colors, as well as metallic gold and silver.

Thermography is used mostly for commercial stationery, such as letterheads, envelopes, announcements, and business cards. It is also used for social stationery, such as wedding invitations and informal cards. A growing use is for greeting cards and original works of art. Thermography is simple, fast, and much less expensive than the intaglio methods it imitates.

EDMUND C. ARNOLD
Syracuse University

THERMOLUMINESCENCE, thûr-mō-lōō-mə-nes′-əns, is the emission of light by certain irradiated solid materials on heating, over and above incandescent emission, or "red heat." It represents a discharge of stored energy derived from ionizing radiation (α, β, or γ-radiation) impinging on the material. Once this stored energy has been discharged, reheating will produce no more such emission without another irradiation. The physics of the phenomenon is poorly understood but is based on excitation of electrons by the radiation to higher energy states where a small proportion is trapped in the rigid atomic lattice. Displacement from a trap may occur by heating. When the electron falls back to the ground state a photon of light is emitted. Electron traps seem to be associated with defects and impurities in the lattice.

The two main applications of thermoluminescence make use of its intensity to measure the radiation dose experienced by a material. The first, thermoluminescent dosimetry, is the estimation of doses given to persons undergoing radiotherapy or exposed to hazardous situations by measuring the thermoluminescence of suitably positioned samples of a material such as lithium fluoride. The second application is in dating geological minerals and archaeological pottery. Firing the pottery removes any existing stored energy from its constituents by causing thermoluminescence. Subsequent radiation from traces of radioactivity in the ceramic itself and in the burial medium builds up energy, which can be measured by measuring the thermoluminescence when the pottery is heated. Independent estimation of the dose rate makes it possible to infer the age of the ceramic. Accuracy is less good than with radiocarbon dating. Geological dating of minerals is more difficult.

JOHN WINTER
University of Pennsylvania

THERMOMETER, a graduated instrument that measures the intensity of heat. The essential criterion for a thermometer is the ability of a device to vary in a known and repeatable manner at various temperatures. Three major temperature scales are currently in use.

(1) The Kelvin, or absolute, scale (° K) with absolute zero as the bottom limit, and 273.15° K and 373.15° K, respectively, as the freezing and boiling points of water, is used for scientific purposes, especially for low temperature physics (see CRYOGENICS). (2) The Celsius, or centigrade, scale (° C), with 0° C and 100° C, respectively, the freezing and boiling points of water, has been adopted throughout most of the world for common usages. (3) The Fahrenheit scale (° F) with 32° F and 212° F, respectively, the freezing and boiling points of water, is used in English-speaking countries.

Since a degree Celsius is of the same magnitude as a degree Kelvin, the only difference between them is in their choice of zero, and it is necessary merely to subtract 273.15 units from ° K to convert to ° C. Conversely, one adds 273.15 units to C to convert to ° K. A degree Fahrenheit is not equal to a degree Celsius, and to convert between the two scales the following formulas must be used: $° F = 9/5 \; ° C + 32$ and $° C = 5/9(° F - 32)$. See also TEMPERATURE.

Development of the Thermometer. The phenomenon of heat was observed and measured for centuries before scientists arrived at an understanding of its nature and properties. Until the time of Lord Kelvin (see KELVIN, LORD) in the 1860's, thermometry was based on empirical knowledge and common sense rather than any acceptable scientific theory.

Thermoscopes. Claims to priority in inventing the thermometer are numerous, and the disputes cannot be settled. There are independent reports of air thermoscopes invented around 1610 by the scientist Galileo, and later by his medical disciple Sanctorius, the cosmologist Robert Fludd, the clockmaker Cornelis Drebbel, and the engineer Salomon de Caus. Though some of these instruments were intended for medical or meteorological purposes and others served merely for amusement, they shared basic features of construction: all were glass tubes open at one end, partially filled with air, set in a basin of water, and crudely graduated with notches or dials. None of the scales were comparable with other instruments, nor accurate from one day to the next, because of changing barometric conditions. The earliest air thermometer corrected for air pressure was described by Guillaume Amontons to the Académie des Sciences in 1702.

Closed-Glass Liquid Thermometers. Leopoldo, Cardinal dei Medici, a cofounder of the Accademia del Cimento, made the first closed-glass liquid thermometers, known as Florentine thermometers, around 1654. These thermometers, widely used in France and England, were graduated into 50, 100, or 300 degrees. They were roughly standardized by the heat of the sun and the cold of ice water, and filled with distilled colored wine. The advantage of a liquid like wine was that its expansion was independent of air pressure. Mercury and water thermometers were also tried by the Florentines but abandoned because their expansion was too small. Later this problem was overcome by making thermometers with finer bores, thereby increasing their sensitivity, and by the middle of the 18th century mercury thermometers had superseded others because of their more uniform expansion.

Calibration of Scales. Attention now turned to standardizing scales of temperature by marking off heat levels of specified natural phenomena. At first a large number of reference points were used, including the equilibrium temperature of ice water and various salts, the melting point of butter or wax, and even the temperature of the basement of the Paris Observatory. Three other fixed points were frequently used, particularly for the four major scales developed in the 18th century: the boiling and freezing points of water, and the normal body temperature.

In 1708, Gabriel Daniel Fahrenheit, an instrument maker from Danzig who practiced in Holland, borrowed from the Danish astronomer Ole Rømer the idea of calibrating thermometers to the melting point of ice and the heat of blood. In 1724, Fahrenheit announced to the Royal Society that he had constructed thermometers in which he had fixed 32° F as the freezing point of water and 96° F as normal body temperature. That his thermometers registered 212° F when water boiled was not originally taken as a fundamental reference point, though it was widely adopted as such by about 1740. The F scale was adopted in England and the Low Countries, but not in France, where the system proposed by René de Réaumur prevailed.

Réaumur initially calibrated his 1730 thermometers on the expansion of alcohol from 1,000 to 1,080 parts by volume as it was heated from the temperature of freezing to the temperature of boiling water. The Réaumur scale was later simplified to register 0° for freezing and 80°

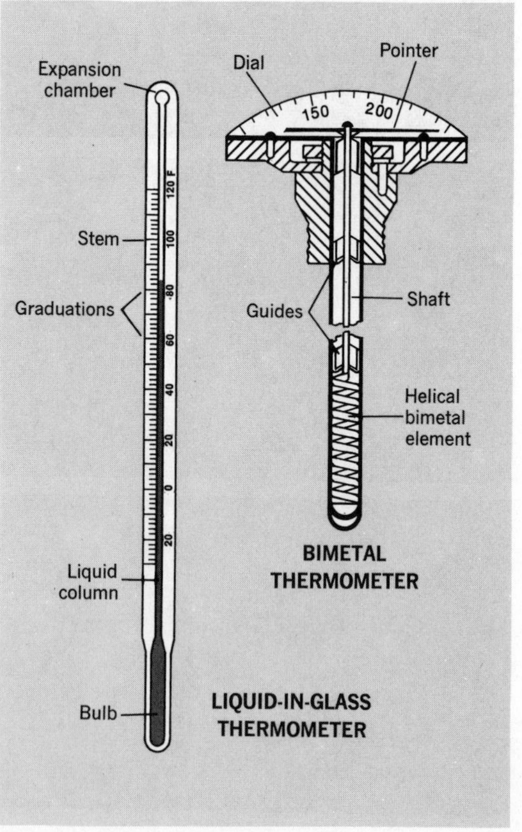

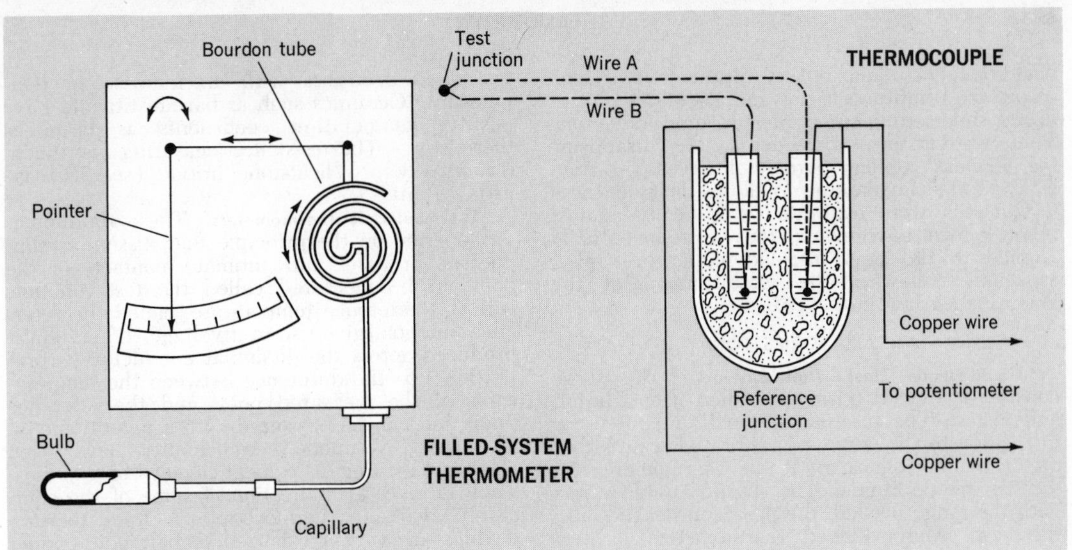

for boiling, regardless of the liquid employed. Joseph Nicolas Delisle invented another scale in 1732, which remained popular in Russia for over a century. Initially, he fixed 0° as the boiling point of water for a mercury thermometer and calibrated the volume lost by contraction of the mercury down to the freezing point of water into one thousand units. In 1738 the Delisle thermometer was recalibrated with 0° as the boiling point and 150° as the freezing point of water. Both Réaumur and Delisle, who initially rejected the use of two arbitrary points for their scale, were led to accept them to permit easy calibration for new instruments.

Less complex in its history was the centigrade scale, now called Celsius, though its adoption in place of the Réaumur scale in France remains a puzzle. Several attempts to transform Delisle's scale to a 100-degree interval were made before the Swedish astronomer Anders Celsius proposed in 1741 to graduate thermometers with 0° as the boiling point of water and 100° as the melting point of snow. In 1745, his friend Carl Linnaeus inverted the scale to give us the now-familiar centigrade scale. An instrument maker in Lyon, named Christin, also adopted this practice independently. Its general use in the 19th century may have been spurred by the French adoption, during their revolution, of the decimal system for all measurable quantities.

Later Developments. The demand for greater accuracy and problems related to thermometric construction forced scientists to devise alternative techniques for measuring temperature. Deformation thermometers based on the expansion of metal rods were tried as early as 1735 and led to the development of bimetallic instruments by the end of the 18th century. These instruments function on the principle that the difference in the rates of expansion of two metal strips welded together produces a bending that can activate a pointer on a dial calibrated against a standard mercury thermometer.

Though convenient as pocket instruments, metallic thermometers were neither as accurate nor as scientifically sound as the new gas thermometers, invented after the establishment in 1802 of Charles' law, which relates the volume and temperature of a gas. When allowance is made for changes in atmospheric pressure, pure gases expand more uniformly as a function of heat increase than liquids do. Gas thermometers also allow measurement of temperatures higher than the upper limits of mercury thermometers (around 350° C). Hydrogen thermometers have an effective upper limit of around 1100° C, and nitrogen thermometers of around 1550° C.

Two kinds of gas thermometers were devised. One was the constant-pressure thermometer, which relies upon volumetric measurement. The other, more popular, was the constant-volume thermometer, based on pressure measurements. By extensive laboratory experiments published in 1847, Henri Regnault set new standards for gas thermometry, with errors of only 0.1° C in the range of 0° to 100° C. Further refinements in 1888 by Pierre Chappuis of the International Bureau of Weights and Measures reduced the error to around 0.002° C for the same range. By supplying mercury thermometers calibrated against his gas thermometers, Chappuis began the process of internationalizing standards. They were not formally accepted until the 1927 General Conference of Weights and Measures, which gave the first official International Practical Temperature Scale, comparing the results of the long history of practical thermometry with the half-century-old thermodynamic scale. Revisions of this Practical Scale are made periodically at international meetings, the latest one held in 1968.

Other useful forms of thermometry were based upon electrical phenomena. The thermocouple, based upon the discoveries of T. J. Seebeck in 1821 and J. C. A. Peltier in 1834, and systematized by Lord Kelvin in 1847, was also adopted for temperatures up to 1000° C, particularly after A. L. Day and R. B. Sosman, in 1911, showed the simple convertibility of the gas thermometer scale to their own platinum and platinum-rhodium thermocouple. The resistance thermometer made of platinum was studied and perfected in 1886 by H. L. Callendar. It found immediate wide use and is now the prime standard thermometer between −259° C and +630° C.

Instruments to measure high temperatures have traditionally been called pyrometers. First devised in the 1780's by the Wedgwoods for the pottery industry, they were extensively used in metallurgical industries during the 19th century. Initially, high temperatures were estimated by recording color changes in ceramic beads. Radiation pyrometers, which measure the intensity of heat radiation, and optical pyrometers, which record the brightness of this radiation, were introduced superseding the cruder ceramic indicators. These were in turn superseded by the "disappearing filament" optical pyrometer developed from E. F. Morse's invention. While at first all these instruments were calibrated empirically against other known instruments, they were eventually aligned to the new thermodynamic principles, especially following the establishment of the Wien-Planck law in the 1910's.

STANDARD FORMS TODAY

Liquid-Filled Glass Thermometers. This type consists of a closed glass tube filled with a liquid and a gas. The position of the liquid meniscus in relation to the engraved calibrated scale either on or behind the stem of the thermometer indicates temperature. The liquid used varies with the range needed, the precision desired, and the cost. Mercury-filled thermometers have a nominal range of −35° to 500° C. For lower temperatures—as low as −200° C—alcohol, penthane, petroleum ether, or other organic liquids colored with a dye are used.

Filled-System Thermometers. These thermometers are all metal and consist of a bulb, a capillary tube, and a mechanical device for the indicator. The fluid, either liquid or gas, changes state or phase with temperature, thereby changing the pressure or the volume in the system and activating the mechanical device, usually a Bourdon tube (see BOURDON GAUGE). These thermometers are commonly found in the home as indoor-outdoor thermometers and in the thermostatic controls of ovens, furnaces, and air conditioners. They have been classified by the Scientific Apparatus Makers Association into various types (see Table 1).

Bimetallic Thermometers. These thermometers depend upon the differential thermal expansion of two metals. The sensing element consists of two metals fastened together and usually wound in a spiral, connected to an indicator by means of gears and levers. A range of −100° to +550° C is possible with an error of less than 1% of the full range. They are most commonly found in homes in the wall thermostat.

Resistance Thermometers. The resistance thermometer is based on the fact that many metals, semiconductors, and ceramics change their electrical resistance with temperature in a known and reproducible way. Three items are necessary to measure temperature with a resistance thermometer: the sensing element, a resistance-measuring instrument, and the electrical wires connecting them.

The resistor, considered as a sensing element, is a metal with a positive temperature coefficient—that is, the resistance of the metal increases with increasing temperature. Other sensors have temperature coefficients at least 1,000 times greater than metals. Metallic oxides of manganese, nickel, cobalt, copper, magnesium, and similar substances, fabricated into small beads or washers, are known as thermistors. They have a negative temperature coefficient—that is, their resistance decreases with an increase in temperature. Ceramics such as barium titanate have positive temperature coefficients as large as thermistors. The resistance-measuring instrument is normally a Wheatstone bridge (see WHEATSTONE BRIDGE).

Table 1—FILLED SYSTEM THERMOMETERS

Class	Principle	Fluid	Range (°C)
I	Volumetric	Liquid	−150 to +315
II	Pressure	Vapor	− 40 to +315
III	Pressure	Gas	−240 to +535
IV	Volumetric	Mercury	− 39 to +535

Thermoelectric Thermometers. These thermometers operate on the principle that dissimilar conductors brought into intimate contact at the point to be measured called the test junction, and at a reference temperature, called the reference junction, give rise to a voltage. The voltage produced across the dissimilar conductors is proportional to the difference between the temperatures of the measured point and the reference point and can be measured with a potentiometer. The most common thermocouples have been classified by the Instrument Society of America. Table 2 gives an indication of some of the commonly available thermocouples. Other thermocouples are very specialized; cobalt/gold-copper is used at cryogenic temperatures, while tungsten-tungsten/26% rhenium operates for very high temperatures.

Table 2—THERMOCOUPLES

Type	Materials	Sensitivity (μV/°C)	Range (°C)
S	Platinum—Platinum + 10% Rhodium	6	0 to +1500
J	Iron—Constantan	26 to 63	−200 to + 800
T	Copper—Constantan	15 to 60	−262 to + 350
K	Chromel—Alumel	15 to 40	−200 to +1375
E	Chromel—Constantan	50 to 80	−200 to +1000

[1] Microvolts per degree C.

Pyrometers. Optical or "disappearing filament" pyrometers that record the brightness of radiant energy consist of a lens system that focuses the target to be measured onto a calibrated lamp with a tungsten filament. The introduction of a calibrated wedge into the optical path changes the apparent color of the target until the target and the filament appear alike. Another type of optical pyrometer uses a varying current for the lamp instead of a wedge. Colored filters of specific wavelengths are often used to make the calibration more precise. The temperature range for optical pyrometers is 500° to 3000° C.

Radiation pyrometers, which measure intensity of heat radiation, have no theoretical upper limit of temperature. Like the optical pyrometer, they use a lens system that focuses the radiant energy of the target on a thermal sensing device. The temperature rise of the sensor is dependent upon the total radiation received and the rate of conducted heat away from the sensor. The sensor may be a thermopile (a number of thermocouples connected in a series), a resistance thermometer, or a bolometer (a thin platinum foil acting as a resistance thermometer). The accuracy of these devices depends upon the emissivity of the surface being measured (see THERMODYNAMICS), smoke or haze that may be between the target and the instrument, the type of glass in the optics, and the calibration of the sensor.

ROGER HAHN
University of California, Berkeley
PIERRE M. HAHN
University of California, Los Angeles

Further Reading: Instrument Society of America, *Temperature: Its Measurement and Control in Science and Industry*, Symposiums, 1939, 1954, 1961, 1971 (Pittsburgh); Middleton, William E. K., *A History of the Thermometer and Its Use in Meteorology* (Baltimore 1966).

THERMONUCLEAR ENERGY is energy produced in certain nuclear fusion reactions. See NUCLEAR ENERGY.

THERMOPILE. See THERMOCOUPLE.

THERMOPLASTIC MATERIALS are those that soften when heated but regain their original properties on cooling. Such materials include the polyvinyl, acrylic, polystyrene, and polyethylene resins.

THERMOPLASTIC RECORDING, the storage of images by forming ripples in the surface of a plastic material, was first introduced by the American physicist William E. Glenn in 1959. Thermoplastic recording provides a high recording speed, high storage capacity, rapid image development, direct optical or electronic readout, and ease of erasure. It is promising for dry photography, high-resolution displays, information storage and retrieval, mapping, and TV broadcasting.

Glenn's recording medium has three layers: a thin thermoplastic with a low melting point, a transparent electrically conductive coating, and a glass substrate. An electron beam sprays charges on the thermoplastic surface in a pattern depending on the image to be stored. The thermoplastic is heated briefly so that electrostatic forces deform the soft plastic and form surface ripples corresponding to the charge pattern, and the ripples are then frozen in by rapidly cooling the thermoplastic. In the 1960's other researchers used a top layer that is both thermoplastic and photoconductive. It is charged by a corona discharge, exposed to light bearing an image, and then deformed to a rippled surface by applying hot air.

In both techniques, a special optical system is needed to project the recorded image. Where a ripple is present, it refracts transmitted light and produces a spot on a screen; where there is no ripple, the screen remains black. Both black-and-white and color images can be projected.

HERBERT R. ANDERSON, JR., *IBM Corp.*

THERMOPYLAE, thûr-mop'ə-lē, Greece, was the site of a battle in 480 B.C. A small group of Greeks under the Spartan King Leonidas fought to the death, heroically delaying the conquest of Athens by perhaps 180,000 Asiatics under Xerxes.

Thermopylae means "hot gates" and is named for adjacent hot springs. It is a pass 86 miles (137 km) northwest of Athens, between Mt. Kallidromon and the sea, which in antiquity nearly reached the foot of the crags.

On the first day, Xerxes sent first his Medes and Cissians to attack, and then his Guard Division, the 10,000 "Immortals." But Leonidas' forces, armored and with longer spears than those of the Persians, held the pass and inflicted severe casualties.

On the second day the Persians fared no better; but that night a local guide led Xerxes' Immortals along hunters' trails a long way round, to reach a track "along the spine of the mountain," as Herodotus says, so that they could attack Leonidas in rear. Leonidas had stationed a thousand men on the mountain to forestall this, but they were ineffective.

In order to gain time for his main body to escape, Leonidas with his royal guard of 300 Spartans and about 2,000 Helots and Boeotians fought to the end. A monument was erected in 1955 at the site of the stand, which is now a mile (1.6 km) from the sea.

This defense was a modest holding action to support the Greek navies, manned by some 65,000 men, whose presence north of Euboea Island kept the Persian fleet at sea, exposed to severe storm damage. Xerxes' armies took Athens. But at the ensuing naval battle of Salamis the weakened Persian fleet was badly beaten. Stranded without naval logistic support, Xerxes withdrew with his main force to Asia.

ANDREW ROBERT BURN
Author of "Persia and the Greeks"

THERMOS BOTTLE. See VACUUM BOTTLE.

THERMOSETTING MATERIALS are those that solidify on heating and cannot be remelted. Such materials include polyurethane, epoxy, alkyd, and phenolic resins.

THERMOSPHERE, thûr'mə-sfir, a temperature zone of the atmosphere, beginning about 50 miles (80 km) above the earth and extending upward indefinitely. Thermosphere temperatures reach above 2,000° F (1,100° C). See ATMOSPHERE.

THERMOSTAT, a type of feedback control that reacts to a change in temperature. The change of temperature affects a sensing element in the thermostat, which in turn sends back an electrical or pressure signal to control a heating or cooling system. Thermostats are used to control the temperature of buildings, water heaters, ovens, electric irons, automobile radiators, and other devices to provide a predetermined constant temperature or safe limits of operation of the equipment.

The first bimetal temperature-responsive device was a "grid-iron" pendulum built in England in 1726 to improve the accuracy of a clock operating under varying temperature conditions. The word "thermostat" was introduced in 1830 by Andrew Ure, a Scottish professor of chemistry, who was issued a patent on what he called "a heat-responsive element consisting of a bar of steel united to zinc by numerous rivets." This bimetallic bar bends with temperature change because of the different expansion rates of the metal strips, and the bending can be used to actuate valves or dampers to control heating or cooling systems.

Bimetal-strip thermostats of improved design now are widely used, although other designs have been developed. One other type has a low-expansion rod contained in a high-expansion tube—for example, a steel rod and nickel tube sealed together at one end. Contraction of the tube moves the free end of the rod, actuating a valve or electric switch. Another group of thermostats uses a volatile liquid contained in a bellows that exerts a variable pressure depending on the temperature of the volatile substance. Refrigeration thermostats are designed on this principle. Thermostats used in homes or small buildings usually are low-voltage electric controls that turn a burner or refrigeration compressor on or off as required. Pneumatic thermostats, which operate from air-pressure signals that are carried in small copper tubes, frequently are used in larger buildings.

JOHN F. SANDFORT
South Dakota State University

THERMOTAXIS, thûr-mə-tak′səs, a reflex movement by a freely motile and usually simple organism in response to a temperature gradient. The term is also sometimes used to mean temperature regulation. See TAXIS.

THERMOTROPISM, thər-mot′rə-piz-əm, an involuntary movement of an organism or part of an organism in response to temperature changes. The term is most often used in botany to refer to the tendency of a plant to react to heat. See TROPISM.

THEROPODA, a group of saurischian, or "reptile hip," dinosaurs that were flesh-eating and bipedal. See DINOSAUR—*Flesh-Eating Bipeds*.

THERSITES, thər-sī′tēz, according to Homer, the ugliest man in the Grecian army that beleaguered Troy. He was a malicious and slanderous brawler whom Ulysses publicly beat and brought to tears for his insulting attack on their commander Agamemnon. Thersites was eventually slain by Achilles for piercing with his spear the eye of the dead queen of the Amazons, Penthesilea, after ridiculing Achilles for having mourned her death.

THESAURUS, thi-sôr′əs, the Latin word for "treasury" or "storehouse," is a book of information about words or concepts. It is most commonly applied to dictionaries of synonyms, the best known of which is Roget's *Thesaurus of English Words and Phrases* (1st ed., 1852). See also SYNONYMS AND ANTONYMS.

THESEUS, thē′sē-əs, was an Athenian hero who was probably mythical, although the ancients regarded him as a historical personage, the first king to establish Athens on a firm basis as a unified city-state. Theseus appears as a character in several Greek tragedies, nearly always embodying Athenian ideals of humaneness and magnanimity. He is also the subject of a biography by Plutarch. For political reasons the figure of Theseus was built up as a kind of Ionian Greek counterweight to the great Dorian hero Hercules (Heracles).

The father of Theseus was King Aegeus of Athens, but, as is common for heroes of mythology, Theseus was said to have been simultaneously begotten by a deity, the sea-god Poseidon. Before the boy's birth Aegeus had to leave the mother, Aethra, in her native Troezen. When Theseus was old enough to lift a stone under which Aegeus had placed a sword and sandals, he set out to join his father in Athens. On his way from Troezen across the Isthmus to Attica, he rid the country of various monsters and robbers, among them Procrustes, who, by stretching or cutting, had been forcing all passersby to fit the exact size of his bed.

In Athens, Theseus volunteered to go as one of seven youths who, along with seven maidens, were sent as tribute to King Minos of Crete. These victims were put into the mazelike Labyrinth to be tracked down and eaten by the monstrous Minotaur, half-man and half-bull. But Ariadne, Minos' daughter, fell in love with Theseus. She gave him a sword and stood holding one end of a skein of thread at the entrance to the Labyrinth while he made his way to the center of the maze, slew the Minotaur, and returned, guiding himself by the thread.

When he started his voyage back from Crete, Theseus took Ariadne with him, but he deserted her on the island of Naxos. The goddess Aphrodite punished this abandonment by making Theseus forget a promise he had made to his father. He had said that if he conquered the Minotaur he would use a white sail on his ship. When the waiting Aegeus saw a black sail, he took it as a sign that his son was dead, and drowned himself in the sea.

After becoming king, Theseus, often aided by his friend Pirithous, performed many exploits, including fighting the Centaurs, repelling an invasion of the Amazons, and trying to abduct the goddess Persephone. Eventually, after he had been imprisoned in Hades for some years, he was driven out of Athens. Sailing for Crete he was shipwrecked on the island of Scyros and was killed by King Lycomedes, who threw him off a cliff.

RICHMOND Y. HATHORN
State University of New York at Stony Brook

THESPIS, thes′pəs, Greek writer and actor of the 6th century B. C., who is generally considered the father of tragedy. He was born in Icaria, Attica, and is said to have won the drama contest in Athens in the 530's. According to Aristotle, Thespis was the first to add an actor to tragedy. Before this time tragedies were simply choral odes performed at festivals honoring the god Dionysus. Thespis supposedly added an individual actor who spoke a prologue and answered the chorus. Thespis is also credited with introducing the use of masks to tragedy. According to Horace, in *Ars poetica*, Thespis went about the countryside in a wagon, giving plays, but this information is generally considered to be erroneous.

THESSALONIANS, Epistles to the, thes-ə-lō′nē-ənz, two letters from St. Paul to the Christian community at Thessalonica in Greece. These epistles are the 13th and 14th books of the New Testament.

Setting and Date. The account of Paul's Second Missionary Journey given in Acts 15:36 to 18:22 includes a description of the founding of the church in Thessalonica (modern Salonika). In response to Paul's vision of an appeal to him from a Macedonian, Paul and his companions sailed across the northern Aegean Sea from Troas to Philippi. They eventually arrived at Thessalonica, where for three sabbaths Paul argued with the Jews in their synagogue that Jesus was the promised Messiah. He met with such success that the Jews who were opposed to him stirred up a mob, forcing Paul and Silas to flee to Beroea. Again the Jews of Thessalonica made trouble, and Paul fled south to Athens by sea, leaving Silas and Timothy behind.

After an unsuccessful mission in Athens, Paul went to Corinth, where Silas and Timothy rejoined him. I Thessalonians 3:6 and Acts 18:5 imply that I Thessalonians was written at this point and that it was followed closely by II Thessalonians.

Modern critical study has accepted the general outline of the story told in Acts. The description of the foundation of the Thessalonian church in I Thessalonians 1 to 2 suggests that Paul is speaking of recent events. There can be little doubt that the letters should be read against the account in Acts 17:1 to 18:17. In that case the reference to Gallio in Acts 18 and other evidence date the Thessalonian correspondence between 50 and 52 A. D., probably in the spring of 51. Most modern critics agree that the letters, assuming their authenticity, were written from Corinth about 51 A. D.

At the same time, certain details in the story of Acts must be corrected by evidence in the letters themselves. For example, it seems unlikely that "three Sabbaths" would be enough to establish a church that could later remain unshaken by persecution. More importantly, the persecution suffered by the Thessalonians was at the hands of Gentiles, not Jews.

Authenticity and Relationship of the Letters. The two letters have met differing fates in modern discussions of whether or not Paul wrote both. There is universal agreement that I Thessalonians was written by Paul. It is also generally agreed to be the oldest of Paul's letters that has been preserved. The problem of authenticity has attached almost exclusively to II Thessalonians, and it has been raised largely because of the difficulty involved in relating the two letters to each other.

Despite the fact that II Thessalonians is not universally accepted, most modern critics regard it as genuine. The stylistic resemblance of the two letters can most simply be explained by assuming they were written by Paul in the same brief period. Some scholars have held that the contrast between the views taken of the last things in the two letters argues for two separate authors. However, this contrast need not be presented as a contradiction. In I Thessalonians Paul wishes to assure his readers that their dead will share in the general resurrection (4:13), while in II Thessalonians he must deny that the Day of the Lord has already come (2:2). These two different aims require a difference of emphasis, but need not imply any change in Paul's teaching.

Content. In order to understand the letters, it is necessary to remember that they were addressed to specific situations. In the case of I Thessalonians the occasion was provided by Timothy's return from Thessalonica (3:6). His report that the church was standing firm despite persecution evoked from Paul a letter of thanksgiving and encouragement. It is more difficult to describe the particular occasion that prompted the writing of II Thessalonians. It is reasonable to suppose, however, that Paul received fresh reports from Thessalonica—for example, in 3:11, the phrase "we hear." He learned that some had given up working and become idle (3:11; and compare I Thessalonians 4:11). In addition he discovered that his own authority had been invoked as warrant for the notion that the Day of the Lord had already come (2:2). If I Thessalonians is a letter of thanksgiving, II Thessalonians is a letter of instruction designed to deal with what Paul heard about events in Thessalonica.

Except for the discussions of the Day of the Lord, there is no extended theological argumentation in the letters. Nevertheless, the thanksgivings and exhortations quite clearly reflect and, in fact, appeal to the Christian tradition Paul delivered to the Thessalonians (I Thessalonians 2:4; 4:1; II Thessalonians 2:15; 3:6). God has elected and called the Thessalonians from idolatry to Himself (I Thessalonians 1:4, 9; 2:12; 4:7; 5:24; II Thessalonians 1:11; 2:14). They, in turn, have responded to the Christian preaching with faith in Christ, who died and was raised (I Thessalonians 1:7–10; 4:14; 5:10). Their life as Christians is characterized by a new living with Christ (I Thessalonians 5:10), by faith, hope, and love (I Thessalonians 1:3; 5:8; II Thessalonians 1:3), and by the reception of the Holy Spirit (I Thessalonians 1:5f.; 4:8; II Thessalonians 2:13). The moral consequences of this life are described by the metaphor of walking (I Thessalonians 2:12; 4:1, 12; II Thessalonians 3:6, 11). Its consequence will be the possession of salvation (I Thessalonians 5:9; II Thessalonians 2:13). This partial list of theological themes reveals nothing that is specifically Pauline.

In the same way the most striking aspect of the eschatological teaching—that is, teaching about the last things and the Second Coming of Christ—found in the letters is its traditional character. The Second Coming of Christ will be accompanied by a command, the voice of the archangel, and the trumpet of God. That Day will come "like a thief in the night" (I Thessalonians 5:2, with which compare Matthew 24:43). II Thessalonians 2:1–12 describes what will happen before the Day of the Lord. The "mystery of lawlessness," though already at work, is now held back by the power or the person "who restrains it." Once he, or it, is removed, the man of lawlessness, or Antichrist, will be revealed, to be slain by Christ at His coming. The restraining power has commonly been identified as the Roman Empire. Others have seen the figure as Paul himself. But regardless of the puzzling problems of identification, all these details suit the general picture of the eschatological drama found in the apocalyptic writings and in the Qumran literature. See also DEAD SEA SCROLLS.

ROWAN A. GREER
Yale Divinity School

THESSALONICA, a city in Greece. The spelling is also transliterated Thessalonike or Thessaloniki. Another form is Salonika. See SALONIKA.

THESSALY, thes'ə-lē, is an administrative region of east-central Greece. Its area is 5,907 square miles (15,299 sq km), and its population (1961) is 695,385. It is separated from Macedonia on the north by Mt. Olympus, the mythological home of the Greek Olympic gods and the

highest mountain (9,550 feet; 2,911 meters) of Greece. Epirus lies to the west beyond the Pindus range, and along the Aegean Sea to the east is the coastal range of Ossa and Pelion. The region of Central Greece and Euboea lies to the south of the Othrys Mountains. The fertile Thessalian plain is drained by the Peneus River, which reaches the Aegean through the picturesque Vale of Tempe. Historically important land routes traverse Thessaly.

There are four departments (nomes) in Thessaly: Larissa, Magnesia, Karditsa, and Trikkala. The largest cities are Larissa in the central plain and Volos at the head of the Gulf of Volos (Pagasai). The chief agricultural products of Thessaly are grain, cotton, and sugar beets.

History. The rich plain of Thessaly was inhabited throughout the long Neolithic period (about 6,000–3,000 B. C.). At some sites, such as Argissa, Dimini, and Sesklo, sophisticated fortification walls and other architectural units existed by late Neolithic times. Many Mycenaean kings to the south were reputed to be descendants of the royal family at Iolchus (Volos), from which Jason and the Argonauts set out to recover the Golden Fleece.

A few families gathered enough power into their hands by the 6th century B. C. to organize Thessaly into a federal state, probably the earliest in Greece. The state was headed by an administrative and military officer called a *tagus*. Rivalries among the aristocratic families as well as the Larissan Aleuadae family's alliance with Persia during the Persian War helped to intensify a decline in the state's power during the 5th century.

Jason of Pherae revived the national state and for a brief period in the early 4th century B. C. was perhaps the most powerful leader in Greece. Thessaly was under the control of the Macedonian kings from 344 B. C., the time of Philip II, until 196 B. C., when Rome reestablished the Thessalian League. In 148 B. C., Thessaly became a part of the Roman province of Macedonia. During the Byzantine period a score of monasteries, known as the Meteora, were established on sheer cliffs. The cliffs lie at the foot of the Pindus Mountains.

JAMES R. WISEMAN
University of Texas

THETFORD MINES is a city in southeastern Quebec, Canada, about 75 miles (120 km) south of Quebec city. The principal industry is the mining of huge asbestos deposits, discovered in 1876. There are also chromium and feldspar mines in the region.

The community formerly was called Kingsville but was renamed for Thetford in Norfolk, England. It became a village in 1892, a town in 1905, and a city in 1912. Population: 22,003.

THETIS, thē'təs, in Greek myth, was a daughter of Nereus and Doris and therefore one of the Nereids (sea nymphs). Because of a prophecy that her son would have more power than his father, a mortal, Peleus, King of Phthiotis, was chosen by Zeus as her husband. Their nuptials were celebrated on Mount Pelion and were honored by the presence of all the gods except Eris, or Discord, who was not invited. To avenge the slight Eris threw in among the company the apple of discord. By Peleus, Thetis became the mother of Achilles.

THI. See TEMPERATURE-HUMIDITY INDEX.

THIAMINE, thī'ə-mēn, is a water-soluble vitamin necessary for growth, carbohydrate metabolism, and the proper functioning of nerves and muscles. Thiamine, also known as vitamin B_1, is most abundant in liver, pork, egg yolk, nuts, whole grains, legumes, and yeast. See VITAMINS—*Water-Soluble Vitamins.*

THIBAULT, Jacques Anatole François. See FRANCE, ANATOLE.

THIBODAUX, tib-ō-dō', a town in southern Louisiana, the seat of Lafourche parish, is 60 miles (96 km) southwest of New Orleans. It is the center of an agricultural region that raises sugarcane, corn, vegetables, and cotton. The town has sugar refineries, foundries, canneries, and ice plants.

Thibodaux, originally named Thibodauxville in honor of Gov. Henry S. Thibodaux of Louisiana, was established as a trading post about 1820. It was incorporated in 1838. Government is by commission. Population: 14,925.

THICK KNEE, any of a family of predominantly nocturnal shorebirds found in the temperate and tropical zones of Europe, Africa, Asia, Australia, and South America and in the semitropical and tropical zone of North America. Thick knees, also known as *stone curlews*, are named for their enlarged intertarsal joint, which actually is equivalent to the mammalian heel.

Thick knees are 14 to 20 inches (35–50 cm) long and have broad heads and large yellow eyes. Their plumage is sandy or grayish brown, usually streaked or spotted with darker brown on the back and paler below. All species have a light superciliary eyebrow, and some species have a dark eye stripe. The wings show prominent dark and light bars.

Some thick knees frequent seacoasts or riverbeds, whereas others prefer woodland, dry rocky scrub, savannah, or desert areas. They are most active at night, when they feed on large insects, worms, mollusks, crustaceans, small vertebrates, and seeds. During the day they rest motionless in low cover and are wary and difficult to ap-

Thick knees, or stone curlews, changing over at nest.

ERIC J. HOSKING

proach. If disturbed, they are reluctant to fly, preferring to run away or hide by crouching down. They need a clear runway to take off, and their flight is silent, strong, and deceptively rapid although not prolonged. Their calls are loud, mournful whistles like those of curlews.

The nest is an unlined bare hollow in the ground. Both parents incubate the two creamy to light-brown spotted eggs. The downy young leave the nest immediately after hatching.

Thick knees make up the family Burhinidae of the order Charadriformes.

GEORGE E. WATSON, *Smithsonian Institution*

THIERS, tyâr, **Louis Adolphe** (1797–1877), French political leader and historian, who led France through the critical reconstruction period after the Franco-Prussian War. Born in Marseille on April 16, 1797, Thiers studied law at Aix-en-Provence and then became a journalist when he went to Paris in 1821. He made a reputation through his articles in a liberal journal, *Constitutionnel,* and he achieved even more fame with his 10-volume *Histoire de la révolution française* (1823–1827), a work that was a literary success and an indirect attack against the reactionary monarchy. In 1830 he helped found an antigovernment paper, *National,* whose success did much to precipitate the July Revolution.

Thiers held several ministerial posts during the July Monarchy (1830–1848). Although he was premier twice, his ill-considered, bellicose policies were unacceptable to King Louis Philippe, who first dismissed Thiers in 1836 for advocating intervention in Spain, and again in 1840 when Thiers' Middle East policy nearly involved France in a war with Britain. Thiers then opposed the regime in the Chamber of Deputies but devoted most of his efforts to his second major work, the 20-volume *Histoire du consulat et de l'empire* (1845–1861). In 1846 he re-emerged as a vigorous government opponent and was about to become premier when the revolution of 1848 broke out.

Elected to the Constituent Assembly, Thiers accepted the republic unenthusiastically and supported Louis Napoléon for the presidency. When he opposed Napoléon's seizure of power in 1851, however, Thiers was exiled. Returning to France after a few months, Thiers did not participate actively in politics until 1863, when he began to figure prominently in efforts to liberalize the empire. He opposed the policy that plunged France into the disastrous war with Prussia but declined to join the emergency government of national defense. Instead he embarked on a diplomatic mission in a vain attempt to solicit support for France.

Leader of France. Thiers was successful, however, first in securing an armistice from German Chancellor Otto von Bismarck and then in personally negotiating an acceptable peace settlement. Chosen "head of the executive power," Thiers next had to restore the government's authority in Paris, which he had deliberately abandoned to the radicals and their revolutionary Commune of 1871. The repression, conducted according to Thiers' own plan, was so severe that it nearly destroyed the working-class movement and greatly exacerbated class antagonisms.

Thiers was then picked as the first president of the yet unformed republic. Although he preferred constitutional monarchy, Thiers believed that the republic would divide France least. His support of the Third Republic, however, caused the monarchist majority in the National Assembly to unite long enough to force Thiers to resign in 1873. By then Thiers' sound administration had enabled France to recover from the war and meet the terms of the peace treaty. When he died in St. Germain-en-Laye on Sept. 3, 1877, most Frenchmen thought of Thiers as the nation's "liberator," for he had delivered France from the German occupiers.

RICHARD T. BIENVENU, *University of Missouri*

THIEU, tyû, **Nguyen Van** (1923–), Vietnamese army officer, who became president of South Vietnam in 1965. He was born in Phan Rang, in what is now South Vietnam, on April 5, 1923. He is popularly referred to as "Thieu," although his surname is Nguyen Van.

After graduating from the Vietnamese military academy in Da Lat in 1948, Thieu studied in France. He fought on the side of the French during the Indochina War of 1946–1954. In 1960 he was given command of the 1st Infantry Division of South Vietnam by the government of President Ngo Dinh Diem.

During the November 1963 coup that overthrew Diem, Thieu led a regiment against the presidential bodyguard. When a 10-man military committee took power in June 1965, Thieu, who was its chairman, became chief of state. He was elected president on Sept. 3, 1967. Thieu's appointment of Gen. Tran Tieu Khiem as prime minister on Sept. 1, 1969, in place of the civilian Tran Van Huong, underlined the military and authoritarian character of his regime.

JOSEPH BUTTINGER
Author of "Vietnam: A Dragon Embattled"

THIGHBONE, also called *femur,* the longest and strongest bone in the human body. See FEMUR.

THIGMOTROPISM, thig-mo'trə-piz-əm, an involuntary movement of an organism or part of an organism in response to the stimulus of physical contact or touch. The term is most often used in botany to refer to a plant's curving toward a solid object. See TROPISM.

THIMANN, Kenneth Vivian (1904–), American botanist who isolated and purified auxin, the plant growth hormone, and studied its function. Inspired by the American botanist Fritz Went's discovery (1928) that a diffusible plant growth substance could be collected from the cut tips of seedlings, Thimann collaborated with Went's associate Herman Dolk. After Dolk's death in 1933, Thimann completed their work, obtaining the pure auxin and identifying it as indole-3-acetic acid in 1934.

Working with the American botanists James Bonner, Went, and Folke Skoog, Thimann proved that auxins control cell elongation, root formation, and bud growth. He also showed that synthetic substances could act as auxins—a finding that led to the development of several important agricultural growth substances.

Thimann was born in Ashford, Kent, England, on Aug. 5, 1904, and received his Ph. D. from Imperial College in London. He taught at the California Institute of Technology from 1930 to 1935 and at Harvard University from 1935 to 1965, when he became provost at the University of California at Santa Cruz.

JOHN F. BENNETT, *Stanford University*

THIMBLE, thim'bəl, a small, usually bell-shaped cap used to protect the needle finger in sewing. Seamstresses use thimbles with a round end and indentations to keep the needle from slipping. Tailors' thimbles are open at the end. A sailmaker's thimble, or "thummel," is a heavy ring worn on the thumb, with a disk attached to push the needle. Ordinary sewing thimbles are made of metal or plastic, but in the past they were made of gold, silver, bone, ivory, leather, or china. The Chinese used them at an early date, and they were probably introduced into Europe in the 17th century by Nicholas van Benschoten of Amsterdam.

THIMBLEWEED is a common name for any of several plants having thimble-shaped flowers or flower heads. Among the plants often called thimbleweed are the coneflower and some anemones and clovers. See ANEMONE; CLOVER; CONEFLOWER.

THIMBU, thim'bōō, is the capital of the Himalayan country of Bhutan. Built in a narrow valley, one of the few valleys of the inner Himalaya, the town is situated on the banks of the Thimbu River at an elevation of 7,950 feet (2,423 meters).

Still under construction in the early 1970's, Thimbu consisted of a small cluster of houses immediately south of Tashi Chho Dzong, a fortified monastery being converted and expanded to house all of Bhutan's administrative departments. The capital will include schools, a hospital, and shopping and entertainment centers. It is already served by Bhutan's first hydroelectric power station and first modern road. Buses using the road link Thimbu with Siliguri, India. Population: (1964 est.) 10,000.

BEATRICE D. MILLER, *Beloit College*
ROBERT J. MILLER, *University of Wisconsin*

THIN-FILM CIRCUITS are microcircuits formed by depositing thin films on a flat supporting base. In one method, a vaporized metal or insulating material passes through a mask and then solidifies as a precisely placed film pattern on a ceramic base. Film thickness ranges from a fraction of a micron to several microns (1 micron = 0.0001 cm). For circuits used in industry, thin-film resistors are formed on a ceramic base as fine metal lines long enough to provide the desired resistance values; a metal such as nichrome or tantalum typically is used for resistors.

Thin-film capacitors are formed by depositing a film of insulating material, such as silicon monoxide, between two thin films of a metal such as copper, aluminum, or tantalum. Metallic interconnections are used to complete the circuit designs. Individual transistors are attached to film networks after the films are deposited; this is done because thin-film semiconductor transistors have been made only in laboratory models.

THIOKOL, thī'ə-kôl, is the trade name for a group of synthetic rubbers that are resistant to oils, hydrocarbons, acids, and mild alkalis. They are used as sealants for fuel cells and machine and electrical parts. Hoses, caulking, printers' rolls, tank linings, gaskets, and cable covering may be made of Thiokol. Thiokol is made by the reaction of polysulfides with ethylene dichloride or dichloroethyl ether.

THIRD CENTURY. Much of the civilized world at the opening of the 3d century A. D. was under the sway or influence of three great imperial systems: the Roman, the Parthian, and the Chinese. Within a few decades all of these empires either cracked or collapsed.

On the death of Marcus Aurelius in 180, the Roman Empire headed into troubled times and, though a dire crisis was forestalled until 235, when the Severan line of emperors came to an end, for almost a half century thereafter the imperial throne was the prize of military commanders. Unity and order were fully restored by Diocletian, who became emperor in 284. His many reforms helped considerably to extend the life of the empire.

The Parthian regime in Iran, racked by revolt for many years, expired in the early 3d century. It was replaced by the Sassanian dynasty, which endured for more than 400 years. In China, the downfall of the Later Han dynasty in 220 marked the close of four centuries of united imperial rule. The ensuing Age of Political Disunity lasted until 589.

The subcontinent of India continued to be politically unstable during the 3d century. But during this period Indian religious and cultural influences began, with lasting effects, to take hold in many parts of Southeast Asia.

HYMAN KUBLIN, *Brooklyn College*

1. Rome

From the beginning of the 3d century down to 235 the Roman Empire was ruled by the dynasty founded by Septimius Severus (reigned 193–211). After the extinction of the Severan house came the Great Crisis of the Roman Empire (235–270). Emperors backed either by the legions or by the Senate followed each other in rapid succession and saw their position challenged by competing army groups. At the same time the empire was attacked on several sides by dangerous foreign foes. Saxons appeared in the English Channel, Franks crossed the Rhine, Goths raided the Aegean area, and the powerful Persian Empire under the new Sassanian dynasty threatened the eastern provinces. Gaul and the East virtually seceded from the empire in the 260's. The cities especially suffered from the wars. After 270, however, the fabric of the Roman Empire was restored by a series of emperors.

CRISIS AND CONSOLIDATION

In the 3d century the Roman Empire lost to the barbarians the territories in the triangle between the upper reaches of the Rhine and Danube rivers (now Baden-Württemberg) and the province of Dacia (now Rumania), north of the lower Danube. In themselves these evacuations of border provinces by the Roman armies were not critical, but the 3d century was also a period of thoroughgoing social, economic, intellectual, and religious upheavals.

Population Decline. At the end of the 3d century, the Roman Empire had a population of about 50 million, compared with about 70 million at the beginning of the 1st century. The populations of Gaul, Italy, and Greece were decimated as a result of foreign and domestic crises, including a plague that raged practically without interruption in the 250's and 260's. The numerical reduction of the total population was especially dangerous because it was coupled with an even greater decline in the Romanized part

ROGER VIOLLET

TRIUMPH of Persian king Shapur I over Roman emperor Valerian in 258 or 259 is commemorated in cliff sculpture at Naqsh-i Rustam, Iran. Shapur (on horse) may have captured Valerian (kneeling) in personal combat.

of the population. To make up for this decline, the imperial government, from the days of Emperor Marcus Aurelius (reigned 161–180), settled large numbers of Germanic prisoners in the Balkan Peninsula and in Gaul.

Social Changes. In the age of the Antonines (138–192) the Roman legions had been recruited primarily from the propertied classes in the cities. Now, in the 3d century, this became increasingly difficult, and the government consequently had to draw on the manpower resources of the least Romanized regions, notably Illyricum (in the Balkan Peninsula). These armies of the 3d century felt a much stronger attachment to the emperors than to the Roman state. In an age of debased currency and inflationary pressures, the emperors attempted to buy the loyalty of the troops by lavish distributions of gold among the soldiers. This mutual bond between emperors and armies strengthened the economic position of the soldiers at the expense of the civilian population and led to the militarization of the Roman Empire. Even the civilian administration of the empire was now largely in the hands of Illyrians, Africans, or Orientals who had previously distinguished themselves in the armed forces. The emperors of the 3d century were regularly proclaimed by the armies, and the Senate normally did nothing but ratify the choice of the legions.

These were not the only social changes in the fabric of the Roman Empire. Ever since the time of Emperor Hadrian (reigned 117–138) the entire military strength had been stationed in fortified places along the frontiers. In the 3d century, Roman resources were no longer sufficient to permit this system of a rigid frontier cordon, and a transition was gradually made to the grouping of armies in depth. The best units were stationed at points far to the rear of the frontiers, at important road junctions from which they could be marched speedily to any point where an invasion occurred. Such strategic places were Aquileia, Milan, and Verona in Italy; Trier in Gaul; and Sirmium in Pannonia. As time passed, the venerable urban centers of the Greco-Roman world, most particularly Rome, as well as the more civilized provinces, lost their importance and were overshadowed by the new garrison cities in the frontier provinces. At the same time the preferential position of Italy in relation to the provinces was erased by the Antonine Constitution (212) which granted Roman citizenship to all freeborn provincials.

Regimentation of the Economy. The military requirements of the 3d century brought about the transition from a free to a regimented economy. The foreign and domestic wars of the 3d century demanded an ever-increasing outlay, but the numbers and the economic resources of the taxpayers, as well as the volume of their economic activity, were constantly on the decline. If the armies were to be paid and equipped and if the cities were to be provisioned, the emperors had to make use of all sorts of compulsory measures to ensure the regular payment of taxes in money and in kind. For this reason the peasants and their descendants were prohibited from leaving their land and often were organized communally to ensure their ability to discharge various obligations. Municipal council members and their families were made responsible for the taxes in their cities. Similarly, the trades considered vital for provisioning the cities, such as shipping and baking, were placed under government control.

Another means of satisfying the increased financial demands of the state was the debasement of the currency: gold coins were reduced in size, and silver coins lost practically all their silver content. The resulting inflation, as well as the intensification of compulsory measures, increased the evils they were designed to remedy: city dwellers abandoned their property, and in Gaul especially peasants banded together in gangs, disturbed the countryside, and forced the emperors of the 3d, 4th, and 5th centuries to undertake military campaigns for the purpose of restoring law and order.

The Restoration. The Roman Empire was saved by the emperors from Aurelian to Constantine the Great. Aurelian (reigned 270–275) reconquered the eastern provinces from the romantic Zenobia, queen of Palmyra, and soon liquidated the "Gallic Empire" in a battle near Châlons. Diocletian (reigned 284–305) reestablished orderly processes of government in an empire torn by decades of civil wars and anarchy. To prevent further usurpations and to provide for the defense of the empire he established the tetrarchy, or system of four emperors: two augusti and two caesars shared the responsibility of defending the empire against foreign and domestic foes. Each of the four emperors had his own court, his own army, and his own civilian administration. Thus the armed forces and the bureaucracy increased in number. At the same time a rigid distinction was introduced between military and civilian authorities, primarily to obviate the danger of further usurpations. For the same reason Diocletian systematized a new court ceremonial borrowed probably from Sassanian Persia and designed to raise the emperor above the level of ordinary mortals. All these reforms intensified the demands of the state on the citizens of the empire, but they succeeded in extending its life.

RELIGION

In this age of insecurity, men were inclined to put their trust in divine help. In the eastern provinces of the empire, local cults, in addition to emperor worship, flourished with increased vigor. Judaism and Christianity were practiced widely. The Oriental cults of Cybele, Isis, Juppiter Dolichenus, and other deities became prominent in the West. All of them commemorated and reenacted the death and resurrection of a god. Even more important in the 3d century was the cult of the Iranian Mithras, whose cave-like sanctuaries are found wherever Roman troops were stationed. The initiates of Mithras saw in their god a power able and willing to protect them in the here and the hereafter, provided only that they lived up to his moral precepts. One Oriental cult, that of the Syrian Sol Invictus (Unconquered Sun) was officially inaugurated at Rome in 274 by Emperor Aurelian in order to provide the nationalities of the empire with a common religious denominator. This is only the most prominent instance of a process of religious syncretism that frequently assimilated the gods of different regions to each other and led to an interchange of their attributes. In the midst of foreign invasions, social upheavals, and economic disasters, men believed in dreams and spirits, practiced magic and astrology, and resorted to all kinds of religious experimentation.

Christianity. The spirit of the age favored the Christian church, which was hierarchically organized, based its teachings in a sacred book, and —unlike all other religions in the Roman Empire with the exception of Judaism—forbade participation in other cults. We hear of Christian martyrs in Egypt and Africa early in the 3d century. During the Great Crisis, the Roman emperors decided to break the resistance of the church to emperor worship. Emperor Decius began a persecution of the Christians (249–251) by calling on all inhabitants of the empire to perform prescribed pagan cult acts. The persecution was resumed by Emperor Valerian in 257. Both emperors met with a violent end, and the persecutions were halted, to flare up for a last time at the beginning of the 4th century. During these persecutions many Christians complied with the demands of the political authorities. However, when Gallienus issued an edict of toleration in 260, the "lapsed" were restored to the church, and afterward pagans came to remember the heroism of the martyrs rather than the weakness of the "lapsed." The persecutions of the 3d century thus strengthened rather than weakened the church.

At the same time the bishops of Rome assumed an increasingly important position in the church; in particular, they took the lead in dealing with heretical opinions that had arisen within it. Most important among these was Monarchianism, which refused to regard Jesus as a second divine person but considered him the incarnation of God the Father. Monarchians were opposed by the proponents of the "Logos theology," for which Jesus was the Logos (or Word of God) incarnate, created by God the Father in time. The controversy was decided by St. Dionysius, who became bishop of Rome probably in 260 and condemned the extremes of both positions. The bishop of Alexandria, also called Dionysius, was forced to give up his doctrine of Jesus' creation in time and to accept the Roman teaching of the eternity of the Son, and in 268 the Monarchian Paul of Samosata, who had become bishop of Antioch, was declared a heretic and deposed. The 3d century also saw the origin and a modest spread of Manichaeism, which reached its highest point only in the 4th and later centuries.

At the end of the 3d century Christianity was still a minority religion, but its adherents must have numbered several millions. It commanded the allegiance of the majority of the population in certain areas, such as Anatolia, and of very sizable minorities in other areas, such as Italy and North Africa.

INTELLECTUAL ACTIVITY

Literature and Historiography. The catastrophic events that befell the ancient world in the 3d century discouraged literary and artistic activity. To offset Christian propaganda, Julia Domna, wife of Septimius Severus, commissioned the orator Philostratus to write the life of a pagan saint and wonder-worker of the 1st century, Apollonius of Tyana. Other types of escapist literature were the Greek romances, of which Longus' *Daphnis and Chloë* is the outstanding example, and Athenaeus' *Deipnosophistai,* with its essays on the fine art of genteel living. Under Alexander Severus (reigned 222–235), Dio Cassius wrote a history of Rome from legendary times to his own day; it is one of the most important sources for Roman imperial history. The greatest and most influential Roman jurists—Papinian, Ulpian, and Julius Paulus—wrote in the early 3d century.

PALMYRA, once a rich caravan city in the Syrian desert, challenged the power of both Persia and Rome in the 3d century. The city was captured by the Romans in 272 and destroyed by them the following year, after it revolted.

PHOTO CICCIONE FROM RAPHO GUILLUMETTE

Philosophy and Theology. The dying paganism of this century produced one philosophical school of considerable originality—Neoplatonism, of which the Egyptian, Plotinus, was the most important representative. He taught at Rome and there wrote his *Enneads* (or groups of nine books). Unlike Plato, Plotinus did not believe in a rigid separation of the intelligible world and the material one. A continuous chain of emanations linked the One (or the Absolute, or God) with the worlds of thought and of matter, and man was declared able to reach the Absolute by an act of what Plotinus called "creative contemplation" or "assimilation with God." The last of the original pagan philosophers thus did not condemn the material world as a prison for the soul but saw in it a beautiful replica of the divine One.

Meanwhile, a fusion of Christian revelation and Platonic philosophy had produced in Alexandria the first great theological system of the church, that of Origen. In 203 he became the head of the Catechetical School at Alexandria. In his work *On First Principles* he explained the Biblical account of creation with the help of the Platonic distinction between the two worlds of form and matter. To Origen, as a Platonist, only incorporeal intelligences had existed from all eternity. Some of these had fallen away from God. For their education and correction the visible world had been created and bodies had been given to them. Their redemption from the material world will come through Christ. The whole process of fall and redemption will be repeated several times, until finally all souls will be united with God. This theological system was clearly Platonic, inasmuch as it considered the visible world a result of the fall of some of the incorporeal intelligences. Origen became the founder of Christian (especially Eastern) theology, although some of his views were later declared heretical. He also wrote a famous apology of the Christian faith (*Contra Celsum*) and compiled the *Hexapla* ("Sixfold"), in which the Hebrew text of the Old Testament was compared with several of its Greek translations.

In the West the church found a fiery apologist in Tertullian and a great defender of orthodoxy and church discipline in St. Cyprian, bishop of Carthage. Yet Latin Christianity had to wait for more than a century until it produced in St. Augustine a theologian of the stature of Origen.

Architecture, Sculpture, and Painting. During the first 70 years of the 3d century, only the emperors were able to undertake large building projects, such as the Arch of Septimius Severus, erected in the Roman Forum, or the Baths of Caracalla, also in Rome. Imperial building activity reached a high point after the restoration of the state, when Diocletian and his colleagues adorned their cities of residence with palaces, baths, and other buildings.

Except for imperial portraits, sculpture in the round was appreciated less and less in the 3d century, while relief work (as on sarcophagi or arches) became ever more frequent. The function of these reliefs was to impress the spectator with the transcendent majesty and power of the persons represented, especially of the imperial family.

Historical events tended to be transformed into ceremonial symbols. Social rank was represented by size, so that the socially more important figures were shown in larger scale than others. Individuals came to be represented frontally rather than in profile, and in their faces emphasis was placed on the spiritual personality (especially the eyes) rather than on auxiliary features. The catacomb paintings and the early Christian sarcophagi show that this "late-classical" style influenced the first artistic expressions of the early church.

PAUL J. ALEXANDER
Author of "The Ancient World to 300 A. D."

2. Middle East

The primary importance of the Middle East in the 3d century lay in its position across the main trade route from China and India, the great luxury producers of the time, to the rich consumer lands of the Mediterranean basin. At the beginning of the century the Iranian section of this route had long been in the hands of the alien Parthians. But the Parthians soon gave way to a new power, the Persian Sassanians.

Political Developments. Sandwiched between two expansionist powers—the Romans to the west and the Kushanas to the east—and subject to chronic dynastic instability, the Parthians were able to defend themselves but lacked the strength and organization to take advantage of military success. Little is known of events in the east. In the west, in Mesopotamia, war between Parthia and Rome in 215–217 ended with the extension of the Parthian frontier to the Euphrates. However, the effort merely exhausted the Parthian kingdom and provided an opportunity for its overthrow.

The final blow came from the vassal kingdom of Persis, whose ruler Ardashir overthrew the last Parthian king in 224 or 226. He established the Sassanian dynasty, named for his grandfather Sassan. The Sassanian empire was more closely knit than the Parthian and, tracing its origins to the Old Persian empire, was eager to reestablish Persia's ancient boundaries. Ardashir and his son Shapur I (reigned 240–272) reduced the weakening Kushana empire to vassaldom, thus extending the Sassanian realm to the Oxus (Amu Darya) and Indus valleys. Shapur conducted several successful campaigns against the Romans, culminating in 258 or 259 with the capture of Emperor Valerian and a large Roman army near Edessa (modern Urfa, Turkey).

Despite these successes, the Persians, like the Parthians and the Romans, lacked the strength for permanent conquest. Shapur was forced to retreat, and the initiative was seized by Palmyra, a rich caravan city situated between the Euphrates and the Mediterranean. Palmyra was nominally a Roman colony, but when its ruler Odenathus defeated Shapur the Romans allowed him to conquer Mesopotamia virtually in his own interest. After his murder in 267 his wife, Zenobia, added Syria, Egypt, and most of Anatolia to the Palmyrene conquests, and a new Middle Eastern power seemed to have been born. But in 272 the short-lived empire collapsed before a Roman attack.

In Persia, the Sassanian kings were distracted by dynastic problems and revolt in the east. Varahran II (reigned 276–293), faced by a rebellious brother and a Kushana revival, yielded Armenia and northern Mesopotamia to Rome in 283. In 297, Narseh (reigned 293–302) was forced to surrender further territory in eastern Armenia, and the century ended with Persia once more on the defensive.

Religion. The Parthians' attitude toward religion was easygoing and tolerant. They themselves had adopted a form of Iranian Mazda-worship but saw no need to persecute other faiths. But Christianity, Buddhism, and other foreign religions became increasingly attractive to Persians, and the new dynasty found in them a universal, international spirit that was totally opposed to their nationalistic revival.

Shapur saw that the empire needed a Persian religion to offer similar attractions. He therefore showed much favor to Mani, a local prophet who preached universal redemption, immortality, and the triumph of good over evil. Under Shapur's successors the policy of support for Manichaeism was reversed, and the national Zoroastrian church was built up in a mood of militant orthodoxy as a partner of the government and a persecutor of heresies. But Manichaeism survived to influence China and medieval Europe.

The Arts. The replacement of the Parthians by the Sassanians brought about a strong creative upsurge in the Middle East. Numerous rock sculptures, metal bowls, stamp seals, coins, and other objects reveal the splendor and confidence of a new national art. In architecture, too, the early Sassanians evolved a style which, like their art, was based on older Iranian traditions but drew freely and effectively on foreign sources. The beginnings of written, as distinct from oral, literature can also be found, starting with the collection and arrangement of sacred books, and extending to epic, moral fable, and scientific works, many from Indian and Greek sources.

Social Organization. The social organization of the Sassanians was based on that of their predecessors, but was much more centralized and efficient. Under the king was a feudal pyramid of nobles of varying degrees, filling administrative positions, providing service in war, and bound by loyalty to the royal house. For these people the benefits of foreign campaigns, flourishing commerce, improved agriculture, and large-scale public works provided a life of luxury and refined ease. But the majority of the people, tied to the soil and barred from social advancement, had little hope of material gain and, with the rejection of Manichaeism, lost spiritual hope as well. The civilization created by the early Sassanians, although brilliant, was shallow and from the beginning contained the seeds of its final destruction.

JAMES G. MACQUEEN
University of Bristol, England

3. South and Southeast Asia

The record of events in South and Southeast Asia in the 3d century is sketchy and uncertain. In India two great empires, the Kushana in the north and the Satavahana in the south, were crumbling. In Southeast Asia the century witnessed the transition from protohistory to history.

The Political Picture. The Kushanas had ruled over extensive parts of northern India and Afghanistan, and under their patronage Buddhism had begun its journey into Central Asia. During the 3d century, Kushana rule was increasingly subverted by numerous Scythian (Shaka) dynasties that rose in central and western India and by scattered republican oligarchies in northern and central India. The Satavahanas, who had controlled the Deccan for nearly two centuries, were rapidly superseded by local dynasties such as the Abhira and the Vishnukundin. Farther south, in the Tamil country, the Pallavas were rising into eminence, while Ceylon, recovering from the aftermath of the Chola invasions of the 2d century, was beginning to enjoy peace, unity, and prosperity under the successors of Gajabahu (reigned 174–196).

In the Indochinese Peninsula, the kingdom of Funan, with its center in Cambodia, was consolidating and extending its power in the valley of the lower Mekong and westward into the Malay Peninsula. A ruler called Fan Shih-man by the

EVENTS OF THE THIRD CENTURY

212 Antonine constitution granted Roman citizenship to all freeborn provincials.
220 Collapse of the Later Han dynasty in China ushered in the Age of the Three Kingdoms (220–265), first phase of a long period of political disunity.
224 or 226 Parthian dynasty in Iran fell, and Sassanian dynasty was established.
235 Great Crisis of the Roman Empire began after murder of Emperor Alexander Severus ended Severan line.
249 Roman Emperor Decius began persecution of Christians.
251 Goths defeated and killed Roman Emperor Decius.
253 or 254 Christian theologian Origen died.
258 or 259 Shapur I of Persia defeated the Romans at Edessa and took Emperor Valerian prisoner.
270 Neoplatonist philosopher Plotinus died.
272 Palmyra fell to the Romans.
275 Death of Emperor Aurelian ended 5-year reign during which he reunited the Roman Empire.
c.277 Persian prophet Mani, founder of Manichaeism, was put to death.
280 Chin dynasty conquered Wu, last of the Three Kingdoms, and briefly reunited China.
284 Diocletian, reorganizer of the Roman Empire, came to the throne.

LOUIS FRÉDÉRIC FROM RAPHO GUILLUMETTE

STATUE OF BUDDHA from Gandhara, in what is now northwestern Pakistan, shows Greek or Roman influence.

Chinese led Funan from about 205 to 225, and he and his successors made extensive conquests and maintained diplomatic contacts with China and India. The Funanese had mastered the technique of draining swamps. As a result, settled agriculture coupled with trade became the basis of their economic power.

In what is now central Vietnam lay the early Cham kingdom of Lin-yi. The Chinese occupation of Tonkin, the Vietnamese homeland to the north of Lin-yi, set in motion a struggle between the Chinese and both Lin-yi and the Vietnamese. Other Southeast Asian states in the 3d century were the kingdoms of Langkasuka and Tambralinga in the Malay Peninsula. On the west coast of Burma, a local dynasty ruled in Arakan.

Cultural Developments. Culturally, the 3d century was of great importance in South and Southeast Asia. In India the new devotional, mystical Mahayana form of Buddhism was clearly ascendant. The Kushans supported it, and under their patronage a unique form of art had come into being. This art, called Gandharan from the district of Gandhara in northwest India, was inspired by Greco-Roman styles and Indian ideals as understood by the Kushanas, who were of Central Asian origin. Gandharan art effectively broke the earlier taboo against depicting the Buddha in plastic form, and workshops in the Peshawar and Mathura regions turned out hundreds of Buddhist icons. A new spirit in Hinduism brought into prominence Vishnu and Shiva as the two great gods of the Hindu revival and reformation. Classical Sanskrit was also coming into its own, and works attributed to the 3d century clearly foreshadow the coming efflorescence.

The 3d century was notable for the spread of Indian cultural influences to most parts of mainland Southeast Asia and to Indonesia. The new ideas were transmitted by Hindu and Buddhist priests and missionaries, traders, and adventurers, who established colonies and intermingled with the local nobilities. The kingdom of Funan, for example, traced its origin to the advent of Indian cultural influences, which were assimilated into an evolving Cambodian civilization.

B. G. GOKHALE
Wake Forest University

4. East Asia

China. As the 3d century opened, the Later (Eastern) Han dynasty, which had reigned for almost 200 years, was disintegrating. Imperial government had virtually broken down, and military strong men wielded power. Were it not for Ts'ao Ts'ao, the ablest of the Later Han generals, the dynasty would doubtless have been overthrown sooner than it was. With his death in 220, the Han regime collapsed. Thus was ushered in the Age of Political Disunity, which prevailed until 589, when the Sui dynasty restored imperial unity. Two of the six dynasties that Chinese historians have recognized as legitimate during this period—the Shu and the Chin (Tsin)—reigned during the 3d century.

Three Kingdoms and Chin Dynasty. With the collapse of the Later Han regime three large kingdoms soon divided up much of the imperial realm among themselves. In the north, occupying the oldest settled areas of China and the most highly developed region in East Asia, the state of Wei was founded by the son of Ts'ao Ts'ao. To the south, with its main centers of power in the lower Yangtse River valley, but extending as far as northern Vietnam, the state of Wu emerged. The state of Shu, ruled by a descendant of a Later Han emperor, was set up in the southwest. These three kingdoms, each aspiring to restore imperial unity, vied for supremacy for about a half century, a period known in Chinese history as the Age of the Three Kingdoms. After Wei had overwhelmed and annexed Shu in 264, a Wei general, Ssu-ma Yen, usurped the throne in 265 and proclaimed the establishment of a new dynasty, the Chin. In 280 he subjugated the southern kingdom of Wu and thereby restored imperial unity. The new and united regime scarcely outlived its founder, however. With his death in 290 the Chin dynasty tottered, finally disappearing in 316.

Traditionally, the larger history of China in the 3d century has been overshadowed by the dramatic events and personalities of the turbulent Age of the Three Kingdoms. The many legends and folktales inspired by the events of the era furnished the substance for a later Chinese literary classic, the *Romance of the Three Kingdoms* (*San Kuo Chih Yen I*).

Philosophy and Religion. During the 400-year span of the Han dynasties (202 B. C.–220 A. D.), Confucian philosophy, entailing the modified teachings of Confucius and his disciples, had won a preeminent position in official and intellectual life. It was during this era that Confucianism was elevated to the status of an official cult and its exponents won for themselves a privileged place in Chinese life. But as the Later Han dynasty declined and the political upheavals of the 3d century set in, Confucian scholarship was arrested and ceased to be a prerequisite of official advancement. The 3d century in China was not philosophically and intellectually sterile.

however. In scattered areas, Confucian patronage and learning continued to endure. But more important for the philosophical growth of the Chinese people, other bodies of thought were now increasingly thrust forward for their attention.

Buddhism, which had seeped inconspicuously into the Chinese empire in Later Han times, now began to take on greater visibility. Stupas, commemorative monuments to the Buddha, were frequently erected in the great cities of the north. New ideas, spiritual and cosmological, which had scarcely occurred to previous generations of Chinese philosophers, turned minds in new and fertile directions. The very vocabulary of Chinese learning was lastingly enriched by the intrusions of Buddhism.

Taoism, representing native streams of Chinese thought, also underwent many fundamental changes during the 3d century. The somewhat recondite teachings of the legendary Lao Tzu and particularly of the master Chuang Tzu had, before the Han period, evoked the interest of few individuals. The process of modification and popularization of Taoism, which had gathered momentum during the era of the Han dynasties, continued with vital effects in the 3d century. More and more, Taoism started to take on beliefs and characteristics that were antithetical to the teachings of the earlier philosophical school. It is likely that some of these changes were due to the influences of Buddhism.

Ethnic Changes. One result of the turbulence of the 3d century was that the composition of the Chinese people was altered. Warriors from non-Chinese tribes to the north and west entered the military service of the warring Chinese armies and intermarried with local Chinese women. Many Chinese migrated from the war zones into the frontier regions of the south and southwest. There they intermarried with local non-Chinese peoples and intensified the Sinification process already under way among these peoples.

Korea and Japan. Little is known about the Korean peninsula and the Japanese islands in the 3d century. The inhabitants of these areas were culturally less developed than the Chinese, who had an imperfect knowledge of them. Several centuries had yet to elapse before the Koreans and Japanese stepped firmly onto the stage of history.

HYMAN KUBLIN
Brooklyn College

Bibliography

Balasz, Étienne, *Chinese Civilization and Bureaucracy: Variations on a Theme* (New Haven 1964).
Cambridge University Press, *The Cambridge Ancient History,* vol. 12 (New York and London 1939).
Coedès, George, *The Making of South East Asia* (Berkeley and Los Angeles 1966).
Fitzgerald, Charles P., *China: A Short Cultural History,* 3d ed. (New York 1965).
Frye, Richard N., *The Heritage of Persia* (Cleveland 1963).
Ghirshman, Roman, *Persian Art: The Parthian and Sassanian Dynasties* (New York 1962).
Goodrich, Luther Carrington, *A Short History of the Chinese People,* 3d ed. (New York 1963).
Hall, Daniel G. E., *A History of South-East Asia,* 3d ed. (New York 1968).
McNeill, William H., *The Rise of the West: A History of the Human Community,* chap. 8 (Chicago 1963).
Majumdar, Ramesh C., ed., *The History and Culture of the Indian People,* vol. 2 (Bombay 1951).
Parker, Henry M. D., *A History of the Roman World, from A. D. 138 to 337,* 2d ed. (New York 1958).
Reischauer, Edwin O., and Fairbank, John K., *East Asia: The Great Tradition* (Boston 1960).
Rostovtzev, Mikhail I., *The Social and Economic History of the Roman Empire,* 2d ed., chaps. 9–12 (New York and London 1957).

THIRD ESTATE, one of the orders into which French society was divided before the French Revolution. The French form of the name is *tiers état.* It included all Frenchmen who were not members of the clergy (First Estate) or the aristocracy (Second Estate). After the Third Estate was legally established as a separate order in the 14th century, it began to take part in the Estates General, a consultative body irregularly convoked by the crown. Led by middle-class lawyers, merchants, and professional men, the Third Estate usually sided with the monarchy against the aristocracy. Although the Third Estate grew in size and economic power, it was unable to acquire political power.

When bankruptcy forced King Louis XVI to convoke the Estates General in 1789, the Third Estate deputies resolved not to meet as a separate order. Defying the King, they urged the other orders to join them and declared themselves a National Assembly. Their determination, the King's indecision, and the popular uprisings of July 1789 enabled the Third Estate to achieve most of its goals by the end of 1789. The National Assembly's constitution of 1791 declared that all Frenchmen were legally equal and thus abolished the three orders as legal entities. See also FRANCE–*History* (Revolution, Consulate, and Empire); FRENCH REVOLUTION.

RICHARD T. BIENVENU
University of Missouri

THIRD INTERNATIONAL. See INTERNATIONAL.

THIRD ORDER. See TERTIARIES.

THIRD REICH. See GERMANY–*History* (*The Third Reich*).

THIRD REPUBLIC. See FRANCE–*The Third Republic, 1870–1940.*

THIRST is a sensation felt in the mouth and throat and associated with the urge to drink. Among the causes of thirst are dehydration of the body tissues, prolonged use of the voice, eating salty, spicy, or sweet foods, feelings of fear or anxiety, and certain diseases, such as diabetes.

In higher animals, including man, thirst and drinking probably are controlled by a center in the brain. Ordinarily this center is stimulated when water is lost in an amount exceeding 1% of the body weight. Death caused by dehydration occurs before water loss exceeds 20% of the body weight, but the rate at which water is lost depends on the temperature of the environment. Thus a person may survive without water for only one or two days in the desert but for a week or more at sea.

A. V. WOLF
College of Medicine, University of Illinois

THIRTEEN COLONIES, the 13 governing units in British North America that, by the Declaration of Independence in 1776, proclaimed themselves the United States of America. They were New Hampshire, Massachusetts, Rhode Island, Connecticut, New York, New Jersey, Pennsylvania, Maryland, Delaware, Virginia, North Carolina, South Carolina, and Georgia. See AMERICAN REVOLUTION; CONTINENTAL CONGRESS; DECLARATION OF INDEPENDENCE; UNITED STATES–*The English Colonies in America, 1607–1763;* and articles on the individual states.

THIRTEENTH CENTURY. The 13th century in Europe was the period in which medieval man's conception of Christendom was most nearly realized. It was characterized by creativity, dynamism, and a search for unity in spiritual, intellectual, and political affairs.

Spiritually, the drive was toward reform, the organization of a Christian order in society, and important missionary activity beyond the confines of Christendom. Intellectually, the universities produced a great synthesis of the religious doctrines of Christianity and the philosophical and scientific traditions of Greek and Arabic culture. Politically, the period came close to establishing a federation of Christian peoples under papal leadership. It witnessed the rise of strong monarchies, the foundation of representative constitutional government, and the growth of self-government in towns. In architecture and sculpture, the Gothic style reached maturity in great cathedrals of unsurpassed beauty. In literature, a popular vernacular prose and poetry developed. Books proliferated as never before. The organization of guilds for religious, political, social, and economic purposes, the growth of a money economy, and the development of new business techniques in an age of economic expansion resulted in prosperity. And this prosperity, occurring during a period of relative peace, made possible the enormous cultural achievements of the century.

JAMES A. CORBETT
University of Notre Dame

THE MONGOL INVASIONS

Eastern Europe and much of Asia bore the onslaught of invading Mongols during the 13th century. In the first three decades the Mongols, under the leadership of Genghis (Chingis) Khan, first conquered the steppes of northern Asia and then flowed west over the chain of rich oasislike city-states of central Asia. There the khanate of Jagatai (Chagadai) became a strategic center of political rivalry. The next stage of Mongol expansion was to overrun Persia and plunder Mesopotamia (1231). Russia was taken in the 1240's, and the Abbasid Caliphate at Baghdad was crushed in 1258. China, the last country to be conquered, was the richest and most populous. Eventually it became the seat of the Great Khan Kublai (Khubilai), under whom the Mongol empire reached its zenith.

Western Europe was saved from invasion when the Mongol armies withdrew from central Europe in 1242 after the death of Ogatai (Ögödei) Khan, the successor of Genghis Khan. Japan, too, escaped invasion, although Mongol-directed armadas were sent against that country in 1274 and 1281. Both invasions of Japan failed when typhoons struck the Mongol fleet.

PAUL V. HYER, *Brigham Young University*

1. Europe

In the medieval world of western Europe, everybody except Jews, the Muslims in Spain, and occasional heretical groups belonged to the one Catholic Church. People were more conscious of belonging to it than to a nation or state.

THE MEDIEVAL CHURCH

The feudalization of the church in the 9th and 10th centuries had resulted in lay control at all levels. The great abuses thus engendered led to the Gregorian Reform of the 11th century, which aimed at freeing the church from lay domination. It involved a revolution in the Carolingian tradition, dating from Charlemagne's coronation by the pope as "emperor of the Romans," whereby the emperor had been the center of Christendom with power to depose bishops, abbots, and popes. Gregory VII (reigned 1073–1085) wanted the church to be recognized as a free and universal spiritual society under the direction of an independent papacy.

MARBURG—ART REFERENCE BUREAU

LE BEAU DIEU, a statue of Christ on a portal of Amiens Cathedral, France, is an example of mature Gothic art. The unknown 13th century sculptor has portrayed Christ as man's redeemer—a noble and majestic figure.

During the 12th century the papacy came to enjoy great international prestige and was in fact the head of a group of Christian nations. Inevitably, it tended to intervene in temporal affairs. The church, with its traditions of the Roman sense for law and order, had become a well-organized society with its own constitution, law, legislative assemblies, and courts throughout Christendom before the territorial feudal states had become strong. Likewise, the church's functions were much more extensive than they are in the modern state. It controlled education, literature, and art, while feudal kings and lords were striving to gain the upper hand over a violent nobility that demanded and fought for local autonomy. Christendom was conceived of as a single body with many members, each having his own functions to perform for the service of the whole. It involved the idea of a hierarchy in which rights and duties and privileges were dependent upon one's function in society.

Papal Political Theory. The papal ascendancy did not occur without challenge, for while papalists said that the empire was within the church, imperialists insisted that the church was within the empire. At the opening of the 13th century, Innocent III (reigned 1198–1216), one of the greatest statesmen and popes of the medieval church, defended the papal cause. Like several of his successors—Gregory IX (reigned 1227–1241), Innocent IV (reigned 1243–1254), and Boniface VIII (reigned 1294–1303)—he was a canon lawyer and sought to give a juridical character to papal doctrine and to define more precisely the nature of the relationship between the spiritual and temporal powers. Building on the canon law codified by Gratian in his *Decretum* (about 1140), Innocent III claimed a broad right to govern the world. But when he intervened in specific cases he said he did so *ratione peccati,* that is, by reason of sin. He made, therefore, a distinction between his power as judge of the moral law and his respect for feudal law. But since political acts are moral acts, it was easy to extend the right of intervention to almost any issue.

This did not mean that the pope was the direct temporal ruler of empire and kingdoms, as he was of the Papal States, nor that he had even there an absolute or totalitarian type of power. He was limited by the natural law, the moral law, and canon and civil law. But he did claim a right to intervene in temporal affairs as supreme judge of the moral law. The claim was made because of the logic inherent in the medieval drive to establish a united peaceful world in which justice and order would prevail. Vassal states, like Spain, Denmark, England, and Hungary, were not subject to direct political control but enjoyed a general protection of the papacy, which they recognized as the center of an international society.

In papal eyes the Christian king or prince was viewed as an official of the one Christian society in a limited area with the responsibility for exercising the temporal power in that area in accordance with the moral law. He would be free of papal intervention if he ruled justly. In medieval political theory there was, consequently, no way to justify absolute power.

Innocent IV developed the theory further by claiming political supremacy over the princes of the earth. Papal doctrine reached its climax in the bull *Unam sanctam* (1302) of Boniface VIII, which restates it in general terms. In order to understand this doctrine we must recognize (1) that it was not an absolute teaching to be asserted at all times and places, but one adapted to a specific historical context and valid only in that context; (2) that while it was supported by many canonists and theologians, it did not receive the unqualified approval of all of them nor of all emperors, kings, and princes; (3) that there was often a wide gulf between theory and practice; and (4) that it was dependent for its effectiveness upon the competence and wisdom of popes and their ability to adapt it to a rapidly changing historical situation. The 13th century therefore marks a turning point, not in the papal claim to be the final judge of the moral law, but in the method of applying it in the new world of national states already developing.

Autonomy of the State. To what extent did the new strong monarchies of the century accept papal intervention? Under the influence of Roman law, many political theorists and lawyers sought to justify the right of the emerging state to exist as an autonomous unit and not simply as an administrative district of the church. French legists, encouraged by King Philip IV, stressed the power of the king at the expense of the pope. The reign of law through control of the king by counselors, a control imposed by the barons, was a 13th century English development leading away from the older emphasis on religious sanctions, such as excommunication and interdict; it foreshadowed the growth of Parliament. With the abuses of the reign of King John, English thinkers sought less to justify the rights of the king than to define and limit them. In the conflict between Emperor Frederick II and the papacy, the imperialists urged a new "caesaropapism," whereby the emperor would be sovereign of the ecclesiastical as well as the political structure of the empire. Frederick's concept of empire was strongly Roman—a peace imposed by the sword, like the ancient Pax Romana. He rejected any papal claims to depose him, though he failed to establish his hegemony over Italy and the papacy. But secular power, defeated in the empire, was actually winning its independence in the form of the Italian city-state.

Amid the welter of claims and counterclaims, St. Thomas Aquinas, the greatest theologian and philosopher of the century, made a fundamental contribution. He knew Aristotle's *Politics* well and adapted its teaching to the medieval context. Aquinas distinguished between the human natural origin of the state, whose function is to provide for the material welfare of man, and the church, which is of divine foundation and ordained to provide for the spiritual welfare of man. Each, therefore, enjoyed an autonomy of its own that the other must respect. This did not mean each was separate from the other and had contradictory objectives. It meant, rather, that since the spiritual end of man, his eternal salvation, was of a higher order than the temporal, the secular power was not free to act in such a way as to hinder or prevent man's attainment of his spiritual end. By recognizing the autonomy of the state, St. Thomas' contribution was not only more in accord with the contemporary character of the French and English monarchies, but it laid the foundation for the theory of the indirect power of the church over the state and pointed in the direction that subsequent political thought would follow.

As the papacy acquired an ever-increasing control of the church, its work multiplied accordingly. This brought about an increase in personnel and a division of labor that paralleled that of the contemporary monarchies. The College of Cardinals usually numbered about 30 in the 13th century. Residing in Rome, it advised the pope and helped him administer the church. Specialization of function resulted in the development of an elaborate chancery, of the camera, or financial administration, and of several special curial courts, such as the Inquisition.

Church Reform. The principal problem of the 13th century church, apart from its effort to make papal supremacy effective, was reform. Innocent III's efforts to unite Christendom under one law express only one aspect of his zeal. His leadership in the Lateran Council of 1215 indicates his desire to improve the discipline of the clergy, meet the threat of heresy, and define the church's position on controversial issues.

The spirit of reform is clearly seen in the extraordinary growth and influence of two new religious orders, the Franciscans and Dominicans. The first, founded by St. Francis of Assisi in 1209, was a challenge to the growing worldliness that resulted from the prosperity of the age. The lovable St. Francis abandoned his fortune to embrace Lady Poverty. Living by begging, he sought to reach the poor and the miserable. His religious order was of a new type and sought to Christianize the masses in the turbulent towns. It tried to change, not the structure of society, but the hearts of men. Thousands came to follow St. Francis, and, in the name of order, the church had to organize them. Many wanted to study and become university teachers, others to become priests and missionaries in foreign lands. All needed some sort of formation. During the first century of the order the Franciscans produced university men of the stamp of St. Bonaventure, Roger Bacon, and Alexander of Hales. As missionaries the Franciscans covered Europe and went to North Africa, the Near and Middle East, and even China.

While St. Francis was attracting men to his simple life of poverty, St. Dominic in 1215 founded the Order of Preachers, or Dominicans, to meet the Albigensian heresy. Dominic realized, after much preaching against the heresy, that the task called for an organized effort. He taught his friars to preach and to teach. They must be thoroughly prepared to meet the arguments of the heretics. The Dominican rule, a development of that of the Canons Regular of St. Augustine, was remarkable not only for meeting the needs of the order, but as an example of representative government.

The Inquisition. The action of the papacy in handling the Albigensian heresy illustrates again the reforming character of the 13th century church. Several heretical movements in southern France and northern Italy are commonly grouped under the name "Albigensianism," from the town of Albi, France. Already strong in the late 12th century, this movement continued to grow in the 13th. Doctrinally it was a revival of the old Manichaeanism that had attracted St. Augustine in his youth. It proclaimed that there were two principles, one of Good and one of Evil. Matter and flesh were the work of the Devil; and God was interested only in spiritual things. These assumptions resulted in some startling conclusions. Albigensians opposed marriage because the birth of children was the work of the Devil. Suicide, preferably by starvation, became a supreme good, for it destroyed an evil body. Such beliefs were so antisocial as to call for stern measures.

The ascetic character of some heretical teaching and practice appealed to many who were shocked by the ignorance and worldliness of so many of the clergy of the time. St. Francis' love of poverty was a similar protest in a sense, but, unlike the heretics, he insisted that reform must be carried out in obedience to and in unity with Rome. The political repercussions were important, since heresy offered an opportunity for the nobility to despoil the church of its property.

ALINARI—ART REFERENCE BUREAU

ST. FRANCIS OF ASSISI, who died in 1226, renounced a comfortable life to embrace poverty. This portrait of the saint, by Cimabue, is from a fresco in the lower church of St. Francis at Assisi, Italy.

Preaching, reasoning, and example failed to check the spread of heresy, as St. Dominic discovered. Episcopal courts likewise failed. Innocent III called for a crusade against the Albigensian Count of Toulouse, deposed him, and invited northern French nobles to defeat him. The intervention of King Louis VIII of France resulted in a military and political victory for the French monarchy and strengthened its hold over southern France. But the heretics remained unconverted. Finally, Pope Gregory IX, in 1231, set up a special court called the Inquisition, which heard cases during the rest of the century. He named Franciscans and Dominicans as inquisitors because of their learning and detachment from worldly things. Innocent III, Gregory IX, and Innocent IV, all first-rate canon lawyers, prescribed the procedure to be used in dealing with heretics and allowed appeals to the popes themselves. Penalties ranged from mild penances to imprisonment, confiscation of property, excommunication, and, after 1254, death—the last carried out by secular courts.

To medieval man, heresy was a crime comparable to treason. It was also viewed as a contagious disease that must be controlled lest it infect the social body and destroy it. Although torture and burning at the stake were unquestionably allowed, these punishments did not shock men who regarded heresy as treason to God, a threat to the social order, and, therefore, a most serious offense. In spite of all the research devoted to this question, we still do not have a clear picture of the actual number who suffered the death penalty in the 13th century. By its end, however, the original drive of the heretical movement had spent itself.

Schism. Another aspect of the vitality of the 13th century church is seen in its efforts to reconcile the Greek Christians, who, in the Roman view, had become schismatic. Innocent III, shocked by the violence and looting that followed the conquest of Constantinople by the Crusaders in 1204, condemned the victors' excesses. However, he organized a hierarchy in the Latin Empire set up after the victory, named a Venetian as patriarch of Constantinople, and sent a papal legate to keep him in line. The zeal, moderation, and sincerity of the Pope were not enough. The bitterness between Greek and Latin, their dogmatic differences, and Innocent's support of the Latin Empire prevented him from winning the confidence of the high Greek clergy and bringing about the desired reunion. It was achieved temporarily at the Council of Lyon in 1274, after the recovery of the Latin Empire by the Greeks. The Patriarch of Constantinople and the Metropolitan of Nicaea, as a result of pressure by the Byzantine Emperor, acknowledged papal supremacy and accepted the Roman creed. But the reunion, celebrated with great ceremony, lasted only seven years, because it was imposed by the Emperor for political reasons and had too little support in the Greek world.

Missionary Activity. Enthusiasm for recovering the Holy Land by Crusades declined after the conquest of Constantinople, but the Crusading ideal remained deeply rooted in the minds of the popes for most of the century. As it waned, the church came to emphasize another approach, which again illustrates its dynamism. St. Francis himself had gone to Egypt and Syria to try to win the Muslims to Christianity. The Franciscans and Dominicans, encouraged by the papacy, sent men eastward. Their efforts to win back heretics and to penetrate the Muslim world at Damascus and Baghdad gave hopes of success for a while, but they were hampered by the fact that the Muslim leaders were more interested in political than religious problems. The friars also worked in North Africa, where schools were set up to help them learn Arabic, but in the 13th as in every other century, Christianity met stubborn resistance in the Muslim world.

In Russia, where the Cumans (Polovtsy) dominated the steppe between the Volga and the Carpathians, the Dominicans converted the Cuman prince and his family in 1227. Evangelization was proceeding fruitfully when the Mongol invasions of 1237–1239 destroyed the work accomplished and created a threat to Christian Europe. A Franciscan mission, led by John of Plano Carpini, reached the Great Khan at the Mongol capital, Karakorum, in 1246. The mission failed to convert the Khan but won a respite for the Christians. Other missions were sent to dissuade the Mongols from further invasions.

In northeastern Europe, the papacy supported the Knights of the Sword, the Teutonic Knights, and the friars in the conquest and conversion of the Baltic area. The whole Baltic coastal region up to and including Finland was evangelized. At the same time the faith was carried southward into the Ukraine.

POLITICAL DEVELOPMENTS

As a result of the Norman Conquest of England in 1066, the political history of France and England became so enmeshed that not until the end of the Hundred Years' War in 1453 were the two countries permanently separated. By the opening of the 13th century, the English kings ruled over all northern and western France, while the Capetian kings of France exercised control over a much smaller area centering on Île de France and Orléanais.

France. In Philip II Augustus (reigned 1180–1223), the French had an energetic and wily king, determined to weaken English power in France. Taking advantage of the absences of Richard the Lion-Hearted and the incompetence of John Lackland, kings of England during his reign, Philip quadrupled the size of his domain at the expense of England in 12 years of war that ended with the Battle of Bouvines in 1214. His son, Louis VIII (reigned 1223–1226), extended royal control to the Mediterranean Sea. In two decades French kings had tipped the balance of power to their own advantage and gained an ascendancy that was challenged but not lost during the Hundred Years' War.

With this political achievement, France reached the peak of its cultural development under Louis IX (reigned 1226–1270), who was later canonized. A gentle man with a passion for justice, he remains the model feudal monarch. He consolidated the gains of his predecessors and strengthened the institutions that made government effective and just. In 1248, against all advice, he led a Crusade to Egypt, where he was captured. With regard to England he preferred peace based on feudal law to warfare and the seizure of the remaining English holdings in France. In his relations with the empire and the papacy he did not hesitate to support Emperor Frederick II when he considered him right, nor to assert his independence of the papacy.

After the less forceful and less competent Philip III the Bold (reigned 1270–1285), France found a strong king in Philip IV the Fair (reigned 1285–1314). Philip IV abandoned the ideal of feudal law in favor of Roman law. Departing from the limited feudal monarchy of Louis IX, he followed the path of absolutism, which Roman law accepted. But the most dramatic events of his reign—the suppression of the Knights Templar and his victory over Pope Boniface VIII—belong to the 14th century.

During the 13th century, which saw France surpass England in power and prepare, at its end, to challenge papal supremacy, the work of government increased enormously. Philip Augustus, after losing his treasure and archives in a battle, built the Louvre as a fortress to house them and made Paris, already an intellectual center of Christendom, the permanent capital of France. By collecting money payments in lieu of feudal services, he was able to build up a royal army strong enough to hold the nobility in check.

The work of the Curia Regis, the king's court, fell more and more into the hands of trained civil and lay officials. Specialization and division of labor led to the formation of the Parlement of Paris, a strictly judicial body. The financial section of the Curia would evolve into the Chamber of Accounts.

France, by virtue of its piecemeal formation, remained a mosaic of lands, gradually absorbed by the crown, but still maintaining a host of local and provincial customs and privileges. Under such conditions it could not develop a common law as did England, which had been conquered and organized as a unit.

England. While France grew from a weak limited monarchy into a strong one with absolutist tendencies, England went from the practically absolute monarchy of John Lackland (reigned 1199–1216) toward a limited one. The loss of English lands on the Continent forced English nobles there to decide whether they would be French or English vassals. By his defeat in France and by his misgovernment and avarice John aroused the clergy and the barons of England to find some way to curb their King. On his return from the defeat at Bouvines, they obliged the King to sign Magna Carta—the Great Charter, called *magna* ("great") because of its length. This was a monumental document in the long history of men's attempt to prevent tyranny by making the ruler obey the law, though in this case the traditional feudal law, which was rapidly becoming unsuited to the times.

English history in the rest of the 13th century involves this same theme and the formation of the English Parliament. After the turbulent reign of King John, Henry III (reigned 1216–1272) gained control of the government. But as his incompetence in political and military affairs became increasingly evident, many of the barons sought some way to control his actions. The influx of French and Italian favorites, the growth of papal taxation, the refusal of the barons to increase the King's income to meet his real needs, and royal extravagance all contributed to producing a cleavage between the King and his baronage. In 1258 the barons presented him with the Provisions of Oxford, which sought to organize an effective check on the King through a council of 15. Henry surrendered completely, and the council functioned for two years before it broke down. The civil war that ensued resulted in the defeat and capture of the King at Lewes by the forces of the barons, led by Simon de Montfort. The latter's death in 1265 and the spirit of conciliation and compromise displayed by Henry's son Edward I (reigned 1272–1307) ended the crisis but not the spirit of reform that had provoked it.

It was against this background of dissatisfaction with the crown and of baronial efforts to establish an effective limited monarchy that Parliament gradually emerged. The word *Parlamentum* came into use in England in the 1240's to describe an instrument of government developed by the king to solve difficult problems of administration, law, and justice that were borderline cases or beyond the competence of existing agencies. Parliament, as a specially solemn meeting of the king's council, took shape in 1258 when the barons imposed some of their own members on it in order to control the king's actions. Such special parliaments, composed of nobles, bishops, judges, and trained civil servants, were numerous in the second half of the century. By the time of Edward I they were in large part a final court of appeal for grievances against local misgovernment and a final place to lodge requests for favors. The English Parliament, at the end of the 13th century, because of the great amount of work that devolved upon it, was staffed by legal experts, clerks, and judges to handle what were primarily questions of administration and justice. Representatives of towns and shires were rarely summoned, and there was no obligation to call them. The barons, unskilled in the technicalities of law and administration, played a minor role. The importance of commoners in Parliament was a development of the 14th century.

Spain. Spanish history in the 12th and 13th centuries centers on the virtual expulsion of the Muslims, who had dominated the Iberian Peninsula since 711. Muslim power was broken permanently at the Battle of Las Navas de Tolosa in 1212, when Spanish and French forces defeated the Almohads, who had established an empire in North Africa. The permanent union, in 1230, of León and Castile permitted the use of the combined forces of the two states against the Muslims, who by 1270 were confined to Granada, where they held out for another two centuries.

As the Muslims were pushed back, towns with extensive privileges were established to hold the newly won land. Self-government became common in Castile. The *cortes,* or assemblies of nobles, clergy, and townsmen, gained the right to approve all extraordinary taxes and to petition the king.

Aragón under James I the Conqueror (reigned 1213–1276) helped to drive back the Muslims in the peninsula and conquered the Balearic Islands from them. James' son, Peter III the Great (reigned 1276–1285), conquered Sicily from the French and made Aragón a great Mediterranean power. But to win support for his conquests, which the nobles opposed, the King had to grant the nobles the General Privilege (1283), a sort of Magna Carta, which strengthened the rights of townsmen and nobility and gave all classes representation in royal councils.

Holy Roman Empire. The history of the Empire in the 13th century is dominated by the conflict between the emperors and the papacy for supreme power and the control of Italy. The sudden death of Emperor Henry VI in 1197 was followed by the election of Otto of Brunswick as king of the Germans by one faction and Philip of Swabia by a rival faction. Pope Innocent III, in 1201, finally recognized the former, who was crowned emperor as Otto IV in 1209. Otto forgot all his promises to the Pope, and invaded and conquered southern Italy. To prevent German domination of the whole peninsula, Innocent III had his ward—the future Frederick II, son of Emperor Henry VI and heir of Sicily—elected king of the Germans. In return for papal support Frederick abdicated his throne of Sicily in favor of his infant son and was proclaimed and crowned king in 1212. The climax of the conflict came at Bouvines in 1214, when Frederick II, allied with Philip Augustus of France, met Otto of Brunswick, who had joined forces with King John of England and the Count of Flanders. The victory of Frederick II and Philip Augustus was decisive in the career of each.

Frederick II won the support of the German nobles by granting them extensive privileges. He gained the approval of the pope by making the German clergy independent of the emperor in Germany and by promising to go on a Crusade. Papal policy seemed to have triumphed. Actually Frederick II, who had been raised in the cosmopolitan Sicily he loved, wanted to recover Sicily and make it the center of his Italo-German empire. This ambition provoked a conflict that lasted until the death of Frederick in 1250. He failed to unite Italy, which remained divided among the rich and independent city-states of the north, the Papal States in the center, and Sicily in the south, the last becoming the object of French and Spanish ambitions.

Germany, after the death of Frederick's son Conrad IV in 1254, was without a king until Rudolf I of Habsburg was chosen in 1273. Devoting himself to his family's fortune rather than to imperial power, Rudolf I laid the foundation of Habsburg wealth by seizing Austria from Ottokar of Bohemia. Germany, with the extensive privileges that had been granted by Frederick II, remained a decentralized country of independent nobles.

The Latin Empire. The Mediterranean, as a result of the Crusades, had become by the 13th century a great area of commerce dominated by the merchants of Venice and Genoa. The capture of Constantinople in 1204 by Crusaders manipulated by Venice gave the Venetians control of the Byzantine Empire's rich capital—a Greek city that had never been conquered since its foundation in 330.

The new Latin Empire thereby founded at the heart of the Greek world, with Count Baldwin of Flanders as its first ruler, was exploited by Venice. Meanwhile, Greek emperors continued to rule the territory they retained in Anatolia. The Latin Empire lasted until 1261, when the Byzantine Emperor Michael VIII Palaeologus put an end to it with Genoese help and restored Greek authority in Constantinople.

SOCIAL AND ECONOMIC LIFE

The development of large feudal states with efficient governments had created large areas within which there was a relative peace. This situation resulted in an increase in the population and permitted the opening of large markets and the revival of industry. The 13th century witnessed a German expansion and colonization eastward and along the Baltic at the expense of the pagan Prussians and Slavs. With the missionaries and traders came Christianity and urban institutions. Within Europe itself a great deal of land was cleared and plowed, marshland was drained, and dikes were built. The interaction of the political, social, and economic factors changed the life of Europe enormously. The overall result was a peace and prosperity that made possible the great cultural developments of the 12th and 13th centuries.

The Decay of Feudalism and Manorialism. During the early 13th century the feudal and manorial organization of society reached its peak and began to decay as a result of the slow but constant erosion that was undermining it. Politically, the nobility, whose function had been to protect and govern in a ruthless world, changed in two ways. As kings recovered sovereignty and were able to assure peace and order, many of the nobles lost their original function and independence. Second, with the growth of trade and town life there was a softening of mores that expressed itself in many ways, and many knights preferred to stay home and enjoy life rather than rush out to battle. The growth of a money economy permitted them to pay scutage, a tax in lieu of military service, to their lord or king, who would then hire mercenaries. Many turned to the life of business by exploiting their lands more fully and taking advantage of the new markets, or they founded towns to profit by the rising prices of real estate and by the taxes to be collected from the townsmen.

For the work of government, kings and lords preferred trained salaried officials to warlike vassals. Unfamiliar with court procedures and complicated legal technicalities, the nobles abandoned the courts more and more to legal experts. Although the nobles had been necessary in a lawless age when government was largely by the sword, they became less useful to governments that needed experts to handle increasingly complex legal, financial, and administrative problems.

The peasantry, too, preferred to convert time-consuming and burdensome labor services into cash payments in order to have greater freedom to dispose of their time and surplus products as they saw fit. With the money the lords could hire laborers and fire them, if inefficient. This commutation of peasant dues and services was well advanced by the 13th century, especially in England.

Life in the New Towns. Between the noble and the peasant a new class emerged in the 12th and 13th centuries—the bourgeoisie, or middle class of the towns. Composed of merchants and artisans, it did not fit into the feudal agrarian world. The rapid increase in number of the middle class caused a social and economic revolution as its members sought to gain economic and political freedom from king or lord by purchase or revolt. The city-states of northern Italy, the free cities of Germany, the communes of France, and the boroughs of England enjoyed varying degrees of self-government, and their townsmen enjoyed a new freedom.

Urban economic life was managed by guilds of merchants and artisans who developed and protected their own interests and those of the towns. Detailed regulations controlled the standards of quality, prices, and wages. But the guilds were religious and social institutions as well, caring for needy members, building hospitals, and celebrating religious holidays and social functions together.

The excitement and freedom of town life attracted many free peasants and serfs. Hundreds of new towns were founded in the 13th century. Such important cities as Berlin, Prague, Danzig (now Gdańsk), and Riga sprang up as German expansion continued eastward and new lands were plowed and settled. It was in the 1200's that the Hansa, a league of German towns, was formed to extend and facilitate trade in the North Sea and Baltic areas.

All during the century, the towns of Flanders were one of the principal economic centers of medieval Europe. They imported a large part of the wool of England and made it into cloth for distribution all over Europe. Champagne had the greatest fairs of the century for merchants traveling from Flanders to Italy. This flourishing urban life undermined the earlier agrarian self-sufficiency and encouraged farmers to produce surpluses to sell in the new markets. Town and countryside complemented each other as never before.

New Financial Practices. The development of a money economy, international trade, and big business led to the development of capitalistic enterprise and new financial techniques. Companies were formed to finance and share the risks involved in long voyages. Marine insurance was well known in the 13th century.

To meet the needs of the expanding economic life a new coinage was needed to replace the traditional silver penny—for centuries the only coin in use. Venice started the reform by minting the big penny, worth twelve of the old ones. France followed with the *gros tournois* (big penny of Tours) and the English with sterling. The florin of Florence and the ducat of Venice were new gold coins that also came into circulation during the century. Deposit banking, letters of credit, bills of exchange, and clearinghouse operations were common. Moneylending became a form of big business with the Italians, the most important moneylenders of the century.

EDUCATION

Intellectually, the great achievement of the 13th century was the completion of the organization of universities and, through them, the integration of ancient Greek and Arabic thought with the religious teachings of the church.

Universities. By the second half of the 12th century, the traditional cathedral and monastic schools could no longer handle the new learning that came into Europe through Latin translations of the philosophical and scientific works of the Greeks and Arabs. A new institution, the university, gradually emerged to meet the new needs.

The two greatest universities of the 13th century were Paris and Bologna. The university of masters and students in Paris was a guild, exempt from all but ecclesiastical jurisdiction, and distinct from the cathedral school out of which it had grown. It had four faculties—arts, theology, law, and medicine—each with its own dean. The arts faculty, the largest, eventually gained the upper hand over the others so that its rector became the superior of the other three deans. Pope Innocent III, in 1215, gave the University of Paris its first regulations. An arts student had to complete six years of study before becoming a master of arts and going on to theology, law, or medicine. The training given, utilizing the method of criticism and doubt, laid the foundations for the development of the scientific tradition that has distinguished Western culture.

The University of Bologna specialized in civil and canon law. It was a lay university, in which the students controlled and regulated everything but the granting of degrees. Bologna trained the civil lawyers who helped to organize the city-state governments of Italy and the canon lawyers who exercised such a great influence on the organization of the church.

Oxford, the first English university, was established in the 12th century and became famous for philosophy and science. The only other university founded in England prior to the 19th century was Cambridge, an offshoot of Oxford. There were no universities in Germany until the 14th century. Salerno and Montpellier were the principal medical schools in Europe.

Most medieval universities were founded and regulated by the papacy, which recognized their importance in raising the intellectual standards of the clergy, in training officials for government, and in coping with the intellectual challenges of the age. The last were momentous because of the rediscovery of Greek and Arab learning in the 12th and 13th centuries.

The Scholastic Synthesis. As the works of Aristotle and their Arab and Jewish commentators became known in the early 13th century—through translations into Latin, made in large part in Sicily and Spain—a clash of ideas between the new learning and traditional Christian thought developed. Accepting as basic that there could be no conflict between the truths known by revelation and those attained by human reason, Christian thinkers tried to harmonize the wisdom of the Greeks and the learning of the Arabs with their own religious doctrines. Believing in the unity and universalism of knowledge, they sought a synthesis of divine and human knowledge.

FRENCH GOVERNMENT TOURIST OFFICE

BOURGES CATHEDRAL, a striking example of French Gothic architecture of the 13th century, resembles a huge, oared ship. The double flying buttresses support the walls that uphold the high vault of the nave.

It was St. Thomas Aquinas who was most successful in working out this synthesis of Aristotelianism and Christian doctrine. His *Summa theologica* represents the greatest theological and philosophical achievement of the century and remains today the fundamental authority and guide for the Roman Catholic Church.

The intense concentration on theology, philosophy, and law—the subjects that preoccupied university minds—tended to smother the humanistic interest in the classics that had flourished in the 12th century. The emphasis on grammar and rhetoric as used by classical authors was weakened by the ascendancy that logic gained as a preparation for higher studies. Latin was learned as a practical tool for the study of theology, philosophy, law, and medicine. A humanistic style was not necessary for such study and was neglected.

ARTS AND SCIENCE

Church Architecture and Decoration. In architecture, the 13th century developed and perfected the Gothic style, which had emerged from Romanesque during the 12th. The 13th is the century of the great Gothic cathedrals, like those of Chartres, Reims, Amiens, and Bourges in France, where Gothic originated. In using the pointed arch, the ogival vault, and the flying buttress, architects and engineers learned that by a careful balancing of thrusts, which concentrated the weight at certain points, they could build churches higher than ever before and devote

JEAN ROUBIER

IN AMIENS CATHEDRAL, the great height of the central aisle helps create an impression of soaring movement, which is typical of Gothic churches. Work on the cathedral was begun in the early 13th century.

larger areas of the wall space to windows. The most beautiful expression of the logic of Gothic is seen in the Sainte Chapelle, built in Paris by Louis IX. It is a church with a roof of stone and walls of glass.

From Île de France and Champagne, Gothic spread throughout Europe to become the dominant style of the century. In Germany, with its strong Romanesque tradition in the Rhineland, Gothic reached its best only in the second half of the century. It was carried by Cistercian and Cluniac monks to Spain.

In England, the Gothic style developed in the late 12th century with the introduction of the pointed arch. Here the naves were narrower and the vaults lower than in contemporary French churches. Choirs were longer, with rectangular ends that permitted large windows in them. The English shunned extensive use of the flying buttress.

The medieval church was not only a place of worship, it was also a school for teaching the people the truths of their faith. When books were so expensive and illiteracy so widespread, the church taught the people through pictures and statuary. In vivid and often amusing ways, the portals and facades portrayed scenes from the Bible and the lives of the saints. By the 13th century sculptors had turned away from the stylized forms of the 12th. There is a human, natural, lifelike character and a combination of dignity, grace, and ease that make 13th century religious sculpture, so rich in symbolism, the most beautiful of the medieval period.

As architects devoted more wall space to windows, the art of stained glass flourished as never before. Glass workers developed their art with a success that seems beyond duplication.

Science. As the translations of Greek and Arabic works became known in Europe, a new interest in science developed. The philosophical notion that everything was composed of a prime matter, common to all things, and of substantial form encouraged the practical idea that it was possible to transmute metals—a theory that modern science has finally confirmed. Chemists were zealous in their efforts to purify the elements and to study their properties. The chemistry that produced the color and gloss of the stained glass windows still amazes. Actually, 13th century chemists were less superstitious and more scientific than their counterparts of the Arab and Greek worlds. The mathematical and engineering knowledge required to build a Gothic cathedral and the accuracy of detail with which animals and plants were carved in stone or portrayed in miniature should warn against superficial conclusions about medieval science.

Leonardo Fibonacci (Leonardo da Pisa) stimulated the development of mathematics and astronomy by introducing the Hindu-Arabic numbers into western Europe in 1202. *The Sphere* of Johannes de Sacrobosco, written early in the 13th century, explains the sphericity of the earth and became a standard compendium of astronomy. More famous was the Franciscan Roger Bacon, erroneously said to have been imprisoned for his interest in science, who emphasized the importance of experimental science, philosophy, and the study of languages for the work of the church.

The knowledge gained by experience and experiment was added to by a number of encyclopedists, like Bartholomaeus Anglicus (Bartholomew the Englishman) and Vincent of Beauvais, who sought to assemble and organize all that was known about nature.

Language and Literature. Latin, the language of the church, chancery, and university, was a living tongue and the medium of a vast literature. Its best literary expression in the 13th century is found in the rhythmic Latin of the liturgy and in such enduring hymns as the *Dies irae,* the *Stabat Mater,* and the *Pange lingua.* Alongside such serious work there were the goliardic lyrics and jingles of students and wandering clerks, which are gay, witty, and often irreverent.

The vernacular languages came of age during the 13th century—a reflection of the growing literacy, leisure, and secular taste of the bourgeoisie. French became an international commercial language. French literature, while continuing to produce *chansons de geste*—epic poems sung by jongleurs to the accompaniment of lyre and harp—became more sophisticated. Romantic literature, as seen in the widely read *Roman de la rose,* composed in the 13th century, was characterized by satire and an extensive use of allegory, a device that writers of popular morality plays also used to personify the virtues and vices. Fabliaux, which were short, humorous, and ribald stories in rhymed verse, became popular among the townsmen. Another characteristic change was the shift from verse to prose. Freed from the limitations of meter and rhyme, authors could give wider scope to their imagination. Many *chansons de geste* and Arthurian tales were rewritten in prose.

The Provençal literature of southern France was dominated by the great lyric poets who flourished in spite of the crusade against the Albigensians. Many sought refuge with Frederick II, who encouraged learned French and Italian poets at his Sicilian court. St. Francis of Assisi, with his love of song and verse, gave impetus to the growth of popular Italian poetry. The two tendencies—the learned and the popular—would fuse in Dante, who was born in 1265.

Anglo-Saxon, which had been smothered by French after the Norman Conquest, began a comeback during the 13th century following England's loss of its Continental fiefs. But no great literature emerged in England until the 14th century.

In Germany, alongside the French *chansons de geste* and romances, which continued to have wide appeal, an original German literature developed. German troubadours, or minnesingers, led by Walther von der Vogelweide, gained wide fame. Early in the century the *Nibelungenlied*, a Christianized form of an old German saga, set the fashion for the literary expression of old German stories.

REPRISE

The achievements of the 13th century—its attempts to establish a Christian order and unity, its dynamism, and its intellectual and artistic vigor—rank it as one of the greatest periods in European history. Before it was over, however, the tremendous drive to build an integrated Christian political and cultural order had lost its impetus, and Europe had begun to show signs of division and disintegration.

JAMES A. CORBETT
University of Notre Dame

2. The Mongol Empire

The emergence of the world's largest empire from the bleak steppes of Mongolia is puzzling to most people. Genghis Khan (1162–1227) united fragmented, feuding clans and tribes that were related but still lacked even the common name "Mongol." But, although it was he who organized and first led the Mongol war machine, its development had taken centuries. Of first importance was the cavalry, consisting of self-reliant herdsmen-warrior-hunters and their sturdy horses. The entire Mongol army probably never numbered more than 250,000 men, but through superb coordination and superior techniques of warfare it was able to dominate large and varied populations for an extended period.

The nomads whom Genghis Khan led out of the steppes had lived in a state of chronic economic instability. Their desire for grain, weapons, cloth, and luxuries was a constant incentive for them to expand into the surrounding settled lands. Their unification in the first decade of the 13th century coincided with a period of disorganization and weakness in the peripheral societies of Asia. After the death of Genghis Khan, his sons and grandsons enlarged his empire. But in the second half of the 13th century it was divided into four main khanates, whose rulers theoretically owed allegiance to the one who had been chosen as great khan. The four divisions were the khanate of the Golden Horde, in Russia; that of the Il-Khans, in Persia; the Jagatai Khanate in Central Asia; and the empire of China.

Most accounts of the Mongol expansion unduly emphasize the terror and slaughter involved. In fact, the conquerors established across Eurasia a *Pax Mongolica*, a period of relative peace opening a new era of East-West cultural and commercial relations. The Mongols drew up an admirable law code, the Great Yasa, and made lasting contributions in administrative structure. Under their comparatively benevolent rule, all religions were tolerated and merchant activity was fostered. Because of the liberal Mongol religious policy, the Muslim peoples were never united in a "holy war" against the invaders.

The Mongols established post roads as the basis of a remarkable system of communications and transportation throughout the empire. During the Mongol period, Chinese technological achievements, such as gunpowder, paper money, printing, porcelain, and medical discoveries began to be introduced to the West. Many foreigners resided in China while it was under Mongol rule. The most noteworthy was Marco Polo, whose travel account contributed to the European notion of a fabulously rich Orient and stimulated the search for routes to the Indies in later years.

PAUL V. HYER, *Brigham Young University*

3. The Islamic World

During the 13th century the political structures and the civilization of Islam were under pressure in the west from Christian Europe and in the east from the Mongols.

The Mediterranean Basin. The efflorescence of medieval Christendom resulting from the cultural achievements of the 12th century, together with the movements across the Mediterranean brought about by the Crusades, meant that the Christian world was now surpassing the Islamic one both in intellectual vitality and in economic progress. In the eastern Mediterranean the political and military effects of this process would not be evident for some centuries to come, for during the 13th century the Muslims ejected the Franks from their last footholds on the Levantine coast. Furthermore, the formation of the powerful Mamluk (Mameluke) Turkish sultanate in Egypt and Syria, followed by that of the Ottoman Turks in Anatolia during the next century, signalized the final failure of the Crusades and erected bastions against European political and cultural expansion in those regions.

The position of Islam in the western Mediterranean was less assured. The Moroccan Almohad dynasty abandoned Spain, the southern part of the peninsula then rapidly fell to the Christians, and before the end of the century the Muslims were reduced to the province of Granada. The local dynasties that succeeded the Almohads in North Africa could do little more against the Spanish than mount occasional raids against them. However, an equilibrium was gradually established in the western Mediterranean region. Commercial contacts between the Muslim and Christian worlds brought considerable prosperity, and the influx of Spanish Muslim refugees into North Africa stimulated economic life in that region.

The Middle East. The central and eastern Islamic lands suffered a cataclysm in the form of the Mongol invasions. They began in 1219 under Genghis Khan and were renewed in 1256 by his grandson, Hülegü (Hulagu), who extinguished the independent but by then moribund Abbasid Caliphate in Baghdad. It seems to have been the provocative behavior of the ruler of the eastern Iranian lands at that time, the Khwarizm Shah, that brought the Mongols westward, but all the Islamic lands between Anatolia and northern India experienced the onslaught. The Mamluks of Egypt, themselves Turkish and thus ethnically akin to a large segment of the Mongols' own troops, halted the invaders in 1260 at Ayn Jalut, Palestine, in one of the world's decisive battles. Three of the four principal Mongol khanates eventually became Muslim—the exception was China—but the ravages of the 13th century dealt severe blows to the fabric of Islamic society and civilization. Nevertheless, the Islamic faith continued to spread in the Inner Asian steppes, in India, Indonesia, West Africa, and Nubia.

As a result of the Mongol invasions, agricultural and economic life in the heartlands of Islam, as far west as the Levant coast, suffered a severe setback. Towns and their rural hinterlands were devastated. In parts of Central Asia and the Iranian lands, tillage was transformed into pasture by the nomads, who settled in these regions. Almost the whole of Transoxiana, some parts of Persia, and much of Anatolia were Turkicized. On the other hand, once the massacres and spoliation ended, the lands under Mongol control benefited to some extent from the *Pax Mongolica.* Long-distance trade across Asia revived, and new influences from the Far East are discernible in Islamic art, especially in ceramics and book illustration. It is probably unfair to attribute the decline of classical Islamic culture to the Mongols, for a decline of interest in new ideas and a contentedness with repeating older patterns of thought and cultural activity are apparent well before their incursions. One important consequence of the Mongol-Turkish invasions was to strengthen the hold of Turkish military dynasties in Muslim lands. By the end of the century Turks held supreme power in almost all the Islamic territories between Egypt and Bengal. Indigenous peoples like the Arabs and Persians served their Turkish masters as officials and as *ulama* (religious scholars).

C. E. Bosworth, *University of Manchester*

USEFULNESS OF ANIMALS is title of manuscript illustrated by various artists of Mongol-ruled Iran.

THE PIERPONT MORGAN LIBRARY

4. China and Korea

The 13th century saw the reunification of China under a Mongol dynasty, which governed the most powerful of the Mongol khanates. The Mongols also conquered Korea, but there the ruling line was permitted to retain the throne.

China. At the beginning of the century, South China was ruled by the Sung dynasty and North China by the Chin, who were Tungusic invaders. Genghis Khan began the conquest of North China in 1211, and after his death in 1227 it was completed by his sons. His grandson Kublai (Khubilai), great khan from 1260, established the Yüan ("origin") dynasty in China and ruled (1271–1294) as emperor in the Chinese style. The dynasty lasted until 1368.

Because of their nomadic, pastoral background, which contrasted strongly with the sedentary agricultural society of the Chinese, the Mongols remained apart—a privileged minority. They ruled through a Chinese bureaucracy recruited by a Chinese chief minister, Yeh-lü Ch'u-ts'ai. However, they gave many of the highest positions to persons who were neither Mongol nor Chinese. One Mongol innovation was the organization of regional governments—forerunners of the provincial administrations. Although Kublai and his successors fostered Confucian ideology and traditional Chinese institutions, the Chinese remained bitter, suspicious, and unreconciled to "barbarian" rule. Thus, the Yüan governed more despotically than most Chinese dynasties.

The Mongols patronized foreign religions, and they themselves favored Lamaism, a form of Buddhism that had developed in Tibet. During this period Christianity made notable gains in China—an archbishopric was organized at Peking—and Islam took permanent root in parts of the country. China influenced both the Islamic world and Europe, though not their religions.

Chinese scholarship and art did not flourish under Mongol rule but did not greatly decline. In Chinese literature, the drama and the novel became important for the first time. The evolution of the drama was due largely to the increased use of the written vernacular, which was closer to common speech than the classical language was, and thus could reach more people. While the dramatic themes were typically Chinese, the performances were influenced by Central Asian traditions. Both dramatists and novelists were mainly Chinese scholars who had turned to these fields because they had less opportunity in official life. The novelists, writing anonymously because of the stigma attached to fiction, gave literary form to traditional tales handed down by professional storytellers. While most Chinese novels in their final form date from a later period, their roots are in the Yüan period.

The *Pax Mongolica* brought China increased trade and relative prosperity. The innovation of paper currency led to a nationwide system of standardized notes. The Grand Canal was enlarged and extended to the lower Yangtze rice areas. On the minus side, graft, corruption and inflation marred the Mongol period.

Korea. The 13th century in Korea was a time of invasion and complete domination by the Mongols. The century opened with the Koryo

MA YÜAN, in his *Walking on a Mountain Path in Spring,* balances areas of bold brushwork with open space. He painted in Sung dynasty China, until sometime after 1225.

PALACE MUSEUM COLLECTION, TAIPEI

dynasty (918–1392) on the throne, but with actual power held by the Ch'oe family. The Mongols invaded in 1231, and after repeated attacks the Koreans surrendered in 1258. The power of the central government was restored and Mongols were placed in the top administrative positions. The Koryo kings, although maintained on the throne, were forced to marry Mongol princesses. Toward the end of the century Korea suffered increasingly from attacks by Japanese pirates.

PAUL V. HYER, *Brigham Young University*

5. Japan

The 1200's were the first full century of Japan's medieval age (1185–1573). It was during this age that provincial warrior, or samurai, families came to supplant the courtier aristocracy of Kyoto as the effective ruling elite of Japan.

Government. In 1185, Minamoto Yoritomo had established a military government at Kamakura in the eastern provinces. This government was known as the Kamakura Shogunate, from the title of *shogun,* or "generalissimo," that Yoritomo received from the imperial court. But despite the rise of the military, the court remained the unchallenged source of government legitimacy.

The Kamakura Shogunate lasted until 1333. During most of the period of this first shogunate of the medieval age, actual ruling power was exercised by the Hojo family. The Hojo were related by marriage to the Minamoto and emerged to prominence after Yoritomo's death in 1199.

During the 13th century, Hojo regents exercised power in the name of titular shoguns. The chief characteristic of Yoritomo's rule had been the force of his own personality. The Hojo, on the other hand, sought to place the shogunate on a more lasting basis by establishing a Council of State in 1225. This institution permitted the other leading chieftains of the east to share in the decision-making process at Kamakura. The Hojo also issued a military code in 1232 that became the model for military law in Japan and remained so until the beginning of the modern era in 1868. See also HOJO.

Religion. The Kamakura period, and the 13th century in particular, witnessed a great religious awakening in Japan. The exclusive and doctrinally complex Buddhist sects of Japan during the previous four centuries proved inadequate for a society beset by the uncertainties and dislocations that accompanied the great shift in rule from courtiers to warriors. In response to the religious needs of the times, a succession of outstanding evangelists, including Honen (1133–1212), Shinran (1173–1262), and Nichiren (1222–1282), came forth with simple formulas of salvation based on faith alone. They founded the Buddhist sects that have since attracted great followings among the Japanese.

A Buddhist sect of quite a different character was introduced to Japan during the early Kamakura period. This was Zen. Rather than salvation through faith, Zen stressed discipline and self-reliance and was especially congenial to the lifestyle of the samurai. In the religiously eclectic fashion of the Japanese, however, most samurai probably sought their ultimate spiritual solace in the salvation sects.

Foreign Relations. The greatest external threat to Japan in premodern times was presented during the 13th century by the Mongol dynasty of China. Outraged at Japan's refusal to accept a subservient, tributary relationship, Kublai Khan sent vast armadas in 1274 and again in 1281 in attempts to invade and humble the island country. On both occasions the Mongols were repulsed by typhoons, which the Japanese called *kamikaze,* or "divine winds," sent to protect their country in time of great peril.

H. PAUL VARLEY, *Author of "The Samurai"*

6. India and Southeast Asia

Just as Genghis Khan was preparing to lead the Mongols out of the inner Asian steppes, the Turks were establishing the first independent Muslim state in India, the Delhi Sultanate. Its founder, Qutb-ud-Din Aibak, was a former slave general of the Turko-Afghan ruler Muhammad Ghuri. In 1206, on Muhammad's death, Qutb-ud-Din succeeded him as independent ruler of the Ghurid possessions in India. Two of Qutb-ud-Din's successors of the new "Slave dynasty," Iltutmish (reigned 1211–1236) and Balban (reigned 1266–1287), consolidated and extended Turkish control over north India. The Slave dynasty was overthrown in 1290 by the founder of the Turkish Khalji dynasty of Delhi.

In south India, the power of the Cholas, once masters of the peninsula, was passing to the Pandyas to the south and the Yadavas to the north. The Pandyas were deeply embroiled in the dynastic affairs of Ceylon. The Yadavas, under Singhana (reigned 1200–1247?) and Krishna (reigned 1247–1261), controlled large areas of the Deccan from their capital, Devagiri (modern Daulatabad, in Maharashtra). Between the

LOUIS FREDERIC, FROM RAPHO GUILLUMETTE

TEMPLE FRIEZE at Somnathpur in southern India depicts a scene from the Hindu epic *Mahabharata*. This richly decorated temple, dating from about 1270, was built by the Hoysala dynasty.

Pandyas and the Yadavas, the Hoysalas rose to temporary eminence during the 13th century.

The constant political turmoil was matched by cultural rivalries between regions and the clash of two world views—Hindu and Muslim. The Hindu caste system had begun to grow more rigid in the face of the Muslim threat, although the assimilation of new ethnic groups into the Hindu social structure continued. Buddhism had already breathed its last in India, and the Hindu cults of Shiva and Vishnu had emerged triumphant. Feudalism had become the dominant pattern in land relations. Commerce prospered only intermittently.

The 13th century was a period of great architectural activity in India. The monumental gateways (*gopuram*) of the Pandyan temples, the exuberance of Orissan architecture (Rajarani and Konarak temples), the exquisite profusion of decoration in the Jain temples at Mt. Abu, Rajasthan, and the vivacity of the Hoysala temples (Halebid Somnathpur) still evoke wonder.

Southeast Asia. Once Kublai Khan had completed the conquest of China, Southeast Asia was directly menaced by the Mongols. In Burma, the Mongol invasions of the last quarter of the 13th century toppled the kingdom of Pagan, which had maintained close contacts with centers of Buddhism in Ceylon. The fall of Pagan was followed by a period of warfare and political division, with Shan dynasties dominant in the north, the seat of former Burman power. In Vietnam, the Mongol visitations were devastating but sporadic. There the dominant historical theme of the 13th century was the struggle between the increasingly aggressive Vietnamese of the north and the Indianized Chams of the south.

In Cambodia, the Khmer empire of Angkor had passed the zenith of its glory. The kings of Angkor were deeply embroiled in conflict with the Chams, and their ambitious building projects, coupled with their wars, placed an almost intolerable burden on the agrarian economy of Cambodia. The Khmers were increasingly challenged by the Thais from the north, who founded an independent state at Sukhothai. Under Rama Khamheng (reigned 1275–1317), Sukhothai greatly expanded its territory and political influence. The Thais borrowed culturally from the Mons to the west and the Khmers to the east. Rama Khamheng encouraged their adoption of Theravada Buddhism.

As the 13th century opened in the island world of Indonesia, the Javanese kingdom of Kediri had become a center of Vishnuite Hindu culture with strong Buddhist elements. In 1222, Kediri was superseded by the new kingdom of Singosari, which patronized a fusion of Shivaite Hinduism and Buddhism. Singosari's greatest ruler, Kertanagara (reigned 1268–1292), established his control over all of Java and extended it to parts of Sumatra, Borneo, and the Moluccas. In 1293 a Mongol expeditionary force landed in Java to punish Kertanagara for having refused to submit to Kublai Khan. However, Kertanagara had been killed by his vassal, the ruler of Kediri. The dead king's son-in-law Vijaya avenged his murder, expelled the Mongols, and founded the kingdom of Majapahit, which became one of the great powers of Southeast Asia.

The two dominant religious systems of Southeast Asia during the 13th century were Theravada Buddhism, spread from Ceylon, and an eclectic worship of Hindu and Buddhist divinities. Pali and Sanskrit literature deeply influenced the literary efforts of Burma, Cambodia, and Java, and the Indian epics *Rāmāyaṇa* and *Mahābhārata*, as well as the Hindu law code of Manu, were integrated into the very core of the cultures of Southeast Asia. The cult of the deification of the king and his identification with Shiva, Vishnu, or a Buddhist deity created an elaborate state ritual with its own complex hierarchy of priests and officials, ascetics, and mystics.

B. G. Gokhale
Wake Forest University

7. Subsaharan Africa

By the 13th century, parts of Africa had long been drawn into the trading concerns of the Mediterranean and Asian worlds. The gold of Africa's western regions, exported across the Sahara from the powerful empire of Ghana and its tributary kingdoms, had fueled the long-distance commerce of the Muslim world by providing the metal for a standard currency. In the 13th century the city-states of southern Europe began to use West African gold for the same purpose. Down the long east coast of Africa, earlier contact with Arab and Indian traders had given rise to the civilization of the Swahili. This enterprising and in some respects brilliant civilization was based on its middleman position between the interior suppliers of gold and ivory and the sea merchants from Arabia, the Persian Gulf, western India, Ceylon, and still farther east.

Africa's participation in far-ranging international trade reflected and was reflected in the general economic and cultural growth of many of its societies. Although the 13th century witnessed the final collapse of the Ghana empire in the Western Sudan, that was partly because of the spread of wealth and the development of social power. The century also saw the rise of a new empire, known as Mali, which not much later was to become larger than Ghana had ever been. Farther east, in the Central Sudan, the empire of Kanem-Bornu was for a while in control of the northern trade routes as far as the Fezzan (southern Tunisia and southwestern Libya) and enjoyed regular contact with northern kingdoms, including the newly founded Mamluk state in Egypt.

The development of African states was associated with other stimuli than that of long-distance trade. Outside its range new kingdoms began to take shape in the upland country of the eastern and central interior, including those that were to develop into the kingdoms of the Hima and Tutsi and, farther south, of the Shona and other Bantu-speaking peoples.

By 1300 the greater part of the African interior had acquired the basic political and cultural formation that European explorers were to discover more than five centuries later.

BASIL DAVIDSON, *Author of "Africa in History"*

8. The Americas

During the 13th century, climatic changes had far-reaching effects on societies in the Americas. Under colder conditions than in previous centuries, Eskimo whale hunters reverted to seal hunting. At the end of the century the Norse settlements in Greenland entered a 200-year decline that led to their extinction. In Wisconsin and Michigan, where the Mississippian cultural pattern had reached a northern limit of expansion, the Indians returned to simpler life patterns. But in Alabama and Georgia, the Temple Mound culture continued to flourish.

In the U. S. Southwest, the peak of Anasazi development (Pueblo III period) lasted from the 11th to the 13th century. Before the end of the 13th, drought and harassment by invading nomadic groups caused the Pueblo farmers to abandon their northern territories for the less exposed zones of the Little Colorado and Rio Grande valleys. However, in the oases of southern Arizona, the Hohokam culture continued to thrive.

There is evidence that on the northern periphery of Mexican civilization the climate was growing drier, and this aridity may have caused migrations of farmers southward into the central plateau. The migrations could in turn explain the fall of the Toltec kingdom, the Chichimec invasions, and the southward shrinkage of agriculture in the early 13th century. Among the groups that settled in central Mexico during this period were the Aztecs.

In the area of Mayan civilization, Mayapán replaced Chichén Itzá as the dominant city of Yucatán at the beginning of the century. To the south, Mexican adventurers subjugated the highland Mayan peoples, establishing the dynasties that were ruling when the Spaniards arrived.

By the 13th century the central Andean sphere of civilization had entered the Bronze Age, and in Peru, Bolivia, and northwestern Argentina bronze supplemented copper for casting tools and weapons. On the north coast of Peru, the Chimu kingdom was rising in the valley oasis of Moche, while at Cuzco, in the highlands, the Inca dynasty began ruling a small tribal state.

PEDRO ARMILLAS, *Author of "The Native Period in the History of the New World"*

EVENTS OF THE THIRTEENTH CENTURY

1204—Crusaders captured Constantinople and founded the Latin Empire.
1206—Mongol leader Temüjin was proclaimed Genghis Khan ("Universal Ruler").
1206—Turks founded first independent Muslim dynasty in India at Delhi.
1208—Crusade against Albigensian heretics in southern France was authorized by Pope Innocent III.
1209—St. Francis founded the Franciscan order.
1212—Battle of Las Navas de Tolosa broke the Muslim hold on Spain.
1214—Battle of Bouvines established France as the leading European power of the 13th century.
1215—Magna Carta, embodying principle of limited monarchy, was signed by King John of England.
1215—Dominican order was founded by St. Dominic.
1215—University of Paris received papal statutes.
1223—Mongols invaded Russia.
1226–1270—Reign of Louis IX (St. Louis) marked the high point of creativity in medieval France.
1231—Inquisition was established by Pope Gregory IX.
1232—Joei Code, the model for military law in Japan until 1868, was issued.
1235—Mali Empire in West Africa was founded.
1238—First Thai state was founded at Sukhothai.
1241—Mongols defeated Poles and Germans at Liegnitz.
1250—Death of Emperor Frederick II signaled end of the medieval struggle between emperors and popes.
1250—Kurdish Ayyubid rulers of Egypt were supplanted by their military slaves, the Mamluks.
1258—Mongols sacked Baghdad and extinguished the line of Abbasid caliphs there.
1260—Mongol penetration toward Egypt was halted by the Mamluks at Battle of Ain Jalut, Palestine.
1266–1273—St. Thomas Aquinas wrote *Summa theologica*, a fundamental work of Roman Catholicism.
1268–1292—Kertanagara ruled kingdom of Singosari in Java, making it Indonesia's leading power.
1271—Kublai Khan founded Yüan (Mongol) dynasty of China.
1273—Election of Rudolf I of Habsburg as Holy Roman emperor ended interregnum that began in 1254.
1281—Typhoon frustrated second and last Mongol attempt to conquer Japan.
1282—Sicilian Vespers revolt foiled Charles of Anjou's ambition to build Mediterranean empire.
1287—Mongols conquered Pagan kingdom of Burma.
1291—Muslims captured Acre, last major stronghold of the Crusaders.
1292–1295—Marco Polo returned to Venice from China.
1296—Philip IV of France and Edward I of England defied Boniface VIII's bull *Clericis laicos*.

Bibliography

Brockelmann, Carl, *History of the Islamic Peoples* (New York 1947).
Coedès, George, *The Making of Southeast Asia* (Berkeley and Los Angeles 1966).
Crump, Charles G., and Jacob, E. F., eds., *Legacy of the Middle Ages* (New York and London 1926).
Davidson, Basil, *A History of East and Central Africa* (New York 1969).
Fage, John D., *A History of West Africa,* 4th ed. (New York and London 1969).
Ganshof, François L., *Feudalism* (New York 1952).
Gernet, Jacques, *Daily Life in China on the Eve of the Mongol Invasions* (New York 1962).
Gilson, Etienne, *History of Christian Philosophy in the Middle Ages* (New York 1955).
Grousset, René, *The Empire of the Steppes* (New Brunswick, N. J., 1970).
Heer, Friedrich, *The Medieval World: Europe 1100–1350* (Cleveland and New York 1961).
Majumdar, Ramesh C., ed., *The History and Culture of the Indian People,* vol. 5 (Bombay 1957).
Pirenne, Henri, *Economic and Social History of Medieval Europe* (New York 1937).
Pirenne, Henri, *History of Europe from the Invasions to the XVIth Century* (New York 1939).
Polo, Marco, *Travels* (many editions).
Rashdall, Hastings, *Universities of Europe in the Middle Ages,* 2d ed. (New York and London 1936).
Reischauer, Edwin O., and Fairbank, J. K., *East Asia: The Great Tradition* (Boston 1960).
Spuler, Bertold, *The Muslim World: A Historical Survey,* vol. 2 (Leiden 1960).
Thorndike, Lynn, *A History of Magic and Experimental Science,* vol. 2 (New York 1923).
Von Hagen, Victor W., *Ancient Sun Kingdoms of the Americas* (Cleveland and New York 1961).
Walsh, James J., *The Thirteenth: Greatest of Centuries,* 12th ed. (New York 1952).

THIRTY-NINE ARTICLES, The. See ARTICLES, THIRTY-NINE.

THIRTY YEARS' WAR, a European conflict fought from 1618 to 1648. It began with a revolt in Bohemia, spread to Germany, and also involved Britain, Spain, the United Provinces of the Netherlands, Denmark, Sweden, and France.

The Holy Roman Empire of the German nation was split up into over 300 principalities and cities, and while most of the princes were peace-loving, a few were ready to take advantage of any situation that would increase their territory or prestige. The empire was, moreover, divided along religious lines—Roman Catholic, Lutheran, and Calvinist. The Peace of Augsburg (1555) gave Catholic and Lutheran princes the right to determine the religion of their subjects, but Calvinists were not legally recognized. Although the possession of church lands was supposedly fixed by this treaty on the basis of the status quo in 1552, there were further confiscations of ecclesiastical properties when the opportunity offered. In 1608 a group of Protestant princes formed a union to protect their interests, and this move was answered in the following year by the founding of a Catholic League. The Emperor was powerless to check these moves, and the functioning of imperial institutions broke down completely.

The interests of foreign states in German affairs were at least as dangerous as the internal political tensions. Britain and the Dutch joined the Protestant Union. The King of Denmark claimed secularized bishoprics in northern Germany and disputed control of the Baltic coast with the King of Sweden.

Spain prepared to reconquer the United Provinces after the expiration of a 12–year truce signed in 1609. An expansion of Spanish power would antagonize France. Most important was the close cooperation of the Habsburg emperors and the Habsburg kings of Spain.

The Bohemian Revolt and the Conquest of the Palatinate, 1618–1623. The opening act of the war was played in an unexpected quarter, the kingdom of Bohemia. In 1617 the Bohemian Diet accepted as king-designate the Habsburg Archduke, Ferdinand of Styria, cousin of Emperor Matthias and an ardent Catholic. On May 23, 1618, a group of Protestant nobles hurled two imperial commissioners and a secretary from a window of the palace in Prague. This defenestration was in protest against the attempts of the Emperor and Ferdinand to centralize the Bohemian government at the expense of the nobility, and to Catholicize a predominantly Protestant land. (See DEFENESTRATION OF PRAGUE.) Protestants of Austria, Moravia, Silesia, and Lusatia, and Gábor Bethlen, the Calvinist prince of Transylvania, joined the revolt against their Habsburg master.

The Bohemian revolt was turned into a German war by the ambitions of two German princes, Frederick V, the Calvinist Elector Palatine of the Rhine, and Maximilian, the Catholic Duke of Bavaria. On Aug. 26, 1619, the Bohemian Diet, having deposed Ferdinand as king of Bohemia, elected Frederick in his place. Two days later, Ferdinand, following the death of Emperor Matthias, was elected emperor with the title of Ferdinand II.

Frederick's acceptance of the Bohemian throne was foolhardy. He hoped for aid from Britain—he was the son-in-law of James I—as well as support from the Protestant Union and the Dutch, but they all disappointed him. The only foreign aid received by the Bohemians was a small mercenary army under the command of the military adventurer Ernst, Count von Mansfeld, whose services were supplied by the anti-Habsburg Duke of Savoy, Charles Emmanuel I.

The Emperor was more fortunate in his search for allies. Spain supplied troops and money. Maximilian of Bavaria, as ardent a Catholic as Ferdinand, head of the Catholic League, and the only German prince with an efficient army, agreed to support the Emperor in return for Frederick's electoral title and territorial compensation. Another German ally was the Lutheran prince John George I, Elector of Saxony, whose hatred of Calvinism was reinforced by the promise of territorial gain.

The Bohemian revolt came to an ignominious end on Nov. 8, 1620, at the Battle of the White Mountain near Prague. Here the forces of the Catholic League, ably commanded by Tilly, afterward Count von Tilly, overwhelmed the Bohemian Army. Frederick, henceforth derisively known as the "Winter King" because of his short royal tenure, took refuge with his family at The Hague. The Emperor executed 27 rebel Bohemian nobles, and Protestantism in Bohemia was permanently suppressed.

Frederick's Bohemian venture played into the hands of Spain. In 1617, Ferdinand, to ensure support for his election as emperor, had promised to turn over the Austrian Habsburg rights in Alsace to the King of Spain. The Palatinate was now the only block of territory that stood in the way of Spanish troops moving up from northern Italy through the Swiss valley of Valtellina for an attack on the Dutch.

A strong army led by the veteran general Ambrogio Spinola, an Italian in Spanish service, marched from the Spanish Netherlands and in September 1621 crossed the Rhine into the Palatinate. Despite the fact that his son-in-law's lands were in danger, James I did little to protect them. A force of 2,000 English volunteers was sent, but by April 1623 the last of them surrendered. The Palatinate was conquered by Spain aided by Bavaria, and the land was ravaged by disease and warfare. The Emperor granted Frederick's title to Maximilian of Bavaria and the province of Lusatia to John George I of Saxony as rewards for their assistance.

The Danish Period, 1624–1629. The Protestant powers, as well as France, were sufficiently alarmed by the Spanish and imperial victories to attempt the formation of an anti-Habsburg coalition. France, with the entry of Cardinal Richelieu into the royal council in 1624, was ready to embark on an aggressive foreign policy. Richelieu's immediate interest, however, was to block the Valtellina to Spanish troops rather than to fight in Germany.

The anti-Habsburg alliance dwindled to Britain, the United Provinces, and Denmark, and of these Christian IV of Denmark bore the brunt of the fighting in Germany. The British King could not get financial assistance from Parliament, and the Dutch were engaged in a desperate struggle with Spain.

Christian had good cause to enter the war because his claims to the important bishoprics of northern Germany were jeopardized by Tilly's army. Nevertheless, the King's decision to enter the war without adequate support from his allies was inexcusable.

To meet the enemy coalition's threat, Emperor Ferdinand II accepted the offer of the Bohemian nobleman Albrecht von Waldstein, commonly known as Wallenstein, to raise an army of 20,000 men. Rewarded with the title of duke of Friedland, Wallenstein was placed in supreme command of the imperial forces in July 1625. His first victory was the defeat of Mansfeld on April 25, 1626, at the Dessau Bridge on the Elbe. Wallenstein pursued Mansfeld into Hungary, and the fleeing soldier of fortune died near Sarajevo while on his way to Venice. Meanwhile, Tilly on Aug. 27, 1626, routed Christian of Denmark's outnumbered army at Lutter am Barenberge. The King's position was hopeless, but he did not sign the Treaty of Lübeck (concluded May 22, 1629) until June 7. It was a moderate peace. Christian retained his hereditary lands and renounced the claims to the German bishoprics for which he had entered the war.

Flushed with victory and encouraged by his Jesuit confessor, Wilhelm Lamormain, Emperor Ferdinand issued the Edict of Restitution on March 6, 1629. By its provisions all ecclesiastical properties taken over by Protestants since 1552 were to be restored to the Catholic Church. The Emperor's power was now so great that it was feared by both Catholic and Protestant princes.

Since this power depended on Wallenstein's army of 100,000 men, the princes demanded the dismissal of the commander in chief. Ferdinand agreed to his great general's discharge on Aug. 13, 1630, at the very time that his most dangerous enemy, the King of Sweden, was consolidating his position in Pomerania.

The Swedish Period, 1630–1634. King Gustavus Adolphus (Gustav II) of Sweden had watched the progress of the German war with increasing alarm. In 1628 he saved the Baltic port of Stralsund from capture by Wallenstein. Now with the defeat of Christian IV, he could no longer delay a full-scale invasion. To Gustavus Adolphus the security of Sweden and the protection of Protestantism were inseparable. They were his objectives when he landed on the Pomeranian coast on July 6, 1630, at the head of a small but well-disciplined army. Except for Stralsund he had no allies, and only his military genius could ensure victory. Not until the signing of the Treaty of Bärwalde on Jan. 23, 1631, did he receive French financial support.

Even the two most important Protestant princes, the electors of Brandenburg and Saxony, opposed his entry into Germany, and they refused to permit passage of his troops through their lands—an action that caused the greatest single catastrophe of the war, the destruction of Magdeburg. On May 20, 1631, the city of Magdeburg, held by a Swedish garrison, was destroyed by assault and fire, after a long siege by Tilly and his lieutenant Gottfried Heinrich, Count zu Pappenheim. Some 20,000 of the city's inhabitants perished.

Tilly refused to accept the Saxon Elector's position of armed neutrality and invaded Saxony, whereupon John George of Saxony reluctantly joined forces with Gustavus Adolphus. On Sept. 17, 1631, the armies clashed at Breitenfeld, near Leipzig. The King of Sweden won an overwhelming victory over Tilly and was hailed throughout Protestant Europe as the Lion of the North sent by God to save the righteous.

Gustavus Adolphus now started on a triumphal march to the Rhine, which he reached at the end of November. Sweden's presence on the Rhine was, however, most displeasing to Richelieu, and relations between King and Cardinal were sorely strained. The deteriorating position on the eastern front forced Gustavus Adolphus to leave the Rhine in March 1632. To save himself, the Emperor had reappointed Wallenstein as supreme commander in December 1631, and the imperial army was growing rapidly, threatening the Saxons who had invaded Bohemia. Tilly also reorganized his forces, defeated a Swedish army at Bamberg, and then moved south.

Gustavus Adolphus caught up with him and on April 15, 1632, won a spectacular victory at the Lech River on the western boundary of Bavaria. Tilly died of wounds suffered in the battle. Bavaria was deliberately devastated and its peasants slaughtered. But Wallenstein outmaneuvered the King, and with superior forces cooped him up in his camp near Nuremberg. An attack by Gustavus Adolphus on Wallenstein's strongly fortified position on September 3 was repulsed. Wallenstein withdrew to Saxony, where he prepared to establish his winter quarters. Gustavus Adolphus followed him, and on Nov. 16, 1632, at Lützen, about 15 miles west of Leipzig, the King of Sweden lost his life in a victorious battle. He had saved German Protestantism and made Sweden a great power.

Christina, the heiress to the Swedish throne, was only six years old when her father died, and the conduct of the war devolved upon Chancellor Axel Gustafsson Oxenstierna, the late King's chief adviser. He formed the Heilbronn League in April 1633, an alliance of German Protestant states, and also renewed the alliance with France. The death of Gustavus Adolphus had, however, irreparably weakened Sweden's position, and Oxenstierna's chief aim became the permanent acquisition of Pomerania. The imperialist cause was also temporarily weakened by Wallenstein's suspicious conduct. The Emperor was finally convinced that Wallenstein plotted treason and therefore gave orders for his seizure dead or alive. On Feb. 25, 1634, Wallenstein was murdered at Eger in Bohemia.

The elimination of Wallenstein ended dissension in the Habsburg camp, while Oxenstierna was unable to obtain the full support of the Heilbronn League. On Sept. 6, 1634, at Nördlingen, an imperial army, reinforced by Spanish forces led by the Cardinal Infante Ferdinand, brother of the Spanish King, Philip IV, defeated a Swedish-German army that was under the command of Marshal Gustaf Horn and Bernhard, Duke of Saxe-Weimar.

The Battle of Nördlingen was as decisive as Breitenfeld. With the exception of a few cities, the conquests of Gustavus Adolphus in southern Germany were lost. John George of Saxony, always a reluctant Swedish ally, signed the Peace of Prague with the Emperor on May 30, 1635. Sorely troubled in conscience, the Emperor virtually suspended the Edict of Restitution in order to obtain peace.

On the other hand, there was no general amnesty, and Calvinists were not by name included in the treaty. Nor was any provision made for the heir of Frederick, the Winter King, who had died shortly after the Battle of Lützen. Nevertheless, the eligible German princes and cities hastened to accept the treaty. The Heilbronn League was shattered, and only two princes, Bernhard of Saxe-Weimar and William of Hesse-Kassel, still remained in arms. The growing strength of Habsburg power finally forced Cardinal Richelieu into open war.

The French Period, 1635–1648. Since he had become chief minister of the French crown in 1624, Richelieu had never deviated from the objectives of his foreign policy: to stop the progress of Spain and to obtain entries into the territories of neighboring states. His first attempt in 1625 to block the Valtellina to Spanish troops had been frustrated by the need to suppress a Huguenot revolt at home. A disputed succession to the Italian duchy of Mantua had provided an excuse for intervention, and French armies had crossed the Alps in 1629 and 1630. The Treaty of Cherasco, signed June 19, 1631, had recognized the French claimant to Mantua. Contrary to the treaty, France had retained the fortress of Pinerolo on the border of Savoy. While the Cardinal had concentrated his warlike efforts in Italy, he had, as has been seen, supported Sweden in Germany. The death of Gustavus Adolphus and the Battle of Nördlingen had removed the danger of Swedish control of the Rhine. But the greater danger of Habsburg control remained, and French troops took over the Alsatian cities that had been captured by Sweden. Lorraine was also occupied. On May 19, 1635, the King of France formally declared war on the King of Spain.

France was poorly prepared for war on a large scale. In the summer of 1636 the combined forces of the Emperor and of Spain invaded France, and Paris itself was in grave danger. Only the stubborn resistance of a portion of the French Army and the difficulties encountered by the Spanish general in provisioning his troops made it possible to force the enemy from French soil. The Swedes fared little better. Although they won a striking victory over a combined Saxon and imperial army at Wittstock in Mecklenburg on Oct. 4, 1636, they were pushed back into Pomerania the following year. When Emperor Ferdinand II died in February 1637, he could still be hopeful that his cause would be victorious. He was succeeded by his son Ferdinand III.

The year 1638 marked the turn of the tide. Two vigorous young Frenchmen rose to military command, the Viscount de Turenne (Henri de La Tour d'Auvergne) and Louis II de Condé, Duke d'Enghien, known later in his life as the Great Condé. The crucial struggle was for control of the Rhine. In its valley, Bernhard of Saxe-Weimar, in cooperation with Turenne, defeated the imperial and Bavarian armies. The climax came with the capitulation of the strategic town of Breisach on Dec. 17, 1638. The loss of Breisach was a great blow to the power of Spain, the Emperor's chief foreign ally, for it cut the Rhine route for Spanish troops marching from Milan to the Netherlands. Then, in October 1639, the sea route to Flanders was severed when the Dutch admiral, Maarten Harpertszoon Tromp, destroyed a large Spanish fleet near Dover. The reconquest of the Dutch Netherlands was now made impossible. Revolts in Catalonia and in Portugal during the year 1640 threatened the very existence of the Spanish monarchy.

Gradually the Emperor's power was further whittled away by military defeats and by the defection of German princes. In July 1641, Frederick William of Brandenburg, who had succeeded his father as elector in the previous year, signed a truce with Sweden. Between 1640 and 1642, France wrested control of Artois and Roussillon from Spain. The deaths of Richelieu on Dec. 4, 1642, and of Louis XIII on May 14, 1643, placed the direction of foreign affairs in the hands of Cardinal Mazarin, who continued his great predecessor's policies.

The first great victory of the new reign was won by d'Enghien on May 19, 1643, at Rocroi on the border of the Spanish Netherlands, where the Spanish infantry was decimated. A Swedish invasion of Saxony forced the elector to sign a truce in September 1645. The following year Bavaria was invaded and devastated by French and Swedish troops, and the country was again overrun in 1648. At Lens, on Aug. 20, 1648, d'Enghien's army shattered the forces of Archduke Leopold, the Emperor's brother and governor of the Spanish Netherlands. A Swedish army besieged Prague. These successive blows forced Ferdinand III to agree to peace.

The Peace of Westphalia. An agreement to begin peace negotiations had been signed by Louis XIII and by the Emperor as early as 1642, but the peace congress did not open until two years later, at the Westphalian towns of Münster and Osnabrück. All the powers were represented except Britain, Poland, Russia, and Turkey. The Emperor treated with France at Münster and with Sweden at Osnabrück. The German states were also represented.

The chief difficulty in the peace negotiations was to satisfy the demands of France and Sweden. France obtained the Habsburg rights in Alsace, but these rights were so complicated that many years passed before the whole of Alsace became French. Strasbourg, its chief city, was seized by Louis XIV as late as 1681. In addition, France received Metz, Toul, and Verdun (for all practical purposes already French), as well as Breisach and Philippsburg. Sweden's demand for the whole of Pomerania was whittled down to western Pomerania. Sweden also obtained Verden, Bremen, and Wismar, and an indemnity of 5 million imperial thalers.

There were a few other territorial changes of concern to the German princes. Frederick William of Brandenburg, although he had a just claim to the whole of Pomerania, was forced to content himself with only the eastern portion. In compensation for the loss of western Pomerania to Sweden, he was granted the bishoprics of Kammin, Halberstadt, and Minden and the right of succession to the archbishopric of Magdeburg. The elector of Brandenburg was now, next to the head of the house of Habsburg, the ruler of the largest territory in the empire. Maximilian of Bavaria retained his electoral title and the Upper Palatinate, while the Lower Palatinate was restored to Charles Louis, the heir of Frederick V (the Winter King of Bohemia), and an eighth electorate was created in his favor.

The solutions found for the religious problems were an extension of the Peace of Augsburg. Calvinism was now recognized, but each prince could still determine the religion of his subjects. The holding of church properties was to be restored to the status quo of Jan. 1, 1624.

The treaties of Münster and Osnabrück, generally known as the Peace of Westphalia, were signed on Oct. 24, 1648. These treaties put an end to the sufferings inflicted by 30 years of warfare, starvation, and pestilence. It has been estimated that the population of Germany sank 40% in the countryside and 33% in the cities, and the material damages are incalculable. Recovery was rapid, however, and the population loss was probably made up for by 1700.

Constitutionally, the Peace of Westphalia strengthened the virtual independence of the princes, while the central authority remained impotent. For the future, this meant that the Habsburg emperors would turn their attention to their hereditary lands in the east, while the few powerful princes, particularly the electors of Brandenburg—the future kings of Prussia and German emperors—would establish states that could compete in the European state system.

In its international aspect, the Peace of Westphalia marked the victory of France and Sweden over the Austrian Habsburgs. France continued the war against Spain until 1659 and was again victorious. The ring of Habsburg territories surrounding France was broken. The recognition of the independence of two states—the United Provinces of the Netherlands and the Swiss Confederation—gave further prestige to the treaty arrangements.

The Thirty Years' War was the last European war in which religious motivation played a role. It is significant that the Pope's solemn protest against clauses of the peace treaties that were injurious to the Catholic Church were ignored by both Catholics and Protestants. Both rejected the claim of a supranational religious authority to interfere in affairs of state.

Until the French Revolution, the Peace of Westphalia was considered to be the basis of the European state system.

See also AUGSBURG, RELIGIOUS PEACE OF; GERMANY—*History* (The Thirty Years' War); SEVENTEENTH CENTURY; WESTPHALIA, PEACE OF.

ELMER A. BELLER
Princeton University

Further Reading: Holborn, Hajo, *A History of Modern Germany*, vol. 1 (New York 1959); Roberts, Michael, *Gustavus Adolphus: A History of Sweden 1611–1632*, 2 vols. (London 1953–1958); Steinberg, Sigfrid H., *The Thirty Years War and the Conflict for European Hegemony, 1600–1660* (London 1966); Wedgwood, Cicely V., *The Thirty Years War* (New Haven 1939).

THISBE. See PYRAMUS AND THISBE.

THISTLE, this'əl, any of various prickly leaved plants of the composite family (Compositae). Thistles are usually tall plants with rounded flower heads. Unlike the daisy, which has flower heads of both disk and ray flowers, the thistle has a flower head composed only of disk flowers. In some thistles, bristles or hairs are mixed in with the disk flowers.

Many thistles are troublesome weeds. The few species that are cultivated are usually grown as ornamental border plants. The Scotch thistle (*Onopordum acanthium*), native to Europe, is also found in North America, where it is a serious pest in the western United States. It grows 9 feet (2.7 meters) tall and bears small lavender flower heads.

Another important European weed that has become naturalized in North America is the Canada thistle (*Cirsium arvense*). This perennial species, ranging in height from 1 to 4 feet (0.3–1.2 meters), has an extensive root system with main roots that grow parallel to the surface of the ground. The leaves are vivid green on the upper surface and woolly on the under surface. The purple flower heads of the Canada thistle are only ½ inch (13 mm) in diameter. Related to the Canada thistle is the bull thistle (*C. vulgare*), a biennial weed of pastures and roadsides throughout the western and northern United States. It reaches a height of 5 feet (1.5 meters) and has purplish flower heads about 2 inches (50 mm) in diameter. Many other thistles belong to the genus *Cirsium*.

T. H. EVERETT

Scotch thistle (*Onopordum acanthium*)

Both the musk thistle (*Carduus natans*) and the Italian thistle (*C. pycnocephalus*) are Eurasian plants that grow as weeds in North America. A related plant, *C. kerneri*, is sometimes cultivated. It ranges in height from 1 to 3 feet (60–90 cm) and bears rosy purple flower heads. The yellow star thistle (*Centaurea solstitialis*) is widespread in California; it is a pesty weed but important as a source of nectar and pollen for bees.

Thistles vary in their reactions to herbicides. For example, the bull thistle is rather susceptible, but the Canada thistle is relatively resistant and the Scotch thistle is extremely resistant.

J. D. YOUNG
U. S. Department of Agriculture

THISTLE, Order of the. See DECORATIONS, MEDALS, AND ORDERS—*Great Britain*.

THOMAS, Saint, one of the 12 apostles of Jesus Christ. Nothing is known about St. Thomas with certainty except what is in the Bible. The Gospels of Matthew, Mark, and Luke, and the Acts of the Apostles merely mention his name in the list of Apostles. John twice refers to Thomas as the one called Twin (11:16; 30:24), which is the meaning of the Aramaic and Syriac word for Thomas and of the Greek Didymus.

The Gospel of John records words spoken by Thomas on three occasions. When Jesus set out for Judaea, where the Jews had recently threatened to stone him (John 10:31), Thomas said to the other Apostles, "Let us also go, that we may die with him" (John 11:16). At the Last Supper, when Jesus said, "And you know the way where I am going," Thomas said, "Lord, we do not know where you are going; how can we know the way?"

Jesus replied, "I am the way and the truth and the life" (John 14: 4–6). After the Resurrection, when Christ first appeared to his Apostles, Thomas was absent. They told him that they had seen Jesus, but Thomas declared that unless he saw and touched Jesus he would not believe. Eight days later, Christ appeared again and invited the doubting Apostle to touch the marks of his wounds. Thomas exclaimed, "My Lord and my God" (John 20: 24–28).

Four apocryphal writings bear the name of Thomas. These spurious works are (1) the lost Gnostic *Gospel of Thomas,* written about 140, of which a Coptic adaptation was found in 1945; (2) the fictional *Thomas Gospel of the Infancy,* dating from before 400; (3) fragments of an *Apocalypse of Thomas;* and (4) the Gnostic-Manichaean *Acts of Thomas* from the early 3d century, which contain a purported account of his travels and missionary efforts. It relates that Thomas preached the Gospel in northern India and died a martyr and that his relics were taken to Edessa, Greece. Later traditions indicate that from Edessa the reputed relics were taken in 1258 to Chios, and thence to Ortona, Italy.

The so-called "St. Thomas Christians" on the Malabar coast of southern India have a tradition, which is questionable, that they are descendants of converts of St. Thomas.

MARION A. HABIG, O. F. M.
St. Augustine Friary, Chicago

THOMAS, tô-mä′, **Ambroise** (1811–1896), French composer, who is noted for his flowing, lyric melody. Charles Louis Ambroise Thomas was born in Metz on Aug. 5, 1811, the son of a musician. He studied at the Paris Conservatory and in 1832 won the Grand Prix de Rome, which enabled him to continue his studies in Italy. Returning to France, he began to compose for the Opéra Comique. His first opera was *La Double Échelle* (1837). In 1871 he succeeded the composer Daniel Auber as director of the Conservatory. Thomas died in Paris on Feb. 12, 1896.

Thomas' best-known opera is *Mignon* (1866). This work, which has a libretto based on Goethe's novel *Wilhelm Meister,* is filled with tuneful melodies, notably *Je suis Titania* and *Connais-tu le pays?* Thomas also achieved success with *Hamlet* (1868) and *Françoise de Rimini* (1882). In addition to operas he wrote a mass, several cantatas, and some chamber music.

THOMAS, Augustus (1859–1934), American playwright, whose local-color plays helped to develop the popular American theater. He was born in St. Louis, Mo., on Jan. 8, 1859. At first a newspaper writer and illustrator, he left journalism to become a playwright.

Thomas' first success, *Alabama* (1891), was followed by a series of plays that included *In Mizzoura* (1893) and his most popular work of that period, *Arizona* (1899). In the early 1900's he wrote satirical comedies, such as *The Earl of Pawtucket* (1903), as well as serious dramas. Among the latter were *The Witching Hour* (1907), *The Harvest Moon* (1909), and his best two plays, *As a Man Thinks* (1911) and *The Copperhead* (1918). Thomas relied on melodramatic situations and theatrical effects to entertain audiences, rarely penetrating a subject or dealing with significant themes. He died in Nyack, N. Y., on Aug. 12, 1934.

BROWN BROTHERS

Dylan Thomas

THOMAS, Dylan (1914–1953), Welsh poet, whose lyric poems are among the most captivating in 20th century romantic verse. Despite ignorance of his native language, Thomas is perhaps the most Welsh of English poets and reflects his Welsh literary heritage in his concepts, images, moods, and rhythms. Having an extraordinarily sensitive ear and a rich, resonant voice, he wrote and read poetry with an unforgettable auditory appeal. He was one of the few modern poets to have gained his first audience through readings—on British Broadcasting Corporation programs, Caedmon recordings, and lecture tours—and only later through printed poems.

Life. Dylan Marlais Thomas was born in Swansea, Wales, on Oct, 27, 1914. From his father, a cultured man and would-be poet, he inherited his intellect and literary abilities, and from his mother, a simple and religious woman, his generosity and Celtic sentimentality. His formal education ended at Swansea Grammar School, where he was undistinguished except for his contributions to the school magazine. He supported himself briefly as a journalist and was intermittently an amateur actor. By 1934 he originated—in style or concept if not in composition—more than half his literary output.

Thomas published his first book, *Eighteen Poems,* in 1934, then moved to London, where he published his second, *Twenty-five Poems,* in 1936. By this time he had won acclaim from the poet Edith Sitwell and others, who praised the variety and originality of his poetic experiments.

Thomas had gained immediate recognition but not wealth, and after his marriage in 1937 to Caitlin Macnamara, his responsibilities as husband, and later as father of three children, rendered more acute his need for money. He wrote radio scripts for the ministry of information and documentaries for the British government. Then, on four lecture tours through America, he gave more than 100 poetry readings. But dissipation and a grueling schedule hindered his literary output, and he published little poetry in his later years.

Thomas' early conviction that he had only a few years to live and his considerable talent as an actor led him to create "instant Dylan"—

the persona of the poet as he thought the public expected him to be. First he assumed the pose of the "consumptive poet" doomed to die young. Later he played the role of the wild Welsh bard damned by women and drink. On Nov. 9, 1953, he died in New York City at the age of 39 of pneumonia superinduced by acute alcoholism.

Writings. Passionately dedicated to his "sullen art," Thomas was a competent, finished, and sometimes intricate craftsman, as the approximately 200 versions of the poem *Fern Hill* attest. His artistry progresses from the early poems, which are relatively complex and obscure in sense and simple and obvious in auditory patterns, to the later poems, which are simple in sense but complex in sounds. Some of the few poems written in his last years are excellent examples of his "moments of magical accident," and thus memorable for their pathos of reminiscence that re-creates through the eyes of the adult the innocence of the child.

Thomas' best poetry is found in *Eighteen Poems, Twenty-five Poems, The Map of Love* (1939), *Deaths and Entrances* (1946), and *In Country Sleep* (1952). The autobiographical sketch *Portrait of the Artist as a Young Dog* (1940), the unfinished novel *Adventures in the Skin Trade* (1955), and the witty play *Under Milk Wood* (1954) are among his best prose works.

LOUISE BAUGHAN MURDY, *Author of "Sound and Sense in Dylan Thomas's Poetry"*

Further Reading: FitzGibbon, Constantine, *The Life of Dylan Thomas* (Boston 1965).

THOMAS, George Henry (1816–1870), American major general, who became famous in the Civil War as "the Rock of Chickamauga." He was born in Southampton county, Virginia, on July 31, 1816. He graduated from the U.S. Military Academy in 1840, and served in the Seminole War in Florida and in the Mexican War, where he distinguished himself at the battles of Monterey and Buena Vista.

When the Civil War came, Thomas remained loyal to the Union. In August 1861 he was commissioned a brigadier general. On Jan. 19, 1862, he won the Battle of Mill Springs, which secured eastern Kentucky for the Union. Promoted to major general, he served in the Perryville campaign and fought at Stones River (Murfreesboro), Dec. 31, 1862, to Jan. 2, 1863, where he was a tower of strength in command of the center of the Union line.

In the Battle of Chickamauga on Sept. 19–20, 1863, his heroic stand on the second day saved the Army of the Cumberland from disaster and earned him his sobriquet. Chosen by Maj. Gen. Ulysses S. Grant to command that army, he led it to victory at Missionary Ridge on Nov. 25, 1863, and throughout Maj. Gen. William T. Sherman's campaign to capture Atlanta.

When General Sherman began his "March to the Sea," Thomas was left with only a small force to face the Confederate army under Gen. John B. Hood, who began a daring advance northward into Tennessee. Hood's failures at Spring Hill and Franklin gave Thomas time to collect a larger force. At Nashville on Dec. 15–16, 1864, he almost annihilated Hood's army.

Thomas died at San Francisco on March 28, 1870. Next to Grant and Sherman, he was undoubtedly the most capable Union leader.

JOSEPH B. MITCHELL
Author of "Decisive Battles of the Civil War"

THOMAS, Isaiah (1749–1831), American publisher. He was born in Boston on Jan. 19, 1749. He was apprenticed to the printer Zechariah Fowle, and worked briefly for newspapers in Nova Scotia and South Carolina. In 1770 he established, with Fowle, the anti-British journal *Massachusetts Spy*, which survived in some form until 1904. During the Revolution, Thomas fought as a minuteman at Lexington and Concord and set up a press in Worcester, Mass., where he published the *Spy*, with editorials supporting the colonists. After the war, Thomas became the leading American publisher, issuing more than 400 books, which were noted for their beauty.

In retirement, Thomas wrote *The History of Printing in America* (1810), which became an early standard work in its field. In 1812 he founded, endowed, and became first president of the American Antiquarian Society. Thomas died in Worcester on April 4, 1831.

THOMAS, Norman (1884–1968), American Socialist leader, who was six times the Socialist party candidate for president of the United States. He championed measures such as unemployment insurance and old age pensions, which seemed radical when first proposed but later became the law of the land.

Thomas was born in Marion, Ohio, on Nov. 20, 1884. After graduating from Princeton University in 1905 and Union Theological Seminary in 1911, he became a Presbyterian minister in New York City. He gave up his pastorate before joining the Socialist party in 1918 so as not to embroil his church in the controversy that surrounded him.

When the United States entered World War I, Thomas, a pacifist, fought for freedom of speech and the rights of conscientious objectors. In 1917 he was a founder of the National Civil Liberties Bureau, which later became the American Civil Liberties Union, and in 1922 he helped organize the League for Industrial Democracy. He also founded and edited *The World Tomorrow*, was an editor of *The Nation* in 1921–1922, and later contributed regularly to the Socialist *New Leader*.

Beginning in 1924, Thomas ran for public office in New York—for governor, mayor, alderman,

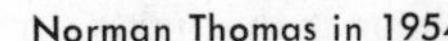

Norman Thomas in 1954

WIDE WORLD

state senator. He was never elected, but his reputation grew. He was the Socialist candidate for president from 1928 to 1948, winning his highest popular vote, 884,781, in 1932. He worked to organize workers and farmers and supported a variety of liberal causes. In Terre Haute, Ind., in 1935, he delivered a famous defense of free speech and free assembly. That year he also fought the Ku Klux Klan in Florida, and in 1938 he received wide publicity for defying the attempt of Mayor Frank Hague to stop a Socialist rally in Jersey City, N. J.

Thomas rejected the old-line Socialist antagonism toward the Soviet Union, but he was disillusioned on a trip there in 1937. He strove to keep America out of World War II, arguing that a war to end fascism was worse than fascism, but after the Japanese attack on Pearl Harbor he gave his support to the war action. He protested the interning of Japanese Americans and mass bombing. Later he endorsed the UN action in Korea but opposed U. S. intervention in Vietnam.

To the end Thomas deprecated violence and remained optimistic about America's future. He was thus overlooked by the new generation of radicals. He died in Huntington, N. Y., on Dec. 19, 1968. His books included *As I See It* (1932), *A Socialist's Faith* (1951), *Great Dissenters* (1961) and *Socialism Re-examined* (1963).

LOUIS FILLER, *Antioch College*

Further Reading: Seidler, Murray B., *Norman Thomas: Respectable Rebel*, 2d ed. (Syracuse, N. Y., 1967).

THOMAS, Seth (1785–1859), American clock manufacturer, whose skill in business organization and production techniques helped change the American clock industry from small-scale craftsmanship to mass production.

Thomas was born in Wolcott, Conn., on Aug. 19, 1785. After very little formal education he was apprenticed to a carpenter. In 1807 he formed a company with Silas Hoadley and Eli Terry, a former peddler who was fascinated with Eli Whitney's idea of interchangeable parts for machines. In three years they produced 4,000 clocks in their water-powered factory in Plymouth, Conn.

In 1812, Thomas set up his own factory in Plymouth Hollow (now Thomaston). In 1814, for $1,000, he bought the rights for manufacturing Terry's "perfected shelf clock," a 30–hour clock with wooden works that became the most popular clock of the era. It sold at first for $15, but the price was reduced to $5 through increased efficiency and sales. In 1838, Thomas began to use brass clock movements. In 1853 he established the Seth Thomas Clock Co., capitalized at $75,000. He died in Plymouth on Jan. 29, 1859.

His son Seth, Jr. (1816–1888) increased the scope of the business to include a wide variety of timepieces and an international market. The firm provides a classic example of the New England family business.

RICHARD D. BIRDSALL, *Connecticut College*

THOMAS, William Isaac (1863–1947), American social scientist who was one of the most important early contributors to social psychology. Thomas was born in Russell county, Va., on Aug. 13, 1863. Between 1894 and 1918, he taught sociology at the University of Chicago. He then engaged in independent research and writing. He died in Berkeley, Calif. on Dec. 5, 1947.

Thomas' writings, which reflect his broad definition of social psychology, include *Source Book of Social Origins* (1909; revised as *Primitive Behavior,* 1937); *The Polish Peasant in Europe and America* (with Florian Znaniecki, 5 vols., 1918–1921); *The Unadjusted Girl* (1923); and *Social Behavior and Personality* (1951).

Thomas insisted on the importance of a scientific orientation and empirical research. He introduced new techniques such as the use of diaries, letters, and other personal documents and autobiographies. His theory focused on the complex interplay of relationships between a person and his environment. He held that the way a person acts in a given situation is determined first by his attitudes as formed by previous experience and second by his definition of the present situation. Thomas suggested that behavior is patterned and can be reduced to four basic forms, the often-cited "four wishes": for security, recognition, new experience, and mastery (or response).

RUTH HEYDEBRAND, *Washington University*

THOMAS, Gospel of. See GOSPELS, APOCRYPHAL.

THOMAS À BECKET. See BECKET.

THOMAS À KEMPIS, ə-kem′pəs (c. 1380–1471), German theologian of the Low Countries who was the reputed author of the *Imitation of Christ.* He is generally considered the most outstanding representative of the late medieval religious movement known as the "Devotio Moderna." Thomas was born at Kempen in present-day Germany. His family name was Hemerken, although he became known by the name of his native village. When he was about 13 he went to Deventer, Netherlands, to attend a school conducted by Florentius Radewijns and the Brethren of the Common Life, a community founded by the Dutch mystic Gerhard Groote. At Deventer, Thomas came under the influence of the "modern devotion," which emphasized the simplicity and sincerity of the earliest Christians.

In 1399, Thomas entered the newly established Augustinian monastery of Mt. St. Agnes near Zwolle, Netherlands, where his older brother John was prior. Except for a brief period (1429–1432), when the monastic community moved to avoid joining in a local dispute against the pope, Thomas spent his whole life at Mt. St. Agnes, where he died and was buried on Aug. 8, 1471. His remains were later transferred to Zwolle.

Ordained a priest about 1414, Thomas subsequently held the positions of procurator, subprior, and novice master. Much of his long life was spent in reading, writing, editing, and copying manuscripts.

Thomas is commonly considered the author of the *Imitation of Christ*, one of the most widely circulated Christian devotional books (see IMITATION OF CHRIST). Thomas was also a prolific writer of sermons, hymns and popular spiritual treatises, religious conferences for monks, contemporary chronicles, as well as biographies, including lives of Groote and Radewijns.

JOHN T. FORD, C.S.C.
The Catholic University of America

THOMAS AQUINAS. See AQUINAS.

THOMASTON, a town in west central Connecticut, is in Litchfield county, on the Naugatuck River, 10 miles (16 km) north of Waterbury. Clocks have been made there since 1812, when the clockmaker Seth Thomas established his business. The town also makes brass and copper sheets and coils, electronic equipment, dies, and glass.

The first settlement was in 1728, as part of Plymouth. The town was separated from Plymouth in 1875 and named for Thomas. Government is by a board of selectmen and town meeting. Population: 6,233.

THOMASTON, a city in western Georgia, the seat of Upson county, is about 60 miles (96 km) south of Atlanta. The area produces beef cattle, dairy products, peaches, pecans, cotton, and lumber. Thomaston manufactures tire cord, sheets, and pillowcases.

The city was incorporated in 1825. Government is by a mayor and council. Population: 10,024.

THOMASVILLE, a city in southern Georgia, the seat of Thomas county, is 220 miles (352 km) south of Atlanta. It is a marketing center for farm products. The city makes clothing, mobile homes, and baked goods. There are meat- and poultry-packing plants. The Archbold Hospital is a medical center for a large area.

Thomasville's annual rose festival attracts thousands of visitors. The region is also notable for hunting, especially for quail, and for lake and pond fishing. The Glen Arven golf course is the fifth oldest in continuous operation in the United States.

Thomasville was founded in 1826. Government is by commission and manager. Population: 18,155.

THOMASVILLE, a town in west central North Carolina, is in Davidson county, about 20 miles (32 km) southwest of Greensboro. Tobacco, corn, and wheat are grown in the surrounding area. Thomasville manufactures furniture, textiles, clothing, plastics, and construction materials. The town was incorporated in 1852. Government is by a council and manager. Population: 15,230.

THOMISM, tō'miz-əm, is one of the two great schools of scholastic philosophy and theology. Thomism derives its name from St. Thomas Aquinas. See AQUINAS, SAINT THOMAS. The other great school is Scotism. See DUNS SCOTUS, JOHN.

THOMPSON, Sir Benjamin (1753–1814), American-born British physicist, diplomat, and social reformer, a man of limitless energy and resources, who managed to carry on a scientific career against a background of constant political intrigue and social reform. He is commonly known by the title Count Rumford.

Thompson was born in Woburn, Mass., on March 26, 1753. After leaving school he served as a physician's apprentice in Boston—and briefly as a schoolmaster. At the age of 19 he married Sarah Walker, the widow of a wealthy and influential Massachusetts colonel. Always ready to exploit a situation, Thompson used his wife's position to secure a major's commission in the New Hampshire militia, probably in return for becoming an informer on revolutionary activities. In 1774 he was tried for sedition by a colonial committee of safety but acquitted for lack of evidence. Throughout 1775, he regularly sent coded messages to the British high command in Boston about insurrectionist schemes in western Massachusetts. Subject to increasing suspicion from the colonists, he sailed for England in 1776, leaving his wife behind.

In London by exaggerating his knowledge of colonial affairs, he became private secretary to the colonial secretary, a post he held for three years. Later George III named him undersecretary of state. With the end of the American Revolution, his value to the crown diminished, and he left England to become aide-de-camp to the Elector of Bavaria. In order to enhance his prestige there, he persuaded George III to knight him. In return, Thompson agreed to spy for the British foreign office. In Germany, Thompson rapidly rose to eminence. He restructured the archaic Bavarian army, became a major general, then minister of war and minister of police. In 1792 he was elevated to the rank of Imperial Count of the Holy Roman Empire (as Count Rumford).

The next 20 years of Thompson's life were creative ones. Equally at home in Paris, Munich, and London, he turned his attention to scientific subjects of both a theoretical and a practical nature. He did pioneering work on heat conduction, radiant heat, and thermometry. He was the first to detect convection currents and to discover that water expands as it cools. His practical work on ventilators, stoves, flues, and lanterns led to many fundamental changes in engineering design.

Thompson's most famous experiments were performed at the munitions works in Munich. Supervising the boring of cannon from brass blocks, he observed that seemingly inexhaustible quantities of heat were being generated. According to the prevailing theory, heat was a substance that was stored in the interstices of bodies, and it could be released by friction. Thompson reasoned that if this theory were true, then the heat in the metal would eventually be used up, and no more heat would be available. Since no amount of boring exhausted the supply of heat, he concluded that heat was not a substance but the mechanical product of motion.

In 1796 he endowed the famous Rumford medals that are awarded by the Royal Society of London and the American Academy of Arts and Sciences for achievements in physics.

Desiring to return to the United States, he conceived a plan in the 1790's for establishing an American military academy. Thompson's past was not easily forgotten, however, and though President John Adams endorsed the plan, he refused to let Thompson return to head the proposed academy. Frustrated by this rebuff, Thompson played an important part in establishing the Royal Institution of London to encourage the promulgation and popularization of science.

Always subject to wanderlust, he left London in 1804 for Paris, where he married Lavoisier's widow. It was not a happy marriage, and they separated in 1807. Thompson died in Auteuil, near Paris, on Aug. 21, 1814.

LAURENS L. LAUDAN, *University of Pittsburgh*

Further Reading: Brown, Sanborn, *Count Rumford: Physicist Extraordinary* (Garden City, N.Y., 1962); Thompson, Sir Benjamin, *The Complete Works of Count Rumford* (Boston 1870–1873); Thompson, James A., *Count Rumford of Massachusetts* (New York 1935).

THOMPSON, Sir D'Arcy Wentworth (1860–1949), Scottish biologist and classicist best known for his work on the mathematical-physical analysis of organic form. His *On Growth and Form* (1917), appearing at a time when the traditional interpretation of morphology in terms of phylogeny and genetics was increasingly unrewarding, established a new approach to the subject by elucidating mathematical aspects of organic form. Thompson analyzed enbryonic development in mathematical-physical terms, described the dynamic and mathematical aspects of functional form, and elaborated a general method to mathematize morphology.

On Growth and Form was a seminal scientific treatise, and many subsequent developments in such diverse fields as developmental biology, marine biology, and paleontology received their original impetus from Thompson's exposition. The work was also a literary achievement, and its impact was enhanced by the beauty and lucidity of Thompson's literary style and the wealth of illustrations from ancient and modern writers.

Thompson was born in Edinburgh, Scotland, on May 2, 1860. He studied at the universities of Edinburgh and Cambridge, and later taught at the University of St. Andrew. He died in London on Jan. 21, 1949.

CHARLES W. BODEMER
University of Washington

THOMPSON, David (1770–1857), Canadian explorer and geographer. He was born in London, England, on April 30, 1770, the son of poor parents, and was educated at the Grey Coat charity school. He was apprenticed to the Hudson's Bay Company at the age of 14. Sent to help build trading posts on Hudson Bay and in the Saskatchewan River country, he gained a good working knowledge of astronomy and surveying. After making reconnaissance tours in the Nelson River and Lake Athabasca areas, he left the Hudson's Bay Company in 1797.

He joined the rival North West Company, which assigned him to determine the relationship of its posts to the new international boundary with the United States. In 1797–1798, Thompson made extensive journeys around the headwaters of the Missouri and Mississippi rivers. In 1804 he transferred his attention westward. He crossed the Rocky Mountains in 1807 through Howse Pass and built Kootenae House, the first trading post on the Columbia River. In 1811 he made his great voyage down the Columbia River, the first white man to travel from its source to its mouth.

Thompson left the West in 1812 and spent the next two years preparing a great map of transportation routes through the vast territory between Lake Winnipeg and the Pacific. From 1816 to 1826 he was employed by the International Boundary Commission to make a survey from the St. Lawrence River to Lake of the Woods. He died in poverty at Longueuil, near Montreal, on Feb. 10, 1857. His narrative of his travels was unpublished until 1916.

D. M. L. FARR, *Carleton University*

THOMPSON, Dorothy (1894–1961), American journalist, who was one of the best-known newspaperwomen of her time. A clergyman's daughter, she was born in Lancaster, N. Y., on July 9, 1894, and graduated from Syracuse University in 1914. Miss Thompson became a correspondent in Europe in the 1920's, winning a wide readership for her reports from Vienna and Berlin. An early critic of Hitler, she was one of the most effective propagandists against his regime. Her column *On the Record,* which she began for the New York *Herald Tribune* in 1936, was later published in some 200 other daily newspapers. Among her books are *The New Russia* (1928), which led her into a dispute with Theodore Dreiser, whom she accused of plagiarizing from it; *A Political Guide* (1938); and *Let the Record Speak* (1939).

Miss Thompson's marriage (1928–1942) to the novelist Sinclair Lewis was the subject of Vincent Sheean's *Dorothy and Red* (1963). She died in Lisbon, Portugal, on Jan. 31, 1961.

THOMPSON, Edward Herbert (1856–1935), American archaeologist, known for his excavation of Maya ruins at Chichén Itzá in Yucatán. He was born in Worcester, Mass., on Sept. 28, 1856. He had no formal training in archaeology, and his later work was the outgrowth of a lifelong interest in Indian lore. He served as American consul in Yucatán from 1885 to 1909, and he devoted his free time to archaeological exploration. He was able to purchase a tract of land that included the site of Chichén Itzá. This tract, which he leased to the Carnegie Institution of Washington, became a center for archaeological research and restoration. His notable discoveries there include the Maya Date Stone and the Sacred Well, a vast oval cavity in rock into which human sacrifices, gold, and precious stones had been thrown in order to propitiate the rain god who was believed to live at its bottom.

Thompson described his work in *The People of The Serpent* (1932). He died in Plainfield, N. J., on May 11, 1935.

PRISCILLA C. WARD
American Museum of Natural History

THOMPSON, Ernest Seton. See SETON, ERNEST THOMPSON.

THOMPSON, Francis (1859–1907), English poet, who wrote the famous religious poem, *The Hound of Heaven.* He was born at Preston, Lancashire, on Dec. 18, 1859. Raised as a devout Roman Catholic, he studied for the priesthood, but his poor health and unstable temperament rendered him unfit for the clergy. After briefly studying medicine, he moved to London in 1885. There, living in poverty and plagued by illness that made him dependent upon opium, he began to write poetry. After submitting verses to the magazine *Merry England,* Thompson was sought out by its editor Wilfrid Meynell, who, with his wife Alice, helped support him for the rest of his life. He died in London on Nov. 13, 1907.

Works. Thompson published three volumes of verse—*Poems* (1893), *Sister Songs* (1895), and *New Poems* (1897). *The Hound of Heaven,* included in *Poems,* describes the religious crisis of a man who is pursued by God's love, at first rejects it, and is finally caught up in it. The poem is in part a record of Thompson's spiritual sufferings in his early London years. Marked by elaborate rhythms, bold diction, and extravagant imagery, it reveals the influence of Crashaw and the Metaphysical poets and also of Shelley and Coventry Patmore. Of Thompson's prose works, his *Essay on Shelley* (1909) is best known.

CLYDE DE L. RYALS
University of Pennsylvania

THOMPSON, Sir John Sparrow David (1844–1894), Canadian prime minister. He was born in Halifax, Nova Scotia, on Nov. 10, 1844. He was called to the bar at the age of 21 and quickly demonstrated capacity. In 1871 he became a Roman Catholic. He was elected to the provincial legislature in 1877 and became premier of Nova Scotia in 1882. His government was defeated in that year, and he then became a puisne justice of the supreme court of Nova Scotia.

Thompson entered federal politics in 1885 as minister of justice in John A. Macdonald's cabinet. He was immediately at the center of controversial questions involving race and religion: the execution in 1885 of Louis Riel, leader of the North-West Rebellion; compensation to the Jesuits in 1888 for the loss of their estates; and the status of the French language in western Canada. Thompson's legal ability was applied to fishery negotiations with the United States and to international copyright.

On Macdonald's death in 1891, Thompson's religion seemed to bar his succession. But when Sir John Abbott retired as prime minister in 1892, Thompson succeeded him. His tenure was short, for he died at Windsor Castle, in England, on Dec. 12, 1894.

G. DE T. GLAZEBROOK, *Author of "A History of Canadian Political Thought"*

THOMPSON, John Taliaferro (1860–1940), American army officer and inventor, whose most famous invention was the Thompson submachine gun (Tommy gun) in 1920. He was born in Newport, Ky., on Dec. 31, 1860, and died in Great Neck, N.Y., on June 21, 1940. Thompson graduated from West Point in 1882, entered the Ordnance Department in 1890, rose to the rank of colonel, and retired in 1914, but returned in World War I to head the Small Arms Division.

During his army career Thompson patented a number of devices for automatic small arms. His submachine gun fired the same cartridge as the standard 0.45 caliber pistol from a clip of 20 rounds or a drum of 50. An air-cooled weapon of very reliable action, it used the delayed blowback principle. Its hitting power and rate of fire made it especially desirable for close fighting. First used in combat by the U.S. Marines in Nicaragua in 1925, it was widely used by U.S. and Allied troops in World War II.

ROBERT S. WOODBURY
Massachusetts Institute of Technology

THOMPSON, Smith (1768–1843), American Supreme Court justice who opposed the nationalism of John Marshall. He voted to uphold state bankruptcy laws in *Ogden* v. *Saunders* (1827) and the power of the courts to require cabinet members to perform their ministerial duties.

Thompson was born on Jan. 17, 1768, in Amenia, N.Y. He graduated from the College of New Jersey (Princeton) in 1788, and was admitted to the New York bar in 1792, practicing in Poughkeepsie, N.Y. Thompson then served as a justice of the state supreme court (1802–1804) and as its chief justice (1814–1818). President Monroe appointed him secretary of the navy in 1818 and named him to the Supreme Court in 1823. Ambitious to be president, Thompson accepted reluctantly. In 1828 he ran unsuccessfully for governor of New York. He died in Poughkeepsie, N.Y., on Dec. 18, 1843.

LEO PFEFFER, *Long Island University*

THOMPSON, William Hale (1869–1944), American political leader, who was mayor of Chicago from 1915 to 1923 and from 1927 to 1931. A vigorous orator, "Big Bill" Thompson, as he was generally known, was one of the most flamboyant figures in municipal politics.

Thompson was born in Boston, Mass., on May 14, 1869, and grew up in Chicago. After eight years as a rancher in the West, he returned to Chicago in 1891 and became active in the real estate business. He entered Republican politics in 1900 as an alderman from Chicago's 2d Ward and was Cook county commissioner from 1902 to 1904. An isolationist during World War I, he established the short-lived America First Foundation in Chicago during the 1920's and attracted national attention with his anti-British speeches.

Thompson's main achievements as mayor were the improvement of city parks and streets and the inauguration of a municipal playground system. But he failed to oust gangster organizations from Chicago, and gang warfare prevailed during his last term. After 1931 his popularity declined, and he was defeated when he ran for governor in 1936. He died in Chicago on March 19, 1944.

THOMPSON INDIANS, American tribe of the Salish linguistic stock. See SALISH INDIANS.

THOMSEN, tôm'sen, **Christian Jürgensen** (1788–1865), Danish archaeologist, known as "the father of European prehistory." He thought of technological development as three successive stages: the Stone, Bronze, and Iron ages.

Thomsen was born in Copenhagen on Dec. 29, 1788. In 1816 the Danish National Museum gave him the task of organizing artifacts accumulated from all parts of Denmark. He classified archaeological finds according to the material of which they were made: stone, bronze, or iron. The three-age system was an outgrowth of this organization. An explanation of the system was published in the museum's catalogue in 1836. It has since been adopted by all archaeologists as a framework for the study of man's prehistory. Thomsen died in Copenhagen on May 21, 1865.

PRISCILLA C. WARD
American Museum of Natural History

THOMSON, Charles (1729–1824), American patriot and political leader. He was born in County Derry, Ireland, on Nov. 29, 1729, and was orphaned during a voyage to New Castle, Del., in 1739. He secured a classical education and taught school in Philadelphia. Thomson was secretary for several Indian conferences in 1756 and 1757, and his narrative on the alienation of the Delaware and Shawnee was published by Benjamin Franklin in London in 1759.

Long active in politics, Thomson emerged in the decade before 1774 as the leader of the merchants, mechanics, and tradesmen opposed to British policies. John Adams called him "the Sam Adams of Philadelphia." Thomson served from 1774 to 1789 as the "perpetual secretary" to Congress. Not having received an office in Washington's administration, he devoted himself to scholarly pursuits at his home in Merion, Pa., where he died on Aug. 16, 1824.

JOHN J. ZIMMERMAN
Kansas State Teachers College

THOMSON, Charles Edward Poulett. See SYDENHAM, 1ST BARON.

THOMSON, Elihu (1853–1937), American inventor and electrical manufacturer. He was born in Manchester, England, on March 29, 1853, and went to the United States in 1858. While teaching in Philadelphia, he and a colleague, Edwin J. Houston, developed basic improvements in various electrical equipment, and in 1883 they founded the Thomson-Houston Electric Company. By 1890 the company had become the chief rival of the Westinghouse company in promoting the use of alternating current (as against direct current advocated by Edison) in systems supplied by central power plants. In 1892 the "battle of the currents" was won by ac when the company merged with the Edison General Electric Company to form the General Electric Company.

Thomson was granted more than 700 patents on his inventions, among them a generator that could deliver three separate alternating currents (1880); resistance welding (1886); the repulsion-type induction motor (1887); and a recording wattmeter (1889). He died in Swampscott, Mass., on March 13, 1937.

KENNETH M. SWEZEY
Author of "Science Shows You How"

THOMSON, Sir George Paget (1892–), English physicist, who shared the Nobel Prize in physics with Clinton Davisson in 1937 "for the experimental discovery of the interference phenomenon in crystals irradiated by electrons." While Davisson used electrons of relatively low velocities, Thomson passed very fast electrons through metal foils in the same way as X rays can be passed through a crystal. The electron radiation was registered on a photographic plate, and a pattern of interference rings was observed. From the radii of the rings it was possible to calculate the corresponding wavelengths and get experimental confirmation of the wave properties of electrons.

Thomson was born in Cambridge, England, on May 3, 1892, the son of the physicist Sir Joseph John Thomson. George Thomson was educated at Trinity College, Cambridge, and served in the Royal Flying Corps during World War I. In 1922 he was appointed professor of physics at Aberdeen. From 1930 until he became master of Corpus Christi College, Cambridge, in 1952, he was professor of physics at the Imperial College of Science in London. He retired from Corpus Christi in 1962.

In World War II, Thomson was chairman of the British commission on atomic energy. He was knighted in 1943. Thomson is the author, with his father, of *The Atom* (1930).

THOMSON, James (1700–1748), Scottish poet, who was a forerunner of the romantic movement in English verse. He was born in Ednam, Scotland, on Sept. 11, 1700. He studied for the ministry at the University of Edinburgh but abandoned theology in 1725 when he moved to England. Thereafter his income was derived from the publication of his poetry and from patronage. He died in Richmond, England, on Aug. 27, 1748.

Thomson composed largely in blank verse at a time dominated by the heroic couplet, a meter used by such friends of his as Alexander Pope. Thomson's best poetry is in *The Seasons*, a series of five poems on nature: *Spring*, *Summer*, *Autumn*, *Winter*, and *A Hymn to the Seasons*. First published serially between 1726 and 1729, they were revised and enlarged until 1746. The description of a snowstorm in *Winter* is widely regarded as the best passage in these poems. *The Castle of Indolence: An Allegorical Poem* (1748) is writing of a very different kind. It begins as a burlesque on Spenser's *The Faerie Queene* and modulates into a serious tale of enchantment.

Thomson also wrote five tragedies, including *Tancred and Sigismonda* (1745). His *The Masque of Alfred* (1740), written with the poet David Mallet and the musician Thomas Arne, contains the famous patriotic poem *Rule, Britannia!*

DAVID F. C. COLDWELL
Southern Methodist University

THOMSON, James (1834–1882), Scottish poet, whose verse was the most pessimistic of the Victorian period. He was born in Port Glasgow on Nov. 23, 1834. His father became paralyzed in 1840 and died in 1853. His mother died in 1842. In 1850 he entered the Royal Military Asylum as an apprentice army schoolteacher and in 1851 was sent to teach in Ireland. There he met the freethinker Charles Bradlaugh. After his discharge from the army for a minor offense, in 1862, Thomson settled in England. With Bradlaugh's aid he found work as a contributor to such magazines as the *National Reformer*, for which he wrote poems, stories, and essays under the pen name "B. V." or "Bysshe Vanolis," from Shelley's middle name and an anagram of the name of the German poet Novalis. In 1872, Thomson visited the United States and in the next year went to Spain as a newspaper correspondent. Plagued by alcoholism and chronic depression, he ultimately quarreled with all his friends. He died in London on June 3, 1882.

Thomson's best-known work is the somber poem *The City of Dreadful Night* (1874), about the futility and loneliness of existence. His other works include *Vane's Story . . . and Other Poems* (1882), *Essays and Phantasies* (1883), and translations of poems by Heine and Leopardi.

DAVID F. C. COLDWELL
Southern Methodist University

THOMSON, Sir Joseph John (1856–1940), English physicist and discoverer of the electron. He was awarded the Nobel Prize in physics in 1906 "in recognition of the great merits of his theoretical and experimental investigations on the conduction of electricity by gases." Born in Cheetham Hill, England, on Dec. 18, 1856, Thomson was educated at Cambridge, with which he had a lifelong association. His earliest investigations concerned the increase in inertia (mass) of a moving electric charge and the behavior of vortex rings.

Thomson's discovery of the electron came about after years of investigating the conduction of electricity by gases in cathode-ray discharge tubes, for which precise measurements only became possible with Roentgen's discovery of X rays in 1895. From studies of the ionization produced by X rays, Thomson became convinced that cathode rays were small charged particles. By early 1897 he had measured their deflection in a magnetic field, as well as the heat they generated, and had concluded that their mass-to-charge ratio was roughly 1,000 times smaller than that of hydrogen ions. He confirmed this conclusion with his famous crossed fields apparatus. By 1899 he had estimated the charge of the electron and proved it to be a universal constituent of matter. Seven years later he proved that the atom contains only a relatively small number of electrons—an essential step toward Rutherford's nuclear atom. In 1912, Thomson showed that the "positive rays" in discharge tubes are atomic and molecular ions, thereby establishing the principles of mass spectroscopy. He also separated the first isotopes known outside the field of radioactivity.

After Thomson became Cavendish professor at Cambridge in 1884 he made what was perhaps his most enduring contribution to physics—the transformation of the Cavendish laboratory into the greatest center of research of the period. Hundreds of outstanding scientists were trained there, eight of whom, among them his son, won Nobel Prizes. The attributes that enabled Thomson to foster such work were his vigorous personality, the example he set, and his conviction that his and his students' research were supremely important. He died in Cambridge on Aug. 30, 1940.

ROGER H. STUEWER
University of Minnesota

THOMSON, Tom (1877–1917), Canadian painter of wilderness scenes. Thomas John Thomson was born in Claremont, Ontario, on Aug. 4, 1877. He spent his childhood on a farm and was virtually self-taught in art. He worked in a photoengraving studio in Seattle in 1901 and as a commercial artist in Toronto in 1905. With the painter A. Y. Jackson he shared a studio and went sketching in Algonquin Park, Ontario. Thomson's first large work was *Northern Lake* (1913). From 1914 he was in the summer a ranger in Algonquin Park, where he did sketches for oil paintings, such as *Northern River* and *Spring Ice*, finished in the winter in Toronto.

Thomson's portrayals of the rugged Canadian north broke with conventional Canadian art, which was dominated by European influence, and inspired the nationalistic landscape painters called the Group of Seven. Thomson was drowned in Canoe Lake, Algonquin Park, on July 8, 1917. See also CANADA—*Art and Architecture*.

Tom Thomson's *The Jack Pine* (1917)

THE NATIONAL GALLERY OF CANADA, OTTAWA

VIRGIL THOMSON was honored by New York University with a medal and citation on his 65th birthday.

WIDE WORLD PHOTOS

THOMSON, Virgil (1896–), American composer and music critic. He was born on Nov. 25, 1896, in Kansas City, Mo., where he studied music with local teachers. After graduating from Harvard in 1923, he taught there for a time and then went to Paris, where he had studied in 1921 under Nadia Boulanger. Living in Paris for many years, he formed friendships with prominent writers and musicians. Gertrude Stein wrote the librettos of his operas *Four Saints in Three Acts* (first performed in 1934) and *The Mother of Us All* (1947). Among Thomson's musical souvenirs of Paris the most notable is *The Seine at Night* (1947) for orchestra. The chamber work *Sonata da Chiesa* (1926) reveals his affinity with "The French Six," a group active in the 1920's.

American themes and scenes are prominent in Thomson's music, particularly the scores for the documentary films *The River* (1937), *The Plough That Broke the Plains* (1936), and *Louisiana Story* (1948); the ballet *Filling Station* (1937); and the *Symphony on a Hymn Tune* (completed in 1928). Such works made Thomson an important figure in the "Americanist" movement, along with Copland, Cowell, and Roy Harris. But Thomson wrote much instrumental and vocal music that is neither nationalistic nor overtly descriptive.

Thomson was music critic for the New York *Herald-Tribune* from 1940 to 1954. His criticism was collected in *The Musical Scene* (1945), *The Art of Judging Music* (1948), and *Music Right and Left* (1951). He also wrote *The State of Music* (1939) and the memoir *Virgil Thomson* (1966).

GILBERT CHASE, *Author of "America's Music"*

THOMSON, William. See KELVIN, LORD.

THOMSON EFFECT, a thermoelectric effect first predicted and experimentally established by William Thomson (later Lord Kelvin) in the 1850's. See THERMOELECTRICITY.

THOMSONITE. See ZEOLITE.

THONGA, tong'gə, a people of southern Africa living primarily in southern Mozambique. Numbering about 1.5 million, they constitute Mozambique's second-largest ethnic group. They are also called Bathonga and Shangana-Tonga.

The Thonga are Negroid in physical appearance. Their language is classified as a major subdivision of the Bantu group of the Niger-Congo family. Many Thonga are Christians.

Agriculture and cattle-raising provide the basis of the Thonga economy. The largest part of the people's income comes from their labor in the mines of South Africa, where 40% of the men work during part of their lifetime.

Little is known of the origins or early history of the Thonga. During the 19th century their homeland was invaded by Nguni-speaking peoples who had migrated from South Africa to escape the spreading power of the Zulu. Soshangane, leader of one of the Nguni groups, conquered the Thonga and established the Gaza empire over them. In 1891 the Thonga came under Portuguese rule.

ROBERT A. LYSTAD
Johns Hopkins University

THOR, thôr, in Norse mythology, was the god of thunder, bringer of rain, provider of abundant crops, and protector of men, especially peasants and farmers. He was the most popular of the gods worshipped in ancient Scandinavia and Germany. Thursday was originally Thor's day.

Thor was conceived of as a mighty hero who warred against a horde of demon giants. His favorite weapon was his hammer, Mjolnir (thunderbolt), which he hurled at the foes of gods and men and which always returned to him. He had iron gloves with which to catch the searing hammer and a magic belt that doubled his great strength. The wheels of his goat-drawn chariot made the sound of thunder as he raced across the sky. Thor's most dangerous adversary, the Midgard (midworld) serpent Jormungandr, cannot be defeated until the time of Ragnarok (doomsday), when the earth and sky will be destroyed and Thor too will perish.

In his great strength and heroic deeds Thor resembles the classic demigod Hercules (Heracles). As god of thunder he has links with the Greek Zeus and the Roman Jupiter.

According to some tales, Thor was the father of Odin, chief of the gods in the Norse pantheon. Other stories, however, made Thor the son of Odin and Frigg (Frigga) or of Odin and Jord. Thor's wives were Iarnsaxa and Sif. His sons were Modi, Magni, and Loride, and his daughter was Thrud. Stories about Thor are found in the *Eddas*.

See EDDAS; SCANDINAVIAN MYTHOLOGY.

BERNARD MANDELBAUM
Bronx Community College, New York

THORACIC DUCT, thə-ras′ik, the large vessel that carries lymph from the intestines and lower parts of the body to a vein in the neck. The lymph is then mixed with the blood and conveyed to the heart. See LYMPH.

THORAX, thôr′aks, in human anatomy, the area of the body between the neck and the abdomen. The thorax, commonly called the chest, contains the lungs, heart, and major blood vessels and is bounded by the ribs, sternum (breastbone), and the thoracic vertebrae of the spine. The floor of the thorax is formed by the diaphragm.

In insects, the term "thorax" denotes the middle section of the body, which bears the insect's wings and legs. In many other arthropods, including spiders, scorpions, lobsters, and horseshoe crabs, the thorax is fused with the head, forming a *cephalothorax*.

THORAZINE, a brand name for chlorpromazine, a drug used for its tranquilizing effects. See TRANQUILIZING DRUGS.

THOREAU, thôr′ō, **Henry David** (1817–1862), American author, who was a younger member of the transcendentalist group that flourished in mid-19th century New England and was probably its best literary artist. His fame rests primarily on his unique masterpiece *Walden*.

Early Life. Thoreau was born in Concord, Mass., on July 12, 1817, and Concord remained the center of his world, although he spent several years of his early childhood in neighboring towns and later lived briefly elsewhere. His college career (1833–1837) at nearby Harvard brought him two gifts—the discovery of the world of books and friendship with Ralph Waldo Emerson, the leader of the transcendental movement (see TRANSCENDENTALISM).

Having read Emerson's essay *Nature* (1836), an expression of the main principles of transcendentalism, the young Thoreau was prepared for the full impact of Emerson's address, *The American Scholar,* delivered before the Phi Beta Kappa Society of Harvard in 1837. In that address Emerson called for leadership of American society by native scholars, who have become self-reliant and independent of the "popular cry" through following the precepts "Know thyself" and "Study Nature."

Thoreau went to live as a member of Emerson's household from 1841 to 1843 and again in 1847–1848. Through this connection he came to know Bronson Alcott, Margaret Fuller, and other members of the Transcendental Club. He helped Emerson edit the transcendental periodical the *Dial* and contributed a number of poems and essays to it. This was his first incentive to authorship and his first outlet, just as the transcendental "fellowship" furnished most of his literary friendships, at least in his early years. But he was a detached participant at best and was never Emerson's disciple in any true sense. As a creative writer, Thoreau is most interesting when farthest removed from Emerson.

Thoreau taught school with his brother John, tried tutoring for a few months, and from time to time was engaged in his father's business of

Henry David Thoreau

BROWN BROTHERS

manufacturing pencils, but his goal was one that could not be fitted to a normal trade or profession. He was a dedicated poet. Authorship of any sort was a precarious way to make a living at that time, and the audience for Thoreau's kind of writing was especially limited.

Middle and Later Years. Thoreau carried out his well-known experiment in living—the residence at Walden Pond, near Concord, from July 4, 1845, to Sept. 6, 1847—partly to determine whether he could support himself in a minimal way by light manual labor and thus have most of his time free for writing. When he left the pond, he had the completed manuscript of *A Week on the Concord and Merrimack Rivers* and an early draft of *Walden*. Thereafter he lived at his family's home in Concord and made a bare living as a handyman so that he might devote himself to writing and still have time for his rambles.

By most of the citizens of Concord, Thoreau was considered an eccentric. His life was marked by whimsical acts and unconventional stands on public issues, but his rare nature lore, unusual manual skills, and keen common sense won the admiration of many who had thought him only an oddity. When he expressed his deepest convictions through dramatic action, he provoked mixed feelings of respect and dismay. His withdrawal to Walden Pond was such an occasion. In protest against the Mexican War and the extension of slavery, he refused in 1845 to pay his taxes and thus forced the Concord jailer to lock him up. This event found expression in his best-known essay *Resistance to Civil Government* (later called *Civil Disobedience* or *On the Duty of Civil Disobedience*), which became highly influential in the 20th century. Near the end of his life Thoreau once again defied society by being almost the first to come to the defense of John Brown's raid on Harpers Ferry (1859). He rang the bell himself at the Concord town hall to call a meeting, and in his *Plea for Captain John Brown*, he exceeded the most fanatical abolitionists. Thoreau died at Concord on May 6, 1862.

Works. Although Thoreau never earned a living by his pen, his works fill 20 volumes. His first book was a spectacular failure. Printed locally at his own expense in 1849, *A Week* sold only 219 of the original 1,000 copies. *Walden* finally appeared in 1854 under the imprint of a leading Boston publisher. Although it received some good reviews, five years were required to dispose of an edition of 2,000 copies. The body of his works intended for publication includes these two books, some poems and numerous essays, and the posthumously published *Excursions* (1863), *The Maine Woods* (1864), *Cape Cod* (1865), and *A Yankee in Canada* (1866).

"A Week on the Concord and Merrimack Rivers." This book usually has been considered Thoreau's most transcendental writing because it is concerned with the quality of experience. In pattern it follows the natural course of the rivers and a literal journey of seven days, but this interpretation is too simple for the complex structure of the work. For one thing, it is a journey back into history, since travelers on these streams move geographically from civilization to primitive country. There is also the outward-bound voyage—against the current, upstream to the source; then the return, rapidly downstream, with the flow of time. Less obvious but more interesting are the symbols suggesting the week of Creation as described in Genesis. For most readers, however, *A Week* remains primarily the discovery of a way back to nature.

"Walden." As a discovery of nature, *A Week* forms an introduction to *Walden*—Thoreau's exploration, through nature, of the life of the spirit. For nearly a century after *Walden*'s publication the main interpretations of this masterpiece treated it as a collection of nature essays, as social criticism, or as literal autobiography. All these approaches throw light on facets of the book, but they leave the central vision untouched.

A recent and much more fruitful tendency is to treat Walden as a created work of art—by one critic, as a poem in prose. Such a reading assumes that the meaning of Walden resides in its language, its structure of images, its symbolism—and is inseparable from them. It is an experience recreated in words for the purpose of getting rid of the world and discovering the self. Finally, an intricate system of circular imagery centers on the pond as a symbol of heaven, the ideal of perfection striven for.

"Journal." Thoreau's contemporary reputation was based on *A Week* and *Walden*, plus a few fine essays like *Walking*, *Wild Apples*, and *Life Without Principle*. The great bulk of his writing consists of his private *Journal*, covering his life from 1837 to 1862, which was not published until nearly 50 years after his death. It is not a diary but an artist's workbook, which records his observations, material for his works, and experiments in a new literary genre of "miniatures." Some critics contend that Thoreau's greatest achievement is this remarkable record of a remarkable man's view of the world. With the publication of the *Journal* (14 vols., 1906), Thoreau came into his own as a major writer.

CHARLES R. ANDERSON
Author of "The Magic Circle of Walden"

Further Reading: Anderson, Charles R., *The Magic Circle of Walden* (New York 1968); id., *Thoreau's World: Miniatures from the Journal* (New York 1971); Harding, Walter, *The Days of Henry Thoreau* (New York 1965); Paul, Sherman, *The Shores of America: Thoreau's Inward Exploration* (Urbana, Ill., 1958); Shanley, J. Lyndon, *The Making of Walden* (Chicago 1957).

THOREZ, tô-rez′, **Maurice** (1900–1964), leader of the French Communist party for 34 years. A miner's son, he was born on April 28, 1900, in Noyelles-Godault. At the Socialist Congress of Tours in 1920 he joined the majority, which founded the French Communist party. He adhered strictly to the Moscow party line and rose rapidly to become secretary general in 1930. He was elected to the Chamber of Deputies in 1932.

Mobilized in 1939, Thorez deserted from the army when the Communist party was outlawed, and he spent the war years in Moscow. He was pardoned in 1944 and returned to parliament in 1945. He was a minister of state and then a deputy prime minister until the Communist members of the government were dismissed in 1947.

After Nikita Khrushchev's denunciation of Stalin in 1956, Thorez kept his party much closer to Stalinism than most other Communist parties. In later life he was incapacitated by strokes, and his functions were assumed by his wife, Jeannette Thorez-Vermeersch, herself a member of parliament and a high Communist official. His autobiography, *Fils du peuple* (1937), was widely used in party propaganda. He died on July 11, 1964, on a Soviet ship sailing for Yalta.

HENRY W. EHRMANN, *Dartmouth College*

THORFINN KARLSEFNI, tôr'fin kärl'sev-ni, Icelandic explorer, who made an expedition to Vinland in the early 11th century. He was born about 980 at Reyniness in the Skagafjord district of Iceland. He is said to have been a seagoing merchant of considerable wealth. His trade route covered Iceland, the British Isles, and mainland Scandinavia. Later he extended his route to Greenland, where he landed about 1001. At Brattahlid he met and married Gudrid, the widow of Thorstein, one of Eric the Red's sons.

Thorfinn, whose nickname *Karlsefni* means "the makings of a man," and Gudrid undertook an expedition to Vinland. They followed the route of Leif Ericson, another son of Eric the Red. Though the prospect of economic gain spurred the voyage, their ultimate goal was permanent settlement. The *Saga of Eric the Red* relates that 160 people sailed in several ships and that, unable to reach Vinland, they tentatively settled on a fjord they named Straumfjord. The *Saga of the Greenlanders* tells, however, of a voyage with about 60 men and 5 women that reached Vinland without incident. Thorfinn remained for three years in Vinland, where his son Snorri was born. After the settlers returned to Greenland, Thorfinn established the homestead of Glaumbaer in Iceland, where he and Gudrid had a second son, Thorbjorn. The date of Thorfinn's death is unknown.

BIRGITTA L. WALLACE
Carnegie Museum

THORIANITE, thôr'ē-ə-nīt, is a rare radioactive mineral consisting of thorium oxide (ThO_2). Its cubic crystals are brown or black, and uranium and rare earths are often present. Thorianite occurs in Ceylon and Madagascar.

THORITE, thōr'īt, is a silicate of thorium. It can vary widely in composition, because uranium, rare earths, lead, and other elements take the place of thorium in the mineral. The uranium and thorium undergo radioactive decay, often causing thorite to alter to a noncrystalline state. Hydration of the mineral also accompanies this process.

Thorite occurs in the igneous rocks known as pegmatites and also as an accessory mineral in other granitic rocks and in sands. It was first found near Brevik, Norway. The material obtained there was analyzed by the Swedish chemist J. J. Berzelius in 1829, resulting in the discovery of the element thorium.

Thorite is found most notably on the island of Madagascar, in New Zealand, western Australia, and, in the United States, in North Carolina, Texas, and Colorado.

Composition: $ThSiO_4$; hardness, 4.5; specific gravity, 4.1–6.7; crystal system, tetragonal.

GEORGE SWITZER, *Smithsonian Institution*

THORIUM, thor'ē-əm, symbol Th, is a soft, radioactive metallic element. It is classified as one of the actinide series of elements. Thorium was discovered in 1828 by the Swedish chemist Jöns Jakob Berzelius and was named after the Norse god Thor.

Uses. The earliest use of thorium was in Welsbach mantles, mainly for gas street lamps, in the late 1800's. These mantles consist of a fabric coated with thorium dioxide and a small amount of cerium oxide, which when heated emits a brilliant light. The Welsbach mantle is still used for outdoor lighting and for interior lighting in areas without electricity.

Although thorium-232 is not fissionable, it can be converted to fissionable uranium-233 by the absorption of neutrons. This is accomplished in a type of nuclear reactor called a breeder reactor. Because the natural abundance of thorium is much greater than that of uranium, the element represents a tremendous potential source of nuclear energy.

Metallic thorium is used as a getter for the removal of nitrogen and oxygen in vacuum tubes. An alloy of thorium and magnesium is used in aircraft and rockets because of its light weight and its strength at high temperatures.

Thorium fluoride is used in the preparation of the metal and in high-temperature ceramics. Thorium oxide is used in ceramics, nuclear fuels, medicine, and electronic equipment. Thorium nitrate is used in medicine and as an analytical reagent. Thorium dioxide, in addition to its use in Welsbach mantles, is used in high-temperature ceramics, as a nuclear fuel, and in optical glass.

Properties. Thorium is located in Group IIIA of the periodic table; its atomic number is 90, and its atomic weight is 232.038. The element melts at about 1750° C (3180° F) and boils at about 3800° C (6900° F). The pure metal is as soft as lead and very ductile. When freshly cut, the metal is lustrous, but it darkens on long exposure to air. Thorium is highly electropositive; it oxidizes in air, and when finely divided, it may ignite spontaneously. Thorium exhibits an oxidation state of +4 in its compounds. There are 13 known isotopes of thorium, ranging from ^{223}Th to ^{235}Th, and all are radioactive. The only isotope found in nature is ^{232}Th, which has a half-life of 1.39×10^{10} years.

Occurrence. Thorium makes up approximately 0.001%–0.002% of the earth's crust. The only commercial source of the element is monazite, a complex radioactive phosphate sand that also contains uranium, cerium, and other lanthanides. Rich deposits of monazite are found in India, Brazil, South Africa, Australia, Malaysia, and the United States. Thorium is also found with niobium, titanium, tantalum, and uranium in minerals such as thorite and thorianite.

Production. There are several methods for producing thorium. The metal may be obtained by reduction of the fluoride, ThF_4, with calcium, using zinc chloride as a flux. It is also prepared by reduction of the oxide or chloride with calcium, magnesium, or sodium. A third method involves the electrolysis of a fused mixture of thorium fluoride, potassium cyanide, and sodium chloride. Thorium may also be recovered as a by-product in processing rare earth elements.

HERBERT LIEBESKIND, *The Cooper Union*

THORN, George Widmer (1906–), American physician and physiologist perhaps best known for his study of the hormones of the adrenal cortex—work that led to a method of treating Addison's disease and to other important advances.

Working with Frank A. Hartman at the University of Buffalo Medical School, Thorn became interested in adrenal cortex extract. He developed a biological assay method useful in purifying the hormone, directed clinical tests of the extract that showed how it affected carbohydrate and mineral metabolism, and recognized its usefulness in treating Addison's disease. Thorn later used adrenal hormone pellets implanted in dogs to determine the rate of absorption and the doses needed to treat adrenal insufficiencies. He also pioneered in the clinical use of ACTH, in ways of detecting adrenal insufficiencies, and in human kidney transplantation.

Thorn was born in Buffalo, N. Y., on Jan. 15, 1906. He received his M. D. degree from the University of Buffalo Medical School in 1929, held positions in the physiology and medicine departments there, and then studied and worked at other universities. In 1942 he was named physician in chief to the Peter Bent Brigham Hospital in Boston and Hersey Professor of the Theory and Practice of Physic at Harvard University. In 1967 he also became Levine Professor of Medicine.

JOHN C. BURNHAM, *Ohio State University*

THORN, the German name for a city now part of Poland. See TORUŃ.

THORN, a name commonly applied to any plant that bears sharp processes on the stem or leaves. Among the plants most often called thorns are the hawthorn and honey locust.

In technical terminology, "thorn" refers only to modified stems. Thorns are thus distinguished from spines, or modified leaves, and prickles, or outgrowths of a leaf or stem. See also STEM.

THORN APPLE is a name for the fruit of the hawthorn or a plant of the genus *Datura.* See DATURA; HAWTHORN.

THORNBILL, any of several species of birds, belonging to quite diverse families, that possess short, slender, sharply pointed, thornlike beaks. Probably the best-known and most numerous thornbills are those of two genera (*Acanthiza* and *Gerygone*) of tree warblers found in Australia, New Zealand, and New Guinea. Small, active birds, they are usually olive-colored above and yellowish below. The yellow-tailed thornbill (*A. chrysorrhoa*) builds a many-chambered, oblong, enclosed nest either among sticks in the margin of the nest of a large bird of prey or at the tip of a small tree branch. The nest opening is on the bottom, and the upper chamber contains the eggs. The female alone incubates the two to four eggs, but the male helps build the nest and feed the young. Because the young of the first brood assist in rearing later broods, these thornbills have unusually persistent family ties. They are classified in the subfamily Malurinae of the Old World warbler family (Sylviidae) in the order Passeriformes.

The red-fronted thornbill (*Phacellodomus rufifrons*) is a South American ovenbird about 6 inches (15 cm) long. Known as "castle builders," they construct many-compartmented, columnar nests that may be 10 feet (3 meters) high and weigh 100 pounds (45 kg). They are classified in the subfamily Synallaxinae of the ovenbird family (Furnariidae), order Passeriformes. Other thornbills are included in three genera (*Chalcostigma, Ramphomicron,* and *Opisthoprora*) of South American hummingbirds of the family Trochlidae.

CARL WELTY, *Beloit College*

An Australian thornbill (*Acanthiza*) in its nest.

JOHN WARHAM

THORNDIKE, thôrn'dīk, **Edward Lee** (1874–1949), American psychologist and educator. He was born in Williamsburg, Mass., on Aug. 31, 1874, and was associated with Teachers College, Columbia University, from 1899 to 1940. He died in Montrose, N. Y., on Aug. 9, 1949.

Thorndike became a leader in the United States in the application of scientific methods of inquiry to psychology and education. Two areas that felt his far-reaching influence were educational psychology and the measurement of mental ability and educational achievement. His system of psychology—earlier called stimulus-response psychology and later connectionism—became a dominant influence on American teaching procedures. His work in the measurement of mental ability and achievement stimulated a half century of research.

The most influential of his publications were the famous "three volumes": *The Original Nature of Man, The Psychology of Learning,* and *Mental Work and Fatigue and Individual Differences and Their Causes* (1913–1914). Other books include *The Psychology of Arithmetic* (1922), *The Measurement of Intelligence* (1926), *Adult Learning* (1928), *The Fundamentals of Learning* (1932), *A Teacher's Word Book of 20,000 Words* (1921, later revised), and *Thorndike-Century Junior Dictionary* (1935).

RICHARD MADDEN, *San Diego State College*

THORNDIKE, Lynn (1882–1965), American historian of the Middle Ages. The guiding theme in Thorndike's historical investigation was that medieval philosophers and scientists were to be judged within the context of the science and thought of their periods. In his 8-volume *History of Magic and Experimental Science* (1923–1958), he presented the thesis that magic was one of the principal roots in the development of experimental science. Also implicit in his studies on medieval science was that the only universal "law of nature" before the law of gravitation was the astrological law of the all-pervading influence of celestial motions on this world.

Thorndike was born in Lynn, Mass., on July 24, 1882. He received his B. A. from Wesleyan University in 1902 and his Ph. D. in 1905 from Columbia University, where he returned to teach in 1924. Through his students his influence on the teaching of history was pervasive. He died in New York City on Dec. 28, 1965.

LONDON TIMES, FROM PICTORIAL PARADE

Dame Sybil Thorndike

THORNDIKE, Dame Sybil (1882–), English actress noted for her dramatic power and great versatility. She was born in Gainsborough, England, on Oct. 24, 1882. She studied music before making her debut as an actress in 1904 with Ben Greet's company, with which she toured England and America until 1907. Beginning in 1908 she was a leading performer at the Manchester Repertory Theatre for several years.

From 1914 to 1918 she played leading roles with the Old Vic Shakespearean company and in succeeding years enhanced her reputation considerably by appearing in such heavily tragic roles as Hecuba, Medea, and Lady Macbeth. She also played the Shavian heroine Candida and created the role of Saint Joan in Shaw's play. For her services to the theater she was made a Dame Commander of the Order of the British Empire in 1931.

In World War II, Dame Sybil toured British mining towns with an Old Vic troupe. After 1945 she maintained her reputation with roles in *Oedipus Rex* (at the Old Vic), *Separate Tables*, and *The Potting Shed*. Her career was bound closely to that of her husband, Sir Lewis Casson (1875–1969), with whom she often appeared.

OSCAR G. BROCKETT, *Indiana University*

THORNTON, Matthew (1714–1803), American physician and legislator, who signed the Declaration of Independence. Born in Ireland in 1714, he was taken to America and received his early education in Worcester, Mass. He studied medicine and began practice in Londonderry, N. H., in 1740. From 1758 to 1788 he was prominent in provincial and state politics, becoming president of the provincial congress in 1775 and a member of the Continental Congress in 1776 and 1778. During the American Revolution, Thornton was colonel of the state militia. He moved to Merrimack, N. H., in 1789 and died in Newburyport, Mass., on June 24, 1803.

JOHN J. ZIMMERMAN
Kansas State Teachers College

THORNTON, William (1759–1828), American architect, who furnished the original design for the U. S. Capitol in Washington, D. C. He was born in the Virgin Islands on May 20, 1759, and attended college in Scotland, where he received an M. D. degree from Aberdeen University in 1784. He never practiced medicine.

In the United States, Thornton was an associate of John Fitch, the inventor of the first operable steamboat, from 1787 to 1790, when he returned to the Virgin Islands. An amateur architect, Thornton went back to the United States in 1792 upon learning of the competition for the design of the national capitol. After winning the competition in 1793, he served as a commissioner of the District of Columbia from 1794 to 1802, during which time he assisted in building the Capitol. He died in Washington on March 28, 1828. See also CAPITOL, UNITED STATES.

THORNTON, a city in north central Colorado, in Adams county, is 4 miles (6 km) north of the center of Denver. It is situated in the Rocky Mountains at an altitude of 5,193 feet (1,582 meters). Thornton is a residential suburb of Denver.

Thornton was incorporated in 1956 and named for Dan Thornton, who was governor of Colorado from 1951 to 1955. Government is by city manager and council. Population: 13,326.

THOROLD, thûr′əld, is a town in southern Ontario, Canada, on the Welland Canal, 8 miles (12 km) west of Niagara Falls, Ont. Its industries, powered by the hydroelectric installations at Niagara Falls, manufacture various types of paper. Thorold's growth has been associated largely with the canal, which rises about 140 feet (52 meters) in a series of locks near the town. Population: 15,065.

THOROUGHBRED, a breed of light horse developed in England through matings originally intended to improve the overall quality of English horses. All modern thoroughbreds descend in the male line from either Matchem (born 1748), Herod (born 1758), or Eclipse (born 1764). They were, respectively, descendants of three eastern sires: the Godolphin Arabian (or Barb), the Byerly Turk, and the Darley Arabian.

A typical racing thoroughbred measures from 15 to 16½ hands (5′0″–5′6″, or 1.5–1.7 meters) high at the withers and weighs from 900 to 1,200 pounds (400–540 kg). Recognized colors of American thoroughbreds are bay (the most prevalent), chestnut, gray, roan, brown, black, and the combinative "dark bay or brown."

Apart from such obvious factors as individual ability, track condition, and weight carried, the speed of a thoroughbred varies according to the distance run. The world record for a quarter mile (402.33 meters) is 20⅘ seconds (43.27 mph, or 69.63 km/hr), while that for 2 miles (3.2 km) is 3 minutes 19⅕ seconds (36.14 mph, or 58.16 km/hr).

WILLIAM ROBERTSON
Editor, "The Thoroughbred Record"

THORPE, thôrp, **Jim** (1888–1953), American football, track, and baseball star, who is considered one of the greatest athletes of all time. A powerful and elusive runner and excellent kicker and passer, his feats in football at the Carlisle (Pa.) Indian School and as a professional are legendary.

At the 1912 Olympic Games he won the de-

CULVER PICTURES

Jim Thorpe

cathlon and pentathlon. King Gustav of Sweden called him "the greatest athlete in the world." When it was later learned that he had played professional baseball, Thorpe had to return his Olympic prizes.

James Francis Thorpe was an American Indian born in Prague, Okla., on May 28, 1888. He played football at Carlisle in 1907 and 1908 and left school to play baseball with the Fayetteville and Rocky Mount teams of the Eastern Carolina League for $15 a week. Thorpe returned to Carlisle in 1911. In one of his greatest football feats, he scored a touchdown and kicked field goals of 23, 45, 37, and 48 yards as Carlisle defeated Harvard 18 to 15. In 1912 he scored 25 touchdowns and 198 points, a record.

Thorpe played the outfield for the New York Giants, Cincinnati Reds, and Boston Braves from 1913 through 1919, batting .252 in 289 games. He played professional football for Canton, Cleveland, Oorang Indians (Marion, Ohio), Toledo, Rock Island, and the New York Giants, and made his last appearance with the Chicago Cardinals in 1929. He became the first president of the American Professional Football Association in 1920. In 1950 Thorpe was voted the best athlete of the first half of the century in an Associated Press poll. He was named to both the college and the professional football halls of fame. He died in Lomita, Calif., on March 28, 1953. Jim Thorpe (formerly Mauch Chunk), a borough in Pennsylvania, was named for him in 1954.

BILL BRADDOCK
New York "Times"

THORVALDSEN, to͝or′väl-sən, **Bertel** (1768/1770–1844), Danish neoclassicist sculptor, who specialized in subjects from Greek and Roman mythology. He was born in Copenhagen, the son of an immigrant Icelandic woodcarver. After attending the Copenhagen Academy of Fine Arts, he won a grant to study in Rome, where he arrived in 1797. The pervasive classical heritage of Rome made a deep and lasting impact on him, and he remained there, with only brief interruptions, until 1838.

In Rome, Thorvaldsen met and was influenced by the Italian sculptor Antonio Canova, whom he soon rivaled as one of the most popular artists of the day. Working in marble, he produced a rich series of reliefs and free-standing works that restated and redefined the ideals of the Greco-Roman spirit. However, although executed with great technical skill, his works, including *Jason* (1803), *Cupid and Psyche* (1804), and *Hope* (1818), are cold and lusterless, lacking in originality and vigor. Thorvaldsen also created designs for monuments to such notables as Copernicus, Pope Pius VII, and Schiller, which were turned out by students and assistants in his Roman studio. In 1838 he settled in Copenhagen, where he died on March 24, 1844. He is buried in the Thorvaldsen Museum in Copenhagen, which houses many of his works as well as his own extensive art collection.

KATHERINE G. KLINE, *"Art News" Magazine*

THOTH, thōth, was an ancient Egyptian god, who appeared most often as an ibis-headed man but was also manifest in the ibis, the dog-headed baboon, and the moon. He was worshiped very early and was one of the deities believed to have ruled Egypt before human kings. On 1st dynasty monuments he is shown in close association with the king. In the 4th dynasty, members of the royal family served as his priests. His place of origin is not known, but from the time of the Middle Kingdom he was most closely

THORVALDSEN'S interest in classical antiquity is exemplified in his study of *Cupid and the Three Graces.*

OLE WOLDBYE, FOR THORVALDSEN MUSEUM

associated with Hermopolis Magna in Upper Egypt.

Thoth was considered the inventor of writing and the patron of scribes and of learning. As "Lord of Time and Reckoner of Years" he was responsible for the calendar and for dispensing long life. The first month of the civil year was named for him. Thoth was also a healer and was well versed in magic. A lover of truth, he stood near the scales at the judgment of the dead to record the innocence or guilt of the deceased.

CAROLINE NESTMANN PECK
Brown University

THOTHMES III. See THUTMOSE III.

THOUGHT CONTROL. See BRAINWASHING; CENSORSHIP; PROPAGANDA.

THOUSAND AND ONE NIGHTS. See ARABIAN NIGHTS.

THOUSAND ISLANDS, an archipelago on the eastern U.S.–Canadian border at the head of the St. Lawrence River. The 1,500 or more islands extend 52 miles (84 km) downstream from the end of Lake Ontario. The international boundary passes through them. Slightly more than half the islands are in Canada. The Thousand Islands Bridge links the United States and Canada over Wellesley and Hill islands.

The islands, which vary greatly in size and appearance, have become a popular vacation center for Americans and Canadians. The larger islands contain farms, golf courses, cottages, and mansions. New York state maintains several state parks in the islands, and Canada a national park. Geologically, the islands are the crests of ancient mountains in the belt of Precambrian rock linking the Adirondack uplands of New York state with the Canadian Shield.

Historically, the Thousand Islands figured in the fur trade, the French and Indian War, the American Revolution, the War of 1812, and the Canadian Rebellion of 1837–1838.

PAUL F. JAMIESON
Editor of "The Adirondack Reader"

THOUSAND OAKS, a city in southwestern California, in Ventura county, is about 30 miles (48 km) west of the center of Los Angeles. It is a center of the aerospace industry, with factories and extensive space research facilities. Electronics and the making of precision instruments and plastics are other important enterprises. California Lutheran College is in Thousand Oaks.

Until the rapid development of its industries in the 1960's, Thousand Oaks was an unincorporated village in a rural area. It was named for its great oak groves. It was incorporated as a city in 1964. Government is by council and manager. Population: 36,334.

THRACE, thrās, is a historic region of the Balkan peninsula, lying partly in Greece, partly in Turkey, and partly in Bulgaria. Thrace as a political and geographical unit in antiquity extended over the eastern part of the Balkan Peninsula, bounded on the north by the Danube River and on the south by the Aegean Sea. It included the Gallipoli Peninsula, which has a history somewhat apart from Thrace in general.

History. The Thracians, who spoke an Indo-European language, originally extended as far

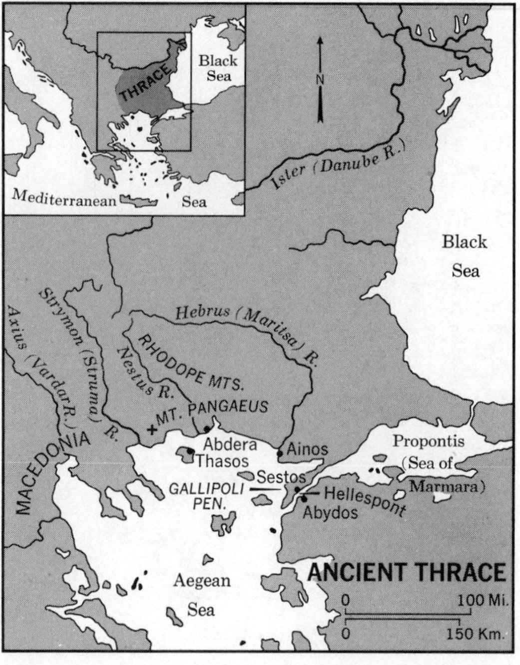

west as the Adriatic Sea, but they lost their lands west of the Axius (Vardar) River to the Illyrians before 1100 B.C. Beginning about 700 B.C. the Greeks began to colonize the coast of Thrace.

The ancient Greeks considered the Thracians not only barbarians, but even slightly ludicrous. The Thracians, like the Macedonians, consciously imitated their Greek neighbors, but with little success, and seem to have possessed almost no cultural refinements. The military prowess of the Thracians, however, was widely respected.

The Persians invaded Thrace in 512 B.C. and occupied the area for the next three decades. When their forces withdrew, the southern Thracian tribes were organized into the Odrysian kingdom, perhaps by Teres I. The vigorous and enterprising Sitalces, son of Teres, figures prominently in the history of the later 5th century. He extended the power of Thracian arms in 429 into the southern Macedonian plain and the valley of the Axius River. The independent states in the mountains of northern Thrace served in his army. Sitalces was killed in battle against the Triballi in 424 and was succeeded by his nephew Seuthes I, who increased the general prosperity and military strength of the kingdom so that it became the most powerful empire between the Adriatic and Black seas.

During this period the Thracian kings levied taxes on the cities in Thrace that had been settled by Greeks. Among the more important of these cities were Ainos (Aenus), Maroneia, and Abdera, home of the philosopher Democritus. The Greeks, especially those from the island of Thasos, mined the gold and silver of Mt. Pangaeus.

The Odrysian kingdom began to decline in power at the end of the 5th century B.C. under King Amatokos, and by 359 it seems to have been divided into three separate monarchies. The western kingdom was conquered by Philip II of Macedonia in 356, and by 342 all of southern Thrace was under Macedonia. Thracian *peltasts*

peltasts (light-armed warriors) served with distinction in the army of Alexander the Great and that of his successor in Thrace, Lysimachus, and often formed mercenary contingents in the Hellenistic period.

After a brief period of independence, Thrace was subjected to a series of invasions by Roman armies in the 1st century B. C. In 46 A. D., Emperor Claudius annexed northern Thrace to the province of Moesia and organized central and southern Thrace into a separate province.

Peninsular Thrace. The Thracian Chersonese, or Gallipoli Peninsula, in Turkey, which forms the European side of the Dardanelles strait (the ancient Hellespont), has a history somewhat distinct from that of Thrace generally. The great flow of traffic through the Hellespont encouraged settlement mainly on the side of the peninsula that faces the straits, and the closeness of some points to the Asian coast made the region still more important strategically. The chief ferry points were at the Greek towns of Sestos, opposite Abydos in Asia near the west end of the straits, and Kallipolis (modern Gallipoli), facing Lampsacus (modern Lâpseki) near the entrance to the Sea of Marmara.

A Thracian tribe called the Dolonkoi inhabited the peninsula in the mid-6th century B. C., and they invited the Athenian Miltiades I to aid them in a war against the Apsinthian Thracians of the plain near Ainos. Miltiades arrived with colonists, founded or refounded several towns at both extremities of the peninsula, and established personal control over both ends of the straits. Miltiades II, nephew of the founder, fled the region in 510 before the threat of a Scythian invasion but returned in 496, again at the invitation of the Thracians. Aegospotami, the site of the great Spartan victory over the Athenian fleet in 405 B. C., was located on the coast between Kallipolis and Sestos.

Athenian dominance in the peninsula was reasserted in the mid-4th century when new groups of colonists were sent there. The wealth of the region, which seems never to have been exceptional, must have come primarily from taxation on traffic and transcontinental transport, and from piloting through the Hellespont.

Thrace From the Byzantine Period to the Present. With the division of the Roman Empire into east and west, Thrace became part of the Eastern, or Byzantine, Empire, although northern Thrace came under Bulgarian control in the 7th century. After the fall of Constantinople in 1453, all Thrace was subject to the Ottoman Empire. In the 19th and 20th centuries, as the Ottoman Empire disintegrated, historic Thrace was divided among three successor states, Greece, Bulgaria, and Turkey. After 1885, "Thrace" was applicable politically only to southern Thrace, divided into Western and Eastern Thrace by the Maritsa River. Turkey controlled Western as well as Eastern Thrace until the Balkan Wars (1912–1913). The present-day boundaries were fixed after several shifts in 1923.

Greek Thrace. The present-day Greek administrative region of Thrace has an area of 3,315 square miles (8,586 sq km). It is separated from Macedonia by the Nestos River on the west and from Turkish Thrace on the east by the Hevros (Turkish, Meric; Bulgarian, Maritsa) River. The Bulgarian border runs along the high Rhodope Mountains to the north. The region is divided into three departments (nomes), Xanthe, Rhodope, and Hevros, whose respective capital cities, Xanthe, Komotine, and Alexandroupolis, are the largest in Thrace. The last is the only important commercial port in Thrace.

There are fertile plains in the region of both Xanthe and Komotine, but the most important is the plain of Orestia-Didymoteikhon, where the Arda and Erythros rivers flow into the Hevros. In the delta of the Hevros, especially to the east of Alexandroupolis, a number of small lakes are used as fish hatcheries. Stock breeding and agriculture are the main occupations of the inhabitants. The chief products are grain, tobacco, and cotton. Population: (1961 census) 356,655.

JAMES R. WISEMAN, *University of Texas*

THRASHER, any of a group of medium-sized songbirds usually found near the ground along the forest edge and in bushy grasslands in North America, Central America, and nearby tropical islands. Like their relatives—catbirds and mockingbirds—they are from 8 to 12 inches (20–30 cm) long and have slender bodies, long curved beaks, long tails, and strong legs and feet. The plumage is usually gray or brown but may be reddish.

Ten species of thrashers (genus *Toxostoma*) range from southern Canada to Mexico and Lower California and one species is found only on Cozumel Island off Yucatán. The brown thrasher (*T. rufum rufum*) with its bright red back and heavily streaked breast is the most familiar species. It feeds on insects and fruits, and its clear sweet song is characterized by the repetition of each note. It winters in the southern United States but migrates north in the spring to breed. Both parents incubate the normal clutch of four pale green eggs spotted with red, and feed the chicks.

Another species often grouped with the thrashers is the Lesser Antilles trembler (*Cinclocerthia ruficauda*), known for its habit of shaking its wings and body. There are about 16 species of thrashers classified in the family Mimidae, order Passeriformes.

JOSEPH BELL
New York Zoological Park

Brown thrasher with young

ALVIN STAFFAN, FROM NATIONAL AUDUBON SOCIETY

THREAD is a highly specialized yarn used in sewing, basting, crocheting, embroidering, and similar work. It is made by the drawing and winding of cotton, silk, or other yarns onto a holding device such as a spool or bobbin. Thread is made from yarn—yarn is not made from thread. The term "thread" is also applied to fine cords—that is, two or more ply, or multiple, yarns twisted together—of any of the major textile fibers. The numbers in cotton thread sizes, such as 40s or 50s, indicate the number of 840-yard hanks of thread needed to total one pound in weight.

Spinning, which is the combining of a number of relatively short fibers into a continuous yarn, is the basic art of threadmaking. Modern threadmaking began about 1754 in England with the development of mechanical spinning. Cotton thread was first produced commercially in 1806 by Patrick Clark of Paisley, Scotland, when Napoleon blockaded Britain and cut off the supply of silk thread used at that time. Cotton thread combined strength with low price and replaced silk and linen thread throughout Britain and Europe. James Coats, also of Paisley, was another pioneer in the manufacture of cotton thread. The Coats and Clark companies, which soon became the major thread companies of Europe, merged in 1952 to form Coats & Clark, Inc. Their trademark, "O. N. T.," established by George Clark in the 1860's, stands for "Our New Thread."

The newest thread is a combination of polyester and cotton. It has a polyester core and a cotton sheathing with a silicone finish. This thread is as fine as an ordinary 60s cotton thread but has the strength of a size 40s thread. It is ideal for smoother sewing of any fabric. It makes more durable seams and has an elasticity that makes it most suitable for durable stretch and durable press fabrics.

GEORGE E. LINTON
Author of "The Modern Textile Dictionary"

THREAD, in machinery. See SCREW.

THREADFIN, any of a family of marine fishes having elongated, free, threadlike filamentous fin rays detached from the anterior part of their pectoral fin. They are also known as *tasselfish.* Most adult threadfins live in tropical seas, usually in shallow water close to shore. Three species are found in waters near the United States: the Pacific threadfin (*Polydactylus approximans*), found from southern California to Peru; the Atlantic threadfin (*P. octonemus*), found from Massachusetts to Florida and around the Gulf of Mexico; and the barbu (*P. virginicus*), found from New Jersey to Brazil. Some species are prized as food fishes.

Threadfin

ROBERT C. HERMES, FROM NATIONAL AUDUBON SOCIETY

The adult threadfin is about 12 inches (30 cm) long and has a conical-shaped snout that extends far beyond the underslung mouth. It has two dorsal fins—the anterior one with spines and the posterior one with soft rays—and a deeply forked tail fin. Young threadfins are pelagic and are often found in abundance in the open sea as far out as 100 miles (161 km).

There are over 20 species of threadfins, classified in several genera, making up the family Polynemidae of the order Perciformes. Their closest relatives are probably the barracudas and the mullets.

DANIEL M. COHEN
U. S. Fish and Wildlife Service

THREADNEEDLE STREET, in central London just north of the river Thames, is famous because the Bank of England, sometimes called the "Old Lady of Threadneedle Street," faces on it. The name is derived from the sign of the Needlemakers Company, which displayed three needles as its emblem. Nothing remains of the company's hall.

THREADWORM, a name commonly applied to many roundworms. Most often it refers to the pinworm (*Enterobium vermicularis*), a common intestinal parasite of man. The worm's eggs, after being ingested, hatch in the small intestine. The larvae migrate to the lower end of the large intestine, and in this region they develop into adults and often cause intense itching of the anus.

THREAT, in criminal law, is a declaration of intent to cause harm to the person, property, or rights of another in order to coerce the victim to engage in specified conduct.

Crimes involving threats include extortion, blackmail, robbery, rape, kidnapping, and the intimidation of public officials or witnesses. The conduct to which the victim is coerced in extortion and robbery is the turning over of property, but these crimes differ in that a robber threatens to inflict immediate, rather than future, harm. In blackmail, the threat is to make public certain facts unless the victim does what is demanded.

Extortion is usually penalized severely, partly because it is characteristic of organized racketeering. Such activity includes the "protection racket," in which periodic payments are coerced from businessmen, and "loansharking," in which money is lent to poor risks at exorbitant interest rates, and collection is ensured by threat of bodily or other injury if the debtor should default. In some situations where an official has power to confer or withhold benefits, it is often difficult to distinguish extortion (coercion) from bribery (collaboration).

RICHARD A. GREEN
Director, American Bar Association Project on Standards for Criminal Justice

THREE-BODY PROBLEM, an unsolved problem in celestial mechanics. It concerns the motions of three spherical bodies that move subject only to their mutual gravitational attraction.

The motions of bodies are governed by Newton's laws of motion and law of gravitation. In the case of two-body systems the problem of determining their motions has been completely solved, but when there are three or more bodies the problem becomes complex, and only a very few special solutions are known.

The most famous solutions are those of the 19th century mathematicians Leonhard Euler and Joseph Lagrange. In one, three bodies lie at the apexes of an equilateral triangle, which can itself pulsate and rotate in space. This configuration apparently can be stable if one body is sufficiently massive relative to the other two. An example is the system of the sun, Jupiter, and the Trojan asteroids (see ASTEROID). In the other solution the three bodies lie in a straight line in special configurations. However, these configurations are not stable and would be broken up by the smallest disturbance.

Most work on the three-body problem is concerned with "satellite" problems, in which one body is at a great distance from the other two, and with "planetary" problems, in which distances are roughly equal but one body is much more massive. In the *restricted problem of three bodies*, one body is assumed to have a mass so small that it does not affect the motions of the other two, which move around one another in circular orbits. The motion of a spacecraft in the earth-moon system is a good approximation of this problem. See CELESTIAL MECHANICS.

J. M. A. DANBY
North Carolina State University

THREE-COLOR PROCESS. See PHOTOENGRAVING—*The Three- and Four-Color Process.*

THREE HOURS, a gathering of Christians on Good Friday for prayer, readings from Scripture, hymns, and meditations or sermons on the seven words or times that Jesus spoke from the cross. The service lasts from noon to 3 P. M., the three hours Jesus was on the cross.

The custom of reading from Scripture and offering prayers on Good Friday was common in the early church. This specific rite, however, was inaugurated in Lima, Peru, in 1687 after an earthquake, originally as an act of penitence. Since then the devotional practice has spread.

THREE KINGDOMS, in Chinese history. The Age of the Three Kingdoms (220–265 A. D.) followed the collapse of the Later Han dynasty. It was marked by the struggles of the successor kingdoms of Wei (north), Shu (west), and Wu (south) for control. It ended when a Wei general established the Chin dynasty, which briefly reunited China. The events of the period are recounted in a classic prose work, the *Romance of the Three Kingdoms.* See also THIRD CENTURY.

THREE KINGDOMS, in Korean history. The first Korean states, which arose between about 100 and 350 A. D., were the kingdoms of Koguryo (north), Paekche (southwest), and Silla (southeast). With Chinese help, Silla united Korea by defeating Paekche in 660 and Koguryo in 668. See also KOREA—*History.*

THREE-MILE LIMIT, once the generally accepted seaward extension of a state's sovereignty. Within these territorial waters sovereignty is subject only to the right of innocent passage by foreign ships. The 3–mile (5–km) width was based on cannon range from the coast. Many states now claim wider belts, some as wide as 200 miles (300 km). See also TERRITORIAL WATERS.

THREE MUSKETEERS, a historical novel by the French authors Alexandre Dumas *père* and Auguste Maquet, published in 1844 under its French title *Les Trois Mousquetaires.* It achieved immediate popularity and has become part of the literary heritage of the many countries into whose languages it has been translated.

Set in the time of King Louis XIII and his minister, Cardinal Richelieu, the novel follows its hero, D'Artagnan, through a series of adventures in love, swordplay, and political intrigue. D'Artagnan, an innocent provincial from Gascony, journeys to Paris to seek his fortune in the service of the king, and with the aid of his sword and three loyal friends, Athos, Aramis, and Porthos—the musketeers of the title—he at last wins admission to the king's guard.

This novel and its two sequels, *Vingt ans après* (1845; *Twenty Years After*) and *Le Vicomte de Bragelonne* (1848–1850), imaginatively recreate some of the aspects of the early and middle 17th century that were most appealing to the French romantic generations. While *The Three Musketeers* is not an aesthetic masterpiece nor important as either a psychological novel or a novel of manners, it is written with verve and immense charm and is capable of involving the reader in its fictitious world. See also ARTAGNAN, SEIGNEUR D'; DUMAS, ALEXANDRE—*Novels.*

RAYMOND GIRAUD, *Stanford University*

THREE RIVERS. See TROIS-RIVIÈRES.

THREE SISTERS, a play in four acts by the Russian dramatist Anton Chekhov, written for the Moscow Art Theater, which first produced it in 1901. The action is muted throughout, and the major events occur offstage. Primary emphasis is on characterization and on mood, which shifts gradually from optimism to joyless acceptance.

The Three Sisters is set in a provincial town far from Moscow. To the Prozorov family (the three sisters Olga, Masha, and Irina and their brother Andrei) Moscow represents all that is missing in their drab lives. Highly educated, they had been brought to the village by their late father, a brigadier general. Olga is a teacher, Masha the wife of a teacher, and Irina a civil servant. Andrei, trained for a professional career, has no outlet for his talents.

The Prozorovs' existence is made bearable by the presence of a military garrison whose officers, especially Vershinin and Tusenbach, provide a link with the world they long for. As the play progresses, Andrei's bride Natasha, the embodiment of all that is crass in provincial society, takes over the management of the household. When the garrison is ordered to leave, the family's last bulwark against vulgarity is gone. But they face the future bravely, hoping that the significance of their frustrated lives will some day be revealed.

OSCAR G. BROCKETT, *Indiana University*

GRANT HEILMAN

Thresher separating grain from straw.

THREEPENNY OPERA, an adaptation of John Gay's *Beggar's Opera* by the German author Bertolt Brecht, with music by Kurt Weill. *The Threepenny Opera* was first performed in Berlin, under its German title *Die Dreigroschenoper,* in 1928 and was given more than 2,000 performances in Germany. An English adaptation by Marc Blitzstein played in New York City from 1954 to 1961, making it the longest-running show in the history of New York theater to that time. Weill's wife, Lotte Lenya, appeared in both the Berlin and New York productions, adding to the popularity of the show by the force of her personality. She also appeared in a film version in 1930.

Brecht's libretto uses Gay's basic story, but updates it and redirects its satire to attack social conditions in pre-World War II Germany. Weill's jazz score, with its popular song *Mack the Knife,* retains only one of the original melodies. See also BEGGAR'S OPERA.

THRESHER SHARK, any of a genus of large sharks with long and powerful tails. They are found in most tropical and temperate seas but usually remain well offshore and below the surface and are not often seen. The common thresher (*Alopias vulpinus*), however, occasionally may be seen at the surface near shallow water along the Atlantic and Pacific coasts of the United States. Thresher sharks, sometimes called "fox sharks," are not known to attack man, but because of their great size and strength they must be considered potentially dangerous.

Thresher sharks may exceed 16 feet (4.9 meters) in length and weigh 1,000 pounds (454 kg). The upper lobe of the asymmetrical tail accounts for about half of the length. The shark uses the tail for propulsion and also to stun the small and medium-sized fishes on which it feeds. Thresher sharks produce many eggs, some of which hatch in the mother's oviducts, but usually only two young are born.

Thresher sharks are classified in the genus *Alopias* of the family Alopiidae of the order Selachii, or Squaliformes.

STEWART SPRINGER
U. S. Fish and Wildlife Service

THRESHING MACHINE, a device formerly used for separating grain from straw and chaff. Before the development of the threshing machine about 1840, the separation was accomplished by trampling with the feet of men or animals or by flailing on threshing floors. The resultant mixture was then tossed into the air and the chaff was blown away by the wind or fanned away.

The principles of impact and abrasion employed in primitive threshing were incorporated in threshing machines. The simple threshing machine had a revolving cylinder with teeth or rasp bars operating against stationary bars called concaves. The space between the revolving and stationary bars was adjustable and set for each type of grain. The unhusked grain was fed between the rotating and stationary bars. The grain or seeds fell through the bars into a collecting pan. More complex machines incorporated devices for cleaning, grain recovery and elevating, and removing and stacking straw. The peripheral speed of the cylinder was regulated so that it was high enough to remove the seed covering, but low enough so as not to crack or otherwise damage the grain. The optimum speed for wheat is between 5,000 and 6,000 feet (1,500 to 1,800 meters) per minute.

At first, animal-powered equipment was used to run threshing machines. It was succeeded by steam engines, internal combustion engines, and electric motors as they become available.

The threshing machine was used in North America and other developed grain-growing areas of the world from 1840 to about 1940. Today the combine, or combined harvester-thresher, has replaced the threshing machine. See COMBINE.

EDGAR LEE BARGER, *Massey-Ferguson, Inc.*
FRANK BUCKINGHAM, *Massey-Ferguson, Inc.*

THRIFT, any of a group of low, mat- or mound-forming perennial plants native to northern temperate regions and southern South America. Thrifts, also called sea pinks, make up the genus *Armeria* of the plumbago, or leadwort, family (Plumbaginaceae). There are about 50 known species, and about one third of them are cultivated. Thrifts grow best in well-drained, sunny locations, and are propagated by seed, division, or cutting.

Thrifts have narrow, linear leaves and red, pink, rose, or white flowers borne in globular heads from 0.5 inch to 2 inches (13–50 mm) in diameter. The common thrift (*A. maritima*) forms a mound about 1 foot (0.3 meter) across and 1 foot high. Its flowers range from pink to white, and the heads are borne on stems from 6 to 10 inches (150–250 mm) long.

ANDREW LEISER
University of California, Davis

THRIPS, any of a large, worldwide order (Thysanoptera) of tiny insects that attack a wide variety of crops, ornamentals, and other plants. Thrips are slender, yellow black, or

Adult female of gladiolus thrips, greatly enlarged.

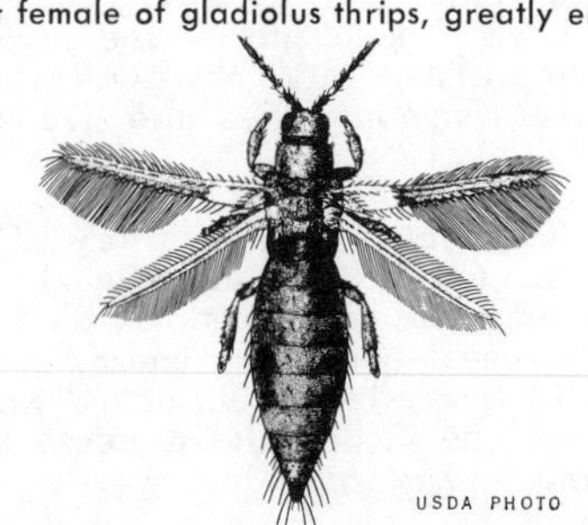

USDA PHOTO

brown insects rarely more than 1/16 of an inch (1.5 mm) long. Some are wingless, but others have four narrow wings that are fringed with tiny hairs.

Female thrips lay their eggs in plants, and the eggs hatch into white or yellow nymphs. Adults and nymphs both suck plant juices. A person bitten by a thrips suffers mild discomfort. Thrips are also beneficial. They aid in the pollination of carrots and certain flowers, and some eat other insect pests.

The onion thrips (*Thrips tabaci*) not only feeds on onion and other plants but transmits to tomatoes and many ornamentals the organism that causes spotted wilt virus disease. The greenhouse thrips (*Heliothrips haemorrhoidalis*) damages greenhouse plants. The pear thrips (*Taeniothrips inconsequens*) causes the buds of fruit trees to shrivel and turn brown. All thrips are controlled with insecticides.

ARLO M. VANCE, *Entomologist*
U. S. Department of Agriculture (Retired)

THROAT, the funnel-shaped passage that connects the cavities of the mouth and nose with the esophagus (gullet) and larynx (voice box). The throat, also known as the *pharynx*, is divided into three major sections: the *nasopharynx*, which opens into the nasal cavities and Eustachian (auditory) tube openings; the *oropharynx*, which opens into the mouth; and the *laryngopharynx*, which opens into the esophagus and larynx. See also ANATOMY, HUMAN; PHARYNX.

THROCKMORTON, throk-môr'tən, **Francis** (1554–1584), English conspirator against Queen Elizabeth I. He was born in Feckenham, Worcestershire, and educated at Oxford University. Sharing his family's zeal for Roman Catholicism, he went in 1580 to the Continent to visit English Catholic leaders in exile. He joined them in formulating plans, involving France and Spain, to invade England in order to reestablish the Catholic religion, free the imprisoned Mary Stuart, and overthrow Elizabeth.

Returning to London in 1583 to act as confidential agent of the conspiracy, he drew up plans of harbors suitable for invasion. Arrested later that year and tortured on the rack at the Tower of London, he confessed to rebellious designs against the queen. He was tried at the Guildhall, convicted of treason, and executed at Tyburn on July 10, 1584.

THROMBIN, throm'bən, is a blood protein that plays a major role in clotting by activating the formation of fibrin. See BLOOD—*Clotting*.

THROMBOPHLEBITIS, throm-bō-flə-bī'təs, is a condition in which an inflammation of a vein has preceded the formation of a blood clot. See PHLEBITIS.

THROMBOPLASTIN, throm-bō-plas'tən, is a blood protein essential for clotting. There are two basic types of thromboplastin, extrinsic and intrinsic. Each is formed by a different set of biochemical activities. See BLOOD—*Clotting*.

THROMBOSIS, throm-bō'səs, is the formation of a blood clot, or thrombus, in a blood vessel or one of the chambers of the heart. Clotting occurs when a blood vessel is damaged or occluded, as in atherosclerosis.

THRONE, a symbol of power and authority, either political or religious, in the form of a stool or chair. It has been in existence since antiquity. In a primitive society, a stool often represents office and power. In more advanced cultures, the seat is frequently elaborate in design and materials in keeping with the ceremony or ritual for which it is intended.

Antiquity. The Bible describes the throne of Solomon as being made of ivory overlaid with gold, with a lion on either side, and a pair of lions guarding each of the six steps approaching the seat. A throne from the tomb of Tutankhamen is on display at the Cairo Museum in Egypt. Numerous ancient Greek and Roman throne chairs, mostly of marble, are extant, and many are depicted in vase and fresco paintings.

The Middle East. The remains of a throne made of rock crystal were found in the ruins of the palace of the Assyrian king Sennacherib. The Byzantine emperors used a throne inspired by Solomon's. It is said to have been surrounded by golden lions who sat up and roared by means of a mechanical device. Shah Abbas I, the Great (1571–1629), of Persia had a marble throne. The 17th century Peacock Throne was one of India's glories at Delhi until it was removed to Persia by Nadir Shah in the 18th century. It was made of two enormous peacock tails that were decorated with precious stones and rested on jeweled, golden feet. It was ascended by silver stairs.

Europe. According to tradition, Dagobert I (died 639), king of the Franks, had a golden throne, a bronze copy of which exists and was used by Bonaparte when he awarded the first decoration of the Legion of Honor in 1804. Bonaparte's own throne was designed by Charles

BRONZE THRONE, thought to be a copy of a golden throne belonging to Dagobert I, King of the Franks.

BIBLIOTHEQUE NATIONALE

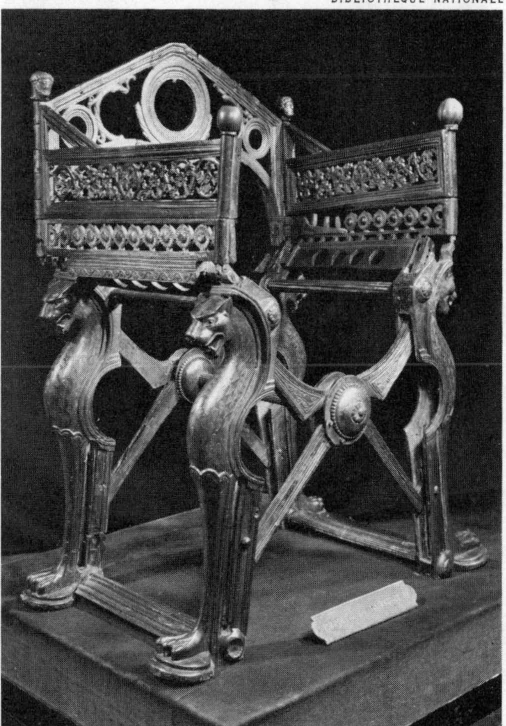

Percier and Pierre Fontaine. It was decorated with an extensive vocabulary of ornamentation borrowed from Egyptian and Roman sources.

The British throne, probably of the 13th century, is a Gothic chair of oak in the House of Lords. It should not be confused with the coronation chair used in the coronation ceremony. An extraordinary coronation throne survives in the Hall of Knights at Rosenborg Castle in Copenhagen, Denmark. Made in Copenhagen about 1665 by Bendix Grodtschilling, it is constructed of ivory and narwhal tusks and decorated with allegorical figures of gilt and bronze. It was used for coronations from 1671 to 1840. A silver throne, now in the Swedish treasury at Stockholm, was made for Queen Christina by Abraham Drentwett at Augsburg about 1650.

The 16th century throne of Czar Boris Godunov, now in the Kremlin in Moscow, is made of wood and covered with gold foil and semiprecious stones, chiefly turquoises. Also in the Kremlin is an elaborate ivory and wood throne in the form of a massive armchair, made for Czar Ivan IV in the 16th century. It was used as the Russian coronation throne until the end of the 19th century. Another dazzling throne in the Kremlin is made of gold, encrusted with 8,000 turquoises, 1,500 rubies, 4 amethysts, and 2 topazes. It was made for the grandfather of Peter the Great.

Religious Thrones. The Chair of St. Peter in St. Peter's Basilica, Rome, symbolizes the authority of the Pope. Every bishop has a throne or cathedra in his own cathedral.

JOSEPH T. BUTLER
Sleepy Hollow Restorations, Tarrytown, N. Y.

Further Reading: Hayward, Helena, ed., *World Furniture* (New York 1965).

TUTANKHAMEN'S THRONE, found in his tomb, is of gold-covered wood. Royal family is portrayed on back.

I. P. P., FROM BLACK STAR

ALVIN STAFFAN, FROM NATIONAL AUDUBON SOCIETY

A wood thrush feeding its young.

THRUSH, any of about 500 species of highly diverse perching birds (order Passeriformes) belonging to two widely distributed families, the true thrushes and the babbling thrushes.

True Thrushes. There are about 300 species of true thrushes classified in 45 genera of the family Turdidae. This group of thrushes includes many well-known birds, among them bluebirds and robins. True thrushes are generally small to medium-sized birds with slender bills, large eyes, and strong legs. Adults commonly are brown but may show black, white, gray, blue, red, green, or other colors. The young usually have speckled plumage.

The greatest number and variety of true thrushes are found in the temperate and tropical zones of the Eastern Hemisphere, but some also are found in North America. They live in forests, grasslands, tundras, deserts, parks, savannas, and on mountains. They eat mostly insects but also feed on fruits and seeds. They are strong fliers, and many northern species are long-distance migrants.

Females generally place their nests in trees, shrubs, cavities, or on the ground. The nests, typically open and cup-shaped, are made of grass, stems, leaves, and moss, sometimes reinforced with mud. The three to six eggs are usually whitish or pale blue and may be spotted. The female alone usually incubates the eggs for 13 or 14 days, and the young fledge in about 12 to 15 days.

Babbling Thrushes. There are about 260 species of babbling thrushes, classified in some 50 genera of the family Timaliidae. They are most abundant in the forests of Southeast Asia but are also found in the forests of Africa and Australia.

Although babbling thrushes vary in size and form, they usually range from 4½ to 14 inches (11–35 cm) in length and have strong, slightly curved bills, short rounded wings, and strong legs. Their insistent unmusical call gives them the name "babblers." They are very different in coloring. Babbling thrushes are poor fliers and travel in restless flocks through thick undergrowth. They usually place their cup-shaped or domed nests in low vegetation or on the ground. The two to seven eggs are white or blue and may be spotted. The young are never spotted.

CARL WELTY, *Beloit College*

THRUSH, in medicine, is a common fungus infection of the inside of the mouth. It is caused by *Candida albicans*, a yeastlike fungus that often lives as a harmless saprophyte on the skin and mucous membranes.

Causes. Thrush affects mainly older adults and infants. In adults it occurs when something upsets the normal ecological balance of microorganisms in the mouth. Such causes include malnutrition, leukemia, diabetes, and the use of steroid hormones, oral contraceptives, and antibiotics, especially the tetracyclines. In infants, thrush occurs when the mother has a *Candida* infection of the vulvovaginal area. The baby is infected during childbirth, and the infection becomes apparent during the second week of life.

Characteristics. Thrush appears as patches of a gray to creamy white material that looks like coagulated milk. When these patches are scraped off gently a bright red mucous membrane, which tends to bleed easily, is revealed. Any part of the tongue, throat, or inside of the cheek may be involved; occasionally the infection spreads to a corner of the mouth, where it appears as a fissure. A diagnosis of thrush is confirmed when scrapings examined under a microscope show the presence of *Candida albicans* organisms.

Treatment. Thrush may be treated by the daily application of a 1% solution of gentian violet to the involved mucous membranes.

STEPHEN E. SILVER, M. D.
Lawrence & Memorial Hosp., New London, Conn.

THRUST is the force produced by a jet exhaust in the direction of motion of the aircraft, rocket, or spacecraft. See ION PROPULSION; JET PROPULSION; ROCKETS.

THUCYDIDES, thōō-sid′ə-dēz (c. 455–c. 400 B. C.), Greek historian. Born in Athens, he was of the aristocratic family that included the generals Miltiades and Cimon and was connected with the royal family of Thrace, where Thucydides had an estate and control of some gold mines. He was raised in Athens during the Golden Age of Pericles. He greatly admired Pericles, contrary to the political tradition of his family, and was obviously well educated in the new style of the Sophists.

Thucydides caught the plague in Athens between 430 and 427 but survived and served in the navy during the early stages of the Peloponnesian War (431–404) between Athens and Sparta. Elected general in 424–423, he was stationed in Thrace, where he failed to prevent the Spartan general Brasidas' seizure of Amphipolis, an Athenian colony, in 422. As a result he was exiled and spent the rest of the war in Thrace or traveling about gathering material for and writing his *History of the Peloponnesian War.* He returned to Athens in 403 after the city fell to the Spartans, but is said to have died in Thrace.

Scope and Composition of the History. The unfinished *History* is divided into eight books. Book I describes the background, causes, and excuses for the war. It includes two long digressions, one outlining the development of early Greece, the other summarizing the events between 479 and 431 and the growth of Athenian power, which Thucydides insists was the true cause of the war. Books II–V (to Chapter 25) contain the narrative of the first 10 years of the war, which started with the Theban attack on Plataea in 431 and ended, more or less as a stalemate, with the Peace of Nicias in 421. The rest of Book V covers the period of nominal but ill-kept peace down to 415. Books VI and VII concentrate on the ill-fated Athenian expedition against Syracuse in Sicily, which ended in complete disaster for Athens in 413. Book VIII recounts the renewed war with Sparta in Greece and the Aegean and the internal troubles of the Athenian government down to late in 411, where it breaks off, apparently in mid-sentence.

There has been much discussion and many different views have been proposed of how and when Thucydides composed his work. He himself states that he conceived the project and started keeping notes before the war began, but it is clear that even the first book had been revised after the end of the war. None of the many theories on the composition can be proven. All that can be said is that the *History* as it exists has a basic unity of ideas and purpose.

Methodology. Thucydides was the first to write a history of strictly contemporary events, and he set for himself very high standards of accuracy. He speaks of the difficulty of checking and reconciling the various versions of an event given by different eyewitnesses and complains about his predecessors: Herodotus, for including too many "mythical" elements and writing primarily to please his audience, and Hellanicus and others for being unclear on chronology. He himself was very precise on the latter, dating by seasons of the year.

He has often been hailed as the first and best of the "scientific" and impartial historians. Perhaps he comes as close as humanly possible to this ideal, even though he has an obvious bias against the Athenian demagogue Cleon, who was probably responsible for his exile, and omitted what seem to be some very important events—such as the tripling of the tribute paid to Athens by its subjects in 425. Some scholars have accused him of misrepresenting events and attitudes because of an aristocratic political bias, but there is evidence to support him. Thucydides states that he composed his *History* to be useful to those who wish to have an exact knowledge of what happened in the past in order to predict or control future events. For future events will resemble those of the past, since human nature stays substantially the same. This is no mere statement that history repeats itself. The important element here is "human nature." Thucydides reflects the Sophists' interest in and emphasis on the individual. To him human nature is the basic causal factor of events and is a constant, so it is useful to know how it has reacted in the past. This is the beginning of psychological positivism.

Psychological Positivism. In this view of history individual motive becomes all-important. To delineate motive and character, Thucydides generally relied upon speeches inserted in the narrative, often in contrasting pairs. He states that, since it was impossible to repeat the exact words spoken, he has written down what the speaker should have said on the occasion, yet keeping as near as possible to the sense of what was actually said. The ambiguity of this statement has led to much debate among modern scholars about the reliability of the speeches.

Thucydides saw three main motivating factors in human behavior: honor, fear, and advantage. He was greatly interested in showing how the war affected the character and motivation of the

Greeks—above all, the Athenians. In the famous *Funeral Speech*, attributed to Pericles at the end of the first year of the war in 431, he portrays the ideal Athens, and the emphasis is certainly upon honor, especially in the relationship of Athens to its subjects. Starkly contrasted with this is the *Melian Dialogue*, supposedly a discussion 15 years later, in 416, between Athenian and Melian officials at a time when Athens was threatening the island of Melos without provocation and forcing it into the Athenian Empire. Here the Athenians argue and act on the basis of fear, greed, and a "might-makes-right" attitude. By "advantage," the third motivation, was meant primarily economic advantage, a concept that Thucydides and his contemporaries certainly understood.

Thucydides points out that these attitudes also arose in the relationships of the Athenians to one another. He stresses the attempt of the demagogue Cleon to set class against class, which led ultimately to the deterioration and temporary destruction of Athenian democracy. One can never know, of course, what Thucydides' final verdict would have been on the Athenians and their loss of the war, but what he did bequeath posterity yields enough insight into man and war to justify his claim that what he had written would endure as "a possession forever."

DONALD W. BRADEEN
University of Cincinnati

Bibliography

Finley, John H., *Thucydides* (Cambridge, Mass., 1942).
Gomme, Arnold W., *A Historical Commentary on Thucydides*, 3 vols. (London 1950–1956).
Grundy, George B., *Thucydides and the History of His Age*, 2d ed., 2 vols. (Oxford, England, 1948).
Romilly, Jacqueline de, *Thucydides and Athenian Imperialism*, tr. by Philip Thody (New York 1964).
Thucydides, *History of the Peloponnesian War*, tr. by Rex Warner, paperback (London 1954).

THUG, a member of a Hindu criminal religious society or caste that is known to have existed as early as the 12th century and probably existed long before that. The term is derived from the Sanskrit *sthag*, meaning "to conceal." The society flourished principally in Uttar Pradesh and Central India, but also to a lesser extent in the Deccan in south central India during the 17th, 18th, and early 19th centuries. In this period the depredations of foreign European powers and the collapse of effective Mogul rule afforded opportunity for the criminal caste to grow.

Origins and History. The society consisted of both Hindu and Muslim units, but the goddess Bhavānī, another name for Kālī, who was sometimes vaguely identified with Fatima, the daughter of Mohammed, or the goddess Lakshmi, was their common cult-object. The Thug cult was centered at the Temple of Kālī at Mirzapur near Benares. A myth involving Kālī grew up to explain the origin of the practices of Thuggee, as the Thug way of life was called. A demon named Rukt Bij-dana, of monstrous size, ate the first men as they were being created. Kālī sought to prevent the destruction of mankind by killing the demon-monster, but a new demon sprang from each drop of blood spilled from Rukt Bij-dana. Wearying of her task, Kālī created two men upon whom she bestowed her *rumal* or handkerchief (symbolic of the work of strangulation), and committed the struggle to them. When they had killed the last demon, Kālī returned the *rumal*, which they offered to give back to her, and commanded them and their descendants to kill all men not related to them. Excluded were certain classes, such as priests, holy men, poets, women, cripples, and water carriers.

The criminal acts performed by the Thugs combined motives of robbery and religious devotion. Victims were selected through divination following a sheep sacrifice. After the robbing, strangling, hacking, and burying of the victims, a sacrificial feast was celebrated. In some cases other methods were used to dispose of the victims, such as poisoning, drowning, and burying alive. The death agony was deliberately prolonged, theoretically so that the goddess might enjoy it.

Thuggee was a hereditary occupation, although the old families were joined from time to time by others. There were degrees of initiation into the society. The preliminary grade of initiation involved fasting, worship, the taking of vows, and, finally, the presentation of the sacred pickax, the tool with which Thug victims were buried as human sacrifices to the goddess. After a probationary period in which the initiate was introduced to his gruesome work, he received a noose purified by holy water.

Suppression. The English first noted the existence of the Thugs in 1799. However, it was not until 1831 that Capt. William Sleeman, the chief agent of Lord William Cavendish Bentinck, governor general of India, declared a "war" on the Thugs. It lasted four years and ended in the virtual annihilation of the Thugs. By gathering elaborate genealogical data, the English authorities were able to track down the related families of the criminal society. By 1861 the lesser Thug gangs had been suppressed, and in 1882 the last known Thug was hanged.

RALPH SLOTTEN, *Dickinson College*

Further Reading: Bruce, George L., *The Stranglers: The Cult of Thuggee and Its Overthrow in British India* (London 1968).

THULE, thōōl, the name given in classical times to the most northerly land, reputedly six days' voyage from Britain. It may have been Norway or Iceland. Thule (pronounced thū'lē or tōō'lē) is now the name of a U. S. Air Force base on Baffin Bay, in northwest Greenland, completed in 1952. Sir John Ross had discovered and named this ice-free area on Baffin Bay in 1818. The Eskimo there, whom Ross called Polar Eskimo, believed they were the only people in the world.

When the American explorer Robert E. Peary visited Thule in 1895, its population was estimated to be 253. Knud Rasmussen, a Danish ethnologist, opened a trading post there in 1910. The Thule Air Force base has facilitated exploration of the north Greenland icecap.

Thule culture is the archaeological name for a pre-European Eskimo culture that once extended from Alaska to Greenland.

J. BRIAN BIRD, *McGill University*

THULIUM, thōō'lē-əm, symbol Tm, is a lustrous metallic element that tarnishes readily in air. It is classified as one of the rare earth, or lanthanide, elements. The element was discovered in 1879 by the Swedish chemist Per Theodor Cleve, who named it for Thule, the ancient name of Scandinavia. Thulium is obtained from the yellowish mineral monazite. The radioactive isotope thulium-170 is used as a source of gamma

THUNDER BAY, Ontario, has huge grain elevators in its port that handle the shipments from farms in the western plains.

ONTARIO DEPARTMENT OF TOURISM AND INFORMATION

rays in portable X-ray units. Thulium oxalate, $Tm_2(C_2O_4)_3 \cdot 6H_2O$, is used for separation of thulium and other lanthanides from metals.

Thulium is located in Group III of the periodic table. Its atomic number is 69, and its atomic weight is 168.934. Thulium melts at about 1600°C (2900°F) and boils at 1727°C (3140°F). It is highly electropositive, reacting slowly with water to liberate hydrogen and burning in air to form the oxide, Tm_2O_3. The oxidation states of the element are +3 and +2. Salts of Tm^{+3} are fairly numerous; they are stable and have a characteristic green color. Salts of Tm^{+2} are unstable and rare. Thulium is separated from the other rare earths by an ion-exchange process.

HERBERT LIEBESKIND, *The Cooper Union*

THUMB. See HAND.

THUN, tōōn, a town in Switzerland, is in Bern canton, 15 miles (24 km) southeast of Bern. It is close to the junction of the central Swiss plateau and the mountains of the Bernese Oberland. An attractive town dominated by its medieval castle, Thun is predominantly German-speaking and Protestant. It is an important tourist center.

The town is on the Aare River, at its exit from the northern end of the narrow Lake of Thun. The lake covers an area of about 18 square miles (47 sq km) and provides excellent sailing. Population: (1968 est.) 35,000.

NORMAN J. G. POUNDS, *Indiana University*

THUNDER is the shock wave of sound produced by the rapid heating of air in a lightning discharge. Sound travels about 1 mile (1.6 km) in 5 seconds, so an observer can roughly calculate his distance from a lightning stroke by noting the time between the stroke and the thunderclap. However, if the lightning follows a curving path, the sound arrives as a rumble because it comes from various distances. The sound also may be reflected from clouds or from the ground. See also LIGHTNING.

THUNDER BAY, a port city in northwestern Ontario, Canada, is at the western Canadian end of Lake Superior, 875 miles (1,400 km) northwest of Toronto. It was created in 1970 by the merging of Fort William, Port Arthur, Neebing, and McIntyre. Thunder Bay is the largest Canadian port in total tonnage handled, and the western terminus of the St. Lawrence Seaway.

The largest industry is the manufacture of timber into lumber, railroad ties, poles, pulp, and paper. Truck trailers, automotive machinery for forest operations, rapid transit and railway cars, and aircraft components are also made.

Grain is one of the principal products shipped. The city's numerous grain elevators, which include one of the largest single-unit elevators in North America, are equipped to hold 110 million bushels (3.8 billion liters) of grain. Iron ore, gold, copper, zinc, nickel, and lead are mined nearby.

Tourists are attracted to the area in increasing numbers. Facilities for hunting and fishing, winter sports, and boating supply year-round diversion. Sibley Provincial Park at the tip of the Sibley peninsula is just across Thunder Bay, for which the city is named. The outline of the peninsula resembles a man in repose, who according to legend is Nanabijou, the Sleeping Giant of Indian folklore.

The first inhabitants of the area were the Ojibwa Indians, whose descendants still live in settlements south of the city. The French explorers Pierre Esprit Radisson and Médard Chouart, Sieur des Groseilliers, probably the first white men to visit the area, arrived about 1656. A trading center and fort were established in 1678. This settlement fell into disuse until 1717 when it was rebuilt and named Fort Kaministikwia. Later abandoned, it was acquired by the North West Fur Trading Company in 1802 and renamed Fort William in 1807. A settlement north of the fort known as the Station sprang up in 1857 as a base for an expedition organized to find a route to open up the West. It was renamed Prince Arthur's Landing in 1869 after Queen Victoria's son and became Port Arthur in 1884 when the town was incorporated. Population: 108,411.

MARGARET HOLLINGSWORTH
Thunder Bay Public Library

THUNDERBIRD, a supernatural figure and concept, which is found generally among North American Indians, but is of particular importance in the Eastern Woodlands, Plains, and Northwest Coast culture areas. Although tribal variations exist, the thunderbird is ordinarily conceived as a huge bird that produces thunder by the beat of its wings and flashes lightning from its mouth or eyes.

Among the Dakota (Sioux) the terms for thunder and the thunderbird are synonymous. The

SMITHSONIAN INSTITUTION

Thunderbird and whale memorial on Vancouver Island.

Ojibwa and other Great Lakes groups regard the thunderbird as the principal power or deity residing in the sky and constantly warring with the underwater powers. Plains tribes conduct sun dances in which the participants represent the cry of young thunderbirds with shrill eagle bone whistles while they face a ceremonial pole supporting a brush nest. In many Indian societies those who receive thunder power in the form of dreams become shamans. The thunderbird motif appears on Indian ceremonial regalia, jewelry, and in the Northwest Coast as carved wooden crests.

STEPHEN E. FERACA
Bureau of Indian Affairs

THUNDERSTORM. See LIGHTNING; METEOROLOGY—THE THUNDERSTORM.

THURBER, thûr′bər, **James** (1894–1961), American humorist and cartoonist, who transformed his experience as an American into superb comedy. He was born in Columbus, Ohio, on Dec. 8, 1894. He described his early life in Columbus in *My Life and Hard Times* (1933) and in many sketches. Partially blinded by a childhood accident, he did not serve in World War I, but he left Ohio State University in 1918 to go to Paris as a code clerk. After the war, he fell back on journalism—which he said is "very much like falling back full-length on a kit of carpenter's tools"—and reported for newspapers in Paris, Columbus, and New York.

James Thurber

UPI

In 1927, Thurber joined the staff of the *New Yorker* magazine, where he found his style and where all but seven of his 22 books first appeared. For his first book, *Is Sex Necessary?* (1929), he collaborated with his fellow staff writer E. B. White. White once rescued and inked in some discarded doodlings by Thurber, and from then on Thurber's drawings became a necessary part of his books. In 1950, Thurber became almost blind. He died in New York City on Nov. 2, 1961.

Work. For the *New Yorker,* Thurber reported the misadventures of a comic antihero incapable of managing shower faucets, used-car salesmen, women, or overcoats. This browbeaten innocent is best represented in *The Middle-Aged Man on the Flying Trapeze* (1935). In Thurber's play *The Male Animal* (1940), written with Elliott Nugent, he is almost victorious.

After *The Last Flower* (1939), a series of drawings that comment bitterly on Western civilization, Thurber returned to writing penetrating comedy of the human condition, notably the story *The Secret Life of Walter Mitty* from *My World and Welcome to It* (1942). He published two collections of modern fables (1939 and 1956) and, though insisting he wrote only about reality, five witty fairy tales for adults—*Many Moons* (1943), *The Great Quillow* (1944), *The White Deer* (1945), *The 13 Clocks* (1950), and *The Wonderful O* (1957).

In *The Thurber Album* (1952) and *The Years with Ross* (1959) the humorist mulls over the past to catch its essence and show its heroes. He published further sketches and stories in *Thurber Country* (1953) and *Lanterns and Lances* (1961).

RICHARD TOBIAS, *Author of "The Art of James Thurber"*

THURGAU, to͝or′gou, is a canton in northeastern Switzerland. Called Thurgovie in French, the canton is a hilly, but not mountainous, region bordered by Lake Constance to the north. Schaffhausen canton is to the northwest, while Zürich and St. Gallen cantons are to the west and south. Thurgau consists essentially of the basin of the Thur River, which enters the canton in the southeast and flows northwest to join the Rhine. North and south of the river are series of hilly ridges that reach a maximum altitude of about 3,280 feet (1,000 meters). Thurgau covers an area of 388 square miles (1,005 sq km).

The canton is a prosperous agricultural region growing grains and fruits, particularly apples and pears. Wine grapes are cultivated near Lake Constance and in the Thur Valley. Most of the population is German-speaking, but there are small French and Italian minorities. Frauenfeld, the capital, is on the Murg River, the principal tributary of the Thur.

The territory of the modern canton was part of the Roman province of Rhaetia until the mid-5th century, when it was overrun by barbarians. During the early Middle Ages it belonged to the counts of Kyburg, passing to the Habsburgs in 1264. Seized by the Swiss states in 1460, Thurgau remained subject to Zürich until 1803, when it received the rights of a self-governing canton. Population: (1968 est.) 187,000.

NORMAN J. G. POUNDS, *Indiana University*

THURINGIA, thōō-rin′jə, is a historical region in Middle Germany with indefinite boundaries lying to the south of the Harz Mountains and between the Werra River on the west and the Saale River on the east. The German form of the name is Thüringen. It was incorporated into East Germany (German Democratic Republic) after World War II.

The Land. Thuringia is a scenic area dominated by the famous Thuringian Forest, which stretches southeast from the Werra Valley for about 62 miles (100 km) until it merges with the Franconian Forest and the Röhn Mountains. The forest varies in width from 6 to 22 miles (10–35 km). Pine and fir trees have largely displaced the former stands of beeches. The forested mountains rise to a characteristic ridge, with the greatest elevation (3,222 feet or 982 meters) at the Beerberg. The mountains form a watershed that sends a number of streams to the Elbe, Weser, and Main-Rhine river basins. There are deposits of lignite, potash, iron ore, copper, cobalt, and slate. The Thuringian basin to the north and east of the forest is a rich agricultural region that produces various kinds of vegetables and fruits.

History. In the early Middle Ages a large Thuringian tribal kingdom developed, but it was conquered by the Franks in 531. The region was Christianized in the 8th century. About 804, Charlemagne established the Thuringian Mark as a protection against the Slavs to the east. The territory was repeatedly partitioned in the feudal conflicts of the Middle Ages. In 1440 most of the area passed to Electoral Saxony, and by a division of lands in 1485 most of it was given to the Ernestine branch of the Wettin family. Under the Ernestines, Thuringia was subdivided into what were known as the Saxe duchies.

During the Reformation, Thuringia became mostly Protestant. Luther for a time was held in protective custody at the Wartburg, a castle where he did much of his translation of the Bible. Through this translation Thuringian speech became the basis for a common High German language.

Thuringia was increasingly influenced by Prussia in the early 19th century and became part of the German Empire in 1871. Under the empire the Thuringian states, as they were commonly called, comprised the Grand Duchy of Saxe-Weimar-Eisenach, the duchies of Saxe-Meiningen, Saxe-Coburg-Gotha, and Saxe-Altenburg, and the principalities of Schwarzburg-Rudolstadt, Schwarzburg-Sondershausen, and Reuss (elder line) and Reuss (younger line). In 1920 these states, except for Coburg, which joined Bavaria, united to form the State of Thuringia in the Weimar Republic. During the era when Hitler was active the Thuringian German Christians were among the most radical of the pro-Nazi church groups.

In 1944, parts of the provinces of Saxony and Hesse-Nassau were added to Thuringia. In 1945, Erfurt replaced Weimar as the capital. The U. S. forces turned the region over to the Russians in July 1945. After World War II it became one of the five states of East Germany. When East Germany abolished these state governments in 1952, most of Thuringia was incorporated into the three districts (*Bezirke*) of Erfurt, Gera, and Suhl.

Ernst C. Helmreich
Bowdoin College

THURLOE, thûr′lō, **John** (1616–1668), English lawyer and diplomat, known as Oliver Cromwell's "Little Secretary of State." He was baptized on June 12, 1616, in Abbot's Roding, Essex. In 1647 he studied law at Lincoln's Inn. Under the patronge of the Puritan parliamentary leader Oliver St. John, Thurloe was appointed secretary to him and Walter Strickland in 1651, when they went on a mission to Holland. In 1652, Thurloe was appointed secretary to the republican Council of State. Entirely trusted by Cromwell, whose sole secretary of state he was for nearly eight years, he was also put in charge of an extensive intelligence system to uncover Royalist plots. It was said that Cromwell carried the secrets of all the powers of Europe at his girdle.

After Oliver's death, Thurloe served Richard Cromwell as the government's chief parliamentary supporter. In 1660 he was reappointed secretary of state and served until just before the Restoration. He died in London on Feb. 2, 1668. His huge correspondence is the main source for information on the Protectorate.

Maurice Ashley
University of Loughborough, England

THURMOND, Strom (1902–), American political leader. James Strom Thurmond was born in Edgefield, S. C., on Dec. 5, 1902. He graduated from Clemson College in 1923, and was admitted to the bar. Entering politics as a Democrat, he became a state senator and a state circuit court judge. He served with distinction in the U. S. Army during World War II.

In 1946, Thurmond was elected governor of South Carolina, and in 1948 he temporarily broke with the national Democrats over President Truman's strong civil rights program. As the States Rights Democratic, or Dixiecrat, nominee for president, Thurmond received 39 electoral votes. (See Dixiecrats.) In 1954 he became the only successful write-in candidate for the U. S. Senate in American history.

In 1964, Senator Thurmond bolted the Democrats and was influential in swinging South Carolina into the Republican presidential column for the first time since 1876. At the 1968 Republican National Convention he persuaded several key Southern delegations to remain loyal to Richard Nixon for the presidential nomination. Thereafter his influence began to wane. Most of his old Dixiecrat region voted for the independent candidate, George Wallace, in the 1968 presidential election, and the Republicans lost heavily in South Carolina state elections. But Thurmond, an outspoken conservative on domestic issues and a "hawk" in foreign affairs, retained his personal popularity in South Carolina.

Ernest M. Lander, Jr., *Clemson University*

THURSDAY, the fifth day of the week, takes its English name from Thor, the god of thunder in Norse mythology. In the Roman planetary week the fifth day honored Jupiter, or Jove, the Roman god of thunder, and the various Germanic tribes observed the same relationship. Thus Thursday is Dies Jovis in Latin and Jeudi in French, while the Scandinavian name is Torsdag and the German is Donnerstag (after Donar, the German form of Thor).

In the Christian religion the Thursday before Easter is called Maundy Thursday, or Holy Thursday. Ascension Day, the 40th day after Easter, is also known as Holy Thursday.

THURSTONE, thûrs′tən, **Louis Leon** (1887–1955), American psychologist, who was a pioneer in mental measurement. He was born in Chicago on May 29, 1887. He was trained as an engineer, taking an M. E. at Cornell, but then shifted to psychology, in which he earned his Ph. D. at the University of Chicago in 1917. He was a member of the faculty at Chicago from 1924 to 1952. He died in Chapel Hill, N. C., on Sept. 29, 1955.

Thurstone was noted for applying mathematical procedures to psychological research. By applying the statistical method known as factor analysis to the results of intelligence tests, he concluded that mental ability is made up of at least seven relatively independent factors. He also developed aptitude tests. His major books were *The Nature of Intelligence* (1924), *The Vectors of Mind* (1935), and *A Factorial Study of Personality* (1944).

THUTMOSE III, thōōt-mō′sə (reigned c. 1490–1436 B. C.), Egyptian pharaoh of the early 18th dynasty, who was perhaps the greatest military leader of ancient Egypt. The son of Thutmose II by a minor queen, he ascended the throne as a child under the regency of Queen Hatshepsut, his stepmother and aunt. But Hatshepsut assumed full kingly titles and for over 20 years ruled as the dominant co-regent, with Thutmose in the minor role. In his 22d year, Thutmose assumed sole power and reigned alone until his death.

Thutmose is best known for his campaigns in southwestern Asia, having personally conducted 16 or 17 in 20 years. During his first, the Egyptians defeated a coalition of Syrian rulers at Megiddo and successfully besieged the city. They then proceeded to what is now Lebanon, where they captured three towns and built a fortress. At the conclusion of his eighth campaign, Thutmose defeated the kingdom of Mitanni and erected a "boundary" stele on the far side of the Euphrates River beside a similar one of his grandfather, Thutmose I.

Less is known about the campaigns to the south, and it is presumed that Thutmose did not personally lead many of them. Nevertheless, Egyptian armies occupied the district below the 4th cataract of the Nile and founded the fortified town of Napata.

At the height of his power Thutmose controlled an empire extending from Thebes some 1,100 miles (1,800 km) to the northeast and 900 miles (1,400 km) to the south. In Asia he governed by means of local princes supervised by resident Egyptian commissioners and a high commissioner for the entire area. In the Sudan a viceroy was assisted by two deputy governors. In Egypt itself, the King was represented by two viziers, one at Thebes and the other probably at Memphis. Thutmose's conquests brought to Egypt masses of tribute to enrich the temples and hordes of captives to be used as slaves.

CAROLINE NESTMANN PECK
Brown University

THWAITES, thwāts, **Reuben Gold** (1853–1913), American editor and archivist. Born in Dorchester, Mass., on May 15, 1853, Thwaites later settled in Wisconsin. He studied at the University of Wisconsin and at Yale, and in 1876 became managing editor of the *Wisconsin State Journal* at Madison. Succeeding Lyman C. Draper as director of the State Historical Society in 1887, Thwaites ably supervised the arrangement of Draper's mammoth collection of early American materials as well as the construction of a large building to house the society and the university library. Dedicated to acquiring rare manuscripts, Thwaites scoured the area gathering papers of old French settlers. He translated and published 73 volumes of *Jesuit Relations and Allied Documents,* completed in 1901. Equally important were his *Original Journals of the Lewis and Clark Expedition* (8 vols., 1904–1905) and *Early Western Travels* (1904–1907) in 32 annotated volumes. Thwaites died in Madison on Oct. 22, 1913.

BERTRAM WYATT-BROWN
Case Western Reserve University

THYESTES, thī-es′tēz, in Greek legend, was the brother of Atreus, king of Mycenae. At a banquet, Atreus served his brother the flesh of two of Thyestes' own sons. See ATREUS.

THYLACINE. See TASMANIAN TIGER.

THYME, tīm, any plant of the genus *Thymus* of the mint family (Labiatae), consisting of about 50 species of small shrubs, one of which is used in cooking. Most species are native to southern Europe, Morocco, and Algeria.

The culinary thyme (*T. vulgaris*) is a southern European perennial. The plant attains a height of 6 to 8 inches (15–20 cm). Its stiff, woody, four-angled branches are hairy and bear small aromatic leaves. The small, two-lipped purple or lilac-colored flowers are borne in clusters at intervals along the flowering stalks. The plant is often grown in rock and herb gardens and is propagated from seeds, cuttings, or by division of the crown.

The tender shoots of the culinary thyme are used either fresh or dried in stuffings, soups, stews, casseroles, and meat dishes. Thyme oil, which is sometimes used in cough medicines, is extracted by distillation of the culinary thyme and another species, *T. zygis.* Thymol, a constituent of the oil, is sometimes used as a topical antifungal medication.

LAWRENCE ERBE
University of Southwestern Louisiana

Thyme (*Thymus vulgaris*)

ROCHE

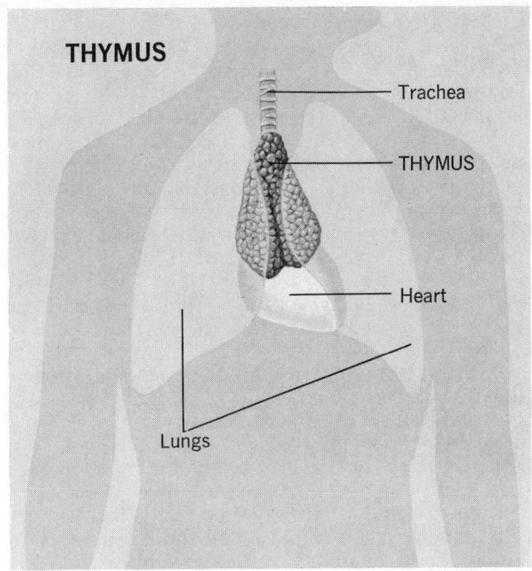

THE THYMUS is usually largest during adolescence, as shown. Following puberty it starts to degenerate.

THYMUS, thī′məs, an organ located in the chest behind the upper part of the sternum (breastbone) and in front of the large blood vessels leading from the heart. The thymus produces cells, sometimes called *thymocytes,* which are a class of lymphocyte. Lymphocytes are found in many other parts of the body, including the blood, bone marrow, lymph, lymph nodes, spleen, and tonsils and in the loose connective tissue of the digestive tract, lungs, and other hollow structures. Lymphocytes from the thymus, like other lymphocytes, play an important role in the process of immunity and in the rejection of transplanted tissues and organs. See also IMMUNITY.

All vertebrate animals have a thymus. In humans it is usually well developed during infancy and childhood. After puberty it decreases in size and importance. In many other species, however, including the rat, mouse, and guinea pig, it remains an important functioning organ throughout life. If the thymus is removed from one of these species soon after birth, severe immunological deficiencies appear, and the animal may die. If the thymus is removed or destroyed after this early period, lymphocytes elsewhere in the body take up the tasks of those from the thymus, and the animal's immunological system does not suffer.

Like the tonsils, the thymus forms in the embryo by the invasion of lymphocytes into the epithelial tissue lining the pharynx. The epithelium giving rise to the thymus lies originally at the sites of the third gill pouches of the developing embryo. From these origins the epithelial cells bud off and migrate to the midline of the chest. Lymphocytes then move toward the displaced epithelial cells and join with them to form the thymus.

The thymus of a calf or other young animal is sometimes eaten as a delicacy known as *sweetbreads.* The pancreas of a young animal is also sometimes sold as sweetbreads.

H. STANLEY BENNETT
University of North Carolina

THYRATRON, thī′rə-tron, a grid-controlled, hot-cathode, gas-filled electron tube for switching electron current. The controlling grid is a screen electrode between the cathode and an anode. With a positive anode voltage, a critical control voltage applied to the grid initiates the development of an ionized, electrically conductive plasma between anode and cathode. Once the tube is conducting, the grid no longer controls the current. The tube is returned to a nonconducting state by interrupting its current by external means.

The thyratron was developed in the 1920's by Irving Langmuir and Albert W. Hull. It is used for controlling the speed of motors, converting power, and generating high-voltage pulses for radar transmitters. In many low-voltage applications the thyratron has been superseded by a semiconductor device called a *thyristor.*

SEYMOUR GOLDBERG, *EG&G, Inc.*

THYROID, an endocrine, or ductless, gland that produces three important hormones. Two of these hormones, L-thyroxine (LT_4) and L-triiodothyronine (LT_3), determine the level of metabolic activity in the body. The third, thyrocalcitonin, counteracts undue hypercalcemia (too much calcium in the blood) and the effects of parathyroid hormone on bone resorption.

Structure. The human thyroid gland consists of two lateral lobes connected by an isthmus. In other mammals the two lobes are separate. The human thyroid lies low in the front of the neck. The recurrent laryngeal nerve courses along the back of the gland, and the parathyroid glands—usually four in number—lie behind the thyroid. In a healthy adult the thyroid weighs about one ounce (30 grams).

The bulk of the thyroid is composed of spherical follicles lined with cuboidal epithelium and filled with colloid, a gelatinous substance containing LT_4, LT_3, and their precursors. Connective tissue continuous with an outer capsule fills the spaces between the follicles and contains

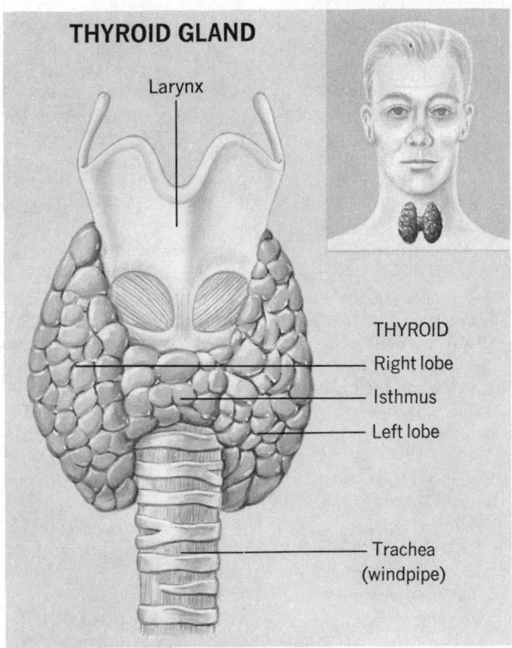

the cells that produce the hormone thyrocalcitonin.

Thyroid Secretion. Normally, the supplies of the hormones LT_4 and LT_3 to the body cells are controlled by a hormone from the hypothalamus (thyrotropin releasing factor, or TRF) and an anterior pituitary hormone (thyroid stimulating hormone, or TSH). In this regulation of hormone production, the hormones themselves serve as signals in negative feedback. The homeostatic mechanisms that control the secretion of thyrocalcitonin are less well defined.

TSH, when released by the anterior pituitary, binds to the cell membranes of the thyroid cells and accelerates the manufacture and release of LT_4 and LT_3. The manufacture of these hormones involves the uptake of inorganic iodide from the blood, the oxidation of iodide to iodine, the iodination of tyrosine (an amino acid) to produce mono- and di-iodotyrosine molecules, and the coupling of mono- and di-iodotyrosine molecules to yield LT_3 or the coupling of two di-iodotyrosine molecules to form LT_4.

Following their release from the thyroid, LT_4 and LT_3 are mostly bound to plasma proteins. Once bound, they dissociate only to a slight degree and provide a steady supply of hormones to the body cells. The manufacture and transport of thyrocalcitonin are not clearly understood.

Diseases and Disorders of the Thyroid.—*Hypothyroidism.* Injury to the hypothalamus-anterior pituitary control system, with the loss of TSH, or the destruction or removal of the thyroid itself, deprives the body of LT_4 and LT_3, causing hypothyroidism, or myxedema. When TSH is absent the myxedema is called secondary. When the fault lies with the thyroid, it is called primary. Both primary and secondary myxedema result in decreased iodine uptake and hormone production and diminished oxygen consumption, which is detectable by low basal metabolism rate values. The person with hypothyroidism complains of dry skin, sleepiness, fatigue, and intolerance to cold. In young children a deficiency of thyroid hormones leads to stunting and cretinism.

The underproduction of thyroid hormones may also be associated with an enlarged thyroid gland, or goiter. Such goiters often result from the blocking of hormone synthesis by inflammatory changes (as in thyroiditis), blocking agents, or by a shortage of iodine. The enlargement of the thyroid in these cases is a consequence of increased TSH, an attempt to restore the supplies of thyroid hormones to normal.

Hypothyroidism is treated by the administration of dessicated thyroid, LT_4, LT_3, or a combination of both hormones.

Hyperthyroidism. Overactivity of the thyroid gland is also associated with goiter. This type of goiter may be caused by stimulation of the gland by long-acting thyroid stimulator (LATS), which is formed as an antibody to thyroid tissue. The goiter also may be caused by one or more nodules or adenomas (tumors) in the thyroid. As a result of overproduction, the basal metabolic rate and heat production rise, producing such symptoms as rapid heartbeat, nervousness, loss of weight despite increased appetite, profuse sweating, and in some an increased protrusion of the eyeballs. Hyperthyroidism is treated by agents that block hormone formation, destruction of thyroid tissue by radioactive iodine, or surgical removal of excess thyroid tissue.

T. S. DANOWSKI, M. D.
Author of "Clinical Endocrinology"

THYROXINE. See THYROID.

TIAHUANACO, tē-ə-wə-nä'kō, one of the prehistoric empires of Peru and Bolivia, flourishing about 1000 A. D. It is an ill-defined civilization that developed in the south-central highlands near Lake Titicaca and seems to have expanded along the highlands and coastal zone of most of Peru in pre-Inca times. It was one of several dynastic states that arose in the Andean region prior to the Spanish Conquest. Tiahuanaco lost political control long before the Inca Empire came to dominate territories that now compose Peru, Ecuador, Bolivia, and the northern part of Chile.

In the same manner as other pre-Spanish civilizations, Tiahuanaco was based on intensive irrigation agriculture and a sharply defined, complex division of labor geared to military conquest and political control of large numbers of people and vast areas. The basic conditions for imperial conquest undoubtedly existed long before the spread of Tiahuanaco civilization, since it is known that ancient Peru underwent several periods of regional development and militaristic expansion—a cyclical development of empires that culminated in the great Inca civilization and was interrupted by the Spanish Conquest. Thus, Tiahuanaco civilization was based on a technology and social organization common to the various peoples of the ancient central Andes and was not an innovative civilization.

The principal archaeological site of Tiahuanaco culture is in the *altiplano* south of Lake Titicaca at an elevation of 12,000 feet (3,657 meters). It is made up of numerous stone buildings, earthen mounds, courts, stairways, reservoirs, and other structures. The complexity and size of

PREHISTORIC MONOLITHS AT TIAHUANACO show the skill of Indian workmen in carving massive stone blocks.

CARL FRANK, FROM PHOTO RESEARCHERS

the site suggest that the large-scale planning and the labor needed to achieve such monumental construction called for strict regimentation of the masses of people by the highest levels of government. Some of the stones used in building parts of this cultural center weighed as much as 100 tons (90 metric tons) and were transported from a quarry 3 miles (4.8 km) distant. Its famous Gateway of the Sun was hewn from a large stone 10 feet (3 meters) high and carved with symbols of human beings, the condor, and the sun god. Stylistic motifs of this sort, characteristic of Tiahuanaco culture, are widespread in the central Andean region and appear not only in stone carvings but in textile designs and ceramics. Such archaeological evidence serves to measure the extension of Tiahuanaco cultural influence and, possibly, political control. It is not known whether the site near Lake Titicaca is actually the center of origin of Tiahuanaco culture or the capital of the empire at its height.

LOUIS C. FARON
State University of New York at Stony Brook

TIBER RIVER, tī′bûr, the longest river in central Italy, known in classical times as Tiberis and in modern Italian as Tevere. It rises in Tuscany, about 40 miles (64 km) east of Florence, and flows generally southward, passing near Perugia and Orvieto. For much of its course it flows alternately across small mountain basins and through narrow, gorge-like valleys. After reaching the Roman Campagna it bends to the southwest, passes through Rome, and reaches the sea at Ostia. The length of the Tiber is 252 miles (405 km), of which only the 20 miles (32 km) from Rome to the sea are navigable. The Tiber is subject to severe winter flooding.

NORMAN J. G. POUNDS
Indiana University

TIBERIAS, tī-bēr′ē-əs, a town in northern Israel, is the capital of the Kinneret subdistrict. It is on the western shore of Lake Tiberias (Sea of Galilee or Kinneret), 30 miles (48 km) east of Haifa. The town is a major winter resort, primarily because of its hot mineral springs. It is also a market center for the collective agricultural settlements of eastern Galilee. The tomb of Maimonides, the Jewish philosopher and physician, and a number of ancient synagogues are located in Tiberias.

Tiberias was founded by Herod Antipas in 26 A.D. near the Biblical site of Rakkath. It was named after the Emperor Tiberius. The majority of the original inhabitants were Jews, and from the 3d century to 637 A.D., when it was taken by the Arabs, the village was the principal center of Talmudic scholarship and the capital of Jewish Palestine. It was captured by the Crusaders in 1099 and, after the 13th century, dwindled in importance. The village was destroyed by an earthquake in 1837. When it was rebuilt, Tiberias was settled chiefly by Jews. In 1948, during the Arab-Israeli war, Arabs inhabiting the village were replaced by Jews.

Nearly half of its population is foreign born, having immigrated after 1948, and 80% of the immigrants from Asian and African countries. Population: (1968 est.) 23,500.

GARY FOWLER
University of Kentucky

TIBERIAS, Lake. See GALILEE, SEA OF.

TIBERIUS, tī-bē′rē-əs (42 B.C.–37 A.D.), was the second Roman emperor. He was born in Rome on Nov. 16, 42 B.C., the son of Tiberius Claudius Nero and Livia. Livia divorced his father in 38 B.C. to marry the future Emperor Augustus. A few months later Livia had her second son, Drusus, by Tiberius Claudius Nero.

When he was nine, Tiberius delivered a public funeral oration for his father. From that time he and his brother Drusus were raised under the tutelage of Augustus. In 20 B.C., in his first significant public act, Tiberius received in the East the standards that Rome had lost to the Parthians. Afterwards Tiberius was groomed as a general. He served in Pannonia and, after Drusus' death in 9 B.C., in Germany.

In 12 B.C., after the death of Augustus' friend Agrippa, Tiberius was forced to divorce his wife Vipsania and to marry Julia, Agrippa's widow and Augustus' daughter. Many believed that Tiberius would be designated as Augustus' successor. In 6 B.C., Tiberius was given a share of the tribunician power, previously held only by the emperor and his heir-designate. But in the same year Tiberius discovered that Augustus secretly hoped that his grandsons, Gaius and Lucius Caesar, would be his heirs. Tiberius haughtily retired to Rhodes, where he remained until 2 A.D., the year Lucius died. In 4, after the death of Gaius, Augustus, who had no other heirs of age, adopted Tiberius and made him his heir. Tiberius was forced to adopt Germanicus, his brother Drusus' son.

Tiberius As Emperor. During the last 10 years of Augustus' reign, Tiberius was virtually coregent. He commanded armies in Germany, Pannonia, and Illyricum. When Augustus died in 14, Tiberius was firmly entrenched and encountered little opposition as emperor, except temporarily among the legions in Germany and Pannonia.

Tiberius' administrative policies were generally wise, and he tried to follow Augustus' precedents. Tiberius adopted a defensive foreign policy and concentrated upon strengthening the imperial frontiers. For the most part his reign was peaceful, and the imperial provinces were governed well. A frugal emperor, he left a wealthy empire.

But Tiberius was a very unpopular emperor. His reign was marred by murderous family quarrels and by his own distrust of the senatorial aristocracy. In 26, Tiberius retired to the isle of Capri and governed from there for the rest of his reign. Until 31 he was under the evil influence of his adviser Sejanus, who encouraged Tiberius' suspicious character. In that year, Sejanus conspired to overthrow Tiberius, but Tiberius detected the conspiracy and inaugurated a reign of terror by executing Sejanus.

His heir, Germanicus, had died in 19 and most members of Germanicus' family died mysteriously or were executed. Tiberius' son Drusus had been poisoned. Tiberius chose as his heir Germanicus' son Caligula, who had been too young to become deeply involved in the political animosities of Tiberius' reign. Romans rejoiced when Tiberius died on March 16, 37, in Campania, and the terror ended.

ARTHER FERRILL, *University of Washington*

Further Reading: Marañón, Gregorio, *Tiberius: The Resentful Caesar*, tr. by Warre B. Wells (New York 1956); Marsh, Frank B., *The Reign of Tiberius* (New York 1931).

EASTFOTO

The Potala, former palace of the Dalai Lamas, dominates the Tibetan capital of Lhasa from atop Red Hill.

TIBET, ti-bet′, is a rugged, mountainous country in Asia, situated in the high plateau area north of the Himalaya. Although occupied by the Communist Chinese since 1950, it has had a long history as an independent state and possesses a distinctive culture. Its strategic location between East, South, and Inner (or Central) Asia has made it on occasion the focus of contention between rival empires, but for the most part it has been allowed to live in "splendid isolation" because of its extreme difficulty of access.

Tibet, or *Bod* in Tibetan, is called *Hsi-tsang* by the Chinese, *Bhot* by the Indians and Nepalis, and *Tobet* by the Mongols. Its capital is Lhasa. Political Tibet, as contrasted with cultural Tibet, consists of three distinct regions: Central Tibet, including the provinces of U (capital, Lhasa) and Tsang (capital, Shigatse); Ngari, or Western Tibet (administrative headquarters, Gartok); and Kham, or Eastern Tibet (administrative headquarters, Chamdo).

Tibetans, or people closely related culturally to them, are found in the Chinese provinces of Szechwan, Kansu, and Chinghai; in the Himalayan states of Nepal, Sikkim, and Bhutan; and in the Ladakh district of Kashmir. The Lhasa government, however, has not exerted political authority over these areas for several centuries.

As the religious center of Lamaistic Buddhism, Tibet has wielded great influence far beyond its ethnic boundaries, particularly in Mongolia and Manchuria and among the Russian Mongol tribes.

1. The Land

The great Tibetan plateau, called the Chang Thang (Northern Plain), stretches for 800 miles (1,300 km) across the country. It is surrounded on all sides by massive, formidable mountain ranges.

Mountains and Rivers. In eastern Tibet, a series of extremely rugged ranges running north-south separate the country from China proper. North of the Chang Thang are the Kunlun Mountains, which average 18,000 to 20,000 feet (5,500–6,100 meters) in elevation, forming an almost impenetrable barrier. On the southern border of Tibet the higher but somewhat more accessible Himalayan crest, averaging above 20,000 feet, is only a slightly less effective barrier to communication with the outside world. Both the Kunlun and Himalaya run east-west, as does the Kailas range, which parallels the Himalaya in southern Tibet for several hundred miles. The Karakoram range forms the boundary between Western Tibet and Ladakh.

Three great South Asian rivers—the Indus, Sutlej, and Brahmaputra (called the Tsangpo in Tibet)—rise in the Lake Manasarowar region of Western Tibet. Two of Southeast Asia's major river systems (the Salween and the Mekong), as well as two of China's largest rivers (the Yangtze and the Hwang), rise in the complex mountain system of northeastern Tibet. Most of the Chang Thang plateau, however, has no river system, although there are numerous brackish lakes.

Climate. The Himalayan chain effectively cuts off the summer monsoon rains, which drench the mountain region to the south of the range. Tibet lies on the dry side of the Himalaya and averages only 5 to 15 inches (125–380 mm) of precipitation annually. Because of Tibet's great elevation —13,000 to 16,000 feet (4,000–4,900 meters) in most of the valleys and plateaus—extreme variations in temperature are common. For example, summer midday temperatures often range up to 75° or 85°F (26°–29°C), with night temperatures falling below freezing.

Plants and Animals. The Chang Thang plateau is a barren wasteland with virtually no trees or bushes. The light precipitation of 10 inches (250 mm) a year does produce a summer grass crop, which is vital to herd grazing in this area. Some of the river valleys in southern Tibet have extensive forests with both conifers and deciduous trees. Cereals, primarily barley and buckwheat, are Tibet's staple crops and form the basic diet.

The animal most closely identified with Tibet is the yak, which is used as a draft animal, a pack animal, and a source of meat and butter. Sheep are also important in the economy. The small but sturdy and sure-footed horses of eastern Tibet, which were used extensively as beasts of burden in trade with China and India, have been much reduced in number. Several wild animals, including the snow leopard and the musk deer, inhabit the Himalayan area in southern Tibet, which is also the home of the legendary *Yeti* (see also ABOMINABLE SNOWMAN).

2. The People

Tibet is inhabited by a Mongoloid people numbering anywhere from 1 to 3 million. No reliable census has ever been taken. A 1963 report from Communist China placed the population of Tibet (as defined in Chinese administrative terms) at 2 million. The office of the exiled Dalai Lama, former ruler of Tibet, estimated the number of Tibetans at 6 million, but this figure presumably includes residents of India, China, Nepal, Sikkim, and Bhutan.

Social Structure. Before Tibetan society was transformed by the Communist Chinese, the most distinctive Tibetan social institution was the monastic system, which dominated political, economic, and social life. It has been estimated that 15% to 20% of the population belonged to one of the numerous Buddhist clerical orders. The Gelugpa (Ge-luk-pa) sect, to which the Dalai Lama and Panchen Lama belong, held the leading position at Lhasa and in the governmental apparatus throughout Tibet. But other important sects, such as the Kargyupa, Sakyapa, Karmapa, Dukpa, and Nyimgmapa, were preeminent in some areas, particularly in eastern Tibet and in Sikkim, Bhutan, and Ladakh. The principal "mother" monasteries of each of these sects had several "daughter" monasteries, with which they had intimate administrative, educational, financial, and, at times, commercial ties. See also DALAI LAMA; PANCHEN LAMA.

The monasteries, some of them very wealthy, derived financial support from various sources. The more important monasteries, such as Ganden, Drepung, Sera, and Tashi Lhunpo, received government endowment, but this was usually only a small proportion of their income. They held extensive landed estates, from which they received rent, and also participated in profitable commercial and moneylending activities. The monasteries were thus the main credit and trading establishments in Tibet.

Within the monasteries, there was a well-defined hierarchical structure. The majority of the monks received only a minimal education, based on the various Buddhist texts, and they provided the necessary unskilled and semiskilled labor besides serving as guards and police. The term *lama*—the Tibetan equivalent of the Sanskrit *guru* ("teacher")—is often applied to all Tibetan monks but more correctly should be used only for incarnate lamas (monks who are embodiments of a divine being) and those monks who had completed the prescribed curriculum in the Buddhist literature. Many of the monks who became high officials in the government or monastic administrative system were from poor families.

In pre-1950 Tibet, there were about 200 noble families, from whose ranks most of the lay government officials were appointed. Several categories of nobility existed: descendants of the old Tibetan dynastic family or regional princely houses; the families of the various Dalai Lamas; and those families that had been ennobled more recently for services to the state or the monastic institutions. Most of the nobility held large private estates by inheritance and occasionally were assigned profitable administrative responsibilities over government estates as part of their official duties. They sometimes played an active role in the trade structure.

There was no Tibetan commercial class as such, outside the monasteries and apart from the nobility, although numerous Tibetans engaged in small-scale local trade as a part-time occupation. Foreign trade, which was very important in the Tibetan economy, was largely the prerogative of the monasteries, the nobility, and the foreign trader communities—Nepali, Ladakhi, Muslim Kashmiri, Bhutanese, Chinese, and Indian.

The common people in Tibet may be divided into two groups: the sedentary agriculturalists, who inhabit the river valleys in southern and southeastern Tibet, and the nomadic pastoralists who are scattered throughout the country but are concentrated most heavily in the northern and northeastern districts. It would appear that relatively few of the agriculturalist class owned land outright. Instead they were granted rights to cultivate lands owned by the monasteries, nobility, or government on condition of the payment of rent or taxes and provision of services (*ulag*). Many also worked as hired laborers on estates or for trade caravans. The nomadic pastoralists, called Drok-pa, mostly practiced seasonal migration, grazing their herds in lowland areas in winter and in mountain pastures in summer.

The first few years of Chinese Communist rule did not significantly alter the social or economic structure in Tibet, except in some of the eastern districts adjacent to China. Following an uprising in 1959, however, the Chinese authorities introduced many radical changes directed at transforming Tibet into a carbon copy of China. Most of the monasteries were closed, the remainder continuing to operate at a mere subsistence level. The nobility lost its privileged status, and many of its members were killed or imprisoned or fled from Tibet.

After a brief initial "land to the tiller" period, the Chinese moved to force both the ag-

TIBETAN HERDSMEN stop work to chat. Cattle raising plays a vital role in the Tibetan economy.

EASTFOTO

EASTFOTO

A YAK DANCE is performed by Tibetans during a celebration in Lhasa. Among the onlookers are many Communist Chinese soldiers.

riculturalists and the nomadic pastoralists into communes. Reports of resistance to this process persist, but the resistance has had to take indirect and subtle forms. The Chinese have also assumed full control over the trading system, both internal and external.

Reports on living conditions in Tibet vary greatly, depending on the source. The Chinese Communists speak of the "liberation" of the Tibetan "serfs" from the "slavery" imposed by the monasteries and "upper stratum" oppressors. The Tibetans in exile decry Chinese "imperialism" and its "cultural genocide" policy. It would appear that the living standards of most Tibetans have declined drastically, in part because of the necessity to support a large Chinese military establishment on limited food resources. Near-famine conditions, once a rarity in Tibet, have been reported regularly. The development of educational and health services by the Chinese is compensation of sorts, but the value of these institutions has been perhaps reduced in the eyes of many Tibetans by their use in destroying Tibet's traditional culture.

Way of Life. Simplicity was the predominant theme of traditional Tibetan life, and even the nobility rarely made ostentatious displays of wealth. Tibetan homes were solid and substantial, usually two or three stories high with the top floor used as the living quarters and the other floors for animals and storage. Most of the houses of the nobility were constructed of stone. Houses of the common people were made of either stone or sun-dried bricks. The nomadic pastoralists dwelt in easily transportable yakskin tents, which were often 30 to 40 feet (9–12 meters) in length.

In dress, class status was indicated more by the quality of the cloth than by differences in style, although the nobility would sometimes don Chinese dress for social occasions. Monks wore a deep-red, ankle-length woolen garment and a hat in the color associated with their particular sect. The dress used by other Tibetans, both men and women, is called a *chuba* and consists of a full gown with long sleeves that reach far below the fingertips. In the summer, cotton cloth is used, the wealthier preferring silk. In the winter, sheepskin cloth lined with lambskin or wadded cotton is common.

Barley flour, called *tsampa*, is the staple food. It is usually mixed with butter and cooked in soup or tea. Meat, curd, and a few fruits and vegetables supplement this simple diet. Tibetans drink large quantities of tea (usually flavored with yak butter and salt) as well as *chang*, a local barley or millet beer.

Insulated from external influences, the Tibetans have developed a distinctive world view that reflects a sense of isolation. A number of their social institutions differ in basic respects from those of surrounding Asian societies. Although marriages, for example, are usually arranged by the parents as in most other Asian countries, the Tibetans practice both polygyny and polyandry, a rare combination. Another example is the disposal of the dead. Cremation is the preferred form, but this is practicable only in the few areas of the country with extensive forests. Elsewhere, the usual practice is to dissect the corpse and expose the remains on hillsides for the vultures and dogs. This practice is not found in any other Buddhist country.

Tibetan festivals invariably are associated with the numerous Buddhist holidays. Often the monasteries serve as the place of celebration. The laity participate and are even assigned important roles on some occasions. The most important festivities are those connected with the new year. They start in February or March and continue for the entire first month of the Tibetan lunar calendar.

Religion. The pre-Buddhist religious system in Tibet, known as Bon, was closely related to Central Asian shamanism. Buddhism probably first entered Tibet in the 4th century A. D. from Kashmir and Nepal. It was adopted as the court religion in the 7th century, but not until the arrival of the great Indian guru Padmasambha a century later did Buddhism seriously challenge Bon as a popular religion. Eventually Buddhism absorbed Bon, after each religion had strongly influenced the other. Such common features of Tibetan Buddhism as the use of oracles, the exorcising of spirits, and the concept of the soul are derived from Bon. The extensive use of prayer wheels is evidence of the influence of Tantrism (see also BUDDHISM). The wheels enclose sheets of paper on which are printed magical sounds called *mantras*, made effective on the divine level when the wheel is turned.

Buddhism gained further impetus in Tibet with the arrival of another great Indian guru, Atisha, in 1042. The division of Tibetan Buddhism into several sects dates from this period. These sects are based for the most part on the extent to which Bon concepts are accepted or rejected or on the school of Indian Buddhism that is followed. Although Padmasambha had founded a monastery in the 8th century, it was only with Atisha that the monastic system spread widely throughout Tibet, finally emerging as the predominant religious institution. A reformation movement, led by the monk Tsongkhapa (1357–1419), the founder of the Gelugpa (Yellow Hat) sect, developed in the 14th century. The Gelugpa sect gradually achieved a preeminent position in Tibetan Buddhism, but one based upon relatively peaceful coexistence with the others. The system continued in this form until about 1960, when the Chinese Communists began a full-scale campaign to undermine and destroy the position of the Tibetan Buddhist institutions. See also LAMAISM.

3. Tibetan Culture

Tibet's physical isolation never excluded external influences because for many centuries the country was one of the channels of communication between South, East, and Central Asia. Even the Tibetan national epic, the *Ge-sar of Ling*, is based on the "Caesar of Rome" story as filtered through Central Asia. But India and China were the primary sources of foreign intellectual and cultural influences, Indian influences predominating until about 1200 and Chinese thereafter. The great achievement of the Tibetans has been their capacity to give outside influences an essentially Tibetan character, fitting them into a uniquely Tibetan cultural mold.

Literature. King Song-tsen Gampo (reigned 627–650) is traditionally credited with the introduction of a written script for the Tibetan language. The script is an adaptation of a northern Indian Gupta alphabet. Prior to this time, there had been a vigorous oral literature, encompassing both the ritualistic and cosmological traditions of the Bon priesthood and the chronologies of the ruling dynasty. Only a small part of this has been preserved in written form, and even it would have disappeared but for the fortunate discovery of a Buddhist cave shrine at Tunhwang, in northwestern China. The shrine contained numerous pre-Buddhist and Buddhist records of the 8th and 9th centuries, including dynastic chronicles, Bon ritual recitations, and early Buddhist texts.

The predominance of Buddhism in Tibetan literature was well established by the 9th century, and from that time on virtually all Tibetan literature was produced by Buddhist monks. The years 800 to 1200 are the period of the "Great Translators," Tibetan scholars who devoted their time to translating the Indian Buddhist texts into the vernacular. In the 13th century, detailed Tibetan commentaries on the Buddhist classics began to appear, and intensive efforts were made to systematize the texts. This culminated in the publication of two voluminous encyclopedic works, the *Kanjur* and *Tenjur*, in the 14th century. The period thereafter was somewhat more creative in character, and numerous original treatises on philosophical and religious themes were written by Tsongkhapa and other great teachers. This scholarship reached its zenith by the 17th century, and few important additions have been made to Buddhist literature. Since 1959, Tibetan refugee monks in India, deprived of their rich monastic libraries, have been seeking to reconstruct the literature of the various sects.

Dance and Drama. A very popular art form in Tibet is the dance drama. Although most of the better-known Tibetan dance dramas, such as the *Cham*, appear to have a secular, or even a Bon origin, a Buddhist interpretation has been superimposed. The *Cham* is a ritual mystery dance that Westerners often incorrectly call a "devil dance" because of the grotesque masks used. It was performed by trained monk dancers at most large monasteries as part of the New Year celebrations. The theme is the invocation of a deity's protection against evil, and usually a small human effigy personifying evil is "slain" and dismembered at the end of the performance. In one such dance, witnessed by the author, the effigy was of Mao Tse-tung.

More secular in character are the *A-che-lha-mo*. These dance dramas, depicting the lives of Tibetans famous for their piety and miraculous achievements, were performed by professional touring troupes. Other very popular forms of dance dramas, often performed by local groups, usually had a religious motif, interpreted from a layman's perspective. One of the best known depicted several of the great Indian gurus as clowns. There were also traveling bards who sang ancient songs, including usually sections of the Ge-sar epic (a remnant of the once vigorous oral tradition), and itinerant monk religious storytellers. All of these traditional forms of entertainment and education have been destroyed or perverted by the Chinese Communists.

Art and Architecture. The earliest Tibetan paintings known to the West date from about 1100. Most of these early works were the product of a rich artistic tradition that developed in the Buddhist shrines and monasteries of Western Tibet. The paintings appear to be in a style then prevalent in northern India, but they are distinctively Tibetan in character and can be recognized as the source of what later became the classic Tibetan art style. Chinese influence entered somewhat later, most notably in the Ming dynastic period (14th–17th century), when subtle changes in both the relationship of figures and the themes depicted can be detected.

The conventional Tibetan religious paintings are usually composed of a symmetrical arrangement of divine figures. The principal deity, painted on a larger scale, is in the center. Under Chinese artistic influence, a freer arrangement is typical, and the main figure may appear among other figures in a lush landscape background. Since the 17th century, art, like literature, has not been particularly creative and original.

The other artistic medium in which Tibetans excelled is metalworking. Initially, Nepali artisans were brought to Tibet in the 13th to 16th centuries to produce the metal ornamental and religious objects required by the monasteries and shrines. Tibetan craftsmanship in this field developed eventually and may even have surpassed the Nepali. Although Indian, Nepali, and Chinese influences are readily apparent in most Tibetan metalwork, here also a distinctive Tibetan style emerged.

In Tibetan architectural styles there is a continuity from the palaces and shrines of the early dynastic period (7th to 9th century) to the monasteries erected nearly a millennium later. External influences are evident in the finishing decoration of the later religious constructions, but the basic structure remained the same: solid stone buildings with inward-sloping walls and flat roofs. A notable example is the Potala, residence of the Dalai Lamas, in Lhasa. One of the most persistent and widespread architectural themes in Tibet is the stupa, a domed structure known locally as a *chorten.* Introduced from India and Nepal at least as early as the 7th century, stupas were originally funeral mounds of religious leaders but later were used primarily to house Buddhist holy relics.

4. The Economy

Sparse natural resources and difficult lines of communication have long hampered the economic development of Tibet. The rugged terrain, dominated by steep mountain ranges and arid plateaus, imposed severe limitations on agriculture. The lack of exportable commodities and the unfeasibility of a substantial entrepôt trade limited Tibet's commercial potential. The Tibetan economy therefore was characterized by a stability that for many centuries amounted to stagnation. The Chinese conquest has changed all this—both for better and worse.

Agriculture. Tibet has a subsistence agricultural system, limited largely to the valleys of the Tsangpo and its tributaries. But even in this comparatively advantaged area, the water supply is uncertain, the soil is poor, and the climate is rigorous. Barley is the staple crop. Millet and buckwheat are grown in the lower valleys. Since 1959 the Chinese have made some basic changes in the organization of the agrarian system through the partial introduction of communes, but these have not had much effect on agricultural production.

BUDDHIST IMAGE with 11 heads and 1,000 arms is richly garmented. Image is in Jokhang Temple, Lhasa.

EASTFOTO

Livestock Raising. Yak herds and sheep flocks have long played a vital role in the Tibetan economy. The herdsmen utilize the higher reaches of the mountain valleys and the vast Chang Thang plains for grazing their herds and flocks. In some areas of Tibet they grow crops in addition. Chinese attempts to establish communes among the nomads have led reportedly to the wholesale slaughter of herds as a form of protest. Guerrilla warfare in nomadic areas also has had a disastrous effect on herds and flocks.

Minerals. One of the Bon vestiges in Tibetan Buddhism is the belief that spirits reside in the earth and are inclined to take revenge on anyone who disturbs them. The Tibet government, therefore, imposed a total prohibition on any mining that involved digging, permitting only placer mining of gold in Western Tibet. Since 1951 the Chinese Communists have conducted extensive geological surveys throughout Tibet. Reports of their investigations indicate that there are substantial mineral resources. Prohibitive transportation and extraction costs have discouraged the exploitation of these resources, but the extensive iron and coal deposits in northeastern Tibet are reported to be in production.

Transportation. There were virtually no roads in Tibet prior to 1951, and the yak or pony was the principal means of transportation. Indeed, the nondevelopment of transportation facilities was a key factor in the Lhasa authorities' isolation policy. Communist China reversed this policy and embarked on a crash program of road construction throughout Tibet after 1951. The emphasis has been on strategic rather than economic factors, the main objective being to improve communications between China and Tibet and to give China access to key points on the Himalayan border. Two motorable roads now connect China with Tibet from the east and one each from the northeast and northwest. The latter, which cuts across the Aksai Chin area, in dispute between India and China, was a prime factor in the brief border war between those two states in 1962. A road system paralleling the Himalaya along its entire distance also has been constructed. In addition, regular air communications have been established between China and Lhasa, and there are military airfields scattered throughout Tibet.

Trade. Small-scale but highly profitable trade with adjacent countries was an important factor in the pre-1951 Tibetan economy. The principal exports were wool and rock salt, most of which was sent to India and Nepal across the Himalayan passes. Tibet's imports consisted of rice, textiles, and various commodities of small bulk but high value from India and the Himalayan border states, and brick tea, silk brocades, and chinaware from China. The deterioration in Sino-Indian relations in 1960 led to an Indian-imposed trade blockade that has virtually ended the traditional trans-Himalayan commerce.

5. Government

What is usually defined as the traditional Tibetan polity is largely the result of developments in the 17th and 18th centuries. In this period, Tibet was transformed into a theocracy, with a religious official as the head of state and with monastic institutions playing a major role in the secular administration. There were, however, civil officials who held broad powers. Indeed, in some periods they dominated the government.

Traditional Government. The Dalai Lama, an incarnate lama of the Gelugpa sect, was the head of the government. He held absolute powers in theory, but in practice he was constrained by a whole set of customary limitations and by the need to operate through the secular administration. Because each Dalai Lama is supposed to be a reincarnation of the previous one and is discovered in childhood, long minorities were an inescapable part of an incarnate lama system. During such period regents were appointed by the Tsongdu (National Assembly). Monastic officials also held posts in the civil administration at the central, provincial, and district levels. One of the four *kalons* (ministers) of the Kashag (executive committee) was usually a monk, and it was also the practice to assign two governors to each province (except Eastern Tibet) and two *dzongpons* (district officers) to each *dzong* (district)—one a civil and the other a monastic official.

The Tsongdu, composed of the leading civil and monastic officials, was usually summoned only during periods of extreme national crisis. The administration was conducted by the Dalai Lama or his regent. Under the *kalons* were several government bureaus, including departments of military affairs, provincial administration, finance, justice, and foreign affairs. There were four provincial headquarters, each with several districts under its jurisdiction. Villages were administered by headmen, some of whom held their post on a hereditary basis.

Communist Administration. The Chinese Communists made their first major change in the Tibetan system of government in 1956, when they established the Preparatory Committee for the Autonomous Region of Tibet, with the Dalai Lama as chairman. They did not abolish the Tibetan administrative system until March 1959, following the outbreak of a major revolt in Lhasa and the flight of the Dalai Lama to India. The Preparatory Committee then assumed responsibility as the governing body in Tibet, with the Panchen Lama (the prelate second in rank to the Dalai Lama) as acting chairman.

In 1964 the Chinese finally moved against what they termed "rule by a lama." The Dalai Lama was denounced as a traitor and was removed as chairman of the Preparatory Committee. The Panchen Lama, until then considered a puppet of the Chinese, was removed as acting chairman. A more compliant Tibetan, Ngabo, was appointed in his place, but he in turn was removed in 1966, possibly in the wake of the Cultural Revolution. Apparently his post was taken over by a Chinese, Gen. Chang Kuo-hua, who had exercised actual power in Tibet since 1959. Chinese cadres now hold almost all administrative posts in Tibet, and virtually all vestiges of the traditional polity has been destroyed, reportedly even at the village level.

The Dalai Lama maintains in India what amounts to a government-in-exile, though it is not defined as such, and he continues to assert his claims as the head of state of Tibet and as the rightful ruler of the Tibetan people. A new constitution proclaimed by the Dalai Lama in 1963 would become effective if Tibet regained its independence. The Dalai Lama would be retained as head of state, succeeded by his own reincarnation, but all other officials would be elected by popular vote.

MUSEUM OF ANTHROPOLOGY, UNIVERSITY OF MICHIGAN

TEMPLE BANNER shows Buddha Gautama (main figure, upper left) and Tsongkhapa (upper right), founder of Gelugpa sect, with two Buddhist deities (below).

6. History

The history of Tibet prior to the 5th century is derived largely from legends and mythology, though some royal grave mounds may yield supportive evidence if subjected to scientific archaeological research. Probably the dynasty that eventually unified Tibet established its authority in the Yarlung area of southern Tibet by the 3d century.

Early History. The most important king of the Tibetan dynasty was Song-Tsen Gam-po, who ascended the throne in 627. By the time of his death 23 years later, he had expanded his empire to include all of Tibet as well as adjacent areas in Nepal, Sikkhim, India, and China. He also moved the capital to Lhasa, a more strategic location on the main routes to China. Song-Tsen Gam-po married a Nepali and a Chinese princess, thus establishing alliances with both states. The two queens are jointly credited with introducing Buddhism into Tibet, and from then on a primitive form of Buddhism was the court religion during the regnum of most of the Tibetan kings.

With the death of Song-Tsen Gam-po in 650, the alliance with the T'ang dynasty in China collapsed, and the next two centuries were marked by widespread though intermittent war between the two states. Tibet was the dominant power in the area under contention, and in 763 a Tibetan army even captured the T'ang capital, Ch'ang-an. In this period Tibet also contended successfully with the powerful Kashmiri kingdom and with the expansionist Islamic states of Central Asia.

The decline and fall of the Tibetan dynasty in the 9th century were due primarily to the confrontation between Buddhist and Bon forces in

Tibet, which created a schism in the royal family and most other noble families as well. The lack of an effective authority at Lhasa led to the emergence of autonomous principalities. Only with the rise of the Mongols under Genghis Khan was a degree of unity restored in Tibet. The Mongol Prince Godan summoned the head of Sakya monastery in Tsang province in 1247 and invested him with temporal powers over Tibet, to be exercised as the viceroy of the Mongol ruler.

This action coincided with the Mongol conquest of China and marked the inauguration of a "teacher-patron" relationship between the Chinese emperor and a Tibetan religious leader. Under this arrangement the lama was responsible for giving spiritual guidance, and the emperor was obligated to provide him with military and political support.

Rise of the Dalai Lamas. With the erosion of Mongol power in China, the authority of the Sakya Lama also declined in Tibet. In the 14th and 15th centuries, powerful noble families in U and Tsang provinces contended for control of Tibet. The facade of centralized authority was usually maintained, but in fact most local rulers enjoyed considerable autonomy. The traditional rivalry between U and Tsang, over which was now superimposed a struggle for religious and political authority among the various Buddhist sects, prevented a centralized polity, particularly in the absence of effective outside intervention by either the Ming dynasty (1368–1644) in China (the successor to the Mongols) or by its Central Asian rivals.

In this period the incarnate lama system developed in Tibet. The third Gelugpa abbot of Drepung monastery, near Lhasa, was recognized as an incarnate and was given the title of Dalai Lama (by which he is best known outside of Tibet) by the Mongolian ruler Altan Khan in 1578. The resulting alliance between the Gelugpa sect and various Mongol rulers had a great impact on Tibetan history. The "Great Fifth" Dalai Lama (1617–1682), with the indispensable assistance of the Qosot Mongol ruler Gushri Khan, conquered Eastern Tibet (1641) and Tsang (1642). His temporal authority was recognized by Gushri Khan and also by the newly established Ch'ing (Manchu) emperor in China, who invited the Dalai Lama to Peking in 1652. This constituted a revival of the "teacher-patron" relationship, which had been set aside during the Ming dynastic period, and also provided the foundation for the relationship between the two countries until the overthrow of the Ch'ing dynasty in 1911.

China's Claims to Authority. A political crisis that emerged in Tibet in the period after the death of the 5th Dalai Lama was due both to internal dissension within Tibet and to the struggle for control of Central Asia between the Ch'ing emperors and various Mongol rulers. This culminated in the first Chinese military expeditions to Tibet in 1717 and 1719 and to the intrusion of a direct Chinese presence there. A Manchu garrison was stationed at Lhasa, and two Manchu *ambans* (residents) were appointed to the Dalai Lama's court.

The proper interpretation of the relationship between the *ambans* and the Tibetan government is still a subject of controversy. The Tibetans define the role of the *ambans* as essentially diplomatic in character, whereas the Chinese insist that *ambans* exercised supervisory functions. In most instances the *ambans* followed a "low posture" policy, the Tibetan authorities enjoyed virtually full autonomy.

By the middle of the 19th century, Chinese influence in Tibet was greatly reduced, partly because of China's defeat in the Opium War (1839–1842) and because of the T'ai-p'ing rebellion (1850–1864) against Ch'ing rule. China played only an observer role in the war between Tibet and the Dogras of Jammu (1841–1842) and the Tibet-Nepal war (1854–1855), and it provided no military assistance. Treaties were concluded

EASTFOTO

TASHI LHUNPO monastery in Shigatse is the residence of the Panchen Lama. Monastery roofs are decorated with Buddhist motifs.

with both adversaries by the Tibetans, and the ultimate sanction given to these agreements by the Peking court was strictly perfunctory.

The crisis in Tibetan-British Indian relations in the last two decades of the 19th century was a far more serious problem for Tibet than China's claims to authority. Lhasa attempted to maintain an isolationist policy, sometimes using China as a shield when this was expedient and other times ignoring Peking completely. But the British could not be frustrated indefinitely by these tactics, and a military force, the Younghusband expedition, made its way to Lhasa in 1904. The 13th Dalai Lama fled to Mongolia, but the Tibetan officials that remained behind concluded an agreement that ended Tibet's isolation, at least on a limited basis.

London's concern over Russian and Chinese reactions to British India's "forward policy" led to a modification of the terms of agreement. The softening of British demands encouraged the Ch'ing court to make one last effort to bring Tibet under control, and Chinese armies were sent into Eastern Tibet (1906–1909) and then to Lhasa (1910). The Dalai Lama fled again, this time to India, but he returned in 1912 following the overthrow of the Ch'ing dynasty and the expulsion of the Chinese forces from Tibet. The Dalai Lama declared Tibet independent in 1913 and moved to solidify his authority over the border districts in Eastern Tibet. This led to intermittent warfare with China, but a de facto boundary, based on the upper Yangtze River for the most part, was secured.

An attempt to settle this dispute was made at the Simla Conference (1913–1914), to which the British, Tibetan, and Chinese governments sent delegates. China refused to ratify the agreement, however, and continued to claim sovereignty over Tibet. Lhasa was able to maintain its independence and even declared its neutrality in World War II.

Tibet Under Communism. The Chinese Communists, after their victory on the mainland in 1949, announced their intention to "liberate" Tibet and to secure China's "traditional boundaries." Peking moved to make good its threat in October 1950, when Chinese forces attacked the Tibetan garrison in Eastern Tibet. Lhasa appealed to the world for support but was rebuffed or ignored. Tibet therefore accepted China's terms, and an agreement was signed in May 1951 in which Tibet recognized Chinese sovereignty in exchange for a guarantee of limited autonomy.

The Chinese army moved into Central Tibet in 1951, but the structure of the Dalai Lama's government was left relatively intact, and Peking agreed to postpone the introduction of basic changes. The Chinese did attempt to bring Eastern Tibet under their direct administrative control, however, and this move led to the outbreak of a widespread revolt in the area in 1956. When hostilities extended into Central Tibet in 1958, the Chinese strongly pressed the Dalai Lama to use his influence to end the rebellion. The situation in Lhasa reached a crisis in March 1959, with a full-scale spontaneous uprising against the Chinese. The Dalai Lama fled to India, and the Chinese successfully crushed the revolt. A new political and administrative system was then introduced, with Tibet defined in 1965 as an "Autonomous Region of the Chinese People's Republic."

PIX

THE 14TH DALAI LAMA of Tibet is received in India by Prime Minister Jawaharlal Nehru (right).

The Chinese Cultural Revolution in 1966–1967 resulted in another political crisis in Tibet. Red Guard units, organized mainly among Chinese party and government officials in Lhasa, indulged in destructive rampages aimed at obliterating "reactionary" Tibetan cultural heritages, such as shrines and monasteries. The Red Guards were opposed by the Chinese military commander in Tibet, Gen. Chang Kuo-hua. After numerous minor clashes in Lhasa, he emerged victorious, and the predominance of Chinese military authority in Tibet was maintained. From the Chinese and Tibetan accounts, it is apparent that this was a struggle for power strictly between Chinese factions. Tibetans played no role in these events and have no part in other forms of political and administrative activity in Tibet.

LEO E. ROSE
University of California, Berkeley

Bibliography

Bell, Charles, *Tibet: Past and Present* (New York and London 1924).
Dalai Lama, XIVth, *My Land and My People* (New York 1962).
Chögyam Trungpa, *Born in Tibet* (New York 1966).
Ginsburgs, George, and Mathos, Michael, *Communist China and Tibet* (The Hague 1964).
Rahul, Ram, *The Government and Politics of Tibet* (Delhi 1969).
Richardson, Hugh, *A Short History of Tibet* (New York 1962).
Shakabpa, Tsepon W. D., *Tibet: A Political History* (New Haven 1967).
Shen, Tsung-lien, and Liu, Shen-chi, *Tibet and the Tibetans* (Stanford 1953).
Snellgrove, David, and Richardson, Hugh, *A Cultural History of Tibet* (New York 1968).
Tucci, Giuseppe, *Tibetan Painted Scrolls* (Rome 1949).

TIBIA, tib'ē-ə, one of the two bones of the leg between the knee and the ankle. See SKELETON.

TIBULLUS, ti-bul'əs, **Albius** (c. 57–19 B.C.), Roman poet of the Augustan age, who, in Ovid's *Tristia,* is placed second in the canon of elegiac poets. Our meager sources indicate that Tibullus belonged to an equestrian family of means and that he owned property in Latium. He was the most prominent member of the literary circle of the general, orator, and historian Marcus Valerius Messala Corvinus, and he and Messala were close friends. In one of his poems Tibullus says that he accompanied Messala on certain military campaigns, but other passages seem to contradict this claim. His death occurred shortly after Vergil's in 19 B.C.

Four books, containing 36 poems, have survived under Tibullus' name, but only the first two, of 16 poems, are considered genuine. The others are thought to be by lesser members of Messala's circle. Tibullus followed Hellenistic themes. He wrote to the usual fickle mistress, whose name is Delia in Book I and Nemesis in Book II. They are probably the same girl. He also included three poems on his love for a young boy. Other themes are Tibullus' hatred of war and love of peace and country life. There is a mood of melancholy and self-pity in most of the poems, emphasized by the poet's simple, graceful Latin.

EDWARD N. O'NEIL
University of Southern California

TIBURÓN, tē-vōō-rôn', an island of northwestern Mexico, is situated in the northern part of the Gulf of California. It is opposite the coast of Sonora, from which it is separated by a narrow channel. The island, whose name means "shark" in Spanish, is about 30 miles (48 km) long and up to 20 miles (32 km) wide and is largely barren. It is mountainous, rising at one point to about 4,000 feet (1,200 meters). Historically, Tiburón is best known as the home of the fierce Seri Indians, who frequently crossed the channel on balsa rafts to wage war against mainland tribes. Only a handful of the Indians remain on the island, which is otherwise virtually unpopulated.

TIC, a brief, sudden movement or twitch that occurs without being stimulated by an external cause. Although many tics occur on the face, they may also occur in other parts of the body, including the neck, shoulders, trunk, arms, and hands. Breathing and speech tics are also common.

The most prominent feature of a tic is its irresistibility, the victim finding it almost impossible to control. This element of compulsion links tics to the compulsive psychoneuroses. If the person is distracted, a tic may be temporarily arrested. Willpower may suppress a tic for a short time, but longer suppression is difficult and may result in malaise.

It is difficult to draw precise lines between tics, bad habits, and more complicated motor-neuroses. Nose-picking, nail-biting, and air-swallowing are closely related to tics. Behind all these actions is a psychic predisposition, and tics often coexist with mental disorders and emotional instability.

The outlook for treating a tic is determined by psychological as well as physical factors. Tics in children can generally be cured, but older people with well-established tics have a less favorable prognosis. In all cases treatment is through psychiatric care.

RAYMOND L. OSBORNE, M. D.
Mount Sinai Hospital, N. Y.

TIC DOULOUREUX, tik dōō-lə-rōō', is a rare disorder of the trigeminal, or fifth cranial, nerve. This nerve carries sensory impulses from parts of the face and mouth to the brain. It also transmits motor impulses to the chewing muscles of the jaw. In tic douloureux the person has intense spasms of pain at places presumably served by branches of the nerve.

In an attack, the victim of tic douleureux is suddenly seized by a most intense and excruciating crescendo of agony in the cheek or jaw. The face becomes twisted with pain on the affected side, and the cheeks redden, the eyes fill with tears, and saliva drools from the parted jaws. As suddenly as it started, the agony disappears. Certain conditions, such as shaving, smiling, talking, chewing, or blowing the nose, may precipitate an attack. Fortunately, attacks do not occur when the person is sleeping. At the onset of the disorder there may be long periods, even months, between attacks, but gradually they occur more and more frequently, finally several times a day.

The cause of tic douloureux is not known and the best method of treating it is the surgical severing of the trigeminal nerve. Drugs may be used as palliative measures in milder cases or when an operation is not advisable.

RAYMOND L. OSBORNE, M. D.
Mount Sinai Hospital, N. Y.

TICAO, tē-kä'ō, in the Philippines, is the smallest of three islands forming Masbate Province. The others are Masbate and Burias. Ticao, which has an area of 129 square miles (334 sq km), lies between the southeastern tip of Luzon and Masbate Island. Mountains on its west coast shelter Masbate harbor. Its southeastern coast guards San Bernardino Strait, one of the chief navigable passages through the eastern Philippines.

Ticao's eastern shores contain a first-class road connecting the island's four municipalities: Batuan, Monreal, San Fernando, and San Jacinto. Inland, small quantities of rice, sugarcane, abaca, and cotton are raised. River gold is panned, but Ticao's gold deposits are not nearly as large as Masbate's. Population: (1970) 65,000.

LEONARD CASPER
Boston College

TICHBORNE CASE, tich'bûrn, English legal proceedings held to determine the identity of a man claiming to be Roger Charles Tichborne, heir to rich estates in Hampshire and a baronetcy. In 1854, Roger was presumed lost at sea. His younger brother Alfred succeeded their father in 1862 as the 11th baronet, but their mother, Lady Tichborne, believed Roger was alive. She produced in 1867 a claimant from Australia. Although he was unlike Roger in important respects and ignorant of his "mother's" given names, she insisted that he was her son. To Lady Tichborne's testimony was added the obstinate belief of half of England in the claimant's rights.

A hearing in the civil action brought to eject Alfred's son Henry, the 12th baronet, opened on May 11, 1871. When it ended on March 5, 1872, the evidence warranted a criminal trial of the claimant for perjury. The trial, which lasted from April 23, 1873, to Feb. 28, 1874, was the longest in English legal history. The claimant was pronounced by a jury to be Arthur Orton, the son of a London butcher. Yet even after Orton's release from prison in 1884, some people still believed him to be Sir Roger.

GEDDES MACGREGOR
Author of "The Tichborne Impostor"

TICINO, ti-chē'nō, is a canton in southern Switzerland. Called Tessin in French and German, it is extremely mountainous and very beautiful. Lying to the south of the main Alpine ranges, the canton has a warmer and sunnier climate than the rest of Switzerland and is very popular as a winter resort.

Ticino is south of the Lepontine and Rhaetian Alps and consists essentially of the upper Ticino Valley and the mountains lying to the west and east. There is also a prolongation to the south that includes parts of lakes Lugano and Maggiore. The Ticino River, which is harnessed for hydroelectric power, flows southward into Italy. West of the Ticino Valley are the Ticino Alps, and to the east are the Adula Alps, whose highest point is 11,175 feet (3,425 meters). To the north the border follows the mountain crest, which dips to 6,929 feet (2,110 meters) at the St. Gotthard pass, leading to the northern cantons.

The canton covers an area of about 1,085 square miles (2,810 sq km), of which about one fourth is forest. Agriculture is of minor importance, except for the cultivation of grape vines. Bellinzona is the cantonal capital. Locarno and Lugano, the only other important towns, are primarily resorts.

Ticino is predominantly Italian-speaking and Roman Catholic. It represents the remains of conquests made south of the Alps by the Swiss cantons in the 15th and early 16th centuries. It was not until 1803, however, that the territory was organized as a full member of the Swiss Confederation. Population: (1968 est.) 237,000.

NORMAN J. G. POUNDS, *Indiana University*

TICINO RIVER, ti-chē'nō, a river in Switzerland and Italy. The Ticino, which is 154 miles (248 km) long, is a source of hydroelectricity in Switzerland and is used for irrigation in Italy. It rises in the Swiss Alps in northwestern Ticino canton and flows southeast and west to enter Lake Maggiore. From the lake it runs southeast to join the Po River below Pavia. Hannibal, after crossing the Alps in 218 B.C., defeated Scipio near the river, called Ticinus by the Romans.

TICK, a large acarine that lives ectoparasitically on the blood of mammals, birds, amphibians, and reptiles. Although ticks are sometimes thought to be insects, they belong to the order Acarina of the class Arachnida. Insects belong to the class Insecta.

Ticks are widely distributed throughout the world but are most abundant in tropical and subtropical regions. They range in body length from the .05 inch (1.2 mm) unengorged *Ixodes soricis* to the 1.1 inch (28 mm) engorged *Amblyomma varium,* the largest species known. Like their close relations the mites, ticks have four pairs of legs. Insects have only three pairs.

Tick Infestation. Common manifestations of tick infestation include illness due to blood loss and tick paralysis. In addition, some ticks are carriers of disease: in man, Rocky Mountain spotted fever, Colorado tick fever, tularemia, and relapsing fever; in domestic animals, anaplasmosis, babesiosis, equine and St. Louis encephalitis, Q fever, spirochetosis, and toxoplasmosis.

In man, tick paralysis is probably the most important disorder caused by ticks. It results from ticks' attaching themselves and feeding along the spinal column or at the base of the skull. A neurotoxin, which is injected into the blood as they feed, is believed to cause the paralysis. Signs of tick paralysis include loss of reflexes, paralysis, and respiratory failure. Although the symptoms are of a progressive nature, they usually disappear rapidly when the ticks are removed, rarely leaving any aftereffects.

A tick should not be removed by pulling it off the body. Instead, a hot object or some alcohol, chloroform, or ether should be applied to its body until the tick releases its mouthparts. Insecticide powders may also be used.

Types of Ticks. Ticks are divided into two major groups: the hard, or scutate, ticks (family Ixodidae) and the soft, or nonscutate, ticks (family Argasidae). Hard ticks are characterized by a hard dorsal scutum that covers the anterior part of the body in the female and immature tick and completely covers the body of the adult male. Hard ticks also have the capitulum (mouthparts) protruding forward. Soft ticks lack a scutum and have a leathery body. Also, the capitulum of soft ticks is in a slightly different position so that it cannot be seen from above.

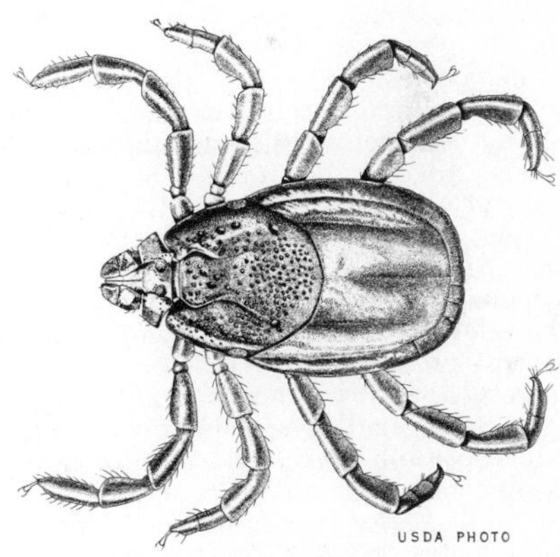

USDA PHOTO

Brown dog tick

Fowl tick

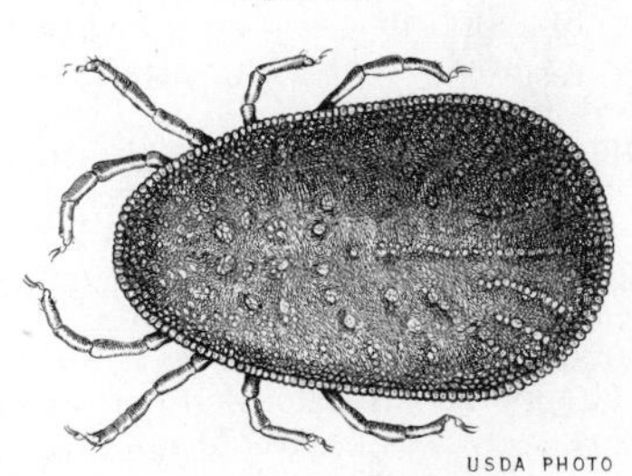

USDA PHOTO

ERIC HOSKING

Tickbird, or red-billed oxpecker

There are 16 species of soft ticks in the United States. Probably the most troublesome are the fowl tick (*Argas persicus*) and the ear tick (*Otobius megnini*). Of the 50 species of hard ticks in the United States the most troublesome include the American dog tick (*Dermacentor variabilis*), the winter tick (*D. albipictus*), the brown dog tick (*Rhipicephalus sanguineus*), the cattle tick (*Boophilus annulatus*), the Gulf coast tick (*Amblyomma maculatum*), and the lone star tick (*A. americanum*).

Life Cycle. The life cycle of a tick varies slightly among the different species but follows a general pattern. Like some insects, ticks have four life cycle stages: egg, larva, nymph, and adult.

In all species the female deposits her eggs on the ground or in sheltered places. Each egg hatches into an active, 6-legged larva, which is sometimes called a *seed tick*. The larva climbs onto a plant or other object and then attaches itself to any suitable host with which it comes in contact. After feeding on the host the larva either remains on the host or drops off and molts into the 8-legged nymph. The nymph then seeks a new host or remains on the same one. After it is engorged with the host's blood, the nymph drops to the ground or remains on the host and molts to the adult stage. Hard ticks have only one nymph stage, but soft ticks may have several.

The adults, after engorging with blood, mate, and the females lay their eggs. Some ticks, such as the fowl tick, lay a few hundred eggs, return to the host for another meal, and then lay more eggs. This process may be repeated several times. Most hard ticks lay a single batch of eggs consisting of 3,000 to 6,000 eggs. Male ticks die after mating and females die after laying their eggs.

An interesting aspect of the life-span is the tick's ability to withstand long periods of time without feeding on a host. Adults of the American dog tick have been kept alive without food for 3 years. Nymphs have survived unfed for more than 6 months and larvae have survived unfed for 11 months. Adults of other species may live as long as 10 years without feeding.

RALPH H. DAVIDSON, *Ohio State University*

TICKBIRD, either of two species of starlings that remove parasitic ticks and insects from the hides of large, hoofed mammals in central, eastern, and southern African grasslands and savannas. They are also known as "oxpeckers."

Both species—the yellow-billed tickbird (*Buphagus africanus*) and the red-billed tickbird (*B. erythrorhynchus*)—are about 9 inches (23 cm) long and have strong, laterally flattened beaks, pointed wings, strong feet with sharp claws, and stiff, longish tails. They have red or red-and-yellow beaks and dark-brown plumage, lighter below.

To find the blood-gorged ticks, flies, and fly larvae on which they feed, tickbirds crawl on the bodies of rhinoceroses, giraffes, buffaloes, and other wild hoofed mammals as well as domestic cattle. The birds nest in cavities in trees or rocks or under the eaves of thatched roofs. The three to five eggs are white, pale blue, or pinkish.

The two species of tickbirds make up the subfamily Buphaginae of the starling family (Sturnidae), order Passeriformes.

CARL WELTY
Beloit College

TICK FEVER is a name applied to several tick-borne diseases. See COLORADO TICK FEVER; TEXAS FEVER.

TICK TREFOIL, tik′ trē′foil, any of a group of mostly tropical weedy plants with small pea-like flowers and jointed pods that cling like burs to clothing and animal fur. Tick trefoils are found throughout the United States except for the Pacific coast.

Nearly all the tick trefoils grow in dry woods and fields, and some are grown as forage plants. They are sometimes also grown in borders and wild gardens.

Tick trefoils make up the genus *Desmodium* of the legume family (Leguminosae). The species *D. purpureum*, also known as beggarweed, is cultivated as a forage and cover crop in the southern United States. The telegraph plant, *D. gyrans*, is an Asian species grown as a curiosity for its jerking leaflets. Two weedy species in the eastern United States are the hoary tick clover, *D. canadense*, and the Spanish tick clover, *D. tortuosum*.

J. A. YOUNG
U. S. Department of Agriculture

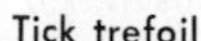

Tick trefoil

JOHN H. GERARD, FROM NATIONAL AUDUBON SOCIETY

TICKELL, tik′əl, **Thomas** (1686–1740), English poet. He was born in Bridekirk and educated at Oxford. His friend the writer Joseph Addison introduced him to the world of letters, and when Addison became secretary of state in 1717 he made Tickell undersecretary. Tickell also served as secretary to the lords justices of Ireland from about 1724 until his death, in Bath on April 23, 1740.

In 1715, Tickell published his translation of the first book of Homer's *Iliad,* at about the same time that Alexander Pope's version appeared. Addison praised Tickell's translation as the better one, and Pope falsely accused Addison of being the real translator. Tickell's other works include a long poem, *Kensington Gardens* (1722), and the ballad *Colin and Lucy.* As a poet, Tickell is remembered chiefly for his elegy to Addison, prefaced to his edition of Addison's works (1721).

TICKING is a rugged, small-twill-weave, loom-finished fabric. It may be recognized by its alternating stripes of white and colored yarns. Loom-finished fabrics (chambray, canvas, denim) are sold as they come from the loom, without further treatment. Typical ticking has a texture of 64 ends (lengthwise yarns) of 12s warp and 50 picks (crosswise yarns) of 14s filling per square inch. It is one of the strongest cottons made and is highly resistant to abrasion.

Hickory stripe is similar to ticking but of lesser quality. It is lower in texture and softer in feel.

GEORGE E. LINTON
Author of "The Modern Textile Dictionary"

TICKNOR, George (1791–1871), American teacher and literary historian. Born in Boston, Mass., on Aug. 1, 1791, into an old and wealthy New England family, he was financially able to pursue his intellectual interests. At 14 he joined Dartmouth's junior class, graduating in 1807. Abandoning law studies, Ticknor toured America and in 1815 began a 4-year visit to Europe. He attended the University of Göttingen, which opened him to the innovations and excitement of German scholarship. Offered a Harvard professorship of French and Spanish literature in 1817, Ticknor mastered the fields by further study in Italy, France, and Spain. His elegant lectures won student favor, but his colleagues, accustomed to a narrow curriculum, resisted Ticknor's efforts to introduce specialized groupings of studies into the undergraduate program. But he did create a separate language department, the basis for curriculum reform in American universities.

Ticknor retired from teaching in 1835 and began his life's work, the *History of Spanish Literature* (3 vols.), published in 1849 and, after a number of editions, placed in definitive form in 1872. Now considered dated, the work easily surpassed previous surveys of the subject. Ticknor died in Boston on Jan. 26, 1871.

BERTRAM WYATT-BROWN
Case Western Reserve University

TICKSEED, any of several plants whose barbed seeds cling to the hair of animals or to clothing and are dispersed in this manner. Tickseeds make up two closely related genera, *Bidens* and *Coreopsis,* of the composite family (Compositae).

Plants of the genus *Bidens* are also commonly known as "tickseeds," "bur marigolds," "sticktights," and "beggar-ticks." Some have daisylike heads of yellow or white ray flowers and yellow disk flowers, while others have only disk flowers. They grow mostly in moist places throughout North America and are seldom raised in flower gardens. Plants of the genus *Coreopsis* are cultivated both as garden and for cut flowers. The annual species sometimes known as "calliopsis" are often raised for their yellow, maroon, and crimson flower heads.

J. A. YOUNG
U. S. Department of Agriculture

TICONDEROGA, ti-kon-dər-o′gə, a village in northeastern New York, in Essex county, is 100 miles (160 km) north of Albany. The surrounding area raises truck and dairy products and apples. The principal industry of the village is fine paper making. Ticonderoga is also an all-year resort.

Strategically situated between Lake George and Lake Champlain, Ticonderoga controlled the route between the Hudson River valley and Canada in the wars of the 18th century. Fort Ticonderoga was built there in 1755, and the area was the scene of fighting by the Indians, French, British, and Americans. A notable encounter was the Battle of Ticonderoga in July 1758, when the French garrison repulsed a British attack on the fort.

Mementos of the past include restored Fort Ticonderoga and its museum and Fort Mount Hope museum. Mt. Defiance, a rocky peak outside the village, is another historic site.

Ticonderoga was settled on the Indian portage between the lakes. Its Indian name, *Cheonderoga,* is sometimes translated as "place between the waters." The first white settlement was made about 1763. Ticonderoga was incorporated as a village in 1889. Government is by mayor and council. Population: 3,568.

COURTNAY KING MORTON
Ticonderoga Public Library

TICUNA, tē-kōō′nə, a tribe of Indians found in the tropical forests of Brazil and Peru in the Upper Amazon region. The Ticuna, or Tucuna, subsist mainly on crops of manioc and maize, by fishing, and by hunting with firearms, which have replaced blowguns—once their major weapons. Ticuna villages are semipermanent, consisting of a large communal house and a few smaller houses. Social and political organization is based on patrilineal kinship ties. Their religion includes the common South American belief in a culture hero-creator. The Ticuna produce bark cloth, baskets, pottery, and dugout canoes, which are supplemented in the 20th century with the importation of some modern materials and implements.

TIDAL BORE. See TIDE–*Tidal Actions.*

TIDAL MARSH, or salt marsh, a sheltered plant-grown shore area periodically flooded by tidal action. A distinction is made between tidal marshes and tidal flats, the latter being sandy or muddy tide-flooded, level areas without plants. Tidal marshes are formed in areas where there is sufficient protection from waves and currents to permit sediments to accumulate and support a growth of seawater-resistant plants.

Tidal marsh soil is a muddy peat composed of the accumulated remains of marsh plants and a mixture of mud and sand brought into the area by tides. It is salty, saturated with water, and usually completely deficient in oxygen (anoxic).

Marsh Plants. Very few plants can live with their roots in oxygen-free salty water. However, some higher plants have adapted to the rigorous marsh conditions by evolving the ability to accumulate salt in their tissues, a condition that resists the high osmotic concentration of seawater, and by developing the capability of transporting oxygen to their roots through their stems.

Two such adapted grasses—smooth cord grass (*Spartina alterniflora*), which grows from mean tide level to high water, and marsh hay (*S. patens*), which grows at high water level—dominate temperate-region tidal marshes. The succulent *Salicornias* (glasswort, samphire) are another conspicuous element of temperate tidal marsh flora. In tropical areas, tidal marshes are dominated by mangrove trees (in Florida, *Rhizophora mangle*). Algae may grow on the surface of the soil, and often photosynthetic purple bacteria are abundant enough to color sandy areas.

Marsh Animals. Fiddler crabs and mud crabs, algae-eating snails of the family Littorinidae, and ribbed mussels are the most conspicuous animals on the surface of the tidal marsh soil. Annelid worms and amphipods are common in the mud. Insects, including mosquitoes and biting flies, are abundant. Among birds and mammals, wrens, sparrows, rails, mice, and, in the Americas, raccoons are regular inhabitants. Killifish and the young of many coastal ocean fishes and invertebrates spend at least part of their life cycle in tidal marshes.

Productivity. Tidal marshes are one of the most productive natural systems on earth. They produce two to ten times more living mass than coastal waters or uplands. This high productivity is maintained by the accumulation of plant nutrients from both land and sea, by the presence of a solid substratum to hold the nutrients and support the plants, by the high rate of turnover of plant and animal materials, and by the combination of both algal and higher plant growth.

JOHN M. TEAL
Woods Hole Oceanographic Institution

TIDAL POWER. See HYDROELECTRIC POWER—*Installed Capacity and Potential Resources;* RANCE TIDAL WORKS.

TIDAL WAVE, an unusually large sea wave produced by an underwater earthquake, a landslide, or volcanic activity. Such waves can be enormously destructive in coastal regions. The term "tidal wave" is a misnomer because the waves have nothing to do with tidal action. The term "tsunami," which has been adopted to avoid this error, is the Japanese word for the phenomenon of seismic sea waves. See also EARTHQUAKE—*Effects of Earthquakes.*

TIDDLYWINKS, a table game for two or more players, consists of snapping, or hopping, plastic disks into a cup. The disks, or winks, are ⅞ inch in diameter and 0.057 inch thick. A larger disk, or tiddly, is used as a shooter. Sets of four winks and a shooter come in different colors. The cup has a diameter of 1½ inches and sides 1½ inches high. Players start with their four winks in line and equidistant from the cup, which is centrally placed. The object of the competition is to be the first player to snap, or hop, four winks into the cup.

Players first draw for order of shooting and choice of color of winks. Then, in turn, each presses the edge of his shooter, held between thumb and forefinger, against the edge of a wink, causing it to snap into the air. If the wink hops into the cup, the player immediately gets an extra turn. If it lands on the table, he takes his next shot from the new location. A wink leaving the table is replaced where it went off the edge. The game requires a considerable amount of manual skill and dexterity to control the flight of the winks.

Players may use a numbered scoring frame that fits around the cup. Numbers are marked in spaces on the frame. A wink into the cup counts 25 while those on the frame count 5 to 15 as indicated and they are not moved again. The player with the highest score wins. The game may be played on a rug or carpet as well as on a table.

FRANK K. PERKINS
Boston "Herald"

SALT MARSH AT LOW TIDE during winter on Cape Cod Bay. The marsh soil is a muddy peat that supports plants that are resistant to the effects of seawater.

NATIONAL FILM BOARD OF CANADA, PHOTOS BY G. BLOUIN

Low and high tide at Parrsboro, Nova Scotia. Tides in the Bay of Fundy area are as high as 70 feet (21 meters).

TIDE, the periodic motion of the waters of the sea, caused by the attractive forces of the moon and the sun. Tidal motion is most readily noted along a beach that is periodically bared at low tide and then covered by the succeeding high tide.

Methods for tidal prediction were developed primarily as an aid to mariners. For example, a ship may ride too deep in the water to clear a sand bar except at high tide. Therefore, tables of predicted tides are needed to supplement the depth data on a nautical chart. Similarly, tidal currents may help or hinder the ship's progress, so that tables of predicted tidal currents may also be needed. In addition, tides are important in many engineering projects, such as pollution studies, harbor channel maintenance, and power generation.

If the earth were moonless, the tides would be caused by the sun alone and would be much simpler to predict. The tides would occur at about the same time each day, and the difference between high and low tide would be considerably smaller. The changes in tidal height from day to day would also be very much smaller, the principal variations being associated with the annual cycles of varying distance and declination of the sun.

TIDAL ACTIONS

Tides are caused primarily by the moon's gravitational attraction and tend to follow the lunar day of 24 hours and 50 minutes, which is the average time between the moon's transits over any given meridian of longitude on earth.

There are two tides a day at most places, marking the passing of the high-water crests below the moon and on the side of the earth opposite the moon. Thus the time between successive high waters averages 12 hours and 25 minutes. At a very few places in the world, such as Port Adelaide on the southern coast of Australia, the solar tide is dominant, and the average time between successive high waters is 12 hours. The range in height between high and low waters is less than a foot in some areas. In others, such as the Bay of Fundy in Nova Scotia, the tidal range may be as great as 50 feet (15 meters).

Kinds of Tides. Tides are ordinarily classified as semidiurnal, diurnal, or mixed.

When there are two high tides and two low tides each lunar day, and the differences in height between pairs of successive high waters and successive low waters are relatively small, the tide is called *semidiurnal.* Tides on the Atlantic coast of the United States are representative semidiurnal tides.

In areas of *diurnal* tides there is only one high tide and one low tide each lunar day, except possibly for a few days during the month when the moon is near the equator. The tide at Pensacola, Fla., on the northern shore of the Gulf of Mexico, is a typical diurnal tide.

With a *mixed* tide, both diurnal and semidiurnal oscillations are important. There is a significant inequality in either the two high-water heights or the two low-water heights in a lunar day, or sometimes in both pairs of heights. The tides along the Pacific coast of the United States are mixed.

Tidal Current. The tide is a three-dimensional phenomenon, affecting water at depth as well as at the surface. Therefore there are horizontal changes, called *tidal currents,* that correspond to the rise and fall of tides.

In river mouths or in straits where the direction of flow is restricted, the tidal current reverses during the lunar day. That is, it flows alternately in opposite directions, with a short period of little or no current at each reversal that is called *slack water.* The tidal current flowing from the ocean into a river is called *flood current,* and the current flowing in the opposite direction is called *ebb current.*

In the ocean there are tidal currents offshore that flow continuously, changing in direction through all points of the compass during a tidal period. These are called *rotary currents.* A diagram showing a series of arrows from a common center, representing the speed and direction of the rotary current each hour, is called a *current rose,* and a curve connecting the ends of the arrows is called a *current ellipse.* Just as with tides, tidal currents may be semidiurnal, diurnal, or mixed.

Bore. The speed of progress of the crest of a tide varies directly as the square root of the water depth over which it is passing. Thus the speed is decreased when the wave enters shallow water. Since the water depth at the trough is more shallow than at the crest, the retardation is greater, and the slope of the wave front is steepened. This means that the time from low tide to high tide becomes less than the following time period from high tide to low tide. In a few estuaries with large tidal ranges and a sloping riverbed, the advance of the low-water

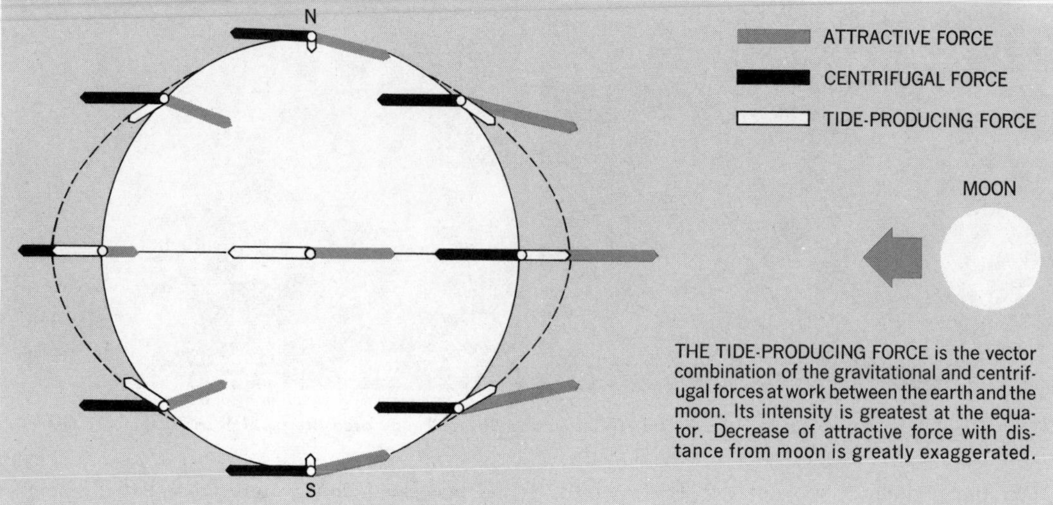

THE TIDE-PRODUCING FORCE is the vector combination of the gravitational and centrifugal forces at work between the earth and the moon. Its intensity is greatest at the equator. Decrease of attractive force with distance from moon is greatly exaggerated.

trough is so retarded that the crest of the rising tide virtually overtakes it. The crest then advances upstream as a turbulent wall of water, called a *bore*. On days when the tide range is large, there is a bore in the Petitcodiac River in the Bay of Fundy.

Nontidal Phenomena. Other phenomena that are sometimes noted on tide gauge records include tsunamis, storm surges, and seiches. A *tsunami*, or "tidal wave," is a series of long waves, usually caused by a seismic displacement of the sea floor. The waves travel across the ocean at speeds as great as 500 miles (800 km) per hour, sometimes building up to destructive heights as they move into the slopes of a coastal region. See also EARTHQUAKE–*Effects of Earthquakes*.

Storm surges are rises in sea level that are caused by hurricane winds piling water onto a coast. A *seiche* is a stationary or standing wave that is caused by strong winds or by changes in atmospheric pressure over closed basins. Seiches have periods ranging from a few minutes to possibly more than an hour.

THE FORMATION OF TIDES

In analyzing the ways in which tides form, it is convenient to study a theoretical "equilibrium tide" by developing a mathematical approach that uses a set of assumptions known to be fictitious. The assumptions specify that the earth is covered by a uniformly deep layer of water, and that these waters respond instantly to the tide-producing forces of the moon and sun to form a "surface of equilibrium," disregarding friction and inertia. Although the actual tides are quite different, this approach permits the determination of the astronomical periods that are important to tides. It thereby facilitates analysis of tide observations and the subsequent predictions based on empirical findings.

Calculation of the tide-producing force can also be simplified if the complex motions of the 3-body earth-moon-sun system are separated into the relatively simpler motions of the 2-body systems of earth-moon and earth-sun.

Tides and the Moon. The moon attracts every particle of matter in the earth, its ocean, and its atmosphere. The attractive force in effect is directed toward the center of the moon and is inversely proportional to the square of the distance between the particle and the moon's center. If the distances of two points on the earth from the moon's center are unequal, the attractive forces at the two points are similarly unequal. The tide-producing force does not represent the attractive force itself. It represents the *difference* in attractive forces, and it varies approximately inversely as the cube of the distance to the center of the moon.

If no other force besides gravitational attraction acted on the earth-moon system, earth and moon would simply come together. However, there is also a centrifugal force at work that is equal and opposite to the gravitational force at the center of the earth. Thus the net force acting on any particle is the vector combination of these two forces. Furthermore, unlike the gravitational force, the centrifugal force is equal and in the same direction for every particle on earth. Whereas the gravitational force is directed toward the center of the moon, the centrifugal force is directed away from the moon in a direction that is always parallel to the imaginary line connecting the centers of the earth and the moon. Where this line intersects the crust of the earth on the moonward side, there is a net force directed toward the moon along the line. Where the line intersects the earth's crust on the side away from the moon, there is a net force directed away from the moon.

If the tide-producing forces at all points on the earth's surface are resolved into vertical and horizontal forces, it is readily demonstrated that the vertical forces in line with the gravitational field of the earth have little effect (see diagram). Instead it is the horizontal forces unopposed by the earth's gravity that draw particles of water over the earth's surface, thereby piling up high-water bulges under and opposite to the moon. That is, the high waters are not caused by any lifting of the water against the force of the earth's gravity, but rather by horizontal tractive forces unopposed by gravity.

Tidal Periods. The simplest concept of the earth-moon system is that the moon revolves around the earth once each month in a circular orbit that is in the plane of the earth's equator. As the earth rotates on its axis once every 24 hours, there is a high-water bulge under the moon, another bulge on the side away from the moon, and a low-water trough on either side of the earth between the bulges. The half lunar day of 12 hours and 25 minutes is the time interval between successive high tides or low tides, and it is the most important period in tidal studies.

In actuality the moon does not go around the earth in a circular orbit, but rather in an elliptical one. Two weeks after it is at *perigee*, the point in its orbit when it is closest to the earth, the moon is at *apogee*, the point farthest from the earth. Because the tide-producing force is inversely proportional to the cube of the distance to the center of the moon, the tidal range is greater than average by about 20% at perigee and smaller than average by about 20% at apogee. To account for this, the tidal mathematician introduces another semidaily tide whose period is such that it is in phase with, or reinforces, the lunar tide at perigee—"perigean tide"—and is out of phase with, or opposed to, the lunar tide at apogee—"apogean tide."

Another complicating factor is that the moon does not remain in the plane of the earth's equator. Instead it moves from an extreme northern declination across the equator to an extreme southern declination and back again, the cycle taking about 27 solar days. When the moon is at its extreme northern or southern declinations, the two tidal bulges are no longer centered on the equator. For example, if the high water under the moon has its maximum in the Northern Hemisphere, the maximum on the opposite side of the earth has its center in the Southern Hemisphere. Thus, as the earth rotates on its axis, a given point on the surface may experience two high—and two low—waters, but they are at different heights. The difference in height caused by the moon's change in declination is called the *diurnal high-water inequality*.

When the moon is at its extreme declination, the larger diurnal ranges—that is, the difference between the heights of the higher high tide and the lower low tide—are called *tropic tides*. The smaller diurnal ranges that occur when the moon is on the equator are called *equatorial tides*.

To simulate the declination period of the moon, the tidal mathematician uses two diurnal tides that are in phase when the moon is at either extreme northern or extreme southern declination and are opposed when the moon is on the equator. The two tides are also such that the sum of their speeds exactly equals the speed of the lunar semidaily tide.

Tides and the Sun. As with the moon, the sun attracts every particle of the ocean and earth. In the earth-sun system there are solar tides under the sun and on the opposite side of the earth. They are smaller and occur at different times than lunar tides. The solar high waters are about 12 hours apart as the earth rotates on its axis. Although the sun's mass is nearly 27 million times the mass of the moon, the distance of its center from the earth is about 390 times that of the moon's distance. Therefore the solar semidaily tide is only 46% that of the lunar semidaily tide.

At new and full moon, both sun and moon are lined up so that the lunar and solar tides reinforce each other. The larger tidal ranges that result are called *spring tides*. In contrast, at first and last quarters of the moon the lunar and solar tides are opposed, and the smaller combined tides that result are called *neap tides*.

The range of the solar tide also varies annually between *perihelion* and *aphelion*, the points in the earth's orbit closest to and farthest from the sun, respectively. In addition a diurnal inequality is introduced because of the annual declinational cycle of the sun. These and other, smaller astronomical refinements are introduced in equilibrium theory by simulated tides of appropriate periods.

Earth and Atmospheric Tides. Unlike the familiar ocean tides, the occurrence of tides in the earth and in the atmosphere is not commonly known. The mechanisms causing these three kinds of tides are quite different.

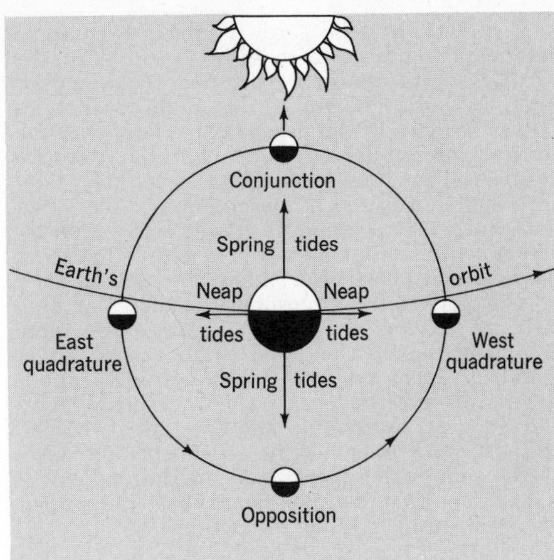

COMBINED EFFECT OF SUN AND MOON on tidal ranges varies according to their positions relative to the earth. Small neap tides occur when the three bodies are aligned. Large spring tides occur when sun and moon are at right angles to the earth.

A TIDAL BULGE of the oceans would occur directly below the moon if the earth were frictionless (A), but the friction of the ocean basins tends to drag the bulge forward as the earth rotates (B). The net result of gravitational pull and friction is that the tidal bulge moves slightly ahead of the moon (C).

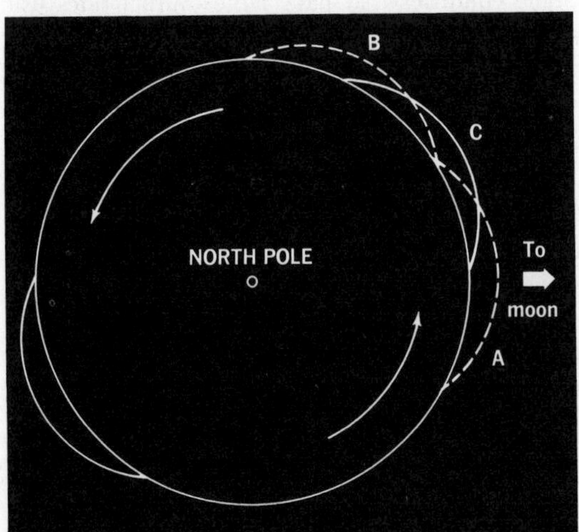

Although the solid earth is subject to periodic deformations similar to those for ocean tides, the particles in the earth's crust cannot be moved freely by horizontal forces into high-tide bulges, as the particles in the oceans can. Therefore the vertical tide-producing forces are the effective mechanism for tides in the solid earth. The tides are usually measured by observation of the variations in the acceleration of gravity and by observation of the variations in the vertical—that is, in the direction in which a plumb line points.

Concerning the atmosphere, analyses of long series of barometric records indicate that there are small lunar tides and significantly larger semidaily solar tides. In low latitudes, atmospheric pressure tends to be high about 10 A. M. and 10 P. M. local time, and low about 4 A. M. and 4 P. M. Although some aspects of the causes of the solar atmospheric tide are unresolved, it is apparent that thermal factors are the principal mechanism causing these tides.

DEVELOPMENT OF TIDAL STUDIES

For centuries tides were measured by visual observations, such as of the level of water on a vertical graduated staff or plank. Automatic tide gauges that record the level of a float in a vertical well are believed to have been introduced about 1830. The float-type gauge is still in general use at most tide stations. Pressure-measuring devices placed on the sea floor have also been developed, but relatively few are yet in use.

Tidal Theory. A few references to tides appear in ancient Greek and Roman writings. Tidal theory essentially originated in the 17th century with Isaac Newton, who applied the laws of gravitation to develop a theoretical equilibrium tide. However, because the connection between the moon and tides was rather obvious, useful tide predictions were produced by rule-of-thumb methods independent of the development of tidal theory. The methods of calculations were considered a family secret to be passed on from father to son. The *Liverpool Tide Tables* by a clergyman named Moses Holden is an outstanding example.

In 1831, John Lubbock used then-existing tidal theory to develop a "nonharmonic" method of tide prediction, as contrasted to the harmonic method described below. He modified time and height predictions of high and low waters based on times of lunar transit by making corrections for the "age" of the moon in the cycle from one new moon to the next, and also by correcting for the declination and parallax of the moon and the sun.

In the late 18th century the French mathematician and astronomer Pierre Laplace formulated the equations of motion for tides on a rotating earth. Subsequent significant contributions were made by George Airy, Lord Kelvin, and George Darwin in Britain and by William Ferrel and Rollin A. Harris in the United States. By the beginning of the 20th century, the tide-prediction technique known as the harmonic method was in general use by the various government tidal agencies throughout the world.

The Harmonic Method. In the harmonic method an observed tide record is first broken down into a number of cosine curves, with each curve representing a significant astronomic period. The derived amplitude and the time lag of each cosine curve apply uniquely to the specific geographic location where the observations were obtained. The individual cosine curves are adjusted in time according to the astronomic events prevailing at the time of the desired predictions. The cosine curves then are added together so that predicted times and heights of high and low waters can be read from the composite cosine curve.

The harmonic method is empirical. It uses equilibrium theory primarily to identify the significant tidal frequencies and to provide a phase reference for each of these frequencies at any time in the past or the future.

The U. S. Coast and Geodetic Survey used 37 tidal constituents—harmonic elements in the mathematical expression for the tide-producing force—on its mechanical tide-predicting machine built in 1910. The gearing on the machine included tidal frequencies ranging from 8 cycles per day to 1 cycle per year. The predicting machine at the Liverpool Tidal Institute included 60 constituents, the greater number being partly related to the nonlinear tides in shallow waters around the British Isles.

Establishment of Datum Planes. In general, tide tables were developed to supplement the depth information on nautical charts. To be able to add chart soundings and table predictions readily by algebraic means, so that depths could be ascertained at a particular time, it became necessary to relate the charts and tables to a particular *datum*, or base reference. There is an international agreement to the effect that the datum of a nautical chart should be so low that the tide seldom, if ever, falls below that level. The practical advantage of such a datum is that the navigator, without consulting a tide table, can count on at least the depth shown on the chart at all times.

However, for various legal and historical reasons, the U. S. Coast and Geodetic Survey does not use a chart datum that low. Instead it uses *mean low water*, the average height of low waters over a 19-year period, on the eastern coast of the United States. On the western coast it uses *mean lower low water*, the average height of the lower of the two low waters each day over a 19-year period—approximately the period required for the regression of the moon's nodes to complete a circuit of 360° in longitude.

Many European countries use *mean low water springs*, or the average low water near times of new and full moon, as their datum. Some countries that have large diurnal tides use *mean Indian spring low water*, which is the average of the lower low tides on days when the moon is new or full and is also near its maximum declination. The name derives from investigation of the tides of India.

TIDAL STUDY TODAY

Methods of tidal analysis and prediction had reached so high a level of achievement by the beginning of the 20th century that procedures remained relatively unchanged for more than 50 years, until the development of electronic computers. Thus, although in 1921 the British oceanographer Arthur Doodson published a greatly expanded study of the equilibrium tide that included about 400 constituents, these additional constituents were not used for practical tide predictions. The increased accuracy from the effort would have been small, and the increased friction in an enlarged mechanical predicting machine would have been too great.

Computer Techniques. In the 1960's changes brought about by the development of electronic computers were made in all aspects of tidal observation, analysis, and prediction. Digital recorders have been installed on automatic tide gauges, providing sequential, point-to-point values of the height of a given tide. These data are routinely processed on computers to calculate the times and heights of high and low waters, mean ranges and inequalities, various tidal planes and monthly extremes, and the lunitidal intervals—the intervals between the moon's transit over the local or Greenwich meridian and the following high or low water.

New analysis procedures have been developed for obtaining the amplitude and phase lag for each constituent of the tide. For example, a "least square" procedure has been programmed for large computers. This procedure solves for all constituents simultaneously, in contrast to the traditional Fourier analysis for one constituent at a time, which eliminates the effects of the other constituents from each result. (See HARMONIC ANALYSIS.) The newer procedure has been found to fit the recorded data somewhat more accurately. In addition, unlike Fourier analysis, it does not require an unbroken sequence of data equally spaced in time.

Electronic computers permit the specification of any frequencies in the prediction process, whereas the mechanical tide-predicting machines were limited to a finite set of frequencies for which appropriate gears were included in the basic design. In both Britain and the United States, studies of the prediction of shallow-water tides by harmonic methods exploited this newly found flexibility, using about 115 tidal constituents to permit more accurate analysis and prediction.

Research studies have used long series of data, for example, a list of 500,000 hourly readings of tidal heights taken over a 50-year period, to establish values of the *continuum*—the "noise," or nonpredictable variations in sea level—as a function of frequency. Determination of these values establishes the limits that may be achieved by even the best predicting procedures. Studies of this kind are also impossible without the use of electronic computers.

In addition, geophysicists Walter Munk of the United States and David Cartwright of Britain developed a "response" method of tide prediction. Weights are computed for a set of time-variable spherical harmonics of the gravitational potential and of radiant flux on the earth's surface to obtain an optimum fit to an observed series of tide heights. For predictions at another time, the same set of weights are then applied to a time series for the gravitational and radiational potentials for the required times.

Study of Worldwide Tidal Patterns. There are ordinarily about 1,000 tide gauges operating around the world at any given time. But for describing global patterns of the tide they could hardly be more poorly distributed. Most of them are at the mouths of harbors and on rivers, places for which tide predictions are a practical necessity. However, because the coastal features may severely modify both the amplitude and the phase of the ocean tide, the harbor and river observations have very limited use in attempts to depict tidal phenomena in the oceans.

Nevertheless, men have attempted for more than a century to use these data, together with data gathered around islands, in preparing cotidal charts and co-range charts of the world. A *cotidal chart* is a set of lines on a chart, each line joining all points at which high water occurs at the same time. Similarly, a *co-range chart* has lines passing through places of equal tidal range. These charts are used in describing only a single harmonic constituent of the tide, so that in theory a chart would be needed for each constituent. In practice, however, charts have been attempted only for the major constituents: the lunar semidaily, solar semidaily, lunar-solar daily, and lunar daily. The principal effort has been applied to lunar semidaily charts, and the preparation of cotidal charts has received more attention than co-range charts.

The most critical aspect of cotidal charts is the location of *amphidromic points*. These are no-tide points from which the radiating cotidal lines progress through all hours of the tidal cycle. Even if there are some islands near these points for which tidal data are available, the "noise" to "signal," or significant data, ratio is large, and hence the data are less reliable when the range of tide is small.

An international program for measuring the tide in deep ocean was initiated in the mid-1960's. Free-fall gauges have been developed that record on the ocean floor and then are recalled to the surface by means of signals. Other bottom-mounted gauges, connected by cables to ships or to the shore, have also produced valuable data. The program to obtain a grid of tide stations covering the world's oceans will take a long time, but the data will be extremely useful for comparison with theoretical numerical studies of the world distribution of tides.

Although tidal characteristics change from place to place, tides in the Atlantic Ocean are basically semidaily, whereas Pacific Ocean tides tend to be mixed. There is some evidence that the tidal range observed on the east coast of the United States varies directly with the width of the continental shelf. Florida is in a somewhat unique tidal environment, having a semidiurnal tide at Miami, a mixed tide at Key West, and a diurnal tide at Pensacola.

Publications. The U. S. Coast and Geodetic Survey publishes annual tide tables for the entire world, in four volumes. Each volume contains daily predictions for key places and tables of time and height differences for secondary sites. There are also two annual volumes of tidal current tables, primarily for places in North America. In addition the survey publishes tidal current charts for a number of major harbors and estuaries. Most of the other important nautical countries publish their own tide tables in various formats.

BERNARD D. ZETLER, *ESSA Atlantic Oceanographic and Meteorological Laboratories, Miami*

Bibliography

Defant, Albert, *Physical Oceanography,* vol. 2 (New York 1961).

Dietrich, Gunter, *General Oceanography: An Introduction* (New York 1963).

Doodson, Arthur T., and Warburg, H. D., *Admiralty Manual of Tides* (London 1941).

Dronkers, Jo J., *Tidal Computations in River and Coastal Waters* (Amsterdam, the Netherlands, 1964).

Macmillan, D. Henry, *Tides* (New York 1966).

Munk, Walter H., and Zetler, Bernard D., "Deep Sea Tides: A Program," *Science,* vol. 158, No. 3803, Nov. 17, 1967.

Schuremen, Paul, *Manual of Harmonic Analysis and Prediction of Tides,* Coast and Geodetic Survey Special Publication No. 98 (Washington 1940).

TIDELAND is land over which the tide daily ebbs and flows. It does not include lands permanently submerged. In Europe, influenced by Roman law, tidelands belong to the state and cannot be alienated (disposed of). In England, title to tidelands belongs to the Crown. When the original 13 American colonies became independent, they assumed sovereign control over their tidelands, and states that later were admitted to the Union were also allowed to assume title. Because the U. S. Constitution does not specifically deny to the states the right to alienate their tidelands, the state legislatures have disposed of much of these areas, subject to the "public trust" principle that preserves to the public the right to navigate, engage in commerce, and fish in these areas.

The actual extent of tidelands is technically determined in certain aspects by federal laws. The federal government has also extended its control to include dredging and erecting of structures in tidal areas.

In *United States* v. *California* (1947) the U. S. Supreme Court ruled that coastal states did not own any of the submerged lands bordering their states. But in 1953, Congress negated this by passing the Submerged Lands Act, extending ownership of the continuous undersea lands to three miles (4.8 km) from a state's "coastline," except for the seaward boundaries of Texas and Florida. These can extend 10.5 miles (16.8 km) into the Gulf of Mexico, as was the case when they entered the Union. The Outer Continental Shelf Lands Act, also passed in 1953, established federal control of the submerged lands seaward of state boundaries, inside the international limit. At issue in federal-state boundary disputes are millions of dollars from oil lease royalties.

JULIUS J. MARKE
New York University Law School

TIDORE, tē-dō'rā, is a mountainous island in the Moluccas, or Spice Islands, of Indonesia. It is about 45 square miles (118 sq km) in area and lies 1 mile (1.5 km) south of Ternate. The northern half of Tidore has some level land along the coast, but the south is dominated by an extinct volcanic peak that rises to 5,676 feet (1,730 meters) above sea level. The fertile lower slopes of the peak support dense tropical forest and crops. Coffee, fruit, tobacco, and spices are the main products of the island.

The Tidorese are predominantly Muslim and speak a language related to Papuan. The island, once the home of a powerful sultanate, came under Portuguese and then Spanish control in the 16th century. It was under Dutch rule most of the time from the 17th century to the mid-20th, when it became part of independent Indonesia. Population: (1961) 58,396.

PETER R. INGOLD, *University of Vermont*

TIECK, tēk, **Ludwig** (1773–1853), German author, who was a major theorist of romanticism in Germany. Johann Ludwig Tieck was born in Berlin on May 31, 1773, and attended the universities of Halle, Göttingen, and Erlangen, concentrating on medieval and Elizabethan studies. The writer Wilhelm Wackenroder encouraged Tieck's interest in nature and in the glories of medieval German art. In 1796–1797, Tieck published his first major work, the largely autobiographical epistolary novel *William Lovell.* In the picaresque novel *Franz Sternbalds Wanderungen* (1798), he celebrated the emotionally satisfying life of the artist.

Tieck's interest in the past is reflected in his *Volksmärchen* (1797), a group of stories and plays, many of which were based on old folktales. Best known of this collection are the play *Der gestiefelte Kater,* a satiric treatment of the Puss-in-Boots story, and *Der blonde Eckbert,* an original, weirdly imaginative narrative.

In Jena in 1799, Tieck met the brothers August Wilhelm and Friedrich von Schlegel, major literary figures of their day. Under their influence he wrote the epic play *Leben und Tod der heiligen Genoveva,* published with other works in *Romantische Dichtungen* (1800). This marked the first use of the word "romantic" in a literary context. Tieck was also connected with August von Schlegel's brilliant translation of Shakespeare's plays. Schlegel, who had begun the project in 1797, gave it up in 1810. Tieck's daughter, Dorothea, later helped complete it under her father's supervision. Chief among Tieck's later romantic works is *Phantasus* (1812–1816), a group of poems, plays, and stories. Toward the end of his life, he turned to realism, with such novellas as *Des Lebens Überfluss* (1839). Tieck died in Berlin on April 25, 1853.

W. T. H. JACKSON, *Columbia University*

TIEN SHAN, tyen shän, a great mountain system in western China and Soviet Central Asia, in part separating the Sinkiang-Uigur autonomous region of China from the Kirghiz republic, USSR. *Tien Shan* means "heavenly mountains" in Chinese.

The mountain system extends some 1,500 miles (2,400 km), from the Kyzyl Kum desert of Soviet Uzbekistan to the western end of the Gobi Desert near the Sinkiang-Kansu-Mongolian border. Its western branches, in the USSR, almost surround the Fergana Valley with its fertile farm lands and modern industrial complex. The eastern outliers in Sinkiang enclose the Turfan Depression, 505 feet (154 meters) below sea level.

Most of the Tien Shan lies within China, dividing Sinkiang into the Dzungaria basin (north) and the Tarim Basin (south). A gap south of Urumchi divides the mountain chain into a western and an eastern section. The latter reaches elevations of over 14,000 feet (4,270 meters), but the highest peaks are in the western section. There, on the Sino-Soviet boundary, Pobeda ("Victory") Peak rises to 24,406 feet (7,439 meters) and Khan Tengri to 22,949 feet (6,995 meters). The Soviet section has deposits of lead, zinc, antimony, mercury, tungsten, copper, petroleum, natural gas, and sulfur. The Chinese part contains petroleum and reportedly also anthracite, lead, zinc, tin, molybdenum, copper, and iron.

FREDERICK HUNG
University of Guelph, Ontario

TIENTSIN, tin'tsin', is the third-largest city in China. Situated on the Hai River about 70 miles (115 km) southeast of Peking and 35 miles (55 km) from the sea, it is accessible to small oceangoing ships. Larger vessels must anchor at the New Port of Tangku, opened in 1952, near the mouth of the river but within the limits of Tientsin (Tianjin) municipality.

The Hai River is formed by the Tzuya and Yungting rivers, which unite at Tientsin and are joined by the Northern Grand Canal. The

METROPOLITAN MUSEUM OF ART, GIFT IN MEMORY OF OLIVER H. PAYNE, 1923

Tiepolo's *Apotheosis of Francesco Barbaro*, painted for the ceiling of the Palazzo Barbaro, in Venice, about 1750.

city is also the junction point of several railroads, which link it with Peking, Manchuria, and the lower Yangtze Valley. As a key point of rail and water transport, Tientsin serves as an outlet for the products of Inner Mongolia and the provinces of northern and northwestern China and is a distributing center for products of southern China. As an international seaport, it handles trade with Japan, the Soviet Union, and various countries of Europe.

The city is highly industrialized. After 1949 over 400 factories were built, expanded, or reconstructed in Tientsin, and special emphasis was given to the development of its metallurgical and metal-fabricating industries. Among the city's chief manufactures besides metal products are cotton and woolen textiles, carpets, food and tobacco products, and chemicals.

Tientsin became a major commercial center after it was opened to foreign trade in 1858. Although geographically in Hopei province, the city is under the jurisdiction of the central government. From 1958 to 1967, however, it was administered as part of Hopei and was the provincial capital. Tientsin has three universities: Hopei, Tientsin, and Nankai. Population: (1964 est.) 4,000,000.

DAVID CHUEN-YAN LAI
University of Victoria, British Columbia

TIEPOLO, tē-ä′pə-lō, **Giovanni Battista** (1696–1770), Italian painter, whose spirited, grandiose, yet graceful frescoes make him the leading figure of the Venetian school of the 18th century.

Life. Tiepolo was born in Venice on March 5, 1696, and was trained there. He is first recorded in the lists of the Venetian painters' guild in 1717, although he had already exhibited work. The monumental wall and ceiling frescoes he created both in his native city and during his frequent travels throughout northern Italy established his international reputation. In 1750, Tiepolo was invited to Würzburg, Germany, to decorate the palace of the prince-bishop. In 1762, accompanied by his son and chief assistant, Giovanni Domenico, he went to Spain at the invitation of Charles III to work on the royal palace. Tiepolo spent the remainder of his life in Madrid, where he died on March 27, 1770.

Work and Style. The best known of Tiepolo's frescoes are the scenes of the story of Anthony and Cleopatra in the Palazzo Labia in Venice (before 1750); the decorations at Würzburg (1750–1753), comprising historical, mythological, and allegorical themes; the frescoes in the Villa Valmarana in Vicenza (1757), consisting of scenes from ancient and Renaissance epics; and the national and dynastic propaganda of the royal palace in Madrid. Tiepolo carried out decorations similar to those in fresco in oil on canvas, such as the *Apotheosis of Francesco Barbaro* (about 1745–1750), a ceiling painting from the Palazzo Barbaro in Venice, now in the Metropolitan Museum, New York. Most of his altarpieces and smaller paintings are in oil. The preparatory drawings and oil sketches for these projects are executed with an exciting freedom that makes them especially attractive to modern tastes. Tiepolo also produced a significant body of etchings, usually of imaginative and often obscure subjects.

Tiepolo was heir to the great pictorial tradition of the Venetian Renaissance. The art of Paolo Veronese in particular provided a model for the development of his style—with its decorative grandeur and controlled rhythm, its light palette and setting of pure and varied color notes against backdrops of sky or architecture. The themes of Tiepolo's paintings are of the highest intellectual and dramatic seriousness, and his figures move with a graceful gravity befitting the baroque tradition. Yet in the lightness of his tones, the exuberance of his forms, and the technical brilliance of his execution, Tiepolo shares certain qualities of the rococo.

DAVID ROSAND, *Columbia University*

Further Reading: Levey, Michael, *Painting in XVIIIth Century Venice* (London 1959); Morassi, Antonio, *G. B. Tiepolo, His Life and Work* (London 1955).

TIERNEY, tēr′nē, **George** (1761–1830), English politician. He was born in Gibraltar on March 20, 1761, the son of a London businessman, and was educated at Eton and Cambridge. At first a supporter of the younger Pitt, he was elected to Parliament as an opponent of the Pitt government in 1789, but lost his seat in 1790. In 1796 the borough of Southwark returned him to Parliament as a reformer and opponent of the war with France. The secession of Whig leaders from Parliament in 1797 left Tierney almost alone in opposition to Pitt, with whom he fought a duel in 1798.

Tierney held minor offices in 1803–1804, 1806–1807, and 1827–1828. From 1818 to 1821 he was leader of the opposition in the Commons, and for the most part he remained in opposition until his death in London on Jan. 25, 1830.

R. G. THORNE
Editor, "History of Parliament 1790–1820"

TIERRA DEL FUEGO, tyer'rä thel fwā'gō, is a group of islands forming the southernmost extension of South America, separated from the mainland by the Strait of Magellan. One large island, the Isla Grande de Tierra del Fuego, occupies two thirds of the total land area of about 27,500 square miles (71,000 sq km). The eastern third of the sparsely populated archipelago belongs to Argentina, and the western two thirds to Chile. The main settlements are Ushuaia, on the Argentine part of the Isla Grande, and Porvenir, on the Chilean part.

Tierra del Fuego is dominated in the south and west by rugged mountains rising to heights of 7,000 feet (2,100 meters). To the northeast, a more gently rolling landscape predominates. Due to the group's extreme southerly, maritime location at about 55° south latitude, the climate is cool, with average temperatures ranging from 50° F (10° C) in summer to 32° F (0° C) in winter. Constant westerly winds bring up to 200 inches (5,000 mm) of rain to the windward western-facing slopes and only 20 inches (500 mm) to the leeward northeast coast.

Ferdinand Magellan discovered the strait that bears his name in 1520, during his momentous circumnavigation of the earth. He named the region Tierra del Fuego ("Land of Fire") because local people were observed carrying fire from place to place, presumably for fear of having their hearth fires go out in such a chilly and sodden land. Sir Francis Drake sighted Cape Horn, the southernmost point of land in the Western Hemisphere, in 1578.

After the 1880's, the less mountainous areas of Tierra del Fuego became used for sheep raising, particularly by the Argentines. A gold rush in the 1890's brought in some European settlers, including Yugoslavs and Italians. The original inhabitants, such as the Ona, Alacaluf, and Yaghan Indians, have dwindled in number. By the mid-20th century, petroleum extraction had joined sheep raising as the area's chief economic mainstay. Population: (1967 est.) 14,000.

KEMPTON E. WEBB
Columbia University

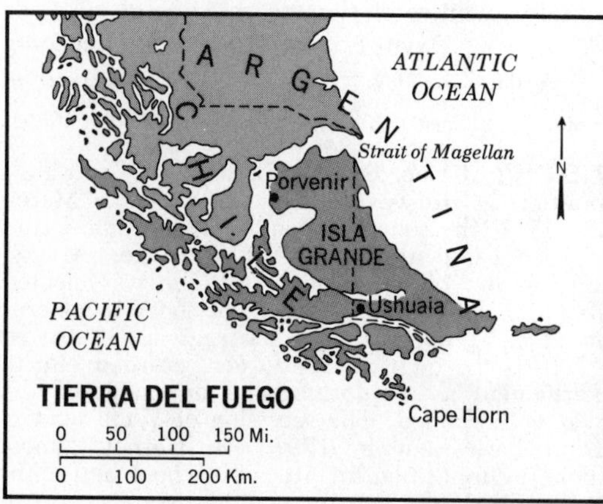

TIFFANY, tif'ə-nē, **Louis Comfort** (1848–1933), American painter, designer, and glassmaker, whose works represent the major U. S. contribution to the art nouveau movement. He was born in New York, N. Y., on Feb. 18, 1848, the son of the jeweler Charles L. Tiffany. Instead of entering the family business, he decided to become a painter. As a youth he studied with George Inness and others and traveled abroad. At intervals during his life he painted in both watercolors and oil, but by the 1870's he showed the interest in the decorative arts through which he eventually achieved fame. His success came not merely through his taste and skill as a designer but also from his business enterprises—design and interior decorating studios, and, most notably, glassworks. In 1918 he established and endowed the Louis Comfort Tiffany Foundation for the benefit of art students. He died in New York City on Jan. 17, 1933.

Tiffany began experimenting with stained glass in 1875, established a glassmaking plant, and eventually devised his own process for the production of an iridescent glass, which he called Favrile glass, but which was better known as "Tiffany glass." The output of his several companies was vast. It included not only glass—bowls, vases, and lampshades, and huge windows and screens for churches and other public buildings—but also metalwork, jewelry, tapestry and rugs, and complete interior ensembles. See also ART NOUVEAU; GLASS AND GLASSWARE—*American Glass* (19th Century).

NICOLAI CIKOVSKY, JR., *University of Texas*

Further Reading: Koch, Robert, *Louis C. Tiffany: Rebel in Glass*, rev. ed. (New York 1966).

TIFFANY GLASS. See GLASS AND GLASSWARE—*American Glass* (19th Century); TIFFANY, LOUIS COMFORT.

TIFFIN, a city in northwestern Ohio, the seat of Seneca county, is on the Sandusky River, about 50 miles (80 km) southeast of Toledo. It produces heavy machinery, pipe fittings, grinding wheels, wire, electrical products, and pottery.

Heidelberg College, a coeducational institution, is in Tiffin. The Seneca County Historical and Archaeological Society has a museum with local history exhibits. In the city is the site of Fort Ball, an army depot in the War of 1812.

A settlement whose name was originally Oakley—changed to Fort Ball in 1824—was begun near the fort in 1817. Tiffin was founded on the south side of the river in 1820 and named for Edward Tiffin, the first governor of Ohio. It was incorporated in 1835 and became a city in 1850. Tiffin is governed by a mayor and council. Population: 21,596.

TIFLIS. See TBILISI.

TIFTON, a city in southern Georgia and the seat of Tift county. It is 191 miles (305 km) south of Atlanta, in an area of diversified agriculture. Tifton's industries produce fertilizers, textiles, shoes, aluminum extrusions, concrete products, and mobile homes. The city is the site of coeducational Abraham Baldwin Junior College, the rural development center of the University of Georgia, and an agricultural research station. Tifton was founded in 1872 and incorporated in 1890. Government is by a city manager and a board of aldermen. Population: 12,179.

TIGER, *Panthera tigris,* is the largest of all cats, with males occasionally reaching a length of 10 feet (3 meters), including a 3-foot (0.9-meter) tail. An average male weighs 420 pounds (190 kg) and a female 300 pounds (136 kg).

Within historic times the range of the tiger spanned 6,000 miles (9,600 km) from eastern Turkey and Iran to India, Burma, Indochina, and Malaya, as well as over much of China, Korea, and Russian Manchuria. Such a vast range implies that tigers are adaptable animals, and indeed they occur in temperate oak forests, dry thorn scrub, humid rain forests, reedbeds, mangrove swamps, and in Manchurian spruce forests where snow may lie deep in the winter. All they need for survival are shade, water, and sufficient prey.

Tigers cannot easily coexist with man. The animals not only inspire fear but also may kill livestock, with the result that they are shot or poisoned. In addition, more and more of their forests have been converted into fields as the human population has increased. Eight races of tiger are recognized by some authorities, and the existence of six of these is endangered. For example, only about 12 Javan tigers remain, and no more than 110 Siberian tigers still exist in the Soviet Far East. Even India, the most famous home of tigers, has only about 2,000 left. The Chinese tiger, once found over much of China, is now probably extinct. Unless all countries protect their tigers and prohibit the current trade in skins, this magnificent cat will surely vanish.

Behavior. Tigers are essentially solitary, although temporary aggregations of several adults and cubs—as many as 7—have been seen together. But being solitary does not imply that they are unsociable. Two animals may meet, greet in typical cat fashion by rubbing cheeks, and then part. Occasionally several animals share a kill. Each tiger inhabits a range of anywhere from 25 to 1,250 square miles (65–3200 sq km), the size depending on the amount of prey. Such ranges overlap extensively. While tigresses tolerate each other and are friendly with males, there is evidence that males generally are antagonistic toward others of their sex. To advertise their presence, tigers roar and leave signs in the form of scent that they spray on bushes and trees.

Reproduction. A tigress becomes sexually mature at the age of 3½ to 4 years. After a gestation period of 98 to 109 days, from 1 to 6 (but usually 2 or 3) cubs are born—blind, helpless, and weighing a mere 3 to 4 pounds (1.4–1.8 kg). These remain hidden in a thicket until the age of 6 to 8 weeks. The cubs do not become fully independent until they are nearly two years old, at which time the tigress may have another litter. Maximum longevity is 20 years.

Food and Hunting. Tigers need an average of about 12 to 15 pounds (5.5–6.8 kg) of meat per day to survive. They kill whatever they can catch, including frogs, fish, and monkeys, but hoofed animals, such as deer, wild pigs, and domestic cattle make up the bulk of their diet. To find prey, tigers pad silently along trails and streambeds, their tawny, black-striped coats blending into the surroundings. Hunting usually under cover of darkness, they stalk close to their quarry before overpowering it after a brief, fast rush. They may hunt in daytime, too, often lying in ambush at waterholes.

Using the strength of its massive forelegs and curved claws to pull an animal down, the cat then kills it either with a bite in the back of the neck or through suffocation by holding the throat. A tiger can consume a prodigious amount of meat in one meal—at least 50 pounds (23 kg). For example, having killed a cow, it will camp beside the carcass, eating at intervals,. After three days it will have consumed all meat, viscera, and skin, leaving only bones and stomach contents. A week may then pass without another meal, for wildlife is so alert that hunts fail more often than not. The tiger leads a life of feast or famine.

Under normal circumstances, tigers are no danger to man. Occasionally they may prey on man, sometimes because a wound prevents them from killing more agile prey or because no other food is available or because they have scavenged on unburied human corpses. Usually, however, they avoid contact with man so assiduously that they are seldom glimpsed.

GEORGE B. SCHALLER
New York Zoological Society

Further Reading: Schaller, George B., and Selsam, Millicent, *Tiger: Its Life in the Wild* (New York 1969).

JEANNE WHITE FROM NATIONAL AUDUBON SOCIETY

SIBERIAN TIGER, found in the Soviet Far East, Korea, and northeastern China, is believed to be nearly extinct in the wild. The International Union for the Conservation of Nature (Red Data Book) estimates the 1970 population at less than 200 animals.

JOHN H. GERARD, FROM NATIONAL AUDUBON SOCIETY

Spotted tiger beetle (*Cicindela sexguttata*)

TIGER BEETLE, any of a group of brightly colored, long-legged, heavily spined beetles. Both the adults and the larvae are predators. The ferocious manner in which they attack and devour their prey has earned them their reputation as miniature tigers.

Often tiger beetles are found congregated in large numbers, greedily eating other insects, worms, and snails. The adults are generally seen flying rapidly in sunlit areas, usually near pools or ponds. The larvae dig short tubes in moist sand, closing the tubes with their heads and holding onto the sides of the tubes with their spines and hooks. When any fairly small animal passes the tube, the larva seizes it, drags it into the tube, and eats it.

The bright colors of tiger beetles make them such favorites among insect collectors that a journal called *Cicindela,* the name of the principal tiger beetle genus, is devoted entirely to the study of these beetles. All tiger beetles belong to the family Cicindelidae, and there are more than 80 species and subspecies in the United States and Canada.

R. H. ARNETT, JR., *Purdue University*

TIGER CAT, a small, spotted, and striped wildcat (*Felis tigrina*), also called the little spotted cat, margay, and kuichua, found from Central America to southern Brazil. It is sometimes confused with the ocelot (*F. pardalis*), but is smaller in size, or with *F. weidii,* most commonly known as the margay.

The tiger cat is grayish yellow, with brownish stripes and large black-bordered oval or round spots and blotches. Along the spine these spots and blotches become elongated and sometimes unite to form continuous chains. Two black lines mark the face from the outer corners of the eyes to the neck. The ears are black, tipped with white. The tiger cat reaches 24 inches (60 cm) in head and body length. Its long, 18-inch (45-cm) tail is a distinctive characteristic.

Tiger cats live in forests, where they usually spend the day resting in the hollows of tree trunks or similar shelters. At night they emerge to hunt for small mammals on the ground or for birds and bird eggs in the trees. They also raid human settlements for domestic fowl. Little is known about the social behavior and reproduction of the tiger cat, but they are assumed to resemble those of the ocelot.

FERNANDO DIAS DE AVILA-PIRES
Museu de Historia Natural, Minas Gerais, Brazil

TIGER LILY, a hardy Asian lily cultivated for its purple-spotted, deep orange-red flowers. The tiger lily (*Lilium tigrinum*), one of the hardiest lilies, is easiest to cultivate. It is native to China, Korea, and Japan and has become naturalized in the northeastern United States.

The tiger lily is often 4 feet (1.2 meters) tall and grows even taller under ideal conditions. The flowers, which may be 4 inches (10 cm) long, have prominent rusty-red stamens. There may be as many as 20 flowers on a single stem. The leaves are glossy green and the stem has purplish-black spots. Small purplish aerial bulblets in the axils of the leaves are a distinctive characteristic of this species.

ANTON KOFRANEK
University of California, Davis

ROCHE

Tiger lily

TIGER MOTH, the common name for any of a large group of brightly colored, stout-bodied moths whose wings are typically orange and black, or sometimes white, marked with black spots or bands. The moths are medium sized, with a wingspan ranging from 1 to 3 inches (25–75 mm).

The larvae, or caterpillars, of the tiger moth are usually covered with long hairs. Unlike those of some hairy caterpillars, these hairs are not connected to stinging glands, and the caterpillars are harmless to touch. Prior to pupation, each larva removes its body hairs with its mouthparts and uses them, along with silk it produces, to weave a flimsy cocoon. Tiger moth larvae are seldom of economic importance. Most species feed on wild plants, but a few eat the leaves of certain fruit and forest trees.

Tiger moths belong to the family Arctiidae, subfamily Arctiinae. They occur throughout the world, and more than 125 species are known in North America alone. Many North American tiger moths belong to the genus *Apantesis.* These species are usually black with orange or yellow streaks. The common red and black woolly bear caterpillar, the larva of the Isabella tiger moth (*Isia isabella*), is found in the New England states. A species widespread throughout the United States is the salt marsh caterpillar (*Estigmene acrea*).

DON DAVIS, *Smithsonian Institution*

TIGER SHARK, a large voracious shark known to attack man. It is common along all tropical and subtropical seacoasts and occasionally wanders far out to sea or into temperate waters. The young, born about 2 or 3 feet (60–90 cm) long in litters of 10 to more than 50, have distinctive black and white stripes in a tigerlike pattern. As the shark grows, sometimes to a length of more than 15 feet (4.6 meters), the stripes fade. The adult is dark gray above and whitish below and has only indistinct markings.

Tiger sharks are indiscriminate feeders. They attack all kinds of prey, including sea turtles, porpoises, and smaller sharks. They also scavenge. There are many authenticated reports of tiger shark attacks on man. The danger of such attacks is reduced, however, by the sharks' tendency to avoid strong light. They move into shallow water chiefly at night, when recreational use of beaches is low. Tiger sharks are taken commercially for their liver oil and for their hide.

MARINELAND OF FLORIDA

Tiger shark

The tiger shark, *Galeocerdo cuvieri,* is classified with other "typical sharks" in the order Galeiformes in the Class Selachii.

STEWART SPRINGER
U. S. Fish and Wildlife Service

TIGEREYE, also called *tiger's-eye,* is a gem variety of quartz. It has a rich golden color, and a beam of reflected light moves from one parallel band to another in the fibrous stone as it is tilted. Carved into cameos, it is one of the most popular gems for men's rings.

Tigereye derives from crocidolite, or blue asbestos, a cross-fiber variety of riebeckite and a member of the amphibole group of minerals. (See CROCIDOLITE.) When the ferrous iron in crocidolite is oxidized to ferric iron, the color changes from bluish to golden, and as the mineral is replaced by silica, it alters to tigereye.

Griqualand West, in South Africa, is virtually the only source of tigereye, although some is found in India.

RICHARD M. PEARL, *Colorado College*

T. H. EVERETT

Tigerflower (*Tigridia pavonia*)

TIGERFLOWER, an erect, Mexican and Guatemalan flower grown for its unusual showy flowers. The tigerflower, *Tigridia pavonia,* also known as peacock flower and Mexican shell flower, belongs to the iris family (Iridaceae).

It grows to a height of 30 inches (7.5 cm) and has smooth, narrow, sword-shaped leaves that may be 18 inches (45 cm) long. The flowers, which may be 6 inches (15 cm) in diameter, have a cup-shaped or saucer-shaped center, three spreading obovate outer segments, and three fiddle-shaped inner segments half the size of the outer ones. The outer segments are bright red, yellow, white, pink, or orange on the limb but red-spotted near the base. The inner segments are orange or yellow and conspicuously spotted or blotched with red, brown, or purple. Each flower lasts only one day.

Tigerflowers are hardy in mild climates and grow best in sandy soil in full sun. They can be grown from seed, bulbs, or bulblets. Bulbs and bulblets should be planted about 6 inches (15 cm) apart and 3 inches (7.5 cm) deep.

ANTON KOFRANEK
University of California, Davis

TIGLATH-PILESER III, tig′lath pī-lē′zər, was king of Assyria from 745 to 727 B. C. The name Tiglath-pileser is the Biblical form of the Assyrian name Tukulti-apil-Esharra. The king was also known as Pulu, or Pul.

Tiglath-pileser usurped the throne at a time of Assyrian weakness. A rival power, Urartu, had cut off the supply of vital commodities, such as horses from Media and metals from Anatolia, and had caused disaffection in northern Syria. After defeating the Aramaean tribes of eastern Babylonia, Tiglath-pileser crushed Urartu and its Syrian allies and extended Assyrian control to southern Palestine, where he aided Ahaz of Judah against Pekah of Israel. Finally, having crushed a rebellion in southern Babylonia, Tiglath-pileser made himself king of Babylon.

With Assyria again a dominant power, Tiglath-pileser moved to secure its position by extensive deportation of conquered peoples and by an elaborate administrative reorganization. Conquered territories, formerly left to tribute-paying rulers, were incorporated under Assyrian governors in a far-reaching bureaucratic system with the king at its head. Tiglath-pileser's conquests and reforms were the basis for the achievements of his Sargonid successors.

JAMES G. MACQUEEN
Author of "Babylon"

GEORGE RAIMONDI, DEPT. OF PARKS, N. Y. C.

Tigon, hybrid offspring of a male tiger and a lioness.

TIGON, tī'gən, or *tiglon,* a cross between a male tiger and a female lion. A cross between a male lion and a female tiger is called a *liger.* Tiger-lion hybrids do not appear in the wild.

TIGRANES I, tig-rā'-nēz, reigned about 95–55 B. C. as king of Armenia. Under his rule Armenia for the first time became a major power. Tigranes (Dikran), after spending his youth as a hostage in Parthia, invaded and occupied large parts of the Parthian kingdom. By 83 B. C. he also controlled much of Mesopotamia and had subdued northern Syria and Cilicia. He then assumed the title "king of kings" and built the splendid new city of Tigranocerta.

His marriage to the daughter of Mithridates of Pontus increased Tigranes' interest in Asia Minor. In 78 he overran Cappadocia. But Rome's war on Mithridates changed Tigranes' fortune. From 69 to 67 the Roman general Lucullus captured Armenia's major cities and forced Tigranes into the Armenian mountains. In 66, Pompey compelled the Armenian king to surrender. Tigranes was allowed to keep a truncated kingdom, and he lived peaceably as a vassal of Rome.

ERICH S. GRUEN
University of California, Berkeley

TIGRIS RIVER, tī'grəs, the principal stream of the Shatt al-Arab river system, in the Middle East. The Tigris (Arabic, Dijla; Turkish, Dicle) is about 1,270 miles (2,045 km) long, and its 43,110-square-mile (111,655-sq-km) drainage basin includes portions of Turkey, Iran, and Iraq. In Iraq, the floodplain of the Tigris forms part of the ancient region known as Mesopotamia, the cradle of civilization in the Middle East and the site of the great Sumerian, Babylonian, and Assyrian states.

The Tigris rises to the east and south of Elâzig in east-central Turkey. As it flows in a southeasterly arc through Iraq, it is fed by numerous tributaries from the Zagros Mountains. The head of the floodplain is near Samarra, and for the next 200 miles (322 km) the river flows through the plain. There is historical evidence of repeated shifts in the river's course, and an extensive network of canals was built to control the recurrent spring floods. South of Kut, floodwaters are diverted into extensive marshes. The Tigris joins the Euphrates above Basra to form the Shatt al-Arab, which flows into the Persian Gulf.

GARY L. FOWLER
University of Kentucky

TIHWA. See URUMCHI.

TIJUANA, tē-wä'nə, is a resort city of northwestern Mexico, in the state of Baja California. It is situated directly south of the U. S. border and the greater San Diego urban complex, on the Pacific coast, in a dry subtropical area.

The city developed around the Rancho de Tia Juana, the largest of six cattle ranches that merged into a village in 1840. In the 1920's, during the Prohibition era in the United States, Tijuana began to attract many tourists, drawn by the availability of alcoholic beverages, a gambling casino, and a racetrack on the outskirts of town at Agua Caliente. Tijuana won a reputation as one of the world's most corrupt cities.

By emphasizing industrialization and family tourism, the city has become a modern industrial center with attractive public buildings and luxury restaurants and lodgings. Its free-port status, instituted in 1933 to permit the import of foreign goods without payment of duty, gave a vital lift to the tourist trade. Most of Tijuana's economy is geared to provide goods and services for American tourists from southern California. The development of new industries, including the production of textiles, electronics, and foodstuffs, has raised the standard of living of its residents. It has also attracted large numbers of young immigrants. Population (1967 estimate): 339,700.

REYNALDO AYALA
San Diego State College

TIKAL, ti-käl', is an ancient Maya city of great archaeological importance, located in the jungles of Peten in western Guatemala. Tikal was a major center of classic Maya culture. The central area covers approximately one square mile (2.59 sq km), while the total extent of the town was several times as great. Its population has been estimated as high as 100,000 at the peak of its power about 600 A. D. Between 800 and 900, the Maya cities were abandoned for reasons still unknown. See also MAYA.

The site contains remnants of major struc-

THE UNIVERSITY MUSEUM

TIKAL'S TEMPLE I, a relic of Guatemala's Maya culture, is set on top of a high terraced pyramid.

tures, referred to as temples and palaces, built on terraced pyramids and grouped around a plaza. The tallest of these structures is 220 feet (67 meters) high. Among the objects discovered at Tikal is the Leyden Plaque, the oldest dated Maya jade object. A thin, carved slab of jade, it has on one side a Maya date corresponding to 320 A. D. On the other it is decorated with an elaborately attired figure. Among other objects the most interesting are carved stelae (commemorative pillars) and stone altars, suggesting Tikal's importance as a ceremonial center.

Exploration and excavation at Tikal was carried on by scientists from the University of Pennsylvania in the 1960's and 1970's.

ERIKA BOURGUIGNON
The Ohio State University

TILAPIA, tə-lā'pē-ə, a genus of cichlid fishes that are becoming increasingly important food fishes. Tilapias are most abundant in Africa but live in almost all tropical and subtropical waters. Although primarily freshwater fishes, they also occur in brackish and salt waters.

Tilapia (*T. mossambica*)

LAURENCE E. PERKINS

Tilapias are usually quite small, less than 2 pounds (.9 kg), and have a tapered dorsal fin. They are often called *African mouthbreeders* because in many species either the male or the female picks up the eggs shortly after they have been deposited and incubates them in the mouth for from 8 to 14 days. The young may later return to the parent's mouth in times of danger.

Tilapias provide a valuable source of protein. They are important food fishes in Africa and in recent years have been introduced and cultured in other countries. Since Tilapias are herbivorous, they have also been used to control aquatic weeds. They are also popular aquarium fishes.

Tilapias are classified in the genus *Tilapia* of the family Cichlidae, order Percopsiformes.

See FISH AND SHELLFISH CULTURE.

R. WELDON LARIMORE
Illinois Natural History Survey

TILBURG, til'bûrg, a city of south-central Netherlands, is in North Brabant province. It is located about 6 miles (10 km) north of the Belgian border and 13 miles (21 km) east of Breda. Lying on the Wilhelmina Canal, Tilburg is connected with the Rhine and Maas rivers.

The city, a long-established market town, developed rapidly during the 19th century into an industrial center. Its products include woolen textiles, leather goods, machinery, and locomotives. There is a textile research center. Also located in Tilburg are a museum of natural history and the Catholic School of Economics. The town hall is the former palace of King William II. Population: (1967 est.) 148,497.

TILDEN, Samuel Jones (1814–1886), American political leader, who as the Democratic presidential candidate in 1876 lost the most controversial election in American history. That loss climaxed a long career in which his reform impulses were frequently overridden by his personal ambition and his ambitions often frustrated by his indecisiveness.

Tilden was born in New Lebanon, N. Y., on Feb. 9, 1814. Precocious but sickly, he was sporadically schooled and tutored. In 1838 he entered law school at New York University, and in 1841 he was admitted to the bar. He became an outstanding corporation lawyer, who mastered the complexities of reorganizing and refinancing railroads. He amassed a fortune in fees, which he augmented by shrewd investments in railroads, iron mines, and real estate

Early Political Career. An ardent Jacksonian in the 1830's, Tilden became a leader in the 1840's of the Barnburners, a Democratic faction committed to free-soil principles. Although a delegate to the Free-Soil National Convention in 1848, he did not follow most Free-Soilers into the new Republican Party. Growing wealthy and conservative, he returned to the Democratic party and abandoned his free soil convictions.

During the Civil War, Tilden's main concerns were neither union nor slavery but the threat of tyranny by a powerful centralized government in Washington. After the war he condemned Radical Reconstruction and in 1868 managed the presidential campaign of Horatio Seymour, governor of New York. From 1866 to 1874, as chairman of the New York State Democratic Committee, Tilden initially cooperated with and later helped destroy the infamous "Tweed ring" that controlled New York City politics. Even after the Republican New York *Times* attacked the ring with damning evidence in July 1871, Tilden, a partisan Democrat, moved cautiously, but in October he examined ring bank accounts and proved that William M. Tweed and his friends had stolen from the city. Members of the ring were promptly arrested. As a member of the state legislature in 1872, Tilden worked to smash the Tweed ring and reform the judiciary, but he characteristically opposed a reform charter for New York City.

Governor and Presidential Candidate. Renowned as a reformer, Tilden was nominated and elected governor of New York in 1874. A meticulous administrator, he reduced expenditures and taxes by introducing economics and eliminating frauds. He destroyed the bipartisan "Canal ring," a group of wealthy politicians who had stolen from the funds necessary to repair and extend the state canal system. His excellent gubernatorial record secured him the 1876 Democratic presidential nomination, with Gov. Thomas A. Hendricks of Indiana as his running mate. The Republicans chose Rutherford B. Hayes of Ohio.

In the bitter campaign that followed, the Democrats attacked Republican corruption in President Grant's administration, while the Republicans accused the Democrats of being disloyal during the war and made issues of Tilden's connections with railroads, his questionable income tax returns, and his health. His slight build, boyish face, weak voice, nervous and awkward actions, and secretive and aloof nature did not inspire voters, but his intellect and reform reputation did. Tilden apparently won the election, but Republican audacity and electoral vote bargaining coupled with Tilden's timidity and procrastination gave the presidency to Hayes. (See HAYES-TILDEN ELECTION.)

In 1880 and 1884 there was sentiment for Tilden's renomination, but he refused both times to be considered. He died in Yonkers, N. Y., on Aug. 4, 1886, a bachelor. Of his $5-million estate, $3 million helped found the New York Public Library.

ARI HOOGENBOOM, *Brooklyn College*

TILDEN, William Tatem, II (1893–1953), American athlete, who was one of the foremost tennis players of all time. Born in Germantown, Pa., on Feb. 10, 1893, he won his first local tennis tournament at the age of seven.

Tilden won the national mixed doubles championship with Mary K. Browne in 1913. Before his graduation from the University of Pennsylvania in 1922, he had won the national doubles title with Vincent Richards in 1918 and the national singles championship in 1920. Thereafter he won the doubles title in 1921–1923 and 1927, and the singles crown in 1921–1925 and 1929. He won the British singles title in 1920, 1921, and 1930. From 1920 until 1930, "Big Bill" Tilden was the top-ranked U. S. player. In Davis Cup play he won 17 of 22 singles matches and shared 4 doubles victories.

Tilden played tennis essentially from the baseline, matching strategy with a cannonball first serve and running backhand and forehand drives. He turned professional in 1931 and for two decades played tournament and exhibition tennis. In an Associated Press poll in 1950, he was voted the greatest tennis player of the first half of the 20th century.

Tilden was also a tennis instructor and made short films on his sport. He wrote numerous books on tennis. *Aces, Places, and Faults* (1938) and *My Story* (1948) are autobiographical. He was voted a member of the National Lawn Tennis Hall of Fame in 1959. Tilden died of a heart attack in Hollywood, Calif., on June 25, 1953.

NEIL L. AMDUR, *New York "Times"*

TILE, a thin slab of fired clay (terra cotta) applied to the interior or exterior surface of a building. The English word "tile" and French *tuile* are derived from the Latin *tegula* ("tile") from the verb *tegere* ("to cover"). Tiles may be used structurally or decoratively to cover roofs, walls, or floors. The composition of the clay and the firing temperature determine whether ceramic tiles will be porous earthenware, similar to brick, or dense porcelain. They may be coated with a vitreous glaze containing mineral oxides that give striking colors.

The term "tile" is extended to include small flat pieces of surfacing material that is not ceramic, such as vinyl, cork, carpet, wood, or stone. The term also refers to ceramic building units that are not flat surfacing pieces, for example, sections of clay pipe.

Ancient. Ceramic tiles, more durable than artifacts of wood, metal, or bone, have provided archaeologists with much information about ancient civilizations. In Egypt the Step Pyramid of Zoser at Sakhara (3d millenium B. C.) was decorated with small blue-glazed faïence tiles fastened by copper wires to the stone walls. Cretan artisans, about 1800 B. C., composed large mosaic scenes with tiny faïence tiles.

The mud-brick ziggurats (temple towers) and palaces of Mesopotamia were faced with brilliant glazed, burnt brick, or brick-shaped tiles set in bitumen. Sometimes the tiles were molded in bas-relief, and they were often fitted together to make stylized designs. Colors included rich blue, red, brown, yellow, and black. An outstanding example of early Mesopotamian tile work was the ziggurat built by the Sumerian ruler Ur-na-mmu in Ur about 2000 B. C. Later, in the 8th century B. C., magnificent tile reliefs adorned the palace of the Assyrian king Sargon II at Dur Sharrukin (Khorsabad). The English scholar D. T. Fyfe said of them, "For precision and delicacy of treatment, fine sense of design and mastery in the rendering of animal form, those reliefs can compare with the architectonic sculpture of any age." Babylon in the 6th century B. C. glowed with tile work, such as that forming gryphons and bulls on the Ishtar Gate and lions bordering the Processional Way.

Persian tile work was also noteworthy, as seen in the frieze of archers from the palace of Darius at Susa (6th century B. C.). Roman tile was used chiefly unglazed on floors or glazed to form mythological scenes on villa walls.

Islamic and Chinese. Islamic architecture, profiting by the traditional skills of Mesopotamian and Persian craftsmen in the areas conquered by Islam, made great use of glazed tile. Buildings in 9th century Samarra in Mesopotamia were adorned with 10-inch square tiles surrounded by oblong hexagonal tiles painted in metallic films of red, green, yellow, or brown luster. Persian tile work was at its height from the 12th to 15th century. The mosques, public buildings, and fine houses of such cities as Rayy, Tabriz, Isfahan, and Veramin were resplendent inside and out with brilliantly glazed wall tiles

CHINESE TILES, carved in bas-relief, from the Nine Dragon Screen, 20 by 100 feet (6 by 30 meters), of brightly colored porcelain, in Peking's Winter Palace.

L. TAGER, FROM BLACK STAR

of different shapes. Often they were blue on white or were lustered in an iridescent golden brown that changed to green, purple, or ruby in the changing light. Large tiles had complete geometric or stylized floral or figural designs, or they had parts of such designs and were combined to form large panels. Smaller monochrome tiles were arranged in geometric mosaics.

Tile was also important in ancient China. Tombs of the Han period (202 B.C.–220 A.D.) were decorated with tiles bearing stamped or molded figures. From the Sung period (10th–13th century) on, vividly glazed tiles covered roofs, walls, and floors of buildings. The roofs of the imperial palace were yellow. Molded wall tiles and the high ridge tiles of the roof, when assembled, formed dragons and other figures.

European. In the 12th century, tile floors began to appear in European cathedrals. They were of encaustic tiles, in which designs in yellow or white clay were inlaid in red-brown tiles and the combination fired to produce a durable surface. Over the centuries, floors of houses came to be made of plain clay tile or, in fine houses, of black and white marble tile.

Spanish architecture, under strong Islamic influence, used tile to such an extent that a Spanish expression for poverty is "To have a house without tiles." Walls were wainscoted in *azulejos* (tiles), which were often blue and white or lustered. They had geometric, stylized floral, or heraldic designs. In Renaissance Spain and Italy, majolica tiles were popular. They were coated with a white tin-enameled glaze on which figures of knights and saints were painted, often in dark blue and yellow.

Italian and Spanish techniques in tile work spread to northern Europe, especially to the Dutch city of Delft. By the mid-17th century, whole walls of Dutch rooms were covered with Delft tiles in a unique Dutch style. Inspired by Chinese porcelain, potters improved the white glazed ground and reduced the area of the usually blue design. Sometimes each tile had a delicate scene painted on it, and sometimes many tiles together formed one large scene. Dutch tiles were exported to England and America to face fireplaces and to Germanic countries to cover the great heating stoves.

The manufacture of Delft tiles is still the

ASSORTED TILES: (left) Turkish tiles with traditional Islamic floral design; (*center*) Delft tile with 17th century soldier; (*right*) modern American tile with molded surface in basket weave pattern.

TURKISH GOVERNMENT INFORMATION OFFICE

MUSEUM OF THE CITY OF NEW YORK

TILE COUNCIL OF AMERICA

basis for modern tile production. Soft clay was pressed into a square mold, trimmed, marked with powered charcoal pounced through the outlines of a design pricked on paper, and then painted with colored glaze. The brushwork varied on different tiles with the same design to avoid monotony. The tile was then sprinkled with *kwaart* (a transparent lead glaze) and fired to fuse the color and the *kwaart* into a smooth surface.

Modern. In the 20th century, tile provides not only color and design but also durable, sanitary, and easily maintained surfaces. It is used on the walls and floors of kitchens, foyers, bathrooms, patios, swimming pools, laboratories, hospitals, and public areas such as subways.

There are various kinds of tile for different purposes. Ceramic wall tile is a glazed tile with a porous, usually white body, made in many shapes and sizes. Most popular is a monochrome 4¼-inch (10.8-cm) square used in bathrooms, kitchens, and hospitals, where sanitation is important. Tiles with distinctive glazes, textures, molded surfaces, and painted designs are sought by decorators for their practicality and beauty.

Ceramic mosaic tile, usually unglazed and in 1- or 2-inch (2.5 or 5-cm) squares, is used for floors and walls indoors and out. Colors are not so vibrant as those of glazed tile. Quarry tile of red or buff clay, commonly in 6- or 9-inch (15- or 23-cm) squares, is used on floors on which there is heavy traffic or where resistance to chemicals is desired. Quarry tile of varied tones or with embossed surfaces is used in residences and public places. Paver tile, similar in size to quarry tile, comes in more colors.

Less generally known is the vital function of electrically conductive ceramic tile. Used in hospital operating and delivery rooms, it conducts static electricity away before it develops into a spark that could ignite inflammable gases.

J. V. Fitzgerald
Director, Tile Council of America

TILEFISH, a brilliantly colored, deepwater marine fish found along the Atlantic coast of North America on the outer part of the continental shelf from Nova Scotia to Chesapeake Bay. It is also found off southern Florida and in the Gulf of Mexico. The tilefish is a delicious food fish.

The tilefish may grow to a length of 42 inches (106 cm) and a weight of 35 pounds (15.8 kg). Its body is stout, laterally compressed, and deep. The head is large, with a projecting lower jaw. Both jaws are equipped with canine teeth followed by bands of smaller teeth. There is a fleshy flap on the back just behind the head and a barbel-like projection at each corner of the mouth. The back and upper sides are bluish to olive green, while the lower sides are yellow or rose and thickly dotted with irregular yellow spots that also appear on the long dorsal fins. The head is reddish on the sides and white on the underside. Tilefish eat invertebrates and fishes and probably spawn in July or August.

The tilefish, *Lopholatilus chamaeleonticeps*, is classified in the family *Branchiostegidae* of the order Perciformes.

William B. Scott, *University of Toronto*

TILL is a mixture of different sizes of glacier-deposited sediment. Tills are unstratified and consist largely of sand-size particles, with some boulders, silt, and clay.

The outer margins of glaciers and ice sheets are marked by hills of terminal moraine composed of till, and a carpet of till covers the land behind the moraine. This till plain often contains glacial boulders, called *erratics*, and smooth hills of till composition, called *drumlins*. Bunker Hill and Breed's Hill in Boston, Mass., are famous examples of drumlins.

Over a long period of time, till may harden into a sedimentary rock called *tillite*. A tillite deposit from the late Paleozoic era of geologic time has been useful in establishing the former existence of the southern supercontinent named Gondwanaland. See also Glacier; Ice Age.

Warren E. Yasso
Teachers College, Columbia University

TILL EULENSPIEGEL. See Eulenspiegel, Till.

TILLETT, til′ət, **Benjamin** (1860–1943), British labor leader, whose personal idealism and evangelistic oratory contributed greatly to the creation of the largest union in Britain, the Transport and General Workers Union. A spokesman for the unskilled workers, Tillett was an early supporter of the idea that trade unions should have social as well as economic goals. He advocated compulsory arbitration as practiced in Australia.

Tillett was born in East Bristol on Sept. 11, 1860. He served in the Royal Navy and the merchant marine and later worked as a teaporter, or dockworker. After organizing a dockers' union, he led the great dock strike of 1899, which greatly improved working conditions. In 1922 his union and other unions merged to form the Transport and General Workers. For many years he served as a member of the general council of the Trades Union Congress, and he was TUC chairman in 1928–1929. He was a founder of the Labour party and served as a member of Parliament for eight years. He died in London on Jan. 27, 1943.

Harvey L. Friedman
University of Massachusetts

TILLETT, til′ət, **William Smith** (1892–), American physician and bacteriologist, who did important research on pneumococci and streptococci bacteria. In the 1920's, Tillett and associates, notably Thomas Francis, Jr., at the Rockefeller Institute Hospital in New York, studied pneumococci bacteria. They discovered the "C fraction" indicator of pathological action in the body and important facts about immune reactions. Later, working with L. R. Christensen and Sol Sherry, Tillett isolated the enzymes streptokinase and streptodornase from the streptococcus organism. These enzymes act as liquefying agents, and Tillett led the way in demonstrating their therapeutic value. In particular, he showed that carefully controlled amounts of streptokinase could be used to dissolve accumulations of pus and fibrin clots.

Tillett was born in Charlotte, N. C., on July 10, 1892. He received his M. D. from Johns Hopkins in 1917. After working at the Rockefeller Institute, he became associate professor of medicine at Johns Hopkins. In 1937 he joined the College of Medicine of New York University as professor of bacteriology. A year later, he became chairman of the department of medicine. He retired in 1958.

John C. Burnham
Ohio State University

TILLEY, til'ē, **Sir Samuel Leonard** (1818–1896), Canadian political leader and one of the fathers of Confederation. He was born in Gagetown, New Brunswick, on May 8, 1818. He was trained as apprentice to a pharmacist and engaged in that business for 20 years. He began his political career in 1850 as a Liberal member of the New Brunswick legislative assembly, with his chief interest in finance.

In 1861, Tilley became premier of New Brunswick and in 1864 was faced with the project for union of the provinces as proposed by the province of Canada. He was its chief advocate in New Brunswick, but anticonfederates secured a large majority in the election of 1865. In 1866 he went to London for the Westminster Conference on settling provisions of the British North America Act (1867). Tilley's efforts led to the victory for Confederation in New Brunswick's 1866 election.

He was minister of customs from 1867 to 1873 in Macdonald's first Canadian cabinet. In 1878, after a term as lieutenant governor of New Brunswick, he became minister of finance in the second Macdonald Cabinet. From 1885 to 1893 he was again lieutenant governor of New Brunswick. He died at Saint John on June 25, 1896.

G. DE T. GLAZEBROOK, *Author of "A History of Canadian Political Thought"*

TILLICH, til'ik, **Paul Johannes Oskar** (1886–1965), German-American philosopher and theologian. The comprehensiveness of his thought, which was both traditional and modern and which built bridges from religious faith to secular activities, made Tillich the most influential theologian of his time in North America.

Life. Tillich was born into the family of a Lutheran pastor in the village of Starzeddel, Prussia, on Aug. 20, 1886. He studied at the universities of Berlin, Tübingen, Halle, and Breslau. In 1912 he was ordained a minister of the Evangelical Lutheran Church. From 1914 to 1918 he was a chaplain in the German Army. After ministering to the wounded and dying and reading Nietzsche's declarations of the "death of God," he concluded that "the traditional concept of God" indeed was dead. Throughout the rest of his career he sought to redefine the concept and to direct men to "the God beyond God."

After the war he taught at the universities of Berlin, Marburg (where he was a colleague of philosopher Martin Heidegger and Biblical scholar Rudolf Bultmann), Dresden, Leipzig, and Frankfurt. He was also an active leader in the Religious Socialist movement in the Weimar Republic. In 1933 he criticized the intimidating actions of Hitler's Brown Shirts at Frankfurt and won "the honor," as he later put it, of being the first non-Jewish professor to be dismissed from a university post by the Nazi government. He went to the United States that same year, knowing no English, to join the faculty of Union Theological Seminary in New York City. He became chairman of the Council for a Democratic Germany and continued his political and social interests. In succeeding years he taught concurrently at Columbia University and the New School for Social Research, and was visiting lecturer at many universities. Retiring from Union at the age of 67, he became a University Professor at Harvard for the next eight years (1954–1962). Then he taught at the University of Chicago until his death there on Oct. 22, 1965.

PICTORIAL PARADE

Paul Tillich

Thought. Tillich's masterpiece was his three-volume *Systematic Theology* (1951, 1957, 1963), the summation of his work of theological reconstruction. But equally impressive to many readers were his more than 30 shorter books in which he ventured into the areas of philosophy, art, depth psychology, political theory, literature, cultural analysis, and autobiography. Such writings he described as "little screws, drilling into untouched rocks." Among the most famous of these are *The Courage to Be* (1952) and *Dynamics of Faith* (1957).

Tillich's "method of correlation" related Christian affirmations to the existential questions arising in human life and history. This method placed Tillich characteristically "on the boundary"—in a favorite phrase. He described himself as living on the boundary between theology and philosophy, church and society, religion and culture, idealism and Marxism, his native and his alien land.

One consequence was that, while he struggled to bring his ideas into systematic coherence, his thought encompassed a dynamism that constantly pushed at the limits of system and prevented its hardening into rigid patterns. He believed in the interdependence of radical skepticism and unassailable faith or "ultimate concern." He combined such diverse traditions as classical ontology, derived from Parmenides, Plato, and Aristotle, with modern romanticism and existentialism. While deeply attached to his own Lutheran heritage, he sought to appropriate insights from the world's religions and philosophies, and he became a theological innovator.

His Protestantism was not a dogmatic position but an affirmation of a "divine and human protest against any absolute claim made for a relative reality."

Tillich did his work in conversation with many of the foremost theologians of his time. In comparison with Reinhold Niebuhr, his close friend, he was more the mystic and ontologist. In comparison with Karl Barth, who emphasized the independence of Christian revelation, Tillich saw the interrelationships between faith and culture. He agreed with Rudolf Bultmann in rejecting literalisms of the past, but believed that religion would always require nonliteral mythological language. His own aim, as he sometimes put it, was to anticipate "a new form of Christianity, to be expected and prepared for, but not yet to be named."

ROGER L. SHINN
Union Theological Seminary, New York City

Further Reading: Adams, James Luther, *Paul Tillich's Philosophy of Culture, Science and Religion* (New York 1965); Kegley, Charles W., and Bretall, Robert W., eds., *The Theology of Paul Tillich* (New York 1952); Lyons, James R., ed., *The Intellectual Legacy of Paul Tillich* (Detroit 1969).

TILLITE. See TILL.

TILLMAN, Benjamin Ryan (1847–1918), American agrarian spokesman and political leader, who served South Carolina as governor and U. S. senator. For promising to "stick my pitchfork" through President Cleveland's ribs, he gained the nickname "Pitchfork Ben."

Tillman was born on Aug. 11, 1847, in Edgefield county, S. C. Although born into the planter class, young Ben did not attend college because of the war and did not serve in the Confederate army because of youth and illness. After 1865 he farmed and prospered until caught in the great agricultural depression of the 1880's.

In 1885, Tillman began the agitation that made him the dominant political force in South Carolina and a leading Southern spokesman. He proclaimed himself the farmers' advocate, but his movement cannot be understood as an uprising of class against class. Although Tillman's oratory at times bespoke radical agrarianism, his platforms demanded nothing more radical than an agricultural college, and he welcomed all classes and occupations into his organization. Rejecting the radical portions of South-wide movements like the Farmers' Alliance or populism, Tillman remained a faithful Democrat and climbed to power within the party. The dominant political leaders had eulogized an idealized past. A new generation responded to Tillman's demands that attention be riveted not on the past but on the present.

Tillman held the governorship for two terms, 1890 to 1894. He accomplished little for the immediate relief of the farmer. His major achievements, which did benefit both farmer and state, were the establishment of Clemson University and Winthrop College.

Tillman is remembered for a strident Negrophobism that emerged largely after 1890. In 1895 he directed the writing of a new state constitution to disfranchise the Negro. While a senator he toured the country lecturing on the evils of the Negro and the need for white rule.

As a senator (1895–1918), Tillman, an agrarian Democrat in an era of business Republicanism, is not associated intimately with important national measures. He was prominent in the movement that gave the agrarians control of the Democratic party in 1896. He helped guide the Hepburn Railroad Rate bill to passage in 1907, and supported President Wilson's war program as chairman of the Senate Naval Affairs Committee. Tillman died in Washington, D. C., on July 3, 1918.

WILLIAM J. COOPER, JR.
Louisiana State University

Further Reading: Cooper, William J., Jr., *The Conservative Regime: South Carolina, 1877–1890* (Baltimore 1968); Simkins, Francis B., *Pitchfork Ben Tillman: South Carolinian* (Baton Rouge, La., 1944).

Benjamin R. Tillman

CULVER PICTURES

TILLODONTIA, til-ə-donch'ē-ə, an extinct group of herbivorous mammals that lived in the late Paleocene and Eocene, about 60 million to 40 million years ago. They were derived from the Condylarthra, an extinct order of primitive ungulates (hoofed mammals), and are sometimes classified in that group. Tillodonts ranged from the size of a woodchuck (marmot) to that of a bear and had bearlike clawed feet. Their skulls somewhat resembled those of rodents, with the second pair of incisors enlarged for gnawing and, in later forms, growing throughout life. The molars were low-crowned, with enamel only above the gum line except on the inside of the lower molars and the outside of the upper molars.

The larger tillodonts lived in North America in the middle Eocene and in Asia to the late Eocene. A smaller, more primitive genus occurred in the early Eocene of Europe and North America and gave rise to a similar-sized form that survived in Asia to the late Eocene.

The order Tillodontia contains one family, the Esthonychidae, with six known genera.

LEIGH VAN VALEN, *University of Chicago*

TILLOTSON, John (1630–1694), English prelate, who was archbishop of Canterbury from 1691 to 1694. Tillotson was born near Halifax, Yorkshire, in October 1630. He graduated from Cambridge University in 1650 and remained to teach as a fellow at Clare College. At the Restoration (1660) he lost his fellowship but was ordained in the Church of England. In 1663 he married Oliver Cromwell's niece, Elizabeth French, and in the same year was appointed preacher at Lincoln's Inn and lecturer at St. Lawrence Jewry in London.

Tillotson's optimistic ethical theism, a reaction against his Puritan background, made him a popular preacher to a generation growing tired of religious controversies. He also preached against Roman Catholicism and Unitarian doctrines. Sermons of 1679–1680 on the latter theme were published to vindicate his orthodoxy in 1693. He was made a Doctor of Divinity in 1666. In 1670 he became a canon and in 1672 dean of Canterbury Cathedral, but he did not give up his London pulpits. In 1689 he welcomed

William of Orange and was appointed by the cathedral chapter to exercise legal jurisdiction for Archbishop Sancroft, who refused to swear allegiance to William and Mary. Appointed dean of St. Paul's, Tillotson took part in the unsuccessful effort in the Convocation of Canterbury to secure the inclusion of nonconformists in the Church of England by amending the prayer book.

Though personally friendly with Sancroft and other nonjurors, Tillotson was finally willing to accept the archbishopric on Sancroft's deprivation in 1691. He was consecrated on May 31, 1691. His brief tenure of the archbishopric was uneventful, but helped to give prestige to his sermons, which were widely read and imitated. He died in London on Nov. 22, 1694.

EDWARD R. HARDY, *Cambridge University*

TILLY, til'ē, **Count von** (1559–1632), Flemish military leader, who was one of the best-known generals of the Thirty Years' War, a struggle shaped by both religious and political issues. Born in February 1559 in Brabant, now in Belgium, Johann Tserclaes von Tilly was educated by the Jesuits and embarked on a military career.

His talent was quickly recognized, and he advanced rapidly. Tilly offered his services to the Holy Roman Emperor Rudolf II in 1594 and was made field marshal in 1605. Although staunchly loyal to Rudolf, Tilly fell out with Matthias, Rudolf's brother and successor. As a result, Tilly took service with Duke Maximilian I of Bavaria, leader of the Catholic faction, who entrusted Tilly with the creation of a military force for the Catholic League.

Thirty Years' War. Campaigning against the Protestants began in 1620, when Tilly occupied lands in upper and lower Austria. From there he moved to Prague, where his victory at White Mountain in November 1620 won the first phase of the Thirty Years' War for Emperor Ferdinand II. When Christian IV of Denmark emerged in 1625 as a menacing champion of northern Protestantism against Habsburg Catholicism, Tilly was permitted to extend the war northward. He dealt Christian a stunning defeat at Lutter am Barenberge in August 1626. When Albrecht Wallenstein, the Emperor's commander, was dismissed, Tilly was given command of the imperial forces in 1630.

Meanwhile, with the invasion of Germany in 1630 by Protestant forces under King Gustavus Adolphus (Gustaf II) of Sweden the war entered a new phase. To head off the Swedish king, Tilly besieged the Protestant city of Magdeburg in 1631 and destroyed it. He then invaded Saxony, where he sustained his first major defeat, at Breitenfeld, near Leipzig, on Sept. 17, 1631. It became clear that Tilly's traditional methods were no match for an innovative leader like Gustavus. In 1632, Tilly gained one more victory, at Bamberg, where he was wounded. Two weeks later, on April 30, 1632, he died near Ingolstadt.

GERALD STRAUSS, *Indiana University*

TILSIT, til'zit, called Sovetsk since its incorporation into the USSR in 1945, is a city in former East Prussia. Part of Kaliningrad oblast of the Russian SFSR, Tilsit is situated on the south bank of the Neman (Niemen) River, which forms the border with the Lithuanian SSR. The city has a paper and pulp mill.

Tilsit grew around a castle fortified in 1288 by the Teutonic Knights, and received a city charter in 1552. It is known for the Peace of Tilsit (1807), in which Napoleon and Czar Alexander I of Russia forced Frederick William III of Prussia to give up his territories west of the Elbe River and most of his Polish possessions, both of which came under Napoleon's control. Prussia regained part of the area after Napoleon's fall in 1815. Population: (1959) 31,900.

THEODORE SHABAD
Editor of "Soviet Geography"

TIMARU, tim'ə-rōō, is a port city in New Zealand, on the east coast of South Island, about 90 miles (145 km) southwest of Christchurch. It is a commercial center for the surrounding farming and sheep-raising district. Its principal exports are frozen foods. Population of urban area: (1966) 27,946.

TIMBER WOLF. See WOLF.

TIMBERLINE, a climatic limit for tree growth. The altitudes at which timberlines occur on mountains generally decrease with increasing distance from the equator. They range downwards from roughly 11,000 to 13,000 feet (3,300 to 4,000 meters) in latitudes near the tropics. Timberline altitudes on mountains also vary greatly with local conditions.

A general timberline, corresponding roughly to the Arctic Circle, occurs in the Northern Hemisphere. The sequence of tree species one observes when climbing toward a mountain timberline is similar to the sequence seen when approaching Arctic regions. See also FOREST.

TIMBUKTU, tim-buk-tōō', a village in Mali on the southern edge of the Sahara, was once an important center of commerce and Islamic culture. It is situated near the northernmost point of the great bend of the Niger River.

Timbuktu (French, *Tombouctou*) was established as a market town about the 11th century. Its location was admirably suited to serve the needs of the fishing and agricultural communities on the middle Niger as well as the caravans from across the Sahara. The town increased in importance during the 14th century when it was part of the ancient kingdom of Mali. Mansa Musa, emperor of Mali, enlarged its mosques, encouraged the establishment of an Islamic school, and enhanced Timbuktu's stature as a repository of Muslim culture. The city reached its peak of prosperity during the heyday of the Songhai empire (15th–16th centuries). A major caravan center, it was a market for gold, slaves, and salt. Chroniclers and religious divines mingled in its bazaar with merchants from North Africa and the Subsaharan regions of modern Ghana and Nigeria.

After Songhai was conquered by Morocco in 1591, Timbuktu began to decline. But its reputation remained to beguile 19th century travelers and 20th century tourists. Several Europeans risked their lives to penetrate the town's Islamic privacy during the early and middle 19th century. The French wrested control of Timbuktu from the Tuareg after a struggle lasting from 1894 to 1905, but little remained of its former glory. Population: (1963) 8,735.

ROBERT ROTBERG, *Author of "A Political History of Tropical Africa"*

TIME. The fact that events take place and things have duration in a dimension called "time" is immediately familiar in human experience. Yet the more deeply the idea of time is explored, the more difficult it becomes. The way man conceives time has changed over the centuries. Today his understanding of time derives from the most advanced fields of physics and astronomy. The first part of this article reviews the changing concepts of the nature of time. The second part describes the ways in which time is determined and measured.

1. The Idea of Time

One of the peculiarities of modern civilization is the importance it attaches to the idea of time. Time is considered a kind of linear progression measured by the clock and the calendar. The tendency is to regard this idea as a necessity of thought, but acquaintance with the beliefs of other civilizations shows that this is not the case.

Evolution of the Idea of Time. Generally speaking, time was not a concept of primary importance in ancient thought. The Greeks tended to regard the cosmic process as a cyclic alternation of opposing forces rather than as a continual evolution. For example, Aristotle stated that even the tendencies of heavy bodies to fall and light bodies to rise are all part of a cyclic process, so that these apparently straight-line motions are in fact circular—like the perpetual circular motion of the heavenly bodies, which had neither beginning nor end.

Aristotle also held that time and motion were independent, movement being measured by time and time by movement. He recognized that time cannot cease, whereas motion can—except for the motion of the heavens—and concluded that time must be associated closely with this motion, which he regarded as the perfect example of uniform motion.

Belief in the cyclic nature of time was widespread in antiquity, and it gave rise to the idea of the Great Year. There were two versions of this idea. In one, the Great Year was considered simply as the period required for the sun, moon, and planets to attain the same positions relative to one another as they had held at some previous given time. This was the sense in which Plato used the idea. On the other hand, the Great Year for Heraclitus signified the period of the world from its formation to its destruction and rebirth. These two versions were combined by the Stoic philosophers. The Stoics believed that when the heavenly bodies returned to the same relative positions they had at the beginning of the world, everything would be restored as it was before and the entire cycle would be renewed in every detail.

Early Christian leaders rigorously disputed the traditional cyclical view of time. Prominent among them was St. Augustine. He laid great emphasis on the idea that the crucifixion of Christ must be regarded as a unique event, not subject to repetition, implying that time is linear rather than cyclic. He was also the pioneer of the study of internal, or mental, time. Dissatisfied with Aristotle's close association of time with motion, Augustine chose to regard time as an activity of the "soul," or mind, endowed with powers of memory, attention, and anticipation.

In the scientific revolution of the 17th century, Isaac Newton took the view that time exists independently not only of human minds but also of all material objects, and that it "flows" uniformly of its own accord. On the other hand his contemporary Leibniz, the German philosopher and mathematician, regarded time simply as the order of succession of phenomena.

The problem of reconciling these different ideas of time was tackled by the German philosopher Immanuel Kant in the 18th century. Kant was an enthusiastic believer in Newton's natural philosophy, but he rejected Newton's idea of time. Instead he argued that time is simply a feature of the way men's minds visualize the external world and is not a characteristic of external reality itself. He reasoned that if time were a characteristic of the world, equally good arguments could be advanced to show both that the world originated and did not originate in time. In view of this contradiction, Kant decided that time does not apply to the universe but only to the way in which men think about the universe.

Concept of Time in Relativity. In the 19th century, as a result of the arguments advanced by geological and biological evolutionists, the modern idea of time as linear advancement finally prevailed over the older, cyclic conceptions. The tempo of everyday life was speeded up, and the temporal aspects of existence were increasingly regarded as of predominating importance. It therefore came as a shock when, in 1905, Albert Einstein pointed out an unsuspected difficulty in the prevailing idea of time and concluded that time depends on the observer in a way not previously imagined, even by Kant.

It had been taken for granted—both by those who followed Kant's ideas and those who did not—that there is a single worldwide time order and that each instant of this order corresponds to a definite contemporaneous state of the whole universe. This, as Einstein observed, was only an assumption. The order in which events are perceived is not always the order in which they are believed to occur. For a simple example, lightning is seen before thunder is heard, but both are manifestations of the same electric discharge in the atmosphere. Yet until Einstein raised the question, it was universally assumed as self-evident that when the rules are found that determine the time of each perception by the time of the event giving rise to it, all events thus perceived must necessarily fall into a definite time-sequence that is the same for all observers.

After much thought on the measurement of time and motion, Einstein came to realize that a person may have an immediate awareness of the simultaneity of two events in his personal experience but have no such awareness when one event is directly experienced and the other occurs at a distance. For example, suppose an explosion were to occur on Mars. An observer on earth records the instant at which he sees the flash. If light traveled instantaneously, the instant of observation on earth would coincide precisely with the instant the explosion was recorded by a hypothetical observer on Mars. However, there is definite experimental evidence that light takes time to travel, so the terrestrial observer must in fact "correct" the time recorded on his watch to make allowance for the time taken by the light to reach him.

In principle, the velocity of light can be determined only if the way to measure time at all places that it traverses is known. But this is precisely what no longer can be known, once the traditional assumption of worldwide simultaneity for all observers is abandoned. To escape this vicious circle, Einstein decided to jettison the classical theory of the measurement of space and time and begin on a totally different basis.

The classical theory, Einstein realized, leads to absurdity when one tries to imagine what would happen when traveling through space at the same velocity as a beam of light. According to the idea of relative motion based on classical theory, the beam of light would then appear to the observer to be at rest. And a vibrating electromagnetic field at rest is a concept in conflict with electromagnetic theory, which Einstein saw no reason to reject. Instead he concluded that the laws of physics—including those concerning the propagation of light—must remain the same for all observers in uniform motion, however fast they may be moving. In particular, the velocity of light in empty space must be the same for all such observers. Since this velocity is finite, it is the classical idea of relative motion that must be modified.

A curious result of Einstein's theory is that, in general, observers in relative motion must assign different times to the same event. Only observers at relative rest can assign the same time to the event. The discrepancy can be illustrated by saying that a clock in relative motion between two other clocks will measure a smaller time interval than will the two clocks at rest, as it passes from one clock to the other. For velocities encountered in everyday life the difference is negligible, but the nearer the relative velocity of the moving clock is to that of light, the greater the difference will be. The relativistic effect has been amply confirmed by experiments with elementary particles moving at nearly the speed of light.

Time, Space-Time, and Causality. The idea of the relativity of time—that is, that time depends on the observer and that there is no absolute measure of duration—entails the relativity of spatial measurement as well. Due to the universal character of the velocity of light, the distance

COMPARATIVE SCALE OF TIME INTERVALS

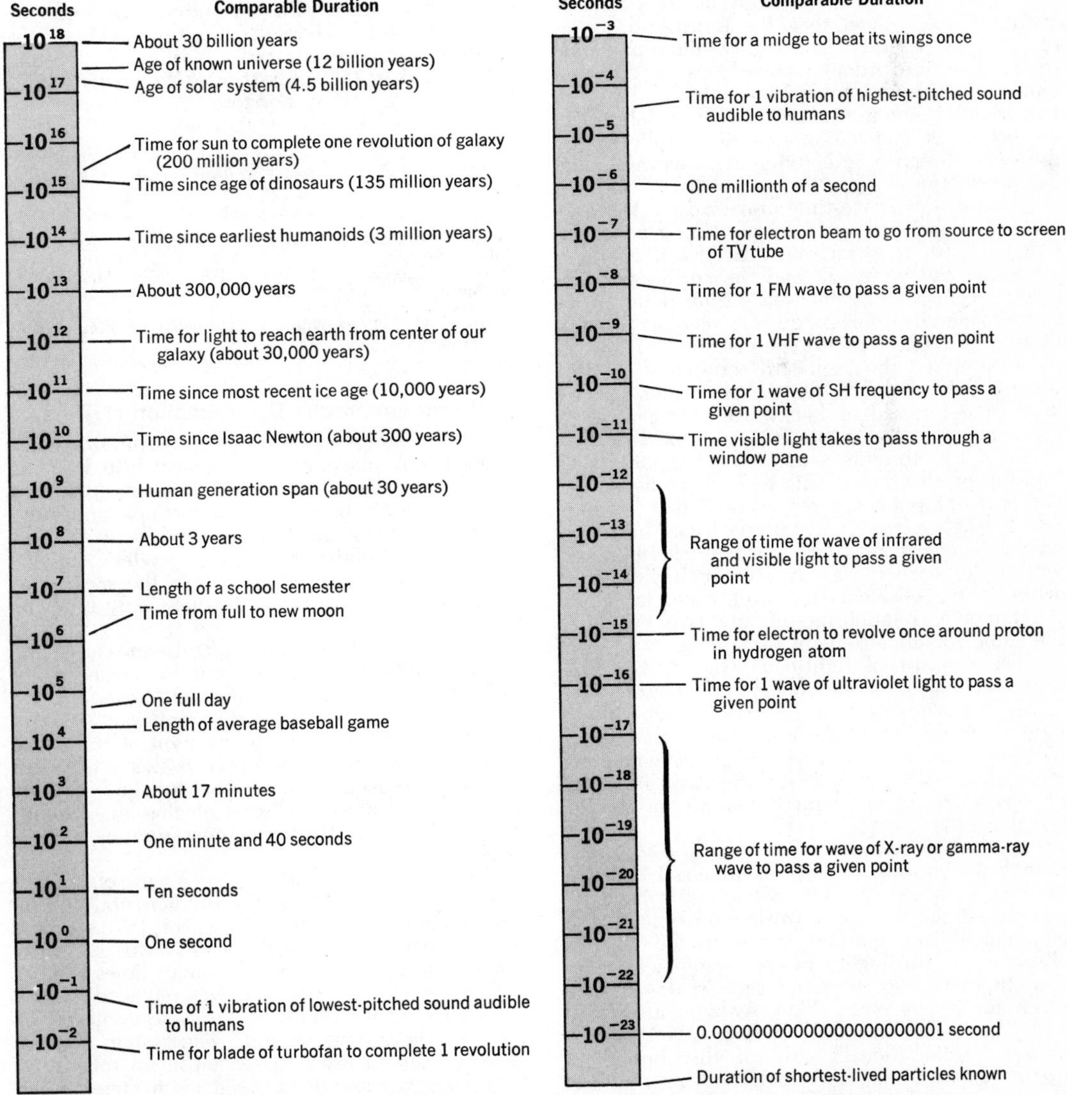

This is a logarithmic scale, in which the time interval increases by a factor of 10 with each division of the scale.

between two places can be measured by the time it takes light to travel from one place to the other. This measurement in turn depends on the observer.

This similarity between space and time is part of the new universal concept introduced by the German mathematician Hermann Minkowski in 1908. If an interval of time is regarded as a kind of "distance" in the time dimension, it can be converted into a distance by being multiplied by c, the velocity of light, thus obtaining the distance light would travel in that time. If the time difference between any two events is T, according to a particular observer, the associated spatial interval is cT. Then if R is the actual distance in space between these events, it can be shown that although both cT and R depend on the particular observer, the difference between cT^2 and R^2 has the same value for all observers in uniform relative motion. This difference is the square of what is called the *space-time interval* between the two events. Space-time is a four-dimensional analog of three-dimensional space, the fourth dimension being the dimension of time.

If the universe is pictured as a system of events in space-time, then the times and spaces of different observers are simply different "cross sections" or individual perspectives of this system. Although the space-time interval between two events is the same according to all observers at rest or in uniform motion, it is split up by different observers into different space and time components.

The idea of space-time also leads to the new concept of forward and backward *light-cones* associated with a given event E. Each of these cones has the vertex E, and the surfaces of the cones are formed by the space-time paths of all conceivable electromagnetic rays passing through that vertex. The forward cone is directed toward the future, and the backward cone converges toward E from the past. Only those events that lie inside the forward or backward light-cone of a given event E are in the future or past of that event in any absolute sense. The temporal relationship of all other events to E depends on the observer. Thus for a given event F that lies outside the light-cones of E, observers can be found who will regard F as later than E, simultaneous with E, or earlier than E. No such ambiguity arises in the classical theory of time, in which the temporal relationship of any two events is the same for all observers.

The concept of light-cones has had a profound influence on the concept of causality because those events that lie inside each other's light cones can be in absolute causal relationship with one another. Einstein later extended his ideas about space-time to include cases in which observers are in accelerated motion in gravitational fields.

Time and the Universe in Modern Cosmology. Although the classical concept of universal time has been undermined, modern cosmologists have reintroduced the idea of a worldwide time that is common to an important but restricted class of observers. According to most cosmological theories, there is a preferential time scale at each place in the universe. This scale is associated with the "local" cosmic standard of rest determined by the "local" bulk of distribution of matter—for example, the center of mass of the stars in our galaxy. The time scales of the observers associated with these local standards of rest, throughout the universe, "fit together" to form one worldwide cosmic time.

It is with reference to this cosmic time that objective meaning can be given to concepts such as the age of the earth, the sun, our galaxy, and even the universe itself. Thus despite the theory of relativity the concept of a cosmic time scale can be retained, even though it is not the time scale of every observer.

According to ideas based on the spectroscopic study of light from distant galaxies, the universe is believed to be expanding, which may imply further limitations on man's idea of time. If the rate of expansion is uniform, the age of the universe would be about 10 billion years, or about twice the age of the sun and the earth. If the rate of expansion is decreasing, the age would be somewhat less. However, if it is increasing, not only would the age be somewhat greater, but there also would be regions receding from our own galaxy at velocities greater than that of light. Hence no light or any other physical influence from such regions could ever reach our galaxy, and no events in the regions could find a place in our time scale. They would lie beyond our "time horizon." Therefore no time scale could comprise all events, and "worldwide" cosmic time would in fact be restricted to events within each observer's time horizon.

See also RELATIVITY; UNIVERSE.

G. J. WHITROW
Imperial College of Science and Technology

Bibliography

Bondi, Hermann, *Relativity and Common Sense* (London 1962).
Fraser, J. T., ed., *The Voices of Time* (New York 1966).
Reichenbach, Hans, *The Philosophy of Space and Time* (New York 1957).
Whitrow, G. J., *The Natural Philosophy of Time* (New York 1962).
Whitrow, G. J., *The Structure and Evolution of the Universe* (New York 1959).

2. Measurement and Determination of Time

In describing an occurrence, one must specify when it took place and how long it lasted. Thus timekeeping involves two concepts. *Epoch* specifies the instant an event occurs, and *time interval* specifies the time elapsed between two events. Civil affairs, navigation, geodetic surveying, and satellite tracking involve the specifying of epoch, whereas physics involves only time interval.

Time Scales. The science of time measurement is concerned with scales of time to which events and time intervals can be referred. Several kinds of scales are used to meet different needs. *Rotational time* is based on the rotation of the earth about its axis. *Ephemeris time* is defined by the motion of the earth about the sun and is used as the time scale of celestial mechanics. *Atomic time* is obtained from the operation of atomic clocks.

Formerly rotational time, or mean solar time, provided both epoch and the fundamental unit of time interval, the second. However, it was found that the earth's rotational speed is variable with respect to ephemeris and atomic times, so in 1956 the mean solar second was replaced by the ephemeris second. This in turn was replaced in 1967 by the atomic second. The system of time measurement in use is based on mean solar time for epoch, whereas it is based upon atomic time for interval.

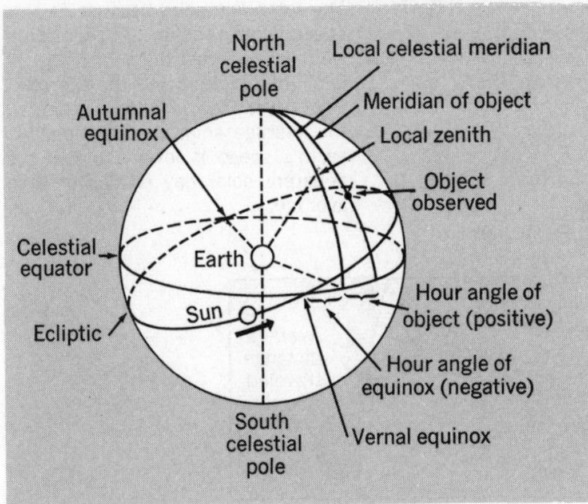

MEASUREMENT OF ROTATIONAL TIME is based on the angular position of celestial objects with respect to the local celestial meridian of a given observer. The angle between this meridian and that of the observed object is the *hour angle* of the object.

ROTATIONAL TIME

The stars, sun, moon, and other celestial bodies are located on an imaginary sphere called the *celestial sphere.* As the earth rotates on its axis the celestial sphere appears to rotate about two fixed points, the north and south celestial poles, at which extensions of the earth's rotational axis would intersect the celestial sphere. Rotational time is described in terms of this sphere.

The measurement of rotational time is based on the angular position of celestial objects with respect to the *local celestial meridian* of longitude for a given observer. The local celestial meridian is a great circle on the celestial sphere, passing through the celestial poles and the observer's zenith, or the point directly overhead. The angular distance—that is, the angle—between the meridian and another great circle passing through the celestial poles and the object being observed is called the *hour angle* of the object. It is given a positive value when the object is west of the meridian, and negative when it is east (see diagram).

The intersection of the plane of the earth's equator with the celestial sphere is called the *celestial equator,* and the intersection of the plane of the earth's orbit with the celestial sphere is called the *ecliptic*. The celestial equator and ecliptic are inclined about 23°27′ to each other, and the two points where they intersect are called the *equinoxes.* One of these, called the *vernal* (or *spring*) *equinox,* is a fundamental reference point for the celestial coordinates of the stars.

Sidereal Time. The stars and sun are seen to rise in the east and set in the west each day. This apparent diurnal motion is the basis of sidereal time, which is defined as the hour angle of the vernal equinox. Sidereal time is determined by noting the instant when a star of known position transits, or crosses, the meridian. See also DAY.

Apparent Sidereal Time. The hour angle of the true sun, as indicated by a sundial, determines apparent solar time. As the earth orbits the sun, the sun appears to move eastward with respect to the stars and equinox. The speed of this motion amounts to a complete revolution of 360° in one year, or nearly 1° per day.

If the sun is at the equinox and also on the meridian in one day, on the next day the sun will be east of the equinox nearly 1°. This means that the sun will not transit the meridian until almost four minutes after the equinox does. Hence the apparent solar day—the time interval between two meridian transits by the true sun—is longer than the sidereal day, which is defined as the interval between two meridian transits by the equinox. The difference between the sidereal day and the solar day varies during the year because the apparent eastward motion of the sun is not uniform. The earth moves about the sun with varying speed in an elliptical orbit. Apparent solar time is not uniform.

Mean Solar Time. The introduction of fairly accurate clocks and watches about 1700 made the use of apparent solar time unsatisfactory, because it is not uniform. Therefore mean solar time was introduced. Mean solar time is determined by the hour angle of a "fictitious" sun that moves uniformly along the celestial equator with virtually the *mean* speed of the true sun, and that has nearly the same hour angle as the true sun. The difference between mean solar

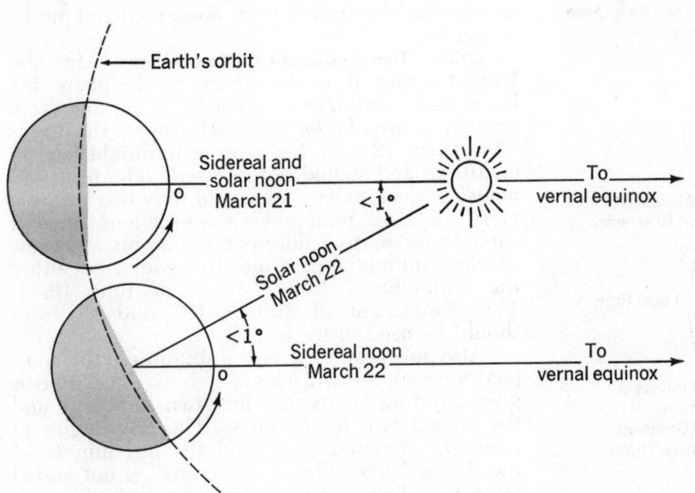

Sidereal and solar day differ in length. If the sun is at the equinox and also on the meridian in one day, then on the next day the sun will be to the east by nearly 1°. Thus the sun will not cross the meridian until about four minutes later the next day, so that the apparent solar day is about four minutes longer than the sidereal day.

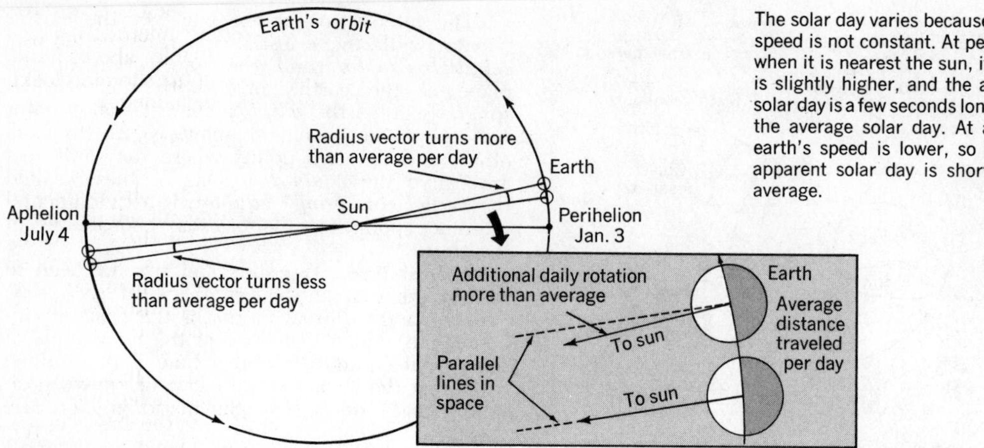

The solar day varies because earth's speed is not constant. At perihelion, when it is nearest the sun, its speed is slightly higher, and the apparent solar day is a few seconds longer than the average solar day. At aphelion earth's speed is lower, so that the apparent solar day is shorter than average.

time and apparent solar time, called the *equation of time*, has a maximum value of about 16 minutes 23 seconds. In one mean solar day, a clock that keeps uniform sidereal time gains 3 minutes 56.555 seconds on a clock keeping mean solar time.

In practice, astronomers determine mean solar time without observing the sun. Stars are observed to obtain uniform sidereal time, and this is transformed into mean solar time by a mathematical formula based on past observations of the sun with respect to the stars.

Local, Standard, and Universal Time. The instant when the equinox or the sun comes to the meridian of a given observer depends on his longitude. Because the earth turns through 360° in 24 hours, the local time for two points will differ by one hour for each 15° difference in longitude. The time is more advanced for the point to the east of the observer.

Up into the 19th century it was the custom to keep local time, but the growth of rapid transportation and communication made this system inconvenient. It was agreed at an international conference in 1884 that the meridian of Greenwich, England, would be adopted as the starting point for reckoning longitude and that the world would be divided into 24 standard time zones. See TIME ZONES.

UNIVERSAL TIME, or Greenwich Mean Time, is based on mean solar time, and uses the longitude of Greenwich, England, as its reference meridian. The difference between an observer's local time and Greenwich Mean Time gives the longitude of the observer.

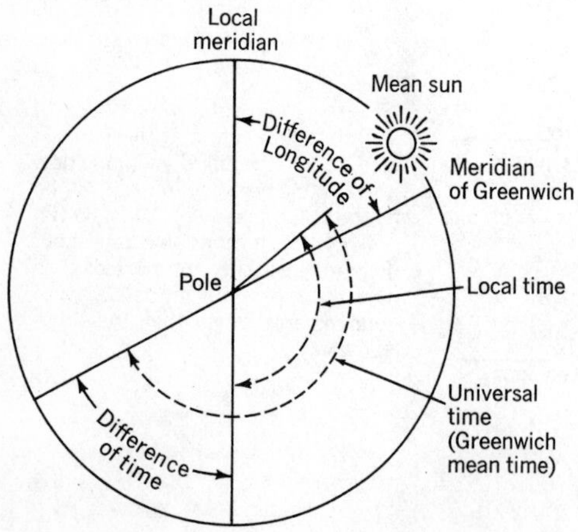

The mean solar time of the Greenwich meridian is used for many scientific and technical purposes to avoid difficulties with local systems. The official name is Universal Time, or UT, but it is often designated Greenwich Mean Time, or GMT. It is used for designating epoch without ambiguity—for example, in worldwide communications and in airflight plans—and is sometimes called "Z."

Observations of star transits made at astronomical observatories first furnish UT in a form known as UTO. This form contains small variations for which corrections are applied by international agreement. UTO is changed to UT1 by correcting for a small variation in longitude caused by polar motion. Correcting for seasonal variations in speed of the earth in its orbit changes UT1 to UT2. In fact, the differences between UTO, UT1, and UT2 are small, generally amounting to less than 0.05 second.

UTC, or *Coordinated Universal Time,* is obtained from atomic clocks that are adjusted in epoch so as to remain close to UT2, within 0.5 second. Beginning Jan. 1, 1972, adjustments are exactly 1 second. For the next few years clocks on UTC will be retarded about once per year. UTC is disseminated widely by means of radio time signals, and these signals ultimately are widely used for setting both household and public clocks.

Other Time-Designation Conventions. In the United States it is customary to designate the hours from midnight to noon by A. M., and from *noon to midnight by* P. M. However, the terms 12 A. M. or 12 P. M. for noon or midnight lead to confusion and should not be used. The term "12 noon" is clear, since it refers to only one possible noon, but "12 midnight" is ambiguous since it could refer to two different midnights. For example, "midnight of June 10" could be either the midnight of June 9-10 or of June 10-11. Thus "midnight of June 9-10" and so forth should be used instead.

Also in order to avoid ambiguities, the military services use a 24-hour system. The time is given by four digits, the first two for hours and the second two for minutes. The day begins at midnight, denoted 0000, and the last minute of the day is 2359. The word "hours" is not added after the digits. Thus 0830 means 8:30 A. M.,

2315 means 11:15 P.M., and the notation "2400 of 10 June" is the same time as "0000 of 11 June."

The 24-hour system is used in continental Europe, and international airline schedules are usually given on this system.

EPHEMERIS TIME AND ATOMIC TIME

The motions of the celestial bodies take place in accordance with the laws of celestial mechanics, first propounded by Isaac Newton in the late 17th century. The theory of relativity formulated by Albert Einstein in the early 20th century introduced slight refinements. Therefore the equations of motion may be written for the orbital motion of the earth about the sun. Solving these equations gives the orbit, which allows the position of the earth to be calculated as a function of time. The time that enters into the equations of motion and into the orbit is called *ephemeris time,* or ET.

Determination of Ephemeris Time. The position of the earth in its orbit is obtained by observation of the position of the sun with respect to the stars, since the earth and sun occupy opposite points in the ecliptic. A table called the *Solar Ephemeris* is computed from the known orbit of the earth. The table gives the position of the sun as a function of ephemeris time, so that ephemeris time may be found by observation of the position of the sun.

The constants that enter into the solution for the earth's orbit have been so chosen that for about two centuries before 1900, the average length of the mean solar second—which is slightly variable—is almost the same as the second of ephemeris time. Nevertheless, the independence of ephemeris time and mean solar time is important. Their difference can be determined only from observation and cannot be predicted from a formula.

Ephemeris time may be obtained from the orbital motion of any planet about the sun or from the motion of a satellite about a primary for which an ephemeris is available. Thus the orbital motions of Venus and Mercury about the sun, and of the moon about the earth, have been used to determine ephemeris time. The times determined in this way are generally consistent, although slight differences exist because of observational error. Hence the motion of the earth about the sun has been chosen as the standard for defining the measure of ephemeris time. The *Tables of the Sun* (1896), developed by the American astronomer Simon Newcomb, are used for this purpose.

In practice, ephemeris time is obtained rapidly from the orbital motion of the moon about the earth. The position of the moon with respect to the stars may be determined with a transit instrument, from occulations, or by photography.

Atomic Time. It has long been known that under certain conditions atoms and molecules emit electromagnetic radiation at fixed frequencies. At about 5×10^{14} cycles per second (cps) the radiation appears as a visible line on the spectrum.

An atomic clock can be constructed if a method can be devised for counting such cycles. This has not been done for visible light because the frequencies are too high, but spectral lines invisible to the eye exist for radio waves of very short wavelength—about 1 centimeter (0.4 inch) —called *microwaves.* For a wavelength of 3 centimeters (1.2 inches), the frequency is about 10^{10} cps. Equipment for generating microwaves and counting cycles became available about 1940. The way was open for developing atomic clocks, although practical problems remained.

ASTRONOMICAL INSTRUMENTS FOR DETERMINING TIME

Rotational time is obtained by observation of the transit across the meridian of an observer, ephemeris time by the position of the sun, moon, or a planet with respect to the stars. The precise determination of rotational and ephemeris times requires specialized astronomical instruments.

Meridian Circle. The meridian circle is a telescope that moves in the plane of the meridian about a horizontal east-west axis. It has an accurately divided circle to indicate elevation. The instrument is used to determine the fundamental positions of the sun, moon, planets, and stars. The *small transit telescope* is mounted like the meridian circle, but it is smaller and its circle is of moderate precision.

PZT and Danjon Astrolabe. The small transit telescope has been mostly superseded at observatories by the photographic zenith tube, or PZT, and the Danjon astrolabe. These instruments have higher accuracy and offer the further advantage of determining latitude also.

The PZT has been used since 1934 by the U. S. Naval Observatory to determine rotational time. The telescope is fixed in position so that it always points to the zenith at the observatory. A basin of mercury, placed underneath the lens at a distance of nearly half the focal length of the lens, reflects the rays of light from a star that crosses the meridian near the zenith. The rays are brought to a focus on a small photographic plate placed about 1 centimeter (0.4 inch) below the lens. The plate moves during the exposure so as to track the star, and signal pulses are transmitted to a clock. The upper part of the instrument and plate are rotated 180° between exposures. Four exposures of about 20 seconds each are made of each of the 16 stars normally observed automatically during the night. By measuring the positions of the images on the plate, it is possible to determine the difference between the clock and rotational time (UT). A PZT is also installed at the Naval Observatory Time Service Substation at Richmond, Fla., and about 12 are in use in other countries.

With the Danjon astrolabe, developed in 1956, an observer visually follows a star of known position. A clock reading is obtained for the instant when the star is at altitude 60°. About 30 stars are observed in a night, and from these observations the difference between the clock and UT can be determined.

Dual-Rate Moon Camera. The dual-rate moon camera was developed in 1951 at the U. S. Naval Observatory to determine ephemeris time from photographic observations of the moon. The camera tracks the moon and stars at their respective rates during a simultaneous 20-second exposure. Measurement of the position of the moon relative to the stars determines ephemeris time.

CLOCKS

Clocks consist essentially of a frequency-control part (frequency is the number of times per second that a repetitive event occurs, such as a pendulum swing) and a part for counting and

NATIONAL BUREAU OF STANDARDS

STANDARD SECOND is based on the oscillation of a cesium-133 atom in a cesium-beam clock (*above*).

indicating oscillations. In a pendulum clock the pendulum is the frequency-control part, and the escapement, gears, dial, and hands are the elements of the counting-and-indicating part. In a common electric clock the frequency-control part is the generator of the electric current being used, and the clock itself consists only of a counting-and-indicating system. Some historical timekeepers, such as the water clock, the sandglass, and the burning candle, indicated only elapsed time. See also CLOCK.

Formerly the rates of even the most precise clocks diverged so much after a while that it was necessary to adjust them in epoch and rate from time to time, in order to conform with rotational time, or UT. Today, however, the frequencies of atomic clocks are of such high stability that they can be used to form a time scale that is independent of rotational time. Indeed, the variation in the speed of rotation of the earth is determined by comparing rotational time with the time provided by atomic clocks.

Pendulum Clocks. Mechanical clocks of low accuracy were constructed as early as the 14th century and possibly earlier. The era of precise timekeeping began with Galileo's discovery, about 1583, that the period of oscillation of a pendulum is nearly independent of the amplitude of the swing. That is, a pendulum will swing back and forth at the same frequency even as the range of the swing is decreasing. About 1656 the Dutch astronomer Christiaan Huygens applied this pendulum principle to the construction of an accurate clock.

In the late 17th century it was also found that a balance wheel controlled by a hairspring would oscillate with a period nearly independent of the amplitude of the oscillation. By the early 18th century both pendulum clocks and hairspring-controlled clocks of fairly good accuracy were being built. By 1930 the rates of the best pendulum clocks were constant to about 0.002 second per day. However, such clocks have been superseded in precise timekeeping by quartz-crystal and atomic clocks.

Electronic Clocks and Quartz-Crystal Oscillators. In an electronic clock, the output frequency of a control oscillator—perhaps 100,000 cycles per second—is introduced and divided electronically to give sharp pulses, one per second. These pulses are the primary time markers of the clock. Other timing markers are produced at rates of 10, 100, 1,000, and 10,000 cps. Hours, minutes, and seconds are displayed in two ways. In some clocks a synchronous motor drives the clock hands, whereas in all-electronic clocks there is no mechanical motion. Instead the display is by means of numbered lights.

A quartz-crystal oscillator is frequently combined with an electronic clock to form a quartz-crystal clock. Quartz and other crystals have elastic and piezoelectric properties—that is, if an electric force is applied to opposite faces of the crystal, the crystal is deformed. Conversely, if the crystal is deformed, an electric force is produced. A quartz crystal can be inserted in an oscillating electric circuit so that its frequency is that of the elastic vibration of the crystal, although this frequency changes slowly with age. The best quartz oscillators have "drift" rates of about 1 part in 10^{11} each day, an acceleration of about 1 microsecond (10^{-6} second) per day per day.

Atomic Clocks. An atomic clock combines an electronic clock with an atomic oscillator. Electromagnetic radiation is produced when an atom or molecule falls from a higher energy state (E_1) to a lower (E_2). The frequency of the radiation is given as $f = (E_1 - E_2)/h$, where h is Planck's constant. See also QUANTUM THEORY.

Ammonia Maser. Experiments carried out in 1947 used two energy states of the ammonia molecule, NH_3, to stabilize electronic oscillators. In 1949 an ammonia-controlled clock was built at the National Bureau of Standards in Washington, D. C. Moderate accuracy was obtained with this device, which used an absorption line of the ammonia spectrum. In 1954 an oscillator was developed that instead used an emission line of ammonia. This device was the maser. The term "maser" stands for "*m*icrowave *a*mplification by *s*timulated *e*mission of *r*adiation." In the maser, molecules that issue from a container are separated magnetically. The molecules in a higher energy state enter a cavity where they fall to a lower state, emitting radiation. See also MASER.

The ammonia maser has high stability, but the frequency it provides is affected somewhat by its adjustment. For nitrogen-14 the frequency is about 23,870,129,300 cps, and for nitrogen-15 it is about 22,789,421,700 cps.

Cesium-Beam Oscillator. An atomic oscillator of very high precision and using a beam of cesium atoms was constructed in 1955 at the National Physical Laboratory at Teddington, England. Although such cesium-beam clocks are complex in theory, they have been produced commercially by several firms in highly accurate, lightweight versions. The frequency remains stable to about ± 2 parts in 10^{12}, and the absolute frequency is correct to about ± 5 parts in 10^{12}.

A joint experiment was carried out in 1955–1958 by the National Physical Laboratory and the U. S. Naval Observatory to determine the frequency of cesium in terms of the second of ephemeris time, as measured with the dual-rate moon camera. The value obtained—9,192,631,770 cps—was adopted in 1967 by the General Conference of Weights and Measures as the definition of the length of the second, in the International System of Units—the modernized metric system.

Hydrogen Maser. The most stable oscillator appears to be the hydrogen maser, developed at Harvard University about 1960. Its stability is about 1 part in 10^{13}, and the frequency is about 1,420,405,751.8 cps. However, the hydrogen maser is more difficult to construct than the cesium-beam oscillator, and some questions remain as to what corrections must be applied to obtain an absolute frequency. For these reasons the oscillations of the cesium atom were instead selected to define the atomic second.

Rubidium Clocks. Atomic clocks using rubidium vapor and employing a principle called "optical pumping" have been constructed. They are light in weight and relatively simple, but the frequency depends on the construction. Thus they are used in fewer applications than are cesium clocks. See LASER for an explanation of optical pumping.

OTHER ASPECTS OF TIME MEASUREMENT

Short time intervals are measured with high precision by electronic counters, which count the cycles produced by an oscillator—say 10^6 per second. A pulse starts the counting, and a second pulse stops it. The time interval between pulses, to the microsecond, is displayed by numerical lights.

Radioactive Dating. Long time intervals must be measured by other means, through the use of radioactivity. Atoms of radioactive elements decay to form other elements or isotopes. For example, uranium eventually decays to lead, and carbon-14 decays to carbon-12. The end products are stable. The decay of uranium, rubidium, and potassium makes it possible to measure very long intervals. The oldest ages thus found are about 3 billion years for some earth rocks and about 4.5 billion years for meteorites and rock samples from the lunar surface.

The decay of carbon-14 enables objects containing former organic matter—for example, paper, wood, and bones—to be dated. The ages that can be established by radiocarbon dating range from about 100 to 100,000 years. See also ARCHAEOLOGY; GEOCHRONOLOGY.

Variations in the Earth's Rotational Speed. Another area involving time measurement is the determination of the variations in the earth's rotational speed. The variations are of three kinds: *secular variation* produced by tidal friction; *irregular variations* probably produced by motions within the earth's core; and *periodic variations* produced chiefly by yearly variations in planetary winds. The secular and irregular variations were discovered by comparison of rotational time with ephemeris time, obtained by means of lunar eclipses, occultations, and meridian observations. Annual variations were found through the use of quartz clocks.

The atomic clock made it possible to study the variations in rotational speed with increased precision. It was formerly thought that the irregular variation consisted of abrupt changes in speed of rotation, but the comparison of rotational time with atomic time since 1955 shows that such changes do not occur. Instead the speed changes continuously, whether accelerating or decelerating. Sudden changes in acceleration occur about every four years. The cause of these changes is not known.

Variations in speed of rotation are best expressed in terms of atomic time, even though atomic clocks date from only 1955. In the last two centuries the duration of a mean solar second with respect to the atomic second has varied as much as ± 5 parts in 10^8, and the difference in accumulated time has amounted to about 50 seconds. The length of the day is increasing about 0.0015 seconds per century.

Worldwide Synchronization. Better methods of transmitting time signals have had to be developed to meet the need for worldwide synchronization of clocks. Thus Universal Time is needed by ships at sea to determine longitude. Beginning in 1904, radio was used to transmit such time signals. Precise time is now transmitted by U. S. naval radio stations around the world, by stations of the National Bureau of Standards, and by radio stations of many other countries. Through international cooperation the signals are closely synchronized, coordination being provided through the International Time Bureau in Paris. An accuracy of about 1 millisecond (10^{-3} second) is provided around the world by these transmissions. The navigational Loran-C transmissions of the U. S. Coast Guard provide an accuracy of about 1 microsecond (10^{-6} second) for receivers within ground range. Naval radio and Loran-C signals are kept in close agreement with the master atomic clock of the Naval Observatory.

The photographic tracking of artificial satellites requires the worldwide synchronization of clocks to 1 millisecond, an accuracy provided by the means just described. However, higher accuracy requirements for satellite and other purposes are forseen for the future. The U. S. Telstar satellite launched in August 1962 was used in long-range experiments to synchronize clocks in the United States and the United Kingdom to 1 microsecond, and the Relay 2 satellite was used in February 1965 to synchronize clocks in the United States and Japan to 0.1 microsecond. In addition, worldwide operational synchronization to 1 microsecond is provided by the Naval Observatory through transport by air of portable, cesium-beam atomic clocks.

Relativity Effects. The time measurement of relativity effects is a final subject to be considered here. According to the concept of time formulated by Isaac Newton in the 17th century, there is a single time reference for all events in the universe. However, according to Einstein's theory of special relativity, formulated in 1905, each inertial system in the universe has its own time parameter. The prerelativity, intuitive concepts of absolute time and absolute simultaneity do not exist in special relativity.

A fundamental consequence of the theory, supported by experiment, follows. Let A, B, and C be similar clocks. A and B are at fixed positions relative to each other and are synchronized. C passes between them, coinciding successively with the positions of A and B. According to relativity theory, the time interval between these coincidences, as measured by clock C alone, will be less than the time interval as measured by the differences in the readings of A and B at the successive coincidences, when clock C passes. The single clock always measures a smaller interval than does the pair, irrespective of whether the single clock or the pair of clocks is considered to be stationary.

Relativity effects are noticeable for particles such as electrons and protons, which can be accelerated to nearly the speed of light. Proposals have been made to measure the effects with atomic clocks, and this will probably be done. See also RELATIVITY.

WILLIAM MARKOWITZ, *Marquette University*

Bibliography

Cowan, Harrison J., *Time and Its Measurement: From the Stone Age to the Nuclear Age* (Cleveland 1958).
Hood, Peter, *How Time is Measured,* 2d ed. (New York 1964).
Nautical Almanac Offices of the United Kingdom and the United States, *Explanatory Supplement to the Astronomical Ephemeris and the American Ephemeris and Nautical Almanac* (London 1961).
Schlegel, Richard, *Time and the Physical World* (New York 1961).
Ward, F. A. B., *Time Measurement* (New York 1967).

TIME, Daylight Saving. See DAYLIGHT SAVING TIME.

TIME CAPSULE, a sealed container holding objects of social and scientific interest and everyday use, with pictures, films, and descriptions of contemporary civilization, to be opened in the distant future. Cornerstones of buildings are often hollowed out to hold such items, continuing a custom practiced in ancient Babylon and Egypt, where inscriptions and statuettes were sealed into temple foundations.

The name "Time Capsule" was adopted by the Westinghouse Electric Corporation for a slim, torpedo-shaped container, 7½ feet (2.3 meters) long, buried in 1938, at a depth of 50 feet (15.2 meters), at the Flushing Meadows site of the New York World's Fair of 1939. At the 1964–1965 New York World's Fair, Westinghouse exhibited and buried a second time capsule. Both are to be opened in 6939 A. D. Expo 67 at Montreal featured a time capsule to be opened in 2067, and Expo '70 at Osaka had a spherical capsule with an inside diameter of 1 meter, to be opened in 6970.

The 1938 and 1965 capsules were glass-lined and filled with nitrogen to prevent the decomposition of the contents. The first capsule was made of a hardened alloy, mainly copper. The other three were stainless steel. As an example of their contents, the 1939 capsule holds more than 100 objects of social, scientific, industrial, and everyday use, as well as extensive microfilms and a newsreel.

A more comprehensive contemporary record, called the Crypt of Civilization, is in a large underground room at Oglethorpe, Ga., sealed in 1940 and to be opened in 8113 A. D.

TIME AND MOTION STUDY. See INDUSTRIAL ENGINEERING.

TIME LOCK. See LOCK.

TIME REVERSAL is an assumed reversal of the normal direction of time, so that it moves from future to past. In exploring this assumption, physicists so far have found that nature is indifferent to the direction of time. One can substitute $-t$ for t in any basic law in physics, and the law will still describe something that could occur in nature. See also SYMMETRY PRINCIPLES; TIME.

TIME ZONE, a zone covering an average of 15° of longitude from pole to pole, and throughout which the same clock time is generally used. With high-speed transportation and almost instantaneous communications, it is most important that the world have an organized and cooperative system of keeping time. If it were not for the standard time zones adopted throughout most of the world, each settled area would have its own local time based on its own longitude.

History. Before telegraphy and railroads were in use, problems of time differences from one community to the next were minimal. Travel was slow, and time changes amounted to hardly more than minor clock adjustments in the course of travel. For example, it takes the noon sun about 12 minutes to pass from Boston to New York, but a traveler in the 18th century would absorb this time difference over a period of three to four days.

With the introduction of the telegraph and the rapid construction of railroads in the middle of the 19th century, the need for a uniform time system soon became apparent. In Europe the railroads at first used the time of their respective capital cities, and differences between that time and local times within a given country were relatively small. In the United States it was impractical for central and western railroads to use the European system and operate on Washington, D. C., time, which would differ by hours from local time. As a result, each railroad developed its own system of time zones, and by the early 1870's over 50 different times were being used. Thus cities functioning on local time, and served by more than one railroad, each on its own time, were centers of considerable confusion. For example, Pittsburgh had five clocks in its station to accommodate the railroads and to show local time. Nevertheless, the systems of time zones developed by the railroads formed the basis of the zones eventually adopted in the United States.

Prior to 1870 some countries had made progress in introducing measures of standard time. By 1850, Britain had established Greenwich Observatory time as standard throughout England, Wales, and Scotland—and for shipping purposes the United States had officially adopted the Greenwich meridian as 0° longitude. American and international scientific societies had committees working on plans to formulate a system of standard time. In a meeting in St. Louis in 1872, U. S. railroads proposed a system of four time zones for their own use, but it was October 1883 before the plan was finally approved, and it was put into operation the following month.

In August 1884 the U. S. Congress authorized President Chester A. Arthur to convene an International Meridian Conference, which would consider a proposal for a system of world time zones and a common zero degree of longitude, and recommend acceptance of it. The conference was held in Washington, D. C., in October 1884. Many of the nations that attended adopted the proposals, and over the following years most of the world has accepted them. The United States itself approved of the plan, and U. S. railroads were already operating on standard time zones, but it was not until 1918 that Congress instructed the Interstate Commerce Commission to establish the actual boundaries between the different zones.

World Time Zones. The basis for the World Time Zones is simply that as the earth rotates,

UNITED STATES TIME ZONES

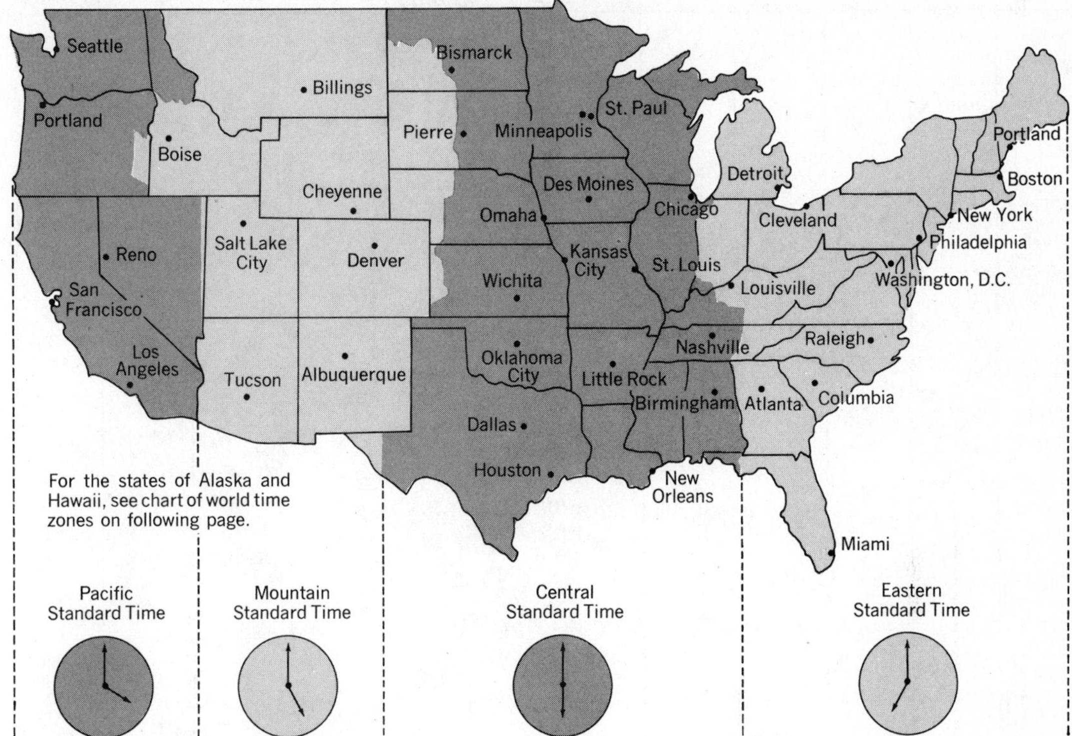

the sun appears to pass through 15° of longitude every hour. Therefore the world is divided into 24 time zones—24 times 15° equals 360°—with each zone one hour ahead of or behind its neighboring zones. All places within a given 15° zone use the same time, which is the time of the central meridian of that zone.

For example, the Greenwich Mean Time Zone, centered on 0° longitude, extends from longitude 7½° W to longitude 7½° E. Successive zones to the east of the Greenwich zone are ahead of Greenwich time by one hour for each 15°. Thus longitude 45° E is three hours ahead of Greenwich time, so that when it is noon at Greenwich, it is 3 P.M. at longitude 45° E. Each zone to the west of Greenwich is one hour behind Greenwich time for each 15° of longitude.

With the Greenwich Mean Time Zone designated as 0 hours, or 00^h, the zones to the east are designated successively as -1^h, -2^h, -3^h, and so forth, and the zones to the west as $+1^h$, $+2^h$, and $+3^h$. These successive zones meet in the opposite hemisphere at the International Date Line, with the zone to the west of the line being -12^h and the zone to the east $+12^h$. A person moving from east to west across the line loses a day—that is, the date moves one day forward—and a person crossing the line from west to east gains a day. The International Date Line is internationally recognized, although it was not officially adopted by the 1884 conference.

U. S. Time Zones. In the United States there are eight official time zones, extending from Atlantic time—60° W, $+4^h$—for Puerto Rico and the Virgin Islands, to Bering time—165° W, $+11^h$—for western Alaska and the Aleutian Islands.

Since the first boundaries were drawn there have been many changes and adjustments. For example, prior to 1941 Georgia was divided by the boundary between the Eastern and Central time zones. As a result of hearings held by the Interstate Commerce Commission, at the request of the state, the line was changed to the Georgia-Alabama boundary, putting Georgia entirely in the Eastern zone. Since the Uniform Time Act of 1966, such adjustments are under the jurisdiction of the Transportation Department.

Time Zone Variations. In theory each World Time Zone boundary would follow a single meridian of longitude from pole to pole, but few zones are so smoothly bounded. Because of political and economic considerations, boundaries are drawn to inconvenience as few people as possible.

A few countries, such as Guyana, Liberia, Mongolia, and Saudi Arabia, have not changed from the use of local time. Other countries have made minor adjustments to bring their time to a half-hour rather than a full hour interval. Newfoundland, Surinam, and Uruguay are on $+3^h30^{min}$, and India's zones are -5^h30^{min} and -6^h30^{min}.

Another variation is the People's Republic of China, which extends through 50° of longitude but uses only a single time, based on the 120th meridian along its eastern seaboard. And Britain, home of the world's adopted standard time, Greenwich Mean Time, uses Central Europe Time, -1^h.

VAN H. ENGLISH, *Dartmouth College*

Further Reading: Harrison, Lucia C., *Sun, Earth, Time, and Man* (Chicago 1960); Strahler, Arthur N., *Physical Geography*, 3d ed. (New York 1969); U. S. Naval Observatory, *The Air Almanac* (Washington, D. C., annually).

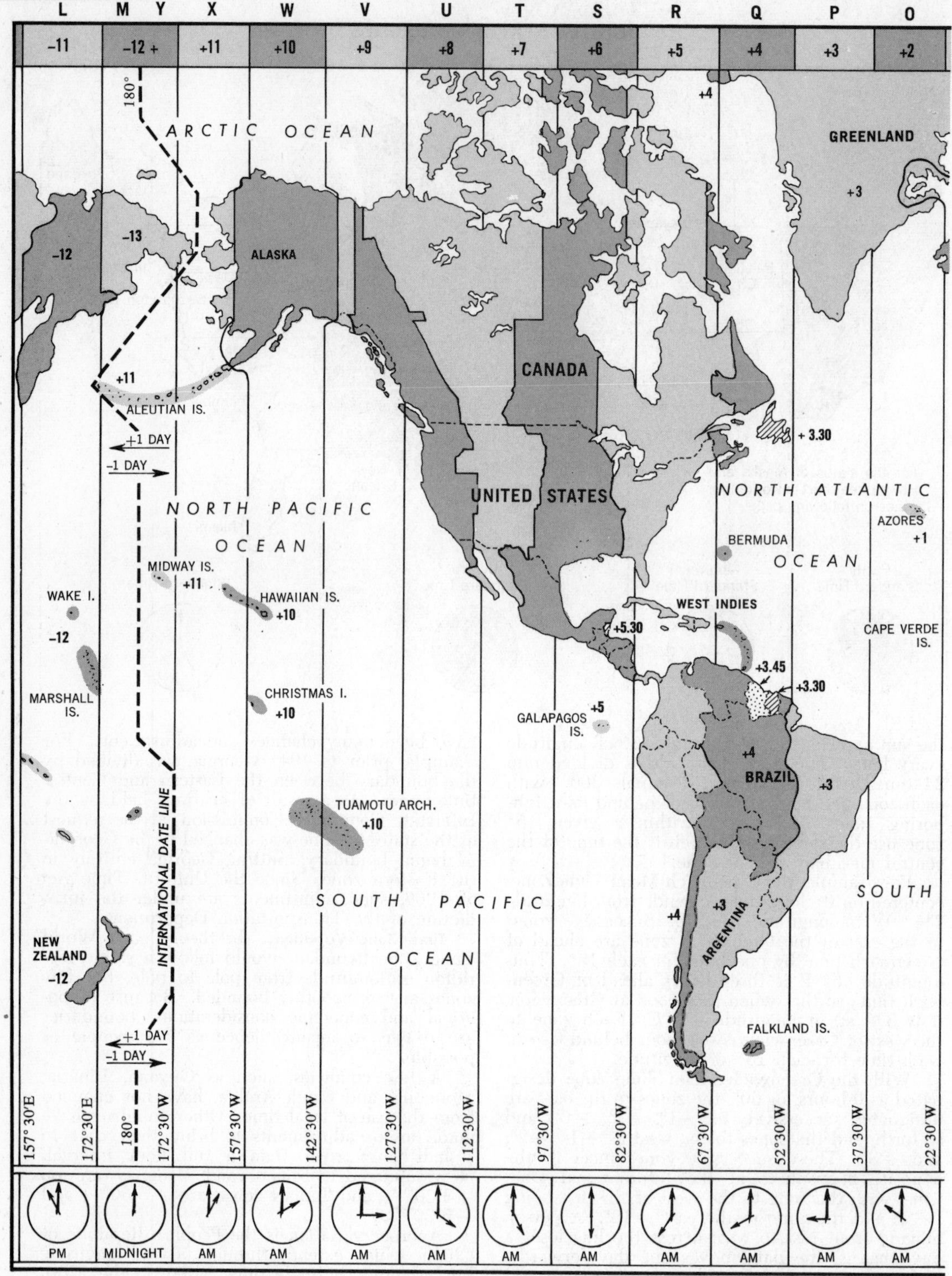

TIME ZONE CHART

SYMBOLS TO SHOW TIME ZONE DIVISIONS

Note: Because of the existence of the "0" time zone, and the irregular time-zone boundaries, the navigational "zone descriptions" indicated at the top of the chart may differ numerically by one or more hours from the Greenwich time difference used in certain localities as noted on the face of the chart.

TIME ZONE

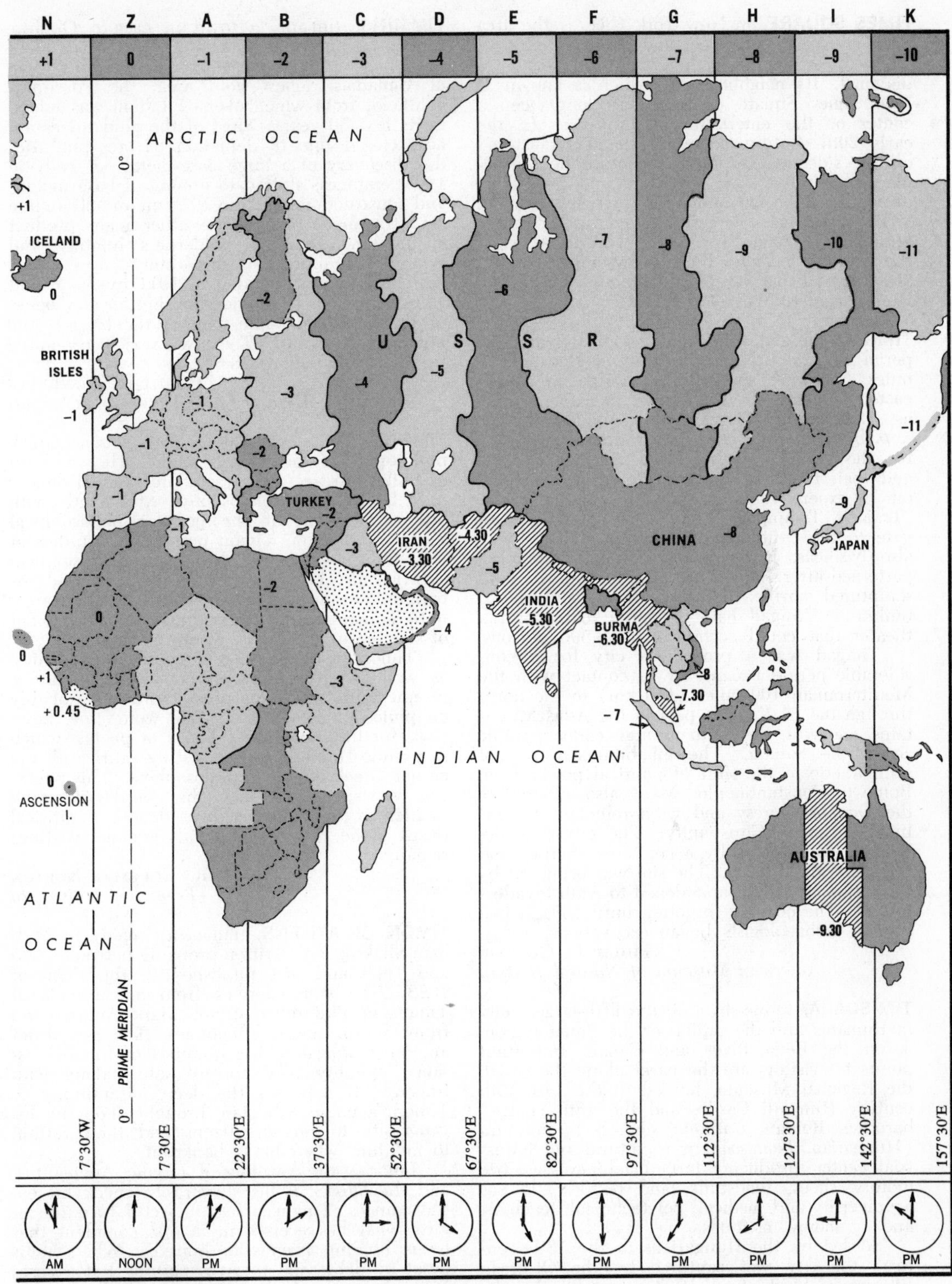

OF THE WORLD

HALF-HOUR ZONES

NO ZONE SYSTEM ADOPTED

Adapted from U. S. Hydrographic Office Chart No. 5192

TIMES SQUARE, in New York City, is the area between West 42d Street and West 47th Street where Broadway and 7th Avenue intersect on a diagonal. Its neighborhood, which is known as "the Times Square district," has long been a center of the entertainment industry. In the early 20th century, scores of theaters clustered on the side streets. Motion picture houses replaced many of these. Writers and publishers of popular songs have offices in the neighborhood.

The area was formerly known as Longacre Square. The name was changed in 1904, when the New York *Times* built a skyscraper on 42d Street from Broadway to 7th Avenue. The *Times* later moved to West 43d Street.

TIMGAD, tim′gad, the largest remains of any imperial Roman city outside Italy, is located 17 miles (27 km) southeast of Batna in northeastern Algeria. It was known in ancient times as Thamugadi. Timgad was founded in 100 A.D. by Emperor Trajan as a retirement location for the soldiers of the Third Augustan legion and their families. Its construction was carried out by expert workmen and artists of the legion. "Trajan's Triumphal Arch," the splendid west gate to the central area, survives. There were also basilicas, markets, and columned temples, patterned after Roman models and adorned with sculptured marble. Besides a library and official buildings, Timgad had 15 public baths and a theater that could accommodate 3,500 persons.

Timgad was a prosperous city for a considerable period because of its contact with the Mediterranian 100 miles (160 km) to the north through the El Kantara pass in the Atlas Mountains, and with the south through caravan traffic across the Sahara. The inhabitants were not sympathetic to the shift of political power from Rome to Constantinople. Many also adhered to the Donatist heresy and were reluctant to embrace orthodox Christianity. The city was destroyed in 534 A.D. by a combined Berber and Spanish-Vandal army. The site was occupied by Byzantine forces but abandoned to Arab invaders in 647. The city lay forgotten until 1881, when French archaeologists began excavations.

PHILIP C. GIFFORD
American Museum of Natural History

TIMIŞOARA, tē-mē-shwä′rä, the fifth-largest city in Rumania and the capital of the Banat region, is on the Bega River and Canal. Important points for visitors are the parks along the canal, the Regional Museum, housed in the 14th-15th century Hunyadi Castle, and the 18th century baroque Roman Catholic church. Timişoara (Hungarian, *Temesvár*) is a cultural and industrial center, producing farm machinery, electric motors, shoes, foodstuffs, and textiles. It has a university and medical, polytechnical, teachers, and agronomy institutes.

Settled by the Hungarians in the 13th century, the city was captured by the Ottoman Empire in 1552. In 1716 it was taken by the Habsburg Empire, under which it became the capital of the Hungarian Banat region and an important trade center. Following World War I, it became a part of Rumania. Because of the mixed Rumanian, Hungarian, and Serbian population in the Banat, control of the city has been disputed. Population: (1966 est.) 175,000.

BARBARA JELAVICH AND CHARLES JELAVICH
Indiana University

TIMMINS, tim′ənz, a town in eastern Ontario, Canada, is on the Mattagami River, 340 air miles (547 km) north of Toronto. It is the chief town of Canada's richest gold area, the Porcupine goldfield, from which over $1 billion was mined in its first 50 years. Most of the gold mines are now closed due to depletion of ore, but after the discovery of a huge base-metal ore body in 1964, emphasis shifted to mining of base metals, and construction began in 1970 on an $80 million zinc treatment plant. The other main product is lumber. There is wilderness hunting and fishing, and tourism is important.

Timmins was founded in 1911 by Noah and Henry Timmins to provide housing for employees of the Hollinger Mine, one of the largest gold mines in the world. The town was incorporated in 1912. Population: 28,542.

GRANT B. CHEVRETTE
Deputy Clerk, Town of Timmins

TIMON, tī′mən (c. 320–c. 230 B.C.), Greek philosopher of the Sophist school. He was born in Philus, Greece, and was a professional dancer until he embraced philosophy. After study with Stilpo, president of the popular philosophical school of Megara, Timon pursued his studies at Elis under Pyrrho, the founder of philosophical skepticism. Then ensued a long period of traveling as a Sophist about the Aegean area, until Timon became the leading literary exponent of skepticism at Athens, where he died.

Timon wrote 60 tragedies and 30 comedies, as well as satyr plays, several epics or satires in epic form, and some prose treatises (probably on philosophical themes). He won fame, however, for his *Silloi,* three books of poems, which in pseudo-Homeric meters wittily satirize all the earlier Greek dogmatic philosophers. This poetry was so successful that the word *sillograph* (writer of *silloi*) is used to denote a satirical poet. Some 80 fragments of Timon's writings remain.

P. R. COLEMAN-NORTON
Princeton University

TIMON OF ATHENS, tī′mən, a tragedy by William Shakespeare, written probably between 1605 and 1609 and first published in the Folio of 1623. The story derives from an account of Timon in Plutarch's life of Mark Antony and from one of Lucian's dialogues. The play, brief and uncomplicated, has qualities of the Renaissance morality play and of satire along with tragedy. It concerns the deep misanthropy of Timon, a noble Athenian, brought about by his generosity to fellow citizens and their refusal to aid him when he is bankrupt.

Ignoring the warnings of a cynic, Apemantus, and the efforts of his steward to check his extravagances, Timon strives in Act I to outdo in gifts what he receives in favors, confident that he is binding friends to himself. When he is beset by debts and receives nothing but excuses from his friends, he holds an ironic feast—covered dishes of water, which he splatters in their faces. Then, cursing all mankind, he retires to a cave near the sea and, while digging there for roots, uncovers gold coins. These he madly gives to a rebel captain, Alcibiades, and to his mistresses, who pass the cave on a march against Athens. Timon begs them to confound and confuse the city and sow consumption and sterility throughout it. Declaring himself "sick of this false world," he then strives to outdo Apemantus in cynicism, spurns his faithful steward, and after denouncing his former friends, goes to the shore to bury himself in the sea.

Because Timon's diatribes parallel various passages in *King Lear*, some critics think that Shakespeare abandoned *Timon* unfinished, having found in *Lear* a larger canvas for the same theme. Others think he was analyzing in *Timon* a tragic flaw characteristic of Greek magnanimity.

ROY W. BATTENHOUSE
Author of "Shakespearean Tragedy"

TIMOR, tē′môr, is a partly Indonesian and partly Portuguese island in the Lesser Sunda group. The southwestern end is included in the Indonesian province of Nusa Tengyara Timur. Portuguese Timor comprises the northeastern end of the island and the enclave of Oé-Cusse on the west coast of the Indonesian section. These territories and the small islands of Ataúro and Jaco to the north constitute Portugal's overseas territory of Timor, which has an area of 5,830 square miles (15,100 sq km). Its capital, Dili, is Timor Island's biggest city.

The Land. The largest of the Lesser Sunda islands, Timor is about 300 miles (500 km) long and has a maximum width of some 60 miles (100 km). The total area is 13,070 square miles (33,851 sq km), the larger portion of which is Indonesian. The land is rocky and mountainous, rising to 9,712 feet (2,960 meters) at Mt. Tata Mailau in Portuguese territory. The seacoast offers few good natural harbors.

Timor has a tropical monsoon climate with a dry season from March to October. Rain falls mostly in December, January, and February, when the northwest monsoon blows.

The island's wildlife includes many Asiatic types, but the plant life is more Australasian than Malaysian in character. The forests tend to be scrubby and thorny, and savannas predominate in the interior.

The People and Their Economy. The island's principal ethnic groups are the Belu in Portuguese Timor and the Atoni and Kupang in Indonesian Timor, who have physical characteristics that are somewhat more Papuan than Indonesian. The majority are animists, but some are Christians or Muslims. There are significant numbers of other Muslims—Buginese, Javanese, Malays, and Arabs—mostly in the coastal areas. The Chinese make up an important minority as traders in the towns. In 1970 about 850,000 people lived in Indonesian Timor and 600,000 in the Portuguese part of the island.

In the interior, agriculture provides little more than subsistence, with maize the staple crop. Rice is cultivated on irrigated terraces near the east coast by Javanese and Malays. The major cash crop is coffee, which is grown on plantations, especially around Kupang. Tea, cacao, tobacco, sugar, rubber, and cotton are also produced on plantations.

The coastal people live chiefly on fishing and the production of copra, obtained from coconuts. They sell tortoiseshells and trepang, which they collect from coral reefs.

History. The Portuguese, who first reached Timor about 1520, founded settlements in order to trade the island's sandalwood. The Dutch conquered what is now Indonesian Timor in 1613–1618. In the following centuries there were numerous disputes and occasional fighting on the island between the two colonial powers. The present borders were settled by treaties signed in 1859, 1893, and 1904 (the last effective in 1914). During World War II the Japanese occupied all of Timor although Portugal was neutral.

Dutch Timor passed to Indonesian control in 1949. Portuguese Timor, at first ruled from Goa, came under the jurisdiction of Macao in 1864. It became a separate colony in 1926 and an overseas province of Portugal in 1951.

WILLIAM Y. DESSAINT
The New University of Ulster

TIMORLAUT ISLANDS. See TANIMBAR ISLANDS.

TIMOSHENKO, tim-ə-sheng′kō, **Semyon Konstantinovich** (1895–1970), Soviet marshal, who led armies in World War II. He was born into a poor peasant family in Furmanka, a village near Odessa, in 1895. Drafted into the czar's army in 1915, he deserted and joined the Bolsheviks in 1917. As a cavalry commander, Timoshenko participated in the Civil War battle of Tsaritsyn in 1918. (See VOLGOGRAD.) From that time dated his close association with Stalin, which facilitated his rise through the army ranks in the 1920's and enabled him to survive—unlike most Bolshevik Civil War commanders—the purges of the 1930's.

Timoshenko was frequently given command in order to rectify the mistakes of others and extricate the Red Army from critical situations. He led the final Soviet offensive in the 1939–1940 war with Finland, breaking enemy resistance by massive artillery and infantry attacks.

Appointed a marshal and commissar for defense in 1940, Timoshenko was responsible for improvements in the organization and training of the Red Army, which included the founding of a new military academy. These reforms contributed to the margin of strength that enabled the Russians to withstand the German assault in 1941. In

August 1941, Timoshenko directed the defensive operations near Smolensk, seriously delaying the German advance on Moscow. In September, he helped to save the remnants of the troops defeated in the Ukraine under Semyon Budenny.

In May 1942, Timoshenko led the abortive Soviet offensive at Kharkov, which had been undertaken against his advice. A military expert rather than a "political general," he was a popular leader during the subsequent victorious campaigns. After the war, Timoshenko headed the Belorussian military district from 1949 to 1960. He died on March 31, 1970, in Moscow, and was buried in the Kremlin wall.

VOJTECH MASTNY
Columbia University

TIMOTHY, Saint, early Christian leader and close associate of the Apostle Paul. He is mentioned in five passages in Acts and in 11 New Testament epistles. Timothy was born in Lycaonia (Asia Minor) of a Gentile father and Jewish mother. He was probably converted by Paul (I Corinthians 4:17) on the latter's first missionary journey to that region. On a return trip Paul persuaded Timothy to join him in his ministry. According to Acts 16:3, Paul circumcised Timothy to avoid giving offense to Jews, who would have considered Timothy Jewish because his mother was a Jewess. Timothy accompanied Paul on part of the apostle's second missionary journey and continued to work with him for many years thereafter.

Paul described him with fatherly affection as one whose devotion was unparalleled (Philippians 2:19–23). He sent him as his deputy on sensitive missions to the churches of Thessalonica and Corinth (I Thessalonians 3:2; I Corinthians 4:17), though he had fears (apparently realized) that Timothy would find it hard to assert his authority in the latter church (I Corinthians 16:10–11). Timothy is mentioned as joint-sender in the salutations of six Pauline letters, which suggests that he had some measure of responsibility for them. He received special tasks during the apostle's final trip to Jerusalem, probably connected with the collection of money for the Christians there from churches in Macedonia and Lycaonia (Acts 19:22; 20:4).

Two of the Pastoral Epistles are addressed to Timothy and represent him as working in Ephesus as Paul's delegate. These two epistles are chiefly responsible for the traditional image of Timothy as an immature young protégé of the apostle. But their historical reliability is doubtful. (See TIMOTHY, EPISTLES TO). A solitary reference to Timothy in the Epistle to the Hebrews (13:23) implies that he was known to the writer and the intended readers of that epistle. The references to him in the other Pauline letters, as well as those in the Acts of the Apostles, indicate that Paul found in Timothy a highly capable fellow minister. Later tradition identifies Timothy as the first bishop of Ephesus. His feast day is celebrated on January 24 in the West and on January 22 by the Eastern Christians.

DAVID M. HAY
Princeton Theological Seminary

TIMOTHY is one of the most widely distributed and commonly grown perennial forage grasses of humid temperate regions. Also known as June grass, Herd's grass, and cattail, it is extensively grown for hay in mixtures with alfalfa, clover,

JANE LATTA

Timothy grass (*Phleum pratense*)

and other forage legumes. In past years it was the standard hay for horses. Timothy is also commonly found in naturalized grassland areas and is frequently used for grazing.

A loosely tufted, somewhat short-lived perennial, timothy ranges in height from 1½ to 4½ feet (0.45–1.35 meters) depending on the variety and the soil conditions. The basal stem nodes are usually very short and swollen or bulbous, and the flower heads are compact cylindrical spikes with crowded spikelets. Timothy grows best in rather heavy, deep, moist soils and can tolerate somewhat wet conditions.

Botanically, timothy is known as *Phleum pratense*. A related species, alpine timothy (*P. alpinum*), is shorter and is widely distributed in mountain regions of Europe, Asia, and North America. It provides excellent forage.

H. A. MACDONALD, *Cornell University*

TIMOTHY, Epistles to, two books in the New Testament that purport to be letters addressed by the Apostle Paul to his younger colleague, Timothy. Because these letters and that addressed to Titus chiefly contain instructions for pastors, the three are commonly called the Pastoral Epistles.

Authorship. The fundamental historical question about all three Pastoral Epistles concerns their authenticity. If they are from Paul, they provide important information about the final period of his life and thought. In the 20th century, however, many scholars have denied that Paul could have written them, chiefly because (1) the Pastorals diverge considerably from the undisputed letters of Paul in vocabulary and style and also in general theological outlook, placing greater emphasis on "good works" and orthodox belief; (2) the church order assumed in these letters seems more highly developed than it probably was in Paul's day; (3) the heresy they condemn fits best with a 2d century date; (4) the situations of Paul, Timothy, and Titus indicated in the Pastorals cannot be easily reconciled with data in Acts and in the other Pauline Letters, and (5) firm evidence of the use of these letters in the church appears rather late (near the end of the 2d century).

Some scholars seek a middle ground between

flatly affirming and flatly rejecting Pauline authorship. Some, for example, urge that these epistles were composed by a secretary who worked on the basis of general instructions from Paul. Others argue that the letters were written some years after Paul's death by one who had access to fragments of genuine letters of the apostle, and that he wove those fragments into his compositions.

The whole problem is famous for its complexity and difficulty. A fully adequate solution to it has yet to appear. Probably, however, the epistles to Timothy and the one to Titus are best regarded as the work of someone who used Paul's name because he believed himself to be faithfully presenting Paul's message for the writer's own time (II Timothy 1:13; 2:2). He was probably a church leader who wrote for the benefit of fellow leaders near the beginning of the 2d century in the area of Asia Minor.

Circumstances of Composition. These letters reflect an era when church leaders needed their duties more sharply defined, ordinary believers required plain moral instruction, and heretics threatened to divide or conquer whole congregations. The heresy (or heresies) to which the epistles allude evidently combined Jewish and Gnostic features. The writer mentions claims to extraordinary knowledge (gnosis) and "godless chatter" about myths and genealogies. Advocating a kind of fanatical dualism, the heretics claimed to be living already in the resurrected state (II Timothy 2:12) and perhaps favored moral libertinism.

Contents. Although some time probably elapsed between the writing of the two epistles —II Timothy many have been written first—they overlap so much in substance that it is best to consider the content of the two together. The author carefully describes the qualifications for several established church offices (bishop, deacon, and widow), and underlines the responsibility of bishops to maintain "sound doctrine." By establishing doctrinal authorities, the early church was in part seeking to cut the ground out from under heterodox teachers.

The writer recommends various measures against heretics, ranging from warning to excommunication. He attempts no detailed refutation of their ideas but castigates them for idle speculation and immorality. Likewise he offers no sustained exposition of what he regards as right belief but only pithy reminders of its essential content. Sometimes these are in the form of quotations of primitive creeds or hymns, as, for example, in I Timothy 3:16 and II Timothy 2:8,9–11. The distinctive Pauline doctrine of justification by grace is insisted on, together with the corollary that God desires all men to be saved.

In opposition to the heretics, the writer affirms the goodness of the material world, the dignity of marriage, and the edibleness of all foods. The lives of believers, he declares, must be pure, disciplined, and respectable. He lists special duties of different classes of Christians (wives and husbands, slaves and rich men) and demands that church leaders set examples of integrity. He notes that believers have positive obligations toward society at large and the state, but reminds his readers that they must be ready if need be to endure persecution as Paul did.

Noteworthy for both moral passion and practicality, these epistles offer vital evidence of the growth of church organization and the struggle against heresy. The fact that they were written in Paul's name facilitated their acceptance, and they in turn helped assure his lasting influence on the mainstream of Christianity.

DAVID M. HAY
Princeton Theological Seminary

Further Reading: Feine, Paul, and Behm, Johannes, *Introduction to the New Testament*, ed. by W. G. Kummel, tr. by A. J. Mattill, Jr. (Nashville, Tenn., 1966); Kelly, John N. D., *A Commentary on the Pastoral Epistles* (Toronto 1963).

TIMPANOGOS CAVE NATIONAL MONUMENT, tim-pə-nō'gəs, is in north central Utah, about 25 miles (40 km) south of Salt Lake City. The cave is actually three caves, connected by short man-made tunnels, in the limestone bulk of Mt. Timpanogos. All the caves display fantastic stalactites, stalagmites, and colorful rock formations. The visitor passes successively through Hansen Cave, Middle Cave, and Timpanogos Cave; from entrance to exit the distance is about ½ mile (0.8 km).

Hansen Cave was discovered in 1887 by Martin Hansen, who owned the land. Timpanogos Cave was found about 1915 and Middle Cave in 1922. The national monument was established in 1922. It covers about 250 acres (100 hectares).

TIMUR, tē-mo͝or' (1336–1405), was a Central Asian conqueror, who sought to restore the empire of Genghis Khan. He was born near Kesh (now Shakhrisyabz, Uzbekistan, USSR) on April 9, 1336. Wounded by an arrow early in his career, he was nicknamed Timur-i Lang (Timur the Lame), corrupted by Europeans into Tamerlane or Tamburlaine.

Rise to Power. Timur belonged to a Turkicized Mongol tribe, the Barlas, which had accompanied Genghis Khan's son Jagatai (Chaghatai) westward and settled in Transoxiana (roughly modern Uzbekistan). This western half of the Jagatai khanate fell under the control of a tribal leader called Qazaghan when Timur was a boy. After Qazaghan's death in 1358, Timur declared himself the vassal of Tughluq-Temür, ruler of Moghulistan (the eastern half of the Jagatai khanate), who invaded Transoxiana. As a reward Timur was made a regional governor.

Rebelling against Tughluq-Temür's son and viceroy, Ilyas Khoja, Timur allied himself with Husain, a grandson of Qazaghan. In 1363 they defeated Ilyas Khoja and expelled him from Transoxiana, setting up a descendant of Jagatai as puppet khan. The next year, they were in turn defeated by Ilyas Khoja, who had now succeeded his father, but he was finally obliged to leave them in peaceful possession of Transoxiana. Their joint rule continued fitfully for several years, Timur often allying himself with Husain's enemies. In 1370 he besieged Husain at Balkh. On capturing and executing his rival, he became sole ruler of Transoxiana under the nominal authority of a new and more tractable Jagatai khan, Soyurghatmish.

First Foreign Conquests. Timur made his capital Samarkand, a city destined to be enriched with the spoils of his conquests. He sought to consolidate his position by campaigns against Khwarizm (Khorezm, Khiva) to the west and Moghulistan to the east. These expeditions into the wild, mountainous country have attracted less attention than the campaigns in the populous

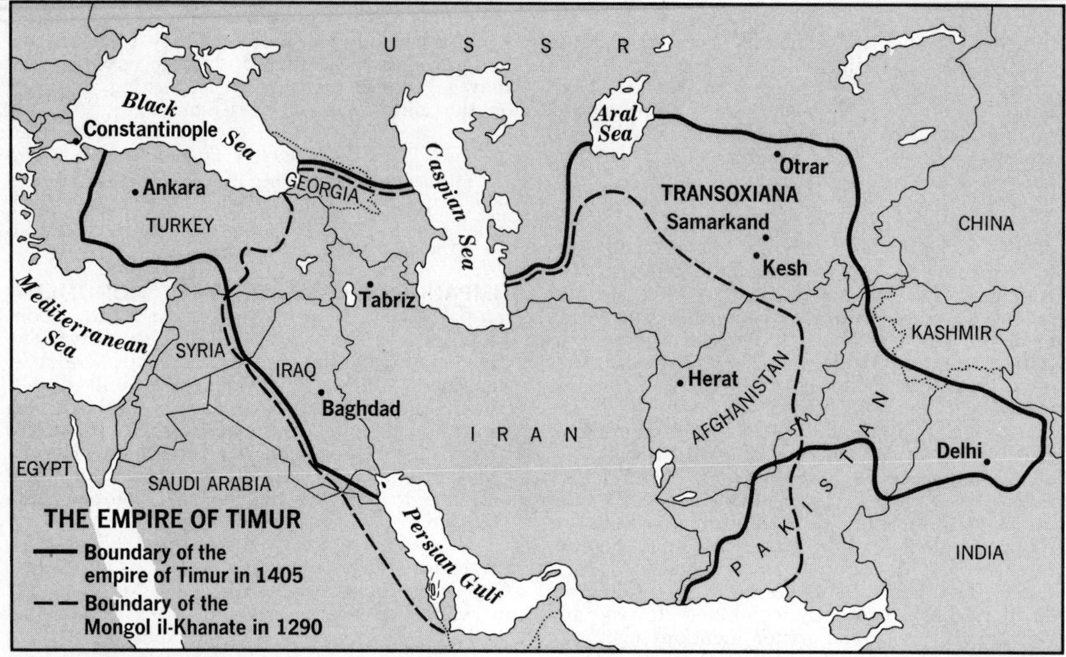

regions of Western Asia, but as military operations were even greater achievements.

In 1381, Timur turned his attention to the southwest, invading Khurasan and receiving the submission of the ruler of Herat. There followed a series of almost annual campaigns, gradually extended farther west into Iraq, Syria, and Anatolia (Turkey). In 1384, however, he was recalled from the west to deal with a threat to his northern frontiers from his former protégé Tokhtamysh (Toqtamish), now ruler of the Golden Horde. Operations against Tokhtamysh and antagonists in Moghulistan occupied Timur for the next four years.

"Five Years' Campaign." Not until 1392 did Timur return to the West to engage in his "five years' campaign," conducted in Iran, Iraq, Anatolia, and southern Russia. In Iran in 1393 he put an end to the Muzaffarid dynasty of Fars by executing most of the surviving princes. He then moved into Iraq, where he occupied Baghdad, and advanced northwards into Caucasia. There in 1395 he again encountered Tokhtamysh, whom he routed in a battle on the Terek River.

Losing track of his fugitive adversary, Timur marched up the Don Valley, attacking and capturing the town of Yelets on the southern border of the Russian principality of Ryazan. He penetrated no farther into the Russian states, aware perhaps of their readiness to defend themselves. Instead he turned back into the territory of the Golden Horde and destroyed its two main centers, Astrakhan and New Sarai, in the winter of 1395–1396. He then marched eastward to Samarkand.

Invasion of India. Timur's invasion of India in 1398, despite its enormous bloodshed and devastation, was little more than a plundering incursion. The vanguard of his army, under one of his grandsons, crossed the Indus River at the beginning of 1398 and captured Multan after a six-months' siege. Timur joined him in the autumn and led the army by the most direct route from Multan to Delhi. On the eve of his decisive victory before the gates of Delhi, he ordered the slaughter of 50,000 prisoners—or, according to some authorities, 100,000. The city was reduced to ruins and did not fully recover for over a century. Timur remained in Delhi for only a fortnight, and by May 1399 he was back in Samarkand.

"Seven Years' Campaign." In 1399, Timur embarked on what was to be the last of his many expeditions, the "seven years' campaign." An invasion of Georgia in 1400 was followed by operations in eastern Turkey and embroilment with the Ottoman Sultan Bayezid I and the Mamluk (Mameluke) sultan of Egypt. Timur invaded Syria, then under Mamluk control, capturing Aleppo in October 1400 and Damascus in March 1401. He next turned his attention for the second time to Baghdad, which was taken in June and its inhabitants massacred.

In February 1402, Timur launched his final attack against Bayezid, whom he defeated and took prisoner at the Battle of Angora (Ankara) on July 20. This crushing defeat of the Ottoman Turks may have delayed their capture of Constantinople, which did not occur until Mehmed II entered the city in May 1453.

By the end of 1402, Timur had reached the Aegean and stormed and sacked Smyrna (İzmir), which was then held by the Knights of St. John. He returned to Samarkand in the summer of 1404 but left it at the end of November to make war on the Ming emperor of China. On Feb. 18, 1405, his Chinese campaign barely under way, Timur died at Otrar, in what is now Soviet Kazakhstan.

Timur's Place in History. Timur was one of history's greatest but cruelest conquerors. At Sabzawar in Afghanistan he had a tower constructed out of 2,000 live men, who were piled one on top of the other and cemented together with bricks and clay. At Sivas in Anatolia, 4,000 of the Armenian defenders of the town were buried alive in fulfillment of his promise that no blood would be shed if they surrendered.

At Isfahan in Iran, he caused the heads of 70,000 persons to be piled up into pyramids. Although Timur patronized the arts and philosophy at his capital, his barbarous acts seem fully to justify Gibbon's conclusion that he "was rather the scourge than the benefactor of mankind."

Timur's empire died with him. His sons and grandsons continued to rule in Transoxiana and Khurasan, sometimes in splendor, but the Timurid dynasty lasted less than a century.

JOHN ANDREW BOYLE
University of Manchester

Bibliography

Barthold, Vasilii, *Four Studies on the History of Central Asia,* tr. by V. Minorsky and T. Minorsky, vols. 1 and 2 (New York, 1956 and 1958).
Grousset, René, *The Empire of the Steppes* (New Brunswick, N. J., 1970).
Hookham, Hilda, *Tamburlaine the Conqueror* (Mystic, Conn., 1962).
Prawdin, Michael, *The Mongol Empire,* 2d ed., tr. by E. Paul and C. Paul (New York 1967).
Vernadsky, George, *The Mongols and Russia* (New Haven, Conn., 1953).

TIMURIDS, tē-mo͝or'idz, descendants of Timur (Tamerlane), ruling in the eastern part of his empire for about 100 years after his death. After the brief reign (1404–1409) of Timur's grandson and successor, Khalil, the throne passed to Timur's fourth son, Shah Rukh (reigned 1409–1447). He ruled directly over Transoxiana and Khurasan and indirectly over western Iran, which was held by various members of the family. The western territory, however, had to be defended constantly against the Turkomans, to whom it was irrevocably lost in the second half of the 15th century.

Shah Rukh's son and successor, Ulugh Beg, was assassinated in 1449 by his own son Abd al-Latif, and he in turn was assassinated a year later. There followed a period of civil war during which Abd al-Latif's cousins Abdallah and Babur gained possession of Transoxiana and Khurasan, respectively. Abdallah was defeated and killed in 1452 by Abu Said, a grandson of Shah Rukh's brother Miran Shah, and on Babur's death in 1457, Abu Said made himself master of Khurasan also. The most energetic of the Timurids, he took the field against both the Moghuls in the east and the Turkomans in the west. With his death in 1489 at the hands of the Turkoman ruler Uzun Hasan, the Timurid realm was once again divided.

Abu Said was succeeded in Transoxiana by his son Sultan Ahmad, who ruled until 1494. Khurasan was governed until 1506 by Husain Baiqara, who belonged to another branch of the family. Soon after the deaths of these two men their territories fell to the Uzbek khan Muhammad Shaibani, who occupied Transoxiana in 1500 and Khurasan in 1507. A nephew of Sultan Ahmad, Babur, was expelled from Fergana by the Uzbeks in 1504, but Babur later invaded India and founded the Mughul (Moghul) dynasty there in 1526.

The Timurids were great patrons of the arts and sciences. Under Shah Rukh, Abu Said, and Husain Baiqara, the city of Herat in Khurasan (now in Afghanistan) was a prominent cultural and intellectual center. Ulugh Beg built an observatory at Samarkand in Transoxiana and collaborated with Persian scholars in compiling astronomical tables.

JOHN ANDREW BOYLE
University of Manchester

TIN is a soft, ductile, silvery white metallic element. The chemical symbol, Sn, is derived from the Latin word for tin, *stannum.*

HISTORY

The earliest use of tin was in the copper-based alloy bronze. The use of bronze probably began before 3000 B.C. in Egypt and Mesopotamia. However, bronze did not become common in these areas until after 2000 B.C. Although copper was readily available in the Middle East, the supply of tin was limited. As tin supplies from Asia Minor (particularly Caucasia) and Persia were exhausted, Phoenician and Greek traders traveled as far as Cornwall in England, Brittany in France, Cantabria in Spain, and central Germany to obtain tin for the Middle East. See also BRONZE; BRONZE AGE.

Tin was mined in Spain from the beginning of the Bronze Age, while the working of mines in France and England began about 500 B.C. Ore was obtained from stream beds and from large underground mines. Examination of ancient furnaces in England and Spain showed that tin of a purity of 99.9% was produced.

Aristotle knew of the existence of gray tin, or "tin pest." In the 1st century A.D. the Roman historian Pliny mentioned the use of lead-tin alloys (solders) for joining metals. Articles of copper coated with tin were also produced by the Romans. However, tinplate, which is tin-coated iron or steel, did not come into wide use until the 1500's in Europe.

USES

Tinplate. The most important use of tin is in the plating of steel. About 40% of the tin produced is used for this purpose. Most tinplate is used in the manufacture of cans for food and drinks. Tin is nontoxic so that it is safe for use in packaging of foods. Tinplated steel has the same good properties as steel, but it also resists corrosion and has the attractive appearance of tin.

The coating of steel may be done by several methods, including electroplating, dipping the object to be plated in molten metal (hot-dipping), or immersion in solutions, such as a sodium stannate-acetate bath, in which plating occurs by chemical reaction. Most tin cans are produced by electroplating.

Alloys. Tin is mechanically weak, so there are few uses for the pure metal. Tin easily forms alloys with many metals, however, and it is used to increase resistance to corrosion and fatigue and to improve malleability. The metals most commonly alloyed with tin are copper, lead, zinc, iron, cadmium, antimony, nickel, cobalt, titanium, and zirconium. Important tin alloys are bronze, pewter, solder, type metal, and Babbitt metal. Some brasses also contain tin.

Bronze. The bronzes are among the oldest known alloys. Originally, the term "bronze" referred to alloys of copper and tin. Now, however, some bronze alloys contain no tin. In bronzes containing tin the tin acts to increase corrosion resistance and improve the mechanical properties of the copper. Tin-containing bronzes are used in high-speed and heavy-duty bearings, steam valve bodies, bushings, wires, rods, electrical contacts, chemical hardware, wire brushes, flexible hose, and springs.

Solder. Solders are low-melting alloys of tin and lead that are used to join pieces of metal.

The most commonly used solder consists of 50% tin and 50% lead. The tin content of other solders ranges from 10% to 97%. Solders that are rich in tin can be applied at lower temperatures than lead-rich alloys. The eutectic alloy, which is the one with the lowest melting point, melts at 183° C (361° F) and contains 63% tin and 37% lead. See also SOLDER.

Pewter. Pewters are alloys of tin with antimony and copper. Although pewters of ancient China and Rome generally contained up to 40% lead, modern pewters usually contain less than 0.5% lead. The lead has been eliminated from the alloy because it is highly toxic and causes the metal to lose its shiny finish. In place of lead, 5% to 8% antimony and 1% copper are used as hardeners. Pewter is used for articles such as vases, tea services, trays, mugs, and candlesticks. See also PEWTER.

Babbitt Metals. Babbitt metals, or bearing metals, are a group of soft alloys that are widely used for bearings. Although the original Babbitt metal consisted mainly of tin, modern bearing metals are generally lead-based alloys containing lesser quantities of tin, antimony, or copper. See also ANTIFRICTION METALS; BABBITT, ISAAC; BABBITT METAL.

Type Metals. Type metals, used for casting printing type, are lead-based alloys containing up to 10% tin and 20% antimony. These metals can be remelted and used repeatedly with little change in properties.

Terneplate. Terneplate consists of a sheet of steel coated with a tin-lead alloy. The percentages of tin and lead in the alloy vary with the type of terneplate involved. Terneplate is used in roofing and in cans for paints and other substances.

Compounds. Tin reacts with a variety of substances to form both inorganic and organic compounds.

Stannic Chloride. Stannic chloride, $SnCl_4$, also known as tin chloride or tin tetrachloride, is used in special coatings, textiles, ceramics, as a bleach for sugar, and in the manufacture of sensitized papers. It is produced by treating tin or stannous chloride with chlorine. The pentahydrate, $SnCl_4 \cdot 5H_2O$, also known as *butter of tin*, is used in place of the anhydrous compound where the presence of water is not objectionable.

Stannic Oxide. Stannic oxide, SnO_2, also known as stannic anhydride, tin peroxide, and tin dioxide, is used in ceramic glazes, putty, as a mordant for textiles, and in the manufacture of milk glass and other glasses. It is found in nature as the mineral cassiterite or it can be produced by melting metallic tin in the presence of air.

Stannous Chloride. Stannous chloride, $SnCl_2$, also known as tin dichloride, is used as a reducing agent in the manufacture of chemicals, dyes, phosphors, and polymers, in galvanizing tin, in silvering mirrors, and as an antisludging agent for lubricating oils. It is produced by dissolving tin in hydrochloric acid. Stannous chloride is soluble in water and alcohol.

Stannous sulfate, $SnSO_4$, also known as tin sulfate, is used in dyeing and in tin-plating. It is produced by the treatment of stannous oxide with sulfuric acid.

Organotin Compounds. Stannous 2-ethylhexoate, $Sn(C_8H_{15}O_2)_2$, is used as a catalyst for the polymerization of the urethane foams and as a lubricant. Stannous oleate, $Sn(C_{18}H_{33}O_2)_2$, is also a polymerization catalyst. Stannous oxalate, SnC_2O_4, is used in dyeing and printing textiles. Other organotin compounds containing up to 50% tin are used as stabilizers in fungicides and insecticides and in plastics.

PROPERTIES

Tin is located in Group IVA of the periodic table. Its atomic number is 50, and its atomic weight is 118.69. The metal melts at 231.9° C (450° F) and boils at 2270° C (4118° F). Tin has valences of +2 and +4. Compounds in which tin is +2 are called *stannous* compounds, and those in which tin is +4 are *stannic*.

Crystalline Structure. Tin has a highly ordered crystalline structure. When a bar of tin is bent, a noise called "tin cry" is produced by the breaking of the crystals.

There are two major crystalline forms of tin. At temperatures below 13.2° C (55.8° F) α tin, or gray tin, is formed. This form crystallizes in the cubic system and has a density of 5.75 g/cc. The β form, which is known as *white tin*, occurs between 13.2° and 161° C (55.8 and 322° F). It has a tetragonal crystal structure and a specific gravity of 7.3. In relatively pure tin the transformation from the β to the α form occurs gradually when the metal is cooled below 13.2° C. The presence of impurities, particularly antimony or bismuth, prevents the transformation altogether. Gray tin has very few uses. The gray form of tin is called "tin pest."

A third crystalline form of tin, called γ tin, may occur between 161° C and the melting point of the element. This form is thought to have a rhombohedral crystal structure and a specific gravity of 6.79 at the melting point. However, the existence of this form is a matter of controversy.

Isotopes. There are 10 stable naturally occurring isotopes of tin and 21 others that are radioactive and can be produced artificially. The isotopes of tin range in atomic weight from ^{108}Sn to ^{132}Sn. The relative concentrations of the naturally occurring isotopes of tin are: ^{120}Sn, 32.9%; ^{118}Sn, 24%; ^{116}Sn, 14.3%; ^{119}Sn, 8.6%; ^{117}Sn, 7.6%; ^{124}Sn, 5.9%; ^{122}Sn, 4.9%; ^{112}Sn, 0.9%; ^{114}Sn, 0.6%; and ^{115}Sn, 0.3%. The radioactive isotopes of tin have half-lives ranging from 2.2 minutes for ^{132}Sn to 100,000 years for ^{126}Sn.

Chemical Reactivity. Hydrogen sulfide attacks metallic tin at temperatures above 100° C (212° F) but has little effect below this temperature. Chlorine, bromine, fluorine, and iodine react vigorously with tin at temperatures above 100° C. Oxygen attacks tin, forming a thin oxide film of SnO_2. Tin reacts slowly with dilute hydrochloric and hydrofluoric acids and rapidly with hydrobromic and nitric acids. Most alkaline solutions attack metallic tin. Tin is not attacked by organic acids in food.

OCCURRENCE

The average concentration of tin in the earth's crust is 40 parts per million (ppm). Soils contain up to 200 ppm, while the average concentration in igneous rocks is 40 ppm. Tin in silicate meteorites averages 5 ppm; in nickel-iron meteorites, 100 ppm; in granite, 80 ppm; in basalt, 4 ppm. In a lunar soil sample the concentration of tin was found to be 0.6 ppm.

Tin is widely distributed in low concentrations throughout the world, but there are only a few deposits large enough to be of commercial importance. These deposits are located in Malaysia, Bolivia, Thailand, Indonesia, Nigeria, the Congo (Kinshasa), and China. The United States has only very low-grade deposits of tin, which are, for the most part, too uneconomical to be worked.

Ores. Cassiterite, SnO_2, also known as *tin stone,* is the main ore of tin and the only one of commercial importance. It is usually brown or black in color and forms tetragonal or ditetragonal-dipyramidal crystals. Other tin-containing minerals are stannite, teallite, canfieldite, franckeite, cylindrite, stokesite, and hielmite.

Types of Deposits. Primary tin ores usually occur in pegmatites, high-temperature veins, or contact-metamorphic deposits in association with granitic rocks. Tungsten, quartz, and white mica are commonly associated with tin ores. Silver or molybdenum is sometimes present in primary tin ores.

About 80% of the world's tin is produced from placer deposits. These deposits are derived from the weathering of the primary lode material, which results in the formation of light particles of gangue and heavy particles of the ore cassiterite. Some of the mixture of gangue and ore is carried by rain into streams, where the light gangue material is easily swept away, and the heavy cassiterite is trapped behind natural obstruction of the stream bed. Tin from placer deposits is generally accompanied by tungsten and iron minerals.

The tin deposits of Malaysia, Thailand, Indonesia, Nigeria, the Congo (Kinshasa), and China are placer deposits. The only important lode deposits are found in Bolivia and in Cornwall, England.

MINING AND CONCENTRATION

Placer deposits are worked by mechanical excavation or by hydraulic mining or dredges if the deposit is underwater. Hydraulic mining involves breaking up the stream bottom with a forceful jet of water from a hose. On a dredge the cassiterite-bearing mud is removed from the bottom of the water course. Concentration of the ore is also performed on the dredge.

Placer tin ores are concentrated by gravity processes because of the high density of the cassiterite, which has a specific gravity of 7 (seven times heavier than water). This may be done in a sluice box or a jig. Large blocks of material must be broken up by tumbling in water before being placed in either the jig or sluice. A sluice box is long and narrow, and the bottom is covered by obstructive bars called riffles. The heavy particles of cassiterite sink to the bottom of the sluice and are trapped behind the riffles, while the light gangue material passes through the box in suspension.

A jig is more compact than a sluice box. It is a hopper-shaped box that is partially divided into two compartments. One compartment has a plunger, while the other has a screen across it near the top. The jig is filled with water. The action of the plunger forces water up through the screen. Ore and water are fed onto the screen. When a pulse of water is forced up through the screen by the plunger, the lighter gangue material becomes suspended in the water and is carried off, while the heavy ore sinks onto the screen. Concentration techniques for placer minerals are very efficient, and the tin ore obtained by these processes contains 70% to 77% cassiterite.

The mining of underground lode deposits is done by block caving, by which the ore is obtained in small pieces. In this process a large block of rock is undercut and broken free from surrounding rock by explosives. As the block settles, it caves in the undercutting tunnels and breaks into small pieces, which are removed through a network of chutes and tunnels in the solid rock below. See also MINING—*Mining Operations.*

The gangue material is removed from the ore by heavy liquid separation. In this process the specific gravity of a heavy liquid is adjusted so that the gangue floats and the heavier cassiterite-rich fraction sinks. During this procedure the mixture is held in cone-shaped vessels or rotating drums. Since cassiterite is a brittle mineral, care must be taken during the preliminary breaking of the ore not to produce fines (very fine particles) that will subsequently be lost as a slime during purification.

METALLURGY

Pretreatment. After concentration, ores from placer deposits contain relatively few impurities and can undergo smelting without pretreatment. However, ores from lode deposits must be treated for the removal of impurities before smelting. These tin concentrates, which may contain only 20% to 60% cassiterite, contain appreciable quantities of iron, sulfur, tungsten, niobium, tantalum, arsenic, lead, copper, and silver. Iron, sulfur, and tungsten are the most troublesome during smelting.

Niobium, tantalum, and tungsten are present in magnetic, iron-rich minerals in tin ores. These materials, along with iron-titanium oxides, may be separated from the nonmagnetic cassiterite by magnetic separation techniques. Some cassiterite will be present in the magnetic fraction. Heat treatment of the magnetic fraction at 600° C (1,112° F) in the presence of sodium carbonate, followed by a water leach, will leave an iron-rich cassiterite residue.

Roasting. An oxidizing roast at 500°C (932° F) may be used to remove arsenic and sulfur. Sulfur is removed as sulfur dioxide and arsenic as arsenic trioxide. A carefully controlled atmosphere must be maintained to prevent the production of arsenic pentoxide, which readily forms nonvolatile arsenates.

Acid Leach. Some elements, including copper, lead, silver, antimony, and bismuth, are made acid-soluble in varying degrees if salt is added to the roasting charge described above. Leaching treatments are expensive and their use may not be practical for some ores. Acid leaching must be followed by a sintering step to impart the proper physical characteristics to the material prior to smelting.

Smelting. High temperatures are required for the smelting of tin. At these high temperatures iron and other impurities that are present will also be reduced. Therefore, it is necessary to use a two-stage smelting process. In the first stage the process is controlled so that only a part of the tin is reduced, thus keeping the concentration of impurities at a minimum. In the second stage the tin-rich slag from the first stage is resmelted. The impure tin metal that is produced by the smelting operations is recycled to the first step for further purification.

Furnaces. The smelting of tin may be carried out in a variety of furnaces. The reverberatory furnace, which is the most commonly used, gives maximum yields from high-grade concentrates because the tin can be drained off as soon as it is reduced. Electric and rotating furnaces, which are used in a few places, can be tapped only from time to time.

Slags. One of the major problems in tin smelting is the tendency for iron to be co-reduced with tin. Iron-rich tin slags are known as *hardhead.* Lime is added to the slagging ingredients because it retards this reaction. Silicon is often added to increase the insolubility of tin by creating an iron-silicon slag phase. A chlorination process is also used, which results in a water-soluble iron phase and insoluble tin products. Tin may also be converted to the volatile sulfides or monoxide, which form the basis of a number of volatilization processes for hardhead treatment.

Refining. After smelting, tin still contains some iron and often arsenic, antimony, copper, lead, and bismuth. Heat treatment and electrorefining are used to purify the metal. Heat treatment is generally used for refining. If an unusually pure grade of tin is required, electrorefining is used.

Heat Treatment. Two types of heat treatments are used in the refining of tin: liquation, or sweating, and boiling, or tossing. The tin may be treated by either method alone or by a combination of the two processes.

Liquation is generally carried out in a reverberatory furnace with a gently sloping hearth. Bituminous coal is used as the fuel. The impure tin is placed at the top of the slope in the furnace, and the temperature is raised to just above the melting point of the element. The tin melts and runs down the slope of the hearth and is collected. This tin is called the first sweat tin. Impurities, such as iron and copper which have higher melting points, and some tin remain as a scum, or dross, at the top of the hearth. The dross is then heated to a higher temperature and a second batch of tin (second sweat tin), which contains a higher concentration of impurities, is collected for retreatment.

In *boiling,* molten tin is stirred in large kettles with poles of green wood. This produces a boiling action that results in the oxidation of impurities and some tin. These metallic oxides form a dross, or scum, which is skimmed off and recycled through the smelting process to recover the tin.

The tin produced by these refining methods is 99.8% pure. More than 97% of the tin is recovered.

Filtration, another refining technique, is used occasionally. In this method an asbestos cloth backed by a perforated plate is used as the filtering apparatus. Filtration is done at a low temperature, so that iron-rich impurities in the melted metal are trapped on the asbestos cloth while the liquid tin passes through the filter and is collected.

Electrorefining. In electrorefining, impure tin metal is cast as anodes and immersed in a complex electrolyte solution. The cathode is made of pure tin. During electrolysis pure tin metal is deposited on the cathode. Silver, copper, bismuth, and antimony do not dissolve in the electrolyte solution, and they appear as slimes coating the anodes. Sulfuric acid and stannous sulfate are added to the electrolyte to prevent lead from being deposited with the tin on the cathode. Iron is not deposited at the cathode; however, a buildup of iron in the electrolyte solution can be harmful because of current-wasting oxidation-reduction reactions involving Fe^{+3} and Fe^{+2}.

Secondary Tin. Secondary tin is tin that is recovered from scrap. The scrap metal from which the tin is obtained is mainly tinplate, bronze, and solder. The scrap is reworked in smelters. Some high-purity tin is produced from the detinning of scrap by chemicals and electrolysis.

WORLD PRODUCTION

In the early 1970's the total world production of tin was approaching 230,000 long tons (253,000 metric tons) annually, including tin recovered from scrap. The leading tin-producing countries are Malaysia, 75,000 long tons (82,500 metric tons); Bolivia, 29,000 long tons (32,000 metrc tons); Thailand, 24,000 long tons (26,400 metric tons); Indonesia, 17,000 long tons (18,700 metric tons); Nigeria, 10,000 long tons (11,000 metric tons); and the Congo (Kinshasa), 7,000 long tons (7,700 metric tons).

Although exact production figures for mainland China and the USSR are not available, it is estimated that China produces more than 20,000 long tons (22,000 metric tons) annually and that the USSR produces 26,000 long tons (28,600 metric tons).

The United States does produce some secondary tin. However, as the world's largest consumer of tin, it must import large quantities of the metal.

For information on the latest production figures for tin, see the article MINING in THE AMERICANA ANNUAL.

J. C. VANLOON
University of Toronto

Further Reading: Hedges, Ernest S., *Tin in Social and Economic History* (New York 1964); Wright, Peter A., *Extractive Metallurgy of Tin* (New York 1966).

TIN PAN ALLEY is that section of a city, especially the Broadway area of New York City, associated with the composers, lyricists, and publishers of popular music. It is also used to refer to the popular music industry in general.

The term, probably derived from "tin pan," slang for a cheap, tinny piano, may have been first used in the early 1900's in a newspaper article about Harry Von Tilzer, composer of *Wait Till the Sun Shines, Nellie.*

While "Tin Pan Alley" suggests music of short-lived appeal and little value—"songs written to order"—it is also associated with such important song writers as George M. Cohan and Irving Berlin.

TIN WARE. See TINWARE.

TINAMIFORMES, an order of birds. See BIRD—*Classification of Birds;* TINAMOU.

TINAMOU, tin′ə-mo͞o, are any of a large group of ground-dwelling game birds found in forests, bushlands, and grasslands from southern Mexico to southern Argentina. Tinamou are from 8 to 21 inches (20–53 cm) long, and although they superficially resemble quail, partridge, and grouse, they are most closely related to the ostrichlike rhea of South America. All species of tinamou have slender, deeply cleft bills and small rounded wings.

A. W. AMBLER, FROM NATIONAL AUDUBON SOCIETY

Crested tinamou, native to southern Argentina.

short legs, and short tails. They are tawny, brown, or gray and are usually streaked, spotted, or barred. Their coloring provides them with excellent camouflage. When in danger, tinamou crouch rather than depend on flight for protection. They tire easily when running or flying.

The tinamou nest is a substantial unlined structure of sticks placed in the ground. The one to ten glossy eggs are green, yellow, blue, or purplish brown. The male tinamou incubates the eggs alone and also cares for the young.

There are over 30 species of tinamou making up the family Tinamidae, order Tinamiformes.

KENNETH E. STAGER
Los Angeles County Museum of Natural History

TINBERGEN, tēn'ber-KHən, **Jan** (1903–), Dutch economist, who shared with Ragnar Frisch the first Nobel Prize in economics, awarded in 1969. Both men were cited for their development of dynamic models in the analysis of economic processes. Such models use mathematical methods to measure economic change.

Tinbergen was born in The Hague on April 12, 1903, and graduated from Leiden University with a degree in physics. He then joined the staff of the Central Bureau of Statistics of the Netherlands, where he specialized in the study of business cycles, an area in which he was later active for the League of Nations. From 1945 to 1955 he was director of the Netherlands Central Planning Bureau. After leaving his government position, he continued to act as adviser to other governments and international organizations, and he retained his teaching post at the Netherlands School of Economics in Rotterdam, to which he had been appointed in 1933.

Tinbergen's major emphasis in his planning work was the construction of models of the Dutch economy that would enable the government to specify targets for economic growth. These models were credited with much of the Netherlands' postwar economic success. Tinbergen's models consistently stressed the need for combining central planning with democratic political methods.

BEN B. SELIGMAN
University of Massachusetts
Author of "Main Currents in Modern Economics"

TINBERGEN, tēn'ber-KHən, **Nikolaas** (1907–), Dutch zoologist who, along with Konrad Lorenz, is often considered a cofounder of ethology, the study of animal behavior based on observations of animals in their natural environment. Tinbergen is probably best known for his analyses of the stimuli that elicit specific behavioral responses in animals. One such response he studied is the pecking, or feeding, response of newly hatched herring gull chicks. The adult gulls have a red spot on the lower beak and Tinbergen found that chicks respond especially to this, and so peck in the right place. Other responses studied, such as the fighting of stickleback fish, show that limited but significant stimuli are used. By comparing related species in different environments, Tinbergen repeatedly showed how responses are adapted to an animal's needs.

Tinbergen also studied the physiological basis of behavior and observed the relationships among different types of behavioral activites. He stressed the importance of certain groups of activities that tend both to occur together and to inhibit other activities. He also developed the concept of out-of-context behavior (displacement activities). An example of this type of activity is the occasional pecking on the ground of cockerels during fights. Tinbergen suggests that displays (threat, courtship) arose from such activities.

Tinbergen was born in The Hague, Netherlands, on April 15, 1907. From 1936 to 1949 he was a lecturer and then a professor of experimental zoology at Leiden University, although he was a political prisoner for a while during World War II. In 1949 he joined the faculty of Oxford University in England and developed ethology in English-speaking countries. His publications include *The Study of Instinct* (1951) and *Social Behavior in Animals* (1953).

MARGARET BASTOCK MANNING
University of Edinburgh

TINCAL, another name for borax. See BORAX.

TINCTURE, in pharmacy, an alcoholic or hydroalcoholic solution containing the active principle of a drug. Tinctures are used as vehicles to dilute and flavor drugs. Some, such as digitalis tincture, may be given orally. Others, such as iodine tincture, may be applied to the skin. Still other tinctures, such as vanilla extract, lemon peel, and sweet orange peel, are commonly used for flavoring.

TINDAL, tin'dəl, **Matthew** (1657–1733), English lawyer, pamphleteer, and deist. Tindal was born in Bere-Ferris, Devonshire. He graduated from Oxford University in 1676, took higher degrees in law, and was a fellow of All Souls' College from 1678 to his death. In 1685 he was admitted to Doctors' Commons, the body of civilian legal experts—that is, experts in Roman, or civil law—in the church and maritime courts.

Under James II he was briefly a Roman Catholic, but he returned to the Church of England early in 1688 and became increasingly hostile to the priesthood, either Roman or Anglican. In 1694 he published a legal opinion that privateers commissioned by King James II could be treated as pirates. In pamphlets he defended religious liberty and the freedom of the press, and launched a satirical attack on the doctrine of the Trinity. *The Rights of the Christian Church* (1706) denied any special position for the clergy.

It caused considerable controversy and was burned by the public hangman in 1710.

In 1729, Tindal's *An Address to the Inhabitants of London and Westminster* replied to a pastoral letter of Bishop Gibson of London attacking current skepticism. Tindal's major work, *Christianity as Old as Creation, or the Gospel a Republication of the Religion of Nature* (1730), written in a sprightly style, reduced religion to belief in God, on rationalistic grounds, and moral duties. It provoked many replies from orthodox churchmen. Tindal died in London on Aug. 16, 1733.

EDWARD R. HARDY
Cambridge University

TINDER is any material that catches fire easily, generally from a spark. Before matches came into common use, most fires were started with tinder, which was ignited by striking flint against steel. In some instances, this process was helped along by the addition of saltpeter or even gunpowder.

Small metal boxes—*tinderboxes*—usually held the tinder and, like flint and steel, were once essential household items. Anyone who might need a fire in his work or for emergencies carried a tinderbox. Charred linen was a common tinder, but most soft, finely divided, inflammable materials would do.

Except in camping and related activities, tinder is rarely used today. For the out-of-doors, many tinders are available. Dry leaves and dry cedar bark make fine tinder.

DONALD N. ZWIEP
Worcester Polytechnic Institute

TINEIDAE, tə-nē′ə-dē, a large, worldwide family of small moths. Probably the best-known members of the family are the three species commonly called "clothes moths." See CLOTHES MOTH.

TINFOIL. See FOIL—*Lead and Tin Foils.*

TINIAN, tin-ē-an′, is an island in the western Pacific Ocean, in the southern Marianas Islands, just southwest of Saipan. It is about 13 miles (21 km) long and 6 miles (10 km) wide, and covers an area of 39 square miles (101 sq km). Most of the inhabitants are Micronesians.

Tinian is part of the U. S. Trust Territory of the Pacific Islands. During World War II, after its capture from the Japanese, the island was a major U. S. air base. Population: (1963) 486.

TINNITUS, tə-nīt′əs, is the sensation of noise in the ear. The noise may be high or low in pitch and may be described as buzzing, ringing, roaring, hammering, hissing, or whistling. It may be continuous or intermittent and may be heard in one ear or both. It may be heard all during the day or only in the quiet of a secluded room. Sometimes it has a rhythm like that of the pulse. Prolonged tinnitus often causes the person to become depressed, and he is so distracted by the noise that he cannot work.

Sometimes tinnitus is caused by impacted ear wax, an inflammation of the ear canal, or an acute inflammation of the middle ear. These conditions interfere with the conduction of sound waves through the ear. Diseases of the inner ear's cochlea or the auditory nerve may also cause tinnitus. Tinnitus may also be caused by disorders that affect the circulation. Such conditions include kidney infections, heart ailments, anemia, arteriosclerosis, and high blood pressure. Tinnitus may also be caused by certain drugs such as quinine and salicylates.

RAYMOND L. OSBORNE, M. D.
Mount Sinai Hospital, N. Y.

TINSTONE is a common name for the tin dioxide mineral, cassiterite. See CASSITERITE.

TINTERN ABBEY, tin′tərn, a famous architectural ruin in southwest England, 8 miles (13 km) south of Monmouth on the west bank of the Wye River. The abbey was founded in 1131 by Walter de Clare for Cistercian monks who came from France. The roofless church that remains was developed between 1220 and 1287. It was completed in the early 14th century. Like so many other small monasteries, this one was dissolved under Henry VIII in 1537.

Although William Wordsworth's poem *Lines composed a Few Miles above Tintern Abbey* (1798) has contributed greatly to its fame, it does not mention the abbey. The existing church is distinguished for its beautiful proportions and graceful architectural detail. It was bought by the British government in 1900.

GORDON STOKES
Author of "English Place-Names"

CULVER PICTURES

TINTERN ABBEY church, dating from the 13th century, displays its graceful lines even in its ruins. It is cared for by the British government.

ALINARI-ART REFERENCE BUREAU

Tintoretto's *St. Mark Rescuing the Slave* (1548).

TINTORETTO, tin-tə-ret′ō, **Jacopo** (1518–1594), Italian painter of the Venetian school, whose dramatically lit, motion-filled canvases make him one of the leading figures of the late Renaissance.

Life. Tintoretto was born Jacopo Robusti in Venice. Because his father was a dyer he was nicknamed Tintoretto, Italian for "little dyer." There is no proof for the traditional view that he was a pupil of Titian. By 1539, Tintoretto was inscribed in the lists of the Venetian painters' guild, and his earliest extant work is dated 1540. He established his reputation in 1548 with his exciting composition of *St. Mark Rescuing the Slave* (Accademia, Venice).

From then on Tintoretto remained, after Titian, the leading artist in Venice, competing with the master himself and eventually succeeding him as official painter to the republic. He headed an extremely active workshop, in which, as customary, his chief assistants were members of his own family—his sons Domenico and Marco and his daughter Marietta. He died in Venice on May 31, 1594.

Work. Most of Tintoretto's work was done for Venetian patrons, and the best of it is still in his native city. For the state he created the decorative cycles in the Ducal Palace, which depict historical events or votive subjects. Since fresco suffered in the humid climate of Venice, Tintoretto worked usually in oil on canvas. The *Coronation of the Virgin,* or *Paradise* (c. 1588), is one of the largest paintings ever executed on canvas.

The Scuola di San Rocco, an extremely rich Venetian confraternity, houses more than 50 monumental canvases by Tintoretto. Ranging in date from 1564 to 1588 and decorating three major rooms, they comprise a continuous pictorial cycle, devoted mainly to scenes of the Virgin and of Christ, as well as of Old Testament prototypes. In 1564, by somewhat devious means, Tintoretto captured the original commission, a ceiling painting of the *Apotheosis of St. Roch.* In a competition for the work he entered a finished picture rather than the requested sketch and then presented it to the confraternity as a gift. Consequently, he was awarded the task of decorating the rest of the building and given membership in the confraternity. He succeeded in transforming the building into a monument to himself and his art.

Style. Tintoretto is the first artist credited with synthesizing the design of Michelangelo and the coloring of Titian, a critical formula for success calculated to resolve the obvious distinctions between the two artistic giants of the 16th century. His art was infused with an unusual physical excitement, a constant movement and tension. Figures are set into motion at angles to the plane of the canvas, moving in and out of the picture in counterpoint to one another, as in *St. Mark Rescuing the Slave.* A major source of inspiration for this figural dialectic was the work of Michelangelo. Tintoretto frequently drew from small copies of that master's sculpture. By significantly selecting unusual views, however, he violated, in effect, Michelangelo's aesthetic principles.

In adapting the free handling of the brush in applying color, which had become part of Venetian tradition, Tintoretto also assumed a radical stance. To Titian's style, in which solid forms were suggested by loosely juxtaposed patches of paint, Tintoretto added an element of

HISTORICAL SOCIETY OF EARLY AMERICAN DECORATION

JANE LATTA

AMERICAN "crooked spout" coffee pot by Oliver Bronson.

ENGLISH tray in elaborate Chippendale-Gothic style.

MEXICAN candleholder in the form of an angel, 20th century.

deliberate speed and action—his long brushstrokes are rarely broad patches of color but have a direction and velocity. The very processes of paint application, the gestures themselves, often seem to be recorded on the surface of his pictures. For this technique his non-Venetian contemporaries harshly criticized his work as sloppily executed and an insult to art.

Tintoretto's mature style depends for its overall compositional unity on this quality of brushwork, as well as on an apparently arbitrary and highly imaginative distribution of tonal values. Only parts of his solid forms are actually illuminated, and these fragmented members, so to speak, are related to one another as parts of the overall design of the composition. This active surface pattern of lights and darks operates in tension with the spatial thrusts of the pictorial illusion. Such powerful dramatic effects, accented by long highlights, are among Tintoretto's most influential contributions to later styles in painting.

DAVID ROSAND, *Columbia University*

Further Reading: Delogu, Giuseppe, *Drawings by Tintoretto* (New York 1969); Tietze, Hans, *Tintoretto, The Paintings* (London 1948).

TINWARE includes objects of pure tin, metals alloyed with tin, and tin-plated iron.

Ancient and Renaissance Tinware. Tin was rare and costly in the ancient world and was esteemed as a protective and hardening metal. The Greeks attributed divine traits to it and called it Hermes and Zeus. Tin deposits in southeast Asia, the Aral Sea area, and Britain's Cornwall led to trade among many peoples.

Bronze Age civilizations made weapons, vessels, and other objects out of bronze, an alloy of copper and tin. In the graves of Andronovo in southern Siberia (2000–1700 B.C.), expertly worked vessels of pure tin were found. An Egyptian grave (1580–1350 B.C.) yielded a tin pilgrim bottle and ring. A necklace of tin beads found in the Low Countries east of the Rhine may have been treasured by Asian migrants about 3000 to 2000 B.C. In the 4th century B.C., Romans had tin-coated copper bowls. Later, Persians ornamented tin vessels with gold.

During the Renaissance in Europe, Italy produced processional lanterns of silver alloyed with tin, which were rubbed with linseed oil to give a pleasing black patina. Bells were cast in tin, and glass mirrors were backed with antimony and tin. In the 15th century, Venetians gilded plates of tin or pewter (a tin alloy) for those who could not afford solid gold. French tin and pewter vessels were engraved in the 16th century, gilded in the 17th. England in the 16th century produced cast tin vessels.

English Tinplate. In the early 18th century in Pontypool, Wales, John Hanbury, inventer of rolling mills, was developing sheet iron. There the Allgoods, father and son, introduced tinplated iron. The Hanbury factory produced boxes, vessels, coffee and tea urns, and varieties of pierced-edge trays. Many trays had simulated tortoiseshell grounds achieved by covering shiny tinplate, or silver-leaf squares randomly set on black, with transparent crimson overlaid by unevenly blended translucent and opaque black and brown. Such grounds were ornamented with scattered nosegays and familiar birds and fruits.

At Birmingham and Wolverhampton (1760–

SEAMED "COFFIN TRAY," ornamented by Oliver Buckley, is an example of early American tinware.

COLLECTION OF HISTORICAL SOCIETY OF EARLY AMERICAN DECORATION

1840) black (japanned) grounds imitated Japanese lacquer. A number of shapes and styles evolved. The most sophisticated were called Chippendale-Gothic. Black or bronze-clouded grounds and finely gilded details—scrolls, vines, curlicues—were combined with painted birds and flowers and leaves with bronze-powder highlights. Painted tinplate was also made in other countries, such as France, where it was known as *tôle*.

American Tinplate. Tinsmiths in 18th and 19th century Maine, Connecticut, New York, and Pennsylvania fashioned unpainted tinware for farm and household use and painted pieces for display. They imported tinplate from England, which kept production methods secret, until 1800, when American production began. Cargo costs and small space on ships limited the size of imported tin sheets. Cut-corner "coffin trays" were small or were seamed. Other tin objects were boxes, punched panels for doors of food cabinets, lanterns, candle-holders, and apple dishes. The crooked-spout coffee pot was designed by Oliver Bronson at the Filley shops in Connecticut.

Grounds were usually black. The Germans in Pennsylvania, however, made crystallized surfaces ranging from orange and yellow to whitish by applying muriatic and sulfuric acids with water to clean, hot tin. Designs on tin were usually floral in the folk tradition, in primary colors without perspective. White bands as background and stylized brushstrokes enhanced the work.

Mexican Tinware. Tinplate art in Mexico resulted about 1650, when the Spanish restricted the use of silver for domestic articles. The Xochiotxin family of Puebla were tinsmiths for generations. In the 20th century, José Sánchez and followers created objects from sheets of shiny unpainted tin. These include chandeliers, sconces, candelabra, tree-shaped, openwork candle shields, and purely ornamental figures. Motifs, such as the rose and pineapple, and techniques are similar to those of Mexican silver. Repoussé and cut-out designs are also common.

MARIA D. MURRAY
Author of "The Art of Tray Painting"

Further Reading: Coffin, Margaret, *The History and Folklore of American Tinware* (New York 1968); DeVoe, Shirley S., *Tinsmiths of Connecticut* (Middletown, Conn., 1968); Lea, Zilla R., ed., *The Ornamented Tray* (Rutland, Vt., 1970); Ramsay, Natalie Allen, ed., *The Decorator Digest* (Rutland, Vt., 1965).

TIP, a small gift of money for service, usually in addition to payment due.

The custom of tipping dates from at least the Roman era and more likely from the first use of coined money, but the origin of the word "tip" is obscure. It may derive from *stipend,* a corruption of the Latin word *stips,* meaning gift. Popular belief holds that tipping originated in 18th century England when the coffeehouse tables of Samuel Johnson's London were equipped with coin boxes labeled *To Insure Promptness.* A coin dropped in the box was supposed to speed service. The coins came to be called by the first letters of the sign, *T. I. P.* or *tip.*

Tipping became prevalent in the American colonies, but after independence and the growth of pride in the young republic, the tip was often condemned as undemocratic and demeaning. Yet tipping persists in the United States and most other countries and in some instances is obligatory.

Travel entails much tipping. Most European hotels and restaurants add a service charge of about 10% to 20% to their bills, and many guests feel impelled to tip over and above this. Taxi drivers, waiters, and ship's stewards all depend on tips for their livelihood.

Airlines have successfully prohibited tipping. Opponents of tipping point to this as proof that the custom of tipping can be eliminated. Efforts to eliminate it in Communist countries have been only partially successful.

GERI TROTTA
Feature and Travel Editor, "Harper's Bazaar"

TIPPECANOE, Battle of, tip-ē-kə-nōō′, fought between U. S. troops and Indians on Nov. 7, 1811, near the junction of the Wabash and Tippecanoe rivers about 60 miles (96 km) northwest of Indianapolis, Ind., near the present town of Battle Ground. From nearby Prophet's Town the Shawnee leader Tecumseh and his brother "the Prophet" were directing an intertribal confederacy against U. S. occupation of lands ceded by the Indians in the Treaty of Fort Wayne (1809).

On the night of November 6, William Henry Harrison, governor of Indiana Territory, brought a force of about 950 U. S. militiamen and soldiers to an encampment near Prophet's Town. Tecumseh was away seeking tribal allies, and the Prophet was in command. Before daybreak the next morning the Indians attacked and seemed about to annihilate the U. S. troops. However, after several hours of intense fighting, the Indians were driven from the field.

Harrison lost about 185 men killed and wounded. The Indian loss was believed to be great. Harrison's men burned Prophet's Town. The legendary "great victory" at Tippecanoe helped elect Harrison U. S. president in 1840.

CARL UBBELOHDE
Case Western Reserve University

TIPPERARY, tip-ə-râr′ē, a county in south central Ireland, is the republic's largest inland county. It has a common boundary with eight counties in the provinces of Munster, Connaught, and Leinster. The Shannon River separates it from the counties of Clare and Galway, and the Suir River forms its boundary with Waterford. The other neighboring counties are Limerick, Cork, Kilkenny, Leix (Laoighis), and Offaly. Tipperary's total area is 1,658 square miles (4,293 sq km).

Near the Galtee (Galty) Mountains in the south is Tipperary's most remarkable geological feature, the limestone caverns known as the Mitchelstown Caves. Much of the county's pastureland is of the highest quality, particularly in the Golden Vein. Cattle rearing and dairying are the main occupations. There are mines at Gortdrum and Silvermines where lead, zinc, silver, copper, barites, and mercury are recovered.

For purposes of local government Tipperary is divided into the North Riding and the South Riding. Thurles is the capital of the North Riding; other towns include Nenagh, Roscrea, and Templemore. Clonmel is the county town of the South Riding and the chief town of Tipperary. Smaller towns include Tipperary town, Carrick-on-Suir, Cahir, and Cashel.

Almost all the towns of Tipperary are market towns. Clonmel produces bacon, cider, plastics, and perambulators. Thurles has a large sugar-processing factory. Tipperary town has a creamery and manufactures linoleum. Nenagh has several industries—the manufacture of woolens, plastics, and aluminum utensils, and flour milling.

Cashel "of the Kings" is one of the most famous towns in Ireland. The Rock of Cashel—the seat of Munster kings beginning in the 4th century—rises 200 feet (60 meters) above the plain. On the summit is Cormac's Chapel, dating from the early 12th century.

Population (1966) of Tipperary town: 4,507; of the county, 122,778.

THOMAS FITZGERALD
Department of Education, Dublin

TIPPETT, tip'ət, **Sir Michael Kemp** (1905–), English composer. He was born in London on Jan. 2, 1905, but grew up in a village in Suffolk. He studied composition and conducting at the Royal College of Music and completed his first symphonic work in the early 1930's. From 1940 to 1951 he was music director at Morley College in London. He attained wide recognition as a composer with *A Child of Our Time* (1941), an oratorio about a youth caught in the machinery of war. The work reflected his own strong humanitarian feelings and his pacificism. Rather than reject the latter, he served a 3-month prison term in 1943 as a conscientious objector.

Tippett's best orchestral works include the Concerto for Double String Orchestra (1939), String Quartet No. 2 (1943), and Symphony No. 2 (1957). His first opera was *The Midsummer Marriage* (1952), and his second, *King Priam* (1962). Tippett was knighted in 1966.

TIPPOO SAHIB. See TIPU SULTAN.

TIPPU TIP, ti-pōō'tip (1820?–1905), was a Swahili-speaking trader in slaves and ivory in the interior of East and Central Africa. He was born in Zanzibar as Hamed bin Muhammad el-Murjebi, the son of an Afro-Arab trader with many commercial connections in the East African interior. The nickname Tippu Tip may mean "blinking eyes."

By about 1850, Tippu Tip was launched on an independent career. His enterprise opened up the areas west and south of Lake Tanganyika to commercial exploitation by Zanzibari-based merchants. By force of arms he effectively dominated a large region extending from Kisangani in the Congo southward to Lake Mweru and eastward to Tabora in Tanzania. Backed by Indian financiers in Zanzibar, he greatly influenced the world market in ivory and slaves.

In 1887, Henry M. Stanley appointed him governor of the eastern Congo on behalf of King Leopold II of Belgium. Other slave traders revolted against Tippu Tip and, during his absence in Zanzibar, a war between Belgians and Arabs effectively subordinated the eastern Congo region to Belgium. Tippu Tip retired to write his memoirs and died in Zanzibar.

ROBERT I. ROTBERG, *Author of "A Political History of Tropical Africa"*

TIPU SULTAN, ti-pōō' (1750–1799), was a Muslim ruler of the predominantly Hindu state of Mysore in southern India. He was born in Mysore on Nov. 10, 1750. Tipu inherited and ably maintained a powerful army and efficient administrative system on the death of his father, Hyder (Haidar) Ali, in 1782.

For much of his reign Tipu was at war with the British East India Company, which was becoming the dominant power in south India. He carried on a war with the British, begun by his father, until 1784. Fighting was resumed in 1790 and continued until 1792, when he was obliged to cede large areas of Mysore to the British and their Indian allies. Mysore was finally completely conquered in 1799, and Tipu was killed on May 4 as British troops stormed his capital, Seringapatam.

P. J. MARSHALL
King's College, University of London

TIRADENTES, tē-rə-dāɴ'tēs (1748–1792), the national hero of Brazil. He was born Joaquim José da Silva Xavier, in the small town of Pombal (now Tiradentes), Minas Gerais, Brazil, on Nov. 12, 1748. At various times in his life he worked as a merchant, dentist, and militia officer. Most often he is known as Tiradentes ("the tooth-puller").

Tiradentes assumed a leading role in the first major conspiracy against Portuguese rule, the "Inconfidência Mineira," which was centered in Minas Gerais at the end of the 18th century. All the conspirators agreed that Brazil should be independent. Beyond that, they could not concur. Tiradentes, who admired the U. S. constitution, advocated a republic.

The conspirators never put their romantic and unrealistic plans into action. Betrayed, they were arrested and imprisoned. Tiradentes maintained that he was the leader of the conspiracy, and, as a result, he was hanged and quartered in Rio de Janeiro on April 21, 1792. The execution created a martyr to Brazilian independence.

E. BRADFORD BURNS
University of California at Los Angeles

TIRANË, tē-rä'nə, the capital of Albania, is located in the central portion of the country, about 20 miles (32 km) from the Adriatic Sea. It is the political, economic, and cultural center of Albania. The city has a university, a national theater, and museums. Because of its rapid expansion after World War II, Tiranë (or Tirana) is modern in appearance, although some buildings remain from its Ottoman past. Government offices front on the central Skanderbeg Square, named for Albania's national hero. The population of Tiranë is 75% Muslim.

Tiranë's postwar growth is due largely to the swift industrialization of the area and to the fact that the city is Albania's administrative center. A major portion of Albania's industrial production is concentrated in the capital city. Among the principal industries are textile and clothing production, food processing, and woodworking. Tiranë is also Albania's main transportation hub, with roads and railroads linking it with its Adriatic port of Durrës and the nation's other major cities.

The city was first mentioned in documents of the 15th century. From this time until 1912 it was part of the Ottoman Empire. In 1920 the city became the capital of independent Albania. During World War II, Tiranë was occupied by Italian and then by German troops. In November 1944, Albanian partisan units liberated the city. In January 1946 the establishment of the socialist government for Albania was proclaimed there. Population: (1963 estimate) 152,500.

BARBARA JELAVICH AND CHARLES JELAVICH
Indiana University

TIRE, a continuous ring, usually of rubber, encircling the rim of a wheel. Tires may be solid, partly solid, or, like the modern passenger-car tire, inflated with air (pneumatic). There are more than 3,500 kinds and sizes of pneumatic tires for passenger cars, trucks, buses, aircraft, farm tractors and implements, motorcycles, and off-the-highway vehicles such as road-building equipment. They range from 1½-pound (680-gram) smooth-contour tires for the tail wheels of airplanes to giant tires weighing more than 3 tons used on earth-moving equipment.

HISTORY

In 1845, Robert William Thomson, a British engineer, discovered and patented the pneumatic principle. This discovery is frequently credited to John Boyd Dunlop, the "father of the tire." Actually Dunlop reinvented the pneumatic tire. He received his patent in 1888.

Thomson worked originally with leather for his treads and built up the tire by hand. The tire was not wholly or readily detachable, and some 70 security bolts were used to fasten it to a wheel. Nevertheless, Thomson by 1850 succeeded in producing a fairly satisfactory light carriage tire. There was not much demand for Thomson's pneumatic tire, but solid rubber tires, which were manufactured in Britain as early as 1846, enjoyed popularity from 1870 until Dunlop's reinvention of the pneumatic tire.

Dunlop was a veterinary surgeon, who lived in Belfast. Spurred by his son's complaint of excessive vibration in his bicycle, Dunlop met the desire for comfort and speed by producing a pneumatic tire. He thus became the second man to apply this principle to wheels but the first to recognize the practicality of fashioning vulcanized rubber and canvas into a light, tubular form.

Dunlop used a solid disk of wood instead of a spoked wheel. His tire consisted of a canvas pocket containing a rubber tube. The tube was protected by outer rubber strips, which were thickened on the running surface. The whole unit formed a D-section tire, which was taped and fastened to the wheel rim by means of rubber solution and by flaps formed for this purpose on the inner canvas jacket. A simple and rather ineffective valve completed the assembly.

Two other names that are closely associated with early tire development are Charles Kingston Welch and William Erskine Bartlett. In 1890, Welch patented the detachable pneumatic tire, which is still in use. In the same year Bartlett developed the beaded-edge tire. Bartlett's tire was secured to the wheel by means of a hooked rim under which the edges of the cover were held in place by compressed air.

TIRE MANUFACTURE

A tire usually consists of rubber, fabric, chemicals, and metal. On the outside is the tread rubber, bordered by the sidewall. On the inside are the fabric plies, which give the tire its strength. In tube tires a thin rubber tube is used beneath the plies. Tubeless tires have a thin layer of soft rubber lining the plies. The rigid base of the tire is the bead, consisting of high-tensile steel wire encased in rubber.

The thick layer of tread rubber is compounded to withstand road wear and to provide traction. The sidewall rubber, which does not touch the ground, is not so thick and is generally made of an abrasion-resistant rubber to provide maximum protection for the structural plies.

Dozens of different chemicals are used in preparing the rubber for use in tires. Sulfur is the basic chemical agent in vulcanization. Zinc oxide, which was used in early compounding to toughen the rubber, is still widely used in tire manufacture. Carbon black came into use for the same purpose in the early 1920's.

The tire's basic strength is derived from its skeletal structure—its layers of rubberized fabric. The fabric also provides the tire's stability and resistance to bruises, fatigue, and heat. Without plies, a tire would be little more than a balloon. Early tires had six plies. The number was reduced to four around 1935 and further reduced to two about 1965. Generally, 4-ply tires are preferred. Fabric makes up about 12% of the weight of a car tire and 15% of a truck tire.

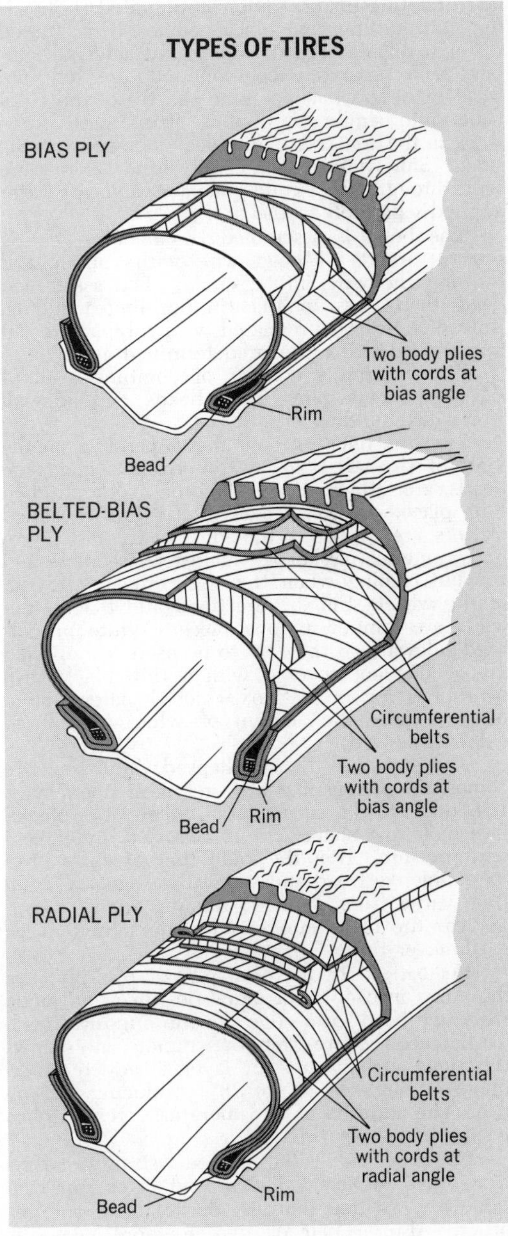

Early tire fabric was made from cotton fibers, and when speeds were slower and loads lighter, the square-woven fabric was adequate. Rayon cord, a synthetic material, was developed in the 1920's and completely replaced cotton. Nylon, another synthetic, appeared during World War II in aircraft tires and by the late 1940's came into use in automobile and truck tires. Polyester cord appeared in the early 1960's.

High-tensile steel wire beads keep the tire in place on the wheel, resisting the various pressures that would force it off. The wires, forming an unstretchable part of the tire, are in effect two rings of steel inside the tire.

Construction. Tire construction varies somewhat among the different manufacturers, but the basic process is approximately the same everywhere.

Natural and synthetic rubber are mixed with chemicals in an internal mixer equipped with large rotating blades. The compounded rubber is fed into milling machines, where it is forced through rollers. Tread rubber and sidewall rubber, each separately compounded, are fed into giant extruders that combine the tread and sidewalls into single continuous strips with tread stock in the center and the black sidewalls on the sides. Sidewalls of white and other colors are sent through a separate machine and are later applied separately to the tire.

The bead is assembled by machine-coating several strands of bead wire with rubber and forming the wire into a circle. The assembled bead then goes to the tire-building machine. Rolls of fabric, impregnated with rubber, are cut in ply-sized strips at a predetermined angle.

Final assembly consists of combining all of the components—plies, tread, beads, and sidewall—on a tire-building drum.

First the plies—the number depending on the kind of tire—are laid on the drum. Then the beads are attached and automatically stitched into place. Strips of calendered fabric, called chafers, are applied to the edges of the last ply to make an effective barrier against air seepage and prevent chafing when the tire contacts the rim of the wheel. Finally, the tread and black sidewalls are applied in one piece. White or colored sidewalls, if they are to be used, are applied last. They are covered with a thin black strip of rubber for protection, which is later buffed off to expose the amount of white or colored sidewall desired.

The drum is then collapsed, and the tire comes off looking like a barrel with open ends. It is taken to the curing room, where it is placed in a mold and shaped and vulcanized under heat and pressure. It is the mold that gives the tire its distinctive tread and sidewall designs. Curing time varies from about 15 minutes for a passenger car tire to as much as 10 hours for a large earthmover tire.

Tire Design. In the cross-ply, or bias-ply, tire the cords in each layer of fabric run at an angle from one bead (rim edge) to the opposite bead. To balance the tire strength symmetrically across the tread center, another layer is added at an opposing angle of 30° to 38°, producing a 2-ply tire. The addition of two more crisscrossed plies results in a 4-ply tire.

Cords in the radial tire run straight across from bead to bead. The second layer runs the same way, so that the plies do not cross one another. Also, a belt of two or more layers is placed circumferentially around the tire underneath the tread.

The bias-belted tire is made much like the conventional bias-ply tire, but it is surrounded by circumferential belts like those in the radial tire.

Of the three types, the radial-ply offers the longest tread life, the best traction, the coolest running, the best gas mileage, and the greatest resistance to road hazards. The bias-ply tire provides a softer, quieter ride and is the least expensive. The bias-belted tire is intermediate between the good-quality bias-ply and the radial tire. It has a longer tread life and is cooler running than the bias ply, and it gives a smoother low-speed ride than the radial.

Belts. Tread wear is caused by abrasion between the surface of the tire tread and the road surface. In belted tires the tread rolls straight over the road surface without lateral motion. In conventional bias-ply tires the path of each point on the tread resembles a cycloid (circular motion) with respect to the road, resulting in lateral, or squirming, movement. This movement causes heat buildup and greatly increases tread wear. The presence of belts restricts tread motion, significantly improving tread life. Tires stabilized with belts permit use of wider treads without producing excessive heat.

Aspect Ratio. Aspect ratio is the relation of tire section height to tire width. Early pneumatic tires were nearly circular in cross section, with a section height almost equal to the width, giving an aspect ratio of close to 100. Over the years, tires have become lower and wider: a conventional passenger-car tire now has an aspect ratio of 83—that is, its height is 83% of its width. A lower aspect ratio provides greater stability for the tire, better handling, greater traction, and increased high-speed capabilities. Racing car tires may have aspect ratios as low as 30.

Tire Materials. If a tire is to perform satisfactorily, the circumferential belt must be relatively nonyielding; that is, it must be made of a high-modulus material. Glass has a much higher modulus than rayon, but the latter gives a smoother ride. Glass also has a tendency to result in broken belt cords, although such breaks have little effect on tire safety. Wire-belted tires often produce harsh rides, but the use of softer wire has reduced this difficulty.

Nylon is the strongest body cord, followed by polyester and rayon. Nylon, however, tends to develop temporary flat spots when the car is parked for any length of time. Polyester and rayon do not flat-spot. Nylon and rayon have a higher thermal threshold—that is, greater heat resistance—than polyester. Nylon is preferred for heavy-duty, off-the-road, and aircraft tires. Polyester offers less noise, better tread wear, and cooler running than nylon.

Rim Design. The straight side rim is universally used today. This rim has flanges that flare outward and serve to keep the tire casing edges from being forced too far sideways. The wire bead reinforcement in the tire holds the tire on the rim by preventing it from slipping over the flanges. The tire and rim must be united into a single structure to support the vehicle load on a cushion of air.

M. E. LERNER
Publisher, "Rubber Age"

Further Reading: French, Tom, "Pneumatic Tyres," *Science Journal*, vol. 5A, pp. 35–39, 1969.

TIRESIAS, tī-rē′sē-əs, in Greek mythology, was a highly renowned blind prophet of Thebes. There are various legends about him. In one he saw Athena bathing, and in anger she blinded him. Later she gave him the power to understand the language of birds.

In another legend the gods blinded him for revealing their secrets, which he had learned from his mother, the nymph Chariclo. A well-known legend concerns his change of sex after he found a pair of snakes and killed the female. Years later in a similar incident he killed the male, and his manhood was restored. Hera and Zeus asked Tiresias whether men or women enjoy love more; when he contradicted Hera by answering "women," she blinded him. Zeus gave him long life and the ability to prophesy.

In literature, Tiresias is a figure in Sophocles' drama *Oedipus Rex*, Tennyson's poem *Tiresias*, and T. S. Eliot's *The Waste Land*.

TÎRGOVIŞTE, tir-gō-vēsh′te, in Rumania, is the capital city of the county (*judet*) of Dîmboviţa. It is in the Ialomiţa River valley, lying 48 miles (77 km) northwest of Bucharest. Tîrgovişte has developed as a tourist center because of its important historical monuments. Of chief interest are the ruins of the palace of Mircea the Old, the 15th century Dealul Monastery, the 16th century Princely Church, and the 17th century Stelea Church. The museum contains an art and archaeology collection of the 14th-17th centuries. Tîrgovişte is also an industrial city, specializing in petroleum products.

First mentioned in the late 14th century, the city was the administrative, political, and cultural center of Wallachia from the 14th to the 17th century, when the capital was moved to Bucharest. Population: (1966 est.) 30,000.

BARBARA JELAVICH and CHARLES JELAVICH
Indiana University

TÎRGU MUREŞ, tir′gōō mōō′resh, a city in central Rumania, is the capital of the county (*judet*) of Mureş. It is in Transylvania, on the Mureş River. Tîrgu Mureş (Hungarian *Vásárhely*) with a population over 50% Hungarian, is a political and cultural center for Rumania's Hungarian minority. It has both Hungarian and Rumanian theaters, a regional art gallery, and the Teleki documentary library, which contains many old manuscripts and rare books important to Transylvanian history. Historical monuments include a fortress, constructed in the 14th century and enlarged in the 16th, and a 15th century Gothic church. Since World War II the city has become a major industrial center, with a sugar refinery, fertilizer and furniture factories, and chemical and food processing plants.

First mentioned in the 14th century, the city passed from Hungarian to Ottoman political control in the 16th century. From the end of the 17th century until 1918, when Rumania acquired Transylvania, it was part of the Habsburg Empire. Population: (1966 est.) 86,000.

BARBARA JELAVICH and CHARLES JELAVICH
Indiana University

TIROL, tə-rōl′, is one of Austria's nine provinces. Tirol, also spelled Tyrol, is in western Austria, east of Vorarlberg. It is concentrated along the Inn and upper Lech river valleys but also includes the completely separate East Tirol. East Tirol became separated when South Tirol was ceded to Italy after World War I. Tirol is part of the eastern Alpine region and has a relatively sunny climate greatly influenced by mild winds. The combination of the climate and the area's spectacular scenery has made it a tourist mecca. Kitzbühel is particularly noted for its ski slopes. Innsbruck is the capital of the province, which has an area of 4,882 square miles (12,645 sq km). About 37% of the area is devoted to pastureland, 33% is forest, 26% is barren, and only 4% is cropland.

Tirol was controlled by the Bavarians and Lombards in the early Middle Ages, was conquered by the Franks in the 8th century, and then came under the counts of Tirol. The Habsburgs obtained most of Tirol by inheritance in 1363 and subsequently added other areas, notably some predominantly Italian-speaking regions in 1803. During the Napoleonic era Tirol came under the domination of the French, who in 1809 suppressed an insurrection started by Andreas Hofer, a Tirolese patriot. Tirol was restored to Austria in 1814. The cession of South Tirol to Italy in 1919 involved not only the Italian-speaking districts, but included some 250,000 Germans. The cession aroused much irredentist feeling in Tirol and has complicated Austro-Italian relations. Population: (1969 est.) 516,500.

ERNST C. HELMREICH, Bowdoin College

TIROS, a weather satellite. See WEATHER BUREAU.

TIRPITZ, tir′pits, **Alfred Peter Friedrich von** (1849–1930), German admiral, who created Germany's high sea fleet in the years preceding World War I. Tirpitz was born at Küstrin, Brandenburg, on March 19, 1849. He entered the Prussian Navy in 1865 and became a torpedo expert. In 1892, as chief of staff to the chief of the naval high command, he convinced his superiors, including Emperor William II, of the need for German naval expansion.

In 1897, Tirpitz became secretary of state of the imperial naval office. He presented to the Emperor a secret memorandum on the composition of the German fleet, naming England as Germany's most dangerous enemy. Beginning in 1898 he piloted a series of navy appropriations through the Reichstag, aiming at parity with England by 1917. The second one in 1900 triggered the Anglo-German naval armaments race.

Tirpitz was made admiral in 1903 and grand admiral in 1911. When World War I came in 1914, Germany had the world's second-strongest fleet. Advocating an offensive naval policy, Tirpitz requested command of the fleet. The appointment was resisted by a cautious naval staff and by Chancellor von Bethmann-Hollweg, and the Emperor refused to override their views. Tirpitz also urged unrestricted submarine warfare, but fearful of international reaction, the government opposed that as well. Frustrated, he resigned on March 15, 1916. In February 1917, however, Germany did begin a policy of unrestricted submarine warfare.

Tirpitz was elected to the Reichstag in 1924 as a member of the German National People's party, but he found politics uncongenial and in 1928 withdrew from public life. He died at Ebenhausen, near Munich, on March 6, 1930.

B. B. SCHOFIELD, *Vice Admiral, Royal Navy*
Author of "British Sea-Power"

TIRSO DE MOLINA, tēr′sō thä mō-lē′nä (1584?–1648), is the pseudonym of the Spanish playwright Gabriel Téllez, who ranks below only Lope de Vega and Calderón among the great dramatists of Spain's Golden Age. Although an adherent of Lope's dramatic theories, he was more concerned than Lope with the psychology of his characters and with social problems.

Life. Tirso was born in Madrid. According to some scholars he was the bastard son of the Duke of Osuna. After studying at the University of Alcalá he entered the Order of Mercy in 1601. He held high posts in this order and, as its chronicler, wrote the *Historia general de la Orden de la Merced* (1639). Between 1616 and 1618 he lived in Santo Domingo, W. I., teaching theology and taking care of the order's affairs there. In 1625 he was chastised by the Council of Castile for what was regarded as the unseemly language and subject matter of some of his plays, and thereafter his playwrighting virtually ceased. He died in Almazán, Spain, in 1648.

Works. Tirso wrote between 300 and 400 plays. About 80 are extant, and of these some 30 are of doubtful authorship. His best-known play, *El burlador de Sevilla y convidado de piedra* (1630), introduced to literature the famous legendary figure Don Juan. The story of this licentious lover, who was impelled to seduce one woman after another, inspired such musicians as Mozart and Richard Strauss, such writers as Molière and Shaw, and such painters as Delacroix. See DON JUAN.

Tirso's dramas fall into three categories: historical works, cloak and sword comedies (*comedias de capa y espada*) that revolve about lively love intrigues, and religious plays. Among the outstanding works usually ascribed to him are *La prudencia en la mujer*, probably the finest historical drama of the Golden Age; *Don Gil de las calzas verdes*, a dazzling example of the *capa y espada* genre; and *El condenado por desconfiado* (1635), a powerful religious play.

Tirso also wrote two collections of prose tales interpersed with plays, *Los cigarrales de Toledo* (1621) and *Deleitar aprovechando* (1635). The stories in both reveal the influence of Boccaccio and Cervantes.

DONALD W. BLEZNICK
University of Cincinnati

Further Reading: McClelland, Ivy L,, *Tirso de Molina: Studies in Dramatic Realism* (Liverpool 1948).

TIRUCHCHIRAPPALLI, ti-rōōt-chi-räp′pəl-li, a city in India, is in Tamil Nadu state, on the Cauvery (Kaveri) River 190 miles (300 km) southwest of Madras. It was formerly called Trichinopoly. The city is dominated by the Rock, a natural formation rising 273 feet (83 meters) above the street level of the extensive fort surrounding it. Tiruchchirappalli is an important rail junction with a large railroad workshop. It manufactures textiles, cement, and cigars, and is the chief market for the produce of the Cauvery delta.

The city's history includes periods when it was the capital of the Chola Empire and of the Naiks of Madura. During the Carnatic Wars of the mid-18th century it was the scene of frequent battles between the French and British. The British acquired the city and surrounding district in 1801. Population: (1961) 249,862.

JOSEPH E. SCHWARTZBERG
University of Minnesota

TIRYNS, tir′ənz, is a prehistoric town in the eastern Greek Peloponnesus, near the Gulf of Argos. It was first excavated by Heinrich Schliemann in 1884–1885, and the work was continued by Wilhelm Dörpfeld and others. The heart of Tiryns was a fortress-palace, on a great limestone rock 59 feet (18 meters) above the surrounding plain. It had massive foundations and walls of roughly dressed stone, 26 feet (8 meters) thick in places, the ruins of which still remain. Most of the population lived on the plain below the fortress but could be protected inside in case of enemy attack.

Although archaeologists found no tombs or rich treasures, Tiryns contained architectural features and decorations that were the heritage of the classical era. The *megaron*, or hall of state, was a rectangular room with four roof-supporting columns around a central hearth and a porch and vestibule at the entrance. This arrangement, and adaptation to a cool climate, appeared later in the plan of the typical Greek temple. The *propylon*, a columned gateway into a fortified area, and column-and-lintel construction were other architectural features. Remnants of fresco decorations—some in the style of the palace at Knossos on Crete—and friezes of alabaster inlaid with blue glass were found.

Together with Mycenae, less than 10 miles (16 km) away, and Troy (both excavated by Schliemann), Tiryns gives evidence of a highly developed land-based civilization. These widespread Helladic peoples (formerly called Mycenaean and dated from 1700 B.C. to 1250 B.C.) interacted with the maritime trade empire in the Aegean Sea that was long controlled by Crete. Located at the head of the Gulf of Argos, Tiryns dominated access to sea routes toward Crete and Egypt, while Mycenae, inland, controlled trade to the north and west. The 14th and 13th centuries B.C. marked the high points of Helladic prosperity and some evidence shows that fleets from Tiryns may have been involved in overseas trading in the later periods. Helladic trade may have influenced the cultures of Bronze Age Europe by way of the Mediterranean and the Rhône and Danube valleys.

In legend, Tiryns was the birthplace of Hercules and was founded by Proteus, brother of King Acrisius of Argos. Proteus is said to have invited the Cyclopes to build the giant walls.

Tiryns was being further strengthened in 468 B.C. when the city was looted and burned by neighboring Argos, and the stronghold was never reestablished. A Byzantine church was later built on part of the site. There is now a village of the same name, with an agricultural school, just to the south.

PHILIP C. GIFFORD, JR.
American Museum of Natural History

TISA RIVER. See TISZA RIVER.

TISCHENDORF, tish′ən-dôrf, **Konstantin von** (1815–1874), German Biblical scholar. Lobegott Friedrich Konstantin von Tischendorf was born in Legenfeld, Saxony, on Jan. 18, 1815. Educated at Leipzig, he was nominally a professor there but devoted his time to research. In 1843 he deciphered *Codex Ephraemi*, a 5th century Greek Bible discovered about 1200.

In 1844 he discovered 43 sheets of a 4th century Greek Bible. With the help of the Russian government he obtained the rest of that manuscript, called *Codex Sinaiticus*, from the monastery of St. Catherine on Mt. Sinai in 1859. Now in the British Museum, it is one of the most important manuscripts of the Bible in Greek.

Tischendorf also edited in 1850 *Codex Amiatinus*, the oldest manuscript (716 A. D.) of the whole Latin Bible. In 1852 he edited the *Codex Claromontanus*, a 6th century manuscript of the epistles of St. Paul in Greek and Latin. By 1869 he had published eight editions of the Greek New Testament with notes on the variant readings. He died in Leipzig on Dec. 7, 1874.

FREDERICK C. GRANT
Union Theological Seminary, N. Y.

TISELIUS, tə-sā′lē-əs, **Arne Wilhelm Kaurin** (1902–1971), Swedish chemist, awarded the Nobel Prize in chemistry in 1948 "for his discoveries in biochemistry and the invention of important laboratory apparatus." Tiselius was born in Stockholm, on Aug. 10, 1902. He received his doctorate from the University of Uppsala. In 1938, Uppsala equipped an institute to aid him in studying the chemistry and physics of life. He died in Uppsala on Oct. 29, 1971.

Tiselius' early work was on electrophoresis, to which he made fundamental contributions. Electrophoresis takes advantage of the fact that when large molecules are in a liquid suspension in an electric field, they become charged by electrostatic induction and will migrate along the direction of the field at a velocity dependent upon their masses. Thus very delicate separations can be made and the products of organic processes studied with great accuracy.

Some biochemical molecules do not react well to electrophoresis. They can be obtained in a pure state by selective adsorption. The best-known adsorption method is chromatography, in which the mixture to be analyzed is passed through a packed column, or along a strip of treated paper, and the constituents absorbed by the column or strip. As in electrophoresis, very delicate and accurate analyses may be performed with this method. It is especially applicable to protein chemistry and to the analysis of protein metabolism. Tiselius carried chromatography to a new height of accuracy and specificity.

L. PEARCE WILLIAMS, *Cornell University*

TISH B'AB, tish′ bäv, a Jewish day of fast commemorating the destruction of the first and second temples in Jerusalem. It is observed on the ninth day of the Jewish month of Av. However, if the 9th of Av falls on the Sabbath, the observance is postponed until the next day. The fast was observed as early as the 6th century B. C., when it commemorated only the destruction of the Temple of Solomon (Zechariah 8:19). Dirges are recited after morning prayer, and readings from the Book of Lamentations form part of the evening service. The fasting restrictions are similar to those of the Day of Atonement (see YOM KIPPUR). Tish B'ab also serves as a day of mourning for other Jewish tragedies.

TISHLER, Max (1906–), American chemist, who made many important contributions to the field of pharmacology. Tishler was born in Boston, Mass., on Oct. 30, 1906. He received a B. S. from Tufts College in 1928 and a Ph. D. from Harvard University in 1934. After several years teaching at Harvard, he joined Merck & Co. in 1937. There he and his colleagues developed methods of synthesizing many vitamins, including vitamins B_2 and K and riboflavin. Tishler also devised practical ways of synthesizing some sulfonamides and several amino acids.

Working with the Nobel laureate Selman A. Waksman, Tishler helped isolate actinomycin in crystalline form, a preparation later used in some cancer treatments. He also directed the production of penicillin and streptomycin. He later took part in the first synthesis of hydrocortisone, and, using very complex methods new to the pharmaceutical industry, developed ways of simplifying the mass production of cortisone and related substances.

In 1957, Tishler became president of Merck Sharp & Dohme Research Laboratories. Under his direction, many new discoveries about drugs for the treatment of heart disease, hypertension, inflammatory diseases, and mental illness have been made. In 1970 he become professor of chemistry at Wesleyan University.

COURTNEY R. HALL, *Queens College, The City University of New York*

TISHRI, tish′rē, is the first month of the Jewish civil year and seventh of the religious year. The New Year (Rosh Hashanah), The Day of Atonement (Yom Kippur), and the Feast of Tabernacles (Sukkot) occur in Tishri. See JEWISH CALENDAR.

TISIPHONE, ti-sif′ə-nē, in classical mythology, was "the blood avenger," one of the avenging goddesses called the Furies. See FURIES.

TISSAPHERNES, tis-ə-fûr′nēz (died 395 B. C.), was a Persian general and diplomat. When he became satrap of Lydia and Caria in 413 B. C., he drew Persia into the Peloponnesian War as an ally of Sparta against Athens, but his preference for intrigue rather than military action made him seem halfhearted. After a revolutionary plot by his brother was discovered, Tissaphernes was displaced in Lydia by Cyrus, the Persian king's younger son.

In 404, Artaxerxes II, elder brother of Cyrus and brother-in-law of Tissaphernes, succeeded to the Persian throne. Tissaphernes first foiled an attempt by Cyrus to murder the new king at his coronation and was then instrumental in the defeat and death of Cyrus at Cunaxa in 401. Having murdered the generals of the Greek mercenary force that had accompanied Cyrus, he harassed the remaining mercenaries (the Ten Thousand) as they retreated under Xenophon. For this he was restored to his command in Anatolia, where the Greek cities refused to recognize him and appealed to Sparta. Frightened by the presence of the Ten Thousand with the Spartan army, Tissaphernes avoided battle, but he was finally defeated near Sardis and assassinated by royal command.

JAMES G. MACQUEEN
University of Bristol, England

TISSUE, in biology, means any aggregation of similar cells that work together to perform a function. Among animal tissues are muscle, epithelium, bone, and blood. Among plant tissues are cork and the food- and water-conducting tissues xylem and phloem.

The scientific study of tissues is known as histology. See ANATOMY—*Microscopic Anatomy* (Histology); HISTOLOGY.

TISSUE CULTURE, a method for the maintenance and growth of cells, tissues, and organs outside the body of a multicellular organism. Tissue culture is widely practiced and of prime importance in almost every area of experimental biology and medicine. It is also of great practical use in such diverse areas as virus vaccine production, the cultivation of orchids, and the diagnosis of nerve tumors.

HISTORY

Early Experiments. The development of modern tissue culture dates from the experiments of the American zoologist Ross Harrison on the growth of nerve cells in 1907. While studying frog nerve tissue embedded in clotted lymph, he observed the outgrowth of the axon, or conducting fiber, from individual nerve cells. During the next two decades, tissue cultures were used in the study of cancer, virus diseases, blood cell development, and the effects of radiation on cells.

The principal method of culture was to take small fragments of tissues and embed them in clotted plasma. Cells that migrated away from the fragments often continued to multiply, and by repeated transference to new containers of plasma they could be maintained for long periods. The best-known example of this type of culture was the chick heart cell culture that was maintained in the laboratory of the French-American surgeon Alexis Carrel for many years.

In the mid-1920's two Britons, the scientist T. S. P. Strangeways and the cell biologist Dame Honor B. Fell, working in Cambridge, England, developed the subspecialty of *organ culture.* The objective of their experiments was to maintain tissues in an organized state so that they would continue to function in the same way they did in the body. Strangeways and Fell were able to culture rudimentary organs from young embryos and follow the patterns of their differentiation and development. They also maintained the adult tissues in their differentiated state. Although this method is limited by the size of the tissue fragments and the length of time they can be maintained, it is still used for studying hormone production and function, virus infection, cell interaction, and other biological phenomena.

In the early 1930's, the American botanist Philip R. White and the French botanist Roger Jean Gautheret independently demonstrated the growth of undifferentiated masses, called *callus,* from bits of meristem (growing) tissue taken from the growing tips of several kinds of plants. For the next three decades, plant tissue culture was mostly limited to studies of tumor induction and to nutritional and metabolic studies. However, after the discovery of plant hormones and the elucidation of their modes of action, plant tissue culture assumed a new significance.

New Culture Techniques. Beginning in the mid-1940's, the American cytologist Wilton Earle and his co-workers at the National Cancer Institute pioneered in a number of technical innovations that helped make cell culture a common laboratory tool. Among these was the development of the *monolayer* technique, which is now the most widely used culture procedure. In this technique, cells are suspended in a suitable fluid culture medium, and portions of the cell suspension are transferred into glass or plastic tubes, bottles, or flasks. If the cells are incubated without being agitated, they migrate to the surface of the vessel where they attach, spread out, and multiply. When a dilute suspension is seeded in this manner and the culture is incubated at the proper temperature, the cells may continue to grow until a complete layer of cells covers the vessel surface. Such cultures have been of great value in research on viruses as well as in assays of drug toxicity.

Other important techniques developed by Earle and his co-workers were replicate culture methods, cell enumeration, the growth of cultures from single cells, and the growth of cells in suspension. The latter technique, first described by the American pathologist George Gey and his co-workers in 1954, has great potential for future culturing of animal and plant cells that produce such important substances as hormones, enzymes, and alkaloids. It may also become the best method for producing virus vaccines.

Improved Culture Media. A major obstacle to the widespread application of tissue culture in the late 1940's was the nature of the culture media required. The nutrients used were salt solutions supplemented with such natural fluids as blood serum and tissue extracts. They were difficult to prepare and maintain free of contamination by microorganisms. The composition of the medium varied from batch to batch and often contained toxic components. Studies of the nutrition of cells in cultures date from the work of the American anatomists and cytologists Margaret and Warren Lewis, which began in 1911. These studies were extended greatly by the Danish bacteriologist Albert Fischer and others during the 1920's, 1930's, and 1940's, but it was not until the late 1940's that enough general information had accumulated to permit the construction of media of known composition that could serve as a base for further studies.

In the early 1950's the American physician and cell biologist Harry Eagle, basing his work on the studies of Fischer, White, Joseph F. Morgan, and others, defined the minimal nutritional requirements for cells in culture. Although the medium designed still required some supplementation, it served as a base for subsequent work. Today many types of cells can be grown in media of known composition, and scientists are continuing to perform sophisticated studies of cell nutrition and metabolism.

Another important development in the production of culture media was the introduction of relatively inexpensive natural products as substitutes for tissue extracts and blood serum. Protein digests from a variety of sources were tested, and several proved to be of great value.

Prevention of Contamination. For many years tissue culture was considered to be useful only for the most painstaking and meticulous workers. This was due in part to the difficulty of maintaining cultures free of contamination by microorganisms. Many tissues used to start cultures were already contaminated, and contamination was common in the biological fluids used for making the culture media. Sterilization by heat, a method commonly used in microbiology, cannot be used for tissue culture since many of the factors required for cell growth are sensitive to heat. Even after tissue cultures were established, the very best aseptic technique was required to prevent contamination during culture procedures. The hazard of contamination increased greatly when cultures were maintained for long periods, or when attempts were made to enlarge the culture. With the introduction of antibiotics in the 1940's, it became possible to incorporate these substances into the culture medium and to prevent contamination in most cases.

The most commonly used antibiotics in tissue cultures are penicillin and streptomycin, which are generally used in combination. The use of antibiotics made possible the large-scale tissue culture program needed to develop and test the Salk polio vaccine. It also enabled scientists to isolate viruses directly from contaminated sources, such as feces. However, because continued use of antibiotics may mask many infections, most workers try to grow cells without the use of antibiotics.

A significant development that has greatly reduced the hazard of contamination is the use of laminar-flow rooms and hoods. In such a room or hood, air that has been filtered and made free of microorganisms is swept over the work areas so as to wash down the microorganisms in the air and thus provide a clean area for working. The development of laminar flow rooms and hoods was a direct by-product of research in space technology.

PRESENT AND FUTURE USES

Cell, tissue, and organ cultures are currently being used for important studies in human genetics, immunity, and cancer. Such cultures are also being used to obtain basic information about memory, aging, and diseases such as arthritis, emphysema, and multiple sclerosis.

Human Genetics. During the 1960's cell culture opened the field of human genetics to a new era of experimentation and analysis. Through studies of cultured white blood cells and skin cells, scientists have been able to link abnormalities of chromosomes with a variety of inherited diseases. These diseases now can be recognized early in life, and patterns of their inheritance can be studied. In some cases chromosomal abnormalities have been associated with birth defects. Such defects can be recognized very early in the development of the fetus by culturing cells obtained from the fluid surrounding the fetus. If the consequences of chromosome abnormalities are serious enough to warrant it, an abortion can be performed.

Tumor Viruses. One of the most important areas of investigation uses culture methods in the search for viruses that cause tumors. Marked advances have been made in studies of animal tumors, and encouraging results have been obtained in the search for viruses that may cause leukemia and breast tumors in humans.

An important finding resulting from studies of animal tumor viruses has been the discovery of a reversal in the basic system of heredity in which DNA directs the synthesis of RNA, which in turn directs protein synthesis. In studies of cells infected with tumor viruses, it was found that virus RNA directs the synthesis of new DNA by taking over the synthetic machinery of the cell.

Immunity. Since the 1950's a great deal has been learned about the cellular basis of immunity to infectious agents. Tissue culture has become an important tool in bringing these studies to a practical conclusion. Similarly, the so-called mixed leukocyte (white blood cell) culture has provided key information on transplantation immunity, which plays a vital role in organ and tissue transplants.

Hybrid Cells. In the early 1960's the French biologist Georges Barski described experiments in which cells grown in mixed culture fused to give rise to heterokaryons, or cells with two kinds of nuclei. When the nuclei divided, all the chromosomes mixed, and a hybrid cell was formed. The rate of nuclear fusion could be greatly increased by adding to the culture a virus that had been inactivated and could not multiply.

The initial experiments with hybrid cells were with cells of different types of mice. Subsequently, many workers produced hybrid cells that included such cell combinations as human-rabbit, human-mouse, and rabbit-chicken. These experiments are important in providing a method for analyzing the expression of genetic information and other aspects of cell behavior.

While the production of animal cell hybrids is of great value in research, reports of similar experiments with plant cells may lead to developments of great practical significance. Since single plant cells can give rise to cultures that can differentiate into normal plants, there is a good chance that new high-yield, disease-resistant varieties may be developed in this way.

Insect Cell Culture. Since the late 1950's a few scientists have cultured insect cells and tissues. Several technical difficulties prevented the widespread use of these systems. Probably the most restrictive feature was the need to use insect body fluid (hemolymph) in the culture medium. This fluid was extremely difficult to prepare and was available only in minute quantities. In the 1960's the Indian scientist K. R. P. Singh and others showed that a number of insect cell cultures could be grown in media very similar to those which are used for growing cells of higher animals.

The ability to culture insect cells and tissues with comparative ease has stimulated several important areas of investigation. Since many insects are carriers of human disease, including virus diseases, it is possible to study patterns of transmission and the mode of reproduction of the infectious agent inside the insect host. Many viruses are known to infect only insects, and several groups of researchers are exploring the possibility of using these viruses in place of DDT and other chemical insecticides to control insect pests. Also, cultured cells might be used to assay certain types of potential control agents. These agents could also be tested on the cells of humans and other animals to determine whether they are toxic.

Plant Propagation. An example of modern plant tissue culture is the propagation of orchids by meristem culture, as originally described by the French scientist Georges Morel in 1960. Callus growth may be repeatedly subdivided to give rise to thousands of cultures. When such cultures are treated with proper plant hormones, each culture can differentiate into a complete orchid plant that blooms normally and is an exact replica of the plant from which the original meristem tissue was taken. Similar methods have been used to cultivate carnations, asparagus, and other plants.

DONALD J. MERCHANT, *Coauthor of "Handbook of Cell and Organ Culture"*

Further Reading: Green, James, ed., *New Developments in Tissue Culture* (New Brunswick, N. J., 1962); Paul, John R., *Cell and Tissue Culture* (Baltimore 1965).

TISSUE TYPING is a method of classifying body tissue antigens based on the presence of these antigens in the white blood cells, or leukocytes. Just as the success of a blood transfusion depends on the compatibility of the donor's and recipient's red blood cell antigens, the success of an organ transplant depends largely on the compatibility of their leukocyte antigens. Because the groups of antigens thus far discovered in human leukocytes also occur in virtually all body tissues, the leukocyte antigen groups can also be called tissue groups. By 1970 about 26 of these groups had been identified.

Compatibility of leukocyte antigens has been found to be of great importance in determining the outcome of kidney, heart, and skin transplants. If the antigen groups of the donor do not match those of the recipient fairly precisely, the transplanted organ may be rejected by the recipient's body. Calculations based on compatibility of red blood cell antigens and leukocyte antigens indicate that only one out of 1,033 prospective transplant recipients has a 95% chance of having a successful transplant.

The logistical problem has stimulated the creation of national and international tissue typing registries that list the leukocyte antigen groups of patients awaiting kidney transplants. When a potential donor is found, a doctor can refer to a registry for the rapid selection of an optimally compatible recipient. The first tissue typing registry, called Eurotransplant, was organized by the Dutch scientist Jon van Rood in 1967. Similar registries that are also currently functioning are Eurotransplant West, which serves France, Spain, and Italy, and Scandiatransplant, which serves Scandinavia. In the United States, a national kidney transplant registry was established in 1969 by Paul I. Terasaki. Within its first year, this registry had been used for more than 250 transplants in which kidneys were transported from donors in one city to recipients in another.

The first leukocyte antigen group, then called Mac, was discovered by the French scientist Jean Dausset in 1958. After 1958, rapid progress was made in the definition of leukocyte antigen groups, largely through an international effort. The participants in this effort included Jon van Rood in the Netherlands, Flemming Kissmeyer-Nielsen in Denmark, Ruggero Ceppellini in Italy, Rose Payne, D. Bernard Amos, Walter Bodmer, Roy Walford, and Paul I. Terasaki in the United States, and Dausset's team in France. At an international workshop held in 1965, Dausset's team reported that the many different antigens behave as if they are components of a very complex genetic system. It proposed that this system be called Hu-1, but it was later changed to HL-A by international agreement.

It is now generally agreed that the HL-A system is the major system of tissue compatibility in humans. Its antigens are determined by a chromosomal region composed of at least two loci. Antigens HL-A 1, 2, 3, 9, 10, and 11 and Da 15, 22, and 25 are determined at the first locus, while antigens HL-A 5, 7, 8, 12, and 13 and Da 18, 20, 23, and 24 are determined at the second. The genes for these antigens occur as alternative alleles at each locus.

FELIX T. RAPAPORT, M. D.
New York University Medical Center

Further Reading: Rapaport, F. T., and Dausset, Jean, *Human Transplantation* (New York 1968).

TISZA, tē'sô, **Count István** (1861–1918), Hungarian government official. Like his father, Kálmán Tisza, who was minister president from 1875 to 1890, István was a Magyar chauvinist and defended the Austro-Hungarian Compromise of 1867. István Tisza was born in Pest on April 22, 1861. He served as minister president and interior minister from 1903 to 1905. When his Liberal party was defeated in 1905, he dissolved it and in 1910 founded the Party of Work. In 1911 he began to publish the *Magyar Figyelö* (Magyar Observer) and in 1913 was reappointed minister president.

In 1914 he temporarily opposed Austria's proposal to invade Serbia. During World War I, he zealously blocked attempts to federalize Austria-Hungary, which would have diminished Hungary's importance. When Emperor Francis Joseph died in 1916, Tisza refused to bow to the demand of the new emperor, Charles I, that voting rights be broadened. Tisza resigned in June 1917 and took a military command in Italy. Toward the war's end he returned to coordinate Hungarian efforts to replace dualism with a simple personal union with Austria. Blamed by the public for Hungary's war misfortunes, he was murdered by a mob in Pest on Oct. 31, 1918, during riots attending Hungary's declaration of independence.

JOSEPH F. ZACEK
State University of New York at Albany

TISZA RIVER, tē'sô, a major tributary of the Danube, in eastern Europe. The Tisza (Tisa in Serbo-Croatian) is formed in the Carpathian Mountains of the Ukrainian SSR by the confluence of the White Tisza and the Black Tisza. It flows westward and then south across the Hungarian Plain. Below Szeged, Hungary, it enters Yugoslavia, joining the Danube above Belgrade. About 450 miles (725 km) of its 800-mile (1,287-km) length are navigable.

TITAN, tī'tən. In Greek mythology, the Titans were the 12 divine children of Uranus (Sky) and Gaea (Earth). One of the Titans, Cronus, castrated his father Uranus and seized the overlordship of the universe. To escape a similar fate Cronus then swallowed his own children, but the last of them, Zeus, eluded him and in his turn established supreme mastery on Mount Olympus. In a tremendous struggle, called the Titanomachy, the Titans attempted to dislodge Zeus and his fellow-Olympians, but were defeated and cast down into Tartarus far below the earth.

In another myth the Titans were incited by Hera to attack Zagreus, Zeus's child, who had been placed by his father on the throne of heaven. Whitening their faces, they stole into Olympus, dismembered the child, and prepared to eat him. But they were smitten to ashes by Zeus' thunderbolts.

The basically similar structure of both myths—the engulfment of the young by the old—indicates the probable origin of these stories in initiation ceremonies. The Titans are mythic counterparts of the older men of the tribe, who often mask or whiten themselves to impersonate death spirits and in this guise lead the boys through the death-and-rebirth rituals of initiation.

RICHMOND Y. HATHORN
State University of New York, Stony Brook

THE *TITANIC* before her maiden voyage, which ended in disaster when she struck an iceberg.

USIA, FROM NATIONAL ARCHIVES

TITAN, tī'tən, is the largest satellite of Saturn. Among the satellites of the solar system, only Jupiter's Ganymede is larger. Titan was discovered by the Dutch astronomer Christiaan Huygens in 1655.

The diameter of Titan is 3,030 miles (4,880 km), equal to the diameter of Mercury and 870 miles (1,400 km) wider than the earth's moon. Its density is about 2.4 that of water, compared to the earth's density of 5.52. The satellite is sixth in order outward from Saturn, orbiting the planet at an average distance of about 759,000 miles (1,222,000 km).

Because of its size and its distance from the sun, Titan has been able to retain an atmosphere. This is the only known atmosphere of a satellite in the solar system. It was first observed in 1908, and in 1943 it was identified spectroscopically as methane. Titan's disk has shown colors and streaks that are indicative of clouds. These observations are quite remarkable when it is noted that the angular size of Titan, as seen from the earth, is only about 0.7 second of arc at best. See also SOLAR SYSTEM.

LAURENCE W. FREDRICK, *University of Virginia*

TITANIA is one of the commercial names used for gem rutile. See RUTILE.

TITANIC, tī-tan'ik. Shortly before midnight on April 14, 1912, the 46,328-ton White Star liner *Titanic,* on her maiden voyage from Southampton to New York, collided with an iceberg off the Banks of Newfoundland. The night was clear, but apparently there was some surface haze. Two hours and forty minutes after the impact, the magnificent new liner—the pride of the British merchant service, the largest and most sumptuously appointed vessel which had ever put to sea—went down with a loss of more than 1,500 lives.

The root cause of this appalling catastrophe, which was accounted at the time "the most terrible shipwreck in history," was simply bad seamanship. Despite all the urgent warnings of ice, by radio and signal-lamp, the *Titanic,* in hopes of an early arrival in New York harbor, continually increased speed and drove that night into the ice track at over 22½ knots (41.7 km/hr).

The *Californian,* the only vessel in the vicinity, lay on the edge of the icefield with her engines stopped, made no attempt to reach the wreck: though rocket after rocket was clearly seen from her bridge. Her radio operator had gone off duty. The Cunard *Carpathia,* however, on receiving the *Titanic's* distress call, at once turned round and steamed at high speed through the ice to the rescue of the survivors.

It is to be observed that though the White Star Line was absolved at the British inquiry, in the High Court—and subsequently on appeal—the charge of negligence was upheld, and the company was ordered to pay heavy damages to the relatives of several of those lost.

Some safety measures prompted by the wreck were creation of the International Ice Patrol, provision of lifeboat space for all persons on a ship, and constant radio watch at sea.

GEOFFREY J. MARCUS
Author of "The Maiden Voyage"

TITANITE, tī'tə-nīt, or *sphene,* is a fairly common silicate of calcium and titanium and a source of the latter metal. It occurs in igneous rocks and in metamorphic rocks, where it is often associated with chlorite. The name "sphene" is derived from a Greek word meaning "wedge," referring to the characteristic shape of the crystals. The crystals may be brown to black, green, or yellow. Composition, $CaTiO(SiO_4)$; hardness, 5–5.5; specific gravity, 3.4–3.55; crystal system, monoclinic.

TITANIUM, tī-tā'nē-əm, symbol Ti, is a light, strong, silvery metallic element. It is classified as one of the transition elements. Titanium was discovered by the British clergyman William Gregor in 1790. Gregor's analysis of a black magnetic sand found near Falmouth, England, yielded a large proportion of a white metallic oxide. In 1795 the German chemist Martin Heinrich Klaproth realized that Gregor's description of the oxide coincided closely with the properties of an oxide that he had isolated from a sample of Hungarian rutile. Klaproth gave the name "titanium" to the metallic element in the oxide.

Uses. The high cost of titanium metal often limits its use to military purposes. Because of its lightness and strength, titanium is used as a structural material in high-speed aircraft, rockets, guided missiles, and recoil mechanisms for artillery. Titanium is often used in the chemical processing industry because of its resistance to corrosion. This resistance is probably due to a thin coating of titanium dioxide, which protects the metal from further corrosion. The metal has unusually good resistance to corrosion by salt water, and so it is used in propeller shafts and other parts exposed to the sea.

Titanium is added to other metals, such as

copper, steel, and aluminum, to affect certain properties. For example, in the manufacture of stainless steel, metallic titanium is used to stabilize the carbon and nitrogen content. Ferrotitanium is added to steel as a deoxidizer.

Titanium dioxide, TiO_2, a white compound, is used in the production of paint pigment, paper, plastics, glass, and ceramics. The presence of titanium dioxide produces the "stars" in star rubies and sapphires.

Titanium hydride, TiH_2, is used in powder metallurgy, in the production of hydrogen, as a getter in vacuum tubes, and in the production of foamed metals. Barium titanate, $BaTiO_3$, is widely used in the electronics industry because of its high dielectric constant. Organic alkali titanates are used as waterproofing agents. Titanium trioxide, TiO_3, is used in dental porcelain. Titanium tetrachloride, $TiCl_4$, is used as a mordant in the textile industry, in artificial pearls, and in titanium pigments. Titanium nitride, TiN, is used in cermets and semiconductor devices. Titanous sulfate, $Ti_2(SO_4)_3$, is used as a reducing agent in the textile industry.

A new nickel–titanium alloy called *nitinol* has been developed, which has the unusual property of regaining its previous shape when heated. First the alloy is shaped and heated to a critical temperature. When the object has cooled, it can be mechanically reshaped. However, when it is then reheated, it will resume its original form. There are numerous potential uses for nitinol, particularly in construction, where areas are often difficult to reach. The alloy could be used to make rivets and cotter pins.

Properties. Titanium is located in Group IVB of the periodic table. Its atomic number is 22, and its atomic weight is 47.90. The element melts at 1675° C (3047° F) and boils at 3260° C (5900° F). Its density is 4.51 g/cc (0.16 lb/cu ft). There are two crystalline forms of titanium. The α form, which is formed at temperatures below 882° C (1620° F), is close-packed hexagonal, and the β form, which is formed above 882° C, is body-centered cubic.

Titanium is as strong as steel but almost 50% lighter. Pure titanium is easily fabricated, but it becomes brittle when contaminated with other elements, such as carbon and nitrogen.

There are nine isotopes of titanium, ranging from ^{43}Ti to ^{51}Ti. Of these, the isotopes ^{46}Ti through ^{50}Ti are stable. Of the titanium found in nature, ^{48}Ti makes up about 74%, ^{46}Ti 7.9%, ^{47}Ti 7.3%, ^{49}Ti 5.5%, and ^{50}Ti 5.3%. The other isotopes, which are radioactive, have half-lives from 0.6 second to approximately 10^3 years.

Titanium exhibits oxidation states of +4, +3, and +2, with Ti^{+4} being the most stable. The metal has a strong affinity for oxygen, carbon, and nitrogen, making it difficult to obtain in the pure state. Titanium will burn in air at about 1200° C (2192° F). It is one of the few metals that will burn in a stream of nitrogen gas. Metallic titanium is readily attacked by concentrated sulfuric and hydrochloric acids, but reacts slowly with the dilute forms of these acids. It is not much affected by nitric acid.

Compounds. A number of titanium oxides can be prepared, including titanium monoxide, TiO; titanium sesquioxide, Ti_2O_3; titanium dioxide, TiO_2; and titanium trioxide, TiO_3. Titanium dioxide is the most stable of these compounds and is found in nature in several minerals. Reduction of titanium dioxide with charcoal produces titanium monoxide. Titanium sesquioxide is produced from the reduction of titanium dioxide. Titanium combines readily with fluorine, chlorine, bromine, and iodine.

Of the various compounds that can be formed, titanium tetrachloride, $TiCl_4$, is the most common. This substance is a liquid at room temperature. Exposure to air results in its decomposition to form corrosive hydrogen chloride gas. The tetrabromide (yellow), the tetraiodide (reddish brown), and the tetrafluoride (white) are all solids at room temperature.

Titanates are compounds of the formula $MTiO_3$, M_2TiO_3, and $M_2Ti_2O_5$, where M represents any of a number of metallic elements, including calcium, magnesium, manganese, barium, and iron. Liquid titanium metal reacts partially with carbon or nitrogen to form TiC and Ti_3N_4. Titanium also reacts with boron, silicon, and other less-common nonmetallic elements.

Extraction. The extraction of titanium from its ores is a relatively slow and costly process, which makes the metal expensive. The most widely used method for obtaining metallic titanium is the Kroll process, which was developed in 1937 by the German scientist William A. Kroll. Until then, it was impossible to obtain large quantities of the pure element because the liquid titanium reacts so readily with nitrogen and oxygen from the air.

In the Kroll process, titanium tetrachloride is prepared by chlorination of the ores ilmenite or rutile. Liquid titanium tetrachloride is then reduced, using metallic magnesium under an inert atmosphere in a sealed reactor. Sometimes, sodium is used instead of magnesium.

The reaction is carried out in a large flat-bottomed steel vessel. The vessel is charged with metallic magnesium, checked for leaks, and filled with argon or helium. The reaction vessel is heated in a furnace to the melting point of magnesium. At this point, liquid titanium tetrachloride is allowed to flow into the vessel. In the reaction that follows, titanium and magnesium chloride are produced. Most of the magnesium chloride liquid is drained from the reaction vessel during the reduction process.

After the reaction is complete, the cooled vessel must be opened in a dry room to prevent contamination of the titanium sponge with moisture. The sponge is usually contaminated with some ferric chloride, as well as magnesium chloride and unreacted magnesium metal. After the sponge has been machined into chips of a manageable size, the impurities are removed by leaching with dilute hydrochloric acid. The sponge, along with any necessary additives, is melted in an electric furnace to form ingots. The ingots are remelted to form the final pure titanium ingot, which can be readily drawn, forged, or rolled.

Very pure titanium can be obtained by the decomposition of titanium tetraiodide at high temperatures and by electrolytic reduction in a fused salt system. These methods work well on a laboratory scale, but they have not been used for commercial production of the metal.

Occurrence. Titanium is the ninth most abundant element in the earth's crust. The average titanium content of igneous rocks is 0.44%, whereas soils contain between 0.5% and 1.5% titanium, depending on location. Lateritic soil (a red soil formed from decayed rock) may contain up to 12% of the element. Natural waters usually contain between 10^{-7}% and 10^{-9}% titanium.

Meteorites have been found to contain 0.13% titanium. Lines characteristic of titanium appear in the spectra of the sun and other stars. Samples of moon rocks have been found to contain about 6% titanium, which is considerably higher than the amount usually found in earth rocks.

Ores. Several different titanium compounds are found in minerals. Three minerals consist of titanium dioxide, TiO_2; while these ores have the same chemical formula, they differ in crystalline structure. Rutile has tetragonal prismatic crystals, brookite has orthorhombic crystals, and octahedrite has tetragonal crystals. Rutile is the only naturally formed titanium dioxide mineral. Brookite and octahedrite form as the result of alteration of other titanium minerals.

Another group of titantium minerals is the titanates. The most important of these is ilmenite, which has hexagonal or rhombohedral crystal structure. Although its formula is usually given as $FeTiO_3$, ilmenite is variable in composition, depending on the concentration of ferric oxide. Other titanate minerals include pseudobrookite, $Fe_2O_3 \cdot 3TiO_2$; pervoskite, $CaTiO_3$; geikielite, $(Mg, Fe)TiO_3$; and pyrophanite, $MnTiO_3$.

The only important titanium-silicate mineral is sphene, which has the formula $CaTiSiO_5$. This mineral, which is also called titanite, cystallizes in the monoclinic system.

Major Deposits. Deposits of titanium minerals are found all over the world. The largest deposits of the metal are in the United States and Australia.

United States. Massive ilmenite deposits are found in Virginia and North Carolina. The titanium dioxide content of the Virginia deposits is about 18.5% and in North Carolina up to 49%. Ilmenite-magnetite deposits are found in New York. These ores contain between 7% and 23% titanium dioxide. Smaller deposits of this type are found in Rhode Island, Minnesota, Wyoming, California, and Montana.

Extensive beach and dune sand deposits of titanium ores are found in the southeastern United States. These are sedimentary deposits probably originating from the Piedmont area of Georgia and the Carolinas. The sands contain approximately 5% rutile and 45% ilmenite. Similar, but smaller, deposits are found in New Jersey, Mississippi, Wyoming, and Montana.

Deposits of rutile in the United States are much less extensive than those of ilmenite or titanium sands. Rutile occurs in commercial quantities in Virginia, and minor rutile ore bodies are found in Arkansas and Florida.

Australia. Australia is the world's largest producer of rutile. Extensive beach deposits containing rutile occur in Queensland. Most of the primary rutile is found in western Australia and in New South Wales. The New South Wales region also has deposits of black sands, which contain ilmenite, monazite, and gold, and consist of about 45% titanium dioxide.

Canada. A number of titanium ore bodies are found in Quebec, where ilmenite-hematite deposits contain between 20% and 30% titanium dioxide. There is also a rutile deposit with ilmenite and sapphirine that contains between 8% and 20% titanium dioxide.

Norway. A rutile deposit in southern Norway contains 10% to 15% titanium dioxide. Southwest Norway has ilmenite ore containing 40% and 45% titanium dioxide.

USSR. Very little detailed information is available about titanium ore deposits in the USSR. There are extensive low-grade deposits throughout the country. A titanium-magnetite ore containing about 14% titanium dioxide is found in the Ilmen Mountains, from which the ore ilmenite derives its name. There are extensive beach sand deposits of titanium in the western Siberian lowlands.

World Production. The largest producers of titanium ores, in order, are the United States, Canada, Australia, Norway, Malaysia, and Finland. The United States produces almost 1 million short tons (900,000 metric tons) of titanium ores annually. Canada produces over 671,000 short tons (610,000 metric tons), and Australia about 615,000 short tons (560,000 metric tons). By the early 1970's world production of titanium ores was about 3.25 million short tons (2,950,000 metric tons).

J. C. VAN LOON
University of Toronto

Bibliography

Abkowitz, Stanley, and others, *Titanium In Industry* (New York 1955).

Barksdale, Jelks, *Titanium: Its Occurrence, Chemistry, and Technology* (New York 1966).

Clark, Robin J. H., *Chemistry of Titanium and Vanadium* (New York 1968).

Codell, Maurice, *Analytical Chemistry of Titanium Metals and Compounds* (New York 1959).

McQuillan, Alan D., and McQuillan, M. K., *Titanium* (London 1956).

TITANOTHERE, tī-tan′ə-thir, a large extinct mammal, vaguely resembling a rhinoceros, that inhabited North America, Asia, and eastern Europe during the Eocene and Oligocene, some 50 million to 30 million years ago. Titanotheres, related to horses, rhinoceroses, and tapirs, are members of the family Brontotheriidae in the order Perissodactyla.

FIELD MUSEUM OF NATURAL HISTORY

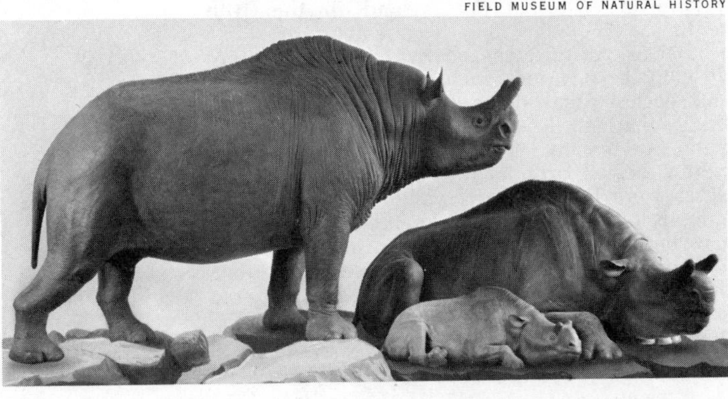

TITANOTHERES, in museum reconstruction, show resemblance to their distant relative the rhinoceros. Now extinct, they lived during the Eocene and Oligocene epochs.

The Oligocene titanotheres were as much as 14 feet (4 meters) long and 8 feet (2.5 meters) high at the shoulders. Their skulls usually were low or even concave on top, and on their snouts they bore roughly Y-shaped horns with bony cores. Titanothere teeth remained relatively primitive, never developing high crowns (high portions above the gum line) or complex patterns, and probably could not withstand a great deal of wear. Accordingly, titanotheres probably ate soft vegetation.

Probable factors leading to the extinction of the titanotheres include the reduction in the area of their presumed river-bottom habitat and the appearance of more efficient, modernized herbivores and carnivores.

LEIGH VAN VALEN, *University of Chicago*

TITCHENER, tich′ən-ər, **Edward Bradford** (1867–1927), British-American psychologist. He was born in Chichester, England, on Jan. 11, 1867. After studying philosophy and physiology at Oxford, he studied physiology and psychology in Wilhelm Wundt's laboratory at Leipzig. Since psychology was virtually unrecognized in his native England, Titchener went to America in 1893, and served for 35 years as professor of psychology at Cornell University. He died in Ithaca, N.Y., on Aug. 3, 1927.

Titchener never entered the mainstream of American psychology, which was then addressing itself to the issues of individual differences and the application of psychology to practical problems. Influenced by Wundt, Titchener adopted what was called the structuralist viewpoint. He sought to explain such problems as feeling and thought in relation to specific aspects of sensory experiences. It was his conviction that understanding the nervous system was the key to understanding any individual's experience. His greatest work was the four-volume *Experimental Psychology* (1901–1905).

MICHAEL G. ROTHENBERG
The City College, New York

TITHE, tīth, the tenth part of produce or other income, paid voluntarily or under the compulsion of law for the benefit of religious institutions, the support of priests and pastors, and the relief of those in need. In western lands tithing is probably derived from the Mosaic prescription of paying tithes for the support of the Levites and the temple service (Numbers 18:21). It was not practiced in the early Christian church but gradually became common by the 6th century. The Council of Tours in 567 and the second Council of Macon in 585 advocated tithing. Tithes were made obligatory by civil law in the Carolingian empire in 765 and in England in the 10th century.

Because of different local circumstances tithes developed in various ways. There were secular and ecclesiastical tithes and personal and real tithes—that is, tithes on income from personal trade, profession, or property. Praedial tithes were tithes on fruits of the soil. Great and small tithes were based on the value of the crops or animals taxed. It became common to substitute a money payment for payment in goods.

Abuses became common, particularly when the right to collect tithes was often given or sold to laymen. Beginning with Pope Gregory VII this practice was declared illegal. Many laymen then presented their tithing rights to monasteries and cathedral chapters. The Reformation did not abolish tithing, and the practice was continued in the Roman Catholic Church and in Protestant countries.

Tithing was abolished in France during the French Revolution (1789) and in other countries was gradually replaced by other forms of taxation. The Roman Catholic Church still prescribes tithes in countries where they are sanctioned by law, and some Protestant bodies consider tithes obligatory. Most religious bodies have abandoned the practice, particularly in the United States, where no system of tithing was ever generally employed after the American Revolution.

JAMES H. SMYLIE
Union Theological Seminary, Richmond, Va.

TITHONUS, tə-thō′nəs, in Greek mythology, was the son of Laomedon, king of Troy. He was the beloved of Eos (Aurora), goddess of the dawn, by whom he had two sons, Emathion and Memnon. Eos induced Zeus to make Tithonus immortal but forgot to ask for eternal youth, and in time he became aged and infirm. Out of pity, Eos changed him into a grasshopper. Tennyson based his poem *Tithonus* (1860) on this legend.

TITI, ti-tē′, a small to medium-sized South American monkey of the genus *Callicebus* (family Cebidae). It lives in forested areas from the southern branches of the Orinoco River in Colombia and Venezuela south to eastern Peru and northern Paraguay; one species, the masked titi (*C. personatus*), inhabits forests in eastern Brazil. The adult titi is commonly between 10 and 15 inches (25–38 cm) in head and body length, with a nonprehensile tail 10 to 20 inches (25–50 cm) long. Coat color ranges from reddish gray to dark brown or black.

Titis feed on fruit, insects, birds' eggs, and birds, and are believed to live in pairs or in family groups. They apparently breed throughout the year. A dusky titi (*C. moloch*) lived to slightly more than 4 years of age in captivity.

LEONARD A. ROSENBLUM, *Director, Primate Laboratory, State University of New York*

Titi (*Callicebus cupreus*)

SAN DIEGO ZOO PHOTO

TITIAN, tish′ən (c. 1480/1490–1576), Italian painter, who was the greatest master of the Venetian school and one of the most renowned figures in the history of art. With Michelangelo he dominated Italian art of the 16th century, excelling especially in the imaginative use of color.

Life. Tiziano Vecellio (Titian) was born in Pieve di Cadore in the Italian Alps. On the evidence of the artist's own testimony in his old age and the subsequent statements of the Vecellio family, it had been accepted that he was born in 1477 and hence died at the impressive age of 99. Modern scholars reject this date as implausible in view of the total absence of documented activity by Titian before 1508.

In the early 1500's Titian may have served an apprenticeship in the workshop of Giovanni Bellini, the greatest Venetian master of the preceding generation. Subsequently he may have studied with Giorgione, the radical innovator of the new era. It is known that in 1508 he worked as the junior collaborator with Giorgione on frescoes (now in fragments) for the facade of the Fondaco dei Tedeschi, the German merchants' center in Venice. It is also known that he completed at least one canvas left unfinished by Giorgione at his death in 1510—*Sleeping Venus* (Gemäldegalerie, Dresden).

In 1511, Titian received payment for frescoes in the Scuola di Sant' Antonio in Padua, his earliest securely datable extant work. He succeeded Bellini as official painter to the Venetian Republic after Bellini's death in 1516.

In the following years Titian's career prospered, and his fame spread beyond Venice. He worked for the courts of Ferrara, Mantua, and Urbino. In 1533 he was appointed court painter to the Holy Roman emperor Charles V, who conferred upon him the rank of Count Palatine as well as the Order of the Golden Spur. Titian was in Rome in 1545–1546 as a celebrated guest and was visited by Michelangelo. In 1547–1548 and again in 1550–1551, he attended the imperial court at Augsburg, where he met Charles' son, the future Philip II of Spain, who became the most important patron of the elderly Titian. As customary, Titian ran a large studio, in which his son Orazio, others of his family, and outsiders assisted him.

In Venice, Titian reigned supreme. Not only was he the most honored painter of the century, but he was also a significant public personality, forming with the writer Pietro Aretino and the sculptor-architect Jacopo Sansovino a triumvirate that dominated the cultural life of the city.

Titian was not an intellectual, but his pictorial interpretations of literary themes are the most sensitive of the Renaissance. He was trained as a painter and never actually practiced any other art, yet his pictures contain sculptural images of his own design, and he was consulted as an expert in architecture. When he died in Venice on Aug. 27, 1576, his fellow Venetian painters planned a public funeral to match in pomp and ceremony the famous obsequies held for Michelangelo by the painters of Florence. This tribute was frustrated, however, by the disastrous plague that was then raging through Venice.

Stylistic Periods. Modern critics have tended to distinguish six phases in the development of Titian's style—a rhythmic system somewhat arbitrary but useful in charting the course of the artist's long career. During the first phase, running to 1516, Titian's style evolved from the soft, poetic traditions of Bellini and Giorgione. His figures assumed a more powerful stature than those of his predecessors, as in the frescoes in Padua and in *Sacred and Profane Love* (c. 1515; Borghese Gallery, Rome).

The second phase, from 1516/1518 to about 1530, includes the series of monumental altarpieces, beginning with the *Assumption of the Virgin* (1516–1518) in the Church of the Frari, Venice. The series continues with the *Madonna of the Pesaro Family* (1519–1526), also in the Frari, and culminates in the *Death of St. Peter Martyr* (1528–1530), destroyed by fire, for the Church of Santi Giovanni e Paolo, Venice. During these years (1518–1523) Titian also painted three mythological subjects for Alfonso d'Este, Duke of Ferrara—*Worship of Venus* (Prado, Madrid), *Bacchanal of the Andrians* (Prado), and *Bacchus and Ariadne* (National Gallery, London). The second phase was a period of tremendous energy, with regard both to Titian's own creative activities and to the character of the compositions themselves. Inspired by classical art and by Michelangelo and other painters of central Italy, Titian achieved a new type of heroic figure design. Further, he gained new control and inventiveness in his handling of color, which became a more dominant and integral element in his work.

The third phase, from about 1530 to about 1540, is often considered a détente in Titian's development. After the creative outburst of the preceding years, he is thought to have retired to a calmer, less dramatic state. This interpretation responds to the highly structured, rectilinear compositions of this decade and the emphasis on the more deliberate painting of natural forms, as in *Venus of Urbino* (1538; Uffizi, Florence) and *Presentation of the Virgin* (1534–1538; Accademia, Venice). During this period Titian also did portraits of such notables as Charles V with his dog (1532; Prado), Cardinal Ippolito de' Medici (1533; Pitti, Florence), and Francis I (1538; Louvre, Paris).

In the fourth phase, from about 1540 to about 1550, Titian was directly confronted with central Italian art, highlighted by his trip to Rome and his meeting with Michelangelo. These years were particularly critical, for now Titian measured his own achievements that emphasized color against the alternative aesthetic tradition of central Italy that stressed form, and he even tried at times to meet it on its own terms. His efforts may be seen in *Cain and Abel, Sacrifice of Isaac,* and *David and Goliath,* all between 1542 and 1544, now in the Church of Santa Maria della Salute, Venice. The most important portrait of this period was that of Charles V on horseback at the Battle of Mühlberg (1548; Prado).

In the fifth phase, 1550 to 1560, Titian resolved the crisis between Venetian and central Italian styles, returning to his native tradition with new confidence and imagination. This is the period of the *poesie,* as Titian called them, for Philip II—pictorial poems combining dramatic action and sensuality, such as in *Danaë* (1554; Prado), *Rape of Europa* (1559; Gardner Museum, Boston), *Venus and Adonis* (versions in the Prado and elsewhere), and *Venus and the Lute-player* (c. 1560; versions in Fitzwilliam Museum, Cambridge, and Metropolitan Museum, New York).

The final phase, from about 1560 to his death, represents a recapitulation of Titian's development but on a new level that was intimately related to his actual methods of painting at that time. Works from this period include the *Martyrdom of St. Lawrence* (Escorial), *Adam and Eve* (Prado), and the *Pietà* (Accademia, Venice). Titian planned the last for his own tomb.

Subject Matter.—*Altarpieces*. Among the most impressive and influential of Titian's early paintings are his altarpieces. According to reports, the huge size and scale of the *Assumption of the Virgin* created a stir within the conservative religious community and even among other painters. But the work was soon accepted as a masterpiece, declaring new directions and possibilities in painting. In this great panel the Virgin is borne aloft within a circular setting of heavenly radiance. Below, the Apostles form a corresponding rectangular block. The bold geometry of the design, related to Raphael's contemporary altarpieces, offers a clear statement of the pictorial principles characteristic of the High Renaissance.

In the *Madonna of the Pesaro Family,* Titian established an unusual precedent in placing the Virgin and Child off the central axis. He took this step not purely to vary an old convention of centrality in altarpieces but also to accommodate the figures to different angles of vision. Such subtle concern for the relationship of a painting to its particular site and to the position of the viewer is typical of Titian.

In the *Death of St. Peter Martyr* the drama of the saint's assassination is set within a landscape dominated by several monumental trees. The theme of figures in a landscape, developed especially by Bellini, had been important in Venetian painting since the later 15th century. Its poetry was further explored by Giorgione, and Titian demonstrated its heroic potential. In the altarpiece the trees assume a significant role in the action itself, accentuating it by their positions within the composition and, in a sense, even participating in the drama through their own dynamic rhythms.

***Mythological Compositions*.** The relationship of figure to landscape is central to Titian's art and is explored in many subjects, especially those from classical mythology that emphasize the reclining female nude. Giorgione's *Sleeping Venus* offered a theme upon which Titian invented variations throughout his career. These extremely sensuous images celebrate in different ways the fullness of nature, the richness of the female form, and, in a more abstract sense, the concept of beauty itself. In the composition of *Venus and the Luteplayer* the introduction of the musician adds a significant dimension. Both the aural and visual perception of beauty are represented. The music of the lute fills the air as the naked form of Venus dominates the canvas. The concept of universal beauty has, of course, foundations in philosophical tradition. Titian, however, gave it tangible form by relating it to human experience, one of the great and influential achievements of his art.

In his treatment of mythological subjects Titian looked to classical sources. The *Worship of Venus, Bacchanal,* and *Bacchus and Ariadne,* all for Alfonso d'Este, are based on ancient texts and are in effect re-creations of classical works of art. The first two closely follow literary descriptions of specific lost Roman paintings. From such archaeological evidence, as it were, Titian created a vital world of natural forms and energies, a celebration of the gods of love and wine, of fertility and frenzy.

The *poesie* for Philip II were based mostly on Ovid's *Metamorphoses.* But the painter did not merely illustrate the lines of the ancient poet. Rather, he imaginatively translated them into a new medium, in the process engaging in certain editing and revision. Thus, for example, in rendering the story of *Venus and Adonis,* he abandoned the text to redefine the dramatic highpoint of the tale, the actual parting of the lovers, a situation absent from the poem.

***Portraits*.** It seems only natural that a painter of such dramatic insight should be a great portraitist as well. Titian endued his sitters with psychological profundity, and just this added dimension, shared to a degree only by Raphael among his contemporaries, elevates Titian above other Renaissance portrait painters. His figures are not set against backdrops, but instead, with softened forms and edges, seem to merge with their surroundings. The shadows playing over their features add an aura of privacy to their moods, and their hands never engage in meaningless or obvious gestures. This approach to the portrait as a psychological world of inner movement and illumination, prepared for by the examples of Leonardo da Vinci and Giorgione, was fully comprehended only by the artist who, more than any other, might be recognized as Titian's heir—Rembrandt. In the monumental portraits of Charles V, above all the equestrian portrait, Titian established the basis for official baroque portraiture of the 17th century.

Technique. One of Titian's followers left a long description of the master's working procedure toward the end of his life. According to this source, Titian began a painting by sketching the composition directly onto the canvas, using a loaded brush for the monochrome underpainting and establishing with just a few strokes the structures of the figures. He turned the picture to the wall for a period of weeks or even months, then scrutinized it critically, adjusted the composition, and corrected whatever faults he found. He repeated this procedure until he judged the canvas finished. In the final stages, Titian is said to have painted with his fingers as much as with the brush.

In recognizing Titian as a master colorist, his contemporaries and later critics were not thinking primarily of the purity, clarity, or intensity of his pigments but of his methods of applying paint. The free, open structure of the painted surface, composed of individual brushstrokes making patches of color, offered an approximation of reality rather than an absolute delineation of form. Much is left to suggestion in that a particular configuration of loosely applied colors requires the viewer to use his imagination to complete the image. Titian's late works seem to speak directly of the painter's medium and craft. On this level in particular they rank with the sculpture of Michelangelo as the most resonant creations of the Renaissance.

David Rosand
Columbia University

Further Reading: Panofsky, Erwin, *Problems in Titian, Mostly Iconographic* (New York 1969); Tietze, Hans, *Titian, the Paintings and Drawings* (London 1950); Valcanover, Francesco, *All the Paintings of Titian* (New York 1960); Wethey, Harold, *Titian, the Religious Paintings* (London 1969).

The Isabella Stewart Gardner Museum, Boston

***Rape of Europa*, by Titian.**

TITIAN

***Francois I, Roi de France*, by Titian.**

The Louvre

***Above:** The Presentation of the Virgin at the Temple* **still hangs on the wall of the Venice Academy for which Titian painted it in the 1530's.**

Anderson-Viollet

TITIAN

Right: **Portrait by Titian of Pietro Aretino, noted Italian satirist and close friend of the artist.**

The Frick Collection, New York

***Below:** Sacred and Profane Love*, **early Titian masterpiece, now in the Borghese Gallery, Rome.**

Bulloz

STERN, FROM BLACK STAR

Indians of the Lake Titicaca region use boats that they have woven from reeds growing along the shores.

TITICACA, Lake, tē-tē-kä′kä, the largest lake in South America and the highest navigable lake in the world, whose surface elevation is 12,500 feet (3,800 meters) above sea level. It is situated in the Andes Mountains at the northern end of the Bolivian Altiplano, on the border with Peru. Extending over 100 miles (160 km) in length, it consists of a larger northwestern section and a smaller southeastern one, connected by a narrow strait. The maximum depth is more than 1,200 feet (365 meters) and the area is 3,140 square miles (8,135 sq km).

Towering above the lake surface are the snow-covered mountain peaks of the Cordillera Real. Although Lake Titicaca is drained at its southern end by the Desaguadero River, it loses more than 90% of its water by evaporation and is therefore quite salty. Along much of its shoreline the lake is shallow and marshy and thick with reeds that the local Aymará Indians use to make woven-reed boats.

The moderating influence of such a large body of water makes possible the cultivation of crops, such as corn, that could not otherwise be grown at such a high altitude. The shores of the lake are rather densely settled, as they have been since the days of the Inca, who conquered the region around 1400 A. D. Earlier, at about the time of Christ, one of the more advanced civilizations of the Western Hemisphere had developed on the south shore of the lake, at Tiahuanaco.

KEMPTON E. WEBB, *Columbia University*

TITLE, in real estate, refers to a combination of legal rights that constitute the full ownership of land or other real property. The subsequent transfers of ownership create a "chain of title" upon which the validity or marketability of the title depends.

The term "title" in Anglo-American law is derived from the use of the same word to designate a royal grant of nobility. Under the English feudal system, ownership in land was transferred by conveying that title of nobility, together with the estate pertaining to it. Despite modern changes in methods of transferring land, the word "title" continues to be used to describe ownership.

Title Search. An examination of the chain of title, called a "title search" is possible because of title recording systems enacted into law in every state of the United States. Recording laws enable a purchaser of land to rely on the title as it appears in the public records. These laws provide that unless a deed is recorded in public records, the deed will be declared void in favor of a subsequent purchaser of the same property who had no knowledge of the prior unrecorded deed.

There are three systems of title recording or registration in use in different states. (1) Under the *Grantor-Grantee Index* system, every sale of real estate is recorded in two sets of alphabetically arranged indexes called a *grantor* (seller) index and a *grantee* (buyer) index. To search a title, a lawyer first looks for the name of the present owner in the grantee index to find when the owner bought the property. He also checks the grantor index to be sure that no sale of the property from the present owner is recorded. The lawyer then repeats the process to find the record of sale from the prior owners, looking back far enough to provide reasonable assurance that there is no break in the chain of title. (2) Under the relatively simple *Tract Index* system, each tract of land in a county is indexed on a separate page that records all transactions for that piece of property. Because of the complexity and expense of converting from the Grantor-Grantee Index to the Tract Index, most states by the 1970's still retained the complicated and inefficient Grantor-Grantee Index system. (3) Under the *Torrens System,* the need for repeating the title search at every sale of the property is eliminated by having an agency of government examine the title, once and for all time, on the basis of which it issues a certificate of registration of title to the owner. See TORRENS SYSTEM.

Title Insurance. No matter how carefully a title search is performed, there are many title defects that may not be discovered and so may create conflicting claims of ownership. For example, if there has been fraud or forgery, or if the deed was signed by a minor or an incompetent person, that deed and all subsequent deeds in the chain of title may be ineffective for passing title and so may provide the basis for an adverse claim of ownership. Homeowners and other purchasers of real estate may obtain protection from loss from such adverse claims by purchasing title insurance.

JEROME G. ROSE, *Rutgers University*
Author, "The Legal Adviser on Home Ownership"

TITLE DEED. See DEED.

TITLE INSURANCE is a contract on the part of a title insurance company to reimburse the insured for any loss that may arise from any undisclosed defect in the insured's title to real estate. In addition, the title insurance company agrees to defend the insured in any claim, valid or not, against the property—an important protection because the expense and time involved in defending against a claim can be considerable.

Title insurance is a single-premium, perpetual policy. It remains in effect as long as the original insured and his heirs own the real estate, whether for a month or a century.

Like other insurance, title insurance assumes unusual but serious perils for the real estate owner. Unlike other insurance, however, it represents protection against hidden defects already in existence on the date the policy is issued rather than against future events. A flaw in title to a parcel of real estate usually grows out of some incident long past that turns up to disturb the present ownership.

In some regions of the United States, little title insurance is sold. Buyers of realty rely instead upon certificates of title issued by attorneys. However, since the certificate of title involves only a title search and investigation of records, it does not afford the same degree of protection that title insurance provides. There are some flaws in title that no amount of checking would ever uncover because they are not in the records. For example, an undiscovered will may create claims against real estate, as may undisclosed marriages and divorces. Also, signatures may be forgeries, or a legally incompetent party may sign a document.

Against all these difficulties, an opinion or certificate of title is no defense. But title insurance will indemnify or protect the insured buyer against loss arising from all such unknown, undiscovered claims not specifically mentioned in the title search report.

Title insurance has the distinction of being one of the few forms of insurance originating in the United States. The first title insurance company was the Real Estate Title Insurance Company of Philadelphia, founded in 1876.

HARRY M. JOHNSON
University of Connecticut

TITMOUSE, any of about 60 species of small, active, gregarious woodland birds found throughout the world except Australia, Polynesia, Madagascar, and the Americas south of Guatemala. Titmice, also called "tits," are most common in the temperate and colder regions of the Northern Hemisphere. Some species are also called "chickadees" in North America.

Titmice are 3 to 8 inches (8–20 cm) long and have short, stout bills whose nostrils are covered with bristles. The feet are short and strong, the wings rounded, and the tails usually long. The plumage, which is alike in both sexes, is olive, brown, gray, or greenish above and white, yellow, or buff below; it is never streaked or barred. Many species have black, white, or blue patterns around the head; a few have crests.

Most titmice feed chiefly on insects but also eat seeds, nuts, and berries. The bird uses its claws to hold a hard seed or nut against a branch and then hammers it with its bill until it opens. A few northern species store food in bark crevices for winter use, while others migrate south in winter. But most are nonmigratory.

A. W. AMBLER, FROM NATIONAL AUDUBON SOCIETY

Tufted titmouse

The nests of titmice vary. Most species use tree cavities, often those abandoned by other birds, and line them with grass, moss, hair, or feathers. Male penduline titmice (Remizinae) of the Old World build complex, finely felted, globular nests with unique tubular side entrances. The clutches vary from 3 or 4 eggs in the tropics to 11 to 16 in the north. The eggs are generally white with gray or brown flecks. The female alone usually incubates the eggs, but in most species both parents feed the young.

Titmice belong to the family Paridae of the order Passeriformes. They are classified in three subfamilies: Parinae, or typical titmice; Aegithalinae, or long-tailed and bush tits; and Remizinae, or penduline titmice.

CARL WELTY, *Beloit College*

TITO, tēt'ō (1892–   ), president of Yugoslavia and creator of the post–World War II republic of Yugoslavia.

Josip Broz was born in Kumrovec, Croatia—then part of Austria-Hungary—on May 25, 1892, of a Roman Catholic peasant family. His mother was Slovene and his father Croatian. After local schooling he became a metalworker. At 18 he joined the Social Democratic party.

During World War I he was conscripted into the Austro-Hungarian Army. In 1915 he was wounded and taken to Russia as a prisoner. He remained there until 1920 and thus experienced the Russian Revolution and the ensuing civil war. He returned to Croatia in 1920 and entered politics. He became a member of the Communist party and in 1927 was secretary of the Zagreb central committee. As the Communist party was outlawed, he spent periods in prison for his political activities. In 1934 he became a member of the party's Politburo. At this time he acquired the code name Tito. In 1936, Tito went to Moscow, where he was associated with the Comintern and its activities. He became secretary general of the Yugoslav Communist party in 1937 and in this capacity was responsible for a party reorganization.

National Leader. Tito's opportunity for action came during World War II when he organized the most successful Balkan resistance movement. His forces, known as the Partisans, were active from the time of the German attack on the Soviet Union in June 1941 until the end of the war. Although the Partisans remained in touch with the Soviet Union, they received more practical aid from the United States and Britain. The Partisans directed their attacks not only against the German and Italian forces, but also against the Chetniks, who supported the royalist Yugoslav government-in-exile. When the Russians entered Belgrade in 1944, Tito and the Partisans were in military control of Yugoslavia.

In 1945, Tito became premier and minister of national defense in a new Yugoslav coalition government. From that time he held the principal position in the Yugoslav state, with control over both the Communist party and the state administration. In 1953 he was elected president, and in 1963 he was made president for life. He has been married three times and has two children.

Policies. In internal affairs Tito was closely associated with three important policies—resistance to Soviet domination, the reconciliation of Yugoslavia's different nationalities, and the reorganization of the economic system to allow more authority to individual industries and to workers' councils. Of these policies the most significant for international affairs has undoubtedly been his independent attitude toward Moscow. From 1948, after a major break with Joseph Stalin, Tito embarked upon an independent course in foreign relations. In subsequent years he not only entered into relations with Western nations but attempted, in cooperation with India and the United Arab Republic, to form a neutralist camp. He also remained on generally good terms with the neighboring socialist states, with the exception of Albania.

BARBARA JELAVICH AND CHARLES JELAVICH
Indiana University

Further Reading: Dedijer, Vladimir, *Tito* (New York 1953); Hoffman, George W. and Neal, Fred W., *Yugoslavia and the New Communism* (New York 1962); Shoup, Paul, *Communism and the Yugoslav National Question* (New York 1968).

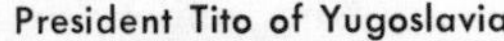
President Tito of Yugoslavia

EASTFOTO

TITOGRAD, tēt'ō-grad, a city in Yugoslavia, is the capital of the constituent republic of Montenegro. About 185 miles (297 km) southwest of Belgrade, it is on the Demovsko Plain at the confluence of the Ribnica and Morača rivers. Formerly called Podgorica, the city was renamed after Tito, then Yugoslav premier, after World War II, when it became the Montenegrin capital. Largely destroyed during the war, the city has been rebuilt in a modern style. It is an important transportation and industrial center.

The city was the birthplace of Stephen Nemanya I, founder of the medieval Serbian dynasty in the 12th century. Titograd was part of the Ottoman Empire from 1474 to 1878, when the Congress of Berlin awarded it to Montenegro. It became part of Yugoslavia after World War I. Population: (1963 est.) 37,000.

BARBARA JELAVICH AND CHARLES JELAVICH
Indiana University

TITRATION, tī-trā'shən, is a technique used in chemical analysis to measure the quantity of a particular substance present in a solution. Titration depends on the chemical reaction between a substance of known concentration (the titrant) and the test substance. The nature of the reaction between the two substances and the ratio in which they combine must be known. Measured quantities of the titrant are then added to the test substance until no further reaction occurs, which means that no test substance is left free in solution. Knowing the reactions involved and the amount of titrant used makes it possible to calculate the amount of test substance that was present in the solution.

Titration is a fast, simple, and very precise technique. Any type of chemical reaction can be used as long as it is rapid, virtually complete, and free of side reactions. The neutralization of an acid by a base is used very frequently—the amount of an acid in a sample is found by titration with a standard base, and vice versa. Metal ions are titrated by complexing agents and sometimes by precipitants. Oxidation-reduction titrations are used for metals and nonmetals and for determining the concentrations of some organic compounds.

In a titration the titrant is added as a standard solution of known concentration. It is generally measured out by volume, but it can also be added by weight. To determine when the titration is complete, a small amount of another substance, called an *indicator,* is added to the mixture of the test substance and titrant. The indicator changes color at the "end point"—that is, the point at which all of the substance being measured has reacted with the titrant. Electrical and other physical methods are also used to locate the end point of the reaction.

HAROLD F. WALTON, *University of Colorado*

TITTLE, tit'əl, **Y. A.** (1926–), American football player, who as quarterback for three National Football League teams ranked as one of the leading passers of his time. With the New York Giants in 1963 he set a league record of 36 touchdown passes in one season. Both the Associated Press and United Press named him all-league quarterback in 1957, 1962, and 1963.

Yelberton Abraham Tittle was born in Marshall, Texas, on Oct. 24, 1926. After graduating from Louisiana State University in 1948, he joined the Baltimore Colts. From 1951 through

1960 he played with the San Francisco 49ers and from 1961 until his retirement as a player in 1964, with the New York Giants. He set league career records of 3,817 passes attempted, 2,118 completed, 28,339 yards gained, and 212 touchdown passes. While maintaining an insurance business in Atherton, Calif., he served as an advisory quarterback coach with the 49ers and switched in 1970 to the Giants.

BILL BRADDOCK, *New York "Times"*

TITUS, tī'təs, **Saint,** leader of the early church and companion of St. Paul. Except for references in the New Testament, little is known about him. Paul opposed the efforts of Judaizing Christians to have Titus, a Gentile Christian, circumcised in accord with the Mosaic law (Galatians 2:3). Paul regarded him as a colleague of exceptional competence and integrity (II Corinthians 7:23; 12:18) and entrusted several missions to him. When the Corinthian church rebelled against Paul, Titus carried a stern letter to the congregation and succeeded in reviving their loyalty to Paul (II Corinthians 7:6–16). Titus later returned to help collect funds for the Jewish Christians in Jerusalem (II Corinthians 8:16–17).

Surprisingly, the Book of Acts, which relates much of Paul's ministry, does not mention Titus. The Pastoral Epistles represent him as working in Dalmatia and Crete. (See TITUS, EPISTLE TO; TIMOTHY, EPISTLES TO). Later tradition records Titus as the first bishop of Crete. His feast is celebrated in the West on Feb. 6 and by Eastern Christians on Aug. 25.

DAVID M. HAY
Princeton Theological Seminary

TITUS, tī'təs (39–81 A.D.), Roman emperor from 79 to 81. Born in Rome on Dec. 30, 39, he was the son of Emperor Vespasian and the older brother of Emperor Domitian. His powerful, aristocratic father provided Titus Flavius Vespasianus with an excellent education. In the reign of Nero, when Vespasian was sent to Palestine to put down the Jewish rebellion, Titus accompanied his father and served as his chief military assistant. Later, while Vespasian plotted elsewhere to become emperor, Titus remained in the east, where he ended the Jewish war by capturing and destroying Jerusalem in 70.

Throughout the reign of Vespasian (69–79), Titus was virtually coemperor and was obviously favored for the throne over his brother Domitian. Titus' reputation was not unblemished. Although the army liked him, he was not especially popular with the civilians in Rome. He carried on a particularly unpopular affair with Berenice, sister of Herod Agrippa I, king of Judaea. There were rumors that he was cruel and that he was guilty of political murders.

Nevertheless Titus became one of Rome's most popular emperors. The historian Suetonius described him as the "delight and darling of mankind." He reversed his father's frugal fiscal policy and spent large sums of money on lavish entertainment of the people. His relations with the Roman senators were good, in part because he refused to permit accusations of treason against any of them. He is reputed to have said on a day during which he had not been generous to anyone: "I have lost a day."

Titus' short, happy reign was unfortunately blighted by three disasters—the famous eruption of Vesuvius (Aug. 24, 79), a fire in Rome, and the plague. Titus used state revenues to alleviate the public's distress and enhanced his popularity as a result. The Colosseum was completed during his reign.

Never trusting his younger brother Domitian, Titus refused to give him responsible positions. Domitian was probably the only Roman who rejoiced when Titus died unexpectedly at the age of 41 on Sept. 13, 81. Suetonius called Titus' death a far greater loss to the world than to Titus himself. His reign, however, was devoid of any spectacular achievement or lasting influence.

ARTHER FERRILL
University of Washington

TITUS, tī'təs, **Epistle to,** the 17th book in the New Testament, ostensibly a letter from the Apostle Paul to his coworker Titus instructing him how to organize church life in Crete. Many modern scholars doubt that Paul wrote the letter, because its language, style, and content differ considerably from the undisputed Pauline letters. Probably this epistle and the two addressed to Timothy are the work of a single author, a disciple of Paul who wrote near the beginning of the 2d century for the benefit of fellow church leaders. (See TIMOTHY, EPISTLES TO). Almost certainly he wrote in Paul's name because he was attempting to restate the apostle's message for his own time and situation.

The chief themes of the epistle are the qualifications and tasks of bishops, the moral standards believers should observe, and the proper measures to take toward heretics. The writer's fundamental concern is the stabilization of church life and thought. He wrote in an age when a fixed episcopal office had developed, and perhaps the terms "bishop" and "elder" are used interchangeably (1:5–7). Bishops are to be models of uprightness and vigorous defenders of "sound doctrine."

The content of orthodox belief is not specified at length, but the author presupposes a Pauline doctrine of justification by grace apart from works. This justification, however, requires believers to strive zealously to lead lives free from sinful passions and devoted to good deeds (2:11–14; 3:4–8). They should display love, gentleness, honesty, and sobriety so as "to adorn the doctrine of God" and win the respect of non-Christians. The epistle attacks heretics who are succeeding in disrupting the churches (1:11). The author chooses not to discuss the content of their teaching but refers cryptically to a "circumcision party," "Jewish myths," and "foolish controversies." Evidently it was a syncretic heresy with Judaizing tendencies. The author denounces the conduct of the heretics as immoral and insists that they be rebuked and, unless they repent, shunned.

DAVID M. HAY
Princeton Theological Seminary

TITUS ANDRONICUS, tī'təs, an-dron'ə-kus, is a tragedy by Shakespeare, first printed in 1594. The play, which is set in late Roman times but is more legendary than historical, draws on mythology for the rape and mutilation of Lavinia, paralleling the tale of Philomela, and for the banquet at which Tamora, like the legendary Thyestes, is served the flesh of her sons.

The play opens with the triumphant return to Rome of Titus Andronicus after 10 years of war with the Goths, bringing as prisoners Tamora, queen of the Goths, and her three sons. Titus is a commanding figure of bravery, who has lost 21 sons in battle and has only 4 remaining sons and a daughter. His Roman sense of honor, however, is his tragic flaw. It induces him, first, to order a public sacrifice of one of Tamora's sons to placate the ghosts of his own slain sons, thus arousing Tamora to plot revenge. Next, when offered the office of emperor, Titus thinks to have greater honor by backing the late emperor's son, Saturninus, overlooking that candidate's guile. Finally, Titus offers the new emperor his daughter, Lavinia, as a bride, disregarding her betrothal to Bassianus, brother of Saturninus. And when his own sons defend Lavinia by helping Bassianus to abduct her, Titus slays one of them. Thus through a flawed sense of honor—a concern more for the reputation of nobility than for its substance—Titus injures himself, his family, and the state.

Out of this beginning all the later horrors of the play arise. The masked villainy of Saturninus and of Tamora and her secret lover, Aaron the Moor, easily victimize Titus and his family, who become metaphorically the doe of the hunt. Bassianus is slain, Lavinia is raped and mutilated, and two of her brothers are trapped into being charged with the crime. Titus is then maneuvered into letting one of his hands be cut off by Aaron, as a supposed ransom for his sons and proof of his "loyalty" to Saturninus, who returns the hand along with the sons' heads. Titus can only brood and take refuge in feigned madness until Tamora unwittingly gives him a chance to slay her sons and cook their bodies in a pie. The subsequent banquet becomes a tumult in which the main characters are slain.

Roy W. Battenhouse
Author of "Shakespearean Tragedy"

TITUSVILLE, tĭt'əs-vil, a city on the east coast of Florida, the seat of Brevard county, is 35 miles (56 km) east of Orlando. It is 8 miles (12 km) northwest of the Kennedy Space Center, across the Indian River, a saltwater lagoon. (See Cape Kennedy.) Titusville's major industry is serving the space program, which caused a fourfold population increase in the community between 1960 and 1966.

Another important industry is packing and shipping citrus fruit. Titusville is in a commercial and sport fishing area. It is also a center for tourism, and has boatyards and marinas that serve pleasure boats plying the Atlantic Intracoastal Waterway which passes down the Indian River.

Col. Henry T. Titus founded the settlement in 1867. It was incorporated as a town in 1886. It is governed by a council, one of whose members is elected mayor, and a city manager. The community grew rapidly during the 1960's, with the population increasing by nearly five times in that period. Population: 30,515.

Jack B. Horton, Jr.
Brevard County Historical Commission

TITUSVILLE, tī'təs-vil, a city in northwestern Pennsylvania, in Crawford county, on Oil Creek, is 41 miles (66 km) southeast of Erie. It is an industrial center, producing specialty steel, forgings, crankshafts, heavy oil-well equipment, lumber, wood products, plastic tile, electronic components, wallpaper, paints, and camper bodies.

The Titusville campus of the University of Pittsburgh offers a 2-year course, and Titusville participates in the vocational-technical education program of Oil City, Pa.

Drake Memorial State Park in Titusville is near the site of the world's first successful oil well, drilled on Aug. 27, 1859, by Col. Edwin L. Drake. It has a working replica of the original well and a museum, opened in 1969, and library with rare documents, artifacts, and mementos of the early days of the oil industry. Narrow dirt roads take visitors into the old oil fields.

Jonathan Titus founded the community in 1796 as a lumbering center. Titusville suffered fires, floods, and explosions that periodically threatened to wipe out the town. As the area's oil fields expanded after the success of the Drake well, Titusville was the center of the independent oil producers' fight against the incursions of the Standard Oil Company. The conflict, which often erupted in violence, ended in 1875 when a Titusville leader became a director of Standard Oil.

Titusville was incorporated as a borough in 1847 and as a city in 1866. It is governed by a manager and council. Population: 7,331.

Patricia C. Schessler
The Franklin "News-Herald"

TIV, tiv, a major ethnic group of northern Nigeria, numbering nearly 1 million. They live along the Benue River and eastward to the Cameroon highlands. The Tiv migrated into their present area from the southeast, and their culture is similar in certain respects to that of several Cameroonian and Congolese peoples.

The Tiv are racially Negroid. Their language belongs to the Niger-Congo family. Primarily farmers, they grow millet, sorghum, and yams as staple foods and benniseed (sesame) and soybeans for cash.

The Tiv society consists of a number of lineages linked together through intermarriage and the sharing of territory and by negotiations and arbitrations conducted by the elders of the family groups. There are no chiefs. The traditional religion remains predominant among the people, although slowly increasing numbers have become Christians. Several Tiv religious cults have actively opposed not only colonial but independent Nigerian political authority.

Robert A. Lystad
Johns Hopkins University

TIVERTON is a town in southeastern Rhode Island, in Newport county, on the Sakonnet River, about 22 miles (35 km) southeast of Providence. It is principally a residential and resort community. Tiverton was incorporated as a town in Massachusetts Bay Colony in 1692. It was annexed to Rhode Island in 1746. In October 1778, Rhode Island troops boarded and captured a British frigate off Tiverton. Government is by selectmen. Population: 12,559.

TIVOLI, ti'və-lē, the Tibur of classical times, is a small Italian hilltop town, located on a spur of the Apennines 18 miles (29 km) northeast of Rome. It lies between the gorge of the Aniene River and the Roman Campagna, across which it commands magnificent views. Known since the days of ancient Rome for its beauty, it was inhabited by many rich Romans. Among these was the Emperor Hadrian, who built a lavish villa on the edge of the plain of the Campagna, below

KOSTICH, FROM MONKMEYER

TIVOLI GARDENS, popular Copenhagen amusement park, is especially appealing at night, when it is brightly illuminated.

the town. Now in ruined condition, the villa is one of the world's most impressive remains of Roman times. Much of its statuary and mosaics are preserved. There are also numerous remains of other villas in the vicinity. A temple devoted to Vesta is now a church.

The ancient buildings in the town were largely replaced by medieval and subsequently by modern structures. Pope Pius II built a castle there in the 15th century, and in the mid-16th century Cardinal Ippolito d'Este built the house with beautiful gardens now known as the Villa d'Este. The town has narrow winding streets and several Renaissance and late medieval churches.

The Aniene River, whose waterfalls remain a major attraction, was the chief source of water supply to the city of Rome, to which water was carried in a system of giant aqueducts. Population: (1961) 25,129.

NORMAN J. G. POUNDS, *Indiana University*

TIVOLI GARDENS, ti′və-lē, an amusement park in Copenhagen, Denmark. These world-famous "pleasure gardens" were laid out on part of the city's old defense works and were opened in 1843 by George Carstensen. They have attracted foreigners as well as Danes ever since.

Among the facilities offered at Tivoli are numerous restaurants and cafés among the trees. Concerts and theatrical performances, including pantomimes and ballets, are scheduled regularly throughout the season, which runs from May to mid-September. There are dance halls and amusement rides. At night, the gardens are attractively illuminated.

In 1944, during the German occupation of Denmark, bomb explosions severely damaged Tivoli. The old Moorish-style concert hall was completely destroyed. In 1956 a new concert hall, in contemporary style, was inaugurated.

TIZARD, tiz′ärd, **Sir Henry Thomas** (1885–1959), British scientist, who was largely responsible for the radar stations around Britain that were such a vital factor at the outset of World War II.

Tizard was born in Gillingham, Kent, on Aug. 23, 1885. He studied chemistry at Oxford and the University of Berlin and was an experimental pilot during World War I. In 1920 he entered government service as assistant secretary of the department of scientific and industrial research, becoming its secretary in 1927. Two years later he was appointed rector of the Imperial College of Science and Technology in London. He remained a part-time government adviser on aeronautical research, and in 1935 he became chairman of the committee responsible for scientific work on air defense. It was in this period that Britain began to prepare its radar defenses.

After Churchill became prime minister in 1940, Tizard's influence diminished, and F. A. Lindemann, later Lord Cherwell, became the government's leading scientific adviser. He and Tizard differed particularly on bombing policy. Tizard wished to concentrate Britain's limited resources on German submarines and bases, but Lindemann advocated the saturation bombing of cities.

In 1942, Tizard gave up most of his government work to become president of Magdalen College, Oxford. In 1947 he became chairman of the government committees for civil and military scientific research. He died in Fareham, Hampshire, on Oct. 19, 1959.

W. A. SMEATON
University College, London

TJIREBON, chir-ə-bôn′, is a port city in Indonesia on the north coast of Java, halfway between Djakarta and Semarang. The port serves the densely populated agricultural plain on which the city is situated. Agricultural goods moving to the city are tobacco, rice, vegetables, oils, sugarcane, cassava, tea, and peanuts. There is some light manufacturing.

The city came under Muslim control in the 16th century, and as the capital of the Sultanate of Tjirebon (Cheribon) it was a stronghold of the Islamic faith. In the 17th century it was a center of opposition to Dutch colonialism. Occupied by the Dutch for most of the period 1673–1949, Tjirebon was transformed into a city of largely European appearance. Population: (1961) 158,299.

PETER R. INGOLD, *University of Vermont*

TLAXCALA, tlä-skäl'ə, is an inland state in central Mexico, east of Mexico City and Mexico state. It is the smallest state in the republic, covering 1,555 square miles (3,914 sq km). Its name is the Nahuatl Indian word for "rocky place." It occupies a high plateau with a mean elevation of 7,000 feet (2,100 meters) and is dominated in the south by a dormant volcano, La Malinche.

With an average of 183 persons per square mile (1960), Tlaxcala is the most densely settled state in Mexico. Afflicted by aridity and soil erosion, it is probably also the poorest and has been losing population. The main economic activities are cattle raising and farming. The land is patched with maguey fields for production of pulque, a fermented beverage.

The capital, also named Tlaxcala, is a picturesque community famous for its textiles. Its Church of San Francisco (1521) is thought to be the oldest in Mexico.

In 1519 the Tlaxcaltec Indians, who were independent of the Aztecs, aided Cortés in conquering Mexico. Population: (1960) 346,699.

REYNALDO AYALA
San Diego State College

TLEMCEN, tlem-sen' is a city in northwestern Algeria near the Moroccan border. It is one of the most traditional of Algerian cities, with a population that is overwhelmingly Muslim and of Berber-Arab origin.

Tlemcen is noted for its leather goods, carpets, wool and silk tapestries, and copperware. Some of these handicrafts have declined under competition from machine-made imports, despite government-sponsorship of workshops to preserve the industries. The city's modern industries include food processing and the manufacture of furniture. Tlemcen is also a market center for local livestock, wool, olives, and wheat. It is located on Algeria's main east-west railroad and highway, and a railroad spur links it with the Mediterranean port of Beni-Saf.

Tlemcen's ancient citadel and sultan's palace and many medieval shops and residences have deteriorated or been partly replaced by later structures. But Tlemcen has a greater proportion of buildings dating from the 12th to the 15th century than any other Algerian town. Among the points of interest are the 14th century Mosque of Sidi Bou Medine and other smaller mosques.

Tlemcen flourished from the 13th to the 15th century as the capital of the Ziyandid dynasty, which ruled most of western Algeria. In this time the city was also a handicraft and cultural center. It later declined, and in the French colonial period (1830–1962) it was surpassed by other Algerian cities. Population: (1965) 82,527.

BENJAMIN E. THOMAS
University of California, Los Angeles

TLINGIT INDIANS, tling'git, an Indian tribe of southeast Alaska. Some authorities consider them a separate linguistic stock, Koluschan, but others group them with the neighboring Haida in the Nadene or Great Athapaskan stock. The Tlingit are representative of the Northwest Coast culture area peoples and are still the largest of such groups.

The traditional Tlingit economy was based primarily on fishing, which supported a complex social and political organization. Large villages of cedar plank houses featured lineage crests (totem poles). Crafts included the making of carved canoes and woven blankets. After the Russians arrived in 1741, the Tlingit were introduced to the fur trade. The trading era permitted the Tlingit to engage in conspicuous displays of wealth (potlatches) and increased slavery.

Many Tlingit still fish or are employed in canneries. In 1970 about 10,000 persons identified as Tlingit lived in southeast Alaska. Many have become highly acculturated.

STEPHEN E. FERACA
Bureau of Indian Affairs

TNT, common name for a powerful, widely used explosive. See TRINITROTOLUENE.

TOAD, any of a genus of about 175 species of warty, land-dwelling, tailless amphibians. Toads are found throughout the world in tropical and temperate land areas, except for Madagascar, Australia, and some Pacific islands. There are about 13 species of true toads in North America.

Toads and frogs together make up the order Salientia, or Anura. There is, however, a great deal of confusion about the terms "toad" and "frog," and all that can be said without question is that members of the genus *Bufo*, family Bufonidae, are "toads."

Description. Toads are commonly 2 or 3 inches (5–7.5 cm) long, but some vary considerably from this range. The oak toad (*Bufo quercicus*) of the southeastern United States seldom attains a length of 1 inch (2.54 cm), but some of the larger species of toads, such as Blomberg's toad (*B. blombergi*), may reach a length of more than 8 inches (20 cm).

Toads typically have a plump body and short legs. Most have horny projections on their hind feet, which aid the toad in "shuffling out" a

American toad, with inflated throat pouch.

HUGH M. HALLIDAY, FROM ANNAN PHOTOS

HAL H. HARRISON, FROM NATIONAL AUDUBON SOCIETY

Fowler's toad (*Bufo woodhousii fowleri*)

shallow burrow in soft soil. They use these burrows as places in which to hide. Toads also usually have warty skin that is thicker than the skin of most frogs and encloses skin glands of several different kinds. The eyes have horizontal pupils. The iris, which has gold and silver markings, is often the brightest part of the toad's body. Most of the common species of toads are brown above with darker brown or black spots and blotches. Some toads, however, are brightly colored. *B. punctatus* has red spots on a light tan or cream-colored background, and *B. viridis* has green spots.

Habitat and Behavior. The thick warty skin allows toads to inhabit drier regions than do their thiner-skinned frog relatives. Toads are often found in fields and gardens as well as more moist meadows and woodlands, from sea level to elevations of 15,000 feet (4,575 meters). As cold weather approaches, toads find a suitable secluded spot and hibernate. They can remain inactive with their body functions slowed for several months.

Short hind limbs prevent toads from making the long leaps characteristic of most frogs. Most toads progress with a series of short hops with which they seem to bounce across the terrain. A few species neither jump nor hop, but walk with a most unfroglike gait, and when in a hurry, scuttle mouselike across the ground.

Adult toads are carnivorous and will eat any moving thing that they can stuff into their gaping mouths. Because most toads are small, their food items are mostly insects. Toads themselves are preyed on by larger carnivorous animals, such as herons and related birds, skunks and other mammals, and a number of snake species.

When toads are disturbed, their skin glands secrete ill-tasting or poisonous substances. The most prominent of the venomous skin glands are the parotoid glands that appear as paired raised areas just behind the eyes. Although numerous animals will eat toads, the toad's parotoid secretions are sufficiently noxious to prevent many other animals from taking them. In most toads, the secretion apparently has no more than a very disagreeable taste. In some of the larger species, however, the secretion is toxic enough to kill a potential predator. Both the marine toad (*B. marinus*) of tropical America and the Colorado river toad (*B. alvarius*) of the southwestern United States have been reported to kill dogs that were unwary enough to have picked the toads up in their mouths.

Toads make up for loss due to predation by having a very high reproductive rate. A female toad commonly lays 20,000 eggs in a single breeding season.

Reproduction. Toads are probably the most prolific of all amphibians. Although they live a mainly terrestrial life, toads must repair to ponds and pools to mate and lay their eggs. During the breeding season, the male takes up position at pond's edge and makes calls that are distinctive of his particular species. These calls serve both to warn other males from encroaching on the spot he has selected and to attract the silent females of his own species. The female toad seldom selects a male of the wrong species even though males of several species may be calling from the same pond. Even to human ears, the calls are as distinctive as bird songs. In fact, a few species such as *B. americanus* and *B. fowleri* of North America are easier to distinguish by their characteristic mating calls than by their physical appearance.

A very few small toads lay as few as 7,000 eggs in the water at breeding time, while some of the larger species lay 30,000 or more eggs at one time. The toad eggs hatch into tailed aquatic larvae, known as *tadpoles*.

In most toads, the tadpole period is short, lasting only a couple of weeks. Unlike adult toads, tadpoles are vegetarians, feeding mainly on green algae.

Economic Value. The insect-eating habits of toads are important to farmers throughout the world. The economic value of the insect controlling effect of a single toad has been variously estimated, with some estimates ranging up to $50 per year. Large tropical toads, in particular, are used for the biological control of insects.

The marine toad, native to Central and South America, is used for the control of sugarcane pests throughout the tropics and has been introduced to many islands of the West Indies as well as to Guam, Hawaii, and New Guinea. The marine toad, which attains a size of 6 to 7 inches (15–17.5 cm), is able to eat not only insects but also mice and other small animals. It is also one of the most prolific of toads, laying as many as 35,000 eggs in a single breeding season. Though some of these eggs and subsequent tadpoles do not survive, many do and prosper, especially on the far-flung islands where they have been artificially introduced and where they have no natural enemies. Under these conditions, the marine toad has increased in numbers to the extent that it too has become a pest.

In some cases, marine toads come out onto roads and are killed in such large numbers that their crushed bodies make the surface of the road dangerously slippery. These toad's booming mating calls create a nuisance, and their highly toxic skin secretions may be dangerous to pets. The results of the widespread introduction of the marine toad are not yet known. It is known, however, that the native fauna of insects as well as that of the native frogs and lizards changes greatly when the population of marine toads increases.

Herndon G. Dowling
The American Museum of Natural History

Further Reading: Cochran, Doris M., *Living Amphibians of the World* (Garden City, N. Y., 1961); Porter, George, *World of the Frog and the Toad* (New York 1967); Wright, Albert H., and Wright, A. A., *Handbook of Frogs and Toads of the United States and Canada*, 3d ed. (Ithaca, N. Y., 1949).

MARINELAND OF FLORIDA

ROBERT HERMES, FROM NATIONAL AUDUBON SOCIETY

TOADFISH is shown above at full length. (*Left*) Head view of oyster toadfish showing its large thick mouth.

TOADFISH, any of a family of small repulsive-looking, slow-moving marine fishes found in warm coastal waters throughout the world. The toadfish's body is thick and short, less than 15 inches (38 cm) long, and the head is large, with a large mouth equipped with strong canine teeth. The eyes are on top of the head and are directed upward. There are two dorsal fins and an anal fin with many rays. Some species (subfamily Thassophryninae) have a highly developed venom delivery apparatus, with poison glands at the bases of two hollow dorsal spines. All toadfishes have a heavy mucous covering, and some have scales. Most are drab in color. Some species (subfamily Porichthyinae), called "midshipmen," have numerous light organs on the body.

Toadfishes are usually found in inshore waters, most often on sand or mud bottoms in crevices or burrows or under rocks. They can live for hours out of water. Vicious and carnivorous, they consume crustaceans, mollusks, and small fishes.

There are more than thirty species of toadfishes, classified in three subfamilies: Batrachoidinae, Porichthyinae, and Thassophryninae of the order Batrachoidiformes.

William B. Scott, *University of Toronto*

TOADFLAX, any of a group of annual and perennial plants with alternate slender leaves that make them resemble flax plants. Toadflaxes make up the genus *Linaria* of the figwort family (Scrophulariaceae) and are not related to flax (*Linum*), which belongs to the family Linaceae.

Toadflaxes are native to Europe, North America, and northern Africa. Many species are grown as garden ornamentals, including *L. maroccana, L. bipartita,* and *L. supena.* These plants have showy flowers that may be white, pink, lavender, purple, yellow, red, or other colors. Some are beautifully bicolored. The yellow toadflax (*L. vulgaris*), also known as butter-and-eggs, is a common wild flower found in meadows and waste places. It has 2-lipped pale yellow flowers that are crowded into dense clusters at the tops of the stems. (See Butter-and-Eggs.)

The bastard toadflaxes (*Comandra*) are not related to the toadflaxes but belong to the sandalwood family (Santalaceae). They have small, white, star-shaped flowers and blunt narrow leaves. They are parasites on the roots of woody plants.

H. A. MacDonald, *Cornell University*

TOADSTOOL is a term often used interchangeably with "mushroom" to denote the large fleshy fruiting body of certain fungi. See Fungus; Mushroom.

TOAST. To toast a person is to propose a drink in his or her honor. In the 16th century it became the fashion in England to add toasted bread to drinks. The term "toast" came to be applied to a drink of honor proposed to some person or sentiment during or at the end of a meal. The word then acquired a broader meaning —for example, a young woman might be called the "toast of the town."

The words used to propose a toast may be short and simple. Some common examples are *sköal!* (Swedish), *à votre santé!* (French), and *prosit!* (German), all of which mean "to your health." At a formal occasion, on the other hand, a toastmaster is chosen to make a short speech each time the company is invited to drink to a guest.

TOBA SOJO, tō-bä sō-jō (1053–1140), Japanese Buddhist priest, who is traditionally identified as the artist of the *Frolicking Animal Scrolls,* four handscroll paintings belonging to Kozanji monastery in Kyoto. He was the son of an imperial councillor and the great-great-grandson of Emperor Daigo. After joining the Tendai Buddhist sect, he took the name of Kakuyu and he received the high ecclesiastical rank of *sojo.* Late in life he retired to Toba in Yamashiro, and from then on he was known as Toba Sojo.

Two of the animal scrolls could not be Toba Sojo's because they were painted in the 13th century. The other two date from the 12th century, but no proof exists that he was the painter. Both in style and subject matter they differ from the religious art of the time. The scrolls are painted in ink brushstrokes of varying intensities and widths and are without color or graded wash—a style borrowed from Buddhist copybooks. Their subject is animals parodying human beings. One scene, a monkey dressed in priestly garb conducting a service before a statue of Buddha that is a frog, seems to be an attack on Buddhism.

Robert Moes
Denver Art Museum

TOBACCO, a plant of the genus *Nicotiana* and a member of the nightshade family (Solanaceae), grown as an annual crop for its leaves. It is unique among its relatives, such as the tomato, potato, and eggplant, in that the nonedible leaf is the commercially important part of the plant. The harvested leaves are dried (cured), fermented slightly, and used for smoking, chewing, and snuffing. They are also used as a source of the insecticidal alkaloid *nicotine.* The use of tobacco, long a controversial matter, has increasingly been condemned by the medical profession. Significant statistical differences between smokers and nonsmokers in the occurrence of lung cancer, heart disease, and other ailments have indicated that smoking may be a cause of these problems. See also SMOKING AND HEALTH.

Consumption. Tobacco consumption is generally highest in industrialized nations. In the middle to late 1960's, Canada led the world in per capita consumption of all tobacco products. Annual use per person over 15 years of age was 10.2 pounds (4.63 kg). The United States followed closely with a per capita consumption of 10.1 pounds (4.58 kg) per year. By contrast, the per capita consumption in Portugal was 2.7 pounds (1.22 kg); in Rhodesia, 2 pounds (0.91 kg); and in India, only 1.8 pounds (0.82 kg).

Cigarettes are the most popular form of tobacco. The number smoked has increased rapidly throughout the world. The use of all other forms of tobacco has tended to be steady or lower, with a few exceptions. Cigar smoking has increased in France, Switzerland, Turkey, and the United States.

Production. Tobacco is a high-value commodity in world trade and within the United States. It is produced in more than 80 countries. Total world production for most of the 1960's averaged about 10.4 billion pounds (5.2 million tons, or 4.7 billion kg) per year. Of this amount the United States produced about 2 billion pounds (1 million tons, or 930 million kg), nearly one fifth of the total annual production. Other major producers are shown in the following table.

United States	2.0 billion lbs	(930 million kg)
China	1.7 billion lbs	(771 million kg)
India	751.0 million lbs	(341 million kg)
USSR	461.0 million lbs	(209 million kg)
Japan	429.0 million lbs	(195 million kg)
Brazil	425.0 million lbs	(193 million kg)

Since 1940, United States production of most tobacco types has been under government control. Total annual production has varied slightly around 2 billion pounds (930 million kg). In the mid-1960's public concern about the effect of cigarette smoking on health caused a decline in the production of cigarette tobacco types.

In the 1960's tobacco ranked fifth in cash value among American farm crops, with growers receiving about $1.2 billion annually. American consumers spent about $10 billion a year on tobacco products, of which about $4.4 billion was for local, state, and federal taxes. In addition, the United States exported about 30% of its production, benefiting its foreign trade balance by more than $500 million.

AVERAGE TOBACCO CONSUMPTION PER ADULT PERSON PER YEAR

Country[1]	Pounds	Kilograms
Canada	10.2	4.63
United States	10.1	4.58
Netherlands	8.7	3.95
Denmark	8.5	3.85
New Zealand	8.1	3.67
Iceland	7.7	3.49
Switzerland	7.5	3.40
Belgium	7.4	3.36
Australia	7.0	3.17
Ireland	6.6	2.99
West Germany	6.4	2.90
United Kingdom	6.1	2.77

[1] *Leading twelve countries.*

COMMON TOBACCO PLANT (*Nicotiana tabacum*). Slender, funnel-shaped flowers are usually light pink.

R. J. REYNOLDS TOBACCO CO.

HISTORY

The two tobacco species of economic importance, *Nicotiana tabacum* and *N. rustica,* were being cultivated by American Indians before Europeans went to the New World. *N. rustica* was the tobacco of tribes east of the Mississippi River and, to a limited extent, of tribes in the southwestern United States and northern Mexico. *N. tabacum* was cultivated from Brazil northward into Central America, through most of Mexico, and in the West Indies. *N. tabacum* brought from Trinidad and from the Orinoco region of South America early replaced *N. rustica* as a crop plant in the English colonies.

Columbus noted that the Indians used tobacco for smoking, chewing, and snuffing. Indians of the Caribbean region smoked the *tobago,* a pipe, from which the word "tobacco" is derived, and also rolled tobacco into crude cigars.

Smoking was introduced into Spain and Portugal about 1550 by sailors returning from the New World. Tobacco seeds were taken to Spain from Santo Domingo about 1559 and to Rome by 1561. The plant was propagated as an ornamental and for its supposed medicinal value. Tobacco was first taken to England from Florida in 1565 by Sir John Hawkins, the English naval

CONNECTICUT DEVELOPMENT COMMISSION

Miles of cheesecloth "tents" 8 feet (2.4 meters) high are erected to protect "shade-grown" cigar-wrapper leaf.

hero. Sir Richard Grenville, the English naval commander, in 1585, and Capt. Ralph Lane, an English colonial administrator, in 1586 brought back tobacco and pipes and thus introduced pipe smoking to England and ultimately to Continental Europe.

By the first decade of the 17th century, tobacco had been introduced into the Palatinate of Germany (now Bavaria), Russia, Turkey, Persia, the west coast of Africa, the Philippines, Japan, and China. Thus tobacco had been introduced to most of the known world before its commercial culture began at Jamestown in 1612. Tobacco use was not universally accepted, and in some parts of the world efforts were made to prohibit it. James I of England placed a punitive tax on tobacco, and severe penalties were imposed on its use in Russia and Turkey—all unsuccessful.

Soon after John Rolfe, husband of Pocahontas, began commercial culture at Jamestown in 1612, tobacco became economically important in the colonies. By 1619, exports to England were substantial. Profits were so great that restrictions on tobacco planting were imposed in 1621 to permit production of food crops. Due to scarcity of money, tobacco became a medium of exchange. It was accepted in payment of taxes and many kinds of debts and was used often to pay the salaries of public officials, colonial militia, and clergymen.

The cigarette came into use in the United States following the Civil War. Introduction of blended tobacco during the first decade of the 20th century popularized cigarette use and led to the greatest expansion of tobacco consumption in history. See also CIGAR; CIGARETTE.

THE PLANT

Tobacco belongs to the genus *Nicotiana,* which contains more than 60 species, most of them native to the New World. All the Old World species are confined to the Australian region. *N. tabacum,* a New World species, is the one grown commercially in most of the world and the only one under commercial production in the United States. *N. rustica,* another New World species, is grown extensively in the USSR and certain Asian countries, though chiefly for local consumption. A few species of *Nicotiana,* such as *N. alata* and *N. sylvestris,* are grown as ornamentals.

Common tobacco, *N. tabacum,* is an annual with perennial tendencies. The plant is 3 to 10 feet (1–3 meters) tall and generally conical in shape. The stem is thick, with few branches. Lateral buds, or suckers, are produced in the leaf axils (the upper angle found between the leaf and the stem). Leaves are stalkless and somewhat oval (ovate, elliptic, or lanceolate), with enormous area in comparison with other crop plants. A single plant may produce as much as 255 square feet (23.5 sq meters) of leaves. Leaf color is light to dark green, becoming a lighter shade or even yellowish green as the leaf matures. Many short-stemmed flowers are borne in a cluster (panicle) at the top of the plant. Most flowers are light pink, but color may vary from white to carmine red. The slender funnel-shaped flowers expand at the top into five lobes. The structure of the flower, which contains five stamens and a pistil, favors self-fertilization. Numerous tiny seeds are contained in a 2-compartment seedpod at maturity.

N. rustica is more strictly an annual than is *N. tabacum.* Also, it is not as tall, and its stem is smaller and less woody. Its leaves are broad with rounded tips (ovate), and very thick and heavy, with clearly defined leaf stalks (petioles). The flower is pale yellow and cylindrical, but thick in shape, with five rounded lobes.

GROWING AND PROCESSING TOBACCO

Requirements for labor are high in tobacco production, exceeding 300 hours per acre (740 hours per hectare).

Culture. Successful tobacco culture depends upon a good supply of well-developed seedlings for transplanting. In the United States these usually are produced in a type of cold frame covered with cheesecloth, plastic, or glass. Tobacco seeds are sprinkled on top of the soil and then tamped firmly into the ground. A high state of fertility and adequate soil moisture must be maintained throughout most of the growing season to ensure vigorous growth.

Tobacco seedlings reach transplant size of 5 to 6 inches (13–15 cm) in 8 to 10 weeks. Transplanting in the southernmost tobacco-growing area begins in late March and extends into June in the north. Thorough soil preparation aids seedlings in gaining an early start in growth, which often determines success or failure of the crop. Generous amounts of commercial fertilizer, and in some cases manure, are used both before transplanting and afterward as a side-dressing (placed near the roots).

The tobacco plant is "topped" (the top removed) when the flower cluster (inflorescence) begins to develop. The purpose is to increase leaf weight and to enhance chemical and physical properties and aroma. Following topping, axillary leaf buds (suckers) begin rapid growth. Formerly, suckers were removed by hand, but they are now controlled with chemical growth regulators.

The tobacco plant is attacked by fungi, bacteria, viruses, nematode worms, and insects. Control of most diseases is centered on the development of disease-resistant tobacco varieties. In certain areas of the United States, economic production of tobacco would not be possible without them. Some varieties are resistant to as many as five diseases. For best results, disease-resistant varieties should be grown in rotation with selected crops other than tobacco. Agricultural chemicals are used to control insects and some of those diseases for which resistant varieties are not available.

Harvesting. Two methods of harvesting—priming and stalk cutting—are employed. Flue-cured and cigar wrapper tobaccos (which are air cured) are primed—that is, leaves are removed as they ripen. All other tobacco is stalk-cut. Before being hung in curing barns, stalk-cut tobacco is speared onto laths ("tobacco sticks"), and prime-harvested leaves are strung on sticks. By another method loose green leaves are compressed into metal racks for bulk curing.

Curing. There are three principal methods, with many variations, of curing tobacco. In *air-curing*, the tobacco is sheltered but cured primarily under natural weather conditions. In *flue-curing*, the tobacco is cured in heated air but not subjected to smoke or odors. Flue-cured tobacco is usually yellowish to reddish orange in color, thin to medium in body, and mild in flavor. In *fire-curing*, the tobacco is cured in heated air, mostly from wood fires, and is in contact with the smoke. A fourth method, curing in open air or direct sunlight, is practiced in Asia and other parts of the world.

During the curing process the leaves lose much of their stored food supply and part of their water content. Complex chemical changes begun during the ripening of the leaves continue until the leaves are dry. These changes include hydrolysis of proteins to amino acids, amines, and ammonia, and hydrolysis of carbohydrates to sugar, then carbon dioxide and water. In flue-curing, the leaf is dried rapidly after the yellow, or bright, color is set, and chemical changes are arrested before completion. The drying process continues for a longer period in fire-curing and even longer in air-curing. The carbohydrate content is essentially depleted during the curing of air-cured tobacco.

Curing barns are 18 to 20 feet (5.5–6 meters) square or are rectangular in shape and of varying size. They may be 18 to 20 feet tall. Well-arranged ventilators permit flow of ambient air around suspended stalks of stalk-cut tobacco or around suspended leaves of flue-cured and cigar wrapper tobacco. Supplemental heat is used on air-cured tobacco during inclement weather.

In both fire-curing and flue-curing, the barns are tightly closed to contain the heat, except for a limited period early in the cure. In fire-curing, heat is supplied by open hardwood fires in the barn. Smoke permeates the tobacco above and escapes around the eaves of the barn. In flue-curing—the term derives from the iron flues formerly used to carry heat through the barn—open-flame gas or oil heaters are used. Bulk-curing, an innovation of flue-curing, involves forcing heated air through lightly compressed leaves in specially constructed curing barns.

Further Processing. To make tobacco suitable for consumption, the cured leaves must be fermented and aged. By this means, the leaves are brought to their peak of odor and aroma, and their harshness or bitter taste is eliminated. This preliminary process must be carefully managed, for inadequate aging or fermentation cannot be overcome in manufacture.

Most tobacco products in the United States contain various amounts of sweeteners, flavorings, or humectants to enhance or modify their natural flavor and aroma. The use of additives is restricted in some countries, notably the United Kingdom.

UNITED STATES TOBACCO INDUSTRY

Flue-cured tobacco is produced in the southeastern Coastal Plain and Piedmont from Virginia to Florida. This type is the major component of American cigarettes, and cigarettes account for about 95% of its use. Flue-cured tobacco is also the principal export type of American tobacco.

Class 2, or fire-cured tobacco, is produced in central and western Virginia and in Tennessee and Kentucky. Varieties of tobacco grown in the fire-cured districts have broad, dark green leaves, heavily drooping and gummy to the touch. After curing, the leaves are light to dark brown in color and strong in flavor. Principal American use is in the manufacture of snuff. In some other countries, it is used in cigars and chewing tobacco.

All other United States tobacco is air-cured and, except for the light air-cured burley and Maryland types, is used principally in cigars. Burley is now widely grown in Kentucky and Tennessee, to a lesser extent in Ohio, Indiana, Virginia, West Virginia, and North Carolina, and its culture has spread to many other countries. The culture of Maryland type tobacco has persisted in the southern part of that state since earliest colonial days.

Cigar tobaccos are classified according to their principal use—that is, as filler, binder, or

TOBACCO TYPES USED IN AMERICAN TOBACCO PRODUCTS

Product	Types used
Cigarettes	Flue-cured, burley, Maryland, imported Turkish
Cigars	Filler, binder, wrapper, imported Cuban and Philippine, some Maryland, fire-cured, dark air-cured
Chewing tobacco	
Plug	Flue-cured, burley, dark air-cured, some fire-cured
Twist	One sucker, burley, fire-cured
Fine-cut	Burley, Green River
Scrap chewing	Cigar leaf
Smoking tobacco (Pipe tobacco, roll-your-own)	Burley, flue-cured, dark air-cured
Snuff	Fire-cured, some dark air-cured

BRUCE ROBERTS, FROM RAPHO GUILLUMETTE

TOBACCO AUCTION. In the southern United States tobacco may be sold in lots at the warehouse, the auctioneer calling bids in a rapid, sing-song voice.

wrapper. All are also used for other products—scrap chewing tobacco accounts for much of the crop not used in cigars.

Cigar tobacco districts of major importance are located in New England, Pennsylvania, Ohio, Wisconsin, Georgia, and Florida. Pennsylvania is the most important state, and Lancaster county the most important county, in the production of cigar filler tobacco. Shade-grown cigar wrapper tobacco is grown in the Connecticut Valley and in northern Florida and southern Georgia. Dark air-cured tobaccos are produced in the Green River area of northern Kentucky, southern Kentucky, and northern Tennessee.

TOBACCO INDUSTRY IN OTHER COUNTRIES

Bright tobacco and "flue-cured" are synonymous terms since cigarettes all over the world are made largely of this type; the production and spread of flue-cured tobacco is linked to popularity of the cigarette. Quality of U. S. tobacco has been the standard foreign producers have tried to emulate. Many countries in Africa and South and Central America, as well as Italy and India, have produced a flue-cured type that is generally inferior to the flue-cured tobacco of the United States.

Many countries have native types of leaf, which are air-cured and consumed in various ways. Local tobaccos in India are smoked in bidis, cigars, cheroots, and hookahs. Brazil also has a large production for local consumption, mostly in the form of dark-tobacco cigarettes. Burley tobacco production has spread to many countries since World War II. Increased burley production in Central and South American countries is occurring at the expense of dark native tobaccos.

With the exception of certain areas in the United States, the world's cigar leaf is produced almost entirely within a belt of 15 degrees latitude on either side of the equator. The finest cigar wrapper is produced in Indonesia in a small area along the coast of Sumatra. Java shares with Cuba the reputation for production of the finest quality cigar filler.

Oriental tobaccos, used for making the finest blended cigarettes, are largely produced in the Balkan countries, particularly Turkey, Greece, Yugoslavia, and Bulgaria. Latakia is an oriental type tobacco, produced in Syria, to which additional flavor has been added. This is accomplished by fumigating the tobacco with smoke by burning species of oak and pine. In a sense, this is similar to fire-cured tobacco.

Fire-cured tobacco is among the least important of tobacco types in the world. Malawi vies with Italy to rank in second place behind the United States in the production of fire-cured tobacco.

E. L. MOORE
Tobacco and Sugar Crops Research Branch
U. S. Department of Agriculture

GLOSSARY

Bright Tobacco—A name for flue-cured tobacco, derived from the bright yellowish color of the tobacco.

Burley—Light air-cured tobacco. Second only to flue-cured tobacco as a component of blended cigarettes in the United States. Burley tobacco plants, which have a unique cream or yellow-green color, originated from a few plants observed in a field of dark green tobacco in Brown County, Ohio, in 1864.

Cavendish—Leaf tobacco, softened, sweetened, and pressed into cakes.

Cutters—Fine cigarette leaf just above the lugs and extending slightly above the middle of the plant.

Homogenized Leaf—Tobacco sheet made from scrap leaf, whole leaf, and some stems, ground finely and made into a paste. The process is patterned after paper making.

Latakia—A highly aromatic smoking tobacco produced in Lebanon and Syria. Its name comes from a seaport in Syria.

Lugs—The bottom 4 to 6 leaves of the plant. Those adjacent to the ground are sometimes called sand lugs.

Maryland—Light air-cured cigarette and smoking tobacco produced in southern Maryland.

Perique—A highly aromatic smoking tobacco produced in St. James Parish, Louisiana, by a unique pressure-cure process. Small quantities are used in fancy smoking tobacco.

Virginia—The flue-cured tobacco of world commerce. The principal component of cigarettes in the United States.

Bibliography

Gage, C. E., *USDA Circular 249* (Washington 1933).

Garner, W. W., *The Production of Tobacco* (Philadelphia and Toronto 1946).

Goodspeed, T. H., *The Genus Nicotiana* (Waltham, Mass., 1954).

Hawks, S. N., Jr., *Principles of Flue-cured Tobacco Production* (Madras 1960).

Indian Central Tobacco Committee, *Indian Tobacco* (Madras 1960).

Lucas, G. B., *Diseases of Tobacco* (New York and London 1965).

Moore, E. L., and others, *North Carolina Agricultural Experiment Station Bulletin 378* (Raleigh, N. C., 1952).

Tobacco Research Council, *Research Paper No. 6,* 2d ed., ed. by D. H. Beese (London 1968).

TOBAGO. See TRINIDAD AND TOBAGO.

TOBEY, tō′bē, **Mark** (1890–), American painter, who developed a style of abstract art known as "white writing" or "white line" painting. He was born in Centerville, Wis., on Dec. 11, 1890. As a young man he worked as a fashion illustrator in Chicago, where he attended the Art Institute. In 1911 he went to New York City, where he took up portrait painting. A turning point in his life came about 1918, when he discovered the Bahai faith, with its stress on the unity of life and world religions. In 1922 he settled in Seattle, Wash., where he taught art and learned the techniques of Chinese calligraphy.

During the 1930's, Tobey traveled extensively, and his firsthand contact in the Far East with Oriental art, philosophy, and religion proved crucial in his artistic development. The "white writing" style of his painting after the mid-1930's clearly derives from Oriental brushwork. His attempts through it to express endless energy-filled space and his view of art as a process of exploration and self-discovery are related to Eastern concepts, but these are joined with features of Western abstract art. By the 1950's, Tobey's works were being shown throughout Europe as well as the United States.

NICOLAI CIKOVSKY, JR.
University of Texas

Further Reading: Seitz, William C., *Mark Tobey* (New York 1962).

TOBIAS, tə-bī′əs, **Channing Heggie** (1882–1961), American Negro leader in interracial cooperation. Tobias was born in Augusta, Ga., on Feb. 1, 1882. He graduated from Paine College in 1902 and then studied for the ministry at Drew University. He returned to Paine College to teach in 1905. From 1911 to 1946 he served the Y.M.C.A., first as student secretary and later as senior secretary of the Colored Men's Department.

Outstanding among Tobias' contributions to good race relations in the 1930's and 1940's were his services as an intermediary between Negroes and the White House. President Truman appointed him a member of the President's Committee on Civil Rights in 1946. Tobias was a trustee of the Phelps Stokes Fund from 1946 to 1953 and also served a number of other agencies that promoted race relations. Tobias died in New York City on Nov. 5, 1961.

LUTHER H. FOSTER, *Tuskegee Institute*

TOBIN, tō′bin, **Daniel Joseph** (1875–1955), American labor leader, who, as president of the Teamsters Union from 1907 to 1952, led it from the early Gompers era of craft unionism into the modern era of industrial unionism.

He was born in Miltown Malbay, County Clare, Ireland, in 1875 and went to Cambridge, Mass., at the age of 14. As a Boston Teamsters leader, Tobin participated in the founding of the International Brotherhood of Teamsters in 1903. He also served the parent American Federation of Labor as treasurer (1917–1928) and as vice president (1935–1955). He was a strong supporter of Samuel Gompers, of the AFL, and of craft unionism. But his Teamsters, ironically, became a stronghold of the industrial type of unionism while still declaring its dedication to the craft type.

Tobin, as an advocate of "business unionism," usually exercised moderation in his demands. He favored voluntary arbitration and almost always used it instead of the strike. He was strongly opposed to compulsory arbitration.

Highly political in his approach to national problems, Tobin was an ardent New Dealer and a close friend of President Franklin D. Roosevelt. He served as chairman of the labor division of the Democratic party in all four of Roosevelt's presidential campaigns. Interested in unionism around the world, he represented the AFL or the U. S. government at many international labor conferences. He died in Indianapolis, Ind., on Nov. 14, 1955.

HARVEY L. FRIEDMAN
University of Massachusetts

TOBIT, Book of, tō′bit, a book regarded as belonging to the Old Testament by Roman Catholic and Eastern Orthodox Christians but to the Apocrypha by Jews and Protestants (see APOCRYPHA). It is preserved from ancient times only in the Greek form in the Septuagint. Although the story is set in Mesopotamia it is not thought to have originated there because of its inaccurate description of the local topography. Most experts assign it to Palestine or Egypt.

Because of irreconcilable differences in details in its several versions it is difficult to reconstruct a single, original form of the story. Probably there was an outline that assumed a fixed sequence about 200 B. C. but still permitted freedom of elaboration in each telling.

Formally the book is a travel narrative. Tobias, son of the suffering but faithful Jew Tobit, recoups the family fortunes by means of a dangerous journey on which he recovers a debt and acquires an heiress wife. In this Tobias is helped by the disguised angel, Raphael, who returns with him and completes the reestablishment of Tobit's fortunes by restoring his sight.

Despite the narrative form this didactic tale belongs with wisdom literature like Proverbs and Job, for it is a guide to right living, not history. This is recognized by the manuscript tradition, which usually places it with the didactic rather than the historical books. It is also indicated by the character of the book itself. It is interested in proverbial wisdom, for example, that is collected in 4:13–19 and 12:6–10, and it draws a moral in chapter 14. Further, its style connects it with the scribal schools that were the custodians of the traditions of wisdom. This is seen in the elaborate speeches and prayers in 3:1–6; 9:15–17; 12:6–15; and 13, and in the imitation of Genesis—for example, Eliezer's journey (Genesis 24) and the Joseph story. This rhetorical and learned style is characteristic of later wisdom literature.

DENNIS J. MCCARTHY, S. J.
Pontifical Biblical Institute, Rome

TOBOGGANING, tə-bog′ə-ning, is the sport of coasting down a snow-covered slope or specially prepared track on a flat, runnerless sled called a toboggan. The vehicle was first used by the North American Indians for hauling supplies and game over the snow, and it serves the same purpose for campers and hunters today. In addition, many participants in winter sports use it for recreation.

Indians made the first toboggans of skins, which they attached to a frame. Later, two or

ERIC M. SANFORD

TOBOGGANNING is an exhilarating pastime that can be enjoyed by people of all ages during the winter season.

three boards lashed together served as a base, with the front end curled up and backward, forming a "hood." A low railing around the sides and back helped keep the goods on the base. Toboggans were narrow so that they could be dragged through the forest by hand or by dogs.

The modern toboggan is constructed of hard, polished woods, and the boards are held together by crosspieces on the nongliding surface. A hand rope around the sides and back helps riders stay on the vehicle. Toboggans vary from 3 to 8 feet (0.91–2.43 meters) in length and from 1½ to 4 feet (0.45–1.21 meters) in width. The longest toboggan will support 4 or 5 riders seated one behind the other, with knees bent and feet straddling the rider ahead. The front rider braces his feet against the hood.

To keep the vehicle on a course without a prepared track or run, the rear rider must guide the toboggan by trailing a foot on one side or the other. Runs were first provided by resorts and country clubs late in the 19th century, the length depending on the terrain available. Rivalry in speed led to tobogganing competitions.

BILL BRADDOCK, *New York "Times"*

TOBRUK, tō-brōōk′, is a port city in northeastern Libya, on the Mediterranean Sea. It has an excellent natural harbor. The city is the trading center for the oases to the south and has several food-processing plants. A pipeline from a major oil field 320 miles (515 km) to the southwest carries oil to Tobruk for transshipment to Europe.

Tobruk was the scene of bitter fighting during World War II. British forces captured the city from the Italians in January 1941 and held it through an 8-month siege by German and Italian troops led by Gen. Erwin Rommel. Tobruk fell to the Germans in June 1942 but was retaken by the British in November. Population: (1964) 15,867.

TOCANTINS RIVER, tō-kən-tēns′, a river of Brazil, is one of the largest tributaries of the Amazon River. It rises in the central plateau of Goiás state and flows northward for about 1,680 miles (2,600 km). It receives the waters of the Araguaia River near São João and empties into the Pará River, a principal distributary of the Amazon, about 50 miles (80 km) southwest of Belém. The Tocantins is 8 miles (13 km) wide at its mouth, spilling bright blue waters into the muddy Pará.

The river is navigable by riverboats in its middle section, upstream from the town of Carolina, and by oceangoing vessels in its lowermost course, up to Tucuruí, which is some 200 miles (320 km) from Belém. In the 1960's construction was begun on a railroad to bypass the rapids upstream from Tucuruí. The Tocantins drains a region that is sparsely populated but that offers promise of future development.

KEMPTON E. WEBB, *Columbia University*

TOCCATA, tə-kot′ə, a musical composition for a keyboard instrument, with full chords and running passages, and often containing a fugue. The word comes from the Italian *toccare,* meaning "to touch," indicating that the notes are quickly played—merely touched, not held.

The toccata originated early in the 16th century. The first pieces usually began with a few chords, to which were added more and more runs and ornamentation. Claudio Merulo (1533–1604) alternated the early free idiomatic style with fugal sections, and Johann Sebastian Bach (1685–1750) developed the form even further along these lines. Bach's Toccata and Fugue in D minor is probably the best-known example.

TOCHIGI, tō-chē-gē, is a prefecture in Japan, in west central Honshu. The prefecture, which has an area of 2,485 square miles (4,970 sq km) includes many fertile plains and a mountainous western section that is part of Nikko National Park. Its capital and chief city is Utsunomiya. The city of Tochigi, a farm marketing center 50 miles (80 km) north of Tokyo, was the capital from 1871 to 1884. Population: (1965) of the prefecture, 1,521,656; of the city, 74,671.

TOCOPHEROL, tō-kof′ə-rôl, also known as vitamin E or the antisterility vitamin, any of six substances essential in the human diet. Because the vitamin is so common, human vitamin E deficiency seldom occurs. The tocopherols are antioxidants, and the symptoms of deficiency are apparently the result of peroxidation of unsaturated fatty acids with subsequent degradation of the membranes of cells and cell organelles. Rats deficient in vitamin E are sterile. In the female, fetal death and reabsorption of the fetuses occur early in pregnancy; in the male the spermatazoa are immotile. These defects can be corrected by administration of the vitamin.

The tocopherols consist of a pair of rings with an attached branched chain. They are designated as α-, β-, γ-, and so forth, tocopherol, and they differ structurally only in the number and position of the methyl groups substituted on the aromatic ring α-tocopherol, which is particularly abundant in wheat germ and cottonseed oils, is the most widely distributed and has the greatest biological activity.

PETER OESPER
St. Lawrence University

TOCQUEVILLE, tōk'vil, **Alexis de** (1805–1859), French historian and political theorist, whose studies of American democracy and the French Revolution were two of the most original and influential books of 19th century social science.

Charles Alexis de Tocqueville was born in Verneuil on July 29, 1805, into a family of Norman aristocrats. Tocqueville studied law and embarked on a judicial career. In 1831 he arranged to be sent to study the U. S. prison system. His observations resulted first in a report on American penitentiaries and then in his first masterpiece, *De La Démocratie en Amérique* (*Democracy in America*), the first parts of which appeared in 1835. The book was an enormous success, and French critics hailed Tocqueville as the greatest political thinker since Montesquieu. See also Democracy in America.

Tocqueville became a member of the Académie des Sciences Morales et Politiques in 1838 and the Académie Française in 1841. In 1839 he was elected to the Chamber of Deputies. Neither his health nor his temperament suited him for political leadership, and he was a cabinet minister only briefly, as foreign minister in 1849. Tocqueville was a moderate liberal who tried to balance equality with liberty. After the Revolution of 1848 broke out, however, he vigorously attacked the socialists, holding them responsible for the violence. He consequently approved of the repressive policies that followed. When Louis Napoléon seized power in 1851, on the other hand, Tocqueville protested and was arrested. After his release he returned to private life, devoting himself to his second masterpiece, *L'Ancien Régime et la révolution* (1856; *The Old Regime and the Revolution*). He died in Cannes on April 16, 1859.

Evaluation. During the 19th century Tocqueville was widely considered one of the foremost proponents of liberalism. His modern reputation rests on his contributions to sociology and history. He himself asserted that his life's goal was "to show man how to escape tyranny." He thought that liberty was threatened by the progress of the "principle of equality" embodied in democratic regimes, but he also believed that the spread of democracy was inevitable and irreversible. He therefore undertook to appraise the threat and the promise of democracy. He concluded that although democracy equalized social classes and fostered wider political participation, it also tended to destroy traditional institutions that could protect the individual from despotic state power. Consequently, he warned that safeguards had to be erected against democracy's potential "tyranny of the majority," which could erode freedom and individuality.

Tocqueville's great historical essay, *The Old Regime and the Revolution*, radically altered the historical interpretation of the French Revolution, for he showed that the Revolution did not constitute a sharp break with the past. He stressed rather the essential continuity between the old regime and the Revolution. He argued that the monarchy's long effort to centralize and rationalize French institutions was completed by the Revolution, which he described as "the sudden and violent termination of a task at which ten generations had labored."

Richard T. Bienvenu
University of Missouri

Further Reading: Herr, Richard, *Tocqueville and the Old Regime* (Princeton 1962).

TODA. See India—*The People* (Tribal Peoples).

TODAI-JI, a temple at Nara, Japan. See Japan—*Architecture* (The Ancient Period).

TODD, Alexander Robertus (1907–), British organic chemist, who was awarded the 1957 Nobel Prize in chemistry for his work on the synthesis of nucleotides.

Todd was born in Glasgow, Scotland, on Oct. 2, 1907. He graduated from the University of Glasgow and received his doctorate from Oxford University in 1933. He joined the faculty of the University of Edinburgh in 1934 and began work on vitamin B_1 (thiamine). In 1936 he joined the Lister Institute of Preventive Medicine in London and carried out an independent synthesis of vitamin B_1 and the related thiochrome and began studies on the structure and synthesis of vitamin E. Two years later, Todd became head of the chemistry department at the University of Manchester, where he completed his work on vitamin E and began studies on the constituents of hashish. He worked on various government projects during World War II. In 1944 he became professor of organic chemistry at Cambridge University and in 1952 chairman of the British Council on Science Policy.

While working on the synthesis of thiamine, Todd realized that it and other B vitamins function as parts of the nucleotides—which are compounds of phosphoric acid, a sugar, and a nitrogenous base—and also function as coenzymes in many biochemical processes in the body. Todd then began to study the synthesis of nucleotides. He produced nucleotides of ribose and deoxyribose sugars with purine and pyrimidine nitrogenous bases, which led to an understanding of the sugar-base portion of nucleotides. Phosphorylation studies then led to the controlled synthesis of nucleotides that functioned as coenzymes and as the building blocks of nucleic acids. This work led to many important advances in chemistry and biochemistry and made it possible to study the implications of the Watson-Crick model of DNA and other nucleic acids more effectively.

Todd was knighted in 1954 and in 1962 was raised to the peerage as Baron Todd of Trumpington.

Aaron J. Ihde
University of Wisconsin

TODD, Thomas (1765–1826), American judge and associate justice of the U. S. Supreme Court. He was born near Dunkirk in King and Queen County, Va., on Jan. 23, 1765. He served briefly in the Revolutionary War and settled in Kentucky, becoming clerk of many conventions then being held to devise a means of separating Kentucky from Virginia. After studying law evenings, he was admitted to the bar. When Kentucky became a state in 1792 he became clerk of its court of appeals. In 1801 he became a judge of that court and in 1806 its chief justice. An expert on real property, he wrote decisions that laid the foundations for Kentucky land law.

Appointed by Jefferson to the Supreme Court in 1807, Todd served 19 years but wrote only a dozen opinions. He aligned himself with John Marshall and concurred in his nationalist decisions. Todd died in Frankfort, Ky., on Feb. 7, 1826.

Leo Pfeffer
Author of "This Honorable Court"

TODY, tō′dē, any of a family of small, colorful birds found in the forests of the West Indies. They are related to kingfishers and motmots. Two species occur on Hispaniola—and one species each on Cuba, Jamaica, and Puerto Rico.

Todies are from 3½ to 4 inches (9–10 cm) long and have relatively long, flattened bills, short tails, and rounded wings. They are generally bright green above and grayish or white below. The flanks are pink or yellow, and in adults, the throat is bright red.

Inquisitive, rather tame birds, todies often perch quietly on low, shaded twigs and dart out to capture insects. They also eat small lizards. In flight, the tody's narrow wing feathers produce a characteristic whirring rattle. Each species also has a distinctive call.

A. W. AMBLER, FROM NATIONAL AUDUBON SOCIETY

Cuban tody (*Todus multicolor*)

Todies use their bills to dig horizontal burrows in an earthbank and then to clear an enlarged nest chamber. Two to four relatively large rounded white eggs are laid. Both parents incubate the eggs and feed the young.

Todies (genus *Todus*) make up the family Todidae of the order Coraciiformes.

George E. Watson, *Smithsonian Institution*

TOE. See Foot.

TOGA, tō′gə, a draped outer garment worn by the citizens of ancient Rome. It was an oblong of wool, which was draped over the left arm, around the back, under the right arm, across the chest, and over the left shoulder. The toga, derived from the Greek himation and the small Etruscan toga, was the mark of the freeborn citizen. In early times it was worn by both sexes and all classes of citizens, but eventually it became the prerogative of aristocratic men. During the republic the toga was enlarged to a semicircle about 6 by 18 feet (2 by 6 meters). Under the empire it became longer and narrower, requiring such complex draping that most aristocrats substituted simpler garments. It was retained, however, for state occasions and for some officials.

The color and quality of the toga indicated the status of the wearer. The *toga pura* (*toga virilis*), of fine white wool, was assumed by youths on reaching manhood. The *toga praetexta,* white with a purple band on the straight edge, was worn by young people and, later, some magistrates. For mourners the *toga pulla,* of dark material, was customary. The *toga picta,* ornately embroidered or painted in purple and gold, was the dress of generals at their triumphal processions and of the emperor.

(LOUVRE) GIRAUDON

Statue of Emperor Tiberius illustrates draping of toga.

Kay Staniland, *Gallery of English Costume Platt Hall, Manchester, England*

TOGLIATTI, tōl-yä′tē, **Palmiro** (1893–1964), Italian Communist leader. A brilliant, pragmatic theoretician, he promoted the doctrine of polycentrism, which holds that each nation should build its own road to communism.

Of lower middle-class origins, he was born in Genoa on March 26, 1893. He obtained a doctorate in law at the University of Turin in 1915. Togliatti soon became a collaborator of Antonio Gramsci in the Socialist party, and in 1921 he joined the faction that founded the Italian Communist party. Repeatedly jailed by the Fascists, Togliatti became in 1926 secretary general in exile of the illegal Communist party. In 1935, with Joseph Stalin's support, Togliatti was appointed secretary of the Communist International (Comintern). Togliatti served in Spain during the Spanish Civil War, fleeing to France at the war's end in 1939. He later took refuge in the Soviet Union. He reentered Italy early in 1944, cooperating at first with the monarchy. He participated in several coalition governments until 1946.

When the leftist parties were ousted from power in 1947, he led, with Pietro Nenni's Socialists, a strenuous opposition to the government. Surviving an attempt on his life in 1948, he continued to lead his party, despite some later opposition from pro-Chinese factions, until his sudden death while on vacation in Yalta, USSR, on Aug. 21, 1964. He was so highly regarded in the Soviet Union that a Russian city, Tolyatti, was named after him.

Sergio Barzanti
Fairleigh Dickinson University

MARC AND EVELYNE BERNHEIM, FROM RAPHO GUILLUMETTE

KINDERGARTEN in Lomé cares for the young children of working mothers. It was set up and is maintained by the government.

TOGO, tō'gō, is a republic in West Africa. From 1919 until it became independent in 1960, it was administered by France, first as a League of Nations mandate and later as a United Nations trust territory. Togo is the second-smallest country in West Africa, after Gambia.

The Land. Togo is situated on the Gulf of Guinea at the center of West Africa's southern coast. It has an area of 21,853 square miles (56,599 sq km). A long and narrow country, it extends 375 miles (600 km) north from the Gulf of Guinea but has a maximum width of only 75 miles (120 km).

Togo is divided into five topographical zones. The southernmost part of the country is a low, smooth sandbar running parallel to the coast of the Gulf of Guinea. It is broken by marshy creeks and coastal lagoons, which often run far inland. North of the coastal lagoons lies the Watyi plateau (*terre de barre*) region, a strip of land 20 to 40 miles (30–60 km) wide and rising to 300 feet (90 meters) above sea level. The next region inland is an undulating plateau that rises gradually to 1,500 feet (450 meters).

North of the plateau the land rises sharply into a range of mountains extending diagonally across Togo from southwest to northeast. In the south these are called the Togo Mountains, whereas in the north they are known as the Atakora Mountains. The range averages 2,000 feet (600 meters) above sea level. North of the mountains stretches a plain cut by a shallow fault extending eastward from Ghana.

Togo has two rather distinct climatic zones. In the south the climate is hot and humid, with mean monthly temperatures of 70°–87°F (21°–31°C). Annual rainfall averages from 30 inches (760 mm) along the coast to 50 inches (1,270 mm) closer to the mountains. Peak rainy periods occur in May-June and September. North of the mountains the climate is generally cooler, with mean monthly temperatures of 67°–72°F (19°–22°C). Annual rainfall averages from 41 inches (1,040 mm) near the mountains to 51 inches (1,300 mm) in the far north. The rainy season extends from May to October.

The People. Togo had an estimated population of 1.8 million in 1969. The majority of its inhabitants are West African Negroid peoples who speak languages of the Twi and southern Nigerian branches of the Kwa subfamily. Descendants of prehistoric Sangoan hunting and gathering peoples, they inhabit the southern and central portions of the country. The peoples living in the northern part of Togo are of Sudanic ancestry and speak languages of the Voltaic subfamily. Their forebears settled in this area during a period of migration westward from the Sudan-Nile region in the 10th to 13th centuries.

Virtually all of Togo's peoples live primarily by subsistence agriculture. There are about 18 major ethnic groups. The most important in the south are the Ewe, the Mina, and the Watyi. In the central region the major peoples are the Akposo, the Kebu, and the Ana. Of the Sudanic peoples in the north, the most important are the Naudeba, the Basari, the Konkomba, the Moba, the Kabré, and the Tem.

The Ewe people have played the major role in the national life of modern Togo. Occupying the southernmost and richest third of the nation, they have become the most numerous, the best educated, and the most prosperous of Togo's peoples. The Ewe are widely employed both in government and the private sector of the economy and lead mostly urban lives. The peoples farther north remain closer to the land, maintain their distinctive, traditional mode of dress—brilliantly colored togas—and have infrequent contact with the larger towns of the south. While striving for modernization, Togolese governments usually respected tribal traditions.

Animism is the predominant religion of about 75% of the Togolese, while an estimated 20% of the population is Christian. There is also a small Islamic community.

Togo has a literacy rate of about 10%. Most of the schools are in the south, but efforts to expand educational facilities in the north have begun. The school attendance rate for Togo as a whole averages 39%, with 73% in Lomé, the capital. About half of the students at all levels attend mission schools.

At the elementary level in the early 1970's there were some 800 schools, 3,000 teachers, and 158,000 students. At the secondary level there were almost 60 schools, 500 teachers, and 12,000 students. There were also 19 technical schools with 70 teachers and 1,800 students. Three teacher training colleges graduated a total of about 400 students each year.

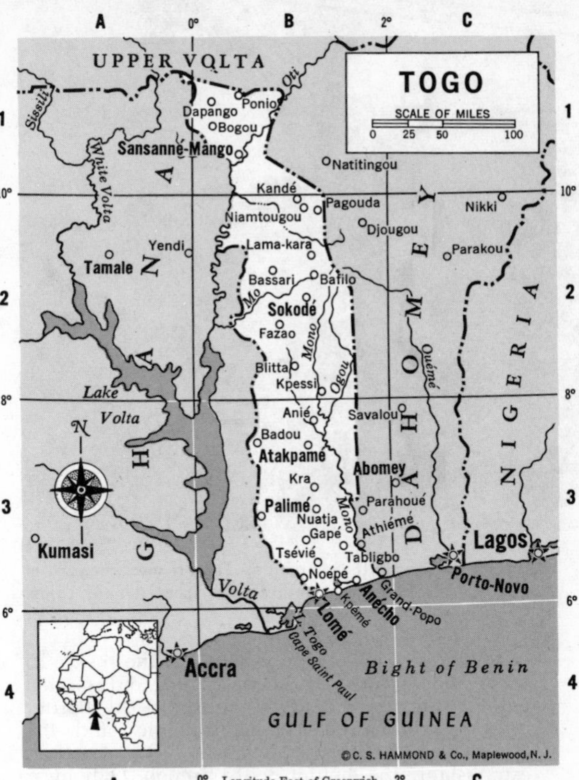

In 1959 the government established the École Togolaise d'Administration, to which candidates with a secondary education are admitted by examination and receive technical training to prepare them for government employment. Since 1965, Togo has been operating, in cooperation with Dahomey, the Institut d'Enseignement Supérieur du Bénin, which teaches literature and law at Lomé and science and medicine at Porto-Novo, Dahomey. Other Togolese students, many on government scholarships, receive higher education abroad.

Togo has about 65 doctors, or one for every 25,000 inhabitants. Most of the physicians work in Lomé.

The Economy. Togo's economy is beset by problems common to many African countries. It is based on only a few products, is hampered by an inadequate transportation system, and is overdependent on foreign aid. Efforts to improve the economy are hindered by the country's lack of natural and financial resources. Thus Togo's economic prospects are clearly limited. However, its economy is diversified enough to protect it somewhat from fluctuations in world prices. Since only about one fourth of the land is under productive cultivation at any one time, agricultural output could be increased substantially.

Agriculture is the main occupation in Togo, involving about 90% of the population and generating about 70% of all exports and 50% of the gross domestic product. Subsistence agriculture is practiced throughout the country on small family farms. Togo's chief export crops are coffee, palm oil kernels, cacao, and cotton. Other important commercial crops include coconuts and peanuts. Togo's forest reserves, covering about 15,000 square miles (39,000 sq km) and including important stands of teakwood, are being exploited.

Important phosphate deposits, with reserves totaling about 100 million tons, were discovered near Lomé in 1953. Phosphate mining was begun in the 1960's, and phosphates have become Togo's most important export, representing about 40% of total exports in value. The Togolese government holds 20% of the shares in the phosphate industry.

In March 1968 an agreement was signed with a U. S. company to begin drilling for petroleum off the coast of Togo. An Italian company is helping to exploit a dolomite deposit at Gnaoulou.

Manufacturing industries make up only a small part of Togo's economy. Industrial activities include the primary processing of phosphates, and cotton and kapok ginning and starch and sugar refining.

Attempts to diversify Togo's agriculture and develop its industry have been hampered by an underdeveloped system of transportation. Roads remain the most important factor affecting transportation. There are about 750 miles (1,200 km) of good roads within the country, but an additional 2,200 miles (3,500 km) of roads are usually passable only during the dry seasons.

There are also about 300 miles (500 km) of government-owned railroad, connecting Lomé with Anécho, Palimé, and Blitta. The phosphate industry is served by its own railroad. Major towns in Togo are linked by a domestic airline, and four international airlines connect Lomé with Paris and major West African cities. The port of Lomé, financed and built mostly by West Germany, was completed in 1968.

Most of Togo's foreign trade is within the franc zone, primarily with France. Other important trading partners include West Germany, the Netherlands, and Belgium. Since independence, Togo has had an average trade deficit of about $12 million a year.

History and Government. Until the 19th century, parts of what is now Togo were under the influence of a succession of powerful kingdoms, which were centered outside Togo's present borders. In the north, in the Upper Volta, the Mossi Empire flourished between the 1200's and the 1800's. In the west, in Ghana, the Ashanti Confederation retained its power until the late 1800's. In the east, the Kingdom of Dahomey thrived from 1625 to 1894.

German Rule. In 1884 a German explorer, Gustav Nachtigal, negotiated a treaty with several Ewe kings at Togoville. The treaty established a German protectorate over an area extending about 15 miles (24 km) along the coast and

INFORMATION HIGHLIGHTS

Official Name: République Togolaise (Republic of Togo).
Head of State: President.
Head of Government: President.
Area: 21,853 square miles (56,599 sq km).
Boundaries: *North,* Upper Volta; *east,* Dahomey; *south,* Gulf of Guinea; *west,* Ghana.
Population: 1,800,000 (1969 est.).
Capital: Lomé (1968 est., 126,000).
Languages: French (official); tribal languages.
Religions: Animism, Christianity, Islam.
Monetary Unit: CFA franc.
Weights and Measures: Metric system.
Flag: Five alternating stripes of green and yellow. A 5-pointed white star is at the center of a red square in upper left corner. See also FLAG.
National Anthem: *Terre de Nos Aïeux* (*Land of Our Fathers*).

MARC AND EVELYNE BERNHEIM, FROM RAPHO GUILLUMETTE

PHOSPHATE MINING provides Togo's most important export. The phosphate deposits are located near Lomé.

3 miles (5 km) inland. During the next 15 years the Germans pushed inland and gained more territory. A treaty establishing the border between Germany's Togoland colony and the British Gold Coast was signed in 1897. Another, establishing the border with French Dahomey, was negotiated in 1899.

During the German period, Lomé was chosen as the capital and a jetty was built there. Three railroads were constructed to link the city with the central region, and a road system was built between principal population centers in the southern half of the country. But German administration was harsh and exploitative. Large numbers of Togolese were jailed or subjected to forced labor.

Mandate and Trusteeship. When World War I began in 1914, British and French colonial troops entered Togoland, and the Germans surrendered unconditionally. The colony was divided provisionally into western and eastern halves, with Lomé and most of the rail lines in the western part under British control. In 1919 the French and British agreed on a new division that gave France control of the entire coastline and the railroad system. The spheres thus established were confirmed in 1922 when the League of Nations issued mandates for their administration and again in 1946 when they were placed under the UN Trusteeship System.

Under both the mandates and the trusteeships, the British administered their sphere as an integral part of their Gold Coast colony. When the Gold Coast became independent in 1957, British Togoland was included in the new state.

The French administered their sphere of Togoland as a separate dependency. Under French administration the port of Lomé was improved, rail lines were extended northward, and the mileage of passable roads was doubled.

In 1955 the French National Assembly approved a statute that loosened French administrative control over Togoland. However, the French government retained some important powers—notably over defense, foreign affairs, and currency. By this time, a number of Togolese political parties had come into existence: the Parti Togolais du Progrès (PTP), headed by Nicholas Grunitzky; the Comité de l'Unité Togolaise (CUT), headed by Sylvanus Olympio; and the Union des Chefs et des Populations du Nord, later to become the Union Démocratique des Populations Togolaises (UDPT). A fourth political group, the Mouvement de la Jeunesse Togolaise (JUVENTO), was initially formed in 1951 as the youthful, militant wing of the CUT, but by 1959 it had assumed the character of a separate opposition party.

On Sept. 10, 1956, the PTP's Grunitzky was appointed by the French to be the first prime minister of the proposed Autonomous Republic of Togo. On October 28 a popular referendum was held to confirm its establishment. According to the French, 71% of the registered voters approved the statute, and France requested the United Nations to terminate Togo's trusteeship status. However, Olympio of CUT lodged a formal protest at the United Nations, claiming that the referendum had been rigged. The United Nations then refused to end Togo's trusteeship status until elections for the proposed legislature were held under UN sponsorship. The elections took place on April 27, 1958, and Olympio's party won 29 of the 46 seats. On May 16, Olympio was installed as prime minister by a unanimous vote of the legislature. In November a resolution ending the trusteeship of Togo was adopted at the U. N. On April 27, 1960, Togo became fully independent.

Independence. After coming to power, Olympio solidified his position, gradually eliminating meaningful opposition parties. However, on Jan. 13, 1963, he was assassinated by a group of Togolese veterans of the French army who, on returning home, had felt frustrated on finding no vacancies for them in the new national army. Shortly after seizing power, the 9-man insurrectionary committee announced that it had called upon Grunitzky to head a provisional regime. Grunitzky abrogated the 1961 constitution and dissolved the National Assembly. He proclaimed a general amnesty and announced that political parties formerly prohibited or restricted could be reestablished. In April representatives of Togo's four parties agreed on a single, evenly divided slate for the new National Assembly, which was approved in elections held on May 7.

Grunitzky served as president for four years. On Nov. 21, 1965, armed civilians occupied the government radio station and announced that "the army" had seized power. However, a detachment of the Togolese army, under Chief of Staff Lt. Col. Étienne Eyadema, recaptured the station and arrested the insurgents.

Eyadema announced that he was negotiating the formation of a new government with Grunitzky, but on Jan. 13, 1967, he instituted direct military rule. Several months later he assumed the country's presidency. He dissolved Togo's four political parties and appointed a committee to draw up a new constitution, promising "free and democratic" elections and a return to civilian government. On Nov. 29, 1969, a new universal political party, the Rassemblement du Peuple Togolais, was formed in Lomé and elected Eyadema as its president.

VICTOR D. DU BOIS
American Universities Field Staff

Further Reading: Lewis, William H., ed., *French-Speaking Africa* (New York 1965); Morgenthau, Ruth S., *Political Parties in French-Speaking West Africa* (New York 1964); Thompson, Virginia, and Adloff, Richard, *French West Africa* (Stanford, Calif., 1957).

TOGO HEIHACHIRO, tō-gō hā-hä-chē-rō (1848–1934), Japanese admiral. He was born in Kyushu on Jan. 27, 1848. He joined the Satsuma provincial navy at the age of 18 and became a cadet in the new imperial Japanese Navy in 1870. After eight years of naval training in England, he was commissioned a lieutenant in 1878.

As commander of the cruiser *Naniwa,* Togo created an international stir at the outbreak of war with China in 1894 by sinking the British steamer *Kowching* while it was carrying Chinese troops. In October 1903, as vice admiral, he was appointed commander in chief of the combined Japanese fleet, a position he held throughout the Russo-Japanese War (1904–1905). During the war he blockaded the Russian Far Eastern naval forces in Port Arthur and Vladivostok, securing the communications of the Japanese armies in Korea and Manchuria. He inflicted a series of defeats on the Russians, culminating in the destruction of their Baltic fleet in the Battle of Tsushima on May 27-28, 1905.

Promoted to admiral in 1904 and to admiral of the fleet in 1913, Togo was chief of the naval staff in 1905–1909 and a member of the high military council for the rest of his life. He was made a count in 1907 and a marquis just before his death in Tokyo on May 30, 1934.

George Fielding Eliot
Author of "Bombs Bursting in Air"

TOGOLAND, tō'gō-land, was a German dependency on the southern coast of West Africa. It was divided between France and Britain in 1919.

A German protectorate on the coast was formed in 1884, when the explorer Gustave Nachtigal signed a treaty with Ewe rulers. Over the next 15 years the Germans pushed inland and gained more territory. After Germany's defeat in World War I, a treaty was signed in Paris in 1919 giving the French control of eastern Togoland and the British control of the western portion. These areas became League of Nations mandates in 1922 and United Nations trusteeships in 1946. In 1956 voters in British Togoland chose unification with an independent Gold Coast, and those two territories became independent as Ghana in 1957. French Togoland acquired independence as Togo in 1960.

Victor D. Du Bois
American Universities Field Staff

TOGRUL, tō-grōōl' (died 1063), Turkish tribal chief who, with his brother Chaghri Beg, founded the Seljuk Empire in Persia in the 11th century. Togrul Beg Muhammad was the grandson of Seljuk, a military leader of the Oghuz (Ghuzz) tribe of the Western Turks, who were nomads living east of the Aral Sea. Togrul (also Toghrıl or Tughrul) was born at the end of the 10th century, about the time that these Turks first accepted Islam. The brothers eventually acceded to the leadership of their tribe, but attacks from other Turkish tribal leaders forced them in 1035 to migrate southward across the Oxus River (Amu Darya) into the Ghaznavid province of Khurasan in search of pasturelands.

So weak was the resistance they met that the migration soon developed into a full-scale Turkish invasion that, under Seljuk leadership, within half a century embraced almost the whole Islamic East. The rule was divided between the brothers, Chaghri governing the eastern regions, Togrul the western. Togrul was proclaimed sultan in Nishapur in 1040, and by 1055 he had delivered Baghdad and the Caliph from the control of the heretical Buwayhids (Buyids). Always eager to appear as the champion of orthodox Islam, he further asserted this identity by marrying a daughter of the Caliph in 1062. Togrul died on Sept. 4, 1063, in Rai, his capital.

John R. Walsh, *University of Edinburgh*

TOJO HIDEKI, tō-jō hē-de-kē (1884–1948), Japanese political and military leader. The premier who ordered the attack on Pearl Harbor in 1941, he personified Japanese militarism.

Tojo Eiku (his name before he became premier) was born in Tokyo on Dec. 30, 1884. The son of an army general, he graduated from the Japanese Military Academy in 1905, and 10 years later completed with honors his studies at the army war college. After World War I, he became an exponent of the theory of total war. As head of the mobilization section of the war ministry, he played an important role in drafting the first general mobilization plans of the imperial army. Committed to the principle that Japan's military strength must be rooted in a developed industrial economy, Tojo urged in the early 1930's the reorganization of the army and, at the same time, the integration of the resources of Manchuria with the economy of Japan.

His remarkable abilities as a staff officer led to rapid promotion. After serving as chief of police affairs of the Kwantung army (the Japanese army in China), he became its chief of staff in 1937. He was appointed vice minister of war in May 1938 and director of military aviation in December. In July 1940, as minister of war, he drafted new mobilization plans that strained diplomatic relations with the United States.

In October 1941 he became premier and took the portfolios of war, education, and commerce and industry. Tojo was a virtual dictator from the Japanese attack on Pearl Harbor on Dec 7, 1941, until his resignation from the government on July 19, 1944, as a result of the American victory at Saipan on July 9. Japan surrendered on Sept. 2, 1945, and nine days later Tojo attempted suicide. Condemned by the International Military Tribunal for crimes against humanity, he was hanged in Tokyo on Dec. 23, 1948.

James B. Crowley, *Yale University*

Further Reading: Browne, Courtney, *Tojo: The Last Banzai* (New York 1967).

TOKAIDO, tō-kī-dō, or "Eastern Sea Route," is the name of the highway that connected Tokyo with Kyoto in premodern Japan. The provinces surrounding this route formed a district that was also called Tokaido. The highway ran along the Pacific coast for the most part, and the scenery and stops along it were depicted by Hiroshige (1797–1858) in his color prints the "Fifty-three Stages of the Tokaido."

This same route is now followed by a national highway and two rail lines—the Tokaido Main Line and the high-speed New Tokaido Line.

TOKAY, tō kā', is a rich, robust, amber-hued wine produced since the Middle Ages near the town of Tokaj, Hungary. The Furmint grape from which true Tokay is made grows only in the Carpathian Mountains, near Tokaj. There are three main types of Tokay: Szamorodni, Aszu, and Eszencia. In its best years, Tokay ranks among the world's greatest natural white wines.

Szamorodni types of Tokay, both sweet and dry, are produced in quantity. In good years some grapes are left on the vines until they become transparent and pucker, bursting with juice. The addition of such grapes to the fermentation cask produces the prized Tokaji Aszu, almost a liqueur. The even rarer Tokaji Eszencia, most of which is used to improve Tokaji Aszu, is made from these grapes alone.

TOKELAU ISLANDS, tō′kə-lou, a group of three coral atolls in the central Pacific Ocean, administered as part of New Zealand. The group lies about 300 miles (500 km) north of Western Samoa. It consists of the atolls of Atafu, Nukunono, and Fakaofo and has a total land area of about 4 square miles (10 sq km). The population has a Polynesian culture, which has been influenced by Samoan contacts. Agriculture and fishing are the basic economies.

The islands were discovered by the British in 1765 and made a British protectorate in 1877. Britain annexed them under the name Union Islands in 1916 and included them in the Gilbert and Ellice Islands Colony. They were placed under New Zealand's administration in 1926. Renamed the Tokelau Islands in 1946, they were included within the territorial limits of New Zealand in 1949. Population: (1966) 1,900.

HOWARD J. CRITCHFIELD
Western Washington State College

TOKEN MONEY means, chiefly, coins containing metal worth substantially less than their monetary, or face, value. Token money differs from *full-bodied coins,* whose metal and monetary values are approximately equal. So long as the value of coins depended on their metal content, there was little opportunity for token coins to circulate. Once social custom had accepted coins purely as a medium of exchange, however, there was little purpose in using costly materials for them, provided that the government conserved their value by avoiding excessive issue. Many countries, including the United States, no longer use full-bodied coins.

In the evolution of U.S. money the copper half-cent and one-cent coins authorized in 1793 initiated the token principle, which was extended to small silver coins in 1853. In 1965, after the market price of silver rose greatly, Congress voted to cease using silver in the 10-cent and 25-cent coins. Only the 50-cent piece has more than a trifling value as metal.

Occasionally, during periods of monetary disturbance, shortages of official coins have created temporary opportunities for private tokens, issued by banks or merchants, to circulate. Such shortages occurred in the United States during the depression years following 1837, during the Civil War, and occasionally at other times in remote areas. Paper currency and bank deposits have occasionally been classed as token money.

PAUL B. TRESCOTT
Southern Methodist University

TOKLAS, tōk′ləs, **Alice B.** (1877–1967), American literary figure, who was a close associate of the author Gertrude Stein. Miss Toklas was born in San Francisco on April 30, 1877. After meeting Miss Stein in Paris in 1907, she became Miss Stein's secretary, cook, and confidante, and together they presided over a literary salon. She gained wide attention with the publication of *The Autobiography of Alice B. Toklas* (1933), which is actually Miss Stein's memoirs. Miss Toklas' own writings include *The Alice B. Toklas Cook Book* (1954), a mixture of recipes and reminiscences, and her autobiography, *What Is Remembered* (1963). She died in Paris on March 7, 1967. See also STEIN, GERTRUDE.

TOKUGAWA, tō-kōō-gä-wä, is the family name of the line of shoguns that governed Japan from 1603 to 1867. The family first appears in historical records of the 1400's as a minor military power in Mikawa province (now Aichi prefecture) and bearing the surname Matsudaira. Ieyasu, who led the house to national preeminence, adopted the name Tokugawa in 1566, claiming descent from the Minamoto clan, the traditional lineage of shoguns. In 1590, after Toyotomi Hideyoshi pacified the country, Ieyasu became the second most powerful man in Japan. After Hideyoshi's death, Ieyasu crushed a coalition supporting the Toyotomi succession and adopted the title of shogun in 1603.

THE TOKUGAWA SHOGUNS

Ieyasu	1603–1605	Ieshige	1745–1760
Hidetada	1605–1623	Ieharu	1760–1786
Iemitsu	1623–1651	Ienari	1787–1837
Ietsuna	1651–1680	Ieyoshi	1837–1853
Tsunayoshi	1680–1709	Iesada	1853–1858
Ienobu	1709–1712	Iemochi	1858–1866
Ietsugu	1713–1716	Yoshinobu	1866–1867
Yoshimune	1716–1745		

Yoshinobu, the 15th and last of the Tokugawa shoguns, resigned his post in 1867 during a national crisis brought on by the presence of Westerners in Japan. After the Meiji Restoration (1868), the Tokugawa family retained only a small holding in the province of Suruga (now Shizuoka prefecture), but later the head of the house was given the rank of prince in the new nobility.

See also IEYASU; IEMITSU; YOSHIMUNE; HITOTSUBASHI YOSHINOBU; EDO PERIOD; JAPAN—*Early Modern History* and sections on the arts.

JOHN W. HALL
Yale University

TOKUSHIMA, tō-kōō-shē-mä, a city in Japan, is on the northeast coast of Shikoku Island at the mouth of the broad Yoshino River. The city is a seaport, railroad junction, and manufacturing center, with modern cotton textile and furniture industries. It is the home of Tokushima University.

The ruins of the city's castle, which was built toward the end of the 16th century, overlook a fine garden that was laid out at about the same time. Tokushima is noted for its Odori Festival, and for its puppet plays (*bunraku*). One of its best-known residents was Wenceslao de Moraes (1851–1929), who settled there after marrying a local girl and wrote many books in Portuguese about Japan.

Tokushima prefecture, of which the city is the capital, has an area of 1,600 square miles (4,143 sq km). It includes the Yoshino Plain, which is its chief agricultural area, and is surrounded by steep mountains. Population (1965): city, 193,233; prefecture, 815,115.

PRUE DEMPSTER
Author of "Japan Advances"

CONSULATE GENERAL OF JAPAN, N. Y.

Downtown Tokyo, looking west from the Edobashi interchange toward Marunouchi financial district (*upper left*).

TOKYO, tō′kyō, the most populous city in the world, is the capital of Japan and the nation's industrial, financial, and cultural center. Twice during the 20th century the city has had to be rebuilt in large part: first after the disastrous earthquake and fire of 1923, and again after the air raids of World War II. Each reconstruction gave the city a more Western appearance.

Tokyo is situated on the Kanto plain of eastern Honshu island, at the head of Tokyo Bay. Its climate is temperate and humid, with a mean temperature of 38.7° F (3.7° C) in January and 77.2° F (25.1° C) in July. The rainiest periods are June-July and September-October.

Central Tokyo is divided into two sections: a western area containing the chief government offices, many educational institutions, and extensive residential sections; and an eastern commercial area. The main industrial zones are in the western suburbs. The ports of Tokyo and Yokohama are now practically one unit, called Keihin; Tokyo handles mainly domestic trade.

The heart of the city is the moated Imperial Palace complex, most of which was destroyed in World War II and subsequently replaced. Just south of the Imperial Palace is the government quarter, site of the gleaming white National Diet Building, where the Japanese legislature (Diet) meets. The tallest building in Japan when completed in 1936, it escaped war damage and today shares prominence with postwar skyscrapers and Tokyo Tower, a 1,092-foot (333-meter) television and radio tower. East of the palace is the Marunouchi section, with headquarters of many banks and businesses. Farther east, beyond Tokyo Station, the hub of Japan's railroad system, is the Nihombashi commercial district. Its main street, Chuo-dori, leads to the Ginza shopping district farther south.

Tokyo has over 800 parks and gardens, some of them of considerable size and beauty. Ueno Park, north of the downtown district, covers 210 acres (85 hectares) and is the site of some of the city's best-known art and science museums. There are also many shrines in Tokyo. The Meiji Shrine, 3 miles (5 km) west of the Imperial Palace, is dedicated to Emperor Meiji (reigned 1867–1912) and his consort. Set amid magnificent gardens, it is one of Tokyo's most popular religious centers, to which millions throng each year. Of the 200 universities and colleges in the metropolis, the University of Tokyo, founded in 1877, is the best known.

Tokyo, originally called Edo ("Estuary Gate"), first appeared in historical records in the 1100's. It rose to importance in 1457, when a fortress was built there. In 1603 it became the administrative seat of the shoguns, military governors of Japan who had more power than the emperor, who resided in Kyoto. After the shogunate was overthrown, Edo became the new imperial capital in 1869 and was renamed Tokyo ("Eastern Capital").

Tokyo's chief executive, the governor, and its legislative body, the Metropolitan Assembly, are both elected by the inhabitants of Tokyo Metropolis. The metropolitan government was created in 1943, when Tokyo Prefecture, including the city of Tokyo and other cities, as well as towns, villages, and rural areas, became Tokyo Metropolis (*Tokyo-to*). The present 23 self-governing wards corresponding to the old city of Tokyo have an area of 221 square miles (572 sq km). The area of Tokyo Metropolis is 824 square miles (2,133 sq km). Population: (1970 est.) of city proper, 8,658,399; of metropolis, 11,109,453.

TOKYO METROPOLIS

As the hub of governmental, commercial, and intellectual activity in a country of more than 100 million people, Tokyo has an enormous magnetism for the Japanese. In the mid-1960's migration to Tokyo Metropolis was about 650,000 a year. However, largely because of dissatisfaction with housing available in the city, nearly as many were leaving the metropolis, about half of them settling in nearby prefectures. Some 30 million people lived within 100 kilometers (62 miles) of Tokyo Station.

The administrative area under the jurisdiction of the Tokyo metropolitan government contains

JAPAN NATIONAL TOURIST ORGANIZATION

THE NATIONAL DIET BUILDING in Tokyo's government quarter is the legislative center of Japan.

the 23 special wards of Tokyo proper, subsidiary political units counted as cities in their own right, 2 counties, and the Izu and Bonin (Ogasawara) islands in the Pacific Ocean. Each working day, approximately 1,500,000 Japanese who live in outlying "bedroom" communities commute as much as 30 miles (50 km) to their jobs. Traffic congestion, housing problems, air pollution, and demands on public utilities are serious, but the metropolitan government is improving these conditions by planning and steady outlays of money.

Transportation. At peak hours, surface transportation is sometimes stalled for many blocks while police untangle the confusion of automobiles, buses, and other vehicles at key intersections. In Tokyo there is an automobile for about every five residents, a relatively small ratio compared with advanced Western countries. A shortage of road space, however, compresses vehicle movement into a few main arteries. Streets occupy only about 10% of the Tokyo city area, compared with 35% in New York, 26% in Paris, and 23% in London. To relieve its traffic congestion, Tokyo has built elevated express highways and multistoried and underground parking garages.

Public transportation is extensive and excellent, but still insufficient. Tokyo's massive internal transportation needs are served by the National Railway and several private railways. There are also subway and bus lines. The city is served by over 40,000 taxis. Among Tokyo's innovations is the world's first public monorail line. It carries passengers between downtown Tokyo and the Haneda international airport, a distance of 7.5 miles (12 km).

TOKYO'S SUBWAY SYSTEM serves a major segment of the 1.5 million commuters who enter the city daily.

JAPAN NATIONAL TOURIST ORGANIZATION

Housing and Utilities. Tokyo's housing problem appears to be soluble only by a dispersal of industry to other cities. In new apartment buildings erected by the government, space is allocated by lottery, and as many as 100 families often apply for each unit. New housing construction averages about 150,000 family units a year, of which about one third are built by government corporations.

The demand on public utilities is similarly overwhelming. When rainfall is below average, there is strict rationing of water in the most crowded neighborhoods. Fewer than 40% of the city's households occupy dwellings that are connected to water mains for sanitary disposal of sewage. Although the city has more than 2,000 parks and playgrounds, they provide the Tokyo citizenry an average of about one square yard (0.84 sq meter) of recreation space apiece.

City Planning. Although city planning was carried out to a certain extent after the earthquake and fire of 1923, a real attack upon Tokyo's problems awaited the preparations for the 1964 Olympic Games. Plans were made well in advance, under the direction of the national and metropolitan governments. In the period 1961–1970 the city undertook public improvement projects that were to cost more than $2 billion. Much of the program was completed before the Olympics began in October 1964. It included the extension of subway lines and the construction of an elaborate system of elevated expressways. Other forward steps included regulations for smoke abatement, the relocation of industrial plants, new housing, and an expanded park program.

Earthquakes and Fires. Quite apart from its normal urban problems, Tokyo lives under the threat of natural disaster. Originally chosen for its military advantages, the site of Tokyo is subject to earth tremors. The great Kanto earthquake, which struck Tokyo on Sept. 1, 1923, was followed by devastating fires and tremendous loss of life.

The development of fireproof building materials and the use of deep pilings below new ferroconcrete buildings are giving Tokyoites a greater sense of security against the threat of destruction by earthquake and fire. But the city is still many years away from reasonable safety. Most of the new construction is in central Tokyo. The poorer sections of the city, with their wood-and-paper houses, can be destroyed in minutes.

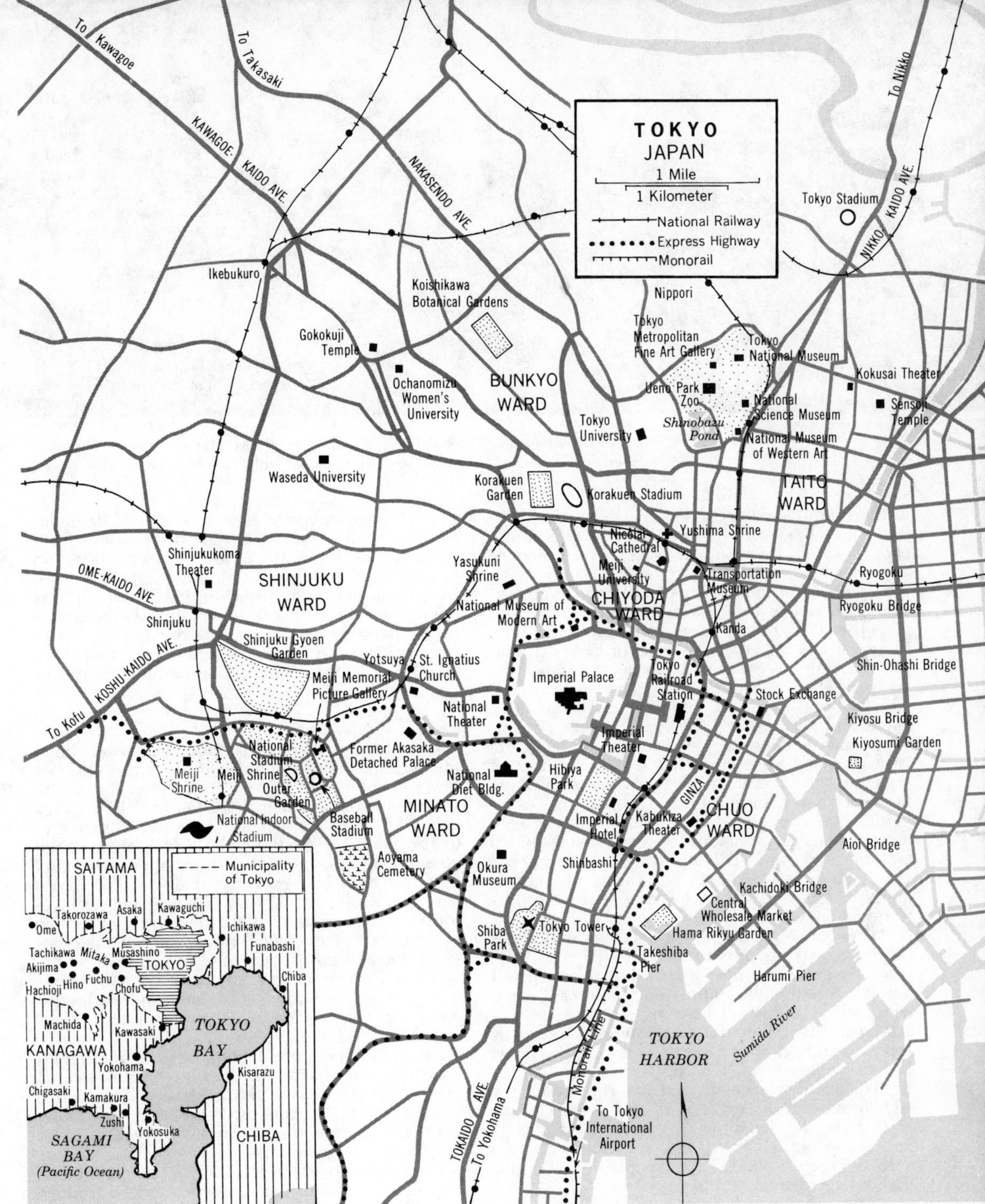

THE ECONOMY

Tokyo's preeminence in Japan's highly productive commercial life had its origin in the growth of a merchant class. The merchants served the needs of the nobles and their large retinues, who congregated around the seat of shogunal power at Edo Castle. The industrial development of Tokyo began with the establishment of a government-operated factory in the mid-1800's, during the last days of shogunal rule. The importation of foreign machinery through the port of Tokyo led to the location of plants in Tokyo to repair and copy the new machines. Wars with China (1894–1895) and Russia (1904–1905) saw the rise of a munitions industry on the shores of Tokyo Bay.

After World War II, the Allied occupation authorities directed all phases of Japan's rehabilitation from their headquarters in Tokyo. It was natural for realistic entrepreneurs to establish their head offices there. Tokyo acquired not only a majority of the industrialists and financiers but also about 10% of the country's population. In 1965, Tokyo accounted for about 13% of Japan's industrial output. Nearly all of the great manufacturing and trading corporations have their head offices in the capital. The banks

NIGEL WATT, FROM PIX

THE IMPERIAL PALACE GROUNDS, situated in the center of Tokyo, are surrounded by a series of moats and high stone walls pierced by several gates.

in the Marunouchi and Nihombashi financial districts and the securities companies on Kabuto-cho, Tokyo's equivalent of Wall Street, finance almost half of the nation's commerce.

Industry. Businessmen from all over the world converge on Tokyo to deal with such famous and powerful Japanese firms as Mitsui and C. Itoh, the great trading combines with branches in major cities on every continent; with Sony, the company that popularized the transistor radio; with Mitsubishi, the shipbuilding and automotive giant; and with Hitachi, Tokyo Shibaura (Toshiba), and Matsushita, leaders in the electric appliance and electronics fields. The makers of Japan's cameras and optical goods—Canon, Nikon, Mamiya, and Yashica—are also located in Tokyo. Within the jurisdictional limits of the Tokyo metropolitan government there are over 80,000 factories and about 230,000 wholesale and retail sales enterprises. About two thirds of Japan's total imports and one third of its exports pass through Tokyo.

Tokyo Port. The port of Tokyo undergoes continual expansion with the filling in of tideland. Several small islands have been constructed out of refuse dumps, and more are planned. They will provide additional berthing space for vessels and space for shore facilities such as railroads and arterial highways. Existing mooring facilities include wharves with berths for vessels up to 20,000 tons displacement and mooring buoys for 10,000-ton ships. Along with the improvement of facilities for handling cargo, the port area is undergoing development as an industrial site, with storage warehouses, power plants, and public housing for pier workers.

Communications. Airlines serving Haneda airport connect Tokyo with other parts of Japan and with major cities abroad. In 1964, Japan inaugurated the world's fastest rail service, and trains now race between Tokyo and Osaka at a top speed of 130 miles (210 km) an hour. High-speed service has been gradually extended.

Tokyoites have a choice of several television channels and radio stations. Tokyo's daily newspaper circulation represents about 17% of Japan's total. *Asahi*, one of the principal newspapers, has one of the largest circulations in the world, with more than 5 million copies sold every day. Tokyo's more than 2,200 publishing houses produce 90% of the 500 million books published annually in Japan.

Telephone service is excellent and includes a direct dialing system to almost all cities. Connection can be made to the United States, to Europe, and to some Asian and Pacific countries by means of the transpacific cable, which was opened in 1964. There is radiotelephone service to all parts of the world. Tokyo has one telephone for every three persons, and there are 70,000 public telephones scattered throughout the city.

GOVERNMENT

As the seat of imperial rule, Tokyo remained under the administrative control of the national government until Oct. 1, 1898, when it became an autonomous municipality. On July 1, 1943, as a World War II efficiency measure, Tokyo Prefecture was abolished and the Tokyo metropolitan government was created with an appointive governor as the chief executive officer. This office was made elective in the postwar political reforms. Each of the cities and wards of Tokyo Metropolis has an elected assembly, but the cities elect their mayors by popular vote while the ward mayors are elected by the respective assemblies. Towns and villages included in the metropolitan governor's jurisdictional area have their own heads, who are elective.

Over all these local bodies is the metropolitan assembly of 126 members, who are elected every four years, as is the governor. The metropolitan assembly has broad powers, including the right to veto the governor's appointment of the three vice-governors and other administrative officers. The governor sets limits on expenditures, and he also has the exclusive right to introduce legislation concerning the budget.

Tokyo's annual budget is equivalent to about 15% of the federal government's expenditures. More than half of the metropolitan revenue is derived from local income taxes and other assessments ranging from the annual fees charged to automobile owners to a levy on patrons of hot-spring mineral baths. The largest items of expenditure are civil engineering and education, followed by welfare projects and the police and fire departments.

SCHOOLS, LIBRARIES, AND MUSEUMS

School attendance through the 9th grade is compulsory in Japan. The national literacy rate, better than 99.9%, is one of the world's highest.

UPI

THE SHOWA PALACE, completed in 1968, is in the Imperial Palace enclosure. View from inner courtyard shows the Seiden, where formal ceremonies are held.

Schools. The Tokyo metropolitan government administers Tokyo Metropolitan University, 4 junior colleges, and more than 150 senior high schools. Junior high schools, primary schools, and kindergartens are operated by wards, cities, and towns. There are also special schools for handicapped children; some of these schools are operated by the metropolitan government and others by local governments. The total enrollment of all the foregoing public institutions exceeds 1.3 million. In addition, over 1 million students attend some 2,200 privately operated institutions from kindergarten up, including nearly 600,000 students in about 90 private universities.

The 13 national universities in Tokyo have a combined enrollment of nearly 50,000 students. One of these institutions supported by the national government is the University of Tokyo, which has been called the Harvard of Japan. See also TOKYO, UNIVERSITY OF.

Competition for admission to the universities is intense, some institutions accepting only one applicant out of every 20 to 40 who take the rigorous entrance examinations. A majority of the successful candidates have taken the entrance tests two or more times before being admitted, and many private tutoring establishments exist specifically for the purpose of preparing these candidates.

More than 40 officially sponsored organizations are engaged in adult education programs in Tokyo, with expert consultants stationed in each political subdivision by the metropolitan board of education. Numerous local centers for self-improvement are maintained by the metropolitan government and by private groups such as the Tokyo Mothers' Association. One of the unusual private education institutions is a school for jockeys, run by the racing associations. Young riders are given general instruction as well as training in horsemanship.

Libraries. Tokyo's public and private library facilities are extensive. The Japanese capital is a city of booklovers, and the numerous second-hand stalls in the Kanda district are always crowded. The National Diet Library is the Japanese equivalent of the Library of Congress in Washington, D. C. The Hibiya Metropolitan Library, in downtown Hibiya Park, contains many rare books of Japanese and Chinese classics and a priceless collection of woodblock prints. It is equipped with a 7-story stockroom, microfilm facilities, an audiovisual hall, and other special rooms, and it can accommodate about 1,100 readers at a time. Local public libraries serve various neighborhoods. The university libraries are rich in research facilities.

Museums and Galleries. Tokyo abounds in museums. The National Museum, in Ueno Park, contains more than 85,000 paintings, sculptures, and various items of antiquity (see also TOKYO NATIONAL MUSEUM). The National Museum of Western Art, also in Ueno Park, specializes in French masterpieces and has 53 works by Rodin among its exhibits. It was built by Le Corbusier in 1959 to house the Matsukata collection of European masterpieces of sculpture and painting, collected by the businessman Matsukata Kojiro (1865–1950). Still another landmark in Ueno Park is the Metropolitan Fine Art Gallery, which is the largest institution of its kind in Japan and is noted for its annual exhibitions of new works by contemporary Japanese and foreign artists.

The Japan Folk Art Museum, in the Meguro district, displays every category of Japanese folk art, from woodblock prints to examples of tableware and kitchen utensils. The Musashino Provincial Museum in Koganei Park contains articles associated with the ancient history of Tokyo. The Nezu Art Museum specializes in fine arts of ancient times, and contains more than 10,000 pieces, including precious items from China.

Other notable museums and galleries include: the National Science Museum; the Transport Museum; the Tsubouchi Memorial Theater Museum, built in 1928 to honor Tsubouchi Shoyo (1859–1935), one of Japan's greatest dramatists; the Okura Antiquities Museum, on the grounds of the Okura Hotel; the Emperor Meiji Memorial Art Gallery; the National Modern Art Gallery; and the Bridgestone Art Gallery. Worthwhile exhibitions of Japanese and Western cultural items are often to be seen in Tokyo's department stores, which are also among the best places to explore Japanese folk arts.

DAILY LIFE

Tokyo offers striking evidence that most Japanese live an existence neither wholly Eastern nor wholly Western. To the casual visitor from abroad, Japan's capital city may convey the impression of being completely Westernized—not essentially different in appearance from New

JAPAN NATIONAL TOURIST ORGANIZATION

ASAKUSA ENTERTAINMENT DISTRICT has many movie theaters, restaurants, bars, and night clubs.

York or London except for the profusion of signs in intricate kanji characters, the system of ideograms adopted from the Chinese. However, many of the signs have been Westernized. For example, all subway stations and the few streets that are named are marked in the Roman alphabet as well as in Japanese. In the main business sections and in many of the small neighborhood shopping areas, the principal stores, banks, offices, and official buildings have signs in English, Japan's second language. Many Japanese products have English brand names, which are shown on the package both in Roman letters and in katakana, the simplified syllabary used for words of foreign derivation for which there is no kanji equivalent. A second syllabary, called hira-gana, is frequently used to reproduce Japanese words phonetically.

The Home. In the average home, the Japanese diet with its basis of rice and fish is generally preferred. However, almost all Japanese except the older generation in rural areas have become accustomed to Western food and the use of the knife, fork, and spoon as well as the traditional *hashi* (chopsticks).

Western clothes are worn on the street and at work by all but a few men, and women and girls wear Western clothing except on special occasions. At the New Year's and other festivals, many Tokyo women wear the kimono, bound around the waist by a sash (*obi*) with an elaborate bow in the back, and split-toed socks (*tabi*) with thonged slippers (*zori*). In their homes, however, a majority of Tokyoites of both sexes discard their Western dress in favor of the comfortable kimono.

Although Western-style furniture is gaining in use, the majority of Tokyo homes retain the traditional straw matting (*tatami*) for the floor, and the low dining table, around which the family sits on cushions. Many Japanese homes in Tokyo lack facilities for bathing. Consequently, the family goes regularly, soap in hand, to the nearest of some 3,000 public bathhouses that also serve more or less as neighborhood clubs.

The beauty-loving Japanese are so fond of gardens that even a tiny plot of grass becomes a garden, simply by the addition of a few stones artistically arranged. In Tokyo, if no ground is available, the average family strives for the effect of a full-sized garden with potted dwarf trees (*bonsai*) and perhaps a miniature landscape on a tray (*bonkei*) in a window.

Western Influence. Much of the so-called Americanization of Tokyo was the natural culmination of the drive to emulate Western progress that took possession of all Japan after 1853. In that year U. S. Commodore Matthew C. Perry and his naval squadron of fire-belching "black ships" visited Japan, awakening the astounded Japanese to the advantages of Western military and industrial techniques and leading to the eventual overthrow of the Japanese variety of feudalism and the restoration of imperial power. Emperor Meiji began to explore ways of putting Japan on an equal footing with the United States and other Western powers. Four years after he established his court in Tokyo, an American school teacher, Horace Wilson, was teaching Japanese boys to play baseball—a game that a generation later was Japan's national sport. But more important than baseball, American industrial, military, and educational methods were being enthusiastically absorbed.

Western governmental systems were being studied, too. The first Diet was elected in 1890 by a limited franchise. The Western ideas of freedom of speech, freedom of association, and equality of the sexes were slowly being accepted, but the rise of the militarist faction in the 1930's undid almost 60 years of steady political and social progress.

The occupation of Japan by U. S. military forces after World War II seems to have had a greater impact on Tokyo than on most cities. Americans form the largest group of Westerners there. American tastes in entertainment and dress have been copied by young Tokyoites, who have also absorbed many American slang expressions into their speech and have adopted certain American habits, such as gum chewing. An expanded advertising and public relations industry is evidence of the impact of the American business community on the Japanese. The leading Tokyo advertising agency, Dentsu, is the largest outside the United States and the fourth largest in the world.

The 7-year U. S. occupation (1945–1952) brought about an abrupt social change in Japan. The destruction, almost overnight, of the ancient concept of the nation as a family with the emperor at its head brought conflict between the older generation and the new. One consequence that was noticeable in Tokyo was the rise of juvenile delinquency with the decline of parental authority. Another has been the growth of radicalism among the young. The freeing of youth from the suffocatingly restrictive conventions of the past has probably been a factor in Japan's vigorous surge forward in every field of intellectual endeavor. Tokyo, as the capital of Japan and center of intellectual life, is in the forefront of this advance.

ENTERTAINMENT

Renowned personalities in every branch of the performing arts may be seen in Tokyo's legitimate theaters and concert halls. Some of the theaters are equipped with individual earphones for translation of dialogue from foreign languages into Japanese, and vice versa. Prices are high for foreign attractions because of the expense of bringing artists from abroad, but the people of Tokyo are so eager to see and hear outstanding talent that tickets are often sold out immediately upon announcement.

Theater and Motion Pictures. While maintaining the traditional theatrical forms like Kabuki and No, which are still popular, the Tokyo stage has become internationalized with regular productions of Shakespeare and contemporary Western playwrights, and of Western musicals with song lyrics and dialogue translated into Japanese for performance by Japanese casts. Famous Western stage directors are occasionally invited to work with Tokyo professional companies.

The all-girl revue has been a feature of the Tokyo theatrical world for decades. The celebrated Shochiku all-girl extravaganza at the huge Kokusai Theater in the Asakusa amusement district of Tokyo features elaborate mechanical effects and massive precision dance numbers bringing several hundred girls on stage at one time. It is reminiscent of the "Rockettes" at New York's Radio City Music Hall, but bigger. Asakusa also has dozens of small theaters, bars, and nightclubs, and amusement parlors devoted exclusively to *pachinko,* a Japanese pinball game.

The most celebrated theater in Tokyo is unquestionably the Kabukiza, near the Ginza. Here are seen plays that have been popular in Japan since the 1600's, performed by highly paid Kabuki actors in gorgeous costumes and elaborate makeup. The National Theater, completed in 1966, also presents Kabuki and other forms of classical drama. Tokyo dramatists have evolved a modern form of drama known as *shingeki* (new theater), with contemporary themes. *Shimpa,* a type of play devised about 1880, falls between Kabuki and *shingeki.*

Tokyo is the headquarters of Japan's motion picture industry, one of the world's largest in number of films produced. Among the most popular Japanese movies are the rousing action films on themes of samurai (warrior) days. These pictures are popularly known as *chambara,* from the sound of swords hitting each other in the frequent battle scenes. Foreign motion pictures are popular, particularly those from Hollywood. Imported films are invariably shown with Japanese subtitles, retaining the original sound track, although foreign television programs almost always have dubbed-in Japanese dialogue.

Music. The Japanese style of music more than holds its own with the Western variety on radio and television programs heard in Tokyo. The three-stringed samisen, the koto, and other Japanese orchestral instruments are commonly heard in the popular theater, on radio and television, and at gatherings featuring geisha, the accomplished female entertainers of traditional Japan. The classic gagaku royal court music, played on antique instruments, and its accompanying dance form, called bugaku, are rarely performed in Tokyo for the general public. They are usually confined to entertainments for the imperial household and its invited guests.

CONSULATE GENERAL OF JAPAN, N. Y.

THE GINZA, Tokyo's best-known shopping street, is noted for its bright lights. *Left* is San-ai Building.

The Japanese have also developed a keen appreciation of old and new forms from the West. Tokyo has several symphony orchestras, and capacity audiences turn out for the frequent visits of leading orchestras, chamber groups, singers, and instrumentalists from other countries. Tokyo also has several opera companies, and the occasional tours of Italian and other opera troupes are eagerly awaited. Western ballet is extremely popular, and Tokyo's numerous ballet companies and schools have provided supporting dancers for visiting stars from the West.

Tokyo's more than 5,000 musical coffeehouses are patronized mostly by younger Japanese, who listen raptly to recorded Western-style music of all types, from the classics to the latest popular tunes of whatever type may be in vogue. Some coffeehouses have orchestras, and a few pass out song sheets to encourage the patrons to sing along with the music.

Sports. Tokyo's sports facilities, enlarged for the 1964 Olympic Games, are among the world's finest. Some of the Olympic structures, particularly the swimming pool and gymnasium buildings designed by Tange Kenzo, are beautiful as well as functional. The National Stadium, where the Olympic track and field events were held, accommodates 85,000 spectators. The city has tracks for horse racing, and there are many fields for baseball. Golf has become so popular that one driving range has three levels. One of the city's many bowling alleys has 250 lanes.

The Judo Kodokan is the world headquarters of the international sport of judo, which originated in Japan. The other popular Japanese sport is sumo, an ancient and highly stylized form of wrestling, whose professional practitioners may weigh more than 300 pounds (136 kg). It is seen at its best in Tokyo's Kuramae Kokugikan arena.

CONSULATE GENERAL OF JAPAN, N. Y.

MEIJI SHRINE is dedicated to the first emperor of modern Japan and his consort. One of Tokyo's most popular religious centers, it is surrounded by a park.

Restaurants and Cabarets. A foreign gourmet once described Tokyo as offering the world's widest variety of superior restaurants. There are over 100,000 eating establishments to choose from, including places that serve Western food, plus about 10,000 bars and cabarets. The Japanese cuisine offers almost unlimited choice. Many Japanese restaurants specialize in one kind of dish prepared many different ways, such as sushi (raw fish on a pedestal of rice), tofu (bean curd), and yakitori (roasted fowl on a skewer), besides the better-known tempura (fried seafood) and sukiyaki (a meat and vegetable stew).

Tokyo's exclusive and expensive restaurants employing geisha entertainers are concentrated in the Shimbashi and Akasaka districts. The city has a great many nightclubs, featuring both Japanese and Western floor shows.

RELIGIOUS LIFE

Most Japanese who have any religious inclinations profess to be Buddhist but also practice Shinto rituals. Most marriages are performed by Shinto rites and most funerals by Buddhist ceremonies. The traditional Japanese home in Tokyo usually has a small Shinto altar on a cabinet or shelf.

The many Shinto shrines in Tokyo are well patronized, especially during the periodic festivals and fairs that lend so much color to the city. On January 1, millions of Tokyoites visit shrines and leave contributions to ensure good fortune for the coming year. November 15 is the festival of *Shichi-go-san* ("Seven-Five-Three"), honoring children seven, five, and three years old. On that day the streets of Tokyo are crowded with children dressed in bright kimonos, on their way to and from the shrines. Before Tango-no-sekku (Boy's Day) on May 5, the city is gay with the huge cloth banners, shaped like carp, flying over households that have male children. Boys are urged to emulate the carp, which shows great strength and courage in its annual struggle upstream.

On any given day, certain leading religious sites, such as the Temple of Kannon (Buddhist goddess of mercy) in the Asakusa section of Tokyo, will be thronged with visitors from outside the city, especially school children on excursions. However, formal religion seems to have lost much of its appeal among the mass of Japanese as a result of the wholesale repudiation of ancient national values after the country's catastrophic defeat in World War II. Long-cherished standards of filial respect, veneration of authority, and reverence for traditional ways were upset. Shinto suffered particularly from the withdrawal of state support under orders of the U. S. occupation authorities.

The shrine festivals that enliven the streets of Tokyo are often said to be observed in the spirit of continuing an attractive folk custom rather than as a religious experience. However, certain ancient forms are scrupulously maintained even in the midst of Tokyo's bustling, superficially Westernized way of life. Such customs as the carrying of portable shrines in street processions and the traditional public dancing for a variety of festivals are acknowledged by enough people to preserve an air of old Japan in the midst of the city's aggressive modernism. The launching of a ship or the opening of an exhibition is always the occasion for silken-robed Shinto priests to appear for incantations before large and respectful gatherings in which motion picture stars and leading businessmen solemnly participate.

HISTORY

Excavations have indicated that the site of Tokyo was inhabited during the Stone Age. The military importance of the site, where the Sumida River empties into Tokyo Bay, led a local warlord by the name of Edo Taro Shigenaga to construct a fort there in the 12th century. The name Edo probably was already in existence and had been adopted by the warrior's family from their place of residence, as was the custom in old Japan.

The place vanished from history until the appearance 300 years later of Ota Dokan, a warrior in the service of Uesugi Sadamasa. Uesugi ruled the Kanto region for the shogun at Kyoto from his military headquarters at Kamakura. He was responsible for protecting the shogunate from forays by unfriendly forces in the north. Accordingly, Ota Dokan erected a fortified castle at the hamlet of Edo. The structure was begun in 1456, and with its completion in 1457, Edo acquired considerable importance. In 1590 the castle came into the possession of Tokugawa Ieyasu, the founder of a new line of shoguns a few years later.

Tokugawa Period. Much of what is now Tokyo was a tidal marsh in the 1500's. Ieyasu immedi-

THE SENSOJI, a temple in the Asakusa section, is reached by a street with colorfully decorated shops. The temple is headquarters of the Kannon Buddhist sect.

JAPAN NATIONAL TOURIST ORGANIZATION

ately began the work of filling in land, a project that continued as the settlement grew from a few hundred thatched huts to a great modern city. After Ieyasu formally assumed the title of shogun in 1603, he moved the military government to Edo. Kyoto, as the residence of the emperor, remained the nominal capital. To prevent vassal lords in distant regions from becoming a threat to the shogunate, Ieyasu required each of these feudal barons, called daimyo, to spend alternate years in Edo. Their families remained there permanently, in effect as hostages. As a result, Edo quickly grew into a bustling city as merchants and artisans congregated to serve the needs of the nobles and their families. The descendants of these tradesmen, the great merchant princes, were to be the true inheritors of Edo.

With the deliberate intent of concentrating the wealth of the nation in his capital, Ieyasu taxed the feudal lords heavily to finance new canals, land reclamation, and new construction. Later the canals were filled in at even greater expense as the price of land went up. Edo came to be a center of the arts as well as of politics and trade. The city's population swelled to a million, and at some time during the Tokugawa period Edo probably became the world's most populous city, a distinction that would later be lost, only to be regained in the second half of the 20th century.

Japan entered its modern era when the 15th and last Tokugawa shogun formally surrendered Edo Castle to imperial forces on May 3, 1868. This ended the military dictatorship. Emperor Meiji moved the royal capital to Edo later that year and took up residence in the castle, which then became the Imperial Palace. The city was renamed Tokyo, meaning "eastern capital."

Imperial Capital. After the Meiji restoration, Tokyo lost half its population. The warrior aristocracy left the capital, followed by many merchants and artisans dependent on samurai patronage. But under the new regime, which encouraged the development of Western technology, commerce revived and the population grew rapidly.

A prefectural government was inaugurated in 1868 and was reorganized in 1871. In 1872, one of the city's numerous conflagrations consumed the daimyo mansions of Marunouchi and the wooden shops that jammed the Ginza. For the next 20 years, Marunouchi reverted to semiwilderness while the Ginza was rebuilt in brick from plans prepared by the British engineer Thomas Waters.

Marunouchi, meanwhile, came into the hands of the Mitsubishi interests, which were later to become a far-reaching financial power. The reconstruction of Marunouchi began in 1892 in the red-brick Gothic architecture of the Victorian period, designed by the British architect Josiah Conder. This area and adjacent Nihombashi, named for a famous bridge from which distances to all points in Japan were measured, became the future financial district and the base of operations for great corporations like Mitsubishi, Mitsui, and Yasuda. The red brick buildings of Marunouchi survived the 1923 earthquake and fire and the bombings of World War II, but were mostly replaced by new ferroconcrete structures in the frantic expansion of Tokyo after 1954.

Destruction and Reconstruction. The earthquake that struck Tokyo and the Kanto Plain at noon on Sept. 1, 1923, and the ensuing holocaust are said to have constituted the worst natural disaster ever visited upon mankind. Some 400,000 houses were burned down in Tokyo. More than a million residents, about 65% of the city's population, were left dead or homeless by the conflagration. The Japanese rebuilt the devastated city in only seven years. The U. S. bombing raids from November 1944 to August 1945, during World War II, were an even greater disaster than the 1923 earthquake and fire. Approximately 800,000 buildings were reduced to ashes, and some 250,000 persons were dead or missing. Evacuation to the countryside had reduced the population by more than half.

After Japan's surrender on Sept. 2, 1945, reconstruction proceeded in stages from makeshift shacks to cheap wooden structures to the new ferroconcrete buildings. In the period preceding the 1964 Olympic Games, an extensive urban development program began with the widening of main traffic arteries and the construction of elevated expressways, subway extensions, and other improvements undertaken with aid from the central government.

ROBERT TRUMBULL
Chief, Tokyo Bureau, "The New York Times"
(1954–1961, 1964–1968)

Further Reading: Japan National Tourist Organization, *The New Official Guide: Japan* (Tokyo 1966); The Tokyo Metropolitan Government, *An Administrative Perspective of Tokyo* (Tokyo 1969). See also JAPAN—*Bibliography*.

TOKYO, University of, the first national university in Japan, founded in 1877. It is under the direction of the ministry of education. The main campus, located in the Hongo section of Tokyo, was established in 1884.

The university has a college of general education and faculties of law, letters, science, and medicine (all founded in 1877) and faculties of engineering (1886), agriculture (1890), economics (1919), education (1949), and pharmaceutical sciences (1958). The graduate school consists of divisions of humanities, education, law and politics, sociology, economics, science, engineering, agricultural sciences, medical sciences, and pharmaceutical sciences. Connected with the university are institutes of Oriental culture, social science, journalism, historiography, medical science, applied microbiology, nuclear study, solid state physics, earthquake and oceanographic research, and space and aeronautical science. There are also an astronomical observatory and a cosmic ray laboratory.

The library has more than 3,500,000 volumes. Enrollment by 1970 was more than 15,000 men and women.

TOMOO MATSUDA, *The University of Tokyo*

TOKYO NATIONAL MUSEUM, Japan's largest museum and one of its three national museums of pre-modern art and archaeology. The others are in Kyoto and Nara. The Tokyo museum's collections include over 86,000 objects, primarily Japanese art from the Stone Age through the Meiji Period (1868–1912). Modern Japanese art is shown at the National Museum of Modern Art, in Tokyo.

The main building of the Tokyo National Museum houses Japanese art from the introduction of Buddhism in 552 A. D. until 1912. The objects are grouped as follows: paintings, sculptures, ceramics, calligraphy, lacquerware, metalwork, prints, and textiles. Exhibits of Japanese archaeology are located in the Hyokeikan, a separate building to the left as one faces the main building. To the right, in the Toyokan, are collections of Chinese, Korean, Central Asian, and South Asian art. The Horyuji Treasure Gallery, behind the Hyokeikan, has an important collection of early Buddhist art from the Horyuji monastery in Nara.

ROBERT MOES
Denver Art Museum

TOLAND, John (1670–1722), Irish philosopher and deist. Toland was born near Londonderry on Nov. 30, 1670. He was baptized a Roman Catholic but became a Protestant before he was 16. He was educated first at Glasgow and then at Leiden and Oxford.

Influenced by the rationalism of his time, he published his famous *Christianity Not Mysterious* (1696), the classic exposition of deism (see DEISM). He returned to Ireland briefly in 1697 and then traveled extensively in Germany and elsewhere on the Continent. His *Life of Milton* (1698) provoked controversy because it questioned the authenticity of parts of the New Testament, while his *Tetradymus* (1720) offered a natural explanation of the miracles recorded in the Gospels. Pantheism was also evident in some of his later writings. Toland died in Putney, England, on Mar. 11, 1722.

POWEL MILLS DAWLEY
The General Theological Seminary, New York

TOLEDO, tə-lēd′ō, a city in northwestern Ohio, the seat of Lucas county, is situated at the southwestern end of Lake Erie, at the mouth of the Maumee River, 96 miles (154 km) west of Cleveland. It is a manufacturing and commercial center, and a port on the St. Lawrence Seaway.

Economy. Toledo's manufacturing is largely for the automotive industry, centered in Detroit, 55 miles (88 km) north of the city. The Jeep is made here. Toledo has extensive oil refineries and is headquarters for four of the nation's leading glass firms. One of them locally manufactures flat glass for cars and buildings.

Toledo is the only port on the Great Lakes with an operating foreign trade zone, and it has giant coal-loading facilities. It has three elevator complexes to supply grain to ocean vessels.

Education and Cultural Life. The University of Toledo has been a state university since 1967. Another state school, the Medical College of Ohio, opened in 1969. Mary Manse College is a Catholic school for women.

The Toledo Museum of Art is noted for its glass collection, housed in a gallery opened in 1970, and for its 17th and 18th century Dutch and French art. The museum has extensive educational facilities, including music classes and a number of concert series. Its concert hall, called the Peristyle, is used by the Toledo Symphony Orchestra and other groups. The Toledo Opera Association performs in the Masonic auditorium, which is also the site of concerts and professional plays. Toledo's zoo is ranked as one of the largest in the United States.

History and Government. The Toledo area was the scene of early fighting. The first white habitation on the site was Fort Industry, built by Gen. Anthony Wayne in 1794, the year he defeated 2,000 Indians at the Battle of Fallen Timbers nearby. Troops in Fort Meigs, which has been restored in a state park, fought off the British and Indians in 1813.

The village of Port Lawrence was established next to Fort Industry in 1817 by a company of speculators. The village of Vistula was begun later a mile away. The two villages decided in 1835 to unite and were incorporated in 1837 as Toledo. The name was suggested by a leader who liked the sound of the Spanish city's name.

Toledo's area was alternately claimed by Michigan and Ohio until the bloodless "Toledo War" of 1835 was settled by the federal government. It awarded the disputed area to Ohio.

Famous men in Toledo history include David Ross Locke, the Toledo *Blade* editor who wrote antislavery satires under the pen name Petroleum V. Nasby; Edward Drummond Libbey, who established a glass factory in Toledo in 1888 and helped to found the Museum of Art; Morrison R. Waite, a chief justice of the United States; Brand Whitlock, a mayor who became ambassador to Belgium; Samuel "Golden Rule" Jones, a businessman who became mayor; James Ashley, a radical Republican congressman who introduced the measure to impeach President Andrew Johnson; Grove Patterson, a *Blade* editor and a founder of the American Society of Newspaper Editors; and Michael Owens, who invented a machine for mass producing glass containers.

Toledo has a city manager government, with a mayor and council. Its present government dates from a charter revision in 1935. Population: (city) 383,818, (urban area) 692,571.

JAMES C. MACDONALD, *The "Blade," Toledo*

HANNA W. SCHREIBER, FROM RAPHO GUILLUMETTE

Toledo, rising above the Tagus River, is dominated by its cathedral (*left*) and the restored Alcázar (*right*).

TOLEDO, tō-lā'thō, historic Spanish city that was once the capital of Spain, is the capital of Toledo province. It lies on the Tagus River, 40 miles (64 km) south of Madrid. Toledo is built on a height, and narrow streets wind down to the river, which curves around the city on three sides.

The historical heritage of Toledo is so rich that the whole city is a veritable museum. It is crowned by a Gothic cathedral begun in 1227 by King Ferdinand III. Many of Toledo's numerous Christian buildings were originally Muslim or Jewish, such as the Tránsito church, formerly a synagogue. The Plaza de Zocodover still has parts of the wall built by the 7th century Visigothic king Wamba and later rebuilt by the Arabs. Several gates of the city date from Moorish times. The Alcázar, a citadel that dominated the city along with the cathedral, was badly damaged during the Civil War of the 1930's but has now been restored.

El Greco's paintings can be seen in many buildings in Toledo, and his former home is now a museum. The church of Santo Tomé houses El Greco's famous painting *Burial of the Count of Orgaz* (1586–1588).

Economy. Metalworking is a leading industry, although it is not so important as in centuries past, when Toledo produced the best swords in Europe. Modern metal products are surgical instruments and shell casings. A secondary enterprise is the making of silk products, particularly ecclesiastical vestments. Most of the city's other commercial life is of a local nature.

History. Romans captured the Carpetani settlement at Toledo in 192 B. C., calling it Toletum. But the town did not assume any great importance until the Visigothic kings made it their capital in the 6th century A. D. In 587, King Reccared and his Arian Gothic followers were converted to the orthodox Catholic Church at Toledo, which was the site of numerous subsequent church councils. The archbishop of Toledo has traditionally been Spain's primate.

In 712 the city fell to Tariq and the Arabs. During the long period of civil strife among the Muslims, Toledo vied with Córdoba and Seville as the capital city of Moorish Spain. Also during this time many Jews and Christians congregated in the cosmopolitan city.

In May 1085, Alfonso VI reconquered Toledo. He was noted for attempting to avoid religious strife between Muslims and Christians, and during his reign many Arabs continued to inhabit his capital, Toledo. In the 13th century Alfonso X, the Wise, established in Toledo his famous school of scholars and translators.

With the coming of the Habsburg dynasty to Spain, Toledo lost some of its importance. After the city fell in 1522 to forces loyal to Emperor Charles V it never regained its stature, and four decades later, under Philip II, a new capital, Madrid, became the seat of government. The French occupied Toledo during the Napoleonic invasion, and much of the Alcázar was burned down. It was subsequently rebuilt.

Toledo not only has figured importantly in Spanish history but also was the national cultural center until Madrid replaced it. It is most closely associated with El Greco, but other great creators were involved in its life. The writers Cervantes and Quevedo laid their stories there. During the romantic period in the 19th century it again became a favorite subject of writers as the embodiment of everything exotic and medieval in the Spanish past.

The Province. Toledo province, located in the historic region of New Castile, has an area of 5,925 square miles (15,445 sq km). The western part is mountainous. To the east the province turns into a plain with rolling hills. It is quite cold in winter and hot in summer. Agriculture and stock raising are the main commercial activities. Population: (1960) of the city, 29,367; (1965 est.) of the province, 516,870.

GREGORY RABASSA, *Queens College, New York*

TOLEDO, Councils of, tō-lā'thō, 18 gatherings, largely of bishops, held at irregular intervals between 400 and 702 to decide issues relating to the Christian Church in Spain. While properly called church councils, they also dealt with some civil problems. They were concerned with the whole Spanish church as well as with particular provinces. They are significant because they show a highly organized church and indicate a close church-state relationship, civil rulers frequently attending them. The third council, held in 589, for example, was important because King Reccared, a recent convert from Arianism, was present. He gave the Spanish church the orthodox direction that was to characterize its future. The entire hierarchy followed his example and professed the orthodox faith.

These councils provide complete information of the Spanish church during its formative, Visigothic period. The councils insisted on clerical celibacy and imposed penalties on those who neglected it. They also settled disputes about the mutual rights of church and state.

PHILIP F. MULHERN, O.P.
St. Mary's Priory, New Haven, Conn.

TOLEDO Y FIGUEROA, tō-lā′thō ē fē-gā-rō′ä, **Francisco Álvarez de** (1515–1582), Spanish viceroy of Peru from 1569 to 1581. Born in Oropesa, Spain, on July 10, 1515, Toledo served in the personal (patrimonial) government of Charles V but held no office under Philip II until the extensive administrative reorganization of the Spanish empire in 1568.

The Great Council that reformed the Council of the Indies (*Consejo de Indias*) also instructed Toledo in the laws and decrees for Peru. After a five-year inspection of the territory, he introduced reforms related to administration, finance, and police. By resettling the Indians in towns, he placed their taxes and labor services under the control of royal officials. He broke the power of the estate landholders (*encomenderos*) and restored viceregal authority. In 1576 he reorganized the University of San Marcos in Lima. After trouble between the Spanish and the Incas, Toledo unjustly executed the rebel Inca, Tupac Amaru. He returned to Spain in 1581 under criticism and died on April 21, 1582.

BENJAMIN F. ZIMDARS
Mary Washington College

TOLERATION ACT, the Act of 1689 passed in England during the reign of William and Mary, granting religious dissenters freedom of worship with certain conditions. Dissenters were allowed to maintain places of worship and to appoint their own ministers. However, they were required to swear allegiance to the crown, and their ministers had to sign the Thirty-nine Articles, with the exception of the two that refer to infant baptism. Quakers were allowed to make an affirmation instead of an oath. Roman Catholics and those who did not believe in the Trinity were not covered by the act.

The purpose of the act was to secure unity among English Protestants against a possible threat of a return of the deposed King James II, a Roman Catholic. Political disqualifications were not removed by the act, and dissenters were not allowed to hold public office until the Occasional Conformity Act of 1711.

TOLKIEN, tol′kēn, **John Ronald Reuel** (1892–1973), English scholar and writer, who is best known for the fanciful trilogy *The Lord of the Rings* (1954–1955) and its prelude *The Hobbit* (1937). He was born in Bloemfontein, South Africa, on Jan. 3, 1892. Tolkien grew up in England and, after graduation from Oxford in 1915, served in World War I and taught at the University of Leeds before returning to Oxford, where he was a professor of Anglo-Saxon and of English language and literature until his retirement in 1959. He died in Bournemouth, England, on Sept. 2, 1973.

WIDE WORLD

J. R. R. Tolkien

Works such as an edition of *Sir Gawain and the Green Knight* (1925; 2d ed., 1968) and the critical study *Beowulf: The Monsters and the Critics* (1936) established Tolkien's reputation as a scholar. But it was through his fiction—notably *The Hobbit* and the trilogy *The Lord of the Rings,* based on a mythology of his own creation—that Tolkien became widely known. Other works include essays, poems, and a play.

Tolkien's popular works reflect his delight in real and imaginary languages, myths, and legends. Many of his heroes are questers, who undertake perilous journeys that result in their own moral growth and in restored health in their lands. Such a quester was the "hobbit" Frodo Baggins—a genial creature resembling both an English countryman and a rabbit. The intricate *Lord of the Rings* tells of a cosmic war between good and evil, in which the forces of good, through suffering and sacrifice, destroy a terrible ring of power and bring harmony to all creation.

CATHARINE R. STIMPSON, *Barnard College*

Further Reading: Isaacs, Neil D., and Zimbardo, Rose A., eds., *Tolkien and the Critics* (Notre Dame, Ind., 1968); Stimpson, Catharine R., *J. R. R. Tolkien* (New York 1969).

TOLL ROADS are roads maintained wholly or in part by fees (tolls) collected from users. The tolls were collected in early times at barriers across the road in the form of turnstiles, often consisting of four pointed sticks called turnpikes. These were later replaced by tollgates. The roads were maintained and often built by a corporation—in the United States, usually a private corporation—chartered by the state.

History. Toll roads originated in England in 1346 and reached their high point there in the early 19th century. Toll roads did not appear in America until after the Revolution—in Virginia in 1785 and in Pennsylvania and Connecticut in 1792. They were built in response to the needs of urban business interests, particularly in sparsely settled rural areas where good roads could not be maintained through taxation.

The great era for toll road construction was 1790–1810. These roads were used until the 1840's. Over 170 turnpike companies were organized in New England from 1792 to 1810, investing more than $5 million in some 3,000 miles (4,800 km) of roads. Among the most famous toll roads were the Philadelphia–Lancaster Turnpike, 62 miles (99 km) long, built at a cost of $7,500 per mile, the Old Post Road connecting New York and Boston, and the Great National Turnpike from Baltimore to Wheeling, W. Va.

The cost of construction varied from $300 to $10,000 per mile, depending on soil, terrain, and the number of bridges needed. To raise these large sums, the road builders sold stock, thus pioneering in the development of the modern corporation. Toll roads aided westward migration, the growth of commercial stagecoach lines, and the development of inland industrial sites. They also led to increased sales of carriages.

Limitations. Although the roads aided general economic advance, most investors in them lost a good part of their money. The roads were a success in moving people and the mails, but, except on short hauls connecting water routes, they were a failure in moving farm produce and heavy industrial goods. Beyond a certain limited economic point, the horse-drawn wagon apparently was too inefficient in carrying freight to yield further profits even over good roads. As toll roads were replaced by state roads and railroads, it became clear that they were economically feasible only in very special or isolated areas.

Revival. The automobile era witnessed a revival of toll roads. Beginning with the Pennsylvania Turnpike, opened in 1940, the movement for superhighway toll roads grew rapidly. It waned as a federally financed interstate highway system began in the mid-1950's.

RICHARD D. BIRDSALL
Connecticut College

TOLLER, tôl′ər, **Ernst** (1893–1939), German expressionist dramatist, who perhaps best typified the generation of German authors that tried to combine literature with political activism. He was born in Samotschin, Posen, Prussia (now Poland) on Dec. 1, 1893. In 1914, he enlisted in the army, but his experiences on the western front, from 1915 to 1916, turned him into a lifelong enemy of war. He was discharged from the army for reasons of health and subsequently went to Munich, where he participated in the Bavarian Revolution of 1918–1919. He was the head of the Bavarian Soviet Republic for seven days (April 7–14) in 1919. As a result he was imprisoned from 1919 to 1924. Between 1924 and 1933 he was involved in various social and political causes. In 1933, when the Nazis seized power, he went into exile and ultimately went to the United States in 1936. During his years in exile he was active in anti-Nazi organizations and gave many speeches. He committed suicide in New York City on May 22, 1939.

Toller's reputation rests mainly on the plays he wrote between 1917 and 1927, including *Die Wandlung* (1919), *Masse-Mensch* (1920), *Hinkemann* (1922), and *Hoppla, Wir Leben!* (1927), most of which are expressionist in style. They deal largely with the themes of political and social revolution. The early plays express faith in human nature and the hope for a peaceful change of the world. In contrast, the later dramas are marked by a tone of pessimism and despair.

JOHN M. SPALEK
Author of "Ernst Toller and His Critics"

TOLMAN, tōl′mən, **Edward Chace** (1886–1959), American psychologist. He was born in West Newton, Mass., on April 14, 1886. He was educated at Massachusetts Institute of Technology and Harvard. After teaching at Northwestern University from 1915 to 1918, he was a member of the faculty of the University of California at Berkeley from 1918 to 1954. He died in Berkeley on Nov. 19, 1959.

Tolman is best known for his modifications of behaviorist psychology. He argued that such theorists as John B. Watson took an overly atomistic view, concentrating on small bits of behavior and explaining everything in terms of conditioned responses. Tolman believed that the whole organism, rather than single actions, is the proper subject matter of psychology. He held that perceptions, ideas, and purposes are key elements in behavior. His molar, or purposive, behaviorism is described in his most important book, *Purposive Behavior in Animals and Men* (1932). See also BEHAVIORISM.

TOLSTOY, tul-stoi′, **Count Aleksei Konstantinovich** (1817–1875), Russian writer, who was noted both as a verse satirist and as the author of several outstanding historical plays. He was born in St. Petersburg on Sept. 5, 1817, and studied at Moscow University. A favorite of Emperor Alexander II, Tolstoy served the government in minor posts. He also travelled widely and spent many years in western Europe. Tolstoy died at Krasny Rog on Oct. 10, 1875.

Tolstoy became famous with the publication (1853–1863) of humorous and satirical poems, written in collaboration with his cousins, the Zhemchuzhnikovs, under the joint pseudonym of "Kozma Prutkov." Although renowned as a humorous poet, he also wrote lyrics as well as narrative verse, including *The Dragon* (1875). His historical novel *Prince Serebryany* (1862) was widely acclaimed.

He is best known outside Russia for his trilogy of historical plays, *The Death of Ivan the Terrible* (1866), *Czar Fyodor Ivanovich* (1868), and *Czar Boris* (1870), marked by their strong dramatic power and fine characterization.

ERNEST J. SIMMONS, *Author, "Leo Tolstoy"*

TOLSTOY, tul-stoi′, **Aleksei Nikolayevich** (1883–1945), Russian novelist and playwright, whose works are among the most popular in the Soviet Union. He was born to a noble family at Nikolayevsk (now Pugachev) on Jan. 10, 1883. Although he studied engineering, he found that he preferred to write. Shortly after the 1917 Revolution he emigrated to western Europe but returned to Russia in 1923 and became a supporter of the Soviet regime. He died in Moscow on Feb. 23, 1945.

Tolstoy began his literary career in 1907 with a volume of poetry, *Lyrics*. However, he soon began to publish novels and short stories distinguished by their brilliant style, original treatment, and striking realism. His two most famous novelistic works are the trilogy *The Road to Calvary* (finished 1941), a vast narrative of Russian life on the eve of World War I, and the three-volume *Peter the Great* (1929–1945), remarkable for its historical realism and vivid characterization. His greatest drama is the two-part play, *Ivan the Terrible* (1942–1943), which gives an idealized portrayal of Ivan.

ERNEST J. SIMMONS, *Author, "Leo Tolstoy"*

CULVER PICTURES

Leo Tolstoy

TOLSTOY, tul-stoi′, **Count Leo** (1828–1910), Russian novelist, moral philosopher, and social reformer, who is renowned as the author of *War and Peace* and *Anna Karenina* and as an outstanding thinker of the 19th century. One of Russia's most beloved novelists, he has been praised by critics for the extraordinary truthfulness and realism of his fiction and for his profound psychological analysis of his characters, such as Natasha Rostova, Prince Andrei Bolkonsky, Pierre Bezukhov, and Anna Karenina. His two most famous rivals, Dostoyevsky and Turgenev, paid him lofty tributes. The first regarded him as superior to any living novelist, and the second called him "great author of the Russian land."

During Tolstoy's lifetime, his fiction was slow to penetrate Western Europe and the United States. Since his death, however, his novels and short stories have been translated into many languages throughout the world, and several have been turned into films.

Such unanimous approval has not always been accorded Tolstoy's many nonfiction works, which have frequently been attacked for their moral absolutism and uncompromising opposition to the established order of things. However, the persuasiveness and brilliant style of the best of these works have been generally recognized, and some discerning modern critics, aware of the peculiar relevance of his reforming views to the major religious, moral, political, and social problems, have begun to credit him with unusual insight and prophetic wisdom.

LIFE

Early Years. Leo (in Russian, Lev) Nikolayevich Tolstoy was born at Yasnaya Polyana, Tula province, Russia, on Sept. 9, 1828, to a family of the gentry. His parents died when he was a child, and he was brought up by female relatives and educated in his early years by foreign tutors. He matriculated at Kazan University in 1844 and did well in some studies. However, he was more interested in social success in the town's high society. In 1847 he left the university, determined to educate himself at Yasnaya Polyana and manage his estate and serfs in a progressive manner. These efforts, later recounted in *A Landowner's Morning* (1856), were unsuccessful, and he spent most of the next few years in the social whirl of Moscow and St. Petersburg. His remarkably frank diary, which he had begun in 1847, reveals his dissatisfaction with this aimless life, as well as his questing, independent mind and his unconventional attempts at self-education.

In 1851, Tolstoy went to the Caucasus to serve as a volunteer in an artillery unit. There he fought bravely against the native hill peoples and, between encounters, completed his first published literary work, the short novel *Childhood* (1852). After receiving a commission in 1854, he was transferred to the army on the Danube and from there to Sevastopol, where he took part in the celebrated siege of that city during the Crimean War. He described these experiences in his popular "Sevastopol" sketches (1855–1856), in which he contrasted the uncomplaining attitude and courage of the common Russian soldiers with the self-interest and false heroics of the officers. At the end of the siege, Tolstoy returned to St. Petersburg and there associated with literary figures among whom he was already well known for his writings. He retired from the army in 1857. Except for two trips abroad in 1857 and 1860–1861, he remained at Yasnaya Polyana during the next five years. There he tended his estate, opened a village school, in which he put into practice his progressive theories of education, wrote textbooks, and founded a pedagogical magazine.

Middle Years. In 1862, Tolstoy married Sofia Andreyevna Bers, who was from a good family, and the next 15 years were the happiest of his life. With all the ardor of his intense nature, he devoted himself to marriage, fathered a large family that eventually reached 13 children, and built up and enlarged his property. During this period he ceased his educational activities and resumed creative writing. He completed a novel, begun years before, *The Cossacks* (1863), as well as his masterpieces *War and Peace* (1865–1869) and *Anna Karenina* (1875–1877).

Prosperous, famous, and seemingly contented with his existence, Tolstoy, in the early 1870's, began to be plagued with agonizing questions about the meaning and purpose of his life. From about 1874 he stubbornly searched for explanations, convinced that without a compelling reason for existence he could not go on living. He turned to religion, and the pivotal point in his conversion came when he believed that he had discovered the true significance of Christ's injunction to "resist not evil"—that is, not to resist those who try to do evil to one. Although he insisted that the Bible contained certain errors and distortions, he found in the teachings of Christ, corrected as he felt they should be if they were to retain their original substance, the explanation of the purpose of life. This aim, he felt, is to serve not our lower, animal nature, but rather the power within us. Our higher nature recognizes its own kinship with that power, he held, and it is that power that enables us to discern what is good. Our reason and conscience flow from it, and the purpose of our conscious life is to do its will. From the Bible he extracted five commandments, which he attributed to Christ. In brief form they are: do not become angry; do not lust; do not bind yourself by oaths; do not resist him that is evil; be good to the just and the unjust.

Last Years. For the rest of his life Tolstoy attempted to abide by these five commandments. The effort brought him into conflict with the state, with the Russian Orthodox Church, which excommunicated him, and with his wife and family. His new faith led him to attack the church for what it preached and to condemn ownership of property as a source of violence. It also induced him to advocate chastity and to abjure war, smoking, intoxicants, and the eating of meat. All forms of violence, he asserted, are wicked. Men should cease living by the work of others and refrain from taking part in the organized violence of governments. He preached charity, disapproved of the artificial culture of the upper classes, and maintained that the social order would improve only when all men learned to love each other.

Tolstoy advocated his new faith in numerous books and articles, most of which, because of government censorship, had to be published abroad and were then smuggled back into Russia. They carried his message to his countrymen and, in translation, to countless people abroad. To his reputation as a great novelist was added international fame as the "conscience of the world." Disciples attempted, with little success, to live according to Tolstoy's precepts. Eventually he came to dislike "Tolstoyism" as an organized movement, for he believed that the kingdom of God is within each man and will manifest itself in individual striving for perfection. He realized that the moral goal he set was often perfection, and he never expected men to attain it. Striving was the end. "We search for mind, powers, goodness, perfection in all this," he wrote in his diary, "but perfection is not given to man in anything. . . ."

During his last years Tolstoy became a world figure, and people from all over Russia and the world visited him to seek the advice of the bearded seer. He dressed simply, often worked with the peasants in the fields, learned to make his own boots, and in general tried to be as self-supporting as possible. Though he wished to renounce all his worldly belongings, his wife persuaded him to deed them to her, especially the valuable copyrights of his writings published before 1880, to be held in trust for their children. Finally, endless bickering with her over property and other matters, as well as a sense of shame at living in comfortable surroundings while he preached a life of poverty and abstention, led Tolstoy, at the age of 82, to depart secretly from his home one night, accompanied only by his faithful physician. It was something he had long wanted to do—to go off alone, to seek freedom from worldly comforts and cares, and thus to come closer to God. A few days later, on Nov. 20, 1910, he died at the tiny railroad station of Astapovo. His body was brought back to Yasnaya Polyana for burial.

WORKS

Early Fiction. Whatever Tolstoy's fame as a moralist and thinker may be, his enduring reputation rests largely on his magnificent literary productions. The early development of his creative art seems to have been a matter of trial and error rather than initial imitation. That is, though he continued and made quite his own the tradition of classical Russian realism begun by Pushkin, there is no marked dependence on preceding Russian authors. He may, however, have been somewhat influenced at the beginning by such foreign writers as Rousseau, Sterne, Stendhal, and later, Thackeray.

A suggestion of his method and approach may be found in the acute self-examinations in Tolstoy's early diary. This kind of searching analysis of the conscious and even subconscious motivation of thought and action appears in his first literary fragment, *A History of Yesterday* (1851), and also in *Childhood*, and its sequels *Boyhood* (1854) and *Youth* (1857). He was skillful in evoking childhood memories, which, when recalled with feeling—as they are—seem infallibly true and charming. He wrote, he said, from the heart and not from the head. Although these initial efforts draw heavily upon personal recollections, there is much sheer invention.

Compared with the work of other major writers, Tolstoy's fiction is unusually autobiographical. This fact is no reflection on his considerable imaginative powers, since the reality of recorded experience and observation that he transformed into art is rendered doubly effective by keen psychological analysis and the meticulous selection of significant detail.

The early Caucasian short stories, *A Raid* (1853), *The Woodfelling* (1855), and *The Memoirs of a Billiard-Marker* (1855), based on Tolstoy's actual experiences in that region, seem to be told merely for their own sake as interesting narratives. But in the short pieces that followed—*Lucerne* (1857), *Albert* (1858), *Three Deaths* (1859), and *Family Happiness* (1859)—he concentrates, in a didactic manner, on moral problems, notably the baseness and vulgarity of the cultured man. The large degree of subjectivism in most of the tales, however, is largely avoided in the stories *Two Hussars* (1856) and *Polikushka* (1863), in which the evil influences of a materialistic society are artistically suggested. It is also avoided in *Kholstomer* (1863; published 1886) a satire on human beings from the point of view of a horse, in which the noble animal's natural life is represented as superior to man's artificial existence. The contrast between natural man and man the spoiled product of civilization is given wonderful artistic expression in *The Cossacks* (1863), a short novel that rounds out Tolstoy's early literary period. The central figure, Olenin, a member of sophisticated society, proves to be no match for the natural, freedom-loving, uninhibited Cossacks, such as old Daddy Yeroshka, one of Tolstoy's most memorable creations.

Later Fiction. Tolstoy's mature art emerged in all its power in his first full-length novel, *War and Peace,* which has frequently been acclaimed by distinguished writers and critics as one of the greatest novels ever written. The work, which is essentially a historical novel, is set in the years between 1805 and 1814 and involves the fortunes of five families: the Rostovs, Bolkonskys, Bezukhovs, Kuragins, and Drubetskoys. Their interrelationships are vividly portrayed against a vast background of Russian social life and the titanic struggle of Napoleon's invasion of Russia. Tolstoy uses the novel to expound his philosophy of history and to theorize on war, thus introducing a didactic quality that may be considered an artistic flaw. There is no doubt that it is the incredibly rich variety of life portrayed, rather than the historical forces integrating it in the grand design of the work, that primarily interests readers.

Tolstoy always contended that it was more difficult to portray real life artistically than to invent fiction, and many of the characters in *War and Peace* are based on members of his family or on friends. Certainly within this novel, life itself is embodied in unforgettable scenes and in scores of vitally realized men and women. None of his other works so justifies his conviction that the aim of an artist is to compel one to love life in all its manifestations. *War and Peace* reveals his uncanny ability to make the ordinary and commonplace seem strange, new, and exciting.

Tolstoy's second full-length novel, *Anna Karenina*, is similar to *War and Peace* in narrative method and style; but it presents a striking contrast to the life-loving optimism of the earlier work, and its plot has more inner unity. Anna's tragedy unfolds slowly and remorselessly before a large audience of the social worlds of two capitals in the 1860's. Nearly all the fully-drawn characters, including the fascinating members of the Oblonsky and Shcherbatsky families, are involved in one way or another with the fate of the two star-crossed lovers, the adulterous Anna and Vronsky, who are effectively compared with the happy lovers, Kitty and Levin. While Tolstoy's characters are always brilliantly and perceptively portrayed, in *Anna Karenina* they are subjected to more intensive psychologizing and to a deeper, more searching moral probing. The novel is one of the great love stories of the world, and it is a measure of the moral balance preserved in the portrayal of the beautiful but tragically erring heroine that he persuades readers to judge her severely but at the same time with compassion.

Fiction After His Conversion. Tolstoy's spiritual crisis overtook him before he finished *Anna Karenina*. After his conversion he tended to devote much of his energy to books and articles on religious, moral, political, and social themes. In 1897, however, he finished *What Is Art?* (1898), an elaborate effort to propound an aesthetic system that would accord with his new moral philosophy and understanding of man's relation to life. In it he developed the thesis that the best literary art is that which "infects" the largest number of people with the loftiest feelings of love and compassion. In the literary works he wrote after his spiritual crisis, he attempted, with few exceptions, to conform to this thesis. At the same time, with inexorable consistency, he relegated his great works of art written before this to the category of "bad art."

Among various short tales done in the new manner, in a bare style and designed to appeal to simple folk as "good universal art," are such little masterpieces as *What Men Live By* (1881), *Two Old Men* (1885), *Evil Allures but Good Endures* (1885), *How Much Land Does a Man Need?* (1886), and *Three Questions* (1903).

Tolstoy's special concern with sex in his new faith in terms of chastity is powerfully reflected in *The Devil* (1889; published posthumously, 1911–1912), a story, based on an incident in Tolstoy's life, of a husband's struggle to overcome his lust for a pretty peasant girl. *The Kreutzer Sonata* (1890) combines an artistic study of a husband's jealousy with a didactic attack on society's sexual education of youth, which he regarded as mendacious.

In some of the works of his later period, Tolstoy came closer to the style, if not the subject matter, of his earlier fiction. Among these works are three outstanding stories: the incomplete *Memoirs of a Madman* (1884; published posthumously, 1911–1912), a rather thinly disguised fictional treatment of the oppressive fear of death that Tolstoy himself had experienced before his conversion; *The Death of Ivan Ilich* (1886), a remarkable account of the hero's mystical conversion when, confronted by death, he discovers the inner light of faith; and the exquisite *Master and Man* (1895), a different treatment of the same theme of mystical illumination, that reminds one of Tolstoy's statement that without simplicity there is no grandeur in art.

Tolstoy's only full-length novel during his old age, *Resurrection* (1899), marks a return to the adorned style and narrative manner of *Anna Karenina*. It concerns the involved relations of the nobleman Nekhlyudov with Katya Maslova, whom he seduces and deserts. Turned out of her home, she is driven to prostitution. Later Nekhlyudov serves as a conscience-stricken juror at the trial in which she is convicted of a crime she did not commit. The work has some outstanding scenes and fine characterizations, but it is marred artistically by its moral preaching and overt satire of social and religious abuses.

Major Nonfiction Works. Out of Tolstoy's great spiritual crisis emerged an extensive body of writing that is a tangible part of his literary experience and reveals his importance as a thinker whose ideas have not lost their significance today.

In *A Confession* (1882), one of the noblest utterances of man, he records the unique and overwhelming inner turmoil of a person extremely perplexed by life's most difficult problem—the relation of man to the infinite. It was followed by *An Examination of Dogmatic Theology* (1891), a vigorous attack on the church; *What I Believe* (1884), a systematic presentation of his views on religion; *What Then Must We Do?* (1902), his account of the Moscow slums, based on an early experience as a census worker, and an elucidation of the causes and cure of social and economic ills; and *The Kingdom of God Is Within You* (1894), the fullest statement of his Christian anarchism and his belief in nonresistance to evil.

These lengthy works, along with many shorter essays, often attack specific governmental and social practices. The use of intoxicants and tobacco is deplored in *Why Do Men Stupefy Themselves?* (1890). Both this work and *I Cannot Be Silent!* (1908), his protest against the execution of revolutionists, are filled with the passionate intensity of his new faith and demonstrate his unusual intellectual capacities and his skill as an astute and convincing logician.

In Tolstoy's search for truth, a compulsive need to achieve the ultimate rational explanation sometimes led him to push theory to the limits of absurdity. However, he never failed to place his faith in the moral development of the people as a final answer to what he regarded as the universal oppression of the many by the few. The ideal human condition, he insisted, must inevitably depend upon the growing moral perfection of each individual through the observance of the supreme law of love and the consequent rejection of every form of violence.

TOLTEC REMAINS include these columns in the form of anthropomorphic figures at Tula, in the State of Hidalgo, some of eight that once held up a temple roof.

Posthumously Published Fiction. Tolstoy withheld publication of a number of works written during the latter part of his life. The best of these were all published in 1911–1912, after his death. *Hadji Murad* is a superb short novel describing a brave Caucasian chief who deserts to the Russians and is killed while trying to see his son in secret. *Father Sergei* is about an aristocrat who conquers his spiritual pride and becomes a hermit-monk. *After the Ball* tells the story of a youth who loses his passion for the daughter of a colonel after the latter orders a soldier clubbed through the ranks for a military offense. *The False Coupon* is a fictional moralistic study of how human goodness can develop out of evil. And *Alyosha Gorshok*, perhaps Tolstoy's last short story, is a perfect artistic gem about a peasant drudge who finds complete contentment in life through service to others.

Plays. Drama was a form of art to which Tolstoy was devoted but in which he was not always successful. His finest play is *The Power of Darkness* (1887), a realistic tragedy of peasant life that reveals the power of evil to beget further evil. *The Fruits of Enlightenment* (1889) is a pleasant comedy that pokes fun at the foibles of aristocratic society.

Two plays were published in the posthumous edition of 1911–1912. These are *The Light Shineth in Darkness,* in which the hero's inability to persuade his family of the rightness of his unconventional beliefs echoes Tolstoy's own situation, and *The Living Corpse,* a convincing psychological dramatization of the strange experience and loving sacrifice of a drunkard. The latter play is suffused with a kindly tolerance of human waywardness and is devoid of the moralizing element that detracts from the enjoyment of some of Tolstoy's works written during his last years. See also ANNA KARENINA; WAR AND PEACE.

ERNEST J. SIMMONS
Author of "Leo Tolstoy"

Bibliography

Editions of Tolstoy's works, in English, include incomplete ones, tr. by Louise and Aylmer Maude (21 vols.; London, 1928–1937) and tr. and ed. by Leo Wiener (24 vols.; Boston, 1904–1905). English translations of individual novels and collections of shorter tales may be found in Everyman Library, Penguin Classics, and Modern Library. A complete Russian edition, including letters, notebooks, and diaries, is in 90 volumes (Moscow 1928–1958).

Biographies

Simmons, Ernest J., *Leo Tolstoy* (Boston 1946).
Tolstoy, Alexandra, *Tolstoy: A Life of My Father* (New York 1953).
Troyat, Henri, *Tolstoy,* tr. by N. Amphoux (New York 1967).

Criticism

Bayley, John, *Tolstoy and the Novel* (London 1966).
Berlin, Isaiah, *The Hedgehog and the Fox* (New York 1954).
Christian, R. F., *Tolstoy: A Critical Introduction* (London 1969).
Lavrin, Janko, *Tolstoy: An Approach* (London 1944).
Noyes, George, *Tolstoy* (New York 1918).
Simmons, Ernest J., *Introduction to Tolstoy's Writings* (Chicago 1968).
Steiner, George, *Tolstoy or Dostoevsky: An Essay in the Old Criticism* (New York 1959).

TOLTEC, tōl′tek. The Toltecs were an Indian people who exercised political domination in central Mexico from about 900 A. D. to about 1200, before the advent of the Aztecs. Their capital was Tollan, now Tula, in the State of Hidalgo. The name "Toltec" is derived from the name of the capital. The actual extent of the Toltec Empire has not been determined, but Toltec influences reached as far south as Yucatán and highland Guatemala. It would seem, however, that this expansion was due to bands led by Toltec war lords acting independently and does not represent the expansion of a unified empire.

The Toltecs were a composite group, formed by Nahua, Otomí, and Nonoalca elements. The Nahua Toltecs, politically the dominant group, had invaded the center of Mexico from a northwesterly direction (possibly from Zacatecas, Jalisco, or the Lerma River basin) around the beginning of the 10th century. The chronicles call them Chichimec Toltecs. The Nonoalca seem to have belonged to the Mazatec and Chocho-Popolocan groups. It is possible that they were carriers of traditions of the Teotihuacán civilization, and represented the culturally dominant element. Chocho-Popoloca and Mazatecs now live in southern Puebla and northern Oaxaca.

The most important figure in Toltec history was Ce Acatl Topiltzin, generally called Quetzalcoatl. It seems, however, that this name was really the title of the highest priest and king and therefore was applied to different men at different times. Ce Acatl Topiltzin founded Tollan, where he established his capital during the second half of the 10th century. His reign was troubled by internal strife between the partisans of the Feathered Serpent god (also called Quetzalcoatl) and those of the god Tezcatlipoca. The sociopolitical background of these religious disturbances was apparently a conflict between theocratic and militaristic tendencies in the organization of the state as well as rivalries among different ethnic groups making up the empire. Ce Acatl Topiltzin was finally forced into exile and went to the Gulf Coast, where he died at the end of the 10th century. Later he was deified and identified in myths with the planet Venus, the morning and evening star.

Studies of evidence by the Mexican ethnologist Wigberto Jiménez Moreno after 1934 and excavations by the archaeologist Jorge Acosta after 1940 made it possible to identify the ruins found on the outskirts of the town of Tula with the ruins of ancient Tollan. The identification of historical Tollan with the ruins of Teotihuacán, formerly accepted by many archaeologists, has been proved wrong. It is clear, moreover, that Teotihuacán antedates the Toltec period.

Features of Tollan include sculptured panels showing jaguars and coyotes, and others of eagles eating human hearts. Architectural details of Tollan are closely paralleled at the Maya center Chichén Itzá.

PEDRO ARMILLAS
State University of New York, Stony Brook

TOLU TREE, tə-lōō′, a tall tropical South American tree that yields a type of balsam used in making perfumes and cough mixtures. The tolu tree reaches a height of 75 feet (23 meters) or more. It has a straight trunk with thick rough bark. The leaves are pinnately compound, with the leaflets arranged alternately. They are oblong in shape and from 2 to 3½ inches (50–90 mm) long. The flowers, which resemble those of the sweet pea, are white or whitish.

The tolu tree, a member of the legume family (Leguminosae), is usually classified as *Myroxylon balsamum* and is divided into two varieties: *M. balsamum balsamum* and *M. balsamum pereirae*. The balsam obtained from the first is called balsam of tolu and that from the latter is called balsam of Peru. Some authorities consider the two trees to be separate species.

J. A. YOUNG, *U. S. Department of Agriculture*

TOLUCA, tə-lōō′kə, is a city in south central Mexico, about 42 miles (67 km) west of Mexico City, in Mexico state, of which it is the capital. Its name is officially Toluca de Lerdo. Though situated at an altitude of 8,000 feet (2,530 meters), the city enjoys mild temperatures. To the south the Nevado de Toluca, an extinct snow-capped volcano, and the mountains around it are covered with evergreen forests exploited for their valuable woods. The fertile Toluca Valley, irrigated by the Lerma River, is an important agricultural area.

After the 1940's, with the tremendous growth of Mexico City, Toluca's economy shifted from a rural to an industrial base. Local industries include food processing and the manufacture of textiles, chemicals, and automobiles. Toluca's development has been partially absorbed into Mexico City, and many of its workers commute between the cities. The famous market in Toluca where Indians sell their handicrafts is popular with tourists. Population: (1960) 77,124.

REYNALDO AYALA, *San Diego State College*

TOLUENE, tol′yə-wēn, is an aromatic hydrocarbon compound with the formula $C_6H_5CH_3$. It is also called *methylbenzene*. Approximately half of the toluene produced is used as a gasoline additive to raise the octane number of gasoline and to reduce the tendency for the fuel to knock in high compression engines. Some toluene is used as a solvent. It is also converted into trinitrotoluene (TNT), primarily for use as a military explosive. Toluene is an important starting material for the manufacture of benzene, benzoic acid, benzaldehyde, phenol, and other chemical products. These include toluene diisocyanate for polyurethane plastics, toluene sodium sulfonate for detergents, and benzyl chloride for pharmaceuticals, insecticides, and dyes.

Toluene is a flammable liquid which solidifies below −95° C (−139° F) and boils at 111° C (232° F). Its density is 0.866 g/ml (54 lb/cu ft) at 20° C. It is only slightly soluble in water but dissolves readily in ethanol, ether, acetone, chloroform, carbon disulfide, and glacial acetic acid.

Toluene was formerly obtained almost exclusively from the coal tar by-product of the coke industry. Now approximately 90% is produced by catalytic reforming of the naphtha fraction from petroleum distillation, using platinum as a catalyst. The product is a mixture of substances sometimes called "platformate." It can be used directly as a gasoline additive or fractionally distilled to separate benzene, toluene, xylene, and other products.

OTTO W. NITZ
Stout State University, Menomonie, Wis.

TOLUIDINE, tə-lōō′ə-dēn, any of three isomeric aminotoluenes with the formula $CH_3C_6H_4NH_2$. All three compounds are used in the manufacture of dyes and other organic chemicals. o-Toluidine is used in printing textiles and to make certain dye colors more resistant to acids.

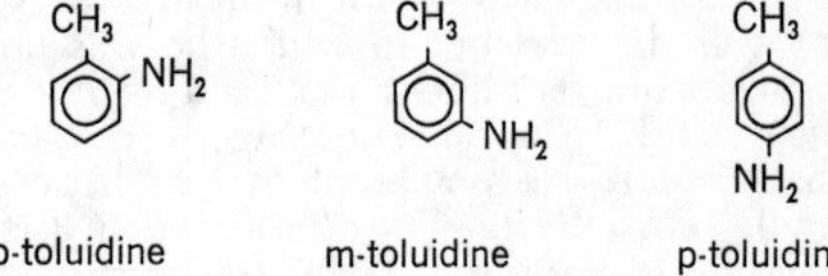

The toluidines are toxic, and their effects on human beings are similar to those of aniline—cyanosis, destruction of blood hemoglobin, dizziness, headache, mental confusion. The compounds may enter the body through inhalation of vapors, swallowing, or skin absorption. Ingestion of relatively small amounts can cause death.

o-Toluidine and m-toluidine are liquids at room temperature, melting at −24° C (11° F) and −30° C (−22° F) respectively. p-Toluidine is a solid, melting at 44° C (111° F). All have boiling points slightly above 200° C (392° F). All are soluble in alcohol and ether but only slightly soluble in water.

o-Toluidine and p-toluidine are produced by heating toluene with nitric and sulfuric acids. The product of this reaction is a mixture of o- and p-nitrotoluene. The mixture is separated, and each nitrotoluene is reduced by iron in the presence of hydrochloric acid to the corresponding toluidine. m-Toluidine is made from p-toluidine by a complicated series of reactions.

OTTO W. NITZ
Stout State University Menomonie, Wis.

TOLYATTI, tō-lyä'tē, is a city in the USSR, in Kuibyshev oblast of the Russian SFSR. Tolyatti (or Togliatti) is situated on the Volga River, near the Kuibyshev dam and hydroelectric station. The city has a large automobile plant, which opened in 1970, producing Fiat-type cars. It also manufactures synthetic rubber and fertilizer.

Tolyatti arose in the 18th century as Stavropol, was moved to higher ground in the 1950's when the Kuibyshev reservoir was filled, and was renamed in 1964 for Palmiro Togliatti, Italian Communist leader. Population: (1970) 251,000.

THEODORE SHABAD
Editor of "Soviet Geography"

TOM JONES, a novel by the English author Henry Fielding, published in 1749. Regarded as Fielding's masterpiece, it unites a classical discipline of form with the boisterous energy of the picaresque novel to realize more fully than Fielding's earlier *Joseph Andrews* his concept of the novel as a "comic epic-poem in prose."

Tom Jones, a foundling, is taken in by Squire Allworthy and raised as a gentleman. The first six books, set in Somersetshire, describe Tom's youthful escapades, his awakening love for Sophia, the daughter of Allworthy's neighbor Squire Western, and his banishment as a result of the machinations of Allworthy's nephew Blifil. The middle six books detail Tom's adventures on the road to London, including his involvement with the amorous Mrs. Waters, and Sophia's flight from home to escape marriage to Blifil. The final six books relate the experiences of Tom and Sophia in London society. Tom eventually ends up in prison, disowned by both Sophia and Allworthy, and apparently guilty of incest when it turns out that Mrs. Waters is actually Jenny Jones, his supposed mother. But Mrs. Waters reveals that Tom's real mother, before her marriage to Blifil's father, was Allworthy's sister Bridget, and Lawyer Dowling exposes Blifil's concealment of his mother's deathbed confession. Tom is restored to favor, and the story ends with the wedding of the hero and heroine.

The novel is remarkable for its diversity of character, incident, and social scene, its robust and witty style, and the generous humanity of its author, who addresses the reader in the prefatory essays to each book. The wonderfully intricate plot dramatizes the complex interaction of appearance and reality in the social and moral spheres, the inescapable chain of causality in all human experience, and the necessity of mature wisdom as the guardian of good nature and virtuous intentions. But the novel's greatness lies finally in the universal largess of its comic vision and its vigorous celebration of the fundamental goodness of human nature.

GLENN W. HATFIELD, *Author of "Henry Fielding and the Language of Irony"*

Further Reading: Battestin, Martin C., ed., *Twentieth Century Interpretations of Tom Jones* (Englewood Cliffs, N. J., 1968).

TOM SAWYER is a novel by Mark Twain, published in 1876. Set in a small Mississippi River town before the Civil War, *The Adventures of Tom Sawyer* deals with the escapades of an imaginative and enterprising boy. Tom plays hooky from school, offends his childhood sweetheart Becky Thatcher, goes on nocturnal sorties with his famous boon companion, Huckleberry Finn, and becomes accidentally involved in the murderous doings of a half-breed criminal named Injun Joe. In the end, Tom is reconciled with Becky Thatcher and with the forces of community law and order, when he testifies to save an innocent man accused of a murder committed by Injun Joe. There are other adventures, including the episode in which he hoodwinks his friends to do his work of whitewashing a fence —a story that has become a literary classic in its own right.

The characters are all drawn clearly. Tom Sawyer himself, the good-natured but irresponsible Huck Finn, the brightly sweet Becky Thatcher, and the simple, faithful, and affectionate Aunt Polly, with whom Tom makes his home, are depicted humorously and with golden sympathy. As a result, the elusive spirit of youth is captured in their history. No matter how melodramatic the plot may wax at times, there is a saline element of sanity and an ironic shrewdness in Twain's treatment of the characters. These qualities maintain the net tone of his narrative this side of farce.

As a deeply nostalgic and poetic re-creation of the author's own youth on the Mississippi, in what he felt was a vanished era, the novel has retained its appeal for successive generations of children and adults and has come to be regarded, along with its sequel, *Huckleberry Finn,* as one of the greatest American novels.

MARKHAM HARRIS
University of Washington

TOM THUMB, General (1838–1883), American midget, who gained international fame as a star of P. T. Barnum's "Greatest Show on Earth." He was born Charles Sherwood Stratton in Bridgeport, Conn., on Jan. 4, 1838. His parents were of normal stature, and he showed no abnormality until at the age of about 6 months he ceased to grow. In 1842, when he was discovered by Barnum, he was somewhat over 2 feet tall and weighed 15 pounds. Later his height increased to

Wedding of "Tom Thumb" and Lavinia Warren in 1863.

CULVER PICTURES

3 feet 4 inches. He was perfectly proportioned, lively, and winsome and was quick to learn singing and dancing. His exhibitions, in which he was billed as "General Tom Thumb," were immensely successful both in the United States and abroad. In 1863 he married Lavinia Warren, also a midget in Barnum's troupe. He died in Middleboro, Mass., on July 15, 1883. See also BARNUM, PHINEAS TAYLOR.

TOM-TOM, a kind of drum. The term refers to the small deep drums used by the American Indian and by primitive peoples native to India and China. Usually such drums are struck by the bare hand to produce a short hollow sound. The term also refers to sets of drums in modern dance bands that imitate primitive tom-toms. Some may be tuned to a high pitch. Others are not tunable.

The tom-tom is sometimes equated with or distinguished from the tam-tam, or gong.

TOMAHAWK, a class of weapons generally associated with North American Indians, the name deriving from an Algonkian term for club. In its broadest sense "tomahawk" embraces wooden clubs and stone axes, but the term came to refer chiefly to metal hatchets made by white artisans for the Indian trade. Most tomahawks were forged of iron with steel edges, but grass, pewter, and even lead were used. English, French, and Dutch axes, modeled after a heavy European type, became immediately popular as trade items with the northeast tribes, but were superseded in the early 18th century by the lighter "belt ax," considered a true tomahawk.

Although the belt ax persisted through the 19th century, coexisting with many other varieties, the three classic tomahawks are the pipe-hatchet combination, the Plains war hatchet, and the spontoon type. The pipe tomahawk, used in both the Eastern Woodlands and Plains areas and particularly desired for ceremonial purposes, featured a small metal pipe bowl opposite the blade. Handles were drilled for smoking purposes. The Plains war hatchet was a clumsy, wide-headed tomahawk, usually with a highly decorated handle. The spontoon type, with a pointed instead of an ax head, was also primarily ceremonial and usually included a pipe bowl. Tomahawks were rarely thrown in combat.

STEPHEN E. FERACA, *Bureau of Indian Affairs*

PIPE TOMAHAWK, a Chickasaw Indian implement made about 1765. This one is 18 inches (46 cm) long.

THE MUSEUM OF THE AMERICAN INDIAN, HEYE FOUNDATION

TOMATO, tə-mā′tō, one of the most widely grown and economically important vegetable crops. Botanically, tomatoes are fruits, but they are commonly referred to as vegetables. They are eaten raw or cooked and are often processed to make tomato paste, sauce, puree, catsup, or juice. Tomatoes are rich in potassium, vitamin A, and vitamin C. A single medium-sized tomato has about 33 calories, just about half the calories of an apple the same size.

The common tomato plant (*Lycopersicum esculentum*) is a member of the nightshade family (Solanaceae) and is closely related to the potato and eggplant. It originated in the highlands of South America near the equator and was introduced to Europe in the mid-1500's. Tomatoes were eaten in Italy as early as 1554 and were grown in English, French, Belgian, and German gardens by the early 1580's. In Italy the tomato was popularly known as the gold apple (*pomi d'oro*), probably because most varieties were yellow. In France it was known as the love apple, probably because it was believed to be an aphrodisiac.

The tomato plant had also been carried northward into North America, but the fruit was thought to be poisonous and not eaten. In the United States tomatoes were not cultivated until the late 1700's and were not widely eaten until about 1900. Today, tomatoes are cultivated commercially in every state of the United States, at an annual value of about $500 million.

THE TOMATO PLANT

The tomato plant may be bushy or vinelike and range in height from 3 to 6 feet (0.9–1.8 meters). Although it is a perennial, it is grown as an annual. Its leaves are composed of many small and large leaflets, and the small yellow nodding flowers are borne in clusters of 3 to 7. Once fruit development starts, it takes 45 to 50 days for the fruits to mature.

The size, shape, and color of the fruits vary according to the variety. Some tomatoes are small and round, somewhat like cherries. Others are shaped like pears or plums, and some are nearly spherical. Still others are very large and flattened, weighing up to 2 pounds (0.9 kg). The flesh may be white, yellow, orange, pink, or red, and the skin may be yellow or colorless. The colorless skin of pink or red tomatoes may appear to be pinkish or reddish because the flesh underneath it is visible.

CULTIVATION AND VARIETIES

Tomatoes are a warm-season crop. Only in warm climates are the seeds planted out-of-doors. In cooler regions the field is set with young plants that have been started several weeks earlier in protected beds or in warmer regions.

Home Garden Cultivation. Tomato plants for home gardens should be planted after the danger of spring frosts has passed. They respond well to fertilizer solutions rich in phosphates and need to be irrigated during periods of dry weather. The plants may be trained on stakes or trellises and mulched with hay, straw, or grass. The plants are spaced 1 to 2 feet (30–60 cm) apart in rows that are 3 to 4 feet (90–120 cm) apart. Among the favorite varieties of the home gardener are Red Cherry, Bonney Best, Marglobe, Jubilee, Rutgers, and Beefsteak.

Commercial Cultivation. Tomatoes for processing are grown mostly in California, where

BURPEE SEEDS

R. A. SCHLEGEL

TOMATO VINES (*left*), with Big Boy and Standard varieties. When grown staked, as here, the vines are less productive than when allowed to sprawl, but the fruit is larger and cleaner. The tomatoes above are Beefsteak, Round, Plum, and Cherry.

they are seeded directly in the field. In the eastern and north central states, fields may be directly seeded or set with plants transported from southern states. Among the best processing varieties are Bouncer, New Yorker, Campbell 1327, VF 145, VF 13L, Red Top, San Marzano, and VF Roma. The VF varieties are resistant to *Verticillium* and *Fusarium* fungi, which cause destructive wilt diseases.

Tomatoes for the fresh market are grown out-of-doors in late fall and winter in Florida. The states producing most of the early spring crop of fresh tomatoes are Florida, Texas, and California. During the early and late summer tomatoes are produced in almost all states. The leading producers are California, New Jersey, Alabama, New York, Pennsylvania, and Michigan. The varieties most often grown commercially for the fresh market include Fireball, Big Boy, Manapal, Floradel, and Pinkshipper.

Greenhouse tomatoes are marketed every month of the year, with peak production in May, June, and July. The center of the greenhouse tomato industry is Cleveland, Ohio. There are also major producing areas near Indianapolis, Ind.; Grand Rapids, Mich.; Toledo, Ohio; Las Vegas, Nev.; and Leamington, Ontario, in Canada. Leading greenhouse varieties include the disease-resistant pink varieties W–R–25, Hybrid–O, and M–R–12, and the red varieties Michigan–Ohio Hybrid, Rapids, Tropic, Manapal, Wolverine 119, and Tuckcross 520.

HARVESTING

Tomatoes are usually ready for harvesting 125 to 135 days after the seedlings emerge from the ground. Because ripening continues after the fruits are picked, tomatoes are usually still somewhat green when harvested.

For hundreds of years tomatoes were harvested by hand. Tomatoes for the fresh market as well as those grown in home gardens and greenhouses are still handpicked, but most tomatoes for processing are harvested by machine. In 1969, 70% of all processing tomatoes raised in the United States were grown in California, and of these, 95% were machine-harvested.

With the advent of mechanical harvesting has come a great change in the types of varieties developed. In order for machine harvesting to be successful, the tomatoes must be firm and resistant to cracking. They should also mature at about the same rate.

PESTS AND DISEASES

Tomatoes are attacked by a wide variety of pests and diseases. Among the insects that destroy tomato plants are flea beetles, aphids, white flies, cutworms, fruit worms, and hornworms. Control of these insect pests includes the raising of resistant varieties and the judicious use of short-acting pesticides such as Malathion and carbaryl (Sevin).

Blossom-end rot results from a deficiency of calcium and can be treated by adding lime to the soil or spraying the leaves with a calcium solution. Maintaining adequate moisture in the soil also controls this disorder.

Many commercial and home-garden varieties of tomatoes are resistant to attack by the fungi *Verticillium* and *Fusarium*. These fungi cause the most destructive tomato wilt diseases. However, other types of fungi are also destructive, causing leaf mold, leaf blight, gray mold, and anthracnose. The control of these diseases relies on the use of fungicides and selecting the best time of planting. The incidence and severity of these fungus diseases are closely related to weather conditions.

Bacterial canker, another serious disease, is transmitted by seeds. The best control measure is the use of certified hot-water treated seed. The tobacco mosaic virus attacks tomatoes, but resistant varieties are available. The virus may also be controlled by fumigation of the soil.

SYLVAN H. WITTWER, *Director, Michigan Agricultural Experiment Station*

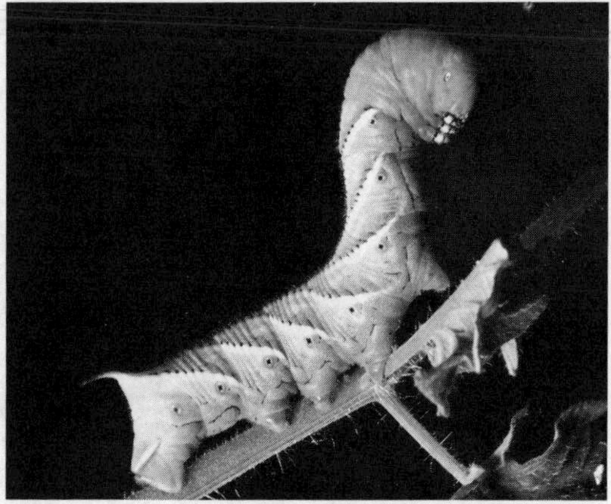

C. G. MAXWELL, FROM NATIONAL AUDUBON SOCIETY

Tomato hornworm

TOMATO HORNWORM, the common name for the larva of the tomato sphinx moth (*Protoparce quinquemaculata*). The tomato hornworm is a pest of several members of the potato family, especially the tomato plant. It reaches a length of 4 inches (100 mm) and is bright green with eight whitish oblique stripes down the side of its body. A prominent back "horn" protrudes from its back near the posterior end.

The adult moth is grayish with long slender wings measuring about 4 or 5 inches (100–125 mm) from tip to tip. It greatly resembles the tobacco sphinx except that it has five pairs of yellowish orange spots along the back of the abdomen. The adult feeds on flower nectar.

The tomato hornworm as well as the tobacco hornworm can be controlled by picking the larvae off the plants or by spraying with insecticides.

DON DAVIS, *Smithsonian Institution*

TOMB, to͞om, a grave or burial place, often constructed of stone or some other long-lasting material. Technically, any burial place can be called a tomb, but the most famous examples are monumental structures built for kings, emperors, or other persons of great importance. The pyramids of Egypt and the Taj Mahal in India are among the greatest such monuments.

Famous Tombs. The pyramids are veritable mountains of stone built in the desert as tombs and memorials for the pharaohs of the Old Kingdom in Egypt (2664–2155 B.C.). Each contains a secret funerary chamber as well as a funerary temple for the cult of the dead. Huge tombs like the pyramids reflect the social stratification of the society that built them. They require the labor of thousands, making great demands on the society's economic resources, and thus can be provided only for the wealthy and powerful.

Among the other famous tombs of antiquity was the Mausoleum, a funerary monument built at Halicarnassus (now in Turkey) in the 4th century B.C., for the region's ruler, Mausolos. The remains of the structure are now in the British Museum. The word mausoleum has become a generic term for tomb.

Perhaps the best-known of all tombs is the Taj Mahal, in Agra, India, a white marble structure, built in the 17th century by the Mogul emperor Shah Jahan, in memory of his wife.

Among famous American tombs is the Tomb of the Unknown Soldier at Arlington National Cemetery. This is a grave marked by a white marble monument. Grant's Tomb, the burial place of General Ulysses S. Grant and his wife in New York City, is a granite mausoleum 165 feet (50 meters) high at its summit.

Burial Practices. Archaeologists get valuable information on the life of ancient peoples from their tombs and burial practices. Ancient forms of tombs include prehistoric mounds or tumuli that were built as individual or collective places of burial. The mounds constructed by the prehistoric Hopewell Indians of Ohio often contained burials, both skeletal and cremated remains of individuals. Such collective burials in effect constitute cemeteries. One of the most remarkable prehistoric cemeteries is the Paracas Necropolis in southern Peru. In this sandy area, a form of natural mummification occurred. The dead are found in individual funerary bundles, of conical shape, up to 5 feet high, containing elaborate textiles, pottery, and with other objects.

Within a tomb, bodies may be placed in simple wooden coffins or more complex containers, such as sarcophagi. A sarcophagus is usually made of stone, though other materials have been used. Sarcophagi vary in size from large coffins to substantial monuments. The ancient Egyptians, who mummified their royal dead, placed them in a series of mummy cases and sarcophagi of human shape and made of a variety of precious materials.

Sarcophagi were placed in tombs or in other buildings, such as temples or churches. Medieval and Renaissance sarcophagi often include a sculptured likeness of the dead person, either lying on the top of the structure or kneeling in an attitude of prayer. A sarcophagus or grave marker in a church can itself be called a tomb. The shrine of St. Thomas à Becket in Canterbury Cathedral was a famous tomb that attracted great numbers of pilgrims in the Middle Ages.

Special areas in churches, or special memorial structures, are set apart for a select group of persons. For example, the great men of Britain are entombed in Westminster Abbey and those of France in the Pantheon. See also CATACOMBS; DEATH CUSTOMS AND RITES; PYRAMID.

ERIKA BOURGUIGNON
The Ohio State University

TOMBALBAYE, tôm-bäl-bä′ye, **François** (1918–), first president of Chad. He was born in the village of Badaya on June 15, 1918, of Protestant parents. He became an assistant teacher after leaving school and took an early interest in trade unionism, becoming president of the Syndicat Autonome du Tchad. After joining the Parti Progressiste Tchadien (PPT), he rose quickly to become an assistant to one of modern Chad's earliest political leaders, Gabriel Lisette.

Tombalbaye held several elected posts under the French administration. He was elected to the Territorial Assembly of Chad in 1952 and again in 1957, when he was also elected to the Grand Council of French Equatorial Africa. He became premier of Chad in 1959.

Soon after the country achieved independence in August 1960, Tombalbaye was elected president. His administration was plagued by problems deriving from the underdevelopment of Chad and by periodic rebellion of the Muslim nomadic peoples of the north. To deal with these problems Tombalbaye obtained substantial French economic aid and military support.

L. GRAY COWAN, *Columbia University*

TOMBSTONE, to͞om′stōn, is a city in southeastern Arizona, in Cochise county, about 69 miles (110 km) southeast of Tucson. It is primarily residential, and many inhabitants work for the U. S. Army Strategic Communications Command at nearby Fort Huachuca. The main economic activity of Tombstone is tourism, related to its past as a lawless silver-mining town.

The site was settled by Ed Schieffelin, a prospector, in 1879. His rich silver finds drew thousands of miners and gamblers. Shootings were common. Boot Hill graveyard was named for the many who died with their boots on. Flooding of the mines in the early 1900's ended the bonanza. The former courthouse is a state historical monument. One of many tourist attractions is the O. K. Corral, where the Earps fought the Clantons. St. Paul's Episcopal Church is the oldest Protestant Church still in use in Arizona.

Tombstone was incorporated as a city in 1881. Government is by mayor and council. Population: 1,283.

DOROTHY M. DOUST
Tombstone Regional Branch Library

JOSEF MUENCH

BOOT HILL, TOMBSTONE, Arizona, is a cemetery holding graves of men who "died with their boots on."

TOMCOD, tom′kod, either of two species of cods found along the coasts of North America. They are primarily bottom-living marine and brackish water fishes, but they can spend their entire life in fresh water. The Atlantic tomcod (*Microgadus tomcod*) occurs from the Gulf of St. Lawrence to Virginia, while the Pacific tomcod (*M. proximus*) is found in waters from Alaska to central California.

An adult tomcod is a small, plump fish, 12 to 13 inches (30–33 cm) long. It has a slender barbel on the tip of the lower jaw, three dorsal fins, two anal fins, and pelvic fins with small tendril-like extensions. The Atlantic tomcod is brown or olive with irregular mottling on the sides and back. The Pacific tomcod is olive or brown above, and white below. Tomcods may deposit 20,000 to 30,000 eggs.

The Atlantic tomcod, a fine food fish, is caught both commercially and for sport on a modest scale, especially during December and January in New England and eastern Canada. The Pacific tomcod, also a fine food fish, is caught only incidentally in trawl-fishing operations.

WILLIAM B. SCOTT
University of Toronto

TOMLINSON, Henry Major (1873–1958), English author. He was born in London on June 21, 1873. After working for a shipping company he joined the staff of the *Morning Leader* in 1904, continuing with the *Daily News* when the two newspapers merged. His first book, *The Sea and the Jungle* (1912), describes a voyage to Brazil. Tomlinson was a war correspondent in France (1914–1917) and from 1917 to 1923 was literary editor of the *Nation* and the *Athenaeum*.

Tomlinson won the French award, the Prix Femina-Vie Heureuse, for his first novel *Gallions Reach* (1927). Among his other novels are *The Snows of Helicon* (1933), *The Day Before* (1939), *Morning Light* (1946), and *The Trumpet Shall Sound* (1957). Tomlinson also wrote several travel books, including *South to Cadiz* (1934) and *The Face of the Earth* (1950). His *A Mingled Yarn: Autobiographical Sketches* appeared in 1953. He died in London on Feb. 5, 1958.

TOMMY ATKINS is a nickname for British soldiers and other rank-and-file personnel. It originated with the use of the name "Thomas Atkins" as a model in filling out printed military forms—like the use of "John Doe."

TOMONAGA SHINICHIRO, tō-mō-nä-gä shēn-ē-chē-rō (1906–), Japanese physicist, who shared the 1965 Nobel Prize in physics with Richard P. Feynman and Julian S. Schwinger "for their fundamental work in quantum electrodynamics with deep-flowing consequences for the physics of elementary particles."

Tomonaga began his research in quantum electrodynamics on graduating from Kyoto University in 1929. He worked under Yoshio Nishina at the Institute of Physical and Chemical Research in Tokyo and, from 1937 through 1939, under Werner Heisenberg in Leipzig, where he wrote his Ph. D. thesis. On returning to Tokyo, he became interested in mesons and developed the intermediate coupling theory to explain the structure of the proton and neutron. In 1942, Tomonaga proposed the covariant formalism of quantum field theory. This, combined with his intermediate coupling theory, enabled him to solve the divergence difficulty in quantum electrodynamics in accordance with the special theory of relativity.

During World War II, Tomonaga turned his attention to microwave systems. He also made the mechanism of magnetron oscillation more understandable by explaining the secular motion of electrons in the split-anode magnetron. In 1949, while at the Institute for Advanced Study in Princeton, N. J., he devised a 1-dimensional model of the many-fermion system in the high density limit. With this work, a new frontier in theoretical physics—the modern many-body problem—was opened up.

Tomonaga's entire academic career was spent at Tokyo Kyoiku University. In 1941 he was appointed professor of physics there, and he was president from 1956 to 1962. He retired in 1969.

N. FUKUDA
Tokyo Kyoiku University

TOMPKINS, tom′kənz, **Daniel D.** (1774–1825), American political leader. Governor of New York and vice president of the United States, he was also a prominent reformer. Tompkins was born in Scarsdale, N. Y., on June 21, 1774. He graduated from Columbia College in 1795, was admitted to the New York bar in 1797, and was elected to the state legislature in 1803. The following year he was elected to Congress but resigned to serve on the New York supreme court.

Tompkins, known popularly as the "farmer's boy," ran successfully for governor in 1807 and was reelected in 1810, 1813, and 1816. A supporter of public education, he also advocated prison reform and better treatment for Indians. Under his aegis, the legislature in 1817 passed an act abolishing slavery in New York by 1827.

Tompkins was U. S. vice president under James Monroe from 1817 to 1825. In 1824, Congress reimbursed him for personal losses in public service, a vindication of charges that as governor he had mismanaged state and federal funds during the War of 1812. He died in Staten Island, N. Y., on June 11, 1825.

LEO HERSHKOWITZ
Queens College, New York

TOMSK, tômsk, a city in the USSR, is the capital of Tomsk oblast in western Siberia. Tomsk is situated on the high east bank of the Tom River, above its junction with the Ob. The city manufactures electrical equipment and ball bearings. It is also an important educational center, with Siberia's oldest university, which was founded in 1888. Tomsk, dating from 1604, was one of the first Russian settlements in Siberia. It became an administrative center of western Siberia in 1804 but was eclipsed early in the 20th century by Novosibirsk, which arose on the newly built Trans-Siberian Railroad.

Tomsk oblast, with an area of 122,400 square miles (317,000 sq km), was a sparsely settled lumbering region until the discovery of oil and gas in the 1960's. Population: (1970) of the city, 339,000; of the oblast, 786,000.

THEODORE SHABAD
Editor of "Soviet Geography"

TON, a unit of mass. The *short ton,* equal to 2,000 avoirdupois pounds, is used in the United States, Canada, and South Africa. The *long ton,* equal to 2,240 avoirdupois pounds, is used in Britain. The *metric ton,* equal to 2,204.632 avoirdupois pounds (1,000 kilograms), is used by most of the other countries in the world. (An avoirdupois pound is a unit of mass equal to 0.45359237 kilogram; the kilogram is a unit of mass equal to the mass of the International Prototype Kilogram.) Ton, pound, and kilogram are also used as units of weight. A weight of 1 ton means a force equal to the pull of the earth on a body whose mass is 1 ton. See also WEIGHTS AND MEASURES.

TONALITY, in music, is the relationship of all tones in a composition in regard to a tonal center. Tonality, in this sense, is related to harmony, in that the individual tones are not separate entities but depend for their meaning on the relationship (harmonics) of one to another and, ultimately, to the dominating tonic tone. Music that is organized outside the tonal system (that is, without a tonal or harmonic center) is known as "atonal music." See ATONAL MUSIC; HARMONY.

TONAWANDA, ton-ə-won′də, is a city in western New York, in Erie county, on the Niagara River and the State Barge Canal, 13 miles (20 km) north of Buffalo. It is part of the Buffalo port of entry. The city manufactures chains, hoists, plastics, paper products, and office supplies.

Tonawanda was incorporated as a village in 1854 and as a city in 1903. Government is by mayor and council. Population: 21,898.

TONE, Wolfe (1763–1798), Irish nationalist hero and revolutionary. Theobald Wolfe Tone was born on June 20, 1763, in Dublin, of middle class Protestant stock. He graduated from Trinity College, Dublin, in 1785, then studied law and in 1789 became a member of the Irish bar.

At Belfast in 1791, Tone, Napper Tandy, and Thomas Russell founded the militant Society of United Irishmen. At first the society agitated for parliamentary reform on the democractic model. Then, inspired by the radical drift of the French Revolution and frustrated by the Irish aristocracy's resistance to change, United Irishmen became republicans and finally adopted revolutionary tactics. Tone and his colleagues used the United Irishmen to bridge the gap between Protestant dissent, particularly in Ulster, and the Roman Catholic majority. He saw the revolutionary potential of Catholic religious, economic, and social grievances and urged complete separation of Ireland from England.

Forced to leave Ireland, Tone arrived in France by way of America in 1796 and persuaded French leaders to invade Ireland. That same year, as an adjutant general, he accompanied a small force commanded by Louis Lazare Hoche. Bad weather prevented a landing, and later attempts at revolution failed in Wexford, Antrim, Down, and Mayo. In 1798, Tone was captured by the English on a French ship off the Donegal coast while making another invasion effort. He was denied a soldier's death by firing squad. Sentenced to hang as a felon, Tone cut his throat in his Dublin prison cell and died on Nov. 19, 1798.

LAWRENCE J. MCCAFFREY
Loyola University, Chicago

TONE is sound considered with reference to its pitch, timbre, duration, and volume. Nearly all tones in music are composite, consisting of several simple constituents having different rates of vibration and known as partial tones. They vibrate according to fixed laws, the pitch depending on the nature of the sonorous body and the mode of producing its vibration. The partial tone having the lowest pitch—and usually the loudest sound—is called the prime, or fundamental, tone; the other partial tones are called accessories, harmonics, or overtones.

Tones differ in quality or timbre according to the number and relative force of their partial tones. A pure tone is a simple harmonic vibration. The seventh tone of a scale is called the characteristic tone. Two tones coalescing are termed combinational. The interval of a major second is called a tone or whole tone. Half of such an interval is a semitone. When a piano key is sounded it produces a note, and the character of that note is a tone. The character of all the notes of an instrument gives the tone of the instrument.

TONE POEM. See SYMPHONIC POEM.

PALACE AT NUKUALOFA, the capital of the Kingdom of Tonga.

LUC BOUCHAGE, FROM RAPHO GUILLUMETTE

TONG, a fraternal organization or, formerly, secret society of Chinese in the United States. In the Cantonese dialect the word denotes a hall or meeting place where family or village elders traditionally made important decisions.

During the latter half of the 19th century most Chinese immigrants to the United States were from the Canton area. Finding their new environment not only different but also restricted and unfriendly, they organized themselves into associations based on their old village relationships. The tongs in the United States were formed primarily to protect and assist their members and to exercise social control over them. Because the range of economic opportunities for Chinese was limited, competition between the tongs soon led to open warfare. Played up by the press, "tong wars" were romanticized in American literature, which provided them with an exaggeratedly lurid background of sinister crimes, opium dens, and bloodthirsty hatchetmen. In 1933 the U. S. government ended the outbreaks by arresting and deporting many tong members and threatening to uproot Chinese settlements in the United States.

Today the tongs support chambers of commerce, consolidated benevolent associations, and other regional associations of the Chinese-American community.

CH'ENG-K'UN CHENG, *University of Hawaii*

TONGA, tōng'ä, is an independent kingdom in the South Pacific Ocean, consisting of about 150 small islands.

The Land. Tonga consists of three island groups and several outlying islands. The Tongatapu, Ha'apai, and Vava'u groups are ancient uplifted coral reefs bordering a continental shelf. Most of the islands are low and featureless, but some—notably Vava'u—are raised and tilted.

To the east is a chain of volcanic islands. One of these, Niuafo'ou, which lies northwest of the main groups, is known to stamp collectors as the "tin-can island" because of the way in which mail was formerly picked up by passing ships. The presence of volcanoes, some of them still active, has caused the nearby coral islands to be repeatedly showered with fertilizing volcanic ash.

Tonga lies in the humid tropics, but its climate varies. In the south it is fairly dry and sometimes cool, whereas in the north the heat and humidity are consistently high. The country occasionally has destructive hurricanes.

The People and Their Economy. Polynesians are believed to have been in Tonga for at least 2,500 years. They numbered about 88,500 in 1970 and have a very high natural growth rate of 3.4% annually. The country's major problems are this population growth and the excessive population densities on several islands. About 17,000 people live in Nukualofa, the capital, situated on Tongatapu, the largest island. The Tongans were converted to Christianity by Wesleyan missionaries in 1822–1845.

Education in Tonga is compulsory for children between the ages of 6 and 14. There are several secondary schools and a teachers' training college. Tongans who are selected for a university education, usually on government scholarships, go primarily to New Zealand, Australia, or Fiji.

Tonga is an agricultural country. It grows most of the food it needs—chiefly yams and taro—and exports copra and bananas.

The islands have a unique land tenure system. Under the law, each male Tongan at 16 years,

INFORMATION HIGHLIGHTS

Official Name: Kingdom of Tonga.
Area: 259 square miles (671 sq km).
Population: 88,500 (1970).
Capital: Nukualofa (1970 population, 17,000).
Languages: Tongan, English.
Religion: Christianity.
Monetary Unit: Pa'anga.
Flag: Red with a red cross in a white canton in upper left hand corner. See also FLAG.

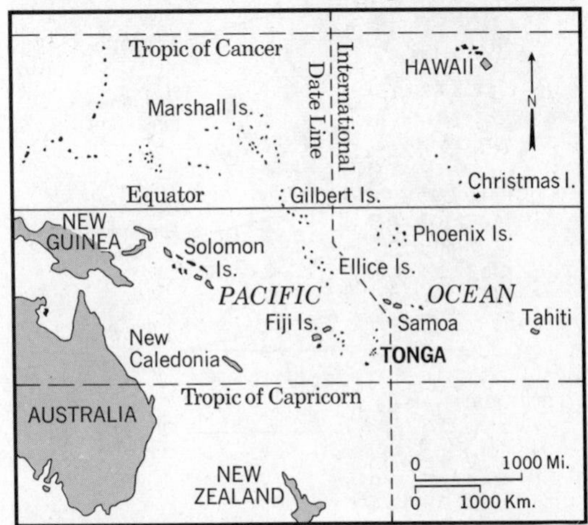

on payment of a small tax, is entitled to lease 8¼ acres (3.3 hectares) of agricultural land plus a village house lot. All land remains the property of the Crown, but some areas are controlled by noble families or by the government, who may sublease it. In practice the land-tenure system does not work as well as was intended. Many Tongans have been unable to obtain allotments, while some hold several illegally.

History. Dutch navigators in the 17th century were the first Europeans to visit Tonga. Capt. James Cook explored the "Friendly Isles," as he named them, in 1777.

During the first half of the 19th century the islands were torn by civil wars, which were ended when George Tupou I became king of all of Tonga in 1845. The kingdom became a British protectorate in 1900. After World War II, British direction was progressively reduced and the Tongans assumed greater control of their own affairs. During the 47-year reign (1918–1965) of Queen Salote, illiteracy and national debt were eliminated. Tonga became independent on June 4, 1970, as a constitutional monarchy under the rule of King Taufa'ahau Tupou IV.

PETER PIRIE, *University of Hawaii*

TONGKING. See TONKIN.

TONGUE, in humans, the muscular organ that fills most of the entire oral cavity (or mouth). The tongue is capable of many motions and configurations and plays a vital role in chewing, swallowing, and speaking. It contains the taste buds and many small salivary glands.

The tongue is generally divided into two major portions. The anterior two thirds is mobile and can be protruded from the mouth. The posterior third, or root, cannot be protruded. It is covered by a mass of lymphoid tissue known as the lingual tonsils.

Structure. The bulk of the tongue is made up of a complex group of transverse and longitudinal muscle bundles and four large muscles that arise elsewhere and extend into the tongue. The structure connecting the anterior portion of the tongue to the floor of the mouth is a thin band of tissue called the lingual frenulum.

The upper surface of the anterior two thirds of the tongue is covered with many tiny structures called papillae. The largest of these, the circumvallate papillae, range in number from 8 to 12 and lie in a V-shaped row just in front of the root portion of the tongue. All papillae house taste buds. When stimulated, the taste buds transmit impulses to the brain over the glossopharyngeal nerve and the chorda tympani branch of the facial nerve.

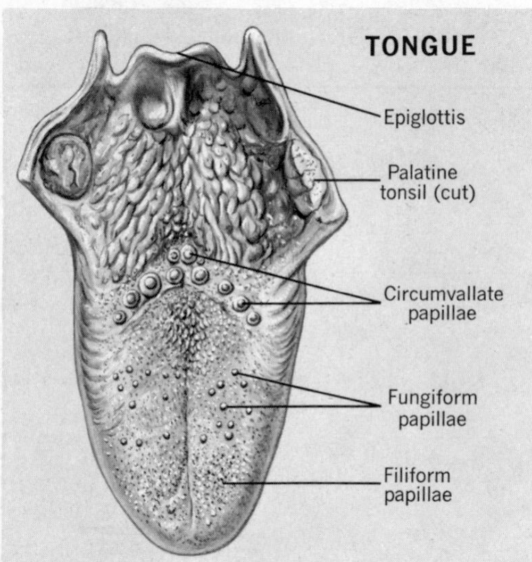

Touch and pain receptors in the tongue are supplied by the lingual nerve and the glossopharyngeal nerve, while motor impulses to the tongue's muscles are transmitted over the hypoglossal nerve. The blood supply to the tongue is carried by the lingual arteries, which are major branches of the external carotid artery.

Tongue Curling. The ability to curl the tongue —that is, to bring the sides of the tongue up to form a tube—is an inherited trait. It is determined by a single dominant gene and is present in about seven out of ten people.

Tongue Diseases and Disorders. The tongue is subject to a variety of diseases and disorders. Glossitis, or inflammation of the tongue, may be a sign of an underlying disease, such as syphilis, pernicious anemia, or a vitamin deficiency.

JAMES R. CHANDLER, M. D.
University of Miami School of Medicine

TONGUE-TIE is a condition in which the mobility of the tongue is restricted. It is usually the result of an abnormally short lingual frenulum, the thin band of tissue connecting the underside of the tongue to the floor of the mouth. When severe, tongue-tie can interfere with swallowing and speech.

Formerly, many articulatory speech disorders were thought to be caused by tongue-tie and in many cases the frenulum was cut. However, it is now believed that tongue-tie only very rarely affects tongue mobility enough to interfere with swallowing or speech.

JAMES R. CHANDLER, M. D.
University of Miami School of Medicine

TONGUE WORM, a bloodsucking parasite of the upper respiratory passages and lungs of many animals. Tongue worms are sometimes considered to be a class—Pentastomida or Linguatulida —of the phylum Arthropoda. Sometimes they are classified as a separate phylum.

Tongue worms require two different hosts, undergoing different stages of their life cycle in each. The most important species in the United States is *Linguatula serrata.* The adults inhabit the nasal and respiratory passages of dogs, foxes, and wolves, and rarely also horses, oxen, sheep, goats, and man. Sneezing and coughing discharge the eggs, and if they land on vegetation they may be eaten by an intermediate host—usually a herbivore such as a rabbit, ox, sheep, horse, pig, rat, guinea pig, or man. After the eggs hatch, the nymphs become encapsulated in the host's visceral organs and remain there for many months. A carnivore becomes infected when it eats the visceral organs of a dead intermediate host. The nymphs then migrate to the host's nasal passages where they develop into adults.

An infected animal may or may not show any symptoms. Sneezing, coughing, difficult breathing, and sometimes vomiting occur. There is no satisfactory treatment for the disease.

KEITH WAYT, D. V. M.
Colorado State University

TONGUES, Gift of, sometimes called glossolalia, is a charism (gift of grace) enabling its recipient to speak in an unaccustomed language. Interpreters disagree about the nature of this gift, which is mentioned in the New Testament. Some understand it as a miraculous but temporary ability to speak in foreign languages. Others consider it an ecstatic's utterances that are incomprehensible to bystanders.

The best-known instance of this gift occurred on the day of Pentecost, when Christ's disciples "were filled with the Holy Spirit and began to speak in strange tongues" (Acts 2:4). Some interpret this event as a gift of elocution, by means of which a person is enabled to speak in an otherwise foreign language. Others consider it as a gift of audition, by means of which those hearing a speaker talking in his own language are enabled to understand him in their own.

The early church considered the gift of tongues a genuine gift of the Holy Spirit. Since such speaking was frequently unintelligible without an interpreter, St. Paul advised regulating its use (I Corinthians 14). In some Pentecostal churches the phenomenon is still common. More traditional and conservative churches are inclined to view talking in tongues with considerable reservations.

JOHN T. FORD, *Catholic University*

TONIC, a medicinal preparation once believed to improve general health and vitality by restoring the normal tone, or condition, of tissues. Tonics were formerly very popular, but they are largely obsolete, and the term itself now seldom appears in pharmacology texts.

There were many different types of tonics, some of which may have improved general health by supplying vitamins and minerals to an individual deficient in these factors. They were, however, highly unlikely to improve general health in persons not suffering from such a deficiency, except perhaps by suggestion. The hematic tonics, which contain iron preparations along with other ingredients, have been replaced by specific iron compounds that are used in the treatment of iron deficiency anemia. Bitter tonics, once claimed to stimulate the appetite, are now seldom used.

ANDRES GOTH, M. D.
University of Texas Southwestern Medical School

TONIC, in music, the keynote of a scale from which the prevailing tonality of a composition is derived. The most obvious use of the tonic is at the end of a tonal (harmonic) composition, where the appearance of the tonic chord, a triad with the tonic in root (bass) position, serves to resolve the harmony, giving the listener a sense of finality. See HARMONY.

TONKA BEAN, tong'kə, the coumarin-yielding seed of several species of trees of the legume family (Leguminosae) native to the upland rain forests of northern Brazil, Surinam, Guyana, and Venezuela. Coumarin is used to scent perfumes, soaps, and cosmetics. It is also used as a flavor enhancer in synthetic vanilla extract and in pharmaceutical preparations and tobacco.

The principal tonka bean of commerce, the Dutch tonka bean, is from *Dipteryx* (or *Cumarouna*) *odorata.* However, since the development of synthetic coumarin, the use of tonka beans as a source of natural coumarin has decreased.

TONKIN, tong'kin', is the former name of the northern part of North Vietnam, the region called Bac Bo by the Vietnamese. The name Tonkin (Tongking) was given to the area by European explorers and missionaries toward the end of the 1500's. Tonkin was then the way the Chinese rendered the name of the city of Dong Kinh (now Hanoi), but it was understood in the West to be the name of a separate Vietnamese state.

Tonkin was the official name of a protectorate set up by the French in northern Vietnam in 1883. The protectorate was one of the five states of French Indochina. See also ANNAM; VIETNAM.

TONKIN GULF RESOLUTION, tong'kin', an action of the U. S. Congress that was used by President Lyndon B. Johnson as the chief constitutional authorization for the escalation of U. S. military involvement in the Vietnam War. The resolution was requested by President Johnson in 1964 after two U. S. destroyers were reportedly fired on in the Gulf of Tonkin by North Vietnamese torpedo boats. It passed 88–2 in the Senate and 416–0 in the House of Representatives. In 1967, Undersecretary of State Nicholas deB. Katzenbach termed the resolution "the functional equivalent of a declaration of war," annoying many legislators who had developed doubts about the wisdom of their support for it.

TONKIN GULF RESOLUTION

SEC. 1. Whereas naval units of the Communist regime in Vietnam, in violation of the principles of the Charter of the United Nations and of international law, have deliberately and repeatedly attacked United States naval vessels lawfully present in international waters, and have thereby created a serious threat to international peace;

Whereas these attacks are part of a deliberate and systematic campaign of aggression that the Communist regime in North Vietnam has been waging against its neighbors and the nations joined with them in the collective defense of their freedom;

Whereas the United States is assisting the peoples of southeast Asia to protect their freedom and has no territorial, military or political ambitions in that area, but desires only that these peoples should be left in peace to work out their own destinies in their own way: Now, therefore, be it

Resolved by the Senate and House of Representatives of the United States of America in Congress assembled, That the Congress approves and supports the determination of the President, as Commander-in-Chief, to take all necessary measures to repel any armed attack against the forces of the United States and to prevent further aggression.

SEC. 2. The United States regards as vital to its national interest and to world peace the maintenance of international peace and security in southeast Asia. Consonant with the Constitution of the United States and the Charter of the United Nations and in accordance with its obligations under the Southeast Asia Collective Defense Treaty, the United States is, therefore, prepared, as the President determines, to take all necessary steps, including the use of armed force, to assist any member or protocol state of the Southeast Asia Collective Defense Treaty requesting assistance in defense of its freedom.

SEC. 3. This resolution shall expire when the President shall determine that the peace and security of the area is reasonably assured by international conditions created by action of the United Nations or otherwise except that it may be terminated earlier by resolution of the Congress.

Disagreement over the resolution after its adoption was rooted in congressional-presidential rivalry respecting authorization to wage war and mounting opposition within Congress to the Vietnam War itself. The Senate repealed the Tonkin Gulf Resolution in 1970. Repeal was unopposed by President Richard Nixon, who asserted that he was not relying on the resolution as authority for his actions in Vietnam but acting on the basis of his power as commander in chief.

RICHARD BUTWELL, *American University*

TONLE SAP, ton′lā sap, a lake in west central Cambodia, is a natural flood reservoir of the lower Mekong River, with which it is connected by the Tonle Sap River. During the high-water season, from June to November, the depth of the Tonle Sap, or "Great Lake," increases from 3–10 feet (1–3 meters) to 30–40 feet (9–12 meters) and its area expands from 1,000 square miles (2,600 sq km) to 3,900 square miles (10,000 sq km). The lake has abundant fish, and the drained floodland produces a rich rice crop.

TÖNNIES, tûn′ēs, **Ferdinand** (1855–1936), German philosopher and sociologist. He was born in Eiderstedt on July 26, 1855. Tönnies (Toennies) received his Ph. D. at the University of Tübingen in 1877, and from 1881 until his removal by the Nazis in 1933, he lectured at the University of Kiel. He died in Kiel on April 11, 1936.

In his major work, *Gemeinschaft und Gesellschaft* (1887; *Community and Society*), Tönnies contrasted two types of social order. The *Gemeinschaft* (communal or rural) society is characterized by the natural or essential will typical of artisans, peasants, women, and youth. In such societies tradition and sentiment are the dominant forces, the family is the basic institution, and social life is valued for its own sake.

In *Gesellschaft* (cosmopolitan) societies, the rational will typical of the businessman, the educated, and those in positions of authority finds its expression in calculated conduct and instrumental social relationships. Law and economic interdependence bind man to man in such urban state societies.

PHILIP J. LEONHARD
City College, New York

TØNSBERG, tûns′bar, is a seaport in southeastern Norway. It is at the head of Tønsberg Fjord, an inlet of Oslo Fjord, and 45 miles (72 km) south of Oslo. Tønsberg, founded in 871, is Norway's oldest city. The ruins of the Tunsberghus, a fortress dating from the 13th century, overlook the city from the top of Slottsfjell (Castle Mountain). A lookout tower built to celebrate the city's millennium is also on the summit. Near the center of the city are mounds marking the site of a regional *ting*, or assembly, of Viking times.

Tønsberg was long one of Norway's principal whaling ports, and one of its main points of interest is the whaling museum. In the early 1970's it ranked as Norway's fourth-largest port of registry for the merchant marine. Shipbuilding and engineering works are the city's leading industries. Tønsberg is the administrative center for Vestfold *fylke*, one of Norway's most prosperous agricultural counties. Population: (1969) 11,354.

VINCENT H. MALMSTRÖM, *Middlebury College*

TONSIL, in popular usage, is the term applied to either of the two oval-shaped masses of lymphoid tissue at either side of the back of the mouth. However, there are actually a number of tonsils, and the pair at the back of the mouth are more precisely known as the *palatine tonsils*. Other tonsils include the *lingual tonsils*, which are on the back portion of the tongue, and the *pharyngeal tonsils*, which are more commonly known as the *adenoids*.

The pharyngeal tonsils are located in the pharynx (throat) at the back of the nose. Bands of lymphoid tissue extending down from the pharyngeal tonsils join a band of lymphoid tissue more or less encircling the throat at the back of the mouth. This irregular band is known as *Waldeyer's ring*.

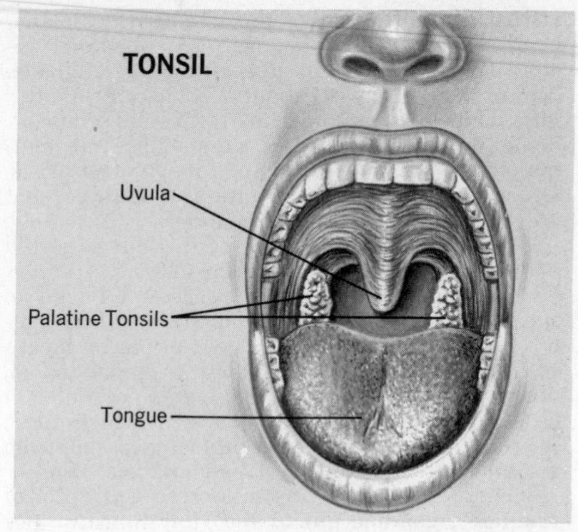

The surface of a tonsil is divided into many deep crypts. The crypts of the palatine tonsils often harbor a variety of bacteria. Although many of these are harmless, others cause infection (tonsillitis). Infection of the palatine tonsils may be chronic or acute and may be related to such diseases as rheumatic heart disease and glomerulonephritis (Bright's disease). When the pharyngeal tonsils become infected or enlarged they may cause ear infections, nasal obstruction, or a loss of hearing due to obstruction of the Eustachian tube, the narrow duct extending from the middle ear to the throat.

Severe tonsillitis is usually treated by the surgical removal of the infected tonsils (tonsillectomy). Usually, it is the palatine tonsils that are removed, but the pharyngeal tonsils are also sometimes removed. An operation in which both the palatine and pharyngeal tonsils are removed is sometimes known as an adenotonsillectomy.

The precise function of the tonsils is not completely known, but they are important in the production of lymphocytes and antibodies. (See IMMUNITY.) For this reason, removal of the tonsils is often avoided, especially if the infection can be treated with drugs.

JAMES R. CHANDLER, M. D.
University of Miami School of Medicine

TONSILLECTOMY, the surgical removal of the tonsils, usually the palatine tonsils. It is usually performed to treat chronic tonsillitis or repeated episodes of acute tonsillitis. Frequently it is combined with the removal of the pharyngeal tonsils (adenoids). These may be removed if they cause ear infections, obstruct the nasal passages, or cause a hearing loss due to obstruction of the Eustachian tube.

In children tonsillectomies are performed under general anesthesia. In adults, local anesthetics are usually used. The palatine tonsils may be removed by a dissecting instrument, or each tonsil may be forced into the aperture of a special instrument and cut from its bed. Generally, the recovery period is short.

JAMES R. CHANDLER, M. D.
University of Miami School of Medicine

TONSURE, a ceremony of shaving part of the head to identify a person as a cleric. The wearing of the tonsure was mandatory for Roman Catholic clergy until 1972, when the ceremony and the wearing of the tonsure were abolished. By local custom the tonsure had not been worn by clergy in the United States and England. Clerical tonsure was common among the clergy of the West since the 6th century. It had several forms, but in modern times consisted of a small shaved circle on top of the head.

TONTI, Henri de. See TONTY, HENRI DE.

TONTINE, ton'tēn, formerly a financial arrangement in which each subscriber to a fund received an annual payment that increased as the number of participants was diminished by death. In some tontines, the last survivor received all. In others, the plan was terminated at a given time and all survivors shared what remained. The term is derived from the name of Lorenzo Tonti, a Paris banker who in 1653 suggested it as a way to raise money for the state, which was to take all capital after the last survivor died. The idea was not used until 1689, when Louis XIV started a fund in which there were 1,400,000 subscriptions. This tontine ended 37 years later with the death of the last survivor, who was drawing an annual dividend 2,300% larger than her investment. Tontine life insurance policies were introduced in the United States in 1868, but they were abandoned after mathematicians developed mortality tables.

TONTY, tôɴ'tē, **Henri de** (1650?–1704), French fur trader and explorer. He was born in Gaeta, Italy, a son of Lorenzo de Tonty (or Tonti), later an Italian émigré to France, who invented the "tontine" system of life annuity. Before going to Canada, Henri participated in several French campaigns, during which he lost his right hand. He arrived in Quebec with La Salle in 1678 and helped him build trading posts on the lower Great Lakes and in the Illinois River valley. In 1682 he accompanied La Salle down the Mississippi River. While his chief was in France, Tonty supervised Midwest trading operations.

During the last decade of the 17th century, a surplus of beaver led French authorities to neglect the area, but Tonty was allowed, as a strategic sign of French presence, to maintain his fort at Pimitoui, near Peoria, Illinois. He joined the Canadian explorer d'Iberville in Louisiana in 1699 and worked to develop trade and keep the peace among the Indians. Tonty typified those who built the French western empire on trade and alliances. He died in Fort Louis on Mobile Bay, Ala., in Sept. 1704.

JAMES S. PRITCHARD
Queen's University, Kingston, Ontario

TOOELE, too͞-el'ə, is a city in northwestern Utah, the seat of Tooele county, about 30 miles (48 km) southwest of Salt Lake City. It is a smelting center in a region of lead, copper, and silver mines. A tunnel 4 miles (6 km) long through the Oquirrh Mountains, which was built between 1937 and 1942, leads to mines in Bingham Canyon. The Tooele ordnance depot of the U.S. Army is south of the city.

Tooele was settled by Mormons about 1850 and was incorporated in 1853. It has a mayor-council government. Population: 12,539.

TOOL, an implement used to modify raw materials for human use. Tools can be considered primarily as extensions of the hand, increasing its speed, power, or accuracy.

The use of tools is not exclusively a human trait, naturally shaped tools being used by insects, birds, and certain mammals. However, tool-using is most characteristic of man. Moreover, toolmaking is almost by definition human. Some authorities believe that this habit distinguishes man from the lower primates and so accord or withhold hominid status on the basis of making or not making tools.

ORIGINS OF TOOLS

Man first used as tools certain natural objects that lay at hand. Evaluation of these earliest tools and of toolmaking men involves distinguishing those stone and bone artifacts shaped by man from those that were shaped by such natural forces as the movement of glaciers. Despite controversy over particular finds, African tools dating from the late Pliocene or early Pleistocene (about two million years ago) are accepted as genuinely manufactured implements. These earliest tools were very crude. They were sometimes only stones—called "pebble tools"—sharpened by removal of a few chips. Other tools were made by splitting bones into useful splinters.

Regardless of details the use and making of tools have transformed man from a comparatively harmless subtropical vegetarian to a ubiquitous predatory semicarnivore. As man evolved he became increasingly dependent on tool-derived power for working, hunting, and fighting.

Tools and weapons were hardly distinguishable in early times. The hand-ax, evidently never hafted (attached to a handle) but held directly in the hand, was as usable as a weapon as it was in digging, scraping, or chopping. Certain specific techniques of tool manufacture, called "traditions" by archaeologists and anthropologists, appeared early, but for more than half of man's history tools were hardly differentiated by function. The few tools were as generalized in use as the modern Latin American machete. The hand-ax was the prime tool of the inhabited world for over 200,000 years during the Lower Paleolithic, the earliest period of the Old Stone Age. Not until the beginning of the Middle Paleolithic period did specialized tools appear in quantity.

In the Upper Paleolithic period many new tools appeared, with functions related to refined stone working, skin dressing, bone working, and woodworking. The tool inventories came to parallel those of historic times. Although the tools were still made of stone, wood, or bone, in conception they are surprisingly modern, many being composite in construction—for example, combining stone and bone parts. Additionally, secondary tools (tools to make tools) supplemented the earlier primary tools at this time.

This article gives an anthropologist's summary of the history of tools from stone and bone forms through bronze, iron, and steel. For information on modern tools consult such articles as BORING MACHINE; DRILL; GRINDING; METALWORKING; and WOODWORKING.

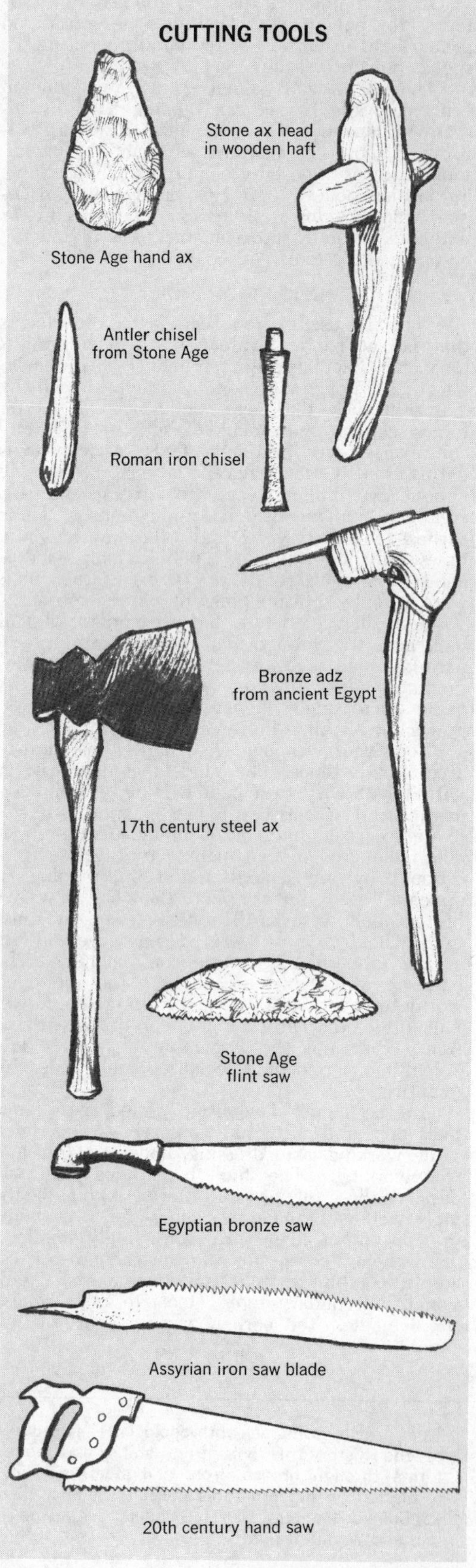

Many types of modern tools date from the Neolithic period (New Stone Age), about 8,000 years ago. Few alterations in basic design have occurred since that period. Neolithic striking tools, and many cutting tools, were hafted. Saws, drills, digging sticks, hoes, and plows are clearly recognizable in archaeological finds. The subsequent introduction of metals changed the style of tools rather than basic conceptions.

CATEGORIES OF TOOLS

Hand tools may be divided into six functional groups—those for striking, cutting, boring, torsion, measuring, and holding. Other functional categorizations are possible. All six categories are found in tools of the Bronze Age (about 3500–1500 B.C.) though torsion and measuring tools are substantially lacking earlier.

Striking Tools. Such striking implements as hammers and punches may be the oldest tools of man. Logically a hammer, doubtless any suitably shaped stone, was prerequisite to chipping the first stone tool. Stone-chipping hammers, carefully shaped, accompanied the refinement of stoneworking techniques, as did punches for the same purpose. At the close of the Paleolithic, hammers were among the tools to acquire handles. Nonmetallic hammers persist today, although with changes in head materials, because resilience of the hammerhead may be necessary for some work. For example, mauls with rawhide faces are used to pound metal parts that would be damaged by a steel head. Stone hammers persist among metalworkers; for example, they are still used in Africa for rough hammering.

Cutting Tools. Axes, adzes, knives, planes, shaves, files, chisels, and saws are very nearly as old as striking tools. The earliest men used stone flakes to butcher game, shape bone tools, and probably to make wooden tools. Primitive axes and choppers—choppers were forerunners of the ax—have been found with these flakes. Despite the names, early axes and choppers were probably used as much for slashing as for chopping.

Ax. The ax developed into one of man's most widely used tools. The Paleolithic hand ax diminished in size, as stoneworking was refined, from the massive styles of the Abbevillean tradition to the small late Acheulean type. With the reduction in size the tool's knifelike character became more obvious. Paleolithic chipped stone axes were followed by Neolithic axes, pecked, ground, and polished into shape. Though more laborious to make, these Neolithic axes were more efficient, especially as they were hafted. At first, heads were fastened to handles by bindings of such materials as hide. Later, holes for shafts were cut through the stone heads.

At the Paleolithic-Neolithic transition period, sometimes called Mesolithic, axes appeared with a tubular antler sleeve joining the head to a bent haft. Socketed axes, with the socket integral with the head, were important during the earlier metal ages. Some medieval axes retained the socket, which now was turned to parallel the cutting edge, eliminating the curved handle. With few exceptions—the broadax of Colonial times and the double-bitted ax, a 19th century American contribution—present-day axes assumed their present forms about three centuries ago.

Adz. The adz has a chisel-edged blade mounted transversely to its handle. For rough dressing of timbers and heavy flooring the adz was unsurpassed until power tools came into use.

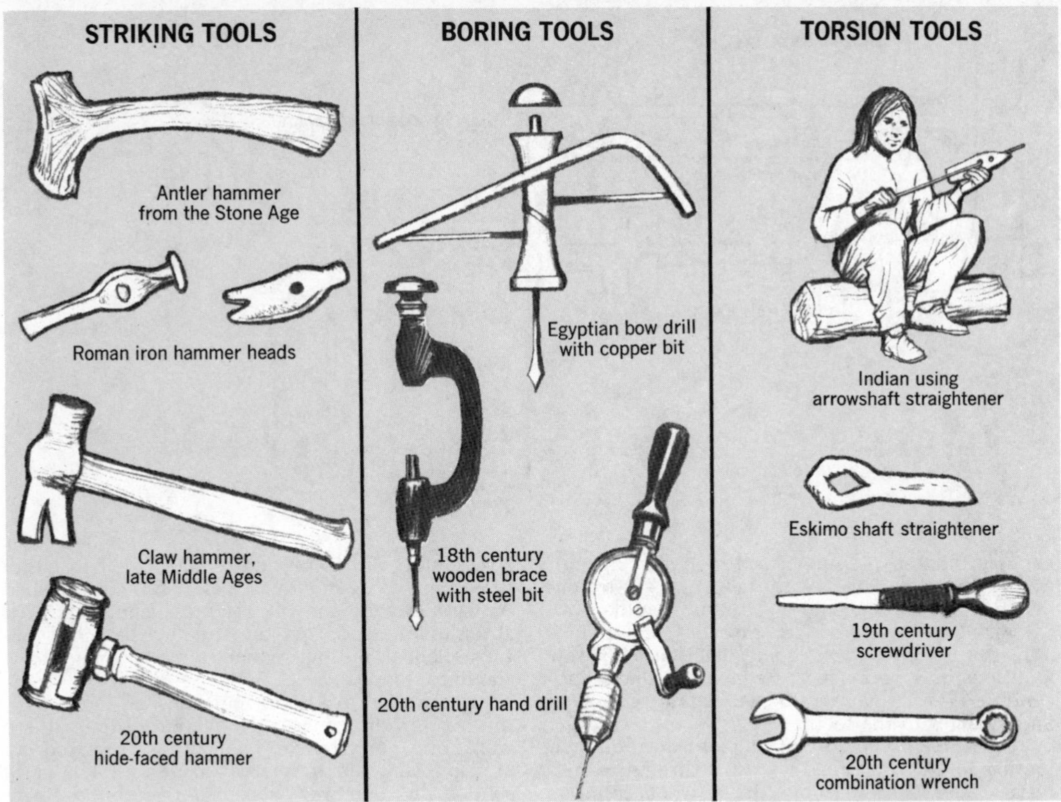

Neither as old nor as ubiquitous as the ax, the adz probably appeared first in the Late Paleolithic and is found among peoples specializing in fine woodwork. Small adzes with stone, shell, or metal blades were used by the New Zealand Maori, by other Pacific peoples, by Northwest Pacific Coast Indians in America, as well as by Europeans. The adz continued to be employed into the 19th century but is now rarely used. Both it and the broadax were made obsolete by modern sawmills.

Shaves, Planes, and Scrapers. These are closely related tools. Scrapers have been found along with the earliest human tools. Though supplanted by metal and glass scrapers in woodworking, stone scrapers persisted in tanneries until recently. Shaves and planes generally cut rather than scrape a surface. Recently drawknives and spokeshaves have fallen out of use. However, in forms substantially unaltered for centuries, they were important until the early 20th century in precision woodworking trades.

Planes offer better control of cutting depth than scrapers and shaves. Blade adjustment was difficult in early wooden planes, which held the blade only with a wedge. Blade-adjusting mechanisms appeared in the 19th century, with a growing use of metal parts. Metal-bodied planes were first known in Roman times but did not persist in common use. For a time a composite plane with metal upper works and a wooden sole was used. Steel planes are now by far the predominant form. As a tool type, planes are comparatively recent and sophisticated. Primitive and early peoples relied heavily on the scraper instead.

Chisels. Chisels first appeared in the Late Paleolithic period, and they continued thereafter. Tanged and socketed metal chisels quickly replaced square-headed stone chisels when metals became available. Many specialized chisels of the 18th and 19th centuries, used for cutting joints, have yielded to machines or have disappeared as joint forms changed.

Files. Comparatively recent tools, files belong to the Iron Age, which began about 1200 B.C. The only comparable primitive tools are rasps formed of stone teeth in a wooden base and used for grating food.

Saws. The long and complex history of saws begins with Paleolithic serrated stone blades, which were possibly not used for woodworking. By the Bronze Age, carpenters used saws, as shown in Egyptian archaeological finds. These were simple, swordlike blades with teeth unraked and unset; the blade was greased and the kerf (the groove cut with the saw) was wedged open to prevent binding.

In sawing, the relationship of blade thickness, degrees of pressure applied, and direction of cutting stroke is vital. A thin blade cut a narrow kerf, conserving wood and having less tendency to bind, but it buckled if pushed too hard. The problems found three solutions. Setting the teeth—bending them alternately left and right—was first done by the Romans. Tapering the blade thickness from edge to back was not done until the 18th century in Europe. Straining the blade in a frame was another Roman innovation. In framed saws the blade was usually mounted on the frame's midline for ripping (cutting the wood in the direction of the grain) or at one side of the frame for crosscutting (cutting the wood across the grain). Both types, especially the latter, underwent refinements in medieval times.

During the frame saw's development the straight, or open, saw continued to be used. In medieval Europe it bore a pistol-grip handle, which later became more curved and made a sharper angle to the blade. Only in the 18th

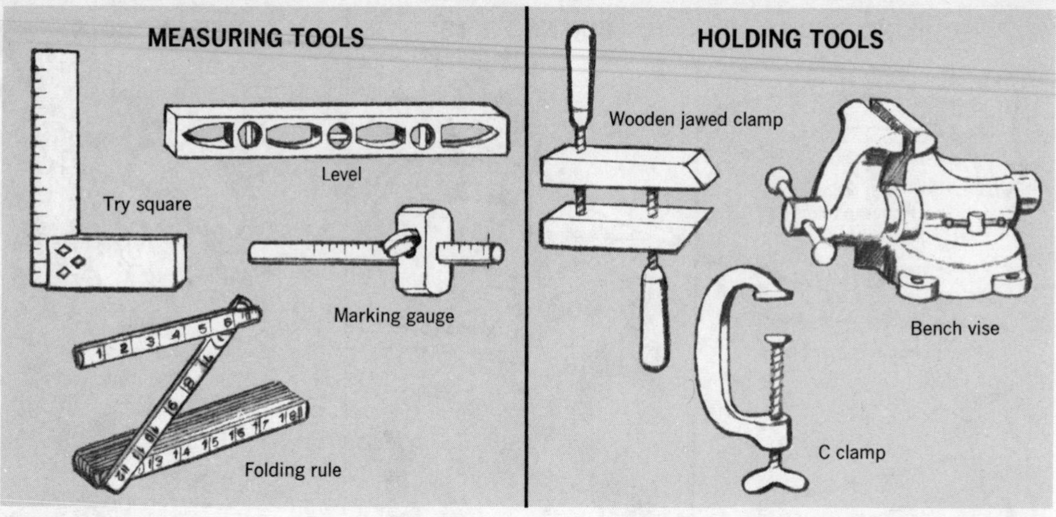

century did the present closed grip first appear. Many Oriental saws, with teeth raked to cut on the pull stroke, had a straight handle.

Virtually every modern saw has an obvious 18th century precursor. Some deletions, but few additions, have occurred. Refinements have concentrated on advances in the quality of steel and changes in the teeth.

Boring Tools. These tools depend on rotational motion to cut or grind their way through a material. The earliest stone drills were splinters of bone or flint blades held in the hand and turned by twisting the wrist back and forth. Later, mounted on a wooden shaft, they were twirled between the palms. Such tools had a characteristic retained by boring tools for thousands of years: their rotation was limited to a few turns before the direction had to be reversed.

Some peoples of the Americas and Asia and some early Europeans employed three other boring tools: the bow drill, the strap drill, and the pump drill. The bow and strap drills both use the principle of wrapping a strip of material, such as hide, around a shaft and working the strip back and forth to rotate the shaft. The pump drill differs in deriving its force from a flywheel set in motion by unwinding twisted cords. All three drills make only a limited number of turns before the rotation is reversed. The palm, bow, and strap drills are suitable for making fire by friction (see FIRE). The pump drill, once common in Europe and the Far East, persists today as a tool of marginal usage.

An unusual drill, surviving today as the spiral ratchet screwdriver in the United States and the fretwork drill in Europe, derives its rotation from movement of a runner along a helically twisted shaft. Though the helix is much older, the drill is about three centuries old in Europe.

The bit brace, dating from the European Middle Ages, was substantially the first form of drill providing continuous unidirectional rotation. The form has remained virtually unchanged, though the material of manufacture has shifted from wood to metals. The first forms used fixed bits. Later braces used simple wooden sockets as bit holders, and these in turn were superseded by adjustable metal chucks.

The last addition to the stock of drilling tools, developed in the early 19th century, was the European geared hand drill.

Drill bits necessarily reflected available materials and rotational characteristics of the motive source. Early bits cut equally well in either direction. Chip removal was first accomplished by withdrawing the bit. Improvements involved straight fluting of the bit and, in the 19th century, helical fluting, which persists today as a standard shape.

In addition to bits for cutting, early men used bits for grinding holes. By Neolithic times these were used on stone. The soft bit carried an abrasive that did the actual grinding. The early solid drills soon were replaced by tubular forms that reduced the labor of making large holes.

Other boring tools—primarily a bit with handle—including brad awls, gimlets, and large augers were turned by hand. Basic forms were established centuries ago, and the bit parallels those used in more elaborate drilling devices.

Torsion Tools. Primarily related to the use of screw threads, torsion tools became common only in the 19th and 20th centuries. The earliest torsion tools were arrow wrenches used by primitive man to straighten projectile shafts. Screwdrivers and wood screws have coexisted since the late 17th century. Wrenches were first made with fixed jaws in the 17th century and later—from the 19th century—with adjustable jaws. Modern wrench sets in standard sizes, depending on standardization of nut and bolt dimensions, are about a century old.

Measuring Tools. Tools for measuring came into common use between medieval and modern times and are the products of sophisticated cultures. Most primitives depended on the eye to plumb and level their work, but they did use peg-and-rope compasses for laying out circular structures. The plumb line, either alone or on A- or T-frames, was used to true virtually all horizontal and vertical lines until factory production of spirit levels in the 19th century. The level is an alcohol-filled glass tube containing a bubble that indicates a horizontal plane by its position. Squares date back to Roman times, but related measuring tools, such as bevel and marking gauges, are probably medieval in origin.

Because carpenters made wooden machinery, curved staircases, and ornamental trim, such tools as compasses and dividers were more common among woodworkers in the past than they are today. Scales and rules were rare until the Middle Ages, when linear measurement standards were applied to common works.

Holding Tools. Vises and clamps, common holding tools, are closely related to the use of other tools. With the work held fast, the workman has both hands free. Otherwise he must hold his work by hand, with his feet (as among some unshod peoples), or with his teeth. The simplest vise was a cleft stick–sometimes with an encircling band. The work might be wedged in a prepared bench, especially for quantity production. The shaving horse, now virtually unknown, combined workbench, clamp, and seat.

We commonly think of the work being stationary while the tool moves, and generally this is true. An exception is the cooper's long plane which was mounted sole uppermost with the stave to be drawn over the blade edge.

In the past each specialized woodworking trade was characterized by its own holding tools, varying with the product, with other tools, and with the way the craftsman sat or stood as he worked.

MECHANIZATION OF TOOLS

An inevitable result of the availability of extrahuman power was the mechanization of tools. Animal power having rarely been applied to tools, mechanization followed the introduction of water power and windpower. Though these natural power sources were tapped after the 12th century, primarily for grinding and pumping, application to the tools discussed probably began in the 16th century.

Early mechanized tools employed few new principles and strongly resembled existing forms. Hammers and saws, readily amenable to powered adaptations, were first. The trip hammers and reciprocating saws that evolved persisted until the 19th century, being improved to strike heavier blows or make multiple cuts. Circular saws and bandsaws, dominant in the 20th century, lack direct hand-tool counterparts and date from the late 18th and mid-19th centuries.

Power boring and routing date from the 19th century, being dependent on suitable rotating machinery and metallurgical advances in drill bits. The power router, though modern, still bears some resemblances to the centuries-old hand router.

Power planers, from the 19th century, called for radical departures from established hand tools. The modern electric hand plane, however, shows a reversion in overall shape toward that of the common hand plane.

The mechanization of tools has been a two-directional evolution. First, machines were developed to accomplish tasks previously done with hand tools, with accompanying changes in form and operation. Second, powered hand tools, based on the small electric motor, were developed from these machines. As a result, most powered hand tools bear only a passing resemblance to the earlier hand tools that they supplanted.

With the advent of powered tools we find changes in tool forms, in the tool inventory, and above all in the attitudes toward tools and work. Many power tools enable a man to work with the skill and precision previously attainable only with years of training and experience.

ROBERT F. G. SPIER, *University of Missouri*

Further Reading: Goodman, W. L., *The History of Woodworking Tools* (London 1964); Mercer, Henry C., *Ancient Carpenter's Tools,* 3d ed. (Doylestown, Pa. 1960); Singer, Charles and others, eds., *A History of Technology,* 5 vols. (New York 1954–1958); Spier, Robert F. G., *From the Hand of Man: Primitive and Preindustrial Technologies* (Boston 1970).

TOOMBS, Robert (1810–1885), American senator and Confederate leader, who remained, after the Civil War, an "unreconstructed rebel." To the end of his life he refused to apply for pardon or take any oath of allegiance.

Toombs was born near Washington, Ga., on July 2, 1810, the son of a well-to-do planter. He attended the University of Georgia, Union College, Schenectady, N. Y., and the University of Virginia law school. Returning to Georgia, he rose rapidly in the legal profession. On the eve of the Civil War, Toombs's fortune, including his landholdings in four states, was estimated at $450,000.

Handsome and imposing, able and outspoken, Toombs became the most powerful political leader in Georgia. After serving in the state legislature for six years, he was elected to the U. S. House of Representatives in 1844 and to the Senate in 1851. Although sensitive on the question of Southern rights, he generally supported the Whig party, which was largely conservative and nationalistic. He worked for the passage of the Compromise of 1850 and fought against a secessionist movement within his state at that time. Amid the growing sectional strife of the 1850's, however, Toombs took an increasingly partisan Southern position. After the election of Abraham Lincoln as President in 1860, Toombs led Georgia out of the Union.

Toombs served the Confederacy as its first secretary of state for five months in 1861, but his restless nature led him into military service. Although a gallant commander, he was constantly critical of President Jefferson Davis and often insubordinate. In March 1863, after being wounded at the battle of Antietam, he resigned his commission of brigadier general and returned home, bitter and frustrated.

At the close of the war, Toombs avoided arrest by federal troops and fled to Europe. He returned to Georgia in 1867 and reestablished his law practice without regaining his citizenship. He opposed carpetbag rule in the state and later fought as strongly against efforts by fellow Georgians to build a new industrial South. His attachments to the past were so strong and his denunciations of post-Reconstruction economic and political trends so extreme that he lost most of his influence. Only as a participant in Georgia's constitutional convention of 1877 and as a legal counsel for the state did he make any significant contributions in this period. Toombs died in Washington, Ga., on Dec. 15, 1885, largely a symbol of the past.

WILLIAM Y. THOMPSON
Louisiana Polytechnic Institute

Further Reading: Thompson, William Y., *Robert Toombs of Georgia* (Baton Rouge, La., 1966).

TOON, tōōn, a tall tropical tree with aromatic red wood that resembles but is softer than mahogany and is used for making furniture. The toon, also called toona, Indian mahogany, and Moulmein cedar, is native to eastern India and Australia. It belongs to the mahogany family (Meliaceae) and is often classified as *Toona ciliata,* but some authorities refer to it as *Cedrela ciliata* or *C. toona.*

The toon reaches a height of 70 feet (21 meters) and has nearly evergreen, pinnate leaves made up of 10 to 20, usually opposite, leaflets. The leaflets range in length from 3 to 6 inches (75–150 mm). The white, honey-scented flowers are borne in drooping clusters. Sometimes they are used as a source of red or yellow dye. Each flower ripens into a winged, seed-containing capsule.

J. A. YOUNG
U. S. Department of Agriculture

TOOTH. See TEETH.

TOOTH SHELL, a marine animal whose shell is shaped like an elephant's tusk but is open at both ends. Tooth shells, also called *tusk shells,* make up the class Scaphopoda of the phylum Mollusca; about 900 species are found throughout the world. The shells range in length from 1/4 inch to 6 inches (6 mm-15 cm). The best-known genus, *Dentalium,* is represented in American waters by about 50 species, most of which are about one inch (25 mm) long and white or yellowish in color.

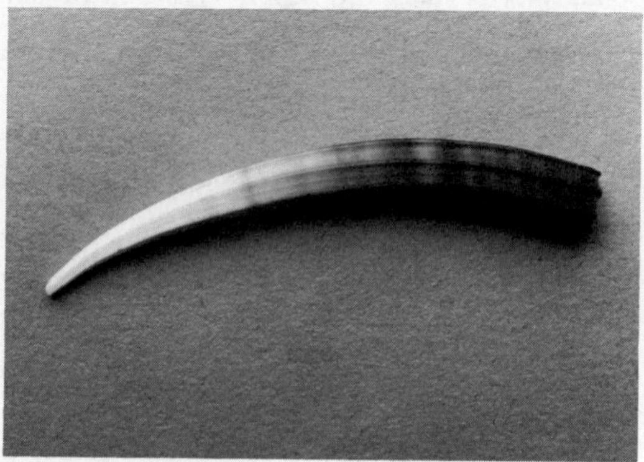

JANE LATTA

Tooth shell (*Dentalium elephantium*)

Before the arrival of European traders, tooth shells were the only form of currency used by the Indians of northwestern America. The cleaned shells were strung together in long bands that sometimes reached a length of 10 feet (3 meters). The shells were also used as nose ornaments.

R. TUCKER ABBOTT
Delaware Museum of Natural History

TOOTHACHE, a pain most often resulting from inflammation and infection of the tooth pulp caused by dental decay. The intensity of a toothache may vary from very mild to excruciating, and it is usually, but not necessarily, related to the depth of the decayed area.

A sharp pain similar to that of an electric shock usually indicates an exposure of the pulp caused by decay or a fracture of the tooth. Intermittent toothache brought on by hot or cold foods or beverages or sweet foods such as candies, jellies, candy breath sweeteners, and cookies indicates early decay or a defective filling or crown. Dull aching pain, which may vary from mild to severe, indicates extension of inflammation and infection into the underlying jawbone. Extensive disease either in a tooth or the jawbone may cause the pain to pulsate, or throb, particularly when the person is lying down. Sometimes a sensitivity of the upper posterior teeth to pressure or chewing is a sign of sinusitis.

Most toothaches can be temporarily alleviated by taking two aspirin. If the decayed area of the tooth is accessible, a small pellet of cotton lightly moistened with oil of cloves and benzacaine will usually give relief until professional treatment is available.

DANIEL A. COLLINS, D. D. S.
Author of "Your Teeth: A Handbook of Dental Care for the Whole Family"

TOOTHACHE TREE is one of the common names for *Aralia spinosa,* a shrub or small tree raised as an ornamental. See ARALIA.

TOOTHPASTE is a preparation for cleaning and polishing the surfaces of the teeth. Toothpastes and tooth powders, known collectively as dentifrices, usually contain many ingredients, including mild abrasives for polishing, binding agents, sudsers (foaming agents), flavorings, and humectants to prevent hardening on exposure to the air.

The abrasives commonly used in dentifrices include calcium carbonate, magnesium carbonate, calcium pyrophosphate, hydroxyapatite tricalcium phosphate, sodium metaphosphate, dicalcium phosphate, charcoal, and bone ash. The effectiveness of the abrasive is determined largely by the hardness, uniformity, and size of the particles. The so-called whitening toothpastes contain relatively larger amounts of these polishing agents and may remove more stains from the teeth. However, they may cause more wear of the tooth surface. The ideal dentifrice produces optimum cleaning and polishing with a minimum of damage to the surfaces of the teeth.

A commonly used binding agent in toothpastes is carrageen. Two widely used sudsers are sodium lauryl sulfate and sodium lauryl sarcosinate. Glycerin is a commonly used humectant. Spearmint, wintergreen, and peppermint are popular flavorings. Saccharin and other sweeteners may also be used, as well as various coloring agents. Some toothpastes also contain fluoride compounds to help prevent dental decay, especially in children.

See also DENTAL HYGIENE.

DANIEL A. COLLINS, D. D. S.
Author of "Your Teeth: A Handbook of "Dental Care for the Whole Family"

TOOTHWORT, to͞oth'wart, any of a group of perennial plants named for the toothlike scales of their white or yellowish creeping rootstocks. Toothworts make up the genus *Dentaria* of the mustard family (Cruciferae). There are about 20 species, and all are native to northern temperate regions. Toothworts are hardy woodland plants that thrive in light, moist soils in partly shaded areas. They are usually propagated by seed and division.

Toothworts have erect stems ranging in height from 6 to 24 inches (15–60 cm). The leaves are pinnately or palmately cut and the white, reddish, or purple flowers are borne in terminal clusters. Probably the most widely cultivated toothwort in the United States is the crinkleroot (*D. diphylla*), with flowers white on the inside and purple on the outside. It ranges from Nova Scotia west to Minnesota and south to South Carolina. Other American species sometimes cultivated are *D. californica,* which is native to California and Oregon, and *D. laciniata* and *D. maxima,* both native to the eastern United States.

ANDREW LEISER
University of California, Davis

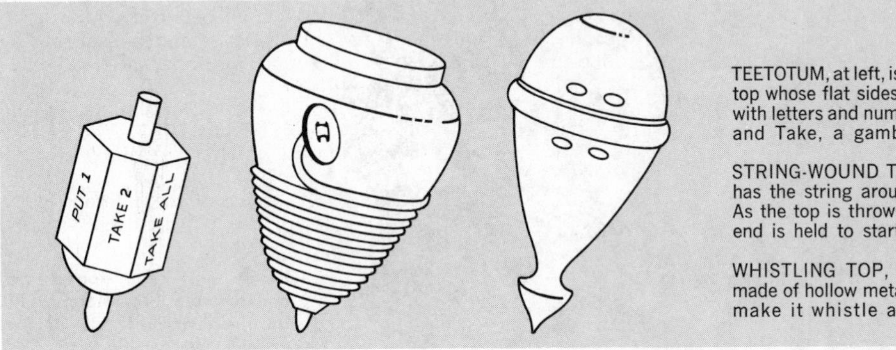

TEETOTUM, at left, is a handspun top whose flat sides are marked with letters and numerals for Put and Take, a gambling game.

STRING-WOUND TOP, center, has the string around its base. As the top is thrown, the string end is held to start it whirling.

WHISTLING TOP, at right, is made of hollow metal. The holes make it whistle as it whirls.

TOOWOOMBA, tə-wŏŏm′bə, is a city in Australia, in southeastern Queensland. It is situated at an elevation of 2,000 feet (600 meters) on the crest of the Main Range, about 85 miles (140 km) west of Brisbane.

Toowoomba is the chief trading center of the Darling Downs, a rich agricultural and pastoral district producing wheat, sorghum, corn, alfalfa, dairy products, and wool. Industries in the city include sawmilling, food processing, and the manufacturing of clothing. There are also a large foundry and engineering workshops.

The city's pleasant subtropical climate and the scenic areas of the surrounding district attract many visitors. Adjacent to the city is a national park area.

Toowoomba is situated on the original route followed by travelers and teamsters moving between the northern and central Darling Downs and Brisbane. The community developed in the 1850's, was incorporated as a town in 1860, and became a city in 1904. Population: (1966) 55,799.

R. M. Younger
Author of "Australia and the Australians"

TOP, essentially a frameless gyroscope, more properly called a spinning top. Because of its seemingly unpredictable behavior, the spinning top has for ages been used throughout the world for gaming and sport by men and boys, and as a toy by children. Its origin is not known. Many games, requiring varying degrees of skill in launching and maneuvering, use tops that are set spinning in one of four ways.

Hand-Spun Top. This top resembles, and possibly was suggested by, the acorn with its cap and stem. Protruding from its head is a spindle, which is twirled between thumb and forefinger or rolled between the palms to set it in motion. The teetotum is a small top of this sort with flat sides marked with symbols indicating *put, take, all,* and *nothing,* and it has long been used as a petty gambling device. Japanese children play with gaily decorated, disk-shaped spindle tops. A Swedish spindle top of bulbous shape is so balanced that it upends itself while in motion to spin on its spindle.

String-Wound Top. The peg top, the best known of this type, has a point or peg of wood or metal. It is launched by throwing it so that a string wound about it is released with a quick snap. A well-launched peg top can reach a speed of 5,000 rpm. Peg tops may be grooved or pierced so they whistle or hum.

The ancient Chinese leveled the head of a conch shell and weighted its tip with lead to make a top. Later, conically shelled marine snails were called top shells. In Japan, where top spinning had become a precise art, the priest top, rounded like the shaved head of a Buddhist priest, is a variation. The striking top, with a sharp metal peg, is launched to split a spinning top.

Whip Top. Set in motion by hand, or by quickly unwinding the short leather or eelskin thong of a light whip that is wound around it, the whip top is kept spinning and is maneuvered by lashing with the whip. In 16th century Europe, top whipping, requiring much skill and energy, was an adult diversion designed to keep the villagers warm in cold weather, and often took place on ice. Overlords gave large whip tops to the peasants. The *potaka* is whipped over artificial ridges of earth by Maori men and boys.

Mechanical Top. Little skill is required to launch a mechanically wound top. The pinch top has a spring that is tightened about a spindle and released by pinching between thumb and fingers. The pump top, spun by the pumping action of a twisted metal ribbon, uses the Archimedean principle of the endless screw. There are many elaborations of these mechanical tops. See also Gyroscope.

Rosemae Wells Campbell
Author of "Tops and Gyroscopes"

TOP SHELL, a marine snail whose shell resembles an inverted toy top. Top shells make up the family Trochidae of the class Gastropoda. There are several hundred species, ranging in size from the ¼-inch (6-mm) *Solariella* of the Arctic seas to the 6-inch (15 cm) *Trochus* of the southwestern Pacific and Indian oceans. The inner layers of the shell are iridescent; the shells of some species of *Trochus* are used to make mother-of-pearl buttons.

All top shells are herbivorous, feeding at night on algae and diatoms. They rasp this food off the bottom by means of a special structure bearing thousands of microscopic teeth. Most shallow-water species live in rock crevices or among kelp. The kelp beds off the coast of California contain about a dozen attractive species of the genus *Calliostoma.*

R. Tucker Abbott
Delaware Museum of Natural History

TOPAZ, tō′paz, is an important industrial and gem mineral consisting of aluminum fluosilicate. Large white masses of topaz are used in the ceramic industry for making spark plug insulators and other heat-resistant products. The name "topaz" is ancient, perhaps coming from a

ORVILLE BRANT, SANTA FE RAILWAY

TOPEKA has open spaces and broad avenues. The state capitol is in the center of this view of the downtown section.

Sanskrit word meaning "fire" or "heat." It originally denoted a different mineral, probably the yellow variety of olivine now known as chrysolite.

Gem topaz is not necessarily yellow, as is commonly thought, but can be blue, pale green, or colorless. The yellow specimens may be heated to become rose pink, and topaz often changes color when exposed to sunlight. Most gems sold as topaz are, in fact, the yellow variety of quartz known as citrine, a less attractive and less valuable stone.

Topaz is commonly found in pegmatite dikes as crystals that weigh up to several hundred pounds. Ordinary granite also may contain small grains of the mineral. The crystals are transparent to translucent and have a perfect cleavage. The action of hot acid gases on solidifying igneous rocks favors the formation of topaz and associated minerals such as fluorite, tourmaline, and cassiterite.

Brazil is the chief supplier of gem topaz, especially a site near Ouro Preto. Russia and Siberia have been noted for fine topaz for centuries. Ceylon and Nigeria are other sources.

Composition, $Al_2SiO_4(OH,F)_2$; hardness, 8; specific gravity, 3.5–3.6; crystal system, orthorhombic.

RICHARD M. PEARL, *Colorado College*

TOPAZOLITE, tō-paz′ə-līt, is a variety of andradite garnet. Its transparent crystals are light yellow or pale gray-green and are sometimes used as gems. Good crystals have been found in the Ala Valley of northern Italy and in California. See also GARNET.

TOPEKA, tə-pē′kə, a city in northeastern Kansas, is the capital of the state and the seat of Shawnee county. It is situated on the Kansas, or Kaw, River, about 135 miles (217 km) northeast of Wichita. It is the third-largest city in Kansas, an industrial center, and an important distribution point in a rich farming area. The skyline has undergone great change as a result of an urban renewal program and the addition of new buildings, including two 17-story office structures, to the downtown business district. A significant development of shopping centers has also occurred. Topeka has attractive tree-shaded residential sections.

The city's manufactures include iron and steel, automobile tires, farm machinery, cellophane, and creamery products. Meatpacking, flour milling, egg packing, publishing and printing, and food processing are also important, and the city has a large grain elevator. The principal offices and machine shops of the Atchison, Topeka & Santa Fe Railroad are in the city.

Among the cultural and educational facilities are Washburn University of Topeka, including the Mulvane Art Center which has painting and sculpture exhibits, and the museum and library of the Kansas State Historical Society, featuring many historical displays and an unusually complete collection of newspaper back files. Topeka has a number of mental care institutions, including the Menninger Foundation, a nonprofit psychiatric center for education, treatment, and research in the field of mental illness; a U. S. Veterans Hospital for psychiatric treatment; the state mental hospital; and the Kansas Neurological Institute.

Topeka's administrative buildings include the state capitol, begun in 1866 but not completed until 1903. Modeled after the national capitol, it contains colorful murals by the Kansas-born painter John Steuart Curry. An extensive plaza development south of the capitol will provide needed space for new government buildings. Other points of interest include Gage Park, which features a rose and rock garden and an excellent zoo. Lake Shawnee, just east of Topeka, has facilities for swimming, fishing, and boating. Forbes Air Force Base is 3 miles (5 km) south of the city.

Topeka was the home of Charles Curtis, the 31st vice president of the United States, and the residence of Alfred M. Landon, the Republican presidential candidate in 1936.

The area around Topeka was opened for settlement in 1854, when Cyrus K. Holliday, a young Pennsylvanian, arrived at the site with some Kansas pioneers to establish a railroad center. The city was founded later in 1854 by antislavery men from New England, and the settlement became a congregation point for free-soil men. Topeka was incorporated as a city in 1857 and was chosen as the state capital when Kansas was admitted to the Union in 1861. The Atchison, Topeka & Santa Fe Railroad, promoted by Holliday, was completed from Atchison to Topeka in 1872.

The city has grown steadily since its founding and, in the 1960's, continued its expansion when many other American cities were losing residents to the suburbs. The city was severely damaged by a flood in 1951 and by a tornado in June 1966. Topeka has the commission form of government, and its mayor is directly elected by the people. Population: 125,011.

JAMES C. MARVIN
Topeka Public Library

TOPHETH, tō'fet, a place in the valley of Hinnom south of Jerusalem where sacrifices to the gods Molech and Baal were common during the Old Testament period. The name "Topheth," or "Tophet," is derived from the Aramaic word for "fireplace" or "hearth." Topheth is generally located near the junction of Wadi er-Rabibi and the brook of Kidron. At this illicit open-air sanctuary, children were sacrificed to the god Molech, or Moloch (Jeremiah 32–35). Other sacrifices were made to the god Baal. Kings Ahaz and Manasseh are mentioned as having sacrificed their children there (II Chronicles 28:3; 33:6). The sanctuary was destroyed by King Josiah during his attempt at religious reform (II Kings 23:10) in the 7th century B.C.

TOPI, tō'pē, an antelope formerly regarded as a distinct species (*Damaliscus korrigum*) but now considered the northern representative of the tsessebe, or sassaby (*D. lunatus*). The topi is found from Senegal east to western Ethiopia and southern Somalia, then south into Tanzania, mostly on short-grass plains. Its color is reddish brown, with a purplish sheen. There is a dark blaze on the face and dark patches on the shoulders and thighs. Both sexes have backwardly curved, ridged horns. Adults weigh from 250 to 300 pounds (113–136 kg) and stand about 50 inches (1.3 meters) high at the shoulders, with the rump distinctly lower.

Topis are almost entirely grazers. They are gregarious, with herds sometimes numbering several hundreds. Rutting males are territorial.

W. F. H. ANSELL, *Department of Wildlife Fisheries and National Parks, Zambia*

TOPIARY, tō'pē-er-ē, is the art of training plants to grow in unnatural, ornamental shapes. It is accomplished by a combination of horticultural techniques, including bending, shearing, and pruning. Evergreen plants are usually most suitable for intricate designs, but any type of plant can be used.

The early Egyptians are known to have clipped trees into columnar forms, but it was the Romans who brought topiary into high art and fashion. Plants were formed into unusual structures, including ships, beasts, and other fanciful designs. Hedges were transformed into elaborate hunting scenes complete with hounds and fox.

Topiary as a part of garden architecture reappeared in the Renaissance and spread throughout Europe and England. Hedges were pruned to resemble fantastic forms or building facades, while elaborately sculpted mazes were common on large estates. In colonial America topiary was generally confined to simpler, low-cut hedges.

The 18th century saw the rise of naturalism in garden art, with the emphasis placed on the natural or ideal shape of the plant. The excesses of topiary, in which every bush and shrub was snipped into an unnatural shape, were ridiculed, and topiary gradually declined and went out of fashion. It remains in modern form in commonly seen geometrically shaped hedges and shrubs. Ivy that is grown on sculpted wire forms represents another contemporary form of topiary.

JULES JANICK, *Purdue University*

Further Reading: Ishimoto, Tatsuo, and Ishimoto, Kiyoko, *The Art of Shaping Shrubs, Trees, and Other Plants* (New York 1966).

PAUL E. GENEREUX

TOPIARY can achieve novel effects, such as this animal, by the training of plants over a wire sculpture.

HEDGE AND TREES have been sheared and pruned to precise geometrical designs in this formal garden.

GOTTSCHO-SCHLEISNER

TOPKAPI SARAYI, tōp-kä′pē sə rä′yē, a museum in Istanbul, Turkey. It was built as a second palace for Mohammed II, and served as a home for the sultans until the 19th century. Construction was completed in 1478. The original structure followed the traditional Turkish plan, grouping living and government quarters around a series of courts, but constant additions and alterations produced an agglomeration of styles. The palace provides an excellent opportunity for the study of Turkish architecture.

The palace became known as Topkapı Sarayı (Cannon Gate Palace) because of its nearness to an old fortified gate. In 1924, under the new regime, it was converted into a museum.

The museum's rich and varied collections include Chinese and Japanese porcelain, as well as Turkish and European porcelain, silver, crystal, and glass. Two libraries contain important collections of rare manuscripts, printed books, incunabula, and decorative bindings. There are other departments with nearly unrivaled collections of calligraphy, Eastern weapons, textiles, Turkish miniatures and tiles, and precious gems.

KATHERINE G. KLINE
"Art News" Magazine

TOPMINNOW, members of a large group of small fishes of the order Cyprinodontiformes. Topminnows are distributed in fresh, brackish, and salt tropical and temperate waters on all continents except Australia. They have only a single dorsal fin, no lateral line pores, and an upturned mouth adapted for obtaining food from surface waters. Many are popular aquarium fishes, and some are used in physiology and genetics research.

Egg-Laying Topminnows. The egg-laying topminnows have small sharp teeth and are classified in the tooth-carp family Cyprinodontidae. Many members of the family are also known as *killifish.* Cyprinodont topminnows are most commonly found in estuaries, lakes, marshes, and quiet streams and are often associated with dense aquatic vegetation. Their upturned mouths may be adaptations not only for feeding but for breathing, permitting the fish to take in well-oxygenated surface water instead of the deeper, oxygen-poor waters of their usual weed-choked, mud-bottomed habitat.

Members of one group of cyprinodont topminnows are known as *annual fishes.* These small, colorful fishes are found in parts of Africa and South America that dry up each year, causing the death of the fishes. Before the dry season, the annual fishes lay eggs that can withstand dessication and hatch to produce a new population the next wet season. Other topminnows, of the genus *Fundulus,* normally spawn in early summer. The eggs adhere to aquatic vegetation and hatch in 8 to 14 days.

Viviparous Topminnows. The viviparous, or livebearing, topminnows are classified in the families Poeçilidae, Goodeidae, and Jenynsiidae. Included in this group are such well-known species as the guppy and the mosquito fish.

R. WELDON LARIMORE
Illinois Natural History Survey

TOPOGRAPHY, tə-pog′rə-fē, is the relief of a land surface, consisting of its contours and features, whether natural or manmade. The art of mapping and charting those features is also called topography. See MAP; SURVEYING.

TOPOLOGY, tə-pol′ə-jē, the branch of mathematics that deals with patterns involving position and relative position. Geometry also deals with position, but the geometer is concerned with measurable quantities such as angles, distances, and areas, whereas the topologist considers only those properties of position that are independent of such magnitudes. For instance, "the two fields are separated by a fence" is a topological statement in that it describes the relative position of the fields without referring to the size of the fields or the height of the fence.

Position and relative position are concepts fundamental to our understanding of the world. The Swiss psychologist Jean Piaget reported that as a child's abstract representation of space develops, the first distinctions he can make are topological ones. For instance, a typical 4-year-old can make the topological distinction between a solid disk and a disk with a hole, while he still cannot make the geometrical distinction between a disk and a square.

The concepts of position and relative position also are fundamental in much of mathematics. Perhaps because they are so basic, their systematic analysis came rather late in the history of mathematics. In 1833, Karl Gauss wrote, "About the *geometria situs,* which Leibniz imagined and at which only a couple of geometers [Leonhard Euler and Alexandre T. Vandermonde] have been allowed to cast a weak glance, we know and possess, after a century and a half, not much more than nothing." *Geometria situs,* the geometry of position, is the term coined by Leibniz in 1679 for a sort of formal vector calculus in which he had great hopes. Euler took over this term for the discipline that later was called *analysis situs* and finally topology.

TWO PROBLEMS IN TOPOLOGY

The Seven Bridges of Königsberg. Part of Euler's "weak glance" is a work appearing in the *Commentaries* of the St. Petersburg Academy of Sciences for 1736. This work, which qualifies as the first published topology article, is entitled *The Solution of a Problem Pertaining to the Geometria Situs.*

Here is the problem in Euler's words: "At Königsberg in Prussia there is an island *A,* called 'der Kneiphof,' and the river surrounding it is divided into two branches, as may be seen in Fig. 1. Over the branches of this river lead seven bridges, *a, b, c, d, e, f,* and *g.* The question is whether one can plan a walk so as to cross each bridge once and not more than once." Euler proved that this is impossible.

Here is his proof. Label the banks of the river by the letters *B, C, D,* as in Fig. 1. Write down the sequence of regions visited, beginning at the starting point of the path. The 1st letter represents the starting point, the 2d letter represents where we land after crossing the 1st bridge,

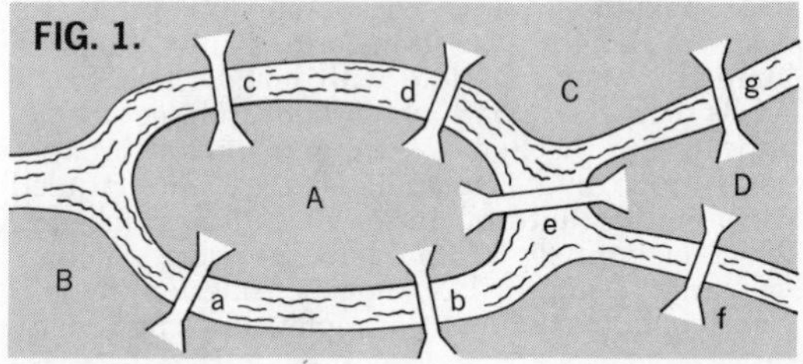

and so forth up to the 8th letter, which represents where we land after crossing the 7th bridge. For instance, the sequence of bridge crossings that begins *acdef* gives a sequence of regions visited that begins *BACADB*.

Now observe that there are five bridges leading to the island *A*. If all five bridges are crossed, the letter *A* will appear in the sequence of regions three times. This is so because one occurrence of *A* will use up at most two bridges. Euler continued his proof: "Since three bridges lead to *B*, *B* must appear twice, and likewise *D* and *C* must occur twice. Therefore, in the series of eight letters, which represents the crossing of the seven bridges, A must appear three times but *B*, *C*, and *D* each twice, which cannot be done in a series of eight letters. This shows that the desired crossing of the seven bridges of Königsberg cannot be carried out."

Euler's method of proof typifies the method of operation of the topologist. Problems in topology usually are not immediately susceptible to mathematical analysis because there is no direct "calculus of position" except in very simple cases. Consequently, most topology problems must first be translated into a domain of mathematics in which one can perform calculations. In this procedure the original topology problem (here, the existence of a path crossing each bridge exactly once) usually is replaced by a combinatorial or algebraic problem (here, the existence of an 8-letter sequence with three *A*'s, two *B*'s, two *C*'s, and two *D*'s). After this translation of the problem the answer may be evident (as in our example), or it may be difficult to find. Also, the translation of the problem often requires great originality and ingenuity.

The Four-Color Problem. These difficulties can be illustrated by the famous 4-color problem, which, despite its elementary character, has never been solved. The problem is as follows.

The statement of the problem is simple. What is the largest number of colors *needed* to color a map so that regions with a common border are never given the same color? It has been proved that five colors are sufficient for any map, and it is easy to find instances where three colors are not sufficient—for example, for New York, Connecticut, Massachusetts, and the Atlantic Ocean. However, in the more than 100 years this problem has been known, no one has been able to prove that four colors are always sufficient or to find a map that requires more than four.

The Königsberg bridge problem and the 4-color problem clearly are topology problems since they are posed in terms of position—paths, crossings, borders. Even more interesting problems occur when topology is applied to questions that arise from another discipline, often one of the other branches of mathematics.

BASIC CONCEPTS OF TOPOLOGY

In order to apply as generally as possible, the theorems of topology are stated about sets that have no structure except the relative position of their elements. Such a set is essentially what is called a *topological space*. The concept of topological space evolved during the 19th century; its present form is due to the German mathematician Felix Hausdorff (1914).

By analogy to geometry, the elements of a topological space are often called *points*. However, just as the number 2 can represent a distance of two miles or a flow of two gallons per hour, a point in a topological space can represent a point in a geometric figure, a whole figure, or a whole system of geometry. It all depends on the application.

FIG. 2.

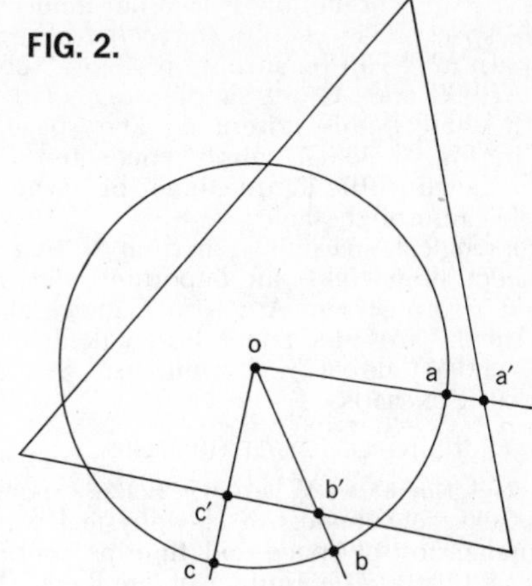

Homeomorphy. In plane geometry, two figures *X* and *Y* are considered the same if they are congruent. This means that there is a way of matching each point of *X* with a point of *Y*, and that this can be done so as to preserve lengths and angles. In topology two spaces *X* and *Y* are considered the same, or *homemorphic,* if points of *X* can be matched with points of *Y* in a way that preserves relative position.

A circle and a triangle are not congruent figures, but they are homeomorphic. To show that they are homeomorphic, we establish a correspondence between points of the circle and points of the triangle by drawing the circle with its center *o* inside the triangle and then matching the points that lie on the same ray emanating from *o* (see Fig. 2). Thus the points *a, b, c* on the circle are matched with the points *a′*, *b′*, *c′* on the triangle. This matching preserves relative position; for instance, point *b* lies between *a* and *c*, and point *b′* lies between *a′* and *c′*.

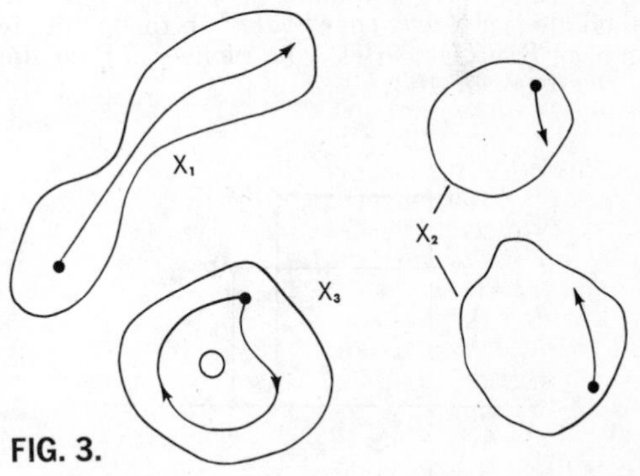

FIG. 3.

In contrast, it is often quite complicated to prove that two spaces are not homeomorphic, and much effort has gone into finding criteria for establishing a proof of this sort. One basic criterion is path connectedness. A space *X* is *path connected* if any two points of *X* can be joined by a path lying in *X*. A path-connected space X_1 and a space X_2, which is not path connected, are represented in Fig. 3.

Another basic criterion is simple connectedness. A space X is *simply connected* if every closed path in X can be shrunk in X to a point. The spaces X_1 and X_2 are simply connected because they meet this criterion. The space X_3 shown in Fig. 3 is not simply connected since the path shown in the figure cannot be shrunk to a point because of the hole.

A topological space is a natural setting for the concept of a *limit,* an important idea first described rigorously by Augustin Cauchy about 1820. Limits are fundamental in calculus and also in understanding real numbers. See also CALCULUS; FUNCTION.

THE TOPOLOGY OF NUMBERS

The Real Numbers. When we make quantitative mathematical models of the physical world, our apprehension of space and time as continua requires us to use a continuum of numbers. The rational numbers do not form a continuum of numbers. For example, the Greeks saw that the length of the diagonal in a unit square cannot be expressed by a rational number. However, one can find rational numbers arbitrarily close to this missing length, such as the sequence 1, 1.4, 1.41, 1.414, and so on. This fact allows one to use certain limits of rational numbers to construct a continuum of numbers called the *real numbers.* This continuum is an infinite line of numbers, called the *real line,* or the *continuum,* and is given the symbol R.

Coordinates. Since distances along a line can be faithfully represented by real numbers, these numbers allow us to calculate positions along a line. For instance, the position of a particle moving along a line can be calculated once we know its law of motion. With the real numbers we can also calculate positions in a plane because, after a choice of coordinate axes, any point P in the plane can be represented by a pair (a,b) of real numbers. Such a pair are called the *cartesian coordinates* of the point, in honor of René Descartes, who pioneered their use in geometry in 1637.

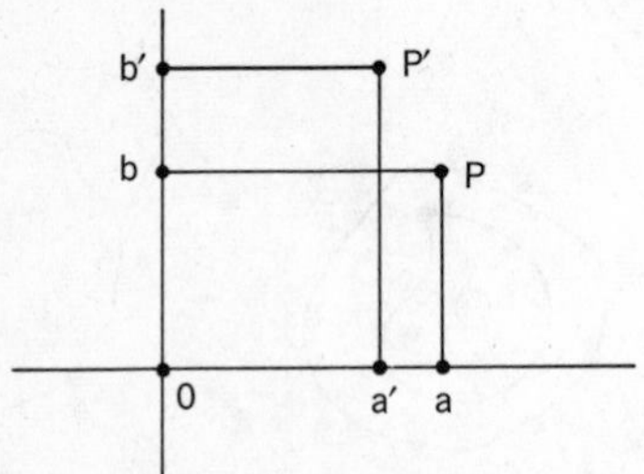

FIG. 4.

The plane with these coordinates is an example of a cartesian product. The *cartesian product* A X B of two topological spaces A and B is the space of pairs (a,b) of points, a from A and b from B, where (a,b) close to (a',b') means that a is close to a', and b is close to b'. A point P' in the plane with coordinates (a',b') will be close to P if and only if a is close to a' and b is close to b' (see Fig. 4). In other words, the plane is homeomorphic to the cartesian product RXR, usually written R^2. Three-dimensional space can be represented as R^3, the space of triples (a,b,c) of real numbers, and so forth for higher dimensional spaces.

MANIFOLDS

The systematic use of these coordinates in physical problems leads to a class of spaces called *topological manifolds,* which were initially investigated by Bernhard Riemann around 1854. Topological manifolds are topological spaces that are locally (in a sense that will be defined) homeomorphic to one of the spaces R, R^2, R^3 . . . of cartesian coordinates.

One-Dimensional Manifolds. We begin with a simple problem: the description of the position of a rigid pendulum that is constrained to move in a plane. The set of positions of such a pendulum is a one-dimensional continuum, since at each point the pendulum can only move clockwise or counterclockwise about its axis. This continuum is different from the real line. In fact, any attempt to describe positions of the pendulum by real numbers ends up either with some positions left undescribed or with several numbers corresponding to the same position. For example, if we assign to each position of the pendulum the number giving the angle in degrees between that position and the vertical downward rest position, counting angles to the right as positive and to the left as negative, the numbers 180 and -180 will both describe the same position, namely, vertical upward.

The correct mathematical model for describing the positions of the pendulum is the circle. To each point on the circle there corresponds exactly one position of the pendulum. This correspondence can be established by considering the pendulum as hung from the center of the circle. If we had needed only to describe positions close to the rest position, the use of real numbers would have been satisfactory because to each real number between -90 and 90 there corresponds exactly one position of the pendulum. In fact, if we stay close to any given position, then we can use an interval of real numbers to describe the positions of the pendulum in an unambiguous way. This situation can be described by saying that *locally*—in the vicinity of any given position—the space of positions of the pendulum is like the space of real numbers. A space that has this local property is called a one-dimensional manifold. Two simple path-connected one-dimensional manifolds are the space R itself and the circle, usually denoted by S^1 (S for sphere, 1 for the dimension). There are many others, but they all exhibit topological peculiarities that will not be dealt with here.

Surfaces. The family of relatively simple manifolds is much larger when we consider two dimensions. Two-dimensional manifolds, or *surfaces,* are spaces locally homeomorphic to the space R^2 of pairs of real numbers. The definition of higher-dimensional manifolds is exactly analogous. For an n-dimensional manifold, we use the n-fold product $RX \ldots XR = R^n$.

For an example of a two-dimensional manifold, we return to the case of the pendulum constrained to move in a plane. From physics we know that, given the position and velocity of the pendulum at one instant of time, it is possible to predict its motion for all succeeding time. The data necessary for this prediction, namely a position and a velocity, can be represented by a point in a two-dimensional manifold. The position, as we have seen, corresponds to a point on the circle. Since the pendulum can only travel forward or backward along this circle, its velocity can be faithfully represented by a real number v, where we consider counterclockwise velocity as positive and clockwise velocity as negative. The position-velocity space, or *phase space*, of the pendulum is therefore the space of pairs (x,v), where x is a point on the circle and v is a real number. In other words, it is the cartesian product $S^1 \times R$. This surface is a cylinder (see Fig. 5).

Topology and Physics: Dynamical Systems. If the pendulum starts at the point (x,v) on the cylinder, its positions and velocities at subsequent times can be thought of as determining a curve, or *orbit*, along which the point representing the state of the pendulum must travel in the phase space. Thus, the physics of the pendulum can be completely represented by a family of curves on the cylinder. Such a family of curves in a phase space is called a *dynamical system*.

In schematically representing these curves for a frictionless pendulum, the cylinder was slit along the line corresponding to $x = 90$ and flattened out as shown in Fig. 6, where curves above the position axis represent counterclockwise motions and the curves below this axis represent clockwise motions. There are two one-point orbits: P, where the pendulum is at rest, and P', where it is standing on its head. Two of the other orbits shown are lines: those passing through the states Q and Q'. In state Q, for example, the pendulum is at the bottom of its swing with just enough momentum to climb up clockwise toward the state P'. The rest of the orbits are circles. Those around P (0,0) correspond to small oscillations of the pendulum. Those above and below P' (180,0) correspond to high-velocity spinning of the pendulum.

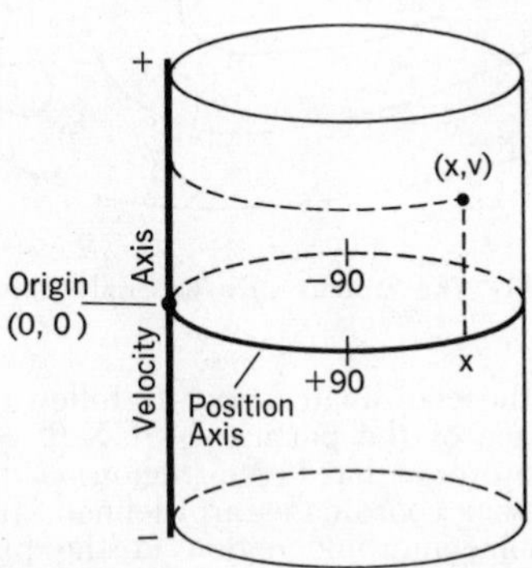

FIG. 5.

The disposition of the various kinds of orbits—that is, the overall qualitative behavior of the physical system—is closely related to the topology of the space. In fact, Henri Poincaré, regarded as the father of modern topology, was led into topology in the 1800's partly as a result of his investigations of the dynamical systems of celestial mechanics.

The Sphere. Another common two-dimensional manifold is the sphere S^2. The surface of the earth is topologically a sphere. The fact that this surface is locally like R^2 gives an overlap between topology and topography (the science of map making). This is so because a map on a page is just a planar representation of part of the earth's surface. Such representations are adequate locally, but there is no way to make a

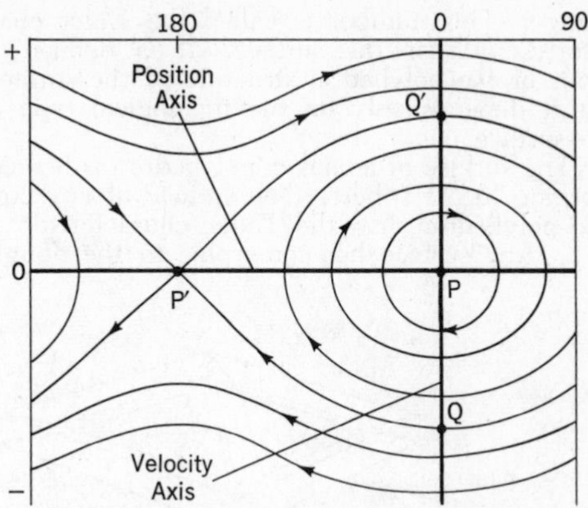

Fig. 6. Behavior of pendulum is represented by orbits.

flat map faithfully represent the whole surface of the earth. This is so because S^2 is not homeomorphic to R^2 or to any part of R^2.

If we return to our example of the pendulum but no longer constrain it to remain in one plane, then the space of positions of the pendulum can be identified with the sphere. If we place the center of the sphere at the point where the pendulum is hung, then to each point on the sphere there corresponds exactly one position of the pendulum (see Fig. 7).

Polyhedra. Other examples of surfaces homeomorphic to the sphere are the surfaces of convex polyhedra. The well-known convex polyhedra are the five regular solids: the tetrahedron (4 vertices, 6 edges, 4 faces), the cube (8, 12, 6), the octahedron (6, 12, 8), the dodecahedron (20, 30, 12), and the icosahedron (12, 30, 20). See also POLYHEDRON.

The Euler Characteristic. Euler noted that the surface of any convex polyhedron satisfies the simple equation $V - E + F = 2$, where V is the number of vertices, E is the number of edges, and F is the number of faces of the convex polyhedron. A nonconvex polyhedron is

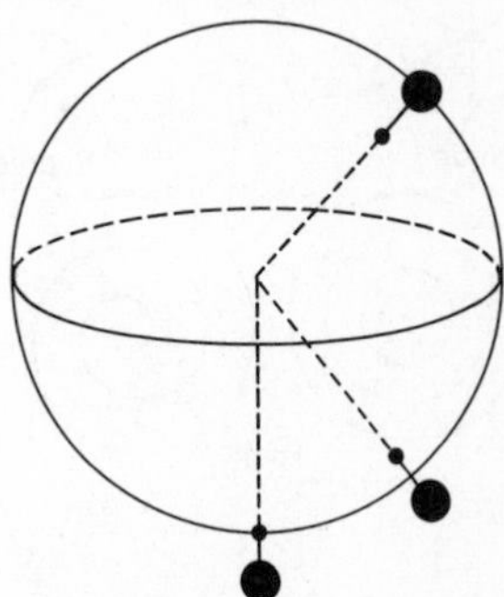

FIG. 7.

shown in Fig. 8. Its doughnut-shaped surface, which can be thought of as made from three triangular prisms stuck end to end, has 9 vertices, 18 edges, and 9 faces. For this surface, $V - E + F = 0$. If two of these polyhedra are joined along a face, the resulting double-doughnut surface has 4 vertices, 32 edges, and 16 faces (see Fig. 9). For the surface of this polyhedron, $V - E + F = -2$.

If a polyhedron is subdivided by adding new vertices or edges, its number $V - E + F$ does not change. This number is called the Euler characteristic, *X*, of the surface. It is defined in terms of the polyhedral structure of the surface, but it depends only on the topological type of the surface.

The surface of a convex polyhedron is homeomorphic to the sphere. The surface of any convex polyhedron has the Euler characteristic $X = 2$. Any surface homeomorphic to the doughnut-shaped surface has $X = 0$. Any surface homeomorphic to the double-doughnut surface has $X = -2$. In general a surface of *genus h*—for instance, the surface of a polyhedron with *h* handles—has $X = 2 - 2h$.

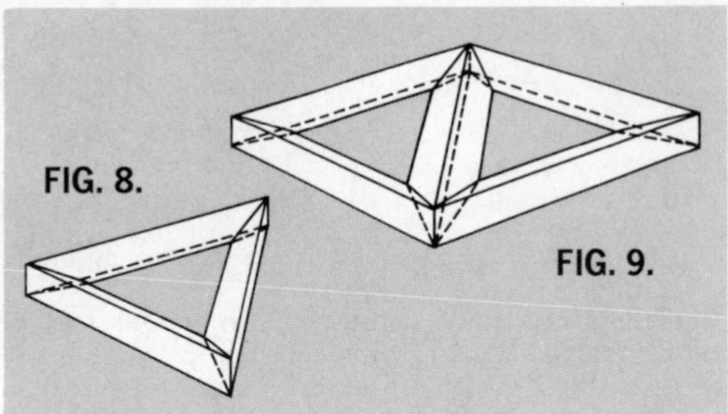

FIG. 8.

FIG. 9.

The Euler Characteristic and Dynamical Systems. The Euler characteristic, which can be defined for topological spaces in general, also appears in the study of dynamical systems. Consider a manifold that carries a family of curves analogous to those shown in Fig. 6. There is a relation between the number and type of singularities of such a family and the Euler characteristic of the manifold. In the case of surfaces, a family of curves may be supposed to have only three types of singularities—nodes, saddle points, and foci (see Fig. 10). In this case the relation, as given by Poincaré in 1885, is $N - S + F =$ Euler characteristic, where *N* is the number of nodes, *S* is the number of saddle points, and *F* is the number of foci. It follows that for a family of curves on S^2, the sum $N + F$ must be at least two, and therefore S^2 has no families of curves without singularities. The fact is sometimes rendered as "you cannot comb the hair on a sphere."

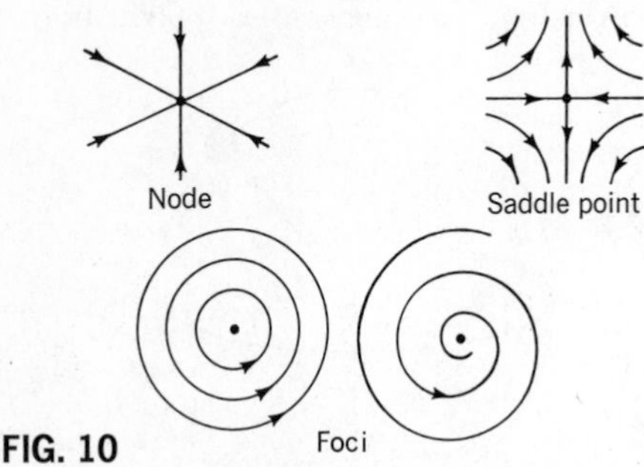

FIG. 10

The Möbius Strip. The Möbius strip, named after the German mathematician August F. Möbius, is the surface formed by slitting the cylinder shown in Fig. 5 and sticking it back together after giving one end a twist (see Fig. 11). One intriguing property of this strip is that it has only one side, whereas the cylinder, the sphere, or the surface of any polyhedron has two sides. If one walks around circle *c* on the strip, one comes back on the opposite side of the surface. This circle is an example of a *nonbounding cycle*, which here means a circle in the surface that is not the boundary of any two-dimensional part of the surface. In contrast, circle *c′* does bound the region *D* of the surface.

The study of nonbounding cycles in surfaces and the study of their higher dimensional analogues is called *homology theory*. Its principles, which are at the center of modern topology, were developed by Riemann, Enrico Betti (1870), and Poincaré (1895).

Higher Dimensional Manifolds. We consider just one example of a higher dimensional manifold—the phase space of the pendulum shown in Fig. 7. We will see that this is a four-dimensional manifold by using a local analogy with the case of a particle moving in the plane. The position and velocity of such a particle are described by four numbers (x, y, v, w), where *x* and *y* are its coordinates in the plane, and *v* and *w* are the components of its velocity in the directions of the coordinate axes. It follows that the phase space of the particle is $R^2 \text{ X } R^2 = R^4$.

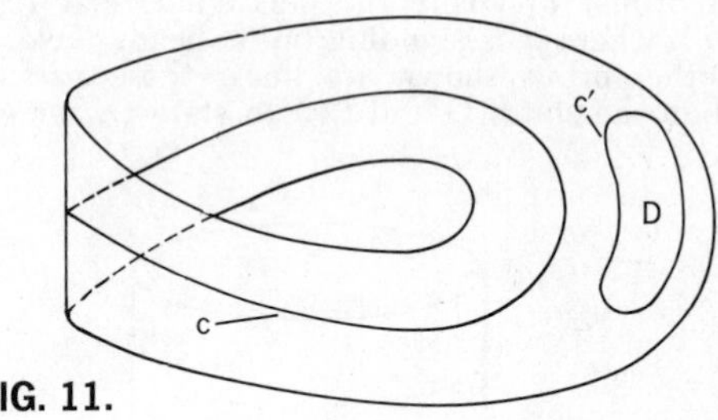

FIG. 11.

Fig. 11. The Möbius strip has only one side.

Suppose now that D is a region on the sphere where planar coordinates are defined, and let *D′* be the homeomorphic region in the plane—that is, the region consisting of the coordinates of points in *D*. If the coordinates are differentiable, then they can be used to calculate the velocity of the pendulum. In fact, that part of the pendulum's phase space where the position is a point in *D* is identical to that part of the particle's phase space corresponding to a position in *D′*. This line of argument shows that the space of pendulum states with positions in *D* is homeomorphic to $D' \text{ X } R^2$ and therefore to $D \text{ X } R^2$. But the total phase space is not homeomorphic to $S^2 \text{ X } R^2$, as the analogy with the planar pendulum might suggest.

A manifold with this sort of local product structure is called a *fiber bundle*. The theory of fiber bundles is an essential part of differential topology, which is a flourishing branch of modern topology. In differential topology, calculus is blended with topology, as in the above case where differentiability of the coordinates is crucial.

ANTHONY PHILLIPS
State University of New York, Stony Brook

Further Reading: Arnold, B. H., *Intuitive Concepts in Elementary Topology* (New York 1962); Kelley, John L., *General Topology* (New York 1955); Lefshetz, Solomon, *Introduction to Topology* (Princeton, N. J., 1949); Milnor, John W., *Topology from the Differentiable Viewpoint* (Charlottesville, Va., 1965).

RELIGIOUS NEWS SERVICE

SCROLLS OF THE TORAH, written in the Hebrew language, are kept in the Ark of every synagogue.

TORAH, tō′rə. In its limited definition, Torah refers to the first five books of the Hebrew Bible. As an all-embracing concept, it means a body of learning and tradition that is of central importance to Judaism.

Defined in its narrowest sense, the Torah is the scroll of parchment, housed in the Ark of every synagogue, upon which is inscribed the first five books of the Bible in Hebrew. These books, often called the Pentateuch, contain among other things a narrative of events from the creation of the world to the death of Moses. According to traditional Judaism, the Torah was given by God to Moses during the revelation that took place on Mount Sinai. However, the subsequent history of the Jewish people is evidence that learning and teaching, which is the literal meaning of Torah, did not end with Moses. Thus, the remaining books of the Hebrew Bible, including the Prophets and the Writings (wisdom literature), while not Torah in the technical sense, are Torah in the spirit of teaching, guidance, law and morality. Likewise, the Talmud, the Midrash, the Responsa literature, the Rabbinic Codes, and even the writings of medieval Jewish philosophers must all be considered part of the great spiritual and moral phenomenon known as Torah.

A distinction must be made between the written Torah and the oral Torah. The former refers to the five books of Moses and signifies the written record of revelation. The latter refers to the principle of continual interpretation of that revelation that has allowed Judaism to survive and grow through the vicissitudes of history.

In the *Sayings of the Fathers*, a Talmudic tractate, one of the rabbis, referring to the Torah, said, "Turn it and turn it over again, for everything is in it, and contemplate it, and wax grey and old over it, and stir not from it, for thou canst have no better rule than this." The Torah is the lifelong occupation of the Jew, and the historic enterprise of Judaism is to learn it, to live it, and to teach it to the world.

In its fullest meaning, Torah is central to the nature of Judaism. Torah is many things—law, ethics, tradition, wisdom, institutions, divine instruction, parental teaching, theology, ordinances, philosophy, a scroll. Above all it is a way of life dictated by the covenant that God established with the people of Israel. It is all of these and infinitely more. The Torah is the *raison d'être* of the Jew. Without it Judaism does not exist. In its all-embracing definition, therefore, the word "Torah" is a synonym for the totality of Judaism.

RONALD B. SOBEL
Rabbi, Temple Emanu-El, New York City

TORBERNITE, tôr′bər-nīt, a hydrous phosphate of uranium and copper, is a minor ore of uranium. Its green crystals, with a pearly to glassy luster, have a hardness of 2 to 2.5 and a specific gravity of 3.2 to 3.6.

TORDESILLAS, Treaty of. See DEMARCATION, LINE OF.

TORGAU, tôr′gou, is a city in East Germany, on the west bank of the Elbe River, 47 miles (76 km) northwest of Dresden. Torgau is a river port and has ceramic and engineering industries. The city's chief monument is the Schloss Hartenfels, a large Renaissance palace built by the electors of Saxony in the 16th and 17th centuries and now used as a museum. The Marienkirche, in which Katharina von Bora, Martin Luther's wife, is buried, was built in the 16th century, as was the city hall.

Founded in the 10th century, the city grew rapidly in the 13th century and later became an important residence of the electors of Saxony. The city played an important role in the history of the Reformation. Luther was frequently in the town, and the Torgau league of Protestant princes was formed in the city in 1526. In 1815, Torgau passed to Prussia. A monument on the Elbe near Torgau commemorates the meeting of Soviet and American troops at the end of World War II. Population: (1968) 21,553.

NORMAN J. G. POUNDS
Indiana University

TORI BUSSHI, tō-rē bōōs-shē, a 7th century Japanese Buddhist sculptor. His exact life dates are not known, but the incised inscription on the halo of his masterpiece, the bronze *Shaka Triad*, is dated 623. It also gives his full title: Shiba Kuratsukuri no Obito Tori Busshi, which means "Shiba Tori, the Buddhist sculptor, head of the Kuratsukuri (family)." Kuratsukuri literally means "saddlemaker," and presumably it was once the family's occupation. Tori's grandfather Kuratsukuri Shiba Tatsuto was Chinese but was naturalized in Japan in 522.

Tori's sculptural style resembles that of the Northern Wei dynasty (386–535) of China. His *Shaka Triad*, in the Horyuji monastery at Nara, consists of Shakyamuni (the historic Buddha) and two attendant bodhisattvas. The main image is very similar to the stone Shakyamuni of Pinyang Chapel, Lungmen, China, which was completed in 523. Although the Wei dynasty style took about 100 years to be transmitted to Japan, via Korea, it remained practically unchanged. Buddhist artisans were required to be faithful to prevailing formulas lest the spiritual efficacy, or magic, of the image be impaired.

ROBERT MOES, *Denver Art Museum*

TORNADO, a small, extremely intense whirlwind formed by a severe thunderstorm. Making a noise like a jet squadron, a tornado descends as a funnel-shaped extension from its parent cloud. If it reaches the ground, its high winds and the sudden drop in air pressure as it passes cause almost complete destruction of everything in its path.

Tornadoes kill thousands of people and destroy property valued at about a billion dollars every year. With their enormous power, they have been known to break trees many feet thick, drive straws into pieces of wood, and lift cattle and even automobiles high into the air.

Occurrence. Although tornadoes are rare, they occur in all parts of the world—with the possible exception of the polar regions. In the United States about 600 or 700 tornadoes are reported each year. They are most prevalent in the region known as "Tornado Alley" that extends through the central plains states.

The storms can occur at all times of the year and at any time of day or night, but are most likely in the spring and summer and in the afternoon and early evening. They usually last only minutes, and their damage paths are only a few hundred feet wide and a few miles long. However, some large tornadoes persist for hours, with paths up to a mile (about 1½ km) wide and hundreds of miles long. Usually the funnel moves—along with the parent thunderstorm—in an easterly direction, at speeds of up to 70 miles (110 km) per hour. Estimates of the wind speed in the funnel itself range from 200 up to 600 miles (320 to 1,000 km) per hour.

Cause. Scientists agree that the tornado's funnel is rendered visible by the cloud of fine waterdrops that condenses in the region of low pressure and temperature that exists in the core of the high-velocity vortex. There are differences of opinion as to why such a vortex should form. Some scientists think that vortexes are caused by vigorous updrafts in a thundercloud, and some think that the cause is falling hail. Others suggest that very intense electrical activity in a storm, as evidenced by unusual lightning displays and by radio and television static, may provide the tornado's energy.

Control. Meteorologists issue tornado alerts when they recognize conditions that are likely to produce the unusually severe thunderstorms that spawn tornadoes. These conditions include warm moist air at low levels, with high winds and cold air at higher levels—a situation that arises along cold fronts and, occasionally, on the periphery of hurricanes. Then, when observers see a funnel cloud or recognize a characteristic "hooklike" echo on weather radar, warnings are broadcast for people to take cover.

Ideas have been proposed for destroying tornadoes by gunfire, rockets, or explosives. It has also been suggested that tornadoes might be prevented by introducing "seeding" agents, electrical conductors, or gases into the parent storms. Such measures have yet to be proved effective, and at present no practicable method of tornado control exists. See also WINDS.

BERNARD VONNEGUT
State University of New York at Albany

Further Reading: Brooks, Edward M., "Tornadoes and Related Phenomena," in *Compendium of Meteorology*, ed. by Thomas F. Malone (Boston 1951); Flora, Snowden D., *Tornadoes of the United States* (Norman, Okla., 1958); Vonnegut, Bernard, "Inside the Tornado," *Natural History Magazine*, vol. 77, April 1968.

A tornado funnel strikes down in Minnesota, raising a cloud of dust and debris as it moves over the land.

ERIC LANTZ, WALNUT GROVE (MINN.) TRIBUNE

TORONTO'S new city hall is a landmark in the downtown area. The design was by the Finnish architect Viljo Revell.

NATIONAL FILM BOARD OF CANADA

TORONTO, tə-ron′tō, the capital of the province of Ontario, is the second-largest city in Canada. Situated on Toronto Bay on the north shore of Lake Ontario, 360 miles (547 km) west of Montreal, it is a major lake port and the commercial, financial, industrial, educational, and cultural center of English-speaking Canada.

The city of Toronto is surrounded by the five boroughs of North York, Scarborough, Etobicoke, York, and East York. The Municipality of Metropolitan Toronto, which encompasses the six municipalities, was created in 1953 by an act of the provincial legislature. It was the first federated system of government of a metropolitan area in North America.

Approaching Toronto from east or west, the visitor is struck by the great number of apartment towers scattered throughout the city. From the air the tall buildings appear to rise from a forest, for the city is planted with trees in most of its residential sections and has thousands of acres of parkland.

Toronto was originally built on the flat land bordering the shore of Lake Ontario. Two miles (3 km) north the land rises about 300 feet (90 meters) to a second plain, which continues to rise gently northward for 30 miles (48 km). These plains, which once formed the shoreline of prehistoric Lake Iroquois, are intersected by the ravines of Ice Age rivers. Two small rivers, the Don in eastern Toronto and the Humber on the western outskirts, run in ancient valleys.

Toronto's main business and shopping area is still concentrated within a mile of the lake front, but large, self-contained shopping plazas have been built in the boroughs. Theaters, nightclubs, and other entertainment centers have remained downtown. The residential areas surround the city core in a great crescent extending 20 miles (32 km) east and 40 miles (64 km) west from Yonge Street, the city's original main street. Toronto was once a city of single-family homes, but today one in four of its citizens lives in a high-rise apartment building. Many of these buildings have replaced the obsolete inner-city buildings and have helped accelerate the reclamation of the older rundown areas of the city.

The Economy. On Bay Street, the heart of Toronto's financial district, business leaders make decisions that affect the mining, pulp and paper, and manufacturing industries from one end of Canada to the other. The Toronto Stock Exchange handles about 70% of all the stock dealings in Canada. Toronto also is headquarters for 5 of Canada's 11 chartered banks and for the T. Eaton Company and the Robert Simpson Company, the country's largest department and mail-order stores.

Toronto is the center of Canadian manufacturing. Important industries include printing and publishing, meatpacking, and the manufacture of electrical machinery, transportation and agricultural equipment, metal products, chemicals, furniture, rubber products, clothing, textiles, paper, beverages, and food products.

Its strategic location makes Toronto a leading distribution point. With the development of the St. Lawrence Seaway, Toronto has become a port of call for vessels from over 60 countries and can handle about 70 vessels at one time.

Transportation. The city is a focal point for the two great transcontinental railroad systems of Canada. Toronto International Airport is expanding to keep up with growing passenger and freight volume. Toronto Island Airport in Toronto Bay handles smaller, private aircraft.

The publicly owned Toronto Transit Commission operates an integrated system of subway trains, streetcars, trolley coaches, and buses. A new rail commuter line, subsidized by the provincial government and operated by the Canadian National Railway, runs for 60 miles (96 km) along the lakeshore between Hamilton and Pickering. The city is crossed by three major limited-access roads.

Education and Cultural Life. The University of Toronto, Canada's largest university, has its main campus in downtown Toronto and satellite colleges in Erindale in the west and Scarborough in the eastern suburbs. Established as a provincial institution in 1850, it has become

WILLIAM FROELICH

CASA LOMA, a fine example of French château architecture, was initially a residence. It is now a museum.

a federation of colleges, professional faculties, and research institutions. York University, with its main campus in North York and a research center in the city, was founded as a municipal institution in 1960 and is Canada's fastest-growing university. Ryerson Polytechnical Institute is also in the city. Toronto is the seat of four of the province's community colleges of applied arts and technology.

Toronto's public library system consists of a large central library with extensive reference and bibliographic services, 65 branch libraries, and a music library. The Royal Ontario Museum, Canada's foremost museum, is internationally known for its Chinese collections and its Sigmund Samuel Canadiana Building. The Art Gallery of Ontario features an extensive program of circulating exhibitions. The Ontario Science Centre, opened in 1969, has a fascinating variety of scientific exhibits. The McLaughlin Planetarium features a circular star theater.

The O'Keefe Centre for the Performing Arts presents Broadway productions and musical and ballet performances. The St. Lawrence Centre, with its Town Hall and theater, is the site of public rallies, recitals, and concerts and is the home of the Repertory Theatre Company. The city is also the home of the Toronto Symphony Orchestra, the Canadian Opera Company, the Festival Singers, and the National Ballet of Canada. Theater productions are frequent and art galleries, jazz clubs, and movie houses are numerous.

Toronto has three daily newspapers—the *Star*, the *Telegram*, and the *Globe and Mail*. It is the headquarters for the Canadian holdings of Lord Thomson of Fleet. It is the center for the Canadian Broadcasting Corporation's English-language television and radio networks and the independent CTV Television Network.

Points of Interest. The Canadian National Exhibition, held each year from mid-August to Labor Day on its 350-acre (141-hectare) lakeside site, is said to be the world's largest annual fair. It brings together agricultural and industrial exhibits and entertainment from many countries.

Black Creek Pioneer Village, 10 miles (16 km) north of downtown Toronto, offers an accurate view of life in Ontario before Confederation. Fort York, the scene of a battle in the War of 1812; Casa Loma, the 98-room castle built in 1911 as a private residence and now a museum, on the heights overlooking old Toronto; and the romanesque old City Hall are landmarks in Toronto. The new City Hall, designed by the Finnish architect Viljo Revell, consists of two semicircular towers surrounding a low central dome. It has become a new landmark. Situated on the edge of Nathan Phillips Square, it is a focal point for rallies, festivals, concerts, protest meetings, and other gatherings.

Sports and Recreation. The new Woodbine and Greenwood race tracks provide horse racing in the summer and autumn. In winter the Maple Leafs of the National Hockey League draw thousands to their games, and skiing, snowmobiling, and skating are popular. Golf and tennis and swimming, and boating on Lake Ontario are spring and summer sports. The Argonauts, Toronto's professional football team, are an autumn attraction.

Government. Toronto's unique federal system of metropolitan government, established by the provincial government in 1953, has been studied by many large cities with administrative problems. The Metropolitan Council is composed of a chairman and 32 councillors (12 from the city of Toronto and 20 from the five boroughs). The numerical basis of the council reflects the principle of representation by population. The chairman is chosen by the council and need not be a councillor of a municipality. Each borough has a mayor and council elected by its residents, and the 32 members of the Metropolitan Council gain their seats by virtue of being elected to local municipal councils. Elections are held every second year.

The metropolitan government is financed by pooling the credit and tax resources of its six member municipalities. All debentures for the metropolitan area are issued by the Metropolitan Corporation for its own capital purposes and on behalf of the six municipalities, the Metropolitan School Board, and the Toronto Transit Commission. The assessment of property for taxation is handled by the government of Ontario. However, each local municipality sets a mill rate to meet its local tax requirements as well as its share of metropolitan tax needs and the needs of the Metropolitan school board. Local boards of education set their own mill rate.

The establishment of the metropolitan form of government has facilitated plans for the orderly development of the area. The pooling of credit resources has made possible the construction of public highways, sewers, and other projects that individual municipalities would have found difficult to finance. The police forces were amalgamated in 1957. Other services, such as libraries, planning boards, emergency service units, public housing and welfare, water supply, parks, public transit, and traffic control, are under metropolitan administration. Fire protection is handled by the several municipalities. Pollution control, a provincial responsibility, is receiving increasing attention.

History. In 1615 the French explorer Étienne Brulé visited the site of Toronto. The French established a trading post here in 1720 and built Fort Rouillé, commonly called Fort

NATIONAL FILM BOARD OF CANADA

The Canadian National Exhibition, held annually on a site by Lake Ontario, draws displays from many nations.

Toronto, in 1750. The fort was destroyed in 1759 to prevent its use by the British.

In 1793, Lt. Gov. John Graves Simcoe selected the site, which he named York, as the capital of the new colony of Upper Canada. The creation of the town of York was primarily a political act, and the needs of government were given paramount consideration. Military roads were built, a fort was established, government buildings were constructed, and generous land grants were made to government administrators. The town grew up slowly around the political and military community. The looting and burning of York following its capture by Americans in 1813 was the excuse for the British attack on Washington in 1814.

When York was incorporated as a city in 1834 under its original name of Toronto, it had a population of 9,000. Three years later William Lyon Mackenzie, Toronto's first mayor, attempted to seize the city during his abortive rebellion against the colonial government. Toronto ceased to be the capital when Upper and Lower Canada were united as the province of Canada in 1841, but it again became the capital in 1849. The two colonies were separated at the time of Confederation in 1867, and Toronto became the seat of government for the new province of Ontario.

The coming of the railway era in the 1850's made Toronto the hub of the province's railway system and stimulated the city's industrialization and commercial growth. Factories and residential areas began to develop in what is now Metropolitan Toronto but which, in the early years of the 20th century, consisted of an unrelated group of 13 communities, including the city of Toronto, 4 adjoining towns, 3 villages, and 5 townships.

Many proposals were offered to solve the crisis in local government faced by the municipalities. In 1953 the Ontario Municipal Board recommended the establishment of a federated metropolitan government to oversee matters of common concern to all 13 municipalities. Metropolitan Toronto was formed in 1954, and in 1967 the municipalities were reduced in number to six, including the city proper and the five boroughs.

In the postwar years a tide of immigrants from Europe, Britain, and the United States arrived in Toronto, and the population rose from 900,000 in 1941 to about 2,000,000 in 1970, of whom one third were born outside Canada. The infusion of new blood has dimmed the white, Anglo-Saxon, Protestant image of "Toronto the Good" but has imparted to its business, outlook, and culture a new and cosmopolitan air. Population: 712,786.

WILLIAM A. MCKAY
University of Toronto

Further Reading: Arthur, Eric, *Toronto, No Mean City* (Toronto 1965); Campeau, Dubarry, *Toronto in Color* (Toronto 1968); Firth, Edith G., *The Town of York, 1815–1834* (Toronto 1966).

TORONTO, University of, a publicly supported university in Toronto, Canada. The first unit of the university was King's College, founded by royal charter in 1827 and closely linked with the Church of England. The college was secularized and became the University of Toronto in 1850. A law of 1853 created University College as the provincial arts and science college of the university. A law of 1887 made possible the federation of three arts colleges—Victoria University (founded by the United Church of Canada), University of Trinity College (Anglican), and St. Michael's College (Roman Catholic)—and three theological colleges—Knox (Presbyterian), Wycliffe (Anglican), and Emmanuel (United Church of Canada). By 1970 four additional constituent colleges—New, Innis, Scarborough, and Erindale—were giving undergraduate instruction in arts and science.

The university has 39 major teaching divisions. Total undergraduate enrollment for the university exceeded 18,000 men and women by 1970. The school of graduate studies has four divisions: humanities, social sciences, physical sciences, and life science. Enrollment is over 6,000.

The university has one of the largest university presses in North America. The library, with more than 3 million volumes, is the largest in Canada.

ETHELYN HARLOW, *University of Toronto*

TORPEDO, any of a genus of rays known for its ability to deliver a strong electric shock. A typical torpedo is *Torpedo nobiliana,* probably the largest electric ray, reaching a length of almost 6 feet (1.8 meters) and a weight of nearly 200 pounds (91 kg). It is found on both sides of the Atlantic from the Carolinas to Nova Scotia and from the Mediterranean to Scotland, usually at depths of 40 fathoms (240 feet) or more. Another species, the smaller *Torpedo californica,* is found along the California coast. The torpedo body is flat and broad and ends in a slender tail. Torpedo eggs hatch in the mother's body and live young are born.

As in all electric rays, the torpedos have an electric organ in each pectoral fin or wing. Each organ is made up of columns of platelike cells modified from muscle tissue. In *Torpedo nobiliana* each organ has more than a thousand columns. The torpedo ray emits pulsed discharges in trains of 10 to 100—all delivered in less than one second to produce a single shock. More than 200 volts have been recorded from torpedos, but such high voltages come only from large torpedos in a healthy and rested condition. After discharging a series of trains, which become progressively weaker, the ray requires a long rest period to regain its full electric powers.

Torpedos produce shock trains at will, either to defend themselves or to immobilize prey. Since torpedos are sluggish and slow swimmers, it was surmised that large torpedos used electric shocks to obtain food because examinations of their stomachs showed the remains of some fast-swimming fishes. This was later confirmed by experiments.

It is theoretically possible for a torpedo shock to be lethal to a diver if he were to grasp a large and fully rested torpedo with both hands simultaneously, but it is extremely unlikely. Torpedos caught in trawl nets usually have exhausted the power of their electric organs by the time they are dumped on deck.

Torpedo rays are classified in the genus *Torpedo.* Along with other electric rays, they are classified in the family Torpedinidae of the order Raiiformes.

STEWART SPRINGER
U.S. Fish and Wildlife Service

The lesser electric ray (*Narcine brasiliensis*) is a member of the torpedo family.

MARINELAND OF FLORIDA

TORPEDO, tôr-pē′dō, a self-propelled weapon designed to detonate an explosive charge under water against the hull of a vessel. Internal mechanical devices provide motive power and control direction and depth. Torpedoes are launched by being dropped from an airplane or ejected from a tube—under water from a submarine or on deck from a surface vessel.

Steam and Electric Torpedoes. Modern torpedoes are of two general types. Steam-propelled models have speeds of 27 to 45 knots and ranges of 4,000 to 25,000 yards (4,367–27,350 meters). The electric-powered models are similar but do not leave the telltale wake created by the exhaust of a steam torpedo.

The steam torpedo consists of four major sections: warhead, air flask, afterbody, and tail. The warhead is a bullet-shaped container filled with a high explosive, normally 400 to 800 pounds (181–363 kg) of TNT. For practice an exercise head is used, filled with water that is forced out by compressed air at the end of the run, allowing the torpedo to rise to the surface and be recovered. This is necessary because of its high cost (at least $20,000).

Propulsion. The steam propulsion system consists of a combustion flask or boiler and a turbine. Alcohol and water are forced into the combustion flask by compressed air in a mixture which, when ignited, forms steam. The steam is directed against the blades of the turbine, which is geared to two shafts carrying propellers that rotate in opposite directions to avert torque. An electric torpedo is propelled by storage batteries and a motor. A small air flask provides power to operate depth and steering mechanisms.

Direction and Depth. The torpedo's direction is controlled by its gyroscope, which is spun electrically. When the horizontal axis of the torpedo is parallel to that of the gyro the weapon will run straight. Should it tend to deviate from its course, the gyroscope, through a series of linkages, operates the vertical rudder to bring the torpedo back to its proper heading. The torpedo can be set for a direction other than that of the launching tube by offsetting the axis of the gyro at the necessary angle. The two axes then come back into parallel early in the torpedo's run.

A torpedo director is necessary to determine the course a torpedo must take to collide with the target. The course and speed of the target, the course of the firing ship, and the torpedo's own speed determine the angle at which the surface tube is set or which is set on the gyro of a torpedo in a fixed tube. To compensate for error in torpedo angle, salvos are fired in spreads to cover the length of the target.

Proper depth to strike the target is maintained by a pendulum-diaphragm combination. The diaphragm is actuated by sea pressure opposed to the counterpressure of a spring equivalent to that of the desired depth. The diaphragm causes the pendulum to tilt, actuating the depth engine that moves the horizontal rudders. Speed is regulated by the rate of fuel and water injected or, in an electric torpedo, by the revolutions per minute of the motor.

Warhead. An exploder mechanism in the warhead ignites the main charge of TNT, which must be set off by a sharp explosion of an unstable substance such as fulminate of mercury. The exploder is armed by a propeller-actuated impeller in the nose, which rotates as the torpedo

TORPEDO of a type employed by destroyers is fired from a barge in U. S. Navy test. An aerial torpedo awaits firing.

OFFICIAL U. S. NAVY PHOTO

runs through the water, moving the detonator into a hole in the warhead. The detonator sets off a booster charge, which in turn explodes the TNT.

Rocket-Propelled Torpedoes. The torpedo remains the major weapon used by submarines against surface ships, but it is also used increasingly against the submarine itself. The modern version in the U. S. Navy is Asroc, a missile-torpedo that became operational in the fleet in 1961. Launched into the air by a surface ship and having a range of 5 miles (9 km), it reenters the water near the target and becomes a homing torpedo. Its sister Subroc, which became operational in 1966, is actually a depth charge capable of being fitted with a nuclear warhead. It is fired from a conventional submarine torpedo tube, rises from the water into the air, returns to the water within a range of 30 miles (56 km) and explodes near the target.

Development. The U. S. Navy in 1970 ordered the Mark 48, usable against ships or submarines. Guided by a wire unreeled from the submarine, it homes in on an enemy vessel acoustically and pursues "intelligently" over 25 miles (40 km).

History. During the Napoleonic Wars the inventor Robert Fulton first demonstrated a method of destroying ships by detonating explosives under water near the hull. There remained the problem of positioning the explosive. Continued efforts resulted in the evolution of two major naval weapons, the mine and the torpedo. The earlier mine, once called the torpedo, is anchored and awaits the moving ship. It is therefore primarily a defensive weapon, for protecting harbors. About 1875, Robert Whitehead, a British engineer, invented an offensive weapon, the automobile torpedo, with steam propulsion, gyroscope direction, and depth setting.

The next problem was the creation of a suitable craft for launching. First came the small torpedo boat, then the destroyer, larger and faster, first designed to repel torpedo boats but then adopted as a launcher itself. It was not, however, until World War I that the torpedo found widespread use. Its launching instrument was the submarine, and it was used against shipping. Total losses of British merchant ships in that war were over 1.5 million tons, while only 60 combat ships were destroyed by torpedoes. The torpedo menace, however, strongly influenced the tactics of Adm. John R. Jellicoe, at Jutland. German ships suffered heavily in that battle from torpedoes fired by British destroyers, while the Germans scored only 2 hits out of 70 fired.

OFFICIAL U. S. NAVY PHOTO

ACOUSTIC-HOMING torpedo, guided by sound, is on course to target. It can track and sink submarines.

British and German coastal motor torpedo boats operated in the English Channel during World War I. The famous PT (patrol torpedo) boat had wide employment in World War II, but experience demonstrated that high-speed motor craft make better gunboats than torpedo boats.

Adm. Bradley Fiske of the U. S. Navy anticipated the torpedo plane as early as 1910. In World War I, aircraft were fitted to drop torpedoes, and ships were converted to carry the planes. One of these ships, the *Engadine*, participated in the Battle of Jutland. H. M. S. *Argus*, commissioned in October 1918, was the first aircraft carrier with torpedo planes that could fly off her deck.

The torpedo plane came into its own as a decisive weapon only in World War II. In November 1940, British torpedo aircraft attacked the Italian fleet at Taranto and put half of its major units out of action for six months. Aircraft carriers on both sides were sunk by torpedoes at the battles of the Coral Sea and Midway. Torpedoes also finally sank the almost impregnable German battleship *Bismarck*.

The campaign of submarine-launched torpedoes against merchant shipping was repeated in World War II by Germany against Britain and by the United States against Japan. Torpedoes almost defeated the British and were a major factor in Japan's defeat. See also SUBMARINE.

JOHN D. HAYES
Rear Admiral, U. S. Navy (Ret.)

TORQUAY, tôr-kē′, is a popular resort in southwest England overlooking Tor Bay in south Devon. It is about 30 miles (48 km) east of Plymouth. The town is built on the south side of a hilly promontory extending into Tor Bay. Its sheltered position and equable climate permit subtropical plants to flourish. The harbor of Torquay is a haven for sailboats and power boats cruising the English Channel.

The remains of Torre Abbey, built during the 12th to 14th centuries, are connected with a more modern building that contains an art gallery. Nearby is a cave, known as Kent's Cavern, which has yielded important archaeological remains. Population: (1961) 54,046.

GORDON STOKES
Author of "English Place-Names"

TORQUE, tôrk, is a measure of the ability of a force to set a body into rotation. It may be either uniform or fluctuating in nature. Torque, also known as the moment of force or turning moment, is commonly measured in units of pound-inches or gram-centimeters, and is equal to the product of the force and the perpendicular distance from the axis of rotation to the point at which the force is applied. It is a vector quantity, which means that it has magnitude, direction, and sense.

Torque is also a measure of a torsional loading on a machine member. This type of torque is a measure of the twist put into the machine member by the various forces acting on it.

Torque is associated with both fixed and rotating bodies. A bolt that has been tightened to prevent any twisting action is an example of the former. An axle turning the wheels of a car is an example of the latter.

In both cases the sum of the applied and reaction torques must equal zero if rotational equilibrium is to exist.

DONALD N. ZWIEP
Worcester Polytechnic Institute

TORQUE CONVERTER, a device used for power transmission in automobiles and similar vehicles to change the torque-speed ratio or mechanical advantage between an input shaft and an output shaft. The term "torque converter" is usually restricted to hydraulic devices, although some mechanical systems—especially gear trains—are widely used as torque converters.

In the hydraulic torque converter, three essential elements are needed: an impeller or pump, a runner or turbine, and a reaction member or stator. Normally, an oil is the working fluid. It is circulated outward from the impeller; inward through the runner; and then through the stator back to the impeller. As the impeller sends the fluid through the runner, the runner is forced to rotate in the same direction as the impeller (while reversing the direction of the fluid), even though there is no mechanical connection between the two. Up to this point, the torque converter resembles a fluid coupling, which consists of an impeller and runner. There is no increase of torque in a fluid coupling, and its output speed varies from its input speed only by the amount of slippage. But in the torque converter there is a stator. When the oil leaves the runner, it enters the stationary stator, whose blades again reverse the direction of its flow so that it aids the rotation of the impeller blades. This change in momentum of the fluid in the impeller results in more torque, with decreasing speed in the runner.

SINGLE-STAGE TORQUE CONVERTER

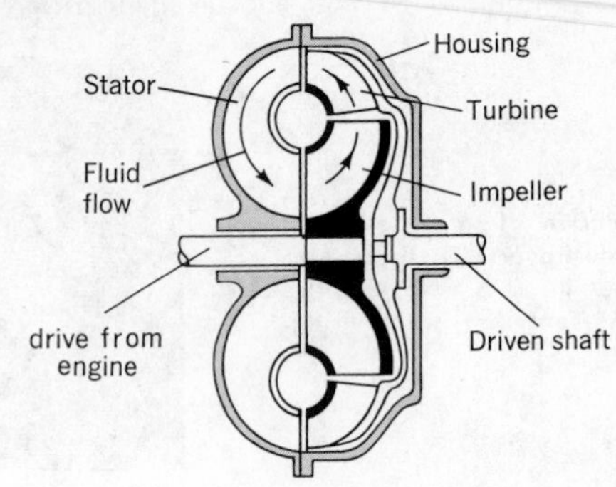

The greatest multiplication of torque takes place when the turbine starts at zero speed. However, a torque converter with the highest operating efficiency does not necessarily have the highest starting efficiency. To get the maximum torque under both starting and operating conditions, it is necessary to modify the design or the system in which the torque converter operates.

Typical modifications to improve overall operating efficiency include adding an impeller, a runner, or a stator with different blade angles. The additional element then operates more or less independently, depending on the conditions and results desired. A second kind of modification involves mounting the stator as a one-way or overrunning clutch. At operating speed the stator in the torque converter free wheels, and the unit then functions as a fluid coupling with a consequent low power loss.

Other modifications involve variable-pitch control of the blades, coupling two or more torque

THREE-STAGE TORQUE CONVERTER

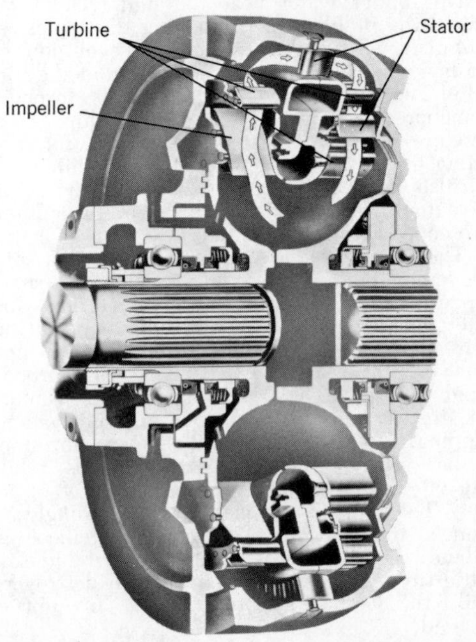

converters in a series, and driving a set of gears, such as a planetary-reduction unit, from the output side of the torque converter. An infinite number of combinations of torque converters, along with gears and clutches and prime movers, is possible. Thus units such as automatic transmissions for automobiles can be designed to be highly flexible with respect both to output speed and torque.

A typical operating torque ratio for a hydraulic torque converter is about 5 or 6 to 1, although higher ratios are not uncommon. The torque transmitted is $T = KN^2D^5$, where D is the outer diameter of the blades in inches, N the impeller speed in rpm, K a design coefficient, and T is in inch-pounds. Efficiency ranges from 65% to 90% at one-quarter to a full load, with some power loss as a result of the operating fluid heating up. In small units, where natural heat dissipation is adequate, this presents no problem. In larger units, however, it is often necessary to provide some sort of cooling apparatus.

DONALD N. ZWIEP
Worcester Polytechnic Institute

Further Reading: Burstall, Aubrey F., *A History of Mechanical Engineering* (Cambridge, Mass., 1965).

TORQUEMADA, tôr-kə-mä′də, **Tomás de** (1420–1498), Spanish inquisitor, who bequeathed to his country and to posterity a tragic legacy of religious fanaticism and cruelty. He was born in Valladolid of noble Castilian parents. At an early age he entered the Dominican convent there, where he earned an enviable reputation for piety and proficiency in theology. Despite his protests, in 1452 he was appointed prior of a Dominican convent in Segovia, a position he filled with distinction for 22 years.

In 1474 he became confessor and counselor of state to Queen Isabella of Castile and her husband, King Ferdinand II of Aragón. Though Torquemada had Jewish blood, he was known for his hostility towards Jews and for his deep suspicion of the New Christians, or *conversos*, many of whom practiced Christianity in public but in private clung to the Jewish faith of their ancestors. These attitudes, as well as his pious rectitude, recommended him to his sovereigns, who regarded religious uniformity as the necessary condition for the unification of Spain under a single royal government.

Inquisitor General. In 1483, when Ferdinand and Isabella obtained papal consent for the unification of the inquisitions of Castile and Aragón, Torquemada was named grand inquisitor general of Spain. As president of the Consejo de la Suprema y General Inquisición, Torquemada gave the Spanish Inquisition its abiding organization and procedure in a series of *Instrucciones* in 1484, 1485, 1488, and 1498. During his term of office, tens of thousands were haled before its courts and at least 2,000 perished at the stake. Exceptionally intolerant, even by the standards of his times, his conduct aroused much protest, but all attempts, even by the papacy, to curb his power proved fruitless. Although ill health forced his retirement in 1494 to the monastery of Santo Tomás, which he had constructed in Ávila, Torquemada remained the inflexible and incorruptible master of the Inquisition until he died at the monastery on Sept. 16, 1498. See also INQUISITION.

J. G. ROWE
University of Western Ontario

TORRANCE, tôr′əns, is a city in southern California, in Los Angeles county, 17 miles (27 km) south of the center of the city of Los Angeles. Torrance is the commercial and financial center of the Southern Bay region of the county. Its principal industries are oil wells, petroleum refining, and the manufacture of steel, electronics, and aircraft.

El Camino Junior College and California State College at Dominguez Hills are in Torrance.

Jared S. Torrance, a Pasadena utilities magnate, employed the landscape architect Frederick Law Olmsted to study the world's best city plans and to plan Torrance as an industrial and residential city. His plan was adopted.

Torrance was founded in 1912 and incorporated as a city in 1921. Government is by city manager and council. Population: 134,584.

RUSSELL J. WEST
Librarian, City of Torrance

TORRENS, Lake, tor′ənz, a large, shallow salt lake in South Australia. It is situated north of Spencer Gulf and forms part of the Torrens rift valley. Covering an area of 2,230 square miles (5,780 sq km), the lake extends about 130 miles (200 km) north-south and is about 30 miles (50 km) wide.

Lake Torrens is frequently nothing more than a salt marsh. It lies in an area that receives less than 8 inches (200 mm) of rain a year. Lake Torrens has no permanent feeder streams or outlet.

TORRENS SYSTEM, tor′ənz, a system of registering title to land that was devised to provide an incontestable title and to avoid repetitive, costly, and time-consuming searches. Originated by Sir Robert Torrens in Australia in 1858 as an alternative to the recording system, it was subsequently adopted in parts of the British Commonwealth and by the 1970's was used in about 20 states of the United States.

In the Torrens system, a property owner files a petition for initial registration of title. Notice, by registered mail and newspaper publication, is then given to all persons known to have an interest in the property. On the basis of a hearing at which a petitioner offers proof of ownership and adverse parties present their claims, a court renders a final judgment by which title to the property is vested in the petitioner if his claim is judged valid. A certificate of registration is then issued and filed in the registrar's office. Thereafter, title to the property is conveyed by a deed and a transfer of the certificate of registration without any additional title search.

Sometimes third parties who had not received notice of the registration proceedings but whose interests in the property were terminated thereby are compensated from an assurance fund derived from fees charged for registration and transfers of title. However, the proceeds of the fund may be insufficient for this purpose. Furthermore, unlike title insurance, the assurance fund does not protect the owner from expenses of defense or losses arising from adverse claims. The combination of this inherent weakness of the system and the opposition of the title insurance industry has resulted in only limited acceptance of the Torrens System in the United States. See also TITLE.

JEROME G. ROSE, *Rutgers University*
Author, "The Legal Adviser on Home Ownership"

TORREÓN, tôr-ē-ōn′, a city in Mexico, in Coahuila state, is an industrial and trade center in the fertile Laguna district. A dry, irrigated oasis on the high plateau of northeastern Mexico, it is a prosperous, fast-growing community and an important railroad junction.

Early in the 20th century, Torreón was a small village where the processing of cotton, candelilla (a wax-producing plant), and guayule (a rubber-producing plant) was the main activity. With the damming of the Nazas River, extensive new areas of cotton cultivation were opened up, and the region became Mexico's first major cotton-producing area. Grape production in neighboring settlements fostered the establishment of viticultural industries. Most of the city's workers are involved in cotton-related industries. There are flour mills, chemical plants, and smelters processing copper, silver, and lead.

Torreón is the seat of the medical school of the University of Coahuila. La Alianza is an important regional market center in the city.

In the 1930's some large ranch holdings were divided into *ejidos,* or communal land properties. Successful as the *ejidos* have been, some families have been relocated in other parts of Mexico because of crowding, increased water salinity, and periods of drought. Population: (1960) 179,901.

REYNALDO AYALA, *San Diego State College*

TORRES BODET, tôr′rās bô-det′, **Jaime** (1902–), Mexican author and government official. He was born in Mexico City on April 17, 1902. He studied at the National University, where he also did postgraduate work in law and was professor of French literature from 1924 to 1928. He then joined the diplomatic service. Torres Bodet was director general of UNESCO (1948–1952) and twice Mexican minister of education (1943–1946, 1958–1964).

Torres Bodet's first book, *Fervor* (1918), is a collection of poems that reflect his admiration for French symbolism and Hispanic modernism. *Poesías* (1926), a collection of the best of his next seven volumes, are less derivative. His prose works include *Margarita de Niebla* (1927; *Margaret of the Mist*), a novel containing elements of fantasy; *Nacimiento de Venus y otros relatos* (1941; *The Birth of Venus and Other Stories*); *Tiempo de arena* (1955; *Sand Time*), a memoir; and *Balzac* (1960). *Obra Poética* (1967) contains his later poetry.

TORRES STRAIT, tôr′əs, is a channel separating Australia and New Guinea and connecting the Arafura Sea on the west with the Coral Sea on the east. The strait is about 95 miles (150 km) wide. Navigation is hazardous because of the shoals and reefs in its waters. Torres Strait was named after the Spanish navigator Luis Vaez de Torres, who discovered it in 1606.

The main islands of the Torres Strait group are peaks of a submerged volcanic range. They include Thursday Island, Prince of Wales Island, and Possession Island, where Capt. James Cook proclaimed British sovereignty over the eastern coast of the Australian continent in 1770. For administrative purposes the islands are included within the Australian state of Queensland. The administrative center is Port Kennedy on Thursday Island. Many of the Torres Strait islanders are members of a distinct ethnic group, with characteristics of the Papuans and Melanesians.

TORREY, tôr′ē, **Charles Turner** (1813–1846), American abolitionist. Born in Scituate, Mass., on Nov. 21, 1813, Torrey was raised by maternal grandparents. He graduated from Phillips Academy and Yale. After pursuing Congregationalist studies, he served various New England churches, but an unstable temperament and a growing antislavery commitment made him ill-suited for parish work. Work on two antislavery papers proved equally uncongenial. In 1842, Torrey was arrested while covering a "Convention of Slaveholders" in Annapolis. Though acquitted, he was again tried in 1844 for helping slaves escape. He died of tuberculosis in the Maryland Penitentiary on May 9, 1846, a martyr, friends claimed, to the cause.

BERTRAM WYATT-BROWN
Case Western Reserve University

TORREY, tôr′ē, **John** (1796–1873), American botanist and teacher, one of the original members of the National Academy of Sciences.

Torrey was born in New York City on Aug. 15, 1796. He was introduced to the study of botany by Amos Eaton. After graduating from the New York College of Physicians and Surgeons in 1818, Torrey spent his leisure time for the next six years in scientific pursuits, particularly botany. He abandoned medicine to teach both chemistry and botany at the College of Physicians and Surgeons and at Princeton. He was a trustee of Columbia College, to which he gave his herbarium and botanical library in 1860.

Torrey was a prolific writer. One of his earliest works was a *Catalogue of Plants Growing Spontaneously Within Thirty Miles of the City of New York.* In 1843 he published an elaborate study of the flora of New York state. He died in New York City on March 10, 1873.

TORRICELLI, tôr-ə-chel′ē, **Evangelista** (1608–1647), Italian scientist and mathematician, best known for the barometric experiments that bear his name. He was born in Faenza, Italy, on Oct. 15, 1608. He studied in Rome about 1630 with Benedetto Castelli, a mathematician trained by Galileo and the founder of hydraulic science. Torricelli wrote to Galileo in 1632, and in 1641 was invited by him, at Castelli's suggestion, to complete certain of his works. Galileo died shortly after Torricelli's arrival at Florence, whereupon the Grand Duke of Tuscany appointed him to Galileo's place as court mathematician.

In 1644, Torricelli published a book on geometry and on motion. It broke important ground in mathematics and provided a firm basis for Galileo's earlier work on mechanics by establishing the principle that connected bodies can move spontaneously only if their common center of gravity moves downward. About the same time he demonstrated the weight of air by experiments with mercury-filled tubes, and correctly distinguished weight and pressure. The priority of his work in geometry and experimental mechanics, though contested by his French contemporaries, is no longer questioned.

Torricelli devoted much time to improving the telescope and microscope. His unpublished works on mathematics included much that later appeared in the calculus, but has only recently been appreciated. He died in Florence on Oct. 25, 1647. His *Academic Lectures* were published posthumously in 1715.

STILLMAN DRAKE, *University of Toronto*

TORRID ZONE is an old geographical term for the equatorial regions lying between the tropics of Cancer and Capricorn. More meaningful temperature zones are now defined on maps by isotherms or by climatic types. See CLIMATE.

TORRIGIANO, tôr-rē-jä′nō, **Pietro** (c. 1470–c. 1528), Italian sculptor, who was the first important Italian artist to work in Renaissance England. He was born in Florence and studied sculpture there, but as a result of a brawl, in which he broke the nose of his fellow artist Michelangelo, he was forced to leave the city. He later went to England, where he executed tombs for King Henry VII and his family. These tombs, in Westminster Abbey, are probably Torrigiano's best work.

In 1526, Torrigiano was in Seville, where he made a terra-cotta bust of Isabella of Portugal. His nude study of St. Jerome and his Virgin and Child are in the Seville Museum. He was given a commission to execute a statue of the Virgin, but on receiving what he considered an inadequate price for it, he smashed it in anger and was imprisoned by the Inquisition on a charge of heresy. He died in prison.

TORRINGTON is a city in northwestern Connecticut, in Litchfield county, on the Naugatuck River, 30 miles (48 km) west of Hartford. It makes needles, sporting equipment, woolens, machinery, and kitchen utensils.

The Torrington branch of the University of Connecticut is in the city. The Torrington Historical Society has a museum with exhibits of local history. John Brown, the abolitionist, was born in Torrington.

In 1732, residents of Windsor, Conn., were granted acreage in the "western lands" by the general court, which ruled that the tract should "ever hereafter be called Torrington," after Torrington, Devonshire, England. The first settlers arrived in 1737, and the town was incorporated in 1740. In 1813 the central area was named Wolcottville, but in 1881 its official name became Torrington.

The city was incorporated in 1923. Government is by mayor and council. Population: 31,952.

CATHERINE C. CALHOUN
Torrington Historical Society

TORSION BALANCE. See BALANCE.

TORSION BAR SUSPENSION. See AUTOMOBILE—*Modern Automobiles.*

TORT, tôrt. Tort law recognizes rights to money damages for injuries caused by civil, or private, wrongs such as traffic accidents, dangerous structures, bursting dams, deleterious food, swindling, or libel. Both parties to tort litigation usually are private persons or business corporations. Assault and battery, false imprisonment, malicious prosecution, negligence, extrahazardous activity, nuisance, and misrepresentation all can result in tort liability. Sometimes misconduct is both a tort and a crime and gives rise to two proceedings, a civil suit and a prosecution.

Background. In the 12th century the distinction between criminal prosecutions and private suits was hazy. Since the 14th century the two have been independently administered. In early common law, torts were likely to be "trespasses with force and arms," such as illegal entry, intentional bodily injuries, or the taking of hostages and chattels. Later a form of action, given the name of "trespass on the case," was recognized. This new form of action was developed to redress negligent injuries, nuisances, frauds, defamations, and malicious prosecutions.

Some Modern Developments. In 1866, Britain's highest court, the House of Lords, redressed damages done by water that flowed out of an artificial lake into nearby coal mines. The opinions were couched in terms of redressing (within certain limits) damages that resulted from bringing onto land substances likely to do damage if they escaped. A modern doctrine states that those engaged in extrahazardous activities are responsible for resulting harm, even though their conduct is careful. This doctrine has had limited but important acceptance, and in some states it has led to the expansion of tort liability for dangerous activities such as blasting and urban storage of inflammable liquids. Courts also have expanded tort liability by eroding special immunities enjoyed by land occupants, local governments, charities, and others. Manufacturers of dangerously defective products who distributed their wares through independent retailers were usually insulated from liability. A 1916 case in New York, however, broke through that limitation and started a contrary trend. In 1962 a New Jersey court held a manufacturer responsible for his defectively made products, regardless of whether he had used due care. These two cases are widely followed.

Legislative Influence. Few torts are statutory. Criminal legislation, however, affects civil responsibility. Proof of violation of a criminal statute often settles an issue of negligence arising in a civil trial. Legislative dissatisfaction with court-made tort law has led to some statutory reforms. Because the courts harshly curtailed liability for work injuries, every state legislature has enacted a workmen's compensation statute.

Since 1930 some writers have urged legislative reform of automobile accident law. Though most states of the United States have statutes intended to ensure motorists' ability to pay for their torts, no legislature has made extensive reforms in substantive automobile accident law. By the 1970's half a dozen statutes had blunted the contributory negligence defense, and two states had set up funds that afford relief to victims of hit-and-run or financially irresponsible drivers. See also DAMAGES.

CLARENCE MORRIS, *University of Pennsylvania Law School, Author of "Morris on Torts"*

TORTILLA, tôr-tē′yə, a name applied to two different foods. In Mexican cooking, a tortilla is a thin pancake made of crushed corn. In Spanish cooking it is a thick hearty omelet containing minced vegetables and sometimes meat.

The Mexican tortilla is sometimes eaten plain, but often it is used to make tacos, enchiladas, and tostadas, or fritos. A taco is a folded tortilla that is filled with chopped beef, chicken, or cheese and then fried. An enchilada is a rolled tortilla filled with similar stuffing and served with a spicy sauce. A tostada is a flat tortilla that is deep fried until it is crisp. It is usually served with a topping of beans, cheese, lettuce, meat, and chopped onions.

BETTY WASON
Author of "The Art of Spanish Cooking"

CY LA TOUR

Galápagos tortoise

JOHN MARKHAM

Forest hinge-back tortoise (*above*) of tropical Africa. (*Below*) Hermann's tortoise, found in southern Europe.

JOHN GERARD, FROM NATIONAL AUDUBON SOCIETY

TORTOISE, tôrt′əs, any of a group of turtles characterized by column-shaped forelimbs with webless toes tightly bound together. Tortoises are terrestrial and are frequently found in dry country.

In the British Isles the term "tortoise" denotes a much larger group. There, all shelled reptiles, except sea turtles, are called "tortoises" or "terrapins." In the United States, however, the term "tortoise" is limited to some 40 species classified in seven genera and making up the family Testudinidae.

Some tortoises are large, attaining weights of 400 and 500 pounds (180-230 kg) or more. Tortoises are adapted for living on land by their club-shaped feet and webless toes. The shell is usually high-domed, and the head can be completely drawn in. They are long-lived, herbivorous, and slow-moving. In the popular imagination, tortoises are symbols of slow movement and longevity; some live to be more than 100 years old.

Fossil records, dating from Eocene times, some 50 million years ago, suggest that tortoises were once abundant even where they are now only feebly represented, especially in North America. This is borne out by their present wide, but sparse, distribution.

Giant Tortoises. Giant tortoises were once common, but today they are found in only two regions—in the Galápagos Islands, 500 to 600 miles (800–960 km) west of Ecuador, and in some islands of the western Indian Ocean. The tortoise populations in these two regions were once great, but they have been decimated by man so that some forms have vanished and others are nearly extinct. The Galápagos tortoise (*Testudo elephantopus*) is usually considered to have 10 subspecies—one on each island. Although there were once several species on the Indian Ocean islands, only *T. gigantea* survives.

African and Madagascan Tortoises. Africa, Madagascar, and a few nearby islands have the greatest variety of tortoises. Three species belonging to two genera (*Testudo* and *Pyxis*) occur in Madagascar, and 18 species, classified in four genera (*Geniochersus, Homopus, Malacochersus,* and *Kinixys*), are distributed throughout Africa. Three species of *Kinixys* tortoises are the only turtles having a hinge in the carapace, or upper shell, which allows them to raise the carapace. The shell of the pancake tortoise (*Malacochersus*) is so flexible that the plastron, or lower shell, moves when the tortoise breathes. This tortoise is somewhat flattened and, if pursued, can hide in a narrow crevice and inflate itself so that it cannot easily be extricated.

North American Tortoises. Three species of gopher tortoises (genus *Gopherus*) are found across much of the southern United States and into northern Mexico. They are interesting because of their burrowing habits. Their burrows are sometimes as long as 40 feet (12 meters) and as much as 10 feet (3 meters) below the surface. Gopher tortoises are popular as pets. See also Gopher Tortoise.

Other Tortoises. About 12 species (genus *Testudo*) occur from southern Europe eastward across southern Asia into Indonesia. Three other species (genus *Testudo*) extend over much of South America east of the Andes and on to Trinidad and the Windward Islands, with one species occurring as far north as Panama.

Clifford Pope
Author of "The Reptile World"

DR. ROSS HUTCHINS
Tortoise beetles

TORTOISE BEETLE, tôrt′əs, any of a group of leaf beetles with beautifully colored, oval, tortoise-shaped bodies. Their attractive hues are partly due to the movement of their internal fluids, which can be seen through the cuticle and which change color as the beetles move from one part of a plant to another. The adults and larvae feed on the foliage of sweet potato plants and other members of the morning glory family. The larvae have a tail-like fork at the end of the body. Cast-off skins and excrement are heaped onto the fork, which is then held over the body as a camouflaging umbrella.

Tortoise beetles belong to the subfamily Cassidinae of the family Chrysomelidae. A common North American species, the argus tortoise beetle (*Chelymorpha cassidae*), has a red or yellow upper surface with 4 or 6 black dots on the front of the thorax and six on each wing case. The underside is black. The stalked eggs of the argus tortoise beetle are laid in groups. The larvae, after hatching, feed alongside the adults. They pupate inside a bluish, waxy moldlike secretion formed on a leaf.

R. H. Arnett, Jr., *Purdue University*

TORTOISESHELL, tôrt′əs-shel, is the conventional name for the horny plates that form the outer layer of the top and bottom shells of the oceanic turtle. The rich, luminous, brown and yellow mottled material is used to make ornamental objects. The best tortoiseshell is that of *Chelo imbricata*, especially from Cuban waters. Less good is that of *Chelo mydas*, from the Mediterranean. The brittle outer layer is removed from the shell by heat and split into its component plates. Under heat the plates become soft and adhesive and can be pressed together side by side or in layers.

Since the 17th century stained horn has been a common substitute for expensive tortoiseshell. About 1900 stained celluloid was introduced. The most frequently used modern substitute is simulated plastic tortoiseshell, which has diminished demand for the natural material.

Tortoiseshell was greatly appreciated by the ancient Romans as a furniture veneer. Muslim workers made tortoiseshell caskets, combs, and knife handles in 11th century Cairo. Almost unknown in medieval Europe, tortoiseshell was later imported from the New World. It was recorded about 1570 that eating and drinking from tortoiseshell vessels was a way to avoid infectious disease.

From the 1620's tortoiseshell was a favorite decorative veneer on baroque furniture. The Parisian cabinetmaker André Charles Boulle made veneers from plaques of tortoiseshell cut by special saws and inlaid with brass, pewter, or copper, or alternatively from metal plaques inlaid with tortoiseshell. So-called Boulle furniture went out of style about 1730 but was much imitated in the 19th century.

From the second half of the 17th century, tortoiseshell has been made into small objects—clock cases, picture and mirror frames, *étuis* (needle cases), toilet sets, ornamental combs (especially for Spanish women), knife handles, and, above all, snuff boxes. In the French technique known as *piqué*, gold or silver designs are laid on tortoiseshell roughened by pricking holes

JANE LATTA
Tortoiseshell purse with mother-of-pearl inlay.

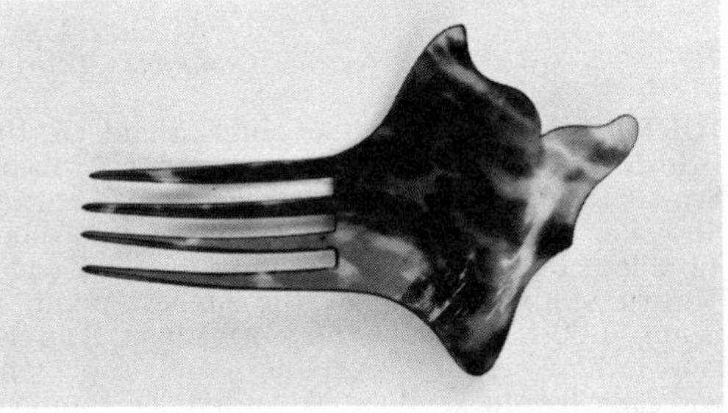
JANE LATTA
Decorative comb made of tortoiseshell.

in it. The emigration of French Protestant craftsmen at the end of the 17th century brought piqué to England and elsewhere. From about 1680, Naples has been a major center of piqué and other tortoiseshell work.

Tortoiseshell has become less and less popular. When snuff went out of favor in the early 19th century, tortoiseshell snuff boxes disappeared. In the 1920's the adoption of short hair by many women greatly reduced the number of high tortoiseshell combs.

R. W. Lightbown
Victoria and Albert Museum, London

TORTOISESHELL BUTTERFLY, any of a widespread group of butterflies named for their attractive tortoiseshell-like patterns of black, deep orangy brown, yellowish brown, and white. The adult butterflies are medium sized with a wingspan ranging from 1½ to 3 inches (37–75 mm). They belong to a larger group of butterflies known as the anglewings because the outer margin of each forewing is angular or notched.

JOHN WARHAM

Tortoiseshell butterfly

The larvae, or caterpillars, of tortoiseshell butterflies are of various colors and usually have bristly spines. They tend to feed in colonies, eating the leaves of a wide variety of trees and nonwoody plants, especially willows, poplars, cherries, and nettles.

Tortoiseshell butterflies belong to the genus *Nymphalis* of the family Nymphalidae. The Compton tortoiseshell (N. *j-album*) is a woodland species ranging from southern Canada to North Carolina. The American tortoiseshell (*N. milberti*) occurs over much the same range but is smaller in size.

DON DAVIS
Smithsonian Institution

TORTOLA, tôr-tō′lə, is the chief island of the British Virgin Islands in the eastern Caribbean Sea. It is less than 4 miles (6 km) northwest of St. John, one of the U. S. Virgin Islands. About 12 miles (19 km) long and 3 miles (5 km) wide, Tortola is hilly. Mt. Sage, the highest point, is nearly 1,800 feet (550 meters) high. The islanders grow fruit, vegetables, and sugarcane and raise livestock. Road Town, on the southern coast, is the main settlement and principal port of entry in the British Virgin Islands group. Tortola has been administered by Britain since 1666, when it was taken from its first European settlers, the Dutch. Population: (1965) 6,762.

TORTUGA ISLAND, tôr-tōō′gə, is an island off the northeastern coast of Hispaniola in the West Indies. Its official name is Île de la Tortue. Part of the Republic of Haiti, it is situated about 5 miles (8 km) north of the Haitian town of Port-de-Paix. It is more than 20 miles (32 km) long and up to 4 miles (6 km) wide and is moderately hilly. A village, occupying the highest ground, is the only population center, although 10,000 or more people live on the small farms that are scattered around the island.

Tortuga was a famous haunt of pirates after 1625. The French buccaneers who gathered there were largely responsible for launching the French conquest of Spanish eastern and northern Hispaniola in the mid-17th century. Later, English pirates used the island as a base for attacks on the shipping of France, Spain, and other countries.

TORTUGAS. See DRY TORTUGAS.

TORTURE is the deliberate infliction of physical pain or psychological anguish. It has been used for a variety of reasons. Perverted or psychotic individuals have tortured victims for the sadistic pleasure of witnessing agony. Societies have used torture to increase the horrors of capital punishment. Officials of government have also used torture as a means of making persons confess crimes or reveal secrets.

Torture and Capital Punishment. From ancient times war prisoners and convicted criminals have been put to death by torture. It was a custom of some American Indian tribes to torment and burn prisoners. The laws of ancient Rome sanctioned crucifixion, and European laws of medieval and early modern times provided for such punishments as burning or drawing and quartering. See CAPITAL PUNISHMENT.

Torture as Part of Criminal Investigation. Perhaps the greatest use of torture throughout history has been as a recognized part of the judicial process, not only as punishment but even more as a means of obtaining information. Greek law allowed authorities who were investigating a crime to torture slaves. Roman law provided that slaves and citizens could be questioned under torture. European countries that followed the Roman system of law allowed courts to order the torture of suspects. The Roman Catholic Church sanctioned the torture of suspected heretics at the orders of inquisitors.

French laws of the 17th century can be cited to illustrate the way European society used torture as part of the system of criminal justice. The criminal ordinance of 1670 permitted the courts to order "preparatory torture" (or "questioning") of an individual for whom there was a "grave" presumption of guilt. The purpose of torture was to secure a confession, which was considered the best possible proof of guilt. The process of questioning was subject to various conditions. Torture could be ordered "with the reservation of entire proof." This meant that, if the suspect maintained his innocence throughout the questioning, he could not be sentenced to death but must receive a lesser penalty. If he was questioned "without the reservation of entire proof" and did not confess, he was set free.

A person who had been convicted and condemned to death could be subjected to a second "questioning." The purpose at this stage was to get him to confess the crime for which he had been condemned or to get information about accomplices.

In England, where Anglo-Saxon rather than Roman law was the model for the legal code of the country, torture was not a regular part of the judicial procedure in the sense that it was in France. English common law recognized only one use of torture. If an accused person refused to plead either guilty or not guilty, he could be subjected to the *peine forte et dure*. The victim was forced to lie on the floor on his back, a board was placed on him, and weights were piled on the plank until he either agreed to make a plea or died. In the English colony of Massachusetts Bay, Giles Cory was subjected to this treatment in 1692 when he refused to plead to a charge of witchcraft.

Although torture was not systematized in England, it was often and openly employed as an extralegal means of extracting information. Under the Tudors and the first two Stuarts, for example, the Star Chamber tortured suspects. Guy

Fawkes and others accused of treason at the time of the Gunpowder Plot were tortured.

Some Methods and Devices. The most commonly used instrument of torture in France seems to have been the boot. In its early crude form, the boot consisted of a number of boards tightly bound around the foot. Wedges were driven between the boards and the foot, creating enough pressure to crush bones. Another variety of this device crushed both the knee and the foot. Still another "boot" was an iron frame that was heated over a fire.

In England the rack was often used. This stretched the body until the bones were pulled from their sockets. The "scavenger's daughter," on the other hand, compressed the body, causing ruptures, hemorrhages, and broken bones.

Other techniques employed in medieval and Renaissance Europe included thumbscrews and iron gauntlets. The water torture consisted in forcing quantities of water down a victim's throat. The strappado was a system of hoisting a suspect in a way that could dislocate his shoulders. His hands were tied behind his back, the rope was run over a pulley, he was lifted off the floor, and weights were hung on his feet. If "extraordinary" questioning was permitted, the rope was struck repeatedly, and the jarring normally resulted in dislocating his shoulder joints. Many of these methods of torture were used by the Inquisition, and particularly savage pain was inflicted in both Protestant and Catholic countries on those charged with witchcraft. It is a surprising fact that large numbers of those whose questioning is recorded did not confess to any crime.

Attempts to Abolish Torture. At various points in history prominent men spoke out against the use of torture in judicial proceedings—Seneca and Justinian in Rome, for example. The 17th century English constitutional lawyer Sir Edward Coke opposed torture, and his work contributed to the Bill of Rights of 1689, which banned cruel and unusual punishment. Voltaire, Montesquieu, and other leaders of the Enlightenment in France argued against judicial torture, as did the Italian criminologist Cesare Beccaria.

Many Western nations followed England and banned torture. The 8th Amendment to the U. S. Constitution forbids cruel and unusual punishments. France abandoned torture as a legal procedure in 1789 and Russia did so in 1801. A papal bull of 1816 forbade the use of torture in Roman Catholic countries. In the 19th century the rejection of torture was viewed as evidence of the progress of Western civilization.

The 20th Century. Modern legal codes do not countenance torture, but all sorts of cruel and coercive practices have continued in use. Police departments in some countries have used the "third degree"—prolonged questioning perhaps accompanied by threats and beating—as a means to force suspects to confess or to furnish evidence against others. To cite an extreme example, the German Nazis used both traditional tortures and scientific cruelties—such as "medical" experiments —in their concentration camps. Guerrilla fighters, and military men trying to suppress irregular forces, have tortured prisoners. Modern techniques include electric shock applied to the genitals. Sophisticated combinations of physical abuse and psychological stress have also been tried. See BRAINWASHING.

LEONARD D. SAVITZ
Temple University

TORUŃ, tôr-o͞on′, is a city in Poland on the right bank of the Vistula River, 118 miles (190 km) northwest of Warsaw. Toruń, at a key crossing of the Vistula, has played a prominent role in the history of Poland. The German form of its name is Thorn. It is in the *województwo* (province) of Bydgoszcz.

The town emerged as an important commercial and market center in the Middle Ages. For a time it was in the hands of the Teutonic Knights, who built a castle there in the 13th century, and it was a member of the Hanseatic League in the 14th century. Toruń became one of the most important commercial cities in Poland, gathering products of central Poland and sending them downriver to the seaport Danzig (now Gdańsk). In this prosperous period many fine Gothic churches and the Gothic town hall were built. Parts of the medieval city wall survive as well.

The city overthrew the Knights' rule in 1454 and passed into Polish possession. It remained Polish until it was annexed by Prussia in the Second Partition of Poland in 1793. It was restored to Poland in 1918.

Toruń's commercial importance declined in modern times as the grain trade declined. The city became a railroad center in the 19th century. Its manufacturing has been much expanded since World War II, and it is now a center of chemical and engineering industries. The Nicolaus Copernicus University, named after the great astronomer born in Toruń, was founded in 1945. Population: (1967 est.) 117,000.

NORMAN J. G. POUNDS
Indiana University

TORUS, tôr′əs, or *anchor ring*, a surface shaped like the inflated inner tube of a tire or like a doughnut. In mathematics a torus is formed in three-dimensional space by rotating a circle about a line that is in the same plane as the circle but does not cut or touch it. For instance, a torus can be formed by rotating the circle $x^2 + y^2 = 1$ about the line $x = 3$. In this case the radius, r, of the circle is 1, and the distance, k, from the center of the circle to the line is 3. This torus has a surface area equal to $4\pi^2(1)(3)$ and a volume equal to $2\pi^2(1)^2(3)$. In general, the surface area of a torus is equal to $4\pi^2rk$, and its volume is equal to $2\pi^2r^2k$.

The torus was mentioned by Archytas of Tarentum and other Greek mathematicians. In modern mathematics deformations of the torus are studied in topology. See also TOPOLOGY.

A TORUS, which resembles an inflated inner tube, is generated by rotating a circle about a distant axis.

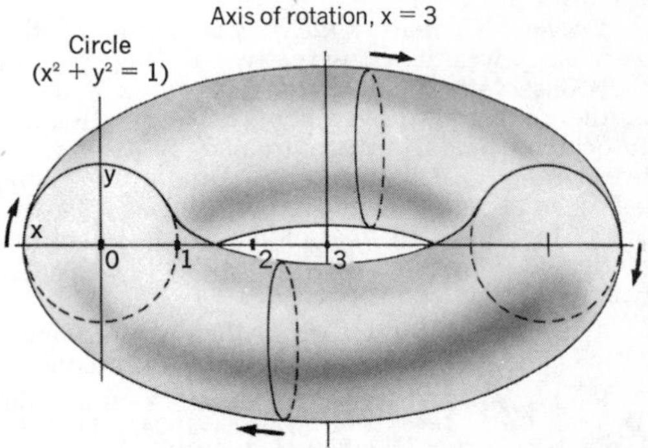

TORY is the former name for the British Conservative party. The name is still used unofficially to refer to Conservatives in Britain. In a political sense it originated in 1680 in the debates over the proposed exclusion of James, Duke of York, from the succession to the throne of England on the ground that he was a Roman Catholic. When the Exclusion Bill was introduced into Parliament, the opposition party, from their protestations of abhorrence, became known as Abhorrers. Soon they were lampooned by their opponents as Tories, and the name stuck.

The original Tories, however, were Irish highwaymen, also called *rapparees,* in the 16th and 17th centuries, and the application of the term to an English political party may have arisen from a belief that the Stuarts were willing to use Irish troops to support their throne. The Tories have always been on the political right, and if the word was first used as a term of abuse, it has long been accepted as an honorable designation.

From Stuart to Hanover. As church and king men the Tories were firm in their support of Charles II, but the Roman Catholic tendencies of James II meant that they had to choose between church and king, so the Jacobite wing hived off, and the now divided party was out of office for some 70 years after the Revolution of 1688. With the accession of George III in 1760 it began to revive. In many ways Toryism was now different from what it had been in Stuart times, for there was more insistence on loyalty to the constitution and to the throne as an institution than to the monarch personally, and very little was now heard about the church.

If the Tories had sacrificed some of their old principles, they retained their devotion to the throne, and, despairing of the restoration of the Stuarts, even the old Jacobite wing was not prepared to transfer its loyalty to the house of Hanover. In the words of Edmund Burke, "They changed their idol but they preserved their idolatry." For his part, George III leaned heavily on the Tories for support. Such an attitude of loyalty to the throne on the part of the English Tories explains why the name Tory was often applied to loyalists during the American Revolution.

In the main, the Tories supported George III for the first 20 years of his reign. The outbreak of the French Revolution brought them support among political moderates, as did the long war against Napoleon. Except for a brief interval, 1806–1807, the Tories were in power until 1830. That year they lost office, the Reform Bill was passed in 1832, and in the ensuing general election the party went down to disaster. Defeat led the party to think of a more popular name, and "Conservative" gradually came into use after 1833.

Revival. Thereafter the official name of the Tory party was the Conservative, or, for a period, the Conservative and Unionist party as a result of the controversy over home rule for Ireland. In Scotland and Northern Ireland the Conservatives prefer to call themselves Unionists. There has been a marked tendency, especially in the press, to revert to the older word, which is shorter and less restrictive. See CONSERVATIVE PARTY; GREAT BRITAIN—*History*.

SIR CHARLES PETRIE, *Author of "The Four Georges: A Revaluation"*

Further Reading: Feiling, Keith G., *A History of the Tory Party, 1640–1714* (London 1924); id., *The Second Tory Party, 1714–1832* (London 1951).

TOSCA, tōs′kä, an opera in three acts by Giacomo Puccini. It was first produced in Rome on Jan. 14, 1900. The libretto, by Giuseppe Giacosa and Luigi Illica, is based on Victorien Sardou's play *La Tosca* (1887). Among the popular arias in the opera are Cavaradossi's *Recondita armonia* and Tosca's *Vissi d'arte.*

The action of *Tosca* takes place in Rome in June 1800. Angelotti, a former consul of the Roman republic, has escaped from prison and takes refuge in the Church of Sant'Andrea della Valle. There he finds a sympathizer, the painter Mario Cavaradossi, who offers to help him. Just then Cavaradossi, the lover of the singer Floria Tosca, hears Tosca's voice outside. She enters and accuses Cavaradossi of having been in conversation with a woman but leaves reassured. A cannon shot announces that Angelotti's escape is known, and Cavaradossi leaves with the fugitive.

The dreaded chief of police, Baron Scarpia, traces Angelotti to the church and decides to use Tosca to trap Angelotti. Cavaradossi is arrested and tortured at the Farnese Palace within the hearing of Tosca, who breaks down and reveals Angelotti's hiding place. Scarpia orders Cavaradossi to be shot, but Tosca bargains for her lover's life; and Scarpia then arranges a mock execution. When Scarpia tries to embrace Tosca in fulfillment of her bargain, she stabs him to death, then hurries to the mock execution on the roof of Sant'Angelo castle. But Scarpia has tricked her—the bullets are real. Realizing that Cavaradossi is dead, Tosca hurls herself to death from the battlements.

HAROLD ROSENTHAL, *Editor of "Opera" Magazine*

TOSCANINI, tos-kə-nē′nē, **Arturo** (1867–1957), Italian symphonic and operatic conductor, who exerted an important influence on 20th century standards of musical performance. By his insistence on strict fidelity to the spirit and artistic intentions of composers—rejecting the views of 19th century romantics who permitted interpretative liberties in the name of expression and artistic freedom—Toscanini made disciplined musicianship and analytical musical studies the basis for performance.

Early Years. Toscanini was born in Parma on March 25, 1867. He was deeply influenced by his father, a tailor, who had served with the patriot Garibaldi and who gave his son a love of democracy that in later years led to Toscanini's denunciation of fascism and nazism.

Educated as a cellist and pianist in the Royal School of Music in Parma, Toscanini made his debut as a conductor in Rio de Janeiro on June 30, 1886, directing *Aïda* as a last-minute replacement for a senior colleague in a touring Italian opera company. His ability was immediately recognized, and during the next dozen years Toscanini developed his career in Italy with engagements of increasing importance. In 1898 he became the music director of La Scala, in Milan, Italy's leading operatic theater.

Later Years and Influence. Increasing artistic dissatisfaction took Toscanini to New York in 1908 as a principal conductor of the Metropolitan Opera. In 1915 he returned to Italy, where he remained in semiretirement until 1919. He toured the United States with the orchestra of La Scala in 1920–1921 and then resumed the directorship of La Scala for eight years. Basic conflicts with the Mussolini government led to his departure in 1929.

NBC
Arturo Toscanini

Toscanini served as guest conductor of the New York Philharmonic (1926–1927) and then as its principal conductor (1928–1936). In 1937, at the age of 70, he was persuaded to direct the NBC Symphony, a new orchestra to be formed especially for his recordings and his broadcast concerts. Thus began 17 years in which Toscanini's musical outlook was deeply impressed on the American public. With the NBC Symphony he toured South America in 1940 and the United States in 1950. His last conducting was at an NBC Symphony recording session on June 5, 1954, and his final years were divided between Italy and New York. Toscanini died in New York City on Jan. 16, 1957.

A champion of the composers who influenced him in his youth, Toscanini was more important in establishing standards for the performance of recognized masterworks than as an innovator. As years passed, his repertory narrowed, but he remained virtually unrivaled in his specialties.

ROBERT C. MARSH, *Author of "Toscanini and the Art of Conducting"*

Further Reading: Antek, Samuel, and Hupka, Robert, *This Was Toscanini* (New York 1963); Sacchi, Filippo, *The Magic Baton*, rev. ed. (New York 1957).

TOSHOGU, tō-shō-gōō, a shrine at Nikko, Japan, built in 1634–1636. It commemorates Tokugawa Ieyasu, the founder of the Tokugawa Shogunate (1603–1867). See also NIKKO.

TOTALITARIANISM is a difficult concept to define, principally because it is confused with authoritarianism, dictatorship, tyranny, and similar concepts that denote oppression of individuals or groups within a social system. Totalitarianism signifies total control over the individual in every aspect of his life. As such, however, a totalitarian regime or order may be either good or bad. For example, parental control over young children approaches pure totalitarianism, and such control obviously can have either beneficent or maleficent effects.

The following baffling questions have arisen with respect to totalitarianism. (1) How can those who seek to impose a totalitarian order tell good from bad, right from wrong? This consideration has been one of the central preoccupations of ancient and modern philosophers, including Plato, Aristotle, Cicero, Aquinas, Kant, and Hegel. (2) To what standards of ethics should one recur for the establishment and maintenance of a totalitarian regime?

Answers to these questions vary. Ancient and medieval theorists concentrated on the perennial question of the essence of justice in the eyes of man and of the gods. The early utilitarians, most notably Jeremy Bentham and James Mill, seemed not to object to totalitarian systems provided that the "greatest happiness for the greatest number" principle would prevail. Utopian socialists, the presumed forebears of the Marxists, emphasized the value of equality and the drastic restructuring of the social order to achieve this same end. Because of these differences as to what goals or ideals should form the basis for total control by the state, examples of totalitarianism are rare. Sparta usually is cited as the ancient example and Nazi Germany and the Soviet Union as modern equivalents.

Scholars generally agree that because of the diversity of man in his inclinations, beliefs, and capacities, totalitarianism necessarily involves coercion and repression. This is why totalitarianism is so often confused with despotism. See also DICTATORSHIP.

GEORGE W. CAREY, *Georgetown University*

Further Reading: Arendt, Hannah, *The Origins of Totalitarianism* (New York 1951); Friedrich, Carl, and Brzezinski, Zbigniew, *Totalitarian Dictatorship and Autocracy* (Cambridge, Mass., 1956).

TOTEM, an animal, plant, or inanimate object with which a social or religious group feels a special affinity and which is often considered to be the mythical ancestor of the group. The word comes from the Ojibwa, an Algonkian tribe of North America. The term *totemism* denotes a form of social organization centered on a totem. Totemism is based on a religious principle that divides mankind and nature into classes and categories and links a particular cultural group with a specific being or thing, which is the totem. The totem is worshiped or esteemed by members of the clan bearing its name. An appropriate myth may explain the role of the totem in the origin of the clan. A totemic animal may not be killed or harmed by those who consider themselves to be its descendants except on certain ritual occasions when it might be eaten sacramentally.

Membership in a totemic clan or lineage is hereditary. It may be matrilineal (through the mother), patrilineal (through the father), or bilateral. Magical rites and observance of special taboos are obligatory. The members of the clan are considered to be related by blood to each other, since they are descendants of the same ancestor. Totemic clans as a rule are exogamous —that is, they must marry outside their own clan. However, clans and exogamy may occur independently of totemism. In social structure, the totem is always the primary basis for group division within a society. Every totemic commu-

MUSEUM OF THE AMERICAN INDIAN, HEYE FOUNDATION

TOTEM POLE carved in 19th century by Haida Indians of Alaska. The three lower figures symbolize the lineage of a tribal chief; the upper, that of his wife.

nity is divided into a set of equivalent social units. These complement each other, sometimes by concentrating, in plant or animal totemism, on different species and always by exchanging marriageable individuals between the social units.

Theory of Origin and Function. The origin of totemism has been discussed by scholars for almost a century, but there is little unity of opinion. The content of totemism and its function differ greatly around the world, making it difficult to set up universal criteria. For American Indian tribes such as the Iroquois, the totem merely denotes group membership. Among the Australian aborigines, membership in a totemic group determines kin groupings, marriage rituals, and type of diet.

Among the earliest scholars concerned with similarity and unity in the practice of totemism, the most prominent were Sir James Frazer in *Totemism and Exogamy* (1910), Sigmund Freud in *Totem and Taboo* (1913), and Émile Durkheim in *Elementary Forms of Religious Life* (1915). Frazer developed three variant theories of the origin of totemism. One, totems are the repository of external souls that are reincarnated in people. Two, totems have a religious-economic base in magical techniques used to ensure the food supply. Three, totems might be used to explain the origin of human life. In general, totemism expressed ritually man's relation to the world of animals and plants around him. For Durkheim, a totem is a form of symbol representing the collective life of a social group, being its basic integrative force. Freud transformed the Oedipus myth into a totemic system, in which the father gives his descendants a name and protection in return for honoring the totem.

Later theories are equally divergent. F. A. R. Radcliffe-Brown feels that the term totemism is applied to a number of diverse institutions in which one common feature is the function of the totem as a basic organizing principle. W. H. R. Rivers defined totemism as a combination of three elements: (1) the social, which is the division of the tribe into totemic groups; (2) the psychological, which is the belief in a kinship between members of the clan; and (3) the ritual, which includes all the taboos and magical practices. Claude Lévi-Strauss finds common elements between totemic groups and castes, grounded in the fact that in both systems the people as individuals identify themselves in terms of their membership in a given group into which they were born.

Totem Poles. Among American Indians, totemism is well developed in many variants. It is best known from the Northwest Coast area, where the tribes of Tlingit, Haida, Tsimshian, and Kwakiutl live. One of the outstanding characteristics of this area is the abundance of carved posts, called totem poles. They are made of cedar tree trunks set up in front or at the side of the doorway, usually rising well above the roof of the house. Some wealthy chieftains set up spectacular totem poles as high as 60 feet (18 meters). The poles are curved in low relief around a cylindrical or half-cylindrical basic form. They show various combinations of animal and human forms piled one on another, representing the heraldic crest of the clan or lineage. The heraldic designs often embody the family history. Most of the carving is painted with accentuated lines. It is often difficult to identify the design, since the artist usually distributes various parts of the animal body around the trunk. New poles are rarely erected, and old poles are disintegrating.

SULA BENET, *Hunter College*

TOTOWA, tō′tō-wə, is a borough in northeastern New Jersey, in Passaic county, 3 miles (5 km) west of Paterson. Its factories make metal products, Swedish steel, precision tools, burial vaults, and cosmetics and process food. The borough is on the site of a camp of George Washington's army in the American Revolution. It was incorporated in 1898. Government is by mayor and council. Population: 11,580.

TOTTORI, tōt-tō-rē, a port city in southwestern Japan, is the capital of Tottori prefecture. The city is situated on the Sendai River, near the Sea of Japan coast, 75 miles (120 km) northwest of Kobe. It is a marketing and distribution center for the prefecture's products, notably lumber, raw silk, and rice, and has textile, woodworking, and paper industries. The city is the home of Tottori University. It is also a health resort featuring hot springs.

The largely mountainous Tottori prefecture, fronting the Sea of Japan, has an area of 1,347 square miles (3,488 sq km). Population (1965): of the city, 108,860; of the prefecture, 579,853.

TOUAREG. See TUAREG.

TOUCAN, tōō'kan, any of a family of large-billed tropical, arboreal birds found from southern Mexico to northern Argentina. The majority of species occur in the Amazon basin. Larger toucans typically inhabit lowland rain forests, while smaller species live at higher altitudes of up to 10,000 feet (3,300 meters).

Toucans are from 12 to 24 inches (30–60 cm) long. They have short, rounded wings, strong legs, and rather long tails. They are known for their enormous beaks that commonly approximate the body in bulk. The beaks are strong, but very light. They are honeycombed with fibers and with delicate struts, or supporting pieces, and are covered with a thin horny sheath. The toucans' tongues are long and straplike with notched edges and bristly tips. The beaks and the plumage are brightly colored with red, yellow, orange, blue, and black pigments, often in varied patterns. The sexes are usually alike in coloring.

THE TOUCAN is known for its very large bill, which it uses in courtship displays as well as in feeding.

FROM NATIONAL AUDUBON SOCIETY
ARTHUR W. AMBLER,

Gregarious birds, toucans in small loose flocks roam treetops and may even roost communally in tree cavities overnight. They seemingly enjoy playing together, jumping, fencing with their beaks, and preening one another's feathers. They are easily tamed. Their varied calls are unmusical buglings, croaks, yelps, mews, chatterings, and billclaps. Some of the smaller species are good mimics. Toucans feed chiefly on fruits and berries, but they also eat insects, small reptiles, and the eggs and young of other birds.

Toucans usually nest in tree cavities or in old woodpecker holes. Both parents incubate the two to four white eggs, which hatch in about 16 days. The hatchlings require three to four weeks to open their eyes and in at least one species six or seven weeks to leave the nest.

There are about 37 species of toucans, classified in five genera, making up the family Ramphastidae of the order Piciformes.

CARL WELTY, *Beloit College*

TOUCH refers to a class of sensations produced by the application of light pressure to the surface of the body. Such sensations result from touching the skin with a thread, twitching a hair, pressing a pencil against the skin, and stroking the skin with the fingers. Closely related to these tactile sensations are those of tickle and vibration.

The sense of touch depends on the arousal of a network of fine nerve endings in the outer layers of the skin. Some of these receptors penetrate the epidermis, whereas others envelop the shafts of hairs. Among the regions with the heaviest concentrations of touch receptors are the tongue, lips, and finger pads. These are the regions most sensitive to feeble stimuli. In the less sensitive regions, such as the back and legs, there are "touch spots," which respond more easily to stimulation than the surrounding skin. Meissner's corpuscles, which are found in the hairless skin of the fingers and toes, may be touch receptors, but they are not essential for touch perception since these structures do not occur in the tongue, lips, and hairy areas of the skin.

Impulses initiated by the touch receptors in the skin travel along chains of sensory nerve fibers. These fibers take several different pathways to the brain's thalamus and finally arrive at the parts of the cerebral cortex that are concerned with perception and awareness. The time between actual stimulation and awareness is shorter for the sense of touch than for the other cutaneous senses.

Warmth, Cold, and Pain. In the hairy areas of the skin, the same general apparatus that is aroused by tactile stimulation also responds to temperature changes and painful stimuli, such as injury to the skin. In the hairless skin of the fingers and toes, other receptors have been found but their roles in skin sensation have not been established. The theories about the end bulbs of Krause responding to cold and the Ruffini corpuscles responding to warmth have not been proven. There is even doubt that the Ruffini corpuscles exist.

DAVID SINCLAIR
Author of "Cutaneous Sensation"

TOUCH FOOTBALL. See FOOTBALL—*Touch Football.*

TOUCH-ME-NOT, any of a large group of widely distributed plants with seedpods that burst open when touched. Touch-me-nots belong to the genus *Impatiens* of the balsam family (Balsaminaceae). They are sometimes also known as jewelweeds.

A common species found in the eastern United States is the orange touch-me-not (*I. capensis*). It is from 2 to 5 feet (0.6–1.5 meters) in height and bears pointed oval leaves. The flowers are orange, usually marked with reddish brown. Another species of the eastern United States is the yellow touch-me-not (*I. pallida*). It is slightly taller than the orange touch-me-not and has yellow flowers often marked with red.

JOHN J. SMITH

Touch-me-not (*Impatiens capensis*)

The name touch-me-not is also applied to the squirting cucumber (*Ecballium elaterium*) of the cucumber family (Cucurbitaceae). It is a trailing plant with oblong greenish fruits that, when ripe, break off from the plant and squirt their seeds. It is found in the Mediterranean area.

TOUCHSTONE is a fine-textured, velvety black variety of quartz, in the submicroscopically crystalline form of chert. It is also known as *Lydian stone* and *basanite*. The even-grained rock often has a high polish.

The name "touchstone" derives from its ancient use in assaying gold and silver alloys. An alloy, or a portion placed on a needle, would be rubbed across the surface of the stone. The color of the resulting streak would be compared to standard streaks of known composition. An expert could judge quite accurately the percentage of precious metal in the alloy.

TOULON, to͞o-lôɴ′, a port on the Mediterranean coast of France, is in Var department, 41 miles (66 km) east of Marseille. Toulon became the leading French naval base because of its magnificent sheltered anchorages. The waterfront, largely destroyed in World War II, has been rebuilt in modern style, but behind it still lie the picturesque narrow 18th century streets of the old town. Behind the city a semicircle of hills is crowned with forts, notably Mont Faron, with its memorial to the Allied landings of 1944.

New industrial areas have been created on the fringe of the city to supplement employment in the naval base, in shipbuilding, and in associated engineering plants. There is a small commercial port and ferry service to Corsica, to Sardinia, and to the Balearic Islands. The city's flourishing commercial activity includes one of the most important wholesale flower markets of France. Increasingly, however, the city has turned toward the tourist trade. Warships have given way to thousands of pleasure craft, and in the suburb of Le Mourillon a magnificent beach resort has been created. The city has spread inland and also along the coast in each direction, forming an agglomeration of about 350,000 people.

History. Henry IV founded the first naval arsenal, which was strengthened and expanded by the Marquis de Vauban in the late 17th century. Bonaparte first distinguished himself as a young artillery officer in the expulsion of a British occupying force in 1793. The naval base reached its peak in the great days of the French colonial empire in the late 19th and early 20th centuries. Its darkest moment was when the fleet was scuttled to prevent seizure by Germans in 1942. Population: (1968 est.) 175,000.

T. H. Elkins
University of Sussex

TOULOUSE, to͞o-lo͞oz′, is a city in southern France. It is on the Garonne River, commanding the ascent southward to the passes of the Pyrenees and Spain. It is linked to the Mediterranean by the 17th century Canal du Midi and to the Atlantic by the Garonne Lateral Canal. It is the capital of Haute-Garonne department and of the Midi-Pyrénées region.

The heart of Toulouse is the spacious Place du Capitole. The 11th–12th century St.-Sernin Basilica, to the north of this square, is one of France's largest and finest Romanesque churches. St.-Étienne cathedral, numerous other churches, former religious houses, and merchants' residences of the medieval and Renaissance periods add to the interest this rosebrick city holds for tourists.

In the 20th century, Toulouse became the center of the French aerospace industry and developed important electronic and chemical plants. Government aerospace research and training establishments and the adjoining Rangueil science campus of the University of Toulouse make the city a leading center of scientific research and education. Since World War II the expansion of the city has been dramatic.

History. An important Gallo-Roman city, Toulouse was the center of a great Visigothic kingdom from about 416 to 508. From the 9th century it was part of the feudal county of Toulouse, and the distinctive language culture of Languedoc flourished. By 1189 its citizens had achieved virtual independence and were governed by *capitouls* (magistrates), but in 1271 the county and city passed to the French crown. From 1470, following a period marked by plague, the Hundred Years' War, and the great Toulouse fire of 1463, the city entered its "golden century" of prosperity and artistic achievement. All local independence vanished with the revolutionary reorganization of 1790, but Toulouse remained the dominant administrative and commercial center between the Massif Central and the Pyrenees. Population: (1968) 370,796.

T. H. Elkins
University of Sussex

TOULOUSE, University of, a public university located in Toulouse, France, supported by the ministry of education.

The University of Toulouse was founded in 1229, drawing faculty members from the University of Paris. Toulouse became noted as a school of law, though other disciplines were also taught. During the French Revolution the government suppressed the university, but separate faculties continued to function and were reconstituted as a university in 1896. The university has faculties of law, letters, medicine and pharmacy, and science. The enrollment in the early 1970's was about 35,000 men and women.

In the late 1960's, as part of a general review of educational policies in France, the university began a period of major reorganization. One aim of the review was to give the university more autonomy in its relations with the ministry of education in Paris.

PHOTO MARJO; MUSÉE TOULOUSE-LAUTREC

MUSÉE TOULOUSE-LAUTREC, ALBI, FRANCE

TOULOUSE-LAUTREC evoked Paris in the 1890's in his lithographed poster (*left*) *Moulin Rouge—La Goulue* (1891) and his oil painting (*right*) *Au Salon de la rue des Moulins* (1894).

TOULOUSE-LAUTREC, too͞-lo͞oz′ lō-trek′, **Henri de** (1864–1901), French painter and lithographer, who chronicled the Parisian night life of the 1890's. Although he was the friend of many of the more eccentric entertainers of the cabarets, theaters, and bars of Montmartre, he maintained in his art the objectivity of an observer, creating an aesthetic work out of their unique physical characteristics but ignoring any social questions that their situation might raise.

Life and Work. Henri Marie Raymond de Toulouse-Lautrec-Monfa, descendant of the counts of Toulouse, was born in Albi in southern France on Nov. 24, 1864. He seemed destined to carry on his father's devotion to horses and falconry until, at 15, two falls left him permanently crippled with dwarfed legs. While convalescing, Toulouse-Lautrec began to study painting, concentrating on horses. In 1882 he went to Paris to study and by 1885 had found a sympathetic environment in Montmartre.

Like Degas before him, Toulouse-Lautrec dealt with unconventional subject matter—the spectacle of contemporary life in some of its livelier aspects. Montmartre in the 1880's and 1890's attracted nearly all the major artists, such as Van Gogh, with whom Toulouse-Lautrec formed a warm friendship. The district was also a center of the world of entertainment, which stressed the bizarre, exaggerated, or provocative. Dissatisfied with professional models, Toulouse-Lautrec turned to performers for subjects and often for company. Avoiding moral judgments, he presented them only as intriguing personalities. Aristide Bruant, whose songs sentimentalized the picturesque slums and their inhabitants, was his friend and appeared on a Toulouse-Lautrec poster in 1893. The artist also portrayed the dancers La Goulue, Valentin le Désossé, and Jane Avril in such works as *La Goulue Entering the Moulin Rouge* (1892; Musée Toulouse-Lautrec, Albi) and the poster of Jane Avril at the Jardin de Paris (1893). Other theatrical subjects include the singers May Belfort and Yvette Gilbert and circus performers, as in *Cirque Fernando: The Equestrienne* (1888; Art Institute, Chicago). He also depicted prostitutes, as in *Au Salon de la rue des Moulins* and *The Inspection* (both 1894; Musée Toulouse-Lautrec), and street people, as in *Friends* (1895; Zurich, private collection).

Toulouse-Lautrec's wealth saved him from the burden of poverty that oppressed most of his friends. He showed little work until 1893, when the Goupil Gallery gave him a one-man exhibition. Although his oils on cardboard, and his sketches and lithographed posters were highly respected by other artists and some critics, his parents felt disappointed and disgraced by his obsession with what one critic called "the larvae of vice and poverty." Gradually alcohol undermined his health, and he died at a family estate, Château de Malromé, on Sept. 9, 1901.

Analysis. Toulouse-Lautrec was as unconventional in his treatment of motion and space as in his subject matter. The traditional conception was that a scene should contain whole figures and summarize one or more events seen at their most significant moments. By contrast, he used the "cut-off" figure to suggest that the scene extends beyond the frame and that the viewer sees an instantaneous or accidental glimpse of a moving object—similar to that caught by a camera. This conception is reflected in the awkward, unposed postures and unusual perspective of such works as the *Cirque Fernando*.

Toulouse-Lautrec's interest in motion and space may be related to the shadow puppet plays of his day and to experiments with early motion pictures. Fascinated by the camera, he frequently copied from photographs, using perspective to create a space that seems to be seen through the eye of a camera. He also admired Japanese prints with their insistent perspective.

Turning away from impressionists' sunshine and natural flesh hues, Toulouse-Lautrec captured artificial theatrical light falling on costumes and sets and on intense, painted faces and dyed hair. His curvilinear, whip-lash contours tending toward abstraction resemble the decorative preoccupation of art nouveau, but he used line more to express action and personality.

Toulouse-Lautrec's lithographed posters for dance halls and theaters have an especially close relationship to the culture of the 1890's. Lithography on a large scale was just coming into use by major artists. Visible everywhere in the streets of Paris, his posters introduced the popular art of Montmartre to the whole city and the work of the artist to the common people. Poster design—with its simple, direct images and strong color contrasts—proved so vital that it soon joined with the decorative patterns of art nouveau to shape later styles of French painting.

HERSCHEL B. CHIPP, *Author of "The Theories of Modern Art"*

Further Reading: Cooper, Douglas, *Toulouse-Lautrec* (New York 1956); Mack, Gerstle, *Toulouse-Lautrec* (New York 1938).

TOUNGOO DYNASTY, toung′go͞o, a line of Burmese rulers from 1486 to 1753. The dynasty was at its height in the period 1531–1581 under Tabinshweti and his son-in-law Bayinnaung.

Prior to 1527 the tiny Burmese princedom of Toungoo was constricted in the narrow Sittang Valley between the warlike Shan kingdom of Ava to the north and the commercially active Mon state of Pegu in the south. In the 1530's its ruler, Tabinshweti, took advantage of tribal attacks on Ava to capture the city of Pegu and make it his capital. He occupied the central Irrawaddy Valley and eventually staged an abortive attack on the Thai capital, Ayuthia. Tabinshweti was assassinated in 1550, however, and the Mons temporarily recovered Pegu.

Bayinnaung, who assumed power at Toungoo in 1551, began a vast military expansion. After taking Pagan in the north and recovering Pegu, he pushed eastward to capture Chiengmai in Thailand and Vientiane in Laos. He took Ayuthia in 1564 and 1569, carrying away vast treasure. European visitors in the 1570's marveled at the splendor of his new capital, Pegu.

Following Bayinnaung's death in 1581, his empire crumbled. The Burmese were forced out of Thailand, and in 1635 the dynasty moved its capital northward to Ava. It survived until 1753, the year after Ava fell to the Mons.

JOHN F. CADY, *Author of "Southeast Asia: Its Historical Development"*

TOURACO, to͝or′ə-kō, or *turaco,* any of a family of large, brilliantly colored, fruit-eating birds widely distributed in Africa south of the Sahara. They are also known as *plantain-eaters.* Touracos inhabit a variety of habitats from arid thornbrush lands and grasslands to dense evergreen forests and are found at all altitudes up to 12,000 feet (3,600 meters).

Touracos are from 15 to 30 inches (38–76 cm) long. Their heads frequently have prominent crests tipped with red or white, and their stubby, curved bills are often colorful. Touraco plumage is loose, fluffy, and brilliant with iridescent blues, violets, and greens. The green coloring is produced by turacoverdin—the only green pigment known to occur in birds. The dazzling red patches found on the wings of many species are caused by turacin, a copper-bearing pigment unique in the animal kingdom.

A. W. AMBLER, NAT. AUDUBON SOC.

Red-crested touraco

Strictly arboreal birds, touracos are extremely agile in scrambling about tree branches; they are, however, poor fliers. They commonly live in small, noisy family groups and feed chiefly on fruits, insects, and grubs. The nest is a crude flat platform of sticks. Both parents incubate the two white or tinted eggs for perhaps 18 days and later feed regurgitated fruit pulp to the young. Touracos make up the family Musophagidae of the order Passeriformes.

CARL WELTY, *Beloit College*

TOURAINE, to͞o-ren′, is a historic province of France. It is renowned for its châteaus, built mostly during the Renaissance, when Touraine was the residence of the French monarchs and aristocrats. Touraine lies astride the Loire Valley in the southern Paris Basin. Most of the modern department of Indre-et-Loire and parts of Loir-et-Cher and Indre occupy the area. The provincial capital was Tours.

The farmland of the rather monotonous Touraine plateau is interrupted by forests, where the kings of France once hunted. By contrast, the valleys of the Loire River and its tributaries are famed for their favorable climate, great fertility, and beauty. The grapes of famous wines like Vouvray are raised on the slopes. The proximity of Paris has encouraged the post-World War II growth of industry.

History. The rich lands once inhabited by the Turons, a Celtic tribe, were also prized from the Roman period into Merovingian and Carolingian times, when pilgrims to the shrine of St. Martin of Tours brought great wealth to the region. After the chaos of the Norman invasions, the feudal county of Tours was disputed by the counts of Blois and Anjou. Control of Touraine went in 1044 to the Angevins, who became kings of England in 1154. The castle of Chinon was their great strongpoint in Touraine.

Philip II Augustus of France regained Touraine in 1205. It was made into a royal duchy. The duchy was again disputed by the English in the Hundred Years' War (1337–1453). In 1429, the young Joan of Arc had her historic meeting with the future Charles VII at Chinon. In the late 1400's and in the 1500's, Touraine was the favorite residence of the French kings. The kings, the nobility, and the rich bourgeois transformed the gloomy feudal castles into the magnificent Renaissance châteaus that are today's tourist attractions. In 1584 the duchy became a province, and in the 17th century, court life moved away to Paris and Versailles. Touraine was divided into departments in 1790.

T. H. ELKINS, *University of Sussex*

TOURANE. See DA NANG.

TOURÉ, too-rā', **Samori** (about 1830–1900), Mandingo warrior chief, who founded a Muslim state in West Africa in the mid-19th century. He was born in Sanankoro, in what is now northern Guinea. Rapidly acquiring a reputation as a warrior, he became king of his native town by 1872. Soon after he declared himself an *almami*, or Muslim religious chief.

Samori (Samory) proceeded to extend his control to the east bank of the upper Niger River, where he came into conflict with French military expeditions. With his supporters he resisted French penetration and was engaged in battle almost continually from 1883 until his death. In 1886, Samori accepted French protection and agreed not to cross the Niger. When instead he attempted to conquer the region eastward to the Black Volta River, he was unsuccessful. Hostilities broke out again with the French in 1891. Samori was forced to retreat, first into what is now the northern Ivory Coast and then to eastern Liberia, where he was captured near the Cavally River on Sept. 29, 1898. He died in exile in Gabon on June 2, 1900.

Samori was the last leader of a sovereign Guinea for more than half a century. But his name lived on in the memory of his compatriots to aid the nationalist movement for independence.

L. GRAY COWAN, *Columbia University*

TOURÉ, too-rā', **Sékou** (1922–), first president of Guinea. He was born on Jan. 9, 1922, in Faranah, to a Muslim family. He was educated at a Koranic school and at 15 was expelled from a technical school for leading a food strike. Later, while working for the French colonial administration, he became a union leader.

In 1947, Touré helped found the African Democratic Rally, an interterritorial political party. Dismissed from his treasury post because of his radical political activities, he became a full-time unionist and organized the Guinean Democratic party. In 1956 he was elected mayor of Conakry and a representative of Guinea to the French National Assembly. The following year he became vice president of Guinea. In 1958, Touré called for a "no" vote on the constitutional referendum establishing the French Community. When Guinea achieved independence in October 1958, he became president.

Touré retained firm control of the party and government. His emphasis on party organization and on the development of mass political consciousness at the expense of economic progress was responsible for the deterioration of standards of living and the limiting of foreign investment. A voluminous writer, Touré published several volumes on the theory and practice of his interpretation of socialism as applied to Guinea.

L. GRAY COWAN, *Columbia University*

TOURISM, the pastime of journeying from home to some other place, near or far, has become big business. The money spent in tourism constitutes the largest single item in world trade, although "tourism," as a budgetary category, is composed of many separate elements. Among these are transportation by air, sea, and land; food, services, accommodations, and entertainment for visitors; and the manufacture and sale of thousands of items, from souvenirs to jet aircraft.

Tourism is often called an invisible export because many nations accumulate large sums in foreign currency by successfully encouraging foreign visitors to travel inside their countries. Tourism accounts for 6% of all the "exports" in the world. Catering to the traveler from abroad is so important that some countries depend on it for half of their foreign-exchange earnings. Some nations that might otherwise register a trade deficit have balanced their international accounts by attracting visitors from abroad.

Growth of Tourism. Such has been the increase in tourism that in some communities it has outstripped all other sources of income. A notable example is Hawaii, which after becoming the 50th state of the United States, vastly increased its tourist facilities. Tourism has outdistanced both sugar—a crop planted since shortly after the arrival of the missionaries in 1820—and pineapples as a source of income. Three fourths of the economy of the U. S. Virgin Islands is based on tourism and travel. In the United States it is estimated that at least 8 million people are directly or indirectly employed in the tourist industry.

Between 1950 and 1970 tourism throughout the world increased in size 10 times. Its growth each year was almost double that of other world "exports." International travel was expected to rise another 70% between 1970 and 1980.

A wide combination of factors were responsible for this enormous growth, among them vastly increased leisure time, early retirement age, the advent of jet travel, and the creation of low-cost means of transport and commensurate low-cost hotels, which have placed travel, both foreign and domestic, within the economic reach of large groups of people, particularly North Americans, Western Europeans, and Japanese.

Before the advent of jets in 1958 an airplane trip from New York to Europe took about 15 hours eastbound and sometimes more than 20 hours westbound; afterward, it took half that time. Able to get more use out of their aircraft, the airlines reduced the cost of flight, or at least held the price line despite severe inflation.

The speed of the jets also opened up new areas, once considered too distant for convenient travel. Traveling around the world by air became popular, and the Far East was opened to masses of travelers. From Afghanistan to East Africa, American-style hotels guaranteed a high standard of comfort, acceptable meals, potable water, and a price within the means of many.

Credit plans offered people the option of traveling on the installment plan: to "Fly now—pay later." Large groups of people found they could charter airplanes and even organize ground tours at costs that were lower than regularly scheduled flights and regular tours.

In the hopes of reaping the benefits that could result from actively soliciting travelers, many governments engaged in large and colorful advertising campaigns in magazines, newspapers, and ultimately in television. In 1969, national governments spent nearly $13 million on advertising in U. S. newspapers, magazines, radio, and television. Government travel offices in many countries not only served their own populations, but sought bookings from travel agents who could send them foreign tourists. Old national grudges and conflicting ideologies were forgotten, and often the combinations were unusual. The Spanish government operates a travel office in Sweden; the Danes try to attract the Germans, their oppressors during World War II. The state of Hawaii opened a travel office in Tokyo; Bulgaria, Czechoslovakia, the USSR, Poland, and Yugoslavia all opened bureaus in the West.

Economic Impact. The earnings that accrue to nations favored by travelers are enormous. U. S. visitors spend about $1 billion each year in Canada and about two thirds as much in Mexico. The first time that more than 1 million Americans descended on one European country in one year was in 1969, when 1,095,000 Americans went to Britain and spent a total of $225 million.

Visitors to the United States from all other countries totaled about 2.2 million in 1968. They spent about $2.86 billion. In 1968–1969, tourism was the primary source of foreign revenue in Israel, Portugal, and Spain; was second in Egypt, Greece, and Italy; and third in Britain, France, South Africa, and Switzerland.

Changing Patterns of Tourism. Much of the overseas travel is by fast jet aircraft. For the first time there were no major liners traveling on regular transatlantic schedules during the winter of 1969–1970. The big liners turned to cruises, and those with imaginative itineraries were able to attract large numbers of passengers.

For example, the S. S. *France,* one of the traditional liners that were able to adapt most successfully to the new vogue in sea travel, celebrated the 200th anniversary of Napoleon's birth by making a cruise to famous places in the history of Bonaparte's life, among them Ajaccio, Corsica, where he was born; Elba, whence he returned for the Hundred Days; and St. Helena, where he died. It was a sellout.

But sea travel was inevitably changing. Travelers liked the concept of flying the relatively long distance from home to the first foreign port and there joining a cruise ship. The New Yorker, for example, could take a winter cruise and still avoid the bad weather and rough seas at the beginning and end of the journey, by flying to Curaçao and boarding his cruise ship there.

To suit that purpose, cruise ship operators and airlines put together packages offering both the flight to a Mediterranean or Caribbean port and a luxury cruise in warm waters. The demand for new cruise ships was so great that shipyards in Helsinki, Finland, had orders for six. The first in this line, the MS *Song of Norway,* entered service in Florida in 1970. These new specialized ships were being called "cruisers."

The arrival of the wide-bodied planes—Boeing's 747 in 1970, to be followed by the DC-10 of McDonnell-Douglas and the L-1011 of Lockheed—inspired U. S. hotelkeepers to expand their facilities abroad. Hilton International, Inter-Continental Hotels, and more moderately priced chains, such as Holiday Inns, TraveLodge, Marriott, and Howard Johnson's, announced vast expansion plans. To ensure hotel rooms for their passengers, airlines moved in the 1960's to link up with hotel chains. Thus Trans World Airlines (TWA) bought Hilton International, and United Airlines affiliated with Western International. American Airlines began to build, buy, or arrange operating contracts for hotels along its prime routes to Acapulco, Hawaii, and beyond to the antipodes. Pan American World Airways had started this trend long before, when it began building hotels in 1946 and formed Inter-Continental Hotels. By 1970 this chain had 48 hotels in 35 countries.

While the railroad network continued to disintegrate in the United States, rail travel flourished in some other countries. The "bullet" trains traveling at high speeds between Tokyo and Osaka were marvels of efficiency, comfort, and dispatch. Similarly, the French National Railroads, with the plush *Mistral* running to the Riviera and other fast trains speeding in comfort to English Channel ports, met with great approbation and success.

The renting of automobiles, which grew in acceptance in the United States in the mid-1950's and expanded rapidly, also became a factor in world travel. As Americans became more sure of themselves outside their own country, they were encouraged to take "fly-drive" trips. Booking bureaus for major car-rental agencies appeared at international airports in most of the countries of the world. The Hertz Corporation keeps a roster of over 50,000 cars stationed at 1,000 locations in the United States, and by 1969 it listed 25,000 cars at 1,200 different places spread over more than 100 other countries. Avis Rent-A-Car has more than 60,000 cars for rent in the United States and has car-rental locations in 57 other countries. Both Hertz and Avis rent cars in the Soviet Union.

Cross-Cultural Effects. This era of widespread travel has had an enormous cultural impact, broadening the tastes of travelers in matters of food, dress, decoration, music, architecture, and automobiles, and giving them much broader political perspectives as well.

While they were being accommodated in almost any corner of the world with all the comforts and appurtenances of home, Americans who traveled abroad also began to appreciate the varied delights of foreign cuisine—French, Italian, German, Spanish, and on to Oriental. The sale of specialty foods zoomed in the United States. European and Japanese restaurants became almost as common a sight as European and Japanese cars. Cross-pollination of taste around the world was furthered by heavily attended world's fairs in Brussels, New York, Montreal, and Osaka.

Americans acquired a taste for foreign artifacts, foreign crafts, and foreign dress. Indian and Oriental influences appeared in both interior design and apparel. The internationalization of American tastes created enthusiasm for traveling performers from other countries, and in turn American theater, orchestras, and performers received wide acclaim in many countries.

Many returned to their own countries enlightened by their stay in other lands and equipped with a better perspective on their homeland and its relation to the rest of the world. Domestic difficulties could be assayed in relation to similar problems in other nations. Moreover, there was the opportunity to view at first hand the chief examples of other forms of government, both of the right and of the left.

History. Pleasure travel in the United States up to and through the 19th century was largely limited to summer excursions to Newport, R. I., and to the spas of Pennsylvania and the Virginias, and was solely for the rich. Taking the waters was, similarly, the prime reason impelling Europeans to undertake tiresome journeys by stagecoach. With the development of the steam engine and comfortable oceangoing ships, traveling abroad became more comfortable, but it remained the prerogative of only a tiny fraction of the population.

The European university student's *Wanderjahr* (traditional year of travel on completing his formal studies) developed into the educational Grand Tour of the young British aristocrat. For Americans of means, the Grand Tour meant a long European trip in which they were conducted to the Swiss Alps, taken for cruises along the Rhine, and shown the indoor and outdoor masterpieces of Venice, Florence, and Rome.

World War I gave many Americans of all economic and social classes their first look at Europe, and set off a popular annual summer migration abroad that was to persist. World War II sent enormous numbers of Americans not only to Europe but also to the Pacific and the Far East. Soldiers and sailors were given leave on Waikiki Beach and the French Riviera, and in London, in Paris, and in Swiss resorts.

That acquaintance with foreign lands and infatuation with foreign ways seemed to be responsible for the travel boom that resulted when normality returned. Small recessions notwithstanding, the boom never subsided. United States citizens were expected to spend $9.4 billion annually on foreign travel in the 1970's.

HORACE SUTTON
Associate Editor, "Saturday Review"

TOURMALINE, to͝or′mə-lən, is a complex silicate of boron and aluminum, with varying amounts of sodium, calcium, iron, lithium, and magnesium. It is strongly pyroelectric and piezoelectric—that is, its crystals develop an electric charge if subjected to heat or pressure, respectively. Because of its piezoelectricity, tourmaline is used in pressure gauges. It also forms beautiful semiprecious gem stones.

Appearance. Tourmaline crystals are usually prismatic. The prism faces tend to be vertically grooved and to round into one another, giving the crystals a peculiar triangular cross section with curved sides. The color depends on the crystal's composition. *Schlorite,* the most common variety, is black and contains much iron, whereas brown tourmaline is magnesium-bearing. Less common lithium-bearing varieties are light red, pink, green, blue, or yellow. The mineral is rarely white or colorless, as in *achroite.* The principal gem varieties are pink to red (*rubellite*), blue (*indicolite*), and green.

The crystals may show several different colors, arranged either in concentric bands around the center or in lengthwise transverse layers. They may also exhibit strong dichroism, showing one color when viewed lengthwise and another color when viewed at a right angle to the first position. See DICHROISM.

Occurrence. Tourmaline commonly occurs in the coarse igneous rocks called granite pegmatites, in association with microcline, quartz, and mica. It also is found in schists and gneisses and crystalline limestones. Gem tourmaline occurs in the state of Minas Gerais, Brazil, on the islands of Madagascar and Elba, and in Mozambique and the Ural Mountains. In the United States, gem varieties are found in Maine, Connecticut, and California.

Composition: $XY_3Al_6(BO_3)_3(Si_6O_{18})(OH)_4$, where X is Na or Ca and Y is Al, Fe, Li, or Mg; hardness, 7–7.5; specific gravity, 3.0–3.5; crystal system, hexagonal.

GEORGE SWITZER
Smithsonian Institution

TOURNAI, to͞or-nā′, is a city in southwestern Belgium, in Hainaut province, on the Scheldt River, about 7 miles (11 km) from the French border. Tournai, called *Doornik* in Flemish, is dominated by the five Romanesque towers of its cathedral. Other monuments include the 12th–14th century belfry, the Renaissance Cloth Hall, and the Pont des Trous, a fortified medieval bridge across the Scheldt. Tournai and its surrounding region have varied textile and clothing industries. Stone quarrying, cement manufacturing, machine building, printing, and food processing are also important. The city is a rail junction on the Lille-Brussels line and is served by the canalized Scheldt.

Tournai was an important Gallo-Roman city, known as Turnacum or Civitas Nerviorum. Childeric, a leader of the Salian Franks and the father of Clovis, was buried there in 481. Clovis first established undisputed control of the area around Tournai before beginning his conquest of Gaul. Medieval Tournai, with its flourishing weavers, merchants, and moneylenders, was an advance base of French influence in Flanders. After numerous changes of rule it passed in 1815 to the United Netherlands, and, when the latter dissolved in 1830, to Belgium. Economic and demographic expansion in the 20th century has been slight. Population: (1967 est.) 33,309.

T. H. ELKINS, *University of Sussex*

TOURNAMENT, a medieval mock battle between armed knights, in which the objective was to demonstrate skill and courage by unhorsing opponents, breaking lances over them, disarming them, or capturing their banners.

The origins of the chivalric tournament are obscure, and satisfactory evidence of its introduction, first in France, is only available from the late 12th century. Thereafter, throughout Europe, combats between knights flourished as military exercise, sport, and spectacle, until these were outmoded in the early 17th century.

Tournaments as Contests. The tournament of the 13th century was generally a violent, haphazard battle between armed groups, but increasingly the contests became formalized. The introduction of the "tilt," a barrier to prevent the collision of the horses, early in the 15th century; the development of heavier armor; the use of lighter "rebated," or blunted, weapons; and the evolution of the international institutions of heraldry all furthered this regulatory process. By the later 15th century the ritualization was elaborated in numerous treatises regulating procedure from the first issue of a challenge by the holders, or challengers, and its acceptance by the comers, or answerers, to the processions into the lists, or combat area, the contest itself, the scoring methods, and award of prizes.

Modes of Combat. Five principal modes of combat had evolved: "jousts royal," or tilting, that is, single combat between mounted knights armed with lances and separated by a tilt; joust-

EDITORIAL PHOTOCOLOR ARCHIVES

TOURS lies on the Loire, which winds through the famous château country of Touraine.

ing at large without the tilt, sometimes performed with unrebated spears; tourney on horseback, fought with swords; barriers, or foot combats, fought with swords or short spears; and, less commonly, mock sieges of fortified places. Challenges were generally *à plaisance* (for pleasure), but when issued *à outrance* (to the very end, or death) they resembled the duel. The most popular form was tilting, with the scoring based on the number of spears broken on an opponent. Attaints, blows delivered legitimately but without breaking the lance, were also taken into account. By the late 16th century most tournaments were confined to ceremonial lance-breaking, though the death of Henry II of France, in 1559, from a tilting injury, showed that even this sport could be dangerous.

Tournament as Pageant. Intrinsically, the tournament was always a dramatic spectacle, and even in the 13th century romantic impersonations were occasionally employed. This aspect was emphasized in the 14th century at the court of Edward III of England, and in the 15th century in the tournaments of René, Duke of Anjou, the Dukes of Burgundy, and the north Italian princes. Allegorical challenges provided literary settings enhanced by semidramatic speeches, culminating in court festivals such as the Accession Day tilts for Elizabeth I of England. There the tournament formed the core of a complex entertainment comprising allegory, music, poetry, and dancing, and helped in the evolution of the opera, court ballet, and court masque. See CHIVALRY.

SYDNEY ANGLO, *University of Wales; Author, "The Great Tournament Roll of Westminster"*

TOURNIQUET, tûr′ni-kət, a device, usually a band of material, that is applied as a last resort to stop profuse bleeding. See FIRST AID.

TOURS, to͝or, a city in France, was the capital of the Touraine region and is now a tourist center for the Loire Valley châteaus. Tours, capital of Indre-et-Loire department, is 145 miles (233 km) southwest of Paris. It is situated at the point where the major Paris-Bordeaux-Spain highway crosses the Loire River, just above the Loire-Cher confluence.

The City. Southward from the 18th century Loire bridge the wide Rue Nationale bisects the town and is the main shopping street. To the west, narrow streets of half-timbered houses surround the two surviving towers of the Basilica of St. Martin, one of the great pilgrimage churches of medieval Europe. It was ruined after the revolution of 1789. In the administrative and professional quarter to the east is the 13th–16th century Cathedral of St. Gatien and the 17th–18th century Archbishop's Palace, now a museum. Residential suburbs have spread north of the Loire, and on the city's southern fringe flood control on the Cher River has made land available for the creation of an impressive "new town."

Tours is the traditional agricultural marketing and retailing center for Touraine, but it has also profited from post–World War II industrial decentralization from Paris. Industrial activities include food processing and manufacturing metal and electrical equipment, pharmaceuticals, and tires. There are large railway yards to the west at St.-Pierre-des-Corps.

History. The original capital of the Turons, a Celtic tribe, was probably north of the Loire. Roman Caesarodunum, south of the river, was succeeded by a Christian bishopric, associated notably with St. Martin in the 4th century, St. Gregory in the 6th, and Alcuin, the English scholar, in the 8th. A prosperous silk industry was devastated by the expulsion of its Protestant craftsmen at the end of the 17th century. Tours was the seat of the French provisional government in 1870, and again, briefly, in 1940. Population: (1968 est.) 128,120. See also TOURAINE.

T. H. ELKINS, *University of Sussex*

TOURS, to͝or, **Battle of,** a decisive engagement in 732 in which forces under Charles Martel, the Frankish mayor of the palace, checked the Muslim advance into France. It is sometimes called the Battle of Poitiers. In 732, Abd ar-Rahman, a Muslim emir, led a large force north from Spain. After sacking Poitiers, the invaders marched toward Tours but were met and defeated by Charles' army. The Muslims never again penetrated so far into France.

TOUSSAINT L'OUVERTURE, to͞o-saɴ′ lo͞o-ver-tür′, **Pierre François Dominique** (c. 1749–1803), Haitian general, who was one of the principal leaders of the slave insurrection that led eventually to the independence of Haiti. His father, Gaou-Guinou, the son of an African king, had been transported as a slave to toil on the sugar plantation of the Count de Noé at Bréda in the French West Indian Colony of St.-Domingue, which occupied the western third of the island of Hispaniola. Toussaint was taught a smattering of French, Latin, geometry, and the Roman Catholic religion by a missionary-trained godfather. The origin of Toussaint's interest in military history is obscure, as is the source of the qualities of leadership that early earned him a position as overseer of the other slaves.

Toussaint joined the slave insurrection of August 1791, though not before ensuring the safe departure of the Noé family from their plantation. His military victories won him the sobriquet of *L'Ouverture* ("Opening"), as a man who, it was said, "makes an opening everywhere." His astuteness and his craftiness in diplomacy—called hypocrisy by his critics—enabled him for many years to outmaneuver other slave leaders, the white and mulatto slaveholders, and French military and civilian officials. After France declared war on Britain (Feb. 1, 1793), he deserted both the French and insurrectionary troops and joined the opposing Spanish army in Santo Domingo, the colony on the eastern part of Hispaniola. When France officially proclaimed emancipation a year later, he rejoined the French army with the rank of brigadier general.

Promoted to lieutenant governor and major general, Toussaint outwitted several French officials who were exploiting the hostility between the "blacks" and the mulattoes in an effort to restore white supremacy. Spain and France made peace in 1795, and three years later Toussaint forced the surrender of British troops that had occupied St.-Domingue since the end of 1793. During the naval war between the United States and France (1798–1800), he received U. S. military and commercial aid against the mulattoes in return for his opposition to the French.

The restoration of peace among France, the United States and Britain was the prelude to the downfall of Toussaint, who had proclaimed himself "First of the Blacks" and governor general for life of the entire island. The peace enabled Napoleon to send some 30,000 troops to restore French sovereignty. The French captured Toussaint in June 1802 and sent him to France, where he died in prison on April 7, 1803. But the French army did not prevail. Haitian independence was declared on Jan. 1, 1804.

RAYFORD W. LOGAN, *Howard University*

TOWAKONI INDIANS (tə-wä′kə-nē), a North American Indian tribe of the Caddoan linguistic stock, closely related to the Wichita Indians. When contacted by the French in the early 18th century, the Towakoni were along the Canadian River in what is now Oklahoma. Their history is primarily associated with the area along the Brazos and Trinity rivers in Texas. The Towakoni made treaties with French, Spanish, Republic of Texas, and U. S. officials.

Although the Towakoni were an agricultural people inhabiting villages of grass thatched houses and maintaining large fields of corn, they were frequently at war with the Osage, Lipan Apache, Comanche, and the Spanish. In the early part of the last century the Towakoni were allied with the Comanche in hostilities against Texas settlers. The group was much reduced by warfare and disease when they joined the Wichita in 1859 in Oklahoma. Descendants of the Towakoni may be found among the Wichita.

STEPHEN E. FERACA, *Author of "Wakinyan: Contemporary Teton Dakota Religion"*

TOWER OF BABEL. See BABEL, TOWER OF.

TOWER OF LONDON, an ancient fortress occupying nearly 13 acres (5 hectares) on the north side of the Thames River in southeast London. The fortress dates from about 1078, when William the Conqueror began erecting the central building, or keep. Because the keep became known as the White Tower, the name "Tower" was applied to the whole fortress that grew up around it. The White Tower was planned for William by Gundulf, a Norman who became bishop of Rochester.

THE TOWER OF LONDON—named for the White Tower, its central feature—has many buildings. It is surrounded by inner and outer walls, seen at right. The White Tower dates from about 1078, the walls from the 13th century.

ROTKIN, P. F. I.

Most of the fortress' walls and fortifications were built in the 13th century. The inner wall, with its 13 towers, was completed in Henry III's reign (1216–1272), and the outer wall in the reign (1272–1307) of Edward I. The modern entrance, completed in 1966, is over a stone causeway crossing the outer moat built by Edward I in 1278.

The Tower was occasionally used as a royal residence until the reign (1603–1625) of James I. It has been used both as a fortress and as a state prison. The first prisoner was Ranulf Flambard, bishop of Durham, one of the original builders of the White Tower. The latest was Rudolf Hess, a Nazi leader, who landed in Britain on an unauthorized mission in 1941.

There are two chapels within the Tower walls: the Norman St. John's Chapel, the oldest church in London, in the White Tower, and St. Peter ad Vincula, which was burned and rebuilt in 1512. Immediately south of the latter is Tower Green, the place of private execution, last used in 1601 for the execution of the Earl of Essex. Public execution took place on Tower Hill, outside the Tower walls.

The Crown Jewels are displayed in the Waterloo Barracks within the walls.

RICHARD E. WEBB
British Information Services, New York

TOWER OF SILENCE, a structure on which the Parsees of India expose the bodies of their dead until the bones have been picked clean by birds. See DEATH CUSTOMS AND RITES.

TOWHEE, tō'ē, any of six species of large, heavy-set, sparrowlike birds found only from central Canada south to Guatemala. Towhees vary in length from 6¾ to 9 inches (17–23 cm). They also vary in coloring from soft shades of tan and brown to contrasting patterns of black, white, and chestnut or black, white, and green.

Living in dense thickets, towhees spend a great deal of time foraging on the ground in search of food. Vegetable matter, primarily seeds, makes up about 70% of their diet, but they also eat many insects. Most towhees move along the ground by means of a bouncing hop, but one species—the green-tailed towhee (*Chlorura chlorura*) of the western mountains—often runs rapidly across the ground with its tail elevated.

The towhee's cup-shaped nest is made of small twigs and has a well-constructed lining of fine grasses, rootlets, and animal hair. The nest is usually placed on the ground or in low bushes. However, the brown towhee (*Pipilo fuscus*) has been known to place its nest 35 feet (11 meters) up in a tree. The two to five towhee eggs are white or bluish white with heavy spotting. Both parents care for the young.

Towhees are classified in the genera *Chlorura* and *Pipilo* of the finch and sparrow family Fringillidae of the order Passeriformes.

KENNETH E. STAGER
Los Angeles County Museum of Natural History

Red-eyed towhee (*Pipilo erythrophthalmus*)

ALLAN D. CRUICKSHANK, FROM NATIONAL AUDUBON SOCIETY

TOWN, in the legal sense, a unit of local self-government. In parts of the United States, mainly New England, the town is a territorial subdivision of a county. See MUNICIPAL GOVERNMENT; TOWN MEETING.

TOWN MEETING, a legislative assembly in which all townspeople may participate. A particularly American governmental institution, it is the most eulogized and least understood example of direct democracy. The town meeting was created by early New Englanders from a maze of antecedents. In modified form it remains the basic unit of local self-government in many towns there, particularly in Maine and Vermont. Outside New England the idea never took hold.

Originally town meetings were held weekly, and all qualified males were expected to attend. This arrangement proved onerous, and ever-increasing powers were delegated to elected administrators known as selectmen. The town meeting became an annual event, usually held in the spring. Special meetings may be called by the selectmen or when requested by a stated number of townspeople.

Agenda, Debate, and Voting. Every town meeting is "warned" by a special notice called the "warrant." No item may be voted on unless it has been included in the agenda by the selectmen or in response to a request by townsmen and then properly posted, published, or otherwise legally made known in advance. The first order of business at the annual meeting is the election of a presiding officer, or moderator, who also presides at any subsequent special meetings during his one-year term. Each item of the warrant is then taken up and either voted on, passed over, postponed, or tabled. Two types of items are usually considered: the election of officers, and such issues as the tax rate, town zoning or planning, and new programs. A slate of officers often is chosen in advance by an informal caucus of the local ruling clique.

Any legal voter, informed or not, may speak at length on a warning item. Voting is usually by a simple "aye" or "nay," by raising hands, or by scribbling on a scrap of paper. Some state laws permit and some require the secret ballot, which many critics consider to be detrimental to the town meeting principles of open debate and democratic consensus.

Analysis. The town meeting operated most effectively in a rural setting. It was once the social event of the year, with friends reviewing issues and all sitting down to a noon meal prepared by a local women's organization. Increasing population and complexity of issues have led some large towns, beginning with Brookline, Mass., in 1915, to adopt a representative town meeting, in which a limited number of elected representatives debate and vote, and which remains open to all. This system preserves the form of the town meeting but not the principle of direct democracy.

Another innovation that attempts to keep the town meeting concept alive in modern society is the so-called "pre-town meeting." It is held on the evening before the prescribed day. Townspeople can attend without losing a day's work and participate in the debate instead of leaving decisions to a small group. The actual town meeting, under these circumstances, is largely devoted to formal voting for officers and on issues that legally must be decided on the specified day.

The question remains whether the town meeting is an anachronism in the face of the need for effective local government. An affirmative answer would mean that America has lost one of its most cherished institutions.

ANDREW E. NUQUIST, *University of Vermont*
Author, "Town Government in Vermont"

TOWNES, Charles Hard (1915–), American physicist, who is best known for his work on the maser. He shared the Nobel Prize in physics in 1964 with the Russian physicists Nikolai Basov and Aleksandr Prokhorov for "fundamental work in the field of quantum electronics, which has led to the construction of oscillators and amplifiers on the maser-laser principle."

Townes was born in Greenville, S. C., on July 28, 1915. He graduated from Furman University in 1935 and received a Ph. D. in physics from the California Institute of Technology in 1939. During World War II he worked on microwave spectroscopy and radar. In 1948 he joined Columbia University, where, from 1950 to 1952, he was director of the Columbia Radiation Laboratory and, from 1952 to 1955, chairman of the physics department.

While teaching at Columbia and training a generation of microwave spectroscopists, Townes continued his work on the microwave spectroscopy of gases, and in 1951 he conceived and, with the help of two students, built the first successful ammonia maser. In 1958 he and A. L. Schawlow outlined the principles of the optical maser and laser in a paper that has stimulated important developments in the field.

In 1959, Townes left Columbia to become director of the Institute of Defense Analysis. Two years later he was made professor of physics and provost of the Massachusetts Institute of Technology. He directed research in nonlinear optics at M. I. T. until 1967, when he became a professor at large at the University of California. There he became engaged in an active program of research in radio and infrared astronomy.

H. J. ZEIGER
Massachusetts Institute of Technology

TOWNSEND, Francis Everett (1867–1960), who originated the Townsend Plan for old-age pensions in the United States during the Great Depression. His plan focused attention on the plight of the aged, assuring inclusion of old-age insurance in the Social Security Act of 1935.

Townsend was born near Fairbury, Ill., on Jan. 13, 1867, graduated from the Omaha Medical College in 1903, and became a general practitioner in Belle Fourche, S. Dak., and in Long Beach, Calif. His experience sensitized him to the problems of poverty. When a change of administration in 1933 cost him his job as assistant medical officer for Long Beach, he spoke out on the hopeless condition of the aged poor.

His plan, outlined in the Long Beach *Press-Telegram* on Sept. 30, 1933, proposed (1) a pension of $150 a month—later $200—to all citizens who retired at age 60 and promised to spend the money within 30 days, and (2) a national sales tax—later a transaction tax—to finance the pension. Intended as a Depression recovery program, the plan was popular, notably among older business and professional people and farmers.

Passage of the Social Security Act strengthened the movement briefly because of the inadequacy of benefit payments. The Townsend movement—organized in local clubs—claimed 5 million members at its peak. But the increasing effectiveness of social security, dissension within the organization, and Townsend's support of the Union Party in the 1936 presidential election contributed to the decline of his movement. By 1941 it ceased to be politically important. Yet Townsend had an undeniable charisma, and he retained a following of one million at his death in Los Angeles on Sept. 1, 1960.

ROBERT L. DANIEL, *Ohio University*

TOWNSHEND, toun'zənd, **Charles** (1675–1738), English political leader. He was born on April 18, 1675, the eldest son of the 1st Viscount Townshend. Succeeding to the peerage in 1687, he took his seat in the House of Lords in 1697 as a Tory, but soon went over to the Whigs. As ambassador at The Hague from 1709 to 1711 he negotiated a treaty with the Dutch for which he was censured by the Tory House of Commons in 1712 for exceeding his instructions.

Appointed secretary of state on the accession of George I in 1714, Townshend took the lead in the new Whig administration, with his brother-in-law, Robert Walpole, as second-in-command in the Commons. Ousted by a court intrigue, he went into opposition with Walpole, with whom he returned to office as lord president in 1720.

From 1722, Townshend and Walpole were the joint heads of the ministry. Townshend, since 1721 secretary of state, was the senior partner because of his greater influence at court. The situation was reversed on George II's accession in 1727. In Walpole's words, the firm of Townshend and Walpole became Walpole and Townshend, whereupon a rupture ensued. Resigning in 1730, Townshend devoted himself to agricultural improvements, notably the use of turnips as a rotation crop, for which he became known as "Turnip Townshend." He died in Raynham, Norfolk, on June 21, 1738.

R. R. SEDGWICK, *Editor*
"History of Parliament 1715–1754"

TOWNSHEND, toun'zənd, **Charles** (1725–1767), English political leader. He was born on Aug. 27, 1725, the second son of the 3d Viscount Townshend. Entering Parliament in 1747, he was a junior lord of trade from 1749 to 1754, when he was promoted to the admiralty board. In 1755 he went into opposition with the elder Pitt, who rewarded him with a sinecure on coming to power in 1756.

On George III's accession in 1760, Townshend became allied with the King's favorite, Lord Bute, who made him secretary-at-war in 1761 and 1st lord of trade in 1763. Declining an offer of the admiralty from Bute's successor, George Grenville, later that year, Townshend was out of office until 1765, when he accepted the post of paymaster general. He retained it under the Rockingham administration. On the formation of the Chatham (Pitt) administration in 1766, he was appointed chancellor of the exchequer. In this capacity, Townshend was responsible for imposing duties on America (see TOWNSHEND ACTS). He died in London on Sept. 4, 1767.

R. R. SEDGWICK, *Editor, "History of Parliament 1715–1754"*

TOWNSHEND ACTS, measures imposed by Britain on its American colonies. Sponsored by Charles Townshend, chancellor of the exchequer, they were passed by Parliament between June 26 and July 2, 1767.

The Revenue Act placed duties on glass, china, red and white lead, painters' colors, paper and pasteboards, and tea imported into America. Its purpose was to provide salaries for some colonial officials so that the provincial assemblies could not coerce them by withholding wages.

A companion measure created a five-man board of customs commissioners, with headquarters in Boston, to collect the duties and provide close supervision of all trade. Haughty and arbitrary, these commissioners rigidly enforced all acts of trade, causing riots in Boston in 1768.

To force New York into compliance with the Quartering Act, Parliament also passed the New York Restraining Act, which, in effect, suspended the provincial legislature until it provided "his Majesty's troops . . . with all such necessaries" as required by British law.

After colonists began to boycott British goods, Parliament altered the revenue measure on March 5, 1770. Duties on all items except tea were repealed. The tea tax was retained because it was the most lucrative and to show Americans that Parliament still had the right to tax them.

ROBERT J. CHAFFIN
Wisconsin State University, Oshkosh

TOWNSHIP, in parts of the United States, a political subdivision of a county. The township in some Eastern and Midwestern states is a unit of local government equivalent to the town in New England. See UNITED STATES—*State and Local Government.*

TOWNSVILLE, a city in Australia, is a commercial center and seaport in northeastern Queensland, on the shore of Cleveland Bay.

Townsville is on the coastal railroad, a branch of which goes westward from the city, through cattle-raising districts, to the important mining center of Mount Isa. Copper ore is treated at an electrolytic refinery. Other industries include food processing, lumber milling, cement works, and railroad maintenance.

Townsville was established after 1865 and became a municipality in 1866. Harbor facilities were constructed when gold was discovered in the hinterland in the 1870's. The city was a base for Australian and U. S. forces during World War II. Population: (1966) 58,847.

R. M. YOUNGER
Author of "Australia and the Australians"

TOWSON, tou'sən, is an unincorporated area in northeastern Maryland, the seat of Baltimore county. It is situated immediately north of the city of Baltimore. Population: 77,809.

TOXEMIA, tok-sē'mē-ə, is any of a wide range of disorders usually caused by the presence of toxic substances in the body. Toxemias are generally serious conditions and require careful hospital management. The kidneys are almost invariably affected. If kidney failure occurs, uremia and heart failure often follow.

There are many causes of toxemia. Patients with severe infections, such as pneumonia, meningitis, cholera, or typhoid fever, may develop toxemias caused by the toxins, or poisons, produced by the invading microorganisms. The ingestion of poisonous chemicals and metals, such as iodine and lead, are also common causes.

Toxemia of pregnancy, also known as eclampsia, is a metabolic disorder of unknown cause. It occurs during the last three months of pregnancy, and among the contributing factors are excessive weight gain and increased salt retention. The symptoms of eclampsia include an increase in blood pressure, the presence of albumin in the urine, and swelling of the face, fingers, and ankles. The woman may also experience visual disturbances, headaches, and abdominal discomfort accompanied by vomiting. Convulsions may also occur. Toxemia of pregnancy occurs in about 5 out of every 100 pregnancies. It is more common in women over the age of 35 and in women who are pregnant for the first time. See also ECLAMPSIA.

REAUMUR S. DONNALLY, M.D.
Washington Hospital Center, Washington, D.C.

TOXICOLOGY, tok-sə-kol'ə-jē, deals with the harmful effects of chemicals on living organisms. Every person comes in contact with a large variety of chemicals, many of which may be harmful if not used properly. In the United States alone, approximately 9,000 deaths are caused by poisoning every year, and it is estimated that there are at least 100 times as many nonfatal cases of poisoning.

Branches of Toxicology. There are three principal branches of toxicology. *Industrial toxicology* studies the harmful effects of chemical pollutants in the air and water, as well as of chemicals present in the working environment and around the home. *Economic toxicology* deals with chemicals used as drugs, food additives, cosmetics, pesticides, and veterinary drugs. *Forensic toxicology* is concerned with the medical-legal aspects of harmful chemicals, especially when death or serious injury results from exposure to them.

Toxicological Classification of Chemicals. Every chemical can be classified according to its potency, or toxicity. The six basic classes of chemicals are extremely toxic, highly toxic, moderately toxic, slightly toxic, relatively nontoxic, and relatively harmless.

"Poison" is defined as a chemical that is highly or extremely toxic. This means that small amounts are capable of producing serious harm or death. A chemical is labeled "poison" if it is known to produce death in 50% of a group of experimental animals within 48 hours after 50 milligrams per kilogram of body weight is given by mouth to each animal. For adult humans, this is equivalent to about one teaspoonful.

Procedures and Techniques. The techniques and procedures for studying the harmful effects of chemicals involve the administration of chemicals to experimental animals or to isolated living cells or tissues. A wide variety of animals are used in toxicological experiments. Among the smaller animals often used are rats, mice, and guinea pigs. The larger animals include monkeys and farm animals.

There are three basic types of toxicological studies. *Acute studies* involve the administration of a chemical only once, followed by observation of the animals for a period of several days. *Prolonged,* or *subacute, studies* involve the repeated administration of a chemical, usually at daily intervals for periods not less than 90 days. *Chronic studies* are conducted for at least a year and sometimes continue for the entire life-span of the experimental animals. In these studies the chemical is administered daily or five days a week.

Only when animal studies are completed and reasonable safety can be assured by extrapolation of the animal data to humans may limited studies be performed on people. Examples of such studies are those for determining the irritating effects of chemicals on human skin.

When chemicals are believed to be the cause of illness or death, samples of the victim's blood or urine or postmortem samples of tissue are submitted to a toxicological chemist. He conducts chemical analyses for detecting the presence of any harmful chemicals and determining their amounts.

TED A. LOOMIS, M. D.
Author of "Essentials of Toxicology"

TOXIN, tok'sən, may mean any poison, but the term is usually applied to poisons produced by living organisms. One of the most potent of all toxins is botulin, which is produced by the bacterium that causes botulism. An example of a toxin produced by higher plants is abrin, which is found in jequirity beans, the seeds of the Indian licorice plant. A well-known type of animal toxin is snake venom. See ANTITOXIN; TOXICOLOGY.

TOXOPLASMOSIS, tok-sō-plaz-mō'sis, is a protozoan infection caused by *Toxoplasma gondii.* This parasite infects a wide range of domestic and wild animals, including pigs, sheep, cattle, dogs, cats, and rabbits. Humans may acquire the parasites by eating infected meat that is not adequately cooked.

Acquired toxoplasmosis is usually asymptomatic but is sometimes characterized by fever, weakness, and enlarged lymph nodes that may remain swollen for months. Sometimes it is characterized by eye disease in one eye. In severe cases of acquired toxoplasmosis there may be complications such as hepatitis, pneumonia, myocarditis, or inflammation of the brain.

If a pregnant woman acquires the organisms, her child may be born with congenital toxoplasmosis. The brain is the organ most often infected in congenital toxoplasmosis, and mental retardation and blindness in one or both eyes often result.

Toxoplasmosis is treated with sulfa drugs and pyrimethamine. Although these drugs are beneficial they carry a high risk of damage to the blood-forming tissues.

VERNON KNIGHT, M. D.
Baylor College of Medicine

THE METROPOLITAN MUSEUM OF ART, ROGERS FUND

EGYPTIAN IVORY mechanical dog of about 400 B. C. The dog's mouth opens by means of lever action.

TOY. Originally, a "toy" was a pretty trifle made for adults rather than children. Some of the earliest dollhouses were elaborate cabinets furnished with decorative miniatures in glass, silver, or porcelain. Religious crèche scenes—with the Nativity group enlarged to include market or street tableaus—encouraged the production of tiny "toy" figures, which sometimes fell into the hands of children. By the 19th century the word came to denote more specifically a child's plaything.

Play is a natural means of learning for young animals. Toys can be seen as the tools of the human child, training him in physical skills, developing his imagination, and stimulating his thinking. A young child will use natural objects as he copies the actions of his parents. A stick becomes a hammer, a gun, a telescope, or a horse. Children do not usually make elaborate toys. It is the adults who from earliest times seem to have elaborated on simple playthings either for fun or for commercial profit.

Toys imitate in miniature the world familiar to children. Toys thus differ according to the part of the world where the children who use them live, the nature of the society, the period of time in which they grew up, and the materials available. Toys are valuable as a record of social history. Most countries are alive to the importance of such history and feature toys in

CYPRIOTE TERRACOTTA horse on wheels with vessels in side panniers, of about 1200–1000 B. C.

THE METROPOLITAN MUSEUM OF ART, THE CESNOLA COLLECTION

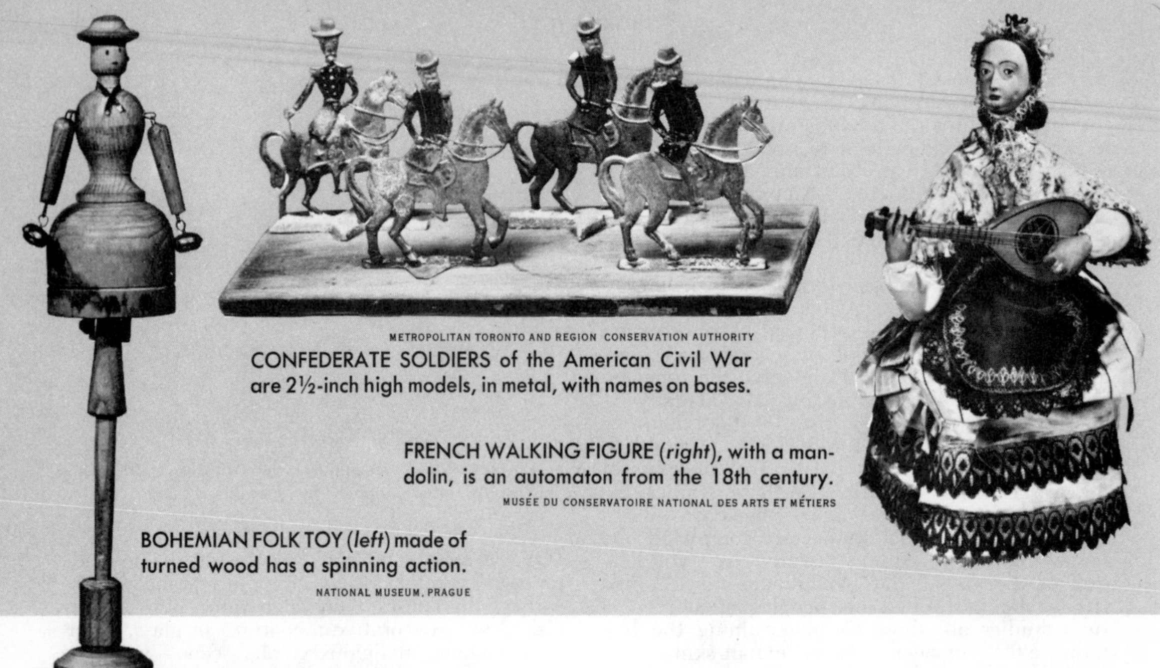

METROPOLITAN TORONTO AND REGION CONSERVATION AUTHORITY

CONFEDERATE SOLDIERS of the American Civil War are 2½-inch high models, in metal, with names on bases.

FRENCH WALKING FIGURE (*right*), with a mandolin, is an automaton from the 18th century.

MUSÉE DU CONSERVATOIRE NATIONAL DES ARTS ET MÉTIERS

BOHEMIAN FOLK TOY (*left*) made of turned wood has a spinning action.

NATIONAL MUSEUM, PRAGUE

THE FITZWILLIAM MUSEUM

JAPANESE MOVABLE TOYS are depicted in a woodcut reproduced on this early 19th century fan.

TOY ELEPHANT dating from about 1829 represents a type of stuffed toy popular with young children.

MUSEUM OF THE CITY OF NEW YORK

museum collections. Dolls portray costumes and fashions of the past. Toy vehicles show the evolution of transportation from carts to carriages to mechanical power. Miniature swords and helmets of the 18th century gave way to a variety of model pistols and rifles a century later, and in the 20th century to space-ray guns in a world of science fiction.

Another example of the relation of toys to social custom is that an underlying religious or superstitious motive frequently prompted the giving of a toy. A silver rattle made in the form of a cross with bells to frighten evil spirits or a coral spur as a talisman against witches were designed both to amuse and protect infants.

Primitive and Ancient Toys. Many children grow up without toys. This was especially the case in primitive societies where children were put to work early. Toys excavated from graves of early civilizations, placed there in belief that they would serve dead children in their afterlife, give valuable clues to the materials and techniques of the period. Simple principles of leverage were used for working toys, and platforms on wheels provided crude pull-along toys as long ago as 3000 B.C. in Egypt. Molded clay was baked in shapes for hollow whistles, rattles in bird, fish, and animal patterns, jointed puppets and dolls, tops, balls, marbles, bowling pins, and gaming counters or beads. Evidence of toys from Greek and Roman times is provided by illustrations on pottery vases, which show children playing with hoops, hobby horses, balls, and knucklebones. Inflated bladders and rubber balls (known in ancient Mexico) added a third dimension to ball play, from which evolved a whole new area of sport.

Pre-Christian literature records that at puberty Greek and Roman children dedicated toys to the shrine of a god or goddess as a sort of ritual relinquishment of childhood. Doll-like images discovered at ancient temples more probably were votive offerings than toys, just as some doll-like figures from Egypt represented fertility tokens.

Oriental Toys. The history of toys goes back as far in the East as in the West. Some of the earliest toys of any civilization were found in

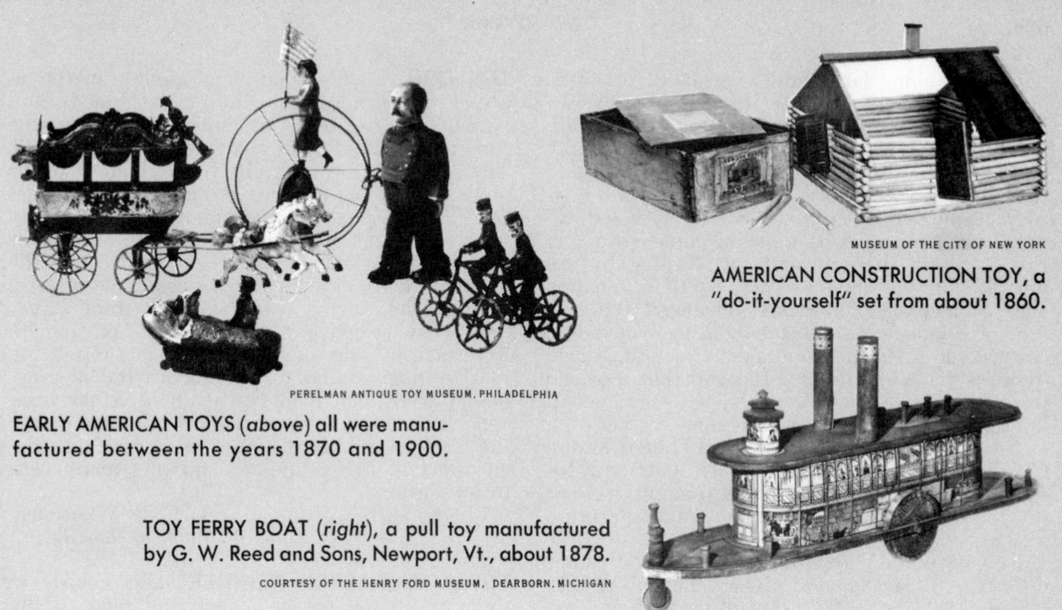

MUSEUM OF THE CITY OF NEW YORK

AMERICAN CONSTRUCTION TOY, a "do-it-yourself" set from about 1860.

PERELMAN ANTIQUE TOY MUSEUM, PHILADELPHIA

EARLY AMERICAN TOYS (*above*) all were manufactured between the years 1870 and 1900.

TOY FERRY BOAT (*right*), a pull toy manufactured by G. W. Reed and Sons, Newport, Vt., about 1878.

COURTESY OF THE HENRY FORD MUSEUM, DEARBORN, MICHIGAN

India. Thirteenth century Chinese paintings of toy peddlers show the great variety and early tradition of folk toys in the East. It is impossible to trace how far back the pattern for some of the clever principles stretches: nodding-head animals, whirring birds on a string, snakes made of jointed wood sections, and weighted tumbler dolls. There also were many novelties made from frail materials such as bamboo, silk, paper, and papier mâché.

The Japanese are great lovers of children. At festivals for girls (March 3) and boys (May 5), new toys are given and family "heirloom" toys displayed. Both are associated with homage to the emperor and remembrance of the past tradition and history of Japan. Interest by foreign collectors has caused a great renaissance in doll making and folk toys. Kite flying is a popular sport in the East. Kites are made in a countless variety of shapes, some imitating birds, reflecting man's original aspirations to conquer space.

Medieval and Early Modern Toys. Medieval toys in Europe matched the society that used them. For the poor classes there were simple folk toys distributed by peddlers or at fair booths. For children of noble birth, noted craftsmen made gifts including dolls with elaborate trousseaus and miniature suits of armor, weapons, and tourney toys. Few early toys survive. Old prints or paintings and written records supply the main evidence of toys popular in medieval Europe. Dolls molded from clay or carved from wood and little pieces of furniture were common. Hobbyhorses, animals, soldiers, tops, rattles, bowling pins, windmills, bubble pipes, stilts, skates, and balls were plentiful. A large toymaking center developed in southern Germany, and records show that guilds were organized among toymakers as early as the 15th century. Nuremberg, with its command of trade routes, became famous for distributing toys made in the surrounding richly forested districts. Fine dolls, Noah's arks, forts, stables, puppets in wood, a variety of musical instruments, small weapons, and dollhouse furnishings became the stock in trade of industry. Advertisements in early New England newspapers show that toys from Europe were among shiploads of goods. By the early 19th century immigrant toymakers were establishing their own skills in America.

The invention of clockwork was adapted to toys, which had previously been powered by physical means (water, sand, hot air, or the hand). In the 18th century there was a vogue for ingenious life-size figures (androids) that played instruments or performed for public exhibition.

In the 19th century, aptly called the "Golden Age of Toys," such automata were adapted as elaborate toys. Walking dolls, moving animals, and performing groups, often with musical accompaniment made their appearance. When the age of steam brought railways, ships, and cars, clockwork replicas followed. Newly found scientific principles were reflected also in such optical toys as the kaleidoscope. The magic lantern with color slides, a 17th century wonder, was reproduced in miniature for the nursery. With the advance of industry, scientific toys taught principles of magnetism, steam power, and elec-

EDUCATIONAL TOYS in the 1970's included kits for building such structures as bridges and geodesic domes.

CREATIVE PLAYTHINGS, PRINCETON AND LOS ANGELES

tricity. Working lathes and even model distilleries and factories ushered in the mechanical age. By the end of the 19th century, miniature railways on tracks were made in Germany, England, and the United States with an engineering skill that appealed to men as well as boys.

Modern Developments. Revolutionary educational methods such as those of Montessori and Froebel, with their precepts of learning by doing, taught that an interested child is a happy one. Kindergarten methods influenced the pattern of toys and introduced building blocks and constructor sets, color mosaics, and educational jigsaws. Games purely for fun and skill replaced those of a dreary "moral" type. Ornamental building bricks in wood and stone came from Germany and log cabins from the United States. Clever construction games were patented—for example, the lovable "Humpty-Dumpty" circus in wood in 1903. Structural metal engineering sets were introduced, such as "Meccano" in Britain in 1901 and "Erector" in the United States in 1913. Boxed games often reflected special technical interests such as chemistry and geology. Sets for glassblowing and experiments in the wireless and the telephone appeared in the early 1920's.

At the end of the 19th century, new factories arose to mass-produce toys, and fine stores were established to sell them. Development of color printing brought a wave of card and paper toys and games. Miniature toy soldiers, first invented in flat relief in Germany in 1775, were rivaled by the hollow-cast models introduced in England in 1893. Except for some model cars and items for collectors, plastic is now used for most miniatures.

In the 20th century, soft toys also became popular. The "Teddy Bear" made his debut in 1903 and has remained a favorite ever since. Advanced thinking in child welfare influenced the shape of toys, and special standards of safety and hygiene are enforced today. Vinyl plastic and foam rubber revolutionized the toy industry, and a special accent on activity and communal toys such as climbing frames, trampolines, splash pools, and sand trays has developed. World War I cut German production of toys and encouraged the United States and Britain to become major centers for the manufacture of toys. However, after World War II Japan became the world's largest producer of toys.

At various times in history, "war toys" have been attacked for teaching children to be aggressive. This concern came to the fore again in the 1960's and 1970's, when educators, sociologists, psychologists, and parents expressed fears over the effects that model guns, miniature tanks, and the like have on children. They believed that violent play might be a factor in the acceptance of violence as a means of settling problems in society. Many toy manufacturers began giving renewed attention to toys that have peaceful educational value, and a new interest developed in using toys to teach school subjects.

See also DOLL.

MARY L. HILLIER
Author of "Pageant of Toys"

Further Reading: Culff, Robert, *The World of Toys* (London 1969); Fritsch, K. E., and Bachmann, M., *An Illustrated History of Toys* (London 1968); Hertz, Louis H., *The Toy Collector* (New York 1969); Hillier, Mary L., *Pageant of Toys* (London 1965); McClintock, Marshall and Inez, *Toys In America* (Washington, D. C., 1961).

TOY DOG, a very small dog used primarily as a pet and companion. About 30 breeds and varieties of toy dogs are known, of which the American Kennel Club recognizes (registers) 16. Toy dogs range in weight from about 2 to 18 pounds (1–8 kg) and are about 6 to 11½ inches (15–29 cm) high at the shoulder. Coats vary greatly in color and may be smooth, rough, or long, or there may be no coat at all, as in the Mexican hairless dog. Toy dogs have diverse origins, but many were derived from larger breeds by selective matings. The Pomeranian, for example, was once a large spitz-type dog.

Toy dogs similar to the modern Italian greyhound were known in Egypt about 5,000 years ago. Toy dogs were present in Europe before the 1300's, and the Chinese were breeding the ancestors of the Pekingese and pug many centuries earlier.

C. G. E. WIMHURST
Author of "Book of Toy Dogs"

TOY MANCHESTER TERRIER, also known as the English toy terrier (black and tan) or the miniature black-and-tan terrier. The toy Manchester terrier, developed by selective breeding of small-sized Manchester terriers, weighs up to

EVELYN M. SHAFER

Toy Manchester terrier

12 pounds (5.4 kg). It resembles the Manchester terrier, except that its ears must be naturally erect rather than either erect, rosebud, or cropped.

In 1938 the Toy Manchester Club of America introduced the name "Toy Manchester" for the breed. Up until 1959 the Manchester terrier and the toy Manchester terrier were registered by the American Kennel Club as separate breeds, although interbreeding was permitted. They are now regarded as a single breed, with two varieties: standard and toy.

THELMA R. CRABTREE
American Manchester Terrier Club

TOYAMA, tō-yä-mä, is a city in west central Honshu, Japan, about 125 miles (200 km) northwest of Tokyo. The chief producer of patent medicines in Japan, it also has cotton, synthetic fiber, and chemical industries. It is the capital of Toyama prefecture. The prefecture, with an area of 1,642 square miles (4,252 sq km), borders the Sea of Japan and has a mountainous interior. The coastal plain is an important rice-growing area. Population (1965): city, 239,810; prefecture, 1,025,465.

TOYNBEE, toin′bē, **Arnold** (1852–1883), English social reformer and economic historian, who had a great effect on English reform movements both by his work and by his example. He was born in London on Aug. 23, 1852, and educated at Balliol College, Oxford, where he became a lecturer in 1878 and bursar in 1881. He died in Wimbledon on March 9, 1883.

Toynbee is noted for his efforts to establish housing, libraries, and parks for the working-class poor of the Whitechapel district of London, where Toynbee Hall is named in his honor. In his lectures to working-class audiences he proposed programs of municipal socialism and encouraged the development of trade unions and cooperatives. His *Lectures on the Industrial Revolution of the Eighteenth Century in England* (published in 1884) was the first work to examine this period as a single historical event.

PHILIP J. LEONHARD
The City College, New York

TOYNBEE, toin′bē, **Arnold J.** (1889–), British historian, who is best known for his monumental *A Study of History*, a philosophical investigation of the origin, growth, and breakdown of civilizations. Toynbee was born in London on April 14, 1889. He graduated from Balliol College, Oxford, trained in the classics. Then he walked for nine months through Crete and the Athos peninsula, musing on the mortality of civilizations. He served in the British foreign office during World Wars I and II and was a delegate at the Paris Peace Conferences in 1919 and 1946.

Toynbee was professor of Byzantine and modern Greek language, literature, and history at the University of London and then became director of studies at the Royal Institute of International Affairs in London. From 1920 to 1946 he helped write the annual volumes of *A Survey of International Affairs*.

Toynbee's 12-volume *A Study of History* appeared between 1934 and 1960. It was published in 1- and 2-volume abridgments in 1946 and 1957, respectively, prepared by D. C. Somervell. Toynbee was inspired to plan the work by his belief that the modern world, beginning in World War I, was entering a time of troubles comparable to those of Greece in the Peloponnesian War.

Toynbee maintains that growth is a process of challenge and response, and success or failure of societies depends on how well they meet human and environmental challenges. Of the 26 civilizations he identifies, 16 are already dead, 3 are arrested, leaving 7 that are recombining into 5: Western; Orthodox Christian, including southeast Europe; Islamic; Hindu; and Far Eastern, including China, Japan, and Korea. Each civilization is studied in stages of genesis, growth, breakdown, and disintegration.

Toynbee's study provoked considerable criticism, mainly for its arbitrary hypotheses, factual errors, and overreliance on religion as a regenerative force. Toynbee's examination of recent history in such books as *Civilization on Trial* (1948) and *The World and the West* (1953) also sparked widespread debate.

For critical evaluations of his work, see M. F. Ashley Montague's *Toynbee and History* (1956), and for Toynbee's reply see *Reconsiderations* (1960).

KENNETH W. THOMPSON, *Author of "Political Realism" and "The Moral Issue"*

TOYOHASHI, tō-yō-hä-shē, is a city in Japan, in Aichi prefecture, about 40 miles (60 km) southeast of Nagoya. The city is a manufacturing center with a large output of silk, cotton, and synthetic textiles. Silkworms are raised extensively in the surrounding countryside.

Toyohashi was formerly a fortified town and stronghold of the Matsudaira clan. It was a station on the historic Tokaido highway between Kyoto and Edo (Tokyo) and is today a stop on the New Tokaido high-speed rail line. Population: (1967) 249,000.

T. H. EVERETT

Toyon (*Heteromeles arbutifolia*)

TOYON, toi′on, an evergreen shrub or small tree of California. The toyon (*Heteromeles arbutifolia* or *Photinia arbutifolia*) is also called the California holly and Christmasberry.

The toyon grows to a height of 30 feet (9 meters) and has shiny, leathery, dark green leaves that are from 2.5 to 6 inches (63–152 mm) long and have sharply toothed edges. The bark is smooth and light gray in color. The 5-petaled white flowers, which are a half inch (13 mm) or less in diameter, are borne in large showy clusters in the late spring. The fruit is a bright red, fleshy, berrylike pome about a third of an inch (6.5 mm) in diameter. It ripens during December and January. The laws of the state of California forbid the gathering of the fruit of the wild toyon.

The Chinese photinia (*Photinia serrulata*) is a close relative of the toyon. Its flowers and fruit are similar to those of the toyon but its leaves are larger and more finely toothed. It is native to China and Taiwan.

RICHARD A. CRILEY
University of Hawaii

TOYOTOMI HIDEYOSHI, tō-yō-tō-mē hē-de-yō-shē (1536–1598), was a Japanese warrior chieftain who unified Japan after a century of extreme decentralization and near-anarchy. He was probably the greatest military genius in his country's history.

Career. Hideyoshi rose to power from the lowest ranks of the army of Oda Nobunaga, a daimyo (regional baron) who imposed his control over much of central Japan. The son of a peasant, Hideyoshi rose to field commander by sheer ability and established himself as a preeminent strategist and battle technician. When Nobunaga was assassinated in 1582 by one of his leading commanders, Hideyoshi avenged his death and resumed the task of unifying Japan.

Like Nobunaga, Hideyoshi made the central provinces his base, and he built his principal fortress in Osaka. In a series of campaigns during the period 1582–1590 he brought all of Japan under his control. His final years were darkened by two disastrous attempts to invade Korea, in 1592 and 1597. He died in 1598 while the second invasion was still in progress and left only an infant son as his successor. Within two years another daimyo, Tokugawa Ieyasu, had emerged as the new military ruler of Japan.

Policies. Hideyoshi employed as his national administrators those daimyo who had been his personal vassals from the days before his rise to power. He maintained control over the other daimyo by means of a variety of techniques, including outright threats, marriage pacts, the shifting of domains, and the retention of hostages.

Although Hideyoshi himself had risen from the peasantry, it was he who ultimately affirmed the strict class division of samurai (warriors) and peasants on a national basis. In a series of decrees, he directed that all peasants should remain in the countryside and engage solely in farming; samurai, on the other hand, should reside in towns in the exclusive service of their warrior overlords. To ensure samurai monopoly of the military profession and to preclude further uprisings among the peasantry, which had been common during the medieval period just ended, Hideyoshi also conducted a national "sword hunt" to confiscate all weapons in the possession of the peasantry.

A unique feature of the 16th century in Japan was the coming of Europeans for the first time. The Portuguese arrived in 1542, and several decades later they were joined by the Spanish. European-style firearms, not previously known to the Japanese, came into great demand among the daimyo, and both Nobunaga and Hideyoshi won important battles with them. These weapons undoubtedly would have changed methods of warfare in Japan even more drastically and would have terminated the feudal fighting privileges of the samurai class. But Western firearms remained in scarce supply until about 1600, when civil conflict was finally brought to an end by the establishment of the lasting Tokugawa hegemony.

Besides firearms, the Europeans brought trade and Christianity to Japan. Following Nobunaga's lead, Hideyoshi authorized official trading ships under special "vermillion seals" and these Japanese craft sailed the waters throughout East and Southeast Asia during the late 16th century. However, he did not regard trade with the Europeans as an unmixed blessing. He became increasingly alarmed by the concomitant proselytizing of Christianity, which he considered socially subversive. Yet Hideyoshi could never bring himself to outlaw Christianity fully and thus risk the loss of European trade.

H. PAUL VARLEY
Author of "The Samurai"

TPN, or triphosphopyridine nucleotide, is a coenzyme involved in the oxidation of foodstuffs in the cell. It is also known as NADP, or nicotinamide adenine dinucleotide phosphate. See NAD.

TRABERT, trā'bûrt, **Tony** (1930–), American tennis player, who was the top-ranked U. S. player in 1953 and in 1955, the year he won the U. S. national singles championship.

Marion Anthony Trabert was born in Cincinnati, Ohio, on Aug. 16, 1930. He began to play tennis at the age of six and won the intercollegiate championship in 1951 while a student at the University of Cincinnati. In 1953 he won the U. S. singles title, dethroning E. Victor Seixas, Jr. The next year he shared the indoor doubles title with Seixas and won the French singles championship. In 1955 his honors included the U. S., British, and French singles crowns, the U. S. indoor singles championship, and, with Seixas, the indoor doubles title. Trabert was a member of the U. S. Davis Cup teams from 1951 through 1955. He began to play professionally in 1955, touring with Pancho Gonzales, and retired in 1963.

NEIL L. AMDUR, *New York "Times"*

TRABZON, trab-zän', a Turkish port on the Black Sea, is known also outside Turkey as Trebizond. Its ancient name was Trapezus. The old city was situated on a high plateau between two deep gorges descending to a bay where formerly the harbor was located. The ruined walls of the citadel that occupied this elevation can still be seen, and today it is the site of a military radar installation. Trabzon is closed in on the south by the lofty arc of the Pontic Mountains, and access to the hinterland is through the Zigana Pass, which connects with routes leading to the eastern provinces and Iran. The coastal road affords good motor communication with the other cities along the Black Sea.

Modern Trabzon is a fairly prosperous city and the capital of the agricultural province of the same name. Its mountainous encirclement has deprived it of a rail link, and it has steadily lost its commercial importance to Samsun.

History. It is as a commercial city that Trabzon figures throughout history, since Greek traders from Sinope first founded a colony there in the 8th century B. C. In the Mithridatic wars of the 1st century B. C. it fell to the Romans. Although captured by the Goths in 260 A. D., it was restored in Byzantine times and became a flourishing center of Christianity.

The Seljuk Turks were never able to penetrate Trabzon, and when the Crusaders captured Constantinople in 1204, a splinter Greek kingdom was established at Trabzon by Alexius Comnenus. It survived until its conquest by the Ottomans in 1461. During this time it remained a busy port for the Black Sea trade of the Genoese and Venetians. Population: (1965), of the city, 65,516; of the province, 595,782. See also TREBIZOND, EMPIRE OF.

JOHN R. WALSH, *University of Edinburgh*

TRACER, Isotopic, an isotope of an element that is used to study the paths of certain atoms or molecules in chemical and biochemical reactions. The isotopes used as tracers must be easily detectable. Most are radioactive. However, stable nonradioactive isotopes are also used, particularly deuterium, or heavy hydrogen, which is detectable by its density, and carbon-13, which is detectable by nuclear magnetic resonance.

Radioactive isotopes of most elements are available and can be used in a great variety of experiments. Isotopes with a very low level of radioactivity can be detected and measured with great precision. When handled with proper precautions, these isotopes present no health threat.

The most widely used radioactive isotope is carbon-14, which was discovered in 1946 by the American chemist Willard F. Libby, and is employed in biochemical experiments. For example, an atom of carbon-14 can be built into a drug molecule at a specific place. It is then possible to see how the drug is broken up in the body by finding which of its products are radioactive. The mechanism of photosynthesis in green plants has been studied in the same manner by using carbon dioxide labeled with carbon-14.

Radioactive iodine is used to observe the movement of iodine in the thyroid gland. Radioactive phosphorus is used to study the metabolism of phosphorus in growing plants. Radioactive isotopes of metals are used to detect wear in engine parts. Isotopes are used in chemistry to study such phenomena as diffusion and solubility of sparingly soluble salts. The movement of sand in an ocean harbor in Argentina was traced by dumping a ton of sand carrying adsorbed radioactive silver and following the spread of radioactivity. See also ISOTOPE.

HAROLD F. WALTON
University of Colorado

TRACERY, trās′ə-rē, in architecture, is a pattern of openings cut through a plane of stone within an arch or created within such an area by interlocking bars of stone. Its primary function is to hold glass in windows. A similar design carved in wood as decoration for screens or choir stalls is also called tracery.

There are two kinds of tracery: plate and bar. Plate tracery characterized the early Gothic period in France during the late 12th and early 13th centuries. At Chartres Cathedral, for example, the clerestory windows of the nave contain circular and partly circular openings pierced through a plate of stone, as cookies are cut from a sheet of dough.

About 1225, plate tracery gave way to bar tracery, as at Amiens Cathedral, with the upper part of the window subdivided by interlocking stone bars. The windows of the Angel Choir at Lincoln Cathedral in the English Decorated period (1250–1350) were filled with geometric designs of circles and segments of circles. These gave way in the early 14th century to curvilinear motifs with reverse curves in the bars—a style widely used in the French Flamboyant period (15th century). About 1350 the Perpendicular style with vertical lines and panels appeared in England, as in the east window of Gloucester Cathedral.

EVERARD M. UPJOHN
Columbia University

TRACHEA, trā′kē-ə, or *windpipe*, the long narrow tube that carries air from the back of the mouth to the bronchi of the lungs. See LUNGS; RESPIRATORY SYSTEM.

TRACHEOPHYTA, trā-kē-of′ə-tə, in modern systems of plant classification, the division that contains all the plants with vascular, or conducting, tissues. These tissues are the xylem, which conducts water through the plant, and the phloem, which carries food materials. The name Tracheophyta is derived from "tracheid," the name of the most common type of xylem cell.

The Tracheophyta comprise four classes: the Psilopsida, containing the oldest and most primitive vascular plants, most of which are known only as fossils from the Devonian period; the Lycopsida, or lycopods, containing the small and inconspicuous lycopodiums and selaginellas as well as the treelike *Lepidodendron* of the Carboniferous period; the Sphenopsida, or horsetails, which have only one living genus, *Equisetum*, although related species lived during the Carboniferous period; and the Pteropsida, containing the ferns, gymnosperms, and the flowering plants (angiosperms). In other systems of plant classification each of these classes is made a separate division of the plant kingdom because it is believed that they evolved independently of each other after their initial separation during Paleozoic times.

CHESTER A. ARNOLD
University of Michigan

TRACHEOTOMY, trā-kē-ot′ə-mē, an incision into the trachea, or windpipe. It is generally performed when a patient's airways are blocked, as by a foreign body or food particle lodged in the larynx. The incision is made at the base of the neck and kept open by a cannula or other narrow tubular object. Although the patient can breathe freely, he cannot speak. When normal breathing is restored, the tube is removed and the incision is closed.

TRACHOMA, trə-kō′mə, is a chronic infectious eye disease caused by *Chlamydia trachomatis*, a microorganism related to bacteria. The disease has long been prevalent in the Mediterranean Basin and in the Orient, and it is estimated that 400 million individuals are infected. Trachoma flourishes in areas that are hot and dry and have a shortage of water and poor hygienic customs. In such areas infection commonly occurs in early childhood and persists throughout life. Often, the disease is aggravated by bacteria that cause conjunctivitis.

It is believed that *Chlamydia trachomatis* is transmitted mainly by contact with an infected eye or its secretions. A closely related infection, inclusion conjunctivitis, is a sexually transmitted disease that may produce the same signs and symptoms as trachoma. Typical early signs of trachoma are follicular conjunctivitis, redness of the eye, and eye exudations. Gradually blood vessels grow downward into the cornea from up above, forming a pannus (vascularized area) that obstructs vision. Scars appear on the conjunctiva of the eyeball and on the lids, which may become deformed. Severe trachoma leads to blindness.

Treatment of trachoma entails the local or systemic administration of tetracyclines. Surgery is necessary to correct lid deformities and replace an opaque cornea. The prevention of trachoma requires early treatment of all infected children, improvements in sanitation and personal hygiene, and an abundant water supply.

ERNEST JAWETZ, M. D.
School of Medicine
University of California

TRACHYTE, trak′īt, is a volcanic rock consisting principally of alkali feldspar, often with crystals of glassy feldspar and other mineral inclusions. It resembles syenite, but it lacks quartz. The rock is commonly banded or streaked.

DON WILKINSON

Teammates exchange batons in a qualifying heat of the sprint relay (4 x 100 meters) at the 1968 Olympic Games.

TRACK AND FIELD

CONTENTS

TRACK AND FIELD is essentially an individual sport comprising contests in foot racing, hurdling, jumping for height or distance, and throwing assorted implements of specified design. Called simply *track* in the United States, the sport is known as *athletics* in Britain and *light athletics* in Germany and the Soviet Union. Track meets may be conducted outdoors or on indoor tracks. The majority of the running events take place on 400-meter or 440-yard ovals and the jumping and throwing (field) events on the infields of the ovals or on an adjacent area. Men and women participate separately, and almost all competitors are amateurs.

The world governing body in track and field is the International Amateur Athletic Federation (IAAF), whose headquarters is in London. Affiliates of this body include the official governing organizations of about 140 countries sponsoring the sport. One such affiliate is the Amateur Athletic Union of the United States (AAU). The IAAF's world championships are contested only in the quadrennial Olympic Games, in which track is the most popular sport.

Track distances are measured in meters and kilometers, except in the United States and parts of the Commonwealth, which follow the English system of measuring in yards and miles. The United States sometimes uses the metric system in national championships and always measures in meters in the Olympic Games tryouts. Britain switched to the metric system for its national championships in 1969. The IAAF lists events in which world records are recognized in both the metric and the English systems (see table). In field events only the metric system is official.

Any number of events constitutes a program, or *meet,* which may be sponsored by a club, college, civic group, or military unit. The program is based on the availability of talent and the limitations of time and facilities. Each country holds district and national championships in whatever events it chooses and may also list records in events not recognized by the IAAF. Hemispheric and regional games are conducted under IAAF sanction every two or four years.

Indoor track, a wintertime activity, expanded in the United States in the early 20th century in large arenas or armories in cities and in field houses on college campuses. The tracks, usually banked wooden ovals, vary from 5 to 12 laps to the mile, as against the common outdoor 4. By the 1950's indoor track had spread, principally to Europe and Japan. Limitations of arenas dictated shorter sprints. Standard races include 60, 600, and 1,000 yards. Activities requiring ample space, such as the discus, javelin, and hammer throws, are not usually contested indoors.

The IAAF does not recognize indoor records, mainly because of the variation in track sizes and surfaces. In the United States the AAU recognizes indoor records made on wood or synthetic-covered wood and has a separate category for indoor records made on outdoor-type surfaces such as clay, cinder, or rubberized asphalt.

Team effort in meets is achieved in two ways: through relay racing and team championships decided by scoring points. Scoring systems vary. The IAAF recommends a 5-3-2-1 system—that is, 5 points for first place, 3 for second, 2 for third, and 1 for fourth. For more than two teams the IAAF suggests a 7-5-4-3-2-1 score. For relay races, the IAAF breakdown is 5-2 for dual meets; 7-4-2 for three-team meets; and 7-5-4-3-2-1 for meets with six teams or more. In the United States, scoring in dual meets is 5-3-1, but 5-0 in relays; 5-3-2-1 for meets involving three or more teams; and 6-4-3-2-1 or 10-8-6-4-2-1 in championships.

Mandatory attire includes shorts and a jersey, or shirt, to which an identifying number must be affixed. Participants may compete in bare feet or in shoes on one or both feet. High jumpers sometimes wear a shoe only on the takeoff foot. The soles of shoes may not be more than one-half inch thick. The heels may not be more than one-quarter inch (6 mm) thicker than the sole, except for race walking, in which a difference of one-half inch (13 mm) is permitted.

Spikes, either detachable or permanently built into the sole and heel of a shoe, have been used by foot racers since the middle of the 19th century. Modern rules permit a maximum of six spikes in the sole and two in the heel. Field events require different arrangements of spikes or no spikes at all. Some hammer throwers prefer the ground-gripping feel of ballet slippers. Road runners on highways must wear spikeless shoes.

1. Running Events

Except for road races and cross-country runs, most outdoor races take place on an oval of crushed rock and cinders with a top dressing of fine cinders mixed with clay loam, volcanic ash, or ground tile. This track needs constant grooming. It churns to mud in rain. In the 1960's all-weather tracks consisting of rubberized asphalt or synthetics of plastics or cellulose were introduced. Such tracks are impervious to weather and spikes and require little maintenance. The first U. S. championships on rubberized asphalt were held in 1963, when Bob Hayes of Florida A & M University became the first man to run 100 yards in 9.1 seconds.

Rules Common to Running Events. Although distances of the running events range from 50 yards to the marathon, some rules are common to all. A line on the ground marks the start and the finish. The finish line is also marked by two white posts between which the runner must pass, and may have a chest-high line of worsted, called the *tape*, stretched between these posts to help the finish judges. Runners in all races not exceeding 880 yards may use *starting blocks*. These must be of rigid design and without springs, so that the runner cannot obtain artificial impetus.

In all races up to and including 880 yards the starter uses the commands "On your marks," when the runners take their places at the starting line, and "Set," when they move into final position. After all are steady, the race begins with the firing of a gun. Above 880 yards, the starter dispenses with the command "Set" and fires the gun when all competitors are steady. In all instances a false start—that is, any runner's movement forward before the shot—brings a warning to the offender. Two false starts disqualify the offender.

Although track competition can be conducted on any surface on which conditions are equal for all entrants, approved tracks are 24 feet (7.3 meters) wide, with 6 lanes of 4 feet (1.2 meters) each, and may be 32 feet (9.7 meters) wide with 8 lanes. A raised curb, 2 inches by 2 inches, marks the inside border of the track. In races run around the track in lanes, each lane is measured separately—the inside lane 12 inches (30 cm) from the curb and other lanes 8 inches (20 cm) from the inside marking. A seemingly uneven start, called a *stagger*, is thus created, since each lane has its own starting line. However, all participants will have run exactly the same distance when they enter the final straightaway. Lanes are used for all races up to and including 440 yards.

In the 880, participants may run in lanes around the first turn and, at a spot clearly marked by a flag, may cut for the *pole* (curb), providing they do not interfere with rivals. In

EVENTS RECOGNIZED BY IAAF

Track Events (metric system)

Running	Hurdling	Relays
60 meters[1]	100 meters[1]	4 × 100 meters*
100 meters*	110 meters	4 × 200 meters*
200 meters*	200 meters*	4 × 400 meters*
400 meters*	400 meters	4 × 800 meters*
800 meters*		4 × 1,500 meters
1,000 meters*		
1,500 meters*	**Race Walking**	
2,000 meters	20 kilometers	**Marathon**
3,000 meters	30 kilometers	42,195 meters
5,000 meters	50 kilometers	(26 miles,
10,000 meters	*two hours of*	385 yards)
20,000 meters	*walking*	
25,000 meters		
30,000 meters		
one hour of	**Steeplechase**	
running	3,000 meters	

Track Events (English system)

Running	Hurdling	Relays
100 yards*	120 yards	4 × 110 yards*
220 yards*	220 yards	4 × 220 yards*
440 yards*	440 yards	4 × 440 yards*
880 yards*		4 × 880 yards*
1 mile*		4 × 1 mile
2 miles		
3 miles	**Race Walking**	
6 miles	20 miles	
10 miles	30 miles	
15 miles		

Field Events

Jumping: High*, Long*, Triple, Pole vault.
Throwing: Discus*, Javelin*, Hammer, Shot put*.

All-Around

Decathlon: 100, 400, and 1,500 meters in running; 110 meters in hurdling; high jump, long jump, and pole vault; and discus throw, javelin throw, and shot put.
Pentathlon (women): 200 meters in running, 100 meters in hurdling, high jump, long jump, and javelin throw.

* *events also contested by women*
[1] *women only*

UPI

PAAVO NURMI, the Flying Finn, wins the 1,500-meter race in a record 3:53.6 at the 1924 Olympics in Paris.

races of 800 meters and longer in which lanes are not used, the start is marked by a curved line from the inside curb to the outside of the track to equalize the distance for each runner. For all races beyond one lap, the firing of a pistol signals the start of the last lap.

Timers use tenth-second watches. For all races above a mile, the time is recorded officially in even tenths. Electrical timing devices are officially approved, but their cost limits their use to such meets as the Olympics. In deference to records already established by manual timing, electrical equipment must have a built-in lag of .05 second. This compensates for slower human reaction to the flash of the starter's gun.

A runner finishes a race when any part of his torso, excluding head, neck, arms, and legs, reaches the finish line. In all major meets a photograph is taken of contestants as they cross the finish line. When judges disagree, and in all close finishes, the photo must be viewed before a placement decision is final.

Track officials must use instruments for measuring the direction and force of the wind if world or national records are to be approved. In all races up to 220 yards and in the long and triple jumps, a record is unacceptable if the favoring wind exceeds 2 meters (6 feet) per second. Officials read the wind gauge for a period of 10 seconds in 100-meter races, 15 seconds in the 110-meter hurdles, 20 seconds in 220-yard straightaway races, and for the last 10 seconds in a 220-yard run around a turn. They read the gauge for 5 seconds in the last 40 meters of the run-up in the long jump and for 35 meters in the triple jump.

Sprints. The 100- and 220-yard races and their meter equivalents are called *sprints,* or *dashes.* At the speed of the best modern quarter milers, the 440-yard race is often considered a prolonged sprint. The 100 is always run on a straight course on one side of a track. Two kinds of 220-yard sprints are run—straightaway or around a turn. Turn races are run in all championships.

The sprints require an explosive burst out of starting blocks, a quick *gather,* or *pickup,* to top speed, and all-out strides to the finish. All sprinters start from a crouch. They get down on all fours, one foot planted ahead of the other in the starting blocks and both hands resting just behind the starting line. The origin of the crouch start, which provides a quicker getaway than the previously used standing start, is attributed to Charles H. Sherrill, who used it in 1888 while a student at Yale. Contemporaries claimed that the crouch start was the invention of professional track runners. To promote races with local champions at county fairs, the professionals offered to handicap themselves by lying on their backs when the starting gun was fired. They then whirled into a crouch to start, nullifying the apparent advantage given to the standing-start rival.

Among top-level competitors, sprint races are often decided by inches, and therefore various finish styles have been tried to gain an edge at the end. With the shrug finish, perfected by Georgetown University's Bernie Wefers at the end of the 19th century, the runner throws one side of the body across the finish, one arm held high and the other arm drawn far back. In the lunge finish, the runner thrusts his chest forward and flings his arms back in the final stride. Charles W. Paddock of Los Angeles, celebrated as the "fastest human" in the 1920's, was famed for his jump finish, a flying leap through the tape. No sprinter appears to benefit from leaving the ground at the finish, however. Most sprinters run through the tape with a forward lean in the final stride. Breathing is not a factor in a sprint. Runners take a deep breath at the command "Set" and do not need another in the 100.

Middle Distance and Distance Runs. In middle distance events, including runs from 400 to 1,000 meters, and in distance events, knowledge of the opposition's capabilities and tactics can suggest the strategy that will give a runner his best chance to win. One competitor pits his intelligence and determination as well as his speed and stamina against another at all stages of the event.

From the one-lap races upward, judgment of pace, or rate of speed, is very important. Practice enables a runner to plan a timetable, running faster or slower at certain portions of the race in order to achieve maximum results for the race as a whole. A rival's tactics often influence or disrupt a plan. Some runners can be drained of their final sprint by being forced to run at a pace to which they are not geared. Some who do not have a "kick," or final sprint, can win on their stamina by running a fast, even pace. This interplay of tactics keeps contestants alert and adds interest for spectators.

During the race a runner tries to avoid having one rival in front of him and another at his side. Thus "boxed," he may be unable to meet the tactics of a leader who suddenly steps up the pace or sprints. He must hope for an opening that will give him clear running room.

A superior runner at one distance may also manifest his excellence at a distance shorter or longer than his specialty. Most great sprinters are equally good at either 100 or 220 yards. A quarter-miler who is also a superior 220-yard sprinter is typed as a 220/440 runner. A quarter-miler may have the range to be outstanding at 880 yards. Ted Meredith, of the University of Pennsylvania, held world records in the 440 for 16 years (1916–1932) and 880 for 14 (1912–1926).

The mile and the 1,500 meters, sometimes called the *metric mile* although it is approximately 120 yards short of a mile, are looked upon as the most glamorous of track races. IAAF lists John Paul Jones as the first official mile record holder. In 1913, Jones ran the mile in 4 minutes 14.4 seconds while a student at Cornell.

Renowned examples of the 880 mile type are Glenn Cunningham of Kansas University, who competed in the 1930's; Jim Ryun, also of Kansas, who was the first schoolboy or teen-ager to better 4 minutes in the mile (1964); and Peter Snell of New Zealand, who raced in the 1960's. Notable world-record milers who also concentrated on the 1,500 meters are John E. Lovelock of New Zealand in the 1930's; Roger Bannister of Britain, the first man to run a mile under 4 minutes, in 1954; and Herb Elliott of Australia in the late 1950's.

Some record holders in the mile and 1,500 meters carried their speed up to 10,000 meters and longer. Foremost among them is Paavo Nurmi of Finland, often cited as the greatest runner of the 20th century. Competing between 1920 and 1932, he bettered world records from 1,500 to 20,000 meters, or about 12½ miles. A stylist with an erect carriage who held his arms chest-high, he perfected an even-pace technique through planned prerace timetables that he maintained by glancing at his watch. It was said of Nurmi that he ran against the clock, not against his opposition. In three Olympic Games he won an unprecedented total of nine gold medals: 10,000 meters on the flat and 10,000 meters individual and team cross country, in 1920; 1,500 and 5,000 meters within one hour, 10,000 meters individual and team cross country, and 3,000-meter team race, in 1924; and 10,000 meters in 1928.

Emil Zátopek of Czechoslovakia set records from 5,000 to 30,000 meters. He achieved an unparalleled feat in winning the 5,000 and 10,000 meters and marathon in the 1952 Olympic Games. No one, though, broke more distance records (two miles up to the one-hour event) than Ron Clarke of Australia in the 1960's. Yet Clarke, competing in the Olympic or British Empire and Commonwealth Games in 1964, 1966, 1968, and 1970, never won an international championship.

Abebe Bikila of Ethiopia was the first distance runner to win successive Olympic marathons—in 1960 and 1964. From Kenya came the first black Africans to achieve Olympic track honors: Kipchoge Keino in the 1,500 meters, Amos Biwott in the steeplechase, and Naftali Temu in the 10,000 meters in the high-altitude games in Mexico City in 1968.

Cross Country, Road Runs, and Marathon. Cross country, road runs (at distances from 15 to 30 kilometers), and the marathon are conducted as separate events—that is, they do not take place on the running track. A cross-country race may start or finish on a regular track, but most of the race takes place over open fields on a surveyed and marked course. Distances for men vary from

UPI

ROGER BANNISTER beats John Landy in first double sub-4-minute mile, at 1954 British Commonwealth Games.

2 miles in high schools and some colleges, to 10,000 meters in national competition, and 7½ miles in international contests. For women, IAAF recommends distances of 2,000 to 5,000 meters, or about 1¼ to 3¼ miles. Runners participate in cross country in the fall, as a training prelude to indoor track, or in early spring as a conditioner for outdoor track. In large measure, though, cross country is a competitive activity itself, deciding individual and team winners.

Teams of seven runners compete in cross country, but only five count in the scoring. Points are allotted according to finishing positions—1 point for first, 2 for second, and so on. The team with the lowest score wins. A perfect team score for finishing in the first five places is 15 points. Five runners of a team must finish to be counted in the team score.

Distance runs from 10,000 meters to the marathon and even farther take place on roadways. Measurement of the length is by a calibrated measuring wheel or bicycle. The marathon, unknown in the ancient Olympics, was devised by a Frenchman named Michel Bréal as a tribute to the legendary feat of a Greek soldier, Pheidippides, who reputedly ran from Marathon to Athens in 490 B.C. to announce the Greek victory over the Persians. The first marathon contested in the 1896 Olympics measured 40,000 meters, or about 24⅞ miles. The standard distance of 26 miles 385 yards is attributed to the desire of the British royal family to see the start of the 1908 Olympic race, which thus began at Windsor Castle and finished in White City Stadium, Shepherd's Bush, London.

Race Walking. Competitive walking as a sport dates from the latter part of the 19th century. At first it was mainly professional, with a staked wager. The British introduced a 7-mile event into their championships in 1866. In the United

States handicap and distance walking races were popular in the 1870's and 1880's. Walking became a part of the Olympic Games in 1908. A 2-mile walk is contested in AAU outdoor championships and 1-mile indoors, but Olympic walking races are at 20 and 50 kilometers.

Race walking involves a heel-and-toe movement. The walker must keep contact with the ground in every stride. Thus, the heel of the forward foot meets the ground before the toe of the other foot leaves the ground. Furthermore, the forward leg for an instant must be straightened, that is, locked at the knee.

Relay Races. In a relay race four contestants constitute a team, and they run separate and consecutive distances, or *legs*. A line, called a *scratch line*, marks the length of each leg. A *baton* is carried in the hand and is relayed from teammate to teammate over the course. The baton, a smooth hollow tube of wood or metal, is not more than 12 inches (28 cm) in length and 4¾ inches (120 mm) in circumference and weighs 1¾ ounces (50 grams). If a runner drops the baton, he must retrieve it. Runners exchange the baton in take-over zones, which are 10 meters long on each side of the scratch line. Sweden introduced the baton as relay equipment in 1912.

In most relays each runner covers an equal distance. When the legs of the relay vary, the race is called a *medley*. Common relays are the 1 mile (4 laps × 440 yards) and the 2 miles (4 × 880). The sprint relays include the 440 yards (4 × 110) and the 880 yards (4 × 220). In the 4-mile relay each runner covers one mile. In the Olympic Games the 400 meter (4 × 100) and the 1,600 meter (4 × 400) are held for men and women. A sprint medley consists of legs of 440, 220, 220, and 880 yards, or a total distance of 1 mile. A distance medley consists of 440 yards, 880 yards, 1,320 yards, and 1 mile. A "Swedish relay" is a medley of 400, 100, 200, and 300 meters, or a medley of 440, 110, 220, and 330 yards.

In the 480-yard shuttle hurdle relay each teammate runs the regular 120-yard high hurdles course, touching off the next hurdler who returns over the course in an adjacent lane. Shuttle relayers do not use a baton.

The first recorded intercollegiate relay race in the United States was a 40 × 440-yard test between teams from the University of Pennsylvania and Princeton University, arranged in 1893. This contest led in 1895 to the first Penn Relay Carnival, a series of mile relay matches. Gradually built up through the years, the annual Penn Relays features relay races at all levels of competition—open, college, school, and women—in addition to other track events. Popular relay competitions conducted annually include the Drake Relays, at Des Moines, Iowa; Kansas Relays, Lawrence, Kans.; Texas Relays, Austin, Texas; and Florida Relays, Gainesville, Fla.

Obstacle Races. Obstacle races are of two kinds—hurdles and steeplechase. Each hurdles race outdoors has a *flight*, or series, of 10 barriers, spaced 10, 20, or more yards apart, depending on the race. The high hurdle, for the 120-yard or 110-meter event is 3 feet 6 inches (about 1 meter) high; for high school contests, it is 3 feet 3 inches high. The low hurdle, for the 220-yard or 200-meter race, an event for women and schoolboys, measures 2 feet 6 inches (76.2 cm) high. The intermediate hurdle for the 440-yard or 400-meter event is 3 feet (91.4 cm) high. For women, the 100-meter race requires a 2-foot 9-inch hurdle. In indoor track, high hurdles races are 50, 60, and 70 yards, with flights of 4, 5, and 6 barriers, respectively.

Hurdles are made of metal, except for a wooden bar across the top, which is 2¾ inches (70 mm) wide and 3 feet 11 inches (1.19 meters) long. Two bases and two uprights support a rectangular frame reinforced by one or more crossbars. The bases face the approaching hurdler, and the uprights are fixed to the ends of the bases. Adjustable weights on each base are so fastened that a force of at least 8 pounds (3.6

WIDE WORLD

MILDRED (BABE) DIDRIKSON, considered to be the greatest U. S. woman athlete (*right*), set world and Olympic records in 80-meter hurdles at the 1932 games in Los Angeles. Her time was 11.7 seconds. She also won the javelin event, with a throw of 43.69 meters (143 ft 4 in) at the games.

kg) applied to the center of the top edge of the wooden bar is required to overturn the hurdle. Total weight of a hurdle shall not be less than 22 pounds ¾ ounces (about 10 kg).

The high hurdles are essentially sprints, not jumps, over obstacles. Proper form places a premium on ability to regain sprint action instantly upon clearing the hurdle. In modern hurdling style, the hurdler throws his lead leg up and straight forward over the barrier. He jackknifes his body from the waist until it is almost parallel to the thigh of the front leg as he snaps it to the ground. Simultaneously, the forward thrust of the opposite arm swiftly brings his trailing leg up and over the crossbar, bent at the knee. Forrest Smithson, of Portland, Ore., used the extended advance-leg form to become the 1908 Olympic champion. Fred W. Kelly, of the University of Southern California, introduced the forward leg snap, or chop, for a quicker landing and an unchecked stride.

A hurdler takes off about 7 feet from each barrier, lands 4 feet beyond it, takes exactly three steps between obstacles in the high hurdles, 7 strides in the low hurdles and, in the intermediate hurdles, 13 or 15 strides, often adjusted to 15 or 17 in the latter stages of a race. Stride control and pace judgment are more essential than hurdling technique in the longer race.

The steeplechase, a 3,000-meter race, includes 35 hurdles in all—28 over 3-foot high wooden barriers, four on each of seven laps—and 7 water jumps, one on each lap. The water jump, placed between the third and fourth hurdle on each lap, is a combination 3-foot high hurdle and a 12-foot jump over a water hole, or *pool*. The water is 2 feet 3½ inches deep at the hurdle, and the depth decreases on a slope upward to ground level at the far end. A contestant may leap over the barriers cleanly, step on them, or hand-vault them. He may clear the water in one bound or land in it. There is usually a run of 270 meters to the first hurdle, 78 meters between hurdles, and 68 meters to the finish.

2. Field Events

Field events include contests in which the participants jump for distance—measured either vertically as in the high jump and pole vault, or horizontally, as in the long and triple jumps—or throw various implements for distance, measured horizontally. Common throwing events are the shot, discus, javelin, and hammer. In addition, the 56-pound and 35-pound weights are sometimes featured in meets in the United States; neither of these weight events is recognized by the IAAF.

For jumpers and vaulters, a landing bed, or *pit*, filled with foam rubber, sawdust, or other soft material protects them from injury when they hit the ground.

High Jump and Pole Vault. In the high jump and the pole vault the judges decide in advance the starting height of the crossbar for the particular meet and the progressively greater heights. Each contestant is allowed three tries to get over the bar at each height. On a third consecutive miss, the jumper is eliminated. He may start at any height selected by the judges; pass, or waive, a height; or, after a miss at one height, take his remaining tries at greater heights. Those who clear a height move on to the next height, until a winner is decided. After any record jump, the officials remeasure the height with a steel tape.

The competitor who clears the greatest height on the fewest attempts wins. But because of frequent ties, the rules state that if two competitors clear the same height in the same number of attempts, then the one who has fewer misses during the entire competition wins. If they are still tied, the competitor with fewer attempts in the competition wins. This last specification leads to strategical and psychological ploys. For instance, a competitor may elect to pass his turn at a critical moment in the competition, risking his chances on his ability to succeed at a greater height.

WIDE WORLD

HARRISON DILLARD (*left*) clears final hurdle of a 60-yard race at the 1951 AAU meet in New York. In the 1940's he won 82 consecutive hurdles races. He won Olympic gold medals in the 100-meter dash and 400-meter relay in 1948, and 110-meter hurdles and 400-meter relay in 1952.

WIDE WORLD

VALERI BRUMEL, Russian track champion, became the world's foremost high jumper in the 1960's.

WIDE WORLD

IOLANDA BALAS, Rumanian Olympic medalist, jumped a record 1.91 meters (6 ft 3 in) in 1961.

In the high jump the contestant may approach the bar any way he wishes and at any speed. The takeoff area, however, must have at least 50 feet (15.2 meters) of level surface for a run-up from any angle within 180°. The uprights, not less than 12 feet (3.7 meters) apart, may be of any rigid material. The horizontal supports for the crossbar are flat and rectangular, pointed toward the opposite upright. Resting thus on the supports, the bar can be dislodged in either direction if touched by a jumper. The uprights extend at least 4 inches (10 cm) above the crossbar, which may be triangular or circular and made of metal or wood. The bar weighs no more than 4 pounds 6½ ounces (about 2 kg).

Styles in takeoff and the layout over the crossbar have departed considerably from the original scissors-kick method, which took the jumper into a sitting position atop the crossbar. George Horine of Stanford University and Edward Beeson of the University of California boosted the record beyond 6 feet 7 inches in 1912 by using the "Western roll." With this style a jumper who takes off from the left foot, kicks up hard with the right leg to elevate the hips. At the top of the jump the whole body is laid out parallel to the ground, face down, and the landing in the pit is on the hands and knees. In the 1940's the "belly straddle" was a popular style. The jumper kicked the right leg upward and over the crosspiece, rotating his face down atop the crossbar. This style required less expenditure of energy in the body lift. Dick Fosbury of the University of Oregon introduced a new technique when he pivoted on the takeoff to clear the crossbar on his back. He won the Olympic title with this method in 1968. Any jump is legal today, provided the jumper takes off from one foot.

In the pole vault the contestant uses a long pole to propel himself over a crossbar. The pole may be of bamboo, metal, or fiber glass, its length and weight dictated by the size and strength of the user. The uprights are at least 12 feet apart, supported by 4-inch-high bases. The crossbar, at least 12 feet 8 inches (about 4 meters) long, rests on round pins that project 3 inches (75 mm) from the uprights. The uprights may be moved up to 2 feet forward or back to satisfy a contestant.

The vaulter, holding the pole in his hand, races down a 125-foot runway at full speed. He plants the pole in a metal or wood vaulting box at the end of the runway and, with the help of the pole and the momentum gained from the run, lifts himself off the ground and over the bar. The vaulting box is fixed into the ground so that all the upper edges are flush with the runway. The angle of the stopboard at the end of the box is 105° to avoid damage to the pole.

Vaulters first used heavy and inflexible hickory, ash, or spruce poles, with an iron prong at the end, which they planted in the earth for the takeoff. They then "climbed the pole" as they lifted themselves off the ground. Climbing was barred in 1890, when the rules decreed that the upper hand on the pole could not be moved after the takeoff. The lighter and more flexible bamboo poles with mushroom-shaped plugs at the end were first used in the 1900 Olympic Games. Cornelius Warmerdam, one of the greatest vaulters, used a bamboo pole. He held the U. S. indoor record of 15 feet 8½ inches from 1943 to 1959 and retired from competition in 1946 after vaulting 15 feet or more in 43 meets.

Bamboo poles gave way to steel and aluminum alloy after World War II, and in the 1960's to fiber glass. With the extreme flexibility and strength of this synthetic, vaulting styles changed drastically. The pole, bending almost 90°, catapults the vaulter aloft more than two feet higher than the record achieved with bamboo or metal.

ERNEST E. SCHWORCK, FROM UPI

BOB SEAGREN, champion U. S. pole vaulter, won 1968 Olympic event with a vault of 5.4 meters (17 ft 8½ in).

UPI

BOB BEAMON, U. S. track star, shattered the long jump world record at the 1968 Olympic Games in Mexico.

Long Jump and Triple Jump. In the long jump (previously called the *running broad jump*) and the triple jump (also known as the *hop, step, and jump*) contestants make three attempts, and each distance is measured. The six leaders, or one more than the number of scoring places, qualify for three more jumps. The best of each contestant's six jumps decides the placings. If two have the same best jump, their second-best jumps resolve the tie.

The facilities for the long and triple jumps include a runway of unlimited length, preferably 130 feet or more; a takeoff board sunk level with the runway, and just beyond it a layer of plasticine to reveal a footprint and thus mark a fault; and a landing area. In the long jump, the takeoff board is 1 meter (3 feet) from the landing area; in the triple jump, 11 meters (36 feet).

In both jumps, the contestants approach the takeoff at full speed and may take off back of the board. The officials measure the jump, however, from the forward edge of the board to the nearest indentation of foot or body in the landing area. A jumper may take off from either foot. On the first jump (hop) of the triple jump, however, he must land on the same foot. On the second jump (step) he lands on the other foot, from which he makes the final jump. During the three jumps the trailing leg may not touch the ground.

Factors Common to Throwing Events. In the throwing events, each contestant is permitted three attempts. Then the six leaders, or one more than the number of scoring places, take three more throws. Each is permitted two minutes for each try. The best throw of each contestant decides the placings.

All events except the javelin are contested from a circle, whose surface is concrete or hard-packed earth or clay. For the shot, hammer, and weights, the area is 7 feet (2.1 meters) in diameter; for the discus, 8 feet 2½ inches (2.5 meters). The surrounding rings are of band iron or steel, the top flush with the ground outside. The area within the circle is sunken by ¾ inch (2 cm). For the shot, a wooden arc-shaped stopboard is fastened to the ground at the front of the ring, the inner edge coinciding with the inner edge of the circle. During the event the competitor may touch the inner edge of the circles, including the stopboard but not the top of it..

A competitor throws the javelin from a runway 98½ to 120 feet (30–36.5 meters) long and 13 feet 1½ inches (4 meters) wide. He makes the throw from behind an arc of wood or metal sunk flush with the ground.

In all throwing events the implement must land within the boundaries of sector lines. In the shot, the sector is approximately 65°, the radii lines starting at the center of the circle and passing the ends of the stopboard. The sectors for the discus, hammer, and weights are 45°. A 29° sector for the javelin is formed by drawing lines from the center of an imaginary circle, of which the arc marking the scratch line is a part, through the ends of the arc where they join the runway lines.

Measurement of throws is made from the inner edge of the circle or arc to the nearest mark made by the implement. Only the head of the hammer and the point of the javelin are counted in determining the distance. The tip of the javelin's metal head must hit the ground first. The contestant may not leave the circle or runway until the implement touches the ground. Hammer and weight throwers may wear gloves.

Shot Put. The men's shot, a solid iron or solid or lead-filled brass ball, weighs 16 pounds (7.257 kg) and measures 110 to 130 mm in diameter. Schoolboys use a 12-pound (5.4-kg) implement, and women an 8-pound 13-ounce (4-kg) shot. Indoors, a leather or plastic-covered shot is used to protect wooden floors.

MEN'S WORLD RECORDS RECOGNIZED BY IAAF

(*s = second, m = minute, h = hour*)

Event	Record	Holder	Country	Date
RUNNING				
100 yards	9.1 s	Robert Hayes	United States	June 21, 1963
		Harry Jerome	Canada	July 15, 1966
		Jim Hines	United States	May 13, 1967
		Charlie Greene	United States	June 15, 1967
		John Carlos	United States	May 10, 1969
220 yards (straightaway)	19.5 s	Tommie Smith	United States	May 7, 1966
220 yards (turn)	20.0 s	Tommie Smith	United States	June 11, 1966
440 yards	44.5 s	John Smith	United States	June 26, 1971
880 yards	1 m 44.6 s	Richard Wohlhuter	United States	May 27, 1973
1 mile	3 m 51.1 s	Jim Ryun	United States	June 23, 1967
2 miles	8 m 14.0 s	Lasse Viren	Finland	Aug. 14, 1972
3 miles	12 m 47.8 s	Emiel Puttemans	Belgium	Sept. 20, 1972
6 miles	26 m 47.0 s	Ron Clarke	Australia	July 14, 1965
10 miles	46 m 04.2 s	Willy Polleunis	Belgium	Sept. 20, 1972
15 miles	1 h 12 m 48.2 s	Ron Hill	United Kingdom	July 21, 1965
1 hour	20,784 meters	Gaston Roelants	Belgium	Sept. 20, 1972
RUNNING (Metric Distances)				
100 meters	9.9 s	Jim Hines	United States	June 20, 1968
		Charlie Greene	United States	June 20, 1968
		Ronnie Ray Smith	United States	June 20, 1968
		Jim Hines	United States	Oct. 14, 1968
		Eddie Hart	United States	July 1, 1972
		Reynaud Robinson	United States	July 1, 1972
200 meters (straightaway)	19.5 s	Tommie Smith	United States	May 7, 1966
200 meters (turn)	19.8 s	Tommie Smith	United States	Oct. 16, 1968
		Donald Quarrie	Jamaica	Aug. 3, 1971
400 meters	43.8 s	Lee Evans	United States	Oct. 18, 1968
800 meters	1 m 43.7 s	Marcello Fiasconaro	Italy	June 27, 1973
1,000 meters	2 m 16.2 s	Jurgen May	East Germany	July 20, 1965
		Franz-Josef Kemper	West Germany	Sept. 21, 1966
1,500 meters	3 m 33.1 s	Jim Ryun	United States	July 8, 1967
2,000 meters	4 m 56.2 s	Michel Jazy	France	Oct. 12, 1966
3,000 meters	7 m 37.6 s	Emiel Puttemans	Belgium	Sept. 14, 1972
5,000 meters	13 m 13.0 s	Emiel Puttemans	Belgium	Sept. 20, 1972
10,000 meters	27 m 38.4 s	Lasse Viren	Finland	Sept. 3, 1972
20,000 meters	57 m 44.4 s	Gaston Roelants	Belgium	Sept. 20, 1972
25,000 meters	1 h 15 m 22.6 s	Ron Hill	United Kingdom	July 21, 1965
30,000 meters	1 h 31 m 30.4 s	Jim Alder	United Kingdom	Sept. 5, 1970
3,000-meter steeplechase	8 m 20.8 s	Anders Gärderud	Sweden	Sept. 14, 1972
HURDLES				
120 yards	13.0 s	Rodney Milburn	United States	June 25, 1971
		Rodney Milburn	United States	June 20, 1973
220 yards	21.9 s	Don Styron	United States	April 2, 1960
440 yards	48.8 s	Ralph Mann	United States	June 20, 1970
110 meters	13.1 s	Rodney Milburn	United States	July 22, 1973
200 meters (straightaway)	21.9 s	Don Styron	United States	April 2, 1960
200 meters (turn)	22.5 s	Martin Lauer	West Germany	July 7, 1959
		Glenn Davis	United States	Aug. 20, 1960
400 meters	48.1 s	John Akii-Bua	Uganda	Sept. 2, 1972
WALKING				
20 kilometers	1 h 25 m 19.4 s	Peter Frenkel	East Germany	July 24, 1972
		Hans-Georg Reimann	East Germany	July 24, 1972
30 kilometers	2 h 14 m 45.6 s	Karl-Heinz Stadmüller	East Germany	April 16, 1972
20 miles	2 h 31 m 33.0 s	Anatoli Vedjakov	USSR	Aug. 23, 1958
30 miles	3 h 56 m 12.6 s	Peter Selzer	East Germany	Oct. 3, 1972
50 kilometers	4 h 03 m 42.6 s	Veniamin Soldatenko	USSR	Oct. 5, 1972
2 hours	26,911 meters	Karl-Heinz Stadmüller	East Germany	April 16, 1972
RELAYS				
440 yards	38.6 s	Univ. of Southern California, U. S. (Earl McCullouch, Fred Kuller, O. J. Simpson, LennoxMiller)		June 17, 1967
800 meters	1 m 21.5 s	Italy (F. Ossola, P. Abeti, L. Benedetti, P. Mennea)		July 21, 1972
1 mile	3 m 2.8 s	Trinidad and Tobago National Team (Lennox Yearwood, Kent Bernard, Edwin Roberts, Wendell Mottley)		Aug. 13, 1968
2 miles	7 m 11.6 s	Kenya (Naftali Bon, Hezekiah Nyamau, Thomas Saisi, Robert Ouko)		Sept. 5, 1970
4 miles	16 m 02.8 s	New Zealand (K. Ross, A. Polhill, R. Taylor, R. Quax)		July 4, 1969
400 meters	38.2 s	United States National Team (Charlie Greene, Mel Pender, Ronnie Ray Smith, Jim Hines)		Oct. 20, 1968
	38.2 s	United States National Team (Larry Black, Robert Taylor, Gerald Tinker, Eddie Hart)		Sept. 10, 1972
1,600 meters	2 m 56.1 s	United States National Team (Vince Matthews, Ron Freeman, Larry James, Lee Evans)		Oct. 20, 1968
3,200 meters	7 m 8.6 s	West German National Team (Manfred Kinder, Walter Adams, Dieter Bogatzki, Franz-Josef Kemper)		Aug. 13, 1966
6,000 meters	14 m 49.0 s	French National Team (Pierre Vervoort, Claude Nicolas, Michel Jazy, Jean Wadoux)		June 25, 1965

MEN'S WORLD RECORDS (Cont.)

Event	Record	Holder	Country	Date
FIELD EVENTS				
High Jump	2.29 meters (7 ft 6¼ in)	Patrick Matzdorf	United States	July 3, 1971
Long Jump	8.90 meters (29 ft 2½ in)	Bob Beamon	United States	Oct. 18, 1968
Triple Jump	17.44 meters (57 ft 2¾ in)	Victor Saneyev	USSR	Oct. 17, 1972
Pole Vault	5.63 meters (18 ft 5¾ in)	Bob Seagren	United States	July 2, 1972
Shot Put	21.82 meters (71 ft 7 in)	Allan Feuerbach	United States	May 5, 1973
Discus Throw	68.40 meters (224 ft 5 in)	Jay Silvester	United States	Sept. 18, 1968
		Richard Bruch	Sweden	July 5, 1972
Hammer Throw	76.4 meters (250 ft 8 in)	Walter Schmidt	West Germany	Sept. 4, 1971
Javelin Throw	94.08 meters (308 ft 8 in)	Klaus Wolfermann	West Germany	May 5, 1973
Decathlon	8,454 points	Nicolai Avilov	USSR	Sept. 8, 1972

In all field events measurements are to a centimeter, or to a quarter of an inch, for all distances up to 100 feet and to 2 centimeters, or to an inch, beyond 100 feet. Only the metric measurement is official. English approximations are given for information only.

WOMEN'S WORLD RECORDS RECOGNIZED BY IAAF

(s = second, m = minute, h = hour)

Event	Record	Holder	Country	Date
RUNNING				
100 yards	10.0 s	Chi Cheng	Rep. of China (Taiwan)	June 13, 1970
220 yards	22.6 s	Chi Cheng	Rep. of China (Taiwan)	July 3, 1970
440 yards	52.2 s	Kathy Hammond	United States	Aug. 12, 1972
880 yards	2 m 2 s	Dixie Willis	Australia	March 3, 1962
		Judy Amoore-Pollock	Australia	July 5, 1967
1 mile	4 m 35.3 s	Ellen Tittel	West Germany	Aug. 20, 1971
60 meters	7.2 s	Betty Cuthbert	Australia	Feb. 27, 1960
		Irina Bochkareva	USSR	Aug. 28, 1960
100 meters	11.0 s	Wyomia Tyus	United States	Oct. 15, 1968
		Chi Cheng	Rep. of China (Taiwan)	July 18, 1970
		Renate Meissner	East Germany	Aug. 2, 1970
		Eva Gleskova	Czechoslovakia	July 1, 1972
		Renate Stecher	East Germany	July 31, 1971
		Renate Stecher	East Germany	July 3, 1972
		Ellen Stropahl	East Germany	July 15, 1972
200 meters	22.4 s	Chi Cheng	Rep. of China	July 12, 1970
		Renate Stecher	East Germany	Sept. 7, 1972
400 meters	51.0 s	Marilyn Neufville	Jamaica	July 23, 1970
		Monika Zehrt	East Germany	July 4, 1972
800 meters	1 m 58.5 s	Hildegard Falck	West Germany	July 11, 1971
1,500 meters	4 m 01.4 s	Ludmilla Bragina	USSR	Sept. 9, 1972
HURDLES				
100 meters	12.5 s	Annelie Ehrhardt	East Germany	June 15, 1972
		Pamela Ryan	Australia	June 28, 1972
200 meters	25.7 s	Pamela Ryan	Australia	Nov. 25, 1971
RELAYS				
440 yards	44.7 s	Tennessee State University (United States) (D. Hughes, D. Wedgeworth, M. Render, I. Davis)		July 9, 1971
880 yards	1 m 35.8 s	Australian Interstate Team (Marion Hoffman, Raelene Boyle, Pamela Kilborn, Jennifer Lamy)		Nov. 9, 1969
1,600 yards	3 m 33.9 s	United States (Kathy Hammond, Mable Fergerson, Madeline Manning Jackson, D. Edwards)		Aug. 12, 1972
400 meters	42.8 s	United States National Team (Barbara Ferrell, Margaret Bailes, Mildrette Netter, Wyomia Tyus)		Oct. 20, 1968
		West Germany (C. Krause, I. Mickler, A. Richter, H. Rosendahl)		Sept. 10, 1972
800 meters	1 m 33.8 s	British National Team (Maureen Tranter, Della James, Janet Simpson, Valerie Peat)		June 24, 1968
1,600 meters	3 m 23.0 s	East Germany (D. Käsling, R. Kühne, H. Seidler, M. Zehrt)		Sept. 10, 1972
		French National Team (Bernadette Martin, Nicole Duclos, Eliane Jacq, Colette Besson)		Sept. 20, 1969
1 mile	3 m 38.8 s	Atoms Track Club (United States) (M. McMillan, L. Reynolds, G. Fitzgerald, C. Toussaint)		July 10, 1971
3,200 meters	8 m 16.8 s	German National Team (E. Tittel, S. Schenk, C. Merten, H. Falck)		July 31, 1971
FIELD EVENTS				
High Jump	1.94 meters (6 ft 4½ in)	Jordanka Blagoyeva	Bulgaria	Sept. 24, 1972
Long Jump	6.84 meters (22 ft 5¼ in)	Heide Rosendahl	West Germany	Sept. 2, 1970
Shot Put	21.03 meters (69 ft 0 in)	Nadyezhda Chizhova	USSR	Sept. 7, 1972
Discus Throw	67.32 meters (220 ft 10 in)	Argentina Menis	Rumania	Sept. 23, 1972
Javelin Throw	65.06 meters (213 ft 5 in)	Ruth Fuchs	East Germany	June 11, 1972
Pentathlon	4,831 points	Burglinde Pollak	East Germany	Aug. 11, 1972

SOURCE: IAAF OFFICIAL RECORDS AS OF SEPT. 30, 1973

UPI

HAL CONNOLLY (*left*), champion hammer thrower, and **AL OERTER**, discus record-breaker, were U. S. Olympic gold medal winners in the 1956 Games. Oerter took discus honors again in the 1960, 1964, and 1968 Games.

A legal stance at the start of the put requires that the shot touch the chin or be close to it. The hand must not be dropped below this position during the action of putting. The contestant thrusts the shot from the shoulder with one hand only. The shot may not be brought behind the line of the shoulders.

Modern shot put technique calls for an opening stance facing the rear of the circle, a low crouch with a pivot and a hop across the circle in the thrust of the shot, and a reverse pivot to stay inside the circle. Parry O'Brien, of the University of Southern California, who in 1954 was the first man to better 60 feet, introduced the technique of facing away from the line of the put.

Discus Throw. The discus, a circular wood or plastic plate with a metal rim, uses 2-inch metal plates in its center set flush with the sides as a means of acquiring the correct weight. Men use a discus at least 8⅕ inches (219 mm) in diameter and 4 pounds 6½ ounces (2 kg) in weight. About 1½ inches thick at the center, it tapers to about ½ inch at the edge. Schoolboys and women throw a discus somewhat lighter in weight and smaller in diameter.

Discus throwing was a popular activity in ancient Greece. Surviving statuary indicates that throwers used a straightforward underhand motion. Athletes before 1900 used a similar style and performed from a pedestal. This early style limited throws to about 100 feet. Performance improved rapidly when the thrower was permitted a spin within a circle. Today the thrower spins around in a circle 1¾ times to gain momentum and releases the discus at arm's length with a sweeping sidearm motion. Record throws now exceed 200 feet.

Javelin Throw. The javelin consists of a shaft of wood or metal, a metal tip with a sharp point, and a cord grip at about the center of gravity of the shaft. For men and schoolboys, the javelin weighs 1 pound 12 ounces (800 grams) and is at least 8 feet 6¼ inches (260 mm) long. Women throw a shorter javelin weighing about 1 pound 5 ounces (600 grams). The contestant holds the javelin by the grip and runs rapidly up to a line, behind which he must release the shaft. He may not turn completely around during the act of throwing and must throw the javelin over his shoulder or upper part of his arm.

Hammer Throw. The hammer consists of a ball, or head, attached to a long handle by a swivel. The head, made of iron or solid or lead-filled brass, has a diameter of 4 to 4¾ inches (102–120 mm). A spring-steel wire handle at least 3 feet 10¼ inches (117.5 mm) long loops at the end to form a rigid handgrip. The implement weighs 16 pounds (about 7.3 kg). To throw, the contestant swings the hammer around his head several times. Then, with the swing of the implement, he makes three turns with his body to gain maximum centrifugal force before he releases it.

Weight Throws. The 35-pound weight has a head of molded lead or lead-filled brass shell. Attached to it through a forged steel eyebolt is a triangular handle of round iron or steel, one-half inch in diameter and no longer than 7½ inches on any of its three sides. The length, including the head, is 16 inches. Specifications for the 56-pound weight are similar.

For either of these weights, the contestant begins with his back to the direction he will throw. With both hands, he grasps the weight by the handle and swings it a few times in front of him to gain momentum. Then, with one complete turn of his body he swings the weight around and up over his shoulder and releases it. The 35-pound weight is an indoor event on AAU and college programs. The 56-pound weight is only thrown outdoors.

3. All-Around Events

A 10-part American invention, called the all-around, was first contested in 1884. It was abandoned in the 1920's and revived as a U. S. championship event in 1950. Contested in one day, the 10 parts (in order of competition) consist of the 100-yard run, shot put, high jump, 880-yard walk, hammer throw, pole vault, 120-yard high hurdles, 56-pound weight throw, long jump, and mile run.

The decathlon and pentathlon, popular versions of the all-round, were introduced at the Olympic Games in Sweden in 1912. Contested in two days, the decathlon comprises the 100-meter run, long jump, shot put, high jump, and 400-meter on the first day; the 110-meter hurdles, discus throw, pole vault, javelin throw, and 1,500-meter run on the second day.

The pentathlon, a one-day event, consists of long jump, javelin, 200 meters, discus throw, and 1,500-meter run. A two-day pentathlon for women first appeared at the 1964 Olympic Games and includes 100-meter hurdles, shot put, and high jump on the first day, and long jump and 200 meters on the second day.

In scoring, points are allotted according to an IAAF scoring table, revised every few years, which awards a specific number of points for each performance. The usual formula is to allot 1,000 points for world records of a given year in the recent past. Less or more points are allotted according to the time, height, or distance by each contestant.

In all-around tests, each contestant gets only three trials in the long jump and throwing events. In the races, each is timed separately, running in groups of four in the short races. Every participant strives against the IAAF book of standards rather than against his opposition. Thus there are no finals as such. A contestant must start in or take a trial in all events in order to be credited with a total score.

4. History of Track and Field

Man learned to run, jump, and throw out of necessity. He ran after his prey or for his life. He jumped from tree to tree and across brooks. He threw rocks and fashioned weapons that could be hurled great distances with considerable accuracy. In time, he turned these exercises into activities for physical well-being and to satisfy an instinct for competition.

No record of such competition appears until 776 B.C., when Coroebus of Elis, a cook, won a foot race in the religious and athletic rites called the Olympic Games, held on the Plain of Elis on Peloponnesus. The first race was about 170 meters long. The Games were celebrated once every four years for 11 centuries thereafter, and longer foot races and a pentathlon were added. With the decline of Greek culture and the conquest of Greece by Rome, the Games were finally terminated in 393 A. D. by Emperor Theodosius I, who regarded them as pagan idolatry.

No further record of athletic games exists until 1154, when open areas in London were set aside for running, jumping, and throwing. Edward III banned these activities in 1330 because they interfered with the practice of archery, a skill essential for war. Athletics were permitted again early in the 15th century and were generally approved from the reign of Henry VIII.

Origins of Modern Track. Amateurs, or "gentlemen," contested races in the London area in the 1820's. In 1837 a 100-yard hurdle race over 10 hurdles originated at Eton College. Sprints and a steeplechase appeared in interclass meets at Eton in 1843. Colleges at Oxford University took up track in 1856, and Cambridge and Dublin universities held contests a year later. Oxford conducted its first track meet for all its undergraduates in 1860. Oxford and Cambridge held the first dual meet on March 5, 1864, a date that marks the beginning of modern track and field as a competitive sport. The mile race was won by Charles B. Lawes, of Cambridge, who ran it in 4 minutes 56 seconds.

Athletes emigrating from Britain introduced track and field to the United States. The start of amateur competition, however, is credited to the New York Athletic Club (NYAC), which was founded in 1868 and held the first track meet on

RANDY MATSON (*left*), U. S. world champion, was the first athlete to put the shot over 21.3 meters (70 ft). JANIS LUSIS (*right*), Russian javelin star, threw 90.1 meters (295 ft 7¼ in) to win the 1968 Olympic event.

WIDE WORLD; TASS, FROM SOVFOTO

November 11 of that year. It was an "indoor" meet conducted in a partly completed unroofed skating rink with a 220-yard track arranged on its dirt floor. This meet marked the first use of spiked shoes in a U. S. track event.

The first national track contests were held in London on March 23, 1866, conducted by the Mincing Lane Athletic Club, which later became the London Athletic Club. British youths took track to Dresden, Germany, in 1874, but many years elapsed before the sport was practiced seriously on the Continent. The Amateur Athletic Association of Britain was formed in 1880 to organize annual championships, which were open to foreigners as well as to British amateurs.

The year 1876 saw the first U. S. National Amateur Championships, sponsored by the NYAC. In the same year, the newly formed Intercollegiate Association of Amateur Athletes of America (IC4–A) conducted its first meet at Saratoga, N. Y., and Horace H. Lee of the University of Pennsylvania became the first U. S. athlete to run 100 yards in 10 seconds. Since that year the IC4–A has conducted annual outdoor championships, except for 1917. It has also sponsored indoor championships every year from 1922.

In 1879 the NYAC led 14 athletic clubs, mostly from the New York–New Jersey area but also including a club from Boston and one from San Francisco, in the formation of the National Association of Amateur Athletes of America (NAAAA) to meet the needs of noncollegiate track and field competitors. This association was superseded by the AAU in 1888, which provided firmer control of amateurs following charges of track abuses by unscrupulous promoters, including the use of "ringers" (athletes competing under assumed names) and recruiting. The AAU subsequently codified rules for amateur sports. The Amateur Athletic Union of Canada dates from the same period.

WILMA RUDOLPH, champion U. S. runner, displays one of three gold medals she won at the 1960 Olympics.

WIDE WORLD

The first international track meet, held in London in 1894 between Oxford and Yale universities, was followed a year later by the first interclub meet, held at Travers Island in New York, between the outstanding athletes of the London and New York athletic clubs. On a one-fifth-mile clay track, the NYAC won all of the 11 events. Michael K. Sweeney increased the high jump record to 6 feet 5⅝ inches, Charles H. Kilpatrick lowered the 880-yard run to 1 minute 53⅖ seconds, and Thomas P. Conneff ran the mile in 4 minutes 15⅗ seconds. These records were unsurpassed for 14 to 17 years.

In 1905 the National Collegiate Athletic Association became the rules-making body for intercollegiate sports in the United States. Annual NCAA track and field championships have been conducted since 1921, with participants limited to full-time college students. An NCAA-backed United States Track and Field Federation, formed in 1962, conducts annual open meets as a challenge to the authority of the AAU.

The International Amateur Athletic Federation (IAAF), world governing body for the sport, was founded in Stockholm in 1912. That year it undertook the first official listing of world records and adopted rules standardizing events for men and tracks.

International and Regional Competitions. The early international contests between British and American athletes preceded the most momentous impetus given to track and field—the first modern Olympic Games, held in Athens in 1896. The revival of the ancient games was due in great part to Baron Pierre de Coubertin, an educator who desired to rehabilitate French youth after the 1870 military debacle against Prussia and who coincidentally was interested in promoting international amity through sports. After a struggling start, the Olympic movement flourished. In 1968 a total of 112 nations competed in the games at Mexico City. From the outset track and field was the heart of the 20-sport Olympic program. See also Olympic Games.

The Olympic Games set the pattern for hemispheric and regional games, which now include the Pan-American Games, European Cup, Asian Games, Pacific Games, South Pacific Games, Central American and Caribbean Games, Mediterranean Games, British Empire and Commonwealth Games, and Americas versus Europe. Special interest meets are also held regularly, such as the Maccabiah Games in Israel, World University Games, and International Paraplegic Games. Dual meets between nations are annual events. Outstanding among these is the U. S.-USSR meet for men and women, inaugurated in Moscow in 1958 and continued alternately in each country. The series was interrupted for political reasons in 1966 but was resumed in 1970.

Organization for Women's Track. For many years after its founding, the IAAF resisted proposals to accept control of women's athletics. An official body became essential as a result of increased interest by women in competing in track and field, and the Fédération Sportive Féminine Internationale (FSFI) was founded in Paris in 1921.

The FSFI conducted the first world championship for women in 1922 in Paris and the second in 1926 in Göteborg, Sweden. The British team won both meets. Between these years, the IAAF, under pressure from the Belgian Athletic Association and other groups, appointed a special commission for women's sports and included in the commission representatives from FSFI. The commission made two recommendations: that the FSFI be delegated to govern women's track under rules to be drawn up by the IAAF, and that the IAAF request the International Olympic Committee to include five track and field events for women in the Olympic Games at Amsterdam.

After considerable debate women were accepted at the 1928 Games under the jurisdiction of the FSFI, and 25 countries sent women's teams. Competitions were held in the 100- and 800-meter runs, 400-meter relay, high jump, and discus throw. The recommendation for dual control of women's track was unpopular, however, and Germany proposed in 1934 that the IAAF assume full responsibility for managing women's competition. Finally, in 1936 the IAAF accepted the role of governing women's track, and the FSFI became extinct. In the 1968 Olympic Games, competition was held in 14 events for women.

From 1928 to 1968, U. S. women won the most first places (19). Their first star was Mildred (Babe) Didrikson, winner of the hurdles and javelin and second in the high jump in 1932. In 1948, Fanny Blankers-Koen, a Dutch housewife and mother, won 4 gold medals: 100, 200, hurdles, and relay. Betty Cuthbert of Australia won 3 gold medals in the sprints and relay in 1956, as did Wilma Rudolph of the United States in 1960. In that year Iolanda Balas of Rumania became the first woman high jumper to clear 6 feet.

Other Developments. The IAAF makes no rules for high school athletes. In the United States, the National Federation of State High School Athletic Associations, founded in 1920, sets the rules for high school track but does not conduct the competition. For example, the 2-mile run is the longest race permitted and, in most cases, an athlete can enter no more than three events. A participant also is limited to one race at 440 yards or more, or no more than two races by a sprinter and a hurdler. Meets are conducted by local groups and state associations. Schoolboys and schoolgirls are eligible to compete in meets conducted by the AAU.

The AAU also fosters an age-group program for participants 9 to 17 years of age. For open competition, it recognizes three divisions: novice, for those who have never won a prize; junior, for those of any age who never have won an AAU or major college title or been selected to compete in open international competition; and senior, for all athletes. For women the AAU has two divisions: girls, up to 16 years of age; and women. For open competition, girls must be 14 years old.

Meets for athletes below high school age are sponsored not only by various districts of the AAU but also by organizations such as the Young Men's Christian Association, the Catholic Youth Organization, and Junior Chamber of Commerce groups.

Improvement in track and field records, witnessed over the years, stems from better year-round training procedures—for example, weight-lifting to strengthen muscles; psychological adjustment to pain; shifting of personal goals as records are bettered; and understanding of oxygen debt and other physiological factors involving expenditure and conservation of energy. An athlete can set his goals at whatever level he chooses and derive benefits from his track and field activity.

UPI

CHI CHENG of Taiwan broke or tied several world sprint records at European and U. S. meets in 1970.

The drive to improve records took on new dimensions after World War II. Athletic clubs in the United States declined as track and field became a part of physical education programs in virtually all high schools and colleges, thus broadening the base of participation. Clubs, however, remain the medium of participation in all other countries. The development of women's track and field is still mainly the burden of clubs and civic groups in the United States.

JESSE ABRAMSON, *Former President Track Writers' Association of New York Director, U. S. Olympic Invitational Track Meet*

Bibliography

Amateur Athletic Union, *The Official AAU Track and Field Handbook and Rules* (New York, annually).

American Association for Health, Physical Education, and Recreation, *Track and Field Guide* (Washington, biennially).

Bresnahan, George T., and others, *Track and Field Athletics*, 7th ed. (St. Louis 1969).

International Amateur Athletic Federation, *Official Handbook* (London, annually).

Jordan, Payton, and Spencer, Bud, *Champions in the Making* (Englewood Cliffs, N. J., 1969).

National Collegiate Athletic Association, *The NCAA Official Track and Field Guide* (Phoenix, annually).

Parker, Virginia, and Kennedy, Robert, *Track and Field Activities for Girls and Women* (Philadelphia 1969).

TRACTARIANISM, trak-târ′ē-ə-niz-əm, the early stage of the Oxford Movement within the Church of England in the 19th century. The name is derived from *Tracts for the Times*, a series of tracts or treatises published by John Henry Newman, John Keble, and others, which opposed both the papacy and Low Church concepts. See ENGLAND, CHURCH OF; OXFORD MOVEMENT.

STEAM TRACTOR of the 1890's, at left, was used to haul lumber. This machine was necessarily huge to accommodate the large boiler needed to generate steam power.

CATERPILLAR TRACTOR COMPANY

TRACTOR, a self-propelled multipurpose vehicle and power unit used in agriculture, road building and other construction work, and transportation. There are about 10 million tractors in use in all parts of the world, with most employed in agriculture. The term "tractor" has been attributed to various sources but is believed to have originated in England in the mid-18th century as a synonym for "traction engine," a self-propelled engine. The term appeared in an 1890 U. S. patent for a tracklaying steam traction engine and about 1900 in advertisements for an American-built traction engine powered by an internal-combustion engine.

Early agricultural steam engines simply provided belt power for threshing machines and similar stationary work but had to be moved from place to place by horses or oxen. During the 1850's successful self-propelled steam plowing engines were developed, and they were steadily improved over the next 50 years. These steam tractors and stationary engines required several men to haul fuel and water, fire the boiler, and operate the controls.

The first gasoline-powered tractors, whose development was stimulated by the need to reduce the size of the operation crew, closely resembled steam tractors. The advance of the gasoline tractor was slow, however, until expiration of the basic patents of the Otto engine—the common automobile engine—in 1890. Tractors using internal-combustion engines were steadily improved from that time on, with sharp reductions in weight and in the size of operating crew compared to early steam-powered units. Some early steam tractors weighed more than 1,000 pounds per horsepower (448 kg per metric hp). The average weight of contemporary agricultural tractors is about 90 to 100 pounds per horsepower (40–45 kg per metric hp).

The number of low-powered tractors has decreased steadily. In the United States, for instance, 90.8% of the tractors built in 1950 had less than 35 horsepower. By 1960 only 17% were under 35 horsepower, and this dropped to 8.4% in 1968. On the other hand, almost 33% of the tractors built in 1968 had 90 or more horsepower.

Diesel engines are capable of producing power efficiently over a wider range of loads and engine speeds than gasoline engines, and diesel fuel generally costs less than gasoline. Since the power and economy advantages of diesel engines are particularly important in larger tractors, the percentage of diesel engines has climbed rapidly as tractor size has increased. In 1955 only 12.5% of American-built tractors had diesel engines, but by 1968 more than 69% were diesel powered. Tractors burning liquid petroleum (lp) gases were introduced in the 1940's.

Basic Functions. Because tractors are basically power sources, they must be equipped with the proper machines or attachments to perform useful work. Tractor power may be utilized in one or more of five basic ways.

(1) Early horse-drawn steam engines transmitted power through an endless belt from a drive pulley on the engine to a similar pulley on the thresher, grinder, pump, or other stationary machine. Many tractors today can be also equipped with belt pulleys to provide stationary power.

(2) With the engines self-propelled, power could be transmitted by traction between drive wheels or tracks and the soil. This permitted the use of implements pulled behind the tractor or mounted on the tractor frame.

(3) In 1918 the "power takeoff" was introduced. With this system, rotary power from the engine can be transmitted through a flexible shaft to drive such field implements as hay balers, combines, and mowing machines. Because power takeoff can also be used to drive stationary machines and is much more convenient than an endless belt, it has largely replaced the belt pulley on newer tractors.

(4) Hydraulic power, available on nearly all new tractors, is generated by oil forced through pipes or hoses by an engine-driven pump to a point of application. Hydraulic lift is obtained by pumping oil into a piston-equipped cylinder, forcing the piston out and raising the attached pull-type or tractor-mounted implement. Reversing the procedure, and removing the oil, lowers the implement. Hydraulic rotary power for machine operation is provided by forcing oil

CRAWLER TRACTOR (*right*), powered by a diesel engine, has a bulldozer attached. This type of earthmover is used chiefly for clearing and leveling land.

MASSEY-FERGUSON, INC.

through a hydraulic motor similar to the engine-driven pump. Other applications of hydraulic power include power steering, power brakes, and raising and lowering seats.

(5) The tractor's electrical system is used in a very minor way to power small electric motors for special applications. Primary uses of tractor electrical power—normally a 12-volt system—are for starting the engine, for lighting, for air conditioning, and for ignition on gasoline engines.

Tractor Types. Evolution of tractor design has resulted in several tractor types, or conformations. These are classified according to arrangement of the tractor frame and traction members (wheels and tracks).

Standard tractors, developed for pulling heavy loads, are characterized by two large rear drive wheels and normally a fixed width between the left and right wheels.

Row-crop tractors were developed in the early 20th century to permit power cultivation of crops, that are planted in rows, such as corn. Row-crop tractors have two rear drive wheels and one of three front-end types: a single narrow tire, which can operate between rows of vegetables or other closely spaced row crops; two closely spaced, narrow front tires—known as a tricycle model; or a wide front axle that, like the rear wheels, is adjustable to match various row spacings for different crops. Row-crop tractors provide high clearance (21 to 26 inches, or 53–66 cm) under the axles and are the most popular type tractor today.

Four-wheel-drive tractors were in volume production by 1930 but never accounted for a significant portion of the market. However, the limited power that can be transmitted through two traction wheels has not been sufficient to meet the demand for higher powered tractors, and the market for 4-wheel-drive machines for agriculture and industry has greatly expanded. Many 4-wheel-drive tractors exceed 100 horsepower in size.

The two basic types of 4-wheel-drive tractors are characterized by their steering systems. The first is steered by pivoting the front or front and rear wheels at the ends of their axles. Steering of the second type, referred to as articulated steering, is done by pivoting front and rear sections of the tractor about a hinge point in the middle of the frame.

Crawler, or track-type, tractors run on endless steel tracks, which provide traction. Since tractor weight is supported by the entire track surface touching the ground, these tractors are well adapted for soft, wet, or sandy soils where wheel tractors would mire down. Crawler tractors are used primarily for earthmoving and industrial applications, although some are also employed in agricultural operations. Field operating speed is relatively slow compared to rubber-tired tractors, which limits their use to pulling extremely heavy loads or to work on steep slopes.

Tool-carrier tractors have found greatest application in Europe and are used by attaching a variety of implements or transport boxes to the tractor frame.

Implement carriers, although similar to tool-carrier tractors, make use of a common engine,

GASOLINE TRACTOR of 1908 used "caterpillar" treads for traction on steeply inclined surfaces.

CATERPILLAR TRACTOR COMPANY

MASSEY-FERGUSON, INC.

FARM TRACTOR with three-point hitch pulls a plow (*left*). The hydraulically controlled three-point hitch (shown in close-up below) transfers the weight of the plow, harrow, or other implement to the tractor's rear wheels for greater traction. The hitch can be raised or lowered as needed, simplifying the task of attaching heavy implements to the tractor.

frame, and wheels to power mounted harvesting machines such as combines, forage harvesters, hay balers, and corn pickers.

Front-wheel-drive tractors were introduced during the early transition from horses to tractors, about 1914 to 1920, and permitted the continued use of old-style horsedrawn implements. The driver sat on the implement to drive the tractor. The steering column, steering wheel, and controls were extended back to the operator's seat on the implement. In some cases the driver even used reins as though he were driving horses. These machines generally did not perform satisfactorily and are now principally museum pieces. Walk-behind garden tillers are a version of this tractor type.

Compact tractors, looking much like scaled-down farm tractors, have been popular for lawn and garden use since the early 1960's. These tractors should not be confused with the generally lower powered riding lawn mowers and walk-behind garden tillers. It is estimated that several million lawn and garden tractors were in use in the United States in 1970.

Most units are powered by 7 to 14 horsepower, single-cylinder gasoline engines, with a few smaller and some larger engines for specialized operations. Some have battery-powered electric motors.

Walk-behind garden tractors with two drive wheels and a variety of rotary or fixed tillage attachments have been available since about 1930. These usually have from one to 10 horsepower and are quite common in Japan and developing Asian countries.

Tractor Testing. In 1919 the Nebraska legislature passed a tractor testing law requiring that all tractors sold in the state be tested and the results published. These tests provide standards for tractor rating and comparison and have attained worldwide recognition. They have also speeded tractor improvements and helped eliminate inferior models.

Three-point Hitch. The 3-point linkage hitch for mounting implements on the tractor was developed by Harry Ferguson, who lived and did his early experimental work in Ireland. One of the major features of the Ferguson system is achieving traction and improved performance through weight transfer from the implement to the rear tractor wheels instead of building excessive weight into the tractor.

Highlights in Tractor Development

1858: Steam plowing engine built by J. W. Fawkes pulled an 8-bottom plow at 3 miles (5 km) per hour in virgin sod.

1873: The Parvins steamer was probably the first American attempt to construct a track-type tractor, although the U. S. patent office records crawler tractor developments in the early 1850's.

1876: Otto patents were issued for an internal-combustion engine.

1889: At least one company built a tractor with an internal-combustion engine.

1908: The first Winnipeg, Canada, tractor trials were held to compare gasoline and steam tractors.

1910–1914: Smaller, lightweight tractors were introduced, and the first tractor demonstration in the United States was held at Omaha in 1911.

1919: The Nebraska Tractor Test law was passed.

1920–1924: A highly successful all-purpose, or row crop, tractor was developed.

1925–1929: The power takeoff was gradually adopted.

1930–1937: The diesel engine was applied to larger tractors. Rubber tires and faster field speeds were introduced. Electric starting and lights were made available. The row-crop, or all-purpose, tractor was generally accepted.

1937–1941: Standardized positions for power takeoff and drawbar were generally accepted by major manufacturers. Liquid was placed in tractor tires to add weight for better traction. Three-point mounting of implements on the rear of the tractor was introduced. Automatic hydraulic draft control was introduced.

1941–1949: Hydraulic controls for pull-type implements were adopted. Tractors burning liquified petroleum gases (LPG) were introduced.

1950–1971: Tractor horsepower increased rapidly. Percentage of diesel tractors increased. Refinements, such as power steering, automatic and hydrostatic transmissions, and transmissions with greater speed selections, became widely available. Automatic weight transfer systems were developed for pull-type implements.

An understanding of the theory of traction and weight transfer makes it easier to understand the function of the 3-point hitch. A tractor is able to pull because of the resistance, or tractive effect, between the tire or crawler track and the surface on which it operates. Two basic factors contribute to traction: friction between the tire and surface, and the shearing of the soil from penetration of the tire lugs. The amount of weight on the wheel affects both the friction and the gripping or penetration of tire lugs.

From the standpoint of traction, it does not matter how the drive wheel weight is obtained. It may come from weight built into the tractor chassis, from cast-iron weights bolted onto the wheels, from water pumped into the tires, or weight from the implement and front end of the tractor transferred temporarily to the drive wheels. The last is the goal of the 3-point hitch.

Heavy draft machines, such as plows and tillers, penetrate into the soil and develop a downward force. By adjustment of the hydraulic lift control valve to maintain the desired draft load on the tractor, this downward force is continuously opposed by the 3-point hitch lift mechanism, transferring force from the implement to the tractor's rear wheels. Balancing the force, or weight, shifted from the implement is a similar amount of weight transferred from the front tractor wheels to the rear drive wheels. As draft load increases, the weight transferred to the rear wheels also increases, providing better traction. As the implement is raised from the ground, the draft load drops to zero, and no more weight is transferred to the rear.

A typical 3-point hitch consists of two lower links attached just below the rear axle of the tractor and a top link attached to a spring-loaded mounting point above the rear axle. The lower links pull, lift, and carry the implement, and the top link senses the implement load and limits the rotation of the implement about its attachment points to the lower links.

Mounted just below the seat is a lift, or rocking, shaft that is rotated by a hydraulic cylinder located inside the tractor. Rotation of the rocking shaft raises and lowers the lower links, and consequently the attached implement. The lower links are vertically adjustable to permit side-to-side leveling of mounted implements. Length of the top link is also adjustable for leveling the implement from front to rear. Certain tractors incorporate draft sensing linkage in the attachment points of the lower links rather than the top link.

The important contribution of the Ferguson system is demonstrated by the fact that more than 90% of the wheel tractors produced throughout the world incorporate 3-point hitches and some form of hydraulic implement control.

EDGAR LEE BARGER AND FRANK BUCKINGHAM
Massey-Ferguson, Inc.

Bibliography

American Society of Agricultural Engineers, *Agricultural Engineers Yearbook,* 17th ed. (St. Joseph, Mich., 1970).
Barger, E. L., Liljedahl, J. B., Carleton, W. M., and McKibben, E. G., *Tractors and Their Power Units,* 2d ed. (New York 1963).
Hunt, Donnell R., *Farm Power and Machinery Management,* 5th ed. (Ames, Iowa, 1968).
Implement and Tractor Red Book, 54th ed. (Kansas City, Mo., 1970).
Jones, Fred R., *Farm Gas Engines and Tractors,* 4th ed. (New York 1963).
Stone, Archie, and Gulvin, Harold, *Machines for Power Farming,* 2d ed. (New York 1967).

TRACY, Spencer (1900–1967), American film star, who was often called an "actor's actor" because of his ability to handle convincingly almost any role. He was born in Milwaukee, Wis., on April 5, 1900. He entered Ripon College in 1921 but soon left to study at the American Academy of Dramatic Arts in New York. Following his first great success on Broadway, in *The Last Mile* (1930), he went to Hollywood and made his film debut later that year in *Up the River.*

In his early films, when his hair was red, Tracy often played the underdog, fighting back with tenacity. Later, as his hair turned white, he became a father figure—reserved and patient but always strong and shrewd. He won the Academy Award for best actor in *Captains Courageous* (1937) and *Boys Town* (1938) and was nominated for it for his roles in other films, including *Father of the Bride* (1950), *Bad Day at Black Rock* (1955), *The Old Man and the Sea* (1958), *Inherit the Wind* (1960), and *Judgment at Nuremberg* (1961). His last film, *Guess Who's Coming to Dinner?,* released posthumously in 1968, was one of nine in which he costarred with his long-time friend Katharine Hepburn. He died in Beverly Hills, Calif., on June 10, 1967.

HOWARD SUBER
University of California, Los Angeles

CULVER PICTURES

Spencer Tracy in *Captains Courageous* (1937)

TRACY, a city in west-central California, in San Joaquin county, is about 60 miles (96 km) west of San Francisco. It is a shipping and trading center for the San Joaquin Valley. The city is the largest asparagus-shipping point in the United States and annually processes and ships thousands of carloads of fresh and canned fruits and vegetables. Tracy's industries make beet sugar, dairy products, alfalfa meal, glass, and paper products. A major U. S. defense distribution depot is in Tracy.

The community was founded in 1878 and was incorporated in 1910. Government is by city manager. The city's population grew from 11,289 in 1960 to 14,724 in 1970.

ARMSTRONG ROBERTS

BULK CARGO that is transported in the holds of freighters is an important segment of world's trading.

TRADE is an exchange of goods and services. "Foreign trade" means commercial exchanges between residents of different sovereign political units. It becomes clearly distinguishable from local or domestic trade only as nations emerge and begin to formulate national commercial policies; then it becomes "international trade."

International trade has reached immense proportions. The value of total world merchandise exports rose to the $300-billion-a-year level for the first time in the early 1970's. To this must be added from $50 billion to $60 billion more annually in transportation, insurance, banking services, travel expenditures, and other expenditures in other countries for "services." These services are also part of international trade, even though discussions of trade are often limited to trade in merchandise.

Trade increases the standard of living for all countries. For some countries foreign markets take a third to a half of total output, and the standard of living depends crucially on the international division of labor that foreign trade permits.

Trade, domestic or foreign, involves at least two parties, at least two products—it is thus distinguished from gifts or grants—and a price, or terms of trade, at which the products are exchanged. Trade is also often associated with credit—that is, deferred payment—because there is usually a considerable period of time between the production of a commodity and its sale for ultimate consumption. The "price" at which an exchange takes place thus may include a number of dimensions—credit terms, degree to which transportation and insurance costs are absorbed by the seller, extent of guarantee and provision of services after the sale, and so on.

Early trade was in the form of barter, an exchange of goods for goods, and much trade in primitive societies is still of this character. The use of money as a medium of exchange emerged very early, however, because traders found it much more convenient to have a unit of account and an easily transportable store of value.

Pricing Methods. Whether trade is barter or involves the use of money, the methods for reaching a mutually agreeable price are much the same. Four methods of determining price can be distinguished: haggling, organized brokerage, auctioning, and posted pricing.

All four methods of pricing are found in trade. Haggling is the dominant form of determining price when there are few buyers and sellers. Organized brokerage generally prevails when a commodity is uniform in quality and there are large numbers of buyers and sellers. Auctioning is used mainly when the commodity is unique and there are several prospective buyers. Posted pricing is used most frequently when there are large numbers of buyers and few sellers, or large numbers of sellers and few buyers.

Haggling. Haggling over the price is a long-established practice in which buyer and seller both name a desired price and then adjust it until a deal can be struck or until it is clear that no mutually agreeable exchange is possible. A variant of this is the so-called silent barter formerly used by traders in dealing with primitive tribes, especially in Africa. Traders arriving by ship would leave a pile of goods on the beach, and then retire to the ship and wait. The other party would inspect the goods and leave another pile of goods to be exchanged for the first. Next the traders on the ship would inspect the offerings. If they liked the exchange, they would take the second pile and leave the first. If they did not, they would return to the ship without disturbing either pile, and wait for another offer, which would be made in the same way as the first.

Organized Brokerage. In large organized markets, such as the international commodity exchanges, the haggling takes place through an intermediary, called a broker. Prospective buyers and prospective sellers of a product indicate to the broker prices and quantities desired. The broker attempts to match buyers and sellers. At the same time the broker indicates to each how the market is developing so that absurd offers are not placed. See also BROKER.

Auctioning. Another method of determining price is auctioning or bidding. Auctions arise when a prospective seller desires to sell his product for the best available price, although he may state a reservation price below which he is unwilling to sell. An auction may proceed by prospective buyers bidding successively higher prices until only one buyer is left in the field. Or it may proceed in reverse, with the auctioneer starting with a high price and gradually dropping it until a buyer announces his willingness to buy. The latter is the so-called Dutch auction, used for sale of flowers. Auctions are especially suitable when unusual items such as antique furniture or paintings are being sold and a standard market price cannot be established, or when highly perishable goods must be sold at whatever they will bring. Closely related is the system of bidding in which a prospective buyer makes known his specific requirements and various potential suppliers then make bids with the low bidder (for comparable quality) winning the contract.

Posted Pricing. In this method of determining price one of the trade partners posts a price and sells or buys all that is asked or offered at that price. Adjustments are made in the posted price from time to time if trade is too low or too high. This mode of pricing is found in the typical Western retail store. It is also found, both on the buying and the selling side, in international commerce.

Benefits of Trade. Trade must be mutually beneficial; otherwise people would not engage in it on a sustained basis. The gain from trade in reproducible commodities arises from differences in production costs between different areas or different groups of people. These differences in costs may arise from differences in underlying productive capability, from differences in the degree of capitalization, or from differences in the tastes of the consuming public. Each country concentrates its production on those goods it can produce relatively cheaply; at the same time trade permits each country to diversify consumption, because goods produced in excess of its requirements are exchanged for goods from elsewhere offering lower cost or greater variety. This "division of labor" among countries leads to greater efficiency in the use of the world's limited resources. The gains from trade grow larger as differences grow larger in the relative costs of production between trading partners. Trade also brings peoples of diverse backgrounds into contact with one another and generally broadens their intellectual horizons.

Political and Social Aspects. The relationship between foreign trade and international politics is a complex one. It used to be said that trade follows the flag, meaning that once political ties were established, trade flourished. Thus two regions might be joined politically, or one country might found colonies or establish political dominance over other areas, and thereby foster trade. But it is perhaps historically more correct to say that the flag follows trade. Political outposts and military forays leading to political dominance often were undertaken to protect lucrative trade routes, to service vessels plying those routes, and to preserve trading monopolies. Thus the British Empire is sometimes said to have been founded "in a fit of absence of mind" while Britain was securing its trading interest.

The technology and social ideas transmitted through trade have often had profound effects on the trading partners. The compass and paper, both of which Europe acquired from the Muslim civilization of northern Africa, provide examples of these effects. Without the introduction of the compass the great explorations of the 15th and 16th centuries would not have been possible. Without paper the invention of the printing press, which was in turn carried to other parts of the world, could not have had the impact it had.

Foreign trade has exposed the traders to different social and political institutions, and these in turn often induced reflection about the institutions at home. Jean Jacques Rousseau and the French naturalists drew inspiration for their political theories from tales of primitive tribes told by traders returning from far-off lands, and the feudal shogunate of Japan eventually collapsed after extensive contact with Western trade and technology. On the morbid side, trade has also transmitted devastating communicable diseases from one society to another. Measles and smallpox often decimated communities in which these diseases had previously been unknown.

Effects of Transportation Advances. The evolution of trade has been closely related to the evolution of transportation. Most trade has always taken place in local markets, less than a day's journey by foot or pack animal from the trader's residence, and this continues to be true. But long-distance trade relied on caravan animals, such as the camel, and on ships propelled by oar or sail. Long-distance trade was revolutionized with the advent of the railroad and the internal combustion engine on land, and at sea by the steam- or diesel-powered metal-hull ship.

One index of the revolution is simply the growth in size of large merchant ships. They rose from the 500-gross ton galleon of the 16th century, to the 2,000-ton clippers plying the seas in the late 19th century, to the 10,000-ton tankers of the late 1930's, to the 100,000-ton-plus tankers and bulk carriers of the early 1970's. With larger size also came greater speed, but the speed of transportation has been changed most markedly by the airplane. It can circumnavigate the world routinely in less than the five days it took to travel from Baltimore to Philadelphia in the late 18th century and in less than 1/500 of the time it took Magellan's men to circumnavigate the globe in 1519–1522. These striking improvements in transportation have affected not only the speed and volume of trade, but also the composition, because goods that were formerly confined to production strictly for local consumption can now be transported economically for long distances.

HISTORY OF TRADE

Ancient Trade. Little is known about the earliest trade. English flint, used to make primitive tools, was widely traded in Europe thousands of years before Christ, and so was salt from mines in central Europe. Amber, a solidified resin originating in the regions around the Baltic Sea and admired for its beauty, has been found in Cretan graves dating as far back as 2500 B.C. Most of this trade must have been overland, but from 1700 B.C. the Cretans traded extensively by sea. The Egyptians, too, ranged far in search of gold, antimony (for rouge and bronze), and slaves. As early as 3000 B.C., Egyptians may have sailed down the African coast as far as the Zambezi River, nearly 5,000 miles (about 8,000 km) away by sea.

The Phoenicians (about 1200 to 300 B.C.) were unexcelled traders. Operating from a narrow coastal strip in the eastern Mediterranean, they built up the large urban centers of Sidon and Tyre as the focal points of land and sea trade extending over a wide area. They had efficient merchant vessels powered by sail and oar, good navigators, and a broad knowledge of sea routes and winds. This knowledge was carefully guarded from potential competitors—Phoenician captains are reported to have sailed for days off route if necessary to throw off a following ship.

Some idea of the wide variety of goods traded by the Phoenicians can be obtained from a description in the Bible (Ezekiel 27) of Tyre around 600 B.C. Silver, iron, lead, and tin from Spain, linen from Egypt, ivory and ebony from central Africa, fine embroidery from Syria, lambs and goats from Arabia, spices and gold from Sheba, and gems, horses, mules, wheat, wine, wool, and slaves are all mentioned as goods traded in Tyre. The Phoenicians established trading centers all around the Mediterranean, including the famous city of Carthage, near modern Tunis, and even on the Atlantic coast. They invented the phonetic alphabet (merchants with widespread interests had to keep careful records) and in the Carthaginian era used the oldest known bills of exchange and mortgages (on ships).

Early trade was attended by large risks—both natural risks such as storms and human risks such as piracy and brigandage—and was hampered by poor transport. Because of risks, trade was limited to easily transportable, high-value products. Trade was based largely on goods derived from natural advantages—the presence of desirable natural resources such as tin, gold, amber, or ebony—but occasionally also on the products of special technology and unique skills, as in the case of Egyptian glass beads and cloth dyed with the famous Tyrean purple. Trade gradually became more broadly based. The Greek city-states were importers of food, and later Rome became heavily dependent on Egypt for grain, which was transported on remarkably large ships. By 500 B.C., centers of "manufacturing" ("fashioning by hand") were established in Greek and Phoenician cities.

By the late Roman era virtually all the Eastern hemisphere was linked by trade. Chinese and Indian products had appeared in Europe earlier, but they probably changed hands many times in passage. But Rome traded directly with China through overland trading caravans, and the high costs and risks of such trade are reflected in the attempt by Emperor Justinian I (reigned 527–565 A.D.) to have silkworms smuggled out of China to start a silk industry in Europe.

Dark and Middle Ages. The incursions of northern tribes into the Roman Empire in the 5th century and the spread of Islam across the Near East and North Africa in the 6th century disrupted trade in the Mediterranean area. Trade became insecure, subject not only to brigandage but also to extortion by local chieftains and feudal lords as a price for protection. Trading activity even became disreputable, and traders were often socially suspect. Organized trade in Europe languished. But it flourished elsewhere, especially between the Arab world and India.

About 650 a canal was dredged between the Nile and the Red Sea, linking the eastern Mediterranean with the Indian Ocean. The Roman Emperor Trajan had built one in 98, but it was unusable by the 3d century. By the end of the 7th century, Arab colonies fringed the west coast of India, and by the middle of the next century large Arab trading communities were established in China.

Although there had been sustained trade between China and the Roman Empire, direct trading contact between Europe and China was not reestablished until the 13th century, when Marco Polo published his famous account of his stay in Shangtu. Oriental goods that found their way to Europe did so through Middle Eastern middlemen. In the meantime Arab trading encompassed not only the Far East, the Indian Ocean, and Central Asia, but also the eastern coast of Africa and, through desert caravan routes, central Africa.

The Crusades, begun in 1096 to wrest the holy cities of Palestine from Arab control, exposed Europeans to the wealth of the Arab world and awakened a strong trading interest. Here was a case where trade followed the flag. Although the military successes of the Crusades were temporary, they opened commerce in both goods and ideas between western Europe and the non-Christian Eastern world.

Rise of Venice and Genoa. The Italian city-states, most notably Venice and Genoa, established dominant positions in this trade. Venice was an important trading link between western Europe and the eastern Roman Empire centered in Constantinople (now Istanbul) after the 7th century, and served as a conduit for Middle Eastern and Oriental goods into Europe. Venice was in a natural position to expand this trade following the Crusades, but its virtual monopoly on trade with the eastern Mediterranean was successfully challenged by Genoa in the 13th century. Genoa also established trading links with the growing manufacturing centers of Flanders and with southern Russia and central Asia by way of the Black Sea.

Some idea of the nature of trade can be gained from the size of ships. In Roman times grain ships of 2,500 tons regularly plied the Mediterranean, and there are reports of ships as large as 6,500 tons. The Arabs used ships in the 2,000-to-3,000-ton class in their Indian trade. But in the Venetian fleet in the 15th century, which consisted of about 3,000 ships, only about 10% of the ships exceeded 700 tons, and most of them were about 200 to 300 tons. Ships used later by the Portuguese to explore Africa and engage in the India trade were also about 200 to 300 tons.

This decline in the size of trading vessels reflected several factors—partly lost technology in shipbuilding, partly the decline in security in the Mediterranean and the desire to spread shipment among several vessels to reduce risk, and partly the reversion of trade from bulk items such as grain to high-value, less bulky luxury goods.

Scandinavian and German Expansions. While the Italian cities were gradually expanding their trading operations eastward, the Scandinavians were exploring westward, and the German cities were extending their operations to the northeast. The Vikings settled Greenland around 1000, and over three centuries of regular commerce followed. The Greenlanders needed timber, iron products, grain, and salt. They exported dairy products, wool, furs, walrus tusks and skins, and the tusk of the narwhal, which was sold in Europe as the horn of a unicorn, thought to have powerful medicinal properties.

Trade with Russia was quantitatively more important. It was carried on by the Hanseatic League, a loose confederation of independent northern European cities formed in the early 13th century. Lübeck eventually became the leading city, but at one time the league had nearly 100 members and operated privileged trading centers from London on the west to Novgorod on the east. The league's main purposes were to provide protection for commercial activity and to acquire and preserve trading privileges from other areas. The Hanseatic League reached the peak of its influence in the late 14th and 15th centuries, but it became increasingly restrictive in its rules governing production and trade. It was further weakened by religious wars in Germany and by the shift of trading activity to the Atlantic coastal ports. See also HANSEATIC LEAGUE.

During the late Middle Ages, Bruges became the leading trade center in northern Europe. It was close to the source of fine Flemish woolens, made from English wool and in heavy demand throughout Europe. This trade brought both Italians from the Mediterranean and Germans from the Baltic. As a result Bruges became a great entrepôt (transshipment center) for trade in goods from all sources.

Innovations in Practices. In this period a number of practices essential for modern trade were advanced. They included conventions regarding commercial contracts, double-entry bookkeeping, risk-sharing through commercial insurance, standard weights and measurements, and, above all, the introduction of paper (far cheaper than parchment) on which business records could be kept.

In 1453, Constantinople fell to the Turks and symbolized the closing of the eastern Mediterranean to western Europe. In fact the Venetians kept their stations in the area for some time, but gradually trade through the Middle East became more difficult. Partly because of these developments, partly because of the tight monopoly that the Venetians maintained on eastern trade, and partly because of religious motives, the Portuguese and Spanish sought routes to the East that bypassed the eastern Mediterranean. Portuguese explorers finally sailed around southern Africa in 1488. In 1498, Vasco da Gama reached India by that route, and in 1514, China was reached by sea. In 1492, Christopher Columbus discovered the West "Indies" for Spain, and in 1519–1522, Ferdinand Magellan's ships sailed around Cape Horn to the Far East and westward back to Spain. These great voyages transformed the pattern and composition of trade and marked the beginning of transoceanic travel.

The Rise of Modern Trade. The new routes to the Far East and the discovery of the New World revolutionized both the geographical pattern and the commodity composition of foreign trade. The great trading centers of the Mediterranean were eclipsed by the growth of new centers farther west, mostly on or near the Atlantic—Lisbon, Antwerp, and Lyon in the 16th century and Amsterdam and London in the 17th century. Trade with India and China and the Spice Islands (now Indonesia) increased greatly, as indicated by the sharp fall in European prices of spices, silks, cotton products, and other Oriental goods.

New Commodities. The commodity composition of trade also changed radically. First of all there were some commodities completely new to Europe—tomatoes, potatoes, cocoa, green beans, and corn were all introduced from the New World—but these were not especially important in foreign trade. In the early 16th century, trade was dominated by the inflow of spices from the Far East and of gold and silver bullion from the Americas. Much silver was transshipped to the Far East in payment for Oriental products, but enough remained in Europe to cause a substantial inflation there. Some European goods were exported to the New World, but because much of the bullion was simply taken, this flow to Europe did not, strictly speaking, represent trade.

Later in the 16th century, cotton calicoes from India displaced spices as the major item in trade with the East, and sugar became the principal import from the Americas. New products transformed European life. Sugar was used in tea, chocolate, and coffee—themselves tropical drinks. Cotton fabrics permitted greater personal cleanliness than did the traditional wool and linen, which were more difficult to wash. And the tobacco habit became nearly universal. Earlier these had all been luxury goods, but the new trade reduced their prices so much that by the late 17th century their use was widespread. Industry was also greatly stimulated by the new trade—sugar refining, calico printing, shipbuilding, and ironmongering (for export) all thrived.

Commercial Organization. The new trade also gave a fillip to commercial organization. Trade voyages were expensive and risky—although very profitable—ventures. The new trade induced the formation of many partnerships and later of joint stock companies to raise the large sums required to launch a voyage and to establish trading centers abroad. Some of the leading groups, such as the East India Company, the Dutch East India Company, and Hudson's Bay Company, gained trade monopolies, established agents and forts in various parts of the world, and even acted as governments. See CHARTERED COMPANIES.

In addition the large flow into Europe of precious metals permitted the greater use of money and reduced the importance of barter within Europe. From the 15th to the 18th century the nations of Europe were being consolidated, with two consequences for trade. First, many of the internal barriers to trade, such as tolls by local rulers and highway robbery—barriers that had plagued trade in the Middle Ages—were reduced as national governments gradually asserted their authority.

Second, the system of *mercantilism* was imposed on foreign trade. This term covers a wide variety of policies, but broadly speaking it involved the use of foreign trade to enrich the home country, both in gold and silver and in employment in manufacturing. The nature and emphasis of mercantilist policies varied from country to country. In Portugal and Spain the focus was on state monopoly of the spice trade and on the accumulation of precious metals. Spain imposed stiff penalties for the export of gold or silver, even though these metals, apart from the export of wool, provided the principal means by which Spain could pay for an increased volume of imports and could carry on its expensive wars in Europe and Africa.

In England, the Netherlands, and France greater emphasis was placed on the establishment and protection of domestic manufacturing. These countries tried to preserve their trading monopolies. For example, England required that all American export goods had to be shipped first to England—in American or English ships—where they paid English duties before they could be exported to their final destinations. It was some of the more abusive features of this mercantilist system which sparked the revolt of the American colonies in 1775. See also MERCANTILISM.

Although the bulk of foreign trade continued to be in basic raw materials and foodstuffs up until the 20th century, trade in manufactured products—especially trade in iron products and textiles—grew rapidly through the 18th and 19th centuries. There was, however, little trade in machinery, which was largely custom built and often subject to export prohibitions to prevent its use by foreign competitors.

A number of technological improvements fostered the growth of trade. Astronomy, geography, and cartography all advanced greatly during the early part of this period, and these advances aided navigation. Ships, though still wooden, grew in size, had improved hull lines, and increased in speed. Transportation within countries also improved because of better roads, canals, and security.

Technological Advances. Large breakthroughs in transportation came in the 19th century with the advent of the railroad, the steamship, the metal hull, and telegraphy. In the mid-19th century, railroads helped open up the great interiors of the United States and Canada, and later in the century they did the same for Argentina and Russia. They made bulk transportation within countries much easier. Two effects were that the agricultural populations of Europe were threatened by imports of grain from North America, and the building of the railroads increased tremendously the demand for iron and steel, especially from Britain.

Sailing ships depended on favorable weather for their journey; the steam engine liberated shipping from the winds. Steam was first used as auxiliary power on a transatlantic voyage in 1819, and the first trip powered principally by steam was made in 1838. Steam power permitted regular scheduling of voyages. Steam also could propel the larger ships that were made possible by the use of iron, and later steel, as a hull material. The first steel-hulled ship traversed the Atlantic in 1879.

Telegraphy and ocean cables—first successfully laid across the Atlantic in 1866 and across the Pacific in 1902—tied buyer and shipper and seller together in quick, reliable communication, reducing risks in commercial decisions. The radio—first used shore-to-ship in 1897 and developed over the following years—improved communication still further, and it permitted importers to know exactly when their goods would land. See also TRANSPORTATION.

Changing Economic Policy. During the 19th century there was an important change in government policies toward trade, away from mercantilist protectionism and toward freer trade—fewer prohibitions and lower duties on foreign trade. This change was most notable in Britain, but it also extended to France and most other European countries. The United States and Canada were exceptions, and both countries increased their tariffs toward the end of the century. See also FREE TRADE.

As a result of improvements in transportation and communication and of reductions in tariffs, foreign trade grew. In rough terms, the value of world exports increased from \$600 million in 1820 to \$5 billion in 1867, to nearly \$20 billion in 1921, and to over \$300 billion in 1971. Price increases accounted for some of this rise, but most of it reflected an increase in the volume of trade. Britain became the preeminent importing and exporting nation, and London became the leading trading and financial center of the world and remained so well into the 20th century.

CURRENT FOREIGN TRADE

International trade grew at the extraordinary rate of 8.1% a year between 1950 and 1970, a rapid rate compared even with the rates of growth during the periods of discovery and of technological revolution in transportation. Much of this rapid growth was due to changes in commercial policies.

Direction of Trade. Despite the rapid growth in trade, the list of leading exporting countries has been remarkably stable since the early part of the 20th century. Eleven of the 15 largest exporting countries at the start of the 1970's were also among the 15 largest in 1913, immediately before World War I began.

The ranking within the "top 15" list has also been quite stable. Britain, the world's largest trading nation throughout the 19th century, yielded this position during World War I to the United States, which has led since that time. In the 1960's, Britain dropped into third place behind West Germany.

Together the 15 most important exporting countries account annually for about 70% of world exports. The countries that lead in exports also tend to lead in total production, although the ranking does not correspond perfectly. Some countries are extremely dependent on trade while others are much less so. The Netherlands, for example, exports 45% of its total output, and Belgium, Switzerland, and Venezuela all export over 30%. In contrast, the USSR exports well under 4% of its total output, and the United States is also relatively self-sufficient.

Much trade, especially among industrial countries, is with contiguous areas. For instance, about two thirds of Canada's exports go to the United States, and Canada is the largest single customer of the United States. Nearly two thirds of the exports of western Europe are to countries within that region, and the same is true of the Communist areas.

Commodity Composition of Trade. The commodity composition of trade shows greater change over time than does the geographical pattern. Many leading commodity groups of 1937 retained their relative importance in the early 1970's, but a number of commodities—wool, rubber, fruits, and alcoholic beverages—ceased to be among the 20 most important groups. Commodity groups added to the "top 20" list by 1970 were apparel, organic chemicals, ships and boats, and aircraft.

The relative position of commodities that retained their prominence from 1937 to 1970 changed markedly. Cotton, coal, and textiles dropped substantially, while machinery and transportation equipment became relatively more important. The rising importance of petroleum is also noteworthy. Since 1960 more than half the tonnage moved by merchant ships in world trade has been in petroleum and its products.

Manufactured products grew in importance from less than 40% of world trade in 1928 to nearly 60% in 1970. This growth took place in spite of a number of transportation improvements that made possible the economical shipment of low-value or perishable goods. Now refrigerated ships permit the movement of fruits and fresh meat, and air cargo even permits shipment of cut flowers. Huge bulk carriers and tankers permit economical shipment of low-grade ores and crude petroleum to distant refineries.

Trade Policy. Since 1945, trade policies have

favored the growth of trade in manufactures. In the late 1940's most countries had severe restrictions on foreign trade. Many of these dated from the Great Depression of the 1930's when one country after another raised its tariffs to protect home industries in the face of declining world demand, thereby actually contributing to the decline. New restrictions on imports were added immediately after the war, partly to help conserve scarce foreign exchange resources and partly to protect industries that had been built up artificially during the war. Raw materials largely escaped these restrictions, for they were needed for production.

During the 1950's a concerted effort was made to reduce these artificial barriers to trade, and as a result the quotas and other controls limiting foreign trade were gradually dismantled. At the same time, a series of tariff reductions took place under the auspices of the General Agreement on Tariffs and Trade (GATT). As quantitative restrictions on trade were being reduced, so were the duties that importers had to pay.

Trade in food products grown in temperate climates did not generally benefit from the postwar trade liberalization. Most industrial countries protect their agricultural communities from foreign competition. And at the same time that tariffs and other barriers to trade in manufactured products in industrial countries were being reduced, they were being raised by many nonindustrial countries that wished to promote domestic manufacturing production. Many experts question the advisability of these policies, arguing that the industries so encouraged will be inefficient and highly uncompetitive and will require protection from imports for many years. Capital equipment is generally exempt from the heavy protection that these countries impose on manufactured imports, however, and in fact their economic policies tend to encourage the importation of such equipment. Often capital equipment is financed under foreign aid programs of the industrial countries.

Institutional Framework. Each sovereign nation is free to establish laws, taxes, and regulations governing its own foreign trade. But nations have found it convenient, particularly after experience with the tariff wars of the 1930's, to agree to rules that limit their own freedom of action in trade matters, and generally to work toward removal of artificial and often arbitrary barriers to trade.

The GATT. These rules are set down in the General Agreement on Tariffs and Trade, a document that was signed by 23 countries in 1947 and whose signatories exceeded 70 countries within 20 years.

The GATT is dedicated to a multilateral, nondiscriminatory trading world, one in which trade problems and trade conflicts are worked out cooperatively and in which each country treats other countries on a par in trade matters. The aim of nondiscrimination is furthered primarily by the "most favored nation" principle, which requires each country to extend to other countries the lowest tariff it charges on imports from any country.

As with most rules, there are important exceptions. Some discriminatory trading arrangements antedated the GATT. These include the British Commonwealth Preference arrangements and the preferential trade agreement between the United States and the Philippines. Other arrangements, such as discrimination against Communist countries—to the point in some cases of outright prohibition of trade—arise from political considerations. Finally, an exception to the rule of nondiscrimination is made for countries that wish to establish customs unions or free trade areas among themselves. This exception is made on the ground that a customs union or free trade area is sometimes a step toward political union. In any case, it is argued, the action advances the objective of removing barriers to trade, which countries may be more ready to do with a limited number of trading partners than they would for the world as a whole.

The GATT lays down certain general principles and sponsors periodic rounds of tariff reductions. In addition, it provides a framework for continuous consultation on trade matters, inquiry into complaints regarding trade policies, adjudication of trade disputes between countries, and arrangement of compensation to countries that feel their trade position has been damaged by the actions of some other country. Often proposed changes in policies or practices affecting trade—for example, health or safety requirements that many countries place on certain products, including imports—can be modified so as not to damage trade while still achieving the objective. See also TARIFFS.

International Forums. The Trade Committee of the Organization of Cooperation and Development provides a forum for technical discussions on trade problems of the industrialized countries. The United Nations Conference on Trade and Development (UNCTAD)—first held in 1964, the largest international conference ever held—and its various working groups provide forums for discussing the special trade problems of less developed countries.

Regional Associations. Since the late 1950's an important influence on the geographic pattern of trade has been the formation of duty-free areas made up of several countries. The largest in economic importance is the European Economic Community, formed in 1957 by Belgium, France, West Germany, Italy, Luxembourg, and the Netherlands, and to come into effect gradually over the following 12 years. The European Free Trade Association, comprising Britain, Scandinavia, Austria, Switzerland, and Portugal, is less ambitious in its overall economic aims but achieved free trade within the region earlier, in 1967. In addition, four countries of Central America formed the Central American Common Market in 1959, and a group of eight Latin American countries agreed in 1960 to form the Latin American Free Trade Association (LAFTA).

The first three of these associations have induced a marked redirection of their trade, which has grown much more rapidly than world trade in general. The proliferation of such trading arrangements does tend to fragment world trade, however, particularly as nonmembers seek forms of association less comprehensive than full membership.

Trade Mechanics. Most international trade today is carried on by private parties—mainly manufacturers and persons and firms specializing in buying and selling abroad. But for some commodities and some countries foreign trade is still conducted extensively or even exclusively by state organizations, especially in the Communist countries, although even they have tended to decentralize responsibility.

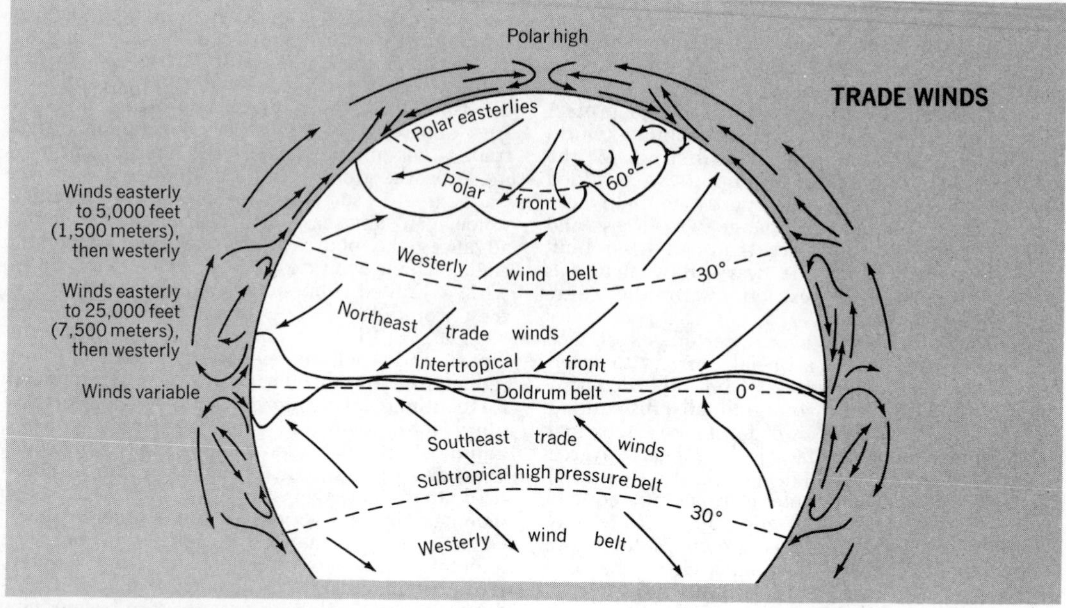

Foreign trade is highly sophisticated and involves many subsidiary services—not only transportation, but also credit, insurance, foreign exchange dealing, and so on. As world trade has grown, so have these related services. Banks often provide many of the services needed by traders, not only supplying credit but also guaranteeing payment, undertaking foreign exchange transactions, insuring against losses that might arise from movements in exchange rates, and the like.

The mere granting of trade credit has to some extent moved out of the banks. Large firms sell to their customers on their own credit. In addition, most countries have established government-sponsored credit institutions, such as the Export-Import Bank and the Commodity Credit Corporation in the United States, to extend or to guarantee longer-term export credits than banks are normally willing to undertake.

DOMESTIC TRADE

As barriers to foreign trade are removed, it will become increasingly like domestic trade. Indeed, there is often little difference between the two, because the distances to be traveled and the other arrangements required for trade—with the exception of foreign exchange dealings—are often the same within a country as they are between countries. Because of the absence of customs frontiers, however, there is less quantitative information about domestic trade than about foreign trade.

The vast improvements in transportation and communications have influenced domestic trade as well as foreign trade. Extensive railway systems have helped to integrate such countries as Canada, India, the USSR, and the United States. Airplanes make increased contact possible with remote and inaccessible parts of many less-developed countries, and these countries are fostering national airlines.

One indication of improved and transformed domestic and international trade is that fresh fruits, formerly available in northern American or European markets for only a month or two each year, can now be purchased the year round. Another indication of improved trade conditions is that countries that once were fragmented economically are increasingly becoming national markets.

RICHARD N. COOPER, *Yale University*
Author of "The Economics of Interdependence"

Bibliography

Ashworth, William, *A Short History of the International Economy since 1850,* 2d ed. (London 1962).
Condliffe, J. B., *The Commerce of Nations* (New York 1950).
Cooper, Richard N., *The Economics of Interdependence* (New York 1968).
General Agreement on Tariffs and Trade (GATT), *International Trade* (Geneva, annually).
General Agreement on Tariffs and Trade (GATT), *Trends in the International Trade* (Geneva 1958).
Haberler, Gottfried, *The Theory of International Trade, with Its Application to Commercial Policy* (London 1936).
Herrmann, Paul, *Conquest by Man* (New York 1954).
Kenen, Peter B., *International Economics,* 2d ed. (Englewood Cliffs, N. J., 1967).
Maizels, Alfred, *Industrial Growth and World Trade* (New York 1963).
United Nations, *Yearbook of International Trade Statistics* (New York, annually).
Woytinsky, Wladimer S., and Woytinsky, E. S., *World Commerce and Governments* (New York 1955).
Yates, P. Lamartine, *Forty Years of Foreign Trade* (London 1959).

For Specialized Study

Bohannan, Paul, and Dalton, George, eds., *Markets in Africa* (New York 1965).
Curzon, Gerald, *Multilateral Commercial Policy: The General Agreement on Tariffs and Trade and Its Impact on National Commercial Policies and Techniques* (London 1965).
Heckscher, Eli, *Mercantilism,* 2 vols. (London 1935).
Johnson, Harry G., *Economic Policies Toward Less Developed Countries* (Washington 1967).
League of Nations, *Industrialization and Foreign Trade* (Geneva 1945).
Polanyi, Karl, and others, *Trade and Market in Early Empires* (Glencoe, Ill., 1957).
Pryor, Frederic L., *The Communist Foreign Trade System* (London 1963).
Rowe, J. W. F., *Primary Commodities in International Trade* (New York 1965).

TRADE ROUTES. See TRADE—*History of Trade.*

TRADE UNION. See CRAFT UNION; LABOR UNION.

TRADE WINDS, the persistently easterly winds—that is, westward-blowing winds—of the earth's tropical regions. They come out of the subtropical high pressure regions centered about 30° latitude north and south, blow from the northeast in the Northern Hemisphere and from the southeast in the Southern Hemisphere, and die out in the doldrums—the belt of low atmospheric pressure at the equator.

The trade winds are the most nearly constant of the various planetary wind systems. Their direction and speed over the oceans vary only slightly from day to day. Thus they have been of great importance to sailing ships, and they were largely responsible for the success of the voyage of Columbus westward across the Atlantic Ocean. The name "trade winds," in fact, comes from the Old English "trade," meaning "path," because of the regular course of the winds. However, the winds are not well defined over continental areas because of the disrupting effects of the rough continental surface.

The air mass of the trade winds is warm and moist. The weather is generally fair, with showers and thundershowers occurring infrequently over the open ocean but more frequently over islands and close to the equatorial low pressure belt. The surface layer of trade wind air is overlain by warmer and much drier air. Thus there is a temperature inversion in the winds—an increase of temperature with height. This temperature inversion tends to suppress vertical currents of air that might form clouds and showers. However, some moisture does move upward, producing the "trade wind cumuli" seen over the ocean in the tropics.

For a description of trade winds in relation to other planetary wind systems, see CLIMATE—*Prevailing Winds and Vertical Air Currents.*

JAMES E. MILLER
New York University

TRADEMARK, any word, name, symbol, or device, or any combination thereof, that is adopted and used by a manufacturer or merchant to identify and distinguish his goods from goods manufactured or sold by others. The law of trademarks deals with not only true trademarks, but also such variations as *service marks, certification marks,* and *collective marks.*

Patents and copyrights are expressly provided for in Article 1, Section 8, of the U. S. Constitution, and the federal government has exclusive control over both. But the law of trademarks is not provided for there, as such. In most instances, federal trademark registration has been based on the "interstate commerce" clause in Section 8. Less often, it is based on foreign or territorial commerce. Hence, there are parallel federal and state registrations of trademarks.

Registration. Applications for federal registration are processed by the U. S. Patent Office, a division of the Department of Commerce. Each of the states also maintains trademark registers. With most business being transacted in interstate commerce, and thus subject to control by Congress, the importance of state trademark registrations has materially lessened.

In the United States all trademark rights require actual usage, not merely intended use, and they are also appurtenant to the goodwill of a business.

Trademarks are divided into strong, or technical, trademarks (as, Kodak, a coined expression) and weak, or descriptive, trademarks (as Jucy, a phonetic variation of "Juicy"). Under the 1946 Federal Trademark Act, often referred to as the Lanham Act, technical marks qualify for the Principal Register; descriptive marks, if valid, appear on the Supplemental Register.

Renewal. A U. S. trademark registration must be renewed every 20 years. Also, in the sixth year after registration, an affidavit of use must be filed, or the registration will be void.

A distinction should be made between trademarks such as Coca Cola, and *trade names,* such as Coca Cola Company. A trade name, identifying a business or occupation, is not registrable.

Variations Registrable Under Trademark Law. These include the *service mark,* used in the sale or advertising of services, such as consulting services and dry cleaning services, or the titles, character names, and other distinctive features of radio and television programs; the *certification mark,* used in connection with the products or services of one or more persons other than the owner of the mark, to certify regional or other origin, quality, or accuracy (such as the Underwriters' Seal of Approval), or to attest that the work or labor on the goods or services were performed by members of a union or other organization; the *collective mark,* a trademark or service mark used by members of a cooperative, an association, or other collective group, such as a mark indicating membership in Rotary.

International Registration. Trademark systems have been adopted in virtually all countries. A U. S. trademark owner seeking to protect his trademark in foreign countries must register it almost always on a country-by-country basis. The United States is not a party to international arrangements such as the Arrangement of Madrid that enables most European businesses to secure "International Registration."

ARTHUR H. SEIDEL, *Coauthor of "Trademarks: Law and Practice"*

TRADES UNION CONGRESS. See GREAT BRITAIN—*Labor.*

TRADING STAMPS are fractional merchandise certificates that business firms give their customers to promote patronage. Some firms give them to employees to encourage performance. Savers paste the gummed certificates into booklets and exchange them for a variety of goods or services at a redemption center maintained by a stamp company.

The trading stamp system has been steadily involved in controversy. In 1916 the U. S. Supreme Court said that "by an appeal to cupidity [stamps] lure to improvidence." Every year, legislatures in the United States and elsewhere consider proposals to outlaw or restrict the use of this promotional tool.

Savers. Trading stamps offer several advantages to savers. They enable consumers to obtain goods for which they would not spend cash. In many families, stamps constitute the housewife's private fund. Savers redeem them for presents, household articles, or something personal. Many certificates are donated to charitable organizations, for which stamp companies make special redemption arrangements.

Users. Supermarkets, gasoline stations, dry cleaners, bowling alleys, and other businesses, typically retailers in crowded fields, give stamps to shoppers in proportion to their purchases. When competitive facilities and offerings, especially prices, are similar, stamps can win customer preference for an enterprise. Stamps attract new customers. Empty spaces in booklets bring them back.

A business using stamps can plan efficiently. It may be able to reduce other promotional expenses and its purchase cost of merchandise. If used effectively, stamps do not necessitate price rises at retail. Stamp offerings speed collections, clear excess inventories, induce referrals, and create goodwill. But the service is relatively inflexible and provokes competitive retaliation.

The Industry. From their inception in 1892 until World War I, trading stamps enjoyed rising popularity in the United States. For the next 35 years they had little vogue. In the early 1950's, however, supermarket chains led a new surge of stamp plan adoptions that did not level off until 1963. Subsequent defections by many supermarkets were offset by growth elsewhere.

Stamp companies distribute catalogs showing the premiums for which their stamps are redeemable. The firms issue stamps, at $1.50 to $2.50 per 1,000, to their business subscribers. The stamp companies earn interest on the cash they receive from subscribers for about nine months before the stamps are redeemed. Paying factory or wholesale prices, efficient stamp companies deliver premiums having an average retail value slightly above $2.50 per 1,000 stamps. An average of 95% of the stamps issued are said to be redeemed.

A handful of companies dominate the U. S. industry, which has sales of less than 0.1% of the gross national product.

HAROLD W. FOX, *DePaul University*
Author of "The Economics of Trading Stamps"

TRAFALGAR, Battle of, trə-fal′gər, fought off Cape Trafalgar, Spain, Oct. 21, 1805, between a British fleet of 27 ships and 5 frigates under Vice Adm. Lord Nelson and a Franco-Spanish fleet of 33 ships and 7 frigates under Adm. Pierre Villeneuve. It resulted in a decisive British victory that deprived France of sea power. Napoleon was therefore forced to follow a continental strategy, and this led eventually to his defeat at Waterloo.

Napoleon's plan for invading England had failed. His main fleet under Villeneuve and that of his Spanish ally were blockaded in Cádiz Bay by Nelson's fleet. Yet he ordered Villeneuve to sail for Naples and at the same time appointed his relief. This spurred Villeneuve to risk battle. Nelson planned, in the event of an enemy sortie, to form his fleet in two divisions. The windward one led by his flagship *Victory* would cut through the enemy's line and bring about a melee around Villeneuve's flagship *Bucentaure*, containing the French van and center. The lee division led by Collingwood's flagship *Royal Sovereign* would encircle and destroy the French rear.

So it happened. Action was joined at noon on October 21, and 4½ hours later the French and Spanish had been defeated with the loss of 15 ships sunk or stranded and 8 taken in prize. French-Spanish casualties were 4,400 dead and 2,545 wounded against British losses of 449 killed and 1,214 wounded. Nelson was fatally wounded but lived to know that victory had been won.

B. B. SCHOFIELD, *Vice Admiral, Royal Navy*
Author of "British Sea Power"

TRAFFIC CONTROL is the scientific effort to bring order and safety to the complex movements of automobiles, trucks, buses, and pedestrians on streets and highways. Traffic control improves traffic operations on existing streets and highways by routing traffic and using a variety of traffic control devices. It also utilizes modern techniques of planning and designing new highways to allow for the habits and abilities of motorists and pedestrians and the characteristics of vehicles.

Increasing reliance on automobile travel has emphasized the need to improve highway transportation in every country. The shift of population and employment to urban areas has led to measures designed to preserve mobility. In addition, a growing concern over the quality of the environment has accented the need to make the best use of existing streets and highways. Improved safety and mobility, together with more efficient use of urban space, call for increasingly sophisticated methods of traffic control.

The motor vehicle dominates movement in urban areas. In most U. S. urban areas, virtually all personal trips take place in cars or buses, and trucks make an average of 100 deliveries annually at each home. Industry throughout the world increasingly relies on truck transport to move finished products. The availability of good highways is one of the strongest considerations in determining where a firm will settle.

TRAFFIC PROBLEMS

Traffic congestion and accidents increase the individual's cost of transportation. Although substantial progress is being made in coping with these problems, rapid urbanization and the increasing use of motor vehicles have led to a series of conditions commonly grouped together as "the traffic problem," a worldwide phenomenon.

Outmoded street systems, inadequate even for horse-and-buggy traffic in large cities, continue to plague traffic movement. In many communities streets were laid out without regard to the different volumes and kinds of traffic that would be generated by the different uses of land. Many older communities were built when it was important to develop streets as cheaply as possible, taking the easiest route between two points even when it was narrow and indirect. These older streets are now part of arterial highway networks and fail to serve the mobility needs of modern traffic and commerce.

The gridiron pattern of streets made it simple to lay out new communities, but it created an excessive number of intersections, each the focal point for conflicts between traffic moving in different directions. In downtown areas the close spacing of the gridiron pattern has made it difficult to coordinate traffic signal timing.

Travel to and from work represents only about one out of every five trips in U. S. cities, but the concentration of this traffic taxes the capacity of road and transit systems. At one time the bulk of work traffic was concentrated on routes leading to the central business districts of cities. It was possible to serve a substantial part of the commuting load with different kinds of transit. Changes in the manufacturing process, calling for use of more ground space, together with the advent of the motor truck, encouraged dispersion of industry. Increasing income permitted widespread ownership of private homes and private cars. Together these developments have stimulated a sharp growth in commuting travel between outlying homes and outlying jobs in metropolitan areas. This development increases the traffic load on suburban road systems, many of them not built to adequate standards. A complicating factor is the multiplicity of local governments in many outlying areas, making the job of coordinating road building especially difficult.

Changed travel habits also contribute to traffic problems. Increased family income and a shorter work week have led to a greater use of recreational and educational facilities. Many of these facilities were located in relatively isolated areas when they were less heavily patronized. Modern traffic strains both the access roads and the parking facilities at such places. In most urban areas, social and recreational trips are increasing at a faster rate than work trips. The condition is most apparent on weekends, when arterial traffic flow and shopping and pleasure traffic combine on many arterial streets.

Off-street parking shortages are gradually being overcome in many central business districts through aggressive construction programs, but the condition is far from cured. Parking authorities have been active in downtown areas, but some older, small-business districts strung out along arterial streets continue to suffer parking shortages. In many cases it is necessary to remove curb parking from these streets, forcing car owners to move their vehicles into nearby residential streets when off-street parking is unavailable. The same situation prevails in older industrial districts where there is insufficient off-street parking.

Truck-loading is increasingly a problem in the centers of cities. In many communities, only trucks are permitted to stop at downtown curbs during the day, but even this restriction is usually inadequate for handling the growing volume of truck deliveries. Lack of off-street loading in older city areas interferes with traffic movement and makes truck operations inefficient and expensive.

Pedestrian-vehicular conflicts continue to be badly handled. Some improvements in traffic controls have been made specifically for the benefit of pedestrians, who are subject to delays and danger from conflicts with turning vehicles, parked cars, and truck loading. In general, however, pedestrians are relatively uncontrolled.

TRAFFIC ENGINEERING

Traffic control through engineering includes four basic techniques: (1) traffic routing, including one-way streets, through streets, reversible streets, and special routing for trucks and buses; (2) traffic regulation, including parking and loading controls, turning controls, speed limits, and freeway operations; (3) traffic control devices, such as signs, signals, and markings; and (4) physical improvements, such as channelization and intersection redesign.

Traffic Routing. The most important step in traffic routing is the determination of the predominant use of each street in a city. This decision will guide further efforts to direct different parts of the traffic stream and different kinds of traffic to roads that are best able to handle them. This also is the basis for building streets to certain physical standards. What finally is developed may be a truck route, a street for through—that is, long-distance—travel, or some other special traffic treatment.

Freeway systems—intended largely for longer trips within urban areas—represent the clearest application of the principle that distinct road systems should be developed to handle different kinds of traffic. Freeways afford control over access from adjoining property and are free of crossings at grade. Most freeways also include high standards of lane width, curvature, lighting, and signs. In the built-up parts of cities freeways generally are either depressed below ground level or elevated. The depressing or elevating of the road permits an adequate number of street crossings and interchanges with local through streets.

Most early freeways were constructed as bypasses to permit through traffic to go around rather than through city centers. In most large cities, however, through traffic is a small proportion of all traffic, and many freeways are now located so as to serve local trips. Freeway systems eventually are expected to make up about 5% of the road mileage within U. S. cities and to handle about half of all traffic.

Through-street systems expedite traffic and provide greater safety. In most cities a system of streets protected by traffic signals or stop signs generally gives motorists using through streets right-of-way over cross traffic and provides positive control at intersections with other through streets. An effective through-street system concentrates traffic on a limited number of high-quality streets, reducing congestion and accidents on other streets. At the same time, a good through-street system provides greater speed for through traffic and generally provides access to a community's freeway system.

Some newer urban areas have applied the through-street concept very broadly. In California, Orange county and its 25 cities, having agreed upon a system of through streets, cooperate in financing street improvements. The county and many of its cities also have joined in a coordinated program of traffic signal timing on these streets and have limited the number of cross streets and driveways. The limitation on cross streets helps to assure that subsequent land development will not reduce the traffic-carrying capacity of the through-street system.

One-way street systems are widely accepted as a way of relieving congestion in downtown areas. These systems also overcome some of the timing problems of closely spaced traffic signals. New York City has adopted this approach on almost all streets and avenues in Manhattan. Similar—although less extensive—systems are common in the central areas of most large U. S. cities and in many smaller cities. The technique has received worldwide acceptance and is particularly helpful where street widening is difficult. One-way streets reduce potential conflicts at intersections and generally improve traffic safety and increase traffic speed.

Reversible streets operate in opposite directions at different times of day. During off-peak periods they may operate as 2-way streets. Washington, D. C., uses this system on several major streets serving the downtown area.

In most cases, however, reversible lanes, rather than entire streets, are employed. Generally the center lane or lanes of a street are "added" to the lanes handling the heaviest direction of traffic flow during peak hours. Markings, signs, or overhead signals advise motorists that the lanes are reversible. Los Angeles and Chicago use this practice on some of their most heavily traveled arteries.

Chicago, St. Louis, and several other cities utilize reversibility on freeways. Two special lanes are set aside in the center of some freeways, to be operated in different directions at different times of day. Because of high speeds on freeways, overhead signals are generally used, together with movable guardrails that prevent traffic from entering these lanes in the wrong direction.

Truck routes in many cities aid commercial traffic by providing streets built to adequate standards for handling heavy vehicles. Good truck routing helps trucks to avoid unnecessary interference with other traffic movement. Noncommercial traffic is generally allowed to use truck routes, except in a few cases where special freeway lanes have been set aside for truck use only.

Special bus lanes are receiving increasing attention as a way of assisting transit. Nashville, New Orleans, and Philadelphia have such lanes in their central areas for use during peak hours.

Traffic Regulation. Traffic engineering procedures also include regulation of parking, loading, turning, pedestrian movement, and speed. Some regulations prohibit parking where street space is necessary for moving traffic. Other regulations allocate scarce curb space among competing uses, such as loading, and short- and long-term parking. Parking regulations sometimes apply only during the peak hours of traffic movement, but, especially in downtown areas, parking is frequently prohibited at all times.

Some cities back up their peak-hour parking restrictions by towing away the cars of offenders. It has been increasingly possible to limit downtown curb parking as construction of off-street parking has made more space available. Most new commercial, industrial, and residential developments are required to provide off-street parking, permitting the prohibition of parking on many outlying arterials. Since 14% of urban accidents involve parked vehicles, the prohibition of curb parking can be an important safety step.

Restrictions on turning are generally applied where turning vehicles create peak-hour congestion or where turns are unsafe at any time. Part-time turn restrictions may be handled through signals, changeable or permanent signs, or police officers.

Pedestrian controls are widely applied at many busy intersections, generally by the use of traffic signals that prohibit walking at certain times during the traffic signal cycle. This reduces pedestrian interference with turning traffic and enhances pedestrian safety by showing when it is unsafe to walk. Pedestrians are also restrained by physical barriers such as chains or fences at points of unusual hazard. Such physical controls are usually applied when lesser warnings have not been adequately followed.

Pavement markings have been widely adopted to guide pedestrians within crosswalks. The safety advantage of such markings is generally believed to result from the grouping together of pedestrians rather than from any protective qualities of the markings themselves.

Speed regulations are among the most widely used of traffic techniques. They advise motorists and police alike of safe speeds under normal conditions. Modern speed zoning is generally based on measurements of the behavior of traffic and is designed to expedite traffic flow rather than to slow down motorists to some arbitrary limit. Speed zoning is far more widely used in the United States than in Europe, where many countries do not impose maximum speed limits on their high-speed rural highways.

Freeway operations constitute a new application of traffic regulation. Freeway congestion has been relieved by metering the traffic using some on-ramps during peak hours or, in some cases, closing ramps entirely at certain times of day. Freeway ramp metering is usually accompanied by messages posted on adjacent streets, advising motorists of alternate routes. Ramp metering is used in Chicago, Detroit, Los Angeles, and Houston.

Advisory messages from lane signals or changeable electric signs—warning, for instance, of fog or ice—are also used on some freeways to inform motorists of conditions on the road ahead. Part of a freeway in Detroit uses such lane signals, and warning signs are widely used on the New Jersey Turnpike.

Traffic Control Devices. The use of signs, signals, and markings in traffic control is gradually changing under the influence of technical advances. Computers and remote sensing devices make it possible to process thousands of bits of information about traffic conditions to help in timing signals or in advising motorists of alternate routes.

These advances permit coordinated operation of traffic signals over wide sections of a city instead of just a single street. Area-wide controls are successfully used in parts of London, Glasgow, and Toronto. Area-wide traffic signal coordination, aimed at reducing congestion, also performs the normal signal functions of sharing rights-of-way among conflicting traffic streams and reducing accident potential.

Traffic signs—useful for indicating the proper way for motorists to operate in traffic, for warning of hazards, and for directing traffic to destinations—are also being improved. Most changes are in the nature of improved materials, often the result of technological advances.

Substantial progress has been achieved in international agreement on traffic control device standards, particularly important in what traffic engineers call "signing"—placing signs along a highway. There is considerable agreement on colors, symbols, and shapes of different types of signs. These international accords will probably lead to a somewhat greater use of symbols in the United States.

Pavement markings, such as centerlines and lane lines, are helpful in directing traffic into desired paths for through movement or for turns. There is a growing use of raised plastic markers as a way of providing long-lasting material under the stress of heavy traffic and for good visibility in rain. Pavement markings continue to be heavily used as a means of getting the most out of existing streets, since motorists make more economical use of street space with markings present.

Physical Improvements. Minor physical betterments, such as channelization and intersection redesign, substantially improve the use of existing streets. Channelization generally consists of raised concrete islands, designed to show the proper path for traffic to follow through complicated or very large intersections, increasing both efficient movement and safety. Intersection redesign is usually aimed at eliminating bottlenecks, such as narrow pavement sections or awkward turns, or at enhancing safety by improving visibility.

Increasing use is being made of downtown pedestrian malls, utilizing some of the techniques learned in shopping center design. The malls are usually developed on the most active shopping streets in a city and are accessible only to pedestrians and emergency and service vehicles. Malls generally have parking at their periphery, as in Fresno and Pomona, Calif., and Kalamazoo, Mich.

Other attempts to alleviate downtown congestion include development of outlying parking lots in connection with transit stops, as is common in Cleveland and Chicago, or through construction of lots near downtown areas with a connecting transit service, as in St. Louis, Mo., and Washington, D. C.

To cope with the problem of trucks in downtown areas, Dallas established a system of underground loading areas at all new buildings. To separate pedestrians and vehicles, Minneapolis and London created extensive pedestrian bridges and second-story sidewalks.

ENFORCEMENT

Safe and efficient traffic movement requires the services of police officers, the courts, licensing officials, and motor vehicle registrars. They are responsible for apprehending and punishing those who fail to observe state and local traffic laws. Laws and enforcement must have public support in order to be effective.

Apprehending violators is simply a first step in improving driver behavior. Depending upon circumstances, courts may require attendance at special schools to improve driver attitudes and skills. At other times, medical tests may be ordered.

Because of the chronic shortage of police, the practice of selective enforcement is generally followed. Under this program police are assigned to locations where problems are known to exist. Police use accident records, frequently analyzed with the aid of a computer, to pinpoint problem locations and to identify conditions that might be improved.

Most traffic enforcement is by city police or state patrol. There has been some shifting of city freeway enforcement responsibilities to state patrol officers, especially in large and complex metropolitan areas. See the *Index* entry TRAFFIC CONTROL.

D. GRANT MICKLE
Highway Users Federation for Safety and Mobility
Coauthor of "Traffic Engineering Handbook"

Bibliography

Eno Foundation, *Traffic Quarterly* (Saugatuck, Conn., current ed.).
Highway Research Board, *Getting the Most from City Streets* (Washington 1967).
Highway Research Board, *Highway Capacity Manual* (Washington 1967).
Institute of Traffic Engineers, *Traffic Engineering* (Washington, current ed.).
Institute of Traffic Engineers, *Traffic Engineering Handbook* (Washington 1965).
Meyer, John R., and others, *Urban Transportation Problem* (Boston 1965).
U. S. Government Printing Office, *Manual on Uniform Traffic Control Devices* (Washington 1961).
World Touring and Automobile Organisation, *Traffic Engineering and Control* (London, current ed.).

TRAGEDY, traditionally, is a form of drama or narrative in which disaster overtakes the hero despite his noble defiance of fate or of the gods. The possibilities of tragedy exist in a world in which man's powers are limited and in which heroism and virtue do not guarantee moral victories. In traditional tragedy, fate, symbolically represented as the inexorable laws of cause and effect, and the gods, who represent transcendent power in the cosmos, combine to destroy the hero who transgresses established codes and natural laws, no matter how virtuous his intentions or mission. The result is an experience that evokes pity and fear for the hero and in which the doomed figure emerges as an affirmation of man's moral potentialities and of his capacity for self-knowledge through suffering.

Aristotelian Concepts. The first major treatise on the nature of tragedy, the *Poetics* (*Peri Poiētikēs;* literally, *On Poetry*) by Aristotle (384–322 B. C.), consists of lecture notes written long after the great age of Greek tragedy (5th century B. C.) had ended. As Aristotle interprets it, tragedy—a term derived from the Greek *tragōidia*, or "goat song," which was associated with ancient ritual dance and song honoring the fertility god Dionysus—presents a plot or story (*mythos*) involving a highly renowned "man who is not eminently good and just, yet whose misfortune is brought about not by vice or depravity, but by some error or frailty" (*hamartia*), traditionally called the "tragic flaw." The tragic action, moving inexorably toward disaster, though not necessarily resulting in the hero's death, concludes with self-discovery and moral revelation. With the restoration of cosmic and social order, the audience experiences a purgation (*katharsis*) of pity and fear.

Critics of Aristotle have often pointed out that the *Poetics* cannot be taken as a set of rules or even as an accurate description of most tragedies. Aristotle's primary intent was to defend tragedy against its condemnation by his former teacher, Plato (428?–?347 B. C.). In *The Republic* and in other dialogues, Plato had attacked tragedy as an irrational depiction of mythological figures with whom an audience erroneously identifies. He held that fantasies in which great and essentially good men, such as Oedipus and Thyestes, are unwittingly destroyed can result only in moral debilitation with a correspondingly disastrous effect on the state. In answer, Aristotle insisted that *katharsis* in tragedy would restore emotional balance to the audience. He further contended that tragedy, by permitting human actions to be fully realized according to the "law of probability or necessity," was more philosophical than history, since it dealt with general truths, not particulars. In short, Aristotle was concerned with providing a rational, philosophical defense, not a primer for dramatists or a yardstick with which to measure the success or failure of actual tragedies. See also POETICS OF ARISTOTLE, THE.

Tragedy in the Middle Ages. In the Middle Ages, tragedy became a moral narrative to warn man against the sin of pride. In such 14th century works as Petrarch's *De viris illustribus* (*Concerning Illustrious Men*) and Boccaccio's *De casibus vivorum illustrium* (*Concerning the Falls of Illustrious Men*) and in John Lydgate's 15th century work *Fall of Princes*, the depiction of sudden disasters served as a reminder of God's omnipotence and man's original sin. Chaucer, in the *Monk's Tale* (one of the *Canterbury Tales*), employs the word "tragedie" to describe a simplified version of ancient drama:

Tragedie is to seyn a certyn storie,
As olde bookes maken us memorie,
Of hym that stood in greet prosperitee,
And is y-fallen out of heigh degree
Into myserie, and endeth wreccedly.

Renaissance Concepts. During the Italian Renaissance, new translations of and commentaries on Aristotle's *Poetics*—unknown in antiquity and neglected in the Middle Ages—gave rise to a neoclassical conception of tragedy. However, the Italians often misinterpreted Aristotle's observations and at times even mistranslated them.

One of the most influential of the Italian commentaries, *Poetices libri septem* (1561; *Poetics*) by Julius Caesar Scaliger (1484–1558), argued that the action of tragedy should be more consistent with our understanding of reality. The Trojan War, for example, cannot be presented within two hours on a stage; hence, drawing inspiration from Aristotle, Scaliger suggests that tragedy confine itself to actions that can be presented more realistically within the time and space limitations of the stage.

Following Scaliger, Lodovico Castelvetro (1505–1571) formulated the famous unities of time, place, and action—the "Weird Sisters" of neoclassic tragedy—which were, like neoclassical theory in general, to influence dramatists and critics through the 18th century. In his *Poetica d'Aristotele* (1570), he stipulated that unity of action could be achieved by depicting "one action of one person, or two actions, which by their interdependence can be counted one"; the unity of time requires that "the time of action ought not to exceed the limit of twelve hours"; and the unity of place should be achieved by setting the action in "a very limited extent of place." But Castelvetro had mistranslated and augmented Aristotle's *Poetics,* for nowhere do we see the unities of time and place in the ancient work. Aristotle merely observes that many tragedies confine their action to one revolution of the sun. Of place he says nothing.

18th Century Theories. Debates over neoclassical theories continued on the Continent and in England for two centuries. By the 18th century, resistance to the rigidity of neoclassical rules had increased considerably. Though a neoclassicist himself, Dr. Samuel Johnson (1709–1784), in the preface of his edition of *The Plays of William Shakespeare* (1765), rejected the unities of time and place as invalid rules, for they confused representation with reality: "The truth is, that the spectators are always in their senses, and know, from the first act to the last, that the stage is only a stage, and that the players are only players." Nor did Johnson believe Shakespeare's mingling of the comic and tragic a grave error, as neoclassical critics had insisted, for "there is always an appeal open from criticism to nature."

In Germany, Gotthold Lessing (1729–1781), in his *Hamburgische Dramaturgie* (1769; *Hamburg Dramaturgy*), agreed with Johnson that Shakespeare had truly understood the unity of action, which involves "change of circumstances, recognition, and suffering." The other so-called "unities" are to be regarded not as rigid laws but as natural consequences of the primary unity regarding action. Indeed, Lessing urged his fellow dramatists to reject the rigidities of French tragedy and adopt the more versatile English forms.

With the growing number of bourgeois tragedies—Lessing was the leading author of such plays in Germany—the older notion of the inevitable destruction of the hero gave way to the romantic belief in redemption and "poetic justice," which rewarded the good and punished the wicked. Thus, audiences in the 18th century became accustomed to drama adapted to their middle-class assumptions and responses. As the French playwright Beaumarchais (1732–1799) remarked in his *Essai sur le genre dramatique sérieux* (1767; *Essay on the Serious Drama*): "The nearer the suffering man is to my station in life, the greater is his claim upon my sympathy."

19th Century Theories. A major challenge to such plays was made by Georg Wilhelm Hegel (1770–1831) in his *Vorlesungen über die Aesthetik* (1835–1838; *Lectures on Aesthetics*), which attacked bourgeois morality as a basis for tragedy. As in Sophocles' *Antigone,* which provided Hegel with his argument, tragedy involves "a conflict of ethical substance," of good against good, both of them partial claims urged as absolutes. Thus, Antigone, who wishes to bury her brother's body, and Creon, who denies that wish because the brother's rebellion against the state prohibits it, are convinced of their absolute duties. This is a conflict of "thesis" and "antithesis," both manifestations of *Geist,* or "spirit," which expresses itself rationally in the cosmos. Tragedy reconciles such a conflict by revealing that neither claim is absolute—the "synthesis." Tragedy, therefore, manifests a dialectical development in human history.

One of the greatest philosophical treatises on tragedy in the 19th century, *Die Geburt der Tragödie* (1872; *The Birth of Tragedy*), by Friedrich Nietzsche (1844–1900), rejects the traditional conception of Greek tragedy as an expression of the Apollonian elements of classicism—order, harmony, and restraint. Nietzsche asserts that such qualities were only the externals, whereas the Dionysian elements of wildness and frenzy, associated with primitive celebrations from which tragedy emerged, provided the emotional experience or inspiration. The "fraternal union" of the two divine elements is the "highest goal of tragedy and of art in general." Nietzsche's view of tragedy is clearly an accommodation between the demands of man's deeper, wilder self to be free of restraint and his need for a form to contain and express those urges.

20th Century Theories. In the 20th century, much critical writing on tragedy has been concerned with its decline and death. Joseph Wood Krutch (1893–1970), in *The Modern Temper* (1929), asserts that tragedy, like religion, provides "a rationality, a meaning, and a justification to the universe" and that it is not "an expression of despair but the means by which [the great ages] saved themselves from it." In the modern world, however, loss of faith in God and man has resulted in a corresponding inability to create tragic experiences comparable to those in past ages. So-called "modern tragedy," Krutch contends, presents the miseries of men who lack exalted spirit and whose disasters are merely depressing. A notable voice in defense of modern tragedy was raised by Arthur Miller, who, in his essay *Tragedy and the Common Man* (1949), argued that the common man may acquire tragic status by "his willingness to throw all he has into the contest, the battle to secure his rightful place in the world."

In *The Death of Tragedy* (1961), George Steiner presided at the interment by tracing the decline of the "organic world view" and the resulting loss of the values and beliefs essential to traditional tragedy. Some critics, such as John Gassner (1903–1967), have provided themselves with new sets of terms to characterize modern plays that depict human disaster—"low tragedy," such as Miller's *Death of a Salesman,* and "high tragedy," such as *Hamlet.* Symbolically, these terms suggest the nature of man's aspirations as well as his achievements.

KARL BECKSON, *Editor of "Great Theories of Literary Criticism"*

Bibliography

Clark, Barrett H., ed., *European Theories of the Drama,* rev. ed. by Henry Popkin (New York 1965).
Corrigan, Robert W., ed., *Tragedy: Vision and Form* (San Francisco 1965).
Kaufmann, Walter, *Tragedy and Philosophy* (Garden City, N. Y., 1968).
Lucas, Frank Laurence, *Tragedy in Relation to Aristotle's "Poetics"* (New York 1928).
Mandel, Oscar, *A Definition of Tragedy* (New York 1961).
Olson, Elder, *Tragedy and the Theory of Drama* (Detroit 1966).

TRAGICOMEDY is a form of drama that combines tragic and comic elements. Although comic elements may be seen in some ancient Greek tragedies, they are generally incidental to the tragic action. The Roman dramatist Plautus, in the prologue to *Amphytryon,* coined the term *tragicomedy* and violated dramatic decorum by introducing kings and slaves into the same play. Yet the work is more farce than tragicomedy.

During the Renaissance, tragicomedy took on a distinctive structure. It included any work that did not end in death but brought some characters near to it. The term had nothing to do with humor or lack of it. Sudden reversals, averted catastrophes, and happy endings were the standard ingredients of the form, which we see in Shakespeare's plays *The Merchant of Venice* and *Measure for Measure.*

In the 19th century, the romantics introduced the grotesque into such plays, thereby influencing modern drama. But the dramas of Henrik Ibsen, notably *Ghosts* (1881) and *The Wild Duck* (1884), and of Anton Chekhov, especially *The Cherry Orchard* (1903), with their touching comic sadness, have revealed the possibilities of the form.

Writers associated with the "theater of the absurd" have been particularly attracted to tragicomedy, although the term seems to be an inaccurate description of their work. Samuel Beckett's *Waiting for Godot* (1953), for example, has neither a comic nor a tragic ending. The play is puzzling, grotesque, and elusive. Yet Beckett calls it a "tragicomedy," a term now often used to describe a variety of dramatic modes.

KARL BECKSON, *Editor of "Great Theories of Literary Criticism"*

TRAGOPAN, trag′ə-pan, any of a genus of mountain pheasants found from Kashmir along the Himalayan range through Burma to central China. They are usually found at elevations from 3,000 to 12,000 feet (915–3,660 meters).

Tragopans are heavily built birds, usually from 20 to 27 inches (51–69 cm) long. The males have a pair of fleshy hornlike structures on the sides of the head. These "horns" can be erected during courtship display. The males also have large biblike neck wattles of brilliant red and cobalt blue that they display during the breeding season. The males are colored with rich red, buff, brown, and black, interspersed with spottings of gray or white, but the females are somberly colored in shades of brown, mottled with black.

Inhabitants of chilly, damp, mountain forests, tragopans feed primarily on buds and leaves obtained high in the trees. They also sometimes eat seeds, berries, and insects. Tragopans differ from other members of their family in their habit of building bulky leaf-and-twig nests high in trees. They also sometimes use a deserted crow's nest. The three to six buff-colored eggs are thought to be incubated by the female alone.

There are five species of tragopans making up the genus *Tragopan* of the family Phasianidae.

KENNETH E. STAGER
Los Angeles County Museum of Natural History

TRAHERNE, trə-hûrn′, **Thomas** (1637?–1674), English poet, prose writer, and clergyman, who is generally regarded as the last of the "metaphysical" poets of 17th century England. The son of a Welsh shoemaker, he was born in Hereford and educated at Oxford. After taking holy orders he retired to a country parish near his birthplace, where he led a life that was quiet and uneventful in its externals. For a time he was in London as chaplain to Sir Orlando Bridgman, Lord Keeper of the Great Seal, but he spent the last years of his life in Herefordshire.

The only work of Traherne's published during his era were the polemical *Roman Forgeries* (1673) and two devotional books, *Christian Ethics* (1675) and *A Serious and Pathetical Contemplation of the Mercies of God* (1699). The bulk of his poetry and his prose meditations, unknown in his own time, were discovered in the 20th century and published as *The Poetical Works* (1903 and 1906), *Traherne's Poems of Felicity* (1910), and *Centuries of Meditations* (1908).

Traherne's poetry is remarkable for its ecstatic and mystical qualities and its preoccupation with the themes of childhood and innocence. But Traherne was a poet of great lines and phrases rather than of achieved artistic wholes, and meter and rhyme meant little to him. His finest accomplishment is the prose *Meditations,* in which his rhapsodic genius was liberated.

FRANK J. WARNKE, *Coeditor of "Seventeenth Century Prose and Poetry"*

TRAIL, a city in southern British Columbia, Canada, is on the Columbia River, 250 miles (about 400 km) east of Vancouver and about 6 miles (9 km) north of the U. S. border. It is one of the greatest mining and smelting centers in Canada. Lead, zinc, silver, cadmium, bismuth, mercury, tin, and iron are mined in the area. Trail's manufactures include steel, hardware, zinc products, chemicals, and fertilizers.

The community was first called Trail Creek Landing, because Trail Creek, which joins the Columbia River here, was a part of the Dewdney Trail, which was traveled in the 1860's by miners en route to nearby goldfields. The town site was surveyed in 1891, and the first smelter was opened in 1895. The city was incorporated in 1910 under the name of Trail. Population: 11,149.

VESELY COMPANY

TRAVEL TRAILER of average size (*above*) is easy to handle on the road and has a spacious interior (*below*).

CAMPING TRAILER (*below*) has beds in the canvas overhangs and sleeps 6 to 8 people. It has an icebox, range, sink, and water pump. For travel, it collapses, the metal roof dropping to rest on the metal sides.

TRAILER, any wheeled vehicle incapable of independent locomotion, designed to be towed. Truck trailers have long played a key role in transportation. Horse trailers and small box trailers have played a lesser role. Specialized trailers for boats have been common since the 1940's. Two other types of vacation trailers are important: the *travel trailer,* of permanent construction and affording fairly comfortable vacation living, and the *camping trailer,* essentially a large tent that folds into a small box. Both are popular in North America and western Europe.

Travel Trailers. The length averages from 10 to about 30 feet (3 to 10 meters), the middle sizes being the most popular. All are 8 feet (2.4 meters) wide and the majority provide standing room inside. The smallest accommodate 2 persons and the largest, 6 to 8.

The body of the trailer is of either streamlined or rectangular construction, the former aerodynamically designed and unusually strong, the latter efficient in its use of interior space and less expensive to manufacture. Virtually all exteriors are aluminum, often protected with a baked enamel finish.

No interior space in travel trailers goes un-

POLORON PRODUCTS, INC.

used. The smallest contain cabinets, a small kitchen, and dining furniture that converts into a bed. Larger models have bathrooms, separate bedrooms, more fully equipped kitchens, and even living rooms. Many also have carpeting, fashionable furniture, wood paneling, and color-coordinated kitchens. Kitchen appliances and a heater operate on butane or propane gas stored under high pressure in 5-gallon tanks located over the coupler joining trailer to towing car.

Many trailer parks provide power, water, and sewer connections. Not all do, however, and so most trailers are self-contained and can operate for weeks without utility connections. Water is stored in a tank and delivered by a small hand or electric pump. Power is provided by storage batteries, sometimes aided by a gasoline generator. Liquid waste is stored in a holding tank until emptied at a dumping station.

Travel trailers are not *mobile homes,* which are relatively permanent residences, too large to be moved often. Migratory workers and military families sometimes live in travel trailers, but the principal use of such trailers is recreational, permitting extended inexpensive travel without the sacrifice of conveniences.

Camping Trailers. Less elaborate than travel trailers, folded camping trailers range in length from 8 to 14 feet (3.4 to 4.3 meters) and in width from 6 to 7 feet (1.8 to 2.1 meters). None exceed 4 feet (1.2 meters) in height when packed. These compact units unfold into large tent-top structures that will sleep 4 to 8. Some models have cooking facilities, chemical toilets, sinks, and attachable rooms with screen walls.

Choosing a Trailer. There are more than 300 U. S. companies manufacturing trailers, making the task of selecting one difficult. Requirements may be defined by determining how much space the family needs, how large and heavy a trailer the family car can pull, how much can be spent for a trailer, how often it will be used, and where it will be stored.

The buyer should visit many dealers and study brochures and recreational-vehicle magazines. A trailer should comply with industry plumbing, heating, and electrical codes, as indicated by the seal of the Trailer Coach Association (TCA), the Recreational Vehicle Institute (RVI), or the state in which the trailer is sold. A trailer should be bought only from a reputable dealer who will fulfill warranty obligations.

Safety. The use of a weight-equalizing hitch with antisway control makes the use of the trailer and towing vehicle much easier to handle. The added weight on the towing vehicle's wheels makes heavier tires advisable. Under no circumstances should a hitch be attached only to the bumper. The hitch should be inspected often.

Almost all trailer brakes are now electrical. Most states require a specially designed breakaway switch that automatically engages the trailer's brakes if it separates from the towing vehicle. A safety chain is required by all states.

Great care must be exercised in the use of butane and propane gas, which are heavier than air and tend to collect in corners and on the floor when there is a leak. Vigorous fanning is the only effective way to clear the gas.

Liability insurance should be bought from the same company that insures the towing vehicle, to avoid conflict in case of accident.

ROBERT H. NULSEN
Author of "Travel Trailer Manual"

ROCHE

Trailing arbutus (*Epigaea repens*)

TRAILING ARBUTUS, är-bū'təs, is a small creeping evergreen shrub with small white or rosy tubular flowers that have a spicy aroma. The trailing arbutus has broad, oval, alternate leaves that range in length from 4/5 of an inch to 3 inches (2–8 cm). They have rounded or lobed bases and stiff hairs on both surfaces. The stems have coarse hairs and grow about a foot (30 cm) long.

The trailing arbutus, *Epigaea repens,* belongs to the heath family (Ericaceae) and is also commonly known as the ground laurel or mayflower. It is found on sandy and peaty soils in the eastern United States from Florida and Mississippi to southern New England, southeastern New York, Pennsylvania, and Ohio. A smooth-leafed form, *E. repens glabrifolia,* occurs from Labrador to Saskatchewan and in the Appalachian uplands to North Carolina. Closely related to the trailing arbutus is *E. asiatica,* a Japanese shrub sometimes planted as an ornamental in parts of the United States.

PETER R. HANNAH
University of Vermont

TRAIN. See LOCOMOTIVE; RAILROADS.

TRAIT, a characteristic element of an individual or a group. Social scientists have applied the trait concept to studies of personality and culture. A personality trait can be identified by observation, testing, or statistical analysis of test results. A distinction is made among cognitive traits, or abilities; temperament traits, such as ego strength; and dynamic traits, or interests and motivations. Another distinction is between surface traits and source traits. A surface trait is a readily observable, repeated pattern of behavior. A source trait is the underlying factor accounting for the surface trait. For example, a person's score on a test can be accounted for by his intelligence and the extent of his education. A trait profile is a significant part of an individual's personality description.

In anthropology, culture traits such as a style of pottery, a tribal myth, or a religious custom are the basic units of a culture. Traits arise through invention within one group or assimilation from another group. See also CULTURE—*Culture as a Way of Life.*

TRAJAN, trā′jən (53–117), Roman emperor, who directed the last major expansion of the Roman Empire. Trajan was born Marcus Ulpius Traianus in Italica, Spain, on Sept. 18, 53. His father, also Marcus Ulpius Traianus, was a distinguished Roman soldier, and his mother was Spanish.

Trajan became consul in 91, and he was governor of Upper Germany in 97 when he was unexpectedly adopted by Emperor Nerva. Nerva had become emperor in 96 after Domitian's assassination. Nerva's position was weak because, as a civilian, he did not have the support of the Roman armies, so he adopted Trajan, a leading general. Nerva died in 98 while Trajan was still in Germany. Trajan, as the new emperor, arrived in Rome in 99 and was well received by the senators and the people. Unlike many of his predecessors Trajan ruled with moderation and respect for the senatorial aristocracy.

His reign was relatively long and also significant. He reduced taxes and increased public services. He extended Nerva's *alimenta,* a public assistance program for farmers and orphans. Under Trajan's benevolent reign Italy prospered, and Trajan became known as *optimus princeps,* Rome's best ruler. Trajan showed his humane sense of responsibility in an exchange of letters with Pliny the Younger.

Foreign Campaigns. Trajan broke with the defensive foreign policy that Roman emperors had generally followed and became the most successfully aggressive Roman emperor. He waged wars in two areas, Dacia and Parthia.

Decebalus, the barbarian king of Dacia (roughly modern Rumania), had fought against Domitian, and in 92 the two rulers had negotiated a peace that left Decebalus firmly in control of Dacia. Trajan refused to accept this settlement of the Danubian frontier, and in 101 he made an invasion that culminated in the surrender of Decebalus in 102 and a treaty.

In 105, Decebalus broke the treaty and invaded the Roman province of Moesia. Trajan decided to destroy the Dacian kingdom, and the Second Dacian War resulted in the permanent conquest of Dacia in 107. Decebalus committed suicide, and Dacia became a Roman province. Trajan's Column in the Forum of Trajan in Rome shows scenes from the Dacian Wars.

During the war with Parthia (113–117), Trajan annexed Armenia and made it a Roman province. To protect Armenia, Trajan decided that it was necessary to destroy Parthia, Rome's traditional enemy along the eastern frontier. In 115 he marched down the Euphrates River, crossed to the Tigris, and took Ctesiphon, the Parthian capital. In 116, Parthians encouraged a Jewish rebellion. By 117, however, Trajan had created two new provinces, Mesopotamia and Assyria.

Trajan became ill in 117 and was returning to Rome when he died in Selinus in Cilicia about August 8. He was succeeded by his nephew Hadrian, who immediately reversed Trajan's aggressive foreign policy in the east. Thus, Trajan's gains were short-lived. Most modern historians agree that Trajan dangerously overextended Roman resources. But the Romans revered Trajan's memory.

ARTHER FERRILL, *University of Washington*

Further Reading: Henderson, Bernard W., *Five Roman Emperors* (New York 1927); Lepper, F. A., *Trajan's Parthian War* (London 1949).

THE NISSEN CORPORATION

THE TRAMPOLINE has a resilient surface on which athletes can rebound to perform tumbling stunts.

TRAMPOLINE, tram-pə-lēn′, an elevated resilient web-constructed bed (mat), used by gymnasts, acrobats, and others as a performing surface. A spring or rubber suspension system anchors the bed to a table-high steel frame, the sides of which are padded to protect the user from injury. The springs attached to the bed cause the performer to continue rebounding upward. The activity that takes place on the apparatus is called trampolining, or rebound tumbling.

Trampolines are constructed in various sizes. A 17- by 10-foot (5.18- by 3-meter) frame is the one often used in national and international competition. For the novice or high school gymnast the standard 15- by 9-foot (4.57- by 2.7-meter) bed is adequate. The minimum size is 12 by 5½ feet(3.6 by 1.65 meters). Modern trampolines can be folded and easily stored.

Professional acrobats performing in circuses popularized rebound tumbling during the 20th century. The activity gained a following in the United States after the U.S. Navy preflight program utilized the trampoline during World War II to improve fliers' coordination and balance. It soon became a popular physical education activity and a competitive event in schools, colleges, and clubs. In 1954 the Amateur Athletic Union recognized rebound tumbling as an independent division and began to conduct meets for both sexes, starting at age 10. The National Association of Intercollegiate Athletics holds competitions for its members. The Fédération Internationale Trampoline decides the routines for world championships.

Trampolining consists of stunts formed from limitless combinations of somersaults and twists. It is an exhilarating sport but should not be attempted without adequate supervision.

GEORGE SZYPULA, *Michigan State University*
Author of "Beginning Trampolining"